RHONDA GUTENBERG / LONELY PLANET IMAGES ©

Budapest, Hungary

3 Hungary's capital (p385) has cleaned up its act in recent years. Gone are those old Soviet-era cars that used to spew their choking blue haze over the flat landscape of Pest. Now, the hills on the Buda side of the city are gleaming, and Pest itself is teeming with energy and life. It's no stretch to say that these days Budapest combines the beauty of Prague and buzz of Berlin into something that's uniquely Hungarian. Fishermen's Bastion, Budapest, below

HOLGER LEUE / LONELY PLANET IMAGES ©

Art Nouveau Architecture in Rīga, Latvia

2 If you ask any Rīgan where to find the city's famous art nouveau architecture (p471), you will get the same answer: 'Look up!' Over 750 buildings (more than any other city in Europe) boast this style – a menagerie of mythical beasts, screaming masks, twisting flora, goddesses and goblins. Much of the city's personality can be gleaned through its architecture. Many of the elaborate apartments stand next to weathered, crumbling facades. Sculpture, Rīga, above

Red Square, Moscow

4 With the gravitational pull of a black hole, Krasnaya ploshchad (p773; Red Square) sucks in every visitor to Russia's capital, leaving them slack jawed with wonder. Standing on the rectangular cobblestoned expanse – surrounded by the candy-coloured swirls of St Basil's cupolas, the red-star-tipped towers of the Kremlin, Lenin's squat granite tomb, the handsome red-brick facade of the State History Museum, and GUM, a grand emporium of consumption – you are literally at the centre of Russia's modern history.

Hiking the High Tatras, Slovakia

5 The rocky, alpine peaks of the High Tatras (p880) in Slovakia are the highest in the Carpathians, with 25 peaks over 2500m. But hikin this impressive little range needn't require an Olympian effort. In the morning, ride a cable car up to 1800 and you can hike along mid-elevation trails, stopping at a log cabin hikers' hut with a restaurant for lunch. A few hours more and you're at a funicular terminus that will take you down to a turn-of-the-20th-century resort village below, well in time for dinner.

Bay of Kotor, Montenegro

6 There's a sense of secrecy and mystery to the Bay of Kotor (p584). Grey mountain walls rise steeply from steely blue waters, getting higher and higher as you progress through their folds to the hidden reaches of the inner bay. Here, ancient stone settlements hug the shoreline, with Kotor's ancient alleyways concealed in its innermost reaches behind hefty stone walls. Talk about drama! But you wouldn't expect anything else of the Balkans, where life is exuberantly Mediterranean and lived full of passion on these ancient streets. Kotor town, right

Prague, Czech Republic

7 Prague's big attractions – Prague Castle and Old Town Square – are highlights of the Czech capital (p276), but for a more insightful look at life two decades after the Velvet Revolution, head to local neighbourhoods around the centre. Working-class Žižkov and energetic Smíchov are crammed with pubs, while elegant tree-lined Vinohrady features a diverse menu of cosmopolitan restaurants. Gritty Holešovice showcases many forms of art, from iconic works from the last century to more recent but equally challenging pieces.

Walking the Old City Walls, Dubrovnik, Croatia

8 Get up close and personal with the city by walking Dubrovnik's spectacular city walls (p254), as history is unfurled from the battlements. No visit is complete without a leisurely walk along these ramparts, the finest in the world and Dubrovnik's main claim to fame. Built between the 13th and 16th centuries, they are still remarkably intact today and the vistas over the terracotta rooftops and the Adriatic Sea are sublime, especially at dusk when the sundown turns the hues dramatic and the panoramas unforgettable.

Wine Tasting in Mileştii Mici or Cricova, Moldova

9 Of Moldova's many fine wineries, Cricova (p567) and Mileştii Mici (p568) are the best known. Both boast underground kingdoms in former limestone mines dating from the 15th century that are among the largest in Europe. Mileştii Mici is the largest, with a Guinness World Record collection of more than two million bottles housed among 200km of tunnels. Both wineries offer excellent tours, done by car, that wind through the cellars and end with tastings and meals. Vineyard, Cricova, right

Black Sea Beaches, Bulgaria

10 Sun, sand and sea might not be what you associate with Eastern Europe, but Bulgaria's Black Sea coast (p183) has plenty of beaches. Resorts like Sandy Beach and Golden Sands attract international tourists with their pristine beaches, nightlife and water-sports, while resort towns Varna and Burgas have long stretches of sand on their doorsteps. If you want to escape the crowds, head south to Tsarevo or Sinemorets or to the far north for peaceful, sandy Kavarna or remote Kamen Bryag. Beach, Varna, left

RICHARD WATKINS / LONELY PLANET IMAGES ©

Taking an Overnight Train Anywhere in Eastern Europe

11 With the windows down and the scenery racing past, there are few modes of transport more pleasurable than the overnight sleeper train (p1018), the best way to get about in Eastern Europe. Whether you're in *platzkart* (3rd class) with Bulgarian peasants drinking *rakia* (fruit brandy) and playing cards while discussing life under communism or enjoying the more private *kupe* (2nd class), this is an essential experience and a great way to avoid paying for a hotel.

MARTIN MOOS / LONELY PLANET IMAGES ©

Steam Yourself Clean in a Banya, Russia

12 The great Slavic tradition of the *banya* (p819), or bathhouse, is as Russian as things come. *Banyas* come in all shapes and sizes, from small wooden huts in backyard gardens to lavish and luxurious venues with hundreds of years of history. Don't be shy, get naked with your friends, expose yourself to brain-melting heat, enjoy a surprisingly pleasant whipping with birch twigs (to remove those toxins, you understand) and then plunge yourself into a pool of freezing water. Rinse, wash, repeat – unforgettable. *Banya* at Lake Baikal, below

Berat, Albania

13 This wine-producing region's town (p57) reigns supreme in terms of Ottoman-style wonder and magic. From the river below, the multi-windowed white and black Unesco-listed houses look down at you. Wander on up the cobblestone paths to see what they're really about and meander through its living and breathing castle area complete with a museum filled with stunning iconography by Onufri. Stay in Berat's Ottoman-style hostel or one of two traditional-homes-turned-hotels and participate in the evening walk along the promenade for a truly enlivening experience. Berat Castle, right

Castles & Mountains of Transylvania, Romania

14 The southern swipe of Transylvania's Carpathian Mountains (p709) is packed with opportunities. There's biking in the Bucegi Mountains, day and multiday hikes in the Făgăraş Mountains, driving on the winding Transfăgărăşan Road, declared to be 'the best road in the world' by BBC's *Top Gear*, and skiing in Sinaia and Poiana Braşov. The area also features the vampiric Bran Castle, the ruins of the 13th-century Râşnov fortress and Peleş Castle. Castle, Hunedoara, left

Crimean Landscapes, Ukraine

15 By and large Ukraine is as flat as a topographically challenged blin (pancake), which makes its bumpy bits all the more special. The limestone mountains of Crimea (p977) reach over 1500m, but their wooded plateaus, abrupt cliffs, lonely peaks and show-stopping views make them prime hiking and biking territory. Bunched up in the south of the peninsula, half the fun is getting beneath the ranges, the soft stone shot through in places with a veritable honeycomb of caves, tunnels and subterranean caverns. Crimean coastline near Sevastopol, right

Ohrid, Macedonia

16 Whether on the way downwards from Ohrid's sturdy medieval castle, coming up through the Old Town's stone laneways or gazing at the restored Plaošnik, every visitor pauses for a few moments at Sveti Jovan at Kaneo, a church set high on a bluff overlooking the lake. This is the prime spot for absorbing Ohrid (p538), the point from where one gazes upon architecture sublime, idling sunbathers and distant fishing skiffs alike – all framed by the rippling green of Mt Galicica to the southeast and the endless expanse of lake stretching out everywhere else. Plaošnik, left

Kraków, Poland

17 As popular as it is, Poland's former royal capital (p625) never disappoints. It's hard to pinpoint why it's so special, but there's an aura of history radiating from the sloping stone buttresses of the medieval buildings in the Old Town that makes its streets seem just right. Add to that the extremes of a spectacular castle and the low-key oh-so-cool bar scene situated within the tiny worn buildings of the Kazimierz back streets, and it's a city you want to seriously get to know. Market Sq, Kraków, above

Mt Triglav & Vršič Pass, Slovenia

18 They say you're not really Slovene until you've climbed Mt Triglav (p925). There's no rule about which particular route you take – there are about 20 ways up – but if you're a novice, ascend with a guide from the Pokljuka Plateau north of Bohinj. If time is an issue and you're driving head for the Vršič Pass (p927), which stands (literally) head and shoulders above the rest and leads from alpine Gorenjska, past Mt Triglav itself and down to sunny Primorska and the bluer-than-blue Soča River in one hair-raising, spine-tingling hour. Julian Alps, Triglav National Park, below

Island Hopping in the Adriatic, Croatia

19 From short jaunts between nearby islands to overnight rides along the length of the Croatian coast, travel by sea is a great and inexpensive way to see the Croatian side of the Adriatic (p237). Take in the scenery of this stunning coastline as you whiz past some of Croatia's 1244 islands, and if you have cash to splash, take it up a couple of notches and charter a sailboat to see the islands in style, propelled by winds and sea currents. Boat anchored off Korčula Island, below

Mostar, Bosnia & Hercegovina

20 If the 1993 bombardment of Mostar's iconic 16th-century stone bridge underlined the heartbreaking pointlessness of Yugoslavia's brutal civil war, its painstaking reconstruction has proved symbolic of a peaceful new era. Although parts of Mostar (p120) are still dotted with shockingly bombed-out buildings, the town continues to dust itself off. Its charming Ottoman quarter has been especially convincingly rebuilt and is once again a delightful patchwork of stone mosques, souvenir peddlers and inviting cafes, and today it's tourists rather than militias that besiege the place.

Český Krumlov, Czech Republic

21 Showcasing quite possibly Europe's most glorious Old Town, for many travellers Český Krumlov (p315) is a popular day trip from Prague. But a rushed few hours navigating the town's meandering lanes and audacious cliff-top castle definitely sells short the CK experience. Stay at least one night to lose yourself in the Old Town's shapeshifting after-dark shadows, and get cosy in riverside restaurants, cafes and pubs. The following morning get active with rafting or canoeing on the Vltava River, before exploring the nearby Newcastle Mountains by horse or mountain bike.

Cycling the Curonian Spit, Lithuania

22 Allegedly created by the sea goddess Neringa, the fragile, narrow sliver of land that is the Curonian Spit (p517) juts out of the Baltic Sea, its celestial origins giving it a somewhat otherworldly ambience and its giant sand dunes earning it the nickname of 'Lithuania's Sahara'. The best way to explore it is by bicycle, riding through dense pine forest from one cheerful fishing village to the next, stopping to sample freshly smoked fish, or – if you're lucky – to glimpse the Spit's elusive wildlife: elk, deer and wild boar.

CHRISTIAN KLEIN / ALAMY

STEPHEN SAKS / LONELY PLANET IMAGES ©

Visegrád, Hungary

23 A lonely, abandoned fortress (p409) high atop the Danube River marks what was once the northern border of the Roman Empire. Long after the Romans decamped, the ancient Hungarian kings, the Ottoman Turks and the Austrian Habsburgs in turn all marked this turf as their own. Climb to the top for some soul-stirring vistas over the surrounding countryside and to ponder for a moment the kingdoms and peoples who have come and gone over 16 centuries of history.

Novi Pazar, Serbia

24 Ambling through the winding streets of Novi Pazar (p850) can be as disorienting as a narghile haze. This southern Serbian town could be anywhere in Turkey: old men in prayer caps solve the world's problems over mud-thick coffees, hijabbed girls giggle in labyrinthine bazaars and the call of the muezzin echoes over Arabic pop blasting from halal grills. Thankfully, the mondo-oddball Hotel Vrbak is there to put you back in place: an acid-flashback rendered in cement, this Communist-era throwback simply screams 'Serbia'.

TONY P EVELING / ALAMY

Toruń, Poland

25 This beautiful Gothic city (p671) has just the right balance between sightseeing and relaxing. Grab a *zapiekanka* (a Polish snack consisting of a toasted roll topped with mushrooms,
cheese and tomato sauce) from the window of the milk bar just off the main square, then saunter
past the locals to check out the curious statues around the square's edge, including a monument
to local hero Copernicus. Finish the day at one of the fancy beer garden decks perched on the
cobblestones. Old Town Market Sq, Toruń, above

need to know

Buses

» While often far from luxurious, buses cover almost all areas of Eastern Europe and are particularly useful for reaching more remote areas.

Trains

» The classic way to get around the region – comfortable trains connect nearly all major cities in the region, and overnight trips are a fantastic experience.

When to Go

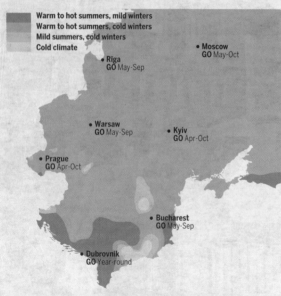

Warm to hot summers, mild winters
Warm to hot summers, cold winters
Mild summers, cold winters
Cold climate

● Moscow
GO May-Oct

● Rīga
GO May-Sep

● Warsaw
GO May-Sep

● Kyiv
GO Apr-Oct

● Prague
GO Apr-Oct

● Bucharest
GO May-Sep

● Dubrovnik
GO Year-round

High Season (Jul-Aug)

» Expect high temperatures and long evenings.

» Hotels will be 30% more expensive and you'll need to book rooms in advance.

» Big draws such as Prague, Budapest and Kraków will be very crowded.

Shoulder (May-Jun & Sep-Oct)

» Crowds and prices drop off.

» The weather remains very pleasant.

» Overall the best time to travel in Eastern Europe.

Low Season (Nov-Apr)

» Hotel prices drop to their very lowest.

» Weather can be decidedly cold and days short.

» Some places, such as resort towns, are like ghost towns.

Your Daily Budget

Budget less than
€40

» Hostel beds for as little as €10

» Self-catering is easy throughout the region

» Take overnight train journeys to save on hotel costs

Midrange
€40-150

» Midrange hotels are everywhere, averaging €50 a night

» Meals in decent restaurants are around €10 per person

» Travel comfortably by train in *kupe* or even 'soft' sleepers

Top end more than
€150

» Top-end hotel rooms start at €150 per night

» In big cities top table meal prices start around €25 per person

» Hire cars start around €30 per day

Driving

» Driving is on the right. Roads are generally good, but be aware that many hire companies limit which countries their hire cars can be taken to.

Ferries

» Ferries connect the Balkans to Italy; Estonia and Russia to Finland; and Ukraine to Turkey. They aren't a common way to get around, however.

Bicycles

» Commonly hired in big cities, though long-distance biking is still something of a novelty.

Planes

» International air routes connect most capitals to neighbouring countries and Western European hubs. Internal flights are less common.

Websites

» **Deutsche Bahn** (www.bahn.de) The best online train timetable for the region.

» **Flycheapo** (www.flycheapo.com) Find out which low-cost airline flies where.

» **Go East Europe** (www.goeasteurope.about.com) Great information and news stories.

» **In Your Pocket** (www.inyourpocket.com) Downloadable Eastern Europe guides.

» **Lonely Planet** (www.lonelyplanet.com/thorntree) Ask other travellers on this message board.

Money

» Countries using the Euro: Estonia, Kosovo, Montenegro, Slovakia and Slovenia.

» Countries not using the Euro: Albania, Belarus, Bosnia and Hercegovina, Bulgaria, Croatia, Czech Republic, Hungary, Latvia, Lithuania, Macedonia, Moldova, Poland, Romania, Russia, Serbia, Ukraine.

» Best currencies to take to countries not using the Euro in order of preference: euro, US dollars, British pounds.

Visas

» EU, US, Canadian, Australian and New Zealand passport holders require no visa for the vast majority of Eastern Europe, though non-EU passport holders will need a visa if they plan to stay more than three months consecutively in the Schengen Area.

» The following countries require some nationalities to have visas: Russia (everyone), Belarus (everyone), Moldova (Australians and New Zealanders), Ukraine (Australians and New Zealanders).

Arriving in EE

Many travellers will arrive in Eastern Europe overland, by train, bus or car from other European transport hubs such as Frankfurt, Berlin or İstanbul.

» **Moscow Domodedovo & Sheremetyevo Airports** Trains – R300, 7am-midnight, every 30 minutes, 40 minutes. Taxi – R1000-1500, best booked in advance

» **Prague Ruzyné Airport** Bus – Airport Express buses cost 50Kč to Prague's train station Taxi – Around 650Kč

What to Take

» Flip-flops (thongs) – very useful on overnight train rides, in hostel bathrooms and for the beach.

» Hiking boots – if you plan to take advantage of Eastern Europe's fantastic and easy walking.

» Ear plugs – helpful anywhere, but especially if you plan to sleep in hostels.

» Notepad and pen – essential for noting down bus times!

» European plug adaptors – Brits, North Americans and Antipodeans will need these.

» An unlocked mobile phone – picking up a local SIM card for making cheap calls is a great way to save.

if you like...

Old Towns

With more cobbled squares, ancient churches and labyrinthine back streets that perhaps the rest of the world combined, there is simply nowhere better in the world to explore old towns than Eastern Europe.

Prague The big daddy of them all; it's hard not to fall instantly in love with the beautifully preserved Staré Město (p276)

Kraków Perhaps Eastern Europe's finest old town is to be found at the heart of Poland's royal capital and miraculous survivor; the incredible Rynek Główny cannot be missed (p627)

Dubrovnik The marble-paved streets of the Stradun and the fantastical city walls are part of the finest old town in the Balkans (p254)

Vilnius Europe's largest baroque old town feels more 'real' than its Baltic neighbours and is a largely unsung draw to tiny Lithuania (p494)

Lviv Western Ukraine's repository of culture is fast becoming a must-see old town on any Eastern European trip (p959)

Beaches

Don't associate Eastern Europe with beaches? You're certainly not alone, but you're definitely wrong – between the Adriatic, Baltic and Black Seas, not to mention pristine lakes and rivers across the region, definitely plan on being able to take it easy on a beautiful stretch of sand during your trip.

Curonian Spit, Lithuania & Russia Technically one long beach, this Unesco World Heritage Site of sand dunes and bracing waters is the best place to swim in the Baltic (p517)

Drymades Beach, Albania The stuff of legend among backpackers, this white-sand beach on Albania's fast-disappearing undeveloped coastline remains the one to head for (p61)

Black Sea Coast, Bulgaria Bulgaria boasts the best beaches on the Black Sea, but we recommend avoiding the big resort towns and heading instead to Sozopol or Sinemorets (p183)

Baltic Beaches, Poland Long, beautiful sandy beaches line the coast from Gdańsk all the way to the German border (boxed text p675)

Castles

Transylvanian fortresses, Bohemian chateaux, Russian kremlins: Eastern Europe offers a huge range of royal dwellings and seats of political power that have survived the centuries amazingly intact.

Bran Castle, Romania Better known as Dracula's Castle despite having fairly tenuous associations with the man himself, this Transylvanian beauty is straight out of a horror movie (p719)

Spiš Castle, Slovakia This impressive site may now be a ruin, but its sheer size and situation makes it one of the most popular sights in Slovakia (p891)

The Moscow Kremlin, Russia The seat of power to medieval tsars and modern tyrants, Moscow's vast Kremlin is unlike anywhere else in the world – breathe in the power as you wander its incredible interior (p772)

Karlštejn Castle, Czech Republic A true piece of fairytale Gothic, this Bohemian beauty near Prague makes for a great day trip (p298)

BRUCE BI / LONELY PLANET IMAGES ©

» Minsk (p78)

Mountains & Hiking

Walkers and mountain lovers will be spoilt rotten in Eastern Europe; it's criss-crossed by mountain ranges, gentle rolling hills and thick forest, and hiking of all levels is never far away. Routes are generally well maintained and infrastructure in and around national parks has been steadily improving.

Slovenský Raj National Park, Slovakia Waterfalls, gorges and thick forests decorate Slovakia's outstanding national park (p892)

Bulgarian Mountains With no fewer than seven mountain ranges within its borders, Bulgaria is a hiker's dream; don't miss the trails around stunning Rila Monastery (p161) or the beautiful Rodopi Mountains (p163)

Zakopane, Poland There's great hiking to be had in Southern Poland's Tatra Mountains, including wonderful emerald-green Lake Morskie Oko (p644)

Zlatibor, Serbia The rolling hills and spectacular views in this corner of Southern Serbia are ideal for gentle hikes (p852)

Relics of Communism

While it may be dead and buried in almost all of the region, there's no denying that communism has more than left its mark on the countries of Eastern Europe. Anyone interested in the history of the 20th century's 'great experiment' will find plenty of monuments and statues to look at, and even the odd communist enclave apparently frozen in time.

Lenin's Tomb, Moscow, Russia Come and see communism's mecca, where a waxy Lenin lies in state on impressive Red Square (p776)

Stalinist Minsk, Belarus Flattened during WWII, the capital city of Belarus was rebuilt in a monolithic Stalinist style during the 1950s and has barely changed since (p78)

Transdniestr, Moldova As relics go, an entire self-proclaimed country is pretty unbeatable, but that's just what you get in this still communist slice of Moldova (p569)

Memento Park, Budapest, Hungary A dumping ground for all of Hungary's unwanted statues of communist leaders and monuments to the great socialist idea; do not miss this amazing collection of follies (p387)

Great Food & Drink

One of the hardest regional stereotypes to break is that going east of Berlin means nothing but cabbage-based delicacies and warm shots of vodka at dinnertime. Nothing could be further from the truth – dive in and enjoy Eastern Europe's surprisingly varied and delicious cuisine.

Istrian delights, Croatia A food-lover's heaven, Istria is packed full of top eateries where slow food is a buzzword and truffles, wild asparagus and fresh seafood are on the menu (p222)

Nordic cuisine, Estonia Excellent dining scenes await in Tallinn, Tartu and Pärnu; don't miss cutting-edge Nordic cuisine at Ö in Tallinn, among others (p356)

Café Pushkin, Moscow, Russia Once famed for food queues, Moscow is now a top culinary destination. Dine in sumptuous elegance at this sublime Moscow institution (p784)

Wine tasting, Moldova Hungary and the Balkans are known for good wines, but for something totally different we recommend you check out the great and largely undiscovered viniculture of plucky little Moldova (p567)

» Plitvice Lakes National Park (p239), Croatia

Extreme Sports

With its wide-open spaces, innovative tourism industries and relative affordability, Eastern Europe has fast become an extreme-sports playground.

Bovec and Bled, Slovenia The unrivalled capital of extreme sports in Eastern Europe is tiny Slovenia, where you can do everything from canyoning to hydrospeeding at Bovec and Bled (p927)

Rafting and kayaking, Bosnia and Hercegovina Fast-flowing rivers provide world-class rafting and kayaking, especially in the Vrbas Canyons between Jajce and Banja Luka (p138)

Sigulda, Latvia The Baltic capital of extreme sports; come here to bobsleigh, bungee jump from a moving cable car and even try out 'aerodium' air blasting (p486)

Bridge diving, Mostar, Bosnia and Hercegovina You too can dive from Mostar's terrifyingly high bridge to the river below after training from the locals (p120)

Spectacular Scenery

So dazzling is Eastern Europe's cultural heritage that many people don't realise how beautiful the region is, taking in everything from sand dunes to dramatic sea cliffs and magnificent national parks where you'll often not even see another visitor.

Plitvice Lakes National Park, Croatia With its shimmering turquoise waters, waterfalls and thick woods, this beautiful spot is one of the region's finest (boxed text p239)

Bohemian Switzerland National Park, Czech Republic Wander in awe past sandstone pinnacles and through spectacular gorges in this breathtaking place (p303)

Cape Kolka, Latvia This desolate moonscape where the Gulf of Rīga meets the Baltic Sea is truly dramatic and hauntingly remote (p484)

Lake Koman ferry, Albania See a part of the world few foreigners ever make it to on this most beautiful ferry ride in Albania's remote and mountainous north (p54)

Art Collections

Art lovers will be bowled over by the art of all forms on offer in this region, itself a kind of warehouse of art history, from the unparalleled wealth of the tsar's collection in St Petersburg to the more modest museums in the former Yugoslavia that miraculously survived the wars of the 1990s.

Hermitage, St Petersburg, Russia Housed in the Winter Palace, this is quite simply one of the world's greatest art collections, stuffed full of treasures from Egyptian mummies to a superb cache of Picassos (p792)

National Gallery, Prague, Czech Republic Inside the Šternberg Palace, this collection of 14th- to 18th-century art is one of the finest in Eastern Europe (p285)

Pinchuk Art Centre, Kyiv, Ukraine For a taste of something truly different visit this extraordinary centre for contemporary art, the pet project of one of Ukraine's most famous businessmen (p951)

State Tretyakov Gallery, Moscow, Russia This fabulous repository of Russian culture is Moscow's best collection of art, spanning an entire millennium, from religious icons to contemporary sculpture (p777)

If you like... Newly independent countries
Make sure you include Kosovo on your trip – this controversial place is Europe's youngest state (p451)

Jewish Heritage

Despite the obliteration of centuries-old Jewish communities throughout Eastern Europe during the Holocaust, the imprint of Jewish culture and heritage remains strongly felt across the region, and many communities are now thriving again.

Sarajevo Haggadah, Bosnia and Hercegovina A priceless Jewish codex that narrowly avoided Nazi capture during WWII and is now said to be the world's most valuable book (p109)

Sugihara House and Foundation, Kaunas, Lithuania The moving house museum of the erstwhile Japanese consul who saved some 6000 Jewish lives by issuing them Japanese visas (p512)

New Synagogue, Szeged, Hungary A refreshingly reborn synagogue being used as a place of worship rather than simply another museum, this spectacular building is testament to Szeged's multicultural heritage (p432)

Oświęcim, Poland Better known to the world as Auschwitz, this chilling site is still an absolute essential for any visitor to Eastern Europe (p636)

Contemporary Architecture

Eastern Europe's architectural heritage is world famous. Gothic Prague, neoclassical St Petersburg and art nouveau Rīga are all must-see destinations, but there's modern architecture too – from the sublime to the ridiculous, the following are some of our favourites.

Museum of Contemporary Art, Zagreb, Croatia Definitely one of the sleekest art museums in the world, this stunner designed by local architect Igor Franić is a stellar example of clever use of light and space (p216)

KUMU, Tallinn, Estonia A world-class concrete-and-glass building holds this excellent art collection; it won the European Museum of the Year award in 2008 (p352)

Slovenian Mountaineering Museum, Mojstrana, Slovenia This brand-new addition to Slovenia's already beautiful mountains gives traditional alpine architecture a modern spin (p926)

National Library of Belarus, Minsk An example of what can only be called post-Soviet hubris, this spaceship-like glass-fronted rhombicuboctahedron has to be seen to be believed (p80)

Nightlife

It's not all stag parties and hen nights in Eastern Europe. Whether it's dancing to cutting-edge international DJs on the dance floors of Moscow or a rather more relaxed party on an Adriatic beach in mid-summer, this is a part of the world that knows how to party.

Moscow, Russia Once famed for its 'face control' (aggressively selective door policies) Moscow is now becoming an essential stop on the clubber's world map with a slew of new democratically run bars and clubs (p786)

Belgrade, Serbia Lonely Planet readers voted Belgrade the best party city in the world in 2009... come here yourself to see why! (p840)

Cluj-Napoca, Romania Cluj's historic back streets house perhaps the friendliest bunch of student party animals anywhere in the world (p731)

Odesa, Ukraine Join the hordes and come to the Black Sea in the summer months to party on down in this post-Soviet petri dish of hedonism and debauchery (p975)

month by month

Top Events

1 **Croatian Carnivals**, February

2 **Czech Beer Festival**, May

3 **St Petersburg White Nights**, June

4 **EXIT Festival**, July

5 **Dragačevevo Trumpet Assembley**, August

January

While it's cold across Eastern Europe, January is a great time to experience the region's winter-wonderland appearance, with everything under blankets of snow. You'll find most towns relatively tourist-free, and hotel prices are rock-bottom.

Great-Value Skiing

Head to Eastern Europe's ski slopes for wallet-friendly prices. After the first week of January most hotels offer their lowest annual rates, making skiing affordable to all. Try the Bosnian slopes at Bjelašnica (p119) and Jahorina (p118) or Bulgaria's Mt Vitosha range (p160) or Bansko (p162).

Empty Streets

Wander around the Old Town of Prague unencumbered by huge groups of tourists and have lesser-known sights and cities across the region pretty much to yourself during January, the quietest time of year.

February

Still cold, but with longer days and the promise of spring around the corner, February sees colourful carnivals held across the region. Low hotel prices and the off-season feel also remain.

Croatian Carnivals

For colourful costumes and nonstop revelry head to Rijeka, where Carnival is the pinnacle of the year's calendar (p232). Zadar and Samobor host colourful Carnival celebrations too, with street dancing, concerts and masked balls. This exciting rite of spring is also celebrated in Ptuj, Slovenia.

March

Spring arrives in the Balkans, while further north the remaining countries of Eastern Europe continue to freeze, though days are often bright and the sun shines.

Vitranc Cup

Anyone who enjoys watching thrilling acrobat-ics on the ski slopes should not miss the excitement of this men's slalom and giant slalom competition (www.pokal-vitranc.com) in Kranjska Gora, Slovenia.

Polish Paganism

Head to Poland in March for the quirky rite of the Drowning of Marzanna, a surviving pagan ritual in which an effigy of the goddess of winter is immersed in water at the advent of spring. The festival, also celebrated as Maslenitsa in Russia, with variants in most other Slavic countries, features lots of bliny (pancakes) to boot.

Hungarian Waltzes

One of Europe's top classical music events is the two-week-long Budapest Spring Festival (www.springfestival.hu) that takes place in late March each year. Concerts are held in a large number of beautiful venues including several stunning churches, the Hungarian State Opera House and the National Theatre.

Kooky Kukeri

Also known as Pesponedelnik, the truly

unique Bulgarian festival of Kukeri features fearsome masked dancers dressed in shaggy fur outfits and adorned with bells parading around the southern town of Shiroka Lâka to ward off evil spirits.

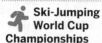

Ski-Jumping World Cup Championships

Held the third weekend in March, this exciting international competition (www.planica.si) in Planica, Slovenia, was the site of a world-record jump of 239m in 2005 and is a must for all adrenalin junkies.

April

Spring has well and truly arrived by April – the Balkans are already enjoying warm, sunny days and, after months of snow, even Russia has finally seen a thaw. Hotel prices outside the Easter holiday period remain low.

Carnival Humorina

April Fool's Day is taken to extremes as Odesa becomes the venue for a one-day street parade. Floats, music, dancing and feasting in the streets are in order to celebrate the city's self-proclaimed status as Ukrainian capital of humour (www.umorina.od.ua, in Russian).

Easter Festival of Sacred Music

Six thematic concerts (www.mhf-brno.cz) with full orchestras take place in three of the oldest churches in Brno, Czech Republic, including the beautiful Ca-

thedral of SS Peter & Paul, in the two weeks following Palm Sunday.

Music Biennale Zagreb

Held since 1961, the Music Biennale Zagreb (www.mbz.hr/eng) is Croatia's most important contemporary music event. It takes place in various venues around the capital over 10 days during mid-April in odd years.

May

An excellent time to visit Eastern Europe, May is sunny and warm and full of things to do, while never too hot or too crowded, though you can still expect the big destinations to feel busy.

International Labour Day

Once bigger than Christmas in the communist world, International Labour Day may have dropped in status since the fall of the wall, but it's still a national holiday in Russia and several other former Soviet republics. You'll find fireworks, concerts and even the occasional military parade on Moscow's Red Square.

Reliving Bulgarian History

Military history fans should not miss the spectacular annual reenactment of the 1876 April Uprising against the Turks in the charming mountain town of Koprivshtitsa, which is bizarrely held on 1 or 2 May (presumably in the hopes of better weather).

Czech Beer Festival

An event most travellers won't want to miss is the Czech Beer Festival (www.ceskypivnifestival.cz), where lots of food, music and – most importantly – some 70 beers from around the country are on offer in Prague from mid- to late May.

Rafting in Bosnia & Hercegovina

After the spring rains May is the time for experienced rafters to head to the fast-flowing river gorges of BiH, but if you're a beginner, stay well away until summer, when conditions are more suitable – see p144.

Music in Prague

Two very different but equally excellent music festivals make May a great time to visit the Czech capital. The three-week-long Prague Spring International Music Festival (www.festival.cz) sees international stars descend for major classical music events, while the Khamoro World Roma Festival (www.khamoro.cz/en) showcases the unique musical traditions of Europe's Roma people.

June

The shoulder season is well underway – it's already summer in southeastern Europe and the sun is barely setting in the Baltic as the solstice approaches. This is definitely one of the best times to travel, if not the best.

⭐ White Nights in the North

By mid-June the Baltic sun only just sinks behind the horizon at night, leaving the sky a grey-white colour and encouraging locals to forget their routines and party hard. The best place to join the fun is in St Petersburg, where balls, classical music concerts and other summer events keep spirits high.

Baltica International Folklore Festival

This festival consists of five days of folk music and dance and rotates between the Baltic capitals; it will be in Rīga (Latvia) in 2012, Tallinn (Estonia) in 2013 and Vilnius (Lithuania) in 2014.

Rose Festivals

A three-day celebration of roses (p173) in Kazanlâk, Bulgaria, culminates in the crowning of a festival queen. Meanwhile, in the Czech Republic, knights, jugglers, musicians and artists roam Český Krumlov during the Five-Petalled Rose Festival (p317), a celebration of the Renaissance period.

St John's Eve & St John's Day

The Baltic region's biggest annual night out is a celebration of midsummer on 23 and 24 June. It's best experienced out in the country, where huge bonfires flare for all-night revellers – see p380 and p490.

July

The middle of summer sees Eastern Europe packed with both people and things to do. Temperatures and prices soar by the end of July, but hotel room rates remain reasonable early in the month.

EXIT Festival

Eastern Europe's most talked about music festival (www.exitfest.org; p846) takes place each July within the walls of the Petrovaradin Fortress in Serbia's second city, Novi Sad. Book early for tickets as big international headlining acts attract music lovers from all over the continent.

Jewish Culture Festival in Kraków

Kraków rediscovers its Jewish heritage during a completely packed week of music, art exhibitions and lectures (www.jewishfestival.pl). Poland's festival is the biggest and most exciting Jewish festival in the region.

Slavyansky Bazaar

Held in the old Russian city of Vitsebsk (in modern Belarus), this festival (www.festival.vitebsk.by/en; p93) is one of the biggest cultural events in the former Soviet Union, featuring theatrical performances, music concerts and exhibits from all over the Slavic world.

Karlovy Vary International Film Festival

The region's own version of Cannes is a far smaller affair than its French cousin, but its reputation grows each year. The festival (www.kviff.com; p304) is held in one of the most beautiful spa towns in the Bohemian Czech Republic, Karlovy Vary, and hundreds of new releases make up the program each year.

Kavarna Rock Fest

Metalheads should make a beeline for Bulgaria's Kaliakra Rock Fest in Kavarna (www.kaliakrarockfest.com, in Bulgarian; p190) to kickstart the Black Sea summer with well-known rock and heavy metal acts.

Ivana Kupala

On 7 July, Ukraine's exhilarating pagan celebration of midsummer involves fire jumping, maypole dancing, fortune telling, wreath floating and strong overtones of sex. Head for the countryside for the real deal.

International Music Festival

Thousands of music lovers congregate in Český Krumlov, Czech Republic, for classical concerts, as well as jazz, rock and folk music, at this impressive month-long July festival (www.festivalkrumlov.cz), which often stretches into August too.

Medieval Festival of the Arts

During July the beautiful Romanian city of Sighişoara hosts open-air concerts, parades and ceremonies, all glorifying medieval Transylvania and taking the town back to its fascinating 12th-century origins.

Ohrid Summer Festival

The month-long Ohrid Summer Festival (www.ohridsummer.com.mk) comprises a wealth of performances ranging from classical, opera and rock acts to theatre and literature, all celebrating Macedonian culture. The best events are held in the town's magical open-air Roman theatre.

 Sarajevo Film Festival

This globally acclaimed festival (www.sff.ba) that grew out of the ruins of the '90s civil war screens commercial and art-house movies side by side in the Bosnian capital.

August

It's easy enough to get away from the crowds and expense, even at summer's height. There's a huge amount to see and do in August, and the weather – from the Baltic coast to the Adriatic – is hot, hot, hot!

Trumpeting Insanity in Serbia

Guča's Dragačevo Trumpet Assembly (www.guca.rs; p852) is one of the most exciting and bizarre events in all of Eastern Europe. Hundreds of thousands of revellers descend on the small Serbian town of Guča to damage their eardrums, livers and sanity over four cacophonous days of revelry.

Sziget Music Festival

A week-long, great-value music festival (www.sziget. hu) held all over Budapest, Sziget features bands from around the world playing at more than 60 venues.

 Don Cento Jazz Festival

A newish jazz event in Kaliningrad, Russia, that is already attracting jazz performers from across Europe, the Don Cento Jazz Festival (www.jazzfestival.ru) is held over three days across the city, with nightclub jams, big concerts and even free open-air sessions.

September

The summer crowds have dropped off somewhat, and prices are no longer sky high, but the great weather remains across the entire region, making September a fantastic time to head for Eastern Europe.

Dance with Slovenian Cows

This Slovenian mid-September weekend of folk dancing, music, eating and drinking in Bohinj marks the return of the cows from their high pastures to the valleys in typically ebullient Balkan style.

Dvořák Autumn

This festival (www. kso.kso.cz) of classical music honours the work of the Czech Republic's favourite composer, Antonín Dvořák. The event is held over three weeks in the spa town of Karlovy Vary.

Adventure Race Montenegro

A two-day mid-September fundraising challenge (www. adventureracemontenegro. com; p585) that incorporates kayaking, mountain biking, hiking and orien-

teering. There's also a one-day event held a week later.

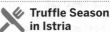 Truffle Season in Istria

Hunt for the prized white truffles that grow in the Croatian forests around Motovun and Buzet in Istria's interior before cooking up the tasty, smelly fungus and eating it in risottos, pastas and omelettes. The season lasts until January.

October

October is still wonderfully warm in the Balkans but already getting cold in the north. Prices remain low, and crowds lessen with each passing day, making it a good time to visit.

Wine Festival

Winemakers, wine tasting, wine buying and wine-enriched folkloric performances in Moldova draw oenophiles and anyone that wants to take advantage of the 10-day visa-free regime Moldova introduces during the festival dates.

November

The days are short and the weather is cold, but you'll have most of Eastern Europe's attractions all to yourself and accommodation is cheap. Head south to the Balkans if you want any chance of sunshine, though!

Sarajevo International Jazz Festival

Held in Sarajevo in early November, this festival (www.jazzfest.ba) showcases local and international jazz musicians.

St Martin's Day Festival

This annual wine festival is held in Zagreb to celebrate the end of the grape harvest as Croatian wineries begin the crushing process. Expect lots of wine, good food and a generally upbeat mood.

December

December is a magical time to visit Eastern Europe: Christmas

decorations brighten up the dark streets and, despite the cold across much of the region, as long as you avoid Christmas and New Year's Eve themselves, prices remain surprisingly low.

Tirana International Film Festival

Each December Tirana holds its annual short and feature film festival (www.tiranafilmfest.com), the only one of its kind in tiny Albania. It's a great way to take stock of Eastern European film-making.

Christmas Markets

Throughout December Eastern Europe heaves with German-style Christmas markets. You'll find these in many cities in the region, though we recommend Bratislava's for its Slovakian charm and beautiful setting – see p865.

 Christmas

Christmas is celebrated in different ways in Eastern Europe: most countries celebrate on Christmas Eve (24 December) with an evening meal and midnight mass. In Russia, Ukraine and Belarus, Christmas falls in January, as per the Gregorian calendar.

 New Year's Eve

Even back when communist officials frowned on Christmas, New Year's Eve remained a big holiday in Eastern Europe. Join the party wherever you are and see in the new year with locals.

itineraries

Whether you've got six days or 60, these itineraries provide a starting point for the trip of a lifetime. Want more inspiration? Head online to lonelyplanet. com/thorntree to chat with other travellers.

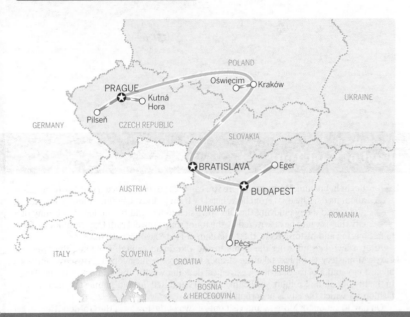

Two Weeks
Essential Eastern Europe

Begin your trip in **Prague**, spending several days absorbing the Old Town, Lesser Side and the magnificent Prague Castle. Don't miss nearby towns such as beer lovers' mecca **Pilzeň** and beautiful **Kutná Hora**.

On day five head by train into Poland and regal **Kraków**, with its gobsmacking Old Town and the vast Rynek Główny. Spending three nights here allows you to get to know the Wawel Castle complex, off-beat Kazimierz and a day trip to harrowing **Oświęcim** (Auschwitz).

On day eight head south to Slovakia, where you'll pass through magnificent scenery in the High Tatras before arriving in **Bratislava**, with its grand castle and wonderful Danube views.

On day 10 take a boat down the Danube to **Budapest**, where you can spend hours in luxurious sulphur baths, explore the famous coffee houses and take in the dazzling art and architecture of the forward-looking Hungarian capital. From here visit the Hungarian countryside – try the baroque city of **Eger**, or **Pécs**, full of relics from the Turkish occupation.

East of East Tour

> Begin in bustling **Warsaw**, where you can see the reconstructed Old Town and learn about its dark history. From here, head by train to **Lviv**, Ukraine's most beautiful city, and spend a day enjoying the Old Town's churches and the undeniable beauty of a city that is yet to be discovered by the tour group crowd. From Lviv, continue by train to fascinating and historic **Kyiv**, the Jerusalem of East Slavonic culture.

After a few days enjoying the sights in the Ukrainian capital, including the awesome Caves Monastery Complex, take the sleeper train to the megalopolis **Moscow**, Europe's biggest city and a place of striking extremes, dazzling wealth and gridlocked traffic. Drink in the history of the Kremlin, see Lenin, St Basil's and Red Sq, and sample the nightlife and fashion for which the city is now rightly famous.

On day 10 get out of Moscow and visit one or two of the towns in the **Golden Ring** to get a sense of the Russian countryside. Next on the agenda is the beautiful baroque and neoclassical architecture of mind-blowing **St Petersburg**. You can easily spend three or four days in the city itself, although there are abundant sights outside it as well, such as the tsarist palaces at **Petrodvorets** or Tsarskoye Selo.

From Russia take the train to Estonia's magical capital where you can soak up the Old Town of medieval **Tallinn** and the rural delights of **Saaremaa** before heading south to Latvia. The Latvian capital **Rīga** boasts Europe's finest collection of art nouveau architecture and is a delightful place to spend a few days. Latvia has plenty of other highlights to offer though, such as the medieval castles and caves of **Sigulda** and the breathtaking Baltic coastline around **Ventspils**. Finally, cross into Lithuania, where a couple of nights in charming **Vilnius** will reveal the Baltic's least known and most underrated capital. From Vilnius make a trip to the huge sand dunes and fragile ecological environment of the amazing **Curonian Spit.** Those who have made the effort to get a visa can then take the train to the isolated republic of Belarus and its Stalinist-style capital **Minsk** before re-entering Poland and heading back to Warsaw.

Four Weeks
The Balkans & Beyond

> Begin in lively little Slovenia, with a cheap flight to charming **Ljubljana**. Indulge in superb scenery and adrenaline-rush mountain sports in the **Julian Alps** before heading south to the Croatian coast and working your way through the beaches along the **Dalmatian coast**. Stop in **Dubrovnik** to explore the Old Town, its vast ramparts and the surrounding islands, which shouldn't be missed. Take a side trip to Bosnia – perhaps a day trip to **Mostar** to see the legendary bridge and the interesting multiethnic community that has enjoyed rejuvenation since the Balkan War, or a night or two in the bustling capital of **Sarajevo**.

Then continue south into Montenegro, one of Europe's youngest countries. Visit the historic walled city of **Kotor**, see the wonderful natural fjord and surrounding hills, and enjoy some of the country's beautiful beaches around **Sveti Stefan** before heading into Albania.

From the northern city of **Shkodra** take a bus straight on to **Tirana**, a mountain-shrouded ramshackle capital on the rise. Make an excursion to historic **Kruja** and the gorgeous Unesco-heritage town of **Berat** before taking a bus through the mountains into little-explored Macedonia, ending up in beautiful **Ohrid**. Spend at least two days here, enjoying the wonderful monastery and swimming in the eponymous lake. Make your way to **Skopje**, Macedonia's fun capital, from where you can head overland into Bulgaria.

Your obvious first stop is **Sofia**, one of Europe's best value capitals and a little known gem. But there's more good stuff to come once you continue east to **Veliko Târnovo**, the awesome ancient capital and university town with a dramatic setting over a fast-flowing river. From here it's an easy bus to the beach at **Varna**, complete with marvellous museums, Roman ruins and open-air nightclubs.

Finally plunge into Romania. Start off in **Bucharest** for excellent food and nightlife and a taste of megalomaniac architecture before heading to mythic Transylvania. Use **Cluj-Napoca** as your base for visiting the region of Maramureş, then head for the medieval superlatives of **Sibiu** and **Braşov** before heading on to the **Danube Delta**, where you can ogle birds, dine on fish and enjoy some of the quietest beaches in Europe.

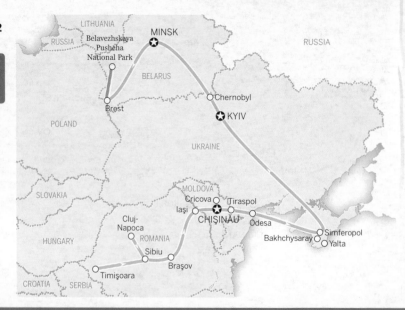

Four Weeks
On The Edge

Begin with a cheap flight from Western Europe to **Timişoara** or **Cluj-Napoca** before getting medieval in **Sibiu** and/or **Braşov** and making a run to lively **Iaşi**, near the Moldovan border.

Here the real adventure starts – cross into Moldova and head for the entertaining capital, **Chişinău**, where partying is a way of life and the excellent local wine is plentiful and cheap, including that from the must-visit vineyards of **Cricova**. Travel into Transdniestr, a country that doesn't officially exist and where the clock has resolutely stopped somewhere in the mid-1980s. In the fascinating 'capital' **Tiraspol** you'll feel as if time has stood still for two decades.

Entering Ukraine, make a beeline for the ethnic melting pot at **Odesa** and enjoy the relaxed pace of the Black Sea and its raucous nightlife during the summer months. If you want to check out the Crimean peninsula, head to **Simferopol**, the area's transport hub. From here you can make a loop around the peninsula to admire the mountainous landscapes, the tsarist-era palaces near **Yalta**, and the fantastic Khan's Palace and monastery at **Bakhchysaray**.

When you have had your fill of sun and sea, head north to **Kyiv**, which demands several days' attention. This modern capital city is at once the ancient seat of Slavic and Orthodox culture and a modern, industrial Soviet city. Don't miss the Caves Monastery Complex and St Sophia's Cathedral. If you dare, book a tour to **Chernobyl**, and become one of the few people in the world to visit the towns nearby to the ill-fated reactor No 4.

The final stop on this tour through the most-remote parts of the region is Belarus, Europe's so-called 'last dictatorship'. Have a blast in monolithic **Minsk** and find a surprising amount going on in a city dominated by huge Stalinist avenues and Soviet memorials. Heading west, stop at **Brest** on the border and use it as a base to visit **Belavezhskaya Pushcha National Park** where you'll be able to see Europe's largest mammal, the zoobr (European bison) as well as a host of other wild beauties before crossing back into the EU.

Four Weeks
The Ionian to the Baltic

This trip takes you from Eastern Europe's south to its northern tip. Arrive in mountainous Albania by ferry from Corfu at the busy port of **Saranda**, then stay the night and try to see the glorious ruins of Butrint right on the Greek border before travelling up the **Ionian Coast** to **Tirana**, perhaps via **Gjirokastra** or **Berat**, two of Albania's loveliest old towns. Spend a day or two exploring the Albanian capital before taking the bus to **Shkodra** and travelling on to Montenegro.

Don't miss lovely **Kotor** and its spectacular setting and old town before picking up an overnight sleeper train to Belgrade from **Bar**. The scenery en route is spectacular, especially around the **Morača Canyon**.

Arriving the next morning in **Belgrade** you'll be struck by how vibrant and rejuvenated the Serbian capital is – it's definitely worth giving it a couple of days. Continue north to **Novi Sad** – if you come in July you might catch the EXIT Festival, held annually in the city's historic hilltop fortress.

Cross into Hungary at pretty **Szeged** and head for **Lake Balaton** for some sublime swimming. Keep surging north into Slovakia, aiming for plucky traveller favourite **Bratislava**, where it's perfectly acceptable to kick back and enjoy the good food and nightlife for a few days before going on to the incredible scenery of **Slovenský Raj National Park**.

Crossing the Tatra Mountains into Poland, travel via **Kraków** to unsung gem **Wrocław**, spending a few days in both before dropping in on beautifully restored **Poznań**. From here, the Baltic is yours. Try any of the towns along the coast: Hel and **Łeba** are both recommended for beaches, wildlife and water sports; **Malbork** is famed for Europe's biggest Gothic castle; while bustling Hanseatic **Gdańsk** (formerly the German Free City of Danzig) is the thriving port city where WWII broke out and Solidarity was born. Next up is the plucky Russian Baltic enclave of **Kaliningrad** – remember to have sorted your visa ahead of time! – spend some time in the decidedly German city, and venture out to see the **Curonian Spit** as well, before flying on to **St Petersburg**, the most northern city in this book, for several days spent in Eastern Europe's most beautiful architectural ensemble.

Two Weeks
Baltic Blast

This trip along the Baltic coast takes you through four very different countries and across a region that few travellers ever get to know beyond the universally loved capital cities of Tallinn, Rīga and Vilnius. Beginning in the gloriously beautiful Baltic city of **St Petersburg** for three nights, see the Hermitage, the Admiralty and vast Nevsky Prospekt's crumbling mansions and palatial residences. For a real palace, head to the superbly restored out-of-town palace of Peter the Great at **Petrodvorets**, itself positioned with glorious views over the Baltic. Travel to **Narva**, walking across the long bridge connecting Russia and Estonia and getting great views of the castle. Carry on to the Estonian capital **Tallinn** for two days and wander the charmingly chocolate box streets of the 14th and 15th century Old Town before heading to the beautiful, remote and pine-forest-clad island of **Saaremaa** for a day or two's exploration. From Saaremaa, head to the inviting Estonian beach resort of **Pärnu** for a slice of Eastern European holiday making (think mud baths, Bacchanalian youth and golden-sand beaches) before continuing south into Latvia. Stop off in cheerful, castle-rich **Sigulda** and spend a day or two walking in tranquil landscapes and thick forests of the **Gauja National Park** before going to **Rīga** for a couple of nights. Latvia's delightful capital, where you can soak up the fantastic architecture, the Old Town and friendly atmosphere, has plenty to keep you interested for several days. Lithuania is next up – and it greets you straight away with its astounding hill of crosses in **Šiauliai**, a must-see even if there's no reason to dawdle. Charming university town **Kaunas** is Lithuania's second city and boasts a leafy old centre and friendly locals, as well as being just a short distance away from the chilling Ninth Fort concentration camp. Finally, end your journey in beautiful **Vilnius**, the country's crowning glory, which boasts the biggest Old Town in the Baltic and is still relatively undiscovered by tour groups. To add to its quirky kudos, don't miss the Frank Zappa memorial or the wonderfully idiosyncratic Užupis Republic, a kernal of counter culture at the city's heart.

Two Weeks
Eastern Europe 101

Only got two weeks and want to see the most you can in such a limited time? This itinerary is for you. Start off by flying to the Polish capital **Warsaw** for one night, seeing the beautifully restored Old Town and eating delicious *pierogi* before taking the train south to **Kraków** for two nights, giving you time to see the Old Town, Wawel Castle and Kazimierz and to do a day trip to **Oświęcim** (Auschwitz) before taking the overnight train to **Prague** for two days of intensive sightseeing – Prague Castle, Charles Bridge, wandering the Malá Strana and the Old Town and tasting genuine Czech Beer in a local brewery. Take another overnight train to **Budapest** for two nights, soak in the glorious Gellért Spa, take a cruise on the Danube, see the magnificent Hungarian Parliament building and wander Castle Hill before yet another overnight train to Romania's much underrated capital, **Bucharest**, where with a one-night stay you can cover the main sights including the amazing Palace of Parliament, wander the small historic centre, and pick up a sense of the city's energy in its bars and clubs. Continue by train to wonderful and much-overlooked **Veliko Târnovo** in Northern Bulgaria for one night, a stunning and unusually located university town and a far more 'everyday' Eastern European town than most national capitals. While here, find the time to see the ancient fortress (and stick around for the nightly summer light show) before finishing up your two weeks by taking the train to **Sofia** for two last nights that will give you a taste of the plucky Bulgarian capital, including the wonderful golden-domed **Alexander Memorial Church**. On your last day take a day trip through the Rila Mountains to the unmissable **Rila Monastery**, the country's holiest site and one of the most important monasteries in Eastern Europe. From here you can fly out of Sofia or continue to bigger air hubs such as nearby Athens and İstanbul to get a flight home.

countries at a glance

Eastern Europe can appear overwhelming at first glance; after all, just two decades ago there were a mere eight countries in a space that today contains 21 independent nations. While the big hitters such as Russia, Poland, the Czech Republic and Romania may need little introduction, below we've summed up each country in one sentence to give you an initial idea of what there is to do there, although of course each place offers far more than we can sum up here. Whether you spend your entire trip in one country or travel between a dozen, you'll be amazed by the sheer variety you'll encounter.

Albania

Beaches ✓✓
Scenery ✓✓✓
Culture ✓✓

Once isolated Albania has some of the last undeveloped coastline on the Mediterranean, its mountains are some of Europe's most spectacular, and the Koman ferry is possibly the region's most beautiful boat ride.
p43

Belarus

History ✓✓
Architecture ✓✓
Nature ✓✓

If communist architecture is your thing, look no further than Minsk, which was rebuilt from rubble after WWII. Belarus also has two superb national parks – the Belavezhskaya Pushcha and the 'lungs of Europe', the Pripyatsky National Park.
p75

Bosnia & Hercegovina

Scenery ✓✓
Adventure Holidays ✓✓✓
History ✓✓

One of the best-known European destinations for active holidays, Bosnia is a great place for kayaking, skiing, hiking and mountain biking. With its mixed Muslim and Christian heritage, it's also a fascinating blend of cultures.
p103

Bulgaria

Hiking ✓✓✓
Architecture ✓✓
Beaches ✓✓

With six mountain ranges within its borders, Bulgaria is a walker's fantasy, while you'll find the best Black Sea beaches on its sandy coastline, and its ancient towns packed full of history.
p147

Croatia

Cuisine ✓✓
Architecture ✓✓✓
Scenery ✓✓✓

A dazzling coastline and thousands of islands, Dubrovnik's legendary Old Town, Diocletian's Palace in Split, the extraordinary Plitvice Lakes National Park and Istria's foodie offerings – you're spoilt for choice in Croatia.
p207

Czech Republic

Old Towns ✓✓✓
Scenery ✓✓
Beer ✓✓✓

Prague's beautiful Old Town is just the tip of the iceberg – Bohemia enjoys spectacular scenery and nowhere else in the world has as much cachet among beer lovers as the breweries in the Czech Republic.
p273

Estonia

Islands & Coastline ✓✓
Architecture ✓✓✓
Culture ✓✓

Tallinn's Old Town is the medieval jewel of Estonia, and walking its narrow streets is like strolling back to the 14th century. With an incredible 1521 islands studding its coastline, Estonia also offers great beaches.
p343

Hungary

Architecture ✓✓
Partying ✓✓✓
Wine ✓✓

Budapest is one of Eastern Europe's most happening party towns, with Pest coming alive in the summer months. Oenophiles will love touring Tokay or tasting Bull's Blood wine in the Valley of Beautiful Women near Eger.
p383

Kosovo

Ottoman Architecture ✓
Monasteries ✓✓
Scenery ✓

Check out Europe's newest and most controversial country. Kosovo's Serbian monasteries date back to the 1300s and have outstanding frescos, while the attractive hills around Peja are ideal for hiking and skiing as well.
p451

Latvia

Architecture ✓✓✓
Castles ✓✓
History ✓✓

With over 750 buildings in Rīga alone, Latvia has the largest collection of art nouveau facades in the world. Crumbling castle ruins abound throughout the pine-peppered terrain, each a testament to a forgotten kingdom.
p462

Lithuania

Scenery ✓✓
Offbeat Attractions ✓✓
Castles ✓✓✓

The Curonian Spit is a wondrous mixture of pine forest and giant sand dunes: Norway meets the Sahara desert. Don't miss Vilnius' Upper Castle, or Trakai Castle, which sits picturesquely in the middle of lake.
p492

Macedonia

Cuisine ✓
Churches ✓✓
Lakes ✓

Macedonia grows arguably the finest sweet peppers in the world, its Byzantine churches contain some of the most important medieval art in the Balkans, and its lakes include Lake Ohrid, a beautiful spot for a dip.
p527

Moldova

Wine ✓✓
Cave Monasteries ✓✓✓
Breakaway Republics ✓✓

Among tiny Moldova's attractions are the breathtaking cave monasteries of Orheiul Vechi, an exceptional wine industry centred on the labyrinthine cellars at Cricova and Mileştii Mici, and the breakaway regions of Transdniestr and Gagauzia.
p557

Montenegro

Scenery ✓✓✓
Historic Sites ✓✓
Outdoor Pursuits ✓✓

Montenegro crams an awful lot into a very small space: jagged mountains, sheer-walled river canyons, extreme sports, long sandy beaches and the spectacular Bay of Kotor, where the mountains dip their toes into the sea.
p581

Poland

History ✓✓✓
Architecture ✓✓✓
Scenery ✓✓

From the southern Tatras to the Great Masurian Lakes of the north, Poland is one of Eastern Europe's most spectacular countries. History and architecture buffs will be similarly overwhelmed by the sheer variety here.
p607

Romania

Mountains ✓✓✓
Saxon Villages ✓✓
Monasteries ✓✓✓

The Carpathian Mountains offer some of Europe's finest hiking, Southern Transylvania's Saxon villages beckon with ancient churches, and the monasteries of Southern Bucovina are among Europe's most outstanding artistic achievements.
p692

Russia

History ✓✓✓
Architecture ✓✓
Art ✓✓✓

Brutal, fascinating, bizarre – there's no rivalling Russia for having a dramatic past. The medieval Kremlin, the Winter Palace and Lenin's Tomb all beg for your attention, while great art collections await in Moscow and St Petersburg.
p769

Serbia

People ✓✓✓
Food ✓✓
Partying ✓✓✓

Between Belgrade's legendary nightclubs and frenetic festivals like Novi Sad's EXIT and Guča's Dragačevo Trumpet Assembly, Serbia is a land of rich hospitality, great food and passionate revelry. Ditch the calorie counting and dig in!
p829

Slovakia

Hiking ✓✓✓
Old Towns ✓✓
Castles ✓✓

From the rocky High Tatra peaks to its lower forested mountain ranges, Slovakia is riddled with hiking trails, hundreds of fortress ruins dot the countryside and medieval walls surround well-preserved old town centres.
p859

Slovenia

Scenery ✓✓✓
Outdoor Sports ✓✓✓
Wine ✓✓

Even serial visitors to Slovenia regularly stop and stare, mesmerised by the sheer beauty of this tiny country. Don't miss Mt Triglav, Vršič Pass, Lake Bled, the Karst, or the Postojna and Škocjan caves.
p907

Ukraine

Monasteries ✓✓
Scenery ✓✓
Extreme Tourism ✓✓✓

Kyiv overflows with ancient gold-domed churches and the huge Caves Monastery complex, which is the city's top experience. Elsewhere the Crimea's craggy mountain range is the biggest draw.
p946

Look out for these icons:

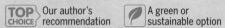

| TOP CHOICE | Our author's recommendation | 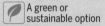 A green or sustainable option | FREE | No payment required |

See the Index for a full list of destinations covered in this book.

On the Road

Albania

Includes »

Best Places to Stay

» Berat Backpackers (p59)
» B&B Tedeschini (p56)
» Hotel Kalemi (p66)

Best Places to Eat

» Kujtimi (p66)
» Era (p50)
» Tradita G+T (p54)

Why Go?

Alps sprout in the background, plains and lakes surround the central mountain ranges, and coastal areas provide the traveller to Albania (or Shqipëria, as the locals call it) with dramatically different cultural and geographical landscapes. City slickers can down coffee in busy, always surprising Tirana before heading to an exhibition or nightclub.

After years of government-enforced isolation, Albanians welcome travellers with sincere hospitality. Upgraded roads swirl past the new houses and bar/restaurant/hotel developments that demonstrate the country's newfound prosperity.

August sees quiet seaside spots morph into loud disco-laden towns where every day is a thumping weekend. Head north and you might spot locals in traditional dress, sworn virgins and shepherds guiding flocks in the otherwise inhospitable mountains.

Albania is unforgettable: donkeys tethered to concrete bunkers, houses crawling up each other to reach the hilltops in Berat and Gjirokastra, and isolated beaches.

When to Go
Tirana

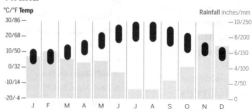

June Enjoy the Mediterranean climate and deserted beaches.

August Beaches are packed and overseas-based Albanians return to holiday with their families.

December See features and shorts at the Tirana Film Festival. Snowshoe to Theth.

Fast Facts

» **Area** 28,748 sq km
» **Capital** Tirana
» **Telephone country code** 355
» **Emergency** police 129, fire 128, ambulance 127

Exchange Rates

Australia	A$1	102.5 lekë
Canada	C$1	101.8 lekë
euro	€1	141.8 lekë
Japan	¥100	116.5 lekë
New Zealand	NZ$1	77.1 lekë
UK	UK£1	159.3 lekë
USA	US$1	97.9 lekë

Set Your Budget

» **Budget hotel** €12-15 per person
» **Two-course meal** €10
» **Museum entrance** €1-3
» **Local beer** €1.50
» **City transport ticket** 30 lekë

Resources

» **Albania-Hotel** (www. albania-hotel.com)
» **Balkanology** (www.balkanology.com/albania)
» **National Tourist Organisation** (www.albaniantourism.com)

Connections

Albania has daily bus connections with Kosovo, Montenegro, Macedonia, Italy (bus and ferry) and Thessaloniki and Athens in Greece. Albania's Saranda is a short ferry trip from Greece's Corfu. Travellers heading south from Croatia can pass through Montenegro to Shkodra (via Ulcinj), and can loop the country before heading into Macedonia via Pogradec or Kosovo via the Lake Koman ferry or new superfast Albania–Kosovo highway.

ITINERARIES

Three Days

Drink frappé at Tirana's trendy Blloku cafes, check oput the museum and art gallery, then spend the night dancing in packed nightclubs. On day two, head up the Djati Express and dine on roast lamb in the clean mountain air of Mt Djati National Park. Return to Tirana in time for the two-hour trip to the Ottoman-era town of Berat. Stay in a character-filled hotel or hostel in the town's old quarters. On day three, Kruja is a good detour on the way to the airport; check out one of the country's best ethnographic museums and buy souvenirs in its authentic little bazaar.

One Week

Spend a day in Tirana, head south to Berat for a few days, then pass through the scenic Llogaraja Pass. Take on beachside Drymades or Jal before making a pit stop at Saranda to prepare for a stroll around Butrint's ruins. Pause at the Blue Eye Spring en route to the Ottoman-era town of Gjirokastra.

Essential Food & Drink

» **Byrek** Pastry with cheese or meat
» **Fergesë** Baked peppers, egg and cheese and occasionally meat
» **Midhje** Wild or farmed mussels, often served fried
» **Paçë Koke** Sheep's head soup usually served for breakfast
» **Qofta** Flat or cylindrical minced-meat rissoles
» **Sufllaqë** Doner kebab
» **Tavë** Meat baked with cheese and egg
» **Konjak** Local brandy
» **Raki** Popular spirit made from grapes
» **Raki mani** Spirit made from mulberries

MONTENEGRO

Peja

Plav

KOSOVO

Valbonë

Theth ⑤
Bajram Curri
Valbonë National Park
Theth National Park
Fierzë
Drin
Lake Fierza

Lake Skadar
Lake Koman
Puka
Kukës
E851

E762
Shkodra
Koman
E851

Tetovo
E65
E65

Lura National Park
Rreshen
Peshkopia
Mavrovo National Park

Milot
E851
MACEDONIA
Drin River
E65

Qafe Shtama National Park
Kruja
Bulqiza
Zall Gjocaj National Park
E65
Mt Dajti National Park
① Tirana

Durrës
E852
E852
Ohrid
Lake Ohrid

Kavaja
E853
Elbasan
Lake Prespa

Divjaka National Park
Shkumbini
Lake Prespa National Park

Lushnja
E853
Kuçova
Mt Tomorri National Park
Korça
Apollonia Fier
Berat ②
▲ ⛰ Mt Tomorri (2415m)
Drenova National Park

Vjosa River
Sazan
Vlora
Këlcyra

Karaburun Peninsula
E853

Llogaraja Pass National Park
Dhërmi
Gjirokastra ②
E90

Drymades ③ Vuno
Himara
Jal
Livadhi
Blue Eye Spring
GREECE

E853
Saranda
Mesopotamia

Ksamil
Ioannina

Butrint National Park ④
Corfu
Kerkira

IONIAN SEA
GREECE

N
0 ___ 40 km
0 ___ 20 miles

TIRANA

☑04 / POP 600,000

Lively, colourful Tirana has changed beyond belief in the last decade from the dull, grey city it once was (see pre-'90s Albanian movies for a glimpse). It's amazing what a lick of paint can do – it covers one ugly tower block with horizontal orange and red stripes, another with concentric pink and purple circles, and plants perspective-fooling cubes on its neighbour.

Trendy Blloku buzzes with well-dressed *nouvelle bourgeoisie* hanging out in bars or zipping between boutiques. Quite where

their money comes from is the subject of much speculation in this economically deprived nation, but thankfully you don't need much of it to have a fun night out in the city's many bars and clubs.

The city's grand central boulevards are lined with fascinating relics of its Ottoman, Italian and communist past – from delicate minarets to loud socialist murals. Tirana's traffic does daily battle with both itself and pedestrians in a constant scene of unmitigated chaos. Loud, crazy, colourful, dusty – Tirana is simply fascinating.

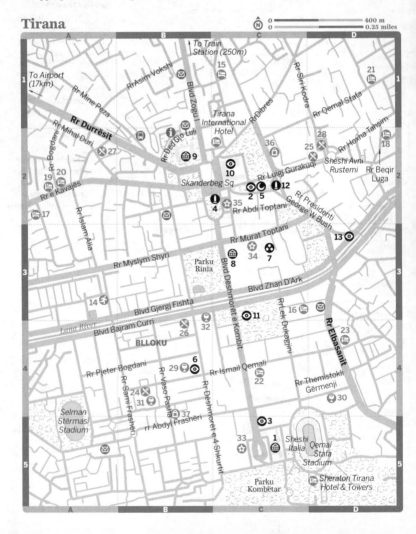

Tirana

◉ Sights & Activities

Running through Tirana is Blvd Zogu I, which becomes Dëshmorët e Kombit as it crosses the Lana River. At its northern end is Tirana's train station, head south and you're at the Tirana University. The main sites of interest are on or very close to this large boulevard, including, roughly halfway along, the orientation point of Skanderbeg Sq.

NORTH OF THE RIVER
Sheshi Skënderbej   SQUARE

Skanderbeg Sq is the best place to start witnessing Tirana's daily goings-on. Until it was pulled down by an angry mob in 1991, a 10m-high bronze statue of Enver Hoxha stood here, watching over a mainly car-free square. Now only the **equestrian statue of Skanderbeg** remains, deaf to the cacophony of screeching horns as cars four-lanes deep try to shove their way through the battlefield below. The square's recent redevelopment may turn the cacophony into a murmur.

Et'hem Bey Mosque   MOSQUE

(☺8am-noon) If you stop to examine Skanderbeg's emblematic goat's-head helmet, the minaret of the 1789–1823 Et'hem Bey Mosque will catch your eye. The small and elegant mosque is one of the oldest buildings left in the city, spared from destruction during the atheism campaign of the late '60s because of its status as a cultural monument. Take your shoes off to look inside at the beautifully painted dome.

Clock Tower   MONUMENT

(Kulla e Sahatit; Rr Luigi Gurakqi; admission 50 lekë; ☺9am-1pm Mon, 9am-1pm & 4-6pm Thu) Behind the mosque is the tall Clock Tower, which you can climb for views of the square. Further on, the socialist realist **Statue of the Unknown Partisan** attracts day labourers waiting for work, some with their own jackhammers – a fitting image of the precarious position of the postcommunist Albanian worker.

Palace of Culture   NOTABLE BUILDING

(Pallate Kulturës; Sheshi Skënderbej) To the east of Sheshi Skënderbej is the white stone Palace of Culture, which has a theatre, shops and art galleries. Construction of the palace began as a gift from the Soviet people in

Tirana

1960 and was completed in 1966, years after the 1961 Soviet-Albanian split.

National History Museum
ART MUSEUM

(Muzeu Historik Kombëtar; Sheshi Skënderbej; admission 200 lekë; ☉10am-5pm Tue-Sat, to 2pm Sun) On the northwestern side of the square is the National History Museum. This, the largest museum in Albania, holds most of the country's archaeological treasures and a replica of Skanderbeg's massive sword (how he held it, rode his horse and fought at the same time is a mystery). The mosaic mural entitled *Albania* adorning the museum's facade shows Albanians victorious and proud from Illyrian times through to WWII. There's a terrific exhibition of icons by Onufri, the renowned 16th-century master of colour. A sombre and controversial gallery devoted to the miseries of the communist regime was being updated at the time of research. Note there's no entry half an hour before closing time.

National Art Gallery
ART GALLERY

(Galeria Kombëtare e Arteve; Blvd Dëshmorët e Kombit; admission 200 lekë; ☉10am-5pm Tue-Sat, to 2pm Sun) The National Art Gallery is packed with bright Soviet realism paintings featuring smiling 'aren't we happy to be here!' workers in their various places of employ. No entry 20 minutes before closing time.

Fortress of Justinian
RUINS

(Rr Murat Toptani) If you turn up Rr Murat Toptani, behind the National Art Gallery, you'll pass the 6m-high walls of the Fortress of Justinian, the last remnants of a Byzantine-era castle. These days half a cinema/nightclub overflows over the top. East from here, on the corner of Rr Presidenti George W Bush and the Lana River, is Tanners' Bridge, a small 19th-century slippery-when-wet stone bridge.

FREE | Mosaic of Tirana
RUINS

(Rr Naim Frashëri 1; www.drkkt.com) It's a little tricky to find (it was only discovered itself in 1972) but this 3rd-century AD mosaic and other surviving relics are proof of an early ancient settlement in Tirana.

SOUTH OF THE RIVER

Pyramid
NOTABLE BUILDING

(Blvd Dëshmorët e Kombit) The Pyramid was designed by Enver Hoxha's daughter and son-in-law and completed in 1988. It was formerly the Enver Hoxha Museum, and more recently a convention centre and nightclub; its white-marble sides are slowly falling apart and it appears that the Pyramid's dis-

integration will be complete before renovation occurs.

Congress Building
NOTABLE BUILDING

(Blvd Dëshmorët e Kombit) Another creation of the former dictator's daughter and son-in-law is the square Congress Building, just a little down the boulevard from the Pyramid. Follow Rr Ismail Qemali two streets north of the Congress Building and enter the once totally forbidden but now totally trendy **Blloku** area. This former Communist Party elite hang-out was opened to the general public for the first time in 1991. Security still guards the **former residence of Enver Hoxha** (cnr Rr Dëshmorët e 4 Shkurtit & Rr Ismail Qemali).

Archaeological Museum
MUSEUM

(Muzeu Arkeologjik; Sheshi Nënë Tereza; admission €1; ☉10.30am-2.30pm Mon-Fri) The staff may bemoan the unrenovated condition of the Archaeological Museum, but it does manage to house an extensive collection of antiquities and provide information about recent archaeological digs.

Martyrs' Cemetery
CEMETERY

At the top of Rr Elbasanit is the Martyrs' Cemetery, where some 900 partisans who died in WWII are buried. The views over the city and surrounding mountains (including Mt Dajti to the east) are excellent, as is the sight of the immense, beautiful and strangely androgynous Mother Albania statue (1972). Hoxha was buried here in 1985 but in 1992 he was exhumed and interred in an ordinary graveyard elsewhere. Catch a municipal bus heading up Rr Elbasanit; the grand driveway is on your left.

🖝 Tours

Get off the beaten track or discover Albania's tourist attractions with the following Tirana-based tour companies:

Albanian Experience
TOURS

(☏2272 055; www.albania-experience.al; Sheraton Tirana Hotel, Sheshi Italia; ☉8.30am-7pm Mon-Fri, 8.30am-5pm Sat) Organises tours of Albania with knowledgeable guides.

Outdoor Albania
TOURS

(☏2227 121; www.outdooralbania.com; Metropol Bldg, Rr Sami Frashëri; ☉9am-5pm Mon-Fri) Excellent trailblazing adventure tour agency offering hiking, rafting, snowshoeing, sea and white-water kayaking and, in summer, hikes through the Alps.

Festivals & Events

Tirana International Film Festival CINEMA
(www.tiranafilmfest.com) This festival is held each December and features both short and feature films from its international competition winners, as well as new cinematic work from Albanian filmmakers.

🛏 Sleeping

Tirana Backpacker Hostel HOSTEL €
(☏068 2167 357; www.tiranahostel.com; Rr Elbasanit 85; dm €12; @) Albania's first hostel opened in 2005 in a 70-year-old villa close to the city centre. Its 25 beds are spread over four rooms and its bathrooms have great showers. It has big balconies, a garden and a cosy outdoor kitchen. Helpful managers can link you in to their summer hostel in Vuno (p62) and Hostel 2, which is also in Tirana.

Milingona HOSTEL €
(☏069 2260 775, 069 2049 836; www.milingona hostel.com; Rr Qemal Stafa 277; dm €12; @) Run by uber-enthusiastic and multilingual sisters Zhujeta and Rozana, Milingona (meaning 'ant') is clean and homey, with a 'never going to leave' terrace up top which, thanks to the sisters' local musical connections, occasionally doubles as a music venue. There's no breakfast but there is an excellent kitchen for self-caterers. They offer bike rental and tours of Tirana, and they'll meet you in Tirana when you arrive.

Hostel Albania HOSTEL €
(☏067 2783 798; www.hostel-albania.com; Rr Beqir Luga 56; dm €11-13; 🅰@🛜) This hostel has small four- and six-person dorms, though the basement's 14-bed dorm (€11) is the coolest spot in summer and dividers hide the fact that there are so many bunks down there. There's room for a couple of tents (€7 per person). Zen space is in the outdoor shoes-off oriental lounge, and a filling breakfast with filter coffee is included. Great information about the local art scene can be found here.

Green House BOUTIQUE HOTEL €€€
(☏2222 632; www.greenhouse.al; Rr Jul Varibova 6; s/d €85/110; 🅰🛜) In a cool spot in Tirana sits this modern hotel with downlit, modern rooms that scream celebrity. Its restaurant is a modern and friendly expat hang-out with a varied menu and a long wine list. It looks up at one of Tirana's quirkiest buildings.

Hotel Nirvana HOTEL €€
(☏2235 270; Rr e Kavajës 96/2; s/d incl breakfast €60/80; 🅰@) With its ostentatious marble staircase and walls dripping with art (apparently this is nothing compared with the owner's house), this hotel may have delusions of grandeur, but thankfully the price remains reasonably humble and the staff are friendly and helpful. Free parking.

Pension Andrea PENSION €€
(☏069 2094 915; Rr Anton Harapi 103; s/d €25/30) Grandmother Gina runs this quiet pension with limited English but loads of enthusiasm. All rooms have TVs and air-con. There's a safe storage area for bicycles. From Rr Jeronim de Rada take the first right down the court; you'll find Gina through the gate on your right.

Freddy's Hostel HOTEL €
(☏068 2035 261, 2266 077; www.freddyshostel. com; Rr Bardhok Biba 75; dm/r €12/32) Freddy's isn't really a hostel (there's no communal area) but the clean, basic bunk-free rooms have lockers and come in different configurations. It's well signposted on a suburban street running parallel to Blvd Zogu I. Can also arrange long-term apartments.

Hotel Serenity HOTEL €€
(☏2267 152; Rr Bogdani 4; d €50; 🅰@) This simple villa-style hotel is in a quiet and central location. Rooms have tiled floors, minibars and TVs and offer excellent value.

Rogner Hotel Europapark Tirana HOTEL €€€
(☏2235 035; www.hotel-europapark.com; Blvd Dëshmorët e Kombit; s €150-180, d €170-200, ste €240-270; 🅰@🏊🛜) With an unbeatable location in the heart of the city, the Rogner is a peaceful oasis with a huge garden, tennis court and free wi-fi in the lobby as well as onsite banks, travel and car-rental agencies. The rooms are spacious and comfortable and have flat-screen TVs.

🍴 Eating

If you thought that cuisine in Tirana's restaurants might be monotonous or that eating out would be a downmarket experience, you were wrong.

Most of the eating and drinking action is at Blloku, a square of some 10 blocks of shops, restaurants, cafes and hotels situated one block west of Dëshmorët and along the Lana River in south Tirana.

TOP CHOICE **Era** TRADITIONAL €
(☏2266 662; Rr Ismail Qemali; mains from 200 lekë; ⏰11am-midnight) Serves traditional Albanian and Italian fare in the heart of Blloku. Be warned: it's hard to move on once you've

eaten here. It's also sometimes quite hard to get a seat. Does delivery and takeaway.

Oda
TRADITIONAL €€

(Rr Luigj Gurakuqi; meals 800 lekë) Bright flashing lights will guide you to this endearing little restaurant down a lane near Sheshi Avni Rustemi. It's up there in the traveller popularity stakes, and offers diners (if there's room) an authentic vibe, interesting Albanian dishes, and extra, extra-strong restaurant-distilled raki.

Pasticeri Française
BAKERY €

(Rr Dëshmorët e 4 Shkurtit 1; breakfast from 300 lekë; ☺8am-10pm; 🛜) It's no wonder this French cafe has a slimming advertisement hanging on its wall; its sweet pastries (and macarons) are irresistible.

Shpia Jon
TRADITIONAL €€

(Rr Kont Urani; meals 800 lekë; ☺7am-10pm, closed Sun) This new restaurant is hidden in a fairly suburban part of town but serves light and fluffy qofte and qifqi (meatballs and rice-balls) and piping-hot tavë (blend of cheese, peppers, tomato and eggplant with an egg). The serves are generous and, bar the moving wall of water in the courtyard, the house is decorated with tradition in mind.

Stephen Centre
CAFE €€

(Rr Hoxhim Tahsim 1; mains 500 lekë; ☺8am-8pm, closed Sun; 🛜) If you like your fries thin, your wi-fi free and the spirit Christian, here's the cafe for you. The accommodation upstairs comes in single-bed configurations (single/double €30/40).

🍷 Drinking

Most of Tirana's nightspots will have you partying on to the wee hours.

Radio
BAR

(Rr Ismail Qemali 29/1) Set back from the street is this very, very cool yet understated bar. Check out the owner's collection of antique Albania-made radios while sipping cocktails with groovy locals.

Charl's
BAR

(Rr Pjetër Bogdani 36) Charl's is a consistently popular bar with Tirana's students because of its ever-varying live music on the weekends, and disco/dance crowd-pleasers the rest of the time. The relaxed vibe is enhanced by the bar's open-air garden.

Kaon Beer Garden
BEER HALL

(Rr Assim Zeneli; ☺noon-1am) For those who hate the hassle of ordering beer after beer,

here's Kaon. Its popular 'keg-on-the-table' approach means it can be hard to get a table in the evening (queuing is normal), but once you get in, it's a pleasant outdoor bar and restaurant in the fancy villa-filled part of town. You won't go hungry; Albanian meals start from 200 lekë. Locally brewed beer comes in standard glasses, or tabletop two- and three-litre 'roxys'.

Sky Club Bar
BAR

(Sky Tower, Rr Dëshmorët e 4 Shkurtit) Start your night here for spectacular city views from the revolving bar on top of one of the highest buildings in town.

☆ Entertainment

There is a good choice of entertainment options in Tirana, in the form of bars, clubs, cinema, performances, exhibitions and even ten-pin bowling. For the low-down on events and exhibitions, check posters around town. For alternative events ask at Milingona hostel and Hostel Albania.

Folie
CLUB

(Rr Murat Toptani) This is where the big-name DJs come to play, and though the crowd can be a little more concerned with being seen than actually enjoying themselves, it's a great outdoor venue for a loud night out.

FREE Marubi Film & Multimedia School
CINEMA

(www.afmm.edu.al; Rr Aleksander Moisiu 76; ☺7pm Thu) Shows free art-house movies on Thursdays during the semester. It's near the last Kino Studio bus stop in the city's northeast.

Kinema Millennium 2
CINEMA

(www.ida-millennium.com; Rr Murat Toptani; tickets 300-500 lekë) Current-release movies that are cheaper the earlier in the day you go. At night it's a nightclub.

Theatre of Opera & Ballet
THEATRE

(☑2224 753; Sheshi Skënderbej; tickets from 300 lekë; ☺performances from 7pm, from 6pm winter) Check the listings and posters outside the theatre for performances.

Academy of Arts
THEATRE

(☑2257 237; www.artacademy.al; Sheshi Nënë Tereza) Classical music and other performances take place throughout the year in either the large indoor theatre or the small open-air faux-classical amphitheatre; both are part of the university. Prices vary according to the program.

🛍 Shopping

Souvenir shops on Rr Durrësit and Blvd Zogu I sell red Albanian flags, red T-shirts, red lighters, bunker ashtrays and lively traditional textiles.

Adrion International Bookshop   BOOKS
(Palace of Culture; ⊙9am-9pm Mon-Sat) The place to head for maps, guides and English-language books.

Market   FOOD & DRINK
(Sheshi Avni Rustemi) Buy fruit, vegetables and deli produce here; nearby Qemal Stafa has second-hand stalls selling everything from bicycles to bedheads.

 Natyral & Organik   FOOD & DRINK
(Rr Vaso Pasha) This tiny store in Blloku not only supports small village producers by stocking their organic olive oil, honey, herbs, tea, eggs, spices, raki and cognac (these make great gifts, but be aware of customs regulations in the countries you're travelling through); it's also a centre for environmental activism.

ℹ Information

Tirana has plenty of ATMs linked to international networks.

ABC Clinic (☏2234 105; www.abchealth.org; Rr Qemal Stafa 260; ⊙9am-1pm Mon, Wed & Fri, 9am-5pm Tue & Thu) Has English-speaking Christian doctors and a range of services, including brief (600 lekë) and normal (1200 lekë) consultations.

DHL (☏2268 755; Rr Ded Gjo Luli 6; ⊙8am-6pm Mon-Fri, 8am-noon Sat) Parcel-sending service.

Hygeia Hospital Tirana (☏2390 000; www.hygeia.al; Tirana-Durrës Hwy) This new Greek-owned private hospital has a 24-hour emergency department.

Post office (☏2228 262; Rr Çameria; ⊙8am-8pm) A shiny and clean oasis in a street jutting west from Sheshi Skënderbej. Smaller offices operate around the city.

Tirana in Your Pocket (www.inyourpocket.com) Has a local team of writers providing up-to-date coverage of Tirana. It can be downloaded free or bought at bookshops, hotels and some of the larger kiosks for 500 lekë.

Tirana tourist information centre (☏2223 313; Rr Ded Gjo Luli; www.tirana.gov.al; ⊙9am-7pm Mon-Fri, 9am-4pm Sat & Sun) Friendly staff make getting information easy at this new-to-Tirana government-run initiative.

ℹ Getting There & Around

A large number of agencies and airline offices sell air and bus tickets along Rr Mine Peza and Blvd Zogu 1, close to the National History Museum.

Air

Nënë Tereza International Airport (Mother Teresa Airport, Rinas airport, Tirana Airport; www.tirana-airport.com.al) is at Rinas, 17km northwest of Tirana. The new, glossy passenger terminal opened in 2006. The Rinas Express airport bus operates an hourly (6am to 6pm) service from Rr Mine Peza on the western side of the National History Museum for 250 lekë one way. The going taxi rate is €17. The airport is 20 minutes' drive away, but plan for possible traffic delays.

Bicycle

This was the main form of transport for Albanians until the early '90s, and it's having a comeback (cyclists seem to make more headway in Tirana's regular traffic snarls). Bike hire is available from several hostels.

Bus

You have the option of buses or *furgons* (minibuses). There is no official bus station in Tirana, though there's a makeshift bus station beside the train station where some buses drop passengers off and depart from. Confusingly, other buses and *furgons* depart from ever-changing places in and around the city, so check locally for the latest departure points. You can almost guarantee that taxi drivers will be in the know; however, you may have to dissuade them from taking you the whole way.

Furgons are usually slightly more expensive than buses and leave when full. Buses for Pristina in Kosovo (€10, five hours, three daily) leave from beside the museum on Blvd Zogu 1. To Macedonia, there are buses via Struga (€13, five hours) to Tetovo (€15, seven to eight hours) and Skopje (€20, eight hours) from the same spot. Buses to Ulcinj (€20) and Budva (€30) in Montenegro depart from 6am in front of the tourist information centre. If you're heading to Athens (€35, 15 hours), buses leave at around either 8am or 7pm from outside the travel agencies on Blvd Zogu 1.

Most bus services are fairly casual; you turn up and pay the driver. However, you can also buy tickets the day before from **Drita Travel and Tours** (☏2251 277; www.dritatravel.com; Rr Ded Gjo Luli) for services to Athens (8am, €35), Montenegro (6am, €30), Kosovo (6am, €10) and Macedonia (7.30pm, €20).

Car

Lumani Enterprise (☏04-2235 021; www.lumani-enterprise.com) is a local car-hire

DOMESTIC BUSES FROM TIRANA

DESTINATION	COST (LEKË)	DURATION (HR)	DISTANCE (KM)
Berat	400	2½	122
Durrës	100	1	38
Elbasan	300	1½	54
Fier	300	2	113
Gjirokastra	1000	7	232
Korça	800	4	181
Kruja	200	½	32
Pogradec	700	3½	150
Saranda	1200	7	284
Shkodra	400	2	116
Vlora	400	4	147

company. International companies in Tirana include the following (each also has an outlet at the airport):

Avis (☎2235 011, 068 2062 161; Rogner Hotel Europapark, Blvd Dëshmorët e Kombit)

Europcar (☎2227 888, 068 2093 908; Rr Durrësit 61)

Hertz (☎2255 028; Tirana Hotel International, Sheshi Skënderbej)

Sixt (☎2259 020, 068 2068 500; Rr e Kavajës 116)

Train

The run-down train station is at the northern end of Blvd Zogu I. Albania's trains range from sort of OK to very decrepit. Albanians travel by train if they can't afford to travel by bus. Seven trains daily go to Durrës (70 lekë, one hour, 36km). Trains also depart for Elbasan (190 lekë, four hours, 2.10pm), Pogradec (2km out of town; 295 lekë, eight hours, 5.30am), Shkodra (145 lekë, 3½ hours, 1.15pm) and Vlora (250 lekë, 5¾ hours, 4.30pm). Check timetables at the station the day before travelling. Purchase tickets before hopping on the train.

Taxi

Taxi stands dot the city, and taxis charge 300-400 lekë for a ride inside Tirana and 600 lekë at night and to destinations outside the city centre. Reach agreement on price with the driver before setting off. **Radio Taxi** (☎377 777), with 24-hour service, is particularly reliable.

AROUND TIRANA

Just 25km east of Tirana is **Mt Dajti National Park** (1611m). It is the most accessible mountain in the country, and many Tiranans go there to escape the city rush and

have a spit-roast lamb lunch. A sky-high, Austrian-made cable car, **Dajti Express** (www.dajtiekspres.com; 700 lekë return; ⊙9am-9pm Tue-Sun), takes 15 minutes to rise to (almost) the top. It's a scenic trip over bunkers, forest, farms and hilltops. Once there, you can avoid all the touts and their minibuses and take the opportunity to stroll through lovely, shady beech and pine forests. There are grassy picnic spots along the road to the right, but if you didn't pack a picnic, try the lamb roast and spectacular views from the wide terrace of the **Panorama Restaurant** (meals 800 lekë).

To get to the Dajti Express departure point, take the public bus from outside Tirana's Clock Tower to 'Porcelain' (30 lekë). From here, it's a 1.5km walk uphill, or you can wait for a free bus transfer. Taxis seem to charge what they want to the Dajti Express drop-off point, but the trip from Tirana should only cost 600 lekë. It's also possible to drive or cycle to the top.

NORTHERN ALBANIA

The northern Albanian landscape has rich wildlife, swamps and lagoons around Shkodra and Lezha and high mountains around Theth in the northeast (named the 'accursed mountains', Bjeshkët e Namuna, in Albanian). Blood feuds may occupy some locals' minds, but pose little risk to tourists (see the boxed text, p53).

Shkodra

📍 022 / POP 91.300

Shkodra (Shkodër), the traditional centre of the Gheg cultural region, is one of the oldest cities in Europe. Rozafa Fortress has stunning views, and the Marubi permanent photography exhibition in town is small but fascinating. A section of town has benefited from sensitive renovations of its historic buildings, and Shkodra's locals are more likely to ride a bicycle than drive a car.

Travellers pass through here on the way between Tirana and Ulcinj in Montenegro, but most use the town as a base for forays into the alpine areas of Theth and Valbonë and the isolated wonder of Lake Koman.

As the Ottoman Empire declined in the late 18th century, Shkodra became the centre of a semi-independent *pashalik* (region governed by a pasha, an Ottoman high official), which led to a blossoming of commerce and crafts. In 1913 Montenegro attempted to annex Shkodra (it succeeded in taking Ulcinj), a move not approved of by the international community, and the town changed hands often during WWI. Badly damaged by an earthquake in 1979, Shkodra was subsequently repaired and is Albania's fourth-largest town. The communist-era Hotel Rozafa in the town centre does little to welcome guests, but it makes a good landmark: restaurants, the information centre and most of the town's sights are close by.

Rozafa Fortress   CASTLE

(admission 200 lekë; ⊘8am-10pm) Three kilometres southwest of Shkodra, near the southern end of Lake Shkodra, is the Rozafa Fortress, founded by the Illyrians in antiquity and rebuilt much later by the Venetians and Turks. The fortress derives its name from a woman named Rozafa, who was allegedly walled into the ramparts as an offering to the gods so that the construction would stand. The story goes that Rozafa asked that two holes be left in the stonework so that she could continue to breastfeed her baby. There's a spectacular wall sculpture of her near the entrance of the castle's **museum** (admission 150 lekë; ⊘8am-7pm). Some nursing women come to the fortress to smear their breasts with the milky water that seeps from the wall during some months of the year. Municipal buses (30 lekë) stop near the turn-off to the castle, and it's a short walk up from there.

Marubi Permanent Photo Exhibition

ART GALLERY

(Rr Muhamet Gjollesha; admission 100 lekë; ⊘8am-4pm Mon-Fri) Hidden behind a block of shops and flats, the Marubi Permanent Photo Exhibition has fantastic photography by the Marubi 'dynasty', Albania's first and foremost photographers. The first-ever photograph taken in Albania is here, taken by Pjetër Marubi in 1858. The exhibition shows fascinating portraits, places and events. Not only is this a rare insight into what things looked like in old Albania, it is also a small collection of mighty fine photographs. To get here, go northeast of the clock tower to Rr Çlirimi; Rr Muhamet

---

FAMILY FEUD WITH BLOOD AS THE PRIZE

The *Kanun* (Code) was formalised in the 15th century by powerful northern chieftain Lekë Dukagjin. It consists of 1262 articles covering every aspect of daily life: work, marriage, family, property, hospitality, economy and so on. Though the *Kanun* was suppressed by the communists, there has been a revival of its strict precepts in northern Albania.

According to the *Kanun*, the most important things in life are honour and hospitality. If a member of a family (or one of their guests) is murdered, it becomes the duty of the male members of that clan to claim their blood debt by murdering a male member of the murderer's clan. This sparks an endless cycle of killing that doesn't end until either all the male members of one of the families are dead, or reconciliation is brokered through respected village elders.

Hospitality is so important in these parts of Albania that the guest takes on a godlike status. There are 38 articles giving instructions on how to treat a guest – an abundance of food, drink and comfort is at his or her disposal, and it is also the host's duty to avenge the murder of his guest, should this happen during their visit. It's worth reading *Broken April*, by Ismail Kadare, a brilliant exploration of people living under the *Kanun*.

Gjollesha darts off to the right. The exhibition is on the left in an unmarked building, but locals will help you find it if you ask.

🛏 Sleeping & Eating

TOP CHOICE **Tradita G&T**

BOUTIQUE HOTEL, TRADITIONAL RESTAURANT **€€**
(Tradita Gegë dhe Toskë; ☎068 2086 056, 2240 537; www.traditagt.com; Rr Skënderbeu 4; s/d/t €35/50/55;👁) Hooray, this restaurant has expanded into a hotel and the rooms are a delight. Family rooms have two levels and basic facilities, and there's a homemade, home-grown breakfast waiting for guests in the morning. The restaurant serves excellent fish dishes (meals 1100 lekë) in an ethnographic museum atmosphere. If you're heading Lake Koman way, the owner can arrange for the bus to pick you up from the hotel.

Hotel Kaduku HOTEL **€**
(HK; ☎42 216; Sheshi 5 Heronjtë; s/d incl breakfast €23/32) This popular hotel is behind Raiffeisen Bank on the roundabout near Hotel Rozafa. Its two wings have been renovated, but the best reason to stay here is for the information provided by staff about getting to and from Theth. If it's full, owners have access to cheap rooms elsewhere.

Piazza Park PIZZA **€**
(Rr 13 Dhjetori; mains 300-1000 lekë) Where the locals return to, night after night, day after day. Once you get past security, people-watch (or be watched) next to the fountains and kids' playground.

Hotel Europa BAR
(Sheshi 2 Prilli) Check out the accursed mountains from the bar on level five of this luxury hotel. Its outdoor ground-floor bar is also a relaxing spot next to a park and playground.

ℹ Information

The **information office** (a stand-alone booth) near Piazza Park is open daily, and until 9pm in summer.

ℹ Getting There & Away

BUS There are hourly *furgons* and buses to and from Tirana (350 lekë, two hours, 6am to 4pm). From Shkodra, *furgons* depart from outside Radio Shkodra near Hotel Rozafa. *Furgons* to Ulcinj in Montenegro leave at 9am and 4pm (600 lekë, two hours) from the other side of the park abutting Grand Hotel Europa. They fill quickly. From Ulcinj, buses leave for Shkodra at 6am and 12.30pm. Catch the 7am bus to Lake Koman (800 lekë, two hours) in time for the wonderful

ferry trip along the lake to Fierza (400 lekë, two hours) near Kosovo. *Furgons* depart for Theth daily at 7am (700 lekë).

TAXI It costs between €40 and €45 for the trip from Shkodra to Uncinj in Montenegro.

TRAIN Trains depart Tirana daily at 1.15pm (145 lekë), and arrive in Shkodra at 4.50pm, but you'll need to be up early to catch the 5.40am train back. *Furgons* meet arriving trains.

Theth & Valbonë

These small villages deep in the 'accursed mountains' are all but deserted in winter (Theth locals head south to live in Shkodra) but come summer, they're a magnet for those seeking beauty, isolation, mystery and adventure. From Theth, three circular hikes are marked out with red and white markers. It's possible to hike in the region without a guide, but they're helpful and you can expect to pay an informal guide between 3000 and 4000 lekë per day. Formal guides charge €50.

The main hike is from Theth to Valbonë (or vice versa). It takes around three hours to trek from Theth's centre (742m) to Valbonë pass (1812m), then a further two hours to the houses of Rragam and 1½ hours along a riverbed to near Bajram Curri.

👁 Sights

Kulla HISTORIC BUILDING
(Theth; admission €1) Visit this 'lock-in tower' in central Theth where men waited, protected, during a blood feud (see boxed text p53).

🛏 Sleeping & Eating

Recent investment has resulted in many of Theth's homes becoming B&Bs (complete with Western-style bathrooms with hot showers). Due to the absence of restaurants in town, families include breakfast, lunch and dinner in the deal. Try www.shkoder -albanian-alps.com (linked with Outdoor Albania, p48) for accommodation.

Guesthouse Mëhill Çarku GUEST HOUSE **€€**
(☎069 3164 211; www.guesthouse-thethi-carku. com; Theth; per person 2500 lekë; ☺Apr-Oct) Book in advance for a bed in this home with thick stone walls, timber floors, a garden and farm.

Guesthouse Tërthorja GUEST HOUSE **€€**
(☎069 3840 990; www.terthorja-guesthouse -tethi.com; Theth; per person lekë 2500) This renovated guest house has a sports field, sports equipment and a resident cow.

On the hillsides, beaches and generally most surfaces in Albania, you will notice small concrete domes (often in groups of three) with rectangular slits. Meet the bunkers: Enver Hoxha's concrete legacy, built from 1950 to 1985. Weighing in at five tonnes of concrete and iron, these little mushrooms are almost impossible to destroy. They were built to repel an invasion and can resist full tank assault – a fact proved by their chief engineer, who vouched for his creation's strength by standing inside one while it was bombarded by a tank. The shell-shocked engineer emerged unscathed, and tens of thousands were built. Today, some are creatively painted, one houses a tattoo artist, and maybe one day the more spectacularly located ones will house tourists.

Hotel Rilindja HOTEL
(☑067 3014 637; www.journeytovalbona.com; Valbonë; r incl breakfast per person €15, per tent €6) Good accommodation and food. The family can organise hikes, picnics and transport.

❶ Getting There & Around

BUS Though Theth is only 70km from Shkodra, expect the occasionally hair-raising *furgon* trip to take four hours. The *furgon* leaves from outside Café Rusi in Shkodra at 7am.

TAXI To Theth from Shkodra by taxi expect to pay €100.

FERRY A popular route is to take the 7am *furgon* from Shkodra to the Koman Ferry, travel by ferry (two hours) then jump on a *furgon* from the ferry to Bajram Curri (20 minutes, 150 lekë) in time for the 2.30pm *furgon* to Valbonë (200 lekë). This route can also be driven (the ferry charges €25 for a car and five people). The *furgon* leaves Valbonë at 7am for Bajram Curri, while the return ferry departs Fierzë at 2pm. If you're heading into Kosovo, it takes roughly 50 minutes to the border by car from the ferry terminal.

CENTRAL ALBANIA

Central Albania crams it all in. Travel an hour or two from Tirana and you can be Ottoman house-hopping in brilliant Berat, musing over ancient ruins in deserted Apollonia or haggling for antiques in an Ottoman bazaar in Kruja.

Kruja

☑0511 / POP 20,000
From the road below, Kruja's houses appear to sit in the lap of a mountain. An ancient castle juts out to one side, and the massive Skanderbeg Museum juts out of the castle itself. The local plaster industry is going

strong so expect visibility-reducing plumes of smoke to cloud views of the Adriatic Sea.

Kruja is Skanderbeg's town. Yes, Albania's hero was born here, and although it was over 500 years ago, there's still a great deal of pride in the fact that he and his forces defended Kruja from the Ottomans until his death. As soon as you get off the *furgon* you're face to knee with a statue of Skanderbeg wielding his mighty sword with one hand, and it just gets more Skanderdelic after that.

At a young age Kastrioti, the son of an Albanian prince, was handed over as a hostage to the Turks, who converted him to Islam and gave him a military education at Edirne in Turkey. There he became known as Iskander (after Alexander the Great) and Sultan Murat II promoted him to the rank of *bey* (governor), thus the name Skanderbeg.

In 1443 the Turks suffered a defeat at the hands of the Hungarians at Niš in present-day Serbia, and nationally minded Skanderbeg took the opportunity to abandon the Ottoman army and Islam and rally his fellow Albanians against the Turks. Skanderbeg made Kruja his seat of government between 1443 and 1468. Among the 13 Turkish invasions he subsequently repulsed was that led by his former commander, Murat II. Pope Calixtus III named Skanderbeg the 'captain general of the Holy See' and Venice formed an alliance with him. The Turks besieged Kruja four times. Though beaten back in 1450, 1466 and 1467, they finally took control of Kruja in 1478 (after Skanderbeg's death).

Kruja's sights can be covered in a few hours, making this an ideal town to visit en route to Tirana's airport.

◉ Sights

Castle CASTLE
(⊘24hr) Inside Kruja's castle grounds are Albania flag sellers, pizza restaurants and an

array of interesting sights, though few actually castle-related.

Skanderbeg Museum
MUSEUM

(admission 200 lekë; ⊙9am-1pm & 4-7pm Tue-Sun) Designed by Enver Hoxha's daughter and son-in-law, this museum opened in 1982, and its spacious seven-level interior displays replicas of armour and paintings depicting Skanderbeg's struggle against the Ottomans. The museum is something of a secular shrine, and takes itself very seriously indeed, with giant statues and dramatic battle murals.

Ethnographic Museum
MUSEUM

(admission 300 lekë; ⊙9am-1pm & 4-7pm, closed Mon) This traditional home in the castle complex below the Skanderbeg Museum is one of the best in the country. Set in an original 19th-century Ottoman house that belonged to the affluent Toptani family, this museum shows the level of luxury and self-sufficiency the household maintained by producing its own food, drink, leather and weapons. They even had their very own mini-*hammam* (Turkish bath) and watermill. The walls are lined with original frescos from 1764. The English-speaking guide's detailed explanations are excellent; offer a tip if you can.

Teqe
CHURCH

A short scramble down the cobblestone lane are the remains of a small *hammam* as well as a functioning *teqe* – a small place of worship for those practising the Bektashi branch of Islam. This beautifully decorated *teqe* has been maintained by successive generations of the Dollma family since 1789. Skanderbeg himself reputedly planted the knotted olive tree at the front.

Bazaar
MARKET

This Ottoman-style bazaar is the country's best place for souvenir shopping and has WWII medical kits, antique gems and quality traditional ware, including beautifully embroidered tablecloths, copper coffee pots and plates. You can watch women using looms to make *kilims* (rugs) and purchase the results.

❶ Getting There & Away

Kruja is 32km from Tirana. Make sure your *furgon* from Tirana (200 lekë) is going to Kruja, not just Fush Kruja, below. It is very easy to reach the airport (100 lekë, 15 minutes) by *furgon* or taxi from here, and it's en route to Shkodra, though you'll need to pull over a bus on the busy Tirana–Shkodra highway as they don't stop in the town itself.

Durrës

Durrës was once Albania's capital. Its 10km-long beach is a lesson in unplanned development; hundreds of hotels stand side by side, barely giving breathing space to the beach and contributing to the urban-waste problem that causes frequent outbreaks of skin infections in swimmers. Despite this, it has some good sights in the older part of town and makes a decent place for day-trippers.

◉ Sights

Archaeological Museum
MUSEUM

(Muzeu Arkeologik; Rr Taulantia; admission 300 lekë; ⊙9am-3pm Tue-Sat, 10am-3pm Sun) The Archaeological Museum on Durrës' waterfront has an impressive collection of artefacts from the Greek, Hellenistic and Roman periods, and guides who will explain it all. Durrës was a centre for the worship of Venus, and the museum has a cabinet full of little busts of the love goddess.

Amphitheatre of Durrës
RUINS

(Rr e Kalasë; admission 300 lekë; ⊙9am-7pm) The Amphitheatre of Durrës was built on the hillside inside the city walls in the early 2nd century AD. In its prime it had the capacity to seat 15,000 to 20,000 spectators, but these days a few inhabited houses occupy the stage, a reminder of its recent rediscovery (in 1966) and excavation. The Byzantine chapel in the amphitheatre has several beautiful mosaics.

🛏 Sleeping & Eating

B&B Tedeschini
TOP CHOICE

B&B €€

(☎224 343, 068 2246 303; ipmcrsp@icc.al.eu.org; Rr Dom Nikoll Kaçorri 5; s/d without bathroom incl breakfast €15/30) This gracious 19th-century former Italian consulate is a homey B&B with airy rooms, containing antique furniture. Owner (and doctor) Alma prepares great breakfasts in the country-style kitchen. From the Great Mosque walk past the town hall and take a right, then a quick left. Use the doorbell next to the green gates.

Hotel Pepeto
HOTEL €€

(☎224 190; Rr Mbreti Monun 3; s/d/ste incl breakfast €25/35/50; ❋@🕏) A well-run (and well-signposted) guest house at the end of a court, just off the square fronting the Great Mosque. The rooms are decent and quiet, some have baths and balconies and the suite is an attic-dweller's dream. There's a spacious lounge and bar area downstairs.

Bar Torra BAR €
(Sheshi Mujo Ulqinaku) This Venetian tower was opened by a team of local artists and was one of the first private cafes in Albania. There are art displays (and cozy nooks) downstairs, and in summer you can gaze around Durrës from the top of the tower.

Picante INTERNATIONAL €
(Rr Taulantia; mains 700-7000 lekë) Upping the trendy ante on the redeveloped waterfront is this stark white restaurant with a chilli theme and good, though budget-stretching, meals.

❶ Getting There & Away

BOAT Agencies around the train station sell tickets for the many ferry lines plying the Durrës–Bari route (single deck €40, eight hours). **Venezia Lines** (☑225 338) has the fastest boat to Bari (€60, 3½ hours). Ferries also depart Durrës for Ancona most days in summer (€65, 17 hours) and at least three days a week throughout the year.

BUS & FURGON *Furgons* (150 lekë, one hour) and buses (100 lekë, one hour) to Tirana leave from beside the train station when they're full. Buses leave for Shkodra at 7.30am and 1.30pm (400 lekë, three hours). In summer, long-distance buses and *furgons* going to and from Saranda, Gjirokastra, Fier and Berat (400 lekë, 1½ hours) bypass this station, picking up and dropping off passengers at the end of Plazhi i Durrësi, east of the harbour, which can be reached by the 'Plepa' orange municipal bus (30 lekë, 10 minutes). In July and August many buses connect Durrës with Pristina in Kosovo (€10, five hours).

TRAIN Six trains a day head to Tirana (70 lekë, one hour, 6.15am, 8.45am, 9.20am, 1.05pm, 3.12pm, 4.45pm and 8.05pm). Trains also depart for Shkodra (1.05pm), Pogradec (6.45am), Elbasan (6.45am, 3.25pm) and Vlore (5.35pm). Check at the station for changes in departure times.

Apollonia

The ruined city of ancient **Apollonia** (admission 700 lekë; ☺9am-5pm) is 12km west of Fier, which is 90km south of Durrës. Apollonia is set on rolling hills among olive groves, and the plains below stretch for kilometres. Apollonia (named after the god Apollo) was founded by Greeks from Corinth and Corfu in 588 BC and quickly grew into an important city-state, which minted its own currency and benefited from a robust slave trade. Under the Romans (from 229 BC) the city became a great cultural centre with a famous school of philosophy.

Julius Caesar rewarded Apollonia with the title 'free city' for supporting him against Gnaeus Pompeius Magnus (Pompey the Great) during the civil war in the 1st century BC, and sent his nephew Octavius, the future Emperor Augustus, to complete his studies here.

After a series of military and natural disasters (including an earthquake in the 3rd century AD that turned the river into a malarial swamp), the population moved southward into present-day Vlora, and by the 5th century AD only a small village with its own bishop remained at Apollonia.

There is far less to see at Apollonia than there is at Butrint, but there are some picturesque ruins within the 4km of city walls, including a small original theatre and the elegant pillars on the restored facade of the city's 2nd-century AD administrative centre. You may be able to see the 3rd-century BC **House of Mosaics** from a distance, though they're often covered up with sand for protection from the elements. Inside the **Museum of Apollonia** complex is the Byzantine monastery and Church of St Mary, which has gargoyles on the outside pillars. Much of the site remains to be excavated, but recent discoveries include a necropolis outside the castle walls with graves from the Bronze and Iron Ages.

❶ Getting There & Away

Apollonia is best visited on a day trip from Tirana, Durrës, Vlora or Berat.

Furgons depart for the site (50 lekë) from Fier's '24th August Bar' (ask locals for directions). From Fier, *furgons* head to Durrës (200 lekë, 1½ hours), Tirana (300 lekë, two hours), Berat (300 lekë, one hour) and Vlora (200 lekë, 45 minutes).

If you'd prefer not to wait for the *furgon*, a taxi will charge 500 lekë one way from Fier.

Berat

☑032 / POP 45,500

A highlight of any trip to Albania is a visit to beautiful Berat. Its most striking feature is the collection of white Ottoman houses climbing up the hill to its castle, earning it the title of 'town of a thousand windows' and helping it join Gjirokastra on the list of Unesco World Heritage sites in 2008. Its rugged mountain setting is particularly evocative when the clouds swirl around the tops of the minarets, or break up to show the icy top of Mt Tomorri.

WHERE'S THE ROOF?

Half-completed houses dot Albania's roadsides, and while many look deserted, the reality is they're being built one level at a time, with immigrants returning each summer armed with more cash to add another level, or to finally put the finishing touch – a roof – on their multilevel home. While the house is a work in progress, look up: you'll most certainly spot a weatherbeaten stuffed teddy bear adorning its highest level. A lost child's toy? No, it's an attempt to ward off the evil eye.

The old quarters are lovely ensembles of whitewashed walls, tiled roofs and cobblestone roads. Surrounding the town, olive and cherry trees decorate the gentler slopes, while pine woods stand on the steeper inclines. In true Albanian style, an elegant mosque with a pencil minaret is partnered on the main square by a large new Orthodox church. Bridges over the Osumi River include a 1780 seven-arched stone footbridge.

In the 3rd century BC an Illyrian fortress called Antipatrea was built here on the site of an earlier settlement. The Byzantines strengthened the hilltop fortifications in the 5th and 6th centuries, as did the Bulgarians 400 years later. The Serbs, who occupied the citadel in 1345, renamed it Beligrad, or 'White City'. In 1450 the Ottoman Turks took the town. After a period of decline, in the 18th and 19th centuries the town began to thrive as a crafts centre specialising in woodcarving.

⊙ Sights

Kalasa   CASTLE
(admission 100 lekë; ◷24hr) The neighbourhood inside the castle's walls still lives and breathes; you'll see old Mercedes-Benz cars struggling up the cobblestone roads to return locals home. If you walk around this busy, ancient neighbourhood for long enough you'll invariably stumble into someone's courtyard thinking it's a church or ruin (no one seems to mind, though). In spring and summer the fragrance of chamomile is in the air (and underfoot), and wildflowers burst from every gap between the stones. The highest point is occupied by the **Inner Fortress**, where ruined stairs lead to a Tolkienesque water reservoir; take a torch (flashlight) and watch your step.

Onufri Museum   ART GALLERY
(admission 200 lekë; ◷9am-1pm & 4-7pm May-Sep, 9am-4pm Oct-Apr, closed Mon) Kala was traditionally a Christian neighbourhood, but fewer than a dozen of the 20 churches remain. The quarter's biggest church, **Church of the**

Dormition of St Mary (Kisha Fjetja e Shën Mërisë), is the site of the Onufri Museum. The church itself dates from 1797 and was built on the foundations of a 10th-century church. Onufri's spectacular 16th-century artworks are displayed on the ground level along with a beautifully gilded iconostasis.

Churches & Chapels   CHURCHES
Ask at the Onufri Museum if you can see the other churches and tiny chapels in Kala, including **St Theodore** (Shën Todher), close to the citadel gates; the substantial and picturesque **Church of the Holy Trinity** (Kisha Shën Triades), below the upper fortress; and the little chapels of **St Mary Blachernae** (Shën Mëri Vllaherna) and **St Nicholas** (Shënkolli). Some of the churches date back to the 13th century. Also keep an eye out for the **Red Mosque**, by the southern Kala walls, which was the first in Berat and dates back to the 15th century.

Chapel of St Michael   CHURCH
Perched on a cliff ledge below the citadel is the artfully positioned little chapel of St Michael (Shën Mihell), best viewed from the Gorica quarter.

Ethnographic Museum   MUSEUM
(admission 100 lekë; ◷9am-1pm & 4-7pm May-Sep, 9am-4pm Oct-30 Apr, closed Mon) Down from the castle, this museum, in an 18th-century Ottoman house that's as interesting as the exhibits. The ground floor has displays of traditional clothes and the tools used by silversmiths and weavers, while the upper storey has kitchens, bedrooms and guest rooms decked out in traditional style. Check out the *mafil*, a kind of mezzanine looking into the lounge where the women of the house could keep an eye on male guests (and see when their cups needed to be filled). There are information sheets in Italian, French and English.

Mosques   NEIGHBOURHOOD
Down in the traditionally Muslim Mangalem quarter, there are three grand mosques. The 16th-century **Sultan's Mosque** (Xhamia

e Mbretit) is one of the oldest in Albania. The **Helveti teqe** behind the mosque has a beautiful carved ceiling and was specially designed with acoustic holes to improve the quality of sound during meetings. The Helveti, like the Bektashi, are a dervish order, or brotherhood, of Muslim mystics. The big mosque on the town square is the 16th-century **Lead Mosque** (Xhamia e Plumbit), so named because of the lead coating its sphere-shaped domes. The 19th-century **Bachelors' Mosque** (Xhamia e Beqarëvet) is down by the Osumi River; look for the enchanting paintings on its external walls. This mosque was built for unmarried shop assistants and junior craftsmen and is perched between some fine Ottoman-era shopfronts along the river.

Activities

Bogove Waterfall
HIKING
Catch the 8am or 9am *furgon* to Bogove via Skrappar, or a later bus to Polican then transfer to a *furgon* to Bogove. Lunch at Taverna Dafinat above the bus stop, then follow the path along the river (starting on the Berat side) to this icy waterfall.

Cobo Winery
WINE TASTING
The Cobo family winery has one of the only cellar doors in Albania, and it's worth checking out. Try its Sheshi i Bardhe, Trebiano, Shesh i Izi and Kashmer wines, and, of course, its Raki me Arra. Any bus/*furgon* heading to Tirana can drop you off at the winery for 100 lekë.

Albanian Rafting Group
RAFTING
(☑069 2035 634; www.albrafting.org) Organises one- and two-day rafting trips along the Osumi River and canyons.

Sleeping & Eating

TOP CHOICE **Berat Backpackers**
HOSTEL €
(☑069 3064 429; www.beratbackpackers.com; Gorica; dm incl breakfast €12; ⊗Apr-Nov) Albania's best backpackers is the brainchild of Englishman Scott; he's transformed a traditional house in the Gorica quarter (across the river from Mangalem) into a vine-clad hostel with a basement bar, alfresco drinking area and a cheery, relaxed atmosphere that money can't buy. There's a shaded camping area on the terrace (€5 per person), two airy dorms with original ceilings, and one excellent-value double room (€13 per person).

Hotel Mangalemi
HOTEL €€
(☑32 093, 068 2429 803; www.mangalemihotel.com; Rr e Kalasë; s/d incl breakfast €20/35) Tomi Mio

(the hotel is known locally as Hotel Tomi) and his son run this iconic hotel in two sprawling Ottoman houses (they recently bought and renovated the house next door). Its terrace restaurant has great Albanian food with bonus views of Mt Tomorri. It's on the left side of the cobblestone road leading to the castle.

Hotel Guva
HOTEL €
(☑30 014; Mangalem; s/d incl breakfast €15/30) The four rooms of this 'new kid on the block' have tremendous views of Gorica, as does its upstairs terrace bar. One room has four single beds for €10 per person. It's a hike up stairs near St Michael.

Bujar's
TRADITIONAL €
(meals 200 lekë) In the market area near the Osumi River you'll find this simple restaurant with cheap and traditional lunches. The restaurant doesn't have menus, just a selection of daily offerings. Look for a single-storey, light-blue building down a lane.

Antigoni
TRADITIONAL €€
(Gorica; mains 600 lekë) This bustling restaurant may have an unusual style of service (some call it ignoring), but the Mangalem and Osumi River views from its upper levels are outstanding, and the food and local wine, when you finally get to order it, is good.

Information

The town's **information centre** (www.bashki aberat.com) is located in the council building, parallel to the Osumi River in new Berat.

Getting There & Away

Buses and *furgons* run between Tirana and Berat (400 lekë, 2½ hours) hourly until 3pm. From Tirana, buses leave from the 'Kombinati' station (catch the municipal bus from Sheshi Skënderbej to Kombinati for 30 lekë). In Berat, buses depart from and arrive at the bus station next to the Lead Mosque. There are buses to Vlora (300 lekë, 2½ hours, until 3pm), Durrës (400 lekë, 1½ hours) and Saranda via Gjirokastra (1000 lekë, six hours, two daily at 8am and 2pm).

SOUTHERN COAST

With rough mountains falling headfirst into bright-blue seas, this area is wild and ready for exploration. Some beaches are jam-packed in August, yet there's plenty of space, peace and happy-to-see-you faces in the low season. With careful government planning, the southern coast could shine. In the meantime, if the rubbish lying next to you on the beach gets you down, you only have to bend your neck a bit to see the snowcapped mountain peaks and wide green valleys zigzagged by rivers.

Vlora

☎033 / POP 124,000

It's here in sunny Vlora (the ancient Aulon) that the Adriatic Sea meets the Ionian, but the beaches are muddy and grubby, and the port town has really outgrown itself. History-buffs should come here for its museums and historic buildings, while beach lovers should hold their horses for horses for Dhermi, Drymades or Jal, all further south.

◉ Sights

Sheshi i Flamurit SQUARE
At Sheshi i Flamurit (Flag Sq), near the top of Sadik Zotaj, a magnificent socialist-realist **Independence Monument** stands proud against the sky with the flag bearer hoisting the double-headed eagle into the blue. Near the base of the monument lies the grave of local Ismail Qemali, the country's first prime minister.

Ethnographic Museum MUSEUM
(Sheshi i Flamurit; admission 50 lekë; ⊗9am-noon Mon-Sat) This ethnographic museum is jam-packed with relics of Albanian life. It's hidden behind an inconspicuous metal fence.

Muzeu Historik MUSEUM
(Sheshi i Flamurit) This antiquities museum opposite the ethnographic museum was undergoing renovation at the time of research.

Muradi Mosque MOSQUE
The 16th-century Muradi Mosque is a small elegant structure made of red and white stone, with a modest minaret; its exquisite design is attributed to one of the greatest Ottoman architects, Albanian-born Sinan Pasha.

National Museum of Independence MUSEUM
(admission 100 lekë; ⊗9am-1pm & 5-8pm) Down by the harbour, the National Museum of Independence is housed in the villa that became the headquarters of Albania's first government in 1912. The preserved offices, historic photographs and famous balcony make it an interesting place to learn about Albania's short-lived, but long-remembered, 1912 independence.

🛏 Sleeping

Hotel Konomi HOTEL €
(☎229 320; Rr e Uji i Ftohtë; r €20) Set on top of a hill with views of the party end of town, this stark former workers' camp is good for the socialist idealism experience. Catch an orange municipal bus to Uji i Ftohtë (30 lekë) and walk along the beach road until the second pedestrian crossing; the stairs start behind the cafe.

ⓘ Information

Colombo Travel & Tours (☎232 377; Hotel Sazani) Books tours and provides information.

ⓘ Getting There & Away

BUS & FURGON Buses (400 lekë, four hours) and furgons (500 lekë, three hours) to Tirana and Durrës (500 lekë, 2½ hours) whiz back and forth from 4am until 7pm. Buses to Saranda (800 lekë, six hours) and on to Gjirokastra (900 lekë, seven hours) leave at 7am and 12.30pm. There are nine buses a day to Berat (300 lekë, two hours). Buses leave from Rr Rakip Malilaj; departures to Athens (€25) and cities in Italy (from €70) depart from Muradi Mosque.

FERRY Vlora to Brindisi in Italy takes around six hours. From Monday to Saturday there are departures from Brindisi at 11pm and Vlora at noon (deck €35).

TRAIN The daily train departs Tirana for Vlora at 4.30pm and Vlora for Tirana at 4.30am (250 lekë, five hours).

Llogaraja Pass National Park

Reaching the pinetree-clad Llogaraja Pass National Park (1025m) is a highlight of travels in Albania. If you've been soaking up the sun on the southern coast's beaches, it seems impossible that after a steep hairpin-bend climb you'll be up in the mountains tucking into spit-roasted lamb and homemade wine. There's great scenery up here, including the *pisha flamur* (flag pine) – a tree resembling the eagle design on the Albanian flag. Watch clouds descending onto the mountain, shepherds on the plains guiding their herds, and thick forests where deer, wild boar and wolves roam. Check out the resident deer at the Tourist Village before heading across the road to the cute family-run cabins at **Hotel Andoni** (☎068 240 0929; cabins 4000 lekë). The family do a wonderful lamb roast lunch (800 lekë) here.

Drymades

As you zigzag down the mountain from the Llogaraja Pass National Park, the white crescent-shape beaches and azure waters lure you from below. The first beach before the alluvial fan is Palasa, and it's one of the last bar/restaurant/hotel free beaches around.

The next beach along is **Drymades beach**. Turn right just after the beginning of the walk down to Dhërmi beach and you'll be on the sealed road that twists through olive groves. After a 20-minute walk you'll be on its rocky white beach.

🛏 Sleeping & Eating

TOP CHOICE **Sea Turtle** CAMPING GROUND €

(☑069 4016 057; per person 1000 lekë; ☺Jun-Sep) This great little set-up is run by two brothers. Each summer they turn the family orange orchard into a vibrant tent city, and the price includes the tent (with mattresses, sheets and pillows), breakfast and a family-cooked dinner (served up in true camp style). Hot showers are under the shade of old fig trees.

Drymades Hotel CAMPING GROUND €

(☑069 2074 000; campsites 700 lekë, cabins incl breakfast 7000 lekë) A constellation of cabins and rooms under the shade of pine trees just a step away from the blue sea. You can stay indoors or camp. There's a bar, restaurant and shaded playground, plus a classic beach bar with a straw roof. Prices halve off peak.

Lollipop CLUB

(Drymades Beach) This very loud beach club (part of an Albanian chain of clubs) has DJs bopping along with their headphones on during long August days and nights, and a certain hammock and cocktail (500 lekë) appeal.

Dhërmi

Dhërmi beach is well and truly under the tourist trance in summer: expect booked-out accommodation and an almost unbearable rubbish problem. Despite this, there is fun to be had, and, if techno isn't your style, peace and quiet to be had, too. It's made up of lovely rocky outcrops, Mediterranean-blue water and tiny coves. The beach is 1.5km below the Vlora–Saranda road, so ask the driver to stop at the turn-off on the Llogaraja side of the village. From here it's an easy 10-minute walk downhill.

🛏 Sleeping & Eating

Hotel Riviera HOTEL €€

(☑068 2633 333; Dhërmi Beach; d €40-80;❄@) This hotel has had a leopardskin-curtain makeover and is now ultra too-cool-for-school, with orange, lime-green and brown walls. The futon-style beds and flat-screen TVs make it all acceptable. An ubercool bar, the Yacht Club, is perched on the water's edge.

Blu Blu HOTEL €€

(☑068 6055 371; Dhërmi Beach; r €80;☺May-Oct; ❄🛜) Hello? Whose stroke of genius is this? Turn left at the bottom of the road to Dhërmi, and follow the road almost to its end. Here you'll find one of the best 'no disco' beachside spots in Albania. Little white cabins with sea views sit among growing banana trees, and the bar/restaurant serves great food. Start your dream day with a freshly squeezed orange juice. Rooms start at €30 in May.

Hotel Luciano RESTAURANT €€

(mains 500 lekë) Sure, the mosaic on the wall of this waterfront pizza and pasta joint says 'no', but it's a resounding 'yes' to its woodfired pizzas. It's the first place you'll find after walking down the hill from the main road.

Himara

☑0393 / POP 4500

This sleepy town has fine beaches, a couple of pleasant Greek seafood tavernas, some hi-tech, good-looking hotels and an interesting Old Town high on the hill. Most of the ethnic Greek population left in the 1990s, but many have returned – Greek remains the mother tongue of its people. The lower town comprises three easily accessible rocky beaches and the town's hotels and restaurants. The main Vlora–Saranda road passes the entrance to the hilltop castle, which, like Berat's, still houses many people. A taxi to the castle from Himara costs 300 lekë.

🛏 Sleeping

Rapo's Resort LUXURY HOTEL €€€

(☑22 856; www.raposresorthotel.com; d €110-140;❄) This top-end resort has smart interior design and sparkling bathrooms, and it also houses a massive swimming pool. For €5 anyone can relax by the pool for the day.

Kamping Himare CAMPING GROUND €

(☑068 5298 940; www.himaracamping.com; per person €4; ☺Jun-Sep) Midnight movies in an open-air cinema add to the appeal of this fairly central camping ground in an olive and orange grove. Tent rate include mattresses, sheets and pillows. Try the restaurant's sublime pancakes (100 lekë) for breakfast.

Manolo BOUTIQUE HOTEL €€
(☑22 375; d €50) Above a cool, but not too cool, bar are four contemporary rooms that show good attention to detail and have sea views.

Kamping Mediterraneo CAMPING GROUND €
(☑067 2184 518; per person incl breakfast & dinner €8) This camping ground is at Livadhi beach, a 30-minute walk north from Himara. The beach's northern water is warmer and sandier, but it's the southern side that houses the camping ground. It's got disco in its soul, so don't expect a quiet night. Taxis here from Himara are 400 lekë.

❶ Getting There & Away

Buses towards Saranda and Vlora pass through Himara in the early morning; check with locals exactly when. The Himara–Saranda bus departs at 1pm from near Manolo.

Vuno & Jal

Less than 10 minutes' drive from Himara is Vuno, a tiny hillside village above a picturesque beach (Jal, pronounced Yal). Outdoor Albania (p48) renovated Vuno's primary school, and each summer its classrooms are filled with blow-up beds and it becomes **Shkolla Hostel** (☑068 3133 451; www.tirana hostel.com; dorm bed €7; ⊘Jul & Aug). What it lacks in infrastructure and privacy it makes up for with its goat-bell soundtrack and evening campfire. From Vuno walk over the bridge and follow the rocky path to your right past the cemetery.

It's a challenging 40-minute signed walk through olive groves to picturesque Jal, or a 5km walk along the main beach road. Jal was a victim of the permit police a few years ago, and since then new structures have taken on a temporary tone. Jal has two beaches; one has free camping while the other has a camping ground set back from the sea (including tent 2000 lekë). Fresh seafood is bountiful in Jal and there are plenty of beachside restaurants in summer.

Saranda

☑0852 / POP 32,000
Saranda has grown rapidly in the past few years; skeletal high-rises crowd around its horseshoe shape and hundreds more are being built in the outlying region. Saranda is bustling in summer – buses are crowded with people carrying swimming paraphernalia and the weather means it's almost obligatory to go for a swim. A daily stream of Corfu holidaymakers take the 45-minute ferry trip to Albania, add the Albanian stamp to their passports and hit Butrint or the Blue Eye Spring before heading back.

The town's name comes from Ayii Saranda, an early monastery dedicated to 40 saints; its bombed remains (including some preserved frescos) are still high on the hill above the town. The town was called Porto Edda for a period in the 1940s, after Mussolini's daughter.

Saranda's stony beaches are quite decent and there are plenty of sights in and around town, including the mesmerising ancient archaeological site of Butrint and the hypnotic Blue Eye Spring. Between Saranda and Butrint, the lovely beaches and islands of Ksamil are perfect for a dip after a day of exploring.

◎ Sights

Synagogue RUINS
(Rr Skënderbeu; ⊘24hr) This 5th-century synagogue is centrally located and is evidence of one of the earliest Balkan-Jewish communities.

Museum of Archaeology MUSEUM
(Rr Flamurit; ⊘9am-2pm & 4-9pm) This office-like building houses a well-preserved mosaic floor in its basement. If you are lucky, you will hear the manager's flute.

Castle of Lëkurësit CASTLE
This former castle is now a restaurant with superb views over Saranda and Butrint lagoon, especially at sunset. A taxi there costs about 1000 lekë return; arrange a time for the driver to pick you up, or it's a 15-minute walk up from the Saranda–Tirana road.

⨮ Sleeping

Hairy Lemon HOSTEL €
(☑069 3559 317; dm incl breakfast €12; ⊛) With a prime 8th-floor location, a clean beach at its base and a friendly, helpful atmosphere, this Irish-run backpacker hostel is a good place to chill out. There's an open-plan kitchen and lounge, and two dorm rooms with fans and sea breezes. Follow the port road for around 10 minutes and continue when it becomes dirt; it's the orange-and-yellow apart-

Over the past years, rampant development combined with land ownership issues have resulted in a fierce crackdown on what are perceived to be 'illegal' buildings throughout the country. Owners of buildings deemed to be constructed illegally (particularly in beachside areas, but including Tirana) are given written notice before the bulldozers and dynamite experts are called in to render the building uninhabitable. The rubble remains long after the bulldozers have gone, making some villages look like an earthquake has hit, though some of the lopsided skeletal remains could be modern art.

ment block on your right, above Dora E Art. Pancakes for breakfast.

Hotel Palma
HOTEL €€

(☎22 929; Rr Mithat Hoxha; s/d incl breakfast €30/50;❄) Right next to the port, this hotel has carpets that don't fit, but some rooms have great views with large balconies and the location is handy. If you're up for it, guests get free entry into the onsite summer disco.

Hotel Gjika
HOTEL €

(☎22 413; Lagjia nr 1; s/d incl breakfast €15/20) Up the hill from the main road is this simple family-run hotel with clean rooms with sea views. It's a quiet spot in a reasonably low-rise neighbourhood and is a good budget option for couples.

Bunker Hostel
HOSTEL €

(☎069 4345 426; dm incl breakfast €12; 🖳) Practically kissing the port, this hostel is run by local Rino (it's also known as Rino's bunker), who has all the past and present gossip of the town (where to find hidden bunkers, for a start). The rooms, however, are bland, the common area is windowless and there is only one bathroom for the 18 beds.

🍴 Eating

Tani
SEAFOOD €

(mains 250-550 lekë) This portside seafood restaurant is run by chef Tani, who prides himself on serving dishes he's invented himself. The oven-baked filled mussels are a cheesy delight, and it's in a cool vine-draped location.

Dropulli
TRADITIONAL €

(cnr Rruga Skënderbeu & Rr Mitro Dhmertika; veg dishes around 300 lekë) A local restaurant that has Albanian holidaymakers returning to it day after day has to be good, and vegetarians will love the melt-in-your-mouth stuffed peppers with tasty rice; ask for it to be served with potatoes.

Beque
TRADITIONAL €

(Sheshi Qendror I Qytetit; mains 300-500 lekë) Listen to the mosque call over the park while eating some of Saranda's cheapest and best Albanian-style food. Try the traditional soup and local seafood, or *tasqebap* (meat in sauce).

Pupi
SEAFOOD €€

(Rr Saranda-Butrint; seafood dishes around 650 lekë) Pupi has an unusual name but serves good seafood dishes on terraces under pine trees. It's on the road to Butrint, after Hotel Grand. In summer diners can take a swim at its private beach.

ℹ️ Information

Four main streets arc around Saranda's bay, including the waterfront promenade that becomes prime *xhiro* (evening walk) territory in the evening. Banks with ATMs line the sea road (Rr 1 Maji) and the next street inland (Rr Skënderbeu).

ZIT information centre (Rr Skënderbeu; ⊙8am-4pm Mon-Fri, 9am-2pm & 4-9pm Sat & Sun Oct-Jun, 8.30am-2pm & 4-10pm Jul-Sep) Saranda's ZIT information centre is the most established in Albania and provides information about transport and local sights. The newer, bigger tourist information centre on the promenade sells travel guides, souvenirs, Ismail Kadare novels and maps.

ℹ️ Getting There & Away

The ZIT information centre opposite the synagogue ruins has up-to-date bus timetables.

Bus

The main bus station is uphill from the ruins on Rr Vangjel Pando. Municipal buses go to Butrint via Ksamil on the hour from 7am to 5pm (100 lekë, 30 minutes), leaving from the roundabout near the port and opposite ZIT. Buses to Tirana (1200 lekë, seven hours) leave at 5am, 6.30am, 8.30am, 9.30am, 10.30am, 2pm and 10pm. The 5.30am Tirana bus takes the coastal route (1200 lekë, nine hours). There are two buses and *furgons* an hour to Gjirokastra's new town (300 lekë, 1½ hours) – they all pass the turn-off to the

Blue Eye Spring. Buses to Himara (600 lekë, two hours) leave at 6am, 2pm, 2.30pm and 3pm, and the daily service to Korça (1200 lekë, eight hours) leaves at 5.30am. Buses to the Greek border near Konispoli leave Saranda at 8am and 11am (200 lekë), otherwise you can reach the Greek border via Gjirokastra.

Ferry

Finikas (☑260 57; finikaslines@yahoo.com; Rr Mithat Hoxha) at the port sells tickets for the **Ionian Cruises** (www.ionian-cruises.com) fast boat, the *Flying Dolphin*, which leaves for Corfu at 10.30am daily except Mondays (€19, 45 minutes). A slower boat departs daily at 4.30pm (€19, 90 minutes) and in summer a third ferry departs Saranda at 12.45pm Tuesday to Sunday and 10.30am Monday. From Corfu there are three ferries: the *Flying Dolphin* departs 9am, *Sotiraquis* at 9.30am and *Kaliopi* at 6.30pm. Greek time is one hour ahead of Albanian time.

Taxi

Taxis wait for customers at the bus stop and opposite Central Park on Rr Skënderbeu. A taxi to the Greek border at Kakavija costs 4000 lekë.

Around Saranda

BUTRINT

The ancient ruins of **Butrint** (www.butrint.org; admission 700 lekë; ☉8am-dusk), 18km south of Saranda, are renowned for their size, beauty and tranquillity. They're in a fantastic natural setting and are part of a 29-sq-km national park. Set aside at least two hours to explore this fascinating place.

Although the site had been inhabited long before, Greeks from Corfu settled on the hill in Butrint (Buthrotum) in the 6th century BC. Within a century Butrint had become a fortified trading city with an acropolis. The lower town began to develop in the 3rd century BC, and many large stone buildings had already been built by the time the Romans took over in 167 BC. Butrint's prosperity continued throughout the Roman period, and the Byzantines made it an ecclesiastical centre. The city went into decline and was abandoned until 1927, when Italian archaeologists arrived. These days Lord Rothschild's UK-based Butrint Foundation helps maintain the site.

As you enter the site the path leads to the right, to Butrint's 3rd-century-BC **Greek theatre**, secluded in the forest below the acropolis. Also in use during the Roman period, the theatre could seat about 2500 people. Close by are the small **public baths**, where geometric mosaics are buried under a layer of mesh and sand to protect them from the elements.

Deeper in the forest is a wall covered with crisp Greek inscriptions, and the 6th-century palaeo-Christian **baptistry** decorated with colourful mosaics of animals and birds, again under the sand. Beyond are the impressive arches of the 6th-century **basilica**, built over many years. A massive **Cyclopean wall** dating back to the 4th century BC is further on. Over one gate is a relief of a lion killing a bull, symbolic of a protective force vanquishing assailants.

The top of the hill is where the **acropolis** once was. There's now a castle here, housing an informative **museum** (☉8am-4pm). The views from the museum's courtyard give you a good idea of the city's layout, and you can see the Vivari Channel connecting Lake Butrint to the Straits of Corfu. There are community-run stalls inside the gates where you can buy locally produced souvenirs.

❶ Getting There & Away

The municipal bus from Saranda to Butrint costs 100 lekë and leaves hourly from 7am to 5pm. It passes through Ksamil.

KSAMIL

Ksamil, 17km south of Saranda, has three small, dreamy islands within swimming distance and dozens of beachside bars and restaurants that open in the summer. The public Saranda–Butrint bus stops twice in the town (100 lekë; leaves hourly 1am to 5pm); either stop will get you to the pristine waters, though if you look closely you'll realise that the sand is trucked in.

Hotel Joni (☑069 2091 554; s/d €15/20) is a clean hotel near the roundabout. There are plenty of 'rooms to rent' in private homes closer to the water and seafood restaurants perch along the beachfront in summer.

BLUE EYE SPRING

Twenty-two kilometres east of Saranda, the **Blue Eye Spring** (Syri i Kaltër; admission per person 50 lekë, per car 200 lekë) is a hypnotic pool of deep-blue water surrounded by electric-blue edges like the iris of an eye. It feeds the Bistrica River and its depth is unknown. It's a pleasant spot; blue dragonflies dash around the water, and the surrounding shady oak trees make a pleasant picnic spot. There's a restaurant and cabins nearby. If you don't mind a 2km walk, any bus travelling between Saranda and Gjirokastra can drop you off at the spring's turn-off. **Terini Travel Agency** (☑24 985; Rr 4 Mitat Haxha, Saranda) by Saranda's port runs bus tours to the spring leaving the port at 10am on Tuesday and Saturday (€15), otherwise try a taxi.

EASTERN ALBANIA

Close to the Greek border and accessible from the Tirana–Athens bus route or from Saranda is the Unesco town of Gjirokastra. Expect bunker-covered mountains, wintertime snowfields and plenty of roads leading to Greece.

Gjirokastra

☑084 / POP 35,000

Defined by its castle, roads paved with chunky limestone and shale, imposing slate-roofed houses, and views out to the Drina Valley, Gjirokastra is an intriguing town described beautifully by local-born author Ismail Kadare (b 1936) in *Chronicles of Stone*. Archaeological evidence suggests there's been a settlement here for 2500 years, though these days it's the 600 'monumental' houses in town that attract visitors. Some of these magnificent houses, a blend of Ottoman and local architectural influence, have caved in on themselves, and Unesco funding is being spent to maintain them. Repairing each roof costs around $US20,000 – a sum out of reach for many of the homes' owners. Gjirokastra-born former dictator Enver Hoxha made sure his hometown was listed as a museum city, but after the fall of the communist regime the houses fell into disrepair.

◉ Sights

Gjirokastra Castle CASTLE
(admission 200 lekë; ☉8am-8pm) The town's moody castle hosts an eerie collection of armoury and is the setting for Gjirokastra's folk festival (held every four or five years). It was built by Ali Pasha of Tepelena. It's an extra 200 lekë to visit its interior **Museum Kombetar** and see prison cells and more armoury. A new museum on the history of Gjirokastra was being planned at the time of research.

Ethnographic Museum MUSEUM
(admission 200 lekë; ☉9am-7pm) This museum houses local homewares and was built on the site of Enver Hoxha's former house.

Zekate House HISTORIC BUILDING
(admission €1) This incredible three-storey house dates from 1811 and has twin towers and a double-arched facade. The owners live next door and collect the payments. Check with the information centre for opening hours.

Bazaar HISTORIC AREA
The 'Neck of the Bazaar' makes up the centre of the Old Town and contains artesian shops that support masters of the local stone- and wood-carving industries. Walk up to find the steps leading to Gjirokastra castle.

⊨ Sleeping

Stay in the scenic Old Town if possible, though there are accommodation options in the new town.

TOP CHOICE **Hotel Kalemi** HOTEL €€
(☑263 724; draguak@yahoo.com; Lagjia Palorto Gjirokastra; r €35; @🛜❄) This delightful, large Ottoman-style hotel has spacious rooms adorned with carved ceilings and large communal areas, including a broad veranda with Drina Valley views. Breakfast (juice, tea, a boiled egg, and bread with delicious fig jam) is included.

Guest House Haxhi Kotoni B&B €
(☑263 526, 069 2366 846; www.kotonihouse.com; s/d incl breakfast €20/25;❄) The fact that these rooms are 220 years old makes up for their small size, and attached bathrooms and air-conditioning are bonuses. Hosts Haxhi and Vita love Gjirokastra and are happy to pass information on, as well as pack picnics for guests' day trips. Ask about fishing trips and hikes. Wheelchair friendly.

Hotel Cajupi HOTEL €€
(☑269 010; www.cajupi.com; s/d incl breakfast €30/40;❄) A revamp has turned this mammoth communist-era hotel into a decent place to stay, though the bathroom blocks the view in some badly planned rooms.

✗ Eating

TOP CHOICE **Kujtimi** TRADITIONAL €
(mains 250-400 lekë; ☉11am-late) On the left-hand side of the path to Fantazia Restaurant is this unassuming outdoor restaurant, run by the Dumi family. Try the *trofte* (fried trout; 400 lekë), the *midhje* (fried mussels; 350 lekë) and the local red wine.

Kurveleshi TRADITIONAL €
(mains 200 lekë; ☉9am-dinner) This small cafe-style restaurant in the neck of the bazaar is

a good spot for lunch. Local specialities include minty rice *qifqi* (200 lekë) and there's beer on tap (60 lekë).

 Information

The new town (no slate roofs here) is on the main Saranda–Tirana road, and a taxi up to or back from the Old Town is 300 lekë.

Information Centre (◯8am-4pm Mon-Fri, 9am-2pm & 4-9pm Sat & Sun Oct-Jun, 8.30am-2pm & 4-10pm Jul-Sep) Opposite Cajupi Hotel behind the statue of the partisans.

 Getting There & Away

Buses pass through the new town on their way to Tirana and Saranda, and *furgons* also go to Saranda (400 lekë, one hour). It takes about an hour to get to the Blue Eye Spring from Gjirokastra; buses to and from Saranda pass by its entrance, which is 2km from the spring itself. Buses to Tirana leave on the hour from 5am – the last one passes through after 11pm.

UNDERSTAND ALBANIA

History

Albanians call their country Shqipëria, and trace their roots to the ancient Illyrian tribes. Their language is descended from Illyrian, making it a rare survivor of the Roman and Slavic influxes and a European linguistic oddity on a par with Basque. The Illyrians occupied the western Balkans during the 2nd millennium BC. They built substantial fortified cities, mastered silver and copper mining, and became adept at sailing the Mediterranean. The Greeks arrived in the 7th century BC to establish self-governing colonies at Epidamnos (now Durrës), Apollonia and Butrint. They traded peacefully with the Illyrians, who formed tribal states in the 4th century BC.

Roman, Byzantine & Ottoman Rule

Inevitably the expanding Illyrian kingdom of the Ardiaei, based at Shkodra, came into conflict with Rome, which sent a fleet of 200 vessels against Queen Teuta in 229 BC. A long war resulted in the extension of Roman control over the entire Balkan area by 167 BC.

Under the Romans, Illyria enjoyed peace and prosperity, though large agricultural estates were worked by slaves. The Illyrians preserved their own language and traditions despite Roman rule. Over time the populace slowly replaced their old gods with the new Christian faith championed by Emperor Constantine. The main trade route between Rome and Constantinople, the Via Egnatia, ran from the port at Durrës.

When the Roman Empire was divided in AD 395, Illyria fell within the Eastern Empire, later known as the Byzantine Empire. Three early Byzantine emperors (Anastasius I, Justin I and Justinian I) were of Illyrian origin. Invasions by migrating peoples (Visigoths, Huns, Ostrogoths and Slavs) continued through the 5th and 6th centuries.

In 1344 Albania was annexed by Serbia, but after the defeat of Serbia by the Turks in 1389 the whole region was open to Ottoman attack. The Venetians occupied some coastal towns, and from 1443 to 1468 the national hero Skanderbeg (Gjergj Kastrioti) led Albanian resistance to the Turks from his castle at Kruja. Skanderbeg won all 25 battles he fought against the Turks, and even Sultan Mehmet-Fatih, the conqueror of Constantinople, could not take Kruja. After Skanderbeg's death the Ottomans overwhelmed Albanian resistance, taking control of the country in 1479, 26 years after Constantinople fell.

Ottoman rule lasted 400 years. Muslim citizens were favoured and were exempted from the janissary system, whereby Christian households had to give up one of their sons to convert to Islam and serve in the army. Consequently many Albanians embraced the new faith.

Independent Albania

In 1878 the Albanian League at Prizren (in present-day Kosovo) began a struggle for autonomy that the Turkish army put down in 1881. Further uprisings between 1910 and 1912 culminated in a proclamation of independence and the formation of a provisional government led by Ismail Qemali at Vlora in 1912. These achievements were severely compromised when Kosovo, roughly one-third of Albania, was ceded to Serbia in 1913. The Great Powers tried to install a young German prince, Wilhelm of Wied, as ruler, but he wasn't accepted and returned home after six months. With the outbreak of WWI, Albania was occupied in succession by the armies of Greece, Serbia, France, Italy and Austria-Hungary.

In 1920 the capital city was moved from Durrës to less vulnerable Tirana. A republican government under the Orthodox priest

Fan Noli helped to stabilise the country, but in 1924 it was overthrown by the interior minister, Ahmed Bey Zogu. A northern warlord, he declared himself King Zogu I in 1928, but his close collaboration with Italy backfired in April 1939 when Mussolini ordered an invasion of Albania. Zogu fled to Britain with his young wife, Geraldine, and newborn son, Leka, and used gold looted from the Albanian treasury to rent a floor at London's Ritz Hotel.

On 8 November 1941 the Albanian Communist Party was founded with Enver Hoxha as first secretary, a position he held until his death in April 1985. The communists led the resistance against the Italians and, after 1943, against the Germans.

The Rise of Communism

In January 1946 the People's Republic of Albania was proclaimed, with Hoxha as president and 'Supreme Comrade'.

In September 1948 Albania broke off relations with Yugoslavia, which had hoped to incorporate the country into the Yugoslav Federation. Instead, it allied itself with Stalin's USSR and put into effect a series of Soviet-style economic plans – raising the ire of the USA and Britain, which made an ill-fated attempt to overthrow the government.

Albania collaborated closely with the USSR until 1960, when a heavy-handed Khrushchev demanded that a submarine base be set up at Vlora. Breaking off diplomatic relations with the USSR in 1961, the country reoriented itself towards the People's Republic of China.

From 1966 to 1967 Albania experienced a Chinese-style cultural revolution. Administrative workers were suddenly transferred to remote areas and younger cadres were placed in leading positions. The collectivisation of agriculture was completed and organised religion was completely banned.

Following the Soviet invasion of Czechoslovakia in 1968, Albania left the Warsaw Pact and embarked on a self-reliant defence policy. Some 60,000 igloo-shaped concrete bunkers (see boxed text, p55) serve as a reminder of this policy. Under the communists, some malarial swamps were drained, hydroelectric schemes and railway lines were built, and the literacy level was raised. Albania's people, however, lived in fear of the Sigurimi (secret police) and were not permitted to leave the country, and many were tortured, jailed or murdered for misdemeanours such as listening to foreign radio stations.

With the death of Mao Zedong in 1976 and the changes that followed in China after 1978, Albania's unique relationship with China also came to an end, and the country was left isolated and without allies. The economy was devastated and food shortages became more common.

Post-Hoxha

Hoxha died in April 1985 and his associate Ramiz Alia took over the leadership. Restrictions loosened (Albania was opened up to tourists in organised groups) but people no longer bothered to work on the collective farms, leading to food shortages in the cities. Industries began to fail and Tirana's population tripled as people took advantage of being able to freely move to the city.

In June 1990, inspired by the changes that were occurring elsewhere in Eastern Europe, around 4500 Albanians took refuge in Western embassies in Tirana. After a brief confrontation with the police and the Sigurimi, these people were allowed to board ships for Brindisi in Italy, where they were granted political asylum.

Following student demonstrations in December 1990, the government agreed to allow opposition parties, and the Democratic Party, led by heart surgeon Sali Berisha, was formed.

The March 1992 elections ended 47 years of communist rule, with parliament electing Sali Berisha president. Former president Alia was later placed under house arrest for writing articles critical of the Democratic government, and the leader of the Socialist Party, Fatos Nano, was also arrested on corruption charges.

During this time Albania switched from a tightly controlled communist regime to a rambunctious free-market free-for-all. A huge smuggling racket sprang up in which stolen Mercedes-Benz cars were brought into the country, and the port of Vlora became a major crossing point for illegal immigrants from Asia and the Middle East into Italy.

In 1996, 70% of Albanians lost their savings when private pyramid-investment schemes, believed to have been supported by the government, collapsed. Riots ensued, elections were called, and the victorious Socialist Party under Nano – who had been freed from prison by a rampaging mob – was able to restore some degree of security and investor confidence.

In 1999 a different type of crisis struck when 465,000 Kosovars fled to Albania as a result of a Serbian ethnic-cleansing campaign. The influx had a positive effect on Albania's economy, and strengthened the relationship between Albania and Kosovo.

For the past decade Albania has found itself in a kind of mini boom, with much money being poured into construction projects and infrastructure renewal. The general election of 2005 saw a return of Berisha's Democratic Party to government, and in 2009 they narrowly won again, forming a coalition with the Socialist Movement for Intergration (LSI). The LSI's leader, Ilir Meta, formerly of the Socialist Party, is Albania's deputy prime minister. Albania managed to manoeuvre itself around the crippling economic crisis that gripped other European countries in 2008 and economic growth has continued. Despite this, infrastructure deficiencies still plague the country.

Albania joined NATO in 2009, and EU membership beckons.

The Albanians

Albania's population is made up of approximately 95% Albanians, 3% Greeks and 2% 'other' – comprising Vlachs, Roma, Serbs, Macedonians and Bulgarians.

Albanians are generally kind, helpful and generous. If you ask for directions, don't be surprised if you're guided all the way to your destination. The majority of young people speak some English, but speaking a few words of Albanian (or Italian, and, on the south coast, Greek) will be useful.

Albanians shake their heads sideways to say yes *(po)* and usually nod and 'tsk' to say no (jo – pronounced 'yo'). Albanians familiar with foreigners often take on the nod-for-yes way, which increases confusion.

The Ghegs in the north and the Tosks in the south have different dialects, music, dress and the usual jokes about each other's weaknesses.

Albanians are nominally 70% Muslim, 20% Christian Orthodox and 10% Catholic, but more realistic statistics estimate that up to 75% of Albanians are nonreligious. Religion was ruthlessly stamped out by the 1967 cultural revolution, when all mosques and churches were taken over by the state. By 1990 only about 5% of Albania's religious buildings were left intact. The rest had been turned into cinemas or army stores, or were destroyed. Albania remains a very secular society.

The Muslim faith has a branch called Bektashism, similar to Sufism, and its world headquarters were in Albania from 1925 to 1945. Bektashi followers go to *teqe* (temple-like buildings without a minaret), which are found on hilltops in towns where those of the faith fled persecution. Most Bektashis live in the southern half of the country.

The Arts

Literature

One Albanian writer who is widely read outside Albania is Ismail Kadare (b 1936). In 2005 he won the inaugural Man Booker International Prize for his body of work. His books are a great source of information on Albanian traditions, history and social events, and exquisitely capture the atmosphere of the country's towns, as in the lyrical descriptions of Kadare's birthplace, Gjirokastra, in *Chronicle in Stone* (1971). *Broken April* (1990), set in the northern highlands before the 1939 Italian invasion, describes the life of a village boy who is next in line in a desperate cycle of blood vendettas.

There is no substantial body of Albanian literature before the 19th century besides some Catholic religious works. Oral epic poetry was the most popular literary form during the period leading up to Albanian independence in 1912. A group of romantic patriotic writers at Shkodra, including Migjeni (1911–38) and Martin Çamaj (1925–92), wrote epics and historical novels.

Perhaps the most interesting writer of the interwar period was Fan Noli (1880–1965). Educated as a priest in the US, Noli became premier of Albania's Democratic government until it was overthrown in 1924, when he returned to head the Albanian Orthodox Church in the US. Although many of his books have religious themes, the introductions he wrote to his own translations of Cervantes, Ibsen, Omar Khayyám and Shakespeare established him as Albania's foremost literary critic.

Cinema

During Albania's isolationist years the only Western actor approved by Hoxha was UK actor Sir Norman Wisdom (he became quite a cult hero). However, with so few international movies to choose from, the local film industry had a captive audience. While much of its output was propagandist, by the

1980s this little country was turning out an extraordinary 14 films a year. Despite a general lack of funds, two movies have gone on to win awards at international film festivals. Gjergj Xhuvani's comedy *Slogans* (2001) is a warm and touching account of life during communist times. This was followed in 2002 by *Tirana Year Zero*, Fatmir Koci's bleak look at the pressures on the young to emigrate.

Another film worth seeing is *Lamerica* (1995), a brilliant and stark look at Albania around 1991. Woven loosely around a plot about a couple of Italian scam artists and Albanians seeking to escape to Italy, the essence of the film is the unshakeable dignity of the ordinary Albanian in the face of adversity.

Renowned Brazilian director Walter Salles *(The Motorcycle Diaries)* adapted Ismail Kadare's novel *Broken April*. Keeping the novel's main theme, he moved the action to Brazil in *Behind the Sun* (2001). *Lorna's Silence* (2008), a film about Albanians living in Belgium, was awarded in the 2008 Cannes Film Festival.

Music

Blaring from cars, bars, restaurants and mobile phones – music is something you get plenty of in Albania. Most modern Albanian music has clarinet threaded through it and a goatskin drum beat behind it. Polyphony, the blending of several independent vocal or instrumental parts, dates from ancient Illyrian times, and can still be heard, particularly in the south.

Visual Arts

One of the first signs of the Albanian arts scene are the multicoloured buildings of Tirana, a project organised by the capital's mayor, Edi Rama, himself an artist. The building's residents don't get a say in the colour or design, and come home to find their homes daubed in spots, paintings of trees, or even paintings of laundry drying under their windowsills.

Remnants of socialist realism adorn the walls and gardens of some galleries and museums, although most were destroyed in a backlash after the fall of the communist government.

One of the most delicious Albanian art treats is to be found in Berat's Onufri Museum (p58). Onufri was the most outstanding Albanian icon painter of the 16th and 17th centuries, and his work is noted for

its unique intensity of colour, derived from natural dyes that are as fresh now as the day he painted with them.

Churches around the country also feature amazing original frescos.

The Landscape

Albania consists of 30% vast interior plains, 362km of coast and a mountainous spine that runs its length. Mt Korab, at 2764m, is Albania's highest peak. Forest covers just under 40% of the country, with Mediterranean shrubs at up to 600m, an oak forest belt between 600m and 1000m, and beech and pine forests between 1000m and 1600m.

The country's large and beautiful lakes include the Balkans' biggest, Lake Shkodra, which borders Montenegro in the north, and the ancient Lake Ohrid in the east (one-third Albanian, two-thirds Macedonian). Albania's longest river is the Drin (280km), which originates in Kosovo and is fed by melting snow from mountains in Albania's north and east. Hydroelectricity has changed Albania's landscape: Lake Koman was once a river, and the blue water from the Blue Eye Spring near Saranda travels to the coast in open concrete channels via a hydroelectricity plant. Agriculture makes up a small percentage of land use, and citrus and olive trees spice up the coastal plains. Most rural householders grow their own food.

National Parks & Wildlife

The number of national parks in Albania has risen from six to 15 since 1966 and include Dajti, Llogara, Tomorri, Butrint, Valbonë and Theth. Most are protected only by their remoteness, and tree-felling and hunting still take place. Hiking maps of the national parks are available, though they can be hard to find (try *Wanderkarte Nordalbanien* for Theth).

Albania's Alps have become a 'must-do' for hikers, and they're home to brown bear, wolf, otter, marten, wild cat, wild boar and deer. Falcons and grouse are also alpine favourites, and birdwatchers can also flock to wetlands at Lake Butrint, Karavasta Lagoon and Lake Shkodra (though the wetlands aren't pristine).

Lake Ohrid's trout is endangered (but still eaten), and endangered loggerhead turtles nest on the Ionian Coast and on the Karaburun

Peninsula, where there have also been sightings of critically endangered Mediterranean monk seals.

Environmental Issues

During communism, there were around 2000 cars in the country. The number of roaring automobiles has since risen to Western European levels and rises by 10% annually. Many of Albania's older cars are diesel Mercedes-Benzes stolen from Western Europe. As a consequence of the explosion, air-pollution levels in Tirana are five to 10 times higher than in Western European countries.

Illegal logging and fishing reached epidemic proportions during the 1990s, and there are signs of it today; fishing for the endangered *koran* trout in Lake Ohrid continues, as does fishing with dynamite along the coast.

Badly maintained oilfields around Fier leak sludge into the surrounding environment, and coastal regions discharge raw sewage into seas and rivers. The rapid development of beach areas has compounded the issue, though projects are in place to improve waste disposal in environmentally sensitive areas like Lake Ohrid.

Albania was practically litter-free until the early '90s, as everything was reused or recycled, but today there's literally rubbish everywhere. Walk around the perimeter of a hotel in a picturesque location and you'll come across its very unpicturesque dumping ground. Some Albanians are doing their bit to improve these conditions, and a 'raising awareness' campaign against litter was started by well-known Albanians in 2010. Several organic food organisations are also trying to make a difference.

Food & Drink

In coastal areas the calamari, mussels and fish will knock your socks off, while high-altitude areas like Llogaraja have roast lamb worth climbing a mountain for.

Offal is popular; *fërgesë Tiranë* is a traditional Tirana dish of offal, eggs and tomatoes cooked in an earthenware pot.

Italian influences mean vegetarians will probably become vegitalians, and many restaurants serve pizza, pasta or grilled and stuffed vegetables.

Most restaurants allow smoking, though some may have designated nonsmoking areas.

Local Drinks

Raki is very popular. The two main types are grape *raki* (the most common) and *mani* (mulberry) *raki*. Ask for homemade if possible *(raki ë bërë në shtëpi)*. If wine is more your cup of tea, seek out the Çobo winery near Berat and its Shesh i bardhe white. Local beers include Tirana, Norga (from Vlora) and Korça. Korça's beer fest takes place each August (www.visit-korca.com). Most days start with an espresso.

SURVIVAL GUIDE

Directory A–Z

Accommodation

With almost every house, bar and petrol station doubling as a hotel you might think you'll never have trouble finding a bed in Albania, and you're right, though seaside towns are often booked out in August.

The number of backpacker hostels has tripled in recent years and you'll find them in Tirana, Vuno, Saranda and Berat. Check for new ones on www.hostelworld.com.

Homestays abound in Theth (www.shkoder-albanian-alps.com). The number of camping grounds is increasing; you'll find them at Himare, Livadhi, Dhërmi and Drymades (from €4 per person). Most have hot showers, onsite restaurants and entertainment.

Prices included are for high season. You can expect the following from Albania's hotels:

€ usually decent and clean; a simple breakfast and wi-fi often included

€€ bigger rooms, onsite restaurant and possibly swimming pool

€€€ include modern decor, fitness centre, satellite TV and swimming pool

Activities

Hiking and adventure sports are gaining popularity in Albania, and **Outdoor Alba-**

SLEEPING PRICE RANGES

» € – under €30 per night for a double room

» €€ – €30 to €100

» €€€ – cheapest double over €100

nia (www.outdooralbania.com) is an excellent organisation at the forefront of the industry. Smaller operatives are starting up: the **Albania Rafting Group** (www.albrafting.org) runs rafting tours of the Osumi River and canyons in Berat. Hiking in the Alps is popular (with and without guides), as is mountain biking around the country.

Beachwise, south of Vlora the sandy Adriatic gives it up for its rockier Ionian counterpart, but the swimming is better and the scenery more picturesque.

Business Hours

If opening hours are not listed in reviews they are as follows:

Banks 9am-3.30pm Mon-Fri

Cafes & Bars 8am-midnight

Offices 8am-5pm Mon-Fri

Restaurants 8am-midnight

Shops 8am-7pm; siesta time can be any time between noon and 4pm

Embassies & Consulates

There is no Australian, New Zealand or Irish embassy in Albania. The following embassies and consulates are in Tirana:

Canada (☑04-2257 275; canadalb@canada.gov.al; Rr Dëshmorët e 4 Shkurti)

France (☑04-2233 750; www.ambafrance-al.org; Rr Skënderbej 14)

Germany (☑04-2274 505; www.tirana.diplo.de; Rr Skënderbej 8)

Netherlands (☑04-2240 828; www.mfa.nl/tir; Rr Asim Zeneli 10)

UK (☑04-2234 973; www.ukinalbania.fco.gov.uk; Rr Skënderbej 12)

US (☑04-2247 285; http://tirana.usembassy.gov; Rr Elbasanit 103)

Food

The average cost of a main course in a restaurant is 100 to 200 lekë for budget (€), 200 to 500 lekë for midrange (€€) and more than 500 lekë for top end (€€€). See also p70.

Gay & Lesbian Travellers

Extensive anti-discrimination legislation became law in 2010, but did not extend to legalising same-sex marriage. Gay and lesbian life in Albania is alive and well but is not yet organised into clubs or organisations. It's no problem to be foreign and affectionate with your same-sex partner in the street, but keep in mind that no couples are overly demonstrative in public in Albania so any public sexual behaviour beyond holding hands and kissing will be a spectacle. Gaydar will serve gay and lesbian visitors well here: you'll have to ask on the street where the parties are. The alternative music and party scene is queer-friendly.

Holidays

New Year's Day 1 January

Summer Day 16 March

Nevruz 23 March

Catholic Easter March or April

Orthodox Easter March or April

May Day 1 May

Bajram i Madh September

Mother Teresa Day 19 October

Bajram i Vogël November

Independence Day 28 November

Liberation Day 29 November

Christmas Day 25 December

Internet Access

If you've brought your own smartphone or laptop you can access free wi-fi around the country. Internet cafes (often dominated by teens playing shoot-'em-up games) cost around 100 lekë per hour.

Money

The lekë is the official currency, though the euro is widely accepted; you'll get a better rate in general if you use lekë. Accommodation is quoted in euros but can be paid in either currency. ATMs (found in most of Albania's towns, bar Theth and small beaches) usually offer to dispense cash in either currency.

Albanian banknotes come in denominations of 100, 200, 500, 1000, 2000 and 5000 lekë. There are five, 10, 20, 50 and 100 lekë coins.

In 1964 the currency was revalued 10 times; prices are sometimes quoted at the old rate (3000 lekë instead of 300). Happily, if you hand over 3000 lekë you will probably be handed 2700 lekë in change.

Albanian lekë can't be exchanged outside the country, so exchange them or spend them before you leave.

Credit cards are accepted only in the larger hotels, shops and travel agencies, and few of these are outside Tirana.

It's polite to leave your change as a tip.

Post

The postal system is fairly rudimentary – there are no postcodes, for example – and it certainly does not enjoy a reputation for efficiency.

Telephone

Albania's country phone code is ☑355 (dial + or 00 first from a mobile phone).

Three established mobile-phone providers are Vodafone, AMC and Eagle, and a fourth licence has been promised. Don't expect isolated areas to have coverage (though Theth does). Prepaid SIM cards cost around 600 lekë and include credit. Calls within the country cost roughly 30 to 60 lekë a minute. Mobile numbers begin with ☑06. To call an Albanian mobile number from abroad, dial ☑+355 then either 67, 68 or 69 (ie drop the 0).

Tourist Information

Tourist information offices operate in Tirana, Shkodra, Saranda, Gjirokastra (www.gjirokastra.org) and Berat (www.bashkia-berat.net). You can purchase city maps of Tirana in bookshops, and maps of Vlora, Saranda, Gjirokastra, Durrës and Shkodra from the respective town's travel agencies or hotels.

Travellers with Disabilities

High footpaths and unannounced potholes make life difficult for mobility-impaired travellers. Tirana's top hotels do cater to people with disabilities, and some smaller hotels are making an effort to be more accessible. The roads and castle entrances in Gjirokastra, Berat and Kruja are cobblestone, although taxis can get reasonably close to the action.

Visas

Visas are not required for citizens of EU countries or nationals of Australia, Canada, New Zealand, Japan, South Korea, Norway, South Africa or the USA. Travellers from other countries should check www.mfa.gov.al. Passports are stamped for a 90-day stay. A €10 entry and exit fee was abolished some years ago; do not be conned into paying this by taxi drivers at border crossings.

Women Travellers

Albania is a safe country for women travellers, but outside Tirana it is mainly men who go out and sit in bars and cafes in the evenings. You may tire of being asked why you're travelling alone.

Getting There & Away

Air

Nënë Tereza International Airport (Mother Teresa Airport, Rinas airport, Tirana Airport; www.tirana-airport.com.al) is 17km northwest of Tirana. There are no domestic flights within Albania. The following airlines fly to and from Albania:

Adria Airways (JP; ☑04-2272 666; www.adria.si) Flies to Madrid, Barcelona, Paris, Zurich, Munich, Frankfurt, Brussels, London, Manchester, Ljubljana, Amsterdam, Copenhagen, Warsaw, Moscow, Stockholm, Sarajevo and Vienna.

Air One (AP; ☑04-2230 023; www.flyairone.it) Flies to Milan.

Albanian Air (LV; ☑04-2235 162; www.albanianair.com) Flies to Pisa, Bologna, Turin, Pisa, Bergamo, Milan, London, Frankfurt, Istanbul, Antalya, Dubai and Jeddah.

Alitalia (AZ; ☑04-2230 023; www.alitalia.com) Flies to Rome, Verona, Turin, Naples, Florence, Genoa, Milan, Catania, Venice, Brussels, London, Madrid, Paris, Barcelona, Amsterdam and Munich.

Austrian Airlines (OS; ☑04-2235 029; www.austrian.com) Flies to Vienna.

BelleAir (LZ; ☑04-2240 175; www.belleair.it) Flies to Pristina, Ancona, Rimini, Forli, Bari, Pescara, Naples, Trieste, Perugia, Milan, Treviso, Turin, Parma, Bologna, Pisa, Florence, Rome, Geneva, Zurich, Stuttgart and Liege.

British Airways (BA; ☑04-2381 991; www.britishairways.com) Flies to London.

Bulgaria Air (FB; ☑04-2230 410; www.air.bg) Flies to Sofia, June to September only.

Lufthansa (LH; ☑04-2258 010; www.lufthansa.com) Flies to Vienna and Munich.

Malév Hungarian Airlines (MA; ☑04-2234 163; www.malev.hu) Flies to Budapest.

Olympic Air (OA; ☑04-2228 960; www.olympicair.com) Flies to Athens.

Turkish Airlines (TK; ☑04-2258 459; www.turkishairlines.com) Flies to İstanbul.

Land

Border Crossings

There are no passenger trains into Albania, so your border-crossing options are buses, *furgons*, taxis or walking to a border and picking up transport on the other side.

Montenegro The main crossings link Shkodra to Ulcinj (Muriqan) and to Podgorica (Hani i Hotit).

Kosovo The closest border crossing to the Koman Ferry terminal is Morina, and further north is Qafë Prush. Near Kukës use Morinë.

Macedonia Use Blato to get to Debar, quiet Qafë e Thanës to the north of Lake Ohrid, or Sveti Naum, near Pogradec, to its south. There's also a crossing at Stenje.

Greece The main border crossing to and from Greece is Kakavija on the road from Athens to Tirana. It's about half an hour from Gjirokastra and 250km west of Tirana, and can take up to three hours to pass through during summer. Kapshtica (near Korça) also gets long lines in summer. Konispoli is near Butrint in Albania's south.

Bus

From Tirana, regular buses head to Pristina, Kosovo; to Struga, Tetovo and Skopje in Macedonia; to Budva and Ulcinj in Montenegro; and to Athens and Thessaloniki in Greece. *Furgons* and buses leave Shkodra for Montenegro, and buses head to Kosovo from Durrës. Buses travel to Greece from Albanian towns on the southern coast and buses to Italy leave from Vlora.

Car & Motorcycle

To enter, you'll need a Green Card (proof of third-party insurance, issued by your insurer); check that your insurance covers Albania.

Taxi

Heading to Macedonia, taxis from Pogradec will drop you off just before the border at Tushëmisht/Sveti Naum. Alternatively, it's an easy 4km walk to the border from Pogradec. It's possible to organise a taxi (or, more usually, a person with a car) from where the Koman Ferry stops in Fierzë to Gjakove in Kosovo. Taxis commonly charge €40 from Shkodra to Ulcinj in Montenegro.

Sea

Two or three ferries per day ply the route between Saranda and Corfu, in Greece, and there are plenty of ferry companies making the journey to Italy from Vlora and Durrës – see those sections for detailed information.

Bicycle

Cycling in Albania is tough but certainly feasable. Expect lousy road conditions including open drains, some abysmal driving from fellow road users and roads that barely qualify for the title. Organised groups head north for mountain biking, and cyclists are even spotted cycling the long and tough Korça–Gjirokastra road. Shkodra, Durrës and Tirana are towns where you'll see locals embracing the bike, and Tirana even has bike lanes.

Bus

The first bus/*furgon* departure is often at 5am and things slow down around lunchtime. There are many buses catering for the crowds along the coast in July and August. Fares are low (eg Tirana–Durrës costs 150 lekë), and you either pay the conductor on board or when you hop off.

Municipal buses operate in Tirana, Durrës, Shkodra and Vlora, and trips cost 30 lekë. Watch your possessions.

Car & Motorcycle

Albania's drivers are not the best in the world, mostly due to the communist era, when car ownership required a permit from the government, and only two were issued to non-party members. As a result, the government didn't invest in new roads, and most Albanians were inexperienced motorists. Nowadays the road infrastructure is improving; there's a super highway from Tirana to Kosovo, and the coastal route from the Montenegro border to Butrint, near Saranda, is in good condition. That said, drivers are still highly unpredictable.

Tourists are driving cars, motorbikes and mobile homes into the country in greater numbers, and, apart from bad roads and bad drivers, the only hazards some report are being caught speeding.

Off the main routes a 4WD is a good idea. Driving at night is particularly hazardous, and driving on mountain 'roads' at any time is a whole new field of extreme sport. Cars, *furgons,* trucks and buses *do* go off the edge.

The **Automobile Club of Albania** (ACA; ☏04- 2257 828; www.aca.al; Rr Ismail Quemali 32/1, Tirana) offers emergency assistance (☏04-2262 263) around the country for 300 lekë per year and has links with international national automobile associations.

Driving Licence

Foreign driving licences are permitted, but it is recommended to have an International Driving Permit as well.

Fuel & Spare Parts

There are petrol stations in the cities and increasing numbers in the country. Unleaded fuel is available along all major roads, but fill up before driving into the mountainous regions. A litre of unleaded petrol costs 150 lekë, eurodiesel is 145 lekë. As the range of cars being driven around Albania increases, so does the availability of spare parts, but it almost goes without saying that if you're driving an old Mercedes-Benz there will be parts galore.

Car Hire

See p52 for car-hire companies operating out of Tirana. Hiring a small car costs from €35 per day, a 4WD costs around €100 per day.

Road Rules

Drinking and driving is forbidden, and there is zero tolerance for blood-alcohol readings.

Both motorcyclists and passengers must wear helmets. Speed limits are as low as 30km per hour in built-up areas and 35km per hour on the edges and there are plenty of speed cameras monitoring the roads. Keep your car's papers with you, as police are active checkers.

Hitchhiking

Though never entirely safe, hitchhiking is quite a common way for travellers to get around – though it's rare to see locals doing it.

Train

Albanians prefer bus and *furgon* travel, and when you see the speed and the state of the (barely) existing trains, you'll know why. However, the trains are dirt cheap and travelling on them is an adventure. Daily passenger trains leave Tirana for Durrës, Shkodra, Fier, Vlora, Elbasan and a few kilometres out of Pogradec. Check timetables at the station in person, and buy your ticket 10 minutes before departure. Albania is not connected to neighbouring countries by train.

Belarus
Беларусь

Best Places to Stay

» Hotel Eridan (p93)
» Hotel Europe (p81)
» Semashko (boxed text, p95)

Best Places to Eat

» Jules Verne (p90)
» Strawnya Talaka (p82)
» Zolotoy Lev (p93)

Why Go?

Eastern Europe's outcast, Belarus lies at the edge of the region and seems determined to avoid integration with the rest of the continent at all costs. Taking its lead from the Soviet Union rather than the European Union, this pint-sized dictatorship may seem like a strange choice for travellers, but its isolation remains at the heart of its appeal.

While the rest of Eastern Europe has charged headlong into capitalism, Belarus allows the chance to visit a Europe with minimal advertising and no litter or graffiti. Outside the monumental Stalinist capital of Minsk, Belarus offers a simple yet pleasing landscape of cornflower fields, thick primeval forests and picturesque villages. The country also offers two excellent national parks and is home to Europe's largest mammal, the zoobr (or European bison). While travellers will always be subject to curiosity, they'll also invariably be on the receiving end of extremely warm hospitality and a genuine local welcome.

When to Go
Minsk

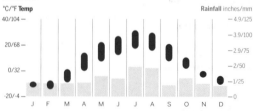

| June-August You won't have to worry about high season: come to escape the crowds elsewhere. | Mid-July Join in Vitsebk's superb Slavyansky Bazaar festival and celebrate all things Slavic. | Early July On 6 July watch the locals celebrate Kupalye, a fortune-telling festival with pagan roots. |

Fast Facts

» **Area** 207,600 sq km

» **Capital** Minsk

» **Telephone code** 375

» **Emergency** fire 01, police 02, ambulance 03

Exchange Rates

Australia	A$1	BR3187
Canada	C$1	BR3165
euro	€1	BR4409
Japan	¥100	BR3620
New Zealand	NZ$1	BR2393
UK	UK£1	BR4953
USA	US$1	BR3045

Set Your Budget

» **Budget hotel room** BR70,000

» **Two-course meal** BR60,000

» **Museum entrance** BR2000

» **Beer** BR1000

» **Minsk metro ticket** BR700

Resources

» **Belarus Embassy in the UK** (www.uk.belembassy. org)

» **Belarus Tourism** (www. eng.belarustourism.by)

Connections

Belarus has good overland links to all its neighbouring countries. Daily trains from Minsk serve Moscow, St Petersburg, Vilnius, Warsaw (via Terespol) and Kyiv; see p102 for more details. Bus services, which tend to be less comfortable, connect Minsk to Moscow, St Petersburg, Kyiv, Warsaw and Vilnius; Vitsebsk to Moscow and St Petersburg; and Brest to Terespol in Poland.

ITINERARIES

Three Days

Spend two days getting to know Minsk – its Stalinist architecture belies a lively and friendly city – before taking a day trip to Dudutki and Mir to get a feel for the charming Belarusian countryside.

One Week

Begin with two nights in Brest, including a day trip to the Belavezhskaya Pushcha National Park, then take a train to Minsk, allowing yourself time for a day trip to Dudutki and Mir before continuing on to historic Vitsebsk.

Essential Food & Drink

» **Belavezhskaya** A bitter herbal alcoholic drink

» **Draniki** Potato pancakes, usually served with sour cream (*smetana*)

» **Kletsky** Dumplings stuffed with mushrooms, cheese or potato

» **Kolduni** Potato dumplings stuffed with meat

» **Manchanka** Pancakes served with a meaty gravy

Map Labels

Gulf of Riga

LATVIA

⊙ Rīga

⊙ Jelgava

Rēzekne

Panevėžys ⊙

⊙ Daugavpils

RUSSIA

LITHUANIA

Daugava (Zapadnaya Dvina)

P18

P46

P133

⊗ Novopolatsk ⊙ Polatsk

Vitsebsk ❹

Kaunas ⊙

Hlybokoye

Bjarezinski Biosphere Reserve

P46

M3

M8

Smolensk ⊙

A141

Vilnius ✈

P45

P28

Neris (Vilija)

M3

Khatyn

E30

⊙ Orsha

Mahileu (Mogilev)

A101

E28

⊗ Maladzechna

⊙ Barysau

Krichev

⊙ Zaslavl ❶ Minsk

❺ Dudutki

Lida ⊗

M6

Mir ❻

P68

E28

P43

Hrodna

Navahrudak (Novogrudak)

P11

Babrujsk

Dnipro (Dniepr)

M8

Białystok ⊗

Slonim

❼ Nyasvizh

Baranavichy ⊙ Slutsk

Zhlobin

Homel

M10

❷ Belevezhskaya Pushcha National Park

P43

Svetlahorsk

POLAND

P136

E30

P31

⊗ Rechitsa

Bug

Brest

Pinsk

M10

Zhytkavichy

Kalinkavichy

Chernihiv

❸ Kobryn

Turau

Pripyat

Mazyr

Terespol

P17

Pripyatsky National Park

Chornobyl Exclusion Zone

Deana

Chornobyl

UKRAINE

Lutsk ⊙

⊙ Rivne

Kyiv ✪

Kyiv Reservoir

Zhytomyr

160 km
100 miles

Belarus Highlights

❶ Get under the skin of **Minsk** (p78), the showpiece of Stalinist architecture, and a friendly and accessible city

❷ Spot a European bison, a brown bear or a wolf at **Belavezhskaya Pushcha National Park** (p91)

❸ Stroll through the mellow pedestrian streets of

cosmopolitan Brest to the epic WWII memorial that is **Brest Fortress** (p87)

❹ Discover the childhood home of painter Marc Chagall in **Vitsebsk** (p92)

❺ Enjoy life at a slow pace while visiting the charming farm-museum in bucolic **Dudutki** (p86)

❻ See the fairytale 16th-century castle at **Mir** (p86) that presides over the tranquil town of the same name

❼ Explore one of the few historical complexes to have survived WWII at **Nyasvizh** (p86), amid beautiful lakes and the picturesque Radziwill Palace Fortress

MINSK MIHCK

♪017 / POP 1.73 MILLION

Minsk will almost certainly surprise you. The capital of Belarus is, despite its thoroughly dreary-sounding name, a progressive and modern place quite at odds with its own reputation. Here fashionable cafes, wi-fi enabled restaurants and crowded nightclubs vie for your attention, while sushi bars and art galleries have taken up residence in a city centre once totally remodelled to the tastes of Stalin. Despite the strong police presence and obedient citizenry, scrape the surface and you'll find that there's more than a whiff of rebellion in the air.

Totally razed to the ground in WWII, Minsk is an ideological statement wrought in stone and cement. With almost no buildings remaining from the pre-war years, there are relatively few traditional sights in the city. Instead though, there are myriad places of interest to anyone fascinated by the Soviet period, and a smattering of cosmopolitan pursuits to keep you entertained come the evening.

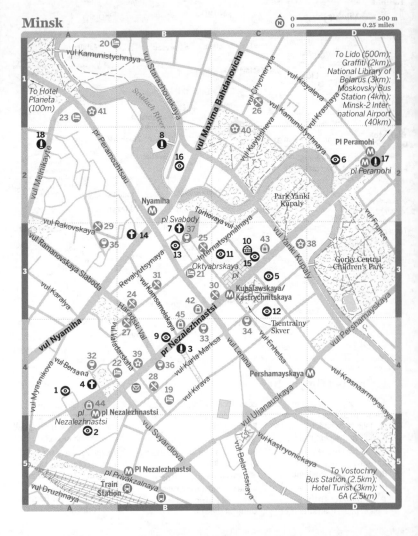

Minsk

⊙ Sights

Razed to the ground in WWII, Minsk retains almost nothing from the pre-war period, and was built anew in the late 1940s and 1950s as a flagship Stalinist city. The result is a remarkably uniform conurbation that is actually strangely attractive, the Stalinist style being far grander and more colourful than the later Soviet architecture of the 1960s and 1970s.

Pl Nezalezhnastsi
SQUARE

The city's central square, pl Nezalezhnastsi (Independence Sq, also called pl Lenina), is dominated by the **Belarusian Government Building** (behind the Lenin statue) on its northern side, and the equally proletarian **Belarusian State University** on the south side. The red-brick Catholic **Church of Sts Simon & Elena** built in 1910 is also here. Its tall, gabled bell tower and attractive detailing are reminiscent of many brick churches in the former Teutonic north of Poland. Beneath the square lies Stolitsa Shopping Centre (p84), a modern three-storey mall where you'll find much of Minsk's best shopping.

Pr Nezalezhnastsi
AVENUE

Heading northeast from pl Nezalezhnastsi is the main part of pr Nezalezhnastsi and the bustling heart of Minsk, including the Soviet-era GUM department store (p84). An entire block at No 17 is occupied by a yellow neoclassical building with an ominous, temple-like Corinthian portal – the **KGB headquarters**. On the other side of the street is a long, narrow park with a **bust of Felix Dzerzhinsky**, the founder of the KGB's predecessor (the Cheka) and a native of Belarus.

Oktyabrskaya Pl
SQUARE

Between vul Enhelsa and vul Yanki Kupaly is a square that is still referred to by its Russian name, Oktyabrskaya pl (in Belarusian, it's pl Kastrychnitskaya). This is where opposition groups gather to protest against Lukashenko from time to time, and it's where they attempted the failed Denim Revolution in March

BELARUS MINSK

Minsk

2006. Here you'll find the impressive, severe **Palats Respubliki** (Palace of the Republic), a concert hall. Also on this square is the classical, multicolumned **Trade Unions Culture Palace**, and next to this is the excellent **Museum of the Great Patriotic War** (☑277 5611; pr Nezalezhnastsi 25a; admission BR2000; ☺10am-6pm Tue & Thu-Sat, 11am-7pm Wed & Sun), where Belarus' horrors and heroism during WWII are exhibited in photographs, huge dioramas and other media. Particularly harrowing are the photographs of partisans being executed in recognisable central Minsk locations. The big sign above the building means 'The feats of the people will live on for centuries'.

Tsentralny Skver SQUARE

Across the street is Tsentralny Skver (Central Sq), a small park on the site of a 19th-century marketplace. The dark-grey building is **Dom Ofitserov** (Officer's Building), which has a tank memorial at the front, devoted to the soldiers who freed Minsk from the Nazis. Beyond this is the lifeless-looking, seriously guarded **Presidential Administrative Building**, from where Alexander Lukashenko rules.

Pl Peramohi SQUARE

Further north pr Nezalezhnastsi crosses the Svislach River and parkland on both sides, before coming into striking pl Peramohi (Victory Sq), marked by a giant **Victory Obelisk** and its eternal flame, which is directly beneath the obelisk underground.

Traetskae Pradmestse OLD TOWN

In lieu of any real remaining Old Town is Traetskae Pradmestse, a pleasant – if tiny – re-creation of Minsk's pre-war buildings on a pretty bend of the river downstream from pl Peramohi. It's worth strolling through for its little cafes, restaurants and shops. At the end of a little footbridge nearby is the evocative Afghan war memorial, **Island of Courage and Sorrow**, more commonly called the Island of Tears. Standing on a small island connected by a walking bridge, it's built in the form of a tiny church, with four entrances, and is surrounded by towering gaunt statues of sorrowful mothers and sisters of Belarusian soldiers who perished in the war between the Soviet Union and Afghanistan (1979–89). Look for the small statue of the crying angel, off to the side – it is the guardian angel of Belarus.

Zaslavsky Jewish Monument MONUMENT

Another extremely moving sight is the Zaslavsky Jewish Monument, rather hidden away in a sunken gully amid trees off vul Melnikayte. It commemorates the sav-

age murder of 5000 Jews from Minsk at the hands of the Nazis on 2 March 1942, and is made up of sculptures of scared men, women and children lining up to be shot, one person even carrying their violin.

Pl Svabody SQUARE

Between vul Internatsyanalnaya and the river is the charming pl Svabody, which contains the baroque, twin-towered Orthodox **Holy Spirit Cathedral**, which was built in 1642 and stands confidently on a small hill. It was once part of a Polish Bernardine convent, along with the **former Bernardine Church** next door, which now houses city archives. The white medieval **ratusha** (town hall) is also on the square and this is a popular place for locals to come for wedding pictures, as you'll no doubt discover.

Sts Peter & Paul Church CHURCH

(vul Rakovskaya 4) Across the vul Lenina overpass is the attractively restored 17th-century Sts Peter & Paul Church, the city's oldest church (built in 1613, looted by Cossacks in 1707 and restored in 1871). Now it is awkwardly dwarfed by the surrounding morose concrete structures.

Church of St Aleksandr Nevsky CHURCH

(vul Kazlova 11) This red-brick church was built in 1898, was closed by the Bolsheviks, re-opened by the Nazis, re-closed by the Soviets and now it's open again. It's said that during WWII, a bomb crashed through the roof and landed plum in front of the altar, but never detonated.

National Library of Belarus LIBRARY

(☑293 2853; old.nlb.by/en; pr Nezalezhnastsi 116; ☺10am-9pm Mon-Fri, 10am-6pm Sat & Sun, closed Sun Jun-Aug; Ⓜ Vostok) For a taste of post-Soviet Belarus, head north of the centre to the new National Library of Belarus, a ghastly piece of Lukashenko-approved hubris. The building is a giant rhombicuboctahedron (look it up!) that is lit at night and contains over two million records as well as art galleries and a **viewing platform** (admission BR3000; ☺1-9pm Tue-Fri, 10am-6pm Sat & Sun) on the 22nd floor.

🛏 Sleeping

Minsk's accommodation scene is generally limited to fusty old Soviet hotels or overpriced four- and five-star places geared to business travellers. A much better option if you're in the city for more than a few days is to rent an apartment. Several agencies offer this service, including **Belarus Rent** (www.belarusrent.com) and **Belarus Apartment**

Just across the bridge over the Svislach River, on the west bank, is the **former residence of Lee Harvey Oswald** (vul Kamyunistychnaya 4); it's the bottom left apartment. The alleged assassin of former US president John F Kennedy lived here for a couple of years in his early 20s. He arrived in Minsk in January 1960 after leaving the US Marines and defecting to the USSR. Once here, he truly went native: he got a job in a radio factory, married a Minsk woman, had a child – and even changed his name to Alek. But soon he returned to the United States and...you know the rest.

Lovers of old coins should stop in at the train station's **left-luggage area**, where there are lockers that (surprise, surprise) date back to the Soviet days – and they still only work with Soviet coins. Pay BR550 and in exchange get two locker 'tokens' – 15-kopek coins from the USSR, some dating back to the 1960s.

(www.belarusapartment.com). Rates range from €40 to €100 per night.

Crowne Plaza Minsk   HOTEL €€€
(☑229 8333; www.hoteleurope.by; vul Internatsyanalnaya 28; r incl breakfast from BR765,000, ste from BR1,019,000; ✳☎⚛) Generally considered to be Minsk's finest hotel, the superb, central and sleek Crowne Plaza is the choice of business people and the pleasantly wealthy. The rooms are large, well appointed and stylish, and the location can't be beaten.

Hotel Europe   HOTEL €€€
(☑229 8333; www.hoteleurope.by; vul Internatsyanalnaya 28; s/d incl breakfast from BR795,000/925,000, ste from BR1,400,000; ✳☎⚛) The first five-star hotel in Belarus opened to great fanfare in 2006, and while there are some horrific crimes against taste being perpetrated in the lobby, the spacious if flouncy rooms can't really be faulted. Service is excellent, and extras such as a fitness centre and a small pool seal the deal.

40 Let Pobedy   HOTEL €
(☑294 7963; vul Azgura 3; s/d from BR64,000/70,000) This slightly out-of-the-way yet central place offers decent, good-value rooms and friendly service. The hotel has made a good effort to modernise itself (even if it is with cheap furnishings) and all the bathrooms have been redone. Cheap wi-fi is available throughout.

Hotel Yubileiny   HOTEL €€
(☑226 9024; fax 226 9171; pr Peramozhtsau 19; unrenovated s/d BR155,000/190,000, renovated s/d BR228,000/275,000;⚛) This centrally located Soviet place is located across the road from Minsk's main athletics stadium and the river. Most of the rooms have been done up, but rooms on the 5th, 7th and 13th floors have

not and are cheaper as a result. The staff are friendly and there's cheap lobby wi-fi.

Hotel Belarus   HOTEL €€
(☑209 7693/7537; www.hotel-belarus.com; vul Starazhouskaya15;s/dinclbreakfastfromBR185,000/228,000;⚛) Just when you thought Minsk couldn't get any more Soviet, along comes the monolithic Hotel Belarus. Set in parkland amid plenty of open space a 15-minute amble from the city centre, this place has undergone little change since it was built, although a swimming pool with a waterslide sets it apart from other hotels of this standard.

Hotel Turist   HOTEL €€
(☑295 4031; Partizansky pr 81; s/d from BR158,000/222,000) Out of the city centre but handily located for the Partizanskaya metro station, this old Soviet place has been partially remodelled. The economy-class rooms, all with bathrooms, are basic but good value for money. Cheap wi-fi is available.

Hotel Planeta   HOTEL €€
(☑226 7855; www.hotelplaneta.by; pr Peramozhtsau 31; s/d incl breakfast from BR215,900/BR266,000; ⚛) On a hill a fair walk from the centre of the city, the Hotel Planeta offers midrange remodelled rooms and a decent standard of service. Nevertheless, an endearing Soviet air remains. There's cheap lobby wi-fi.

Hotel Minsk   HOTEL €€€
(☑209 9062; www.hotelminsk.by; vul Nezalezhnastsi 11; s/d incl breakfast BR540,000/620,000, ste from BR888,000; ✳✳☎) Excellently located, the city's long-standing hotel of choice has now been eclipsed by newer five-star hotels. It's still a solid option, though the mattresses are in need of replacement, and there's free wi-fi in the lobby only.

✕ Eating

Minsk has a decent eating scene and plenty of choice – don't believe the hype about food in Belarus; in the capital, at least, you'll eat well. Consider reserving tables at weekends.

TOP CHOICE Strawnya Talaka — TRADITIONAL €€
(vul Rakovskaya 18; mains BR10,000-60,000; ⊘10am-6am) This relaxed and cosy place is the best restaurant in Minsk for an authentic local meal, and also has handy long opening hours. Try the hare in bilberry sauce or just a bowl of ham and bean soup with fabulous *deruni* (potato pancakes).

Vino y Comida — TAPAS BAR €€€
(vul Internatsyanalnaya; tapas BR8,000-20,000, mains BR25,000-50,000; ⊘11am-midnight) This stylish new addition to Minsk's dining scene serves up good tapas from a large menu that encompasses all the classics, as well as offering a range of meaty *platos calientes* and excellent paella (BR60,000 to BR80,0000).

Pizza Tempo — PIZZA €€
(🗹292 1111; www.pizzatempo.by; vul Karla Marksa 9; mains BR8000-25,000; ⊘8am-11pm) This chain of seven pizzerias is spread across the city, with each restaurant stylishly decorated and enjoying a relaxed vibe. Citywide delivery is available and the pizza is the best we've found in Minsk.

Bistro de Luxe — BISTRO €€€
(Haradsky Val 10; mains BR20,000-40,000; ⊘8am-midnight; 🛜) Housed in a pleasant light-bathed space with chandeliers, sleek brasserie-style furnishings and aspirational toilets, Bistro de Luxe is a current favourite of the fashionable in Minsk. There's free wi-fi, excellent coffee and a full menu that leans towards Italian. Breakfast is served daily until midday.

Gurman — RUSSIAN €€
(🗹290 6774; vul Kamyunistychnaya 7; mains BR6000-40,000; ⊘8am-11pm) This Minsk institution specialises in many varieties of delicious, freshly made *pelmeni* (Russian-style ravioli) and also offers a wide selection of pastas and even curries. The light and airy premises and friendly staff make this well worth the wander from the metro. It's worth booking a table for dinner.

Byblos — LEBANESE €€
(vul Internatsyanalnaya 21; mains BR10,000-25,000; ⊘noon-midnight) What this Lebanese-style place lacks in authenticity it makes up for in value, quick service and an English menu. Great for an easy lunch; the kebabs and hummus are decent enough, given that you're in Belarus, and there's great people-watching from the enclosed terrace.

Mirsky Zamak — TRADITIONAL €€€
(Haradsky Val 9; mains BR15,000-70,000; ⊘noon-midnight Sun-Thu, to 2am Fri & Sat) The 'Mir Castle' is a friendly place, as traditionally decked out as possible given its location in a Soviet residential block to one side of the KGB. Hearty, meaty Belarusian dishes are served up and loud live music is performed each evening from 8pm.

Lido — CANTEEN €
(pr Nezalezhnastsi 49/1; mains BR2000-5000; ⊘8am-11pm Mon-Fri, 11am-11pm Sat & Sun) This excellent place is a real lifesaver for a quick and filling meal. The large cafeteria has a huge array of food on display, so it's easy for non-Russian speakers: just point at what you want. Lunchtime is always packed, but it's usually easy to find a seat among the curious faux-medieval village decor.

Tsentralny Magazin — SUPERMARKET €
(2nd fl, pr Nezalezhnastsi 23; ⊘9am-11pm) A large, Western-style grocery store with plenty of supplies for self-caterers.

🍷 Drinking

Bars

Rakovsky Brovar — MICROBREWERY
(vul Vitsebskaya 10; ⊘noon-midnight) Minsk's first microbrewery is housed in an enormous central venue and shows no sign of losing its popularity. There's a full menu here too (mains BR12,000 to BR40,000), although most people come here for after-work drinks and stay late amid the raucous atmosphere.

U Ratushi — PUB
(vul Gertsena 1; ⊘10am-2am) This multilevel pub-style restaurant, right across from the *ratusha* (town hall), is packed with a raucous, fun-loving crowd on weekends (there is often a small cover charge for live bands). Book ahead for weekends, or come really early.

Drozhzhi United — IRISH PUB
(vul Sverdlova 2; ⊘9am-2am) Centrally located, Minsk's Irish pub is instantly recognisable to anyone who has ever been an expat, anywhere. There's good food, Guinness on tap and a friendly atmosphere.

Cafes

The best cafes in Minsk include the sleek **News Café** (vul Karla Marksa 34; ⊘8am-midnight; 🛜), where free wi-fi (only until 7pm), good

Between the Soviet, post-Soviet, Russian and Belarusian names for streets and places in Belarus things can get confusing. In this chapter we use Belarusian street and place names, as this is almost universally how they are written on signposts (in Cyrillic of course – so you'll still have to transliterate). However, almost everyone will tell you the Russian names for streets, so there's room for real confusion. When giving addresses we use the abbreviations vul (*vulitsa*), pr (*praspekt*) and pl (*ploshcha*) to denote street, avenue and square. Russian speakers will call these *ulitsa*, *prospekt* and *ploshchad* respectively, but again, the Belarusian versions are used on street signs in nearly all cases.

Minsk is particularly confusing in this respect. To honour the great Belarusian renaissance man, the city's main thoroughfare was once called pr Francyska Skaryny, but in 2005 Lukashenko changed it to 'Independence Avenue': pr Nezalezhnastsi (pr Nezavisimosti in Russian). Similarly pl Peramohi (Victory Sq) is often referred to as its Russian variant, pl Pobedy.

Metro stop and town square pl Lenina also goes by its post-Soviet name, which switches 'Lenin' for 'Independence': ploshcha Nezalezhnastsi (pl Nezavisimosti in Russian). Metro change station and main town square Oktyabrskaya pl (its Russian name) is sometimes called pl Kastrychnitskaya (the Belarusian version of the same name). Enjoy!

coffee and full meals make for a great hangout, and the bizarre next-door **My English Granny** (vul Karla Marksa 36; ☉9am-11pm; 🛜), a cafe that has pulled off the incredible feat of making kitschy Victoriana look trendy, where you'll get a lovely pot of tea and some good cakes, as well as meals and a great breakfast selection. Two other slightly more bohemian options are sister cafes **Stary Mensk** (pr Nezalezhnastsi 14; ☉10am-11pm) and **London** (pr Nezalezhnastsi 18; ☉10am-11pm), which both serve hot drinks and are favoured by Minsk's intellectual crowd.

☆ Entertainment

Performing Arts

A pleasant hangover from Soviet times is that performing arts are of very good quality and tickets are cheap.

To buy advance tickets or to find out what's on, head to the **central ticket office** (pr Nezalezhnastsi 13; ☉9am-7pm). There are more places for tickets in the underground crossing in the centre. Same-day tickets are often available only from the performance venues.

Don't miss the highly respected **National Academic Opera & Ballet Theatre** (📞234 8074; pl Parizhskoy Kamunni 1; ☉ticket office 9am-1pm & 2-6pm Mon-Fri), where there are several different operas performed each month; performances take place at 7pm on Thursday, Saturday and Sunday. The **Belarusian State Circus** (📞226 1008; pr Nezalezhnastsi 32) was being renovated at the time of research, but should be open again in 2011.

Nightclubs

Minsk has a surprisingly good selection of nightlife and there's plenty going on in town to keep night owls busy.

Graffiti   UNDERGROUND BAR
(www.graffiti.by; pr Kalinina 16; cover BR10,000-20,000; ☉11am-11pm, to 2am Fri & Sat) For something more contemporary and underground, Graffiti offers nightly concerts from local bands and big weekend parties popular with an anti-Luka crowd. It's a 10-minute walk from the Park Chelyuskintsev metro station, head up Vul Tolbukhina, turn right onto vul Knorina and then left into vul Belinskogo and Graffiti can be found in the unlikely-looking industrial building on the corner.

Overtime   NIGHTCLUB
(pr Peremozhtsau 4; cover free-BR40,000; ☉6pm-6am) Currently the hippest place in town despite its premises being better suited for use as a venue for a high school disco, this club attracts a chic and monied crowd of local glitzy gals and their muscley boyfriends. Dress up to get in – face control can be tough.

6A   GAY CLUB
(Partizansky Pr 6a; cover BR5000; ☉10pm-3am; Ⓜ Proletarskaya) The only gay club in Minsk is a curious but friendly Soviet throwback in a building where time appears to have stood still since the 1970s. A unique experience.

Bela Vezha   NIGHTCLUB
(📞284 6922; pr Masherava 17; cover BR20,000-40,000; ☉11pm-5am Tue-Sun) This nightclub has a space-aged theme, plays house and

pop and has lots of live acts. Its labyrinthine corridors contain a huge 24-hour casino, an expensive restaurant and a big dance floor.

Bronx
NIGHTCLUB

(288 1061; pr Masherava 17/1; cover BR10,000-50,000; noon-5am Thu-Sat, noon-2am Sun-Wed) Bronx is favoured by a very young crowd and is a relaxed and fun space. Special guest bands and DJs from abroad show up at the sleek, ultramodern warehouse-style space, where there are billiards, dance floors and fashion shows.

🔒 Shopping

Minsk's shopping scene is far from mind-blowing, but the locals love nothing more than to revel in consumerism. If you want a general browse, a good place to start is the **Stolitsa Shopping Centre** (pl Nezalezhnastsi; 10am-10pm), a three-level subterranean mall housing much of the capital's swanki-est shops.

Souvenirs from Belarus tend to be alco-holic, but there are other options beyond buying vodka. At many grocery shops you'll find candies with old-fashioned wrappers steeped in nostalgia for a Soviet childhood. Belarus is also known for its straw crafts, which include dolls and wooden boxes in-tricately ornamented with geometric pat-terns of the stuff. Linens and other woven textiles unique to Belarus are also popular handicrafts. These are easily found in city department stores, hotel lobbies and at **Min-sky Vernisazh** (Oktyabrskaya pl; 8am-6pm Tue-Sun), a souvenir market right next to the Museum of the Great Patriotic War where you can haggle for local art, folk crafts and other rather garish traditional items. Other recommended shops include **Podzemka** (pr Nezalezhnastsi 43; 10am-8pm Mon-Sat, 11am-6pm Sun), an underground bohemian shop-cum-art-gallery that sells all sorts of goodies you won't find anywhere else including an excellent range of DVDs, funky artistic piec-es and handmade jewellery.

It's also worth checking the department stores, such as **GUM** (pr Nezalezhnastsi 21) and **TsUM** (pr Nezalezhnastsi 54) or the **Tsentral-naya Kniharnya** (pr Nezalezhnastsi 19) book-shop for souvenirs.

ℹ Information

Internet Access

Free wi-fi can be had in top-end hotels (buy a coffee in the lobby and try to look like a guest) or **My English Granny** (p82), **Bistro de Luxe** (p82)

and until 7pm at **News Café** (p82). The most ac-cessible internet cafes include the following:

Internet Café (train station; 9am-7am) Use-fully located club on the 3rd floor of the city's railway station.

Soyuz Online (2nd fl, vul Krasnaarmeyskaya 3; 24hr) Large internet cafe in the centre of town. Food and drinks available. Go up the steps to the Dom Ofitserov and enter the far door near the tank monument.

Tetris Internet Café (vul Frunze 3; 8am-9pm)

Internet Resources
Minsk in Your Pocket (www.inyourpocket.com/belarus) Has a free Minsk guide to down-load, which is regularly updated; it's also avail-able in hard copy from some hotels.

Left Luggage
Train station (lockers BR500, luggage room BR1000; 24hr) Downstairs is a well-signed place, with a fiendishly complex system. To use the lockers, put your stuff in an empty one, select a code on the inside of the door, put a token in, shut the door. Use your second token to open the locker again. Ask staff to help if you're confused (you probably will be) – or pay a little extra to use the luggage room.

Medical Services
24-hour Pharmacy (pr Nezalezhnastsi 16)
EcoMedservices (207 7474; www.ems.by; vul Tolstoho 4; 8am-9pm) The closest thing to a reliable, Western-style clinic. Dental services are offered here too.

Money
ATMs can be found throughout the city. Many ATMs offer US dollars or euros, if for some rea-son you need foreign currency (don't take out dollars or euros just to change them to roubles though; you'll pay the exchange rate twice). Big hotels all have exchange bureaus, and a handful can cash travellers cheques.

Post
DHL and UPS have offices based in the major hotels, including Hotel Yubileiny (p81).

Central post office (pr Nezalezhnastsi 10; 7am-11pm) In the centre of town.

Tourist Information
Travel agencies can provide information but of course they want you to book tours. There is no official tourist information centre in Minsk.

Travel Agencies
Alatan Tour (227 7417; www.welcome belarus.com; vul Internatsionalnaya 33b) A reliable English-speaking outfit that offers visa support, hotel bookings, guide services and drivers.

Belarus Tour Service (☎200 5675; www.hotelsbelarus.com; vul Rozi Lyuksemburg 89) Visa support, hotel bookings and transfers.

Belintourist (☎226 9971; www.belintourist.by; pr Peramozhtsau 19) The state-run tourist agency does visa support, city tours and trips to Mir, Dudutki, Nyasvizh and Belavezhskaya Pushcha National Park – as well as offering all kinds of tours including hunting trips, skiing trips and a 28-day 'Say Goodbye to Asthma' tour.

Top Tour (☎202 8404; en.toptour.by; Hotel Orbita, pr Pushkina 39) Visa support, hotels, interpreters and tours.

Vokrug Sveta (☎226 8392; vokrugsveta.by; vul Internatsyanalnaya 10) Another good agency offering visa support, accommodation, excursions and interpreters.

❶ Getting There & Away

Air

International flights entering and departing Belarus do so at the **Minsk-2 international airport** (☎006, 279 1300; www.airport.by), about 40km east of Minsk. Some flights to the former Soviet Union depart from the smaller **Minsk-1 airport** (☎006; vul Chkalova 38), only a few kilometres south of the city centre.

Bus

There are three main bus stations, and you can buy tickets for anywhere at any of them. To ask which station you're departing from in Russian is 'v ka-*kom* av-toh-vak-*za*-le ot-prav-*lye*-ni-ye'. The **MinskTrans** (www.minsktrans.by) website also gives full timetable information, though it's in Russian only. From Minsk, international services include buses to Vilnius, Warsaw, Kyiv, Moscow and St Petersburg.

Moskovsky bus station (☎219 3622; vul Filimonava 63) Near Maskouskaya metro station, about 4km east of the city.

Tsentralny bus station (☎227 0473; vul Bobruyskaya 6) By the train station.

Vostochny bus station (☎247 4984; vul Vaneeva 34) To get here from the train station (or metro Pl Lenina), take bus 8 or trolley 20 or 30; get off at 'Avtovokzal Vostochny'.

Car & Motorcycle

You can hire cars from the following places:

Avis (☎347 7990; www.avis.by; Hotel Belarus, vul Storozhevskaya 15)

Europcar (☎209 9009; www.europcar.by; Hotel Minsk, pr Nezalezhnastsi 11)

Hertz (☎209 9091; www.hertz.com; pr Nezalezhnastsi 11)

Train

The busy and modern **Minsk train station** (☎105, 225 7000; ☺24hr) is pretty easy to deal with. Very basic food and complex left-luggage services are available here, as well as an internet cafe on the 3rd floor, ATMs and exchange facilities. Buy domestic and CIS tickets here.

Domestic train ticket office (☎225 6271; pr Nezalezhnastsi 18; ☺9am-8pm Mon-Fri, 9am-7pm Sat & Sun) Tickets for domestic and CIS (Commonwealth of Independent States) destinations.

International train ticket office (☎213 1719; vul Bobruyskaya 4; ☺9am-8pm) Advance tickets for non-CIS destinations; located to the right of the train station.

❶ Getting Around

See p102 for information on car rentals.

To/From the Airport

From Minsk-2 airport, a 40-minute taxi ride into town should cost anywhere from BR80,000 to BR120,000, depending on your bargaining skills. There are buses and *marshrutky* (minibuses; BR5000, 90 minutes, hourly) that bring you to the city centre, though you can get out at the first metro station (Uruchye) to get elsewhere in the city. From Minsk-1 airport, take bus 100 to the centre; it goes along pr Nezalezhnastsi.

INTERNATIONAL TRAINS FROM MINSK

DESTINATION	PRICE PLATZKART/KUPE	DEPARTURES	DURATION (HR)
Berlin	BR423,000 *kupe* only	1 daily	16
Kyiv	BR106,0000/167,000	1 daily	12
Moscow	BR100,0000/195,000	multiple daily	11
Prague	BR485,000 *kupe* only	3 times a week	21
St Petersburg	BR108,0000/211,000	1 daily	14
Vilnius	BR25,000/58,000	2 daily	4
Warsaw	BR205,000 *kupe* only	1 daily	10

Public Transport

Minsk's metro is simple: just two lines with one transfer point at the Kastrychnitskaya-Kupalauskaya interchange on pr Nezalezhnastsi – and operates until just after midnight. One token *(zheton)* costs BR700.

Buses, trams, trolleybuses and the metro operate from 5.30am to 1am. *Marshrutki* cost about BR1000 to BR1500 per ride and are generally quicker than other overground transport methods. Popular bus 100 comes every five to 15 minutes and plies pr Nezalezhnastsi as far as Moskovsky bus station. You can buy a ticket from the person on board wearing a bright vest. Once you get the ticket, punch it at one of the red buttons placed on the poles.

Taxi

For taxis, ☎081 is the state service and almost always has cars available, while ☎007 is private, the cheapest and has the best service (less likely to rip off foreigners) but cars are sometimes not available during peak times. You can also hail one from the street. Unlike in Russia, private cars don't usually stop for passengers.

AROUND MINSK

Leave Minsk for an easy taste of the gently appealing Belarusian countryside, to a world where instead of mobile-phone shops and sushi bars, the few stores you'll see will have names like 'Bread' and 'Shoes', dating from a bygone era of no choice. Don't miss the fairytale castle at Mir or your chance to taste a slice of traditional village life at Dudutki.

To really immerse yourself in rural life, consider trying **Rural Belarus** (☎205 0465; www.ruralbelarus.by), a nonprofit association of B&Bs that offers dozens of homestays throughout the country.

Dudutki ДУДУТКІ

☎01713

Tasting delicious farm-made sausages, cheese and bread is only a small part of the experience of a visit to the **open-air interactive museum** (☎133 0747; www.dudutki.by; adult/child incl tastings BR25,000/7000; ⏲10am-4pm Tue-Wed, 10am-5pm Thu-Sun) of Dudutki, located 40km south of Minsk. This completely self-sufficient farm offers horse riding, sleigh rides, demonstrations of ceramic making, blacksmithing and more. You'll be offered fresh *salo* (tallow) with garlic, salt and rye bread; pickles dipped in honey; and homemade moonshine – all scrumptious.

There are two daily buses (one hour, BR7000 each way) to Dudutki from Minsk's Vostochny bus station at 9.40am and 12.55pm, with return buses at 2.20pm and 5.40pm. Otherwise, contact Valeria's **Dudutki Tur** (☎017-251 0076; dudutki@telecom.by), which can organise private transport.

Nyasvizh НЯСВІЖ

☎01770 / POP 15,000

The magical old buildings of Nyasvizh make it a great place to get in touch with Belarus' past – one that elsewhere has all too often been destroyed as military campaigns flattened the country. This quiet but green and attractive town 120km southwest of Minsk is one of the oldest in the country, dating from the 13th century. It reached its zenith in the mid-16th century while owned by the mighty Radziwill magnates.

The **Farny Polish Roman Catholic Church** was built between 1584 and 1593 in early baroque style and features a splendidly proportioned facade. Inside, the frescos have been restored to their former elaborate glory.

Just beyond the church is the red-brick arcaded **Castle Gate Tower**. Constructed in the 16th century, the tower was originally part of a wall and gateway controlling the passage between the palace and the town. Here there's an **excursion bureau** (vul Leninskaya 19; ⏲8am-5pm Mon-Fri) where you pay to enter the fortress grounds (BR5000). Guided tours (BR50,000) for one to 25 people last about 1½ hours and are available in either Russian or Belarusian.

Further on is a causeway leading to the beautiful **Radziwill Palace Fortress** (1583), the main sight in Nyasvizh. In Soviet times it was turned into a sanatorium but restoration was nearing completion at the time of research. There are English and Japanese gardens to stroll in here, as well as an eternal flame in the attractive lakeside park, commemorating those who died in WWII.

From Minsk's Vostochny bus station, there are two daily buses to/from Nyasvizh (BR12,000, 2½ hours).

Mir МІР

☎01596 / POP 2500

The charming small town of Mir, 85km southwest of Minsk, is dominated by the impossibly romantic 16th-century **Mir Castle** (☎23 035; admission BR10,000; ⏲10am-5pm) that overlooks a small lake at one end of the town. It was once owned by the powerful Radziwill princes and has been under Unesco protection since 1994. Sadly, today the exterior is the highlight of the castle as almost all the original contents have been removed. Even though it's worth a walk around the small areas open to visitors, there's little to see here. Guided tours in Russian are offered (BR55,000 for one to 10 people). The town of Mir itself is a delightful backwater.

The small, friendly **Hotel Mir** (☑ 23 851; pl 17ogo Sentyabrya 2; s/d BR47,150/72,300) is the only place to stay in town. You'll find it on the charming town square, across the way from the bus station. Breakfast is not included, but there is a cafe here and a restaurant on the other side of the square.

From Minsk's Vostochny and Tsentralny bus stations, there are buses to Navahrudak (Novogrudok in Russian) that stop in Mir (BR10,000 to BR12,000, 2½ hours, hourly).

Khatyn ХАТЫНЬ

☑ 01774

The hamlet of Khatyn, 60km north of Minsk, was burned to the ground by Nazis on 22 March 1943. Of a population of 149 (including 85 children), only one man, Yuzif Kaminsky, survived. The site is now a sobering **memorial** (☑ 55 787; ☉ 9am-5pm Tue-Sat); tours are offered in Russian. More information can be found at www.khatyn.by. There's also an exhibit of photographs (admission BR2000).

There's no public transport to Khatyn from Minsk, but a taxi will cost around BR150,000 for the return journey. Pricey trips are organised by **Belintourist** (p84).

SOUTHERN BELARUS

Leave Minsk and you're quickly in another world. The concrete landscape gives way to pastoral scenes and undulating flat green plains rich in simple bucolic beauty – a river wending its way gently past thick forests, fields of cornflowers in bloom and small villages populated entirely by pensioners. It's not dramatic, but this is the 'real' Belarus.

The south of Belarus is dominated by Brest, a lively and attractive border town with a more European feel than Minsk. The star attraction nearby is the wonderful Belavezhskaya Pushcha National Park, which can be visited in a day trip from Brest, or –

even better – on an overnight trip where you stay in the park itself. There's also the excellent Pripyatsky National Park for those *really* wanting to get off the beaten path.

Brest БРЭСТ

☑ 0162 / POP 312,000

After visiting Minsk you'd be forgiven for thinking you'd arrived in another country when you get off the train in Brest. This prosperous and cosmopolitan border town looks far more to the neighbouring EU than to Minsk. It has plenty of charm and has performed a massive DIY job on itself over the past few years.

The city's main sight is the Brest Fortress, a moving WWII memorial where Soviet troops held out far longer than expected against the Nazi onslaught in the early days of Operation Barbarossa.

⊙ Sights

Brest Fortress   MUSEUM COMPLEX
(Brestskaya krepost; pr Masherava; admission free) Very little remains of Brest Fortress. Certainly don't come here expecting a medieval turreted affair – this is a Soviet WWII memorial to the devastating battle that resulted when German troops advanced into the Soviet Union in the early days of Operation Barbarossa in 1941. The large complex occupies a beautiful spot at the confluence of the Buh and Mukhavets Rivers, a 20-minute walk from the town centre or a short hop on the hourly 17 bus from outside the Hotel Intourist.

The fortress was built between 1838 and 1842, but by WWII it was used mainly as a barracks. The two regiments bunking here when German troops launched a surprise attack in 1941 defended the fort for an astounding month and became venerated as national legends thanks to Stalin's propaganda machine.

The **Brest Fortress main entrance** is its most iconic building – a huge socialist star formed from concrete. Sombre music accompanies you through the tunnel, and as you leave it, on the left and past a small hill, you'll see some **tanks** and, straight ahead, the stone **Thirst statue**, which depicts a water-starved soldier crawling for a drink. After you cross a small bridge, to your right are the brick ruins of the **White Palace**, where the 1918 Treaty of Brest-Litovsk – which marked Russia's exit from WWI – was signed. Further to the right is the **Defence of Brest Fortress Museum**

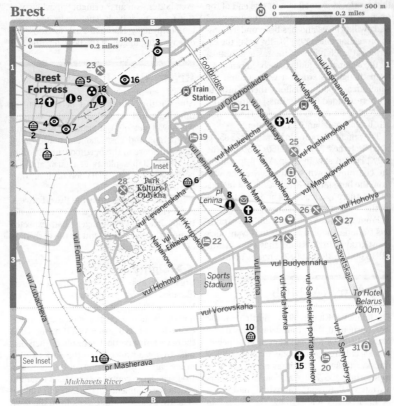

(adult/student BR2420/1450; ⊘9am-6pm). Its extensive and dramatic exhibits demonstrate the plight of the defenders. There's also a small collection of weaponry from 18th- to 20th-century warfare for which a separate ticket is required (BR2000).

Behind the museum is Café Tsitadel (p90), the only eating option here.

On the other side of the fortress is a collection of **cannons**. Behind this area is the entrance to the new **Brest Art Museum** (admission BR2250; ⊘10am-6pm Wed-Sun), which holds art done by Brest citizens, and some local crafts.

Heading to the **main monuments** – a large stone soldier's head projecting from a massive rock, entitled 'Valour', and a sky-scraping obelisk – you'll see an eternal flame and stones bearing the names of those who died (several are marked 'unknown'). Sombre orchestral music is played here too to ensure you are suitably moved.

Behind the Valour rock is the attractive, recently renovated Byzantine **Nikalaivsky Church**, the oldest church in the city, which dates from when the town centre occupied the fortress site. It holds regular services.

To the south is **Kholmskie Gate**; its bricks are decorated with crenulated turrets and its outer face is riddled with hundreds of bullet and shrapnel holes. Beyond the Kholmskie Gate is the **Bereste Archaeological Museum** (admission BR2500; ⊘9am-6pm), a large covered archaeological site where peasant and artisan huts from the 12th to 14th centuries have been uncovered.

Museum of Confiscated Art   MUSEUM
(vul Lenina 39; admission BR1500; ⊘10am-5.30pm Tue-Sun) There are a couple of excellent museums in the city centre. The most interesting is the Museum of Confiscated Art, where there's an extraordinary display of icons, paintings, jewellery and other valuables that were seized from smugglers trying to get

them across the border to Poland during the 1990s. Items on display are of unknown origin, hence their display in a museum rather than a return to their rightful owners.

Museum of Railway Technology MUSEUM
(pr Masherava 2; admission BR5000; ◷9am-6pm Wed-Sun May-Oct, 9am-5pm Wed-Sun Nov-Apr) Another interesting sight is the outdoor Museum of Railway Technology, where there's a superb collection of locomotives and carriages dating from 1903 (the *Moscow–Brest Express* with shower rooms and a very comfy main bedroom) to 1988 (far more proletarian Soviet passenger carriages). You can go inside many of them, so train enthusiasts and children love this place.

History of Brest Museum MUSEUM
(vul Levaneiskaha 3; admission BR14,000; ◷10am-5.15pm Tue-Sat) In an unassuming white building, the two-storey History of Brest Museum has a small exhibit on the city in its different guises throughout history, including an excellent model of the Brest Fortress in its heyday.

Other Sights

With its gold cupolas and yellow-and-blue facades, the breathtakingly detailed 200-year-old Orthodox **St Nikolaiv Church** (cnr vul Savetskaya & vul Mitskevicha) is one of many lovely churches in Brest. On pl Lenina, a **Lenin statue** points east towards Mos-

cow; though it appears more to be pointing across the street accusingly at the 1856 **St Christopher's Polish Catholic Church**. The peach-and-green **St Simeon Cathedral** (cnr pr Masherava & vul Karla Marksa) was built in 1865 in Russian-Byzantine style (the gold on the cupolas was added in 1997).

🛏 Sleeping

All hotels listed here have cheap wi-fi in their lobbies.

TOP CHOICE **Hotel Molodyozhnaya** HOTEL €€
(☎21 63 76; vul Kamsamolskaya 6; s/d BR92,300/141,720) This is the newest and least Soviet of Brest's hotels – a small and very centrally located place a short walk from the station. The rooms are comfortable and clean, all have private facilities and the welcome is almost warm.

Hotel Buh HOTEL €
(☎23 64 17; vul Lenina 2; s/d without bathroom BR64,000/96,000, with bathroom BR90,000/146,000; ☎) The cheapest and oldest of Brest's hotels is also the best choice for some character – the brightly painted Stalin-era foyer is a highlight and service is friendly. The renovated rooms with private bathrooms are often booked up in advance though, leaving the older facility-free rooms as the only option.

Hotel Belarus
HOTEL €€

(☎22 16 48; bresttourist@tut.by; bul Shevchenko 6; s/d incl breakfast BR102,000/150,000) This large block on a busy avenue leading out of the city centre is a little further out than the other hotels, and its rooms overlooking the main road can be very loud at night. Other than that, it's fine – simple but clean rooms with basic bathrooms contain TV, fridge and phone.

Vesta Hotel
HOTEL €€

(☎23 71 69; hotelvesta@tut.by; vul Krupskoi 16; s/d from BR89,000/111,000, ste BR212,000-456,000) Identical to its sister Soviet hotels in town, the Vesta does, however, boast a side-street location, making it far more peaceful than the other options. Its rooms are also somewhat more spacious, but largely identical, with TV and phones.

Hotel Intourist
HOTEL €€

(☎20 05 10; www.brestintourist.com; pr Masherava 15; s/d incl breakfast BR114,020/177,200, ste BR224,800-320,000) In a slightly better location than Hotel Belarus, the Intourist nevertheless has distinctly less friendly reception staff and its cavernous reception remains determinedly dark. Rooms are passable, though, with modernised facilities on almost every floor, and there are good city views.

Eating & Drinking

Brest has plenty of takeaways and fast food on offer, particularly around the pedestrianised area of vul Savetskaya. There's also a passable **supermarket** (vul Savetskaya 48; ☺8am-11pm) in the centre. At the fortress itself there's only the decidedly mediocre **Café Tsitadel** (☺9am-6pm) to cater for you – it's best to bring a packed lunch if you want to eat while you visit.

TOP CHOICE **Jules Verne**
FINE DINING €€

(vul Hoholya 29; mains BR12,000-50,000; ☺noon-midnight) It's almost a miracle that such a great restaurant exists in Brest. Decked out like a gentleman's club and with a travel theme, this dark, atmospheric joint manages to be refined without being stuffy. It serves up cracking dishes – from mouthwatering curries and a range of French cooking to sumptuous desserts and the best coffee in town. Don't miss it.

Retro Pizza
PIZZA €€

(vul Savetskaya 49; pizzas BR15,000-25,000) As well as decent pizza, there are good salads, pasta dishes and grills available at this spacious and light restaurant furnished with some wonderful Soviet-era technological

dinosaurs – check out the huge radio at the entrance. Delivery is possible.

Traktir U Ozera
TRADITIONAL €€

(Park Kultury i Otdykha; mains BR12,000-45,000) This old-style Russian inn (*traktir*) by the lake in Brest's main park has plenty of charm, although it's perhaps better for an evening meal than a daytime one, as it rather squanders its lakeside position and is surprisingly dark inside. Dishes range from steaks and kebabs to sushi and grills. For something simpler in equally pleasant surroundings, there's an open-air cafe serving up kebabs and beer outside.

Pizzeria
PIZZA €

(vul Pushkinskaya 20; pizzas BR10,000-18,000) It's not well signed, but you can pretty much follow your nose into the building through a garish bakery and then down the stairs. Surprisingly good thin-crust pizzas are made to order and consumed in this basement place while dubbed Mexican soap operas entertain the diners. Salads and fries are available as well.

Pub House
PUB

(vul Hoholya; ☺10am-midnight) This friendly and rustic wooden bar offers up a selection of beers from all over Europe, as well as showing sports events and serving decent food too. It's by far the most pleasant place for a drink in town.

Shopping

Souvenirs can be bought on the 1st floor of the city's **TsUM** (pr Masherava 17; ☺9am-9pm Mon-Sat, 9am-7pm Sun), although the selection is fairly limited. Local bra and underwear merchants **Milavitsa** (www.milavitsa.by; vul Pushkinskaya 21) continue to do a busy trade at their popular shop.

Information

24-hour pharmacy (vul Hoholya 32)

Belarusbank (pl Lenina) Currency exchange, Western Union and a nearby ATM.

Beltelekom (pr Masherava 21; internet per hr BR1500; ☺7am-10.30pm) You can make long-distance calls here, as well as use the internet cafe or the cheap wi-fi for those with laptops.

Brest Intourist (☎22 55 71, 20 10 71; www.brestintourist.com; pr Masherava 15; ☺9am-6pm Mon-Fri) Inside Hotel Intourist; the superfriendly English-speaking staff can arrange city tours including 'Jewish Brest' and overpriced trips to the Belavezhskaya Pushcha National Park.

City Emergency Hospital (☎23 58 38; vul Lenina 15)

Cyber Brest (3rd fl, vul Kamsamolskaya 36; per hr BR2000; ☺9am-midnight) Internet access at your choice of 50 computers; follow the footprints to the top floor.

Post office (pl Lenina)

❶ Getting There & Around

The **train station** (☎005) has on-site customs. Trains leave for Minsk (BR15,000/25,000 platzkart/kupe, four hours) several times daily. When taking a train from Brest, note that the platform nearest the city centre is for eastbound trains (ie towards Minsk and Russia); the next one is for trains heading west (towards Poland). To get to the city from the train station, you'll have to mount a steep flight of steps from the platform; once you're up, go right on the overpass. It's a short walk, but a taxi into town should be no more than BR10,000.

The **bus station** (☎004, 114) is in the centre of town and has both left-luggage lockers and an internet cafe. There are five daily buses to Minsk (BR33,000 to BR40,000, five hours), 10 daily to Hrodna (BR27,000 to BR41,000, five hours) and a service to Vilnius on Friday and Sunday (BR60,000, eight hours).

For a taxi, call ☎061 or have your hotel call for you.

Around Brest

A Unesco World Heritage site some 60km north of Brest, **Belavezhskaya Pushcha National Park** (☎01631-56 370) is the oldest wildlife refuge in Europe and is the pride of Belarus. Half the park's territory lies in Poland, where it's called Białowieża National Park (p623).

Some 1300 sq km of primeval forest survives here. It's all that remains of a canopy that eight centuries ago covered northern Europe. Some oak trees here are over 600 years old and some pines at least 300 years old.

At least 55 mammal species, including deer, lynx, boars, wild horses, wolves, elk, ermines, badgers, martens, otters, mink and beavers, call this park home, but the area is most celebrated for its 300 or so European bison, the continent's largest land mammal. These free-range zoobr – slightly smaller than their American cousins – were driven to near extinction (the last one living in the wild was shot by a hunter in 1919) and then bred back from 52 animals that had survived in zoos. Now a total of about 3000 exist, of which over 300 are wild in the Belavezhs-

kaya Pushcha. Amazingly you can pay to shoot them – '300 is enough' according to park wardens, who want to control their numbers due to the vast amount of foliage these enormous beasts consume.

There's a **nature museum** (admission BR3000; ☺9am-5pm) that gives a great introduction to the species living in the park and *volerei* (enclosures; admission BR3000), where you can view bison, deer, bears, boars and other animals (including the rare hybrid Tarpan horse, a crossbreed of a species that was also shot into near extinction).

There are a few different options for overnight stays, all of which are best arranged through Brest Intourist (p90). Camping requires permission but costs BR15,000 per person. The **Kamyanyuki Hotel Complex** (☎01631-56 497; Kamyanyuki; s/d incl breakfast BR68,000/80,000) includes a serviceable hotel next to the nature museum in the eponymous village just outside the national park. Rooms are remodelled, and have bathrooms and balconies. Other options include **Dom Grafa Tushkevicha**, a guesthouse better for families or other small groups, and the historic **Viskuli Hotel**, where Lukashenko often stays. Book these through Brest Intourist as they aren't used to people just turning up. There's a restaurant in the Kamyanyuki Hotel Complex, as well as a couple of other cafes serving up simple *shashlyk* (meat kebabs) and bliny.

It's entirely possible (and a great deal cheaper) to see the national park without taking a guided tour, although if you don't speak Russian you may miss some interesting commentary on trips through the woods and in the museum. From Brest take one of the six daily *marshrutky* or buses to Kamyanyuki (BR18,000, one hour 20 minutes) and walk from the village to the clearly visible reserve buildings. Once there you can walk around the park yourself, or even better, hire a bike from the museum (BR3000 per hour). On some days individuals with private cars or taxis are allowed to drive along the set route for tours in the reserve, although usually you'll have to join a tour bus, which runs one to three times a day from the museum (BR14,000, 1½ hours) depending on demand.

An altogether easier option is to book a day trip with Brest Intourist. This includes transport, the services of an English-speaking guide, and museum and park entry fees, although at BR600,000, it's expensive unless you share the cost with a couple of other people.

PRIPYATSKY NATIONAL PARK

One of the best-kept secrets in Belarus is the excellent **Pripyatsky National Park** (☎02353-75 644, 75 173; www.npp.by, in Russian; vul Leninskaya 127, Turau), a relatively untouched swathe of marshes, swampland and floodplains known locally as 'the lungs of Europe'. Flora and fauna particular to wetlands are found here, including more than 800 plant species, some 50 mammal species and more than 200 species of birds.

At the park headquarters and museum you can tour a great display of the flora and fauna specific to the area, and make all the arrangements you need. Excursions range from one day to a week, and can include extended fishing, hunting and boating expeditions deep into the marshlands. Cruises on the river are particularly recommended.

Park staff can also put you up at one of their guest houses in town, arrange accommodation in a private home or, even better, put you up in the middle of the park itself. Several comfy cottages have been kitted out with kitchens and saunas and are set in sublimely peaceful settings. The park organises winter ice-fishing expeditions (followed by vodka and a sauna, of course) and many summer activities. Prices vary, but generally a person need only spend about €75 per day, including accommodation, three meals and guided tours.

From the UK, **Nature Trek** (www.naturetrek.co.uk) offers a well-regarded eight-day guided birdwatching trip to the park each May that costs UK£1200 all-inclusive from London.

From Minsk there are at least two daily buses to Turau (BR18,000, four to seven hours), plus one daily *marshrutka* (BR30,000, four hours) from Minsk's Vostochny bus station.

NORTHERN BELARUS

In the north of the country, Vitsebsk is the most obviously appealing destination for travellers, with its dramatic river, a clutch of lovely churches and the artistic heritage bequeathed to it by Marc Chagall. Also of interest is lovely Hrodna, one of the few towns in the country not destroyed in WWII.

Vitsebsk BIЦeбск

☎0212 / POP 365,000

The historic city of Vitsebsk (known universally outside Belarus by its Russian name, Vitebsk) lies a short distance from the Russian border and almost 300km from Minsk. Unlike the Belarusian capital, Vitsebsk has survived the whippings of history to some degree, making it one of the country's most historically and culturally significant places.

Clustered around the steep banks of the Dvina River, the city is today most famous for being the childhood home of the painter Marc Chagall, who grew up and studied here before moving to St Petersburg, where his career began. With its relaxed atmosphere, attractive centre and diverting museums, Vitsebsk makes for a pleasant side trip or stopover on the way through to Russia.

Coming into Vitsebsk, you may be inclined to turn around and leave again, as the grey suburbs and heavy industry on the city's outskirts are particularly unappealing. The main drag, inventively named vul Lenina, runs parallel to the Dvina River, while the perpendicular Kirovsky Bridge crosses the river and leads via vul Kirova to the train and bus stations.

⊙ Sights

Chagall Museum   MUSEUM
(www.chagall.vitebsk.by; vul Punta 2; admission BR5000, tours BR15,000; ⊙11am-7pm Tue-Sun Mar-Sep, Wed-Sun Oct-Feb) The first museum on every itinerary should be the excellent Chagall Museum, which was established in 1992 and displays collections of Chagall lithographs – his illustrations for the Bible (1956–60), designs to accompany Gogol's *Dead Souls* (1923–25) and graphic representations of the 12 tribes of Israel (1960). Downstairs there's a space for temporary exhibits. Sadly there aren't more Chagall painting in Belarus, as his work was banned by the Soviet government, which even rejected a cache of paintings bequeathed to them by the artist himself.

Marc Chagall House Museum   MUSEUM
(vul Pokrovskaya 11; admission BR5000; ⊙11am-7pm Tue-Sun) Across the river a good 20-minute walk away from the Chagall Museum is the Marc Chagall House Museum, where the artist lived as a child for 13 years between 1897 and 1910 – a period beautifully evoked in his autobiography, *My Life*. The simple, small house contains photographs of Chagall and his family, various Jewish knick-

knacks and some period furniture, and leads out into a garden. It's very evocative of a simple Jewish-Russian childhood.

Art Museum
MUSEUM

(☑36 22 31; vul Lenina 32; admission BR5000; ⊙10am-6pm Tue-Sun) The grand halls of the Art Museum are decked out with mainly local art, both old and new. There are numerous 18th- to 20th-century works, including those by Repin and Makovsky. A highlight is the collection of very moving realist scenes of early-20th-century Vitsebsk street life by Yudel Pyen. Of the 793 paintings he donated to the city before he died, only 200 have survived, most of them held here.

Churches
CHURCHES

While Vitsebsk does not have many churches of note, there is a pair of very different **Orthodox churches** on the eastern bank of the Dvina, near the main bridge on vul Zamkovaya. Nearby too is the lovely **Svyato-Voskresensky Church**, on the corner of vul Lenina and vul Zamkovaya, a reconstruction of a magnificent 18th-century church with gorgeous frescos on its facade and golden onion domes.

🎊 Festivals & Events

Slavyansky Bazaar
FESTIVAL

(Slavic Bazaar; www.festival.vitebsk.by) This popular festival is held in mid-July, and brings in dozens of singers and performers from Slavic countries for a week-long series of concerts. The annual event attracts tens of thousands of visitors, creating a huge party.

🛏 Sleeping

TOP CHOICE
Hotel Eridan
HOTEL €€

(☑36 24 56; www.eridan-vitebsk.com; vul Savetskaya 21/17; s/d/ste incl breakfast BR140,000/220,000/280,000; ✳) The best-value hotel in town is handy for the Chagall Museum and well located in the middle of the Old Town. With pleasant wooden furniture, high ceilings, cheap lobby wi-fi and rooms that are well equipped (albeit done out rather gaudily), this place has just the charm so lacking in the standard-issue Soviet hotels you'll stay in elsewhere.

Hotel Luchesa
HOTEL €€

(☑29 85 00; www.luchesa.by; pr Stroiteley 1; s/d incl breakfast from BR173,000/198,000; ✳@) The top business hotel in town is the four-star Luchesa, housed in a modern building some way south of the city centre. It's well run and has comfy – if fairly standard – modern rooms in varying shades of brown with cheap wi-fi.

Hotel Vitebsk
HOTEL €

(☑35 92 80; vul Zamkovaya 5/2a; s BR62,000-116,000, d BR82,000-155,000) This is the standard-issue Soviet hotel-block option complete with violent green rooms and minute lifts. For an overnight stay the hotel is passable and centrally located by the Kirovsky Bridge. The cheaper rooms need to be booked in advance. There's also a popular nightclub in the building.

🍴 Eating & Drinking

Zolotoy Lev
TRADITIONAL €€

(vul Suvorova 20/13; mains BR10,000-25,000; ⊙noon-midnight) The smartest place in town is the expansive golden lion. There's a charming interior (when the TV is off), a large menu offering traditional Belarusian cuisine, and a spacious outdoor area serving up *shashlyk* and beer.

Vitebsky Traktir
INN €

(vul Suvorova 4; mains BR7000-20,000; ⊙noon-midnight) What else would you expect to find in a dark cellar oozing centuries of Slavic tradition? Why, sushi of course. This decent place has lots of charm, even if it is a little too dark for its own good. A traditional Belarusian menu and European dishes are also available.

Zolotoy Drakon
CHINESE €€

(vul Krylova 8; mains BR10,000-20,000; ⊙noon-midnight) The golden dragon is a surprisingly good Chinese restaurant complete with a Chinese chef, a relaxed atmosphere and a full menu with some dodgy English translations.

Kofeynya
CAFE

(vul Suvorova 2) This small coffeehouse next door to the Vitebsky Traktir serves up the best coffee in town, as well as a large selection of teas and cake.

Café Melody
BAR

(vul Lenina 65; ⊙11am-midnight) Vitsebsk's answer to the Hard Rock Café is a surprisingly cool place, even if instead of Hendrix's guitar it only has a worn copy of Macca's *Flowers in the Dirt* LP reverently displayed. During the day a young crowd drinks coffee and eats cake to a rocking soundtrack, while at night cocktails are served up and there's often live music.

ℹ Information

There are ATMs on vul Lenina, although there always seems to be a queue for their services.

Internet Centre (vul Mayakovskaya 3; per hr BR1860; ☺10am-10pm) On a small square off vul Lenina and behind the Svyato-Voskresenesky Church.

Post office (vul Lenina) Offers international phone calls and internet access.

❶ Getting There & Away

Vitsebsk is on one of the major railway lines heading south from St Petersburg into Ukraine. There are two or three daily trains to Minsk (BR16,000 to BR25,000, 4½ to six hours) and one to St Petersburg (BR132,000, 13 hours). There's also a daily train to both Moscow (BR87,000, 11 hours) and Brest (BR56,000, 11 hours).

There are approximately hourly to two-hourly buses or *marshrutky* to Minsk (BR20,000 to BR25,000, four to five hours).

❶ Getting Around

While Vitsebsk is larger than most other regional centres, the city is pleasant to explore on foot. Buses ply the 1.5km main drag from the bus and train stations into town; get off just after crossing the Dvina and you'll be only 500m from the Art Museum.

UNDERSTAND BELARUS

History

Arrival of the Slavs

Evidence of a human presence in Belarus goes back to the early Stone Age. Eastern Slavs from the Krivichi, Dregovichi and Radimichi tribes arrived here in the 6th to 8th centuries AD. The principalities of Polatsk (first mentioned in 862), Turau (980), Pinsk and Minsk were formed, all falling under the suzerainty of Prince Vladimir's Kyivan Rus by the late 10th century. The economy was based on slash-and-burn agriculture, honey farming and river trade, particularly on the Dnyapro River (Dnepr in Russian), a vital link between Byzantium and the Nordic Varangians.

Lithuanian & Polish Control

Belarus means 'White Russia', a name determined by the fact that it is the one part of Rus that, while conquered by the Mongols in 1240, was never settled by them. The term 'white' refers therefore to the purity of the people, who unlike their Muscovite cousins, never intermarried.

In the 14th century, the territory of modern-day Belarus became part of the Grand Duchy of Lithuania. It was to be 400 years before Belarus came under Russian control, a period in which Belarusians became linguistically and culturally differentiated from the Russians to their east and the Ukrainians to their south.

After Lithuania became Roman Catholic following the uniting of its crown with Poland's in 1386, the Belarusian peasantry remained Orthodox but were reduced to serf status. Lithuania nonetheless permitted its subjects a fair degree of autonomy, even using Belarusian as its state language during the early 15th century – an important fact for patriotic Belarusians today as proof of their historical legitimacy. All official correspondence, literature, doctrines and statutes at the time were written in Belarusian.

In 1596 the Polish authorities arranged the Union of Brest, which set up the Uniate Church (also known as Ukrainian Catholic or Greek Catholic), bringing much of the Orthodox Church in Belarus under the authority of the Vatican. The Uniate Church insisted on the pope's supremacy and Catholic doctrine, but permitted Orthodox forms of ritual.

Over the next two centuries of Polish rule, Poles and Jews controlled trade and most Belarusians remained peasants. Only after the three Partitions of Poland (1772, 1793 and 1795–96) was Belarus absorbed into Russia.

Tsarist Rule

Under Russian rule, a policy of Russification was pursued, and in 1839 the Uniate Church was abolished, with most Belarusians returning to Orthodoxy. The Russian rulers and the Orthodox Church regarded Belarus as 'western Russia' and tried to obliterate any sense of a Belarusian nationality. Publishing in the Belarusian language was banned.

The economy slowly developed in the 19th century with the emergence of small industries such as timber milling, glass-making and boat-building. However industrial progress lagged behind that of Russia, and poverty in the countryside remained at such a high level that 1.5 million people – largely the wealthy or educated – emigrated in the 50 years before the Russian Revolution in 1917, mostly to Siberia or the USA.

During the 19th century Belarus was part of the Pale of Settlement, the area where Jews in the Russian Empire were required to settle. The percentage of Jews in many Belarusian cities and towns before WWII was between 35% and 75%. The vast majority of

HRODNA

If you're entering Belarus from northern Poland, or if you have extra time in the country, think about visiting Hrodna (Grodno in Russian). It was one of the few Belarusian cities that *wasn't* bombed during WWII, so it's rife with old wooden homes and, although it's a major city, it definitely has a 'big village' sort of feel to it. The city's best hotel by far is the privately run, superfriendly **Semashko** (☎0152-75 02 99; www.hotel-semashko.ru/en; vul Antonova 10; s/d incl breakfast from BR160,000/240,000; @✉), which you should reserve in advance due to its popularity. The hotel added a new building in 2008, giving it far more space and a rather more modern feel, but the high standards remain the same. The room price includes use of the Oasis sauna and its small pool. Trains between Minsk and Hrodna leave five times a day (BR15,000, six hours), although *marshrutky* from Minsk's Vostochny bus station do the trip much faster and far more regularly (BR30,000, three hours).

Belarusians remained on the land, poor and illiterate. Due to their cultural stagnation, their absence from positions of influence and their historical domination by Poles and Russians, any sense among Belarusian speakers that they were a distinct nationality was very slow to emerge. Nonetheless, Belarusian intellectuals were part of a wave of nationalism across Europe and it was in the 19th century that the concept of Belarusians as a distinct people first emerged.

World Wars & the Soviet Union

In March 1918, under German occupation during WWI, a short-lived independent Belarusian Democratic Republic was declared, but the land was soon under the control of the Red Army, and the Belarusian Soviet Socialist Republic (BSSR) was formed. The 1921 Treaty of Rīga allotted roughly the western half of modern Belarus to Poland, which launched a program of Polonisation that provoked armed resistance by Belarusians. The eastern half was left to the Bolsheviks, and the redeclared BSSR was a founding member of the USSR in 1922.

In the 1920s the Soviet regime encouraged Belarusian literature and culture, but in the 1930s under Stalin, nationalism and the Belarusian language were discouraged and their proponents ruthlessly persecuted. The 1930s also saw industrialisation, agricultural collectivisation, and purges in which hundreds of thousands were executed – most in the Kurapaty Forest, outside Minsk.

In September 1939 the Red Army seized western Belarus from Poland. When Nazi Germany invaded Russia in 1941, Belarus was on the front line and suffered greatly.

German occupation was savage and partisan resistance widespread until the Red Army drove the Germans out in 1944, with massive destruction on both sides. Hundreds of villages were destroyed, and barely a stone was left standing in Minsk. At least 25% of the Belarusian population (over two million people) died between 1939 and 1945. Many of them, Jews and others, died in 200-plus concentration camps; the third-largest Nazi concentration camp was set up at Maly Trostenets, outside Minsk, where over 200,000 people were executed.

Western Belarus remained in Soviet hands at the end of the war, with Minsk developing into the industrial hub of western USSR and Belarus becoming one of the Soviet Union's most prosperous republics.

The 1986 Chernobyl disaster (p990), just over the border in Ukraine, was most profoundly felt by the people of Belarus. The radiation cloud released left about a quarter of the country seriously contaminated, and its effects are still felt today, particularly in the southeastern regions of the country.

Post-Soviet Belarus

On 27 July 1990, the republic issued a declaration of sovereignty within the USSR. On 25 August 1991 a declaration of full national independence was issued. With no history whatsoever as a politically or economically independent entity, the country of Belarus was one of the oddest products of the disintegration of the USSR.

Since July 1994 Belarus has been governed by Alexander Lukashenko, a former collective-farm director. His nickname throughout the country and beyond is Bat'ka (Papa). His presidential style has been seen by many as autocratic and authoritarian, and the country was declaimed an 'outpost of tyranny' by former US Secretary of State Condoleezza

Rice. Lukashenko has on several occasions altered the constitution (the referenda were criticised by the EU and the OSCE), rendering the parliament essentially toothless and extending both his term and the number of times he can hold the presidency. Media distribution is handled by the state, so independently produced publications are easily quashed. Online publications are all that is left for independent Belarusian media, and even those are on shaky ground as internet access is increasingly state controlled, and antigovernment sites are routinely blocked.

On 19 March 2006, Lukashenko officially won another five-year term as president, with 83% of the vote and 98% voter turnout. However, newspapers such as the *Guardian* have claimed that his opponents – the most popular being European-styled Alexander Milinkevich – were harassed and deprived of public venues throughout the campaign. On the night of the 19th, thousands of protesters turned out on the city's main square for what was being termed as the Denim Revolution – a 'mini-maydan' echoing what happened in Kyiv 1½ years earlier. A peaceful tent city started, and hundreds of people, mostly students, withstood freezing temperatures for almost a week. But once the international media left the scene to cover Ukrainian parliamentary elections, protesters were beaten and arrested by riot police.

Belarus Today

Lukashenko's relationship with Russia deteriorated sharply in 2007–8, following a spat with Russian energy giant Gazprom over gas price hikes and Russia's war with Georgia, of which the Belarusian government was sharply critical. This was followed by an apparent two-year thaw in relations between the EU and Minsk. Despite having slapped a travel ban on Lukashenko and consistently rejected the legitimacy of his electoral victories, the EU, wanting to draw Minsk from Moscow's orbit, waved the carrot of billions in economic aid if the 2010 elections were declared free and fair, and invited Belarus to join the EU's 'Eastern Partnership' program. Lukashenko likewise appeared keen to make new friends in the West, even hiring Margaret Thatcher's former PR guru, Tim Bell, to whitewash his country's terrible human rights record and change its woefully bad image abroad. Indeed, during 2010 many began to believe that things were slowly changing in Belarus.

Playing Moscow off against the EU has long been a survival mechanism for Lukashenko, but this one was masterful. Fearful of losing one of its very last remaining European allies, Russia agreed to continue providing Belarus with low-cost gas just before the presidential elections in December 2010, alleviating Minsk's need to have the election pronounced fair by EU observers.

The elections of December 2010 were by any standard a travesty; that they should happen in Europe in the 21st century is simply extraordinary. Lukashenko won a truly implausible 79% of the vote, all OSCE election monitors rejected the results out of hand, and protestors on the main square in Minsk were violently dispersed, leaving more than 600 people in jail, including several of the opposition candidates, many of whom were allegedly beaten and abducted from the street and even their hospital beds.

Belarus remains a tightly controlled, repressive and violent police state at the time of writing, and, as a leaked diplomatic cable published by Wikileaks in December 2010 succinctly puts it, 'Lukashenko intends to stay in power indefinitely and sees no reason to change his course'.

The Belarusians

There are approximately 9.6 million people in Belarus, of which 81.2% are Belarusian, 11.4% Russian, 4% Polish and 2.4% Ukrainian, with the remaining 1% consisting of other groups. This results in a rather homogeneous population. Prior to WWII, 10% of the national population was Jewish, and in cities like Minsk, Hrodna and Brest Jews made up between one-third and three-quarters of the population. They now make up about 0.3% of the country's population.

Generally speaking, Belarusians are quiet, polite and reserved people. Because they tend to be shy, they seem less approachable than Russians and Ukrainians, but they are just as friendly and generous (often more so) once introductions are made.

Atheism is widespread. Of believers, 80% are Eastern Orthodox and 20% are Roman Catholic (about 15% of the Catholics are ethnic Poles). During the early 1990s the Uniate Church (an Orthodox sect that looks to Rome, not Moscow) was re-established and now it has a following of over 100,000 members. There's also a small Protestant minority, the remnant of a once-large German population.

Art, Literature & Music

Assumed by many to be Russian or French, surrealist painter Marc Chagall (1887–1985) was actually born and grew up in Belarus and is by far the country's best-known artist. Born to a Jewish family in a village near Vitsebsk in 1887, Chagall lived and trained there before moving to St Petersburg aged 20 and then to Paris in the 1930s to set the world alight with his surrealist images and trademark flying people. His family home is now a small museum (see p92), although there are very few Chagalls in Belarus today – the Soviet government clearly didn't think much of his work, refusing multiple offers of canvases from the artist during his lifetime.

The hero of early Belarusian literary achievement was Francysk Skaryna. Born in Polatsk but educated in Poland and Italy, the scientist, doctor, writer and humanist became the first person to translate the Bible into Belarusian. He also built the first printing press in the country. In the late 16th century the philosopher and humanist Symon Budny printed a number of works in Belarusian. The 19th century saw the beginning of modern Belarusian literature with works by writers and poets such as Maxim Bohdanovich, Janka Kupala and Jakub Kolas.

The band Pesnyary has been extremely popular since the 1960s for putting a modern twist on traditional Belarusian folk music. Acclaimed Belarusian rock bands include Lyapis Trubetskoi and NRM. The Soviet Union's answer to Elton John, Boris Moiseev, was born in a prison in Mogilev, Belarus, even though, like most modern Belarusian acts, he sings in Russian. Dima Koldun, Belarus' entry to the 2007 Eurovision Song Contest, remains the country's most famous singer today, performing widely throughout Eastern Europe.

Environment

It's safe to say that Belarus does not enjoy a wildly exciting geography. It's a flat country, consisting of low ridges dividing broad, often marshy lowlands with more than 11,000 small lakes. In the south are the Pripet Marshes, Europe's largest marsh area, dubbed locally the 'lungs of Europe' because air currents passing over it are re-oxygen-ated and purified by the swamps. Around 6.4% of Belarusian land is protected.

Because of the vast expanses of primeval forests and marshes, Belarusian fauna abounds. The most celebrated animal is the zoobr (European bison), the continent's largest land mammal. It was hunted almost to extinction by 1919, but was fortunately bred back into existence from 52 animals that had survived in zoos. Now several hundred exist, mainly in the Belavezhskaya Pushcha National Park (p91), a Unesco World Heritage site. It is the oldest wildlife refuge in Europe, the pride of Belarus and the most famous of the country's five national parks. The *pushcha* (wild forest) went from obscurity to the front page in late 1991 as the presidents of Belarus, Russia and Ukraine signed the death certificate of the USSR – a document creating the Commonwealth of Independent States (CIS) – at the Viskuli dacha here.

Trips to Belarusian national parks and biosphere reserves, including arranged activities and camping or hotel stays, are possible; contact a tourist agency (p84) in Minsk for all but the Belavezhskaya, which is best arranged with Brest agencies (p90).

The 1986 disaster at Chernobyl has been the defining event for the Belarusian environment. The dangers of exposure to radiation for travellers, particularly in the areas covered in this guide, are almost nonexistent. Ironically, the exclusion zone has proved a boon for nature – the absence of human habitation seems to have done more to improve biodiversity than a nuclear explosion appears to have done to damage it. For more about Chernobyl, see p990.

Food & Drink

Belarusian cuisine rarely differs from Russian cuisine (see p821), although there are a few uniquely Belarusian dishes. *Draniki* are the Belarusian version of *olad'i* (potato pancakes); *kolduni* are potato dumplings stuffed with meat; and *kletsky* are dumplings stuffed with mushrooms, cheese or potato. *Manchanka* are pancakes served with meat gravy.

Belavezhskaya is a bitter herbal alcoholic drink. Of the Belarusian vodkas, Charodei is probably the most esteemed (but can be hard to find). Other popular souvenir-quality vodkas are Belarus Sineokaya and Minskaya. Beer is a much-loved drink in Belarus too. Local brews are decent, although most bars now serve imported lager from the EU.

Although the cuisine is largely meat-based, and the concept of vegetarianism is not exactly widespread, it is possible to find some dishes without meat, although eating vegan will be considerably more difficult.

Restaurants and bars usually open around 10am and, with few exceptions, close between 10pm and midnight. There is no nationwide ban on smoking, though most bars and restaurants have nonsmoking areas.

SURVIVAL GUIDE

Directory A–Z

Accommodation

While budget and midrange accommodation standards in Belarus tend to be lower than in Western Europe, they are still generally acceptable and often better than in Russia or Ukraine. Top-end places, of which there are a few in Minsk, are usually more expensive and of a lower standard than what you would expect from a top-end place in the West.

Our price ranges for a double room are budget (€; less than BR100,000), midrange (€€; BR100,000 to BR300,000) and top end (€€€; more than BR300,000).

A fledgling B&B association, **Rural & Ecotourism** (☑017-251 0076; www.ruralbelarus. by), was started by the woman who runs Dudutki (p86) and offers the chance to do homestays all over the country.

All rooms in this chapter have private bathrooms unless otherwise indicated; prices given are for the high season for a room only (unless otherwise indicated, breakfast is not included). Smoking in hotel rooms usually occurs in Belarus; only top-end hotels tend to offer nonsmoking rooms.

Farmers and villagers are usually generous about allowing campers to pitch a tent on their lot for an evening. Outside national parks you may camp pretty much anywhere, although camping in or near a city is asking for trouble from the police.

Activities

Belarus is flat, but visitors can still enjoy skiing. About 20km from Minsk is the Raubichy Olympic Sports Complex, where you can enjoy some great cross-country skiing, while downhill skiing and snowboarding are possible at **Logoisk** (☑01774-53 758, 53 298; www.logoisk.by) and the newer **Silichy** (☑01774-50 285; www.silichy.by), both about 30km from Minsk. Belintourist (p85) does skiing and other activity-related tours.

Business Hours

Banks 9am-5pm Mon-Fri

Offices hours 9am-6pm Mon-Fri

Shops 9am or 10am-9pm Mon-Sat, to 6pm Sun if open at all

Some businesses will close for lunch, which is usually for an hour and occurs anytime between noon and 2pm. Restaurants and bars usually open between 10am and midday and close between 10pm and midnight.

Embassies & Consulates

There is no representation for Canada, Australia, New Zealand or the Netherlands in Belarus.

France (☑017-299 1800; www.ambafrance-by.org; pl Svabody 11, Minsk)

Germany (☑017-217 5900; www.minsk.diplo.de; vul Zakharava 26, Minsk)

Moldova (☑017-289 1441; vul Belarusskaya 2, Minsk)

Romania (☑017-203 8097; per Moskvina 4, Minsk)

Russia Brest (☑0162-23 78 42; vul Pushkinskaya 10, Brest); Minsk (☑017-222 4985; vul Novolvilenskaya 1a, Minsk)

UK (☑017-210 5920; www.ukinbelarus.fco.gov.uk; vul Karla Marksa 37, Minsk)

Ukraine Brest (☑0162-22 04 77; vul Vorovskaha 19, Brest); Minsk (☑/fax 017-283 1989/91; vul Staravilenskaya 51, Minsk)

USA (☑017-210 1283; http://minsk.usembassy.gov; vul Staravilenskaya 46, Minsk)

Festivals & Events

The night of 6 July is **Kupalye**, a celebration with pagan roots when young girls gather flowers and throw them into a river as a method of fortune-telling, while everyone else sits by lake or riverside fires drinking beer.

Belarus' best-loved cultural event is the Slavyansky Bazaar, held in Vitsebsk; see p93 for details.

Food

Price ranges are: budget (€; under BR5000), midrange (€€; BR5,000 to 15,000) and top end (€€€; over BR15,000).

Gay & Lesbian Travellers

Homophobia is rife in Belarus, even though gay sex acts were legalised in 1994. Despite this, Slavic laissez-faire attitudes mean that you don't have to look hard to find gay life, the details of which flourish on the internet, and at Minsk's one gay club, 6A, and at ever-changing venues that are gay-friendly or have gay nights. As travellers, gay and lesbian couples are unlikely to horrify locals by asking for a double room, but otherwise discretion is advisable. Websites to check out include www.gay.by (in Russian only) and the Russian site gay.ru, which has a section in English and includes information about Belarus.

Holidays

New Year's Day 1 January

Orthodox Christmas 7 January

International Women's Day 8 March

Constitution Day 15 March

Catholic & Orthodox Easter March/April

Unity of Peoples of Russia and Belarus Day 2 April

International Labour Day (May Day) 1 May

Victory Day 9 May

Independence Day 3 July

Dzyady (Day of the Dead) 2 November

Catholic Christmas 25 December

Internet Access

A new presidential decree introduced in 2010 made Belarusian internet laws by far the tightest in Europe. Legally, all internet cafes now need to make a note of your name and passport number before allowing you to surf, so bring your passport out with you if you plan to use the web. While some Minsk cafes and hotels offer free wi-fi, it's still far from the norm, and most hotels offer wi-fi access via paid cards you buy at the lobby (usually requiring your passport and name as well). These cards are very cheap, however (around €1 per hour), and connections are generally good.

Insurance

All visitors to Belarus are required to possess medical insurance to cover the entire period of their stay. It is unlikely you will ever be asked for it, but you may have to purchase the official policy at border posts if you don't have documentation to prove you're insured.

Insurance is not required for holders of transit visas.

Language

Despite the fact that almost all official signage is in Belarusian, advertising and conversation on the street are both almost universally in Russian. This creates a rather strange dichotomy between what you see and hear; for example, if you ask somebody the name of the street you're on and are told it's ulitsa Krasnaya (Russian), you'll find that the street sign calls it vulitsa Chyrvonaya (Belarusian). Confused? You will be. In this guide we've used the Belarusian names for streets, to match the local signage.

Some basic English is usually spoken by younger people, but standards of language teaching in schools generally remains low, particularly outside bigger cities.

Money

The Belarusian rouble (BR) is the national currency, and the money's wide spectrum of bill denominations is overwhelming to the newcomer. There are BR10, BR20, BR50, BR100, BR500, BR1000, BR5000, BR10,000, BR20,000, BR50,000 and BR100,000 notes. There are no coins, so you'll quickly acquire a thick wad of largely worthless notes. Ensure you change any remaining roubles before leaving Belarus, as it's almost impossible to exchange the currency outside the country.

ATMs and currency-exchange offices are not hard to find in Belarusian cities. Major credit cards are accepted at many of the nicer hotels, restaurants, and supermarkets in Minsk, but travellers cheques are not worth the effort. Some businesses quote prices in euros or US dollars (using the abbreviation Y.E.), but payment is only accepted in roubles.

Post

The word for post office is *pashtamt* in Belarusian, or *pochta* in Russian. Mail important, time-sensitive items is with the Express Mail Service (EMS), at most main post offices.

Telephone

Numbers listed in this chapter are nearly all landlines that need to be dialled with the city or town's regional code before them if you're calling from another part of Belarus. The mobile-phone market is divided between four companies, of which Velcom (www.velcom.by) and MTS (www.mts.by) are the dominant players. Anyone with an unlocked mobile-phone handset can buy a SIM card for next to nothing (bring your passport and have an address in Belarus).

To dial a Minsk landline number from a Minsk landline number, just dial the number; from a local mobile phone, press ✆8 017 or ✆375 17 and then dial the number.

To dial from one Minsk mobile number to another, dial ✆8 029 for Velcom, MTS and Diallog (the most common providers) or ✆8 025 for BeST.

To make an intercity call from a land phone, dial ✆8 (wait for the tone), the city's area code (including the 0) and the number; from a mobile, do the same, and if it doesn't work, try dialling ✆+375 and the area code without the 0, then the number.

To make an international call from a landline phone, dial 8 (wait for the tone), 10, then the country code, area code and number; from a mobile, press +, then dial the country code, area code and number.

If your local mobile phone is on roaming, call a Belarusian landline by dialling ✆+375 and the area code without the 0; to call a Belarusian mobile, dial ✆+375 29 and the number (or ✆+375 25 for calls to BeST phones).

To phone Belarus from abroad, dial ✆375 followed by the city code (without the first zero) and number.

For operator enquiries, call ✆085 (it's serviced 24 hours); a few of the staff speak English.

Visas

Belarusian visa regulations change frequently, so check by telephone with your nearest Belarusian embassy for the latest details. While most embassies have visa information on their websites, be aware that they are not always up to date.

Nearly all visitors require a visa, and arranging one before you arrive is usually essential. Visas on arrival are only issued at the Minsk-2 international airport, but they are expensive and are just as much hassle, so it's well worth getting one in advance for peace of mind (it's rare but not unheard of for people to have problems getting visas at the airport).

Applications

By far the simplest – although also the most expensive – way to get a visa is to apply through a visa agency. Alternatively, you can take a faxed or emailed confirmation from your hotel to the nearest Belarusian embassy and apply for one yourself.

Tallinn, Rīga and Vilnius have numerous travel agencies specialising in Belarusian visas.

Visa costs vary depending on the embassy you apply at and your citizenship. Americans pay more, but typically transit visas cost around €65, single-entry visas cost about €90 and to get either of those in 48 hours rather than five working days, count on paying double.

There are four main types of visa.

Tourist Visa

Tourist visas are issued if you have an invitation from an accredited Belarusian travel agency or a hotel reservation voucher. Single-entry and double-entry visas are valid for 30 days.

Guest Visa

The guest visa (also known as a 'private visa') is excellent if you're a citizen of the EU, Canada, South Africa, Australia or New Zealand. New regulations mean that you simply need to provide the name and address of a local friend or contact you'll be staying with (though in fact you can stay in a hotel or a rented apartment) and you can receive a visa. Guest visas are valid for 30 days and can only be single entry. The disadvantage is that many embassies are apparently unaware of these relatively new rules and are still demanding an official invitation from an individual, which is how the private visa used to work.

Business Visa

Business visas are issued to those invited to Belarus by a business. Business visas are for 90 days and can also be multi-entry.

Transit Visa

If you are passing through Belarus and won't be in the country for more than 48 hours, you can apply for a transit visa, for which no invite or voucher is necessary. You simply have to show a train or air ticket to prove your need to transit through Belarus. The possession of a valid Russian visa is not enough to serve as a transit visa. Transit visas are not available at the border.

Registration

If you are staying in Belarus for more than five working days, you must have your visa officially registered. Hotels do this automatically and the service is included in the room price. They will stamp the back of your white landing card, which you will need to keep and show to immigration agents upon departure. In theory you'll be fined if you don't provide proof of registration for every day of your stay; in practice, proof of one day is good enough. If you're staying at a short-term let apartment, the owner will usually have a connection at a local hotel and will organise your registration for you. Note that if you're staying for fewer than five working days, there is no need to register.

If you've received a personal invitation, you'll need to find the nearest *passportno-vizovoye upravleniye* (passport and visa department; PVU, formerly OVIR), though this will be time consuming and your host will need to come with you. The simplest place to register your visa in this case is at Minsk's **PVU main office** (☑017-231 9174; pr Nezalezhnastsi 8, Minsk).

An easier way to get this done is to pay for one night's stay at a cheap hotel where the staff will register your visa – you don't even have to spend the night there if you have accommodation elsewhere, though don't make this clear to the staff.

Getting There & Away

Once you have your visa in your passport, the process of entering Belarus is relatively simple. Ensure you fill out one of the white migration cards in duplicate before presenting your passport to the immigration officer.

Air

Belarus' two international airports are both in Minsk. Most flights are handled at **Minsk-2 international airport** (☑006, 279 1300; www.airport.by), about 40km out of the city. Some flights to the former Soviet Union depart from the smaller **Minsk-1 airport** (☑006; vul Chkalova 38), only a few kilometres south of the city centre.

Belarus' national airline is **Belavia** (☑017-210 4100; www.belavia.by; vul Nyamiha 14, Minsk), which has flights to London, Paris, Frankfurt, Berlin, Vienna, Rome, Milan, Tel Aviv and many Eastern European capitals.

The following are the main international airlines that fly to Minsk:

Aeroflot (www.aeroflot.com)

Air Baltic (www.airbaltic.com)

Air Zena Georgian Airways (www.airzena.com)

Austrian Airlines (www.aua.com)

Czech Airlines (www.lot.com)

El Al (www.elal.co.il)

Estonian Air (www.estonian-air.ee)

Etihad Airways (www.etihad.com)

LOT Polish Airlines (www.lot.com)

Lufthansa (www.lufthansa.com)

Turkish Airlines (www.turkishairlines.com)

Land

Bus

Bus travel is a common and fast way to enter the country, although long queues at border crossings are not uncommon. Immigration and customs control will normally come aboard the bus and check all passengers, and you may be asked to get off for luggage searches. The most frequently used international bus services are the quick four-hour trip between Vilnius (Lithuania) and Minsk, and the seven-hour trip between Minsk and Bialystok (Poland). See p102 for details on bus services from Minsk and p91 for services from Brest.

Car & Motorcycle

If you're driving your own vehicle, there are 10 main-road routes into Belarus via border stations through which foreigners can pass. International Driving Permits are recognised in Belarus. Roads in Belarus are generally very good and main motorways are wonderfully light on traffic, although the main M1/E30 motorway gets busy with long-distance trucks travelling between Russia and the EU in both directions. Signage is excellent throughout the country, although usually only in Cyrillic. On intercity road trips, fill up with fuel when exiting the city; fuel stations may be scant before you hit the next big town.

Train

Trains are usually a more comfortable but slightly slower way to travel than bus. From Minsk there are services to Russia, Lithuania and Poland, plus connections to the rest of Europe via Brest. You can also get to Russia from Vitsebsk.

Getting Around

Air

There are no domestic airline services in Belarus.

Bicycle

Belarus' flat landscape and generally good-quality roads makes it perfect for cyclists, although it's not a common mode of transport for locals and drivers still have a long way to go before they could be called cycle-friendly. You can rent mountain bikes from several locations around the Svisloch River in Minsk.

Bus

Bus services cover much of the country, and are generally a reliable, if crowded, means of transportation. You can always buy tickets on the day, usually before you board, at the bus-station ticket desk. As in Russia, normal bus services are supplemented by *marshrutka* routes.

Car & Motorcycle

It's perfectly possible to hire a car in Minsk (see p102), though cars are usually old and badly maintained. Look them over carefully and check the spare tyre before you drive off.

The Brest–Vitsebsk highway (Brestskoye shosse; E30/M1) is an excellent two-laner, but there are frequent tollbooths (they only charge cars with foreign licence plates).

Drivers from the USA or EU can use their own country's driving licence for six months. Cars drive in the right-hand lane, children 12 and under must sit in a back seat, and your blood-alcohol level should be 0%. Fuel is usually not hard to find, but try to keep your tank full, and it would even be wise to keep some spare fuel as well.

You will be instructed by signs to slow down when approaching GAI (road police) stations, and not doing so is a sure-fire way to get a substantial fine. You may see GAI signs in Russian or in Belarusian.

Train

Train is a popular and scenic way to travel between the major towns of Belarus, though the bus network is far more extensive and prices are similar. Travelling by train is an excellent way to meet locals, with whom you'll be sharing compartments. Bring along some food to share and you'll make friends in no time.

Bosnia & Hercegovina

Includes »

Why Go?

This craggily beautiful land retains some lingering scars from the heartbreaking civil war in the 1990s. But today visitors will more likely remember Bosnia and Hercegovina (BiH) for its deep, unassuming human warmth and for the intriguing East-meets-West atmosphere born of fascinatingly blended Ottoman and Austro-Hungarian histories.

Major drawcards are the reincarnated antique centres of Sarajevo and Mostar, where rebuilt historical buildings counterpoint fashionable bars and wi-fi–equipped cafes. Elsewhere Socialist architectural monstrosities are surprisingly rare blots on predominantly rural landscapes. Many Bosnian towns are lovably small, wrapped around medieval castles and surrounded by mountain ridges or cascading river canyons. Few places in Europe offer better rafting or such accessible, inexpensive skiing.

When to Go

Sarajevo

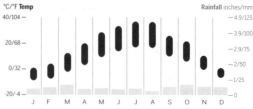

Spring Beat the heat in Herzegovina, blooming flowers in Bosnia, peak-flowing rivers.

Summer Accommodation fills up but for beginners the rafting is best in July.

Mid-December to mid-March Olympic-standard skiing. Prices drop in late March.

Best Places to Stay

Best Places to Eat

Fast Facts

» **Area** 51,129 sq km

» **Capital** Sarajevo

» **Telephone country code** 387

» **Emergency** ambulance 124, fire 123, police 122, roadside assistance 1282, 1288

Exchange Rates

Australia	A$1	1.41KM
Canada	C$1	1.40KM
euro	€1	1.95KM
Japan	¥100	1.60KM
New Zealand	NZ$1	1.06KM
UK	UK£1	2.20KM
USA	US$1	1.35KM

Set Your Budget

» **Budget hotel room** 60KM

» **Two-course meal** 17KM

» **Museum entrance** 1.50KM to 5KM

» **Beer** 2KM to 3KM

» **City transport ticket** 1.80KM

Resources

» **BiH Tourism** (www.bhtourism.ba)

» **Bosnian Institute** (www.bosnia.org.uk)

» **Office of the High Representative** (www.ohr.int)

Connections

Regular buses link the Croatian coast to Mostar and Sarajevo plus there's a little-publicised Trebinje–Dubrovnik service. Trains link Sarajevo to Zagreb, Belgrade and Budapest-Keleti, the only direct overland link to Hungary. There are numerous bus connections to Serbia and Montenegro from Sarajevo, Višegrad and Trebinje.

ITINERARIES

Six days

Arriving from Dubrovnik (coastal Croatia), roam Mostar's Old Town and join a day tour visiting Počitelj, Blagaj and the Kravice waterfalls. After two days in Sarajevo head for Jajce then bus down to Split (Croatia). Or visit Višegrad en route to Mokra Gora and Belgrade (Serbia).

Two weeks

As above, but add quaint Trebinje and (if driving) historic Stolac between Dubrovnik and Mostar. Ski or go cycling around Bjelašnica, visit the controversial Visoko pyramid and old-town Travnik en route to Jajce, and consider adding in some high-adrenaline rafting from Banja Luka, Bihać or Foča.

Essential Food & Drink

» **Ćevapčići** Grilled minced meat formed into cylindrical little *ćevapi* or patty-shaped *pljeskavica*.

» **Ćevabdžinica** *Ćevapi* specialist-eateries but almost all restaurants serve them along with *šnicla* (steak/schnitzel), *kotleti* (normally veal), *ražnjići* (shish kebab), *pastrmka* (trout) and *ligne* (squid).

» **Dolme** Cabbage leaves or vegetables stuffed with minced meat.

» **Ionac** Cabbage and meat hotpot.

» **Hurmastica** Syrup-soaked sponge fingers.

Bosnia & Hercegovina Highlights

1 Nose about Mostar's atmospheric Old Town seeking ever-new angles from which to photograph young men throwing themselves off the magnificently rebuilt **Stari Most** (Old Bridge; p120)

2 Raft dramatic canyons down one of BiH's fast-flowing rivers – whether from **Foča** (p131), **Bihać** (p138) or **Banja Luka** (p136)

3 Ski the 1984 Olympic pistes at **Jahorina** (p118) or **Bjelašnica** (p119) or explore the wild uplands behind them

4 Potter around the timeless Turkish- and Austrian-era pedestrian lanes of **Sarajevo** (p106), sample its fashionable cafes and eclectic nightlife or gaze down on the mosque-dotted, red-roofed cityscape from Biban restaurant

SARAJEVO

♩ 033 / POP 737,000

In the 1990s Sarajevo was on the edge of annihilation. Today it's a cosy, vibrant capital with humanity, attractive contours and East-meets-West ambience that are increasingly making it a favourite summer traveller destination. And in winter it's brilliantly handy for some of Europe's best-value skiing.

The city is tightly wedged into the steep, narrow valley of the modest Miljacka River. Attractive Austro-Hungarian–era avenues Ferhadija/Maršala Tita and Obala Kulina Bana converge at the very atmospheric Baščaršija, 'Turkish Town'. Surrounding slopes are fuzzed with red-roofed Bosnian houses and prickled with uncountable minarets, climbing towards green-topped mountain ridges. Westward, Sarajevo sprawls for over 10km through Novo Sarajevo and dreary Dobrijna past contrastingly dismal ranks of bullet-scarred apartment blocks. At the westernmost end of the tramway spine, affluent Ilidža gives the city a final parkland flourish.

History

Romans had bathed at Ilidža's sulphur springs a millennium earlier, but Sarajevo was officially 'founded' by 15th-century Turks. It rapidly grew wealthy as a silk-importing entrepôt and developed considerably during the 1530s when Ottoman governor Gazi-Husrevbey lavished the city with mosques and built the covered bazaar that still bears his name (see p107). In 1697 the city was burnt by Eugene of Savoy's Austrian army. When rebuilt, Sarajevo cautiously enclosed its upper flank in a large, fortified citadel, the remnants of which still dominate the Vratnik area.

The Austro-Hungarians were back more permanently in 1878 and erected many sturdy central European-style buildings. However, their rule was put on notice by Gavrilo Princip's fatal 1914 pistol shot that killed Archduke Franz Ferdinand, plunging the world into WWI.

Less than a decade after hosting the 1984 Winter Olympics, Sarajevo endured an infamous siege that horrified the world. Between 1992 and 1995, Sarajevo's heritage of six centuries was pounded into rubble and its only access to the outside world was via a metre-wide, 800m-long tunnel under the airport (p112). Bosnian Serb shelling and sniper fire killed over 10,500 Sarajevans and wounded 50,000 more. Uncountable white-stoned graveyards on Kovači and up near Koševo Stadium are a moving testimony to those terrible years.

The Entities of Bosnia & Hercegovina

Plunge into the pedestrianised 'Turkish' lanes of **Baščaršija** and the street cafes of **Ferhadija**. From the spot where a 1914 assassination kicked off WWI cross the cute **Latin Bridge** for a beer at **Pivnica HS** or dinner overlooking the city rooftops at **Biban**.

Next day ponder the horrors of the 1990s siege era at the moving **History Museum** and unique **Tunnel Museum**. Recover with a drink at eccentrically Gothic **Zlatna Ribica** and a feisty gig at **Bock/FIS**.

⊙ Sights & Activities

BAŠČARŠIJA & AROUND

The bustling old Turkish quarter is a warren of marble-flagged pedestrian lanes with open courtyards full of mosques, copper workshops, jewellery shops and inviting little restaurants. The area's charms are best discovered by untargeted wandering between the many street cafes.

Pigeon Square   NEIGHBOURHOOD
(Map p110) Nicknamed Pigeon Sq for all the birds, Baščaršija's central open space centres on the **Sebilj**, an ornate 1891 drinking fountain. It leads past the lively (if tourist-centric) coppersmith alley, **Kazandžiluk**, to the picturesque garden-wrapped 16th-century **Baščaršija mosque** (Bravadžiluk) and the six-domed **Bursa Bezistan** (www.muzejsarajeva.ba; Abadžiluk 10; admission 2KM; ⊙10am-6pm Mon-Fri, 10am-3pm Sat). Originally a silk-trading bazaar, this 1551 stone building is now a museum with bite-sized overviews of the city's history and a compelling model of Sarajevo as it looked in 1878.

Gazi-Husrevbey Vakuf Buildings
    ARCHITECTURAL ENSEMBLE
(Map p110) Ottoman governor Gazi-Husrevbey's splendid 16th-century complex includes a **madrassa** (religious school; Saraći 33-49), a stone-vaulted **covered bazaar** and the imposing **Gazi-Husrevbey Mosque** (www.vakuf-gazi.ba; Saraći 18; admission 2KM; ⊙9am-noon, 2.30-4pm & 5.30-7pm May-Sep, closed Ramadan). Its cylindrical minaret contrasts photogenically with the elegant stone **clock tower** across Mudželeti Veliki alley.

Old Orthodox Church   CHURCH
(Map p110; Mula Mustafe Bašeskije 59; ⊙8am-6pm Mon-Sat, 8am-4pm Sun) This outwardly austere little 1740 stone church has an impressive gilded iconostasis (wall of icons) and a three-room **cloister-museum** (admission 2KM; ⊙8am-3pm Tue-Sun) displaying historic icons, old manuscripts and church paraphernalia.

BJELAVE & VRATNIK

Svrzo House   HOUSE-MUSEUM
(Svrzina Kuća; Map p110; ☏535264; Glođina 8; admission 2KM; ⊙10am-6pm Mon-Fri, 10am-3pm Sat). This brilliantly restored 18th-century house-museum retains its courtyards and *doksat* (overhanging box windows).

Vratnik   NEIGHBOURHOOD
(Map p108) For great views over town continue up towards the once-vast Vratnik Citadel, built in the 1720s and reinforced in 1816. Its **Kula Ploče tower** (Ploča bb; admission 2KM; ⊙10am-6pm Mon-Fri, 10am-3pm Sat) houses a fascinating little museum to BiH's first president Alija Izetbegović and allows access to a short city-wall walk (exit at Kula Širokac tower). But the best panoramas are from the grassy-topped **Yellow Bastion** (Žuta Tabija; Jekovac bb). Minibus 55 runs to Vratnik.

FERHADIJA & AROUND

In summer, street cafes fill virtually every open space around Ferhadija, a pedestrianised avenue lined with grand Austro-Hungarian buildings. There's also plenty of sternly triumphalist early-20th-century architecture along Maršala Tita beyond an **eternal flame** that commemorates victims of WWII. The city's socially harmonious pre-1990s past is well illustrated by the close proximity of three places of worship.

Catholic Cathedral   CHURCH
(Katedrala; Map p110; Trg Fra Grge Martića 2; ⊙9am-4pm) The 1889 neo-Gothic Catholic Cathedral is where Pope John Paul II served mass during his 1997 visit.

Orthodox Cathedral   CHURCH
(Saborna Crkva; Map p110; Trg Oslobođenja) The large 1872 Orthodox Cathedral, built in Byzantine-Serb style, is artfully lit at night.

Jewish Museum   MEDIEVAL SYNAGOGUE
(Map p110; Mula Mustafe Bašeskije 40; admission 2KM; ⊙10am-6pm Mon-Fri, 10am-1pm Sun) More religiously open-minded than most of Western Europe in its day, the 15th-century Ottoman

BOSNIA & HERCEGOVINA

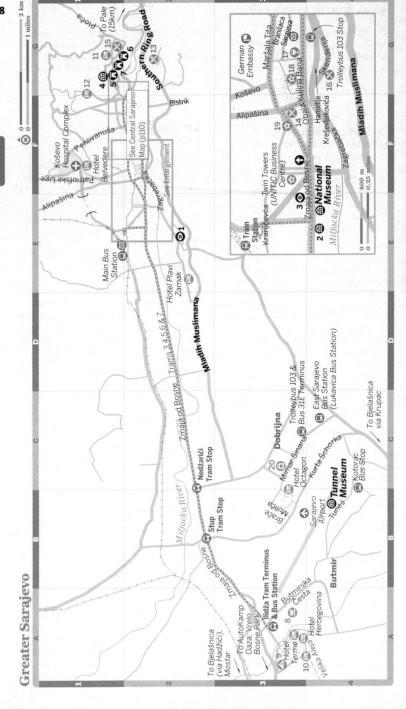

BOSNIA & HERCEGOVINA SARAJEVO

Greater Sarajevo

Empire offered refuge to the Sephardic Jews who had been evicted en masse from Spain in 1492. While conditions varied, Bosnian Jews mostly prospered, until WWII that is, when most of the 14,000-strong community fled or were murdered by Nazis. The community's story is well told in this 1581 Sephardic synagogue that still sees active worship during Rosh Hashana (Jewish New Year).

THE RIVERBANK

National Library ARCHITECTURAL MONUMENT
(Map p108) Bosnia's once-glorious National Library started life as the 1892 City Hall (Vijećnica). A century later it was deliberately hit by a Serb incendiary shell and its irreplaceable collection of manuscripts and Bosnian books was destroyed. Today the building is just a skeleton with scaffolding partly hiding its storybook Moorish facades. However, long overdue reconstruction work has finally restarted.

Sarajevo 1878–1918 Museum
 HISTORICAL MUSEUM
(Map p110; Zelenih Beretki 2; admission 2KM; ⊙10am-6pm Mon-Fri, 10am-3pm Sat) This one-room exhibition examines the city's Austro-Hungarian-era history and the infamous 1914 assassination of Franz Ferdinand that happened right outside, ultimately triggering WWI.

Obala Kulina Bana HISTORICAL STREET
The riverside drive is patchily flanked with fine Austro-Hungarian–era buildings, including the **main post office** (Map p110; Obala

Kulina Bana 8; ⊙7am-8pm Mon-Sat) with its soaring interior and old-fashioned brass counter-dividers. Next door, the **University Rectorate** (Map p110; Obala Kulina Bana 7) is similarly grand. Across the river the Gothic Revival-style **Academy of Arts** (Map p108; Obala Maka Dizdara) looks like a mini version of Budapest's magnificent national parliament building.

NOVO SARAJEVO

During the 1992–95 siege, the wide road from the airport (Zmaja od Bosne) was dubbed 'sniper alley' because Serb gunmen in surrounding hills could pick off civilians as they tried to cross it. The distinctive, pudding-and-custard coloured **Holiday Inn** (Map p110; www.holidayinn.com/sarajevo; Zmaja Od Bosne 4) famously housed most of the embattled journalists covering that conflict.

National Museum MUSEUM
(Zemaljski Muzej Bosne-i-Hercegovine; Map p108; www.zemaljskimuzej.ba; Zmaja od Bosne 3; adult/student 5/1KM; ⊙10am-5pm Tue-Fri, 9am-1pm Sat, 10am-2pm Sun) Large and very impressive, the National Museum is a quadrangle of four splendid neoclassical buildings purpose-built in 1913. The ancient history section displays Illyrian and Roman carvings in a room that looks dressed for a toga party. Upstairs, peep through the locked, high-security glass door of room 37 to glimpse the world-famous **Sarajevo Haggadah**, a 14th-century Jewish codex estimated to be worth around a billion US dollars. Geraldine

Central Sarajevo

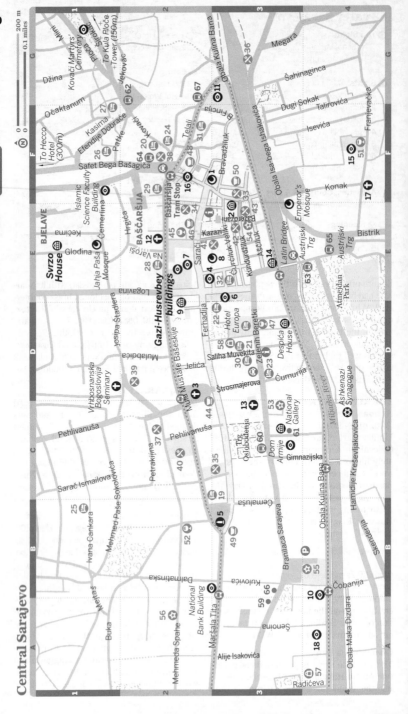

Brooks' 2007 historical novel *People of the Book* is a part-fictionalised account of how the Nazis failed to grab it during WWII.

Across a peaceful botanical garden are sections on natural history and minerals, plus an ethnography building with mannequin scenes of traditional Bosnian life set in gorgeous wooden interiors rescued from real 19th-century houses. At the front are some exceptional medieval *stećci* (carved grave slabs).

History Museum MUSEUM
(Map p108; Zmaja od Bosne 5; foreigner/local 4/2KM; ☉11am-7pm Mon-Fri, 10am-2pm Sat & Sun) More than half of the small but engrossing History Museum 'non-ideologically' charts the course of the 1990s conflict. Affecting personal exhibits include ID cards of 'lost' medics, examples of food aid, stacks of Monopoly-style 1990s dinars and a makeshift siege-time 'home'. The effect is emphasised by the building's miserable and still partly war-damaged 1970s

Central Sarajevo

architecture. Directly behind, the amusingly tongue-in-cheek **Tito Cafe** (www.caffetito.ba; ⊘7am-midnight) comes replete with Tito photos, stormtrooper-helmet lampshades and garden seating amid WWII artillery pieces.

ILIDŽA & BUTMIR

 Tunnel Museum   WAR MUSEUM
(Map p108; Tuneli 1, Butmir; admission 5KM; ⊘9am-3pm, closed some Sun in winter) For much of the 1990s' war, Sarajevo was virtually surrounded by hostile Serb forces. Butmir was the last Bosniak-held part of the city still linked to the outside world. However, between Butmir and Sarajevo lies the airport runway. Although it was supposedly neutral and under tenuous UN control, crossing it would have been suicidal during the conflict. The solution, in extremis, was a hand-dug 800m tunnel beneath the runway. That alone proved just enough to keep Sarajevo supplied with arms and food during the three-year siege. Most of the tunnel has since collapsed, but this unmissable museum retains a 20m section and gives visitors just a glimpse of its hopes and horrors. Photos are displayed around the shell-pounded house that hides the tunnel entrance and there's a 20-minute video wordlessly showing footage of city bombardment and the wartime tunnel experience.

Joining a Sarajevo city tour (organised by most hostels) is generally cheaper than coming by taxi and your guide can add a lot of useful insight. Alternatively take tram 3 to Ilidža (35 minutes, 11km from Baščaršija), then switch to the Kotorac bus (10 minutes, twice hourly). Get off at the last stop, walk across the bridge, then turn immediately left down Tuneli for 600m.

Termalna Rivijera   SWIMMING
(Map p108; www.terme-ilidza.ba/en; Butmirska Cesta 18; adult/child Mon-Fri 13/10KM, Sat & Sun 15/12KM; ⊘9am-10pm Sun-Fri, 9am-2am Sat) A complex of indoor and outdoor swimming pools 500m east of Ilidža tram terminus.

Vrelo Bosne   PARK
The focus of this extensive park is a pretty patchwork of lush mini-islands where the source of the Bosna River is a hole in a rocky cliff. While it's not worth a special trip from central Sarajevo, if you're staying in Ilidža the park makes a pleasant outing accessible by horse-cart or on foot along Velika Aleja, a

tree-lined pedestrian avenue stretching 3km from Ilidža's main hotel area.

☞ Tours

A 90-minute, €7 **Sarajevo Discovery** (☑061190591; www.sarajevo-discovery.com) walking tour departs daily at 5pm from the main tourist office. Book ahead from either tourist office for the daily Tunnel Tour (€12, 2pm) and excellent three-hour 'Times of Misfortune' (€25, 11am), visiting sites related to the 1990s conflict.

Assuming a minimum group size, many hostels also offer tunnel and/or city tours, often fascinatingly accompanied by siege survivors.

For trips further afield, ecotourism specialist **Green Visions** (☑717290; www.sarajevo-travel.ba; opposite Radnića 66; ⊘9am-5pm Mon-Fri) offers a wide range of weekend and tailor-made hiking trips into the Bosnian mountains and villages.

✸ Festivals & Events

Baščaršijske Noći (Baščaršija Nights; www.bascarsijskenoci.ba) Wide-ranging arts fest lasting all July.

Jazz Festival (www.jazzfest.ba) Local and international jazz in early November.

Sarajevo Film Festival (www.sff.ba) Globally acclaimed with commercial and arthouse movies, most with English subtitles. Held in late July

🛏 Sleeping

CITY CENTRE

Hotel Michele   BOUTIQUE GUEST HOUSE €€€
(Map p110; ☑560310; www.hotelmichele.ba; Ivana Cankara 27; r €75-105, apt €120-150) Behind the exterior of a contemporary townhouse, this marvellously offbeat eight-room guest house excites with a lobby-bar full of portraits and elegant furniture and follows up with accommodation that's mostly in vast, exotically furnished apartments with antique if sometimes mismatching furniture. Recent celebrity guests have included Morgan Freeman and Kevin Spacey.

Hotel Kovači   NEO-TRADITIONAL HOUSE-HOTEL €€
(Map p110; ☑573700; www.hotelkovaci.com; Kovači 12; s/d/tr/apt €50/70/90/100; ❀🕄) This wonderfully central family hotel blends a chic, understated modernism with the basic design of a traditional *doksat* house, its fresh white rooms softened with photos

of 19th-century Sarajevo on protruding panels.

Hotel Central
SPORTS HOTEL €€€

(Map p110; ☑561800; www.hotelcentral.ba; Cumurija 8; s\d/tr 200/240/300KM; ❋✿🖤) Behind the grand Austro-Hungarian facade, most of this newly renovated 'hotel' is in fact an amazing three-floor gym complex with professional-standard cardio and weight rooms and a big indoor pool with hot tub and saunas. All this along with qualified sports training staff is included in the rates for the 15 huge, fashionably appointed guest rooms leading off corridors painted lugubriously deep purple.

Hotel Hecco
HOTEL €€

(Map p108; ☑273730; www.hotel-hecco.net; Medresa 1; s/tw/d/tr/apt 80/110/130/150/160KM; @✿) Twenty-nine bright, airy rooms lead off an artfully designed warren of corridors that are dotted with armchairs and feel a little like a Mondrian painting in three dimensions. Staff are obliging, there's limited car parking but no lift and only the top floor has air-con. Minibus 58 stops outside.

Residence Rooms
HOSTEL €

(Map p110; ☑200157; www.residencerooms.ba; 1st fl, Saliha Muvekita 1; dm/d €15/40; @✿) High ceilings, ample common areas and widely spaced beds in the dorms all make for a convivial hostel experience and there are plenty of lively bars within stumbling distance.

HCC Sarajevo Hostel
HOSTEL €

(Map p110; ☑503294; www.hcc.ba; 3rd fl, Saliha Muvekita 2; dm 25-29KM, s/d 40/65KM; @✿) This sociable new hostel has a brilliant kitchen and a smaller communal TV lounge/lobby with DVDs to watch and a guitar to strum. Don't be put off by the speakerphone entrance and four flights of ragged access stairs.

Sobe Divan
BUDGET ROOMS €

(Map p110; ☑061420254; Brandžiluk 38; tw €30) Above an Ali Baba's cave of a restaurant, these 10 twin rooms are painted in sunny Provencal colours and are all equipped with new, private bathrooms. There's no reception or common room, but at such bargain prices one can't complain. Off season, single use is just €15.

Haris Hostel
HOSTEL €

(Map p108; ☑232563; www.hyh.ba; Vratnik Mejdan 29; dm €15; @✿) If you can handle the sweaty 10-minute climb from town, Haris is a friendly budget choice with three six-bed dorms sharing a decent kitchen, sitting area

and a rough concrete terrace with rooftop views and occasional barbeques. Check availability at the hostel's **Old Town office** (Map p110; Kovači 7; ⊙8am-7pm Mon-Fri, 8am-4pm Sat).

Hotel Art
BUSINESS HOTEL €€

(Map p110; ☑232855; www.hotelart.ba; Ferhadija 30a; s/d 165/186KM; ❋@✿P) Wrought-iron bedsteads and Persian rugs contrast with the functional plastic-wood veneer furniture in pastel-toned rooms that come with in-room computer, safe and trouser press.

Villa Wien
BUSINESS HOTEL €€

(Ćurčiluk Veliki 3; d 146KM) More original, slightly cheaper and just as central as the co-run Hotel Art, it has six indulgently pseudo–*belle époque* rooms above the Wiener Café. Check in at the main hotel.

City Boutique Hotel
BOUTIQUE HOTEL €€

(Map p110; ☑566850; www.cityhotel.ba; Mula Mustafe Bašekije 2; r €67-71 Fri-Sun, €101-112 Mon-Thu; ❋✿) Contemporary, designer rooms in rectilinear modernist style feature striking colours and backlit ceiling panels. There's a 6th-floor self-serve lounge-cafe and rooftop terrace with limited views. Busy road outside.

Hotel Safir
FAMILY HOTEL €€

(Map p110; ☑475040; www.hotelsafir.ba; Jagodića 3; s/d €60/82; ✿) Off stairways featuring vibrantly colour-suffused flower photos, well-tended rooms come with little window mirrors, conical basins and beam-me-up-Scotty shower booths. Six out of eight have a kitchenette.

Hotel Telal
MINI-HOTEL €

(Map p110; ☑525125; www.hotel-telal.ba; Abdesthana 4; s/d/tr/apt €25/35/45/60)

Reception feels a little claustrophobic but the rooms are unexpectedly smart and well tended for the price.

Ljubičica Hostel — BUDGET ACCOMMODATION €
(Map p110; ☑232109, 061131813; www.hostel ljubicica.net; Mula Mustafe Bašeskije 65; dm €10, homestay s/d from €15/20; ☺5.30am-11pm, 8am-10pm winter) This agency can usually find you a homestay room somewhere within the old city and has several sites with packed-full dorms. The dorms at Mula Mustafe Bašeskije 49 are new but as functional as you'd expect for €10. Numerous other cheap options lie within 100m.

ILIDŽA

Several grand yet well-priced hotels lie in green, pleasant Ilidža. Parking is easier here than downtown but it's a 35-minute tram-ride from Sarajevo's old centre.

TOP CHOICE Casa Grande — ELEGANT HOTEL €€
(Map p108; ☑639280; www.casagrande-bih.com; Velika Aleja 2; s/d/tr/q 68/113/138/165KM; ✱☎P) Designed like an aristocratic 1920s villa, the Casa Grande sits amid the plane trees right at the start of Ilidža's classic avenue, Velika Aleja. Rooms range from spacious to huge and are remarkably luxurious for the price. Expect satellite TV, 30-nozzle full-body shower pods and framed (if sometimes dreadful) imitations of 'classic' art.

AutoKamp Oaza — CAMPING GROUND €
(☑636140; hoteloaza@live.com; per person 10KM plus per tent/car/campervan 7/8/12KM) Tree-shaded camping and caravan hookups (electricity 3KM extra) tucked behind the Hotel Imzit, 1.5km west of Ilidža tram terminus.

Eating

CITY CENTRE

Mala Kuhinja — FUSION €€
(Map p110; ☑061144741; www.malakuhinja.ba; Josipa Štadlera 6; meals 15-20KM; ☺9am-6pm Mon-Fri, 9am-5pm Sat) There's no menu at this tiny, fusion-food gem where TV celebrity chef Muamer Kurtagic asks you what you fancy, hands you a shot of homemade *loza* (local grappa) and sets about creating culinary magic. Sit at the three-stool 'bar' to watch the show in all its glory. Reservations advisable.

Karuzo — VEGETARIAN, SEAFOOD €€
(Map p110; ☑444647; www.karuzorestaurant.com; Dženetića Čikma 2; veg mains 15-18KM; ☺noon-3pm Mon-Fri, 6-11pm Mon-Sat) This friendly

little restaurant, styled vaguely like a yacht's interior, is one of the few places in Bosnia to offer a meat-free menu. This includes imaginative vegetarian meals like spicy chickpea pockets with tahini sauce and a range of fish dishes (17KM to 35KM) and sushi (3KM to 5KM per piece). The owner is both waiter and chef so don't be in a hurry.

Dveri — BOSNIAN €€
(Map p110; ☑537020; www.dveri.co.ba; Prote Bakovića 10; meals 10-16KM; ☺10am-11pm; ✱) A narrow, easily missed streetfront entrance leads through into this tourist-friendly 'country cottage' eatery hung with loops of garlic, corn cobs and gingham-curtained windows. Inky risottos or veggie-stuffed eggplant wash down a treat with 6KM glasses of the house red, an excellent Hercegovinian Blatina. Beware if offered 'homemade bread': it's good but costs 5KM extra.

To Be or Not to Be — ECCLECTIC €€
(Map p110; ☑233265; Čizmedžiluk 5; meals 10-22KM; ☺11am-11pm) Arched metal shutters creak open to reveal a tiny two-table room lovably decorated in traditional Bosnian style. Try the daring, tongue-tickling steak in chilli chocolate (20KM). The name, with 'Not to Be' crossed out as a message of positivity, was originally a poster slogan for the 1994 Sarajevo Winter Festival, held against all odds during the siege.

Inat Kuća — CLASSIC BOSNIAN €€
(Spite House; Map p110; ☑447867; www.inatkuca. ba; Velika Alifakovac 1; mains 12-20KM, snacks 10KM) In a classic Ottoman-era house, this Sarajevo institution is a veritable museum piece with a great riverside terrace. The menu tells the story of its odd name but much of the typical Bosnian food (stews, *dolme*) is pre-prepared and slightly lacklustre.

GREATER SARAJEVO

Hot Wok Café — ASIAN FUSION €€
(Map p108; ☑203322; Maršala Tita 12; meals 12-17KM; ☺11am-11pm Mon-Fri, 11am-1am Sat) Pull up an over-tall stool-seat and watch the chef wok up your meal on an antique stove that contrasts with the *Kill Bill* modernism of the decor. The menu is pun-tastic and the Southast Asian fusion food is full of unexpected flavour combinations that confuse the palate but leave you wanting to lick the plate.

Biban — BOSNIAN €€
(Map p108; ☑232026; Hošin Brijeg 95a; mains 7-16KM; ☺10am-10pm) Biban offers panoramic city views similar to those from better-

known Park Prinčeva, but it's cheaper and more relaxed without the latter's scurrying army of waistcoated waiters. Perfectly cooked squid (13KM) and various Bosnian dishes come in generously sized portions. Walk 600m uphill from Park Prinčeva, turning left after Nalina 15.

Park Prinčeva   BOSNIAN €€€
(Map p108; ☎222708; www.parkprinceva.ba; Iza Hidra 7; meals 12-23KM; ☺9am-11pm) Like Bono and Bill Clinton before you, gaze down from this picture-perfect ridgetop perch for fabulous views of Sarajevo's rooftops, mosques and twinkling lights. Get there by minibus 56 from Latin Bridge.

Quick Eats

Close to Pigeon Sq you'll find a Konzum Supermarket, a 24-hour bakery and dozens of street-terrace cafes. For inexpensive snack meals look along Bradžiluk or Kundurdžiluk where the best-known *ćevabdžinica* (albeit not the sexiest) is **Željo** (Map p110; Kundurdžiluk 17 & 20; ćevapi 3-7KM; ☺8am-10pm).

Markale   MARKET
(Map p110; Mula Mustafe Bašeskije; ☺7am-5pm Mon-Sat, 7am-2pm Sun) The central market comprises the covered 1894 Gradska Tržnica hall selling meat and dairy goods while across a busy road is Markale's huddle of vegetable stalls. Marketgoers were massacred here on several occasions by Serb mortar attacks in the 1990s, including a 1995 assault that proved a 'last straw', triggering NATO air strikes against the forces besieging Sarajevo.

Butik-Badem   SWEETS, NUTS
(Map p110; Abadžiluk 12; ☺8am-11pm) This super little health-food shop sells luscious *lokum* (Turkish delight; per kg 6KM to 10KM), nuts and a variety of tempting snack foods by weight.

🍷 Drinking

As chilly April melts into sunny May, terraces blossom and central Sarajevo becomes one giant street cafe.

Bars

Zlatna Ribica   BAR
(Map p110; Kaptol 5; ☺10am-2am) This marvellously Gothic cafe-bar is loaded with eccentricities, including drinks menus hidden away in old books that dangle from lampshades. The uniquely stocked toilet will have you laughing out loud. Expect soft jazz and free nibbles, perhaps grapes or dried figs.

Pivnica HS   BREWERY BAR-RESTAURANT
(Map p110; Franjevačka 15; ☺10am-1am) If Willy Wonka built a beer hall it might look like this. It's the only place you can be sure of finding excellent Sarajevskaya dark beer (brewed next door) and there's superb food too (pastas 8KM, mains from 13KM).

Pravda   COCKTAILS & COFFEE
(Map p108; www.pravda.ba; Radićeva 4c; ☺8am-midnight) Choose from marigold-patterned chill-out sofas or white-enamel perch-stools, then strike your pose amid Sarajevo's gilded youth. Oh no, don't say they've all gone next door to Cafe Nivea?!

City Pub   PUB
(Map p110; Despićeva bb; ☺8am-2am) Despite a could-be-anywhere pub interior, this friendly place is a very popular meeting point, with occasional live music.

Barhana   RAKIJA, PIZZERIA
(Đugalina 8; ☺10am-midnight) A selection of flavoured local shots (from 3KM) served in a hidden courtyard off a lane with several other bar-restaurants.

Cafes

Kuća Sevdaha   CAFE
(Map p110; www.artkucasevdaha.ba/en/; Halači 5; ☺10am-11pm) Sip Bosnian coffee, juniper sherbet or rose water while nibbling local sweets and listening to the lilting wails of *sevdah*, traditional Bosnian music. The ancient building that surrounds the cafe's glassed-in fountain courtyard is now used as a museum celebrating great 20th-century *sevdah* performers (admission 2KM).

Caffe Divan   CARAVANSERAI
(Map p110; Morića Han, Saraći 77; ☺8am-midnight) Relax in wicker chairs beneath the wooden beams of a gorgeous, historic caravanserai courtyard whose stables now contain an alluring Iranian carpet shop.

Hecco Deluxe   CAFE
(Map p110; www.heccodeluxe.com; 10th fl, Ferhadije 2; coffee 2-3KM, mains 8-25KM; ☺7am-11pm) For memorable 360-degree views of the city centre take the lift to the 9th-floor Hecco Deluxe Hotel, then climb the stairs one floor further. Good coffee, no alcohol.

Alfonso   COFFEE HOUSE
(Map p110; Trg Fra Grge Martica 4; ☺8am-11pm) Great espressos served at open-air pavement seating that sprawls around the Catholic cathedral, or inside where a hip interior includes a catwalk between cushioned

sunken seat spaces. Music gets louder after dark.

Dibek
HUBBLE-BUBBLE BAR

(Map p110; Laledžina 3; ⊙8am-11pm) Smoking a hookah (*nargile* water pipe; 10KM) is back in fashion as you'll see in this DJ-led bar on a super-quaint little Old Town square.

☆ Entertainment
Nightclubs & Live Music

Bock/FIS
ALTERNATIVE/URBAN

(Map p108; www.bock.ba; Musala bb; ⊙6pm-2am) There's no easy-to-spot sign for this little basement venue, where you might find live punk or alternative bands on weekdays and 'urban' party music at weekends.

The Club
DJS, LIVE MUSIC

(Map p108; ☑550550; www.theclub.ba; Maršala Tita 7; beer 4KM; ⊙10am-4am) This subterranean trio of stone cavern rooms includes a restaurant that serves till 3am (with live Serbian folk music), a lounge that would seem better suited to a gentlemen's club, and a bar where DJs or cramped live concerts pull in crowds after midnight (entrance 5KM includes drink). Around the back, Pivnica Sarajevo has a cushioned garden-bar.

Club Jež
TURBOFOLK

(Map p110; www.jez.ba; Zelenih Beretki 14; drinks 2.50KM; ⊙6pm-late) This intimate stone-vaulted cavern club heaves with young local revellers overdosing on turbofolk. Cover charges (around 3KM) include one drink.

Sloga
STUDENT DISCO

(Map p110; Seljo, Mehmeda Spahe 20; beer from 4KM; ⊙8pm-3am) This cavernous, blood-red club-disco-dance hall caters to an excitable, predominantly student crowd but dancing is oddly impeded by rows of tables (only moved on Mondays for salsa night). Cover charge 5KM at weekends.

Hacienda
DJ-BAR, RESTAURANT

(Map p110; www.placetobe.ba; Bazerdzani 3; ⊙10am-very late) The not-quite Mexican food could be spicier. Not so the ambience at 2am, by which time this cane-ceilinged cantina has metamorphosed into one of the Old Town's most happening nightspots. Several other bars in the block are equally buzzing.

Performing Arts

National Theatre
PERFORMING ARTS

(Narodno Pozorište; Map p110; ☑221682; www.nps. ba; Obala Kulina Bana 9; tickets from 10KM; ⊙box office 9am-noon & 4-7.30pm) Classically adorned with fiddly gilt mouldings, this proscenium-arched theatre hosts a ballet, opera, play or philharmonic concert virtually every night from mid-September to mid-June.

Shopping

Baščaršija's pedestrian lanes are full of jewellery stalls and wooden-shuttered souvenir shops flogging slippers, Bosnian flags, carpets, archetypal copperware and wooden spoons, though if you're heading to Mostar, you might find prices better there. The attractive, one-street, stone-domed **Gazi-Husrevbey Covered Bazaar** (Map p110; www. vakuf-gazi.ba; ⊙8am-8pm Mon-Fri, 9am-2pm Sat) sells relatively inexpensive souvenirs, fake brand-name bags and sunglasses (from 5KM).

Some Sarajevo bookshops still stock the darkly humorous *Sarajevo Survival Guide* (23.40KM), originally published during the 1992–3 siege, as well as guidebooks, magazines and English-language books on ex-Yugoslavia.

BuyBook (Map p108; ☑716450; www.buybook. ba; Radićeva 4; ⊙9am-10pm Mon-Sat)

Šahinpašić (Map p110; ☑667210; www. btcsahinpasic.com; Vladislava Skarića 8; ⊙9am-9pm Mon-Sat)

❶ Information
Internet Access

Albatros (Map p110; Sagradžije 27; per hr 2KM; ⊙10am-midnight)

Internet Caffe Baščaršija (Map p110; Aščiluk bb; per hr 2KM; ⊙7am-midnight)

Internet Resources

Sonar (www.sonar.ba) Has listings and information.

Medical Services

Klinički Centar Univerziteta Sarajevo (Map p108; ☑297000; 1st fl, DIP Bldg, Stepana Tomića bb; ⊙8am-2pm Mon-Fri) VIP (ie English-speaking) Clinic within the vast Koševo Hospital complex. Take bus 14 from Dom Armije to Hotel Belvedere and then walk 300m northwest.

Money

There are ATMs outside the bus station, inside the airport and sprinkled all over the city centre. There's nowhere to exchange money at the stations but several banks on Ferhadija around the Catholic Cathedral can oblige. **UniCredit Bank** (Map p110; Zelenih Beretki 24; ⊙8am-6pm

Mon-Fri, 8.30am-1pm Sat) changes travellers cheques.

Tourist Information

Tourist information centre (Map p110; ✆220724; www.sarajevo-tourism.com) Baščaršija (Saраči 58; ⏱10am-2pm & 3-8pm Mon-Fri, 10am-4pm Sat-Sun); Main office (Zelenih Beretki 22a; ⏱9am-5.30pm Mon-Fri, 9am-3pm Sat) Helpful with maps, brochures and ready answers for many an awkward question. Recommended daily walking and war-era city tours.

❶ Getting There & Away

Air

Sarajevo's modest international **airport** (Map p108; ✆234841; www.sarajevo-airport.ba; Kurta Šchorka 36) is about 12km southwest of Baščaršija. For flight details see p145.

BUSES FROM SARAJEVO

DESTINATION	STATION	PRICE (KM)	DURATION (HR)	DEPARTURES
Banja Luka	M	31	5	5am, 7.45am, 9.15am, 2.30pm, 3.30pm, 4.30pm, 6.30pm
	L	31	5	9.30am, 11.30am
Bihać	M	42	6½	7.30am, 1.30pm, 10pm
Belgrade	M	47	7½	6am
	L	40-55	8-11	8am, 9.45am, 12.30pm, 3pm, 10pm
Dubrovnik	M	44	7	7.15am, 10am, plus 2.30pm, 10.30pm summer
Foča	L	9	1½	7.45am, 9.30am, 11am, 6.25pm; or use Trebinje & Višegrad services
Herceg Novi	M	49	7½	11am (summer only)
Jajce	ML	23.50	3½	take Banja Luka buses
Ljubljana	M	92	8½	8.40pm Tue, Fri, Sun
Mostar	M	18	2½	15 daily
Munich	M	134	19	8am
Niš	L	46	11	8.40am, 6pm
Novi Pazar	M	32	7-8	9am, 3pm, 6pm, 9pm, 10pm
Pale	L	3.50	40min	12 daily Mon-Fri, 3.15pm only Sat & Sun
	M	5.40	25min	7am, 10am, 2pm
Podgorica	L	35	6	8.15am, 2pm, 10.30pm
Split (via Mostar)	M	51	7½	10am, 9pm, plus 7am in summer
Split (via Livno)	M	51	7¼	6am via Livno
Travnik	M	15.50	2	nine daily
Trebinje	L	26	5	7.45am, 1pm, 4.05pm (via Sutjeska National Park)
Tuzla	M	20	3¼	nine daily
Visoko	M	5.70	50min	at least hourly by Kakanj bus
Vienna (Beč)	M	100	14½	11.15am
Zagreb	M	54	9½	6.30am, 12.30pm, 10pm
	M	54	8½	9.30am via Bosanski Brod

M = main bus station, L = East Sarajevo Bus Station

Bus

Sarajevo's **main bus station** (Map p108; ☑213100; Put Života 8) primarily serves locations in the Federation, Croatia and Western Europe. Most services to the Republik Srpsk (RS) and Serbia leave from **East Sarajevo Bus Station** (Map p108; ☑057-317377; Nikole Tesle bb), commonly known as Lukovica bus station. The latter lies way out in the suburb of Dobrinja, 400m beyond the western terminus stop of trolleybus 103 and bus 31E. To some destinations, buses leave from both stations.

Train

From the **train station** (Map p108; ☑655330; Put Života 2) useful services include:

Belgrade (33KM, nine hours) Departs 11.35am.

Budapest (105.90KM, 12 hours) Departs 6.55am, routed via Doboj, Šamac and Osijek (Croatia). Returns from Budapest-Keleti at 9.45am.

Mostar (9.90KM, three hours) Departs 7.05am and 6.18pm on trains bound for Ploče (23.50KM, four hours) on the Croatian coast.

Zagreb (58.90KM, 9½ hours) Trains depart 10.42am and 9.27pm. There is no longer any couchette service.

❶ Getting Around

To/From the Airport

Bus 36 departs from directly opposite the terminal but only runs to Nedžarići (part way along the Ilidža–Baščaršija tram line) and at best runs only twice an hour. More frequent and convenient trolleybus 103 and bus 31E both run to the centre, picking up around 700m from the terminal. To find the stop turn right out of the airport then take the first left. Shimmy right-left-right past Hotel Octagon, then turn right at the Panda car wash (Brače Mulića 17). Just before the Mercator Hypermarket (Mimar Sinana 1) cross the road and take the bus-trolleybus going back the way you've just come.

Airport taxis charge at least 7KM to Ilidža and 25KM to Baščaršija.

Bicycle

Rent-A-Bike (☑062547364; www.girbikerental. com.ba; Dženitića Čikma bb; per hr/day/week 3/15/50KM; ⊙9am-2pm & 3.30-9pm Wed-Mon)

Car

One-way systems and parking are awkward and Baščaršija is largely pedestrianised. Many hotels advertising parking have just a few spaces available. However, while central Sarajevo isn't driver-friendly, a car certainly makes it much easier to reach the surrounding mountain areas. Many hotels have their own small car-rental agencies. See also p146.

Public Transport

Many lines (including tram 1, trolley 103 and minibus 56) operate 6am to 11pm daily, but some stop after 7pm, and all have reduced services on Sunday. For timetables, click 'Redove Voznje' on www.gras.co.ba then select mode of transport.

Single-ride tickets, 1.60/1.80KM from kiosks/ drivers, must be stamped once aboard. Inspectors have no mercy on 'ignorant foreigners'. Day tickets (5.60KM) are valid on almost all buses, trams and trolleybuses. They're sold at the kiosk facing the Catholic Cathedral.

USEFUL ROUTES

Tram 3 (every four to seven minutes) From Ilidža passes the Holiday Inn then loops one way (anticlockwise) around Baščaršija. Last tram back to Ilidža departs around midnight.

Tram 1 (every 12 to 25 minutes) Does the same loop as the more frequent Tram 3 but starts from the train station (from where you could alternatively walk to the nearest Tram 3 stop in about seven minutes).

Trolleybus 103 (every six to 12 minutes) Runs along the southern side of the city from Austrijski Trg passing near Green Visions en route to Dobrinja (30 minutes). Handy for East Sarajevo (Lukovica) bus station and the airport.

Bus 31E (three per hour, 6.30am to 10pm) Vijećnica to Dobrinja (for Lukovica bus station).

Taxi

All of Sarajevo's taxis have meters; **Žuti Taxis** (Yellow Cab; ☑663555) actually turn them on. Taxis cost 2KM plus about 1KM per kilometre. Handy central taxi ranks are near Latin Bridge, Hotel Kovači and outside Zelenih Beretki 5.

AROUND SARAJEVO

Mountains rise directly behind the city, offering convenient access to winter skiing or summer rambles but landmine dangers remain, so stick to well-used paths.

Jahorina

☑057

Jahorina's mixture of open grasslands, forested patches and wide views makes it the most visually attractive of BiH's three main ski resorts. The world-class pistes at this **resort** (www.oc-jahorina.com; ski pass per half/ full day 20/30KM, ski-set rentals per day 25-40KM) were designed for the 1984 Winter Olympics. All accommodation is within 300m of one of Jahorina's six main ski lifts.

In summer you can rent mountain bikes from Hotel Termag (per half/full day 7/10KM).

🛏 Sleeping & Eating

Hotels are widely strung out along 2.5km of wiggling lane. This starts with a little seasonal shopping 'village' where you'll find the cheaper *pansions* (all closed out of season). The Termag Hotel is 300m above, then around 1km beyond the road S-bends past the Hotel Dva Javora and the post office. Beyond the still-ruined Hotel Jahorina the lane tunnels beneath Rajska Vrata before dead-ending at the top of the Skočine Lift. Quoted ski-season rates are for mid-January to March with half board; summer rates include breakfast only.

Termag Hotel   SKI HOTEL €€€
(☎270422; www.termaghotel.com; s/d/ste 115/152/200KM, ski season from d/ste 240/300KM; 🛜🏊Ⓟ) Within an oversized mansion built in Scooby Doo Gothic style, the Termag is a beautifully designed fashion statement where traditional ideas and open fireplaces are given a stylish, modernist twist. Rooms use thick wooden boards to artistic effect and many have glowing bedside tables. Underground parking available.

Rajska Vrata   RESTAURANT, ROOMS €€
(☎272020; www.jahorina-rajskavrata.com; mains 7-14KM) Beside the longest piste in town, this perfect alpine ski-in cafe-restaurant has rustic sheepskin benches around a centrally flued real fire. The cosy pine-walled bedrooms (doubles/triples €50/75) are only available in summer.

Hotel Dva Javora   SKI HOTEL €€
(☎270481;   www.hoteldvajavora.com;   s/d/tr €24/40/56, ski season from €38/62/86; 🛜) Above a seasonal shopping centre, the modern lobby bar has glowing fireplaces. The rooms, while fairly plain, come with new pine beds and clean checkerboard bathrooms. In season, apartments sleeping up to six people cost just €72 without meals.

Pansion Sport   SKI LODGE €€
(☎270333; www.pansion-sport.com; s 39-92KM, d 54-124KM; ⊙19 Dec-10 Apr) Pleasant Swiss chalet–style guest house at the bottom 'village area' of the resort.

ℹ Getting There & Away

Jahorina is 13km from Pale, or alternatively 27km from Sarajevo via a scenic mountainside lane. Buses run in ski season only, departing from Pale (3KM, 25 minutes) at 7am and 2pm and returning at 8am and 3pm. Some winter weekends buses depart Sarajevo's main bus station at 9am, returning at 3.45pm. A taxi from Pale costs 30KM.

Bjelašnica

☎033

BiH's second Olympic ski field rises above the two-hotel resort of **Bjelašnica** (www.bjelasnica.ba; ski pass per day/night/week 30/18/200KM), around 30km south of Sarajevo. In summer Bjelašnica's numerous apartments mostly lie empty but you can still rent bicycles (per hour/day 4/25KM) from the excellent new **Hotel Han** (☎584150; www.hotelhan.ba; summer 70/100KM, winter 105/170KM; 🛜), a stylish yet reasonably priced 2010 construction facing the main piste. For groups it can also arrange hiking and quad biking.

Fronted by what looks like a giant Plexiglas pencil, the friendly but older **Hotel Maršal** (☎584100; www.hotel-marsal.ba; d/ste €54/80, winter from €80/110; @) rents skis, boots and poles (guests/nonguests per day 15/20KM) in season.

The good-value, brand-new **Hostel Feri** (☎775555; www.feri.ba; Veliko Polje; per person 42.60-67KM, s 64-100KM; 🛜) charges the same per person whether you're in a double or six-bedded room, all unexpectedly luxurious for a 'hostel' with flat-screen TV and wi-fi. It's set in a meadow 5km northwest of Bjelašnica, too far from the lifts for downhill skiing but other assorted sporting activities are available.

Minibus 85 leaves from Sarajevo's Ilidža bus station on Monday, Tuesday and Saturday at 8am plus 4pm Friday. It returns from Bjelašnica around 10.15am Monday and Saturday (not Tuesday) and 6.15pm Friday. On weekends in ski season there's also a 9am bus from Sarajevo's National Museum, returning at 4pm.

HERCEGOVINA

Hercegovina is the part of BiH that no one in the West ever mentions, if only because they can't pronounce it. The arid, Mediterranean landscape has a distinctive beauty punctuated with barren mountain ridges and photogenic river valleys. Famed for its fine wines and sun-packed fruits, Hercegovina is sparsely populated, but it has several

UMOLJANI

If you're driving, don't miss exploring the web of rural lanes tucked away in the grassy uplands above Bjelašnica. Although most villages here suffered severely in the war, with little traditional architecture left, their mountain settings are truly lovely. Try heading for **Umoljani village** (16km from Bjelašnica), where there's rustic accommodation (single/twin/triple/quad 20/40/60/80KM) available in a new, three-bedroom log house behind the cute little **Restoran Studeno Vrelo** (☎061709540; coffee/snack 1.50/5KM). The approach road to Umoljani is beautiful and there are *stećci* just above the road around 2.5km before the village. The road to **Milišići** has even more dramatic views. **Green Visions** (www.sarajevo-travel.ba) organises summer weekend trips to war-spared **Lukomir**, the nation's highest and most isolated village.

intriguing historic towns and the Adriatic coast is just a skip away.

Mostar

☎036 / POP 94,000

At dusk the lights of numerous millhouse restaurants twinkle across gushing streamlets. The impossibly quaint Kujundžiluk 'gold alley' bustles joyously with trinket sellers. And in between, the Balkans' most celebrated bridge forms a truly majestic stone arc between reincarnated medieval towers. It's a magical scene.

Meanwhile, behind the cobbled lanes of the attractively restored Ottoman quarter, a less palatable but equally unforgettable 'attraction' lies in observing the devastating urban scars that still recall the city's brutal 1990s conflict all too vividly.

Add in a selection of day trips for which Mostar makes an ideal base and it's not surprising that this fascinating little city is starting to attract a growing throng of summer visitors.

History

Mostar means 'bridge-keeper', and the crossing of the Neretva River here has always been its raison d'être. In the mid-16th century, Mostar boomed as a key transport gateway within the powerful, expanding Ottoman Empire. Some 30 *esnafi* (craft guilds) included tanners (for whom the Tabhana was built), and goldsmiths (hence Kujundžiluk, 'gold alley'). In 1557, Suleyman the Magnificent ordered a swooping stone arch to replace the suspension bridge whose wobbling had previously terrified tradesmen as they gingerly crossed the fast-flowing Neretva River. The beautiful Stari Most (Old Bridge) that resulted was finished in 1566 and came to be appreciated

as one of the era's engineering marvels. It survived the Italian occupation of WWII, but after standing for 427 years the bridge was destroyed in November 1993 by Bosnian Croat artillery in one of the most poignant and depressingly pointless moments of the whole Yugoslav civil war.

Ironically Muslims and Croats had initially fought together against Serb and Montenegrin forces that had started bombarding Mostar in April 1992. However, on 9 May 1993, a bitter conflict erupted between the former allies. Bosnian Croat forces expelled many Bosniaks from their homes: some were taken to detention camps, others fled across the Neretva to the very relative safety of the Muslim east bank. For two years the two sides swapped artillery fire and the city was pummelled into rubble.

By 1995 Mostar resembled Dresden after WWII, with all its bridges destroyed and all but one of its 27 Ottoman-era mosques utterly ruined. Vast international assistance efforts rebuilt almost all of the Unesco-listed old city core, including the classic bridge, painstakingly reconstructed using 16th century–style building techniques and stone from the original quarry. However, nearly two decades after the conflict, significant numbers of shattered buildings remain as ghostlike reminders. The psychological scars will take generations to heal and the city remains oddly schizophrenic, with two bus stations, two postal systems and, until very recently, two fire services – one Bosniak and the other Croat.

◉ Sights

Stari Most   MEDIEVAL BRIDGE

The world-famous **Stari Most** (Old Bridge) is the indisputable visual focus that gives Mostar its special magic. The bridge's pale stone magnificently throws back the golden glow of sunset or the tasteful nighttime floodlighting. Numerous well-positioned cafes and restaurants, notably behind the **Tabhana** (an Ottoman-era enclosed courtyard), tempt you to admire the scene from a dozen varying angles. Directly west in a semicircular gunpowder tower is the **Bridge-Divers' Clubhouse** (admission 2KM; ◷10am-dusk, variable). Its members are an elite group of young men who will plunge 21m off the bridge's parapet into the icy Neretva River below once their hustlers have collected enough photo money from onlookers. If you want to jump yourself (from €25), they can organise a wet suit and basic training (highly advisable). When you're ready to go, two divers wait below in case of emergencies. Visiting the clubhouse you can read a few information boards about the bridge's history and descend for a brief glimpse of the unadorned Turkish jail-pit below. The tower's top two floors house a separate exhibition of around 50 black-and-white photos depicting city life during the war – great but hardly justifying the extra 5KM entry fee.

Across the bridge, the **Old Bridge Museum** (adult/student 5/3KM; ◷11am-2pm winter, 10am-6pm summer, closed Mon) has two parts, both offering only sparse exhibits. First you climb up a five-storey stone defence tower for partial views and interesting but limited displays about the bridge's context and construction. Climb back down to walk through the bridge's archaeological bowels, emerging on Kujundžiluk. There's a slow-moving 15-minute video of the bridge's destruction/reconstruction but a better-paced DVD is shown (and for sale, €10) at the free-admission **Galerija Sava Neimarevic** in a former mosque right on the bridge's southwest parapet.

The annual bridge-diving competition is held in July.

Old Town   NEIGHBOURHOOD

Layered down a mini-valley around the quaint little **Crooked Bridge** (Kriva Ćuprija), stairways link quaint old houses and stone mills, now mostly used as restaurants. Above, pretty old shopfronts line **Prječka Čaršija** and **Kujundžiluk**, the picturesque cobbled alleys that join at Stari Most. Entered from a gated courtyard, the originally 1618 **Koski Mehmed Paša Mosque** (Mala Tepa 16; mosque/mosque & minaret 4/8KM; ◷8am-7pm Apr-Oct, 9am-3pm Nov-Mar) has interior decor that lacks finesse, but climbing its claustrophobic minaret offers commanding Old Town panoramas.

Braće Fejića   NEIGHBOURHOOD

Mostar's main shopping street, Braće Fejića, links the modest **Tepa Vegetable Market** (◷6.30am-2pm) to **Trg Musala**, once the grand heart of Austro-Hungarian Mostar, now scarred by the war-ruined shell of Hotel Neretva (under reconstruction). Braće Fejića's architecture is predominantly banal but features the expertly rebuilt 1557 **Karađozbeg Mosque** (mosque/mosque & minaret 4/8KM; ◷9am-7pm Apr-Oct, 9am-5pm Nov-Mar, closed during prayers) with its distinctive lead-roofed wooden veranda and four-domed madrassa annexe (now a clinic). The early-17th-century **Roznamedži Ibrahimefendi Mosque** was the only mosque to survive the 1993–5 shelling relatively unscathed. Its associated **madrassa**, demolished in 1960, has also been rebuilt and hosts shops and a cafe.

Down a side lane, the charmingly ramshackle **Bišćevića Ćošak** (Turkish House; ☎550677; Bišćevića 13; admission 4KM; ◷9am-3pm Nov-Feb, 8am-8pm Mar-Oct) is a 350-year-old Ottoman-Bosnian home with a colourfully furnished interior sporting a selection of traditional metalwork and carved wooden furniture. For interesting comparisons also visit the grander 18th/19th-century **Muslibegović House** (admission 4KM; ◷10am-6pm mid-Apr–mid-Oct), which now doubles as a boutique hotel (see p124).

Former Front Line   WAR DAMAGE

It's thought-provoking and intensely moving to see that over 15 years after the conflict, many buildings are still bullet pocked and some remain skeletal wrecks. Several of these lie along Mostar's former front line across which Croat and Muslim communities bombarded each other during the civil war. Every year more are restored but you'll still see several tragic ruins around Spanski Trg, including the bombed-out nine-storey tower that was once **Ljubljanska Banka** (Kralja Zvonimira bb).

Bajatova   NEIGHBOURHOOD

The little **Museum of Hercegovina** (http://muzejhercegovine.com; Bajatova 4; admission 5KM; ◷8am-2pm Mon-Fri, 10am-noon Sat) is housed in the former home of Džemal Bijedić, an ex-head of the Yugoslav government who died in mysterious circumstances in 1978. There are small archaeological and ethnographic sections plus a well-paced 10-minute film featuring pre- and post-1992 bridge-diving plus war footage that shows the moment Stari Most was blown apart.

Mostar

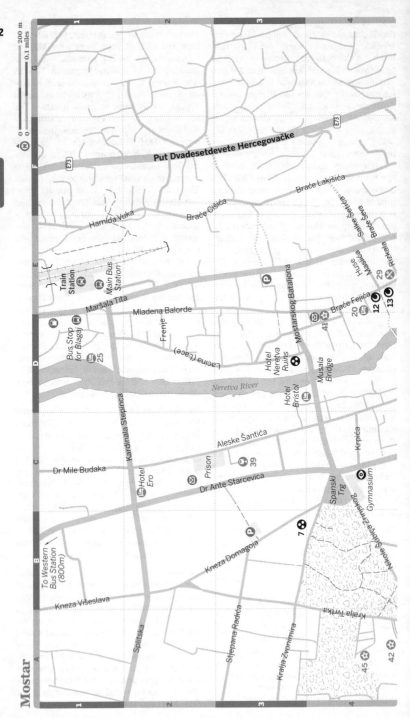

200 m
0.1 miles

Put Dvadesetdevete Hercegovačke

E73

E73

Braće Lakišića

Braće Ćišića

Hamida Vuka

Salke Šehtića

Braće Ševe

Huse Maslića

Rizitala

29

Train Station

Main Bus Station

Mostarskog Bataljona

Braće Fejića

12

13

Maršala Tita

Mladena Balorde

20

41

Bus Stop for Blagaj

25

Frenje

Lacina (Lace)

Hotel Neretva Ruins

Musala Bridge

Neretva River

Hotel Bristol

Kardinala Stepinca

Aleske Šantića

Dr Mile Budaka

Prison

39

Hotel Ero

Dr Ante Starcevica

Spanski Trg

Krpića

Gymnasium

To Western Bus Station (800m)

Kneza Domagoja

7

Nikole Šubića Zrinjskog

Kneza Višeslava

Splitska

Stjepana Radića

Kralja Zvonimira

Kralja Tvrtka

42

45

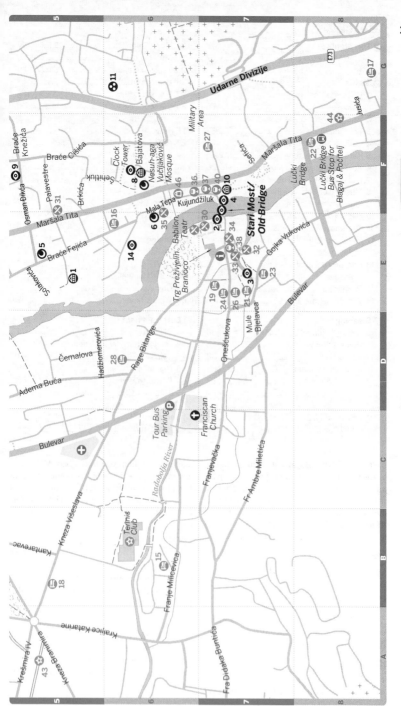

Stairway lane **Bajatova** climbs on towards the M17 with an underpass leading towards the site of a once imposing **Orthodox church** almost totally destroyed by Croat shelling in 1993. The site is currently fenced off for planned reconstruction but when accessible it offers extensive city views.

🕝 Tours

Some homestays and hostels offer walking tours around town and/or great-value €25 day trips visiting Blagaj, Međugorje, Počitelj and the Kravice waterfalls. **Almira Travel** (☑551873; www.almira-travel.ba; Mala Tepa 9) offers alternative options including wine-tasting tours in a range of European languages.

🛏 Sleeping

If you're stumped for accommodation the tourist information centre (p127) and travel agencies can help you find a bed. Most budget options are in people's homes without reception or full-time staff, so calling ahead is wise. In low season some are virtually dormant but you might get a whole room for the dorm price.

TOP CHOICE **Muslibegović House**

HERITAGE HOUSE **€€**
(☑551379; www.muslibegovichouse.com; Osman Đikća 41; s/d/ste €50/85/100; ❄🅰) In summer, tourists pay to visit this restored 18th-century Ottoman courtyard house. But it's simultaneously an extremely convivial boutique homestay-hotel. Room sizes and styles vary significantly, mixing excellent modern bathrooms with elements of traditional Bosnian, Turkish or even Moroccan design, notably in rooms 2 and 3. Double rooms cost €70 during low season.

Hotel Old Town
BOUTIQUE HOTEL €€

(☑558877; www.oldtown.ba; Rad Bitange 9a; d/tr from 160/240KM; ❄️ⓟ🛜) This super-central boutique hotel is designed to look like a typical Bosnian house and sports handmade, specially designed wooden furniture. Meanwhile its state-of-the-art ecofriendly energy-saving systems include waste-burning furnaces for water-heating and air circulation to save on air-con wastage. Deluxe rooms (single/double 190/280KM) are marginally larger than standard ones.

Hostel Majdas
HOUSE-HOSTEL €

(☑061382940, 062265324; www.hostelmajdas. com; 1st fl, Franje Milicevica 39; dm/d without bathroom €12.90/27; ❄️@🛜) By sheer force of personality, and a very human awareness of traveller needs, the host family has transformed this once dreary tower-block apartment into Mostar's cult hostel. Space is tight in the colour-coordinated bunk dorms and little communal areas, but it's a great place to meet fellow travellers; there are lockers, FAQ and cultural-tip sheets, €3 laundry, a book exchange and a taxi sign-up sheet. Sharp-witted Bata runs popular full-day regional tours several times weekly (€25).

Pansion Oscar
BUDGET ROOMS €

(☑580237; Oneščukova 33; s/d €30/40, s/d/tr/q without bathroom €20/30/45/60; ❄️) This brilliantly located family *pansion* has six rooms in two reconstructed Old Town houses, separated by parasol-shaded summer seating. The cheaper but more appealing rooms are set into sloping eaves. Two of the unsophisticated en suites share a balcony. The lovely contoured garden below becomes a *nargile* (hubble-bubble) cafe in summer, but there's no indoor sitting room or internet.

Motel Emen
OLD TOWN ROOMS €€

(☑581120, 061848734; www.motel-emen.com; Oneščukova 32; s/d/tr/q 82/124/154/212KM; ❄️@) The term 'motel' is quite misleading for what are in fact six tastefully appointed new rooms above a restaurant on one of Old Mostar's most popular pedestrian lanes. The decor has an understated chic and prices are reasonable for such a prized address. Room 103 (double 144KM) has a large private terrace.

Kriva Ćuprija
MILLHOUSE ROOMS €€

(☑550953; www.motel-mostar.ba; s/d/apt from €30/55/65; ❄️) Soothe yourself with the sounds of gushing streams in new, impeccably clean (if not necessarily large) rooms ranged above this stone millhouse restaurant overlooking the Crooked Bridge. The new annexe, **Kriva Ćuprija 2** (Maršala Tita 186) is stylish and features two hot tubs on a rear deck but it lacks the perfect location of the original and is right beside a busy main road.

Shangri-La
B&B €€

(☑551819; www.shangrila.com.ba; Kalhanska 10; d without/with breakfast €34/44; ❄️🛜ⓟ) Charming English-speaking hosts are welcoming but not intrusive, while their four rooms are better appointed than those of many Mostar hotels. Quiet yet very central with limited free (if awkward) parking.

Motel Deny
MINI-HOTEL €€

(☑578317; www.mdmostar.com; Kapetanovina 1; s/d/tr 70/100/150KM May-Sep, 60/90/130KM Oct-Apr; ❄️🛜ⓟ) Four of the six neat, well-furnished rooms overlook the Old Town's mill area, the best balcony views being from the smallest rooms (102 and 202). At night the lobby flickers alluringly with candlelight.

Hotel Pellegrino
APARTMENT HOTEL €€

(☑062969000, 061480784; www.hotel-pellegrino. ba; Faladžića 1c; r €50-120; ❄️) Above a large, neo-Tuscan restaurant-lounge (guests only), expansive rooms have excellent anti-allergenic bedding and kitchenette. Each room has its own oddity, be it a giant black lacquer vase, a bundle-of-twigs lamp or a whole-cow mat.

Villa Fortuna
B&B €€

(☑551888; www.villafortuna.ba; Rade Bitange 34; s/d/tr €30/40/55, incl breakfast €35/50/70; ❄️🛜ⓟ) Seven fresh, air-con rooms with elements of pseudo-aged 'country' furniture are set above Fortuna Travel in a hidden courtyard with gated parking for small cars. The backyard sitting area is decorated with old Bosnian metalwork.

Hostel Nina
FAMILY HOSTEL €

(☑061382743; www.hostelnina.ba; Čelebica 18; dm/ s/d without bathroom €10/15/20; @❄️) Popular homestay-hostel run by an obliging English-speaking lady whose husband, a war survivor and former bridge jumper, runs regional tours that often end up over bargain beers at his bar in the Tabhana. Note that the overflow annexe is in a dowdy apartment block across town near the Rondo.

Pansion Aldi
HOUSE-HOSTEL €

(☑552185, 061273457; www.pansion-aldi.com; Lačina 69a; dm/d without bathroom €10/20; ❄️@ⓟ) Handy for the bus station, this family-run hostel has 17 beds in five large if simple rooms; all but one is double, with air-con. There's a shared kitchenette and three small toilet-shower cubicles. A highlight is the riverside garden terrace where a small splash pool is installed among the roses in summer.

Hostel Miturno HOSTEL €

(☑552408; www.hostel-miturno.ba, www.miturno.ba; Braće Felića 67; dm/d €10/20; ❅☏) Run by a youthful, music-loving crew, this central mini-hostel has a handful of rooms and small dorms above a main-street shop. The TV room-lobby is cramped but colourful and social.

✖ Eating

Cafes and restaurants with divine views of the river cluster along the riverbank near Stari Most. Although unapologetically tourist-oriented, their meal prices are only a *maraka* or two more than any ordinary dive. Along Mala Tepe and Braće Fejića you'll find a morning vegetable market, supermarkets and several inexpensive places for *ćevapi* and other Bosnian snacks.

Restaurant Bella Vista BOSNIAN €€

(Tabhana; pizzas 7-10KM, mains 8-18KM) Along with Restaurants Babilon and Teatr next door, the Bella Vista has stupendous terrace views across the river to the Old Town and Stari Most. The food might be less impressive than the views, but some of the set 'tourist menus' are excellent value.

Konoba Stari Mlin BOSNIAN €

(Jusovina bb; meals 5-12KM; ☺8am-10pm) Down a hidden stairway, this millhouse restaurant includes one table tucked into a rocky alcove and several more on a tree-shaded terrace looking up at the crooked bridge, albeit across a litter-strewn stream. Exceptionally good-value meals include garlic calf's liver with French fries (5KM) and well-cooked trout (10KM) and the house white wine (per litre 15KM) is better than many competitors'.

Hindin Han FISH, BOSNIAN €€

(Jusovina bb; fish 10-18KM, grills 6-12KM; ☺11am-11pm) Perched pleasantly but not spectacularly high above a side stream, this rebuilt historic building can be beaten for views but rarely for the quality of its fish meals.

Šadrvan BOSNIAN €€

(Jusovina 11; meals 10-20KM) On a quaint, vine- and tree-shaded corner where the pedestrian lane from Stari Most divides, this tourist favourite has tables set around a trickling fountain made of old Turkish-style metalwork. The menu covers all Bosnian bases and takes a stab at some vegetarian options.

Meat-free *đuveć* (KM7) tastes like ratatouille on rice.

Urban Grill ČEVABDŽINICA €

(www.urbangrill.ba; Mala Tepa; 5/10 ćevapi 3.50/6KM; ☺8am-11pm) Can *ćevapi* ever be cool? They think so here. And hidden away beneath the hip main servery is a little terrace with an unexpectedly excellent Old Bridge view.

ABC ITALIAN €

(☑061194656; Braće Fejića 45; pizza & pasta 6-9KM, mains 12-15KM; ☺8am-11pm Mon-Fri, noon-11pm Sat & Sun) Above a popular cakeshop-cafe, this relaxed pastel-toned Italian restaurant is decorated with photos of old Mostar and dotted with aspidistras. Pizzas are bready but the pastas come with an extra bucketful of parmesan. Try plate-lickingly creamy Aurora tortellini.

Eko-Eli BOSNIAN PIES €

(Maršala Tita 115; mains 2-3KM; ☺7am-11pm) Typical Bosnian snacks including *krompirača*, *sirnica*, *burek* and *zeljanica* are cooked fresh over hot coals and served up for pennies at sit-and-scoff tables. Zero luxury and no tourists.

🍷 Drinking

Ali Baba CAVE BAR

(Kujundžiluk; ☺24hr Jun-Sep, closed winter) Take a cavern in the raw rock, add colourful low lighting, fat beats and sensibly priced drinks and hey presto, you've got this wacky party bar. A dripping tunnel leads out to a second entrance on Maršala Tita.

OKC Abrašević ALTERNATIVE BAR

(☑561107; www.okcabrasevic.org; Alekse Šantića 25) This understatedly intellectual smoky box of a bar offers Mostar's most vibrantly alternative scene and has an attached venue for offbeat gigs. It's hidden away in an unsigned courtyard on the former front line. Draft beer from 2KM. Hours vary.

Bijeli Bar BAR-CAFE

(Stari Most 2; ☺7am-11pm) The ubercool main lounge zaps you with wicked white-on-white Clockwork Orange decor. Meanwhile, around the corner the same bar owns an utterly spectacular perch-terrace from which the old bridge and towers appear from altogether new angles. The latter is entered from Maršala Tita, through a wrought-iron gate marked Atelje Novalić: cross the Japanese-style garden and climb the stone roof-steps.

Caffe Marshall BAR-CAFE

(Oneščukova bb; ☻8am-midnight) Minuscule box bar with an electronic jukebox and a ceiling draped with musical instruments.

Wine & More WINE-TASTING CAFE

(Mala Tepa; ☻9am-11pm) Play Bacchus, sampling Trebinje's famous Turdoš Monastery wines (per glass 5KM) at barrel tables on the Old Town's time-polished stone stairways. Inside the icon decor is less interesting.

☆ Entertainment

OKC Abrašević hosts occasional concerts and Ali Baba fills its summer cave with contemporary dance sounds, particularly on weekend party nights. There are several DJ cafes and nightclubs in a mall area near the Rondo.

Club Oxygen NIGHTCLUB

(www.biosphere.ba/biosfere-stranice-oxigen-en. html; Braće Fejića bb; ☻variable) Oxygen has movie nights, DJ-discos and Mostar's top live gigs. In summer its rooftop SkyBar takes over as the place to party.

Dom Herceg Stjepan Kosaća
CULTURAL CENTRE

(☑323501; Rondo; ☎) Diverse shows and concerts include occasional touring operas, ballets and theatre from Croatia. There's a weekend turbofolk club behind.

Pavarotti Music Centre STUDIO VENUE

(☑550750; Maršala Tita 179) Originally funded by the famous tenor as a post-war rehabilitation program, this music school and recording studio has a cafe and holds occasional concerts in its open courtyard.

🔒 Shopping

The stone-roofed shop-houses of Kujundžiluk throw open metal shutters to sell colourfully inexpensive Turkish and Indian souvenirs including glittery velveteen slippers (€7), pashmina-style wraps (from €5), fezzes (€5), *boncuk* (evil-eye) pendants and Russian-style nested dolls. Look for pens fashioned from old bullets and watch while master coppersmith **Ismet Kurt** (Kujundžiluk 5; ☻9am-8pm) hammers old mortar-shell casings into works of art.

ℹ Information

Most businesses accept euros and Croatian kuna as well as marakas. Along Braće Fejića are banks, ATMs, a pharmacy, supermarkets and two internet cafes (both in side lanes). Mostar website include the **Hercegovina Tourist Board** (www.hercegovina.ba) and **Visit Mostar** (www. visitmostar.org).

Bosniak post office (Braće Fejića bb; ☻8am-8pm Mon-Fri, 8am-6pm Sat)

Croat post office (Dr Ante Starčevića bb; ☻7am-7pm Mon-Sat, 8am-noon Sun)

Europa Club (Huse Maslića 10; per hr 1KM; ☻7am-midnight) Internet cafe beneath a stationery shop.

Tourist information centre (☑397350; Trg Preživjelih Branioco; ☻9am-9pm Jun-Sep, 10am-6pm Oct, closed Nov-May)

ℹ Getting There & Around

Air

Mostar airport (code OMO; ☑350992; www. mostar-airport.ba), 6km south of town off the Čapljina road, has no scheduled flights.

BUSES FROM MOSTAR'S MAIN BUS STATION

DESTINATION	PRICE (KM)	DURATION (HR)	DEPARTURES
Banja Luka (via Jajce)	25	6	1.30pm
Belgrade	53	11	7.30pm, 9pm
Čapljina	6	40min	twice-hourly Mon-Fri, six daily Sun
Dubrovnik	27	3-4	7am, 10.15am, 12.30pm
Herceg Novi	46	4½	7am
Sarajevo	18	2½	hourly 6am-3pm plus 6.15pm & 8.30pm
Split	31	4½	7am, 10.15am, 12.50pm, 11.25pm
Stolac	6	1	hourly till 6.15pm
Trebinje (via Nevesinje)	21	3	6.15am Mon-Sat, 3.30pm, 5.30pm
Vienna	110	12	8.30am
Zagreb	43	9½	7am, 9am, 8.15pm

Bicycle

Polo Travel (☑061547827; Trg Preživjelih Bra-nioco; ☺9am-9pm) rents bicycles (per half/full day €10/15).

Bus

Most long-distance buses use the **main bus station** (☑552025; Trg Ivana Krndelja) beside the train station. However, Renner buses to Stolac, a 4.30pm bus to Split (25KM) and seven weekday services to Međugorje (4KM, 45 minutes) start from the inconveniently located, half-built **western bus station** (Autobusni Kolodvor; ☑348680; Vukovarska bb). Yellow **Mostar Bus** (☑552250; www.mostarbus.ba/linije.asp) services to Blagaj start from opposite the train station and pick up passengers more conveniently at the Lučki Most stop.

Car

Hyundai Rent-A-Car (☑552404; www.hyundai.ba; main bus station; per day/week from 75/390KM; ☺8am-6pm Mon-Fri, 9am-noon Sat) hire charges include full insurance without deductible and free option to drop off in Sarajevo. Add 17% tax in some cases and 30KM extra to collect or drop off the car after hours.

Train

Trains to Sarajevo (9.90KM, 2¾ hours) depart at 7.59am and 6.40pm daily, puffing alongside fish farms in the dammed gorge of the pea-green Neretva River before struggling up a series of switchbacks behind Konjic to reach Sarajevo after 65 tunnels.

Around Mostar

By joining a tour or hiring a car you could visit Blagaj, Počitelj, Međugorje and the Kravice waterfalls all in one day.

BLAGAJ
☑036 / POP 4000

The most iconic sight in pretty Blagaj village is a very picturesque, half-timbered **Tekija** (Dervish House; ☑573221; admission 4KM; ☺8am-10pm) standing at the foot of a soaring cliff that's topped, way above, by the **Herceg Stjepan Fortress** ruins. The Tekija's ground floor is used as a souvenir shop and cafe but upstairs the wobbly wooden interior entombs two Tajik 15th-century dervishes and attracts pious pilgrims. Outside, the surreally blue-green Buna River gushes out of a cave in the cliff base and flows past a series of riverside restaurants linked by footbridges.

Walking to the Tekija takes 10 minutes from the seasonal **tourist information booth** (☑061687575; blagaj_city@yahoo.com; ☺10am-7pm

in season), which rents bicycles. Easy to miss behind a stone wall en route is the artistically appointed **Oriental House** (Velagomed, Velagic House; ☑572712; Velagicevina bb; admission 2KM), an 18th-century Ottoman homestead ensemble set behind island-meadow gardens. Hours are sporadic. At times they have been known to rent out guest rooms. Otherwise try the friendly unmarked **Kayan Pansion** (☑572299; nevresakajan@yahoo.com; per person €10; ✳), offering two well-kept four-bed rooms above a family home. It's unmarked, set back across a side road opposite the octagonal 1892 **Sultan Sulejman Mosque**.

Camp Bara (☑061627803; www.camp-bara.com) is just a scraggy patch of riverside grass with two simple bathrooms down a steep, narrow lane. It overlooks a fish farm but it's a cheap, central spot for camping.

Mostar Bus (www.mostarbus.ba/linije.asp) routes 10, 11 and 12 from Mostar all run to (or very near) Blagaj (2.10KM, 30 minutes), with 16 services on weekdays but only a handful at weekends. There's no direct public transport from Blagaj to Počitelj.

MEĐUGORJE
☑036 / POP 4300

On 24 June 1981 a vision appeared to six local teenagers in Međugorje (www.medjugorje.hr). What they believe they saw was a manifestation of the Holy Virgin. As a result, this formerly poor wine-making backwater has been utterly transformed into a bustling Catholic pilgrimage centre and continues to grow even though Rome has not officially acknowledged the visions' legitimacy. Today Međugorje has that odd blend of honest faith and cash-in tackiness that is reminiscent of Lourdes (France) or Fatima (Portugal) but there's little of beauty here and for nonpilgrims a one-hour visit often proves ample to get the idea. The town's focus is double-towered 1969 **St James' Church** (Župna Crkva). In a garden 200m behind that, the mesmerising **Resurrected Saviour** (Uskrsli Spasitej) is a masterpiece of contemporary sculpture showing a 5m-tall metallic Christ standing crucified yet cross-less, his manhood wrapped in scripture. At times the statue's right knee 'miraculously' weeps a colourless liquid that pilgrims queue to dab onto specially inscribed pads.

A 3km (5KM) taxi ride away at **Podbrdo** village, streams of the faithful climb **Brdo Ukazanja** (Apparition Hill). Red-earth paths studded with sharp stones access a white statue of the Virgin Mary marking the site of the original 1981 visions. If you're fit you could nip up and back in 20 minutes but pilgrims spend an hour or more contemplating and praying at way stations, a few walking barefoot in deliberately painful acts of penitence.

Download artists'-eye town maps from the **tourist association** (www.tel.net.ba/tzm -medjugorje/1%20karta100.jpg).

POČITELJ
☑036 / POP 350

This stepped Ottoman-era fortress village is one of the most picture-perfect architectural ensembles in BiH. Cupped in a steep rocky amphitheatre, it was systematically despoiled in the 1990s conflicts but its finest 16th-century buildings are now rebuilt, including the **Šišman Ibrahim Madrassa**, the 1563 **Hadži Alijna Mosque** and the 16m **clock tower** (Sahat Kula). The upper village culminates in the still part-ruined **Utvrda** (Fort) containing the iconic octagonal **Gavrakapetan Tower**.

Two lovely new pine-walled **apartments** (d/tr €40/60; ✸) just beside the city gate-tower include breakfast on a vine-shaded view-terrace. Pre-book through English-speaking **Mediha Oruč** (☑062481844), summer only. Year-round, Razira Kajtaz offers simple **homestay rooms** (☑826468, 062230023; per person €10) in an unlabelled, stone-roofed house with partial air-con.

Muta Restaurant (snacks 5-7KM, mains 12-20KM) serves schnitzels, *dolme* or trout in a stonewalled house opposite the mosque. The vine-shaded terrace is great for a drink.

Počitelj is right beside the main Split–Mostar road, 5km north of Čapljina. Mostar–Split and Mostar–Čapljina buses pass by, but southbound only the latter (roughly hourly on weekdays) will usually accept Počitelj-bound passengers. If day-tripping in

summer, arrive early to avoid the heat and the Croatian tour groups.

KRAVICE WATERFALLS
In spring this stunning mini-Niagara of 25m cascades pounds itself into a dramatic, steamy fury. In summer the falls themselves are less impressive but surrounding pools become shallow enough for swimming. The falls are 15 minutes' walk from a car park that's 4km down a dead-end road turning off the M6 (Čapljina–Ljubuški road) at km42.5. There's no public transport.

Neum

Driving between Split and Dubrovnik, don't forget your passport as you'll pass through BiH's tiny toehold of Adriatic coastline. Buses often make a refreshment break on the Neum bypass (kuna accepted), but Neum itself is crammed with concrete apartment-hotels and the Adriatic is more inviting elsewhere in neighbouring Croatia.

Stolac
☑036 / POP 12,000

Backed by a steep, bald mountain ridge, the attractive castle town of Stolac was the site of Roman Diluntum (3rd century AD). A prominent citadel from the 15th century, Stolac suffered serious conflict in 1993. The displaced population has returned and several of the town's greatest historical buildings have been painstakingly reconstructed, though war damage is still painfully evident.

In the town centre, the 1735 **Šarić House** faces memorable mural-fronted **Čaršija Mosque**, rebuilt to look just like the 1519 original. A derelict supermarket in front is less photogenic. Upstream are several picturesque but increasingly ruinous 17th-century stone **mill-races**. Downstream, the tree-lined main street, Hrvatske-Brante (aka Ada), passes a diagonal switchback lane that leads up to the hefty **castle ruins**. Around 300m further is another group of historic buildings, some rebuilt. Across the bridges, views of the castle site are most memorable from near the Auro petrol station, 50m south of the graffiti-covered bus station.

Beside the Mostar road 3km west of Stolac, **Radimlja Necropolis** (admission free) looks at first glimpse like a marble quarryman's yard, and the backdrop of dreary cafes and low-rise

20th-century buildings doesn't help. On closer inspection the group of around 110 blocks are actually some of Bosnia's most important *stećci* grave-markers (see p142), though only a few have outstanding carvings.

Stolac's only hotel, **Villa Ragusa** (☎853700; s/d/tr 35/70/105KM), offers unremarkable but spruced up old rooms just across a small bridge from the town centre.

Except on Sunday, buses run from Mostar to Stolac at least hourly. The intriguing Stolac-Trebinje road crosses a war-scarred former no-man's-land passing the still bombed-out hilltop hamlet of Žegulja. There's no bus link but you might persuade the town's one taxi to take you to Ljubinje (20km), from where a 4.30pm bus runs to Trebinje (10KM, 1½ hours).

EASTERN BOSNIA & HERCEGOVINA

To get quickly yet relatively easily off the main tourist trail, try linking Sarajevo or Mostar to Dubrovnik via Trebinje, or head to Belgrade via Višegrad. For much of these journeys you'll be passing through the Republika Srpska, where's it's fascinating to hear about BiH's 1990s traumas from the 'other side'.

Trebinje
☎059 / POP 36,000

A beguiling quick stop between Dubrovnik (28km) and Višegrad (or Mostar), Trebinje has a small, walled **Old Town** (Stari Grad) where inviting, unpretentious cafes offer a fascinating opportunity to meet friendly local residents and hear Serb viewpoints on divisive recent history. Old Town ramparts back onto the riverside near a 19th-century former Austro-Hungarian barracks which now houses the eclectic **Hercegovina Museum** (www.muzejhercegovine.org; Stari Grad 59; admission 2KM; ⊙8am-2pm Mon-Fri, 10am-2pm Sat).

Parts of Trebinje feel a little like southern France, nowhere more so than on the lovely stone-flagged **Trg Svobode**, which is shaded by plane and chestnut trees and lined with street cafes with wrought-iron overhangs.

Trebinje's 1574 **Arslanagić Bridge** (Perovića Most) is a unique double-backed structure sadly let down by the unexotic

suburban location (700m northeast of Hotel Leotar) to which it was moved in the 1970s.

For phenomenal views take the 2km winding lane leading east of Hotel In to hilltop **Hercegovacka Gracanica**, where the compact but eye-catching **Presvete Bogorodice Church** was erected in 2000 to rehouse the bones of local hero Jovan Dučić. Its design is based on the 1321 Gračanica monastery (p456) in Kosovo, a building that's symbolically sacred to many Serbs.

🛏 Sleeping

TOP CHOICE **Hotel Platani** BOUTIQUE HOTELS €€ (www.hotelplatani.info; Trg Svobode; s/d/tr old building 71/104/126KM, new building 82/134/157KM; ❄🐾) The Platani consists of two outwardly similar buildings with iconic glass and wrought-iron overhangs that help give Trebinje's tree-lined main square its Gallic character. Rooms in the old building are unimpeachably clean but slightly dated. However, in the new building they're contrastingly stylish and contemporary with Klimt-esque art works. Highly recommended.

Hotel Porto Bello GUEST ROOMS €€ (☎223344; www.portobellotrebinje.com; s/d €30/45; ❄@) Five try-hard rooms with decent facilities but without much character above a restaurant within the walls of the Old Town.

Hotel In MOTEL €€ (☎261443; www.etagehotel.com; Dušanova; s/d/tr 60/90/120KM; ❄P) Across the river near the hospital, the 'In' is set back from the main road so it's quieter than its parent, Motel Etage. Brand new at the time of research, it was clean and fresh but without particular interest and some rooms were a squeeze.

🍴 Eating & Drinking
Pizza Castello ITALIAN €
(☎260245; Trg Travunije 3; pizzas 6-12KM; ⊙8am-11pm Mon-Sat, 6-11pm Sun) Castello's terrace is great for people-watching, jovial hosts Snezhan and Dušan speak great English, and the thin-crust pizza is excellent. Castello is on the left as you enter the Old Town square from the Platani.

Galerija Veritas CAFE
(Stari Grad 17; ⊙9am-11pm) This brick-domed vaulted cavern cafe has a beamed upper level and a floating barge-bar terrace on the river at the back, partly beneath the Kameni Bridge.

Azzovo CAFE
(Stari Grad 114; ☺8am-11pm Mon-Sat, 10am-11pm Sun) Old Town blues-oriented bar with ceilings of bamboo and vine stems.

ℹ Information

Balkan Investment Bank (Preobraženska 6; ☺8am-3.30pm Mon-Fri, 8am-11.30am Sat) Changes money, has an ATM.

Online City Map (www.trebinje.info/trebinje/mape/plan-grada.html)

Tourist office (☏273410; Jovan Dučića bb; www.trebinjeturizam.com; ☺8am-8pm Mon-Fri, 8am-3pm Sat) Facing the Hotel Platani near the Old Town's western gate.

ℹ Getting There & Away

The '**bus station**' (Vojvode Stepe Stepanovića) is simply a pair of bus shelters in a parking area. Walk north then immediately east (200m) to find the Old Town's west gate.

Trebinje To Višegrad

Trebinje–Belgrade and Trebinje–Sarajevo buses pass through the glorious **Sutjeska National Park** (www.npsutjeska.srbinje.net, in Bosnian), where the magnificent grey rock sides of the Sutjeska canyon rise like Chinese paintings either side of the road. Further north the canyon opens out near an impressively vast concrete **Partizans' Memorial** commemorating the classic WWII battle of Tjentište. Mountaineers and hikers can explore more of the national park's scenic wonders with extreme-sports outfit **Encijan** (☏211220, 211150; www.pkencijan.com; Kraljapetra-I 1; ☺9am-5pm Mon-Sat), based in **Foča**. It also organise world-class **rafting** on the Tara River that cascades out of Europe's deepest canyon (across the Montenegrin border) then thunders over 21 rapids (class III to class IV in summer, class IV to class V in April).

Višegrad
☏058 / POP 20,000

Višegrad is internationally famous for its 10-arch **Mehmet Paša Sokolović Bridge**, built in 1571 and immortalised in Andrić's classic *Bridge on the Drina*. Celebrated Sarajevo-born film director Emir Kusturica is reportedly planning a movie based on the Andric book with filming to coincide with long-overdue repair work to the great bridge's foundations (probably 2012). Filming may create a stone ethno-village in Višegrad to be used first as a set and later as a tourist resort much as happened with Drvengrad (www.mecavnik.info) in Serbia.

The town is otherwise architecturally unexciting but it's set between some of Bosnia's most impressive river canyons. If you're driving, there's a great **viewpoint** 3.6km down a side road to Ruda that branches off the Višegrad–Goražde highway 9km south of town.

Boat trips (from 30KM per person including lunch) from Višegrad depart around 10am in summer, and will probably become more frequent in coming years but for now pre-booking is usually essential. Check details with the helpful **tourist office** (☏620821, 620950; www.visegradturizam.com; ☺8am-4pm Mon-Fri, 8am-3pm Sat) near the southern end of the old bridge. The website has a town map.

BUSES FROM TREBINJE

There are no longer buses to Stolac or Herceg Novi.

DESTINATION	PRICE (KM)	DURATION (HR)	DEPARTURES
Belgrade (via Višegrad)	48	11	8am, 6pm
Dubrovnik	10	45min	10am Mon-Sat (returns at 1.30pm)
Foča	18	2½	take Belgrade, Pale or Sarajevo bus
Ljubinje	10	1½	2.10pm Mon-Fri, 7pm daily
Mostar (via Nevesinje)	20	3	6.15am, 10am, 2.30pm
Novi Sad	53	12	5.30pm
Pale	28	4½	5am
Podgorica (via Nikšič)	33	3½	8.30am, 3pm, 4.30pm
Sarajevo	26	4	5am, 7.30am, 11am

Reconstructed in 2010, the narrow-gauge railway to Mokra Gora (Serbia) links up with the popular **Šargan 8 tourist train** (see p853). Daily services could start by the time you read this, allowing a stop at the historic **Dobrun Monastery** (km11.5, Višegrad–Belgrade road). From outside that complex looks like a latter-day hacienda hotel but the site is of deeply historical resonance for Serbs as Karađorđe hid here immediately before launching the 1804 Serb uprising. The monastery was almost entirely destroyed in WWII but the original porch of the central 14th-century chapel survives.

Sleeping & Eating

Hotel Višegrad   HOTEL €€
(631051; www.hotel.visegrad24.info; Trg Palih Boraca; s/d/tr 49/83/123KM) Behind a sickly yellow facade, the Višegrad is ideally central and staff are helpful but despite a 2009 renovation it remains less than luxurious. Rooms are clean enough but showers are feeble and power points are wantonly inconvenient. Its restaurant (mains 7KM to 14KM) is a blandly boxlike affair pumping out loud Europop but the terrace has picture-perfect views of the classic bridge and the kitchen produces unexpectedly excellent dinners, with fresh trout at just 30KM per kg. Two other motels are both around 1km from the centre, and there's a third at km8 on the Dobrun road.

ⓘ Getting There & Away

A bus station is planned near the 'new bridge' 1.5km northeast of centre. Until it's built, buses to Foča (9.30am), Banja Luka (8am), Užice (11.30am and 6pm via Dobrun and Mokra Gora) and the 5.15am bus to Belgrade start from outside the Hotel Višegrad. Other buses, which are in transit through town, stop briefly near the north side of the old bridge and at Motel Okuka (1km northeast of the centre) where some make a refreshment break. Such routes include Trebinje (via Foča and Sutjeska National Park) at 10am and 11.15pm, Sarajevo at 4am and 12.45pm, Niš around 9.20pm and Belgrade at 9.45am, 1.30pm and 10.45pm.

CENTRAL & WESTERN BOSNIA

West of Sarajevo lies a series of mildly interesting historic towns, green wooded hills, rocky crags and dramatic rafting canyons. The area offers ample opportunities for exploration and adrenaline-rush activities.

Visoko

032 / POP 17,000

Once the capital of medieval Bosnia and the spiritual centre of the controversial Bosnian Church, this unremarkable leather-tanning town had been largely forgotten during the 20th century. Then Bosnian archaeologist Semir Osmanagic hatched a bold theory that Visoko's 250m-high Visočica Hill is in fact the **World's Greatest Pyramid** (Sun Pyramid; www.piramidasunca.ba; admission 2KM) built approximately 12,000 years ago by a long-disappeared superculture. Other nearby hills are mooted to be lesser pyramids too, and archaeologists are busily investigating prehistoric subterranean labyrinths, notably the **Tunnel Ravne** (062730299; admission 5KM; call ahead), of which over 200m can already be visited on guided hard-hat tours.

The mainly forested 'Sun Pyramid' does indeed have a seemingly perfect pyramidal shape when viewed from some angles (despite a long ridge at the back) and plates of bafflingly hard ancient 'concrete' found here are cited as having once covered the hill, creating an artificially smoothed surface. Visits to the site's **archaeological excavations** (admission 2KM) start with a stiff 20-minute climb from an info point-ticket booth near Bistro Vidikovac, itself around 15 minutes' walk from Visoko bus station. Start by crossing the river towards the **Motel Piramida-Sunca** (731460; www.motelpiramidasunca.co.ba; 6th fl, Musala 1; s/d/tr/q 50/80/120/160KM;) and turn immediately left down Visoko's patchily attractive main street, Alije Izetbegovića, passing the excellent if semidormant **Hotel Centar** (061108427; www.hotelcentar.ba; s/d 70/130KM, apt 110-160KM; call ahead;). Renamed Čaršijska, the street then curves to point directly towards the pyramid summit. After the bazaar veer left into Tvrtka/Mule Hodžić then, opposite Mule Hodžić 25, climb steeply up winding Pertac/Fetahagića, turning left at the top. The info point is just beyond.

ⓘ Getting There & Away

Visoko is a stop for buses between Sarajevo (5.70KM, 50 minutes) and Kakanj (4.70KM, 35 minutes) running 18 times daily (seven times Sundays). For Travnik and Jajce, direct buses depart Visoko at 8.10am, 9.50am, 2.10pm and 4.10pm or change in Zenica (14 buses on weekdays).

Dotted among the faceless industrial towns of virtually untouristed northeastern Bosnia are several very photogenic medieval castle ruins.

» **Doboj** The city is an ugly railway junction but the castle hosts costumed festivals and there's a great little cafe-tower.

» **Gradačac** Gradačac town centre is dominated by a partly reconstructed castle with a restaurant on top.

» **Srebrenik** Truly dramatic crag-top setting 6km east of Srebrenik town.

» **Tešanj** Powerful ruins rise above a loveable Old Town square.

» **Vranduk** Small ruins set in BiH's most idyllic castle village, around 10km north of Zenica.

Travnik

030 / POP 27,500

Once the seat of Bosnia's Turkish viziers (Ottoman governors), Travnik is now best known for its sheep cheese – and as the birthplace of Nobel prize–winning author Ivo Andrić, who set his classic *Bosnian Chronicle* here. It's a pleasant place to briefly break the journey between Sarajevo and Jajce, and in winter there's skiing at nearby Vlašić. Funnelled through the narrow, forest-sided Lavša Valley, Travnik straddles the M5 highway, paralleled by the main commercial street, Bosanska. To find Bosanska from the bus station, exit through the platform-side yellow fencing, turn left and walk four minutes east continuing when Prnjavor becomes a footpath alley just beyond the BHT/post office building. You should emerge on Bosanska near the dome-sheltered **Viziers' Turbe**, the best known of several Travnik tomb posts. Turn right here to find the helpful **tourist office** (511588; www.tzsbk.com; Bosanska 75; 8am-4pm Mon-Fri) facing the distinctive **Sahat Kula** stone clocktower. Turn left for all other sights.

Sights & Activities

Stari Grad   FORTRESS RUINS
(adult/student 2/1.50KM; 8am-8pm May-Sep, 9am-6pm Oct & Apr)

Towards the town's eastern end, a sizeable castle ruin encloses a reconstructed multi-sided keep that houses a modest museum featuring local costumes and sketching the area's history. Around the castle site lies Travnik's most attractive historical district. At its base, **Plava Voda** (Blue Water) is a picturesque gaggle of summer restaurants beside a merrily gurgling stream criss-crossed by small bridges.

Many Coloured Mosque   HISTORIC MOSQUE
(Šasend Džamija; Bosanska 203) Built in 1757 and reconstructed a century later, its famous facade murals have faded but the mosque is remarkable for the *bezistan* (mini-bazaar) built into the arches beneath the main prayerhouse. Behind the mosque is a pedestrian underpass beneath the M5 from which Varoš leads up to Stari Grad.

Ivo Andrić Museum   MEMORIAL MUSEUM
(518140; Zenjak 13; adult/student 2/1.50KM; 9.30am-5pm) Readers who enjoyed *Bosnian Chronicle* might like this old-style house designed to simulate Andrić's birthplace. Labels are in Bosnian but the enthusiastic curator speaks English. The museum is one block off Bosanska (north between 171 and 169).

Vlašić   SKI RESORT
(www.babanovac.net; ski passes per day/night/week 19/12/120KM) This three-lift ski field is above Babanovac village, 27km northwest of Travnik.

Sleeping

Central hotels suffer from road rumble as do half a dozen other motels strung 10km along the eastbound M5.

CENTRAL TRAVNIK
Motel Aba   HOTEL €
(511462; www.aba.ba; Šumeća 166a; s 35-40KM, d/tr/q 50/70/80KM;) Handily near to Plava Voda, Aba provides highly acceptable, unfussy en suite rooms at unbelievably reasonable prices. There's free wi-fi and limited free parking but breakfast costs 10KM extra.

The stairs and road noise are minor niggles but it's fabulous value.

Hotel Lipa
HOTEL €€

(☑511604; Lažajeva 116; s/d/tr 52/84/111KM) Neat, if blandly remodelled, little rooms lead off the dingy corridors at this Yugoslavian-era hotel, but at least the location is relatively central, directly behind the Viziers' Turbe.

VLAŠIĆ

Blanca
RESORT & SPA €€€

(☑519900; www.blancaresort.com; s €52-165, d €74-242, tr €132-273) Right at the base of the ski-jump, this 2010 complex uses wooden chalet elements to soften an overall sense of poised designer cool. Guests get free use of four different saunas, the indoor swimming pool has recliner chairs at view windows and unlike virtually every other Vlašić hotel it's open year round. 'Classic' rooms have no view whatsoever while 'superior' rooms are huge. 'Premium' rooms strike the best balance.

Hotel Central
SKI HOTEL €€

(☑540165; www.hotel-central-vlasic.net; per person 52-82KM) Homey, seasonal ski hotel that's about the nearest Vlašić gets to 'budget accommodation'.

✕ Eating

Along Bosanska you'll find supermarkets, bakeries and several shops (such as number 157) selling Travnik's trademark white cheese (*Travnički Sir*).

Restaurant Divan
TRADITIONAL BOSNIAN €€

(Zenjak 13; meals 5-16KM; ☉9am-11pm) Dine on fish, squid or Bosnian grills around the piano in thick-walled, timber-beamed rooms beneath the Ivo Andrić museum or in the enclosed courtyard behind.

Lutvina Kahva
HISTORIC CAFE €

(Plava Voda; ćevapi 2-7KM, mains 9-11KM; ☉7am-10pm) Decorated with copperware, this Moorish cube of cafe featured in Andrić's novel and has perfectly situated streamside seating.

Konoba Plava Voda
TRADITIONAL BOSNIAN €€

(Šumeće bb; meals 5.50-15KM; ☉7am-10pm) Three restaurants, all called Plava Voda, each have lovely summer terraces overlooking the attractive springs area. This one offers an English menu and generous portions.

❶ Getting There & Away

Travnik's **bus station** (☑792761) is off Sehida (the M5 highway) around 500m west of centre.

Jajce

☑030 / POP 30,000

Above an impressive waterfall, Jajce's fortified Old Town climbs a steep rocky knoll to the powerful, ruined castle where Bosnia's medieval kings were once crowned. The surrounding array of glorious mountains, lakes and canyons make Jajce a great exploration base, while curious catacombs and a Mithraic temple might intrigue fans of mysterious 'lost' religions. But don't expect too much from the town centre; despite the surrounding fortifications, it's a mainly banal collection of 20th-century architecture.

◉ Sights

Old Town Jajce's attractions can be seen in a two-hour ramble, assuming you can locate the sites' various keyholders.

Catacombs
MEDIEVAL CARVINGS

(Svetog Luke bb; admission 1KM) Built around 1400, this two-level half-lit crypt is small and roughly hewn but notable for the boldly sculpted sun and crescent moon motif, a rare surviving memorial to the independent

BUSES FROM TRAVNIK

DESTINATION	PRICE (KM)	DURATION (HR)	DEPARTURES
Bihać	26-32	6	6, 6.50am, 9.30am, 3.30pm, 4.20pm, 11.50pm
Babanovac	4	45min	7.15am, 11.30am, 6pm, 7.30pm
Jajce	8-12.70	1½	7.25am, 11.10am, 5.15pm, plus all Bihać buses
Sarajevo	15.50	2	about hourly till noon, 3.40pm, 6.20pm, 7.10pm
Split (via Bugojno)	23-31	4½	up to 6 daily
Zenica	4.50-7	1	25 daily

Bosnian Church. Tito is said to have hidden here during 1943. Request the key from the little cafe-hairdresser opposite, which is built onto the side of the sturdy round **Bear Tower** (Medvjed Kula).

Tvrđava   FORTIFIED CITADEL
To explore the remnant Old Town, walk up past the **Tower of St Luke**, a 15th-century campanile attached to a now ruined church. Turn right at the tiny, boxlike Dizdar Džamija (Women's Mosque) and climb stairs to the portal of the sturdy main **fortress** (adult/child 1/0.50KM; ☉10am-7pm). Inside is mostly bald grass but the ramparts offer sweeping views of the valleys and crags that surround Jajce's urban sprawl.

From the **Velika Tabija** (Gornja Mahala) a further section of citadel wall descends to the **Midway Tower** (Mala Tabija) facing the attractively renovated **Old Kršlak House**.

Waterfalls   VIEWPOINT
Jajce's impressive 21m-high **waterfalls** mark the confluence of the Pliva and Vrbas Rivers. For the classic tourist-brochure photo, cross the big Vrbas bridge and turn left on the Banja Luka road. Walk 500m, then at the third lay-by on the left climb over the low crash barrier and double back 150m down a footpath through the pinewoods to the viewpoint.

Mithraeum   ANCIENT SCULPTURE
(Mitrasova 12) Hidden in a drab 20th-century building are remnants of a 4th-century sculpture featuring Mithras fighting a bull watched by an audience of ladies and centurions. Once worshipped in a now-mysterious, forgotten religion, Mithras was a pre-Zoroastrian Persian sun god 'rediscovered' by mystical Romans. Peep in through the glassless window with a torch or request the key from the tourist booth (1KM per person).

AVNOJ Museum   SOCIALIST HISTORY
(admission 2KM; ☉9am-5pm) In 1943 the second congress of Antifascist Council of the People's Liberation of Yugoslavia (AVNOJ) formulated Yugoslavia's postwar socialist constitution. This momentous event occurred in a banal Jajce building rather like a school hall on whose stage now stands a large brooding statue of partisan Tito made of gold-painted polystyrene. Sparse photographic info boards have partial translations in barely intelligible English.

Plivsko Jezero   LAKES
Some 5km west of Jajce, wooded mountains reflect idyllically in the picture-perfect Pliva

Lakes (Plivsko Jezero). A water-meadow park between the two contains a superquaint collection of 17 miniature **watermills** that form one of Bosnia's most photographed scenes. Take Jezero-bound buses to Plaža Motel (km91 on the M5), then walk 15 minutes back along the lakeside. Plaža Motel rents **rowing boats** (per hr 6KM). Rent bicycles at AutoKamp (per hr/day 2/10KM; ☉7am-11pm).

🛏 Sleeping & Eating

Eko-Pliva (✆564100, 065632110; www.plivatourism.ba) and the tourist information booth can both arrange simple **homestays** (per person 20-30KM). One such is **Pašagina Avlija's place** (✆657048; per person €10) right beside the Bear Tower.

CENTRAL JAJCE

Hotel Stari Grad   CENTRAL HOTEL €€
(✆654006; www.jajcetours.com; Svetog Luke 3; s/d 57/84KM, apt 82-154KM; ✳@🛜) Although it's not actually old, beams, wood panelling and a heraldic fireplace give this comfortable little hotel a look of suavely modernised antiquity. Beneath the part-glass floor of the appealing lobby-restaurant (mains 10KM to 14KM) are the excavations of an Ottoman-era *hammam* (Turkish bath).

Hotel Tourist 98   URBAN MOTEL €€
(✆658151; www.hotel-turist98.com; Kraljice Katerine bb; s/d/tr/q 58/86/109/138KM; ✳) This bright-red box beside Jajce's big hypermarket offers new, very straightforward rooms with pearl-in-shell lamps. Four apartments (from 122KM) have air-con.

LAKES AREA

Plaža Motel   LAKESIDE MOTEL €
(✆647200; www.motel-plaza.com; s/d 40/70KM, pizza 7-11KM, mains 9-14KM) Clean, inexpensive rooms, but the main attraction is dining on trout, pizza or *ćevapi* right at the waterfront beside the hotel's small jetty.

AutoKamp   CAMPING GROUND €
(www.jajcetours.com; campsite per person from 10KM; ☉mid-Apr–Sep) Well-maintained site set 300m back from the lake and watermills.

🍸 Drinking

Travnik Gate   CAFE-BAR
(Sadije Softića 1; ☉7am-11pm) This unpretentiously local bar is hidden in the bare stone tower of the medieval Travnik Gate. Enter through the historic Omerbegović House,

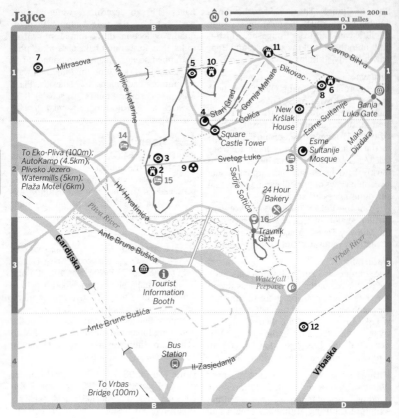

the first unmarked wooden door on Sadije Softića, and climb.

ℹ Information

Several central banks change money and have ATMs.

Network (Trg Jajačkih Branitelja; internet per hr 2KM; ⊗8.30am-midnight)

Tourist information booth (☑658268; ⊗9am-6pm Mon-Fri, 10am-6pm Sat May-Sep) Off season the office moves into the AVNOJ Museum building.

ℹ Getting There & Away

See the table, opposite.

Banja Luka

☑051 / POP 232,000

Probably Europe's least-known 'capital' (of the Republika Srpska since 1998), Banja

Luka is lively more than lovely but it's a fine base for organising rafting, canyoning, cycling or hiking on landmine-free trails in the surrounding countryside. To organise any of the above contact **Guideline** (☑466411; www.guidelinebl.com; Cerska 54; ⊗9am-5pm) or discuss things with the enthusiastic **tourist office** (☑232760; www.banjaluka-tourism.com; Kralja Petra 87; ⊗8am-6pm Mon-Fri, 9am-2pm Sat). The latter is conveniently central on the city's main drag (Kralja Petra) opposite the iconic 1933 Hotel Palace. Mountain bikes can be rented from **Cycling Shop** (Gundulićeva 106; per hr/day 2/15KM), 1.3km northeast. You can download extensive if slightly dated city listings from http://www.inyourpocket.com/bosniaherzegovina/banja-luka.

Historic Banja Luka was ravaged by a 1969 earthquake then, late in the civil war, was flooded by Serb refugees from Croatia who dynamited over a dozen historic mosques. The most famous of these, the **Ferhadija**

Jajce

Džamija, is now being painstakingly reconstructed using traditional masonry techniques. On the riverside directly southeast are the chunky walls of a large, squat 16th-century **castle** (kaštel) enclosing parkland. Summer festivities held here include the famous **Demofest** (www.demofest.org), a playoff competition between up-and-coming raw garage bands held in late July.

Otherwise, the only two central blocks with much architectural appeal are around the memorable **Orthodox Church of Christ Saviour** (Crkva Hrista Spasitelja); its brick belltower looks like a Moroccan minaret on Viagra.

🛏 Sleeping & Eating

Running parallel to Kralja Petra, there are cheap snack bars in courtyards off Veselina Maslaše and many street cafes on its northern extension, Bana Milosavlevica.

Vila Vrbas BOUTIQUE HOTEL €€
(☎433840; Brace Potkonjaka 1; s/d/ste 70/110/120KM; ❈🛜) Polished new rooms above an upmarket restaurant peep through the plane trees at the castle ramparts from across the river.

Hotel Atina BUSINESS HOTEL €€
(☎334800; www.atinahotel.com; Slobodana Kokanovica 5; web rate s/d 140/180KM, walk-in rate s/d/apt 102/104/204KM; ❈🛜) Smart without undue extravagance; the main features are stylish rectilinear fittings and a helpfully central yet quiet location just east of the castle.

Hostel Banja Luka HOUSE-HOSTEL €
(☎065831131; www.hostelbanjaluka.com; Srpskih Ustanika 26; dm/tw/tr without bathroom €10/20/30; 🛜) Guests pay per person in four simple two- or three-bed rooms above the Pigal Cafe. The kitchen is tiny and the location blandly suburban but owner Vladimir's brimming enthusiasm for Banja Luka is contagious. His place is 1.7km southeast of the castle with bakeries, ATMs, forest hikes, an internet cafe and the Guideline office all within easy walking distance. Take bus 14 from the centre or 14B from the bus station alighting at 'Integral'.

City Smile Hostel HOSTEL €
(☎214187; www.citysmilehostel.com; Skendera Kulenovića 16; dm 22KM; 🛜) Bunk beds can be tight packed at this small hostel but there's a decent kitchen and sitting area and it's only

BUSES FROM JAJCE

DESTINATION	PRICE (KM)	DURATION (HR)	DEPARTURES
Banja Luka	8.50-12	1½	7.30am, 9.15am, 1pm, 4.20pm, 5.20pm, 6.50pm
Bihać	19-25	3½	8.30am, 11.15am, 12.30pm, 5.25pm
Jezero	1.5-2	15min	7.30am, 8.30am, 11.30am, 12.30pm, 4.30pm
Mostar	18.50-25	4	2.20pm, 6.15pm
Sarajevo	23.50	3½	7am, 9.15am, 10.20am, 5.15pm
Split	30.50	4½	6am (from Split departs at 12.30pm)
Travnik	8-12.70	1¼	take Zenica or Sarajevo buses
Zenica	14	2¼	8.15am, 8.50am, 1.40pm, 3.15pm, 3.50pm
Zagreb	36	8½	10am, 11.15am, 12.30pm

BUSES FROM BANJA LUKA

DESTINATION	PRICE (KM)	DURATION (HR)	DEPARTURES
Belgrade	41.5	5¾-7½	many 5am-5pm plus 9pm & 11.30pm
Bihać	20	3	5.30am, 7.30am, 1pm, 2pm
Jajce	11.50	1½	6.40am, 7.45am, 1pm, 2pm, 4pm
Sarajevo	31	5	6.30am, 7.45am, 2.30pm, 4pm, 5pm, 12.30pm
Zagreb	31	7	3.15am, 6.30am, 8.45am, 9.10am, 11.30am, 4pm, 5.30pm

800m south of the centre. The entrance is hidden on Duška Koščige.

ⓘ Getting There & Away

The **airport** (☑535210; www.banjaluka-airport. com) is 22km north. That's 50KM by taxi or a 1.2km walk east of the Gradiška bus route (1.50KM). **Adria Airlines** (www.adria.si) connects four times weekly via Ljubljana to much of Europe. BH Airlines flies to Zürich (thrice weekly).

The **main bus and train station** (☑315555; Prote N Kostića 38) are together, 3km north using buses 6, 8 or 10 from near Hotel Palace.

Useful rail connections include Zagreb (27KM, 4¼ hours) at 3.49pm and Sarajevo (24.70KM, five hours) at 1.15pm.

Around Banja Luka

VRBAS CANYONS

Between Jajce and Banja Luka the Vrbas River descends through a series of lakes and gorges that together form one of BiH's foremost adventure-sport playgrounds. **Karanovac Rafting Centre** (☑882085, 065420000; www.guidelinebl.com), 11km from Banja Luka by bus 8A, is a reliable, well-organised outfit offering guided **canyoning** (€25), **kayaking** and especially top-class **rafting** (€33 per person). Rafting requires at least four people but joining a group is usually easy enough in summer and some weekends there's a rare opportunity for some floodlit **night-rafting**.

Set 800m off the road at **Krupa** (25km), where a pretty set of cascades tumbles down between little wooden mill-huts, nearby canyons and grottoes attract mountaineers and cavers. The Jajce road winds steeply on past a high dam overlooked by the rocky knob of what was once **Bočac Citadel**.

Bihać

☑037 / POP 80,000

In central Bihać, a closely clumped **church tower**, **turbe** and 16th-century stone **tower-museum** (☑223214; admission 2KM; ☺call ahead) look very photogenic viewed through the trees across gushing rapids. But that's about all there is to see here apart from nearby **Fethija Mosque**, converted from a rose-windowed medieval church in 1595. Bihać could make a staging post for reaching Croatia's marvellous Plitvice Lakes (www.np-plitvicka-jezera.hr; p239) just 30km away. Otherwise grab a map and brochure from Bihać's **tourist booth** (www.tzusk. net; Bosanska 1; ☺8am-4pm) or from the Hotel Park opposite. Then head out into the lovely Una Valley, preferably on a raft!

⊙ Sights & Activities

Una River VALLEY
In the lush green gorges of the **Una Valley**, the adorable Una River goes through varying moods. Sections are as calm as mirrored opal, others gush over widely fanned rapids or down pounding cascades, most dramatically at **Štrcački Buk**. There are lovely watermill restaurants at **Bosanska Krupa** and near **Otoka Bosanska**. Up 4km of hairpins above the valley, spookily Gothic **Ostrožac Fortress** (☑061236641; www.ostrozac.com; admission 1KM; ☺8am-6pm) is the most inspiring of several castle ruins. Phone the caretaker for admission.

Various adventure-sports companies offer rafting (€27 to €52, six person minimum) and kayaking. Each has its own campsite and provides transfers from Bihać since none are central. Try **Una Kiro Rafting** (☑361110; www.una-kiro-rafting.com; Golubić), **Una-Aqua** (☑061604313; www.una-aqua. com; Račić) or **Bjeli Una Rafting** (☑380222,

061138853; www.una-rafting.ba; Klokot). The festive **Una Regatta** in late July sees hundreds of kayaks and rafts following a three-day course from Kulen-Vakuf to Bosanska Krupa via Bihać.

For caving, climbing, cycling and canyoning contact extreme-sports club **Limit** (061144248; www.limit.co.ba; Džanića Mahala 7, Bihać).

Sleeping & Eating
CENTRAL BIHAĆ

Villa Una GUEST HOUSE €€
(311393; villa.una@bih.net.ha; Bihaćkih Branilaca 20; s/d/tr 52/74/96KM, superior s/d 62/84KM; ❄️🛜🅿️) In this very friendly *pansion* homey standard rooms (some with air-con) suffer from road noise but much newer 'superior' rooms are quiet and well appointed with little balconies and great showers. It's halfway between the bus station and the Una Bridge; the frontage is painted to look half-timbered.

Hotel Paviljon RESTAURANT, ROOMS €€
(220882; www.hotel-paviljon.com; Una Bridge; s/d 69/125KM; ❄️🛜) Red carpet and two-colour woods give a strikingly modern feel to 13 new if sometimes cramped rooms above central Bihać's most polished riverside restaurant (grills 3KM to 8KM, mains 7KM to 23KM). It's set in parkland beside the main Una Bridge. Several rooms have semiprivate riverview terraces.

Opal Exclusive RIVERSIDE HOTEL €€
(228586, 224182; www.hotelopalexclusive.net; Krupska bb; s/d/apt 89/138/192M; ❄️🛜🅿️) The staff are gruffly uncommunicative and getting here you'll pass briefly through a rather off-putting area of town just north of the centre. However, the spacious rooms are the best in central Bihać, and there are paintings in gilt frames, indulgent settees on the landings and lovely river views.

Motel Avlija MINI-HOTEL €€
(220882; www.avlija-motel.ba; Trg Maršala Tita 7; s/d/tr/apt 59/111/131/132KM; ❄️🛜) Pleasantly crafted new guest rooms set above a busy cafe-bar behind the central, well-marked UniCredit Bank.

Restaurant River Una WATERSIDE RESTAURANT €€
(310014; Džemala Bijedića 12; mains 12-17KM; ⏰7am-11pm) Fish 'fly' inside this pseudo-rustic restaurant situated just across the Una Bridge from central Bihac, but it's the summer seating right at the water's edge

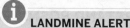

LANDMINE ALERT 139

The Bihać area was mined during the war so stick to paths and concreted areas.

that puts it one step ahead of several nearby rivals.

UNA VALLEY

TOP CHOICE **Kostelski Buk** RIVERSIDE HOTEL €€
(302340; www.kostelski-buk.com; M14, Kostela; s/d from 63/96KM; ❄️🛜🅿️) The Louis XVI chairs, copper-coloured curtains and leather-padded doors might be a little glitzy for some tastes but the rooms are superbly equipped, amply sized and come with artistic bronze-coloured panelling that's somewhere between Klimt and William Morris. Beds have luxurious mattresses worthy of a five-star hotel. The cosiest of three restaurants (mains 10KM to 18KM) overlooks some waterfall rapids and serves excellent seafood platters (30KM for two people) washed down with a very good Hercegovinian Riesling (per 500ml 9KM). It's 9km from Bihać towards Banja Luka.

Motel Estrada FAMILY HOTEL €
(531320; Ostrožac; s/d 30/40KM) Homestay-style en suite rooms in the fifth unmarked house on the left up the Prečići road; 300m southwest of Ostrožac castle.

Getting There & Away
Disguised as a mini-casino, Bihać's **bus station** (311939) is 1km west of the centre, just off Bihaćkih Branilaća. Destinations include:

Banja Luka (20KM, three hours) Departs 5.30am, 7.30am, 1pm and 3pm via Bosanska Krupa and Otoka Bosanska.

Kostela (2.50KM, 10 minutes) Use Cazin-bound buses, 10 times daily on weekdays, 8.50am, 11.30am and 3.30pm Saturday, 3.30pm only Sunday. Use same buses for Ostražac (3.50KM, 25 minutes).

Plitvice Jezero Take the 7am Slunjski bus to Grabovac (10KM, 45 minutes, no service Sunday), cross the road to the AutoKamp then catch the 8.45am shuttle to the lake park's entrance gate.

Sarajevo (42KM, seven hours) Departs 12.45am, 7.30am, 2.30pm and 10pm, via Travnik.

Zagreb (21-24KM, 2½ hours) Departs 4.45am (no service Sunday), 10.20am, 2pm and 4.45pm.

BOSNIA & HERCEGOVINA BIHAĆ

UNDERSTAND BOSNIA & HERCEGOVINA

History

Be aware that much of BiH's history remains highly controversial and is seen very differently according to one's ethno-religious viewpoint.

In AD 9 ancient Illyrian Bosnia was conquered by the Romans. Slavs arrived from the late 6th century and were dominant by 1180, when Bosnia first emerged as an independent entity under former Byzantine governor Ban Kulina. BiH had a patchy golden age between 1180 and 1463, peaking in the late 1370s when Bosnia's King Tvtko gained Hum (future Hercegovina) and controlled much of Dalmatia.

Blurring the borderline between Europe's Catholic west and Orthodox east, sparsely populated medieval Bosnia had its own independent church. This remains the source of many historical myths, but the long-popular idea that it was 'infected' by the Bulgarian Bogomil heresy is now largely discounted.

Turkish Ascendancy

Turkish raids whittled away at the country throughout the 15th century and by the 1460s most of Bosnia was under Ottoman control. Within a few generations, easygoing Sufi-inspired Islam became dominant among townspeople and landowners, many Bosnians converting as much to gain civil privileges as for spiritual enlightenment. However, a sizeable proportion of the serfs (*rayah*) remained Christian. Bosnians also became particularly prized soldiers in the Ottoman army, many rising eventually to high rank within the imperial court. The early Ottoman era also produced great advances in infrastructure, with fine mosques and bridges built by charitable bequests. Later, however, the Ottomans failed to follow the West's industrial revolution. By the 19th century the empire's economy was archaic, and all attempts to modernise the feudal system in BiH were strenuously resisted by the entrenched Bosnian-Muslim elite. In 1873 İstanbul's banking system collapsed under the weight of the high-living sultan's debts. To pay these debts the sultan demanded added taxes. But in 1874 BiH's harvests failed, so paying those taxes would have meant starving. With nothing left to lose the mostly Christian Bosnian peasants revolted, leading eventually to a messy tangle of pan-Balkan wars.

Austro-Hungarian Rule

These wars ended with the farcical 1878 Congress of Berlin, at which the Western powers carved up the western Ottoman lands. Austria-Hungary was 'invited' to occupy BiH, which was treated like a colony even though it theoretically remained Ottoman under sovereignty. An unprecedented period of development followed. Roads, railways and bridges were built. Coal mining and forestry became booming industries. Education encouraged a new generation of Bosnians to look towards Vienna. But new nationalist feelings were simmering: Bosnian Catholics increasingly identified with neighbouring Croatia (itself within Austria-Hungary) while Orthodox Bosnians sympathised with recently independent Serbia's dreams of a greater Serbian homeland. In between lay Bosnia's Muslims (40%), who belatedly started to develop a distinct Bosniak consciousness.

While Turkey was busy with the 1908 Young Turk revolution Austria-Hungary annexed BiH, undermining the aspirations of those who had dreamed of a pan-Slavic or greater Serbian future. The resultant scramble for the last remainders of Ottoman Europe kicked off the Balkan Wars of 1912 and 1913. No sooner had these been (unsatisfactorily) resolved than the heir to the Austrian throne was shot dead while visiting Sarajevo. One month later Austria declared war on Serbia and WWI swiftly followed.

World Wars, Communism & Political Tension

WWI killed an astonishing 15% of the Bosnian population. It also brought down both the Turkish and Austro-Hungarian empires, leaving BiH to be absorbed into proto-Yugoslavia.

During WWII, BiH was occupied partly by Italy and partly by Germany, then absorbed into the newly created fascist state of Croatia. Croatia's Ustaše decimated Bosnia's Jewish population, and they also persecuted Serbs and Muslims. Meanwhile a pro-Nazi group of Bosnian Muslims committed their own atrocities against Bosnian Serbs while Serb Četniks and Tito's Communist Partizans put up some stalwart resistance to the Germans (as well as fighting each other). The BiH mountains proved ideal territory for Tito's flexible guerrilla army, whose greatest victories are still locally commemorated with vast memorials. In 1943, Tito's antifascist council meeting at Jajce (p135) famously formulated a constitution for an inclusive postwar, socialist Yugoslavia. BiH was granted republic status within that Yugoslavia but up until 1971 (when *Muslim* was defined as a Yugoslav 'ethnic group'), Bosniaks were not considered a distinct community and in censuses had to register as Croat, Serb or 'Other/Yugoslav'. Despite considerable mining in the northeast and the boost of the 1984 Sarajevo Winter Olympics, BiH's economy remained relatively undeveloped.

The 1990s Conflict

In the post-Tito era, as Yugoslavia imploded, religio-linguistic (often dubbed 'ethnic') tensions were ratcheted up by the ultranationalist Serb leader Slobodan Milošević and equally radical Croatian leader Franjo Tuđman. Although these two were at war by spring 1991, they reputedly came up with a de facto agreement in which they planned to divide BiH between breakaway Croatia and rump Yugoslavia.

Under president Alija Izetbegović, BiH declared independence from Yugoslavia on 15 October 1991. Bosnian Serb parliamentarians wanted none of this and withdrew to set up their own government at Pale, 20km east of Sarajevo. BiH was recognised internationally as an independent state on 6 April 1992 but Sarajevo was already under siege both by Serb paramilitaries and by parts of the Yugoslav army (JNA).

Over the next three years a brutal and extraordinarily complex civil war raged. Best known is the campaign of ethnic cleansing in northern and eastern BiH creating the 300km 'pure'-Serb Republika Srpska (RS). But locals of each religion will readily admit that 'there were terrible criminals on our side too'. In western Hercegovina the Croat population armed itself with the help of neighbouring Croatia, eventually ejecting Serbs from their villages in a less reported but similarly brutal war.

Perhaps unaware of the secret Tuđman-Milošević understanding, Izetbegović had signed a formal military alliance with Croatia in June 1992. But by early 1993 fighting had broken out between Muslims and Croats, creating another war front. Croats attacked Muslims in Stolac and Mostar, bombarding their historic monuments and blasting Mostar's famous medieval bridge into the river. Muslim troops, including a small foreign mujahedin force, desecrated churches and attacked Croat villages, notably around Travnik.

UN Involvement

With atrocities on all sides, the West's reaction was confused and erratic. In August 1992, pictures of concentration-camp and rape-camp victims (mostly Muslim) found in northern Bosnia spurred the UN to create Unprofor, a protection force of 7500 peacekeeping troops. Unprofor secured the neutrality of Sarajevo airport well enough to allow the delivery of humanitarian aid, but overall proved notoriously impotent.

Ethnic cleansing of Muslims from Foča and Višegrad led the UN to declare safe zones around the Muslim-majority towns of Srebrenica, Župa and Goražde. But rarely has the term 'safe' been so misused. When NATO belatedly authorised air strikes to protect these areas, the Serbs responded by capturing 300 Unprofor peacekeepers and chaining them to potential targets to keep the planes away.

In July 1995 Dutch peacekeepers could only watch as the starving, supposedly 'safe' area of Srebrenica fell to a Bosnian Serb force led by the infamous Ratko Mladić. An estimated 8000 Muslim men were slaughtered in Europe's worst mass killings since WWII. Miraculously, battered Goražde held out thanks to sporadically available UN food supplies. By this stage, Croatia had renewed its own internal offensive, expelling Serbs from the Krajina region of Croatia in August 1995. At least 150,000 of these dispossessed people then moved to the Serb-held areas of northern Bosnia.

Finally, another murderous Serb mortar attack on Sarajevo's main market (Markale) kickstarted a shift in UN and NATO politics. An ultimatum to end the Serbs' siege of Sarajevo was made more persuasive through two weeks of NATO air strikes in September 1995. US president Bill Clinton's proposal for a peace conference in Dayton, Ohio, was accepted soon after.

The Dayton Agreement

While maintaining BiH's pre-war external boundaries, Dayton divided the country into today's pair of roughly equally sized 'entities' (see the boxed text, p142), each with limited autonomy. Finalising the border required considerable political and cartographic creativity and was only completed in 1999 when the last sticking point, Brčko, was belatedly given a self-governing status all of its own. Meanwhile BiH's curious rotating tripartite presidency has been kept in check by the EU's powerful High Representative (www.ohr.int).

ℹ WHAT'S IN A NAME?

Geographically Bosnia and Hercegovina (BiH) comprises Bosnia (in the north) and Hercegovina (pronounced Her-tse-GO-vina, in the south), although the term 'Bosnian' refers to anyone from BiH, not just from Bosnia proper. Politically, BiH is divided into two entirely different entities. Southwest and central BiH falls mostly within the Federation of Bosnia and Hercegovina, usually shortened to 'the Federation'. Meanwhile most areas bordering Serbia, Montenegro and the northern arm of Croatia are within the Serb-dominated Republika Srpska (abbreviated RS). A few minor practicalities (stamps, phonecards) appear in different versions and the Cyrillic alphabet is more prominent in the RS but these days you'll often struggle to notice which one you're in.

For refugees (1.2 million abroad, and a million displaced within BiH), the Dayton Agreement emphasised the right to return to (or to sell) their pre-war homes. International agencies donated very considerable funding to restore BiH's infrastructure, housing stock and historical monuments.

An embarrassing problem post-Dayton was the failure to find Ratko Mladić and the Bosnian Serb leader Radovan Karadžić (president of the RS until July 1996). Both were due to face trial as war criminals. Despite five million dollar rewards offered for their arrest, Karadžić was only apprehended in 2008, while Mladić remains at large, probably protected by supporters who perceive him to be an honest patriot.

Bosnia & Hercegovina Today

Less radically nationalist politicians now run the RS, while under EU and American pressure BiH has centralised considerably in a movement away from the original Dayton 'separate powers' concept. BiH now has a unified army and common passports. Both entities now have indistinguishable car licence plates and use the same currency, albeit with banknotes in two variants. Many (though by no means all) refugees have returned and rebuilt their pre-war homes.

Deep scars remain and the communities remain socially divided but violence has long since stopped. Today economics is the greatest concern for most Bosnians. Those few socialist-era factories that weren't destroyed in the 1990s conflicts have downsized to fit tough 21st-century global realities. New 'business-friendly' government initiatives, including a recent wave of privatisations, are eyed with suspicion; the populace fears growing corruption. People assume that one day BiH will join the EU, though for many, nearby Slovenia's experience suggests that EU membership will just push up prices and make life harder. 'Life's tough' one war widow told us, 'but at least there's peace'.

The People of Bosnia-Hercegovina

Bosniaks (Bosnian Muslims, 40% of the population), Bosnian Serbs (Orthodox Christians, 31%) and Bosnian Croats (Catholics, 15%) differ by religion but are all Southern Slavs. Physically they are indistinguishable (so the term 'ethnic cleansing' applied so often during the war, should more accurately have been called 'religio-linguistic forced expulsions'). The pre-war population was mixed, with intermarriage common in the cities. Stronger divisions have inevitably appeared since the 'ethnic cleansing' of the 1990s. The war resulted in massive population shifts, changing the size and linguistic balance of many cities. Bosniaks now predominate in Sarajevo and central BiH, Bosnian Croats in western and southern Hercegovina, and Bosnian Serbs in the RS, which includes Istochno (East) Sarajevo and Banja Luka. Today social contact between members of the three groups remains limited and somewhat wary. Religion is taken seriously as a badge of 'ethnicity' but spiritually most people are fairly secular.

The Arts
Crafts

BiH crafts from *kilims* (woollen flat-weaves) to copperware and decoratively repurposed bullet casings are widely sold in Mostar's Kujundžiluk and Sarajevo's Baščaršija. *Stećci* (singular *stećak*) are archetypal Bosnian forms of oversized medieval gravestones. The best-known examples are found at Radimlja near Stolac. However, those collected outside Sarajevo's National Museum are finer, while a group near Umoljani has a much more visually satisfying setting.

Literature

Bosnia's best-known writer, Ivo Andrić (1892–1975), won the 1961 Nobel Prize in Literature. With extraordinary psychological agility, his epic novel, the classic *Bridge on the Drina*, retells 350 years of Bosnian history as seen through the eyes of unsophisticated townsfolk in Višegrad. His *Travnik Chronicles* (aka *Bosnian Chronicle*) is also rich with human insight, though its portrayal of Bosnia is through the eyes of jaded 19th-century foreign consuls in Travnik.

Many thought-provoking essays, short stories and poems explore the prickly subject of the 1990s conflict, often contrasting horrors against the victims' enduring humanity. Quality varies greatly but recommended collections include Miljenko Jergović's *Sarajevo Marlboro* and Semezdin Mehmedinović's *Sarajevo Blues*.

Movies

The relationship between two soldiers, one Muslim and one Serb, caught alone in the same trench during the Sarajevo siege was the theme for Danis Tanović's Oscar-winning 2002 film *No Man's Land*. The movie *Go West* takes on the deep taboo of homosexuality as a wartime Serb-Bosniak gay couple become a latter-day Romeo and Juliet. *Gori Vatra* (aka *Fuse*) is an irony-packed dark comedy set in the pretty Bosnian castle town of Tešanj just after the war, parodying efforts to hide corruption and create a facade of ethnic reintegration for the sake of a proposed visit by US president Bill Clinton.

Music

Sevdah (traditional Bosnian music) typically uses heart-wrenching vocals to recount tales of unhappy amours, though singing it was once used as a subtle courting technique. Sarajevo has an annual jazz festival (November). The post-industrial city of Tuzla has vibrant rap and metal scenes.

The Landscape

BiH is predominantly mountainous. The mostly arid south (Hercegovina) dips one tiny toe of land into the Adriatic Sea at Neum then rises swiftly into bare limestone uplands carved with deep grey canyons. The central mountain core has some 30 peaks rising between 1700m and 2386m.

Further north and east the landscape becomes increasingly forested with waterfalls and alpine valleys, most famously in the magnificent Sutjeska National Park. In the far northeast the peaks subside into rolling bucolic hills flattening out altogether in the far north.

SURVIVAL GUIDE

Directory A–Z

Accommodation

Except in hostels, all quoted room prices assume a private bathroom and breakfast unless otherwise indicated.

Our price ranges for a double room are budget (€; less than 80KM), midrange (€€; 80KM to 190KM) and top end (€€€; more than 190KM).

High season means June to September generally but late December to early March in ski resorts. In Mostar and Sarajevo summer prices rise 20% to 50% and touts appear at the bus stations.

Accommodation Types

Homestays Somebody's spare room. Slip-on shoes and plentiful clean socks are a boon since it's normal courtesy to remove footwear on entering a private house. Hosts will provide slippers.

Hostels Usually bunk rooms in a semi-converted private home. Many lack signs but can be booked through international hostel-booking sites. Essentially Mostar and Sarajevo only.

Hotels Often inhabiting the husk of old Tito-era concrete monsters, many are now elegantly remodelled but some remain gloomy and a little forbidding.

> ### BOOKS
>
> *Bosnia: A Short History* by Noel Malcolm is a very readable introduction to the complexities of Bosnian history. In *Not My Turn To Die* by Savo Heleta the memoirs of a besieged family at Goražde give insights into the strange mixture of terror, boredom and resignation of the 1990s conflict.
>
> **BuyBook** (www.buybook.ba) produces several regional guidebooks.

GAY & LESBIAN TRAVELLERS

Although homosexuality was decriminalised per se in 1998 (2000 in the RS), attitudes remain very conservative. Sarajevo's only high-profile LGTB event (the Queer Festival of 2008) was violently attacked by anti-gay protesters. **Association Q** (www.queer.ba) nonetheless attempts to empower the self-reliance of the gay community in BiH and the English-language **Gay Romeo** (www.gayromeo.com) chat site reportedly has several hundred Sarajevo members.

Motels Generally new and suburban and ideal for those with cars. However, occasionally the term simply implies a lower midrange hotel so don't automatically assume there's parking.

Pansions Anything from a glorified homestay to a little boutique hotel.

Ski Hotels Between Christmas and 15 January availability is very stretched and prices will be around 50% higher. Some demand minimum stays during ski season, though since the economic downturn this rule is being less rigorously enforced. Most close during low season.

Activities

Skiing Inexpensive yet world-class at Jahorina, Bjelašnica or Vlašić.

Rafting Reaches terrifyingly difficult class V in April/May but is more suitable for beginners in summer. Top spots are around Foča, Bihać and Banja Luka.

Hiking and mountain biking Compromised since the 1990s by the presence of landmines, but many upland areas and national parks now have safe, marked trails. Ecotourism organisation Green Visions (p112) offers seasonal hiking excursions from Sarajevo.

Business Hours

Office hours 8am-4pm Mon-Fri

Banks 8am-6pm Mon-Fri, 8.30am-1.30pm Sat

Shops 8am-6pm daily

Restaurants 11.30am-10.30pm, often later in summer.

Whatever signs might say, actual restaurant closing time depends on customer demand more than fixed schedules. Restaurants opening in the morning usually operate as a cafe only until lunchtime.

Dangers & Annoyances

Landmines and unexploded ordnance, still thought to affect around 3% of BiH's area, caused nine deaths and 19 recorded injuries in 2009. Stick to asphalt/concrete surfaces or well-worn paths in affected areas and don't enter war-damaged buildings. **BHMAC** (www.bhmac.org) has more information.

Food

The average cost of a main courses in a restaurant is under 8KM for budget (€), 8KM to 15KM for midrange (€€) and more than 15KM for top end (€€€).

Holidays

Major Islamic festivals are observed in parts of the Federation where the Feast of Sacrifice is known as Kurban Bajram and the end-of-Ramadan celebration is Ramazanski Bajram. Orthodox Easter (variable) and Christmas (6 January) are observed in the RS. Western Easter (variable) and Christmas (25 December) are celebrated in the Federation. Nationwide holidays:

New Year's Day 1 January

Independence Day 1 March

May Day 1 May

National Statehood Day 25 November

Internet Access

Most hotels and some cafes now offer wi-fi; it's free unless otherwise mentioned.

LANGUAGE

The people of BiH speak essentially the same language but it's referred to as 'Bosnian' (Bosanski) in Muslim parts, 'Croatian' (Hrvatski) in Croat-controlled areas and 'Serbian' (Српски) in the RS. The Federation uses the Latin alphabet. The RS uses predominantly Cyrillic (Ћирилица) but Latin (Latinica) is gaining wider parallel usage there too. Brčko uses both alphabets equally.

Key Bosnian phrases: *zdravo* (hello); *hvala* (thanks); *molim* (please).

Maps

Freytag & Berndt's very useful if flawed 1:250,000 BiH road map costs 12KM in Sarajevo bookshops. City maps are patchily available from bookshops, kiosks or tourist information centres. Many cities post town plans on their websites.

Money

ATMs Machines accepting Visa and MasterCard are ubiquitous.

Cash Bosnia's convertible mark (KM or BAM) is pronounced *kai-em* or *maraka* and divided into 100 fenig. It's tied to the euro at approximately €1=1.96KM. Many businesses unblinkingly accept euros and for minor purchases you'll often get a favourable 1:2 rate. Croatian kuna are accepted in some places too.

Travellers cheques Exchange usually requires the original purchase receipt.

Post

BiH fascinates philatelists by having three parallel postal organisations, each issuing their own stamps: **BH Post** (www.bhp.ba) and **Srpske Poste** (www.filatelija.rs.ba) for the RS, and the Croat **HP Post** (www.post.ba) based in western Mostar.

Telephone

Mobile-phone companies BH Mobile (☎061- and ☎062-), HT/EroNet (☎063-) and M-Tel (☎065-) all have virtually nationwide coverage.

Phonecards (10KM) for payphones are sold at post offices and some street kiosks. Beware that different cards are required for the Federation and for RS.

Country code ☎387

International operator ☎1201

Local directory information ☎1188

Travellers with Disabilities

Bosnia's most charming townscapes are full of stairways and steep, rough streets that are very awkward if you're disabled. A few places have wheelchair ramps in response to all the war wounded, but smaller hotels won't have lifts and disabled toilets remain extremely rare.

Visas

Stays of under 90 days require no visa for citizens of most Europeans countries and Australia, Brunei, Canada, Japan, Malaysia, New Zealand, Singapore, South Korea, Turkey and the USA. Other nationals should see www.mva.ba for visa details and where to apply. For South Africans that's London or Tripoli! Visas usually require a letter of invitation or a tourist-agency voucher of EU, and most other European, countries.

Getting There & Away

Air

As an alternative to flying direct, consider budget flights to Dubrovnik, Split or Zagreb (Croatia) and connecting to BiH by bus or train.

Airlines

Adria (JP; www.adria.si) Via Ljubljana (also serves Banja Luka).

Austrian (OS; www.austrian.com) Via Vienna.

BH Airlines (JA; Map p110; ☎033-550125, 768335; www.bhairlines.ba; Branilaca Sarajeva 15, Sarajevo; ☺9am-5pm Mon-Fri, 9am-2pm Sat) Pronounced 'Bay-Ha', this is the national carrier. It flies from Sarajevo to Belgrade, Copenhagen, Frankfurt, Gothenburg, İstanbul, Stockholm, Vienna and Zürich. Some Frankfurt and Vienna services go via Banja Luka.

Croatia Airlines (OU; www.croatiaairlines.com) Via Zagreb.

germanwings (4U; www.germanwings.com) Stuttgart and Köln-Bonn.

JAT (JU; Map p110; www.jat.com) Via Belgrade.

Lufthansa (LH; www.lufthansa.com) Via Munich.

Malév (MA; www.malev.com) Via Budapest.

Norwegian (DY; www.norwegian.no) Weekly to Stockholm.

Turkish (TK; www.thy.com) Via İstanbul.

Land

Bus

There are buses to Zagreb and/or Split (Croatia) at least daily from most towns in the Federation and to Serbia and/or Montenegro from many RS towns. Buses to Vienna and Germany run several times weekly from bigger BiH cities.

Car & Motorcycle

Drivers need Green Card insurance and an EU or International Driving Permit. Transiting Neum in a Croatian hire car is usually hassle-free.

Train

The modest international network links Sarajevo to Belgrade, Zagreb (via Banja Luka), Budapest (via Osijek, Croatia) and to Ploče (coastal Croatia via Mostar).

Getting Around

Bicycle

For tough cyclists BiH's calm if hilly secondary routes can prove a delight. Several mountain areas now have suggested off-road trails for mountain bikers but beware of straying off-route: landmines remain a danger.

Bus

Frequency drops drastically at weekends on shorter-hop routes, some stopping altogether on Sundays.

Bus stations pre-sell tickets but it's normally easy enough to wave down any bus en route. Advance reservations are sometimes necessary for overnight routes or at peak holiday times.

Fares are around 7KM per hour travelled. Return tickets can prove significantly cheaper than two singles but you'll be inconveniently limited to one specific company. Expect to pay 2KM extra per stowed bag. Most bus station ticket offices have a 'garderob' for left luggage (from 2KM).

Car & Motorcycle

There's minimal public transport to BiH's most spectacular remote areas so having wheels can really transform your trip. Bosnian winding roads are lightly trafficked and a delight for driving if you aren't in a hurry. **BIHAMK** (📞222 210; bihamk.ba; Skenderija 23, Sarajevo; annual membership 25KM; ⊗8am-4.30pm Mon-Fri, 9am-noon Sat) offers road as-

sistance and towing services (call 📞1282 or 📞1288).

Hire

International chains are represented while smaller local outfits are often based at hotels. Most companies add 17% VAT. A good deal is **Hyundai Rent-A-Car** (www.hyundai.ba; from 75/390KM per day/week); its standard rates include full insurance, theft protection and CDW. Pick up/drop off is possible at Mostar, Sarajevo or Sarajevo airport without extra charge for open-jaws.

Road Rules

Drive on the right. First-aid kit, warning triangle and spare bulb-kits are compulsory.

Blood-alcohol limit 0.031%

Headlights Must be kept on day and night

LPG Availability very limited

Parking Awkward in Mostar and Sarajevo, contrastingly easy elsewhere. In town centres expect to pay 1KM per hour to an attendant.

Petrol Typically around 2.05KM per litre (Federation), 1.95KM (RS)

Seatbelts Compulsory

Snow chains Compulsory on some mountain roads (November to April) and wherever snow is over 5cm deep

Speed limits 100kmh (dual carriageways), 80kmh (rural), 60kmh or less (in town). Absurdly slow limits are often posted with no obvious logic but police spot-checks are common.

Winter Tyres Compulsory mid-November to mid-April

Train

Trains are slower and less frequent than buses but generally around 30% cheaper. **RS Railways** (www.zrs-rs.com/red_voznje.php) has full, up-to-date rail timetables.

Bulgaria България

Includes »

Best Places to Eat

» Dream House (p156)

» Pri Yafata (p156)

» Malâk Bunardzhik (p167)

» Chiflika (p183)

» Casanova (p193)

Best Places to Stay

» Red House (p155)

» Dedo Pene (p163)

» Hotel Romantica (p166)

» Hotel Bolyarski (p177)

» Hotel California (p193)

Why Go?

Tucked into the southeastern corner of Europe, Bulgaria is best known for its long Black Sea coast, speckled with historic seaside towns, remote beaches and brash clubland resorts. But elsewhere you'll find wild, heavily forested and hugely varied landscapes ideal for hiking, cycling, mountaineering and wildlife watching, as well as a number of modern ski resorts.

Across Bulgaria you'll find churches and monasteries full of vibrant icons and presided over by white-bearded priests, picturesque villages of timber-framed houses and cobbled lanes – seemingly lost in time – and dramatic reminders of the country's ancient heritage, from Thracian tombs and Roman ruins to medieval fortresses, Ottoman mosques and communist monuments slowly crumbling away into history.

Bulgaria's cities, too, reward visitors with treasure-filled museums and galleries and relaxed, cafe-sprinkled parks. Getting around is easy and still remarkably cheap, so brush up your Cyrillic, buy a bus ticket and get ready to explore.

When To Go

Sofia

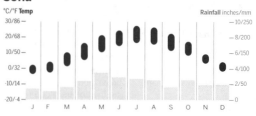

January Skiing in Bansko or down Mount Vitosha is just the thing.

March–May The fine spring weather welcomes folk and music festivals across the country.

June–September Spend lazy days on the Black Sea beaches and the nights at Bulgaria's best clubs.

Fast Facts

» **Area** 110,910 sq km

» **Capital** Sofia

» **Telephone country code** 359

» **Emergency** 112

Exchange Rates

Australia	A$1	1.44lv
Canada	C$1	1.42lv
euro	€1	1.95lv
Japan	¥100	1.64lv
New Zealand	NZ$1	1.07lv
UK	UK£1	2.22lv
USA	US$1	1.36lv

Set Your Budget

» **Budget hotel room** 40lv

» **Two-course meal** 10lv

» **Museum entrance** 4-10lv

» **Beer** 1.80lv

» **City transport ticket** 1lv

Resources

» **BG Maps** (www.bgmaps.com)

» **Bulgaria Travel** (www.bulgariatravel.org)

» **Beach Bulgaria** (www.beachbulgaria.com)

» **City Info Guide** (www.cityinfoguide.net)

Connections

Although Sofia has international bus and train connections, it's not necessary to backtrack to the capital if you're heading to Bucharest or İstanbul. From central Veliko Târnovo, for example, there are daily trains both ways – and much of the country offers overnight buses to İstanbul. Heading to Greece or Belgrade by train means going through Sofia; for Skopje, you'll need to catch a bus from there, too.

ITINERARIES

One Week

Start off with a full day in Sofia, visiting the Archaeological Museum and Borisova Gradina, then take the bus to Veliko Târnovo for a few days of sightseeing and hiking. For the rest of the week, head to Varna for some sea and sand.

Two Weeks

After a couple of days in Sofia, catch a bus to Plovdiv and wander the cobbled lanes of the Old Town. From there, take a day trip to visit the Roman spa town of Hisar or Bachkovo Monastery. After a few days in Plovdiv, make for the coast, staying a couple of nights in ancient Sozopol. Head north to overnight in Varna then get a connection to Ruse for a glimpse of the Danube and some fine museums, and finish in Veliko Târnovo.

Essential Food & Drink

» **Banitsa** The ultimate Bulgarian street-snack, the *banitsa* is a flaky cheese pasty, often served fresh and hot.

» **Kebabche** There's no escaping this thin, grilled pork sausage, a staple of every *mehana* in the country. *Kyufte* is a round, flat, burger-like variation of the same, sometimes filled with cheese.

» **Tarator** On a hot day there's nothing better than this delicious chilled cucumber and yoghurt soup, served with garlic, dill and crushed walnuts.

» **Beer** You're never far from a cold beer in Bulgaria. Zagorka, Kamenitza and Shumensko are the most popular nationwide brands, but look for regional brews, too.

» **Wine** They've been producing wine here since Thracian times, and there are some excellent varieties to try, including the unique, blood-red Melnik.

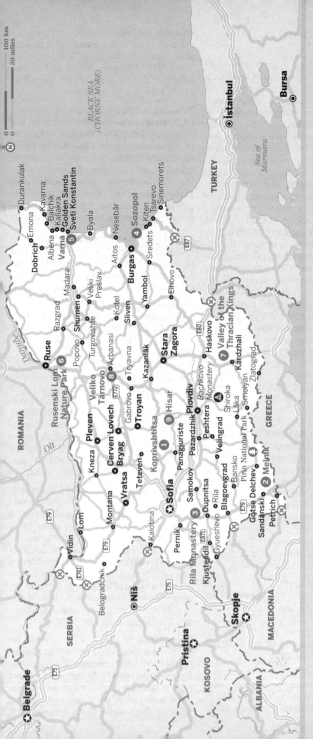

Bulgaria Highlights

1 Go back in time through the National Revival houses in **Koprivshtitsa** (p172)

2 Sip a glass or two of refreshing Bulgarian vino in the wine town of **Melnik** (p161)

3 Explore the luminous artistic and religious treasures of Bulgaria's most revered monastery at **Rila** (p161)

4 Relax on the sands of the Black Sea at **Sozopol** (p194)

5 Go clubbing, take in the Summer Festival and stroll through Primorski Park in cosmopolitan **Varna** (p184)

6 Discover the wild landscapes and rich bird and animal life of the **Rusenski Lom Nature Park** (p183)

7 Learn about Thracian heritage at **Perperikon** (p171) and in the **Valley of Thracian Kings** (p173)

8 Visit the Tsars' medieval stronghold in **Veliko Tärnovo** (p174)

9 Take the waters in the peaceful spa town of **Hisar** (p169)

SOFIA СОФИЯ

♪02 / POP 1.3 MILLION

Bulgaria's capital, Sofia is an energetic and largely modern city at the base of towering Mt Vitosha, but probably not the first place you think of when Eastern Europe comes to mind. Don't expect to uncover the 'new Prague' here; there's a lingering Soviet tinge to the city, with its blocky architecture and stubborn Red Army monuments, but there are also some fine parks, absorbing museums, beautiful churches and a buzzing nightlife scene.

Settled perhaps 7000 years ago by the Thracian Serdi tribe, and later called Serdica by the Romans, Sofia (Greek for 'holy wisdom') was a market town of 1200 residents when it became the nation's unlikely capital in 1879. The city grew rapidly over the following decades, but sadly much of the centre was destroyed in WWII bombing raids, and post-war Stalinist reconstruction cared little for aesthetics.

Most visitors to Bulgaria will arrive in Sofia and quickly move on, but if you have the time, it's worth spending at least a couple of days in this underrated city: you may end up staying longer than you thought.

◉ Sights

Sofia is a pleasingly compact city and most, if not all, of the main sights are easily reached on foot.

PLOSHTAD ALEKSANDER NEVSKI

Aleksander Nevski Church   CHURCH
(pl Aleksander Nevski; admission free; ⊘7am-7pm) This awesome, gold-domed church is the pride of Sofia, constructed between 1882 and 1912 in neo-Byzantine style as a memorial to the 200,000 Russian soldiers who died fighting for Bulgarian independence in the Russo-Turkish War (1877–78). Inside, giant brass chandeliers hang from the smoky ceilings high above, while naturalistic and faded murals of saints adorn the walls.

Aleksander Nevski Crypt   ART GALLERY
(adult/student 6/3lv; ⊘10.30am-5.30pm Wed & Fri-Sun, 10am-6.30pm Tue & Thu) To the left of the church's main entrance, a door leads down to the crypt, which now houses Bulgaria's biggest and best collection of icons, stretching back to the 5th century.

Sveta Sofia Church   CHURCH
(ul Parizh; ⊘7am-7pm summer, 7am-6pm winter) Sveta Sofia Church is the capital's oldest, and gave the city its name. Inside the much-restored red-brick church, you can see evidence of its earlier incarnations through glass panels in the floor. Outside are the Tomb of the Unknown Soldier and an eternal flame, and the grave of Ivan Vazov, Bulgaria's most revered writer.

National Gallery for Foreign Art ART GALLERY
(ul 19 Fevruari 1; adult/student 4/2lv; free last Mon of month; ⊘11am-6.30pm Wed-Mon) To the east of Aleksander Nevski Church, the faintly musty, echoing halls of this imposing gallery hold a varied collection of artworks, ranging from Indian woodcarvings and African tribal masks on the ground floor to several galleries of paintings upstairs, including some minor sketches by Matisse and Renoir.

SOFIA CITY GARDEN & AROUND

This well-manicured park a couple of blocks southwest of pl Aleksander Nevski is frequented by chess-players and bordered by cafes and a handful of attractions.

Archaeological Museum   MUSEUM
(pl Nezavisimost; adult/student 10/2lv; ⊘10am-6pm May-Oct, 10am-5pm Tue-Sun Nov-Apr) Housed in a former mosque, dating from 1496, this fascinating museum is a treasure trove of Thracian and Roman oddments. Facing the entrance is a century-old reproduction of the Madara horseman, while the downstairs gallery displays Roman tombstones, Thracian armour and a 4th-century AD mosaic floor from the Sveta Sofia Church. Upstairs you can see the unnervingly lifelike bronze head of a 4th century BC Thracian king, with coloured glass eyes and fine copper eyelashes, found near Shipka in 2004.

Party House & the President's Building
                        HISTORIC BUILDINGS
Across the street from the Archaeological Museum is the unmistakable giant white **Party House** (look for the ghostly impression of the partly chiselled-away hammer and sickle on the front) and the **President's Building** (both closed to the public), the site of the **changing of the guards**. Here, on the hour during daylight hours, you can watch as soldiers in rather natty uniforms goose-step their way to their sentry boxes.

Royal Palace   ART GALLERY
(ul Tsar Osvoboditel) The former Royal Palace is now home to two museums. The squeaky-floored **National Art Gallery** (adult/student 6/3lv; ⊘10am-6pm Tue-Sun) offers a seemingly endless parade of Bulgarian oils, mainly from the 1880s to the 1940s and including

works by Vladmir Dimitrov (look for his psychedelic *Peasant Wedding*) and Impressionist landscapes of Sofia by Nikola Petrov. Upstairs are several galleries of Bulgarian sculptures.

Sharing the palace, the **Ethnographical Museum** (adult/student 3/1lv; ⊘10am-6pm Tue-Sun) displays folk costumes, carpets and carvings, and often has long-term thematic exhibitions.

FREE Sofia City Art Gallery   ART GALLERY
(ul General Gurko 1; ⊘10am-7pm Tue-Sat, 11am-6pm Sun) On the south side of the park, the Sofia City Art Gallery is well worth a peek for its regular temporary exhibitions, ranging from 19th-century portraits to contemporary video installations.

National Museum of Natural History
MUSEUM
(www.nmnhs.com; bul Tsar Osvoboditel 1; adult/student 4/2lv; ⊘10am-6pm) Bulgaria's oldest museum was founded in 1889, originally to house Prince Ferdinand's collection of stuffed birds. Today you can take a close look at everything from cases of pinned ants and mounted hummingbirds to stuffed bears and apes, and there's also a display of minerals and crystals, and an enormous ammonite. English labelling throughout.

PLOSHTAD SVETA NEDELYA & AROUND

FREE Sveta Nedelya Cathedral   CHURCH
(pl Sveta Nedelya) At the heart of pl Sveta Nedelya is the striking Sveta Nedelya Cathedral, built between 1856 and 1863. Colourful murals line the walls while the supposedly miracle-working relics of a medieval Serbian king lie next to the altar. Communists bombed the church in 1925 in an attempt to kill Tsar Boris III; over 120 people died, but Boris survived.

Sveta Petka Samardjiska Church   CHURCH
(admission 4lv; ⊘7.30am-7.30pm) Just north of the cathedral, accessed via an underpass, this small church pokes up its 14th-century steeple amid a sea of traffic. There are some faded 16th century murals inside.

North on bul Maria Luisa, you'll see the renovated **Tsentralni Hali**, a stylish shopping mall dating from 1909, while on the opposite side of the road stands the unmistakable 16th century **Banya Bashi Mosque** (admission free; ⊘dawn-dusk). Behind the mosque are the ornate red-and-gold **mineral baths** (aka Turkish baths). They've been closed for

an achingly slow renovation for many years and are unlikely to reopen to the public again anytime soon ('I don't think they will ever open to us again,' says one local, 'the authorities want to keep it for their own parties.') Behind the baths, on ul Ekzarh Iosif, is a **hot water spring complex** where locals fill bottles from gushing spouts.

A couple of blocks west is the **Sofia Synagogue** (ul Ekzarh Iosif 16; ⊘9am-4pm Mon-Fri, 10am-2pm Sun), the largest Sephardic synagogue in Europe.

BULEVARD VITOSHA & PLOSHTAD BULGARIA

Bulevard Vitosha   NEIGHBOURHOOD
Extending south of pl Sveta Nedelya, towards its towering namesake, Mt Vitosha, this central section of bul Vitosha is now a car-free strip with Sofia's ritziest shops, along with a few trendy coffee bars. After a kilometre it reaches **Ploshtad Bulgaria**, an elongated tree-lined plaza popular with skateboarders and dotted with alfresco bars and popcorn and ice-cream vendors.

Monument to the Bulgarian State
MONUMENT
At the northern end of Ploshtad Bulgaria is the Monument to the Bulgarian State. Now fenced off, the socialist-era eyesore was erected in 1981 to celebrate the 1300th anniversary of the first Bulgarian Empire, but it has been slowly falling apart for years. It's surrounded by panels on which local teens practise their graffiti skills; competitions are sometimes held here. Beyond is the gigantic **NDK** (National Palace of Culture) complex, the city's main concert and trade fair venue. Take the lift up to access the usually open **viewing deck**.

SQUAT SHOPS

In the capitalist fervour that followed the fall of communism, Sofia saw an outbreak of the *klek* (squat shop), a basement-level shop that sells snacks and drinks out of a little window. Despite the advance of Western-style boutiques, these legacies of the transition – when expanding a basement window was cheaper and quicker than overhauling a ground-floor apartment – remain across Sofia. Just look for Sofians bent over and holding their backs in pain.

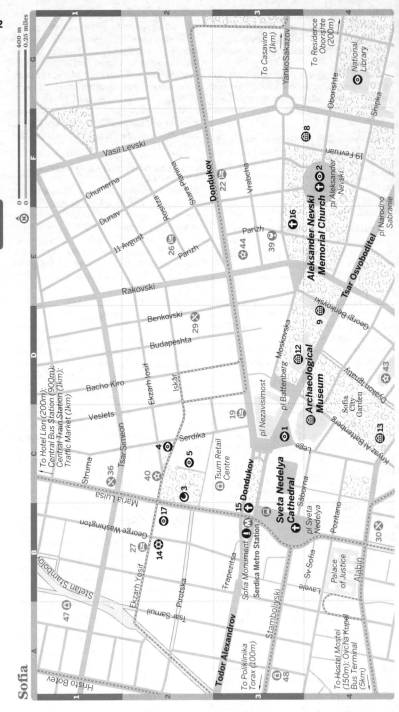

Sofia

152

400 m
0.25 miles

To Casavino
(1km)

To Residence
Oborishte
(200m)

YankoSakazov

National
Library

Oborishte

Shipka

8

Vasil Levski

Chumerna

Dunav

11 Avgust

Rositza

Stara Planina

Dondukov

22

Vrabcha

19 Fevruari

pl Aleksander
Nevski

2

**Aleksander Nevski
Memorial Church**

16

Parizh

44

39

Tsar Osvoboditel

26

Parizh

Rakovski

Benkovski

Georgi Benkovski

9

pl Narodno
Sabranie

29

Budapeshta

Moskovska

12

**Archaeological
Museum**

Dyakon Ignatiy

43

Bacho Kiro

Ekzarh Iosif

Iskar

pl Battenberg

pl Nezavisimost

Sofia
City
Garden

Veslets

13

Knyaz Al Battenberg

Struma

36

Tsar Simeon

Serdika

Dondukov

4

40

5

19

1

Lege

Maria Luisa

3

Tsum Retail
Centre

15 Dondukov

**Sveta Nedelya
Cathedral**

Saborna

17

George Washington

27

14

Trapezitsa

Sofia Monument

Serdika Metro Station

pl Sveta
Nedelya

Sv Sofia

Lavele

Pozitano

30

Stefan Stambolov

Ekzarh Yosif

Pirotska

Tsar Samuil

Stamboliyski

Sv Sofia

Palace
of Justice

Alabin

47

Todor Alexandrov

To Poliklinika
Torax (100m)

48

To Hostel Mostel
(150m); Ovcha Kupel
Bus Terminal
(5km)

Hristo Botev

To Hotel Lion (200m);
Central Bus Station (900m);
Central Train Station (1km);
Traffic Market (1km)

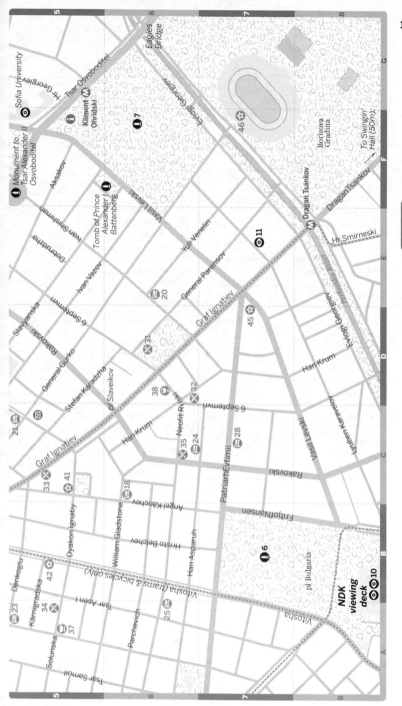

BORISOVA GRADINA & AROUND

Monument to the Soviet Army   MONUMENT
A few blocks southeast of pl Aleksander Nevski is a Monument to the Soviet Army. Built in 1954 to celebrate Russia's second liberation of Bulgaria in 1944, the monument features several statue groups of determined, gun-waving soldiers and smiling, industrious workers. It guards the entrance of the massive **Borisova Gradina Park**, with more socialist remnants.

Red House   ART GALLERY
(www.redhouse-sofia.bg; ul Lyuben Karavelov 15) The Red House is a lively cultural centre, with a busy program covering everything from heavyweight political debates and lectures (often in English) to film screenings, concerts and dance performances. Many events are free. The house once belonged to the sculptor Andrey Nikolov (1878–1959) and some of his works are displayed in the **Nikolov Hall** (admission free; ◷3-7pm Tue-Sat) here.

⚲ Courses

Institute of Foreign Languages   LANGUAGE
(☑971 7162; www.deo.uni-sofia.bg; ul Kosta Lulchev 27) At Sofia University; offers Bul-

garian-language courses (private tutors for 19lv per hour; three-week courses 599lv).

🛏 Sleeping

New hotels and hostels are constantly appearing. We've focused on more intimate ones that are within walking distance of central sights. Prices shift seasonally and business hotels often cut prices at weekends and in August. Some travel agents can find private accommodation.

Hotel Niky
HOTEL €€

(☑952 3058; www.hotel-niky.com; ul Neofit Rilski 16; s/d incl breakfast from €40/45; ✳@) Niky offers 23 smart rooms and suites, all with tiny kitchenettes, aimed mainly at business travellers. The central location and reasonable prices means it's often full, so book ahead. There's also a good restaurant.

TOP CHOICE / Red House
B&B €€

(☑988 8188; www.redbandb.com; ul Lyuben Karavelov 15; s/d incl breakfast from €25/40; @) This cultural house keeps six fairly spartan but clean wood-floored rooms (with shared bathrooms) upstairs. They're all different shapes and sizes, and it can be a little noisy with so much going on here. However, where else would you get an in-house museum and theatre? Maintaining the Bohemian atmosphere, breakfast doesn't start till 10.15am.

Residence Oborishte
BOUTIQUE HOTEL €€€

(☑814 4888; www.residence-oborishte.com; ul Oborishte 63; s/d incl breakfast from €100/120; ⊝✳🖿) A bright-red '30s-era home with its own bistro, the Residence has nine rooms with cherry-wood flooring, antique-style furnishings and lots of space. The penthouse (€170) has a view over the Aleksander Nevski Church. Prices drop by 20% at weekends.

Grand Hotel Sofia
LUXURY HOTEL €€€

(☑811 0810; www.grandhotelsofia.bg; ul General Gurko 1; r incl breakfast from €215; P✳🖿) Overlooking the Sofia City Garden, this certainly is a very grand place, with 109 tastefully furnished rooms, liveried doormen and a couple of very good restaurants. Prices usually drop at weekends.

Canapé Connection
HOSTEL €

(☑441 6373; www.canapeconnection.com; ul Yuri Venelin 2; dm incl breakfast €11-14; @) Run by three young travellers, Canapé is a new place with eight- and four-bed dorms (one en suite) with smart wooden bunks and wooden floors. Homemade *banitsa*, pancakes and croissants are on the breakfast menu.

Arte Hotel
HOTEL €€€

(☑402 7100; www.artehotelbg.com; bul Dondukov 5; s/d from €60/82; ✳🖿) Across the road from the old Party House, this 25-room hotel has bright rooms with lots of pine and an orange-and-cream colour scheme. All have flat-screen TVs and fridges.

Ethno Hostel
HOSTEL €

(☑0878 345 845; www.ethnohostel.com; ul Tsar Ivan Assen II 33; dm incl breakfast €11; @) Though a little out of the way, east of the city centre, Ethno has a relaxed, friendly, hippy-ish vibe, with a cosy lounge, log fire, colourful wall paintings, and bongos, guitars and even a double bass for some late-night jamming.

Hostel Gulliver
HOSTEL €

(☑987 5210; www.gulliver1947-bg.com; bul Dondukov 48; dm/s/d incl breakfast 18/38/48lv; @) Conveniently located just a couple of blocks north of pl Aleksander Nevski, Gulliver is a clean and brightly furnished little hostel with a couple of five-bed dorms and four doubles (one en suite). All rooms have TVs and fridges. Laundry costs 6lv per load.

Hostel Mostel
HOSTEL €

(☑0889 223 296; www.hostelmostel.com; ul Makedoniya 2; dm incl breakfast €8-13, s €22, d €30-39; @) One of Sofia's most popular hostels, Mostel fills the 1st floor of an old tavern with a choice of six- and eight-bed dorms as well as doubles, triples and one single (some en suite). There are comfy sofas, a pool table, wooden veranda and 42-inch plasma TV.

Hotel Lion
HOTEL €€

(☑917 8400; www.sofia.hotelslion.bg; bul Maria Luisa 60; s/d from €59/69; ✳🖿) Overlooking the Lions Bridge, this is a neat, modern hotel with 33 comfortable, variously sized rooms and a restaurant. It's handy for the bus and train stations, but on a busy road intersection.

Scotty's Boutique Hotel
BOUTIQUE HOTEL €€

(☑983 6777; www.scottyshotel.eu; ul Ekzarh Iosif 11; s/d from €70/90; ✳🖿) This gay-friendly place has 16 colourful rooms named after cities – 'Paris' is particularly bright, the orange 'San Francisco' gets a small balcony, while 'Cape Town' is done out with zebra print. The cheapest are a bit small.

Sofia Guesthouse
HOSTEL €

(☑403 0100; www.sofiaguest.com; ul Patriarh Evtimii 27; dm/d incl breakfast €9/30; ✳@) Filling a little house in a private garden just off the busy street, this hostel has a travel agent plus bright but rather small rooms with their own bathrooms. Dorms are clean but, again, there's not a lot of room.

Kervan Hostel
HOSTEL €

(☎983 9428; www.kervanhostel.com; ul Rositza 3; dm/d incl breakfast €10/30; ☎) Clean and friendly, the Kervan has an entry lined with antique radios and a 'Spanish' tiled kitchen. Free tea and coffee is on hand and bikes are available for hire for €10 per day.

Hotel Enny
HOTEL €

(☎983 4395; www.enyhotel.com; ul Pop Bogomil 46; s/d from 25/40lv) A back-up in the centre, the Enny has simple rooms (some small, all without air-con or fan) that can get you to the next day OK. Most have shared bathrooms.

Art Hostel
HOSTEL €

(☎987 0545; www.art-hostel.com; ul Angel Kânchev 21a; dm/s/d incl breakfast €11/28/38; @) They claim it's 'like joining a family for a few days', and this Boho hang-out has plenty of character, with various arty types knocking about, a back garden and a cool basement bar. The dorms are a bit cramped though, with triple bunks.

Hotel Diter
HOTEL €€

(☎989 8998; www.diterhotel.com; ul Han Asparukh 65; s incl breakfast weekday/weekend €78/68, d €98/88; ❇@) Built in 1895, this sky-blue house was once home to Bulgarian writer Todor Vlaykov – and now his descendants have opened the doors for a simple but comfortable business-type hotel, with a decent restaurant.

✗ Eating

Sofia has, by far, the country's most cosmopolitan and varied dining scene. Appealing new places are popping up constantly – try between bul Vitosha and ul Rakovski.

A refurbished covered market, **Tsentralni Hali** (cnr bul Maria Luisa & ul Ekzarh Iosif; ☺7am-10pm) has three floors busy with fruit and vegetables, fresh bread and cakes, ice cream, wine and olives. On the upper level is a small food court with outlets selling sandwiches, pizzas and beer.

TOP CHOICE ▷ **Pri Yafata**
BULGARIAN €€

(ul Solunska 28; mains 5-15lv) Decked out like a rustic tavern, with agricultural tools, vintage rifles and flagons hanging off the walls, Pri Yafata might seem a bit over the top, but the food is excellent. The lengthy menu offers hearty pork, chicken, duck and fish dishes, and the lamb sausages (8.90lv)

are particularly good. They also have a big choice of *rakias* to try (around 3.20lv).

Trops Kâshta
BULGARIAN €

(bul Maria Luisa 26; mains from 3lv; ☺8am-8.30pm) For cheap, fast, fresh cafeteria-style food, like *kebabche* and moussaka, this busy place doesn't disappoint. There's another branch in the basement of Tsentralni Hali.

TOP CHOICE ▷ **Dream House**
VEGETARIAN €

(ul Alabin 50a; mains 3-8lv) Offering Sofia's best meatless dining, this friendly, pea-green restaurant has a relaxed atmosphere, with a seasonal menu featuring the kind of inspired veggie and vegan choices that are hard to find in Bulgaria. Organic buckwheat pancakes, stir-fries, soups and almond milk desserts are among the options.

Olive's
INTERNATIONAL €€

(ul Graf Ignatiev 12; mains 7-18lv) With jokey vintage advertising posters on the walls and newspaper-style menus, Olive's is a quirky place that serves up tasty dishes ranging from simple pasta and burger meals to Mediterranean-influenced concoctions such as cod with pesto (12lv) and chorizo sausages.

Krâchme Divaka
BULGARIAN €

(ul 6 Septemvri 41a; mains 3-7lv; ☺24hr) In an appealing old house, this restaurant is a good choice for traditional Bulgarian food. Dishes include wine-soaked kebab with mashed potatoes (4.60lv), a filling potato cream soup (2.20lv) and grilled trout (6.90lv). There are plenty of vegetarian options, but they do seem overfond of dill and garlic.

Sofi French Bakery
BAKERY €

(ul Rakovski 161; salads 4.90lv; ☺8.30am-8.30pm Mon-Sat, 9am-7pm Sun) This cute little takeaway bakery has some of the best cakes in town, and does meal deals such as a croissant and a coffee for 2.70lv or a salad and drink for 6lv. There are a couple of stand-up tables inside.

Chaina
TEAHOUSE €

(ul Benkovski 11; mains 4.50-9lv; ☺10am-11pm Mon-Sat) This arty teahouse, decked out with vintage sofas and oil paintings, doubles as a vegetarian restaurant, with various salads and pastas dominating the menu. Teas start at 1.90lv.

⚲ Drinking

Look in the free weekly *Programata* magazine for listings. Open-air bars abound in city parks and squares like Ploshtad Bulgaria and Borisova Gradina; those in search of a pricey little coffee can try open-air cafes along bul Vitosha.

Pri Kmeta
PUB

(ul Parizh 2; ⊗noon-4am) In a big cellar behind the Sveta Sofia Church, this is Sofia's only microbrewery, complete with gleaming copper vats in the corner. They produce four home-brews (500ml from 2.60lv) including a cloudy wheat beer and a strong dark beer, which are also served by the metre (from 20.60lv).

Fresh Break
CAFE

(ul Solunska 43; ⊗8am-8pm) If you're after a nonalcoholic pick-me-up, try this juice bar that offers a variety of freshly made milkshakes (from 1.95lv) and fresly squeezed juices (3lv to 5lv). They also do muffins, sandwiches and salads.

Hambara
PUB

(ul 6 Septemvri 22; ⊗8pm-late) Located in a two-level cellar lit only by candles, this rather secretive place is unsigned, down a dark and dingy path; you might have to knock on the door to be let in.

Upstairs
BAR

(bul Vitosha 18; ⊗10am-2am) Upstairs is the air-kissing, in-crowd hang-out, where you can sip cocktails on a designer sofa with chill-out music playing in the background.

☆ Entertainment

Sofia has the best clubs in the country, playing everything from the cheesiest *chalga* to more familiar house and pop. If that's not your style, there are plenty of venues to enjoy live music, and more than a handful of cinemas.

Swingin' Hall
CLUB

(bul Dragan Tsankov 8; ⊗Tue-Sun) Probably Sofia's best live-music venue, with jazz, blues and rock shows taking over the cellar-styled club.

Escape
CLUB

(ul Angel Kânchev 1; cover 10lv; ⊗10pm-late Thu-Sun) Sofia's favoutite central disco, Escape has various theme nights including Britpop parties, hip-hop and drum'n'bass night.

ID Club
GAY & LESBIAN

(bul Vitosha 18; ⊗9pm-5am Tue-Sat) ID is a big, glittering gay club with three bars, theme nights, cabaret and a playlist including everything from house to *chalga*.

Cinema City
CINEMA

(bul Stamboliyski 101; tickets 5-9lv) On the top floor of the Mall of Sofia, this is a modern

multiscreen cinema showing the latest Hollywood releases.

Odeon
CINEMA

(bul Patriarh Evtimii 1; tickets 4lv) This is a great art-house cinema, showing older films, often black and white classics, on long runs.

Dom na Kinoto
CINEMA

(ul Ekzarh Iosif 37; tickets 4-7lv) One of the smaller and older cinemas, the Dom shows mainly Bulgarian and European movies, with Bulgarian subtitles.

National Opera House
OPERA

(☏987 1366; www.operasofia.com; ul Vrabcha 1; ⊗ticket office 9.30-6.30pm Mon-Fri, 10.30-6pm Sat & Sun) In a grand neoclassical building, Sofia's opera house stages regular operatic performances, as well as occasional ballet and classical music concerts.

🛍 Shopping

The year-round daily **fleamarket** (pl Aleksander Nevski) is a ragbag of genuine antiques, touristy junk, modern artworks and plenty of fakes – be very wary of the Soviet and Nazi knick-knacks. Most stuff is way overpriced though.

Stenata
OUTDOOR GEAR

(ul Bratya Miladinovi 5; ⊗10am-8pm Mon-Fri, 10am-6pm Sat) A great outfitter for the woodsbound, with a two-floor selection of camping, hiking and rock-climbing gear.

Casavino
FOOD & DRINK

(bul Yanko Sakazov 42; ⊗9am-10pm) One of three branches in Sofia, Casavino offers a vast range of Bulgarian wines and spirits, as well tipples from South America.

Ladies Market
MARKET

(ul Stefan Stambolov; ⊗dawn-dusk) So called because traditionally this was where country women came to sell their farm produce, this is still Sofia's liveliest market with countless stalls selling fruit, vegetables, meat, clothing and household goods.

ℹ Information

Dangers & Annoyances

Inspectors on public transport make a beeline for foreigners; fines are issued to those who don't punch a tram ticket for both themself *and* their bag. Be very careful when using taxis as Sofia has an abundance of crooked taxi drivers, as well as technically legal taxi firms charging extortionate rates (check the rear window for prices); some of these adopt names very similar to the reputable OK Supertrans company, deliberately to deceive

BUS FARES FROM SOFIA

TO	COST (LV)	DURATION (HR)	FREQUENCY (PER DAY)
Bansko	13-14	3	5
Belogradchik	15	4	2
Burgas	22-28	6	8-11
Kârdzhali	20	4	10-12
Kazanlâk	16	3	5
Koprivshtitsa	10	2	3-6
Melnik	13	3	1
Nesebâr	28	7	3
Plovdiv	12	2	25
Ruse	15	4½	14
Shumen	28	5	9
Smolyan	23	4½	6
Sozopol	25	6	2
Varna	25-30	6	20
Veliko Târnovo	18	3½	26-27
Vidin	16	4½	7-8

– even locals get caught. Some moneychangers advertise one rate outside, then a worse one in tiny print inside the changing booth. Sofia also has a large stray-dog population, but they are rarely aggressive during the day – most likely they're exhausted from their regular all-night barking sessions. Watch out for dog poo, too.

Internet Access

There are plenty of free wi-fi spots across the city, including in many restaurants and hotels, but just one internet cafe: **Garibaldi** (ul Graf Ignatiev 6; per hr 3.30lv; ⏱8.30am-midnight).

Medical Services

Poliklinika Torax (☎91285; www.thorax.bg; bul Stamboliyski 57; ⏱24hr) Good private clinic west of the centre.

Tokuda Hospital (☎403 4000; www.tokuda bolnica.bg; bul Nikola Vaptsarov 51b; ⏱24hr) Modern, Japanese-run private hospital with English-speaking staff.

Money

Most foreign-exchange booths are along bul Vitosha, bul Maria Luisa and bul Stamboliyski run nonstop.

Unicredit Bulbank (ul Lavele & ul Todor Aleksandrov; ⏱8.30am-6pm Mon-Fri)

Tourist Information

Sofia Tourist Information Centre (☎491 8345; Sofia University underpass; ⏱8am-8pm) Lots of free leaflets and maps, and helpful English-speaking staff.

Getting There & Away

Air

At **Sofia airport** (☎937 2211; www.sofia-airport. bg), terminal 2 receives most international flights, though some charter flights still use terminal 1. In terminal 2's arrival hall there's an information booth, ATM, foreign exchange and car rental.

Bus

DOMESTIC BUSES Sofia's modern **central bus station** (www.centralnaavtogara.bg; bul Maria Luisa 100; ⏱24hr), located next to the train station, is filled with stands of competing bus companies and can be a bit hectic, but there's a 24-hour information desk to help you, plus **left luggage** (small/big bag per day 5/7lv; ⏱24hr). The OK Supertrans Taxi stand at the door is dependable. Many international buses, and a few domestic ones, leave from the wilder Traffic Market, between the station and train station.

All go from the central bus station and times are frequent (generally every hour) unless otherwise noted. Some Black Sea towns have less frequent services outside of summer.

Two buses connect Sofia with the Rila Monastery (10lv, 2½ hours), leaving at 10.20am and 6.20pm from the **Ovcha Kupel bus terminal** (Zapad; bul Tsar Boris III). Reach the station by tram 5 from pl Makedoniya, west of the centre on ul Alabin (it's a 20-minute ride).

INTERNATIONAL BUSES Most international buses are handled by the stands at the Traffic Market, between the bus station and train station. **Matpu** (www.matpu.com) sells tickets for Skopje and Ohrid in Macedonia. **Union-Ivkoni** (www.union-ivkoni.com) runs buses to Budapest, and other stands sell tickets for Belgrade, Bratislava, Prague and other European destinations.

MTT (bul Maria Luisa 84; www.mttsofia.com) sends at least one daily bus to Thessaloniki, five weekly to Athens and one weekly to Patras. There are several daily buses to İstanbul from the central station.

Macedonia-bound buses cross at Gyueshevo–Deve Bair; Belgrade-bound buses from Sofia cross at Kalotina–Dimitrovgrad, Serbia (most travellers prefer the train on this route).

Train

Sofia's **central train station** (bul Maria Luisa) is a bit confusing, though departures and arrivals are listed in English on a large computer screen on the main floor, where there's an information booth (but usually no English), plus **left luggage** (per bag per day 2-3lv; ⏰6am-11pm). You buy same-day tickets for Vidin, Ruse and Varna on the main floor, and all other domestic destinations downstairs. Advance tickets are available at another office downstairs.

DOMESTIC Sample 2nd-class train fares for direct routes:

Burgas (21.50lv, 6½ to 7½ hours, six daily)

Gorna Oryakhovitsa (15.50lv, 4½ hours, 10 daily) Near Veliko Târnovo.

Plovdiv (10.20lv, 2½ hours, 12 daily)

Ruse (20.40lv, 6½ hours, four daily)

Varna (25.20lv, seven to eight hours, six daily)

Vidin (12.60lv, 5½ hours, three daily)

Reaching Veliko Târnovo (16.30lv, five to six hours) requires a change (usually in Gorna Oryakhovitsa), sometimes getting onto a slow ordinary train, which may be late; about six times a day trains are timed to link for easy transfers.

INTERNATIONAL Two daily trains go to Bucharest; the *Trans Balkan* (No 462) leaves in the morning, the *Bulgaria Express* (No 382) in the evening. The Sofia–Athens train (No 361) travels to Thessaloniki and Athens, leaving daily at 5.05pm.

The *Balkan Express* (No 491) leaves at night for İstanbul. The same train goes in the reverse direction during the day to Belgrade and then on to Budapest and Vienna. The Sofia–Belgrade Train (No 292) leaves nightly.

International tickets can be purchased at the **Rila Bureau** (☑932 3346; ⏰24hr) in the northern part of the station's main floor, or at its **centre office** (☑987 0777; ul General Gurko 5; ⏰7am-7.30pm Mon-Fri, 7am-6.30pm Sat).

❶ Getting Around

To/From the Airport

An **OK Supertrans Taxi** (☑973 2121) booth in the arrivals hall arranges metered cabs to the centre (about 10lv to 12lv). Outside is a bus stop, where bus 284 leaves for a stop along bul Vasil Levski, near Sofia University (a bookshop in the arrival hall sells bus tickets). Minibus 30 travels between bul Maria Luisa and the airport (1.50lv).

Car & Motorcycle

Most travel agents rent cars. Local agents include the following:

Bulgaria Car Rental (☑400 1060; www.bulgariacarrent.com; ul Orfei 9)

Motoroads (☑0885 370 298; www.motoroads.com; ul Sveti Kiprian 279, Mladost 2)

Tany Rent-a-Car (☑970 8500; www.tany97.com; ul Chehov 69)

Public Transport

Sofia's trams, buses and metro line run from 5.30am to 11pm and use the same ticket system. A single ride is 1lv and a day pass 4lv. Blue ticket booths are near most stops. Single-ride tickets must be validated once you board; disguised officials fine those without them. You *must* punch a separate ticket for a big bag.

Trams 1 and 7 connect the bus station and train station with the centre. Minibuses ply many useful city routes at 1.50lv per ride; number 5 goes to the train station, 30 goes to the airport and 21 takes you to Boyana.

Sofia's expanding metro line currently stretches from the western suburbs to the city centre, including the Serdica station near ploshtad Sveta Nedelya and Kliment Ohridski station, near Sofia University. Construction (meaning lots of road closures) is likely to continue into 2012 and beyond.

Taxi

Sofia's taxis have a reputation for overcharging foreigners. **OK Supertrans Taxi** (☑973 2121) runs on the meter.

AROUND SOFIA

In addition to the following, many visitors decide to travel to Rila Monastery (p161) as a day trip.

Vitosha ВИТОША

The feather in Sofia's cap is this 23km by 13km mountain range (part of Vitosha Nature Park: www.park-vitosha.org), just south of the city. At summer weekends, many Sofians come to hike, picnic and pick berries. In winter, it's the nearest skiing to the capital.

🏃 Activities

The mountain has dozens of well-marked **hiking trails**. It's worth paying 5lv for the Cyrillic trail map *Vitosha Turisticheska Karta* (1:50,000), available in Sofia. Popular ones include the steep 90-minute trip up Mt Cherni Vrâh (2290m) from Aleko; a three-hour trek east of Mt Sredets (1969m) from Aleko past Goli Vrâh (1837m) to Zlatni Mostove; and a three-hour hike from Boyana Church past a waterfall to Zlatni Mostove.

The **skiing**, from mid-December to April, covers 29km of the mountain; it's generally cheaper here than ski resorts (about 30lv for a lift ticket) and you can ski higher (the peak is 1800m). Rental equipment is available; try to avoid busy weekends.

Most people reach the mountain by chairlift. **Dragalevtsi** has two chairlifts, located a few kilometres up from the village bus stop (walk via the creekside) – one lift goes to Bai Krâstyo, the second to Goli Vrâh (1837m). The other option is the six-person gondola at **Simeonovo**, which runs from Friday to Sunday (closed in April), and goes to Aleko, a popular hike/ski hub. It's possible to go up either Dragalevtsi or Simeonovo, hike 30 minutes, and return down the other.

ℹ️ Getting There & Away

About 2km south of the NDK in Sofia, the useful **Hladilnika bus stop** (ul Srebârna), just east of bul Cherni Vrâh, has several Vitosha-bound buses. Bus 122 leads directly to the Simeonovo gondola. Bus 64 goes to Dragalevtsi centre and on to Boyana. Get to Hladilnika bus stop by tram 9, just east of the NDK.

Boyana БОЯНА

Once a separate village (now officially a part of Sofia), hillside Boyana has a couple of interesting attractions. The **National Historical Museum** (www.historymuseum.org; bul Vitoshko Lale 16; adult/student 10/1lv, combined ticket with Boyana Church 12lv, guide 20lv; ⊙9.30am-6pm Tue-Sun Apr-Oct, 9am-5.30pm

Tue-Sun Nov-Mar) is housed in a 1970s presidential palace. It's an exhaustive collection chronicling the history of Bulgaria from earliest times, with displays including Neolithic flints, Thracian jewellery, costumes, furniture and weaponry. Unfortunately there are many reproductions of original pieces and a disappointing lack of context.

Built between the 11th and 19th centuries, the colourful, Unesco-protected **Boyana Church** (ul Boyansko Ezero; adult/student 10/1lv, combined ticket with National Historical Museum 12lv, guide 10lv; ⊙9.30am-5.30pm Apr-Oct, 9am-5pm Nov-Mar), 1.5km south of the historical museum, is Bulgaria's most revered medieval church, and only allows 10-minute visits. The 90 colourful murals date from 1259, and are considered among the finest examples of medieval Bulgarian art. They include the oldest known portrayal of St John of Rila (Ivan Rilski) and portraits of Tsar Konstantin Asen and Queen Irina.

Minibus 21 from the city centre (flag one down on bul Patriarh Evtimii) will drop you right outside the museum gates, and continues from there to Boyana Church. Tram 9 goes down ul Hristo Botev from the centre to Hladilnika bus stop, where bus 64 goes past the museum to the east then within 200m of the church.

There are a couple of good hotels out here if you want to stay. The **Casa Boyana** (✆805 0800; www.casaboyana.com; ul Ivanitza Dantchev 23; s/d from €70/80; P ✳ @), near the Boyana Church, is a four-star boutique hotel with a very good restaurant, gym, business centre and stylish rooms with mountain views.

RILA & PIRIN MOUNTAINS

These two mountain chains snuggle up to the Greek border south of Sofia, and are made of serious Alps-like rocky-topped peaks full of rewarding hikes. It's here that one of Bulgaria's most famous sites, Rila Monastery, stands guarded by mountains, while Melnik is a favourite spot for wining weekends.

🏃 Activities

Most hiking paths are well signed. For Rila hikes, the monastery is a possible starting point, with four trails meeting others higher up. Day hikes are certainly possible and *hizhas* (mountain huts) are spaced three to nine hours apart. For longer hikes, it's best to start up at Malîovitsa (southwest from

Samokov), where you can reach the Sedemte Ezera (Seven Lakes).

Pirin hikes are generally tougher than Rila ones, with more abrupt slopes. In summer it's better to end walking down to Melnik.

Also see www.rilanationalpark.org and www.pirin-np.com.

Rila Monastery
РИЛСКИ МАНАСТИР
☎07054

Bulgaria's most famous monastery (admission free; ◷6am-9pm), set in a forested valley 120km south of Sofia, is a popular destination for day trippers from around the region. The murals here, painted by Zahari Zograf, are some of Bulgaria's finest, and there are plenty of hiking trails in the nearby Rila Mountains.

Day trips to Rila from Sofia range from about €20 to €80 or more. There are usually direct buses from Sofia, but it sometimes requires a change.

First built in 927, and heavily restored in 1469, the monastery helped to keep Bulgarian culture and language alive during Ottoman rule. A fire engulfed most buildings in 1833, but they were rebuilt shortly thereafter.

The entrance to the monastery is from the west at Dupnitsa Gate, and around the east side at Samokov Gate. The 300 monks' cells fill four levels of colourful balconies overlooking the large courtyard. Built in the 1830s, the Nativity Church (Church of Rozhdestvo Bogorodichno) contains 1200 magnificent murals. Tsar Boris III's tomb – actually containing only his heart – is to the right when you enter. Nearby, the 23m stone Hrelyu Tower is all that remains from the 14th century.

The Ethnographic Museum (admission 3lv; ◷8am-5pm) houses many ornate woodwork pieces, including the double-sided Rila Cross, with 140 tiny biblical scenes.

If you have time, hike up to the Tomb of St Ivan (Grobyat na Sv Ivan Rilski). To reach the start of the 15-minute hike up the clearly marked trail, walk about 3.7km east on the road, behind the monastery.

You can stay in the monastery's rooms (☎2208; r 30-60lv); the attendant often leaves mid-afternoon. There are also a couple of nearby hotels, plus camping and bungalows at riverside Zodiak (☎2291; campsites 10lv, d from 30lv), 2km past the monastery. The nearest hizha is about a six-hour walk up.

Rila village, 21km away, has a hotel, ATM and an information centre.

ℹ Getting There & Away

One daily direct bus connects the monastery with Sofia's Ovcha Kupel bus terminal (10lv, 2½ hours), leaving at 10.20am, with one returning at 3pm. There are also five daily buses to nearby Rila village (2lv, 30 minutes), where you can catch hourly buses to Blagoevgrad (1.80lv, 25 minutes).

Melnik МЕЛНИК
☎07437 / POP 275

Officially Bulgaria's smallest town, tiny Melnik – hidden by jutting pyramid-style claysand mountains at the dramatic southwest end of the Pirins – is one of the country's most famous wine centres, and also has great day hikes. Family-run *mehanas* (tavern restaurants) boast their own barrels of blood-red Melnik, the unique local varietal, which is sold in plastic jugs on the dirt streets.

A century ago, Melnik was home to 20,000 people– mostly Greeks – until much of it burned down during the 1912–13 Balkan Wars. The population never recovered, and you can still see the ruins of many old family homes on the village outskirts. From the bus stop, roads run on either side of a largely dry creek into town. There's no bank or ATM here.

◉ Sights

Mitko Manolev Winery　　　　WINERY
(admission incl tasting 2lv; ◷9am-dusk) Follow the main road east, and up, to the 250-year-old Mitko Manolev Winery. The manager – nicknamed 'Shestaka' for his six-fingered hand – is happy to talk wine (in English) and sell glasses of his red and white wine for 2lv, in a pleasant setting with wooden stools overlooking Melnik.

Kordopulov House　　　HISTORIC BUILDING
(admission 2lv; ◷9am-6pm) Also at the eastern end of the village is the Kordopulov House, a giant revival-period home with exquisite carved wooden ceilings and a huge wine cellar down below.

🏃 Activities

The best half-day hike is the trip to the hilltop Rozhen Monastery, 10km east by road (or about 4km by hiking trail). Built in 1217 and redone in the mid-18th century, the monastery has a mural-filled church and is connected by a trail through the mountains with Melnik (about one hour downhill).

Consider taking one of the few daily buses up to Rozhen village (or a share taxi for about 6lv), then walk 800m up to the monastery and back down to Melnik. Signs point west, going behind the monastery. The trail gets slippery after rains.

More exploring can be done closer to Melnik, too. Framing the village to the south is **Nikolova Gora**, a flat-top hill scattered with ruins. A sign points up from across the Rodina Hotel. About 15 minutes up, signs point left and right. To the right, you'll pass the battered 13th-century **St Nicola Church** and, further on, the dramatic cliffside, 13th-century **Despot Slav Fortress**. Back the other way, the trail looks over Melnik, reaching the **St Mary Spileotisa Monastery** (which draws pilgrims on 31 August); the trail heading back on the opposite side of the hill goes to another monastery. You'll need about two hours in all.

🛏 Sleeping

Most of the traditional-style private homes let out simple rooms with shared bathroom from 10lv or 12lv per person.

Hotel Slavova Krepost HOTEL €€
(☑0889 414 001; www.slavovakreposthotel.com; d incl breakfast Mon-Thu €25, Fri-Sun €35; ✴@) In the village centre, the rooms at this modern, National Revival–style hotel have a contemporary style, and there's a restaurant and wine cellar stocked with the produce of Slavova's own vineyard. Guests are treated to a free wine-tasting session on arrival.

Hotel Despot Slav HOTEL €€
(☑248; www.melnik.bg; s/d incl breakfast 50/70lv) On the main strip heading towards the winery, this hotel has cool, airy rooms with wooden floors and ceilings, and a traditional *mehana*.

Hotel Elli Greco HOTEL €€
(☑2233; www.elligreco.eu; r incl breakfast 80lv; P✴✴) One of Melnik's bigger hotels, Elli Greco has spacious modern rooms and excellent facilities, including an outdoor pool, garden, children's playground and spa centre, as well as a restaurant serving Greek and Bulgarian cuisine.

🍴 Eating

All the above hotels have very good restaurants open to nonguests. Another popular *mehana* is **Mencheva Kâshta** (mains 7-20lv; ⊙10am-11pm), a homely tavern halfway to the winery that serves up hearty Bulgarian dishes including local specialities such as trout.

ℹ Getting There & Away

One daily direct bus connects Melnik with Sofia (13lv, three to four hours).

Bansko БАНСКО

☑0749 / POP 9200

A once quaint, historic mountain town, Bansko has swelled with overdevelopment in recent years, with tacky modern resorts cosying up to Mt Vihren (2914m) and a property boom that has seen numerous apartment blocks and holiday homes erected all around the resort, and extended ski slopes and facilities built as part of the town's unsuccessful bid for the 2014 Winter Olympics. 'Bansko is ruined, all for money,' was the considered opinion of one local, but it's not all bad: the cobbled Old Town is still pleasant to wander around, and Bansko's famously festive *mehanas* are a joy.

Bansko celebrates its folk dances and music during the **Celebration of Bansko Traditions** in mid-May. The **Pirin Sings Folk Festival** is staged nearby in August every five years (next scheduled for 2015). The annual **International Jazz Festival** takes place in the second week of August.

◉ Sights

Kâshta-Museum of Nikola Vaptsarov
MUSEUM
(pl Nikola Vaptsarov; admission 3lv; ⊙9am-noon & 2-5pm) This museum, dedicated to a romantic local poet, is set in his childhood home. Vaptsarov was executed for his antifascist poetry in 1942 and the exhibtion here chronicles his life and works.

Sveta Troitsa Church CHURCH
(pl Vûzhrazhdane; ⊙8am-6pm) Built in the 1830s, the Sveta Troitsa Church is particularly striking for its 30m-high belltower – a Bansko landmark – and its wooden interior and faded murals.

🏃 Activities

The ski season in Bansko lasts from mid-December to April, though the first snows tickle the mountains in late September. And it's good skiing. There are two major mountains – the lower **Chalin Valog** and the bigger **Shiligarnika**, higher up – with 26km of runs (7km of night skiing, too). A lift pass for all four lifts is 50lv for a day, ski rental is 30lv per day, and snowboard gear is 50lv. For old-school lifts, and shorter lines, take the bus 6km east to **Dobrinishte**, which a

NARROW-GAUGE TRAIN RIDE

Few visitors reach or leave Bansko by train, but if you have the time, the wonderful narrow-gauge line to Septemvri (5.60lv, five hours, four daily) offers one of the country's most scenic rides. The little carriage trundles slowly north towards the Sofia–Plovdiv main line at unremarkable Septemvri, with fantastic views and lots of tunnels along the way. One of the stops, Avramovo, is the highest station in the Balkans.

some point may merge with Bansko's lifts into one mega-slope.

Paths to the Pirin Mountains are accessed just south of town. In summer minibuses go to Banderitsa (about 4lv, three daily) to access trails to lakes and *hizhas*.

🛏 Sleeping

There are plenty of hotels and guesthouses in town, but book way ahead during ski season, when prices are sometimes 50% higher.

TOP CHOICE **Dedo Pene** HOTEL €
(☏88348; www.dedopene.com; ul Buynov 1; s/d 30/50lv, winter 35/60lv) Dating from 1820, this lovely renovated old home overlooks a narrow cobbled lane near the Sveta Troitsa church. It has just eight cosy rooms with wooden floors and ceilings, and fireplaces that may be lit in winter. The attached folksy tavern serves its own wine.

Hotel Avalon HOTEL €
(☏88399; www.avalonhotel-bulgaria.com; ul Eltepe 4; s/d €18/20, winter €30/45; ⊘closed Apr, May & late Nov; @) This friendly, British-run hotel offers light, restful rooms and is big with the budget crowd. The owners offer ski lessons and excursions, and there's a sauna in the basement.

Spa Hotel Villa Roka LUXURY HOTEL €€
(☏88337; ul Glazne 37b; s/d from €23/31, winter from €34/48; P✳🖥🏊) One of the smarter places in town, the Roka has 89 minimalist-style rooms, suites and maisonettes with balconies, and a fully equipped spa centre and pool.

🍴 Eating

The most appealing *mehanas* – with wood-beamed ceilings, hanging vines and live bands – are just north of the square, including **Kasapinova Kâshta** (ul Sandanski 4; mains from 5lv; ⊘noon-midnight).

❶ Information

Pick up maps at the **tourist information centre** (☏88580; www.bansko.bg; pl Nikola Vaptsarov; ⊘9am-5pm), which often keeps irregular hours.

❶ Getting There & Away

Buses and trains stop about 300m north of the central pl Nikola Vaptsarov, reached along ul Todor Aleksandrov. From the square ul Pirin goes south to pl Vûzhrazhdane and on to the ski lifts and, 2km further, the Pirin National Park entrance.

From the **bus station** (☏88420; ul Patriarh Evtimii), frequent buses go to Sofia (14lv, three hours) and Blagoevgrad (7lv, one hour), while one or two go to Plovdiv (12lv, 3½ hours).

The **train station** (ul Akad Yordan Ivanov) is next to the bus station.

THRACIAN PLAIN & THE RODOPIS

Sitting in the wide-open Thracian plain, Plovdiv lies just within the cusp of the thickly forested Rodopi Mountains rising to the south. Like the Pirin and Rila, the Rodopis have good hikes, and offer culturally rich villages to top it all off. Smolyan is a key Rodopi hub, from where you can travel further into the Rodopi range or east to out-of-the-way Kârdzhali to see the Thracian remains of Perperikon.

🏃 Activities

Shiroka Lâka, 24km northwest of Smolyan, is a good base for hikes. A popular one is the five-hour hike south to Golyam Perelik (where there's a *hizha*) or there's a two-day hike from Shiroka to Trigrad via Mugla (a mountain village with accommodation). The international trail E8 plies the Rodopis.

Trail maps (5lv each) split the Rodopis into the western and eastern ranges.

Plovdiv ПЛОВДИВ
☏032 / POP 375,000

Bulgaria's second city, and one of its oldest, Plovdiv has a rich cultural heritage and an impressive roll-call of attractions, including the still-functioning Roman theatre, art galleries, ancient churches and mosques. The cobbled lanes of the hilltop 'Old Town' are especially rewarding, with a number of restored National Revival–era houses to visit.

Plovdiv was first settled as early as 5000 BC by Thracians, who built a fortress on

Nebet Tepe hill. It was occupied by the Macedonians, under Philip II, who founded the city of Philippopolis here in 342 BC, which in turn became known as Trimontium under the Romans, Pupulden under the Bulgarians and Filibe under the Turks. Plovdiv remained, briefly, in Ottoman hands after the rest of Bulgaria gained its independence in 1878, thus missing its likely elevation to capital city, and kicking off a rivalry with Sofia that exists to this day – to start a colourful conversation, ask proud locals what they think of Sofia.

◉ Sights

Most of Plovdiv's main attractions are in or around the Old Town, and can be seen in a day.

OLD TOWN

Revival-era wooden-shuttered homes lean over narrow cobbled lanes in this hilly neighbourhood, and about a dozen renovated *kâshta* (traditional homes) are now kept as museums. Also here are several art galleries, a couple of museums and some of Plovdiv's most interesting churches.

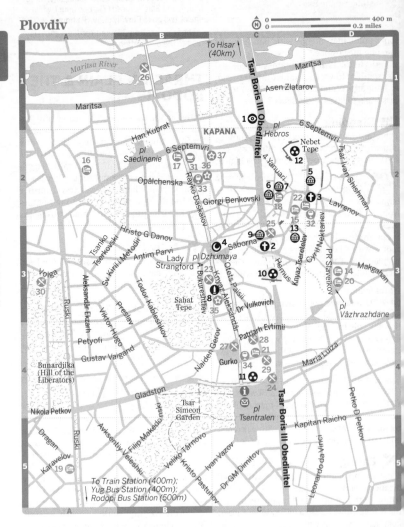

Plovdiv

Ethnographical Museum
MUSEUM

(ul Dr Chomakov 2; adult/student 5/1lv; ☺9am-noon & 2-5.30pm Tue-Thu & Sat-Sun, 2-5.30pm Fri) Housed in one of the Old Town's most striking buildings, dating from 1847, the Ethnographical Museum is worth visiting for its restored rooms and beautifully carved wooden ceilings alone. Exhibits include traditional costumes, musical instruments, beekeeping and wine-making equipment, and apparatus used for distilling attar of roses.

State Gallery of Fine Arts
ART GALLERY

(ul Sâborna 14; admission 3lv, free on Thu; ☺9.30am-12.30pm & 1-5.30pm Mon-Fri, from 10am Sat & Sun) This gallery houses an outstanding display of works by Bulgarian artists such as Goshka Datsov and Georgi Mashev, as well as more modern paintings and sculptures.

Hindliyan Kâshta
HISTORIC BUILDING

(ul Artin Gidikov 4; adult/student 5/1lv; ☺8.30am-4.30pm) Dating from 1835, this is probably the most rewarding of the National Revival houses. Its walls are adorned with colourful landscape paintings and it's filled with exquisite period furniture.

Gallery of Mexican Art
ART GALLERY

(ul Artin Gidikov 11; adult/student 2/1lv; ☺9.30am-5.30pm Mon-Fri, 10am-5pm Sat & Sun) For something completely different, this time-warp 1846 house has displays of 1970s Mexican woodcuts, serigraphs and copies of pre-Columbian art downstairs (a gift to the communist state in 1981), and paintings by local artist Tsanko Lavrenov upstairs, including his dramatic *Twenty Years of Socialist Construction*.

Ruins of Eumolpias
ANCIENT SITE

(ul Dr Chomakov; admission free; ☺24hr) The top of Nebet Tepe hill was the site of a Thracian settlement dating from around 5000 BC; the strategic location was later used by Macedonians, Romans, Byzantines, Bulgarians and Turks, so it's difficult to make much sense of the higgledy-piggledy walls, trenches and boulders that cover the area, but there are great views over the town.

Roman Theatre
ANCIENT SITE

(admission 3lv; ☺10am-5pm) A more impressive site, and one of Plovdiv's landmarks, is the amazing Roman Theatre. It's easily seen from the cafe set up outside the gates, but entry lets you tread on worn steps approaching

BULGARIA PLOVDIV

Plovdiv

their 2000th birthday. The theatre holds various events from June to August.

Church of Sveta Bogoroditsa CHURCH

(ul Sâborna 40) One of the Old Town's most active churches is the 19th-century Sveta Bogoroditsa, with a huge pink clock tower; note the murals of Turkish soldiers harassing chained Bulgarians inside.

Philipopolis Art Gallery ART GALLERY

(ul Sâborna 29; admission 3lv; ◷10am-7pm) Located in the 1865 Hadzhi Aleko House, this private gallery displays paintings by some of the leading lights of 19th- and 20th-century Bulgarian art. Temporary exhibitions of contemporary artists are also held here, and there's a garden restaurant at the back.

Church of Sveti Konstantin & Elena CHURCH

(ul Sâborna 24) Near the Ethnographical Museum, this mural-filled church is Plovdiv's oldest, dating from the 4th century, though most of what you see today was rebuilt in 1832. It contains a particularly fine iconostasis, painted by Zahari Zograf, with images of Adam and Eve.

Icon Museum MUSEUM

(ul Sâborna 22; adult/student 2/1lv; ◷9.30am-12.30pm & 1-5.30pm Mon-Fri, from 10am Sat & Sun) Next door to the Church of Sveti Konstantin & Elena, this small museum has a wonderful collection of luminous icons, dating from the 15th century onwards.

Dzhumaya Mosque MOSQUE

(Friday mosque; pl Dzhumaya; admission free; ◷dawn-dusk) The recently renovated Dzhumaya Mosque was once the largest of Plovdiv's 50 Ottoman mosques, and is one of the oldest in the Balkans, dating back to 1368, though it was reconstructed in 1784. The interior is simply adorned with a few painted flowers.

Outside, a modern **statue of Philip II of Macedon** (Alexander the Great's dad) looks over a small section of the **Roman stadium ruins**, consisting of a few rows of seats.

Centre for Contemporary Art ART GALLERY

(Chifte Banya; pl Hebros; adult/student 1/0.50lv; ◷during exhibitions 2-6pm Tue-Sun) North of the Old Town, this 16th-century Turkish baths with its multiple crumbly, domed-ceiling rooms makes a surreal exhibition space for temporary modern art exhibitions.

🛏 Sleeping

Plovdiv's hotels are always busy, but are often full during the international trade fairs (May and September) – rates can rise outrageously in these periods.

TOP CHOICE Hotel Romantica BOUTIQUE HOTEL €€
(✆622 675; www.hotelromantica.net; ul Gurko 17; r incl breakfast from 70lv; ❋ 🖥) Tucked down a small side-street off the main drag, the Romantica occupies a grand old ochre building adorned throughout with reproduction Impressionist paintings, and offering six large and tastefully furnished rooms. Most have small kitchen areas as well as TVs. The English-speaking staff are super-friendly, and you'll be treated to a different breakfast each morning.

Hotel Hebros LUXURY HOTEL €€€

(✆260 180; www.hebros-hotel.com; ul Stoilov 51; s/d incl breakfast €99/119; ❋ 🖥) Those looking for a classic Old Town sleep should opt for this inviting 10-room inn fully decked out in 19th-century style. There's a back courtyard, spa and sauna, plus one of Plovdiv's best restaurants.

Raisky Kat Hostel HOSTEL €

(✆268 849; www.raiskykat.hostel.com; ul Slaveikov 6; dm/d incl breakfast €10/24; @) With just five rooms, each with two or three single beds, this peaceful, family-run Old Town hostel is more like a cosy little hotel, and is well placed for sightseeing. Breakfast is served in the flagstone courtyard.

Hotel Renaissance BOUTIQUE HOTEL €€

(✆266 966; www.renaissance-bg.com; pl Vâzhrazhdane 1; s/d incl breakfast from €59/69; ❋ @) About halfway between the New and Old Towns, this attractive boutique hotel has just five colour-coordinated rooms with hand-painted walls.

Hotel Leipzig HOTEL €€

(✆654 000; www.leipzig.bg; bul Ruski 70; s/d incl breakfast from 69/78lv; P ❋ @) This recently remodelled communist-era tower block has gone all funky '60s retro, with lots of purple and pink, flowery wallpaper and animal-print upholstery. It makes a bold statement, and rooms are large and comfortable, with plasma TVs and fridges.

Plovdiv Guesthouse HOSTEL €

(✆622 432; www.plovdivguest.com; ul Sâborna 20; dm/s/d incl breakfast May-Sept €10/28/36, Oct-Apr €10/20/23; ◷ ❋ @) Home to Penguin Travel, this pink Old Town house has a couple of large dorms and a selection of twin rooms. There's a lounge and communal kitchen. It's strictly no smoking and no alcohol.

Notice that big-eared bloke on the main drag of ul Knyaz Aleksandâr? The seated statue on the central steps is a tribute to wisecracker **Milyu**, a legendary *zavek* (wanderer) from the early '70s of Plovdiv. Milyu, who died in 1974, was famous for coming to unsubtly 'listen in' to various conversations and pass on things he heard.

Another new cult character popular these days is the bearded '**Stefchu Avtografa**', who is trying to get into the Guinness Book of World Records for collecting the most autographs. Don't be surprised if he finds you. To quote one local: 'He's not exactly normal, but we love him.'

Hotel Ego   BUSINESS HOTEL €€
(☑636 261; www.hotelego.info; ul Eliezer Kaleff 2; s/d incl breakfast 59/74lv; ⓟ❋☗) The Ego is a modern business hotel on a quiet lane just north of bul 6 Septemvri. The 26 rooms and suites are a bit clinical, but clean and bright, with sparkly bathrooms. There's also a bar, sauna and spa.

Hiker's Hostel   HOSTEL €
(☑0885 194 553; www.hikers-hostel.org/pd; ul Sâborna 53; dm €7-10lv, d €25; ☗) This cosy backpacker stop occupies a little house in the Old Town, with clean dorms and comfy communal areas. The laid-back staff can arrange excursions. Breakfast is 2lv extra.

Hotel Elite   HOTEL €€
(☑624 537; www.hotel-elite.eu; ul Raiko Daskalov 53; s/d 49/59lv; @) A simple and reasonably central hotel, the Elite has small, clean rooms with TV and views of the Imaret mosque. There's cheap internet access downstairs, but no breakfast.

✗ Eating

In the underpass off pl Tsentralen, **Bani-charnitsa** (pizzas 1-1.50lv, banitsa 0.90lv; ⊗6am-6pm Mon-Sat) is a very popular takeaway bakery. The best spot for kebabs or falafel is **Alaeddin** (ul Naiden Gerov; kebabs 1.70lv, falafel 1.50lv; ⊗24hr).

TOP CHOICE **Malâk Bunardzhik**   BULGARIAN €
(ul Volga 1; mains 4-11lv; ⊗9am-midnight) Half hidden in the park up from bul Ruski, this restaurant, with tables set in quiet, leafy courtyard, is a great place for traditional Bulgarian food like *kebabche* and *tarator* soup, and hearty pork, chicken and fish dishes. There's occasional live music in the evenings.

Gusto   PIZZA €
(ul Otets Paisii 26; mains 6-15lv; ⊗9am-1am) Pizzas and pasta dishes (both very good) seem to be the mainstays at this busy place, but

there are plenty of alternatives on the menu, including steaks, chicken, duck and fish. The outdoor seats fill up quickly in the evenings.

Hemmingway   FINE DINING €€
(☑267 350; ul Gurko 10; mains 8-24lv; ⊗9am-1am) If you've had enough of shopska salad and *kebabche*, Hemmingway provides a cool, relaxing atmosphere and a vaguely Mediterranean menu. Meals include risottos, grilled chicken, duck dishes and scallops, or you could just sit back with a daiquiri and listen to the pianist tinkling in the corner.

Bulgarska Kâshta   BULGARIAN €
(ul Sâborna 31; mains 4-10lv; ⊗11.30am-3am) Traditional dishes like *gyuvech*, a kind of claypot stew with cheese and vegetables (5lv to 7lv) and *patatnik*, a mix of potato and bacon (5lv), are served at rustic outdoor tables or in a cosy interior.

Chilli   CAFE €
(Maritsa Bridge; mains 3-6lv; ⊗11am-8pm) On the pedestrian bridge over the Maritsa, this simple cafeteria offers cheap dishes like chicken chops, sausages, soups and fish, with great river views. It's best for lunch, as things tend to dry up later in the day.

Dreams   CAFE €
(pl Stambolov; cakes from 3lv) You'll struggle to find a free seat at this outdoor cafe, famous for its desserts, sandwiches and cocktails.

🍷 Drinking

Chocolate   CAFE
(ul Daskalov 48; cocktails 3-3.50lv ⊗7am-11pm Mon-Fri, 9am-11pm Sat-Sun) With outdoor seating both sides of the road, this place serves a colourful range of both alcoholic and non-alcoholic cocktails, as well as light meals.

Vinalia   WINE BAR
(cnr ul Knyaz Aleksândar & ul Gurko; wine 3lv per glass; ⊗10am-midnight) This central wine bar

BULGARIA PLOVDIV

offers a huge list of Bulgarian wines to sip while munching your way through various tapas dishes (from 3.90lv). Bottles cost from 9lv to 80lv.

Marmalad
BAR

(ul Bratya Pulievi 3; cocktails 3lv; ☺9am-2am) On a side lane, trendy Marmalad has cream leather booths and stools on old wooden floors. It's popular with local dress-uppers who sip cocktails here before heading to the clubs.

King's Stable
BAR

(ul Sâborna; cocktails 3.50lv; ☺8.30am-2am Apr-Sep) This great open-air bar – behind a host of Old Town buildings – serves drinks and snacks at a leisurely pace.

☆ Entertainment

Much of the nightlife lingers around the Kapana district, around ul Benkovski north of Dzhumaya mosque. Find club, restaurant and cinema listings in *Programata* and *Plovdiv Guide* (both free).

Petnoto
CLUB

(ul Yoakim Gruev 36) Petnoto claims an underground status and features local bands and DJs plus jazz sessions on Monday evenings and rock on Thursdays.

Infi Folk Deluxe
CLUB

(ul Bratya Pulievi 4) With a name that cheesy, there's no prizes for guessing that this is the place to go for full-on *chalga,* with live performances most nights. It's a popular student hang-out.

Caligula
GAY & LESBIAN

(ul Knyaz Aleksandâr 30) Off the main strip, Plovdiv's only gay club appeals to folks of all stripes.

❶ Information

Foreign-exchange offices and ATMs abound along ul Knyaz Aleksandâr and also on ul Ivan Vazov.

Internet access is available (to nonguests) at Hotel Elite and Plovdiv Guesthouse.

Main post office (pl Tsentralen; ☺7am-7pm Mon-Sat, 7-11am Sun) Has several computers with online access, and phone booths on the ground floor (open 7am to 10pm).

Tourist information centre (☏656 794; www.plovdiv-tour.info; pl Tsentralen; ☺9am-6pm Mon-Fri, 10am-2pm Sat & Sun) Next to the post office, it can help find private accommodation.

Unicredit Bulbank (ul Ivan Vazov 4; ☺8am-6pm Mon-Fri)

❶ Getting There & Away

Bus

Plovdiv has three bus stations: the main **Yug bus terminal** (ul Hristo Botev), 100m northeast of the train station; the more modern **Rodopi bus terminal**, reached by underground passageway from the train station; and the **Sever bus terminal**, 1.5km north of the river. The Yug and Rodopi bus stations both hold bags for 1lv per day.

Sample fares follow; buses leave/arrive at Yug unless otherwise noted:

Bansko (12lv, four hours, three daily)

Burgas (20lv, four hours, four daily)

Hisar (3.20lv, one hour, every one to two hours)

Kârdzhali (12lv, 2½ hours, every two hours) From Rodopi.

Kazanlâk (9lv, two hours, three daily) From Sever.

Koprivshtitsa (10lv, two hours, one daily) Departs 4.30pm from Sever.

Smolyan (9lv, 2½ hours, hourly 6am to 7pm except noon) From Rodopi.

Sofia (12lv, two hours, once or twice hourly 6am to 8pm)

Varna (26lv, seven hours, two daily)

Veliko Târnovo (15lv, 4½ hours, four daily) From Sever.

Buses to Athens go via Sofia. There's also at least six daily buses to İstanbul.

Train

Plovdiv's **train station** (bul Hristo Botev) serves the Sofia–Burgas line and has 24-hour luggage storage (3lv per piece per day).

A dozen or so daily trains go to Sofia (10.20lv, 2½ hours).

There are also direct services to Burgas (13.40lv, 4½ to five hours, five daily), Veliko Târnovo (11lv, five hours, one daily) and Varna (16.70lv, 6½ hours, four daily). Other destinations may mean a change in Stara Zagora.

A nightly train to İstanbul (49lv, 11 hours) leaves at 9.35pm. The train to Belgrade requires a change in Sofia. For international tickets, go to nearby **Rila Bureau** (☏643 120; bul Hristo Botev 31a; ☺7.30am-7.30pm Mon-Fri, 8am-6pm Sat summer, 7.30am-5.30pm Mon-Fri, 8am-5pm Sat winter).

❶ Getting Around

It's easy to get around Plovdiv's centre by foot. On arrival, take bus 7, 20 or 26 in front of the train station (1lv; buy ticket on board) and exit on ul Tsar III Obedinitel past the tunnel to reach the Old Town.

Around Plovdiv

About 20km south of Plovdiv is the **Asenovgrad Fortress**, a renovated mountaintop fortress built in the 11th century. It's about 4km south of the unremarkable town of Asenovgrad on the road to Smolyan.

Another 7km south (past the Chepelarska Gorge), **Bachkovo Monastery** (admission free; ☻6am-10pm) is Bulgaria's second biggest, founded in 1083 and restored in the 17th century. In Bachkovo's central courtyard, the 17th century **Church of Sveta Bogoroditsa** houses murals by Zahari Zograf and an icon of the Virgin, which legend claims was painted from life by St Luke, though it dates from the 14th century. A smaller courtyard contains the rarely open **Church of Sveti Nikolai** built in 1836 and decorated with a striking Last Judgement scene, again by Zograf. There are several hiking trails nearby, indicated on a signboard near the monastery entrance.

Bachkovo is an easy day trip from Plovdiv. Catch one of the frequent buses to Smolyan and ask to be dropped off near the Bachkovo entrance (there are a couple of restaurants and lots of souvenir stalls heading uphill).

Buses to Asenovgrad (3lv, 30 minutes, at least hourly from 6.50am to 6.20pm) leave from Plovdiv's Yug Bus Terminal but there is no public transport to the fortress.

Hisar ХИСАР

☑0337 / POP 10,000

Hisar, also known as Hisarya, has been a therapeutic spa centre since Roman times, when it was named Diokletianopolis, after the Emperor Diocletian. It's a small, peaceful town, with attractive public gardens and 22 active mineral springs, whose waters are alleged to have all kinds of benefits, from 'breaking down fat tissue' to 'stimulating gastric secretion', and there are always crowds of locals filling up bottles at each fountain. There are numerous clinics and pharmacies dotted around, and most hotels offer spa treatments of some sort.

Hisar also has the most extensive and impressive Roman ruins in Bulgaria, which are all free to explore, including lengthy walls, vast gateways and bath houses. They seem to be all over town, but there are no explanations anywhere.

From the bus station, head down the main road (ul Hristo Botev) for around 100m and turn right, following the sign to the 'Archaeological Reserve'; you'll soon arrive at the **Momina Salza Park**, where one of the main springs is located, in a rather grand classical colonnade. There are scattered ruins in the park, including a Roman bath house. Hisar's **Archaeological Museum** (ul Stamboliyiski 8; admission 2lv; ☻8-11.30am & 1-4.30pm Tue-Sun) is well hidden, off one of the dusty side streets opposite the park (head up ul Markov and turn left). It has a few local finds, a scale model of the Roman town and folk costumes.

There are plenty of hotels if you want to stay. The **Hotel Galeri** (☑62085; www.hotelgaleri.net; ul Gurko 15; s/d from 50/55lv; ✸@✉) is an excellent-value modern hotel complex with indoor and outdoor pools and spa centre. The nearby **Hotel Chinar** (☑62299; www.hotelchinar.bg; ul Vasil Petrovich 5; s/d from 80/90lv; ✸☏) has a relaxed ambience, spa and very good restaurant.

The **Natsional** (ul Gurko 12; mains 5-15lv) is a relaxed *mehana* restaurant set around a flowery courtyard, offering the usual nourishing Bulgarian grills and stews.

There are several buses daily from Hisar to Plovdiv (3.20lv, one hour), one to Sofia, leaving at 3.50pm (16lv, three hours) and one to Veliko Tărnovo at 8.45am (15lv, 3½ hours), going via Kazanlâk (9lv, two hours).

Smolyan СМОЛЯН

☑0301 / POP 32,800

Very long and very narrow, Smolyan is a convenient Rodopi hub surrounded by steep, forested mountains. Despite the pretty rural setting, the town itself (a modern amalgamation of four villages) is a fairly lacklustre place with no real centre, but it does have a couple of interesting attractions, and all-important bus links into deeper, more rewarding Rodopi villages.

Buses arrive near the west end of long bul Bulgaria (at the 'old centre'). About 200m to the east it becomes a pedestrian thoroughfare, where you'll find banks and ATMs.

Another 1km east on bul Bulgaria, near the museums, is the **tourist office** (☑62 530; www.smolyan.com; bul Bulgaria 5; ☻9am-5.30pm Mon-Fri), with handouts on hikes and accommodation.

◉ Sights

Planetarium MUSEUM

(☑83 074; www.planetarium-sm.org; admission 10lv, minimum 5 visitors; ☻English shows 2pm)

Hisar has been famous for its steaming mineral water for centuries, but how did these springs first materialise? Well, according to a typically colourful local legend, this is how the the **Momina Salza** spring came into being; a beautiful, and very virtuous, local woman spurned the advances of a powerful Ottoman lord, and as punishment for this slight, he took her prisoner and forced her to serve food naked at a banquet for a few of his chums, no doubt twirling his moustache and laughing cruelly as she did so. As she approached him, she whacked him over the head with a tray of sweets, killing him. The woman was immediately taken away and burned at the stake, and, as she was enveloped in the flames, her tears fell to the ground, and a hot spring gushed forth, and still flows today.

Bulgaria's biggest public observatory, Smolyan's Planetarium features a domed-ceiling 'space odyssey' show (about 40 minutes, also in French and German).

Historical Museum MUSEUM
(pl Bulgaria 3; adult/student 5/3lv; ⊙9am-noon & 1-5pm Tue-Sun) This interesting museum, up several flights of steps behind the civic centre, fills three floors with local Thracian finds, traditional musical instruments and folk costumes, including hairy *Kuker* outfits.

🛏 Sleeping

The tourist office arranges private accommodation (about 20lv per person). Ask about camping areas in the hills outside town.

Three Fir-Tree House B&B €
(✆64 281; www.trieli.hit.bg; ul Srednogorets 1; s/d 30/40lv; @) The motherly owner of this charming small hotel speaks English and German, and serves up wonderful homemade breakfasts for 5lv. Rooms are clean and simple, with tiled floors and shared bathrooms. It's down the steps at the western end of bul Bulgaria.

Hotel Luxor BUSINESS HOTEL €€
(✆63 317; www.luxor-bg.com; bul Bulgaria 51; s/d incl breakfast €21/31; P✳@) This shiny three-star business hotel is a bit bland, but has spacious rooms and a good range of amenities including a restaurant, sauna and gym.

🍴 Eating

There are plenty of restaurants along bul Bulgaria offering the usual choice of pizzas or sausagey Bulgarian standards. For something a bit more special, try **Riben Dar** (✆63 220; ul Snezhanka 16; mains 6-12lv), around 800m north of bul Bulgaria in a complex with a cobbled courtyard and small lake. It specialises in fresh local fish

❶ Getting There & Around

Hourly buses leave Smolyan's **bus station** to Plovdiv (9lv, 2½ hours), stopping in Pamporovo. Smolyan has less-frequent links into the mountains, including half a dozen buses to Shiroka Lâka (about 4lv, 40 minutes).

A few buses leave for Sofia each day (28lv, four hours).

Buses to Kârdzhali (10lv to 12lv, three hours) leave twice daily from the **Ustovo bus station**, 10km east, reached by city bus 3.

City buses 1 and 2 go from the bus station past the pedestrian mall and museums.

Shiroka Lâka & Around
ШИРОКА ЛЪКА

✆03030 / POP 850

Pretty Shiroka Lâka, 24km west of Smolyan, is famed for its hump-backed bridges and picturesque National Revival–era houses. It's a small, quiet place, and everything of interest can be seen on a day trip. The best time to visit is the first Sunday in March, when locals adorn shaggy fur costumes during the **Kukeri Festival**.

The **tourist office** (✆233; www.rhodope.net; ul Kapitan Petko Voivoda 48; ⊙9am-5pm Tue-Sat), 100m east of the bus stop, sells maps and books private rooms.

The **Church of the Assumption**, built in 1834, is worth a look for the gleefully ghoulish fresco on the front showing a funeral procession attended by dancing devils, as well as the calmer saintly icons inside.

The village makes an excellent base for hiking and there are plenty of routes in the forested hills around. One goes a few hours up to **Gela village**; another goes up **Mt Perelik**.

About 36km east, **Trigrad** is a tiny village near the lovely Trigrad gorge, where you can take a tour of an impressive **cave** (admission 3lv; ⊙9am-5pm May-Sep). Opening times can change, though; check with the tourist office in Shiroka Lâka before you go. You can hike a few hours to **Yagodina** village, home to the region's longest cave. Buses to Trigrad go via Devin.

There are several small guesthouses around the village. **Kâshta James** (⌨0887 136 207 www.shirokalaka.com; s/d incl breakfast 40/60lv) is a renovated historical building with homely, traditional-style rooms and a tavern.

Buses between Devin and Smolyan stop here.

Kârdzhali & Around
КЪРДЖАЛИ

☑0361 / POP 45,000

A spread-out industrial town with two dammed lakes and a diverse mix of Turks and Bulgarians, Kârdzhali (named after a 17th-century Turkish general) remains far removed from most itineraries, and has little of interest in itself. However, it's a good jumping-off point for visiting Thracian archaeological sites in the region, and there's a border-crossing with Greece at Zlatograd, about 55km south.

◉ Sights

Regional History Museum   MUSEUM
(ul Republikanska 4; adult/student 2/1lv; ◷9am-noon & 1-4.30pm Tue-Sun) Housed in a grand 1930s building designed to be a Muslim *madrasa* (Islamic school), this museum has an interesting collection of Perperikon relics (and others from Thracian and Roman sites), plus some ethnographical and geological exhibits – most are signed in English.

Perperikon   ANCIENT SITE
(Перперикон; www.perperikon.bg; admission free) The recently rediscovered (and expanding) excavation site of Perperikon is about 20km east of town (brown signs lead the way). Atop a rocky bluff (a 15-minute walk up) are stunning indications of Thracian (and later Roman) life on a site first inhabited 7000 years ago. There's much to see: dug-out water tanks, tombs and walls – all supposedly part of the Temple of Dionysus and the location where Alexander the Great's destiny was prophesised.

You can go by a couple of daily buses to the nearby village of Gorna Krepost, where it's a 2km walk south to the turn-off, and 750m up to the parking lot.

Tatul   ANCIENT SITE
(Татул) About 27km southwest (east of Momchilgrad town) is the recent find of Tatul, an arched Thracian above-ground tomb reached by a short dung-splattered trail (there are lots of shepherds here). Apparently the first settlement here was around 6000 years ago. You'll need your own transport to get here.

🛏 Sleeping

Hotel Perperikon   HOTEL €€
(☑67 140; www.perperikonbg.com; ul Volga 3; s/d incl breakfast from 90/100lv; ℗✱@✱) This smart, modern and security-conscious hotel in downtown Kârdzhali offers the best facilities in town, with bright, attractive rooms, outdoor pool and terrace, restaurant and guarded parking lot.

Hotel Kârdjali   HOTEL €€
(☑82 354; www.hotel-kardjali.com; bul Belomorski 68; s/d incl breakfast €18/29; ✱@) Across from the bus station, about 1km south of the centre, Hotel Kârdjali has simple, modern rooms and friendly staff. There's also a small gym and sauna.

❶ Getting There & Around

From Kârdzhali bus station, buses go every two hours to Plovdiv (12lv, 2½ hours) and a couple daily to Smolyan (10lv to 12lv, three hours), which goes to Smolyan's Ustovo bus station, 10km east of main bus station.

CENTRAL BALKANS

Crossing Bulgaria's belly, this broad swipe of lovely mountains – called the Stara Planina – is striped with hiking trails and dotted with towns in 19th-century revival style. Some hiking paths can also be cross-country skied or cycled. Historic Veliko Târnovo is the most convenient stop, while windswept hubs (Kazanlâk and Shumen) are more off the beaten track. Check www.staraplanina.org for more information.

Some travellers find themselves changing trains or buses in the Stara Planina's outer reaches at Stara Zagora.

Koprivshtitsa
КОПРИВЩИЦА

☑07184 / POP 2700

About 85km east of Sofia (and about two centuries back in time), Koprivshtitsa is a unique museum-town, with almost 400 restored and protected historic buildings standing gracefully over quaint cobbled lanes. The village was the setting for the key 20 April 1876 Uprising against the Turks, and seems to have stood still ever since. It isn't exactly the easiest place to get to by public transport, but it's a peaceful and charming place to while away an afternoon.

The **re-enactment of the April Uprising** (curiously held on 1 May or 2 May) and the **Folklore Days Festival** (mid August) are popular events.

The **tourist information centre** (☑2191; pl 20 April; ☺9.30am-7pm summer, 10.30am-4.30pm winter) arranges horse-riding trips and sells town and hiking maps (3.50lv). There's an ATM next to the bus station.

◎ Sights

Six of Koprivshtitsa's traditional homes are now 'house museums', and an excellent value **combo ticket** (adult/student 5/2lv) will get you into them all; otherwise it's 3/1lv each. All are open 9am to 5.30pm summer, and 9am to 5pm winter, with Monday or Tuesday off (see listings).

Benkovski House   HISTORIC BUILDING
(ul Georgi Benkovski 5; ☺closed Tue) Exhibits on a cavalry commander killed in a Turkish ambush in 1876; there's a statue of him on horseback above the house.

Debelyanov House   HISTORIC BUILDING
(ul Dimcho Debelyanov 6; ☺closed Mon) This picturesque house with a lovely garden was once home to Dimcho Debelyanov, the 'tender poet' killed in WWI.

Kableshkov House   HISTORIC BUILDING
(ul Todor Kableshkov 8; ☺closed Mon) The home of the man said to have fired the first shot of the 1876 April Uprising, with beautiful wood-carvings and many interesting old photos.

Karavelov House   HISTORIC BUILDING
(ul Hadzhi Nencho Palaveev 39; ☺closed Tue) Three-section home where the brothers Karavelov grew up.

Lyutov House   HISTORIC BUILDING
(Topalov House; ul Nikola Belovezhdov 2; ☺closed Tue) The most colourful of the homes, with vibrant walls and ceilings.

Oskelov House   HISTORIC BUILDING
(ul Gereniloto 4; ☺closed Mon) One of the grandest examples of National Revival architecture in town, once home to a wealthy merchant.

🛏 Sleeping

The tourist office can help arrange private rooms (30lv to 45lv).

Hotel Dzhogolanova Kâshta   HOTEL €€
(☑2911; www.kopri-dk.com; ul Hadzhi Nencho Palaveev 89; s 42-68lv, d 50-80lv; @) Near the Benkovski House, this place has a selection of 11 brightly furnished rooms, suites and duplex apartments, and there's a good restaurant on site, too.

Hotel Borimechkova Kâshta   PENSION €
(☑0888 631 446; www.borimechkova-kashta.dir.bg; ul Hadzhi Nencho Palaveev 36; d 40lv) This traditional old home has five simple but cosy rooms with wooden ceilings and TVs. It's just off the main street, set in a peaceful garden with a BBQ.

Hotel Panorama   HOTEL €€
(☑2035; www.panoramata.com; ul Georgi Benkovski 40; s/d incl breakfast 45/60lv) A friendly English-speaking family runs this hotel about 300m south of the centre. There are lovely views and rooms are well kept and comfortable.

✗ Eating

Traditional *kâshtas* serve meaty meals and are found on side streets, some keeping seasonal hours. One good choice is **Dyado Liben** (ul Hadzhi Nencho Palaveev; dishes from 3lv), occupying a wonderful 1852 home.

❶ Getting There & Away

The **bus station** sends buses every couple of hours to Sofia's Traffic Market (10lv, two hours). A 6.30am bus (2pm on Sunday) leaves for Plovdiv (10lv, two hours).

Koprivshtitsa's **train station** is 10km north of town, and there's a connecting bus service, which can be irregular outside summer. At the time of research, extensive work on the rail line meant there were no direct trains to Sofia; there are normally three or four daily trains to Sofia (2½ hours) and one to Burgas (five hours); for Plovdiv, you have to change in Karlovo.

Kazanlâk & Around
КАЗАНЛЪК
☑0431 / POP 82,500

Although hardly the most attractive or outwardly interesting town in Bulgaria, slightly scruffy Kazanlâk is worth a stopover as a base for exploring the 'Valley of Roses' to the west and the 'Valley of Thracian Kings' a few kilometres north. The June bloom ushers in the annual three-day **Rose Festival** (www.rose-fes tival.com; finishing the 1st Sun in Jun) culminating in the crowning of the festival queen. Kazanlâk's most rewarding draws, though, are the nearby Thracian sites, including 40 tombs.

The central pl Sevtopolis is about 400m north of the train and bus stations (via ul Rozova Dolina), with banks, an internet cafe and the **tourist information centre** (☑62817; ul Iskra 4; ⊗8am-1pm & 2-6pm Mon-Fri).

◉ Sights
IN KAZANLÂK
Iskra Museum & Art Gallery MUSEUM
(ul Slaveikov 8; adult/student 3/1lv; ⊗9am-5pm) A couple of blocks north of pl Sevtopolis, the Iskra Museum & Art Gallery has plenty of local archaeological finds, including pottery and jewellery from the region's many Thracian tombs. Upstairs is a gallery of Bulgarian paintings. Staff can help you visit some of the Thracian tombs (not listed here) that are otherwise kept locked up.

Tyulbe Park ANCIENT SITE
Kazanlâk's Tyulbe Park (about 300m northeast of the centre) houses the remarkably well-preserved 4th-century BC domed **Thracian Tomb** (admission 20lv; ⊗9am-5pm Apr-Oct), a Unesco World Heritage site with paintings of chariot races and feasting; only 20 people per day can visit, and it's often closed. If it is, or you don't want to part with 20lv, you can visit the nearby **tomb copy** (admission 3lv; ⊗9am-5pm Apr-Oct), which looks identical to the untrained eye.

Museum of the Roses MUSEUM
(ul Osvobozhdenie; adult/student 3/1lv; ⊗9am-5pm Apr-Oct) At the northern end of Kazanlâk, 2.5km towards Shipka, you can stop by the Museum of the Roses, a small exhibition on the history of rose cultivation, with a shop selling rose oil products.

VALLEY OF THRACIAN KINGS
Mogila ANCIENT SITE
Outside town lie 1500 Thracian *mogila* (burial mounds), though only a few have been excavated. The only one keeping regular hours is **Golyama Kosmatka** (Shipka village; adult/student 3/1lv; ⊗9am-5pm Apr-Oct), with three chambers where the 5th-century BC tomb of Seuthes III was found in 2004. The king's gold wine cups, wreath and bronze armour were discovered here, along with an exquisite bronze head, identified as coming from a statue of Seuthes, ritually buried at the tomb entrance. You can see a replica here;

the original is now at Sofia's Archaeological Museum (p150). Contact the Iskra Museum about getting a guide (and keys) to visit other tombs in the area, such as **Svetitsa**, which also yielded rich gold treasures.

🍴 Sleeping & Eating
Hotel Teres HOTEL €€
(☑64272; www.hotelteres.com; ul Nikola Petkov; s/d incl breakfast 50/64lv; 🕸@) Located near the entrance to Tyulbe Park, this is a friendly modern place with cosy rooms.

Hotel Palas HOTEL €€
(☑62311; www.hotel-palas.com; ul Petko Stainov 9; s/d 80/110lv; ⊖🕸🛜🍴) One of Kazanlâk's classier hotels, the Palas has good-sized rooms, a spa centre and an excellent restaurant.

You can find pizzerias and cafes around pl Sevtopolis in Kazanlâk, including **New York Bar & Grill** (pl Sevtopolis; pizza from 5lv).

❶ Getting There & Away
Kazanlâk's **bus station** (ul Kenali) sends a handful of daily buses to Sofia (16lv, three hours), Veliko Târnovo (15lv to 20lv, three hours) and Plovdiv (9lv, two hours). City bus 6 goes to Shipka village.

Across the street, Kazanlâk's **train station** (ul Sofronii) sends six daily trains to Sofia (10.40lv, 3½ hours) and two to Burgas (10.40lv, three hours).

Veliko Târnovo
ВЕЛИКО ТЪРНОВО
☑062 / POP 72,000
Clinging to a sharp S-shaped gorge split by a snaking river, Veliko Târnovo is one of the real highlights of Bulgaria. This medieval capital (1185–1393) and major university town is a pleasure to explore, despite the seemingly endless traffic and curious lack of pedestrian crossings. It's filled with days of potential, including hill hikes, hill towns, hill climbs and the most impressive ruined citadel in the country.

From the Yug Bus Terminal, ul Hristo Botev climbs north to ul Nezavisimost and the town centre. A taxi should cost no more than 3lv.

The **International Folklore Festival** takes place in Veliko Târnovo over three weeks in late June and early July, with traditional music and dance performances staged around town.

BULGARIA CENTRAL BALKANS

Veliko Târnovo

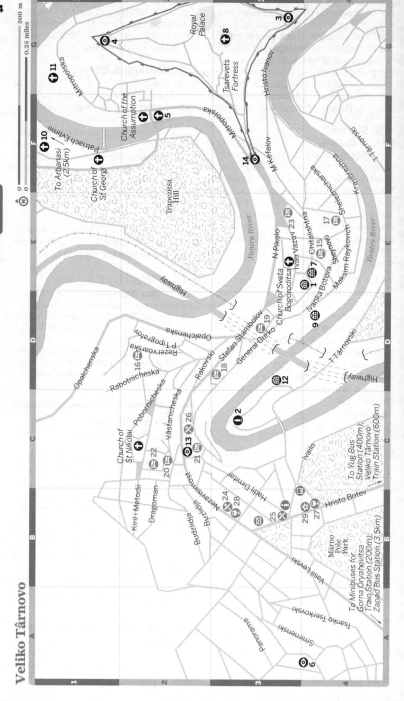

Sights

Veliko Târnovo has many attractions clamouring for your cash, but if you're pressed for time, the Tsarevets Fortress is by far the most worthwhile. The town's museums, most charging a rather steep 6lv a go, are perhaps less of a must-see.

Fun walks are free though. A great one goes up to the nearby village of Arbanasi. In town, be sure to walk along ul Gurko, Veliko Târnovo's oldest street, which twists its way along the gorge.

Tsarevets Fortress   ANCIENT SITE
(adult/student 6/2lv; ☺8am-7pm Apr-Sep, 9am-5pm Oct-Mar) About a kilometre from the centre, this mammoth fortress sprawls over a large and commanding site. What you see today – a triangular, high-walled fortress with the remains of more than 400 houses and 18 churches – was largely built between the 5th and 12th centuries.

Be careful when wandering around: there are lots of holes, broken steps, loose stonework and unfenced drops. Also, as signs around the complex warn, 'don't walk on the fortress walls, as there is a probability of falling down.' And indeed there is.

From the **main gate**, follow the left wall past a **watch tower** to the northern end where you can see **execution rock**, from where convicted traitors were hurled into the river below. Back south, a giant Bulgarian flag flies from the ruined **Royal Palace**, which has several empty rooms you can

look around. Its high-up neighbour is the renovated **patriarch's complex**. Inside the church are ugly grey, modern murals, while at the back of the church there's a **scenic elevator** (2lv), whisking you to the top for panoramic views of the fortress. Back near the main gate, you can follow the south wall to the **Baldwin Tower**, named after naughty Baldwin of Flanders, who led a Crusader army against Christian Constantinople in 1204, declared himself Byzantine Emperor, and was imprisoned and executed here a year later after invading Bulgaria.

Buses 20, 400 and 110 make the trip between the centre and the site.

MUSEUMS

Archaeological Museum   MUSEUM
(ul Ivan Vazov; adult/student 6/2lv; ☺9am-6pm Tue-Sun) Down a flight of steps from ul Ivan Vazov, this museum has an interesting but poorly labelled collection, running from prehistoric flint tools and Roman pots downstairs to more visually arresting medieval chainmail, weapons and gold jewellery upstairs. You can't miss the colourful patriotic murals depicting Bulgarian tsars on the stairwell.

Museum of National Revival   MUSEUM
(ul Ivan Vazov; adult/student 6/2lv; ☺9am-6pm Wed-Mon) Next door to the Archaeological Museum, this building was where the 1872 National Assembly was held, producing the country's first constitution. It's full of photos,

documents and portraits of local and national worthies.

Sarafkina Kâshta
MUSEUM

(ul General Gurko 88; adult/student 6/2lv; ⊙9am-6pm Mon-Fri) This two-storey former banker's home, built in 1861, displays period furnishings, traditional costumes and photographs of the old town.

State Art Gallery
ART GALLERY

(Asenovtsi Park; adult/student 3/1lv, free on Thu; ⊙10am-6pm Tue-Sun) This large gallery, set dramatically on the little finger of land poking into the Yantra, holds two floors of Bulgarian paintings, including a permanent collection of Veliko Târnovo landscapes and Italian sketches by local artist Boris Denev. In front stands the huge 1985 **Asenevs Monument** depicting medieval Bulgarian tsars.

CHURCHES & MONASTERIES

Forty Holy Martyrs Church
CHURCH

(ul Mitropolska; adult/student 5/1lv; ⊙9am-5.30pm) The Asenova quarter has many churches. Walking there from the Tsarevets gate, you first pass the Forty Holy Martyrs Church. It dates from 1230, and King Kaloyan's tomb was found here in 2004, but so much is reconstructed that feeling the history takes imagination.

St Peter & St Paul Church
CHURCH

(ul Mitropolska; adult/student 4/2lv; ⊙9am-6pm) Probably more rewarding for most is the St Peter & St Paul Church, it's past the bridge. Inside are fragments of murals from the 14th to 17th centuries.

St Dimitâr Church
CHURCH

(ul Patriarh Evtimii) Across the wooden pedestrian bridge, you can reach the often-closed, Byzantine-influenced St Dimitâr Church, Veliko Târnovo's oldest church, where the Assen brothers launched their rebellion in 1185. Ask at the Tsarevets gate about unlocking churches if they're closed.

⚡ Activities

Most of the hostels offer excursions and various outdoor activities.

Ask at the tourist centre about horse riding in Arbanasi and rock climbing and hiking trails in the area.

Trapezitsa
ROCK CLIMBING

(☏635 823; www.trapezitca1902.com; ul Stefan Stambolov 79; ⊙9am-6pm Mon-Fri) True to its website, Trapezitsa dates from 1902, arranges rock-climbing trips, sells a climbing guide

(6lv) and can point you to local climbing or biking clubs. Nearby climbs include Trinity Monastery and Usteto (2km south).

Gorgona
CYCLING

(☏601 400; www.gorgona-shop.com, in Bulgarian; ul Zelenka 2; ⊙10am-1pm & 2-7pm Mon-Fri, 10am-2pm Sat) For biking options, Gorgona rents out mountain bikes (10lv per day) and helmets (2lv per day) and knows good trails to ride. Head up the steps across ul Nezavisimost from the post office.

🛏 Sleeping

Be wary of the touts offering private rooms at the bus and train stations; these places are often far from the centre and you're probably better off going to a reputable hostel, most of which offer free pick-ups from the stations.

Nomads Hostel
HOSTEL €

(☏603 092; www.nomadshostel.com; ul General Gurko 27; dm incl breakfast 20-22lv, s 40lv, d 50-54lv; ✳@) The only air-conditioned hostel in town, Nomads enjoys a quiet and picturesque location on historic ul Gurko, with all rooms facing the river down below, and a balcony to sit out on.

Phoenix Hostel
HOSTEL €

(☏603 112; www.phoenixhostel.com; ul Daskalov 12; dm/d incl breakfast 20/50lv; @⊜) Run by a welcoming, well-travelled British couple, this sociable hostel occupies a lovely old timber-framed house in the Varosha district, with a peaceful common room (pointedly with no TV) and kitchen. Various day trips can be arranged.

TOP CHOICE Hotel Bolyarski
HOTEL €€

(☏613 200; www.bolyarski.com; ul Stefan Stambolov 53a; s/d incl breakfast from 70/110lv; ℙ✳☎≋) In the centre of town, Bolyarski has large, comfortable rooms, many with fantastic views over the river gorge. It's a bargain at this price, and there's a gym staffed by friendly instructors, spa and pool downstairs, and a terrace restaurant.

Studio Hotel
LUXURY HOTEL €€

(☏604 010; www.studiohotel-vt.com; ul Todor Lefterov 4; s/d incl breakfast from 89/90lv; ✳@) The 13-room Studio boasts some surprisingly chic rooms with black carpet and bold wallpaper. Some have fantastic fortress views, and breakfast is served on a breezy outside terrace.

Ivan's House
PENSION €

(☏0886 438 370; www.ivanovata-kashta.com; ul Vâstanicheska 5; s/d/apt 25/40/50lv; ✳) On a cobbled side street in the town centre, Ivan's is good value. It feels like staying in a private home, with a choice of small, simple but bright rooms, all with bathrooms and TVs, and guests have use of a kitchen.

Hikers Hostel
HOSTEL €

(☎0889 691 661; www.hikers-hostel.org; ul Rezevoarska 91; campsites/dm/d incl breakfast 14/20/52lv; 🛜) Way up a steep cobbled path, this small hostel is a hike to reach but has superb views – the upstairs balcony, with couches, looks onto the fortress's light show. There are a couple of tents on the patio if you want to sleep alfresco.

Hostel Mostel
HOSTEL €

(☎0897 859 359; www.hostelmostel.com; ul Iordan Indjeto 10; campsites/dm/s/d incl breakfast 18/20/46/60lv; @) Just 150m from the Tsarevets Fortress, Mostel has bright dorms, as well as a few en suite doubles. There's a BBQ in the garden, bar and lounge, and home-made meals are available.

Beiskata Kâshta
BOUTIQUE HOTEL €€

(☎602 090; www.beiskata.com; ul Chitalishtna 4; r incl breakfast 60-130lv; ❋@) With a traditional tavern at the front, this historic seven-room guesthouse has understated antique-style furnishings and a cosy atmosphere.

Hotel Kiev
HOTEL €€

(☎600 572; www.hotelkiev.eu; ul Velchova Zavera 4; s/d 40/55lv; ❋) The Kiev occupies a stately 1930s building in the town centre and offers fairly plain but large rooms that are quite good value. Staff are helpful and there's a neat little lobby bar.

✖ Eating

Gastronomes will find slim pickings in Veliko Târnovo, but there are a few OK restaurants scattered around the centre.

Ego Pizza
PIZZA €

(ul Nezavisimost 17; pizzas 5-10lv) This spacious place is a very popular spot for pizzas, with an outdoor terrace overlooking the river. Service is quick and pizzas are huge. Alternatives include chicken and pork dishes.

Mehana Gurko
BULGARIAN €

(ul General Gurko 33; mains 4-7lv) This traditional-style tavern, downstairs from the hotel of the same name, serves up predictable Bulgarian favourites like *kyufte* (meatballs), soups and salads in relaxed, folksy surroundings.

H Bogart
BULGARIAN €

(ul Hristo Botev; mains 4-9lv) Opposite the tourist office, this cheery place offers a big menu

of Bulgarian standards, plus pizzas and fish. Best are the *gyuvetcheta* dishes (clay-pot meals), available in meat or veggie versions (4lv to 6lv). They have some weird salad ideas though: the 'English' salad features carrots and bananas.

🍷 Drinking

Martin McNamara
PUB

(ul Nezavisimost 25; ⊘noon-late) This buzzing basement Irish pub has regular live music on Fridays and Saturdays, as well as jam sessions and party nights.

City Pub
PUB

(ul Hristo Botev 15; ⊘noon-1am) This big, brassy pub near the tourist office is popular with local students and sometimes has live music.

☆ Entertainment

Follow students to the latest clubs, such as **Spider** (ul Hristo Botev; admission 2-3lv), a two-floor dance club with dance areas around a barstool centre; access through a plain brown door next to the City Pub.

ℹ Information

Era Internet (off ul Hristo Botev; per hr 1.20-1.40lv; ⊘24hr)

Main post office (ul Nezavisimost)

Postbank (ul Hristo Botev)

Tourist information centre (☎622 148; www.velikoturnovo.info; ul Hristo Botev 5; ⊘9am-6pm Mon-Fri, Mon-Sat summer) Helpful English-speaking staff can help book accommodation and rent cars.

ℹ Getting There & Away

Bus

Veliko Târnovo has three bus stations. **Yug Bus Terminal** (ul Hristo Botev), a 15-minute walk downhill from the centre, and the bus stand of **Etap Adress** (Hotel Etâr, ul Ivailo 2) serve most bigger, long-distance destinations. For buses to Sofia (18lv, 3½ hours) or Varna (16lv, 3½ hours), it's easiest to catch one of the 10 daily stopping at Etap Adress, which also sends buses to Shumen (13lv, two hours). Yug serves these destinations, and sends one daily bus to Burgas (20lv to 26lv, about four hours) at 7.30am, a midday bus with a quick transfer in Ruse to Bucharest and a night bus to İstanbul.

There are several daily buses to Ruse (10lv, 2½ hours), three to Plovdiv (15lv, 4½ hours) and a few to Burgas from the **Zapad Bus Terminal**, 4km west of the centre, which also has buses to regional destinations including Tryavna and Gabrovo. Bus 10, among others, heads west to the terminal from ul Vasil Levski.

Train

Veliko Târnovo's small **train station**, 1.5km south of town, sends about five direct trains a day to Ruse (5.90lv to 6.80lv, about three hours), one to Plovdiv (11lv, five hours) and eight to Tryavna (3.80lv, 45 minutes). There are five daily trains to Sofia (16.30lv, five to six hours), and four to Varna (12.50lv, four or five hours) require a change at the busier **Gorna Oryakhovitsa train station**, 13km north of town. Minibuses along ul Vasil Levski, or bus 10 east from the centre, head there every 10 or 15 minutes; a taxi is about 10lv.

An overnight train to İstanbul (14 hours) and mid-morning train to Bucharest (six hours) stop in Veliko Târnovo. Buy international tickets at **Rila Bureau** (☑622 130; ul Tsar Kolyan; ☺8amnoon & 1-6.30pm Mon-Fri), in the alley behind the information centre.

There's a walkway from the train platform (away from station) that connects to an underpass leading to ul Hristo Botev. Catch bus 4, 5, 13, 30 or 70 heading south from outside the station to reach the centre. A taxi will cost about 5lv.

Around Veliko Târnovo

With your own set of wheels, there are plenty of interesting and easy day-trip options around Veliko Târnovo. Besides those places already mentioned here, you could try the historic hill town of **Elena** (37km southeast), the stark Roman ruins of **Nikopolis-ad-Istrum** (admission 4lv; 20km north) and the valley hiking trails (and eerie caves) at **Emen** (27km northwest).

Several of the hostels in town run organised day trips and activities, and rent bikes.

ARBANASI АРБАНАСИ
♩062 / POP 1500

In Târnovo's glory years, the walled villas of hilltop Arbanasi, 4km to the northeast, housed much of the king's royal entourage. It's still an affluent area, filled with very swish private villas.

The one site most worth seeking out is the 16th-century **Nativity Church** (adult/student 6/2lv; ☺9am-5pm), 200m west of the bus stop. Inside it bursts with colourful, floor-to-ceiling murals depicting 3500 separate figures in 2000 scenes, including the evocative 'wheel of life'. The elegant iconostases were carved by master craftsmen from Tryavna.

You can reach Arbanasi via a 90-minute **hiking trail**. Walk through the Asenova Quarter on the west side of Tsarevets then cross a pedestrian bridge; the trail begins below the bridge.

The enticingly named **Wine Palace Hotel** (☑600 610; www.winpalace.net; s/d from 58/68lv; ❋❷❄), about 300m north of the bus stop, doesn't disappoint, with a choice of snug rooms, spa centre, pool and traditional-style restaurant, where, of course, you can try an array of local wines.

It's about 5lv to reach Arbanasi by taxi from Veliko Târnovo. Some Gorna Oryakhovitsa–bound minibuses leave from ul Vasil Levski in Veliko Târnovo stop in Arbanasi (all come within a 700m walk of the centre).

PREOBRAZHENSKI MONASTERY
ПРИОБРАЖЕНСКИ МАНАСТИР

Dating from 1360, this hilltop **monastery** (admission 2lv) can be reached via the Ruse road, 6km north of the centre, or by a 90-minute hike beginning near the Hikers Hostel (turn right on a path going through a small playground). Its location – on a cliff below a higher wall – is gorgeous, as are the murals by Zahari Zograf (of Rila Monastery fame). The giant boulders strewn around the compound are narrow misses from a 1991 earthquake. Looking west, you can see hilltop **Sveta Troitsa convent**.

DRYANOVO MONASTERY ДРЯНОВСКИ МАНАСТИР

Set beside a bubbling stream beneath limestone cliffs, this charming **monastery** (admission free; ☺9am-6pm) lies some 24km south of Veliko Târnovo. It was founded in the 12th century, but has been destroyed and rebuilt a number of times over the centuries. Behind is the **Bacho Kiro cave** (short/long tour 2/4lv; ☺9am-6pm Apr-Oct, 10am-4pm Nov-Mar), a damp, 3600m-long cave, featuring awesome stalactites and stalagmites. Guides take you through a well-lit 700m-long section.

Above is a **hiking trail** that links Dryanovo with nearby village Bozhentsite (15km). For a 45-minute loop, go left upstream from the monastery to a dark swimming hole, and up some *steep* steps to an overview near a Roman road; it continues on to the cave entrance.

There are bungalows and a small hotel nearby, and along the river a leafy open-air *mehana* serving Bulgarian food. Gabrovo-bound buses will stop at the turn-off (if requested), about 5km south of the town of Dryanovo, from where it's a 1.5km walk to the monastery.

TRYAVNA ТРЯВНА
♩0677 / POP 12,000

Bulgaria's pretty-as-a-postcard woodcarving capital, Tryavna is around 40km southwest of Veliko Tărnovo and is a visual delight of cobbled streets and beautifully restored National Revival architecture. Some of the houses are open to the public, showing off the intricate carvings inside.

From the neighbouring bus and train stations, walk along ul Angel Kânchev 400m (over the creek) to the centre, where you'll find a **tourist information centre** (☑2247; www.tryavna.bg; ul Angel Kânchev 33; ⊚9am-noon & 2-5pm Mon-Fri). Several hiking trails loop to nearby villages.

The town has about a dozen signed museums, traditional homes and churches to see. Some of the smaller places are closed on Mondays and Tuesdays. West of the tourist office, you'll find the **Archangel Michael Church** (admission 1lv), with elaborate woodcarvings and icons, and **Staroto Shkolo** (ul Angel Kânchev 7; admission 3lv; ⊚9am-6pm), an art museum in a former school, next to the chiming clock tower. It also displays a collection of timepieces.

Over the arched bridge to ul Slaveikov, 150m past the antiques shops, is the **Daskalov House** (ul Slaveikov 27; admission 3lv; ⊚9am-6pm), now home to Bulgaria's only dedicated museum of woodcarving, with many fine examples from the Tryavna school.

In the centre, **Hotel Hilez** (☑66 920; www.hilez.tryavna.biz; ul Stara Planina 17; s/d €45/60; ✹@) is a bright modern hotel with a restaurant.

From Veliko Tărnovo, it's best taking the train (3.80lv, 45 minutes). Otherwise there are frequent buses from Gabrovo (3lv, 25 minutes).

ETÂR ЕТЪР
☑066

Around 8km south of the town of Gabrovo, **Etâr Ethnographic Village Museum** (☑801 838; adult/student 4/2lv, guided tour in English 12lv; ⊚9am-6pm May-Sep, 9am-4.30pm Oct-Apr), is an interesting open-air museum complex with water-powered mills and National Revival–style buildings, plus workshops where you can watch traditional craftsmen and women at work, and buy their products, such as rugs, wood carvings, knives and pottery. There are also occasional concerts and music recitals.

If you want to stick around, the **Strannopriemnitsa Hotel** (☑810 580; www.etar.org/hotel; s/d incl breakfast 41/71lv) has a selection of bright, simple rooms with TVs right at the entrance to the complex, as well as a restaurant.

Buses go to/from Gabrovo every 20 to 45 minutes.

Shumen ШУМЕН
☑054 / POP 103,000

Usually bypassed by tourists on the way to or from the coast, Shumen lacks the quaint cobbles and National Revival prettiness of other towns. It does have an awful lot of greying concrete, but it's an easy-going place with some worthwhile museums, a park, an ancient fortress, grandiose communist monuments and plenty of cafes. It's also handy for nearby attractions like the Madara Reserve and the ruins of the medieval capital of Veliki Preslav.

The main square, pl Osvobozhdenie, is about 1km west of the neighbouring bus and train stations on bul Slavyanksi. Here you'll find ATMs, cafes, a post office and the **tourist information centre** (☑857 773; www.shumen.bg; bul Slavyanski 17; ⊚9am-5pm Mon-Fri).

⊙ Sights

Founders of the Bulgarian State Monument   MONUMENT

(admission 3lv; ⊚9am-7pm) The cubist-style Founders of the Bulgarian State Monument welcomes those who climb the 1.3km from the centre (or take a taxi). Its incredible horseback figures peer down from between crevices like stone Don Quixotes. The monument (ambitiously described as 'Europe's largest triptych mosaic') was built in 1981 to commemorate Bulgaria's 1300th birthday. There's rarely anyone around to sell you a ticket.

Shumen Fortress   ANCIENT SITE

(adult/student 3/1lv; ⊚9am-5pm Mon-Fri) On a hilltop 6km west of the centre, this massive fortress stands on a site dating back to the Iron Age, which has been occupied by Thracians, Romans and Byzantines; its golden age was in the 12th century but it was destroyed during the unsuccessful 1444 Crusade led by King Ladislas of Hungary against the Turks. A road marked 'Pametnik Sâzdateli na Bâlgarskata Dârzhava' meanders 3km to the Founders monument.

Tombul Mosque   MOSQUE

(☑802 875; ul Rakovski 21; admission 2lv; ⊚9am-6pm) The impressive 18th-century (and still active) Tombul Mosque, 500m southwest of pl Osvobozhdenie, is one of the largest on the Balkan peninsula, with a dramatic 25m-high dome and 40m-high minaret.

🛏 Sleeping & Eating

There are a couple of *mehana* restaurants on ul Tsar Osvoboditel.

Hotel Rai HOTEL €€
(📞802 670; www.hotel-rai.eu; ul Ohrid 26a; s/d €20/28; ✱@) In a quiet spot a few blocks south of pl Osvobozhdenie, the pink-and-yellow Rai is a welcoming family hotel with neatly furnished and very colourful rooms.

Hotel Solo HOTEL €€
(📞981 571; www.hotelsolo-bg.com; ul Volov 2; s/d incl breakfast €26/35; ✱@) Just off the main pedestrian thoroughfare in the town centre, the Solo has seven smart rooms with TVs and fridges, and there's a big outdoor terrace.

Acktion Center BUSINESS HOTEL €€
(📞801 081; www.acktioncenter.com; ul Drumev 12; r/apt 50/75lv; P✱@) North of the centre, this place has stylish rooms and apartments with a minimalist black-and-white decor scheme and some very cool bathrooms. There's also a gym, solarium and beauty centre.

ℹ Getting There & Away

Numerous buses en route to Sofia (28lv, 4½ hours) and Varna (10lv, 1½ hours) stop in Shumen. At least four buses daily go to Ruse (9lv, 2½ hours) and Veliko Târnovo (13lv, two hours).

Around nine daily direct trains leave for Varna (6.20lv, 1¾ hours), five for Sofia (17.70lv, 6½ hours), one to Plovdiv (16.70lv, 7½ hours) and one to Veliko Târnovo (8.10lv, 2½ hours). Trains to Ruse (8.30lv, 3½ hours) require a change in Kaspichan.

Madara МАДАРА

📞05313 / POP 1300

Off the main highway between Shumen and Varna, Madara is a simple village that's home to the original, endlessly reproduced horseman figure that appears on Bulgaria's stotinki coins. The enigmatic 23m bas-relief on a sheer rock wall at the **Madara National Historical & Archaeological Reserve** (admission 4lv; ⊙8am-7.30pm summer, 8am-5pm winter) depicts a horseman spearing a lion. It's believed to date from the 8th century, though some argue it's much older.

Afterwards follow a trail north and up 378 steps to a mountaintop **fortress**.

From Shumen, 16km west, buses reach Madara village (2lv, 30 minutes) five times daily, the last returning around 6.30pm. You can also take the train (1.50lv, five daily). From Madara village follow the road towards the mountain (just east), and take the left fork; it's a 2km walk slightly uphill.

Ruse РУСЕ

📞082 / POP 175,00

There's more than a touch of *mitteleuropa* grandness in Ruse (roo-*say*) that's not seen elsewhere in Bulgaria, boasting as it does a wealth of imposing, belle-époque architecture festooned with masks and swags, and neatly trimmed, leafy squares – as if a little chunk of Vienna had broken off and floated down the Danube. There are a few interesting museums to look around, and the nearby Rusenski Lom Nature Park is well worth exploring if you have the time.

The bus and train stations are at the end of ul Borisova, 2km south of the city centre.

Ruse's **March Days Music Festival** is held in the last two weeks of March.

⊙ Sights

A combined ticket for six city museums costs 5lv, but is valid only for one day.

Roman Fortress of Sexaginta Prista
ANCIENT SITE
(ul Tsar Kaloyan 2; adult/student 2/1lv; ⊙8.30am-noon & 1-5.30pm Tue-Sat) Near the river, you can explore the remains of this once mighty Roman fort, built around 70AD and housing some 600 soldiers at its peak. Apart from a few crumbling walls and columns, there's not much to see today, but the enthusiastic custodian will show you around and bring it to life. Sadly, a planned hotel next door has halted further promising excavations. There's also a WWII German bunker, where a few finds are kept. The more important pieces are now in the town's History Museum.

History Museum MUSEUM
(pl Battenberg 3; adult/student 4/1lv; ⊙9am-6pm) Exhibits start with 6000-year-old bone amulets and boomerangs, and continue through time with Thracian bronze helmets, Roman statues and 19th-century fashions. Most impressive, though, is the magnificent Borovo Treasure, a collection of silver cups and jugs decorated with Greek gods, from the 5th century BC.

Profit-Yielding Building NOTABLE BUILDING
(pl Svoboda) This huge, gloriously titled neo-baroque building dominates the western end of pl Svoboda. Built between 1898 and

BULGARIA RUSE

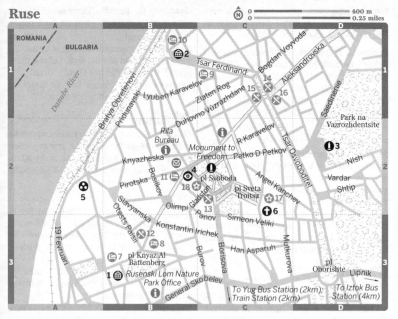

Ruse

⊕ Sights

1 History Museum	B3
2 Museum of the Urban Lifestyle in Ruse	B1
3 Pantheon of the National Revival	D2
4 Profit-Yielding Building	B2
5 Roman Fortress of Sexaginta Prista	A2
6 Sveta Troitsa Church	C2

⊜ Sleeping

7 Charlino Plaza	B3
8 Cosmopolitan	B3
9 English Guest House	C1
10 Riga Hotel	B1
11 Splendid Hotel	B2

✕ Eating

12 Chiflika	B3
13 Friendly House	C2
14 Gradski Hali	C1
15 Hlebozavod Ruse	C1
16 Ostankino	C1

✪ Entertainment

| 17 Ruse Opera House | C2 |
| 18 Sava Ognyanov Drama Theatre | B2 |

1902 by Viennese architects, it was intended as a home for the Dramatic Theatre (which is still here) and several shops. The rents from these were used to fund local schools, hence the name. These days it also houses a few restaurants.

Sveta Troitsa Church   CHURCH
(pl Sveta Troitsa; admission free; ⊙7am-6pm) At the eastern end of pl Sveta Troitsa, this church was built in 1632. Following the Ottoman rule that churches should be as unobtrusive as possible, the nave is below ground level,

with steps leading down from the entrance. It has a fine, gilt wood iconostatis and wooden pillars painted to look like marble, as well as some large and well-preserved icons.

Museum of the Urban Lifestyle in Ruse
     MUSEUM
(ul Tsar Ferdinand 39; adult/student 4/1lv; ⊙9am-noon & 1-5.30pm Mon-Sat) North of the centre, you can take a quick peek into the past in this elegant townhouse, built in 1866. Upstairs, there are a few recreated period rooms (heavy furniture, chandeliers, lots of

lace etc) while downstairs there are temporary exhibitions on social themes such as childhood and education.

Pantheon of the National Revival MONUMENT
(ul Tsar Osbvoboditel; adult/student 2/1lv; ⊙8.30am-noon & 1-5.30pm Sun-Thu) East of the city centre, at the entrance to a large park, the gold-domed Pantheon of the National Revival houses the tombs of 453 19th-century revolutionary heroes and an eternal flame.

Promenade PARK
Strangely, Ruse seems to turn its back to the Danube, but there is a scruffy promenade that offers views across the water to Romania, and you can access the shore at various points. The bobbing plastic bottles, oil discharged from the many passing boats and general gunk suggest that it's probably best not to join the speedo-sporting pensioners taking a dip in the far from blue Danube, though.

🛏 Sleeping

Charlino Plaza HOTEL €€
(✆825 707; www.charlino-plaza.com; ul Kaloyan 24; s/d from 60/80lv; P❄️@🛜) Occupying a grand, Viennese-style mansion near the History Museum, the Charlino has a selection of restful rooms and suites, all with TVs and fridges. There's also a restaurant, bar and garden.

English Guest House B&B €
(✆875 577; www.the-english-guest-house.com; ul Rayko Daskalov 33; s/d from 35/50lv; ❄️🛜) A few blocks north of pl Svoboda, this British-run hotel offers cosy, brightly furnished rooms in a renovated mansion that once belonged to Todor Zhivkov, Bulgaria's last communist leader. It's a fun place where guests can mingle over some free tea in the garden, and there are plans to install a cinema and gym.

Cosmopolitan BUSINESS HOTEL €€€
(✆805 063; www.cosmopolitanhotelbg.com; ul Dobri Nemirov 1-3; s/d incl breakfast from 80/150lv; ❄️🛜🏊) This modern business hotel has all the facilities and comforts you would expect, including a spa centre, pool and restaurants. Rooms are stylish, some with terraces, but it's a big place, and the labyrinthine layout can be confusing.

Riga Hotel HOTEL €€
(✆822 042; www.hotel-riga.com; bul Pridunavski 22; s 40-78lv, d 60-98lv; P❄️) This communist-era monolith may have seen better days, and the cheapest rooms don't have air-con, but the better, renovated rooms are good value, and those on the upper floors have panoramic

views over the Danube. There are also a few restaurants including a pleasant garden cafe.

Splendid Hotel HOTEL €€
(✆825 972; www.splendid.rousse.bg; ul Aleksandrovska 51; s/d from 46/56lv; ❄️@) Off the main square, the Splendid has slightly dated rooms with narrow single beds or doubles, all with TVs. Breakfast is 6lv extra.

🍴 Eating

There are plenty of open-air cafes and snacks to find on ul Aleksandrovska. For groceries, head northwest on ul Aleksandrovska 200m from pl Svoboda to **Gradski Hali** (ul Aleksandrovska 93; ⊙8am-10pm)

TOP CHOICE **Chiflika** BULGARIAN €€
(ul Otets Paisii 2; mains 6-20lv) Set in several rooms decorated like an old-world tavern, this is the best place in town to sample authentic Bulgarian cuisine such as soups, clay-pot meals, grills and fish, as well as more adventurous dishes like lamb's intestines and 'Granny's Rag Carpet' (a mixed meat stew, apparently).

Ostankino BULGARIAN €
(ul Alexandrovska 76; mains 3-8lv; ⊙8.30am-midnight) Typical cheap and hearty Bulgarian food including sausages, grills, chicken steaks and fish are served at this busy cafe with outdoor tables.

Friendly House CAFE €
(ul Gladston 1; mains 5-10lv) This cheerful, brightly lit, two-level place has a varied menu including grills, chicken hotpot, couscous, spaghetti and kebabs, which will do for a quick lunch.

Hlebozavod Ruse STREET FOOD €
(ul Aleksandrovska; banitsa 0.70lv; ⊙6.30am-7pm Mon-Fri, 6.30am-2pm Sat) Ruse's best takeaway *banitsa* draws locals all day.

ℹ Information

Internet Dexter (ul Duhovno Vûzrazhdane 10; per hr 1.50lv; ⊙24hr)

Post office (pl Svoboda)

Tourist information centre (✆824 704; ul Aleksandrovska; ⊙9am-6pm Mon-Fri, 9.30am-12.30pm & 1-6pm Sat & Sun) Helpful English-speaking staff and a handful of free brochures.

Unicredit Bulbank (cnr ul Alexandrovska & pl Svoboda)

ℹ Getting There & Away

Ruse's **Yug Bus Terminal** (ul Pristanishtna) has frequent daily buses heading to Sofia (18lv to

22lv, five hours) and Veliko Târnovo (10lv, two hours). There are also a few buses to Varna (16lv, 3½ hours), stopping in Shumen (6lv, 1½ hours). A couple of companies, including **Ovanesovi**, send buses to Bucharest (three hours). There is at least one daily bus to İstanbul (13 hours), run by **Union-Ivkoni**.

Two or three daily buses to Cherven and Ivanovo in Rusenski Lom Nature Park leave from **Iztok Bus Terminal**, 4.5km east of the centre; taxi there or take bus 2 or 13 from near the pl Oborishte roundabout.

The **train station**, next to Yug, has three daily trains to Sofia (17.20lv, seven hours), three to Veliko Târnovo (5.90lv, 2½ to 3½ hours) and two to Varna (11lv, four hours). International tickets are sold from the Rila Bureau here. Trains leave for Bucharest (three hours) at the unreasonable hour of 3.15am or the perfectly reasonable 3pm. The daily train for İstanbul (60lv) leaves at 3.15pm.

Rusenski Lom Nature Park ПРИРОДЕН ПАРК РУСЕНСКИ ЛОМ

Spread over the Rusenski Lom, Beli Lom and Malki Lom rivers in the Danube plain southwest of Ruse, this stunning nature park is a superb spot for birdwatching, with 172 species recorded here, including golden eagles, Egyptian vultures and eagle owls. The 3408-hectare park of winding rivers and cliffside hiking paths is also home to wolves, hamsters and 24 species of bat, as well as rare plant species, although most visitors come for the unique cave churches. There are plans to expand the park (apparently) by *10* times, to more than 33,000 hectares.

Before heading out, call by Ruse's **Rusenski Lom Nature Park Office** (☑872 397; www.lomea.org; ul General Skobelev 7; ☉9am-5pm Mon-Fri). Helpful staff can arrange accommodation and suggest hikes, and sell useful 1:50,000 maps (3lv). Summertime **canoe trips** can be organised too; contact them for details and prices.

◉ Sights

Ivanovo Rock Monastery MONASTERY
(St Archangel Michael; ☑0889 370 006; adult/student 4/1lv; ☉9am-noon & 1-6pm) Four kilometres east of Ivanovo (where there's an info centre with brochures; see www.ivanovo.bg), the park's most famous attraction was built into a 16m-long cave in the 13th century and contains colourful, well-preserved 14th century murals, including a Last Supper scene. Today it's on Unesco's World Heritage list.

From the village of Bozhichen, 4km northeast of Ivanovo, there's a 6km hiking trail that hugs the river on a two-hour walk back to Ivanovo. Get a trail map from the office in Ruse.

Citadel Ruins RUINS
(adult/student 4/0.5lv; ☉9am-noon & 1-6pm) In the lovely valley village of Cherven, about 14km southeast of Ivanovo, the spread-out remains of this 6th-century citadel sit atop a cliff at a sharp bend in the river.

Orlova Chuka Cave CAVE
About 22km southeast of Ivanovo, the 13km long Orlova Chuka Cave is filled with a huge bat colony (with 25 bat species); visitors can make a 1.5km loop, though it's usually closed when bats are breeding (around May and June).

🛏 Sleeping

Many villages offer homestays, including Ivanovo, Cherven and Koshov. Next to Ivanovo train station, **Kladenitsa** (☑0899 773 288; www.hotel-kladeneca.com; ul Olimpiyska 22; r per person 20lv) provides simple rooms with shared bathroom and meals. Next to Orlova Chuka cave, an unnamed **hizha** (☑0886 003 233; www.orlovachuka.eu; dm 8-10lv) has basic bunk-bed rooms, a communal kitchen and a restaurant.

❶ Getting There & Away

It's easiest to visit with your own wheels. Buses from Ruse's Iztok bus terminal go a few times daily to Cherven via Ivanovo and Koshov, while eight trains from Ruse reach Ivanovo (2.80lv, 25 minutes). Hiking trails link villages throughout the park.

BLACK SEA COAST

Every summer brings the annual race to Bulgaria's 378km coastline, the Black Sea's best expanse of golden sand on blue water, and one of the country's main draws. The package tourists fly into Varna or Burgas and then travel on to the overpriced and overdeveloped resorts like Sunny Beach or Golden Sands; most independent travellers reach the Black Sea at Varna by train or bus.

There's much to see, of course. Burgas makes a good base for visiting the ancient towns of Nesebâr and Sozopol, and Balchik is an easy day trip from Varna. For quieter nooks, head north of Kavarna or make your way to Sinemorets, near the Turkish border. Travelling to the far north or south, though, requires plenty of time, or your own transport.

Varna BAPHA

♬ 052 / POP 357,000

Cosmopolitan Varna, with its long sandy beaches, Roman ruins, museums and legendary nightlife, was established as Bulgaria's first seaside resort in 1921, with the still-going **Summer Festival** following a few years later. Briefly called 'Stalin' after WWII, Varna's origins stretch back 6000 years or so to the Thracians, while 6th-century BC Greek colonists founded the city of Odessos here; the name Varna first appeared under Byzantine rule in the 6th century AD.

The **Varna Summer International Festival**, which dates from 1926, features all sorts of music and street performances between May and October.

◉ Sights & Activities

Beaches   BEACH

Starting just steps from the train station, the Varna city **beach** is 8km long. The south beach (with its pool complex, water slides and cafes) has a quite popular stretch; the central beach has thinner sand patches and is dominated by clubs; beyond is a rocky area lined with restaurants and further north there are some wider and more attractive areas of sand as well as an outdoor **thermal pool** with year-round hot water where locals take a daily dip. The blue-flag **Bunite Beach** north of here is one of the better places to stretch out, although there's a big private section, with a beach bar and tacky plastic coconut trees, where you can get a sunbed for 7lv, a double bed for 20lv or a 'VIP pavilion' (a canvas tent) for a cool 50lv. Elsewhere, beach bars rent loungers and umbrellas for about 5lv.

Just in from the beach is **Primorski Park**, a vast expanse of greenery dotted with statues, open-air cafes and popcorn vendors.

Archaeological Museum   MUSEUM

(ul Maria Luisa 41; adult/student 10/2lv; ⊙10am-5pm Tue-Sun Apr-Sep, 10am-5pm Tue-Sat Oct-Mar) Housed in a grand old two-storey building, this large museum is among Bulgaria's best, displaying more than 100,000 artefacts covering 6000 years of local history.

The exhibits start off with pottery and flints from the now submerged Neolithic settlements around Varna Lake, highlighted by 6500-year-old gold jewellery, said to be the oldest worked gold in the world. Other interesting exhibits include Roman surgical implements, Hellenistic statues and, inevitably, a floor full of icons.

Roman Thermae   ANCIENT SITE

(cnr ul Han Krum & ul San Stefano; adult/student 4/2lv; ⊙10am-5pm May-Oct, 10am-5pm Tue-Sat Nov-Apr) Wedged between the St Anastasios Orthodox Church and modern housing, the ruins of the 2nd- century AD Roman Thermae are the biggest in Bulgaria, but there's not much information inside. You can just about make out the various bathing areas, and peer into the furnaces, where slaves kept the whole enterprise going.

City History Museum   MUSEUM

(ul 8 Noemvri 5; adult/student 4/2lv; ⊙10am-5pm Tue-Sun) This vine-covered building, just behind some partially excavated **Roman bath ruins**, focuses on the city's 19th- and 20th-century past, with displays of old photos, postcards and souvenirs from its early resort days, plus reconstructions of long-gone local shops.

Ethnographic Museum   MUSEUM

(ul Panagyurishte 22; adult/student 4/2lv; ⊙10am-5pm Tue-Sun Apr-Sep, 10am-5pm Tue-Fri Oct-Mar) Housed in an 1860 National Revival building, the Ethnographic Museum is a complex of traditional buildings. Inside are agricultural tools, antique fishing and wine-making equipment, and colourful folk costumes.

Cathedral of the Assumption of the Virgin   CHURCH

(pl Mitropolitska Simeon) The blocky, gold-onion-domed Cathedral of the Assumption of the Virgin was built in the 1880s and is a much-cherished symbol of the city. The bright murals and stained glass windows date from the 1950s.

🛏 Sleeping

During high season (June to September), there are plenty of private accommodation options. Locals carrying cardboard signs advertising spare rooms hang around the train station, charging around 15lv per person, but check the location first so you don't end up in some distant suburb. In summer, there are accommodation bureaux in the main bus and train stations offering private apartments. Other places that can help:

Isak (♬602 318; info@accommodatebg.com; train station; r from 12lv; ⊙9am-9.30pm May-Sep) Books rooms in private homes plus self-contained flats from around 30lv.

Global Tours (☎601 085; www.globaltours-bg. com; ul Knyaz Boris I 67; ⊙8am-8pm Mon-Fri, 10am-6pm Sat & Sun Jun-Sep, 9am-6pm Mon-Fri Oct-May) Finds apartments from around €18 per day.

Modus Hotel   LUXURY HOTEL €€€
(☎660 910; www.modushotel.com; ul Stefan Stambolov 46; s/d from €110/120; P☀☎) This very chic, new boutique hotel has stylish rooms with flat-screen TVs and a gym, sauna and smart bistro on site. Rates drop by €30 between Friday and Sunday.

Grand Hotel London   LUXURY HOTEL €€€
(☎664 100; www.londonhotel.bg; ul Musala 3; s/d incl breakfast from €120/140; P☀☎) The *grande dame* of Varna's hotel scene was established in 1912, and is a stylish if slightly chintzy place, with lots of heavy curtains and potted ferns. It's recently undergone a refit and has an excellent restaurant as well as a gym, sauna and 'wellness centre'.

Victorina (☎603 541; http://victorina.borsabg. com; Tsar Simeon 36; s/d in private apartment from 25/35lv; ⊙9am-6pm Mon-Sat, 10am-3pm Sun) Operates a window bureau across from the train station. Note that cheaper rooms may be far from the centre. It also offers numerous excursions.

Hotel Acropolis   HOTEL €
(☎603 108; www.hotelacropolis.net; ul Tsar Ivan Shishman 13; s incl breakfast 40-50lv, d incl breakfast 50-60lv; P☀☎) On a residential street across the road from the beach, the Acropolis is a friendly, family-run hotel with small, simple but clean rooms with modern bathrooms.

Hotel Astra   HOTEL €
(☎630 524; hotel_astra@abv.bg; ul Opalchenska 9; s/d from 40/50lv; ☀☎) The Astra is a peaceful family hotel on a leafy central street with 10 decent-sized rooms with polished wood floors, TVs and fridges. Some rooms have balconies and there's a small summer garden.

Hotel Hi   HOTEL €€
(☎657 777; www.hotel-hi.com; ul Han Asparuh 11; s/d incl breakfast from €45/60; ☀☎) Say hello to this new boutique hotel in a quiet location just south of ul Knyaz Boris, featuring cool, stylish rooms with plasma TVs and bright bathrooms.

Yo Ho Hostel   HOSTEL €
(☎0886 382 905; www.yohohostel.com; ul Ruse 23; dm/d €11/15; @) With a vaguely piratey theme, this is a laid-back, fairly central hostel run by four local guys who organise interesting day trips as well two-night rafting

excusions (€75 per person, including professional guide, equipment and meals).

X Hostel   HOSTEL €
(☎0885 049 084; www.xhostel.eu; Evksinograd 19, 16th Rd, Sveti Konstantin; dm/s/d €11/14/28; ☀@☎) About 10km north of Varna, on the southern edge of the Sveti Konstantin resort, the X has a small pool, garden and restaurant, sea views and regular party nights and movies. Get off the bus 1km south of the main Sveti Konstanti stop (by the Opet gas station), then follow the signs 600m to 'Villa Waikiki'.

Flag Hostel   HOSTEL €
(☎0897 408 115; www.varnahostel.com; ul Bratya Shkorpil 13a; dm incl breakfast €9; ☎) Recently relocated to its third premises in nine years, the British-run Flag is a popular choice, offering bright, clean dorms with single beds (no bunks), a free beer on arrival and modern shared bathrooms.

Voennomorski Club   HOTEL €€
(☎617 965; ul Vladislav Varenchik 2; s 25-48lv, d 72lv; ☀) Occupying the top two floors of the sky-blue Naval Club building, rooms at the 'BNK' are a little dated and cheerless, but the central location is convenient. The cheaper singles don't have air-con.

Art Hotel   HOTEL €€
(☎657 600; www.arthotelbg.com; ul Preslav 59; s/d from 35/54lv; ☀@) Just off the main square, this is a functional hotel with 11 small tiled rooms with TVs. It's reasonably priced for Varna though.

✕ Eating

In summer, there's a string of restaurants along the seafront, just north of the nightclubs, offering seafood and traditional Bulgarian and Italian menus. **Mandarin** (ul 27 Yuli 68; ⊙9am-midnight) is a handy little supermarket that sells all the basics.

Mr Baba   SEAFOOD €€
(☎614 629; off bul Primorski; mains 8-25lv; ⊙8am-midnight) For something a bit different, climb aboard this replica landlocked sailing ship near the port for some tasty seafood such as octopus risotto (17.90lv), shark, trout and sea bass. Chicken and pork dishes are available (from 9lv) if you're not in a fishy mood.

Tanasi   GREEK €
(☎601 138; ul Bratya Shkorpil 16; mains 5-15lv) This welcoming Greek restaurant has fresh white linen indoors, plus less formal outdoor seating. Featured dishes include

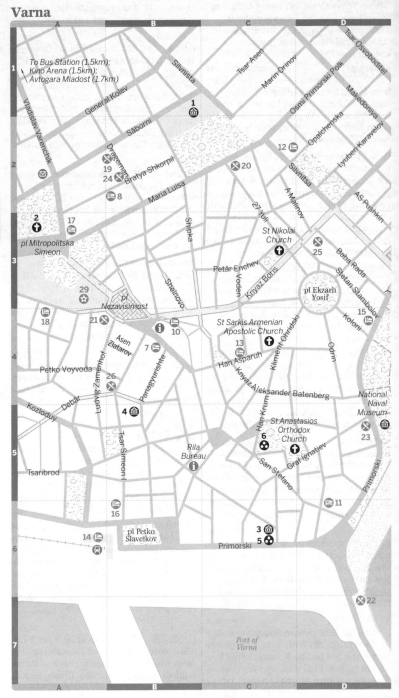

To Bus Station (1.5km);
Kino Arena (1.5km);
Avtogara Mladost (1.7km)

Vladislav Varenchik

General Kolev

Saborni

Silvnista

Tsar Asen

Marin Drinov

Tsar Osvoboditel

Osmi Primorski Polk

Makedoniya

Opalchenska

Lyuben Karavelov

1

Dragoman

19
24

Bratya Shkorpil

8

Maria Luisa

Shipka

Silvnitsa

A Malinov

AS Pushkin

20

12

27 Yuli

St Nikolai Church

2

pl Mitropolitska Simeon

17

Petâr Enchev

Voden

Knyaz Boris

25

Baba Rada

Stefan Stambolov

29

pl Nezavisimost

Stelnovo

pl Ekzarh Yosif

Koloni

18

21

10

St Sarkis Armenian Apostolic Church

15

Asen Zlatarov

7

13

Kliment Ohridski

Ogrin

Petko Voyvoda

Ludvig Zamenhof

26

Panagyurishte

Han Asparuh

Knyaz Aleksander Batenberg

National Naval Museum

Kozloduy

Debâr

4

Tsar Simeon I

Han Krum

St Anastasios Orthodox Church

6

23

Tsaribrod

Rila Bureau

San Stefano

Graf Ignatiev

11

16

14

pl Petko Slaveikov

3
5

Primorski

Primorski

22

Port of Varna

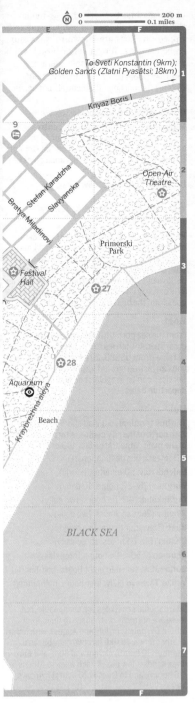

stuffed aubergines, roast lamb 'Cretan style' and various fish.

Pri Monahinite FINE DINING €€
(ul Primorski 47; mains 8-22lv) For a bit more class, try this well-regarded restaurant, in a one-time nunnery's courtyard. It's big on grilled meats (lots of fish and lamb) that come with more style than your average tavern.

La Pastaria ITALIAN €
(ul Dragoman 25; mains 6-15lv) This cosy little Italian place with chequered tablecloths serves up a good choice of pizza and pasta dishes, as well as seafood dishes like squid (9lv).

Trops Kâshta BULGARIAN €
(bul Knyaz Boris I 48; dishes 3-5lv) This bright branch of the dependable nationwide chain

offers cheap Bulgarian staples. There's no English menu; just point at whatever takes your fancy, and hope you haven't chosen tripe soup.

Morsko Konche
PIZZA €

(pl Nezavisimost; pizzas 5-10lv) This cheap and cheerful pizzeria has seats on the square in front of the opera house and a big menu of traditional and more eccentric pizzas, including one topped with bananas. Grills, salads and beer are also served.

Vinagi Topli Zakuski
STREET FOOD €

(cnr ul Tsar Simeon & ul Debâr; banitsa 0.90lv; ⊙6am-6.30pm Mon-Fri, 7am-2pm Sat & Sun) This simple window-counter bakery – its name means 'always hot breakfasts' – draws queues for its freshly made *banitsa*.

🍷 Drinking & Entertainment

In summer, a beach nightlife zone – mostly grouped about 400m north along the beach – opens its doors on the beach. There are a few good 'chill-out' bars clustered near the south end.

Along the beachfront pathway known as Kraybrezhna Aleya, you'll find clubs like Exit (⊙10pm-4am) and Copacabana (⊙10pm-5am), and plenty of summer-only beach-bars. Check for the latest listings in *Programata*.

Varna Opera Theatre
OPERA

(☑650 555; www.operavarna.bg; pl Nezavisimost 1) If you're looking for something more cultural, this company stages regular performances.

Kino Arena
CINEMA

(www.kinoarena.com; bul Vladislav Verenchik 138; tickets 5-15lv) The 10 screens at the Kino show the latest Hollywood films. It's in the Grand Mall Varna shopping centre, right behind the main bus station.

ℹ Information

The free, monthly, English-language *Varna City Guide* has useful general information and restaurant and bar listings.

Dangers & Annoyances

Every summer visitors lose cameras, bags and even towels left on the beach; go in groups and have someone keep an eye on them. Avoid the overpriced shops and kiosks along the main city centre thoroughfares, and outlets along the beachfront: you'll find more reasonable prices for basics like bottled drinks at shops in the backstreets. Black market money-changers still hang around pl Nezavisimost. Don't change money on the street; it's illegal and you are sure to be ripped off. Taxis are known to con visitors, so be cautious. Your hotel or hostel will be able to direct you to reliable operators.

Internet Doom (ul 27 Yuli 13; per hr 1.60lv; ⊙24hr) Get online at this central spot behind the St Nikolai church.

Main post office (ul Sâborna 36)

Municipal tourist information centre (☑602 907; www.vtc.bg; pl Musala; ⊙9am-7pm Mon-Sat May-Sep, 9am-6pm Mon-Sat Oct-Apr) Hands out some leaflets, maps and copies of the useful *Varna City Guide*.

Unicredit Bulbank (ul Slivinitsa)

ℹ Getting There & Away

Air

Varna airport (www.varna-airport.bg), 8km northwest of the centre, sees charter flights in summer and all-year flights to Sofia, operated by both Bulgaria Air and Wizz Air; prices are competitive but vary wildly, starting from as little as 27lv one way if you book in advance. Bus 409 goes from the bus station; a taxi is about 15lv.

Boat

From the sea port, **UKR Ferries** (www.ukrferry. com) operates ferries to Ilyichevsk, near Odesa, Ukraine (from US$80, 20 hours), from where you can pick up onward ferries to Georgia. Services can be irregular; check the website for departure dates.

Bus

The **bus terminal** (bul Vladislav Varenchik 158), 2km north of the city centre, is three stops north of the main cathedral on bus 409 or 148.

Domestic bus destinations:

Balchik (5lv, 50 minutes, hourly)

Burgas (12lv, 2½ hours, 10 daily)

Durankulak (9lv, 1½ hours, two daily)

Plovdiv (26lv, six hours, two daily)

Ruse (15lv, four hours, five daily)

Shabla (6lv, 1½ hours, three daily)

Shumen (7.50lv, 1½ hours, three daily)

Sofia (30lv, seven to eight hours, half-hourly)

Veliko Târnovo (17lv, four hours, half-hourly)

International schedules are changeable, but there are normally daily buses to Bucharest (about 6½ hours) in July and August, with fewer at other times; **Nisikli** has two daily buses to İstanbul (10 hours) at 9am and 8pm; and **Euro-lines** sends a few buses each week to Athens (26 hours), and to Odesa (20 hours) five days a week.

Minibus

The **minibus terminal** (Avtogara Mladost; ul Do-brovoltsi 7), 200m west of the bus station (cross the street via an underpass and go left 50m, then right past the next block), sends minibuses hourly to Burgas (12lv), and to Albena and Bal-chik (5lv) from about 7am to 7pm. Less-frequent services go to Nesebâr (via Sunny Beach; 10v).

Minibuses also leave for Albena (5lv) from the more convenient stop at ul Maria Luisa.

Train

Direct train services from the **main train sta-tion** (bul Primorski) link Varna to Sofia (21.90lv, seven to eight hours, six daily), Plovdiv (16.70lv, 6½ to 7½ hours, four daily), Ruse (11lv, 3¾ hours, two daily) and Gorna Oryakhovitsa (for Veliko Târnovo; 11.80lv, 3½ hours, five daily).

There are two daily trains to Bucharest (30lv, 13 hours), one requiring a 2¾-hour wait in Ruse, and a night train requiring a five-hour wait in Ruse in the middle of the night. International tickets must be purchased at **Rila Bureau** (✆632 348; ul Pre-slav 13; ⊗8.30am-5.30pm Mon-Fri, 8am-3.30pm Sat), a few minutes' walk from the station.

❶ Getting Around

Local bus routes are listed on the Domino city map; tickets are sold on the bus for 1lv. Some taxi drivers overcharge – make sure the meter is on.

Between June and September a hop-on-hop-off **Varna City Tour Bus** (24hr ticket 19lv) runs around 19 stops in town and beyond, with multi-lingual commentary. Buy tickets on board or at your hotel.

Global Tours (✆601 085; www.globaltours-bg. com; ul Knyaz Boris I 67; ⊗8am-8pm Mon-Fri, 10am-6pm Sat & Sun Jun-Sep, 9am-6pm Mon-Fri Oct-May) rents out cars from €35 per day.

North Coast

North of Varna you'll find a succession of big seaside resorts, starting with sedate Sveti Konstantin, famous for its spa treatments, before you hit the big beasts of Golden Sands and Albena, better known for their clubs, pubs and water sports. After historic Balchik the coastline opens up into a steppe of farmland that meets rocky seashores and less-visited villages such as Kamen Bryag.

VARNA TO BALCHIK

Just 9km north of Varna, Sveti Konstantin is a lovely area of elms, pines and oaks, with a twee little monastery, and lots of midrange resort hotels. From Varna, take bus 8 from ul Maria Luisa. See p187 for information about X Hostel, located here. A more comfortable

option in the resort is the **Estreya Palace Hotel** (✆052 361 135; www.hotelestreya.com; s/d 70/108lv; ❇❇) with large rooms, pool and spa.

Another 9km north is **Golden Sands** (Zlatni Pyasâtsi), a brasher resort with a busy 4km beach lined with burger stands, bungee trampolines and a Ferris wheel. In the nearby hills, **Aladzha Monastery** (adult/student 5/2lv; ⊗9am-6pm May-Oct, 9am-4pm Tue-Sat Nov-Apr) is a 13th-century rock monastery with a pleas-ant forest hike to interesting catacombs, 600m away.

Buses 109, 209, 309 and 409 pass near Golden Sands. It might be worth taking a taxi to the monastery, then following the blue or gold signs marking trails down to Golden Sands; otherwise hop off the bus just past the monastery turn-off and walk up (about one hour). In summer, the Varna City Tour Bus swings by here.

Another 15km north, the road winds past **Albena**, a purpose-built resort with a more thoughtful plan of development, and a shady camping ground Gorska Feya, 500m south.

Minibuses leave hourly for Albena from Varna (5lv, 30 minutes), continuing on to Balchik.

BALCHIK БАЛЧИК
✆0579 / POP 12,000

Balchik is a small, pretty town and fishing port huddled below white chalk cliffs. It's a low-key holiday spot that feels like a breath of fresh sea air after the ugly artificial resorts further to the south, whose lights can be seen winking across the bay at night. There's not much of a beach, but there are good connec-tions to interesting towns to the north.

The bus stop is 1km above the historic centre, where you'll find ATMs, waterside restaurants and car-rental agents.

In the 1920s, when the region was part of Romania, King Ferdinand built the **Sum-mer Palace of Queen Marie & Botanical Gardens** (Dvorets; admission 10lv; ⊗8am-8pm May–mid-Oct, 8.30am-6.30pm mid-Oct–Apr) for his English wife as a place of solitude and contemplation. The modestly sized palace shows off Marie's eccentric tastes, mixing Islamic and Bulgarian revival styles. The formal, themed gardens feature a watermill, chapel, winery and some 600 species of flo-ra, including cacti.

In the town centre, the **Irish Rover** (✆0888 510 530; www.balchikirish.com; ul Primor-ska 27; s/d July-Aug €15/30, Sept-Jun €10/20; @) has cosy en suite rooms with TVs, above a popular pub and restaurant.

For a more sophisticated ambience, try the waterfront **Mistral** (☎71130; www.hotel mistralbg.com; ul Primorska 8b; s/d from €40/45; ❄️🛜), a four-star hotel with large, sea-facing rooms and a very good restaurant. Prices double in July and August.

There are frequent minibuses to Varna (5lv, one hour). Two daily buses leave at 11am and 5.30pm for Kaliakra Cape (5lv, 45 minutes), returning at 1pm and 7pm.

KALIAKRA CAPE & AROUND НОС КАЛИАКРА

The area's most arresting scene is at this 2km-long, 70m-high headland topped by the **Kaliakra Nature Reserve** (admission 3lv; ⏱24hr) poking into the Black Sea about 30km northeast of Balchik. At the heart of the site are ruins dating from the 4th century-BC Thracian town of Thirisi, which was rebuilt as Kaliakra (or 'Beautiful') in the 13th century. A couple of kilometres north (past the whirling wind-power mills) is a small beach at **Bolata**.

Kaliakra is 12km east of **Kavarna** (aka 'Heavy Metal Capital of the World'), which hosts the annual **Kavarna Rock Fest** on the last weekend of July. Kavarna's waterfront is around 3km downhill from town and can be reached by hourly buses from the bus station. The sandy beach, watched over by impressive white cliffs, has a couple of beach bars and fish restaurants, but not much else.

Two daily buses go from Balchik to Kaliakra, but many more go to Kavarna, where there are a few more buses to Kaliakra during the day.

KAMEN BRYAG (STONE BEACH) & AROUND КАМЕН БРЯГ

North of Kaliakra, a beachside road continues, taking in a few mostly undeveloped towns (and the unremarkable resort at Rusalka) along the rocky seashore stretching north to Romania.

The highlight, 18km north, is Kamen Bryag, a quiet town along cliffs and the seaside site **Yailata** (admission 1.50lv), featuring 5th century BC cave dwellings and the remains of a Byzantine fortress. Some rock climbers come to the area for rope-free climbs above the water.

There's a guesthouse and restaurant, and many homes offer private rooms. You'll need your own transport to get here.

The lake in **Durankulak**, 33km north (on the main highway), is popular for birdwatching. From here, you can get a taxi to the 24-hour Romanian border (about 5lv), and walk to Vama Veche, Romania.

Central Coast

Dominating the coastal strip between Varna and Burgas – often a mountainous ride, generally inland away from the water – is the huge, club-land resort of Sunny Beach and its ancient, church-filled neighbour, Nesebâr. A few surprises can be found via out-of-the-way rough roads too.

VARNA TO BURGAS

Byala, about 54km south of Varna, is a basic town of 2100 people, set on the rising hills above the beach. Some 4km north – on a dirt road past rolling hills of vineyards – is the more attractive **Karadere beach**. Varna–Burgas buses pass by Byala.

About 13km south (past the small beach town of Ozbor, where buses stop), a road heads east a couple of kilometres towards the largely untouched **Irakli beach**, with a guesthouse and a couple of bungalows.

For the best views, a rough road rambles from Irakli for 8km up to hillside **Emona**. The trans-Bulgarian Mt Kom–Emine Cape hike (E3) ends here, and a very rough dirt road leads down to a small beach. The road curves inland, bypassing Sunny Beach and Nesebâr, and continues on 31km into Burgas.

NESEBÂR НЕСЕБЪР

☎0554 / POP 9360

Packed tightly onto a small rocky peninsula 37km northeast of Burgas, Nesebâr is a Unesco World Heritage site, founded as Mesembria by Greek colonists in 512 BC but most famous today for its numerous (though mostly ruined) Byzantine-era churches. It's certainly picturesque, but hardly a well-kept secret. In summer, the Old Town's narrow cobbled lanes are lined with countless kitschy souvenir shops selling everything from baseball caps and T-shirts to fake perfumes and watches, and thronged with shuffling hordes of snap-happy day trippers from the nearby resorts. However, there's plenty to see, and it's much less frantic in the evenings.

◉ Sights & Activities

A **combined ticket** (7-10lv) is available at the Archaeological Museum, giving access to the museum itself plus between one and three other sights.

Archaeological Museum
MUSEUM

(www.ancient-nessebar.org; ul Mesembria 2; adult/
student 4/2lv; ⊙9am-7pm Mon-Fri, 9am-6pm Sat
& Sun summer, 9am-1.30pm & 2-6pm Mon-Sat
winter) Nesebâr's interesting Archaeological
Museum has a varied collection of Thracian,
Hellenistic and Roman-era artefacts, including a 2nd-century BC statue of Hecate (the
goddess of witchcraft and fertility), gold jewellery, Greek tombstones and icons.

CHURCHES
There were once around 80 churches in
Nesebâr, built between the 6th and 14th
centuries. Most of those that remain are now
ruins (and free to explore), while some now
house commercial art galleries and a couple
more charge entry fees. Characteristic of the
Nesebâr design are horizontal bands of white
stone and red brick and green ceramic discs.

St Stefan Church
CHURCH

(ul Ribarska; adult/student 5/2lv; ⊙9am-6pm Mon-
Fri, 9am-1pm & 1.30-6pm Sat & Sun) The best preserved is this 11th century church adorned
with colourful 300-year-old murals and an
elaborate 16th-century iconostasis.

Old Metropolitan Church
CHURCH

(ul Mitropolitska) At the centre of town, the
vast and impressive shell of this church is
surrounded by cafes and artists' stalls.

St John Aliturgetos Church
CHURCH

(ul Mena) Overlooking the harbour to the
south, this earthquake-battered building is
set on a cliff and provides a picturesque setting for summertime concerts.

Christ Pantokrator Church
CHURCH

(ul Mesembria) Another well-kept church is
this 14th century example, notable for its
unusual frieze of swastikas, an ancient solar
symbol. It's now an art gallery.

BEACHES
A promenade runs along the rocky coast
(and a small beach on the east end), with
great views looking back at Sunny Beach.

South Beach
BEACH

Around 1.5km west of the peninsula, in the
'new town', is this long stretch of sand where
you can try jet-skiing, water-skiing, windsurfing and other watery activities.

A regular toy-train style trolley (3lv) trundles along the coast road between Nesebâr
and Sunny Beach's 8km stretch of sand.

⊨ Sleeping
Some hotels operate only between May and
September; high-season July and August

prices (listed here) are often about 75%
higher than other periods.

Hotel Tony
HOTEL €

(☎42403, 0889 268 004; ul Kraybrezhna 20; r from
40lv; P❋) Half of the 12 clean and airy rooms
have sea-facing balconies, and all have TVs
and sparkling new bathrooms. It's a real bargain for Nesebâr, and the place if often full in
summer. The owner speaks English.

Prince Cyril Hotel
HOTEL €

(☎42220; hotelprincecyril@gmail.com; ul Slavyanska 9; d/apt 50/70lv; ❋) On a quiet cobbled
lane away from the souvenir shops and
bustle, the Prince Cyril is a friendly place
with a variety of mostly large rooms, all with
TV and fridge. A couple of the bigger apartments have terraces. Breakfast, served in a
restaurant down the road, is 5lv extra.

Royal Palace Hotel
HOTEL €€

(☎46490; www.nessebarpalace.com; ul Mitropolitska 19; s/d 100/120lv; P➡❋☎) One of the classier hotels in town, the Royal Palace offers 26
neat rooms, including some with disabled
access, as well as a good restaurant. Prices
drop by about 20% out of high season.

✗ Eating
Nesebâr has an abundance of cheesy, overpriced restaurants; avoid the places with
touts (often dressed as sailors or chefs) trying to reel in passers-by for an in-and-out
mediocre meal. The further from the gates,
the better it gets. Try Pri Shopi (ul Neptun
12; mains 7-15lv), which does a good range of
grills, steaks and fish dishes, including light
lunch dishes like mussels and rice (7lv); or
the nearby Tangra (ul Neptun; mains 7-20lv),
good for local fish.

❶ Information
Unicredit Bulbank (ul Mesembria; ⊙8.30am-
5pm Mon-Fri) has an ATM. The tourist information centre (☎42611; www.visitnessebar.org;
ul Mesembria 10; ⊙9am-5.30pm May-Oct) sells
some glossy brochures, but is often closed.

❶ Getting There & Away
From outside the Nesebâr gate, buses go to
Burgas (5lv, 40 minutes) every 40 minutes. Five
minibuses head to Varna (10lv, two hours). Most
Varna–Burgas buses stop 2km west on the main
highway. There are also a few daily buses to
Sofia (28lv, seven hours).

Bus 1 goes regularly to Sunny Beach (1lv), or if
you don't mind looking goofy, there's a colourful
trolley along the seafront (3lv).

Nesebâr

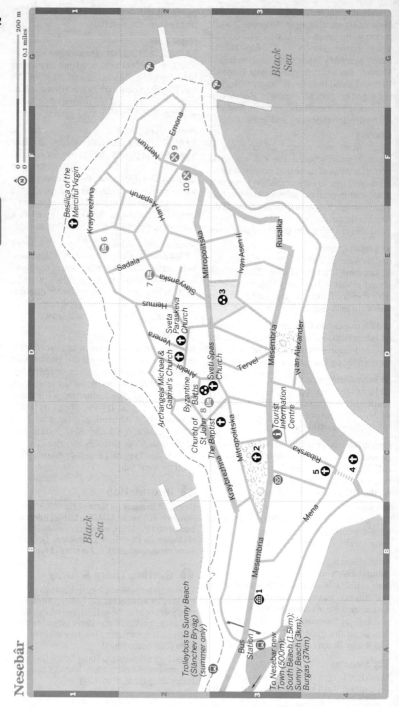

0 200 m
0 0.1 miles

Black Sea

Basilica of the Merciful Virgin

Kraybrezhna

Emona

Neptun

Han Asparuh

Mitropolitska

Ivan Asen II

Rusalka

Sadala

Hemus

Slavyanska

Sveta Paraskeva Church

Venera

Ahelon

Archangels Michael & Gabriel's Church

Byzantine Baths

Sveti Spas Church

Church of St John The Baptist

Mesembria

Ivan Alexander

Tervel

Mitropolitska

Tourist Information Centre

Ribarska

Kraybrezhna

Mena

Mesembria

Black Sea

Trolleybus to Sunny Beach (Slánchev Bryag) (summer only)

Bus Station

To Nesebar new Town (500m);
South Beach (1.5km);
Sunny Beach (3km);
Burgas (37km)

Nesebâr

Burgas БУРГАС

🖉056 / POP 229,000

Bulgaria's 'other' Black Sea city is often unfavourably compared with the more dynamic Varna, but while Burgas is hardly a must-see tourist stopover, it has a certain relaxed, un-touristy charm, a perfectly good beach, an extensive seaside park and a handful of small museums worth looking over. Some decent hotels plus good transport links also make it a practical base for exploring nearby resorts such as Sozopol and Nesebâr.

◉ Sights & Activities

Burgas Beach BEACH

Burgas' 2km-long beach isn't the best the Black Sea has to offer, but the northern end, at least, is clean and patrolled by lifeguards in summer. It's lined with many beach bars and fish restaurants, and umbrellas and loungers can be hired. Running along the beach is the leafy, flower-filled **Maritime Park**, which has a predictably graffiti covered communist monument, as well as lots of statues, fountains and a couple of bars.

Archaeological Museum MUSEUM

(ul Bogoridi 21; adult/student 3/1lv; ⊙9am-6pm Mon-Fri, 10am-6pm Sat) Probably the best of the handful of museums in town is this one, displaying Thracian jewellery, Greek statues and Roman pottery; look out for the flashy earrings and necklace that belonged to a Thracian priestess called Lesseskepra.

Ethnographical Museum MUSEUM

(🖉842 587; ul Slavyanska 69; adult/student 3/1lv; ⊙9am-12.30pm & 1.30-5.40pm) Also worth a visit with two floors of folk costumes and crafts.

🛏 Sleeping

TOP CHOICE **Hotel California** BOUTIQUE HOTEL €€

(🖉531 000; www.burgashotel.com; ul Lyuben Karavelov 36; s/d incl breakfast 60/70lv; ❄🏠) This smart new boutique hotel on a quiet side street about five minutes' walk west of the city centre is a winner, with large rooms featuring colourful wall prints and especially soft mattresses. Guests get a 20% reduction in the excellent restaurant.

Grand Hotel Primoretz LUXURY HOTEL €€€

(🖉812 345; www.hotelprimoretz.bg; ul Knyaz Al Battenberg 2; s/d from 164/184lv; ❄🏠🏊) This gigantic, resort-style, five-star hotel overlooks the quieter end of the beach and has pretty much everything you would expect, including indoor and outdoor pools, a spa and a couple of restaurants.

Hotel Chiplakoff HOTEL €€

(🖉829 325; www.chiplakoff.com; ul Ferdinandova 88; s/d incl breakfast from €30/35; ❄@) Around a 10-minute walk west of the centre, this attractively renovated mansion dating from the 1920s is a good deal, with spacious, modern rooms and a pizzeria downstairs.

Fotinov Guest House HOTEL €€

(🖉0878 974 703; www.hotelfotinov.com; ul Konstantin Fotinov 22; s/d €36/41; ❄🏠) This central 11-room hotel is a handy option, with multilingual staff, small but neat rooms and even a sauna. Laptops can be hired at reception to take advantage of the in-house wi-fi.

Burgas Hostel HOSTEL €

(🖉825 854; elanbase@gmail.com; ul Slavyanska 14; dm/d incl breakfast €10/25; @) The only hostel in town didn't bother with a fancy name. It's a simple but clean place with five- and eight-bed dorms, plus a couple of doubles (one en suite) and a small lounge and kitchen.

✖ Eating

There are several snack bars selling kebabs, *banitsa*, hot dogs, pizza slices, ice cream and so on along ul Bogoridi, and cheap restaurants along the beach where you can sample a dish of the locally caught small, battered *safrid* fish for around 3lv.

TOP CHOICE **Casanova** ITALIAN €€

(ul Knyaz Al Battenberg 14; mains 7-20lv) Set in the leafy courtyard of a grand century-old house, Casanova specialises in tasty Italian food, including pizza, pasta and risotto, as well as more sophisticated lamb and fish dishes. They also have an extensive wine list (bottles 12lv to 72lv).

Vodenitsata
BULGARIAN €

(Water Mill; mains from 4lv) One of the better beachfront places, this traditional tavern offers the usual hearty grills and soups in summer.

BMS
CAFE €

(ul Aleksandrovska 20; mains 2.50-4lv; ⊗8am-10pm) This self-service, cafeteria-style chain restaurant serves up cheap eats like soups, sausages and moussaka, as well as some tasty desserts, including a creamy 'biscuit cake'.

☆ Entertainment

The hippest beach club is **Barcode**, with comfy sofas and cocktails and visiting DJs. Elsewhere you'll find plenty of open-air cafe-bars along ul Bogoridi and ul Aleksandrovska.

Party Club (ul Bogoridi 36; ⊗5pm-late) is a cavernous basement bar with live music.

❶ Information

If you can read Cyrillic, the free local edition of *Programata* has listings of weekly events.

Bulbank (ul Aleksandrovska)

Internet Club (ul Knyaz Boris 6; per hr 1.50lv; ⊗9am-midnight)

Post office (ul Tsar Petâr)

Tourist Information Centre (☐825 772; Opera House underpass, ul Hristo Botev; ⊗9am-6.30pm Mon-Fri) English-speaking staff hand out brochures and maps and can help with car rental.

❶ Getting There & Away

Air

Wizz Air connects Burgas' airport (8km north) with London's Luton three times weekly. Bus 15 (1lv, 15 minutes) heads to/from Yug Bus Terminal every half-hour from 6am to 11pm.

Bus

Most buses and minibuses use the **Yug Bus Terminal** (cnr ul Aleksandrovska & ul Bulair). However, buses from Varna and central Bulgaria usually drop off Burgas passengers at the **Zapad Bus Terminal**, 2km west of the centre. City bus 4 connects the two.

Buses from Yug go to Varna (12lv, 2½ hours) half-hourly from 6.30am to 7pm. About eight buses go daily to Sofia (22lv to 28lv, six hours), most of which stop in Plovdiv (20lv, four hours), several go to Ruse (28lv, 4¾ hours) and two to Veliko Târnovo (26lv, 4½ hours).

Yug also serves nearby beach towns, with frequent services to Nesebâr (5lv, 45 minutes) and Sozopol (4lv, 40 minutes) and a few daily

to Kiten, Pomorie, Tsarevo and other smaller resorts.

Enturtrans/Istanbul Seyahat (ul Bulair 22) sells tickets for Bulgarian destinations and two or three daily buses to İstanbul (50lv, seven hours).

Train

The **train station** (ul Ivan Vazov) sells tickets to Sofia (18.30lv, seven to eight hours, seven daily) and Plovdiv (13.40lv, four to five hours, five daily). Trains to Ruse (15.50lv, 6½ hours, one daily) require a change in Kaspichan.

The train to Bucharest (11 hours, twice weekly) running from June to August, requires a quick transfer in Ruse; the train continues on to Kiev and Moscow. Buy international tickets at **Rila Bureau** (⊗8am-4pm Mon-Fri, 8am-2.30pm Sat) in the station.

South Coast

The finest sandy beaches dot the coast south from Sozopol to the Turkish border, though some come with less-appealing modern beach resorts that cater mostly to Bulgarians and Eastern European visitors. It helps to have wheels, but you can reach more-rewarding spots (like Sinemorets) by bus, too.

SOZOPOL СОЗОПОЛ
☐0550 / POP 4650

A curling peninsula of cobbled streets, sandy beaches and simple fish restaurants, Sozopol was founded by Greek settlers in the 7th century BC, and named Apollonia Pontica, in honour of the god Apollo. It was renamed Sozopolis ('City of Salvation') under Byzantine rule. Today, it's a hugely popular seaside resort, but it has a calmer, less-in-your-face atmosphere than its more boisterous rival to the north, Nesebâr. In early September, the town hosts the **Apollonia Festival**, a 10-day festival of music and theatre.

◉ Sights & Activities

Beaches
BEACH

Sozopol has two good beaches – the smaller **town beach**, which gets very crowded, and the much longer **Harmanite Beach** which has water slides, paddle boats and volleyball nets, as well as plenty of beach bars and restaurants. At the southern end of this beach you can see the remnants of stone sarcophagi from the ancient **Apollonia Necropolis**, which was recently excavated by archaeologists.

Archaeological Museum
MUSEUM

(ul Han Krum 2; admission 4lv; ⊘8.30am-6pm, closed Sat & Sun winter) There are a few low-key museums in the Old Town, including the Archaeological Museum, which displays ancient anchors and amphorae dredged from the seabed. Recent finds from the Apollonia Necropolis and St Ivan's Island are also on show.

Southern Fortress Wall & Tower Museum
ANCIENT SITE

(ul Milet 40; adult/student 4/3lv; ⊘9.30am-8pm Jul-Aug, 9.30am-5pm May-Jun & Sep-Oct) This consists of reconstructed walls and walkways along the rocky coastline, and a 4th-century BC well that was once part of a temple to Aphrodite. All this is free to explore – the couple of mostly empty rooms you get to see for your four leva are something of an anticlimax.

St Ivan's Island
CRUISE

In summer, it's possible to hire a sea taxi for tours or to go to swimming spots, such as around the 6.6-sq-km St Ivan's Island, just offshore. The island itself (the largest in the Black Sea) is out of bounds though; archaeological excavations are ongoing on the site of a medieval monastery, and in 2010 a reliquary allegedly containing bones of St John the Baptist was discovered here.

Between July and early September there are regular hour-long **night cruises** (adult/child 10/6lv) at 6pm, 7.30pm and 8.15pm. Boat day trips to Nesebâr cost 50lv per person. To hire a boat, look for 'sea taxis' at the port.

🛏 Sleeping

Most hotels are found in the New Town, though there are a couple of smaller family-run establishments in the Old Town, and during summer many houses here offer private accommodation (from 20lv).

Art Hotel
HOTEL €€

(☑24081; www.arthotel-sbh.com; ul Kiril i Metodii 72; d incl breakfast 70-100lv; ❉@) This peaceful Old Town house, belonging to the Union of Bulgarian Artists, has unfussy rooms with balconies overlooking the sea and a good terrace restaurant.

Hotel Villa List
HOTEL €€

(☑22235; www.hotellist-bg.com; ul Yani Popov 5; s/d incl breakfast 71/119lv; ❉@☷) With its dramatic setting overlooking the sea in the New Town, plus indoor and outdoor pools and a spa centre, the Villa List is a popular choice. There's even a rooftop 'nude terrace' for that all-over tan. Prices drop as much as 50% in low season.

Sasha Hristov's Private Rooms
PENSION €

(☑23434; ul Venets 17; r without bathroom 25lv) This peaceful old family home is located near the end of the peninsula, opposite the Art Gallery in the Old Town. There are four cosy rooms with terraces and a shared kitchen.

🍴 Eating

Locally sourced fish, naturally enough, features heavily on local restaurant menus. Sozopol's best restaurants are along ul Morksi Skali at the tip of the Old Town peninsula, including **Di Valli** (ul Morski Skali 35; mains 7-18lv), which offers wonderful sea views and dishes such as squid and trout, as well as pasta, duck and chicken.

There are also several cheap fish restaurants at the harbourside, such as **Bizhou** (ul Kraybrezhna; mains 4-9lv) and outlets serving up pizzas and burgers along Harmanite Beach in the New Town.

ℹ Information

Internet Club Escape (ul Ropotomo; per hr 2.50lv; ⊘9am-2am) Check your emails in the New Town.
Investbank (ul Apollonia)

ℹ Getting There & Away

Buses and minibuses leave the **bus terminal** (ul Han Krum) for Burgas (5lv, 40 minutes, half-hourly 6am to 9pm) all year. In summer buses go to Primorsko (3.50lv) and Kiten (4lv) to the south. Stands in New Town sell tickets to Sofia (28lv, seven hours).

SOZOPOL TO TSAREVO

Just south of Sozopol, an inland road rambles past undeveloped **Stork Beach** (Alepu), a protected beach backed by marsh that sees thousands of storks in August.

The bustling resort towns of **Primorsko** (22km south of Sozopol) and **Kiten** (5km further south) attract mostly Bulgarian holidaymakers; neither is that atmospheric, but both have fine beaches and plenty of mid-range hotels.

TSAREVO ЦАРЕВО
☑0590

Twelve kilometres south of Kiten, Tsarevo was once a popular holiday retreat for Bulgaria's royal family. It's a peaceful and uncommercialised fishing town, stretched out along a rocky peninsula, with a small beach on its north side and a quiet park at the east end of town, affording a grand view over the Black Sea.

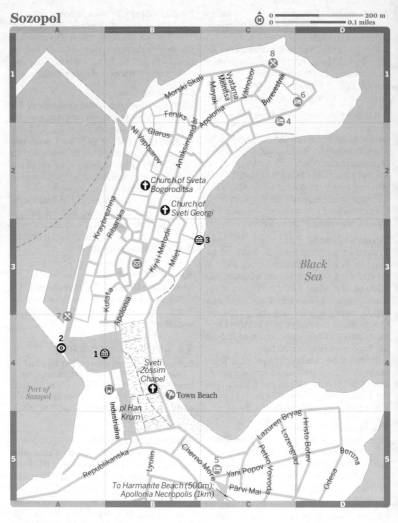

a few hotels and ongoing construction. The setting's lovely, on a wide peninsula looking over the blue sea. About 1.5km south of the bus stand is an attractive gold-sand beach; an even better, completely undeveloped beach is further on, via a short walk over the rocky cliffs.

A third (sometimes nude) beach is back toward the town entrance, where you can take boat trips into the marshy riverway of the **Strandzha Nature Park**. A 90-minute ride on the Veleka River is 15lv, including a walk up a bluff south of town.

Hotel Zebra (☎55 111; www.hotel-zebra.com; ul Khan Asparuh 10; s/d Jul-Aug €30/38, s/d Sept-Jun from €23/28; P❄@☎) is a good choice if you fancy staying, offering large rooms with balconies, a pool and restaurant, near the Sea Gardens.

Sunhouse (☎52 193; www.sunhousebg.com; ul Kraymorska 2; s/d from 28/35lv; ❄@) is a cheaper but still inviting guesthouse with various sized rooms, all with balconies and sea views.

SINEMORETS СИНЕМОРЕЦ
☎0590

The road gets bumpier as you press on south 20km to this spread-out village of new villas,

Sozopol

Dayana Beach Hotel (☎65503; www.dayana beach.com; s/d €25/35; ❄ 🗐 ⛱) is a modern hotel close to the central beach. The 23 bright rooms come with TVs, fridges and balconies, and there's an inviting outdoor pool, terrace and restaurant.

NORTHWEST BULGARIA

Bulgaria's little horn – jutting up between Romania and Serbia – is a bit of a backwater that's way off the usual tourist trail, which is surprising. Curved to the northeast by the Danube, it's seen plenty of military struggles, and prehistoric forces that forged stunning rock formations and gorges that make for great hiking and rock climbing. The train from Sofia goes past impressive **Iskâr Gorge**, south of Mezdra.

Vidin ВИДИН

☎094 / POP 68,000

Tucked snugly into a bend of the Danube, Vidin is a sleepy (and sometimes eerily deserted) place that doesn't receive too many foreign visitors, but it's an historic town with one of Bulgaria's best-preserved medieval fortresses, and the long, leafy park stretching along the riverside is a pleasant spot for an afternoon amble. There are a few outdoor bars here, a crumbling communist monument and even a tiny sandy beach.

The modern pedestrianised town centre, centered on pl Bdin, is a few minutes' walk north of the bus and train station, and has a few banks with ATMs.

◉ **Sights**

Baba Vida Museum-Fortress HISTORIC BUILDING
(adult/student 4/2lv, combined ticket with Archaeological Museum 5lv; ☺8.30am-5pm Mon-Fri, 9.30am-5pm Sat & Sun) About 1km north of the centre, the Baba Vida Museum-Fortress is largely a 17th-century Turkish upgrade of 10th-century Bulgarian fortifications, which in turn were built upon the ruins of the 3rd-century Roman fort of Bononia. Surrounded by a (now dry) moat, the fort is remarkably well preserved and is often used as a movie set. There's little to see inside, and not much in the way of explanations, but it's still an atmospheric place. Watch out for uncovered holes, dodgy stone stairways and the unfenced sheer drops on the top; there are many opportunities to break a leg here.

Archaeological Museum MUSEUM
(ul Tsar Simeon Veliki 12; adult/student 4/2lv; ☺9am-noon & 1.30-5.30pm Tue-Sat) Housed in the former Turkish prison, this small museum holds a scrappy collection of Neolithic flints, Roman statue fragments, medieval swords and 19th-century rifles. There's no English labelling and it's probably only worth a quick look if you've bought the combined ticket with the Baba Vida fortress (5lv).

🛏 **Sleeping**

Anna-Kristina Hotel HOTEL €€
(☎606 038; www.annakristinahotel.com; ul Baba Vida 2; d incl breakfast from 80lv; ❄ 🗐 ⛱) Occupying a century-old Turkish bathhouse, the Anna-Kristina offers 21 spacious rooms and suites, as well as a summer-only outdoor pool (10lv extra). It enjoys a pleasant, quiet setting in the riverside park and staff are friendly and helpful.

Hotel Staryat Grad HOTEL €€
(☎600 023; www.oldtownhotel.dir.bg; ul Knyaz Boris I 2; s/d incl breakfast 60/80lv; ❄🗐) Also known as the Old Town Hotel, this newish place has just eight tastefully furnished rooms in a renovated townhouse just inside the Old Town *Stambol Kapia* gateway.

Hotel Bononia HOTEL €
(☎606 031; www.hotelbononia.com; ul Bdin 2; s/d 33/39lv; ❄🗐) This boxy socialist-era hotel has been nicely spruced up and offers neat, if small, modernised rooms, and there's a busy restaurant attached. Breakfast is 5lv extra.

🍴 **Eating**

There are a few basic restaurants in the riverside park offering cheap standard dishes like grills and salads. For something more substantial, try **Classic Pizzeria** (ul Aleksandar II 25; mains 5-10lv), which, in addition to pizzas, also serves chicken, steaks and local fish dishes. It's right opposite the Port Authority building.

ⓘ Getting There & Away

Ten or more daily buses connect Vidin's Aleksiev bus station with Sofia (15lv to 16lv, four hours); most are operated by **Aleksiev**, which also runs one daily bus to Pleven (16lv, four hours), leaving at 8.30am, from where you can get onward links to other towns in central and northern Bulgaria. At least two daily buses go from the public bus station across the road to Belogradchik (4lv, 1¼ hours), but times and frequency change throughout the year. A couple of buses daily head for Bregova, at the Serbian border; you can walk across and catch the train for Belgrade.

Three fast trains leave from the train station, across from the bus station, to Sofia (12.60lv, 4¾-5½ hours) at 5.50am, 12.30pm and 3.55pm.

The bridge across the Danube to Calafat, Romania, may be completed by 2012; meanwhile a ferry goes every hour or two from 3km north of town. For foot passengers it's €3; cars are €18 to €22.

Belogradchik
БЕЛОГРАДЧИК

☏ 0936 / POP 5640

Reached by side roads, tranquil little Belogradchik is surrounded by weird and wonderful rock formations; jagged stone figures, carved by prehistoric seas, stand atop a rising mountain, looking like petrified giants, looming over a fort built originally by Romans, then extended by Bulgarians, and then Turks. It's a quiet, out-of-the-way kind of place, but is becoming more popular with both Bulgarian and foreign tourists.

The main sight here is the impressive **Kaleto Fortress** (admission 4lv; ◷9am-6pm Jun-Sep, 9am-5pm Oct-May), 1km past the central square (where you can find ATMs). The Romans first set up a fort here in the 1st century AD, which was subsequently built upon and enlarged by Byzantines, Bulgarians and Turks, who greatly extended it in the early 19th century. There are great views over the town below and of the rock formations behind. A hiking trail goes from the village central square past many formations and up around the fort above.

About 25km north, **Magura Cave** (admission 4lv; ◷10am-3pm) is worth a trip for a memorable, hour-long, unguided walk past stalagmites on sometimes slippery walk-

ways, and 4500-year-old rock paintings. Drakite Guesthouse arranges rides here (about 25lv); taxis are about 10lv more.

◉ Sleeping & Eating

Drakite Guesthouse   GUEST HOUSE **€**
(☏ 3930; www.drakite.com; ul Treti Mart 37; s/d from 25/35lv; ☏) Run by a helpful English-speaking local who can organise fishing trips and transport, there are five simple but comfortable rooms with views over mountains; those with bathrooms cost slightly more. The whole place can be hired for 175lv per day.

Hotel Skalite   HOTEL **€€**
(☏ 094 691 210; www.skalite.bg; pl Vazrazhdane 2; s/d weekday 80/100lv, s/d weekend 90/110; ✱❀☏) This is the smartest place in town, with comfy modern rooms, sparkly bathrooms, a spa, pool, restaurant and bars.

For meals, there are a few places around, but it's worth following the road between Hotel Skalite and the central square 1.5km to **Hanche Madona** (◷10am-2am), a friendly spot built into a giant boulder. It serves typical Bulgarian BBQ dishes.

ⓘ Getting There & Away

In summer, three or four daily buses connect Belogradchik with Vidin (4lv, 1¼ hours). From Sofia, the Vidin-bound train stops at nearby **Gara Oroshets**, 15km east, where a bus for Belogradchik (1.50lv) meets most oncoming trains daily (except Saturday).

UNDERSTAND BULGARIA

History
Becoming Bulgaria

Thracians moved into the area of modern Bulgaria by around 5000 BC, and Greek colonists from the south began settling cities on the Black Sea coast from the 7th century BC on. By AD 100 Bulgaria was part of the Roman Empire. The first Slavs migrated here from the north in the 5th century AD, and the first Bulgarian state was formed in AD 681.

The fierce Bulgars first reached these areas from their expansive territories between the Caspian and Black Seas. By the time the Byzantine Empire conquered Bulgaria in 1014, the first state had created a language, the Cyrillic alphabet and a national church.

It's a name you'll see on street signs and public buildings in every Bulgarian town, and the matinee idol looks will soon become familiar from the countless moustachioed, gazing-into-the-distance statues across the country; a bit like Che Guevara but with neater hair. It's Vasil Levski, the 'Apostle of Freedom' and Bulgaria's undisputed national hero.

Born Vasil Ivanov Kunchev in Karlovo in 1837, Levski (a nickname meaning 'Lion') originally trained as a monk, but in 1862 fled to Belgrade to join the revolutionary fight against the Turks, led by Georgi Rakovski. A few years later he was back, travelling incognito around Bulgaria, setting up a network of revolutionary committees. Levski, who believed in the ideals of the French Revolution, was a charismatic and able leader of the independence movement, but he was captured in Lovech in December 1872, and was hanged in Sofia in February 1873; the Levski Monument marks the spot where he died.

Bulgaria gained independence from Constantinople in 1185, and this second kingdom, based in Veliko Târnovo, lasted until the Ottomans took control in 1396.

Under the Ottomans

The next 500 years were spent living 'under the yoke' of Ottoman rule. The Orthodox Church persevered by quietly holing up in monasteries. Higher taxes for Christians saw many convert to Islam.

During the 18th and 19th centuries, many 'awakeners' are credited with reviving Bulgarian culture. By the 1860s several revolutionaries (including Vasil Levski – see the boxed text – and Hristo Botev) organised *cheti* (rebel) bands for the unsuccessful April Uprising of 1876. With Russia stepping in, the Turks were defeated in 1878, and Bulgaria regained its independence.

War & Communism

With eyes on lost Macedonia, following a series of painful Balkan Wars (including WWI), Bulgaria surprisingly aligned with Nazi Germany in WWII with hopes to expand its borders. Famously, however, Tsar Boris III said 'no' to Hitler, refusing to send Bulgaria's Jewish population to concentration camps, sparing up to 50,000 lives.

Towards the end of the war, the communist Fatherland Front gained control of Bulgaria, and Georgi Dimitrov became the first leader of the People's Republic in 1946. The royal family were exiled. A programme of rapid industrialisation and collectivisation followed and under Todor Zhivkov, the country's leader from 1954–1989, Bulgaria became one of the most repressive of the Eastern Bloc regimes, and the most loyal of Russia's client states, even proposing to join the USSR in 1973.

Modern Bulgaria

The communists were finally ousted in 1989, although reforming as the Socialist Party, they were re-elected into office the following year. In 2001, history was made when the former king, Simeon II, was elected as Bulgaria's prime-minister; the first former monarch to return to power in Eastern Europe. Bulgaria joined NATO in 2004 and the EU in 2007, but low wages, organised crime and corruption are sources of continual complaint and anguish.

The Bulgarians

The population of Bulgaria is 7.2 million, and continues to shrink – it has been estimated that 1.5 million people have left the country over the last 20 years. Bulgarians and Slavs constitute roughly 85% of the population, with the largest minorities being Turks (9%) and Roma (4.5%).

There are around 200,000 Pomaks – Muslims of Slavic origin – in the villages of the Rodopi Mountains, although many consider themselves to be ethnic Turks and others claim to be descended from ancient Balkan tribes converted by Arab missionaries a thousand years ago, but nobody knows for sure. There's also a small Jewish population of about 5000, mostly living in Sofia. During the communist era Bulgaria was officially atheist. These days, about 83% of the population are Orthodox Christian and 12% are Muslim (almost all of these are Sunni).

Art & Architecture
Music

Bulgaria has an impressive musical tradition, stretching back more than a thousand

IVAN VAZOV

Bulgaria's most loved author is Ivan Vazov (1850-1921), the revolutionary poet who wrote the stirring novel, Under The Yoke (1893) set at the time of the 1876 April Uprising against the Ottomans. This patriotic tale is Bulgaria's best-known work of literature, and has been translated into more than 30 languages. The novel has also been made into a film; as well as being a thrilling drama of heroism and self-sacrifice, the story of down-trodden villagers rising up against their oppressors (with the Russian army waiting to come to the rescue) was perfect material for communist propagandists, and the 1952 movie made by Dako Dakovski became one of Bulgaria's most popular films.

Vazov's other works include collections of nationalistic poetry such as *Epic of the Forgotten* (1884) about Bulgaria's struggles against Turkish occupation, and *It Will Not Perish* (1920).

years. Bulgarian ecclesiastical music is powerfully evocative, especially Orthodox chants and choral music.

Traditional music – played with *gaida* (bagpipes), *tambura* (four-stringed lute) and *tâppan* (drum) – is widespread. Turn on a TV and you'll see several channels dedicated to endless folk singing.

One very popular form of modern music you simply can't avoid is *chalga,* a vaguely Oriental-sounding, warbling folk-pop, often with a scantily clad female vocalist. It's brash, cheesy (often self-consciously so) with pretty naff lyrics, and many Bulgarians will visibly cringe at the mention of it. 'Please don't think this is what Bulgarian music is about!' winced one local, 'It's junk!' However, the continuing success of *chalga* stars and *chalga* clubs suggests many Bulgarians *do* quite like it, even if they'd rather not admit it. One of the most popular *chalga* performers, Azis – a gay, white-bearded transvestite – has sold more CDs than nearly any other Bulgarian artist.

Architecture

Bulgaria's 19th-century National Revival saw many town makeovers with quaint, traditionally styled *kâshta* buildings (with whitewashed walls, wood shutters, wood-carved ceilings and hand-woven carpets) built close alongside cobbled streets. This massive source of Bulgarian pride is evident in many towns, most notably Koprivshtitsa and Shiroka Lâka.

Visual Arts

Bulgaria's most treasured art graces the walls of medieval monasteries and churches, such as Boyana Church (p160) near Sofia, Arbanasi's Nativity Church (p178) and the paintings by Zahari Zograf (1810–53) at Rila Monastery (p161).

Renowned Bulgarian artists include Vladimir Dimitrov (1882–1960), an exponent of fauvism often referred to as 'The Master', whose very colourful paintings of country folk can be seen in galleries all over the country, and sculptor Andrey Nikolov (1878–1959) whose works include the stone lion at Sofia's Tomb of the Unknown Soldier.

The most famous contemporary Bulgarian artist is Christo Javacheff (aka 'Christo'), who specialises in wrapping polypropylene sheeting around well-known buildings like Berlin's Reichstag.

Natural Bulgaria

Bulgaria lies in the heart of the Balkan Peninsula, stretching 502km from the Serbian border to the 378km-long Black Sea coast.

Bulgaria is one-third mountains. The Stara Planina (also known as the Balkan Mountains) stretch across central Bulgaria. In the southwest are three higher ranges: the Rila Mountains, south of Sofia (home to the country's highest point, Mt Musala, 2925m); the Pirin Mountains, just south towards Greece; and the Rodopi Mountains to the east.

Although Bulgaria has some 56,000 kinds of living creature – including 400 bird species and one of Europe's largest bear populations – most visitors see little wildlife, unless venturing deep into the thickets and mountains. Popular birdwatching spots near the Black Sea include Burgas Lakes, west of Burgas, and Durankulak Lake, near the Romanian border.

Bulgaria has three national parks (Rila, Pirin and Central Balkan) and 10 nature parks, all of which offer some protection to the environment (and have tourist potential). The

EU has funded a number of projects to offer more protection, particularly along the Black Sea Coast and the Rodopi Mountains. Also see www.bulgariannationalparks.org.

Local Cuisine

Staples & Specialities

Fresh vegetables and dairy products form the basis of Bulgarian cuisine, which has been heavily influenced by Turkish and Greek cookery. Pork is the most widely used meat, and chicken, veal and tripe are also popular. Locally sourced fish also appears on menus on the coast or inland towns with well-stocked rivers. A seemingly endless variety of salads are available everywhere; the most popular is the *shopska* (tomatoes, onions, cucumbers and cheese). *Tarator* is a delicious chilled soup made with thin youghurt, diced cucumbers and walnuts.

Main dishes are mostly grilled, pork, lamb and chicken – such as the *kebabche* (spicy meat sausages) – or heavier stews such as *kavarma*. *Gyuvech* is a tasty meat or vegetable stew, served in a hot clay pot. Side dishes (such as boiled potatoes or cheese-covered chips) are ordered separately.

Vegetarians have plenty of choice. As well as salads, most restaurants serve yoghurt- or vegetable-based soups and several egg dishes. Well-made pizza, served by the slice or whole, is everywhere.

Bulgarians have an inordinate fondness for cheese, which is odd seeing as there are only two varieties: *kashkaval* (yellow, hard) and *sirene* (white, crumbly). One or the other seems to appear on virtually every meal.

Other less savoury ingredients that show up on Bulgarian menus include tripe soup (*shkembe chorba*), tongue (*ezik*) and brain (*mozâk*).

Drinks

Coffee is served everywhere, normally in espresso form, while tea (*chai*) is usually herbal; if you want black tea, ask for *cheren chai*. For a cooling beverage, try a glass of *ayran*, a chilled, slightly salty yoghurt drink.

Beer (*bira* or *pivo*) is ubiquitous and cheap. Big brands include Zagorka, Kamenitza and Shumensko. Domestically produced red and white wine is also abundant. Melnik, Gamza and Mavrud are leading Bulgarian red grape varieties, and Dimyat, Traminer and Muscat are some of the whites.

Rakia is the national spirit, a powerful clear type of brandy made from grapes or, occasionally, from plums. There are countless brands available, and it's normally drunk with ice as an aperitif or with light meals.

SURVIVAL GUIDE

Directory A–Z

Accommodation

Accommodation listings in this guide have been ordered by our preference. You'll find a budget room for less than 50lv a double; midrange doubles will cost somewhere between 50lv and 80lv and top-end places tend to cost more than 80lv. Prices listed in this chapter are for the high season.

Camping & Huts

Camping grounds normally consist of wooden cabins in a patch of forest and are usually quite simple, but cheap. Camping outside camping grounds is technically illegal and potentially dangerous.

Hizhas (mountain huts) dot the high country and range in quality. Most are very basic places intended only for a one-night stopover. Many are now privately run (and cost about 10lv to 30lv per person); some more remote ones are free. Most Bulgaria maps show these. In July and August, you may wish to reserve ahead at an agency.

Hostels

Hostels still aren't that common in Bulgaria, and are currently only found in the bigger cities of Sofia, Veliko Tårnovo, Plovdiv, Varna and Burgas. Expect to pay 18lv to 24lv per person in a dorm, including free breakfast and internet use; many have private rooms as well.

Hotels

Generally hotel rooms have private bathrooms, TV and a fan if not air-conditioned, and most include breakfast in the price. Most double rooms have twin beds. Average rates for a budget hotel are around 30lv for a single and 40lv for a double.

Nonsmoking rooms are rare outside the more modern, top-end hotels.

Watch out for hotels advertising *pochivka* ('rest') rates, which means two-hour slots used by prostitutes seeking privacy.

Private Rooms

Travellers on a budget can rent private rooms *(stai pod naem),* often offered by agencies, signed homes or English-speaking touts at train and bus stations. Rates range from 10lv or 15lv per person in smaller towns, to 35lv or more in places such as Sofia, Plovdiv and Varna. Cheaper places tend to be far from the city centre.

Activities

Bulgaria's mountains have more than 37,000km of hiking trails, some of which can be cross-country skied or cycled; nearly all lead to *hizhas* with dorm or private rooms and cafes. There are excellent opportunities for mountain climbing, caving, skiing and snowboarding.

Before setting out, drop by the expert consultants at **Zig Zag Holidays** (☎980 5102; www.zigzagbg.com; bul Stamboliyski 20V; ☺9.30am-6.30pm Mon-Fri) for tips and maps (particularly Domino's excellent trail maps). They also offer caving, rock-climbing, hiking, cycling and snowshoeing excursions.

Other companies offering interesting activities include:

» Crazy Sharks (www.dive-bg.com) – Certified PADI diving courses

» Cycling Bulgaria (www.cycling.bg) – Multi-day mountain-bike tours

» Hiking in Bulgaria (www.bghike.com) – Guided hiking trips

» Horse Riding Holidays (www.horse ridingholidaysbulgaria.com) – Day rides in the Stara Planina region

» Horseriding in Bulgaria (www. horseridingbulgaria.com) – Horse-back tours around Bulgaria

» Motoroads (www.motoroads.com) – Self-guided motorcycle tours and adventure activities

» Neophron (www.birdwatchingbulgaria.net) – Birdwatching, botany, bear-viewing and wildlife photography tours

Books

» Lonely Planet *Bulgaria* – More comprehensive coverage of the country.

» *The Rose of the Balkans* (Ivan Ilchev) – A readable historical overview of Bulgaria.

» *Under The Yoke* (Ivan Vazov) – A patriotic tale based around the 1876 Uprising against the Turks, and available in a recent English translation.

Business Hours

Banks 8.30am-5.30pm Mon-Fri

Shops 9am-6pm daily

Post Offices 8.30am-5pm Mon-Sat

Restaurants 10am-11pm

Museums 10am-5pm

Dangers & Annoyances

You're unlikely to face major problems in Bulgaria. Pickpocketing or beach grab-and-runs can happen in summer, particularly on Varna's beach. There are plenty of rogue taxi drivers waiting to rip off foreigners; always use a reputable firm, and, if possible, ask your hotel to call your cab. If you're a non-smoker, there's bad news: chain-smoking seems to be Bulgaria's top pastime, and smoking is allowed in most places, including restaurants and bars (inside and out).

Discount Cards

Most museums offer up to 75% discounts for students with valid ID.

Usit Colours (www.usitcolours.bg; Sofia Map p152; ☎02-981 1900; ul Vasil Levski 35; ☺9.30am-6.30pm Mon-Fri, 10.30am-4pm Sat; Veliko Târnovo Map p175; ☎062-601 751; pl Slaveikov 7; ☺9.30am-6.30pm Mon-Fri; 10.30am-4pm Sat) issues student cards for 10lv.

Embassies & Consulates

New Zealanders can turn to the UK embassy for assistance, or contact their **consulate general** (☎210-6874 700; 268 Kifissias Ave, Halandri) in Athens.

All of the below are in Sofia unless stated:

Australia (☎02-946 1334; austcon@mail.orbi-tel.bg; ul Trakia 37) Main office in Athens.

Canada (☎02-969 9710; general@canada-bg. org; ul Moskovska 9)

France (☎02-965 1100; www.ambafrance-bg. org; ul Oborishte 27-29)

Germany (☎02-918 380; www.sofia.diplo.de; ul Frederic Joliot-Curie 25)

Greece (☎02-843 3085; www.info.greek embassy-sofia.org; ul San Stefano 33)

Hungary (☎02-963 1136; ul 6 Septemvri 57)

Ireland (☎02-985 3425; info@embassyofire-land.bg; ul Bacho Kiro 26-30)

Macedonia (☎02-870 1560; ul Frederic Joliot-Curie 19)

Poland (☎02-987 2610; www.polamba-bg.org; ul Han Krum 46)

Romania (☎02-971 2858; bul Mihai Eminescu 4)

Russia (☎02-963 0912; www.russia.bg; bul Dragan Tsankov 28)

Serbia (☎02-946 1633; www.emb-serbia.com; ul Veliko Tărnovo 3)

Turkey (☎02-935 5500; bul Vasil Levski 80)

UK (☎02-933 9222; www.british-embassy.bg; ul Moskovksa 9)

USA (☎02-937 5100; www.bulgaria.usembassy. gov; ul Kozyak 16)

Food

Price ranges are: budget (€; under 10lv), mid-range (€€; 10lv to 20lv) and top end (€€€; over 20lv).

Gay & Lesbian Travellers

Homosexuality is legal in Bulgaria, but Bulgaria is far from openly tolerant (a 2008 poll found 80% of the nation had 'negative attitudes' towards homosexuality). There are a few gay clubs in Sofia, Varna and Plovdiv listed in this chapter, as well as low-key venues elsewhere. Some gay events are starting to appear, including Sofia's Gay Pride parade in June and Varna's Gay Week in September. Useful websites include:

» **Bulgarian Gay Organization Gemini** (www.bgogemini.org)

» **Bulgayria** (www.gay.bg)

» **Sofia Gay Guide** (http://sofia.gayguide.net)

Internet Access

Wi-fi access is now common in larger towns and cities, and is often free in hotels and restaurants. Hostels often have computers for guest use. Internet cafes have become less common in recent years, but most big towns will have at least one.

Legal Matters

Bulgaria is a member of the EU and more or less follows the same legal system as the rest of Europe. You need to be 21 years old to rent a car, and over 18 in order to drink alcohol.

Money

Many Bulgarian hotels and travel agencies list their prices in euros, which is roughly 2:1 to the lev; prices in this chapter reflect local quotes. Note that all businesses will accept either currency. Bulgaria won't be adopting the euro during the life of this book.

Cash

The local currency, the lev (lv), comprises 100 stotinki. It's been pegged to the euro (roughly 2:1) since January 2002. Banknotes come in denominations of two, five, 10, 20 and 50 leva, and coins in one, two, five, 10, 20 and 50 stotinki and one lev.

Money Changers

Foreign-exchange offices are abundant. Note that some occasionally post more-attractive rates outside, then put the real rates in tiny print inside a booth. Ask before handing over cash. US dollars, pounds sterling and euros are the best currencies to carry.

Travellers Cheques

American Express and Thomas Cook cheques in US dollars and euros can be cashed at many banks.

Public Holidays

New Year's Day 1 January

Liberation Day (National Day) 3 March

Orthodox Easter Sunday & Monday March/April; one week after Catholic/Protestant Easter

St George's Day 6 May

Cyrillic Alphabet Day 24 May

Unification Day (National Day) 6 September

Bulgarian Independence Day 22 September

National Revival Day 1 November

Christmas 25 and 26 December

Telephone

Nearly all Mobika and BulFon telephone booths use phonecards *(fonkarta)*, available at news-stands for 5lv to 25lv, for local or international calls.

GSM mobile phones can be used in nearly all places in Bulgaria. M-tel, Globul and Vivatel are the operators. Telephone numbers have different codes (eg ☎087 and ☎088).

To ring Bulgaria from abroad, dial the international access code then ☎359, followed by the area code (minus the first zero) then the number.

To call direct from Bulgaria, dial ☎00 followed by the country code.

Travellers with Disabilities

Unfortunately, Bulgaria is not an easy destination for travellers with disabilities. Uneven and broken footpaths are common in towns and wheelchair-accessible toilets and ramps are rare outside the more expensive hotels.

The Center for Independent Living (www.cil.bg) in Sofia may be worth contacting for advice.

Toilets

Most toilets in Bulgaria are of the modern, sit-down variety, though squat toilets do exist. Public toilets are not common, and are not always very clean. You can usually find public toilets near bus and train stations. More modern (and free) toilets can be found in shopping malls.

Visas

Citizens of other EU countries, as well as citizens of Australia, Canada, Israel, Malaysia, New Zealand and the USA, do not need a visa for stays of up to 90 days. Other nationals should contact the Bulgarian embassy in their home countries for current visa requirements.

Getting There & Away

Bulgaria is well-connected by air, rail and road to neighbouring countries and the rest of the world. Flights, tours and rail tickets can be booked online at lonelyplanet.com/bookings.

Entering Bulgaria

There are minimal border formalities for EU, US, Australian, Canadian and New Zealand citizens.

PASSPORT

There are no restrictions on any foreign passport holder entering Bulgaria.

Air

AIRPORTS & AIRLINES

Bulgaria's chief airports are in Sofia (www.sofia-airport.bg), Varna (www.varna-airport.bg) and Burgas (www.bourgas-airport.com). The vast majority of international flights arrive in, and depart from, Sofia. No additional departure tax is levied outside the price of your ticket. Airlines flying to/from Bulgaria:

Aeroflot (SU; www.aeroflot.ru)

Aerosvit (AEW; www.aerosvit.com)

Air France (AF; www.airfrance.com)

British Airways (BA; www.britishairways.com)

Bulgaria Air (FB; www.air.bg)

ČSA (OK; www.czechairlines.com)

easyJet (EZY; www.easyjet.com)

LOT Polish Airlines (LO; www.lot.com)

Lufthansa (LH; www.lufthansa.com)

Malév (MA; www.malev.com)

Turkish Airlines (TK; www.turkishairlines.com)

Wizz Air (WZZ; www.wizzair.com)

Land

BUS

International tickets to destinations across Eastern Europe (and beyond) are available at practically any bus station in the country. Prices aren't set, so it's worth checking a few companies.

You will need to get off the bus at international borders for passport checks. The cost of visas is not included in the price of the bus ticket; check before you go if you need to buy in advance or whether you can purchase a visa, if needed, at the border crossing.

CAR & MOTORCYCLE

Drivers bringing cars into Bulgaria are asked to pay a 'road fee' (vignette) from €5 per week.

TRAIN

There are a number of international trains from Bulgaria, including services to Romania, Greece and Turkey. Sofia is the main hub, although trains stop at other towns. The daily *Trans Balkan,* running between Budapest and Thessaloniki, stops at Ruse, Gorna Oryakhovitsa (near Veliko Tãrnovo) and Sofia. The *Balkan Express* normally goes daily between Belgrade and İstanbul, with stops in Sofia and Plovdiv. The *Bulgaria Express* to Bucharest leaves from Sofia.

Tickets for international trains can be bought at any government-run **Rila Bureau** (www.bdz-rila.com; ⊘most closed Sun) or at some stations' dedicated ticket offices (most open daily) at larger stations with international connections.

River

There is a daily ferry service across the Danube River from Vidin.

Sea

Ferries connect Varna (p189) with Ilyichevsk (Ukraine) in summer, but the service can be irregular.

Getting Around

Air

Bulgaria Air (www.air.bg) flies between Sofia and Varna daily; it also flies to

Burgas. **Wizz Air** (www.wizzair.com) also flies between Sofia and Varna.

Bicycle

Heavy traffic means bicycles are not advisible as a mode of transport in most Bulgarian cities. Traffic is relatively light outside the cities, but winding curves in the mountains and/or potholes everywhere can be obstacles.

Bulgaria has very few bike-rental options: Try hostels in Sofia and Veliko Tárnovo.

Bus

Buses (public and private) and minibuses connect all cities and major towns, and there are numerous private companies. The website of **Sofia Central Bus Station** (www.centralnaavtogara.bg) has comprehensive information (in English) on domestic bus routes. Intercity buses are normally modern and comfortable. Local buses are usually older but fine for shorter trips.

Some major companies include:

» **Biomet** (www.biomet.bg) Services between Sofia, Varna, Veliko Tárnovo and Burgas

» **Enturtrans** (www.enturtrans.com) Runs from Burgas to Sofia, Ruse and Pleven

» Etap-Grup (www.etapgroup.com) Most major inter-city routes

» **Union-Ivkoni** (www.union-ivkoni.com) Most major initer-city routes

Bus stations have a confusing array of private bus booths advertising overlapping destinations. Most bus stations have a left-luggage service with long (but not 24-hour) opening hours.

Note that some bus stations are inconveniently located far from the city centre and some cities, like Plovdiv, have more than one; make sure you know which station your bus is heading to.

Car & Motorcycle

Rental prices in Bulgaria are reasonable and will include unlimited kilometres and should include some car insurance, but always check.

To rent, you normally need to be 21 and have a driving licence from your own country. Generally prices should include the 20% VAT. If not, ask about paying in cash to waive it.

Most intercity roads are well signed in Cyrillic and Latin alphabets and conditions are normally good. On smaller roads, you may have to negotiate big bumps. Passing through some larger towns can take time, as signs often follow unwieldy circuits around the housing blocks and industrial zones; sometimes it's easier to go through the centre.

If oncoming cars flick their lights, it's likely a police speed trap is around the corner (the west-bound entry to Sofia is notorious for police traps). Speed limits are well signed: usually 130km/h on main highways and 90km/h on smaller ones. Town speed limits are 50km/h unless otherwise noted.

To drive on Bulgarian roads you need to purchase and display a 'vignette', available at border-crossings and post offices. It costs from €5 per week, but the price depends on your vehicle.

Train

Trains – all run by the Bulgarian State Railways (BDZh) – are generally cheaper but take a little longer than buses. The rail network is extensive and trains are normally very reliable. However, carriages are often pretty old, uncomfortable and poorly maintained. More modern trains are slowly being introduced on some routes such as Sofia-Plovdiv and Sofia–Kyustendil.

Ekspresen (express) and *bârz* (fast) trains way out-speed the slow *pâtnicheski* (passenger, or ordinary) trains, which don't offer much savings for their time loss.

All prices in this chapter are for 2nd-class seats (with eight seats per cabin); 1st-class seats, which cost roughly 20-30% extra, have six seats per cabin, and for some routes see far fewer people; it's definitely worth paying for 1st-class on longer journeys.

Most Europe-wide rail passes can be purchased in Bulgaria, but will not be good value for getting around the country.

Bring what food or water you'll need for the trip. Many train stations are poorly signposted, and in Cyrillic only, and no announcements are made on board.

Croatia

Best Places to Stay

» Arcotel Allegra (p215)

» Hotel Peristil (p243)

» Lešić Dimitri Palace (p250)

» Hotel Bellevue (p257)

Best Places to Eat

» Vinodol (p215)

» Konoba Batelina (p228)

» Foša (p239)

» Konoba Trattoria Bajamont (p244)

Why Go?

Croatia has been touted as the 'new this' and the 'new that' for years since its re-emergence on the tourism scene, but it's now clear that it's a unique destination that holds its own and then some: this is a country with a glorious 1778km-long coast and a staggering 1244 islands. The Adriatic coast is a knockout: its sapphire waters draw visitors to remote islands, hidden coves and traditional fishing villages, all while touting the glitzy beach and yacht scene. Istria captivates with its gastronomic delights and wines, and the bars, clubs and festivals of Zagreb, Zadar and Split remain little-explored gems. Eight national parks showcase primeval beauty with their forests, mountains, rivers, lakes and waterfalls. Punctuate all this with dazzling Dubrovnik in the south – just the right finale. Best of all, Croatia hasn't given in to mass tourism: there are pockets of authentic culture and plenty to discover off the grid.

When to Go
Zagreb

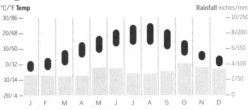

July & August Lots of sunshine, warm sea and summer festivals. Many tourists and highest prices.

June Best time to visit: beautiful weather, fewer people, lower prices, the festival season kicks off.

May & September Good weather, few tourists, full local events calendar, great for hiking.

Fast Facts

» **Area** 56,538 sq km

» **Capital** Zagreb

» **Telephone country code** 385

» **Emergency** ambulance 194, fire 193, police 192, roadside assistance 1987

Exchange Rates

Australia	A$1	5.32KN
Canada	C$1	5.29KN
euro	€1	7.36KN
Japan	¥100	6.04KN
New Zealand	NZ$1	4.01KN
UK	UK£1	8.27KN
USA	US$1	5.08KN

Set Your Budget

» **Budget room** 450KN

» **Two-course meal** 150KN

» **Museum entry** 10-40KN

» **Beer** 15KN

» **City transport ticket** 10KN

Resources

» **Adriatica.net** (www.adriatica.net)

» **Croatian National Tourist Board** (www.croatia.hr)

Connections

Croatia is a convenient transport hub for southeastern Europe and the Adriatic. Zagreb is connected by train and/or bus to Venice, Budapest, Belgrade, Ljubljana and Sarajevo. Down south there are easy bus connections from Dubrovnik to Mostar and Sarajevo (Bosnia and Hercegovina), and to Kotor (Montenegro). There are a number of ferries linking Croatia with Italy, including routes from Dubrovnik to Bari, and Split to Ancona.

ITINERARIES

One week

After a day in dynamic Zagreb, delving into its simmering nightlife, fine restaurants and choice museums, head down to Split for a day and night at Diocletian's Palace, a living part of this exuberant seafront city. Then hop over to chic Hvar and windsurf in pretty Bol on Brač. Next take it easy down the winding coastal road to magnificent Dubrovnik, for the final two days, taking a day trip to Mljet or the nearby Elafiti Islands.

Two weeks

After two days in Zagreb, head to Istria for a three-day stay, with Rovinj as the base, and day trips to Pula and Poreč. Go southeast next to the World Heritage–listed Plitvice Lakes National Park, a verdant maze of turquoise lakes and cascading waterfalls. After a quick visit, move on to Zadar, a real find of a city: historic, modern, active and packed with attractions. Then go on south to Split for a day or two. From here, take ferries to Hvar, Brač and then Korčula, spending a day or more on each island before ending with three days in Dubrovnik and an outing to Mljet.

Essential Food & Drink

» **Ćevapčići** Small spicy sausages of minced beef, lamb or pork.

» **Pljeskavica** An ex-Yugo version of a hamburger.

» **Ražnjići** Small chunks of pork grilled on a skewer.

» **Burek** Pastry stuffed with ground meat, spinach or cheese.

» **Rakija** Strong Croatian brandy comes in different flavors, from plum to honey.

» **Beer** Two top types of Croatian *pivo* (beer) are Zagreb's Ožujsko and Karlovačko from Karlovac.

ZAGREB

📵 01 / POP 779,145

Everyone knows about Croatia's coast and islands, but a mention of the country's capital still draws the question: 'Is it worth going to?' Here is the answer: Zagreb is a great destination, with culture, arts, music, architecture, gastronomy and everything else that make a quality capital.

Visually, Zagreb is a mixture of straight-laced Austro-Hungarian architecture and rough-around-the-edges socialist structures; its character is a sometimes uneasy combination of these two elements. This mini metropolis is made for strolling, drinking coffee in the permanently full cafes, popping into museums and galleries, and enjoying the theatres, concerts and cinema. It's a year-round outdoor city: in spring and summer everyone scurries to Jarun Lake in the southwest to swim, boat or dance the night away at lakeside discos, while in autumn and winter Zagrebians go skiing at Mt Medvednica, only a tram ride away, or hiking in nearby Samobor.

History

Zagreb's known history begins in the medieval times with two hills: Kaptol, now the site of Zagreb's cathedral, and Gradec. When the two merged in the mid-16th century, Zagreb was born.

The space now known as Trg Josipa Jelačića became the site of Zagreb's lucrative trade fairs, spurring construction around its edges. In the 19th century the economy expanded and cultural life blossomed with the development of a prosperous clothing trade and a rail link connecting Zagreb with Vienna and Budapest.

Between the two world wars, working-class neighbourhoods emerged in Zagreb between the railway and the Sava River, and new residential quarters were built on the southern slopes of Mt Medvednica. In April 1941, the Germans invaded Yugoslavia and entered Zagreb without resistance. Ante Pavelić and the Ustaše moved quickly to proclaim the establishment of the Independent State of Croatia (Nezavisna Država Hrvatska), with Zagreb as its capital.

In postwar Yugoslavia, Zagreb (to its chagrin) took second place to Belgrade but continued to expand. Zagreb was made the capital of Croatia in 1991, the same year that the country became independent.

⊙ Sights

As the oldest part of Zagreb, the Upper Town (Gornji Grad) offers landmark buildings and churches from the earlier centuries of Zagreb's history. The Lower Town (Donji Grad) has the city's most interesting art museums and fine examples of 19th- and 20th-century architecture.

UPPER TOWN

Cathedral of the Assumption of the Blessed Virgin Mary CHURCH
(Katedrala Marijina Uznešenja; Kaptol; ⊙10am-5pm Mon-Sat, 1-5pm Sun) Kaptol Sq is dominated by the twin neo-Gothic spires of this 1899 cathedral, formerly known as St Stephen's. Elements of an earlier medieval cathedral, destroyed by an earthquake in 1880, can be seen inside, including 13th-century frescoes, Renaissance pews, marble altars and a baroque pulpit. Note that you might be turned away if you're not dressed appropriately: no bare legs or shoulders.

Dolac Market MARKET
(⊙6am-3pm Mon-Sat, 6am-1pm Sun) Zagreb's colourful Dolac is just north of Trg Josipa Jelačića. This buzzing centre of Zagreb's daily activity since the 1930s draws in traders

---

ZAGREB IN TWO DAYS

Start your day with a stroll through Strossmayerov Trg, Zagreb's oasis of greenery. While there, take a look at the Strossmayer Gallery of Old Masters and then walk to Trg Josipa Jelačića, the city's centre. Head up to Kaptol for a look at the Cathedral of the Assumption of the Blessed Virgin Mary, the focus of Zagreb's (and Croatia's) spiritual life. While you're in the Upper Town, pick up some fruit at the Dolac market. Then get to know the work of Croatia's best sculptor at Meštrović Atelier and take in a contemporary art exhibition at Galerija Klovićevi Dvori. See the lay of the city from the top of Lotrščak Tower and then enjoy a bar-crawl along Tkalčićeva.

On the second day, tour the Lower Town museums, reserving two hours for the Museum Mimara, then have lunch at Tip Top. Early evening is best at Trg Petra Preradovića before dining at one of the Lower Town restaurants and sampling some of Zagreb's nightlife.

Croatia Highlights

1 Gape at the Old Town wall of **Dubrovnik** (p253), which surrounds luminous marble streets and finely ornamented buildings

2 Admire the Venetian architecture and vibrant nightlife of **Hvar Town** (p247)

3 Indulge in the lively and historic delights of Diocletian's Palace in **Split** (p240)

4 Explore the lakes, coves and island monastery of **Mljet** (p251)

5 Stroll the cobbled streets and unspoiled fishing port of **Rovinj** (p222)

6 Take in the wild landscapes of **Rt Kamenjak** (p226) cape near Pula

7 Marvel at the turquoise lakes and waterfalls in **Plitvice Lakes National Park** (boxed text, p237)

Zagreb

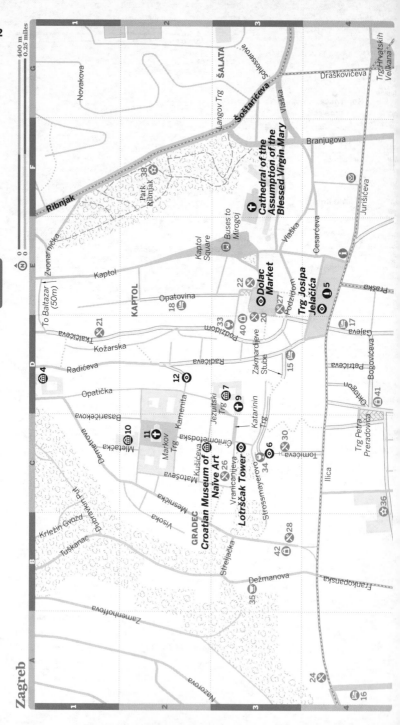

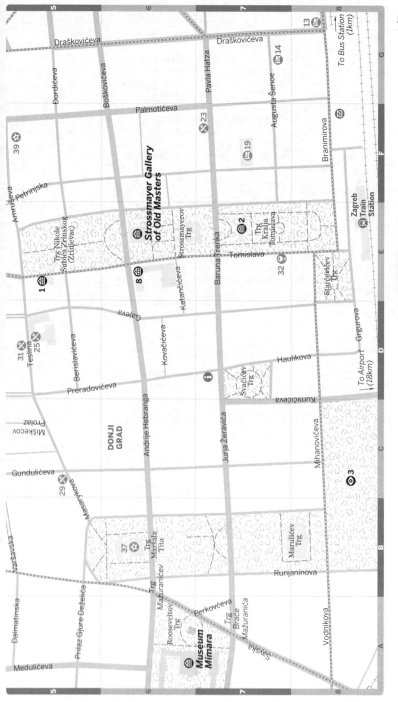

213

CROATIA ZAGREB

To Bus Station
(1km)

Draškovićeva

Draškovićeva

13

14 Pavla Hatza

Augusta Šenoe

Branimirova

Palmotićeva

23

39

19

Amruševa

Petrinjska

Strossmayer Gallery
of Old Masters

Trg Nikole
Šubića Zrinskog
(Zrinjevac)

Strossmayerov
Trg

2

Trg
Kralja
Tomislava

Zagreb
Train
Station

8

Baruna Trenka

Tomislava

32

Katančićeva

Starčevićev
Trg

Gajeva

Grgurova

To Airport
(18km)

Berislavićeva

Kovačićeva

Haulikova

31

25

Teslina

Preradovićeva

Andrije Hebranga

Juria Žerawića

Starčićev
Trg

Kumičićeva

Mihanovićeva

Miškecov
Prolaz

DONJI
GRAD

3

Gundulićeva

29

Masarykova

Trg Maršala
Tita

37

Marulićev
Trg

Varšavska

Runjaninova

Dalmatinska

Prilaz Gjure Deželića

Roosveltov
Trg

Mažuranićev Trg

Perkovčeva

Trg
Braće
Mažuranića

Savska

Vodnikova

Meduliceva

Museum
Mimara

Zagreb

from all over Croatia who flog their products here. The main part of the market is on an elevated square; the street level has indoor stalls selling meat and dairy products and, towards the square, flower stands.

Lotrščak Tower HISTORIC BUILDING
(Kula Lotrščak; Strossmayerovo Šetalište 9; adult/concession 10/5KN; ⊙10am-8pm) From Radićeva 5, off Trg Jelačića, a pedestrian walkway called Stube Ivana Zakmardija leads to this medieval tower, which can be climbed for a sweeping 360-degree view of the city. The nearby **funicular railway** (4KN), which was constructed in 1888, connects the Lower and Upper Towns.

St Mark's Church CHURCH
(Crkva Svetog Marka; Markov Trg; ⊙7.30am-6.30pm) Its colourful tiled roof makes this Gothic church one of Zagreb's most emblematic buildings. Inside are works by Ivan Meštrović, Croatia's most famous modern

sculptor. You can only enter the anteroom during the listed opening hours; the church itself is open during Mass.

Meštrović Atelier ART GALLERY
(Mletačka 8; adult/concession 30/15KN; ⊙10am-6pm Tue-Fri, to 2pm Sat & Sun) This 17th-century building, the former home of Croatia's most recognised artist, Ivan Meštrović, now houses an excellent collection of some 100 sculptures, drawings, lithographs and furniture created by the artist.

Galerija Klovićevi Dvori ART GALLERY
(www.galerijaklovic.hr; Jezuitski Trg 4; adult/concession 30/20KN; ⊙11am-7pm Tue-Sun) Housed in a former Jesuit monastery, this is the city's most prestigious space for exhibiting modern Croatian and international art.

Stone Gate LANDMARK
Make sure you take a peek at this eastern gate to medieval Gradec Town, now a shrine.

According to legend, a great fire in 1731 destroyed every part of the wooden gate except for the painting of the *Virgin and Child* by an unknown 17th-century artist.

City Museum MUSEUM
(Muzej Grada Zagreba; www.mgz.hr; Opatička 20; adult/concession 20/10KN; ⊙10am-6pm Tue-Fri, 11am-7pm Sat, 10am-2pm Sun) Check out the scale model of old Gradec, atmospheric background music and interactive exhibits that fascinate kids. There are summaries in English in each room of the museum, which is in the former Convent of St Claire (1650).

Croatian Museum of Naïve Art MUSEUM
(Hrvatski Muzej Naivne Umjetnosti; www.hmnu. org; Ćirilometodska 3; adult/concession 20/10KN; ⊙10am-6pm Tue-Fri, to 1pm Sat & Sun) If you like Croatia's naïve art or want a good intro to it, head to this small museum. It houses over 1000 paintings, drawings and some sculpture by the discipline's most important artists.

LOWER TOWN
Trg Josipa Jelačića SQUARE
Zagreb's main orientation point and its geographic heart is Trg Josipa Jelačića. It has an **equestrian statue** of Jelačić, the 19th-century *ban* (viceroy or governor) who led Croatian troops into an unsuccessful battle with Hungary in the hope of winning more autonomy for his people. The square is Zagreb's principal meeting point; sit in one of the cafes for quality people-watching.

Museum Mimara MUSEUM
(Muzej Mimara; Rooseveltov Trg 5; adult/concession 40/30KN; ⊙10am-7pm Tue-Fri, to 5pm Sat, to 2pm Sun) Ante Topić Mimara donated his diverse collection to Croatia. Housed in a neo-Renaissance palace, it includes icons,

glassware, sculpture, Oriental art and works by renowned painters such as Rembrandt, Velázquez, Raphael and Degas.

Strossmayer Gallery of Old Masters MUSEUM
(Strossmayerova Galerija Starih Majstora; www. mdc.hr/strossmayer; Trg Nikole Šubića Zrinskog 11; adult/concession 10/5KN; ⊙10am-7pm Tue, to 4pm Wed-Fri, to 1pm Sat & Sun) Inside the neo-Renaissance Croatian Academy of Arts and Sciences, it showcases the impressive fine-art collection donated to Zagreb by Bishop Strossmayer in 1884. When it's closed, enter the interior courtyard to see the Baška Slab (1102) from Krk Island, one of the oldest inscriptions in the Croatian language.

Archaeological Museum MUSEUM
(Arheološki Muzej; www.amz.hr; Trg Nikole Šubića Zrinskog 19; adult/concession 20/10KN; ⊙10am-5pm Tue, Wed & Fri, to 8pm Thu, to 1pm Sat & Sun) The fascinating Archaeological Museum has a wide-ranging display of artefacts from prehistoric times through to the medieval period. Behind the museum is a garden of Roman sculpture turned into a pleasant open-air cafe in the summer.

Gallery of Modern Art ART GALLERY
(Moderna Galerija; www.moderna-galerija.hr; Andrije Hebranga 1; adult/concession 40/20KN; ⊙10am-6pm Tue-Fri, to 1pm Sat & Sun) With a glorious display of Croatian artists of the last 200 years, it offers an excellent overview of Croatia's vibrant arts scene.

Art Pavilion ART GALLERY
(Umjetnički Paviljon; www.umjetnicki-paviljon.hr; Trg Kralja Tomislava 22; adult/concession 30/15KN; ⊙11am-7pm Tue-Sat, 10am-1pm Sun) The yellow Art Pavilion in a stunning 1897 art nouveau building presents changing exhibitions of contemporary art. It shuts down from mid-July through late August.

FREE THRILLS

Though you'll have to pay to get into most of Zagreb's galleries and museums, there are some gorgeous parks and markets to be enjoyed for nowt – and there's always window shopping!

» Taste bits of food for free at Dolac – but don't be too cheeky!

» Smell the herbs at the Botanical Gardens.

» Enjoy the long walks around Maksimir Park.

» See the magnificent Mirogoj cemetery.

» Pop inside the gorgeous baroque Jesuit Church of St Catherine and the ever-renovated cathedral.

MARKET DAYS

The Sunday **antiques market** (⊘9am-2pm) on Britanski Trg is one of central Zagreb's joys, but to see a flea market that's unmatched in the whole of Croatia, you have to head to **Hrelić** (⊘7am-3pm). This huge open space is packed with anything – from car parts, cars and antique furniture to clothes, records, kitchenware, you name it. Shopping aside, it's also a great place to experience the truly Balkan part and chaotic fun of Zagreb – Roma music, bartering, grilled-meat smoke and general gusto. If you're going in the summer months, take a hat and slap on sunscreen – there's no shade. Take bus 295 to Sajam Jakuševac from behind the train station.

Botanical Garden   GARDEN
(Botanički Vrt; Mihanovićeva bb; admission free; ⊘9am-2.30pm Mon-Tue, 9am-7pm Wed-Sun Apr-Oct) Laid out in 1890, the garden has 10,000 plant species, including 1800 tropical flora specimens. The landscaping has created restful corners and paths that seem a world away from bustling Zagreb.

OUTSIDE THE CENTRE

Museum of Contemporary Art   MUSEUM
(Muzej Suvremene Umjetnosti; www.msu.hr; Avenija Dubrovnik 17; adult/concession 30/15KN, free 1st Wed of month; ⊘11am-7pm Tue-Sun, 11am-10pm Thu) Housed in a dazzling functionalist building by local architect Igor Franić, this swanky new museum in Novi Zagreb, across the Sava River, puts on solo and thematic group shows by Croatian and international artists. The year-round schedule is packed with film, theatre, concerts and performance art.

Mirogoj   CEMETERY
(⊘6am-8pm Apr-Sep, 7.30am-6pm Oct-Mar) A 10-minute ride north of the city centre on bus 106 from the cathedral (or a half-hour walk through leafy streets) takes you to one of Europe's most beautiful cemeteries. This verdant resting place was designed in 1876 by Austrian-born architect Herman Bollé, who created numerous buildings around Zagreb. The sculpted and artfully designed tombs lie beyond a majestic arcade topped by a string of cupolas.

Maksimir Park   PARK
(Maksimirska bb; www.park-maksimir.hr; ⊘9am-dusk) Another green delight is Maksimir Park, a peaceful wooded enclave covering 18 hectares; it is easily accessible by trams 4, 7, 11 and 12. Opened to the public in 1794, it was the first public promenade in southeastern Europe. There's also a modest **zoo** (www.zoo.hr; adult/child 30/20KN; ⊘9am-8pm) here.

☞ Tours

ZET   BUS TOURS
(www.zet.hr) Zagreb's public transportation network operates open-deck tour buses (70KN) departing from Kaptol on a hop-on hop-off basis from April through September.

Zagreb Inside   WALKING TOURS
(www.zagrebinside.com) Runs weekly thematic tours (adult/student 90KN/70KN) such as Women of Zagreb and Do You Speak Croatian?, which teaches you basic language skills. The meeting point is outside the tourist info centre; no tours in August.

Blue Bike Tours   BIKE TOURS
(www.zagrebbybike.com) Has three-hour tours (170KN) departing twice daily.

✬✬ Festivals & Events

For a complete listing of Zagreb events, see www.zagreb-convention.hr.

Music Biennale Zagreb   MUSIC
(www.mbz.hr) Croatia's most important contemporary music event is held during odd-numbered years, in April.

Queer Zagreb Festival   GAY & LESBIAN
(www.queerzagreb.org) Camp out and party in late April/early May, with theatre, film, dance and music.

T-Mobile INmusic Festival   MUSIC
(www.t-mobileinmusicfestival.com) A three-day extravaganza every June, this is Zagreb's highest-profile music festival, with multiple stages by the Jarun Lake.

World Festival of Animated Film   FILM
(www.animafest.hr) This prestigious festival has been held in Zagreb since 1972, now annually in June.

Cest is D'Best   STREET FESTIVAL
(www.cestisdbest.com) In early June, it features five stages around the city centre, around 200 international performers and

acts that include music, dance, theatre, art and sports.

Eurokaz
THEATRE

(www.eurokaz.hr) The International Festival of New Theatre showcases innovative theatre troupes and cutting-edge performances from around the world in the second half of June.

International Folklore Festival
FOLKLORE

(www.msf.hr) Each July, it features folk dancers and singers from Croatia and other European countries, plus free workshops in dance, music and art.

Zagreb Summer Evenings
MUSIC

A cycle of concerts in the Upper Town each July, with the atrium of Galerija Klovićevi Dvori and the Gradec stage used for the performances of classic music, jazz, blues and world tunes.

🛏 Sleeping

Zagreb's accommodation scene has been undergoing a small but noticeable change with the arrival of some of Europe's low-cost airlines: the budget end of the market is consequently starting to get a pulse. Although the new hostels cater mainly to the backpacker crowd, it's a good beginning. For midrangers and those wanting more privacy and a homey feel, there are private rooms and apartments.

Prices stay the same in all seasons but be prepared for a 20% surcharge if you arrive during a festival, especially the autumn business fair in mid- to late September.

If you intend to stay in a private house or apartment, try not to arrive on Sunday, because most of the agencies will be closed. Prices for doubles run from about 300KN and studio apartments start at 400KN per night. There's usually a surcharge for one-night stays. Some agencies:

Evistas (☑48 39 554; www.evistas.hr; Augusta Šenoe 28; s from 210KN, d/apt 295/360KN) Recommended by the tourist office.

InZagreb (☑65 23 201; www.inzagreb.com; Remetinečka 13; apt 471-616KN) Centrally located apartments with a minimum three-night stay. The price includes bike rental, wireless internet and pick-up and drop-off from the train and/or bus station.

Never Stop (Nemoj Stati; ☑091 637 8111; www.nest.hr; Crvenog Križa 31; apt 430-596KN) Has apartments in the centre of town, with a minimum three-night stay.

Arcotel Allegra
BOUTIQUE HOTEL €€€

(☑46 96 000; www.arcotel.at/allegra; Branimirova 29; s/d from 730/840KN; P🖳❄@⑤) Zagreb's first designer hotel has a marble-and-exotic-fish reception and airy rooms where bed throws come with printed faces of Kafka, Kahlo and other iconic personalities. There's a top-floor spa, and a good onsite restaurant. Look out for summer specials.

Hotel Dubrovnik
HOTEL €€€

(☑48 63 555; www.hotel-dubrovnik.hr; Gajeva 1; s/d from 980/1200KN; P❄⑤) Smack on the main square, this glass city landmark has 245 elegant units with old-school classic style and, from some, great views of the square.

Hotel Ilica
HOTEL €€

(☑37 77 522; www.hotel-ilica.hr; Ilica 102; s/d/apt 349/449/749KN; P❄⑤) A great central option, with quiet rooms ranging from super kitsch to lushly decorous. Trams 6, 11 and 12 stop right outside the entrance, or walk down buzzy Ilica for 15 minutes.

Hobo Bear Hostel
HOSTEL €

(☑48 46 636; www.hobobearhostel.com; Medulićeva 4; dm/d from 122/400KN;❄@⑤) Inside a duplex apartment, this sparkling seven-dorm hostel has exposed-brick walls, hardwood floors, free lockers, kitchen, common room and book exchange. Three doubles are across the street.

Krovovi Grada
PENSION €

(☑48 14 189; Opatovina 33; s/d 200/300KN;@⑤) Basic but charming, this restored old house is set back from the street a minute from bustling Tkalčićeva. Rooms have creaky floors, vintage furniture and grandma blankets. Get the upstairs room for vistas of Old Town rooftops.

Fulir Hostel
HOSTEL €

(☑48 30 882; www.fulir-hostel.com; Radićeva 3a; dm 130-140KN; @⑤) Seconds away from Trg Josipa Jelačića, the Fulir has 28 beds, friendly owners, self-catering (it's right by Dolac market), lockers, a DVD-packed common room and free internet, tea and coffee.

Buzzbackpackers
HOSTEL €

(☑23 20 267; www.buzzbackpackers.com; Babukićeva 1b; dm/d from 130/450KN;❄@⑤) Out of the centre but clean with bright rooms, free internet, a shiny kitchen and a BBQ area. Take tram 4 or 9 from the train station to the Heinzelova stop, from where it's a short walk. The owners also run an apartment-style hostel in the city centre.

Omladinski Hostel
HOSTEL €

(✆48 41 261; www.hfhs.hr; Petrinjska 77; 6-/3-bed dm 113KN, s/d 203/286KN; 🛜) Although spruced up not too long ago, this socialist-era spot still maintains a bit of its old gloomy feel. The rooms are sparse and clean; it's central and the cheapest in town.

✖ Eating

You'll have to love Croatian and (below par) Italian food to enjoy Zagreb's restaurants, but new places are branching out to include Japanese and other world cuisines. The biggest move is towards elegantly presented haute cuisine at haute prices, many with a slow-food twist.

You can pick up excellent fresh produce at Dolac market.

TOP CHOICE Vinodol
CROATIAN €€

(Teslina 10; mains from 70KN) Well-prepared Central European fare much loved by local and overseas patrons. On warm days, eat on the covered patio entered through an ivy-clad passageway off Teslina. Highlights include the succulent lamb or veal and potatoes *under peka* (baked in a coal oven).

Tip Top
SEAFOOD €€

(Gundulićeva 18; mains from 55KN; ⊘Mon-Sat) The excellent Dalmatian food is served by wait staff sporting old socialist uniforms. Every day has its own set menu of mainstays; the Thursday octopus goulash is particularly tasty.

Amfora
SEAFOOD €

(Dolac 2; mains from 40KN; ⊘to 3pm Mon-Sat, to 1pm Sun) This locals' lunch fave serves super-fresh seafood straight from the market across the way, paired with off-the-stalls veggies. It's a hole-in-the-wall place with a few tables outside and an upstairs gallery with a market vista.

Kerempuh
CROATIAN €€

(Kaptol 3; mains from 75KN; ⊘lunch Mon-Sun) Overlooking Dolac market, this is a fabulous place to taste well-cooked and simple Croatian cuisine. The set menu changes daily, according to what the chef picked out at the market.

Prasac
MEDITERRANEAN €€€

(✆48 51 411; Vranicanijeva 6; mains from 87KN; ⊘Mon-Sat) Creative Mediterranean fare is conjured up by the Croatian-Sicilian chef at this intimate spot with wooden beamed ceilings. The market-fresh food is superb but the service slow and the portions small. Reserve ahead.

Stari Fijaker 900
CROATIAN €

(Mesnička 6; mains from 50KN; ⊘closed Sun evening summer) Tradition reigns in the kitchen of this restaurant-beer hall with a decor of banquettes and white linen, so try the homemade sausages, bean stews and *štrukli* (dumplings filled with cottage cheese), or one of cheaper daily dishes.

Ivica i Marica
CROATIAN €€

(Tkalčićeva 70; mains from 70KN) Based on the Hansel and Gretel story, this restaurant-cake shop is made to look like the gingerbread house from the tale, with waiters clad in traditional costumes. It has veggie and fish dishes plus meatier fare. The cakes and *štrukli* are great.

Konoba Čiho
SEAFOOD €€

(Pavla Hatza 15; mains from 80KN) An old-school Dalmatian *konoba* (simple family-run establishment), where, downstairs, you can get fish (by the kilo) and seafood grilled or stewed. Try the wide range of *rakija* (grape brandy) and house wines.

Vallis Aurea
CROATIAN €

(Tomićeva 4; mains from 37KN; ⊘Mon-Sat) This true local eatery has some of the best home cooking you'll find in town, so it's no wonder it gets chock-a-block at lunchtime for its *gableci* (traditional lunches). Right by the lower end of the funicular.

Karijola
PIZZA €

(Kranjčevićeva 16a; pizzas from 42KN) Locals swear by the thin-crust crispy pizza churned out of a clay oven at this no-frills spot. Pizzas come with high-quality ingredients such as smoked ham, top olive oil, cherry tomatoes, rocket and oyster mushrooms. It's near the Cibona Tower (take tram 12 from the main square, direction Ljubljanica).

Baltazar
CROATIAN €€€

(Nova Ves 4; mains from 120KN; ⊘Mon-Sat) Meats – duck, lamb, pork, beef and turkey – are grilled and prepared the Zagorje and Slavonia way in this upmarket old-timer. The summer terrace is the place to dine under the stars.

Nova
VEGETARIAN €€

(Ilica 72; mains from 60KN; ⊘Mon-Sat) This elegant macrobiotic restaurant is the place for those of the vegan persuasion, with great-value set menus.

Pingvin
SANDWICH STAND €

(Teslina 7; ⊘9am-4am Mon-Sat, 6pm-2am Sun) This quick-bite institution, around since 1987, offers tasty designer sandwiches and salads which locals savour on a handful of bar stools.

Rubelj FAST FOOD €
(Dolac 2; mains from 25KN) One of the many Rubeljs across town, this Dolac branch is a great place for a quick portion of *ćevapi* (small spicy sausage of minced beef, lamb or pork).

Drinking

In the Upper Town, the chic Tkalčićeva throbs with bars and cafes. In the Lower Town, Trg Petra Preradovića (known locally as Cvjetni Trg) is the most popular spot for street performers and occasional bands in mild weather. One of the nicest ways to see Zagreb is to join in on the *špica* – Saturday-morning pre-lunch coffee drinking on the terraces along Bogovićeva, Preradovićeva and Tkalčićeva.

TOP CHOICE **Bacchus** BAR
(www.bacchusjazzbar.hr; Trg Kralja Tomislava 16) You'll be lucky if you score a table at Zagreb's funkiest courtyard garden – lush and hidden in a passageway. After 10pm, the action moves indoors, inside the artsy subterranean space that hosts jazz concerts, poetry readings and oldies' nights.

Booksa COFFEE HOUSE
(www.booksa.hr; Martićeva 14d; ⊘11am-8pm Tue-Sun, closed 3 weeks from late Jul) Bookworms and poets, writers and performers, oddballs and artists and other creative types come to chat over coffee, buy books and hear readings at this lovely bookshop. There are English-language readings too. It's a 10-minute stroll east of the main square.

Stross BAR
(Strossmayerovo Šetalište) From June to September a makeshift bar is set up at the Strossmayer promenade in the Upper Town, with cheap drinks and live music most nights. Come for the mixed-bag crowd, great city views and leafy ambience.

Cica BAR
(Tkalčićeva 18) This tiny storefront bar is as underground as it gets on Tkalčićeva. Sample one or – if you dare – all of 15 kinds of *rakija* (homemade brandy) that the place is famous for.

Velvet CAFE
(Dežmanova 9; ⊘8am-10pm Mon-Fri, to 3pm Sat, to 2pm Sun) Stylish spot for a good cup of java and a quick bite amid the minimalist chic interior decked out by owner Saša Šekoranja, Zagreb's hippest florist.

☆ Entertainment

Zagreb doesn't register highly on a nightlife Richter scale, but it does have an ever-developing art and music scene. Its theatres and concert halls present a variety of programs throughout the year. Many are listed in the monthly brochure *Zagreb Events & Performances,* which is available from the main tourist office

Nightclubs

Nightclub entry ranges from 20KN to 100KN. Clubs open around 10pm but most people show up around midnight. Most clubs open only from Thursday to Saturday.

Aquarius CLUB
(www.aquarius.hr; Jarun Lake) A truly fab place to party, this enormously popular spots opens onto a huge terrace on the lake. During summer, Aquarius sets up shop at Zrće on Pag.

Močvara CLUB
(www.mochvara.hr, in Croatian; Trnjanski Nasip bb) In a former factory on the banks of the Sava River, 'Swamp' is one of the best venues in town for the cream of alternative music and attractively dingy charm.

KSET CLUB
(www.kset.org, in Croatian; Unska 3) Located in the neighbourhood of Trnje, this is Zagreb's best music venue, with anyone who's anyone performing here – from ethno to hip-hop acts.

Jabuka CLUB
(Jabukovac 28) 'Apple' is an old-time favourite, with 1980s hits played to a 30-something crowd that reminisces about the good old days when they were alternative. It's in the leafy residential neighborhood of Tuškanac.

Medika CLUB
(www.pierottijeva11.org; Pierrotijeva 11) This artsy venue in an old pharmaceutical factory, just to the west of Savska, is the city's first legalized squat, with concerts, art exhibits and parties fuelled with cheap beer.

Purgeraj CLUB
(www.purgeraj.hr; Park Ribnjak 1) Live rock, blues and avant-garde jazz is on the music menu at this funky space. The popular Saturday night hosts a fusion of disco, funk, pop and '80s.

Gay & Lesbian Venues

The gay and lesbian scene in Zagreb is finally becoming more open than it has previously been, although 'freewheeling' it isn't. Many gay men discreetly cruise the south beach around Jarun Lake and are welcome in most discos.

David
GAY & LESBIAN

(www.sauna-aquateam.hr; Ulica Ivana Broza 8a; ☺5-11pm) This men-only sauna, bar and video room, to the west of Savska, is a popular spot on Zagreb's gay scene. The day ticket is 80KN.

Rush Club
GAY & LESBIAN

(Amruševa 10) A younger gay and lesbian crowd mixes at this fun club in the city centre, with free entry on Thursday and themed nights such as karaoke.

Sport

Basketball is popular in Zagreb, home to Cibona basketball team. Pay homage to the team's most famous player at the **Dražen Petrović Memorial Museum** (☎48 43 333; www.cibona.com; Savska 30; tickets for games 20-100KN), located south along Savska, on a small square just to the west. Games take place frequently; tickets can be purchased at the door or online at www.cibona.com.

Dinamo is Zagreb's most popular football (soccer) team and it plays matches at **Stadion Maksimir** (Maksimirska 128; tickets from 30KN), on the eastern side of Zagreb. Games are played on Sunday afternoons between August and May. Take trams 4, 7, 11 or 12 to Bukovačka.

Performing Arts

Make the rounds of the theatres in person to check their programs. Tickets are usually available for even the best shows.

Croatian National Theatre
THEATRE

(☎48 88 418; www.hnk.hr; Trg Maršala Tita 15) This neo-baroque theatre, established in 1895, stages opera and ballet performances.

Vatroslav Lisinski Concert Hall
LIVE MUSIC

(☎61 21 166; www.lisinski.hr; Trg Stjepana Radića 4) The city's most prestigious venue for symphony concerts, jazz and world music performances. It's tucked away behind the main train station.

Croatian Music Institute
LIVE MUSIC

(☎48 30 822; Gundulićeva 6a) Another good venue for classical music concerts, it often feature Croatian composers performed by Croatian musicians.

Shopping

Ilica is Zagreb's main shopping street.

TOP CHOICE / **Prostor**
CLOTHING & ACCESSORIES

(www.multiracionalnakompanija.com; Mesnička 5; ☺noon-8pm Mon-Fri, 10am-3pm Sat) A fantastic little art gallery and clothes shop, featuring some of the city's best independent artists and young designers. In a courtyard off Mesnička.

Bronić Sisters
CLOTHING

(www.bronic.biz) Don't miss the versatile textured interpretations of multitalented twins Josipa and Marijana, who sell their inspired garments and accessories at their home studio.

Natura Croatica
FOOD & DRINK

(www.naturacroatica.com; Skalinska 2a) All-natural Croatian products and souvenirs – from handcrafted soaps and fragrant bath oils to *rakija*, wines, chocolates, jams and spices.

Sherrif & Cherry
CLOTHING

(www.sheriffandcherry.com; Medvedgradska 3) Snag a par of revamped and super-trendy Yugo-era Startas trainers at this boutique-creative studio headed up by Rovinj-born designer Mauro Massarotto. Continue north along Tkalčićeva for five minutes.

Profil Megastore
BOOKS

(Bogovićeva 7; ☺9am-10pm Mon-Sat) Inside an entryway, this most atmospheric of Zagreb bookstores has a great selection of books (many in English) and a nice cafe.

ⓘ Information

Discount Cards

Zagreb Card (www.zagrebcard.fivestars.hr; 24/72hr 60/90KN) Provides free travel on all public transport, a 50% discount on museum and gallery entries, plus discounts in some bars and restaurants, and on car rental. The card is sold at the main tourist office and many hostels, hotels, bars and shops.

Emergency
Police (☎45 63 311; Petrinjska 30)

Internet Access

Several cafes around town offer free wi-fi, including Booksa.
Sublink (www.sublink.hr; Teslina 12; per hr 15KN; ☺9am-10pm Mon-Sat, 3-10pm Sun) The city's first cybercafe remains its best.

Left Luggage

Garderoba bus station (1st 4hr 20KN, then per hr 2.50KN; ☺5am-10pm Mon-Sat, 6am-10pm Sun); train station (lockers per 24hr 15KN; ☺24hr)

Medical Services

Dental Emergency (☎48 03 200; Perkovčeva 3; ⏲24hr)

KBC Rebro (☎23 88 888; Kišpatićeva 12; ⏲24hr) East of the city, it provides emergency aid.

Pharmacy (☎48 16 198; Trg Josipa Jelačića 3; ⏲24hr)

Money

There are ATMs at the bus and train stations, the airport, and at numerous locations around town. Some banks in the train and bus stations accept travellers cheques. Exchange offices can be found in many locations around town.

Post

Main post office (☎48 11 090; Jurišićeva 13; ⏲7am-8pm Mon-Fri, 7am-1pm Sat) Has a telephone centre.

Tourist Information

Main tourist office (☎48 14 051; www. zagreb-touristinfo.hr; Trg Josipa Jelačića 11; ⏲8.30am-9pm Mon-Fri, 9am-6pm Sat & Sun) Distributes free city maps and leaflets, and sells the Zagreb Card.

Plitvice National Park office (☎46 13 586; Trg Kralja Tomislava 19; ⏲8am-4pm Mon-Thu, 8am-3.30pm Fri) Has details and brochures mainly on Plitvice but also on Croatia's other national parks.

Seasonal tourist office annex (airport; ⏲9am-9pm Mon-Fri, 10am-5pm Sat & Sun Jun-Sep) By International Arrivals.

Tourist office annex (train station; ⏲8.30am-8pm Mon-Fri, 12.30-6.30pm Sat & Sun) Same services as the main tourist office.

Travel Agencies

Atlas Travel Agency (☎48 07 300; www. atlas-croatia.com; Zrinjevac 17) Tours around Croatia.

Croatia Express (☎49 22 237; Trg Kralja Tomislava 17) Train reservations, car rental, air and ferry tickets, hotel bookings and a daily trip to the beach from June to September (90KN round trip to Crikvenica).

ⓘ Getting There & Away

Air

For information about international flights to and from Croatia, see p268.

Zagreb Airport (☎45 62 222; www.zagreb-air port.hr) Located 17km southeast of Zagreb, this is one of the country's major airports, offering a range of international and domestic services.

Bus

Zagreb's **bus station** (☎060 313 333; www. akz.hr; Avenija M Držića 4) is 1km east of the train station. Trams 2, 3 and 6 run from the bus station to the train station. Tram 6 goes to Trg Josipa Jelačića.

Before buying a bus ticket, ask about the arrival time – some of the buses take local roads and stop in every town en route.

International destinations include Belgrade (199KN to 204KN, six hours, six daily), Munich (352KN, 9½ hours, two daily), Sarajevo (188KN to 244KN, seven to eight hours, four to five daily) and Vienna (250KN, five to six hours, two daily).

Train

The **train station** (☎060 333 444; www.hznet. hr) is in the southern part of the city. As you come out of it, you'll see a series of parks and pavilions directly in front of you, which lead into

DOMESTIC BUSES FROM ZAGREB

DESTINATION	FARE (KN)	DURATION (HR)	DAILY SERVICES
Dubrovnik	215-228	9½-11	9-10
Korčula	239	11	1
Krk	163-194	3-4½	8
Mali Lošinj	267-284	5-6	3
Plitvice	72-83	2-2½	11
Poreč	150-221	4-4½	11
Pula	162-185	3½-5½	14-17
Rijeka	104-155	2½-3	20-25
Rovinj	146-185	3-6	9-11
Split	165-181	5-8½	32-34
Zadar	99-138	3½-5	31

DESTINATION	FARE (KN)	DURATION (HR)	DAILY SERVICES
Banja Luka	100	4½	2
Belgrade	159	6½	4
Budapest	223	6-7	3
Ljubljana	100	2½	7
Mostar	282	11½	1
Munich	674	8½-9	3
Plŏe	313	13½	1
Sarajevo	222	9½	2
Venice	303	7½	1
Vienna	446	5½-6½	2

the town centre. It's advisable to book train tickets in advance because of limited seating.

Domestic trains head to Rijeka (97KM, four to five hours, five daily), Split (166KM, 5½ to eight hours, five daily) and Zadar (161KM, eight hours, one daily).

Getting Around

Zagreb is a fairly easy city to navigate. Traffic is bearable and the efficient tram system should be a model for other polluted, traffic-clogged European capitals.

To/From the Airport

BUS The Croatia Airlines bus to the airport (30KN) leaves from the bus station every half-hour or hour from about 5am to 8pm, and returns from the airport on the same schedule.

TAXI Costs between 150KN and 300KN.

Car

Zagreb is a fairly easy city to navigate by car (boulevards are wide and parking in the city centre, although scarce, costs 12KN per hour). Watch out for trams buzzing around.

Motorists can call **Hrvatski Autoklub** (HAK; Croatian Auto Club; ☑ 46 40 800; www.hak. hr; Avenija Dubrovnik 44) on ☑ 987 for help on the road.

International car-hire companies include **Budget Rent-a-Car** (☑ 45 54 936; www.budget.hr; 1. Pile 1 and at airport) and **Hertz** (☑ 48 46 777; www.hertz.hr; Vukotinovićeva 4). Local companies usually have lower rates; try **H&M** (☑ 37 04 535; www.hm-rentacar.hr; Grahorova 11), which also has a desk at the airport.

Public Transport

Public transport is based on an efficient network of trams, although the city centre is compact enough to make them unnecessary.

Buy tickets at newspaper kiosks for 8KN. Tickets can be used for transfers within 90 minutes, but only in one direction. Note that you can ride the tram for free two stations in each direction from the main square.

A *dnevna karta* (day ticket), valid on all public transport until 4am the next morning, is available for 25KN at most newspaper kiosks.

Make sure you validate your ticket when you get on the tram by inserting it in the yellow box.

Taxi

Zagreb's taxis all have meters, which begin at 19KN and then ring up 7KN per kilometre. On Sunday and at night (10pm to 5am) there's a 20% surcharge. Waiting time is 50KN per hour. The baggage surcharge is 3KN per bag.

You'll have no trouble finding idle taxis, usually at blue-marked taxi stops, or you can call for one at ☑ 060 800 800.

ISTRIA

☑ 052

Continental Croatia meets the Adriatic in Istria (Istra to Croats), the heart-shaped 3600-sq-km peninsula just south of Trieste in Italy. While the bucolic interior of rolling hills and fertile plains attracts artsy visitors to its hilltop villages, rural hotels and farmhouse restaurants, the verdant indented coastline is enormously popular with the sun'n'sea set. Vast hotel complexes line much of the coast and its rocky beaches are not Croatia's best, but the facilities are wide-ranging, the sea is clean and secluded spots are still plentiful.

The coast, or 'Blue Istria', as the tourist board calls it, gets flooded with tourists in summer, but you can still feel alone and undisurbed in 'Green Istria' (the interior), even in mid-August. Add acclaimed gastronomy (starring fresh seafood, prime white truffles, wild asparagus, top-rated olive oils and award-winning wines), sprinkle it with historical charm and you have a little slice of heaven.

Poreč

POP 17,460

Poreč (Parenzo in Italian) sits on a low, narrow peninsula halfway down the western coast of Istria. The ancient Roman town is the centrepiece of a vast system of resorts that stretch north and south, entirely devoted to summer tourism. While this is not the place for a quiet getaway (unless you come out of season), there is a World Heritage-listed basilica, a medley of Gothic, Romanesque and baroque buildings, well-developed tourist infrastructure and the pristine Istrian interior within easy reach.

◉ Sights

The compact Old Town, called Parentium by the Romans, is based on a rectangular street plan. The ancient Decumanus with its polished stones is the main street running through the peninsula's middle, lined with shops and restaurants. Hotels, travel agencies and excursion boats are on the quay, Obala Maršala Tita, which runs from the small-boat harbour to the tip of the peninsula.

Euphrasian Basilica   CHURCH
(Eufrazijeva bb; admission free, belfry 10KN; ⊙7am–8pm Apr–mid-Oct or by appointment) The main reason to visit Poreč is the 6th-century Euphrasian Basilica, one of Europe's finest intact examples of Byzantine art. What packs in the crowds are the glittering wall mosaics in the apse, veritable masterpieces featuring biblical scenes, archangels and martyrs. The belfry affords an invigorating view of the Old Town.

Also worth a visit is the adjacent **Bishop's Palace** (admission 10KN; ⊙10am-7pm Apr–mid-Oct or by appointment), which contains a display of ancient stone sculptures, religious paintings and 4th-century mosaics from the original oratory.

Trg Marafor   SQUARE
Trg Marafor is where the Roman forum used to stand and public gatherings took place. West of this rectangular square, inside a small park, are the ruins of the 2nd-century **Temple of Neptune**, dedicated to the god of sea.

Sveti Nikola   ISLAND
From May to October passenger boats (adult/child 20/10KN) travel to Sveti Nikola, the small island that lies opposite Poreč harbour. They depart every 30 minutes (from 6.45am to 1am) from the wharf on Obala Maršala Tita.

Activities

Many recreational activities are to be found outside the town in either Plava Laguna or Zelena Laguna. For details, pick up the annual *Poreč Info* booklet from the tourist office.

From May to early October, a tourist train operates regularly from Šetalište Antuna Štifanića by the marina to Plava Laguna (15KN) and Zelena Laguna (15KN). An hourly passenger boat makes the same run from the ferry landing (15KN).

The well-marked paths make **cycling** and **hiking** a prime way to explore the region. The tourist office issues a free map of roads and trails. You can rent a bike at agencies around town for about 70KN per day.

There is good **diving** in and around shoals and sandbanks in the area, as well as at the nearby *Coriolanus*, a British Royal Navy warship that sank in 1945. At **Diving Centre Poreč** (☑433 606; www.divingcenter-porec.com), boat dives start at 110KN (more for caves or wrecks) or 310KN with full equipment rental.

🛏 Sleeping

Accommodation in Poreč is plentiful but gets booked ahead of time, so advance reservations are essential if you come in July or August.

If you want to find private accommodation, consult the travel agencies we've listed (p222). Expect to pay between 200KN and 250KN for a double room in the high season or 280KN to 350KN for a two-person apartment, plus a 30% surcharge for stays of less than four nights. There are a limited number of rooms in the Old Town, where there's no parking. Look for the *Domus Bonus* certificate of quality in private accommodation.

Valamar Riviera Hotel   LUXURY HOTEL €€€
(☑408 000; www.valamar.com; Obala Maršala Tita 15; s 990-1400KN, d 1300-1990KN; P❄@) This new harbourfront property is a swanky four-star choice, with a private beach on Sveti Nikola. Look out for specials and packages.

Hotel Hostin
HOTEL €€

(☑408 800; www.hostin.hr; Rade Končara 4; s/d 683/966KN; **P** ❄ @ ☎) At this charmer, in verdant parkland steps from the bus station, each room has a balcony. There's an indoor swimming pool, and a pebble beach only 70m away.

Hotel Poreč
HOTEL €

(☑451 811; www.hotelporec.com; Rade Končara 1; s/d 475/720KN; ❄) While the rooms inside this concrete box have uninspiring views over the bus station and the shopping centre opposite, they're acceptable and an easy walk from the Old Town.

Camp Zelena Laguna
CAMPING GROUND €

(☑410 700; www.plavalaguna.hr; Zelena Laguna; per adult/campsite 55/77KN; ⊙Apr-Sep; ☎) Well equipped for sports, this camping ground 5km from the Old Town can house up to 2700 people. It has access to many beaches, including a naturist one.

✗ Eating

A large supermarket and department store are situated next to Hotel Poreč, near the bus station.

Peterokutna Kula
INTERNATIONAL €€

(Decumanus 1; mains from 70KN) Inside the medieval Pentagonal Tower, this upmarket restaurant has two alfresco patios in a stone vault, and a roof terrace. It serves a full spectrum of fish and meat but has erratic service.

Dva Ferala
ISTRIAN €

(Obala Maršala Tita 13a; mains from 60KN) Savour well-prepared Istrian specialities, such as *istarski tris* for two – a copious trio of homemade pastas – on the terrace of this pleasant *konoba*.

Nono
PIZZA €

(Zagrebačka 4; pizzas 40-80KN) Nono serves the best pizza in town, with puffy crusts and toppings such as truffles. Other dishes are tasty too.

Buffet Horizont
SEAFOOD €

(Eufrazijeva 8; mains from 30KN) For cheap and tasty seafood snacks like sardines, shrimp and calamari, look out for this yellow house with wooden benches outside.

🍺 Drinking & Entertainment

Lapidarium
BAR

(Svetog Maura 10) This gorgeous bar with a large courtyard has a series of antique-filled inner rooms. Wednesday is jazz night in summer, with alfresco live music.

Byblos
CLUB

(www.byblos.hr; Zelena Laguna bb) On Fridays, celeb guest DJs such as David Morales crank out house tunes at this humongous open-air club, one of Croatia's hottest places to party.

Torre Rotonda
CAFE-BAR

(Narodni Trg 3a) Take the steep stairs to the top of the historic Round Tower and grab a table at the open-air cafe to watch the action on the quays.

ℹ Information

You can change money at any of the many travel agencies or banks. There are ATMs all around town.

Atlas Travel Agency (☑434 933; www.atlas -croatia.com; Eufrazijeva 63) Books excursions.

CyberM@c (Mire Grahalića 1; per hr 42KN; ⊙10am-10pm) A full-service computer centre.

Di Tours (☑432 100; www.di-tours.hr; Prvomajska 2) Finds private accommodation.

Left luggage (per hour 6KN; ⊙7am-8.30pm) At the bus station.

Medical Centre (☑451 611; Maura Gioseffija 2)

Post office (Trg Slobode 14; ⊙8am-noon & 6-8pm Mon-Fri, 8am-noon Sat) Has a telephone centre.

Sunny Way (☑452 021; sunnyway@pu.t-com. hr; Alda Negrija 1) Specialises in boat tickets and excursions to Italy and around Croatia.

Tourist office (☑451 293; www.to-porec.com; Zagrebačka 9; ⊙8am-9pm Mon-Sat, 9am-1pm & 6-9pm Sun)

ℹ Getting There & Away

From the **bus station** (☑432 153; Rade Končara 1) just outside the Old Town, behind Rade Končara, there are buses to Rovinj (42KN, 45 minutes, six daily), Zagreb (218KN, four hours, seven daily), Rijeka (85KN, two hours, seven daily) and Pula (54KN, one to 1½ hours, eight daily).

There are four fast catamarans to Venice daily in high season (two hours) by **Commodore Cruises** (www.commodore-cruises.hr), **Astarea** (☑451 100) and **Venezia Lines** (www.venezia lines.com). Prices range from 225KN to 474KN for a one-way journey, and 300KN to 880KN for return trip. **Ustica Line** (www.usticalines.it) runs catamarans to Trieste every day except Monday (160KN, 1½ hours).

Rovinj

POP 14,234

Rovinj (Rovigno in Italian) is coastal Istria's star attraction. While it can get overrun with tourists in the summer months and residents are developing a sharp eye for maximising their profits (by upgrading the hotels and restaurants to four-star status), it remains one of the last true Mediterranean fishing ports. Fishermen haul their catch into the harbour in the early morning, followed by a horde of squawking gulls, and mend their nets before lunch.

The massive Church of St Euphemia, with its 60m-high tower, punctuates the peninsula. Wooded hills and low-rise hotels surround the Old Town, which is webbed by steep, cobbled streets and piazzas. The 13 green, offshore islands of the Rovinj archipelago make for a pleasant afternoon away, and you can swim from the rocks in the sparkling water below Hotel Rovinj.

◉ Sights

The Old Town of Rovinj is contained within an egg-shaped peninsula, with the bus station just to the southeast. There are two harbours – the northern open harbour and the small, protected harbour to the south.

Church of St Euphemia   CHURCH
(Sveta Eufemija; Petra Stankovića; ⊙10am-6.30pm May-Oct, sporadic hours rest of year) The town's showcase is the imposing Church of St Euphemia that dominates the Old Town from its hilltop location. Built in 1736, it's the largest baroque building in Istria, reflecting the period during the 18th century when Rovinj was its most populous town, an important fishing centre and the bulwark of the Venetian fleet.

Inside the church behind the right-hand altar, don't miss the marble **tomb of St Euphemia**, Rovinj's patron saint martyred in AD 304, whose body mysteriously appeared in Rovinj according to legend. The mighty 60m **bell tower** is topped by a copper statue of St Euphemia, which shows the direction of the wind by turning on a spindle. You can climb it for 10KN.

Batana House   MUSEUM
(Pina Budicina 2; adult/child 10/5KN, with guide 15KN; ⊙10am-3pm & 7-11pm Jun-Aug, 10am-1pm Tue-Sun Sep-May, closed Jan & Feb) On the harbour, Batana House is a multimedia museum dedicated to the *batana*, a flat-bottomed fishing boat that stands as a symbol of Rovinj's seafaring and fishing tradition.

Grisia   HISTORIC AREA
Lined with galleries where local artists sell their work, this cobbled street leads uphill from behind the elaborate 1679 **Balbi Arch** to St Euphemia. The winding narrow back-streets around Grisia are an attraction in themselves. Windows, balconies, portals and squares are a pleasant confusion of styles – Gothic, Renaissance, baroque and neoclassical. On the second Sunday in August each year, Grisia becomes an open-air **art exhibition**, with anyone from children to professional painters displaying their work.

Heritage Museum   MUSEUM
(www.muzej-rovinj.com; Trg Maršala Tita 11; adult/concession 15/10KN; ⊙10am-2pm & 6-10pm Tue-Fri, 10am-2pm & 7-10pm Sat & Sun) In a baroque palace, it contains a collection of contemporary art and old masters from Croatia and Rovinj, as well as archaeological finds and a maritime section. Hours are shorter outside summer.

Punta Corrente Forest Park   PARK
Follow the waterfront on foot or by bike past Hotel Park to this verdant area, locally known as Zlatni Rat, about 1.5km south. It's covered in oak and pine groves and boasts 10 species of cypress. You can swim off the rocks or just sit and admire the offshore islands.

🏃 Activities

Most people hop aboard a boat for **swimming**, **snorkelling** and **sunbathing**. In summer, there are hourly boats to Sveta Katarina (return 30KN, 10 minutes) and to Crveni Otok (return 40KN, 15 minutes). They leave from just opposite Hotel Adriatic and also from the Delfin ferry dock near Hotel Park.

Nadi Scuba Diving Centar (✆813 290; www.scuba.hr) and **Petra** (✆812 880; www.diving petra.hr) offer daily boat dives. The main attraction is the **Baron Gautsch wreck**, a 1914 Austrian passenger steamer sunk in 40m of water.

Biking around Rovinj and the Punta Corrente Forest Park is a superb way to spend an afternoon. You can rent bikes at many agencies around town, for about 20KN per hour or 60KN per day.

👉 Tours

Most travel agencies in Rovinj sell day trips to Venice (400KN to 500KN), Plitvice (550KN to 600KN) and Brijuni (380KN to 430KN). There are also fish picnics (250KN), panoramic cruises (100KN) and boat outings to Limska Draga Fjord (150KN). These can be slightly cheaper if booked through one of the independent operators that line the waterfront; **Delfin** (✆848 265) is reliable.

For kayaking, such as an 8km jaunt around the Rovinj archipelago, book a trip through **Istrian Kayak Adventures** (☑095 838 3797; Carera 69).

🛏 Sleeping

Rovinj has become Istria's destination of choice for hordes of summertime tourists, so reserving in advance is strongly recommended. Prices have been rising steadily and probably will continue to do so.

If you want to stay in private accommodation, there is little available in the Old Town, plus there is no parking and the cost is higher. Double rooms start at 220KN in the high season, with a small discount for single occupancy; two-person apartments start at 330KN. Out of season, prices go down considerably.

The surcharge for a stay of less than three nights is up to 50% and guests who stay only one night are sometimes punished with a 100% surcharge during summer months. You can book directly through a travel agency.

Except for a few private options, most hotels and camping grounds in the area are managed by **Maistra** (www.maistra.com), including Rovinj's swankiest hotel, **Monte Mulini** (www.montemulinihotel.com).

TOP CHOICE **Hotel Heritage Angelo D'Oro**
BOUTIQUE HOTEL **€€€**
(☑840 502; www.rovinj.at; Via Švalba 38-42; s/d 916/1580KN; P☀️🔁) In a renovated Venetian townhouse, the 23 plush rooms and suites of this boutique hotel have lots of antiques plus mod cons aplenty. There's a tanning room, bikes for rent and a lush interior terrace, a great place for a drink amid ancient stone.

Casa Garzotto GUEST HOUSE **€€**
(☑814 255; www.casa-garzotto.com; Via Garzotto 8; s/d 758/1010KN; P☀️🔁) Each of the four studio apartments inside this historic town house has original details like fireplaces and wooden beams. There are two annexes nearby: one with more basic rooms (650KN) and another with four-person apartments (1440KN).

Vila Lili HOTEL **€€**
(☑840 940; www.hotel-vilalili.hr; Mohorovičića 16; s/d 380/788KN;☀️@) Bright rooms have all the three-star perks, including air-con and minibars, in a small modern house a short walk out of town. There are also a couple of pricier suites.

Hotel Adriatic HOTEL **€€**
(☑803 510; www.maistra.com; Pina Budicina bb; s/d 676/1007KN;☀️@🔁) The location right on the harbour is excellent and the rooms spick-and-span and well equipped, but on the kitschy side. The pricier sea-view rooms have more space.

Porton Biondi CAMPING GROUND **€**
(☑813 557; www.portonbiondi.hr; per person/tent 41/24KN; ⊙Mar-Oct) This camping ground that sleeps 1200 is about 2km from the Old Town.

🍴 Eating

Most of the restaurants that line the harbour offer the standard fish and meat mainstays at similar prices. For a more gourmet experience, you'll need to bypass the water vistas. Note that many restaurants shut their doors between lunch and dinner.

Picnickers can get supplies at the supermarket next to the bus station or at one of the Konzum stores around town.

TOP CHOICE **Ulika** ISTRIAN **€€**
(Vladimira Švalbe 34; mains from 80KN) For an evening snack of local cheese, cured meats and tasty small bites, head to this tiny tavern a few doors down from Angelo D'Oro.

Kantinon SEAFOOD **€**
(Alda Rismonda 18; mains from 53KN) A fishing theme runs through this high-ceilinged canteen that specialises in fresh seafood at low prices. The Batana fish plate for two is great value, as are the set menus.

La Puntulina MEDITERRANEAN **€€€**
(☑813 186; Svetog Križa 38; mains from 100KN) Sample creative Med cuisine on three alfresco terraces. Pasta dishes are more affordable (from 80KN). At night, grab a cushion and sip a cocktail on the rocks below this converted townhouse. Reservations recommended.

Veli Jože SEAFOOD **€**
(Svetog Križa 3; mains from 50KN) Graze on good Istrian standards, either in the eclectic interior crammed with knick-knacks or at the outdoor tables with water views.

🍷 Drinking & Entertainment

While there are plenty of spots for a quiet drink during the day, come night most action takes place at **Monvi Centar** (www.monvicenter.com; Luja Adamovića bb), a stroll out of the centre. This entertainment complex has lounge bars, restaurants and clubs that regularly host open-air concerts and celebrity DJs.

Havana BAR
(Aldo Negri bb) Tropical cocktails, Cuban cigars, straw parasols and the shade of tall pine trees make this open-air cocktail bar

DESTINATION	FARE (KN)	DURATION	DAILY SERVICES
Dubrovnik	589	15hr	1
Labin	80	2hr	3
Poreč	41	45min	11
Pula	38	50min	23
Rijeka	94	3hr	8
Split	416	11hr	1
Trieste, Italy	88	2hr	3
Zagreb	193	5hr	10

a popular spot to chill and watch the ships go by.

Piassa Granda WINE BAR
(Veli Trg 1) This stylish little wine bar with red walls and wooden beamed ceilings has 150 wine labels, mainly Istrian. Try the truffle grappa and the delicious snacks and salads.

Valentino BAR
(Svetog Križa 28) Premium cocktail prices on the terrace of this high-end cocktail and champagne spot include fantastic sunset views, on the water's edge.

ⓘ Information

There's an ATM next to the bus-station entrance, and banks all around town. Most travel agencies will change money.

Futura Travel (☑817 281; www.futura-travel. hr; Matteo Benussi 2) Private accommodation, money exchange, excursions and transfers.

Globtour (☑814 130; www.globtour-turizam.hr; Alda Rismonda 2) Excursions, private accommodation and bike rental.

Left luggage (per day 6KN; ☺6am-8pm Mon-Fri, 7.45am-7.30pm Sat & Sun) *Garderoba* is at the bus station. Note the half-hour breaks at 9.15am and 4.40pm.

Medical Centre (☑813 004; Istarska bb)

Planet (☑840 494; www.planetrovinj.com; Svetog Križa 1) Doubles as an internet cafe (6KN per 10 minutes) and has a printer. Good bargains on private accommodation, too.

Post office (Matteo Benussi 4; ☺7am-8pm Mon-Fri, to 2pm Sat)

Tourist office (☑811 566; www.tzgrovinj. hr; Pina Budicina 12; ☺8am-10pm Jun-Sep, 8am-3pm Mon-Fri, 8am-1pm Sat Oct-May) Just off Trg Maršala Tita, it has plenty of brochures and maps.

ⓘ Getting There & Away

The bus station is just to the southeast of the Old Town.

Pula

POP 60,000

The wealth of Roman architecture makes the otherwise workaday Pula (ancient Polensium) a standout among Croatia's larger cities. The star of the Roman show is the remarkably well-preserved Roman amphitheatre, which dominates the streetscape and doubles as a venue for summer concerts and performances. Historical attractions aside, Pula is a busy commercial city on the sea that has managed to retain a friendly small-town appeal. A series of beaches and good nightlife are just a short bus ride away at the resorts that occupy the Verudela Peninsula to the south. Further south along the indented shoreline, the Premantura Peninsula hides a spectacular nature area, the protected cape of Kamenjak.

◉ Sights

The oldest part of the city follows the ancient Roman plan of streets circling the central citadel. Most sights are clustered in and around the Old Town, as well as on Giardini, Carrarina and Istarska as well as the Riva, which runs along the harbour.

Roman Amphitheatre ANCIENT SITE
(Arena; Flavijevska bb; adult/concession 40/20KN; ☺8am-9pm summer, 9am-8pm spring & autumn, 9am-5pm winter) Pula's most famous and imposing sight is this 1st-century amphitheatre overlooking the harbour northeast of the Old Town. Built entirely from local limestone, the amphitheatre with seating for up

to 20,000 spectators was designed to host gladiatorial contests. In the chambers downstairs is a small **museum** with a display of ancient olive oil equipment. Every summer the **Pula Film Festival** is held here, as are pop and classical concerts.

Temple of Augustus   RUINS

(Forum; adult/concession 10/5KN; ⊙9am-8pm Mon-Fri, 10am-3pm Sat & Sun summer, or by appointment) This is the only visible remnant from the Roman era on Forum, Pula's central meeting place from antiquity through the Middle Ages. This temple, erected from

Pula

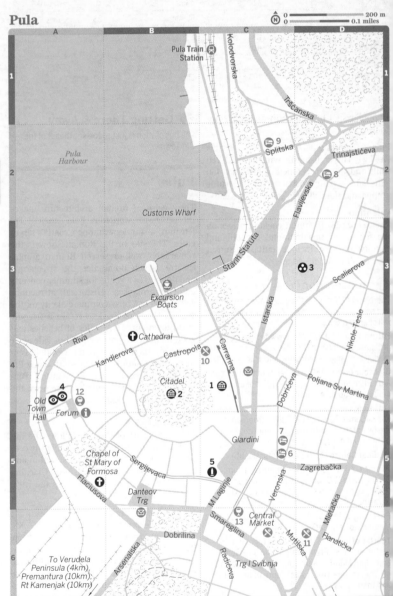

2 BC to AD 14, now houses a small historical museum with captions in English.

Archaeological Museum
MUSEUM

(Arheološki Muzej; Carrarina 3; adult/concession 20/10KN; ⊘9am-8pm Mon-Sat, 10am-3pm Sun May-Sep, 9am-2pm Mon-Fri Oct-Apr) This museum presents archaeological finds from all over Istria. Even if you don't enter the museum, be sure to visit the large **sculpture garden** around it, and the **Roman theatre** behind. The garden, entered through 2nd-century twin gates, is the site of concerts in summer.

Triumphal Arch of Sergius
RUINS

Along Carrarina are Roman walls, which mark the eastern boundary of old Pula. Follow these walls south and continue down Giardini to this majestic arch erected in 27 BC to commemorate three members of the Sergius family who achieved distinction in Pula.

Museum of History
MUSEUM

(Povijesni Muzej Istre; Gradinski Uspon 6; adult/concession 15/7KN; ⊘8am-9pm Jun-Sep, 9am-5pm Oct-May) In a 17th-century Venetian fortress on a hill above the Old Town's centre, it has meagre exhibits that deal mostly with the maritime history of Pula, but the views from the citadel walls are worth a stop.

Beaches

Pula is surrounded by a half-circle of rocky beaches, each one with its own fan club. The most tourist-packed are undoubtedly those surrounding the hotel complex on the **Verudela Peninsula**, although some locals will dare to be seen at the small turquoise-coloured **Hawaii Beach** near the Hotel Park.

For seclusion, head out to the wild **Rt Kamenjak** (www.kamenjak.hr, in Croatian; pedestrians & cyclists free, per car/scooter 25/15KN; ⊘7am-10pm) on the Premantura Peninsula, 10km south of town. Istria's southernmost point, this gorgeous, entirely uninhabited cape has wildflowers (including 30 species of orchid), 30km of virgin beaches and coves, and a delightful beach bar, **Safari** (snacks 25-50KN; ⊘May-Sep), half-hidden in the bushes near the beach, about 3.5km from the entrance to the park. Watch out for strong currents if swimming off the southern cape.

Windsurf Bar (www.windsurfing.hr) in Premantura rents bikes and windsurfing equipment (board and sail from 70KN per hour). Take city bus 26 from Pula to Premantura (15KN), then rent a bike to get inside the park.

🏃 Activities

At the **Orca Diving Center** (☑224 422; Hotel Histria) on the Verudela Peninsula, you can arrange boat and wreck dives. In addition to windsurfing, **Windsurf Bar** (☑091 512 3646; www.windsurfing.hr; Camping Village Stupice) in Premantura offers biking (250KN) and kayaking (300KN) excursions.

An easy 41km **cycling trail** from Pula to Medulin follows the path of Roman gladiators. Check out **Istria Bike** (www.istria-bike.com), a tourist board–run website outlining trails, packages and agencies that offer biking trips.

🛏 Sleeping

Pula's peak tourist season runs from the second week of July to late August. During this period it's wise to make advance reservations. The tip of the Verudela Peninsula, 4km southwest of the city centre, has been turned into a vast tourist complex replete with hotels and apartments.

Any travel agency can give you information and book you into one of the hotels, or you can contact **Arenaturist** (☑529 400; www.arenaturist.hr; Splitska 1a).

The travel agencies in Pula can find you private accommodation, but there is little available in the town centre. Count on paying from 250KN to 490KN for a double room and from 300KN to 535KN for a two-person apartment. You can also browse the list of private accommodation at www.pulainfo.hr.

Hotel Scaletta
HOTEL €€

(☑541 599; www.hotel-scaletta.com; Flavijevska 26; s/d 505/732KN;❀Ⓟ๏) There's a friendly family vibe here, the recently spruced up rooms have tasteful decor and a bagful of trimmings (such as minibars), and the restaurant serves decent food. Plus it's just a hop and a skip from town.

Hotel Galija
HOTEL €€

(☑383 802; www.hotelgalija.hr; Epulonova 3; s/d 505/732KN;❀๏) A stone's throw from the market in the town centre, this small family-run hotel has comfortably outfitted rooms that come in different sizes and colours, some with hydromassage showers.

Hotel Omir
HOTEL €

(☑218 186; www.hotel-omir.com; Dobricheva 6; s/d 450/600KN;๏) The best budget option smack in the heart of town, Hotel Omir has modest but clean and quiet rooms with TV. The more expensive units have air-con. There's no elevator.

Riviera Guest House
HOTEL €

(☑211 166; www.arenaturist.hr; Splitska 1; s/d 350/555KN) This once grand property in a neo-baroque 19th-century building is in dire need of a thorough overhaul. The saving grace: it's in the centre and the front rooms have water views.

Youth Hostel
HOSTEL €

(☑391 133; www.hfhs.hr; Valsaline 4; dm 117KN; caravan 137KN;@) This hostel overlooks a beach in Valsaline Bay, 3km south of central Pula. There are dorms and caravans split into two tiny four-bed units, each with bathroom. To get here, take bus 2A or 3A to the 'Piramida' stop, walk back towards the city to the first street, then turn left and look for the hostel sign.

Camping Stoja
CAMPING GROUND €

(☑387 144; www.arenacamps.com; Stoja 37; per person/tent 57/34KN; ☉Apr-Oct) The closest camping ground to Pula, 3km southwest of the centre, has lots of space on the shady promontory, with a restaurant and diving centre. Take bus 1 to Stoja.

✕ Eating

There are a number of decent eating places in the city centre, although most locals head out of town for better value and fewer tourists.

TOP CHOICE **Milan**
MEDITERRANEAN €€

(www.milan1967.hr; Stoja 4; mains from 70KN) An exclusive vibe, seasonal speciali-

ties, four sommeliers and even an olive-oil expert on staff all create one of the city's best dining experiences. The five-course fish menu is well worth it.

Vodnjanka
ISTRIAN €

(Vitezića 4; mains from 40KN; ☉closed Sat dinner & Sun) Locals swear by the real-deal home cooking at this cash-only no-frills spot. Its small menu concentrates on simple Istrian dishes. To get here, walk south on Radićeva to Vitezića.

Konoba Batelina
SEAFOOD €€

(Cimulje 25, Banjole; mains from 70KN; ☉dinner) The superb food that awaits at this family-run tavern is worth a trek to the village of Banjole, 3km east of Pula. The owner, fisherman and chef David Skoko, dishes out seafood that's some of the best, most creative and lovingly prepared you'll find in Istria.

Kantina
INTERNATIONAL €€

(Flanatička 16; mains from 70KN; ☉Mon-Sat) The beamed stone cellar of this Habsburg building has been redone in a modern style. The ravioli Kantina, stuffed with *skuta* (ricotta) and prosciutto, are delicious.

Jupiter
PIZZA €

(Castropola 42; pizzas 25-84KN) The thin crusts here would make any Italian mama proud; the pasta is yummy, too. There's a terrace upstairs and a 20% discount on Wednesday.

♟ Drinking & Entertainment

You should try to catch a concert in the spectacular amphitheatre; the tourist office has schedules. Although most of the nightlife is out of the town centre, in mild weather the cafes on the Forum and along the pedestrian streets Kandlerova, Flanatička and Sergijevaca are lively people-watching spots.

TOP CHOICE **Scandal Express**
CAFE-BAR

(Ciscuttijeva 15) Mingle with a mixed-bag crowd of locals at this popular gathering spot with a cool train carriage vibe, lots of posters and smoking allowed.

Cabahia
BAR

(Širolina 4) This artsy hideaway in Veruda has a cosy wood-beamed interior, eclectic decor, dim lighting, South American flair and a great garden terrace out the back. It hosts concerts and gets packed on weekends.

Rojc
ART CENTRE

(Gajeva 3) For the most underground experience, check the program at this converted army barracks, just south of the city centre,

DESTINATION	FARE (KN)	DURATION	DAILY SERVICES
Dubrovnik	557	15hr	1
Poreč	50-65	1-1½hr	14
Rovinj	35	45min	20
Split	387-392	10hr	3
Zadar	255	7hr	3
Zagreb	170-216	4-5½hr	15

that houses a multimedia art centre and art studios with occasional concerts, exhibitions and other events.

Cvajner   CAFE
(Forum 2) Snag a prime alfresco table at this artsy cafe right on the buzzing Forum and check out rotating exhibits in the funky interior that showcases works by up-and-coming local artists.

ℹ Information

Active Travel Istra (☑215 497; www.activa-istra.com; Scalierova 1) Excursions around Istria, adventure trips and concert tickets.

Hospital (☑376 548; Zagrebačka 34)

IstrAction (☑383 369; www.istraction.com; Prilaz Monte Cappelletta 3) Offers half-day tours to Kamenjak and around Pula's fortifications as well as medieval-themed full-day excursions around Istria.

Left luggage (Garderoba; per hr 2.50KN; ⊙4am-10.30pm Mon-Sat, 5am-10.30pm Sun) At the bus station, however, hours are unreliable.

Main post office (Danteov Trg 4; ⊙7.30am-7pm Mon-Fri, to 2.30pm Sat) You can make long-distance calls here. Check out the cool staircase inside!

MMC Luka (Istarska 30; per hr 25KN; ⊙8am-midnight Mon-Fri, 8am-3pm Sat) Internet access.

Tourist Ambulance (Flanatička 27; ⊙8am-9.30pm Mon-Fri Jul & Aug)

Tourist information centre (☑212 987; www.pulainfo.hr; Forum 3; ⊙8am-9pm Mon-Fri, 9am-9pm Sat & Sun) Knowledgeable staff here provide maps, brochures and schedules of events in Pula and around Istria. Pick up *Domus Bonus*, a booklet listing the best-quality private accommodation in Istria.

ℹ Getting There & Away

Boat
Pula's harbor is located west of the bus station. **Jadroagent** (☑210 431; www.jadroagent.hr;

Riva 14; ⊙7am-3pm Mon-Fri) has schedules and tickets for boats connecting Istria with the islands and south of Croatia.

Commodore Cruises (☑211 631; www.commodore-travel.hr; Riva 14) sells tickets for a catamaran between Pula and Zadar (100KN, five hours), which runs five times weekly from July through early September and twice weekly in June and late September. There's a Wednesday boat service to Venice (430KN, 3½ hours) between June and September.

Bus
From the Pula **bus station** (☑060 304 091; Trg 1 Istarske Brigade bb), located 500m northeast of the town centre, there are buses heading to Rijeka (77KN to 88KN, two hours) almost hourly. In summer, reserve a seat a day in advance.

Train
The train station is near the sea, less than 1km north of town. There is one direct train daily to Ljubljana (144KN, 4½ hours) and three to Zagreb (140KN, nine hours), but you must board a bus for part of the trip, from Lupoglav to Rijeka.

ℹ Getting Around

The city buses of use to visitors are 1, which runs to Camping Stoja, and 2A and 3A to Verudela. The frequency varies from every 15 minutes to every half-hour (from 5am to 11.30pm). Tickets are sold at *tisak* (newsstands) for 6KN, or 11KN from the driver.

KVARNER REGION

☑051

The Kvarner Gulf (Quarnero in Italian) covers 3300 sq km between Rijeka and Pag Island in the south, protected by the Velebit Range in the southeast, the Gorski Kotar in the east and the Učka massif in the northwest. Covered with luxuriant forests, lined with beaches and dotted with islands, the region has a mild gentle climate and a wealth of vegetation.

The metropolitan focus is the busy commercial port of Rijeka, Croatia's third-largest city, only a few kilometres from the aristocratic Opatija Riviera. The islands of Krk, Rab, Cres and Lošinj offer picture-perfect Old Towns just a ferry ride away, as well as plenty of beaches for scenic swimming.

Rijeka

POP 137,860

While Rijeka (Fiume in Italian) doesn't quite fit the bill as a tourist destination, it does offer an insightful glimpse into the workaday life of Croatia's largest port. Most people rush through en route to the islands or Dalmatia but, for those who pause, a few assets await. Blend in with the coffee-sipping locals on the bustling Korzo pedestrian strip, stroll along the tree-lined promenade that fronts the harbour, and visit the imposing hilltop fortress of Trsat. Rijeka also boasts a burgeoning nightlife, and hosts Croatia's biggest and most colourful Carnival celebration every year.

Much of the centre contains the ornate, imposing public buildings you would expect to find in Vienna or Budapest, evidence of the strong Austro-Hungarian influence. The industrial aspect is evident from the boats, cargo and cranes that line the waterfront. As one of Croatia's most important transportation hubs, Rijeka has buses, trains and ferries that connect Istria and Dalmatia with Zagreb.

Korzo runs through the city centre, roughly parallel to Riva (seafront). The intercity bus station is at the western edge of Riva. The train station is a five-minute walk west of the intercity bus station, along Krešimirova.

◉ Sights

Trsat Castle & Church   CASTLE
(adult/concession 15/5KN; ◷9am-8pm May-Oct, to 5pm Nov-Apr) High on a hill above the city is this semi-ruined 13th-century fortress that houses two galleries and great vistas from the open-air cafe. During the summer, the fortress features concerts and theatre performances. The other hill highlight is the **Church of Our Lady of Trsat** (Crkva Gospe Trsatske; Frankopanski Trg; ◷8am-5pm), a centuries-old magnet for believers that showcases an apparently miraculous icon of Virgin Mary.

City Tower   MONUMENT
Rijeka's main orientation point is this distinctive yellow tower on the Korzo, originally a gate from the seafront to the city and one of the few monuments to have survived the devastating earthquake of 1750.

Maritime & History Museum   MUSEUM
(Pomorski i Povijesni Muzej Hrvatskog Primorja; www.ppmhp.hr; Muzejski Trg 1; adult/concession 10/5KN; ◷9am-8pm Mon-Fri, to 1pm Sat) Housed in the Hungarian-style Governor's Palace, this museum gives a vivid picture of life among seafarers, with model ships, sea charts, navigation instruments and portraits of captains.

Astronomical Centre   ASTRONOMICAL CENTRE
(Astronomski Centar; www.rijekasport.hr; Sveti Križ 33; ◷8am-11pm Tue-Sat) High on a hill in the city's east, Croatia's first astronomical centre is a striking modern complex encompassing an observatory, planetarium and study centre. Catch bus 7A from the centre.

Museum of Modern & Contemporary Art   MUSEUM
(Muzej Moderne i Suvremene Umjetnosti; www. mmsu.hr; Dolac 1; adult/concession 10/5KN; ◷10am-1pm & 6-9pm Mon-Fri, 10am-1pm Sat) On the 2nd floor of the University Library, this small L-shaped museum puts on high-quality rotating shows, from street photography to contemporary Croatian artists.

✯✯ Festivals & Events

The **Rijeka Carnival** (www.ri-karneval.com.hr) is the largest in Croatia, with two weeks of pageants, street dances, concerts, masked balls, exhibitions and parades. It occurs anywhere between late January and early March, depending on when Easter falls.

Hartera (www.hartera.com) is an annual electronic music festival with DJs and artists from across Europe. It's held in a former paper factory on the banks of the Rječina River over three days in mid-June.

🛏 Sleeping

Prices in Rijeka hotels generally stay the same year-round, except at popular Carnival time, when you can expect to pay a surcharge. There are few private rooms in Rijeka itself; the tourist office lists these on its website. Opatija is a much better choice for accommodation.

Best Western Hotel Jadran   HOTEL €€
(✆216 600; www.jadran-hoteli.hr; Šetalište XIII Divizije 46; s/d from €97/114; P⊕❄@శ) Located 2km east of the centre, this attractive four-star hotel has seaview rooms where you can revel in the tremendous Adriatic vistas from

your balcony right above the water. There's a tiny beach below.

Youth Hostel
HOSTEL €

(✆406 420; www.hfhs.hr; Šetalište XIII Divizije 23; dm/s/d 165/192/330KN; ☺@🛜) In the leafy residential area of Pečine 2km east of the centre, this renovated 19th-century villa has clean, spacious (if plain) rooms and a communal TV area. Reserve ahead.

Hotel Neboder
HOTEL €€

(✆373 538; www.jadran-hoteli.hr; Strossmayerova 1; s/d from €63/79; P✱@) This modernist tower block offers small, neat and modish rooms, most with balconies and amazing views; only the superior rooms have air-conditioning.

Hotel Continental
HOTEL €€

(✆372 008; www.jadran-hoteli.hr; Andrije Kačića Miošića 1; s/d/ste €72/90/110; P✱@) At this landmark hotel, the ground-floor reception and bar areas are dated and staff can be uninterested. That said, the recently renovated rooms are comfortable and the location excellent.

Eating

If you want a meal on a Sunday, you'll be relegated to either fast food, pizza or a hotel restaurant, as nearly every other place in Rijeka is closed.

Foodies should consider heading to the nearby village of Volosko, 2km east of Opatija, where there's a clutch of fantastic restaurants.

For self-caterers, there's a large supermarket between the bus and train stations, and a **city market** (btwn Vatroslava Lisinskog & Trninina) open till 2pm daily (noon Sunday). Also check out **Mlinar** (Grdenićeva 27) bakery for delicious filled baguettes, wholemeal bread, croissants and *burek*.

Na Kantunu
SEAFOOD €€

(Demetrova 2; mains from 45KN) If you're lucky enough to grab a table at this tiny lunchtime spot on an industrial stretch of the port, you'll be treated to superlative daily catch.

Kukuriku
FINE DINING €€

(✆691 519; www.kukuriku.hr; Trg Matka Laginje 1a, Kastav; 6-course meals 380-550KN; ☺closed Mon Nov-Easter) Among the pioneers of the slow-food movement in Croatia, this gastronomic destination in the Old Town of Kastav, Rijeka's hilltop suburb, offers delectable meals amid lots of rooster-themed decoration. It's worth the splurge and the trek on bus 18 from Rijeka or buses 33 and 37 from Opatija.

Zlatna Školjka
SEAFOOD €€

(Kružna 12; mains 65-95KN) Savour the superbly prepared seafood and choice Croatian wines at this classy maritime-themed restaurant. The adjacent **Bracera**, by the same owners, serves crusty pizza, even on Sunday.

Restaurant Spagho
ITALIAN €

(Ivana Zajca 24A; mains from 40KN) A stylish, modern Italian with exposed brickwork, art and hip seating that offers delicious, filling portions of pasta, pizza, salads, and meat and fish dishes.

🍷 Drinking

The main drags of Riva and Korzo are the best bet for a drink, with everything from lounge bars to no-nonsense pubs.

Gradina
CAFE

(Trsat; 🛜) Set in the grounds of the castle, this happening cafe-bar with chill-out music, great views and friendly service would rate anywhere.

Karolina
BAR

(Gat Karoline Riječke bb) Occupying a striking glass structure on the waterfront, this destination bar is good for daytime coffee and for hanging out with the in-crowd to DJ-spun music on summer nights.

Hemingway
BAR

(Korzo 28) This stylish venue for coffee-sipping, cocktail-drinking and people-watching pays homage to its namesake with large B&W photos of the white-bearded one.

❶ Information

There are ATMs and exchange offices along Korzo and at the train station.

Erste Club (Korzo 22; ☺7am-11pm Mon-Sat, 8am-10pm Sun) Four terminals where you can surf the net for free for short periods. There's free wireless access along Korzo and in parts of Trsat.

Hospital (✆658 111; Krešimirova 42)

Left luggage intercity bus station (per day 15KN; ☺5.30am-10.30pm); train station (per day locker 15KN; ☺4.30am-10.30pm) The bus-station *garderoba* is at the cafe next door to the ticket office.

Post office (Korzo 13; ☺7am-8pm Mon-Fri, to 2pm Sat) Has a telephone centre and an exchange office.

Tourist Information Centre (✆335 882; www.tz-rijeka.hr; Korzo 33a; ☺8am-8pm Mon-Sat) Has good colour city maps, lots of brochures and private accommodation lists.

Rijeka

CROATIA KVARNER REGION

To Opatija
(14km)

To Tirsat Castle
& Church (1.8km)

To Train Station
(1.8km)

Franje Brentinija

Milana Smokvine

Andrije Kačića Miošica

Rječina River

Cindrića

Šetalište Vladimira Nazora

Park Nikole Hosta

Kalvarija

Ivana Grohovca

Fašizma

Školjić

Agatićeva

Pava Rittera Vitezovica

Fiumara

Mrtvi Canal

Žrtava

Laginjina

Muzejski Trg

Gornja Vrata

Grivica

Đure Šporera

Trg

Užarska

Ante Starčevića

Sokolkula

Jelačićev Trg

Scarpina

Veslarska

Menzelova

Slavka

Pomerio

Ivana Dežmana

Frana Supila

Frana Kurelca

Slogrinkula

Kovačka

Trg Riječke Revolucije

Petra Zoranića

Trg Ivana Koblera

Adamićeva

Matije Gupca

Ivana Zajca

Kazališni Park

Trninina

Vatroslava Lisinskog

Verdijeva

Dolac

Korzo

Zanonova

Adamićeva

Splitska

Riva N

Riva Zagrebačka

Riva Boduli

Trpimirova Jadranski Trg

Zadarska

Ciottina

Trg Žabica

Rijeka Harbour

Rijeka Harbour

Rijeka

ⓘ Getting There & Away

Boat

All ferries depart from the new ferry terminal.

Jadroagent (☎211 626; www.jadroagent.hr; Trg Ivana Koblera 2) Has information on all boats around Croatia.

Jadrolinija (☎211 444; www.jadrolinija.hr; Riječki Lukobran bb; ⊙8am-8pm Mon-Fri, 9am-5pm Sat & Sun) Sells tickets for the large coastal ferries that run all year between Rijeka and Dubrovnik on their way to Bari in Italy, via Split, Hvar, Korčula and Mljet.

Bus

If you fly into Zagreb, there is a Croatia Airlines van that goes directly from Zagreb airport to Rijeka daily (155KN, 3.30pm, two hours). It goes back to Zagreb from Rijeka at 5am. There are three daily buses to Trieste (50KN, 2½ hours) and one daily bus to Ljubljana (170KN, five hours). To get to Plitvice (130KN, four hours), you have to change in Otočac.

The **intercity bus station** (☎060 302 010; Trg Žabica 1) is west of the town centre.

Car

AMC (☎338 800; www.amcrentacar.hr; Lukobran 4) Based in the new ferry terminal building, has cars starting from 243KN per day.

Dollar & Thrifty Rental Car (☎325 900; www.subrosa.hr) Has a booth inside the intercity bus station, also competitively priced.

Train

The **train station** (☎213 333; Krešimirova 5) is a ten-minute walk east of the city centre. Seven daily trains run to Zagreb (100KN, four to five hours). There's one daily connection to Split (170KN, eight hours), though it involves a change at Ogulin. Two direct daily services head to Ljubljana (98KN, three hours) and one daily train goes to Vienna (319KN to 525KN, nine hours).

ⓘ Getting Around

Taxis are very reasonable in Rijeka (if you use the right firm). **Cammeo** (☎313 313) cabs are modern, inexpensive, have meters and are highly recommended; a ride in the central area costs 20KN.

Opatija

POP 7872

Opatija stretches along the coast, just 15km west of Rijeka, its forested hills sloping down to the sparkling sea. It was this breathtaking location and the agreeable all-year climate that made Opatija the most fashionable seaside resort for the Viennese elite during the days of the Austro-Hungarian empire. The grand residences of the wealthy have since been revamped and turned into upscale hotels, with a particular accent on spa and health holidays. Foodies have been flocking from afar too, for the clutch of terrific restaurants in the nearby fishing village of Volosko.

CROATIA OPATIJA

BUSES FROM RIJEKA

DESTINATION	FARE (KN)	DURATION (HR)	DAILY SERVICES
Dubrovnik	357-496	12-13	3-4
Krk	56	1-2	14
Pula	92	2¼	8
Rovinj	86	1-2	4
Split	253-324	8	6-7
Zadar	161-203	4-5	6-7
Zagreb	137-155	2¼-3	13-15

Opatija sits on a narrow strip of land sandwiched between the sea and the foothills of Mt Učka. Ulica Maršala Tita is the main road that runs through town; it's lined with travel agencies, ATMs, restaurants, shops and hotels.

◉ Sights & Activities

Lungomare
SEAFRONT

The pretty Lungomare is the region's showcase. Lined with plush villas and ample gardens, this shady promenade winds along the sea for 12km from Volosko to Lovran. Along the way are innumerable rocky outgrowths – a better option than Opatija's concrete beach.

Villa Angiolina
HISTORIC BUILDING

(Park Angiolina 1; ⊙9am-1pm & 4.30-9.30pm Tue-Sun summer, shorter hr rest of yr) The restored Villa Angiolina houses the **Croatian Museum of Tourism**, a grand title for a modest travel-related collection of old photographs, postcards, brochures and posters. Don't miss a stroll around the park, overgrown with gingko trees, sequoias, holm oaks and Japanese camellia, Opatija's symbol.

Učka Nature Park
NATURE RESERVE

Opatija and the surrounding region offer some wonderful opportunities for hiking and biking around the Učka mountain range; the tourist office has maps and information.

⌕ Sleeping & Eating

There are no real budget hotels in Opatija, but there's plenty of value in the midrange and top end. Private rooms are abundant but a little more expensive than in other areas; expect to pay around 170KN to 240KN per person.

Maršala Tita is lined with serviceable restaurants that offer pizza, grilled meat and fish. The better restaurants are away from the main strip. Head to nearby Volosko for fine dining and regional specialities.

Villa Ariston
HOTEL €€

(✆271 379; www.villa-ariston.com; Ulica Maršala Tita 179; s 350-480KN; d 600-800KN; P✳@�) With a gorgeous location beside a rocky cove, this historic hotel with period charm has celeb cachet in spades (Coco Chanel and the Kennedys are former guests).

Hotel Opatija
HOTEL €€

(✆271 388; www.hotel-opatija.hr; Trg Vladimira Gortana 2/1; r €52-66; P✳✼@) The setting in a Habsburg-era mansion is the star at this large hilltop three-star with comfortable rooms, an amazing terrace, a small indoor seawater pool and lovely gardens.

Medveja
CAMPING GROUND €

(✆291 191; medveja@liburnia.hr; per adult/tent 44/32KN; ⊙Easter–mid-Oct) It lies on a pretty pebble cove 10km south of Opatija and has apartments and mobile homes for rent too.

Istranka
ISTRIAN €

(Bože Milanovića 2; mains from 55KN) Graze on flavourful Istrian mainstays like *maneštra* (vegetable and bean soup) and *fuži* (hand-rolled pasta) at this rustic-themed tavern in a small street just up from Maršala Tita.

Bevanda
MEDITERRANEAN €€€

(Zert 8; mains from 180KN) A marble pathway leads to this gorgeous restaurant, which has a huge ocean-facing terrace with Grecian columns and a short modern menu featuring terrific fresh fish and meat dishes.

🍷 Drinking & Entertainment

Opatija is a pretty sedate place, its Viennese-style coffee houses and hotel terraces popular with the mature clientele, though there are a few stylish bars. Check out the slightly bohemian **Tantra** (Lido), which juts out into the Kvarner Gulf, and **Hemingway** (Zert 2), the original venue of what is now a nationwide chain of sleek cocktail bars.

❶ Information

Da Riva (✆272 990; www.da-riva.hr; Ulica Maršala Tita 170) A good source for private accommodation and excursions around Croatia.

Linea Verde (✆701 107; www.lineaverde-croatia.com; Andrije Štangera 42, Volosko) Specialist agency with trips to Učka Nature Park and gourmet tours around Istria.

Tourist office (✆271 310; www.opatija-tourism.hr; Ulica Maršala Tita 128; ⊙8am-10pm Mon-Sat, 5-9pm Sun Jul & Aug, 8am-7pm Mon-Sat Apr-Jun & Sep, 8am-4pm Mon-Sat Oct-Mar) This office has lots of maps, leaflets and brochures.

❶ Getting There & Away

Bus 32 runs through the centre of Rijeka along Adamićeva to the Opatija Riviera (18KN, 15km) as far as Lovran every 20 minutes daily until late in the evening.

Krk Island
POP 16,400

Croatia's largest island, 409-sq-km Krk (Veglia in Italian) is also one of the busiest in the summer. It may not be the most beautiful or lush island in Croatia – in fact, it's largely overdeveloped and stomped over – but its decades of experience in tourism make it an easy place to visit, with good transport connections and well-organised infrastructure.

ℹ Getting There & Around

The Krk toll bridge links the northern part of the island with the mainland, and a regular car ferry links Valbiska with Merag on Cres (passenger/car 18KN/115KN, 30 minutes) in summer.

Krk is also home to **Rijeka airport** (www.rijeka-airport.hr), the main hub for flights to the Kvarner region, which consist mostly of low-cost and charter flights during summer.

Rijeka and Krk Town (56KN, one to two hours) are connected by nine to 13 daily bus services. Services are reduced on weekends.

Six daily buses run from Zagreb to Krk Town (179KN to 194KN, three to four hours). Note that some bus lines are more direct than others, which will stop in every village en route. **Autotrans** (www.autotrans.hr) has two quick daily buses.

Out of the summer season, all services are reduced.

KRK TOWN
POP 3373

The picturesque Krk Town makes a good base for exploring the island. It clusters around a medieval walled centre and, spreading out into the surrounding coves and hills, a modern development that includes a port, beaches, camping grounds and hotels.

◎ Sights

Highlights include the Romanesque **Cathedral of the Assumption** (Trg Svetog Kvirina) and the fortified **Kaštel** (Trg Kamplin) facing the seafront on the northern edge of the Old Town. The narrow cobbled streets that make up the pretty old quarter are worth a wander, although they're typically packed.

🛏 Sleeping & Eating

There is a range of accommodation in and around Krk, but many hotels only open between April and October. Private rooms can be organised through any of the agencies, including **Autotrans** (221 661; www.autotrans-turizam.com; Šetalište Svetog Bernardina 3) in the bus station.

Hotel Marina   BOUTIQUE HOTEL €€€
(221 357; www.hotelikrk.hr; Obala Hrvatske Mornarice 6; r 890-1606KN; P🌐@🛜) The only hotel in the Old Town, with a prime waterfront location and 10 deluxe contemporary units.

Bor   HOTEL €€
(220 200; www.hotelbor.hr; Šetalište Dražica 5; s/d from 290/581KN; ⏱Apr-Oct; P🛜) The 22

rooms are modest and without trimmings at this low-key hotel, but the seafront location amid pine forests makes it a worthwhile stay.

Autocamp Ježevac   CAMPING GROUND €
(221 081; camping@valamar.com; Plavnička bb; per adult/campsite 47/59KN; ⏱mid-Apr–mid-Oct) Beachfront camping ground with shady pitches located on old farming terraces, with good swimming and barbecue sites. It's a 10-minute walk southwest of town.

Konoba Nono   CROATIAN €
(Krčkih Iseljenika 8; mains from 40KN) Savour local specialities like *šurlice* (homemade noodles) topped with goulash or scampi, just a hop and a skip from the Old Town.

Galija   PIZZA €
(www.galija-krk.com; Frankopanska 38; mains from 45KN) Munch your margarita or vagabondo pizza, grilled meat or fresh fish under beamed ceilings of this convivial part-*konoba*, part-pizzeria.

ℹ Information

The **seasonal tourist office** (220 226; www.tz-krk.hr, in Croatian; Obala Hrvatske Mornarice bb; ⏱8am-8pm Mon-Sat, 8am-2pm Sun Jun-Oct & Easter-May) distributes brochures and materials, including a map of hiking paths, and advice in many languages. Out of season, go to the **main tourist office** (220 226; Vela Placa 1; ⏱8am-3pm Mon-Fri) nearby. You can change money at any travel agency and there are numerous ATMs around town.

The bus from Rijeka stops at the station (no left-luggage office) by the harbour, a few minutes' walk from the Old Town.

DALMATIA

Roman ruins, spectacular beaches, old fishing ports, medieval architecture and unspoilt offshore islands make a trip to Dalmatia (Dalmacija) unforgettable. Occupying the central 375km of Croatia's Adriatic coast, Dalmatia offers a matchless combination of hedonism and historical discovery. The jagged coast is speckled with lush offshore islands and dotted with historic cities.

Split is the largest city in the region and a hub for bus and boat connections along the Adriatic, as well as home to the late-Roman Diocletian's Palace. Nearby are the early Roman ruins in Solin (Salona). Zadar has yet more Roman ruins and a wealth of churches. The architecture of Hvar and Korčula recalls the days when these islands

LOŠINJ & CRES ISLANDS

Separated by an 11m-wide canal (with a bridge), these two highly scenic islands in the Kvarner archipelago are often treated as a single entity. On Lošinj, the more populated of the two, the pretty ports of Mali Lošinj and Veli Lošinj, ringed by pine forests and lush vegetation, attract plenty of summertime tourists. Consequently, there are varied sleeping and eating options. The waters around Lošinj are the first protected marine area for dolphins in the entire Mediterranean, watched over by the Mali Lošinj-based **Blue World** (www.blue-world.org) NGO.

Wilder, more barren Cres has a natural allure that's intoxicating and inspiring. Sparsely populated, it's covered in dense primeval forests and lined with a craggy coastline of soaring cliffs, hidden coves and ancient hilltop towns. The northern half of Cres, known as Tramuntana, is prime cruising terrain for the protected griffon vulture; see these giant birds at **Eco-Centre Caput Insulae** (www.supovi.hr), an excellent visitor centre in Beli on the eastern coast. The main seaside settlements lie on the western shore of Cres, while the highlands showcase the astounding medieval town of Lubenice.

The main maritime port of entry for the islands is Mali Lošinj, which is connected to Rijeka, Pula, Zadar and Venice in the summer. A variety of car ferries and catamaran boats are run by **Jadrolinija** (www.jadrolinija.hr), **Split Tours** (www.splittours.hr) and **Venezia Lines** (www.venezialines.com).

were outposts of the Venetian empire. None can rival majestic Dubrovnik, a cultural and aesthetic jewel, while magical Mljet features isolated island beauty.

Zadar

☑ 023 / POP 73,442

Boasting a historic Old Town of Roman ruins and medieval churches, cosmopolitan cafes and excellent museums, Zadar is really beginning to make its mark. It's not too crowded and has two unique attractions: the sound-and-light spectacle of the Sea Organ and Sun Salutation, which need to be seen and heard to be believed.

It's not a postcard-perfect kind of place. Stroll the Old Town and you'll pass unfortunate Yugo-era office blocks juxtaposed with elegant Hapsburg architecture – this is no Dubrovnik. Zadar is a working town, not a museum piece, and a key transport hub with superb ferry connections to Croatia's Adriatic islands, Kvarner, southern Dalmatia and Italy.

It's also recently been dubbed Croatia's 'city of cool' for its clubs, bars and festivals run by international music stars.

◉ Sights & Activities

Sea Organ & Sun Salutation   LANDMARK
Zadar's incredible **Sea Organ** (Morske Orgulje), designed by local architect Nikola Bašić, has a hypnotic effect. Set within the perforated stone stairs that descend into the

sea is a system of pipes and whistles that exudes wistful sighs when the movement of the sea pushes air through it.

Right next to it is the **Sun Salutation** (Pozdrav Suncu), another wacky and wonderful Bašić creation. It's a 22m circle cut into the pavement, filled with 300 multilayered glass plates that collect the sun's energy during the day, and, together with the wave energy that makes the Sea Organ's sound, produce a trippy light show from sunset to sunrise.

Church of St Donat   CHURCH
(Crkva Svetog Donata; Šimuna Kožičića Benje; admission 12KN; ◔9am-9pm May-Sep, 9am-4pm Oct-Apr) This circular 9th-century Byzantine structure was built over the Roman forum. Slabs from the ancient forum are visible in the church and there is a pillar from the Roman era on the northwestern side. In summer, ask about the musical evenings held here (featuring Renaissance and early baroque music).

Museum of Ancient Glass   MUSEUM
(www.mas-zadar.hr; Poljana Zemaljskog Odbora 1; adult/concession 30/10KN; ◔9am-9pm May-Sep, 9am-7pm Mon-Sat Oct-Apr) Zadar's newest attraction is this well-designed museum, which explains the history and invention of glass with thousands of pieces on display: tools, blowpipes and early vessels from Egypt and Mesopotamia, goblets, jars, vials, jewellery and amulets.

St Simeon's Church CHURCH
(Crkva Svetog Šime; Trg Šime Budinica; ⊘8am-noon & 6-8pm Jun-Sep) Reconstructed in the 16th and 17th centuries on the site of an earlier structure, this church has a 14th-century sarcophagus, a masterpiece of medieval goldsmith work.

Cathedral of St Anastasia CATHEDRAL
(Katedrala Svete Stošije; Trg Svete Stošije; ⊘8am-noon & 5-6.30pm Mon-Fri) The 13th-century Romanesque Cathedral of St Anastasia has some fine Venetian carvings in the choir stalls and a **belltower** (10KN) that you can climb for stunning Old Town views.

Museum of Church Art MUSEUM
(Trg Opatice Čike bb; adult/concession 20/10KN; ⊘10am-12.45pm & 6-8pm Mon-Sat, 10am-noon Sun) In the Benedictine monastery opposite St Donatus, this impressive museum offers two floors of elaborate gold and silver reliquaries, marble sculptures, religious paintings, icons and embroidery.

Beaches BEACHES
You can swim from the steps off the promenade and listen to the sound of the Sea Organ. There's a swimming area with diving boards, a small park and a cafe on the coastal promenade off Zvonimira. Bordered by pine trees and parks, the promenade takes you to a beach in front of Hotel Kolovare and then winds on for about a kilometre up the coast.

☞ Tours

Travel agencies offer boat cruises to Telašćica Bay and the beautiful Kornati Islands, which include lunch and a swim in the sea or a salt lake. **Aquarius Travel Agency** (☎212 919; www.juresko.hr; Nova Vrata bb) charges 250KN per person for a full-day trip or ask around on Liburnska Obala (where the excursion boats are moored).

Organised trips to the national parks of Paklenica, Krka and Plitvice Lakes are also popular.

⁂ Festivals & Events

Between July and September, the Zadar region showcases some of the globe's most celebrated electronic artists, bands and DJs. The ringmaster for these festivals is the Zadar-based **Garden** bar, but the festivals are held in nearby Petrčane up the coast, 10km north of town. The original event, the **Garden Festival** (www.thegardenzadar.com) has been running since 2006. By 2010, four other festivals (Soundwave, Suncebeat, Electric Elephant and Stop Making Sense) had joined the Petrčane party.

🛌 Sleeping

Most visitors head out to the 'tourist settlement' at Borik, 3km northwest of Zadar, on the Puntamika bus 5 or 8 (8KN, every 20 minutes from the bus station, hourly on Sunday). Here there are hotels (most dating from the Yugo days), a hostel, a camping ground, big swimming pools, sporting opportunities and numerous *sobe* (rooms) signs; you can arrange a private room through a travel agency in town.

Hotel Bastion BOUTIQUE HOTEL €€€
(☎494 950; www.hotel-bastion.hr; Bedemi Zadarskih Pobuna 13; s/d/ste from 905/1140/

WORTH A TRIP

PLITVICE LAKES NATIONAL PARK

Midway between Zagreb and Zadar, **Plitvice Lakes National Park** (☎751 015; www.np-plitvicka-jezera.hr; adult/concession Apr-Oct 110/80KN, Nov-Mar 80/60KN; ⊘7am-8pm) comprises 19.5 hectares of wooded hills and 16 turquoise lakes, all connected by a series of waterfalls and cascades. The mineral-rich waters carve new paths through the rock, depositing tufa (new porous rock) in continually changing formations. Wooden footbridges follow the lakes and streams over, under and across the rumbling water for an exhilaratingly damp 18km. Swimming is not allowed. Your park admission (prices vary by season) is valid for the entire stay and also includes the boats and buses you need to use to see the lakes. There is hotel accommodation only onsite, and private accommodation just outside the park. Check the options with the Plitvice National Park office in Zagreb (p218).

We've received complaints regarding bus transport to Plitvice: note that not all Zagreb–Zadar buses stop here, as the quicker ones use the motorway. Check schedules at www.akz.hr. The journey takes three hours from Zadar (75KN to 89KN) and 2½ hours from Zagreb (62KN to 70KN), and there are 10 daily services. Luggage can be left at the **tourist information centre** (⊘7am-8pm) at the park's main entrance.

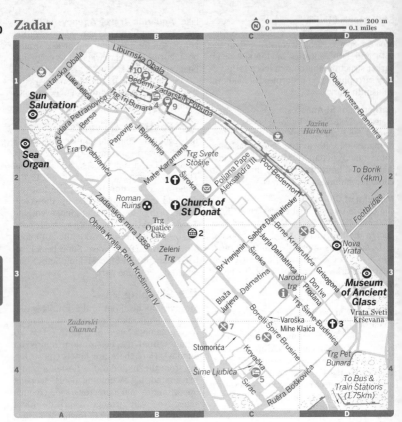

0   200 m
0   0.1 miles

1290KN; ❄ @ 🛜) Built over the remains of a fortress at the heart of the Old Town, the Bastion radiates character, with a pleasing art deco design theme, 28 well-finished rooms, and a top-drawer restaurant and basement spa.

Villa Hrešć   PENSION €€
(☎337 570; www.villa-hresc.hr; Obala Kneza Trpimira 28; s 550-650KN; d 750-850KN; P ❄ 🛜) This condo-style villa is about a 20-minute walk from Zadar's historic sights. There's a coastal garden with an Old Town vista, and good-value rooms and apartments with attractive decor. Some also have massive terraces.

Venera Guest House   PENSION €
(☎214 098; www.hotel-venera-zd.hr; Šime Ljubića 4a; d 350-450KN) A modest guest house that has two things going for it: a good location on a quiet street in the Old Town and friendly family owners.

Student Hostel   HOSTEL €
(☎224 840; Obala Kneza Branimira bb; dm 147KN; ☉Jul & Aug) This student dormitory turns into a hostel in July and August. It's centrally located – right across the footbridge – and has no-frills three-bed rooms and shared bathrooms.

Autocamp Borik   CAMPING GROUND €
(☎332 074; per adult 38-56KN, per campsite 94-146KN; ☉May-Oct) A good option for those who want easy access to Zadar, this camping ground is steps away from the shore at Borik. Pitches are shaded by tall pines and facilities are good.

✖ Eating
Zadar's morning **market** (☉6am-3pm) is one of Croatia's best.

Foša   FINE DINING €€€
(www.fosa.hr; Kralja Dmitra Zvonimira 2; mains from 85KN) A classy place with a gorgeous terrace

Zadar

jutting out into the harbour and a sleek interior. Start by tasting the olive oils, and move on to a grilled Adriatic fish of your choice, and mean meat dishes too.

Zalogajnica Ljepotica CANTEEN €
(Obala Kneza Branimira 4b; mains from 35KN) The cheapest place in town prepares three to four dishes a day (think risotto, pasta and grilled meat) at knockout prices in a no-frills setting.

Trattoria Canzona ITALIAN €
(Stomorića 8; mains from 40KN) Simple, enjoyable trattoria with pavement tables laid with gingham tablecloths. Best for an inexpensive meal; it has very substantial and juicy gnocchi.

Na po ure DALMATIAN €
(Borelli Špire Brusine 8; mains from 40KN) Hungry? This unpretentious family-run *konoba* is the place to sate that appetite with from-the-heart Dalmatian cooking: grilled lamb, calves' liver and fresh fish served with potatoes and vegetables.

🍷 Drinking & Entertainment

Zadar has pavement cafes, lounge bars, boho bars and everything in between. Head to the district of Varoš on the southwest side of the Old Town for interesting little dive bars popular with students and arty types.

Garden BAR
(www.thegardenzadar.com; Bedemi Zadarskih Pobuna; ⊙late May-Oct) One of the reasons many of Croatia's youngsters rate Zadar as 'a really cool place' is this remarkable bar-club-garden-restaurant perched on top of the old city walls. It's owned and run by UB40's producer Nick Colgan and drummer James Brown. Daytime is relaxed; the real fun begins at night.

Arsenal BAR
(www.arsenalzadar.com; Trg Tri Bunara 1) A large renovated shipping warehouse now hosts this brilliant cultural centre, with a large lounge bar-restaurant-concert hall in the centre that has a small stage for live music and shows.

❶ Information

Aquarius Travel Agency (☑212 919; www.juresko.hr; Nova Vrata bb) Books, accommodation and excursions.

Geris.net (Federica Grisogona 8 1; per hr 25KN) The city's best cybercafe.

Hospital (☑315 677; Bože Peričića 5)

Left luggage (Garderoba; per day 15KN) bus station (⊙6am-10pm Mon-Fri); Jadrolinija dock (⊙7am-8.30pm Mon-Fri, to 3pm Sat); train station (⊙24hr)

Miatours (☑/fax 212 788; www.miatours.hr; Vrata Svetog Krševana) Arranges excursions and accommodation.

Post office (Poljana Pape Aleksandra III; ⊙7.30am-9pm Mon-Sat, to 2pm Sun) You can make phone calls and there's an ATM.

Tourist office (☑316 166; www.tzzadar.hr; Mihe Klaića 5; ⊙8am-10pm Mon-Fri, to 9pm Sat & Sun Jun-Sep, 8am-8pm Oct-May) Publishes a good colour map and the free *Zadar City Guide*.

❶ Getting There & Away

Air

Zadar's airport, 12km east of the city, is served by **Croatia Airlines** (☑250 101; www.croatiaairlines.hr; Poljana Natka Nodila 7) and **Ryanair** (www.ryanair.com). A Croatia Airlines bus meets all flights and costs 20KN. For a taxi, call the very efficient and cheap **Lulić** (☑494 494).

Boat

On the harbour, **Jadrolinija** (☑254 800; Liburnska Obala 7) has tickets for all local ferries. Buy international tickets from **Jadroagent** (☑211 447; jadroagent-zadar@zd.t-com.hr; Poljana Natka Nodila 4), just inside the city walls.

Bus

The **bus station** (☑211 035; www.liburnija-zadar.hr, in Croatian) is a 10-minute walk southeast of the harbour and the Old Town and has daily buses to Zagreb (95KN to 143KN, 3½ to seven hours, every 30 minutes). Buses marked 'Poluotok' run from the bus station to the harbour.

Train

The **train station** (☑212 555; www.hznet.hr; Ante Starčevića 3) is adjacent to the bus station. There are six daily trains to Zagreb, but the journey time is very slow indeed; the fastest take over eight hours.

Split

☑021 / POP 188,694

The second-largest city in Croatia, Split (Spalato in Italian) is a great place to see Dalmatian life as it's really lived. Free of mass tourism, this always buzzing city has just the right balance of tradition and modernity. Step inside Diocletian's Palace – a Unesco World Heritage site and one of the world's most impressive Roman monuments – and you'll see dozens of bars, restaurants and shops thriving amid the atmospheric old walls where Split life has been going on for thousands of years. Split's unique setting and exuberant nature make it one of the most delectable cities in Europe. The dramatic coastal mountains are the perfect backdrop to the turquoise waters of the Adriatic and you'll get a chance to appreciate the gorgeous Split cityscape when making a ferry journey to or from the city.

The Old Town is a vast open-air museum and the new information signs at the important sights explain a great deal of Split's history. The seafront promenade, Obala Hrvatskog Narodnog Preporoda, better known as Riva, is the best central reference point.

History

Split achieved fame when Roman emperor Diocletian (AD 245–313) had his retirement palace built here from 295 to 305. After his death the great stone palace continued to be used as a retreat by Roman rulers. When the neighbouring colony of Salona was abandoned in the 7th century, many of the Romanised inhabitants fled to Split and barricaded themselves behind the high palace walls, where their descendants continue to live to this day.

⊙ Sights

DIOCLETIAN'S PALACE

Diocletian's Palace   HISTORIC AREA

Facing the harbour, Diocletian's Palace is one of the most imposing Roman ruins in existence. Don't expect a palace though, nor a museum – this palace is the living heart of the city, and its labyrinthine streets are packed with people, bars, shops and restaurants.

It was built as a strong rectangular fortress, with walls measuring 215m from east to west, 181m wide at the southernmost point and reinforced by square corner towers. The imperial residence, mausoleum and temples were south of the main street, now called Krešimirova, connecting the east and west palace gates.

Town Museum   MUSEUM

(Muzej Grada Splita; www.mgst.net; Papalićeva 1; adult/concession 10/5KN; ⊙9am-9pm Tue-Fri, 9am-4pm Sat-Mon) Built for one of the many noblemen who lived within the palace in the Middle Ages, the Papalić Palace that houses the museum is considered a fine example of late-Gothic style. Its three floors showcase a tidy collection of artefacts, paintings, furniture and clothes from Split; captions are in Croatian. Shorter hours outside summer.

Ethnographic Museum   MUSEUM

(Etnografski Muzej; www.etnografski-muzej-split.hr, in Croatian; Severova 1; adult/concession 10/5KN; ⊙9am-9pm Mon-Fri, 9am-1pm Sat) This mildly interesting museum has a collection of photos of old Split, traditional costumes and memorabilia of important citizens, housed in two floors and an attic. For great Old Town views, make sure you climb the staircase that leads to the terrace on the southern edge of the vestibule. Shorter hours outside summer.

Cathedral of St Domnius   CHURCH

(Katedrala Svetog Duje; Kraj Svetog Duje 5; admission free; ⊙8am-8pm Mon-Sat, 12.30-6.30pm Sun Jun-Sep, sporadic hrs Oct-May) On the eastern side of the Peristil, Split's cathedral was built as Diocletian's mausoleum. The oldest monuments inside are the remarkable 13th-century scenes from the life of Christ carved on the wooden entrance doors. The choir is furnished with 13th-century Romanesque seats that are the oldest in Dalmatia. The **treasury** (admission 10KN) is rich in reliquaries, icons, church robes and illuminated manuscripts. You can climb the Romanesque **belfry** (admission 10KN).

Peristil   SQUARE

This picturesque colonnaded square, with a neo-Romanesque cathedral tower rising above, is a great place for a break in the sun. The **vestibule**, an open dome above the ground-floor passageway at the southern end of the Peristil, is overpoweringly grand and cavernous.

Temple of Jupiter
RUIN

(admission 5KN; ⊗8am-8pm Jun-Sep) The temple once had a porch supported by columns, but the one column you see today dates from the 5th century. Below the temple is a crypt, which was once used as a church.

Basement Halls
MONUMENT

(adult/concession 25/10KN; ⊗9am-9pm Jun-Sep, shorter hrs Oct-May) Although mostly empty, the rooms and corridors underneath Diocletian's Palace emit a haunting sense of timelessness that is well worth the price of the ticket.

OUTSIDE THE PALACE WALLS

Gregorius of Nin
LANDMARK

(Grgur Ninski) This 10th-century statue is of the Croatian bishop who fought for the right to use old Croatian in liturgical services. Notice that his left big toe has been polished to a shine – it's said that rubbing the toe brings good luck.

Gallery of Fine Arts
MUSEUM

(Galerija Umjetnina Split; www.galum.hr; Kralja Tomislava 15; adult/concession 20/10KN; ⊗11am-7pm Tue-Sat, 10am-1pm Sun) Split's newest museum in a former hospital exhibits nearly 400 works of art spanning almost 700 years. Upstairs is the permanent collection; temporary exhibits downstairs change every few months. The cafe has a terrace overlooking the palace.

OUTSIDE CENTRAL SPLIT

Archaeological Museum
MUSEUM

(Arheološki Muzej; www.armus.hr; Zrinsko-Frankopanska 25; adult/concession 20/10KN; ⊗9am-2pm & 4-8pm Mon-Sat) North of town, this is a fascinating supplement to your walk around Diocletian's Palace and around ancient Salona. The history of Split is traced from Illyrian times to the Middle Ages, in chronological order, with explanations in English.

Meštrović Gallery
ART GALLERY

(Galerija Meštrović; Šetalište Ivana Meštrovića 46; adult/concession 30/15KN; ⊗9am-7pm Tue-Sun May-Sep, shorter hrs Oct-Apr) At this stellar art museum, below Marjan to the west of the city centre, you'll see a comprehensive, nicely arranged collection of works by Ivan Meštrović, Croatia's premier modern sculptor.

Marjan
NATURE RESERVE

For an afternoon away from the city buzz, Marjan (178m) is the perfect destination. This hilly nature reserve offers trails through fragrant pine forests, scenic lookouts and ancient chapels. There are different ways

of reaching Marjan. One is to hike straight up from the Meštrović Gallery. Otherwise, you can start closer to the centre, from the stairway (Marjanske Skale) in Varoš, right behind the Church of Sveti Frane. Alternatively, walk along the seafront of Marjan to get to some quiet beaches, such as Kašjuni cove.

Bačvice
BEACH

The most popular city beach is on the eponymous inlet. This biggish pebbly beach has good swimming, a lively ambience, a great cafe-bar and plenty of water games. There are showers and changing rooms at both ends of the beach.

✦ Festivals & Events

This traditional February **Carnival** event sees locals dressing up and dancing in the streets for two very fun days. Otherwise known as Split Day, the 7 May **Feast of St Duje** involves much singing and dancing all around the city. From mid-July to mid-August, the **Split Summer Festival** (www.splitsko-ljeto.hr) features opera, drama, ballet and concerts on open-air stages.

🛏 Sleeping

Good budget accommodation has become more available in Split in the last couple of years but it's mostly hostels. Private accommodation is again the best option,and in the summer you may be deluged at the bus station by people offering *sobe* (rooms available). Make sure you are clear about the exact location of the room or you may find yourself several bus rides from the town centre.

The best thing to do is to book through one of the travel agencies, but there is little available within the heart of the Old Town. Expect to pay between 200KN and 400KN for a double room; in the cheaper ones you will probably share the bathroom with the proprietor.

Hotel Peristil
HOTEL €€€

(✆329 070; www.hotelperistil.com; Poljana Kraljice Jelene 5; s/d 1000/1200KN;❄@☎) This lovely hotel overlooks the Peristil, in the midst of Diocletian's Palace, with its 12 gorgeous rooms – all with hardwood floors, antique details, good views and warm service.

Hotel Bellevue
HOTEL €€

(✆345 644; www.hotel-bellevue-split.hr; Bana Josipa Jelačića 2; P@) This atmospheric old classic has seen better days, but it remains one of the more dreamy hotels in town, with its regal patterned wallpaper, dark-brown

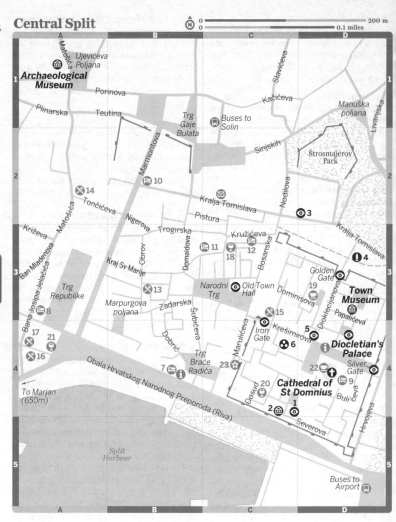

CROATIA DALMATIA

wood, art deco elements, billowing curtains and faded but well-kept rooms.

Villa Varoš PENSION **€**
(☎483 469; www.villavaros.hr; Miljenka Smoje 1; d/ste 500/800KN; ✳🔊) Owned by a New Yorker Croat, Villa Varoš, just to the west of Bana Josipa Jelačića, is central, the rooms are simple, bright and airy, and the apartment is excellent (with a well-equipped kitchen, Jacuzzi and small terrace).

Hotel Adriana HOTEL **€€**
(☎340 000; www.hotel-adriana.com; Obala Hrvatskog Narodnog Preporoda 8; s/d 700/1000KN;

✳🔊) Good value, excellent location. The rooms are not massively exciting, with navy curtains and beige furniture, but some have sea views – a real bonus in Split's Old Town.

Silver Central Hostel HOSTEL **€**
(☎490 805; www.silvercentralhostel.com; Kralja Tomislava 1; dm 150-180KN; ✳@🔊) In an upstairs apartment, this light yellow-coloured boutique hostel has four dorm rooms, free internet and cable TV in the pleasant lounge. There's another hostel, **Silver Gate** (☎322 857; www.silvergatehostel.com; Hrvojeva 6; dm 165KN), near the food market, with the same facilities.

Split Hostel Booze & Snooze HOSTEL €
(342 787; www.splithostel.com; Narodni Trg 8; dm 150-180KN; ❄@☎) Run by a pair of Aussie Croat women, this party place at the heart of town has 25 beds in four dorms, a terrace, book swap and free internet. Their brand-new outpost, **Fiesta Siesta** (Kružićeva 5; dm 150-180KN, d 440-500KN; ❄@☎) has five sparkling dorms and one double above the popular Charlie's Backpacker Bar.

✖ Eating

TOP CHOICE **Konoba Trattoria Bajamont**
DALMATIAN €
(Bajamontijeva 3; mains from 60KN; ⊙closed dinner Sun) At this one-room joint with a handful of tables and no sign above the door, the menu features excellent Dalmatian mainstays, such as small fried fish, squid-ink risotto and *brujet* (seafood stew with wine, onions and herbs, served with polenta).

Kod Fife DALMATIAN €
(Trumbićeva Obala 11; mains from 40KN) Dragan presides over a motley crew of sailors, artists and misfits who drop in for his simple, Dalmatian home cooking (especially the *pašticada*), and his own brand of grumpy slow but loving hospitality. Go west of the Riva, which turns into Trumbićeva Obala.

Perun DALMATIAN €€
(Senjska 9; mains from 70KN) This adorable spot in Varoš has a leafy terrace amid ancient stone, a rustic low-key vibe and seafood (and meat) done *na gradele* (on the grill), depending on what's fresh that day.

Šperun SEAFOOD €€
(Šperun 3; mains from 70KN) A sweet little restaurant decked out with rustic details, this favourite among the foreigners churns out decent Dalmatian classics. **Šperun Deva** across the street is a charming corner bistro with a few tables outside, offering breakfasts and a great daily menu (from 50KN).

Makrovega VEGETARIAN €
(Leština 2; mains from 40KN; ⊙9am-8pm Mon-Fri, to 5pm Sat) A meat-free haven with a clean, spacious (nonsmoking!) interior and delicious buffet and à la carte food that alternates between macrobiotic and vegetarian.

Galija PIZZA €
(Tončićeva 12; pizzas from 20KN) The most popular place on Split's pizza scene for several decades now, it's the sort of joint that locals take you to for a simple but good meal.

Art & Čok SANDWICH BAR €
(Obrov 2; sandwiches from 14KN; ⊙Mon-Sat) Excellent sandwiches on handcrafted bread.

Try the *porchetta* (aromatic pork, roasted red peppers and gherkins).

 Drinking & Entertainment

Split is great for nightlife, especially in the spring and summer months. The palace walls are generally throbbing with loud music on Friday and Saturday nights.

Žbirac CAFE
(Bačvice bb) This beachfront cafe is like the locals' open-air living room, a cult hang-out with great sea views, swimming day and night, and occasional concerts.

Bifora CAFE-BAR
(Bernardinova 5) A quirky crowd of locals frequents this artsy spot on a lovely little square, much loved for its intimate low-key vibe.

Ghetto Club BAR
(Dosud 10) Head for Split's most bohemian bar in an intimate courtyard amid flowerbeds, a trickling fountain, great music and a friendly atmosphere.

Galerija CAFE-BAR
(Vuškovićeva bb) Catch up with friends in the granny-chic interior, with pretty floral sofas and armchairs, paintings and little lamps everywhere.

Luxor CAFE-BAR
(Kraj Sv Ivana 11) Touristy, yes, but having coffee in the courtyard of the cathedral is great: cushions are laid out on the steps and you can watch the locals go about their business.

Vidilica CAFE
(Nazorov Prilaz 1) Worth the climb up the stone stairs through the ancient Varoš quarter for a sunset drink at this hilltop cafe with amazing city and harbour views.

Libar CAFE-BAR
(Trg Franje Tuđmana 3) A relaxed place away from the palace buzz, this little spot has a lovely upper terrace, great breakfasts and tapas all day.

Fluid BAR-CLUB
(Dosud 1) This chic spot is a jazzy party bar. Right up the stairs, which get jammed with people on weekend nights, the sleek **Puls** draws more of an electronic-music crowd.

 Information

Discount Cards
Split Card (1 day 35KN) Get the Split Card for one day and you can use it for three days without paying anything extra. You get free and reduced admissions to Split attractions and discounts on car rental, restaurants, shops and hotels.

Internet Access
Several cafes around town offer free wi-fi access, including Luxor.
Backpackers Cafe (☑338 548; Obala Kneza Domagoja 3; per hr 30KN; ☉7am-9pm) Also sells used books and provides information for backpackers. There's happy hour for internet between 3pm and 5pm, when it's 50% off.

Left Luggage
Garderoba bus station (1st hr 5KN, then 1.50KN per hr; ☉6am-10pm); train station (per day 15KN; ☉6am-11.30pm)

Medical Services
KBC Firule (☑556 111; Spinčićeva 1) Split's hospital.

Money
You can change money at travel agencies or the post office. There are ATMs around the bus and train stations and throughout the city.

Post
Main post office (Kralja Tomislava 9; ☉7.30am-7pm Mon-Fri, 7.30am-2.30pm Sat)

Tourist Information
Croatian Youth Hostel Association (☑396 031; www.hfhs.hr; Domilijina 8; ☉8am-4pm Mon-Fri) Sells HI cards and has information about youth hostels all over Croatia.
Tourist office (☑345 606; www.visitsplit.com; Peristil; ☉8am-8.30pm Jul-Aug, 8am-8.30pm Mon-Sat, 8am-1.30pm Sun Jun & Sep, 9am-5pm Mon-Fri Oct-May) Has information on Split and sells the Split Card.

Travel Agencies
Atlas Airtours (☑343 055; www.atlasairtours.com; Bosanska 11) Tours, private accommodation and money exchange.
Maestral (☑470 944; www.maestral.hr; Boškovića 13/15) Monastery stays, horseback-riding excursions, lighthouse holidays, hiking, sea kayaking and more.
Turist Biro (☑347 100; www.turistbiro-split.hr; Obala Hrvatskog Narodnog Preporoda 12) Its main area is private accommodation.

Getting There & Away
Air
Split airport (www.split-airport.hr) is 20km west of town, just 6km before Trogir. **Croatia Airlines** (☑362 997; www.croatiaairlines.hr; Obala Hrvatskog Narodnog Preporoda 9; ☉8am-8pm Mon-Fri, 9am-noon Sat) operates

one-hour flights to Zagreb several times a day and a weekly flight to Dubrovnik.

A couple of low-cost airlines fly to Split, including **Easyjet** (www.easyjet.com) and **germanwings** (www.germanwings.com).

Boat

Jadrolinija (☑ 338 333; Gat Sv Duje bb), in the large ferry terminal opposite the bus station, handles most of the coastal ferry lines and catamaran boats that operate between Split and the islands. There is also the twice-weekly ferry service between Rijeka and Split, which goes on to Bari (406KN) in Italy. Four times weekly a car ferry goes from Split to Ancona in Italy (361KN, nine to 11 hours).

In addition to Jadrolinija's boats, there is a fast passenger boat, the **Krilo** (www.krilo.hr), that goes to Hvar Town (22KN, one hour) daily and on to Korčula (55KN, 2¾ hours).

SNAV (☑ 322 252; www.snav.it) has daily ferries to Ancona (Italy) from mid-June through September (five hours) and to Pescara (Italy) from late July through August (6½ hours). Also departing to Ancona from Split are **BlueLine** (www. blueline-ferries.com) car ferries (from 333KN per person, 450KN per car, 10 to 12 hours).

Car ferries and passenger lines depart from separate docks; the passenger lines leave from Obala Lazareta and car ferries from Gat Sv Duje. You can buy tickets from either the main Jadrolinija office in the large ferry terminal opposite the bus station, or at one of the two stalls near the docks. In summer it's necessary to reserve at least a day in advance for a car ferry and you are asked to appear several hours before departure.

Bus

Advance bus tickets with seat reservations are recommended. Most buses leave from the main **bus station** (☑ 060 327 777; www.ak-split.hr) beside the harbour.

Bus 37 goes to Split airport and Trogir (20KN, every 20 minutes), also stopping at Solin; it leaves from a local bus station on Domovinskog Rata, 1km northeast of the city centre, but it's faster and more convenient to take an intercity bus heading north to Zadar or Rijeka.

Train

There are five daily trains between Split **train station** (☑ 338 525; www.hznet.hr; Obala Kneza Domagoja 9) and Zagreb (179KN to 189KN, 5½ to eight hours), which is just behind the bus station, two of which are overnight. There are also two trains a day from Split to Zadar (88KN, five hours) via Knin.

ℹ Getting Around

Buses by **Pleso Prijevoz** (www.plesoprijevoz. hr) and **Promet Žele** (www.split-airport.com.hr) depart to Split airport (30KN) from Obala Lazareta several times daily. You can also take bus 37 from the local bus station on Domovinskog Rata (20KN, 50 minutes).

Buses run about every 15 minutes from 5.30am to 11.30pm. A one-zone ticket costs 10KN for one trip in central Split; it's 20KN to the surrounding districts. You can buy tickets on the bus and the driver can make change.

Trogir

☑ 021 / POP 12,995

Gorgeous and tiny Trogir (formerly Trau) is beautifully set within medieval walls, its streets knotted and maze-like. It's fronted by a wide seaside promenade lined with bars and cafes and luxurious yachts docking in the summer. Trogir is unique among Dalmatian towns for its profuse collection of Romanesque and Renaissance architecture (which flourished under Venetian rule), and this,

BUSES FROM SPLIT

DESTINATION	FARE (KN)	DURATION (HR)	DAILY SERVICES
Dubrovnik	105-157	4½	20
Međugorje*	100	3-4	4
Mostar*	114	3½-4½	8
Pula	397	10-11	3
Rijeka	305	8-8½	11
Sarajevo*	190	6½-8	4
Zadar	120	3-4	27
Zagreb	185	5-8	29

*Bosnia & Hercegovina

along with its magnificent cathedral, earned it status as a World Heritage site in 1997.

Trogir is an easy day trip from Split and a relaxing place to spend a few days, taking a trip or two to nearby islands.

◉ Sights

The heart of the Old Town, which occupies a tiny island in the narrow channel between Čiovo Island and the mainland, is a few minutes' walk from the bus station. After crossing the small bridge near the station, go through the north gate. Trogir's finest sights are around Narodni Trg to the southeast. Most sights can be seen on a 15-minute walk around this island.

Cathedral of St Lovro CHURCH
(Katedrala Svetog Lovre; Trg Ivana Pavla II; admission 20KN; ⊙8am-8pm Mon-Sat, 2-8pm Sun Jun-Sep, shorter hrs Oct-May) The showcase of Trogir is this three-naved Venetian cathedral built from the 13th to 15th centuries. Its glory is the Romanesque portal of *Adam and Eve* (1240) by Master Radovan, the earliest example of the nude in Dalmatian sculpture. Enter the building through an obscure back door to see the richly decorated **Renaissance Chapel of St Ivan** and the choir

stalls, pulpit and **treasury**, which contains an ivory triptych. You can climb the 47m cathedral **tower** for a delightful view.

Kamerlengo Fortress FORTRESS
(Tvrđava Kamerlengo; admission 15KN; ⊙9am-9pm May-Oct) Once connected to the city walls, the fortress was built around the 15th century. Today it hosts concerts during the Trogir Summer festival.

Town Museum MUSEUM
(Gradski Muzej; Kohl-Genscher 49; admission 15KN; ⊙10am-5pm Jul-Sep, shorter hrs Oct-May) Housed in the former Garagnin-Fanfogna palace, the museum has five rooms which exhibit books, documents, drawings and period costumes from Trogir's long history.

❶ Information

Atlas Trogir (☑881 374; www.atlas-trogir.hr; Obala Kralja Zvonimira 10) This travel agency arranges private accommodation and runs excursions.

Portal Trogir (☑885 016; www.portal-trogir. com; Obala Bana Berislavića 3) Finds private accommodation; rents bikes, scooters and kayaks; books excursions and has an internet corner.

WORTH A TRIP

SOLIN (SALONA)

The ruin of the ancient city of Solin (known as Salona by the Romans), among the vineyards at the foot of mountains just northeast of Split, is the most interesting archaeological site in Croatia. Salona was the capital of the Roman province of Dalmatia from the time Julius Caesar elevated it to the status of colony. It held out against the barbarians and was only evacuated in AD 614 when the inhabitants fled to Split and neighbouring islands in the face of Avar and Slav attacks.

Begin your visit at the main entrance near Caffe Bar Salona, where you'll see an info-map of the complex. **Tusculum Museum** (admission 20KN; ⊙9am-7pm Mon-Sat, 9am-1pm Sun Jun-Sep, 9am-3pm Mon-Fri, 9am-1pm Sat Oct-May) is where you pay admission for the entire archaeological reserve (you'll get a brochure with a map) as well as for the small museum with interesting sculpture embedded in the walls and in the garden. Some of the highlights inside the complex include **Manastirine**, the fenced area behind the car park, a burial place for early Christian martyrs prior to the legalisation of Christianity; the excavated remains of **Kapljuč Basilica** – one of the early Christian cemeteries in Salona – and the 5th-century **Kapjinc Basilica** that sits inside it. Also look out for the **covered aqueduct** from the 1st century AD; the 5th-century **cathedral** with an octagonal **baptistery**; and the huge 2nd-century **amphitheatre**.

The ruins are easily accessible on Split city bus 1 (12KN), which goes directly to Caffe Bar Salona (sit on the right side and look out for the blue and white sign pointing to Salona) every half-hour from Trg Gaje Bulata.

From the amphitheatre at Solin it's easy to continue on to Trogir by catching a westbound bus 37 from the nearby stop on the adjacent highway (buy a four-zone ticket for 20KN in Split if you plan to do this). If, on the other hand, you want to return to Split, use the underpass to cross the highway and catch an eastbound bus 37.

❶ Getting There & Away

City bus 37 from Split (28km) leaves half-hourly from the local bus station, with a stop at Split airport en route to Trogir. You can buy the four-zone ticket (20KN) from the driver. There are boats to Split four times daily (20KN), from Čiovo island (150m to the left of the bridge).

Southbound buses from Zadar (130km) will drop you off in Trogir, as will most northbound buses from Split going to Zadar, Rijeka and Zagreb.

Hvar Island

📞 021 / POP 11,459

Hvar is the number-one carrier of Croatia's superlatives: it's the most luxurious island, the sunniest place in the country and, along with Dubrovnik, the most popular tourist destination. Hvar is also famed for its verdancy and its lavender fields, as well as other aromatic herbs such as rosemary.

The island's hub and busiest destination is Hvar Town, estimated to draw around 30,000 people a day in the high season. It's odd that they can all fit in the small bay town, but fit they do. Visitors wander along the main square, explore the sights on the winding stone streets, swim on the numerous beaches or pop off to get into their birthday suits on the Pakleni Islands, but most of all they party at night. There are several good restaurants and a number of top hotels, as well as a couple of hostels.

Car ferries from Split deposit you in Stari Grad but local buses meet most ferries in summer for the trip to Hvar Town. The town centre is Trg Sv Stjepana, 100m west of the bus station. Passenger ferries tie up on Riva (seafront promenade), the eastern quay.

◎ Sights & Activities

Franciscan Monastery & Museum
MONASTERY

(admission 20KN; ⊙9am-1pm & 5-7pm Mon-Sat) At the southeastern end of Hvar Town you'll find this 15th-century Renaissance monastery, with a wonderful collection of Venetian paintings in the adjoining church and a cloister garden with a cypress tree said to be more than 300 years old.

Arsenal
HISTORIC BUILDING

(Trg Svetog Stjepana; admission arsenal & theatre 20KN; ⊙9am-9pm) Smack in the middle of Hvar Town is the imposing Gothic arsenal, and upstairs is Hvar's prize, the **Renaissance theatre** built in 1613 – reported to be the first theatre in Europe open to plebs and aristocrats alike.

Cathedral of St Stephen
CHURCH

(Katedrala Svetog Stjepana; Trg Svetog Stjepana; ⊙30min before twice-daily Mass) Forming a stunning backdrop to Trg Sv Stjepana, the cathedral was built in the 16th and 17th centuries at the height of the Dalmatian Renaissance.

Fortica
FORTRESS

(admission 20KN; ⊙8am-9pm Jun-Sep) On the hill high above Hvar Town, this Venetian fortress (1551) is worth the climb up to appreciate the sweeping panoramic views. The fort was built to defend Hvar from the Turks, who sacked the town in 1539 and 1571. There's a lovely cafe at the top.

🛏 Sleeping

Accommodation in Hvar Town is extremely tight in July and August: a reservation is highly recommended. Try the travel agencies for help. Expect to pay anywhere from 150KN to 300KN per person for a room with a private bathroom in the town centre. Outside the high season you can negotiate a better price.

Hotel Riva
LUXURY HOTEL €€€

(📞750 100; www.suncanihvar.com; Riva bb; s/d 1401/1497KN; ❄@) Now the luxury veteran on the Hvar Town lodging scene, this 100-year-old hotel has 54 smallish contemporary rooms and a great location right on the harbour, perfect for watching the yachts glide up and away.

Hotel Croatia
HOTEL €€

(📞742 400; www.hotelcroatia.net; Majerovica bb; s/d 810/1080KN; P🛜@❄) Only a few steps from the sea, this medium-size, rambling 1930s building sits among gorgeous, peaceful gardens. The rooms are simple and fresh, many with balconies overlooking the gardens and the sea.

Luka's Lodge
HOSTEL €

(📞742 118; www.lukalodgehvar.hostel.com; Lučica bb; dm 140KN; d per person 120-175KN; @🛜❄) Friendly owner Luka takes good care of his guests at this homey hostel a five-minute walk from town. All rooms come with fridges, some with balconies. There's a living room, two terraces and a kitchen.

Green Lizard
HOSTEL €

(📞742 560; www.greenlizard.hr; Ulica Domovinskog Rata 13; dm 140KN; d per person 120-175KN; ⊙Apr-Oct; @🛜) This private hostel is a friendly and cheerful budget option, a short walk from the ferry. Dorms are simple and clean, there's a communal kitchen and laundry service and a few doubles with private and shared facilities.

Camping Vira
CAMPING GROUND €

(☎741 803; www.campingvira.com; per adult/campsite 50/87KN; ☉May–mid-Oct; 🛜) This four-star camping ground on a wooded bay 4km from town is one of the best in Dalmatia. There's a gorgeous beach, a lovely cafe and restaurant, and a volleyball pitch. The facilities are well kept.

🍴 Eating

The pizzerias along the harbour offer predictable but inexpensive eating. Self-caterers can head to the supermarket next to the bus station, or pick up fresh supplies at the next-door vegetable market.

Konoba Menego
DALMATIAN €€

(Put Grode bb; tapas-style dishes 45-70KN) At this rustic old house, everything is decked out in Hvar antiques and the staff wear traditional outfits. Try the marinated cheeses and vegetables, prepared the old-fashioned Dalmatian way.

Konoba Luviji
DALMATIAN €€

(mains from 70KN) Food churned out of the wood oven at this wine-focused tavern is simple, unfussy and tasty. Downstairs is the *konoba* where Dalmatian-style tapas is served; the upstairs restaurant has Old Town and harbour views.

Zlatna Školjka
FINE DINING €€€

(Petra Hektorovića 8; www.zlatna.skoljka.com; mains from 120KN) This slow-food family-run hideaway stands out for its creative fare conjured up by a local chef-celebrity. Try the unbeatable *gregada*, traditional fish stew with lobster and sea snails; order in advance.

🍷 Drinking

Hvar has some of the best nightlife on the Adriatic coast.

Falko Bar
BEACH BAR

(☉10am-10pm mid-May–mid-Sep) A 20-minute seafront walk from the town centre, past Hula Hula, brings you to this adorable hideaway in a pine forest just above the beach. Think low-key artsy vibe, homemade *rakija*, hammocks and occasional concerts, exhibits and other fun events.

Carpe Diem
BAR-CLUB

(www.carpe-diem-hvar.com; Riva) This swanky harbourfront spot is the mother of Croatia's coastal clubs, with house music spun nightly by resident DJs. The new **Carpe Diem Beach**

on the island of Stipanska is the hottest place to party (June to September), with daytime beach fun and occasional full-moon parties.

Hula-Hula
BEACH BAR

(www.hulahulahvar.com) THE spot to catch the sunset to the sound of techno and house music, Hula-Hula is known for its apres-beach party (4pm to 9pm) where all of young trendy Hvar descends for sun-downer cocktails. To find it, head west along the seafront.

V-528
CLUB

(www.v-528.com; ☉from 9.30pm) A former fortress on the slope above the seafront, this open-air venue has a stunning look, great sound system, DJ-fuelled parties and an oxygen room in an ancient chapel.

ℹ️ Information

Atlas Hvar (☎741 911; www.atlas-croatia.com) On the western side of the harbour, it finds private accommodation.

Clinic (☎741 300; Sv Katarine) Medical clinic about 700m from the town centre.

Del Primi (☎095 998 1235; www.delprimi-hvar .com; Burak 23) Travel agency specialising in private accommodation.

Francesco (Burak bb; per hr 30KN; ☉8am-midnight) Internet cafe and call centre.

Pelegrini Tours (☎742 743; www.pelegrini -hvar.hr; Riva bb) Private accommodation, boat tickets to Italy with SNAV and Blue Line, excursions (daily trip to Pakleni Otoci), and bike, scooter and boat rental.

Secret Hvar (☎717 615; www.secrethvar.com) Great offroad tours of the island's scenic interior, with abandoned villages, dramatic canyons and endless lavender fields.

Tourist office (☎742 977; www.tzhvar.hr; ☉8am-2pm & 3-9pm Jun & Sep, 8am-2pm & 3-10pm Jul-Aug, 8am-2pm Mon-Sat Sep-May) On Trg Svetog Stjepana.

ℹ️ Getting There & Away

The local Jadrolinija car ferry from Split calls at Stari Grad (47KN, two hours) six times a day in summer months. Jadrolinija also has a catamaran daily to Hvar Town (22KN, one hour). In addition, **Krilo** (www.krilo.hr), the fast passenger boat, travels once a day between Split and Hvar Town (22KN, one hour) in the summer months; it also goes to Korčula (55KN, 2¾ hours). You can buy tickets at Pelegrini Tours.

There are at least 10 car ferries (fewer in the low season) running from Drvenik, on the mainland, to Sućuraj (16KN, 35 minutes) on the tip of Hvar Island. The **Jadrolinija agency** (☎741 132; www. jadrolinija.hr) is beside the landing in Stari Grad.

There are also connections to Italy in the summer season. The Jadrolinija ferries that operate between Rijeka and Dubrovnik call at Hvar twice a week during summer, stopping in Stari Grad before continuing on to Korčula, Dubrovnik and ultimately Bari in Italy. During the summer, two Jadrolinija ferries per week go from Stari Grad to Ancona in Italy. **SNAV** (www.snav.com) and **BlueLine** (www.blueline-ferries.com) also run regular boats to Ancona from Hvar Town. Pelegrini Tours in Hvar sells these tickets.

ℹ Getting Around

Buses meet most ferries that dock at Stari Grad and go to Hvar Town (25KN, 50 minutes). A taxi costs from 150KN to 350KN. **Radio Taxi Tihi** (☏098 338 824) is cheaper if there are a number of passengers to fill up the minivan.

Korčula Island

☏020 / POP 16,200

Rich in vineyards and olive trees, the island of Korčula was named Korkyra Melaina (Black Korčula) by the original Greek settlers because of its dense woods and plant life. As the largest island in an archipelago of 48, it provides plenty of opportunities for scenic drives, particularly along the southern coast.

Swimming opportunities abound in the many quiet coves and secluded beaches, while the interior produces some of Croatia's finest wine, especially dessert wines made from the *grk* grape cultivated around Lumbarda. Local olive oil is another product worth seeking out.

On a hilly peninsula jutting into the Adriatic sits Korčula Town, a striking walled town of round defensive towers and red-roofed houses. Resembling a miniature Dubrovnik, the gated, walled Old Town is crisscrossed by narrow stone streets designed to protect its inhabitants from the winds swirling around the peninsula.

The big Jadrolinija car ferry drops you off either in the west harbour next to the Hotel Korčula or the east harbour next to Marko Polo Tours. The Old Town lies between the two harbours. The large hotels and main beach lie south of the east harbour, and the residential neighbourhood Sveti Nikola (with a smaller beach) is southwest of the west harbour. The town bus station is 100m south of the Old Town centre.

◉ Sights

Other than following the circuit of the city walls or walking along the shore, sightseeing in Korčula centres on Trg Sv Marka (St Mark's Sq).

St Mark's Cathedral   CHURCH

(Katedrala Svetog Marka; Statuta 1214; ⊘9am-9pm Jul & Aug, Mass only Sep-Jun) Dominating Trg Svetog Marka, the 15th-century Gothic-Renaissance cathedral features two paintings by Tintoretto (*Three Saints* on the altar and *Annunciation* to one side).

Town Museum   MUSEUM

(Gradski Muzej; ☏711 420; Statuta 1214; admission 15KN; ⊘9am-9pm daily Jun-Aug, 9am-1pm Mon-Sat Sep-May) The 16th-century Gabriellis Palace opposite the cathedral houses the museum, with exhibits of Greek pottery, Roman ceramics and home furnishings, all with English captions.

Marco Polo Museum   MUSEUM

(Ulica De Polo; admission 15KN; ⊘9am-7pm Jun-Sep, 10am-4pm May & Oct) It's said that Marco Polo was born in Korčula in 1254; you can visit what is believed to have been his house and climb the tower for an eagle's-eye vista over the Korčula peninsula and Adriatic.

Treasury Museum   MUSEUM

(Statuta 1214; admission 15KN; ⊘9am-7.30pm Mon-Sat May-Nov) Located in the 14th-century Abbey Palace, this museum with its hall of Dalmatian art is worth a look.

☞ Tours

Both Atlas Travel Agency and Marko Polo Tours offer a variety of boat tours and island excursions, including day trips to Mljet. In summer, water taxis at the east harbour collect passengers to visit **Badija Island**, which features a historic 15th-century Franciscan Monastery, plus **Orebić** (p250) and the nearby village of **Lumbarda**, both of which have sandy beaches.

🛏 Sleeping & Eating

Korčula's hotel scene is on the bulky and resort side. If you don't fancy staying in any of the big hotels, a more personal option is a guest house. Atlas Travel Agency and Marko Polo Tours arrange private rooms (from 250KN in high season).

Lešić Dimitri Palace   BOUTIQUE HOTEL €€€

(☏715 560; www.lesic-dimitri.com; Don Pavla Poše 1-6; apt 2731-8741KN; ❋⊜☏) Exceptional in every way (including its rates). Spread over several town mansions, the six 'residences' have been finished to an impeccable standard, while keeping original detail.

OREBIĆ

Orebić, on the southern coast of the Pelješac Peninsula between Korčula and Ploče, offers better beaches than those found at Korčula, 2.5km across the water. The easy access by ferry from Korčula makes it the perfect place to go for the day. The best beach in Orebić is Trstenica cove, a 15-minute walk east along the shore from the port.

In Orebić the ferry terminal and the bus station are adjacent to each other. Korčula buses to Dubrovnik, Zagreb and Sarajevo stop at Orebić.

Hotel Bon Repos   HOTEL €€
(☎726 800; www.korcula-hotels.com; d 524KN; P⚡❄@🐾) On the road to Lumbarda, this huge decent-value hotel has manicured grounds, a large pool overlooking a small beach and water-taxi service to Korčula Town.

Villa DePolo   APARTMENTS €
(☎711 621; tereza.depolo@du.t-com.hr; Svetog Nikole bb; d 330KN;❄🐾) These small, simple but attractive modern rooms (and one apartment) come with comfortable beds; one has a terrace with amazing views. It's a short walk from the Old Town.

Pansion Hajduk   PENSION €
(☎711 267; olga.zec@du.t-com.hr; d from 430KN; ❄⚡🐾) It's a couple of kilometres from town on the road to Lumbarda, but you get a warm welcome, air-conditioned rooms with TVs and even a swimming pool.

Autocamp Kalac   CAMPING GROUND €
(☎711 182; www.korculahotels.com; per person/ campsite 54/48KN; ☺May-Oct) This attractive camping ground with tennis courts is a 30-minute walk away from the Old Town, in a dense pine grove near the beach.

TOP CHOICE | **Konoba Komin**   DALMATIAN €€
(☎716 508; Don Iva Matijace; mains from 45KN) This family-run *konoba* looks almost medieval, with its *komin* (roaring fire), roasting meat, ancient stone walls and solid wooden tables. The menu is simple and delicious and the space tight so book ahead.

LD   FINE DINING €€
(☎715 560; www.lesic-dimitri.com; Don Pavla Poše 1-6; mains from 45KN) Korčula's finest restaurant, with tables right above the water, offers a modern, metropolitan-style menu and many wonderful Croatian wines.

Konoba Maslina   DALMATIAN €€
(Lumbarajska cesta bb; mains from 50KN) Everything you'd want from a rural *konoba*; this traditional place 3km out of town on the road to Lumbarda offers honest country cooking – fresh fish, lamb and veal, and local ham and cheese.

🛈 Entertainment

Between June and September there's **moreška sword dancing** (tickets 100KN; ☺9pm Mon & Thu) by the Old Town gate; performances are more frequent during July and August. The clash of swords and the graceful movements of the dancers/fighters make an exciting show. The tourist office, Atlas and Marko Polo Tours sell tickets.

🛈 Information

There are several ATMs around town, including one at HVB Splitska Banka. You can also change money at the post office or at any of the travel agencies.

Atlas Travel Agency (☎711 231; atlas -korcula@du.htnet.hr; Trg 19 Travnja bb) Represents American Express, runs excursions and finds private accommodation.

Hospital (☎711 137; Kalac bb) About 1km past the Hotel Marko Polo.

Kantun Tours (☎715 622; www.kantun-tours. com; Plokata 19 Travnja bb) Probably the best-organised and largest agency, it offers private accommodation, excursions, car hire and boat tickets. Also has luggage storage.

PC Centrar Doom (Obvjeknik Vladimir DePolo; per hr 25KN) Internet access and cheapish international phone calls.

Tourist office (☎715 701; www.korcula.net; Obala Franje Tuđmana 4; ☺8am-3pm & 5-8pm Mon-Sat, 9am-1pm Sun Jul-Aug, 8am-2pm Mon-Sat Sep-Jun) On the west harbour; an excellent source of information.

🛈 Getting There & Away

Transport connections to Korčula are good. There are buses to Dubrovnik (85KN, three hours, one to three daily) and one to Zagreb (239KN, 11 hours). Book ahead in summer.

The island has two major entry ports by boat – Korčula Town and Vela Luka. All the Jadrolinija ferries between Split and Dubrovnik stop in Korčula Town. There's a **Jadrolinija office** (☎715 410) about 25m down from the west harbour.

There's a daily fast boat, the **Krilo** (www.krilo. hr), which runs from Split to Korčula (55KN, 2¾ hours) all year round, stopping at Hvar en route. Jadrolinija runs a passenger catamaran daily from June to September from Split to Vela Luka (60KN, two hours), stopping at Hvar. There's also a regular afternoon car ferry between Split and Vela Luka (45KN, three hours) that stops at Hvar most days.

From the Pelješac Peninsula, regular boats link Orebić and Korčula. Passenger launches (15KN, 10 minutes, 13 daily June to September, at least five daily rest of year) sail to Korčula Town. Car ferries (17KN, 15 minutes, at least 14 daily year-round) also run this route, but use the deeper port of Dominče, 3km away from Korčula Town. (As bus connections are poor and taxis fares are extortionate – 80KN for a 3km journey – try to use the catamaran boats if you're on foot.)

Scooters (291KN for 24 hours) and boats (580KN per day) are available from **Rent a Đir** (☑711 908; www.korcula-rent.com; Biline 5).

Mljet Island

☑020 / POP 1232

Of all the Adriatic islands, Mljet (Meleda in Italian) may be the most seductive. Much of the island is covered by forests and the rest is dotted with fields, vineyards and villages. The northwestern half of the island forms **Mljet National Park**, where lush vegetation, pine forests and two saltwater lakes offer a scenic hideaway. It's an unspoiled oasis of tranquillity that, according to legend, capti-vated Odysseus for seven years.

The island is 37km long, and has an av-erage width of about 3km. The main points of entry are Pomena and Polače, two tiny towns about 5km apart.

Most people visit the island on excursions from Korčula or Dubrovnik, but it is possible to take a passenger boat from Dubrovnik or come on the regular ferry from Dubrovnik and stay a few days for hiking, cycling and boating.

◉ Sights & Activities

The highlights of the island are **Malo Jez-ero** and **Veliko Jezero**, the two lakes on the island's western end connected by a channel. In the middle of Veliko Jezero is an islet with a 12th-century **Benedictine monastery**, which contains a pricey but at-mospheric restaurant.

There's a boat from Mali Most (about 1.5km from Pomena) on Malo Jezero that leaves for the island monastery every hour at 10 minutes past the hour. It's not pos-sible to walk right around the larger lake as there's no bridge over the channel con-

necting the lakes to the sea. If you decide to swim it, keep in mind that the current can be strong.

Renting a bicycle (20/100KN per hour/day) is an excellent way to explore the na-tional park. Several places including Hotel Odisej in Pomena have bikes. Be aware that Pomena and Polače are separated by a steep hill. The bike path along the lake is an easier and very scenic pedal, but it doesn't link the two towns. You can rent a paddleboat and row over to the monastery but you'll need stamina.

The island offers some unusual oppor-tunities for **diving**. There's a Roman wreck dating from the 3rd century in relatively shallow water. The remains of the ship, in-cluding amphorae, have calcified over the centuries and this has protected them from pillaging. There's also a German torpedo boat from WWII and several walls to dive. Contact **Kronmar Diving** (☑744 022; Hotel Odisej).

🛏 Sleeping & Eating

The Polače tourist office arranges private accommodation (from around 260KN per double), but it's essential to make arrange-ments before peak season. You'll find more *sobe* signs around Pomena than Polače, and practically none at all in Sobra. Restaurants rent out rooms too.

Stermasi APARTMENTS €
(☑098 939 0362; Saplunara; apt 401-546KN; P✻) On the 'other' side of Mljet, these apartments are ideal for those wanting to enjoy the simple life and natural beauty of the island. Well presented and bright, the nine modern units have terraces or private balcony. Sandy beaches are on your doorstep and the onsite restaurant is one of Dalmatia's best.

MLJET: INS & OUTS

Sightseeing boats from Korčula and the Dubrovnik catamarans arrive at Polače wharf in high season; Jadrolinija fer-ries use the port of Sobra close to the centre of the island. The entry point for **Mljet National Park** (www.np-mljet. hr; adult/concession 90/40KN) is be-tween Pomena and Polače. Your ticket includes a bus and boat transfer to the Benedictine monastery. If you stay overnight on the island you only pay the park admission once.

Soline 6
HOTEL €€

(☑744 024; www.soline6.com; Soline; d 546KN) This very green place is the only accommodation within the national park, with everything built from recycled products, organic waste composted, waterless toilets and no electricity. The four studios are modern and equipped with private bathrooms, balconies and kitchens.

Camping Mungos
CAMPING GROUND €

(☑745 300; www.mungos-mljet.com; Babino Polje; per person 52KN; ☺May-Sep) Close to the beach and the lovely grotto of Odysseus, this camping ground has a restaurant, currency exchange and a mini-market.

Hotel Odisej
HOTEL €€€

(☑744 022; www.hotelodisej.hr; Pomena; d from 580KN; P☺✳@☎) The only conventional hotel option in Mljet isn't great. A lingering Yugo flavour endures, service can be stone-faced and decor is little changed from the 1970s. That said, rates are not outrageous and it's rarely booked up.

Melita
DALMATIAN €€

(www.mljet-restoranmelita.com; St Mary's Island, Veliko Jezero; mains from 60KN) A more romantic (and touristy) spot can't be found on the island – this is the restaurant attached to the church on the little island in the middle of the big lake.

❶ Information

The **tourist office** (☑744 186; www.mljet.hr; ☺8am-1pm & 5-7pm Mon-Sat, 9am-noon Sun Jun-Sep, 8am-1pm Mon-Fri Oct-May) is in Polače and there's an ATM next door (and another at Hotel Odisej in Pomena). There are free brochures and a good walking map for sale.

Babino Polje, 18km east of Polače, is the island capital. It's home to another **tourist office** (☑745 125; www.mljet.hr; ☺9am-5pm Mon-Fri) and a post office.

❶ Getting There & Away

Jadrolinija ferries stop only at Sobra (32KN, two hours) but the **Melita catamaran** (☑313 119; www.gv-line.hr; Vukovarska 34, Dubrovnik) goes to Sobra (22KN, one hour) and Polače (50KN, 1½ hours) in the summer months, leaving Dubrovnik's Gruž harbour twice daily (9.15am and 6.15pm) and returning daily from Polače at 4pm and twice daily from Sobra (6.15am and 4.40pm). You *cannot* reserve tickets in advance so get to the harbour ticket office well in advance in high season to secure a seat. Tour boats from Korčula also run to Polače harbour in high season. Infrequent buses connect Sobra and Polače.

Dubrovnik

☑020 / POP 29,995

No matter whether you are visiting Dubrovnik for the first time or if you're returning again and again to this marvellous city, the sense of awe and beauty when you set eyes on the Stradun (the Old Town's main street) never fades. It's hard to imagine anyone, even the city's inhabitants, becoming jaded by its marble streets and baroque buildings, or failing to be inspired by a walk along the ancient city walls that once protected a civilised, sophisticated republic for five centuries and that now look out onto the endless shimmer of the peaceful Adriatic.

History

Founded 1300 years ago by refugees from Epidaurus in Greece, medieval Dubrovnik (Ragusa until 1918) shook off Venetian control in the 14th century, becoming an independent republic and one of Venice's more important maritime rivals, trading with Egypt, Syria, Sicily, Spain, France and later Turkey. The double blow of an earthquake in 1667 and the opening of new trade routes to the east sent Ragusa into a slow decline, ending with Napoleon's conquest of the town in 1808.

The deliberate shelling of Dubrovnik by the Yugoslav army in 1991 sent shockwaves through the international community but, when the smoke cleared in 1992, traumatised residents cleared the rubble and set about repairing the damage. Reconstruction has been extraordinarily skilful.

After a steep postwar decline in tourism, Dubrovnik has bounced back and become a major tourist destination once again.

❂ Sights

All the sights are in the Old Town, which is closed to cars. Looming above the city is Srđ Hill, which is connected by cable car to Dubrovnik. The main street in the Old Town is Placa (better known as Stradun).

OLD TOWN

City Walls & Forts
LANDMARK

(Gradske Zidine; adult/concession 70/30KN; ☺9am-6.30pm Apr-Oct, 10am-3pm Nov-Mar) No visit to Dubrovnik would be complete without a leisurely walk around the spectacular city walls, the finest in the world and Dubrovnik's main claim to fame. Built between the 13th and 16th centuries, they are still intact today. They enclose the en-re city in a protective veil more than 2km long and up to 25m high, with two round and 14 square towers, two corner fortifications and a large fortress. The views over the town and sea are great – this walk could be the high point of your visit. The main entrance and ticket office to the walls is by the **Pile Gate**. You can also enter at the **Ploče Gate** in the east (a wise move at really busy times of day).

War Photo Limited
PHOTO GALLERY
(www.warphotoltd.com; Antuninska 6; admission 10KN; ☺9am-9pm daily Jun-Sep, 9am-3pm Tue-Sat, 9am-1pm Sun May & Oct) An immensely powerful experience, this state-of-the-art photographic gallery has changing exhibitions curated by the gallery owner and former photojournalist Wade Goddard. In addition to temporary shows, there's a permanent exhibition on the upper floor devoted to the war in Yugoslavia. It closes between November and April.

Franciscan Monastery & Museum
MONASTERY
(Muzej Franjevačkog Samostana; Placa 2; adult/concession 30/15KN; ☺9am-6pm) Inside the monastery complex is a mid-14th-century **cloister**, one of the most beautiful late-Romanesque structures in Dalmatia. Further inside is the third-oldest functioning **pharmacy** in Europe, in business since 1391. The small monastery **museum** has a collection of relics, liturgical objects and pharmacy items.

Dominican Monastery & Museum
MONASTERY
(Muzej Dominikanskog Samostana; off Ulica Svetog Dominika 4; adult/concession 20/10KN; ☺9am-6pm May-Oct, to 5pm Nov-Apr) This imposing 14-century structure in the northeastern corner of the city is a real architectural highlight, with a forbidding fortress-like exterior that shelters a rich trove of paintings from Dubrovnik's finest 15th- and 16th-century artists.

Rector's Palace
PALACE
(Pred Dvorom 3; adult/concession 35/15KN, audio guide 30KN; ☺9am-6pm May-Oct, to 4pm Nov-Apr) This Gothic-Renaissance palace built in the late 15th century houses a museum with furnished rooms, baroque paintings and historical exhibits. Today, the atrium is often used for concerts during the Summer Festival.

Cathedral of the Assumption of the Virgin
CHURCH
(Stolna Crkva Velike Gospe; Poljana M Držića; ☺morning & late-afternoon Mass) Completed in 1713 in a baroque style, the cathedral is notable for its fine altars. The cathedral **treasury**

(Riznica; adult/concession 10/5KN; ☺8am-5.30pm Mon-Sat, 11am-5.30pm Sun May-Oct, 10am-noon & 3-5pm Nov-Apr) contains relics of St Blaise and a number of religious paintings.

Sponza Palace
PALACE
The 16th-century Sponza Palace was originally a customs house, then a minting house, a state treasury and a bank. Now it houses the State Archives and the **Memorial Room of the Defenders of Dubrovnik** (☺10am-10pm Mon-Fri, 8am-1pm Sat), a heartbreaking collection of portraits of young people who perished between 1991 and 1995.

St Blaise's Church
CHURCH
(Crkva Svetog Vlahe; Luža Sq; ☺morning & late-afternoon Mass Mon-Sat) Imposing church built in 1715 in a baroque style; the ornate exterior contrasts strongly with the sober residences surrounding it.

Onofrio Fountain
MONUMENT
One of Dubrovnik's most famous landmarks, the Onofrio Fountain was built in 1438 as part of a water-supply system that involved bringing water from a well 12km away.

Serbian Orthodox Church & Museum
CHURCH
(Muzej Pravoslavne Crkve; Od Puča 8; adult/concession 10/5KN; ☺9am-2pm Mon-Sat) This 1877 Orthodox church has a fascinating collection of icons dating from the 15th to 19th centuries.

Synagogue
SYNAGOGUE
(Sinagoga; Žudioska 5; admission 10KN; ☺10am-8pm May-Oct Mon-Fri, to 3pm Nov-Apr) The oldest Sephardic and second-oldest synagogue in the Balkans, dating back to the 15th century, has a small museum inside.

Orlando Column
MONUMENT
This popular meeting place used to be the spot where edicts, festivities and public verdicts were announced.

EAST OF THE OLD TOWN

TOP CHOICE ‣ Cable Car
CABLE CAR
(Petra Krešimira IV; www.dubrovnikcable car.com; adult/concession 40/20KN; ☺9am-10pm Tue-Sun May-Oct, shorter hrs Nov-Apr) Reopened after 19 years, the cable car whisks you from just north of the city walls up to Mount Srđ in under four minutes, for a stupendous perspective from a lofty 405m, down to the terracotta-tiled rooftops of the Old Town and the island of Lokrum, with the Adriatic Sea and distant Elafiti islands filling the horizon.

CROATIA DALMATIA

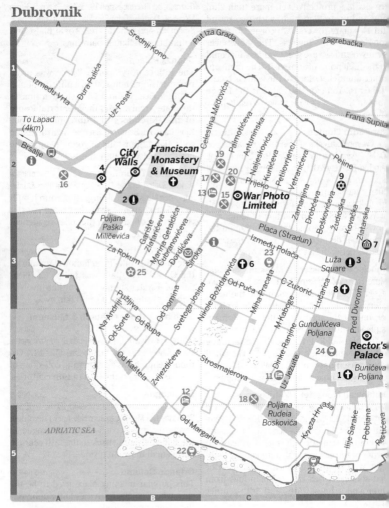

THE COAST

Banje Beach, not far from Ploče Gate, used to be the most popular city beach, though it's less popular now a section has been roped off for the exclusive EastWest Club. Just southeast is **Sveti Jakov**, a good local beach that doesn't get rowdy. Buses 5 and 8 will get you here. The nicest beach that's walkable from the Old Town is below Hotel Bellevue. **Lapad Bay** brims with hotel beaches that you can use without a problem; try the bay by Hotel Kompas. A little further on is the good shallow **Copacabana Beach** on Babin Kuk peninsula. In

the Old Town, you can also swim below the two Buža bars.

An even better option is to take the ferry that shuttles hourly in summer to lush **Lokrum Island** (return 40KN, last boat back 6pm), a national park with a rocky nudist beach (marked FKK), a botanical garden and the ruins of a medieval Benedictine monastery.

🏃 Activities

Navis Underwater Explorers (☏099 35 02 773; www.navisdubrovnik.com; Copacabana Beach) offers recreational dives (including the wreck of the *Taranto*) and courses.

Contact **Adriatic Kayak Tours** (☏091 72 20 413; www.adriatickayaktours.com; Zrinsko Frankopanska 6) for kayak excursions (from a half-day paddle to a week-long trip).

Tours

Dubrovnik Walks   CITY TOURS
(☏095 80 64 526; www.dubrovnikwalks.com) Excellent guided walks in English. One-hour Old Town tours (70KN) run twice daily.

Adriatic Explore   TOURS
(☏323 400; www.adriatic-explore.com; Bandureva 4) Day trips to Mostar and Montenegro (both 380KN) are very popular; excursions

to Mljet, Korčula and the Elafiti Islands (250KN) are also offered.

257

Festivals & Events
The **Feast of St Blaise** is held on 3 February, and **Carnival** is also held in February.

Dubrovnik Summer Festival (www.dubrovnik-festival.hr) is a major cultural event over five weeks in July and August, with theatre, music and dance performances at different venues in the Old Town.

Sleeping
Private accommodation is generally the best option in Dubrovnik, which is the most expensive destination in Croatia. Beware the scramble of private owners at the bus station and ferry terminal: some provide what they say they offer while others are scamming. Expect to pay from 300KN for a double room, and from 500KN for an apartment in high season.

OLD TOWN

TOP CHOICE ┃ **Karmen Apartments** APARTMENT €€
(☏323 433, 098 619 282; www.karmendu.com; Bandureva 1; apt 437-1165KN;❅❄) Run by an Englishman who has lived in Dubrovnik for decades, these four inviting apartments with plenty of character enjoy a great location a stone's throw from Ploče harbour. Book well ahead.

Fresh Sheets HOSTEL €
(☏091 79 92 086; www.igotfresh.com; Sv Šimuna 15; dm/d 210/554KN; ❄@❄) The only hostel in the Old Town is a warm, welcoming place right by the city walls; all rooms and reception areas are painted in zany colours and there's space for socialising downstairs. It's run by a party-hard crew who organise legendary booze-ups.

Hotel Stari Grad BOUTIQUE HOTEL €€€
(☏322 244; www.hotelstarigrad.com; Od Sigurate 4; s/d 1180/1580KN; ❄❅❄) This Old Town hotel is all about location – it's very close to the Pile Gate and just off the Stradun. Its eight rooms are smallish but neat and attractive. Staff are sweet and views from the rooftop terrace are dramatic.

Apartments Amoret APARTMENTS €€
(☏091 53 04 910; www.dubrovnik-amoret.com; Dinke Ranjine 5; apt 655-874KN;❄❅❄) Spread over three historic buildings in the heart of the Old Town, Amoret offers 11 high-quality renovated studio apartments with wi-fi, elegant

CROATIA DUBROVNIK

decor, a dash of art, parquet wood flooring and kitchenette-style cooking facilities.

OUTSIDE THE OLD TOWN

Hotel Bellevue　　　　LUXURY HOTEL €€€
(☑330 000; www.hotel-bellevue.hr; Petra Čingrije 7; d from 1835KN; P🚫❄🏊@🛜) Ignore the dated tinted-glass frontage; this is a very classy hotel, positioned on a cliff over the Adriatic, boasting all balconied rooms. The restaurant, Vapor, is top-notch and there's a gem of a beach below, accessible by the hotel's lift. It's a 15-minute walk west of the Pile Gate.

Begović Boarding House　　　PENSION €
(☑435 191; www.begovic-boarding-house.com; Primorska 17; dm/r/apt 146/292/364KN; P@) A steep walk uphill from Lapad harbourfront, this welcoming family-run place has smallish but clean pine-trimmed rooms, some opening out onto a communal garden with amazing views. There's free pick-up from the bus or ferry, free internet, a kitchen and excursions.

YHA Hostel　　　　　HOSTEL €
(☑423 241; dubrovnik@hfhs.hr; Vinka Sagrestana 3; dm 148KN; @) Its location is pretty good, in a quiet area 1km west of the Old Town.

This mid-sized hostel has decent, spacious if plain dorms (and one double) and a rooftop terrace. Rates include breakfast. Book ahead.

Hotel Ivka　　　　　HOTEL €€
(☑362 600; www.hotel-ivka.com; Put Sv Mihajla 21; s/d 585/760KN; P❄@🛜) Modern three-star hotel with spacious modern rooms that have wooden floors and free wi-fi; most come with balconies, too. Comfort levels are high given the prices. It's closer to Lapad and the ferry terminal than the Old Town, but on a regular bus route.

✖ Eating

Weed out tourist traps and choose carefully, and you'll find fabulous food in the Old Town.

Lucín Kantun　　　　CROATIAN €€
(☑321 003; Od Sigurate bb; meals around 140KN) A modest-looking place with shabby-chic decor, a few pavement tables and some of the most creative food in Dubrovnik. Everything on the short mezze-style menu is freshly cooked from an open kitchen so you may have to wait a while at busy times.

Wanda

ITALIAN €€€

(☑098 94 49 317; www.wandarestaurant.com; Prijeko 8; mains from 70KN) This is a very classy Italian, with good Croatian wines and dishes such as osso buco with saffron risotto and beautifully crafted pastas. Eat from the fixed-priced tasting menus (150KN to 580KN) to see what the chefs are really capable of.

Dubravka 1836

CAFE €€

(www.dubravka1836.hr; Brsalje 1; mains from 49KN) This place has arguably Dubrovnik's best dining terrace, right by the Pile Gate with stunning wall and sea views. Though it draws quite a touristy clientele, locals still rate the fresh fish, risottos and salads, pizza and pasta.

Nishta

VEGETARIAN €

(www.nishtarestaurant.com; Prijeko bb; mains from 59KN; ⊙ closed Mon) A casual enjoyable vegetarian restaurant, Nishtu raids the globe for dishes so you'll find miso soup, nachos, Indian food, Thai curries and chow mein.

Buffet Skola

CAFE €

(Antuninska 1; snacks from 17KN) For a quick bite between sightseeing spots, you can't do better. The ham and cheese sandwich is the thing to order.

🍷 Drinking

Buža

BAR

(Ilije Sarake) Finding this isolated bar-on-a-cliff feels like a discovery as you duck and dive around the city walls and finally see the entrance tunnel. It showcases tasteful music and a mellow crowd soaking up the vibes, views and sunshine.

Buža II

BAR

(Crijevićeva 9) Just a notch more upmarket than the original, this one is lower on the rocks and has a shaded terrace where you can snack on crisps, peanuts or sandwiches.

The Gaffe

PUB

(Miha Pracata bb) The busiest place in town, this huge pub has a homey interior, a long covered side terrace and friendly staff.

Troubadur

BAR

(Bunićeva Poljana 2) Come to this corner bar, a legendary Dubrovnik venue, for live jazz concerts in the summer.

EastWest Club

BAR-CLUB

(www.ew-dubrovnik.com; Frana Supila bb) By day this outfit on Banje Beach rents out beach chairs and umbrellas and serves drinks to the bathers. When the rays lengthen, the cocktail bar opens.

☆ Entertainment

TOP CHOICE **Lazareti**

CULTURAL CENTRE

(www.lazareti.com; Frana Supila 8) Dubrovnik's best cultural centre, Lazareti hosts cinema nights, club nights, live music, gigs and pretty much all the best things in town.

Open-Air Cinema

CINEMA

(Kumičića, Lapad) In two locations, it's open nightly in July and August with screenings starting after sundown. Also at Za Rokom in the Old Town.

❶ Information

There are numerous ATMs in town, in Lapad and at the ferry terminal and bus station. Travel agencies and post office will also exchange cash.

Atlas Travel Agency (www.atlas-croatia.com) Gruž Harbour (☑418 001; Obala Papa Ivana Pavla II 1); Pile Gate (☑442 574; Sv Đurđa 1) Organises excursions within Croatia and to Mostar and Montenegro. Also finds private accommodation.

Hospital (☑431 777; Dr Roka Mišetića) A kilometre south of Lapad Bay.

Left luggage (Garderoba; 1st hr 5KN, then each hr 1.50KN; ⊙4.30am-10pm) At the bus station.

Main post office (cnr Široka & Od Puča)

Netcafé (www.netcafe.hr; Prijeko 21; per hr 30KN) This cybercafe has fast connections, CD/DVD burning, wi-fi, photo printing and scanning.

OK Travel & Trade (☑418 950; okt-t@du.t-com.hr; Obala Stjepana Radića 32) Near the Jadrolinija ferry terminal.

Tourist office (www.tzdubrovnik.hr; ⊙8am-8pm daily Jun-Sep, 8am-3pm Mon-Fri, 9am-2pm Sat Oct-May) bus station (☑417 581; Obala Pape Ivana Pavla II 44a); Gruž Harbour (☑417 983; Obala Stjepana Radića 27); Lapad (☑437 460; Šetalište Kralja Zvonimira 25); Old Town (☑323 587; Široka 1); Old Town 2 (☑ 323 887; Ulica Svetog Dominika 7) Maps, information and the indispensable *Dubrovnik Riviera* guide. The smart new head office that's under construction just west of the Pile Gate should open by the time you read this.

❶ Getting There & Away

Air

Daily flights to/from Zagreb are operated by **Croatia Airlines** (☑01-66 76 555; www.croatia airlines.hr). Fares vary between 270KN for promo fares and around 760KN for flexi fares. The trip takes about an hour. Croatia Airlines also operate nonstop flights to Frankfurt and seasonal routes to cities, including Rome, Paris and Amsterdam.

Dubrovnik airport is served by over 20 other airlines from across Europe.

Boat

A twice-weekly **Jadrolinija** (☎ 418 000; www. jadrolinija.hr; Gruž Harbour) coastal ferry heads north to Korčula, Hvar, Split, Zadar and Rijeka. There's a local ferry that leaves Dubrovnik for Sobra and Polače on Mljet (60KN, 2½ hours) throughout the year; in summer there are two ferries a day. Several daily ferries run year-round to the outlying Elafiti Islands of Koločep, Lopud and Šipan.

Ferries also go from Dubrovnik to Bari, in southern Italy; there are six a week in the summer season (291KN to 401KN, nine hours) and two in the winter months.

Jadroagent (☎ 419 000; Obala Stjepana Radića 32) books ferry tickets and has information.

Bus

The Jadrolinija ferry terminal and the bus station are next to each other at Gruž, several kilometres outside of the Old Town.

Buses out of Dubrovnik **bus station** (☎ 060 305 070; Obala Pape Ivana Pavla II 44a) can be crowded, so book tickets ahead in summer.

Split–Dubrovnik buses pass briefly through Bosnian territory, so keep your passport handy for border-crossing points.

All bus schedules are detailed at www.libertas dubrovnik.hr.

❶ Getting Around

Čilipi international airport (www.airport -dubrovnik.hr) is 24km southeast of Dubrovnik. Atlas buses (35KN) leave from the main bus station irregularly, supposedly two hours before Croatia Airlines domestic flights, but it's best to check the latest schedule at the Atlas travel agency by the Pile Gate. Buses leave the airport for Dubrovnik bus station (via the Pile Gate in this direction) several times a day and are timed to coincide with arrivals. A taxi costs around 240KN.

Dubrovnik's buses run frequently and generally on time. The fare is 10KN if you buy from the driver but only 8KN if you buy it at a kiosk.

UNDERSTAND CROATIA

History

Croatia has a long and torrid history, which has helped define the Croats and contributed much to the fabric of the country. Since time immemorial, people have come and gone, invading, trading and settling. For long periods, the Croats have been ruled by and have fought off others – Venetians, Ottomans, Hungarians, Habsburgs, the French, the Germans. The creation of Yugoslavia after WWII brought some semblance of unity into the south Slavic nations. Yet it didn't last long. After the death of Yugoslav leader Tito in 1980, Yugoslavia slowly disintegrated, and a brutal civil war ensued.

War & Peace

With political changes sweeping Eastern Europe, many Croats felt the time had come to separate from Yugoslavia and the elections of April 1990 saw the victory of Franjo Tudman's Croatian Democratic Union (Hrvatska Demokratska Zajednica; HDZ). On 22 December 1990 a new Croatian con-

BUSES FROM DUBROVNIK

DESTINATION	FARE (KN)	DURATION (HR)	DAILY SERVICES
Korčula	95	3	2
Kotor	96	2½	2-3
Mostar	105	3	3
Orebić	84	2½	2
Plitvice	330	10	1
Rijeka	357-496	13	4-5
Sarajevo	210	5	2
Split	122	4½	19
Zadar	174-210	8	8
Zagreb	250	11	7-8

stitution was promulgated, changing the status of Serbs in Croatia from that of a 'constituent nation' to a national minority.

The constitution's failure to guarantee minority rights and mass dismissals of Serbs from the public service stimulated the 600,000-strong ethnic Serb community within Croatia to demand autonomy. In early 1991 Serb extremists within Croatia staged provocations designed to force federal military intervention. A May 1991 referendum (boycotted by the Serbs) produced a 93% vote in favour of independence, but when Croatia declared independence on 25 June 1991, the Serbian enclave of Krajina proclaimed its independence from Croatia.

Under pressure from the EC (now the EU), Croatia declared a three-month moratorium on its independence, but heavy fighting broke out in Krajina, Baranja (the area north of the Drava River opposite Osijek) and Slavonia. The Serb-dominated Yugoslav People's Army intervened in support of Serbian irregulars, under the pretext of halting ethnic violence.

When the Croatian government ordered a blockade of 32 federal military installations in the republic, the Yugoslav navy blockaded the Adriatic coast and laid siege to the strategic town of Vukovar on the Danube. During the summer of 1991, a quarter of Croatia fell to Serbian militias and the Yugoslav People's Army.

In early October 1991 the federal army and Montenegrin militia moved against Dubrovnik to protest the blockade of their garrisons in Croatia, and on 7 October the presidential palace in Zagreb was hit by rockets fired by Yugoslav air-force jets in an unsuccessful assassination attempt on President Tuđman. When the three-month moratorium on independence ended, Croatia declared full independence. On 19 November the city of Vukovar fell after a bloody three-month siege. During six months of fighting in Croatia 10,000 people died, hundreds of thousands fled and tens of thousands of homes were destroyed.

To fulfil a condition for EC recognition, in December the Croatian Sabor (Parliament) belatedly amended its constitution to protect minority groups and human rights. A UN-brokered ceasefire from 3 January 1992 generally held. In January 1992 the EC, succumbing to strong pressure from Germany, recognised Croatia. This was followed three months later by US recognition; in May 1992 Croatia was admitted to the UN.

The fighting continued until the Dayton Accord, signed in Paris in December 1995, recognised Croatia's traditional borders and provided for the return of eastern Slavonia, which was effected in January 1998. The transition proceeded relatively smoothly, but the two populations still regard each other with suspicion.

Although the central government in Zagreb has made the return of Serb refugees a priority in accordance with the demands of the international community, Serbs intending to reclaim their property face an array of legal impediments.

Franjo Tuđman's combination of authoritarianism and media control, and tendency to be influenced by the far right, no longer appealed to the postwar Croatian populace. By 1999 opposition parties united to work against Tuđman and the HDZ. Tuđman was hospitalised and died suddenly in late 1999, and planned elections were postponed until January 2000. Still, voters turned out in favour of a centre-left coalition, ousting the HDZ and voting in the centrist Stipe Mesić, who held the presidential throne for ten years.

Croatia on the Cusp

Sitting between the Balkans and Central Europe, Croatia has been suffering from something of a love-hate-love affair with the EU and its neighbours as well as with its own politicians.

The biggest drama in Croatia's contemporary politics took place in July 2009 when the then prime minister Ivo Sanader announced his resignation and withdrawal from politics out of the blue and, rumours had it, went off sailing on his yacht. The parliament quickly approved his deputy, former journalist Jadranka Kosor, as prime minister; she was the first woman in Croatia's history to hold this post. In a move unpopular with the opposition, Kosor formed the government with pretty much the same cabinet members as Sanader's.

A major change happened in Croatia when Ivo Josipović of the opposition party, the Social Democratic Party of Croatia (SDP), won the presidential election in January 2010, beating the independent candidate Milan Bandić (Zagreb's mayor, who is serving his fourth term) with 60.26% of the vote in the runoffs. He was inaugurated as Croatia's third president in February 2010. Many Croats see Josipović as ineffective, a puppet of a corrupt regime. Others regard him as pro-European, in his (some say weak) attempts to employ a zero-tolerance policy towards corruption and inspire foreign investment.

Membership talks with the EU continue, as Croatia deals with the repercussions of global recession on its home turf as well as widespread governmental corruption and elements of rabid nationalism. It aims to join the EU in 2012, although that largely depends on negotiations and the accession treaty being ratified by the 27 members.

Attitudes towards Croatia joining the EU are divided. Many people are enthusiastic, though the enthusiasm has dropped with what some locals see as 'an endless list of rules' presented to the country. Predictably, it's the younger generations who are more geared towards joining the EU; the older generations lament the loss of industrial and agricultural independence that will inevitably happen when the country joins up.

It remains to be seen whether Croatia will manage to clean up its act. Until then, Croatia is still on the brink of Europe, which is part of its appeal and its curse.

The People of Croatia

According to the most recent census (2001), Croatia had a population of roughly 4.5 million people, a decline from the prewar population of nearly five million. Some 59% live in urban areas. About 280,000 Serbs (50% of the Serbian population) departed in the early 1990s; an estimated 110,000 have returned. In the postindependence economic crunch, 120,000 to 130,000 Croats emigrated, but a roughly equal number of ethnic Croat refugees arrived from Bosnia and Hercegovina and another 30,000 or so came from the Vojvodina region of Serbia. Italians are concentrated in Istria, while Albanians, Bosniaks and Roma can be found in Zagreb, Istria and some Dalmatian towns. The largest cities in Croatia are Zagreb (780,000), Split (188,700), Rijeka (138,000), Osijek (85,200) and Zadar (73,500).

Religion

According to the most recent census, 87.8% of the population identified itself as Catholic, 4.4% Orthodox, 1.3% Muslim, 0.3% Protestant and 6.2% others and unknown. Croats are overwhelmingly Roman Catholic, while all Serbs belong to the Eastern Ortho-

dox Church, a division that has its roots in the fall of the Roman Empire.

It would be difficult to overstate the extent to which Catholicism shapes the Croatian national identity. The Church is the most trusted institution in Croatia, rivalled only by the military. Religious holidays are celebrated with fervour and Sunday Mass is strongly attended.

Food & Drink

Croatian food is a savoury smorgasbord of taste, echoing the varied cultures that have influenced the country over the course of its history. You'll find a sharp divide between the Italian-style cuisine along the coast and the flavours of Hungary, Austria and Turkey in the continental parts.

Staples & Specialities

Zagreb and northwestern Croatia favour the kind of hearty meat dishes you might find in Vienna. Juicy spit-roasted and baked meat features *janjetina* (lamb), *svinjetina* (pork) and *patka* (duck), often accompanied by *mlinci* (baked noodles) or *pečeni krumpir* (roast potatoes).

Coastal cuisine is typically Mediterranean, using a lot of olive oil, garlic, fresh fish and shellfish, and herbs. Along the coast, look for lightly breaded and fried *lignje* (squid) as a main course. For a special appetiser, try *paški sir,* a pungent hard cheese from the island of Pag. Dalmatian *brodet* (stewed mixed fish served with polenta) is another regional treat.

Istrian cuisine has been attracting international foodies for its long gastronomic tradition, fresh foodstuffs and unique specialities. Typical dishes include *maneštra,* a thick vegetable-and-bean soup, *fuži,* hand-rolled pasta often served with truffles or game meat, and *fritaja* (omelette often served with seasonal vegies). Istrian wines and olive oil are highly rated.

It's customary to have a small glass of brandy before a meal and to accompany the food with one of Croatia's many wines. Croatians often mix their wine with water, calling it *bevanda. Rakija* (brandy) comes in different flavours. The most commonly drunk are *loza* (grape brandy), *šljivovica* (plum brandy) and *travarica* (herbal brandy).

The two top types of Croatian *pivo* (beer) are Zagreb's Ožujsko and Karlovačko from

Karlovac. You'll probably want to practise saying *živjeli!* (cheers!).

Where to Eat & Drink

Most restaurants cluster in the middle of the price spectrum – few are unbelievably cheap and few are exorbitantly expensive. A restaurant *(restoran)* is at the top of the food chain, generally presenting a more formal dining experience. A *gostionica* or *konoba* is usually a traditional family-run tavern. A *pivnica* is more like a pub, with a wide choice of beer. A *kavana* is a cafe. Self-service cafeterias are quick, easy and inexpensive, though the quality of the food tends to vary.

Restaurants are open long hours, often noon to 11pm (some midnight), with Sunday closings outside of peak season.

Vegetarians & Vegans

Outside of major cities like Zagreb, Rijeka, Split and Dubrovnik, vegetarian restaurants are few but Croatia's vegetables are usually locally grown and quite tasty. *Blitva* (swiss chard) is a nutritious side dish often served with potatoes. The hearty *štrukli* (baked cheese dumplings) are a good alternative too.

The Arts

Literature

Croatia's towering literary figure is 20th-century novelist and playwright Miroslav Krleža (1893–1981). His most popular novels include *The Return of Philip Latinovicz* (1932), which has been translated into English.

Some contemporary writers worth reading include expat writer Dubravka Ugrešić, best known for her novels *The Culture of Lies* and *The Ministry of Pain*. Slavenka Drakulić's *Café Europa – Life After Communism* is an excellent read, while Miljenko Jergović's *Sarajevo Marlboro* and *Mama Leone* powerfully conjure up the atmosphere of life in pre-war Yugoslavia.

Music

Although Croatia has produced many fine classical musicians and composers, its most original musical contribution lies in its rich tradition of folk music. The instrument most often used in Croatian folk music is the *tamburica,* a three- or five-string mandolin that is plucked or strummed. Translated as 'group of people', *klapa* is an outgrowth of church-choir singing. The form is most pop-

FESTIVALS
263

In July and August there are summer festivals in Dubrovnik, Split, Pula and Zagreb. Dubrovnik's summer music festival emphasises classical music, with concerts in churches around town, while Pula hosts a variety of pop and classical stars in the Roman amphitheatre and also hosts a film festival. Mardi Gras celebrations have recently been revived in many towns with attendant parades and festivities, but nowhere is it celebrated with more verve than in Rijeka.

ular in rural Dalmatia and can involve up to 10 voices singing in harmony.

There's a wealth of homegrown talent on Croatia's pop and rock music scene. Some of the most prominent pop, fusion and hip-hop bands are Hladno Pivo (Cold Beer), Pips Chips & Videoclips, TBF, Edo Maajka, Vještice (The Witches), Gustafi and the deliciously insane Let 3.

Visual Arts

Vlaho Bukovac (1855–1922) was the most notable Croatian painter in the late 19th century. Important early-20th-century painters include Miroslav Kraljević (1885–1913) and Josip Račić (1885–1908). Post-WWII artists experimented with abstract expressionism but this period is best remembered for the naive art that was typified by Ivan Generalić (1914–92). Recent trends have included minimalism, conceptual art and pop art. Contemporary Croatian artists worth checking out include Lovro Artuković, Sanja Iveković, Dalibor Martinis, Andreja Kulunčić, Sandra Sterle and Renata Poljak.

Environment

Croatia is shaped like a boomerang: from the Pannonian plains of Slavonia between the Sava, Drava and Danube Rivers, across hilly central Croatia to the Istrian peninsula, then south through Dalmatia along the rugged Adriatic coast.

The narrow Croatian coastal belt at the foot of the Dinaric Alps is only about 600km long as the crow flies, but it's so indented that the actual length is 1778km. If the 4012km of coastline around the offshore islands is added to the total, the length becomes 5790km. Most of the 'beaches' along this jagged coast consist of slabs of rock sprinkled with naturists. Don't come expecting to find sand, but the waters are sparkling clean, even around large towns.

Croatia's offshore islands are every bit as beautiful as those off the coast of Greece. There are 1244 islands and islets along the tectonically submerged Adriatic coastline, 50 of them inhabited. The largest are Cres, Krk, Mali Lošinj, Pag and Rab in the north; Dugi Otok in the middle; and Brač, Hvar, Korčula, Mljet and Vis in the south.

Wildlife

Deer are plentiful in the dense forests of Risnjak National Park, as are brown bears, wild cats and *ris* (lynx), from which the park gets its name. Occasionally a wolf or wild boar may appear but only rarely. Plitvice Lakes National Park, however, is an important refuge for wolves. A rare sea otter is also protected in Plitvice, as well as in Krka National Park.

The griffon vulture, with a wingspan of 2.6m, has a permanent colony on Cres, and Paklenica National Park is rich in peregrine falcons, goshawks, sparrow hawks, buzzards and owls. Krka National Park is an important migration route and winter habitat for marsh birds as well as rare golden eagles and short-toed eagles.

National Parks

When the Yugoslav federation collapsed, eight of its finest national parks ended up in Croatia. These have a total area of 96,135 sq km, of which 74,260 sq km is land and 21,875 sq km is water. 7.94% of the entire surface of Croatia is protected land.

The dramatically formed karstic gorges and cliffs make Paklenica National Park along the coast a rock-climbing favourite. More rugged is the mountainous Northern Velebit National Park, a stunning patchwork of forests, peaks, ravines and ridges that backs northern Dalmatia and the Šibenik-Knin region. The abundant plant and animal life, including bears, wolves and deer, in the Plitvice Lakes National Park between Zagreb and Zadar has warranted its inclusion in Unesco's list of World Natural Heritage sites. Both Plitvice Lakes and Krka National Parks (near Šibenik) feature a dramatic series of cascades and incredible turquoise lakes.

The Kornati Islands consist of 140 sparsely inhabited and vegetated islands, islets and reefs scattered over 300 sq km – an Adriatic showpiece easily accessible on an organised tour from Zadar. The northwestern half of the island of Mljet has been named a national park due to its two highly indented saltwater lakes surrounded by lush vegetation. The Brijuni Islands near Pula are the most cultivated national park since they were developed as a tourist resort in the late 19th century and were the getaway paradise for Tito.

Environmental Issues

The lack of heavy industry in Croatia has had the happy effect of leaving its forests, coasts, rivers and air generally fresh and unpolluted, but, as ever, an increase in investment and development brings forth problems and threats to the environment. With the tourist boom, the demand for fresh fish and shellfish has risen exponentially. As it is no longer possible to fish their way out of the problem, the only alternative for Croats is to grow their own seafood. The production of farmed sea bass, sea bream and tuna (for export) is rising substantially, resulting in environmental pressure along the coast. In particular, Croatian tuna farms capture the young fish for fattening before they have a chance to reproduce and replenish the wild fish population.

Coastal and island forests face particular problems. The dry summers and brisk *maestrals* (strong, steady westerly winds) also pose substantial fire hazards along the coast.

SURVIVAL GUIDE

Directory A–Z

Accommodation

In this chapter, budget accommodation (€) includes camping grounds, hostels and some guest houses, and costs up to 450KN for a double. Midrange accommodation (€€) costs 450KN to 800KN a double, while the top end (€€€) starts from 800KN and can go as high as 4000KN per double. Reviews are listed in order of preference. For hotels, we list the starting B&B price in high season.

Note that private accommodation is a lot more affordable in Croatia; it's very often great value. If you don't mind foregoing hotel facilities, it's a great way to go about vacationing in Croatia.

Note that many establishments add a 30% charge for less than three-night stays and include 'residence tax', which is around

7KN per person per day. Prices in this book do not include the residence tax.

Along the coast, accommodation is priced according to four seasons, which vary from place to place:

November to March The cheapest months. There may only be one or two hotels open in a coastal resort but you'll get great rates – often no more than 350KN for a double in a good three-star hotel and 250KN in a lesser establishment.

April, May and October Generally the next-cheapest months.

June and September The shoulder season.

July and August Book in advance (especially along the coast) and count on paying top price, especially in the peak period, which starts in late July and lasts until mid- or late August.

Camping

Nearly 100 camping grounds are scattered along the Croatian coast. Camping grounds are generally open from mid-April to mid-September, give or take a few weeks. The exact times change from year to year, so it's wise to call in advance if you're arriving at either end of the season.

Nudist camping grounds (marked FKK) are among the best, as their secluded locations ensure peace and quiet. Bear in mind that freelance camping is officially prohibited. A good site for camping information is www.camping.hr.

Hostels

The **Croatian YHA** (☑01-48 29 291; www.hfhs. hr; Savska 5/1, Zagreb) operates youth hostels in Rijeka, Dubrovnik, Punat, Zadar, Zagreb and Pula. Nonmembers pay an additional 10KN per person per day for a stamp on a welcome card; six stamps entitle you to membership. The Croatian YHA can also provide information about private youth hostels in Krk, Zadar, Dubrovnik and Zagreb.

Prices given in this book are for the high season in July and August; prices fall the rest of the year.

Hotels

Hotels are ranked from one to five stars with most in the two- and three-star range. Features such as satellite TV, direct-dial phones, high-tech bathrooms, minibars and air-con are standard in four- and five-star hotels, and one-star hotels have at least a bathroom in the room. Many two- and three-star hotels offer satellite TV but you'll find better decor in the higher categories. In August, some hotels may demand a surcharge for stays of less than three or four nights, but this is usually waived during the rest of the year, when prices drop steeply. In Zagreb prices are the same all year.

Breakfast is included in the prices quoted for hotels in this chapter, unless stated otherwise.

Private Rooms

Private rooms or apartments are the best-value accommodation in Croatia. Service is excellent and the rooms are usually extremely well kept. You may very well be greeted by offers of *sobe* (rooms) or *apartmani* (apartments) as you step off your bus and boat, but rooms are most often arranged by travel agencies or the local tourist office. Booking through an agency will ensure that the place you're staying in is officially registered and has insurance.

It makes little sense to price shop from agency to agency, since prices are fixed by the local tourist association. Whether you deal with the owner directly or book through an agency, you'll pay a 30% surcharge for stays of less than four or three nights and sometimes 50% or even 100% more for a one-night stay, although you may be able to get them to waive the surcharge if you arrive in the low season. Some will even insist on a seven-night minimum stay in the high season.

Whether you rent from an agency or rent from the owners privately, don't hesitate to bargain, especially for longer stays.

Activities

There are numerous outdoorsy activities in Croatia.

Cycling Croatia has become a popular destination for cycle enthusiasts. See www.bicikl.hr and www.pedala.com.hr.

Diving Most of the coastal and island resorts mentioned in this chapter have dive shops. For more info see the **Croatian Association of Diving Tourism** (www.croprodive.info), **Croatian Diving Federation** (www.diving-hrs.hr, in Croatian) and **Pro Diving Croatia** (www.diving.hr).

Hiking For information about hiking in Croatia, see the **Croatian Mountaineering Association** (www.plsavez.hr).

Kayaking and rafting Zagreb-based **Huck Finn** (www.huck-finn.hr) is a good contact for sea and river kayaking packages as well as rafting.

Rock climbing and caving For details, contact the **Croatian Mountaineering Association** (www.plsavez.hr) or check its speleological department website at www.speleologija.hr.

Windsurfing For info about windsurfing in Croatia, see www.hukjd.hr or www.windsurfing.hr.

Yachting A good source of information is the **Association of Nautical Tourism** (Udruženje Nautičkog Turizma; ☑051-209 147; Bulevar Oslobođenja 23, Rijeka), which represents all Croatian marinas.

Business Hours

Banks 9am-7pm Mon-Fri, 8am-1pm or 9am-2pm Sat

Bars 9am-midnight

Offices 8am-4pm or 9am-5pm Mon-Fri, 8am-1pm or 9am-2pm Sat

Restaurants noon-11pm or midnight, closed Sun out of peak season

Shops 8am-8pm Mon-Fri, to 2pm Sat

Embassies & Consulates

The following are all in Zagreb.

Albania (☑01-48 10 679; Jurišićeva 2a)

Australia (☑01-48 91 200; Kaptol Centar, Nova Ves 11)

Bosnia & Hercegovina (☑01-45 01 070; Torbarova 9)

Bulgaria (☑01-46 46 609; Nike Grškovića 31)

Canada (☑01-48 81 200; Prilaz Gjure Deželića 4)

Czech Republic (☑01-61 77 246; Radnička Cesta 47/6)

France (☑01-48 93 600; Andrije Hebranga 2)

Germany (☑01-63 00 100; Ulica Grada Vukovara 64)

Hungary (☑01-48 90 900; Pantovčak 257)

Ireland (☑01-63 10 025; Miramarska 23)

Netherlands (☑01-46 42 200; Medveščak 56)

New Zealand (☑01-46 12 060; Vlaška 50a/V)

Poland (☑01-48 99 444; Krležin Gvozd 3)

Romania (☑01-46 77 550; Mlinarska ulica 43)

Serbia (☑01-45 79 067; Pantovčak 245)

Slovakia (☑01-48 77 070; Prilaz Gjure Deželića 10)

Slovenia (☑01-63 11 000; Alagovićeva 30/annex)

UK (☑01-60 09 100; I Lučića 4)

USA (☑01-66 12 200; Thomasa Jeffersona 2)

Food

Price ranges are: budget (€; under 50KN), midrange (€€; 50KN to 80KN) and top end (€€€; over 80KN).

Gay & Lesbian Travellers

Homosexuality has been legal in Croatia since 1977 and is tolerated, but not welcomed with open arms. Public displays of affection between same-sex couples may be met with hostility, especially beyond the major cities.

Exclusively gay clubs are a rarity outside Zagreb, but many of the large discos attract a mixed crowd. Raves are also a good way for gay men and women to meet. On the coast, gay men gravitate to Rovinj, Hvar, Split and Dubrovnik, and tend to frequent naturist beaches.

In Zagreb, late April/early May is the **Queer Zagreb Festival** (www.queerzagreb.org) and the last Saturday in June is Gay Pride Zagreb day. Gay-friendly venues are listed throughout this book.

Most Croatian websites devoted to the gay scene are in Croatian only, but a good starting point is http://travel.gay.hr.

Holidays

New Year's Day 1 January

Epiphany 6 January

Easter Monday March/April

Labour Day 1 May

Corpus Christi 10 June

Day of Antifascist Resistance 22 June; marks the outbreak of resistance in 1941

Statehood Day 25 June

Homeland Thanksgiving Day 5 August

Feast of the Assumption 15 August

Independence Day 8 October

All Saints' Day 1 November

Christmas 25 & 26 December

Money

Credit Cards

Amex, MasterCard, Visa and Diners Club cards are widely accepted in large hotels, stores and many restaurants, but don't count on cards to pay for private accommodation or meals in small restaurants. You'll find ATMs accepting MasterCard, Maestro, Cirrus, Plus and Visa in most bus and train stations, airports, all major cities and most small towns.

Lonely Planet's *Croatia* is a comprehensive guide to the country.

Interesting reads about Croatia include Rebecca West's *Black Lamb and Grey Falcon*, a classic travel book which recounts the writer's journeys through Croatia, Serbia, Bosnia, Macedonia and Montenegro in 1941. British writer Tony White retraced West's journey in *Another Fool in the Balkans* (2006), juxtaposing modern life in Serbia and Croatia with the region's political history. *Croatia: Travels in Undiscovered Country* (2003), by Tony Fabijančić, recounts the life of rural folks in a new Croatia. *Plum Brandy: Croatian Journeys* by Josip Novakovich is a sensitive exploration of his family's Croatian background.

Currency

Croatia uses the kuna (KN). Commonly circulated banknotes come in denominations of 500, 200, 100, 50, 20, 10 and five kuna. Each kuna is divided into 100 lipa. You'll find silver-coloured 50- and 20-lipa coins, and bronze-coloured 10-lipa coins.

Tax

Travellers who spend more than 740KN in one shop are entitled to a refund of the value-added tax (VAT), which is equivalent to 22% of the purchase price. In order to claim the refund, the merchant must fill out the Tax Cheque (required form), which you must present to the customs office upon leaving the country. Mail a stamped copy to the shop within six months, which will then credit your credit card with the appropriate sum.

Tipping

If you're served well at a restaurant, you should round up the bill, but a service charge is always included. Bar bills and taxi fares can also be rounded up. Tour guides on day excursions expect to be tipped.

Telephone

Mobile Phones

If you have an unlocked 3G phone, you can buy a SIM card for about 50KN. You can choose from four network providers: VIP (www.vip.hr), T-Mobile (www.t-mobile.hr), Tomato (www.tomato.com.hr) and Tele2 (www.tele2.hr).

Phone Codes

To call Croatia from abroad, dial your international access code, then ☎385 (the country code for Croatia), then the area code (without the initial 0) and the local number.

To call from region to region within Croatia, start with the area code (with the initial zero); drop it when dialling within the same code.

Phone numbers with the prefix ☎060 are either free or charged at a premium rate, so watch the small print. Phone numbers that begin with ☎09 are mobile phone numbers.

Phonecards

To make a phone call from Croatia, go to the town's main post office. You'll need a phone card to use public telephones. Phonecards are sold according to *impulsa* (units), and you can buy cards of 25 (15KN), 50 (30KN), 100 (50KN) and 200 (100KN) units. These can be purchased at any post office and most tobacco shops and newspaper kiosks.

Tourist Information

Croatian National Tourist Board (www.croatia.hr) is a good source of info. There are regional tourist offices that supervise tourist development, and municipal tourist offices that have free brochures and information.

Travellers with Disabilities

Due to the number of wounded war veterans, more attention is being paid to the needs of disabled travellers in Croatia. Public toilets at bus stations, train stations, airports and large public venues are usually wheelchair accessible. Large hotels are wheelchair accessible, but very little private accommodation is. Bus and train stations in Zagreb, Zadar, Rijeka, Split and Dubrovnik are wheelchair accessible, but the local Jadrolinija ferries are not. For further information, get in touch with **Hrvatski Savez Udruga Tjelesnih Invalida** (☎01-48 12 004; www.hsuti.hr; Šoštarićeva 8, Zagreb), the Croatian union of associations for physically disabled persons.

Visas

Citizens of the EU, USA, Canada, Australia, New Zealand, Israel, Ireland, Singapore and the UK do not need a visa for stays of up to 90 days. South Africans must apply for a 90-day visa in Pretoria. Contact any Croatian embassy, consulate or travel agency abroad for information.

Getting There & Away

Getting to Croatia is becoming ever easier, especially if you're arriving in summer. Low-cost carriers are finally establishing routes to Croatia, and a plethora of bus and ferry routes shepherd holidaymakers to the coast.

Air

There are direct flights to Croatia from a number of European cities; however, there are no nonstop flights from North America to Croatia.

There are several major airports in Croatia.

Dubrovnik (www.airport-dubrovnik.hr) Non-stop flights from Brussels, London (Gatwick), Manchester, Hannover, Frankfurt, Cologne, Stuttgart and Munich

Pula (www.airport-pula.com) Nonstop flights from Manchester and London (Gatwick).

Rijeka (www.rijeka-airport.hr) Nonstop flights from Cologne and Stuttgart.

Split (www.split-airport.hr) Nonstop flights from London, Frankfurt, Munich, Cologne, Prague and Rome.

Zadar (www.zadar-airport.hr) Nonstop flights from London, Brussels, Munich, Bari, Dublin and more.

Zagreb (www.zagreb-airport.hr) Direct flights from all European capitals, plus Hamburg, Stuttgart and Cologne.

Land

Croatia has border crossings with Hungary, Slovenia, Bosnia & Hercegovina, Serbia and Montenegro.

Bus

Buses run to destinations throughout Europe.

From Austria, **Eurolines** (www.eurolines.com) operates buses from Vienna to several destinations in Croatia.

Rijeka €43, nine hours, two weekly

Split €51, 11½ hours, two weekly

Zadar €43, 8¼ hours, two weekly

Zagreb €32, five to seven hours, two daily (one direct, the other via Varaždin)

Bus services between Germany and Croatia are good, and fares are cheaper than the train. All buses are handled by **Deutsche Touring GmbH** (www.deutsche-touring.de); there are no Deutsche Touring offices in Croatia, but numerous travel agencies and bus stations sell its tickets.

Scheduled departures to/from Germany:

Istria From Frankfurt weekly; from Munich twice weekly.

Split From Cologne, Dortmund, Frankfurt, Main, Mannheim, Munich, Nuremberg and Stuttgart daily; from Berlin (via Rijeka) twice a week.

Rijeka From Berlin twice weekly.

Zagreb From Cologne, Dortmund, Frankfurt, Main, Mannheim, Munich, Nuremberg and Stuttgart daily; from Berlin four times a week.

Trieste in Italy is well connected with the Istrian coast. Note that there are fewer buses on Sundays. In addition to the following, there's also a bus from Padua that passes Venice, Trieste and Rovinj and ends up in Pula (235KN, six hours). It runs Monday to Saturday.

Dubrovnik 410KN, 15 hours, one daily

Rijeka 65KN, two hours, five daily

Rovinj 88KN, three hours, two daily

Poreč 69KN, two hours, three daily

Pula 105KN, 2½-3¾ hours, six daily

Split 279KN, 10½ hours, two daily

Zadar 188KN, 7½ hours, one daily

For Montenegro, there are three daily buses from Kotor to Dubrovnik (100KN, 2½ hours) that starts at Bar and stops at Herceg Novi.

There are six daily buses from Zagreb to Belgrade, Serbia (199KN to 204KN, six hours). At Bajakovo on the border, a Serbian bus takes you on to Belgrade.

Slovenia is well connected with the Istrian coast. Buses from Ljubljana head to Rijeka (180KN, 2½ hours, two daily), Rovinj (173KN, four hours, three daily) and Split (310KN, 10 hours, one daily). There's also one bus each weekday that connects Rovinj with Koper (87KN, 2¾ hours), stopping at Poreč, Portorož and Piran.

Car & Motorcycle

If you rent a car in Italy, many insurance companies will not insure you for a trip into

Croatia. Border officials know this and may refuse you entry unless permission to drive into Croatia is clearly marked on the insurance documents.

Most car-rental companies in Trieste and Venice are familiar with this requirement and will furnish you with the correct stamp. Otherwise, you must make specific inquiries.

Train

There are two daily and two overnight trains between Vienna and Zagreb, via Slovenia and via Hungary. The price is between €47 and €57 and the journey takes between 5¾ and 6½ hours.

For BiH, trains from Sarajevo service Ploče (via Mostar and Banja Luka; €13, four hours, two daily) and Zagreb (€30, 9½ hours, two daily)

There are three trains daily from Munich, Germany to Zagreb (€39 to €91, 8½-nine hours) via Salzburg and Ljubljana. Reservations are required southbound but not northbound.

There are three daily trains from Zagreb to Budapest, Hungary (€30 return, six to seven hours).

Between Venice, Italy and Zagreb (€25 to €40, 7½ hours), there is one direct train at night and several more that run through Ljubljana.

Four daily trains connect Zagreb with Belgrade, Serbia (159KN, 6½ hours).

From Slovenia, trains run from Ljubljana to Rijeka (100KN, 2½ hours, two daily) and Zagreb (100KN to 160KN, 2½ hours, seven daily).

Sea

Regular boats from the following companies connect Croatia with Italy:

Blue Line (www.blueline-ferries.com)

Commodore Cruises (www.commodore -cruises.hr)

Emilia Romagna Lines (www.emiliaromag nalines.it)

Jadrolinija (www.jadrolinija.hr)

Split Tours (www.splittours.hr)

SNAV (www.snav.com)

Termoli Jet (www.termolijet.it)

Ustica Lines (www.usticalines.it)

Venezia Lines (www.venezialines.com)

Getting Around

Air

Croatia Airlines (☎01-66 76 555; www.croa tiaairlines.hr) is the only carrier for flights within Croatia. There are daily flights between Zagreb and Dubrovnik, Pula, Split and Zadar.

Bicycle

Cycling can be a great way to explore the islands. Relatively flat islands such as Pag and Mali Lošinj offer the most relaxed biking, but the winding, hilly roads on other islands offer spectacular views. Bicycles are easy to rent along the coast and on the islands. Some tourist offices, especially in the Kvarner and Istria regions, have maps of routes and can refer you to local bike-rental agencies. Even though it's not fully translated into English yet, www.pedala.hr is a great reference for cycling routes around Croatia.

Boat

Jadrolinija Ferries

Jadrolinija operates an extensive network of car ferries and catamarans along the Adriatic coast. Ferries are a lot more comfortable than buses, though somewhat more expensive.

Services operate year-round, though they are less frequent in winter. Cabins should be booked a week ahead. Deck space is usually available on all sailings.

You must buy tickets in advance at an agency or a Jadrolinija office. Tickets are not sold on board. In summer months, you need to check in two hours in advance if you bring a car.

Somewhat mediocre fixed-price menus in onboard restaurants cost about 100KN; the cafeteria only offers ham-and-cheese sandwiches for 30KN. Do as the Croatians do: bring some food and drink with you.

Local Ferries

Local ferries connect the bigger offshore islands with each other and with the mainland, but you'll find many more ferries going from the mainland to the islands than from island to island.

On most lines, service is less frequent between October and April. Extra passenger boats are added in the summer; these are usually faster, more comfortable and more expensive.

On some shorter routes (eg Jablanac to Mišnjak), ferries run nonstop in summer and advance reservation is unnecessary.

Buy tickets at a Jadrolinija office or at a stall near the ferry (usually open 30 minutes prior to departure). There are no ticket sales on board. In summer, arrive one to two hours prior to departure, even if you've already bought your ticket.

Cars incur a charge; calculated according to the size of car, and often very pricey. Reserve as far in advance as possible. Check in several hours in advance. Bicycles incur a small charge.

There is no meal service; you can buy drinks and snacks on board. Most locals bring their own food.

Bus

Bus services are excellent and relatively inexpensive. There are often a number of different companies handling each route so prices can vary substantially. Luggage stowed in the baggage compartment under the bus costs extra (7KN a piece, including insurance).

Bus Companies

The companies listed here are among the largest.

Autotrans (☎051-660 300; www.autotrans. hr) Based in Rijeka. Connections to Istria, Zagreb, Varaždin and Kvarner.

Brioni Pula (☎052-535 155; www.brioni. hr) Based in Pula. Connections to Istria, Trieste, Padua, Split and Zagreb.

Contus (☎023-315 315; www.contus.hr) Based in Zadar. Connections to Split and Zagreb.

Croatiabus (☎01-61 13 213; www.croatiabus.hr) Connecting Zagreb with towns in Zagorje and Istria.

Samoborček (☎01-48 19 180; www.samo borcek.hr) Connecting Zagreb with towns in Dalmatia.

Tickets & Schedules

At large stations, bus tickets must be purchased at the office, not from drivers. Try to book ahead to be sure of a seat, especially in the summer.

Departure lists above the various windows at bus stations tell you which window sells tickets for your bus. On Croatian bus schedules, *vozi svaki dan* means 'every day' and *ne vozi nedjeljom i blagdanom* means 'no service Sunday and holidays'.

Some buses travel overnight, saving you a night's accommodation. Don't expect to get much sleep, though, as the inside lights will be on and music will be blasting the whole night. Take care not to be left behind at meal or rest stops, which usually occur about every two hours.

Car & Motorcycle

Croatia has recently made a major investment in infrastructure, the highlight of which is a new motorway connecting Zagreb with Split. The 'autoroute' is expected to reach Dubrovnik at some stage. Zagreb and Rijeka are now connected by motorway, and an Istrian motorway has shortened the travel time to Italy considerably.

Although the new roads are in excellent condition, there are stretches where service stations and facilities are few and far between.

Car Hire

In order to rent a car you must be 21 or over, with a valid driving licence and a valid credit card.

Independent local companies are often much cheaper than the international chains, but the big companies offer one-way rentals. Sometimes you can get a lower car-rental rate by booking the car from abroad, or by booking a fly-drive package.

Car Insurance

Third-party public liability insurance is included by law with car rentals, but make sure your quoted price includes full collision insurance, known as a collision damage waiver (CDW). Otherwise, your responsibility for damage done to the vehicle is usually determined as a percentage of the car's value, beginning at around 2000KN.

Driving Licence

Any valid driving licence is sufficient to drive legally and rent a car; an international driving licence is not necessary.

The **Hrvatski Autoklub** (HAK; Croatian Auto Club; ☎01-46 40 800; www.hak.hr; Avenija Dubrovnik 44, Zagreb) offers help and advice. For help on the road, you can contact the nationwide **HAK road assistance** (Vučja Služba; ☎987).

On the Road

Petrol stations are generally open from 7am to 7pm and often until 10pm in summer. Petrol is Eurosuper 95, Super 98, normal or

Prague Saints
BAR

(Map p278; ☑222 250 326; www.praguesaints.cz; Polska 32; Vinohrady; ⓐ11 to Vinohradská tržnice) This bar is a good intro to what's happening on the Prague gay scene. The vibe is low-key, friendly and inclusive; an ideal first stop in town.

Termix
DANCE CLUB

(Map p278; www.club-termix.cz; Trebízckého 4A, Vinohrady; ☺8pm-5am Wed-Sun; ⓐ11 to Vinohradská tržnice) A friendly mixed gay-and-lesbian scene with an industrial/high-tech vibe. Wednesdays are good fun with retro Czech pop.

Valentino
DANCE CLUB

(Map p278; www.club-valentino.cz; Vinohradská 40, Vinohrady; ☺from 11am; ⓐ11 to Vinohradská tržnice) Welcome to Prague's gay superclub, with three floors concealing two dance areas, four bars and rooms with exceedingly low lighting.

Cinemas

Most films are screened in their original language with Czech subtitles (české titulky), but Hollywood blockbusters are often dubbed into Czech (dabing); look for the labels 'tit.' or 'dab.' on listings. Tickets are around 180/140Kč for adult/child.

Kino Světozor
ART HOUSE

(Map p282; ☑224 946 824; www.kinosvetozor.cz; Vodičkova 41, Nové Město; ⓜMůstek) Your best bet for Czech films with English subtitles; under the same management as Kino Aero but more central. Plus it includes a cool DVD and movie poster shop.

Kino Aero
ART HOUSE

(off Map p278; ☑271 771 349; www.kinoaero.cz; Biskupcova 31, Žižkov; ⓐ1, 9, 16 to Ohrada) This art-house cinema has themed weeks and retrospectives; often screens films with English subtitles.

Palace Cinemas
MAINSTREAM

(Map p282; www.palacecinemas.cz; Slovanský dům, Na příkopě 22, Nové Město; ⓜnám Republiky) A 10-screen multiplex showing current Hollywood films.

🔒 Shopping

Near the Old Town Sq, explore the antique shops of Týnská and Týnská ulička.

Pivní Galerie
BEER

(Map p278; www.pivnigalerie.cz; U Průhonu 9, ☺noon-8pm Tue-Fri; ⓐ1, 3, 5, 25 to U Průhonu) Just a quick tram ride from central Prague, you can purchase beers from across the Czech Republic – we counted around 170 from

more than 30 breweries. Note the limited opening hours, so head to the Pivovarský Klub bar/restaurant/beer shop (p292) if you're in town from Saturday to Monday.

Kubista
DESIGN

(Map p282; www.kubista.cz; Ovocný trh 19, Staré Město; ⓜnám Republiky) Kubista specialises in limited-edition reproductions of distinctive cubist furniture and ceramics, and designs by masters of the form such as Josef Gočár and Pavel Janák. It also has a few original pieces for serious collectors with serious cash to spend.

Modernista
DESIGN

(Map p282; www.modernista.cz; Celetná 12, Staré Město; ☺11am-7pm; ⓜnám Republiky) This classy showcase of Czech cubism, art deco and similar design features covetable but reasonably affordable ceramics, jewellery, posters and books. Downstairs a renovated vaulted Gothic space provides the ultimate showcase for larger, but equally desirable, examples of home and office furniture and lighting.

Botanicus
COSMETICS

(Map p282; Týn 3, Staré Město; ⓜnám Republiky) Prepare for sensory overload in this popular old apothecary, which sells natural health and beauty products in slightly nostalgic packaging. The scented soaps, herbal bath oils and shampoos, fruit cordials and handmade paper products are made from herbs and plants grown on an organic farm east of Prague.

Big Ben Bookshop
BOOKS

(Map p282; www.bigbenbookshop.com; Malá Štupartská 5, Staré Město; ⓜnám Republiky) English-language books about Prague and the Czech Republic.

Bontonland
MUSIC

(Map p282; Václavské nám 1, Nové Město; ⓜMůstek) Contemporary and traditional Czech music.

Granát Turnov
JEWELLERY

(Map p282; www.granat.eu; Dlouhá 28-30, Staré Město; ⓜnám Republiky). Has gold and garnet pieces plus more affordable gold-plated silver and vltavín (a dark-green semiprecious stone).

Manufaktura
HANDICRAFTS

(Map p282; www.manufaktura.biz; Melantrichova 17, Staré Město; ⓜStaroměstska) Sells traditional Czech handicrafts, wooden toys and handmade cosmetics.

Moser
CRYSTAL

(Map p282; www.moser-glass.com; Na příkopě 12, Nové Město; ☺10am-8pm Mon-Fri, to 7pm Sat &

Sun; Mnám Republiky) Top-quality Bohemian crystal.

ℹ️ Information

Dangers & Annoyances

Pickpockets work the crowds at the astronomical clock, Prague Castle and Charles Bridge, and on the central metro and tramlines, especially crowded trams 9, 22 and 23.

Most taxi drivers are honest, but some operating from tourist areas overcharge their customers (even Czechs). Phone a reputable taxi company or look for the red and yellow signs for the 'Taxi Fair Place' scheme, indicating authorised taxi stands.

The park outside the main train station is a hang-out for dodgy types and worth avoiding late at night.

Emergency

If your passport or valuables are stolen, obtain a police report and crime number from the **Prague 1 Police Station** (☏224 222 558; Jungmannovo nám 9, Nové Mesto; ⏱24hr; MMůstek). You'll need this for an insurance claim. There's usually an English-speaker on hand. The emergency phone number for the police is ☏158.

Internet Access

Many hotels, bars, fast-food restaurants and internet cafes provide wi-fi hotspots.

Globe Cafe & Bookstore (www.globebook store.cz; Pštrossova 6, Nové Město; per min 1.50Kč; ⏱9.30am-midnight; MKarlovo nám)

Mobilarium (Rathova Pasaž, Na příkopě 23, Nové Město; per min 1.50Kč; ⏱10am-7pm Mon-Fri, 11am-6pm Sat; Mnám Republiky)

Medical Services

Canadian Medical Care (☏235 360 133, after hours 724 300 301; www.cmcpraha. cz; Veleslavínská 1, Veleslavín; ⏱8am-6pm Mon, Wed & Fri, to 8pm Tue & Thu; 🚊20, 26 to Veleslavínská from MDejvická) Expat centre with English-speaking doctors, 24-hour medical aid and a pharmacy.

Na Homolce Hospital (☏257 271 111, after hours 257 272 527; www.homolka.cz; 5th fl, Foreign Pavilion, Roentgenova 2, Motol; 🚊167 from MAnděl) Prague's main casualty department.

Polyclinic at Národní (☏222 075 120; 24hr emergencies 720 427 634; www.poliklinika. narodni.cz; Národní třída 9, Nové Město; ⏱8.30am-5pm Mon-Fri; 🚊Národní Třída) English-, French- and German-speaking staff.

Praha lékárna (☏224 946 982; Palackého 5, Nové Město; MMůstek) A 24-hour pharmacy; for emergency service after business hours, ring the bell.

Money

The major banks are best for changing cash, but using a debit card in an ATM gives a better rate of exchange. Avoid směnárna (private exchange booths), which advertise misleading rates and have exorbitant charges.

Post

Main post office (Jindřišská 14, Nové Město; ⏱2am-midnight; MMůstek) Collect a ticket from the automated machines outside the main hall (press 1 for stamps and parcels, 4 for Express Mail Service – EMS).

Tourist Information

The **Prague Information Service** (Pražská informační služba, PIS; ☏12 444, in English and German; www.praguewelcome.cz) provides free tourist information with good maps at the following locations:

PIS Malá Strana Bridge Tower (Map p278; Charles Bridge; ⏱10am-6pm Apr-Oct; 🚊12, 20, 22, 23 to Malostranské nám)

PIS Old Town Hall (Map p282; Staroměstské nám 5, Staré Město; ⏱9am-7pm Mon-Fri, to 6pm Sat & Sun Apr-Oct, to 6pm Mon-Fri, to 5pm Sat & Sun Nov-Mar; MStaroměstská) The main branch.

PIS Rytirská (Map p282; Rytirská 31; ⏱9am-7pm Apr-Oct, 9am-6pm Nov-Mar; MMůstek)

PIS Train station (Praha hlavní nádraží; Map p282; Wilsonova 2, Nové Město; ⏱9am-7pm Mon-Fri, to 6pm Sat & Sun; MHlavní nádraží)

If you're venturing beyond Prague, **Czech Tourism** (Map p282; www.czechtourism.com; Staroměstské nám, Staré Město; ⏱9am-5pm Mon-Fri; MStaroměstská) has an office in Prague's Old Town Square.

ℹ️ Getting There & Away

Bus

The main terminal for international and domestic buses is **Florenc bus station** (ÚAN Florenc; Map p278; Křižíkova 4, Karlín; MFlorenc), 600m northeast of the main train station. Short-haul tickets are sold on the bus, and long-distance domestic tickets are sold in the newly renovated central hall.

Some regional buses depart from near metro stations Anděl, Dejvická, Černý Most, Nádraží Holešovice, Smíchovské Nádraží or Želivského, and some departures to České Budějovice or Český Krumlov depart from the Ná Knížecí or outside the outside Roztyly metro station. Check timetables and departure points at www.idos.cz.

Main bus companies:

Eurolines (☏245 005 245; www.elines.cz; Florenc bus station) Buses to all over Europe.

Megabus (☏775666 140; www.megabus.cz; Můstek metro station, Florenc bus station)

Links Prague with Karlovy Vary, Plzeň and Brno; also services throughout Europe.

Student Agency (📞800 100 1300; www.student agency.cz) Central Prague (Ječná 37; Nove Město); Florenc (Florenc bus station) Links major Czech cities; also services throughout Europe.

Key services from Florenc:

Brno 200Kč, 2½ hours, hourly

České Budějovice 213Kč, 2¾ hours, four daily

Český Krumlov 160Kč, three hours, seven daily

Karlovy Vary 140Kč, 2¼ hours, eight daily

Kutná Hora 120Kč; 1¼ hours, six daily

Plzeň 90Kč, 1½ hours, hourly

Train

Prague's main train station is **Praha-hlavní nádraží** (Map p282; 📞221 111 122; Wilsonova, Nové Město; M Hlavní nádraží). At the time of research Praha-hlavní nádraží was undergoing major redevelopment. Check signage for the current locations of domestic and international ticket counters. Also buy train tickets and get timetable information from **ČD Centrum** (⊘6am-7.30pm) at the southern end of level 2 in Praha-hlavní nádraží.

Some international trains stop at Praha-Holešovice station on the northern side of the city, while some domestic services terminate at Praha-Smíchov south of Malá Strana. Check timetables and departure points at www.idos.cz.

Key services from Praha-hlavní nádraží:

Brno 316Kč, three hours, frequent

České Budějovice 213Kč, 2¾ hours, four daily

Karlovy Vary 294Kč, 3½ hours, four daily

Kutná Hora 100Kč, one hours, six daily

Plzeň 90Kč, 1½ hours, hourly

🛈 Getting Around

To/From the Airport

Prague's Ruzyně airport is 17km west of the city centre. There are several options for travel to/from central Prague.

The **Airport Express** (50Kč; ⊘5am-10pm) bus service goes directly to the upper level of Prague's main train station (Praha-hlavní nádraží) from where you can access the metro system. Luggage is free on this service; buy your ticket from the driver. Another option is to catch it only as far as the Dejvická metro station (30Kč).

Cedaz Minibus (📞220 111 111; www.cedaz.cz; ⊘every 30min 7.30am-7pm) leaves from outside arrivals; buy your ticket from the driver. The minibus stops at the **Czech Airlines** (V Celnici 5; M nám Republiky) office near the Hilton around nám Republiky (120Kč) or further out at the Dejvická metro station (90Kč). You can also get a Cedaz minibus from your hotel or any other

address (480Kč for one to four people, 960Kč for five to eight).

Otherwise, see the Dopravní podnik (DPP) desk in arrivals and take bus 119 (26Kč, 20 minutes, every 15 minutes) to the end of the line (Dejvická), then continue by metro into the city centre (another 10 minutes; no extra ticket needed). You'll also need a half-fare (13Kč) ticket for your backpack or suitcase if it's larger than 25cm x 45cm x 70cm.

AAA Taxis (📞14 014; www.aaataxi.cz; around 650Kč) are reputable and the drivers speak good English. To the airport should be around 600Kč.

Bicycle

City Bike (📞776 180 284; www.citybike-prague. com; Královodvorská 5, Staré Město; per day 500Kč; ⊘9am-7pm May-Sep; M Staroměstská)

Car & Motorcycle

Challenges to driving in Prague include cobblestones, trams and one-way streets. Try not to arrive or leave on a Friday or Sunday afternoon or evening, when Prague folk are travelling to and from their weekend houses.

Central Prague has many pedestrian-only streets, marked with Pěší Zoná (Pedestrian Zone) signs, where only service vehicles and taxis are allowed; parking can be a nightmare. Meter time limits range from two to six hours at around 50Kč per hour. Parking in one-way streets is normally only allowed on the right-hand side.

Public Transport

All public transport is operated by **Dopravní podnik hl. m. Prahy** (DPP; 📞800 191 817; www. dpp.cz), with information desks at **Ruzyně airport** (⊘7am to 7pm) and in four metro stations – **Muzeum** (⊘7am to 9pm), **Můstek** (⊘7am to 6pm), **Anděl** (⊘7am to 6pm) and **Nádraží Holešovice** (⊘7am to 6pm) – where you can get tickets, directions, a multilingual system map, a map of Noční provoz (night services) and a detailed English-language guide to the whole system.

Buy a ticket before boarding a bus, tram or metro. Tickets are sold from machines at metro stations and major tram stops, at news-stands, Trafiky snack shops, PNS and other tobacco kiosks, hotels, all metro station ticket offices and DPP information offices.

A jizdenka (transfer ticket) is valid on tram, metro, bus and the Petřín funicular and costs 26Kč (half-price for six- to 15-year-olds); large suitcases and backpacks (anything larger than 25cm x 45cm x 70cm) also need a 13Kč ticket. Kids under six ride free. Validate (punch) your ticket by sticking it in the little yellow machine in the metro station lobby or on the bus or tram the first time you board; this stamps the time and date on it. Once validated, tickets remain valid for 75 minutes from the time of stamping, if validated between 5am and 10pm on weekdays, and for 90 minutes at other times. Within this period, you can make unlimited transfers between all types of public transport (you don't need to punch the ticket again).

There's also a short-hop 18/9Kč adult/child ticket, valid for 20 minutes on buses and trams, or for up to five metro stations. Being caught without a valid ticket entails a 400Kč on-the-spot fine (100Kč for not having a luggage ticket).

Tickets for 24 hours (100Kč) and three/five days (330/500Kč) are also available. If you're staying for longer and will be travelling a lot, consider a monthly pass (550Kč). All passes must be validated on first use only. Before shelling out on a pass, note that much of central Prague can be explored on foot.

The metro operates from 5am to midnight daily. Line A runs from northwest Prague at Dejvická to the east at Depo Hostivař; line B runs from the southwest at Zličín to the northeast at Černý Most; and line C runs from the north at Letňany to the southeast at Háje. Line A intersects line C at Muzeum, line B intersects line C at Florenc and line A intersects line B at Můstek.

After the metro closes, night trams (51 to 59) and buses (501 to 512) travel about every 40 minutes. Check if one of these services passes near where you're staying.

Taxi

Try to avoid getting a taxi in tourist areas such as Wenceslas Sq and outside the main train station. To avoid being ripped off, phone a reliable company such as **AAA** (☑14 014; www.aaaradiotaxi.cz) or **City Taxi** (☑257 257 257; www.citytaxi.cz). Both companies also offer online bookings.

Prague runs the 'Taxi Fair Place' scheme, with authorised taxis in 49 locations around key tourist areas. Look for the yellow and red signs. Drivers can charge a maximum of 40Kč flagfall plus 28Kč per kilometre and 6Kč while waiting, and must announce the estimated price in advance. On this basis any trip within the city centre should be around 170Kč.

AROUND PRAGUE

You can visit the following places on day trips using public transport.

Karlštejn

Erected by the Emperor Charles IV in the mid-14th century, **Karlštejn Castle** (☑274 008 154; www.hradkarlstejn.cz; Karlštejn; ☉9am-6pm Tue-Sun Jul & Aug, to 5pm May, Jun & Sep, to 4pm Apr & Oct) crowns a ridge above Karlštejn village. It's a 20-minute walk from the train station.

The highlight is the **Chapel of the Holy Rood**, where the Bohemian crown jewels were kept until 1420. The 55-minute guided tours (in English) on **Route I** costs 250/150Kč per adult/child. **Route II**, which includes the chapel (June to October only), are 300/200Kč adult/child and must be pre-booked. See online for details.

Trains from Praha-hlavní nádraží station to Beroun stop at Karlštejn (49Kč, 45 minutes, hourly).

Konopiště

The assassination of the heir to the Austro-Hungarian throne, Archduke Franz Ferdinand d'Este, sparked off WWI. For the last 20 years of his life he hid away southeast of Prague in his country retreat at **Konopiště Chateau** (www.zamek-konopiste.cz; Benešov; ☉9am-5pm Tue-Sun May-Aug; to 9am-4pm Tue-Fri, to 5pm Sat & Sun Sep; 9am-3pm Tue-Fri, to 4pm Sat & Sun Apr & Oct).

Three guided tours are available. **Tour III** (adult/child 300/200Kč) is the most interesting, visiting the archduke's private apartments, unchanged since the state took over the chateau in 1921. **Tour II** (adult/child 200/130Kč) takes in the **Great Armoury**, one of Europe's most impressive collections.

The castle is a testament to the archduke's twin obsessions of hunting and St George. Having renovated the massive Gothic and Renaissance building in the 1890s, Franz Ferdinand decorated his home with some of his 300,000 hunting kills. About 100,000 of them adorn the walls, marked with when and where it was slain. The **Trophy Corridor** and **Chamois Room** (both on Tour III) are truly bizarre.

His collection of St George–related artefacts includes 3750 items, many displayed in the **Muzeum sv Jiří** (adult/child 30/15Kč) at the front of the castle. From June to September weekend concerts are sometimes held in the castle's grounds.

Konopiště is 2.5km west of Benešov. There are direct trains from Prague's Hlavní nádraží (main train station) to Benešov u Prahy (68Kč, 1¼ hours, hourly). Buses depart from Florenc or the Roztyly metro station to Benešov on a regular basis (42Kč, 1¼ hours).

Local bus 2 (11Kč, six minutes, hourly) runs from a stop on Dukelská, 400m north of the train station (turn left out of the station, then first right on Tyršova and first left) to the castle car park. Or it's a 30-minute walk. Turn left out of the train station, go left across the bridge over the railway, and follow Konopištská street west for 2km.

Kutná Hora

In the 14th century, the silver-rich ore under Kutná Hora gave the now-sleepy town an importance in Bohemia second only to Prague. The local mines and mint turned out silver *groschen* for use as the hard currency of central Europe. The silver ore ran out in 1726, leaving the medieval townscape largely unaltered. Now with several fascinating and unusual historical attractions, the Unesco World Heritage–listed town is a popular day trip from Prague.

In early June, the town hosts an **International Music Festival** (www.mfkh.cz), with chamber-music recitals in venues including the soaring Cathedral of St Barbara.

◉ Sights

TOP CHOICE **Sedlec Ossuary** CHURCH
(www.kostnice.cz; Zamecka 127; adult/child 50/30Kč; ⊙8am-6pm Apr-Sep, 9am-noon & 1-5pm Oct & Mar, 9am-noon & 1-4pm Nov-Mar) From Kutná Hora hlavní nádraží, walk south for 10 minutes to the remarkable Sedlec Ossuary. When the Schwarzenberg family purchased Sedlec monastery in 1870, a local woodcarver got creative with the bones of 40,000 people from the centuries-old crypt. Skulls and femurs are strung from the vaulted ceiling, and the central chandelier contains at least one of each bone in the human body.

From the Kutná Hora bus station catch bus 1B and get off at the 'Tabak' stop. A tourist minibus also shuttles between the Ossuary and the Cathedral of St Barbara.

Cathedral of St Barbara CHURCH
(www.chramsvatebarbory.cz; Jakubská ulice; adult/child 50/30Kč; ⊙9am-6pm Apr-Oct, 10am-4pm Nov-Mar) The Gothic cathedral of St Barbara rivals Prague's St Vitus in magnificence, its soaring nave culminating in elegant, six-petalled ribbed vaulting. The ambulatory chapels preserve original 15th-century frescos, some showing miners at work.

Old Town HISTORIC AREA
The Old Town lies south of **Palackého nám**, the main square. From the square's western end, Jakubská leads to **Church of St James** (1330). Further east is the **Italian Court** (Vlašský dvůr; Havlíčkovo nám 552; adult/child 100/80Kč; ⊙9am-6pm Apr-Sep, 10am-4pm

Oct-Mar), the former Royal Mint. Florentine craftsmen began stamping silver coins here in 1300. It houses a mint museum and a 15th-century **Audience Hall** with 19th-century murals depicting the election of Vladislav Jagiello as King of Bohemia in 1471 and the Decree of Kutná Hora being proclaimed by Wenceslas IV and Jan Hus in 1409.

Czech Silver Museum MUSEUM
(www.cms-kh.cz; adult/child 70/40Kč, English-speaking guide 400Kč; ⊙10am-6pm Jul & Aug, 9am-5pm Apr-May & Sep-Oct, closed Mon year-round) From the southern side of St James Church, Ruthardská leads to the **Hrádek** (Little Castle), a 15th-century palace housing the Czech Silver Museum. Don a miner's helmet to join the 1½-hour **Way of Silver tour** (adult/child 120/80Kč) through 500m of medieval mine shafts beneath the town. Kids need to be at least seven for this tour. A combination ticket for the museum and the mine tour (adult/child 140/90Kč) is also available.

Jesuit College HISTORIC BUILDING
Beyond the Hrádek is a 17th-century former Jesuit college, with a terrace featuring 13 **baroque statues** of saints, inspired by those on Prague's Charles Bridge. The second one along of a woman holding a chalice is St Barbara, the patron saint of miners and Kutná Hora.

⏝ Sleeping

Penzión u Kata PENSION €
(☎327 515 096; www.ukata.cz; Uhelná 596; s/d/tr 500/760/1140Kč; ⓟ@⊛) You won't lose your head over the rates at this good-value family hotel called the 'Executioner'. Bikes can be hired for 200Kč per hour and it's a short stroll from the bus station. Downstairs is a welcoming Czech beer hall and restaurant.

Hotel u Vlašského dvora HOTEL €€
(☎327 514 618; www.vlasskydvur.cz; 28 Řijna 511; s/d 1190/1500Kč; @⊛) Brightly coloured rooms linger just off Kutná Hora's main square, and a cooked breakfast downstairs in the almost-hip cafe makes a nice change from the usual cheese and sliced meat buffet.

✗ Eating & Drinking

Pivnice Dačický BEER HALL €
(Rakova 8; mains 100-250Kč) Try Kutná Hora's dark beer at this traditional beer hall. Rustle up three drinking buddies and order the Gamekeepers Reserve, a huge platter that demands at least a second beer. There are six different brews available, so try not to miss the bus back to Prague.

Kutná Hora

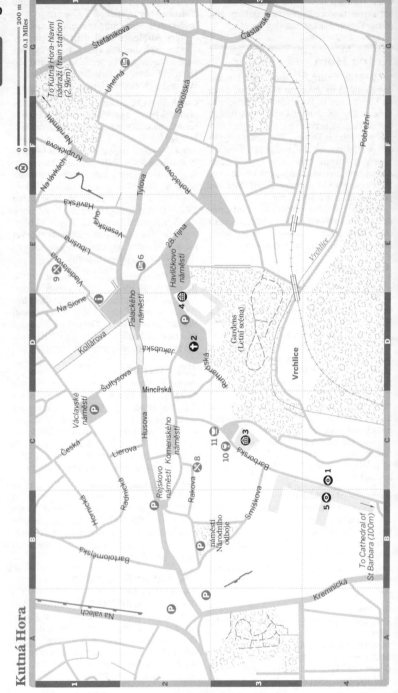

To Kutná Hora-hlavní nádraží (train station) (2.9km)

Na náměti

Štefánikova

Uhelná 7

Čáslavská

Sokolská

Krupičkova

Na lávkách

Havlířská

Vladislavova 9

Libušina

Veselého

Tylova

Rohácova

28. října

6

Havlíčkovo náměstí

Na Sione

Palackého náměstí

Kollárova

Jakubská

4

2

Ruthardská

Mincířská

Gardens (Letní scéna)

Vrchlice

Václavské náměstí

Šultysova

Husova

Česká

Lierova

Komenského náměstí

11

10

3

Barborská

Hornická

Radnická

Rejskovo náměstí

Rakova 8

Smíškova

1

5

Bartolomějská

náměstí Národního odboje

Na valech

Kremnická

To Cathedral of St Barbara (100m)

Vrchlice

0 200 m
0 0.1 Miles

Kutná Hora

U Sňeka Pohodáře   PIZZA €
(Vladislavova 11; pizza 100-130Kč) Kutná Hora's best Italian flavours are at this cosy local favourite that's very popular for takeout or dine-in pizza and pasta. And no, we don't know why it's called the 'Happy Snail'.

Kavárna Mokate   CAFE €
(Baborská 7; coffee & cake 70-80Kč; ☺8.30am-9.30pm Mon-Thu, 9am-midnight Fri & Sat, noon-7pm Sun) It's not just good coffee at this place with rustic tiled floors, and mismatched furniture from your last student flat – a global array of teas complements yummy cakes.

Baborska   BAR
(Baborská 35; ☺4pm-1am Mon-Thu, 4pm-3am Fri-Sat, 4-10pm Sun) Cosy, cosmopolitan and crafting very good cocktails, Baborska is a lively spot if you do decide to miss that last bus back to Prague.

❶ Information

The **information centre** (☎327 512 378; www.kutnahora.cz; Palackého nám 377; ☺9am-6pm Apr-Sep, 9am-5pm Mon-Fri, 10am-4pm Sat & Sun Oct-Mar) books accommodation, provides internet access (1Kč per minute) and rents bicycles (220Kč per day).

❶ Getting There & Away

Kutná Hora hlavní nádraží (the main train station) is 3km northeast of the Old Town centre. The bus station is more conveniently located on the Old Town's northeastern edge.

BUS There are about six direct buses a day, on weekdays only, from Prague's Florenc bus station to Kutná Hora (62Kč, 1¼ hours). A few also travel from Prague Černý Most metro station. A bus leaves Prague Florenc at 8.10am for an early start.

TRAIN There are direct trains from Prague's Hlavní nádraží (main train station) to Kutná Hora-hlavní nádraží (98Kč, 55 minutes, seven daily). Each has a good connection by local train (10Kč, eight minutes) to Kutná Hora-město station, adjacent to the old town.

❶ Getting Around

On weekdays local bus 1 runs between the bus station and the main train station (Kutná Hora-hlavní nádraží) every 30 minutes; get off at the Sedlec-Tabak stop (beside a big church) for Sedlec Ossuary. Look for the 'Kostnice' sign.

On weekends, the route is served by bus 7 (every one to two hours). Buy your ticket (9Kč) from the driver. A taxi from the station into town costs around 100Kč.

During summer a special tourist minibus (40Kč per person) travels a loop including the train station, the Sedlec Ossuary, and the Cathedral of St Barbara.

BOHEMIA

The ancient land of Bohemia makes up the western two-thirds of the Czech Republic. The modern term 'bohemian' comes to us via the French, who thought that Roma came from Bohemia; the word *bohémien* was later applied to people living an unconventional lifestyle. The term gained currency in the wake of Puccini's opera *La Bohème* about poverty-stricken artists in Paris.

Terezín

The massive fortress at Terezín (Theresenstadt in German) was built by the Habsburgs in the 18th century to repel the Prussian army, but the place is better known as a notorious WWII prison and concentration camp. Around 150,000 men, women and children, mostly Jews, passed through en route to the Auschwitz-Birkenau extermination camps: 35,000 of them died here of hunger, disease or suicide, and only 4000 ultimately survived. From 1945 to 1948 the fortress served as an internment camp for the Sudeten Germans, who were expelled from Czechoslovakia after the war.

Terezín also played a tragic role in deceiving the world about the ultimate goals of the

Nazi's 'Final Solution'. Official visitors were immersed in a charade, with Terezín being presented as a Jewish 'refuge', complete with shops, schools and cultural organisations – even an autonomous Jewish 'government'. As late as April 1945, Red Cross visitors delivered positive reports.

The **Terezín Memorial** (www.pamatnik -terezin.cz) consists of the Museum of the Ghetto in the Main Fortress, and the Lesser Fortress, a 10-minute walk east across the Ohře River. Admission to one part costs 160/130Kč per adult/child; a combined ticket is 200/150Kč. Ask at the ticket office about historical films in the museum's cinema.

The **Museum of the Ghetto** (◑9am-5.30pm) records daily life in the camp during WWII, through moving displays of paintings, letters and personal possessions. Entry to the Museum of the Ghetto includes entry to the Magdeburg Barracks and vice versa.

Around 32,000 prisoners, many of them Czech partisans, were incarcerated in the **Lesser Fortress** (◑8am-6pm Apr-Oct, to 4.30pm Nov-Mar). Take the grimly fascinating self-guided tour through the prison barracks, workshops, morgues and mass graves, before arriving at the bleak execution grounds where more than 250 prisoners were shot.

At the **Magdeburg Barracks** (cnr Tyršova & Vodárenská; ◑9am-6pm Apr-Oct, to 5.30pm Nov-Mar), the former base of the Jewish 'government', are exhibits on the rich cultural life – including music, theatre, fine arts and literature – that flourished against this backdrop of fear. Most poignant are the copies of *Vedem* ('In the Lead') magazine, published by 100 boys from 1942 to 1944. Only 15 of the boys survived the war.

❶ Getting There & Away

Buses (80Kč, one hour) leave hourly from outside Prague's Holešovice metro station. Most continue on to Litoměřice, the nearest town. The last bus back to Prague from Terezín usually leaves at 6.20pm. Frequent buses (9Kč, 10 minutes) link Litoměřice to Terezín.

Litoměřice

POP 25,100

Founded by German colonists in the 13th century, Litoměřice prospered in the 18th century as a royal seat and bishopric. The town centre features picturesque buildings and churches, some designed by the locally born baroque architect Ottavio Broggio.

The Old Town lies across the road to the west of the train and bus stations, guarded by the remnants of the 14th-century town walls. Walk along Dlouhá to the central square, Mírové nám.

◉ Sights

The main square is lined with Gothic arcades and facades dominated by the tower of **All Saints Church**, the step-gabled **Old Town Hall** and the distinctive **House at the Chalice** (Dům U Kalicha), housing the present town hall. Sprouting from the roof is a copper chalice, the traditional symbol of the Hussite church. The slim baroque facade at the square's elevated end is the **House of Ottavio Broggio**.

Along Michalská on the square's southwest corner is another Broggio design, the **North Bohemia Fine Arts Gallery** (Michalská 7; adult/child 32/18Kč; ◑9am-noon & 1-5pm Tue-Sun) with the priceless Renaissance panels of the Litoměřice altarpiece.

Turn left on Michalská and follow Domská to Domské nám on Cathedral Hill, passing the baroque **St Wenceslas Church**, on a side street to the right. Atop the hill is the town's oldest church, the 11th-century **St Stephen Cathedral**.

Follow the arch on the cathedral's left and descend down steep and cobbled Máchova. At the foot of the hill turn left then first right, up the zigzag steps to the **Old Town walls**. Follow the walls right to the next street, Jezuitská, then turn left back to the square.

🏃 Activities

The **Porta Bohemica 1** (www.osobni-lod.cz; adult 60-160Kč, child 30-80Kč; ◑daily July-Aug, Thu-Sun Jun & Sep, Fri-Sun May) operates cruises on the Labe River. **Cruise One** (7 hours; ◑Mon, Wed, Fri & Sat) runs north to Lovosice, Velké Žernoseky, Píštany and Ústí nad Labem, while **Cruise Two** (7 hours, ◑Tue, Thu, Sun) cruises south to Roudnice nad Labem and Šétí. Costs vary depending on the destination from Litoměřice, and there is full restaurant and bar service on board.

🛏 Sleeping

U Svatého Václava PENSION €
(☑416 737 500; www.upfront.cz/penzion; Svatovaclavská 12; s/d 750/1300Kč) Beside St Wenceslas Church, this popular haven has well-equipped rooms, hearty cooked breakfasts and owners whose English is better than they think.

Pension Prislin
PENSION €

(☎416 735 833; www.prislin.cz; Na Kocandě 12; s/d/tr/q 800/1100/1500/1800Kč) Pension Prislin has a friendly dog called Baltimore and a switched-on owner who's decorated his pension in bright colours. The spacious apartments take up to five travellers.

✖ Eating & Drinking

Radniční sklípek
CZECH €€

(Mírové nám 21; mains 150-280Kč) Keep your head down in this underground labyrinth that does great grills accompanied by a mainly local wine list. In summer, the meaty action spills onto the main square.

U Štěpána Pizzeria
PIZZA €

(Dlouhá 43; pizza 45-145Kč) Around 300m from the downhill end of the square, this spot has a monk as a logo, but there's definitely nothing frugal about the pizza toppings.

Gurmănie
CAFE €

(Novobranská 14; snacks 70-1000Kč; ⊙9am-5pm Mon-Fri, 9am-3pm Sat; 🛜) At the top end of the square, Gurmănie has tasty ciabatta sandwiches and tortilla wraps, plus salads and pasta. Say *ahoj* to Litoměřice's best coffee.

ℹ Information

The **information centre** (☎416 732 440; www.litomerice.cz; Mírové nám 15/7; ⊙9am-6pm May-Sep, 8am-4pm Mon-Fri & 8-11am Sat Oct-Apr) in the town hall books accommodation and runs walking tours. Internet is available; for wi-fi grab a coffee at the Gurmănie cafe.

ℹ Getting There & Away

Buses (80Kč, one hour) leave approximately hourly from outside Prague's Holešovice train station. Most stop first in Terezín. There are also frequent bus connections between Litoměřice and Terezín (9Kč, 10 minutes).

Bohemian Switzerland National Park

The main road and rail route between Prague and Dresden follows the fast-flowing Labe (Elbe) River, gouging a sinuous, steep-sided valley through a sandstone plateau on the border between the Czech Republic and Germany. The landscape of sandstone pinnacles, giddy gorges, dark forests and high meadows is the Bohemian Switzerland National Park (Národní park České Švýcarsko),

named after two 19th-century Swiss artists who settled here.

⊙ Sights & Activities

Just south of the German border, **Hřensko** is a cute village of half-timbered houses crammed into a sandstone gorge where the Kamenice River joins the Labe. It's overrun with German day trippers at summer weekends, but upstream, peaceful hiking trails begin.

A signposted 16km (five to six hours) circular hike explores the main sights. From Hřensko's eastern end a trail leads via ledges, walkways and tunnels through the mossy chasms of the **Kamenice River Gorge**.

Two sections – **Edmundova Soutěska** (Edmund's Gorge; ⊙9am-6pm May-Aug, Sat & Sun only Apr, Sep & Oct) and **Divoká Soutěska** (Savage Gorge; ⊙9am-5pm May-Aug, Sat & Sun only Apr, Sep & Oct) – have been dammed. Continue by punt and a ferryman through a canyon 5m wide and 50m to 150m deep. Each ferry trip costs 60/30Kč per adult/child.

A kilometre beyond the end of the second boat trip, a blue-marked trail leads uphill to the Hotel Mezní Louka. Across the road, a red-marked trail continues through the forest to the spectacular rock formation **Pravčická Brána** (www.pbrana.cz; adult/child 75/25Kč; ⊙10am-6pm Apr-Oct), the largest natural arch in Europe. Crouched beneath is the **Falcon's Nest**, a 19th-century chateau housing a national park museum and restaurant. From here the red trail descends westward back to Hřensko.

The area is also popular with climbers. Ask at the Hřensko information office about climbing day trips, and hire gear from **Hudy Sport** around 400m up the Kamenice River Gorge road.

🛏 Sleeping & Eating

Pension Lugano
PENSION €

(☎412 554 146; www.hrensko-lugano.cz; Hřensko; s/d 500/1000Kč) A cheerful place in the centre of Hřensko serving terrific breakfasts at a riverside restaurant.

Hotel Mezní Louka
HOTEL €

(☎412 554 220; www.mezni-louka.cz; Mezní Louka 71; s/d 900/1450Kč) In the hills, this is a 19th-century hiking lodge with a decent restaurant (mains 90Kč to 170Kč).

Camp Mezní Louka
CAMPING GROUND €

(☎412 554 084; r.kolarova@npcs.cz; campsites per tent/bungalow 110/510Kč) Across the road from Hotel Mezní Louka.

If you have a car, base yourself in either Janov or Jetřichovice. In Janov **Pension Pastis** (☑142 554 037; www.pastis.cz; Janov 22; s/d 540/1080Kč; ☎) has an excellent restaurant; in Jetřichovice try **Pension Dřevák** (☑412 555 015; s/d incl breakfast 700/1050Kč), housed in a 19th-century wooden building. Bookings can be made at www.ceskosaske-svycarsko.cz.

❶ Information

The **Hřensko information office** (☑414 554 286; www.ceskosaske-svycarsko.cz; ☺9am-6pm Apr-Oct) is on the corner of the road from Děčín.

❶ Getting There & Away

Boat

From May to September, the **Poseidon** (www.labskaplavebni.cz) travels along the Labe River from Děčín to **Hřensko** (adult/child 100/50Kč; ☺9.30am Mon-Fri, 9am & 1pm Sat-Sun) and back to **Děčín** (adult/child 120/60Kč; ☺10.30am Mon-Fri, 10am & 2pm Sat-Sun). **Return tickets** (adult/concession 180/80Kč) are also available. From mid-April to September it's also possible to travel by river from Hřensko to Bad Schandau and Königstein in Germany on MS *Sächsiche Schweiz*.

Bus

From Prague, take a bus from Florenc (120Kč, 1¾ hours, five daily) to Děčín. Buses run every two hours from Děčín to Hřensko (22Kč, 30 minutes) and from Děčín via Česká Kamenice or Hřensko to Jetřichovice, Vysoká Lípa or Mezná.

Train

Catch a Dresden-bound train and get off at Bad Schandau (280Kč, two hours, eight daily), in Germany, and then a local train back to Schöna on the German bank of the river opposite Hřensko. From the station, a ferry (20Kč, three minutes, 6am to 10pm April to September, 8am to 6pm October to March) crosses to Hřensko on demand.

❶ Getting Around

In summer, keep an eye out for the big red **Nationalpark Express**, a heritage double-decker bus that crosses over from Germany and provides regular transport to Pravčická Brána and Mezní Louka.

Karlovy Vary

POP 60,000

Karlovy Vary is the closest the Czech Republic has to a glam resort, but it's still glam with a small 'g', and it's popular with the Zimmer frame set. Well-heeled hypochondriacs, increasingly from Russia and the Middle East, make the pilgrimage to try to enjoy courses of 'lymphatic drainage' and 'hydrocolonotherapy' – all activities that should be outlawed under several international agreements. And every spa season sees more and more signage in Russia's Cyrillic alphabet. Maybe the town should be called Karlovy Varygrad instead.

If you're really keen to discover the dubious pleasures of a steam inhalation session or a sulphur bath, you'll need to make a prior appointment. If not, there's good hiking in the surrounding hills, and a busy arts and entertainment programme.

The **Karlovy Vary International Film Festival** in early July is well worth attending. More than 200 films are shown, tickets are easy to get, and a funky array of concurrent events (including buskers and world music concerts) give this genteel town a much-needed annual energy transfusion.

◉ Sights

Mill Colonnade   HISTORIC BUILDING

At the central spa district is the neoclassical Mill Colonnade (Mlýnská Kolonáda), with occasional summer concerts. Other elegant colonnades and 19th-century spa buildings are scattered along the Teplá River, with the 1970s concrete Hotel Thermal spoiling the effect slightly.

FREE **Hot Springs**   SPRINGS

Purchase a *lázeňský pohárek* (spa cup) and some *oplátky* (spa wafers) and sample the various hot springs. Infocentrum has a leaflet describing the 12 springs in the 'drinking cure', ranging from the **Rock Spring** (Skalní Pramen), which dribbles just 1.3L per minute, to the robust **Geyser Vřídlo**, which spurts 2000L per minute in a 14m-high jet. The latter is housed in the 1970s **Geyser Colonnade** (Vřídelní Kolonáda; ☺10am-6pm Mon-Fri, to 4pm Sat & Sun).

To look inside the old spa buildings without enduring the dubious rigours of *proktologie* and *endoskopie,* nip into **Spa No 3** (Lázně III) just north of the Mill Colonnade.

The most splendid spa building is the restored **Spa No 1** (Lázně I) at the south end of town, dating from 1895 and once housing Emperor Franz Josef's private baths. Across the river is the baroque **Grandhotel Pupp**, a former meeting place of European aristocrats.

Diana Funicular Railway   CABLE CAR

(one way/return adult 40/70Kč, child 20/35Kč; ☺9am-6pm) North of the Grandhotel Pupp, a narrow alley leads to the bottom station of the Diana Funicular Railway, which climbs 166m to great views from the **Diana Look-**

As Monty Python asked: 'Do you get wafers with it?' In Karlovy Vary the answer is a re-sounding 'yes', with locals prescribing the following method of taking your spring water: have a sip from your *lázeňský pohárek* (spa cup), then dull the sulphurous taste with a big, round sweet wafer called *oplátky*; these are sold for 12Kč each at spa hotels, speciality shops and at a stall in front of the Hotel Thermal. Steer clear of the fancy chocolate or hazelnut flavours, though; they're never as crunchily fresh and warm as the standard flavour. *Oplátky* are also a big hit in Mariánské Lázně.

out Tower. It's a pleasant walk back down through the forest.

Moser Glass Museum　　　　MUSEUM
(Sklářské Muzeum Moser; www.moser-glass.com; Kpt Jaroše 19; adult/child 80/50Kč; ☺9am-5pm) Just out of town, Moser Glass Museum has more than 2000 items on display. Afterwards get hot under the collar at the adjacent **glassworks** (adult/child 120/70Kč; ☺9am-2.30pm). Combined tickets (adult/child 180/100Kč) are also available.

🏃 Activities

Castle Spa (Zámecké Lázně; ☑353 222 649; www.edengroup.cz; Zámechý vrch; treatments from €30; ☺7.30am-7.30pm Mon-Fri, from 8.30am Sat & Sun) is a modernised spa centre, complete with a subterranean thermal pool. It still retains a heritage ambience.

For a cheaper paddle head to the **open-air thermal pool** (per hr 80Kč; ☺8am-8pm). Follow the 'Bazén' signs up the hill behind Hotel Thermal.

🎉 Festivals & Events

Karlovy Vary International Film Festival (www.kviff.com) is held in early July, **Karlovy Vary Folklore Festival** in early September, and the classical music festival, **Dvořák Autumn**, in September.

🛏 Sleeping

Accommodation is pricey, and can be tight during weekends and festivals; definitely book ahead. Infocentrum can find hostel, pension and hotel rooms. Consider staying in Loket and visiting Karlovy Vary as a day trip.

Hotel Maltézsy Kříž　　　　HOTEL €€
(☑353 169 011; www.maltezskykriz.cz; Stará Louka 50; s/d/apt €69/117/133; @⸛) Oriental rugs and wooden floors combine at this spiffy recent opening with cosy rooms and a more spacious double-storeyed apartment. Bathrooms are decked out in warm earth tones.

Hotel Boston　　　　HOTEL €€
(☑353 362 711; www.boston.cz; Luční vrch 9; s/d 1850/1950Kč; ⸛⸛) Tucked away down a quiet lane, this family-owned hotel has relatively spacious rooms decorated in bright colours with new bathrooms. The flash cafes of Stará Louka are just around the corner.

Hotel Ontario　　　　HOTEL €€
(☑353 222 091; www.hotelontario.cz; Zámecký vrch; s/d 2450/2850Kč; P@⸛) Look forward to great views and just maybe Karlovy Vary's friendliest team on reception. They call the stylishly appointed lodgings 'rooms', but they're actually compact apartments. The hotel is a stiff five-minute walk uphill.

Hotel Kavalerie　　　　HOTEL €
(☑353 229 613; www.kavalerie.cz; TG Masaryka 43; s/d from 950/1225Kč; P) Friendly staff abound in this cosy spot above a cafe. It's located near the bus and train stations, and nearby eateries can help you avoid the spa district's high restaurant prices. Rooms are starting to look a bit worn, but it's still OK value in an expensive destination.

Chebský dvůr　　　　PENSION €
(☑353 229 332; www.volny.cz/egerlaender; Tržíště 39; s/d 950/1300Kč) Simple and clean rooms above a Czech–German restaurant.

🍴 Eating & Drinking

La Scala　　　　ITALIAN €
(Jaltská 12; mains 120-190Kč) Karlovy Vary's best Italian flavours are hidden downstairs under an office building. Kick off your night with a drink in their stylish bar. Good-value lunch specials are 90Kč.

Tandoor　　　　INDIAN €
(IP Pavlova 25; mains 120-180Kč; ⸛) Located under a block of flats, Tandoor turns out the winning combo of authentic Indian flavours, smooth, creamy lassis and Gambrinus beer for just 28Kč. Vegetarian options abound, and if you're after a serious chilli hit, order the chicken phall (140Kč).

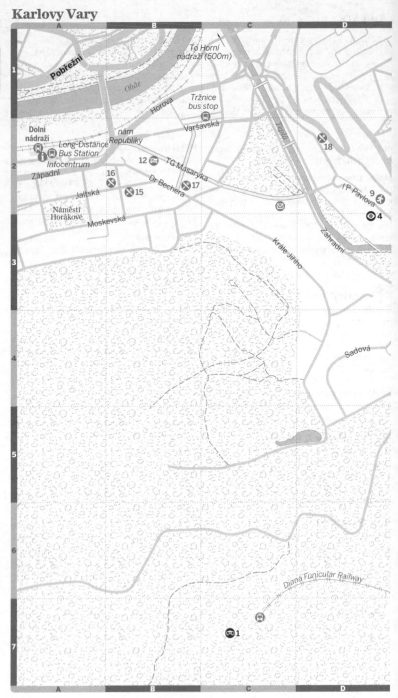

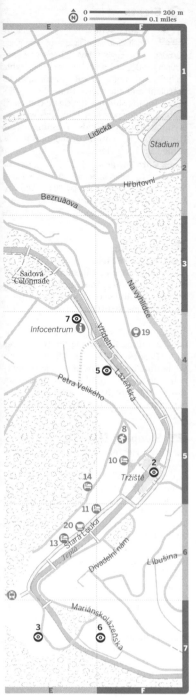

Kus　　　　　　　　　　　　　　　　CAFE €

(Bělehradská 8; snacks 50-70Kč; ⊙7am-5pm Mon-Fri) This cosy cafe and bakery serves salads, pasta and homemade desserts with an organic and vegetarian tinge.

Rad's Baguettes　　　　　　　　BAKERY €

(cnr Zeyerova & Dr Bechera; baguettes 30-40Kč; ⊙7am-6pm Mon-Fri, 8am-noon Sat) Just say no to the high prices of local restaurants with tasty salads and filled baguettes at Rad's.

Cafe Elefant　　　　　　　　　　CAFE €

(Stará Louka 30; coffee 50Kč) Classy old-school spot for coffee and cake. A tad touristy, but still elegant and refined.

Bernard　　　　　　　　　　　　　PUB

(Ondřejská 120/14) Live jazz occasionally features at this cosy pub with a backstreets location. If not, there's always the sunny terrace to look forward to.

🛈 Information

Infocentrum (www.karlovyvary.cz) Dolní nádraží (☏353 232 838; Západni; ⊙9am-6pm Mon-Fri,

10am-5pm Sat & Sun); Spa No 3 (☎353 321 176; ⊗10am-5pm) Loads of information on the town, plus maps, accommodation help and internet (2Kč per minute).

Moonstorm Internet (TG Masaryka 31; per min 2Kč; ⊗9am-9pm)

❶ Getting There & Away

BUS **Student Agency** (www.studentagency.cz) and **Megabus** (www.megabus.cz) run frequent buses to/from Prague Florenc (from 100Kč, 2¼ hours, eight daily) departing from the main bus station beside Dolní nádraží train station. There are direct buses to Plzeň (92Kč, 1½ hours, hourly). Buses to/from Loket, a recommended base for visiting Karlovy Vary, run throughout the day (28Kč, 20 minutes).

TRAIN Karlovy Vary has two train stations: Dolní nádraží (Lower Station), beside the main bus station, and Horní nádraží (Upper Station), across the Ohře River to the north. There are direct (but slow) trains from Karlovy Vary to Prague Holešovice (294Kč, 3½ hours). The train journey to Mariánské Lázně (60Kč, 1¾ hours) is slow but scenic.

❶ Getting Around

Prague trains arrive at Horní nádraží. Take bus 11, 12 or 13 (12Kč) from across the road to the Tržnice bus stop; bus 11 continues to Divadelní nám in the spa district. Alternatively it's 10 minutes on foot.

The Tržnice bus stop is three blocks east of Dolní nádraží and the main bus station, in the middle of the town's modern commercial district. Pedestrianised TG Masaryka leads east to the Teplá River; from here the old spa district stretches upstream for 2km along a steep-sided valley.

Loket

POP 3200

Nestled in a bend of the Ohře River, Loket is a gorgeous little place that's attracted many famous visitors from nearby Karlovy Vary. A plaque on the facade of the Hostinec Bílý Kůň on the chocolate-box town square commemorates Goethe's seven visits.

Most people visit Loket as a day trip from Karlovy Vary, but it's also a sleepy place to ease off the travel accelerator for a few days, especially when the day trippers have all departed. Loket also makes a good base for visiting Karlovy Vary.

In the second half of July, the annual **Loket Summer Cultural Festival** (www. loketfestival.info) features classical music and opera on an outdoor stage near the river, with the castle as a dramatic backdrop.

◉ Sights

TOP CHOICE **Loket Castle** CASTLE
(adult/child with English-speaking guide 90/60Kč, with English text 80/45Kč; ⊗9am-4.30pm Apr-Oct, to 3.30pm Nov-Mar) Highlights include two rooms of the town's lustrous porcelain and the views from the castle's tower. During summer the castle courtyard is also used for occasional live gigs with everything from local bands to visiting reggae DJs. Ask at Infocentrum or the local musos at the Lazy River Hostel.

Black Gate Tower LOOKOUT
(Černá Věž; TG Masaryka; admission 20Kč; ⊗10am-5pm Jul & Aug, Fri-Sun only May, Jun & Sep) Loket's striking tower houses a small art gallery and wine shop, and offers some tip-top photo opportunities.

⚡ Activities
HIKING & RAFTING

Ask at Infocentrum about short walks in the surrounding forests. You can also walk from Karlovy Vary to Loket along a 17km (three-hour) blue-marked trail, starting at the Diana lookout.

Karlovy Vary is also the destination for one-day rafting trips along the Ohře River with **Dronte** (☎274 779 828; www.dronte. cz). Rafting on the Ohře is a quieter alternative to Český Krumlov and the Vltava River. Costs are from 1100Kč to 1600Kč per person, including transport. Ask at Infocentrum.

🛏 Sleeping & Eating

Lazy River Hostel HOSTEL €
(☎776 235 417; www.hostelloket.com; Kostelní 61; dm/d/tr 300/800/1200/Kč; @🛜) The welcoming Lazy River Hostel has a heritage ambience with ancient wooden floors and Old Town views. The friendly owners have a castle-full of ideas for day trips, so look forward to staying longer than planned.

Penzion Ve Skalé PENSION €
(☎352 624 936; www.penzionveskale.cz; Nádražní 232, 61; s/d 650/1200Kč; 🅿🛜) Spacious and romantic rooms feature at this pension up the hill from the train station. You're forgoing an Old Town location, but the excellent-value rooms compensate.

Pizzeria na Růžka PIZZA €
(cnr TG Masaryka & Kostelní; pizza 100-140Kč) Has a Mediterranean ambience and excellent thin-crust wood-fired pizzas. The sunny terrace is popular with cyclists.

Hrnčírna Galerie Café
CAFE €

(TG Masaryka 32; ☺2-6pm Fri-Sun; @) This funky main-square cafe conceals an art space for local artists and a cosy garden. Loket's best coffee and internet access comes as standard.

Pivovar Sv Florian
BEER HALL €

(TG Masaryka 81) In the basement of the restored Hotel Císař Ferdinand, enthusiastic locals brew one of Bohemia's best beers. Ask about their nightly terrace barbecues during summer.

❶ Information

Infocentrum (☏352 684 123; www.loket. cz; TG Masaryka 12; ☺10.30am-5pm) can book accommodation and has internet access.

❶ Getting There & Away

Frequent bus departures link Karlovy Vary to Loket (28Kč, 20 minutes). The bus arriving from Karlovy Vary stops across the bridge from the Old Town. Walk across the bridge to reach the castle, accommodation and tourist information.

Plzeň

POP 175,000

Plzeň (Pilsen in German) is the hometown of Pilsner Urquell (Plzeňský prazdroj), the world's original lager beer. 'Urquell' (in German; *prazdroj* in Czech) means 'original source' or 'fountainhead', and the local style is now imitated across the world.

Pilsner Urquell is now owned by international conglomerate SAB-Miller, and some beer buffs claim the brew's not as good as before. One taste of the town's tasty *nefiltrované pivo* (unfiltered beer) will have you disputing that claim, and the original brewery is still an essential stop for beer aficionados.

The capital of West Bohemia is a sprawling industrial city, but has an attractive Old Town wrapped in tree-lined gardens. Plzeň's industrial heritage includes the massive Škoda Engineering Works. These armament factories were bombed heavily during WWII and now make machinery and locomotives.

Plzeň is an easy day trip from Prague, but the buzzing pubs and smaller microbreweries of this university town also reward an overnight stay.

❍ Sights

Brewery Museum
MUSEUM

(www.prazdroj.cz; Veleslavínova 6; guided tour adult/child 120/90Kč, with English text 90/60Kč; ☺10am-5pm) The Brewery Museum is in a medieval malt house. A **combined entry** (adult/child 250/130Kč) that includes the Pilsner Urquell Brewery is also available.

Pilsner Urquell Brewery
BREWERY

(www.prazdroj.cz; guided tour adult/child 150/80Kč; ☺10am-5pm) Beer fans should make the pilgrimage east across the river to the famous Pilsner Urquell Brewery. Visiting the hallowed brewery involves travelling deep into a series of tunnels, with the ultimate reward of a superior, just-tapped glass on Pilsner Urquell.

WORTH A TRIP

MARIÁNSKÉ LÁZNĚ & CHODOVÁ PLANÁ

For a more relaxed Bohemian spa experience than bustling Karlovy Vary, consider Mariánské Lázně. Perched at the southern edge of the Slavkov Forest (Slavkovský Les), the spa town formerly known as Marienbad drew such luminaries as Goethe, Thomas Edison and King Edward VII. Even old misery-guts Franz Kafka was a regular visitor, enjoying the pure waters and getting active on the walking trails that criss-cross the rolling forest. In contemporary times the appeal of spa services, heritage hotels and gentle exercise is complemented by a busy summertime cultural program, including mid-August's **Chopin Music Festival** (www.chopinfestival.cz). You can also catch a local bus (18Kč, 20 minutes) to nearby Chodová Planá and bath in giant hoppy tubs of lager in the Czech Republic's first (and still the best) **beer spa** (www.chodovar.cz).

From Prague, Mariánské Lázně can be reached by train (238Kč, five hours) on trains to Cheb from Prague's main train station (Praha-hlavní nádraží). Buses (170Kč, three hours) run from Prague's Florenc bus station. There are also trains (101Kč, 1½ hours, eight per day) and buses (80Kč, one hour, four daily) to/from Plzeň. From the adjacent bus and train stations at the southern end of Mariánské Lázně, catch trolleybus 5 to the spa area's main bus stop. The **information office** (www.marianskelazne.cz) is 200m uphill on the left.

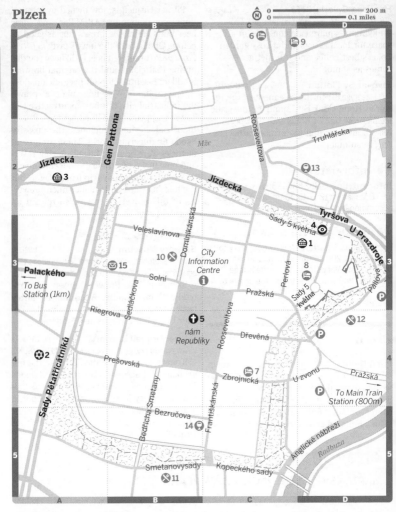

Plzeň

N 0 ————— 200 m
0 ————— 0.1 miles

Plzeň Historical Underground HISTORIC AREA
(www.plzenskepodzemi.cz; adult/child 90/60Kč;
⊙10am-5pm) In previous centuries beer was
brewed, stored and served in the tunnels
beneath the Old Town. Take a 30-minute
guided tour through 500m of tunnels at the
Plzeň Historical Underground. The temperature is a chilly 10°C, so wrap up and bring
a torch (flashlight). Tours begin at the Brewery Museum.

Great Synagogue SYNAGOGUE
(Sady Pětatřicátníků 11; adult/child 55/35Kč;
⊙10am-6pm Sun-Fri Apr-Oct) The Great Synagogue, west of the Old Town, is the third-
largest in the world – only those in Jerusalem and Budapest are bigger. It was built in
the Moorish style in 1892 by the 2000 Jews
who lived in Plzeň at the time. An English
guide costs 500Kč extra. The building is often used for concerts and art and photography exhibitions.

Patton Memorial Pilsen MUSEUM
(Podřežni 10; adult/child 60/40Kč; ⊙9am-1pm &
2-5pm Tue-Sun) North of the Great Synagogue
is the Patton Memorial Pilsen, with an interesting and poignant display on the liberation of Plzeň in 1945 by the American army
under General George Patton.

Plzeň

St Bartholomew Church CHURCH
(adult/child 20/10Kč; ◎10am-4pm Mon-Fri) In summer people congregate at the outdoor beer bar in nám Republiky, the sunny Old Town square, beneath the Gothic Church of St Bartholomew. Inside the 13th-century structure there's a Gothic *Madonna* (1390) on the high altar and fine stained-glass windows. Climb the 102m church **tower** (adult/child 30/10Kč; ◎10am-6pm, weather dependent), the highest in Bohemia, for great views of Plzeň's rugged sprawl.

🛏 Sleeping

Hotel Rous BOUTIQUE HOTEL €€
(☎602 320 294; www.hotelrous.cz; Zbrojnicka 113/7; s/d from 1690/2290Kč; ▣@⏐) This 600-year-old building incorporates the warmth of the original stone walls with modern furnishings. Bathrooms are art deco cool in black and white. Breakfast is taken in a garden cafe concealed amid remnants of Plzeň's defensive walls. Downstairs, the Caffe Emily serves the hotel's very own microbrewed beer.

Pension Stará Plzeň PENSION €
(☎377 259 901; www.pension-sp.cz; Na Roudné 12; s/d from 875/1250Kč; ▣@⏐) Rooms are light and sunny with skylights, wooden floors and huge beds. A newly completed addition has transformed old stables into spacious accommodation with high ceilings. Cross the river north on Rooseveltova, veer right into Luční and turn left into Na Roudné.

Pension City PENSION €
(☎377 326 069; www.pensioncityplzen.cz; Sady 5 května 52; s/d 1050/1400Kč; ▣⏐) On a quiet, central street near the river, the City is popular with both local and overseas guests. Welcoming English-speaking staff are a good source of local information. Rooms are showing a bit of wear and the wi-fi is patchy, but the buffet breakfast continues to be one of Bohemia's best.

Euro Hostel HOSTEL €
(☎377 259 926; www.eurohostel.cz; Na Roudne 13; dm 350-400Kč; ⏐) In newly renovated rooms in the associated Hotel Roudna, the Euro Hostel is Plzeň's best budget accommodation. The location is around five minutes' walk from the main square. The hostel has a quiet vibe – save your partying for Prague or Česky Krumlov. Cross the river north on Rooseveltova, veer right into Luční and turn left into Na Roudné.

🍴 Eating & Drinking

Dominik Rock Cafe CAFE €
(Dominikánská 3; mains 130Kč; ◎10am-11pm Mon-Wed, to 2am Thu, to 4am Fri, 1pm-2am Sat, 1pm-10pm Sun) Get lost in the nooks and crannies of this vast student hang-out. There's cool beats all day every day, and excellent beer, pizza and sandwiches are served in the nicely grungy beer garden.

Měšťanská Beseda CAFE
(Kopeckého sady 13) Cool heritage cafe, sunny beer garden, expansive exhibition space and occasional arthouse cinema – Měšťanská Beseda is hands-down Plzeň's most versatile venue. The beautifully restored Viennese-style coffee house is perfect for a leisurely coffee and cake. Check out who's performing at the attached theatre.

Slunečnice VEGETARIAN €
(Jungmanova 10; baguettes 70Kč; ◎11am-10pm; ⏐) Fresh sandwiches, self-service salads and vegetarian dishes are available here. For around 120Kč you can buy a heaped plate. The fresh juice and smoothie bar is another tasty distraction.

PLZEŇ'S OTHER BEERS

Pilsner Urquell may enjoy the international reputation, but beer fans should also seek out these other examples of West Bohemian hoppy goodness.

» Groll Pivovar (Truhlářska 10; mains 100-200Kč) Enjoy a beer garden lunch at this recently opened microbrewery. Their own beers are complemented by well-priced steaks and salads. From Sady 5 května, cross over busy Tyršova to Truhlářska.

» Caffe Emily (Hotel Rous, Zbrojnicka 113/7; mains 120-200Kč) Another beer garden – this time tucked into the old city walls – and another couple of local brews to try.

» Restaurace Gondola (Hotel Gondola, Pallova 12; mains 115-220Kč) Plzeň's Purkmistr brewery (www.purkmistr.cz) has a suburban location, so the best bet for visitors is to try their beers at the centrally located restaurant at the Hotel Gondola. Ask about their regular seasonal brews.

Na Parkanu PUB €

(Veleslavínova 4; mains 100-150Kč) Attached to the Brewery Museum, Na Parkanu lures a mix of tourists and locals with good-value meals and a summer garden. Don't leave without trying the *nefiltrované pivo* (unfiltered beer). It's not our fault if you stay for another.

Music Bar Anděl LIVE MUSIC

(Bezručova 7; ✎) By day a coolly hip cafe, the Anděl is transformed after dark into a rocking live-music venue featuring the best of touring Czech bands and occasional international acts. It also has a good vegetarian menu.

ℹ Information

American Center Plzeň (Dominikánská 9; per hr 60Kč; ◷10am-10pm) Internet access.

City Information Centre (www.plzen.eu) nám Republiky (městské informační středisko; ☎378 035 330; nám Republiky 41; ◷9am-6pm); train station (☎972 524 313; ◷9am-7pm Apr-Sep, to 6pm Oct-Mar)

ℹ Getting There & Away

Express buses run to/from Prague Florence (90Kč, 1½ hours, hourly). Buses also link Plzeň to Karlovy Vary (84Kč, 1¾ hours, five daily) and Mariáns ké Lázně (80Kč, 1¼ hours, four daily).

Fast trains link Plzeň and Prague hlavní nádraží (147Kč, 1½ hours, eight daily), České Budějovice (174Kč, two hours, five daily) and Mariánské Lázně (101Kč, 1½ hours, eight per day)

ℹ Getting Around

The main bus station is west of the centre on Husova. Plzeň-hlavní nádraží, the main train station, is on the eastern side of town, 10 minutes' walk from nám Republiky, the Old Town square. Tram 2 (12Kč) goes from the train station through the centre of town and on to the bus station.

České Budějovice

POP 100,000

After Plzeň, conduct the ultimate Bohemian beer taste test at České Budějovice (Budweis in German), the home of Budvar lager. The regional capital of South Bohemia is also a picturesque medieval city. Arcing from the town square are 18th-century arcades leading to bars that get raffishly rowdy at weekends.

◉ Sights

Nám Přemysla Otakara II HISTORIC AREA

The broad expanse of Nám Přemysla Otakara II, centred on the **Samson Fountain** (1727) and surrounded by 18th-century arcades, is one of the largest town squares in Europe. On the western side stands the baroque **town hall** (1731), topped with figures of the cardinal virtues: Justice, Wisdom, Courage and Prudence. On the square's opposite corner is the 72m-tall **Black Tower** (adult/child 25/15Kč; ◷10am-6pm daily Jul & Aug, closed Mon Apr-Jun, Sep & Oct), dating from 1553.

The streets around the square, especially Česká, are lined with old burgher houses. West near the river is the former **Dominican monastery** (1265) with a tall tower and a splendid pulpit. Adjacent is the **Motorcycle Museum** (Piaristické nám; adult/child 50/20Kč; ◷10am-6pm Apr-Oct), with a fine collection of Czech Jawas and WWII Harley-Davidsons. The **Museum of South Bohemia** (Jihočeské Muzeum; adult/child 60/30Kč; ◷9am-5.30pm Tue-Sun) showcases history, books, coins, weapons and wildlife.

Budweiser Budvar Brewery BREWERY

(www.budvar.cz; cnr Pražská & K Světlé; adult/child 100/50Kč; ◷9am-5pm Mar-Dec, closed Sun & Mon Jan-Feb) The Budweiser Budvar Brewery is

3km north of the main square. Group tours run every day and the 2pm tour (Monday to Friday only) is open to individual travellers. The highlight is a glass of real-deal Budvar deep in the brewery's chilly cellars. Catch bus 2 to the Budvar stop (12Kč).

In 1876 the founders of American brewer Anheuser-Busch chose the brand name Budweiser because it was synonymous with good beer. Since the late 19th century, both breweries have used the name, but in mid-2010 the European Union ruled that Anheuser-Busch were unable to register the brand name 'Budweiser' in the EU.

🛌 Sleeping

TOP CHOICE **Residence u černé věž** APARTMENTS €€
(☎725 178 584; www.residenceucerne veze.cz; U Černé věž 13; apt from 2300Kč; ❄P🛜) Four centrally located townhouses have been given a thoroughly 21st-century makeover to create 18 furnished, self-contained apartments. The decor is crisply modern with high ceilings, spotless bathrooms and fully equipped kitchens. Rates exclude breakfast.

Hotel Savoy HOTEL €€
(☎387 201 719; www.hotel-savoy-cb.cz; B Smetany; s/d/tr 1350/1850/2350Kč; P@🛜) The newish Savoy has a quiet location just outside the Old Town and spacious, modern rooms with art deco furniture – trust us, the combination works. The younger English-speaking crew at reception can recommend CB's best pubs and restaurants.

Hotel Budweis BOUTIQUE HOTEL €€
(☎389 822 111; www.hotelbudweis.cz; Biskupská 130/3; s/d 2490/2990Kč; ❄P🛜) A restored heritage building and an absolute riverside location make the newly opened Budweis the flashest place to stay in town. All areas are nonsmoking, and the city's interesting historical precinct is just metres away.

Penzión Centrum PENSION €
(☎387 311 801; www.penzioncentrum.cz; Biskupská 130/3; s/d 1000/1400Kč; P🛜) Huge rooms with queen-size beds and crisp linen make this an excellent reader-recommended spot near the main square. Right next door there's a good vegetarian restaurant.

Cafe Hostel HOSTEL €
(☎387 204 203; Panská 13; www.cafehostel.cz; dm 350Kč; 🛜) Simple and central dorm accommodation above a buzzy cafe and bar. Look forward to lots of local knowledge and regular live music in the evenings.

Ubytovna u nádraží HOTEL €
(☎972 544 648; www.ubytovna.vors.cz; Dvořákova 161/14; s 420-460Kč, d 640-690Kč; ❄🛜) A renovated tower block a few hundred metres from the bus and train stations has simple accommodation with shared bathrooms. Rates exclude breakfast but shared kitchens are available.

🍴 Eating

Greenhouse VEGETARIAN €
(Biskupská 130/3; meals 120Kč; ⏱8am-5pm Mon-Fri; 🖉) České Budějovice's best vegetarian flavours are at this modern self-service cafe. The healthy array of soups, salads and casseroles changes daily, with wraps and baguettes for smaller appetites. Here's your best chance to try organic beer as well.

Fresh Salad & Pizza PIZZA €
(Hroznová 21; salads 70-90Kč, pizza 100-140Kč) This lunch spot with outdoor tables does exactly what it says on the tin: healthy salads and (slightly) less healthy pizza dished up by a fresh and funky youthful crew.

Indická (Gateway of India) INDIAN €
(Piaristická 28; mains 110-170Kč; ⏱closed Sun) From Chennai to České comes respite for travellers wanting something different. Request spicy because they're used to dealing with slightly timid Czech palates. Daily lunch specials (80Kč to 100Kč) are good value.

Pekarna Rolo BAKERY €
(Dr Stejskala 7; ⏱7.30am-6pm Mon-Fri, 7am-noon Sat) Excellent baked goods, open sandwiches and fresh fruit cover all the bases for an on-the-go combination of eating and strolling.

🍺 Drinking

TOP CHOICE **Masné kramý** BEER HALL €€
(Krajinská 13; mains 140-240Kč) The best place in town for a cold Budvar is this beer hall in České Budějovice's 16th-century meat markets. Try the hard-to-find Budvar Super Strong, or the superb unfiltered yeast beer, *kroužkovaný ležák*. Tuck yourself away in one of the cosy booths and enjoy all this hoppy goodness with lashings of hearty Czech food.

CK Solnice CAFE €
(www.bazilika.cz; Česká 141/66) This cafe and versatile performance space could be the most bohemian venue in all of South Bohemia. It's got an arty, student vibe, České Budejovice's best espresso and cold beer, and an eclectic programme of art, music

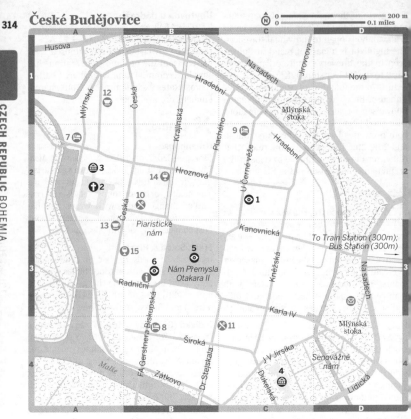

and dance throughout the year. Check the website for what's on.

Cafe Hostel CAFE €
(Panská 13; ☎) This cosy cafe and bar features occasional DJ sets and live music. The scruffy rear garden could charitably be described as a work in progress. Upstairs are a couple of simple, but spotless, dorm rooms.

Singer Pub BAR
(Česká 55) With Czech and Irish beers, plus good cocktails, don't be surprised if you get the urge to rustle up something on the Singer sewing machines on every table. If not, challenge the regulars to a game of *foosball* with a soundtrack of noisy rock.

ℹ Information

There's free access at the Municipal Information Centre and wi-fi at Cafe Hostel.

Municipal Information Centre (Městské Informační Centrum; ☎386 801 413; www.c-budejovice.cz; nám Přemysla Otakara II 2; ⏰8.30am-6pm Mon-Fri, 8.30am-5pm Sat, 10am-4pm Sun May-Sep, 9am-5pm Mon-Fri, to 1pm Sat Oct-Apr; @) books tickets, tours and accommodation.

ℹ Getting There & Away

BUS Česká Budějovice's bus station is 300m southeast of the train station above the Mercury Central shopping centre on Dvořákova.

The bus to Brno (220Kč, 3½ hours) travels via Telč (92Kč, two hours). Buses regularly shuttle south to Český Krumlov (32Kč, 45 minutes) and north to Prague's Na Knížecí Metro station (152Kč, 2¼ hours).

TRAIN From the train station it's a 10-minute walk west down Lannova třída, then Kanovnická, to nám Přemysla Otakara II, the main square. There are trains from České Budějovice to Prague (213Kč, 2½ hours, hourly) and Plzeň (174Kč, two hours, five daily). Frequent trains trundle to Český Krumlov (46Kč, 45 minutes).

České Budějovice

Sights

1	Black Tower	C2
2	Dominican Monastery	A2
3	Motorcycle Museum	A2
4	Museum of South Bohemia	C4
5	Samson Fountain	B3
6	Town Hall	B3

Sleeping

	Cafe Hostel	(see 12)
7	Hotel Budweis	A2
8	Penzión Centrum	B4
9	Residence u černé věž	C2

Eating

	Fresh Salad & Pizza	(see 3)
	Greenhouse	(see 8)
10	Indická (Gateway of India)	B2
11	Pekarna Rolo	C4

Drinking

12	Cafe Hostel	A1
13	CK Solnice	A3
14	Masné Kramý	B2
15	Singer Pub	B3

Heading for Vienna (620Kč, four hours, two daily) you'll have to change at České Velenice, or take a direct train to Linz (420Kč, 2¼ hours, one daily).

Hluboká nad Vltavou

Hluboká nad Vltavou's neo-Gothic **chateau** (www.zamek-hluboka.eu; ⊙9am-5pm Jul & Aug, closed Mon Apr-Jun & Sep-Oct), was rebuilt by the Schwarzenberg family in 1841–71 with turrets and crenellations inspired by England's Windsor Castle. The palace's 144 rooms remained in use up to WWII.

There are three English-language tours available. **Tour 1** (adult/child 220/150Kč) focuses on the castle's public areas, while **Tour 2** (adult/child 230/150Kč) goes behind the scenes in the castle apartments. **Tour 3** (adult/child170/80Kč) explores the kitchens. The park is open throughout the year (no admission charge).

The **information centre** (☎387 966 164; www.visithluboka.cz; Masarykova 35) can assist with finding accommodation, but Hluboká is an easy day trip from České Budějovice by local bus (18Kč, 20 minutes, two hourly).

Český Krumlov

POP 14,600

Crowned by a stunning castle, Český Krumlov's glorious Renaissance and baroque buildings enclosed by a meandering arc of the Vltava River, producing a captivating Old Town of narrow lanes and footbridges.

The town's original Gothic fortress was rebuilt as an imposing Renaissance chateau in the 16th century. Since the 18th century the town's appearance has been largely unchanged, and careful renovation and restoration has replaced the architectural neglect of the communist era. In 1992 Český Krumlov was granted Unesco World Heritage status.

For too many travellers, Český Krumlov is just a hurried day trip, but its combination of dazzling architecture and watery fun on the Vltava deserve more attention. After dark in the Old Town is a magical time, and you can easily fill three days by adding a day trip to the nearby Newcastle mountains area.

During summer, busloads of day-tripping tourists pour in, but either side of July and August, the town is (slightly) more subdued and secluded. Come in winter to experience the castle blanketed in snow.

Sights

TOP CHOICE **Český Krumlov Castle** CASTLE

(☎380 704 721; www.castle.ckrumlov.cz; ⊙9am-6pm Tue-Sun Jun-Aug, to 5pm Apr, May, Sep & Oct) The Old Town, almost encircled by the Vltava River, is watched over by Český Krumlov Castle and its ornately decorated **Round Tower** (50/30Kč). Three different guided tours are on offer: **Tour I** (adult/child 240/140Kč) takes in the Renaissance and baroque apartments that the aristocratic Rožmberk and Schwarzenberg families called home; **Tour II** (adult/child 180/110Kč) visits the Schwarzenberg apartments used in the 19th century; and the **Theatre Tour** (adult/child 380/220Kč; ⊙10am-4pm Tue-Sun May-Oct) explores the chateau's remarkable rococo theatre, complete with original stage machinery. Wandering through the courtyards and gardens is free.

The path beyond the fourth courtyard leads across the spectacular **Most ná Plášti** to the castle gardens. A ramp to the right leads to the **former riding school**, now a restaurant. The relief above the door shows cherubs offering the head and boots of a vanquished Turk – a reference to Adolf von Schwarzenberg, who conquered the Turkish

Český Krumlov

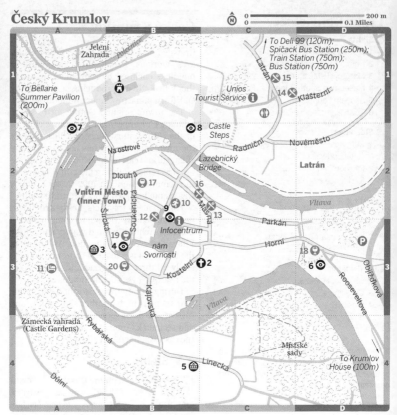

fortress of Raab in the 16th century. From here the Italian-style **Zámecká zahrada** (castle gardens) stretch away towards the **Bellarie summer pavilion**.

Nám Svornosti
SQUARE

Across the river is nám Svornosti, the Old Town square, overlooked by the Gothic **Town Hall**. Above the square is the striking Gothic **Church of St Vitus** (1439).

Egon Schiele Art Centrum
ART GALLERY

(www.schieleartcentrum.cz; Široká 70-72; adult/child 120/700Kč; ☺10am-6pm) The Egon Schiele Art Centrum is an excellent gallery showcasing the Viennese painter Egon Schiele (1890–1918). The attached **cafe** (☺10am-7pm) is appropriately arty and has a good selection of Moravian wines.

Fotoateliér Seidel
MUSEUM

(www.seidel.cz; Linecká 272; admission 130K; ☺9am-4pm) The Fotoateliér Seidel presents a retrospective of the work of local photographers Josef Seidel and his son František. Especially poignant are the images recording early 20th-century life in nearby mountain villages.

Eggenberg Brewery
BREWERY

(www.eggenberg.cz; Latrán 27; tours with/without tasting 130/100Kč; ☺tours 11am) The Eggenberg Brewery is also where most canoeing and rafting trips end. Relive your experiences on the Vltava's gentle rapids in the brewery's beer garden. Book brewery tours at Infocentrum.

🏃 Activities & Tours

Maleček
RIVER RAFTING

(☎380 712 508; http://en.malecek.cz; Rooseveltova 28; ☺9am-5pm) Rents out canoes, rafts and rubber rings. A one-hour splash in a two-person canoe costs 400Kč, or you can rent a canoe for a full day trip down the river from Rožmberk (850Kč, six to eight hours).

Český Krumlov

Sebastian Tours   SIGHTSEEING
(☏607 100 234; www.sebastianck-tours.com; 5 Května Ul, Plešivec; per person 599Kč) Offers southern Bohemia on guided tours, including stops at Hluboká nad Vltavou and České Budějovice.

Expedicion   ADVENTURE
(☏607 963 868; www.expedicion.cz; Soukenická 33; ⊙9am-6.30pm) Offers bike rental (280Kč a day), horse riding (300Kč an hour) and action-packed day trips (1680Kč, including lunch) incorporating horse-riding, fishing, mountain biking and rafting in the Newcastle mountains.

Krumlov Tours   WALKING TOUR
(☏723 069 561; www.krumlovtours.com; nám Svornosti; per person 200-250Kč) Has walking tours with regular departure times; good for solo travellers.

Oldřiška Baloušková   WALKING TOUR
(oldriskab@gmail.com) Offers tailored walking tours for 450Kč per hour. It's recommended you contact her by email a few days before you arrive in town.

⚜ Festivals & Events

Infocentrum sells tickets to most festivals.

Five-Petalled Rose Festival   FOLK CULTURE
In mid-June; features two days of street performers, medieval games.

Chamber Music Festival   CLASSICAL MUSIC
Late June to early July.

Český Krumlov International Music Festival   CLASSICAL MUSIC
(www.festivalkrumlov.cz) July to August.

Jazz at Summer's End Festival   JAZZ
(www.jazz-krumlov.cz) Mid-September.

⌂ Sleeping

Pension Sebastian   PENSION €
(☏608 357 581; www.sebastianck.com; 5 Května Ul, Plešivec; s/d/tr incl breakfast 1090/1250/1590Kč; ⊙Apr-Oct; P🖼) An excellent option just 10 minutes' walk from the Old Town, and therefore slightly cheaper. Larger four-bed rooms (1780Kč) are good for families and there's a pretty garden for end-of-day drinks and diary writing. The well-travelled owners also run tours of the surrounding region.

Krumlov House   HOSTEL €
(☏380 711 935; www.krumlovhostel.com; Rooseveltova 68; dm/d/tr 300/750/1350Kč; ✳🖼) Perched above the river, Krumlov House is friendly and comfortable and has plenty of books, DVDs and local info to feed your inner backpacker. Lots of suggestions for day trips, too.

Hostel Skippy   HOSTEL €
(☏380 728 380; www.skippy.wz.cz; Plesivecka 123; dm/d 300/650Kč) Smaller and less boisterous than some other CK hostels, Skippy is more like staying at a friend's place. The creative owner, 'Skippy', is an arty muso type, so you might be surprised with an impromptu jam session in the front room.

Pension Rožmberk Royale   PENSION €
(☏380 727 858; www.pensionroyale.cz; Rožmberk nad Vltavou; s/d 800/1300Kč; P🖼) This pension has an absolute riverfront location in the sleepy village of Rožmberk nad Vltavou. A castle looms above the village, and it's a short, scenic bus ride (28Kč, 35 minutes, seven daily) from Český Krumlov. A pleasant stroll just around the river reveals a good fish restaurant.

Dilettante's Hangout   PENSION €
(☏728 280 033; www.dilettanteshangout.com; Plesivecke nám 93; r 890-990Kč; ⊜) Don't be fooled by the bland exterior: inside this intimate

BOHEMIAN ROOTS – TÁBOR

The Old Town of Tábor was a formidable natural defence against invasion. Six centuries ago, the Hussite religious sect founded Tábor as a military bastion in defiance of Catholic Europe. Based on the biblical concept that 'nothing is mine and nothing is yours, because everyone owns the community equally', all Hussites participated in communal work, and possessions were allocated equally in the town's main square. This exceptional nonconformism gave the word 'bohemian' the connotations we associate with it today. Religious structures dating from the 15th century line the town square, and it's possible to visit the 650m stretch of underground tunnels the Hussites used for refuge in times of war.

Today Tábor is an ideal overnight refuge from Prague if the tourist throngs of the Czech capital are wearing you down. The annual **Tabor Meetings Festival** is held on the second weekend in September. Expect medieval merriment with lots of food, drink and colourfully dressed locals celebrating their Hussite heritage. See www.tabor.cz for more information.

Penzión Alfa (☑381 256 165; www.pensionalfa.cz; Klokotská; s/d/tr 570/900/1300Kč; ☎) occupies a cosy corner just metres from the main square. Downstairs get your Geronimojo back at the funky Native American–themed cafe. Right on the main square, the **Hotel Nautilus** (☑380 900 900; www.hotelnautilus.cz; Žižkovo nám 20; s/d from €96/116; ᴘ☎) is a splurgeworthy and very cool boutique hotel.

Travel to Tábor by bus, either from Prague Florenc (92Kč, 1½ hours, eight daily) or České Budějovice (62Kč, one hour, 15 daily).

---

homestay are two romantic and arty rooms decorated with mementos of the artistic owner's global wanderings. Both rooms are unique, but each is equally cosy and eclectic. Owner Matya and her kids are great hosts.

Pension Kapr　　　　　　　PENSION €
(☑602 409 360; www.penzionkapr.cz; Rybářská 28; s 1000Kč, d 1220-1600Kč; ᴘ@☎) OK, it may be named after a fish (carp), but this riverside pension with exposed bricks and 500 years of history has a quiet location and wonderful views of the Old Town. The lovely rooms with whitewashed walls and wooden floors are all named after the owners' children.

Castle View Apartments　　APARTMENTS €€
(☑731 108 677; http://accommodation-cesky -krumlov.castleview.cz; Satlavska 140; d 2000-3500Kč) Furnished apartments are better value than top-end hotels in Český Krumlov. Castle View has seven apartments with spacious bathrooms and decor combining sophistication and romance in equal measure. Five of the apartments can sleep up to five people. Infocentrum can also recommend other furnished apartments.

Kemp Nové Spolí　　CAMPING GROUND €
(☑380 728 305; www.kempkrumlov.cz; campsites per person 50Kč; ☺Jun-Aug; ☎) Located on the Vltava River about 2km south of town, it has basic facilities but an idyllic location. Take bus 3 from the train or bus station to the

Spolí mat. šk. stop; otherwise it's a half-hour walk from the Old Town.

✗ Eating

Laibon　　　　　　　VEGETARIAN €
TOP CHOICE (☑728 676 654; Parkán 105; mains 100-180Kč) Candles and vaulted ceilings create a great boho ambience in the best little vegetarian teahouse in Bohemia. The riverside setting's pretty fine as well. Order the blueberry dumplings for dessert and don't miss the special 'yeast beer' from the Bernard brewery. Ask David, the well-travelled owner, where he's headed next.

Láb　　　　　　　　　　CZECH €
(nám Svornosti; mains 110-160Kč) CK's best pub is hidden away on the edge of the main square. The kitchen also serves other more touristy eateries, but you're guaranteed a cheaper, and more local, experience here. Apparently the local mayor is a big fan of the good-value 80Kč lunch menu.

U Dwau Maryí　　　　　　CZECH €
(☑380 717 228; Parkán 104; mains 110-220Kč) The 'Two Marys' medieval tavern recreates old recipes and is your best chance to try dishes made with buckwheat and millet: all tastier than they sound. Wash the food down with a goblet of mead (a drink made with honey) or a 21st-century pilsner. In summer it's a tad touristy, but the stunning riverside castle views easily compensate.

Nonna Gina
PIZZA €

(✆380 717 187; Klášterní ul 52; pizza & pasta 90-170Kč) Authentic Italian flavours from the authentic Italian Massaro family feature in this pizzeria down a quiet lane. Grab an outdoor table and pretend you're in Naples.

Deli 99
CAFE €

(Latrán 106; snacks 50-80Kč; ☺7am-7pm Mon-Sat, 8am-5pm Sun; 🛜) Bagels, sandwiches, organic juices and wi-fi all tick the box marked 'Slightly Homesick Traveller'.

Potraviny
SUPERMARKET €

(Latrán 55) Self-catering central, especially if you're going rafting.

🍸 Drinking

Na louži
PUB

(Kájovská 66) Nothing's changed in this wood-panelled *pivo* parlour for almost a century. Locals and tourists pack Na louži for huge meals and tasty dark beer from the Eggenberg brewery.

Divadelní Klub Ántré
CAFE

(✆602 336 320; Horní Braná 2; ⊜🛜) This non-smoking arty cafe–bar in the town theatre has a sprawling terrace overlooking the river. There's free wi-fi, and it's always worth dropping by to see if any music gigs are scheduled.

Cikánská jizba
CZECH €€

(✆380 717 585; Dlouhá 31; mains 140-230Kč; ☺3pm-midnight Mon-Sat) At the 'Gypsy Room' there's live Roma music at the weekends to go with the menu of meaty Czech favourites.

La Bohème
BAR

(Soukenická; ☺from 5pm) With art deco styling, La Bohème is your best bet for a quieter spot with good cocktails. From 5pm to 8pm, there's a 30% 'Happy Hour' discount.

ℹ Information

Infocentrum (✆380 704 622; www.ckrumlov.cz; nám Svornosti 1; ☺9am-6pm) Transport and accommodation info, maps, internet access (5Kč per five minutes) and audio guides (100Kč per hour). A guide for disabled visitors is available.

Unios Tourist Service (✆380 725 110; www.visitceskykrumlov.cz; Zámek 57; ☺9am-6pm) Accommodation bookings and an internet cafe.

ℹ Getting There & Away

Student Agency (www.studentagency.cz) buses depart frequently from Prague Ná Knížecí (180Kč, three hours) via České Budějovice. In July and August this route is very popular and booking a couple of days ahead is recommended.

The main bus station is east of the town centre, but if you're arriving from České Budějovice or Prague get off at the Špičák bus stop (the first in the town centre, just after you pass beneath a road bridge). Local buses (32Kč, 50 minutes, seven daily) run to České Budějovice, for onward travel to Brno or Plzeň (see www.idos.cz).

Direct shuttle buses to Austria are offered by several companies. For a train, you'll need to first head to České Budějovice.

Šumava

The Šumava region's forested hills stretch for 125km along the border with Austria and Germany. Before 1989 the range was divided by the Iron Curtain, a line of fences, watchtowers, armed guards and dog patrols between Western Europe and the communist East. In a different era, the hills are now popular for hiking, cycling and cross-country skiing. The best English-language websites are www.sumava.com and www.czech-mountains.eu/sumava-en, especially for hiking and cycling.

The **Povydří trail** along the Vydra (Otter) River in the northern Šumava is one of the national park's most popular walks. It's an easy 7km hike along a deep, forested river valley between Čeňkova Pila and Antýgl. Buses run between Sušice and Modrava, stopping at Čeňkova Pila and Antýgl.

Around the peak of **Boubín** (1362m), the 46-hectare *prales* (virgin forest) is the only part of the Šumava forest that is largely untouched by human activity. The trailhead is 2km northeast of the zastávka Zátoň train stop (not Zátoň town train station) at Kaplice, where there is car parking as well as basic camping facilities. From here it's an easy 2.5km to U pralesa Lake on a blue and green marked trail. Remain on the blue trail for a further 7.5km to reach the summit of Boubín. Return by following the trail southwest. The complete loop takes about five hours.

If you'd rather use wheels, the **Šumava Trail** is a weeklong bike ride through dense forests and past mountain streams from Český Krumlov to Domažlice.

Trains runs from České Budějovice (123Kč, three hours) and Český Krumlov (85Kč, 1¾ hours) to Volary. From May to August, buses cover a similar route (88Kč, two hours).

From Volary, trains continue north to Strakonice via Zátoň (30Kč, 30 minutes, four daily) and Kubova Huť (37Kč, 35 minutes, four daily).

SLAVONICE

Barely hanging onto the Czech Republic's coat-tails (the border with Austria is just 1km away), Slavonice is a little town any country would be proud to own. Slavonice's initial prosperity during the Thirty Years' War produced two squares dotted with stunning Renaissance architecture. Economic isolation followed when the main road linking Prague and Vienna was diverted in the 18th century, and in the 20th century Slavonice's proximity to the Cold War border with Austria maintained its isolation. The town's architectural treasures were spared the socialist makeover other parts of the country endured, and now (once the Austrian day trippers have left) Slavonice resurrects its compellingly moody atmosphere like nowhere else.

Slavonice is on a little-used train line from Telč (45Kč, one hour). The sleepy **tourist office** (☎384 493 320; www.mesto-slavonice.cz) is on the main square, nám Miru. Just off nám Miru, **Beśidka** (☎606 212 070; www.besidka.cz; d 1490Kč; ☎) has spacious loft-style rooms and a cosmopolitan downstairs cafe that might just serve the Czech Republic's best wood-fired pizzas. Try to visit on a weekday as it's often booked by in-the-know Prague expats at weekends.

The Povydří trail is best approached from Sušice, which can be reached by direct bus from Prague Ná Knížecí (123Kč, 2½ hours, two daily). Another bus links Sušice with Čeňkova Pila and Antýgl (50Kč, one hour, two or three daily).

Adršpach-Teplice Rocks

The Czech Republic's most extraordinary scenery lies near Poland, in a protected landscape region known as the Adršpach-Teplice Rocks (Adršpašsko-Teplické skály). Thick layers of stratified sandstone have been eroded and fissured by water and frost to form giant towers and deep, narrow chasms. Discovered by mountaineers in the 19th century, the region is popular with rock climbers and hikers. Sandy trails lead through pine-scented forests and loop through the pinnacles, assisted occasionally by ladders and stairs.

In summer the trails are busy; book accommodation at least a week ahead. In winter (snow lingers to mid-April) you'll have the area mainly to yourself, but some trails may be closed. Try to avoid weekends, when Polish busloads visit en masse.

There's a small **information office** (☎491 586 012; www.skalyadrspach.cz; ☺8am-12.30pm & 1-5pm Apr-Oct) near the Adršpach train station.

◉ Sights & Activities

Two main formations – **Adršpach Rock Town** (Adršpašské skalní město) and **Teplice Rock Town** (Teplické skalní město) – comprise a single nature reserve. At each entrance there's a **ticket booth** (adult/child 60/30Kč; ☺8am-6pm Apr-Nov) with handy 1:25,000 trail maps on offer. Outside the official opening hours, entry is free. It's an additional 25Kč for a boat trip on a compact lake secreted in the rocks. Buy tickets on the boat.

If you're pushed for time, walk the **green loop trail** (1½ hours), starting at Adršpach and progressing through deep mossy ravines and soaring rock towers to the Great Lookout (Velké panorama). Admire the view of pinnacles escalating above the pines, before threading through the Mouse Hole (Myší dírá), a vast vertical fissure barely a shoulder-width wide.

The **blue loop trail** (2½ hours), starting at Teplice, passes a metal staircase leading strenuously to Střmen, a rock tower once occupied by an outlaw's timber castle, before continuing through the area's most spectacular pinnacles to the chilly ravine of Siberia (Sibiř).

An excellent **day hike** (four to five hours), taking in the region's highlights, links the head of the Teplice trail, beyond Sibiř, to Adršpach via the Wolf Gorge (Vlčí rokle). Return from Adršpach to Teplice by walking along the road (one hour) or by train (10 minutes).

To experience the rock towns more closely, contact Tomas Pycha at **Tomadventure** (☎775 158 538; www.tomadventure.org, climbing instruction per hr 300Kč). Climbing tuition for beginners to advanced is available, and Tomas also rents out bicycles for 250Kč per day.

🛏 Sleeping & Eating

Pension Dita   PENSION **€**
(☎606 611 640; www.pensiondita.cz; per person 250-400Kč; ℗☎) This just may be the most

welcoming pension in East Bohemia, with spacious attic rooms including small kitchenettes. Their snazzy new garden bungalows are especially comfortable. Dita is a 10-minute walk from the Teplice rock town, and one minute from a good restaurant.

Hotel Javor
HOTEL €€
(☏491 586 182; www.hotel-adrspach.cz; s/d 1400/1800Kč; P@🌐) Located just out of Adršpach, the Javor has 41 smart rooms decked out in modern furniture with skylights galore. Downstairs the restaurant also achieves a lighter touch with good mixed grills, salads and pasta.

Skalní Mlýn
PENSION €
(☏491 586 961; www.skalni-mlyn.cz; s/d/tr 600/1200/1800Kč) In a quiet setting between Teplice and Adršpach, this restored river mill has rustic rooms, a good restaurant and friendly dogs who like to be fed furtively under the table. Four-person log cabins (2400Kč) are available from July to September.

ℹ Getting There & Away
There are direct buses from Prague's Černý Most metro station to Trutnov (160Kč, 2¾ hours, hourly). From Trutnov catch a train to Teplice nad Metují-Skály (46Kč, 1¼ hours) via Adršpach (40Kč, one hour). Note that some express trains do not stop at Teplice nad Metují-Skály, so change to a local train at Teplice nad Metují or walk. Buses also run from Trutnov to Teplice nad Metují-Skály (46kč, one hour) and Adršpach (36Kč, 50 minutes). Check www.idos.cz for timetables.

MORAVIA

Away from the tourist commotion of Prague and Bohemia, Moravia provides a quietly authentic experience. Olomouc and Telč are two of the country's prettiest towns, and bustling Brno serves up Czech urban ambience without the tourists. Mildly active travellers can explore the stunning landscapes of the Moravian Karst region, and everyone can celebrate with a good vintage from the Moravian wine country.

Brno
POP 387,200
Brno's attractions may not seem obvious after the showy buzz of Prague, but after a short stay you'll see the traditional Moravian reserve melting away in the Old Town's bars and restaurants. Leave the touristy commotion back in Prague, and you'll have Brno's stellar array of museums and galleries almost to yourself. Despite having a population of less than 400,000, Brno behaves just like the confident, cosmopolitan capital (ie of Moravia) that it is.

⊙ Sights & Activities
Ask at the tourist information office about Brno's many other excellent museums and art galleries.

Špilberk Castle
CASTLE
(www.spilberk.cz; ⊙9am-5pm Tue-Sun). Founded in the early 1200s, Brno's castle was lived in by the Czech kings before being transformed into a military fortress in the 18th century. In this form the castle became 'home' to enemies of the Austro-Hungarian Empire, with a multinational band of rebels incarcerated in the so-called Prison of Nations. The prison closed in 1853, but was reopened by the occupying Nazis in WWII.

The castle is now home to **Brno City Museum** (exhibitions adult/child 70/50Kč). The two most popular exhibitions are **From Castle to Fortress**, on the castle's history, and **Prison of Nations**, on the role Špilberk played in the 18th and 19th centuries. Other exhibitions of the focus on the history, art and architecture of Brno. A combined ticket (adult/child 120/60Kč) gives access to all displays.

Špilberk's **casemates** (kasematy; adult/child 70/35Kč), the dark corridors beneath the bastions, also can be visited. In Špilberk's time as the 'Prison of Nations', the casemates were reserved for the toughest and most dangerous of prisoners.

After the gloom of the casemates, lighten up in the exquisite **baroque pharmacy** (adult/child 30/15Kč; ⊙9am-6pm Tue-Sun May-Sep) dating from the mid-18th century, or climb the **lookout tower** (adult/child 30/15Kč).

The castle is approachable only on foot, up a steepish hill through the quiet gardens.

Capuchin Monastery
MONASTERY
(Kapucínské nám 5; adult/child 60/30Kč, English text 40Kč extra; ⊙9am-noon & 1pm-4.30pm May-Sep, closed Mon mid-Feb–Apr & Oct–mid-Dec) The Capuchin Monastery's well-ventilated crypt allows the natural mummification of dead bodies. On display are the desiccated corpses of 18th-century monks, abbots and local notables, including chimney-sweeper Barnabas Orelli, who is still wearing his boots. In the glass-topped coffin in a separate room is Baron von Trenck – soldier, adventurer, gambler and womaniser.

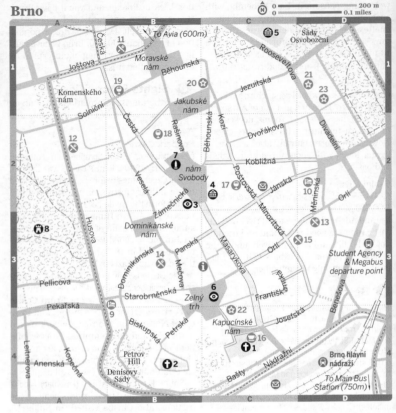

Museum of Romany Culture   MUSEUM

(Muzeum romské kultury; www.rommuz.cz; Bratislavská 67; adult/child 40/20Kč; ◷10am-5pm Tue-Fri, closed Mon & Sat) This excellent museum provides an overdue positive showcase of Romany culture. Highlights include music-packed videos, and period photographs from across Europe. There's a good cafe and musical concerts are held occasionally. This part of town can be dangerous after dark, but it's a safe area to walk in during the day.

Parnassus Fountain   MONUMENT

The sloping **Zelný trh** (Cabbage Market) is the heart of the Old Town, and where live carp were sold from the baroque Parnassus Fountain (1695) at Christmas. The fountain is a symbolic cave encrusted with allegorical figures. Hercules restrains three-headed Cerberus, watchdog of the underworld, and the three female figures represent the ancient empires of Babylon (crown), Persia (cornucopia) and Greece (quiver of arrows).

Cathedral of SS Peter & Paul   CHURCH

From the top of the Cabbage Market take Petrská to Petrov Hill. Climb the **tower** (adult/child 35/30Kč; ◷11am-6pm Mon-Sat, from 11.45am Sun) or descend into the **crypt** (adult/child 20/10Kč; ◷as per tower). At the foot of the cathedral is a charming courtyard cafe.

Nám Svobody   SQUARE

The city's main square combines mainly 19th-century buildings with a few older monuments. The **plague column** dates from 1680, and the **Dům Pánů z Lipé** (House of the Lords of Lipé) at No 17 is a Renaissance palace (1589–96) with a 19th-century *sgraffito* facade and arcaded courtyard (now filled with shops). On the square's eastern side is the quirky **House of the Four Mamlases**, dating from 1928 and with four moronic 'Atlas' figures struggling to hold the building and their loincloths up at the same time.

Brno

Mendel Museum　　　　　　　　　MUSEUM
(www.mendel-museum.com; Mendlovo nám 1; adult/
child 60/30Kč; ☉10am-5pm Tue-Sun) Gregor
Mendel (1822–84), the Augustinian monk
whose studies of peas and bees at Brno's
Abbey of St Thomas established modern ge-
netics, is commemorated in the Mendel Museum, housed in the abbey itself. Catch tram
1 from the train station to Mendlovo nám.

Vila Tugendhat　　　　　NOTABLE BUILDING
(☎545 212 118; www.tugendhat.eu; Černopolni 45)
Brno is dotted with cubist, functionalist and
internationalist buildings, and one of the
finest is the functionalist Vila Tugendhat designed by Mies van der Rohe in 1930. At the
time of research, this amazing Unesco World
Heritage–listed family home was closed for
significant restoration work. Check the website, phone ahead or ask at the Brno tourist information office for the latest status.

When it does reopen, booking ahead will be
mandatory.

🎉 Festivals & Events

Festival of Sacred Music　　CLASSICAL MUSIC
(www.mhf-brno.cz) Held around Easter in
Brno's old churches.

Ignis Brunensis Fireworks Festival
　　　　　　　　　　　　　　　　　FIREWORKS
(www.ignisbrunensis.cz) International pyro-
technics action in late May.

Moto Grand Prix　　　　　　MOTORSPORT
(www.motogp.com) World-renowned motorcycle race in mid-August. Accommodation
is regularly booked out.

🛏 Sleeping

Accommodation increases in cost and demand when major trade fairs are on, especially in mid-April and mid-September (see
www.bvv.cz for a calendar of trade fairs).
Most hotel websites also list the specific
dates when their rates increase.

Hotel Europa　　　　　　　　HOTEL €€
(☎545 421 400; www.hoteleuropa.cz; trída kpt
Jaroše 27; s/d from 1360/1600Kč; ⓟ@🖥) Art
nouveau touches and excellent service in reception give way upstairs to spacious rooms
with modern bathrooms. The breakfast
spread is one of Brno's best. Look forward to
a quiet tree-lined location a 15-minute stroll
from central Brno.

Comsa Brno Palace　　　　LUXURY HOTEL €€€
(☎532 156 777; www.comsabrnopalace.com;
Šilingrovo nám 2; r from €149; ⓟ@🖥) Five-star
heritage luxury comes to Brno at the recently opened Comsa Brno Palace. The lobby
blends glorious 19th-century architecture
with thoroughly modern touches, and the
spacious rooms are both contemporary and
romantic. The location on the edge of Brno's
old town is excellent.

Hotel Omega　　　　　　　　HOTEL €
(☎543 213 876; www.hotelomega.eu; Křídlovická
19b; s/d 950/1450Kč; ⓟ🖥) In a quiet neighbourhood, 1km from the centre, this tourist
information favourite has spacious rooms
with modern pine furniture. A couple of
three- and four-bed rooms cater to travelling
families, and breakfast comes complete with
castle views. Catch tram 1 from the train station to the Václavská stop.

Penzion Na Starém Brně　　　PENSION €
(☎543 247 872; www.pension-brno.com; Mendlovo nám 1a; s/d incl breakfast 960/1290Kč; ⓟ) An

atmospheric Augustinian monastery conceals five compact rooms that come reader-recommended. Just metres away there's a Moravian wine bar. Catch tram 1 from the train station to Mendlovo nám.

Hostel Fléda HOSTEL €
(✆533 433 638; www.hostelfleda.com; Štefánikova 24; dm/tw from €12/32; @⊚) One of Brno's best music clubs also offers funky and colourful rooms a quick tram ride from the centre. A nonsmoking cafe and good bar reinforce a social vibe. Catch tram 1 or 6 to the Hrnčírská stop. It's not recommended if you're looking for a quiet night, though.

Travellers' Hostel HOSTEL €
(✆542 213 573; www.travellers.cz; Jánská 22; dm 290Kč; ⊘Jul & Aug) Set in the heart of the Old Town, this place provides the most central cheap beds in the city – for July and August anyway.

🍴 Eating

TOP CHOICE **Rebio** VEGETARIAN €
(Orli 16; mains 80-120Kč; ⊘8am-7pm Mon-Fri, 10am-3pm Sat; ⚕) Healthy risottos and veggie pies stand out in this self-service spot that changes its tasty menu every day. Organic beer and wine is available, and there's another **branch** (Mečova 2; ⊘9am-9pm Mon-Fri, 11am-8pm Sat-Sun) on the 1st floor of the Velký Spalicek shopping centre.

Avia MEDITERRANEAN €
(Botanická 1; mains 90-140Kč) Avia's buzzy but elegant dining room is tucked underneath a striking functionalist Hussite church in a leafy suburb. The oft-changing menu presents robust Mediterranean flavours including risotto, grilled eggplant with feta cheese, and Tuscan-style soup. Wines from the nearby Moravian vineyard region regularly feature. Catch tram 1 or 6 to the Antonínská stop, turn left into Smetanova and then right into Botanická.

Hansen CZECH €€
(Besední dům, Komenského nám 8; mains 160-300Kč) Modern interpretations of classic Czech cuisine feature at the gloriously elegant restaurant in the headquarters of the Brno Philharmonic. The spacious alfresco terrace is the city's most romantic place for a meal, all at prices a fraction of far-off, touristy Prague.

Brabander INTERNATIONAL €€
(Joštova 4; mains 150-340Kč) This cellar restaurant serves up innovative food – on a Brno scale anyway – with a lighter Mediterranean

and Asian touch. A good wine list adds to the appeal of one of Brno's best.

Spolek CAFE €
(Orli 22; mains 70-100Kč; ⊘closed Sun) The service is unpretentious at this cool, studenty haven with interesting salads, soups, pasta and wine.

🍺 Drinking

Pivnice Pegas PUB
(Jakubská 4) *Pivo* melts any Moravian reserve as the locals become pleasantly noisy. Don't miss the *Pšeničné pivo* (unfiltered wheat beer) with a slice of lemon. Good luck finding a table, or grab a spot at Brno's longest bar.

Cafe Tungsram CAFE
(Kapucínské nám 7/531; ⊘8am-10pm Mon-Sat, 10am-9pm Sun) This arty cafe mixes minimalist style and a heritage ambience; check out the restored floor tiles. Brno's best coffee is provided by a guy who really knows his stuff, and beer and wine is available for later in the day.

Zelená Kočka PUB
(Solniční 1; ⊛) Tasty beers from the tiny Dalešice brewery are the main drawcard at this relaxed spot in central Brno, but the food is damn good too and it's all nonsmoking. And no, we don't know why it's called the 'Green Cat'.

Starobrno Brewery PUB
(Hlinky 160/12) Brno's longest-established brewery is at its best in the beer garden on a warm summer's evening – especially if there is a band playing live music. Catch tram 1 from the train station to Mendlovo náměstí.

Minach CAFE
(Poštovská 6; per chocolate 13Kč; ⊘10am-7pm Mon-Sat, from 2pm Sun) More than 50 kinds of handmade chocolates and bracing coffee make this an essential mid-morning or mid-afternoon detour.

⭐ Entertainment

Brno offers excellent theatre and classical music. Find entertainment listings in the free monthly *Metropolis*, ask at the tourist information office or see the website of the **Národní Divadlo Brno** (National Theatre Brno; www.ndb.cz). Tickets for performances at the Reduta and Janáček Theatres can be obtained through the **Theatre Booking Office** (✆542 321 285; www.ndb.cz; Dvořákova 11; ⊘8am-5.30pm Mon-Fri, 9am-noon Sat). For tickets to rock, folk and classical concerts, visit the **Central Booking Office** (☑542 210 863; Běhounská 17; ☉10am-6pm Mon-Fri).

Fléda   CLUB
(www.fleda.cz; Štefánikova 24; ☉to 2am) DJs, Brno's up-and-coming bands and occasional touring performers all rock the stage at Brno's best music club. Catch tram 1 or 6 to the Hrnčírská stop.

Klub Desert   CLUB
(www.dodesertu.com; Rooseveltova 24; ☉5pm-3am Mon-Thu, 10am-3am Fri, 5pm-2am Sat-Sun) Part cool bar and cafe and part intimate performance venue, Klub Desert features Brno's most eclectic live late-night line-up. Gypsy bands, neo-folk – anything goes.

Janáček Theatre   THEATRE
(Janáčkovo divadlo; Sady Osvobození) Opera and ballet are performed at this modern theatre.

Reduta Theatre   CLASSICAL MUSIC
(Reduta divadlo; Zelný trh 4) The restored Reduta showcases Mozart's work (he played there in 1767).

❶ Information

Cyber Cafe (Velký Spalicek shopping centre, Mečova 2; per hr 60Kč; ☉9am-11pm) There's a wi-fi hotspot throughout the surrounding shopping centre.

Lékárna Koliště (☑545 424 811; Koliště 47) A 24-hour pharmacy.

Tourist information office (Kulturní a Informační Centrum; KIC; ☑542 211 090; www.ticbrno.cz; Radnická 8; ☉8am-6pm Mon-Fri, 9am-5.30pm Sat & Sun Apr-Sep, 9am-5pm Sat, 9am-3pm Sun Nov-Mar) Sells maps and books accommodation. Free internet up to 15 minutes.

Úrazová nemocnice (☑545 538 111; Ponávka 6) Brno's main hospital.

❶ Getting There & Away

AIR ČSA (www.csa.cz) flies from Prague daily. **Ryan Air** (www.ryanair.com) four times a week from London and **Wizz Air** (www.wizzair.com) three times a week from London. Brno's **Tuřany Airport** (☑545 521 302; www.airport-brno.cz) is 7.5km southeast of the train station.

BUS There are frequent buses from Brno to Prague (200Kč, 2½ hours, hourly), Bratislava (135Kč, 2¼ hours, hourly) and Vienna (180Kč, two hours, five per day). The departure point is either the main bus station or near the train station opposite the Grand Hotel. Check your ticket. Private companies **Student Agency** (☑841 101 101; www.studentagency.cz) and **Megabus** (☑234 704 977; www.megabus.cz) both leave from their ticket booths north of the train station.

TRAIN Run to Prague (316Kč, three hours) every two hours. Direct Eurocity trains from Brno to Vienna (1¾ hours, five daily) arrive at Vienna's Südbahnhof. There are frequent trains to Bratislava in Slovakia (two hours), and direct trains to Berlin (7½ hours), Dresden (five hours) and Hamburg (10 hours) in Germany.

See www.idos.cz for bus and train information.

❶ Getting Around

Bus 76 runs from the train station and bus station to the airport (22Kč). A taxi will cost around 300Kč.

Buy public transport tickets from vending machines, news-stands or at the **DPMB Information Office** (☑543 174 317; www.dpmb.cz; Novobranská 18; ☉6am-6pm Mon-Fri, 8am-3.30pm Sat). Tickets valid for 15/60/90 minutes cost 18/22/24Kč, and allow unlimited transfers; 24-hour tickets are 68Kč. A 10-minute, no-transfer ticket is 14Kč. For taxis, try **City Taxis** (☑542 321 321).

Around Brno

SLAVKOV U BRNA

Slavkov u Brna is better known in history by its Austrian name, Austerlitz. On 2 December 1805 the Battle of the Three Emperors was fought here, when Napoleon Bonaparte's Grande Armée defeated the combined forces of Emperor Franz I (Austria) and Tsar Alexander I (Russia). During lulls in the fighting, Napoleon stayed at **Slavkov Chateau** (zámek Slavkov; www.zamek-slavkov.cz; chateau tours adult/child 60/40Kč, in English 105/85Kč; ☉9am-4pm Jun-Aug, Tue-Sun only May & Sep-Nov). As well as tours of the chateau's luxuriant interiors, visitors can experience the multimedia **Virtual Battle exposition** (adult/child 70/50Kč). Promising '3-D virtual reality' but delivering a slightly enhanced PowerPoint presentation, it does illuminate the surrounding terrain on which the battle was fought.

The battle was decided at **Pracký kopec**, 12km west of Slavkov, now marked by the **Cairn of Peace** (Mohyla míru; adult/child 75/35Kč; ☉9am-6pm Jul & Aug, 9am-5pm May, Jun & Sep, 9am-5pm Tue-Sun Apr, 9am-3.30pm Tue-Sun Oct-Mar) with a museum on the conflict that claimed 20,000 lives. Annual re-enactments take place around 2 December.

Slavkov is 21km east of Brno and reached by bus (36Kč, 25 minutes) or train (42Kč, 35 minutes). Pracký kopec is awkward to reach by public transport. Take a local train from Brno to Ponětovice (28Kč, 20 minutes) and walk 3.5km southeast through Prace.

MORAVIAN KARST

A good day trip from Brno, the limestone plateau of the Moravian Karst (Moravský kras) is riddled with caves and canyons carved by the subterranean Punkva River. There's a car park at **Skalní Mlýn** with an information desk and ticket office. A **mini-train** (adult/child return 70/60Kč; ☉Apr-Sep) travels along the 1.5km between the car park and the caves. Otherwise it's a 20-minute stroll through forest.

The **Punkva Caves tour** (Punkevní jeskyně; www.smk.cz; adult/child160/80Kč; ☉8.20am-3.50pm Apr-Sep, 8.40am-2pm Mon-Fri & 8.40am-3.40pm Sat & Sun Oct, 8.40am-2pm Tue-Sun Nov-Mar) involves a 1km walk through limestone caverns to the bottom of the **Macocha Abyss**, a 140m-deep sinkhole. Small, electric-powered boats then cruise along the underground river back to the entrance. At weekends and in July and August tickets for cave tours can sell out in advance, so book ahead online.

Beyond the Punkva Caves entrance, a **cable car** (adult/child return 80/70Kč, combined tourist train & cable-car ticket 120/100Kč) travels to the upper rim of the Macocha Abyss. Afterwards, wander down on the blue-marked trail (2km).

Kateřinská Cave (Kateřinská eskyně; adult/child 70/50Kč; ☉8.20am-4pm Apr-Sep, to 2pm Oct, 10am, noon & 2pm Feb-Mar) is 300m from the Skalní Mlýn car park. Usually less crowded, the 40-minute tour explores two massive chambers.

From Brno trains run to Blansko (35Kč, 30 minutes, hourly). Buses depart from Blansko bus station (across the bridge from the train station) to Skalní Mlýn (16Kč, 15 minutes, five daily April to September). You can also hike an 8km trail from Blansko to Skalní Mlýn (two hours).

Olomouc

POP 105,000

While show-offs Prague, Karlovy Vary and Český Krumlov are constantly praised, Olomouc goes quietly about its authentically Moravian business, and emerges as the Czech Republic's most underrated destination.

An Old Town rivalling Prague's Old Town Sq combines with the graceful campus of the country's second-oldest university. Moravia's most impressive religious structures play host to a thrilling history and one of the Czech Republic's best museums. And, with tourist numbers at a relative trickle, Olomouc is a great-value destination.

◉ Sights & Activities

HORNÍ NÁM & AROUND

TOP CHOICE **Holy Trinity Column** MONUMENT

The Unesco World Heritage–listed Holy Trinity Column (Sousoší Nejsvětější trojice), built between 1716 and 1754, is a baroque structure reminiscent of a Buddhist stupa. The square is ringed by historic facades and features two of the city's six baroque fountains.

Town Hall HISTORIC BUILDING

The splendid Town Hall was built in 1378, though its present appearance and **tower** (admission 15Kč; ☉tours 11am & 3pm Mar-Oct) date from 1607. Don't miss the **astronomical clock** on the north side, remodelled in communist style so that each hour is announced by ideologically pure workers instead of pious saints. The best display is at noon. In front of the town hall, a brass model of Olomouc will help you get your bearings.

St Moritz Cathedral CHURCH

Down Opletalova is the immense, Gothic St Moritz Cathedral (chrám sv Mořice), built slowly from 1412 to 1530. The cathedral's peace is shattered every September with an International Organ Festival; the cathedral's own organ is Moravia's mightiest.

DOLNÍ NÁM & AROUND

Church of the Annunciation of St Mary CHURCH

The 1661 Church of the Annunciation of St Mary (kostel Zvěstování Panny Marie) has a beautifully sober interior, in contrast to the square's other two attractions: the opulent 16th-century Renaissance **Hauenschild Palace** (not open to the public), and the **Marian Plague Column** (Mariánský morový sloup).

St Michael Church CHURCH

Picturesque lanes thread northeast to the green-domed St Michael Church (kostel sv Michala). The baroque interior includes a rare painting of a pregnant Virgin Mary. Draped around the entire block is an active **Dominican seminary** (Dominikánský klášter).

NÁM REPUBLIKY & AROUND

Nám Republiky HISTORIC AREA

The original Jesuit college complex, founded in 1573, stretches along Universitní and into nám Republiky, and includes the **Church of St Mary of the Snows** (kostel Panny Marie Sněžné), with many fine frescos.

Olomouc Museum of Art ART GALLERY

(Olomoucký muzeum umění; www.olmuart.cz; Densova 47; adult/child 50/25Kč; ⊙10am-6pm Tue-Sun) This gallery has an excellent collection of 20th-century Czech painting and sculpture. Admission includes entry to the Archdiocesan Museum.

Bomb Shelter HISTORIC STRUCTURE

(admission 20Kč; ⊙2pm Thu, 10am, 1pm & 4pm Sat mid-May–mid-Sep) Olomouc is all about centuries-old history, but this more recent relic of the Cold War is also worth exploring on a guided tour. The shelter was built between 1953 and 1956 and was designed to shelter a lucky few from the ravages of a chemical or nuclear strike. Book at the tourist information office.

Regional History Museum MUSEUM

(Vlastivědné muzeum; www.vmo.cz; nám Republiky 5; adult/child 40/20Kč; ⊙9am-6pm Tue-Sun Apr-Sep, 10am-5pm Wed-Sun Oct-Mar) The Regional History Museum has historical, geographical and zoological displays.

VÁCLAVSKÉ NÁM & AROUND

To the northeast, the pocket-sized Václavské nám has Olomouc's most venerable buildings, with one converted into perhaps the Czech Republic's finest religious museum.

Archdiocesan Museum MUSEUM

(www.olmuart.cz; Václavské nám 3; adult/child 50/25Kč; ⊙10am-6pm Tue-Sun) The early 12th-century Přemysl Palace (Přemyslovský palác) is now the Archdiocesan Museum with treasures from the 12th to the 18th centuries, when Olomouc was the Moravian capital. A thoughtful makeover showcases the site's diverse architecture from several centuries, and many of the ecclesiastical treasures are superb. Admission includes entry to the Olomouc Museum of Art.

St Wenceslas Cathedral CHURCH

(Václavské nám; ⊙9am-2pm Tue, Thu & Sat, 9am-4pm Wed & 11am-5pm Sun) Originally a Romanesque basilica first consecrated in 1131, the adjacent St Wenceslas Cathedral (dóm sv Václava) was rebuilt several times before having a 'neo-Gothic' makeover in the 1880s.

⚲ Tours

Olomouc Tours (☑775 345 570; www.olomouc tours.com; by donation Jul & Aug, rest of year 200Kč) offers two-hour walking tours led by the guys from Poet's Corner Hostel. They leave from the astronomical clock daily at 10am in July

and August. During other months you'll need to book. Cycling tours (350Kč, two hours) are also available.

✦ Festivals & Events

The **Olomouc Beer Festival** (www.beerfest. cz) is one of the Czech Republic's biggest. Held in June, with around 20 different breweries and loads of live folk, blues and rock, it's pretty well Beervana for curious hopheads.

Much more sedate is **Flora Olomouc** (www.flora-ol.cz), a world-renowned horticultural exhibition and fair in August.

⊨ Sleeping

Poet's Corner HOSTEL €

(☑777 570 730; www.hostelolomouc.com; 3rd fl, Sokolská1; dm/s/tw/tr/q350/650/900/1200/1600Kč; ❀⊚) Aussie owners Greg and Francie are a wealth of local information at this friendly and well-run hostel. Bicycles can be hired for 100Kč per day. In summer there's a two-night minimum stay, but Olomouc's definitely worth it.

Penzion Na Hradě PENSION €€

(☑585 203 231; www.penzionnahrade.cz; Michalská 4; s/d 1590/1790; ❀⊚) Tucked away in the robust silhouette of St Michael church, this designer pension has sleek, cool rooms and professional service creating a contemporary ambience in the heart of the old town.

Pension Křivá PENSION €€

(☑585 209 204; www.pension-kriva.cz; Křivá 8; s/d 1450/1950Kč; ⊚) This new opening gets a lot of things right: spacious rooms with cherry-wood furniture, flash bathrooms with even flasher toiletries, plus a cosy cafe downstairs. The quiet laneway location doesn't hurt either.

Ubytovna Marie HOSTEL €€

(☑585 220 220; www.ubytovnamarie.cz; třída Svobody 41 5; r per person 500Kč; ❀⊚) Spick-and-span (if spartan) double and triple rooms with shared bathrooms and kitchens make this new spot popular with long-stay overseas students. Significant discounts kick in after five nights.

✕ Eating & Drinking

TOP CHOICE **U kašny** CZECH €

(Dolní nám 43; mains 120-250Kč) Your first choice – cosy cellar bar or breezy garden bar – is easy. After that, indecisive travellers may take some time selecting one of the rotating mix of excellent beers from smaller

Olomouc

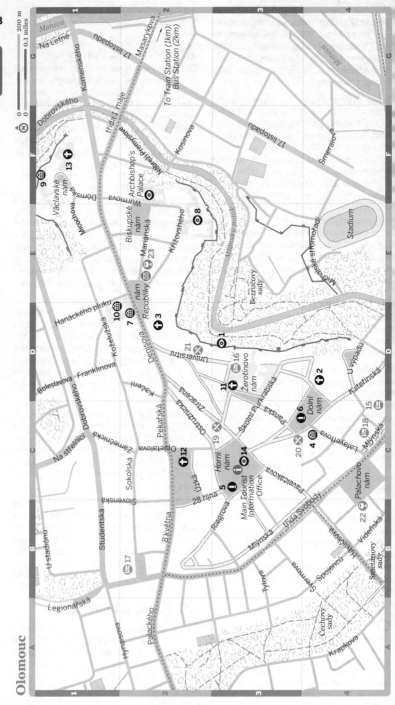

Na Letné

Moravа

Dobrovského

Komenského

17. listopadu

třída 1 máje

Masarykova

To Train Station (1km);
Bus Station (2km)

Morava

17. listopadu

Šmeralovа

Stadium

Michalské stromořadí

Bezručovy
sady

Mlýnský potok

13

9

Václavské
nám

Mlčochova

Domská

Wurmova

Biskupské
nám

Archbishop's
Palace

Náměstí Přemysla

Kosinovа

Mariánská

Křížkovského

8

nám
Republiky

23

Hanáckého pluku

Koželužská

Denisova

10

7

3

1

21

Univerzitní

16

Žerotínovo
nám

11

2

U výpadu

Kateřinská

15

Boleslavova

Franklinova

Kačení

Zámečnická

Zlatá
ulička

Pekařská

Ostružnická

Školní

Purkrabská

Panská

6

Dolní
nám

Lafayettova

18

Mlýnská

Na střelnici

Opletalova

12

19

5

14

Horní
nám

Main Tourist
Information
Office

4

20

Pavelčákova

Slovenská

Sokolská

Studentská

U stadiónu

8 května

Úzká

28. října

Riegrova

Mlýnská

třída Svobody

Tylova

Šantova

Spojenců

22

Palachovo
nám

Havlíčkova

Videňská

Smetanovy
sady

17

Legionářská

Palackého

Hynaisova

Dobrovského

Čechovy
sady

Krapkova

Olomouc

regional breweries. U kašny's meals are deliciously meaty, and don't miss Moravia's best *bramboráčky* (potato pancakes).

Cafe 87 CAFE
(Denisova 87; chocolate pie 40Kč, coffee 40Kč; ⊙8am-9pm) Locals flock to this funky cafe beside the Museum of Art for coffee and the famous chocolate pie. Some locals still prefer the dark chocolate to the white chocolate. Maybe one day we'll be convinced. It's a top spot for breakfast too.

Hanácacká Hospoda CZECH €
(Dolní nám 38; mains 100-180Kč) In the same building as the Hauenschild Palace, the menu lists everything in the local Haná dialect. It's worth persevering because the huge Moravian meals are tasty and supreme

value. Don't worry – they have an English menu if you're still coming up to speed with Haná.

Vila Primavesi INTERNATIONAL €€
(☏777 749 288; Universtiní 7; mains 180-250Kč; ⊜) In an art nouveau villa that played host to Austrian artist Gustav Klimt in the early 20th century, Vila Primavesi is Olomouc's newest eatery. On summer evenings enjoy meals like tuna steak and risotto in the lovely gardens. Lunch specials are good value. Phone ahead for dinner.

Green Bar VEGETARIAN €
(Ztacená 3; meals 100Kč; ⊙10am-5pm Mon-Fri, to 2pm Sat; ⊜⊿) Around 100Kč will get you a feast of salads, couscous and vegie lasagna at this self-service vegetarian cafe. It's popular with overseas students.

Moritz BEER HALL €
(Nešverova 2; mains 100-180Kč; ⊜) This microbrewery and restaurant is a firm local favourite. We reckon it's a combination of the terrific beers, good-value food and a praiseworthy 'No smoking' policy. In summer, the beer garden's the only place to be.

Svatováclavský Pivovar BEER HALL €
(Mariánská 4; meals 100-200Kč; ⊜) Relocated to spacious digs in Olomouc's university precinct, the city's 'other' microbrewery also has a praise-worthy nonsmoking policy. Try the zingy *hefeweizen* (wheat beer) with the gloriously pungent Olomouc cheese and potato fritters. Occasionally the brewmasters have a crack at conjuring up seasonal beers, including a very interesting *višňové pivo* (cherry beer).

ⓘ Information

Slam.cz (Slovesnská 12; per min 1Kč; ⊙9am-9pm) Includes wi-fi for laptop travellers.

Tourist information office (Olomoucká informační služba; ☏585 513 385; www.olomouc-tourism.cz; Horní nám; ⊙9am-7pm) Sells maps and makes accommodation bookings. Audio guides (150Kč for three hours) include a map detailing 28 points of interest.

ⓘ Getting There & Away

Frequent buses link Olomouc with Brno (92Kč, 1¼ hours) and Prague's Florenc bus station (220Kč, 3¾ hours).

Five direct fast trains (130Kč, 1½ hours) link Brno and Olomouc daily. Trains from Prague (3210Kč, 3¼ hours) leave from Praha-hlavní nádraží. Faster SC Pendolino trains (510Kč, 2¼ hours) stop at Olomouc en route to Ostrava.

From Olomouc to Poland there are two direct trains to Warsaw at 12.37am and 12.54pm daily (six hours), and one to Kraków at 12.37am (4½ hours).

Direct trains link Olomouc to Košice at 1.54pm (5½ hours) in Slovakia, but for Bratislava you'll need to change at Břeclav.

ⓘ Getting Around

The main train station (hlavní nádraží) is 2km east of the old town, over the Morava River and its tributary the Bystřice (catch tram 2, 4 or 6 for the town centre). The bus station is 1km further east (catch tram 4 to town).

Telč

POP 6000

Telč is a quiet town, with a gorgeous old centre ringed by medieval fish ponds and unspoilt by modern buildings. Unwind with a good book and a glass of Moravian wine at one of the local cafes.

The bus and train stations are a few hundred metres apart on the eastern side of town. A 10-minute walk along Masarykova leads to nám Zachariáše z Hradce, the Old Town square.

Telč's **tourist information office** (☑567 243 145; www.telc-etc.cz; nám Zachariáše z Hradce 10; ☉8am-5pm Mon-Fri, 10am-5pm Sat & Sun; @) books accommodation in private homes (around 300Kč to 400Kč per person). Internet access is 1Kč per minute.

⦿ Sights

Nám Zachariáše z Hradce   TOWN SQUARE
In a country full of gorgeous Old Town squares, Telč's Unesco World Heritage–listed and cobblestoned nám Zachariáše z Hradce may outshine the lot. When the day trippers have departed, the Gothic arcades and elegant Renaissance facades are a magical setting.

Water Chateau   CASTLE
(www.zamek-telc.cz; ☉9am-5pm Tue-Sun May-Sep, to 4pm Apr & Oct) At the square's northwestern end is the Water Chateau. The one-hour **Tour A** (adult/child110/70Kč, in English 210Kč) visits the Renaissance halls, while 45-minute **Tour B** (adult/child 80/50Kč; ☉9am-5pm Tue-Sun May-Sep only) visits the private apartments, inhabited by the aristocratic owners until 1945. At the castle's entrance is the **Chapel of All Saints**, where trumpeting angels guard the tombs of Zacharias of Hradec, the castle's founder, and his wife.

⏺ Sleeping

Accommodation can be hard to get and expensive during the annual **Prázdniny v Telči folk music festival** in late July and early August. Book ahead.

Penzion Kamenné Slunce   PENSION €
(☑732 193 510; www.kamenne-slunce.cz; Palackého 2; s/d/apt 600/900/2000Kč; ☺) Lots of brick, exposed beams and warm wooden floors make this a very welcoming spot just off the main square. Hip bathrooms with colourful tiles are further proof of Telč's coolest place to stay.

Hotel Pangea   HOTEL €
(☑567 213 122; www.pangea.cz; Na Baště 450; s/d 1200/1400Kč; P❄@☎☀) Huge buffet breakfasts and loads of facilities make the functional Pangea good value. Outside July and August, rates fall by up to 30%. Ask for a room down the lane away from the occasional road noise.

Penzión Danuše   PENSION €
(☑567 213 945; www.telc-etc.cz/cz/privat/danuse; Hradebni 25; s/d 500/1000Kč, 4-bed apt 2000Kč) Discreet wrought-iron balconies and wooden window boxes provide a touch of class just off the main square.

✖ Eating & Drinking

Šenk Pod Věží   CZECH €
(Palackého 116; mains 110-200Kč) Sizzling grills and tasty pizza are the big drawcards at this cosy and traditional restaurant tucked under the tower. The outdoor terrace has views of a couple of domesticated deer.

Kavarná Antoniana   CAFE €
(nám Zachariáše z Hradce; coffee & cake 70Kč) Documentary photography from around Moravia will get you planning your next destination at this modern refuge from the Renaissance glories outside. Have a coffee or something stronger.

Pizzerie   PIZZA €
(☑567 223 246; nám Zachariáše z Hradce 32; pizza 80-140Kč) Top-notch pizzas and to-die-for town square views.

U Marušky   BAR
(☑605 870 854; Palackého) Telč's hipper younger citizens crowd this buzzy bar for cool jazz and tasty eats.

ⓘ Getting There & Around

Five buses daily travel from Prague Florenc to Telč (150Kč, three hours). Buses between České

Budějovice and Brno also stop at Telč (100Kč, two hours, two daily).

Trains (43Kč, one hour) rumble south to the beautiful village of Slavonice on a little-used branch line. It's a great way to connect two of the Czech Republic's loveliest villages.

Hračky Cyklo Sport (nám Zachariáše z Hradce 23; per day 100Kč; ⊗8am-5pm Mon-Fri, 9am-noon Sat) rents out bicycles, and you can hire **rowboats** (per 30min 20Kč; ⊗10am-6pm Jul & Aug) from outside the East gate.

Moravian Wine Country

Heading south from Brno to Vienna is the Moravian wine country. Czech wine has improved greatly since the fall of communism in 1989, with small producers concentrating on the high-quality end of the market. Czech red wines, such as the local speciality Svatovavřinecké (St Lawrence), are mediocre, but dry and fruity whites can be good, especially the Riesling *(Vlašský Ryzlink)* and Müller-Thurgau varietals.

There are lots of *vinné sklepy* (wine cellars), *vinoteky* (wine shops) and *vinárny* (wine bars) to explore, as well as spectacular chateaux. The terrain is relatively flat, so cycling is a leisurely way to get around. See www.wineofczechrepublic.cz for touring routes and more information.

MIKULOV
POP 7600

Described by Czech poet Jan Skácel as a 'piece of Italy moved to Moravia by God's hand', Mikulov is an excellent base for exploring the neighbouring Lednice-Valtice Cultural Landscape. The nearby Palavá Hills are a mecca for hiking and cycling.

Topped with an imposing chateau and studded with a legacy of baroque and Renaissance façades, Mikulov deserves its growing popularity amid the burgeoning Moravian wine country. And once you've experienced enough pretty Renaissance architecture, the legacy of Mikulov's once-thriving Jewish community is a compelling alternative. See the box, p334, for more opportunities to explore Moravia's Jewish heritage.

If you're travelling from Brno to Vienna, Mikulov is a good stopping-off point.

◉ Sights & Activities

A pleasant way to visit smaller, local vineyards across the rolling countryside is by bicycle on the **Mikulov Wine Trail**. The

Mikulov tourist office can recommend a one-day ride that also takes in the nearby chateaux at Valtice and Lednice. Bicycles and additional cycle touring information are available from **Top Bicycle** (⊅519 513 745; www.topbicycle.com; Náměstí 24/27). Ask at the travel agency opposite the tourist office.

Mikulov Chateau   CASTLE
(⊅519 309 019; www.rmm.cz; adult/concession 70/35Kč; ⊗9am-5pm Tue-Sun May-Sep, to 4pm Apr & Oct) Torched by the retreating German army in February 1945, Mikulov's spectacular castle has now been painstakingly restored. Three separate tour routes detail the history of the aristocratic Dietrichstein family (40Kč), the archaeology of Roman and German civilisation in the nearby Palavá Hills (30Kč), and the history of viticulture in the area (30Kč). In the cellar is the largest wine barrel in central Europe, made by Kryštof Secht of Brno in 1643.

Jewish Quarter   HISTORIC AREA
The hub of Mikulov's historical Jewish quarter is the former **synagogue** (synagóga; ⊗519 510 255; Husova 11; adult/concession 20/10Kč; ⊗1-5pm Tue-Sun mid-May–Oct), now used as an exhibition space. The **Jewish Cemetery** (Židovský hřbitov; adult/concession 20/10Kč; ⊗9am-5pm Mon-Fri Jul-Aug), founded in the 15th century, is off Brněnská. There are tours every half-hour. An 'instructive trail' now runs through the Jewish quarter, with information plaques in English. You can pick it up at the end of Husova near Alfonse Muchy. Above the Jewish quarter is **Goat Hill** (Kozí hrádek) topped with a 15th-century **lookout tower** (admission 20Kč; ⊗9am-6pm Apr-Oct).

Holy Hill   LANDMARK
(Svatý kopeček). The 1km path to this 363m peak is through a nature reserve and past grottos depicting the Stations of the Cross to the compact **Church of St Sebastian**. The blue-marked trail begins at the bottom of the main square on Svobody. The whitewashed church and the white limestone on the hill almost give it a Mediterranean ambience. Ask at the tourist information about other walking trails in the nearby Pavlovské hills.

🛏 Sleeping

TOP CHOICE **Hotel Templ**   BOUTIQUE HOTEL €€
(⊅519 323 095; www.templ.cz; Husova 50; s/d from 1390/1650Kč, apt 2490Kč; 🐾) Here you'll find discreetly furnished rooms and a selection of stylish restaurants in a restored Renaissance mansion. It's also an excellent

place to learn about the local wines. Each room is named after flowers or birds found in the nearby Palavá Hills.

Penzion Fontána Mikulov
PENSION €

(☎519 510 241; www.fontana.euweb.cz; Piaristů 6; s/d/tr 500/650/950Kč) By day this friendly couple run the local stationery shop. After hours the focus is on the clean and colourful rooms attached to their house. Buy a bottle of local wine and fire up the garden barbecue for dinner.

Fajká Penzion
PENSION €

(☎732 833 147; www.fajka-mikulov.cz; Alfonse Muchy 18; s/d 400/800Kč) Bright, newly decorated rooms sit above a cosy wine bar. Out back is a garden restaurant if you really, really like the local wine.

Eating & Drinking

Petit Café
CAFE €

(Náměstí 27; crepes 40-70Kč; ☎) Tasty crepes and coffee are dished up in a hidden courtyard meets herb garden. Later at night have a beer or a glass of wine.

Restaurace Templ
CZECH €€

(☎519 323 095; Husova; mains 130-240Kč; ☎) The best restaurant in town is matched by a fine wine list specialising in local varietals. Choose from the either the more formal (nonsmoking) restaurant or the more relaxed wine garden.

Vinařské Centrum
WINE BAR

(Náměstí 11; ☺9am-6pm Mon-Sat, 10am-5pm Sun) This winebar and retail shop has an excellent range of local wines available in small tasting glasses (15Kč to 50Kč), plus whole bottles when you've made up your mind.

ℹ Information

Tourist office (☎519 510 855; www.mikulov. cz; Nám 30; ☺8am-6pm Mon-Fri, 9am-6pm Sat & Sun Jun-Sep; 8am-noon & 12.30-5pm Mon-Fri, 9am-4pm Sat-Sun Apr, May & Oct; 8am-noon & 1-4pm Mon-Fri Nov-Mar) Organises tours (including specialist outings for wine buffs) and accommodation, and has internet access (1Kč per minute).

ℹ Getting There & Away

There are five buses daily from Mikulov to Lednice (35Kč, one hour), and five daily from Brno (62Kč, 1¾ hours). From Brno, Tourbus travel through Mikulov en route to Vienna.

There are eight daily trains from Znojmo (62Kč, one hour) and Břeclav (43Kč, 30 minutes), some which have direct connections with Brno and Bratislava. Some trains also link from Břeclav to Vienna. See www.idos.cz.

LEDNICE & VALTICE

A few kilometres east of Mikulov, the **Lednice-Valtice Cultural Landscape** consists of 200 sq km of woodland, artificial lakes and avenues dotted with baroque, neoclassical and neo-Gothic chateaux. Effectively Europe's biggest landscaped garden, it was created over several centuries by the dukes of Liechtenstein and is now a Unesco World Heritage site.

The massive neo-Gothic **Lednice Chateau** (☎519 340 128; www.zamek-lednice.com; ☺9am-6pm Tue-Sun May-Aug, to 5pm Tue-Sun Sep, to 4pm Sat & Sun only Apr & Oct) was the Liechtensteins' summer palace. Studded with battlements, pinnacles and gargoyles, it gazes across an island-dotted artificial lake. **Tour 1** (adult/child 120/70Kč, 45 min) visits the major rooms, while **Tour 2** (adult/child 120/70Kč, 45 min) concentrates on the Liechtenstein apartments. Both tours last 45 minutes. Alternatively visit the gardens for free, or cruise on a **pleasure boat** (☺9.30am-5pm Jul & Aug, Tue-Sun May, Jun & Sep, Sat & Sun Apr & Oct). Routes take you from the chateau to an incongruous minaret (adult/child 80/40Kč) or from the minaret to nearby Janův castle (adult/child 120/60Kč).

During summer the **Birds of Prey show** (www.zayferus.cz; adult/child 90/45Kč) presents birds soaring and hunting above Lednice's meadows.

Valtice's huge baroque chateau houses the **National Wine Salon** (Národní salon vín; ☎519 352 072; www.salonvin.cz; Zámek 1; ☺9.30am-5pm Tue-Thu, 10.30am-6pm Fri, 10.30am-5pm Sat-Sun Jun-Sep). The cellars of the chateau are the place to buy and try local wines. Tasting programs cost from 120Kč to 250Kč or, if 'stickies' are your thing, for 399Kč you can sample nine equally lusciously dessert wines. Unfortunately you'll need at least five thirsty and likeminded travellers.

ℹ Getting There & Away

There's around five buses per day from Mikulov to Lednice, and regular buses shuttle the short distance between Lednice and Valtice (14Kč, 15 minutes). If you get an earlyish start from Mikulov, it's a good day trip to catch the bus to Lednice, another bus to Valtice and then catch the train back to Mikulov.

Regular trains link Mikulov to Valtice (22Kč, 15 minutes) and Břeclav (38Kč, 30 minutes) with connections to Brno, Bratislava and Vienna.

Moravia, the eastern part of the modern Czech Republic, has a rich Jewish heritage dating back to 13th century. According to a 1930 census, 356,830 people in the Czechoslovak region identified themselves as Jewish by religion. However, by the end of WWII, it's estimated that the Nazi regime had killed around 263,000 of these people.

More than seven decades later, awareness of Moravia's centuries-old Jewish history is increasing, and several towns and villages are essential stops for heritage travellers.

Mikulov's former Jewish precinct stands in melancholy contrast to the beautiful scenery surrounding the town, while the Moravian villages of Boskovice and Třebíč feature two of Central Europe's best-preserved Jewish ghettos.

The undoubted highlight of **Boskovice** is the beautifully restored **Maoir Synagogue** (admission 30Kč; ⊙9am-5pm Tue-Fri & 1-5pm Sat-Sun May-Sep, 1-5pm Sat-Sun Apr & Oct), originally built in 1698 and decorated with exquisite baroque frescoes in the 18th century. Download the 'Jewish Town' PDF from www.boskovice.cz for more information.

Boskovice is best reached by regular buses from either Brno (48Kč, 50 minutes) or Olomouc (63Kč, 1½ hours).

Southwest of Boskovice, **Třebíč** (www.trebic.cz) was another historical centre of Judaism in Moravia, but the Jewish population was annihilated during WWII, with only 10 of Třebíč's 281 Jews surviving the war. The Jewish quarter is now a Unesco World Heritage site, and the riverside district's winding alleys are studded with historical structures, including the restored **Rear Synagogue** (adult/concession 40/20Kč; ⊙10am-noon & 1-5pm) with an excellent historical model of the ghetto. Around 600m north of the ghetto, the 17th-century **Jewish cemetery** (⊙8am-8pm Sun-Fri May-Sep, 8am-6pm Mar, Apr & Oct, 9am-4pm Nov-Feb) is the largest in the country with more than 11,000 graves, the oldest dating from 1641.

Třebíč is easily reached by bus from Brno (70Kč, 1½ hours) or Telč (40Kč, 45 minutes). The town is also visited on tours operated by Prague-based **Wittman Tours** (www.wittman-tours.com).

UNDERSTAND CZECH REPUBLIC

History

Over the centuries, the Czechs have been invaded by the Habsburgs, the Nazis and the Soviets, and the country's location has meant domestic upheavals have not stayed local for long. Their rejection of Catholicism in 1418 resulted in the Hussite Wars. The 1618 revolt against Habsburg rule ignited the Thirty Years' War, and the German annexation of the Sudetenland in 1938 helped fuel WWII. The liberal reforms of 1968's Prague Spring led to tanks rolling in from across the Eastern Bloc, and the peaceful ousting of the government during 1989's Velvet Revolution was a model for freedom-seekers everywhere.

Bohemian Beginnings

Ringed by hills, the ancient Czech lands of Bohemia and Moravia have formed natural territories since earliest times. Slavic tribes from the east settled and were united from 830 to 907 in the Great Moravian Empire.

Christianity was adopted after the arrival in 863 of the Thessalonian missionaries Cyril and Methodius, who created the first Slavic (Cyrillic) alphabet.

In the 9th century, the first home-grown dynasty, the Přemysls, erected some huts in what was to become Prague. This dysfunctional clan gave the Czechs their first martyred saints – Ludmila, killed by her daughter-in-law in 874, and her grandson, the pious Prince Václav (or Good 'King' Wenceslas; r 921–29), murdered by his brother Boleslav the Cruel.

The Přemysls' rule ended in 1306, and in 1310 John of Luxembourg came to the Bohemian throne through marriage, and annexed the kingdom to the German empire. The reign of his son, Charles IV (1346–78), who became Holy Roman Emperor, saw the first of Bohemia's two 'Golden Ages'. Charles founded Prague's St Vitus Cathedral, built Charles Bridge and established Charles University. The second was the reign of Rudolf II (1576–1612), who made Prague the capital of the Habsburg Empire and attracted artists, scholars and scientists to his court. Bohemia and Moravia remained under Habsburg dominion for almost four centuries.

Under the Habsburg Thumb

In 1415 the Protestant religious reformer Jan Hus, rector of Charles University, was burnt at the stake for heresy. He inspired the nationalist Hussite movement that plunged Bohemia into civil war (1419–34).

When the Austrian and Catholic Habsburg dynasty ascended the Bohemian throne in 1526, the fury of the Counter-Reformation was unleashed after Protestants threw two Habsburg councillors from a Prague Castle window. This escalated into the Catholic -Protestant Thirty Years' War (1618–48), which devastated much of Central Europe.

The defeat of the Protestants at the Battle of White Mountain in 1620 marked the start of a long period of forced re-Catholicisation, Germanisation and oppression of Czech language and culture.

National Reawakening

The Czechs started to rediscover their linguistic and cultural roots at the start of the 19th century, during the so-called *Národní obrození* (National Revival). Overt political activity was banned, so the revival was culturally based. Important figures included historian Josef Palacký and composer Bedřich Smetana.

An independent Czech and Slovak state was realised after WWI, when the Habsburg empire's demise saw the creation of the Czechoslovak Republic in October 1918. Three-quarters of the Austro-Hungarian empire's industrial power was inherited by Czechoslovakia, as were three million Germans, mostly in the border areas of Bohemia (the *pohraniči*, known in German as the Sudetenland).

The Czechs' elation was to be short-lived. Under the Munich Pact of September 1938, Britain and France accepted the annexation of the Sudetenland by Nazi Germany, and in March 1939 the Germans occupied the rest of the country (calling it the Protectorate of Bohemia and Moravia).

Most of the Czech intelligentsia and 80,000 Jews died at the hands of the Nazis. When Czech paratroopers assassinated the Nazi governor Reinhardt Heydrich in 1942, the entire town of Lidice was wiped out in revenge.

Communist Coup

After the war, the Czechoslovak government expelled 2.5 million Sudeten Germans – including antifascists who had fought the Nazis – from the Czech borderlands and confiscated their property. During the forced marches from Czechoslovakia many were interned in concentration camps and tens of thousands died.

In 1947 a power struggle began between the communist and democratic forces, and in early 1948 the Social Democrats withdrew from the postwar coalition. The result was the Soviet-backed coup d'état of 25 February 1948, known as *Vítězný únor* (Victorious February). The new communist-led government established a dictatorship, which resulted in years of oppression. In the 1950s thousands of noncommunists fled the country. Others were captured and imprisoned, and hundreds were executed or died in labour camps.

Prague Spring & Velvet Revolution

In April 1968 the new first secretary of the Communist Party, Alexander Dubček, introduced liberalising reforms to create 'socialism with a human face' – known as the 'Prague Spring'. Censorship ended, political prisoners were released and economic decentralisation began. Moscow was not happy, but Dubček refused to buckle and Soviet tanks entered Prague on 20 August 1968, closely followed by 200,000 Soviet and Warsaw Pact soldiers.

Many Communist Party functionaries were expelled and 500,000 party members lost their jobs after the dictatorship was re-established. Dissidents were summarily imprisoned and educated professionals were made manual labourers.

The 1977 trial of the underground rock group the Plastic People of the Universe (for disturbing the peace at an unauthorised music festival) inspired the formation of the human-rights group Charter 77. The communists saw the musicians as threatening the status quo, but others viewed the trial as an assault on human rights. Charter 77's group of Prague intellectuals, including the playwright–philosopher Václav Havel, continued their underground opposition throughout the 1980s.

By 1989 Gorbachev's perestroika and the fall of the Berlin Wall on 9 November raised expectations of change. On 17 November an official student march in Prague was smashed by police. Daily demonstrations followed, culminating in a general strike on 27 November. Dissidents led by Havel formed the Anti-Communist Civic Forum

The films of Jan Hrebejk (b 1967) – *Musíme si pomáhat* (Divided We Fall, 2000), *Pupendo* (2003) and *Horem pádem* (Up and Down, 2004) – all cover different times in the country's tumultuous 20th-century history.

Jiří Menzel's take on writer Bohumil Hrabal's *I Served the King of England* (2006) enjoyed art-house success, and *Občan Havel* (Citizen Havel, 2008) is a fascinating documentary about Václav Havel. A recent critical and box office hit was *Kajínek* (2010), a thriller about the Czech Republic's most notorious hit man.

Buy Czech films on DVD at Kino Světozor in Prague (p295).

and negotiated the resignation of the Communist government on 3 December, less than a month after the fall of the Berlin Wall.

A 'Government of National Understanding' was formed, with Havel elected president on 29 December. With no casualties, the days after 17 November became known as *Sametová revoluce* (the Velvet Revolution).

Velvet Divorce

Following the end of communist central authority, antagonisms between Slovakia and Prague re-emerged. The federal parliament granted both the Czech and Slovak Republics full federal status within a Czech and Slovak Federated Republic (ČSFR), but this failed to satisfy Slovak nationalists.

Elections in June 1992 sealed Czechoslovakia's fate. Václav Klaus' ODS took 48 seats in the 150-seat federal parliament, while 24 went to the Movement for a Democratic Slovakia (HZDS), a left-leaning Slovak nationalist party led by Vladimír Mečiar.

In July the Slovak parliament declared sovereignty, and on 1 January 1993 Czechoslovakia ceased to exist for the second time. Prague became capital of the new Czech Republic, and Havel was elected its first president.

A New Country

Thanks to booming tourism and a solid industrial base, the Czech Republic enjoyed negligible unemployment and by 2003 Prague enjoyed Eastern Europe's highest standard of living. However, capitalism also meant a lack of affordable housing, rising crime and a deteriorating health system.

The Czech Republic became a member of NATO in 1999, and joined the EU on 1 May 2004. With EU membership, greater numbers of younger Czechs are now working and studying abroad, seizing opportunities their parents didn't have. The Czech Republic is scheduled to adopt the euro in 2012.

People & Religion

The population of the Czech Republic is 10.2 million; 95% of the population are Czech and 3% are Slovak. Only 150,000 of the three million Sudeten Germans evicted after WWII remain. A significant Roma population (0.3%) is subject to hostility and racism, suffering from poverty and unemployment.

Most Czechs are atheist (39.8%) or nominally Roman Catholic (39.2%), but church attendance is low. There are small Protestant (4.6%) and Orthodox (3%) congregations. The Jewish community (1% in 1918) today numbers only a few thousand.

Czech Literature

Franz Kafka and other German-speaking Jewish writers strongly influenced Prague's literary scene in the early 20th century.

After WWI Jaroslav Hašek devoted himself to lampooning the Habsburg empire. His folk masterpiece *The Good Soldier Švejk* is a riotous story of a Czech soldier during WWI.

Bohumil Hrabal (1914–97), one of the finest Czech novelists of the 20th century, wrote *The Little Town Where Time Stood Still*, a gentle portrayal of the machinations of small-town life.

Milan Kundera (b 1929) is the most renowned Czech writer internationally, with his novel *The Unbearable Lightness of Being* being adapted as a film. His first work, *The Joke*, explores the communist era's paranoia.

Art & Music

Though he is associated with the French art nouveau movement, Alfons Mucha's (1860–1939) heart remained at home in Bohemia. Much of his work reflects themes of Slavic suffering, courage and cross-nation brotherhood.

TOP PLACES TO TRY CZECH BEER

There is an increasing number of excellent Czech regional beers also worth investigating. Buy the *Good Beer Guide to Prague & the Czech Republic* by long-time Prague resident Evan Rail. In Prague it's available at Shakespeare & Sons (www.shakes.cz) or the Globe Bookstore & Cafe (www.globebookstore.cz).

Keep up to date with Evan's ongoing investigation of the Czech beer scene at www.beerculture.org. Here's our pick to get you started on your hoppy way.

» Pivovarský Klub (p292), Prague
» Groll Pivovar (p312), Plzeň
» Pivovar Sv Florian (p309), Loket
» Pivnice Pegas (p325), Brno
» Moritz (p330) & Svatováclavský Pivovar (p330), Olomouc

David Černý (b 1967) is a contemporary Czech sculptor. For more on his confrontational work, see the box, p285.

Bedřich Smetana (1824–84), an icon of Czech pride, incorporated folk songs and dances into his classical compositions. Antonín Dvořák's (1841–1904) most popular works include the symphony *From the New World,* his *Slavonic Dances* of 1878 and 1881, the operas *The Devil & Kate* and *Rusalka,* and his religious masterpiece *Stabat Mater.*

More recently, the Plastic People of the Universe played a role in the Velvet Revolution, and still stage the occasional live gig. Newer bands to watch for include Please the Trees and Sunshine Caravan. Gipsy.cz are a successful hip-hop group drawn from the Czech Republic's Roma community.

Czech Cuisine

The classic Bohemian dish is *knedlo-zelo-vepřo* – bread dumplings, sauerkraut and roast pork. Also look out for *cesneková* (garlic soup), *svíčková na smetaně* (roast beef with sour-cream sauce and cranberries) and *kapr na kmíní* (fried or baked carp with caraway seed).

A *bufet* or *samoobsluha* is a self-service cafeteria with *chlebíčky* (open sandwiches), salads, *klobásy* (spicy sausages), *špekáčky* (mild pork sausages), *párky* (frankfurters), *guláš* (goulash) and of course *knedlíky.*

A *pivnice* is a pub without food, while a *hospoda* or *hostinec* is a pub or beer hall serving basic meals. A *vinárna* (wine bar) has anything from snacks to a full-blown menu. The occasional *kavárna* (cafe) has a full menu, but most only serve snacks and desserts. A *restaurace* is any restaurant.

In Prague and other main cities, you'll find an increasing number of excellent vegetarian restaurants, but smaller towns remain limited. There are a few standard *bezmasá jídla* (meatless dishes) served by most restaurants. The most common are *smažený sýr* (fried cheese) and vegetables cooked with cheese sauce.

For non-smoking premises, look out for signs saying *Kouření zakázano.*

Beer & Wine

One of the first words of Czech you'll learn is *pivo* (beer). Most famous are Budvar and Pilsner Urquell, but there are many other local brews to be discovered.

Most beer halls have a system of marking everything you eat or drink on a small piece of paper that is left on your table, then totted up when you pay (say *zaplatím, prosím* – I'd like to pay, please).

The South Moravian vineyards around the town of Mikulov produce improving *bílé víno* (white wines).

The Landscape

The landlocked Czech Republic is bordered by Germany, Austria, Slovakia and Poland. The land is made up of two river bsins: Bohemia in the west, drained by the Labe (Elbe) River flowing north into Germany; and Moravia in the east, drained by the Morava River flowing southeast into the Danube. Each basin is ringed by low, forest-clad hills, notably the Šumava range along the Bavarian–Austrian border in the southwest, the Krušné hory (Ore Mountains) along the northwestern border with Germany, and the Krkonoše mountains along the Polish border east of Liberec. The country's highest peak, Sněžka (1602m), is in the Krkonoše.

South Bohemia has hundreds of linked fishponds and artificial lakes, and East Bohemia is home to the striking 'rock towns' of the Adršpach-Teplice Rocks.

Environment

Single-minded industrial development policies during successive communist governments caused environmental havoc for decades. Since the Velvet Revolution, policies have changed significantly, and standards have increased to meet EU regulations. Private involvement in environmental projects is adding to progress. Groups include the **Friends of Nature Society** (www.novyprales.cz), which is active in returning forested areas to indigenous vegetation.

SURVIVAL GUIDE

Directory A–Z

Accommodation

Outside the peak summer season, hotel rates can fall by up to 40%. Booking ahead – especially in Prague – is recommended for summer and around Christmas and Easter. There is no law banning smoking in rooms, but a growing number of midrange and top-end options can provide nonsmoking accommodation.

PRICE RANGES

In this chapter prices quoted are for rooms with a private bathroom and a simple breakfast, unless otherwise stated. The following price indicators apply (for a high-season double room):

€€€ more than 3700Kč

€€ 1600Kč to 3700Kč

€ less than 1600Kč

CAMPING

Most campsites are open from May to September only and charge around 80Kč to 100Kč per person. Camping on public land is prohibited. See **Czech Camping** (www.czechcamping.com) and **Do Kempu** (www.czech-camping.com) for information and online booking.

HOSTELS

Prague and Český Krumlov are the only places with a choice of backpacker-oriented hostels. Dorm beds costs around 450Kč in Prague and 350Kč to 450Kč elsewhere. Booking ahead is recommended. **Czech Youth Hostel Association** (www.czechhostels.com) offers information and booking for Hostelling International (HI) hostels.

PRIVATE ROOMS & PENSIONS

Look for signs advertising private rooms (*privát* or *Zimmer frei*). Most tourist information offices can book for you. Expect to pay from 450Kč to 550Kč per person outside Prague. Bathrooms are usually shared.

Pensions (*penzióny*) are small, often family-run, accommodation offering rooms with private bathroom and breakfast. Rates range from 1000Kč to 1500Kč for a double room (1900Kč to 2500Kč in Prague). See **Czech Pensions** (www.czechpension.cz).

HOTELS

Hotels in central Prague, Český Krumlov and Brno can be expensive, but smaller towns are usually significantly cheaper. Two-star hotels offer reasonable comfort for 1000Kč to 1200Kč for a double, or 1200Kč to 1500Kč with private bathroom (around 50% higher in Prague). It's always worth asking for a weekend discount in provincial Czech cities and towns. See **Czech Hotels** (www.czechhotels.net), **Czech Hotels.cz** (ww.czechhotels.cz), **Discover Czech** (www.discoverczech.com) and **Sleep in Czech** (www.sleepinczech.com)

Business Hours

Banks 8.30am-4.30pm Mon-Fri

Bars 11am-midnight

Museums & Castles Usually closed Mon year-round

Restaurants 11am-11pm

Shops 8.30am-6pm Mon–Fri, 8.30am-noon Sat

Embassies & Consulates

Most embassies and consulates are open at least 9am to noon Monday to Friday. All of the following are in Prague.

Australia (☎221 729 260; www.australia.pl/wsaw/Pragueaddres.html; 6th fl, Klimentská 10, Nové Město) Honorary consulate for emergency assistance only. The Australian Embassy in Warsaw covers the Czech Republic.

Austria (📞257 090 511; www.aussenminister ium.at/prag; in German & Czech; Viktora Huga 10, Smíchov)

Bulgaria (📞222 211 258; bulvelv@mbox.vol.cz; Krakovská 6, Nové Město)

Canada (📞272 101 800; www.canada.cz; Muchova 6, Bubeneč)

France (📞251 171 711; www.france.cz, in French & Czech; Velkopřerovské nám 2, Malá Strana)

Germany (📞257 113 111; www.deutschland.cz, in German & Czech; Vlašská 19, Malá Strana)

Hungary (📞233 324 454; huembprg@vol.cz; Českomalínská 20, Bubeneč)

Ireland (📞257 530 061; www.embassyofireland. cz; Tržiště 13, Malá Strana)

Netherlands (📞224 312 190; www.netherlands embassy.cz; Gotthardská 6/27, Bubeneč)

New Zealand (📞222 514 672; egermayer@ nzconsul.cz; Dykova 19, Vinohrady) Honorary consulate providing emergency assistance only; the nearest NZ embassy is in Berlin. Visits only by appointment.

Poland (www.ambpol.cz) consulate (📞224 228 722; konspol@mbox.vol.cz; Vúžlabině 14, Strašnice); embassy (📞257 099 500; Valdštejnská 8, Malá Strana) Go to the consulate for visas.

Russia (📞233 374 100; embrus@tiscali.cz; Pod Kaštany 1, Bubeneč)

Slovakia (📞233 113 051; www.slovakemb.cz, in Slovak; Pelléova 87/12, Bubeneč)

South Africa (📞267 311 114; www.saprague.cz; Ruská 65, Vršovice)

UK (📞257 402 111; www.britain.cz; Thunovská 14, Malá Strana)

Ukraine (; 📞233 342 000; emb_cz@mfa.gov.ua; Charlese de Gaulla 29, Bubeneč)

USA (📞257 022 000; www.usembassy.cz; Tržiště 15, Malá Strana)

Food

Restaurants open as early as 11am and carry on till midnight; some take a break between lunch and dinner. In this chapter, the following price indicators apply (for a main meal):

€€€ more than 500Kč

€€ 200Kč to 500Kč

€ less than 200Kč

For information on Czech cuisine, see p337.

Gay & Lesbian Travellers

Homosexuality is legal in the Czech Republic, but Czechs are not yet used to seeing public displays of affection; it's best to be discreet. For online information including links to accommodation and bars see the following:

Prague Saints (www.prague saints.cz) Information on Prague's gay scene; they also run a popular bar (p295).

Prague Gay Guide (www.prague.gayguide.net)

Holidays

New Year's Day 1 January; also anniversary of the founding of the Czech Republic.

Easter Monday March/April

Labour Day 1 May

Liberation Day 8 May

SS Cyril and Methodius Day 5 July

Jan Hus Day 6 July

Czech Statehood Day 28 September

Republic Day 28 October

Struggle for Freedom and Democracy Day 17 November

Christmas 24 to 26 December

Internet Access

Accommodation, bars and restaurants with shared internet terminals (@) or wi-fi (📶) are indicated throughout the chapter. Most Czech accommodation now offers wi-fi access, and internet cafes remain common throughout the country. An increasing number of Infocentrum (tourist information) offices also offer internet access. Data transfer speeds are generally good; rates are around 1Kč per minute.

Money
ATMS

ATMS linked to the most common global banking networks can be easily located in all major cities, and smaller towns and villages.

CASH & CREDIT CARDS

The Czech crown (Koruna česká; Kč) has appreciated against other currencies in recent years and Prague is no longer a budget destination. Keep small change handy for use in public toilets, telephones and tram-ticket machines, and try to keep some small denomination notes for shops, cafes and restaurants. Changing larger notes from ATMs can be a problem.

Credit cards are widely accepted in petrol stations, midrange and top-end hotels, restaurants and shops.

EXCHANGING MONEY

Use ATMs or to change cash and get a cash advance on credit cards at the main banks. Beware of *směnárna* (private exchange offices), especially in Prague – they advertise misleading rates, and often charge exorbitant commissions or 'handling fees'. There is no black market for currency exchange, and anyone who offers to change money in the street is dodgy.

TIPPING

- **Bars** Leave small change as a tip
- **Restaurants** Optional, but increasingly expected in Prague; round the bill up the next 20Kč or 30Kč (5% to 10%)
- **Taxi drivers** As per restaurants

Post

The Czech Republic has a reliable postal service. Mail can be held at Prague Poste Restante, Jindřišská 14, 11000 Praha 1, Czech Republic.

Telephone

All Czech phone numbers have nine digits; dial all nine for any call, local or long distance. Buy phonecards from post offices and news-stands from 1000Kč.

Mobile-phone coverage (GSM 900) is excellent. If you're from Europe, Australia or New Zealand, your own mobile phone should be compatible. Purchase a Czech SIM card from any mobile-phone shop for around 500Kč (including 300Kč of calling credit). Local mobile phone numbers start with the following; 601 to 608 and 720 to 779. The Czech Republic's country code is ☎420.

Tourist Information

ABC Prague (www.abcprague.com) English-language news.

Czech Tourism (www.czechtourism.com) Official tourist information.

Czech.cz (www.czech.cz) Informative government site on travel and tourism, including visa requirements.

IDOS (www.idos.cz) Train and bus timetables.

Mapy (www.mapy.cz) Online maps.

Prague Information Service (www.praguewelcome.cz) Official tourist site for Prague.

Travellers with Disabilities

Ramps for wheelchair users are becoming more common, but cobbled streets, steep hills and stairways often make getting around difficult. Public transport is still problematic, but a growing number of trains and trams have wheelchair access. Major tourist attractions such as Prague Castle also offer wheelchair access. Anything described as *bezbarierová* is 'barrier free'.

Prague Integrated Public Transport (www.dpp.cz) See the 'Barrier Free' information online.

Prague Wheelchair Users Organisation (Pražská organizace vozíčkářů; ☎224 827 210; www.pov.cz, in Czech; Benediktská 6, Staré Město)

Visas

The Czech Republic is part of the Schengen Agreement, and citizens of most countries can spend up to 90 days in the country in a six-month period without a visa. For travellers from some other countries, a Schengen Visa is required; you can only do this from your country of residence. Check www.czech.cz for the latest information.

Getting There & Away

Located in the geographic heart of Europe, the Czech Republic is easily reached by air from key European hubs or overland by road or train from neighbouring countries.

Flights, tours and rail tickets can be booked online at www.lonelyplanet.com/travel_services.

Entering the Czech Republic

With an economy that depends heavily on tourism, the Czech Republic has wisely kept red tape to a minimum for foreign visitors. If you're travelling overland into the Czech Republic, or have already flown into a European hub like Frankfurt or Amsterdam, note that under the Schengen Agreement there's no border control between the Czech Republic and other member countries.

Air

Most international flights arrive in Prague, with Frankfurt, Amsterdam or Munich being the most relevant major European hubs if flying from Asia, Oceania or North America.

The Czech Republic's second city, Brno, receives flights regular flights from London. **Czech Airlines** (www.czechairlines.com) has a good safety record and is a member of the Skyteam airline alliance. International airports:

Prague-Ruzyně Airport (www.prg.aero)

Brno-Tuřany Airport (www.airport-brno.cz)

Land

The Czech Republic has border crossings with Germany, Poland, Slovakia and Austria.

BUS

Prague's main international bus terminal is Florenc bus station. The peak season for bus travel is mid-June to the end of September, with daily buses to major European cities. Outside this season, frequency falls to two or three a week. Neighbouring international destinations are listed below.

Between them, **Student Agency** (www.studentagency.eu), **Tourbus** (www.tourbus.cz) and **Eurolines** (www.elines.cz) cover services across Europe. Private shuttle buses also link Český Krumlov with Vienna, Linz and Salzburg. Bus services to/from Prague:

Berlin €29, 4½ hours, daily

Bratislava €14, 4¼ hours, several daily

Dresden €23, 2¼ hours, daily

Frankfurt €60, 7½ hours, daily

Košice €19.50, 10 hours, four daily

Munich €35, 5¼ hours, two daily

Vienna €24, 4½ hours, several daily

Warsaw 890Kč, 12 hours, three per week

Bus services to/from Brno:

Bratislava €10, two hours, several daily

Košice €15.50, seven hours, four daily

Krakow 702Kč, five hours, weekly

Vienna €8, two hours, several daily

Warsaw 1026Kč, 10 hours, weekly

CAR & MOTORCYCLE

In order to use Czech motorways, motorists need to buy a *nálepka* (motorway tax coupon), which are on sale at border crossings and petrol stations. See www.ceskedalnice. cz for more information. Drivers must also have their passport, vehicle registration papers and the 'green card' that shows they carry at least third-party liability insurance (see your domestic insurer about this).

TRAIN

International train tickets can be purchased online with **České Dráhy** (Czech Railways; www cd.cz). International trains arrive at Prague' main train station (Praha-hlavní nádraží or Praha hl. n.), or the outlying Holešovice (Praha Hol.) and Smíchov (Praha Smv.) stations, as well as Brno's main train station.

Inter-Rail (Zone D) passes are valid in the Czech Republic, and in 2009 the country became part of the Eurail network.

As well as those listed below, there are also services between České Budějovice and Linz, and from Olomouc to Warsaw and to Krakow. Train services to/from Prague:

Berlin 737Kč, five hours, daily

Bratislava 500Kč, 4¼ hours, several daily

Dresden 483Kč, 2¼ hours, several daily

Frankfurt 1245Kč, seven hours, two daily

Munich €35, six hours, two daily

Vienna 483Kč, five hours, several daily

Warsaw 477Kč, 8½ hours, two daily

Train services to/from Brno:

Bratislava 210Kč, 1½ hours, several daily

Vienna 229Kč, two hours, several daily

Getting Around

Air

The Czech Republic is compact and internal flights are limited. **Czech Airlines** (☎800 310 310; www.czechairlines.com) links Prague with Brno, Karlovy Vary, Ostrava and Brno.

Bicycle

The Czech Republic offers excellent opportunities for cycle touring and has many dedicated trails. See http://www.czech.cz/en/67105-cycling for information.

Cyclists should be careful as minor roads are often narrow and potholed. In towns, cobblestones and tram tracks can be a dangerous combination, especially after rain. Theft can be a problem so always lock up your bike.

It's easy to transport your bike on Czech trains. Purchase your train ticket and then take it with your bicycle to the train luggage office.

Bus

Within the Czech Republic, buses are often faster, cheaper and more convenient than trains. Many bus routes have reduced frequency (or none) at weekends. Buses occasionally leave early so get to the station at least 15 minutes before the official departure time. Check bus timetables and prices at www.idos.cz. Main bus companies:

CSAD (✆information line 900 144 444) The national bus company links cities and smaller towns.

Megabus (www.megabus.cz) Links Prague with Karlovy Vary, Brno and Plzeň.

Student Agency (www.studentagency.cz) Has destinations including Prague, Brno, České Budějovice, Český Krumlov, Karlovy Vary and Plzeň.

DECIPHERING THE TIMETABLES

» Crossed hammers means the bus runs on *pracovní dny* (working days; ie Monday to Friday only).
» A Christian cross means the bus runs on Sundays and public holidays.
» Numbers in circles refer to particular days of the week (1 is Monday, 2 Tuesday etc).
» *Jede* means 'runs'.
» *Nejede* means 'doesn't run'.
» *Jede denne* means 'runs daily'.
» *V* is 'on', *od* is 'from' and *do* is 'to' or 'until'.

Car & Motorcycle
DRIVING LICENCE
Foreign driving licences are valid for up to 90 days. Strictly speaking, licences that do not include photo identification need an International Driving Permit as well, although this rule is rarely enforced.

FUEL
Leaded petrol is available as *special* (91 octane) and *super* (96 octane), and unleaded as *natural* (95 octane) or *natural plus* (98 octane). The Czech for diesel is *nafta* or just *diesel*. *Autoplyn* (LPG gas) is available in every major town but at very few outlets.

HIRE
Small local companies offer better prices, but are less likely to have fluent, English-speaking staff. It's often easier to book by email than by phone. Typical rates for a Škoda Fabia are around 700Kč a day, including unlimited kilometres, collision-damage waiver and value-added tax (VAT). Bring your credit card as a deposit. A motorway tax coupon is included with most rental cars. Local operators in Prague:

Secco Car (✆220 802 361; www.seccocar.cz; Přístavní 39, Holešovice)

Vecar (✆224 314 361; www.vecar.org; Svato-vítská 7, Dejvice)

ROAD RULES
Driving is on the right hand side of the road, and road rules reflect the rest of Europe.
» A vehicle must be equipped with a first-aid kit and a red and white warning triangle.
» Using seat belts is compulsory.
» Drinking and driving is forbidden (the blood alcohol level is zero).
» Speed limits are 30km/h or 50km/h in built-up areas, 90km/h on open roads and 130km/h on motorways.
» Motorbikes are limited to 80km/h.

Police can hit you with on-the-spot fines of up to 2000Kč for speeding and other traffic offences (be sure to insist on a receipt).

Local Transport
Local transport is very affordable, well organised and runs from around 4.30am to midnight daily. Purchase tickets in advance from news-stands and vending machines. Validate tickets in time-stamping machines on buses and trams and at the entrance to metro stations.

Tours
Ave Bicycle Tours (www.bicycle-tours.cz) Cycle touring specialists.

E-Tours (www.etours.cz) Nature, wildlife and photography tours.

Greenways Travel Club (www.visitgreen ways.com) From cycling and walking to beer and wine, Czech glass and Czech music tours.

Top Bicycle (www.topbicycle.com) Biking and multisport tours.

Train
Czech Railways provides efficient train services to almost every part of the country. See www.idos.cz and www.cd.cz for fares and timetables.

TICKETS
The sales clerks at ticket counters outside of Prague may not speak English, so write down your destination with the date and time you wish to travel. If you're paying by credit card, let them know *before* they issue the ticket. Ticket categories:

EC (EuroCity) Fast, comfortable international trains, stopping at main stations only, with 1st- and 2nd-class coaches; supplementary charge of 60Kč; reservations recommended. Includes 1st-class only SC Pendolino trains that run from Prague to Olomouc, Brno and Ostrava, with links to Vienna and Bratislava.

Ex (express) As for IC, but no supplementary charge.

IC (InterCity) Long-distance and international trains with 1st- and 2nd-class coaches; supplement of 40Kč; reservations recommended.

Os *(osobní)* Slow trains using older rolling stock that stop in every one-horse town; 2nd-class only.

R *(rychlík)* The main domestic network of fast trains with 1st- and 2nd-class coaches and sleeper services; no supplement except for sleepers; express and *rychlík* trains are usually marked in red on timetables.

Sp *(spěšný)* Slower and cheaper than *rychlík* trains; 2nd class only.

Estonia

Includes »

Best Places to Stay

» Pädaste Manor (p375)

» Villa Hortensia (p354)

» Toomarahva Turismitalu (p362)

» Antonius Hotel (p366)

» Georg Ots Spa Hotel (p374)

Best Places to Eat

» nAnO (p356)

» Ö (p356)

» Altja Kõrts (p362)

» Sadhu Cafe (p375)

» Supelsaksad (p372)

Why Go?

These are heady days for Estonia. In only one generation this diminutive country has shaken off the dead weight of the Soviet era and turned its focus to the West, and to promises of a richer, shinier future. In recent years it's claimed EU membership and rather miraculously joined the eurozone, and now it's celebrating its return to the world stage: proud, independent, economically robust and tech-savvy.

And the world is tuning in to low-key, lovely Estonian charms, an irresistible blend of Eastern European and Nordic. Soaking up Tallinn's long white nights and medieval history, or exploring the country's island-studded coastline, are joys to be savoured. National parks provide plenty of elbow-room, quaint villages evoke a timeless sense of history, and uplifting song festivals celebrate age-old traditions.

The 20th century was full of twists and turns for Estonia, but it's now primped and primed and waiting to shine in the spotlight.

When to Go
Tallinn

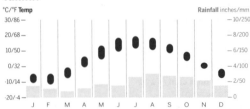

April–May See the country shake off winter's gloom.

June–August White nights, beach parties and loads of summer festivals.

December Christmas markets, mulled wine and long cosy nights.

Fast Facts

» **Area** 45,226 sq km

» **Capital** Tallinn

» **Telephone country code** 372

» **Emergency** 112 (ambulance and fire), 110 (police)

Exchange Rates

Australia	A$1	€0.72
Canada	C$1	€0.71
Japan	¥100	€0.82
New Zealand	NZ$1	€0.54
UK	UK£1	€1.12
USA	US$1	€0.69

Set Your Budget

» **Budget hotel room** €40

» **Two-course meal** €10-15

» **Museum entrance** €3-5

» **Beer** €2.50-3

» **Tallinn transport ticket** €1

Resources

» **VisitEstonia.com** (www.visitestonia.com)

» **Tallinn Tourism** (www.tourism.tallinn.ee)

» **Estonia Public Broadcasting News** (http://news.err.ee/)

» **Estonica** (www.estonica.org)

Connections

Estonia is well connected for visiting the neighbours. It's an easy northern addition to Eastern European roaming, as plenty of daily buses connect with destinations in Latvia and Lithuania. There's the option of following the white nights to Scandinavia – Tallinn has daily ferry connections to/from Stockholm and Helsinki. If you're hearing the siren call of Russia, nightly trains connect Tallinn and Moscow, and plenty of daily buses run between Tallinn or Tartu and St Petersburg.

ITINERARIES

Five days

Hit Tallinn at a weekend to get in your sightseeing and partying, then head east to Lahemaa National Park or southwest to the island of Saaremaa – two (or four) wheels will offer the chance to really explore.

Two weeks

There'll be time to explore Tallinn more deeply; a retreat to Lahemaa National Park or Saaremaa could also be on your agenda. If the weather's fine, opt for fun in the sun in Pärnu, then get back to nature at Soomaa National Park, and finish with a pub crawl with local students in Tartu.

Essential Food & Drink

» **Vana Tallinn** A syrupy, sweet liqueur of indeterminate origin, best served in coffee, over ice or in champagne. There's also a cream version.

» **Pork and potatoes** Prepared in a hundred different ways.

» **Verivorst** (blood sausage) – call it black pudding and it might sound more palatable.

» **Berries and mushrooms** Seasonal delights freshly picked from the forests – in summer and autumn, respectively.

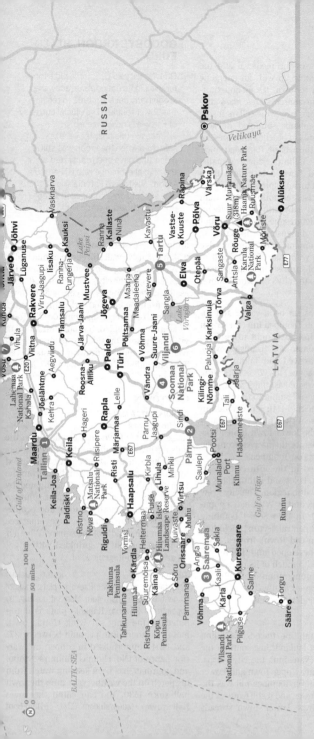

Highlights

1 Find medieval bliss exploring **Tallinn's Old Town** (p345), then unwind at leafy, lovely Kadriorg Park

2 Get sand in your shorts in **Pärnu** (p369), Estonia's summertime mecca

3 Escape to the island of **Saaremaa** (p374) for castles, coastlines and spas

4 Have a natural encounter worth writing home about in **Soomaa National Park** (p373)

5 Further your local education among the bars

and cafes of **Tartu** (p364), Estonia's second city

6 Let your hair down with 20,000 music lovers at **Viljandi Folk Music Festival** (p373)

7 Beat a retreat from Tallinn to chill out in rustic **Altja** (p362) in Lahemaa National Park

8 Wave to Russia from the castle in bordertown **Narva** (p363)

TALLINN

POP 400,000

Today's Tallinn fuses the medieval and the cutting edge to come up with an energetic new mood all of its own. It's an intoxicating mix of ancient church spires, glass-and-chrome skyscrapers, cosy wine cellars inside 15th-century basements, sun-filled Raekoja plats, and bike paths to beaches and forests – with a few Soviet throwbacks for added spice.

The jewel in Tallinn's crown remains its two-tiered Old Town, a 14th- and 15th-century jumble of turrets, spires and winding streets. Most tourists see nothing other than this cobblestoned labyrinth of intertwining alleys and picturesque courtyards, but Tallinn's modern dimension – its growing skyline, shiny shopping malls, cutting-edge art museum, the wi-fi that bathes much of the city – is a cool surprise and harmonious counterbalance to the city's old-world allure.

History

In 1219 the Danes set up a castle and installed a bishop on Toompea hill (the origin of the name Tallinn is thought to be from *Taani linn*, Estonian for 'Danish town'). German traders arrived and Tallinn joined the Hanseatic League in 1285, becoming a vital link between east and west. The Danes sold northern Estonia to the German knights and by the mid-14th century Tallinn was a major Hanseatic town. The merchants and artisans in the lower town built a fortified wall to separate themselves from the bishop and knights on Toompea.

Prosperity faded in the 16th century as Swedes, Russians, Poles and Lithuanians all fought over the Baltic region. The city grew in the 19th century and by WWI had a population of 150,000. In 1944 Soviet bombing destroyed several central sectors, including a small section on Old Town's fringes. After WWII, industry developed and Tallinn expanded quickly, with much of its population growth due to immigration from Russia. Politically and economically, Tallinn is the driving force of modern Estonia.

◉ Sights

Tallinn spreads south from the edge of Tallinn Bay on the Gulf of Finland. Just south of the bay is Old Town (Vanalinn), the city's heart. It divides neatly into Upper Town and Lower Town. Upper Town on Toompea hill was the medieval seat of power, and it still features the parliament buildings. Lower Town spreads

---

GOODBYE KROON, HELLO EURO

On 1 January 2011, Estonia bid a fond farewell to its national currency, the kroon (introduced in 1992 to replace the Soviet rouble). The official currency of Estonia is now the euro.

Prices in this chapter were researched when the kroon was still in place, and have been converted at the official exchange rate (€1 = 15.65 kroon). Visitors to Estonia should therefore expect some changes to listed prices as the euro settles in.

---

around the eastern foot of Toompea, and a 2.5km defensive wall still encircles much of it.

A belt of green parks around Old Town follows the line of the city's original moat defences. Radiating from this old core is New Town, dating from the 19th and early 20th centuries.

There are loads of sights inside Old Town to keep you occupied, but only a fraction of visitors make it outside the medieval town walls. Chart-topping drawcards outside Old Town include Kadriorg Park and KUMU art museum.

OLD TOWN

RAEKOJA PLATS & AROUND

Raekoja plats SQUARE

Raekoja plats (Town Hall Sq) has been the pulsing heart of Tallinn life since markets began here in the 11th century. It's ringed by pretty pastel-coloured buildings from the 15th to 17th centuries, and dominated by the Gothic town hall. Throughout summer, outdoor cafes implore you to sit and people-watch; come Christmas, a huge pine tree stands in the middle of the square. Whether bathed in sunlight or sprinkled with snow, it's always a photogenic spot.

Town Hall HISTORIC BUILDING

(www.tallinn.ee/raekoda; Raekoja plats; adult/student €4/2; ⊙10am-4pm Mon-Sat Jul-Aug, by appointment Sep-Jun) Raekoja plats is dominated by the only surviving Gothic town hall in northern Europe, built between 1371 and 1404. Immortalised in copper, the warrior figure of Old Thomas, Tallinn's symbol and guardian, has been keeping watch from his perch on the weathervane atop the town hall since 1530. You can climb the **town hall tower** (adult/student €3/1; ⊙11am-6pm

May–mid-Sep) for fine Old Town views. A tiny and atmospheric cafe, **Tristan ja Isolde**, is tucked inside on the ground level.

Town Council Pharmacy HISTORIC BUILDING
(Raeapteek; Raekoja plats 11; ☺10am-6pm Tue-Sat) The Town Council Pharmacy, on the northern side of Raekoja plats, is another ancient Tallinn institution; there's been a pharmacy or apothecary's shop here since at least 1422, though the present facade is from the 17th century.

Holy Spirit Church CHURCH
(adult/concession €1/0.50; ☺9am-5pm Mon-Sat May-Sep, 10am-3pm Mon-Fri Oct-Apr) Duck through the arch beside the Town Council Pharmacy into the narrow **Saiakang** (White Bread Passage), which leads to the striking 14th-century Gothic Holy Spirit Church. Its luminous blue-and-gold clock (on the facade, just to the right of the entry) is the oldest in Tallinn. The lavish carvings inside the church date from 1684.

VENE & AROUND

Vene STREET
Several 15th-century warehouses and merchant residences surround Raekoja plats, notably when heading towards the street of Vene (meaning 'Russian' in Estonian, and named for the Russian merchants who traded here). Vene is home to some gorgeous passageways and courtyards – the loveliest being **Katariina käik** (Vene 12), home to artisans' studios and a decent Italian restaurant, and **Masters' Courtyard** (Vene 6), a cobblestoned delight partially dating from the 13th century that's filled with craft stores and a sweet cafe and *chocolaterie*.

Tallinn City Museum MUSEUM
(www.linnamuuseum.ee; Vene 17; adult/student €3.20/1.90; ☺10am-6pm Wed-Mon Mar-Oct, to 5pm Nov-Feb) A medieval merchant's home houses the City Museum, which traces Tallinn's development from its beginnings through to 1940 with some quirky displays and curious artefacts.

PIKK & LAI

Pikk STREET
From the Holy Spirit Church you can stroll along Pikk (Long Street), which runs north to the **Great Coast Gate** – the medieval exit to Tallinn's port. Pikk is lined with the 15th-century houses of merchants and gentry, as well as the buildings of several old Tallinn guilds. Check out the fabulous sculpted facade of the 1911 **Draakoni Gallery** (Pikk 18).

Estonian History Museum MUSEUM
(www.eam.ee; Pikk 17) This museum is set in the 1440 building of the Great Guild, to which the most important merchants belonged. Closed at the time of research but due to re-open in mid-2011, the museum's exhibits feature Estonian history up to the 18th century, and contain ceramics, jewellery and archaeological delights. The branch of the museum dealing with Estonia's history from the 18th century onwards is outside the town centre, on the beachside promenade Pirita tee.

St Olaf's Church CHURCH
At the northern end of Pikk stands an important Tallinn landmark, the gargantuan St Olaf's Church (entry at Lai 50). Anyone unafraid of a bit of sweat should head up to the **observation tower** (adult/student €2/1; ☺10am-6pm Apr-Oct), halfway up the church's 124m structure; it offers the city's best views of Old Town. First built in the early 13th century, the church was once the world's tallest building (it used to tower 159m before several fires and reconstructions brought it down to its present size).

Former KGB headquarters HISTORIC BUILDING
(Pikk 59) Just south of St Olaf's is the former KGB headquarters, whose basement windows were sealed to conceal the sounds of interrogations.

Fat Margaret BASTION, MUSEUM
The Great Coast Gate is joined to Fat Margaret, a rotund 16th-century bastion that protected this entrance to Old Town. Inside the bastion is the **Maritime Museum** (www.meremuuseum.ee; Pikk 70; adult/student €3.20/1.60; ☺10am-6pm

---

TALLINN IN TWO DAYS

Get your bearings by heading to **Raekoja plats** to climb up the **town hall tower**. Follow this with an in-depth exploration of the streets down below – museums, shops, churches, courtyards, whatever takes your fancy. That night treat yourself to a medieval feast at **Olde Hansa** or modern Estonian cuisine at **Ö**.

On the second day, do what most tourists don't – step out of Old Town. Explore the neighbourhood of **Kadriorg**, with its old homes, sprawling park and superb museums, or consider a **cycling tour** with the folks from the Traveller Info Tent or City Bike.

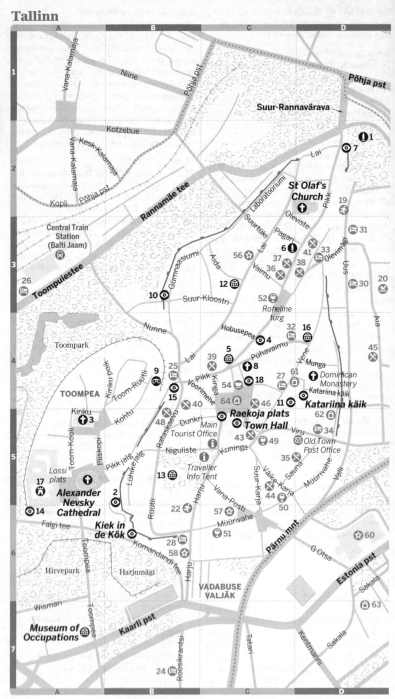

ESTONIA TALLINN

A B C D

Põhja pst

Niine

Suur-Rannavärava

Kotzebue

Lai

①1

⊚7

St Olaf's
Church

Laboratooriumi

Oleviste

Pikk

19

Pagari

①31

Central Train
Station
(Balti Jaam)

Suurtüki

Lai

6①

41

33

Olevimägi

Uus

26

Toompuiestee

Gümnaasiumi

Aida

56⊗

37

38

①30

20

Vaimu

36

10⊚

Suur-Kloostri

12🏛

52

Roheline
turg

Ara

Nunne

Hobusepea

4

32

16🏛

Toompark

39

5

Pühavaimu

Vene

Munga

45

Lai

9

25

Pikk

①8

27

61

Dominican
Monastery

Kiriku põik

Toom-Rüütli

Voorimehe

18

Katariina käik

TOOMPEA

15

Kinga

54

11⊚

Katariina käik

Kohtu

40

64

46

62

Kiriku

①3

Dunkri

Rataskaevu

Raekoja plats

Viru

34

Toom-Kooli

Pikk jalg

48

Main
Tourist Office

Town Hall

Old Town
Post Office

Piiskopi

Niguliste

Kuninga

43⊗

49

35

Sauna

Müürivahe

Valli

Lühike jalg

13🏛

Traveller
Info Tent

Harju

Suur-Karja

Väike-Karja

Lossi
plats

17

①

2

Vana-Posti

44

50

⊗14

Alexander
Nevsky
Cathedral

22⊗

57

60

Falgi tee

Rüütli

28🏛

Müürivahe

①51

Kiek in
de Kõk

Komandandi tee

58⊗

Pärnu mnt

Estonia pst

Hirvepark

Harjumägi

Harju

VADABUSE
VALJÄK

Sakala

Wismari

Toompea

63

Museum of
Occupations🏛

Kaarli pst

Roosikrantsi

Tatari

Sakala

Kentmanni

24🏛

A B C D

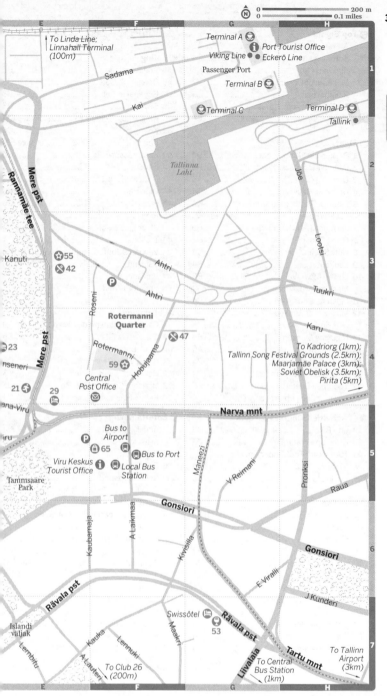

N

0   200 m
0   0.1 miles

Terminal A

To Linda Line;
Linnahall Terminal
(100m)

Port Tourist Office

Viking Line ● ● Eckerö Line

Passenger Port

Sadama

Terminal B

Kai

Terminal C

Terminal D

Tallink ●

Tallinna
Laht

Mere pst

Rannamäe tee

Joe

Lootsi

Kanuti

55

42

Ahtri

Roseni

Tuukri

Ahtri

Karu

Rotermanni
Quarter

47

Mere pst

Rotermanni

Hobujaama

To Kadriorg (1km);
Tallinn Song Festival Grounds (2.5km);
Maarjamäe Palace (3km);
Soviet Obelisk (3.5km);
Pirita (5km)

23

nseneri

59

Central
Post Office

21

29

ana-Viru

Narva mnt

iru

Bus to
Airport

65

Bus to Port

Viru Keskus
Tourist Office

Local Bus
Station

Maneezi

V Reimani

Pronksi

Raua

Tammsaare
Park

Gonsiori

Kaubamaja

A Laikmaa

Kivisilla

Gonsiori

Gonsiori

Rävala pst

E Viralli

Islandi
väljak

Swissôtel

Rävala pst

J Kunderi

Lembitu

Kauka

Lennuki

Maakri

53

Liivalaia

Tartu mnt

To Tallinn
Airport
(3km)

A Lauteri

To Club 26
(200m)

To Central
Bus Station
(1km)

Wed-Sun). The exhibits are ho-hum, but there are nice views from the rooftop.

Broken Line Monument   MONUMENT

Just beyond Fat Margaret stands the Broken Line monument, a black, curved slab in memory of victims of the *Estonia* ferry disaster. In September 1994, 852 people died when the ferry sank en route from Tallinn to Stockholm.

Museum of Applied Art & Design   MUSEUM

(Lai 17; adult/student €2.60/1.30; ⏱11am-6pm Wed-Sun) While Pikk was the street of traders, Lai, running roughly parallel, was the street of artisans, whose traditions are recalled in this museum. You'll find an excellent mix of historical and contemporary ceramics, glass, rugs, and metal- and leather-work.

Lower Town Wall   TOWN WALL

Suur-Kloostri leads to a long and photogenic stretch of the Lower Town Wall, which has nine towers along Laboratooriumi. Here, as well as at various points around the town wall, you can enter the towers.

NIGULISTE

Niguliste Museum   MUSEUM

(www.ekm.ee; Niguliste 3; adult/student €3.20/1.90; ⏱10am-5pm Wed-Sun) The Gothic St Nicholas' Church (Niguliste Kirik) is another of the city's medieval treasures. Dating from the 13th century, the church is now known as the Niguliste Museum and houses artworks from medieval Estonian churches. The acoustics are first-rate, and organ recitals are held here most weekends (4pm Saturday and Sunday; entry with museum ticket).

TOOMPEA

A regal approach to Toompea hill is through the red-roofed 1380 **Pikk jalg Gate Tower** at the western end of Pikk in Lower Town, and then heading uphill along Pikk jalg (Long Leg). Alternatively, a winding stairway connects Lühike jalg (Short Leg), off Rataskaevu, to Toompea.

Alexander Nevsky Cathedral   CHURCH

(Lossi plats; ⏱8am-8pm) The 19th-century Russian Orthodox cathedral greets you at the top of Toompea in all its onion-domed splendour. Orthodox believers still come here in droves, as do tourists who ogle the interior's mosaics and icons. The cathedral was built as a part of Alexander III's policy of Russification, and is sited strategically across from Toompea Castle, Estonia's traditional seat of power.

Toompea Castle   HISTORIC BUILDING

(Lossi plats) The Riigikogu (Parliament) meets in the pink baroque-style building

FANCY A VIEW?   351

Here's a run-down on the best places for a bird's-eye view of Tallinn.

» Fancy a freebie? **Toompea** has superb viewpoints on Kohtu and off nearby Toom-Kooli.

» Fancy a climb? Head up either the **town hall tower** or the tower of **St Olaf's church**.

» Fancy a coffee? On the 4th floor of the Solaris centre, **Komeet** (www.kohvikkomeet.cee; Estonia pst 9) has a dazzling array of cakes and a leafy view to Old Town.

» Fancy a cocktail? On the 30th floor of the Swissôtel, fancy-pants **Horisont Restaurant & Bar** (www.horisont-restoran.com; Tornimäe 3) offers outstanding panoramas (and prices to match).

» Fancy a sweat? Book a sauna at **Club 26** on the 26th floor of a hotel and with first-class city vistas.

opposite the Orthodox cathedral; it was an 18th-century addition. Nothing remains of the original 1219 Danish castle; three of the four corner towers of its successor, the Knights of the Sword's Castle, are still standing. The finest of these towers is the 14th-century **Pikk Hermann** (Tall Hermann) at the southwestern corner, from which the Estonian flag flies. A path leads down from Lossi plats through an opening in the wall to the **Danish King's Courtyard**, where in summer artists set up their easels.

Kiek in de Kök   TOWER

(☎644 6686; http://linnamuuseum.ee/kok/en; Komandandi tee; adult/student €4.50/2.60; ⏱10.30am-5pm Oct-Mar, to 6pm Tue-Sun Nov-Feb) Kiek in de Kök, a formidable cannon tower built in about 1475, houses a museum documenting the birth of Tallinn, its bastions and its military events. Its name is Low German for 'Peep into the Kitchen' – from the upper floors of the tower, medieval voyeurs could see into Old Town kitchens. Departing from the tower are tours that take in the **17th-century tunnels** connecting bastions, built by the Swedes to help protect the city (tours adult/student €5.75/3.20, bookings essential).

ROTERMANNI QUARTER

One of Tallinn's recent developments has seen the restoration and reinvigoration of the Rotermanni Quarter, a former factory complex that sits between Old Town and the passenger port. It's now home to offices and apartments, shops and restaurants, and a quirky collection of studios and galleries. In summer the Rotermanni väljak – the square behind the cinema – hosts a farmers market (Wednesday to Saturday) and a craft market (Sunday).

Dome Church   CHURCH
(Toomkirik; Toom-Kooli 6; ⏰9am-5pm Tue-Sun) Toompea is named after the Lutheran Dome Church, founded in 1233. There is actually no dome – the nickname is a corruption of the Estonian word *toom*, itself borrowed from the German word *Dom*, meaning cathedral. The austere interior features finely carved tombs and coats of arms from Estonia's noble families. From the Dome Church, follow Kohtu to the city's favourite **lookout** over Lower Town.

Museum of Occupations   MUSEUM
(www.okupatsioon.ee; Toompea 8; adult/student €1.90/1; ⏰11am-6pm Tue-Sun) This museum, just downhill from Toompea, has a worthwhile display about Estonia's 20th-century occupations. Photos and artefacts illustrate five decades of oppressive rule, under both the Nazis and the Soviets. Displays are good, but it's the videos (lengthy but enthralling) that leave the greatest impression – and the joy of a happy ending. Head to the basement to check out the graveyard of Soviet-era monuments.

KADRIORG
To reach the lovely, wooded **Kadriorg Park**, 2km east of Old Town along Narva mnt, take tram 1 or 3 to the last stop. As well as the museums outlined below, there are other, smaller museums in the park, plus a playground and a fine cafe.

Kadriorg Palace   ART MUSEUM
Kadriorg Park and its centrepiece, Kadriorg Palace (1718–36), were designed for Peter the Great's wife Catherine I (Kadriorg means 'Catherine's Valley' in Estonian). Kadriorg Palace is now home to the **Kadriorg Art Museum** (www.ekm.ee; Weizenbergi 37; adult/student €4.15/2.25; ⏰10am-5pm Tue-Sun May-

Sep, 10am-5pm Wed-Sun Oct-Apr). The 17th- and 18th-century foreign art is mainly unabashedly romantic, and the palace unashamedly splendid.

KUMU   ART MUSEUM
(Kunstimuuseum, Art Museum of Estonia; www.ekm.ee; Weizenbergi 34; adult/student €5.75/3.20; ⏰11am-6pm Tue-Sun May-Sep, 11am-6pm Wed-Sun Oct-Apr) KUMU opened in this futuristic Finnish-designed seven-storey building to rave reviews in early 2006, and in 2008 it won the title European Museum of the Year from the European Museum Forum. It's a spectacular structure of limestone, glass and copper, nicely integrated with the landscaping, and it contains the largest repository of Estonian art, plus constantly changing contemporary exhibitions. There's a cafe restaurant and gallery shop on-site.

TOWARDS PIRITA
Buses 1A, 8, 34A and 38 all run between the city centre and Pirita, stopping on Narva mnt near Kadriorg Park.

Pirita tee   PROMENADE
Jutting north of Kadriorg alongside the sea coast towards Pirita is Pirita tee, Tallinn's seaside promenade. Summer sunsets around midnight are particularly romantic from here, and it's a popular cycling and rollerblading area.

Tallinn Song Festival Grounds   AMPHITHEATRE
(Lauluväljak; Narva mnt) North of Kadriorg you come to Tallinn Song Festival Grounds, an impressive amphitheatre that hosts song festivals and big-name concerts. In 1988, 300,000 Estonians squeezed in for one songfest and publicly demanded independence during the 'Singing Revolution'.

Maarjamäe Palace   MUSEUM
This 1870s neo-Gothic 'palace' is home to the second branch of the **Estonian History Museum** (www.eam.ee; Pirita tee 56; adult/student €2.90/1.60; ⏰10am-5pm Wed-Sun); the first, dealing with pre-18th-century history, is in Old Town. This branch does a particularly good job of detailing the twists and turns of 20th-century Estonian history. There's a park outside featuring old Soviet statues.

Soviet obelisk   MONUMENT
(Pirita tee) Heading further north, you pass the foreboding Soviet obelisk, locally dubbed 'the Impotent's Dream'. It's the focal point of a 1960 Soviet war memorial that's now more crumbling than inspiring.

Pirita Yacht Club
YACHT CLUB

Just before Pirita tee crosses the Pirita River, a side road leads to Pirita Yacht Club and the Tallinn Olympic Yachting Centre, near the mouth of the river. This was the base for the sailing events of the 1980 Moscow Olympics.

Pirita beach
BEACH

North of the bridge is 3km-long, white-sand Pirita beach, which is *the* place to shed your clothes in Tallinn summertime. It's easily the city's largest and most popular beach; it's backed by wooded parkland that's popular for walking and cycling.

Pirita Convent
RUINS

(www.piritaklooster.ee; Kloostri tee; adult/student €1.30/0.65; ⊙10am-6pm Apr-May & Sep-Oct, 9am-7pm Jun-Aug, noon-4pm Nov-Mar) On the other side of Pirita tee from the beach are the ruins of the 15th-century Convent of St Birgitta, the perfect place for a ramble. The 10-day **Birgitta Festival** (www.birgitta.ee) sees atmospheric choral, opera and classical concerts staged here in August.

SOUTHWEST OF OLD TOWN

Tallinn Zoo
ZOO

(www.tallinnzoo.ee; Paldiski mnt 145; adult €3.20-5.75, child €1.90-2.90; ⊙9am-5pm Mar-Apr & Sep-Oct, 9am-7pm May-Aug, 9am-3pm Nov-Feb) About 4.5km southwest from Old Town, Tallinn Zoo boasts the world's largest collection of mountain goats and sheep (!), plus around 350 other species of feathered, furry and four-legged friends. Avoid Mondays, when some exhibits are closed. It's best reached by bus 22 or trolleybus 6.

Estonian Open-Air Museum
MUSEUM

(www.evm.ee; Vabaõhumuuseumi tee 12; adult €3-6, child €1.50-3; ⊙buildings 10am-6pm May-Sep, grounds 10am-8pm May-Sep, 10am-5pm Oct-Apr) North of the zoo is the Rocca al Mare neighbourhood and its open-air museum. Most of Estonia's oldest wooden structures, mainly farmhouses but also a chapel (1699) and a windmill, are preserved here. Every Saturday and Sunday morning from June to August there are folk song-and-dance shows; if you find yourself in Tallinn on Midsummer Eve, come here to witness the traditional celebrations, bonfire and all. There's also an old wooden tavern serving traditional Estonian cuisine (open year-round). Bus 21 runs here from the train station.

🏊 Activities

Water Parks

Water parks are big business in Estonia; the biggest in Tallinn is the **Kalev Spa Waterpark** (www.kalevspa.ee; Aia 18; 2½hr visit adult/family €9.60/25.90; ⊙6.45am-9.30pm Mon-Fri, 8am-9.30pm Sat & Sun), just outside Old Town. For serious swimming there's an Olympic-size indoor pool, but there are plenty of other ways to wrinkle your skin, including waterslides, jacuzzis, saunas and a kids' pool. There's also a gym and day spa.

Saunas

Saunas are an Estonian institution and come close to being a religious experience. If you're looking to convert, splurge at **Club 26** (☑631 5585; www.club26.ee; Liivalaia 33; per hr before/after 3pm €19.20/38.40; ⊙7am-10pm), on the 26th floor of the Radisson Blu Hotel Olümpia, with correspondingly outstanding views. There are two private saunas here, each with plunge pool and tiny balcony. Food and drink can be ordered to complete the experience; book online.

Beaches

The most popular beaches are at **Pirita** (p353) and **Stroomi** (4km due west of the centre, or a 15-minute ride on bus 40). You can hire rowing boats and canoes for exploring at **Pirita Rowboat Rental** (Kloostri tee 6, Pirita; per hr from €10; ⊙10am-10pm May-Sep), beside the bridge over the river.

Sea-kayaking

From June to August, **360° Adventures** (☑5555 8785; www.360.ee) offers twice-weekly guided kayaking trips giving you four hours out on Tallinn Bay (€30) and a new perspective on Tallinn's sights. No previous kayaking experience is required. The company also offers bog-walking excursions (see the website).

Ice-skating

Rug up warm to join the locals at the scenic outdoor ice rink, **Uisuplats** (www.uisuplats.ee; Harju; per hr €3.50-4.50; ⊙10am-10pm Nov-Mar).

👣 Tours

Traveller Info Tent
WALKING & CYCLING

(☑5554 2111; www.traveller.ee; Niguliste) Runs entertaining, good-value walking and cycling city tours – including a free, two-hour walking tour of the capital, departing at noon daily. Three-hour bike tours (€10) take in the town's well-known eastern attractions (Kadriorg, Pirita etc), or more offbeat areas to the west. There's also a pub crawl (€10, including drinks). From June to August, the tours run daily from the tent itself; the rest of the year they need to be booked in advance via email or phone (minimum three participants). Winter tours are weather dependent.

City Bike WALKING & CYCLING
(☎511 1819; www.citybike.ee; Uus 33) Has a great range of Tallinn tours, by bike or on foot, as well as tours to Lahemaa National Park. Two-hour cycling tours (€16) of the capital run year-round and cover 16km, heading out towards Kadriorg and Pirita.

EstAdventures SMALL TOURS
(☎5385 5511; www.estadventures.ee) A small company offering diverse, offbeat tours – four-hour walking tours of Tallinn (€15), plus full-day excursions further afield (€45) to Lahemaa, Haapsalu and Tartu. Operates May to September.

Tallinn City Tour BUS TOURS
(☎627 9080; www.citytour.ee; 24hr pass €16) Runs red double-decker buses that give you quick, easy, hop-on, hop-off access to the city's top sights. Buses leave from Mere pst, just outside Old Town.

✯ Festivals & Events
For a complete list of Tallinn's festivals, visit culture.ee (www.culture.ee) and the 'Experience' pages of Tallinn (www.tourism.tallinn.ee). Expect an extra-full calendar of events in 2011 as Tallinn celebrates its status as a European City of Culture; check Tallinn 2011 (www.tallinn2011.ee).

Big-ticket events include the following:

Jazzkaar MUSIC
(www.jazzkaar.ee) Jazz greats from around the world converge on Tallinn in mid-April for this two-week festival; there are smaller events in autumn and around Christmas.

Old Town Days HISTORY
(www.vanalinnapaevad.ee) Week-long festival in early June featuring dancing, concerts, costumed performers and plenty of medieval merrymaking on nearly every corner of Old Town.

Õllesummer MUSIC
(Beer Summer; www.ollesummer.ee) Popular ale-guzzling, rock-music extravaganza over four days in early July at the Song Festival Grounds.

Black Nights Film Festival FILM
(www.poff.ee) Films and animations from all over the world. Estonia's biggest film festival brings life to cold winter nights from mid-November to mid-December.

Estonian Song & Dance Celebration SONG & DANCE
(www.laulupidu.ee) Convenes every five years and culminates in a 30,000-strong traditional choir; due in Tallinn in 2014.

Baltica International Folklore Festival FOLK
(www.cioff.org) A week in June of music, dance and displays focusing on Baltic and other folk traditions, this festival is shared between Rīga, Vilnius and Tallinn; it's Tallinn's turn to play host again in 2013.

🛏 Sleeping
Old Town has the top lodgings, with plenty of atmospheric rooms set in beautifully refurbished medieval houses – though you'll pay a premium for them. Midrange and budget hotels are scarcer in Old Town; apartment-rental agencies have the best midrange deals. In recent times there's been an explosion of hostels competing for the attention of backpackers. Most of them are small, friendly and laid-back; they're largely found in Old Town, but few offer private rooms.

The website Tallinn (www.tourism.tallinn.ee) has a full list of options. Whatever your preference, be sure to book in advance in summer. As ever, look for good deals on the internet.

TOP CHOICE **Villa Hortensia** APARTMENTS €€
(☎504 6113; www.hoov.ee/villa-hortensia.html; Masters' Courtyard, Vene 6; apt s €38.30-76.70, d €51.50-102.25; @) Villa Hortensia is a small collection of apartments in the Masters' Courtyard, off Vene. This sweet, cobblestoned courtyard has been a labour of love for Jaan Pärn, architect turned jeweller (his studio shop acts as reception) and the man responsible for the restoration of the ancient buildings. There are six apartments here (the website has pics) – four split-level studio ones, with private bathroom, kitchenette, table and chairs and access to a shared communal lounge. The two larger apartments are the real treats, with balconies, TVs, kitchenettes and loads of character. This place offers unbelievable value in a superb location – book ahead.

Tallinn Backpackers HOSTEL €
(☎644 0298; www.tallinnbackpackers.com; Olevimägi 11; dm €9-13; @🐭) In a perfect Old Town location and staffed by backpackers who are more than happy to party with guests, this 26-bed place has a global feel and a roll-call of traveller-happy features: happy hours,

heap dinners, free wi-fi and internet, lockers, free sauna, snazzy bathrooms, bike rental and day trips to nearby attractions. The staff organise pub crawls and city tours that anyone can join, and a shuttle bus to Rīga. Private rooms are available at the offshoot **Viru Backpackers** (☑644 6050; 3rd fl, Viru 5; s/d/tw with shared bathroom €25/36/36/48), which has less atmosphere but a good central location; its only downside is the shortage of bathrooms.

Hotel Telegraaf
HOTEL €€€

(☑600 0600; www.telegraafhotel.com; Vene 9; s/d/ste from €119/139/259; P@🛜🛜🏊) This upmarket hotel, in a converted 19th-century former telegraph station, delivers style in spades. It boasts a spa and a small swimming pool, gorgeous black-and-white decor, a pretty courtyard, an acclaimed restaurant, and smart, efficient service. 'Superior' rooms are at the front of the house, with a little more historical detail (high ceilings, parquetry floors), but we prefer the marginally cheaper executive rooms, for their bigger proportions and sharper decor.

Old House Hostel & Guesthouse
GUESTHOUSES €

(☑641 1464; www.oldhouse.ee; Uus 22 & Uus 26; dm/s/tw without bathroom from €19/29/42; P@🛜) Although one is called a hostel, these twin establishments feel much more like cosy guest houses, and they're a long way from earning the 'party hostel' tag. Instead, they offer homey, old-world decor (think antiques, plants, lamps and bedspreads, with minimal bunks) to appeal to the more mature budgeteer. Dorms and private rooms are available in both (all bathrooms are shared); guest kitchen, living room, wi-fi and parking are quality extras.

Nordic Hotel Forum
HOTEL €€

(☑622 2900; www.nordichotels.eu; Viru väljak 3; €86-150; P@🛜🏊) The Forum shows surprising style and personality for a large, business-style hotel – witness the artwork on the hotel's facade and the trees on the roof. It stands out among its competitors for the facilities, laid on thick (including a lovely 'relaxation centre' with saunas and indoor pool); welcoming staff; and prime location.

Bern Hotel
HOTEL €€

(☑680 6630; www.bern.ee; Aia 10; s/d from €84/94; ✳@🛜) One of a rash of newer hotels on the outskirts of Old Town, Bern is named after the Swiss city to indicate 'hospitality and high quality'. It's nothing special from the

outside, but rooms are petite and modern, with great attention to detail for the price. Nice extras include robes and slippers, aircon, minibar, hairdryer and toiletries. Online deals can see rooms for under €60.

Hotel Schnelli
HOTEL €€

(☑631 0100; www.gohotels.ee; Toompuiestee 37; r €70-86; P@🛜) This modern hotel at the train station isn't just for train travellers. The block-boring building is home to small but fresh and functional rooms, and offers decent value a short walk from Old Town; rates include buffet breakfast, parking and wi-fi. Non-trainspotters should opt for a room in the Green Wing, with views to the park opposite and Old Town beyond; cheaper Blue Wing rooms overlook the station.

Euphoria
HOSTEL €

(☑5837 3602; www.euphoria.ee; Roosikrantsi 4; dm €8.90-14.40, d without bathroom €35.20; P@🛜) So laid-back it's almost horizontal, this backpacker hostel, just south of Old Town, has adopted some very '60s hippie vibes and given them a modern twist. It's a fun place to stay, with a sense of traveller community – especially if you like hookah pipes, bongo drums, jugglers, musos, artists and impromptu late-night jam sessions (pack earplugs if you don't).

Schlössle Hotel
HOTEL €€€

(☑699 7700; www.schloesslehotel.com; Pühavaimu 13/15; d from €150; @🛜) The individually designed rooms are a delight in this elegant, five-star medieval complex in the heart of Old Town.

Flying Kiwi
HOSTEL €

(☑5821 3292; www.flyingkiwitallinn.com; Nunne 1; dm €9-13.50, tw & d €23-40, tr with bathroom €40.50-51; @🛜) This relaxed, friendly hostel, newly purchased by a Kiwi couple, is not far from the train station. It's up two flights of stairs.

Apartment Agencies

The capital has dozens of apartments for rent – a great alternative for those who prefer privacy and self-sufficiency. Try the following agencies:

Ites Apartments
APARTMENTS €€

(☑631 0637; www.ites.ee; Harju 6; per night €58-130) Friendly and efficient bunch offering several apartments in Old Town and its surrounds. There are discounts for stays of more than one night, and car rental can be arranged.

Old House
APARTMENTS €€

(☑641 1464; www.oldhouse.ee; office at Uus 26; per night €69-249) As well as a guest house and hostel, Old House has 19 beautifully furnished apartments throughout Old Town, including two spectacular three-bedroom options.

 Eating

With headquarters in Old Town, Tallinn's restaurant scene has unbeatable atmosphere – whether you want to dazzle a date or just soak up the medieval digs al fresco, you'll find plenty of choices. There aren't too many bargains, however – expect the kind of prices you'd pay in any European capital. A word to the wise: lunchtime specials offer the best deals.

TOP CHOICE ### nAnO
CAFE €

(☑5552 2522; Sulevimägi 5; meals around €5; ⏱lunch Mon-Fri) There's no real sign to indicate you've found this place, nor are there firm hours, or a written menu. Instead, this is a whimsical world concocted by Beatrice, an Estonian model, and Priit, her DJ husband, who welcome guests into part of their home – rooms eclectically furnished with astounding colour and flair. Beatrice and Priit feed diners wonderfully fresh, home-style meals along the lines of herb-filled borsch, Russian-style pastries and pasta with in-season chanterelles or salmon. It's a treat for all the senses. Call ahead to check hours – at research time there was talk of opening for dinner too.

Ö
MODERN ESTONIAN €€€

(☑661 6150; Mere pst 6e; www.restoran-o.ee; mains €17-24) No, we can't pronounce it either, but award-winning Ö has carved a unique space in Tallinn's culinary world. With angelic chandelier sculptures, and charcoal-and-white overtones, the dining room is an understated work of art – as are the meals coming out of the kitchen. Ö harvests and promotes seasonal local produce, making sorbets from collected berries and smoking its own meats and fish. The result is something quite special; bookings are advised.

Olde Hansa
MEDIEVAL €€

(www.oldehansa.ee; Vana turg 1; mains €10-23) With peasant-garbed servers labouring beneath large plates of wild game in candlelit rooms, medieval-themed Olde Hansa is the place to indulge in a gluttonous feast. And if the medieval music, communal wooden tables, and thick aromas of red wine and roast meats sound a bit much, take heart – the chefs have done their research, produc-

ing historically authentic fare. It may sound a bit cheesy and touristy, but even the locals rate this place.

Vapiano
ITALIAN €

(Hobujaama 10; pizza & pasta €4-8) Choose your pasta or salad from the appropriate counter and watch as it's prepared in front of you. If it's pizza you're after, you'll receive a pager to notify you when it's ready. This is 'fast' food done healthy, fresh and cheap. The restaurant itself is big, bright and buzzing, with huge windows, high tables and shelves of potted herbs. There's a second branch inside the Solaris Centre.

Sfäär
INTERNATIONAL €€

(www.sfaar.ee; Mere pst 6E; mains €8-14) This new, warehouse-style space is populated by Tallinn's beautiful people enjoying the simple but high-quality menu (from warm trout salad to red curry and chicken), cocktails, funky decor and smooth tunes. But multi purpose Sfäär is not just a cafe–restaurant-bar – it's also a store, selling wine, clothes, homewares and the odd gourmet product.

Bonaparte Café
CAFE €

(Pikk 45; pastries €1, meals €2.90-8.30) Flaky croissants and raspberry mousse cake are just a few of the reasons why Bonaparte ranks as Tallinn's best patisserie. It's also a supremely civilised breakfast or lunch stop, with the likes of French onion soup and Niçoise salad on the menu. And the quiches – *très magnifique!*

Chedi
ASIAN €€€

(☑646 1676; www.chedi.ee; Sulevimägi 1; mains €12.50-24) If you can't get a booking at top Asian restaurants at home, console yourself at sleek, sexy Chedi. UK chef Alan Yau (of London's Michelin-starred Hakkasan and Yauatcha) consulted on the menu, and some of his trademark dishes are featured here. The pan-Asian food is exemplary – try the delicious crispy duck salad or sublime roasted silver cod.

Kompressor
PANCAKES €

(Rataskaevu 3; pancakes €2.60-3.70) Under an industrial ceiling you can plug any holes in your stomach with cheap pancakes of the sweet or savoury persuasion. The smoked cheese and bacon is a treat, but don't go thinking you'll have room for dessert. By night, this is a decent detour for a budget drink. It's low on aesthetics but high on value.

Von Krahli Aed
INTERNATIONAL €

(Rataskaevu 8; mains €4-10) You'll find more greenery on your plate at this rustic, plant-filled restaurant than at other eateries in Tallinn ('Aed' means Garden). The menu embraces fresh flavours and wins fans by noting gluten-, lactose- and egg-free options, and there are creative vegetarian choices too.

Vanaema Juures   TRADITIONAL ESTONIAN €€
(Rataskaevu 10/12; mains €8-16) Food just like your grandma used to make (if she was Estonian). 'Grandma's Place' rates as a top choice for traditional, homestyle Estonian fare. The antique-furnished, photograph-filled dining room has a formal air, and the menu has plenty of options aside from pork and sauerkraut.

Troika   RUSSIAN €€
(Raekoja plats 15; soup or pelmeni €5-6.30, mains €8.80-16.80) Tallinn's most cheerful Russian restaurant is an experience in itself. Head to the *trahter,* the somewhat cheesy, folksy country tavern (at ground level), for a plate of delicious *pelmeni* (Russian-style ravioli stuffed with meat), bliny or a bowl of borsch, or stop in for an ice-cold shot of vodka poured from on high.

Angel   GAY CAFE €
(Sauna 1; mains €4-10; ⊘5pm-2am Mon-Thu, 5pm-6am Fri & Sat, 5pm-1am Sun) One of Tallinn's most diverse crowds gathers at this 2nd-floor restaurant, upstairs from Tallinn's best gay nightclub. A loungelike feel provides a warm setting for the eclectic menu (salads, pastas and an unbeatable cheeseburger). Best of all, the kitchen stays open until late.

Pizza Grande   PIZZA €
(Väike-Karja 6; small pizzas & pasta €3.10-4.40) Local students vote this their favourite pizza spot. Enter from the courtyard and check the lengthy menu, where some left-of-centre topping combos (chicken, shrimps, blue cheese and peach?) stand alongside the tried-and-true.

Self-catering

There's a small, 24-hour grocery store, **Kolmjalg** (Pikk 11), in Old Town. For first-rate picnic fodder, stock up at **Bonaparte Deli** (Pikk 47; ⊘10am-7pm Mon-Sat). Otherwise, try **Rimi** (Aia 7), a supermarket on the outskirts of Old Town; or **Kaubamaja Toidumaailm** (Viru Keskus, Viru väljak 4), in the basement of Viru Keskus shopping centre.

Drinking
Bars & Pubs

Whether you seek a romantic wine cellar, a chic locals-only lounge or a raucous pub full of pint-wielding punters, you'll find plenty to choose from.

TOP CHOICE **Hell Hunt**   PUB
(Pikk 39) See if you can score a few of the comfy armchairs out the back of this trouper of the pub circuit. Beloved by discerning locals of all ages, it boasts an amiable air and reasonable prices for local-brewed beer and cider, plus decent pub grub. Don't let the menacing-sounding name put you off – it actually means 'Gentle Wolf'.

Drink Bar & Grill   PUB
(Väike-Karja 8) You know a bar means business when it calls itself Drink. This popular place takes its beer seriously (serving drops from all over the world), and offers plenty of beer-friendly accompaniments: cheap lunches, traditional pub grub, happy hour from 5pm to 7pm, big-screen sports, quiz nights. It's a fun place to do as the name suggests.

Clazz   LIVE MUSIC
(www.clazz.ee; Vana turg 2) Behind the cheesy name (a contraction of 'classy jazz') is an increasingly popular restaurant–bar, featuring live music almost every night (cover charge varies), and food served into the wee hours. Sunday is salsa night (with free dance classes starting at 8pm). On other nights it could be DJs or bands – jazz, blues, Brazilian etc (check the website).

Gloria Wine Cellar   WINE BAR
(Müürivahe 2) This mazelike cellar has a number of nooks and crannies where you can secrete yourself with a date and/or a good bottle of Shiraz. The dark wood, antique furnishings and flickering candles add to the allure.

Cafes

Tallinn's Old Town is so packed with absurdly cosy cafes that you can spend your whole trip wandering from one coffee house to the next. In most the focus is on coffee, tea, cakes and chocolates – there's usually considerably less effort put into savoury snacks. These places often stay open until midnight, dispensing post-dinner sweets and treats.

Kehrwieder   CAFE
(Saiakang 1; ⊘8am-midnight or 1am) Sure there's seating on Raekoja plats, but inside the city's cosiest cafe is where ambience is found in spades – you can stretch out on a couch, read by lamplight and bump your head on the arched ceilings.

Cafe-Chocolaterie de Pierre
CAFE

(Masters' Courtyard, Vene 6; ☺9am-10pm) Nestled inside the picturesque Masters' Courtyard, this snug, antique-filled cafe makes you feel like you're hiding away at your granny's place. It's renowned for its delectable handmade chocolates – they're impossible to resist.

Park Café
CAFE

(A Weizenbergi 22; ☺10am-8pm Tue-Sun) At the western entrance to Kadriorg Park is this sweet slice of Viennese cafe culture. If the sun's shining, the al fresco tables by the pond might just be our favourite place in town.

☆ Entertainment

Tallinn is small as capitals go and the pace is accordingly slower than in other big cities, but there's lots to keep yourself stimulated, whether in a nightclub, laid-back bar or concert hall. Buy tickets for concerts and main events at **Piletilevi** (www.piletilevi.ee; Viru Keskus, Viru väljak 4), which has a number of central locations. Events are posted on city centre walls and advertised on flyers found in shops and cafes.

Nightclubs

Club Hollywood
CLUB

(www.club-hollywood.ee; Vana-Posti 8; ☺from 11pm Wed-Sat) A multilevel emporium of mayhem, this is the nightclub that draws the largest crowds. Plenty of tourists and Tallinn's young party crowd mix it up to international and local DJs. Wednesday night is ladies' night (free entry for women), so expect to see loads of guys looking to get lucky.

Bon Bon
CLUB

(www.bonbon.ee; Mere pst 6e; ☺10pm-5am Fri & Sat) With enormous chandeliers and a portrait of Bacchus overlooking the dance floor, Bon Bon is renowned for its chichi attitude. It attracts a 25- to 30-something A-list clientele who want to party in style. Frock up to fit in.

Club Privé
CLUB

(www.clubprive.ee; Harju 6; ☺11pm-6am Wed-Sat) Tallinn's most progressive club is at its busiest on Saturdays. Global DJs attract a club-savvy local and foreign crowd after something more cutting-edge than the likes of Club Hollywood. Minimum age is 20 on Friday and Saturday.

Angel
GAY CLUB

(www.clubangel.ee; Sauna 1; ☺11pm-5am Fri & Sat) Open to all sexes and orientations, this mainly gay club is one of the liveliest spots in town. There is strict door control, however, and women may struggle to get in on busy nights. Check the website for party nights.

Performing Arts

The places listed tend to stage performances in Estonian only, save of course for modern dance shows or the rare show in English or other languages. *Tallinn in Your Pocket* (www.inyourpocket.com) lists major shows; other good sources of information are **culture.ee** (www.culture.ee), **Eesti Kontsert** (www.concert.ee) and **Eesti Teatri Agentuur** (www.teater.ee).

Estonia Concert Hall & National Opera
CONCERT HALL

(☎concert hall 614 7760, opera 683 1215; www.concert.ee & www.opera.ee; Estonia pst 4) The city's biggest concerts are held in this double-barrelled venue. It's Tallinn's main theatre, and also houses the Estonian national opera and ballet.

City Theatre
THEATRE

(Tallinna Linnateater; ☎665 0800; www.linnateater.ee; Lai 23) The most beloved theatre in town always stages something memorable. Watch for its summer plays on an outdoor stage or in different Old Town venues.

Cinemas

Films are shown in their original language, subtitled in Estonian and Russian. Night-time and weekend tickets cost around €4.15 to €4.80 (daytime sessions are slightly cheaper).

Katusekino
OUTDOOR CINEMA

(www.katusekino.ee; Viru Keskus, Viru väljak 4; ☺May-Sep) In the warmer months, a fun outdoor cinema is set up on the rooftop of Viru Keskus shopping centre. It screens an eclectic list (cult classics, as well as interesting new releases). Screen times depend on sunset – anything from 9pm (September) to 11pm (July) – but food and drinks are available from 6pm.

Artis
ARTHOUSE CINEMA

(www.kinoartis.ee; Estonia pst 9) Inside the new Solaris Centre but somewhat tricky to find, this arthouse cinema shows European, local and independent productions.

Solaris Kino
CINEMA

(www.cinamon.ee; Estonia pst 9) Inside the new Solaris Centre, with mostly mainstream offerings.

Coca-Cola Plaza
CINEMA

(www.forumcinemas.ee; Hobujaama 5) Modern 11-screen cinema playing the latest Hollywood releases. Located behind the post office.

🔒 Shopping

Inside Old Town, dozens of small shops sell Estonian-made handicrafts, linen, leather-bound books, ceramics, jewellery, silverware, stained glass and objects carved from limestone, or made from juniper wood. Look for signs for *käsitöö* (handicrafts). These are all traditional Estonian souvenirs – as is a bottle of Vana Tallinn, of course. In summer a **souvenir market** is set up daily on Raekoja plats.

Katariina Gild   HANDICRAFTS
(Katariina käik, Vene 12) This photogenic laneway is home to a number of artisans' studios where you can happily browse and potentially pick up some beautiful pieces, including stained glass, ceramics, textiles, patchwork quilts, hats, jewellery and leather-bound books.

Masters' Courtyard   HANDICRAFTS
(Vene 6) Rich pickings here, with the courtyard home not only to a cosy cafe–*chocolaterie* but also small stores selling quality ceramics, jewellery, knitwear, candles, and wood and felt designs.

Knit Market   KNITWEAR
(Müürivahe) Along the Old Town wall there are a dozen or so vendors praying for cool weather and selling handmade linens, scarves, sweaters, mittens, beanies and socks.

Solaris Centre   SHOPPING MALL
(www.solaris.ee; Estonia pst 9; ⊙9am-11pm) A newcomer to Tallinn's shopping scene, Solaris hosts a handful of boutiques, an excellent bookstore, popular restaurants, and both mainstream and arthouse cinemas.

Viru Keskus   SHOPPING MALL
(www.virukeskus.com; Viru väljak 4; ⊙9am-9pm) Tallinn's showpiece shopping mall, aka Viru Centre, lies just outside Old Town. It's home to mainstream fashion boutiques, a great bookstore (Rahva Raamat, with two quality on-site cafes), and a tourist information desk. In summer there's a rooftop cinema. The bus terminal for local buses is in the basement.

ℹ️ Information

Discount Cards

Tallinn Card (www.tallinncard.ee; 1-/2-/3-day card €24/28/32) Offers free rides on public transport, admission to museums, free excursions and discounts at restaurants (cheaper children's cards are available). It can be purchased from the information desks of the Tallinn tourist information centre and from a number of hotels.

Internet Access

Tallinn is flooded with wi-fi, but if you're not packing a laptop you'll find the city light on internet cafes. Most hostels and hotels will offer a computer for guests to use, or try the following:

Bookingestonia.com (2nd fl, Voorimehe 1; per hr €3) Booking agency with computers; hidden just off Raekoja plats.

Estonian National Library (Tõnismägi 2) Free access, but some bureaucracy involved.

Metro Internet (basement, Viru Keskus, Viru väljak 4; per hr €1.60) By the bus terminal under Viru Keskus.

Media

Tallinn in Your Pocket (www.inyourpocket.com) The king of the region's listings guides has up-to-date information on everything to do with arriving, staying and having fun in Tallinn and other cities in Estonia. Its booklets are on sale at bookshops or can be downloaded free from its website.

Medical Services

Apteek 1 (Aia 7; ⊙9am-8.30pm Mon-Fri, 9am-8pm Sat, 9am-6pm Sun) One of many well-stocked *apteek* (pharmacies) in town.

East Tallinn Central Hospital (☑622 7070, emergency department 620 7040; Ravi 18) Has a full range of services and a 24-hour emergency room.

First-Aid hotline (☑697 1145) English-language advice on treatment, hospitals and pharmacies.

Money

Foreign-currency exchange is available at any large bank *(pank)*, transport terminals, exchange bureaux, the post office and major hotels, but check the rate of exchange. For better rates, steer clear of the small Old Town exchanges. Banks and ATMs are widespread.

Tavid (Aia 5) Reliably good rates. A night-time exchange window is open 24 hours, but rates aren't as good as during business hours.

Post

Stamps can be purchased from any kiosk in town.

Central post office (Narva mnt 1) Entrance beside Nordic Hotel Forum.

Old Town post office (Viru; ⊙10am-6pm Mon-Fri, 10am-4om Sat & Sun) Small branch in Old Town.

Telephone

You can buy chip cards from news stands to use for local and international calls at any of the blue phone boxes scattered around town. Otherwise, post offices, supermarkets, phone-company stores (in the shopping centres) and some kiosks sell cheap mobile-phone starter kits with prepaid SIM cards (from €3.20).

Tourist Information

Tallinn tourist information centre (☑645 7777; www.tourism.tallinn.ee; cnr Kullassepa & Niguliste; ☺9am-5pm Mon-Fri, 10am-3pm Sat Oct-Apr, 9am-6pm or later Mon-Fri, 10am-5pm Sat & Sun May-Sep) A block south of Raekoja plats, the main tourist office has a full range of services. Note there are also information desks at the port (Terminal A), and inside Viru Keskus shopping centre. None of these centres books accommodation.

Traveller Info Tent (www.traveller-info.com; Niguliste; ☺9am-9pm or 10pm Jun-Aug) Stop by this fabulous source of information, set up by young locals in a tent opposite the official tourist information centre. It produces an invaluable map of Tallinn with recommended places, dispenses lots of local tips, keeps a 'what's on' board that's updated daily, and operates entertaining, well-priced walking and cycling tours.

Travel Agencies

Booking Estonia (☑5618 3909; www.bookingestonia.com; 2nd fl, Voorimehe 1) Hidden just off Raekoja plats, this small, helpful agency can book bus, train and ferry tickets (no commission), and help arrange accommodation and car rental. Also offers luggage storage and internet access (per hour €3).

Union Travel (☑627 0621; Lembitu 14) Close to the Radisson Blu Hotel Olümpia. Can help arrange visas to Russia, but these take 10 working days to process and there are restrictions on who can apply outside their country of residence. It's best to arrange Russian visas in your home country, prior to travelling.

ⓘ Getting There & Away

Air

For information on international flights to Estonia, see p382. Year-round, **Avies Air** (U3; ☑630 1370; www.avies.ee) flies daily from Tallinn to the island of Hiiumaa, while **Estonian Air** (OV; ☑640 1163; www.estonian-air.ee) connects Tallinn and Saaremaa, and Tallinn and Tartu.

Tallinn airport (TLL; ☑605 8888; www.tallinn-airport.ee) is just 4km southeast of the city centre on Tartu mnt.

Boat

FINLAND A fleet of ferries carries more than two million people annually across the 85km separating Helsinki and Tallinn. There are dozens of crossings made every day (ships two to 3½ hours; hydrofoils approximately 1½ hours). Note that in high winds or bad weather, hydrofoils are often cancelled; they operate only when the sea is free from ice, while larger ferries sail year-round.

All companies provide concessions, allow pets and bikes (for a fee) and charge higher prices for peak services and weekend travel. Expect to pay around the price of an adult ticket extra to take a car. There's lots of competition, so check the companies for special offers and packages.

Operators include the following:

Eckerö Line (☑664 6000; www.eckeroline.ee; Terminal A) Sails back and forth once daily year-round (adult one-way €19 to €23, three to 3½ hours).

Linda Line (☑699 9333; www.lindaliini.ee; Linnahall Terminal) Small, passenger-only hydrofoils up to seven times daily late March to late December (adult €19 to €45, 1½ hours).

Tallink (☑640 9808; www.tallinksilja.com; Terminal D) At least five services daily in each direction, year-round. The huge *Baltic Princess* takes 3½ hours; newer high-speed ferries take two hours. Adult prices cost from €26 to €44.

Viking Line (☑666 3966; www.vikingline.ee; Terminal A) Operates a giant car ferry, with two departures daily (adult €22 to €39, 2½ hours).

SWEDEN **Tallink** (☑640 9808; www.tallinksilja.com) sails every night between Tallinn's Terminal D and Stockholm, via the Åland islands (cabin berth from €144, 16 hours). Book ahead.

Bus

For bus information and advance tickets for Estonian and international destinations, go to the **Central Bus Station** (Autobussijaam; ☑12550; Lastekodu 46), about 2km southeast of Old Town. Tram 2 or 4 will take you there, as will bus 17, 23 or 23A.

Ecolines (☑614 3600; www.ecolines.net) and **Eurolines** (☑680 0909; www.luxexpress.eu) have offices at the bus station, but you can easily book online, or **Bookingestonia.com** (☑5618 3909; www.bookingestonia.com; 2nd fl, Voorimehe 1) in Old Town will book and issue your bus tickets for no commission.

Ecolines connects Tallinn with several cities in central and eastern Europe. Lux Express, the Eurolines operator within the Baltic countries, has direct services connecting Tallinn with Rīga (from €10.50, 4½ hours, eight or nine daily) and Vilnius (from €26.40, nine to 11 hours, seven daily via Rīga). Buses leave Tallinn for St Petersburg eight or nine times daily (from €22, seven to nine hours), passing through bordertown Narva en route. Lux Express offers different classes of buses – the most expensive have free hot drinks and wi-fi and plush leather seats.

The useful website **BussiReisid** (www.bussireisid.ee) has times, prices and durations for all national bus services.

Car & Motorcycle

There are 24-hour fuel stations at strategic spots within the city, and on major roads leading to and from Tallinn.

Your hotel can often arrange car rental. Many companies have their office at the airport and will deliver a car to you.

Advantec (☑520 3003; www.advantage.ee; Tallinn airport) Cars from €38 per day (cheaper for longer rentals).

Bulvar (☑503 0222; www.bulvar.ee; Regati pst 1) From €25 per day (good deals for longer rentals).

Hertz (www.hertz.ee) city centre (☑611 6333; Ahtri 12); Tallinn airport (☑605 8923; Tallinn Airport)

Train

The **Central Train Station** (Balti Jaam; www.baltijaam.ee, in Estonian; Toompuiestee 35) is on the northwestern edge of Old Town, a short walk from Raekoja plats via Nunne, or three stops on tram 1 or 2, heading north from the Mere pst stop.

Train travel is not as popular as bus travel in Estonia, so domestic routes are quite limited (as are international options).

There are no rail connections to Riga, Vilnius or St Petersburg; however, an overnight train runs every evening in either direction between Moscow and Tallinn (€121 in a four-berth compartment, 15 hours) operated by **GO Rail** (☑631 0044; http://tickets.gorail.ee).

ℹ Getting Around

To & From the Airport

Bus 2 runs every 20 to 30 minutes (6am to around 11pm) from A Laikmaa, next to Viru Keskus; the bus stop is opposite, not out front of, the Tallink Hotel. From the airport, bus 2 will take you to the centre. Tickets are €1.60 from the driver (or cheaper from a kiosk); journey time depends on traffic but rarely takes more than 20 minutes.

A taxi between the airport and the city centre should cost about €7.50 to €8.

To & From the Ferry Terminals

Tallinn's sea-passenger terminal is at the end of Sadama, a short, 1km walk northeast of Old Town. Bus 2 runs every 20 to 30 minutes between the bus stop by Terminal A and A Laikmaa in the city centre; if you're heading to the terminal, the bus stop is out the front of the Tallink Hotel. Also from the heart of town (around the Viru Keskus transport hub), trams 1 and 2, and bus 3 go to the Linnahall stop, by the Statoil Petrol Station, five minutes' walk from terminals A, B and C, and the Linda Line terminal.

Terminal D is at the end of Lootsi, better accessed from Ahtri; bus 2 services the terminal (the same bus route that services terminal A and the airport).

A taxi between the city centre and any of the terminals will cost about €5.

Bicycle

As well as offering city cycling and walking tours, **City Bike** (☑511 1819; www.citybike.ee; Uus 33; rental per hr/day/week €2.30/13/51.10) can take care of all you need to get around by bike, within Tallinn, around Estonia or throughout the Baltic region.

Public Transport

Tallinn has an excellent network of buses, trams and trolleybuses that usually run from 6am to midnight. The major local bus station is on the basement level of Viru Keskus shopping centre; local buses may also terminate their route on the surrounding streets, just east of Old Town. All local public transport timetables are online at **Tallinn** (www.tallinn.ee).

The three modes of local transport all use the same ticket system. Buy *piletid* (tickets) from street kiosks (€0.96, or a book of 10 single tickets for €6.39) or from the driver (€1.60). Validate your ticket using the machine or hole puncher inside the vehicle – watch a local to see how this is done. One-/three-/10-day paper tickets are available for €4.40/7.35/13.10, but can only be bought from kiosks. The Tallinn Card (p359) gives you free public transport in the city.

Taxi

Taxis are plentiful in Tallinn. Oddly, taxi companies set their own rates, so flag fall and per-kilometre rates vary from cab to cab – prices should be posted in each taxi's right rear window. If you merely hail a taxi on the street, there's a chance you'll be overcharged. To save yourself the trouble, order a taxi by phone: try **Krooni Takso** (☑1212, 638 1212) and **Reval Takso** (☑621 2111).

NORTHEASTERN ESTONIA

This region has received much less attention from tourists than more popular destinations such as Pärnu and Tartu, and shows a different side to Estonia. As you head east from Lahemaa, the vast majority of the population is Russian-speaking, which adds another flavour to the Estonian cultural mosaic, and some places feel like Soviet relics.

Lahemaa National Park

The perfect country retreat from the capital, Lahemaa takes in a stretch of coast deeply indented with peninsulas and bays, plus 475 sq km of pine-fresh forested hinterland. Visitors are well looked after: there are cosy guesthouses, restored manor houses, remote camping grounds along the sea and an extensive network of pine-scented forest trails.

◉ Sights & Activities

There is an unlimited amount of sightseeing, hiking, cycling and boating to be done here; remote islands can also be explored. The park has several well-signposted nature trails and cycling paths winding through it. The small coastal towns of Võsu, **Käsmu** and (to a lesser extent) **Loksa** are popular seaside spots in summer. Käsmu is a particularly enchanting village, one of Estonia's prettiest.

Lahemaa also features historic manor houses. Park showpiece **Palmse Manor** (www. palmse.ee; adult/concession €4.80/3.20; ⊙10am-6pm or 7pm), next to the visitors centre, was once a wholly self-contained Baltic German estate, while the pink-and-white neoclassical **Sagadi Manor** (www.sagadi.ee; adult/concession €2.60/1.30; ⊙10am-6pm May-Sep, by appointment Oct-Apr) was built in 1749. There are also other manor houses at **Kolga** and **Vihula** – Vihula's is now part of a 'country club' featuring activities, a spa, restaurants and pricey accommodation (www.vihulamanor.com).

🛏 Sleeping & Eating

Palmse Manor and Sagadi Manor have good sleeping and eating options on the estates, while the fishing village of Altja offers a rural idyll.

ALTJA

TOP CHOICE ⟩ **Toomarahva Turismitalu**

CAMPING, GUESTHOUSE **€**

(☑325 2511; www.toomarahva.ee; Altja; campsites per person €3, r without bathroom €38.40, apt €64; 🛜) A farmstead with thatch-roofed wooden outhouses, and a garden full of flowers and sculptures, this gem of a place offers a gorgeous taste of rural Estonia. There's a yard for camping, a barn full of beds serving as a summer dorm for groups, plus rooms in converted stables (the 'apartment' has kitchen facilities). There is a rustic sauna and bikes for rent. Ülle, the friendly owner, also offers catering. Signage is minimal – it's located opposite the yard of the Altja Kõrts.

Altja Kõrts TRADITIONAL INN **€€**
(Altja; mains €4.15-12.15) Set in an old wooden farmhouse, this rustic place serves delicious plates of home cooking. Don't be deterred by the menu's first page, listing crisp pig's ears and black pudding as starters. Read on for more appetising options like juniper-grilled salmon, or pork roulade flavoured with horseradish and herbs. End on a high note with fresh blueberry pie (seasonal).

SAGADI

Sagadi Manor Hotel & Restaurant

HOTEL, RESTAURANT **€€**

(☑676 7888; www.sagadi.ee; dm €16, s/d from €57.50/76.70; @🛜) With its whitewashed exterior and hanging flower baskets, this hotel on the Sagadi estate offers a cheerful welcome. On the ground floor are fresh new rooms opening onto small patios and a courtyard. Upstairs rooms are older and marginally cheaper. Sagadi also has a 35-bed hostel in the old steward's house. The hotel's 2nd-floor **restaurant** (mains €4-16) offers meals ranging from a club sandwich to baked rabbit stew. Bike rental is available.

ℹ Information

Lahemaa National Park visitor centre (☑329 5555; www.lahemaa.ee; ⊙9am-6pm or 7pm daily mid-Apr–mid-Oct, 9am-5pm Mon-Fri mid-Oct–mid-Apr) is in Palmse, 7km north of Viitna in the park's southeast, next door to Palmse Manor. Here you'll find the essential map of Lahemaa, as well as information on accommodation, hiking trails, island exploration and guide services.

ℹ Getting There & Away

Hiring a car is a good way to reach and explore the areas inside the park; alternatively you can take a tour from Tallinn (see p354 for some tour operators). **City Bike** (☑511 1819; www.citybike. ee; Uus 33, Tallinn) runs a minibus tour of Lahemaa (€49) that takes in Palmse, Sagadi, Altja, Võsu and Käsmu villages. It runs daily in summer and four times a week from mid-October to mid-May. If you feel like getting closer to nature, it also offers bus transport to the park and supply of a bike and maps for self-guided exploration (€49). Talk to the staff about itinerary building and transfers if you fancy spending a few days discovering the park by bike.

Otherwise, for public transport exploration you'll need patience and plenty of time up your sleeve. The best starting point for buses to destinations within the park is the town of Rakvere, about halfway between Tallinn and Narva. Regular buses connect Rakvere with Tallinn (€5.50, 1½ hours, 20 per day). From Rakvere buses run to the park

Narva & Around

POP 67,000

Estonia's easternmost town is separated from Ivangorod in Russia only by the thin Narva River and is almost entirely populated by Russians. Although the most outstanding architecture was destroyed in WWII, Estonia's third-largest city is an intriguing place to wander, as you'll find no other place in Estonia quite like it. The centre has a melancholy, downtrodden air; the prosperity evident in other parts of the country is harder to find here (though it does exist in some pockets, most notably the brash shopping centres along Tallinna mnt). Narva is a place that will have you scratching your head at times: is it a Russian city on the wrong side of the border? Is it Estonia (and Europe's) easternmost point, or Russia's westernmost town?

◎ Sights

Narva Castle   CASTLE

Restored after WWII, imposing Narva Castle (Peterburi mnt), guarding the Friendship Bridge over the river to Russia, dates from Danish rule in the 13th century. It faces Russia's matching Ivangorod Fortress across the river, creating a picturesque face-off that's best captured from the park below the **Swedish Lion monument**, behind the Narva Hotel at Puškin 6. The castle houses the **Narva Museum** (www.narvamuuseum.ee; adult/concession €3.80/2.60; ⊙10am-6pm, closed Mon & Tue Sep-May).

Narva-Jõesuu   BEACH RESORT

About 13km north of Narva is the resort of Narva-Jõesuu, popular since the 19th century for its long golden-sand beach backed by pine forests. There are impressive early 20th-century wooden houses and villas here, as well as spa hotels. It's a popular spot for holidaying Russians after some quality beach time.

🛏 Sleeping & Eating

King Hotel   HOTEL €€

(☑357 2404; www.hotelking.ee; Lavretsovi 9; s/d from €37/47; @�) Not far north of Narva's town centre (and with a few similarly priced sleeping and eating options in the immediate vicinity) is Narva's best hotel choice, with snug modern rooms and an excellent on-site **restaurant** (mains €6.60-18). For something

different, try the lamprey (a local fish from the Narva River).

Pansionaat Valentina   GUESTHOUSE €

(☑357 7468; www.valentina.ee; Aia 49, Narva-Jõesuu; r €25.60-51.10; @�) Behind the big Meresuu Spa & Hotel in Narva-Jõesuu, metres from the beach, is this handsome, salmon-coloured guesthouse offering rooms and cottages in immaculate grounds. It's family friendly, with plenty of facilities, including bike rental, tennis courts, sauna, barbecue and cafe. Be sure to admire the breathtaking intricacy of the historic villa right next door.

Castell   RESTAURANT €€

(Narva Castle; Peterburi mnt; mains €9.90-17.90) Inside the castle grounds, this medieval-styled restaurant-bar offers up a big menu of dubiously titled dishes ('Mystery of the River Depths', 'Bravery of the Military Field' etc).

❶ Information

The extremely efficient **tourist information centre** (☑356 0184; http://tourism.narva.ee; Puškini 13; ⊙10am-6pm Mon-Fri, 10am-4pm Sat & Sun mid-May–mid-Sep, 9am-5.30pm Mon-Fri mid-Sep–mid-May) is in the city centre; it has an ATM and currency exchange as neighbours. It's a few minutes' walk from the Estonia–Russia border crossing.

❶ Getting There & Away

Narva is 210km east of Tallinn on the road to St Petersburg, which is a further 130km away. Around 20 daily buses travel between Tallinn and Narva (€8.30 to €11.50, three to four hours), and one train (€7.40, 3¾ hours) runs daily. There are also up to 10 daily Tartu–Narva buses (€7 to €10.20, 2½ to 3½ hours). Buses to St Petersburg (from Tallinn and Tartu) and night trains from Tallinn to St Pete stop in Narva to pick up passengers. The bus and train stations are located together at Vaksali 25, opposite the Russian Orthodox Voskresensky Cathedral. Walk north up Puškini to the castle (500m) and the centre.

Bus 31 runs about hourly to connect Narva with Narva-Jõesuu (€1, 20 minutes), as do numerous *marshrutky* (minibuses) without set timetables.

SOUTHEASTERN ESTONIA

Set with rolling hills, picturesque lakes and vast woodlands, the southeast sings with some of Estonia's prettiest countryside. It also contains one of the country's most important cities: the vibrant university centre of Tartu.

Tartu

POP 102,000

If Tallinn is Estonia's head, Tartu may well be its heart (and possibly its university-educated brains, too). Tartu lays claim to being Estonia's spiritual capital – locals talk about a special Tartu *vaim* (spirit), created by the time-stands-still, 19th-century feel of many of its wooden-house-lined streets, and by the beauty of its parks and riverfront.

Small and provincial, with the Emajõgi River flowing through it, Tartu is Estonia's premier university town, with students making up nearly one-fifth of the population. This injects a boisterous vitality into the leafy, historic setting and grants it a surprising sophistication for a city of its size.

Tartu was the cradle of Estonia's 19th-century national revival and it escaped Sovietisation to a greater degree than Tallinn. Today visitors to Estonia's second city can get a more authentic depiction of the rhythm of Estonian life than in its glitzier cousin to the north (and accompanied by far fewer tourists, too). In addition to galleries and cafes, there are good museums here; the city is also a convenient gateway to exploring southern Estonia.

⊙ Sights & Activities

Raekoja plats   MAIN SQUARE

At the town centre on Raekoja plats is the **town hall** (1782–89), topped by a tower and weathervane, and fronted by a fountain and statue of students kissing under an umbrella – an apt, light-hearted symbol of Tartu. At the other end of the square is the wonderfully skew-whiff building housing the **Tartu Art Museum** (Raekoja plats 18; adult/student €2.20/1; ⊙noon-6pm Wed-Sun). In between are loads of cafes and al fresco tables.

Tartu

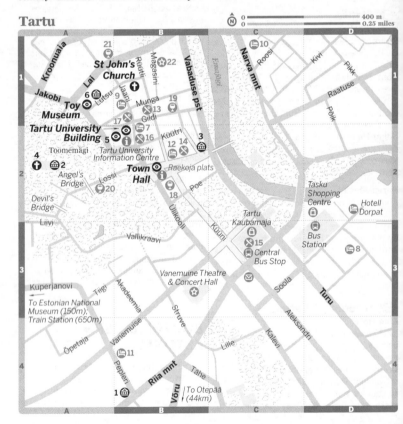

Tartu University
UNIVERSITY

The city's university was founded in 1632 by the Swedish king; the grand, neoclassical main **university building** (www.ut.ee; Ülikooli 18) dates from 1804. It houses the **University Art Museum** (€1.30; ⊙11am-5pm Mon-Fri) and entertaining **Student's Lock-Up** (€0.65; ⊙11am-5pm Mon-Fri), where 19th-century students were held for their misdeeds.

St John's Church
CHURCH

(Jaani Kirik; Jaani 5; ⊙10am-6pm Tue-Sat) North of the university stands the magnificent Gothic St John's Church, which features elaborate brickwork and dates back to at least 1323. It's noteworthy for its rare terracotta sculptures in niches around the main portal. Climb the 135 steps of the 30m-high **observation tower** (adult/child €1.60/0.95) for a great bird's-eye view of Tartu.

Toomemägi
PARK

Rising to the west of Raekoja plats is the splendid Toomemägi (Cathedral Hill), landscaped in the manner of a 19th-century English park and perfect for a stroll. The 13th-century Gothic Tartu **cathedral** (Toomkirik) at the top was rebuilt in the 15th century, despoiled during the Reformation in 1525, and partly rebuilt in 1804–07 to accommodate the university library, which is now the **Museum of University History** (adult/student €1.60/1; ⊙11am-5pm Wed-Sun).

Estonian National Museum
MUSEUM

(www.erm.ee; Kuperjanovi 9; adult/student €1.30/1, admission free Fri; ⊙11am-6pm Tue-Sun) As the major repository of Estonia's cultural heritage, Tartu has an abundance of first-rate museums. Among them is the absorbing Estonian National Museum – small, sweet and proud (much like the country itself), it traces the history, life and traditions of the locals.

KGB Cells Museum
MUSEUM

(Riia mnt 15b; adult/student €1.30/0.65; ⊙11am-4pm Tue-Sat) The former KGB headquarters now houses this sombre and highly worthwhile museum. Chilling in parts, it gives a fascinating rundown of deportations during the Soviet era and life in the gulags. Entrance is on Pepleri.

TOP CHOICE Toy Museum
MUSEUM

(www.mm.ee; Lutsu 8; adult/child €1.90/0.30;) The best place to pass a rainy few hours is in the enchanting Toy Museum, showcasing dolls, model trains, rocking horses, toy soldiers and tons of other desirables dating back a century or so. It's all geared to be nicely interactive – exhibits in pull-out drawers, toys to play with – and there's a kids' playroom too. The adjacent courtyard house is home to fun characters and props from Estonian animated films. Down the road is the affiliated **Theatre House** (www.teatrikodu.ee; Lutsu 2; adult/child €1/0.65;

Tartu

⊙11am-6pm Wed-Sun), a newly restored children's theatre (performances are usually in Estonian). In the basement is a small, sweet museum showcasing theatre puppets of the world. Have a coin ready for the amazing animation as you enter.

✦ Festivals & Events

Tartu regularly dons its shiniest party gear and lets its hair down – good events to circle in your calendar include the following. Check out **Kultuuriaken** (http://kultuuriaken.tartu.ee) for more.

Tartu Ski Marathon SPORTS
(www.tartumaraton.ee) Tartu hosts this 63km race in mid-February, drawing around 4000 competitors to the region's cross-country tracks. The same organisation hosts a range of sporting events (such as cycling road races, mountain-bike races and running races) in and around Tartu throughout the year.

Tartu Student Days STUDENT CELEBRATIONS
(www.studentdays.ee, in Estonian) Catch a glimpse of modern-day student misdeeds at the end of April, when they take to the streets to celebrate term's end. A second, smaller version occurs in mid-October.

Hansa Days Festival HISTORY
(www.hansapaevad.ee) Crafts, markets, family-friendly performances and more commemorate Tartu's Hanseatic past over three days in mid-July.

tARTuFF FILM
(www.tartuff.ee) For one week in August, a big outdoor cinema takes over Raekoja plats. Screenings (with arthouse leanings) are free, plus there are docos, poetry readings and concerts.

🛏 Sleeping

TOP CHOICE **Antonius Hotel** HOTEL €€
(☑737 0377; www.hotelantonius.ee; Ülikooli 15; s/d/ste from €75/93/245; 🛜) Opened in 2009, Antonius has brilliantly raised the bar for Tartu's top-end accommodation. Sharing the same owners as Pärnu's Ammende Villa, this 16-room boutique hotel sits plumb opposite the university main building and is loaded with antiques and period features, from the library with fireplace to the suites with antique stoves. Breakfast is served in the vaulted cellar (which by night is a romantic restaurant); the summertime terrace is delightful. Service is first-class.

Tartu Student Village Hostels
STUDENT RESIDENCES €
(☑742 7608; www.tartuhostel.eu; s/d €22.40/32; 🛜) Narva dorm (Narva mnt 27); Pepleri dorm (Pepleri 14) These student residences offer outstanding value in prime central locations – Pepleri is south of the river, Narva opposite parklands north of the city centre. The Narva option has five two-room apartments, each with its own living room, bathroom and kitchenette. Pepleri's standard rooms are smaller, minus the living room, but larger apartments are available (for €51). Narva has a sauna for hire, while Pepleri has a laundry and a pub on-site. Advance reservations are a must.

Terviseks Backpackers HOSTEL €
(☑565 5382; terviseksbackpackers@gmail.com; top fl, Raekoja plats 10; dm/r from €15/30; @🛜) In a brand-new, fully renovated location smack in the heart of town, this true backpackers refuge (run by a Brit and a Canadian) offers dorms, private rooms, shiny new facilities and lots of switched-on info about the cool places in town. You couldn't be better placed for a chilled-out good time.

Tampere Maja GUESTHOUSE €€
(☑738 6300; www.tamperemaja.ee; Jaani 4; s/d/tr/q from €40/60/88/110; @🛜) Maintained by the Finnish city of Tampere (Tartu's sister city), this cosy guesthouse in the town's old quarter features six warm, light-filled guestrooms ranging in size. Breakfast is included, and each room has cooking facilities; two-room suites sleep up to four. And it wouldn't be Finnish if it didn't offer an authentic sauna (open to non-guests).

Hotel Tartu HOTEL €€
(☑731 7728; www.tartuhotell.ee; Soola 3; budget s/d/tr €32/32/48, s/d €48/74; @🛜) In a handy location across from the bus station and shiny new Tasku shopping centre, this hotel offers rooms from the Ikea school of decoration – low-frills and modern. The 'hostel' is actually six spotless, older-style hotel rooms (shared bathrooms in the corridor) sleeping three. Reception wins brownie points for having laptops on loan for guests to check their emails.

✕ Eating & Drinking

The most central **supermarket** (⊙9am-10pm Mon-Sat, 9am-7pm Sun) is in the basement of the Tartu Kaubamaja shopping centre.

Tsink Plekk Pang ASIAN €€
(Küütri 6; dishes €4.20-19) Behind Tartu's funkiest facade (look for the stripy paintwork) and set over three floors is this cool Chinese-fla-

voured restaurant–lounge, named after the zinc buckets suspended from the ceiling as lampshades. You'll need time to peruse the huge, veg-friendly menu – there are plenty of well-priced noodles and soups, plus a decent Indian selection and even a handful of Japanese dishes. Or simply stop by to enjoy drinks with a DJ-spun soundtrack on weekends.

La Dolce Vita ITALIAN €€
(Kompanii 10; pizza & pasta €5-8.50, mains €6-16) Thin-crust pizzas come straight from the wood-burning oven at this cheerful, family-friendly pizzeria. It's the real deal, with a big Italian menu of bruschetta, pizza, pasta, gelati etc and classic casual decor (red-and-white checked tablecloths, Fellini posters – tick).

University Café CAFE €
(Ülikooli Kohvik; Ülikooli 20; mains €3.50-12.50; ⊙cafeteria 8am-7pm Mon-Fri, 10am-4pm Sat & Sun, cafe noon-11pm Mon-Thu, noon-1am Fri & Sat, noon-8pm Sun) Some of the most economical meals in town are waiting for you at the ground-floor cafeteria, which serves up decent breakfasts and a simple daytime buffet (per 100g €0.60 to €0.75). Upstairs is a labyrinth of elegantly decorated rooms, both old-world grand and cosy, where artfully presented dishes are served.

Crepp CAFE €
(Rüütli 16; crepes €2.60-3.20) Locals seem to love this place, and its warm, stylish decor belies its bargain-priced crepes (of the sweet or savoury persuasion, with great combos like cherry-choc and almonds). Upstairs and open in the evening, **Trepp** (⊙7pm-2am Mon-Thu, 7pm-3pm Sat & Sun) is a popular watering hole, also offering meals (and the all-important happy hour from 7pm to 9pm).

Püssirohukelder PUB €€
(Lossi 28; mains €4-17) Set in a cavernous old gunpowder cellar under a soaring, 10m-high vaulted ceiling, this is both a boisterous pub and a good choice for meaty meals (lots of pork options). When the regular live music kicks in later in the night (sometimes with a cover charge), you'll find the older crowd withdrawing to the more secluded wine cellar, which serves tapas-style snacks.

❶ Information
Post office (Riia 4)

Tartu in Your Pocket (www.inyourpocket.com) More great info from this listings guide; available in bookshops or online.

Tartu tourist information centre (☑744 2111; www.visittartu.com; town hall, Raekoja plats; ⊙9am-6pm Mon-Fri, 10am-5pm Sat, 10am-3pm Sun mid-May–mid-Sep, 9am-5pm Mon-Fri, 10am-2pm Sat mid-Sep–mid-May) This friendly office has local maps and brochures, and loads of other city info. It can also book accommodation and tour guides, sell you souvenirs and get you online (free internet access available).

❶ Getting There & Away
From the **bus station** (☑12550; Turu 2), daily buses run to/from Tallinn (€8 to €10, 2½ to 3½ hours) about every 15 to 30 minutes from 6am to 9pm. Four or five daily trains also make the journey (€6.70, 2½ to three hours).

Tartu is the main hub for destinations in south and southeastern Estonia, and has frequent connections with all other towns, including some nine buses a day to Pärnu (€9 to €10, 2½ to 3½ hours).

There are two daily buses connecting Tartu with St Petersburg (from €21.40, 7½ hours) – one involves a change of bus in Narva.

Otepää
POP 2100

The small hilltop town of Otepää, 44km south of Tartu, is the centre of a scenic area beloved by Estonians for its hills and lakes, and hence its endless opportunities for sports – hiking, cycling and swimming in summer, and cross-country skiing in winter.

◉ Sights
Church CHURCH, MUSEUMS
Otepää's pretty 17th-century church is on a hilltop about 300m northeast of the bus station. It was in this church in 1884 that the Estonian Students' Society consecrated its new blue, black and white flag, which later became the flag of independent Estonia. The former vicar's residence (across the road from the church) now houses two **museums**, one dedicated to the story of the flag and the other to local skiing.

Linnamägi HILL
The tree-covered hill south of the church is Linnamägi (Castle Hill), a major stronghold from the 10th to 12th centuries. There are traces of old fortifications on top and good views of the surrounding country.

Pühajärv LAKE
The best views are along the shores of the 3.5km-long Pühajärv (Holy Lake), just southwest of town. A 12km nature trail and a bike path encircle the lake, making it a lovely spot

STUDENT LIFE IN TARTU

The world over, students gravitate to cheap meals and booze, and Tartu is no different. Many of the cafes on Raekoja plats cater to impoverished students with great-value weekday lunch deals for around €2.50 (check out **Sõprade Juures** at number 12, with large/small daily dishes for €3.10/2.10). In the evening, down cheap beer (a half-litre for around €1.60) alongside students at dive bars like tiny basement **Möku** (Rüütli 18) and industrial-chic **Zavood** (Lai 30). Other popular drinking spots include **Illegaard** (Ülikooli 5), a laid-back pub where you're likely to encounter foreign students studying in Tartu, and the incomparable **Genialistide Klubi** (www.genklubi.ee; behind Lai 37) – an all-purpose 'subcultural establishment' that encompasses music, cinema, theatre, cafe, library, stores – be sure to check it out (enter from Magasini). For more tips on tapping into local student life, the staff at Terviseks Backpackers are generally in the know.

for a walk. It's a 30-minute (2.3km) walk from Otepää township (via Pühajärve tee) to the northern tip of the lake, where there's a walk to a picturesque **beach park** that's popular with summer swimmers; rowboats can be hired. The lake was blessed by the Dalai Lama and a small monument on the eastern shore commemorates his visit in 1991.

🏃 Activities

It would be a shame not to take advantage of some of the outdoor activities the region has to offer. To rent bikes, rollerblades, skis and snowboards, or to take a bike or canoe tour, contact **Fan Sport** (☑507 7537; www.fansport. ee), which has three offices inside the larger hotels in Otepää. **Toonus Pluss** (☑505 5702; www.toonuspluss.ee) specialises in canoeing trips in the area; tailor-made trips can combine canoeing with hiking and mountain biking. Ask at the tourist office for more options – there's everything from golf to snowtubing or snowmobile safaris.

🛏 Sleeping & Eating

Low season here is April to May and September to November; at this time hotel prices are about 10% to 15% cheaper.

Bernhard Spa Hotel　　　　　HOTEL €€
(☑766 9600; www.bernhard.ee; Kolga tee 22a; s/d weekdays €67/80, weekends €80/99; @🛜🏊)
Tucked away in a private setting, this handsome hotel offers balconies and forest views from all rooms. There's a good on-site restaurant and a beautifully appointed spa; the *pièce de résistance* is the small, heated outdoor pool – a delight in winter as snow falls.

Edgari　　　　　　　　　GUESTHOUSE €
(☑766 6550; karnivoor@hot.ee; Lipuväljak 3; r per person €19.20; 🛜) A good-value place to stay right in town, this guesthouse has a mix of

hostel-style rooms (shared bathroom and kitchen, communal lounge), plus studio apartments with kitchenette and private bathroom. Downstairs is a tavern and small food shop.

Pühajärve Spa Hotel　　　　　HOTEL €€
(☑766 5500; www.pyhajarve.com; Pühajärve tee; s/d weekdays €53/67, weekends €61/77; @🛜🏊)
In a plum lakeside location and with lovely sprawling grounds, this is the best-equipped place in town: there's a day spa, indoor pool, bowling alley, gym, tennis courts and bike rental. It's a pity the rooms are so tired and dreary, however. Still, there are good eating options – best of all is the **pub** (mains €3.80-9.60); catch a few rays on its outdoor terrace, or shoot some pool inside. Also check out the views from the cafe tower.

ℹ Information

The point where Valga mnt and Tartu mnt meet is the epicentre of the town, with the bus station here, alongside the **tourist information centre** (☑766 1200; www.otepaa.ee; Tartu mnt 1; ⊙10am-5pm Mon-Fri, 10am-4pm Sat & Sun mid-May–mid-Sep, 10am-5pm Tue-Fri, 10am-4pm Sat mid-Sep–mid-May).

Behind the tourist info centre is the triangular main 'square', Lipuväljak; in this area you'll find the main town services.

ℹ Getting There & Away

Buses connect Otepää with Tartu (€2.20 to 3.20, 40 minutes to 1¼ hours, at least 10 daily) and Tallinn (€3.20, 3½ hours, one daily).

WESTERN ESTONIA

As well as a tourist-magnet coastline come summer, the western half of the country houses Estonia's most popular resort town, sweet country villages, a vast national park and a handful of islands – developed or remote and windswept, take your pick.

Pärnu

POP 44,000

Local families, young party-goers, and German and Finnish holidaymakers join together in a collective prayer for sunny weather while strolling the golden-sand beaches, sprawling parks and picturesque historic centre of Pärnu (*pair*-nu), Estonia's premier seaside resort.

Come summer, the town acts as a magnet for party-loving Estonians – in these parts, its name alone is synonymous with fun in the sun (one hyperbolic local described it to us as 'Estonia's Miami'!). Yet youth and bacchanalia aren't the only spirits moving through town. Most of Pärnu is actually quite docile, with leafy streets and expansive parks intermingling with turn-of-the-century villas that reflect the town's past as a resort capital of the Baltic region. Older visitors from the Baltics, Finland and Eastern Europe still visit, seeking rest, rejuvenation and Pärnu's vaunted mud treatments.

⊙ Sights & Activities

Pärnu Beach   BEACH
The wide, golden-sand beach and Ranna pst, the beachside avenue whose buildings date from the early 20th century, are among Pärnu's finest attractions. Note the handsome 1927 neoclassical **Mudaravila** (Ranna pst 1), a symbol of the town's history. The legendary mud baths that once operated here are closed, awaiting restoration.

A curving path stretches along the sand, lined with fountains and park benches perfect for people-watching. The beach itself is littered with volleyball courts and tiny changing cubicles. Back from the sand, a park holds plenty of picnic tables.

From June to August you can rent bikes from **Tõruke Rattarent** (502 8269; cnr Ranna pst & Supeluse; bike per hr/day/week €2.70/10/43). For €1 they'll deliver a bike to you, year-round.

Veekeskus   WATER PARK
(445 1166; www.terviseparadiis.ee; Side 14; day ticket adult/concession €19/13; ⊙10am-10pm) At the far end of the beach, Estonia's largest water park, Veekeskus, beckons with pools, slides, tubes and other slippery fun. It's a big family-focused draw, especially when bad

weather ruins beach plans. It's part of the huge Tervise Paradiis spa hotel complex.

Rüütli   HISTORIC STREET
The main thoroughfare of the historic centre is Rüütli. Just off the main street is the **Red Tower** (Punane Torn; Hommiku 11), the city's oldest building, which dates from the 15th century; despite its name, it's actually white. A handicrafts market sets up inside and nearby.

Parts of the 17th-century Swedish moat and ramparts remain at the western end of Rüütli; the tunnel-like **Tallinn Gate** (Tallinna Värav), which once marked the main road to Tallinn, pierces the point where the rampart meets the western end of Kuninga.

🛏 Sleeping

In summer it's well worth booking ahead; outside of high season you should be able to snare yourself a good deal. Prices listed below are for high season (websites list off-season rates, which can be up to 40% lower).

Netti   GUESTHOUSE €€
(516 7958; www.nettihotel.ee; Hospidali 11-1; ste €77-103; 🐾) Anni, your host at Netti, is a ray of sunshine, and her three-storey guesthouse, comprising four two-room suites, positively gleams under her care. The suites sleep two to four, have some kitchen facilities and are bright and breezy (reminiscent of the '80s). The downstairs sauna area is a lovely place to unwind after a hard day at the beach.

Hommiku Hostel   GUESTHOUSE €€
(445 1122; www.hommikuhostel.ee; Hommiku 17; dm/s/d €19.20/38.30/57.50; 🐾) Hommiku is far more like a hotel than a hostel (except for its prices). This modern place has handsome rooms with private bathrooms, TV and kitchenettes; some also have old beamed ceilings. It's in a prime in-town position, with good eateries as its neighbours.

Inge Villa   GUESTHOUSE €€
(443 8510; www.ingevilla.ee; Kaarli 20; s/d €70.30/86.30; 🐾) In a prime patch of real estate not far back from the beach you'll find lovely Inge Villa, a 'Swedish–Estonian villahotel'. Its 11 rooms are simply decorated in calming tones with Nordic minimalism at the fore. The garden, lounge and sauna seal the deal. Closed November to February.

Ammende Villa   HOTEL €€€
(447 3888; www.ammende.ee; Mere pst 7; r/ste from €180/242; 🐾) If money's no object, this is where to spend it. Class and luxury abound in this exquisitely refurbished 1904

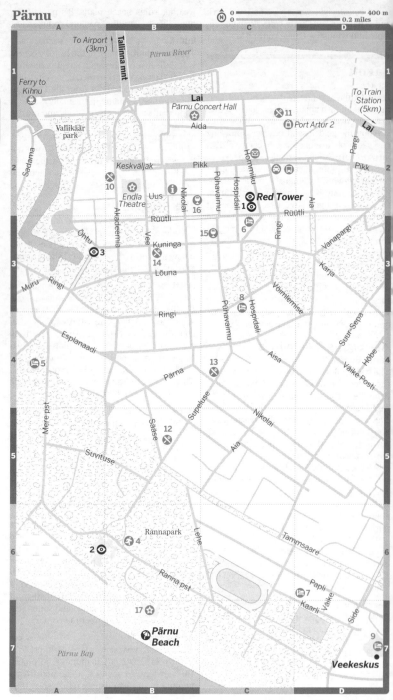

art nouveau mansion, which lords it over handsomely manicured grounds. The gorgeous exterior is matched by an elegant lobby, individually antique-furnished rooms and top-notch service.

Camping Konse　　　CAMPING, GUESTHOUSE **€**
(☑5343 5092; www.konse.ee; Suur-Jõe 44a; campsites €4 plus per person €4, r without/with bathroom €39/55; @☏) Perched on a spot by the river only 1km east of Old Town (off Lai), Konse offers campsites and a variety of rooms (half with private bathroom, half with shared facilities, all with kitchen access). It's not an especially charming spot but there is a sauna, and bike and rowboat rental. Open year-round.

✕ Eating & Drinking

The most central supermarket is **Port Artur Toidukaubad** (☺9am-10pm) inside the Port Artur 2 complex, off Pikk and opposite the bus station.

TOP CHOICE **Supelsaksad**　　　CAFE **€**
(cnr Supeluse & Nikolai; meals €5-11) The street of Supeluse is lined with lovely old wooden villas, and this one houses a gorgeously colourful cafe – what your granny's place might have looked like if she was prone to bold colours and a riot of stripes and prints. The menu holds an appealing mix of wraps, salads and pastas, and, if you eat all your veggies, make a beeline for the

bountiful cake display. Drop by in the evening for a glass of wine on the terrace.

Si-si　　　ITALIAN **€€**
(Supeluse 21; pizza/pasta €4.80-8.30, mains €8.90-17.20) Beachside dining in Pärnu is disappointingly bland, but a walk up Supeluse presents appealing options, including this Italian restaurant–lounge. Inside is smart white-linen dining, outside is a stylishly relaxed terrace. There's a good selection of gourmet pizzas and the all-important tiramisu.

Trahter Postipoiss　　　RUSSIAN **€€**
(Vee 12; mains €5.40-20.50) This 19th-century postal building houses a rustic tavern, with excellent Russian cuisine, a convivial crowd and imperial portraits watching over the proceedings. The spacious patio opens during summer, and there's live music at weekends. Opt for the signature 'pork chop Postipoiss' – loaded with onions, bacon and dill pickles and served with a shot of vodka.

Ammende Villa　　　RESTAURANT **€€**
(☑447 3888; Mere pst 7; cafe meals €4-10, restaurant mains around €17.50; ☺breakfast 7-10am Mon-Fri, 8-11am Sat & Sun) Non-guests can get a taste of life at this art nouveau gem by joining in the breakfast buffet (€13) – a splendid spread of salmon, fresh fruit and Champagne (bookings advised). Otherwise, various salons and the beautiful garden terrace are great spots to dine, or you can simply stop by for a glass

of bubbles and a cheese platter. To help unleash your inner sophisticate, weekly jazz concerts are held on the lawn in summer.

Mõnus Margarita　　　　　TEX-MEX €€
(Akadeemia 5; mains €4-16) Big, colourful and decidedly upbeat, as all good Tex-Mex places should be – but if you're looking for heavy-duty spice, you won't find it here. Fajitas, burritos and quesadillas all score goals, plus there are margaritas and tequilas for the grown-ups and a play area for the kids.

Piccadilly　　　　　CAFE-WINE BAR €
(Pühavaimu 15) Piccadilly offers down-tempo bliss in plush surroundings, plus a top wine selection, and an extensive range of coffee, tea and hot choc. Savoury food begins and ends with quiche – here it's all about the sweeties, including moreish cheesecake and handmade chocolates.

Veerev Õlu　　　　　PUB
(Uus 3a) The 'Rolling Beer' (named after the Rolling Stones) wins the award for friendliest and cosiest pub. It's a tiny rustic space with lots of good vibes, cheap beer and the occasional live rock-folk band (with compulsory dancing on tables, it would seem).

Sunset Club　　　　　CLUB
(www.sunset.ee; Ranna pst 3; ⊙Fri & Sat Jun-Aug) In a grandiose seafront building dating from 1939, Pärnu's biggest and most famous nightclub has an outdoor beach terrace and a sleek multifloor interior with plenty of cosy nooks for when the dance floor gets crowded. Imported DJs and bands, plus a young crowd, keep things cranked until the early hours.

ℹ Information

Pärnu in Your Pocket (www.inyourpocket.com) More great info from this listings guide; available in bookshops or online.

Pärnu tourist information centre (☏447 3000; www.visitparnu.com; Uus 4; ⊙9am-6pm daily mid-May–mid-Sep, 9am-5pm Mon-Fri, 10am-2pm Sat & Sun mid-Sep–mid-May) Pick up maps and brochures, or use the internet (free for first 15 minutes). Staff will book accommodation or car hire for a €2 fee.

Post office (Pikk) Inside the Port Artur 1 complex, opposite the bus station.

ℹ Getting There & Away

About 25 daily buses connect Pärnu with Tallinn (€5.75 to €8, two hours), and nine services connect Pärnu with Tartu (€9 to €9.60, 2½ to three hours). Tickets for a multitude of other destinations, including Rīga and beyond, are available at the Pärnu **bus station ticket office** (☏12550; Ringi), across from the bus station.

There are also two daily Tallinn–Pärnu trains (€5.40, 2¾ hours), though the train station is an inconvenient 5km east of the town centre, down Riia mnt.

Viljandi
POP 20,000

One of Estonia's most charming towns, Viljandi, 90km east of Pärnu, is a relaxed place to stop for a day or more. It's a good spot to use as a base for exploring the country's largest flood plain and bog area (no laughing!), and the town itself, settled since the 12th century, has a gentle 19th-century flow to it. The **tourist information centre** (☏433 0442; www.viljandimaa.ee; Vabaduse plats 6; ⊙10am-6pm Mon-Fri, 10am-3pm Sat & Sun mid-May–mid-Sep, 10am-5pm Mon-Fri, mid-Sep–mid-May) is one of Estonia's finest, with local maps and information in loads of languages; it also has info on Soomaa National Park.

A highlight is visiting **Castle Park** (Lossimäed), which sprawls out from behind the tourist information office. A picturesque green area with spectacular views over Lake Viljandi, the park contains the ruins of a 13th- to 15th-century castle founded by the German Knights of the Sword, which are open for all to muck about in. The excellent **Kondase Keskus** (www.kondase.ee; Pikk 8; adult/student €1/0.30; ⊙10am-5pm Wed-Sun) is the country's only art gallery devoted to naive art.

Easily the biggest event on the calendar is the hugely popular four-day **Viljandi Folk Music Festival** (www.folk.ee/festival), held in late July and renowned for its friendly relaxed vibe and impressive international line-up (incorporating traditional folk, folk rock and world music). It's the country's biggest music festival, with some 20,000-plus festival-goers. Pop into the new **Estonian Traditional Music Centre** (www.folk.ee), in Castle Park, to see if there are any concerts being held during your visit.

On one of Viljandi's loveliest streets, the small, six-room **Hostel Ingeri** (☏433 4414; www.hostelingeri.ee; Pikk 2c; s €22.40, d €32-38.40; ⊛) offers seriously good value with its bright, comfortable rooms, all with TV and bathroom. Plant life, sauna, a small gym and a kitchen for guest use make it a good home away from home, while the parkside location couldn't be better.

The terrace overlooking the park is one drawcard of the tavern-style **Tegelaste**

Tuba (Pikk 2b; mains €3.80-5.10), but so are the comfy interiors on cold, rainy days. Estonian handicrafts enliven the walls and a diverse crowd enjoys the wide-ranging menu of soups, salads and meaty mains.

Around 12 daily buses connect Viljandi with Tallinn (€6.40 to €9, two to 2½ hours). There are about 10 daily buses to/from Pärnu (€5.10 to €6.40, 1½ to two hours) and up to 13 to/from Tartu (€4.15 to €5.10EEK, one to two hours).

Soomaa National Park

Some 40km west of Viljandi is **Soomaa National Park**, a rich land of bogs, marsh, crisscrossing rivers and iron-rich black pools of water, perfect for a quick summer dip. Much more interesting than what the word 'bog' implies, this 37,000-hectare park is full of quirky opportunities, from a walk through the swampland landscape or a single-trunk canoe trip down one of the rivers, to an unforgettable sauna atop a floating raft.

The **Soomaa National Park visitor centre** (☑435 7164; www.soomaa.ee; ☺10am-6pm May-Sep, 10am-4pm Tue-Sat Oct-Apr) is 22km west of the village of Kõpu, itself 20km west of Viljandi. You can also call into the **Viljandi tourist office** (☑433 0442; www.viljandi.ee; Vabaduse plats 6) to pick up maps and brochures.

Soomaa.com (☑506 1896; www.soomaa.com), a local company promoting ecotourism and sustainable development, offers the best way to explore the park. It has a fabulous range of year-round activities; transfers from Pärnu are available. The Wilderness Experience **day trip** includes river canoeing and walking on peat bog (€50 from Soomaa, €70 from Pärnu; runs from May to September). There are also guided and self-guided canoeing, beaver-watching, bog-shoeing and mushroom-picking experiences and, in winter, kick-sledding, cross-country-skiing, ice-fishing and snowshoeing excursions. Independent adventurers can rent gear such as tents and sleeping bags, as well as canoes. Accommodation in nearby guesthouses can be arranged, as can the rental of our favourite Soomaa treat, the floating sauna atop the Raudna River. You'll need to contact Soomaa.com in advance to arrange your itinerary; check the website for all the options.

There is no public transport to Soomaa National Park.

Saaremaa

POP 36,000

For Estonians, Saaremaa (literally 'Island Land') is synonymous with space, spruce, peace and fresh air – and killer beer. Estonia's largest island (roughly the size of Luxembourg) still lies covered in thick pine and spruce forests, and juniper groves, while old windmills, slender lighthouses and tiny villages appear unchanged by the passage of time. There's also a long history of beer home-brewing, and a large beer festival, Õlletoober (www.olletoober.ee), takes place here in mid-July.

During the Soviet era, the entire island was off limits (due to a radar system and rocket base). This unwittingly resulted in a minimal industrial build-up and the protection of the island's rural charm.

To reach Saaremaa you must first cross Muhu, the small island where the ferry from the mainland docks; Muhu is connected to Saaremaa by a 2.5km causeway. Kuressaare, the capital of Saaremaa, is on the south coast (75km form the ferry terminal) and is a natural base for visitors – it's here, among the upmarket hotels, you'll understand where the island got its nickname, 'Spa-remaa'.

☉ Sights & Activities

Bishop's Castle   CASTLE
The island's most distinctive landmark is the striking, fortress-style Bishop's Castle (1338–80), located at the southern end of Kuressaare and ringed by a moat. It looks like it was plucked from a fairy tale, and now houses the **Saaremaa Museum** (www.saaremaamuuseum.ee; adult/concession €3.20/1.60; ☺10am-6pm May-Aug, 11am-6pm Wed-Sun Sep-Apr). You can hire a rowboat at **Lossikonn** (Allee 8) to float idly along the moat.

Angla   WINDMILLS
Angla is 40km north of Kuressaare, en route to the small harbour at Triigi. Just off the main road at Angla is a photogenic group of five **windmills**. Two kilometres away, along the road opposite the windmills, is **Karja Church**, a striking 14th-century German Gothic church.

Kaali   METEORITE CRATER
At Kaali, 18km from Kuressaare, is a 110m-wide, water-filled **crater** formed by a meteorite at least 3000 years ago. In ancient Scandinavian mythology the site was known as the sun's grave. It's Europe's largest and

most accessible meteorite crater, but looks mighty tiny up close!

Sõrve Peninsula   LANDSCAPES
Saaremaa's magic can really be felt along the Sõrve Peninsula, jutting out south and west of Kuressaare. This sparsely populated strip of land saw some of the heaviest fighting in WWII, and some bases and antitank defence lines still stand. A bike or car trip along the coastline provides some of the most spectacular sights on the island; several daily buses from Kuressaare also head down the coast of the peninsula.

🛏 Sleeping
The tourist information office can organise beds in private apartments throughout the region; farm stays are also available across the island. Hotel prices are up to 40% cheaper from September through to April.

Georg Ots Spa Hotel   HOTEL €€
(📞455 0000; www.gospa.ee; Tori 2, Kuressaare; d €89; @🖨🛜🏊) Easily one of the country's nicest large hotels, the Georg Ots (named after a renowned Estonian singer) has fresh modern rooms with enormous king-sized beds, CD-player and a warm but minimalist design. Most rooms have balconies, and there's a pool, fitness centre and spa services just down the hall, as well as top nosh at the hotel's restaurant. Apartments are also available (see the website), and families are very well catered to.

Karluti Hostel   GUESTHOUSE €
(📞501 4390; www.karluti.ee; Pärna 29, Kuressaare; r without bathroom per person €12.80-16; 🛜) Lovely Tiia is your host at this cheerful

---

CLEAN & GREEN

Saaremaa is waking up to the potential of its clean, green image. Organic farms and cottage industries focusing on quality local produce are popping up, and many open their doors to the public. In summer you can make organic soap at **GoodKarma** (www.goodkarma.ee), sample local mustards at **Mustjala Mustard** (www.mustjala-mustard.com), or pick your own fruit at various farms. Other places offer horse riding, farm activities and accommodation. Visits generally need to be arranged beforehand; pick up a copy of *Saare County Open Organic Farms* brochure and map, or download it from www.saaremahe.ee.

---

yellow guesthouse, set in a large garden on a quiet residential street close to the centre. Three spotless rooms house seven beds (book ahead for summer) and there's kitchen access. Bike and car rental can also be arranged.

Veskimaja Hoov   STUDIO APARTMENT €
(📞5567 3438; www.veskimaja.webs.com; Uus 29, Kuressaare; r €32-41.50; 🛜) Next door to Veski Trahter tavern and surrounded by a vast and gorgeous garden, this bright room (with bathroom and kitchenette) offers excellent value. As a bonus, the creative owners (one a cook with a great bakery at the rear of the Kuressaare market) are a mine of knowledge on local life.

🍴 Eating & Drinking
RAE Supermarket (Raekoja 10, Kuressaare; ⏱9am-10pm) is the best grocery store. It's behind the tourist information centre.

Sadhu Cafe   CAFE €
(Lossi 5, Kuressaare; meals €4.80-8) Kuressaare's chill-out spot adds a touch of spice to the main street. It's a true travellers cafe, decked out with textiles and artefacts from India – and the menu takes a few cues from there too, alongside local dishes like Saaremaa lamb stew and a wild-boar burger. It runs from breakfast to late-night drinks on the garden terrace, and offers a weekday lunch special at €2.60 – what's not to like?

Veski Trahter   TRADITIONAL ESTONIAN €
(Pärna 19, Kuressaare; mains €3.80-10.50) Sure, it's a little touristy (the folk performances on summer evenings are a dead giveaway), but this tavern inside an 1899 windmill emphasises quality and ambience, with plenty of hearty local fare such as wild boar in juniper-berry marinade, flavoured beers and Saaremaa cheeses.

La Perla   ITALIAN €€
(Lossi 3, Kuressaare; mains €6.10-12.50) A pearl of a menu makes dining at this popular Italian restaurant a warming Mediterranean treat. Swing from bruschetta to tiramisu via all manner of pizza, pasta and grilled meats, preferably accompanied by a cheeky glass of Italian red.

John Bull Pub   PUB
(Pärgi 4, Kuressaare) In the park surrounding the castle, this pub (not particularly English, despite its name) has a great moatside deck, a menu of cheap'n'cheerful pub classics, and

SPLURGE

Pädaste Manor (☎454 8800; www.padaste.com; Muhu; r from €190; @☎) wins our vote as Estonia's finest place to bed down. On a manicured bayside estate in Muhu's south, this boutique resort encompasses an exquisitely restored manor house, a fine-dining restaurant called Alexander (many claim it's Estonia's best), a spa and a brasserie. The attention to detail is second to none, from the private cinema in the carriage house to the antique furnishings and from the Muhu embroidery to the spa treatments using local herbs, mud and honey. Even if you're not staying at Pädaste, you can stop by for a meal at the manor restaurant (book ahead) or, in summer, at the beautifully sited Sea House Terrace (open noon to 7pm June to August).

our favourite feature – a bar made from an old Russian bus.

ⓘ Information

Kuressaare's **tourist information office** (☎453 3120; www.kuressaare.ee; Tallinna 2; ☺9am-7pm Mon-Fri, 9am-5pm Sat, 10am-3pm Sun May-Sep, 9am-5pm Mon-Fri Oct-Apr) can help you make the best of your stay. Pick up maps outlining nature trails, cycling trails, craft and heritage excursions.

More information is online at **Saaremaa** (www.saaremaa.ee).

ⓘ Getting There & Around

A year-round vehicle ferry runs throughout the day from Virtsu on the mainland to the island of Muhu, which is joined by causeway to Saaremaa; see **Saaremaa Laevakompanii** (www.laevakompanii.ee) for ferry schedules and prices.

Around 14 direct buses travel daily between Tallinn and Kuressaare (€12.80 to €14.40, 3½ to 4¼ hours), via the ferry. Three buses run daily to/from Tartu (€14 to €16, 5½ to 6½ hours), and four to/from Pärnu (€13, three to 3½ hours).

Consider flying – you may just find a fare comparable with a bus ticket. **Estonian Air** (OV; ☎640 1163; www.estonian-air.ee) flies up to nine times a week year-round between Tallinn and Kuressaare (from €14, 45 minutes).

UNDERSTAND ESTONIA

History
Early History

It's commonly held that in the mid-3rd millennium BC, Finno-Ugric tribes came from either the east or south to the territory of modern-day Estonia and parts of Latvia, and mixed with the tribes who had been there from the 8th millennium BC. They were little influenced from outside until German trad-

ers and missionaries, followed by knights, were unleashed by Pope Celestinus III's 1193 crusade against the 'northern heathens'. In 1202 the bishop of Rīga established the Knights of the Sword to convert the region by conquest; southern Estonia was soon subjugated, and the north fell to Denmark.

Foreign Rule

After a crushing battle with Russian prince and military leader Alexander Nevsky in 1242 on the border of present-day Estonia and Russia, the Knights of the Sword were subordinated to a second band of German crusaders, the Teutonic Order, which by 1290 ruled the eastern Baltic area as far north as southern Estonia, as well as most of the Estonian islands. Denmark sold northern Estonia to the Livonian Order (a branch of the Teutonic Order) in 1346, placing Estonians under servitude to a German nobility that lasted till the early 20th century. Although Sweden and Russia would later rule the region, German nobles and land barons maintained great economic and political power. The Hanseatic League (a mercantile league of medieval German towns bound together by trade) encompassed many towns on the routes between Russia and the west, which prospered under the Germans, although many Estonians in rural areas were forced into serfdom.

By 1620 Estonia had fallen under Swedish control. The Swedes consolidated Estonian Protestantism and aimed to introduce universal education; however, frequent wars were devastating. After the Great Northern War (1700–21), Estonia became part of the Russian Empire. Repressive government from Moscow and economic control by German powers slowly forged a national self-awareness among native Estonians. Serfs were freed in the 19th century, and their improved education and land-ownership rights also helped promote national culture and welfare.

Independence

With the Treaty of Brest-Litovsk, the Soviets abandoned the Baltic countries to Germany in March 1918, although Estonian nationalists had originally declared independence on 24 February. The resulting War of Independence led to the Tartu Peace Treaty on 2 February 1920, in which Russia renounced territorial claims to Estonia.

Damaged by the war and hampered by a world slump and disruptions to trade with the USSR, independent Estonia suffered economically even as it bloomed culturally. Prime Minister Konstantin Päts declared himself president in 1934 and ruled Estonia as a relatively benevolent dictator while also quietly safeguarding the USSR's interests.

Soviet Rule & WWII

The Molotov-Ribbentrop Pact of 23 August 1939, a non-aggression pact between the USSR and Nazi Germany, secretly divided Eastern Europe into Soviet and German spheres of influence. Estonia fell into the Soviet sphere and by August 1940 was under occupation. Estonia was 'accepted' into the USSR after fabricated elections and within a year more than 10,000 people in Estonia had been killed or deported. When Hitler invaded the USSR in 1941, many saw the Germans as liberators, but during their occupation about 5500 people died in concentration camps. Some 40,000 Estonians joined the German army to prevent the Red Army from reconquering Estonia; nearly twice that number fled abroad.

Russia annexed Estonia after WWII. Between 1945 and 1949 agriculture was collectivised, industry was nationalised and 60,000 more Estonians were killed or deported. An armed resistance led by the Metsavennad (Forest Brothers) fought Soviet rule until 1956.

With postwar industrialisation, Estonia received an influx of immigrant workers from Russia, Ukraine and Belarus, all looking for improved living conditions but having little interest in local language and customs. Resentment among Estonians grew as some of these immigrants received prized new housing and top job allocations. In the second half of the 20th century, within the USSR, Estonia developed the reputation of being the most modern and European of all the republics, mainly due to its proximity to Finland, and enjoyed a relatively high standard of living.

New Independence

On 23 August 1989, on the 50th anniversary of the Molotov-Ribbentrop Pact, an estimated two million people formed a human chain across Estonia, Latvia and Lithuania, calling for secession from the USSR. Independence came suddenly, however, in the aftermath of the Moscow putsch against Gorbachev. Estonia's declaration of complete independence on 20 August 1991 was recognised by the West immediately, and by the USSR on 6 September.

In October 1992 Estonia held its first democratic elections, which brought to the presidency the much-loved Lennart Meri, who oversaw the removal of the last Russian troops in 1994. The decade after independence saw the government focusing on radical reform policies, and on gaining membership to the EU and NATO. The sweeping transformations on all levels of society saw frequent changes of government, however, and no shortage of scandal and corruption charges. Yet despite this, the country came to be seen as *the* post-Soviet economic miracle. In 2004, Estonia officially entered both NATO and the EU, although troubled relations with its big easterly neighbour are of ongoing concern.

Recent years saw the Estonian economy riding a huge boom; however, the brakes were slammed on by the global financial crisis, with the country falling sharply into recession in 2008. The government slashed public spending to counter the crisis. Economic recovery was strong in 2009–10, and in January 2011, Estonia took the euro as its official currency. It became only the third ex-communist state to make the switch (after Slovenia and Slovakia), and is the first former Soviet republic to have done so. This move highlights the country's resolve to look west, catch up with its Nordic neighbours, and not to look back (nor east).

The People of Estonia

In the 1930s native Estonians made up 88% of the population. This began to change with the Soviet takeover; migration from other parts of the USSR occurred on a mass scale from 1945 to 1955. Today only 69% of the people living in Estonia are ethnic Estonians. Russians make up 26% of the population, with 2% Ukrainian, 1% Belarusian and 1% Finnish. Ethnic Russians are concentrated in the industrial cities of the northeast, where in some places (such as Narva) they make up around 95% of the population. Russians also have a sizeable presence in Tallinn (39%). While much is made of tension between Estonians and Russians, the two communities live together in relative harmony, with only occasional flare-ups, such as the violence that followed the decision to move a Soviet war memorial from the centre of Tallinn in 2007.

Estonians are closely related to the Finns, and more distantly to the Sami (indigenous Laplanders) and Hungarians; they're unrelated to the Latvians and Lithuanians, however, who are of Indo-European heritage. Estonians are historically a rural people, wary of outsiders and stereotypically most comfortable when left alone. Women are less shy and more approachable than men, though both exude a natural reticence and distance in social situations. In general, the younger the Estonian, the more relaxed, open and friendly they'll be.

Historically Estonia was Lutheran from the early 17th century, though today only a minority of Estonians profess religious beliefs, and there's little sense of Estonia as a religious society. The Russian community is largely Orthodox, and brightly domed churches are sprinkled around eastern Estonia. There are an estimated 10,000 Muslims in Estonia and about 2500 Jews. In 2007 the Jewish community celebrated the opening of its first synagogue (in Tallinn) since the Holocaust.

Arts

Literature

Estonian was traditionally considered a mere 'peasants' language' rather than one with full literary potential, and as a result the history of written Estonian is little more than 150 years old.

Estonian literature grew from the poems and diaries of Kristjan Jaak Peterson, who died when he was but 21 years old in 1822. His lines 'Can the language of this land/carried by the song of the wind/not rise up to heaven/and search for its place in eternity?' are engraved in stone in Tartu, and his birthday (14 March) is celebrated as Mother Tongue Day.

Until the mid-19th century, Estonian culture had been preserved only by way of an oral folk tradition among the peasants. Many of these stories were collected around 1861 to form the national epic *Kalevipoeg* (The Son of Kalev), by Friedrich Reinhold Kreutzwald, which was inspired by Finland's *Kalevala*. The *Kalevipoeg* relates the

adventures of the mythical hero, and ends in his death, his land's conquest by foreigners and a promise to restore freedom. The epic played a major role in fostering the national awakening of the 19th century.

Lydia Koidula (1843–86) was the poet of Estonia's national awakening, and first lady of literature. Anton Hansen Tammsaare (1878–1940) is considered the greatest Estonian novelist for his *Tõde ja Õigus* (Truth and Justice), written between 1926 and 1933. Eduard Vilde (1865–1933) was a controversial early 20th-century novelist and playwright who wrote with sarcasm and irony about parochial mindsets.

Jaan Kross (1920–2007) is the best-known Estonian author abroad, and several of his most renowned books, including *The Czar's Madman* and *The Conspiracy and Other Stories,* have been translated into English. Tõnu Õnnepalu and Andrus Kivirähk are two important figures in modern Estonian literature.

Music

Estonia has a strong and internationally well-respected classical-music tradition, and is most notable for its choirs. The Estonian Boys Choir has been acclaimed the world over. Hortus Musicus is Estonia's best-known ensemble, performing mainly medieval and Renaissance music. Estonian composer Arvo Pärt is among the world's most renowned living composers for his haunting sonic blend of tension and beauty, creating outwardly simple but highly complex musical structures.

See **estmusic.com** (www.estmusic.com) for detailed listings and streaming samples of Estonian musicians of all genres; it's a worthwhile site, despite not being particularly up to date.

CAN I BUY A VOWEL PLEASE?

Intrigued by the national language? Fancy yourself a linguist? If you're keen to tackle the local language, bear in mind that Estonian has 14 cases, no future tense and no articles. And then try wrapping your tongue around the following vowel-hungry words:

» *jäääär* – edge of the ice

» *töööö* – worknight (can also be *öötöö*)

» *kuuuurija* – moon researcher

» *kuuüür* – monthly rent

And then give this a go: '*Kuuuurijate töööö jäääärel*', or 'a moon researcher's worknight at the edge of the ice'!

The Landscape

With an area of 45,226 sq km, Estonia is only slightly bigger than Denmark or Switzerland. It is part of the East European Plain, and is extremely flat, though it's marked by extensive bogs and marshes. At 318m, Suur Munamägi (Great Egg Hill) is the highest point in the country – a mere molehill for those of you from less height-challenged terrain. There are more than 1400 lakes, the largest of which is Lake Peipsi (3555 sq km), straddling the Estonia–Russia border. Swamps, wetlands and forests make up half of Estonia's territory. There are more than 1500 islands along the 3794km-long, heavily indented coastline and they make up nearly 10% of Estonian territory.

The Baltic Glint is Estonia's most prominent geological feature. These 60-million-year-old limestone banks extend 1200km from Sweden to Lake Ladoga in Russia, forming impressive cliffs along Estonia's northern coast; at Ontika the cliffs stand 50m above the coast.

Most of the population of Estonia's rare or protected species can be found in one of the several national parks, nature reserves and parks. There are beavers, otters, flying squirrels, lynxes, wolves and brown bears in these areas. White and black storks are common in southern Estonia.

Estonia's western islands and national parks boast some of the most unspoilt landscapes in Europe, and with the exception of the country's northeast (where Soviet-era industry is concentrated), Estonian levels of air pollution are low by European standards. Almost 20% of Estonia's lands (more than double the European average) are protected to some degree.

Since independence there have been major clean-up attempts to counter the effects of Soviet-era industrialisation. In the industrialised northeast of Estonia toxic emissions have been reduced, and new environmental impact legislation aims to minimise the effects of future development. However, heavy oil-shale burning in the northeast keeps air-pollution levels there high.

Estonian Cuisine

Did someone say 'stodge'? Baltic gastronomy has its roots planted firmly in the land, with livestock and game forming the basis of a hearty diet. The Estonian diet relies on *sealiha* (pork), other red meat, *kana* (chicken), *vurst* (sausage) and *kapsa* (cabbage); potatoes add a generous dose of winter-warming carbs to a national cuisine often dismissed as bland, heavy and lacking in spice. Sour cream is served with everything but coffee, it seems. *Kala* (fish), most likely *forell* (trout) or *lõhe* (salmon), appears most often as a smoked or salted starter. *Sült* (jellied meat) is likely to be served as a delicacy as well. At Christmas time *verivorst* (blood sausage) is made from fresh blood and wrapped in pig intestine (joy to the world indeed!). Those really in need of a culinary transfusion will find blood sausages, blood bread and blood dumplings available in most traditional Estonian restaurants year-round.

Õlu (beer) is the favourite alcoholic drink in Estonia and the local product is very much in evidence. The best brands are Saku and A Le Coq, which come in a range of brews. *Viin* (vodka) and *konjak* (brandy) are also popular drinks. Vana Tallinn, a seductively pleasant, sweet and strong (40% to 50% alcohol) liqueur of unknown extraction, is an integral part of any Estonian gift pack.

Where to Eat

At mealtimes, seek out a *restoran* (restaurant) or *kohvik* (cafe); both are plentiful. In addition, a *pubi* (pub), *kõrts* (inn) or *trahter* (tavern) will usually serve hearty, traditional meals. Nearly every town has a *turg* (market), where you can buy fresh produce.

Is it only the Estonians who could turn the gentle pleasure of riding a swing into an extreme sport? (Well, frankly, we're surprised the New Zealanders didn't think of it first.) From the weird and wacky world of Estonian sport comes *kiiking*, invented in 1997. Kiiking sees competitors stand on a swing and attempt to complete a 360-degree loop around the top bar (with their feet fastened to the swing base and their hands to the swing arms). The inventor of kiiking, Ado Kosk, observed that the longer the swing arms, the more difficult it is to complete a 360-degree loop. Kosk then designed swing arms that can gradually extend, for an increased challenge. In competition, the winner is the person who completes a loop with the longest swing arms – the current record stands at a fraction over 7m! If this concept has you scratching your head, head to **Eesti Kiikingi Liti** (www.kiiking.ee) to get a visual version of the whole thing and find out where you can see it in action (or even give it a try yourself).

Many Estonians have their main meal at lunchtime, and accordingly most establishments have excellent-value set lunches. The main cities burst with sophisticated restaurants, funky eateries, cool bars and cosy cafes; while they often command Western European city prices, eating in the provinces is cheap.

Restaurants are generally open from noon to midnight; cafes often open at 8am or 9am and close by 10pm. Bars are open from noon to midnight Sunday to Thursday, and noon to 2am on Friday and Saturday. Food shops and supermarkets are open until 10pm every day. Unless otherwise noted, listings in this chapter follow these general rules.

Smoking is not permitted in restaurants, bars, nightclubs and cafes, although it is permitted on outdoor terraces or in closed-off smoking rooms.

SURVIVAL GUIDE

Directory A–Z
Accommodation
Places are listed in our Sleeping sections in order of preference. In the budget category, you'll find backpackers' lodgings, hostels and basic guesthouses (many with shared bathrooms). A dorm bed generally costs €10 to €15. Midrange listings run the gamut from family-run guesthouses to large hotel rooms (private bathroom and breakfast generally included). Top-end listings comprise historic hotels, spa resorts and charming places offering something particularly special (such as antique-filled rooms or ocean views).

There are a few *kämpingud* (camping grounds; open from mid-May to September) that allow you to pitch a tent, but most consist of permanent wooden huts or cabins, with communal showers and toilets. Farms and homestays offer more than a choice of rooms; in many cases meals, a sauna and a range of activities are available. There's a search engine at **Visitestonia.com** (www.visitestonia.com) for all types of accommodation throughout the country.

The peak tourist season is from June through August. If you come then, you should book well in advance. This is essential in Tallinn and in popular summertime destinations such as the islands and Pärnu.

PRICE RANGES
All prices listed in this chapter are high-season prices and for rooms that have private bathroom, unless otherwise stated.

€ less than €40

€€ €40 to €130

€€€ more than €130

Activities
Many travel agencies can arrange a variety of activity-based tours of Estonia. A detailed list of companies keeping tourists active can be found at **Turismiweb.ee** (www.turismiweb.ee).

For energetic, ecofriendly activities, contact **Reimann Retked** (☏511 4099; www.retked.ee). The company offers a wide range of sea-kayaking excursions, including overnight trips and four-hour paddles out to Aegna island, 14km offshore from Tallinn (€28.80). Other possibilities include diving, rafting, bog walking and snowshoeing, as well as kick sledding on sea ice, frozen lakes or in snowy forest; most arrangements need

DRINKING WATER

Official travel advisories detail the need to avoid tap water in the Baltic countries and drink only boiled or bottled water, but locals insist the tap water is safe. Some visitors may wish to buy bottled water simply because they prefer the taste. In consideration for the environment, buy locally sourced and bottled water, rather than imports. In Estonia you can return recyclable bottles to vending machines at supermarkets for the return of a deposit – it won't make you rich, but it will help the environment.

a minimum of eight to 10 people, but smaller groups should enquire as you may be able to tag along with another group.

City Bike (☑511 1819; www.citybike.ee; Uus 33, Tallinn) can take care of all you need to get around by bike.

Business Hours

In the larger cities some cafes stay open until midnight dispensing coffee and after-dinner sweet treats. Exceptions to the following standard hours are listed in the text.

Banks 9am-4pm Mon-Fri

Bars noon-midnight Sun-Thu, noon-2am Fri & Sat

Cafes 8 or 9am-10pm

Clubs 10pm-4am Thu-Sat

Post offices 8am-6pm Mon-Fri, 9am-3pm Sat

Shops 9 or 10am-6 or 7pm Mon-Fri, 10am-4pm Sat & Sun

Supermarkets 9 or 10am-10pm

Restaurants noon-midnight

Discount Cards

There are frequent student, pensioner and group discounts on transport, in museums and in some shops upon presentation of accredited ID.

Embassies & Consulates

For up-to-date contact details of Estonian diplomatic organisations, as well as foreign embassies and consulates in Estonia, check the website of the **Estonian Ministry of Foreign Affairs** (www.vm.ee).

All the following embassies and consulates are in Tallinn unless otherwise indicated.

Canada (☑627 3311; www.canada.ee; 2nd fl, Toom-Kooli 13)

Finland (☑610 3200; www.finland.ee; Kohtu 4)

France (☑616 1610; www.ambafrance-ee.org; Toom-Kuninga 20)

Germany (☑627 5300, www.tallinn.diplo.de; Toom-Kuninga 11)

Ireland (☑681 1888; www.embassyofireland.ee; 2nd fl, Vene 2)

Japan (☑631 0531; www.japemb.ee; Harju 6)

Latvia (☑627 7850; embassy.estonia@mfa.gov.lv; Tõnismägi 10)

Lithuania (☑616 4991; http://ee.mfa.lt; Uus 15)

Netherlands (☑680 5500; www.netherlandsembassy.ee; Rahukohtu 4-I)

Russia Narva (☑356 0652; narvacon@narvacon.neti.ee; Kiriku 8); Tallinn (☑646 4175; www.rusemb.ee; Pikk 19)

Sweden (☑640 5600; www.sweden.ee; Pikk 28)

UK (☑667 4700; www.britishembassy.ee; Wismari 6)

USA (☑668 8100; www.usemb.ee; Kentmanni 20)

Festivals & Events

Estonia has a busy festival calendar celebrating everything from religion to music, art to film, beer to ghosts. Peak festival fun is in summer, with a highlight being midsummer festivities. A good list of upcoming major events nationwide can be found at **culture.ee** (www.culture.ee). See also our listings of prime Tallinn festivals, p354, and Tartu events, p366.

The biggest occasion in Estonia is **Jaanipäev** (St John's Day; 24 June), a celebration of the pagan midsummer or summer solstice. Celebrations peak on the evening of 23 June and are best experienced far from the city along a stretch of beach, where huge bonfires are lit for all-night parties.

Food

Eating options are listed in order of preference; prices indicate the cost of a main meal.

€ below €10

€€ €10 to €20

€€€ more than €20

Gay & Lesbian Travellers

While open displays of same-sex affection are infrequent in Estonia, the overall attitude is more of openness than antagonism. There's not much dedicated information online in

English – try the website **Cafe HMSX** (www. hmsx.info, in Estonian), with links to venues in its top banner. Otherwise, your best starting point for information on the scene may be Tallinn's Angel nightclub and restaurant.

Holidays

New Year's Day 1 January

Independence Day 24 February

Good Friday March/April

Spring Day 1 May

Whitsunday Seventh Sunday after Easter; May/June

Victory Day (1919; Battle of Võnnu) 23 June

Jaanipäev (St John's Day; Midsummer's Day) 24 June

Day of Restoration of Independence 20 August

Christmas Day 25 December

Boxing Day 26 December

Internet Access

There are approximately 1140 wi-fi areas throughout Estonia, with 355 in Tallinn alone; many of these are free. You'll find wi-fi hot spots in hotels, pubs, libraries, petrol stations, urban parks and elsewhere; visit **wifi.ee** (www.wifi.ee) for a list of locations.

Money

On 1 January 2011, Estonia joined the eurozone. The euro is now Estonia's currency, and the country has bid a very fond farewell to its kroon (EEK); the official rate is €1 = 15.65EEK.

Credit cards are widely accepted. Most banks (but not stores and restaurants) accept travellers cheques, but commissions can be high.

Tipping in service industries has become the norm, but generally no more than 10% is expected.

Post

Mail service in and out of Estonia is highly efficient. To post a letter up to 50g anywhere in the world costs €0.58.

Telephone

There are no area codes. All landline numbers have seven digits; mobile numbers have seven or eight digits, and begin with ☑5.

Estonia's country code is ☑372.

Visas

EU citizens can spend unlimited time in Estonia, while citizens of Australia, Canada, Japan, New Zealand, the USA and many other countries can enter visa-free for a maximum 90-day stay over a six-month period. Travellers holding a Schengen visa do not need an additional Estonian visa. For more information, check out the website of the **Estonian Ministry of Foreign Affairs** (www.vm.ee).

Getting There & Away

Air

The national carrier **Estonian Air** (OV; ☑640 1163; www.estonian-air.ee) links Tallinn with approximately 15 cities in Europe. Other airlines serving **Tallinn airport** (TLL; ☑605 8888; www.tallinn-airport.ee) include **airBaltic** (BT; ☑17107; www.airbaltic.com), offering flights to Vilnius and Rīga, and **Finnair** (AY; ☑626 6309; www.finnair.com), with frequent links to Helsinki. Budget airlines serving Tallinn include **Ryanair** (FR; www.ryanair.com), new in 2011, and **easyJet** (U2; www.easyjet.com).

Tartu airport (TAY; ☑605 8888; www.tartu-airport.ee) is now connected by air to Rīga with airBaltic, and Stockholm and Tallinn with Estonian Air.

Land

BUS

Buses are the cheapest way of reaching the Baltics; see p382 for further details on international buses.

CAR & MOTORCYCLE

From Finland, put your vehicle on a Helsinki–Tallinn ferry. If approaching Estonia from the south or Western Europe, be sure to avoid crossing through Kaliningrad or Belarus – you'll need hard-to-get visas for these countries, and are likely to face hassles from traffic police and encounter roads in abominable condition.

TRAIN

There are international trains between Tallinn and Moscow; see p383.

Sea

Ferries run to Finland and Sweden from Tallinn; see p360.

Getting Around

Air

Avies Air (☑630 1370; www.avies.ee) and **Estonian Air** (☑640 1163; www.estonian-air.ee) provide domestic flights.

Bicycle

The flatness and small scale of Estonia, and the light traffic on most roads, make it good cycling territory. On the islands you will see cyclists galore in summer. Most bring their own bicycles, but there are plenty of places where you can rent a bicycle, including Tallinn's **City Bike** (☑511 1819; www.citybike.ee; Uus 33), which also offers plenty of useful advice.

Bus

Buses are a good option, as they're more frequent and faster than trains, and cover many destinations not serviced by the limited rail network. For detailed bus information and advance tickets, contact Tallinn's **Central Bus Station** (Autobussijaam; ☑12550; Lastekodu 46). The website **BussiReisid** (www.bussireisid.ee) has schedules and prices for all national bus services.

Car & Motorcycle

An International Driving Permit (IDP) is useful; otherwise, carry your national licence bearing a photograph. It's compulsory to carry your vehicle's registration papers and accident insurance, which can be bought at border crossings. Fuel and service stations are widely available.

Traffic drives on the right-hand side of the road, and driving with any alcohol in your blood is illegal. Seatbelts are compulsory, and headlights must be on at all times while driving. Speed limits in built-up areas are 50km/h; limits outside urban areas vary from 70km/h to 110km/h. Be on the lookout for signs, as these limits are often strictly enforced.

Train

Trains are slower and rarer than buses; the most frequent trains service the suburbs of Tallinn and aren't much use to travellers. Regional train schedules are listed at **Edelaraudtee** (www.edel.ee).

7000Ft to 8500Ft for a double, and 10,000Ft to 13,000Ft for a small apartment. Two brokers are **Best Hotel Service** (Map p394; ☎318 4848; www.besthotelservice. hu; V Sütő utca 2; ☉8am-8pm) and **To-Ma Travel Agency** (Map p394; ☎353 0819; www. tomatour.hu; V Október 6 utca 22; ☉9am-noon & 1-8pm Mon-Fri, 9am-5pm Sat & Sun).

BUDA

Lánchíd 19   BOUTIQUE HOTEL **€€€**
(Map p391; ☎419 1900; www.lanchid19hotel.hu; I Lánchíd utca 19; s/d/ste from €120/140/300; ✷@) This boutique number facing the Danube won a design award in 2008. Its facade features images created by special sensors that reflect the movement of the Danube, and its rooms are equally impressive, containing distinctive artwork and unique chairs designed by art students. Seasonal discounts on the hotel website can bring the price of a double down to €75 a night.

Back Pack Guesthouse   HOSTEL **€**
(Map p388; ☎385 8946; www.backpackbudapest. hu; XI Takács Menyhért utca 33; beds in yurt 3000Ft; dm large/small 3800/4500Ft, d 11,000Ft; @) A hippyish, friendly place, though relatively small, with around 40 beds. There's a lush garden in the back with a hammock stretched invitingly between trees. Take bus 7 to Tétényi út (from Keleti train station) or tram 18 to Móricz Zsigmond Kő'rtér to catch bus 7 to Tétényi út (from Déli train station).

Danubius Hotel Gellért   LUXURY HOTEL **€€**
(Map p394; ☎889 5500; www.danubiusgroup. com/gellert; XI Szent Gellért tér 1; s/d/ste from €80/145/240; ✷@⟰) Peek through the doors of this turn-of-the-20th-century grand dame, even if you don't choose to stay here. The 234-room, four-star hotel has loads of character, and its famous thermal baths (p387) are free for guests. Prices depend on your room's view and the quality of its bathroom.

Papillon Hotel   HOTEL **€**
(Map p388; ☎212 4750; www.hotelpapillon. hu; II Rózsahegy utca 3/b; s/d/tr/apt from €44/54/69/78; ✷@⟰) This small 20-room hotel in Rózsa-domb has a delightful back garden with a small swimming pool, and some rooms have balconies. There are also four apartments available in the same building, one of which has a lovely roof terrace.

Burg Hotel   HOTEL **€€**
(Map p391; ☎212 0269; www.burghotelbuda pest.com; I Szentháromság tér 7-8; s/d/ste from €105/115/134; ✷@) Prices have crept up here at the Burg, located at the centre of Castle Hill, just opposite Matthias Church. Ask for a room overlooking Matthias Church for a truly historic wake-up view. The 26 partly

Central Pest

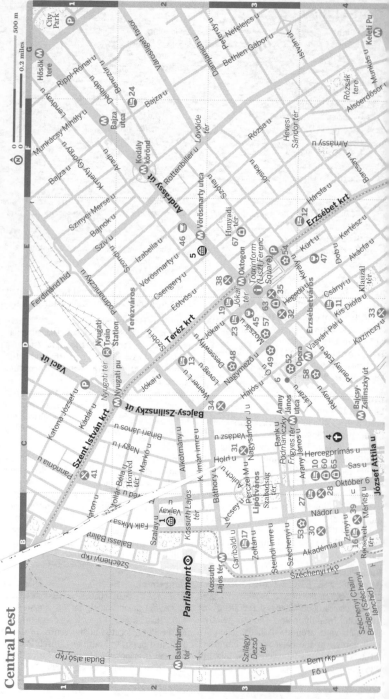

500 m
0.2 miles

City Park

Hősök tere M

Rippl-Rónai u

Benczúr u

Delibáb u

Lendvay u

Munkácsy Mihály u

Kmetty György u

Bajza u

Aradi u

Szondi u

Szív u

Bajnok u

Szinyei Merse u

Bajza u

Kodály körönd M

Rottenbiller u

Szófia út

Andrássy út

Munkácsy u

Bajza utca

Bethlen Gábor u

Damjanich u

Peterdy u

Nefelejcs u

István u

Rózsák tere

Munkás út

Keleti Pu

Alsóerdősor u

Rózsa u

Hevesi Sándor tér

Almássy u

Jósika u

Hársfa u

Kertész u

Dob u

Akácfa u

Csányi u

Kis Diófa u

Klauzál tér

Kazinczy út

Erzsébet krt

Erzsébetváros

Izabella u

Vörösmarty u

Csengery u

Eötvös u

Jókai u

Liszt Ferenc (Square)

Oktogon M

Teréz krt

Teréz krt

Terézváros

Vörösmarty M

Ifjúsági

Szófia út

Kürt u

Hegedü u

Vasvári Pál u

Pauleny Ede u

Révay u

Bajcsy-Zsilinszky út M

Nagymező u

Mozsár u

Hajós u

Dessewffy u

Lázár u

Opera M

Arany János utca M

Bank u

Podmaniczky

Frigyes tér

Arany János u

Hercegprímás u

Sas u

Október 6

Nádor u

Zrínyi u

Roosevelt tér

Mérleg u

József Attila u

Széchenyi Chain Bridge (Széchenyi lánchíd)

Akadémia u

Steindl Imre u

Vécsey u

Garibaldi u

Zoltán u

Balassi Bálint u

Falk Miksa u

Szalay u

Stollár Béla u

Báthory u

Perczel M u

Szabadság tér

Lipótváros

Nagysándor u

Hold u

Alkotmány u

Kálmán Imre u

Markó u

Bihari János u

Nagy u

Vadász u

Alkotmány u

Kádár u

Katona József u

Pannónia u

Szent István krt

Vaci út

Nyugati Train Station M

Ferdinánd híd

Podmaniczky u

Nyugati tér M

Nyugati pu

Jókai u

Szófia u

Jókai tér

Meiner L u

Lővölde tér

Váci út

Balaton u

Honvéd tér

Kossuth Lajos tér

Vécsey u

Parliament

Kossuth Lajos tér

Batthyány tér M

Szilágyi Dezső tér

Bem rkp

Budai alsó rkp

Széchenyi rkp

Fő u

Szilágyi Dezső tér

1
1
2
3
3
4

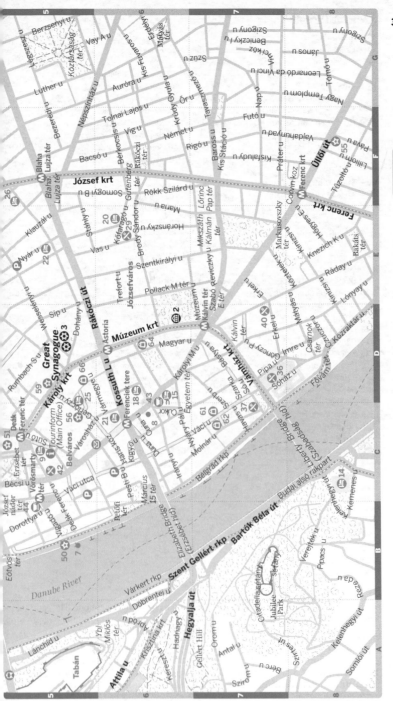

HUNGARY BUDAPEST

refurbished rooms are fairly ordinary, but location is everything here.

Büro Panzió PENSION €
(Map p391; ☎212 2929; www.buropanzio.hu; II Dékán utca 3; s/d/tr/q from €34/43/59/72; ✵◉) This pension looks basic from the outside, but its 10 compact rooms are comfortable

and have TV and telephone. The central Moszkva tér transportation hub – metro stop, tram stations – is seconds away.

Hotel Kulturinnov HOTEL €€
(Map p391; ☎224 8102; www.mka.hu; I Szentháromság tér 6; s/d/tr €64/80/96;✵) A small hotel sitting in the belly of the grandiose

(Map p394; ☎322 4098; VI Liszt Ferenc tér 11;
☽10am-6pm Mon-Fri)

Travel Agencies

Discover Budapest (Map p394; ☎269 3843;
www.discoverbudapest.com; VI Lázár utca 16;
☺9.30am-6.30pm Mon-Fri, 10am-4pm Sat &
Sun) Visit this one-stop shop for helpful tips
and advice, accommodation bookings, internet
access, and cycling and walking tours.

Vista (☎429 9760; www.vista.hu; VI Andrássy
utca 1; ☺9.30am-6pm Mon-Fri, to 2.30pm Sat)
Good choice for all travel needs, both for inbound
travellers (room bookings, sightseeing tours) and
outbound (travel tickets, package tours).

ⓘ Getting There & Away

Air

The main international carriers fly in and out
of Terminal 2 at Budapest's **Ferihegy International Airport** (☎1-296 7000; www.bud.hu),
24km southeast of the centre on Hwy 4; low-cost
airlines use the older Terminal 1 next door. For
carriers flying to Hungary, see p449.

Boat

Mahart PassNave (www.mahartpassnave.hu;
Belgrád rakpart ☎484 4013; Vigadó tér Pier
☎484 4005), with two docks, runs ferries and
hydrofoils from Budapest. A hydrofoil service
on the Danube River between Budapest and
Vienna (5½ to 6½ hours) operates daily from
late April to early October; passengers can
disembark at Bratislava with advance notice
(four hours). Adult one-way/return fares for
Vienna are €89/109 and for Bratislava €79/99.
Students with ISIC cards receive about a €20
discount, and children between two and 14 years
of age travel for half price. Boats leave from the
Nemzetközi hajóállomás (International Ferry
Pier).

There are ferries departing at 10.30am daily for
Szentendre (one way/return 1490/2235Ft, 1½
hours) from May to September, decreasing to 9am
departures on weekends only in April and October.

Vác (one way/return 1990/2990Ft, 40 minutes), Visegrád (one way/return 2690/3990Ft,
one hour) and Esztergom (one way/return
3290/4990Ft, 1½ hours) can be reached by fast
hydrofoil from Budapest at 9.30am at weekends
between May and September (and also on Friday
from June to August). There are also slower
daily ferries at 8am from Budapest to Vác (one
way/return 1490/2235Ft, 2½ hours), Visegrád
(one way/return 1590/2385Ft, 3½ hours) and
Esztergom (one way/return 1990/2985Ft, 5½
hours) between June and August. Services run
on Friday and weekends in May, and weekends
only in September.

When day-tripping to the Danube Bend by
ferry, remember to check the return departure
time when you arrive at your destination. Most
sail to Budapest between 4.30pm and 6.45pm.

Bus

Volánbusz (☎382 0888; www.volanbusz.hu),
the national bus line, has an extensive list of
destinations from Budapest. All international
buses and some buses to/from southern Hungary use **Népliget bus station** (Map p388; IX
Üllői út 131). **Stadionok bus station** (Map p388;
XIV Hungária körút 48-52) generally serves
places to the east of Budapest. Most buses to
the northern Danube Bend arrive at and leave
from the **Árpád híd bus station** (Map p388;
off XIII Róbert Károly körút). All stations are on
metro lines, and all are in Pest. If the ticket office
is closed, you can buy your ticket on the bus.

INTERNATIONAL BUSES FROM BUDAPEST

DESTINATION	PRICE (FT)	DURATION (HR)	FREQUENCY
Bratislava, Slovakia	3700	4	1 daily
Florence, Italy	22,900	14	3 weekly
Frankfurt, Germany	14,900	14	1 daily
London, UK	29,900	25	6 weekly
Munich, Germany	15,900	10	4 weekly
Paris, France	24,900	22	3 weekly
Prague, Czech Republic	10,900	7½	3 weekly
Rijeka, Croatia	12,900	8¼	1 weekly
Rome, Italy via Florence	26,900	19	3 weekly
Sofia, Bulgaria	12,500	12	3 weekly
Subotica, Serbia	3900	4½	2 daily
Vienna, Austria	5900	3½	5 daily

DESTINATION	PRICE (€)	DURATION (HR)
Berlin, Germany	45	12
Bratislava, Slovakia	17	2½
Bucharest, Romania	75	13-15
Frankfurt, Germany	75	15
Kyiv, Ukraine, via Csop & continuing to Moscow	96	24
Ljubljana, Slovenia	40	8½
Munich, Germany	60	7-9
Prague, Czech Republic	40	7
Sofia, Bulgaria	78	18
Thessaloniki, Greece	90	23
Venice, Italy	54	14
Vienna, Austria	25	3
Warsaw, Poland	60	12
Zürich, Switzerland	80	12

Car & Motorcycle

Car rental is not recommended if you are staying in Budapest. The public transport network is extensive and cheap, whereas parking is scarce and road congestion is high.

If you want to venture into the countryside, travelling by car is an option. Daily rates start at around €60 per day with unlimited kilometres. If the company does not have an office at the airport, it will usually provide free pick-up and delivery within Budapest or at the airport. All the major international chains have branches in Terminal 2 at Ferihegy airport.

Two good local options:

Recent (☑453 0003; www.recentcar.hu; ☺9am-6pm) Reliable outfit.

Fox Autorent (☑382 9000; www.foxautorent. com; ☺8am-6pm) Another good bet.

Train

The Hungarian State Railways, MÁV, administers the country's extensive rail network. Contact the **MÁV-Start passenger service centre** (☑06 40 494949; www.mav-start.hu) for 24-hour information on domestic train departures and arrivals. The website has a useful timetable (in English) for planning routes. Fares are usually noted for destinations within Hungary.

Buy tickets at one of Budapest's three main train stations. Always confirm your departure station when you buy your tickets, since stations can vary depending on the train.

Keleti train station (Eastern; Map p388; VIII Kerepesi út 2-4) handles international trains from Vienna, including the express Railjet trains, and most other points west, plus domestic trains to/from the north and northeast. For some international destinations, as well as domestic ones to/from the northwest and the Danube Bend, head for **Nyugati train station** (Western; Map p394; VI Nyugati tér). For trains bound for Lake Balaton and the south, go to **Déli train station** (Southern; Map p391; I Krisztina körút 37). All train stations are on metro lines.

ⓘ Getting Around

To/From the Airport

The simplest way to get to town is to take the **Airport Minibus** (☑296 8555; www.airport shuttle.hu; one way/return 2990/4990Ft) directly to the place you're staying. Buy tickets at clearly marked stands in the arrivals halls.

An alternative is travelling with **Zóna Taxi** (☑365 5555), which has a monopoly on airport taxis. Fares to most central locations range from 5200Ft to 6000Ft. Of course, you can take any taxi to the airport, and several companies offer a flat fare (between 4800Ft and 5400Ft) to/from Ferihegy.

The cheapest (and slowest) way to get into the city centre from Terminal 2A and 2B is to take city bus 200 (320Ft, or 400Ft on the bus), which terminates at the Kőbánya-Kispest metro station. Look for the stop on the footpath between terminals 2A and 2B. From its final stop, take the M3 metro into the city centre. The total cost is 640Ft to 800Ft. Bus 93 runs from Terminal 1 to Kőbánya-Kispest metro station.

Trains also link Terminal 1 with Nyugati station. They run between one and six times an hour between 4am and 11pm and cost 365Ft (or around 600Ft if you board the hourly IC train). The journey takes 20 minutes.

Boat

From May to August, the **BKV passenger ferry** (Map p388; ☑258 4636; www.bkv.hu) departs from Boráros tér Terminus beside Petőfi Bridge, south of the centre, and heads for III Pünkösdfürdő in Óbuda, a 2¼-hour trip with 14 stops along the way. Tickets (adult/concession 900/450Ft from end to end) are sold on board. The ferry stop closest to the Castle District is Batthyány tér, and Petőfi tér is not far from Vörösmarty tér, a convenient place to pick up the boat on the Pest side.

Public Transport

Public transport is run by **BKV** (☑258 4636; www.bkv.hu). The three underground metro lines (M1 yellow, M2 red, M3 blue) meet at Deák tér in Pest. The HÉV suburban railway runs north from Batthyány tér in Buda. A *turista* transport pass is only good on the HÉV within the city limits (south of the Békásmegyer stop). There's also an extensive network of buses, trams and trolleybuses. Public transport operates from 4.30am until 11.30pm, and 35 night buses run along main roads.

A single ticket for all forms of transport is 320Ft (60 minutes of uninterrupted travel on the same metro, bus, trolleybus or tram line *without* transferring/changing). A transfer ticket (490Ft) is valid for one trip with one validated transfer within 90 minutes. The three-day *turista* pass (3850Ft) or the seven-day pass (4600Ft) make things easier, allowing unlimited travel inside the city limits. Keep your ticket or pass handy; the fine for 'riding black' is 6000Ft on the spot, or 12,000Ft if you pay later at the **BKV Office** (☑258 4636; VII Akácfa utca 18; ☉6am-8pm Mon-Fri, 8am-1.45pm Sat).

Taxi

Taxi drivers overcharging foreigners in Budapest has been a problem for some time. Never get into a taxi that lacks an official yellow licence plate, the logo of the taxi firm and a visible table of fares. If you have to take a taxi, it's best to call one; this costs less than if you flag one down. Make sure you know the number of the landline phone you're calling from, as that's how the dispatcher establishes your address (though you can call from a mobile as well). Dispatchers usually speak English. **City Taxi** (☑211 1111), **Főtaxi** (☑222 2222) and **Rádió Taxi** (☑377 7777) are reliable companies. Note that rates are slightly higher at night. Tip about 10% of the fare to reward good service.

North of Budapest, the Danube breaks through the Pilis and Börzsöny Hills in a sharp bend before continuing along the Slovak border. The Roman Empire had its northern border here, and medieval kings ruled Hungary from majestic palaces overlooking the river at Esztergom and Visegrád. East of Visegrád the river divides, with Szentendre and Vác on different branches. Today the easy access to historic monuments, rolling green scenery – and vast numbers of souvenir craft shops – lure many day-trippers from Budapest.

Szentendre

☑26 / POP 23,500

Once an artists' colony, now a popular day trip 19km north of Budapest, pretty little Szentendre (*sen*-ten-dreh) has narrow, winding streets and is a favourite with souvenir-shoppers. The charming old centre has plentiful cafes and art-and-craft galleries, and there are a few Serbian Orthodox churches, dating from the time when Christian worshippers fled here centuries ago to escape the Turkish invaders, that are worth checking out. Expect things to get crowded in summer and at weekends. Outside town is the largest open-air village museum in the country.

◉ Sights

Fő tér PUBLIC SQUARE

Begin your sightseeing at the colourful Fő tér, the town's main square. Here you'll find many structures from the 18th century, including the 1763 **Memorial Cross** (Emlékkereszt) and the 1752 Serbian Orthodox **Blagoveštenska Church** (Blagoveštenska Templom; admission 300Ft; ☉10am-5pm Tue-Sun), which is small but stunning.

All the pedestrian lanes surrounding the square burst with shops, the merchandise spilling out into displays on the streets.

Margit Kovács Ceramic Collection MUSEUM

(Kovács Margit Kerámiagyűjtemény; Vastagh György utca 1; adult/concession 1000/500Ft; ☉10am-6pm) Downhill to the east of the square, off a side street on the way to the Danube, is the Margit Kovács Ceramic Collection. Kovács (1902–77) was a ceramicist who combined Hungarian folk, religious and modern themes with a hint of Gothic to create her figures.

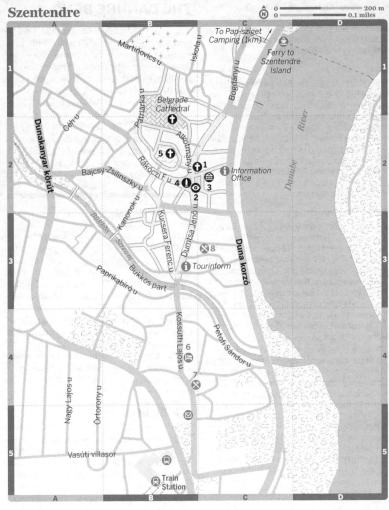

Parish Church of St John

CHURCH

(Szent Janos Plébánia Templom; Várhegy) Uphill to the northwest from the square, a narrow passageway leads up from between Fő tér 8 and 9 to Castle Hill (Vár-domb) and the Parish Church of St John, rebuilt in 1710, from where you get great views of the town and the Danube.

Open-Air Ethnographic Museum

OPEN-AIR MUSEUM

(Szabadtéri Néprajzi Múzeum; www.skanzen.hu; Sztaravodai út; adult/concession 1400/700Ft; ☺9am-5pm Tue-Sun late Mar-Oct) Don't miss the extensive Open-Air Ethnographic Museum, 3km outside town. Walking through the fully furnished ancient wooden and stone homes, churches and working buildings brought here from around the country, you can get a real sense of what rural life was – and sometimes still is – like in different regions of Hungary. In the centre of the park stand Roman-era ruins. Frequent weekend festivals offer you a chance to see folk costumes, music and dance, as well as home crafts. To get here, take the hourly buses marked 'Skansen' from stop 7 at the town's bus station.

Szentendre

🛏 Sleeping & Eating

Seeing Szentendre on a day trip from Budapest is probably your best bet. The town can be easily covered in a day, even if you spend a couple of hours at the open-air museum. For private rooms in town, visit the Tourinform office. Being a tourist town, there are plenty of places to grab a bite to eat.

Mathias Rex　　　　　　　PENSION €€
(☎505 570; www.mathiasrexhotel.hu; Kossuth Lajos utca 16; s/d 10,000/15,000Ft) Attractive, family-run pension about 10 minutes' walk from Fő tér. The spotless rooms are done out in high-quality dark woods and crisp linens. Guests have use of the backyard garden, and the cellar restaurant is one of the best in this part of town.

Pap-sziget Camping　　　CAMPING GROUND €
(☎310 697; www.pap-sziget.hu; camp sites per adult/concession 1200/700Ft, tents 3000Ft, bungalows from 11,000Ft; ⊗May–mid-Oct;🛉) Large shady trees, a sandy beach and numerous tent and caravan sites. Bungalows are basic. Take bus 11 from Szentendre.

Erm's　　　　　　　　　　HUNGARIAN €
(Kossuth Lajos utca 22; mains around 2000Ft) This unpretentious spot a bit away from the day-tripper throng serves very good Hungarian specialities like fish stew, and even some vegetarian choices. The simple wooden tables dressed in lacy cloth are reminiscent of yesteryear.

Palapa　　　　　　　　　　HUNGARIAN €
(☎302 418; Batthyány utca 4; mains 1500-3000Ft; ⊗5pm-midnight Mon-Fri, noon-midnight Sat & Sun) For a change from Hungarian cuisine, try the Mexican-inspired cooking here.

ℹ Information

There are no left-luggage offices at the HÉV train or bus stations.

Main post office (Kossuth Lajos utca 23-25) Across from the bus and train stations.

OTP Bank (Dumtsa Jenő utca 6) Just off Fő tér.

Silver Blue (Dunakanyar Körút 14; per hr 400Ft; ⊗10am-8pm Mon-Sat) Internet cafe near the train and bus terminals.

THE AQUATIC HIGHWAY

No other river in Europe is as evocative as the Danube. It has been immortalised in legends, tales, songs, paintings and movies, and has played an essential role in the cultural and economic life of millions of people since the earliest human cultures settled along its banks.

Originating in Germany's Black Forest, the river cuts an unrelenting path through – or along the border of – 10 countries, and after 2800km empties itself into the Black Sea in Romania. It is second only in length to the Volga in Europe (although, at 6400km, the Amazon dwarfs both) and, contrary to popular belief, is green-brown rather than blue. Around 2400km of its length is navigable, making it a major transport route across the continent.

Even though only 12% of the river's length is located in its territory, Hungary is greatly influenced by the Danube. The entire country lies within the Danube river basin, and being so flat, it is highly prone to flooding. As early as the 16th century, massive dyke systems were built for flood protection. However, it's hard to stop water running where it wants to – as recently as 2006 the river burst its banks, threatening to fill Budapest's metro system and putting the homes of 32,000 people in danger.

Despite the potential danger the river is much loved, and has even been awarded its own day. On 29 June every year cities along the Danube host festivals, family events and conferences in honour of the mighty waterway. If you'd like to join in, visit www.danube-day.org for more information.

THE MUMMIES OF VÁC

Between 1731 and 1801 the original crypt of Vác's Dominican church functioned as a place of burial for the general public, but it was later bricked up and forgotten. The micro-climatic conditions underground were perfect for mummification – a cool temperature and minimal ventilation allowed the bodies of the deceased to remain in exceptional condition for centuries. When renovation work on the church began in 1994, the crypt was rediscovered. Of the 262 bodies exhumed over the ensuing months, 166 were easily identified through church records. It was a goldmine for historians; the clothing, jewellery and general appearance of the corpses helped to shed light on the burial practices and the local way of life in the 18th century.

The majority of mummies now reside in the vaults of the Hungarian National Museum (p392) in Budapest but three are on display in the **Memento Mori exhibition** in Vác, near the Dominican church. It also showcases some colourfully painted coffins, clothes and jewellery of the deceased, a registry of those buried and a brief history of the church and its crypt.

Tourinform (⌨317 965; szentendre@tourin-form.hu; Bercsényi utca 4; ⏱9.30am-4.30pm Mon-Fri year-round, 10am-2pm Sat & Sun mid-Mar–Oct) Hands out maps and can make recommendations on shopping, dining and hotel rooms. In 2010 the office moved to this temporary location on a side street just along the Duna korzó. It wasn't clear at the time of research if the office would still be here or would move back to its former location (Dumtsa Jenő utca 22).

❶ Getting There & Away

The most convenient way to get to Szentendre is to take the commuter HÉV train from Buda's Batthyány tér metro station to the end of the line (one way about 450Ft, 45 minutes, every 10 to 15 minutes).

For ferry services from Budapest, see p450.

Vác

⌨27 / POP 33.300

Lying on the eastern bank of the river, Vác (*vahts*) is an unpretentious town with interesting historic relics, from its collection of baroque town houses to its vault of 18th-century mummies. It's also the place to view glorious sunsets over the Börzsöny Hills reflected in the Danube.

Vác is an old town. Uvcenum – the town's Latin name – is mentioned in Ptolemy's 2nd-century *Geographia* as a river crossing on an important road. The town's medieval centre and Gothic cathedral were destroyed during the Turkish occupation; reconstruction under several bishops in the 18th century gave Vác its present baroque appearance.

◉ Sights

Március 15 tér   PUBLIC SQUARE

Március 15 tér, the main square, has the most colourful buildings in Vác. At the centre of the square, you'll find a **crypt** (Március 15 tér; adult/concession 500/250Ft; ⏱9am-5pm Tue-Sun May-Sep), the only remnant of the medieval St Michael's Church. It contains a brief history of the church and town in the Middle Ages.

Dominating the square is the **Dominican church** (Fehérek temploma; Március 15 tér 19). The church is best known for holding a cache of fascinating mummies (see boxed text, above), a small collection of which remain on view at the nearby **Memento Mori** (Március 15 tér 19; adult/concession 1000/500Ft; ⏱10-5pm Tue-Sun) exhibition. Also worth seeking out is the 1764 **Town Hall** (Március 15 tér 11), considered a baroque masterpiece. Opposite is the former **Bishop's Palace** (Március 15 tér 6). Next door, the **Vác Diocesan Museum** (Március 15 tér 4; adult/concession 500/200Ft; ⏱2-6pm Wed-Fri, 10am-6pm Sat & Sun) displays a tiny portion of the treasures the Catholic Church amassed in Vác over the centuries.

Triumphal Arch   MONUMENT

North of the main square is the Triumphal Arch (Diadalív-kapu), the only such structure in Hungary. It was built by Bishop Migazzi in honour of a visit by Empress Maria Theresa and her husband Francis of Lorraine in 1764. From here, dip down one of the narrow side streets (such as Molnár utca) to the west for a stroll along the Danube. The **old city walls** and Gothic **Pointed Tower** (now a private home) are near Liszt Ferenc sétány 12.

FREE | **Vác Cathedral** CHURCH
(Váci székesegyház; ☺10am-noon & 1.30-5pm Mon-Sat, 7.30am-7pm Sun) Tree-lined Konstantin tér to the southeast is dominated by colossal Vác Cathedral, which dates from 1775 and was one of the first examples of neoclassical architecture in Hungary.

🛏 Sleeping & Eating

Vác is an easy day trip from Budapest, but there are some accommodation and dining options if you want to stay over.

Fónagy & Walter PENSION €
(☎310 682; www.fonagy.hu; Budapesti főút 36; r 9000Ft) Fónagy & Walter is a pension of the 'homely' variety – rooms are lovingly prepared, and the wine selection from the private cellar is outstanding.

Vörössipka BOUTIQUE HOTEL €€
(☎501 055; okktart@netelek.hu; Honvéd utca 14; s/d 9000/14,000Ft) If Fónagy & Walter is full, consider this plain hotel located away from the centre. Rooms lack character, but they're clean and definitely adequate for a night.

Váci Remete HUNGARIAN €€
(☎302 199; Fürdő utca; mains 2100-3600Ft) Worth seeking out for lunch or dinner. This eatery impresses with views of the Danube from its handsome terrace, a top-notch wine selection and a fine choice of Hungarian specialities.

Duna Presszó CAFE €
(Március 15 tér 13) Duna is the quintessential cafe: dark-wood furniture, chandeliers and the occasional resident drunk. If you are looking for cakes and arguably even better coffee, head to **Chococafe** (Március 15 tér 20) in a far corner of the square, next to the carillon.

☆ Entertainment

Imre Madách Cultural Centre THEATRE
(☎316 411; Dr Csányi László körút 63) This circular centre can help you with what's on in Vác, such as theatre, concerts and kids' shows.

❶ Information

Main post office (Posta Park 2) Off Görgey Artúr utca.

Matrix (Rév köz; per hr 280Ft; ☺9am-1pm Mon-Fri) Small internet cafe.

OTP Bank (Dunakanyar shopping centre, Széchenyi utca)

Tourinform (☎316 160; www.tourinformvac.hu; Március 15 tér 17; ☺10am-7pm Mon-Fri, 10am-2pm Sat mid-Jun–Aug, 9am-5pm Mon-Fri, 10am-noon Sat Sep–mid-Jun) Helpful English-speaking staff. Located on the main square.

❶ Getting There & Away

Car ferries (1460/420/420/350Ft per car/bicycle/adult/concession, every 15 to 30 minutes 6am to 8pm) cross over to Szentendre Island; a bridge connects the island's west bank with the mainland at Tahitótfalu. From there hourly buses run to Szentendre. You can also catch half-hourly buses (500Ft, 50 minutes) and trains (600Ft, 40 minutes) from Vác to Budapest.

Visegrád

☎26 / POP 1700

The spectacular vista from the ruins of Visegrád's (*vish*-eh-grahd) 13th-century citadel, high on a hill above a curve in the Danube, is what pulls visitors to this sleepy town. The first fortress here was built by the Romans as a border defence in the 4th century. Hungarian kings constructed a mighty citadel on the hilltop, and a lower castle near the river, after the 13th-century Mongol invasions. In the 14th century a royal palace was built on the flood plain at the foot of the hills, and in 1323 King Charles Robert of Anjou, whose claim to the local throne was being fiercely contested in Buda, moved the royal household here. For nearly two centuries Hungarian royalty alternated between Visegrád and Buda.

The destruction of Visegrád came first at the hands of the occupying Turks and then at the hands of the Habsburgs, who destroyed the citadel to prevent Hungarian independence fighters from using it. All trace of the royal palace, situated close to the town centre not far from the riverbank, was lost until 1934 when archaeologists, by following descriptions in literary sources, uncovered the ruins that you can visit today.

The small town has two distinct areas: one to the north around the Mahart ferry pier and another, the main town, about 1km to the south, near the Nagymaros ferry.

❍ Sights & Activities

Royal Palace RUIN
(Királyi Palota; Fő utca 29; adult/concession 1100/550Ft; ☺9am-5pm Tue-Sun) The partial reconstruction of the royal palace, near the main town, only hints at the structure's former magnificence. Inside, a small museum is devoted to the history of the palace and its excavation and reconstruction. To find the palace from the Mahart ferry, walk south in the direction of the Nagymaros ferry about

400m and turn in toward town to find Fő utca. The entrance is across from a children's playground.

Solomon's Tower   MUSEUM
(Salamon Torony; adult/concession 700/350Ft; ☉9am-5pm Tue-Sun May-Sep) North of the main town and just a short walk from the Mahart ferry port, the ruin of Solomon's Tower was once part of a lower castle used to control river traffic. These days, the tower houses the royal palace's original Gothic fountain along with some town-history exhibits. To find the tower from the Mahart ferry, cross the road and then turn left onto a paved path, walking uphill.

Visegrád Citadel   RUIN
(Visegrád Cittadella; adult/concession 1400/700Ft; ☉9.30am-5.30pm daily mid-Mar–mid-Oct, 9.30am-5.30pm Sat & Sun mid-Oct–mid-Mar) From just beyond Solomon's Tower, you can climb a very steep path uphill to the Visegrád Citadel directly above. While the citadel (1259) ruins themselves are not as spectacular as their history, the view of the Danube Bend from the walls is well worth the climb. An alternative, less steep path leads to the citadel from the town centre area. Find the trail behind the Catholic church on Fő tér.

🛏 Sleeping & Eating
As with the other towns in the Danube Bend, Visegrád is an easy day trip from Budapest, so it's not necessary to stay over. **Visegrád Tours** (☎398 160; Rév utca 15; ☉8am-5.30pm), a travel agency in the town centre, provides information and books private rooms for around 5000Ft per person per night.

Hotel Honti   PENSION €
(☎398 120; www.hotelhonti.hu; Fő utca 66; s/d from €40/55; @) Honti is a friendly pension filled with homey rooms. Its large garden and table tennis are available for guest use, and bicycles can be hired for 2000Ft per day.

Reneszánsz   HUNGARIAN €€
(☎398 081; Fő utca 11; mains 2000-4000Ft) Step through this restaurant's doors to be greeted by a medieval banquet and men in tights with silly hats. If you're in the right mood, it can be quite a hoot. The convenient location is right across the street from the Mahart ferry port.

Don Vito Pizzeria   ITALIAN €
(Fő utca 83; mains 1300-2200Ft) This handsome pizza and pasta joint in the town centre offers a relaxing terrace out back or a more formal – and air-conditioned – main dining room inside.

ℹ Getting There & Away
Frequent buses go to Visegrád from Budapest's Árpád híd bus station (600Ft, 1¼ hours, hourly), the Szentendre HÉV station (400Ft, 45 minutes, every 45 minutes) and Esztergom (400Ft, 40 minutes, hourly).

For ferry services from Budapest, see p450.

Esztergom
☑33 / POP 31,000
It's easy to see the attraction of Esztergom, even (or especially) from a distance. The city's massive basilica, sitting high above the town and Danube River, is an incredible sight, rising magnificently from its rural setting.

The significance of this town is even greater than its architectural appeal. The 2nd-century Roman emperor-to-be Marcus Aurelius wrote his famous *Meditations* while he camped here. In the 10th century, Stephen I, founder of the Hungarian state, was born and crowned at the cathedral. From the late 10th to the mid-13th centuries Esztergom served as the Hungarian royal seat. In 1543 the Turks ravaged the town and much of it was destroyed, only to be rebuilt in the 18th and 19th centuries.

◉ Sights & Activities

FREE Esztergom Basilica   CHURCH
(Esztergomi Bazilika; www.bazilika-esztergom.hu; Szent István tér 1; ☉6am-6pm) Hungary's largest church is the Esztergom Basilica. Perched on Castle Hill, its 72m-high central dome can be seen for many kilometres around. Reconstructed in the neoclassical style, much of the building dates from the 19th century; the oldest section is the red-marble 1510 **Bakócz Chapel** (Bakócz Kápolna). The **treasury** (kincsház; adult/concession 800/400Ft; ☉9am-4.30pm Mar-Oct, 11am-3.30pm Sat & Sun Nov & Dec) contains priceless objects, including ornate vestments and the 13th-century Hungarian coronation cross. If you're fit and up for a challenge, climb up to the massive **cupola** (admission 500Ft; ☉9am-4.45pm) for some amazing views of the river and town below. Among those buried in the **crypt** (altemplom; admission 200Ft; ☉9am-4.45pm) under the cathedral is Cardinal Mindszenty, who was imprisoned by the communists for refusing to allow Hungary's Catholic schools to be secularised.

Castle Museum
MUSEUM

(Vár Múzeum; adult/concession 840/420Ft; ⊙10am-6pm Tue-Sun Apr-Oct, 10am-4pm Tue-Sun Nov-Mar) At the southern end of the hill is the Castle Museum, inside the reconstructed remnants of the medieval royal palace (1215), which was built upon previous castles. The earliest excavated sections on the hill date from the 2nd to 3rd centuries.

Watertown
HISTORICAL DISTRICT

Southwest of the cathedral along the banks of the Little Danube, narrow streets wind through the Víziváros (Watertown) district, home to the 1738 **Watertown Parish Church** (Víziváros Plébánia Templom) at the start of Berényi Zsigmond utca. The **Christian Museum** (Keresztény Múzeum; www.christianmuseum.hu; Berényi Zsigmond utca 2; adult/concession 800/400Ft; ⊙10am-6pm Wed-Sun May-Oct, 11am-3pm Tue-Sun Nov, Dec, Mar & Apr) is in the adjacent Primate's Palace (1882). The stunning collection of medieval religious art includes a statue of the Virgin Mary from the 11th century.

Szent István strandfürdő'
SWIMMING POOL

(Kis-Duna sétány 1; adult/concession 1100/800Ft; ⊙9am-7pm May-Sep) Just east of the Little Danube are outdoor thermal pools and stretches of grass 'beach'.

Aquasziget Esztergom
WATER PARK

(Táncsics Mihály utca 5; admission 2950Ft, after 4pm 2100Ft; ⊙9am-8pm May-Sep) This modern water park, with pools and water slides, is a bit livelier than the Szent István pool and great for kids. You'll find it on the opposite side of the Little Danube canal from the main town, just across the Bottyán Bridge.

🍽 Sleeping & Eating

Although frequent transportation connections make Esztergom an easy day trip from Budapest, you might want to stop a night if you are going on to Slovakia. Contact Gran Tours (p413) about private rooms (3000Ft to 4000Ft per person) or apartments (from 9000Ft).

Self-caterers can shop at the **Match** (Bajcsy-Zsilinszky utca; ⊙6.30am-8pm Mon-Fri, 6.30am-6pm Sat, 8am-noon Sun), next to the OTP Bank, or the small town **market** on Simor János utca.

Ria Panzió
PENSION €€

(⊉313 115; www.riapanzio.com; Batthyány Lajos utca 11; s/d 9000/12,000Ft; ⊛) This is a family-run place in a converted town house just down from the basilica. Relax on the terrace or arrange an adventure through the own-

ers: you can rent a bicycle or take a water-skiing trip on the Danube in summer. The owners are friendly; our only gripe was the lacklustre breakfast.

Alabárdos Panzió
PENSION €€

(⊉312 640; www.alabardospanzio.hu; Bajcsy-Zsilinszky utca 49; s/d 8500/11,000Ft) Alabárdos isn't flashy but it does provide neat, tidy and sizeable accommodation. Offers unexpected extras like a laundry room and a small beauty parlour on the premises. The location is great if you want to be close to the cathedral: the hotel is at the base of Castle Hill.

Gran Camping
CAMPING GROUND €

(⊉411 953; www.grancamping-fortanex.hu; Nagy-Duna sétány 3; camp sites per adult/concession/tent/tent & car 1300/700/1100/1400Ft, bungalows 16,000-22,000Ft, dm/d/tr 2900/13,000/14,000Ft; ⊙May-Sep;⊛) Small but centrally located, this camping ground has space for 500 souls in various forms of accommodation, as well as a good-size swimming pool. It's a 10-minute walk along the Danube from the cathedral.

Padlisán
HUNGARIAN €

(⊉311 212; Pázmány Péter utca 21; mains 1500-3000Ft) With a sheer rock face topped by a castle bastion as its backdrop, Padlisán has a dramatic setting. Thankfully its menu doesn't let the show down, featuring modern Hungarian dishes and imaginative salads.

Múzeumkert
HUNGARIAN €

(Batthyány Lajos utca 1; mains 1800-3600Ft) A combination restaurant and cocktail bar, just down from the Csú'ló'k Csárda, serves very good Hungarian dishes by day (try the tender veal stew in paprika sauce); by night it morphs into one of the few places near the basilica where you can relax over a beer or cocktail till late.

Csülök Csárda
HUNGARIAN €

(Batthyány Lajos utca 9; mains 1800-3600Ft) The Pork Knuckle Inn – guess the speciality here – is a charming eatery popular with visitors and locals alike. It serves up good home cooking (try the bean soup), in huge portions.

ⓘ Information

OTP Bank (Rákóczi tér 2-4) Does foreign-exchange transactions.

Post office (Arany János utca 2) Just off Széchenyi tér.

Gran Tours (⊉502 001; Széchenyi tér 25; ⊙8am-5pm Mon-Fri, 9am-noon Sat Jun-Aug, 8am-4pm Mon-Fri Sep-May) The best source of information in town.

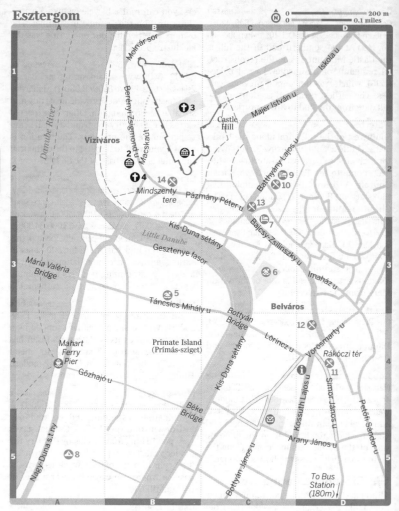

ℹ Getting There & Away

Buses run to/from Budapest's Árpád híd bus station (700Ft, 1½ hours) and to/from Visegrád (400Ft, 45 minutes) at least hourly. Hourly buses also link Esztergom to Szentendre (800Ft, 1½ hours).

The most comfortable way to get to Esztergom from Budapest is by rail. Trains depart from Budapest's Nyugati train station (1100Ft, 1½ hours) at least hourly. Cross the Mária Valéria Bridge into Štúrovo, Slovakia, and you can catch a train to Bratislava, which is 1½ hours away.

For ferry services from Budapest, see p450.

NORTHWESTERN HUNGARY

A visit to this region is a boon for anyone wishing to see remnants of Hungary's Roman legacy, medieval heritage and baroque splendour. This swath of land was fortunate in largely avoiding the Ottoman destruction wrought on the country in the 16th and 17th centuries. Its seminal towns – Sopron and Győr – managed to save their medieval centres from total devastation, and exploring their cobbled streets and hidden courtyards is a magical experience. They also house a

Esztergom

ornucopia of baroque architecture, some-
hing rare in Hungary. Equally rewarding
are reminders of Roman settlement, and the
egion's natural beauty.

Győr

🚊 96 / POP 130,000

Not many tourists make the effort to stop at
Győr (German: Raab), which is all the more
reason to visit. This large city with the tricky
name (pronounced *jyeur*) is a surprisingly
splendid place, with a medieval heart hidden behind a commercial facade.

Midway between Budapest and Vienna,
Győr sits at the point where the Mosoni-
Danube, Rábca and Rába Rivers meet. This
was the site of a Roman town named Ar-
rabona. In the 11th century, Stephen I established a bishopric here, and in the 16th
century a fortress was erected to hold back
the Turks. The Ottomans captured Győr in

1594 but were able to hold on to it for only
four years. For that reason Győr is known as
the 'dear guard', watching over the nation
through the centuries.

⊙ Sights & Activities

Bécsí kapu tér PUBLIC SQUARE
The enchanting 1725 **Carmelite Church**
(Karmelita Templom; Bécsi kapu tér) and many
fine baroque palaces line riverfront Bécsí
kapu tér. On the northwestern side of the
square are the fortifications built in the 16th
century to stop the Turks. A short distance
to the east is **Napoleon House** (Napoleon-ház;
Király utca 4), named after the French military
leader (see boxed text below). Walk the old
streets and stop in at a pavement cafe or
two.

FREE | **Basilica** CATHEDRAL
(Bazilika; Apor Vilmos püspök tere; ⊙8am-
noon & 2-6pm) North up Káptalan-domb
(Chapter Hill), in the oldest part of Győr, is
the solid baroque Basilica. Situated on the
hill, it was originally Romanesque, but most
of what you see inside dates from the 17th
and 18th centuries. Don't miss the Gothic
Héderváry Chapel (Hédervary-kápolna)
at the back of the cathedral, which contains
a glittering 15th-century gold bust of King
(and St) Ladislas.

Diocesan Treasury & Library MUSEUM
(Egyházmegyei Kincstár és Könyvtár; adult/conces-
sion 700/400Ft; ⊙10am-4pm Tue-Sun Mar-Oct)
East of the Basilica is the Diocesan Treasury
& Library. Of particular value in its collection are the Gothic chalices and Renaissance mitre embroidered with pearls, but
stealing the show is the precious library,
containing almost 70,000 volumes printed
before 1850. At the bottom of the hill on
Jedlik Ányos utca is the **Ark of the Cove-
nant** (Frigyláda), a statue dating from 1731.
From here you can head north to a bridge
overlooking the junction of the city's three
rivers.

NAPOLEONIC PAUSE

France's Napoleon Bonaparte once spent a night in Hungary – in Győr to be precise. The
vertically challenged military commander slept over at Király utca 4, due east of Bécsi
kapu tér, on 31 August 1809. The building is now called Napoleon-ház (Napoleon House),
appropriately enough. And why did Bonaparte choose Győr to make his grand entrée into
Hungary? The city was near the site of the Battle of Raab, which had taken place just 11
weeks earlier between Franco-Italian and Austrian–Hungarian armies. Bonaparte's side
won, and an inscription on the Arc de Triomphe in Paris still recalls 'la bataille de Raab'.

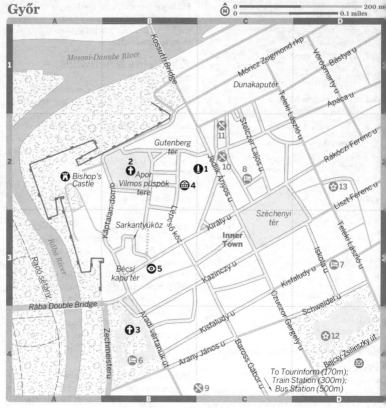

Mosoni-Danube River

Bishop's Castle

Gutenberg tér

Apor Vilmos püspök tere

Sarkantyúköz

Bécsi kapu tér

Rába River

Radó sétány

Rába Double Bridge

Inner Town

Széchenyi tér

To Tourinform (170m); Train Station (300m); Bus Station (500m)

Győr

⊙ Sights

1 Ark of the Covenant	C2
2 Basilica	B2
3 Carmelite Church	B4
4 Diocesan Treasury & Library	B2
5 Napoleon House	B3

⊜ Sleeping

6 Hotel Klastrom	B4
7 Kertész Pension	D3
8 Soho Café & Pension	C2

⊗ Eating

9 Kaiser Supermarket	C4
10 La Máreda	C2
11 Matróz	C2

⊛ Entertainment

12 Győr National Theatre	D4
13 Rómer Ház	D2

Rába Quelle SWIMMING POOL
(☑514 900; Fürdő tér 1; adult/concession per day 2400/1800Ft; per 3hr 1950/1550Ft; ☉thermal baths 9am-8.30pm, pool 8am-8pm Mon-Sat) The water temperature in the pools at thermal bath Rába Quelle ranges from 29°C to 38°C. You can also take advantage of its fitness and wellness centres.

⚝ Festivals & Events

Győr has a couple of festivals held every summer that are worth catching. The **Hungarian Dance Festival** (www.magyartanc fesztival.hu) is held in late June, and the **Győr Summer Cultural Festival** runs from late June to late July.

⊨ Sleeping & Eating

The **Kaiser supermarket** (Arany János utca 16; ☉7am-7pm Mon-Fri, 6.30am-3pm Sat, 8am-1pm Sun) is the place to head for self-catering purposes. Széchenyi tér, the town's outsized

PANNONHALMA ABBEY

Take half a day and make the short trip from Győr to the ancient and impressive **Pannonhalma Abbey** (Pannonhalmi Főapátság; ☑570 191; www.bences.hu; Vár utca 1; foreign-language tours adult/student/family 2500/1500/6000Ft; ☉9am-4pm Tue-Sun Apr & Oct–mid-Nov, 9am-5pm daily Jun-Sep, 10am-3pm Tue-Sun mid-Nov–Mar), now a Unesco World Heritage site. Most buildings in the complex date from the 13th to the 18th centuries; highlights include the Romanesque basilica (1225), the Gothic cloister (1486) and the impressive collection of ancient texts in the library. Because it's an active monastery, the abbey must be visited with a guide. English and German tours leave at 11.20am and 1.20pm from April to September, with an extra tour at 3.20pm from June to September. Between October and March, foreign-language tours must be booked in advance.

There are buses to the abbey from Győr at 8am, 10am and noon (around 400Ft, 30 minutes, 21km).

central square, is the perfect place to people-watch over a coffee or ice-cream cone.

Hotel Klastrom　　BOUTIQUE HOTEL **€€€**
(☑516 910; www.klastrom.hu; Zechmeister utca 1; s/d/tr 12,500/17,500/20,000Ft;@) This delightful three-star hotel occupies a 300-year-old Carmelite convent south of Bécsi kapu tér. Rooms are charming and bright, and extras include a sauna, a solarium, a pub with a vaulted ceiling, and a restaurant with seating in a leafy and peaceful garden.

Kertész Pension　　PENSION **€€**
(☑317 461; www.kerteszpanzio.com; Iskola utca 11; s/d/tr/q 8000/12,000/14,100/16,000Ft) The 'Gardener' has very simple rooms on offer, but it's well located in downtown Győr and staff couldn't be friendlier.

Soho Café & Pension　　PENSION **€**
(☑550 465; www.sohocafe.hu; Kenyér köz 7; s/d/tr 7000/10,000/13,000Ft) Győr's cheapest in-town pension has simple no-frills rooms and two big pluses: it's just a block from Széchenyi tér and has a ground-floor cafe with free wi-fi, friendly staff, and good coffee and beer.

TOP CHOICE **Matróz**　　HUNGARIAN **€**
(☑336 208; Dunakapu tér 3; mains 1100-2200Ft) Matróz makes the best damn fish dishes around, from warming carp soup to delicate pike-perch fillets. The handsome vaulted brick cellar, complete with dark-blue tiled oven and nautical memorabilia, completes this wonderful little eatery.

La Maréda　　INTERNATIONAL **€€**
(☑510 982; Apáca utca 4; mains 1600-3500Ft) If the wait for a table is too long over at Matróz, try this upmarket bistro that serves Hungarian specialties like duck and turkey

breast but adds a gourmet touch (such as topping the turkey breast with baked apple and smoked cheese).

☆ Entertainment

A good source of information for what's on in Győr is the free magazine *Győri Est*.

Győr National Theatre　　THEATRE
(Győri Nemzeti Színház; ☑520 600; Czuczor Gergely utca 7) The celebrated Győr Ballet and the city's opera company and philharmonic orchestra all perform at this modern venue. Tourinform can help with performance schedules.

Rómer Ház　　BAR & CINEMA
(☑550 850; www.romerhaz.eu; Teleki László utca 21) One-stop shop for entertainment, featuring an independent cinema upstairs, and regular live concerts and club nights down in the dungeon.

❶ Information

Darius Café (Czuczor Gergely utca 6; per hr 210Ft; ☉1-9pm Mon-Fri, 3-10pm Sat) Internet access on several computers in a convivial atmosphere and decent coffee to boot.

Main post office (Bajcsy-Zsilinszky út 46; ☉8am-6pm Mon-Fri) There's a branch office at the main train station.

OTP Bank (Baross Gábor 16)

Tourinform (☑311 771; www.gyortourism.hu; Árpád út 32; ☉9am-6pm Jun-Aug, 9am-5pm Mon-Fri, 9am-1pm Sat Sep-May) Small but helpful tourist office located in a small kiosk astride Baross Gábor utca.

❶ Getting There & Away

Buses travel to Budapest (2480Ft, two hours, hourly), Pannonhalma (460Ft, 30 minutes, half-hourly), Esztergom (1830Ft, 2½ hours, one daily) and Balatonfüred (1800Ft, 2½ hours, six daily).

Győr is well connected by express train to Budapest's Keleti and Déli train stations (2480Ft, 1½ hours, half-hourly), and 10 daily trains connect Győr with Vienna's Westbahnhof (6000Ft, 1½ hours).

Sopron

99 / POP 59,000

Sopron (*shop*-ron) is an attractive border town with a history that stretches back to Roman times and beyond. It boasts some well-preserved Roman ruins and a fetching medieval square, bounded by the original town walls, that invites an hour or two of aimless meandering. That said, in summer it's teeming with day-trippers from Austria (Vienna is only 70km away) who come here for inexpensive dental work and the inevitable *kaffee und kuchen* before and after. This is one place in Hungary where any scrap of high-school German you can pull out will be amply rewarded. On our visit, even the tourist office couldn't muster any English.

The Mongols and Turks never got this far so, unlike many Hungarian cities, numerous medieval buildings remain in use. The town's close history with Austria goes

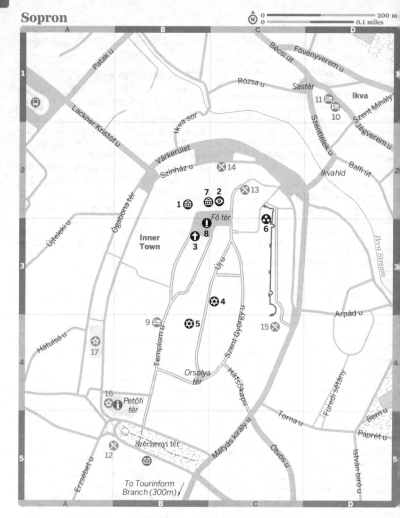

Sopron

back centuries and Sopron could easily have landed on the other side of the border if it weren't for a referendum in 1921 in which town residents voted to remain part of Hungary. The rest of Bürgenland (the region to which Sopron used to belong) went to Austria. The area is known for its good red wines, such as Kékfrancos, and once you've strolled through the quiet backstreets, you can opt for a glass or two at a local cafe or restaurant.

Sopron Festival Weeks (www.prokultura. hu) runs from late June to mid-July.

◉ Sights & Activities

Fő tér   PUBLIC SQUARE
Fő tér is the main square in Sopron; there are several museums, monuments and churches scattered around it. At the time of research much of the square was fenced off as workers were repairing the cobblestones; several attractions, including the massive **Firewatch Tower** (Tűztorony), were closed. It wasn't clear if the tower would reopen by 2011, but be prepared for some minor inconveniences. The 60m-high tower rises above the Old Town's northern gate and is visible from all around. The building is a true architectural hybrid: the 2m-thick square base, built on a Roman gate, dates from the 12th

century, the middle cylindrical and arcaded balcony was built in the 16th century and the baroque spire was added in 1680. If it's open, you can climb to the top for views of the Alps. In the centre of Fő tér is the 1701 **Trinity Column** (Szentháromság Ozlop). Just off the square, along the town wall, are the small **open-air ruins** (admission free; ◷24hr), with reconstructed Roman walls and 2nd-century houses dating from the time when Sopron was a tiny Roman outpost known as Scarbantia. On the north side of the square are Storno House and Fabricus House, each holding a pair of museums.

Storno House   MUSEUM
(Storno Ház; Fő tér 8) This house has a so-so exhibit on Sopron's more recent history on the 1st floor, but the floor above holds the more worthy **Storno Collection** (adult/concession 1000/500Ft; ◷10am-6pm Tue-Sun Apr-Sep, 2-6pm Tue-Sun Oct-Mar), displaying the interiors of a successful 19th-century family who furnished their apartment with priceless found objects from the Romanesque and Gothic periods.

Fabricius House   MUSEUM
(Fabricius Ház; Fő tér 6) Fabricius is home to a fascinating **archaeological exhibition** (adult/concession 700/350Ft; ◷10am-6pm Tue-Sun Apr-Sep, 10am-2pm Tue-Sun Oct-Mar), with stone sculptures and other remains recovered from Roman times. Upstairs, there is an exhibition dedicated to **urban apartments** (adult/concession 800/400Ft; ◷10am-6pm Tue-Sun Apr-Sep, 10am-2pm Tue-Sun Oct-Mar), where you can see how Sopron's residents lived in the 17th and 18th centuries.

Goat Church   CHURCH
(Kecske Templom; Templom utca 1; admission free; ◷8am-9pm mid-Apr–Sep, 8am-6pm Oct–mid-Apr) Near the centre of Fő tér is the 13th-century Goat Church, whose name comes from the heraldic animal of its chief benefactor. Just off the main nave is the **Chapter Hall** (Káptalan Terem), part of a 14th-century Franciscan monastery, with frescos and stone carvings.

Synagogues   SYNAGOGUES
The **New Synagogue** (Új Zsinagóga; Új utca 11) and **Old Synagogue** (Ó Zsinagóga; Új utca 22; adult/concession 600/300Ft; ◷10am-6pm Tue-Sun May-Oct), both built in the 14th century, are reminders of the town's once substantial Jewish population. The latter contains a museum of Jewish life.

🛏 Sleeping & Eating

For self-catering supplies, head for **Match** (Várkerület 100; ⊙6.30am-7pm Mon-Fri, 6.30am-3pm Sat) supermarket.

TOP CHOICE **Wieden Pension** PENSION €
(☎523 222; www.wieden.hu; Sas tér 13; s/d/tr/apt from 7700/10,900/12,900/11,900Ft;@) Sopron's cosiest pension is located in an attractive old town house within easy walking distance of the Inner Town. The rooms are sparsely furnished but comfortable; the friendly reception desk will go out of its way to make you feel at home.

Hotel Wollner BOUTIQUE HOTEL €€
(☎524 400; www.wollner.hu; Templom utca 20; s/d/apt from €75/90/110;@) A worthy splurge option in the heart of the Old Town, with elegant period doubles hidden away in a 300-year-old baroque town palace. The courtyard restaurant is one of the best in town.

Jégverem Pension PENSION €
(☎510 113; www.jegverem.hu; Jégverem utca 1; s/d 6900/8900Ft) An excellent and central bet, with five suitelike rooms in an 18th-century ice cellar in the Ikva district. Even if you're not staying here, try the terrace restaurant for enormous portions of pork, chicken and fish dishes.

Vákació Vendégház HOSTEL €
(☎338 502; www.vakacio-vendeghazak.hu; Ady Endre út 31; dm 2800Ft) Cheap lodgings not far west of the town centre. Rooms are clean and furnished with two to 10 beds; bus 10 will drop you off not far from the front door. Phone in advance for reservations; note the reception opens only at 4pm.

Graben HUNGARIAN €
(Várkerület 8; mains 1000-1800Ft) The secluded garden terrace is a welcoming lunch or dinner spot for well-prepared Hungarian dishes, including fresh lightly baked pike-perch. In winter dine below in a Gothic cellar.

Generális-Corvinus INTERNATIONAL €
(Fő tér 7-8; mains 1100-2100Ft) This large restaurant is in reality two eateries – one serving decent Hungarian cuisine, the other acceptable pizzas. The tables on the main square are a welcome respite for refreshment and people-watching.

Dömörői CAFE €
(Széchenyi tér 13) In a city that takes its cultural cues from Vienna, what could be more natural than a Viennese-style coffeehouse? Arguably the best ice cream in town.

☆ Entertainment

Ferenc Liszt Conference & Cultural Centre CONCERT HALL
(Liszt Ferenc Kulturális Központ; ☎517 517; Liszt Ferenc tér) A concert hall, cafe and exhibition space all rolled into one. The information desk has the latest on classical music and other cultural events in town.

Petőfi Theatre THEATRE
(☎517 517; www.prokultura.hu; Petőfi tér 1) This beautiful building with mosaics on its facade is Sopron's leading theatre.

🛈 Information

Main post office (Széchenyi tér 7-10)

OTP Bank (Várkerület 96a)

Tourinform main branch (☎517 560; sopron@tourinform.hu; Liszt Ferenc utca 1; ⊙9am-6pm daily mid-Jun–Aug, 9am-5pm Mon-Fri & 9am-noon Sat Sep–mid-Jun); southern branch (☎505 438; Deák tér 45; ⊙9am-5pm Mon-Fri, 9am-noon Apr-Oct) Both branches offer free internet access and a plethora of tourist information.

🛈 Getting There & Away

There are two buses a day to Budapest (3300Ft, 3¾ hours), and seven to Győr (1500Ft, two hours). The bus station is northwest of the Old Town on Lackner Kristóf utca.

Trains run to Budapest's Keleti train station (3500Ft, 2¾ hours, eight daily) via Győr. You can also travel to Vienna's Meidling station (4200Ft, three hours, up to 15 daily), pending reconstruction of Vienna's Südbahnhof sometime in 2012.

LAKE BALATON

Central Europe's largest expanse of fresh water is Lake Balaton, covering 600 sq km. The main activities include swimming, sailing and sunbathing, but the lake is also popular with cyclists lured here by the more than 200km of marked bike paths that encircle the lake.

The southern shore is mostly a forgettable jumble of tacky resorts, with the exception of party town Siófok. The northern shore however, is yin to the southern's yang. Here the pace of life is more refined, and the forested hills of the Balaton Uplands National Park create a wonderful backdrop. Historical towns such as Keszthely and Balatonfüred dot the landscape, while Tihany, a peninsula cutting the lake almost in half, is home to an important historical church.

Siófok

📱84 / POP 23,900

Siófok (*shee*-a-folk) is officially known as 'Hungary's summer capital' – unofficially it's called 'Hungary's Ibiza'. In July and August, nowhere in the country parties as hard or stays up as late as this lakeside resort, which attracts an ever-increasing number of international DJs and their avid followers. Outside the summer months Siófok returns to relative normality.

Greater Siófok stretches for some 17km, as far as the resort of Balatonvilágos (once reserved exclusively for communist honchos) to the east and Balatonszéplak to the west.

◉ Sights & Activities

There are rowing boats and sailing boats for hire at various locations along the lake, including Nagy Strand. Lake cruises run from late May to mid-September, generally daily at 10am, 11.30am, 1pm, 2.30pm, 4pm and 5.30pm. There are additional cruises at 11am, 2pm and 4pm daily from late April to late May.

Water Tower   MONUMENT
(víztorony; Szabadság tér) The town's wooden water tower, built in 1912, affords an impressive view out over the town and lake beyond. As we were researching this guide the tower was closed for renovation. It was expected to reopen by 2012.

Nagy Strand   BEACH
(adult/concession 1000/500Ft) Nagy Strand, 'Big Beach', is centre stage on Petőfi sétány; free concerts are often held here on summer evenings. There are many more managed swimming areas along the lakeshore, which cost around the same as Nagy Strand.

Galerius   SWIMMING POOL
(📱506 580; www.galerius-furdo.hu, in Hungarian; Szent László utca 183; pools adult/concession 2900/2500Ft, sauna & pools 3400Ft; ⊙9am-9pm) Galerius is 4km west of downtown Siófok. It offers a plethora of indoor thermal pools, saunas and massages.

🛌 Sleeping & Eating

Prices quoted are for the high season in July and August. Tourinform can help find you a private room (prices starting around €15 per person), or an apartment for slightly more.

TOP CHOICE / **Mala Garden**   BOUTIQUE HOTEL €€€
(📱506 687; www.malagarden.hu; Petőfi sétány 15a; r 21,900-36,900Ft;❄) Most of Siófok's accommodation options pale in comparison with this gorgeous boutique hotel. It's reminiscent of Bali, with Indonesian art lining the walls, a small manicured flower garden at the rear of the hotel and an excellent restaurant serving Asian cuisine.

Hotel Yacht Club   BOUTIQUE HOTEL €€
(📱311 161; www.hotel-yachtclub.hu; Vitorlás utca 14; s/d €52/112; ❄@☁) Overlooking the harbour is this excellent little hotel with cosy rooms, some of which have balconies overlooking the lake, and a modern wellness centre. Bicycles can be hired.

Siófok Város College   HOSTEL €
(📱312 244; www.siofokvaroskollegiuma.sulinet.hu; Petőfi sétány 1; dm 2700Ft) Close to the action in central Siófok, it's hard to beat this basic college accommodation for price and location.

Roxy   INTERNATIONAL €
(Szabadság tér; mains 1200-3000Ft) Pseudo-rustic restaurant–pub in the commercial centre at Szabadság tér attracts diners with a wide range of international dishes and surprisingly imaginative Hungarian mains.

☆ Entertainment

South Balaton Cultural Centre (📱311 855; Fő tér 2), Siófok's main cultural venue stages concerts, dance performances and plays. However, most visitors to Siófok are interested in more energetic entertainment. Turnover of bars and clubs is high, but the following manage to attract punters year after year:

Flőrt   CLUB
(www.flort.hu; Sió utca 4) Well-established club with visiting DJs and light shows.

Palace   CLUB
(www.palace.hu; Deák Ferenc utca 2) Hugely popular club. Accessible by free bus that leaves from the Palace cafe along the beach promenade (Petőfi sétány).

Renegade   BAR
(Petőfi sétány 9) Wild pub near the beach; table dancing and live music are common.

❶ Information

Main post office (Fő utca 186)

OTP Bank (Szabadság tér 10a)

Tourinform (📱310 117; tourinform@siofokportal. hu; Fő utca 174-176; ⊙8am-7pm Mon-Fri, 10am-7pm Sat & Sun mid-Jun–mid-Sep, 8am-4pm

Mon-Fri, 9am-noon Sat mid-Sep–mid-Jun). Hands out city maps and can advise on and book rooms in season starting at about 3500Ft per person. Note the office is normally based in an old *víztorony* (water tower), but was temporarily relocated inside the Atrium shopping centre (until late 2011) while the water tower undergoes repair work.

❶ Getting There & Away

From April to October, at least four daily passenger ferries run between Siófok and Balatonfüred (1360Ft, 50 minutes), some of which carry on to Tihany. Up to eight ferries follow the same route in July and August.

The bus and train stations are in Millennium Park just off Fő utca. Buses serve a lot of destinations from Siófok, but you'll find the more frequent train connections of more use. Trains to Nagykanizsa pass through all the resorts on the southern edge of the lake, and there are several daily train connections to and from Budapest (2160Ft, two hours).

Balatonfüred

☑87 / POP 13,000

Walking the hillside streets, you'll catch glimpses of the easy grace that 18th- and 19th-century Balatonfüred (*bal*-ah-tahn fuhr-ed) enjoyed. In those days the wealthy and famous built large villas on its tree-lined streets, hoping to take advantage of the health benefits of the town's thermal waters. In more recent times, the lake frontage has received a massive makeover and now sports the most stylish marina on the lake. The hotels here are a bit cheaper than those on the neighbouring Tihany peninsula, making this a good base for exploring. Most of the action, including the beaches, hotels and restaurants, are clustered along the shoreline.

◉ Sights & Activities

Cruises   BOAT RIDES

The park along the central shore, near the ferry pier, is worth a promenade. You can take a one-hour **pleasure cruise** (☑342 230; www.balatonihajozas.hu; ferry pier; adult/concession 1400/600Ft) four times a day, from late May to mid-September. The **retro disco boat** (disco hajo; ☑342 230; www.balatonihajozas.hu; ferry pier; cruise 1800Ft), a two-hour cruise with music and drinks, leaves at 9pm Tuesday, Thursday and Friday.

Kisfaludy Strand   BEACH

(Aranyhíd sétány; adult/concession 550/350Ft; ◷8am-6pm mid-May–mid-Sep) Along the foot-

path 800m northeast of the pier, Kisfaludy Strand is a relatively sandy beach. You can explore the waterfront by bike (see p422).

Kossuth Forrásvíz   SPA

The heart of the old spa town is Gyógy tér, where Kossuth Forrásvíz (Kossuth Spring, 1853) dispenses slightly sulphurous water that people actually drink for health. Don't stray far from a bathroom afterwards.

🛏 Sleeping

Prices fluctuate throughout the year and usually peak between early July and late August; high-season prices are quoted here. **SunCity Tours** (☑06 30 947 2679; Csokonai utca 1) can help with finding you a place, as can **Fontaine Room Service** (☑343 673; Honvéd utca 11). There are lots of houses with rooms for rent on the streets north of Kisfaludy Beach.

Hotel Blaha Lujza   BOUTIQUE HOTEL €€

(☑581 219; www.hotelblaha.hu; Blaha Lujza utca 4; s/d €40/60) This was once the holiday home of the much-loved 19th-century Hungarian actress–singer Blaha Lujza. Its rooms are a little compact but very comfy.

Villa Balaton   BOUTIQUE HOTEL €

(☑788 290; www.balatonvilla.hu; Deák Ferenc utca 38; s/d 6250/12,500Ft) The large, bright rooms of this pastel-yellow villa uphill from the lake are available for rent. Each has its own balcony overlooking a sunny garden and grapevines, and guests can make use of the well-equipped kitchen.

Füred Camping   CAMPING GROUND €

(☑580 241; fured@balatontourist.hu; Széchenyi utca 24; camp sites per adult/concession/tent 1600/1200/5500Ft, bungalows/caravans from 17,000/23,000Ft; ◷mid-Apr–early Oct) Sprawling beachfront complex 1km west of the centre, with water-sport rentals, swimming pools, tennis courts, a restaurant and a convenience store.

✗ Eating & Drinking

La Riva   FINE DINING €€

(Zákonyi Ferenc sétány 4; mains 1500-4000Ft) Taking pride of place on the modern marina's waterfront is La Riva, a restaurant that combines imaginative cooking and the prospect of a relaxed table over the water. Pasta and pizza are the mainstays of the menu, but don't overlook the daily blackboard specials.

Balaton   HUNGARIAN €

(Kisfaludy utca 5; mains 1000-3000Ft) This cool, leafy oasis amid all the hubbub is set back

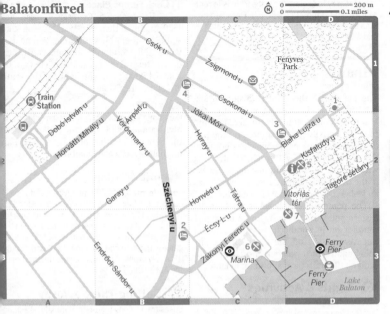

Balatonfüred

from the lake in a shaded park area. It serves generous portions and, like so many restaurants in town, has an extensive fish selection.

Stefánia Vitorlás　　　　　　　HUNGARIAN €
(Tagore sétány 1; mains 1500-3000Ft) Enormous wooden eatery sitting right on the lake's edge at the foot of the pier. Watch the yachts sail in and out of the harbour while enjoying Hungarian cuisine and local wine.

Karolina　　　　　　　　　　　CAFE €
(Zákonyi Ferenc sétány 4) Karolina, just to the left of La Riva, is a sophisticated cafe–bar

that serves excellent coffee, teas and local wines.

ℹ Information

OTP Bank (Petőfi Sándor utca 8)

Post office (Zsigmond utca 14; ⊙8am-4pm Mon-Fri)

Tourinform (☑580 480; balatonfured@tourin form.hu; Kisfaludy utca 1; ⊙9am-7pm Mon-Fri, to 6pm Sat, to 1pm Sun Jul & Aug, 9am-5pm Mon-Fri, to 1pm Sat Jun & Sep, 9am-4pm Mon-Fri Oct-May) Helpful tourist office.

ℹ Getting There & Around

The adjacent bus and train stations are on Dobó István utca, about 1km uphill from the lake. Buses to Tihany (250Ft, 30 minutes) leave every 30 minutes or so throughout the day. Several buses daily head to the northwestern lakeshore towns including Keszthely (1200Ft, 1½ hours).

Budapest-bound buses (2400Ft) depart from Balatonfüred four times daily and take between two and three hours to get there. Trains (2480Ft, three daily) take about as long. There are a number of towns on the train line with 'Balaton' or 'Füred' somewhere in their name, so double-check which station you're getting off at.

From April to September, half a dozen daily ferries ply the water from Balatonfüred to Tihany (1040Ft, 30 minutes) and Siófok (1360Ft, 50 minutes).

A good way to explore the waterfront is to rent a bike from **Tempo 21** (☑480 671; Deák Ferenc utca 56; per hr/day 350/2400Ft; ☻9am-6pm mid-May–mid-Sep).

Tihany

☑87 / POP 1500

The place with the greatest historical significance on Lake Balaton is Tihany (*tee-hah-nee*), a hilly peninsula jutting 5km into the lake. Activity here is centred on the tiny town of the same name, which is home to the celebrated Abbey Church. Contrasting with this are the hills and marshy meadows of the peninsula's nature reserve, which has an isolated, almost wild feel to it.

The peninsula has beaches on both its eastern and western coasts and a big resort complex on its southern tip. However, you can easily shake off the tourist hordes by going hiking. Bird-watchers, bring your binoculars: the trails have abundant avian life.

⊙ Sights & Activities

Abbey Church CHURCH
(Apátság Templom; adult/concession 800/400Ft; ☻9am-6pm May-Sep, 10am-5pm Apr & Oct, 10am-3pm Nov-Mar) You can spot twin-towered Abbey Church, dating from 1754, from a long way off. Entombed in the crypt is the abbey's founder, King Andrew I. The admission fee includes entry to the attached **Abbey Museum** (Apátsági Múzeum). Behind the church a path leads to outstanding views.

Open-air Folk Museum MUSEUM
(Szabadtéri Néprajzi Múzeum; Pisky sétány 10; adult/concession 400/300Ft; ☻10am-6pm May-Sep) Follow the pathway along the ridge north from the church in the village to reach the tiny Open-air Folk Museum.

⊨ Sleeping & Eating

Tihany is an easy day trip (by bus or boat) from Balatonfüred, so there's no reason to stay over unless you're hiking. If you are looking for lodgings, one option is to look for a '*zimmer frei*' (German for 'room for rent') sign on the small streets north of the church.

Adler BOUTIQUE HOTEL €€
(☑538 000; www.adler-tihany.hu; Felsőkopaszhegyi utca 1a; r €45-56, apt €72-99; ❄❋) Features large, whitewashed rooms with balconies, and there's a spa bath, sauna and restaurant on the premises.

Ferenc Pince HUNGARIAN €
TOP CHOICE (☑448 575; Cserhegy 9; mains from 1500Ft; ☻noon-11pm Wed-Mon) About 2km south of the Abbey Church, Ferenc is a wine- and food-lover's dream. During the day, its terrace offers expansive views of the lake, while at night the lights of the southern shore are visible.

Rege Café CAFE
(Kossuth Lajos utca 22; ☻10am-6pm) From its high vantage point near the Abbey Church, this modern cafe has an unsurpassed panoramic view of Lake Balaton.

ⓘ Information

Tourinform (☑448 804; tihany@tourinform.hu; Kossuth Lajos utca 20; ☻9am-7pm Mon-Fri, 10am-6pm Sat & Sun mid-Jun–mid-Sep, shorter hours rest of year) sells hiking maps and film, and provides tourist information. Note that the office is tricky to find from the main road, though it's easily visible from just beyond the front of the Abbey Church.

ⓘ Getting There & Away

Buses travel along the 14km of mostly lakeside road between Tihany village and Balatonfüred's train and bus stations (280Ft, 30 minutes) at least 13 times a day.

The harbour where ferries heading to and from Balatonfüred dock is a couple of kilometres downhill from the village of Tihany, which occupies a bluff on the eastern edge of the peninsula. Passenger ferries sail between Tihany and Balatonfüred from April to September (1040Ft, 30 minutes, six daily). You can follow a steep path up to the village from the pier to reach the Abbey Church.

Keszthely

☑83 / POP 21,800

At the very western end of the Balaton sits Keszthely (*kest*-hey), a place of grand town houses and a gentle ambience far removed from the lake's tourist hot spots. Its small, shallow beaches are well suited to families, and there are enough accommodation options to suit most holidaymakers. Of its handful of museums and historical buildings, nothing tops the Festetics Palace, a lavish baroque residence. The town lies just over 1km northwest of the lake and with the exception of a few guesthouses, almost everything stays open year-round. If you visit in May, you might catch the town's annual Balaton Festival.

The bus and train stations, side by side at the end of Mártírok útja, are fairly close to

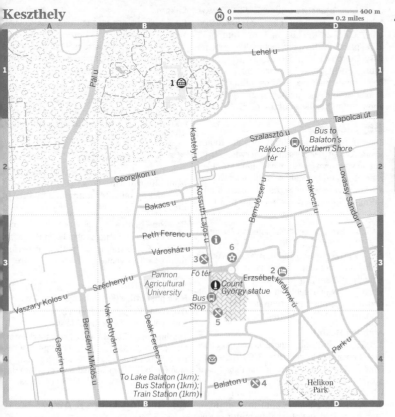

Keszthely

⊚ **Sights**

1 Festetics Palace B1

🛏 **Sleeping**

2 Bacchus C3

🍴 **Eating**

3 CBA C3

4 Lakoma C4

5 Pelso Café C4

☺ **Entertainment**

6 Balaton Theatre C3

the water. The beaches and the ferry pier lie to the southeast through a small park. The main commercial centre, where everything happens, is about 500m north of the bus and trains stations uphill, along the main street, Kossuth Lajos utca.

⊙ Sights & Activities

Festetics Palace   PALACE

(Festetics Kastély; ☎312 190; Kastély utca 1; adult/concession 2000/1000Ft; ◷9am-6pm Jul & Aug, 10am-4pm Sep-Jun) The glimmering white, 100-room Festetics Palace was first built in 1745; the wings were extended out from the original building 150 years later. About a dozen rooms in the one-time residence have been turned into a museum. Many of the decorative arts in the gilt salons were imported from England in the mid-1800s. The **Helikon Library** (Helikon Könyvtár), in the baroque south wing, is known for its 100,000 volumes and its hand-carved furniture, crafted by a local artisan. To reach the palace, follow Kossuth Lajos utca, the long pedestrian street in the centre of the Old Town.

Lakeside Area   BEACH

The lakeside area centres on the long ferry pier. From March to October you can take

a one-hour **pleasure cruise** (☎312 093; www.
balatonihajozas.hu; ferry pier; adult/concession
1400/600Ft) on the lake at 11am, 1pm, 3pm
and 5pm daily. If you're feeling like a swim,
City Beach (Városi Strand) is just to the
southwest of the ferry pier, near plenty of
beer stands and food booths. **Libás Beach**
(Libás Strand) is smaller and quieter. It's
about 200m northeast of the pier.

🛌 Sleeping

Tourinform can help find private rooms
(from 3500Ft per person). Otherwise, strike
out on your own (particularly along Móra Ferenc utca) and keep an eye out for '*szoba kiadó*' or '*zimmer frei*' signs (Hungarian and
German, respectively, for 'room for rent').

Bacchus   HOTEL €€
(☎510 450; www.bacchushotel.hu; Erzsébet királyné
utca 18; s/d/apt 12,300/16,500/24,800Ft) Bacchus' central position and immaculate rooms
make it a popular choice with travellers.
Equally pleasing is its atmospheric cellar,
which is divided between a fine restaurant
and a wine museum (admission free, open
11am to 11pm) where tastings are available.

Ambient Hostel   HOSTEL €
(☎06 30 460 3536; http://hostel-accommodation.
fw.hu; Sopron utca 10; dm/d from 3500/7800Ft;@)
Only a short walk north of the palace is a
hostel with basic, cheap dorms, each of
which comes with its own bathroom. Laundry service is available 3pm to 5pm, from
Monday to Friday. Note that reception closes
by 9.30pm, so be sure to call ahead if your
train or bus gets you in later than that.

Tokajer   B&B €
(☎319 875; www.pensiontokajer.hu; Apát utca 21;
s/d/apt from €33/50/70; ✳@✳) Spread over
four buildings in a quiet area of town, Tokajer has slightly dated rooms, but they're
still in good condition. Extras include a
mini-wellness centre and free use of bicycles.

Castrum Camping   CAMPING GROUND €
(☎312 120; www.castrum.eu; Móra Ferenc
utca 48; camp sites per adult/concession/tent
1400/1000/2000Ft; ☉Apr-Oct;✳) North of the
stations, this large camping ground is green
and spacious and has a big pool.

🍴 Eating

If you need groceries, shop while admiring
the beautiful stained-glass windows of the
CBA (Kossuth Lajos utca 35) supermarket, just at
the intersection Kossuth Lajos utca and Fő ter.

Lakoma   HUNGARIAN €
(☎313 129; Balaton utca 9; mains 1000-2600Ft)
With a good fish selection, grill/roast specialities and a back garden that transforms
itself into a leafy dining area in the summer
months, it's hard to go wrong.

Pelso Café   CAFE €
(Fő tér; coffee & cake from 300Ft; ☉9am-9pm; 📶)
This modern two-level cafe at the southern
end of the main square does decent coffee,
cake and cocktails. Has free wi-fi.

☆ Entertainment

The biweekly *ZalaEst* booklet, available
from Tourinform, is a good source of
information on entertainment activities in
Keszthely.

Balaton Theatre   THEATRE
(☎515 230; www.balatonszinhaz.hu, in Hungarian;
Fő tér 3) Catch the latest in theatre performances at this venue on the main square.

ℹ Information

Main post office (Kossuth Lajos utca 48)

OTP Bank (Kossuth Lajos utca 38) Facing a
small park near the centre of town.

Tourinform (☎314 144; keszthely@tourinform.
hu; Kossuth Lajos utca 28; ☉9am-8pm Mon-
Fri, to 6pm Sat mid-Jun–mid-Sep, 9am-5pm
Mon-Fri, to 12.30pm Sat mid-Sep–mid-Jun) Has
information on the whole Lake Balaton area.

ℹ Getting There & Away

The future of **Balaton airport** (☎554 060; www.
flybalaton.com), 15km southwest of Keszthely at
Sármellék, was unclear as this book was being
researched. The airport has served as a convenient hub for incoming budget flights from Germany and the UK but has recently experienced
financial problems.

Back on the ground, buses from Keszthely to
Hévíz (220Ft, 15 minutes) leave at least every 30
minutes during the day. Other places served by
buses include Balatonfüred (1200Ft, 1½ hours,
seven daily) and Budapest (3300Ft, three hours,
seven daily). The bus is faster than the train for
reaching Budapest.

Keszthely is on a railway branch line linking
the lake's southeastern shore with Budapest
(3500Ft, four hours, six daily). To reach towns
along Lake Balaton's northern shore by train,
you have to change at Tapolca (380Ft, 30 minutes, hourly).

From April to September, **Balaton Shipping
ferries** (www.balatonihajozas.hu) link Keszthely
with Badacsonytomaj (1560Ft, two hours, four
daily) and other, smaller lake towns.

SOUTH CENTRAL HUNGARY

Southern Hungary is a region of calm, a place to savour life at a slower pace. It's only marginally touched by tourism, and touring through the countryside is like travelling back in time. Passing through the region, you'll spot whitewashed farmhouses whose thatched roofs and long colonnaded porticoes decorated with floral patterns seem unchanged over the centuries.

Historically, the area bordering Croatia and Serbia has often been 'shared' between Hungary and these countries, and it's here that the remnants of the 150-year Turkish occupation can be most strongly felt.

The region is bounded by the Danube River to the east, the Dráva River to the south and west, and Lake Balaton to the north. It's generally flat, with the Mecsek and Villány Hills rising in isolation from the plain. The weather always seems to be a few degrees warmer here than in other parts of the country; the sunny clime is great for grape-growing, and oak-aged Villány reds are well regarded.

Pécs

☑72 / POP 156,000

Blessed with a mild climate, an illustrious past and a number of fine museums and monuments, Pécs (pronounced *paich*) is one of the most pleasant and interesting cities to visit in Hungary. For those reasons and more – a handful of universities, the nearby Mecsek Hills, a lively nightlife – many travellers put it second only to Budapest on their Hungary must-see list.

Lying equidistant from the Danube to the east and the Dráva to the south, Pécs enjoys a microclimate that lengthens the summer and is ideal for viticulture and fruit production. An especially fine time to visit is during a warm *indián nyár* (Indian summer), when the light seems to take on a special quality.

Pécs' history stretches back nearly 2000 years and the city remains marked by the dynasties that have come and gone. The Roman settlement of Sopianae on this site was the capital of the province of Lower Pannonia for 400 years. Christianity flourished here as early as the 4th century, and in 1009 Stephen I made Pécs a bishopric. The Mongols swept through here in 1241, prompting the authorities to build massive city walls, parts of which are still standing.

The Turkish occupation began in 1543 and lasted nearly a century and a half, lending Pécs an Ottoman patina that's immediately visible at the Mosque Church that stands at the heart of the city's main square.

In recognition of Pécs' remarkable past, as well as its cultural and geographic proximity to the Balkans, the city was named a European Cultural Capital in 2010. That designation helped to bring millions of euros of investment into the historic core and helped the city to rejuvenate its impressive coterie of museums.

⊙ Sights & Activities

The main sights are clustered in three areas: Széchenyi tér, Dóm tér (dominated by the Basilica of St Peter) and Káptalan utca, Pécs' 'museum street'.

FREE **Mosque Church** CHURCH
(Mecset Templom; Széchenyi tér; ⊙10am-4pm mid-Apr–mid-Oct, shorter hours rest of year) The curiously named Mosque Church dominates the city's central square. It has no minaret and has been a Christian place of worship for a long time, but the Islamic elements inside, such as the mihrab on the southeastern wall, reveal its original identity. Constructed in the mid-16th century from the stones of an earlier church, the mosque underwent several changes of appearance over the years – including the addition of a steeple. In the late 1930s the building was restored to its medieval form.

Hassan Jakovali Mosque MOSQUE
(Hassan Jakovali Mecset; adult/concession 500/250Ft; ⊙9.30am-6pm Wed-Sun late Mar-Oct) West along Ferencesek utcája, you'll pass the ruins of the 16th-century Turkish **Pasa Memi Baths** (Memi Pasa Fürdője) before you turn south on Rákóczi utca to get to the 16th-century Hassan Jakovali Mosque. Though wedged between two modern buildings, this smaller mosque is more intact than its larger cousin, the Mosque Church, and comes complete with a minaret. There's a small museum of Ottoman history inside.

Zsolnay Porcelain Museum MUSEUM
(Zsolnay Porcélan Múzeum; Káptalan utca 2; adult/concession 700/350Ft; ⊙10am-5pm Tue-Sun) From the northern end of Széchenyi tér, climb Szepessy Ignéc utca and turn left (west) on Káptalan utca, a street lined with museums and galleries. The Zsolnay Porcelain Museum is on the eastern end of this strip. English translations provide a good history of

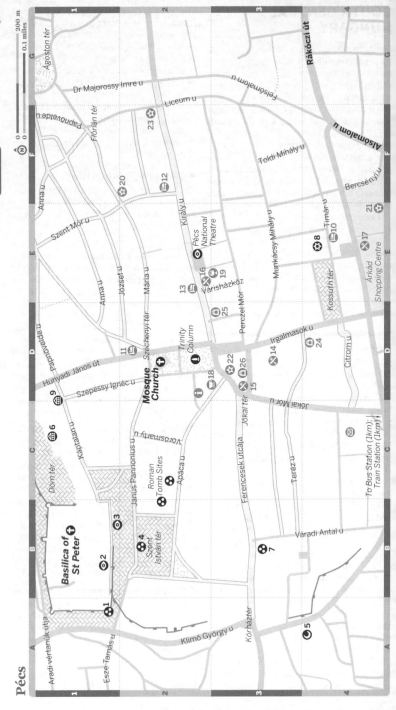

Pécs

0   0   200 m
0   0.1 miles

Ágoston tér

Dr Majorossy Imre u

Papnövelde u

Flórián tér

Liceum u

Felsőmalom u

Rákóczi út

Anna u

Szent Mór u

Anna u

József u

Mária u

Király u

Toldi Mihály u

Munkácsy Mihály u

Bercsényi u

Alsómalom u

23

20

12

Pécs National Theatre

16
19
13
Várisházköz

25

Timár u

8

10

21

17

Arkád Shopping Centre

Kossuth tér

Szent Mór u

Trinity Column

11

Széchenyi tér

Mosque Church

18

22
26
15
14

Irgalmasok u

24

Perczel Mór

Citrom u

Hunyadi János út

Szepessy Ignéc u

Papnövelde u

9

6

Dóm tér

Káptalan u

Janus Pannonius u

Vörösmarty u

Roman Tomb Sites

Apáca u

Basilica of St Peter

2

3

4
Szent István tér

1

Esze Tamás u

Aradi vértanúk útja

Klimó György u

Kórház tér

Ferencesek utcája

Jókai tér

Teréz u

Jókai Mór u

Váradi Antal u

7

5

To Bus Station (1km);
Train Station (1km)

Pécs

the artistic and functional ceramics produced from this local factory's illustrious early days in the mid-19th century to the present.

TOP CHOICE ⟩ Modern Hungarian Art Gallery
ART GALLERY
(Modern Magyar Képtár; Káptalan utca 4; adult/ concession 700/350Ft; ◎noon-6pm Tue-Sun Apr-Oct, 10am-4pm Tue-Sun Nov-Mar) At the excellent Modern Hungarian Art Gallery you can get a comprehensive overview of Hungarian art from 1850 till today. In 2010 the museum hosted a groundbreaking exhibition on 1920s and early '30s Bauhaus architecture, and Pécs' contribution to it.

Basilica of St Peter
CHURCH
(Szent Péter Bazilika; Dóm tér; adult/concession 800/500Ft; ◎9am-5pm Mon-Sat, 1-5pm Sun) At Dóm tér the walled bishopric complex contains the four-towered Basilica of St Peter. The oldest part of the building is the 11th-century crypt. The 1770 **Bishop's Palace** (Püspöki Palota; adult/concession 1500/700Ft; ◎tours 2pm, 3pm & 4pm Thu late Jun–mid-Sep) stands in front of the cathedral. Also near the square is a nearby 15th-century **barbican** (barbakán), the only stone bastion to survive from the old city walls.

Cella Septichora Visitors Centre
RUINS
(Janus Pannonius utca; adult/concession 1200/ 600Ft; ◎10am-6pm Tue-Sun) On the southern side of Dom tér is the Cella Septichora Visitors Centre, which illuminates a series of early Christian burial sites that have been on Unesco's World Heritage list since 2000. The highlight is the so-called **Jug Mausoleum** (Korsós Sírkamra), a 4th-century Roman tomb whose name comes from a painting of a large drinking vessel with vines.

Early Christian Tomb Chapel
RUINS
(Ókeresztény sírkápolna; Szent István tér 12; adult/ concession 400/200Ft; ◎10am-6pm Tue-Sun) Across Janus Pannonius utca from the Cella Septichora Visitors Centre, the early Christian tomb chapel dates from about AD 350 and has frescos of Adam and Eve, and Daniel in the lion's den.

Synagogue
SYNAGOGUE
(zsinagóga; Kossuth tér; adult/concession 500/300Ft; ◎10am-noon & 12.45-5pm Sun-Fri May-Oct) Pécs' beautifully preserved 1869 synagogue is south of Széchenyi tér.

🛏 Sleeping

Tourinform can help book private rooms, which start at around 4000Ft per person.

Hotel Főnix
BOUTIQUE HOTEL €€
(☎311 680; www.fonixhotel.hu; Hunyadi János út 2; s/d 7100/11,300Ft; ❄@) Odd angles and sloping eaves characterise the asymmetrical Hotel Főnix. Rooms are plain and those on the top floor have skylights.

Palatinus City Center
HOTEL €€

(☎889 400; www.danubiushotels.com; Király utca 5; s/d from €75/104; ✳@) For art nouveau glamour, Palatinus is *the* place in Pécs. An amazing marble reception has a soaring Moorish-detailed ceiling. It's a shame that the rooms are not as luxurious, but still, in Pécs, it's as plush as it gets.

Hotel Diána
PENSION €€

(☎328 594; www.hoteldiana.hu; Tímár utca 4a; s/d/tr from 11,350/16,350/20,350Ft; ✳@) This very central pension offers 20 spotless rooms, comfortable kick-off-your-shoes decor and a warm welcome.

Nap Hostel
HOSTEL €

(☎950 684; www.naphostel.com; Király utca 23-25; dm/d from 2500/11,000Ft;@) Clean, friendly hostel has dorms and a double room on the 1st floor of a former bank. There's also a large kitchen. Enter from Szent Mór utca.

✗ Eating & Drinking

Pubs, cafes and fast-food eateries line pedestrian-only Király utca. Another good bet is tiny and more intimate Jókai tér. Get self-catering supplies at the **Interspar** (Bajcsy-Zsilinszky utca 11; ⊙7am-9pm Mon-Thu & Sat, 7am-10pm Fri, 8am-7pm Sun) supermarket in the basement of the Árkád shopping centre.

TOP CHOICE **Az Elefánthoz**
ITALIAN €

(☎216 055; Jókai tér 6; mains 1600-2100Ft) With its welcoming terrace overlooking Jókai tér and quality Italian cuisine, this place is a sure bet for first-rate food in the centre. Has a wood-fired stove for pizzas, though the pasta dishes are also worth a look.

Corso
FINE DINING €€€

(☎525 198; Király utca 14; mains 2400-4600Ft) One of Hungary's top restaurants and arguably the most prestigious meal in town. Dining is on two levels, with the top featuring refined Hungarian cooking with Italian and French influences. The ground floor is slightly less expensive, but equally good. Here the focus is on traditional Hungarian dishes.

Áfium
BALKAN €

(☎511 434; Irgalmasok utca 2; mains 1400-1900Ft; ⊙11am-1am) With Croatia and Serbia so close, it's a wonder that more restaurants don't offer cuisine from south of the border. Don't miss the bean soup served covered with a top of freshly baked bread. Decently priced set lunches during the week.

Korhely
INTERNATIONAL €

(Boltív köz 2) This popular *csapszék* (tavern) has peanuts on the table, shells on the floor, a half-dozen beers on tap and a sort of 'retro socialist meets Latin American' decor.

Coffein Café
CAFE €

(Széchenyi tér 9) For the best views across Széchenyi tér to the Mosque Church and Király utca, find a perch at this cool cafe done up in the warmest of colours.

☆ Entertainment

Pécs has well-established opera and ballet companies as well as a symphony orchestra. Tourinform has schedule information. The free biweekly *Pécsi Est* also lists what's on around town.

House of Artists
EXHIBITION SPACE

(Művészetek Háza; ☎522 834; www.pmh.hu, in Hungarian only; Széchenyi tér 7-8) This is a cultural venue that hosts classical-music performances. A schedule is posted outside.

Bóbita Puppet Theatre
THEATRE

(Bóbita Bábszínház; ☎210 301; www.bobita.hu; Mária utca 18) Lively puppet theatre with a varied program aimed at audiences of all ages. At the time of research there were plans afoot to move the theatre to a new location a bit further from the centre.

Cyrano Lounge
CLUB

(Czindery utca 6; ⊙8pm-5am Fri & Sat) A popular nightclub next to the big Árkád shopping centre.

Varázskert
OUTDOOR CLUB

(Király utca 65-67; ⊙6pm-3am summer) Big open-air beer garden and late-hours music club at the far end of Király utca.

🔒 Shopping

Pécs has been known for its leatherwork since Turkish times, and you can pick up a few bargains around the city. Try **Blázek** (☎332 460; Teréz utca 1), which deals mainly in handbags and wallets. **Zsolnay** (☎310 220; Jókai tér 2) has a porcelain outlet south of Széchenyi tér. **La Gourmet** (Király utca 8) specialises in wines from Pécs and nearby Villány.

ℹ Information

There are plenty of banks and ATMs scattered around town.

Main post office (Jókai Mór utca 10) In a beautiful art nouveau building (1904) with a colourful Zsolnay porcelain roof.

Tourinform (☏213 315; pecs@tourinform.hu; Széchenyi tér 1; ☺8am-6pm Mon-Fri, 10am-3pm Sat & Sun Jun-Aug, 8am-5.30pm Mon-Fri, 10am-2pm Sat May, Sep & Oct, 8am-4pm Mon-Fri Nov-Apr) Tons of local info, including lists of hotels and museums. The office can help book private rooms, advise on transport and rent bikes. Note that Tourinform was planning to move in 2011, but did not know where.

Webforrás (Boltív köz 2; per hr 420Ft) Just off Király utca is an internet cafe.

❶ Getting There & Away

Buses for Harkány (500Ft, 40 minutes) leave regularly throughout the day. At least five buses a day connect Pécs with Budapest (3600Ft, 4½ hours), three with Siófok (2480Ft, three hours) and eight with Szeged (3400Ft, 4½ hours).

Pécs is on a main rail line with Budapest's Déli train station (4400Ft, three hours, nine daily). One daily train runs from Pécs to Osijek (two hours) in Croatia, with continuing service to the Bosnian capital, Sarajevo (nine hours).

SOUTHEASTERN HUNGARY

Like the Outback for Australians or the Old West for Americans, the Nagyalföld (Great Plain) holds a romantic appeal for Hungarians. Images of shepherds guiding their flocks with moplike *puli* dogs and cowboys riding across the *puszta* (plain) are scattered throughout the nation's poetry and painting. The Great Plain covers some 45,000 sq km east and southeast of Budapest. Beyond its big-sky-country appeal, the Great Plain is also home to cities of graceful architecture, winding rivers and easygoing afternoons.

Kecskemét

☏76 / POP 107,000

Located about halfway between Budapest and Szeged, Kecskemét (*kech*-kah-mate) is a green, pedestrian-friendly city with interesting art nouveau architecture. Colourful buildings, fine small museums and the region's excellent *barackpálinka* (apricot brandy) beckon. And Kiskunsági Nemzeti Park, the *puszta* of the Southern Plain, is right at the back door. Day-trip opportunities include hiking in the sandy, juniper-covered hills, a horse show at Bugac or a visit to one of the area's many horse farms. Note that central Kecskemét is made up of squares that run into one another, and consequently it's hard to tell them apart.

◉ Sights

Szabadság tér   PUBLIC SQUARE

The square's eclectic buildings include the Technicolor art nouveau style of the 1902 **Ornamental Palace** (Cifrapalota; Rákóczi út 1), recently refurbished and covered in multicoloured majolica tiles. The palace houses the **Kecskemét Gallery** (Kecskeméti Képtár; adult/concession 320/160Ft; ☺10am-5pm Tue-Sun), with its fine interiors and a small collection of modern Hungarian paintings.

Kossuth tér   PUBLIC SQUARE

Kossuth tér is dominated by the massive 1897 art nouveau **Town Hall** (Városháza), which is flanked by the baroque **Great Church** (Nagytemplom; Kossuth tér 2; ☺9am-noon & 3-6pm Tue-Sun, mornings only Oct-Apr) and the earlier **Franciscan Church of St Nicholas** (Szent Miklós Templom), parts of which date from the 13th century. Nearby is the magnificent 1896 **József Katona Theatre** (Katona József Színház; Katona József tér 5), a neo-baroque performance venue with a statue of the Trinity (1742) in front of it.

Hungarian Folk Craft Museum   MUSEUM

(Népi Iparmüvészeti Múzeum; Serfőző utca 19a; adult/concession 400/200Ft; ☺10am-5pm Tue-Sat Feb-Nov) The Hungarian Folk Craft Museum has a definitive collection of regional embroidery, weaving and textiles, as well as some furniture, woodcarving and agricultural tools. A few handicrafts are for sale at the entrance.

🛏 Sleeping

Tourinform can help you locate the numerous colleges that offer dormitory accommodation in July and August.

Fábián Panzió   PENSION €

(☏477 677; www.panziofabian.hu; Kápolna utca 14; s/d from 9000/12,000Ft; ❇@⊛) The world-travelling family that owns this small guesthouse know how to treat a visitor well. The exceptionally friendly staff help their guests plan each day's excursions, teapots are available for in-room use, wireless internet is free and bikes are available for hire.

Hotel Három Gúnar   BOUTIQUE HOTEL €€

(☏483 611; Batthyány utca 1; s/d 10,500/14,900Ft; ❇) Four multihued town houses – flowerboxes and all – have been transformed to contain 49 smallish rooms (the best are Nos 306 to 308). Simple veneer

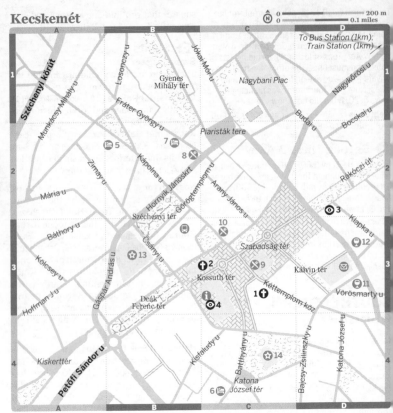

N 0 ——— 200 m
0 ——— 0.1 miles

furnishings in the rooms are less cheery than the exterior facade. There's an onsite restaurant.

Teachers' College HOSTEL €
(Tanítóképzö Kollégium; ☎486 977; loveikollegium@tfk.kefo.hu; Piaristák tere 4; s/d 2500/5000Ft; ☺mid-Jun–Aug) A good choice among the academic accommodation options, with a central location.

✖ Eating

Liberté Étterem HUNGARIAN €€
(☎509 175; Szabadság tér 2; mains 1200-3200Ft) Artistic presentations come with your order, whether it's the traditional stuffed cabbage or the mixed sautéed chicken with aubergine. This is modern Hungarian done well. Its outside tables have some of the best seats in town for people-watching. Our only gripe is the 10% service charge automatically added to the tab, so there's no need to leave a tip.

Lordok HUNGARIAN €
(Kossuth tér 6-7; mains 400-700Ft; ☺7am-11pm) This popular self-service canteen and adjoining trendier coffeeshop does triple duty as a cheap and tasty lunch option, a place for a midafternoon caffeine break and comfortable spot for an after-dinner beer or cocktail.

Italia ITALIAN €
(☎484 627; Hornyik János körút 4; mains 1200-1400Ft) More fast food than restaurant, so a better choice for something quick and cheap than a meal to remember.

🍷 Drinking

For drinks the Western-themed pub **Wanted Söröző** (Csányi János körút 4; ☺10am-midnight Mon-Sat, from 4pm Sun) sits handily across from the more alternative **Black Cat Pub** (Csányi János körút 6; ☺11am-midnight Sun-Thu, to 2am Fri & Sat), making for quite the convivial corner.

Kecskemét

☆ Entertainment

Tourinform has a list of what concerts and performances are on, or check out the free weekly magazine *Kecskeméti Est*.

József Katona Theatre THEATRE
(Katona József Színház; ☎483 283; Katona József tér 5) Experience operettas and symphony performances in this grand 19th-century building. Tourinform can let you know if something's happening during your trip.

Bling Bling Nights CLUB
(www.blingblingnights.hu; Malom, Korona tér 2) Hip-hop, house, R&B – the nightclub atop Malom Shopping Centre is definitely eclectic. Most of the action occurs on weekend nights, but occasional parties happen throughout the week as well.

❶ Information

Lordok Internetpont (Kossuth tér 6-7; per hr 720Ft; ☺9am-10pm) Internet access. Find the entrance in a shopping passage behind the Lordok canteen and coffeeshop.

Main post office (Kálvin tér 10)

OTP Bank (Malom Centre, Korona utca 2)

Tourinform (☎481 065; kecskemet@tour inform.hu; Kossuth tér 1; ☺8am-7pm Mon-Fri, 10am-8pm Sat & Sun Jul-Aug, 8am-6pm

Mon-Fri Sep-Jun) In the northeastern corner of the large Town Hall. Rents bikes and can advise on outings to the nearby Kiskunsági National Park.

❶ Getting There & Away

The main bus and train stations are opposite each other in József Katona Park. Frequent buses depart for Budapest (1700Ft, 1½ hours, hourly) and for Szeged (1700Ft, 1¾ hours, hourly). A direct rail line links Kecskemét to Budapest's Nyugati train station (1900Ft, 1½ hours, hourly) and Szeged (1650Ft, one hour, hourly).

Kiskunsági Nemzeti Park

Totalling 76,000 hectares, **Kiskunsági Nemzeti Park** (Kiskunság National Park; www. knp.hu) consists of half a dozen 'islands' of protected land. Much of the park's alkaline ponds and sand dunes are off limits. Bugac (*boo*-gats) village, about 30km southwest of Kecskemét, is the most accessible part of the park.

The highlight of a trip here is a chance to see a popular **horse show** (admission 1400Ft; ☺12.15pm May-Oct), where the horse herders race one another bareback and ride 'five-in-hand'. It's a breathtaking performance in which one *csikós* (cowboy) gallops five horses at full speed while standing on the backs of the rear two.

There are also several nature and educational hiking trails in the vicinity, with explanatory sign-posting in English, where you can get out and see this amazing ecosystem of dunes and bluffs and swamps.

The only problem, and it's a formidable one if you don't have your own wheels, is trying to get here. There's a morning bus to Bugac from Kecskemét (600Ft, 50 minutes) that goes daily at 11am, but it won't get you there in time for the 12.15pm show. Alternatively, you could plan to spend the night in Bugac, leaving on the bus the first day, hiking in the afternoon, and then returning to Kecskemét the second day after the horse show on the 3.50pm bus.

If you've got your own transportation, follow route 54 out of Kecskemét in the direction of Soltvadkert. Turn off the road at the 21km marker and follow a dirt track a couple of kilometres toward Bugacpuszta and then follow signs to the **Karikás Csárda** (☎575 112; Nagybugac 135; mains 1600-2100Ft; ☺8am-8pm May-Oct), a kitschy but decent restaurant that also doubles as a ticket and information booth to the horse show and small **herder museum** (admission free; ⊘10am-5pm May-Oct). You can get to the show by foot or ride a **horse-drawn carriage** (adult/concession incl horse show 3000/1800Ft; ⊘11.15pm May-Oct). The Tourinform office in Kecskemét can help plan an outing to the national park; the owners of the Fábián Panzió in Kecskemét are another good source of information on how best to access the park and the horse show.

One overnight option in the park, though it's not very close to the horse show, is **Somodi Tanya** (📞377 095; www.samoditanya.hu; Fú'ló'pháza; r per person about 2000Ft), a lovely dude ranch with crisp, clean rooms where you can ride horses or just laze around and look at the sky.

Szeged

📞62 / POP 170,000

Szeged (*seh*-ged) is a bustling border town with a handful of historic sights that line the embankment along the Tisza River and a clutch of sumptuous art nouveau town palaces that are in varying states of repair and disrepair. It's also a big university town, which means lots of culture, lots of partying and an active festival scene that lasts throughout the year.

For centuries, the city's perch at the confluence of the Maros and Tisza Rivers brought prosperity and growth. That happy relationship turned sour in 1879, when the Tisza overflowed its banks, wiping out much of the central city. Most of the historic architecture you see today dates from the late 19th and early 20th centuries.

The **Szeged Open-Air Festival** (📞541 205; www.szegediszabadteri.hu) is held in Dom tér from mid-July to late August.

⊙ Sights & Activities

TOP CHOICE **New Synagogue** SYNAGOGUE
(Új Zsinagóga; www.zsinagoga.szeged.hu; Gutenberg utca 13; adult/concession 400/300Ft; ⊘10am-noon & 1-5pm Sun-Fri Apr-Sep, 10am-2pm Sun-Fri Oct-Mar) To the west of the centre, the New Synagogue is the most beautiful Jewish house of worship in Hungary and is still in use. An ornate blue-and-gold painted interior graces the 1903 art nouveau building.

Ferenc Móra Museum MUSEUM
(Móra Ferenc Múzeum; www.mfm.u-szeged.hu; Roosevelt tér 1; adult/concession 700/350Ft; ⊘10am-5pm Tue-Sun) The huge, neoclassical Ferenc

Móra Museum overlooks the Tisza River. It contains a colourful collection of folk art from Csongrád County with descriptions in several languages and an exhibit of 7th-century gold work by the Avar, a mysterious people who are thought to have originated somewhere in Central Asia. The best exhibit showcases an even more obscure group, the Sarmatians, who originated in present-day Iran.

FREE **Dom tér** PUBLIC SQUARE
The city's ecclesiastical heart is dominated by the twin-spired **Votive Church** (Dom tér; admission free; ⊘9am-5pm Mon-Sat, 1-5pm Sun), which was pledged following the 1879 flood but not finished until 1930. While the exterior is something of an architectural monstrosity, the interior is impressive, with a gigantic nave and an organ that boasts more than 11,000 pipes. Next door is the tiny, Romanesque **Demetrius Tower** (admission free; ⊘by appointment), the city's oldest structure, and the last remnants of a church built here in the 11th century. For appointments, inquire at the local Tourinform office (p435). There's also a small **Church Museum** (Dom tér 5; adult/concession 100/50Ft; ⊘10am-6pm Tue-Sat), where you can see religious artefacts through the ages from around the plains. Running along three sides of the square is the **National Pantheon** (Nemzeti Emlékcsarnok; admission free;

Szeged

⊙24hr), with statues and reliefs of 80 Hungarian notables.

Pick Salami & Szeged Paprika Museum
MUSEUM

(Pick Szalámi és Szegedi Paprika Múzeum; Felső Tisza-part 10; www.pickmuseum.hu; adult/concession incl salami tasting & paprika sample 880/660Ft; ⊙3-6pm Tue-Sat) Just north of the Old Town ring road is the Pick Salami & Szeged Paprika Museum. Two floors of exhibits show traditional methods of salami production. There's a small gift stand in the museum and a butcher shop around the corner in this factory building.

🛏 Sleeping

Hotel Korona BOUTIQUE HOTEL €€
(☎555 787; www.hotelkoronaszeged.hu; Petőfi Sándor sgt 4; s/d 14,000/18,000Ft;❄) This modern, clean, well-run hotel comes as a pleasant surprise after seeing so many other family-owned hotels in converted villas that simply don't hold up. Firm mattresses, thick cotton sheets, sparkling baths and the big buffet breakfast all justify the premium room rate. Ask for a quiet room facing the courtyard. Free parking at the back.

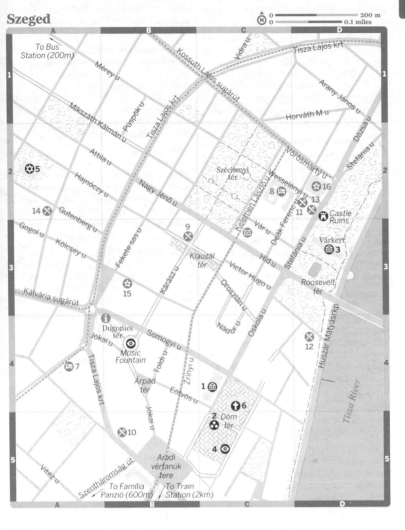

Szeged

Tisza Hotel
BOUTIQUE HOTEL €€€

(☎478 278; www.tiszahotel.hu; Széchenyi tér 3; s/d classic 14,500/19,000Ft; superior 18,200/23,000Ft;❄) Top-notch hotel with an old-world feel off central Széchenyi tér. Superior rooms have air-conditioners and mini-bars, as well as antique throw rugs, wooden floors and big wooden beds. Splurge option.

Família Panzió
PENSION €€

(☎441 122; www.familiapanzio.hu; Szentháromság utca 71; s/d/tr 8400/11,200/14,000Ft;❄) This family-run guesthouse with contemporary furnishings in a great Old Town building is often booked up. The reception area may be dim, but rooms have high ceilings and loads of light.

Partfürdő
CAMPING GROUND €

(☎430 843; Közép-kikötő sor; camp sites per person/tent 990/380Ft, r 5400-6900Ft, bungalows 8000-12,000Ft; ☺mid-May–Sep;☀) This green, grassy camping ground is across the river in New Szeged. Bungalows sleep up to four people. Gets kind of crazy during the open-air festival in midsummer.

✗ Eating & Drinking

Port Royal Étterem
INTERNATIONAL €

(☎547 988; Stefánia 4; mains 1500-2300Ft; ☺11am-midnight Mon-Thu, to 2am Fri & Sat, to 11pm Sun) There's an unmistakeable nautical theme running through this popular restaurant and cocktail bar. Maybe it's the suspended boat above the bar or the wooden planks for flooring. Whatever, it works. The modern kitchen turns out tasty traditional dishes, international faves and veggie options. Cocktails are served till 2am Friday and Saturday.

Halászcsárda
HUNGARIAN €€

(☎555 980; Roosevelt tér 14; mains 2200-3600Ft) An institution that knows how to prepare the best fish dish in town – whole roasted pike with garlic, accompanied by pan-fried frog legs and fillet of carp soup. Although there are white tablecloths and waiters are dressed to the nines, the outdoor terrace is pretty casual.

Taj Mahal
INDIAN €

(Gutenberg utca 12; mains 1700-2300Ft) Pleasantly authentic Indian–Pakistani restaurant, just a couple of metres from the New Synagogue.

Agni
VEGETARIAN €

(Tisza Lajos körút 76; mains 800-1100Ft; ☺11am-7pm Mon-Fri) Daily lunch specials round out the menu at this little vegetarian restaurant. Try the substantial paprika-and-mushroom stew with millet. Closed weekends.

A Cappella
CAFE €

(Kárász 6, cnr Kárász utca & Klauzál tér) Giant sidewalk cafe with a full range of cakes, ice creams and frothy coffee concoctions.

Grand Café
CAFE €

(Deák Ferenc utca 18; ☺2pm-midnight Mon-Fri, 5pm-2am Sat & Sun) Climb up to the 2nd floor to find this small but trendy cafe–bar with a decidedly '60s feel. They also hold regular screenings of classic films.

☆ Entertainment

Szeged's status as a university town means that there's a vast array of bars, clubs and other nightspots, especially around Dugonics tér. Nightclub programs are listed in the free *Szegedi Est* magazine.

Szeged National Theatre
THEATRE

(Szegedi Nemzeti Színház; ☎479 279; www.szinhaz.szeged.hu, in Hungarian; Deák Ferenc utca 12-14) Since 1886, this venue has been the centre of cultural life in the city. Opera, ballet and drama performances take to its stage. Szeged is known throughout Hungary for the quality of its contemporary dance.

Jazz Kocsma
LIVE MUSIC

(Kálmány Lajos 14; ☺4pm-2am Mon-Sat) The kind of small, smoky music club that no self-respecting university town would be without. Gets pretty crowded during the academic year for live music on Friday and Saturday nights. Things slow down considerably in summer, but still worth searching out for a drink.

Reök Palace
EXHIBITION SPACE

(☎541 205; www.reok.hu, in Hungarian; Tisza Lajos körút 56) Art nouveau palace that's been polished up to its original lustre and now hosts regular photography and visual arts exhibitions as well as occasional theatre and dance.

❶ Information

Cyber Arena (Deák Ferenc utca 24-26; per hr 500Ft; ☺24hr) Internet access with Skype set-ups and cheap international phonecards.

Main post office (Széchenyi tér 1)

OTP Bank (Klauzál tér 4)

Tourinform (☎488 699; http://tip.szegedvaros.hu; Dugonics tér 2; ☺9am-5pm Mon-Fri, to 1pm Sat) Tourist office hidden in a courtyard.

❶ Getting There & Around

The train station is south of the city centre on Indóház tér; from here, tram 1 takes you along Boldogasszony sugárút into the centre of town. The bus station, on Mars tér, is west of the centre within easy walking distance via pedestrian-only Mikszáth Kálmán utca.

Buses run to Pécs (3360Ft, 4¼ hours, seven daily) and Debrecen (3890Ft, five hours, two daily). Buses run to the Serbian city of Subotica up to four times daily.

Szeged is on the main rail line to Budapest's Nyugati train station (3000Ft, 2¾ hours, hourly); trains also stop halfway along in Kecskemét (2100Ft, 1¼ hours, hourly). You have to change in Békéscsaba (1600Ft, two hours, half-hourly) to get to Arad in Romania.

NORTHEASTERN HUNGARY

If ever a Hungarian wine were world-famous, it would be tokay (occasionally spelled *tokaj*). And this is where it comes from, a region of Hungary containing microclimates conducive to wine production. The chain of wooded hills in the northeast constitutes the foothills of the Carpathian Mountains, which stretch along the Hungarian border with Slovakia. Though you'll definitely notice the rise in elevation, Hungary's highest peak of Kékes is still only a proverbial bump in the road at 1014m. The highlights here are wine towns Eger and Tokaj, and Szilvásvárad – the Hungarian home of the snow-white Lipizzaner horse.

Eger

📍 36 / POP 58,300

Filled with wonderfully preserved baroque architecture, Eger (*egg*-air) is a jewelbox of a town containing gems aplenty. Explore the bloody history of Turkish conquest and defeat at its hilltop castle, climb a Turkish minaret, hear an organ performance at the ornate basilica...but best of all, go from cellar to cellar in the Valley of Beautiful Women (yes, it's really called that), tasting the celebrated Bull's Blood wine from the region where it's made.

It was here in 1552 that Hungarian defenders, led by local hero Captain István Dobó, temporarily stopped the Turkish advance into Western Europe and helped preserve Hungary's identity (see boxed text, p438). However, the persistent Ottomans returned in 1596 and finally captured Eger Castle. They were evicted nearly 100 years later, in 1687.

In the 18th century, Eger played a central role in Ferenc Rákóczi II's attempt to overthrow the Habsburgs, and it was then that a large part of the castle was razed by the Austrians. Eger has some of Hungary's finest architecture, especially examples of Copf (Zopf in Hungarian), a transitional style between late baroque and neoclassicism found only in central Europe.

⊙ Sights & Activities

Eger Castle   FORTRESS
(Egri Vár; www.egrivar.hu; Vár 1; adult/concession incl museum 1300/650Ft; ⊙9am-6pm Tue-Sun Apr-Oct, 10am-4pm Tue-Sun Nov-Mar) The most striking attraction, with the best views of town, is Eger Castle, a huge walled complex at the top of the hill off Dósza tér. It was first fortified after an early Mongol invasion in the 13th century; the earliest ruins on site are the foundations of St John's Cathedral, built in the 12th century and destroyed by the Turks. The excellent **István Dobó Castle Museum** (Dobó István Vármuzeum), inside the Bishop's Palace (1470) within the castle grounds, explores the history and development of the castle and the town. Other onsite exhibits such as the **Waxworks** (Panoptikum; adult/concession 450/300Ft) and the **Minting Exhibit** (Éremverde; adult/concession 400/250Ft) cost extra. Even on days when the museums are closed, you can walk around the grounds and battlements and enjoy the views if you buy a *sétaljegy* (strolling ticket, adult/concession 700/350Ft).

Minaret   MINARET
(Knézich Károly utca; admission 200Ft; ⊙10am-6pm Apr-Oct) A 40m-high minaret, minus the mosque, is allegedly Europe's northernmost remains of the Ottoman invasion in the 16th century. You can climb to the top with a great view of the castle, though the 97 steep steps provide a pretty good workout.

FREE **Minorite Church**   CHURCH
(Minorita Templom; Dobó István tér; admission free; ⊙9am-5pm Tue-Sun) The Minorite Church, built in 1771, is a glorious baroque building. In the town's main square, in front of the church, are statues of national hero István Dobó and his comrades-in-arms routing the Turks in 1552.

Eger Basilica   CHURCH
(Egri Bazilika; Pyrker János tér 1) The first thing you see as you come into town from the bus or train station is the mustard-coloured, neoclassical basilica, with its gigantic pillars. It was built in 1836 and is free to enter. You can tour the caverns below the basilica to see the archbishop's enormous former wine cellar at the **Town Under the Town** (Pyrker János tér; adult/concession 950/500Ft; ⊙10am-8pm Apr-Sep,

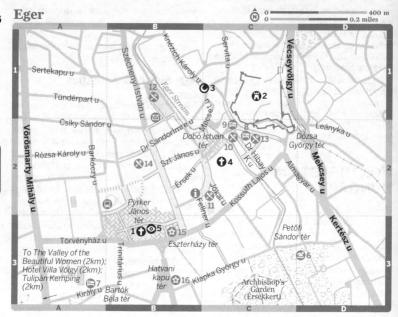

10am-5pm Oct-Mar) exhibition. Most tours are given only in Hungarian, though it might be worth it on a hot day, anyway, since the cellar remains chilly year-round. Bring a sweater.

City Thermal Baths   BATHHOUSE
(Városi Térmalfürdő; ☑ 413 356; Fürdő utca 1-3; adult/ concession 1600/1400Ft; ⊙ 6am-8pm Apr-Oct, 9am-7pm Nov-Mar) The Archbishop's Garden was once the private reserve of papal princes, but today it is open to the public. Inside the park, the City Thermal Baths has open-air and covered pools with different temperatures and mineral contents. From June to August you can pay 1000Ft extra to get into the modern 'adventure' complex with bubbling massage pools and a castle-themed kids' pool.

FREE **Szépasszony völgy**   WINE CELLARS
(Valley of the Beautiful Women; off Király utca) To sample Eger's wines, visit the extravagantly named 'Valley of the Beautiful Women', home to dozens of small wine cellars that truck in, store and sell Bull's Blood and other regional red and white wines. It's about 1km southwest of the town centre. Walk the horseshoe-shaped street through the valley and stop in front of one that strikes your fancy and ask '*megkosztólhatok?*' to taste their wares (around 220Ft per decilitre). If you want wine to go, you can bring an empty bottle and have

it filled for about 500Ft per litre. The cellar's outdoor tables fill up on a late summer afternoon as locals cook *gulyás* in the park and strains from a gypsy violinist float up from the restaurants at the valley's entrance. A taxi back to the centre costs about 1200Ft.

🛏 Sleeping

Tourinform has a glossy booklet of accommodation, including private rooms, for the city and the surrounding area.

Hotel Senator Ház   BOUTIQUE HOTEL **€€€**
(☑ 411 711; www.senatorhaz.hu; Dobó István tér 11; s/d 17,900/23,000Ft; ✳) Warm and cosy rooms with traditional 19th-century period furnishings fill the upper floors of this delightful 18th-century inn on Eger's main square. The ground-floor reception area could easily moonlight as a history museum. The hotel's terrace restaurant is *the* place in town for dinner alfresco, usually accompanied by live music.

Dobó Vendégház   BOUTIQUE HOTEL **€€**
(☑ 421 407; www.vendeghaz.hu; Dobó utca 19; s/d 9000/13,000Ft) A pleasant and affordable guest house, just a few steps from Eger's main square. The rooms are large and airy, with big wooden beds and fresh white-cotton linens. Some rooms open onto shared balconies off the back with pretty views towards

Eger

town. Take a look at 3a. The friendly reception speaks only halting English at best, but a little sign language goes a long way.

Hotel Villa Völgy BOUTIQUE HOTEL €€€
(☎321 664; www.hotelvillavolgy.hu; Tulipánkert utca 5; s/d 3-star 14,900/20,900Ft, 4-star 20,900/24,900Ft; ⊛) A classy, modern villa with a big outdoor swimming pool that's a welcome splurge, especially if you're travelling with children in the hot summer. Adults will appreciate the close proximity to the 'Valley of the Beautiful Women' wine cellars. Rooms come in three- and four-star options, with the latter offering in-room safes, minibars and air-conditioning. Enclosed parking costs 1000Ft per night.

Barók Tér Panzió PENSION €
(☎515 556; www.bartokpanzio.com; Bartók Béla tér 8; s/d 6000/9000Ft) Big, cool rooms in summer, and the location is convenient to both the in-town sights and the wine cellars of the Valley of Beautiful Women. Rates include breakfast.

Tulipán Kemping CAMPING GROUND €
(☎311 542; Szépasszony völgy utca 71; camp sites per person/tent 1940Ft, bungalows 6000Ft;⊛) Many of the camping sites here are in an open, shadeless field, but you're surrounded

by vineyards and are stumbling distance from the valley wine cellars.

✗ Eating & Drinking

At the base of the 'Valley of Beautiful Women' (Szépasszony völgy utca), outside town, you'll find several small terrace *büfé* (snack bars) that have all the Hungarian favourites and plenty of wine (or beer) to wash it all down with. In the centre, there are lots of cafes along pedestrianised Széchenyi István utca. A good strip for dining is along Dobó István tér, heading up toward the castle. The area is known for its *pistrang* (trout) dishes.

Head to the covered **market** (piac; Katona István tér; ◷6am-6pm Mon-Fri, to 1pm Sat, to 10am Sun) to buy fruit, vegetables, meat and bread.

TOP CHOICE **Palacsintavár** CREPERIE €
(Dobó István utca 9; mains 1600-1800Ft) Pop art lines the walls, and groovy music provides the soundtrack to this eclectic eatery. *Palacsintak* (crêpelike pancakes) are served with an abundance of fresh vegetables and range in flavour from Asian to Italian, and even local versions that feature hot peppers and chicken livers. Try to time your arrival for off-meal times, as the wait at the lunch and dinner rush hours can stretch to an hour or more.

Szántófer Vendéglő HUNGARIAN €€
(☎517 298; Bródy utca 3; mains 1500-2400Ft) One of the better choices in town for hearty, homestyle Hungarian food. Farming equipment and cooking utensils hang on the walls, and the covered courtyard out back is perfect for escaping the heat.

Capri Pizza ITALIAN €
(☎410 877; Bajcsy-Zsilinszky utca 4; mains 900-1400Ft) An ordinary pizzeria that will do in a pinch if you're looking for something quick, cheap and central.

Bikavér Borház BAR €
(Dobó István tér 10) After dinner, head to this tastings bar just across from the Senator Ház hotel for a nightcap or two of some of the region's best wines, served by the glass or the bottle. The waiters can guide you with the right selection, and bring along a plate of cheese or grapes to help you cleanse your palate. They also sell bottles to take home.

✪ Entertainment

The Tourinform office can tell you what concerts and musicals are on. The free *Egri Est* magazine has nightlife listings.

HUNGARY EGER

AS STRONG AS A BULL

The story of the Turkish attempt to take Eger Castle is the stuff of legend. Under the command of István Dobó, a mixed bag of 2000 soldiers held out against more than 100,000 Turks for a month in 1552. As every Hungarian kid in short trousers can tell you, the women of Eger played a crucial role in the battle, pouring boiling oil and pitch on the invaders from the ramparts.

If we're to believe the tale, it seems that Dobó sustained his weary troops with a ruby-red vintage of the town's wine. When they fought on with increased vigour – and stained beards – rumours began to circulate among the Turks that the defenders were gaining strength by drinking the blood of bulls. The invaders departed, and the legend of Bikavér (Bull's Blood) was born.

Géza Gárdonyi Theatre　　　　THEATRE
(Gárdonyi Géza Színház; ☑310 026; Hatvani kapu tér 4) Dance, opera and drama are staged at this theatre.

Broadway Studio　　　　CLUB
(Pyrker János tér 3; ◷10pm-6am Tue & Sat) This bizarre, cavernous dance club beneath the cathedral's steps parties hard weekends. Check kiosks around town for events. Expect to pay a cover of 800Ft to 1000Ft.

❶ Information

Egri Est Café (Széchenyi István utca 16; per hr 300Ft; ◷11am-midnight Sun-Thu, to 2am Fri & Sat) Cafe-bar with internet access.

OTP Bank (Széchenyi István utca 2)

Post office (Széchenyi István utca 22; ◷8am-8pm Mon-Fri, to 1pm Sat)

Tourinform (☑517 715; eger@tourinform.hu; Bajcsy-Zsilinszky utca 9; ◷9am-5pm Mon-Fri, to 1pm Sat & Sun, closed Sun mid-Sep–mid-Jun) Offers guided historical tours at weekends (300Ft per person). Good source for information on nearby Szilvásvárad.

❶ Getting There & Away

The main train station is a 15-minute walk south of town, on Vasút utca, just east of Deák Ferenc utca. Egervár train station, which serves Szilvásvárad and other points north, is a five-minute walk north of the castle along Vécseyvölgy utca. The bus station is west of Széchenyi István utca, Eger's main drag.

Hourly buses make the trip from Eger to Szilvásvárad (500Ft, 45 minutes). Other destinations include Kecskemét (2200Ft, 4½ hours, three daily) and Szeged (3500Ft, 5¾ hours, two daily). To get to Tokaj by bus, you have to go past it to Nyíregyháza and get another bus back.

Up to seven direct trains a day head to Budapest's Keleti train station (2300Ft, 2½ hours). Otherwise, Eger is on a minor train line linking Putnok and Füzesabony, so you have to change

at the latter for Debrecen (2160Ft, three hours). You can also catch a local train to Szilvásvárad (640Ft, one hour, six daily).

Tokaj

☑47 / POP 5100

The sweet and sultry wines produced here have been around for centuries, thanks to the area's volcanic soil and unique microclimate, which promotes the growth of *Botrytis cinerea* (noble rot) on the grapes. The result is Tokaji Aszú, a world-class dessert wine.

Today Tokaj (*toke*-eye) is a picturesque little town of old buildings, wine cellars and nesting storks. The 66-sq-km Tokaj-Hegyalja wine-producing region, a microclimate along the southern and eastern edges of the Zemplén Hills, was declared a World Heritage site in 2002.

Tokaj is divided into two areas: a larger commercial area near the Millennium Hotel, and a smaller, more pedestrian-friendly part further beyond. It's here where you'll find the Tourinform office, several pensions, the museum and the best wine cellars.

◉ Sights & Activities

Rákóczi Cellar　　　　WINE CELLAR
(Rákóczi Pince; Kossuth tér 15; ◷11am-8pm) Head to the 600-year-old Rákóczi Cellar for a tasting and a tour. Bottles of wine mature underground in the long cavelike corridors (one measures 28m by 10m). A flight of six Tokaj wines costs about 3000Ft. The correct order of sampling Tokaj wines is: Furmint, dry Szamorodni, sweet Szamorodni and then the Aszú wines, moving from three to six *puttony,* the measurement used for sweetness. Six, by the way, is the sweetest.

Tokaj Museum

MUSEUM

(Tokaji Múzeum; Bethlen Gábor utca 13; adult/concession 600/300Ft; ⊙10am-5pm Tue-Sun) The Tokaj Museum leaves nothing unsaid about the history of Tokaj, the region and its wines.

Great Synagogue

SYNAGOGUE

(Nagy Zsinagóga; Serház utca 55; admission 200Ft) The eclectic 19th-century Great Synagogue was used as a German barracks during WWII, but it's once again gleaming after a thorough renovation.

🛏 Sleeping & Eating

Private rooms on offer along Hegyalja utca are convenient to the train station and are surrounded by vineyards. There are several camping grounds spread out along the banks of the Tisza River across from the town centre.

Millennium Hotel

BOUTIQUE HOTEL €€

(☑352 247; www.tokajmillennium.hu; Bajcsy-Zsilinszky utca 34; s/d 12,900/14,900Ft; 🌐@) Equidistant from the train station and town centre; the only drawback to this hotel's location is the busy road out front. Pleasant beer garden, though.

Huli Panzió

PENSION €

(☑352 791; www.hulipanzio.hu; Rákóczi út 16; s/d 4000/8000Ft;🌐) Bright and simple pension with 12 down-to-earth rooms. Enjoy breakfast (800Ft) at the ground-floor restaurant.

Vaskó Panzió

PENSION €

(☑352 689; http://vaskopanzio.fw.hu; Rákóczi út 12; r 8000Ft) The supremely central Vaskó has eight cute rooms, and windowsills bedecked with flowerpots. It's above a private wine cellar and the proprietor can organise tastings. Breakfast costs an additional 700Ft per person.

Tisza Camping

CAMPING GROUND €

(☑06 30 432 8242; Strand 1; per person tent sites/ bungalows 1000/1700Ft; ⊙Apr-Oct) Nothing special, but you'll find shady tent sites and basic bungalows adjacent to the river.

Degenfeld

HUNGARIAN €€

(☑552 006; Kossuth tér 1; mains 1950-3650Ft) Expert wine pairings accompany each exquisite dish, such as duck leg in honey-mustard sauce or pork medallions in pepper sauce. Also sells Degenfeld's own wines, including local favourite 'Fortissimo 2008' for 3200Ft per bottle.

Fakapu

HUNGARIAN €

(Rákóczi út 27; mains 1000-1650Ft) Just what you'd expect in Tokaj: a cute terrace–wine cellar that offers simple Hungarian soups, stews and plates of smoked meats to accompany wine tastings. Great choice for a light (and mostly liquid) lunch.

🛍 Shopping

You can buy wine at any of the places mentioned for tasting, or stop at the **Furmint Vinotéka** (☑353 340; Bethlen Gábor utca 12; ⊙9am-6pm) wine shop for a large local selection.

ℹ Information

Tourinform (☑552 070; www.tokaj-turizmus. hu; Serház utca 1; ⊙9am-6pm Mon-Fri, 10am-7pm Sat & Sun Jun-Aug, 9am-5pm Mon-Fri Sep-May) Just off Rákóczi út. Hands out a handy booklet of wine cellars in the area and organizes weekend 'wine bus' tours (from 3200Ft per person) with visits to two or three wineries, depending on the day.

ℹ Getting There & Away

Trains arrive 1200m south of the town centre; walk north on Baross Gábor utca and turn left on Bajcsy-Zsilinszky út, which turns into Rákóczi út, the main thoroughfare. The bus station is more convenient, in town on Seráz utca.

No direct buses connect Tokaj with Budapest or Eger; train travel is your best option here. Up to 10 trains a day head west to Budapest Keleti (3840Ft; 2½ hours), and at least one train daily goes east to Debrecen (1650Ft, two hours).

Debrecen

☑52 / POP 215,000

Flanked by the golden Great Church and historic Aranybika Hotel, the main square of Hungary's second city is quite pretty; a surprise given the unattractive industrial zones and apartment blocks you pass when arriving by bus or train. During summer, street festivals fill the pedestrian core with revellers, and the city's array of museums and its town thermal baths will keep you busy for a day or two. The Debrecen Flower Carnival happens in late August; Debrecen Jazz Days is in September.

The area around Debrecen (*deb*-re-tsen) has been settled since the earliest times. Debrecen's wealth, based on salt, the fur trade and cattle-raising, grew steadily through the Middle Ages and increased during the Turkish occupation. Debrecen played a pivotal role in the 1848 nationalist revolt, and it experienced a major building boom in the late 19th and early 20th centuries.

HUNGARY DEBRECEN

A ring road, built on the city's original earthen walls, encloses the Belváros, or Inner Town. This is bisected by Piac utca, which runs northward from the train station (Petőfi tér) to Kálvin tér, site of the Great Church and Debrecen's centre. The bus station (Külső-Vásártér) is on the 'outer marketplace' at the western end of Széchenyi utca.

☉ Sights & Activities

Great Church
CHURCH

(Kálvin tér; adult/concession 350/250Ft; ☺9am-4pm Mon-Fri, 9am-1pm Sat, noon-4pm Sun Apr-Oct, 10am-1pm Mon-Sat, 11.30am-1pm Sun Nov-Mar) Many of the town's big sights are at the northern end of Piac utca, including the yellow neoclassical Great Church. Built in 1821, it has become so synonymous with Debrecen that mirages of its twin clock towers were reportedly seen on the Great Plain early last century. Climb the 210 steps to the top of the west clock tower for grand views over the city.

Reformed College
MUSEUM

(Református Kollégium; Kálvin tér 16; adult/concession 700/350Ft, English-language tours 3500Ft; ☺10am-4pm Tue-Sat, to 1pm Sun) North of the church stands the 1816 Reformed College, the site of a prestigious secondary school and theological college since the Middle Ages. It houses exhibits on religious art and sacred objects (including a 17th-century chalice made from a coconut) and on the school's history.

Aquaticum
BATHHOUSE

(www.aquaticum.hu; adult/concession 2100/1600Ft; ☺10am-10pm) You can wander along leafy trails and rent a paddle boat (per hr 1000Ft; ☺9am-8pm Jun-Aug) in Nagyerdei Park, north of the centre. But the main attraction here is Aquaticum, a complex of 'Mediterranean Enjoyment Baths' offering all manner of slides and waterfalls, spouts and grottoes within its pools.

🛏 Sleeping

Loads of dormitory accommodation is available in July and August; ask at Tourinform for details.

Aquaticum Wellness Hotel
BOUTIQUE HOTEL €€

(☎514 111; www.aquaticum.hu; Nagyerdei park 1; s/d €105/140; ❋@≈) Kids' programs, babysitting, bike rental, spa services, a swimming pool, and loads of other amenities make Aquaticum attractive to both adults and children. Room rates include breakfast and dinner, as well as access to all of the spas and pools.

Aranybika
HOTEL €€

(☎508 600; www.civishotels.hu; Piac utca 11-15; s/d from €40/60; ❋≈) Try as we might, we just can't give this landmark art nouveau hotel on the central square an enthusiastic thumbs up. The historic exterior has been spruced up by the Civis hotel chain, which owns the property, but the rooms remain stubbornly stuck in the communist 1970s, with drab carpets and plain, proletarian furnishings. On the plus side, the location is unbeatable, the reception desk is helpful, and the property admittedly does have a faded retro charm. Plump for the 'superior' rooms, which are larger and cooler than standard.

Szï Panzió
PENSION €

(☎322 200; www.szivpanzio.hu; Szív utca 11; r 7800Ft) The chief advantage at this out-of-the way guesthouse is its proximity to both the rail and bus stations (about 300m from both). The area is a little depressing, but the rooms themselves are clean and quiet, and some even have air-conditioning.

Maróthi György College
HOSTEL €

(☎502 780; Blaháné utca 15; s/d 3500/7000Ft) Right across from a large church, this is a central place to stay. Rooms are fairly basic (containing just a bed and a desk), and facilities are shared. There are simple kitchens available, along with a courtyard and a basketball court for guest use.

🍴 Eating & Drinking

There's a grocery shop (Piac utca 75; ☺24hr) within walking distance of the train station and a small covered fruit and vegetable market (Csapó utca; ☺5am-3pm Mon-Sat, to 11am Sun) right in the centre.

Trinacria da Tano e Pippo
ITALIAN €€

(☎416 988; Batthyány utca 4; mains 1500-3500Ft) Upscale trattoria that serves well-prepared pasta dishes, including homemade raviolis, as well as very good wood-fired pizzas. Call ahead to reserve a table on the terrace in summer.

Eve's Café and Lounge
CAFE €

(☎322 222; Simonffy utca 1b; sandwiches 800-1000Ft) Pleasantly upscale cafe serves breakfasts as well as very good sandwiches and salads throughout the day. Pedestrianised Simonffy utca is the nicest spot in the centre to sit back with a coffee and people-watch.

Csokonai Söröző
HUNGARIAN €€

(☎410 802; Kossuth utca 21; mains 1800-3200Ft) Medieval decor, sharp service and excellent

Hungarian specialities all help to create one of Debrecen's best eating experiences. This cellar pub–restaurant also serves the odd international dish, like turkey enchiladas with beans.

Klári Salátabár   VEGETARIAN €

☑ 412 203; Bajcsy-Zsilinszky utca 3; per 100g 150-350Ft; ⊗9am-7pm Mon-Fri) Tiny, canteen-like salad bar serves salad greens and vegetables by weight as well as a range of fried foods, like mushrooms, cheese and fish.

☆ Entertainment

Pick up a copy of the biweekly entertainment freebie *Debreceni Est* (www.est.hu) for music listings. For bars and late-night cafes, check out Simonffy utca. For clubs, most of the action is along Bajcy-Zsilinszky.

Csokonai Theatre   THEATRE

☑ 455 075; www.csokonaiszinhaz.hu; Kossuth utca 10) Three-tiered gilt balconies, ornate ceiling frescos, and elaborate chandeliers: the Csokonai is everything a 19th-century theatre should be. Musicals and operas are staged here.

Jazz Klub   BAR

(Bajcsy-Zsilinszky utca 4) This subterranean music bar has a big open-air terrace out back in summer. It's a good place to relax over an evening beer.

Cool Music and Dance Club   CLUB

(Bajcsy-Zsilinszky utca 1-3; cover charge 500-800Ft) DJs spin house and techno tunes here most weekends; Fridays see frequent theme parties.

ⓘ Information

Data Net Cafe (Kossuth utca 8; per hr 480Ft; ⊗9am-midnight) Internet and cheap international calls.

Ibusz (☑ 415 555; Révész tér 2; ⊗8am-5pm Mon-Fri, 9am-1pm Sat) Travel agency renting private apartments.

Main post office (Hatvan utca 5-9)

OTP Bank (Piac utca 16 & 45) Both have ATMs.

Tourinform (☑ 412 250; http://portal.debrecen.hu) town hall office (Piac utca 20; ⊗9am-8pm Mon-Fri, 9am-5pm Sun Jun-Aug, 9am-5pm Mon-Fri Sep-May); summer booth (Kossuth tér; ⊗10am-6pm Jun-Sep)

ⓘ Getting There & Away

Buses are quickest if you're going directly to Eger (2300Ft, 2½ hours) or Szeged (3400Ft, five hours, three daily).

Frequently departing trains will get you to Budapest (4000Ft, 3¼ hours) and Tokaj (1650Ft,

1½ hours). The night train from Budapest to Moscow stops here at 9.36pm.

UNDERSTAND HUNGARY

History
Pre-Hungarian Hungary

The plains of the Carpathian Basin attracted waves of migration, from both east and west, long before the Magyar tribes decided to settle there. The Celts occupied the area in the 3rd century BC, but the Romans conquered and expelled them just before the Christian era. The lands west of the Danube (Transdanubia) in today's Hungary became part of the Roman province of Pannonia, where a Roman legion was stationed at the town of Aquincum (now called Óbuda). The Romans brought writing, planted the first vineyards and built baths near some of the region's many thermal springs.

A new surge of nomadic tribespeople, the Huns, who lent Hungary its present-day name, arrived on the scene with a leader who would become legendary in Hungarian history. By AD 441, Attila and his brother Bleda had conquered the Romans and acquired a reputation as great warriors. This reputation still runs strong and you will notice that many Hungarians carry the name Attila, even though the Huns have no connection with present-day Hungarians and the Huns' short-lived empire did not outlast Attila's death (453), when remaining tribespeople fled back from whence they came. Many tribes filled the vacuum left by the Huns and settled in the area, such as the Goths, Longobards and the Avars, a powerful Turkic people who controlled parts of the area from the 5th to the 8th centuries. The Avars were subdued by Charlemagne in 796, leaving space for the Franks and Slavs to move in.

The Conquest

Magyar (Hungarian) tribes are said to have moved in around 896, when Árpád led the alliance of seven tribes into the region. The Magyars, a fierce warrior tribe, terrorised much of Europe with raids reaching as far as Spain. They were stopped at the Battle of Augsburg in 955 and subsequently converted to Christianity. Hungary's first king and its patron saint, István (Stephen), was crowned on Christmas Day in 1000, marking the foundation of the Hungarian state.

Medieval Hungary was a powerful kingdom that included Transylvania (now in Romania), Transcarpathia (now in Ukraine), modern-day Slovakia and Croatia. Under King Matthias Corvinus (1458–90), Hungary experienced a brief flowering of Renaissance culture. However, in 1526 the Ottomans defeated the Hungarian army at Mohács and by 1541 Buda Castle had been seized and Hungary sliced in three. The central part, including Buda, was controlled by the Ottomans, while Transdanubia, present-day Slovakia and parts of Transcarpathia were ruled by Hungarian nobility based in Pozsony (Bratislava) under the auspices of the Austrian House of Habsburg. The principality of Transylvania, east of the Tisza, prospered as a vassal state of the Ottoman Empire.

Habsburg Hegemony & the Wars

After the Ottomans were evicted from Buda in 1686, the Habsburg domination of Hungary began. The 'enlightened absolutism' of the Habsburg monarchs Maria Theresa (r 1740–80) and her son Joseph II (r 1780–90) helped the country leap forward economically and culturally. Rumblings of Hungarian independence surfaced off and on, but it was the unsuccessful 1848 Hungarian revolution that really started to shake the Habsburg oligarchy. After Austria was defeated in war by Prussia in 1866, a weakened empire struck a compromise with Hungary in 1867, creating a dual monarchy. The two states would be self-governing in domestic affairs, but act jointly in matters of common interest, such as foreign relations. The Austro-Hungarian monarchy lasted until WWI.

After WWI and the collapse of the Habsburg Empire in November 1918, Hungary was proclaimed a republic. But she had been on the losing side of the war. The 1920 Treaty of Trianon stripped the country of more than two-thirds of its territory – a hot topic of conversation to this day.

In 1941 Hungary's attempts to recover lost territories saw the nation go to war on the side of Nazi Germany. When leftists tried to negotiate a separate peace in 1944, the Germans occupied Hungary and brought the fascist Arrow Cross Party to power. The Arrow Cross immediately began deporting hundreds of thousands of Jews to Auschwitz. By early April 1945 Hungary was defeated and occupied by the Soviet army.

Communism

By 1947 the communists assumed complete control of the government and began nationalising industry and dividing up large estates among the peasantry. On 23 October 1956, student demonstrators demanding the withdrawal of Soviet troops were fired upon. The next day Imre Nagy, the reformist minister of agriculture, was named prime minister. On 28 October Nagy's government offered an amnesty to all those involved in the violence and promised to abolish the hated secret police, the ÁVH (known as ÁVO until 1949). On 4 November Soviet tanks moved into Budapest, crushing the uprising. By the time the fighting ended on 11 November, thousands had been killed. Then the reprisals began: an estimated 20,000 people were arrested; 2000 were executed, including Nagy; another 250,000 fled to Austria.

By the 1970s Hungary had abandoned strict central economic control in favour of a limited market system, often referred to as 'Goulash Communism'. In June 1987 Károly Grósz took over as premier and Hungary began moving towards full democracy. The huge numbers of East Germans who were able to slip through the Iron Curtain by leaving via Hungary contributed to the eventual crumbling of the Berlin Wall.

The Republic

At their party congress in February 1989 the Hungarian communists agreed to surrender their monopoly on power. The Republic of Hungary was proclaimed in October, and democratic elections were scheduled for March 1990. Hungary changed its political system with scarcely a murmur, and the last Soviet troops left the country in June 1991.

The painful transition to a full market economy resulted in declining living standards for most people and a recession in the early 1990s, but the early years of the 21st century saw astonishing growth. Hungary became a member of NATO in 1999 and the European Union (EU) in 2004.

In December 2007 Hungary joined the Schengen zone of European countries, abandoning border controls with its EU neighbours Austria, Slovakia and Slovenia. Late in 2008, reeling from the fallout of the global financial crisis, Hungary was forced to approach the International Monetary Fund for economic assistance, though the economy began a modest recovery in 2010. Hungary originally aimed to adopt the euro by

2010, but the effects of the crisis have since obliged the government to delay adoption for several more years.

People

Some 10.2 million people live within the national borders, and another five million Hungarians and their descendants are abroad. The estimated 1.45 million Hungarians in Transylvania constitute the largest ethnic minority in Europe, and there are another 530,000 in Slovakia, 293,000 in Serbia, 156,000 in Ukraine and 40,500 in Austria.

Ethnic Magyars make up approximately 93% of the population. Many minority groups estimate their numbers to be significantly higher than official counts. There are 13 recognised minorities in the country, including Germans (2.6%), Serbs and other South Slavs (2%), Slovaks (0.8%) and Romanians (0.7%). The number of Roma is officially put at 1.9% of the population, though some sources place the figure as high as 4%.

Of those Hungarians declaring religious affiliation, about 52% are Roman Catholic, 16% Reformed (Calvinist) Protestant, 3% Evangelical (Lutheran) Protestant, and 2.6% Greek Catholic and Orthodox. Hungary's Jews number around 100,000, down from a pre-WWII population of nearly eight times that amount.

Literature & the Arts

The history of Hungarian highbrow culture includes world-renowned composers such as Béla Bartók and Franz Liszt, and the Nobel Prize–winning writer Imre Kértesz and his innovative contemporary Peter Esterházy. Hungary's proximity to classical-music hub Vienna, as well as the legacy of the Soviet regard for the 'proper arts', means that opera, symphony and ballet are high on the entertainment agenda, and even provincial towns have decent companies.

For the more contemporary branches of artistic life, Budapest is the focus, containing many art galleries and theatre and dance companies. The capital is also a centre for folk music and crafts that have grown out of village life or minority culture.

Literature

Hungary has some excellent writers, both of poetry and prose. Sándor Petőfi (1823–49) is Hungary's most celebrated poet. A line from his work *National Song* became the rallying cry for the War of Independence between 1848 and 1849, in which he fought and is commonly thought to have died.

Contemporary Hungarian writers whose work has been translated into English and are worth a read include Tibor Fischer, Péter Esterházy and Sándor Márai. The most celebrated Hungarian writer is the 2002 Nobel Prize winner Imre Kertész. Among his novels available in English are *Fateless* (1975), *Detective Story* (1977), *Kaddish for an Unborn Child* (1990) and *Liquidation* (2003). Another prominent contemporary writer, who died in 2007 at age 90, was Magda Szabó (*Katalin Street,* 1969; *The Door,* 1975).

Classical & Traditional Music

As you will no doubt see from the street names in every Hungarian town and city, the country celebrates and reveres its most influential musician, composer and pianist Franz (or Ferenc) Liszt (1811–86). The eccentric Liszt described himself as 'part Gypsy', and in his *Hungarian Rhapsodies,* as well as in other works, he does indeed weave Romani motifs into his compositions.

Ferenc Erkel (1810–93) is the father of Hungarian opera, and his stirringly nationalist *Bánk Bán* is a standard at the Hungarian State Opera House in Budapest. Béla Bartók (1881–1945) and Zoltán Kodály (1882–1967) made the first systematic study of Hungarian folk music; both integrated some of their findings into their compositions.

Hungarian folk musicians play violins, zithers, hurdy-gurdies, bagpipes and lutes on a five-tone diatonic scale. Look out for Muzsikás, Marta Sebestyén, Ghymes (Hungarian folk band from Slovakia) and the Hungarian group Vujicsics, which mixes in elements of southern Slav music. Another folk musician with eclectic tastes is the Paris-trained Bea Pálya, who combines such sounds as traditional Bulgarian and Indian music with Hungarian folk.

Romani music, found in restaurants in its schmaltzy form (best avoided), has become a fashionable thing among the young, with Romani bands playing 'the real thing' in trendy bars till the wee hours: it's a dynamic, hopping mix of fiddles, bass and cymbalom (a stringed instrument played with sticks). A Romani band would never be seen without the tin milk bottle used as a drum, which gives Hungarian Roma music its characteristic sound. It's reminiscent of traditional Indian music, an influence that perhaps harks back to the Roma's Asian roots. Some modern Romani music groups – Kalyi Jag (Black Fire) from northeastern Hungary, Romano Drom (Gypsy Road) and Romani Rota (Gypsy Wheels) – have added guitars, percussion and even electronics to create a whole new sound.

Klezmer music (traditional Eastern European Jewish music) has also made a comeback in the playlists of the young and trendy.

Pop music is as popular here as anywhere. Indeed, Hungary has one of Europe's biggest pop spectacles, the annual Sziget Music Festival (p393). It has more than 1000 performances over a week and attracts an audience of up to 385,000 people. Popular Hungarian musical artists to look out for include pop singers Magdi Rúzsa and Laci Gáspár and pop/folk band Nox.

Visual Arts

Favourite painters from the 19th century include realist Mihály Munkácsy (1844–1900), the so-called painter of the plains, and Tivadar Kosztka Csontváry (1853–1919). Győző Vásárhelyi (1908–97), who changed his name to Victor Vasarely when he emigrated to Paris, is considered the 'father of op art'. Contemporary painters to keep an eye out for include Árpád Müller and the late Endre Szász (1926–2003).

In the 19th and early 20th centuries, the Zsolnay family created world-renowned decorative art in porcelain. Ceramic artist Margit Kovac (1902–77) produced a large number of statues and ceramic objects during her career. The traditional embroidery, weavings and ceramics of the nation's *népművészet* (folk art) endure, and there is at least one handicraft store in every town.

Environment

The Landscape

Hungary occupies the Carpathian Basin to the southwest of the Carpathian Mountains. Water dominates much of the country's geography. The Duna (Danube River) divides the Nagyalföld (Great Plain) in the east from the Dunántúl (Transdanubia) in the west. The Tisza (597km in Hungary) is the country's longest river, and historically has been prone to flooding. Hungary has hundreds of small lakes and is riddled with thermal springs. Lake Balaton (596 sq km, 77km long), in the west, is the largest freshwater lake in Europe outside Scandinavia. Hunga-

ry's 'mountains' to the north are merely hills, with the country's highest peak being Kékes (1014m) in the Mátra Range.

Wildlife

There are a lot of common European animals in Hungary (deer, hares, wild boar and foxes), as well as some rare species (wild cat, lake bat and Pannonian lizard), but most of the country's wildlife comes from the avian family. Hungary is a premier European spot for bird-watching. Around 75% of the country's 480 known vertebrates are birds, for the most part waterfowl attracted by the rivers, lakes and wetlands. The rare black stork, a smaller, darker version of its common cousin, also spends time in Hungary on its migration from Africa to Europe.

National Parks

There are 10 national parks in Hungary. Bükk Nemzeti Park, north of Eger, is a mountainous limestone area of forest and caves. Kiskunsági Nemzeti Park and Bugac, near Kecskemét, and Hortobágy Nemzeti Park (www.hnp.hu) in the Hortobágy Puszta (a World Heritage site), outside Debrecen, protect the unique grassland environment of the plains.

Environmental Issues

Environmental disaster struck Hungary in 2010, when toxic industrial sludge from an aluminium factory in Ajka, in western Hungary, broke through barriers and leeched into local rivers. Initial fears that the sludge would contaminate the Danube proved unfounded and the sludge should pose no hazard to visitors. In spite of the spill, there's been a marked improvement in both the public's awareness of environmental issues and the government's dedication to environmental safety.

Food & Drink

Hungarian Cuisine

The omnipresent seasoning in Hungarian cooking is paprika, a mild red pepper that appears on restaurant tables as a condiment beside the salt and black pepper, as well as in many recipes. *Pörkölt,* a paprika-infused stew, can be made from different meats, including *borju* (veal), and usually it has no vegetables. *Galuska* (small, gnocchi-like dumplings) are a good accompaniment to soak up the sauce. The well-known *paprikas csirke* (chicken paprikash) is stewed chicken in a tomato, cream and paprika sauce; it's

THE GRAND PRIX

The Hungarian Formula One Grand Prix, held in late July or early August, is the year's biggest sporting event. The **Hungaroring** (www.hungaroring.hu) track is 19km north of Budapest, in Mogyórod, but hotels in the capital fill up and prices skyrocket during the event.

not as common here as in Hungarian restaurants abroad. *Töltött káposzta* (cabbage rolls stuffed with meat and rice) is cooked in a roux made with paprika, and topped with sour cream, as is *székelygulyás* (stewed pork and sour cabbage). Another local favourite is *halászlé* (fisher's soup), a rich mix of several kinds of poached freshwater fish, tomatoes, green peppers and (you guessed it) paprika.

Leves (soup) is the start to any main meal in a Hungarian home; some claim that you will develop stomach disorders if you don't eat a hot, daily helping. *Gulyás* (goulash), although served as a stew outside Hungary, is a soup here, cooked with beef, onions and tomatoes. Traditional cooking methods are far from health-conscious, but they are tasty. Frying is a nationwide obsession, and you'll often find fried turkey, pork and veal schnitzels on the menu.

For dessert you might try the cold *gyümölcs leves* (fruit soup) made with sour cherries and other berries, or *palincsinta* (crêpes) filled with jam, sweet cheese or chocolate sauce. A good food-stand snack is *lángos,* fried dough that can be topped with cheese and/or *tejföl* (sour cream).

Where to Eat & Drink

An *étterem* is a restaurant with a large selection, formal service and formal prices. A *vendéglő* is smaller and more casual, and serves home-style regional dishes. The overused term *csárda,* which originally meant a rustic country inn with Romani music, can now mean anything – including 'tourist trap'. To keep prices down, look for *étkezde* (a tiny eating place that may have a counter or sit-down service), *önkiszolgáló* (a self-service canteen), *kínai gyorsbüfé* (Chinese fast food), *grill* (which generally serves gyros or kebabs and other grilled meats from the counter) or a *szendvicsbar* (which has open-faced sandwiches to go).

For this guide, budget eating is defined as establishments charging up to around 2500Ft per main course. Midrange are places where most mains cost between 2500Ft and 4000Ft. Top end is anything above that.

Wine has been produced in Hungary for hundreds of years, and you'll find it available by the glass or bottle everywhere. There are plenty of pseudo-British/Irish/Belgian pubs, smoky *sörözök* (Hungarian pubs, often in a cellar, where drinking is taken very seriously), *borozók* (wine bars, usually a dive) and nightclubs, but the most pleasant place to imbibe a cocktail or coffee may be in a cafe. A *kávéház* may primarily be an old-world dessert shop, or it may be a bar with an extensive drinks menu; either way they sell alcoholic beverages in addition to coffee. In spring, pavement tables sprout up alongside the new flowers.

Vegetarians & Vegans

Traditional Hungarian cuisine and vegetarianism are definitely not a match made in heaven. However, things are changing and there are places even in the provinces that serve good vegetarian meals. Where there are no vegetarian restaurants, you'll have to make do with what's on the regular menu or shop for ingredients in the markets.

Some not very light but widely available dishes for vegetarians to look for are *rántott sajt* (fried cheese), *gombafejek rántva* (fried mushroom caps), *gomba leves* (mushroom soup) and *túrós* or *káposzta csusza* (short, wide pasta with cheese or cabbage). *Bableves* (bean soup) usually contains meat.

SURVIVAL GUIDE

Directory A–Z

Accommodation

Hungary has a wide variety of lodging options, ranging from youth hostels and camping grounds at the low end, to private rooms, pensions (*panziók*), hotels and luxury boutiques at the high. Prices are highest in Budapest, and the high season for lodging typically runs from April to October and the Christmas and New Year holidays. For this guide, budget accommodation is defined as under 10,000Ft per double per night in the provinces (under 15,000Ft in Budapest). Midrange is between 10,000Ft and 15,000Ft in the countryside (15,000Ft and 30,000Ft in Budapest). Top end is anything above that.

Hungary's camping grounds are listed in Tourinform's *Camping Hungary* map and

HABITS & CUSTOMS

The Magyar are a polite people and their language is filled with courtesies. To toast someone's health before drinking, say *egéségére* (*egg*-eh-shaig-eh-ray), and to wish them a good appetite before eating, *jo étvágat* (*yo* ate-vad-yaht). If you're invited to someone's home, always bring a bunch of flowers and/or a bottle of good local wine.

brochure (www.camping.hu). Facilities are generally open May to October and can be difficult to reach without a car.

The **Hungarian Youth Hostels Association** (MISZSZ; www.miszsz.hu) keeps a list of year-round hostels throughout Hungary. In general, year-round hostels have a communal kitchen, laundry and internet service, and sometimes a lounge; a basic bread-and-jam breakfast may be included. Having an HI card is not required, but it may get you a 10% discount. A useful hostel website with online booking (only in Hungarian) is www.hihostels.hu.

From July to August, students vacate college and university dorms, and administration opens them to travellers. Facilities are usually – but not always – basic and shared. Local Tourinform offices can help you locate such places.

Renting a private room in a Hungarian home is a good budget option and can be a great opportunity to get up close and personal with the culture. Prices outside Budapest run from 3500Ft to 6000Ft per person per night. Tourinform offices can usually help with finding these; otherwise look for houses with signs reading *'szoba kiadó'* or *'Zimmer frei'*.

An engaging alternative is to stay in a rural village or farmhouse, but only if you have wheels: most of these places are truly remote. Contact Tourinform, the **National Federation of Rural & Agrotourism** (FATOSZ; ☎1-352 9804; VII Király utca 93) or the **Centre of Rural Tourism** (☎1-321 2426; www.falutur.hu; VII Dohány utca 86) in Budapest.

Activities

Canoeing For canoeists, **Ecotours** (☎030-606-1651; www.ecotours.hu) leads seven-day Danube River canoe-camping trips (tent rental and food extra) for about €600, as well as shorter Danube Bend and Tisza River trips.

Cycling Hungary's flat terrain makes it ideal for cycling. **Velo-Touring** (☎1-319 0571; www.velo-touring.hu) has a great selection of seven-night trips in all regions, from a senior-friendly Danube Bend tour (€689) to a bike ride between spas on the Great Plain (€847). Lake Balaton is circled by a long cycling track that takes four to five days to complete at a leisurely pace.

Hiking/Birdwatching Hiking enthusiasts may enjoy the trails around Tihany at Lake Balaton, the Bükk Hills north of Eger or the plains at Bugac Puszta south of Kecskemét. Birdwatchers could explore these same paths or take a tour with **Birding Hungary** (www.birdinghungary.com).

Horseback Riding There's a helpful HNTO *Riding in Hungary* booklet on equestrian tourism, or you could contact the **Hungarian Equestrian Tourism Association** (MLTSZ; ☎1-456 0444; IX Ráday utca 8, Budapest). **Pegazus Tours** (☎1-317 1644; www.pegazus.hu; V Ferenciek tere 5, Budapest) organises horse-riding tours.

Spas Hungary has more than 100 thermal baths open to the public. For locations, ask Tourinform for the *Spa & Wellness* booklet. For more about Budapest spas, check out www.spasbudapest.com.

Business Hours

Banks 9am-5pm Mon-Fri, 9am-noon Sat

Museums 9am or 10am-5pm or 6pm Tue-Sun

Restaurants roughly 11am-midnight

Courses

Debreceni Nyári Egyetem (Debrecen Summer University; ☎52-532 595; www.nyariegyetem.hu; Egyetem tér 1, Debrecen) is the best-known school for studying Hungarian. It organises intensive two- and four-week courses during July and August and 80-hour, two-week advanced courses during winter. The **Debrecen Summer University Branch** (☎1-320 5751; www.nyariegyetem.hu/bp; V Báthory utca 4) in Budapest also offers courses.

Discount Cards

The **Hungary Card** (☎1-266 3741; www.hungary card.hu; 7900Ft) gives 50% discounts on six return train fares and some bus and boat travel, free entry to many museums, up to 20% off selected accommodation, and 50%

off the price of the Budapest Card (p402). It's available at Tourinform offices.

Embassies & Consulates

Embassies in Budapest (phone code ☎1) include the following.

Australia (☎457 9777; XII Királyhágó tér 8-9)

Austria (☎479 7010; VI Benczúr utca 16)

Canada (☎392 3360; II Ganz utca 12-14)

Croatia (☎354 1315; VI Munkácsy Mihály utca 15)

France (☎374 1100; VI Lendvay utca 27)

Germany (☎488 3500; I Úri utca 64-66)

Ireland (☎301 4960; V Szabadság tér 7-9)

Netherlands (☎336 6300; II Füge utca 5-7)

Romania (☎384 0271; XIV Thököly út 72)

Serbia (☎322 9838; VI Dózsa György út 92/a)

Slovakia (☎460 9010; XIV Stefánia utca 22-24)

Slovenia (☎438 5600; II Cseppkő utca 68)

South Africa (☎392 0999; II Gárdonyi Géza út 17)

UK (☎266 2888; V Harmincad utca 6)

Ukraine (☎422 4122; XII Nógrádi út 8)

USA (☎475 4400; V Szabadság tér 12)

Food

Price ranges are budget (€; under 2500Ft), midrange (€€; 2500Ft to 5000Ft) and top end (€€€; over 5000Ft).

Gay & Lesbian Travellers

Budapest has a large and active gay population, and Pécs and Szeged also have sizeable gay scenes. Check the **Budapest GayGuide. net** (www.gayguide.net) for up-to-date information on gay-friendly clubs and accommodation, as well as a small list of venues in the countryside. **Labrisz** (www.labrisz.hu) is a lesbian association with a good website with a small English-language section.

Media

Budapest has two English-language newspapers: the weekly *Budapest Times* (www. budapesttimes.hu), with interesting reviews and opinion pieces, and the business-oriented bi-weekly *Budapest Business Journal* (http:// bbj.hu). Both are available on newsstands.

Money

The unit of currency is the Hungarian forint (Ft). Coins come in denominations of five, 10, 20, 50, 100 and 200Ft, and notes are denominated in 500, 1000, 2000, 5000, 10,000

and 20,000Ft. ATMs are everywhere, even in small villages, though some UK readers have reported problems with UK credit and debit cards. It's always best to check with your home bank before leaving to avoid disappointment. Tip waiters, hairdressers and taxi drivers approximately 10% of the bill.

Post

Postcards and small letters mailed within Europe cost 210Ft. To addresses outside Europe, expect to pay 240Ft. Mail addressed to poste restante in any town or city will go to the main post office *(főposta)*. When collecting poste-restante mail, look for the sign *'postán maradó küldemények'*.

Public Holidays

New Year's Day 1 January

1848 Revolution Day 15 March

Easter Monday March/April

International Labour Day 1 May

Whit Monday May/June

St Stephen's Day 20 August

1956 Remembrance Day 23 October

All Saints' Day 1 November

Christmas Holidays 25 and 26 December

Telephone

Hungary's country code is ☎36. To make an outgoing international call, dial ☎00 first. To dial city-to-city (and all mobile phones) within the country, first dial ☎06, wait for the second dial tone and then dial the city code and phone number. All localities in Hungary have a two-digit city code, except for Budapest, where the code is ☎1.

In Hungary you must always dial ☎06 when ringing mobile telephones, which have specific area codes depending on the telecom company: **Pannon GSM** (☎06 20; www. pgsm.hu), **T-Mobile** (☎06 30; www.t-mobile.hu) or **Vodafone** (☎06 70; www.vodafone.hu).

Consider buying a rechargeable SIM card. All of the major telephone companies offer some kind of prepaid SIM plan for around 4000Ft where you get a local number and calls, texts and data downloads are charged at local rates. These often include credit built into the card. Once the credit is exhausted, you can buy recharge cards at mobile-phone stores and supermarkets.

There's also a plethora of phonecards for public phones on offer, including T-Com's **Barangoló**, which comes in denominations of 1000Ft and 5000Ft; **NeoPhone** (www.neo phone.hu), with cards also valued at 1000Ft, 2000Ft and 5000F; and **Pannon**, offering cards for 1000Ft, 3000Ft and 5000Ft. It can cost as little as 8Ft per minute to call the USA, Australia and New Zealand using such cards. Telephone boxes with a black-and-white arrow and red target on the door and the word '*Visszahívható*' display a telephone number, so you can be phoned back.

Tourist Information

The **Hungarian National Tourist Office** (HNTO; www.hungarytourism.hu) has a chain of over 140 **Tourinform** (☎hotline 1-438 8080; www.tourinform.hu) information offices across the country. These are the best places to ask general questions and pick up brochures.

Travellers with Disabilities

Hungary's record in this regard is so-so. Wheelchair ramps and toilets fitted for people with disabilities do exist, though not as commonly as in Western Europe. Audible traffic signals are becoming more common in big cities. For more information, contact the **Hungarian Federation of Disabled Persons' Associations** (MEOSZ; ☎1-388 5529; www.meoszinfo.hu, in Hungarian; III San Marco utca 76) in Budapest.

Visas

EU citizens do not need visas to visit Hungary and can stay indefinitely. Citizens of the USA, Canada, Israel, Japan, New Zealand and Australia do not require visas to visit Hungary for stays of up to 90 days.

Check with the **Ministry for Foreign Affairs** (www.mfa.gov.hu) for an up-to-date list of which country nationals require visas.

Getting There & Away

Air

Airports & Airlines

The vast majority of international flights land at **Ferihegy International Airport** (☎1-296 7000; www.bud.hu) on the outskirts of Budapest. **Balaton airport** (www.flybalaton.com) is another possible arrival destination, though as we were researching this guide, the airport's future was in doubt. It is located 15km southwest of Keszthely near Lake Balaton. Hungary's national carrier is **Malév Hungarian Airlines** (MA; ☎06 40 212121; www.malev.hu).

Major airlines, aside from Malév, servicing Hungary:

Aeroflot (SU; www.aeroflot.com)

Air Berlin (AB; www.airberlin.com)

Air France (AF; www.airfrance.com)

Alitalia (AZ; www.alitalia.com)

Austrian Airlines (OS; www.aua.com)

British Airways (BA; www.ba.com)

CSA (OK; www.csa.cz)

easyJet (EZY; www.easyjet.com)

El Al (LY; www.elal.co.il)

EgyptAir (MS; www.egyptair.com)

Finnair (AY; www.finnair.com)

germanwings (4U; www.germanwings.com)

LOT Polish Airlines (LO; www.lot.com)

Lufthansa (LH; www.lufthansa.com)

Ryanair (FR; www.ryanair.com)

SAS (SK; www.flysas.com)

Tarom (RO; www.tarom.ro)

Turkish Airlines (TK; www.thy.com)

Wizz Air (W6; www.wizzair.com)

Land

Hungary's entry into the Schengen zone means that there are no border controls with Austria, Slovakia and Slovenia. Standard border procedures exist with Ukraine, Romania, Serbia and Croatia.

There are excellent land transport connections with Hungary's neighbours. Most of the departures listed are from Budapest, though other cities and towns closer to the various borders can also be used as springboards.

Bus

Most international buses arrive at the Népliget bus station in Budapest. **Eurolines** (www.eurolines.com), in conjunction with its Hungarian affiliate, **Volánbusz** (☎1-382 0888; www.volanbusz.hu), is the international bus company of Hungary. Useful international buses include those from Budapest to Vienna, Bratislava in Slovakia, Subotica in Serbia, Rijeka in Croatia, Prague in the Czech Republic and Sofia in Bulgaria. For more details, see p450.

Car & Motorcycle

Foreign driving licences are valid for one year after entering Hungary. Drivers of cars and riders of motorbikes also need the vehicle's registration papers. Third-party insurance is compulsory for driving in Hungary; if your car is registered in the EU, it's assumed you have it. Other motorists must show a Green Card or buy insurance at the border.

Travel on Hungarian motorways requires pre-purchase of a highway pass (E-vignette). Unlike many other countries, this is not a sticker, but rather your licence-plate number is entered into a computer database where it can be screened by highway-mounted surveillance cameras. Passes are available at border stops. Prices are 1530Ft for four days, 2550Ft for 10 days and 4200Ft for one month.

Train

The Hungarian State Railways, MÁV (☎1-444 4499; www.mav-start.hu) links up with international rail networks in all directions, and its schedule is available online.

Eurail passes are valid, but not sold, in Hungary. EuroCity (EC) and Intercity (IC) trains require a seat reservation and payment of a supplement. Most larger train stations in Hungary have left-luggage rooms open from at least 9am to 5pm. There are three main train stations in Budapest, so always note the station when checking a schedule online.

Some direct train connections from Budapest include Austria, Slovakia, Romania, Ukraine (continuing to Russia), Croatia, Serbia, Germany, Slovenia, Czech Republic, Poland, Switzerland, Italy, Bulgaria and Greece. See p451 for details.

Ticket and information offices are located at rail stations.

River

A hydrofoil service on the Danube River between Budapest and Vienna operates daily from late April to early October; passengers can disembark at Bratislava with advance notice. See p450 for more details.

Getting Around

Note that Hungary does not have any scheduled internal flights.

Boat

In summer there are regular passenger ferries on Lake Balaton and on the Danube from Budapest to Szentendre, Vác, Visegrád and Esztergom. Details of the schedules are given in the relevant destination sections.

Bus

Domestic buses, run by the Volán (www.volan. eu) association of coach operators, cover an extensive nationwide network.

Timetables are posted at stations and stops. Some footnotes you could come across include *naponta* (daily), *hétköznap* (weekdays), *munkanapokon* (on work days), *munkaszüneti napok kivételével naponta* (daily except holidays) and *szabad és munkaszüneti napokon* (on Saturday and holidays). A few large bus stations have luggage rooms, but these generally close by 6pm.

Car & Motorcycle

Most cities and towns require that you pay for street parking (usually 9am to 6pm workdays) by buying temporary parking passes from machines. Most machines take only coins (so keep a lot handy); place the time-stamped parking permit on the dashboard. The cost averages about 200Ft an hour in the countryside and up to 400Ft on central Budapest streets. Parking fines average about 3500Ft.

Automobile Associations

The so-called 'Yellow Angels' of the Hungarian Automobile Club do basic breakdown repairs for free if you belong to an affiliated organisation such as AAA in the USA or AA in the UK. You can telephone 24 hours a day on ☎188 nationwide.

Fuel & Spare Parts

Ólommentes benzin (unleaded petrol 95/98 octane) is available everywhere. Most stations also have *gázolaj* (diesel).

Hire

In general, you must be at least 21 years old and have had your licence for at least a year to rent a car. Drivers under 25 sometimes have to pay a surcharge. Rental agencies are common in large cities and at Budapest airport. Local rental rates are relatively high, and if you plan on renting a car during your stay, you're best advised booking online before you travel.

Road Rules

The most important rule to remember is that there's a 100% ban on alcohol when you are driving, and this rule is strictly enforced.

Using a mobile phone while driving is prohibited in Hungary. *All* vehicles must have their headlights switched on throughout the day outside built-up areas. Motorcyclists must have their headlights on at all times.

Hitching

In Hungary, hitchhiking is legal except on motorways. Hitchhiking is never an entirely safe way to travel and we don't recommend it, but if you're willing, **Kenguru** (www.kenguru.hu) is an agency that matches riders with drivers.

Local Transport

Public transport is efficient and extensive, with bus and, in many towns, trolleybus services. Budapest and Szeged also have trams, and there's an extensive metro and a suburban commuter railway in Budapest. Purchase tickets at newsstands before travelling and validate them once aboard. Inspectors do check tickets, especially on the metro lines in Budapest.

Train

MÁV (☑06 40 494 949; www.mav-start.hu) operates reliable train services on its 8000km of tracks. Schedules are available online, and computer information kiosks are popping up at rail stations around the country. Second-class domestic train fares range from 150Ft for a journey of less than 5km to about 4000Ft for a 300km trip. First-class fares are usually 25% more. IC trains are express trains, the most comfortable and modern. *Gyorsvonat* (fast trains) take longer and use older cars; s*zemélyvonat* (passenger trains) stop at every village along the way. Seat reservations *(helyjegy)* cost extra and are required on IC and some fast trains; these are indicated on the timetable by an 'R' in a box or a circle (a plain 'R' means seat reservations are available but not required).

In all stations a yellow board indicates departures *(indul)* and a white board arrivals *(érkezik)*. Express and fast trains are indicated in red, local trains in black. In some stations, large black-and-white schedules are plastered all over the walls.

Most train stations have left-luggage offices that are open at least from 9am to 5pm.

If you're travelling with a bicycle, many trains now transport bikes in cars marked with a bicycle symbol. When buying tickets, let the ticket seller know you are bringing a bike. Bike fare is normally half the regular passenger fare.

Consider purchasing the Hungary pass from Eurail, available to non-European residents only, before entering the country. It costs US$99/139 for five/10 days of 1st-class travel in a 15-day period, and US$75/89 for youths in 2nd class. Children aged five to 11 pay half price. You would, however, need to use it a lot to get your money's worth.

Kosovo

Best Places to Stay

» Hotel Sara (p453)
» Hotel Royal (p453)

Best Places to Eat

» Renaissance-2 (p456)
» Tiffany (p456)

Why Go?

Everyone loves a newborn, and since 2008, when Kosovo declared independence, large letters spelling 'NEWBORN' have graced a section of pavement in Pristina. The location, between the secure offices of the UN and a shopping mall featuring ubiquitous European clothing stores and a sky-clawing crumbling concrete monument, tells it all. Kosovo is finding its feet. Staff from international organisations glam up Pristina's restaurants, cafes and bars, as do talented Kosovars who are taking their seats for the ride forward.

Barbs of its past are impossible to miss: roads are dotted with memorials featuring etchings of those killed in 1999, when Serbia stripped Kosovo of its autonomy and initiated ethnic cleansing. Kosovo's modern architectural standouts may stand out for all the wrong reasons, but what the rebuilt country lacks in style, it makes up for with its mountain-backed towns, hiking opportunities and 13th-century Serbian monasteries, all no more than a couple of hours' drive from its capital.

When to Go
Pristina

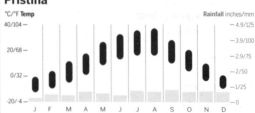

December–April The skiing's good in these months.

July The Ship Film Fest brings short films to Peja.

August It's a sweat-free summer as temperatures hover in the mid-20s°C.

Fast Facts

» **Area** 10,887 sq km

» **Capital** Pristina

» Telephone area code 381

» **Emergency** police 92, fire 93, ambulance 94

Exchange rates

Australia	A$1	€0.75
Canada	C$1	€0.74
Japan	¥100	€0.89
New Zealand	NZ$1	€0.57
UK	UK£1	€1.18
USA	US$1	€0.74

Set Your Budget

» **Budget accommodation** €10 to €15 per person

» **Two-course meal** €10-20

» **Museum entrance** €1 to €3

» **Local beer** Peja €2

Resources

» **Balkan Insight** (www.balkaninsight.com)

» **Balkanology** (www.balkanology.com)

» **Balkans Peace** Park (www.balkanspeacepark.org)

Connections

Kosovo has good bus connections between Albania, Montenegro and Macedonia, and there's a train line from Pristina to Macedonia's capital, Skopje. If you plan to go to Serbia but entered Kosovo via Albania, Macedonia or Montenegro, officials at the Serbian border will deem that you entered Serbia illegally and you will not be let in.

ITINERARIES

Two to Three Days

Fine dining and museum finding in Pristina, a visit to Gračanica Monastery and a curl through the mountains to Prizren's Ottoman sights.

One Week

After two or three days in the capital, loop to Prizren for castle views and its ethnographic museum, then Peja for monasteries, markets and mountain strolling.

Essential Food & Drink

» **Byrek** Pastry with cheese or meat

» **Duvěc** Baked meat and vegetables

» **Fli** Flaky pastry pie served with honey

» **Kos** Goat's-milk yogurt

» **Pershut** Dried meat

» **Qofta** Flat or cylindrical minced-meat rissoles

» **Raki** Locally made spirit, usually made from grapes

» **Tavě** Meat baked with cheese and egg

» **Vranac** Red wine from the Rahovec region of Kosovo

Kosovo Highlights

1 See the sights in Pristina's Ottoman-styled **bazaar area** (p453)

2 Breathe deep at Peja's Saturday **cheese market** (p457)

3 Buy local wine and cheese at the serene 14th century **Decani monastery** (p457)

4 Get your photo taken next to Pristina's **'Newborn' monument** (p453)

5 Trek around the **Rugova mountains** (p457)

PRISTINA

📞 038 / POP 500,000

Pristina is a city in recovery, and it's managing to mix lazy boulevards with zigzagging Ottoman-style streets, while stamping almost every corner with statues of persons important to Kosovo (Clinton, Mother Teresa, Albright). The biggest stamp of all is letters spelling the word NEWBORN – an announcement in monumental form that Pristina is indeed in its infancy.

⊙ Sights

BAZAAR AREA

The streets are narrow and twisting and the sights are many in this area, which is reminiscent of a Turkish bazaar.

Ethnographic Museum   HISTORIC BUILDING

(Rr Iliaz Agushi; admission €2.50; ⊙10am-4pm) Follow the signs to locate this well-kept 'how we lived' Ottoman house.

Kosovo Museum   MUSEUM

(Sheshi Adam Jashari; admission €3; ⊙10am-4pm Tue-Sat) A written plea to have antiquities returned from Serbia greets visitors; while you're waiting, see modern exhibits upstairs (celebrating America's support for Kosovo when we visited) and delicate 6000-year-old statues on the ground floor. It's occasionally closed without explanation.

Mosques   MOSQUE

Fronting the museum is the 15th-century **Carshi Mosque**. Nearby, the **Sultan Mehmet Fatih Mosque** (the 'Big Mosque') was built by its namesake around 1461, converted to a Catholic church during the Austro-Hungarian era and refurbished again during WWII. **Jashar Pasha Mosque** has vibrant interiors that exemplify Turkish baroque style.

Clock Tower   LANDMARK

This 26m tower makes a good point of reference. The **Great Hamam** nearby is being renovated.

Pristina

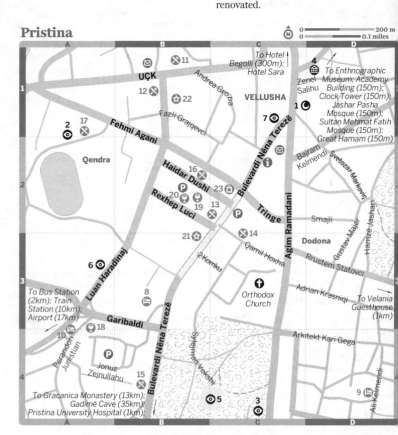

0 — 200 m
0 — 0.1 miles

To Hotel Begolli (300m); Hotel Sara

UÇK

VELLUSHA

Andrea Gropa

Zenel Salihu

To Enthnographic Museum; Academy Building (150m); Clock Tower (150m); Jashar Pasha Mosque (150m); Sultan Mehmat Fatih Mosque (150m); Great Hamam (150m)

Fazli Grajqevci

Fehmi Agani

Qendra

Bulevardi Nëna Terezë

Bajram Kelmendi

Svetozar Markoviç

Haidar Dushi

Rexhep Luci

Tringe

Agim Ramadani

Smajli

Dodona

Gustav Majer

Hamze Jashari

Z. Korniku

Qamil Hoxha

Rrustem Statovci

Luan Haradinaj

Orthodox Church

Adrian Krasniqi

To Velania Guesthouse (1km)

To Bus Station (2km); Train Station (10km); Airport (17km)

Garibaldi

Parandoni Jushtian

Bulevardi Nëna Terezë

Sylejman Vokshi

Arkitekt Kari Gega

Jonuz Zejnullahu

To Gracanica Monastery (13km); Gadime Cave (35km); Pristina University Hospital (1km)

Ali Kelmendi

he gates of the government buildings at he northern end of Bul Nëna Terezë bear hostlike **photos of the missing** – a stark eminder of how recently Pristina was in urmoil.

National Library LIBRARY
www.biblioteka-ks.org; ⊙7am-8pm Mon-Fri, 7am-pm Sat) The National Library, completed in 982 by Croatian Andrija Mutnjakovic, must e seen to be believed (think gelatinous eggs vearing armour).

FREE **Kosovo Art Gallery** ART GALLERY
(www.kosovaart.com; Agim Ramadani; ⊙9am-5pm) Behind the National Library, his gallery is a welcoming place featuring he works of local artists.

FREE **Independence House of Kosovo**
HISTORIC BUILDING
⊙10am-4pm Mon-Sat) This small house oppo-ite the stadium is devoted to former presi-lent Ibrahim Rugova and Kosovo's recent ndependence movement.

🛏 Sleeping

Hotel Royal HOTEL €€
220 902; www.royalhotel-pr.com; Pashko Vaso 3; /d incl free breakfast €80/92; @P) In a central, ively part of the city, Hotel Royal provides comfortable luxury accommodation.

Hotel Sara HOTEL €€
236 203; www.hotelsara-medi.com; Rr Maliq Pash Gjinolli; s/d incl free breakfast €35/50) At-ention haters of cushy velour couches and ooms drenched in chintz: this hotel is for

you. Simple, stylish rooms have timber-inspired floors. There's a lift.

Velania Guesthouse PENSION €
(531 742, 044 167 455; http://guesthouse-ks.net/eng/vlersimet.html; Velania 4/34; s/d €15/20; @) This bustling guesthouse is spread over two buildings in an affluent part of town. The jovial professor who runs it loves a chat and could double as your grandfa-ther. The hike up to it is much more fun in a taxi (€1.50).

Hotel Afa HOTEL €€
(225 226; www.hotelafa.com; Ali Kelmendi 15; s/d €75/92; ✳@) Spacious rooms have robot-style showers, and returning guests have inspired the owners to build a brand-new hotel next door.

Hotel Begolli HOTEL €€
(244 277; www.hotelbegolli.com; Rr Maliq Pash Gjinolli 8; s/d incl breakfast €40/50, ste €60; ✳@🛜) While it may have gone overboard with its '90s-style furniture, Begolli is a pleasant, rather sprawling place to stay. The suite has two bedrooms and is good value.

Grand Hotel HOTEL €€€
(220 210; www.grandhotel-pr.com; Bul Nëna Ter-ezë; s/d €70/100, ste €300-1000; @🛜) In three words: don't stay here. It really should have lost four of its five stars years ago.

🍴 Eating
Head to **Maxi Supermarket** (Rr Rexhep Luci; ⊙7am-midnight) for groceries.

Pristina

GRAČANICA MONASTERY & GADIMË CAVE

Explore beyond Pristina by heading southeast to Gračanica Monastery or south to Gadimë Cave. Dusty fingers of sunlight pierce the darkness of **Gračanica Monastery** (⊙6am-5pm), completed in 1321 by Serbian King Milutin. It's an oasis in a town that is the cultural centre of Serbs in central Kosovo. Take a Gjilan-bound bus (€0.50, 15 minutes, every 30 minutes); the monastery's on your left. Rumours abound that bus drivers won't let you on or off if you tell them where you're going, so be discreet.

Famed for helictites, **Gadimë Cave** (Shpella Mermerit; admission €2.50; ⊙9am-7pm) is visited with a guide who enthusiastically points out shapes like a hand, an elephant head and various body parts.

Buses go to Gadimë (€1, 30 minutes, every half-hour) via Lipjan. Or take a Ferizaj-bound bus, get dropped at the Gadimë turn-off and walk the 3km to town.

Renaissance-2 TRADITIONAL €€
(☎044 118 796; meals €15; ⊙6-11pm) Hidden in a lane opposite Radio Kosovo, this is possibly the classiest 'all you can eat and drink' restaurant you'll ever find (if you can find it). The starters (baked peppers, divine dips and beans) get usurped by the tender mains (your choice of fish, chicken or beef).

Tiffany TRADITIONAL €
(mains €6; ⊙8am-11pm Mon-Sat, 6-11pm Sun) No menu, no pizza and no pasta (it's official!). Pay up and enjoy the day's grilled special (whatever's fresh that day) and oven-baked bread. It's off Fehmi Agani, opposite the sports stadium.

de Rada Brasserie TRADITIONAL €
(Rr UÇK 50; mains €7; ⊙8am-midnight Mon-Sat) The sort of place you wish you could afford in Paris. Nibble on calamari in surrounds bursting with olden-day photos.

Pishat TRADITIONAL €
(☎245 333; Rr Qamil Hoxha 11; mains €6; ⊙8am-11pm Mon-Sat, noon-11pm Sun) Sample Albanian dishes at this indoor/outdoor spot which is often packed with expats and discerning locals.

Home INTERNATIONAL €
(Rr Migjeni, mains €6; ⊙7am-11pm Mon-Sat, 11am-11pm Sun) A chicken-laden menu, longish wine list and an eggplant tower for vegetarians.

Select CANADIAN CAFE €
(Rr Fehmi Agani 1/1; breakfasts €4.5) A breakfast and brunch menu worth getting excited about: try the buttermilk pancakes with maple syrup.

🍷 Drinking

There's a slight madness to Pristina's drinking scene; places are hip one minute and empty the next. Try 2 Korriko for 'spill-out in-the-street' summer drinking.

Tingell Tangell BA
(Rr Rexhep Luci) Hidden away at the base of a block of flats is this cool and quirky drinking spot. When its terrace was bulldozed recently (planning issues) it was back up in mere days.

Strip Depot COCKTAIL BA
(Rr Rexhep Luci 6/10) Has nothing to do with stripping but lots to do with cocktails and conversation.

Publicco BA
(Rr Garibaldi 7) A suave option for coffee and cocktail seekers.

☆ Entertainment

Kino ABC CINEMA
(www.kinoabc.info; Rr Rexhep Luci 1; ⊙8am-midnight) Two cinemas (ABC and ABC1 which is on R Luan Haradinaj) usually show a couple of movies daily.

🛍 Shopping

Library Dukagjini BOOKS
(Bul Nëna Terezë 20; ⊙8am-8pm Mon-Sat) Sells maps, language and history books and novels

ℹ Information

Barnatore Pharmacy (Bul Nëna Terezë; ⊙8-10pm)

Pristina University Hospital (Bul I Dëshmorët)

PTK Post (www.ptkonline.com) Agim Ramadani (Agim Ramadani; ⊙8am-10pm Mon-Sat); Rr UÇK (Rr UÇK 66; ⊙8am-10pm Mon-Sat) Post and phone services.

Turist Kosovo (☎232 999, 237 777; www.turistkosova.net; Bul Nëna Terezë 25a; ⊙8am-7pm Mon-Fri, 8am-1pm Sat) Travel agent.

Getting There & Around

Air

Taxis charge €25 for the 20-minute, 18km trip to **Pristina Airport** (www.airportpristina.com). **Kosova Airlines** (☎038-249 185; www.flyksa.com) has an office in the Grand Hotel. **MCM Travel** (☎242 424; info@mcm.travel; Bul Nëna Terezë; ⏰9am-8pm) is an airline agent.

Bus

The **bus station** (Stacioni I Autobusëve; Rr Lidja e Pejes) is 2km southwest of the centre off Bul Bil Klinton. Taxis to the centre should cost €2. International buses from Pristina include Serbia's Belgrade (€20, six hours, 11pm) and Novi Pazar (€5, three hours, 10am); Sarajevo (Bosnia and Hercegovina) via Novi Pazar (€23, 4pm); Durres and Tirana, Albania (€10, five hours), Skopje, Macedonia (€5, 1½ hours, every 30 minutes 5.30am to 5pm); Podgorica, Montenegro (€15, seven hours, 5.45pm, 7pm and 7.30pm); Linz, Austria (€50, 14 hours) and İstanbul (€30, 20 hours).

Taxi

Local taxi trips cost a few euro; the meter starts at €1.50. A good operator is **Radio Taxi Victory** (☎044 111 222, 555 333). Fares for unofficial taxis must be negotiated beforehand.

Train

Trains run from Pristina to Peja (€3, two hours, 7.50am and 4.30pm) and, internationally, Skopje in Macedonia (€4, three hours, 7.10am).

AROUND PRISTINA

Not far in distance, but worlds away from the chaotic capital, the smaller towns of Peja and Prizren offer a different pace and a new perspective. The easy journey through the countryside is an experience in itself.

Peja (Peć)

☎039

Peja is flanked by sites vital to Orthodox Serbians, with a Turkish-style bazaar at its heart. The Lumbardhi River torrents through town in winter and the surrounding mountains are ripe for trekking in summer.

Sights

Patriachate of Peć MONASTERY
(☎044 15 07 55; ⏰9am-6pm) This church and monastery is a slice of Serbian Orthodoxy. Multilingual Mrs Dobrilla may be able to show you around. It's a ten-minute walk from town along the river and guarded by NATO's Kosovo Force (KFOR; you may need to hand in your passports for the duration of your visit).

Cheese Market MARKET
The town's bustling bazaar makes you feel like you've turned left into İstanbul. Farmers gather here on Saturday mornings with wooden barrels of goat's cheese, so follow your nose.

Ethnological Museum MUSEUM
(Sheshi i Republikës; admission €1; ⏰9am-noon & 3pm-7pm Tue-Sat, 9am-4pm Sun) This Ottoman house is filled with local traditional crafts.

> DON'T MISS
>
> **DECANI MONASTERY**
>
> This regal **monastery** (Rr Ul St Manastirit, Decani; ⏰11am-1pm & 4-6pm), 15km south of Peja, is one of Kosovo's highlights. Buses go to Decani from Peja (€1, 30 minutes, every 15 minutes) on their way to Gjakovë. It's a pleasant 2km walk to the monastery from the bus stop. The onsite shop sells delicious monastery-made cheeses and wines. Keep to the roads – KFOR warns of UXO (unexploded ordnance) in the area.

Sleeping & Eating

Dukagjini Hotel HOTEL €€
(☎429 999; www.hoteldukagjini.com; Sheshi I Dëshmorëve 2; s/d €30/40; ❄📶) Enjoying its third recent name change and undergoing an extensive renovation when we visited, its rooms have character and a riverside breakfast is included.

Hotel Gold HOTEL €€
(☎434 571; Rr Eliot Engl 122/2; s/d €40/50; @) Decent rooms packed with ostentatious furniture.

Semitronix Centre TRADITIONAL €
(Mbretëresha Teutë; meals €4; ⏰7am-11pm) There's sky-high views and good food at this rooftop restaurant.

Information

Rugova Experience (☎432 352; Mbretëreshë Teuta; www.rugovaexperience.org) Maps and plenty of information about Peja's local trekking opportunities.

ⓘ Getting There & Away

BUS Frequent buses run to Peja (€4, 90 minutes, every 20 minutes) from Pristina. International buses link Peja with Ulqinj (10am, 11am) and Podgorica in Montenegro (9.30am, 10am and 11am).

TRAIN Trains depart Peja for Pristina at 5.30am and 11.10am (two hours) and depart Pristina for Peja at 7.50am and 4.30pm.

Prizren

♫029 / POP 70,000

Picturesque Prizren shines with postindependence euphoria, and its old town is worth setting aside a few hours to visit.

Prizren's 15th-century **Ottoman bridge** has been superbly restored. Nearby is **Sinan Pasha Mosque** (1561), which renovations are resurrecting as a central landmark in Prizren. Have a peak inside the nonfunctioning **Gazi Mehmed Pasha Baths**.

The **Orthodox Church of the Virgin of Leviša** is not exactly welcoming – it's surrounded by barbed wire.

The **Ethnological Museum** (admission €1; ☉11am-7pm Tue-Sun) is where the Prizren League (for Albanian autonomy) organised itself in 1878.

There is naught to see at the 11th-century **Kalaja**, but the 180-degree views over Prizren from this fort are worth the walk. On the way, more barbed wire surrounds **Saint Savior Church**, hinting at the fragility of Prizren's remaining relics.

Stay at stylish **Hotel Centrum** (♫230 530; www.centrumprizren.com; Rr Bujtinat 1; s/d €40/50; ☎). There's a vibrant strip of bars and eateries on the castle side of the river, and **Tabu Jazz Bar** is a popular hang-out near the path to the castle.

Prizren is well connected to Pristina (€3, 90 minutes, every 10 to 25 minutes), Peja (€3, 90 minutes, six daily) and Albania's Tirana (€10, four hours).

UNDERSTAND KOSOVO

History

In the 12th century Kosovo was the heart of the Serbian empire, until Turkish triumph at the pivotal 1389 Battle of Kosovo ushered in 500 years of Ottoman rule.

Serbia regained control in the 1912 Balkan War. In WWII the territory was incorporated into Italian-controlled Albania and liberated in October 1944 by Albanian partisans. After decades of neglect, Yugoslavia granted Kosovo de facto self-government status in 1974.

In 1989 the autonomy Kosovo enjoyed under the 1974 constitution was suspended by Slobodan Milošević. Ethnic Albanian leaders declared independence from Serbia in 1990. War broke out in 1992 – that same year, Ibrahim Rugova was elected as the first president of the self-proclaimed Republic of Kosovo. Ethnic conflict heightened and the Kosovo Liberation Army (KLA) was formed in 1996.

In March 1999 a US-backed plan to return Kosovo's autonomy was rejected by Serbia, which moved to empty the province of its non-Serbian population. Nearly 850,000 Kosovo Albanians fled to Albania and Macedonia. After Serbia refused to desist, NATO unleashed a bombing campaign on 24 March 1999. In June, Milošević agreed to withdraw troops, air strikes ceased, the KLA disarmed and the NATO-led KFOR (Kosovo Force; the international force responsible for establishing security in Kosovo) took over. From June 1999, Kosovo was administered as a UN–NATO protectorate.

Kosovo caught the world's attention again in 2004 when violence broke out in Mitrovica; 19 people were killed, 600 homes were burnt and 29 monasteries and churches were destroyed in the worst ethnic violence since 1999.

UN-sponsored talks on Kosovo's status began in February 2006 and Kosovo's parliament declared Kosovo independent on 17 February 2008. Seventy-one UN member states recognise Kosovo's independence, but the Serbian prime minister, Vojislav Koštunica, stated that 'as long as the Serb people exist, Kosovo will be Serbia'.

In June 2008 a new constitution transferred power from the UN to the government of Kosovo. Kosovo Serbs established their own assembly in Mitrovica.

In July 2010 the International Court of Justice ruled that Kosovo's declaration of independence did not violate international law; however, Serbia's president reiterated that Serbia would 'never recognise the unilaterally proclaimed independence of Kosovo'.

Fatmir Sejdiu became president after Ibrahim Rugova's death in 2006, but resigned in September 2010 after Kosovo's

NEWSPAPERS

» *Pristina Insight* (€1; www.prishtina insight.com), a newspaper run by the Balkan Investigative Reporting Network, gives exactly what its title says.

onstitutional court declared he was in 'serious breach' of the constitution by maintaining a party post while in office. Hashim Thaci is Kosovo's prime minister.

People & Religion

The population was estimated at 1.8 million in 2010; 92% are Albanian and 8% are Serb (mostly living in enclaves), Bosniak, Gorani, Roma, Turks, Ashkali and Egyptians. The main religions are Muslims (mostly Albanians), Serbian Orthodox and Roman Catholic.

Arts

Former president Ibrahim Rugova was a significant figure in Kosovo's literary scene; his presidency of the Kosovo Writers' Association was a step towards presidency of the nation.

Kosovar music bears the imprint of five centuries of Turkish rule; high-whine flutes carry tunes above goat-skin drumbeats. Architecture also shows Islamic influence, mixed with Byzantine and vernacular styles.

The visual-arts scene is re-emerging after troubled times; visit Kosovo Art Gallery (p453) to check it out.

Environment

Kosovo is broadly flat but surrounded by impressive mountains, the highest being Deravica (2656m). Most of Kosovo's protected area is in Šara National Park, created in 1986.

Among the estimated 46 species of mammal in Kosovo are bears, lynx, deer, weasels and the endangered river otter. Around 220 bird species live in or visit Kosovo, including eagles and falcons. Waterbird numbers have declined in recent decades.

Pollutants emitted from infrastructure hit by NATO bombs have affected Kosovo's biodiversity. Industrial pollution, rapid urbanisation and over-harvesting of wood threaten ecosystems.

Food & Drink

'Traditional' food is generally Albanian – most prominently, stewed and grilled meat and fish. *Kos* (goat's-cheese yogurt) is eaten alone or with almost anything. Turkish kebabs and *đuveč* (baked meat and vegetables) are common. The local beer is Peja (from Peja). International presence has brought world cuisines to the capital. Outside Pristina, however, waiters respond to vegetarian requests with thigh-slapping laughter. Requests for nonsmoking areas will be met with the same reaction.

SURVIVAL GUIDE

Directory A–Z

Accommodation

Apart from a few high-standard hotels, expect either mid-range hotels or cheap rooms above bars. Our price ranges for a double room are budget (€; less than €30), midrange (€€; €30 to €70) and top end (€€€; more than €70).

Business Hours

Reviews include hours only if they differ significantly from these.

Banks 8am-5pm Mon-Fri, until 2pm Sat

Bars 8am-11pm (on the dot if police are cracking down)

Shops 8am-6pm Mon-Fri, until 3pm Sat

Restaurants 8am-midnight

Dangers & Annoyances

Check government travel advisories before travelling to Kosovo. Sporadic violence occurs in North Mitrovica. Unexploded ordnance (UXO) has been cleared from roads and paths but you should seek KFOR advice before venturing off beaten tracks.

Make sure your insurance covers you for travel in Kosovo.

Embassies & Consulates

There are no embassies for New Zealand, Australia or Ireland in Kosovo. The following are all in Pristina:

France (☎038-224 588; pristina-amba@diplomatie.gouv.fr; Ismail Qemajli 67, Dragodan)

Germany (☎038-254 500; www.konsulate.de; Azem Jashanica 17)

Netherlands (☎038-516 101; nl_kosovo@yahoo.com; Xhemajl Berisha 12, Velania)

Switzerland (☎038-248 088; www.eda.admin.ch/pristina; Ardian Krasniqi 11; ⊙8.15am-12.30pm, 1.30pm-4.30pm Mon-Fri)

UK (☎038-254 700; www.ukinkosovo.fco.gov.uk; Ismail Qemajli 6; ⊙8.30am-5pm Mon-Thu, 8.30am-1.30pm Fri)

USA (☎038-59 59 3000; http://pristina.usembassy.gov; Arberia, Nazim Hikmet 30; ⊙8am-5pm Mon-Fri)

Food

The average cost of a main course in a restaurant is under €5 for budget (€), €5 to €15 for midrange (€€) and €15 to €30 for top end (€€€). See also p459.

Holidays

New Year's Day 1 January

Independence Day 17 February

Kosovo Constitution Day 9 April

Labour Day 1 May

Europe Holiday 9 May

Note that traditional Islamic holidays are also observed.

Internet Resources

Pristina in Your Pocket (www.inyourpocket.com/city/pristina.html) is a downloadable guide; it's also available at Library Dukagjini (p456) for €4.

Money

Kosovo's currency is the euro; arrive with small denominations. ATMs are common and established businesses accept credit cards.

Post

PTK post and telecommunications offices operate in Kosovo's main towns.

Telephone

Kosovo's country code is ☎381.

Vala (www.valamobile.com) and Zmobile (www.zmobileonline.com) have SIM cards that are effectively free; the €5 fee includes €5 worth of credit.

Visas

Visas are not required; check www.mfa-k net for changes. Upon arrival, you get a 9C day entry stamp.

If you wish to travel between Serbia an Kosovo you'll need to enter Kosovo fror Serbia first; see the boxed text, p452.

Getting There & Away

Air

Pristina International Airport (☎038-595 123; www.airportpristina.com) is 18km from th centre of Pristina.

AIRLINES

Adria Airways (JP; ☎038-543 411/285; www.adria.si) Flies to Sarajevo, Warsaw, Stockholm, Copenhagen, London, Amsterdam, Brussels, Frankfurt, Paris, Munich, Zürich, Barcelona, Ljubljana and Venice.

Air Berlin (AB; www.airberlin.com) Flies to Düsseldorf, Hamburg, Frankfurt, Munich, Zürich and Geneva.

Austrian Airlines (OS; ☎038-548 435, 038-502 456; www.aua.com) To Vienna.

British Airways (BA; ☎038-548 661; www.britishairways.com) To London.

Croatia Airways (OU; ☎038-233 833; www.croatiaairlines.com) Flies to Amsterdam, Brussels, Copenhagen, Frankfurt, London, Munich, Paris, Split, Zagreb, Vienna and Zürich.

Edelweiss (ED; www.edelweissair.ch) Flies to Zürich and Genf.

Germania Airlines (ST; www.flygermania.de) Flies to Düsseldorf, Stuttgart, Munich and Dortmund.

germanwings (4U; www.germanwings.com) Flies to London, Cologne, Hanover, Berlin, Leipzig, Dresden, Stuttgart and Munich.

Malév (MA; ☎038-535 535; www.malev.hu) To Budapest.

Montenegro Airlines (YM; ☎038-242 424; www.montenegroairlines.com) To Podgorica.

Meridiana (IG; ☎038-5958 123; www.meridiana.it) To Verona.

Swiss (LX; 038-243 446; www.swiss.com) To Zürich.

Turkish Airlines (TK; ☎038-247 711/696; www.turkishairlines.com) To İstanbul.

Land

See p457 for details of international bus trips between Kosovo and various destinations. There's a train to Skopje from Pristina (€4, three hours, 7.10am).

Border Crossings

Albania To get to Albania's Koman Ferry use Morina, and further north is Qafë Prush. The busiest border is Morinë.

Macedonia Blace from Pristina and Jazince from Prizren.

Montenegro The main crossing is on the road between Rozaje and Peja.

Serbia Due to outbreaks of violence, travellers are advised to be extra vigilant if entering Kosovo at Leposavic or Zubin Potok. Other borders include Banja and Jarninje.

Getting Around

Bus

Buses stop at distinct blue signs, but can be flagged down anywhere. A 90-minute bus trip in Kosovo will cost you around €4.

Car

Rental-car agencies include **Europcar** (☑381-38 541 401; www.europcar-ks.com). Hard-to-spot potholes make road conditions difficult. Serbian-plated cars have been attacked in Kosovo, and rental companies do not let cars hired in Kosovo travel to Serbia and vice versa. European Green Card vehicle insurance is not valid in the country.

Train

The train system is stretching itself to routes including Pristina–Peja (€3, 1½ hours, 7.50am and 4.30pm) and Pristina–Skopje (€4, three hours, 7.10am). Locals generally catch buses.

Latvia

Best Places to Stay

» Hotel Bergs (p476)

» Europa Royale (p476)

» Naughty Squirrel (p475)

» Neiburgs (p475)

Best Places to Eat

» Istaba (p478)

» Aragats (p478)

» Ostas Skati (p478)

Why Go?

Tucked between Estonia to the north and Lithuania to the south, Latvia is the meat of the Baltic sandwich. We're not implying that the neighbouring nations are slices of white bread, but Latvia is the savoury middle, loaded with colourful fillings. Thick greens take the form of Gauja Valley pines. Onion-domed cathedrals sprout above local towns. Cheesy Russian pop blares along coastal beaches. And spicy Rīga adds an extra zing as the country's cosmopolitan nexus and unofficial capital of the entire Baltic.

If that doesn't whet your appetite, hear this: the country's under-the-radar profile makes it the perfect pit stop for those seeking something a bit more authentic than the over-run tourist hubs further afield. So, consider altering your Eastern European itinerary and fill up on little Latvia instead of big-ticket destinations Prague, Vienna or – dare we say it – Hungary.

When to Go

Riga

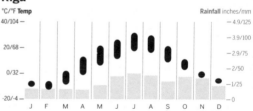

December to January Celebrate the holidays in the birthplace of the Christmas tree

Mid-June to August Summer starts with an all-night solstice romp; then it's off to the beach

September Refusing to let summer go, Rīgans sip lattes under heat lamps at al fresco cafes.

Connections

Latvia is the link in the Baltic chain, making Rīga a convenient point between Tallinn and Vilnius. Long-distance buses and trains also connect the capital to St Petersburg, Moscow and Warsaw, and ferry services shuttle passengers to Stockholm and the German towns of Rostock and Lübeck. Rīga is the hub of airBaltic, which offers direct service to more than 50 European cities. See p491 for details.

ITINERARIES

Three Days

Fill your first two days with a feast of Rīga's architectural eye candy, and spend your third day hiking betwixt Sigulda's castles, sunbathing in scintillating Jūrmala or snapping photos of Rundāle's opulent palace.

One Week

After a few days in the capital, swing by Jūrmala on your way up the horn of Cape Kolka for saunas, sunsets and solitude. Glide through western Latvia comparing its ultrabucolic townships to Rundāle's majestic grounds, then blaze a trail across eastern Latvia for a rousing trip back in time spiced with adrenaline sports.

Essential Food & Drink

» **Black Balzām** Goethe called it 'the elixir of life'. The jet-black, 45% proof concoction is a secret recipe of more than a dozen fairy-tale ingredients including oak bark, wormwood and linden blossoms. A shot a day keeps the doctor away, so say most of Latvia's pensioners. Try mixing it with glass of cola to take the edge off.

» **Mushrooms** Not a sport but a national obsession; mushroom picking takes the country by storm during the first showers of autumn.

» **Alus** For such a tiny nation there's definitely no shortage of *alus* (beer) – each major town has its own brew. You can't go wrong with Užavas (Ventspils' contribution).

» **Smoked fish** Dozens of fish shacks dot the Kurzeme coast – look for the veritable smoke signals rising above the tree line. Grab 'em to go; they make the perfect afternoon snack.

» **Kvass** Single-handedly responsible for the decline of Coca-Cola at the turn of the 21st century, Kvass is a beloved beverage made from fermented rye bread. It's surprisingly popular with kids!

AT A GLANCE

» **Currency** lats (Ls)

» **Language** Latvian, Russian

» **Money** ATMs all over Rīga and smaller cities; banks open Mon-Sat

» **Visas** none required for stays of up to 90 days for Australian, Canadian, New Zealand and US citizens

Fast Facts

» **Area** 64,589 sq km

» **Capital** Rīga

» **Telephone country code** 371

» **Emergency** ☑112

Exchange Rates

Australia	A$1	€0.5Ls
Canada	C$1	€0.5Ls
euro	€1	€0.7Ls
Japan	¥100	€0.59Ls
New Zealand	NZ$1	€0.39Ls
UK	UK£1	€0.8Ls
USA	US$1	€0.48Ls

Set Your Budget

» **Budget hotel room** 25Ls

» **Two-course meal** 10Ls

» **Museum entrance** 1.50Ls

» **Beer** 1.20Ls

» **City transport ticket** 0.70Ls

Resources

» **1188** (www.1188.lv)

» **Latvia Institute** (www.li.lv)

» **Latvia Tourism Development Agency** (www.latvia-tourism.lv)

Latvia Highlights

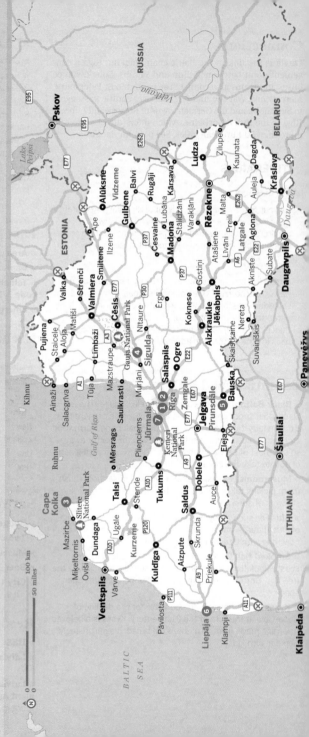

1 Click your camera at the menagerie of gargoyles, beasts, goddesses and twisting vines that inhabits the surplus of **Riga's art nouveau architecture** (p475).

2 Lose yourself in the maze of cobblestones, church spires and gingerbread trim that is **Old Riga** (p464).

3 Listen to the waves pound the awesomely remote **Cape Kolka** (p484), which crowns the desolate Kurzeme coast.

4 Swing through **Sigulda** (p487) on a bungee cord.

5 Sneak away from the capital and indulge in aristocratic decadence at **Rundāle Palace** (p483).

6 Wander past gritty Soviet tenements and gilded cathedrals in the crumbling Karosta district of port-ly **Liepāja** (p485).

7 Hobnob with Russian jetsetters in the heart of **Jūrmala's** (p483) swanky spa scene.

RĪGA

POP 790,000

'The Paris of the North', 'The Second City that Never Sleeps' – everyone's so keen on qualifying Latvia's capital, but regal Rīga does a hell of a job of holding its own. For starters, the city has the largest and most impressive showing of art nouveau architecture in Europe. Nightmarish gargoyles and praying goddesses adorn more than 750 buildings along the stately boulevards radiating out from the city's castle core. The heart of the city – Old Rīga – is a fairytale kingdom of winding wobbly lanes that beat to the sound of clicking stilettos, beer garden brouhahas and rumbling basement discotheques.

Although some Latvians lament the fact that they are an ethnic minority in their own capital, others are quick to point out that Rīga was never a 'Latvian' city. Founded in 1201 by the German Bishop Albert von Buxhoevden (say that three times fast) as a bridgehead for the crusade against the northern 'heathens', Rīga was a stronghold for the Knights of the Sword, a member of the Hanseatic League and an important trading junction between Russia and the West. When Sweden snagged the city in 1621, it grew into the largest holding of the Swedish empire (even bigger than Stockholm). Soon the Russians ploughed through, and by the mid-1860s Rīga was the world's biggest timber port. The 20th century saw the birth of cafes and salons, which were bombed to high hell in WWI and suppressed by the Nazis during WWII. Somehow, Rīga's indelible international flavour managed to rise up from the rubble; even as a part of the USSR the city was known for its forward thinking and thriving cultural life.

Today, Rīga's cosmopolitan past has enabled the city to adjust effortlessly to an evolving global climate, making it more than just the capital of Latvia – it's the cornerstone of the Baltic.

◎ Sights

OLD RĪGA (VECRĪGA)

RĀTSLAUKUMS

TOP CHOICE **Blackheads' House** HISTORIC BUILDING
(Melngalvju House; Map p468; Rātslaukums 7; http://nami.riga.lv/mn; admission 2Ls; ⊙10am-5pm Tue-Sun) Touristy Rātslaukums is home to the postcard-worthy Blackheads'

House, built in 1344 as a veritable fraternity house for the Blackheads guild of unmarried German merchants. The house was decimated in 1941, and flattened by the Soviets seven years later. Somehow the original blueprints survived and an exact replica was completed in 2001 for Rīga's 800th birthday.

Museum of the Occupation of Latvia
MUSEUM
(Latvijas okupācijas muzejs; Map p468; ☑6721 2715; www.omf.lv; Latviešu Strēlnieku laukums 1; admission by donation; ⊙11am-6pm) Ironically inhabiting a Soviet bunker, this museum carefully details Latvia's Soviet and Nazi occupations between 1940 and 1991. Exhibits are well curated and intriguing, though the focus on minutia can be slightly tedious for those without pre-existing knowledge of Latvian political history.

Mentzendorff's House
HISTORIC BUILDING
(Mencendorfa nams; Map p468; ☑6721 2951; www.mencendorfanams.com; Grēcinieku iela 18; admission 1Ls; ⊙10am-5pm Wed & Fri-Sun, noon-7pm Thu) Once the home of a wealthy German noble, the 17th-century Mentzendorff's House offers insight into Rīga's history of shipping excess through the everyday trappings of an elite merchant family.

Town Hall
HISTORIC BUILDING
(Map p468; Rātslaukums) Facing the Blackheads' House across the square is the Town Hall, also rebuilt from scratch in recent years. A statue of Rīga's patron saint **St Roland** stands between the two buildings. It's a replica of the original, erected in 1897, which now sits in St Peter's.

PĒTERBAZNĪCA LAUKUMS

St Peter's Lutheran Church
CHURCH
(Sv Pētera baznīca; Map p468; www.peterbaznic. lv; Skārņu iela 19; admission 3Ls; ⊙11am-6pm Tue-Sun) Rīga's skyline centrepiece is gothic St Peter's Lutheran Church, thought to be around 800 years old. Don't miss the view from the spire, which has been rebuilt three times in the same baroque form. Legend has it that in 1667 the builders threw glass from the top to see how long the spire would last. A greater number of shards meant a very long life. The glass ended up landing on a pile of straw and didn't break – a year later the tower was incinerated. When the spire was resurrected after a bombing during WWII, the ceremonial glass chucking was repeated, and this time it was a smash hit. The spire is 123.25m high, but the lift whisks you up only to 72m.

Start in the heart of the city, getting lost amid the twisting cobbled alleys that snake through medieval **Old Rīga** (p464). Snap shots of the photogenic **Blackheads' House** (p464), and scout out some Latvian grub. Walk off the calories in the afternoon while checking out the city's surplus of **art nouveau architecture** (see p478), then clink evening drinks at one of the city's hipster dens (p479). After midnight, drop by **Pelmeņi XL** (p477) to binge on a late-night snack of Russian dumplings.

On day two, fine-tune your bargaining skills at the **Central Market** (p469). Then try firing a round with an AK47 in a former **Soviet fallout shelter** (p474). After sunset, snag tickets to a show at the **National Opera House** (p480) or bar-hop your way through Old Rīga (don't forget to try **Black Balzām**). End the night with a well-deserved cocktail at **Skyline Bar** (p479) overlooking the twinkling urban lights below.

Museum of Decorative Arts & Design
MUSEUM

(Dekoratīvi lietiškās mākslas muzejs; Map p468; ☑6722 7833; www.dlmm.lv; Skārņu iela 10/20; admission 0.70-3Ls; ⊙11am-5pm Tue & Thu-Sun, to 7pm Wed) Behind St Peter's church sits another impressive religious structure – the former **St George's Church** – that is now the Museum of Decorative & Applied Arts, highlighting Latvia's impressive collection of woodcuts, textiles and ceramics. The building's stone foundations date back to 1204, when the Livonian Brothers of the Sword erected their castle here.

KALĒJU IELA & MĀRSTAĻU IELA
Zigzagging **Kalēju iela** and **Mārstaļu iela** are dotted with poignant reminders of the city's legacy as a wealthy northern European trading centre. Several of the old merchants' manors have been transformed into museums like the **Latvian Photography Museum** (Latvijas fotogrāfijas muzejs; Map p468; ☑6722 2713; www.fotomuzejs.lv; Mārstaļu iela 8; admission 1.50Ls; ⊙10am-5pm Wed & Fri-Sun, noon-7pm Thu), which displays unique photographs from 1920s Rīga.

Don't forget to look up at the curling vines and barking gargoyles adorning several art nouveau facades (p475) including **Rīga Synagogue** (Map p468; Peitavas iela 6/8), the only active Jewish house of worship in the capital. The structure was restored in a 'sacral art nouveau' style at the end of 2009 after a generous infusion of money from the EU.

LĪVU LAUKUMS
This bustling square is lined by a colourful row of 18th-century buildings – most of which have been turned into rowdy restaurants and beer halls. The 19th-century Gothic exterior of the **Great Guild** (Lielā gilde; Map p468; Amatu iela 6) encloses a sumptuous merchants' meet-

ing hall, built during the height of German power in the 1330s. The fairy-tale castle next door is the **Small Guild** (Mazā gilde; Map p468; Amatu iela 5), founded during the 14th century as the meeting place for local artisans.

Don't miss the **Cat House** (Kaķu māja; Map p468; Miestaru iela 10/12), named for the spooked black cat sitting on the roof. According to legend, the owner was rejected from the local Merchants' Guild across the street, and exacted revenge by placing a black cat on the top of his turret with its tail raised towards the esteemed Great Guild hall.

DOMA LAUKUMS
Dome Cathedral
CHURCH

(Doma baznīca; Map p468; ☑6721 3213; www.doms. lv; Doma laukums 1; admission 2Ls; ⊙9am-5pm) The centrepiece of expansive Doma Laukums is Rīga's enormous Dome Cathedral. Founded in 1211 as the seat of the Rīga diocese, it is still the largest church in the Baltics. The floor and walls of the huge interior are dotted with old stone tombs. In 1709, the cholera and typhoid outbreak that killed a third of Rīga's population was blamed on a flood that inundated the crypt. The cathedral's pulpit dates from 1641 and the huge, 6768-pipe organ was the world's largest when it was completed in 1884 (it's now the fourth largest). Mass is held at noon on Sundays, and at 8am every other day of the week.

Museum of the History of Rīga & Navigation
MUSEUM

(Rīgas vēstures un kuģniecības muzejs; Map p468; ☑6735 6676; www.rigamuz.lv; Palasta iela 4; admission 3Ls; ⊙11am-5pm Fri-Tue, noon-7pm Thu) The Museum of the History of Rīga & Navigation, the Baltics' oldest museum, is situated in the monastery's cloister at the back of the Dome Cathedral complex. Founded in 1773, the exhibition space features a permanent collection of artefacts from the Bronze Age all the way up to WWII.

Three Brothers   HISTORIC BUILDING
(Trīs brāļi; Map p468; Mazā Pils iela 17, 19 & 21) Located behind Doma Laukums, the Three Brothers exemplifies Old Rīga's diverse collection of old architectural styles. Number 19 (built in the 17th century) is now the **Rīga Museum of Architecture** (Latvijas arhitektūras muzejs; Map p468; www.archmuseum. lv; admission by donation; ⊙9am-5pm Mon-Fri). Note the tiny windows on the upper levels – Rīga's property taxes during the Middle Ages were based on the size of one's windows.

St Jacob's Cathedral   CHURCH
(Sv Jēkaba katedrāle; Map p468; Klostera iela) Latvia's first Lutheran services were held in St Jacob's Cathedral, which has an interior dating back to 1225. Today it is the seat of Rīga's Roman Catholic archbishopric.

PILS LAUKUMS

Rīga Castle   CASTLE
(Rīgas pils; Map p468; Pils laukums 3) In the far corner of Old Rīga near the Vanšu bridge, verdant **Pils Laukums** sits at the doorstep of Rīga Castle. Originally built as the headquarters for the Livonian Order, the foundation dates to 1330 and served as the residence of the order's grand master. This canary yellow bastion is home to Latvia's president and boasts two museums. The **Museum of Foreign Art** (Ārzemju mākslas muzejs; ☑6722 6467; www.amm.lv; admission 2.50Ls; ⊙11am-5pm Tue-Sun) exhibits Latvia's largest treasury of international artwork dating back to the 14th century, and the **History Museum of Latvia** (Latvijas vēstures muzejs; ☑6722 1357; www.history-museum.lv; admission 2Ls; free Wed; ⊙10am-5pm Tue-Sun) traces the history of Latvia and its people from the Stone Age to present day.

Exhibition Hall Arsenāls   ART GALLERY
(Mākslas muzejs Arsenāls; Map p468; ☑6735 7527; www.lnmm.lv/en/arsenals; Torņa iela 1; admission 2.50Ls; ⊙noon-6pm Tue, Wed & Fri, to 8pm Thu, to 5pm Sat & Sun) Constructed in 1832 in Russian Late Empire style, the building was originally used as a warehouse. Today it features a variety of international art exhibitions and houses the finalists of the Purvītis Art Prize – most prestigious in Latvia, named for Vilhelms Purvītis the 'father of Latvian Painting'.

Saeima   NOTABLE BUILDING
(Map p468; Jēkaba iela 11) Sharing a block with Arsenāls, Latvia's Parliament lives in a Florentine Renaissance structure originally commissioned as the Knights' House of the German landlords.

TORŅA IELA
The entire north side of handsome **Torņa iela** (Map p468) is flanked by the custard-coloured **Jacob's Barracks** (Jēkaba Kazarmas; Torņa iela 4), built as an enormous warehouse in the 16th century. Tourist-friendly cafes and boutiques now inhabit the refurbished building. On the other side of the street, find **Trokšnu iela**, Old Rīga's narrowest *iela* (street), and the **Swedish Gate** (Zviedru vārti; Torņa iela 11), which was built in 1698 while the Swedes were in power. The cylindrical **Powder Tower** (Pulvertornis; Smilšu iela 20) dates back to the 14th century, and is the only survivor of the 18 original towers that punctuated the old city wall. In the past it served as a prison, torture chamber and frat house. Today it is the **Museum of War** (Kara muzejs; www.karamuzejs. gov.lv; Smilšu iela 20; admission free; ⊙10am-6pm Tue, Wed & Fri-Sun, 11am-7pm Thu).

CENTRAL RĪGA (CENTRS)

ESPLANADE & AROUND

Freedom Monument   MONUMENT
(Map p468; Brīvības bulvāris) Affectionately known as 'Milda', Rīga's Freedom Monument was erected in 1935 where a statue of Russian ruler Peter the Great once stood. A copper female Liberty tops the soaring monument, holding three gold stars representing the

---

OH CHRISTMAS TREE

Rīga's Blackheads' House was known for its wild parties; it was, after all, a clubhouse for unmarried merchants. On a cold Christmas Eve in 1510, the squad of bachelors, full of holiday spirit (and other spirits, so to speak), hauled a great pine tree up to their clubhouse and smothered it with flowers. At the end of the evening, they burned the tree to ground in an impressive blaze. From then on, decorating the 'Christmas Tree' became an annual tradition, which eventually spread across the globe (as you probably know, the burning part never really caught on).

An octagonal commemorative plaque, inlaid in cobbled Rātslaukums, marks the spot where the original tree once stood.

LATVIA

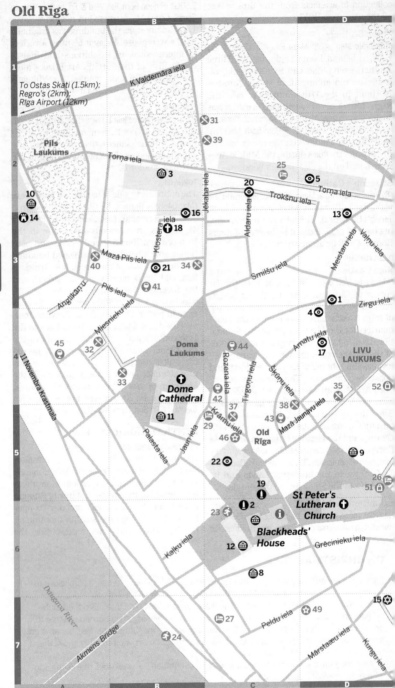

To Ostas Skati (1.5km);
Regro's (2km);
Rīga Airport (12km)

Pils
Laukums

K Valdemāra iela

Torņa iela

Jēkaba iela

Trokšņu iela

Torņa iela

Klostera iela

Aldaru iela

Smilšu iela

Meistaru iela

Vaļņu iela

Zirgu iela

Maza Pils iela

Pils iela

Anglikāņu

Miesnieku iela

Amatu iela

LIVU
LAUKUMS

Doma
Laukums

Rozena iela

Tirgoņu iela

Skārņu iela

Mazā Jaunavu iela

Dome
Cathedral

Krāmu iela

Old
Rīga

Jauņ iela

Palasta iela

Pagasta iela

11 Novembra Krastmala

Daugava River

Akmens Bridge

St Peter's
Lutheran
Church

Blackheads'
House

Kaļķu iela

Grēcinieku iela

Peldu iela

Mārstaņu iela

Kungu iela

LATVIA RĪGA

original cultural regions of Latvia: Kurzeme, Vidzeme and Latgale. Two soldiers stand guard at the monument throughout the day and perform a modest changing of the guard every hour on the hour from 9am to 6pm.

A second spire, the **Laima Clock** (Laimas pulkstenis), sits between Milda and the entrance to Old Rīga. Built in the 1920s as a gentle way to encourage Rīgans not to be late for work, the clock is now used as the preferred meeting place for young Latvians.

Latvian National Museum of Art   MUSEUM
(Latvijas Nacionālais mākslas muzejs; Map p472; ☑6732 5051; www.lnmm.lv; K Valdemāra iela 10a; admission 3Ls; ⊙11am-6pm Tue-Sun) Sitting within the Esplanāde's leafy grounds, this impressive gallery features pre-WWII Russian and Latvian art displayed among the Soviet grandeur of ruched net curtains, marble columns and red carpets. The structure was purpose-built at the turn of the 20th century.

Russian Orthodox Cathedral   CHURCH
(Pareizticīgo katedrāle; Map p472; Brīvības bulvāris 23) At the far end of the Esplanade near Hotel Latvija, this stunning 19th-century cathedral majestically rises above the trees with its gilded cupolas. During the Soviet era the church was used as a planetarium.

CENTRAL MARKET DISTRICT

TOP CHOICE **Central Market**   MARKET
(Centrāl tirgus; Map p472; www.centraltirgus.lv; Nēģu iela 7; ⊙7am-5pm Sun & Mon, to 6pm Tue-Sat) Haggle for your huckleberries at the Central Market, housed in a series of mammoth zeppelin hangars constructed for the Germans during WWI. Check out the seafood pavilion for locally adored herring and smoked eel, or swing by the produce section for chilled sauerkraut juice – a traditional hangover remedy. It's a fantastic spot to assemble a picnic lunch and do some people watching.

Akadēmijas Laukums   SQUARE
Just beyond the soaring hangars of the Central Market lies Akadēmijas Laukums, home to the **Academy of Science** (Map p472; Zinātņu Akadēmija; www.lza.lv; Akadēmijas laukums 1; ⊙9am-8pm). Also called 'Stalin's Birthday Cake', this is Rīga's Russified Empire State Building. Those with an eagle eye will spot hammers and sickles hidden in the convoluted facade. A mere 2Ls grants you admission to the observation deck on the 17th floor.

Don't miss the moving **Holocaust Memorial** nearby. A large synagogue once occupied this street corner until it was burned

LATVIA

Old Rīga

to the ground during WWII with the entire congregation trapped inside. No one survived.

Spīķeri NEIGHBOURHOOD
(off Map p472; www.spikeri.lv) The shipping yard behind the Central Market is the latest district to benefit from a generous dose of gentrification. These crumbling brick warehouses were once filled with swinging slabs of hanger meat; these days you'll find hip cafes and start-up companies. Stop by during the day to check out **Kim?** (☑6722 3321; www.kim.lv; Maskavas iela 12/1; admission free; ☺2-7pm Wed-Fri, noon-7pm Sat & Sun) – an experimental art zone that dabbles in contemporary media – or come in the evening to peruse the surplus of farm produce at the **night market** (Maskavas iela 12; ☺9pm-dawn).

QUIET CENTRE

Just when you thought that Old Rīga was the most beautiful neighbourhood in town, the city's audacious art nouveau district swoops in to vie for the prize. Check out p475 for more info.

TOP CHOICE Rīga Art Nouveau Centre MUSEUM

(Rīgas jūgemdstila muzejs; Map p472; ☑6718 1465; www.jugendstils.riga.lv; Alberta iela 12; admission 2.50Ls, English tour 10Ls; ☉10am-6pm Tue-Sun) If you're curious about what lurks behind Rīga's imaginative art nouveau facades, then it's definitely worth stopping by. Once the home of Constantīns Pēkšēns (a local architect responsible for more than 250 of the city's buildings), the centre has been completely restored to resemble a middle-class apartment from the 1920s. Note the geometric frescos, rounded furniture, original stained glass in the dining room, and the still-functioning stove in the kitchen. Don't miss the free 10-minute video detailing the city's distinct decor, and check out the centre's website for details about the art nouveau walking routes around town. Enter from Strēlnieku iela; push No 12 on the doorbell.

Janis Rozentāls & Rūdolfs Blaumanis' Museum MUSEUM

(Map p472; ☑6733 1641; Alberta iela 12; admission 1Ls; ☉11am-6pm Wed-Sun) Follow the wonderfully lavish stairwell up to the fifth floor to find the former apartment of Janis Rozentāls, one of Latvia's most celebrated painters. Enter from Strēlnieku iela; push No 9 on the doorbell.

Jews in Latvia MUSEUM

(Map p472; ☑6728 3484; www.jews.lv; Skolas iela 6; admission by donation; ☉noon-5pm Sun-Thu) This small and rather informal space briefly recounts the city's history of Jewish life until 1945 through artefacts and photography. Rīga's Jewish population (unlike that of Vilnius) was very much integrated into the rest of society. You'll find a teeny kosher cafe in the basement (entrance on Dzirnavu iela) selling traditional treats like *challa* bread and gefillte fish.

OUTLYING NEIGHBOURHOODS

Those who venture beyond Rīga's inner sphere of cobbled alleyways and over-the-top art nouveau will uncover a handful of other neighbourhoods that help paint a full picture of this cosmopolitan capital.

Latvian Ethnographic Open-Air Museum MUSEUM

(Latvijas etnogrāfiskais brīvdabas muzejs; www.brivdabasmuzejs.lv; Brīvības gatve 440; adult/child 2/1Ls; ☉10am-5pm) If you don't have time to visit the heart of the Latvian countryside, then a stop at the Latvian Ethnographic Open-Air Museum is recommended. This vast stretch of forest contains more than 100 wooden buildings from all over Latvia. Take bus 1 to the 'Brīvdabas muzejs' stop.

Andrejsala NEIGHBOURHOOD

(www.andrejsala.lv) At first glance, Andrejsala looks like an abandoned port littered with outdated Soviet parts. A closer glimpse reveals a sprouting artists' colony amid grungy warehouses. Check out **Peldošā Darbnīca** (Floating Cafeteria; ☑2617 7133; www.peldosadarbnica.lv; ☉10am-6pm Mon-Fri), a three-storey floating workshop the doubles as a creative space and cafeteria. The **Museum of Naive Art** (☑6770 3240; www.noass.lv; ☉noon-7pm Tue-Sun May-Sep) allows curious visitors to sneak a look at the work of untrained creative types. At the time of research plans were underway to develop a

---

DON'T MISS

ART NOUVEAU IN RĪGA

If you ask any Rīgan where to find the city's world-famous art nouveau architecture, you will always get the same answer: 'Look up!' More than 750 buildings in Rīga (more than any other city in Europe) boast this flamboyant and haunting style of decor; and the number continues to grow as myriad restoration projects get underway. Art nouveau is also known as Jugendstil, meaning 'youth style', named after a Munich-based magazine called *Die Jugend,* which popularised the design on its pages.

Art nouveau's early influence was Japanese print art disseminated throughout Western Europe, but as the movement gained momentum, the style became more ostentatious and freeform – design schemes started to feature mythical beasts, screaming masks, twisting flora, goddesses and goblins. The turn of the 20th century marked the height of the art nouveau movement, as it swept through every major European city from Porto to Petersburg.

The art nouveau district (known more formally as the 'Quiet Centre') is anchored around **Alberta iela** (check out 2a, 4 and 13 in particular), but you'll find fine examples all throughout the city. Don't miss the renovated facades of **Strēlnieku 4a** and **Elizabetes 10b** and **33,** then check out the highly informative **Rīga Art Nouveau Centre** (p471).

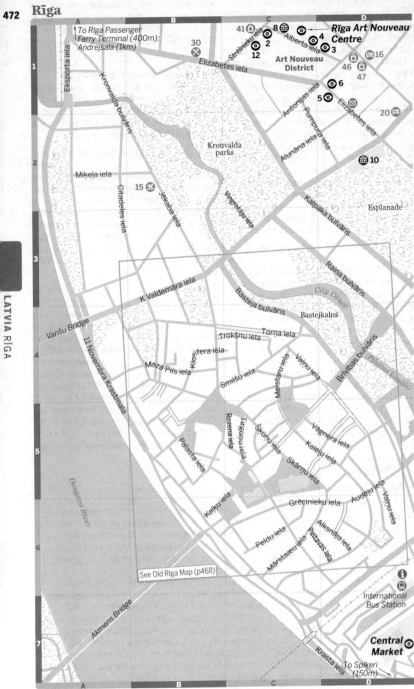

To Rīga Passenger Ferry Terminal (400m); Andrejsala (1km)

Rīga Art Nouveau Centre

Art Nouveau District

Eksporta iela

Kronvalda bulvāris

Strēlnieku iela

Elizabetes iela

41
8
2
12
4
3
30
46
47
16
6
5
20

Antonijas iela

Pumpura iela

Elizabetes iela

Alunāna iela

Kronvalda parks

Mikeļa iela

Citadeles iela

Jēkaba iela

15

Vingrotāju iela

10

Kalpaka bulvāris

Esplanade

Raiņa bulvāris

City Canal

K Valdemāra iela

Basteja bulvāris

Bastejkalns

Vanšu Bridge

11 Novembra Krastmala

Torņa iela

Trokšņu iela

Klostera iela

Maza Pils iela

Smilšu iela

Meistaru iela

Valņu iela

Brīvibas bulvāris (Pilsētas kanāls)

Vāgnera iela

Rozena iela

Tirgoņu iela

Skārņu iela

Kaļēju iela

Skārņu iela

Palasta iela

Daugava River

Kaļķu iela

Grēcinieku iela

Audēju iela

Valņu iela

Peldu iela

Mārstaļu iela

Alksnāja iela

Peitavas iela

See Old Rīga Map (p468)

International Bus Station

Akmens Bridge

Central Market

To Spīķeri (150m)

Krasta iela

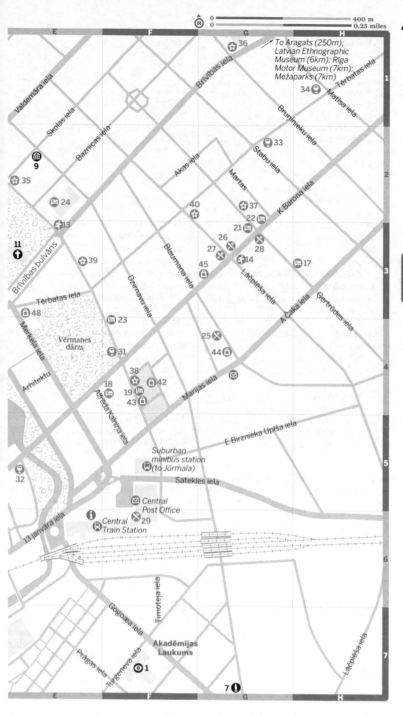

E F G H

0 400 m
0 0.25 miles

N

To Aragats (250m);
Latvian Ethnographic
Museum (6km); Rīga
Motor Museum (7km);
Mežaparks (7km)

LATVIA

Brīvības iela

Tērbatas iela

Matīsa iela

Bruņinieku iela

Stabu iela

Valdemāra iela

Skolas iela

Baznīcas iela

Akas iela

Martas

K Barona iela

Brīvības bulvāris

Dzirnavu iela

Blaumaņa iela

Lāčplēša iela

A Čaka iela

Ģertrūdes iela

Tērbatas iela

Merķeļa iela

Vērmanes
dārzs

Arhitektu

Alfrēda Kalniņa iela

Marijas iela

E Birznieka Upīša iela

Satekles iela

Suburban
minibūs station
(to Jūrmala)

Central
Post Office

13 Janvāra iela

Central
Train Station

Gogoļa iela

Timoteja iela

Lāčplēša iela

Prāgas iela

Turgeņeva iela

Akadēmijas
Laukums

36
34
33
9
35
24
13
11
40
37
22
21
26
27
28
45
14
17
39
48
23
25
44
31
38
18
42
19
43
32
29
1
7

contemporary art museum in an abandoned electrical powerstation (à la Tate Modern in London). Follow Kronvalda bulvaris 1.5km north of Old Rīga, or take tram 7 from the Freedom Monument to the end of the line.

Rīga Motor Museum   MUSEUM
(Rīgas motormuzejs; ☑6709 7170; www.motormuzejs.lv; Eizenšteina iela 6; admission 1.50Ls; ⊙10am-6pm) The stars of this collection include the cars that once belonged to Soviet luminaries like Gorky, Stalin and Khrushchev, complete with irreverent life-sized figures of the men themselves. The museum is 8km outside the city centre near the Mežciems suburb. Take bus 21 to the Pansionāts stop.

Mežaparks   NEIGHBOURHOOD
Woodsy Mežaparks (literally 'Forest Park' in Latvian), 7km outside the centre, is Europe's oldest planned suburb. Built by the Germans in the 20th century, this 'garden city' was the go-to neighbourhood for wealthy merchants looking to escape the city's grimy industrial core. The area is home to the **Rīga National Zoo** (Zoologiskais dārz; www.rigazoo.lv; Meža prospekts 1; adult/child 4/3Ls; ⊙10am-6pm), which features the usual cast of Noah's ark.

Activities
Regro's   SHOOTING RANGE
(off Map p468; ☑6760 1705; Daugav-grīvas iela 31; bullets 0.80-2Ls; ⊙10am-7pm Mon-Sat, by appointment Sun) The ambience at Regro's is reason enough to visit: a dingy Soviet fallout shelter adorned with posters of rifle-toting models wearing fur bikinis. Choose from a large selection of retro firearms (including Kalashnikovs) to aim at your paper cut-out of

James Bond. You pay by the bullet. Take the Vanšu bridge across the river, pass Ķīpsala, and take your first right until you hit a petrol station. Also accessible by tram 13. Don't forget your passport.

Taka Spa SPA
(Map p472; ☑6732 3150; www.takaspa.lv; Kronvalda bulvāris 3a; treatments from 15Ls; ☺10am-9pm Mon-Fri, 10am-7pm Sat & Sun) You don't have to run all the way to Jūrmala to see some serious spa action. Taka Spa is one of Rīga's standout spots to get pampered in the traditional Latvian style: getting whipped by dried birch branches while sweating it out in temperatures beyond 40°C. Sounds relaxing...

☞ Tours

Swarms of operators offer tours around Rīga and daytrips to nearby attractions like Rundāle Palace and Sigulda. Check out www.jugendstils.riga.lv for touring routes focusing on the city's clutch of art nouveau architecture.

E.a.t. Riga HISTORY
(☑2246 9888; www.eatriga.lv) Not a foodie's tour – these walking and bicycle jaunts (from 25Ls) give visitors a chance to sneak behind the (iron) curtain and see the 'real Rīga'.

Riga By Canal CITY
(Map p468; ☑6750 9974; www.kmk.lv; adult/child 5/3Ls; ☺9am-11pm) Enjoy a different perspective of the city aboard the 100-year-old *Darling*, a charming wooden canal cruiser.

Rīga City Tour CITY
(☑2665 5405; www.citytour.lv; tour 10Ls) Hop-on-hop-off double-decker bus that winds through the capital.

Riga Out There CULTURE
(Map p472; ☑2938 9450; www.rigaoutthere.com) Organises loads of tours, day trips and activities for tourists, from AK-47 shooting to late-night pub-crawls. It also runs funky apartment-style accommodation (30Ls) from its office.

✹✵ Festivals & Events

Check out www.rigatourism.lv for a complete list of local events.

Rīga Opera Festival MUSIC
(www.opera.lv; ☺Jun) The National Opera's 10-day event featuring performances by local and world-renowned talent.

Baltā Nakts ART
(www.baltanakts.lv; ☺Sep) 'White Night' mirrors Paris' nightlong showcase of artists and culture around the city.

Arsenāls International Film Forum FILM
(www.arsenals.lv; ☺Sep) An annual film festival showcasing more than 100 movies relating to experiential and interactive themes.

🛏 Sleeping
OLD RĪGA (VECRĪGA)

Naughty Squirrel HOSTEL €
(Map p468; ☑2646 1248; www.naughtysquirrelbackpackers.com; Kalēju iela 50; dm/d 8/30Ls; @☎) Kalēju iela 50 has been the address of several hostel incarnations, and the Naughty Squirrel is by far the best yet. Brilliant slashes of bright paint and cartoon graffiti have breathed new life into the city's capital of backpacker-dom, which buzzes as travellers rattle the foosball table and chill out in the TV room. Sign up for regular pub-crawls, adrenaline day trips to the countryside, or summer barbecues.

Neiburgs BOUTIQUE HOTEL €€€
(Map p468; ☑6711 5522; www.neiburgs.com; Jaun iela 25/27; s/d/ste incl breakfast from 100/130/170Ls; ✳@☎) Beautiful Neiburgs blends contemporary touches (think patterned accent walls and chrome in bathroom) with carefully preserved details (like curling crown moulding) for its signature blend of boutique-chic style. Try for a room on one of the higher floors – you'll be treated to a colourful clutter of gabled roofs and twisting medieval spires. The in-house restaurant is exceptionally popular with locals. Go for the 'Business Lunch' – it's so well priced you'll think the waiter left a zero off the bill!

Ekes Konventas HISTORIC HOTEL €€
(Map p468; ☑6735 8393; www.ekeskonvents.lv; Skārņu iela 22; d incl breakfast €57; ☎) Not to be confused with Konventa Sēta next door, the 600-year-old Ekes Konventas oozes wobbly medieval charm from every crooked nook and cranny. Curl up with a book in the adorable stone alcoves on the landing of each storey. Breakfast is served in the mod cafe down the block.

Blue Cow Barracks HOSTEL €
(Map p468; ☑2773 6700; www.bluecowbarracks.com; Torņa iela 4-2B; dm/d €10/35Ls; @☎) Run by the same people at Naughty Squirrel, this is an excellent, though smaller and more intimate hostel in the historic Jacob's Barracks on the other side of Old Rīga.

Old Town Hostel
HOSTEL €

(Map p468; ☑6722 3406; www.rigaoldtownhostel.lv; Vaļņu iela 43; dm/d 7/30Ls; @🛜) The cosy English-style pub on the ground floor doubles as the hostel's hang-out space, and if you can manage to lug your suitcase past the faux bookshelf door and up the twisting staircase, you'll find spacious dorms with chandeliers and plenty of sunlight. Private rooms are located in another building near the train station.

Friendly Fun Franks
HOSTEL €

(Map p468; ☑2599 0612; www.franks.lv; 11 Novembra Krastmala 29; dm/d from 5.90/40Ls; @🛜) If you want to party, look no further than this bright orange stag-magnet, where every backpacker is greeted with a hearty hello and a complimentary pint of beer. The staff offer free 'What to Do' tours of Rīga, beach parties and Saturday trips to Sigulda. Accommodation must be booked in advance.

CENTRAL RĪGA (CENTRS)

TOP CHOICE Hotel Bergs
BOUTIQUE HOTEL €€€

(Map p472; ☑6777 0900; www.hotelbergs.lv; Elizabetes iela 83/85; ste from €164; ✳@🛜P) A refurbished manor house embellished with Scandi-sleek design, Hotel Bergs embodies the term 'luxury' from the lobby's mix of sharp lines, rococo portraits and tribal reliefs, to the spacious suites lavished with high-quality monochromatic furnishings worthy of a magazine spread. Countless other treats await, like a custom-composed sleeping soundtrack in the room's CD player, and an endless supply of complimentary Acqua Panna. Our favourite – the 'pillow service' – allows guests to choose from an array of different bed pillows based on material and texture. Be sure to check out the in-house restaurant – the menu of refined Latvian fare reads like an ode to your tastebuds, and all seasonal items are locally sourced.

Europa Royale
HISTORIC HOTEL €€€

(Map p472; ☑6707 9444; www.europaroyale.com; K Barona iela 12; s/d/ste incl breakfast €79/89/189; ✳@🛜) Once the home of media mogul Emīlija Benjamiņa (Latvia's version of Anna Wintour), this ornate manse retains much of its original opulence with sweeping staircases and stately bedrooms. In fact, when Latvia regained its independence, the house was initially chosen to be president's digs but the government didn't have enough funds for the restoration. There are 60 large rooms, yet guests will feel like they're staying at their posh aunt's estate.

Radisson Blu Hotel Elizabete
HOTEL €€€

(Map p472; ☑6778 5555; www.radissonblu.com/elizabetehotel-riga; Elizabetes iela 73; d incl breakfast from €85; ✳@🛜P) The newest link in the Radisson Blu chain is a flash address designed by an up-and-coming London architectural firm. The facade is an eye-catching mix of chrome, steel and giant sheets of glass, and the interior continues to impress: stylish furnishings and clever floor plans give the rooms a cosy-yet-trendy feel.

Albert Hotel
HOTEL €€

(Map p472; ☑6733 1717; www.alberthotel.lv; Dzirnavu iela 33; s/d incl breakfast €64/69; ✳@🛜P) The boxy, metallic facade starkly contrasts with the surrounding art nouveau gargoyles, but the interior design is undeniably hip, paying tribute to the hotel's namesake, Albert Einstein. The patterned carpeting features rows of atomic energy symbols, and the 'do not disturb' doorknob danglers have been replaced with red tags that read 'I'm thinking'.

Radisson Blu Hotel Latvija
HOTEL €€€

(Map p472; ☑6777 2222; www.radissonblu.com/latvijahotel-riga; Elizabetes iela 55; d incl breakfast from €79; ✳@🛜🏊) During the height of the Soviet regime, the Hotel Latvija was a drab monstrosity in which several floors were devoted to monitoring the various goings-on of the hotel's guests. The room keys weighed several kilos, as they were outfitted with conspicuous listening devices. Today, after a much-needed facelift, the era of espionage is long gone; it's all swipe-cards and smiley service now. Don't miss the views from the Skyline Bar on the 26th floor (p479).

Hotel Valdemārs
HOTEL €€

(Map p472; ☑6733 4462; www.valdemars.lv; Valdemāra iela 23; s/d incl half board from €50/60; ✳@🛜) Modern Hotel Valdemārs is a great find geared towards the Scandinavian market – rooms feel efficient yet homey, in an upmarket Ikea kind of way. Don't forget to give away the flower adorning the bureau in your room – it's a Latvian tradition!

Krišjānis & Ģertrūde
B&B €€

(Map p472; ☑6750 6604; www.kg.lv; K Barona iela 39; s/d/tr incl breakfast €35/45/55; @🛜) Step off the bustling intersection into this quaint, family-run B&B adorned with still lifes of fruit and flowers. It's best to book ahead since there are only six cosy rooms. Enter from Ģertrūdes iela.

B&B Rīga
APARTMENT €€

(Map p472; ☎6727 8505; www.bb-riga.lv; Ģertrūdes iela 43; s/d €39/49; @☎) Snug, apartment-style accommodation comes in different configurations (suites with lofted bedrooms are particularly charming), and are scattered throughout a residential block.

KB
B&B €

(Map p472; ☎6731 2323; www.kbhotel.lv; K Barona iela 37; s/d/tr 19/21/23Ls; @☎) This great find in the pinch-a-penny category is located up a rather opulent marble staircase. The rooms are simple but well appointed, and there's a modern communal kitchen.

✗ Eating

Check out p489 for details about eating in Latvia.

OLD RĪGA (VECRĪGA)

If you're self-catering, there's a branch of Rimi (www.rimi.lv; Audēju iela 16), a reputable supermarket chain, in Old Rīga's Galerija Centrs shopping mall.

Pelmeņi XL
FAST FOOD €

(Map p468; Kaļķu iela 7; dumpling bowls 0.86-2.50Ls; ☺9am-4am) A Rīga institution for backpackers and undiscerning drunkards, this extra-large cafeteria stays open extra-late serving up huge bowls of *pelmeņi* (Russian-style ravioli stuffed with meat) amid Flintstones-meets-Gaudi decor (you'll see). There's a second location in the central train station.

Dorian Gray
CAFE €€

(Map p468; www.doriangray.lv; Mazā Muzeja iela 1; mains 3.60-8Ls) With seating purchased from a car-boot sale, random pillows scattered about, and cracked crimson brick crumbling off the walls, Dorian Gray might just be (rather ironically) the least image-obsessed place in town. Down-to-earth wait staff serve curious concoctions like chicken stuffed with shrimp and a strange carrot cake that could more appropriately be defined as a dessert salad. Swing by for weekly movie nights and brunch-time screenings of *Ugly Betty*.

V. Ķuze
CONFECTIONER €

(Map p468; www.kuze.lv; Jēkaba iela 20/22; coffee & cake from 1.20Ls) Vilhelms Ķuze was a prominent entrepreneur and chocolatier while Latvia flirted with freedom between the world wars. When the Soviets barged in he was promptly deported to Siberia where he met his maker. Today, Ķuze Chocolates is up and running once more, and this charm-ing cafe-cum-confectioner functions not only a memoriam to dear Vilhelms but also as a tribute to the colourful art nouveau era when arcing furniture and geometric nature motifs were en vogue.

Rozengrāls
MEDIEVAL €€€

(Map p468; www.rozengrals.lv; Rozena iela 1; mains 4.50-19.20Ls) Remember 500 years ago when potatoes weren't the heart and soul of Latvian cuisine? We don't, but Rozengrāls does – this candlelit haunt takes diners back a few centuries offering medieval game (sans spuds) served by costume-clad waiters.

Boulangerie Bonjour
BAKERY €

(Map p468; www.boulangeriebonjour.lv; Jēkaba iela 20/22; mains 2-5Ls; ☺7am-8pm Mon-Fri, 10am-6pm Sat & Sun) Barnyard murals and custard mouldings confirm the provincial theme at this popular snackery. And just in case it wasn't clear from the name that this place is French run, there are oddly placed photos of Gérard Depardieu on the wine menu.

Gutenbergs
LATVIAN €€

(Map p468; www.gutenbergs.eu; Doma laukums 1; mains 5.90-11.90Ls; ☺May-Oct) Go one better than dining with a view – dine *in* the view! The Hotel Gutenbergs' rooftop terrace in the heart of Old Rīga squats between sky-scraping spires and gingerbread trim. Potted plants, cherubic statues and trickling fountains contribute to a decidedly Florentine vibe, although the menu focuses on local favourites.

Vecmeita ar kaki
LATVIAN €€

(Spinster & Her Cat; Map p468; Mazā Pils iela 1; mains 3.10-9.90Ls) This cosy spot across from the president's palace specialises in cheap Latvian grub and meaty mains. In warmer weather, patrons dine outside on converted sewing-machine tables.

Ķiploku Krogs
INTERNATIONAL €€

(Garlic Bar; Map p468; Jēkaba iela 3/5; mains 3.40-9.80Ls) Vampires beware – *everything* at this joint contains garlic, even the ice cream. The menu is pretty hit-and-miss, but no matter what, it's best to avoid the garlic pesto spread – it'll taint your breath for days (trust us). Enter from Mazā Pils.

Šefpavārs Vilhelms
FAST FOOD €

(Chef William; Map p468; Šķūņu iela 6; pancake rolls 0.65Ls) Customers of every ilk are constantly queuing for a quick nosh – three blintze-like pancakes smothered in sour cream and jam equals the perfect backpacker's breakfast.

CENTRAL RĪGA (CENTRS)

Self-caterers should try **Rimi** (www.rimi.lv; K Barona iela 46) in the Barona Centrs shopping mall or check out the **Central Market** (p469).

TOP CHOICE **Istaba** CAFE €€
(Map p472; ☑6728 1141; K. Barona iela 31a; mains 3-10Ls; ☺Mon-Sat) Owned by local chef and TV personality Mārtiņš Sirmais, the 'Room' sits in the rafters above a like-named gallery space adorned with trendsetting bric-a-brac. In summer you can dine on the street-side veranda, though we prefer heading upstairs to grab a seat in the mob of discarded lamps and sofas. There's no set menu – you're subject to the cook's fancy – but it's all about flavourful and filling portions served on mismatched dishware. Reservations are recommended.

Aragats GEORGIAN €€
(☑6737 3445; Miera iela 15; mains 4-8Ls; ☺Tue-Sun) Ignore the plastic shrubbery – this place is all about sampling some killer cuisine from the Caucasus. Start with an appetiser of pickled vegetables – the perfect chaser for your home-brewed *chacha* (Georgian vodka). Then make nice with the matronly owner as she dices up fresh herbs at your table to mix with the savoury lamb stew. At the end of the meal men should pay for the women at the table, especially since the women's menus don't have any of the prices listed!

Ostas Skati GOURMET €€
(☑2000 9045; www.foodandbeverages.lv; Matrožu iela 15; mains 6.50Ls; ☺8.30am-midnight) Known around town as the 'democratic restaurant' for its recession-proof prices, Ostas Skati was once a staff caf that's now been jazzed up by trendy mood lighting and stocked with attractive serving staff. Expertly presented Latvian dishes include Daugava catfish and home-smoked trout. Don't miss the cup of scrumptious curd-cream and strawberry jam for dessert – enjoy it on the riverside deck during the summer months.

Meta-Kafe CAFE €
(www.metakafe.lv; Maskavas iela 12/1; mains 2.90-4.70Ls; 🖄) Safely tucked away from those who aren't in the know, this hipster hangout occupies one of the renovated spaces in the newly trendy Spīķeri neighbourhood. Stencil scribbles adorn the spots on the walls that aren't hidden behind shelves of art books. Sip your house wine out back in the concrete courtyard or join the headphoneed loiterers inside as they slurp soups and mess around on their MacBooks.

Vincents FINE DINING €€€
(Map p472; ☑6733 2634; www.restorans.lv; Elizabetes iela 19; mains 13-20Ls; ☺6-11pm Mon-Sat) Ask any older Rīgan – they'll all tell you that Vincents is the top spot in town. So it's no surprise that it's also the most expensive. Apparently when Queen Elizabeth spent a day in town, she ate both her lunch and dinner here, and other world figures have followed suit. The head chef is a stalwart of the Slow Food movement, and crafts his ever-changing menu amid eye-catching van Gogh–inspired decor (hence the name).

LIDO Atpūtas Centrs LATVIAN €
(LIDO Recreation Centre; www.lido.lv; Krasta iela 76 mains 2-6.50Ls) If Latvia and Disney World had a love child it would be the LIDO Atpūtas Centrs – an enormous wooden palace dedicated to the country's coronary-inducing cuisine. Servers dressed like Baltic milkmaids bounce around as patrons hit the rows of buffets for classics like pork tongue and cold beet soup. Take the free bus from Ratslaukums or tram 3, 7 or 9 and get off at the 'LIDO' stop. There's a handful of miniature LIDO restaurants dotted around the city centre for those who don't have time to make it out to the mothership.

Osīriss CAFE €€
(Map p472; K Barona iela 31; mains 3-9Ls; ☺8am-midnight; 🖄) Despite Rīga's mercurial cafe culture, Osiriss continues to be a local mainstay. The green faux-marble tabletops haven't changed since the mid-'90s and neither has the clientele: angsty artsy types scribbling in their Moleskines over a glass of red wine.

Charlestons INTERNATIONAL €€€
(Čarlstons; Map p472; www.charlestons.lv Blaumaņa iela 38/40; mains 5-19Ls; 🖄) If you're up to your elbows in pork tongue, Charlestons is a sure bet to get rid of the meat sweats. Lounge around the terraced courtyard in the heart of a residential block and feast on delicious platters such as Norwegian salmon, sautéed duck and the best Caesar salad in the Baltic.

🍺 Drinking

If you want to party like a Latvian, assemble a gang of friends and pub-crawl your way through the city, stopping at colourful haunts for rounds of shots, belly laughter and, of course, Black Balzāms. On summer evenings, nab a spot at one of the city's many beer gardens.

OLD RĪGA (VECRĪGA)

Cuba Cafe
BAR

(Map p468; www.cubacafe.lv; Jauņ iela 15; ☎) An authentic mojito and a table overlooking Doma laukums is just what the doctor ordered after a long day of sightseeing. On older days, swig your caipirinha inside amid dangling Cuban flags, wobbly stained-glass lamps and the murmur of trumpet jazz.

La Belle Epoque
BAR

(French Bar; Map p468; Mazā Jaunavu iela 8) Students flock to this boisterous basement bar to power down its trademark 'apple pie' shots (1Ls). The Renoir mural and kitschy *Moulin Rouge* posters seem to successfully ward off stag parties.

Nekādu Problēmu
BEER GARDEN

(No Problem; Map p468; www.nekaduproblemu. lv; Doma laukums) This sea of sturdy patio ware enlivens Doma laukums in the warmer months as the rousing fits of live music bounce off the cathedral walls. Sample more than 20 types of draught beer, and the food's pretty darn good too.

Paldies Dievam Piektdiena Ir Klāt
BAR

(Thank Goodness It's Friday; Map p468; www.piek diena.lv; 11 Novembra Krastmala 9) No relation to the fried-food-slinging American chain, this 'TGIF' rescues locals from bitter winter nights with loud Caribbean decor, appropriately attired barkeeps and fruity shooters.

Aptieka
BAR

(Pharmacy Bar; Map p468; Mazā Miesnieku iela 1) Antique apothecary bottles confirm the subtle but stylish theme at this popular drinking haunt run by a Latvian–American.

CENTRAL RĪGA (CENTRS)

TOP CHOICE Pērle
BAR-CAFE

(Tērbatas iela 65) Pērle is where outmoded technology goes to die a stylish rockstar death. It's everything you'd want in a neighbourhood hipster hangout: discarded gameboys, racks of vintage tweed, a massacre of mannequin parts and designer lattes... with Baileys. Oh, and everything's for sale. Naturally.

Skyline Bar
HOTEL BAR

(Map p472; Elizabetes iela 55; ☎) A must for every visitor, glitzy Skyline Bar sits on the 26th floor of the Reval Hotel Latvija. The sweeping views are the city's best, and the mix of glam spirit-sippers makes great people-watching under the retro purple lighting.

Gauja
BAR

(Map p472; www.gauja.je; Tērbatas iela 56) Step off the street and into time-warped Gauja – a small bar decked out in Soviet-style decor. Hunker down amid period furnishings for a rousing duel on the retro chessboard, or link together the set of wooden dominos while unique beats soar above (the owners have their own recording studio).

Apsara
TEA HOUSE

(Map p472; Elizabetes iela 74) A charming wooden pagoda in the heart of Vērmanes dārzs, Apsara is a veritable library of rare teas imported from beyond the Himalayas. Daintily sip your imported brews while relaxing on the floor amid a sea of pastel pillows. There a couple of locations around town including a branch tucked into an old medieval building at Skārņu iela 22 (Map p468).

☆ Entertainment

Nightclubs

Nabaklab
CLUB

(Map p468; www.nabaklab.lv; Meierovica bulvaris 12) Imagine if your favourite alternative radio station opened a nightspot that played its signature blend of experimental tunes and electronica. Well, you're in luck – Naba's (93.1FM) club space attracts the city's boho hobos with its DJ-ed beats, vintage clothes racks, art gallery and cheap beer in the quaint Soviet-style den.

Pulkvedim Neviens Neraksta
CLUB

(No-one Writes to the Colonel; Map p468; www. pulkvedis.lv; Peldu iela 26/280) There's no such thing as a dull night at Pulkvedis. The atmosphere is 'warehouse chic', with pumping '80s tunes on the ground floor and trance beats down below.

Club Essential
CLUB

(Map p472; www.essential.lv; Skolas iela 2) Essential is a spectacle of beautiful people boogying to some of Europe's top DJ talent. Overzealous security aside, this two-storey complex is your safest bet if partying till dawn is your mission.

Moon Safari
CLUB

(Map p468; www.moonsafari.lv; Krāmu iela 2) Beds in the 'VIP room' and a pet snake at the bar? It's all pretty suggestive, but the 2Ls cocktails and colourful karaoke booth lure a young Erasmus crowd for all-night shenanigans.

Golden
GAY & LESBIAN

(Map p472; www.mygoldenclub.com; Ģertrūdes iela 33/35; admission 3-5Ls) It's all about smoke

LATVIA

and mirrors (literally) at Rīga's most 'open' venue. However, if you're looking for a thriving gay scene, better pick another city.

Performing Arts

National Opera House OPERA
(Map p468; ☑6707 3777; www.opera.lv; Aspazijas bulvāris 3) The pride of Latvia boasting some of the finest opera in all of Europe (and for the fraction of the price of other countries). Mikhail Baryshnikov got his start here.

Dome Cathedral LIVE MUSIC
(Doma baznīca; Map p468; ☑6721 3213; www.doms.lv; Doma laukums 1) Twice-weekly short organ concerts (Wednesday and Saturday evenings) and lengthier Friday night performances are well worth attending.

Great Guild LIVE MUSIC
(Map p468; ☑6722 4850; www.lnso.lv; Amatu iela 6) Home to the acclaimed Latvian National Symphonic Orchestra. Classical music and jazz scats are often heard from the window.

New Rīga Theatre THEATRE
(Jaunais Rīgas Teātris; Map p472; ☑6728 0765; www.jrt.lv; Lačplēša iela 25) Contemporary repertory theatre.

Dailes Theatre THEATRE
(Map p472; ☑6727 0463; www.dailesteatris.lv; Brīvības iela 75) Rīga's largest modern theatre. Retains a lot of its original architectural elements from the Soviet era.

Cinemas

Catching a movie is a great way to spend a rainy day in Rīga (trust us, there are many). Tickets cost between 2Ls and 4Ls.

Kino Rīga CINEMA
(Map p472; www.kinoriga.lv; Elizabetes iela 61) The Baltic's first cinema hosts myriad film festivals. Worth stopping by to check out the over-the-top mess of baroque styling (think gilded palm trees and chubby cherubs).

K Suns CINEMA
(Map p472; www.kinogalerija.lv; Elizabetes iela 83/85) An artsy movie house projecting mostly indie films on its one screen.

🛒 Shopping

Street sellers peddle their touristy wares outside St Peter's church. Keep an eye out for the beautiful Namēju rings worn by Latvians around the world as a way to recognise one another.

Madam Bonbon ACCESSORIE
(Map p472; www.madambonbon.lv; Alberta iela 1-7a) Carrie Bradshaw's died and gone to heaven every surface in this old-school art nouveau apartment features some sort of foot furniture. Squeeze into the stiletto on the baby grand piano, or go for the boot behind th teapot on the kitchen table.

Sakta Flower Market MARKE
(Map p472; Tērbatas iela 2a) Open extra-late fo those midnight mea culpas when you'v gotta bring a gift home to your spouse afte a long evening out with friends.

Upe MUSI
(Map p468; www.upett.lv; Vāgnera iela 5) Classica Latvian tunes play as customers peruse tra ditional instruments and CDs of local folk rock and experimental sounds.

Latvijas Balzāms FOOD & DRIN
(Map p468; www.lb.lv; Audēju iela 8) A popula chain of liquor stores selling the trademar Latvian Black Balzām. There's anothe branch on Blaumaņa iela (Map p472) an another on K Barona iela (Map p472) alon with several others around town.

Robert's Books BOOK
(Map p472; http://robertsbooksriga.com; Antonija iela 12) Robert used to write for the *Econo mist*; these days he calls Rīga home an tends to his small collection of used Englis books. Traditional textiles and beeswax car dles are also on offer. Enter on Dzirnavu iela

Jāņa Sēta BOOK
(Map p472; www.mapshop.lv; Elizabetes iela 83/85 The largest travel bookstore in the Balti overflows with a bounty of maps, souveni photo books and Lonely Planet guides.

Art Nouveau Riga SOUVEN
(www.artnouveauriga.lv; Strēlnieku iela 9) Pu chase a variety of art nouveau–related sou venirs, from guidebooks and postcards t stone gargoyles and bits of stained glass.

The following shops are located in Berg Bazārs (Map p472; www.bergabazars.lv; Dzirnav iela 84), a maze of upmarket boutiques orbi ing the five-star Hotel Bergs:

Emihla Gustava Shokolahde FOOD & DRIN
(Map p472; www.sokolade.lv) Latvia's finest chocolate shop doubles as a cafe. The fruit-stuffed truffles are divine, but don't miss the mud-thick hot chocolate.

Garage AF
(Map p472; www.garage.lv) A gallery and souvenir shop featuring upmarket handicraft

esigned by Latvian artists. In the evening doubles as a wine bar.

ℹ Information

nternet Access

very hostel and hotel has some form of internet connection available to guests. Internet cafes re a dying breed in Rīga and they're usually illed with 12-year-olds blasting cybermonsters.

lik Kafe (Merķeļa iela 1; per 30min/1hr 45/0.85Ls; ⊙24hr) Conveniently located near le train station above McDonald's. Second cation at Kaļķu iela 11.

ledia & Websites

iga in Your Pocket (www.inyourpocket.com/tvia/riga) Handy city guide published every ther month. Download a PDF version or pick p a copy at most midrange or top-end hotels ree). The tourist offices and several book-hops also have copies (2Ls).

iga this Week (www.rigathisweek.lv) An xcellent (and free) city guide available at virtu-lly every sleeping option in town. Published very second month.

igaInSight (www.rigainsight.com) New con-ibution to Rīga's clutch of miniguides. Free opies are available practically everywhere ncluding the airport's arrival terminal.

gaNOW! (www.bestriga.com) A magazine eaturing the city's best spots. Complimentary ppies are available at most midrange and top-nd hotels. The website has similar info.

ledical Services

RS (☎6720 1003; www.ars-med.lv; Skola la 5) English-speaking doctors and 24-hour onsultation available.

loney

here are scores of ATMs scattered around the apital. Withdrawing cash is easier than trying to xchange travellers cheques or foreign curren-es; exchange bureaux often have lousy rates nd most do not take travellers cheques.

larika (Brīvības bulvāris 30) Offers 24-hour urrency exchange services with reasonable ates. Second location at Dzirnavu 96.

'ost

hose blue storefronts with 'Pasta' written on em aren't Italian restaurants – they're post ffices. See www.pasts.lv for more info.

entral post office (Brīvības bulvaris 32; ⊙7.30am-8pm Mon-Fri, 8am-6pm Sat, 10am-pm Sun) International calling and faxing ervices available.

ost office (Elizabetes iela 41/43; ⊙7.30am-pm Mon-Fri, 8am-4pm Sat)

Tourist Information

Tourism information centre (☎6730 7900; www.rigatourism.com; Rātslaukums 6; ⊙9am-6pm) Gives out excellent tourist maps and walking tour brochures. Staff can arrange accommodation and book day trips. Sells concert and opera tickets in summer. Satellite tourism offices can be found at the train station, bus station and airport. Buy the **Rīga Card** (www.rigacard.lv; 24hr card 10Ls), which offers discounts on sights and restaurants, and free rides on public transportation.

ℹ Getting There & Away

Air

Rīga airport (Lidosta Rīga; off Map p472; www.riga-airport.com, Marupes pagast) is in the suburb of Skulte, 13km southwest of the city centre. See p491 for info on airlines flying into the capital.

Boat

Rīga's **passenger ferry terminal** (off Map p472; ☎6732 6200; www.portofriga.lv; Eksporta iela 3a), located about 1km downstream (north) of Akmens Bridge, offers service to Stockholm aboard **Tallink** (☎6709 975; www.tallink.lv). **DFDS Ferry Lines** (☎6735 3523; www.lisco. lv; Zivju iela 1) and **Ave Line** (☎6709 7999; www.aveline.lv; Uriekstes 3) leave from the Vecmīgrāvja cargo terminal (further down the Daugava) for Travemünde (Lübeck), Germany. Service is often suspended in the colder months.

Bus

Buses depart from Rīga's **international bus station** (Rīgas starptautiskā autoosta; Map p472; www.autoosta.lv; Prāgas iela 1), located behind the railway embankment just beyond the southeastern edge of Old Town. International destinations include Tallinn, Vilnius, Warsaw, Pärnu, Kaunas, St Petersburg and Moscow. Try one of following companies:

Ecolines (☎6721 4512; www.ecolines.net)

Eurolines Lux Express (☎6778 1350; www. luxexpress.eu)

Nordeka (☎6746 4620; www.nordeka.lv)

Domestic services from Rīga include the following:

Bauska 2Ls, 1¼ hours, every 30 minutes from 6.30am to 11pm

Cēsis 2.60Ls, two hours, every 30 minutes from 7.30am to 9.30pm

Kolka 4Ls to 5Ls, 3½ to 4½ hours, five daily from 7.20am to 5.15pm

Kuldīga 4.10Ls, 2½ to 3¼ hours, hourly from 7am to 8pm

Liepāja 5.50Ls to 6.50Ls, four hours, every 45 minutes from 6.45am to 7.30pm

LATVIA

Sigulda 1.80Ls, one hour, every 30 minutes from 7am to 9.30pm

Ventspils 4.70Ls, three to four hours, hourly from 7am to 10.30pm

Train

Rīga's **central train station** (centrālā stacija; Map p472; Stacijas laukums) is convenient to Old Rīga and Centrs, and is housed in a conspicuous glass-encased shopping centre near the Central Market. Give yourself extra time to find the ticket booths, as they are scattered throughout the building and sometimes tricky to find.

The city's network of handy suburban train lines makes day tripping to Jūrmala (0.95Ls, 30 minutes, two hourly), Sigulda (1.55Ls, 70 minutes, hourly) and Cēsis (2.30Ls, 1¾ hours, five daily) quite convenient. Purchase tickets to the aforementioned destinations at windows 7 to 12.

Rīga is directly linked by long-distance trains to Daugavpils (4¾ hours), Moscow (16½ hours), St Petersburg (13¼ hours) and Pskov (8½ hours). Visit www.ldz.lv to view the timetables and prices for long-haul international and domestic trains. Train service is not convenient to any destinations in western Latvia.

❶ Getting Around

To/From the Airport

There are three means of transport connecting the city centre to the airport. The cheapest option is bus 22 (0.70Ls), which runs every 15 minutes and stops at several points around town including the Stockmanns complex and the Daugava River (near Friendly Fun Franks hostel). Passengers who carry luggage onto public transportation (with the exception of bus 22) need a 'luggage ticket' (0.10Ls; available from the driver). AirBaltic runs lime-green minibuses (3Ls) from the airport to a selection of midrange hotels in Central Rīga. Lime-green taxis cost a flat rate of 9Ls from the airport (expect your taxi driver to keep 1Ls as 'tip' if you hand him a 10Ls note); cabbies run the meter when heading *to* the airport (figure around 7.70Ls from Central Rīga with light traffic).

Bicycle

Zip around town with **Baltic Bikes** (Map p468; ✆6778 8333; www.balticbike.lv; per hr/day 0.70/6Ls). A handful of stands are conveniently positioned around Rīga and Jūrmala; simply choose your bike, call the rental service and receive the code to unlock your wheels.

Car & Motorcycle

For information on car rentals, see p492. Motorists must pay 5Ls per hour to enter Old Town – tickets must be purchased in advance at Statoil stations or foreign exchange bureaus.

Public Transport

Most of Rīga's main tourist attractions are within walking distance of one another, so you might never have to use the city's convoluted network of tramlines, trolleybus paths and bus routes. Tickets cost 0.70Ls (0.50Ls if you buy your ticket ahead of time from an automated machine or newsstand). A three-day unlimited transport pass can be purchased for 5.70Ls. City transport runs daily from 5.30am to midnight. Some routes have an hourly night service. For Rīga public transport routes and schedules visit www.rigassatiksme.lv

Taxi

Taxis charge 0.40Ls to 0.50Ls per kilometre (oftentimes 0.50Ls to 0.60Ls between 10pm and 6am). Insist on having the meter on before you set off. Meters usually start running at 1Ls to 1.50Ls. Don't pay more than 4Ls for a short journey (like crossing the Daugava for dinner in Ķīpsala). There are taxi ranks outside the bus and train stations, at the airport, and in front of a few major hotels in Central Rīga, like Radisson Blu Hotel Latvija.

AROUND RĪGA

It's hard to believe that long stretches of flaxen beaches and shady pine forests lie just 20km from Rīga's metropolitan core. The highway connecting Rīga to Jūrmala (Latvia's only six-lane road) was known as '10 Minutes in America' during Soviet times because locally produced films set in the US were always filmed on this busy asphalt strip.

Jūrmala

POP 54,930

The Baltics' version of the French Riviera, Jūrmala is a long string of townships with stately wooden beach estates belonging to Russian oil tycoons and their supermodel trophy wives. Even during the height of communism, Jūrmala was always a place to *sea* and be seen. Today, at summer weekends, vehicles clog the roads when jetsetters and day-tripping Rīgans flock to the resort town for some serious fun in the sun.

If you don't have a car or bicycle, you'll want to head straight to the heart of the action – the townships of Majori and Dzintari. A 1km-long pedestrian street, Jomas iela, connects these two districts and is considered to be Jūrmala's main drag.

◎ Sights & Activities

Jūrmala's first spa opened in 1838, and since then, the area has been known far and wide

RUNDĀLE PALACE

If you only have time for one day trip out of Rīga, make it **Rundāle Palace** (Rundāles pils; ✆6396 2274; www.rundale.net; short/long route 2.50/3.50Ls, photography permit 1Ls; ⊗10am-7pm May-Oct, 10am-5pm Nov-Apr), 75km south of the capital near the tiny town of Bauska. The architect of this sprawling monument to aristocratic ostentation was the Italian baroque genius Bartolomeo Rastrelli, best known for designing the Winter Palace in St Petersburg. About 40 of the palace's 138 rooms are open to visitors, as are the wonderfully landscaped gardens.

Most tour operators run frequent day trips to the palace (figure 20Ls per person); it's best to rent a car if you plan on reaching Rundāle under your own steam. You can also take a bus from Rīga to Bauska (2Ls, 70 minutes, twice hourly), then switch to one of the nine daily buses (0.35Ls) connecting Bauska to the palace (Pilsrundāle), 12km away.

as the spa capital of the Baltic countries. Treatments are available at a variety of big-name hotels and hulking Soviet sanatoriums further along the beach towards Ķemeri National Park. Many accommodation options offer combined spa and sleeping deals.

Wooden Houses   HISTORIC BUILDING
Besides the beach and spa scene, Jūrmala's main attraction is its colourful art nouveau wooden houses, distinguishable by frilly awnings, detailed facades and elaborate towers. There are more than 4000 fairytale-like structures (most are lavish summer cottages) found throughout Jūrmala, but you can get your fill of wood by taking a leisurely stroll along Jūras iela, which parallels Jomas iela between Majori and Dzintari. The houses are in various states of repair; some are dilapidated and abandoned, some are beautifully renovated and others are brand new. Download the detailed 'Routes along the historical centres of Jurmala' brochure from www.jurmala.lv for more info.

Baltic Beach Spa   SPA
(✆6777 1446; www.balticbeach.lv; Jūras iela 23/25; day-use/massages from 10/35Ls; ⊗8am-10pm) The Baltic Beach Spa is the largest treatment centre in the Baltic, with three rambling storeys full of massage rooms, saunas, yoga studios, swimming pools and Jacuzzis. The 1st floor is themed like a country barn and features invigorating hot-and-cold treatments in which one takes regular breaks from the steam room by pouring buckets of ice water over one's head à la Jennifer Beals in *Flashdance*.

Ķemeri National Park   NATURE RESERVE
(✆6714 6819; www.kemeri.gov.lv) Beyond Jūrmala's stretch of celebrity summer homes lies a verdant hinterland of sleepy fishing villages, quaking bogs and thick forests. At the

end of the 19th century Ķemeri was known for its curative mud and spring water, attracting visitors from as far away as Moscow.

🛏 Sleeping & Eating

Jūrmala has a wide selection of lodging options – very few of them are good value. If penny pinching's your game, do a day trip to Jūrmala and sleep in Rīga. Check out www.jurmala.lv for additional lodging options across a wider spectrum of wallet sizes.

Hotel MaMa   BOUTIQUE HOTEL €€€
(✆6776 1271; www.hotel mama.lv; Tirgonu iela 22; d/apt from €185/213; @☞P) The bedroom doors have thick, mattress-like padding on the interior (psycho-chic?) and the suites themselves are a veritable blizzard of white drapery. A mix of silver paint and pixie dust accent the ultramodern furnishings and amenities. If heaven had a bordello, it would probably look something like this. The in-house restaurant has a special menu for dogs (no joke), and check out the 'Adam and Eve' bathrooms with a fun surprise on the ceiling.

Orizzonte   GOURMET €€€
(www.orizzonte.lv; Baznīcas iela 2B; mains 5-19Ls) Located directly along the sandy shores in Jūrmala's Dubulti district, Orizzonte is a fantastic place to watch the sun dip below the Bay of Rīga. After dark it's all out white-cloth tabletops, candlelight and gentle strums of the guitar in the corner.

ⓘ Information

Tourism information centre (✆6714 7902; www.jurmala.lv; Lienes iela 5; ⊗9am-7pm Mon-Fri, 10am-5pm Sat, 10am-3pm Sun) Located across from Majori train station. Staff can assist with accommodation bookings and bicycle rentals.

Getting There & Away

Two to three trains per hour link central Rīga to the sandy shores of Jūrmala (0.95Ls). Take any train bound for Dubulti, Sloka or Tukums and disembark at Majori station (30 to 35 minutes). Minibuses (1.10Ls) are also a common mode of transportation. From Jūrmala catch a ride along the street at Majori train station. In Rīga, minibuses depart from the suburban minibus station (Map p472) across the street from the main entrance to the train station. Motorists driving the 15km into Jūrmala must pay a 1Ls toll per day, even if they are just passing through. Keep an eye out for the multilane self-service toll stations sitting at both ends of the resort town.

WESTERN LATVIA

Just when you thought that Rīga was the only star of the show, in comes western Latvia from stage left, dazzling audiences with a whole different set of talents. While the capital wows the crowd with intricate architecture and metropolitan majesty, Kurzeme (Courland in English) takes things in the other direction: vast expanses of austere landscapes.

It's hard to believe that desolate Kurzeme was once the bustling Duchy of Courland. During the 17th century, Duke Jakob, Courland's ruler, flexed his imperial muscles by colonising Tobago and the Gambia. He even had plans to colonise Australia! (Needless to say, that didn't quite work out...)

Cape Kolka (Kolkasrags)

Enchantingly desolate and hauntingly beautiful, a journey to Cape Kolka (Kolkasrags) feels like a trip to the end of the earth. During Soviet times the entire peninsula was zoned off as a high-security military base – the dusty road between Ventspils and Kolka was a giant aircraft runway. The region's development was subsequently stunted, and today the string of desolate coastal villages has a distinct anachronistic feel – as though they've been locked away in a time capsule.

The village of Kolka is nothing to write home about, but the windswept moonscape at the waning edge of the cape (just 1km away) could have you daydreaming for days. It's here that the Gulf of Rīga meets the Baltic Sea in a very dramatic fashion. A monument to those claimed by treacherous waters marks the entrance to the beach near a small information booth. The poignant stone slab, with its haunting anthropomorphic silhou-

ette, was erected in 2002. If you plan to stay the night, Ūši (☎2947 5692; www.kolka.info; s/d 16/22Ls, camping per person 2.50Ls), across from the Russian Orthodox church, has two simple but prim rooms and a spot to pitch tents in the flower-filled garden.

Getting There & Away

The easiest way to reach Cape Kolka is by private vehicle (adventurous types can bike), but buses are also available. To reach the town of Kolka, buses either follow the Gulf Coast Rd through Dundaga, or they ply the route through Talsi and Dundaga (inland). There are five daily buses that link Rīga and Kolka town (4Ls to 5Ls, three to four hours).

Kuldīga

POP 12,180

If Kuldīga were a tad closer to Rīga it would be crowded with day-tripping camera-clickers. Fortunately, the town is located deep in the heart of rural Kurzeme, making its quaint historic core the perfect reward for more intrepid travellers. In its heyday, Kuldīga served as the capital of the Duchy of Courland (1596–1616) and was known as the 'city where salmon fly' – during spawning season salmon would swim upstream, and when they reached Ventas Rumba (the widest waterfall in Europe) they would jump through the air attempting to surpass it.

Kuldīga was badly damaged during the Great Northern War and was never able to regain its former lustre. Today, this blast from the past is a favourite spot to shoot Latvian period-piece films – 29 movies and counting...

Kuldīga's best hotel, Hotel Metropole (☎6335 0588; Baznīcas iela 11; d/ste incl breakfast 44/50Ls; @), rolls out the red carpet up its mod concrete stairwell to charming double-decker bedrooms overlooking the town's main drag, pedestrian Liepājas iela. Long ago, guests used to receive a lady with their room – needless to say, things have changed quite a bit since then.

At Dārziņš Bakery (Baznīcas iela 15; snacks 0.10-2Ls; 8am-6pm Mon-Fri, to 3pm Sat) the cashier calculates your bill with an amber abacus. Try the sklandu rausis (0.22Ls), an ancient Cour carrot cake. Pagrabiņš (Baznīcas iela 5; mains 3-7Ls), with its charming brick alcoves and wafting '60s rock, lurks in the cellar beneath the information centre in what used to be the town's prison.

ℹ Information

ourist information centre (☎6332 2259;
www.visit.kuldiga.lv; Baznīcas iela 5; ☺9am-6pm
Mon-Sat, 10am-2pm Sun May-Aug, 9am-5pm
Mon-Fri rest of year) The helpful office in the
ld town hall provides brochures.

ℹ Getting There & Away

uses run to/from Rīga (4.10Ls to 4.70Ls, 2½ to
½ hours, 12 daily), Liepāja (2.50Ls to 2.80Ls,
¾ hours, seven daily), Ventspils (1.80Ls to 2Ls,
¼ hours, six daily) and Talsi (2.10Ls to 2.40Ls,
½ hours, four daily).

Ventspils

POP 44,000

abulous amounts of oil and shipping mon-
y have turned Ventspils into one of Latvia's
most beautiful and dynamic towns. And although locals coddle their Užavas beer and
laim that there's not much to do, tourists
will find a weekend's worth of fun in the
orm of brilliant beaches, interactive muse-
ms and winding Old Town lanes.

The city's biggest draws are state-of-the-art
museum in the 13th-century **Livonian Or-
ler Castle** (☎6362 2031; www.ventspilsmuzejs.
v; Jāṇa iela 17; adult/child 1.50/0.75Ls; ☺10am-6pm
ue-Sun), and the **House of Crafts** (☎6362
174; Skolas iela 3; admission 0.60Ls; ☺10am-6pm
ue-Fri, 10am-3pm Sat) where you can watch lo-
al artisans spin yarns (literally).

Our favourite spot to spend the night,
Kupfernams (☎6362 6999; kupfernams@inbox.
v; Kārļa iela 5; s/d 26/37Ls) sits in an inviting
wooden house at the centre of Old Town.
he cheery rooms with slanted ceilings sit
bove a fantastic restaurant and a trendy
air salon (which doubles as the front desk).
Grab a bite at **Melanis Sivēns** (Jāṇa iela 17;
meals 3-8Ls), a medieval-style restaurant on
he castle grounds.

ℹ Information

ourism information centre (☎6362 2263;
www.tourism.ventspils.lv; Dārza iela 6; ☺8am-
pm Mon-Fri, 10am-5pm Sat, 10am-3pm Sun)
ocated in the ferry terminal. Pick up the handy
Walking Routes brochure detailing four scenic
ours through town.

ℹ Getting There & Away

'entspils is served by buses to/from Rīga
4.70Ls, three to four hours, hourly), Liepāja
3.30Ls to 4.10Ls, two to three hours, six daily)
nd Kuldīga (1.80Ls to 2Ls, 1¼ hours, six daily).
here is no train service.

Scandlines (☎6779 6900; www.scandlines.
lt) runs ferries five times weekly to Nynashamn,
Sweden (60km from Stockholm) and twice
weekly to Travemünde (Rostock), Germany.
Plans are in the works to run a ferry between
Ventspils at Montu harbour on the Estonian island of Saaremaa. **Finnlines** (www.finnlines.de)
operates a twice-weekly ferry service between
St Petersburg, Russia, and Lübeck, Germany.

Liepāja

POP 84,000

For the last decade, Liepāja has been searching for its identity like an angsty teenager.
The city's growing pains are evident in the
visual clash of gritty warehouses and tricked-
out nightclubs. The local tourist office calls
Liepāja 'the place where wind is born', but
we think the city's rough-around-the-edges
vibe is undoubtedly the city's biggest draw.

Start in the Karosta district, 4km north of
the city centre, where you'll find a particularly dour collection of **Soviet tenements** min-
gling with the gilded cupolas of **St Nicholas
Orthodox Maritime Cathedral**. Daily multilingual tours lead visitors through **Karosta
Prison** (Karostas cietums; ☎2636 9470; www.
karostascietums.lv; Invalīdu iela 4; tours 2.50Ls, 2hr
shows 5.50Ls, sleepovers 8Ls; ☺10am-6pm May-
Sep, by appointment Oct-Apr), which was used
to punish disobedient Russian soldiers. Sign
up to be a prisoner for the night and subject
yourself to regular bed checks and verbal
abuse by guards in period garb. For those
only wanting a pinch of masochism, there
are abridged two-hour 'reality shows'.

You'll either adore or abhor spending a
night at **Hotel Fontaine** (☎6342 0956; www.
fontaine.lv; Jūras iela 24; r 15-35Ls; @☎P), a
funky hostelry whose reception doubles as
a secondhand knick-knack shop. The 20-
odd rooms are stuffed to the brim with rock
memorabilia, dusty oriental rugs, Soviet
propaganda and anything else deemed appropriately offbeat.

For a night out on the town, try **Latvia's
1st Rock Café** (www.pablo.lv; Stendera iela
18/20; mains 2.50-4.50Ls), a pseudo-industrial
mega-complex, or **Fontaine Palace** (www.
fontainepalace.lv; Dzirnavu iela 4), an always
open rock house luring loads of live
acts and crowds of sweaty fanatics. The
attached **Fontaine Delisnack** (mains 3-8Ls)
was designed with the inebriated partier in
mind: the burgers, nachos and pizzas are a
foolproof way to sop up those vodka shots
downed earlier in the evening.

LATVIA VENTSPILS

❶ Information

Tourist information centre (☑6348 0808;
www.liepaja.lv; Rožu laukums 5; ☉9am-7pm
Mon-Fri, 10am-6pm Sat, 10am-3pm Sun Jun–
mid-Sep, 9am-5pm Mon-Fri, 10am-3pm mid-
Sep–May) Offers walking tour maps. Can help
with accommodation bookings.

❶ Getting There & Away

Buses run to/from Kuldīga (2.50Ls to 2.80Ls,
1¾ hours, seven daily), Ventspils (3.30Ls to
4.10Ls, two to three hours, six daily) and Rīga
(5.50Ls to 6.50Ls, four hours, every 45 minutes). Liepāja and Rīga are also connected by an
infrequent train service (departing Liepāja on
Monday and Saturday).

Scandlines (☑6779 6900; www.scandlines.
lt) runs ferries twice weekly from Liepāja to
Travemünde (Rostock), Germany.

EASTERN LATVIA

When Rīga's urban hustle fades into a pulsing hum of chirping crickets, you've entered
eastern Latvia. Known as Vidzeme, or 'the
Middle Land', to locals, the country's largest
region is an excellent sampler of what Latvia
has to offer. Most tourists head to **Gauja National Park** (Gaujas nacionālais parks; www.gnp.
gov.lv), the country's oldest preserve, where
forest folks hike, bike or paddle through the
thicketed terrain, and history buffs ogle at the
generous sprinkling of castles throughout.

Sigulda

POP 10,780

With a name that sounds like a mythical ogress, it comes as no surprise that the
gateway to the Gauja is an enchanting little
spot with delightful surprises tucked behind
every dappled tree. Locals proudly call their
pine-peppered town the 'Switzerland of Latvia', but if you're expecting the majesty of
a mountainous snowcapped realm, you'll
be rather disappointed. Instead, Sigulda
mixes its own exciting brew of scenic trails,
extreme sports and 800-year-old castles
steeped in colourful legends.

◉ Sights

If you've just arrived from the train or bus
station, walk down Raina iela to linden-
lined Pils iela until you reach **Sigulda New
Castle** (Pils iela 16), built in the 18th century
during the reign of German aristocrats.
Check out the ruins of **Sigulda Medieval**

Castle (Pils iela 18) around back, which wa
constructed in 1207 by the Order of th
Brethren of the Sword, but now lies mostl
in ruins after being severely damaged dur
ing the Great Northern War.

Follow Ainas iela to the rocky precipice an
take the **cable car** (☑6797 2531; www.bungee.l
Poruka iela 14; 1-way weekday/weekend 2/2.50L
☉10am-7.30pm Jun-Aug, to 4pm May-Sep) over th
scenic river valley to **Krimulda Manor** (www
krimuldapils.lv; Mednieku iela 3), an elegant esta
currently used as a rehabilitation clinic. Visi
the crumbling ruins of **Krimulda Medieva
Castle** (Krimuldas iela) nearby, then follow th
serpentine road down to **Gūtmaņa Cav**
where you can read myriad inscription
carved into the cavern walls.

Walk up the hill to find the **Turaid
Museum Reserve** (☑6797 1402; www.turaid
-muzejs.lv; Turaidas iela 10; admission 3Ls; ☉10am
6pm May-Oct, to 5pm Nov-Apr), home to a beau
tiful 13th-century castle that was erecte
over an ancient Liv stronghold.

🏃 Activities

Extreme Sports

If you're looking to test your limits with a bev
of adrenaline-pumping activities, then you'v
come to the right place. Sigulda's 1200m ar
tificial **bobsled track** (☑6797 3813; bobtrase@
lis.lv; Šveices iela 13; ☉noon-7pm Sat & Sun) wa
built for the former Soviet bobsleigh team. I
winter you can fly down the 16-bend track a
80km/h in a five-person **Vučko tourist bo**
(ride per person 7Ls), or try the real Olympia
experience on the hair-raising **winter bo**
(ride per person 35Ls). Summer speed fiends ca
try the wheeled **summer sled** (ride per perso
7Ls) without booking in advance.

If the bobsled isn't enough to make yo
toss your cookies, take your daredevil sh
nanigans to the next level and try a 43m **bun
gee jump** (☑2921 2731; www.bungee.lv; Poruk
iela 14; Fri/weekend jumps 20/25Ls; ☉6.30pm
last jump Fri-Sun May-Oct) from the cable ca
that glides high over the Gauja River.

The one-of-a-kind **aerodium** (☑283
4400; www.aerodium.lv; 2min weekday/weeken
15/18Ls; ☉6-8pm Tue-Fri, noon-8pm Sat & Sur
is a giant wind tunnel that propels partic
pants up into the sky as though they ar
flying.

Hiking, Cycling & Canoeing

Sigulda is prime hiking territory, so brin
your *spiekis* (walking stick)! Check ou
www.sigulda.lv for a detailed list of trail
and cycling routes.

Makars Tourism Agency (☑2924 4948; www.makars.lv; Peldu iela 1) runs a campsite and arranges one- to three-day water tours round the park. Less intrepid paddlers can hire canoes and rubber boats seating between two and six people starting at 10Ls per day.

🛏 Sleeping & Eating

Click on www.sigulda.lv for additional lodging and dining options.

Livkalns B&B €
(☑6797 0916; www.livkalns.lv; Pēteralas iela; s/d from 15/25Ls) No place is more romantically rustic than this idyllic retreat next to a pond on the forest's edge. The rooms are pine-fresh and sit among a campus of adorable thatch-roof manors. The cabin-in-the-woods-style restaurant is fantastic.

Kaķu Māja LATVIAN €
(Pils iela 8; www.cathouse.lv) The 'Cat House' is the top spot around town for a cheap bite. In the **bistro** (mains from 2Ls), point to the ready-made dishes that tickle your fancy, then hunker down on one of the inviting picnic tables outside. For dessert, visit the attached bakery to try out-of-this-world pastries and pies. On Friday and Saturday nights, the restaurant at the back busts out the disco ball until the wee hours of the morning. Apartment-style **accommodation** (d 30Ls) is also available.

ℹ Information

Gauja National Park Visitors Centre (☑6780 4388; www.gnp.gov.lv; Baznīcas iela 7; ⊙9am-6pm) Can arrange tours, backcountry camping and other accommodation. Cycle and hiking trail maps also available.

Tourism information centre (☑6797 1335; www.sigulda.lv; Raiņa iela 3; ⊙10am-7pm May-Sep, to 5pm Oct-Apr) Has an internet kiosk and mountains of helpful information about activities and accommodation. Ask about the *Sigulda Spiekis* discount card.

ℹ Getting There & Around

See p491 for details on travelling to/from Rīga. Buses also run between Sigulda and Cēsis (1.40Ls, 45 minutes).

Sigulda's attractions are quite spread out; bus 12 links all of the sights, and plies the route seven times daily (more on weekends). Bus times are posted at the stations and on the info centre's official website.

Cēsis
POP 17,700

Cēsis' unofficial moniker, 'Latvia's most Latvian town', pretty much holds true, and day trippers will be treated to a mosaic of quintessential country life – a stunning Livonian castle, soaring church spires, cobbled roads and a lazy lagoon – all wrapped up in a bow like an adorable adult Disneyland.

In 1209 the Knights of the Sword founded the fairytale-like **Cēsis Castle** (Cēsu pils) with its two stout towers at the western end. To enter, visit **Cēsis History & Art Museum** (Cēsu Vēstures un mākslas muzejs; Pils laukums 9; admission 3Ls; ⊙10am-5pm Tue-Sun) in the adjoining 18th-century 'new castle' painted salmon pink.

Province (☑6412 0849; www.provincecesis.viss.lv; Niniera iela 6; d from 30Ls) pops out from the surrounding Soviet-block housing with its cute, celery-green facade. The rooms are simple and spotless, and there's a cafe on ground floor slinging a variety of international eats.

ℹ Information

Tourist information centre (☑6412 1815; www.tourism.cesis.lv; Pils laukums 9; ⊙10am-6pm Jun-Aug, to 5pm Sep-May) Pick up a map, check email or arrange bike rentals.

ℹ Getting There & Away

See p491 for details on travelling to/from Rīga. Buses also run between Cēsis and Sigulda (1.40Ls, 45 minutes).

UNDERSTAND LATVIA

History
The Beginning

The first signs of modern people in the region date back to the Stone Age, although Latvians descended from tribes that migrated to the region around 2000 BC. Eventually, four main Baltic groups evolved: the Selonians, the Letts (or Latgals), the Semigallians and the Cours. The latter three lent their names to Latvia's principal regions: Latgale, Zemgale and Kurzeme. The country's fourth region, Vidzeme (Livland), borrowed its name from the Livs, a Finno-Ugric people unrelated to the Balts.

A Piece of the European Puzzle

In 1201, at the behest of the Pope, German crusaders conquered Latvia and founded Rīga. They also founded the Knights of the Sword, and made Rīga their base for subjugating Livonia. Colonists from northern Germany followed, and during the first period of German rule Rīga became the major city in the German Baltic, thriving from trade between Russia and the West, and joining the Hanseatic League (a medieval merchant guild) in 1282.

The 15th, 16th and 17th centuries were marked with battles and disputes about how to divvy up what would one day become Latvia. After a 'golden' period of Swedish rule, the Russians conquered the area during the Great Northern War (1700–21) and held the former fiefdom for two centuries.

A Taste of Freedom

Out of the post-WWI confusion and turmoil arose an independent Latvian state, declared on 18 November 1918. By the 1930s, Latvia had achieved one of the highest standards of living in all Europe. Initially, the Soviets were the first to recognise Latvia's independence, but the honeymoon didn't last long. Soviet occupation began in 1939 with the Molotov–Ribbentrop Pact. Nationalisation, killings and mass deportations to Siberia followed. Latvia was occupied partly or wholly by Nazi Germany from 1941 to 1945, during which time an estimated 175,000 Latvians were killed or deported.

Soviet Rule

When WWII ended, the Soviets marched back in claiming to 'save' Latvia from the Nazi invaders. A series of deportations and mass killings began anew as the nation was forced to adapt to communist ideology. The first public protest against Soviet occupation was on 14 June 1987, when 5000 people rallied at Rīga's Freedom Monument to commemorate the 1941 Siberia deportations. On 23 August 1989, two million Latvians, Lithuanians and Estonians formed a 650km human chain from Vilnius, through Rīga, to Tallinn, to mark the 50th anniversary of the Molotov–Ribbentrop Pact. Although an all-important Moscow coup failed in 1991, the attempt rocked the Soviet just enough for Latvia to finally break free.

Looking Towards Today

The country declared independence on 2 August 1991 and on 17 September 1991 Latvia, along with its Baltic brothers, joined the UN. After a game of prime minister roulette and a devastating crash of the country's economy, Latvia finally shook off its antiquated Soviet fetters, and on 1 May 2004 the EU opened its doors to the fledgling nation.

Latvia registered the highest economic growth in the EU from 2004 to 2007, which later proved to be a curse when the national bank imploded during the so-called Global Economic Crisis. The nation is proudly (but slowly) marching back towards stability, but a recent shift in politics might be the prelude to a strengthening trade relationship with Russia rather than the EU.

The People of Latvia

Casual hellos on the street aren't common but Latvians are a friendly and welcoming bunch. Some will find that there is a bit of guardedness in the culture, but this caution, most likely a response to centuries of foreign rule, has helped preserve the unique language and culture through changing times. Today, Latvians readily embrace the changes in their globalising country – classic hipster trappings are worn like uniforms of some world-wise army; locals even have their own version of Facebook. Although you'll mostly hear either Latvian or Russian, most locals do speak a fair bit of English – especially the younger generations.

Most Latvians are members of the Lutheran Church, although ancient pagan traditions still influence daily life. These pre-Christian beliefs are centred on nature-related superstition, and although they seem incongruous when juxtaposed with Christian ideals, Latvians have done a good job of seamlessly uniting the two. Midsummer's Day, or Jāņi as it's commonly known, is the most popular holiday in Latvia. The solstice was once a sunlit night of magic and sorcery, and today everyone flocks to the countryside for an evening of revelry.

Of Latvia's 2.27 million citizens, only 60% are ethnically Latvian. Russians account for 29% of the total population and make up the ethnic majority in most major cities, including the capital. Unlike Latvians, they are mostly members of the Roman Catholic, Old Believer and Orthodox churches.

The Land That Sings

Latvians often wax poetic about their country, calling it 'the land that sings'. It seems to be in the genes; locals are blessed with unusually pleasant voices, and their canon of traditional tunes is the power source for their indomitable spirit. Latvians (along with their Baltic brothers) literally sang for their freedom from the USSR in a series of dramatic protests known as the 'Singing Revolution' and today the nation holds the Song and Dance Festival, which unites thousands upon thousands of singers from across the land in splendid harmony.

In 2003 the Song and Dance Festival was inscribed on Unesco's list of 'Oral and Intangible Heritage of Humanity' masterpieces.

Latvia's Dining Scene

For centuries in Latvia, food equalled fuel, energising peasants as they worked the fields, and warming their bellies during bone-chilling Baltic winters. Today, the era of boiled potatoes and pork gristle has begun to fade, as food becomes more than a necessary evil. Although it will be a few more years before globetrotters stop qualifying local restaurants as being 'good by Latvia's standards', the cuisine scene has improved by leaps and bounds over the last couple of years.

Lately the Slow Food movement has taken the country by storm. Seasonal menus feature carefully prepared, environmentally conscious dishes using organic produce grown in Latvia's ample farmland. Beyond the sphere of upmarket eats, many joints still embrace the literal sense of the term 'slow food', with tortoise-speed service.

As the country's dining scene continues to draw its influence from a clash of other cultures, tipping is evolving from customary to obligatory. A 10% gratuity is common in the capital, and many restaurants are now tacking the tip onto the bill.

SURVIVAL GUIDE

Directory A–Z
Accommodation

Expect to pay up to 25Ls (€35) for a budget double room; figure between 5Ls and 10Ls for a dorm bed. You'll spend between 25Ls

(€35) to 50Ls (€75) for something in the mid-range category, and big spenders will drop upwards of 50Ls (€75) on top-end digs. We highly advise booking ahead during summer. Prices listed here for the high season; rates drop significantly in the colder months.

All rooms in this chapter are en suite unless otherwise stated. Most hotels in Latvia have a mix of smoking and nonsmoking accommodation.

Visit www.hotels.lv for more info about Latvia's hospitality industry. Check out www.camping.lv for details on pitching a tent.

Business Hours

Standard business hours are 10am to 6pm Monday to Friday and 10am to 5pm Saturday, though many shops tend to stay open until 7pm or later. Smoking is prohibited in all indoor public venues including restaurants and bars.

Restaurants and cafes Open daily around 11am or noon and close at 11pm.

Bars Open daily around 11am or noon and close at midnight from Sunday to Thursday and at around 3am on Friday and Saturday.

Clubs Venues start filling up at 11pm and close around 6am from Wednesday to Saturday. In warmer months you'll often find that clubs are open from Sunday to Tuesday as well.

Embassies & Consulates

The following embassies are in Rīga:

Australia (☑6722 4251; Tomsona iela 33-1)

Belarus (☑6732 5321; www.belembassy.org/latvia; Jēzusbaznīcas 12)

Canada (☑6781 3945; www.latvia.gc.ca; Baznīcas iela 20/22)

Estonia (☑6781 2020; www.estemb.lv; Skolas iela 13)

France (☑6703 6600; www.ambafrance-lv.org; Raiņa bulvāris 9)

Germany (☑6708 5100; www.riga.diplo.de; Raiņa bulvāris 13)

Ireland (☑6703 9370; www.embassyofireland.lv; Alberta iela 13)

Lithuania (☑6732 1519; www.lv.mfa.lt; Rūpniecības iela 24)

Netherlands (☑6732 6147; www.netherlandsembassy.lv; Torņa iela 4)

Russia (☑6733 2151; www.latvia.mid.ru; Antonijas iela 2)

Sweden (☎6768 6600; www.swedenabroad.com/riga; Pumpura iela 8)

UK (☎6777 4700; www.ukinlatvia.fco.gov.uk/en; Alunāna iela 5)

USA (☎6703 6200; www.riga.usembassy.gov; Raiņa bulvāris 7)

Festivals & Events

Latvians enjoy any excuse to party, especially during the summer months. Check out www.culture.lv for a yearly listing of festivals and events across the country. Latvia's biggest event, the **Song and Dance Festival**, is held every five years. It was last held in 2008.

Food

Price ranges are: budget (€; under 5Ls), mid-range (€€; 5Ls to 10Ls) and top end (€€€; over 10Ls).

Holidays

The website of the **Latvia Institute** (www.li.lv) has a page of special Latvian remembrance days.

New Year's Day 1 January

Easter in accordance with the Western Church calendar

Labour Day 1 May

Restoration of Independence of the Republic of Latvia 4 May

Mothers' Day second Sunday in May

Whitsunday a Sunday in May or June in accordance with the Western Church

Līgo & Jāņi 23 & 24 June; St John's Day & Summer Solstice festival

National Day 18 November; anniversary of proclamation of Latvian Republic, 1918

Christmas Holiday 24-26 December

New Year's Eve 31 December

Internet Access

Almost all accommodation in Rīga offers some form of internet access. Hotels in smaller cities have been doing a good job of following suit. Internet cafes are a dying breed, as many restaurants, cafes and bars now offer wireless connections.

Lattelecom (www.lattelecom.lv), Latvia's main communications service provider, has set up wi-fi beacons at every payphone around the city. Users can access the internet from within a 100m radius of these phone booths. To register for a Lattelecom password and username, call ☎9000 4111, or send an SMS with the word 'WiFi' to ☎1188

Money

Latvia's currency, the lats, was introduced in March 1993. The lats (Ls) is divided into 100 santīms. The national bank, **Latvijas Bankas** (Latvian Bank; www.bank.lv), posts the lats' daily exchange rate on its website. Many of Rīga's hotels publish their rack rates in euros. Although Estonia has ascended to the euro, Latvia still has quite a way to go.

Post

Latvia's official postal service website (www.post.lv) can answer any of your mail-related questions, including shipping and stamp prices. Service is reliable; mail to North America takes 10 days and within Europe about a week.

Telephone

Latvian telephone numbers have eight digits; landlines start with '6' and mobile (cell) numbers start with '2'. To make any call within Latvia, simply dial the eight-digit number. To call a Latvian telephone number from abroad, dial the international access code, then the country code for Latvia (371) followed by the subscriber's eight-digit number.

Telephone rates are posted on the website of the partly state-owned **Lattelecom** (www.lattelecom.lv), which enjoys a monopoly on fixed-line telephone communications in Latvia.

Mobile phones are available for purchase at most shopping malls around Rīga and other major cities. If your own phone is GSM900-/1800-compatible, you can purchase a prepaid SIM-card package and top-up credit from any Narvesen superette or Rimi grocery store. The most popular plan is **ZZ by Tele2** (Tele-divi; www.tele2.lv; SIM-card 0.99Ls).

Calls on a public phone are made using cardphones called *telekarte,* which come in different denominations and are sold at post offices, newspaper stands and superettes.

Visas

Holders of EU passports do not need a visa to enter Latvia; nor do Australian, Canadian, New Zealand and US citizens, if staying for less than 90 days. For information on obtaining visas (and seeing if you need one), visit www.mfa.gov.lv/en.

Getting There & Away

Air

Rīga airport (Lidosta Rīga; ☎1187; www.riga-air port.com), about 13km southwest of the city centre, houses Latvia's national carrier, airBaltic (☎9000 1100; www.airbaltic.com), which offers direct flights to more than 50 destinations within Europe including Amsterdam, Berlin, Brussels, Copenhagen, Helsinki, Oslo, Rome, Stockholm and Vienna.

Other carriers with year-round direct flights to Rīga include:

Aeroflot (☎6724 0228; www.aeroflot.lv)

Aerosvit (☎6720 7502; www.aerosvit.com)

Belavia (☎6732 0314; www.belavia.by)

City Airline (www.cityairline.com)

Czech Airlines (☎6720 7636; www.czechair lines.lv)

Finnair (☎6720 7010; www.finnair.com)

LOT (☎6720 7113; www.lot.com)

Lufthansa (☎6750 7711; www.lufthansa.com)

Norwegian (www.norwegian.no)

Ryanair (www.ryanair.com)

Tarom (www.tarom.ro)

Turkish Airlines (☎6721 0094; www.turkish airlines.com)

Uzebkistan Airways (☎6732 4563; www. uzairways.com)

Wizz Air (☎9020 0905; www.wizzair.com)

Land

In 2007 Latvia acceded to the Schengen Agreement, which removed all border control between Estonia and Lithuania. Carry your travel documents with you at all times, as random border checks do occur.

BUS

See p491 for details.

CAR

Rental cars are allowed to travel around the Baltic at no extra fee. See p492 for details.

TRAIN

Several train routes link Rīga to destinations in other countries; see p492 for details.

SEA

Latvia is connected to a number of destinations by sea. See p491 for details on services to/from Rīga, and p491 for details on services to/from Ventspils.

Getting Around

Bus

Buses are much more convenient than trains if you're travelling beyond the capital's clutch of suburban rail lines. Updated timetables are available at www.1188.lv. See p491 for more details.

Car & Motorcycle

Driving is on the right-hand side. Headlights must be on at all times. Be sure to ask for 'benzene' when looking for a petrol station – gāze means 'air'.

You'll find the usual suspects when it comes to renting a vehicle; however, several small businesses in Rīga offer cheaper options than the international companies at the airport – expect cash-only transactions and free delivery anywhere in the capital. Rentals range from €30 to €60 per day, depending on the type of car and time of year. The number of automatic cars in Latvia is limited. Companies usually allow you to drive in all three Baltic countries but not beyond.

AddCar Rental (☎2658 9674; www.addcar rental.com)

Auto (☎2958 0448; www.carsrent.lv)

EgiCarRent (☎2953 1044; www.egi.lv)

Train

Most Latvians live in the large suburban ring around Rīga, hence the city's network of commuter rails makes it easy for tourists to reach day-tripping destinations. Latvia's further attractions are best explored by bus. All train schedule queries can be answered at www.1188.lv.

Lithuania

Includes »

Why Go?

The Baltic countries have a reputation for their dour ways, but this image fades when you enter rebellious Lithuania, a country blessed with boundless energy and studded with reminders of its turbulent history.

It may be a dot on Europe's map, but that didn't stop Lithuania from becoming a mighty empire in the 1400s, its territory extending beyond Kursk in the east and all the way to the Black Sea in the south. Even today Lithuanians brim with pride and confidence befitting their mighty heritage.

From the baroque spires and effortless charm of Vilnius' vibrant streets and the ancient ruins of Kernavė to the ghostly sand dunes of the Curonian Spit and the lakes and forests of the southeast, Lithuania has it all. More and more travellers are making their way to this tiny country with an earthy vibe, where pagan roots run deep and Catholic passion lives on.

Best Places to Stay

» Palanga Hotel (p516)
» Narutis (p501)
» Miško Namas (p521)
» Litinterp Guesthouse (p518)

Best Places to Eat

» Борщ! (p502)
» Ararat (p518)
» Lokys (p503)

When to Go
Vilnius

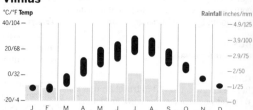

April Some of the world's best jazz performers are at the Kaunas International Jazz Festival.

June & July Partake in the pagan Midsummer festival, with in Kernavė.

September Vilnius City Days, a celebration of the capital with street theatre, music and fashion.

Connections

Buses, trains and ferries provide numerous travel options to Lithuania's neighbouring countries.

Vilnius is a hub for buses to Poland, Latvia, Estonia, Belarus and Russia's Kaliningrad; from Kaunas there are buses to Latvia, Estonia and Kaliningrad, and the latter may also be reached from Klaipėda and the Curonian Spit.

Trains serve Russia, Poland and Belarus from the capital, but there are no rail connections to Latvia or Estonia. Sweden and Germany can be reached by ferry from Klaipėda, Lithuania's international port.

ITINERARIES

Three Days

Devote two days to exploring the baroque heart of Vilnius, then day-trip to Trakai for its spectacular island castle and the homesteads of the Karaite people, stopping off at Paneriai on the way.

One Week

Spend four nights in Vilnius, with day trips to both Trakai and the Soviet sculpture park near Druskininkai. Travel cross-country to Šiauliai and the Hill of Crosses, then spend two or three days exploring some serious nature on the Curonian Spit. Head back east via Klaipėda and Kaunas.

Essential Food & Drink

» **Potato creations** Try the *cepelinai* (potato dough zeppelin stuffed with meat, mushrooms or cheese), *bulviniai blynai* (potato pancakes), *žemaičių blynai* (heart-shaped mashed potato stuffed with meat and fried), or the *vedarai* (pig intestine stuffed with potato).

» **Beer snacks** No drinking session is complete without a plate of smoked pigs' ears and *kepta duona* (deep-fried garlicky breadsticks).

» **Beetroot delight** Cold, creamy *šaltibarščiai* (beetroot soup) is a summer speciality, served with a side of fried potatoes.

» **Unusual meat** Try the game specialities, such as beaver stew and bear sausages.

» **Smoked fish** A Curonian Spit speciality; the *rukytas unguris* (smoked eel) is particularly good.

» **Beer and mead** Šytutys, Utenos and Kalnapilis are top beers; *midus* (mead) is a honey-tinged nobleman's drink.

AT A GLANCE

» **Currency** litas (Lt)

» **Language** Lithuanian

» **Money** ATMs all over

» **Visas** Not required for citizens of the EU, Australia, Canada, Israel, Japan, New Zealand, Switzerland or the US

Fast Facts

» **Area** 65,303 km

» **Capital** Vilnius

» **Telephone country code** 370

» **Emergency** 112

Exchange Rates

Australia	A$1	2.54Lt
Canada	C$1	2.44Lt
euro	€1	3.45Lt
Japan	¥100	2.85Lt
New Zealand	NZ$1	1.87Lt
UK	UK£1	3.87Lt
USA	US$1	2.32Lt

Set Your Budget

» **Budget hotel room** 180Lt

» **Two-course meal** 50Lt

» **Museum entrance** 5Lt

» **Beer** 8Lt

» **Bicycle hire (per day)** 40Lt

Resources

» **In Your Pocket** (www.inyourpocket.com)

» **Lithuania's Museums** (www.muziejai.lt)

» **Tourism in Lithuania** (www.tourism.lt)

VILNIUS

POP 544,200

Vilnius, the baroque bombshell of the Baltics, is a city of immense allure. As beautiful as it is bizarre, it easily tops the country's best-attraction bill, drawing tourists to it with a confident charm and a warm, golden glow that makes one wish for long, midsummer evenings every day of the year.

At its heart is Europe's largest baroque Old Town, so precious that Unesco added it to its World Heritage list in 1994. Its skyline, pierced by (almost) countless Orthodox and Catholic church steeples, appears like a giant bed of nails from the basket of a hot-air balloon. Adding to the intoxicating mix is a combination of cobbled alleys, hilltop views, breakaway states and traditional artists' workshops.

Vilnius feels tiny, but that's a bit deceptive because the suburban sprawl that surrounds Old Town is a fairly typical Soviet-style

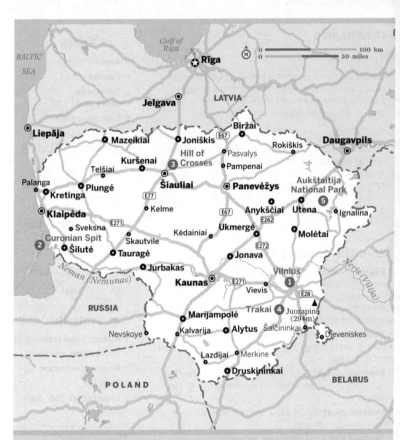

Lithuania Highlights

1 Explore beautiful baroque **Vilnius** (p494) with its cobbled streets, skyline of church spires, and bars and bistros

2 Breathe the pure air within the fragrant pine

forests and high sand dunes of the enchanting **Curonian Spit** (p519)

3 Hear the wind breathe between the thousands of crosses on the eerie **Hill of Crosses** (p514) in Šiauliai

4 Wander wonderful **Trakai** (p507), home of the Karaite people and a stunning island castle

5 Berry-pick, bathe and boat in **Aukštaitija National Park** (p509)

Spend your first day taking in the magic of the **Old Town**. Start off at the **Gate of Dawn**, then spend a few hours snaking your way towards **Cathedral Sq**. Climb **Gediminas Hill** for sunset, and crown the day with a meal at **Lokys**.

On day two, devote some time to the **Museum of Genocide Victims** and explore the old **Jewish quarter**. Then cross the Vilnia River into bohemian **Užupis**, where another fine sunset panorama beckons at **Tores**.

LITHUANIA

mess of snarled traffic, car dealerships and concrete.

History

Legend has it that Vilnius was founded in the 1320s when Lithuanian Grand Duke Gediminas dreamt of an iron wolf that howled with the voices of 100 wolves – a sure sign to build a city as mighty as their cry. In fact, the site had already been settled for 1000 years.

Despite the threat of attacks from the Teutonic Knights and Tatars, Vilnius prospered during the Middle Ages and by the end of the 16th century it was among Eastern Europe's biggest cities. It became a key Jewish city by the 18th century and an isolated pocket of Poland after WWI, but WWII rang the death knell for its Jewish population.

Soviet rule scarred Vilnius' skyline with residential high-rises, but since independence it has fast become a modern European city. In 1994 its Old Town became a Unesco World Heritage site.

◎ Sights

Vilnius is a compact city, and most sights are easily reached on foot. Those visiting for a couple of days will scarcely move out of the Old Town, where souvenir stalls, folk-artist workshops and designer boutiques jostle for attention with a treasure trove of architectural gems. Stay a couple more days and the New Town – with its museums, shops and riverside action – beckons.

GEDIMINAS HILL & CATHEDRAL SQUARE

Gediminas Hill   LANDMARK

Vilnius was founded on 48m-high Gediminas Hill, topped since the 13th century by the oft-rebuilt **Gediminas Tower**. There are spectacular views of the Old Town from the top of the tower, which houses the **Upper Castle Museum** (adult/child 5/2Lt; ⊘10am-7pm) containing medieval arms and exhibits on Lithuania's 1990 proclamation of inde-

pendence, reached by **funicular** (adult/child 3/2Lt; ⊘10am-7pm) located at the rear of the Museum of Applied Arts. From here you'll also see the white **Three Crosses** on a hill to the east, erected in memory of three crucified monks.

Cathedral Square   HISTORIC AREA

At the base of Gediminas Hill sprawls Cathedral Sq (Katedros aikštė), dominated by **Vilnius Cathedral** (⊘7am-7.30pm, mass Sun 8am, 9am, 10am, 11.15am & 6.30pm) and its 57m-tall **belfry**, a Vilnius landmark. The square buzzes with local life, especially during Sunday morning mass. Amuse yourself by hunting for the secret *stebuklas* (miracle) tile; if found it can grant you a wish if you stand on it and turn around clockwise. It marks the spot where the 650km Tallinn–Vilnius human chain, protesting against Soviet rule, ended in 1989.

The first wooden cathedral, built here in 1387–88, was in Gothic style but has been rebuilt many times since then. The most important restoration was completed from 1783 to 1801, when the outside was redone in today's classical style. The interior retains more of its original aspect. Its showpiece is the baroque **St Casimir's Chapel**, with white stucco sculptures and frescos depicting the life of St Casimir (Lithuania's patron saint), whose silver coffin lies within.

Museum of Applied Arts   MUSEUM

(www.ldm.lt; Arsenalo gatvė 3a; adult/student 6/3Lt; ⊘11am-6pm Tue-Sat, 11am-4pm Sun) The Museum of Applied Arts, in the old arsenal at the foot of Gediminas Hill, houses temporary exhibitions, such as the treasures of Gediminas Palace, alongside a permanent collection showcasing 15th- to 19th-century Lithuanian sacred art. Much of it was discovered in Vilnius cathedral only in 1985, after being hidden in the walls by Lithuanian soldiers in 1655 after Vilinus was about to be stormed by Russian soldiers.

Central Vilnius

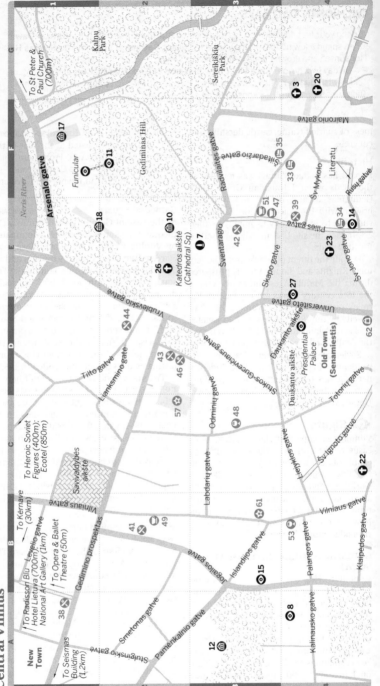

New Town

To Radisson Blu Lietuva (700m); Levelio gatve (1km); Hotel Lietuva (700m); National Art Gallery

To Kernave (30km)

To Opera & Ballet Theatre (50m)

To Seismas Building (1.2km)

To Heroic Soviet Figures (400m); Ecotel (850m)

Noris River

Arsenalo gatve

Kalnų Park

To St Peter & Paul Church (700m)

Sereikiškių Park

Gediminas Hill

Funicular

Katedros aikštė (Cathedral Sq)

Šventaragio

Vrublevskio gatve

Tilto gatve

Liamksmino gatve

Smetonas gatve

Stuflinskio gatve

Paměnkalinio gatve

Gedimino prospektas

Vilniaus gatve

Savivaldybes aikšte

Odminių gatve

Strikos-Gucevičiaus gatve

Labdariu gatve

Islandijos gatve

Jogelios gatve

Palangos gatve

Klaipedos gatve

Kalinausko gatve

Vilniaus gatve

Lietuvkos gatve

Šv Ignoto gatve

Totoriu gatve

Daukanto aikšte

Presidential Palace

Daukanto aikšte

Universiteto gatve

Skapo gatve

Pilies gatve

Šv Jono gatve

Old Town (Senamiestis)

Radvilaites gatve

Šiltadarzio gatve

Maironio gatve

Šv Mykolo

Rusu gatve

Literatų

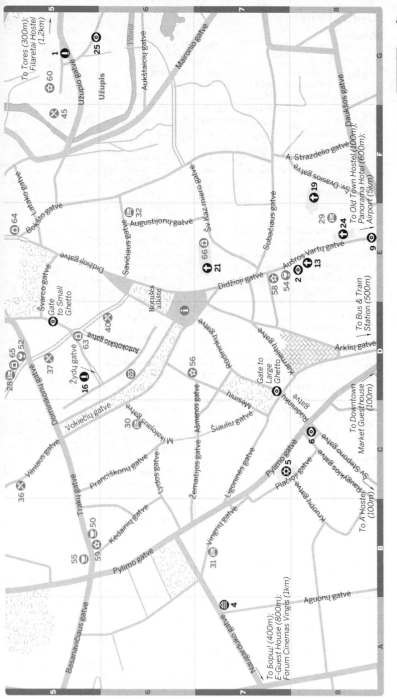

497

LITHUANIA

To Tores (300m);
Filaretai Hostel
(1.2km)

1

25

60

45

Užupis

Užupio gatve

Aukštaičių gatve

Maironio gatve

Vilnia

A. Strazdelio gatve

To Old Town Hostel (100m);
Daukšos gatve
Panorama Hotel (600m);
Airport (5km)

Šv. Dvasios gatve

19

29

24

9

Aušros Vartų gatve

13

2

54

58

Subačiaus gatve

Šv. Kaz miero gatve

66

21

Didžioji gatve

Augustijonų gatve

32

Savičiaus gatve

Latako gatve

Bokšto gatve

64

Didžioji gatve

Rotušes
aikšte

i

To Bus & Train
Station (500m)

Arklių gatve

Svarco gatve

Gate to Small
Ghetto

Antokolskio gatve

40

Žydų gatve

63

16

28

65

52

37

Dominikonų gatve

Vilniaus gatve

36

Karmelitų gatve

Gate to
Large
Ghetto

Rūdninkų gatve

Mesinu

56

Rudninku gatve

Asmenos gatve

Žemaitijos gatve

M Kailojaus gatve

30

Vokiečių gatve

Lydos gatve

Prancišconų gatve

Trakų gatve

50

55

59

Kedamų gatve

Pylimo gatve

To Downtown
Market Guesthouse
(100m)

Šv Stepono gatve

Pylimo gatve

5

6

Plačioji gatve

Kniopų gatve

To A Hostel (100m);
To Daugyklos gatve
Downtown
Market Guesthouse
(100m)

Šiaulių gatve

Ligonnes gatve

Vingrių gatve

31

Pylimo gatve

Basanavičaus gatve

Naugarduko gatve

4

Aguonų gatve

To Борис! (400m);
E Guest House (800m);
Forum Cinemas Vingis (1km)

National Museum of Lithuania MUSEUM
(www.lnm.lt; Arsenalo gatvė 1; adult/child 5/2Lt;
⏱10am-5pm Tue-Sat, 10am-3pm Sun) Sitting
stoically nearby, the National Museum of
Lithuania is guarded by a proud statue of
Mindaugas, the first and only king of Lithuania. Inside are exhibits looking at Lithuanian ethnographic and cultural life from
the 13th century to WWII, including some
superb temporary exhibitions.

Gediminas Palace PALACE
At the square's eastern end is an **equestrian
statue of Gediminas**, built on an ancient
pagan site. Behind it stands the **Royal Palace** (Valdovų rumai), which buzzed with
masked balls, gay banquets and tournaments in the 16th century. But in 1795 the
Russians occupied Lithuania and demolished the palace along with the Lower Castle
and city defence wall.

Having been rebuilt brick by brick, this palace of incredible dimensions has risen from the ashes to mark the millennium anniversary of the first mention of Lithuania in writing. Renovations of the interior won't be completed until June 2011, after which the palace will house a museum with displays detailing the reconstruction project and a treasure trove of Gothic and baroque archaeological finds – ceramics, glassware, weaponry and jewellery – discovered during the excavation work and currently on display at the Museum of Applied Arts.

St Peter & Paul Church   CHURCH

(Antakalnio gatvė 1; ☉6.30am-7pm) East of Cathedral Sq, magnificent St Peter & Paul Church is one of Vilnius' finest baroque churches. It's a treasure trove of sparkling white stucco sculptures of real and mythical people, animals and plants, with touches of gilt, paintings and statues. The decoration was done by Italian sculptors between 1675 and 1704.

OLD TOWN

Eastern Europe's largest Old Town deserves its Unesco status. The area stretches 1.5km south from Cathedral Sq and the eastern end of Gedimino prospektas.

Vilnius University   HISTORIC BUILDING

(www.vu.lt; Universiteto gatvė 3; adult/student 5/1Lt; ☉9.30am-5.30pm Mon-Sat) The students of Vilnius University attend classes on a spectacular campus featuring 13 courtyards framed by 15th-century buildings and splashed with 300-year-old frescos.

Founded in 1579 during the Counter-Reformation, Eastern Europe's oldest university was run by Jesuits for two centuries and became one of the greatest centres of Polish learning before being closed by the Russians in 1832. It reopened in 1919.

The library here, with five million books, is Lithuania's oldest and may be visited only with a guide. The university also houses the world's first Centre for Stateless Cultures (www.statelesscultures.lt/eng/apie.php), established for those cultures that lack statehood, such as Jewish, Roma and Karaimic (Karaite) cultures, in its history faculty.

You need to go through the university entrance on Universiteto gatvė (and pay the admission fee) to access St John's Church (☉10am-5pm Mon-Sat), a baroque gem. It was founded in 1387 – well before the university arrived – and its 17th-century bell tower is the highest structure in Old Town.

Gate of Dawn   HISTORIC BUILDING

Located at the southern border of the Old Town, the 16th-century Gate of Dawn (Aušros Vartai) is the only one of the town wall's original nine gates still intact. The gate houses the Chapel of the Blessed Virgin Mary (☉6am-7pm, mass 9am Mon-Sat, 9.30am Sun) and the black-and-gold 'miracle-working' Virgin Mary icon. A gift from the Crimea by Grand Duke Algirdas in 1363, it is one of the holiest icons in Polish Catholicism, and the faithful arrive in droves to offer it whispered prayer. Look up as you're exiting the Old Town and you can spot the icon through the window of the chapel.

Churches   CHURCH

There are four stunning churches in the immediate vicinity of the Gate of Dawn. Catholic St Teresa's Church (Aušros Vartų gatvė 14) is early baroque (1635–50) outside with a predominantly rococo interior. Roughly behind it is the big, pink, domed 17th-century Orthodox Church of the Holy Spirit (Aušros Vartų gatvė 10), Lithuania's chief Russian Orthodox church and another fine baroque specimen. Directly across the street, through a late baroque archway known as the Basilian Gates (Aušros Vartų gatvė 7), is the dilapidated Holy Trinity Church. And further up Aušros Vartų gatvė, on the eastern side, is ravishing St Casimir's Church (Aušros Vartų gatvė), the oldest of Vilnius' baroque masterpieces. It was built by Jesuits (1604–35) and under Soviet rule was a museum of atheism.

Pilies gatvė   NOTABLE STREET

Cobbled Pilies gatvė – the hub of tourist action and the main entrance to the Old Town from Cathedral Sq – buzzes with buskers, souvenir stalls and the odd beggar. At No 26 stands the House of Signatories (admission 2Lt; ☉10am-5pm Tue-Sat, 10am-3pm Sun), where the act granting Lithuania independence in 1918 was signed.

Vokiečių gatvė   NOTABLE STREET

Vokiečių gatvė, the Old Town's main commercial street, makes a good jumping-off point for explorations of the old Jewish quarter (see boxed text p501); it offers fine views of several churches. Peering north from Vokiečių you'll spot St Catherine's Church (Vilniaus gatvė 30), displaying Vilnius' trademark peach baroque style.

VILNIUS' WACKY STATUES

Peruse Vilnius' statues – don't pass over the chance to see the world's first **Frank Zappa memorial** (Kalinausko gatvė 1), the oversized **egg statue** (cnr Šv Stepono & Raugyklos gatvė) on a nest of real twigs, or the **heroic Soviet figures** (Kalvarijų gatvė) symbolising Youth, Labour and Military Glory along Green Bridge. In the breakaway republic of Užupis, marvel at the trumpet-blowing **Angel** (Užupio gatvė).

UŽUPIS

The cheeky streak of rebellion that pervades Lithuania flourishes in this district, located just east of the Old Town. In 1998 the resident artists, dreamers, squatters and vagabonds declared the district a breakaway state known as the **Užupis Republic**. The state has its own tongue-in-cheek president, anthem, flags and a 41-point **Užupis Republic constitution** that, among other things, gives inhabitants the right to cry, the right to be misunderstood and the right to be a dog. Read the entire thing in nine languages on a wall on Paupio gatvė.

The best time to visit Užupis is April Fool's Day. Mock border guards set up at the main bridge into town and stamp visitors' passports and a huge party rages all day and all night. However, it's worth visiting any time of year for its galleries, craft workshops and bohemian vibe.

Just over Užupis' northern bridge you'll find baroque **Bernardine Church** and pint-sized Gothic **St Anne's Church**, essentially fused together like mismatched Siamese twins.

NEW TOWN

TOP CHOICE **Museum of Genocide Victims**
MUSEUM
(www.genocid.lt/muziejus; Aukų gatvė 2a; adult/child 6/3Lt, audioguide 10Lt; ⊙10am-6pm Wed-Sat, to 5pm Sun) Called the 'KGB Museum' by locals, the building facing the square used to be the notorious KGB headquarters and prison from 1940 to 1991. The detailed exhibits deal with the Soviet oppression of the Lithuanian people, the post-WWII Lithuanian resistance movement and the mass deportation of locals to Siberia.

However, there is almost no mention of the fact that this was also the Gestapo headquarters between 1941 and 1944, or of their role in the genocide of much of the city's Jewish population.

Names of those who were murdered in the prison are carved into the stone walls outside – note how young many victims were. Inside, inmate cells and the execution cell where prisoners were shot or stabbed between 1944 and the 1960s can be visited.

Gedimino prospektas NOTABLE STREET
Vilnius' 19th-century New Town boasts a true European boulevard in Gedimino prospektas. It's a grand road with Vilnius Cathedral at one end and the silver-domed **Church of the Saint Virgin's Apparition** (A Mickevičiaus 1) at the other. Much of Gedimino becomes a pedestrian street outside working hours, when fashionable types flock here to see, be seen and peruse the sundry Western brands on display in the shop fronts.

National Art Gallery ART GALLERY
(www.ndg.lt; Konstitucijos gatvė 22; adult/child 6/3Lt; ⊙noon-7pm Tue, Wed, Fri & Sat, 1-8pm Thu, noon-5pm Sun) North of Gedimino prospektas, across the river, the cubelike building houses some of the best work by Lithuanian artists from the 20th and 21st century within its spacious, minimalist interior. Excellent temporary exhibitions are held in the basement.

Seimas NOTABLE BUILDING
At the west end of Gedimino prospektas is the **Seimas** (parliament) building. Further along lies pleasant **Vingis Park**, and beyond that the 326m-tall **TV Tower** (Sausio 13-osios gatvė 10; adult/child 21/9Lt; ⊙observation deck 10am-10pm), where wooden crosses remember the victims of 13 January 1991, killed by Soviet tanks. Take trolleybus 1, 3, 7 or 16 to the Televizijos Bokštas stop.

✷ Festivals & Events

A comprehensive list of festivals is at www.vilniusfestivals.lt.

Lygiadienis PAGAN
Pagan carnival marking spring equinox, held in March.

Vilnius Festival MUSIC
Classical music, jazz and folk concerts in Old Town courtyards in June.

Vilnius City Days ARTS
Music, performing arts and fashion festival, the beginning of September.

🛏 Sleeping

For tips on booking accommodation in Vilnius, see p523.

Narutis   LUXURY HOTEL €€€
(☑5-212 2894; www.narutis.com; Pilies gatvė 24; r/ste from 470/746Lt; ❄@☎P) Impossibly stylish and beautiful hotel in an impeccable central location combines 16th-century frescoes and wooden beams with touches of modern decadence, such as the spa and the *hamam* (Turkish bath) in some suites. Impeccable service and a restaurant serving expertly prepared international dishes complete the experience.

Domus Maria   GUEST HOUSE €€
(☑5-264 4880; www.domusmaria.lt; Aušros Vartų gatvė 12; s/d/tr/q 250/300/329/369Lt; @P) Positively unique and immensely popular, this guest house within a monastery captures the soul of Vilnius without capturing too much of your hard-earned cash. It stays true to its monastic origins with wide-arched corridors and spartan white rooms.

Jimmy Jumps House   HOSTEL €
(☑60788235; www.jimmyjumpshouse.com; Savičiaus gatvė 12-1; dm from 37Lt; d without bathroom 110Lt; @☎) Word is spreading fast about the Canadian-owned newcomer on the hostel scene in a superb central location.

The free walking tour, themed pub crawls, Machine Gun Tour and free breakfast more than make up for the modest-sized dorms.

Litinterp   B&B €
(☑5-212 3850; www.litinterp.lt; Bernardinų gatvė 7-2; s/d/tr without bathroom 80/140/180Lt, with bathroom 100/160/210Lt, apt 280Lt; ☺office 8.30am-7pm Mon-Fri, 9am-3pm Sat) This bright, clean and friendly establishment has a wide range of options in the heart of the Old Town. Rooms with shared bathroom can be a little cramped, but those with en suite are generously large. Guests can check in after office hours providing they give advance notice.

Apia Hotel   HISTORIC HOTEL €€
(☑5-212 3426; www.apia.lt; Sv Ignoto gatvė 12; s/d/tr 136/150/182Lt; @☎P) This smart, friendly, family-run hotel may be housed in a restored 17th-century building in the heart of the Old Town, but its facilities are truly modern. There is satellite TV and wi-fi access in each of the nine rooms and you can choose courtyard or cobbled-street views.

Hotel Rinno   HOTEL €€
(☑5-262 2828; www.rinno.lt; Vingrių gatvė 25; s/d from 260/320Lt; @☎P) Rinno is tops – its staff are exceptionally helpful and polite; its rooms are first rate; its location, between the

---

JEWISH VILNIUS

Dubbed by Napoleon the 'Jerusalem of the north', Vilnius had one of Europe's most prominent Jewish communities until Nazi brutality wiped it out (with willing assistance from the ethnic Lithuanian communities).

The old Jewish quarter lay in the streets west of Didžioji gatvė, including present-day Žydų gatvė (Jews St) and Gaono gatvė, named after Vilnius' most famous Jewish resident, Gaon Elijahu ben Shlomo Zalman (1720–97), a sage who could recite the entire Talmud by heart at the age of six.

A good place to start your tour is the **Centre for Tolerance** (www.jmuseum.lt; Naugarduko gatvė 10; adult/child 5/2Lt; ☺10am-6pm Mon-Thu, 10am-4pm Fri & Sun), a beautifully restored former Jewish theatre that houses thought-provoking historical displays and occasional art exhibitions. The **Holocaust Museum** (Pamėnkalnio gatvė 12; adult/child 5/2Lt; ☺9am-5pm Mon-Thu, 9am-4pm Fri, 10am-4pm Sun), in the so-called Green House, is a moving museum detailing the horror suffered by Lithuanian Jews in an 'unedited' display of horrific images and letters. Nearby, the **Jewish Community of Lithuania** (www.litjews.org; Pylimo gatvė 4; admission free; ☺10am-5pm Mon-Fri) is another source of information – pick up a copy of the country's only Jewish newspaper, *Jerusalem of Lithuania*, here.

Vilnius' only remaining synagogue, the **Choral Synagogue** (Pylimo gatvė 39; donations welcome; ☺10am-2pm Sun-Fri), was built in a Moorish style in 1903 and survived only because the Nazis used it as a medical store.

For a more casual glimpse of Jewish life, walk down Žydų gatvė to the **memorial bust of Gaon Elijahu** (Žydų gatvė 3), imagining how life once was. There's a map of the two main Jewish ghettos during WWII at Rūdninkų gatvė 18, which used to be the single gate to the largest ghetto.

Old Town and the train and bus stations, is handy; and its price is a bargain. Breakfast is served in the pleasant, and private, backyard.

Shakespeare BOUTIQUE HOTEL €€€
(☎5-266 5885; www.shakespeare.lt; Bernardinų gatvė 8/8; s/d from 363/600Lt; ❄@) Striving to be the best of boutique hotels, Shakespeare is a refined Old Town gem that evokes a cultured, literary feel with its abundance of books, antiques and flowers. Each room pays homage to a different writer – in name and design.

Downtown Market Guesthouse B&B €
(☎67985476; www.downtownmarket.lt; Pylimo gatvė 57; r from 190Lt; 📶) Located next to the downtown market, this refurbished little guest house has just six individually decorated doubles, from the pink 'Flea Market' to the lime-green 'Flower Market'. The staff are friendly, the location is very central and the filling breakfast is made from organic produce.

Hostelgate HOSTEL €
(☎63832818; www.hostelgate.lt; Mikalojaus gatvė 3; dm 39-42Lt, d/tr 110/140Lt;@) Under a new name, this central little hostel is still a grand choice for travellers where the owner goes out of his way to make the guests feel welcome. There's free internet access, tea, coffee and lockers, but no breakfast (there is a kitchen).

Radisson Blu Hotel Lietuva BUSINESS HOTEL €€€
(☎5-272 6272; www.radissonblu.com/lietuvahotel-vilnius; Konstitucijos prospektas 20; s/d/ste from 410/480/830Lt; ❄@) The burly, bustling, 22-storey Radisson Blu is the antidote to Vilnius' plethora of quaint boutique hotels, with well-appointed business-class rooms, the best casino in Vilnius and a rare fitness centre that's worthy of the name. The top-floor SkyBar has the city's best views.

Filaretai Hostel HOSTEL €
(☎5-215 4627; www.filaretaihostel.lt; Filaretų gatvė 17; dm/s/d without bathroom 34/70/100Lt;@📶) This chilled-out hostel occupies a quaint old villa in Užupis. It's clean and quiet, and there's a laundry and kitchen for guest use. Take bus 34 from the bus station to the Filaretų stop.

E-Guest House GUEST HOUSE €€
(☎5-266 0730; www.e-guesthouse.lt; Ševčenkos gatvė 16; s/d/tr from 200/228/280Lt;@) Gleaming white, inside and out, this professional hotel has a fitness hall and sauna among other perks. It's a little out of the centre but real value for money. Breakfast is an extra 8Lt, and guests receive a 20% discount at the restaurant next door.

Ecotel BUSINESS HOTEL €
(☎5-210 2700; www.ecotel.lt; Slucko gatvė 8; s/d/tr 100/197/211Lt; ❄@) In a quiet part of town, Ecotel is a steal, with simple but smart furnishings filling its squeaky-clean rooms, in which bathrooms have heated towel rails. There is a computer with free internet access in the lobby as well.

Panorama Hotel HOTEL €€
(☎5-273 8011; www.hotelpanorama.lt; Sodų gatvė 14; s/d from 298/330Lt;@P) The somewhat shabby Soviet-era chocolate-brown tiled facade of this hotel near the train station hides a bright, stylish and airy interior. An added bonus is the fabulous view of the Old Town.

Old Town Hostel HOSTEL €
(☎5-268 5967; www.oldtownhostel.lt; Aušros Vartų gatvė 20-15a; dm 35Lt, d/tr without bathroom 110/144Lt;@📶) Perfect location near the Old Town and the train station, with kitchen facilities but little atmosphere.

A Hostel HOSTEL €
(☎5-215 0270; www.ahostel.lt; Šv Stepono gatvė 15; 10-/6-bed dm 34/48Lt, s/d 107/120Lt;@📶) Modern, squeakier than squeaky-clean hostel near the train station.

Eating

Whether it's curry, *cepelinai* (gut-busting meat and potato zeppelins) or *kepta duona* (fried bread sticks oozing garlic) you want, Vilnius has a mouthwatering selection of local and international cuisine.

Борщ! UKRAINIAN €
(Algirdo gatvė 5-2; mains 11-25Lt) This bright new Ukrainian restaurant somehow manages to combine traditional flavours with a minimum of stodge. The menu is not extensive, but everything – from the superb signature borsch, to the sweet and savoury *pelmeni* and *vareniki* (dumplings), to the meat dishes – is innovatively prepared with great attention to both taste and presentation. Wash it down with the sublime homemade *kvas* (a mildly alcoholic drink made from fermented bread).

Lokys LITHUANIAN €€
(Stiklių gatvė 8; mains 24-58Lt) Dine like a medieval noble at one of Vilnius's best-loved cellar restaurants. The game dishes range from the traditional – such as quail in blackberry sauce and venison carpaccio – to the unusu-

al (beaver stew, and 'cold noses'; blueberry dumplings), but all are superbly prepared. The herbal wine makes a fine accompaniment to any meat dish.

Sue's Indian Raja
INDIAN €€

(Odminių gatvė 3; mains 22-48Lt) Whoever said that you need to go to Britain (or India) for a proper curry? Loved by expats and visitors alike, this fine eating establishment next door to the Indian embassy serves large portions of expertly flavoured Indian dishes, such as the sublime butter chicken, and there's a good range of veg options. If they claim that a dish is spicy, trust them!

Bistro 18
INTERNATIONAL €€

(Stiklių gatvė 18; mains 25-44Lt) Bistro 18 is a breath of fresh air in Vilnius' restaurant scene. The service is friendly, polite and attentive, the decor is minimalist yet comfortable, the food is imaginative, international and flavoursome, and the wine list features bottles from as far away as the Antipodes. At around 26Lt, the lunch menu is a bargain and the homemade meatballs are superb.

Tres Mexicanos
MEXICAN €

(Tilto gatvė 2; mains 18-28Lt) Like a ray of sunshine in the bleak Baltic winter, this cheerful little Mexican-run restaurant with a jolly yellow interior packs some proper heat with a selection of authentically spicy enchiladas, tacos and burritos. This may the best stop for *mole poblano* this side of the Atlantic. Veg dishes available.

Balti Drambliai
VEGETARIAN €

(Vilniaus gatvė 41; mains 10-17Lt) The 'White Elephant' whips up a vegan and veggie storm, offering pancakes, pizzas, Indian curries and tofu-based dishes to hungry (and mostly dreadlocked) non-meat-eaters. Its lively courtyard is also good for a drink, and its cavernous basement hosts reggae and raga gigs at weekends.

Zoe's Bar & Grill
INTERNATIONAL €€

(Odminių gatvė 3; mains 25-58Lt) A restaurant can't always get away with trying to cover too many culinary bases. Zoe's, however, manages to pull it off, with the likes of fabulous tender steaks and spicy Thai stir-fries and soups. The staff are delightful.

Forto Dvaras
LITHUANIAN €

(Pilies gatvė 16; mains 22-24Lt) Perpetually popular folk-themed restaurant that's in danger of turning its patrons into something visually resembling its signature dish, the *cepelinai*. It's among the best in the city, as are

There are few eateries in bohemian Užupis, but most of them are noteworthy. Mountain lodge-style **Tores** (Užupio gatvė 40; mains 27-50Lt) has good international food and atmosphere, but the main reason to come is for the stunning panorama of Gediminas Castle and the cathedral across the Vilnia River valley.

Užupio Kavinė (Užupio gatvė 2; mains 17-43Lt), right on the river as you enter Užupis, doubles as the republic's headquarters and is a legendary spot known for its arty clientele and good cheap breakfasts. Ask the bartender for a copy of the Užupis constitution in English.

the potato pancakes and the *šaltibarščiai* (beetroot soup).

Kalvarijų market
MARKET €

(Kalvarijų gatvė 61; ⏱7am-5pm Tue-Sun) Fresh fruit, honey, smoked eel and other cheap staples located north of the Neris River.

Pomodoro
ITALIAN €

(Jogailos gatvė 4; mains 15-22Lt) Inexpensive, generous portions of delicious pizza and pasta.

Soprano
ICE CREAM €

(Pilies gatvė 3) Get lickin' with fruit-topped *gelato Italiano* by the cone (4Lt).

Čili Pica
PIZZA €

(Gedimino prospektas 23; mains 19-35Lt) The ubiquitous pizza chain spread far and wide in Lithuania.

Supermarkets are everywhere: **Iki** (Sodų gatvė 22, bus station) and **Maxima** (Mindaugo gatvė 11; ⏱24hr) are leading chains.

Drinking

Vilnius' riotous party culture centres on clubs in the cold months and outdoor cafes in the summer. At weekends, many cafes turn into clubs and many restaurants turn into raucous bars.

Cozy
CAFE

(Dominikonų gatvė 10) Cozy has been a hot address in Vilnius for years and will probably continue to be so for years to come. It has something for everyone; street level is a lounge-style cafe–restaurant with a chef who cooks until late, while local DJs spin tunes downstairs to a discerning crowd from Thursday to Saturday.

AJ Šokoladas
CAFE

(Pilies gatvė 8) Pick a selection of chocolates, lovingly made in Trakai, indulge in a cup of decadently thick molten chocolate, or sample a selection of delectable cakes. The brandy-infused chocolate cake with marzipan is heaven on a plate.

In Vino
WINE BAR

(Aušros Vartų gatvė 7) This is the bar of the moment, with one of the loveliest courtyards in the city. Excellent wines, expensive tapas (25Lt to 45Lt) and a few mains. Arrive early in summer to secure a table, then watch the place fill to overflowing.

Franki Pub
PUB

(Vilniaus gatvė 37) Serving up live blues and folk music by night, and hosting international acts during the Singers-Songwriters' Festival, this intimate, candlelit pub fills up early at weekends. The food is nothing special, but the atmosphere more than makes up for it.

SkyBar
BAR

(Konstitucijos prospektas 20) It may look – and feel – like an airport lounge, but nothing can beat the panoramas of this dangerously popular bar on the 22nd floor of the Radisson Blu Hotel Lietuva. DJs spin tunes on Friday and Saturday.

Būsi Trečias
BEER HALL

(Totorių gatvė 18) Microbrewery that brews hit-and-miss beer (the almond-flavoured one is a mistake you'll only make once) but with a raucous beer-hall atmosphere. Popular with locals and beginning to appear on pub-crawl lists.

Skonis ir Kvapas
TEA HOUSE

(Trakų gatvė 8) Heaven for tea connoisseurs, this stylish courtyard cafe knows how to make a great cuppa. Choose from around 100 teas from across the globe and a sublime array of creamy homemade cakes.

Coffee Inn
COFFEE HOUSE

(Vilniaus gatvė 17) The Lithuanian answer to Starbucks offers freshly made wraps, cookies and excellent grilled vegetable sandwiches. There are also branches at Trakų gatvė 7, Gedimino prospektas 9 and Pilies gatvė 3.

☆ Entertainment

In Your Pocket (www.inyourpocket.com) publishes a list of movie theatres as well as listings for opera, theatre, classical music and other big events. Most such venues close for the summer. The tourist offices also post events listings.

The tourist office publishes events listings, as does the *Baltic Times* (www.baltic times.com), a local English-language paper.

Cinemas

Mostly popular Hollywood films are screened in English with Lithuanian subtitles at the 12-screen **Forum Cinemas Vingis** (www.forumcinemas.lt; Savanorių prospektas 7).

Performing Arts

Opera & Ballet Theatre
OPERA

(☑5-262 0727; www.opera.lt; Vienuolio gatvė 1) Classical productions in a grand, gaudy building near the river.

National Philharmonic
CLASSICAL MUSIC

(☑5-266 5233; www.filharmonija.lt; Aušros Vartų gatvė 5) The country's most renowned orchestras perform here.

Lithuanian National Drama Theatre
THEATRE

(www.teatras.lt; Gedimino Prospektas 4) This theatre stages national and international productions in Lithuanian.

Nightclubs

Vilnius has a thriving nightlife. Expect cover charges on most nights and gorillas on the doors.

Pabo Latino
CLUB

(www.pabolatino.lt; Trakų gatvė 3) This sultry-red club specialises in live Latin music and strong cocktails. Put on your dancing shoes, fortify your liver, and be prepared for a fun night out with some of the city's most beautiful people.

Brodvėjus
LIVE MUSIC

(www.brodvejus.lt; Mėsinių gatvė 4) The place to come for occasionally good live bands and cheesy tunes, or a quieter drink upstairs. It's hugely popular with older expats, students, local lookers and travel-guide writers.

Stopkė
CLUB

(Užupio gatvė 2a) A ramshackle artwork of a place, this irreverent art gallery turns into a live music space by night, favoured by the alternative and arty crowd. Find it next to the most colourful building in Užupis, by the river.

Soho
GAY & LESBIAN

(www.sohoclub.lt; Švitrigailos gatvė 7/16) Since Men's Factory went largely straight, this is now the main haunt for Vilnius' gay community. Leap into the limelight on the stage or the dance floor, or chill out in one of the mini halls or the mirrored VIP balcony.

Woo

CLUB

(www.woo.lt; Vilniaus gatvė 22) Escape the mainstream at Woo, a basement club below Radvilos' Palace, with a young, alternative crowd. Resident DJs spin drum'n'bass, techno and funk to a backdrop of VJ art, and jazz sessions occasionally fill the space.

🛍 Shopping

Amber (often described as 'Baltic gold') and linen are two commodities worth tracking down in Lithuania. The Old Town's main thoroughfare, running from Pilies gatvė to Aušros Vartų gatvė, is something of a bustling craft market/tourist trap, with its fair share of stores selling both amber and linen.

Aldona Mickuvienė

WOVEN GOODS

(Žydų gatvė 2-10) Colourful wedding sashes woven in the neighbouring workshops. Buy a readymade sash or order one with your name on it. Each sash takes a full day or more to weave.

Linen & Amber Studio

SOUVENIRS

(www.lgstudija.lt; Pilies gatvė 10) An excellent selection of both amber and linen articles and very helpful staff.

Lino Namai

LINEN

(www.siulas.lt; Pilies gatvė 38) An extensive range of linen creations for the home and the body.

Ona

CRAFTS

(Šv Kazimiero gatvė 12) Stocks a range of original, ecologically friendly jewellery, paintings and other crafts produced by small-scale local artists.

Akademinė Knyga

BOOKS

(Universiteto gatvė 4) Some translated Lithuanian works, small foreign literature section, and Lonely Planet travel guides.

Mint Vinetu

BOOKS

(Šv Ignoto gatvė 16/10) The largest selection of English-language titles in Vilnius.

ℹ Information

Internet Access

A growing number of cafes, restaurants and hotels have free wi-fi zones; check www.wifi.lt for more information.

Collegium (Pilies gatvė 22-1; per hr 6Lt; ⊘8am-8pm)

Taškas (Jasinskio gatvė 1/8; per hr 5Lt; ⊘24hr)

Left Luggage

Ask for the *bagažinė* (left-luggage room).

Bus station (per bag per 12hr 3Lt; ⊘5.30am-9pm Mon-Sat, 7am-8pm Sun)

Train station (per bag per 12hr 3-6Lt; ⊘24hr)

Medical Services

Baltic-American Medical & Surgical Clinic (☎234 2020; www.bak.lt; Nemenčinės gatvė 54a; ⊘24hr) English-speaking health care inside Vilnius University's Antakalnis hospital, northeast of town.

Main pharmacy (Gedimino Vaistinė, Gedimino prospektas 27; ⊘8am-10pm Mon-Fri, 10am-5pm Sat & Sun)

Money

Vilnius is littered with ATMs and banks, and most offer the usual exchange, money transfer, travellers cheques and cash-advance services. Many are concentrated on Vokiečių gatvė.

Keitykla Exchange (Parex Bankas; www.keitykla.lt; Geležinkelio gatvė 6; ⊘24hr) Currency exchange with ATM near the train station. Parex Bankas is Lithuania's Amex representative.

Post

Branch post office (Vokiečių gatvė 7)

Central post office (Gedimino prospektas 7)

Tourist Information

Vilnius tourist information centre (www.vilnius-tourism.lt; ⊘9am-6pm Mon-Fri, 10am-4pm Sat & Sun) Town Hall (☎5-262 6470; Didžioji gatvė 31); train station (☎5-269 2091); Vilniaus gatvė (☎5-262 9660; Vilniaus gatvė 22) Friendly centres with a wealth of glossy brochures and general information. They also give out the free *Vilnius Visitor's Guide*, arrange tour guides and book accommodation (hotel reservation fee of 6Lt applies).

ℹ Getting There & Away

Air

For information on air transport to and from Lithuania, see p525.

Bus

From the **bus station** (☎1661; Sodų gatvė 22), **Eurolines** (☎5-233 5277; www.eurolines.lt), **Ecolines** (☎5-262 0020; www.ecolines.net) or one of the affiliated smaller carriers run services to the following international destinations:

Berlin via Riga and Tallinn 310Lt, 34 hours, four daily

Kaliningrad 65Lt, 7½ hours, daily

Moscow 156Lt, 16 hours, daily

Rīga 60Lt, 4½ hours, at least four daily

St Petersburg 153Lt, 16 hours, four daily

Tallinn 116Lt, 10½ hours, up to five daily

Warsaw 59Lt, nine hours, one daily

DOMESTIC BUSES FROM VILNIUS

DESTINATION	COST (LT)	DURATION (HR)	FREQUENCY
Druskininkai	30	2	10 daily
Kaunas	25	1¾	2-3 hourly
Klaipėda	64	4-5½	15 daily
Palanga	69	4¼-6	7 daily
Šiauliai	47	3	up to 12 daily

There are a couple of weekly buses from Vilnius to Kyiv and a handful of Western European cities, including London and several German cities.

Car & Motorcycle

The big international car-rental agencies are well represented at Vilnius airport. Try **Avis** (☏5-232 9316; www.avis.lt) or **Budget** (☏5-230 6708; www.budget.lt). You'll save a ton of money by renting from a local operator. Charismatic **Rimas** (☏69821662) rents older cars at the lowest rates in town.

Train

From the **train station** (☏5-233 0088; www.litrail.lt; Geležinkelio gatvė 16), Vilnius is linked by regular direct trains to the following international destinations. Note that you'll need a Belarus visa for the Moscow train; for Warsaw, a change in Šeštokai is required.

Moscow 185Lt, 14¾ to 15¾ hours, up to three daily

St Petersburg from 146Lt, 13½ to 18 hours, twice daily

Kaliningrad from 84Lt, 6½ to 7½ hours, up to five daily

Minsk from 74Lt, four to 4½ hours, up to seven daily

Warsaw from 130Lt, 8½ hours, one daily

You can lumber from Vilnius to a few domestic destinations:

Kaunas 15Lt, 1 to 1¾ hours, up to 17 daily

Klaipėda 51.20Lt, 4 ½ to five hours, three daily

Šiauliai 34.80Lt, 2½ hours, three daily

Ignalina (14Lt, 1½ to 1 ¾ hours, six daily)

Trakai (6.20Lt, 35 minutes, up to nine daily)

ⓘ Getting Around

To/From the Airport

Vilnius International Airport (☏5-273 9305; www.vno.lt; Rodūnios Kelias 2) lies 5km south of the centre. Bus 1 runs between the airport and the train station; bus 2 runs between the airport

and the northwestern suburb of Šeškinė. A shuttle train service runs from the train station every 30 minutes between 6.30am and 7.30pm (2Lt).

A taxi from the airport to the city centre should cost around 50Lt.

BICYCLE VeloCity (☏5-261 2671; www.velo -city.lt; Bernardinų gatvė 10; ⊙10am-7pm) rents bicycles for 10/40Lt per hour/day, provides information on cycling routes and arranges biking tours of the city. The one-hour city tour is free, while the four-hour tour costs 50Lt. There's a 15% discount for ISIC card holders.

CAR & MOTORCYLE There are numerous guarded paid car parks around town. Avoid parking on unlit streets overnight; car break-ins are on the increase.

PUBLIC TRANSPORT Unless you're heading well out of the Old Town, you won't have much need for public transport in Vilnius. Tickets for buses, trams and trolleybuses cost 2Lt at news kiosks and 2.50Lt direct from the driver; punch tickets on board in a ticket machine or risk a 60Lt on-the-spot fine.

TAXI Taxis officially charge 4Lt per kilometre and must have a meter. Drivers often try to rip tourists off, especially if flagged down on the street. You can phone a taxi (☏1409, 1411, 1818, 1445, no prefix needed), or queue up at one of the numerous taxi ranks. Popular spots are outside the train station and at the southern end of Vokiečių gatvė.

AROUND VILNIUS

A fairytale castle and ancient castle mounds lie within easy reach of the capital. You can also take the sombre trip to Paneriai.

Paneriai

Between July 1941 and August 1944, the Nazis, aided by Lithuanian accomplices, exterminated 100,000 people, around 70,000 of whom were Jewish, at this site, 10km southwest of central Vilnius.

From the entrance a path leads to the small **Paneriai Museum** (☑68081278; Agrastų gatvė 17; ☉9am-5pm Wed-Sat). Nearby are two monuments – one Jewish (marked with the Star of David), the other one Soviet (an obelisk topped with a Soviet star).

Paths lead from here to grassed-over pits where the Nazis burnt the exhumed bodies of their victims to hide the evidence of their crimes.

There are nearly two dozen trains daily from Vilnius to Paneriai station (2Lt, eight to 11 minutes). From the station, it's a 1km walk southwest along Agrastų gatvė into the forest to reach the site.

Trakai

POP 5400

With its red-brick fairytale castle, Karaite culture, quaint wooden houses and pretty lakeside location, Trakai is a must-see within easy reach of the capital.

The Karaite people are named after the term *Kara,* which means 'to study the scriptures' in both Hebrew and Arabic. The sect originated in Baghdad and practises strict adherence to the Torah (rejecting the rabbinic Talmud). In around 1400 the grand duke of Lithuania, Vytautas, brought about 380 Karaite families to Trakai from Crimea to serve as bodyguards. Only 60 remain in Trakai today and their numbers – about 280 in Lithuania – are dwindling rapidly.

This area has protected status as the **Trakai Historical National Park** (www.seniejitrakai.lt). The **tourist information centre** (☑528-51934; www.trakai.lt; Vytauto gatvė 69; ☉9am-5pm Mon, to 6pm Tue-Fri, to 3pm Sat & Sun) sells maps, books accommodation, and has information on fishing, sailing, scuba diving, horse riding and a range of other activities.

◉ Sights

Karaimų gatvė 30 is a beautifully restored early 19th-century **Kenessa** (prayer house) of the Karaites, which is often closed. The ruins of Trakai's **Peninsula Castle**, built from 1362 to 1382 by Kęstutis and destroyed in the 17th century, are near the Sacral Art Exhibition.

Island Castle   HISTORIC BUILDING

(www.trakaimuziejus.lt;   adult/student   &   child 12/6Lt, camera 4Lt;   ☉10am-7pm May-Sep) Trakai's trophy piece is the fairytale Island Castle, occupying a small island in Lake Galvė. A footbridge links the Island Castle to the shore. The red-brick Gothic castle, painstakingly restored from original blueprints, dates from the late 14th century when Prince Kęstutis, father of Vytautas, once ruled the area. Vytautas completed what his father started in the early 1400s and died in the castle in 1430. In summer the castle courtyard is a magical stage for concerts and plays.

Trakai History Museum   MUSEUM

(www.trakaimuziejus.lt;   adult/student   &   child 12/6Lt, camera 4Lt;   ☉10am-7pm May-Sep) The museum branch inside the castle's cellars and tower tells the history of the castle, and has hoards of coins, weaponry and some interactive displays.

The museum has two other branches in town. The **Sacral Art Exhibition** (Kestučio gatvė 4; adult/student & child 4/2Lt), which was closed for renovation at the time of research, houses a small but very fine collection of precious reliquaries and monstrances. The **Karaite Ethnographic Exhibition** (Karaimų etnografinė paroda; Karaimų gatvė 22; adult/student & child 4/2Lt, camera 4Lt, guided tour 30Lt; ☉10am-6pm Wed-Sun) provides a good introduction to the fascinating Karaite culture.

WORTH A TRIP

EUROPOS PARKAS

Hooked on modern art? Fancy seeing the works of some of the world's leading artists in an innovative setting? Then look no further; the **Europos Parkas sculpture park** (www.europosparkas.lt; ☉10am-sunset; adult/student/child 21/14/7Lt; guided tour 100Lt) is located only 19km from Vilnius, at the geographical centre of Europe.

The open-air art gallery comprises almost 100 sculptures by the likes of Sol LeWitt and Dennis Oppenheim. You can visit the exhibits either on foot or by bicycle, which you can rent at the entrance.

To get here, take trolleybus 5 from the Vilnius bus station towards Žirmūnai and alight at the Žalgirio bus stop. Then take the bus marked 'Skirgiškės' (4Lt, 30 minutes, up to four daily) and tell the driver to drop you off at the entrance to the park.

🛏 Sleeping

Kempingas Slėnyje　　CAMPING GROUND €
(☎528-53380; www.camptrakai.lt; Slėnio gatvė 1; adult/car/tent 20/8/20Lt, summer house for 3 people 100Lt, d/tr/q without bathroom 80/100/110Lt, cottage for 2-6 people 220-300Lt, d in guest house 170Lt) This sublime complex, popular with Lithuanian families, is 5km out of Trakai on the northern side of Lake Galvė. Pitch your tent by the lake or stay in wooden cabins or the spectacular guest house with lakeside balconies. Activities include horse riding, biking, canoeing and hot-air balloon rides.

Trakai National Sports & Health Centre
　　　　　　　　　　　　　　SPORTS CENTRE €
(Trakų Poilsio ir pramogų centras; ☎528-55501; sportocentras@mail.lt; Karaimų gatvė 73; s/d 120/140Lt) Rooms here are basic but big and clean, and half have wonderful lakeside views. There's also a decent eatery with huge terrace attached overlooking the lake, as well as boats, canoes and pedalos for hire and a lakeside sauna.

🍴 Eating

There are two good options for trying out Karaite food – especially *kibinai*, meat-stuffed pastries that are similar to empanadas.

Kibininė (Karaimų gatvė 65; kibinai 3.80-7Lt) has a dreamy location right on the lake and features venison *kibinai*, while **Kybynlar** (Karaimų gatvė 29; mains 18-34Lt) has a more Turkic feel. The writing on the wall is in the endangered Karaim language.

Buy picnic supplies at **Iki** (Vytauto gatvė 56), opposite the tourist information centre.

Getting There & Away

Up to nine daily trains (6.20Lt, 35 minutes) travel between Trakai and Vilnius. Trakai's bus station (closer to the castle than the train station) is served by frequent Alytus-bound buses (5.60Lt, 40 minutes, twice hourly).

Kernavė

Deemed an 'exceptional testimony to some 10 millennia of human settlements in this region' by Unesco, which made it a World Heritage site in 2004, Kernavė is the 'Pompeii of Lithuania' and a must-see. Thought to have been the spot where Mindaugas (responsible for uniting Lithuania for the first time) celebrated his coronation in 1253, the rural cultural reserve comprises five old hill fort mounds and the archaeological remains of a medieval town.

The fascinating heritage of the **Kernavė Cultural Reserve** (Kernavės kultūrinio rezervato; www.kernave.org; admission free; ⊙dawn-dusk) can be explored in the **Archaeological & Historical Museum** (Archeologijos ir istorijos muziejus; ☎382-47385; Kerniaus gatvė 4a) after May 2011, when it reopens following extensive renovations. **Guided tours** (per person 20Lt; ⊙10am-5.30pm Tue-Sat Apr-Oct) of the area are still available by prior arrangement, otherwise the area is free to explore at your leisure.

You can light bonfires, honour the setting sun and wash yourself in morning dew (deemed to have magical powers) during the overnight **Dew Feast** on 23 June, or take part in medieval fun and frolics – axe throwing, catapulting, mead making, knight tournaments, music making and so on – during the three-day **International Festival of Experimental Archaeology** in mid-July.

To reach Kernavė, 35km northwest of Vilnius in the Neris Valley, follow the road through Dūkštos from Maisiagala on the main road north to Ukmergė or take a bus from Vilnius (12Lt, one hour, up to five daily; fewer on weekends).

EASTERN & SOUTHERN LITHUANIA

The mythical forests and famous spas of eastern and southern Lithuania make easy day trips from Vilnius – although outdoor enthusiasts should not hesitate to spend more time here camping, cross-country skiing, canoeing, hiking, bird-watching or berry-picking.

Aukštaitija National Park

Lithuania's first national park (founded in 1974) is a 400-sq-km wonderland of rivers, lakes, centuries-old forests and tiny villages still steeped in rural tradition. Around 70% of the park comprises pine, spruce and deciduous forests, inhabited by elk, deer, wild boar, storks and white-tailed and golden eagles. Its highlight is a network of 126 lakes, the deepest being Lake Tauragnas (60.5m deep).

The park is mainly for lovers of the outdoors, with nine fully equipped campsites located by the lakes, and biking, canoeing, kayaking and parachute jumping among the activities on offer. However, there are also ome cultural attractions, including several ettlements that are protected ethnograph-c centres. For those interested in getting deeper under the skin of this enchanting area, the **Aukštaitija National Park Office** (☎386-53135, 386-47478; www.anp.lt; ☺9am-6pm Mon-Sat) in Palūšė, 5km away from Ignalina, has everything you need to know, including park maps (17Lt) and free internet access. The **tourist office** (☎386-52597; www. gnalinatic.lt; Ateites gatvė 23; ☺8am-6pm Mon-Fri, 10am-3pm Sat) in Ignalina, the main gateway own to the park, can also help with information and accommodation.

To get here jump on a train from Vilnius o Ignalina (14Lt, 1½ to 1¾ hours, six daily); from there one morning bus travels to Palūšė (2.70Lt, Friday to Monday).

Druskininkai

POP 24,755

Druskininkai, 130km south of Vilnius, is Lithuania's most famous health resort. In recent years it has gained notoriety as he home of the Soviet sculpture museum known as Grūto Parkas (p510), somewhat controversial due to its kitsch re-creation of a concentration camp and fondness for communist memorabilia.

People have been taking in the incredibly salty waters in this leafy riverside town since the 18th century. Today there's a mix of both Soviet-style and more modern treatments to be had if you're in the mood for pampering. The magical powers of local mineral water can be tested at the Dzūkija Fountain inside he **Mineralinio Vandems Biuvetė** near the Nemunas River, or not far north at the **Fountain of Beauty** (Grožio šaltinis) – one slurp of the shockingly salty water promises eternal beauty. The **tourist information cen-**

tre (www.info.druskininkai.lt) former train station (☎313-60800; Gardino gatvė 3; ☺8.15am-5.15pm Mon-Fri) town centre (☎313-51777; Čiurlionio gatvė 65; ☺10am-6.45pm Mon-Sat, 10am-5pm Sun) can help you out with accommodation and information on the town's dozens of spas, including the brand-new **Aqua Park** (www. akvapark.lt). An excellent **camping ground** (☎313-60800; Gardino gatvė 3a; ☺May-Oct) with tents (25Lt) and cabins (120Lt) is next door to the train station information centre.

There are up to 10 daily buses between Druskininkai and Vilnius, and hourly buses to/from Kaunas (30Lt, two hours).

CENTRAL LITHUANIA

Most view Lithuania's nondescript interior as little more than something you need to cross to get to the west coast or Latvia, but it does offer a few worthwhile diversions, including the country's signature tourist attraction, the Hill of Crosses in Šiauliai.

Kaunas

POP 352,279

Kaunas, a sprawling city on the banks of the Nemunas River, has a compact Old Town, an array of artistic and educational museums, and a rich history all of its own. Its sizeable student population provides it with plenty of vibrant, youthful energy, and its rough edges give it that extra bit of spice lacking in many of Lithuania's provincial towns and urban expanses.

The capital of Lithuania in the dark days between the two world wars, Kaunas is enjoying a renaissance of sorts as Ryanair has made the city its Lithuanian hub, although

---

DON'T MISS

GRŪTO PARKAS

Chances are you've come to Druskininkai to see the **sculpture park** (www.grutoparkas. lt; adult/6-15yr 20/10Lt, audioguide 46Lt; ☺9am-8pm), 8km west of town in the village of Grūtas. The park has been an enormous hit since it opened to much fanfare in 2001. The sprawling grounds, designed to look like a concentration camp, contain 53 statues of Lenins, Stalins and other communist heroes, exhibits on Soviet oppression of Lithuania, and loudspeakers bellowing Soviet anthems. The statues once stood confidently in parks or squares across the country.

If you're going straight to Grūto Parkas, ask to be let off at Grūtas, then walk the final 1km to the park along a well-signposted road. Bus 2 runs from the Druskininkai bus station directly to the park (3Lt, up to eight daily; fewer at weekends).

Kaunas

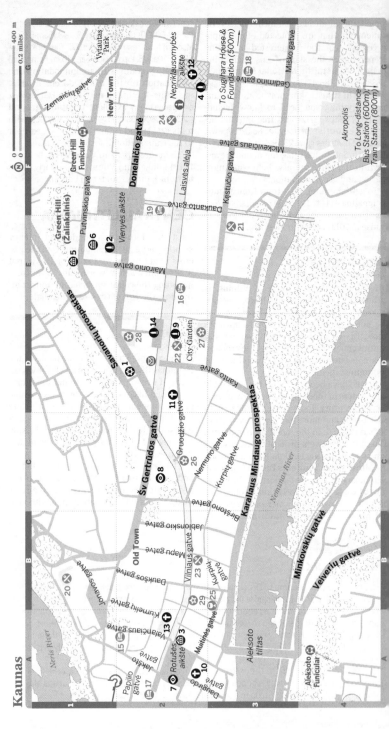

most people who fly in here head straight to Vilnius.

Kaunas is a convenient overnight stop-over and, in the warmer months, a decent place to experience the real Lithuania away from the crowds of Vilnius. A great time to visit is in April, when the city comes alive during the four-day **International Jazz Festival** (www.kaunasjazz.lt).

⊙ Sights

OLD TOWN

Rotušės aikštė   SQUARE
In the lovely Old Town, most streets lead to Rotušės aikštė (Central Sq). Surrounding the square are 15th- and 16th-century German merchants' houses. The 18th-century, white baroque former city hall is now the **Palace of Weddings**. The southern side of the square is dominated by the 18th-century twin-towered **St Francis church**.

St Peter & Paul Cathedral   CHURCH
(Vilniaus gatvė 1) St Peter and Paul Cathedral on the northeastern corner of the square owes much to baroque reconstruction, but its early 15th-century Gothic-shaped windows remain. Outside the cathedral's south wall is the **tomb of Maironis**, one of Lithuania's most revered poets.

Kaunas Photography Gallery   ART GALLERY
(Vilniaus gatvė 2; adult/student 4/2Lt; ⊙11am-6pm Tue-Fri, 11am-5pm Sat & Sun) On the eastern corner of the square, this bright and modern new gallery stages excellent photographic exhibitions by contemporary Lithuanian and international photographers.

Presidential Palace of Lithuania
                        HISTORIC BUILDING
(Vilniaus gatvė 33; adult/student 4/2Lt; ⊙11am-5pm Tue-Sun, gardens 8am-9pm daily) Near the eastern edge of the Old Town is the former Presidential Palace of Lithuania. The country was run from here between 1920 and 1939.

NEW TOWN

Kaunas expanded east from the Old Town in the 19th century, giving birth to the modern centre and its striking 1.7km-long pedestrian street, Laisvės alėja, which today is lined with trees, bars, shops and restaurants.

Museum of Devils   MUSEUM
(Putvinskio gatvė 64; adult/child 6/3Lt; ⊙11am-5pm Tue-Sun) The superb Museum of Devils contains more than 2000 devil statuettes from the mythologies of countries around the world. Note the satanic figures of Hitler and Stalin, formed from tree roots and performing a deadly dance over Lithuania.

City Garden
GARDEN

Near the western end of Laisvės alėja you'll find City Garden (Miestos Sodas), where the **Romas Kalanta memorial** takes the form of several stone slabs. Kalanta was a Kaunas student who set himself on fire on 14 May 1972 in protest at tyrannical communist rule. Nearby stands a statue of **Vytautas the Great**.

St Michael the Archangel Church
CHURCH

The white, neo-Byzantine St Michael the Archangel Church (1893) dominates the eastern end of Laisvės alėja from its position on the adjacent Nepriklausomybės aikštė (Independence Sq). On the same square, the **statue of Man**, modelled on Nike the Greek god of victory, caused a storm of controversy when his glorious pose exposing his manhood was unveiled.

St Gertrude's Church
CHURCH

(Laisvės alėja 101a) Tucked away in a courtyard off Laisvės alėja is St Gertrude's Church, a Gothic gem of a church.

Choral Synagogue
SYNAGOGUE

(Ožeškienės gatvė 13; admission free; ⊙5.45-6.30pm Mon-Fri, 10am-noon Sat) Not far north of New Town's main artery is the pale-blue Choral Synagogue, a functioning house of worship.

Freedom Monument
MONUMENT

North of Laisvės alėja, Vienybės aikštė (Unity Sq) contains the Freedom Monument, which honours 16 February 1918, the day Lithuania declared independence. It was erected in 1928. It was destroyed during the Stalin era, and rebuilt and put back in place on 16 February 1989.

National Čiurlionis Art Museum
ART GALLERY

(Putvinskio gatvė 55; adult/child 6/3Lt; ⊙11am-5pm Tue-Sun) The National Čiurlionis Art Museum has an extensive collection of the romantic symbolic paintings of Mikalojus Konstantinas Čiurlionis (1875–1911), Lithuania's beloved artist and composer.

OUT OF TOWN

Ninth Fort
MUSEUM

(Žemaičių plentas 73; adult/child 5/3Lt; catacombs with guide 10Lt; ⊙10am-6pm Wed-Mon) The 19th-century Ninth Fort, 7km north of Kaunas, was used by the Russians in WWI to defend their western frontier against Germany. During WWII the Nazis murdered an estimated 80,000 people, mostly Kaunas Jews, here. The excellent museum, comprising the old fort and a half-bunker/half-church, cov-

ers deportations of Lithuanians by the Soviets as well as the fort's other uses.

Take bus 23 from Jonavos gatvė, alight at the Forto Muziejus stop and take the pedestrian crossing under the motorway.

Sugihara House & Foundation
MUSEUM

(Vaižganto gatvė 30; adult/child 10/5Lt; ⊙10am-5pm Mon-Fri, 11am-4pm Sat & Sun) East of here, the Sugihara House and Foundation tells the story of Chiune Sugihara, the Japanese consul to Lithuania (1939–40), known as 'Japan's Schindler', through a series of photos, artefacts and video recordings. He saved 6000 lives by issuing transit visas (against orders) to Polish and Lithuanian Jews who faced the advancing Nazi terror.

🛏 Sleeping

Kaunas
BUSINESS HOTEL €€

(☎37-750 850; www.kaunashotel.lt; Laisvės gatvė 79; s/d/ste from 255/310/350Lt; ❇@🛜🏊🞩) A superb central location, every creature comfort imaginable and a top-class onsite restaurant make this smart hotel a popular upmarket choice. Balconies overlooking the pedestrian street are ideal for people-watching and you can work off your excess *cepelinai*-induced calories in the swimming pool and fitness centre.

Apple Hotel
HOTEL €€

(☎37-321 404; www.applehotel.lt; Valančiaus gatvė 19; s/d 170/230Lt; @🞩) Fans of minimalism will love the quirky, cheerful Apple. Spot the green-apple motif on your pillows and on the silk wall hangings that add a splash of colour to the otherwise white rooms.

Kauno Arkivyskupijos Svečių Namai
B&B €

(☎37-322 597; kaunas.lcn.lt/sveciunamai; Rotušės aikštė 21; s/d/tr from 80/120/140Lt; @) This charming guest house, run by the Lithuanian Catholic Church, sits snugly between centuries-old churches overlooking the Old Town square. Rooms are spartan but spacious, and management employs a number of eco-friendly practices, including energy-saving lightbulbs and recycling. Breakfast is not included.

Metropolis
HOTEL €

(☎37-205 992; www.metropolishotel.lt; Daukanto gatvė 21; s/d/tr/q 110/140/185/240Lt; 🛜) This graceful old dame is looking a bit frayed these days, but she still displays some of her past grandeur. Sculpted-stone balconies overlook a leafy street, a hefty wooden turnstile door sweeps guests into a lobby with moulded ceiling, and the rooms are spacious with high ceilings.

Litinterp   B&B €
(☑37-228 718; www.litinterp.lt; Gedimino gatvė 28/7; s/d/tr from 120/160/210Lt; ⊘office 8.30am-7pm Mon-Fri, 9am-3pm Sat) Not a lot of character, but rooms are cheap, clean and functional, and the staff are superfriendly and knowledgeable about the town.

✗ Eating

It's no Vilnius, but Kaunas' restaurant scene is gradually improving, and food tends to be cheaper than in the capital. Central supermarkets include **Iki** (Jonavos gatvė 3) and **Maxima** (Kęstučio gatvė 55).

Senieji Rūsiai   LITHUANIAN €€
(Vilniaus gatvė 34; mains 25-50Lt) Easily the tastiest street terrace at which to dine, drink and soak up the Old Town. Its candlelit 17th-century cellar has great grilled meats and a wide selection that includes game dishes, trout and the ubiquitous potato pancakes.

55°   FINE DINING €€
(Laisvės alėja 79; mains 22-50Lt) Exemplary service and expertly executed international and Lithuanian dishes attract a well-heeled crowd to this cellar restaurant named after the alcohol content of Lithuania's traditional moonshine, *samanė*. Learn how it's made as you dine.

Miesto Sodas   INTERNATIONAL €€
(Laisvės alėja 93; mains 24-36Lt) One of Kaunas' trendiest eateries, Miesto Sodas has more than passable steaks, a decent international menu and, rarity of all rarities, a salad bar. Siena nightclub in the basement is a great place to watch Žalgiris basketball games.

Žalias Ratas   LITHUANIAN €
(Laisvės alėja 36b; mains 9-35Lt) Tucked away behind the tourist office is this pseudo-rustic inn where staff don traditional garb and bring piping-hot, belly-filling fare to eager customers.

🍸 Drinking

BO   BAR
(Muitinės gatvė 9) The laid-back 'Blue Orange' attracts an alternative student set and gets crammed to overflowing on weekends. Its own brew is a tasty but potent offering, and there's live music some nights.

Avilys   MICROBREWERY
(Vilniaus gatvė 34) The last bastion of some of Lithuania's best beer since the Vilnius branch closed down. Descend into the cellar

to sample the excellent light and dark beers, as well as honey ale.

☆ Entertainment

Latino Baras   CLUB
(www.latinobaras.lt; Vilniaus gatvė 22; ⊘Fri & Sat) Latin music, occasional dance lessons, multiple rooms and beautiful young things combine to make Latino Baras a standout club for many locals.

BarBar'a   CLUB
(www.barbarabar.lt; Vliniaus gatvė 56; ⊘Thu-Sat) Swanky new basement club popular with the trendy young crowd. Excellent cocktails served to the soundtrack of quality homegrown and international DJs.

Kaunas Philharmonic   CLASSICAL MUSIC
(www.kaunofilharmonija.lt; Sapiegos gatvė 5) This is the main concert hall for classical music.

Kaunas Musical Theatre   OPERA
(www.muzikinisteatras.lt; Laisvės alėja 91) This 1892 building hosts operettas from September to June.

❶ Information

Casinos have 24-hour currency exchanges. All major banks cash travellers cheques.

Baitukas (www.baitukas.lt; K Donelaičio gatvė 26; per hr 6Lt; ⊘8am-7pm Mon-Fri, 10am-6pm Sat) New Town internet cafe.

Kaunas Guide (www.kaunastic.lt) Annual city guide with useful addresses and phone numbers, given away at the tourist office, airport, bus and railway station.

Kaunas in Your Pocket (www.inyourpocket. com) Annual city guide featuring detailed listings, sold in hotels, tourist offices, art galleries and news kiosks for 6Lt.

Main post office (Laisvės alėja 102)

SEB Bankas (Laisvės alėja 82) Has an ATM.

Tourist office (☑37-323 436; www.kaunas tic.lt; Laisvės alėja 36; ⊘9am-6pm Mon-Fri, 10am-6pm Sat, 10am-3pm Sun) Books accommodation, sells maps and guides, arranges bicycle rental (50Lt per day plus 5Lt for lock) and guided tours of the Old Town (40Lt, 4pm Thursday mid-May to September).

Ūkio Bankas (Maironio gatvė 25) Has an ATM.

❶ Getting There & Around

Air

Kaunas International Airport (☑37-399 307; www.kaunasair.lt; Savanorių prospektas) is 12km north of the Old Town in the suburb of Karmėlava. To get there take minibus 120 from the big stop at Šv Gertrūdos gatvė (2.50Lt), or bus 29 from the stop on Vytauto prospektas (1.50Lt). For information on international flights, see p525.

Bus

Major international services to/from Kaunas are operated by **Eurolines** (☑37-202 020; www.eurolines.lt) and **Ecolines** (☑37-202 022; www.ecolines.net). International destinations from the **long-distance bus station** (☑37-409 060; Vytauto prospektas 24) include Warsaw (59Lt, seven hours, daily), Kaliningrad (128Lt, five hours, daily), Rīga (54Lt, five hours, daily) and Tallinn (110Lt, nine hours, daily).

Domestic routes include the following:

Druskininkai (30Lt, two to three hours, 12 daily)

Klaipėda (50Lt, 2¾ hours, up to 18 daily)

Palanga (54Lt, 3¼ hours, up to 9 daily)

Šiauliai (35Lt, three hours, up to 18 daily)

Vilnius (25Lt, 1¾ hours, up to three per hour)

Train

From the **train station** (☑37-221 093; Čiurlionio gatvė 16) there are trains to/from Vilnius (from 15Lt, 1¼ to 1¾ hours, up to 17 daily) and to/from Šiauliai (22Lt, 2½ hours, one daily).

Šiauliai

POP 126,215

Lithuania's fourth-largest city is a work in progress. Formerly a shabby place on the outskirts of a massive Soviet military air-field, Šiauliai has been cleaning up its act (and its main street) in the recent past and transforming into a city with a buzz about it. Its biggest drawcard is the incredible Hill of Crosses, 10km to the north.

Get your bearings at the **tourism information centre** (☑41-523 110; www.siauliai.lt/tic; Vilniaus gatvė 213; ⊙9am-6pm Mon-Fri, 10am-4pm Sat), which sells maps and guides (including cycling itineraries to the Hill of Crosses), makes accommodation bookings and has internet access (1Lt per 15 minutes).

⊙ Sights & Activities

TOP CHOICE | Hill of Crosses   MONUMENT

Lithuania's most incredible, awe-inspiring sight is the legendary Hill of Cross-es (Kryžių kalnas), 10km north of Šiauliai. The sound of the breeze tinkling through the myriads of tiny crosses festooned upon the thousands of larger crosses, which appear to grow on the hillock, is eerie and unmissable. Each and every cross represents the amaz-ing spirit, soulfulness and rebellious nature of the Lithuanian people.

Legend says the tradition of planting crosses began in the 14th century. The cross-es were bulldozed by the Soviets, but each night people crept past soldiers and barbed wire to plant more, risking their lives or freedom to express their national and spiri-tual fervour. Today the Hill of Crosses is a place of national pilgrimage.

Some of the crosses are devotional, others are memorials (many for people deported to Siberia) and some are finely carved folk-art masterpieces.

Head north up highway A12, then travel 2km east from a well-marked turn-off (the sign says 'Kryžių kalnas 2'). You can rent a bike from the tourist information centre (5Lt per hour) and pedal out here, or take a Joniškis-bound bus (2.70Lt, 10 minutes, up to nine daily) get off at the 'Domantai' stop and then walk for 15 minutes along the sign-posted eastbound road. A round-trip taxi with half an hour to see the crosses should cost around 50Lt.

Vilniaus gatvė   NOTABLE STREET

Vilniaus gatvė is the city's main pedestrian drag and a great place to stroll or plop down in a streetside cafe and watch the world go by. It's also a free wi-fi zone.

Museums   MUSEUMS

Šiauliai's list of eccentric museums is im-pressive. In the centre you'll find the **Ra-dio & TV Museum** (Vilniaus gatvė 174; adult/child 2/1Lt; ⊙10am-6pm Wed-Fri, 11am-5pm Sat & Sun) and **Bicycle Museum** (Vilniaus gatvė 139; adult/child 6/3Lt; ⊙10am-6pm Tue-Fri, 11am-5pm Sat). Nearby, the **Photography Museum** (Vilniaus gatvė 140) was closed for renovation at the time of research. A little east of central Šiauliai is the **Museum of Cats** (Žuvininku gatvė 18; adult/child 4/2Lt; ⊙10am-5pm Tue-Sat), which houses feline memorabilia (includ-ing a stained-glass cat window) and two live cats.

Sundial   MONUMENT

(cnr Salkausko gatvė & Ežero gatvė) The city's quirky symbol is a bizarre golden sundial, topped by a gleaming statue of an archer. It stands on the edge of the city's peaceful cem-etery, about five minutes' walk north from the centre.

🛏 Sleeping & Eating

Šiauliai College Youth Hostel   HOSTEL €

(☑41-523 764; www.jnn.siauliukolegija.lt; Tilžės gatvė 159; s/d/tr 50/70/90Lt) This former col-lege has been renovated with EU funds to create a spanking-clean and sparkling hostel with kitchen and lounge with satellite TV. The staff at reception speak only rudimentary English, but they do their very best to help.

Šiauliai   HOTEL €
(41-437 333; www.hotelsiauliai.lt; Draugystės prospektas 25; s/d/tr from 105/160/195Lt; @) The town's old 14-storey Soviet hotel has enjoyed recent renovations both inside and out, leaving it with pleasant rooms of varying shapes and sizes, dressed in pale yellow and brown. The views are still as great as ever.

Juonė Pastuogė   LITHUANIAN €
(Aušros 31a; mains 9-32Lt) A country-and-western style music club–tavern with an enormous garden and an imaginative menu including the likes of ostrich steak, hearty country stews, the ubiquitous *cepelinai* and vegetarian pancakes.

❶ Getting There & Away
Šiauliai is roughly 140km from both Kaunas and Vilnius. With your own wheels you could feasibly visit the Hill of Crosses as a day trip from either.

Bus
Services from the **bus station** (41-525 058; Tilzes gatvė 109) include the following:
Kaunas 35Lt, three hours, up to 21 daily
Klaipėda 35Lt, 3½ hours, up to six daily
Rīga 34Lt, 2½ hours, up to six daily
Tallinn 61Lt, 7½ hours, one daily
Vilnius 47Lt, three hours, up to 12 daily

Train
From the **train station** (41-203 445; Dubijos gatvė 44) there are trains to Vilnius (35Lt, 2½ hours, three daily), Kaunas (22Lt, 2½ hours, one daily) and Klaipėda (from 23Lt, two to three hours, five daily).

WESTERN LITHUANIA

Lithuania's lively west coastline is only 99km long but it packs plenty of firepower, with a thriving port city, a thumping party town and its crown jewel, the starkly beautiful, sand dune–covered Curonian Spit – a Unesco World Heritage site. Toss in a few fine festivals, add a dollop of German history and there will be plenty to keep you occupied in this wonderful part of the world.

Palanga
POP 17,600
Downright dull by winter, beachside Palanga, just 25km north of Klaipėda, becomes Lithuania's undisputed party capital in the summer months.

The **tourist information centre** (460-48811; www.palangatic.lt; Kretingos gatvė 1; 9am-7pm Mon-Fri & 10am-4pm Sat & Sun mid-Jun–Aug, 9am-5pm Mon-Fri & 10am-2pm Sat Sep–mid-Jun) adjoins the tiny bus station, east of Palanga's lengthy main artery, pedestrian Basanavičiaus gatvė.

◎ Sights
Botanical Park   PARK
For a peaceful escape from the crowds of Basanavičiaus gatvė, walk or cycle south along Meilės alėja, the main beachfront path, to Palanga's Botanical Park, where you'll discover lush greenery and swans gliding on still lakes. The park's highlight is the **Amber Museum** (Vytauto gatvė 17; adult/student 8/4Lt; 10am-8pm Tue-Sat, to 7pm Sun), inside the sweeping former palace of the noble Polish Tyszkiewicz family, with its collection of over 25,000 pieces of 'Baltic Gold'.

Antanas Mončys House Museum   MUSEUM
(Daukanto gatvė 16; adult/student 4/2Lt; noon-5pm Tue, 2-9pm Wed-Sun) Near the Botanical Park, you'll find the unusual Antanas Mončys House Museum, with a collection of the Lithuanian sculptor's finest works in wood and stone, all of which you can touch.

🛏 Sleeping & Eating
Room rates change by the week in summer. For cheap digs try haggling with one of the dozens of locals who stand at the eastern end of Kretingos gatvė touting *nuomojami kambariai* (rooms for rent). Expect to pay 40Lt to 110Lt per head.

Palanga Hotel   LUXURY HOTEL €€€
(460-41414; www.palangahotel.lt; Birutės gatvė 60; d/ste 750/900Lt, 2-room apt 1850Lt; ❄@ 🛜🔁P) If you want to do it in style, look no further than this swish hotel of glass and wood surrounded by 80-year-old pine trees. Indulge in one of the many spa treatments and sample the restaurant's celebrated flambé dishes.

Vila Ramybė   BOUTIQUE HOTEL €€
(460-54124; www.vilaramybe.lt; Vytauto gatvė 54; s/d/apt 160/200/400Lt; @🛜) Pristine little boutique hotel near the centre, with

rooms ranging from spacious singles to two-bedroom apartments with their own terrace. The bar on the premises is one of the friendliest in town.

Ema GUEST HOUSE €€
(☎460-48608; www.ema.lt; Jūratės gatvė 32; s/d from 130Lt/240) This basic guest house has stripped-back rooms in every pastel colour known.

Žuvinė SEAFOOD
(Basanavičiaus gatvė 37a; mains 22-45Lt) An upmarket restaurant-cum-library specialising in fresh fish and seafood

1925 Baras CAFE
(Basanavičiaus gatvė 4; mains 25-48Lt) A rustic wood-panelled cafe and bar.

❶ Getting There & Away

There are regular daily buses to the following destinations:

Vilnius 67Lt, 4¼ hours, up to 12 daily

Kaunas 53Lt, 3¼ hours, up to 11 daily

Klaipėda 5.20Lt, 45 minutes, every 20 minutes

Šiauliai 34Lt, three hours, up to 10 daily

Liepaja 12Lt, 1¼ hours, up to three daily

Rīga 52Lt, 4½ hours, two daily

Klaipėda

POP 182,716

Gritty Klaipėda is Lithuania's main port city and boasts a fascinating history as the East Prussian city of Memel. While many visitors use it merely as a stopover on their way to the Curonian Spit, it has enough attractions of its own to warrant lingering a day or two.

◎ Sights

Castle CASTLE
West of Old Town are the remains of Klaipėda's old moat-protected castle. The **Klaipėda Castle Museum** (www.mlimuziejus. lt; Pilies gatvė 4; adult/child 6/3Lt, combined ticket History Museum of Lithuania Minor 10Lt; ⊙10am-6pm Tue-Sat) inside the one remaining tower tells the castle's, and Klaipėda's, story from the 13th to 17th centuries. The visit is worth it for the atmospherically lit fort interior. To get to the museum, walk through the Klaipėda State Sea Port Authority building and a ship repair yard.

Old Town HISTORIC AREA
What little remains of Klaipėda's **Old Town** (most of it was destroyed in WWII) is wedged between the Danė River and Tur-

gaus gatvė. There are several well-preserved old German half-timbered buildings in the vicinity of Teatro aikštė (Theatre Sq), which is Klaipėda's spiritual heart.

The square's dominant building is the **Drama Theatre** (Teatro aikštė 2), where in 1939 Hitler announced from the balcony the incorporation of Memel into Germany. Occupying the middle of the square is the much-loved **statue of Ännchen von Tharau** – a character from a love poem thought to have been written by the 17th-century German poet Simon Dach. The statue is a replica of the original, which was destroyed during the war.

History Museum of Lithuania Minor
MUSEUM
(Didžioji Vandens gatvė 6; adult/child 5/2Lt; ⊙10am-6pm Tue-Sat) Extremely worthwhile museum detailing the history of the area, with exhibits ranging from hoards of coins to nautical history to recreation of traditional dwellings, though it would benefit from more English captioning. Excellent temporary photographic exhibitions held upstairs.

✦ Festivals

Sea Festival NAUTICAL
(www.jurossvente.lt) The city celebrates its nautical heritage each July with a flamboyant Sea Festival that draws crowds for a weekend of concerts, parties, exhibitions and nautical manoeuvres.

⌂ Sleeping

Litinterp Guesthouse B&B €
(☎46-410 644; www.litinterp.lt; Puodžių gatvė 17; s/d/tr without bathroom 90/160/210Lt, with bathroom 110/180/240Lt; ⊙8.30am-7pm Mon-Fri, 10am-3pm Sat; ☎) This accommodation agency arranges B&B in Klaipėda, Palanga and along the Curonian Spit. The 16 rooms in its own guesthouse are cheerful and comfortable, and breakfast is delivered in a basket.

Amberton Klaipėda LUXURY HOTEL €€€
(☎46-404 372; www.ambertonhotel.com; Naujoji Sodo gatvė 1; s/d/ste from 320/540/1000Lt; ❄@ ☎≋P) Choose from sturdy and comfortable rooms in the 12-storey red-brick monstrosity or their newer deluxe cousins in the celebrated 'K-Centre' next door. Lose yourself amid the restaurants, bars, tennis courts and casinos of this self-proclaimed 'City Within the City'.

Preliudija Guesthouse GUEST HOUSE €€
(☎46-310 077; www.preliudija.com; Kepėjų gatvė 7; s/d from 180/210Lt; @) Snug in an Old Town

house dating to 1856, this guest house – a rare breed in Klaipėda – is charming. Rooms are minimalist and modern; each has a single fresh flower in a vase, and a sparkling bathroom.

Klaipėda Travellers Hostel HOSTEL **€**

(☑46-211 879; www.Klaipėdahostel.com; Butkų Juzės gatvė 7/4; dm/d 44/88Lt; @🛜) This friendly hostel close to the bus station looks terrible from the outside but is homely and pleasant inside, though facilities are few.

✖ Eating & Drinking

Self-caterers can head directly for **Iki** (Mažvydo alėja 7/11) and **Ikiukas** (Turgaus gatvė) supermarkets.

TOP CHOICE **Ararat** ARMENIAN **€€**

(Liepų gatvė 48a; mains 20-30Lt) Arguably one of the best places to eat in town, this restaurant specialises in superbly flavoured Armenian dishes against a backdrop of bright-coloured rugs and photos of Mount Ararat. Try the eggplant with cottage cheese and the grilled meats, and finish off with a lump of hot, sweet *pakhlava* washed down with traditional Armenian herbal tea.

Kurpiai BAR **€€**

(Kurpių gatvė 1a; mains 20-40Lt) Kurpiai's cobbled terrace and dark old-world interior make it not only one of the best places in town to sample ostrich steak, fresh trout and a wide range of pork, beef and vegetarian dishes, but also a top spot to catch live jazz, which is either extremely good or dire.

Senoji Hansa LITHUANIAN **€**

(Kurpių gatvė 1; mains 17-28Lt) If you're hankering after some filling potato pancakes, or meat dishes served by attentive staff, then this Old Town restaurant in a charming location fits the bill perfectly. It's a crying shame that the lively summer terrace is squished into an alleyway, though.

Memelis MICROBREWERY **€**

(Žvejų gatvė 4) This red-brick brewery and restaurant by the river has been in operation since 1871 and is popular with the city's expat community. Interior is old-style beer hall; outside is industrial-feel riverside terrace, and the beer is very good indeed.

Pizza Bombola PIZZA **€**

(H Manto gatvė 1; mains 15-22Lt) Popular with a local crowd, this bright spot on the corner of one of the city's busiest streets serves consistently decent pizzas.

ℹ Information

The **tourist office** (☑46-412 186; www.Klaipėdainfo.lt; Turgaus gatvė 7; ☺9am-7pm Mon-Fri, 10am-4pm Sat & Sun) is exceptionally efficient, selling maps, arranging accommodation and renting bicycles (10/40Lt per hour/day plus 200Lt deposit). The internet here costs 1Lt per 15 minutes.

ℹ Getting There & Away

Boat

The **International Ferry Port** (☑46-395 051; www.dfdslisco.lt; Perkėlos gatvė 10) is 3km south of the New Ferry Terminal. **DFDS Seaways** (☑46-393 600; www.dfdslisco.com; J Janonio gatvė 24) runs passenger ferries to/from Kiel (from €46, six weekly, 23 hours) and Sassnitz (from €37, three weekly, 18 hours) in Germany and Karlshamn, Sweden (€62, 14 hours, daily).

Krantas Travel (☑46-395 233; www.krantas.lt; Teatro gatvė 5) sells ferry tickets to Kiel, Karlshamn, and Sassnitz.

Passenger ferries to the Smiltynė ferry landing on the Curonian Spit leave from the **Old Castle Port** (www.keltas.lt; Žvejų gatvė 8), near the castle, west of the Old Town. Ferries leave every half-hour in the high season and cost 2.90Lt (10 minutes). Vehicles must use the **New Port** (Nemuno gatvė 8; per car 10Lt), 3km south of the passenger terminal. Services depart at least hourly.

Take bus 1 (2Lt) to both the New Port (10 minutes) and the International Ferry Port (30 minutes).

Bus

The major operators are **Eurolines** (☑46-415 555) and **Ecolines** (☑46-310 103).

Buses leave from Klaipėda **bus station** (☑46-411 547; Priestočio gatvė).

Train

From the **train station** (☑46-313 677; Priestočio gatvė 1), 150m from the bus station, there are trains to Vilnius (51Lt, 4½ to five hours, three daily) and Šiauliai (from 23Lt, two to three hours, five daily).

Curonian Spit

POP 3100

This magical sliver of land, dangling off the western rump of Lithuania, hosts some of Europe's most precious sand dunes and a menagerie of elk, deer and avian wildlife. Just 3.8km at its widest point, the spit looks positively brittle on a map, but it seems much sturdier, thanks to the pine forests that cover 70% of its surface. A few dunes rise high above those forests, creating a surreal effect.

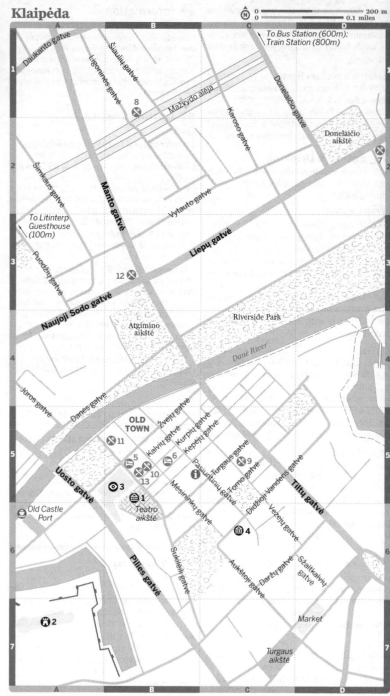

N 0 ——————————— 200 m
0 ——————————— 0.1 miles

To Bus Station (600m);
Train Station (800m)

Daukanto gatvė

Šiaulių gatvė

Ligoninės gatvė

Donelaičio gatvė

8

Mažvydo alėja

Keroso gatvė

Donelaičio
aikštė

7

Simkaus gatvė

Manto gatvė

Vytauto gatvė

To Litinterp
Guesthouse
(100m)

Puodžių gatvė

Liepų gatvė

Naujoji Sodo gatvė

12

Atgimino
aikštė

Riverside Park

Dané River

Jūros gatvė

Danės gatvė

OLD
TOWN

Žvejų gatvė

Kurpių gatvė

Kalvių gatvė

Kepėjų gatvė

11

5

6

10

13

Pašiuntinių gatvė

Turgaus gatvė

9

Tomo gatvė

Uosto gatvė

3

1

Teatro
aikštė

Mėsininkų gatvė

Didžioji Vandens gatvė

Vežėjų gatvė

Tiltų gatvė

Old Castle
Port

4

Pilies gatvė

Sukilėlių gatvė

Aukštoji gatvė

Daržų gatvė

Šaltkalvių
gatvė

2

Market

Turgaus
aikštė

Klaipėda

The fragile spit, which Unesco recognised as a World Heritage site in 2000, has faced a number of environmental threats over the years, beginning with the clear-felling of its forests in the 16th century. Lately the dunes have been eroding rapidly and tourism is exacerbating the problem.

The entire Curonian Spit was Prussian territory until WWI. These days the spit is divided roughly evenly between Lithuania and Russia's Kaliningrad region in the south. Lithuania's share of the spit is protected as **Curonian Spit National Park** (www.nerija.lt).

Administratively, the Lithuania side is divided into two regions: the township of Smiltynė, which is part of Klaipėda; and the Neringa municipality, which contains the villages of Juodkrantė, Pervalka, Preila and touristy Nida.

❶ Getting There & Away

To get to the spit you need to take a ferry or bus from Klaipėda or take the Kaliningrad–Klaipėda bus.

From Smiltynė, buses and microbuses (9Lt, one hour, at least six times daily) run regularly to/from the **Nida bus station** (☑469-54859; Naglių gatvė 18e) via Juodkrantė (4Lt, 15 to 20 minutes).

SMILTYNĖ

Smiltynė is where the ferries from Klaipėda dock. On summer weekends Klaipėda residents cram Smiltynė, flocking to its beaches and to the delightful **Lithuanian Sea Museum** (☑46-490 754; www.juru.muziejus.lt; adult/student 12/6Lt; ☉10.30am-6.30pm Tue-Sun), which features a large aquarium, nautical history exhibits, seal and sea-lion shows and the star attraction – spectacular dolphin shows at the dolphinarium (closed for reconstruction at the time of research).

JUODKRANTĖ

Juodkrantė is a quiet, spread-out settlement with everything a traveller needs. The most popular activity in the village is one of Neringa's trademark activities: buying and tasting freshly caught and smoked fish, which is sold from several wooden houses along the main road, Rėzos gatvė (look for the *žuvis* signs).

Top of the strange sights list is **Raganų Kalnas (Witches' Hill)**, a spooky sculpture trail through gorgeous forest with large, fairytale Lithuanian wooden carvings created by local artists.

Less than 1km south of Juodkrantė is one of Neringa's must-see attractions, a massive **colony of grey herons and cormorants**. Wooden steps lead from the road to a viewing platform where the panorama of thousands of nests amid pine trees – cormorants to the north, herons to the south – is breathtaking. In March and April the air

BUSES FROM KLAIPĖDA

DESTINATION	COST (LT)	DURATION (HR)	FREQUENCY
Kaliningrad via Nida	46	4½	daily
Kaunas	50	2¾	up to 18 daily
Liepāja	22	2¾	daily
Palanga	5.20	45 minutes	every 20 minutes
Šiauliai	35Lt	3½	up to six daily
Vilnius	64Lt	4-5½	up to 15 daily

is thick with birds carrying huge sticks to build their nests, and in May the cacophony rises to a deafening crescendo as the chicks are born.

In Juodkrantė stay at the marvellously rustic **Vila Flora** (☑469-53024; www.vilaflora. lt; Kalno gatvė 7a; s/d 200/260Lt), which also serves up some of the best food on the spit (mains 25Lt to 48Lt). For tasty fish dishes and an excellent view of the pier, try **Vela Bianca** (Liudviko Rėzos gatvė 1; mains 27-50Lt), the airy yacht-club restaurant.

NIDA
Neringa's southernmost settlement is the charming village of Nida, which slumbers much of the year but in summer becomes Neringa's tourist nerve centre.

Bankas Snoras (Naglių gatvė 27) has a currency exchange and ATM opposite the bus station. The **tourist information centre** (☑469-52345; www.visitneringa.com; Taikos gatvė 4; ◷10am-7pm Mon-Fri, to 6pm Sat, 10am-3pm Sun) books accommodation (5Lt fee) and stocks loads of useful information on walks, bike rides, fishing-boat trips and more.

◉ Sights & Activities
Nida's architecture is a mix of classic German half-timbered construction, quaint wooden houses with frilly eaves and intricate facades, and intricate, brightly painted weather vanes.

TOP CHOICE **Parnidis Dune**   LANDMARK
The Curonian Spit's awe-inspiring sand dunes are on full display from the smashed-granite sundial atop the 52m-high Parnidis Dune. The panorama of coastline, forests and the spit's most stunning dune extending towards Kaliningrad to the south is unforgettable. You can walk up here from town along a **nature trail** through the forest at the southern end of Naglių gatvė or drive via Taikos gatvė. Make sure you don't stray from the wooden boardwalk as the dune is very fragile.

Museums   MUSEUMS
Check out the restored 19th-century fisherman's cottage that is the **Ethnographic Museum** (Naglių gatvė 4; adult/child 2/1Lt; ◷10am-6pm); the excellent little **Amber Gallery** (Pamario gatvė 20; adult/child 4/2Lt; ◷9am-8pm), a combined museum and shop featuring some stunning amber pieces of all colours; and the **Neringa History Museum** (Pamario gatvė 53; adult/child 2/1Lt; ◷10am-6pm), with its evocative displays on

fishing, catching crows (biting their necks to kill them and washing away the taste with vodka), and wading into the surf after a storm, armed with a net, to trawl for amber.

Cycling   CYCLING
An excellent way to see the spit is by bicycle. A flat **cycling trail** runs all the way from Nida to Smiltynė, and you stand a good chance of seeing wild boar or other wildlife at any point along the path. There are bicycles for hire (around 40Lt per 24 hours) on almost every street corner in Nida; some allow you to leave your bike in Smiltynė or Juodkrantė and bus back to Nida.

🛏 Sleeping & Eating
The tourist information centre can help arrange accommodation in private houses, but contact the centre weeks in advance for summer bookings. In winter expect steep discounts on prices listed here.

Miško Namas   GUEST HOUSE €€
(☑469-52290; www.miskonamas.com; Pamario gatvė 11-2; d 249Lt, 2-/4-person apt 318/331Lt; @) A beautiful wooden guest house with a 180-year-old twisting wooden staircase. Every room here has its own fridge, sink, kettle and satellite TV, and a couple have balconies. Self-cater in the cosy communal kitchen.

Kambarių nuoma   GUEST HOUSE €€
(☑469-52256; http://nida.w3.lt; Lotmiškio gatvė 7; s/d 120/200Lt; @) Guest house in a superb location – a minute's walk from the sea. There's an immaculate kitchen and dining area and the owners go out of their way to make you feel welcome.

Nidos Kempingas   CAMPING GROUND €-€€
(☑469-52045; www.kempingas.lt; Taikos gatvė 45a; per tent 17-28Lt, per person 17-22Lt, per car 10-15Lt, d from 250Lt, 4-/6-bed studios with garden 350/490Lt; ❄) Set in pine forest, 15 minutes' walk from Nida, this camping ground has accommodation to suit all budgets. There are also bikes for hire, a swimming pool and tennis courts.

Kuršis   LITHUANIAN €
(Naglių gatvė 29; mains 16-25Lt) Open year-round, this popular bar–restaurant serves hearty Lithuanian staples, such as potato pancakes, excellent cold beetroot soup and meat and fish dishes. Order the beer snack platter only if you intend to share.

UNDERSTAND LITHUANIA

History

Birth & Death of the Lithuanian Empire

Lithuania's history is a story of riches to rags and then back to riches again. It all started when ancient tribes fanned out across the Baltics to take advantage of the region's plentiful amber deposits. In 1009 those tribes were sufficiently assimilated for Lithuania to be mentioned for the first time in writing.

By the 12th century Lithuania's peoples had split into two tribal groups: the Samogitians (lowlanders) in the west and the Aukštaitiai (highlanders) in the east and southeast. In the mid-13th century Aukštaitiai leader Mindaugas unified Lithuanian tribes to create the Grand Duchy of Lithuania, of which he was crowned monarch in 1253 at Kernavė.

It was the Lithuanian leader Gediminas who pushed Lithuania's borders south and east between 1316 and 1341. In 1386 marriage forged an alliance with Poland against the Teutonic Order – Germanic crusaders who were busy conquering much of the region – that lasted 400 years. The alliance defeated the German knights in 1410 at the battle of Grünwald in Poland, ushering in a golden period during which Vilnius was born and Lithuania became one of Europe's largest empires.

But Lithuania was destined to disappear off the maps of Europe. In the 18th century, the Polish–Lithuanian state was so weakened by division that it was carved up by Russia, Austria and Prussia (successor to the Teutonic Order) in the partitions of Poland (1772, 1793 and 1795–96).

Lithuania in the 20th Century

Vilnius was a bastion of Polish culture in the 19th century and a focus of uprisings against Russia. It also became an important Jewish centre; Jews made up almost half of its 160,000-strong population by the early 20th century.

Lithuanian nationalists declared independence on 16 February 1918, with Kaunas proclaimed the capital, as Polish troops had annexed Vilnius from the Red Army in 1920. Lithuania's first president, Antanas Smetona, ruled the country with an iron fist during this time.

In 1940, after the Molotov–Ribbentrop Pact, Lithuania was forced into the USSR. Within a year, 40,000 Lithuanians were killed or deported. Up to 300,000 more people, mostly Jews, died in concentration camps and ghettos during the 1941–44 Nazi occupation, many of them at Paneriai.

The USSR ruled again between 1945 and 1991. An estimated 250,000 people were murdered or deported to Siberia while armed partisans resisted Soviet rule from the forests. This bloody period of resistance, which petered out in 1953, is chronicled in Vilnius' Museum of Genocide Victims and a number of smaller museums around the country.

The Push for Independence

In the late 1980s Lithuania led the Baltic push for independence. The popular front, Sajūdis, won 30 seats in the March 1989 elections for the USSR Congress of People's Deputies. Lithuania was the first Soviet republic to legalise noncommunist parties. In February 1990 Sajūdis was elected to form a majority in Lithuania's new Supreme Soviet (now the parliament), which on 11 March declared Lithuania independent.

Moscow marched troops into Vilnius and cut off Lithuania's fuel supplies. On 13 January 1991, Soviet troops stormed key buildings in Vilnius. Fourteen people were killed at Vilnius' TV tower and Lithuanians barricaded the Seimas (their parliament). In the wake of heavy condemnation from the West, the Soviets recognised Lithuanian independence on 6 September 1991, bringing about the first of the Baltic republics.

Life after the Soviet Union

The last Soviet troops left the country on 31 August 1993. Lithuania replaced the rouble with the litas, joined NATO in April 2004, and entered the EU a month later. True to form, bold Lithuania forthrightly ratified the EU constitution in November 2004, becoming the first of the 25 EU member countries to do so.

Lithuania's enthusiasm for the EU continues unabated. In a mid-2008 poll, 70% of the population still viewed EU membership optimistically. Many are keen on the euro, but the EU currency won't be introduced here until at least 2014. As with everything, EU membership has its downside: members of the country's younger generation are leaving in droves for the greener pastures of the UK and Ireland. Yet Lithuania still remains a country of optimism.

The Lithuanians

Lithuania is easily the most ethnically homogeneous population of the three Baltic countries, with Lithuanians accounting for 83.5% of the total population. Poles form 6.7% and Russians 6.3%. The remaining 3.5% comprises various nationalities from Eastern Europe and further afield.

Compared with their reticent neighbours in Latvia and Estonia, Lithuanians are an outgoing, cheeky bunch. That has led some to call them the 'Spanish of the Baltics'. Others call them the 'Italians of the Baltics', citing their fierce pride – a result of the many brutal attempts to eradicate their culture and the memories of their long-lost empire.

Lithuania was the last pagan country in Europe, which explains why so much of its religious art, national culture and traditions have raw pagan roots. Today the country is 70% to 80% Roman Catholic by most estimates, with strong Lutheran and Russian Orthodox minorities.

The Arts

Lithuania's best-known national artist will always be Mikalojus Konstantinas Čiurlionis (1875–1911), a painter who also composed symphonic poems and piano pieces. The best collection of his paintings is in the National Čiurlionis Art Museum in Kaunas.

Lithuania has a thriving contemporary art scene. Vilnius artists created the tongue-in-cheek Užupis Republic, which hosts alternative art festivals, fashion shows and exhibitions in its breakaway state.

Music is at the heart of the Lithuanian spirit, and Lithuania is the jazz giant of the Baltics, with its highlight the Kaunas International Jazz Festival.

Lithuanian fiction began with the late-18th-century poem 'Metai' (The Seasons) by Kristijonas Donelaitis. Antanas Baranauskas' 1860 poem 'Anykščiai Pine Forest' uses the forest as a symbol of Lithuania. Literature suffered persecution from the tsarist authorities, who banned the use of the Latin alphabet between 1864 and 1904.

Several major Polish writers grew up in Lithuania and regarded themselves as partly Lithuanian, most notably Adam Mickiewicz (1798–1855), the inspiration for 19th-century nationalists, whose great poem 'Pan Tadeusz' begins 'Lithuania, my fatherland...'

Environment

Lush forests and more than 4000 lakes mark the landscape of Lithuania, a country that is largely flat with a 100km-wide lowland centre. Forest covers a third of the country and contains creatures such as wild boar, wolves, deer and elk. Aukštaitija National Park is one place where these beasts roam, although you are unlikely to encounter them without a guide. You're more likely to spot a stork – Lithuania has Europe's highest concentration of storks, and their nests crop up in the unlikeliest places.

A huge amount of EU money is being sunk into cleaning up Lithuania's environment, which continues to suffer from years of Soviet mismanagement and indifference.

For years the hot potato has been the Ignalina Nuclear Power Plant, 120km north of Vilnius. One of two reactors similar in design to Chernobyl was closed in December 2004, and the final shutdown of the plant took place in 2009 at a massive cost of €3.2 billion. There are plans to build a new nuclear power station on the same site.

Lithuania faces the threat of large-scale pollution from a recently discovered arsenal of decomposing chemical weapons. About 40,000 bombs and mines lie on the seabed 70 nautical miles off Klaipėda, where Soviet forces sank German ships, and the cargo from these ships could threaten the fragile coastline of the Curonian Spit. The spit is also threatened by the D-6 oil field in the Kaliningrad region, 22km from the coast and 500m downstream from the Lithuania–Russia border. Oil rigs are currently being operated by Lukoil in the area.

Greenhouse gases have been on the rise in recent years. Among the main sources of air pollution are city transport and industrial sites. Additionally, the delicate biodiversity of Lithuania's forests is under threat due to mismanagement and illegal logging.

To do your part for the environment, camp only in designated areas and, when required, keep to the marked trails on the sand dunes of the Curonian Spit and in other national parks.

Lithuanian Cuisine

Unbuckle your belts for the gastronomic delights of good, hearty Lithuanian cooking. The food was tailor-made for peasants out working the fields, so it's seriously stodgy comfort eating rather than delicate morsels. Based on potatoes, meat and dairy goods, it's not ideal for vegetarians, so we've tried to list options for those who shun the pleasures of pigs trotters and pork knuckles.

The national dish is the hearty *cepelinai* (zeppelins): airship-shaped parcels of gluey potato dough stuffed with cheese, *mesa* (meat) or *grybai* (mushrooms). It comes topped with a rich sauce made from onions, butter, sour cream and bacon bits. Another artery-hardening favourite is sour cream–topped *kugelis,* a dish that bakes grated potatoes and carrots in the oven. *Koldūnai* are hearty ravioli stuffed with meat or mushrooms, and *virtiniai* are stodgy dumplings. *Šaltibarščiai* is a creamy beetroot soup served cold in the summer.

Lithuanians drink their share of *alus* (beer) and it's all pretty good. The most popular brand is Švyturys, but try Utenos, Kalnapilis and Gubernija as well. No beer is complete without the world's most fattening bar snacks, *kepta duona* (deep-fried black bread with garlic) and smoked pigs' ears.

Midus (mead) originated in the Middle Ages but is making a comeback these days. It's made of honey boiled with water, berries and spices, then fermented with hops.

Since 2007 there has been a total country-wide ban on smoking in restaurants and bars.

SURVIVAL GUIDE

Directory A–Z

Accommodation

Vilnius has a serious room crunch so book ahead in the high season. In coastal locations such as Palanga and the Curonian Spit rooms fill up months ahead in summer. Peak-season prices are around 30% higher than off-season prices. Prices are higher in Vilnius. Some hotels offer cheaper weekend rates in the off-season. Smoking is still generally accepted in Lithuania, but this is slowly changing. Expect most hotels to offer a handful of nonsmoking rooms.

Our price ranges for a double room are budget (€; up to 200Lt), midrange (€€; 200Lt–450Lt) and top end (€€€; more than 450Lt).

BUDGET

The budget price range covers camping grounds, youth hostels, budget hotels and guesthouses. Vilnius has numerous youth hostels and budget accommodation is easy to come by outside the capital. Camping grounds are often basic, but gradually improving.

Many budget guest houses now offer free internet or wi-fi. Budget guesthouse rooms may be en suite and some have TVs and refrigerators. Breakfast is included in the price unless stated otherwise.

MIDRANGE

In Vilnius and other cities it's becoming easier to find good business hotels and guest houses in this price range. These may include renovated and upgraded old Soviet hotels. Facilities may include air-con, fitness facilities, free wi-fi, and good onsite restaurants.

TOP END

There is no shortage of excellent top-end lodgings in Vilnius, Kaunas, Palanga and Klaipėda. This includes boutique hotels in renovated historic buildings and smart business hotels. Expect a full range of creature comforts, multilingual staff, fine dining onsite, gyms, swimming pools, Jacuzzis and air-con.

Business Hours

Opening hours given in the chapter are for peak season. Off season, museums, businesses and tourist offices work reduced hours on weekends or are closed altogether.

Banks 9am-5pm Mon-Fri

Bars 11am-midnight Sun-Thu, 11am-2am Fri & Sat

Clubs 10pm-5am Thu-Sat

Post offices 8am-8pm Mon-Fri, 10am-9pm Sat, 10am-5pm Sun

Restaurants noon-11pm; later on weekends, especially in cities

Shops 9am or 10am-7pm Mon-Fri; earlier closing Sat

Discount Cards

If you're planning on intensive sightseeing in the capital within a short period of time, it may be worth your while to get a Vilnius City Card (52/110Lt for 24/72 hours). For full details of participating museums, restaurants, shops and tour companies, see www.vilnius-tourism.lt.

Benefits include free travel on local buses and trolleybuses, free entry to numerous museums, and discounts on tours, accommodation, restaurants and shopping.

Embassies & Consulates

The following embassies and consulates are in Vilnius.

Australia (☎5-212 3369; australia@consulate.lt; Vilniaus gatvė 23)

Belarus (☎5-213 2255; www.lithuania.bel embassy.org; Muitinės gatvė 41)

Canada (☎5-249 0950; www.canada.lt; Jogailos gatvė 4)

Denmark (☎5-264 8760; www.ambvilnius. um.dk; T Kosciuškos gatvė 36)

Estonia (☎5-278 0200; www.estemb.lt; A Mickevičiaus gatvė 4a)

France (☎5-212 2979; www.ambafrance-lt.org; Švarco gatvė 1)

Germany (☎5-210 6400; www.wilna.diplo.de; Z. Sierakausko gatvė 24/8)

Ireland (☎5-262 9460; vilniusembassy@dfa.ie; Gedimino gatvė 1)

Latvia (☎5-213 1260; www.latvia.lt; Čiurlionio gatvė 76)

Netherlands (☎5-269 0072; www.netherlands embassy.lt; Jogailos gatvė 4)

Poland (☎5-270 9001; www.wilno.polemb.net; Smėlio gatvė 22a)

Russia (☎5-272 1763; www.lithuania.mid.ru; Latvių gatvė 53/54)

UK (☎5-246 2900; ukinlithuania.fco.gov.uk; Antakalnio gatvė 2)

USA (☎5-266 5500; www.usembassy.lt; Akmenų gatvė 6)

Food

Price ranges are: budget (€; under 45Lt), midrange (€€; 45Lt to 65Lt) and top end (€€€; over 65Lt).

Holidays

New Year's Day 1 January

Independence Day 16 February; anniversary of 1918 independence declaration

Lithuanian Independence Restoration Day 11 March

Easter Sunday March/April

Easter Monday March/April

International Labour Day 1 May

Mothers Day First Sunday in May

Feast of St John (Midsummer) 24 June

Statehood Day 6 July; commemoration of coronation of Grand Duke Mindaugas

Assumption of Blessed Virgin 15 August

All Saints' Day 1 November

Christmas 25 & 26 December

Internet Access

Internet use has developed at a staggering pace in Lithuania's urban areas., and free wi-fi hot spots are found all over Vilnius and other cities. There are few internet cafes, but many hotels, guest houses and hostels now offer free internet connections or wi-fi.

Money

The Lithuanian litas (the plural is litai; Lt) is divided into 100 centai. It is pegged to the euro at the rate of 3.45Lt per euro. On 1 January, 2014 Lithuania is expected to trade in its litas for the euro.

All but the smallest Lithuanian towns have at least one bank with a functional ATM. Most big banks cash travellers cheques and exchange most major currencies, and credit cards are widely accepted.

Telephone
Mobile phones

It's relatively inexpensive to call home using another European mobile in Lithuania. Local prepaid SIM cards make it cheaper to call within the country. Mobile companies **Bitė** (www.bite.lt), **Omnitel** (www.omnitel.lt) and **Tele 2** (www.tele2.lt) sell prepaid SIM cards.

Phone codes

To call Lithuania from abroad, dial ☎370 then city code, followed by phone number. To call cities within Lithuania, dial ☎8 followed by city code and phone number.

To make an international call dial ☎00 before country code. To call a mobile phone within Lithuania, dial ☎8 followed by the three-digit code and mobile number, and to call a mobile from abroad dial ☎370 instead of ☎8.

Phonecards

Public telephones are increasingly rare given the widespread use of mobiles. They only accept phonecards, which are sold in denominations of 10/15/20/30Lt at newspaper kiosks.

Visas

Citizens from the EU, Australia, Canada, Israel, Japan, New Zealand, Switzerland and the US do not require visas for entry into Lithuania if staying for less than 90 days.

For information on other countries and obtaining a visa, visit www.migracija.lt.

Getting There & Away

The Europe-wide budget-airline explosion hasn't left Lithuania untouched. Kaunas, not Vilnius, is the destination for budget flights, though Vilnius is well served by numerous international flights, and plentiful rail, ferry and bus services make travel to neighbouring countries straightforward.

Since Lithuania's become a member of the EU, entering the country is unlikely to present any problems for most visitors. However, those crossing overland from Russia or Belarus can expect delays at the border.

Air

There are direct flights to Lithuania from a number of European cities, though none from North America to Lithuania.

There are three airports in Lithuania accepting international traffic.

Kaunas International Airport (www.kaunasair.lt) Nonstop flights to London, Edinburgh, Frankfurt, Oslo, Milan, Paris, Stockholm and Dublin, among others

Vilnius International Airport (www.vno.lt) Nonstop flights to London, Vienna, Moscow, Frankfurt, Paris, Warsaw, Dublin, Brussels and Prague, among others.

Palanga Airport (www.palanga-airport.lt) Nonstop flights to Copenhagen.

Airlines

The reliable national airline, **airBaltic** (www.airbaltic.com) runs direct flights between Vilnius and about a dozen Western European destinations, as well as from Palanga to Riga.

Major international carriers with direct flights to Vilnius:

Aer Lingus (☑5-252 5010; www.aerlingus.com)

Austrian Airlines (☑5-210 5030; www.austrian.com)

Czech Airlines (☑5-215 1503; www.czechairlines.com)

Estonian Air (☑5-232 9300; www.estonian-air.com)

Finnair (☑5-252 5010; www.finnair.com/lt)

LOT (☑5-273 9000; www.lot.com)

Lufthansa (☑5-232 9292; www.lufthansa.com)

SAS (www.flysas.com)

Land

Border crossings

Lithuania has border crossings with Latvia, Poland, Belarus and Russia. You must have a valid visa for entering both Belarus and Russia (Kaliningrad).

Bus

The main international bus companies operating in Lithuania are **Eurolines** (www.eurolines.lt) and **Ecolines** (www.ecolines.net). Sample destinations and prices:

Kaliningrad 65Lt, 7½ hours, daily

Rīga 60Lt, 4½ hours, at least four daily

Tallinn 116Lt, 10½ hours, up to five daily

Warsaw 59Lt, nine hours, one daily

Car & Motorcycle

Coming from the south, you're looking at a 30-minute to one-hour wait at the two Polish border crossings (Ogrodniki and Budzisko). Lines at the Latvian border are generally nonexistent. Have your passport, insurance and registration documents ready.

If you're planning on crossing into Russia (Kaliningrad) or Belarus in a rental car, check your rental conditions very carefully – most rental companies forbid this.

Train

Vilnius is linked by regular direct trains to Moscow, St Petersburg, Kaliningrad and Minsk; see www.litrail.lt. You'll need a Belarus visa for the Moscow train. Sample destinations and prices:

Kaliningrad from 84Lt, 6½ to 7½ hours, up to five daily

Minsk from 74Lt, four to 4½ hours, up to seven daily

Moscow 185Lt, 14¾ to 15¾ hours, up to three daily

St Petersburg from 146Lt, 13½ to 18 hours, twice daily

Sea

International ferry services depart from Klaipėda. Destinations include Germany and Sweden. See p519 for details.

Getting Around

Air

At the time of research, there were no domestic flights serving Lithuania.

Bicycle

Two-wheeled exploration of certain parts of the country is particularly rewarding as Lithuania is flat and its once-disastrous roads have much improved.

Bicycles are easy to rent on the Curonian Spit and all the major cities. Most tourist offices have maps of cycle routes and rent bicycles, and there are designated cycling lanes in the big cities and along the Curonian Spit.

Information about bike touring in Lithuania can be found on **BaltiCCycle** (www.bicycle.lt).

Bus

Lithuania is covered by an extensive network of buses and minibuses. There are several different companies handling each route so prices can vary. The most comfortable tend are Eurolines and Ecolines; free wi-fi and hot drinks are included in ticket price.

Ecolines (www.ecolines.net) Serves large cities and international destinations.

Eurolines (www.eurolines.com) Serves large cities and international destinations.

Kautra (www.kautra.lt) Serves most destinations within Lithuania.

Toks (www.toks.lt) Serves most destinations within Lithuania.

Car & Motorcycle

You can drive from any point in Lithuania to another in a couple of hours. Modern four-lane highways link Vilnius with Klaipėda (via Kaunas) and Panevėžys. See p526 for car-hire companies in Vilnius.

The speed limit in Lithuania is 50km/h in cities and 90km/h to 110km/h on highways. On the A1 (E85) between Vilnius and Kaunas, the speed limit is always 100km/h. Headlights must be switched on at all times, and winter tyres must be fitted between 1 November and 1 March.

It is useful to have an International Driving Permit (IDP), but your home-country licence with a photograph will suffice.

Local Transport

The main form of local transport is buses and route taxis (although the bigger cities also have well-developed tram and trolleybus systems).

A ride costs between 1.20 and 2Lt, with a small discount if you buy tickets from a *Lietuvos Spauda* kiosk. Punch your ticket in one of the punch boxes inside the vehicle or risk a fine.

Train

There are daily suburban train departures from Vilnius to Šiauliai, Kaunas, Ignalina, Klaipėda and Trakai. Trains are less frequent than buses. Suburban trains are reasonably comfortable.

For information about schedules, prices and services, contact **Lithuanian Rail** (www.litrail.lt).

Macedonia Македонија

Best Places to Eat

» Restaurant Lyra (p534)

» Stara Gradska Kuča
(p534)

» Letna Bavča Kaneo (p542)

Best Places to Stay

» Hotel Radika (p538)

» Villa Dihovo (p545)

» Hotel Pelister (p532)

» Chola Guest House (p544)

Why Go?

Macedonia is hard to beat. Part Balkan and part Mediterranean, and offering impressive ancient sites and buzzing modern nightlife, the country packs in much more action, activities and natural beauty than would seem possible for a place its size.

In summer, try hiking, mountain biking and climbing in remote mountains, or explore the Old Towns of Skopje, the capital, and Ohrid, noted for its sublime Byzantine churches and an immense lake great for swimming. Winter offers skiing and food-and-grog festivities.

Macedonia retains an undiscovered feel that is somewhat lacking elsewhere in Europe, as visitors will discover among the hospitable, laid-back locals. Agriculture remains vital, as seen by the endless vineyards, watermelon pyramids, hanging red peppers and tobacco plains dotted with storks' nests. Although infrastructure impatiently awaits upgrading, travelling is cheap, easy and hassle-free.

When to Go
Skopje

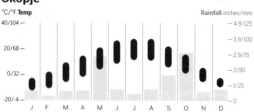

June–August
Enjoy the Ohrid Summer Festival's concerts and dive into Ohrid's 34km-long lake

September & October Get into Skopje's Beer Fest, Jazz Festival and harvest celebrations

December–February Ski Mavrovo and enjoy Macedonia's winter carnivals

Fast Facts

» **Area** 25,713 sq km

» **Capital** Skopje

» **Telephone country code** 389

» **Emergency** 194 (ambulance)

Exchange Rates

Australia	A$1	45MKD
Canada	C$1	44MKD
euro	€1	61MKD
Japan	¥100	51MKD
New Zealand	NZ$1	34MKD
UK	UK£1	69MKD
USA	US$1	43MKD

Set Your Budget

» **Hotel room in Skopje** 2500MKD

» **Two-course meal** 320MKD

» **Beer in bar** 120MKD

» **Skopje bus fare** 25MKD

» **Petrol (1L)** 70MKD

Resources

» **Macedonian Information Agency** (www.mia.com.mk)

» **Exploring Macedonia** (www.exploringmacedonia.com)

Connections

From Skopje, buses serve Sofia, Belgrade, Budapest, Pristina, Tirana, İstanbul, Thessaloniki and more. Thessaloniki's also the terminus for a train serving Belgrade via Skopje. Other ground borders include Novo Selo – near Strumica – for southern Bulgaria, and Lake Ohrid's border with Albania, past Sveti Naum Monastery.

ITINERARIES

One Week

Spend two nights in Skopje, visiting its Čaršija (old quarter), with historic churches, mosques and an Ottoman castle. Then travel southwest to Ohrid, with its nightlife, Old Town and lake. After two days, continue to cultured Bitola, and explore ancient Heraclea and Pelister National Park.

Two Weeks

After Skopje, Ohrid and Bitola, return via Kruševo, a historically significant mountain town, before visiting Prilep and the nearby Byzantine churches; finish with sampling wines in the Tikveš wine region and ancient Stobi.

Essential Food & Drink

» **Ajvar** Sweet red pepper sauce; accompanies meats and cheeses

» **Šopska salata** Tomatoes, onions and cucumbers topped with flaky soft *sirenje* (white cheese)

» **Uviač** Rolled chicken or pork wrapped in bacon and filled with melted yellow cheese

» **Skopsko** and **Dab lagers** Macedonia's favourite brews

» **Rakija** Grape-based firewater, useful for a toast (and cleaning cuts and windows!)

» **Vranec** and **Temjanika** Macedonia's favourite red- and white-wine varietals

SKOPJE СКОПЈЕ

02 / POP 670,000

Skopje in winter is enveloped by fog – symbolic of the conspiratorial overtones of a small Balkan city still haunted by the intrigues of foreign diplomats and chronic recriminations of rival political parties.

All the better, then, that these subtleties will be lost on most visitors. Skopje also offers Ottoman- and Byzantine-era wonders, like the 15th-century Kameni Most (Stone Bridge), Čaršija (old Turkish bazaar), Sveti Spas Church, with its ornate, hand-carved iconostasis, and the nearby Tvrdina Kale

Macedonia Highlights

1 Gaze out over Ohrid from the **Church of Sveti Jovan at Kaneo** (p539), immaculately set on a bluff above the lake

2 Unwind in historic **Skopje** (p529), combining Ottoman and Byzantine architecture with nightlife

3 Enjoy the Old World ambience of **Bitola** (p544)

and visit nearby Pelister National Park

4 Explore wineries, archaeological sites and lakes in the **Tikveš wine region** (p548)

5 Experience the serenity of the cliff-top **Zrze Monastery** (p547) near Prilep, with sweeping views of the Pelagonian Plain and priceless Byzantine artworks

6 Hit the slopes at **Mavrovo** (p537), site of Macedonia's premier ski resort in the west

7 Head to the offbeat village of **Dihovo** (p545) in Pelister National Park to leap boulders in the little Sapungica River, or scale the loftier nearby peaks

SKOPJE IN...

One Day

After a morning coffee on Skopje's **Ploštad Makedonija** (main square), cross the Vardar River on the **Kameni Most** (Stone Bridge) into the Old Town, the **Čaršija**. Here peruse Turkish mosques, converted *hammam*s and churches, as well as the new Holocaust Memorial Center, before ascending the **Tvrdina Kale Fortress** (Ottoman castle), where the Turks ruled for centuries; the ramparts offer impressive views. Then enjoy dinner and drinks in the new town or in the Čaršija.

Three Days

After seeing the Old Town sights, get another perspective from the forested **Mt Vodno**, flanking Skopje. Up here visit the Byzantine **church of Sveti Pantelejmon**. Along the cafe-lined ul Makedonija see the **Memorial House of Mother Teresa** and **Museum of the City of Skopje**.

    Lake Matka, west of Skopje, has a striking canyon and forests offering hiking trails and monastic grottos. Later, celebrate with live music complemented by beer or superb local wines at the **Čaršija's** stylish nightspots.

Fortress, Skopje's guardian since the 5th century. And, with its bars, clubs and galleries, the city has modern culture too.

◉ Sights

The Čaršija houses Skopje's main historic sights. Other museums are on the Vardar's southern shore, where cafes line pedestrianised ul Makedonija. Buzzing Ploštad Makedonija (Macedonia Sq) stands smack by the Ottoman stone bridge (Kameni Most), which accesses the Čaršija.

PLOŠTAD MAKEDONIJA & THE SOUTH BANK

Ploštad Makedonija   SQUARE

This square contains audacious new statues dedicated to various national heroes, plus smaller works depicting quotidian urban life. From here, stroll or cycle along the river bank, or relax in a river-facing cafe.

FREE **Memorial House of Mother Teresa**
                                          MUSEUM

(www.memorialhouseofmotherteresa.org; ul Makedonija bb; ⊙9am-8pm Mon-Fri, to 2pm Sat-Sun) Located in a two-storey structure, the Memorial House of Mother Teresa displays memorabilia from the life of the famed Catholic nun of Calcutta, born in Skopje in 1910.

FREE **Museum of the City of Skopje**
                                          MUSEUM

(Mito Hadživasilev Jasmin bb; ⊙9am-3pm Tue-Sat, to 1pm Sun) Ul Makedonija ends at the worthwhile city museum – exhibitions include ancient and Byzantine finds from Tvrdina Kale.

It's in the old train station; the stone fingers of its **clock** were frozen at 5.17am on 27 July 1963, the moment when Skopje's great earthquake struck, and they remain so today.

NORTH BANK & ČARŠIJA

Čaršija   OTTOMAN BAZAAR

Across the **Stone Bridge** (Kameni Most), the Čaršija reveals Skopje's Ottoman past, in its architecture and largely Muslim Albanian and Turkish population. On the left, the 1886 **Church of Sveti Dimitrija** (⊙9am-6pm) is a three-aisled structure. Behind the church stands the brand-new **Holocaust Memorial Center of the Jews from Macedonia** (www.holocaustfund.org, 11 Mart bb admission free, ⊙9am-5pm Tue-Sun;) opened in March 2011, it commemorates the all-but-lost Sephardic Jewish culture of Macedonia through a range of educational photos, wall texts, maps and video. Some 98% of Macedonian Jews (7148 individuals in total) perished in the Holocaust. Across from it, the double domes of the **Daut Paša Baths** (1466), once the Balkans' largest Turkish bath, rise unmistakably. The **City Art Gallery** (Kruševska 1a; admission 100MKD; ⊙9am-3pm Tue-Sun), also housed here, displays modern art. Another old bath turned art gallery is the **Čifte Amam** (admission 50MKD; ⊙9am-4.45pm Mon-Fri, to 3pm Sat, to 1pm Sun) The Čaršija ends at **Bit Pazar**, a big, busy vegetable market purveying bric-a-brac, household goods and anything random.

Sveti Spas Church   CHURCH

(Makarie Frc/vkoski 8; admission 100MKD; ⊙8am-3pm Tue-Sun) Past the Čaršija's shops, teahouses and bars, ul Samoilova accesses the intriguing Sveti Spas Church. Built partially underground (the Turks banned churches from being taller than mosques), it boasts a wood-carved iconostasis 10m wide and 6m high, built by early 19th-century master craftsmen Makarije Frčkovski and the brothers Petar and Marko Filipovski.

Outside, the **Tomb and Museum of Goce Delčev** contains the remains of Macedonia's foremost national hero. Leader of the VMRO (Internal Macedonian Revolutionary Organisation), Delčev was killed by Turks in 1903.

Museum of Macedonia   MUSEUM
(www.musmk.org.mk; Čurčiska 86; admission 50MKD; ☉9am-5pm Tue-Sun) Documenting neolithic through communist times, this museum contains an ethnographical exhibition, plus ancient jewellery and coins, icons and wood-carved iconostases. Opposite, archaeological items decorate **Kuršumli An** (1550), once an Ottoman *caravanserai* (inn), now used for concerts and films.

Sultan Murat Mosque   MOSQUE
On the other side of bul K Misirkov from Bit Pazar, **Sultan Murat mosque** (1436) features a distinctive, red-tipped clock tower and Ottoman *madrasa* (Islamic school) remains.

KALE & AROUND

Mustafa Paša Mosque   MOSQUE
(Samoilova bb) Above Sveti Spas, the 1492 Mustafa Paša Mosque exemplifies magnificent Ottoman architecture, with a lawn, garden and fountain.

FREE **Tvrdina Kale Fortress**   FORTRESS
(☉daylight hours) Opposite Mustafa Paša Mosque, Tvrdina Kale Fortress, built in the 6th century AD by the Byzantines, still conceals archaeological finds from neolithic to Ottoman times. The ramparts offer great views over the city and river.

Museum of Contemporary Art   MUSEUM
(www.msuskopje.org.mk; Samoilova bb; admission 100MKD; ☉10am-5pm Tue-Sat, 9am-1pm Sun) Further on from Tvrdina Kale Fortress, the Museum of Contemporary Art displays works by Macedonian and world-famous artists (there's even a Picasso).

MT VODNO & AROUND

Mt Vodno   MOUNTAIN
Framing Skopje to the south, Mt Vodno is popular with hikers, though a gondola up the mountainside for cheaters is being planned. Two restaurants stand at Sredno (Middle) Vodno (taxis drive here for 150MKD). Hiking trails to the mountain top access the 66m-high **Millenium Cross** (2002), the world's largest, which is illuminated at night.

Sveti Pantelejmon Monastery   MONASTERY
Further west along Vodno, in Gorno Nerezi village, the Sveti Pantelejmon Monastery (1164) is among Macedonia's most significant churches. Its remarkable Byzantine frescos, like the *Lamentation of Christ,* depict a pathos and realism predating the Renaissance by two centuries. It's 5km from Skopje's centre (by taxi, 140MKD) and offers great views.

MACEDONIA

AROUND SKOPJE

A half-hour drive, or slightly longer city bus trip, accesses tranquil **Lake Matka**. Although crowded at weekends, this idyllic spot beneath the steep Treska Canyon is excellent, offering hiking, rock climbing, caving (€10) and ancient churches in its forested environs. On-site restaurants provide nourishment and lake views.

In summer 2010 visiting European divers discovered that Matka's caverns are nearing the continental record (218m deep); future explorations may prove Lake Matka to be Europe's deepest.

Matka's traditional link with the Virgin Mary (Matka means 'womb' in Macedonian) is accentuated by grotto shrines like **Sveta Bogorodica**. From here a steep path reaches **Sveti Spas**, **Sveta Trojca** and **Sveta Nedela** – the last, a 4km walk (around 1½ hours). These caves once sheltered ascetics and anti-Ottoman revolutionaries.

After the **Church of Sveti Nikola**, beyond the dam and across the bridge, visit the frescoed **Church of Sveti Andrej** (1389). The adjoining mountaineering hut **Matka** (☎3052 655; per bed 500MKD) offers guides, climbing gear and accommodation.

From Skopje get here by driving, taking a taxi (350MKD) or catching bus 60 along bul Partizanski Odredi (50MKD, 40 minutes, hourly).

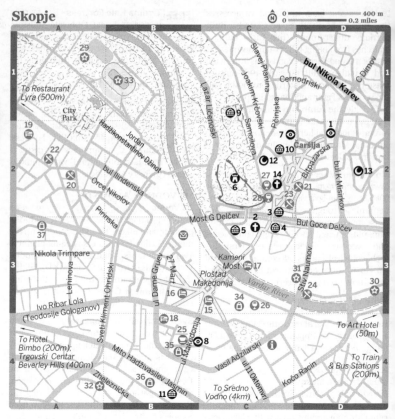

✦ Festivals & Events

Skopsko Leto
(www.dku.org.mk) Comprises art exhibitions, performances and concerts in summer.

Pivolend
(www.pivolend.com.mk) Held in September at Kale, this event features rock acts and DJs – plus numerous international beers.

Skopje Jazz Festival
(www.skopjejazzfest.com.mk) This October festival always features at least one world-renowned artist.

May Opera Evenings
In May, this event and **Off-Fest** (www.offest.com.mk) combine world music and DJ events.

Taxirat Festival
Good rock bands sometimes feature at this December festival.

🛏 Sleeping

Skopje accommodation is overpriced. Old Town accommodation ranges from suspiciously seedy to outrageously expensive; better deals are within a five-minute walk, taxi or bus ride from the centre.

Hotel Pelister   BOUTIQUE HOTEL **€€**
(☎3239 584; www.pelisterhotel.com.mk; Ploštad Makedonija; s/d/apt from €59/65/85; ✳@🛜) Located above the eponymous restaurant (both until recently called 'Dal Met Fu'), Pelister has well-designed rooms with great views; however, its central address means it can be noisy.

Hotel Square   BUDGET HOTEL **€€**
(☎3225 090; www.hotelsquare.com.mk; 6th fl, Nikola Vapcarov 2; s/d/tr €45/60/75; ✳@) Well situated high above the action, the Square offers cosy, well-kept and modern rooms. The balcony cafe offers great views. An optional breakfast (€5 extra) is in **Café Trend**

below. Look for the signposted business–apartment block off Ploštad Makedonija.

Art Hostel   HOSTEL €
(☎3223 789; www.art-hostel.com.mk; Ante Hadz/vimitkov 5; dm/s/d €12/25/40; ✳@☎) In its brand-new location only a five-minute walk from the train and bus stations in a little neighborhood along the River Vardar, Art Hostel remains Skopje's most popular choice for backpackers. It has clean, if slightly cramped, six-bed dorms and small private rooms, shared bathrooms that are clean and new, friendly service, free wifi and a big common area bar. It's in easy walking distance of both the train and bus and the city centre. The relaxed vibe is enhanced by a billiards table and low-lit outdoor balcony with couches.

Tim's Apartments   APARTMENTS €€
(☎3237 650; www.tims.com.mk/; Orce Nikolov 120; s/d/apt €69/89/110; ✳@☎) Near the park,

Tim's has 10 classy rooms and seven apartments with kitchenettes.

Hotel TCC Plaza   LUXURY HOTEL €€€
(☎3111 807; www.tccplaza.com; Vasil Glavinov 12; s/d/ste €95/115/144; ℗✳@☎⌘) This central, five-star hotel offers spacious, well-lit rooms and suites, plus a spa centre with a modest swimming pool, and fitness and massage services.

Hotel Bimbo   HOTEL €€
(☎3214 517; www.hotelbimbo.com.mk; 29 Noemvri 63; s/d incl breakfast €40/55; ✳@) Basic but clean rooms, with a cosy breakfast nook. It's in a residential area near Skopje's centre.

Hotel Stone Bridge   LUXURY HOTEL €€€
(☎3244 900; www.stonebridge-hotel.com; Kej Dimitar Vlahov 1; s/d/apt €138/159/259; ℗✳@☎) This deluxe hotel across the Stone Bridge has sophisticated rooms graced with stylised Ottoman furnishings, though it's arguably overpriced.

Eating

Skopje's restaurants work until midnight; nonsmoking laws are strictly enforced. *Skara* (grilled meat) is popular, as well as international cuisine. For breakfast, try *burek* (white cheese, spinach or ground meat in filo pastry) with drinking yoghurt.

The Čaršija has *kebapčilnici* (beef kebab restaurants) – the lurid, lesser-visited ones can prove unsafe for the belly, though.

Stara Gradska Kuča
MACEDONIAN €€
(Pajko Maalo 14; mains 250-400MKD; ⊗8am-midnight) This restored traditional house has a warm ambience, an excellent assortment of traditional Macedonian dishes and, sometimes, live Macedonian music.

Restaurant Lyra
FINE DINING €€€
(Nikola Tesla 11; mains 350-500MKD; ⊗9am-midnight) One of Skopje's fancier establishments, Lyra has a subdued atmosphere, excellent service and wine list, and inventive Macedonian and international dishes.

Restaurant Pelister
INTERNATIONAL €€
(Ploštad Makedonija; mains 280-350MKD; ⊗7.30am-midnight) It might strike tourists as, well, touristy, but this big square-front place (previously Dal Met Fu) is appreciated by locals for its light pastas, cheerful staff and preening position behind big windows. There's a self-serve salad bar for vegetarians.

Kebapčilnica Destan
KEBABS €
(ul 104 6; 10 kebabs for 120MKD) Skopje's best beef kebabs, accompanied by seasoned grilled bread, are at this classic Čaršija place.

Idadija
SKARA €€
(Rade Koncar 1; mains 180-250MKD) In the quiet Debar Maalo neighbourhood's *skara* corner, Idadija has been serving excellent grills for 80 years.

Restaurant Roulette
SKARA €€
(Simeon Kavrakirov 9a; mains 150-250MKD) The best restaurant near the train and bus stations, this local favourite on a residential side street does good grilled meats.

Papu
MACEDONIAN €€
(Djuro Djakovic 63; mains 250-400MKD) The tastes and decor of old Kruševo are preserved at this lovely place studded with stone arches and antiques and filled with the sounds of cascading water.

Pivnica An
MACEDONIAN, INTERNATIONAL €€€
(Čaršija; mains 300-500MKD) You're paying for the ambience at this 'beerhouse' located in a restored Ottoman building's sumptuous courtyard (while tasty, the food is over-priced).

Drinking

Popular new nightspots are now breathing life into the Old Town. Cafes and bars work until 1am on summer weekends, though nightclubs continue until late.

While the average price for a beer in most places is 70MKD to 100MKD – an espresso less – the popular newer bars are, alas, suffering from severe price inflation.

Vinoteka Temov
WINE BAR
(Gradište 1-a; ⊗9am-midnight Mon-Thur, to 1am Fri-Sun) Skopje's best wine bar, in a restored wood building near Sveti Spas, exudes ambience. A vast (but pricey) wine list presents the manifold flavours of Macedonia's vineyards, while live traditional and classical guitarists often play.

La Bodeguito Del Medio
LATIN BAR
(Kej 13 Noemvri; ⊗9am-1am) Known to locals as 'the Cuban', this gregarious riverfront place does do Cuban food – but it's best at night, when the long bar is lined with carousers and inventive cocktails.

Old Town Brewery
BEER HALL
(Gradište 1; ⊗10am-1am Mon-Fri, to 3am Fri-Sun) This beer bar above Vinoteka Temov is Skopje's only place for a yard of beer, and the selection is good (though pricey). In summer, the benches spill outside, where bands cover classic rock.

Café di Roma
CAFE
(Makedonija; ⊗8am-1am) This stylish place opposite the Memorial House of Mother Teresa does Skopje's best espresso and other caffeinated drinks, hot and cold.

Café Trend
CAFE
(Ploštad Makedonija; ⊗8am-1am) Aspiring socialites mix with (and gossip about) local celebrities at this slick square-side place.

Entertainment

Skopje is among southeastern Europe's clubbing hot spots, hosting well-known international DJs; see www.skopjeclubbing.com.mk.

Colosseum
NIGHTCLUB
(www.colosseum.com.mk; City Park in summer, under train station in winter) This is Skopje's biggest and most popular club, along with **Element** (www.element.com.mk; City Park).

When international DJs appear, tickets run 250MKD to 500MKD.

Multimedia Center Mala Stanica
GALLERY CAFE

(www.nationalgallery.mk; Zheleznička 18; ⊙9am-midnight) Featuring arty, ornate decor, the National Art Gallery's cafe hosts temporary exhibitions and live music.

Club Castro
ROCK BAR

(train station; ⊙8pm-4am) This sweaty student favourite under the train station offers live rock, reggae and ska.

Hard Rock
ROCK BAR

(Kej Dimitar Vlahov bb; ⊙10pm-4am) Popular late at night, Hard Rock features DJs and, sometimes, live bands.

Universal Hall
LIVE MUSIC

(☑3224 158; bul Partizanski Odredi bb) Hosts classical, jazz, pop and kids' performances.

Macedonian National Theatre
THEATRE

(☑3114 060; www.mnt.com.mk; Kej Dimitar Vlahov bb) In a communist-era building, the theatre hosts opera, ballet and classical music.

Kino Milenium
CINEMA

(☑3120 389; www.kinomilenium.mk, in Macedonian; Gradski Trgovski Centar) Skopje's central movie theatre.

Kino Ramstore
CINEMA

(Ramstore Mall, Mito Hadživasilev Jasmin bb) This Skopje cinema is smaller than Kino Milenium.

🛍 Shopping

Čaršija sells jewellery, traditional carpets, dresses and more. Bit Pazar sells fruit, vegetables and things you're less likely to need. The **Gradski Trgovski Centar** (11 Oktomvri) and **Ramstore** (Mito Hadživasilev Jasmin bb) are major malls. **Trgovski Centar Bunjakovec** (bul Partizanski) and **Trgovski Centar Beverly Hills** (Naroden Front) are smaller shopping centres.

Ikona
HANDICRAFTS

(Luj Paster 19; ⊙9am-9pm Mon-Fri, to 4pm Sat) 'Traditional' souvenirs, including icons, archaeological replicas, pottery, painted boxes and folk dolls.

Lithium Records
MUSIC

(www.lithiumrecords.com.mk; Gradski Trgovski Centar; ⊙8.30am-8pm Mon-Sat) Lithium sells Macedonian and international CDs, plus concert and festival tickets.

ℹ Information

Dangers & Annoyances

Skopje is basically safe. Drivers are creatively reckless, though; be wary of cars and unexpected cracks and holes on pavements. Roma children's begging can be frustrating – hapless visitors are occasionally besieged by juvenile gangs sticking their hands into loose pockets. Inebriated folks leaving bars late at night may also attract these unfortunate, exploited children.

Skopje's wild dogs are less troublesome than before, though joggers and cyclists are still fair game.

Emergency

These numbers are valid nationwide. By law, any working mobile phone (even one lacking prepaid credit) can call them.

Ambulance (☑194)

Fire Brigade (☑193)

Police (☑192)

Roadside Assistance (☑196)

Internet Access

Find free wi-fi internet in cafes, restaurants, hotels and on some bus routes through the city centre. Internet cafes exist around the centre and at the train and bus stations.

Medical Services

City hospital (☑3130 111; 11 Oktomvri 53; ⊙24hr)

Neuromedica private clinic (☑3133 313; 11 Oktomvri 25; ⊙24hr)

Money

ATMs and *menuvačnici* (exchange offices) abound.

Menuvačnica Euro (Gradski Trgovski Centar; ⊙9am-8.30pm Mon-Sat)

Post & Telephone

The **Main Post Office** (☑3141 141; Orce Nikolov 1; ⊙7am-7.30pm Mon-Sat, 7.30am-2.30pm Sun) is 75m northwest of Ploštad Makedonija. Others are opposite the train station, in the Gradski Trgovski Centar and in Ramstore.

The train-station branch houses a telephone centre. Some kiosks (newsagents) have private telephones.

Tourist Information

City of Skopje Bureau for Tourism and Information (www.skopje.mk; Vasil Adzilarski bb; ⊙8.30am-4.30pm Mon-Fri) Skopje's tourism office offers useful info.

Travel Agencies

Go Macedonia (www.gomacedonia.com.mk; Trgovski Centar Beverly Hills lok 32, Naroden

TRANSPORT FROM SKOPJE

Domestic Buses

DESTINATION	COST (MKD)	DURATION (HR)	DAILY DEPARTURES
Bitola	470	3	12
Gostivar	200	1	12
Kavadarci	250	2	7
Kruševo	380	3	3
Makedonski Brod	330	3	5
Mavrovo	330	2	7 Mon-Fri, 2 Sat-Sun
Negotino	210	2½	11 Mon-Fri, 9 Sat-Sun
Ohrid	520	3	11
Prilep	380	2½	14

International Buses

DESTINATION	COST (MKD)	DURATION (HR)	DAILY DEPARTURES
Belgrade	1400	10	12
İstanbul	2560	12	5
Ljubljana	3750	14	1
Pristina	320	2	12
Sofia	1040	5½	5
Thessaloniki	1280	4	1 Mon, Wed & Fri
Zagreb	3150	12	1

Domestic Trains

DESTINATION	COST (MKD)	DURATION (HR)	DAILY DEPARTURES
Bitola	200	4	3
Gevgelija	185	2½	3
Kičevo	136	2	3
Kumanovo	59	40 min	4
Negotino	132	2	3
Prilep	166	3	3

Front 19) Arranges hiking, cycling, caving and winery tours.

Macedonia Travel (www.macedoniatravel.com; Orce Nikolov 109/1, lok 3) Does tours, including trips to Jasen Nature Reserve, and discounted air tickets.

Websites

Lonely Planet (www.lonelyplanet.com) has useful links. Other recommended English-language websites:

Skopjeonline.com.mk General info, including local attractions, shopping and entertainment

Skopje.gov.com Skopje's official website

Skopje.mk Official website of Skopje's tourism office

 Getting There & Away

Air

Alexander the Great Airport (www.airports.com.mk; Aerodrom Aleksandar Veliki), 21km east of Skopje, handles most international flights. However, flying into Sofia or Thessaloniki and travelling to Skopje by ground is often cheaper.

Airlines flying to/from Skopje:

Adria Airways (www.adria.si)

Austrian Airlines (www.austrian.com)

Croatia Airlines (www.croatiaairlines.hr)

JAT (www.jat.com)

Macedonian Airlines (MAT, IN; www.mat.com.mk)

SkyWings (www.skywings.info)

Turkish Airlines (www.thy.com)

Bus

Skopje's **bus station** (www.sas.com.mk; bul Jane Sandanski), with ATM, exchange office and English-language info, adjoins the train station.

Buses to Ohrid go via Kičevo (three hours, 167km) or Bitola (four to five hours, 261km) – book ahead in summer. One boxed text above lists several domestic routes while the one below lists international routes. Most inter-city buses are air-conditioned and are generally faster than trains, though more expensive too.

Train

The **train station** (Zheleznička Stanica, bul Jane Sandanski) serves local and international destinations. Northbound trains pass through Kumanovo for Serbia. The southbound service transits Veles; from here, one line continues south through Gevgelija for Greece, while the other forks southwest through Prilep for Bitola.

Another line serves eastern Macedonian towns, while a lesser-used western line terminates at Kičevo. The domestic train routes boxed text below has further details.

International train routes serve Thessaloniki (920MKD, 4½hrs, two daily) and Belgrade (1300MKD, eight to 10 hours, two daily). There's also one line to Pristina.

🛈 Getting Around

TO/FROM THE AIRPORT There's (still) no airport bus. Taxi prices should be signposted; they're around 1000MKD to 1200MKD. To avoid miscommunications, inspect the written rates with the driver present. Note that you are entitled to be taken to Skopje on the aftopat (highway) – drivers will occasionally try and persuade passengers to go on back-road adventures, just to avoid paying tolls.

BICYCLE Bike lanes on major streets, and along the Vardar River's north bank, let you cycle (or roller-blade) across town. For basic bike rental (10MKD per hour for a classic, basket-fronted contraption), bring your passport to the rental booth, located near the parking lot on Ploštad Makedonija's western end.

BUS Skopje city buses cost 25MKD to 35MKD and congregate under the bus and train stations, behind the enclosed area where intercity buses depart. Bus 22 usefully cuts through the city centre and down bul Partizanski Odredi.

CAR Daily rental prices start at 26,000MKD. Try **Budget Car Rental** (Mito Hadživasilev Jasmin bb).

TAXI Skopje's base rate is 50MKD, and drivers use their meters. Central destinations cost 50MKD to 100MKD. **Lotus** has spiffy, air-conditioned cars, and **Naše Taxi** is also good. Legit cabs usually have the five-digit ordering phone number (starting with 🖉151) emblazoned somewhere. Various dubious cabs hover near Bit Pazar; worse are the pushy drivers working outside (and sometimes inside) the bus and train stations – they're happy to cheat locals and tourists alike. Avoid being cheated by instead hailing passing cabs heading in your direction.

WESTERN MACEDONIA

Western Macedonia gets most of Macedonia's visitors, and no wonder – its mountain ranges provide a stunning backdrop, running south from Šar Planina to the gentler Jablanica range, ending with the 34km-long Lake Ohrid.

Lying outstretched southward, and flanked by Galičica National Park, the lake's dotted with coastal and upland villages. Ohrid town itself boats manifold historic sites, a lovely old quarter and summer cultural events and nightlife.

Mavrovo National Park
МАВРОВО НАЦИОНАЛЕН ПАРК

🖉042

Mavrovo's ski resort is Macedonia's biggest, though the rarefied air and stunning vistas are great year-round. It comprises 730 sq km of birch and pine forest, gorges, karst fields and waterfalls, plus Macedonia's highest peak, Mt Korab (2764m). Located up a winding road southwest of Gostivar, Mavrovo lies near the must-see Sveti Jovan Bigorski Monastery and Galičnik, famous for its traditional village wedding.

👁 Sights & Activities

Zare Lazarevski Ski Centre   SKI RESORT
(🖉489 002; www.zarelaz.com; ⊙8am-10pm) Macedonia's top ski resort, with average snow cover of 70cm and slopes from 1860m to 2255m, Zare Lazarevski offers ski rental (600MKD), lift tickets (800MKD/3500MKD

per day/week) and a ski school. The Hotel Bistra (p538) is nearest the slopes. Mavrovo's also good for summer hiking.

Sveti Jovan Bigorski Monastery MONASTERY
Off the Debar road, Sveti Jovan Bigorski is a Byzantine monastery dating from 1020, where an icon of Sveti Jovan Bigorski (St John the Forerunner, ie St John the Baptist) miraculously appeared. Since then it's been rebuilt often – the miraculous icon occasionally reappearing. The impressive church also houses Jovan's alleged forearm.

However, Bigorski's main attraction is its awe-inspiring iconostasis. The final of just three such iconostases carved by local craftsmen Makarije Frčkovski and the brothers Filipovski between 1829 and 1835, this colossal work depicting biblical scenes is enlivened with 700 tiny human and animal figures. Gazing up at this enormous, intricate masterpiece is breathtaking. After finishing, the carvers allegedly flung their tools into the nearby Radika River – ensuring that the secret of their artistic genius would be washed away forever.

Galičnik TRADITIONAL VILLAGE
Up a winding, tree-lined road ending in a rocky moonscape 17km southwest of Mavrovo, almost depopulated Galičnik features traditional houses rising from the mountainside. It's placid except for 12 and 13 July, when the **Galičnik Wedding** sees one or two lucky couples wed here. Visit, along with 3000 happy Macedonians, and enjoy eating, drinking, traditional folk dancing and music.

🛏 Sleeping & Eating

If staying for the wedding, book ahead. Go Macedonia (p535) arranges Galičnik Wedding trips that include transport, guided activities, local accommodation and monastery tours.

TOP CHOICE **Hotel Radika** SPA HOTEL €€
(📞223 300; www.radika.com.mk; Lenovo village; s/d/apt €39/59/69; P☀🏠) Just 5km from Mavrovo, this ultraposh spa hotel is perfect for pampering, with numerous massage treatments and excellent rooms. Prices fall considerably in summer. Nondrivers should take a taxi from Gostivar (600MKD), on the Skopje–Ohrid road.

Sveti Jovan Bigorski MONASTERY €
(📞478 675; per person €5) The self-catering dormitories here are under reconstruction – check ahead.

Hotel Srna SKI LODGE €€
(📞388 083; www.hotelsrnamavrovo.com; Mavrovo; s/d/apt €20/40/60; ☀✹@) The smaller Srna, 400m from the chairlifts, has breezy, clean rooms.

Hotel Bistra SKI LODGE €€
(📞489 002; www.bistra.com; Mavrovo; s/d €65/90; P☀✹🏠☀) The Bistra has comfortable, clean rooms and amenities (restaurant, bar, pool, fitness centre, sauna) for cultivating that ski-lodge glow, plus jacuzzis in the deluxe rooms. Prices fall in summer. It also runs the simpler **Hotel Ski Škola** (s/d €20/40) and **Hotel Mavrovski** (s/d €20/40); guests can use the Bistra's facilities.

ℹ Getting There & Away

Southbound buses reach Mavrovo Anovi (2km away) en route to Debar (120MKD, seven daily), or while travelling north to Tetovo (140MKD, five daily) and Skopje (180MKD, three daily).

For Sveti Jovan Bigorski Monastery, drive; alternatively, buses transiting Debar for Ohrid or Struga will drop you at the entrance.

Ohrid ОХРИД

📞046 / POP 55,700
Sublime Ohrid is Macedonia's prime destination, with its atmospheric old quarter with beautiful churches stacked up a graceful hill, all topped by a medieval castle overlooking serene, 34km-long Lake Ohrid. Nearby, mountainous Galičica National Park offers pristine nature, while secluded beaches dot the lake's eastern shore.

Ohrid and its beaches are packed from 15 July to 15 August, when the popular summer festival is held. For more tranquillity, try June or September.

Lake Ohrid, 300m deep and three million years old, shared by Macedonia (two-thirds) and Albania (one-third), is among Europe's deepest and oldest. Although usually calm, during storms Ohrid seethes with steely-grey whitecaps evoking the sea.

History

Fourth-century-BC Lychnidos ('city of light' in Ancient Greek, evincing the lake's clarity) hugged the Via Egnatia connecting Constantinople with the Adriatic. Under Byzantium, it became a trade, cultural and ecclesiastical centre.

Slavic migrations created the name Ohrid (from *vo rid*, or 'city on the hill'). Bulgarian Slavs arrived in 867, and the Ohrid literary school – the first Slavic university – was established by 9th-century Saints Kliment and Naum. Macedonia's Christianisation specifically and Slavic literacy in general were expedited when Kliment created the Cyrillic alphabet.

Ohrid became the stronghold of Bulgarian Cars Simeon (r 893–927) and Samoil (r 997–1014). When the Byzantines defeated Samoil, Ohrid was reclaimed. Ottoman Turks conquered Ohrid (and Macedonia), in the late 14th century. In 1767 Greek intrigue caused the abolition of Ohrid's archbishopric – a long-lasting grievance for both Macedonians and Bulgarians. Today, the restored archbishopric represents the Macedonian Orthodox Church's highest office.

◉ Sights

Ohrid churches charge 100MKD admission. Churches and museums are closed on Monday.

To see Ohrid's sights in the most efficient and least exhausting way, start at the **Gorna Porta** (Upper Gate), about 80MKD from centre by taxi.

Church of Sveta Bogorodica Perivlepta
CHURCH

(admission 100MKD; ⊙9am-1pm & 4-8pm) Just inside the Gorna Porta, this 13th-century Byzantine church has vivid biblical frescos and an **icon gallery** (Gorna Porta; ⊙9am-2pm & 5-8pm, closed Mon) highlighting the founders' artistic achievements.

FREE Classical Amphitheatre AMPHITHEATRE
Straight from Gorna Porta, Ohrid's impressive Classical Amphitheatre was built for theatre; the Romans later removed 10 rows to accommodate gladiators. It hosts Summer Festival (p539) performances.

Car Samoil's Castle
MEDIEVAL CASTLE

(30MKD; ⊙9am-6pm Tue-Sun) The massive, turreted walls of the 10th-century Car Samoil's Castle indicate the power of the medieval Bulgarian state. Ascend the narrow stone stairways to the ramparts for fantastic views.

Plaošnik
CHURCH

(admission free; ⊙9am-6pm) Down a wooded path below the castle looms Plaošnik, also called the church of Sveti Kliment i Pantelejmon. This 5th-century basilica was restored in 2002 according to its Byzantine design – an almost unprecedented feat. The multidomed church has glass floor segments revealing original foundations. It houses St

Kliment's relics, with intricate 5th-century mosaics outside.

Just across, **4th-century church foundations**, replete with Early Christian mosaics of flora and fauna, stand under a protective roof.

Church of Sveti Jovan at Kaneo
CHURCH

(admission 50MKD; ⊙9am-6pm) The stunning sight of the 13th-century Church of Sveti Jovan at Kaneo, set on a cliff over the lake, emerges at the wooded path's end. It's possibly Macedonia's most photographed structure, and it's a wonderful place to relax. Peer down into the azure waters and you'll see why medieval monks found spiritual inspiration here. The small church has original frescos behind the altar.

Sveta Sofija Cathedral
CHURCH

(Car Samoil bb; 100MKD;⊙10am-8pm) Ohrid's grandest church, 11th-century Sveta Sofija is supported by columns and decorated with elaborate Byzantine frescos. Its superb acoustics mean it's often used for concerts.

Come by the road running down from Kaneo, past the Old Town's lovely houses, or along the new overwater walking bridge, beginning on the beach south of Kaneo.

National Museum
MUSEUM

(Car Samoil 62; admission 50MKD; ⊙9am-4pm & 7-11pm Tue-Sun) Near Sveta Sofija, the 1827 National Museum features distinctive white-and-brown architecture. The **Robev Residence** houses ancient epigraphy and the **Urania Residence** opposite has an ethnographic display.

Sveta Bogorodica Bolnička & Sveti Nikola Bolnički
CHURCHES

Ohrid's two other frescoed 14th-century churches are open infrequently (ask at the museum). *Bolnica* means hospital in Macedonian; during plagues visitors faced 40-day quarantines here.

Činar
PLANE TREE

Stroll ul Sveti Kliment Ohridski, lined with cafes and shops, to reach this enormous, 900-year-old plane tree – a likeable Ohrid landmark.

✯ Festivals & Events

Balkan Festival of Folk Dances & Songs
This July festival draws regional folkloric groups.

Ohrid Summer Festival
(☏262 304; www.ohridsummer.com.mk) Features classical and opera concerts, theatre and dance.

Ohrid

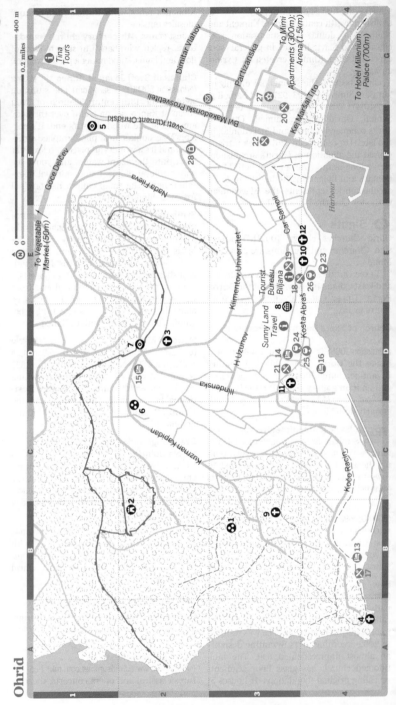

Sveti Naum–Ohrid swimming marathon This 30km event is usually in August.

Macedonian language course (www.ukim.edu.mk/smjlk; €850) This three-week course, run each August by the SS Cyril & Methodius University, attracts international students. It includes language lessons, cultural excursions and accommodation, and is, by all accounts, great fun.

🛏 Sleeping

Private rooms or **apartments** (per person €5-10) are advertised by the sign 'sobi' (rooms) – search, or ask agencies like Sunny Land Tourism (p542) or Tourist Bureau Biljana (p542). Since quality varies, shop around – and do avoid the pushy people who wait outside the bus station to pounce on arriving travellers.

Vila Sveta Sofija HOTEL €€
(☑254 370; www.vilasofija.com.mk; Kosta Abraš 64; s/d €35/60, ste €80-120; ❄@) This opulent getaway combines traditional furnishings with chic modern bathrooms in an old Ohrid mansion near Sveta Sofija.

Villa Lucija RENTED ROOMS €€
(☑265 608; www.vilalucija.com.mk; Kosta Abraš 29; s/d/apt €15/25/40; ❄@) Lucija has fantastic Old Town ambience and lovingly decorated, breezy rooms with lake-view balconies.

Stefan Kanevče Rooms RENTED ROOMS €
(☑234 813; apostolanet@yahoo.co.uk; Kočo Racin 47; per person €10) Near Kaneo beach, this atmospheric 19th-century house boasts carved wooden ceilings and good hospitality.

Mimi Apartments APARTMENT €
(☑250 103; mimioh@mail.com.mk; Strašo Pinđur 2; r incl breakfast 800MKD) Spacious, centrally located private rooms with fridge.

Villa Forum HOTEL €€
(☑267 060; www.villaforumohrid.com.mk; Kuzman Kapidan 1; s/d/apt €25/60/70; ❄@) This luxurious Gorna Porta hotel has well-furnished, comfortable rooms with sparkling bathrooms.

Hotel Millenium Palace HOTEL €€€
(☑263 361; www.milleniumpalace.com.mk; Kej Maršal Tito bb; s/d/ste/apt €49/70/99/149; ❄🛜≋) Odd-looking on the outside but nice inside, this waterfront hotel has business-class rooms, gym, sauna and indoor swimming pool with cocktail bar. Suites have lake-view terraces.

🍴 Eating

Old Town restaurants are best; self-caterers have **Tinex supermarket** (bul Makedonski Prosvetiteli) and the **vegetable market** (Kliment Ohridski).

Don't order Ohrid's endemic trout – it's endangered and (supposedly) protected from fishing, and dearer than the *mavrovska* and *kaliforniska* varieties.

TOP CHOICE **Letna Bavča Kaneo** SEAFOOD €
(Kočo Racin 43; fish 100-300MKD) This simple 'summer terrace' on Kaneo beach is inexpensive and great. A fry-up of diminutive *plasnica* fish, plus salad, feeds two. Swim from the restaurant's dock and soak up the summer sun.

Restaurant Antiko MACEDONIAN €€
(Car Samoil 30; mains 350-600MKD) In an old Ohrid mansion, the famous Antiko has great traditional ambience and pricey, but good, traditional dishes.

Pizzeria Leonardo PIZZA €
(Car Samoil 31; pizzas 200-350MKD) Ohrid's best pizza is served here – it's popular with locals too.

Restoran Belvedere SKARA €
(Kej Maršal Tito 2; mains 300MKD) Try the excellent *skara* (grilled meats) here, where outdoor tables extend under a leafy canopy.

Restoran Sveta Sofija MACEDONIAN €€€
(Car Samoil 88; mains 300-500MKD) This upscale restaurant opposite Sveta Sofija serves traditional fare and more than 100 Macedonian wines.

Drinking & Entertainment

Aquarius CAFE
(Kosta Abraš bb; ☉10am-1am) Ohrid's original lake-terrace cafe, Aquarius remains cool for a midday coffee and is lively at night.

Liquid CAFE
(Kosta Abraš 17; ☉9am-1am) This hip, chill-out place near Aquarius also has a lake-front patio and is good for a relaxed drink.

Jazz Inn BAR
(Kosta Abraš 74; ☉10pm-4am) This dark, late-night bar plays predominantly jazz and funk.

Cuba Libre BAR
(Kosta Abraš; ☉10pm-4am) This festive, Old Town bar and club is perennially popular.

Arena NIGHTCLUB
(cnr Jane Sandanski & Karpoš Vojvoda; ☉10pm-4am) Sweaty, packed pop and rock nightclub Arena is 1.5km from town.

Dom na Kultura CULTURAL HALL
(Grigor Prličev; admission 50-100MKD) The house of culture holds cultural events and houses Ohrid's movie theatre.

Shopping

Bisera PEARLS
(Sveti Kliment Ohridski 60; ☉9am-1pm & 6-10pm) From his little shop, friendly Vane Talev continues a family tradition started in 1924: making the unique Ohrid pearls. Prices range from €25 for a simple piece to €600 for an elaborate necklace.

Information

Internet Café Inside (Amam Trgovski Centar, bul Makedonski Prosvetiteli; per hr 60MKD; ☉9am-1am) Located in a mall near Ploštad Sveti Kliment Ohridski.

Ohrid.com (www.ohrid.com.mk) Municipal website.

Post Office (bul Makedonski Prosvetiteli; ☉7am-8pm Mon-Sat)

Sunny Land Tourism (www.sunnylandtourism.com; Car Samoil, by the National Museum; ☉9am-7pm) Led by local expert Zoran Grozdanovski, Sunny Land finds accommodation and arranges various tours and activities in Ohrid and beyond.

Telephone centre (bul Makedonski Prosvetiteli; ☉7am-8pm Mon-Sat)

Tina Tours (bul Turisticka 66; ☉9am-6pm) Full-service travel agency opposite Ohridska Banka.

Tourist Bureau Biljana (www.beyondohrid.com; Car Samoil 38; ☉10am-midnight) Provides general info, accommodation and outdoor activities.

Getting There & Away

Air

Ohrid's **St Paul the Apostle Airport** (www.airports.com.mk), 10km north, mostly handles summertime charter flights. Take a taxi (300MKD).

Bus

From the **bus station** (7 Noemvri bb), 1.5km east of the centre, buses serve Skopje, either via Kičevo (520MKD, three hours, 11 daily) or (the longer route) via Bitola; for Bitola itself, 10 daily buses run (210MKD, 1¼ hours). Buses to Struga (50MKD, 14km) leave every 30 minutes. In summer, reserve ahead for Skopje buses. Some *kombi* (minibuses) and taxis wait outside Tina Tours for intercity destinations.

International buses serve Belgrade (via Kičevo; 1820MKD, 15 hours, one daily). A 7pm bus serves Sofia (1450MKD, eight hours). For Albania, take a bus to Sveti Naum (110MKD, 29km). Cross the border and take a cab (€5, 6km) to Pogradeci. An Ohrid–Sveti Naum taxi costs 900MKD.

Around Ohrid

🔊046

South of Ohrid, a long, partly wooded coast conceals pebble beaches, historic churches and villages, and camping spots. In summer the big, resort-style hotels and beaches are crowded and dirty, but beyond them things improve.

In summer buses and *kombi* operate frequently up to Gradište; further destinations such as Trpejca, Ljubaništa and Sveti Naum are served less frequently.

◉ Sights & Activities

Beaches stretch down Ohrid's southern shore – unfortunately, in summer they're extremely overcrowded and unclean. Water clarity improves only after **Peštani** (12km from Ohrid); the village has an ATM but is ugly from overdevelopment.

The wooded **Gradište camping ground**, 2km further, is popular with sunbathing students who enjoy the beachside DJ parties at night. There's a fascinating **Neolithic Settlement Museum** here, with artefacts from a 4000-year-old site where Ohrid's ancestors lived on stilt huts built into the lake bed.

Trpejca ТРПЕЈЦА   FISHING VILLAGE
Further on lies Trpejca, cupped between a sloping hill and tranquil bay. Ohrid's last traditional fishing village, it features clustered houses with terracotta roofs and a white-pebble beach. At night, the sounds of crickets and frogs are omnipresent.

Trpejca has limited services, though in midsummer its small beach gets very crowded. The superb waters offer excellent swimming, and forested Mt Galičica's just opposite.

From Trpejca, boats visit **Sveta Bogorodica Zahumska Church** (simply called Sveti Zaum), 2.5km south, on a wooded beach near the lake's deepest part (294m). Its unusual frescos date from 1361. Fishermen or Ohrid travel agencies organise trips.

Sveti Naum Monastery СВЕТИ НАУМ
                                    MONASTERY
Splendid Sveti Naum Monastery, 29km south of Ohrid, lies before the Albanian border above a sandy beach. Built by Naum, a contemporary of St Kliment, this post-Byzantine monastery became an educational centre. Naum's Church of the Holy Archangels (AD 900) was replaced by the 16th-century **Church of Sveti Naum**; this multidomed, Byzantine-style structure on

a cliff, surrounded by roses and preening peacocks, boasts 16th- and 19th-century **frescos**.

Inside, drop an ear to the **tomb of Sveti Naum** to hear his muffled heartbeat. Outside, a **wishing well** collects spare denars. From the wall, lake views are excellent.

Sveti Naum has one of Ohrid's only sandy beaches, with good swimming, and a hotel.

Galičica National Park   PARK
The rippling, rock-crested Mt Galičica separates Lake Ohrid from Lake Prespa. Galičica's peaks top 2000m. This national park comprises 228 sq km of territory and features endemic plants and trees. Try hiking or paragliding here.

Visit **Elšani**, 10km from Ohrid (if driving, turn left uphill by **Elešec camping ground**). The village offers good hiking and excellent lake views at its 19th-century **Church of Sveti Ilias**.

🛏 Sleeping & Eating

Coastal accommodation and restaurants mostly work summer only; private accommodation (per person 300–600MKD) is generally plentiful.

Hotel Sveti Naum   HOTEL €€€
(📞283 080; www.hotel-stnaum.com.mk; Sveti Naum; s/d/ste from €37/74/116; ❄@) This fancy hotel with restaurant works year-round. Rooms are luxurious, if dated; lake-view rooms cost €20 extra.

Risto's Guest House   GUESTHOUSE €€
(📞285 464, 075977930; elshani@mt.net.mk; Elšani village; s/d/tr incl breakfast €15/24/32; 🛜) This relaxing guesthouse has spacious and clean rooms. Most have private baths, all have lake-view balconies. Home-cooked meals are available (€12 per person). Call for free pick up from Ohrid.

Vila DeNiro   RENTED ROOMS €€
(📞070212518; Trpejca; d/apt €25/50; ❄@) Trpejca's only modern place, this yellow mansion is located where the walkway downhill diverges. It offers three doubles and an en suite apartment.

Camping Ljubaništa   CAMPING GROUND €
(📞283 240; per tent 800MKD; ☺May-Oct) This camping ground 27km from Ohrid on a sandy beach is good for families and solitude-seekers, though facilities are quite dated.

Gradište Camping   CAMPING GROUND €
(📞285 920; Gradište; per tent 1000MKD; ☺May-Oct) Party-minded campers should head

here, 14km from Ohrid. Both camping grounds have shops and eateries.

Restoran Ribar
SEAFOOD €

(Trpejca; fish per person 300-600MKD; ⊙10am-midnight) Right on Trpejca's waterfront, Ribar serves local fish, meat and coffees.

❶ Getting There & Away

Frequent buses and *kombi* ply the Ohrid–Sveti Naum route in summer, as far as Gradište. Services are less frequent to Trpejca, Ljubaništa and Sveti Naum. In Ohrid, wait for *kombi* by Tina Tours (p542), opposite Ohridska Banka. These operate in summer until 2am.

Taxis are expensive; however, during summer some charge bus-ticket rates when filling up fast (check with the driver).

Boat tours from Ohrid to Sveti Naum (350MKD return) are traditionally held, though stricter safety laws may restrict them. Rates for village boat trips vary.

CENTRAL MACEDONIA

Macedonia's diverse central region is among its wildest, most unexplored areas, flush with mountains, canyons, vineyards and caves. It also offers plenty of culture and significant historical sites.

Bitola БИТОЛА

🕿047 / POP 95,400

With elegant buildings and beautiful people, elevated Bitola (660m) has a sophistication inherited from its Ottoman days as the 'City of Consuls'. Its 18th- and 19th-century colourful townhouses, Turkish mosques and cafe culture make it Macedonia's most intriguing and liveable major town. An essential experience is sipping a coffee and people watching along the pedestrianised Širok Sokak ('Wide Street' in Turkish – still called ul Maršal Tito officially).

◉ Sights & Activities

Church of Sveti Dimitrij
CHURCH

(11 Oktomvri bb; ⊙7am-6pm) This Orthodox church (1830) has rich frescos, ornate lamps and a huge iconostasis.

Širok Sokak
PEDESTRIAN STREET

(ul Maršal Tito) Bitola's **Catholic church** is staid but conspicuous amid the Širok Sokak's multicoloured facades. Enjoying the **cafe life** here while the beautiful people promenade past is an essential Bitola experience.

Mosques
MOSQUES

Bitola's 16th-century **Yeni**, **Isak** and **Yahdar-Kadi Mosques**, all between the Dragor River and the Stara Čaršija (Old Bazaar), testify to Ottoman times, as does the enormous **Clock Tower** (Saat Kula).

Stara Čaršija
BAZAAR

During Ottoman times, the Stara Čaršija boasted around 3000 clustered artisans shops; though today only about 70 different trades are conducted, it's still worth a peek.

✷ Festivals & Events

The **Bit Fest** (June to August) features concerts, literary readings and art exhibits. The **Ilinden Festival** (2 August), honouring the Ilinden Uprising of 1903, is celebrated with food and music.

The **Manaki Brothers Film Festival** (www.manaki.com.mk; late Sep-early Oct) screens independent foreign films. It honours Milton and Ianachia Manaki, the Balkans' first film-makers (1905). The **Inter Fest** features classical-music performances in the cultural centre and Bitola Museum.

⊨ Sleeping & Eating

Chola Guest House
GUESTHOUSE €

(🕿224 919; www.chola.mk; Stiv Naumov 80; s/d €12/20; 🐾) This quiet place in an old mansion has clean, well-kept and pretty rooms with colourful modern bathrooms. Ask the taxi driver for Video Club Dju (directly opposite the Chola).

Via Apartments
APARTMENTS €

(🕿075246261; www.via.mk; Elpida Karamandi 4; s/d €12/24; ❋🐾) These clean, well-designed apartments are right downtown and share a kitchen, laundry room, lounge and outdoor patio.

Hotel De Niro
HOTEL €€

(🕿229 656; www.hotel-deniro.com; Kiril i Metodij 5; s/d/ste €35/50/80; ❋🐾) The central yet discreet De Niro has two locations: one has snazzy rooms in the old Bitola style and an Italian restaurant, the other is minimalist in design with a popular pub below (light sleepers take note).

Hotel Milenium
HOTEL €€

(🕿241 001; h.milenium@t-home.mk; Marsal Tito 48; s/d/ste/apt €39/66/80/99; ❋🐾) Atriums with splashes of stained glass, smooth marble opulence and historical relics channel old Bitola. The spacious rooms have sparkling bathrooms. Great value, and right on the Širok Sokak.

Hotel Epinal
HOTEL €€

(☏224 777; www.hotelepinal.com; Maršal Tito bb; s/d €49/69; P❄☀) The ageing Epinal rises unpromisingly over Bitola but is actually quite nice – especially considering its swimming pool, jacuzzi and gym.

El Greko
PIZZA €

(cnr Maršal Tito & Elipda Karamandi; mains 180-320MKD; ⊙10am-1am) This popular Sokak Kaverna and pizzeria has great beer-hall ambience.

🍷 Drinking & Entertainment

Basa
BAR

(⊙10pm-2am) Get your groove on at this dark-lit bar on a side street off ul Leninova, behind Centar na Kultura. It plays house music and local and Western pop.

Porta Jazz
BAR

(Maršal Tito; ⊙8am-midnight) Porta Zazz is a popular, funky place that's packed when live local jazz and blues bands appear.

Pivnica
BAR

(Hotel De Niro, Kiril i Metodij 5; ☏noon-1am) The Hotel De Niro's subterranean bar, Pivnica, is a fun nightspot.

Nightclub Rasčekor
NIGHTCLUB

(⊙10pm-4am) The best Bitola nightclub is the slick Rasčekor, near the train station.

ℹ Information

Širok Sokak is a wi-fi hot spot, with nearby internet cafes.

Baloyannis Tours (☏220 204, 075207273; Solunska 118; ⊙8am-6pm Mon-Sat) Provides city tours and outdoor adventure trips (with prior notice).

Tourist information centre (bitola-tourist-info@t-home.mk; Sterio Georgiev 1; ⊙9am-5pm Mon-Sat) Friendly info centre.

ℹ Getting There & Away

The **bus** and **train stations** (Nikola Tesla) are adjacent, 1km south of the centre. Buses serve Skopje (470MKD, 3½ hours, 12 daily) via Prilep (130MKD, one hour), Kavadarci (280MKD, two hours, five daily), Strumica (460MKD, four hours, two daily) and Ohrid (210MKD, 1¼ hours, 10 daily).

For Greece, take a taxi to the border (450MKD) and find a cab to Florina or a Bitola cab driver who will go to Florina (3000MKD).

Three daily trains serve Skopje (210MKD) via Prilep (66MKD) and Veles (154MKD).

Macedonia's oldest national park (1948) covers 125 sq km on its third-highest mountain range, the quartz-filled Baba massif. Eight peaks top 2000m, crowned by Mt Pelister (2601m). Two glacial lakes, Pelisterski Oči (Pelister's Eyes), provide chilly refreshment.

Pelister's 88 tree species include the rare five-leafed Molika pine. It also hosts endemic Pelagonia trout, deer, wolves, chamois, wild boars, bears and eagles.

MALOVIŠTE

Down in the foothills, old Vlach villages like Malovište preserve rustic ambience and traditional architecture – though not restaurants or guesthouses.

Malovište's cobblestone laneways require good shoes. A 30-minute walk (2.5km) from the frescoed **Church of Sveta Petka** (1856) reaches the secluded **Church of Sveta Ana**.

To reach Malovište from Bitola, drive 4km west towards Resen, and turn at Kazani. Take the first left, and then another left through a tunnel and proceed straight.

DIHOVO ДИХОВО

Only 5km from Bitola, the 830m-high mountainside hamlet of Dihovo is a base for Pelister hikes, with appealing stone houses and the icon-rich **Church of Sveti Dimitrije** (1830). Dihovo's **outdoor swimming pool** is basically a very large basin containing ice-cold mountain-spring waters, rushing from the boulder-filled Sapungica River.

For summer **hiking trips** or winter **skiing**, see Petar Cvetkovski of Villa Dihovo. From Bitola, a taxi costs 120MKD to 150MKD.

Villa Dihovo
GUESTHOUSE €€

(☏070544744; www.villadihovo.com; pay as you like; P✉) One of Macedonia's most remarkable guesthouses, the Villa Dihovo consists of three traditionally decorated rooms in the 80-year-old home of ski instructor Petar Cvetkovski and family. It's signposted inside the first long driveway after Dihovo centre's restaurant, and it has a big flowering lawn great for kids. The only fixed prices are for the homemade wine, beer and *rakija* (firewater); all else, room price included, is your choice.

Villa Patrice
RENTED ROOMS €€

(☏075466878; s/d 900/1440MKD) This friendly family-run place offers spacious and well-maintained rooms. It's a 5-minute walk from the centre off the road towards the pool.

Restoran Idela   SKARA €€
(mains 250-400MKD; ☺6am-midnight) Idela has a hunting-lodge feel and does great *skara*.

Prilep ПРИЛЕП

☎048 / POP 76,800

A hard-working, dusty, tobacco town, Prilep sits along the Pelagonian Plain, surrounded by weird, jagged-rock formations. It does have some decent eating and drinking options along its smart new square thronged with locals in evening. Prilep attractions include the craggy castle of 14th-century Macedonian King Marko and the magnificent nearby clifftop monasteries of Treskavec and Zrze.

⊙ Sights & Activities

Some 2km from town, **King Marko's Towers** (Markovi Kuli) rise from a sharp cliff. Fortified since ancient times, this unique defensive position offers great views. The fortress was famously commanded by King Marko (r 1371–95), a semiautonomous despot under the Turks, whose suzerainty extended into today's northern Greece. Although killed in battle while conscripted by Turks, King Marko's still commemorated in Macedonian (and Serbian) folk songs, which celebrate his superhuman strength.

Prilep's marketplace, the **Čaršija**, houses artisans shops and is, along with the nearby **Clock Tower**, a relic of Ottoman times. Prilep's well-kept centre – flush with new squares, fountains, statues (and a duck pond for kids) – has become a national example. There's a robust cafe and bar scene, with live bands playing outdoors in summer.

The **theatre festival** (June–July) has performances at the Dom na Kultura. The popular midsummer **Prilep beer festival** attracts thousands for prodigious consumption of beer and *skara* (grilled meat) while serenaded by well-known Balkan musical acts.

🛏 Sleeping

Hotel Sonce   HOTEL €€
(☎401800; www.makedonskosonce.com; Aleksandar Makedonski 4/3a; r incl breakfast 1240/2480MKD P✳@🛜≋) The Sonce has decent rooms, a restaurant and a small outdoor swimming pool (used by locals too, for a fee).

Hotel Crystal Palace   HOTEL €€€
(☎418 000; www.kp.mk; Leninova 184; s/d/t €35/59/83; P✳@🛜) Near the train station Prilep's four-star institution has well appointed rooms.

✗ Eating & Drinking

Pizzeria Leone   PIZZA €€
(Goce Delcev 30; pizzas 200-350MKD; ☺11am-midnight) This central place does great pizzas.

Porta Club Restaurant   RESTAURANT €€
(Republikanska 84; mains 300-450MKD; ☺10am-midnight) A spacious, well-lit bistro, the Porta Club does fancy grills and good fish.

Virus   ROCK BAR
(Borka Taleski bb) Pop, house and live rock are played here; ambience is sustained by classic touches like weathered wooden stairs, ornate print wallpaper, old paintings and little balcony tables.

❶ Getting There & Away

From Prilep's **bus station** (Sotka Gorgioski) buses serve Skopje (380MKD) via Negotino and Veles; Kavadarci (190MKD, 1½ hours, two daily) is also served. Buses head south to Bitola (130MKD, 10 daily), some continuing to Ohrid (380MKD).

Prilep's on the Bitola–Skopje train line (three daily trains).

DON'T MISS

HERACLEA LYNCESTIS

Heraclea Lyncestis (admission 100MKD, photos 500MKD; ☺9am-3pm winter, to 5pm summer), 1km south of Bitola (70MKD by taxi), is among Macedonia's best archaeological sites. Founded by Philip II of Macedon, Heraclea became commercially significant before Romans conquered (168 BC), and its position on the Via Egnatia kept it prosperous. In the 4th century Heraclea became an episcopal seat, but Goths and then Slavs sacked it during the next two centuries.

See the Roman baths, portico and amphitheatre, and the striking Early Christian basilica and episcopal palace ruins, with beautiful, well-preserved floor mosaics. They're unique in depicting endemic trees and animals.

KRUŠEVO

No town is as close to Macedonia's heart as Kruševo (pop 6000), situated 1200m on a mountain top between Bitola and Prilep. Historically linked with the Vlach minority, Kruševo is commemorated each 2 August – the date on which, in 1903, an anti-Ottoman rebellion succeeded, if briefly, in establishing the first Balkan republic.

Although the 'Ilinden Uprising' was swiftly crushed, Kruševo survived and boasts cultural offerings like the **Nikola Martinovski Gallery** (Nikola Gurkevič bb; ⊘9am-4pm Tues-Sun), exhibiting works by this local painter, and the **Churches of Sveti Nikola** (1905) and **Sveti Jovan** (1897), containing impressive ecclesiastical architecture and icons.

In winter, Kruševo's **ski centre** offers gentle slopes great for beginners. **Hotel Montana** (☑048 477 121; Hotelska zona bb; s/d 1740/2140MKD) offers slope-side accommodation. Additionally, several modern private apartments are available (check locally).

On 16 October 2007 Kruševo lost a local son and national musical icon, Toše Proeski; aged just 26, the singer died in a tragic car crash. Toše was admired for his booming voice and seductive good looks, but was also respected for his humanitarian work for children. Each year, thousands of fans visit the **Toše Proeski memorial**, near the cemetery of Kruševo's local heroes on the town's northern hill; lined with flowers, photos, icons and gifts from children, it's a moving open shrine commemorating the love and affection Macedonians still feel for the late singer.

The walk downhill back into town passes Kruševo's cobbled lanes and lovely houses (some historically listed). Near the church-side square, local sausage and other *skara* is served at **Restoran Sape** (Ilindenska bb; mains 120-250MKD; ⊘9am-midnight), while **Pizza Skar** (Shula Mina 38; ⊘10am-midnight; 80-220MKD) does good pizzas. For a drink, try **Club Planet** (ul Toše Proeski bb; ⊘8am-2am), a classic cafe and bar with elegant green-trim wood furnishings, where the late Proeski celebrated with friends.

Kruševo gets buses from Prilep, Bitola and Skopje.

Treskavec Monastery
МАНАСТИР ТРЕСКАВЕЦ

Ten kilometres above Prilep, this 13th-century monastery rises from Mt Zlato (1422m), a bare massif replete with twisted rock formations. Its vivid frescos, including a rare depiction of Christ as a boy, line the 14th-century **Church of Sveta Bogorodica**, built over a 6th-century basilica. Earlier Roman remains are visible inside, along with graves, inscriptions and monks' skulls.

Treskavec offers **accommodation** (☑070918339; per person 200MKD) and food.

A paved road is planned; till then, drive to the paved road's end, unless you have a 4WD for the final rocky kilometres. If so, start from Prilep's cemetery and turn uphill at the sign marked 'Manastir Sveta Bogorodica, Treskavec'.

Alternatively, to hike up, drive or take a taxi to Dabnica and follow the cobbled track towards Mt Zlato; after the fountain, a path reaches Treskavec (two hours total; 4.5km).

Zrze Monastery
МАНАСТИР ЗРЗЕ

Some 26km northwest of Prilep, towards Makedonski Brod, the 14th-century **Monastery of the Holy Transfiguration-Zrze** (☑048 459 400; Manastir Sveto Preobrazhenije-Zrze; admission free; ⊘8am-5pm) rises like a revelation from a secluded clifftop. The monastery's tranquil position set around a spacious lawn, with views over the outstretched Pelagonian Plain, is stunning. At dawn, a low-lying fog sometimes shrouds the plain in marble.

During Ottoman times, Zrze underwent periods of abandonment, rebuilding and plunder but remained an important spiritual centre for centuries. Its unusual 17th-century **Church of Ss Petar and Paul** contains important frescos and icons.

At time of research, Zrze was planning accommodation. Visitors can enjoy coffee with the kind monks and a tour of the church, with its priceless frescos and icons. While today the museum in Skopje houses Zrze's most famous icon, the *Holy Mother of God*

Pelagonitsa (1422), a large copy remains in the church.

On the adjacent hillside, excavations continue on Zrze's precursor: a **5th-century basilica**. More information about it might become available as the monks continue investigating.

Get here by driving towards Makedonski Brod and turning at Ropotovo village; several villages lie between it and the monastery (take the left-hand turn at Kostinci). Zrze is infrequently signposted. The dirt roads are well built but worsen at nearly deserted Zrze village, beneath the mountain. From here, walk 2km uphill to the monastery, or drive if with a 4WD vehicle.

Tikveš Wine Region

Macedonia's winery heartland, Tikveš features rolling vineyards, lakes, caves and mountains, plus archaeological sites and churches. It's especially beautiful at dusk, when the fading sunlight suffuses soft hills laden with millions and millions of grapes.

The region has produced wine since the 4th century BC. Tikveš local grapes generally retain an ideal sugar concentration (17% to 26%). Travel agencies arrange tastings; alternatively, prearrange with the wineries.

KAVADARCI КАВАДАРЦИ
☏043 / POP 38,700

Just west of the road and rail hub of Negotino, Kavadarci is fittingly dusty and agricultural, though it is improving its services. Attractions include wine tastings, monasteries, museums and Lake Tikveš, good for boating and bird watching.

◉ Sights & Activities

FREE **Kavadarci Museum**　　　MUSEUM
(7 Septembri 58; ⊙8.30am-4.30pm Mon-Sat) Ancient finds, some depicting wine bacchanalia, are kept here.

Tikveš Winery　　　WINERY
(☏414 304; www.tikves.com.mk; 29 Noemvri 5; ⊙10am-5pm) Massive Tikveš Winery, southeastern Europe's biggest (established 1885), produces 29 quality wines. Winery tours visit the facilities and include a tasting.

Vinoteka David　　　WINERY
(cnr Cano Pop Ristov & Ilindenska; ⊙8am-1pm & 5-7pm) Central Vinoteka David has regional wines.

Kavadarci Wine Carnival　　　WINE FESTIVAL

Visit during the Kavadarci Wine Carnival (5–7 September) for the costumed parade, public wine tasting and merrymaking.

🛏 Sleeping & Eating

Hotel Uni Palas　　　HOTEL €€
(☏419 600; Edvard Kardelj bb; s/d incl breakfast €36/56; 🅿@) This comfortable, modern hotel by the bus station has well-appointed rooms with hydro-massage showers, and a popular cafe – plus an additional location with similar rooms but less central.

Restoran Exclusive　　　MACEDONIAN €€
(bul Makedonija 66; mains 250-450MKD; ⊙9am-midnight) About 100m from Uni Palas, Kavadarci's best wine restaurant serves Macedonian and international dishes.

ℹ Getting There & Away

From Kavadarci, buses serve Skopje (250MKD, seven daily), Prilep (190MKD, one hour, two daily) and Bitola (280MKD, five daily). For Negotino, use local buses (30MKD, 15 minutes, six daily) or take a taxi (200MKD).

AROUND KAVADARCI

Three kilometres southwest of Kavadarci, past **Vataša**, the **Monastery of Sveti Nikola** sits alongside a forested river and displays rare 16th-century frescos.

Created in 1968 by damming the Crna River, nearby **Lake Tikveš** is surrounded by scrubland and stark cliffs, dotted with medieval hermitage frescos and circled by eagles and hawks. Being artificial, it has no endemic species, though it seems the monster catfish – weighing up to 200kg – has become pretty territorial since Comrade Tito first dispatched them into the 100m depths.

The 32km-long lake lies 11km southwest of Kavadarci; turn south at **Vozarci** to reach the small beach.

To arrange half-day **boat trips** with skippers and an English-speaking guide, check in Kavadarci at the Hotel Uni Palas or, failing that, the local municipality building. Some Skopje travel agencies also arrange tours. Large groups use the 40-seater boat (4000MKD per group) while small groups use a regular fishermen's caique (1800MKD).

The tour navigates the lake's widest stretches for 20km, visiting the 14th-century **Pološki Monastery** (also called Polog Monastery), inhabited by a single nun. The monastery's **Church of Sveti Gjiorgji**

Thickly forested mountains dotted with pristine rivers, seriously deep caves, winding lakes, delicious honey sold by the comb, rumours of secret, communist-era military tunnels and even a dilapidated ammunition factory...what more could one ask for?

Makedonski Brod (pop 3500) is admittedly a sleepy place; north of it, however, the **Poreče region** and **Jasen Nature Reserve** (www.jasen.com.mk), hosting endangered European brown bats and the rare lynx, are for nature lovers Jasen is bisected by artificial Lake Kozjak, running lazily north to the Treska River and Lake Matka.

The enormous cave entrance of **Pešna** – reputedly Europe's biggest – is 7km east of Brod and looms beside the main road, a five-minute walk down the wooded path starting inside the gate. Fortuitously enough, a relaxing restaurant stands by the road, on sculpted lawns and offering pagoda seating. **Meana Dedo Ilija** (80-150MKD; ⊙8am-1am) serves great meats and local fish. Inexpensive bungalow accommodation is being prepared (check ahead). From Brod, taxis cost 350MKD.

Monastirec is a traditional village with a beautiful monastery (a one-hour, 4km, hike uphill or a 20-minute drive on an asphalt road) 17km east of Brod.

Good eats and basic accommodation in Monastirec exist at **Riben Restoran-Motel Izvor** (☏045 279 200; cvetanovskivlado@yahoo.com; fish 200-400MKD; ⊙10am-10pm), peacefully set alongside the Treska River. The stuffed bear on the wall and live trout swimming in the pools will fascinate kids. (Choose your fish and they'll cook it.)

Izvor has simple, clean rooms with double beds (600MKD) and others with shared bath (400MKD). Hike the riverside trail or stroll through the village itself, set in a bowl surrounded by verdure. Several daily *kombi* (minibuses) connect Brod with Monastirec (60MKD). Taxis run 400MKD.

The more adventurous should visit **Belica** village. Its local river (Belica Reka) flows with pristine, frigid water from mountain springs – the trout here is a protected endemic species. Belica's lingering elderly residents are a hardy bunch indeed, and services are few.

Speleological expeditions, however, do visit; central Macedonia's caves are still largely unexplored and have aroused excitement. Belica's mountaineers' hut (*planinarski dom*) offers accommodation – arrange your stay with the **Macedonian Speleological Federation** (☏023 165 540; www.speleomacedonia.org.mk). These dangerous caverns are locked except during expeditions.

Makedonski Brod is usually accessed via the Kičevo–Prilep road running west to east; from Skopje, three daily *kombi* travel here (330MKD, three hours) via Kičevo. However, Brod is actually only 57km from Skopje; a direct road along Lake Kozjak is being built, and those with a 4WD can already tackle it.

Brod lacks accommodation, though services like shops, restaurants and ATMs exist. The **opština** (municipality; www.mbrod.gov.mk) near the police station can provide useful information.

---

was built by Serbian emperor Stefan Dušan (r 1331–55), and features expressive frescos of saints and of the emperor himself.

Ringed by rugged cliffs, the lake offers **bird watching** (look out for the royal eagle, bearded vulture and white Egyptian vulture). Sometimes **fishing** is possible, though reeling in the obese catfish from the muddy depths might require a hydraulic lift. You can try **swimming**, but be mindful of the strong currents, steep drop-offs and rocks near the shore.

OTHER WINERIES

Grkov Winery   WINERY
(☏043 400 565; pericajovevski@urbaninvest.com.mk; Krnjavo) Enjoying a spectacular vineyard setting in **Krnjavo**, this winery is 26km south of Kavadarci. Call ahead for organised tours and tastings. It's challenging to reach; after **Garnikovo** village, turn left at the large yellow road sign containing many printed destinations. Continue straight, and a dirt road uphill leads to the winery. If you reach the settlement below, you've missed this road.

Bovin Winery WINERY
(☑043 365 322; www.bovin.com.mk; Industriska bb; ⊙10am-5pm) This winery in Negotino has won numerous awards. Tours include extensive tastings.

Elenov Winery WINERY
(☑043 367 232; vinarija_elenov@t-home.com.mk; Ivo Lola Ribar bb, Demir Kapija) Visit this winery at the southeastern edge of the wine region, by the magnificent **Demir Kapija Gorge**. It's visible on the western side of the north-south E75 hwy. Dating from 1928, it was Serbian king Aleksandar's official wine cellar, and it organises tastings.

Popova Kula Winery WINERY
(in Skopje; ☑02 3228 781; Demir Kapija; d/ste €60/120) Also in Demir Kapija, up an 800m dirt road past the cemetery, is possibly Macedonia's most aesthetically pleasing winery, with great views over vineyards and the gorge from a traditionally decorated tasting room. For overnights, call ahead to book one of the modern, traditionally accentuated rooms here.

Disan Hills Winery WINERY
(☑043 362 520, 070384325; ristov@mt.net.mk; Dolni Disan) Around 5km south of Negotino, in the village of Dolni Disan, Disan Hills is set amid vineyards and is run by people who put heart and soul into crafting limited quantities of high-quality wine. Tastings can be arranged.

STOBI СТОБИ
The ruins of Roman Stobi occupy a valley beside the E75 hwy, 9km northwest of Negotino. The **site** (admission 100MKD; ⊙9am-5pm), discovered in 1861, is organised, with running descriptions of the major ruins. There's a snack bar and gift shop selling replicas and wines.

Established in the 7th century BC, Stobi grew under the Macedonians and Romans, even hosting an ancient Jewish population (synagogue foundations lie beneath Christian basilica remains). Although important as a Byzantine archbishopric, Stobi was sacked by Goths in 479 and further doomed by earthquake in 518.

Start at the **Roman amphitheatre** (on the left) and clamber up further for Stobi's best **mosaics**. The path continues past well-marked ruins, including **ancient sanctuaries** to gods. At the end, turn right to the enormous **city walls**. Excavations continue.

UNDERSTAND MACEDONIA

History

Historical or geographical Macedonia is divided between the Republic of Macedonia (38%), Greek Macedonia (51%) and Bulgaria's Pirin Macedonia (11%). For its people their history is a source of great pride but also a heavy burden. The post-Yugoslav experience has seen existential pressure from neighbours constantly challenging the Macedonian identity. Macedonia's history is too complex for simple answers; remember that many people have strong opinions.

Ancient Macedonians & Romans

The powerful Macedonian dynasty of King Philip II (r 359–336 BC) dominated the Greeks and other powers. His son, Alexander the Great, spread the empire to India before dying in 323 BC, his empire soon dissolving amid infighting. In 168 BC, Rome conquered Macedonia; its position on the Via Egnatia from Byzantium to the Adriatic, and the Axios (Vardar River) from Thessaloniki up the Vardar Valley, kept cities prosperous.

The Apostle Paul famously brought Christianity to Macedonia. With the Roman Empire's division in AD 395, Macedonia came under Constantinople and Greek-influenced Orthodox Christianity.

The Coming of the Slavs & the Macedonian Cars

The 7th-century Slavic migrations intermingled Macedonia's various peoples. In 862 two Thessaloniki-born monks, St Cyril and St Methodius, were dispatched to spread orthodoxy and literacy among the Slavs of Moravia (in modern-day Czech Republic). Their disciple, St Kliment of Ohrid, modified their Glagolitic script, creating the Cyrillic alphabet. With St Naum, he propagated literacy in Ohrid (the first Slavic university) in the late 9th century.

Byzantium and the Slavs could share a religion but not political power. Chronic wars unfolded between Constantinople and the expansionist Bulgarian state of Car Simeon (r 893–927) and Car Samoil (r 997–1014). Prespa and Ohrid in Macedonia became their strongholds, until Byzantine Emperor Basil II defeated Samoil at the Battle of Belasica (near today's Strumica, in eastern Macedoia) in 1014. According to legend (probably only that), he blinded 14,000 of Samoil's men.

After Belasica, Byzantium retook Macedonia. However, the Serbian Nemanjid dynasty's growth allowed Serbia to expand into Macedonia. After Emperor Stefan Dušan (r 1331–55) died, Serbian power waned. The Ottoman Turks soon arrived, ruling until 1913.

Ottoman Rule & the Macedonian Question

The Ottomans introduced Islam and Turkish settlers. Skopje became a trade centre, and beautiful mosques, *hammam*s and castles were built. However, even though the Turks were ruling, Greeks wielded considerable power. In 1767, Greek intriguing caused the abolition of the seven-centuries-old Ohrid archbishopric. Greek priests started opening schools and building churches, to the resentment of locals. Bulgaria and Serbia also sought Macedonia. The lines were drawn.

In Macedonia, Western European ethnic nationalism collided violently with the Ottomans' civil organisation by religion (not ethnicity). Europe's great powers intervened after the Russo-Turkish War of 1877–78, when the Treaty of San Stefano awarded Macedonia to Bulgaria. However, fearing Russia, Western powers reversed the decision with the Treaty of Berlin, fuelling 40 years of further conflict.

Macedonia remained Ottoman after the Treaty of Berlin, but the 'Macedonian question' persisted. With the empire's days numbered, various Balkan powers sponsored revolutionary groups. In 1893, the Internal Macedonian Revolutionary Organisation (in Macedonian, Vnatrešna Makedonska Revolucionerna Organizacija, or VMRO) formed. VMRO was divided between 'Macedonia for the Macedonians' propagandists and a pro-Bulgarian wing.

In the St Elijah's Day (Ilinden) Uprising (2 August 1903), Macedonian revolutionaries declared the first Balkan republic, in Kruševo; the Turks crushed it 10 days later. Although nationalist leader Goce Delčev had died months earlier, he's considered Macedonia's national hero.

In 1912 the Balkan League (Greece, Serbia, Bulgaria and Montenegro) declared war on Turkey (the First Balkan War). Macedonia was the prime battleground. The Turks were expelled, but a dissatisfied Bulgaria turned on its former allies in 1913 (the Second Balkan War). Defeated, Bulgaria allied with Germany and Austria in WWI, reoccupying Macedonia and prolonging the suffering of the local population.

The Yugoslav Experience

In WWI, Bulgaria lost, and Macedonia was divided between Greece and the new Kingdom of Serbs, Croats and Slovenes (Royalist Yugoslavia). Belgrade would ban the Macedonian name and language – disgruntled VMRO elements helped Croat nationalists assassinate Serbian King Aleksandar in 1934.

During WWII, Josip Broz Tito's Partisans resisted the Bulgarian–German occupation. Tito promised Macedonians republican status within communist Yugoslavia but was disinterested in their aspirations; Partisans seeking to fight for Greek-controlled Macedonia were shot as an example to the others. Nevertheless, in the 1946–49 Greek Civil War, some ethnic Macedonians joined the communists fighting Royalists. The communist defeat forced thousands, including many children (known as the *begalci*, meaning 'refugees'), to flee Greece.

After WWII, Tito redistributed Macedonia's wealth. Nationalisation of property and industry ruined villages, with farmers deprived of flocks. Tito's concrete monstrosities sheltered the newly urbanised populations. Nevertheless, some nation-building overtures were made, such as a Macedonian grammar in 1952 and the Macedonian Orthodox Church's creation in 1967 – the 200th anniversary of the Ohrid archbishopric's abolition.

Macedonia after Independence

In a referendum on 8 September 1991, 74% of Macedonians voted to split from Yugoslavia. In January 1992 the Republic of Macedonia declared independence. Unlike Yugoslavia's other breakaway republics, Macedonian President Kiro Gligorov negotiated the Yugoslav army's peaceful withdrawal.

Greece, however, was enraged. Macedonia's first flag bore the Vergina star – the ancient Macedonian royal symbol – and Athens argued that the Macedonian name itself was sacrosanct to Greece. The Macedonians emphatically denied Greek allegations that they secretly had claims on northern Greece.

Greek lobbying brought a 'provisional' name, the Former Yugoslav Republic of Macedonia (FYROM), for the country's UN admission in April 1993. When the USA (following six EU countries) recognised FYROM in February 1994, Greece retaliated with an economic embargo. In November 1995, Macedonia changed its flag and agreed to future negotiations, and the embargo ended.

In the 1990s 'transition' period, an oligarchical system arose amid shady privatisations, deliberate bankrupting of state-owned firms and dubious pyramid schemes. Worse, tensions were simmering with Macedonia's restive ethnic Albanians. During the 1999 NATO bombing of Serbia, Macedonia sheltered more than 400,000 Kosovo Albanian refugees; this hospitality, however, only emboldened the Ushtria Člirimtare Kombetare (UČK; National Liberation Army), which started a war in early 2001. The conflict lasted six months. The ensuing Ohrid Framework Agreement granted more minority language and national symbol rights, along with quota-based public-sector hiring.

Implementing the Framework Agreement proved difficult, though, especially concerning power decentralisation and municipal rezoning. The agreement stipulated more rights where minorities comprised 20% of the population.

Towards Europe

Macedonia is an EU-membership candidate, with deep participation in NATO peacekeeping missions abroad. However, at the time of research, Greece continued to block Macedonia's EU and NATO hopes, citing the unresolved name issue – frustrating Macedonians and many foreign leaders. Further, the ingrained patronage system and sluggish economy both persist, and the gap between rich and poor is increasing. Ethnic and religious divisions also continue to widen.

People

At the time of research, Macedonia was expecting a new census to be held in the autumn of 2011. In 2004, the population of 2,022,547 was divided thus: Macedonians (66.6%), Albanians (22.7%), Turks (4%), Roma (2.2%), Serbs (2.1%) and others (2.4%). Most Serbs live near the Serbian border, while most Albanians live in the northern and western towns nearest Kosovo and Albania. The Vlachs, descendants of ancient Romans long assimilated into Macedonian-ness, historically hail from Bitola and Kruševo. Turks live in Skopje, western Macedonia and elsewhere. Many of the disadvantaged Roma are mostly urban, surviving through begging and odd jobs.

Religion

Most Macedonians are Orthodox Christians with some Macedonian-speaking Muslims (the so-called Torbeši and Gorani). Turks are Muslim, like most Albanians; however Catholic Albanians exist (Mother Teresa, born here as Agnes Gonxha Bojaxhiu, is a famous example). A Jewish community of 200 people descends from Sephardic Jews who fled Spain after 1492. Sadly, approximately 98% of their ancestors – over 7200 people – were deported to Nazi concentration camps by Bulgarian occupiers in WWII. The community holds a Holocaust commemoration ceremony every 11 March.

The Macedonian Orthodox Church isn't recognised by some neighbouring Orthodox countries, but it's active in church-building and restoration work. Although Macedonians don't attend church services often, they do stop to light a candle, kiss icons and pray.

Music & Dance

Macedonian folk instruments include the *gajda*, a single-bag bagpipe, played solo or accompanied by a drum, the *tapan*, played with different sticks for different tones. Other instruments include the *kaval* (flute), *tambura* (small lute with two pairs of strings) and *zurla* (a double-reed horn, accompanied by the *tapan*). The *Čalgija* music form, involving clarinet, violin, *darabuk* (hourglass-shaped drum) and *doumbuš* (banjo-like instrument) is representative. Macedonian music employs the 7/8 time signature.

Macedonian traditional dancing includes the *oro* circle dance. The male-only *Teškoto oro* ('difficult dance'), accompanied by *tapan* and *zurla*, is performed in traditional costume. The *Komitsko oro* symbolises the anti-Turkish struggle, while the *Tresenica* is for women.

The Ministry of Culture (www.culture. in.mk) lists performance dates and venues. National folk-dance ensemble Tanec (02 2461 021; www.tanec.com.mk; Vinjamin Macukovski 7, Skopje) tours worldwide.

Macedonian musicians have won international acclaim: pianist Simon Trpčevski, opera singer Boris Trajanov, jazz guitarist Vladimir Četkar and percussionists, the Tavitjan Brothers. Especially beloved is Toše Proeski, a charismatic singer who died tragically in

2007; aged just 26, Proeski was admired not only for his music but also for his humanitarian work.

The Land

Located where the Continental and Mediterranean climate zones converge, Macedonia (25,713 sq km) is mostly plateau (600m to 900m above sea level), with more than 50 mountain peaks topping 2500m. The Vardar River passes Skopje and runs into the Aegean Sea. Lakes Ohrid and Prespa are two of Europe's oldest tectonic lakes (around three million years old); at 300m, Ohrid is the Balkans' deepest lake. International borders are largely mountainous, including Šar Planina, near Kosovo in the northwest; Mt Belasica, in the southeast, bordering Greece; and the Osogovski and Maleševski ranges near Bulgaria. Macedonia's highest peak, Mt Korab (Golem Korab; 2764m), borders Albania in the Mavrovo National Park.

Wildlife

Macedonia's eastern Mediterranean and Euro-Siberian vegetation contains pine-clad upper slopes, while lower mountains feature beech and oak. Vineyards dominate the central plains. Endemic fauna includes the *molika* tree, a subalpine pine unique to Mt Pelister, and the rare *foja* tree on Lake Prespa's Golem Grad island.

Macedonia's alpine and low Mediterranean valley zoological zones contain fauna such as bears, wild boars, wolves, foxes, chamois and deer. The rare lynx inhabits Šar Planina and Jasen Nature Reserve. Blackcaps, grouse, white Egyptian vultures, royal eagles and forest owls inhabit woodlands. Lake birds include Dalmatian pelicans, herons and cormorants. Storks (and their huge nests) are prominent. Macedonia's national dog, the *šar planinec*, is a 60cm tall sheepdog that will fight bears and wolves.

Lakes Ohrid, Prespa and Dojran are separate fauna zones, due to territorial and temporal isolation. With 146 endemic species, Ohrid is a living fossil-age museum – its endemic trout predates the last Ice Age. Ohrid also has whitefish, gudgeon and roach, plus a 30-million-year-old snail genus, and the mysterious Ohrid eel, which arrives from the Sargasso Sea to live for 10 years before returning to breed and die; its offspring restart the cycle.

National Parks

Macedonia's national parks are Pelister (near Bitola), Galičica (between Lakes Ohrid and Prespa) and Mavrovo (between Debar and Tetovo). Pelister and Galičica are part of a tri-border protected area involving Albania and Greece. Hiking in summer and skiing at Mavrovo in winter are fantastic. All parks are accessible by road; none requires tickets or permits.

Environmental Issues

Lake Ohrid's endemic trout is an endangered species. Do the right thing and choose from three other varieties *(mavrovska, kaliforniska* or *rekna)* instead – they're just as tasty and cheaper.

Despite new laws, littering continues and recycling is rare.

Food & Drink

Macedonia's specialities combine Ottoman and central European tastes. *Ajvar* is a sweet red-pepper sauce; *lutenica* similar, but with hot peppers and tomatoes. Macedonia's national salad, *šopska salata*, features tomatoes and cucumbers topped with *sirenje* (white cheese). *Čorba* (soup) and *tavče gravče* (oven-cooked white beans) are other specialities.

Skara (grilled meat) includes spare ribs, beef *kebapci* (kebabs) and *uviač* (rolled chicken or pork stuffed with yellow cheese) and remains popular, though 'international' cuisine is widespread.

For breakfast, try *burek* (cheese, spinach or minced meat in filo pastry) accompanied by drinking yoghurt or *kiselo mleko* ('sour milk', like yoghurt).

Bitter Skopsko Pivo is Macedonia's leading beer. The national firewater, *rakija,* is a strong grape spirit, delicious served hot with sugar in winter. *Mastika,* like ouzo, is also popular. Macedonians make home-made brandies from cherries and plums. The Tikveš region produces excellent wines.

SURVIVAL GUIDE

Directory A–Z

Accommodation

Skopje's hotels are expensive; agencies find private rooms. Ohrid and villages have budget and midrange choices; book ahead for July to August, Orthodox Christmas (7 January), Orthodox Easter and during festivals or carnivals.

PRICE RANGES

In this chapter prices quoted are for rooms with a private bathroom unless otherwise stated. The following price indicators apply (for a high-season double room):

€   less than €50

€€   €50 to €80

€€€   more than €80

Activities

Zare Lazarevski ski centre in Mavrovo National Park has Macedonia's best skiing. Popova Šapka ski centre, near Tetovo, will hopefully resume operations – check locally.

Mavrovo, Galičica and Pelister National Parks and **Jasen Nature Reserve** (www.jasen.com.mk) have great hiking and wildlife.

Near Skopje, Lake Matka offers wooded walks, boating and caving. Lake Ohrid offers swimming and boating, or you could bird watch on Lakes Prespa and Tikveš. Paragliding is great on Mt Galičica near Ohrid and in Kruševo.

Travel agencies in Skopje, Ohrid and Bitola run outdoors tours. The website of the mountaineering association **Korab Mountain Club** (www.korab.org.mk/indexen.html) details 14 mountain routes.

Business Hours

Banks 7am-5pm Mon-Fri

Businesses 8am-8pm Mon-Fri, to 2pm Sat

Post offices 6.30am-8pm

Dangers & Annoyances

The all-pervasive fear of a draft (*promaja*), which causes otherwise sane Macedonians to compulsively shut bus windows on sweleringly hot days, is without doubt the most incomprehensible and aggravating thing foreigners complain about here – fight for your rights, or suffer in silence.

Skopje's detestable bus and train station taxi drivers practically pull you out of the train and should be ignored. Roma children's begging and occasional pickpocketing attempts can irritate. Littering remains a problem, and the ban on selling alcohol in shops after 7pm (9pm in summer) also vexes.

Embassies & Consulates

All offices are in Skopje.

Australia (☑023 061 114; www.serbia.embassy.gov.au/bgde/home.html; austcon@mt.net.mk; Londonska 11b)

Canada (☑023 225 630; www.embassypages.com/missions/embassy16494; honcon@unet.com.mk; bul Partizanski Odredi 17a)

France (☑023 118 749; www.ambafrance-mk.org; Salvador Aljende 73)

Germany (☑023 093 900; www.skopje.diplo.de/Vertretung/skopje/mk/Startseite.html; dtboskop@on.net.mk; Lerinska 59)

Netherlands (☑023 129 319; www.nlembassy.org.mk; Leninova 69-71)

Russia (☑023 117 160; www.russia.org.mk (no English); embassy@russia.org.mk; Pirinska 44)

UK (☑023 299 299; http://ukinmacedonia.fco.gov.uk/en; beskopje@mt.net.mkI; Dimitrie Čupovski 26)

USA (☑023 116 180; http://macedonia.usembassy.gov; Samoilova bb)

Food

In this chapter the following price indicators apply (for a main meal):

€   less than 150MKD

€€   150MKD to 300MKD

€€€   more than 300MKD

Money

Macedonian denars (MKD) come in 10-, 50-, 100-, 500-, 1000- and 5000-denar notes, and one-, two-, five-, 10- and 50-denar coins. Denars are nonconvertible abroad. Euros are usually accepted. While some hotels quote euro rates, payment in denars is acceptable.

Macedonian exchange offices *(menuvačnici)* work commission-free. ATMs are widespread, except in villages, and using them for cash is the best idea, considering that credit card fraud, even in well-respected hotels, restaurants and shops, occasionally occurs. Avoid travellers cheques.

Post

Mail to Europe and North America takes seven to 10 days. Certified mail *(preporačeno)* is more expensive – fill out and keep the small green form. Letters to the USA cost 38MKD, to Australia 40MKD and to Europe 35MKD. Skopje has global shipping companies.

Public Holidays

New Year's Day 1 January

Orthodox Christmas 7 January

Orthodox Easter Week March/April

Labour Day 1 May

SS Cyril and Methodius Day 24 May

Ilinden Day 2 August

Republic Day 8 September

1941 Partisan Day 11 October

Telephone & Fax

The country code for Macedonia is ✆389. Internet cafes offer cheap international phone service. Public telephone cards sold in kiosks or post offices in units of 100 (200MKD), 200 (300MKD), 500 (650MKD) or 1000 (1250MKD) offer good value for domestic calls. Drop the initial zero in city codes and mobile prefixes (✆07) when calling from abroad.

Macedonia's largest provider is T-Mobile, followed by One and VIP.

Major post offices do international faxing – lawyers' offices, more cheaply.

Tourist Information

Travel agencies are best, though some towns have information offices; see the information section of specific towns.

Travellers with Disabilities

City streets' random holes challenge the wheelchair-bound; most historical sites and old quarters aren't wheelchair-friendly. Expensive hotels may provide wheelchair ramps. Buses and trains lack disabled access.

Visas

Three-month visa-free stays are allowed for passport holders from Australia, Canada, the EU, Iceland, Israel, New Zealand, Norway, Switzerland, Turkey and the USA. Visas are required for most other countries. Visa fees average from US$30 for a single-entry visa and US$60 for a multiple-entry visa. Check www.mfa.gov.mk for updated information.

Getting There & Away

Air

Alexander the Great Airport (✆023 148 651), 21km from Skopje, is Macedonia's main airport, with Ohrid's **St Paul the Apostle Airport** (✆046 252 820) mostly used for summer charters. See www.airports.com.mk for information, including timetables and weather conditions. Exchange offices, and hotel-booking and car-rental services, are at Skopje's airport.

For the list of airlines flying to/from Macedonia, see p555.

Land

Of the four border crossings between Macedonia and Albania, Kafasan–Qafa e Thanës, 12km southwest of Struga, is busiest, followed by Sveti Naum–Tushëmishti, 29km south of Ohrid. Blato, 5km northwest of Debar, and Stenje, on Lake Prespa's southwestern shore, are less used.

For Bulgaria, Deve Bair (90km from Skopje, after Kriva Palanka) is on the road to Sofia. The Delcevo crossing (110km from Skopje) leads to Blagoevgrad, while the southeastern Novo Selo crossing, 160km from Skopje beyond Strumica, accesses Petrich.

The Blace border crossing 20 minutes north from Skopje accesses Kosovo, as does Tetovo's Jazince border point.

For Serbia, Tabanovce is the major road/rail crossing. Pelince, 25km northeast, is less frequently used.

BUS

Buses serve Balkan and other European cities. See the boxed text, p536, for details.

CAR & MOTORCYCLE

A Green Card endorsed for Macedonia is required; see p1016 for more.

TRAIN

Macedonia's antiquated railway serves Greece, Serbia and Kosovo, and is the cheapest and most iconic way to go. See **Macedonian Railway** (www.mz.com.mk) or p556 for details.

Getting Around

Bicycle

Cycling is popular as traffic is light in rural areas, though mountains and reckless drivers are common.

Bus

Skopje is well connected to domestic destinations (p536). Larger buses are new and air-conditioned, *kombi* (minibuses) usually not. During summer, book ahead for Ohrid.

Car & Motorcycle

If you have the correct documentation and aren't violating laws, don't worry if stopped at random police checkpoints.

AUTOMOBILE ASSOCIATIONS

AMSM (Avto Moto Soyuz na Makedonija; ☑023 181 181; www.art.com.mk, in Macedonian; Ivo Ribar Lola 51, Skopje) offers road assistance, towing services and information (in German, English and Macedonian), with branches nationwide.

DRIVING LICENCE

National drivers licences are respected, though an International Driving Permit is best.

FUEL & SPARE PARTS

Petrol stations are prevalent except in rural areas. Unleaded and regular petrol cost about 70MKD per litre, while diesel costs around 50MKD per litre.

HIRE

Skopje's rental agencies include international biggies and local companies. Ohrid has many, other cities fewer. Sedans average €60 daily, including insurance. Bring your passport, drivers licence and credit card.

INSURANCE

Rental agencies provide insurance (€15 to €25 a day, depending on vehicle type; the nonwaivable excess is €1000 to €2500). Green Card insurance is accepted, third-party insurance, compulsory.

ROAD RULES

Drive on the right. Speed limits are 120km/h (motorways), 80km/h (open road) and 50km/h to 60km/h (in towns). Speeding fines start from 1500MKD. Seatbelt and headlight use is compulsory. Cars must (on paper, at least) carry replacement bulbs, two warning triangles and a first-aid kit. From 15 November to 15 March snow chains are useful. Motorcyclists and passengers must wear helmets. Police are vigilant on speeding, drink driving (blood alcohol limit 0.05%) and headlight use. Fines are payable immediately.

Taxi

Taxis are inexpensive. Skopje base rates are 50MKD; in smaller cities, 30MKD to 40MKD. For some intercity routes, taxis collect four people before going – the individual cost is similar to the cost of a bus ticket.

Train

Major lines are Tabanovce (on the Serbian border) to Gevgelija (on the Greek border), via Kumanovo, Skopje, Veles, Negotino and Demir Kapija; and Skopje to Bitola, via Veles and Prilep. Smaller Skopje–Kičevo and Skopje–Kočani lines exist. See p556 for details.

Moldova

Why Go?

Moldo-who? The country is only vaguely known in Europe and is all but anonymous to the rest of the world; travel blogs about Moldova – consistently ranked near the bottom of the World Database of Happiness – are more often written by melancholy Peace Corps volunteers than tipsy revellers enjoying what is arguably the best-value wine-drinking (ad)venture on the planet. More sober tourist attractions are few but outstanding, such as the dramatic and beautiful cave monasteries and the always petulant breakaway republic of Transdniestr, still plugging along as one of Europe's top (and most notorious) idiosyncratic wonders. Chişinău's unexpectedly superb dining and clubbing options have been known to extend a few visits as well.

Although Moldova is a perpetual contender for the 'poorest country in Europe' designation, prices here, particularly for accommodation, can be surprisingly high. Coming from Romania, expect to pay about the same for almost everything.

When to Go

Chisinau

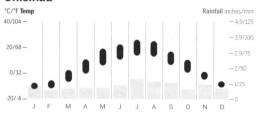

June Parks and restaurant terraces fill with freed students, as do markets with fresh produce.

July High season, what there is of it, hits its peak with hiking, wine tours and camping all in full operation.

October The Wine Festival is on the second Sunday in October, with a 10-day visa-free interval.

Fast Facts

» **Area** 33,851 sq km

» **Capital** Chişinău

» **Telephone code** 373

» **Emergency** police 902, ambulance 903

Exchange Rates

Australia	A$1	12.14 lei
Canada	C$1	11.97 lei
euro	€1	16.53 lei
Japan	¥100	13.88 lei
New Zealand	NZ$1	9.13 lei
UK	UK£1	18.74 lei
USA	US$1	11.51 lei

Set Your Budget

» **Budget hotel room** 500 lei

» **Two-course meal** 160 lei

» **Museum entrance** 15 lei

» **Beer** 25 lei

» **City transport ticket** 2 lei to 3 lei

Resources

» **Fest** (www.fest.md)

» **Moldova Azi** (www.azi.md)

» **Moldova.org** (www.moldova.org)

Connections

International connections from Moldova are little better than provincial calibre. Daily trains from Chişinău head to Iaşi and Bucharest, as well as branching out into Ukraine, some continuing to Minsk, St Petersburg and Moscow. Buses run similar routes, though transiting Transdniestr when going to Odesa (Ukraine) is discouraged. Buses from Chişinău to Transdniestr are frequent, but the 'border' crossing has historically been unpredictable; see the boxed text (p570) for details.

ITINERARIES

One week

Arrive in Chişinău – buy and uncork several bottles of wine to fuel partying...erm, civilised wine tasting. Use Chişinău as your base, making a trip out to the cave monastery at Orheiul Vechi. Take a tour around a big-name vineyard.

Two weeks

Follow the one-week itinerary, then spend a few memorably surreal days in Transdniestr, the country that doesn't officially exist. Tack on a few smaller vineyard tours around Chişinău, purchasing your customs limit, before returning home.

Essential Food & Drink

» **Wine** Cricova, Mileştii Mici and Cojuşna wineries and others offer the most fulfilling and inexpensive wine tours in the world.

» **Fresh produce** There's nothing else available, and thank goodness, because Moldova is essentially one big, very rewarding farmers market.

» **Muşchi de vacă/porc/miel** A cutlet of beef/pork/lamb.

» **Piept de pui** Chicken breast.

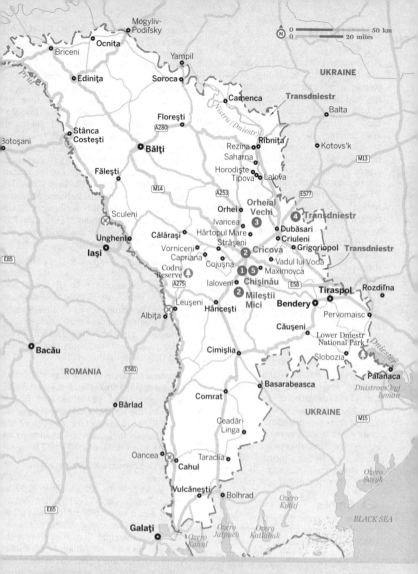

Moldova Highlights

1 Stroll the admirably green streets and parks, then sample the religion-changing nightlife of **Chişinău** (p559)

2 Designate a driver for tours of the world-famous wine cellars at **Mileştii Mici** (p568) and **Cricova** (p568)

3 Detox at the fantastic cave monastery, burrowed by 13th-century monks, at **Orheiul Vechi** (p568)

4 Go *way* off the beaten path in the self-styled 'republic' of **Transdniestr** (p569), a surreal, living homage to the Soviet Union

5 Gorge on the many excellent **dining** options found in Chişinău (p563)

CHIŞINĂU

☑22 / POP 785,000

Newly arrived visitors to Moldova, a country routinely found at the bottom of European economic indicator rankings, may suffer initial confusion when seeing Chişinău's fashionably dressed inhabitants exiting flashy cars, strutting down boutique-lined avenues and talking into state-of-the-art mobile phones, as they head to lunch in fancy restaurants. Sizeable incoming cash flow from emigrants working abroad accounts for some of this paradoxical affluence, but there's the well off and then there's the dubiously well connected – individuals who are clearly above the law and shamelessly conduct themselves as such. While these occasional, disquieting sightings may distract visitors, citizens of this vibrant, good-natured city have long since dismissed such oddities in favour of what really counts: having a good time.

First chronicled in 1420, Chişinău (*kish*-i-now in Moldovan, *kish*-i-nyov in Russian) became a hotbed of anti-Semitism in the early 20th century. Later Chişinău was the headquarters of the USSR's southwestern military operations during Soviet rule. Between 1944 and 1990 the city was called Kishinev, its Russian name, which is still used by some of the few travel agencies abroad who actually know where it is.

In 2007, Chişinău elected then 28-year-old Liberal Party vice-president Dorin Chirtoacă as its mayor, a small victory for the anti-communist coalition. However, a dubious party switch by a former Chirtoacă ally returned the city-council majority to communist hands, where it remains as of this writing.

◉ Sights

Lacking in pulse-quickening 'must-sees', Chişinău is simply a pleasant city to wander about and discover as you go – with frequent cafe breaks and all-you-can-carry wine and champagne shopping sprees. It was heavily bombed during WWII, and little remains of its historic heart. Still, there are some great museums and parks, and the communist iconography merging with symbols of Moldovan nationalism is intriguing.

Parcul Catedralei & Grădina Publică Ştefan cel Mare şi Sfînt   PARKS

Chişinău's best-known parks diagonally oppose each other, forming two diamonds at the city's core. The highlights of **Parcul Catedralei** (Cathedral Park) are the city's main

Orthodox Cathedral, with its lovely bell tower (1836), and the Holy Gates (1841), also known as Chişinău's own **Arc de Triomphe**. On the northwestern side of the park is a colourful 24-hour **flower market**. **Grădina Publică Ştefan cel Mare şi Sfînt** (Ştefan cel Mare Park) is a first-rate strolling and people-watching area. Ştefan was Moldavia's greatest medieval prince and ubiquitous symbol of Moldova's brave past. His **statue** (1928) lords it over the entrance. Both parks have spotty but free wi-fi. **Government House**, where cabinet meets, is the gargantuan building opposite the Holy Gates. The parliament convenes in **Parliament House** (B-dul Ştefan cel Mare 123) further north. Opposite this is the ominous **Presidential Palace**, conspicuous photography of which will elicit a security response.

National Archaeology & History Museum
MUSEUM

(www.nationalmuseum.md; Str 31 August 1989; admission/photo/video 15/15/40 lei; ☉10am-6pm Sat-Thu) The grandaddy of Chişinău's museums contains archaeological artefacts from Orheiul Vechi, including Golden Horde coins, Soviet-era weaponry and a huge WWII diorama on the 1st floor.

National Museum of Fine Arts   ART MUSEUM

(Muzeul de Arte Plastice; Str 31 August 1989, 115; adult/student 15/10 lei; ☉10am-6pm Tue-Sun) Opposite the **National Library**; browse the interesting collection of contemporary European (mostly Romanian and Moldovan) art, folk art, icons and medieval knick-knacks.

National Ethnographic & Nature Museum   MUSEUM

(Str M Kogălniceanu 82; adult/child 15/10 lei; ☉10am-6pm Tue-Sun) The highlight of this massive and wonderful exhibition is a life-size reconstruction of a dinothere (an elephant-like mammal that lived during the Pliocene Epoch – 5.3 million to 1.8 million years ago) skeleton, discovered in the Rezine region in 1966. Allow at least an hour to see the museum's pop art, taxidermied animals and exhibits covering geology, botany and zoology. An English-language tour – arranged in advance – costs 100 lei.

Pushkin Museum   HISTORIC HOUSE

(Str Anton Pann 19; admission 15 lei; ☉10am-4pm Tue-Sun) Northeast of the central parks, this is where Russian poet Alexander Pushkin (1799–1837) spent three years exiled between 1820 and 1823. It was here that he wrote *The Prisoner of the Caucasus* and other

Sightseeing options are engaging but thin and easily covered in a half-day amble. Spend both nights ensconced in Chişinău's legendary nightlife.

On your first day eat at the outstanding **Vatra Neamului** before moving on to cocktails at **Déja Vu**. Dance the night away at **City Club**.

On your second day get a hearty breakfast at **Cactus Café**. Wander through the **National Archaeology and History Museum** and **National Museum of Fine Arts**, then find a nice spot in one of the city's excellent, wi-fi enabled parks to rest up. Finally, do it all again until 6am at **Star Track**.

classics – that is, when he wasn't involved in the amorous intrigues, hard drinking and occasional violence of his social circles in what was then a distant rough-around-the-edges outpost of the Russian empire. You can step in and view his tiny cottage, filled with original furnishings and personal items. An English-language tour costs 50 lei. If the gate is locked, knock on the nearby window.

National Army Museum OUTDOOR MUSEUM
(cnr Str 31 August 1989 & Str Tighina; admission/photo 2/3 lei; ☺9am-8pm Tue-Sun) This small open-air military exhibition displays Soviet-made tanks, fighter planes and other military toys inherited by Moldova's armed forces.

☞ Tours

Chişinău Brewery BEER
(☎929 243; www.berechisinau.md, in Moldovan; Str Uzinelor 167) Just east of the centre in Ciocana, the Chişinău Brewery offers free, one-hour tours that include a short video and a surprisingly generous tasting.

🛏 Sleeping

Check out **Marisha** (www.marisha.net) for cheap homestays and apartments in Chişinău.

TOP CHOICE | **Chişinău Hostel** HOSTEL €
(☎069-711 918; www.chisinau-hostel.ucoz.com; Str Arborilor 5/4, behind Malldova; dm/d 157/410 lei; 🛜📶) Moldova's only proper hostel is about a 25-minute walk south from the centre. This comfortable, well-run place offers lockers, breakfast, shared kitchen, Wii, laundry (32 lei), and tours to wineries and Transdniestr. A number of maxitaxis stop here from the centre and all stations; ask for 'Malldova'. A taxi ride will cost 35 to 40 lei. It's a popular place, so book ahead.

Adresa APARTMENTS €€
(☎544 392; www.adresa.md; B-dul Negruzzi 1; apt 395-1100 lei; ☺24hr) For short- or long-term stays, this reliable agency offers a great alternative to hotels, renting out one- to three-room apartments throughout the city. It's a memorable way to live as the locals do, using rusty lifts or climbing disagreeable staircases. Still, they're all safe, comfortable and clean. Most aren't right in the city centre but are a short taxi ride away.

Hotel Codru HOTEL €€€
(☎208 104; www.codru.md; Str 31 August 1989, 127; incl breakfast s 1237-1550 lei, d 1400-1710 lei, ste 3115 lei; 🛜) Get through the ho-hum lobby and enjoy paradoxically nice rooms that become downright luxurious when you reach 'eurostandard' classification. Wi-fi, balconies and immaculate bathrooms complete the package. There's an on-site restaurant, where the continental breakfast is served.

Hotel Cosmos HOTEL €€
(☎542 757; www.hotel-cosmos.com; Piaţa Negruzzi 2; s/d 492/622 lei, with air con 622/781 lei; ❄🛜) Rooms are reasonably priced in this concrete hulk, with decent beds, newish baths and grubby balconies overlooking the bedlam in Piaţa Negruzzi. Downstairs there's a shopping centre, full-service desk and internet cafe. Wi-fi is in the lobby and select rooms.

Flowers HOTEL €€€
(☎277 262; www.hotelflowers.md; Str Anestiade 7; s/d 2200/2515 lei; ➔❄@🛜) This 40-room hotel is a good splurge. Enormous rooms equipped with wi-fi, minibar and high ceilings are exquisitely decorated with tasteful restraint, incorporating paintings by local artists and, of course, a small jungle's worth of plants and flowers.

Hotel Turist HOTEL €
(☎220 637; B-dul Renaşterii 13; s 500-700 lei, d 450-560 lei; 🛜) For a kitsch blast of the Soviet past, try this place, overlooking a giant Soviet memorial to communist youth. The socialist mural on its facade is prime photo-op material. The doubles are all unrenovated

MOLDOVA

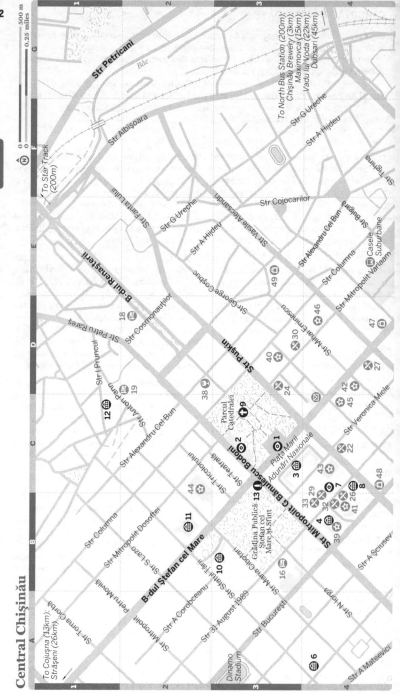

Central Chişinău

500 m
0.25 miles

To Cojuşna (13km);
Străşeni (26km)

To Toma Ciorba

B-dul Renaşterii

Str Petricani

Str Albişoara

To Star Track
(200m)

To North Bus Station (200m);
Chişinău Brewery (3km);
Maximovca (15km);
Vadu lui Vodă (22km);
Dubăsari (45km)

Str G Ureche

Str A Hîjdeu

Str Tighina

Str Cojocarilor

Str Panta Lupului

Str G Ureche

Str A Hîjdeu

Str Vasile Alecsandri

Str Alexandru Cel Bun

Str Buiucani

Casele
Suburbane

Str Columna

Str Mitropolit Varlaam

Str George Coşbuc

Str Cosmonauţilor

Str Petru Rareş

Str I Pruncul

Str Anton Pann

Str Alexandru Cel Bun

Str Puşkin

Str Mihai Eminescu

Str Alexandru Cel Bun

Str Veronica Micle

Str Columna

Str Trioloutlui

Str Teatrală

Parcul
Catedralei

Piaţa Marii
Adunări Naţionale

Str Mitropolit G Bănulescu Bodoni

Grădina Publică
Ştefan cel
Mare şi Sfînt

Str A Sciusev

Str Mitropolit Dosoftei

Str Columna

Str S Lazo

B-dul Ştefan cel Mare

Str Mitropolit Petru Movila

Str A Corobceanu

Str 31 August 1989

Str Maria Cibotari

Str Steluţ Tării

Str Bucureşti

Str N Iorga

Dinamo
Stadium

Str A Mateevici

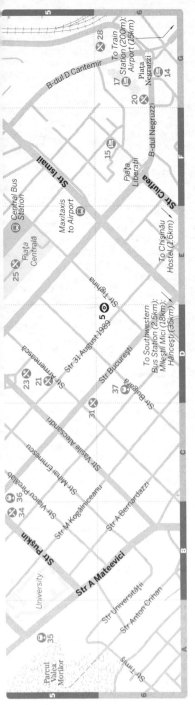

and spare, but just fine. More expensive rooms have refrigerators, air-con and balconies. Breakfast is 55 lei.

Hotel Zarea HOTEL €
(☎227 625; Str Anton Pann 4; r 560-700 lei, without bathroom 270-390 lei) This drab high-rise has dour, smoky rooms that are appropriately priced. There's a bar and billiard club. Breakfast isn't included. Higher-priced doubles have air-con.

✗ Eating
The assortment of great places to eat in Chişinău far exceeds the space we have to list them. These are some of our favourites, but we encourage you to explore others that look interesting.

TOP CHOICE **Vatra Neamului** INTERNATIONAL €€€
(Str Bucureşti 67; mains 90-207 lei) The slightly formal crystal glasses are offset by the unfailingly genial staff. A long menu of imaginatively dressed-up meats – including rabbit and duck, grilled dishes and copious vegetarian options – may prompt repeated visits. Enter via the door on Str Puşkin.

Grill House INTERNATIONAL €€€
(Str Armeneasca 24; mains 70-250 lei) Outstanding dishes are produced by attentive servers from the glassed-in, fire-oven kitchen. Creative pasta dishes complement the array of hearty meat and fish. Meat salads like chicken liver with quail eggs or ravioli stuffed with chicken liver in truffle sauce go for 124 lei. Skip the outrageously priced foreign wine for a Moldovan variety. Go down the atmospheric alley off the sidewalk.

Carmelo ITALIAN €€
(Str Veronica Micle 1/1; pasta 80-150 lei, pizzas 75-150 lei) Italian-run; these guys serve up excellent pasta dishes and filling, thin crust pizza. The *secondi* (meat plates) are special-occasion prices.

Beer House INTERNATIONAL €€
(B-dul Negruzzi 6/2; mains 68-190 lei) This brewery-cum-restaurant has four delicious home-brewed beers and a superb menu, warming up with chicken wings and peaking at rabbit or chicken grilled in cognac. The relaxed ambience and impeccable service add to the charm.

Symposium FRENCH €€
(Str 31 August 1989, 78; mains 80-170 lei) Regarded as one of the city's top dining experiences in terms of elegance and refinement, coupled with reasonable prices. The French-style

MOLDOVA

MOLDOVA CHIŞINĂU

cuisine is succulent, including lamb in a white wine mushroom sauce and a long list of desserts like chocolate crepes and fried bananas in cognac sauce.

Oraşul Vechi MOLDOVAN €€€
(Old City; ☑225 063; Str Armenească 24; mains 45-300 lei) This stylish restaurant with chandeliers, classic paintings and a fireplace has nightly live piano. The juicy grilled pork in wine sauce is 98 lei.

Cactus Café CAFE €€€
(www.cactus.md; Str Armenească 41; mains 95-225 lei; ☞) The 'Wild West meets urban bohemian' interior decor here will stun wine-fogged patrons into thinking they've been zapped to Brooklyn during the night. Extravagant breakfasts (30 to 70 lei), vegetarian meals and daring plates like 'fois gras with cauliflower puree and mushroom sauce' (240 lei) don't help to dull the sensation.

Pani Pit MOLDOVAN €€
(31 August 1989, 115; www.ten.md; mains 80-180 lei) Peasant waitresses serve omelettes and pancakes, along with the usual Moldovan menu of beef, pork and chicken. Choose the classy dining room or the large terrace, with cushioned cast-iron chairs, vines and a small waterfall. If the front is locked, enter through the terrace around the side.

Green Hills Café CAFE €€
(B-dul Ştefan cel Mare 77; mains 55-130 lei) Though the large selection of meat and vegetable dishes are delicious, most come for a quick fix – great coffee, cocktails or beer, and, of course, people-watching on the city's main drag. There's a second branch, **Green Hills Restaurant** (Str 31 August 1989, 76).

Café Vijelios CAFE €
(Str Puşkin 22; mains 10-22 lei) This cafeteria serves surprisingly succulent food priced for the impoverished university crowd.

Celentano

PIZZA €

(Str Puşkin 30; pizzas 20 lei, plus toppings) Popular for its locally unique build-your-own-pizza offer (our chicken and onion pizza was 36 lei). It also does fruit and chocolate shakes.

Delice d'Ange

CAFE €

(Str 31 August 117/2) Dazzling pastries and great coffee (25 lei). There's a tree and children's play area upstairs.

Green Hills Market

SUPERMARKET €

(B-dul D Cantemir 6) The newest and most central location of the Green Hills Market chain. Sprawling and modern, it's comparable to any Western supermarket chain.

Opa

GREEK €€

(Str Mitropolit Varlaam 88; mains 60-190 lei) A Greek grill with several types of souvlaki, salads and the best baklava in Chişinău.

Central market

MARKET €

(Piaţa Centrală; ☺7am-5pm) Since 1825 this market has been the scene of lively price haggling for fresh meat and produce. Brave the crowds for its fresh food and singular ambience.

🍷 Drinking

Robin Pub

PUB

(Str Alexandru cel Bun 83; mains 72-195 lei; ☺11am-midnight) A friendly, affordable local-pub feel reigns in this tastefully decorated hang-out. The extravagant menu includes omelettes, pastas, a tuna steak and delectable crêpes suzette for dessert.

Coliba Studenţilor

BAR

(Str A Mateevici; ☺8am-11pm) This student hang-out, opposite the university, is quiet during summer, but during the school year the terrace is a good place to bump into eager English speakers.

Dublin Irish Pub

PUB

(Str Bulgară 27; mains 55-150 lei; ☺noon-11pm) Rather expensive, but one of the few places in town where you can get a pint of Guinness (70 lei).

Déja Vu

COCKTAILS

(Str Bucureşti 67; ☺11am-2am) A true cocktail bar, with a tantalising drinks menu. There's also a small dining hall serving meals.

☆ Entertainment

Posters listing what's on are displayed on boards outside the city's various theatres.

Nightclubs

Chişinău parties in earnest every weekend, but in some of the larger clubs be prepared for body searches, metal detectors and tough-guy posturing from goonish doormen.

City Club

CLUB

(Str 31 August 1989, 121; ☺10pm-6am) In the alley next to the Licurici Puppet Theatre, this 2nd-floor club consistently ranks as one of the hippest places in town.

Star Track

CLUB

(Str Kiev 7; ☺10pm-4am Tue-Sun) Located about 1km northeast of the centre, with a dark interior that offers comfortable sofas and make-out booths where one can ogle dance performances by scantily clad men and women. Under Star Track is the less titillating but equally popular Military Pub.

Booz Time

DANCING

(Str 31 August 1989, 117; ☺9pm-3am) A popular bar with theme nights like salsa dancing (Thursday) and Retro Sundays.

Performing Arts

Opera & Ballet Theatre

BALLET

(B-dul Ştefan cel Mare 152; ☺box office 10am-2pm & 5-7pm) This venue is home to the esteemed national opera and ballet company. Grab a bite at Andy's Pizza outside the entrance before the show.

Chekhov Drama Theatre

LIVE THEATRE

(Teatrul Dramatic A Cehov; Str Pârcălab 75) Plays in Russian are performed at the Chekhov Drama Theatre, situated where Chişinău's choral synagogue was located until WWII.

Organ Hall

CONCERTS

(Sala cu Orgă; B-dul Ştefan cel Mare 79) Classical concerts and organ recitals are held at this hall, next to the Mihai Eminescu National Theatre. Performances start at 6pm; tickets are sold at the door.

Mihai Eminescu National Theatre

LIVE THEATRE

(B-dul Ştefan cel Mare 79; ☺box office 11am-6.30pm) Contemporary Romanian productions can be seen at this theatre, founded in 1933.

National Palace

LIVE THEATRE

(Palatul Naţional; Str Puşkin 21; ☺box office 11am-5pm) Various cabarets, musicals and local theatre group productions are performed here.

Philharmonic Concert Hall

CONCERTS

(Str Mitropolit Varlaam 78) Moldova's National Philharmonic is based here.

Sport

Moldovans are big football fans and Chişinău has three stadiums to prove it. The new **Zimbru Stadium** is the city's first European regulation football stadium, located in the Botanica district. **Dinamo Stadium** (Stadionul Dinamo) is north of the city centre on Str Bucureşti. Moldovans like football so much, in fact, there's an American football team called the Chişinău Barbarians, who hold occasional matches, in full gear.

 Shopping

Cricova   WINE
(B-dul Ştefan cel Mare 126; ☺10am-7pm Mon-Fri, to 6pm Sat, to 4pm Sun) One of several outlets for the Cricova wine factory. It stocks numerous types of shockingly affordable wine and champagne (only 23 lei to 70 lei each).

Mileştii Mici   WINE
(www.milestii-mici.md; Str Vasile Alecsandri 137; ☺9am-8pm Mon-Fri) The outlet store for the Mileştii Mici wine cellars. Table wine is sold in litre bottles – 9 lei for white, 12 lei for red. There's another location at the airport.

Galeria L   ART
(Str Bucureşti 64; ☺10am-6pm Mon-Fri, to 5pm Sat, to 4pm Sun) Holds temporary art exhibitions, and sells small works of art and souvenirs crafted by local artists.

 Information

Dangers & Annoyances

The odd Bucharest-style restaurant pricing scam has been reported. Never order anything, particularly wine, without confirming the price *in writing* (eg on the menu) to avoid surprises on the bill. If you've been victimised, keep all receipts and report it to the police.

Cross streets with care – according to locals, hapless pedestrians are mowed down by recklessly driven ministers' cars on an almost weekly basis.

Travellers are required to have their passports with them *at all times*. Cheeky police are prone to random checks.

Medical Services

Contact the US embassy (p578) for a list of English-speaking doctors.

Municipal Clinical Emergency Hospital
(☏emergency 903, information 248 435; Str Toma Ciorba 1; ☺24hr) Provides a variety of emergency services and a good likelihood of finding English-speaking staff.

Felicia (B-dul Ştefan cel Mare 62; ☺24hr) Well-stocked pharmacy.

Internet Access

There's free wi-fi at Parcul Catedralei and Grădina Publică Ştefan cel Mare şi Sfînt.

Internet (Hotel Cosmos, Piaţa Negruzzi 2; per hr 7 lei; ☺24hr)

Moldtelecom Plaza (cnr B-dul Ştefan cel Mare & Str Ismail; free wi-fi)

Money

There are ATMs all over the city centre, in all the hotels and in shopping centres. Currency exchanges are concentrated around the bus and train stations, and also along B-dul Ştefan cel Mare.

Deghest (Str Mitropolit G Bănulescu Bodoni 43) Has the best exchange rates in the city.

Eximbank (B-dul Ştefan cel Mare 6; ☺9am-5pm Mon-Fri) Can give you cash advances in foreign currency.

Victoriabank (Str 31 August 1989, 141; ☺9am-4pm Mon-Fri) Amex's representative in Moldova.

Post

Central post office (B-dul Ştefan cel Mare 134; ☺8am-7pm Mon-Sat, to 6pm Sun) There is also a post office on Aleea Gării (open to 8pm).

Telephone

Central telephone office (B-dul Ştefan cel Mare 65; ☺8am-8pm) Book international calls inside the hall marked 'Convorbiri Telefonice Internaţionale'. Faxes and telegrams can also be sent from here. Receive faxes at ☏549 155.

Travel Agencies

There's no tourist information centre in Moldova, but there are plenty of agencies where you can get information. Most offer discounted rates in some hotels.

Sometimes travel agencies take a while to reply to emails (if ever). A better bet for pre-trip contact are independent operators like **Radu Sargu** (☏069-138 953; www.moldova-travel. com) or **Natalia Raiscaia** (☏079-578 217; www. domasha.net) for apartment rentals, local information and assistance.

Solei Turism (☏271 314; www.solei.md; B-dul Negruzzi 5; ☺8am-6pm Mon-Sat, 9am-5pm Sun) A very efficient organisation, can book accommodation and transport tickets. Multiday excursions to monasteries and places of interest, incorporating rural homestays.

Valery Bradu (☏079-462 986; valbradu@yahoo. com) A recommended tour guide and driver.

 Getting There & Away

Air

Moldova's only airport of significance is **Chişinău international airport** (KIV;

525 111; www.airport.md), 15.5km southeast of the city centre. For more information on airlines servicing Chişinău, see p580.

Bus

Chişinău has three bus stations. The **North Bus Station** (Autogara Nord; www.autogara.md), northeast of the centre where Str Ismail and Str Tudor Vladimirescu meet, is where nearly all domestic and international lines depart, except Transdniestr-bound lines, which depart from the Central Bus Station. Services include regular buses to Soroca, Bălţi and Rezina. There are daily buses to Moscow (580 lei, 30 hours), St Petersburg (810 lei, 33 to 36 hours) and Kyiv (257 lei, 11 hours). Avoid buses that transit Transdniestr through to Odesa (90 lei, five to six hours): opt instead for the longer, but less unpredictable, route through Palanca. You can buy advance tickets here or from a tiny office at the train station. The information booth charges 1 leu per question.

Domestic and international maxitaxis operate from the **Central Bus Station** (Autogara Centrală; Str Mitropolit Varlaam), behind the central market. Maxitaxis go to Tiraspol (29 lei, ½ hours) and Bendery (25 lei) every 20 to 35 minutes from 6.30am to 6.30pm, with reduced services until 10pm. Buses to Bucharest are 225 lei to 280 lei (12 hours). There are buses half-hourly from 9.15am to 10pm to Orhei (19 lei), leaving from the 'Casele Suburbane' terminal about 100m west of Central Station.

Bus services to/from Comrat, Hânceşti and other southern destinations use the **Southwestern Bus Station** (Autogara Sud-vest; cnr Şoseaua Hânceşti & Str Spicului), approximately 2.2km from the city centre. Daily local services include hourly buses to Comrat (36 lei) in Gagauzia and six to Hânceşti (10 lei). A fleet of buses and maxitaxis head to Iaşi, Romania (110 lei, four hours); a few continue on to Braşov and Cluj-Napoca. **Eurolines** (222 827; www.eurolines.md), with an office at the train station, operates a few buses to Western Europe, including once-weekly runs to Berlin and Warsaw, Braşov (four weekly), Constanţa and Ukraine. Three weekly buses head to Paris.

Train

International routes departing from Chişinău's sparkling new **train station** (Aleea Gării), located just southeast of Piaţa Negruzzi, off B-dul Iurii Gagarin, include three daily trains to Moscow (four-bed sleeper 1275 lei to 1515 lei, 28 to 32 hours), three daily trains to Kyiv (545 lei to 670 lei, 14 hours), one each to St Petersburg (1441 lei, 40 hours) and Bucharest (785 lei, 14 hours), and three to Lviv (645 lei, 18 hours), and three weekly services to Minsk (743 lei, 25 hours). To get to Budapest, you must change in Bucharest. **Left luggage** (5am–midnight) costs 11 lei per day.

ℹ Getting Around

To/From the Airport

Maxitaxi 165 departs every 20 minutes from Str Ismail, across from Eximbank near the corner of B-dul Ştefan cel Mare for the airport (3 lei). Coming from the airport, this is the last stop.

Car & Motorcycle

Loran Car Rental (243 710; www.lorancar. md; Hotel Codru, Str 31 August 1989, 127) From €29 (460 lei) per day for a Dacia Logan, including insurance. Payments in cash (euros or lei) or by credit card; a deposit is required.

Public Transport

BUS/MAXITAXI Route 45 runs from the Central Bus Station to the Southwestern Bus Station, as does maxitaxi 117 from the train station. Bus 1 goes from the train station to B-dul Ştefan cel Mare. Trolleybuses (running by overhead wire) 1, 4, 5, 8, 18 and 22 go to the train station from the city centre. Buses 2, 10 and 16 go to the Southwestern Bus Station. Maxitaxis 176 and 191 go to the North Bus Station from the city centre. Tickets costing 2 lei for buses and 1 leu for trolleybuses are sold onboard. Most routes in town and to many outlying villages are served by nippy maxitaxis (3 lei per trip, pay the driver). Maxitaxis run regularly between 6am and 10pm, some with reduced service until midnight.

TAXI Many official and unofficial taxis do not have meters or prices listed on the door and taxi-stand drivers may occasionally try to rip you off. Ordering a taxi (1448, 1433, 1422, 1407) is best. If you decide to hop in off the street, agree on a price to your destination before getting in the car.

MOLDOVA CRICOVA

AROUND CHIŞINĂU

Even the furthest reaches of Moldova are a reasonable day trip from Chişinău, though that's not to say an overnight somewhere isn't a good idea. Get out of the capital and you'll find a far more tranquil atmosphere.

Cricova

Of Moldova's many fine wineries, **Cricova** (022-441 204; www.cricova.md; Str Ungureanu 1; 8am-4pm) is arguably the best known. Its underground wine kingdom, 15km north of Chişinău, is one of Europe's biggest. Some 60km of the 120km-long underground limestone tunnels – dating from the 15th century – are lined wall-to-wall with bottles. The most interesting part of the tour is the wineglass-shaped cellar of collectible bottles, including 19 bottles of Gerhing's wines, a 1902 bottle of Becherovka, a 1902 bottle of Evreiesc de Paşti from Jerusalem and pre-WWII French red wines.

Cricova wines and champagnes enjoy a high national and international reputation. Legend has it that in 1966 astronaut Yuri Gagarin entered the cellars, re-emerging (with assistance) two days later. Russian prime minister Vladimir Putin celebrated his 50th birthday here.

You must have private transport and advance reservations to get into Cricova or you can arrange for staff to pick you up in Chişinău. Tours range from 45 minutes to 2½ hours (250 lei to 1350 lei per person), with increasing tastings and food as the price climbs.

Once you've finished at Cricova, head to the much-awarded **Acorex vineyard** (www.acorex. net; ⊙9am-6pm), just down the hill. There's no tour, but the shop sells limited lines not available in most stores or outside Moldova.

Mileştii Mici

While Cricova has the hype, **Mileştii Mici** (☎022-382 333; www.milestii-mici.md; 2hr tour 250 lei, tour, tasting & lunch 500-900 lei per person; ⊙9am-5pm Mon-Fri) has the goods. Also housed in a limestone mine, these are *the* largest cellars in Europe (over 200km of tunnels). They were recognised by Guinness in 2005 for having the largest wine collection in the world (1.5 million bottles), though the collection has now surpassed the two-million-bottle mark.

Excellent-value tours, done by car, wind down through the cellars with stops at notable collections and artistically executed tourist points, terminating at the elegantly decorated restaurant 60m below ground. These tours are striking, while being refreshingly informal and hilarious. Tour groups must have a minimum of four people – though this is negotiable – while a Saturday/Sunday tour must have a minimum of 15 people.

Cojuşna

Just 13km northwest of Chişinău, **Cojuşna** (☎022-615 329, 69-300 043; Str Lomtadze 4; ⊙8am-6pm) winery, in the village of the same name, offers spunky, friendly and affordable tours, though the setting is moribund in comparison to Cricova and Mileştii Mici.

Cojuşna will need advance warning if you want a tour in English. Tours of one to three hours (246 lei to 377 lei per person) include a gift bottle, tastings and a hot meal at the top end. Prices rise significantly on weekends. Drop-ins are possible, but staff aren't always free to open the very worthwhile wine-tasting rooms, decorated with wooden furniture carved by a local boy and his father. However, you can always buy wine (20 lei to 280 lei per bottle) from the shop.

From Chişinău, catch one of the frequent maxitaxis leaving from Calea Eşilor (take trolleybus 1, 5 or 11 up B-dul Ştefan cel Mare to the Ion Creangă university stop) and get off at the Cojuşna stop. Ignore the fork on the left marked 'Cojuşna' and walk or hitch the remaining 2km along the main road to the vineyard entrance, marked again by a 'Cojuşna' sign and a whitewashed Jesus-on-the-cross. The winery is about 200m from the road.

Orheiul Vechi

Ten kilometres southeast of Orhei lies Orheiul Vechi ('Old Orhei', marked on maps as the village of Trebujeni), unquestionably Moldova's most fantastic sight. It's certainly among its most picturesque places.

The **Orheiul Vechi Monastery Complex** (Complexul Muzeistic Orheiul Vechi; ☎0235-34 242; admission 15 lei; ⊙9am-6pm Tue-Sun), carved into a massive limestone cliff in this wild rocky, remote spot, draws visitors from around the globe.

The **Cave Monastery** (Mănăstire în Peşteră), inside a cliff overlooking the gently meandering Răut River, was dug by Orthodox monks in the 13th century. It remained inhabited until the 18th century, and in 1996 a handful of monks returned to this secluded place of worship and are slowly restoring it. You can enter the cave via an entrance on the cliff's plateau.

Ştefan cel Mare built a fortress here in the 14th century, but it was later destroyed by Tartars. In the 18th century the cave-church was taken over by villagers from neighbouring Butuceni. In 1905 they built a church above ground dedicated to the Ascension of St Mary. The church was shut down by the Soviets in 1944 and remained abandoned throughout the communist regime. Services resumed in 1996.

Ancillary attractions include remnants of a 15th-century defence wall surrounding the monastery complex, an **ethnographic** museum in the nearby village of Butuceni and newly opened caves across the valley.

You'll find the headquarters on the main road to the complex where you park and purchase your tickets for the complex. You can also arrange guides and get general information.

It's forbidden to wear shorts and women must cover their heads while inside the monastery.

Orheiul Vechi Monastery Headquarters (☑0235-56 912; d 450 lei) has six pleasant rooms and a small restaurant. The rooms facing the monastery have spine-tingling balcony views. There's no proper meals served here, including breakfast, though meals can be arranged at the pensions in nearby Butuceni.

From Chișinău, daily buses depart from the Central Bus Station for Butuceni or Trebujeni (20 lei, about one hour) at 10.20am, 3pm and 6.15pm. Return trips run daily at 6am and 4.45pm, with an additional bus at noon Friday to Sunday.

Soroca

POP 27,423

Soroca is the Roma 'capital' of Moldova, but people come here to see the outstanding **Soroca fortress** (☑069-323 734; adult/student/guided tour 3/2/100 lei; ◎9am-1pm & 2-6pm Wed-Sun May-Oct, low season by appointment). Part of a medieval chain of military fortresses built by Moldavian princes between the 14th and 16th centuries to defend Moldavia's boundaries, the fortress was founded by Ștefan cel Mare and rebuilt by his son, Petru Rareș, in 1543–45.

The fortress is administered by the **Soroca Museum of History and Ethnography** (☑0230-22 264; Str Independentei 68; adult/student 3/2 lei; ◎10am-4pm Tue-Sun, low season by appointment). This well-designed museum is a real treat; its 27,000 exhibits cover archaeological finds, weapons and ethnographic displays.

Hotel Central (☑0230-23 456; www.soroca-hotel.com; Str Kogalniceanu 20; s 400 lei, d 500-600 lei; 🛜) is modern if simple, with bare overwhelmingly blue rooms, decent beds and small, clean bathrooms. The 'delux' rooms (750 lei) have refrigerators and air-con. Signs point the way here from the centre. Across the street is the **Nistru Hotel** (☑0230-23 783; Str Mihiel Malmut 20; s 100-300 lei, d 300-400 lei), with simple, bright rooms that are a sizeable step down, but fairly priced.

There are 12 daily buses to Soroca from Chișinău's North Bus Station (2½ hours).

TRANSDNIESTR

POP 555,500

The self-declared republic of Transdniestr (Pridnestrovskaya Moldavskaya Respublika, or PMR in Russian), a narrow strip of land covering 3567 sq km on the eastern bank of the Nistru River is, according to its residents, one of the world's last surviving bastions of communism.

Political jibber-jabber and historic ethnic boundaries notwithstanding, Moldova maintains that Transdniestr was illegally grabbed from its sovereign territory. With Russia's support, Transdniestr effectively won its 'independence' during a bloody civil war in the early 1990s. A tenuous, bitter truce has ensued ever since.

Travellers will be stunned by this idiosyncratic region that has developed its own currency, police force, army and borders, controlled by Transdniestran border guards. Russian is the predominant language. Transdniestrans boycott the Moldovan independence day and celebrate their own independence day on 2 September.

Until very recently, a visit to the area meant submitting to sometimes expensive, organised bribe shakedowns with border officials, but at the time of research reports of such instances had noticeably decreased. It's still a good idea to take a few precautions, though; see the boxed text on p570.

Rumours and political weirdness aside, visits here can be quite pleasant, and the surreal atmosphere is unforgettable.

History

Igor Smirnov was elected president of Transdniestr in 1991, following the region's declaration of independence four months earlier. Most of the time the region pushes for full independence or to join with Russia, though the idea of creating a Moldovan federation, with proportionate representation between Moldova, Transdniestr and Gagauzia, has also been floated (and promptly rejected by Chișinău).

Neither Smirnov's presidency nor the Transdniestran parliament is recognised by the Moldovan – or any other – government. The Russian 14th army, headquartered in Tiraspol since 1956, covertly supplied Transdniestran rebels with weapons during the civil war. The continued presence of a Russian

BORDERS SANS BOREDOM

We used to receive frequent reader feedback reporting disturbing hijinks at Transdniestran border crossings, mainly at the popular crossings at Bendery on the Moldovan side and Pervomaisc on the Ukrainian side, where organised intimidation was used to separate travellers from their money. Accusations of incomplete paperwork or invented transgressions (such as carrying a camera) led to ludicrous 'fines' of up to €200 and beyond. Some of the alleged offences bordered on the absurd, such as not having visas (unnecessary) or letters of invitation, acquired at the 'Transdniestran embassy' (nonexistent).

Though at the time of research it was too early to confidently declare anything, it appeared as if the bribe-factory atmosphere had noticeably cooled. Though you probably won't be invited into a hut with several looming, armed guards to discuss your infraction(s) and haggle over how high a 'fine' you should pay, for the time being it's probably still a good idea to employ a few precautions. Chiefly, it's best not to carry ridiculous amounts of cash – in any currency. The less cash you have, the smaller the proposed bribe is likely to be. Professional-looking cameras, particularly video cameras, may still cause some grumbling.

Transiting the republic during a Moldova–Ukraine journey used to guarantee a bribe stare down. Unless you intend to stop and visit Transdniestr, it's still recommended that you circumnavigate the region by passing through the southeast village of Palanca. Many buses, tired of the border hassles, take this route by default. If you opt to transit Transdniestr during a Moldova–Ukraine journey, we recommend taking the bus over a maxitaxi, as maxitaxi schedules and drivers can be unreliable.

All that said, if you enter Transdniestr on public transport and are detained, often your best defence is calm and patience. Let the maxitaxi leave you behind. Another will be along shortly. Even the most persistent guards will eventually get tired of dealing with you, particularly if their tactics don't appear to be working. Worst-case scenario, you'll be stonewalled at a mirthfully small bribe offer (say €5 or 80 Moldovan lei) or you'll be sent back to where you came from.

Entry-permit prices/requirements change frequently. At the time of writing, permits were 'officially' 20 Moldovan lei (about 17 Transdniestran rubles or €1.25), available *at the border* no matter what the guys on duty playfully tell you. For stays of less than 10 hours, you don't need to pay this fee.

If you're staying for more than 24 hours, you'll need to register with **OVIR** (☑533-55 047; ul Kotovskogo 2a; ⊙9am-noon Mon, 9am-noon & 1-4pm Tue & Thu, 1-3pm Fri). Registration is free. Go down the alley and enquire at the rear white building with the red roof. Oh, and 'men must wear pants'! Seriously. Outside OVIR business hours go to the **Tiraspol Militia Office** (☑533-34 169; Roza Luxemburg 66; ⊙24hr) where registration is possible, but you'll probably be asked to check in at the OVIR office the following working day anyway. Some hotels will register you automatically.

'operational group' in Transdniestr today is seen by locals as a guarantee of their security.

The Ministry of State Security (MGB), a modern-day KGB, has sweeping powers, and has sponsored the creation of a youth wing, called the Young Guard, for 16- to 23-year-olds.

Alongside a number of agreements between Moldova and Transdniestr since 1991, there have been countless moves by both sides designed to antagonise or punish the other. In 2003, a piqued Smirnov slapped exorbitant tariffs on all Moldovan imports, instantly halting trade over the 'border' and making life more difficult for ordinary people on both sides. He later had phone connections severed between the two regions for a few weeks.

While Smirnov is becoming increasingly mistrusted by his 'electorate', a large subsection of locals still refuse to criticise their government. Political and economic attitudes aside, popular opinion still strongly supports independence from Moldova.

On 6 July 2006, a bomb blast on a local bus in Tiraspol killed eight people. Transdniestran politicians were quick to blame 'Moldovan provocateurs', though it was eventually revealed that an amateur bomb-maker had lost control of his merchandise.

After hastily abolishing the presidential term limit that he himself established,

Smirnov was elected to a fourth five-year term as president with a 'reported' 82.4% of the vote in December 2006.

For more practical details about visiting the country, see p569.

Tiraspol

☑ 533 / POP 157,000

The sights are ho-hum and the accommodation iffy; nevertheless, this is one of the most mind-bending, surreal and distinctly memorable places in Europe.

Tiraspol (from the Greek, meaning 'town on the Nistru'), 70km east of Chişinău, is the second-largest city in Moldova – sorry – make that the largest city and capital of Transdniestr! Glorifying all things Soviet, this veritable Lenin-loving theme park is starting to show capitalist cracks. Meanwhile, questionable business dealings from the tiny elite widen the divide between the haves and the have-nots.

The city was founded in 1792 following Russian domination of the region. According to the 2004 Transdniestran census, its inhabitants consist of Moldovans (32%), Russians (30%) and ethnic Ukrainians (29%), with groups of Bulgarians, Poles, Gagauz, Jews, Belarusians and others making up the final 9%.

◉ Sights

Tiraspol National United Museum HISTORY MUSEUM
(ul 25 Oktober 42; admission 25 rubles; ⊘10am-5pm Sun-Fri) The closest thing to a local history museum, it features an exhibit focusing on poet Nikolai Zelinsky, who founded the first Soviet school of chemistry. Opposite is the **Presidential Palace**, from which Igor Smirnov rules his mini-empire. Loitering and/or photography here is likely to end in questioning and a guard-escorted trip off the property.

War Memorial MEMORIAL
At the western end of ul 25 Oktober stands a Soviet armoured tank, from which the Transdniestran flag flies. Behind is the **War Memorial** with its Tomb of the Unknown Soldier, flanked by an eternal flame in memory of those who died on 3 March 1992 during the first outbreak of fighting. On weekends, it's covered in flowers left by wedding-day brides.

Kvint factory BRANDY FACTORY
(http://kvint.biz; ul Lenina 38) The Kvint factory is one of Transdniestr's prides and joys –

since 1897 it's been making some of Moldova's finest brandies. Buy the least expensive cognac in Europe (starting at less than €2!) either near the front entrance of the plant or at the **Kvint shop** (ul 25 Oktober 84; ⊘24hr).

House of Soviets LANDMARK
(Dom Sovetovul; ul 25 Oktober) The House of Soviets, towering over the eastern end of ul 25 Oktober, has Lenin's angry-looking bust peering out from its prime location. Inside is a **memorial** to those who died in the 1992 conflict. Close by is the military-themed **Museum of Headquarters** (ul Kommunisticheskaya 34; admission/photo 2/5 rubles; ⊘8.30am-5pm Mon-Sat), which was closed for renovations at the time of research.

Kirov Park CITY PARK
Further north along ul Lenina, towards the bus and train stations, is Kirov Park, with a **statue** of the Leningrad boss who was assassinated in 1934, conveniently sparking mass repressions throughout the USSR.

🛏 Sleeping & Eating

You must register at **OVIR** (ul Kotovskogo No 2A; ⊘9am-noon Mon, 9am-noon & 1-4pm Tue & Thu, 1-3pm Fri) in central Tiraspol if staying more than 24 hours (see the boxed text, p570). Visit www.marisha.net to arrange a homestay.

Stay at Lena's APARTMENT €
(☑72 536; lena_lozinskiy@inbox.ru; ul pereulok Naberezhnyi 1, apt 79; per person 120-180 rubles) Lena has a cosy two-room apartment with enviable views over Konstityutsii (the main square) and the languorous traffic on ul 25 Oktober. There's 24-hour hot water and a full kitchen. She can also arrange other rooms or full apartments around Tiraspol.

Hotel Aist HOTEL €€
(☑73 776; pereulok Naberezhnyi 3; d 250-550 rubles) Despite a derelict exterior, this is a decent hotel. The more expensive rooms have luxuries such as hot water and TV. Lower-class rooms have shared showers. No breakfast.

Kumanek UKRAINIAN €€
(ul Sverdlova 37; mains 21-89 rubles; ⊘9am-11pm; 🛜) Mainly Ukrainian food, though there's a smattering of European dishes as well, including dumplings, pancakes, fish, pork, mutton, chicken and veal. The speciality is the village-style pork (stuffed with mushrooms, onion and garlic, then breaded and fried). The countryside home decor is kitschy both inside and out.

Eilenburg   GERMAN €

(pereulok Naberezhnyi 1; mains 25-110 rubles;
☺11am-midnight) A medieval-themed German restaurant, with girls in dirndl dresses, stone walls, a suit of armour and, coin-
cidentally, decent food. Choose from beef
stroganoff, quail, rabbit, ostrich, salmon,
quail-egg omelettes, and pancakes topped
with red caviar (27 rubles). There's a short
veg menu.

7 Fridays   CAFE €

(ul 25 Oktober 112; mains 23-66 rubles; ☺11am-
midnight; ☎) A popular cafe serving all manner of meat, salads, soups, and, erm, sushi. A
sashimi platter is 342 rubles (we dare you).
Menus are Russian only, but there are pictures to point at.

☆ Entertainment

Snejok/Plazma Nightclub   BAR/CLUB

(ul Lenina; ☺terrace 9am-midnight, club 9pm-4am
Tue-Sun) A neighbouring bar and club arrangement. The bar terrace is a popular
drinking and football-watching locale. Move
next door when dancing starts at 9pm.

Baccarat   CLUB

(ul 25 Oktober 50; Sat admission 50 rubles; ☺5pm-
4am) A stylish hang-out with expensive
drinks and indoor/outdoor seating. Feverish
dancing starts late.

🛍 Shopping

Sheriff Fan Shop   SOUVENIRS

(ul 25 October 69; ☺10am-7pm) Buy jerseys and
memorabilia if you're a fan of the Moldovan league champions – or a fan of total
monopolies.

❶ Information

Antica Pharmacy (ul 25 October; ☺24hr)

Central telephone office (ul Karl Marx 149;
☺8am-8pm) Through the far-left door you can
buy phonecards (10 rubles to 25 rubles) and
use internet (per hour 5.50 rubles; ☺10am-
10pm). You can also buy phone cards at any
Sheriff Market.

Gasprom Bank (ul 25 Oktober 76; ☺9.15am-
8.30pm Mon-Sat) Changes money. There's an
ATM at ul 25 Oktober 85 that dispenses Transdniestran rubles.

Internet (ul 25 October 76; per hr 6 rubles;
☺24hr) Below Gasprom Bank.

Post office (ul Karl Marx 149; ☺7.30am-7pm
Mon-Fri) Won't be of much use to you unless
you want to send postcards to all your friends
in Transdniestr.

❶ Getting There & Away

Bus

You can only pay for tickets to destinations in
Transdniestr with the local currency, but will be allowed to pay in Moldovan lei/Ukrainian hryvnia for
tickets to Moldova/Ukraine. Buy tickets inside the
left-hand door of the station. From Tiraspol there
is one daily bus to Bălţi (Moldova; 72 rubles, six
hours), eight daily to Odesa (Ukraine; 37.25 rubles,
three hours) and one daily to Kyiv (Ukraine; 186
rubles, 14 hours). Buses/maxitaxis go to Chişinău
(26.70 rubles) nearly every half-hour from 5.10am
to 6.10pm. Trolleybus 19 (1.50 rubles) and quicker
maxitaxis 19 and 20 (2.50 rubles) cross the bridge
over the Dniestr to Bendery.

Train

One daily train goes to Moscow, via Kyiv, leaving
promptly at 2.06am (3rd/2nd class 735/1250
rubles, 26 hours). At the time of research, it
was reported that Transdniestr passenger train
service, suspended since 2006, would resume.
A schedule was not provided; the 2006 schedule
included seven daily trains to Chişinău, three to
Odesa, two to Moscow and Minsk and one to St
Petersburg.

Bendery

📞552 / POP 97,027

Bendery (sometimes called Bender, and previously known as Tighina), on the western
banks of the Dniestr River, is the greener,
more aesthetically agreeable counterpart to
Tiraspol. Despite civil war bullet holes still
decorating several buildings – Bendery was
hardest hit by the 1992 military conflict with
Moldova – the city centre is a breezy place.

During the 16th century Moldavian prince
Ştefan cel Mare built a large defensive fortress here on the ruins of a fortified Roman
camp. In 1538 the Ottoman sultan, Suleiman
the Magnificent, conquered the fortress and
transformed it into a Turkish *raia* (colony),
renaming the city Bendery, meaning 'belonging to the Turks'. During the 18th century Bendery was seized from the Turks by
Russian troops who then massacred Turkish Muslims in the city. In 1812 Bendery fell
permanently into Russian hands. Russian
peacekeeping forces remain here to this day.

◉ Sights

Tighina Fortress   FORTRESS

(📞51 210; admission/tour 17/30 rubles) Bendery's
main sight is this massive Turkish fortress,
built in the 1530s to replace a 12th-century
fortress built by the Genovese. Until recently
an off-limits Transdniestran military training

ground, the fortress can now be toured by private car.

Memorial Park PARK

At the entrance to the city, close to the famous **Bendery-Tiraspol bridge**, is a memorial park dedicated to local 1992 war victims. An eternal flame burns in front of an armoured **tank**, from which flies the Transdniestrian flag. Haunting **memorials** to those killed during the civil war are also scattered throughout many streets in the city centre.

🛏 Sleeping & Eating

A three-tier pricing system is intact here, with one price for locals, another for Moldovans, Ukrainians and Belarusians, and a third for all other foreigners. Prices quoted here are for 'other foreigners'.

Prietenia Hotel HOTEL €€

(☑29 660; ul Tkachenko 18; d 260-800 rubles) The large rooms and thin beds here are fairly priced. At 300 rubles, the business-class rooms – essentially a renovated standard room – are the best deal. Some rooms have balconies with a river view and only the brand-new deluxe rooms have air-con. The complex includes a sauna, billiards room and 'nightclub'. Breakfast is included with all but standard-class rooms.

Breeze GRILL €

(cnr ul Kalinina & ul Lenina; mains 14-28 rubles; ⊙8am-11pm; 🕷) Located in the park across from the department store, this small restaurant has a popular terrace, where grilled-meat dishes are the favourite. It also doubles as a hang-out and bar, with beer starting at 9 rubles.

❶ Information

Central department store (cnr ul Lenina & ul Kalinina; per hr 4 rubles; ⊙9am-8pm)

Currency exchange (ul Sovetskaya) Change money here; located next to the central market. There's an ATM at ul Lenina 5.

Pharmacy (cnr ul Suvorova & ul S Liazo; ⊙8am-9pm)

Telephone office (cnr ul S Liazo & ul Suvorova; ⊙8am-12.30pm, 2pm-5.30pm & 7pm-9pm) International telephone calls can be booked from here. It also has internet (per hour 5.50 rubles, available 9am to 12.20pm and 2pm to 9pm).

❶ Getting There & Around

Train

One daily train goes to Moscow, via Kyiv, leaving at approximately 2am. At the time of research, it was reported that Transdniestr passenger train service, suspended since 2006, would resume. A schedule was not provided; the 2006 schedule included at least 15 daily trains to Chişinău, including ones continuing on to Moscow and Odesa.

Bus

There are buses and maxitaxis every half-hour or so to Chişinău (22.60 rubles, 1½ hours) from 6am to 11pm, and one daily direct to Comrat (41 rubles), though many others go to Comrat, via several stops. Trolleybus 19 for Tiraspol (1.50 rubles) departs from the bus stop next to the main roundabout at the entrance to Bendery; maxitaxis also regularly make the 20-minute trip (2.50 rubles). There are nine daily buses to Odesa (41 rubles, three hours) and one to Kyiv (190 rubles, 14 hours) departing at 4pm. Local maxitaxis (2.50 rubles) leave from the currency exchange near the central market.

UNDERSTAND MOLDOVA

History

As with so many countries in the region, Moldova's history consists of being continually sliced, diced, tossed and wrested by one invading force after another. A political and cultural tug-of-war between Russia and Romania continues to this day

Bessarabia, part of the Romanian principality of Moldavia, was annexed in 1812 by the Russian empire. In 1918, after the October Revolution, Bessarabia declared its independence. Two months later the newly formed Democratic Moldavian Republic united with Romania. Russia never recognised this union.

Then in 1924 the Soviet Union created the Moldavian Autonomous Oblast on the eastern banks of the Nistru River, and incorporated Transdniestr into the Ukrainian Soviet Socialist Republic (SSR). A few months later the Soviet government renamed the oblast the Moldavian Autonomous Soviet Socialist Republic (Moldavian ASSR). During 1929 the capital was moved to Tiraspol from Balta (in present-day Ukraine).

In June 1940 the Soviet army, in accordance with the terms of the secret protocol associated with the Molotov-Ribbentrop Pact, occupied Romanian Bessarabia. The Soviet government immediately joined Bessarabia with the southern part of the Moldavian ASSR – specifically, Transdniestr – naming it the Moldavian Soviet Socialist Republic (Moldavian SSR). The remaining northern part of the Moldavian ASSR was

WORTH A TRIP

GAGAUZIA

The region of Gagauzia (Gagauz Yeri) covers 1832 sq km of noncontiguous land in southern Moldova. This Turkic-influenced Christian ethnic minority (pop 171,500) forfeited full independence for autonomy, being subordinate to Moldova constitutionally and for foreign relations and defence. It comprises three towns and 27 villages.

Gagauzi Muslim antecedents fled here from the Russo-Turkish wars in the 18th century. They were allowed to settle in the region in exchange for their conversion to Christianity. Their language is a Turkish dialect, with its vocabulary influenced by Russian Orthodoxy, as opposed to the Islamic influences inherent in Turkish. Gagauz look to Turkey for cultural inspiration and heritage.

Comrat, Gagauzia's capital, is little more than an intriguing cultural and provincial oddity. In 1990 Comrat was the scene of clashes between Gagauz nationalists and Moldovan armed forces, preceded by calls from local leaders for the Moldovan government to hold a referendum on the issue of Gagauz sovereignty. Local protesters were joined by Transdniestran militia forces, who are always game for a bit of clashing.

The captivating **Comrat Museum** (☎238-22 694; pr Lenina 164; admission 5 lei; ⊙9am-4pm Tue-Sat) is a dizzying hotchpotch of mundane to fascinating items, seemingly collected from townspeoples' attics, including photos of noteworthy locals, books, historical newspaper clippings, costumes, tools, weapons, musical instruments, foreign currency, gifts from visiting dignitaries, furniture and models.

There are five daily return buses from Chişinău to Comrat (36 lei). From Comrat there is one daily direct bus via Bendery to Tiraspol, and others that make frequent stops.

---

returned to the Ukrainian SSR (present-day Ukraine). Bessarabia suffered terrifying Sovietisation, marked by the deportation of 300,000 Romanians.

World War II

During 1941 allied Romanian and German troops attacked the Soviet Union, and Bessarabia and Transdniestr fell into Romanian hands. Consequently, thousands of Bessarabian Jews were sent to labour camps and then deported to Auschwitz. In August 1944 the Soviet army reoccupied Transdniestr and Bessarabia. Under the terms of the Paris Peace Treaty of 1947, Romania had to relinquish the region and Soviet power was restored in the Moldavian SSR.

Once in control again the Soviets immediately enforced a Sovietisation program on the Moldavian SSR. The Cyrillic alphabet was imposed on the Moldovan language (a dialect of Romanian) and Russian became the official state language. Street names were changed to honour Soviet communist heroes, and Russian-style patronymics were included in people's names.

In July 1949, 25,000 Moldovans were deported to Siberia and Kazakhstan, and in 1950–52 Leonid Brezhnev, then first secretary of the central committee of the Moldovan Communist Party, is said to have personally supervised the deportation of a quarter of a million Moldovans.

Independence & Ethnic Tension

Mikhail Gorbachev's policies of *glasnost* (openness) and *perestroika* (restructuring) from 1986 paved the way for the creation of the nationalist Moldovan Popular Front in 1989. Moldovan written in the Latin alphabet was reintroduced as the official language in August 1989. In February and March 1990 the first democratic elections to the Supreme Soviet (parliament) were won by the Popular Front. Then in April 1990 the Moldovan national flag (the Romanian tricolour with the Moldavian coat of arms in its centre) was reinstated. Transdniestr, however, refused to adopt the new state symbols and stuck to the red banner.

In June 1990 the Moldovan Supreme Soviet passed a declaration of sovereignty. After the failed coup attempt against Gorbachev in Moscow in August 1991, Moldova declared its full independence and Mircea Snegur became the democratically elected president in December 1991. Moldova was granted 'most-favoured nation' status by the USA in 1992, qualifying for International Monetary Fund (IMF) and World Bank loans the same year.

Transdniestr's newly emerging desire for autonomy spawned the Yedinstvo-Unitatea

Unity) movement in 1988 to represent the interests of the Slavic minorities. This was followed in November 1989 by the creation of the Gagauz Halki political party in the south of Moldova, where the Turkic-speaking Gagauz minority was centred. Both ethnic groups' major fear was that an independent Moldova would reunite with Romania.

The Gagauz went on to declare the Gagauz Soviet Socialist Republic in August 1990. A month later the Transdniestrans declared independence, establishing the Dniestr Moldovan Republic. In presidential elections, Igor Smirnov came out as head of Transdniestr, Stepan Topal head of Gagauzia.

Whereas Gagauzia didn't press for more than autonomy within Moldova, Transdniestr settled for nothing less than outright independence.

Civil War

In March 1992 Moldovan president Mircea Snegur declared a state of emergency. Two months later full-scale civil war broke out in Transdniestr, when Moldovan police clashed with Transdniestran militia, backed by troops from Russia, in Bendery (then called Tighina). An estimated 500 to 700 people were killed and thousands wounded in events that shocked the former Soviet Union.

A ceasefire was signed by the Moldovan and Russian presidents, Snegur and Boris Yeltsin, in July 1992. Provisions were made for a Russian-led, tripartite peacekeeping force comprising Russian, Moldovan and Transdniestran troops to be stationed in the region. Troops remain there today, maintaining an uneasy peace. Transdniestr continues to aggravate Chişinău and generate the occasional statement of concern from the EU.

EU Aspirations

While Moldova is keen to join the ranks of the EU, two major obstacles still block its path: the country's mounting foreign debt and its inadequate economic growth.

Moldova is widely regarded as one of the most corrupt nations in Europe. Average household income remains low, and with roughly one-third of the country's GDP comprised of monies sent home from emigrants working abroad, an unproductive economic dependency is developing, which will require long-term domestic cultivation to counteract. Even nationalists grudgingly admit that Moldova's economy may never flourish unless it's anchored to a stronger economic entity (ie Romania).

Romania's 2007 entrance into the EU transformed the Moldovan border into the EU's eastern frontier. After an initial period of isolated-feeling Moldovans waiting in demoralising lines to get Romanian visas, Romania eased border restrictions, ostensibly to alleviate visitation for cross-border relatives.

In April 2009, violent protests broke out after election results showed the Communist Party dubiously retaining its power with 50% of the vote. Though the Organization for Security and Co-operation in Europe gave the election a reluctant thumbs up, protestors claimed election fraud, charging that votes had been cast by deceased persons and those working abroad. In what was described as a 'young people's revolt', the crowd threw stones at police and later stormed parliament and the Presidential Palace, stealing and destroying files and computers. Police response was severe – 200 people were arrested, with widespread reports of police station/prison beatings and withholding of information on who was being held and where.

Romania, claiming it wanted to prevent 'a new Iron Curtain', responded by starting a fast-track program to grant dual citizenship to Moldovans. This controversial move alarmed EU member states, worried about a spike in migrant workers. Moldova's then-president Vladimir Voronin accused Romania of backing the protesters and trying to destabilise the country.

In early 2010, Moldova's newly elected Western-leaning government, led by Prime Minister Vlad Filat, signed an order to remove nearly 360km of the communist-era barbed-wire fence separating Moldova from Romania. Romania soon responded by promising €100 million in development aid and doubling the number of scholarships for Moldovan students wanting to study in Romania.

People & Religion

With 4.3 million inhabitants, Moldova is the most densely populated region of the former Soviet Union. Moldovans make up 78.2% of the total population, Ukrainians constitute 8.4%, Russians 5.8%, Gagauz 4.4%, Bulgarians 1.9%, and other nationalities such as Belarusians, Poles and Roma compose 1.3%.

Most Gagauz and Bulgarians inhabit southern Moldova. In Transdniestr, Ukrainians and Russians make up 58% of the region's population; Moldovans make up 34%. It is one of the least urbanised countries in Europe.

Moldova stays on course with the region's religious leanings; the vast majority are Eastern Orthodox (98%), with the recovering Jewish community (1.5%) at a distant second. Baptists and 'other' make up the remaining 0.5%.

Arts

Folk Art

There is a wealth of traditional folk art in Moldova, with carpet making, pottery, weaving and carving predominating.

Traditional dancing in Moldova is similar to the dances of other Eastern European countries. Couples dance in a circle, a semicircle or a line to the sounds of bagpipes, flutes, panpipes and violins.

Music & Art

Two of Moldova's most prolific modern composers are Arkady Luxemburg and Evgeny Doga, who have both scored films and multimedia projects, as well as written songs, concertos, suites and symphonies. Dimitrie Gagauz has for over three decades been the foremost composer of songs reflecting the folklore of the Turkic-influenced Gagauz population of southern Moldova.

The biggest name in Moldovan painting is Mihai Grecu (1916–98), who co-founded the National School of Painting and was also a poet and free love advocate. In sculpture,

Anatol Coseac today produces some highly original woodworks.

Environment

Tiny and landlocked, Moldova is a country of gently rolling steppes, with a gradual sloping towards the Black Sea. With one of the highest percentages of arable land in the world, Moldova is blessed with rich soil. Fields of grains, fruits and sunflowers are characteristic of the countryside. Moldova counts some 16,500 species of animals (460 of which are vertebrates) as its citizens.

There are five scientific reserves (totalling 19,378 hectares) and 30 protected natural sites (covering 22,278 hectares). The reserves protect areas of bird migration, old beech and oak forests, and important waterways. Codru Reserve, Moldova's oldest, boasts 924 plant species, 138 kinds of birds and 45 mammals; this is the most frequently visited reserve.

A great effort has been made by environmental groups to protect Moldova's wetland regions along the lower Prut and Nistru Rivers.

Never heavily industrial, Moldova faces more issues of protection and conservation than pollution. The majority of its 3600 rivers and rivulets were drained, diverted or dammed, threatening ecosystems.

Food & Drink

In Moldova, some Russian influences have meant that pickled fruits and vegetables are popular, as are Russian meals such as

---

MAKE NEW FRIENDS

What with their friendly, outgoing disposition, you shouldn't have any trouble winning acquaintances in Moldova. However, if you want to be instantly embraced, and possibly kissed, steer the conversation towards music, then casually drop these names: Zdob şi Zdub and Gândul Mâţei.

Zdob şi Zdub (zdob-shee-zdoob; www.zdob-si-zdub.com) have been together since 1995, working Moldovan audiences into a lather with their Romanian-folk-meets-the-Red-Hot-Chilli-Peppers sound fusion. In 2005 the group achieved a stunning sixth-place finish in the Eurovision Song Contest. These days they tour so ferociously that poor Moldova hardly hears from them. You're more likely to catch a show in Romania.

Gândul Mâţei (gun-dool muts-ehee; www.myspace.com/gandulmatei) nimbly run the gamut from lounge music to Coldplay-esque ballads to rocking *hard*. They're starting to break out of the Moldovan market, but still gig regularly in Chişinău.

Both bands have a very strong following in Moldova, and locals between the ages of 15 and 35 are guaranteed to become unwound with breathless reverence at the mere mention of their names. Moreover, their shows are fabulous and a highly recommended experience.

pelmeni (Russian-style ravioli stuffed with meat). A Turkic influence has arguably been strong here; in the south you may find the delicious Gagauz *sorpa,* a spicy ram soup.

Though things have improved slightly in recent years, vegetarians will find their meals limited. Locally grown fresh fruit and veg is always a bonus, but expect to find few vegetarian choices. We've pointed them out when we've found them.

Moldova produces excellent wines and brandies. Reds are called *negru* and *roşu,* white is *vin alb,* while *sec* means dry, *dulce* is sweet and *spumos* translates as sparkling.

Across the country, restaurants can be expected to stay open until at least 11pm nightly. Outside of Chişinău you'll be lucky to find a decent restaurant and may be stuck with hotel dining rooms, bars or cafeterias.

Nonsmoking awareness has yet to gain serious traction in Moldvoa. Some restaurants will offer nonsmoking sections, but in general it's still a carcinogenic free-for-all.

SURVIVAL GUIDE

Directory A–Z

This is the Moldova directory. See page 579 for the Transdniestr directory.

Accommodation

Chişinău has a good range of hotels. Most towns have small hotels that have survived from communist days. Basic singles or doubles with a shared bathroom cost €25 to €35 per room in Chişinău, but outside the capital rooms will usually be €12 to €20. Midrange rooms cost €44 to €80, and top-end rooms are €90 to €180. Unless noted otherwise, all accommodation options have private bathrooms and include breakfast in the price. Some hotels may offer nonsmoking rooms, but in general smoking occurs everywhere.

You will be asked to briefly present your passport upon registration; they may keep it for several hours in order to register it.

Camping grounds *(popas turistic)* are practically nonexistent in Moldova. The good news is that wild camping is allowed anywhere unless otherwise prohibited.

The idea of homestays in Moldova is in its infancy. Check **Marisha** (www.marisha.net) for a growing list of options. Many 'hostels' are merely converted apartments with four to six beds in a room.

Business Hours

Only places noticeably deviating from these hours will be noted in individual listings.

Banks 9am-3pm Mon-Fri

Businesses 8am-7pm Mon-Fri, until 4pm Sat

Shops 9am or 10am-6pm or 7pm Mon-Sat

Museums 9am-5pm Tue-Sun

Restaurants 10am-11pm

Embassies & Consulates

Following is a list of countries with embassies or consulates in Chişinău.

France (☎22-200 400; www.ambafrance.md; Str Vlaicu Pircalab 6)

Germany (☎22-200 600; ambasada-germana@riscom.md; Str Maria Cibotari 35)

Romania embassy (☎22-228 126; www.chisinau.mae.ro; Str Bucureşti 66/1); consulate (☎22-237 622; Str Vlaicu Pircalab 39)

Russia (☎22-234 942; www.moldova.mid.ru; B-dul Ştefan cel Mare 153)

Turkey (☎22-242 608; tremb@moldova.md; Str Valeriu Cupcea 60)

UK (☎22-225 902; www.ukinmoldova.fco.gov.uk; Str Nicolae Iorga 18)

Ukraine (☎22-582 151; www.mfa.gov.ua, in Ukrainian; Str V Lupu 17)

USA (☎22-408 300; http://moldova.usembassy.gov; Str A Mateevici 103)

Food

Price ranges are: budget (€; under 100 lei), midrange (€€; 100 lei to 170 lei) and top end (€€€; over 170 lei).

Gay & Lesbian Travellers

Before Moldova repealed its Soviet antigay law in 1995, it was one of only four European countries to still criminalise homosexuality. Now Moldova has among the most progressively liberal laws on the continent: homosexual activity is legal for both sexes at 14, the same age as for heterosexual sex. In 2003 the government adopted a National Human Rights Plan that would see the prohibition of discrimination against homosexuals enshrined in law. In reality persecution of homosexuals is largely ignored. Chişinău's annual Gay Pride parade (theoretically in May) was banned for five years running, and in 2008 it was cancelled on the eve of the event citing safety concerns for the participants.

The president of the Swedish national gay group RFSL, Sören Juvas, was beaten in Chişinău in May 2009. The group accused 'police in civilian clothing or men who had been informed by the police'. The 2010 rally was once again banned, though workshops and other events proceeded.

Needless to say, homosexuality is still a hushed topic, and politicians still get away with antigay rhetoric. While most people take a laissez-faire attitude towards the notion of homosexuality, being visibly out is likely to attract unwanted attention. For more information, visit www.gay.md.

Money

Moldovan lei come in denominations of 1, 5, 10, 20, 50, 100, 200 and 500 lei. There are coins for 1, 5, 10, 25 and 50 bani (there are 100 bani in a leu).

Note that the breakaway Transdniestran republic has its own currency, which is useless anywhere else in the world (see p569).

It's easy to find ATMs in Chişinău, but not in other towns in Moldova. Eximbank will cash travellers cheques and give cash advances on major credit cards. Shops and restaurants will not accept travellers cheques. While credit cards won't get you anywhere in rural areas, they are widely accepted in larger department stores, hotels and most restaurants in cities and towns.

Post

From Moldova, it costs 7 lei to 8.5 lei to send a postcard or letter under 20g to Western Europe, Australia and the USA.

DHL (www.dhl.com) is the most popular international courier service in the region. It has offices in Chişinău and Tiraspol. See its website for details.

Public Holidays

Moldova has the following national holidays:
New Year's Day 1 January
Orthodox Christmas 7 January
International Women's Day 8 March
Orthodox Easter April/May
Victory (1945) Day 9 May
Independence Day 27 August
National Language Day 31 August

Telephone

Moldtelecom, the wonderfully named state-run telephone company, sells pay cards that can be used to dial any number within Moldova only. To make an international call using a prepaid card, you need to use a private company like Treitelecom. These are good for local calls too.

Mobile-phone service in Moldova is provided by Chişinău-based Moldcell (run by Moldtelecom) and the ubiquitous Orange (www.orange.md). Moldova's country code is ☎373.

Visas

Since 1 January 2007 citizens of EU member states, USA, Canada and Japan no longer need visas. Everyone else is still on the hook, though. Furthermore, Australians, New Zealanders and South Africans all require an invitation from a company, organisation or individual. When acquiring a visa in advance, payments to the consulates are usually in the form of a bank deposit at a specified bank.

Visas can be easily acquired on arrival at Chişinău airport or, if arriving by bus or car from Romania, at three border points: Sculeni (north of Iaşi); Leuşeni (main Bucharest–Chişinău border); and Cahul. Visas are not issued at any other border crossings nor when entering by train. Citizens of countries requiring an invitation must present the original document (copies/faxes not accepted) at the border if buying a visa there.

In 2002 Moldova started instituting a visa-free regime for all foreigners wishing to partake in its Wine Festival (second Sunday in October). These visa-free visits cannot exceed 10 days. Those nationalities ordinarily needing invitation letters must still acquire them.

An HIV/AIDS test is required for foreigners intending to stay in Moldova longer than three months. Certificates proving HIV-negative status must be in Russian and English.

Check the **Ministry of Foreign Affairs** (www.mfa.gov.md) website and follow the link for Consular Affairs for the latest news on the visa situation.

COSTS & REGISTRATION
The price of a single-/double-entry tourist visa valid for one month is US$40/50 or 511/639 lei. Single-/double-entry transit visas valid for 72 hours are US$20/40 or 256/511 lei. Special rates apply for tourist groups of more than 10 persons, and for children, the handicapped and the elderly.

Visas can be processed within a day at the **Moldovan consulate** (☑40-21-410 9826; Str C Constantinescu 47, Bucharest) in Romania. Applications must be made between 8.30am and 12.30pm Monday to Friday. After paying for the visa at a specified bank in the city centre, you then collect your visa between 3pm and 4pm the same day.

SURVIVAL GUIDE

Directory A–Z

This is the Transdniestr directory. See p577 for the Moldova directory.

Language
The official state languages in Transdniestr are Russian, Moldovan and Ukrainian. Students in schools and universities are taught in Russian and the local government and most official institutions operate almost solely in Russian. All street signs are written in Russian and sometimes Ukrainian.

Media
The predominantly Russian Transdniestran TV is broadcast in the republic between 6am and midnight. Transdniestran Radio is on air during the same hours. Bendery has a local TV channel that airs 24 hours.

The two local newspapers are in Russian. The *Transdniestra* is a purely nationalist affair advocating the virtues of an independent state; *N Pravda* is marginally more liberal.

Money
The only legal tender is the Transdniestran ruble (TR). Officially introduced in 1994, it quickly dissolved into an oblivion of zeros. To keep up with inflation, monetary reforms introduced in January 2001 slashed six zeros

from the currency, with a new TR1 banknote worth one million rubles in old money. Some taxi drivers, shopkeepers and market traders will accept payment in US dollars – or even Moldovan lei or Ukrainian hryvnia – but generally you'll need to get your hands on some rubles (US$1 = 9.40 rubles, €1 = 11.60 rubles).

Spend all your rubles before you leave, as no one honours or exchanges this currency outside Transdniestr, though you might find takers in Chişinău, from where Transdniestr-bound maxitaxis depart, if you get stuck with a large amount.

Post
Transdniestran stamps featuring local hero General Suvorov can only be used for letters sent within the Transdniestran republic and are not recognised anywhere else. For letters to Moldova, Romania and the West, you have to use Moldovan stamps (available in Transdniestr, but less conveniently than in Moldova).

Getting There & Away

Entering and leaving Moldova is usually a breeze. Moldovan border guards are no longer genuinely surprised to see foreign tourists – though they still haven't learned how to smile.

Flights, tours and rail tickets can be booked online at www.lonelyplanet.com/travel_services.

Air

Airports & Airlines
Moldova's only airport of significance is **Chişinău International** (KIV; ☑22-525 111; www.airport.md), 15.5km south of the city centre.

Aerotour (UN; ☑22-542 454; www.transaero. md; B-dul Ştefan cel Mare 3, Chişinău) Has two flights daily to Budapest, one or two flights daily to Bucharest and four flights weekly to Prague.

Air Moldova (9U; ☑22-830 830; www.airmoldova.md; B-dul Negruzzi 10, Chişinău) Flights between Chişinău and Bucharest five days a week, as well as several cities in Western Europe.

Austrian Airlines (OS; ☑22-244 083; www. austrianair.com)

Carpatair (V3; ☑22-549 339; www.carpatair. com) Flies to Timişoara six times weekly.

Moldavian Airlines (2M; ☑22-549 339; www.mdv.md; B-dul Ştefan cel Mare 3, Chişinău) Located in the Air Service travel centre (www.airservice.md). Offers two daily flights to Budapest, from where it has connections to other European destinations.

Tarom Romanian Air Transport (RO; ☑22-541 254; www.tarom.ro; B-dul Ştefan cel Mare 3, Chişinău; ☺9am-5pm) Flies to Bucharest once or twice daily.

Transaero (UN; ☑542 454; www.transaero.md) Flies between Chişinău and Bucharest.

Turkish Airlines (TK; ☑22-27 85 25; www.turkishairlines.com)

Land

Bus

Moldova is well linked by bus lines to central and Western Europe; for more details, see p580. While not as comfortable as the train, buses tend to be faster, though not always cheaper.

For bus journeys between Chişinău and Odesa, we advise taking the route going through the southeast Palanca border crossing, circumnavigating Transdniestr.

Car & Motorcyle

The Green Card (a routine extension of domestic motor insurance to cover most European countries) is valid in Moldova. Extra insurance can be bought at the borders.

Train

From Chişinău, there are three daily trains to Lviv (Ukraine) and Moscow. Westbound, there are nightly trains to Romania and beyond.

There's an overnight service between Bucharest and Chişinău; at 12 hours, the journey is longer than taking a bus or maxitaxi (the train heads north to Iaşi, then south again), but is more comfortable if you want to sleep. For more details, see p580.

Getting Around

Bicycle

Moldova is mostly flat, making cycling an excellent way of getting around. That is, it would be if it weren't for the bad condition of most of the roads, and for the lack of infrastructure – outside of Chişinău, you'll have to rely on your own resources or sense of adventure (and trying to enlist help from friendly locals) if you run into mechanical trouble.

Bus & Maxitaxi

Moldova has a good network of buses running to most towns and villages. Maxitaxis, which follow the same routes as the buses, are quicker and more reliable.

Car & Motorcycle

In Chişinău, travel agencies can arrange car hire, or try Loran Car Rental (see p581). Be wary, however, as the roads are in poor condition. EU and US driving licences are accepted here; otherwise, bring both your home country's driving licence and your International Driving Permit (IDP), which is recognised in Moldova.

The intercity speed limit is 90km/h and in built-up areas 60km/h; the legal blood alcohol limit is 0.03%. For road rescue, dial ☑901. The **Auto Club Asist** (ACM; ☑22-465 543; www.autoclub.md) can inform you of all regulations and offer emergency assistance (this is a members-only service).

Local Transport

In Moldova, buses cost 2 lei, trolleybuses 1 leu and city maxitaxis 3 lei.

Taxi

In Moldova, there are official (and unofficial) taxis, often without meters, both of which may try to rip you off. It's best to call a taxi. A taxi ride to anywhere inside Chişinău is unlikely to cost more than 65 lei. You should agree upon a price before getting in the car.

Montenegro Црна Гора

Best Places to Eat

» Restoran Stari Mlini (p588)

» Knez Konoba (p590)

» Konoba Feral (p585)

» Stari Most (p595)

» Restoran Kod Marka (p593)

Best Places to Stay

» Palazzo Radomiri (p588)

» Vila Drago (p591)

» Aman Sveti Stefan (p591)

» Eko-Oaza Suza Evrope (p601)

Why Go?

Imagine a place with sapphire beaches as spectacular as Croatia's, rugged peaks as dramatic as Switzerland's, canyons nearly as deep as Colorado's, *palazzi* as elegant as Venice's and towns as old as Greece's. Then wrap it up in a Mediterranean climate and squish it into an area two-thirds the size of Wales, and you start to get a picture of Montenegro.

More adventurous travellers can easily sidestep the peak-season hordes on the coast by heading to the rugged mountains of the north. This is, after all, a country where wolves and bears still lurk in forgotten corners.

Montenegro, Crna Gora, Black Mountain: the name itself conjures up romance and drama. There are plenty of both on offer as you explore this perfumed land, bathed in the scent of wild herbs, conifers and Mediterranean blossoms. Yes, it really is as magical as it sounds.

When to Go

Podgorica

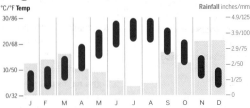

°C/°F Temp · Rainfall inches/mm

June Beat the peak-season rush but enjoy the balmy weather; Boka Navy Day in Kotor.

September Warm water, still, but fewer bods to share it with; the Adventure Race takes off.

October The leaves turn golden, making a rich backdrop to walks in the national parks.

Fast Facts

- » **Area** 13,812 sq km
- » **Capital** Podgorica
- » **Telephone area code** 382
- » **Emergency** police 122, fire 123, ambulance 124

Exchange Rates

Australia	A$1	€0.75
Canada	C$1	€0.74
Japan	¥100	€0.89
New Zealand	NZ$1	€0.89
UK	UK£1	€1.18
USA	US$1	€0.74

Set Your Budget

- » **Budget hotel room** €10 to €15 per person
- » **Two-course meal** €8 to €20
- » **Museum entrance** €1 to €5
- » **Beer** €1.50

Resources

- » **Black Mountain** (www.montenegroholiday.com)
- » **Visit Montenegro** (www.visit-montenegro.com)

Connections

Many travellers make the most of the proximity of Dubrovnik's Čilipi airport to Herceg Novi to tie in a visit to Croatia with a Montenegrin sojourn. At the other end of the coast, Ulcinj is the perfect primer for exploring Albania and is connected by bus to Shkodra. Likewise, Rožaje captures elements of Kosovar culture and is well connected to Peć. A train line and frequent bus connections make a trip to Montenegro's closest cousins in Serbia a breeze. Montenegro shares a longer border with Bosnia and Hercegovina (BiH) than any of its neighbours. There are plenty of crossings for drivers, as well as regular bus services from towns. Towns with onward international transport include Herceg Novi, Kotor, Tivat, Bar, Ulcinj and Podgorica.

ITINERARIES

One week

Base yourself in the Bay of Kotor for two nights. Drive through Lovc'en to Cetinje, then the next day continue to Šćepan Polje via Ostrog Monastery. Go rafting the following morning and spend the night in Podgorica. Head to Virpazar for a boat tour of Lake Skadar and then take the scenic lakeside road to Ulcinj. Finish in Sveti Stefan.

Two weeks

Follow the itinerary above, but allow extra time in Kotor, Lake Skadar and Sveti Stefan. From Šćepan Polje head instead to Žabljak and then to Biogradska Gora National Park before continuing to Podgorica.

Essential Food & Drink

- » **Njeguški pršut i sir** Smoke-dried ham and cheese from the heartland village of Njeguši.
- » **Ajvar** Spicy spread of fried red peppers and eggplant, seasoned with garlic, salt, vinegar and oil.
- » **Kajmak** Soft cheese made from the salted cream from boiled milk.
- » **Kačamak** Porridge-like mix of cream, cheese, potato and buckwheat or cornflour.
- » **Riblja čorba** Fish soup, a staple of the coast.
- » **Crni rižoto** Black risotto, coloured with squid ink.
- » **Ligne na žaru** Grilled squid, sometimes stuffed (*punjene*) with cheese and smoke-dried ham.
- » **Jagnjetina ispod sača** Lamb cooked (often with potatoes) under a metal lid covered with hot coals.
- » **Rakija** Domestic brandy, made from nearly anything. The local favourite is grape-based *loza*.
- » **Vranac** Local red wine varietal.
- » **Krstač** Local white wine varietal.

Montenegro Highlights

1 Marvelling at the majesty and exploring the historic towns hemmed in by the limestone cliffs of the **Bay of Kotor** (p583)

2 Driving the vertiginous route from Kotor to the Njegoš Mausoleum at the top of **Lovćen National Park** (p593)

3 Enjoying the iconic island views while lazing on the sands of **Sveti Stefan** (p590)

4 Seeking the spiritual at peaceful **Ostrog Monastery** (p598)

5 Floating through paradise, rafting between the kilometre-plus walls of the **Tara Canyon** (p600)

6 Wandering through primeval forest mirrored in a tranquil alpine lake at **Biogradska Gora National Park** (p599)

7 Splashing through the floating meadows of water lilies garlanding vast **Lake Skadar** (p595)

BAY OF KOTOR

Coming from Croatia, the Bay of Kotor (Boka Kotorska) starts simply enough, but as you progress through fold upon fold of the bay and the surrounding mountains get steeper and steeper, the beauty meter gets close to bursting. It's often described as Southern Europe's most spectacular fjord, and even though the label's not technically correct, the sentiment certainly is.

Herceg Novi Херцег Нови

☎ 031 / POP 12,700

It's easy to drive straight through Herceg Novi without noticing anything worth stopping for, especially if you've just come from Croatia with visions of Dubrovnik still dazzling your brain. However, just below the uninspiring roadside frontage hides an appealing Old Town with ancient walls, sunny squares and a lively atmosphere. The water's cleaner here near the mouth of the bay, so the pebbly beaches and concrete swimming terraces are popular.

◉ Sights

Stari Grad HISTORIC AREA
Herceg Novi's Old Town is at it's most impressive when approached from the pedestrian-only section of ul Njegoševa, paved in the same shiny marble as Dubrovnik and lined in elegant, mainly 19th-century buildings. The street terminates in cafe-ringed **Trg Nikole Đurkovića**, where steps lead up to an elegant crenulated **clocktower** (1667) that was once the main city gate. Just inside the walls is **Trg Herceg Stjepana** (commonly called Belavista Sq), a gleaming white piazza that's perfect for relaxing, drinking and chatting in the shade. At its centre is the Orthodox **Archangel Michael's Church** (built 1883–1905), its lovely proportions capped by a dome and flanked by palm trees. Its Catholic counterpart, **St Jerome's** (1856), is further down the hill, dominating **Trg Mića Pavlovića**.

Kanli-Kula FORTRESS
(Bloody Tower; admission €1; ☺8am-midnight) The big fort visible from the main road was a notorious prison during Turkish rule (roughly 1482–1687). You can walk around its sturdy walls and enjoy views over the town. The bastion at the town's seaward edge, **Fortemare**, was rebuilt by the Venetians during their 110-year stint as overlords.

Savina MONASTERY
(Manastirska 21; ☺6am-8pm) From its hillside location in the town's eastern fringes, this peaceful Orthodox monastery enjoys wonderful coastal views. It's dominated by the elegant 18th-century **Church of the Dormition**, carved from pinkish stone. Inside there's a gilded iconostasis but you'll need to be demurely dressed to enter (no shorts, sleeveless tops or bikinis). The smaller church beside it has the same name but is considerably older (possibly from the 14th century) and has the remains of frescoes. The monastery is well signposted from the highway.

Regional Museum MUSEUM
(www.rastko.rs/rastko-bo/muzej/index_e.html, Mirka Komnenovića 9; admission €1.50; ☺9am-6pm Mon-Sat) Apart from the building itself (a fab bougainvillea-shrouded baroque palace with absolute sea views), this little museum's highlight is its impressive icon gallery.

FREE **Španjola** FORTRESS
The fortress high above the town, on the other side of the main road, was started and finished by the Turks but named after the Spanish (yep, in 1538 they had a brief stint here as well). If the graffiti and empty bottles are anything to go by, it's now regularly invaded by local teenagers.

🏃 Activities

Herceg Novi is shaping up as the best base for arranging active pursuits, largely due to a network of expats running professional, customer-focused, environmentally aware businesses.

Black Mountain OUTDOOR PURSUITS
(☎067-640 869; www.montenegroholiday.com; bus station) An agency that can arrange pretty much anything active, including diving, rafting, hiking, paragliding, boat trips and excursions. It offers mountain-bike tours (about €20 per person) and hires out bikes (€10 per day).

Kayak Montenegro KAYAKING
(☎067-887 436; www.kayakmontenegro.com; Šetalište Pet Danica bb; hire 1/4/8hr €5/15/25) Another excellent outfit run by expats, Kayak Montenegro rents kayaks and offers paddling tours across the bay (half/full day €35/45, including equipment), as well as day trips to explore Lake Skadar from Rijeka Crnojevića.

DON'T MISS

ADVENTURE RACE MONTENEGRO

Started by a bunch of British expats operating outdoor-adventure businesses out of Herceg Novi, the **Adventure Race** (www.adventureracemontenegro.com) should be high on the agenda for anyone who fancies themselves an action man or wonder woman. Held in late September/early October, there are now two separate events. The Coastal Challenge is one day of kayaking, mountain biking, hiking and orienteering amid the exceptional scenery of the Bay of Kotor. For the truly hardcore, the Expedition Challenge is a gruelling two-day, almost nonstop, team-based race that also includes rafting and traversing the northern mountains in the night. It started in 2010, and organisers hope it will join the international circuit as one of the toughest races of its kind in Europe.

Yachting Club 32 EQUIPMENT HIRE
(www.yachtingclub32.com; Šetalište Pet Danica 32) Yachting Club 32 hires jet skis (per 20 minutes €50), paddleboats (per hour €8) and mountain bikes (hour/three hours/day €3/6/15). Windsurfing and parasurfing is also offered.

🛏 Sleeping

In summer there are often people around the bus station touting private accommodation. Black Mountain (p583) can fix you up with rooms starting from around €12 per person, although most of its apartments are more expensive.

Hotel Perla HOTEL €€
(☑031-345 700; www.perla.me; Šetalište Pet Danica 98; low season s €56-80, d €70-100, high season s €104-163, d €130-204;❄️🅿️🛜) It's a 15-minute stroll from the centre but if it's beach you're after, Perla's possie is perfect. The helpful staff speak excellent English and the front rooms of this medium-sized modern block have private terraces and sea views.

Camp Full Monte CAMPING GROUND €
(☑067 899 208; www.full-monte.com; campsites per person €10; ☺May-Sep) Hidden in the mountains near the Croatian border, this small British-run camping ground offers solar-generated hot water, odourless composting toilets and a whole lot of seclusion. If you hadn't guessed already, clothing is optional. Tents (with full bedding) can be hired for an additional €5 to €15 per person and meals can be arranged (€6.50).

Izvor HOSTEL €
(☑069-397 957; www.izvor.me; dm €12; 🅿️🛜) Four simple shared rooms open out to a terrace overlooking the bay on the slopes above Igalo. The charming young owner speaks excellent English and there's a traditional restaurant (mains €4 to €9) downstairs. There's even a waterfall.

🍴 Eating

If you want to take on the local women in a tussle for the best fresh fruit and vegetables, get to the **market** (Trg Nikole Đurkovića; ☺6am-3pm Mon-Sat, 6am-noon Sun) before 8am.

Konoba Feral TRADITIONAL €€
(Šetalište Pet Danica 47; mains €8-15) Feral is a local word for a ship's lantern, so it's seafood (not wild cat) that takes pride of place on the menu. The grilled squid is amazing and comes with a massive serving of seasonal vegetables and salads.

Portofino ITALIAN €€
(Trg Herceg Stjepana; breakfast €2.50-5, mains €6-16) Its blissful location in Herceg Novi's prettiest square makes it tempting to linger here all day, which is exactly what the local expat community seems to do. The menu features creamy pastas and the town's best steaks.

ℹ Information

You'll find banks with ATMs around Trg Nikole Đurkovića, while ul Njegoševa has the post office and an internet cafe.

Tourist Office (www.hercegnovi.travel; Šetalište Pet Danica bb; ☺9am-11pm May-Sep)

ℹ Getting There & Around

Bus

Buses stop at the station on the highway, just above the Old Town. There are frequent servies to Kotor (€3.50, one hour), Budva (€5, 1¾ hours) and Podgorica (€8, three hours). International services include Dubrovnik (€10, two hours, two daily), Sarajevo (€24, seven hours, four daily) and Belgrade (€30, 13 hours, nine daily).

Car

A tortuous, often gridlocked, one-way system runs through the town, so you're best to park on the highway. If you're driving to Tivat or Budva, it's usually quicker to take the **ferry** (car/motorcycle/passenger €4/1.50/free; ☺24hr) from Kamenari

(15km northeast of Herceg Novi) to Lepetane (north of Tivat). Queues can be long in summer.

Boat

Taxi boats ply the coast during summer, charging about €7 to the beaches on the Luštica Peninsula.

Perast Пераст

Looking like a chunk of Venice that has floated down the Adriatic and anchored itself onto the bay, Perast hums with melancholy memories of the days when it was rich and powerful. This tiny town boasts 16 churches and 17 formerly grand *palazzi*, one of which has been converted into **Perast Museum** (adult/child €2.50/1.50; ◷9am-6pm Mon-Sat, to 2pm Sun) and showcases the town's proud seafaring history.

The 55m belltower belongs to **St Nicholas' Church**, which also has a **museum** (admission €1; ◷10am-6pm) containing relics and beautifully embroidered vestments.

Just offshore are two peculiarly picturesque islands. The smaller St George's Island (Sveti Đorđe) rises from a natural reef and houses a Benedictine monastery shaded by cypresses. Boats (€5) regularly head to its big sister, Our Lady of the Rock Island (Gospa od Škrpjela), which was artificially created in the 15th century. Every year on 22 July the locals row over with stones to continue the task. Its magnificent church was erected in 1630.

Perast makes an atmospheric and peaceful base from which to explore the bay. Several houses rent rooms or you can try the **Hotel Conte Nautilus** (☎032-373 687; www.hotel-conte. com; apt €70-250;❋🖘), where options range from deluxe studios to two-bedroom seaview apartments in historic buildings around St Nicholas' Church. Its wonderful restaurant (mains €6 to €16) serves fresh fish with lashings of romance on a waterside terrace.

Not far from Perast, **Risan** is the oldest town on the bay, dating to at least the 3rd century BC. Signposts point to some superb **Roman mosaics** (admission €2; ◷8am-8pm 15 May-15 Oct), discovered in 1930.

Kotor Котор

◷032 / POP 13,500

Those prone to operatic outbursts may find themselves launching into Wagner at their first glimpse of this dramatically beautiful town. Its sturdy walls – started in the 9th century and tweaked until the 18th – arch steeply up the slopes behind it. From a distance they're barely discernable from the mountain's grey hide but at night they're spectacularly lit, reflecting in the water to give the town a golden halo. Within those walls lie labyrinthine marbled lanes, where churches, shops, bars and restaurants surprise you on hidden piazzas.

Kotor's funnel-shaped Stari Grad (Old Town) sits between the bay and the lower slopes of Mt Lovćen. Newer suburbs surround the town, linking up to the old settlements of Dobrota to the north and Muo to the west.

◉ Sights

The best thing to do in Kotor is to get lost and found again in the maze of streets. You'll soon know every corner, as the town is quite small, but there are plenty of churches to pop into and many coffees to be drunk in the shady squares.

Trg od Oružja SQUARE
Stepping through the main entrance, **Vrata od Mora** (Sea Gate, 1555), onto Trg od Oružja (Square of Arms) you'll see a strange stone pyramid in front of the **clock tower** (1602) that was once used as a pillory to shame wayward citizens.

St Tryphon Cathedral CHURCH
(Trg Sv Tripuna; admission €1.50; ◷8.30am-7pm) The town's most impressive building is the Catholic cathedral, originally built in the 12th century but reconstructed after several earthquakes. The cathedral's gently hued interior is a masterpiece of Romanesque architecture, with slender Corinthian columns alternating with pillars of pink stone, thrusting upwards to support a series of vaulted roofs. Its gilded silver-relief altar screen is considered Kotor's most valuable treasure.

Town Walls FORTRESS
(admission €2) The energetic can make the 280m ascent via 1350 steps up the fortifications for unforgettable views and a huge sense of achievement. There are entry points near the North Gate and Trg od Salata.

Maritime Museum MUSEUM
(Trg Bokeljske Mornarice; adult/child incl audioguide €4/1; ◷8am-7pm Mon-Sat, 9am-1pm Sun) Kotor has a proud history as a naval power and the Maritime Museum celebrates it with three storeys of displays housed in a wonderful early-18th-century palace.

⊨ Sleeping

Although the Stari Grad is a charming place to stay, you'd better pack earplugs. In summer the bars blast music onto the streets

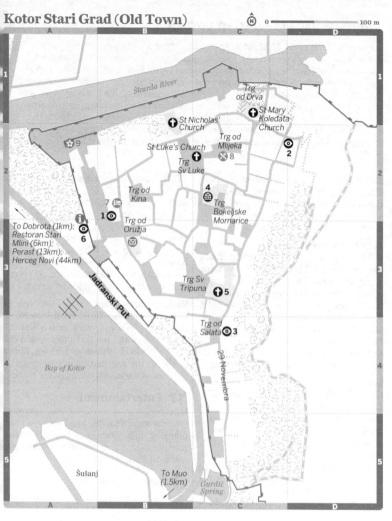

Kotor Stari Grad (Old Town)

◉ Sights

1	Clock Tower	B2
2	Entry to town walls	D2
3	Entry to town walls	C4
4	Maritime Museum	C2
5	St Tryphon Cathedral	C3
6	Vrata od Mora	A3

🛏 Sleeping

7	Meridian Travel Agency	B2

🍴 Eating

8	Restoran Stari Grad	C2

🎭 Entertainment

9	Maximus	A2

DETOUR: BACK ROAD TO MT LOVĆEN

Looming above Kotor is Mt Lovćen. The journey to this ancient core of the country is one of the country's great drives. Take the road heading towards the Tivat tunnel and turn right just past the graveyard (there's no sign). After 5km, follow the sign to Cetinje on your left opposite the fort. From here there's 17km of good but narrow road snaking up 25 hairpin turns, each one revealing a vista more spectacular than the last. Take your time and keep your wits about you; you'll need to pull over and be prepared to reverse if you meet oncoming traffic. From the top the views stretch over the entire bay to the Adriatic. At the entrance to Lovćen National Park you can continue straight ahead for the shortest route to Cetinje or turn right and continue on the scenic route through the park.

until 1am every night and rubbish collectors clank around at 6am. Some of the best options are just out of Kotor in quieter Dobrota and Muo. Enquire about private accommodation at the city's information booth.

TOP CHOICE **Palazzo Radomiri**   HOTEL €€
(☎032-333 172; www.palazzoradomiri. com; Dobrota; s €60-170, d €80-240; ☺Mar-Sep; ❄P❄☎) Exquisitely beautiful, this honey-coloured early 18th-century *palazzo* has been transformed into a first-rate boutique hotel. Some rooms are bigger and grander than others (hence the variation in prices), but all 10 have sea views and luxurious furnishings. Guests can avail themselves of a small workout area, sauna, pool, private jetty and bar.

Euro   PENSION €
(☎069-047 712; lemaja1@t-com.me; Muo 33; r €20-25 per person; ❄) On the Muo waterfront, this traditional stone building with a small private beach enjoys possibly the best views of Kotor. The top two floors have a scattering of differently configured rooms, some of which share bathrooms. The owner's an ex-footballer turned assistant coach for the national side and speaks excellent English. If there are a few of you, enquire about booking a floor.

Meridian Travel Agency   PRIVATE ROOMS €
(☎032-323 448; www.meridiandmc.me) In the lane behind the clock tower, this agency has rooms on its books at around €15 to €30 per person and can also book hotels.

🍴 Eating & Drinking

The Old Town is full of small bakeries, takeaway joints and cafe-bars that spill into the squares and are abuzz with conversation during the day. All chitchat stops abruptly in the evening, when speakers are dragged out onto the ancient lanes and the techno is cranked up to near ear-bleeding volumes.

TOP CHOICE **Restoran Stari Mlini**   TRADITIONAL €€€
(☎032-333 555; www.starimlini.com; Jadranska Put, Ljuta; meals €11-21) It's well worth making the 7km trip to Ljuta, just past Dobrota, for this magical restaurant set in and around an old mill by the edge of the bay. If you've got time and don't mind picking out bones, order the Dalmatian fish stew with polenta for two. The steaks are also excellent, as are the bread, wine and service.

Restoran Stari Grad   TRADITIONAL €€
(Trg od Mlijeka; mains €8-18) Head through to the stone-walled courtyard, grab a seat under the vines and get absolutely stuffed full of fabulous food – the serves are huge. Either point out the fish that takes your fancy or order from the traditional à la carte menu.

☆ Entertainment

Maximus   NIGHTCLUB
(www.discomaximus.com) Montenegro's most pumping club comes into its own in summer, hosting big-name international DJs and local starlets.

ℹ Information

You'll find a choice of banks with ATMs, an internet cafe and the post office on the main square, Trg od Oružja.

Tourist information booth (www.kotor.travel; ☺8am-8pm) Outside Vrata od Mora.

ℹ Getting There & Away

Bus

The bus station is to the south of town, just off the road leading to the Tivat tunnel. Buses to Herceg Novi (€3.50, one hour), Tivat (€2, 20 minutes), Budva (€3, 40 minutes) and Podgorica (€7, two hours) are at least hourly.

Boat

Azzurra Lines (www.azzurraline.com) ferries connect Kotor with Bari, Italy (€65, nine hours, weekly July to August).

Tivat Тиват

📞 032 / POP 9,450

In the process of a major makeover, courtesy of the multimillion-dollar redevelopment of its old shipyard into the **Porto Montenegro** (www.portomontenegro.com) superyacht marina, Tivat is becoming more schmick each year. Already the waterfront has been cleaned up, with a new crop of trendy bars and restaurants filling in the gaps between the old stone buildings on the promenade. It's still got a long way to go before it rivals Kotor for charm, but it's a pleasant place to stop.

There are a lot of sweet villages and beaches to explore on the coast between here and Kotor and on the Luštica Peninsula. The helpful **tourist office** (www.tivat.travel; Palih Boraca 8; ⏰8am-9pm Mon-Sat, 8am-noon Sun) can advise you on some terrific walks.

🛏 Sleeping & Eating

Hotel Villa Royal   HOTEL **€€**
(📞032-675 310; villaroyal@t-com.me; Kalimanj bb; s €42-65, d €68-102, apt €102-141; ❄@🛜) A bright modern block with clean rooms and friendly staff.

Prova   RESTAURANT, BAR **€€**
(Šetalište Iva Vizina 1; mains €7-14) Shaped like a boat with chandeliers that look like mutant alien jellyfish, this upmarket eatery is the very epitome of the new, increasingly chic Tivat. Excellent pasta.

ℹ Getting There & Away

Air

Tivat airport (www.montenegroairports.com) is 3km south of town and 8km through the tunnel from Kotor. Major local and international rental-car companies have counters here. The nearest bus stop is about 1km towards Tivat from the terminal. Taxis cost less than €10 to Tivat, around €15 to Kotor and around €20 to Budva.

Bus

Buses to Kotor (€2, 20 minutes) stop outside a silver kiosk on Palih Boraca. The main stop for longer trips is inconveniently located halfway between Tivat and the airport.

ADRIATIC COAST

Much of Montenegro's determination to reinvent itself as a tourist mecca has focused firmly on its gorgeous Adriatic coastline. In July and August it seems that the entire Serbian world and a fair chunk of its northern Orthodox brethren can be found crammed onto this scant 100km stretch. Avoid these months and you'll find a charismatic set of fortified towns and fishing villages to explore, set against clear Adriatic waters and Montenegro's mountainous backdrop.

Budva Будва

📞033 / POP 10,100

The poster child of Montenegrin tourism, Budva – with its atmospheric Old Town and numerous beaches – certainly has a lot to offer. Yet the child has quickly moved into a difficult adolescence, fuelled by rampant development that has leeched much of the charm from the place. In the height of the season the sands are blanketed with package holidaymakers from Russia and the Ukraine, while by night you'll run the gauntlet of glorified strippers attempting to cajole you into the beachside bars. It's the buzziest place on the coast if you're in the mood to party.

Apart from the Old Town, hardly any streets have names and even fewer have signs. The main beachside promenade is pedestrianised Slovenska Obala, which in summer is lined with fast-food outlets, beach bars, travel agencies hawking tours, internet cafes and a fun park.

👁 Sights & Activities

Stari Grad   HISTORIC AREA
Budva's best feature and star attraction is the Stari Grad (Old Town) – a mini-Dubrovnik with marbled streets and Venetian walls rising from the clear waters below. Much of it was ruined by two earthquakes in 1979 but it has since been completely rebuilt and now houses more shops, bars and restaurants than residences. At its seaward end, the **Citadel** (admission €2; ⏰9am-midnight May-Nov) offers striking views, a small museum and a library full of rare tomes and maps. In the square in front of the citadel is a cluster of interesting churches. Nearby is the entry to the **town walls** (admission €1; ⏰9am-5pm).

Archaeological Museum   MUSEUM
(Petra I Petrovića 11; adult/child €2/1; ⏰9am-10pm) This museum shows off the town's ancient and complicated history – dating back to at least 500 BC – over three floors of exhibits.

FREE **Museum of Modern Art**   GALLERY
(Cara Dušana 19; ⏰8am-2pm & 5-9pm Mon-Fri, 5-9pm Sat) Also in Stari Grad, this attractive gallery stages temporary exhibitions.

Montenegro Adventure Centre PARAGLIDING
(☎067-580 664; www.montenegrofly.com; Lapčići) The Montenegro Adventure Centre offers plenty of action from its perch high above Budva. Rafting, hiking, mountain biking and accommodation can all be arranged, as well as paragliding from launch sites around the country. An unforgettable tandem flight landing 750m below at Bečići beach costs €65.

🛏 Sleeping & Eating

Hotel Astoria HOTEL €€€
(☎033-451 110; www.astoriamontenegro.com; Njegoševa 4; s €99-190, d €105-230; 🌫@) Water shimmers down the corridor wall as you enter this chic boutique hotel hidden in Stari Grad's fortifications. The rooms are on the small side but they're beautifully furnished. The seaview suite is spectacular and the wonderful guest-only roof terrace is Budva's most magnificent dining area.

Hotel Kangaroo HOTEL €€
(☎033-458 653; www.kangaroo.co.me; Velji Vinogradi bb; s €32-40, d €48-64; 🌫P🌐) Bounce into a large clean room with a desk, excellent bathroom and either a terrace or mountain views at this midsized hotel that's a hop, skip and jump from the beach. The owners once lived in Australia, hence the name and the large 3D mural of Captain Cook's *Endeavour* in the popular restaurant below. Attached is a hip new bar for tapas and cocktails, with DJs until midnight on Friday and Saturday – so pack earplugs if you're an early-to-bed type.

Knez Konoba RESTAURANT €€
(Mitrov Ljubiše bb; mains €9-15) Hidden within Stari Grad's tiny lanes, this atmospheric eatery has only three outdoor tables and a handful inside. The traditional dishes are a little more expensive than most but they're beautifully presented and sometimes accompanied with free shots of *rakija* (local brandy).

Saki Apartmani HOTEL €
(☎067-368 065; www.saki-apartmani.com; IV Proleterska bb; dm/d €10/30; 🌫P🌐) Good, clean, cheap apartments and dorm rooms in a quiet location.

Hippo Hostel HOSTEL €
(☎033-458 348; www.hippohostel.com; IV Proleterska 37; dm €10; P@🌐) Social hostel with overgrown garden and buzzy atmosphere.

ℹ Information

The post office and a cluster of banks are on and around ulica Mediteranska.

Tourist office (www.budva.travel; Njegoševa bb; ⊙9am-9pm Mon-Sat May-Oct) Has brochures on sights and accommodation.

ℹ Getting There & Away

The **bus station** (☎033-456 000; Ivana Milutinovića bb) has regular services to Herceg Novi (€5, 1¾ hours), Kotor (€3, 40 minutes), Petrovac (€2.50, 30 minutes) and Cetinje (€3, 40 minutes). **Meridian Rentacar** (☎033-454 105; www.meridian-rentacar.com; Mediteranski Sportski Centar) is opposite the bus station.

You can flag down the Olimpia Express (€1.50) from the bus stops on Jadranska Put to head to Bečići (five minutes) or Sveti Stefan (20 minutes). They depart every 30 minutes in summer and hourly in winter.

Sveti Stefan Свети Стефан

Gazing down on impossibly picturesque Sveti Stefan, 5km south of Budva, provides the biggest 'wow' moment on the entire coast. And gazing on it is all most people will get to do as this tiny island – connected to the shore by a narrow isthmus and crammed full of terracotta-roofed dwellings dating from the 15th century – was nationalised in the 1950s and the whole thing is now a luxurious resort.

Sveti Stefan is also the name of the settlement that's sprung up onshore. From its steep slopes you get to look down at that iconic view all day – which some might suggest is even better than staying in the surreally glamorous enclave below. On the downside, parking is difficult, there are lots of steps and there's little in the way of shops.

The general public can access the main Sveti Stefan beach, which faces the island. From the beach there's a very pleasant walk north to the cute village of **Pržno** where there are some excellent restaurants and another attractive, often crowded beach.

🛏 Sleeping & Eating

TOP CHOICE **Vila Drago** HOTEL €€
(☎033-468 477; www.viladrago.com; Slobode 32; r low season €35-65, high season €60-100; 🌫@🌐) The only problem with this place is that you may never want to leave your terrace, as the views are so sublime. The super-comfy pillows and fully stocked bathrooms are a nice touch, especially at this price. Watch the sunset over the island from the grapevine-covered terrace restaurant (mains €5 to €15) and enjoy specialities from the lo-

cal Paštrovići clan, like roast suckling pig (€15 per kilogram).

Aman Sveti Stefan
RESORT €€€

(☏033-420 000; www.amanresorts.com; ste €700-2500; ❄️P🏊📶) Truly unique, this iconic island resort offers 50 luxurious suites that showcase the stone walls and wooden beams of the ancient houses. Amazingly there's still a village feel, with cobbled lanes, three churches, lots of indigenous foliage and an open-air cafe on the main piazza. But it's a village where you can order a cocktail by a cliff's-edge swimming pool or slink away for an indulgent massage – and it's not open to the general public. Back on the shore, **Villa Miločer** has a further eight suites in a former royal palace facing lovely Miločer Beach through a curtain of wisteria. This and nearby Queen's Beach are reserved for use by the resort's guests. The public can access the main Sveti Stefan beach and avail themselves of three eateries: the **Olive Tree** at the beach's north end, the **Beach Cafe** at Miločer and **Queen's Chair**, perched on a wooded hill facing Budva.

Vila Levantin
APARTMENTS €€

(☏033-468 206; levantin@t-com.me; Vukice Mitrović 3; r €30-90; ❄️P🏊📶) Modern and nicely finished, with red stone walls, blue-tiled bathrooms and an attractive plunge pool on the terrace, Levantin has a range of rooms and apartments at extremely reasonable prices. There's a travel agency attached which can sort you out with tours or rooms in private houses.

ℹ️ Getting There & Away

Olimpia Express buses head to and from Budva (€1.50, 20 minutes) every 30 minutes in summer and hourly in winter, stopping on Ulica Slobode near the Vila Drago.

Petrovac Петровац

The Romans had the right idea, building their summer villas on this lovely bay. The pretty beachside promenade is perfumed with the scent of lush Mediterranean plants, and a picturesque 16th-century **Venetian fortress** guards a tiny stone harbour. This is one of the best places on the coast for families: the accommodation is reasonably priced, the water's clear and kids roam the esplanade at night with impunity.

In July and August you'll be lucky to find an inch of space on the town beach but wander south and there's cypress- and oleander-lined **Lučice Beach** and beyond it the 2.5km-long sweep of **Buljarica Beach**.

🛏️ Sleeping & Eating

Hotel W Grand
HOTEL €€

(☏033-461 703; www.wgrandpetrovac.com; s/d low season €48/64, high season €78/104; P❄️@📶) Spacious rooms painted in warm colours and comfortable beds are the hallmark of this modern midsized hotel. Eat up the views from the terrace while tucking into the brilliant breakfast buffet.

Konoba Bonaca
RESTAURANT €€

(mains €8-15) On the main beach drag, this traditional restaurant focuses mainly on seafood but the local cheeses and olives are also excellent. Grab a table under the grapevines on the terrace and gaze out to sea.

Mornar Travel Agency
PRIVATE ROOMS €

(☏033-461 410; www.mornartravel.com; Nerin bb) An excellent local agency offering private accommodation from €23 per person.

ℹ️ Getting There & Away

Petrovac's bus station is near the top of town. Regular services head to Budva and Bar (both €2, 30 minutes).

Bar Бар

☏030 / POP 13,800

Dominated by Montenegro's main port and a large industrial area, Bar is unlikely to be anyone's highlight, but it is a handy transport hub welcoming trains from Belgrade and ferries from Italy. More interesting are the ruins of Stari Bar (Old Bar) in the mountains behind.

⊙ Sights

Stari Bar
RUINS

(adult/child €1/0.50; ⊙8am-8pm) Impressive Stari Bar, Bar's original settlement, stands on a bluff 4km northeast, off the Ulcinj road. A steep cobbled hill takes you past a cluster of old houses and shops to the fortified entrance where a short dark passage pops you out into a large expanse of vine-clad ruins and abandoned streets overgrown with grass and wild flowers. A small **museum** just inside the entrance explains the site and its history. The Illyrians founded the city in around 800 BC. It passed in and out of Slavic and Byzantine rule until the Venetians took it in 1443 and held it until it was taken by the Ottomans in 1571. Nearly all the 240 buildings now lie in ruins, a result of Montenegrin shelling, when the town was captured in 1878.

Buses marked Stari Bar depart from the centre of new Bar every hour (€1).

King Nikola's Palace MUSEUM
(Šetalište Kralje Nikole; admission €1; ⊙8am-2pm & 5-11pm) Presenting an elegant facade to the water, King Nikola's Palace has been converted into a museum housing a collection of antiques, folk costumes and royal furniture. Its shady gardens contain plants cultivated from seeds and cuttings collected from around the world by Montenegro's sailors.

🛏 Sleeping & Eating

Hotel Princess HOTEL €€€
(📞030-300 100; www.hotelprincess-montenegro.com; Jovana Tomaševića 59; s/d low season €70/100, high season €80/120; ✳@☎P☎) The standards aren't quite what you'd expect for the price, but this resort-style hotel is the best option in town. Make the most of it at the private beach, swimming pool and spa centre.

Konoba Spilja RESTAURANT €
(Stari Bar bb; mains €3-15) So rustic you wouldn't be surprised if a goat wandered through, this is a terrific spot for a traditional meal after exploring Stari Bar.

❶ Information

There are banks with ATMs around ul Maršala Tita and ul Vladimira Rolovića.

Accident & Emergency Clinic (📞124; Jovana Tomeševića 42)

Post office (Jovana Tomeševića bb)

Tourist information centre (Obala 13 Jula bb; ⊙8am-8pm Jul & Aug, 8am-4pm Mon-Sat Sep-Jun) Helpful staff with good English; stocks useful brochures listing sights and private accommodation.

❶ Getting There & Away

The bus station and adjacent train station are 1km southeast of the centre. Bus destinations include Podgorica (€4, seven daily) and Ulcinj (€2.50, three daily). Trains head to Virpazar (€2, 20 minutes, 10 daily), Podgorica (€3.60, one hour, 10 daily) and Kolašin (€8.20, 2½ hours, five daily).

Montenegro Line (📞030-311 164; www.montenegrolines.net) ferries to Bari (€55, nine hours, three weekly) and Ancona (€66, 11 hours, twice weekly in summer) in Italy, and **Azzurra Lines** (www.azzurraline.com) ferries to Bari (€65, nine hours, weekly in summer), leave from the **ferry terminal** (Obala 13 Jula bb) near the centre. You can book your Montenegro Lines ferry tickets here and there's a post office. Azzurra Lines can be booked at **Mercur** (📞030-313 617; Vladimir Rolovića bb).

Ulcinj Улцињ

📞030 / 10,900

If you want a feel for Albania without actually crossing the border, buzzy Ulcinj's the place to go. The population is 72% Albanian and in summer it swells with Kosovar holidaymakers for the simple reason that it's nicer than most of the Albanian seaside towns. The elegant minarets of numerous mosques give Ulcinj a distinctly Eastern feel, as does the music echoing out of the kebab stands.

For centuries Ulcinj had a reputation as a pirate's lair. By the end of the 16th century as many as 400 pirates, mainly from Malta, Tunisia and Algeria, made Ulcinj their main port of call – wreaking havoc on passing vessels and then returning to party up large on Mala Plaža. Ulcinj became the centre of a thriving slave trade, with people – mainly from North Africa – paraded for sale on the town's main square.

You'll find banks, internet cafes, supermarkets, pharmacies and the post office on Rr Hazif Ali Ulqinaku.

◉ Sights & Activities

Stari Grad HISTORIC AREA
The ancient Stari Grad overlooking Mala Plaža is still largely residential and somewhat dilapidated – a legacy of the 1979 earthquake. A steep slope leads to the Upper Gate, where there's a small **museum** (admission €1; ⊙6am-1pm & 4-9pm Tue-Sun) just inside the walls, containing Roman and Ottoman artefacts.

Beaches BEACHES
Mala Plaža may be a fine grin of a cove but it's hard to see the beach under all that suntanned flesh in July and August. You're better off strolling south, where a succession of rocky bays offer a little more room to breathe. **Ladies' Beach** (admission €1.50) has a strict women-only policy, while a section of the beach in front of the Hotel Albatross is clothing optional.

The appropriately named **Velika Plaža** (Big Beach) starts 4km southeast of the town and stretches for 12 sandy kilometres. Sections of it sprout deckchairs but there's still plenty of relatively empty space. To be frank, this large flat expanse isn't as picturesque as it sounds and the water is painfully shallow – great for kids but you'll need to walk a fair way for a decent swim.

On your way to Velika Plaža you'll pass the murky **Milena canal**, where local fishermen use nets suspended from long willow rods attached to wooden stilt houses. The effect is remarkably redolent of Southeast Asia. There are more of these contraptions on the banks of the **Bojana River** at the other end of Veliki Plaža.

D'olcinium Diving Club
DIVING
(2067-319 100; www.uldiving.com; 2 dives incl equipment €40) Divers wanting to explore various wrecks and the remains of a submerged town should contact the D'olcinium Diving Club. It also hires snorkelling (€3) and diving (€15) gear.

Sleeping

Dvori Balšića & Palata Venezia
HOTEL €€€
(2030-421 457; www.hotel-dvoribalsica-montene gro.com; Stari Grad; s/d €65/100; 🖳🗟) These grand stone *palazzi* are reached by the cobbled lanes and stairs of the Old Town – not great if you're lugging luggage but very atmospheric nonetheless. The sizeable rooms all have kitchenettes, romantic sea views , and stucco and dark wooden interiors.

Hotel Dolcino
HOTEL €€
(2030-422 288; www.hoteldolcino.com; Hazif Ali Ulqinaku bb; s/d €40/50; 🖳🗟) You can't quibble over the exceptionally reasonable prices of this modern business-orientated mini hotel in the centre of town. The quieter rooms at the back have spacious terraces, although the small front balconies are great for watching the passing parade. Signs instruct guests not to flush toilet paper; a rarity in 21st-century Montenegro.

Real Estate Travel Agency
PRIVATE ROOMS €
(2030-421 609; www.realestate-travel.com; Hazif Ali Ulqinaku bb) Obliging English-speaking staff can help you find private rooms, apartments or hotel rooms. They also rent cars, run tours, organise diving trips and sell maps of Ulcinj.

Eating

TOP CHOICE Restoran Kod Marka
SEAFOOD €€
(2030-401 720; Bojana River; mains €7-10) Not actually in Ulcinj but well worth the 14km drive, this memorable fish restaurant is one of several that jut out over the Bojana River just before the bridge to Ada Bojana. The specialty, *riblja čorba* (fish soup, €2.50), is sublime: served in a metal pot that will fill your bowl twice over.

Restaurant Pizzeria Bazar
TRADITIONAL, PIZZA €
(Hazif Ali Ulqinaku bb; mains €4-10) An upstairs restaurant that's a great idling place when the streets below are heaving with tourists. People-watch in comfort as you enjoy a plate of *lignje na žaru* (grilled squid), the restaurant's speciality.

❶ Getting There & Away
The bus station is on the northeastern edge of town just off Bul Vëllazërit Frashëri. Services head to Bar (€2.50, 30 minutes, three daily), Podgorica (€6, one hour, four daily), Shkodra (Albania; €6, 90 minutes, two daily) and Pristina (Kosovo; €22.50, eight hours, three daily).

593

CENTRAL MONTENEGRO

The heart of Montenegro – physically, spiritually and politically – is easily accessed as a day trip from the coast but it's well deserving of a longer exploration. Two wonderful national parks separate it from the Adriatic and behind them lie the two capitals, the ancient current one and the newer former one.

Lovćen National Park
Ловћен

Directly behind Kotor is Mt Lovćen (1749m), the black mountain that gave Crna Gora (Montenegro) its name (*crna/negro* means 'black' and *gora/monte* means 'mountain' in Montenegrin and Italian respectively). This locale occupies a special place in the hearts of all Montenegrins. For most of its history it represented the entire nation – a rocky island of Slavic resistance in an Ottoman sea. The old capital of Cetinje nestles in its foothills.

The national park's 6220 hectares are home to 85 species of butterfly, and 200 species of birds and mammals, including endangered brown bears and wolves. It's criss-crossed with well-marked hiking paths.

The **National Park Office** (www.nparkovi. co.me; Ivanova Korita bb; ⊘9am-5pm Apr-Oct, shorter hrs winter) is near its centre and offers accommodation in four-bedded bungalows (€40). If you're planning some serious walking, buy a copy of the *Lovćen Mountain Touristic Map* (scale 1:25,000), available from the office and park entries.

Lovćen's star attraction is the magnificent **Njegoš Mausoleum** (admission €3) at the top of its second-highest peak, Jezerski Vrh (1657m). Take the 461 steps up to the

MONTENEGRO LOVĆEN NATIONAL PARK

entry, where two granite giantesses guard the tomb. Inside, under a golden mosaic canopy, a 28-tonne Vladika Petar II Petrović Njegoš rests in the wings of an eagle, carved from a single block of black granite. The actual tomb lies below and a path at the rear leads to a dramatic circular viewing platform.

If you're driving, the park can be approached from either Kotor or Cetinje (entry fee €2). The back route between the two shouldn't be missed (see the boxed text on p588).

Cetinje Цетиње

☎041 / POP 15,200

Rising from a green vale surrounded by rough, grey mountains, Cetinje is an odd mix of former capital and overgrown village, where single-storey cottages and stately mansions share the same street. Pretty Njegoševa is a partly traffic-free thoroughfare lined with interesting buildings, including the **Presidential Palace** and various former embassies marked with plaques. Everything of significance is in the immediate vicinity. There's a **tourist information centre** (⊙8am-7pm) on Novice Cerovića.

◉ Sights

National Museum of Montenegro MUSEUMS (Narodni muzej Crne Gore; combined ticket adult/child €10/5; ⊙9am-5pm, last admission 4.30pm) This is actually a collection of five museums housed in a clump of important buildings. A joint ticket will get you into all of them or you can buy individual tickets.

Two are housed in the former parliament (1910), Cetinje's most imposing building. The fascinating **History Museum** (Istorijski Muzej; Novice Cerovića 7; adult/child €4/2) is very well laid out, following a timeline from the Stone Age to 1955. There are few English signs but the enthusiastic staff will walk you around and give you an overview before leaving you to your own devices.

Upstairs is the equally excellent **Art Museum** (Umjetnički Muzej; adult/child €4/2). There's a small collection of icons, the most important being the precious 9th-century *Our Lady of Philermos,* which was traditionally believed to have been painted by St Luke himself. Elsewhere in the gallery all of Montenegro's great artists are represented, with the most famous having their own separate spaces. Expect a museum staff member to be hovering as you wander around.

While the hovering at the Art Museum is annoying, the **King Nikola Museum** (Muzej kralja Nikole; Trg Kralja Nikole; adult/child €5/2.50) can be downright infuriating. Entry is only by guided tour, which the staff will only give to a group, even if you've pre-paid a ticket and they've got nothing else to do. Still, this 1871 palace of Nikola I, last sovereign of Montenegro, is worth the hassle.

The castle-like **Njegoš Museum** (Njegošev Muzej; Trg Kralja Nikole; adult/child €3/1.50) was the residence of Montenegro's favourite son, prince-bishop-poet Petar II Petrović Njegoš. The hall was built and financed by the Russians in 1838 and housed the nation's first billiard table, hence the museum's alternative name, Biljarda. The bottom floor is devoted to military costumes, photos of soldiers with outlandish moustaches and exquisitely decorated weapons. Njegoš's personal effects are displayed upstairs.

When you leave Biljarda, turn right and follow the walls to the glass pavilion housing a fascinating large scale **relief map** (adult/child €1/0.50) of Montenegro created by the Austrians in 1917.

Occupying the former Serbian embassy, the **Ethnographic Museum** (Etnografski Muzej; Trg Kralja Nikole; adult/child €2/1) is the least interesting of the five, but if you've bought a joint ticket you may as well check it out. The collection of costumes and tools is well presented and has English notations.

Cetinje Monastery MONASTERY (⊙8am-6pm) It's a case of three times lucky for Cetinje Monastery, having been repeatedly destroyed during Ottoman attacks and rebuilt. This sturdy incarnation dates from 1785, with its only exterior ornamentation being the capitals of columns recycled from the original building, founded in 1484.

The chapel to the right of the courtyard holds the monastery's proudest possessions: a shard of the True Cross and the mummified right hand of St John the Baptist. The hand's had a fascinating history, having escaped wars and revolutions and passing through the hands of Byzantine emperors, Ottoman sultans, the Knights Hospitalier, Russian tsars and Serbian kings. It's now housed in a bejewelled golden casket by the chapel's window, draped in heavy fabric. The casket's only occasionally opened for veneration, so if you miss out you can console yourself that it's not a very pleasant sight.

The monastery **treasury** (admission €2; ⊙8am-4pm) is only open to groups, but if you are persuasive enough and prepared to wait around, you may be able to get in. It holds a wealth of fascinating objects that form a blur as you're shunted around the rooms by one of the monks. These include jewel-encrusted vestments, ancient handwritten texts, icons, royal crowns and a copy of the 1494 *Oktoih* (Book of the Eight Voices), the first book printed in Serbian.

If your legs, shoulders or cleavage are on display, you'll either be denied entry or given an unflattering smock to wear.

🛏 Sleeping & Eating

Accommodation in Cetinje is limited and there are only a few proper restaurants.

Hotel Grand   HOTEL €€
(☑041-231 651; www.hotelgrand.me; Njegoševa 1; s €46-60, d €66-80) 'Fading grandeur' would be a more accurate moniker but aside from a few pigeons roosting in the walls, Cetinje's only hotel is an OK place to stay. The polished parquet floors, comfy beds and new linen certainly help.

Vinoteka   ITALIAN €
(Njegoševa 103; mains €3-12) The wood-beamed porch looking onto the garden is such a nice spot that the excellent and reasonably priced pizza and pasta feels like a bonus – the decent wine list even more so.

ℹ Getting There & Away

Cetinje is on the main highway between Budva and Podgorica and can also be reached by a glorious back road from Kotor via Lovćen National Park. Buses stop at Trg Golootočkih Žrtava, two blocks from the main street. Buses leave every 30 minutes for Podgorica (€3) and hourly for Budva (€3).

Lake Skadar National Park
Скадарско Језеро

The Balkans' largest lake, dolphin-shaped Lake Skadar (Shkodra) has its tail and two-thirds of its body in Montenegro and its nose in Albania. Covering between 370 and 550 sq km (depending on the time of year), it's one of the most important reserves for wetland birds in the whole of Europe. The endangered Dalmatian pelican nests here, along with 256 other species, while 48 known species of fish lurk beneath its smooth surface. On the Montenegrin side, an area of 400 sq km has been protected by a national park since 1983. It's a blissfully pretty area, encompassing steep mountains, hidden vil-

lages, historic churches, clear waters and floating meadows of waterlilies.

The **National Park Visitors Centre** (www. nparkovi.co.me; Vranjina bb; admission €2; ⊙8am-4pm) is on the opposite side of the causeway heading to Podgorica from Virpazar. This modern facility has excellent displays about all the national parks, not just Lake Skadar, and sells park entry tickets (per day €4) and fishing permits (per day €5). In the busy months, various tour operators set up kiosks in the vicinity, hiring rowboats and speedboats with drivers.

Just along the causeway are the remains of the 19th-century fortress **Lesendro**. The busy highway and railway tracks prevent land access to the site.

RIJEKA CRNOJEVIĆA ПИЈЕКА ЦРНОЈЕВИЋА

The northwestern end of the lake thins into the serpentine loops of the Crnojević River and terminates near the pretty village of the same name. It's a charming, tucked-away kind of place, accessed by side roads that lead off the Cetinje–Podgorica highway. There's a history display in the **National Park Visitors Centre** (admission €1; ⊙10am-6pm), which occupies four wooden huts that jut out over the river on stilts.

You wouldn't expect it but this sleepy place is home to one of Montenegro's best restaurants. **Stari Most** (☑033-239 505; fish per kg €30-50) is well located on the marble riverside promenade, looking towards the photogenic arched stone bridge (1854) from which it derives its name. Fish, particularly eel, is the speciality here and the fish soup alone is enough to justify a drive from Podgorica.

VIRPAZAR ВИРПАЗАР

This little town, gathered around a square and a river blanketed with waterlilies, serves as the main gateway to the national park. Most of the boat tours of the lake depart from here, so the tranquillity is shattered at around 10.30am, when the tour buses from the coast pull in. There's a **National Park kiosk** by the marina that sells entry tickets and fishing permits but doesn't offer much information.

The **Pelikan Hotel** (☑020-711 107; www. pelikan-zec.com; d/tr €58/81;❉) is a one-stop shop offering accommodation, an excellent traditional restaurant (main €5 to €12) and 2½-hour boat tours that explore the lake's northern reaches (usually around €10 per person, depending on numbers). The rooms are clean and have nice views over the square, although some of them are tiny.

Virpazar doesn't have a bus station but buses on the Bar–Podgorica route stop here. The decrepit train station is off the main road, 800m south of town. There are 10 services daily to Bar (€2, 20 minutes) and Podgorica (€2.20, 40 minutes).

MURIĆI МУРИЋИ

The southern edge of the lake is the most dramatic, with the Rumija Mountains rising precipitously from the water. From Virpazar there's a wonderful drive following the contours of the lake through the mountains towards the border before crossing the range and turning back towards Ulcinj. About halfway, a steep road descends to the village of Murići. This is one of the lake's best swimming spots. Local boatmen offer trips to the monasteries on the nearby islands for around €10 per hour.

The **Murići Vacation Resort** (069-688 288; www.nacionalnipark-izletistemurici.com; per person €37) has simple log cabins nestled within an olive grove. A decent ablutions block is shared and the price includes three meals in the shady outdoor restaurant (mains €5 to €9). It also organises **lake tours** (€16) that visit the islands and Virpazar.

Podgorica Подгорица

020 / POP 136,500

Podgorica's never going to be Europe's most happening capital but if you can get past the sweltering summer temperatures and concrete apartment blocks you'll find a pleasant little city with lots of green space and some excellent galleries and bars.

The city sits at the confluence of two rivers. West of the broad Morača is what passes for the business district. The smaller Ribnica River divides the eastern side in two. To the south is Stara Varoš, the heart of the former Ottoman town. North of the Ribnica is Nova Varoš, an attractive, mainly low-rise precinct of late 19th-century and early 20th-century buildings housing a lively mixture of shops and bars. At its centre is the main square, Trg Republika.

Sights

FREE **Podgorica Museum & Gallery**

MUSEUM

(Marka Miljanova 4; 9am-8pm) Despite Cetinje nabbing most of the national endowment, the new capital is well served by the Podgorica Museum and Gallery. There's an interesting section on the city's history, including antiquities surviving from its Roman incarnation, Doclea. The gallery features changing exhibitions; look out for Petar Lubarda's large canvas *Titograd* (1956) in the foyer.

FREE **Centre for Contemporary Art**

GALLERIES

The Centre for Contemporary Art operates two galleries in Podgorica. The bottom two floors of the former royal palace **Dvorac Petrovića** (Llubljanska bb; 9am-2pm & 4-9pm Mon-Fri, 10am-2pm Sat) are given over to high-profile exhibitions, while the top floor has an oddball collection of miscellanea. Temporary exhibitions are also staged in the small **Galerija Centar** (Njegoševa 2; 9am-2pm & 5-9pm Mon-Fri, 10am-2pm Sat).

Hram Hristovog Vaskrsenja CHURCH

(Temple of Christ's Resurrection; Bul Džordža Vašingtona) This immense church is an indicator of the healthy state of Orthodoxy in Montenegro. It's still incomplete after 17 years' construction, but its large dome, white stone towers and gold crosses are a striking addition to Podgorica's skyline.

Sleeping

Most visitors to Podgorica are here for business, either commerce or government-related. Hotels set their prices accordingly and private accommodation isn't really an option.

Hotel Evropa HOTEL €€

(020-623 444; www.hotelevropa.co.me; Orahovačka 16; s/d €55/90;) It's hardly a salubrious location, but Evropa is handy to the train and bus stations and offers good clean rooms with comfortable beds, writing desks and decent showers. Despite its diminutive size there's a sauna and fitness room.

Hotel Eminent HOTEL €€€

(020-664 646; www.eminent.co.me; Njegoševa 25; s/d €80/130, apt €90-140;) Given its location and excellent facilities, the Eminent seems to be set up for business people keen on an after-work tipple. The front rooms can be noisy but the comfortable mezzanine apartments open onto a covered veranda at the back.

Eating & Drinking

Head to the **little market** (Moskovska bb) or the **big market** (Bratstva Jedinstva bb) for fresh fruit and vegetables.

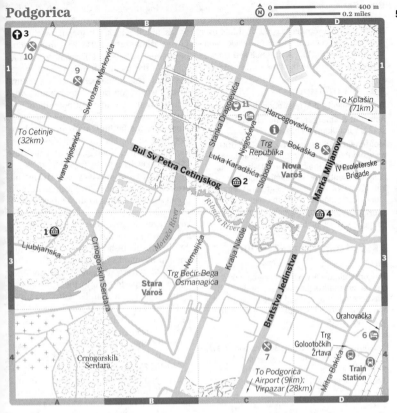

Podgorica

⊙ Sights

🛏 Sleeping

✕ Eating

⊙ Drinking

Leonardo　　　　　　　　　ITALIAN €€

(Svetozara Markovića bb; mains €5-16) Leonardo's unlikely position at the centre of a residential block makes it a little tricky to find but the effort's well rewarded with accomplished Italian cuisine. The pasta dishes are delicious and reasonably priced, given the upmarket ambience, while the €5 pizzas should leave even those on a budget with a Mona Lisa smile.

Laterna　　　　　　　　　PIZZA €

(Marka Miljanova 41; mains €4-13; ⊙9am-midnight Mon-Sat) Farm implements hang from the rough stone walls, creating a surprisingly rustic ambience in the centre of the city. A selection of meat and fish grills is offered but it's hard to go past the crispy-based pizza – it's quite possibly Montenegro's best.

Buda Bar   BAR
(Stanka Dragojevića 26; ⊙8am-2am) A golden
Buddha smiles serenely as you meditate over
your coffee or cocktail. This is one slick watering hole; the tentlike semi-enclosed terrace
is the place to be on balmy summer nights.

Information

You'll find plenty of ATMs around the inner city.
Accident & Emergency clinic (Hitna Pomoć;
☑124; Vaka Djurovića bb)
Montenegro Adventures (☑020-208 000;
www.montenegro-adventures.com; Jovana
Tomaševića 35) The commercial wing of the
nonprofit Centre for Sustainable Tourism
Initiatives (www.cstimontenegro.org) organises
tours, accommodation and the like.
Tourist Organisation Podgorica (TOP; www.
podgorica.travel; Slobode 47)

ⓘ Getting There & Around

Air
Podgorica airport (www.montenegroairports.
com) is 9km south of the city. A shuttle bus (€3)
runs between the airport and Trg Republika roughly
every 30 minutes. Airport taxis have a standard €15
fare to the centre.

Bus
Podgorica's **bus station** (Trg Golootočkih Žrtava;
⊙5am-10pm) has a left-luggage service, ATM and
services to all major towns, including Herceg Novi
(€9, three hours), Kotor (€7, two hours) and Ulcinj
(€6, one hour).

Car
The major rental-car agencies all have counters at
Podgorica airport. Excellent local agency **Meridian Rentacar** (☑020-234 944; www.meridian
-rentacar.com; Bul Džordža Vašingtona 85) also
has a city office.

Train
Don't expect English or much help from the information desk at the **train station** (Trg Golootočkih
Žrtava 13; ⊙5am-11pm), but timetables are
posted. Destinations include Bar (€2.60, one hour,
10 daily), Virpazar (€2.20, 40 minutes, 10 daily),
Kolašin (€4.80, 1½ hours, five daily) and Belgrade
(1st/2nd class €29/20, 7½ hours, three daily).

Ostrog Monastery
Манастир Острог

Resting in a cliff-face 900m above the Zeta
valley, the gleaming white **Ostrog Monastery** is the most important site in Monte-
gro for Orthodox Christians. Even with its
masses of pilgrims, tourists and trashy souvenir stands, it's a strangely affecting place.

Leaving the main Podgorica–Nikšić highway 19km past Danilovgrad, a narrow road
twists uphill for 7km before it reaches the
Lower Monastery (1824). In summer you'll
be greeted with sweet fragrances emanat-
ing from the mountain foliage. The church
has vivid frescos and behind it is a natural
spring, where you can fill your bottles with
deliciously fresh water and potentially benefit from an internal blessing as you sup it.
From here the faithful, many of them barefoot, plod up another two steep kilometres to
the main shrine. Nonpilgrims and the pure
of heart may drive to the upper car park.

The **Upper Monastery** (the really impressive one) is dubbed 'Sv Vasilije's miracle',
because noone seems to understand how it
was built. Constructed in 1665 within two
large caves, it gives the impression that it
has grown out of the very rock. Sv Vasilije
(St Basil), a bishop from Hercegovina,
brought his monks here after the Ottomans
destroyed Tvrdos Monastery near Trebinje.
Pilgrims queue to go into the atmospheric
shrine where the saint's fabric-wrapped
bones are kept. To enter you'll need to be
wearing a long skirt or trousers (jeans are
fine) and cover your shoulders.

One of the only nonsmoking establishments in the country, the **guest house**
(☑067-405 258; dm €4) near the Lower Monastery offers tidy single-sex dorm rooms,
while in summer many pilgrims lay sleeping
mats in front of the Upper Monastery.

There's no public transport but numerous
tour buses head here from all of the tourist
hot spots. Expect to pay €20 for a day trip
from the coast.

NORTHERN MOUNTAINS

This really is the full Monte: soaring peaks,
hidden monasteries, secluded villages, steep
river canyons and a whole heap of 'wild
beauty', to quote the tourist slogan. It's well
worth hiring a car for a couple of days to get
off the beaten track – some of the roads are
truly spectacular.

Kolašin Колашин
☑020 / POP 3000
Kolašin is Montenegro's main mountain
resort. Although the skiing's not as reliable
as Durmitor, Kolašin's much easier to get to
(it's just off the main highway, 71km north

of Podgorica) and has far ritzier accommodation. Like most ski towns it looks a lot prettier under a blanket of snow but even in summer it's a handy base for exploring Biogradska Gora National Park or other parts of the Bjelasica Mountains.

Most things of interest, including the banks and post office, are set around the two central squares (Trg Borca and Trg Vukmana Kruščića) and the short street that connects them (ul IV Proleterske).

🏃 Activities

Kolašin 1450 Ski Resort SKIING
(☑020-717 848; www.kolasin1450.com; skiing half-day/day/week pass €12/20/104) Located 10km east of Kolašin, at an elevation of 1450m, this ski centre offers 30km of runs (graded green, blue, red and black) reached by various ski lifts, as well as a cafe and restaurant in attractive wooden chalets. You can hire a full ski or snowboard kit for €13 per day and there are shuttle buses from the Hotels Lipka and Bianca in the township; they're free if you're a hotel guest or if you purchase your ski pass from the hotel. The ski season lasts roughly from December to mid-April but the centre stays open in summer for hikers and offers guided quad-bike trips up the mountain (per half-hour €30).

Hiking HIKING
Three marked hiking paths start from Trg Borca and head into the Bjelasica mountains. From the ski centre there's a 16km, five-hour loop route through the forest to Mt Ključ (1973m) and back.

Explorer Tourist Agency OUTDOOR PURSUITS
(☑020-864 200; www.montenegroexplorer.co.me; Mojkovačka bb) Located near the bus station, this agency specialises in action-packed holidays. It can arrange hiking, skiing, rafting, mountain biking, canyoning, caving, mountain climbing, jeep safaris, horse riding, paragliding and fishing expeditions. Mountain bikes can also be hired (per day/week €30/100).

🛏 Sleeping

Hotel Lipka HOTEL €€
(☑020-863 200; www.hotellipka.com; Mojkovačka 20; s €65-120, d €86-168; 🛜) Going for the designer-rustic look, this modern 72-room hotel is fitted out in wood and stone and liberally scattered with peasant artefacts – there's a spinning wheel in reception, should you get the urge. It's all finished to a very high and comfortable standard.

ℹ Information

Tourist office (Trg Borca 2; ⊘8am-4pm) When it's open (it's often not) this impressive wooden information centre, very prominently located on the main street, can help arrange private accommodation, hotels, hiking, rafting, mountain biking and guided jeep tours.

ℹ Getting There & Away
Bus
The **bus station** (Mojkovačka bb) is a shed on the road leading into town about 200m from the centre. There are regular services to Podgorica (€5).
Train
You'll see the town laid out below Kolašin's train station; it's a 1.5km walk to the centre. Five trains head to and from Podgorica (€4.80, 1½ hours) each day. Buy your tickets on the train.

Biogradska Gora National Park Биоградска Гора

Nestled in the heart of the Bjelasica Mountain Range, this pretty national park has as its heart 1600 hectares of virgin woodland – one of Europe's last three remaining primeval forests. The main entrance to the park is between Kolašin and Mojkovac on the Podgorica–Belgrade route. After paying a €2 entry fee you can drive the further 4km to the lake.

You can hire rowboats (per hour €5) and buy fishing permits (per day €20) from the **park office** (www.nparkovi.co.me) by the carpark. Nearby there's a **camping ground** (small/large tent €3/5) with basic squat toilets and a cluster of 11 new windowless log cabins, each with two beds (€20). The ablutions block for the cabins is much nicer. **Restoran Biogradsko Jezero** (mains €5.50-9.20) has a wonderful terrace where you can steal glimpses of the lake through the trees as you tuck into a traditional lamb or veal dish.

The nearest bus stop is an hour's walk away at Kraljevo Kolo and the nearest train station is a 90-minute walk away at Štitarička Rijeka.

Durmitor National Park Дурмитор
☑052 / POP 4900

Magnificent scenery ratchets up to the stupendous in this national park (€2 entry fee per day), where ice and water have carved a dramatic landscape from the limestone. Some 18 glacial lakes known as *gorske oči* (mountain eyes) dot the Durmitor range, with the largest, **Black Lake** (Crno Jezero), a pleasant 3km walk from Žabljak. The rounded mass of **Međed** (The Bear; 2287m) rears up behind the lake flanked by others of the park's 48 peaks over 2000m, including the highest, **Bobotov Kuk** (2523m). In winter (December to March) Durmitor is Montenegro's main ski resort; in summer it's a popular place for hiking, rafting and other active pursuits.

The park is home to enough critters to cast a Disney movie, including 163 species of bird, about 50 types of mammals and purportedly the greatest variety of butterflies in Europe.

Žabljak, at the eastern edge of the range, is the park's principal gateway and the only town within its boundaries. It's not very big and nor is it attractive, but it has a supermarket, post office, bank, hotels and restaurants, all gathered around the parking lot that masquerades as the main square.

🏃 Activities

Rafting
RAFTING

Slicing through the mountains at the northern edge of the national park like they were made from the local soft cheese, the **Tara River** forms a canyon that at its peak is 1300m deep. By way of comparison, Colorado's Grand Canyon is only 200m deeper.

Rafting along the river is one of the country's most popular tourist activities, with various operators running trips daily between May and October. The river has a few rapids but don't expect an adrenaline-fuelled white-water experience. You'll get the most excitement in May, when the last of the melting snow still revs up the flow.

The 82km section that is raftable starts from Splavište, south of the impressive 150m-high Tara Bridge, and ends at Šćepan Polje on the Bosnian border. The classic two-day trip heads through the deepest part of the canyon on the first day, stopping overnight at Radovan Luka. Most of the day tours from the coast traverse only the last 18km from Brstanovica – this is outside the national park and hence avoids hefty fees. You'll miss out on the canyon's depths but it's still a beautiful stretch, including most of the rapids. The buses follow a spectacular road along the Piva River, giving you a double dose of canyon action.

If you've got your own wheels you can save a few bucks and avoid a lengthy coach tour by heading directly to Šćepan Polje. It's

important to use a reputable operator; in 2010, two people died in one day on a trip with inexperienced guides. At a minimum make sure you're given a helmet and life-jacket – and make sure you wear them.

One good operator is **Kamp Grab** (☑040-200 598; www.tara-grab.com; half-day tour incl lunch €45), with lodgings blissfully located 8km upstream from Šćepan Polje. To get there, you'll need to cross the Montenegrin side of the border crossing and hang a right (tell the guards you're heading to Grab); the last 3.5km is unsealed.

Tara Tour (☑069-086 106; www.tara-tour.com) offers an excellent half-day trip (with/without breakfast and lunch €40/30) and has a cute set of wooden chalets in Šćepan Polje with squat toilets and showers in a separate block; accommodation, three meals and a half-day's rafting costs €55.

Hiking
HIKING

Durmitor is one of the best-marked mountain ranges in Europe. Some suggest it's a little too well labelled, encouraging novices to wander around seriously high-altitude paths that are prone to fog and summer thunderstorms. Check the weather forecast before you set out, stick to the tracks and prepare for sudden drops in temperature. Paths can be as easy as a 4km stroll around the Black Lake.

Skiing
SKIING

On the slopes of **Savin Kuk** (2313m), 5km from Žabljak, you'll find the main ski centre. Its 3.5km run starts from a height of 2010m and is best suited to advanced skiers. On the outskirts of town near the bus station, **Javorovača** is a gentle 300m slope that's good for kids and beginners. The third centre at **Mali Štuoc** (1953m) has terrific views over the Black Lake, Međed and Savin Kuk, and slopes to suit all levels of experience.

One of the big attractions for skiing here is the cost: day passes are around €15, weekly passes are €90, and ski lessons cost between €10 and €20. You can rent ski and snowboard gear from **Sport Trade** (Vuka Karadžića 7, Žabljak) for around €10 per day.

Tara Bungy
BUNGEE JUMPING

(☑067-9010 020; www.bungy.me; jump €79; ☺Jun-Sep) Hurl yourself off the elegant 172m Tara Bridge under the supervision of experienced operators from the UK Bungee Club.

📍 Sleeping

Eko-Oaza Suza Evrope CABINS €
(📞069-444 590; ekoaozatara@gmail.com; Do-
brilovina; cabin low/high season €25/50; 🅿) Situated 25km west of Mojkovac at the beginning
of the arm of the park that stretches along
the Tara River, this family-run 'eco oasis' consists of four comfortable wooden cabins, each
sleeping six people. From here you can hike
up the mountain and stay overnight in a hut
near the glacial Lake Zaboj (1477m). Home-
cooked meals are provided on request.

MB Hotel HOTEL €€
(📞052-361 601; mb-turist@yahoo.com; Tripka
Ðakovića bb, Žabljak; s/d €30/57; 🅿🛜) In a
quiet backstreet halfway between the town
centre and the bus station, this little hotel
offers decent midrange rooms and an attractive restaurant and bar. The restaurant
even has a nonsmoking section – something even less likely to be seen in these
parts than wolves.

Autokamp Mlinski Potok Mina
CAMPING GROUND €
(📞069-497 625; camp sites per person €3, dm €10)
With a fabulously hospitable host (there's
no escaping the *rakija* shots), this is a basic camping ground above the National Park
Visitors Centre. The owner's house can sleep
12 guests in wood-panelled rooms and he has
another house sleeping 11 by the Black Lake.

ℹ Information

Durmitor National Park Visitor Centre (www.
nparkovi.co.me; Jovana Cvijića bb; ⊙9am-5pm
Mon-Fri) On the road to the Black Lake, this
centre includes a wonderful micromuseum
focusing on the park's flora and fauna. The
knowledgeable English-speaking staff sell local
craft, maps and hiking guidebooks.

ℹ Getting There & Away

The most reliable road to Žabljak follows the
Tara River west from Mojkovac. In summer this
70km route takes about 90 minutes. If you're
coming from Podgorica the quickest route is
through Nikšić and Šavnik, but the road can be
treacherous in winter. The main highway north
from Nikšić follows the dramatic Piva Canyon
to Šćepan Polje. There's a wonderful back road
through the mountains from the highway near
Plužine to Žabljak, but it's impassable as soon as
the snows fall.

There's a petrol station near the bus station at
the southern end of Žabljak on the Nikšić road.
Buses head to Belgrade (€18, nine hours, two
daily) and Podgorica (€8, 3½ hours, three daily).

UNDERSTAND MONTENEGRO

History

Like all the modern states of the Balkan peninsula, Montenegro has a long, convoluted
and eventful history. History is worn on the
sleeve here and people discuss 600-year-old
events (or their not-always-accurate versions of them) as if they happened yester-
day. Events such as the split of the Roman
Empire, the subsequent split in Christianity
between Catholic and Orthodox, and the
battles with the Ottoman Turks still have a
direct bearing on the politics of today.

Before the Slavs

The Illyrians were the first known people to
inhabit the region. By 1000 BC they had established a loose federation of tribes across
much of the Balkans. By around 400 BC the
Greeks had established some coastal colonies and by AD 10 the Romans had absorbed
the entire region into their empire. In 395
the Roman Empire was split into two halves,
the western half retaining Rome as capital,
the eastern half, which eventually became
the Byzantine Empire, centred on Constantinople. Modern Montenegro lay on the fault
line between the two entities.

In the early 7th century, the Slavs arrived
from north of the Danube. Two main Slavic
groups settled in the Balkans: the Croats
along the Adriatic coast and the Serbs in the
interior. With time most Serbs accepted the
Orthodox faith, while the Croats accepted
Catholicism.

First Slavic Kingdoms

In the 9th century the first Serb kingdom,
Raška, arose near Novi Pazar (in modern
Serbia) followed shortly by another Serb
state, Duklja, which sprang up on the site of
the Roman town of Doclea (present-day Podgorica). Initially allied with Byzantium, Duklja eventually shook off Byzantine influence
and began to expand. Over time Duklja came
to be known as Zeta, but from 1160 Raška
again became the dominant Serb entity. At
its greatest extent it reached from the Adriatic to the Aegean and north to the Danube.

Expansion was halted in 1389 at the battle
of Kosovo Polje, where the Serbs were defeated by the Ottoman Turks. Thereafter the
Turks swallowed up the Balkans and the Serb
nobility fled to Zeta, on Lake Skadar. When

they were forced out of Zeta by the Ottomans in 1480 they established a stronghold in the mountains at Cetinje on Mt Lovćen.

Montenegro & the Ottomans

This mountainous area became the last redoubt of Serbian Orthodox culture when all else fell to the Ottomans. It was during this time that the Venetians, who ruled Kotor, Budva and much of the Adriatic Coast, began calling Mt Lovćen the Monte Negro (Black Mountain), which lends its name to the modern state. Over time the Montenegrins established a reputation as fearsome warriors. The Ottomans opted for pragmatism, and largely left them to their own devices.

With the struggle against the Ottomans, the previously highly independent tribes began to work collaboratively by the 1600s. This further developed a sense of shared Montenegrin identity and the *vladika,* previously a metropolitan position within the Orthodox Church, began mediating between tribal chiefs. As such, the *vladika* assumed a political role, and *vladika* became a hereditary title: the prince-bishop.

While Serbia remained under Ottoman control, in the late 18th century the Montenegrins under *vladika* Petar I Petrović began to expand their territory, doubling it within the space of a little over 50 years.

A rebellion against Ottoman control broke out in Bosnia and Hercegovina (BiH) in 1875. Montenegrins joined the insurgency and made significant territorial gains as a result. At the Congress of Berlin in 1878 Montenegro and Bosnia officially achieved independence.

In the early years of the 20th century there were increasing calls for union with Serbia and rising political opposition to the ruling Petrović dynasty. The Serbian king Petar Karadjordjević attempted to overthrow King Nikola Petrović and Montenegrin-Serbian relations reached their historic low point.

The Balkans Wars of 1912–13 saw the Montenegrins joining the Serbs, Greeks and Bulgarians and succeeding in throwing the Ottomans out of southeastern Europe. Now that Serbia and Montenegro were both independent and finally shared a border, the idea of a Serbian-Montenegrin union gained more currency. King Nikola pragmatically supported the idea on the stipulation that both the Serbian and Montenegrin royal houses be retained.

The Two Yugoslavias

Before the union could be realised WWI intervened. Serbia quickly entered the war and Montenegro followed in its footsteps. Austria-Hungary invaded Serbia shortly afterwards and swiftly captured Cetinje, sending King Nikola into exile in France. In 1918 the Serbian army reclaimed Montenegro, and the French, keen to implement the Serbian-Montenegrin union, refused to allow Nikola to leave France. The following year Montenegro was incorporated in the Kingdom of the Serbs, Croats and Slovenes, the first Yugoslavia.

Throughout the 1920s some Montenegrins put up spirited resistance to the union with Serbia. This resentment was increased by the abolition of the Montenegrin church, which was absorbed by the Serbian Orthodox Patriarchate.

During WWII the Italians occupied the Balkans. Tito's Partisans and the Serbian Chetniks engaged the Italians, sometimes lapsing into fighting each other. Ultimately, the Partisans put up the best fight and with the diplomatic and military support of the Allies, the Partisans entered Belgrade in October 1944 and Tito was made prime minister. Once the communist federation of Yugoslavia was established, Tito decreed that Montenegro have full republic status and the border of the modern Montenegrin state was set. Of all the Yugoslav states, Montenegro had the highest per-capita membership of the Communist Party and it was highly represented in the armed forces.

The Union & Independence

In the decades following Tito's death in 1980, Slobodan Milošević used the issue of Kosovo to whip up a nationalist storm in Serbia and ride to power on a wave of nationalism. The Montenegrins largely supported their Orthodox co-religionists. In 1991 Montenegrin paramilitary groups were responsible for the shelling of Dubrovnik and parts of the Dalmatian littoral. In 1992, by which point Slovenia, Croatia and BiH had opted for independence, the Montenegrins voted overwhelmingly in support of a plebiscite to remain in Yugoslavia with Serbia.

In 1997 Montenegrin leader Milo Djukanović broke with an increasingly isolated Milošević and immediately became the darling of the West. As the Serbian regime became an international pariah, the Montenegrins increasingly wanted to re-establish their distinct identity.

In 2000 Milošević lost the election in Serbia. Meanwhile Vojislav Koštunica came to power in Montenegro. With Milošević now toppled, Koštunica was pressured to vote for a Union of Serbia and Montenegro. In theory this union was based on equality between the two republics; however, in practice Serbia was such a dominant partner that the union proved unfeasible from the outset. In May 2006 the Montenegrins voted for independence. Since then the divorce of Serbia and Montenegro has proceeded relatively smoothly. Montenegro has rapidly opened up to the West and has instituted economic, legal and environmental reforms with a view to becoming a member of the EU.

The People of Montenegro

In the last census (2003) 43% of the population identified as Montenegrin, 32% as Serb, 8% as Bosniak (with a further 4% identifying as Muslim), 5% as Albanian, 1% as Croat and 0.4% as Roma. Montenegrins are the majority along most of the coast and the centre of the country, while Albanians dominate in the southeast (around Ulcinj), Bosniaks in the far east (Rožaje and Plav), and Serbs in the north and Herceg Novi.

Religion and ethnicity broadly go together in these parts. Over 74% of the population is Orthodox (mainly Montenegrins and Serbs), 18% Muslim (mainly Bosniaks and Albanians) and 4% Roman Catholic (mainly Albanians and Croats).

In 1993 the Montenegrin Orthodox Church (MOC) was formed, claiming to revive the autocephalous church of Montenegro's bishop-princes that was dissolved in 1920 following the formation of the Kingdom of Serbs, Croats and Slovenes. The Serbian Orthodox Church doesn't recognise the MOC and still control most of the country's churches and monasteries.

Visual Arts

Montenegro's visual arts can be divided into two broad strands: religious iconography and Yugoslav-era painting and sculpture. The nation's churches are full of wonderful frescoes and painted iconostases (the screen that separates the congregation from the sanctuary in Orthodox churches). Of the modern painters, an early great was Petar Lubarda (1907–74), whose stylised oil paintings included themes from Montenegrin history.

Environment

The Land

Montenegro is comprised of a thin strip of Adriatic coast, a fertile plain around Podgorica and a whole lot of mountains. The highest peak is Kolac (2534m) in the Prokletije range near Albania. Most of the mountains are limestone and karstic in nature and they shelter large swathes of forest and glacial lakes. Rivers such as the Tara, Piva and Morača have cut deep canyons through them. The oddly shaped Bay of Kotor is technically a drowned river canyon, although it's popularly described as a fjord. Lake Skadar, the largest in the Balkans, spans Montenegro and Albania in the southeast.

Wildlife

Among the mammals that live in Montenegro are otters, badgers, roe deer, chamois, foxes, weasels, moles, groundhogs and hares. Bears, wolves, lynxes and jackals are much rarer sights. Tortoises, lizards and snakes are easier to find and you might spot golden and imperial eagles, white-headed vultures and peregrine falcons above the peaks. The rare Dalmatian pelican nests around Lake Skadar, along with pygmy cormorants, yellow heron and whiskered tern.

National Parks

Montenegro has five national parks covering a total area of 1075 sq km: Lovćen, Durmitor, Biogradska Gora, Lake Skadar and the recently declared Prokletije.

Environmental Issues

For a new country, especially one recovering from a recent war, Montenegro has made some key moves to safeguard the environment, not the least declaring itself an 'ecological state' in its constitution. Yet in the rush to get bums on beaches, the preservation of the nation's greatest selling point sometimes plays second fiddle to development.

The country currently imports 40% of its electricity and ideas mooted for increasing supply have included flooding part of the Morača canyon to build new hydroelectric power stations.

There's little awareness of litter as a problem. It's not just the ubiquitous practice of throwing rubbish out of car windows; we've seen waitresses clear tables by throwing refuse straight into a river and we've heard reports of train employees doing the same. Along the coast, fly-tipping of rubble from building sites is a problem. On an encouraging note, recycling is now established in Herceg Novi and the hunting of the nation's endangered bear population has recently been banned.

Food & Drink

Loosen your belt; you're in for a treat. Eating in Montenegro is generally an extremely pleasurable experience. By default, most of the food is local, fresh and organic, and hence very seasonal. The only downside is a lack of variety. By the time you've been here a week, menu déjà vu is likely to have set in.

The food on the coast is virtually indistinguishable from Dalmatian cuisine: lots of grilled seafood, garlic, olive oil and Italian dishes. Inland it's much more meaty and Serbian influenced.

The village of Njeguši in the Montenegrin heartland is famous for its *pršut* (dried ham) and cheese. Anything with Njeguški in its name is going to be a true Montenegrin dish and stuffed with these goodies.

In the mountains, meat roasted *ispod sača* (under a metal lid covered with hot coals) comes out deliciously tender. You might eat it with *kačamak,* a cheesy, creamy cornmeal or buckwheat dish – heavy going but comforting on those long winter nights.

On the coast, be sure to try the fish soup, grilled squid (served plain or stuffed with *pršut* and cheese) and black risotto (made from squid ink). Whole fish are often presented to the table for you to choose from and are sold by the kilogram.

Fast-food outlets and bakeries *(pekara),* serving *burek* (meat- or spinach-filled pastries), pizza slices and *palačinke* (pancakes) are easy to find. Anywhere that attracts tourists will have a selection of restaurants and *konoba* (small family-run affairs). There is generally no distinction between a cafe and bar. Restaurants open at around 8am and close around midnight, while cafe-bars may stay open until 2am or 3am.

Eating in Montenegro can be a trial for vegetarians and almost impossible for vegans. Pasta, pizza and salad are the best fallback options. Nonsmoking sections are a rumour from distant lands that have yet to trouble the citizens of Montenegro.

Local Drinks

Montenegro's domestic wine is eminently drinkable and usually the cheapest thing on the menu. Vranac and Krstač are the indigenous red and white grapes, respectively. Nikšićko Pivo (try saying that after a few) is the local beer and a good thirst-quencher. Many people distil their own *rakija* (brandy), made out of just about anything (grapes, pears, apples etc). They all come out tasting like rocket fuel.

The coffee is universally excellent. In private houses it's generally served Turkish-style, 'black as hell, strong as death and sweet as love'.

SURVIVAL GUIDE

Directory A–Z

Accommodation

Prices are very seasonal, peaking in July and August on the coast. In this chapter we've listed indicative ranges. Our price ranges for a double room are budget (€; less than €30 per night for the cheapest double room), midrange (€€; €30 to €90) and top end (€€€; more than €90).

The cheapest options are rooms in private houses and apartment rentals. These can be arranged through travel agencies or, in season, you may be approached at the bus stop or see signs hanging outside of houses. Facilities at camping grounds tend to be basic, often with squat toilets and limited water. The national parks have cabin-style accommodation.

An additional tourist tax (less than €2 per night) is added to the rate for all accommodation types. For private accommodation it's sometimes left up to the guest to pay it, but it can be nigh on impossible finding the right authority to pay it to (the procedure varies from area to area). Theoretically you could be asked to provide white accommodation receipt cards (or copies of invoices from hotels) when you leave the country, but in practice this is rarely required.

Activities

Hooking up with activity operators can be difficult due to language difficulties, lack of permanent offices and out-of-date websites. Luckily there are some excellent travel agencies who will do the legwork for you, including Black Mountain in Herceg Novi (p583) and Montenegro Adventure Centre in Budva.

Business Hours

Business hours in Montenegro are a relative concept. Even if hours are posted on the doors of museums or shops, they may not be heeded. Reviews don't list opening hours unless they differ from the following:

Banks Usually 8am-5pm Mon-Fri, until noon Sat

Cafe-bars 8am-midnight (later in high season in busy areas)

Restaurants 8am-midnight

Shops 8am or 9am to 8pm or 9pm; often closed in late afternoon

Embassies & Consulates

The following are all in Podgorica, unless otherwise stated.

Albania (☏020-652 796; Zmaj Jovina 30)

BiH (☏020-618 105; Atinska 58)

Croatia Kotor (☏032-323 127; Trg od Oružja bb); Podgorica (☏020-269 760; Vladimira Ćetkovića 2)

France (☏020-655 348; Atinska 35)

Germany (☏020-667 285; Hercegovačka 10)

Italy (☏020-234 661; Bul Džordža Vašingtona 83)

Serbia (☏020-667 305; Hercegovačka bb)

UK (☏020-618 010; Ulcinjska 8)

USA (☏020-410 500; Ljubljanska bb)

Food

Price ranges: budget (€; under €5), midrange (€€; €5 to €10) and top end (€€€; over €10).

Gay & Lesbian Travellers

Although homosexuality was decriminalised in 1977 and discrimination outlawed in 2010, attitudes to homosexuality remain hostile and life for gay people is extremely difficult. Many gay men resort to online connections (try www.gayromeo.com) or take their chances at a handful of cruisy beaches. Lesbians will find it even harder to access the local community.

Money

Montenegro uses the euro (€). You'll find banks with ATMs in all the main towns, most of which accept Visa, MasterCard, Maestro and Cirrus. Don't rely on restaurants, shops or smaller hotels accepting credit cards.

Tipping isn't expected, although it's common to round up to the nearest euro.

Public Holidays

New Year's Day 1 and 2 January

Orthodox Christmas 6, 7 and 8 January

Orthodox Good Friday & Easter Monday April/May

Labour Day 1 May

Independence Day 21 and 22 May

Statehood Day 13 July

Telephone

The international access prefix is ☏00 or + from a mobile. Mobile numbers start with 06. Local SIM cards are good if you're planning a longer stay. The main providers are T-Mobile, Telenor and M:tel.

Women Travellers

Other than a cursory interest shown by men towards solo women travellers, travelling is hassle free and easy. In Muslim areas some women wear a headscarf but most don't.

Getting There & Away

Air

Montenegro has two international **airports** (www.montenegroairports.com) – **Tivat** (TIV; ☏032-617 337) and **Podgorica** (TGD; ☏020-872 016) – although most tourists arrive via Croatia's Dubrovnik airport, which is very near the border. While various airlines run summer charter flights, the following airlines have regular scheduled flights to/from Montenegro.

Adria Airlines (JP; ☏020-201 201; www.adria. si; Ivana Vujoševića 46, Podgorica) Ljubljana to Podgorica.

Austrian Airlines (OS; ☏020-606 170; www. austrian.com) Vienna to Podgorica (operated by Tyrolean).

Croatia Airlines (OU; ☏020-201 201; www. croatiaairlines.com; Ivana Vujoševića 46, Podgorica) Zagreb to Podgorica.

JAT Airways (JU; ☏020-664 750; www.jat. com; Njegoševa 25, Podgorica) Belgrade to Tivat and Podgorica.

Malév Hungarian Airlines (MA; ☏020-667 480; www.malev.com) Budapest to Podgorica.

Montenegro Airlines (YM; ☏020-664 411; www.montenegroairlines.com; Slobode 23, Podgorica) Belgrade and Moscow to Tivat; Bari, Belgrade, Brussels, Frankfurt, Ljubljana, London, Milan, Moscow, Naples, Niš, Paris, Pristina, Skopje, Vienna and Zürich to Podgorica.

Moskovia Airlines (3R; ☏033-455 967; www. moskovia.aero; Mediteranska 23, Budva) Moscow to Tivat and Podgorica.

S7 Airlines (S7; ☏7-495-777-99-99; www.s7.ru) Moscow to Tivat and Podgorica.

Turkish Airlines (TK; ☏020-653 108; www. turkishairlines.com) Istanbul to Podgorica.

Land

Border Crossings

Albania The main crossings link Shkodra to Ulcinj (Sukobin) and to Podgorica (Hani i Hotit).

BiH The main checkpoints are at Sitnica, Dolovi and Šćepan Polje.

Croatia There's a busy checkpoint on the Adriatic highway between Herceg Novi and Dubrovnik; expect delays in summer. A longer-distance but often quicker checkpoint is Kobila, on the tip of the Prevlaka peninsula.

Kosovo The main crossing is on the road between Rožaje and Peć.

Serbia The busiest crossing is north of Bijelo Polje near Dobrakovo, followed by the checkpoint northeast of Rožaje and another east of Pljevlja.

Bus

There's a well-developed bus network linking Montenegro with the major cities of the region. Podgorica is the main hub but buses stop at most other big towns as well. For some indicative prices, see p585.

Car & Motorcycle

Drivers are recommended to carry an International Driving Permit (IDP) as well as their home country's driving licence. Vehicles need Green Card insurance or insurance must be bought at the border. A €10 ea (valid for one year) is charged on foreig cars entering the country.

Train

Montenegro's only working passenger train line starts at Bar and heads into Serbia. For details on the train to Belgrade, see p598.

Sea

For details on ferries to Italy from Kotor and Bar, see p588 and p592.

Getting Around

Bicycle

Cyclists are a rare species, even in the cities. Don't expect drivers to be considerate. Wherever possible, try to get off the main roads.

Bus

The local bus network is extensive and reliable. Buses are usually comfortable and air conditioned, and are rarely full. It's slightly cheaper to buy your ticket on the bus rather the station, but a station-bought ticket theoretically guarantees you a seat. Luggage carried below the bus is charged at €1 per piece.

Car & Motorcycle

Independent travel by car or motorcycle is an ideal way to gad about and discover the country; some of the drives are breathtakingly beautiful. Traffic police are everywhere, so stick to speed limits and carry an IDP. Allow more time than you'd expect for the distances involved, as the terrain will slow you down.

The major international car-hire companies have a presence in various centres. **Meridian Rentacar** (☏020-234 944; www.meridian -rentacar.com), which has offices in Budva, Bar, Podgorica and the airports, is a reliable local option; one-day hire starts from €45.

Train

Željeznica Crne Gore (www.zcg-prevoz.me) runs the only passenger train line, heading north from Bar. The trains are old and can be hot in summer but they're priced accordingly and the route through the mountains is spectacular. Useful stops include Virpazar, Podgorica and Kolašin.

Centrum Medyczne LIM (☏22 458 7000; www.cm-lim.com.pl; 3rd fl, Marriott Hotel, Al Jerozolimskie 65/79) Offers specialist doctors, laboratory tests and house calls.

Dental-Med (☏22 629 5938; ul Hoża 27) A central dental practice.

Hospital of the Ministry of Internal Affairs & Administration (☏22 508 2000; ul Wołoska 137) A hospital preferred by government officials and diplomats.

Money

Banks, foreign-exchange offices *(kantors)* and ATMs are easy to find around the city centre. *Kantors* open 24 hours can be found at Warszawa Centralna train station and the airport, but exchange rates at these places are about 10% lower than in the city centre. Avoid changing money in the Old Town, where the rates can be even lower.

American Express (Marriott Hotel, Al Jerozolimskie 65/79; ☺7am-11pm)

Post

Main post office (Map p614; ul Świętokrzyska 31/33; ☺24hr)

Tourist Information

Each tourist office provides free city maps and free booklets, such as the handy *Warsaw in Short* and the *Visitor*, and sells maps of other Polish cities; offices also help with booking hotel rooms.

Free monthly tourist magazines worth seeking out include *Faces* and *Welcome to Warsaw*. The comprehensive *Warsaw Insider* (9.90zł) and *Warsaw in Your Pocket* (5zł) are also useful.

Tourist office (☏22 19431; www.warsawtour. pl) Old Town (Map p612; Rynek Starego Miasta 19; ☺9am-9pm May-Sep, 9am-7pm Oct-Apr); Okęcie airport (☺8am-8pm May-Sep, 8am-7pm Oct-Apr); main hall of Warszawa Centralna train station (Map p614; ☺8am-8pm May-Sep, 8am-7pm Oct-Apr).

Warsaw Tourist Information Centre (Map p612; ☏22 635 1881; www.wcit.waw.pl; pl Zamkowy 1/13; ☺9am-6pm Mon-Fri, 10am-6pm Sat & Sun) Helpful privately run tourist office in the Old Town.

Travel Agencies

Orbis Travel (☏22 827 7140; ul Bracka 16)

Our Roots (☏22 620 0556; ul Twarda 6) Offers Jewish heritage tours.

Trakt (☏22 827 8068; www.trakt.com.pl; ul Kredytowa 6) Guided tours of Warsaw and beyond.

 **Getting There & Away**

Air

The **Warsaw Frédéric Chopin airport** (www. lotnisko-chopina.pl) is more commonly called Okęcie airport.

The useful tourist office is on the arrivals level of Terminal 2.

At the arrivals level there are ATMs and several *kantors*. There are also car-rental companies, a left-luggage room and a newsagent where you can buy public transport tickets.

Domestic and international flights can be booked at the **LOT office** (☏0801 703 703; Al Jerozolimskie 65/79), or at any travel agency. Other airlines are listed on p689.

Bus

Warsaw has two major bus stations for PKS buses. **Dworzec Zachodnia** (Western Bus Station; Map p611; www.pksbilety.pl; Al Jerozolimskie 144) handles domestic buses heading south, north and west of the capital, including up to 11 daily to Częstochowa (41zł, 3½ hours), 13 to Gdańsk (53zł, six hours), seven to Kraków (48zł, six hours), 11 to Olsztyn (35zł, 4½ hours), 15 to Toruń (42zł, four hours), five to Wrocław (54zł, seven hours) and five to Zakopane (60zł, eight hours). This complex is southwest of the city centre and adjoins the Warszawa Zachodnia train station. Take the commuter train that leaves from Warszawa Śródmieście station.

Dworzec Stadion (Stadium Bus Station; Map p611; www.pksbilety.pl; ul Sokola 1) adjoins the Warszawa Stadion train station. It is also easily accessible by commuter train from Warszawa Śródmieście. Dworzec Stadion handles some domestic buses to the east and southeast, including 16 daily to Lublin (23zł, three hours), four to Białystok (33zł, 3½ hours) and three to Zamość (35zł, 4¾ hours).

International buses depart from and arrive at Dworzec Zachodnia or, occasionally, outside Warszawa Centralna. Tickets are available from the bus offices at Dworzec Zachodnia, from agencies at Warszawa Centralna or from any of the major travel agencies in the city. **Eurolines Polska** (www.eurolinespolska.pl) operates a huge number of buses to destinations throughout Eastern and Western Europe; some sample routes include Amsterdam (225zł, 22 hours, four weekly), Cologne (200zł, 20½ hours, daily), London (300zł, 27 hours, four weekly), Paris (260zł, 26½ hours, four weekly), Rome (370zł, 28 hours, three weekly) and Vienna (175zł, 13 hours, four weekly).

Train

Warsaw has several train stations, but the one that most travellers will use is **Warszawa Centralna** (Warsaw Central; Map p614; Al Jerozolimskie 54). Refer to the relevant destination sections in this chapter for information about services to/from Warsaw.

Warszawa Centralna is not always where trains start or finish, so make sure you get on or off promptly; and guard your belongings against pickpocketing and theft at all times.

The station's main hall houses ticket counters, ATMs and snack bars, as well as a post office, newsagents and a tourist office. Along the underground mezzanine level leading to the platforms are several *kantors* (one of which is open 24 hours), a **left-luggage office** (⏲7am-midnight), lockers, eateries, outlets for local public transport tickets, internet cafes and bookshops.

Tickets for domestic and international trains are available from counters at the station (but allow at least an hour for possible queuing). Tickets for immediate departures on domestic and international trains are also available from numerous, well-signed booths in the underpasses leading to Warszawa Centralna.

Some domestic trains also stop at Warszawa Śródmieście station, 300m east of Warszawa Centralna, and Warszawa Zachodnia, next to Dworzec Zachodnia bus station.

❶ Getting Around

To/From the Airport

The cheapest way of getting from the airport to the city centre is bus 175, which leaves every 10 to 15 minutes and travels via Warszawa Centralna train station and ul Nowy Świat, terminating at Plac Piłsudskiego, about a 500m walk from Castle Sq in the Old Town. If you arrive in the wee hours, night bus N32 links the airport with Warszawa Centralna every 30 minutes.

The taxi fare between the airport and city centre is from 40zł to 45zł. Official taxis displaying a name, telephone number and fares can be arranged at the official taxi counters at the international arrivals level.

Car

Warsaw traffic isn't fun, but there are good reasons to hire a car for jaunts into the countryside. Major car-rental companies are listed in the local English-language publications, and include **Avis** (☑22 650 4872; www.avis.pl), **Hertz** (☑22 500 1620; www.hertz.com.pl) and **Sixt** (☑22 511 1550; www.sixt.pl). For more details about car hire, see p690.

Public Transport

Warsaw's public transport operates from 5am to 11pm daily. The fare (2.80zł) is valid for one ride only on a bus, tram, trolleybus or metro train travelling anywhere in the city.

Warsaw is the only place in Poland where ISIC cards get a public-transport discount (of 48%).

Tickets are available for 60/90 minutes (4/6zł), one day (9zł), three days (16zł), one week (32zł) and one month (78zł). Buy tickets from kiosks (including those marked 'RUCH') before boarding, and validate them on board.

A metro line operates from the suburb of Ursynów (Kabaty station) at the southern city limits to Młociny in the north, via the city centre (Centrum), but is of limited use to visitors. Local commuter trains head out to the suburbs from the Warszawa Śródmieście station.

Taxi

Taxis are a quick and easy way to get around – as long as you use official taxis and drivers use their meters. Beware of unauthorised 'Mafia' taxis parked in front of top-end hotels, at the airport, outside Warszawa Centralna train station and in the vicinity of most tourist sights.

MAZOVIA & PODLASIE

After being ruled as an independent state by a succession of dukes, Mazovia shot to prominence during the 16th century, when Warsaw became the national capital. The region has long been a base for industry, the traditional mainstay of Poland's second-largest city, Łódź. To the east of Mazovia, toward the Belarus border, lies Podlasie, which means 'land close to the forest'. The main attraction of this region is the impressive Białowieża National Park.

Łódź

POP 745,000

Little damaged in WWII, Łódź (pronounced woodge) is a lively, likeable place with a wealth of attractive art nouveau architecture, and the added bonus of being off the usual tourist track. It's also an easy day trip from Warsaw. Łódź became a major industrial centre in the 19th century, attracting immigrants from across Europe. Though its textile industry slumped in the post-communist years, the centrally located city has had some success in attracting new investment in more diverse commercial fields.

Many of the attractions are along ul Piotrkowska, the main thoroughfare. You'll find banks and *kantors* here, and on ul Kopernika, one street west. You can't miss the bronze statues of local celebrities along ul Piotrkowska, including pianist Artur Rubenstein, seated at a baby grand. The helpful **tourist office** (⏲8am-7pm Mon-Fri, 10am-4pm Sat & Sun May-Oct, 8am-6pm Mon-Fri, 10am-2pm Sat Nov-Apr) hands out free tourist brochures.

◉ Sights

As Łódź is famous for being the centre of Poland's cinema industry (giving rise to the nickname 'Holly-Woodge'), film buffs will find some attractions of interest here. Along ul Piotrkowska near the Grand Hotel, you can follow the **Walk of Fame**, a series of star-shaped plaques honouring Polish stars and directors such as Roman Polański.

Cinematography Museum MUSEUM

(www.kinomuzeum.pl; Plac Zwycięstwa 1; adult/concession 8/5zł; ☉10am-4pm Tue, Wed & Fri, 11am-6pm Thu, Sat & Sun) Three blocks east of ul Piotrkowska's southern pedestrian zone. Worth a look both for its collection of old cinema gear and its mansion setting.

Historical Museum of Łódź MUSEUM

(ul Ogrodowa 15; adult/concession 8/5zł, free Sun; ☉10am-2pm Mon, 2-6pm Wed, 11am-4pm Tue, Thu, Sat & Sun) Northwest of Plac Wolności, at the north end of the main drag.

Manufaktura MALL

(www.manufaktura.com; ul Karskiego 5) Close by the Historical Museum is this fascinating shopping mall and entertainment centre constructed within a massive complex of historic red-brick factory buildings.

Dętka TOUR

(Plac Wolności 2; adult/concession 5/3zł; ☉noon-7pm Thu-Sun Jun-Sep) Guided tours every half-hour through the old brick sewer system beneath the city's streets, with exhibits en route. Operated by the Historical Museum.

Herbst Palace MUSEUM

(ul Przędzalniana 72; adult/concession 7/4.50zł, free Thu; ☉noon-5pm Wed, Thu & Fri, 11am-4pm Tue, Sat & Sun) Stately home, which has been converted into an appealing 19th-century art museum. It's accessible by bus 55 heading east from the cathedral at the southern end of ul Piotrkowska.

Jewish Cemetery CEMETERY

(www.jewishlodzcemetery.org; ul Bracka 40; admission 4zł, free first Sun of month; ☉9am-5pm Sun-Thu & 9am-3pm Fri Apr-Oct, 9am-3pm Sun-Fri Nov-Mar) One of the largest in Europe. It's 3km northeast of the city centre and accessible by tram 6 from a stop one block north of Plac Wolności to its terminus at Strykowska. Enter from ul Zmienna.

🛏 Sleeping & Eating

The tourist office can provide information about all kinds of accommodation.

Youth Hostel HOSTEL €

(☎42 630 6680; www.yhlodz.pl; ul Legionów 27; dm 18-30zł, s/d from 45/70zł) This place is excellent, so book ahead. It features nicely decorated rooms in a spacious old build-ing, with free laundry and a kitchen. It's 250m west of Plac Wolności.

Hotel Savoy HOTEL €€

(☎42 632 9360; www.hotelsavoy.com.pl; ul Traugutta 6; s/d from 130/272zł) Well positioned just off central ul Piotrkowska, with simple but spacious, light-filled rooms with clean bathrooms.

Hotel Centrum HOTEL €€

(☎42 632 8640; www.centrumhotele.pl; ul Kilińskiego 59; s/d from 207/308zł) A little further east, offers neatly renovated rooms in a communist-era behemoth, handy for the Łódź Fabryczna train station.

Chłopska Izba POLISH €€

(☎42 630 8087; ul Piotrkowska 65; mains 11-37zł; ☉noon-11pm) On ul Piotrkowska is this restaurant with folksy decor, serving up tasty versions of all the Polish standards.

Esplanada EUROPEAN €€

(☎42 630 5989; ul Piotrkowska 100; mains 19-45zł) A vibrant eatery serving quality Polish and German cuisine in an attractive historic venue.

❶ Getting There & Away

From the **airport** (www.airport.lodz.pl), which can be reached by city buses 55, 65 and L (2.40zł, 20 minutes), there are flights via Ryanair to several British and Irish destinations, including London (at least daily) and Dublin (twice weekly). There are no domestic flights.

From the convenient Łódź Fabryczna train station, 400m east of the city centre, you can travel to Warsaw (33zł, 1½ hours, hourly), Częstochowa (25zł, two hours, four daily) and Kraków (40zł, 4½ hours, two daily). From the Łódź Kaliska train station, 1.2km southwest of central Łódź and accessible by tram 12 from the city centre, trains go to Warsaw (35zł, 1¾ hours, four daily), Częstochowa (35zł, two hours, seven daily), Kraków (51zł, five hours, four daily), Wrocław (46zł, four hours, five daily), Poznań (31zł, 4½ hours, five daily), Toruń (37zł, 2½ hours, 12 daily) and Gdańsk (56zł, seven hours, five daily). Buses head in all directions from the bus terminal, next to the Łódź Fabryczna train station.

Białowieża National Park

Once a centre for hunting and timber-felling, Białowieża (Byah-wo-*vyeh*-zhah) is now Poland's oldest national park. Its significance is underlined by Unesco's unusual recognition of the reserve as both a Biosphere Reserve *and* a World Heritage Site. The forest contains over 100 species of birds, along with elk, wild boars and wolves. Its major drawcard is the magnificent European bison, which was once extinct outside zoos, but has been successfully reintroduced to its ancient home.

◉ Sights & Activities

The logical visitor base is the charming village of **Białowieża**. The main road to Białowieża from Hajnówka leads to the southern end of Palace Park (the former location of the Russian tsar's hunting lodge), then skirts around the park to become the village's main street, ul Waszkiewicza.

European Bison Reserve   ZOO

(Rezerwat Żubrów; adult/concession 6/3zł; ⊘9am-5pm May-Sep, 8am-4pm Tue-Sun Oct-Apr) An open-plan zoo containing many mighty bison, as well as wolves, strange horse-like tarpans and mammoth żubrońs (hybrids of bison and cows). Entrance to the reserve is just north of the Hajnówka–Białowieża road, about 4.5km west of the PTTK office – look for the signs along the *żebra żubra* (bison's rib) trail, or follow the green or yellow marked trails. Alternatively, catch a local bus to the stop at the main road turn-off (3zł) and walk a kilometre to the entrance, but ask the driver first if the bus is taking a route past the reserve.

Strict Nature Reserve   FOREST

(adult/concession 6/3zł; ⊘9am-5pm) The main attraction is the Strict Nature Reserve, whose boundaires begin about 1km north of Palace Park. It can only be visited on a three-hour tour with a licensed guide along an 8km trail (165zł for an English-speaking guide). Guides (in many languages) can be arranged at the PTTK office or any travel agency in the village. Note that the reserve does close sometimes due to inclement weather.

Although this is the only chance to encounter bison in their natural habitat, the creatures can be shy of visitors and you may not see them at all; visit the European Bison Reserve if you want a guarantee of spotting *żubry*. Even without bison for company, however, being immersed in one of Europe's last remnants of primeval forest is a special experience.

A comfortable way to visit the nature reserve is by horse-drawn cart (three hours), which costs 150zł in addition to guide and entry fees and holds four people. Otherwise, it may be possible (with permission from the PTTK office) to visit the reserve by bicycle (with a guide). A shop near the PTTK office hires out bikes (35zł per day), as do several hotels and pensions.

Palace Park   PARK

(⊘daylight hr) The elegant Palace Park is only accessible on foot, bicycle or horse-drawn cart across the bridge from the PTTK office. English-language signage explains its natural and historic features of interest.

Natural History Museum   MUSEUM

(adult/concession 12/6zł; ⊘9am-4.30pm) Within Palace Park is this excellent museum, with displays on local flora and fauna. There's a viewing tower (6zł), which you can climb for leafy vistas.

🛏 Sleeping & Eating

There are plenty of homes along the road from Hajnówka to Białowieża offering private rooms for about 40/70zł for singles/doubles.

Pokoje Gościnne BPN   HOTEL €

TOP CHOICE (☑85 682 9729; hotel@bpn.com.pl; s/d 120/130zł) Sparkling three-star option slap bang in the middle of Palace Park, with a good restaurant next door. Even the tsar would have been happy to lay his head here as an alternative to his old hunting lodge. Breakfast is 20zł extra.

Hotel Żubrówka   HOTEL €€€

(☑85 681 2303; www.hotel-zubrowka.pl; ul Olgi Gabiec 6; s/d from 380/420zł; ✷) Just across the way from the PTTK office, this is the town's best hotel. It's eccentrically decorated with animal hides, a working miniature water wheel, and pseudo cave drawings along the corridors. Rooms are predictably clean and comfortable, and there's a cafe, restaurant and nightclub on the premises, along with a sumptuous new swimming pool and wellness centre.

Paprotka Youth Hostel   HOSTEL €

(☑85 681 2560; www.paprotka.com.pl; ul Waszkiewicza 6; dm from 30zł, s/d 50/102zł) One of the best in the region. The rooms are light and spruce, with high ceilings and potted plants; the bathrooms are clean, and the kitchen is excellent. There's a washing machine as well.

Pension Gawra   HOTEL €

(☑85 681 2804; www.gawra.bialowieza.com; ul Polecha 2; d/tr from 130/150zł) A quiet, homey place with large rooms lined with timber in a hunting lodge-style, overlooking a pretty garden just behind the Hotel Żubrówka. The doubles with bathrooms are much more spacious than those without.

Pensjonacik Unikat   HOTEL €

(☑85 681 2774; www.unikat.bialowieza.com; ul Waszkiewicza 39; s/d 110/140zł) A bit too fond

after midnight. It also has a more civilised courtyard, open from 2pm.

Rdza
CLUB
(Map p626; www.rdza.pl; ul Bracka 3/5; ⊙7pm-late) This basement club attracts some of Kraków's more sophisticated clubbers, with its Polish house music bouncing off exposed brick walls and comfy sofas. Guest DJs start spinning at 9pm.

Performing Arts

Stary Teatr
THEATRE
(Map p626; ☎12 422 4040; www.stary-teatr.pl, in Polish; ul Jagiellońska 5) This accomplished theatre company offers quality productions. To overcome the language barrier, pick a Shakespeare play you know well from the repertoire, and take in the distinctive Polish interpretation.

Teatr im Słowackiego
OPERA/THEATRE
(Map p626; ☎12 422 4022; www.slowacki.krakow.pl, in Polish; Plac Św Ducha 1) This grand place, built in 1893, focuses on Polish classics, large theatrical productions and opera.

Filharmonia Krakowska
CLASSICAL MUSIC
(Map p626; ☎12 422 9477; www.filharmonia.krakow.pl; ul Zwierzyniecka 1) Hosts one of the best orchestras in the country; concerts are usually held on Friday and Saturday.

Cinemas

Two convenient cinemas are **Kino Sztuka** (Map p626; cnr ul Św Tomasza & ul Św Jana) and **Kino Pod Baranami** (Map p626; Rynek Główny 27), the latter located within a courtyard off the Main Market Sq.

Shopping

The place to start (or perhaps end) your Kraków shopping is at the large **souvenir market** within the Cloth Hall, selling everything from fine amber jewellery to tacky plush dragons.

Galeria Plakatu
ART
(Map p626; ⊙012 421 2640; www.cracowpostergallery.com; ul Stolarska 8; ⊙11am-6pm Mon-Fri, 11am-2pm Sat) Fascinating examples of Polish poster art can be purchased here.

EMPiK
BOOKS
(Map p626; Rynek Główny 5; ⊙9am-10pm) For foreign newspapers, magazines, novels and maps.

Sklep Podróżnika
BOOKS
(Map p626; ul Jagiellońska 6; ⊙11am-7pm Mon-Fri, 10am-3pm Sat) For regional and city maps, as well as Lonely Planet titles.

Jarden Jewish Bookshop
BOOKS
(Map p629; ul Szeroka 2) Located in Kazimierz; is well stocked with titles on Poland's Jewish heritage.

❶ Information

Discount Cards
Kraków Tourist Card (www.krakowcard.com; 2/3 days 50/65zł) Available from tourist offices, the card includes travel on public transport and entry to many museums.

Internet Access
Greenland Internet Cafe (ul Floriańska 30; per hr 4zł; ⊙9am-midnight)

Klub Garinet (ul Floriańska 18; per hr 4zł; ⊙9am-10pm)

Money
Kantors and ATMs can be found all over the city centre. It's worth noting, however, that many *kantors* close on Sunday, and some located near Rynek Główny and the main train station offer terrible exchange rates – check around before proffering your cash. There are also exchange facilities at the airport, with even less attractive rates.

Post
Main post office (Map p626; ul Westerplatte 20; ⊙8am-8pm Mon-Fri, 8am-2pm Sat)

Tourist Information
Two free magazines, *Welcome to Cracow & Małopolska* and *Visitor: Kraków & Zakopane* are available at upmarket hotels. The *Kraków in Your Pocket* booklet (5zł) is also very useful, packed with entertaining reviews of local sights and eateries.

Tourist office ul Św Jana (Map p626; ☎12 421 7787; www.karnet.krakow.pl; ul Św Jana 2; ⊙10am-6pm); Cloth Hall (Map p626; ☎12 433 7310; Rynek Główny 1; ⊙9am-7pm May-Sep, 9am-5pm Oct-Apr); northeastern Old Town (Map p626; ☎12 432 0110; ul Szpitalna 25; ⊙9am-7pm May-Sep, 9am-5pm Oct-Apr); southern Old Town (Map p629; ☎12 616 1886; Plac Wszystkich Świętych 2; ⊙9am-7pm May-Sep, 9am-5pm Oct-Apr); Wawel Hill (Map p629; ul Powiśle 11; ⊙9am-7pm); Kazimierz (Map p629; ☎12 422 0471; ul Józefa 7; ⊙9am-5pm); Nowa Huta (☎12 643 0303; Os Słoneczne 16; ⊙10am-2pm Tue-Sat); airport (☎12 285 5431; John Paul II International airport, Balice; ⊙9am-7pm) Helpful city-run service; the office at ul Św Jana 2 specialises in cultural events.

❶ Getting There & Away

For information on travelling from Kraków to Zakopane or Oświęcim (for Auschwitz-Birkenau), refer to the relevant destination sections.

Air

The **John Paul II International airport** (www.
lotnisko-balice.pl) is more often called Balice airport, after the suburb in which it's located, about
15km west of the Old Town. The airport terminal
hosts several car-hire desks, along with currency
exchanges offering unappealing rates. To get to
the Old Town by public transport, step aboard the
free shuttle bus to the nearby train station, from
the sign marked 'PKP' outside the airport. Buy
tickets on board the train from a vending machine
(7zł) or the conductor (8zł) for the 17-minute train
journey to Kraków Główny station.

LOT flies between Kraków and Warsaw several
times a day, and offers direct connections from
Kraków to Frankfurt, Munich, Paris and Vienna,
with flights to New York and Chicago during the
summer months. Bookings for all flights can
be made at the **LOT office** (☑ 0801 703 703; ul
Basztowa 15). There are also domestic flights
via Jet Air to Poznań (three weekly) and Gdańsk
(twice weekly).

A range of other airlines, including several
budget operators, connect Kraków to cities in
Europe, including an array of destinations across
Britain and Ireland. There are direct flights daily
to and from London via easyJet and Ryanair. Dublin is serviced daily by Ryanair and Aer Lingus.

Bus

If you've been travelling by bus elsewhere in
Poland, Kraków's modern main **bus terminal** (ul
Bosacka 18) will seem like a palace compared to
the usual facility. It's located on the other side of
the main train station from the Old Town. Taking
the train will generally be quicker, but buses of
interest to visitors run to Lublin (40zł, five hours,
six daily), Zamość (44zł, seven hours, four daily)
and Cieszyn on the Czech border (18zł, three
hours, seven daily).

Train

The lovely old **Kraków Główny train station**
(Plac Dworcowy), on the northeastern outskirts
of the Old Town, handles all international trains
and most domestic rail services. The railway
platforms are about 150m north of the station
building, and you can also reach them from the
adjacent Galeria Krakowska shopping mall.

Each day from Kraków, 20 trains head to
Warsaw, most of them fast Express InterCity
services (110zł, 2½ hours). There are also 17
trains daily to Wrocław (48zł, 4¾ hours), 10 to
Częstochowa (33zł, 2¼ hours), six to Łódź (40zł,
4½ hours), 14 to Poznań (56zł, 7½ hours), eight
to Toruń (58zł, eight hours), nine to Zakopane
(35zł, 3½ hours), 14 to Przemyśl (46zł, four
hours) and two to Lublin (53zł, 4¾ hours). The
10 services to Gdynia via Gdańsk are evenly split
between five TLK trains (68zł, 13 hours) and five
much faster Express InterCity services (129zł,
nine hours).

Oświęcim

POP 40,800

Few place names have more impact than
Auschwitz, which is seared into public consciousness as the location of history's most
extensive experiment in genocide. Every
year hundreds of thousands visit Oświęcim
(osh-*fyen*-cheem), the Polish town that give
its German name to the infamous Nazi
death camp, to learn about its history and to
pay respect to the dead.

Established within disused army barracks
in 1940, Auschwitz was initially designed to
hold Polish prisoners, but was expanded into
the largest centre for the extermination of
European Jews. Two more camps were subsequently established: Birkenau (Brzezinka,
also known as Auschwitz II), 3km west of
Auschwitz; and Monowitz (Monowice), several kilometres west of Oświęcim. In the course
of their operation, between one and 1.5 million people were murdered in these death
factories – about 90% of these were Jews.

Auschwitz   MEMORIAL

Auschwitz was only partially destroyed by
the fleeing Nazis, so many of the original
buildings remain as a bleak document of
the camp's history. A dozen of the 30 surviving prison blocks house sections of the
State Museum Auschwitz-Birkenau (☑ 33
844 8100; www.auschwitz.org.pl; admission free;
⊙ 8am-7pm Jun-Aug, 8am-6pm May & Sep, 8am-
5pm Apr & Oct, 8am-4pm Mar & Nov, 8am-3pm
Dec-Feb). In 2007, Unesco decided to adopt
the wordy title Auschwitz Birkenau – German Nazi Concentration and Extermination
Camp (1940–45) for its World Heritage listing of the site, in order to make it clear that
conquered Poland had taken no part in Auschwitz's establishment or operation.

About every half-hour, the cinema in the
visitors centre at the entrance shows a
15-minute documentary **film** (adult/conces-
sion 3.50/2.50zł) about the liberation of the
camp by Soviet troops on 27 January 1945.
It's shown in several languages throughout
the day; check the schedule at the information desk as soon as you arrive. The film is not
recommended for children under 14 years
old. The visitors centre also has a cafeteria,
bookshops, a *kantor* and a left-luggage room.

Some basic explanations in Polish, English
and Hebrew are provided on-site, but you'll
understand more if you buy the small *Auschwitz Birkenau Guide Book* (translated into
about 15 languages) from the visitors centre.

Between May and October it's compulsory to join a tour if you arrive between 10am and 3pm. English-language **tours** (adult/concession 39/30zł, 3½ hours) of Auschwitz and Birkenau leave at 10am, 11am, 1pm and 3pm daily, and can also occur when a group of 10 people can be formed. Tours in a range of other languages can be arranged in advance.

Auschwitz is an easy day trip from Kraków. However, if you want to stay overnight, **Centre for Dialogue and Prayer** (☑33 843 1000; www.centrum-dialogu.oswiecim. pl; ul Kolbego 1; campsite per person 25zł, s/d 104/208zł) is 700m southwest of Auschwitz. It's comfortable and quiet, and the price includes breakfast. Most rooms have en suites, and full board is also offered.

| FREE | **Birkenau** | MEMORIAL |

(⊘8am-7pm Jun-Aug, 8am-6pm May & Sep, 8am-5pm Apr & Oct, 8am-4pm Mar & Nov, 8am-3pm Dec-Feb) Birkenau, otherwise known as Auschwitz II, was where the murder of huge numbers of Jews took place. This vast (175 hectares), purpose-built and grimly efficient camp had more than 300 prison barracks and four huge gas chambers complete with crematoria. Each chamber held 2000 people and electric lifts raised the bodies to the ovens. The camp could hold 200,000 inmates.

Although much of the camp was destroyed by retreating Nazis, the size of the place, fenced off with barbed wire stretching almost as far as the eye can see, provides some idea of the scale of this heinous crime. The viewing platform above the entrance provides further perspective. In some ways, Birkenau is even more shocking than Auschwitz and there are fewer tourists. There is no compulsory tour requirement at Birkenau in the warmer months.

❶ Getting There & Away

Auschwitz-Birkenau is usually visited as a day trip from Kraków.

From Kraków Główny train station, 12 mostly slow trains go to Oświęcim (13zł, 1½ hours) each day, though more depart from Kraków Płaszów train station.

Far more convenient are the approximately hourly buses each day to Oświęcim (11zł, 1½ hours) departing from the bus station in Kraków, which either pass by or terminate at the museum. The return bus timetable to Kraków is displayed at the Birkenau visitors centre. There are also numerous minibuses to Oświęcim from the minibus stands off ul Pawia, next to Galeria Krakowska.

Every half-hour from 11.30am to 4.30pm between 15 April and 31 October, buses shuttle passengers between the visitor centres at Auschwitz and Birkenau (buses run to 5.30pm in May and September, and until 6.30pm June to August). Otherwise, follow the signs for an easy walk (3km) or take a taxi. Auschwitz is also linked to the town's train station by local buses every 30 to 40 minutes.

Most travel agencies in Kraków offer organised tours of Auschwitz (including Birkenau), from 90zł to 120zł per person. Check with the operator for exactly how much time the tour allows you at each site, as some run to a very tight schedule.

Lublin

POP 350,000

If the crowds are becoming too much in Kraków, you could do worse than jump on a train to Lublin. This attractive eastern city has many of the same attractions – a beautiful Old Town, a castle, and good bars and restaurants – but is less visited by international tourists.

Though today the city's beautifully preserved Old Town is a peaceful blend of Gothic, Renaissance and baroque architecture, Lublin has an eventful past. In 1569 the Lublin Union was signed here, uniting Poland and Lithuania; and at the end of WWII, the Soviet Union set up a communist government in Lublin, prior to the liberation of Warsaw.

◉ Sights & Activities

OLD TOWN

Lublin Castle   CASTLE

This substantial fortification, standing on a hill at the northeastern edge of the Old Town, has a dark history. It was built in the 14th century, then rebuilt as a prison in the 1820s. During the Nazi occupation, more than 100,000 people passed through its doors before being deported to the death camps. Its major occupant is now the **Lublin Museum** (www.zamek-lublin.pl; ul Zamkowa 9; adult/concession 7.50/5.50zł; ⊘9am-4pm Wed-Sat, 9am-5pm Sun). On display are paintings, silverware, porcelain, woodcarvings and weaponry, mostly labelled in Polish. Check out the alleged 'devil's paw-print' on the 17th-century table in the foyer, linked to a local legend.

At the eastern end of the castle is the gorgeous 14th-century **Chapel of the Holy Trinity** (adult/concession 7.50/5.50zł; ⊘9am-4pm Tue-Sat, 9am-5pm Sun), accessible via the museum. Its interior is covered with polychrome Russo-Byzantine frescos painted in 1418 – possibly the finest medieval wall paintings in Poland.

POLAND MAŁOPOLSKA

Lublin

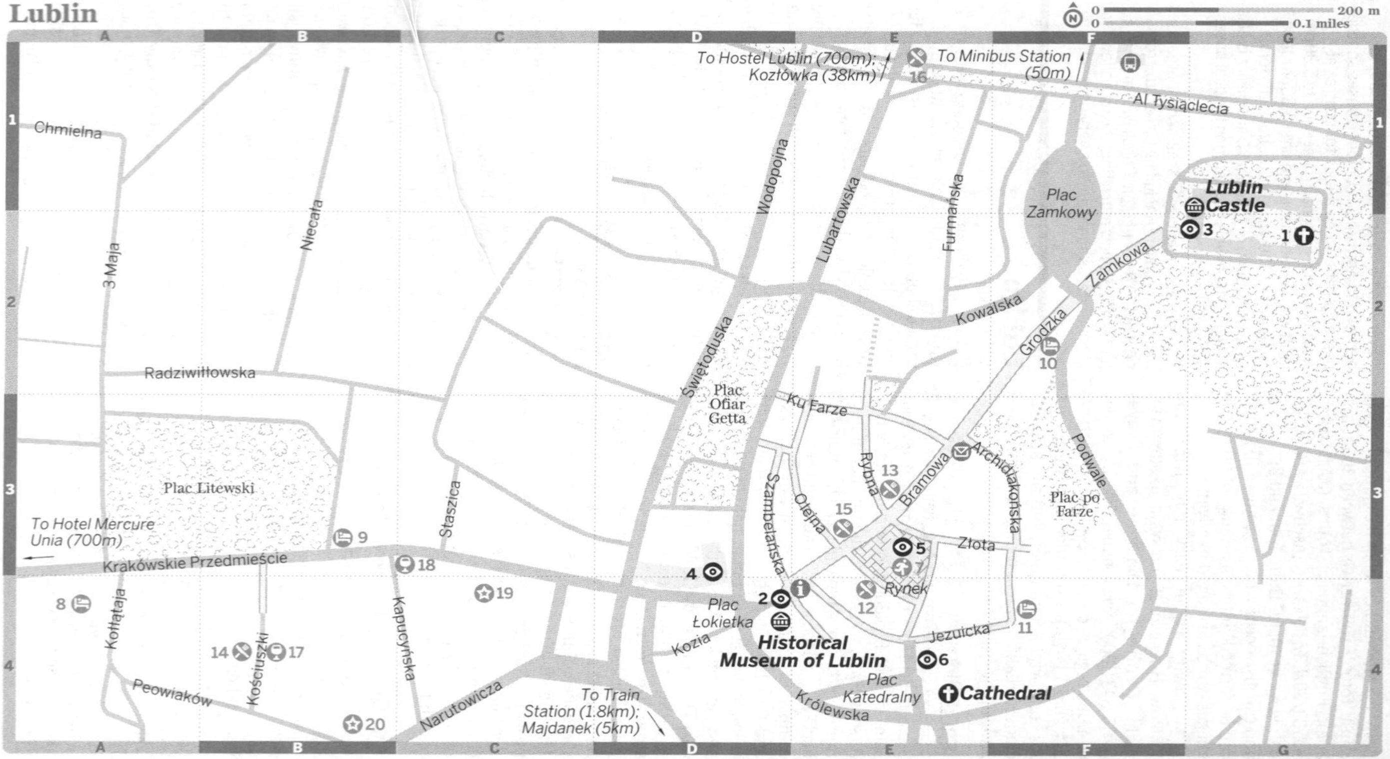

N

200 m
0.1 miles

Lublin Castle

1

3

Al Tysiąclecia

To Minibus Station
(50m)

To Hostel Lublin (700m);
Kozłówka (38km)

16

Plac
Zamkowy

Zamkowa

Furmańska

Kowalska

Grodzka

Archidiakońska

Podwale

Plac po
Farze

10

Lubartowska

Złota

11

Jezuicka

Bramowa

Rybna

Rybna

5

Rynek

7

Jezuicka

6

Cathedral

13

12

Wodopojna

Świętoduska

Ku Farze

15

Olejna

Szambelańska

**Historical
Museum of Lublin**

2

Plac
Katedralny

Plac
Królewska

Plac
Ofiar
Getta

Plac
Łokietka

Kozia

4

Namiwnicza

To Train
Station (1.8km);
Majdanek (5km)

Staszica

19

Niecała

Kapucyńska

18

9

20

Radziwiłłowska

Plac Litewski

Krakówskie Przedmieście

Kościuszki

14

17

Peowiaków

3 Maja

Kołłątaja

To Hotel Mercure
Unia (700m)

8

Chmielna

Underground Route   WALKING TOUR
(Rynek 1; adult/concession 10/7zł; ⊗10am-4pm)
This 280m trail winds its way through connected cellars beneath the Old Town, with historical exhibitions along the way. Entry is from the neoclassical **Old Town Hall** in the centre of the pleasant Market Sq (Rynek) at approximately two-hourly intervals; check with the tourist office for exact times.

Historical Museum of Lublin   MUSEUM
(Plac Łokietka 3; adult/concession 3.50/2.50zł; ⊗9am-4pm Wed-Sat, 9am-5pm Sun) Situated within the 14th-century **Kraków Gate**, a remnant of medieval fortifications, this institution displays documents and photos relating to the city's history. Daily at noon, a bugler plays a special tune atop the **New Town Hall** opposite the gate (if you like bugling, don't miss the annual National Bugle Contest here on 15 August).

Cathedral   CHURCH
(Plac Katedralny; ⊗dawn-dusk) Located near the Trinitarian Tower is this 16th-century place of worship and its impressive baroque frescos. The painting of the Virgin Mary is said to have shed tears in 1949, so it's a source of pride and reverence for local believers.

Archdiocesan Museum   MUSEUM
(Plac Katedralny; adult/concession 7/5zł; ⊗10am-2.30pm Tue-Fri. 10am-5pm Sat & Sun) This museum of sacred art also offers expan-

sive views of the Old Town, as it's housed within the lofty Trinitarian Tower (1819).

MAJDANEK

FREE **Majdanek State Museum** MEMORIAL
(www.majdanek.pl; ⊗9am-4pm) About 4km southeast of the Old Town is one of the largest Nazi death camps, where some 235,000 people, including more than 100,000 Jews, were massacred. Barracks, guard towers and barbed wire fences remain in place; even more chilling are the crematorium and gas chambers.

A short explanatory **film** (admission 3zł) can be seen in the visitors centre, from which a marked 'visiting route' (5km) passes the massive stone **Monument of Fight & Martyrdom** and finishes at the domed **mausoleum** holding the ashes of many victims.

Trolleybus 156 and bus 23 depart from a stop near the Bank Pekao on ul Królewska, and travel to the entrance of Majdanek.

🛏 Sleeping

TOP **Grand Hotel Lublinianka** HOTEL €€€
CHOICE (☎81 446 6100; www.lublinianka.com; ul Krakowskie Przedmieście 56; s/d from 300/360zł; ❄) The swankiest place in town includes free use of a sauna and spa. The cheaper (3rd-floor) rooms have skylights but are relatively small, while 'standard' rooms are spacious and have glitzy marble bathrooms.

CZĘSTOCHOWA

This pilgrimage destination 114km northwest of Kraków is dominated by the graceful **Paulite Monastery of Jasna Góra** (☎34 365 3888; www.jasnagora.pl; admission free; ⊙dawn-dusk), sited atop a hill in the centre of town. Founded in 1382, it's the home of the *Black Madonna*, a portrait claimed to be the source of miracles. In recognition of these feats, in 1717 the painting was crowned Queen of Poland. It's well worth a day trip to the monastery to check out its three museums, and of course to meet the *Black Madonna*.

Częstochowa has regular train connections with Kraków, Łódź, Warsaw, Zakopane and Wrocław. For more details, browse Lonely Planet's *Poland* country guide, visit www. info.czestochowa.pl, or step into the Częstochowa **tourist office** (☎34 368 2250; Al Najświętszej Marii Panny 65; ⊙9am-5pm Mon-Sat).

One room is designed for wheelchair access, and there's a good restaurant on-site.

Hotel Waksman
HOTEL €€

(☎81 532 5454; www.waksman.pl; ul Grodzka 19; s/d 200/220zł) This small gem is excellent value for its quality and location. Just within the Grodzka Gate in the Old Town, it offers elegantly appointed rooms with different colour schemes, and an attractive lounge with tapestries on the walls.

Hostel Lublin
HOSTEL €

(☎79 288 8632; www.hostellublin.pl; ul Lubartowska 60; dm 40zł, r 95zł) The city's first modern hostel is situated within a former apartment building and contains neat, tidy dorms, a basic kitchenette and a cosy lounge. Take trolleybus 156 or 160 north from the Old Town.

Hotel Europa
HOTEL €€€

(☎81 535 0303; www.hoteleuropa.pl; ul Krakowskie Przedmieście 29; s/d from 380/420zł, ste 1150zł; ❆) Central hotel offering smart, thoroughly modernised rooms with high ceilings and elegant furniture, in a restored 19th-century building. Two rooms are designed for wheelchair access, and there's a nightclub downstairs.

Hotel Mercure Unia
HOTEL €€

(☎81 533 2061; www.orbis.pl; Al Racławickie 12; s/d from 275/315zł; ❆) This business hotel is big, central and convenient, and offers all modern conveniences, though it's lacking in atmosphere. There's a gym, bar and restaurant on the premises. Breakfast is 35zł extra per person.

Dom Nauczyciela
HOTEL €€

(☎81 533 8285; www.lublin.oupis.pl/hotel; ul Akademicka 4; s/d from 134/162zł) Value-packed accommodation in the heart of the university quarter, west of the Old Town. Rooms have old-fashioned decor but are clean, with good

bathrooms. Some rooms have views over the city, and there are bars and eateries nearby.

Youth Hostel
HOSTEL €

(☎81 533 0628; ul Długosza 6; dm 32zł, d 72zł) Modest but well run. Simple rooms are decorated with potted plants, and there's a kitchen and a pleasant courtyard area with seating. It's 100m up a poorly marked lane off ul Długosza; take the second left turning when walking down from ul Racławickie.

Camping Marina
CAMPING €

(☎81 745 6910; www.graf-marina.pl, in Polish; ul Krężnicka 6; per tent 16zł, cabins from 70zł) Lublin's only camping ground is serenely located on a lake about 8km south of the Old Town. To get there, take bus 25 from the stop on the main road east of the train station.

Lubelskie Samorządowe Centrum Doskonalenia Nauczycieli
HOSTEL €

(☎81 532 9241; www.lscdn.pl; ul Dominikańska 5; dm 52zł) This place is in an atmospheric Old Town building, and has rooms with between two and five beds. It's good value and often busy, so book ahead.

✗ Eating & Drinking

There's a supermarket located near the bus terminal.

TOP CHOICE Magia
INTERNATIONAL €€

(☎81 532 3041; ul Grodzka 2; mains 20-65zł; ⊙noon-midnight) Charming, relaxed restaurant with numerous vibes to choose from within its warren of dining rooms and large outdoor courtyard. Dishes range from tiger prawns and snails to deer and duck, with every sort of pizza, pasta and pancake between.

Oregano
MEDITERRANEAN €€

(☎81 442 5530; ul Kościuszki 7; mains 19-50zł; ⊙noon-11pm) This pleasant, upmarket restaurant specialises in Mediterranean cuisine, featuring pasta, paella and seafood. There's a well-organised English menu, and the chefs aren't scared of spice.

Biesy POLISH €€
(☎81 532 1648; Rynek 18; mains 12-47zł) Atmospheric cellar eatery with multiple nooks and crannies. Its tasty speciality is large pizza-like baked tarts with a variety of toppings.

Pizzeria Acerna PIZZA €
(☎81 532 4531; Rynek 2; mains 10-35zł) The Acerna is a popular eatery on the main square, serving cheap pizzas and pasta in dazzling variations.

Tamara Café CAFE-BAR €€
(ul Krakówskie Przedmieście 36) This cafe-bar takes its *vino* very seriously. Whether you're a cultured wine connoisseur, a courtyard cocktail fancier, or a hungry tippler who wants some vodka with (or in) your meal, pull up a chair.

Caram'bola Pub PUB €
(ul Kościuszki 8; ☺10am-late Mon-Fri, noon-late Sat & Sun) This pub is a pleasant place for a beer or two. It also serves inexpensive bar food, including Lublin's ubiquitous pizzas.

☆ Entertainment

Club Koyot CLUB
(ul Krakowskie Przedmieście 26; ☺5pm-late Wed-Sun) This club is concealed in a courtyard and features live music or DJs most nights.

Kino Bajka CINEMA
(ul Radziszewskiego 8) If you'd prefer a movie to music, this art house cinema is located in the university district.

Teatr im Osterwy THEATRE
(☎81 532 4244; ul Narutowicza 17) Lublin's main theatrical venue, which features mostly classical plays.

❶ Information

Main post office (ul Krakowskie Przedmieście 50; ☺24hr)

Net Box (ul Krakowskie Przedmieście 52; per hr 5zł; ☺9am-9pm Mon-Fri, 10am-8pm Sat, 2-6pm Sun) Internet access in a courtyard off the street.

Tourist office (☎81 532 4412; www.loit.lublin. pl; ul Jezuicka 1/3; ☺9am-7pm Mon-Fri, 10am-5pm Sat & 10am-4pm Sun May-Sep, 9am-5pm Mon-Fri & 10am-4pm Sat Oct-Apr) Lots of free brochures, including the city walking-route guide *Tourist Routes of Lublin*, which includes a chapter outlining the *Heritage Trail of the Lublin Jews*.

❶ Getting There & Away

From the **bus terminal** (Al Tysiąclecia), opposite the castle, buses head to Białystok (43zł, 5½ hours, five daily), Kraków (42zł, 5½ hours, five daily), Olsztyn (48zł, 8¾ hours, three daily), Przemyśl (32zł, four hours, four daily), Zakopane (56zł, nine hours, four daily), Zamość (16zł, two hours, hourly) and various destinations within Warsaw (30zł, three hours, at least hourly). Private minibuses also head to various destinations, including Zamość (12zł, 1½ hours, half-hourly), from the **minibus station** north of the bus terminal.

The **train station** (Plac Dworcowy) is 1.2km south of the Old Town and accessible by bus 1 or 13. When leaving the station, look for the bus stop on ul Gazowa, to the left of the station entrance as you walk down the steps (not the trolleybus stop). Alternatively, trolleybus 150 from the station is handy for the university area and the youth hostel. Ten trains go daily to Warsaw (37zł, 2½ hours), two travel to Kraków (53zł, 4¾ hours) and one heads to Przemyśl (44zł, four hours).

Around Lublin

The hamlet of **Kozłówka** (koz-*woof*-kah), 38km north of Lublin, is famous for its sumptuous late-baroque **palace**, which houses the **Museum of the Zamoyski Family** (☎81 852 8310; www.muzeumzamoyskich.pl; adult/concession for entry to all sections 24/12zł; ☺10am-4pm Tue-Sun mid-Mar–Oct, 10am-3pm Nov–mid-Dec). The collection in the **main palace** (adult/concession 16/8zł) features original furnishings, ceramic stoves and a large collection of paintings. You must see this area on a Polish-language guided tour, whose starting time will be noted at the top of your ticket. An English-language tour (best organised in advance) costs an extra 52zł. The entrance fee to this section also includes entry to the 1907 **chapel**.

Even more interesting is the incongruous **Socialist-Realist Art Gallery** (adult/concession 6/3zł), decked out with numerous portraits and statues of communist-era leaders. It also features many idealised scenes of farmers and factory workers striving for socialism. These stirring works were originally tucked away here in embarrassment by the communist authorities, after Stalin's death led to the decline of this all-encompassing artistic style.

From Lublin, there's one morning bus that passes through Kozłówka on the way to Puławy, departing at 8.30am (8zł, 50 minutes). Alternatively, you can catch one of the frequent buses from Lublin to Lubartów, then take one of the regular minibuses that pass Kozłówka from there.

A bus heads back to Lublin from Kozłówka around 3.30pm, and another around 6.30pm. Double-check bus timetables before you visit the museum so you can plan your departure accordingly. If you get stuck, take a minibus to Lubartów, from where there is regular transport back to Lublin.

Zamość

POP 66,500

While most Polish cities' attractions centre on their medieval heart, Zamość (*zah-moshch*) is pure Renaissance. The streets of its attractive, compact Old Town are perfect for exploring, and its central market square is a symmetrical delight, reflecting the city's glorious 16th-century origins.

Zamość was founded in 1580 by Jan Zamoyski, the nation's chancellor and commander-in-chief. Designed by an Italian architect, the city was intended as a prosperous trading settlement between Western Europe and the region stretching east to the Black Sea.

In WWII, the Nazis earmarked the city for German resettlement, sending the Polish population into slave labour or concentration camps. Most of the Jewish population of the renamed 'Himmlerstadt' was exterminated.

The splendid architecture of Zamość's Old Town was added to Unesco's World Heritage list in 1992. Since 2004, EU funds have been gradually restoring Zamość to its former glory.

◉ Sights

Great Market Square　　HISTORIC SQUARE
The Great Market Sq (Rynek Wielki) is the heart of Zamość's attractive Old Town. This impressive Italianate Renaissance square (exactly 100m by 100m) is dominated by the lofty, pink **town hall** and surrounded by colourful arcaded burghers' houses, many adorned with elegant designs. The **Museum of Zamość** (ul Ormiańska 30; adult/concession 6/3zł; ⊘9am-4pm Tue-Sun) is based in two of the loveliest buildings on the Rynek and houses interesting exhibits, including paintings, folk costumes, archaeological finds and a scale model of the 16th-century town.

Cathedral　　CHURCH
(ul Kolegiacka; ⊘dawn-dusk) Southwest of the square, this mighty 16th-century holy place hosts the tomb of Jan Zamoyski in the chapel to the right of the high altar. The **bell tower** (admission 2zł; ⊘May-Sep) can be climbed for good views of the historic cathedral bells and the Old Town. In the grounds,

the **Sacral Museum** (admission 2zł; ⊘10am-4pm Mon-Fri & 10am-1pm Sat & Sun May-Sep, 10am-1pm Sun Oct-Apr) features various robes, paintings and sculptures.

Synagogue　　SYNAGOGUE
(ul Pereca 14) Before WWII, Jewish citizens accounted for 45% of the town's population (of 12,000) and most lived in the area north and east of the palace. The most significant Jewish architectural relic is this Renaissance place of worship, built in the early 17th century. At the time of research it was under renovation, being converted into a cultural centre and Jewish museum that should be open by the time you read this.

Bastion　　FORTIFICATION
(ul Łukasińskiego) On the eastern edge of the Old Town is the best surviving bastion from the original city walls. You can take a **tour** (adult/child 5/3zł; ⊘8am-6pm) through the renovated fortifications, checking out displays of military gear and views over the city. Tickets must be bought from the tourist office in Great Market Sq, and the tour only runs when a minimum of 10 people have gathered.

Zamoyski Palace　　PALACE
This former palace (closed to the public) lost much of its character when it was converted into a military hospital in the 1830s. To the north of the palace stretches a beautifully landscaped **park**. To its south is the **Arsenal Museum** (ul Zamkowa 2; adult/concession 6/3zł; ⊘9am-4pm Tue-Sun), housing an unremarkable collection of cannons, swords and firearms.

⊨ Sleeping

Hotel Zamojski　　HOTEL €€€
(☑84 639 2516; www.orbis.pl; ul Kołłątaja 2/4/6; s/d 237/355zł; ❄) The best joint in town is situated within three connected old houses, just off the square. The rooms are modern and tastefully furnished, and there's a good on-site restaurant and cocktail bar, along with a fitness centre.

Hotel Arkadia　　HOTEL €€
(☑84 638 6507; www.arkadia.zamosc.pl; Rynek Wielki 9; s/d from 140/160zł) With just nine rooms, this compact place offers a pool table and restaurant in addition to lodgings. It's charming but shabby, though its location right on the market square is hard to beat.

Pokoje Gościnne OSiR　　HOSTEL €
(☑84 677 5460; ul Królowej Jadwigi 8; dm 24zł; s/d/tr 90/125/150zł) Located in a sprawling sport-

POLAND MAŁOPOLSKA

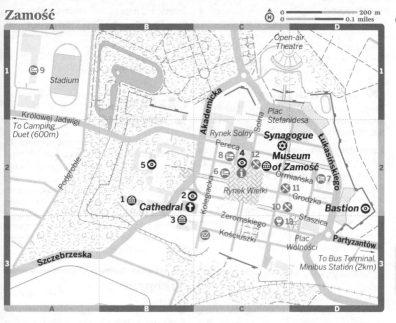

Zamość

ing complex, a 15-minute walk west of the Old Town, and packed with old trophies and students playing table tennis. Rooms are plainly furnished, clean and comfortable, although the bathrooms fall short of the ideal.

Hotel Jubilat HOTEL **€€**
(☏84 638 6401; www.hoteljubilat.pl; ul Kardynała Wyszyńskiego 52; s/d from 136/177zł) An acceptable, if slightly drab, place to spend the night, right beside the bus station. It couldn't be handier for late arrivals or early departures, but it's a long way from anywhere else. It has a restaurant and fitness club.

Hotel Renesans HOTEL **€€**
(☏84 639 2001; www.hotelrenesans.pl; ul Grecka 6; s/d from 156/222zł) It's ironic that a hotel named after the Renaissance is housed in the Old Town's ugliest building. However, it's central and the rooms are surprisingly modern and pleasant.

Camping Duet CAMPING GROUND **€**
(☏84 639 2499; ul Królowej Jadwigi 14; s/d 75/90zł; ❄) West of the Old Town, Camping Duet has neat bungalows, tennis courts, a restaurant, sauna and Jacuzzi. Larger bungalows sleep up to six.

Youth Hostel HOSTEL €
(☑84 638 9500; ul Zamoyskiego 4; dm 15zł; ☺Jul-Aug) You can find this hostel in a school building 1.5km east of the Old Town, not far from the bus terminal. It's basic but functional and very cheap.

Eating & Drinking

For self-caterers, there's the handy **Lux mini-supermarket** (ul Grodzka 16; ☺7am-8pm Mon-Sat, 8am-6pm Sun) near the Rynek.

Restauracja Muzealna POLISH €€
(☑84 638 7300; ul Ormiańska 30; mains 14-27zł; ☺11am-10pm Mon-Sat, 11am-9pm Sun) Subterranean restaurant in an atmospheric cellar below the main square, bedecked with ornate timber furniture and portraits of nobles. It serves a better class of Polish cuisine at reasonable prices, and has a well-stocked bar.

Bar Asia POLISH €
(ul Staszica 10; mains 5-9zł; ☺8am-5pm Mon-Fri, 8am-4pm Sat) For hungry but broke travellers, this old-style *bar mleczny* is ideal. It serves cheap and tasty Polish food, including several variants of *pierogi* (dumplings), in a minimally decorated space.

Corner Pub PUB
(ul Żeromskiego 6) This cosy Irish-style pub is a good place to have a drink. It has comfy booths and the walls are ornamented with bric-a-brac such as antique clocks, swords and model cars.

ⓘ Information

K@fejka Internetowa (Rynek Wielki 10; per hr 3zł; ☺9am-5pm Mon-Fri, 10am-2pm Sat) Internet access.
Main post office (ul Kościuszki)
Tourist office (☑84 639 2292; Rynek Wielki 13; ☺8am-6pm Mon-Fri & 10am-5pm Sat & Sun May-Sep, 8am-5pm Mon-Fri & 9am-2pm Sat Oct-Apr) Sells the glossy *Zamość – A Short Guidebook* (9.50zł).

ⓘ Getting There & Away

The **bus terminal** (ul Hrubieszowska) is 2km east of the Old Town and linked by frequent city buses, primarily buses 0 and 3. Daily buses go to Kraków (44zł, seven hours, four daily), Warsaw (35zł, 4¾ hours, three daily) and Lublin (16zł, two hours, hourly).

Quicker and cheaper are the minibuses that travel every 30 minutes between Lublin and Zamość (12zł, 1½ hours). They leave from the minibus station opposite the bus terminal in Zamość and from a corner north of the bus terminal in Lublin. Check the changeable timetable for departures to other destinations, including Warsaw and Kraków.

Ela Travel (☑84 639 3001; ul Grodzka 18) sells international bus and air tickets.

CARPATHIAN MOUNTAINS

The Carpathians (Karpaty) stretch from the southern border with Slovakia into Ukraine, and their wooded hills and snowy mountains are a beacon for hikers, skiers and cyclists. The most popular destination here is the resort town of Zakopane in the heart of the Tatra Mountains (Tatry). Elsewhere, historic regional towns such as Przemyśl and Sanok offer a relaxed pace and unique insights into the past.

Zakopane

POP 27,300
Nestled at the foot of the Tatra Mountains, Zakopane is Poland's major winter sports centre, though it's a popular destination year-round. It may resemble a tourist trap, with its overcommercialised, overpriced exterior, but it also has a relaxed, laid-back vibe that makes it a great place to chill for a few days, even if you're not planning on skiing or hiking.

Zakopane played an important role in sustaining Polish culture during the foreign rule in the 19th century, thanks to the many artistic types who settled during this period.

◉ Sights & Activities

Mt Gubałówka MOUNTAIN
Mt Gubałówka (1120m) offers excellent views over the Tatras and is a popular destination for tourists who don't feel overly energetic. The **funicular** (adult/concession one way 10/8zł, return 15/12zł; ☺8am-10pm Jul & Aug, 8.30am-6pm Apr-Jun & Sep, 8.30am-6pm Oct & Nov) covers the 1388m-long route in less than five minutes, climbing 300m from the funicular station, which is just north of ul Krupówki.

Tatra Museum MUSEUM
(ul Krupówki 10; adult/concession 7/5.50zł, free Sun; ☺9am-5pm Tue-Sat, 9am-3pm Sun) Check out exhibits about regional history, ethnography and geology here, along with displays on local flora and fauna.

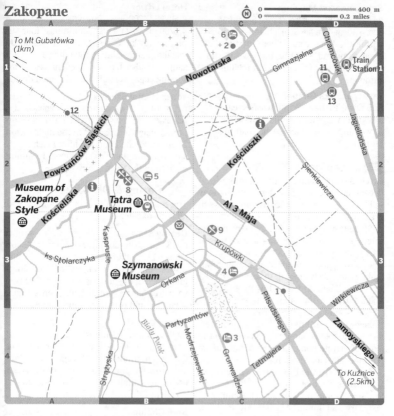

Zakopane

◉ Top Sights

Museum of Zakopane Style	A3
Szymanowski Museum	B3
Tatra Museum	B2

Activities, Courses & Tours

1	Sport Shop & Service	C3
2	Sukces Ski Rental	C1

🛏 Sleeping

3	Carlton	C4
4	Hotel Litwor	C3
5	Hotel Sabała	B2

6	Youth Hostel Szarotka	C1

✖ Eating

7	Czarny Staw	B2
8	Pstrąg Górski	B2
9	Stek Chałupa	C3

☕ Drinking

10	Appendix	B2

Transport

11	Bus Station	D1
12	Funicular Station	A1
13	Minibus Station	D1

Museum of Zakopane Style   MUSEUM
(ul Kościeliska 18; adult/concession 7/5.50zł;
⊙9am-5pm Wed-Sat, 9am-3pm Sun) Fittingly
housed in the 1892 Villa Koliba, the first
house to be designed by artist and architect Stanisław Witkiewicz in the distinctive architectural style which became the
trademark of Zakopane in the late 19th
century.

Szymanowksi Museum　　MUSEUM
(ul Kasprusie 19; adult/concession 6/3zł, free Sun; ⏱10am-4pm Tue-Sun) This institution within the Villa Atma is dedicated to the great composer Karol Szymanowski, who once lived here. It hosts piano recitals in summer.

Jaszczurówka Chapel　　CHURCH
(ul Balzera) Perhaps Witkiewicz's greatest design achievement is this attractive place of worship, located along the road to Morskie Oko.

🛏 Sleeping

Given the abundance of private rooms and decent hostels, few travellers actually stay in hotels. The tourist office usually knows of great bargains in guest houses.

Some travel agencies in Zakopane can arrange private rooms, but in the high season they may not want to offer anything for less than three nights. Expect a double room (singles are rarely offered) to cost about 80zł in the high season in the town centre, and about 60zł for somewhere further out.

Locals offering private rooms may approach you at the bus or train stations; alternatively, just look out for signs posted in the front of private homes – *noclegi* and *pokoje* both mean 'rooms available'.

Like all seasonal resorts, accommodation prices fluctuate considerably between low season and high season (December to February and July to August). Always book accommodation in advance at peak times, especially on weekends. The following rates are for high season.

TOP CHOICE | **Hotel Sabała**　　HOTEL €€€
(☎18 201 5092; www.sabala.zakopane.pl; ul Krupówki 11; s/d from 340/440zł; 🐾) Built in 1894 but thoroughly up-to-date, this striking timber building has a superb location overlooking the picturesque pedestrian thoroughfare. It offers cosy, attic-style rooms, and there's a sauna and solarium on the premises. A candlelit restaurant has views of street life.

Carlton　　HOTEL €€
(☎18 201 4415; www.carlton.pl; ul Grunwaldzka 11; s/d/tr 100/200/300zł) Good-value pension in a grand old house away from the main drag, featuring light-filled rooms with modern furniture. There's an impressive shared balcony overlooking the road, and a big comfy lounge lined with potted plants.

Hotel Litwor　　HOTEL €€€
(☎18 202 4200; www.litwor.pl; ul Krupówki 40; s/d 476/595zł; 🐾🌊) This sumptuous four-star place, with large, restful rooms, has all the usual top-end facilities, including a gym and sauna. It also has an excellent restaurant serving classy versions of traditional dishes.

Youth Hostel Szarotka　　HOSTEL €
(☎18 201 3618; www.szarotkaptsm.republika.pl; ul Nowotarska 45; dm 40zł, d 100zł) This friendly, homey place gets packed in the high season. There's a kitchen and washing machine on-site. It's on a noisy road about a 10-minute walk from the town centre.

🍴 Eating & Drinking

The main street, ul Krupówki, is lined with all sorts of eateries.

Czarny Staw　　GRILL €€
(☎18 201 3856; ul Krupówki 2; mains 12-46zł; ⏱10am-1am) Offers a tasty range of Polish dishes, including a variety of dumplings, and much of the menu is cooked before your very eyes on the central grill. There's a good salad bar, and live music most nights.

Pstrąg Górski　　SEAFOOD €€
(☎18 206 4613; ul Krupówki 6; mains 15-30zł; ⏱9am-10pm) This self-service fish restaurant, done up in traditional style and overlooking a narrow stream, serves some of the freshest trout, salmon and sea fish in town. It's excellent value.

Stek Chałupa　　POLISH €€
(☎18 201 5918; ul Krupówki 33; mains 12-32zł; ⏱8am-midnight) Big friendly barn of a place, with homey decor and waitresses in traditional garb. The menu features meat dishes, particularly steaks, though there are vegetarian choices among the salads and *pierogi*.

Appendix　　CAFE-BAR
(ul Krupówki 6; ⏱11am-midnight) A mellow venue for an alcoholic or caffeine-laden drink, hidden away above the street with an ambient old-meets-new decor. It hosts live music most weekends.

ℹ Information

Centrum Przewodnictwa Tatrzańskiego (Tatra Guide Centre; ☎18 206 37 99; ul Chałubińskiego 42a; ⏱9am-3pm) Arranges English- and German-speaking mountain guides.

Księgarnia Górska (ul Zaruskiego 5) Bookshop in the reception area of the Dom Turysty PTTK, sells regional hiking maps.

Main post office (ul Krupówki; ⊙7am-8pm Mon-Fri, 8am-2pm Sat)

Tourist office (☑18 201 2211) Bus station (ul Kościuszki 17; ⊙9am-5pm daily Jul & Aug, 9am-5pm Mon-Fri Sep-Jun); Town (ul Kościeliska 7; ⊙9am-5pm daily Jul & Aug, 9am-5pm Mon-Fri Sep-Jun) These offices offer advice, sell hiking and city maps, and can also arrange rafting trips down the Dunajec River.

Widmo (ul Galicy 6; per hr 5zł; ⊙7.30am-midnight Mon-Fri, 9am-midnight Sat & Sun) Internet access.

❶ Getting There & Away

From the **bus terminal** (ul Chramcówki), PKS buses run to Kraków every 45 to 60 minutes (18zł, two hours). Two private companies, **Trans Frej** (www.trans-frej.com.pl, in Polish) and **Szwagropol** (www.szwagropol.pl, in Polish), also run comfortable buses from here (18zł) at the same frequency. At peak times (especially weekends), you can buy your tickets for the private buses in advance from offices a short distance west of the bus station in Zakopane. Tickets are also available in Kraków from **Fogra Travel** (ul Pawia 12). The minibus station opposite the bus terminal is most useful for journeys to towns within the Tatra Mountains.

From Zakopane, PKS buses also head to Lublin (56zł, nine hours, four daily), Sanok (42zł, 6½ hours, one daily), Przemyśl (45zł, nine hours, one daily) and Warsaw (60zł, eight hours, five daily). Two daily buses head to Poprad in Slovakia (18zł). PKS buses – and minibuses from opposite the bus terminal – regularly travel to Lake Morskie Oko and on to Polana Palenica. To cross into Slovakia, get off this bus/minibus at Łysa Polana, cross the border on foot, and take another bus to Tatranská Lomnica and the other Slovak mountain towns.

From the **train station** (ul Chramcówki), nine trains a day go to Kraków (35zł, 3½ hours), two to Częstochowa (48zł, 5½ hours), four to Lublin (56zł, nine hours), two to Gdynia via Gdańsk (70zł, 16 hours), one to Łódź (56zł, 8¼ hours), one to Poznań (60zł, 11½ hours) and four to Warsaw (58zł, 8½ hours).

Tatra Mountains

The Tatras, 100km south of Kraków, are the highest range of the Carpathian Mountains, providing a dramatic range of rugged scenery that's a distinct contrast to the rest of Poland's flatness. Roughly 60km long and 15km wide, this mountain range stretches across the Polish–Slovak border. A quarter is in Poland and is mostly part of the Tatra National Park (about 212 sq km). The Polish Tatras contain more than 20 peaks over 2000m, the highest of which is Mt Rysy (2499m).

⊙ Sights & Activities

Cable Car to Mt Kasprowy Wierch CABLE CAR
(www.pkl.pl; adult/concession return 42/32zł; ⊙7am-9pm Jul & Aug, 7.30am-5pm Apr-Jun, Sep & Oct, 9am-4pm Nov) The cable-car trip from Kuźnice (2km south of Zakopane) to the summit of Mt Kasprowy Wierch (1985m) is a classic tourist experience enjoyed by Poles and foreigners alike. At the end of the trip, you can get off and stand with one foot in Poland and the other in Slovakia. The one-way journey takes 20 minutes and climbs 936m. The cable car normally shuts down for two weeks in May, and won't operate if the snow and, particularly, the winds are dangerous.

The view from the top is spectacular (clouds permitting). Two chairlifts transport skiers to and from various slopes between December and April. A restaurant serves skiers and hikers alike. In summer, many people return to Zakopane on foot down the Gąsienicowa Valley, and the most intrepid walk the ridges all the way across to Lake Morskie Oko via Pięciu Stawów, a strenuous hike taking a full day in good weather.

If you buy a return ticket, your trip back is automatically reserved for two hours after your departure, so buy a one-way ticket to the top (32zł) and another one down (26zł), if you want to stay longer. Mt Kasprowy Wierch is popular; so in summer, arrive early and expect to wait. PKS buses and minibuses to Kuźnice frequently leave from Zakopane.

Lake Morskie Oko LAKE
The emerald-green Lake Morskie Oko (Eye of the Sea) is among the loveliest lakes in the Tatras. PKS buses and minibuses regularly depart from Zakopane for Polana Palenica (30 minutes), from where a road (9km) continues uphill to the lake. Cars, bikes and buses are not allowed up this road, so you'll have to walk, but it's not steep (allow about two hours one way). Alternatively, take a horse-drawn carriage (50/30zł uphill/downhill, but very negotiable) to within 2km of the lake. In winter, transport is by horse-drawn four-seater sledge, which is more expensive. The last minibus to Zakopane returns between 5pm and 6pm.

Hiking HIKING
If you're doing any hiking in the Tatras get a copy of the *Tatrzański Park Narodowy* map (1:25,000), which shows all hiking trails in the area. Better still, buy one or more of

the 14 sheets of *Tatry Polskie*, available at Księgarnia Górska (p646) in Zakopane. In July and August these trails can be overrun by tourists, so late spring and early autumn are the best times. Theoretically you can expect better weather in autumn, when rainfall is lower.

Like all alpine regions, the Tatras can be dangerous, particularly during the snow season (November to May). Remember the weather can be unpredictable. Bring proper hiking boots, warm clothing and waterproof rain gear – and be prepared to use occasional ropes and chains (provided along the trails) to get up and down some rocky slopes. Guides are not necessary because many of the trails are marked, but they can be arranged in Zakopane (see p646) for about 350zł per day.

There are several picturesque valleys south of Zakopane, including the **Dolina Strążyska**. You can continue from the Strążyska by the red trail up to **Mt Giewont** (1909m), 3½ hours from Zakopane, and then walk down the blue trail to Kuźnice in two hours.

Two long and beautiful forested valleys, the **Dolina Chochołowska** and the **Dolina Kościeliska**, are in the western part of the park, known as the Tatry Zachodnie (West Tatras). These valleys are ideal for cycling. Both are accessible by PKS buses and minibuses from Zakopane.

The Tatry Wysokie (High Tatras) to the east offer quite different scenery: bare granite peaks and glacial lakes. One way to get there is via cable car to **Mt Kasprowy Wierch**, then hike eastward along the red trail to Mt Świnica (2301m) and on to the Zawrat pass (2159m) – a tough three to four hours from Mt Kasprowy. From Zawrat, descend northwards to the Dolina Gąsienicowa along the blue trail and then back to Zakopane.

Alternatively, head south (also along the blue trail) to the wonderful **Dolina Pięciu Stawów** (Five Lakes Valley), where there is a mountain refuge 1¼ hours from Zawrat. The blue trail heading west from the refuge passes Lake Morskie Oko, 1½ hours from the refuge.

Skiing
SKIING

Zakopane boasts four major ski areas (and several smaller ones) with more than 50 ski lifts. Mt Kasprowy Wierch and **Mt Gubałówka** offer the best conditions and the most challenging slopes in the area, with the ski season extending until early May. Lift tickets cost 10zł for one ride at Mt Kasprowy Wierch, and 2zł on the smaller lift at Mt Gubałówka. Alternatively, you can buy a day

card (100zł) at Mt Kasprowy Wierch, which allows you to skip the queues. Purchase your lift tickets on the relevant mountain.

Another alternative is the **Harenda chairlift** (☎18 206 4029; www.harendazakopane. pl; ul Harenda 63; ⊙9am-6pm) just outside Zakopane, in the direction of Kraków. A one-way/return ticket is 7/10zł.

Ski equipment rental is available at all facilities except Mt Kasprowy Wierch. Otherwise, stop off on your way to Kuźnice at the **ski rental** place near the Rondo in Zakopane. Other places in Zakopane, such as **Sukces Ski Rental** (☎18 206 4197; ul Nowotarska 39) and **Sport Shop & Service** (☎18 201 5871; ul Krupówki 52a), also rent ski gear.

🛏 Sleeping

Tourists are not allowed to take their own cars into the park; you must walk in, take the cable car or use an official vehicle owned by the park or a hotel or hostel.

Camping is also not allowed in the park, but eight PTTK mountain refuges/hostels provide simple accommodation. Most refuges are small and fill up fast; in midsummer and midwinter they're invariably packed beyond capacity. No one is ever turned away, however, though you may have to crash on the floor if all the beds are taken. Don't arrive too late in the day, and remember to bring along your own bed mat and sleeping bag. All refuges serve simple hot meals, but the kitchens and dining rooms close early (sometimes at 7pm).

The refuges listed here are open all year, but some may be temporarily closed for renovations or because of inclement weather. Check the current situation at the **PTTK office** (☎18 201 2429; ul Krupówki 12) in Zakopane.

Kalatówki Mountain Hotel HOTEL €€
(☎18 206 3644; www.kalatowki.pl; s/d from 81/154zł) This large and decent accommodation is the easiest to reach from Zakopane. It's a 40-minute walk from the Kuźnice cable-car station.

Dolina Pięciu Stawów Hostel HOSTEL €
(☎18 207 7607; www.piecstawow.pl; dm 30-35zł) This is the highest (1700m) and most scenically located refuge in the Polish Tatras.

Hala Kondratowa Hostel HOSTEL €
(☎18 201 9114; dm 28zł) This place is about 30 minutes beyond Kalatówki on the trail to Giewont. It's in a terrific location and has a great atmosphere, but it is small.

Roztoka Hostel HOSTEL €
(☎18 207 7442; dm 28-30zł) Hikers wishing to traverse the park might want to begin here. It's accessible by the bus or minibus to Morskie Oko.

Morskie Oko Hostel HOSTEL €
(☎18 207 7609; www.schroniskomorskieoko.pl; dm 27-49zł) An early start from Zakopane would allow you to visit Morskie Oko in the morning and stay here at night.

Dunajec Gorge

An entertaining and leisurely way to explore the Pieniny Mountains is to go **rafting** (www.flisacy.com.pl) on the Dunajec River, which winds along the Polish–Slovak border through a spectacular and deep gorge.

The trip starts at the wharf (Przystan Flisacka) in Sromowce-Kąty, 46km northeast of Zakopane, and you can finish either at the spa town of Szczawnica (adult/concession 44/22zł, 2¼ hours, 18km), or further on at Krościenko (adult/concession 53/27zł, 2¾ hours, 23km). The raft trip operates between April and October, but only starts when there's a minimum of 10 passengers.

The gorge is an easy day trip from Zakopane. Catch a regular bus to Nowy Targ (5zł, 30 minutes, hourly) from Zakopane to connect with one of five daily buses (7zł, one hour) to Sromowce-Kąty. From Szczawnica or Krościenko, take the bus back to Nowy Targ (8zł, one hour, hourly) and change for Zakopane. Krościenko has frequent bus links with Szczawnica, and two buses travel daily between Szczawnica and Kraków (15zł, 2½ hours). You can also return to the Sromowce-Kąty car park by bus with the raftsmen.

To avoid waiting around in Sromowce-Kąty for a raft to fill up, organise a trip at any travel agency in Zakopane, or at the tourist office. The cost is around 90zł per person, and includes transport, equipment and guides.

Sanok

POP 39,400

Nestled in a picturesque valley in the foothills of the Bieszczady Mountains, Sanok has been subject to Ruthenian, Hungarian, Austrian, Russian, German and Polish rule in its eventful history. Although it contains an important industrial zone, it's also a popular base for exploring the mountains.

The helpful **tourist office** (☎13 464 4533; www.sanok.pl; Rynek 14; ⌚9am-5pm Mon-Fri year-round, 9am-1pm Sat & Sun May-Oct) on the market square is the best place to find brochures on Sanok's attractions. You can check email at **Prox** (ul Kazimierz Wielkiego 6; per hr 3zł) further west.

Sanok is noted for its unique **Museum of Folk Architecture** (www.skansen.mblsanok.pl; ul Rybickiego 3; adult/concession 10/6zł; ⌚8am-6pm May-Sep, 8am-2pm Oct-Apr), which features architecture from regional ethnic groups. Walk north from the town centre for 2km along ul Mickiewicza and ul Białogórska, then cross the bridge and turn right. Back in the centre of town, the **Historical Museum** (ul Zamkowa 2; adult/concession 10/7zł; ⌚8am-noon Mon, 9am-3pm Tue-Sun) is housed in a 16th-century castle and contains an impressive collection of Ruthenian icons, along with a modern art gallery.

Sanok's surrounding villages are attractions in their own right, as many have lovely old churches. The marked **Icon Trail** takes hikers or cyclists along a 70km loop, passing by 10 village churches, as well as attractive mountain countryside. Trail leaflets and maps (in English, German and French) are available from the tourist office, as well as information on other themed trails, including a Jewish heritage route.

Find convenient budget accommodation at **Hotel Pod Trzema Różami** (☎13 463 0922; www.podtrzemarozami.pl; ul Jagiellońska 13; s/d 80/100zł), about 300m south of the market square. Further south (another 600m) and up the scale is **Hotel Jagielloński** (☎13 463 1208; www.hoteljagiellonski.bieszczady24.pl; ul Jagiellońska 49; s/d 120/160zł), with distinctive wooden furniture, parquetry floors and a good restaurant. Sanok's most comfortable option is **Hotel Sanvit** (☎13 465 5088; www.sanvit.sanok.pl; ul Łazienna 1; s/d 130/175zł), just west of the market square, with bright, modern rooms, shining bathrooms, spa treatments and a restaurant.

Karczma Jadło Karpackie (☎13 464 6700; Rynek 12; mains 8-25zł) is an amenable, down-to-earth bar and restaurant on the market square. A good place to have a drink, alcoholic or otherwise, is **Weranda Caffe** (ul 3 Maja 14; ⌚10am-10pm), a cosy cafe-bar with a fireplace, and outdoor seating in summer.

The bus terminal and adjacent train station are about 1km southeast of the market square. Three buses go daily to Przemyśl (12zł, two hours), and one to Zakopane (42zł, 6½ hours). Buses also head regularly to

LAKE SOLINA

In the far southeastern corner of Poland, wedged between the Ukrainian and Slovak borders, lies **Lake Solina**. This sizeable reservoir (27km long and 60m deep) was created in 1968 when the San River was dammed. Today it's a popular centre for water sports and other recreational pursuits.

Polańczyk is the best place to base yourself. This pleasant town on the lake's western shore offers a range of attractions, including sailing, windsurfing, fishing and beaches. There are also numerous hotels and sanatoriums offering spa treatments.

There are regular buses from Sanok to Polańczyk each day. For more details, check out Lonely Planet's *Poland* country guide, visit www.karpaty.turystyka.pl or step into the local **tourist office** (☑13 470 3028; ul Wiejska 2, Polańczyk).

Kraków and Warsaw. Train journeys to these destinations, however, may require multiple changes.

Przemyśl

POP 66,400

Everything about Przemyśl (*psheh*-mishl) feels big: its sprawling market square, the massive churches surrounding it, and the broad San River flowing through the city.

Luckily the area of most interest to visitors – around the sloping **Market Sq** (Rynek) – is compact and easily explored. The **tourist office** (☑16 675 2164; www. przemysl.pl; ul Grodzka 1; ☺8am-6pm Mon-Fri & 9am-5pm Sat & Sun Apr-Sep, 9am-5pm Mon-Fri & 10am-2pm Sat Oct-Mar) is situated above the southwest corner of the square.

About 350m southwest of the square are the ruins of a 14th-century **castle** (ul Zamkowa), built by Kazimierz Wielki. In a modern building just northeast of Rynek, you can learn about the history of the surrounding region at the **National Museum of the Przemyśl Lands** (Plac Joselewicza; adult/concession 8/4zł; ☺10am-3pm Tue-Sat, 11am-3pm Sun).

For variety, visit the curious **Museum of Bells and Pipes** (ul Władycze 3; adult/concession 5/3zł; ☺10am-3pm Tue-Sat, 11am-3pm Sun) in the old Clock Tower, where you can inspect several floors worth of vintage bells, elaborately carved pipes and cigar cutters (the city has long been famous across Poland for manufacturing these items). From the top of the tower there's a great view.

Przemyśl has a selection of inexpensive accommodation, including the central **Dom Wycieczkowy Podzamcze** (☑16 678 5374; ul Waygarta 3; dm 25zł, s/d 47/68zł), on the western edge of the Old Town. Its rooms have seen

some wear, but it's pleasant enough for the price.

More comfort is available at **Hotel Europejski** (☑16 675 7100; www.hotel-europejski.pl; ul Sowińskiego 4; s/d/ste 110/140/170/210zł) in a renovated old building facing the attractive facade of the train station. An impressive staircase leads to simple, light rooms with high ceilings. Another option is **Hotel Gromada** (☑16 676 1111; www.gromada.pl; ul Wybrzeże Piłsudskiego 4; s/d 186/249zł), a big, business-friendly chain hotel west of the Old Town.

A worthy place to eat is **Restauracja Piwnica Mieszczańska** (☑16 675 0459; Rynek 9; mains 7-30zł), on the Rynek. It must be Poland's only cellar restaurant with access to a skylight, and is decorated with mini-chandeliers and lace tablecloths. The bourgeoisie platter (three kinds of meat) will interest ardent carnivores, and there's a reasonable selection of soups and fish dishes.

Restauracja Dominikańska (☑16 678 2055; Plac Dominikański 3; mains 5-25zł; ☺10am-10pm) is an elegantly appointed eatery at the quieter northeastern corner of the Market Sq, serving affordable Polish classics.

If you fancy a drink, **Bistro Absynt** (Plac Dominikański 4), on the northwest corner of Rynek, is a relaxed space from which to sip and people-watch.

From Przemyśl, buses run to Lviv (95km) in Ukraine several times a day and regularly to all towns in southeastern Poland, including Sanok (12zl, two hours, three daily). Trains run to Lublin (44zł, four hours, one daily), Kraków (46zł, four hours, 14 daily) and Warsaw (56zł, 6¾ hours, three daily), and stop here on the way to/from Lviv. The bus terminal and adjacent train station in Przemyśl are about 1km northeast of the Rynek.

SILESIA

Silesia (Śląsk, *shlonsk*, in Polish) is a fascinating mix of landscapes. Though the industrial zone around Katowice has limited attraction for visitors, beautiful Wrocław is a historic city with lively nightlife, and the Sudeten Mountains draw hikers and other nature lovers.

The history of the region is similarly diverse, having been governed by Polish, Bohemian, Austrian and German rulers. After two centuries as part of Prussia and Germany, the territory was largely included within Poland's new borders after WWII.

Wrocław

POP 632,000

When citizens of beautiful Kraków enthusiastically encourage you to visit Wrocław (*vrotswahf*), you know you're onto something good. The city's delightful Old Town is a gracious mix of Gothic and baroque styles, and its large student population ensures a healthy number of restaurants, bars and nightclubs.

Wrocław has been traded back and forth between various rulers over the centuries, but began life in the year 1000 under the Polish Piast dynasty and developed into a prosperous trading and cultural centre. In the 1740s it passed to Prussia, under the German name of Breslau. Under Prussian rule, the city became a major textile manufacturing centre, greatly increasing its population.

Upon its return to Poland in 1945, Wrocław was a shell of its former self, having sustained massive damage in WWII. Though 70% of the city was destroyed, sensitive restoration has returned the historic centre to its former beauty.

◉ Sights

OLD TOWN

TOP CHOICE **Gnomes of Wrocław**　　　　STATUES
See if you can spot the diminutive statue of a gnome at ground level, just to the west of the Jaś i Małgosia houses; he's one of over 150, which are scattered through the city. Whimsical as they are, they're attributed to the symbol of the Orange Alternative, a communist-era dissident group that used ridicule as a weapon, and often painted gnomes where graffiti had been removed by the authorities. You can buy a gnome map (5zł) from the tourist office and go gnome-spotting.

Market Square　　　　HISTORIC SQUARE
In the centre of the Old Town is Poland's second-largest old market square (after Kraków), known in Polish as the Rynek. It's an attractive, rambling space, lined by beautifully painted facades and with a complex of old buildings in the middle. The southwestern corner of the square opens into **Salt Place** (Plac Solny), once the site of the town's salt trade and now home to a 24-hour flower market.

City Dwellers' Art Museum　　　　MUSEUM
(adult/concession 7/5zł; ◎10am-5pm Tue-Sat, 10am-6pm Sun) The beautiful town hall (built 1327–1504) on the southern side of the square has stately rooms on show, with exhibits featuring the art of gold and the stories of famous Wrocław inhabitants.

Jaś i Małgosia　　　　HISTORIC BUILDINGS
(ul Św. Mikołaja) In the northwestern corner of the market square are two attractive small houses linked by a baroque gate. They're a couple better known to English speakers as Hansel and Gretel.

Church of St Mary Magdalene　　　　CHURCH
(ul Łaciarska; ◎9am-4pm Mon-Sat) One block east of the Rynek is this Gothic church with a Romanesque portal from 1280 incorporated into its southern external wall. Climb the 72m high tower and its connected **bridge** (adult/concession 4/3zł; ◎10am-8pm Apr-Oct) for a lofty view.

Church of St Elizabeth　　　　CHURCH
(ul Elżbiety 1; admission 5zł; ◎9am-6pm Mon-Fri, 11am-5pm Sat, 1-5pm Sun) Behind houses and gnomes is this monumental 14th-century church with its 83m-high tower, which you can climb for city views.

EAST OF THE OLD TOWN

Panorama of Racławice　　MONUMENTAL ARTWORK
(www.panoramaraclawicka.pl; ul Purkyniego 11; adult/concession 20/15zł; ◎9am-5pm Tue-Sun May-Oct, 9am-4pm Tue-Sun Nov-Apr) Wrocław's pride and joy (and major tourist attraction) is this giant 360-degree painting of the 1794 Battle of Racławice, in which the Polish peasant army, led by Tadeusz Kościuszko, defeated Russian forces intent on partitioning Poland. Created by Jan Styka and Wojciech Kossak for the centenary of the battle in 1894, the painting is an immense 114m long and 15m high, and was brought here by Polish immigrants displaced from Lviv after WWII. Due to the communist government's uneasiness about glorifying a famous Russian defeat, however,

POLAND WROCŁAW

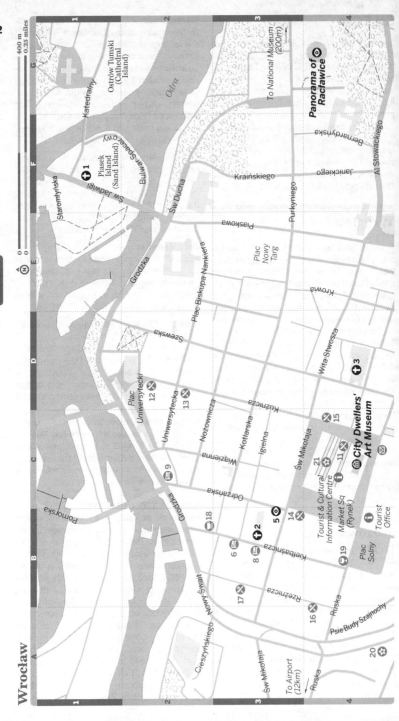

Wrocław

POLAND SILESIA

Ostrów Tumski
(Cathedral
Island)

Katedralny

Odra

Piasek Island
(Sand Island)

Staromłyńska

Św Jadwigi

Bulwar Spacerowy

Grodzka

Św Ducha

To National Museum
(200m)

Panorama of
Racławice

Krainskiego

Piaskowa

Purkyniego

Bernardyńska

Janickiego

Al Słowackiego

Plac Biskupa Nankiera

Plac
Nowy
Targ

Szewska

Krowia

Witta Stwosza

Plac
Uniwersytecki

Uniwersytecka

Nożownicza

Kotlarska

Igielna

Kuźnicza

Kuźnicza

12

13

Więzienna

Szewska

15

City Dwellers'
Art Museum

3

Grodzka

Odrzańska

9

21

11

Św Mikołaja

Tourist & Cultural
Information Centre

Market Sq
(Rynek)

Tourist
Office

18

Kiełbaśnicza

6

8

2

5

14

19

Plac
Solny

Cieszyńskiego Nowy Świat

Rzeźnicza

17

16

Ruska

Św Mikołaja

To Airport
(12km)

Ruska

Psie Budy Szajnochy

20

Pomorska

652

0   400 m
0   0.25 miles

the panorama wasn't re-erected until 1985, in a circular building east of the Old Town.

Obligatory tours (with audio in English, French, German, Spanish, Russian and other languages) run every 30 minutes between 9am and 4.30pm from April to November, and 10am and 3pm from December to March. The ticket also allows entry to the National Museum on the same day.

National Museum   MUSEUM
(www.mnwr.art.pl; Plac Powstańców Warszawy 5; adult/concession 15/10zł, free Sat; ⊙10am-4pm Wed-Fri & Sun, 10am-6pm Sat) Near the Panorama, this museum exhibits Silesian medieval art, and a fine collection of modern Polish painting. Entry is included with a ticket to the Panorama.

ECCLESIASTICAL DISTRICT
Cathedral of St John the Baptist   CHURCH
(Plac Katedralny; ⊙10am-6pm Mon-Sat, except during services) This Gothic cathedral has a unique lift to whisk you to the top of its **tower** (adult/concession 5/4zł) for superb views. Next door to the cathedral is the **Archdiocesan Museum** (Plac Katedralny 16; adult/concession 3/2zł; ⊙9am-3pm Tue-Sun) of sacred art.

Church of Our Lady on the Sand   CHURCH
(ul Św Jadwigi; ⊙erratic) North of the river is Piasek Island (Sand Island), where you'll find this 14th-century place of worship with lofty Gothic vaults and a year-round nativity scene.

Church of the Holy Cross & St Bartholomew   CHURCH
(Plac Kościelny; ⊙9am-6pm) Cross the small bridge to Ostrów Tumski (Cathedral Island), a picturesque area full of churches, and walk to this two-storey Gothic structure, built between 1288 and 1350.

Botanical Gardens   GARDENS
(ul Sienkiewicza 23; adult/concession 7/5zł; ⊙8am-6pm Apr-Oct) North of the cathedral are these charming gardens, where you can chill out among the chestnut trees and tulips.

SOUTH OF THE OLD TOWN
Historical Museum   MUSEUM
(www.mmw.pl; ul Kazimierza Wielkiego 35; adult/concession 15/10zł; ⊙10am-5pm Tue, Wed, Fri & Sat, 1-8pm Thu, 10am-6pm Sun) Housed in a grand former palace, this institution highlights the main events in Wrocław's thousand-year history, and includes an art collection covering the past two centuries.

Wrocław

Passage   MONUMENT
(corner of ul Świdnicka & ul Piłsudskiego) This fascinating sculpture depicts a group of pedestrians being swallowed by the pavement, only to re-emerge on the other side of the street.

✦ Festivals & Events

Jazz on the Odra International Festival
                                           MUSIC
(www.jnofestival.pl) February/March

Musica Polonica Nova Festival   MUSIC
(www.musicapolonica nova.pl, in Polish) May

Wratislavia Cantans   MUSIC
(www.wratislaviacantans.pl) September

Wrocław Marathon   SPORT
(www.wroclawmaraton.pl) September

🛏 Sleeping

Hotel Patio   HOTEL €€
(☎71 375 0400; www.hotelpatio.pl; ul Kiełbaśnicza 24; s/d from 249/279zł; 🌐) Pleasant lodgings a short hop from the main square, housed within two buildings linked by a covered sunlit courtyard. Rooms are clean and light, sometimes small but with reasonably high ceilings. There's a restaurant, bar and hairdresser on-site.

Nathan's Villa Hostel   HOSTEL €
(☎71 344 1095; www.nathansvilla.com; ul Świdnicka 13; dm from 40zł, r from 150zł) This comfortable 96-bed place is conveniently placed about 150m south of the Rynek. It does accept

noisy Polish school groups in addition to backpackers, so check before you check in.

Art Hotel   HOTEL €€
(☎71 787 7100; www.arthotel.pl; ul Kiełbaśnicza 20; s/d from 270/310zł; 🌐) Elegant but affordable accommodation in a renovated apartment building. Rooms feature tastefully restrained decor, quality fittings and gleaming bathrooms. Within the hotel is a top-notch restaurant, and there's a fitness room to work off the resultant kilojoules.

Hostel Babel   HOSTEL €
(☎71 342 0250; www.babelhostel.pl; ul Kołłątaja 16; dm from 45zł, d 140zł) A tatty old staircase leads up to pleasant budget accommodation. Dorms are set in renovated apartment rooms with ornate lamps and decorative ceilings. Bathrooms are shiny clean, and guests have free access to a kitchen and washing machine. There's a DVD player for rainy days.

Hotel Tumski   HOTEL €€€
(☎71 322 6099; www.hotel-tumski.com.pl; Wyspa Słodowa 10; s/d from 260/380zł) This is a neat hotel in a peaceful setting overlooking the river, offering reasonable value for money. It's ideal for exploring the lovely ecclesiastical quarter, and there's a good restaurant attached.

Hotel Zaułek   HOTEL €€
(☎71 341 0046; www.hotelzaulek.pl; ul Garbary 11; s/d from 260/330zł) Run by the university, this guest house accommodates just 18 visitors in a dozen homey rooms. The 1pm checkout is a plus for heavy sleepers, and weekend

prices are a steal. Breakfast is an additional 12zł, and half and full board is available.

Hotel Europejski
HOTEL €€

(☎71 772 1000; www.silfor.pl; ul Piłsudskiego 88; s/d 179/219zł) Apparently a leopard can change its spots – the formerly drab Europejski is now a smart business hotel. Rooms are clean and bright, and very handy for the train station. Breakfast is an extra 25zł.

MDK Youth Hostel
HOSTEL €

(☎71 343 8856; www.mdk.kopernik.wroclaw.pl; ul Kołłątaja 20; dm from 27zł, d from 72zł) Not far from the train station, this is a basic place, located in a grand mustard-coloured building. Some dorms are huge and beds are packed close together. It's almost always full, so book ahead.

Hotel Europeum
HOTEL €€€

(☎71 371 4500; www.europeum.pl; ul Kazimierza Wielkiego 27a; s/d 320/350zł; ❇) Business-oriented hotel with stylish rooms in a great location near the Market Sq. Rates drop dramatically at weekends.

Old Town Apartments
APARTMENTS €€

(☎22 351 2260; www.warsawshotel.com; ul Nowy Świat 29/3, Warsaw; apt from €55) Warsaw-based agency with modern, fully furnished one-bedroom apartments around Wrocław's Market Sq. Weekly rates are available.

✴ Eating & Drinking

TOP CHOICE
Restauracja JaDka
POLISH €€€

(☎71 343 6461; www.jadka.pl; ul Rzeźnicza 24/25; mains 46-82zł; ⊙noon-10pm) Arguably the best restaurant in town, presenting impeccable modern versions of Polish classics amid elegant table settings in delightful Gothic surrounds. There's loads of character in the interior, with tables bearing lacy white tablecloths dotted beneath brick archways, illuminated by low-lit lamps.

Bazylia
CAFETERIA €

(Plac Uniwersytecki; mains 2.15zł per 100g; ⊙8am-7pm) Inexpensive and bustling modern take on the classic *bar mleczny*, in a curved space with huge plate-glass windows overlooking the venerable university buildings. The menu has a lot of Polish standards such as *bigos* and *gołąbki*, and a decent range of salads and other vegetable dishes. Everything is priced by weight at the same rate; order and pay at the till before receiving your food.

Darea
KOREAN €€€

(☎71 343 5301; ul Kuźnicza 43/45; mains 26-60zł; ⊙noon-11pm) With management at the LG Electronics factory in nearby Kobierzyce top-heavy with Koreans, it was inevitable that Wrocław would produce a place serving dishes like *bibimbab* and *bulgogi*. You won't find better Korean anywhere in Poland.

La Scala
ITALIAN €€

(☎71 372 5394; Rynek 38; mains 16-140zł) Offers authentic Italian food and particularly good desserts. Some dishes are pricey, but you're really paying for the location. The cheaper trattoria at ground level serves good pizza and pasta.

Mexico Bar
MEXICAN €€

(☎60 090 4577; ul Rzeźnicza 34; mains 16-35zł; ⊙11am-midnight) Compact, warmly lit restaurant featuring sombreros, backlit masks and a chandelier made of beer bottles. There's a small bar to lean on while waiting for a table. All the Tex-Mex standards are on the menu, but book at least two days ahead for a table on weekends.

Karczma Lwowska
POLISH €€€

(☎71 343 9887; Rynek 4; mains 26-41zł; ⊙11am-midnight) Has a great spot on Market Sq, with outdoor seating in summer, and offers the usual meaty Polish standards in a space with a rustic rural look. It's worth stopping by to try the beer, served in ceramic mugs.

Bar Wegetariański Vega
VEGETARIAN €

(☎71 344 3934; Rynek 1/2; mains 5-7zł; ⊙8am-7pm Mon-Fri, 9am-5pm Sat & Sun) This is a cheap cafeteria in the centre of the Rynek, offering vegie dishes in a light green space. Good choice of soups and crepes. Upstairs there's a vegan section, open from noon.

Pub Guinness
PUB

(Plac Solny 5; ⊙noon-2am) No prizes for guessing what this pub serves. A lively, fairly authentic Irish pub, spread over three levels on a busy corner. The ground-floor bar buzzes with student and traveller groups getting together, and there's a restaurant and beer cellar as well. A good place to wind down after a hard day's sightseeing.

Cafe Artzat
CAFE

(ul Malarska 30) This low-key cafe just north of the Church of St Elizabeth is one of the best places in town to recharge the batteries over coffee or tea and a good book.

☆ Entertainment

Check out the bimonthly *Visitor* (free and in English) for details of what's on in this important cultural centre. It's available from the tourist office and upmarket hotels.

TOP CHOICE **PRL** BAR/CLUB

(Rynek Ratusz 10; ⊙noon-late) The dictatorship of the proletariat is alive and well in this tongue-in-cheek venue inspired by communist nostalgia. Disco lights play over a bust of Lenin, propaganda posters line the walls, and red menace memorabilia is scattered through the maze of rooms. Descend to the basement – beneath the portraits of Stalin and Mao – if you'd like to hit the dance floor. Tuesday is karaoke night.

Teatr Polski THEATRE

(☑71 316 0777; www.teatrpolski.wroc.pl; ul Zapolskiej 3) Wrocław's main theatrical venue stages classic Polish and foreign drama.

Filharmonia CLASSICAL MUSIC

(☑71 342 2001; www.filharmonia.wroclaw.pl; ul Piłsudskiego 19) This place hosts concerts of classical music, mostly on Friday and Saturday nights.

Kino Helios CINEMA

(www.heliosnet.pl; ul Kazimierza Wielkiego 19a) If you're after a movie, head to this modern multiplex screening English-language films.

❶ Information

Internet Netvigator (ul Igielna 14; per hr 3zł; ⊙9am-midnight)

Main post office (Rynek 28; ⊙6.30am-8.30pm Mon-Sat)

Tourist office (☑71 344 3111; www.wroclaw-info.pl; Rynek 14; ⊙9am-9pm Apr-Oct, 9am-7pm Nov-Mar)

Tourist & Cultural Information Centre (☑71 342 0185; www.wroclaw-info.pl; ul Sukiennice 12; ⊙10am-8pm) Handles cultural ticket sales and offers internet access.

W Sercu Miasta (ul Przejście Żelaźnicie 4; per hr 5zł; ⊙10am-11pm Mon-Fri, 10am-9pm Sat, noon-11pm Sun) Internet access down a laneway in the middle of Rynek.

❶ Getting There & Away

Air

From **Copernicus airport** (www.airport.wroclaw.pl), LOT flies frequently between Wrocław and Warsaw. It also heads daily to Brussels and Frankfurt, and twice daily to Munich. Tickets can be bought at the **LOT office** (☑0801 703 703; ul Piłsudskiego 36). Jet Air also links Wrocław to Gdańsk.

A range of budget carriers connect Wrocław with other European cities, including several British and Irish regional destinations. Ryanair and Wizz Air fly daily to London, while Ryanair heads five times a week to Dublin.

The airport is in Strachowice, about 12km west of the Old Town. The half-hourly bus 406 and infrequent night bus 249 link the airport with Wrocław Główny train station and the bus terminal.

Bus

The **bus terminal** (ul Sucha 11) is south of the main train station, and offers five daily buses to Warsaw (44zł, seven hours). For most other travel, however, the train is more convenient.

Train

The **Wrocław Główny train station** (ul Piłsudskiego 105) was built in 1856 and is a historical monument in itself. Every day, trains to Kraków (48zł, 4¾ hours) depart every one or two hours, with similarly frequent services to Warsaw (118zł, 5½ hours), usually via Łódź. Wrocław is also linked by train to Poznań (37zł, 2½ hours, at least hourly), Częstochowa (37zł, three hours, four daily), Toruń (51zł, five hours, two daily) and Szczecin (56zł, five hours, seven daily). Note that when travelling to/from Wrocław at the weekend, you'll be in competition with thousands of itinerant university students, so book your ticket as soon as possible.

Sudeten Mountains

The Sudeten Mountains (Sudety) run for more than 250km along the Czech–Polish border. The Sudetes feature dense forests, amazing rock formations and deposits of semiprecious stones, and can be explored along the extensive network of trails for **hiking** or **mountain biking**. The highest part of this old eroded chain is Mt Śnieżka (1602m).

Szklarska Poręba, at the northwestern end of the Sudetes, offers superior facilities for **hiking** and **skiing**. It's at the base of Mt Szrenica (1362m), and the town centre is at the upper end of ul Jedności Narodowej. The small **tourist office** (☑75 754 7740; www.szklarskaporeba.pl; ul Jedności Narodowej 1a; ⊙8am-4pm Mon-Fri, 9am-5pm Sat & Sun) has accommodation info and maps. Nearby, several trails begin at the intersection of ul Jedności Narodowej and ul Wielki Sikorskiego. The red trail goes to **Mt Szrenica** (two hours) and offers a peek at **Wodospad Kamieńczyka**, a spectacular waterfall.

Karpacz to the southeast has more nightlife on offer, although it attracts fewer serious mountaineers. It's loosely clustered along a 3km road winding through Łomnica Valley at the base of Mt Śnieżka. The **tourist office** (☑75 761 8605; www.karpacz.pl; ul Konstytucji 3 Maja 25) should be your first port of call. To reach the peak of Mt Śnieżka on foot, take one of the trails (three to four hours) from Hotel Biały Jar. Some of the trails pass by one of two splendid postglacial lakes: **Mały Staw** and **Wielki Staw**.

The bus is the fastest way of getting around the region. Every day from Szklarska Poręba, about three buses head to Wrocław (29zł, 3½ hours) and one train plods along to Warsaw (60zł, 11½ hours). From Karpacz, get one of hourly buses to Jelenia Góra (8zł, 40 minutes), from where buses and trains go in all directions.

For the Czech Republic, take a bus from Szklarska Poręba to Jakuszyce (5zł, 15 minutes), cross the border on foot to Harrachov (on the Czech side) and take another bus from there.

WIELKOPOLSKA

Wielkopolska (Greater Poland) is the region where Poland came to life in the Middle Ages, and is referred to as the Cradle of the Polish State. As a result of this ancient eminence, its cities and towns are full of historic and cultural attractions.

The royal capital moved from Poznań to Kraków in 1038, though Wielkopolska remained an important province. Its historic significance didn't save it from international conflict, however, and the region became part of Prussia in 1793. Wielkopolska rose against German rule at the end of WWI and became part of the reborn Poland. The battles of WWII later caused widespread destruction in the area.

Poznań

POP 556,000

No one could accuse Poznań of being too sleepy. Between its regular trade fairs, student population and visiting travellers, it's a vibrant city with a wide choice of attractions. There's a beautiful Old Town at its centre, with a number of interesting museums, and a range of lively bars, clubs and restaurants. The surrounding countryside is also good for cycling and hiking.

Poznań grew from humble beginnings, when 9th-century Polanian tribes built a wooden fort on the island of Ostrów Tumski. From 968 to 1038 Poznań was the de facto capital of Poland. Its position between Berlin and Warsaw has always underlined its importance as a trading town, and in 1925 a modern version of its famous medieval trade fairs was instituted. The fairs, filling up the city's hotels for several days at a time, are the lynchpin of the city's economy.

As it's at the heart of Wielkopolska, Poznań makes a good transport hub from which to explore the region.

◎ Sights

OLD TOWN

Poznań's Old Town is centred on its attractive and ever-busy **Old Market Sq** (Stary Rynek), lined with restaurants and bars. There are several small museums of varying degrees of interest dotted around the square, in its central buildings and nearby; ask at the tourist office for the full list.

Historical Museum of Poznań   MUSEUM
(Stary Rynek 1; adult/concession 5.50/3.50zł, free Sat; ⊙9am-3pm Tue-Thu, noon-9pm Fri, 11am-6pm Sat & Sun) Located within the Renaissance **town hall** (built 1550–60), this museum displays splendid period interiors. If you're outside the building at noon, look up. Every midday two mechanical metal goats above its clock butt their horns together 12 times, echoing an improbable centuries-old legend of two animals escaping a cook and fighting each other in the town hall tower.

Wielkopolska Military Museum   MUSEUM
(Stary Rynek 9; adult/concession 5.50/3.50zł, free Sat; ⊙9am-3pm Tue-Thu, noon-9pm Fri, 11am-6pm Sat & Sun) Exhibits of arms from Poland's many conflicts over the centuries, dating from the 11th century to the present.

Museum of Musical Instruments   MUSEUM
(Stary Rynek 45; adult/concession 5.50/3.50zł, free Sat; ⊙9am-3pm Tue-Thu, noon-9pm Fri, 11am-6pm Sat & Sun) Large though unimaginative collection of music-making devices, displayed over multiple levels.

Franciscan Church   CHURCH
(ul Franciszkańska 2; ⊙8am-8pm) This 17th-century church, one block west of the square, has an ornate baroque interior,

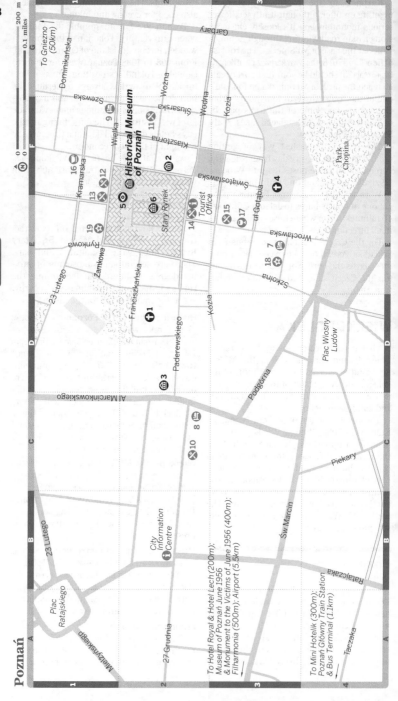

Poznań

POLAND WIELKOPOLSKA

Plac Ratajskiego

Plac Wiosny Ludów

Park Chopina

Stary Rynek

Historical Museum of Poznań

City Information Centre

Tourist Office

Mielżyńskiego

23 Lutego

27 Grudnia

Al Marcinkowskiego

Paderewskiego

Franciszkańska

Zamkowa

Rynkowa

Kramarska

Wielka

Szewska

Dominikańska

Woźna

Wodna

Ślusarska

Klasztorna

Świętosławska

ul Gołębia

Wrocławska

Szkolna

Kozia

Kozia

Podgórna

Piekary

Św Marcin

Ratajczaka

Taczaka

Garbary

To Gniezno (50km)

To Hotel Royal & Hotel Lech (200m); Museum of Poznań June 1956 & Monument to the Victims of June 1956 (400m); Filharmonia (500m); Airport (5.5km)

To Mini Hotelik (300m); Poznań Główny Train Station & Bus Terminal (1.1km)

0.1 miles

200 m

Poznań

complete with wall paintings and rich stucco work.

Parish Church of St Stanislaus   CHURCH
(ul Gołębia 1; ⊙erratic) Two blocks south of the Old Market Sq is this large, pink, baroque place of worship with monumental altars dating from the mid-17th century.

WEST OF THE OLD TOWN
Monument to the Victims of June 1956
MONUMENT
(Plac Mickiewicza) Emotive memorial to the dead and injured of the massive 1956 strike by the city's industrial workers, which was crushed by tanks. It's in a park west of the prominent Kaiserhof building.

National Museum: Paintings & Sculpture Gallery   MUSEUM
(Al Marcinkowskiego 9; adult/concession 10/6zł, free Sat; ⊙9am-3pm Tue-Thu, noon-9pm Fri, 11am-6pm Sat & Sun) This museum branch displays mainly 19th- and 20th-century Polish paintings.

Museum of Poznań June 1956   MUSEUM
(ul Św Marcin 80/82; adult/concession 4/2zł, free Sat; ⊙9am-5pm Tue-Fri, 10am-4pm Sat & Sun) In the Zamek Cultural Centre within the Kaiserhof, there's more detail to be uncovered of the 1956 strike.

Palm House   GREENHOUSE
(ul Matejki 18; adult/concession 5.50/4zł; ⊙9am-5pm Tue-Sat, 9am-6pm Sun) This huge greenhouse (built in 1910) contains 17,000 species of tropical and subtropical plants. It's located in Park Wilsona, 1km southwest of the train station.

NORTH OF THE OLD TOWN
Citadel Park   HISTORIC PARK
This park, about 1.5km north of the Old Town, was once the site of a 19th-century Prussian citadel, where 20,000 German troops held out for a month in February 1945. The fortress was destroyed by artillery fire but the site now incorporates both the **Poznań Army Museum** (Al Armii Poznań; admission free; ⊙9am-4pm Tue-Sat, 10am-4pm Sun) and the nearby **Poznań Citadel Museum** (Al Armii Poznań; adult/concession 4/2zł, free Fri; ⊙9am-4pm Tue-Sat, 10am-4pm Sun).

EAST OF THE OLD TOWN
Ostrów Tumski   HISTORIC AREA
This river island is dominated by the monumental, double-towered **Poznań Cathedral** (ul Ostrów Tumski), originally built in 968. The Byzantine-style **Golden Chapel** (1841) and the mausoleums of Mieszko I and Boleslaus the Brave are behind the high altar. Opposite the cathedral is the 15th-century Gothic **Church of the Virgin Mary** (ul Panny Marii 1/3). The island is 1km east of the Old Town (take any eastbound tram from Plac Wielkopolski).

Lake Malta   RECREATIONAL ZONE
Some 1.6km east of the Old Town is this body of water, a favourite weekend destination for Poles. It holds sailing regattas, outdoor concerts and other events in summer, and in winter there's a ski slope in operation.

  A fun way to visit the lake is to take tram 4, 8 or 17 from Plac Wielkopolski to the Rondo Śródka stop on the other side of Ostrów Tumski. From the nearby terminus, you can catch a miniature train along the **Malta**

Park Railway (ul Jana Pawła II; adult/concession 5/3.50zł; ⊙10am-6.30pm Apr-Oct), which follows the lake's shore to the **New Zoo** (ul Krańcowa 81; adult/concession 11/7zł; ⊙9am-7pm Apr-Sep, 9am-4pm Oct-Mar). This sprawling institution houses diverse species, including Baltic grey seals, in a pine forest environment.

🎪 Festivals & Events

The largest trade fairs take place in January, June, September and October.

Poznań Jazz Fair   MUSIC
March

St John's Fair   CULTURAL
Cultural festival in June.

**Malta International Theatre
Festival**   THEATRE
(www.malta-festival.pl) June

🛏 Sleeping

During trade fairs, the rates of Poznań's accommodation dramatically increases. A room may also be difficult to find, so it pays to book ahead. Prices given here are for outside trade fair periods.

Check out **Biuro Zakwaterowania Przemysław** (☑61 866 3560; www.przemyslaw. com.pl; ul Głogowska 16; s/d from 60/90zł, apt from 180zł; ⊙8am-6pm Mon-Fri, 10am-2pm Sat), an accommodation agency not far from the train station. Rates for weekends and stays of more than three nights are cheaper than the prices quoted here.

TOP CHOICE **Hotel Stare Miasto**   HOTEL €€
(☑61 663 62 42; www.hotelstaremiasto. pl; ul Rybaki 36; s/d 215/340zł; ▣) Elegant, value-for-money hotel with a tasteful chandeliered foyer and a spacious breakfast room. Rooms can be small, but are clean and bright with lovely starched white sheets. Some upper rooms have skylights in place of windows.

Rezydencja Solei   HOTEL €€
(☑61 855 7351; www.hotel-solei.pl; ul Szewska 2; s/d 199/299zł) Temptingly close to the Old Market Sq, this tiny hotel offers small but cosy rooms in an old-fashioned residential style, with wallpaper and timber furniture striking a homey note. The attic suite is amazingly large and can accommodate up to four people.

Frolic Goats Hostel   HOSTEL €
(☑61 852 4411; www.frolicgoatshostel.com; ul Wrocławska 16/6; dm from 50zł, d 170zł) Named after the feisty goats who fight above the town hall clock, this hostel is aimed squarely at the international backpacker. There's a washing machine on the premises, bike hire is available for 30zł per day and room rates are unaffected by trade fairs. Enter from ul Jaskółcza.

Hotel Rzymski   HOTEL €€
(☑61 852 8121; www.hotelrzymski.pl; Al Marcinkowskiego 22; s/d from 250/310zł) Offers the regular amenities of three-star comfort, and overlooks Plac Wolności. The decor has a lot of brown, and rooms aren't quite as grand as the elegant facade suggests, but they're a decent size.

Mini Hotelik   HOTEL €
(☑61 633 1416; Al Niepodległości 8a; s/d from 65/129zł) Like it says on the label, this is a small place in an old building between the train station and the Old Town. It's basic but clean, with colourfully painted chambers. Some rooms share a bathroom. Enter from ul Taylora.

Youth Hostel No 3   HOSTEL €
(☑61 866 4040; ul Berwińskiego 2/3; dm 35zł) Cheap lodgings about a 15-minute walk southwest of the train station along ul Głogowska, adjacent to Park Wilsona. It's a basic 'no frills' option, but fills up fast with students and school groups. There's a 10pm curfew.

Hotel Royal   HOTEL €€€
(☑61 858 2300; www.hotel-royal.com.pl; ul Św Marcin 71; s/d 320/420zł) This is a gorgeous place set back from the main road. Rooms have huge beds and sparkling bathrooms.

Hotel Lech   HOTEL €€
(☑61 853 0151; www.hotel-lech.poznan.pl; ul Św Marcin 74; s/d 200/295zł) Hotel Lech has standard three-star decor, but rooms are relatively spacious and the bathrooms are modern. Flash your ISIC card for a discount.

🍴 Eating & Drinking

Tapas Bar   SPANISH €€
(☑61 852 8532; Stary Rynek 60; mains 18-72zł; ⊙noon-midnight) Atmospheric place dishing up authentic tapas and Spanish wine in a room lined with intriguing bric-a-brac including jars of stuffed olives, Mediterranean-themed artwork and bright red candles. Most tapas dishes cost 18zł to 22zł, so forget the mains and share with friends.

Cymes   JEWISH €€
(☑61 851 6638; ul Woźna 2/3; mains 20-29zł; ⊙1-10pm) If you're tired of pork for dinner, this ambient Jewish restaurant is the logical place to go. The interior is warm and cosy, done out like a residential dining room with

GNIEZNO

If you're staying in Poznań, it's worth checking out historic Gniezno, one of Poland's oldest settlements. It was probably here that Poland's Duke Mieszko I was baptised in 966, the starting point of Catholicism's major role in the nation's story. In 1025, Bolesław Chrobry was crowned in the city's cathedral as the first Polish king. Gniezno probably also functioned as Poland's first capital before Poznań achieved that honour, though history is murky on this point.

Whatever the case, Gniezno makes a good day trip from Poznań, or a short stopover. Setting out from its attractive broad **market square**, you can investigate its historic **cathedral**, dating from the 14th century, and a **museum** dedicated to Poland's origins, situated on the nearby lakeside.

An hour north of Gniezno is the Iron Age village of **Biskupin**, unearthed in the 1930s and partly reconstructed. Passing by it is a **tourist train** that links the towns of Żnin and Gąsawa, both of which have regular bus transport to Gniezno. Gniezno itself is linked to Poznań by frequent trains and buses throughout the day.

For more details, check out Lonely Planet's *Poland* country guide, visit www.turystyka.powiat-gniezno.pl, or drop into Gniezno's **tourist office** (☑61 428 4100; ul Tumska 12).

ceramic plates on the walls. On the menu are various poultry and fish dishes, including a whole goose for eight people, to be ordered 24 hours beforehand.

Gospoda Pod Koziołkami POLISH €€
(☑61 851 7868; Stary Rynek 95; mains 12-27zł; ⊙11am-10pm) Homey bistro within Gothic arches on the ground floor, and a grill in the cellar. The menu is crammed with tasty Polish standards, including some distinctively Wielkopolska specialities.

Bar Caritas CAFETERIA €
(☑61 852 5130; Plac Wolności 1; mains 6-12zł; ⊙8am-7pm Mon-Fri, 10am-5pm Sat, noon-5pm Sun) You can point at what you want without resorting to your phrasebook at this cheap and convenient milk bar. There are many variants of *naleśniki* (crepes) on the menu. Lunchtimes get crowded, so be prepared to share a table.

Sioux AMERICAN €€
(☑61 851 6286; Stary Rynek 93; mains 24-100zł; ⊙noon-11pm) As you'd expect, this is a Western-themed place, complete with waiters dressed as cowboys. Bizarrely named dishes such as 'Scoundrels in Uniforms from Fort Knox' (chicken legs) are on the menu, along with lots of steaks, ribs, grills and enchiladas.

Proletaryat BAR
(ul Wrocławska 9; ⊙1pm-2am Mon-Sat, 3pm-2am Sun) Small, red communist nostalgia bar with an array of socialist-era gear on the walls, including the obligatory bust of Lenin

in the window, and various portraits of the great man and his comrades. Play 'spot the communist leader' while sipping a boutique beer from the Czarnków Brewery.

Bodega CAFE-BAR
(ul Żydowska 4) On a street populated with cafes, Bodega's sleek modern lines stand out. The geometrically sharp interior is composed of mellow chocolate and gold tones, with candles on the tables. Good coffee is accompanied by sweet temptations.

Trattoria Valpolicella ITALIAN €€
(☑61 855 7191; ul Wrocławska 7; mains 23-66zł; ⊙1-11pm) Serves a wide variety of pasta and other Italian specialities, well suited to a glass of vino, in convincingly rustic Mediterranean surroundings.

Bar Wegetariański VEGETARIAN €
(☑61 851 0410; ul Rybaki 10; mains 5-20zł; ⊙11am-6pm Mon-Fri, 11am-3pm Sat) This cheap eatery offers tasty meat-free dishes, including its signature wholemeal crepes stuffed with mushrooms and cabbage.

☆ Entertainment

Lizard King LIVE MUSIC
(Stary Rynek 86; ⊙noon-2am) Simultaneously happening and laid-back, this venue is in prime position on the Old Market Sq. Friendly crowds sit drinking and eating in the split-level space, casting the occasional glance at the lizard over the bar. There's live music later in the week, mostly rock, jazz or blues, usually from 9pm.

Czarna Owca CLUB

(ul Jaskółcza 13; ☺noon-2am Mon-Fri, 5pm-2am Sat) Literally 'Black Sheep', this is a popular club with nightly DJs playing a mix of genres including R&B, house, rock, Latin, soul and funk. There's a disco night on Friday and a retro night on Tuesday.

Teatr Wielki THEATRE

(☑61 659 0280; www.opera.poznan.pl; ul Fredry 9) The main venue for opera and ballet.

Filharmonia CLASSICAL MUSIC

(☑61 853 6935; www.filharmonia.poznan.pl; ul Św Marcin 81) Offers classical concerts at least weekly.

ⓘ Information

City Information Centre (☑61 851 9645; ul Ratajczaka 44; ☺10am-7pm Mon-Fri, 10am-5pm Sat) Handles bookings for cultural events.

Main post office (ul Kościuszki 77; ☺7am-8pm Mon-Fri, 8am-3pm Sat)

Tourist office (☑61 852 6156; Stary Rynek 59; ☺9am-8pm Mon-Sat, 10am-6pm Sun May-Sep, 10am-6pm Mon-Fri Oct-Apr)

Tunel (Poznań Główny train station; per hr 5zł; ☺24hr) Internet access beneath the train station concourse.

ⓘ Getting There & Away

From **Poznań airport** (www.airport-poznan. com.pl), LOT flies at least three times a day to Warsaw, twice daily to Frankfurt and twice daily to Munich. Tickets are available from the **LOT office** (☑0801 703 703) at the airport or from **Orbis Travel** (☑61 851 2000; Al Marcinkowskiego 21).

There are also five domestic flights a week via Jet Air to each of Kraków and Gdańsk. A vast array of other European cities are serviced from Poznań, including London via Wizz Air and Ryanair (at least daily); Dublin via Ryanair (four times a week); and Copenhagen via SAS (five times a week). The airport is in the western suburb of Ławica, 7km from the Old Town and accessible by bus L from the main train station, or buses 48, 59 and night bus 242 from the 'Bałtyk' stop near Rondo Kaponiera.

The **bus terminal** (ul Towarowa 17) is a 10-minute walk east of the train station. However, most destinations can be reached more comfortably and frequently by train.

The busy **Poznań Główny train station** (ul Dworcowa 1) offers services to Kraków (56zł, 7½ hours, 14 daily), Szczecin (42zł, 2½ hours, at least hourly), Gdańsk and Gdynia (53zł, six hours, eight daily), Toruń (25zł, two hours, eight daily), Wrocław (37zł, 2½ hours, at least hourly) and Warsaw (51zł, 3½ hours, at least hourly).

POMERANIA

Pomerania (Pomorze in Polish) is an attractive region with diverse drawcards, from beautiful beaches to architecturally pleasing cities. It covers a large swathe of territory along the Baltic coast, from the German border in the west, to the lower Vistula Valley in the east. A sandy coastline stretches from Gdańsk to western Szczecin, and Toruń lies inland. Pomerania was fought over by Germanic and Slavic peoples for a millennium, before being incorporated almost fully within Poland after WWII.

Gdańsk

POP 456,000

Port cities are usually lively places with distinctive personalities, and Gdańsk is no exception. From its busy riverside waterfront to the Renaissance splendour of its charming narrow streets, there's plenty to like about this coastal city.

And few Polish cities occupy such a pivotal position in history as Gdańsk. Founded more than a millennium ago, it became the focus of territorial tensions when the Teutonic Knights seized it from Poland in 1308. The city joined the Hanseatic League in 1361, and became one of the richest ports in the Baltic through its membership of the trading organisation. Finally, the Thirteen Years' War ended in 1466 with the Knights' defeat and Gdańsk's return to Polish rule.

This to-and-fro between Germanic and Polish control wasn't over, however – in 1793 Gdańsk was incorporated into Prussia, and after the German loss in WWI it became the autonomous Free City of Danzig. The city's environs are where WWII began, when the Nazis bombarded Polish troops stationed at Westerplatte. Gdańsk suffered immense damage during the war, but upon its return to Poland in 1945, its historic centre was faithfully reconstructed.

In the 1980s, Gdańsk achieved international fame as the home of the Solidarity trade union, whose rise paralleled the fall of communism in Europe. Today it's a vibrant city and a great base for exploring the Baltic coast.

◉ Sights

MAIN TOWN

Royal Way HISTORIC ROUTE

The historic parade route of Polish kings runs from the western **Upland Gate** (built

ŚWIEBODZIN

If you're a lover of the bizarre, you could do worse than take a day trip to the town of Świebodzin, 100km west of Poznań. In November 2010 a local priest and a group of enthusiastic followers managed to erect a 33m-high **statue of Jesus Christ** (taller than the one in Rio) on a hilltop overlooking the town. The project caused great controversy among Catholics across the nation, and media reports suggested the 400-tonne figure was built cheaply on insufficient foundations – so if you're interested in seeing it, it might be better to get there sooner rather than later.

Świebodzin is on the busy railway line between Poznań and Berlin, with three direct train connections from Poznań each day.

in the 1770s on a 15th-century gate), onward through the **Foregate** (which once housed a torture chamber) and **Golden Gate** (1614), and east to the Renaissance **Green Gate** (1568). Along the way it passes through beautiful **ul Długa** (Long Street) and **Długi Targ** (Long Market).

Amber Museum MUSEUM
(www.mhmg.gda.pl/bursztyn; adult/concession 10/5zł, free Tue; ⊙10am-2.30pm Tue, 10am-3.30pm Wed-Sat, 11am-3.30pm Sun) Following the royal lead and starting from the Upland Gate, walk east to the Foregate. Within this structure, you can visit this museum, wherein you can marvel at the history of so-called 'Baltic gold'.

State Archaeological Museum MUSEUM
(ul Mariacka 25/26; adult/concession 6/4zł, free Sat; ⊙8am-4pm Tue-Fri, 10am-4pm Sat & Sun) When you reach the Green Gate, step through and follow the riverside promenade north to the 14th-century **St Mary's Gate**, which houses an overly generous number of formerly diseased ancient human skulls, displays of amber, and river views from the adjacent **tower** (admission 3zł).

St Mary's Church CHURCH
(⊙8.30am-6pm, except during services) From St Mary's Gate, stroll west along picturesque ul Mariacka and admire the gracious 17th-century burgher houses and amber shops. At the western end of the street is this gigantic 14th-century place of worship. Watch little figures troop out at noon from its 14m-high astronomical clock, adorned with zodiacal signs. You can also climb the 405 steps of the **tower** (adult/concession 5/3zł) for a giddy view over the town.

Central Maritime Museum MUSEUM
(ul Ołowianka 9-13; one section adult/concession 8/5zł, all sections 18/10zł; ⊙10am-4pm) On the waterfront north of St Mary's Gate, you'll

find the 15th-century **Gdańsk Crane**, the largest of its kind in medieval Europe and capable of hoisting loads of up to 2000kg. It's part of a maritime history museum which has a presence on both sides of the Motława. Its branch on the east bank offers a fascinating insight into Gdańsk's seafaring past, including the **Sołdek Museum Ship**, built here just after WWII.

Dom Uphagena MUSEUM
(ul Długa; adult/concession 10/5zł, free Tue; ⊙10am-3pm Tue, 10am-4pm Wed-Sat, 11am-4pm Sun) This historic 18th-century residence features ornate furniture.

Historical Museum of Gdańsk MUSEUM
(ul Długa 47; adult/concession 10/5zł, free Tue; ⊙10am-3pm Tue, 10am-4pm Wed-Sat, 11am-4pm Sun) Inside the towering Gothic town hall is this institution depicting photos of old Gdańsk, and the damage caused to the city during WWII.

Neptune's Fountain FOUNTAIN
Near the town hall is this decorative fountain (1633), which legend says once gushed forth *goldwasser*, the iconic Gdańsk liqueur.

Artus Court Museum MUSEUM
(ul Długi Targ 43/44; adult/concession 10/5zł, free Tue; ⊙10am-3pm Tue, 10am-4pm Wed-Sat, 11am-4pm Sun) Merchants used to congregate in this building, which boasts lavish interior decoration. Also note the adjacent **Golden House** (1618), which has a strikingly rich facade.

Free City of Danzig Historical Zone
MUSEUM
(ul Piwna 19/21; admission 5zł; ⊙11am-6pm) Small but intriguing display of items from the interwar era when Gdańsk operated as a 'free city', independent of both Poland and Germany.

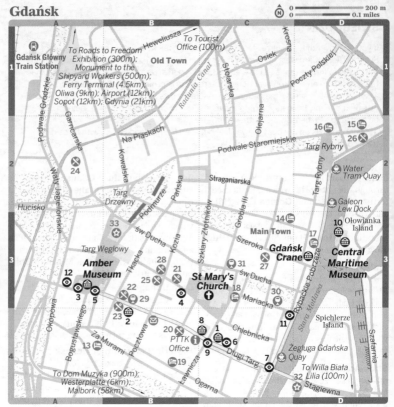

OLD TOWN

Almost totally destroyed in 1945, the Old Town has never been completely rebuilt, but contains some gems worth visiting.

TOP CHOICE **Roads to Freedom Exhibition**

MUSEUM

(ul Wały Piastowskie 24; adult/concession 6/4zł; ⊙10am-4pm Tue-Sun) At the north end of the Old Town is this excellent museum. Its exhibits chart the decline and fall of Polish communism and the rise of the Solidarity trade union. It's a place that anyone interested in Gdańsk's history should visit.

Monument to the Shipyard Workers

MONUMENT

(Plac Solidarności) A short walk further north, this soaring structure stands at the entrance to the Gdańsk Shipyards. It was erected in late 1980 in memory of 44 workers killed during the riots of December 1970, and was the first monument in a communist regime to commemorate the regime's victims.

OLIWA

Park Oliwski GARDENS

(ul Cystersów; ⊙8am-8pm) Some 9km northwest of the Main Town is the towering **Oliwa Cathedral**, located within this lovely set of gardens. It was built in the 13th century with a Gothic facade and a long, narrow central nave. The famous baroque organ is used for recitals each hour between 10am and 3pm Monday to Saturday in July and August. There's an **Ethnographic Museum** (ul Cystersów 19; adult/concession 8/5zł; ⊙10am-5pm Tue-Sun) housed in the nearby Old Granary, and the **Modern Art Gallery** (adult/concession 9/6zł; ⊙10am-5pm Tue-Sun) can be found in the former Abbots' Palace.

To reach the park, take the commuter train to the Gdańsk Oliwa station (3.10zł). From there, it's a 10-minute walk; head (west) up ul

Poczty Gdańsk, turn right (north) along the highway and look for the signs (in English) to 'Ethnographic Museum' and 'Cathedral'.

WESTERPLATTE

World War II Memorial   MEMORIAL

WWII began at 4.45am on 1 September 1939, when the German battleship *Schleswig-Holstein* began shelling the Polish naval post at this location, 7km north of Gdańsk's Main Town. The 182-man Polish garrison held out against ferocious attacks for a week before surrendering.

The enormity of this event is marked by a hilltop **memorial** (admission free; ⊘24hr), a small **museum** (ul Sucharskiego 1; adult/concession 3/2zł; ⊘9am-4pm May-Sep) and **ruins** remaining from the Nazi bombardment.

Bus 106 (25 minutes) goes to the park every 15 minutes from a stop outside the main train station in Gdańsk. Alternatively, see p668 for details of excursion boats from the Main Town to Westerplatte.

✯ Festivals & Events

International Organ Music Festival MUSIC (www.gdanskie-organy.com, under Concerts) June to August

International Street & Open-Air Theatre Festival   THEATRE (www.feta.pl) July

Sounds of the North Festival   MUSIC (www.nck.org.pl) Folkloric music festival in July/August

St Dominic's Fair   SHOPPING (www.mtgsa.pl, under Jarmark Św Dominika) Annual shopping fair in August.

International Shakespeare Festival THEATRE (www.shakespearefestival.pl) July/August

🛏 Sleeping

Accommodation can be tight in the warmer months. If you're having trouble finding accommodation, check with the PTTK office. Also consider staying in nearby Sopot (p668) or Gdynia (p669).

TOP CHOICE **Dom Zachariasza Zappio** HOSTEL € (☎58 322 0174; www.zappio.pl; ul Świętojańska 49; dm 45zł, s/d 92/158zł) At long last there's a hostel in the Main Town, located in an atmospheric former convent building next to St John's Church. Rooms are brightly furnished with contemporary furniture, and there's a fantastic beer garden.

Kamienica Gotyk
HOTEL €€

(☑60 284 4535; www.gotykhouse.eu; ul Mariacka 1; s/d 280/310zł) This Gothic guest house claims to be Gdańsk's oldest residence. Inside, the rooms are compact but neat, with clean bathrooms. The location is impressive, with St Mary's Church and the cafes and shops of ul Mariacka just outside the door.

Happy Seven Hostel
HOSTEL €

(☑58 320 8601; www.happyseven.com; ul Grodzka 16; dm from 45zł, d 150zł) New hostel in which each dorm has a light-hearted theme, including the 'Travel' dorm plastered with maps and the soothing green 'Jungle' dorm. The cool retro lounge contains a games console.

Kamienica Zacisze
APARTMENT €€€

(☑69 627 4306; www.apartments.gdansk.pl; ul Ogarna 107; apt from 350zł) Set within a quiet courtyard off the street, this communist-era workers' dormitory building has been transformed into a set of light, airy apartments for up to six people. Each apartment has high ceilings, a fully equipped kitchen and loads of space. Excellent value for the location and quality.

Dom Muzyka
HOTEL €€

(☑58 326 0600; www.dommuzyka.pl; ul Łąkowa 1/2; s/d/ste 220/310/460zł; ✴) Gorgeous white rooms with arched ceilings and quality furniture, inside the Music Academy some 300m east of the city centre. From July to August, a second wing of the building offers cheaper student-style accommodation. It's hard to spot from the street; head for the door on the city end of the courtyard within the big yellow-brick building.

Apartments Poland
APARTMENT €€

(☑58 346 9864; www.apartmentpoland.com; apt €30-70) A company with renovated properties scattered through the Tri-City Area (Gdańsk/Sopot/Gdynia), including a number in central Gdańsk. Some are big enough for families or other groups. Be aware of the additional electricity charge, based on a meter reading, when checking out.

Dom Harcerza
HOTEL €

(☑58 301 3621; www.domharcerza.pl; ul Za Murami 2/10; dm 39zł, s/d from 75/140zł) The rooms are small but cosy at this place, which offers the best value and location for any budget-priced hotel. It's popular (so book ahead), and can get noisy when large groups are staying here. There's a charming old-fashioned restaurant on the ground floor.

Hostel Targ Rybny
HOSTEL €

(☑58 301 5627; www.gdanskhostel.com.pl; ul Grodzka 21; dm 55zł, d from 150zł) Hostel overlooking the quay on the Motława River. It's a little cramped and starting to show its age, but is sociable, with a comfy lounge area. It also offers bike rental (20zł per day).

Camping Nr 218 Stogi
CAMPING GROUND €

(☑58 307 3915; www.kemping-gdansk.pl; ul Wydmy 9; per person/tent 13/6zł, cabins 60-130zł; ☺May-Sep) This camping ground is only 200m from the beach in the seaside holiday centre of Stogi, about 5.5km northeast of the Main Town. Tidy cabins sleep between two and five people, and facilities include a volleyball court and children's playground. Take tram 8 or 13 from the main train station in Gdańsk.

Willa Biała Lilia
HOTEL €€

(☑58 301 7074; www.bialalilia.pl; ul Spichrzowa 16; s/d 250/320zł) The White Lily Villa is an attractive accommodation choice a short walk east of the Main Town on Spichlerze Island. Rooms are neat and clean, and the staff are helpful.

Hotel Hanza
HOTEL €€€

(☑58 305 3427; www.hanza-hotel.com.pl; ul Tokarska 6; s/d/ste from 695/745/985zł; ✴) The Hanza is attractively perched along the waterfront near the Gdańsk Crane, and offers elegant, tasteful rooms in a modern building. Some rooms have enviable views over the river.

✖ Eating

For self-catering, visit **Kos Delikatesy** (ul Piwna 9/10; ☺24hr) in the Main Town.

Restauracja Pod Łososiem
POLISH €€€

(☑58 301 7652; ul Szeroka 52/54; mains 40-70zł; ☺noon-10pm) This is one of Gdańsk's oldest and most highly regarded restaurants, and is particularly famous for its salmon dishes and the gold-flecked liqueur *goldwasser*, which was invented here. Red-leather seats, brass chandeliers and a gathering of gas lamps fill out the posh interior.

Euro
EUROPEAN €€

(☑58 305 2383; ul Długa 79/80; mains 12-110zł) This elegant eatery is an antidote to the tourist traps along ul Długa, with its fine timber furniture and tasteful decor. The menu ranges widely, from humble *pierogi* to sturgeon in a champagne sauce.

U Dzika
POLISH €€

(☑58 305 2676; ul Piwna 59/61; mains 15-39zł; ☺11am-10pm) Pleasant eatery with a nice outdoor terrace, specialising in *pierogi*. If you're feeling adventurous, try the Fantasy Dumplings, comprising cottage cheese, cinnamon, raisins and peach.

Czerwone Drzwi　　　　INTERNATIONAL **€€**
(☑58 301 5764; ul Piwna 52/53; mains 18-65zł; ☺noon-10pm) Step through the Red Door into a relaxed, refined cafe atmosphere, which helps you digest the small but interesting menu of *pierogi*, pasta and Polish classics.

Bar Mleczny Neptun　　　　CAFETERIA **€**
(ul Długa 33/34; mains 2-13zł; ☺7.30am-7pm Mon-Fri, 10am-6pm Sat & Sun) This joint is a cut above your run-of-the-mill milk bar, with potted plants, lace curtains, decorative tiling and old lamps for decor.

Green Way　　　　VEGETARIAN **€**
(☑58 301 4121; ul Garncarska 4/6; mains 4-12zł; ☺10am-8pm Mon-Fri, noon-7pm Sat & Sun) Popular with local vegetarians, this eatery serves everything from soy cutlets to Mexican goulash in an unfussy green-and-orange space. There's another, more central, branch at ul Długa 11.

Przystań Gdańska　　　　POLISH **€€**
(☑58 301 1922; ul Wartka 5; mains 15-32zł) An atmospheric place to enjoy outdoor dining, with a view along the river to the Gdańsk Crane. Serves Polish classics and a range of fish dishes.

🍺 Drinking

Spiritus Sanctus　　　　BAR
(ul Grobla I 13; ☺5-10pm) If you're tired of beer and vodka, head for this stylish wine bar opposite St Mary's Church. While you're enjoying your Slovenian white or Croatian red, you can marvel at the amazing decor, a jumble of abstract art and classic objets d'art.

Cafe Ferber　　　　CAFE-BAR
(ul Długa 77/78; ☺9.30am-late) It's startling to step straight from Gdańsk's historic main street into this very modern cafe-bar, dominated by bright red panels, a suspended ceiling and boxy lighting. Partake of breakfast, well-made coffee, international wines and cocktail creations, such as the *szary kot* (grey cat).

Kamienica　　　　CAFE-BAR
(ul Mariacka 37/39) The best of the bunch on ul Mariacka is this excellent two-level cafe with a calm, sophisticated atmosphere and the best patio on the block. It's as popular

for daytime coffee and cakes as it is for a sociable evening beverage.

☆ Entertainment

Miasto Aniołów　　　　CLUB
(www.miastoaniolow.com.pl, in Polish; ul Chmielna 26) The City of Angels covers all the bases – late-night revellers can hit the spacious dance floor, crash in the chill-out area, or hang around the atmospheric deck overlooking the Motława River. Nightly DJs play disco and other dance-oriented sounds.

State Baltic Opera Theatre　　　　OPERA
(☑58 763 4912; www.operabaltycka.pl; Al Zwycięstwa 15) This place is in the suburb of Wrzeszcz, not far from the train station at Gdańsk Politechnika.

Teatr Wybrzeże　　　　THEATRE
(☑58 301 1328; www.teatrwybrzeze.pl, in Polish; ul Św Ducha 2) Next to the Arsenal is the main city theatre. Both Polish and foreign classics (all in Polish) are part of the repertoire.

ℹ Information

Almatur (☑58 301 2424; Długi Targ 11) Travel agency.

Jazz 'n' Java (ul Tkacka 17/18; per hr 6zł; ☺10am-10pm) Internet access.

Kawiarnia Internetowa (Cinema City, ul Karmelicka 1; per hr 6zł; ☺9am-12.30am Mon-Sat, 9.30am-12.30am Sun) Free coffee over 30 minutes' access.

Main post office (ul Długa 22; ☺24hr)

Orbis Travel (☑58 301 4544; ul Podwale Staromiejskie 96/97) Travel agency.

PTTK office (☑58 301 1343; www.pttk-gdansk. pl; ul Długa 45; ☺10am-6pm Mon-Fri, 8.30am-4.30pm Sat & Sun)

Tourist office (☑58 301 4355; www.got.gdansk. pl; ul Heweliusza 29; ☺8am-4pm Mon-Fri) Well-concealed from the casual visitor, but helpful.

ℹ Getting There & Away

Air
From **Lech Wałęsa airport** (www.airport. gdansk.pl), LOT has at least five daily flights to Warsaw, and at least three daily to Frankfurt and Munich. Tickets can be bought at the **LOT office** (☑0801 703 703; ul Wały Jagiellońskie 2/4).

Gdańsk is also connected to a plethora of other European cities, including London via Ryanair and Wizz Air (at least daily); Dublin via Ryanair (daily); and Copenhagen via SAS (up to three daily).

The airport is accessible by bus 110 from the Gdańsk Wrzeszcz local commuter train station, or bus 210 or night bus N3 from outside the

Gdańsk Główny train station. Taxis cost 45zł to 55zł one way.

Boat

Polferries (www.polferries.pl) offers daily services between Gdańsk and Nynäshamn (19 hours) in Sweden in summer (less frequently in the low season). The company uses the **ferry terminal** (ul Przemysłowa 1) in Nowy Port, about 5km north of the Main Town and a short walk from the local commuter train station at Gdańsk Brzeźno. Orbis Travel and the PTTK office in Gdańsk provide information and sell tickets.

Between April and October, **Żegluga Gdańska excursion boats** (www.zegluga.pl) leave regularly from the dock near the Green Gate in Gdańsk for Westerplatte (adult/concession return 45/22zł). Further north along the dockside, you can board the Galeon Lew (adult/concession return 40/22zł), a replica 17th-century galleon, for hourly cruises to Westerplatte. Just north of the galleon is the Water Tram, a ferry which heads to Hel (18/9zł, three daily) each weekend during May, then daily from June to August. Bicycles cost an extra 3zł to transport.

Bus

The **bus terminal** (ul 3 Maja 12) is behind the main train station and connected to ul Podwale Grodzkie by an underground passageway. Useful bus destinations include Frombork (17zł, three hours, two daily), Warsaw (52zł, six hours, nine daily) and Świnoujście (63zł, 8½ hours, one daily).

Train

The city's main train station, **Gdańsk Główny** (ul Podwale Grodzkie 1), is conveniently located on the western outskirts of the Old Town. Most long-distance trains actually start or finish at Gdynia, so make sure you get on/off quickly here.

Each day 10 trains (mainly Express InterCity services) head to Warsaw, (114zł, 5½ hours). There are also trains to Malbork (16zł, 1¼ hours, at least hourly), Elbląg (20zł, 1½ hours, 10 daily), Olsztyn (37zł, three hours, six daily), Giżycko (51zł, five hours, two daily), Kraków (129zł, eight hours, 10 daily), Poznań (51zł, 4¾ hours, seven daily), Toruń (39zł, four hours, 11 daily) and Szczecin (56zł, 5½ hours, four daily). Trains also head to Białystok (58zł, 7¾ hours, two daily) and Lublin (63zł, nine hours, two daily).

❶ Getting Around

The local commuter train – the SKM – runs every 15 minutes between 6am and 7.30pm, and less frequently thereafter, between Gdańsk Główny and Gdynia Główna train stations, via Sopot and Gdańsk Oliwa train stations. (Note: the line to Gdańsk Nowy Port, via Gdańsk Brzeźno, is a separate line that leaves less regularly from Gdańsk Główny.) Buy tickets at any station and validate them in the yellow boxes at the platform entrance, or purchase them prevalidated from vending machines on the platform.

Around Gdańsk

Gdańsk is part of the so-called Tri-City Area including Gdynia and Sopot, which are easy day trips from Gdańsk.

SOPOT
POP 38,600

Since the 19th century, Sopot, 12km north of Gdańsk, has been one of the Baltic coast's most fashionable seaside resorts. It has an easy-going atmosphere, good nightlife and long stretches of sandy beach.

◉ Sights & Activities

From the tourist office, head down ul Bohaterów Monte Cassino, one of Poland's most attractive pedestrian streets, past the surreal **Crooked House** (Krzywy Domek; ul Bohaterów Monte Cassino 53) shopping centre to Poland's longest pier (515m), the famous **Molo** (www.molo.sopot.pl; adult/concession 4.30/2.20zł; ☺8am-dusk Apr-Sep). Various attractions and cultural events can be found near and along the structure.

Opposite Pension Wanda, the **Sopot Museum** (ul Poniatowskiego 8; adult/concession 5/3zł, free Thu; ☺10am-4pm Tue-Fri, 11am-6pm Sat & Sun) has displays recalling the town's 19th-century incarnation as the German resort of Zoppot.

🛏 Sleeping & Eating

There are no real budget options in Sopot, and prices increase during the busy summer season. Bistros and cafes serving a wide range of cuisines sprout up in summer along the promenades.

Zhong Hua Hotel HOTEL **€€€**
(📞58 550 2020; www.hotelchinski.pl; Al Wojska Polskiego 1; s/d 310/350zł) Attractive accommodation in a striking wooden pavilion on the seafront. The foyer is decked out in Chinese design, with hanging lanterns and beautiful timber furniture. The theme extends to the small but pleasant rooms, with views of the water.

Hotel Eden HOTEL **€€**
(📞58 551 1503; www.hotel-eden.com.pl; ul Kordeckiego 4/6; s/d 200/300zł) One of the less expensive places in town. It's a quiet, old-fashioned pension with high ceilings, classic furniture and recently renovated bathrooms, overlooking a park one street from the beach.

Willa Karat II

HOTEL €€

(☑58 550 0742; www.willakarat.pl; ul 3 Maja 31; s/d 150/250zł) Cosy budget lodgings a few blocks from the beach, with light, spacious rooms and clean bathrooms, and plants decorating the corridors. There's a kitchen and dining area for guest use. From the train station, walk right along ul Kościuszki, then left along ul 3 Maja towards the coast.

Mandarynka

BAR €€

(ul Bema 6; ☉noon-10pm) One street south of the main drag, this is a very cool confection of timber tables, scarlet lampshades and huge orange cushions. There's a food menu, and a DJ in action upstairs most nights.

Pension Wanda

HOTEL €€€

(☑58 550 3038; ul Poniatowskiego 7; s/d 280/360zł) The Wanda is a homey place with light, airy rooms, in a handy location about 500m south of the pier. Some rooms have sea views.

Cafe del Arte

CAFE

(ul Bohaterów Monte Cassino 53) This classy cafe, within the Crooked House, is a great place to enjoy coffee, cake and ice cream surrounded by artistic objects in the combined cafe-gallery.

❶ Information

Tourist office (☑58 550 3783; www.sopot. pl; ul Dworcowa 4; ☉9am-7pm Jun-Aug, 10am-6pm Sep-May) About 50m from the Sopot train station.

❶ Getting There & Away

From the **Sopot train station** (ul Dworcowa 7), local SKM commuter trains run every 15 minutes to Gdańsk Główny (4.50zł, 15 minutes) and Gdynia Główna (3.10zł, 10 minutes) train stations. Excursion boats leave several times a day (May to September) from the Sopot pier to Hel (adult/concession return 30/20zł). The Water Tram also links Sopot with Hel (16/8zł, three daily) each weekend during May, then daily from June to August.

GDYNIA

POP 249,000

As a young city with a busy port atmosphere, Gdynia, 9km north of Sopot, is less atmospheric than Gdańsk or Sopot. It was greatly expanded as a seaport after this coastal area (but not Gdańsk) became part of Poland following WWI. However, it's worth dropping into on a day trip.

◉ Sights & Activities

From the main Gdynia Główna train station on Plac Konstytucji, follow ul 10 Lutego east for about 1.5km to the **Southern Pier**.

Moored on the pier's northern side are two interesting museum ships. First up is the curiously sky-blue destroyer **Błyskawica** (adult/concession 8/4zł; ☉10am-4.30pm Tue-Sun), which escaped capture in 1939 and went on to serve successfully with Allied naval forces throughout WWII.

Beyond it is the beautiful three-masted frigate **Dar Pomorza** (adult/concession 8/4zł; ☉10am-6pm daily Jul-Sep, 10am-4pm Tue-Sun May, Jun & Oct), built in Hamburg in 1909 as a training ship for German sailors. There's information in English on the dockside.

A 20-minute walk uphill (follow the signs) from Teatr Muzyczny on Plac Grunwaldzki (about 300m southwest of the start of the pier) leads to **Kamienna Góra**, a hill offering wonderful views.

⌱ Sleeping & Eating

Gdynia is best visited as a day trip, but there are some reasonable accommodation options. There are several cheap eateries in the city centre, and upmarket fish restaurants along the pier.

Willa Lubicz

HOTEL €€€

(☑58 668 4740; www.willalubicz.pl; ul Orłowska 43; s/d from 340/380zł) If you're looking for style, you could try this quiet, upmarket place with a chic 1930s ambience at the southern end of town; Gdynia Orłowo is the nearest train station. Third-floor rooms have views of the sea.

Hotel Antracyt

HOTEL €€

(☑58 620 1239; www.hotel-antracyt.pl; ul Korzeniowskiego 19; s/d from 180/220zł) Located in the southern part of central Gdynia, on a hill in an exclusive residential area, with fine views over the water.

China Town Hotel

HOTEL €

(☑58 620 9221; ul Dworca 11a; s/d 100/140zł) Inexpensive lodgings can be found here, opposite the train station. The rooms are plain but serviceable for a night, though singles are very small.

Bistro Kwadrans

POLISH €€

(☑58 620 1592; Skwer Kościuszki 20; mains 12-18zł; ☉9am-10pm Mon-Fri, 10am-10pm Sat, noon-10pm Sun) On the north side of the square between ul 10 Lutego and the pier, this is a great place for tasty Polish food. It also serves up pizzas, including an improbable variant involving banana and curry.

ℹ Information

Tourist office (☎58 622 3766; www.gdynia.pl; ul 10 Lutego 24; ☺9am-6pm Mon-Sat, 9am-4pm Sun May-Sep, 9am-5pm Oct-Apr) About 150m east of the main train station.

ℹ Getting There & Away

Local commuter trains link Gdynia Główna train station with Sopot (3.10zł) and Gdańsk (4.50zł) every 15 minutes. From the same station, trains run hourly to Hel (15zł, two hours) and half-hourly to Lębork (16zł, one hour), where you can change for Łeba. From the small bus terminal outside, minibuses also go to Hel (14zł, two hours, six daily).

Stena Line uses the **Terminal Promowy** (ul Kwiatkowskiego 60), about 5km northwest of Gdynia. It offers twice-daily services between Gdynia and Karlskrona (10½ hours) in Sweden. Take bus 150 from ul Władysława IV.

Between May and September, excursion boats leave Gdynia's Southern Pier to Hel (adult/concession one way 45/30zł, return 60/42zł), from a point beyond the Dar Pomorza.

HEL
POP 3900

Never was a town more entertainingly named – English speakers can spend hours creating amusing twists on 'to Hel and back', or 'a cold day in Hel'. In fact, this old fishing village at the tip of the Hel peninsula north of Gdańsk is an attractive place to visit, and a popular beach resort. The pristine, wind-swept **beach** on the Baltic side stretches the length of the peninsula. On the southern side, the sea is popular for **windsurfing**; equipment can be rented in the villages of **Władysławowo** and **Jastarnia**.

The **Fokarium** (ul Morska 2; admission 2zł; ☺8.30am-dusk), off the main road along the seafront, is home to endangered Baltic grey seals. It also has a good souvenir shop for those 'I'm in Hel' postcards to send to friends back home. The 15th-century **Gothic church**, further along the esplanade, houses the **Museum of Fishery** (ul Nadmorski 2; adult/concession 6/4zł; ☺10am-4pm Tue-Sun).

Visitors often stay in private rooms offered within local houses (mostly from May to September), at about 90zł per double. **Captain Morgan** (☎58 675 0091; www.captainmorgan.hel.org.pl; ul Wiejska 21; d 100zł) also offers plain, clean rooms, and good seafood in a quirky pub stuffed with maritime memorabilia.

To Hel, minibuses leave every hour or so from the main train station in Gdynia (14zł, two hours). Several trains depart from Gdynia (15zł, two hours, hourly), and from May to September from Gdańsk (23zł, three hours, six daily). Hel is also accessible by excursion boat from Gdańsk, Sopot and Gdynia – see the Getting There & Away section for each of these destinations for details.

MALBORK
POP 38,300

The magnificent **Malbork Castle** (☎55 647 0800; www.zamek.malbork.pl; adult/concession 37/27zł; ☺9am-7pm Tue-Sun May-Aug, 10am-5pm Tue-Sun Apr & Sep, 10am-3pm Tue-Sun Oct-Mar) is the centrepiece of this town, 58km south-east of Gdańsk. It's the largest Gothic castle in Europe, and was once known as Marienburg, headquarters of the Teutonic Knights. It was constructed by the order in 1276 and became the seat of their Grand Master in 1309. Damage sustained in WWII has been repaired since the conflict's end, and it was placed on the Unesco World Heritage List in 1997. The entry fee includes a compulsory Polish-language tour, along with an audio-guide offering a tour in English and other languages (you pick up this item from a separate booth next to the castle gate). Alternatively, an English-speaking guide can be obtained for 210zł. On Mondays there's a limited tour for a bargain basement 8zł.

Hotel Grot (☎55 646 9660; www.grothotel.pl; ul Kościuszki 22d; s/d 199/289zł) is classy accommodation for its price range, with contemporary furniture and an impressive restaurant. It's set back off the street in the town centre.

Hotel Zamek (☎55 246 0220; www.hotelprodus.pl; ul Starościńska 14; s/d 200/300zł) is inside a restored medieval building in the Lower Castle. The rooms are a bit old-fashioned, but the bathrooms are up-to-date. The restaurant has character, but can be crowded with tour groups.

The **Youth Hostel** (☎55 272 2408; www.ssm malbork.webpark.pl, in Polish; ul Żeromskiego 45; dm 28zł, d 62zł) is a reasonable budget option in a local school about 500m south of the castle.

Restauracja Piwniczka (☎55 273 3668; ul Starościńska 1; mains 11-89zł; ☺10am-7pm) is an atmospheric cellar restaurant beneath the west wall of the castle.

The castle is 1km west of the train and bus stations. Leave the train station, turn right, cut across the highway, head down ul Kościuszki and follow the signs. Malbork is an easy day trip by train from Gdańsk (16zł, 1¼ hours, at least hourly). Malbork is also connected to Olsztyn (33zł, two hours, six daily), and eight trains head daily to Toruń (21zł, three hours), including three operated by private company Arriva.

Toruń

POP 206,000

The first thing to strike you about Toruń, south of Gdańsk, is its collection of massive red-brick churches, looking more like fortresses than places of worship. The city is defined by its striking Gothic architecture, which gives its Old Town a distinctive appearance and its promotional slogan: *gotyk na dotyk* (touch gothic). The city is a pleasant place to spend a few days, offering a nice balance between a relaxing slow pace and engaging entertainment diversions.

Toruń is also famous as the birthplace of Nicolaus Copernicus, a figure you cannot escape as you walk the streets of his home town – you can even buy gingerbread men in his likeness. The renowned astronomer spent his youth here, and the local university is named after him.

Historically, Toruń is intertwined with the Teutonic Knights, who established an outpost here in 1233. Following the Thirteen Years' War (1454–66), the Teutonic Order and Poland signed a peace treaty here, which returned to Poland a large area of land stretching from Toruń to Gdańsk.

Toruń was fortunate to escape major damage in WWII, and as a result is the best-preserved Gothic town in Poland. The Old Town was added to Unesco's World Heritage List in 1997.

◎ Sights

Old Town Market Square   HISTORIC AREA
The starting point for any exploration of Toruń is the Old Town Market Sq (Rynek Staromiejski). It's the focal point of the Old Town, lined by elegant facades and dominated by the massive 14th-century **Old Town Hall**.

In front of the town hall is an elegant **statue of Copernicus**. Look for other interesting items of statuary around the square, including a dog and umbrella from a famous Polish comic strip, a donkey that once served as a punishment device, and a fabled violinist who saved Toruń from a plague of frogs.

Regional Museum   MUSEUM
(www.muzeum.torun.pl; Rynek Staromiejski 1; adult/concession 10/6zł; ☺10am-6pm Tue-Sun May-Sep, 10am-4pm Tue-Sun Oct-Apr) Within the town hall, this institution features a fine collection of 19th- and 20th-century Polish art. Other displays recall the town's guilds, and there's an exhibition of medieval stained glass and religious paintings. Climb

the 40m-high **tower** (adult/concession 10/6zł; ☺10am-4pm Tue-Sun Apr, 10am-8pm Tue-Sun May-Sep) for great views.

House of Copernicus   MUSEUM
(ul Kopernika 15/17; adult/concession 10/7zł; ☺10am-6pm Tue-Sun May-Sep, 10am-4pm Tue-Sun Oct-Apr) In 1473, Copernicus was allegedly born in the brick Gothic house that now contains this fairly dull museum, presenting replicas of the great astronomer's instruments (though there's now some doubt he was really born here).

More engaging, if overpriced, is the museum's short **audiovisual presentation** (adult/concession 12/7zł) regarding Copernicus' life in Toruń; and the extravagantly titled **World of Toruń's Gingerbread** (adult/concession 10/6zł). Visitors are guided by a costumed medieval townswoman and given the chance to bake their own *pierniki* (gingerbread). A combined ticket to any two of the three attractions costs 18/11zł.

Cathedral of SS John the Baptist & John the Evangelist   CHURCH
(ul Żeglarska; adult/concession 3/2zł; ☺9am-5.30pm Mon-Sat, 2-5.30pm Sun Apr-Oct) One block south of the Old Town Market Sq is this place of worship with its massive **tower** (adult/concession 6/4zł) and bell, founded in 1233 and completed more than 200 years later. No sightseeing allowed during services.

Teutonic Knights' Castle Ruins   RUINS
(ul Przedzamcze; adult/concession 6/4zł, free Mon; ☺10am-6pm Mar-Oct, 10am-4pm Nov-Feb) East of the remnants of the Old Town walls are the ruins of the Teutonic Castle, destroyed in 1454 by angry townsfolk protesting against the knights' oppressive regime.

Far Eastern Art Museum   MUSEUM
(Rynek Staromiejski 35; adult/concession 7/4zł, free Wed; ☺10am-6pm Tue-Sun May-Sep, 10am-4pm Tue-Sun Oct-Apr) The richly decorated, 15th-century **House Under the Star**, with its baroque facade and spiral wooden staircase, contains this collection of art from Asia.

Explorers' Museum   MUSEUM
(ul Franciszkańska 11; adult/concession 8/5zł, free Wed; ☺11am-6pm Tue-Sun May-Sep, 10am-4pm Tue-Sun Oct-Apr) A street back from the Old Town Market Sq is this small but interesting display of artefacts from the collection of inveterate wanderer Antonio Halik.

Ethnographic Museum   MUSEUM
(ul Wały Sikorskiego 19; adult/concession 14/9zł; ☺9am-4pm Wed & Fri, 10am-5pm Tue, Thu-Sun)

POLAND POMERANIA

Toruń

200 m
0.1 miles

To Toruń Miasto Train Station (400m)

Vistula

Wola Zamkowa

Szpitalna
św Jakuba
Ślusarska
Rynek Nowomiejski
Browarna
Przedmiarska

15
20
7
5

Królowej Jadwigi
Wielkie Garbary

New Town
6

Jęczmienna

Małe Garbary

13

Strumykowa
Podmurna
Mostowa
23
Przedzamcze
11
17

Bulwar Filadelfijski

To Bus Terminal (500m)
Zaułek Prosowy

Szczytna
Szeroka
św Jana
Clasna
Łazienna

Old Town
Statue of Copernicus

Podmurna
Szewska

Cathedral of SS John the Baptist & John the Evangelist

Żeglarska
Kopernika
Bankowa

Tourist Office
Regional Museum
Rynek Staromiejski
4
2
21
18
3
Rabiańska
10
12
22

Chełmińska

Fosa Staromiejska

16
Panny Marii
Różana
14
19
8
9

Ducha Świętego

Piekary
Piekary
Piekary

1
24

Waly Sikorskiego
Fosa Staromiejska

Franciszkańska

Fosa Staromiejska

To Toruń Glówny Train Station (2km)

Al Jana Pawła II

Toruń

In a park just north of the Old Town is this showcase of traditional customs, costumes and weapons.

Sleeping

Toruń is blessed with a plentiful number of hotels within converted historic buildings in its Old Town; but as they're fairly small, it pays to book ahead.

Green Hostel HOSTEL €
(56 561 4000; www.greenhostel.eu; ul Małe Garbary 10; s/d 50/100zł) It may be labelled as a hostel, but there are no dorms. Instead, this new budget accommodation boasts shiny inexpensive rooms, a kitchen and a pleasant lounge. Great option for the price.

Hotel Pod Czarną Różą HOTEL €€
(56 621 9637; www.hotel czarnaroza.pl; ul Rabiańska 11; s/d 170/210zł) 'Under the Black Rose' is spread between a historic inn and a newer wing facing the river, though its interiors present a uniformly clean up-to-date look. Some doubles come with small but functional kitchens.

Orange Hostel HOSTEL €
(56 652 0033; www.hostelorange.pl; ul Prosta 19; dm 30zł, s/d 50/90zł) The wave of Polish hostels for the international backpacker has finally swept over sleepy Toruń. Orange is in a handy location, its decor is bright and cheer-

ful, and its kitchen is an impressive place to practise the gentle art of self-catering.

Hotel Petite Fleur HOTEL €€
(56 621 5100; www.petitefleur.pl; ul Piekary 25; s/d 210/270zł) Just opposite the Gotyk, the Petite Fleur offers fresh, airy rooms in a renovated old town house, some with exposed original brickwork and rafters. It also has a French cellar restaurant.

Hotel Pod Orłem HOTEL €€
(56 622 5024; www.hotel.torun.pl; ul Mostowa 17; s/d from 130/165zł) This hotel is great value, and although the rooms are smallish, have squeaky wooden floors and some contain poky bathrooms, the service is good and it's central. The foyer and corridors are fun with their jumble of framed pop-art images and old photos.

Camping Nr 33 Tramp CAMPING GROUND €
(56 654 7187; www.mosir.torun.pl; ul Kujawska 14; camping per person 9zł, tents 6-12zł, s/d from 50/65zł; May-Sep) There's a choice of cabins or hotel-style rooms at this camping ground on the edge of the train line, along with an on-site snack bar. It's a five-minute walk west of the main train station.

Hotel Retman HOTEL €€
(56 657 4460; www.hotelretman.pl; ul Rabiańska 15; s/d 190/250zł) Attractively decorated accommodation offering spacious, atmospheric rooms with red carpet

and solid timber furniture. Downstairs is a good pub and restaurant.

Hotel 1231 HOTEL €€€

(☑56 619 0910; www.hotelesolaris.pl; ul Przedzamcze 6; s/d 340/400zł) Elegant four-star accommodation in the shadow of the Old Town walls, with pleasantly appointed rooms and a cellar restaurant and bar.

Hotel Gotyk HOTEL €€

(☑56 658 4000; www.hotel-gotyk.com.pl; ul Piekary 20; s/d 190/270zł) Housed in a fully modernised 14th-century building just off the Old Town Market Sq, rooms are very neat, with ornate furniture and high ceilings, and all come with sparkling bathrooms.

✖ Eating & Drinking

Toruń is famous for its *pierniki*, which come in a variety of shapes, and can be bought at **Sklep Kopernik** (☑56 622 8832; Rynek Staromiejski 6).

⌐TOP⌐ Gospoda Pod Modrym Fartuchem
CHOICE POLISH, INDIAN €€

(☑56 622 2626; Rynek Nowomiejski 8; mains 16-30zł; ⊘10am-10pm) This pleasant, unpretentious 15th-century pub on the New Town Sq has been visited by Polish kings and Napoleon. The usual meat-and-cabbage Polish dishes are joined by an array of Indian food, including a good vegetarian selection.

Bar Mleczny Pod Arkadami CAFETERIA €

(ul Różana 1; mains 1-9zł; ⊘9am-7pm Mon-Fri, 11am-6pm Sat & Sun) This classic milk bar is just off the Old Town Market Sq, with a range of low-cost dishes. It also has a takeaway window serving a range of tasty *zapiekanki* (toasted rolls with cheese, mushrooms and tomato sauce) and sweet waffles.

Parmis MIDDLE EASTERN €

(☑56 621 0607; ul Mostowa 7; mains 8-23zł; ⊘noon-midnight) A splash of Middle Eastern cuisine in northern Poland, in a cheerful venue decorated with colourful lanterns. The menu contains many variants of kebabs, along with soups, salads and pizzas.

Tantra BAR

(ul Ślusarska 5; ⊘5pm-late) This astonishingly decorated bar is done out in an Indian and Tibetan theme and layered with cloth and other artefacts from the subcontinent. Sit on the cushion-strewn divans, order a drink from the long list and meditate on the infinite.

Manekin POLISH €

(☑56 621 0504; Rynek Staromiejski 16; mains 8-15zł) Vaguely Wild West decor adorns this inexpensive central restaurant specialising in *naleśniki* (crepes). It offers a variety of filled pancakes, including vegetarian options.

Kona Coast Café CAFE

(ul Piekary 22; ⊘7.30am-7pm Mon-Fri, 10am-9pm Sat, 10.30am-5pm Sun) Serves excellent freshly ground coffee, along with homemade lemonade, chai and various cold drinks. There's also a light meal menu.

☆ Entertainment

Piwnica Pod Aniołem LIVE MUSIC

(Rynek Staromiejski 1) Set in a splendid spacious cellar in the Old Town Hall, this bar offers live music some nights. Check the posters outside for the latest gigs.

Koci Ogon CLUB

(ul Rabiańska 17; ⊘5pm-2am Sun-Thu, 5pm-4am Fri & Sat) This is a lively cellar club with rock DJs most nights from 9pm.

Teatr im Horzycy THEATRE

(☑56 622 5222; Plac Teatralny 1) The main stage for theatre performances.

Dwór Artusa CLASSICAL MUSIC

(☑56 655 4929; Rynek Staromiejski 6) This place often presents classical music.

Nasze Kino CINEMA

(www.naszekino.pl, in Polish; ul Podmurna 14) Cool little arthouse cinema embedded within part of the Old Town wall, its single screen showing a range of non-Hollywood films.

❶ Information

Ksero Uniwerek (ul Franciszkańska 5; per hr 3zł; ⊘8am-7pm Mon-Fri, 9am-4pm Sat) Internet access.

Main post office (Rynek Staromiejski; ⊘24hr)

Tourist office (☑56 621 0931; www.it.torun.pl; Rynek Staromiejski 25; ⊘9am-4pm Mon & Sat, 9am-6pm Tue-Fri, 10am-2pm Sun) Offers useful advice and hires out handheld MP3 players with English-language audio tours of the city (10zł per four hours).

❶ Getting There & Away

The **bus terminal** (ul Dąbrowskiego) is a 10-minute walk north of the Old Town, but most places can be reached more efficiently by train.

The **Toruń Główny train station** (Al Podgórska) is on the opposite side of the Vistula River and linked to the Old Town by bus 22 or 27 (get off at the first stop over the bridge). Some trains stop at the more convenient **Toruń Miasto train station** (Plac 18 Stycznia), about 500m east of the New Town.

From the Toruń Główny train station, there are trains to Poznań (25zł, two hours, eight daily), Gdańsk and Gdynia (39zł, four hours, 11 daily), Kraków (58zł, eight hours, eight daily), Łódź (37zł, 2½ hours, 12 daily), Olsztyn (27zł, 2½ hours, eight daily), Wrocław (51zł, five hours, two daily) and Warsaw (48zł, three hours, 10 daily). There are also eight daily trains to Malbork (21zł, three hours), including three operated by private company Arriva. Trains travelling between Toruń and Gdańsk often change at Bydgoszcz, and between Toruń and Kraków you may need to get another connection at Inowrocław.

Szczecin

POP 406,000

Szczecin (*shcheh-cheen*) is the major city and port of northwestern Poland. Massive damage in WWII accounts for the unaesthetic mishmash of new and old buildings in the city centre, but enough remains to give a sense of the pre-war days. The broad streets and massive historic buildings bear a strong resemblance to those of Berlin, for which Szczecin was once the main port as the German city of Stettin. Szczecin may not have the seamless charm of Toruń or Wrocław, but it's worth a visit if you're travelling to/from Germany.

◉ Sights

Szczecin Underground

HISTORIC SHELTER

(☎91 434 0801; www.schron.szczecin.pl; ul Kolumba 1/6; admission 15zł; ☺noon) At the train sta-

tion you can join a fascinating guided tour which takes you through a German-built bomb shelter that later became a Cold War fallout shelter. Pay at the Centrum Wynajmu i Turystyki office.

FREE **Castle of the Pomeranian Dukes**

CASTLE

(ul Korsazy 34; ☺dawn-dusk) This huge and austere castle was originally built in the mid-14th century, then was enlarged in 1577 and rebuilt after major damage from airborne bombing in WWII. Its **Castle Museum** (adult/concession 4/3zł, free Thu; ☺10am-6pm Tue-Sun) explains the building's convoluted history, with special exhibitions mounted from time to time.

Museum of the City of Szczecin MUSEUM

(ul Mściwoja 8; adult/concession 10/5zł, free Thu; ☺10am-6pm Tue-Fri, 10am-4pm Sat & Sun) A short walk south from the castle is the attractive 15th-century Old Town Hall, which contains a museum dedicated to the history of the city. Nearby is the charmingly rebuilt Old Town with its cafes, bars and clubs.

Kino Pionier 1909 HISTORIC BUILDING

(www.kino-pionier.com.pl, in Polish; ul Wojska Polskiego 2) Possibly the oldest continuously operating cinema in the world, having opened in 1909 – though there's a Danish rival that may be one year older. Either way, it's both a historic site and an atmospheric place to catch a film, about 400m west of the tourist office past Plac Zwycięstwa.

POLAND SZCZECIN

WORTH A TRIP

BALTIC BEACHES

Between Gdańsk and the western city of Szczecin, there are numerous seaside towns with unpolluted waters, offering fine sandy beaches during summer. Here are a few places for a sunbathing detour on your journey west along the Baltic coast towards the German border:

» **Łeba** Pleasant holiday town with wide sandy beaches, also the gateway to Słowiński National Park and its ever-shifting sand dunes.

» **Ustka** Once the summer hang-out of German Chancellor Otto von Bismarck, this fishing port is full of atmosphere.

» **Darłowo** A former medieval trading port with an impressive castle, and two beaches linked by a pedestrian bridge over a river.

» **Kołobrzeg** This coastal city offers historic attractions, spa treatments and Baltic cruises.

» **Międzyzdroje** A popular seaside resort and the gateway to Wolin National Park.

» **Świnoujście** On a Baltic island shared with Germany, this busy port town boasts a long sandy shore and pleasant parks.

For more details, check out Lonely Planet's *Poland* country guide, or www.poland.travel.

🛏 Sleeping & Eating

Hotel Campanile HOTEL €€
(☎91 481 7700; www.campanile.com; ul Wyszyńskiego 30; r 273zł) Neat and spacious rooms in a handy position for everything: the Old Town, the train and bus stations, and the central shopping zone.

Youth Hostel PTSM HOSTEL €
(☎91 422 4761; www.ptsm.home.pl; ul Monte Cassino 19a; dm 24zł, d from 54zł) This hostel has clean, spacious rooms and is 2km northwest of the tourist office. Catch tram 1 north to the stop marked 'Piotr Skargi', then walk right one block.

Hotelik Elka-Sen HOTEL €€
(☎91 433 5604; www.elkasen.szczecin.pl; Al 3 Maja 1a; s/d 120/180zł) Simple, light-filled rooms in a basement location in the centre of town. Just south of the tourist office, enter from the side street.

Camping PTTK Marina CAMPING GROUND €
(☎91 460 1165; www.campingmarina.pl; ul Przestrzenna 23; per person/tent 15/9zł, s/d 80/120zł) On the shore of Lake Dąbie – get off at the Szczecin Dąbie train station and ask for directions (2km).

Haga DUTCH €€
(☎91 812 1759; ul Sienna 10; mains 12-24zł) This informal place in the Old Town produces excellent Dutch-style filled pancakes from a menu listing more than 400 combinations.

Karczma Polska Pod Kogutem POLISH €€
(☎91 434 6873; Plac Lotników 3; mains 16-67zł) Northwest of Al Niepodległości, this restaurant serves top-notch traditional Polish food. Roast rabbit in hazelnut sauce, anyone?

ℹ Information

The **tourist office** (☎91 434 0440; Al Niepodległości 1; ⊙9am-5pm Mon-Fri, 10am-2pm Sat) is helpful, as is the **cultural & tourist information office** (☎91 489 1630; ul Korsazy 34; ⊙10am-6pm) in the castle. The **post office** (Al Niepodległości 41/42) and banks can be found along Al Niepodległości, the main street.

ℹ Getting There & Away

The **airport** (www.airport.com.pl) is in Goleniów, 45km northeast of the city. A shuttle bus (18zł) operated by **Interglobus** (☎91 485 0422; www.interglobus.pl) picks up from stops outside the LOT office and the train station before every flight, and meets all arrivals. Alternatively, a taxi should cost around 120zł.

LOT flies between Szczecin and Warsaw three times a day. Book at the **LOT office** (☎0801 703 703; ul Wyzwolenia 17), about 200m from the northern end of Al Niepodegłości. International flights on Ryanair include London (four weekly), Liverpool (twice weekly) and Dublin (twice weekly). Oslo (twice weekly) is reached via Norwegian.

The **bus terminal** (Plac Grodnicki) and the nearby **Szczecin Główny train station** (ul Kolumba) are 600m southeast of the tourist office, though bus departures are of limited interest. Trains travel regularly to Poznań (42zł, 2½ hours, at least hourly), Gdańsk (56zł, 5½ hours, four daily) and Warsaw (58zł, six hours, six daily). Trains also head north to Świnoujście (19zł, two hours, hourly).

Another way to reach Świnoujście is via **ferry** (☎91 488 5564; www.wodolot-szczecin.pl; ul Jana z Kolna 7; adult/concession €14/7; ⊙Apr-Sep), which travels daily from a quay north of the castle across the waters of the Szczeciński Lagoon (1¼ hours).

Advance tickets for trains and ferries are available from **Orbis Travel** (☎91 434 2618; Plac Zwycięstwa 1), about 200m west of the main post office.

WARMIA & MASURIA

The most impressive feature of Warmia and Masuria is its beautiful postglacial landscape dominated by thousands of lakes, linked to rivers and canals, which host aquatic activities like yachting and canoeing. This picturesque lake district has little industry, and remains unpolluted and attractive, especially in summer. Like much of northern Poland, the region has changed hands between Germanic and Polish rulers over the centuries.

Elbląg-Ostróda Canal

The longest navigable canal still used in Poland stretches 82km between Elbląg and Ostróda. Constructed between 1848 and 1876, this waterway was used to transport timber from inland forests to the Baltic. To overcome the 99.5m difference in water levels, the canal utilises an unusual system of five water-powered slipways so that boats are sometimes carried across dry land on rail-mounted trolleys.

Usually, **excursion boats** (⊙May-Sep) depart from both Elbląg and Ostróda daily at 8am (adult/concession 90/70zł, 11 hours), but actual departures depend on available passengers. For information, call the **boat** operators (☑Elbląg 55 232 4307, Ostróda 89 646 3871; www.zegluga.com.pl).

Pensjonat Boss (☑55 239 3729; www.pens jonatboss.pl; ul Św Ducha 30; s/d 160/230zł) is one of several small hotels in Elbląg's Old Town, offering comfortable rooms above its own bar. **Camping Nr 61** (☑55 641 8666; www.camp ing61.com.pl; ul Panieńska 14; per person/tent 12/5zł, cabins d 60zł; ⊙May-Sep), right at Elbląg's boat dock, is a pleasant budget option. In Ostróda, try **Hotel Promenada** (☑89 642 8100; www. hotelpromenada.pl; ul Mickiewicza 3; s/d 160/200zł), 500m east of the bus and train stations.

Elbląg is accessible by frequent trains from Gdańsk (20zł, 1½ hours, 10 daily), Malbork (7zł, 30 minutes, hourly) and Olsztyn (17zł, 1½ hours, 10 daily); and by bus from Frombork (9zł, 45 minutes, at least hourly). Ostróda is regularly connected by train to Olsztyn (9zł, 40 minutes, hourly) and Toruń (23zł, two hours, eight daily), and by bus to Elbląg (15zł, 1½ hours, at least hourly).

Frombork

POP 2500

It may look like the most uneventful town in history, but Frombork was once home to the famous astronomer Nicolaus Copernicus. It's where he wrote his ground-breaking *On the Revolutions of the Celestial Spheres,* which established the theory that the earth travelled around the sun. Beyond the memory of its famous resident, it's a charming, sleepy settlement that was founded on the shore of the Vistula Lagoon in the 13th century. It was later the site of a fortified ecclesiastical township, erected on Cathedral Hill.

The hill is now occupied by the extensive **Nicolaus Copernicus Museum** (ul Katedralna 8), with several sections requiring separate tickets. Most imposing is the red-brick Gothic **cathedral** (adult/concession 6/3zł; ⊙9.30am-5pm Mon-Sat May-Sep, 9am-4pm Mon-Sat Oct-Apr), constructed in the 14th century. The nearby **Bishop's Palace** (adult/concession 5/3zł; ⊙9am-4pm Tue-Sun) houses various exhibitions on local history, while the **belfry** (adult/concession 6/3zł; ⊙9.30am-5pm May-Aug, 9am-4pm Sep-Apr) is home to an example of Foucault's pendulum. A short distance from the main museum, the **Hospital of the Holy Ghost** (adult/concession 5/3zł; ⊙10am-4pm Tue-Sat) exhibits historical medical instruments and manuscripts.

Dom Familijny Rheticus (☑55 243 7800; www.domfamilijny.pl; ul Kopernika 10; s/d 88/120zł) is a small, quaint hotel with cosy rooms and good facilities, a short walk to the east of the bus stop. Breakfast is an extra 15zł.

Camping Nr 12 (☑55 243 7744; ul Braniewska 14; per person/tent 7/10zł, dm 25zł, d 58zł; ⊙May-Sep) is a camping ground at the eastern end of town, on the Braniewo road. It has basic cabins and a snack bar on the grounds.

The bus station is on the riverfront about 300m northwest of the museum. Frombork can be directly reached by bus from Elbląg (9zł, 45 minutes, at least hourly) and Gdańsk (17zł, three hours, two daily). The best place to get on and off is the bus stop directly below the museum on ul Kopernika.

Olsztyn

POP 176,000

Olsztyn (*ol*-shtin) is a pleasant, relaxed city whose rebuilt Old Town is home to cobblestone streets, art galleries, cafes, bars and restaurants. As a busy transport hub, it's also the logical base from which to explore the region, including the Great Masurian Lakes district.

It's also another city on the Copernicus trail, as the great astronomer once served as administrator of Warmia, commanding Olsztyn Castle from 1516 to 1520. From 1466 to 1772 the town belonged to the kingdom of Poland. With the first partition of the nation, Olsztyn became Prussian then German Allenstein, until it returned to Polish hands in 1945.

◎ Sights

Old Town   HISTORIC DISTRICT

Olsztyn's attractive historic centre was rebuilt after WWII destruction, and centres on the **Market Sq** (Rynek). One of its most striking features is the **High Gate**, a surviving fragment of the 14th-century city walls.

Museum of Warmia & Masuria   MUSEUM

(ul Zamkowa 2; adult/concession 9/7zł; ⊙9am-5pm Tue-Sun May-Aug, 10am-4pm Tue-Sun Sep-Apr) West of the square, the 14th-century Castle of the Chapter of Warmia contains this historical museum. Its exhibits star Copernicus, who made some astronomical observations here in the early 16th century, along with collections of coins, art and armour.

Cathedral of St James the Elder   CHURCH

(ul Długosza) The red-brick Gothic cathedral to the east dates from the 14th century, and its 60m tower was added in 1596. The interior is an appealing blend of old and new decoration, including the bronze main doors which depict Pope John Paul II's visit in 1991.

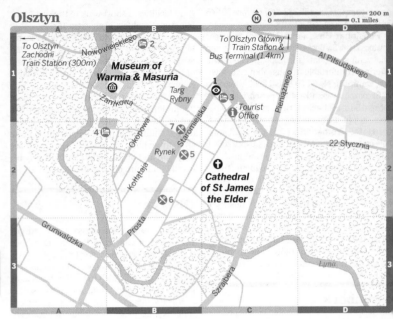

🛏 Sleeping

Polsko-Niemieckie Centrum Młodzieży

HOTEL €€

(☎89 534 0780; www.pncm.olsztyn.pl; ul Okopowa 25; s/d/ste from 195/250/350zł) This place is situated next to the castle. The rooms (some with views of the castle) are plain, but have gleaming bathrooms. There's a good sunlit restaurant off the foyer.

Hotel Pod Zamkiem

HOTEL €€

(☎89 535 1287; www.hotel-olsztyn.com.pl; ul Nowowiejskiego 10; s/d from 160/220zł) Charmingly old-fashioned pension, featuring an extravagant stairwell constructed of dark timber carved with German text; avoid the damp ground-floor rooms. It's near the castle.

Hotel Wysoka Brama

HOTEL €

(☎89 527 3675; www.hotelwysokabrama.olsztyn.pl; ul Staromiejska 1; s/d from 55/70zł) Offers cheap but basic rooms in a very central location next to the High Gate.

🍴 Eating

Restauracja Staromiejska

POLISH €€

(☎89 527 5883; ul Stare Miasto 4/6; mains 15-45zł; ⊙10am-10pm) In classy premises on the Rynek, this restaurant serves quality Polish standards at reasonable prices. There's a range of *pierogi* and *naleśniki* on the menu.

Bar Dziupla

POLISH €

(☎89 527 5083; Rynek 9/10; mains 9-25zł; ⊙8.30am-9pm) This small place is renowned among locals for its tasty Polish food, such as *pierogi*. It also does a good line in soups.

Restauracja Hammurabi

MIDDLE EASTERN €

(☎89 534 0513; ul Prosta 3/4; mains 7-40zł; ⊙11am-11pm Fri & Sat, 11am-9pm Sun-Thu) The Hammurabi offers some inexpensive Middle Eastern choices in a cheerful Arabian setting, along with pizzas and steaks.

ℹ️ Information

The **tourist office** (☎89 535 3565; ul Staromiejska 1; ⊙8am-5pm Mon-Fri & 10am-3pm Sat & Sun May-Sep, 8am-4pm Mon-Fri Oct-Apr) is next to the High Gate, and can help with finding accommodation.

For snail mail, go to the **main post office** (ul Pieniężnego; ⊙6am-7pm); for cybermail, visit the **library** (ul Stare Miasto 33; free; ⊙9am-6.30pm Mon-Fri, 9am-2pm Sat) in the centre of the Market Sq.

ℹ️ Getting There & Away

From the **bus terminal** (ul Partyzantów), useful buses travel to Białystok (46zł, five hours, six daily) and Warsaw (32zł, four hours, 11 daily).

Trains depart from **Olsztyn Główny train station** (ul Partyzantów) to Kętrzyn (16zł, 1½ hours, seven daily), Giżycko (19zł, two hours, seven daily), Białystok (48zł, 4½ hours, two daily), Warsaw (44zł, four hours, four daily), Gdańsk (37zł, three hours, six daily) and Toruń (27zł, 2½ hours, eight daily).

Note that a smaller train station, **Olsztyn Zachodni** (ul Konopnickiej), is located nearer to the Old Town, about 300m west of the castle along ul Nowowiejskiego and ul Konopnickiej; but you're unlikely to find services such as taxis here.

Great Masurian Lakes

The Great Masurian Lakes district east of Olsztyn has more than 2000 lakes, which are remnants of long-vanished glaciers, and surrounded by green hilly landscape. The largest lake is Lake Śniardwy (110 sq km). About 200km of canals connect these bodies of water, so the area is a prime destination for yachties and canoeists, as well as those who love to hike, fish and mountain-bike.

The detailed *Wielkie Jeziora Mazurskie* map (1:100,000) is essential for anyone exploring the region by water or hiking trails. The *Warmia i Mazury* map (1:300,000), available at regional tourist offices, is perfect for more general use.

🏃 Activities

The larger lakes can be sailed from Węgorzewo to Ruciane-Nida, while canoeists might prefer the more intimate surroundings of rivers and smaller lakes. The most popular kayak route takes 10 days (106km) and follows rivers, canals and lakes from Sorkwity to Ruciane-Nida. Brochures

explaining this route are available at regional tourist offices. There's also an extensive network of **hiking** and **mountain-biking** trails around the lakes.

Most travellers prefer to enjoy the lakes in comfort on **excursion boats**. Boats run daily (May to September) between Giżycko and Ruciane-Nida, via Mikołajki; and daily (June to August) between Węgorzewo and Ruciane-Nida, via Giżycko and Mikołajki. However, services are more reliable from late June to late August. Schedules and fares are posted at the lake ports.

ŚWIĘTA LIPKA

This village boasts a superb 17th-century **church** (⊙7am-7pm), one of the purest examples of late-baroque architecture in Poland. Its lavishly decorated organ features angels adorning the 5000 pipes, and they dance to the organ's music. This mechanism is demonstrated several times daily, and recitals are held Friday nights from June to August.

Ask any of the regional tourist offices for a list of homes in Święta Lipka offering private rooms. There are several eateries and places to drink near the church.

Buses run to Kętrzyn every hour or so, but less often to Olsztyn.

WOLF'S LAIR

An eerie attraction at Gierłoż, 8km east of Kętrzyn, is the **Wolf's Lair** (Wilczy Szaniec; ☎89 752 4429; www.wolfsschanze.pl; adult/concession 12/6zł; ⊙8am-dusk). This was Hitler's wartime headquarters for his invasion of the Soviet Union, and his main residence from 1941 to 1944.

In 1944 a group of high-ranking German officers tried to assassinate Hitler here. The leader of the plot, Claus von Stauffenberg, arrived from Berlin on 20 July for a regular military staff meeting. A frequent guest, he entered the meeting with a bomb in his briefcase. He placed it near Hitler and left to take a prearranged phone call, but the briefcase was then unwittingly moved by another officer. Though the explosion killed and wounded several people, Hitler suffered only minor injuries. Von Stauffenberg and some 5000 people allegedly involved in the plot were subsequently executed.

On 24 January 1945, as the Red Army approached, the Germans blew up Wolfsschanze (as it was known in German), and most bunkers were at least partly destroyed. However, huge concrete slabs – some 8.5m thick – and twisted metal remain. The **ruins**

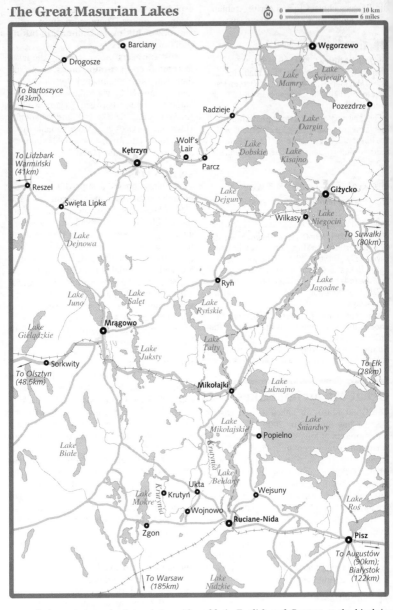

are at their most atmospheric in winter, with fewer visitors and a thick layer of snow.

A large map is posted at the entrance, with features of interest clearly labelled in English (Hitler's personal bunker, perhaps aptly, is unlucky number 13). Booklets outlining a self-guided walking tour are avail-

able in English and German at the kiosk in the car park. The services of English-speaking guides are also available for 50zł.

Hotel Wilcze Gniazdo (☎89 752 4429; kontakt@wolfsschanze.pl; s/d 70/100zł), situated in original buildings within the complex, is fairly basic but adequate for one night. A restaurant is attached.

Catch one of several daily PKS buses (5zł, 15 minutes) from Kętrzyn to Węgorzewo (via Radzieje, not Srokowo) and get off at the entrance. Contact the Kętrzyn **tourist office** (☑89 751 4765; ul Mickiewicza 1; ☺8am-3.30pm Mon-Fri) for updated transport details.

GIŻYCKO
POP 29,600

Giżycko (ghee-*zhits*-ko) is the largest lakeside centre in the region, set on the northern shore of Lake Niegocin. Near the main square (Plac Grunwaldzki) is the very helpful **tourist office** (☑87 428 5265; www.gizycko.turystyka.pl; ul Wyzwolenia 2; ☺9am-5pm Mon-Fri, 10am-2pm Sat May-Sep, 9am-5pm Mon-Fri Oct-Apr).

A notable historic site is the 19th-century **Boyen Fortress** (ul Turystyczna 1; adult/concession 6/3zł; ☺9am-6pm), built by the Prussians to defend the border with Russia.

Sailing boats are available from **Almatur** (☑87 428 5971; ul Moniuszki 24), 700m west of the fortress, and at **Centrum Mazur** (☑87 428 3871; ul Moniuszki 1) at Camping Nr 1 Zamek.

Wama Tour (☑87 429 3079; ul Konarskiego 1) rents out bicycles (30zł per day), and Hotel Zamek has kayaks (8zł per hour). **Żegluga Mazurska** (☑87 428 2578; ul Kolejowa 8) operates excursion boats, and you can arrange car rental through **Fiat Autoserwis** (☑87 428 5986; ul 1 Maja 21).

Sleeping & Eating

Hotel Cesarski   HOTEL €€
(☑87 732 7670; www.cesarski.eu; Plac Grunwaldzki 8; s/d 180/250zł) Formerly the favoured accommodation of Prussian royals and known as the Kaiserhof, this renovated hotel is great value for its quality and central location.

Hotel Zamek   HOTEL, CAMPING GROUND €
(☑87 428 2419; www.cmazur.pl; campsite per person 15zł, dm 26zł, r from 180zł; ☺May-Oct) This combined hotel and camping ground provides a decent standard of accommodation for the price, and hires out bikes for 12zł per hour.

Boyen Fortress Youth Hostel   HOSTEL €
(☑87 428 2959; dm 16-20zł; ☺Jul & Aug) Has a character-packed location within the battlements, and offers the usual basic but clean facilities.

Kuchnie Świata   INTERNATIONAL €
(☑87 429 2255; Plac Grunwaldzki 1; mains 9-46zł) A good dining choice is this cheery red-and-orange space serving up an eclectic range of dishes, including pizza and pasta, along with *placki ziemniaczane* and other Polish favourites.

🛈 Getting There & Away
From the train station, on the southern edge of town near the lake, trains run to Kętrzyn (7zł, 30 minutes, eight daily), Olsztyn (19zł, two hours, seven daily) and Gdańsk (51zł, five hours, two daily).

From the adjacent bus terminal, buses travel regularly to Mikołajki (11zł, one hour, hourly), Olsztyn (20zł, 2¾ hours, eight daily) and Warsaw (39zł, five hours, eight daily).

MIKOŁAJKI
POP 3800

Mikołajki (mee-ko-*wahy*-kee), 86km east of Olsztyn, is a great base for exploring the lakes, and it's a picturesque little village in its own right. The **tourist office** (☑87 421 6850; www.mikolajki.pl; Plac Wolności 3; ☺10am-6pm Jun-Aug, 10am-6pm Mon-Sat May & Sep) is in the town centre. In the colder months you can source tourist information from the **town council offices** (ul Kolejowa 7; ☺7am-3pm Mon-Fri Oct-Apr).

Sailing boats and kayaks can be hired from **Cicha Zatoka** (☑87 421 6275; Al Spacerowa 1) at the waterfront on the other side of the bridge from the town centre, and also from the appropriately named **Fun** (☑87 421 6277; ul Kajki 82).

Lake Śniardwy and **Lake Łuknajno** are ideal for cycling. The tourist office can provide details and maps, and bikes can be rented from Pensjonjat Mikołajki (30zł per day).

Sleeping & Eating
You'll find pensions and homes offering private rooms dotted along ul Kajki, the main street leading around Lake Mikołajskie; more pensions can be found along the roads to Ruciane-Nida and Ełk. There are plenty of eateries situated along the waterfront and around the town square to cater for high-season visitors.

Pensjonat Mikołajki   HOTEL €€
(☑87 421 6437; www.pensjonatmikolajki.prv.pl; ul Kajki 18; s/d from 120/180zł) An attractive place to stay, with timber panelling and a prime lakefront location. Some rooms have balconies overlooking the water.

Camping Nr 2 Wagabunda CAMPING GROUND €
(☑87 421 6018; www.wagabunda-mikolajki.pl; ul Leśna 2; per person/tent 14/14zł, cabins from 110zł; ☺May-Oct) Across the bridge, this

camping ground is 1km southwest of the town centre.

Pizzeria Królewska   PIZZA €
(☑87 421 6323; ul Kajki 5; mains 10-25zł; ⊙noon-10pm) A reasonable pizza restaurant open year-round, in cosy cellar premises.

❶ Getting There & Away

From the **bus terminal** (Plac Kościelny) next to the bridge, two buses go to Olsztyn (16zł, two hours) each day. Otherwise, get a bus (8zł, 40 minutes, hourly) to Mrągowo and change there for Olsztyn. Buses also go hourly to Giżycko (11zł, one hour), and two daily to Warsaw (41zł, five hours). A private company, **Agawa** (☑69 825 6928) runs an express service daily to Warsaw year-round, departing from the bus terminal.

UNDERSTAND POLAND

History

Poland's history started with the Polanians (People of the Plains). During the early Middle Ages, these Western Slavs moved into the flatlands between the Vistula and Odra Rivers. Mieszko I, Duke of the Polanians, adopted Christianity in 966 and embarked on a campaign of conquest. A papal edict in 1025 led to Mieszko's son Bolesław Chrobry (Boleslaus the Brave) being crowned Poland's first king.

Poland's early success proved fragile, and encroachment from Germanic peoples led to the relocation of the royal capital from Poznań to Kraków in 1038. More trouble loomed in 1226 when the Prince of Mazovia invited the Teutonic Knights to help convert the pagan tribes of the north. These Germanic crusaders used the opportunity to create their own state along the Baltic coast. The south had its own invaders to contend with, and Kraków was attacked by Tatars twice in the mid-13th century.

The kingdom prospered under Kazimierz III 'the Great' (1333–70). During this period, many new towns sprang up, while Kraków blossomed into one of Europe's leading cultural centres.

When the daughter of Kazimierz's nephew, Jadwiga, married the Grand Duke of Lithuania, Jagiełło, in 1386, Poland and Lithuania were united as the largest state in Europe, eventually stretching from the Baltic to the Black Sea.

The Renaissance was introduced to Poland by the enlightened King Zygmunt during the 16th century, as he lavishly patronised the arts and sciences. By asserting that the earth travelled around the sun, Nicolaus Copernicus revolutionised the field of astronomy in 1543.

The 17th and 18th centuries produced disaster and decline for Poland. First it was subject to Swedish and Russian invasions, and eventually it faced partition by surrounding empires. In 1773 Russia, Prussia and Austria seized Polish territory in the First Partition; by the time the Third Partition was completed in 1795, Poland had vanished from the map of Europe.

Although the country remained divided through the entire 19th century, Poles steadfastly maintained their culture. Finally, upon the end of WWI, the old imperial powers dissolved, and a sovereign Polish state was restored. Very soon, however, Poland was immersed in the Polish-Soviet War (1919–1921). Under the command of Marshal Jozef Piłsudski, Poland had to defend its newly gained eastern borders from longtime enemy Russia, now transformed into the Soviet Union and determined to spread its revolution westward. After two years of impressive fighting by the outnumbered Poles, an armistice was signed, retaining Vilnius and Lviv within Poland.

Though Polish institutions and national identity flourished during the interwar period, disaster soon struck again. On 1 September 1939, a Nazi blitzkrieg rained down from the west; soon after, the Soviets invaded Poland from the east, dividing the country with Germany. This agreement didn't last long, as Hitler soon transformed Poland into a staging ground for the Nazi invasion of the Soviet Union. Six million Polish inhabitants died during WWII (including the country's three million Jews), brutally annihilated in death camps. At the war's end, Poland's borders were redrawn yet again. The Soviet Union kept the eastern territories and extended the country's western boundary at the expense of Germany. These border changes were accompanied by the forced resettlement of more than a million Poles, Germans and Ukrainians.

Peacetime brought more repression. After WWII, Poland endured four decades of Soviet-dominated communist rule, punctuated by waves of protests, most notably the paralysing strikes of 1980–81, led by the Solidarity trade union. Finally, in the open elections of 1989, the communists fell from power and in 1990 Solidarity leader Lech Wałęsa became Poland's first democratically elected president.

The post-communist transition brought radical changes, which induced new social hardships and political crises. But within a decade Poland had built the foundations for a market economy, and reoriented its foreign relations towards the West. In March 1999, Poland was granted full NATO membership, and it joined the EU in May 2004.

In the 2007 parliamentary elections, Poles decisively rejected the Eurosceptic policies of the Law and Justice party's government, eccentrically headed by the twin Kaczyński brothers as president (Lech) and prime minister (Jarosław). The new centrist government of prime minister Donald Tusk's Civic Platform set a pro-business, pro-EU course, and Lech Kaczyński looked certain to lose the presidential election set for late 2010.

Fate intervened in a shocking manner, however, as Kaczyński was killed in an air crash in April 2010, during an attempted landing at Smolensk, Russia. He had been en route to a commemoration of the Soviet massacre of Polish officers in the nearby Katyń forest in 1940. Also killed in the crash were numerous senior military and government officials, along with relatives of the Katyń victims. The Polish public was stunned by the scale of the tragedy, and campaigning for the following election was subdued. Although the late president's twin brother Jarosław made a surprisingly good showing, in July 2010 Tusk's party ally Bronisław Komorowski was elected as president.

The Poles

For centuries Poland was a multicultural country, home to large Jewish, German and Ukrainian communities. Its Jewish population was particularly large, and once numbered more than three million. However, after Nazi genocide and the forced resettlements that followed WWII, the Jewish population declined to 10,000 and Poland became an ethnically homogeneous country, with some 98% of the population being ethnic Poles.

More than 60% of the citizens live in towns and cities. Warsaw is by far the largest urban settlement, followed by Kraków, Łódź, Wrocław, Poznań and Gdańsk. Upper Silesia (around Katowice) is the most densely inhabited area, while the northeastern border regions remain the least populated.

Between five and 10 million Poles live outside Poland. This émigré community, known as 'Polonia', is located mainly in the USA (particularly Chicago).

Poles are friendly and polite, but not overly formal. The way of life in large urban centres increasingly resembles Western styles and manners. However, Poles' sense of personal space may be a bit cosier than you are accustomed to – you may notice this trait when queuing for tickets or manoeuvring along city streets.

In the countryside, a more conservative culture dominates, evidenced by traditional gender roles and strong family ties. Both here and in urban settings, many Poles are devoutly religious. Roman Catholicism is the dominant Christian denomination, adhered to by more than 80% of Poles. The Orthodox church's followers constitute about 1% of the population, mostly living along a narrow strip on the eastern frontier.

The election of Karol Wojtyła, the archbishop of Kraków, as Pope John Paul II in 1978, and his triumphal visit to his homeland a year later, significantly enhanced the status of the church in Poland.

The overthrow of communism was as much a victory for the Church as it was for democracy. The fine line between the Church and the state is often blurred in Poland, and the Church is a powerful lobby on social issues. Some Poles have grown wary of the Church's influence in society and politics, but Poland remains one of Europe's most religious countries, and packed-out churches are not uncommon.

Arts
Literature

Poland has inherited a rich literary tradition dating from the 15th century, though its modern voice was shaped in the 19th century, during the long period of foreign occupation. It was a time for nationalist writers such as the poet Adam Mickiewicz (1798–1855), and Henryk Sienkiewicz (1846–1916), who won a Nobel Prize in 1905 for *Quo Vadis?* This nationalist tradition was revived in the communist era when Czesław Miłosz was awarded a Nobel Prize in 1980 for *The Captive Mind*.

At the turn of the 20th century, the avant-garde 'Young Poland' movement in art and literature developed in Kraków. The most notable representatives of this movement were writer Stanisław Wyspiański (1869–1907), also famous for his stained-glass work; playwright Stanisław Ignacy Witkiewicz

(1885–1939), commonly known as Witkacy; and Nobel laureate Władysław Reymont (1867–1925). In 1996 Wisława Szymborska (b 1923) also received a Nobel Prize for her poetry.

Music

The most famous Polish musician was undoubtedly Frédéric Chopin (1810–49), whose music displays the melancholy and nostalgia that became hallmarks of the national style. Stanisław Moniuszko (1819–72) injected a Polish flavour into 19th-century Italian opera music by introducing folk songs and dances to the stage. His *Halka* (1858), about a peasant girl abandoned by a young noble, is a staple of the national opera houses.

On a more contemporary note, popular Polish musicians you might catch live in concert include the controversial Doda (pop singer); Feel (pop-rock band); Łzy (pop-rock band); Indios Bravos (reggae band); and Kasia Cerekwicka (pop singer). Poland's equivalent of the Rolling Stones is Lady Pank, a rock band formed in 1982 and still going strong.

Visual Arts

Poland's most renowned painter was Jan Matejko (1838–93), whose monumental historical paintings hang in galleries throughout the country. Wojciech Kossak (1857–1942) is another artist who documented Polish history; he is best remembered for the colossal painting *Panorama of Racławice,* on display in Wrocław (p651).

A long-standing Polish craft is the fashioning of jewellery from amber. Amber is a fossil resin of vegetable origin that comes primarily from the Baltic region, and appears in a variety of colours from pale yellow to reddish brown. The best places to buy it are Gdańsk, Kraków and Warsaw.

Polish poster art has received international recognition; the best selection of poster galleries is in Warsaw and Kraków.

Cinema

Poland has produced several world-famous film directors. The most notable is Andrzej Wajda, who received an Honorary Award at the 1999 Academy Awards. *Katyń*, his moving story of the Katyń massacre in WWII, was nominated for Best Foreign Language Film at the 2008 Oscars. Western audiences are more familiar with the work of Roman Polański, who directed critically acclaimed films such as *Rosemary's Baby* and *Chinatown*. In 2002 Polański released the incredibly moving film *The Pianist*, which was filmed in Poland and set in the Warsaw Ghetto of WWII. The film went on to win three Oscars and the Cannes Palme d'Or. The late Krzysztof Kieślowski is best known for the *Three Colours* trilogy. The centre of Poland's movie industry, and home to its prestigious National Film School, is Łódź.

The Landscape

Geography

Poland covers an area of 312,685 sq km, approximately as large as the UK and Ireland put together, and is bordered by seven nations and one sea.

The northern edge of Poland meets the Baltic Sea. This broad, 524km-long coastline is spotted with sand dunes and seaside lakes. Also concentrated in the northeast are many postglacial lakes – more than any country in Europe, except Finland.

The southern border is defined by the mountain ranges of the Sudetes and Carpathians. Poland's highest mountains are the rocky Tatras, a section of the Carpathian Range it shares with Slovakia. The highest peak of the Polish Tatras is Mt Rysy (2499m).

The area in between is a vast plain, sectioned by wide north-flowing rivers. Poland's longest river is the Vistula (Wisła), which winds 1047km from the Tatras to the Baltic.

About a quarter of Poland is covered by forest. Some 60% of the forests are pine trees, but the share of deciduous species, such as oak, beech and birch, is increasing.

National Parks & Animals

Poland's fauna includes hare, red deer, wild boar and, less abundantly, elk, brown bear and wildcat. European bison, which once inhabited Europe in large numbers, were brought to the brink of extinction early in the 20th century and a few hundred now live in Białowieża National Park (p623). The Great Masurian Lakes district (p679) attracts a vast array of bird life, such as storks and cormorants. The eagle, though rarely seen today, is Poland's national bird and appears on the Polish emblem.

Poland has 23 national parks, but they cover less than 1% of the country. No permit is necessary to visit these parks, but most have small admission fees. Camping in the parks is sometimes allowed, but only at specified sites. Poland also has a network of less strictly preserved areas called 'landscape parks', scattered throughout the country.

The Cuisine

Staples & Specialities

Various cultures have influenced Polish cuisine, including Jewish, Ukrainian, Russian, Hungarian and German. Polish food is hearty and filling, abundant in potatoes and dumplings, and rich in meat.

Poland's most famous dishes are *bigos* (sauerkraut with a variety of meats), *pierogi* (ravioli-like dumplings stuffed with cottage cheese, minced meat, or cabbage and wild mushrooms) and *barszcz* (red beetroot soup, better known by the Russian word *borscht*).

Hearty soups such as *żurek* (sour soup with sausage and hard-boiled eggs) are a highlight of Polish cuisine. Main dishes are made with pork, including *golonka* (boiled pig's knuckle served with horseradish) and *schab pieczony* (roast loin of pork seasoned with prunes and herbs). *Gołąbki* (cabbage leaves stuffed with mince and rice) is a tasty alternative.

Placki ziemniaczane (potato pancakes) and *naleśniki* (crepes) are also popular dishes.

Poles claim the national drink, *wódka* (vodka), was invented in their country. It's usually drunk neat and comes in a number of flavours, including *myśliwska* (flavoured with juniper berries), *wiśniówka* (with cherries) and *jarzębiak* (with rowanberries). The most famous variety is *żubrówka* (bison vodka), flavoured with grass from the Białowieża Forest. Other notable spirits include *krupnik* (honey liqueur), *śliwowica* (plum brandy) and *goldwasser* (sweet liqueur containing flakes of gold leaf).

Poles also appreciate the taste of *zimne piwo* (cold beer); the top brands, found everywhere, include Żywiec, Tyskie, Lech and Okocim, while regional brands are available in every city.

Where to Eat & Drink

The cheapest place to eat Polish food is a *bar mleczny* (milk bar), a survivor from the communist era. These no-frills, self-service cafeterias are popular with budget-conscious locals and backpackers alike. Up the scale, the number and variety of *restauracja* (restaurants) has ballooned in recent years, especially in the big cities. Pizzerias have also become phenomenally popular with Poles. And though Polish cuisine features plenty of meat, there are vegetarian restaurants to be found in most cities.

Menus usually have several sections: *zupy* (soups), *dania drugie* (main courses) and *dodatki* (accompaniments). The price of the main course may not include a side dish – such as potatoes and salads – which you choose (and pay extra for) from the *dodatki* section. Also note that the price for some dishes (particularly fish and poultry) may be listed per 100g, so the price will depend on the total weight of the fish or meat. In this guide, budget (€) restaurant mains start below 10zł, midrange (€€) mains cost between 10zł and 25zł, and top-end (€€€) mains start above 25zł.

Poles start their day with *śniadanie* (breakfast); the most important and substantial meal of the day, *obiad,* is normally eaten between 2pm and 5pm. The third meal is *kolacja* (supper). Most restaurants, cafes and cafe-bars are open from 11am to 11pm. It's rare for Polish restaurants to serve breakfast, though milk bars and snack bars are open from early morning. In the Eating sections of this chapter, only nonstandard restaurant hours are listed.

Smoking is common in bars and restaurants, though there have been unsuccessful proposals to ban it from public spaces. However, many restaurants offer nonsmoking options.

SURVIVAL GUIDE

Directory A–Z

Accommodation

In Poland, budget (€) accommodation includes camping grounds, dorms, or doubles costing up to 150zł; midrange (€€) accommodation will cost between 150zł and 350zł a double; and top-end digs (€€€) will set you back upwards of 350zł per night. Unless otherwise noted, rooms have private bathrooms and the rate includes breakfast.

Camping

Poland has hundreds of camping grounds, and many offer good-value cabins and bungalows. Most open May to September, but some only open their gates between June and August.

Hostels

Schroniska młodzieżowe (youth hostels) in Poland are operated by Polskie Towarzystwo Schronisk Młodzieżowych (PTSM;

www.ptsm.org.pl), a member of Hostelling International. Most only open in July and August, and are often very busy with Polish students; the year-round hostels have more facilities. These youth hostels are open to all, with no age limit. Curfews are common, and many hostels close between 10am and 5pm.

A growing number of privately operated hostels operate in the main cities, and are geared towards international backpackers. They're open 24 hours and offer more modern facilities than the old youth hostels, though prices are higher. These hostels usually offer free use of washing machines, in response to the near-absence of laundromats in Poland.

A dorm bed can cost anything from 25zł to 75zł per person per night. Single and double rooms, if available, start at about 150zł a night.

Hotels
Hotel prices often vary according to season, especially along the Baltic coast, and discounted weekend rates are common.

If possible, check the room before accepting. Don't be fooled by hotel reception areas, which may look great in contrast to the rest of the establishment. On the other hand, dreary scuffed corridors can sometimes open into clean, pleasant rooms.

Accommodation (sometimes with substantial discounts) can be reliably arranged via the internet through www.poland4u.com and www.hotelspoland.com.

Mountain Refuges
Polskie Towarzystwo Turystyczno-Krajoznawcze (PTTK; www.pttk.pl) runs a chain of *schroniska górskie* (mountain refuges) for hikers. They're usually simple, with a welcoming atmosphere, and serve cheap, hot meals. The more isolated refuges are obliged to accept everyone, so can be crowded in the high season. Refuges are normally open all year, but confirm with the nearest PTTK office before setting off.

Private rooms & apartments
Some destinations have agencies (usually called *biuro zakwaterowania* or *biuro kwater prywatnych*), which arrange accommodation in private homes. Rooms cost about 100/130zł per single/double. The most important factor to consider is location; if the home is in the suburbs, find out how far it is from reliable public transport.

During the high season, home owners also directly approach tourists. Also, private homes in smaller resorts and villages often have signs outside their gates or doors offering a *pokoje* (room) or *noclegi* (lodging).

In Warsaw, Kraków, Wrocław and Gdańsk, some agencies offer self-contained apartments, which are an affordable alternative to hotels and allow for the washing of laundry.

Activities
Hikers can enjoy marked trails across the Tatra Mountains (p647), where one of the most popular climbs is up the steep slopes of Mt Giewont (1894m). The Sudeten Mountains (p656) and the Great Masurian Lakes district (p686) also offer good walking opportunities. National parks worth hiking through include Białowieża National Park (p623), Kampinos National Park just outside Warsaw, and Wielkopolska National Park outside Poznań. Trails are easy to follow and detailed maps are available at most larger bookshops.

As Poland is fairly flat, it's ideal for cyclists. Bicycle routes along the banks of the Vistula River are popular in Warsaw, Toruń and Kraków. Many of the national parks – including Tatra (near Zakopane) and Słowiński (near Łeba) – offer bicycle trails, as does the Great Masurian Lakes district. For more of a challenge, try cycling in the Bieszczady ranges around Sanok (p649). Bikes can be rented at most resort towns and larger cities.

Zakopane (p644) will delight skiers from December to March, and facilities are cheaper than the ski resorts of Western Europe. Other sports on offer here include hang-gliding and paragliding. Another place to hit the snow is Szklarska Poręba (p656) in Silesia.

Throngs of yachties, canoeists and kayakers enjoy the network of waterways in the Great Masurian Lakes district (p679) every summer; boats are available for rent from all lakeside towns, and there are even diving excursions. Windsurfers can head to the beaches of the Hel peninsula (p670).

Books
God's Playground: A History of Poland, by Norman Davies, offers an in-depth analysis of Polish history. The condensed version, *The Heart of Europe: A Short History of Poland,* also by Davies, has greater emphasis on the 20th century. *The Polish Way: A Thousand-Year History of the Poles and their Culture,* by Adam Zamoyski, is a superb cultural overview. The wartime Warsaw Rising is vividly brought to life in Norman Davies' *Rising '44,* and *The*

Polish Revolution: Solidarity 1980-82, by Timothy Garton Ash, is entertaining and thorough. *Jews in Poland* by Iwo Cyprian Pogonowski provides a comprehensive record of half a millennium of Jewish life. Evocative works about rural life in interwar Poland include Bruno Schultz's *Street of Crocodiles* and Philip Marsden's *The Bronski House*.

Business Hours

Banks 8am-5pm Mon-Fri, sometimes 8am-2pm Sat

Cafes & restaurants 11am-11pm

Shops 10am-6pm Mon-Fri, 10am-2pm Sat

Nightclubs 9pm-late

Dangers & Annoyances

Poland is a relatively safe country, and crime has decreased significantly since the immediate post-communism era. Be alert, however, for thieves and pickpockets around major train stations, such as Warszawa Centralna. Robberies have been a problem on night trains, especially on international routes. Try to share a compartment with other people if possible.

Theft from cars is a widespread problem, so keep your vehicle in a guarded car park whenever possible. Heavy drinking is common and drunks can be disturbing, though rarely dangerous.

As Poland is an ethnically homogeneous nation, travellers of a non-European appearance may attract curious glances from locals in outlying regions. Football (soccer) hooligans are not uncommon, so avoid travelling on public transport with them (especially if their team has lost!).

Embassies & Consulates

All diplomatic missions listed are located in Warsaw unless stated otherwise.

Australia (☑22 521 3444; www.australia.pl; ul Nowogrodzka 11)

Belarus (☑22 742 0710; www.belembassy.org/poland; ul Wiertnicza 58)

Canada (☑22 584 3100; www.canada.pl; ul Matejki 1/5)

Czech Republic (☑22 525 1850; www.mzv.cz/warsaw; ul Koszykowa 18)

France Warsaw (☑22 529 3000; www.ambafrance-pl.org; ul Piękna 1); Kraków consulate (☑12 424 5300; www.cracovie.org.pl; ul Stolarska 15, Kraków)

Germany Warsaw (☑22 584 1700; www.warschau.diplo.de; ul Jazdów 12); Kraków consulate (☑12 424 3000; www.warschau.diplo.de; ul Stolarska 7, Kraków)

Ireland (☑22 849 6633; www.irlandia.pl; ul Mysia 5)

Japan (☑22 696 5000; www.pl.emb-japan.go.jp; ul Szwoleżerów 8)

Lithuania (☑22 625 3368; www.lietuva.pl; ul Ujazdowskie 14)

Netherlands (☑22 559 1200; www.nlembassy.pl; ul Kawalerii 10)

New Zealand (☑22 521 0500; www.nzembassy.com/poland; Al Ujazdowskie 51)

Russia (☑22 849 5111; http://warsaw.rusembassy.org; ul Belwederska 49)

Slovakia (☑22 525 8110; www.mzv.sk/varsava; ul Litewska 6)

South Africa (☑22 625 6228; warsaw.consular@foreign.gov.za; ul Koszykowa 54)

Ukraine (☑22 622 4797; www.ukraine-emb.pl; Al Szucha 7)

UK Warsaw (☑22 311 0000; http://ukinpoland.fco.gov.uk; ul Kawalerii 12); Kraków consulate (☑12 421 7030; http://ukinpoland.fco.gov.uk; ul Św Anny 9, Kraków)

USA Warsaw (☑22 504 2000; http://poland.usembassy.gov; Al Ujazdowskie 29/31); Kraków consulate (☑12 424 5100; http://poland.us embassy.gov; ul Stolarska 9, Kraków)

Food

Price ranges: budget (€; under 10zł), midrange (€€; 10zł to 25zł) and top end (€€€; over 25zł).

Gay & Lesbian Travellers

Since the change of government in 2007, overt homophobia from state officials has declined; though with the Church remaining influential in social matters, gay acceptance in Poland is still a work in progress. The gay community is becoming more visible, however, and in 2010 Warsaw hosted **EuroPride** (www.europride.com), the first time this major gay festival had been held in a former communist country.

In general though, the Polish gay and lesbian scene remains fairly discreet. Warsaw and Kraków are the best places to find gay-friendly bars, clubs and accommodation. The free tourist brochure, the *Visitor*, lists a few gay nightspots, as do the **In Your Pocket** (www.inyourpocket.com) guides.

A good source of information on gay Warsaw and Kraków is online at www.gay guide.net. **Lambda** (☎22 628 5222; www.lamb dawarszawa.org) is a national gay rights and information service.

Internet Access

Internet access is near universal in Polish accommodation: either as wireless access, via on-site computers, or both. As a result, individual accommodation with internet access has not been denoted as such in this chapter.

In the unlikely event that your lodgings are offline, you'll likely find an internet cafe nearby; expect to pay between 3zł and 5zł per hour. Also, some forward-thinking city councils have set up wireless access in their main market squares.

Internet Resources

Commonwealth of Diverse Cultures (www.commonwealth.pl) Outlines Poland's cultural heritage.

Poland.pl (www.poland.pl) News and a website directory.

Poland Tourism Portal (www.poland.travel) Useful official travel site.

Polska (www.poland.gov.pl) Comprehensive government portal.

VirtualTourist.com (www.virtualtourist. com) Poland section features postings by travellers.

Visit.pl (www.visit.pl) Accommodation booking service for Poland and beyond.

Media

The *Warsaw Business Journal* is aimed at the business community, while *Warsaw Insider* has more general-interest features, listings and reviews. *Warsaw Voice* is a weekly English-language news magazine with a business slant.

The free *Welcome to...* series of magazines covers Poznań, Kraków, Toruń, Zakopane and Warsaw monthly.

Recent newspapers and magazines from Western Europe and the USA are readily available at EMPiK bookshops, and at newsstands in the foyers of upmarket hotels.

Poland has a mix of privately owned TV channels, and state-owned nationwide channels. Foreign-language programs are painfully dubbed with one male voice covering all actors (that's men, women and children) and no lip-sync, so you can still hear the original language underneath.

Most hotels offer English-language news channels.

Money

Poland is obliged by the terms of its accession to the EU to adopt the euro as its currency at some point in the future; but it's not likely to happen until at least 2015.

In the meantime, the nation's currency is the złoty (*zwo*-ti), abbreviated to zł (international currency code PLN). It's divided into 100 groszy (gr). Denominations of notes are 10, 20, 50, 100 and 200 (rare) złoty, and coins come in one, two, five, 10, 20 and 50 groszy, and one, two and five złoty.

Bankomats (ATMs) accept most international credit cards and are easily found in the centre of all cities and most towns. Banks without an ATM may provide cash advances over the counter on credit cards.

Private *kantors* (foreign-exchange offices) are everywhere. They require no paperwork and charge no commission, though rates at *kantors* near tourist-friendly attractions or facilities can be poor.

Travellers cheques are more secure than cash, but *kantors* rarely change them, and banks that do will charge a commission. A better option is a stored value cash card, which can be used in the same manner as a credit card; ask your bank about this before leaving home.

Post

Postal services are operated by Poczta Polska; the Poczta Główna (Main Post Office) in each city offers the widest range of services.

The cost of sending a normal-sized letter (up to 20g) or a postcard to other European countries is 3zł, rising to 3.50zł for North America and 4.50zł for Australia.

Public Holidays

Poland's official public holidays:

New Year's Day 1 January

Easter Sunday March or April

Easter Monday March or April

State Holiday 1 May

Constitution Day 3 May

Pentecost Sunday Seventh Sunday after Easter

Corpus Christi Ninth Thursday after Easter

Assumption Day 15 August

All Saints' Day 1 November

Independence Day 11 November

Christmas 25 and 26 December

Telephone

Polish telephone numbers have nine digits, with no area codes. To call Poland from abroad, dial the country code ☑48, then the Polish number. The international access code when dialling out of Poland is ☑00. For help, try the operators for local numbers (☑913), national numbers and codes (☑912), and international codes (☑908), but don't expect anyone to speak English.

The three mobile-telephone providers are Orange, Era and Plus GSM. Prepaid accounts are cheap by Western European standards, and are easy to set up at local offices of these companies.

Most public telephones use magnetic phonecards, available at post offices and kiosks in units of 15 (9zł), 30 (15zł) and 60 (24zł). The cards can be used for domestic and international calls.

Travellers with Disabilities

Poland is not set up well for people with disabilities, although there have been significant improvements over recent years. Wheelchair ramps are only available at some upmarket hotels, and public transport will be a real challenge for anyone with mobility problems. However, many hotels now have at least one room especially designed for disabled access – book ahead for these. There are also some low-floor trams running on the Warsaw and Kraków public transport networks. Information on disability issues is available from **Integracja** (☑22 530 6570; www.integracja.org).

Visas

EU citizens do not need visas to visit Poland and can stay indefinitely. Citizens of Australia, Canada, Israel, New Zealand, Switzerland and the USA can stay in Poland up to 90 days without a visa.

However, since Poland's entry into the Schengen zone in December 2007, the 90-day visa-free entry period has been extended to all the Schengen countries; so if travelling from Poland through Germany and France, for example, you can't exceed 90 days in total. Once your 90 days is up, you must leave the Schengen zone for a minimum 90 days before you can once again enter it visa free.

South African citizens do require a visa. Other nationals should check with Polish embassies or consulates in their countries for current visa requirements. Updates can be found at the website of the **Ministry of Foreign Affairs** (www.msz.gov.pl).

Getting There & Away

Air

The majority of international flights to Poland arrive at Warsaw's Okęcie airport, while other important airports include Kraków, Gdańsk, Poznań and Wrocław. The national carrier **LOT** (☑0801 703 703, 22 19572; www.lot.com) flies to all major European cities.

Other major airlines flying to/from Poland:

Aeroflot (☑22 650 2511; www.aeroflot.com)

Air France (☑22 556 6400; www.airfrance.com)

Alitalia (☑22 692 8285; www.alitalia.it)

British Airways (☑22 529 9000; www.ba.com)

easyJet (☑0703 203 025; www.easyjet.com)

KLM (☑22 556 6444; www.klm.pl)

Lufthansa (☑22 338 1300; www.lufthansa.pl)

Malév (☑22 697 7474; www.malev.hu)

Ryanair (☑0703 303 033; www.ryanair.com)

SAS (☑22 850 0500; www.flysas.com)

Wizz Air (☑0703 503 010; www.wizzair.com)

Land

Since Poland is now within the Schengen zone, there are no border posts or border-crossing formalities between Poland and Germany, the Czech Republic, Slovakia and Lithuania. Below is a list of major road border crossings with Poland's non-Schengen neighbours that accept foreigners and are open 24 hours.

Belarus (South to north) Terespol, Kuźnica Białostocka

Russia (West to east) Gronowo, Bezledy

Ukraine (South to north) Medyka, Hrebenne, Dorohusk

If you're going to Russia or Lithuania and your train/bus passes through Belarus, you need a Belarusian transit visa and you must get it in advance; see p100.

Bus

International bus services are offered by dozens of Polish and international companies. One of the major operators is **Eurolines Polska** (☑32 351 2020; www.eurolinespolska.pl), which runs buses in all directions.

Car & Motorcycle

To drive a car into Poland, EU citizens need their driving licence from home, while other nationalities must obtain an International Drivers Permit in their home country. Also required are vehicle registration papers and liability insurance (Green Card). If your insurance is not valid for Poland you must buy an additional policy at the border.

Train

Trains link Poland with every neighbouring country and beyond, but international train travel is not cheap. To save money on fares, investigate special train tickets and rail passes (see p1019). Domestic trains in Poland are significantly cheaper, so you'll save money if you buy a ticket to a Polish border destination, then take a local train.

Do note that some international trains to/from Poland have been linked with theft. Keep an eye on your bags, particularly on the Berlin–Warsaw, Prague–Warsaw and Prague–Kraków overnight trains.

Sea

For ferry services from Gdańsk and Gdynia see p668 and p669, respectively. There are also car and passenger ferries from the Polish town of Świnoujście, operated by the following companies:

Polferries (www.polferries.pl) Offers daily services from Świnoujście to Ystad (eight hours) in Sweden, every Saturday to Rønne (5¼ hours) in Denmark, and four days a week to Copenhagen (12 hours).

Unity Line (www.unityline.pl) Runs daily ferries between Świnoujście and the Swedish ports of Ystad (seven hours) and Trelleborg (seven hours).

Any travel agency in Scandinavia will sell tickets for these services. In Poland, ask at any Orbis Travel office. In summer, passenger boats ply the Baltic coast from Świnoujście to Ahlbeck, Heringsdorf, Bansin and Zinnowitz in Germany.

Getting Around

Air

LOT (☎0801 703 703, 22 19572; www.lot.com) flies several times a day from Warsaw to Gdańsk, Kraków, Poznań and Wrocław. Another Polish airline, **Jet Air** (☎22 846 8661; www.jetair.pl), serves the same airports.

Bicycle

Cycling is not great for getting around cities, but is often a good way to travel between villages. If you get tired, it's possible to place your bike in the luggage compartment at the front or rear of slow passenger trains (these are rarely found on faster services). You'll need a special ticket for your bike from the railway luggage office.

Bus

Buses can be useful on short routes and through the mountains in southern Poland; but usually trains are quicker and more comfortable, and private minibuses are quicker and more direct.

Most buses are operated by the state bus company, PKS. It provides two kinds of service from its bus terminals *(dworzec autobusowy PKS)*: ordinary buses (marked in black on timetables); and fast buses (marked in red), which ignore minor stops.

Timetables are posted on boards, and additional symbols next to departure times may indicate the bus runs only on certain days or in certain seasons. Terminals usually have an information desk, but it's rarely staffed with English speakers. Tickets for PKS buses are usually bought at the terminal, but sometimes also from drivers. Note that the quoted bus frequencies in this chapter relate to the summer schedule.

The price of bus tickets is determined by the length, in kilometres, of the trip. Minibuses charge set prices for journeys, and these are normally posted in their windows or at the bus stop.

Car & Motorcycle
Fuel & Spare Parts

Petrol stations sell several kinds of petrol, including 94-octane leaded, 95-octane unleaded, 98-octane unleaded and diesel. Most petrol stations are open from 6am to 10pm (from 7am to 3pm Sunday), though some operate around the clock. Garages are plentiful. Roadside assistance can be summoned by dialling ☎981 or ☎22 9637.

Hire

Major international car-rental companies, such as **Avis** (www.avis.pl), **Hertz** (www.hertz.pl) and **Europcar** (www.europcar.com.pl), are represented in larger cities and have smaller offices at airports. Rates are comparable to full-price rental in Western Europe.

Rental agencies will need to see your passport, your local driving licence (which must be held for at least one year) and a credit card (for the deposit). You need to be at least 21 or 23 years of age to rent a car; sometimes 25 for a more expensive car.

Road Rules

The speed limit is 130km/h on motorways, 100km/h on two- or four-lane highways, 90km/h on other open roads and 50km/h in built-up areas. If the background of the sign bearing the town's name is white you must reduce speed to 50km/h; if the background is green there's no need to reduce speed (unless road signs indicate otherwise). Radar-equipped police are very active, especially in villages with white signs.

Unless signs state otherwise, cars may park on pavements as long as a minimum 1.5m-wide walkway is left for pedestrians. Parking in the opposite direction to traffic flow is allowed. The permitted blood alcohol level is a low 0.02%, so it's best not to drink if you're driving. Seat belts are compulsory, as are helmets for motorcyclists. Between October and February, all drivers must use headlights during the day (and night!).

Train

Trains will be your main means of transport. They're cheap, reliable and rarely overcrowded (except for July and August peak times). **Polish State Railways** (PKP; www.pkp.pl) operates trains to almost every place listed in this chapter. A private company, **Arriva** (www.arriva.pl), also operates local services in the eastern part of Pomerania.

Train Types

Express InterCity trains only stop at major cities and are the fastest way to travel by rail. These trains require seat reservations.

Down the pecking order are the older but cheaper **TLK trains** (*pociąg TLK*). They're slower and more crowded, but will likely be the type of train you most often catch. TLK trains do not normally require seat reservations, except at peak times.

InterRegio trains run services between adjoining regions of Poland, and often operate less frequently at weekends.

At the bottom of the hierarchy, slow **passenger trains** (*pociąg osobowy*) stop by every tree at the side of the track that could be imagined to be a station, and are best used only for short trips. Seats can't be reserved.

Classes & Fares

Express InterCity and TLK trains carry two classes: *druga klasa* (2nd class) and *pierwsza klasa* (1st class), which is 50% more expensive. Most 2nd-class and all 1st-class carriages have nonsmoking compartments.

Note that the quoted train fares in this chapter are for a second-class ticket on a TLK train, or the most likely alternative if the route is mainly served by a different type of train. Frequencies are as per the summer schedule.

In a couchette on an overnight train, compartments have four/six beds in 1st/2nd class. Sleepers have two/three people (1st/2nd class) in a compartment fitted with a washbasin, sheets and blankets. *Miejsca sypialne* (sleepers) and *kuszetki* (couchettes) can be booked at special counters in larger train stations; prebooking is recommended.

Timetables

Train *odjazdy* (departures) are listed at train stations on a yellow board and *przyjazdy* (arrivals) on a white board. Ordinary trains are marked in black print, fast trains in red. The letter 'R' in a square indicates the train has compulsory seat reservation.

The timetables also show which *peron* (platform) it's using. The number applies to *both* sides of the platform. If in doubt, check the platform departure board or route cards on the side of carriages, or ask someone.

Full timetable and fare information in English can be found on the PKP website.

Ticketing

If a seat reservation is compulsory on your train, you will automatically be sold a *miejscówka* (reserved) seat ticket. If you do not make a seat reservation, you can travel on *any* train (of the type requested) to the destination indicated on your ticket on the date specified.

Your ticket will list the *klasa* (class); the *poc* (type) of train; where the train is travelling *od* (from) and *do* (to); the major town or junction the train is travelling *prez* (through); and the total *cena* (price). If more than one place is listed under the heading *prez* (via), ask the conductor *early* if you have to change trains at the junction listed or be in a specific carriage (the train may separate later).

If you get on a train without a ticket, you can buy one directly from the conductor for a small supplement (7zł) – but do it right away. If the conductor finds you first, you'll be fined for travelling without a ticket. You can always upgrade from 2nd to 1st class for a small extra fee (7zł), plus the additional fare.

Romania

Best Places to Eat

» Bella Muzica (p715)
» Felinarul Café (p725)
» Lugano (p730)
» Grand Plaza (p726)
» B+B (p746)

Best Places to Stay

» Hotel Amzei (p703)
» Hotel Traian (p743)
» Pension Casa Leone (p733)
» Felinarul Hostel (p725)
» Casa Cu Cerb (p721)

Why Go?

Singularly beautiful, beguilingly simple and utterly fascinating, Romania's urban evolution has had little effect on its predominantly rural landscape, where aesthetically stirring hand-ploughed fields, sheep-instigated traffic jams and homemade-plum-brandy stills endure. The Carpathian Mountains offer relatively uncrowded hiking, cycling and skiing. Transylvania's Saxon towns are time-warp strolling grounds for Gothic architecture, Austro-Hungarian legacies and Vlad 'Ţepeş' Dracula shtick. The fishies – and the birds that chomp them – thrive in the Danube Delta. Bucolic and wooden Maramureş has the 'merry cemetery', while Unesco-listed painted monasteries dot southern Bucovina. And, for the record, the big cities are a blast, too.

The antics of a tiny number of con artists and beggars have birthed exaggerated stories about Romanians, but you're far less likely to be the victim of crime here than in much of Western Europe. Enjoy the friendliness of a new generation with no vivid memories of Nicolae Ceauşescu.

When to Go
Bucharest

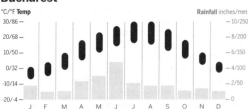

May Some of the best festivals: Sibiu Jazz, Transylvania Film Festival and Bucharest Carnival.

June Mountain hiking starts in mid-June, roughly when the Transfăgărăşan Road opens.

August Folk festivals: National Romanian, Hora de la Prislop, and Fundata's Mountain Festival.

Connections

Trains, buses and maxitaxis swarm around every available border crossing.

Trains depart Bucharest for destinations including Sofia, Budapest, Chişinău, İstanbul, Belgrade, Kyiv, Minsk and Moscow – the latter three via Suceava. Bucharest also has long-haul buses to Western European destinations, and daily maxitaxi services to Sofia.

Budapest can be easily reached by bus or train from Oradea, Timişoara and Cluj-Napoca.

Suceava has one daily bus to Chernivtsi, Ukraine, as well as Chişinău, though entering Moldova is easier from Iaşi. Timişoara buses go all over Western Europe, including Spain, Italy and Sweden. Nearly every major city has a bus service to İstanbul.

ITINERARIES

One week

Spend a day viewing the parts of Bucharest that survived Ceauşescu, then take a train to Braşov – Transylvania's main event – for castles, activities and beer at streetside cafes. Spend a day in Sighişoara's medieval citadel, then catch a train back to Bucharest or on to Budapest.

Two weeks

Arrive in Bucharest (plane) or Timişoara (train), then head into Transylvania, devoting a day or two each at Braşov, Sighişoara and Sibiu. Tour southern Bucovina's painted monasteries, then continue to Kiev, Chişinău or Bucharest.

Essential Food & Drink

» **Mămăligă** Essentially a cornmeal mush that's boiled or fried, sometimes topped with sour cream and/or cheese.

» **Ciorbă** A soup that's a mainstay of the Romanian diet and a powerful hangover remedy.

» **Muşchi de vacă/porc/miel** A cutlet of beef, pork or lamb.

» **Piept de pui** Chicken breast.

» **Wine** The best Romanian wines include Cotnari, Murfatlar, Odobeşti, Târnave and Valea Călugărească.

» **Ţuică** A once-filtered clear brandy made from fermented fruit (the tastiest and most popular is plum ţuică), usually 30 proof. Palincă is similar, only it's filtered twice and is usually around 60 proof.

BUCHAREST

POP 2.1 MILLION

Many Romanians slam it, and some travellers depart visibly stunned after a couple of days (or a single drive through the increasingly gridlocked centre), but Bucharest is an intriguing and evolving mix of eras. Wide boulevards with century-old villas, which once earned it the debatable moniker 'Paris of the East', mingle with deviously hidden 18th-century monasteries, unsightly communist-built housing blocks and statement-making

Romania Highlights

❶ Ascend castles and mountains (and castles on top of mountains), using the Gothic medieval town of **Brașov** (p714) as a base

❷ Follow the Unesco World Heritage conga line of painted monasteries in **Southern Bucovina** (p745)

❸ Soak in **Sibiu** (p723), the beautifully restored Saxon town and 2007 European Capital of Culture

❹ Explore the medieval citadel of **Sighișoara** (p719), Dracula's birthplace

❺ Rewind a few centuries and immerse yourself in **Maramureș** (p737), Europe's last thriving peasant society

❻ Row through the tributaries and the riot of nature in the **Danube Delta** (p756)

❼ Trace the heroic 1989 revolution to tenacious **Timișoara** (p732)

❽ Enter the **Bucegi Mountains** (p713), where novices can bike or hike the flat plateau

❾ Hit a midsummer music fest and soak in some counter-culture vibes at **Vama Veche** (p757)

government headquarters – some still riddled with statement-making bullet holes from the 1989 revolution. Just two decades after his demise, in a transformation that's rich in poetic justice, Ceauşescu's intended legacy is being smothered by stylish people, fast cars and a nightlife scene that's as happening as any in Western Europe. The country's top museums are here, and there are plenty of green parks providing escape from encroaching capitalism and the repellent effects of newly affordable cars. Ongoing development and gentrification of the crumbling historic centre has resulted in an attractive entertainment district.

◉ Sights

Bucharest's museums are some of the best in Romania and will delight those with the requisite stamina. Historic Calea Victoriei roars with heavy vehicles and aspiring street racers, but it's a scenic thoroughfare and it connects the two main squares of the city: Piaţa Victoriei in the north and Piaţa Revoluţiei in the centre. Follow the river east to where it goes under the sprawling Piaţa Unirii.

CEAUŞESCU'S BUCHAREST

An entire suburb of historic buildings was smashed when Nicolae Ceauşescu returned from tours of Pyongyang and Beijing in the 1980s, suffering from some righteous reverse-culture shock. Feverish reconstruction ensued in Bucharest (and eventually all of Romania), which is particularly evident along **Bulevardul Unirii** in southern Bucharest. Romania's 'Champs-Élysées' is a chaotic, fountain-lined 3.2km boulevard – deliberately pipping Paris' by a resounding 6m (take that Frenchies!). Stroll just north into the historic centre (see p695) to get a sense of what was once here.

Patriarchal Cathedral   CHURCH
(Catedrala Patriahală; Map p696; Str Dealul Mitropoliei) From central **Piaţa Unirii** (under which the city's crippled Dâmboviţa River flows), look southwest to the Patriarchal Cathedral, the centre of Romanian Orthodox faith, built between 1656 and 1658. It triumphantly peeks over once-grand housing blocks on B-dul Unirii designed to 'hide' the city's churches. One such fatality is the **Antim Monastery** (Mănăstirea Antim; Map p696; Str Antim), which dates from 1715. It's northwest, just one block before the boulevard ends.

National Museum of Contemporary Art
                              CONTEMPORARY ART
(Muzeul Naţionalde Arta Contemporana; Map p696; www.mnac.ro; Calea 13 Septembrie; adult/student

5 lei/free; ⊘10am-6pm Wed-Sun) At the back of the Palace of Parliament is the superb National Museum of Contemporary Art. The four-floor exhibition space features eclectic European art – including installation and video – and is one of Eastern Europe's most provocative spaces. There's a top-floor open-air cafe. As you make your way back to B-dul Unirii, note the half-finished **National Institute for Science & Technology** (Map p696; cnr B-dul Libertăţii & Calea 13 Septembrie), one of several half-done or abandoned buildings in Bucharest.

Palace of Parliament   HISTORIC BUILDING
(Palatul Parlamentului; Map p696; ☎021-311 3611; B-dul Naţiunile Unite; adult/student with ID 25 lei/free; ⊘10am-3.45pm) Anchoring B-dul Unirii is the mother of all white elephants: the Palace of Parliament, the world's second-largest administrative building (after the US Pentagon). Built in 1984 (and still unfinished), the building's 12 storeys and 3100 rooms cover 330,000 sq metres, and cost an estimated €3.3 billion. The hefty ticket price doesn't buy you a particularly informative or inspiring tour, but the hourly 45-minute tours are the only way to see a handful of the opulent marble rooms, finishing at the balcony that Ceauşescu didn't live long enough to speak from. Facing the Palace of Parliament from B-dul Unirii, the entrance is around to the right (a 12-minute walk). Tour reservations are required. Call one or two days in advance or try between 9am and 9.30am for a last-minute, same-day spot. Passports or international IDs are required to enter.

FREE **Ghencea Civil Cemetery**   CEMETERY
(Cimitriul Civil Ghencea; Map p696; Calea 13 Septembrie; ⊘8am-8pm) A 45-minute lacklustre walk west of the Palace of Parliament (or take bus 385 from outside the Parliament ticket office on B-dul Naţiunile Unite) leads to Ghencea Civil Cemetery, where you can morbidly seek out the final resting spots of Nicolae Ceauşescu (row I-35, marked with a red cross, to the left of the entry path) and his wife Elena (H25, to the right of the entry path), both executed on Christmas Day in 1989.

HISTORIC QUARTER

Piaţa Universităţii   SQUARE
Some of the most heart-wrenching antiprotester violence of the 1989 revolution took place at **Piaţa Universităţii** (Map p700), which straddles Bucharest's most evocative streets. Horrified journalists watched from their viewpoint inside the Hotel Inter-Continental as tanks rolled over Romanian

Bucharest

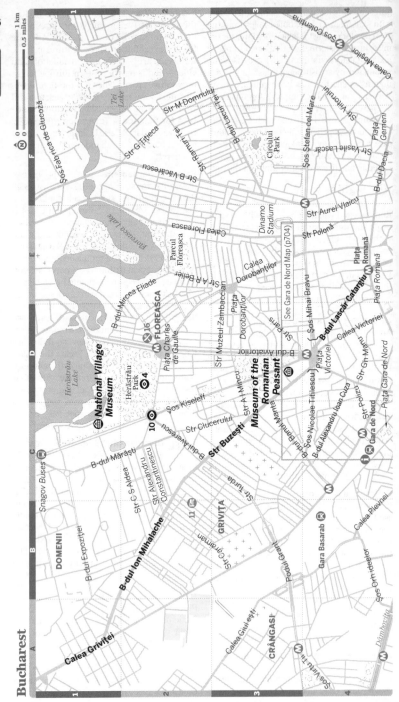

Calea Griviței

DOMENII

B-dul Expoziției

B-dul Ion Mihalache

Calea Griulești

CRÂNGASI

Șos Virtu Titi

Dâmbovița

Șos Orhideelor

B-dul Mărăști

Str C S Aldea

Str Alexandru Constantinescu

Snagov Buses

GRIVIȚA

Str O Pora

Str Braiman

Str Turda

Podul Grant

Gara Basarab

Calea Plevnei

Calea Gara de Nord

Piața Gara de Nord

Gara de Nord

Str Polizu

Str Gh Manu

B-dul Alexandru Ioan Cuza

Șos Nicolae Titulescu

Șos Banu Manta

Str Buzești

B-dul Averescu

Șos Kiseleff

Str Clucerului

National Village Museum

Herăstrău Lake

Herăstrău Park

Tei Lake

Șos Fabrica de Glucoză

Str Ramuri Tei

Str M Domnului

B-dul Lacul Tei

Floreasca Lake

B-dul Mircea Eliade

Piața Charles de Gaulle

FLOREASCA

Parcul Floreasca

Str A R Belier

Calea Floreasca

Str G Țițeica

Str B Văcărescu

Circului Park

Șos Ștefan cel Mare

Str Vasile Lascăr

Piața Gemeni

B-dul Dacia

Str Aurel Vlaicu

Str Polonă

Piața Romană

Piața Dorobanților

Calea Dorobanților

Str Muzeul Zambaccian

Str Paris

Șos Mihai Bravu

Dinamo Stadium

See Gara de Nord Map (p704)

B-dul Lascăr Catargiu

Piața Romană

Calea Victoriei

Piața Victoriei

B-dul Aviatorilor

Museum of the Romanian Peasant

Str A I Mincu

Șos Viilorului

Str Mihai Bravu

Calea Moșilor

Șos Colentina

See Gara de Nord Map (p704)

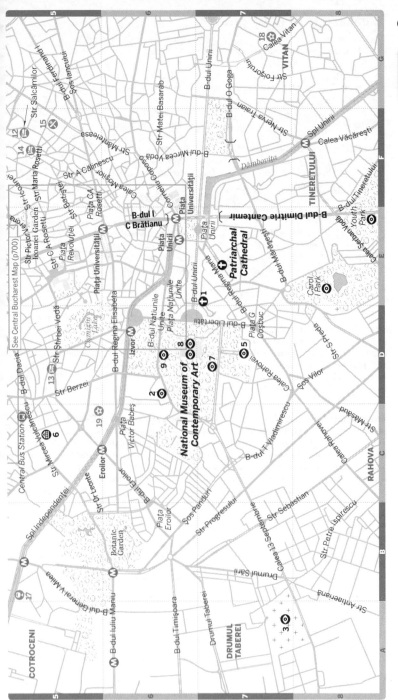

Bucharest

protestors and soldiers shot into the crowds. Scour the area and you'll find bullet marks in some buildings and 10 stone crosses commemorating those killed. A **black cross** and **plaque** on the wall at B-dul Nicolae Bălcescu 18 marks the spot where the first protestor, Mihai Gătlan, died at 5.30pm on 21 December 1989.

Around Piaţa Universităţii   HISTORIC AREA
Much of the historic centre lies in the blocks to the southwest of the square. A good access way is along **Calea Victoriei**, built in 1692 under Brâncoveanu's orders to link the centre with his summer palace in Mogoşoaia, 14km northwest. Three blocks south of the square is **Stradă Lipscani**, its newly cobblestoned portions being early benefactors of central Bucharest's long-awaited gentrification efforts. Smart shops, pubs, restaurants and cafes have duly followed. At the time of writing, intriguing Roman ruins uncovered during street resurfacing stood fenced-off but sadly exposed to people with rubbish-disposal deficiencies. Another block south is the ritzy **Economic Consortium Palace** (Casa de Economii şi Consemnaţiuni), designed by French architect Paul Gottereau between 1894 and 1900.

National History Museum   MUSEUM
(Muzeul National de Istorie a Romaniei; Map p700; ☏021-311 3356; www.mnir.ro; Calea Victoriei 12; adult/student 8/2 lei; ☉10am-6pm Wed-Sun) Despite ongoing, snail-paced renovations, it's worth seeing for the dismantled replica of the 2nd-century 40m Trajan's Column: its 2500 characters retell the Dacian Wars against Rome. (Go to panel 18 to see decapitated heads.) There's also a gold-crammed treasury. It's housed in the neoclassical former Post Office Palace (1894).

FREE **Stavropoleos Church**   CHURCH
(Map p700; Str Stavropoleos) On a street meaning 'town of the cross', the church dates from 1724 and is one of Bucharest's most atmospheric. The ornate courtyard, filled with tombstones and relics from the city's demolished churches, is probably the most peaceful spot in central Bucharest.

Old Princely Court   RUINS
(Palatul Voievodal; Map p700; Curtea Veche; Str Franceză 21-23; admission 3 lei; ☉10am-5pm) The heart of the historic centre is the busted-up Old Princely Court from the 15th century, with a **Vlad Ţepeş statue** out the front.

Jewish History Museum   MUSEUM
(Muzeul de Istorie al Comunitaţilor Evreieşti din România; Map p700; Str Mămulari; admission by donation; ☉9am-1pm Sun-Wed & Fri, to 4pm Thu) Just east of Piaţa Unirii, the interesting Jewish History Museum is housed in a colourful synagogue that dates from 1836 (rebuilt in 1910). Exhibits (in English and Romanian) outline Jewish contributions to Romanian

history, which not all Romanians know about. In 1941, 800,000 Jews lived in Romania; today only 10,000 remain. You need your passport to enter.

PIAŢA REVOLUŢIEI

National Art Museum   ART GALLERY
(Muzeul Naţional de Artă; Map p700; www.mnar.arts.ro; Calea Victoriei 49-53; combination ticket 15 lei, 1st Wed of month free; ⊙11am-7pm Wed-Sun) Housed in the early-19th-century Royal Palace, the National Art Museum is a super three-part museum. The north door leads to the **Gallery of Romanian Art** (adult/student 10/5 lei), with hundreds of icons saved from communist-destroyed churches and many paintings, including arresting portraits by Nicolae Grigorescu. Also in the building is the small **Treasures of Roman Art** (adult/student 10/5 lei). The south door leads to the absorbing **Gallery of European Art** (adult/student 8/4 lei), a 12,000-piece collection largely assembled from Tsar Carol I's collection, which covers all things from Rembrandt and Bartolomeo to Rodin and Monet.

Revolution Sites   HISTORIC SITES
The scene of Ceauşescu's infamous last speech of 21 December 1989 was on the balcony of the former **Central Committee of the Communist Party building** (Map p700; Str Academiei). Sensing irreparable doom amid cries of 'Down with Ceauşescu', he briefly escaped in a helicopter from the roof. Meanwhile, the crowds were riddled with bullets, and many died. The **building shell** (Map p700; cnr Str DI Dobrescu & Str Boteanu) is all that remains of the former home of the hated Securitate after it was destroyed by protestors in 1989. Now a modern glass structure stands inside it; you can see strik-

ing revolution photos while sipping fancy coffee in the basement IO Coffee Bar (p706).

Athénée Palace   HISTORIC BUILDING
(Str Episcopiei 1-3) Just to the north of the National Art Museum is the Athénée Palace, so evocatively captured in its postrevolutionary, prostitute-teeming state by Robert Kaplan in *Balkan Ghosts*. Designed to outdo Paris in 1918, the hotel later served as a hotbed for Romania's 'KGB', the Securitate. Now Hilton has cleaned it up – and priced its rooms beyond their worth.

Romanian Athenaeum   HISTORIC BUILDING
(Ateneul Român; Map p700; admission 7.50 lei) Just east is the grand domed Romanian Athenaeum, which hosts prestigious concerts. Built in 1888, this is where George Enescu made his debut in 1898. Today it's home to the George Enescu Philharmonic Orchestra. Hours vary.

FREE **Cişmigiu Garden**   PARK
Just west is the locally loved Cişmigiu Garden, with shady walks, cafes and a ridiculous number of benches on which to sit and stare at Bucharestians going by.

NORTHERN BUCHAREST

Bucharest's most luxurious villas and parks line the grand avenue **Şoseaua Kiseleff** (Map p696), which begins at Piaţa Victoriei. A leafy walk north of the Piaţa takes you to two wonderful museums that pay tribute to Romania's rural heart.

Museum of the Romanian Peasant   MUSEUM
(Muzeul Țăranului Român; Map p704; Şos Kiseleff 3; adult/student 6/1.50 lei; ⊙10am-6pm Tue-Sun) About 200m north of Piaţa Victoriei, the Museum of the Romanian Peasant is so

---

FREE THRILLS

Bucharest's sprawl means worthwhile free activities are prohibitively distant from one another, but if you happen to be in the area, here are a few you can add to your itinerary:

» Wander the **historic centre** (p695) admiring the crumbling, restored and under-restoration streets and buildings.

» Take a break in the atmospheric courtyard at **Stavropoleos Church** (p698), dating from 1724 and possibly central Bucharest's most serene spot.

» Escape the car-horn refrain at the **Triumphal Arch** (p702) in the exquisite walking and picnicking grounds of **Herăstrău Park** (p702).

» Pay your disrespects to the final resting places of Nicolae and Elena Ceauşescu at **Ghencea Civil Cemetery** (p695).

» Enjoy the heat retreat and Bucharestian-watching in the heroically tended **Cişmigiu Garden** (p699).

Central Bucharest

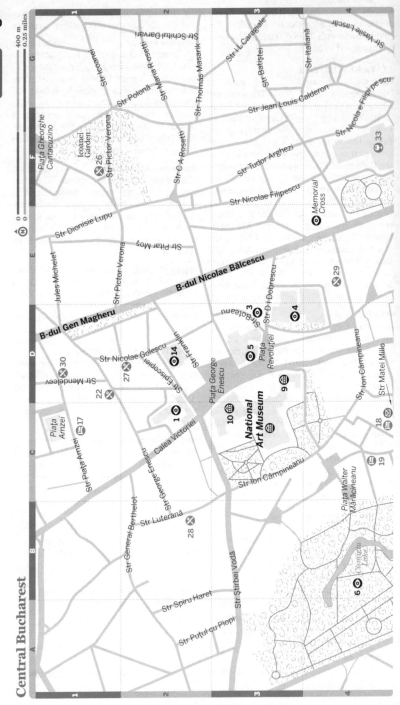

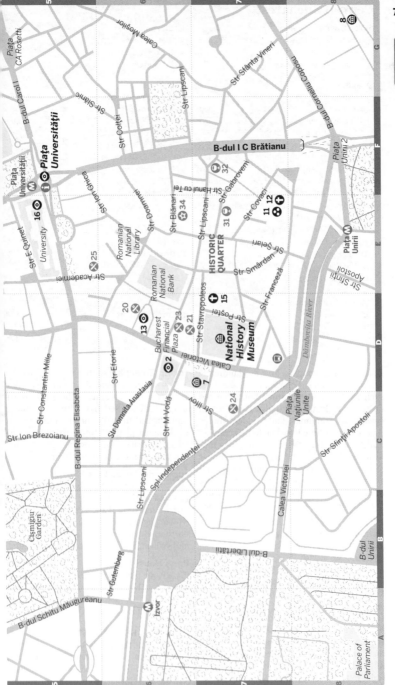

good you may want to hug it. Handmade cards (in English) personalise exhibits, such as a full 19th-century home located upstairs, a heartbreakingly sweet room devoted to grandmas, and 'hidden' rooms that you're ushered to via hand-scrawled directions. Don't miss the (rare) communism exhibit downstairs, with a portrait of Romanian leader Gheorghiu-Dej as well as busts of Lenin and a painting where he might, almost, be smiling. An 18th-century Transylvanian church is in the back lot, as is the museum's gift shop.

National Village Museum   OUTDOOR MUSEUM
(Muzeul Naţional al Satului; Map p696; www.muzeul
-satului.ro; Şos Kiseleff 28-30; adult/student 6/3 lei; ◷9am-7pm Tue-Sun, to 5pm Mon) Adjoining Herăstrău Park, but accessed via Şos Kiseleff, is this terrific open-air collection of several dozen homesteads, churches, mills and windmills that have been relocated from rural Romania. At times in July and August, artisans in traditional garb show off various rural trades. Souvenirs are pricey: unless you're desperate, wait and buy these items while you're roaming the country.

FREE **Triumphal Arch**   LANDMARK
(Arcul de Triumf; Map p696) About 2km north of Piaţa Victoriei is the 1935–36 Triumphal Arch, based on the Paris monument and devoted to WWI and the reunification of Romania in 1918. Traffic roars by, so it's tricky to reach. The viewing platform has sporadic, unposted opening hours.

FREE **Herăstrău Park**   PARK
(Parcul Herăstrău; Map p696) Pathways just east of the Triumphal Arch lead to the lovely Herăstrău Park (Parcul Herăstrău), which hugs the chain of lakes that stripe northern Bucharest. There are plenty of cafes and you can rent pedal boats and rowboats.

Press House   LANDMARK
(Casa Presei Libre; off Map p696) At the north end of Şos Kiseleff is the Stalinesque Press House, built in 1956. Note the hammer and sickle imprint midway up the tower.

WESTERN BUCHAREST

National Military Museum   MUSEUM
(Muzeul Militar Naţional; Map p696; Str Mircea Vulcănescu 125-127; adult/student 5/2.5 lei; ◷9am-5pm Tue-Sun) Not far from the train station,

the pinky-peach Military Museum doubles nicely as a Romanian history museum. Note the 1988 communist mural in the entry; out the back is a superb hangar with Aurel Vlaicu's famed 1911 plane, which Romanians insist made the first 'real' flight.

Sleeping

In an attempt to lure tourists back during the recession, accommodation prices in Bucharest dropped significantly in 2010. It's impossible to say how long these deals will last. Budget options in the centre have improved, though the tranquillity of staying out of the centre may be worth the commute. The grotty Gara de Nord area has some cheaper options. Breakfast is included unless otherwise noted.

TOP CHOICE **Butterfly Villa Hostel** HOSTEL €
(Map p696; ☎021-314 7595; www.villabutterfly.com; Str Stirbei Voda 96; dm 50-54 lei, d 116 lei; ❄@☎) One of Bucharest's best hostels, it's run by a German-Romanian couple and has lounge-y spaces, a kitchen and a small courtyard to kick back in. Dorms have four to eight beds and there's one double room available. Laundry is 10 lei per load. About a 15-minute walk from the train station.

TOP CHOICE **Vila Arte** BOUTIQUE HOTEL €€
(Map p696; ☎021-210 1035; www.vilaarte.ro; Str Vasile Lascăr 78; s/d 253/295 lei; ⊖❄☎) This newly renovated villa has been transformed into a superb boutique hotel stuffed with original art that really pushes the envelope on design and colour. The services are top drawer and the helpful reception makes every guest feel special. The 'Ottoman' room is done in an updated Turkish style, with deep red spreads and oriental carpets. It's nonsmoking throughout. Rooms discounted on weekends.

Hotel Amzei HOTEL €€€
(Map p700; ☎021-313 9400; www.hotelamzei.ro; Str Piaţa Amzei 8; s/d 436/480 lei; ⊖❄☎) This tastefully reconstructed villa just off of Calea Victoriei has 22 rooms on four floors. The wrought-iron atrium in the lobby lends a refined feel. The rooms are in a more restrained contemporary style, but everything about the place screams quality. Wi-fi is in lobby and 1st floor only. Standard class rooms go fast.

Midland Youth Hostel 2 HOSTEL €
(Map p696; ☎021-314 5323; www.themidlandhostel.com; Str Biserica Amzei 22; dm 50-60 lei; @☎) Reasonably central and very spacious (micro-bathrooms notwithstanding), amenities include a TV room, kitchen, free internet/

wi-fi, lockers, laundry (5 lei) and bike rental. Dorms range from six to 14 beds. Try to get one away from the street.

Hotel Carpaţi HOTEL €€
(Map p700; ☎021-315 0140; www.hotelcarpatibucuresti.ro; Str Matei Millo 16; s/d without bathroom 128/180 lei, d with bathroom 240 lei; ☎) This popular central option has 40 recently renovated rooms – some rather tiny and creaky – and a great breakfast served with a little pomp in the Paris-style lobby lounge. All rooms have TV and sink. Wi-fi in the lobby only.

Hotel Opera HOTEL €€€
(Map p700; ☎021-312 4857; www.hotelopera.ro; Str Ion Brezoianu 37; s/d 300/340 lei; ❄@☎) Set on a backstreet corner, this 33-room, faintly art deco, music-themed hotel enjoys membership in Top Hotels Group, and offers, among other things, Mercedes airport transfer. The rooms are small but nicely arranged. There's a tiny computer station (no printer). Street parking.

Golden Tulip HOTEL €€€
(Map p704; ☎021-212 5558; www.goldentulipbucharest.com; Calea Victoriei 166; s/d 375/420 lei; ❄@☎) Rooms are kitted out in wood, with a splash of red furniture and strong IKEA influences. Full-wall glass windows provide great views of the street bustle, though vehicle noise is audible. Enjoy top-end hotel amenities like slippers, toiletry baskets and in-room coffee and tea. Rates drop 20% Friday to Sunday.

Central Hostel HOSTEL €
(Map p696; ☎021-610 2214; www.centralhostel.ro; Str Salcâmilor 2; dm/d from 55/160 lei; @☎) This converted villa in a quiet neighbourhood east of the centre has clean rooms with new beds, a kitchen, laundry (8 lei), lockers and patio seating under a vine shade.

Casa Albă CAMPING GROUND €
(off Map p696; ☎021-230 4525; www.casaalba.ro; Alea Privighetorilor 1-3; campsites per person 40 lei, bungalows with shared/private showers 80/90 lei) This camping ground is 12km north of the centre. Take bus 301 north from Piaţa Romană and get off at 'Restaurant Baneasa' stop; the entrance is across the road. Driving from the centre, pass IKEA, exit before the next bridge and take the second right on Alea Privighetorilor. It's 600m on the left. Bungalows have shared toilets.

Funky Chicken HOSTEL €
(Map p696; ☎021-312 1425; www.funkychickenhostel.com; Str Gen Berthelot 63; dm 40-45 lei; ☎) Just a couple of blocks from Cişmigiu Garden, this bare-bones but pleasant hostel

Gara de Nord

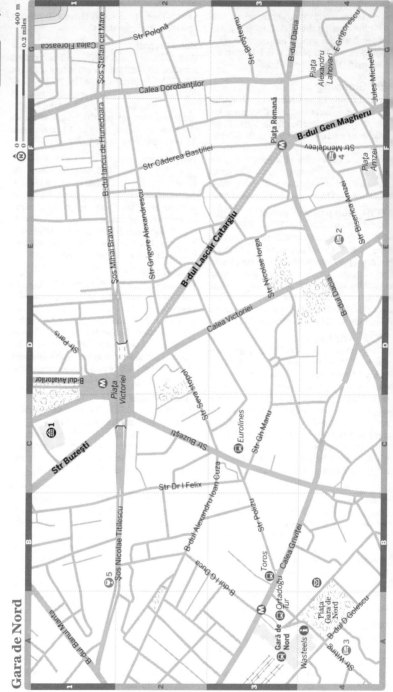

Gara de Nord

occupies a historic home on a shady street. Its three dorm rooms sleep 18. No breakfast, but there's a kitchen.

Hotel Das President   HOTEL **€€**
(Map p704; ☎021-311 0535; www.daspresident. ro; B-dul Dinacu Golescu 29; s/d without bathroom 90/150, s/d with bathroom 110/170 lei; ❉🐾) It's nothing special, but ideal for a sleep during a train layover or before an early departure. Rooms are small and basic, as are the beds, though there's a tiny balcony and TV.

🍴 Eating

TOP CHOICE / **Sale e Pepe**   ITALIAN **€€**
(Map p700; Str Luterană 3; pizza 8-29 lei; ◷10am-midnight Mon-Fri, 3pm-midnight Sat & Sun) This tiny pizza/pasta place specialises in crunchy thin-crust pizzas – and for once in Romania, they don't undercook them. Pizza 'Pepperoni' comes topped with sliced red pepper and spicy sausage, and served with hot sauce on the side on request. There's dining on two levels, with the more popular seating upstairs. They do breakfast, too.

TOP CHOICE / **Caru cu Bere**   ROMANIAN **€€€**
(Map p700; ☎021-313 7560; www.carucu bere.ro; Str Stavropoleos 3-5; mains 15-60 lei; 🐾) Despite a decidedly tourist-leaning atmosphere, with servers in peasant costumes and sporadic Roma song-and-dance numbers, Bucharest's oldest beer house continues to draw in a strong local crowd. The colourful belle époque interior and stained-glass windows dazzle. Try the mixed sausage platter (for two!), which, while delicious, has enough grease for a month. Dinner reservations recommended.

Burebista   GRILL **€€**
(Map p696; Calea Moşilor 195; mains 11-60 lei; ◷noon-midnight) With dark-shaded patio seats outside, and tree-trunk tables and furs inside, the rustic Burebista endeavours to grill every meat on the continent, including hare, quail, pheasant, duck, wild boar and 'bear with mustard sauce'. They do excellent salads, too.

Crama Blanduziei   ROMANIAN **€€**
(Map p700; Str Academiei 2; mains 20-30 lei; ◷11am-11pm) In a great location just on the fringe of Lipscani, it has a traditional dining room and a more relaxed terrace. In summer, it's a good spot for a casual night of grilled meats, salad and bottles of beer. The three-course lunch menu (20 lei) is a good deal.

Bistro Vilacrosse   BISTRO **€€**
(Map p700; Pasajul Macca; mains 14-20 lei) The small Vilacrosse borrows its style heavily from Parisian side streets, with sepia tones and wood floors, though paradoxically, the service here is friendly and quick! The food's good too, including a wine-spattered Transylvania pork fillet on a bed of French fries and roasted cabbage. A few vegetarian options.

Trattoria il Calcio   ITALIAN **€€**
(Map p700; Str Mendeleev 14; mains 22-46 lei) This upmarket Italian chain is run by 'Romania's George Best' (football legend Gino Lorgucescu), complete with framed *Futbol* journals from the 1960s on the walls. The food's great, with hearty meals and good salads. It gets busy at lunch.

Count Dracula Club   ROMANIAN **€€€**
(Map p700; ☎021-312 1353; www.count-dracula. ro; Spl Independenţei 8a; mains 22-88 lei; ◷4pm-midnight) Even the hardest backpacker has to occasionally submit to kitsch like this: a spooky home with blood-dripping walls, Transylvania-themed rooms, impaled heads, hands reaching through walls, and blood-red lights. Plus, Drac himself shows up for a show at 9.30pm on Tuesdays and Fridays. Pull the bell chain to enter.

City Grill   ROMANIAN **€€**
(Map p700; www.citygrill.ro; Str Lipscani 12; mains 11-49 lei; 🐾) Enviably situated in the increasingly pleasant Lipscani area (requisite terrace included), City Grill defies the chain stereotype with great Romanian food and likeable staff. Some vegetarian options and assorted salads.

Grădina Verona   CAFE **€**
(Map p700; Str Pictor Verona 13-15; ◷9am-1am) This garden oasis hidden behind the Cărtureşti bookshop serves standard-issue but excellent espresso drinks and some of the wackiest ice-tea infusions ever concocted in Romania, like peony flower, mango and lime (it's not bad).

IO Coffee Bar
CAFE €

(Map p700; Str Demetru I Dobrescu 5; 🛜) Looking out from a blown-out ruin of the 1989 clash at nearby Piaţa Revoluţi, this cafe has backlit wall-length B&W prints of the 1989 scene and candles on the table. Nights and weekends the volume rises with jazz and dance music.

La Mama
ROMANIAN €€

(Map p700; Str Episcopiei 8; mains 15-25 lei) This highly popular Romanian chain restaurant (think local version of TGIF) is, to coin a phrase, what it is. Come for platters of well-done local dishes, heavy on meat and potatoes, at reasonable prices for the centre of town. The terrace is a pleasant spot for a summertime lunch.

Casa Veche
PIZZA €

(Map p700; Str George Enescu 15; pizzas 16-23 lei) With courtyard seats under vines, and traditional upstairs seating, this place offers great-quality crispy pizzas and a winner setting near the centre.

Snack Attack!
CAFE €

(Map p700; Str Ion Câmpineanu 10; sandwiches 8 lei; ⊘7.30am-8pm Mon-Fri, to 2pm Sat) Fresh, cheap takeaway panini and salads (including hummus and tabouli with tortillas).

🍸 Drinking

Bucharest's budding bar scene is liveliest in the Str Lipscani area. Piaţas Universităţii and Unirii bustle with revellers at the weekend.

Fire Club
BAR

(Map p700; Str Gabroveni 12) This big red-brick room usually has groups of students crouching on stools around small tables with bottles of Tuborg in hand. Rock and punk shows are staged in the basement.

La Motoare
BAR

(Map p700; B-dul Nicolae Bălcescu 2; ⊘2pm-3am Mon-Fri, to 4am Sat & Sun) Huge with uni students, this lively open-deck bar on the 5th floor of the Ion Luca Caragiale National Theatre fits hundreds, with benches and big pillows in the seating areas. It fills early on nice days. Rumours abound of its eventual demise (who ever heard of putting a bawdy rock club on top of a national theatre?), but it was still alive and kicking when we passed through.

Harley
BAR

(Map p700; cnr Str Lipscani & Str Zarafi; ⊘3pm-3am) Just around the corner from Fire Club, it's quite an adventure to find with all the renovation (and demolition) work going on in the area, but worth it for the chilled bar vibe and an emphasis on alt rock and metal.

Dubliner
PUB

(Map p696; Şos Nicolae Titulescu 18; ⊘9am-2am) This is a long-time expat hang-out, with draught Guinness and football games attracting a grab bag of fans. Locals tend to stick with the streetside tables, while sports fans linger by the TVs or dartboard inside. The Dubliner's steak sandwich is super, but priced for foreign budgets.

☆ Entertainment

Şapte Seri (Seven Evenings; www.sapteseri.ro) and 24-Fun are free, weekly entertainment listings magazines (in Romanian). For information on seeing the philharmonic at the Romanian Athenaeum, see p699.

Other entertainment options:

Hollywood Multiplex
CINEMA

(Map p696; Bucureşti Mall, Calea Vitan 55-59; tickets 13-21 lei) A multiscreen jobbie.

Club A
CLUB

(Map p700; Str Blănari 14; ⊘9pm-5am Thu-Sun) Run by students and beloved by all who go there, A cheap beer and rock tunes fill the house until 5am Friday and Saturday nights.

Piranha Club
CLUB

(Map p696; www.clubpiranha.ro; Spl Independenţei 313; ⊘10am-late) About 2.5km west of the centre, this unique jungle lodge-type place has piranhas in aquariums, gazebos decked out like country homes, and pretty good food. There are often live shows. It's south of the river, a couple of hundred metres west of the Grozăveşti metro station.

National Opera House
OPERA

(Opera Română; Map p696; ☎021-313 1857; B-dul Mihail Kogălniceanu 70) Stages full-scale operas in a lovely building. Tickets start at 8 lei.

🛍 Shopping

For beautifully made (though pricey) woven rugs, table runners, national Romanian costumes, ceramics and other local crafts, don't miss the excellent folk-art shop inside the Museum of the Romanian Peasant (p699).

ℹ Information

The best Bucharest map, available at bus ticket stands, is the 100% Planul Oraşului Bucureşti Map (1:200,000; 11 lei), listing all transport routes.

Dangers & Annoyances

Bucharest's stray dogs (aka 'community dogs') number around 100,000. Though they're largely docile, bites are not uncommon – in the first three months of 2010, more than 2000 people were reportedly bitten in Bucharest. In January 2011, a woman was mauled by a pack of stray dogs and later died of her injuries. Avoid packs of dogs and be especially careful around parked cars or bushes at night, where you could inadvertently startle a sleeping dog. If bitten, go to a hospital within 24 hours for antirabies injections.

Rare encounters with fake police (aka 'tourist police') are still being reported. If accosted by dubious officials, insist on being escorted to the nearest station before producing passports, money etc.

A classic (and bafflingly tolerated) annoyance is taxi drivers charging extortionate prices. The worst are those in and around Gara de Nord. We've heard of travellers paying 500 lei for a 17-lei ride! Legit taxis will have prices printed on the side of the car, usually the door, ranging from 1.30 to 1.50 lei per kilometre. The taxis camped at the airport charge 3.50 lei. Watch for creative punctuation: 'TARIF1.3,5 lei/km', looks like a very economical 1.3 lei/km at first glance, until you learn that it means 'Tarif 1 costs 3.5 lei/km'.

Sometimes English-speaking drivers approach travellers at the train station, claiming to be from a hostel, then charge sky-high rates for the ride. Unless you have previously arranged transport with your accommodation, don't take a ride with anyone claiming to be from a hostel or hotel. Wasteels (p708) can usually call for a taxi from the train station if you don't have a phone to call one of the reliable companies listed on p767.

Emergency
Ambulance ☑973

Police (☑955, central station 021-311 2021)

Internet Access

Nearly all hotels and hostels have internet access. Cafes with wi-fi are common.

Argo Internet (cnr B-dul Regina Elisabeta & Calea Victoriei; per hr 5.90 lei)

Green Hours Internet (Calea Victoriei 120; per hr 4 lei) Popular internet cafe adjacent to the Green Hours jazz club.

Medical Services
Emergency Clinic Hospital (☑021-317 0121; Calea Floreasca 8; ☺24hr) Bucharest's best state hospital.

Finesse (Clinica Stomatologica; ☑021-313 4781; www.finesse-dent.ro; Str Hristo Botev 7; ☺10am-8pm Mon-Fri, to 4pm Sat) Dentist.

Sensi-Blu (B-dul Nicolae Bălcescu 7; ☺24hr) Reliable pharmacy chain with countless locations.

Money

Currency-exchange bureaux are everywhere, though it's better to change money at a bank or stick to the ATM. Avoid the currency-exchange counters at the airport: there are ATM machines in the arrivals hall.

ING (Map p700; B-dul Nicolae Bălcescu 22) Bank.

Post
Central post office (☑021-315 9030; Str Matei Millo 10; ☺7.30am-8pm Mon-Fri) Collect poste restante mail here.

Telephone

RomTelecomm cards (from 10 lei) are available at news-stands. Most phone booths are neglected, but should still work. You'll have no problem finding a shop selling Orange or Vodaphone SIM cards for your mobile phone – try a central street like B-dul Magheru.

Tourist Information
Info Tourist Point (Gara de Nord; ☑0371-155 063; www.infotourist.ro; ☺9am-9pm) Bucharest finally joined the rest of the universe in 2010, opening two proper tourist information offices, offering maps, brochures and multilingual assistance. The second location is in the **Piața Universității underpass** (☺9am-6pm Mon-Fri, 10am-1pm Sat).

WORTH A TRIP

DRACULA'S FINAL RESTING PLACE

It's the tomb of infamous tyrant Vlad Țepeș that lures visitors to **Snagov** (about 40km north of Bucharest), although there's also a large lake and leisure complex. Devour the legend of Dracula by visiting the grave where his headless torso is said to lie, buried in the famous 16th-century **church and monastery**, on an island in Snagov Lake.

Most visitors go by organised day trip – and hostels like Butterfly Villa Hostel (p703) in Bucharest arrange these, usually dropping by **Căldărușani Monastery**. It's also possible to go by maxitaxi, leaving hourly from Piața Universității via Piața Romana, Piața Presei and the Press House in Bucharest (8 lei each way).

Wasteels (☎021-317 0370; www.wasteels. ro; Gara de Nord; ☺8am-7pm Mon-Fri) Conveniently located on the left side of the exit hallway of the train station, Wasteels can help with train reservations, and possibly call you a reliable taxi.

❶ Getting There & Away

Air

Romania's national airline is **Tarom** (Transporturile Aeriene Române; www.tarom.ro) airport (☎021-317 4444); city centre (☎021-337 0400; Spl Independenţei 17; ☺8.30am-7.30pm Mon-Fri, 9am-2pm Sat). See p766 for details of international flights to Romania, and p767 for domestic-flight information.

Henri Coanda airport (aka Otopeni; ☎021-204 1000; www.otp-airport.ro; Şos Bucureşti-Ploieşti), located 16.5km north of Bucharest on the road to Braşov, is where most international flights arrive. There are **information desks** (☎021-204 1220; ☺24hr) in both terminals.

Domestic, charter and a few budget airlines use **Băneasa airport** (☎021-232 0020; Şos Bucureşti-Ploieşti 40), 8km north of the centre.

Bus

DOMESTIC BUSES Bucharest's bus system is frankly a mess, scarred by ever-changing departure locations, companies and schedules. Try checking www.cdy.ro or asking your hotel to help with the latest. Or stick with the train.

The most popular routes are the maxitaxis to Braşov (30 lei, 2½ hours), which stop in Sinaia (26 lei), Buşteni and Predeal on the way. Some continue on to Sighişoara (54 lei, five hours). **C&I** (off Map p696; ☎021-256 8039; Str Ritmului 35) runs these from its office 3.25km east of Piaţa Romana: from metro station Piaţa Iancului, go south for one block on Şoseaua Mihei Bravu (toward Maxbet Casino) and right on B-dul Ferdinand. It's up two blocks on the left. Buses 69 and 85 go there from Gara de Nord.

Every 45 minutes or so, maxitaxis head for Constanţa (50 lei, 3½ hours) from the so-called **Central Bus Station** (Autogara; Map p696), which is located about 350m southeast of the train station.

INTERNATIONAL BUSES The biggest name in international buses is **Eurolines** (☎021-316 3661; www.eurolines.ro; Str Buzeşti 44; ☺24hr), which links many Western European destinations with Bucharest. Services include four weekly buses to Athens (300 lei, 22 hours), three weekly to Berlin (490 lei, 32 hours) and to Rome (350 lei, 37 to 40 hours), a daily bus to Vienna (300 lei, 25 hours) and several weekly to Paris (440 lei, 39 hours). Working with Eurolines, **Atlassib** (www.atlassib.ro) handles Italian destinations.

Double T (☎021-313 3642) has daily service to Ruse, Bulgaria (43 lei, 2½ hours) leaving at 3.50pm, which continues on to Pleven and Sofia (107 lei, eight hours).

Those who are Turkey-bound have several options leaving from around Gara de Nord, including **Ortadoğu Tur** (☎021-318 7538; Str Gara de Nord 6-8) and **Toros** (☎021-233 1898; Calea Griviţei 134-136). The 12-hour trip costs about 200 lei one way.

Car & Motorcycle

Bucharest offers some of the country's cheapest car-rental rates. Major car-rental agencies can be found at the Henri Coanda airport arrivals hall. Cheapest are **D&V** (☎021-201 4611, 0788-998 877; www.dvtouring.ro) and **Autonom** (www. autonom.com), offering the Dacia Logan for 126 lei per day (including unlimited mileage and insurance, minimum two days); it falls to 104 lei per day if you rent for more than a week. The tinier Daewoo Matiz goes for 90 lei and 72 lei, respectively.

Hourly parking rates apply in the centre, particularly off Piaţa Victoriei and Piaţa Universităţii – pay at the machine or look for the wardens in yellow-and-blue uniforms. In many places you can just pull onto the streetside.

DOMESTIC TRAINS FROM BUCHAREST

DESTINATION	PRICE (LEI)	DURATION (HR)	DAILY DEPARTURES
Braşov	42	2½	frequent
Cluj-Napoca	58	10	5
Costanţa	39	2-4	frequent
Iaşi	58	7	6
Sibiu	49	7	3
Sighişoara	43	5½	frequent
Suceava	58	7	6
Timişoara	68	8½	6
Tulcea	47	6	2

Train

Gara de Nord (Map p704; ☎021-319 9539; Piaţa Gara de Nord 1) is the central station for national and international trains. Call ☎021-9521 or ☎021-9522 for reservations. It has two halls where same-day tickets can be purchased. Facing the station, the one to the right sells 1st- and 2nd-class domestic tickets; the one to the left sells international (marked 'casa internaţionale') and 1st-class domestic tickets. At night, if you don't have a ticket, you have to pay 1 leu to enter the station. **Left luggage**, located in the hallway leading to the front exit, is 3/6 lei for small/large bags.

Tickets can also be purchased at **Agenţia de Voiaj CFR office** (www.cfr.ro; Str Domnita Anastasia 10-14; ⊘7.30am-7.30pm Mon-Fri, 9am-1.30pm Sat). A seat reservation is compulsory if you are travelling with an Inter-Rail or Eurail pass. Wasteels (p708) on the platform can help out, too. International tickets must be bought in advance.

Check the latest train schedules on either www.cfr.ro or the reliable German site www.bahn.de.

Daily international services include three trains to Budapest's Keleti station (180 lei, 13 to 15 hours); two trains to Sofia (130 lei, 11 hours) and Gorna Oryakhovitsa (near Veliko Târnovo, Bulgaria; 6½ hours); and one train each to Belgrade (130 lei, 12 hours), Chişinău (113 lei, 12 hours), Vienna (250 lei, 16 to 17 hours), İstanbul (240 lei, 20 hours), Kyiv (290 lei, 31 hours) and Moscow (380 lei, 47 hours).

❶ Getting Around
To/From the Airport

BUS To get to Henri Coanda (Otopeni) or Băneasa airport, take bus 783 from the city centre, departing every 15 minutes between 5.37am and 11.23pm (every half-hour at weekends) from Piaţas Unirii and Victoriei and every *piaţa* in between. The Piaţa Unirii stop is on the south side.

Buy a ticket, valid for a return trip (or two people one way) for 7 lei at any RATB (Régie Autonome de Transport de Bucureşti) bus-ticket booth near a bus stop. Once inside the bus remember to feed the ticket into the stamping machine.

Băneasa is 40 to 60 minutes from the centre, depending on traffic; get off at the 'aeroportul Băneasa' stop. Henri Coanda is about 50 to 70 minutes from the centre. The bus stops outside the departures hall then continues to arrivals.

To get to the centre from Henri Coanda, catch bus 783 from the downstairs ramp outside the arrivals hall; you'll need to buy a ticket from the stand at the north end of the waiting platform (to the right as you exit).

TAXI Taking a reputable taxi from the centre to Otopeni should cost no more than 40 to 65 lei.

Fly Taxi and other specially approved companies monopolise airport transfers to the centre, though at 3.5 lei per kilometre it's a fleecing. Alternatively, walk down to the 'Departures' doors and jump into a regular taxi arriving from the city as it drops people off. Look for prices on the door (about 1.30 lei to 1.50 lei) or agree on a fixed price. Avoid the illegal taxis with no posted prices or meters.

TRAIN Train services to Henri Coanda leave 10 minutes past the hour from Gara de Nord from 5am to 11pm. The journey (6 lei, 45 minutes) includes a short shuttle-bus ride from the train terminus to the airport.

Public Transport

You can buy tickets (1.30 lei) for buses, trams and trolleybuses at any **RATB** (www.ratb.ro) street kiosk, marked 'casa de bilete' or simply 'bilete'. Punch your ticket on board or risk an on-the-spot fine.

Public transport runs from 5am to about 11pm (reduced service on Sunday). There's some info online. The *100% Planul Oraşului Bucareşti Map* is a good map with routes.

Bucharest's metro dates from 1979 and has four lines and 49 stations. Trains run every five to seven minutes during peak periods and about every 20 minutes off-peak between 5.30am and 11.30pm.

To use the metro, buy a magnetic-strip ticket at the subterranean kiosks inside the main entrance to the metro station. Tickets valid for two/10 journeys cost 2.50/8 lei. A one-month unlimited travel ticket costs 25 lei. A one-day unlimited-ride ticket is 5 lei.

Opt for a cab with a meter, and avoid the guys outside Gara de Nord. It's best to call one, or have a restaurant or hotel call for you. Reputable companies include **Cobalcescu** (☎021-9451), **CrisTaxi** (☎021-9461) and **Meridian** (☎021-9444). Check that the meter is on; rates are posted on the door.

TRANSYLVANIA

After a century of being name-checked in literature and cinema, the word 'Transylvania' enjoys instant, worldwide recognition. The mere mention of it conjures waves of imagery: mind-bending mountains, Gothic castles, fortified churches, dusty peasant villages, spooky moonlight and a roll-call of bloodthirsty, shape-shifting creatures with wicked overbites.

Unexplained puncture wounds to the neck notwithstanding, Transylvania is all those things and more. The Carpathian Mountains are indeed spectacular, with its

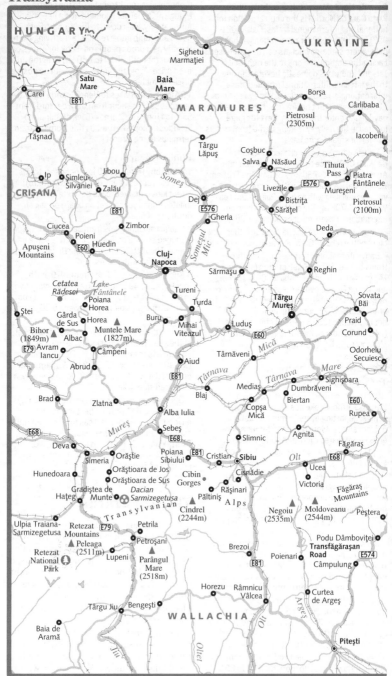

hiking cited as being second only to Switzerland. Valleys are dotted with Saxon towns and fortified churches from the Middle Ages. The well-beaten paths up to Bran and Peleş castles are absolutely worth the crowd-rage. And Dracula's face will stare back at you from a variety of coffee mugs and T-shirts.

Ancient walls, cobblestones, singular architecture and trendy streetside cafes pepper the towns of Braşov, Sighişoara and Sibiu – Transylvania's 'Big Three' – the last of which is still aglow from its tenure as an EU 'Cultural Capital' in 2007. For a little less 'ahhhh', and a little more 'aiii!', the booming student town Cluj-Napoca is where you'll find the country's most agreeable nightlife.

However, it's said that true Romania begins only when you get to the villages. Get some wheels and venture out on your own to the more remote Saxon villages, where two horse carts are a traffic jam.

Sinaia

POP 14,600

Build an eye-popping castle and they will come. Little did King Carol I know that Peleş Castle – his decadent summer residence doubtlessly designed to invoke wretched envy in visiting royal counterparts – would eventually be overrun by busloads of gawking tourists. Situated on the Bucharest–Braşov highway, it's difficult to avoid this defining sight, as evidenced by the state of the car park. There are plenty of supplementary century-old buildings throughout town, too, with a few now serving as hotels.

Sinaia is set within an exquisite, fir-clad scrap of the towering Bucegi Mountains, offering ski runs and hiking trails for year-round fun. It's a little hectic, but wait for the buses to leave or time your visit for mid-autumn or spring, and you'll find the resort's peaceful side.

Sinaia is alleged to have gained its name from Romanian noble Mihai Cantacuzino, who, following a pilgrimage to Mt Sinai in Israel in 1695, founded the Sinaia Monastery. It developed into a major resort after King Carol I selected the area for his summer residence in 1870.

◉ Sights

Peleş Castle   CASTLE

(tours adult/child 20/5 lei; ⊙11am-5pm Tue, 9am-4.15pm Wed-Sun) Romania's monarchy debuted in a blaze of pomp through Peleş

WORTH A TRIP

CURTEA DE ARGEŞ

Curtea de Argeş has a humble, likeable charm, enriched by the captivating treasures left over from being a princely seat in the 14th century. Its church is considered to be the oldest monument preserved in its original form in Wallachia. The city's storied monastery, home to the Episcopal cathedral, sculpted from white stone, is unique for its chocolate-box architecture and the important royal tombs it hides.

The ruins of the **Princely Court** (Curtea Domnească; adult/student/camera 3/1/5 lei), which originally comprised a church and palace, are in the city centre. The church was built in the 14th century by Basarab I, whose statue stands in the square outside the entrance to the court. Basarab died in 1352. His burial place near the altar in the princely church at Curtea de Argeş was discovered in 1939. The princely court was rebuilt by Basarab's son, Nicolae Alexandru Basarab (r 1352–68), and completed by Vlaicu Vodă (r 1361–77). While precious little remains of the palace today, the 14th-century church (built on the ruins of a 13th-century church) is almost perfectly intact.

The fantastical **Episcopal cathedral** (Mănăstirea Curtea de Argeş; adult/child 2/1 lei) was built between 1514 and 1526 by Neagoe Basarab (r 1512–21) with marble and mosaic tiles from Constantinople. Legend has it that the wife of Manole, the master stonemason, was embedded in the church's walls, in accordance with a local custom obliging the mason to bury a loved one alive within the church to ensure the success of his work. Manole told his workers that the first wife to bring their lunch the next day would be entombed. The workers duly went home and warned their women – and so Manole's wife arrived first.

The current edifice dates from 1875 when French architect André Lecomte du Nouy was brought in to save the monastery, which was in near ruins. The white marble tombstones of King Carol I (1839–1914) and his poet wife Elizabeth (1853–1916) lie to the right of the entrance. To the left of the entrance are the tombstones of King Ferdinand I (1865–1927) and British-born Queen Marie (1875–1938) whose heart, upon her request, was put in a gold casket and buried in her favourite palace in Balcic in southern Dobrogea. Following the ceding of southern Dobrogea to Bulgaria in 1940, however, her heart was moved to a marble tomb in Bran. Neagoe Basarab and his wife are also buried in the *pronaos*.

In the park across the road lies **Manole's Well**. Legend has it that Manole tried – and failed – to fly from the monastery roof when his master, Neagoe, removed the scaffolding to prevent him building a more beautiful structure for anyone else. The distant natural spring marks the hapless stonemason's supposed landing pad.

There are nine daily trains running to/from Piteşti (3.90 lei, one hour). Change at Piteşti for all train routes. State buses run from the bus station to/from Braşov (one daily at 10am). Bucharest service runs five times a day on weekdays and three per day on weekends. A daily maxitaxi to Bucharest via Piteşti leaves at 8am from outside Hotel Posada.

Castle, a 20-minute walk up from the centre. King Carol I's vision of fairy-tale turrets rising above acres of green meadows and grand reception halls in Moorish, Florentine and French styles is still awe-inspiring a century later. Endless heavy woodcarved ceilings and gilded pieces induce crossed eyes. Worthwhile (and compulsory) tours take in the 1st floor only – note the ground-breaking central vacuuming system.

Pelişor Palace   PALACE
(compulsory tours adult/child 10/2.50 lei; ⊙9am-5pm Wed-Sun) About 100m up the hill from the castle, the German-medieval Pelişor Palace has a hard time competing with its neighbour. Built by King Carol to house his nephew (and future king) Ferdinand (1865–1927) and wife Marie (who didn't get on well with King Carol and loathed Peleş) its art nouveau style is certainly less showy. The popular Marie died in the arched gold room upstairs.

🏃 Activities

The ski season runs from December through March. Resorts rent skis and snowboards for 43 to 52 lei per day; lift tickets are sometimes bundled by number of trips. Near the cable car, **Snow** (Str Cuza Voda 2a; ⊙9am-6pm) rents out skis and snowboards for 35 lei per day, and bikes for 12/60 lei per hour/day. Skis can also be rented at Cota 1400.

Mountain bikes can be hired at the **bike outlet** (Str Octavia Goga 1; per hr 16 lei; ⊙8am-5pm).

🛏 Sleeping

Travel agencies around town can find you a room in one of the countless pensions, which start at 100 lei. In the Bucegi Mountains there are several cabanas that (purportedly) always have a space for a hiker in need of winks. Some have no electricity.

Hotel Caraiman HOTEL €€
(☑0244-313 551; B-dul Carol I nr. 4; palace@rdslink.ro; s/d/apt 155/205/260 lei; 🐾) Of the faded-glory, century-old hotels (and Sinaia teems with them), we like the large rooms at the 1881 red-and-white Caraiman most – for being less royal ball and more rustic and laid-back.

Hotel Economat HOTEL €€
(☑0244-311 153; www.apps.ro; Aleea Peleşului 2; s/d from 90/180 lei) Just outside the Peleş gate, this place has decent rooms in a setting lovely enough that first-time visitors have been known to mistake it for the castle! There are a few 'Villa Turistica' choices, the best being the two-star Corpul Villa (doubles with shared/private bathroom 100/160 lei).

Marami Hotel HOTEL €€
(☑0244-315 560; www.marami.ro; Str Furnica 52; s/d/ste 160/180/200 lei; ❄🐾) The chalet-style frame looks a little cheap, but this is probably Sinaia's best midrange option. The vibe is slightly art deco and dorm-y with a hint of IKEA. Request a balcony room. Sauna, gym and Jacuzzi access are included.

🍴 Eating

There are a few fast-food stands and pizza places along B-dul Carol I.

Irish House INTERNATIONAL €€
(www.irishhouse.ro; B-dul Carol I nr 80; mains 17-32 lei) There's Guinness on tap (9 lei), green ceilings, and a few token Irish dishes on the menu, including an 'Irish Breakfast' (11 lei). But this place fills for its good Romanian food and reasonably priced pizzas.

Snow ROMANIAN €€
(Str Cuza Voda; mains 15-47 lei) Snow gets busiest with ski and bike rentals, but its outdoor-indoor Romanian restaurant does decent fare, including a few vegetarian dishes.

ℹ Information

The Tourist Information Centre gives away great area maps. Better is the SunCart *Sinaia* map (10 lei), which also includes Buşteni.

Banca Transilvania (B-dul Carol I nr 14) Has a 24-hour ATM; foreign-exchange service is next door.

Central post office (B-dul Carol I 3; ⊙7am-8pm Mon-Fri, 8am-1pm Sat)

Dracula's Land (☑0244-311 441; mihneasutu@yahoo.com; B-dul Carol I nr 14; ⊙9am-5pm) It

---

WORTH A TRIP

BUCEGI MOUNTAINS

Sinaia and Buşteni (5km to the north) are the principal gateways to this stunning (and popular) mountain range that boasts skiing, mountain biking and exceptional hiking fun on a plateau situated on the Transylvania–Wallachia border. Hikes are well marked, and some make for great cycling, though things can get harsh when winds and weather rush over the plateau.

From Sinaia, a 30-person **cable car** (one way to Cota 1400/Cota 2000 13/23.50 lei; return 26/47 lei; ⊙9am-5pm) leaves half-hourly to two station points (Cota 1400 and Cota 2000), but lines stack for a couple of hours in summer (roughly mid-June to mid-September); get there by 7am. Buşteni's **cable-car station** (adult/child one way 29/16 lei; ⊙8.30am-5pm Wed-Mon, 10.30am-5pm Tue) is another access point.

It's possible to hike from the top to Bran – it's about five hours' hike from atop Cota 2000 to Cabana Omul, and another five downhill into Bran. It's a *very* rough hike going up from Bran. Day or overnight trips require the 1:70,000 Dimap trail map of Bucegi, which has trail-marker details.

There are cabanas up here, but most visitors go as a day trip. Talk to Snow (p712) in Sinaia about ski runs and cycling trails, or to get equipment.

Transylvania Adventure (www.adventuretransylvania.com) offers eight-day cycling trips (including bike, meals and accommodation) from mid-May to mid-October for about 3400 lei.

hides its tacky name from the street (its sign merely says 'Tourist Office'), but the chummy blokes inside can help find a villa or hotel room for you, arrange hiking guides or change money.

Salvamont (☑0244-313 131, nationwide 0-SALVAMONT; Primărie, B-dul Carol I) Inside the tourist information centre and at Cota 2000 chairlift station; 24-hour mountain-rescue service.

Sinaia tourism information centre (☑0244-315 656; www.info-sinaia.ro; B-dul Carol I 47; ◉8.30am-4.30pm Mon-Fri) Lots and lots of information and brochures and maps, but it can't book rooms.

Telephone office (◉10am-6pm Mon-Fri, to 2pm Sat) In the same building as the central post office. The public fax line is ☑0244-314 010.

❶ Getting There & Away

Sinaia is on the Bucharest–Braşov rail line – 126km from the former and 45km from the latter – so jumping on a train to Bucharest (27 lei, 1½ hours) or Braşov (12 lei, one hour) is a cinch.

Buses and maxitaxis run every 45 minutes between roughly 6am and 10pm from the train station to Azuga (4 lei, 10 minutes) and Buşteni (3 lei, 20 minutes); some go all the way to Bucharest (24 lei, 1½ hours) or Braşov (9 lei, one hour). Rates are less than the train, and the trip is quicker, but there's little room for luggage. Pay the driver or seek out the bored guy wandering by the taxis with a laminated ID.

Braşov

POP 278,000

Braşov (Brassó in Hungarian) is Romania's ground-zero tourist destination for very good reason. Ringed by perfect mountains and verdant hills (never mind the faux-Hollywood 'Braşov' sign up there), the city is adorned with baroque facades, bohemian outdoor cafes and the lovely Piaţa Sfatului –

one of Romania's finest squares. The agreeable locals are seemingly impervious to the increasing number of visitors each summer. The city is a joy to wander, good food is easy to find and innumerable day trips can be launched from here: hiking or skiing in the Bucegi Mountains, castling in Bran, Râsnov and Sinaia, and more.

Braşov started out as a German mercantile colony named Kronstadt. At the border of three principalities, it became a major medieval trading centre. The Saxons built some ornate churches and town houses, protected by a massive wall that still remains.

◉ Sights

Though sorely lacking in decent museums, drifting through Braşov's medieval glory is arresting enough.

Piaţa Stafalui SQUARE
A good starting point for a walk is central **Piaţa Stafalui**, where witches were once burned and prisoners tortured in the gold **Council House** (Casa Sfatului), which dates from 1420; listen closely when passing (we hear that a caretaker hastily quit after hearing 'ghostly screams' from the tower at night). The building also houses the good tourist information centre and unmemorable **Braşov Historical Museum** (adult/student 7/1.50 lei).

Black Church CHURCH
(Biserica Neagră; adult/child 6/3 lei; ◉10am-5pm Mon-Sat) Looming from the south, the Gothic Black Church, built between 1384 and 1477, gained its name after a 1689 fire blackened its walls. It's noticeably less black these days after an over-ambitious scrub down. Inside the church (supposedly the largest Gothic place of worship between Vienna and İstanbul) you can view apse statues moved from outside and 120 fabulous Turkish rugs – merchants' gifts after Ottoman shopping sprees. Organ

---

BEARS!

About 6000 black and brown bears call Romania home, and many have taken to making day trips into Braşov from the surrounding hills. In recent years, uncollected rubbish bins (and in rare cases, kitchen cabinets) in Braşov have become new feeding areas for bears, delighting some tour operations that champion 'bear-watching' tours to rubbish dumps. Many are against it, as it can be dangerous for bears to become accustomed to associating food with the human presence and, well, it's not very 'natural'.

Unfortunately, headline-grabbing bear attacks have occurred in the area. In 2009 a policeman was killed by a brown bear outside a mountain village. In 2008 a man was 'ripped to shreds' while sleeping on a bench near Braşov's centre. The previous year, a woman was mauled to death and two others injured while on a mountain hike 40km south of the city. In 2005 a bear rampaged a picnic area on the outskirts of town, killing one and injuring nine.

recitals on the 4000-pipe instrument are usually held in July and August (6pm on Tuesdays, Thursdays and Saturdays; 6 lei).

Mt Tâmpa   MOUNTAIN
You can't miss the 'Braşov' sign that looks over town from Mt Tâmpa. This regrettable publicity ploy appeared in 2004 and was enlarged (and floodlit) in 2007. One local laughed it off: 'Do they think I'm too old to remember where I am?' To reach it, take the **Tâmpa cable car** (Telecabina; one way/return 10/20 lei; ⊙9.30am-5pm Tue-Sun), well worth it for the stunning views of town and access to a few hiking trails. From the cable-car station, you'll notice that a substantial portion of the original town wall still encircles the centre. A couple of blocks west is the cobblestoned **Stradă Sforii**, one of Europe's narrowest 'streets'.

St Nicholas' Cathedral   CHURCH
(St Nicolae din Scheii; ⊙6am-9pm) The black-spired Orthodox cathedral, accessed from Piaţa Unirii, dates from the 14th century and is home to the small **Romanian School Museum** (Prima Scoala Romaneasca; adult/student 5/3 lei).

Black Tower & White Tower   LOOKOUT
Leave time to look out over the centre from the two towers on the hillside just west of the centre – popular when the setting sun puts a golden hue on Braşov. The **Black Tower** (Turnul Neagru) and **White Tower** (Turnul Alba), which are actually both rather white, are reached by a lovely promenade alongside the western city walls and a rushing stream. A side road leads to the promenade from about 200m south of the Black Church.

⭐ Festivals & Events
If you're here in April, look out for the **Juni Pageant**. In December Braşov holds its **De la Colind la Stea** festival.

🛌 Sleeping
All three hostels are near Piaţa Unirii, and reached by bus 51 from the train station. Each offers a variety of similarly priced castle/village tours.

TOP CHOICE **Bella Muzica**   HOTEL €€
(☑0268-477 956; www.bellamuzica.ro; Piaţa Sfatului 19; s/d 220/270 lei; ✳🕏) The terrific 25-room Muzica has very stylish rooms with soft lighting, textured orange walls and old-style wood desks to write poems on. Cable internet only in some areas.

Kismet Dao Hostel   HOSTEL €
(☑0268-514 296; www.kismetdao.ro; Str Neagoe Basarab 8; dm/d 43/130 lei; @🕏) At the time of writing, Kismet Dao was in the process of moving to a larger building. From the train station, take bus 51 for four stops or 4 for five stops. Get off the bus, turn left, cross Str Iuliu Maniu at the lights and follow Str Agriselor. Cross B-dul Eroilor and continue uphill. The hostel is on the right. A taxi from the station should cost about 7 lei.

Curtea Braşoveană   HOTEL €€
(☑0268-472 336; www.curteabrasoveana.ro; Str Băilor 16; s/d 210/260 lei; ✳@🕏) In a 100-year-old house, these rooms are modern and immaculate, some with exposed brick and wood ceilings. Buffet breakfast and sauna included.

Casa Kermany   PENSION €
(☑0368-436 068; Str Nicolae Bălcescu 26; s/d/apt 130/140/160 lei; 🕏) This central and good-value place has smallish rooms, decent beds and an inner courtyard that insulates from the street noise. The apartment is larger, with a mini-kitchen.

Rolling Stone Hostel   HOSTEL €
(☑0268-513 965; www.rollingstone.ro; Str Piatra Mare 2a; dm 35-50 lei, r from 118 lei; @🕏) Run by the high-energy Bolea family, the Stone is a homey, friendly place. They also have off-site private apartments. It's about 600m south of Schei Gate – walk through Piaţa Unirii, past Casa Românesca restaurant (on the right side), then continue for one short block and turn right on Str Piatra Mare.

Hotel Postăvarul   HOTEL €
(☑0268-477 448; Str Republicii 62; s/d 60/80 lei; 🕏) Despite its 1910 German design, the gloriously faded grandeur of this 46-room hotel completes, by accident, a stereotypical vision of a 'Transylvanian hotel' – inside floors creak under green-and-white arched doors. This dated, mysterious hotel is not for everyone, but rooms are vacuumed daily and have private toilets; shared showers are down the hall. Its adjoining Hotel Coroana is overpriced. No breakfast.

Hotel Aro Sport   HOTEL €
(☑0268-478 800; Str Sfântu Ioan 3; s/d without bathroom 56/78 lei) These boxy rooms evoke classic Eastern Europe travel – a sink in the corner and a shower down the hall. They're surprisingly clean and bright though, the staff are lovely, and the price is right. No breakfast.

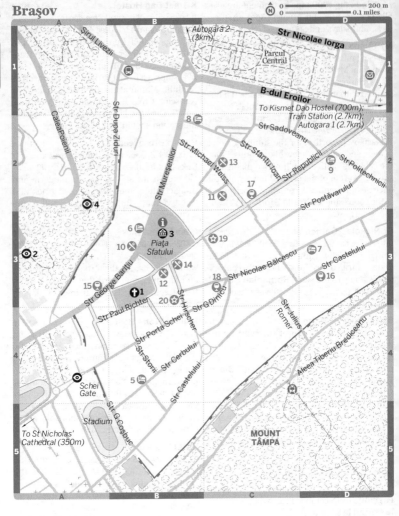

0   200 m
0   0.1 miles

Autogară 2
(3km)

Str Nicolae Iorga

Parcul
Central

B-dul Eroilor

To Kismet Dao Hostel (700m);
Train Station (2.7km);
Autogara 1 (2.7km)

Str Sadoveanu

Str Dupa Ziduri

Str Muresenilor

Str Michael Weiss

Str Stantu Ioan   Str Republicii

Str Politechniei

Str Postavarului

Piaţa
Sfatului

Str George Baritiu

Str Nicolae Bălcescu

Str Castelului

Str Paul Richter

Str Porta Schei

Str Cerbului

Str Castelului

Str Hirscher

Str G Dimcu

Str Julius
Romer

Aleea Tiberiu Brediceanu

Schei
Gate

Stadium

To St Nicholas'
Cathedral (350m)

**MOUNT
TÂMPA**

Calea Poienii

Sirul Livezii

Gabriel Hostel   HOSTEL €

(☏0744-844 223; Str Vasile Saftu 41a; dm 30-43 lei;
d with bathroom 120 lei; @⌨) This 30-bed place
was under renovation during our visit; it
should be completed by the time you arrive.
Beds and bathrooms are all new, though
there's no kitchen (this may change) and no
breakfast. It's about 1km south of Schei Gate.
If you don't find Gabriel at the train station,
take bus 51 to the last stop.

Beke Guesthouse   PENSION €

(☏0268-511 997; Str Cerbului 32; r without bathroom per person 40-50 lei) A lovely Hungarian-
speaking couple runs this handful of spartan
rooms that overlook a vine-covered courtyard. Often they'll bring by a jug of homemade wine. There's no breakfast, no sign,
and no English spoken.

✗ Eating

TOP
CHOICE **Prato**   ITALIAN €€€

(www.prato.ro; Str Michael Weiss 11;
mains 19-54 lei) An extensive Italian menu
includes a savoury fettuccini with salmon, cream sauce and red caviar. Budget-
conscious people will want to aim for the
weekday all-you-can-eat brunch (25 lei).

TOP CHOICE **Bella Muzica** ROMANIAN, MEXICAN **€€€**
(☎0268-477 956; Str Gheorghe Bariţu 2; mains 18-69 lei) Pretty much everyone's local favourite, this lovely cavernous basement restaurant of red brick and candlelight serves up a few Mexican dishes, but keeps the focus on very tasty Romanian fare. Staff bring a welcome shot of *ţuică,* excellent chips and salsa, and a 'music menu' for requests – the list includes 'best ballads' by Uriah Heap, Celine Dion, the Boss and Floyd.

Restaurant Transylvania ROMANIAN **€**
(Str Castelului 106; mains 6-38 lei) Probably the best value and comprehensively delicious Romanian fare in town. *Ciorbas* (soups) start at 3 lei and a litre of house wine is only 16 lei. The menu of the day (soup, main, salad), served noon to 5pm, is 15 lei.

Bistro de l'Arte BISTRO **€€**
(www.bistrodelarte.ro; Piaţa Enescu 11; mains 12-28 lei) On the ground floor of a cosy 15th-century building, the Bistro serves small meals – sandwiches, fish, spaghetti and breakfasts. There are excellent loose teas and wi-fi access.

Casa Româneasca ROMANIAN **€€**
(Piaţa Unirii; mains 12-26 lei) Deep in the Schei district, away from trolling tourists, this casa serves tasty *sarmalute cu mamaliguta* (boiled beef rolled with vegetables and cabbage; 15 lei).

Restaurant Gustari ROMANIAN **€€**
(Piaţa Sfatului 14; mains 12-28 lei) Despite the questionable tourist-trap location, Gustari keeps it simple – no flashiness, just savoury Romanian food at correct prices.

The terrace view is fantastic. It does great *sarmale* (16 lei).

Pasta Pizza Venezia PIZZA **€€**
(Str Hirscher 2; pastas & pizzas 10-24 lei) Wall-sized Venetian paintings and soft lighting help this cosy Italian restaurant fill before its similar-themed and named neighbours.

Spar SUPERMARKET **€**
(Str Nicolae Bălcescu; ⊘24hr) A fully stocked supermarket next to the indoor-outdoor fruit and vegetable market.

🍷 **Drinking**

Deane's Irish Pub & Grill PUB
(Str Republicii 19) Though they have a street-side terrace, the real atmosphere is in the basement, where the smoky pub checklist has been painstakingly filled, including live music, a proper pub menu and a darts room.

Za Pub PUB
(Str Grigoras Dinicu 6; 🛜) A good place for foosball, darts, Guinness (12 lei), cocktails (10 lei to 12 lei) and a variety of live music on Saturdays. Friday is karaoke night. Happy hour is 9am to 1pm.

Cramă WINE SHOP
(Str George Bariţa 20; ⊘9.30am-8pm Mon-Fri, 9am-2pm Sat) A well-hidden alley/basement joint, it sells wine from 5 lei per litre for red, and 4.50 lei for white.

Crama Vinoteca WINE SHOP
(Str Castelului 106; litre of wine 4.50-7.50 lei; ⊘10am-7pm Mon-Fri, to 3pm Saturday) Under Restaurant Transylvania, it has barrels and barrels of

Romanian wine, plus empty litre and half-litre bottles to fill and take to your own drinking spot. The very smooth *pălincă* is 25 lei per litre – enough to flatten the whole hostel.

☆ Entertainment

Gheorghe Dima State Philharmonic

LIVE MUSIC

(Str Hirscher 10) Performs mainly between September and May. Tickets can be purchased at the **Agenţia de Teatrală** (☎0268-471 889; Str Republicii 4; ◷10am-5pm Tue-Fri, to 2pm Sat).

ℹ Information

You'll find numerous ATMs, banks and currency exchange offices on and around Str Republicii and B-dul Eroilor.

Active Travel (☎0268-477 112, www.active travel.ro; Str Republicii 50; ◷10am-6pm Mon-Fri, 10am-1pm Sat) Leads hiking, mountain-biking and cultural tours, and rents out bikes (three/24 hours 25/50 lei).

Aventours (☎0268-472 718; www.discov eromania.ro; Str Paul Richter 1; ◷10am-3pm Mon-Fri) This small agency, led by English-speaking guides, offers great tailor-made tours (particularly mountain-based ones) and oodles of information on the area.

Central post office (Str Iorga Nicolae 1)

County Hospital (☎0268-333 666; Calea Bucureşti 25-27; ◷24hr) Northwest of the centre.

Extreme Adventure (☎0723-990 776; www. extremeadventure.ro) As advertised, hiking, mountain-biking, climbing, skiing and heliskiing adventures are on offer.

Iulian Cozma (☎0744-327 686; www.mountain guide.ro) Guides multiday hiking and skiing in southern Transylvania.

Raiffeisen Bank (Piaţa Sfatului) Gives cash advances on Visa and MasterCard.

Romona Cazacu (☎0723-191 755, www. myromania.com.ro) An English- and French-speaking guide, leading Saxon tours, multiday hikes and cultural walking tours in Bucovina and Maramureş.

Salvamont (☎0725-826 668, nationwide ☎0-SALVAMONT) Emergency rescue for the mountains.

Tibi (Str Gheorghe Bariţiu 8; per hr 2.40 lei) Internet access.

Tourist information centre (www.brasovcity. ro; Piaţa Sfatului 30) In the gold city council building, the English-speaking staff can point you to tour services, offer free brochures and track down hotel vacancies.

ℹ Getting There & Around

Bicycle

Doua Roti (☎0268-470 207; Str Nicolae Bălcescu 55; ◷8.30am-5pm Mon-Fri, 9am-1pm Sat) A bike shop selling used bikes from 200 lei.

Bus

Maxitaxis and microbuses are the best way to reach places near Braşov, including Bran, Râşnov and Sinaia. Otherwise it's generally better to go by train.

The most accessible station is **Autogara 1**, next to the train station, a ramshackle lot with a booming maxitaxi business (hourly jobs ply the Târgu Mureş–Sighişoara–Braşov–Buşteni–Bucharest route) and some long-distance buses. From 6am to 7.30pm maxitaxis leave every half-hour for Bucharest (32 lei, 2½ hours), stopping in Buşteni and Sinaia. About four or five maxitaxis leave daily for Sibiu (20 lei, 2½ hours), stopping in Făgăraş town and Iaşi (48 lei, six to seven hours). Bus 51 goes to/from the centre (pre-buy your ticket). In the centre, catch it in Piaţa Unirii or anywhere on Str Nicolae Bălcescu.

Autogara 2 (Calea Făgăraşului), 4km west of the train station, sends half-hourly buses to Râşnov (2.50 lei, 25 minutes) and Bran (4 lei, 40 minutes) from roughly 6.30am to 11.30pm. A dozen daily buses go to Zărneşti (4 lei, one hour), with fewer on weekends. Take bus 12 to/from the centre (it stops at the roundabout just north of the station).

Car & Motorcycle

Autonom (☎0268-415 250; www.autonom. com) usually has the best car hire prices (Daewoo Matiz from 120 lei per day, with significant discounts for long-term rentals) and will deliver a car to you anywhere inside Braşov free of charge.

Transilvania Travel (☎0268-477 623; www. transilvaniatravel.com; Str Republicii 62; ◷10am-6pm Mon-Fri, to 2pm Sat) also hires cars (Dacia Logan starting at 128 lei per day).

Taxi

Taxi drivers seem pretty honest in Braşov. A couple of good agencies are **Martax** (☎0268-313 040) and **Tod** (☎0268-321 111). Taking a taxi to the 'Three Castles' in Bran, Râşnov and Sinaia costs about 253 lei, including waiting time.

Train

Advance tickets are sold at the **Agenţia de Voiaj CFR** (Str 15 de Noiembre 43; ◷8am-7.30pm Mon-Fri).

Daily domestic train services include the following (prices are for 2nd-class seats on rapid trains): at least hourly to Bucharest (42 lei, 3½ hours), a dozen to Sighişoara (36 lei, 2½ hours), two to Sibiu (50 lei, four hours) and 10 to Cluj-Napoca (65 lei, six hours). For Iaşi, transfer in Ploiesti or Bucharest (96 lei, nine hours).

International links include three daily trains to Budapest (seat/sleeper 150/200 lei, 14 hours), one to Vienna (seat/sleeper 210/281 lei, 18 hours) and one daily train each to Prague (sleeper 461 lei, 21 hours) and İstanbul (seat/sleeper 206/234 lei, 19 hours).

Left luggage is 7 lei per day. From the station, take bus 51 to the centre.

Around Braşov

Sights

Bran Castle CASTLE
(www.brancastlemuseum.ro; adult/student 12/6 lei; ⏲9am-7pm Tue-Sun, noon-7pm Mon May-Sep, 9am-5pm Tue-Sun Oct-Apr) Though Vlad Ţepeş only dropped by once in the 15th century (maybe), it's hard to skip this so-called 'Dracula's castle', 30km south of Braşov. The atmospheric Bran Castle dates from 1378. At first look, the 60m-high castle, set on a rocky outcrop between facing hills, certainly seems like a Hilton for the undead, but the inside – full of tour groups – is somewhat anticlimactic. Queen Marie summered here frequently in the 1920s, as highlighted by exhibits inside.

Bran's **Sâmbra Oilor** festival is held here in September.

Râşnov fortress FORTRESS
(Cetatea Râsnov; admission 10 lei; ⏲9am-8pm May-Oct, to 6pm Nov-Apr) Râşnov, 12km toward Braşov, doubles the castle action with the tempting ruins of the 13th-century Râşnov fortress. From the central square, steps lead up the hill where inclined alleys and a museum await.

Sleeping

Pensiunea Stefi PENSION €
(☎0721-303 009; www.hotelstefi-ro.com; Piaţa Unirii 5; r 90 lei; @📶) This five-room guesthouse, behind the giant red gate in the main square, has carpeted rooms, sauna, fitness centre and a wading pool. Breakfast is 14 lei.

Vila Bran HOTEL €
(☎0268-236 866; www.vilabran.ro; Str Principală 238; r 120-140 lei; 📶) This 103-room, 12-building complex is unflinchingly touristy – three restaurants, tennis court, fitness centre, billiards, flying fox, indoor basketball court – but the view of the hills is worth it. No breakfast.

Getting There & Away

Buses marked 'Bran-Moeciu' (4 lei, 40 minutes) depart every 40 minutes from Braşov's Autogara 2. Return buses to Braşov leave Bran from roughly 7am to 6pm in winter, to 10pm in summer. All buses to and from Braşov stop at Râşnov.

From Bran there are five or six buses daily to Zărneşti (3.5 lei, one hour).

Sighişoara

POP 32,300

Most famously known as the spot where Vlad 'Ţepeş' Dracula scampered about when impaled Turks were just a twinkle in his eye, this dreamy, medieval citadel town is a destination in its own right. Sighişoara (Schässburg in German, Segesvár in Hungarian) has brightly coloured, half-a-millennium-old town houses bordering hilly cobbled streets, and church bells that clang atmospherically in the early hours. Cute museums uncover the colourful local history. Over the low hills flanking the town are pastures and forests leading to traditional Saxon villages. Bus tours overwhelm the citadel in summer, often prompting backpackers to flee after one day, but a night here is highly recommended.

Sighişoara's **Medieval Festival of the Arts** takes place in July. Good day trips from Sighişoara include Saxon Land towns or a day (or two) in the half-Hungarian town of Târgu Mureş.

Sights

Blink and you'll miss the tiny sign announcing that you can visit the History Museum, the medieval arms collection and the Torture Room Museum for a combo ticket price of 17 lei. The quiet, minuscule **Piaţa Cetăţii** is the heart of old Sighişoara. It was here that markets and public executions were held. Hidden away behind the 15th-century **Church of the Dominican Monastery** (Biserica Mănăstirii), across from the museum, is a **Vlad Ţepeş statue**, showing the legend with his trademark 1980s porno moustache.

Citadel Complex MUSEUMS
Sighişoara's primary sights are clustered in the compact, delightfully medieval **citadel** – perched on a hillock and fortified with a 14th-century wall, to which 14 towers and five artillery bastions were later added. Today the citadel, which is on the Unesco World Heritage list, retains just nine of its original towers (named for the guilds in charge of keeping them up) and two of its bastions.

Entering the citadel, you pass under the massive **clock tower** (Turnul cu Ceas), which dates from 1280. Inside the great little **History Museum** (Piaţa Muzeului 1; adult/child

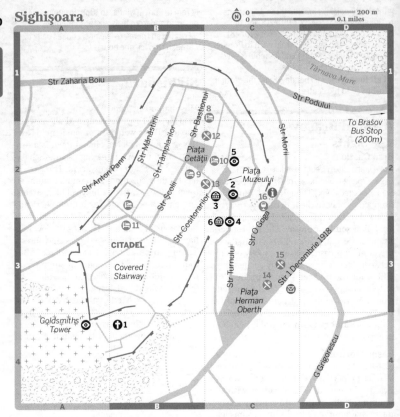

10/2.50 lei; ⊙9am-5.30pm Tue-Fri, 10am-5.30pm Sat & Sun), Sighi's tale is told in small rooms off the steps winding up to the 7th-floor lookout, which has superb panoramic views.

Under the clock tower on the right (if heading out of the Old Town) is the small, dark **Torture Room Museum** (adult/student 4/1 lei; ⊙9am-5.30pm Tue-Fri, 10am-5.30pm Sat & Sun), which shows how fingers were smashed and prisoners burned with coals. If it's closed, ask at the medieval arms collection for entry.

Towards Piața Cetății on the left, the small **Collection of Medieval Arms** (adult/student 6/1.50 lei; ⊙9am-5.30pm Tue-Fri, 10am-5.30pm Sat & Sun) has four rooms devoted to medieval helmets, shields, crossbows and maces.

Church on the Hill CHURCH
(Biserica din Deal; Bergkirche; ⊙mid-Apr–Oct) From the square, turn left up Str Școlii to the 172 steps of the **covered stairway** *(scara acoperit)* to this 429m-high Gothic Lutheran church, dating from 1345, with an atmospheric German cemetery just behind.

🛏 Sleeping

Bed & Breakfast Kula PENSION € `[TOP CHOICE]`
(☎0265-777 907; Str Tâmplarilor 40; r per person 65 lei; @) This 400-year-old home in the citadel has large rooms with classic ceramic wood-fire heaters. It's run by a heartwarmingly kind English-speaking family, who can rent you a bike (30 lei). There are six rooms, plus an apartment in a nearby 500-year-old house. Dinner, including wine and țuică, is available with advance notice (30 lei per person).

Nathan's Villa HOSTEL €
(☎0265-772 546; www.nathansvilla.com; Str Libertății 8; dm 43-50 lei; @🛜) This popular choice, with laundry (10 lei) and a bar, is efficiently run and often has the best nightlife

Sighişoara

in town. It's about 500m west of the train station. Open from March to December.

Casa Cu Cerb   HOTEL €€

(Stag House; ☎0265-774 625; Str Şcolii 1; s/d 194/259 lei; 🛜) The first thing you see walking into this all-restored 1693 building is Prince Charles' mug – he stayed here for a few days in 2002. It's a good choice, with cast-iron bed frames and rattan rugs by the TV sitting area. Prices drop in low season.

Casa Saseasca   HOTEL €

(☎0265-772 400; www.casasaseasca.com; Piaţa Cetăţii 12; s/d 115/125 lei; 🛜) A great value place for the location, its spartan rooms have painted wood furniture, TVs and decent

beds. There's no breakfast, but they have a cafe with an inner courtyard.

Gia Hostel   HOSTEL €

(☎0722-490 003; www.hotelgia.ro; Str Libertăţii 41; dm/r from 35/95 lei; @🛜) Backing the railway line, about 300m west of the station, these rooms recently enjoyed a complete and thoughtful redecoration. There's lots of good services, including an hour's free internet and kitchen/grill access.

Burg Hostel   HOSTEL €

(☎0265-778 489; www.burghostel.ro; Str Bastionului 4-6; dm 40 lei, s/d without bathroom 70/90 lei, with bathroom 80/95 lei; 🛜) This slightly sterile hostel has functional rooms with various bed counts. Breakfast is 12 lei. There's an internet cafe in the basement.

Pensiune Cristina & Pavel   PENSION €

(☎0744-119 211; cristinafaur2003@yahoo.de; Str Cojocarilor 1; dm/s/d 40/80/100 lei; Ⓟ) Another inviting budget option in this quiet corner of the citadel is this home with four simple rooms and one dorm. They do laundry, arrange trips to Făgăraş Biertan and other Saxon villages, and rent out bikes (40 lei). Breakfast is 10 lei and there's a self-catering kitchen available.

Aquaris Camping   CAMPING GROUND €

(☎0265-772 110; www.aquariscamp.net; Nicolae Titulescu 2-4; per tent site/car 15/5 lei, hut without bathroom 50 lei, apartment 140 lei; 🛜) About a 10-minute walk from both the train station and the citadel, the bare huts are larger than average with good beds. Shared bathrooms are of camping-ground standard, while apartments are typical three-star affairs. There's a pool on site. No breakfast. From the station, head west (right) and turn left on Str Gării, then left on Str Saguna. It's signed on the left.

🍴 Eating

Rustic   ROMANIAN €

(Str 1 Decembrie 1918; mains 6-20 lei; ⏱8am-midnight Mon-Sat, noon-midnight Sun) Rustic

---

WORTH A TRIP

POIANA BRAŞOV

Braşov's skiers prefer this **mountain** (www.poiana-brasov.ro), 14km from Braşov and reached by an easy bus trip, over Sinaia's. Ski rental starts at 26 lei per day, an all-day pass is about 250 lei and a five-trip pass is 120 lei. There are good intermediate runs, and a couple of advanced slopes, plus hiking trails in summer. The ski season runs from December to March.

Bus 20 leaves from B-dul Eroilor in front of the County Library in Braşov every half-hour for Poiana Braşov (4 lei), from where it's a 20-minute walk to the slopes.

ZĂRNEŞTI

This windswept town at the edge of the lovely, rugged Piatra Craiului National Park can seem *Twilight Zone*–calibre eerie, but locals are particularly nice, and Zărneşti provides an excellent springboard to nearby hikes.

The 14,800-hectare **Piatra Craiului** and its twin-peaked **Piatra Mică** (Stone of the Prince; no jokes) rise northwest of town. The national park office has outstanding maps detailing hiking loops. The yellow vertical-stripe signs leading from the road either west or south of town mark a four- or five-hour trip that goes through the gorge where Jude Law got shot in *Cold Mountain*. A 30km multiday hike goes along the ridge for about 25km (there are shelters, but no food), finishing at Podul Dambovitei.

The **Piatra Craiului National Park Office** (☎0268-223 165; www.pcrai.ro; Str Topliţei 150; ⊙8am-4pm Mon-Thu, to 2.30pm Fri) is in a bizarrely located but gorgeously set structure about 2km towards the mountains (west) from the centre of town; follow the 'Plaiu Foii' sign at the bus stop roundabout, then go left at the fork. It has excellent maps and guides available (from 82 lei per day).

Pensuine Fabius (☎0742-010 498; Str Dr Senchea 7; r 65 lei) is run by a lovely family (that includes *two* priests). The five-room Fab offers semirustic rooms with TV and private bath. From the bus stop, go a block on Str Baiulescu, then right on Str Dr Senchea.

About a dozen buses leaving weekdays for Autogara 2 in Braşov (4 lei, one hour), and about half that at weekends. About five or six daily buses head to Bran (4 lei, 40 minutes).

---

indeed. A wood-and-brick 'man's man' bar-restaurant is down from the citadel, and its *ciorba ţaraneasca de porc* (countryside pork soup) will erase the hangover acquired at Nathan's Villa. Eggs are served all day.

La Perla Pizzeria
PIZZA €€

(Piaţa Hermann Oberth 15; pizzas 10-19 lei; 🛜) The wood-fired pizza here is arguably the best in town. Sit on the terrace and enjoy 500ml sangria for 7.50 lei or retreat to the three-level dinning/lounge area. They do breakfast, too.

Café International & Family Centre
CAFE €

(Piaţa Cetăţii 8; mains 7-11 lei; ⊙8.30am-7.30pm Mon-Sat Jun-Sep, 9am-6pm Mon-Sat Oct-May; 🛜) This two-room cafe, with chairs in the square, is an ideal lunch spot with daily-made mostly vegetarian fare, including quiches, salads (in summer) and lasagne, plus desserts.

Casa Dracula
ROMANIAN €€€

(Str Cositorarilor 5; mains 23-66 lei) This three-room, candlelit restaurant, in which Vlad Ţepeş reputedly lived until the age of four, is too tempting to pass by. There's plenty of juicy meats on the menu, but it's OK to come for a red wine only (4 lei).

❶ Information

There are numerous exchange offices lining Str 1 Decembrie 1918. Banca Transilvania has a 24-

hour ATM in the citadel, between Piaţa Cetăţii and Muzeulul. There are internet points in Burg Hostel.

Café International & Family Centre (☎0265-777 844; Piaţa Cetăţii 8; internet per hr 5 lei; ⊙8am-8pm Mon-Sat Jun-Sep, 1-7pm Mon-Sat Oct-May; 🛜) Internet access. Volunteer staff of this nonprofit agency double as a tourist office (in summer only); they arrange walking tours and can point you to area hikes.

Cultural Heritage Centre (☎0788-115 511; www.dordeduca.ro; Str Muzeului 6; ⊙10am-6pm Tue-Sun) Rents out bikes (4.30 lei per hour) and offers guided tours of Sighişoara and the fortified churches. They have maps of the city and region.

Eye Tours (☎0721-176 299; www.eye-tours. com) Offers day trips to nearby villages and hiking tours.

Post office (Str 1 Decembrie 1918; ⊙7.30am-7.30pm Mon-Fri) In a funny yellow-panel building.

Tourist information (☎0265-770 415; Str O Goga; ⊙10am-4pm Mon-Fri, 9am-1pm Sat) Can book beds.

❶ Getting There & Away

The **train station** is about 1km northeast of the citadel. A dozen trains daily connect Sighişoara with Braşov (28 lei, two hours), 10 of which continue on to Bucharest (43 lei, 4½ hours). Five daily trains go to Cluj-Napoca (39 lei, 3½ hours). You'll need to change trains in Mediaş to reach Sibiu (10 lei, 2½ hours). Three daily trains go to Budapest (138 lei, nine hours); the night one has a sleeper (from 226 lei). **Left luggage** is 4.60 lei per day.

Next to the train station on Str Libertăţii, the **bus station** sends buses to Făgăraş (14 lei, three hours, one daily) and Sibiu (14 lei, 2½ hours, four daily). Buses to Braşov (32 lei, 2½ hours) pause at the bus stop by the Romstal store on the corner of Str Podului and Str Iorga. Reservations are required (☏0265-250 702).

Saxon Land

Sighişoara, Sibiu and Braşov – the 'Saxon Triangle' if you will – enclose an area loaded with undulating hills and cinematic villages. These yesteryear villages, some sitting at the ends of rather nasty dirt roads, frequently have outstanding fortified churches dating from the 12th century. Even just a kilometre or two off the Braşov–Sibiu highway you'll find a world where horse carriages and walking are generally the only ways anyone gets around, and where a car – any car – gets stares.

Popular destinations include **Biertan** (28km southwest of Sighişoara) and **Viscri** (about 40km east). The former has the added attraction of the Cramă Biertan (wine cellar) on Richiş Rd just outside of town selling bottles starting at 5 lei, while the latter misses most tour buses. Call **Carolina Fernolend** (☏0740-145 397) to arrange private accommodation in Viscri (about 115 lei per person including breakfast and dinner) and a look at the church.

Bus services are infrequent. Rent a car in either Sibiu or Sighişoara. You can also arrange a taxi for the day.

Sibiu

POP 154.500

Crumbling, car-rattling old Sibiu, despite being the capital and most culturally active of the Transylvanian Saxon towns, was once frequently overshadowed by Braşov, Sighişoara and Cluj-Napoca. Then the EU designated it as a 'Capital of Culture' for 2007. Now freshly scrubbed, painted and cobblestoned, the pedestrian areas are frame-worthy from any angle and every third building has been declared a historic monument. Unique 'eyelid' rooftop windows wink from pastel buildings as you sip drinks in Romania's most serene, car-free squares. Some locals liked the old Sibiu better – falling roof tiles, ankle-twisting cobblestones

and all – but there's no arguing that new Sibiu is beaut.

Founded in the 12th century on the site of the former Roman village of Cibinium, Sibiu (Hermannstadt to the German Saxons, Nagyszében to Hungarians) served as the seat of the Austrian governors of Transylvania under the Habsburgs from 1703 to 1791, and again from 1849 to 1867.

◉ Sights
TOWN CENTRE

North of the centre is interesting Lower Town, reached from under the photogenic **Liar's Bridge** (1859) facing Piaţa Mică. It's worth walking along the 16th-century **city walls** and watchtowers, accessible a few blocks southeast of Piaţa Mare, along Str Cetăţii.

A combo ticket for the History, Brukenthal and Pharmacy museums and others is 30/7.5 lei per adult/student.

History Museum   HISTORY MUSEUM
(Str Mitropoliei 2; adult/child 17/5 lei) Just west of here is the lovely Primăria Municipiului (1470), now the newly reopened History Museum. Serious coin went into the swanky new displays, some behind glass in moody corridors. They start at the Palaeolithic age and sweep through all the epochs, displaying tools, ceramics, bronze, jewellery, life-sized home scenes, costumes and furniture. Other sections hold exhibits of guild work (including glassmaking, brasswork and carpentry), an armoury, Roman artefacts and a treasury.

Brukenthal Museum   ART GALLERY
(www.brukenthalmuseum.ro; Piaţa Mare 5; adult/student 12/3 lei) The Brukenthal Museum is the oldest and probably finest art gallery in Romania. Founded in 1817, the museum is in the baroque palace (1785) of the former Austrian governor, Baron Samuel Brukenthal (1721–1803). There are excellent collections of 16th- and 17th-century Flemish, Italian, Dutch, French, Austrian and Romanian paintings, including a giant painting of Sibiu from 1808.

Biserica Evanghelică   CHURCH
(Evangelical Church; Piaţa Huet) Nearby, on Piaţa Huet, is the Gothic Biserica Evanghelică, built from 1300 to 1520. For renovations lasting until 2015, there's scaffolding covering the four magnificent baroque funerary monuments and the 1772 organ with 6002 pipes (the largest in southeast Europe). In

ROMANIA TRANSYLVANIA

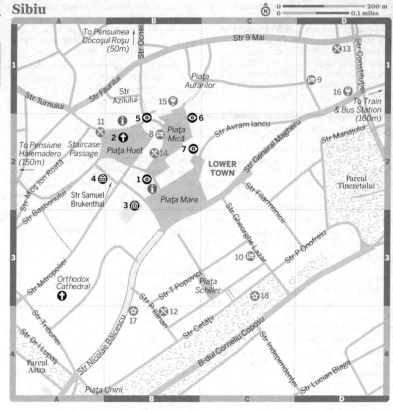

summer, organ concerts (5 lei) are held every Wednesday (6pm) and Sunday (10pm). The tomb of Mihnea Vodă cel Rău (Prince Mihnea the Bad), son of Vlad Țepeș, is in a closed-off section behind the organ (ask for entry). This prince was murdered in front of the church in 1510. You can climb the **church tower** (adult/child 3/2 lei); ask for entry at Casa Luxemburg.

Turnul Sfatului TOWER

(Council Tower; admission 2 lei) The expansive Piața Mare was the very centre of the old walled city. A good start for exploring the city is to climb to the top of the 1588 Turnul Sfatului, which links Piața Mare with its smaller sister square, Piața Mică.

Banca Agricola LANDMARK

(Piața Mare 2) The square's most impressive building is the Banca Agricola, which now houses the town hall and tourist information centre.

Pharmaceutical Museum MUSEUM

(adult/child 6/1.50 lei) On Piața Mică, this three-room collection is packed with pills, powders and scary medical instruments.

OUTSIDE TOWN CENTRE

TOP
CHOICE **Museum of Traditional Folk Civilization** MUSEUM

(Muzeul Civilizației Populare Tradiționale Astra; Calea Rășinarilor 14; adult/child 15/3.50 lei) Sibiu's highlight is 5km south of the centre. The sprawling Museum of Traditional Folk Civilization is an open-air museum with a growing collection of over 120 traditional dwellings, mills and churches brought from around the country and set among two small lakes and a small zoological garden. There's a restaurant with creekside bench seating. Trolleybus 1 from the train station goes here (get off at the last stop and keep walking for less than 1km, or take the hourly Rășinari tram). A taxi is about 12 lei one way. The museum may stay open until 8pm, weather permitting.

🛏 Sleeping

If you get caught without a bed, pick up a free copy of *Şapte Seri* for a full list of pensions and hotels.

TOP CHOICE **Felinarul Hostel** HOSTEL €
(☎0269-235 260; www.felinarulhostelsibiu.ro; Str Felinarul 8; dm/d without bathroom 50/100 lei; @🛜) Setting the bar for boutique hostels everywhere, this friendly 14-bed sanctuary is roughly midway between the train station and the centre. The Romanian-Irish husband and wife team have put a lot of thought into the design, including tasteful German, Hungarian and Romanian influences. They do organic breakfasts (included) and there's an excellent cafe. Laundry is 10 lei.

Flying Time Hostel HOSTEL €
(☎0369-730 179; www.sibiuhostel.ro; Str Gheorghe Lazar 6; dm 42-55 lei, d from 130 lei; @🛜) In an 18th-century building designed to stay naturally cool, this place has 'classic' furniture and decor courtesy of an interior designer's brain splatter. There's great beds, a flowery inner courtyard cafe and a downstairs pub with live music. Laundry is 10 lei.

Happy Day Pension PENSION €
(☎0269-234 985; www.pensiuneahappyday.ro, in Romanian; Str Lungă 2; s/d 100/125 lei; 🛜) It's a brisk 10-minute walk from the centre, but with perks like a full English breakfast (included), this place shapes up as an excellent budget value. The diminutive bathrooms are actually quite nice and little touches like oriental pillows and welcome chocolates atop great beds add to the appeal.

Casa Luxemburg HOTEL €€
(☎0269-216 854; www.kultours.ro; Piaţa Mică 16; s/d/tr from 240/270/330 lei; 🛜) It's a little dormy, but this seven-room job overlooks the Evangelical Church and Piaţa Mică. Complimentary fruit, water and chocolate awaits in each room. They have additional off-site rooms (single/double 190/220 lei) without breakfast.

Pensiunea Cocoşul Roşu PENSION €
(☎0369-427 482; www.cocosulrosu.ro; Str Ocnei 19; s/d 80/100 lei; 🛜) Behind a thick door and down a long atmospheric alley are eight immaculate rooms surrounding a nice patio. Breakfast is 15 lei.

Pensiune Halemadero PENSION €
(☎0269-212 509, Str Măsarilor 10; d/tr without bathroom 80/120 lei) Family-run four-room deal in Lower Town. Rooms are old-school, with TV and three or four beds. The family runs a beery patio cafe. No breakfast.

🍴 Eating

TOP CHOICE **Felinarul Café** INTERNATIONAL €€
(Str Felinarul 8; mains 7-25 lei; ⊙cafe noon-midnight Tue-Sat, kitchen noon-3pm & 5pm-11pm Tue-Sat) The rotating menu includes chicken in green curry, extravagant salads, shark (yes, shark), buffalo wings and what is almost certainly the best cheeseburger in Eastern Europe. They serve excellent coffee, tea and Romanian wines by the glass or bottle.

Butoiul de Aur ROMANIAN €€€
(Str Turnului 3; mains 10-63 lei) Built into the fortifications, and said to be Romania's oldest

restaurant, it has a typical Romanian menu served with care and flair. Despite the fancy atmosphere, most prices are only moderate. There's a short vegetarian menu.

Grand Plaza　　　　　　　　ROMANIAN €
(Str 9 Mai 60; mains 9-20 lei) Just around the corner from Felinarul Hostel, this is no-nonsense Romanian cuisine at great prices – meats are 9 lei to 13 lei, soups 6 lei and salads 3 lei. The *ciolan de porc cu iahnie de fasole* (smoked knuckle of pork with beans, 15 lei) is quite the spectacle. They do omelettes (4 lei to 8 lei) and a three-course menu of the day (15 lei).

Crama Sibiul Vechi　　　　　ROMANIAN €€
(Str P Ilarian; mains 18-32 lei) This popular, evocative, smoky brick-cellar spot off the main crawl reels in locals for its tasty Transylvanian armoury of *ciorba* (soup), mutton, sausages, beef and fish. There's live music most nights.

Pizzeria La Reggina　　　　　　PIZZA €€
(Piaţa Mica 8; pizzas 7-25 lei) Among the chain of cafes serving pizza in Piaţa Mica, this place wins for both sheer variety and quality. Not to be confused with Go In next door.

🍷 Drinking

Piaţa Mică is Sibiu's drinking headquarters.

Music Club　　　　　　　　　　BAR
(Piaţa Mica 23) Descend two flights of stairs and just as you think you're entering the second dungeon, you emerge on to an outdoor terrace. Order cocktails (12 lei to 15 lei) using buttons on the tables. There's live music every Thursday, and other random nights.

Kulturkafe　　　　　　　　　　CAFE
(Piaţa Mică 16) Good table spots on the square, slightly more grown-up inside.

Art Café　　　　　　　　　　　CAFE
(www.galeria-artvo.ro; General Magheru 45) A basement joint with coffee, beer and mixed drinks; it sometimes stages jazz and dance events. It has a very open vibe.

☆ Entertainment

Sibiu's **International Astra Film Festival** is held in May.

Agenţia de Teatrală　　　　TICKET OFFICE
(☎0369-101 578; Str Nicolae Bălcescu 17; ⊙11am-6pm Mon-Fr, to 3pm Sat) Tickets for major events are sold here.

Philharmonic　　　　　　PHILHARMONIC
(☎0269-210 264; www.filarmonicasibiu.ro; Str Cetăţii 3-5) A big cultural player that's hosted classical orchestral concerts since 1949.

ℹ Information

ATMs are located all over the centre.

Banca Comercială Română (Str Nicolae Bălcescu 11) Gives cash advances.

Casa Luxemburg (☎0269-216 854; www.kultours.ro; Piaţa Mică 16) Travel agent offering loads of city tours (25 lei to 58 lei, minimum four people) and day trips (about 200 lei), bike rental (35 lei per day), audioguides (25 lei to 58 lei) and a useful free Sibiu map.

Central post office (Str Mitropoliei 14; ⊙7am-8pm Mon-Fri, 8am-1pm Sat)

Tourist information centre (☎0269-208 913; www.sibiu.ro; Piaţa Mare 2; ⊙9am-5pm Mon-Fri, to 1pm Sat & Sun) On the ground floor of the new city hall. Staff can help with bus schedules and book accommodation.

ℹ Getting There & Around

Air

Sibiu airport (☎0269-229 161; Sos Alba Iulia 73) is 5km west of the centre. Trolleybus 8 runs between the airport and the train station.

Blue Air (www.blueair-web.com) Budget airline that flies to Madrid, London and Stuttgart.

Carpatair (☎0269-229 161; www.carpatair.com) Has an office at the airport. Flies to Germany and Italy via Timişoara.

Tarom (☎0269-211 157; Str Nicolae Bălcescu 10; ⊙9am-12.30pm & 1.30-7pm Mon-Fri, 9am-1pm Sat) Has daily flights to Bucharest (from 222 lei one way), Munich (945 lei) and Vienna (1811 lei).

Bus

The **bus station** (Piaţa 1 Decembrie 1918) is opposite the train station. Bus and maxitaxi services include Braşov (20 lei, 2½ hours, two daily), Bucharest (48 lei, 5½ hours, three to four daily), Cluj-Napoca (28 lei, 3½ hours, three daily) and Timişoara (45 lei, six hours, two daily).

Car & Motorcycle

Autonom (☎0269-235 538; www.autonom.com; Str Nicolae Bălcescu 1; ⊙9am-6pm Mon-Fri) typically has the best rates, from 120 lei per day for a Daewoo Matiz. They also have an office at Sibiu airport.

Taxi

To call a taxi dial ☎0269-953.

Train

Sibiu lies at an awkward rail junction; sometimes you'll need to change trains. But there are three to Bucharest (49 lei, six to eight hours) and three to Timişoara (47 lei, 6½ hours). At the time of writing, service to Braşov was limited to one daytime run (50 lei, four hours) due to bridge repairs. Buy tickets at the station or at **Agenţia de Voiaj**

CFR office (Str Nicolae Bălcescu 6; ⊙7am-8pm Mon-Fri). **Left Luggage** is 4 lei per day.

Trolleybus 1 connects the train station with the centre, but it's only a 450m walk along Str General Magheru.

Făgăraş Mountains

The Făgăraş Mountains cut a serrated line south of the main Braşov–Sibiu road, sheltering dozens of glacial lakes. The famed **Transfăgărăşan Road** (generally open only from June to September due to snow), declared by the guys at *Top Gear* to be the 'best road in the world', cuts north–south through the range. No buses ply the route.

Despite its name, Făgăraş town (pop 43,900) is not the prime access point to the Făgăraş Massif. Most hikers head south to the mountains from the town of Victoria.

Cluj-Napoca

POP 306,000

'Club-Napoca' isn't as picturesque as its Saxon neighbours, but it's famed for its dozens of cavernous, unsnooty discos filled with agreeable students. Even outside the clubs, Cluj is one of Romania's most energised and welcoming cities – our dentist invited us to live music later that evening. Its attractions aren't staggering, and the screaming traffic ruins that which is attractive, but it's a 'real' city where everything's going on (football, opera, espresso, heated politics, trams), with a few surprise nuggets. It's also a great base for renting a car (far more cheaply than Braşov) and serves as a perfect staging area for excursions into Maramureş.

Cluj-Napoca holds the **International Folk Music & Dance Festival of Ethnic Minorities in Europe** in August.

History

In AD 124, Roman Emperor Marcus Aurelius elevated the Dacian town of Napoca to a colony. From 1791 to 1848, and again after the union with Hungary in 1867, Cluj-Napoca served as the capital of Transylvania.

In the mid-1970s the old Roman name of Napoca was added to the city's official title to emphasise its Daco-Roman origin. In the 1990s, then-mayor Gheorghe Funar furthered this nationalism (painting rubbish bins in Romanian colours), embarrassing many locals.

☉ Sights

TOWN CENTRE

St Michael's Church   CHURCH

The vast 14th-century St Michael's Church dominates Piaţa Unirii. The neo-Gothic tower (1859) topping the Gothic hall church creates a great landmark. Outside is a huge equestrian **statue** (1902) of the famous Hungarian king Matthias Corvinus (r 1458-90), who was born here. At night compare the half-hearted lighting on this with the elaborate lighting of the namesake Romanian hero on **Piaţa Avram Iancu** three blocks east.

Pharmaceutical Museum   MUSEUM

(Str Regele Ferdinand 1; adult/child 5.20/3.10 lei; ⊙10am-4pm Mon, Tue, Wed & Fri, noon-6pm Thu) The small three-room Pharmaceutical Museum is in Cluj's first apothecary (1573). Old glass cases housing grounded mummy dust, 18th-century aphrodisiacs and medieval alchemy symbols are brought to life by the

---

HIKING FROM VICTORIA

The Făgăraş Massif is regarded as the most dazzling section of the Carpathian Mountains, and holds arguably some of the best hiking in Europe. The rocky wilderness, featuring well-trodden paths and excellent cabins, is enriched by wildlife and more than 40 glacial lakes. Plan your trip for August and September to rule out heavy snow encounters – though a dusting is always possible.

Take a bus or train to Ucea (on the Braşov–Sibiu road), from where you can catch a bus (or walk the 7km) to **Victoria**. From here you can hike to **Cabana Turnuri** (1520m; 20 beds) in about six hours. The scenery is stunning once you start the ascent. The next morning head for **Cabana Podragu** (2136m; 68 beds), three to four hours south.

Cabana Podragu makes a good base if you want to climb **Mt Moldoveanu** (2544m), Romania's highest peak. It's a tough uphill climb, but the views from the summit are unbeatable. Otherwise, hike eight hours east, passing by Mt Moldoveanu, to Cabana Valea Sambetei (1407m). From Cabana Valea Sambetei you can descend to the railway in Ucea, via Victoria, in a day.

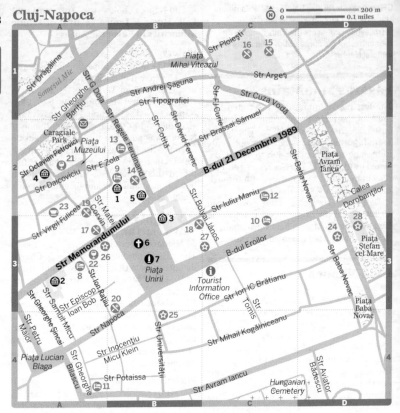

hilarious guide, who ushers you around as if showing off game-show prizes.

Emil Racoviţa Institute of Speleology
MUSEUM

(Str Sextil Puşcariu 10) The institute is finally settled in its new location, but still suffers sporadic closing periods. The much travelled scientist Racoviţa opened the world's first cave institute in Cluj in 1920.

National Art Museum
ART GALLERY

(Piaţa Unirii 30; admission 4 lei; ⊙10am-5pm Wed-Sun) Facing Piaţa Unirii is the interesting National Art Museum, housed inside the baroque Banffy Palace (1791).

National History Museum of Transylvania
MUSEUM

(Str Constantin Daicoviciu 1; adult/child 6/3 lei) Just off lovely Piaţa Muzeului is the National History Museum of Transylvania, filled with ghoulish remains of ancient tombs and many Roman pieces. It was undergoing major renovation during our last visit.

Ethnographic Museum of Transylvania
MUSEUM

(Muzeul Etnografic al Transilvaniei; www.muzeul-etnografic.ro; Str Memorandumului 21; adult/student 6/3 lei) Freshly renovated, the Ethnographic Museum of Transylvania has two floors of well-presented displays featuring tools, weapons, hand crafts, toys and household items with detailed descriptions in English. It also runs an **open-air ethnographic museum** (adult/student 6/3 lei; ⊙closed Apr), with 14 traditional buildings; take bus 27 to Hoia forest from the train station or bus 30 from the centre.

OUTSIDE TOWN CENTRE

Museum of Zoology
MUSEUM

(Str Clinicilor 5-7; adult/student 2/1 lei; ⊙9am-3pm Mon-Fri, 10am-2pm Sat & Sun) In the 'student ghetto' west of the centre, inside the Biology and Geology Faculty you'll find the surpris-

Cluj-Napoca

ROMANIA CLUJ-NAPOCA

ingly rewarding Museum of Zoology, an L-shaped lab that looks like it hasn't changed in five decades. From Str Clinicilor, veer left through the brick gate.

Alexandru Borza Botanic Gardens　GARDEN
(Str Republicii 42; adult/student 4/2 lei) Just south of the museum, head past fast-food joints up Str Bogdan P Haşdeu to Str Pasteur to reach the fragrant 1930 Alexandru Borza Botanic Gardens, with shaded green lawns and a super Japanese garden.

Hungarian cemetery　CEMETERY
Just east of the gardens, most easily reached from Str Avram Iancu down the hill, is an immense, memorable Hungarian cemetery (*Házsongárdi temető*).

Citadel　FORTRESS
For an overall view of Cluj-Napoca, climb up the 1715 citadel (*cetatea*), northwest of the centre.

🏃 Activities & Courses

Access　LANGUAGE
(☎0264-420 476; www.access.ro; Str Ţebei 21, 3rd fl; ⊙10am-6pm Mon & Thu, 2-8pm Tue-Wed, 2-6pm Fri) Offers Romanian-language courses.

Clubul de Cicloturism Napoca　CYCLING
(office@ccn.ro; Cluj-Napoca) Can offer bike-rental advice.

Green Mountain Holidays　HIKING
(www.greenmountainholidays.ro) Offers guided hikes in the Apuseni Mountains.

🛏 Sleeping

TOP CHOICE **Retro Hostel**　HOSTEL €
(☎0264-450 452; www.retro.ro; Str Potaissa 13; dm/s/d/tr from 44/85/125/180 lei; @☎) On a quiet lane amid 16th-century citadel wall fragments, the Retro is one of Romania's best hostels. Dorms are a little tight and there are only a couple of bathrooms, but the chatty and tirelessly helpful staff offer good-value day trips. Breakfast is 14 lei.

Transylvania Hostel　HOSTEL €€
(☎0264-443 266; www.transylvaniahostel.com; Str Iuliu Maniu 26; dm 47-65 lei, d 170 lei; ⊜@☎) This centrally located, 50-bed place is disarmingly welcoming, with all the next-gen hostel attributes: PCs, wi-fi, home theatre, games room with ping pong, large self-catering kitchen and combo sauna/massage showers inspired by *Star Trek*. The privates feel a bit overpriced.

City Center Hostel　HOSTEL €
(☎0264-594 454; www.citycenterhostel.com; Str Ion Ratiu 2; dm 51-67 lei, d without bathroom 75 lei; ❋☎) With natural lighting via skylights on the ground level, this bright place has new beds and thoughtfully decorated common

TÂRGU MUREŞ (MAROSVÁSÁRHELY)

The biggest map-dot in Transylvania's Székely Land, home to Romania's ethnic Hungarian population, Târgu Mureş' worn Habsburg-style architecture and Hungarian accent gives it a different feeling from surrounding towns.

Piaţa Trandafirlor, its lengthy central square, begs to be strolled with a camera at the ready. At the southwestern end, the **Culture Palace** (adult/student 9/3.50 lei) is Târgu Mureş' beloved landmark and top attraction. Inside its glittering, tiled, steepled roof is an often-used concert hall and several worthwhile museums (all included in the entry price). The best is the **Hall of Mirrors** (Sala Oglinzi), with 12 stained-glass windows lining a 45m hallway – a lengthy tape in various languages explains the folk tales portrayed in each. The **History Museum** (1st floor) houses many large late-19th- and early-20th-century paintings, while the **Archaeological Museum** (2nd floor) explains, in English, Dacian pieces found in the region. The **tourist information centre** (www.cjmures.ro/turism; ◷8am-8pm Tue-Thu, to 4pm Mon & Sat) is on the ground floor, offering free maps and information on the region.

Târgu Mureş is well connected by bus and maxitaxi to Sighişoara (9 lei, 1½ hours, 18 daily), Cluj-Napoca (20 lei, 2½ hours, five daily) and Sibiu (15 lei, three hours, two daily).

spaces. As advertised, it's extremely central, just off busy Str Memorandumului.

Vila Eunicia
HOTEL €

(☏0264-594 067; www.vilaeunicia.ro, in Romanian; Str Emile Zola 2; s/d 100/150; ❄☎) Furniture is a bit dated in some rooms, and beds are firm, but it doesn't get much more central than this 10-room option. Rear-facing rooms are blissfully quiet but front-facing rooms suffer from noise pollution. Breakfast (20 lei) is delivered to your room.

Fulton
HOTEL €€

(☏0264-597 898; www.fulton.ro; Str Sextil Puşcariu 10; s 170-210 lei, d 196-236 lei; @☎) This faded back-street boutique inn has earth-tone striped walls, wrought-iron bed frames, and a laid-back covered patio bar. Has a central location, and plug-in and wi-fi internet are free.

Hotel Meteor
HOTEL €€

(☏0264-591 060; www.hotelmeteor.ro; B-dul Eroilor 29; s/d 133/177 lei; ☎) This is a slightly worn, modern hotel. Some rooms are quite small, but staff are nice and there's laundry service. The restaurant's alley tables mean night-time noise in good weather.

Pensiunea Junior
PENSION €

(☏0264-432 028; www.pensiune-junior.ro; Str Cări Ferate 12; s/d 100/130 lei; ☎) Rooms are simple on a loud street 100m east of the train station. It's prohibitively distant from the centre, but it's perfect for layovers or early departures. Rooms 1 and 7 are away from traffic noise. No breakfast.

Camping Făget
CAMPING GROUND €

(☏0264-596 227; campsites per person 10 lei, 2-person huts 73 lei) This hilltop collection of OK cabanas and tent sites is 7km south of the centre. Take bus 35 to the end of the line, from where it's a 2km marked hike.

✗ Eating

TOP CHOICE **Lugano**
ITALIAN €€€

(☏0264-594 593; Str General Eremia Grigorescu 51; mains 12-45 lei) This ritzy little Italian restaurant is the best at the pasta game, with no pizza to clutter the menu or a long wine list. The seafood menu is filled with trout and tuna. Head east on Str Gheorghe Bariţiu along the river, then cross the river at the first bridge. The road bends left and becomes Str General Eremia Grigorescu.

Tokyo
JAPANESE €€

(Str Marinescu 5; sushi & rolls from 15 lei) Full meal prices are very high by Romanian standards, but the sushi is surprisingly good. To get here go south on Str Gheorghe Bilascu, then turn right on Str Ion Creangă. It's on the left after about 300m.

Pizzeria New Croco
PIZZA €€

(www.newcroco.ro; Str V. Babeş 12; pizzas 11-34 lei) They have pasta too, but they do great woodfired pizza, piling on the toppings with American zeal. Exhibit A: 'Pizza Bomba', with mozzarella, mushrooms, salami, ham, sausage, onion, peas, olives, carrots, sweet peppers, tomatoes, eggs and sweetcorn.

Kablooie! They deliver, too. You'll pass it on the way to Tokyo.

Restaurant Matei Corvin ROMANIAN €€
(Str Matei Corvin 3; mains 16-42 lei) The hefty, leather-bound, multilingual menus could press pulp out of oranges, but these tourist-trap alarm bells will be silenced when you sample the competently prepared Romanian and international cuisine. The three-course 'Tourist Menu' is 20 lei (summer only).

Hotel Agape CAFE €
(Str Iuliu Maniu 6; mains 7 lei) Has a Romanian-style, glass-roofed cafeteria on the ground floor.

Gogoaşa Înfuriată BAKERY €
(Str Memorandumului 4; www.gogoasainfuriata.ro) The Krispy Kreme of Romania, this place serves up legendary pastries.

Cafeteria Nicola BAKERY €
(Str Regele Ferdinand 13; pastries 1-3 lei) A lazy coffee and sinful pastries can be enjoyed at this tiny place.

Speed/Alcatraz CAFE €
(Str Napoca 4-6; pizzas/sandwiches 6/14 lei; ⊙24hr) Busy fast-food place with good seating options, including some in the 'Al Capone' jail cages.

Central Market MARKET €
For fresh produce, visit this bustling, indoor market, behind the Complex Commercial Mihai Viteazul shopping centre, which also houses the **Oncos** supermarket.

🍷 Drinking
Many subterranean clubs and bars are spread throughout the centre: it pays to explore. The 'student ghetto', southwest of Cluj-Napoca's centre (on and off Str Piezişă – reached by Str Clinicilor about 300m from Piaţa Lucian Blaga), teems with lively open-air bars.

L'Atelier Café BAR
(Str Memorandumului 9, 1st fl; 🛜) Furniture made of cardboard, doors for tables and pumping indie music can be found in this eccentric, hip place.

Euphoria Irish Pub PUB
(Piaţa Muzeului 4) A popular, exposed-brick cellar pub, serving Guinness (12 lei) and showing football on giant TVs.

Umbra de Noapte CAFE
(www.umbradenoapte.com; Str Georges Clemenceau 7; ⊙noon-11pm) Sip coffee, wine, beer or choose from 11 kinds of absinthe in this Goth-themed cafe. The tiny vampire and fantasy library encourages one to linger.

☆ Entertainment
Şapte Seri (www.sapteseri.ro) and *24-Fun* are free biweekly booklets listing all the latest goings-on (in Romanian).

Janis CLUB
(☎0724-652 647; www.janis.ro; B-dul Eroilor 5; ⊙9pm-6am) When you ask a local about the best nightlife, this sweaty cave is invariably the first place they blurt out. Standard club nights with DJs and general bedlam are jazzed up with frequent theme nights and, yes, karaoke contests. Cover charges vary depending on events, ranging from 20 lei to free.

Diesel CLUB
(Piaţa Unirii 17) Walk past the hipsters in the all-glass entry and go downstairs into a cavernous room with red-spotlit tables and 15-lei gin and tonics.

Cinema Arta CINEMA
(Str Universităţii 3) Screens Hollywood films in English. Tickets cost about 8 lei.

Agenţia de Teatrală TICKET OFFICE
(☎0264-595 363; Piaţa Ştefan cel Mare 14; ⊙11am-5pm Tue-Fri) Sells tickets for theatre and opera, which hit the stage at the **National Theatre Cluj-Napoca** (Piaţa Ştefan cel Mare 2-4).

ℹ Information
Most cafes have free wi-fi.

Banca Comercială Română (Str Gheorghe Bariţiu 10-12) Gives cash advances and changes travellers cheques.

Blade Net (Str Iuliu Maniu 17; per hr 2.40 lei) Internet access.

Central post office (Str Regele Ferdinand 33; ⊙7am-8pm Mon-Fri, 8am-1pm Sat)

Green Mountain Holidays (☎0744-637 227; www.greenmountainholidays.ro) Terrific ecotourism agency providing activity-filled trips in the Apuseni Mountains.

Pan Travel (☎0264-420 516; www.pantravel. ro; Str Grozavescu 13; ⊙9am-5pm Mon-Fri) This top-notch outfit can book accommodation and car rental (from 108 lei per day), provide guides and arrange Maramureş trips. It's best to make contact ahead of time.

Tourist Information Office (☎0264-452 244; www.primariaclujnapoca.ro, in Romanian; B-dul Eroilor 6-8; ⊙8.30am-5pm Mon-Fri, 10am-5pm Sat) New, slick and in very capable hands, they have maps, brochures and information on events, restaurants and accommodation.

Transylvania Ecological Club (Clubul Ecologic Transilvania; ☑0264-431 626; www.green agenda.org) Grassroots environmental group focusing on ecotravel in the region.

❶ Getting There & Around

Air

Tarom has two to five daily direct flights to Bucharest (one way/return from 250/400 lei). Tickets can be bought at the airport (8km east of town, reached by bus 8) or in town at **Tarom** (☑0264-432 669; Piaţa Mihai Viteazul 11; ⊗8am-8pm Mon-Fri, 9am-2pm Sat). Budget carrier **Wizz Air** (www.wizzair.com) flies to London, Paris, Rome, Barcelona and more.

Bus

Bus services from **Autogara 2** (Autogara Beta), 350m northwest of the train station (take the overpass), include the following: Braşov (40 lei, one daily), Bucharest (58 lei, 7½ hours, three daily), Budapest (80 lei, several daily), Suceava (45 lei, four daily) and Sibiu (28 lei, 3½ hours, eight daily). There is no Autogara 1. Budapest-bound maxitaxis stop at the international bus station there and finish at the Budapest airport.

Car

Pan Travel (☑0264-420 516; www.pantravel.ro; Str Grozavescu 13; ⊗9am-5pm Mon-Fri) and **Autonom** (☑0264-590 588; www.autonom.ro; Str Victor Babes 10) offer Dacias and Matiz starting at 108 lei per day.

Taxi

Diesel Taxi (☑0264-953/946) Well-regarded, local company.

Train

The **Agenţia de Voiaj CFR** (☑0264-432 001; Piaţa Mihai Viteazul 20; ⊗8am-8pm Mon-Fri, 9am-1.30pm Sat) sells domestic and international train tickets in advance.

CRIŞANA & BANAT

The areas of Crişana (north of the Mureş River) and Banat (to the south) once merged imperceptibly with Vojvodina (Serbia) and Hungary's Great Plain; until 1918 all three regions were governed jointly. This legacy can still be appreciated in spirit and in the weathered Habsburg architecture in Oradea, Arad and Timişoara.

The nearby Apuşeni Mountains offer skiing, caving, gorges and waterfalls, while a pair of so-so hot-spring resorts (Băile Felix and Băile Herculane) promise to undo any damage done while partaking in the former.

Timişoara

POP 312,000

Tenacious Timişoara stunned the world – though not as much as it stunned the Ceauşescus – as the birthplace of the 1989 revolution. Beaming residents refer to it as 'Primul Oraş Liber' (First Free Town). A charming Mediterranean air pervades Romania's fourth-largest city, which is accentuated by regal Habsburg buildings and a thriving cultural and sports scene. Being in the west, and having infinitely better tourist resources than Bucharest, Timişoara is a far superior overland point of arrival for first-time Romania visitors.

◉ Sights

Piaţa Victoriei   SQUARE
Begging to be photographed with your widest lens is Piaţa Victoriei, a beautiful pedestrian mall with shops and cafes. The National Theatre & Opera House (p735) sits at its head and a column topped with the classic scene of **Romulus and Remus** feeding from

TRAINS FROM CLUJ-NAPOCA

DESTINATION	PRICE (LEI)	DURATION (HR)	DAILY DEPARTURES
Braşov	46	4	6
Bucharest	58	10	5
Budapest (Hungary)	117	5	2
Iaşi	57	9	3
Oradea	31	2¼-4	12
Sibiu	39	4	1
Sighişoara	39	3½	6
Suceava	47	7	3
Timişoara	49	7	6

ORADEA

A few kilometres east of the Hungarian border, Oradea was ceded to Romania in 1920 and has since taken on an air of faded grandeur, but it's a lovely place to stop while heading in or out of Hungary.

Oradea's Piaţa Unirii is one of the best surviving representations of the Austro-Hungarian Empire's 19th-century romantic style. The 1784 Orthodox **Biserica cu Lună (Moon Church)** has an unusual lunar mechanism on its tower that adjusts position in accordance with the moon's movement. In the centre stands an equestrian **statue of Mihai Viteazul**, the prince of Wallachia (r 1593–1601), who is said to have rested in Oradea in 1600. East of this statue, overlooking the Crişul Repede River, you'll find the magnificent **Vulturul Negru** (Black Vulture; 1908) hotel and covered arcade.

Across the bridge in Piaţa Republicii is the magnificent neoclassical **Teatrul de Stat** (State Theatre), designed by Viennese architects Fellner and Hellmer in 1900. To the east is the long, pedestrianised Calea Republicii, lined with bookshops and cafes.

The **Catedrala Romano-Catolică** (Roman Catholic Cathedral; 1780) is the largest in Romania. The adjacent **Palatul Episcopia Ortodoxă** (Episcopal Palace; 1770), with 100 fresco-adorned rooms and 365 windows, was modelled after Belvedere Palace in Vienna. It houses the **Muzeul Ţării Crişului** (Museum of the Land of the Criş Rivers), with history and art exhibits relevant to the region.

Oradea Hostel (☑0751-246 861; www.oradeahostel.com; Tudor Vladimescu 40; dm 42 lei; @) is an amiably managed 20-bed jobbie with free laundry, self-catering kitchen, terrace, wine-cellar bar and common room with foosball and TV. **Restaurant Vegetarian Cris** (Str George Enescu 30; mains 6-12 lei; ⊗9am-9pm Sun-Thu, to 5pm Fri, closed Sat; ☜) was Romania's first vegetarian restaurant and offers a tantalisingly cheap menu of soups, stuffed peppers, minced-lentil balls, macaroni and cabbage, pumpkin schnitzel and walnut haggis.

---

the mother wolf bulls-eyes the centre. This is where thousands of demonstrators gathered on 16 December 1989 following the siege on László Tökés' house. A memorial plaque on the front of the Opera House today reads: 'So you, who pass by this building, will dedicate a thought for free Romania.'

Banat History Museum   MUSEUM
(Muzeul Banatului; Piaţa Huniade 1; adult/student 2/1 lei) Just east of the *piaţa* is the 15th-century **Huniades Palace**, housing the Banat History Museum, which is worth visiting for its displays on natural history, geology, armour, weapons, archaeology, ceramics, tools and scale-model countryside shelters.

Metropolitan Cathedral   CHURCH
Towering over Piaţa Victoriei's southwestern end is the 1946 Romanian Orthodox Metropolitan Cathedral with unique electrical bells. Next to the cathedral is Parcul Central, and just south of it the Bega Canal.

Tökés Reformed Church   CHURCH
(Biserica Reformată Tökés; Str Timotei Cipariu 1) The 1989 revolution began on 15 December 1989 at the Tökés Reformed Church, off B-dul 16 Decembrie just southwest of the

centre, where Father László Tökés spoke out against the dictator.

Piaţa Libertăţii and the **Primăria Veche** (Old Town Hall; 1734) lie north. Piaţa Unirii is Timişoara's most picturesque square, featuring a baroque 1754 **Roman Catholic Cathedral** and the 1754 **Serbian Orthodox Cathedral**. Housed in the city's oldest remaining 18th-century bastion, the **Banat Ethnographic Museum** was closed for renovations during our last pass.

🛏 Sleeping

TOP CHOICE **Pension Casa Leone**   PENSION €€
(☑0256-292 621; www.casaleone.ro; B-dul Eroilor 67; s/d/tr 120/140/180 lei; @☜) This lovely 16-room pension offers exceptional service and individually decorated rooms. They give city tours (20 lei per person) and rent out bikes (20 lei per day), and give a 5% discount to holders of this book. Take tram 8 from the train station and alight at the Deliblata station, or call ahead to arrange transport.

Youth Hostel   HOSTEL €
(☑0256-490 469; djt.timis@yahoo.com; Piaţa Huniade 3, entrance on Str M Eminescu; dm per

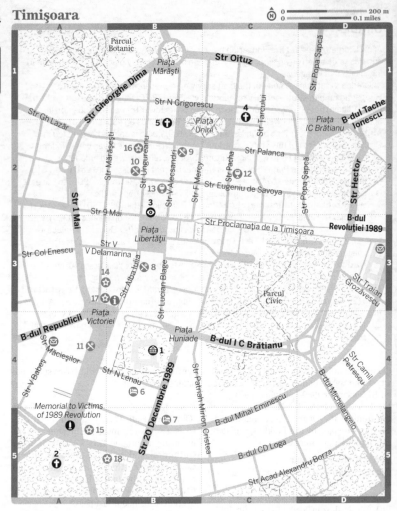

person under/over 35 50/70 lei) An institutional but ideally located youth hostel run by the county's youth department, it's situated just a block off of Piața Victoriei. It's generally clean, but the blankets and beds may test some travellers. Book in advance since it tends to fill up. No breakfast.

Camping International CAMPING GROUND €
(☎0256-208 925; campinginternational@yahoo.com; Aleea Pădurea Verde 6; sites per tent 20 lei, chalets s/d/q 92/126/220 lei) Nestled in the Green Wood forest on the opposite side of town from Timișoara-Nord train station,

the main entrance of this excellent camping ground is on Calea Dorobanților. From the station catch trolleybus 11 to the end of the line. The bus stops less than 50m from the camping ground. The site has a restaurant, and chalets have central heating.

Hotel Central HOTEL
(☎0256-490 091; www.hotel-central.ro; Str N Lenau 6; s/d 160/180 lei; ☀) Aging, unforgiving beds, but otherwise modern and comfortable. There's a big complimentary breakfast and secure parking (5 lei per day).

Timişoara

Hotel Cina Banatul　　　　　　　　HOTEL
(☎0256-490 130; B-dul Republicii 3-5; s/d
120/140 lei) Still the best-value pad in the
centre, with clean, modern rooms.

✕ Eating

Casa cu Flori　　　　　　ROMANIAN €€
(Str Alba Iulia 1; mains 18-28 lei) This is one of the
best-known restaurants in the city and for
good reason: excellent high-end Romanian
cooking comes with refined service at moderate prices. In nice weather, climb three
flights to the flower-lined rooftop terrace.

Restaurant La Savoya　　ROMANIAN €€
(Str Eugeniu de Savoya 18; mains 14-35 lei) This
seven-table casual place gets extremely busy
with suits at lunch for its good-value menu.
The long wine menu is pricey, but beers start
at 5 lei. With its size, the cigarette smoke can
be a bit overwhelming.

Intermezzo　　　　　　　　ITALIAN €€
(Piaţa Unirii; mains 24-36 lei) This place has
great pizzas and even better pastas. Dine
on the terrace on Piaţa Unirii or in the
cellar restaurant.

Restaurant Lloyd　　　　　ROMANIAN €€
(www.lloyd.ro; Piaţa Victoriei 2; mains 15-50 lei)
Exquisite international-Romanian menu of
steaks, shark, smoked salmon and a spit-
roast joint, served on a leafy terrace. Live
music most nights.

Drinking

Bottles of the local Timişoreana Pils beer sell
for about 4 lei at any of the lovely terrace
cafes lining Piaţ Unirii and Piaţa Victoriei,
where you can while away the time or plot
the next revolution.

Piranha　　　　　　　　　　BAR €
(Str V Alecsandri 5; ⊙9am-4am; ☎) This is a full
cafe-bar with house music and a 'vodka red
bull' special for only 7 lei. Arrive early on
weekends to get one of the giant puffy couches fronting aquarium tables filled with fish.

Java Coffee House　　　　　　CAFE €
(Str Pacha 6; ⊙24hr) A dark, cosy coffee
shop. Hot sandwiches (7 lei) are available
across the street at Java Snack House.

☆ Entertainment

Cinema Timiş　　　　　　　　CINEMA
([Piaţa Victoriei 7; tickets 6 lei) Movies are
screened in their original language.

Komodo　　　　　　　　　　CLUB
(Str Ungureanu 9) So trendy it hurts, this
large, colourfully lit eclectic bar has
techno-house DJs on weekends.

Club 30　　　　　　　　　　CLUB
(Piaţa Victoriei 7; h6pm-3am Fri & Sat) Cruise to
the blues in this jazz joint inside Cinema
Timiş. Popular 'oldies' nights bring out
young and old alike.

Agenţia Teatrală　　　　TICKET OFFICE
(☎0256-201 117; Str Mărăşeşti 2; ⊙10am-1pm &
5-7pm Tue-Sun) Buy tickets (adults/students
20/10 lei) for performances at the following venues.

State Philharmonic Theatre　　LIVE MUSIC
(Filharmonica de Stat Banatul; B-dul CD Loga
2) Classical concerts. Tickets can also be
bought at the box office inside.

National Theatre & Opera House　OPERA
(Teatrul Naţional şi Opera Română; Str Mărăşeşti 2)

ⓘ Information

Farmado Pharmacy (Piaţa Victoriei 7)

Info Centru Turistic (☎0256-437 973, www.
timisoara-info.ro; Str Alba Iulia 2) This great
tourism office can assist with accommodation

DON'T MESS WITH TIMIŞOARA

Even at the height of his power, Ceauşescu never liked Romania's westernmost metropolis. The dictator's visits to the city were few, brief and required surreptitious, dread-fuelled travel and sleeping arrangements to allay his assassination concerns. So, when the Securitate overplayed its hand in the already truculent city by trying to deport popular Hungarian pastor and outspoken Ceauşescu critic László Tőkés, the dictator should have sensed disaster looming. However, like most megalomaniacs, he didn't grasp the full scale of his folly until he was being shoved in front of a firing squad, looking genuinely stunned, 10 days later on Christmas Day 1989.

It all started on 15 December 1989 when a group of Tőkés' parishioners formed a human chain to protect him from arrest. It soon mushroomed and lost all focus (many of the protesters at the initial rally mistakenly thought they were demonstrating for religious freedom, not for the defence of Tőkés) and peaked as a full-scale, anti-communist revolt on 20 December. Overconfident Ceauşescu actually left Romania during this time for a visit to Iran, leaving his wife Elena and various subordinates to cope with the escalating protests.

When Ceauşescu returned to Romania a few days later, the situation was critical. Factory workers, armed with clubs brought in by Party officials to crush the demonstrations, spontaneously joined the protesters in Piaţa Operei (today's Piaţa Victoriei), chanting antigovernment slogans and singing an old Romanian anthem ('Wake up, Romanians!') banned since the communists took power in 1947. The crowd, now over 100,000 strong, overpowered and then commandeered some of the tanks that had previously fired on demonstrators. Protests later ensued in Bucharest and around the country and Ceauşescu's fate was sealed.

Despite the events in Timişoara leading to the revolt being somewhat confused and directionless, there's no denying that the people were primed for rebellion. While other cities are said to have mounted similar revolts in the weeks and months before, only to be hastily subdued by Securitate forces, it was the tenacious Timişoarans who first successfully defied their government, leading to the undignified downfall of their least favourite guest.

and trains, and provide maps and Banat regional info.

Post office (B-dul Revoluţiei 2; ☉8am-7pm Mon-Fri, to noon Sat)

Telephone office (Str N Lenau; ☉9am-6pm Mon-Fri, to 1pm Sat; @☎) Has fax facilities, plus free internet.

Unicredit Tiriac Bank (Piaţa Victoriei 2)

Volksbank (Str Piatra Craiului 2)

❶ Getting There & Away

Air

The airport is 12km east of the centre. **Tarom** (☎0256-200 003; B-dul Revoluţiei 1989 3-5; ☉8am-8pm Mon-Fri, 9am-2pm Sat) has two to six daily direct flights to Bucharest (starting at 241 lei) and several weekly international flights.

Timişoara is the hub of **Carpatair** (www.carpatair.ro), with direct service to nine key Romanian cities as well as a growing list of international destinations.

Austrian Airlines (☎0256-490 320; www.aua.com/ro) has daily flights to Vienna starting at €200 (about 850 lei) plus taxes.

Bus

The small, shabby **autogara** (B-dul Maniu Iuliu 54), 3.5km southwest of the centre, has six platforms where slow state buses depart for Arad (14 lei, five daily), Sibiu (43 lei, six hours, two daily) and Rimincu Valcea.

International buses leave from the Autogara Est (East Bus Station), which is merely a few kiosks cluttered outside the east train station. **Atlassib** (☎0256-226 486) goes to Rome (340 lei), Barcelona (382 lei) and even Sweden. **Eurolines** (☎0256-288 132; timisoara.ag@eurolines.ro) goes to Budapest (200 lei, three weekly) and Madrid, among others. **Murat** (☎0744-144 326, no English) goes to İstanbul every Monday (250 lei).

Train

All major train services depart from **Gara Timişoara-Nord** (Northern train station; Str Gării 2), 3km west of the centre. Purchase tickets in advance from the **Agenţia de Voiaj CFR** (cnr Str Măcieşilor & Str V Babeş; ☉7am-8pm Mon-Fri). Daily trains include six to Bucharest (90 lei, 8½ hours), five to Cluj-Napoca (49 lei, six to seven hours), eight to Băile Herculane (41 lei, three hours), one to Baia Mare (49 lei, six hours) via Arad and three sadistically slow runs to Iaşi

(85 lei, 16 hours). Additionally, three go to Budapest (105 lei) and one to Belgrade (60 lei).

MARAMUREŞ

Dismount from the horse-drawn cart and tip your chauffer in cigarettes: you've found one of the last places where rural European medieval life remains intact, where peasants live off the land as countless generations did before them. Even Romanians joke that nothing has changed here for 100 years. Welcome to Maramureş (www.visitmaramures.ro).

Having inconceivably flown under the radar during the collectivisation of the 1940s, systemisation of the '80s and the Westernisation of the '90s, the region is finding that newly imposed EU regulations are starting to cramp its medieval peasant style. Yet nothing short of an occupying force is going to touch the hand-built wooden churches, traditional music, colourful costumes and timeless festivals. Villagers' homes are still fronted with traditional, giant, ornately carved wooden gates. Ear-smoking, 100-proof *ţuică* stills percolate in the shed, usually tended by a rosy-cheeked patriarch. Mirthful sights of villagers with pitchforks in one hand and mobile phones in the other notwithstanding, sensations of time travel and escapism punctuate most visits here.

Sighetu Marmaţiei

POP 44,200

Being the northernmost significant town in Romania, Sighet (as it's known locally) still gives off a whiff of provincial air, despite the area's nominally increasing tourism popularity and gentrification. Its name is derived from the Thracian and Dacian word *seget* (fortress).

The town is famed for its vibrant **Winter Festival**. Its former maximum-security prison is now open as a sobering and informative museum (see the box, p739).

◎ Sights

On Piaţa Libertăţii, the **Hungarian Reformed Church** was built during the 15th century. Close by is the 16th-century **Roman Catholic Church**.

Just off the square is Sighet's only remaining **synagogue** (Str Bessarabia 10). Before WWII there were eight synagogues serving a large Jewish community, which comprised 40% of the town's population.

Elie Wiesel House   HISTORIC BUILDING

The Jewish writer and 1986 Nobel Peace Prize winner, Elie Wiesel, who coined the term 'Holocaust', was born in (and later deported from) Sighet. His house is on the corner of Str Dragoş Vodă and Str Tudor Vladimirescu. Along Str Gheorghe Doja, there is a **monument** (Str Mureşan) to the victims of the Holocaust.

Village Museum   MUSEUM

(Muzeul Satului; ☎0262-314 229; Str Dobăieş 40; adult/child/photo 4/2/4 lei) Allow two to three hours to wander through the incredible constructions at the open-air Village Museum, southeast of Sighet's centre. Children love the wood dwellings, cobbled pathways and 'mini villages'. You can even stay overnight in tiny wooden cabins (20 lei) or pitch a tent (5 lei per person).

Maramureş Ethnographic Museum

MUSEUM

(Piaţa Libertăţii 15; adult/student 4/2 lei) Displays colourful folk costumes, rugs and carnival masks.

🛏 Sleeping

For homestays in the area, check out www.ruraltourism.ro and www.pensiuni.info.ro.

TOP CHOICE | **Casa Iurca**   PENSION €€

(☎0262-318 882; www.casaiurca.ro; Str Dragos Voda 14; r 150 lei; ❄️🛜) Charming, immaculate wood-trimmed rooms surround this private courtyard oasis, which is easily the best-value place in the region. The on-site Romanian restaurant is exceptional (mains 10 lei to 32 lei). The neighbouring **annex** (s 92 lei, d 185-218 lei) has great rooms as well.

Cobwobs Hostel   HOSTEL €

(☎0745-615 173; Str 22 Decembrie 1989 nr; dm/d without bathroom 40/100 lei) Run by an English-Romanian couple, this home-turned-hostel arranges tours of the area and offers dinners (36 lei) in its garden. Breakfast is 16 lei. You can also camp on their property (20 lei per person).

Motel Buţi   HOTEL €

(☎0262-311 035; Str Ştefan cel Mare 6; s/d/tr 100/120/180 lei; @🛜) Spotless, recently renovated rooms. There's a bar and pool table downstairs. Internet is 5 lei per hour; wi-fi is free.

Hotel Coroana   HOTEL €

(☎0262-311 610; Piaţa Libertăţii 8; s/d/apt 80/100/150 lei) The long, dark hallways open into bright, basic rooms. Being

Maramureş

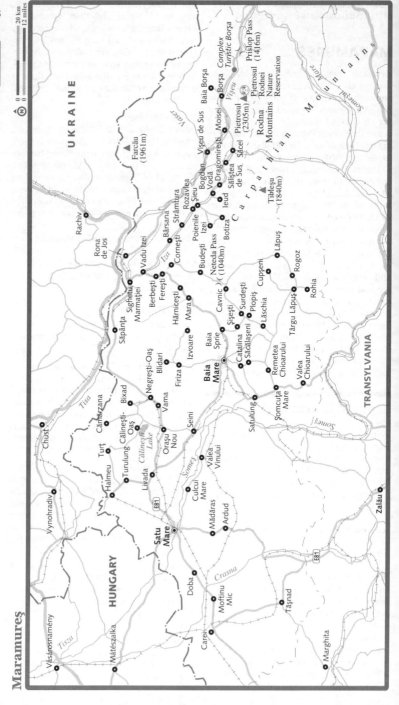

In May 1947 the communist regime embarked on a reign of terror, slaughtering, imprisoning and torturing thousands of Romanians. While many leading prewar figures were sent to hard-labour camps, the regime's most feared intellectual opponents were interned in Sighetu Marmaţiei's maximum-security prison. Between 1948 and 1952, about 180 members of Romania's academic and government elite were imprisoned here.

Today four white marble plaques covering the barred windows of the prison list the 51 prisoners who died in the Sighet cells, notably the academic and head of the National Liberal Party (PNL), Constantin Brătianu; historian and leading member of the PNL, Gheorghe Brătianu; governor of the National Bank, Constantin Tătăranu; and president of the National Peasants' Party (PNŢ), Iuliu Maniu.

The prison, housed in the old courthouse, was closed in 1974. In 1989 it reopened as the **Muzeu al Gândirii Arestate** (Museum of Arrested Thought; Str Corneliu Coposu 4; adult/student 6/3 lei). Photographs are displayed in the torture chambers and cells.

smack-bang in the centre of Sighet, you're paying for location more than comfort.

Eating & Drinking

Casa Veche ROMANIAN €€
(Str Juliu Maniu 27; mains 14-30 lei) A popular local restaurant with a large terrace, it serves great Romanian dishes plus big salads and arguably the best pizza in town. The lunch special is good value at 10 lei.

David's BAR €
(Str Ioan Mihaly de Apşa 1; mains 11-25 lei) The alpha-bar on Sighet's main street, with a menu of salads, pizza, hamburgers, veggie burgers and meat.

Information

ATM (Piaţa Libertăţii 8) Outside Hotel Tisa.

Banca Română (Calea Ioan Mihaly de Apşa 24) ATM, plus cash transfer and exchange facilities.

InfoTur/MTMM office (☎0262-312 552; Piaţa Libertăţii 21; ☺9am-4pm Mon-Fri) A small office administered by the EU to promote development in the Carpathians.

Post & telephone office (Str Ioan Mihaly de Apşa 39) Opposite the Maramureş Museum.

Getting There & Away

There's a car/foot bridge from Sighet to Ukraine, though at the time of writing there was no public transport using this crossing.

Bus

The **bus station** (Str Gării; ☺closed Sun) is opposite the train station. There are several local buses daily to Baia Mare (10 lei), Satu Mare (20 lei), Borşa (18 lei), Budeşti (5 lei), Călineşti (4 lei) and Vişeu de Sus (10 lei), and one bus daily to each of Bârsana, Botiza, Ieud and Mara.

Train

Advance tickets are sold at the **Agenţia de Voiaj CFR** (Piaţa Libertăţii 25; ☺7am-8pm Mon-Fri). There's one daily fast train each to Timişoara (75 lei, 12 hours), Bucharest (75 lei, 12 hours), Cluj-Napoca (39 lei, six hours) and Arad (65 lei, 11½ hours).

Valea Izei

POP 3000

The Valea Izei (Izei Valley) follows the Iza River eastward from Sighetu Marmaţiei to Moisei. A tightly knit procession of quintessential Maramureş peasant villages nestle in the valley, all featuring the region's famed elaborately carved wooden gates and tall wooden churches.

Gradually developing tourism in the region provides visitors the opportunity to sample traditional cuisine or try their hand at woodcarving, wool weaving and glass painting.

In mid-July Vadu Izei, together with the neighbouring villages of Botiza and Ieud, hosts the **Maramuzical Festival**, a lively four-day international folk-music festival.

VADU IZEI

Vadu Izei, at the confluence of the Iza and Mara Rivers 6km south of Sighetu Marmaţiei, serves as the gateway to valley excursions and homestays.

Casa Muntean (☎0766-755 267; www.casamuntean.ro; Str Dumbrava 505; r without bathroom per person 37 lei; @☂) rents out rooms and arranges tours starting at 200 lei per group (one to four people) per day. The lovely **Ramona Ardelean** (☎0744-827 829; www.pensiuneaardelean.ro; s/d without breakfast 100/120 lei) also arranges guided tours in

SĂPÂNȚA

Unassuming Săpânța village has one of the most singular attractions in Romania: the **Merry Cemetery** (admission & camera each 5 lei), famous for the colourfully painted, epitaph-inscribed wooden crosses adorning its tombstones. Shown in art exhibitions across Europe, the crosses attract legions of visitors who marvel at the gentle humour and human warmth that created them.

Off the main road, a new wooden church claiming to be the tallest wooden structure in Europe (75m) has been built – with a stone base.

Eight buses a day go to/from Sighetu Marmației.

French and English (105 lei full day, plus 1.25 lei per kilometre), as well as picnics, woodcarving and icon-painting workshops, and homestays.

BÂRSANA

From Vadu Izei continue southeast for 12km to Bârsana. Dating from 1326, the village acquired its first church in 1720 (its interior paintings were done by local artists). The Orthodox **Bârsana Monastery** is a popular pilgrimage spot in Maramureș. It was the last Orthodox monastery to be built in the region before Serafim Petrovai, head of the Orthodox church in Maramureș, converted to Greco-Catholicism in 1711.

ROZAVLEA

Continue south though Strâmtura to Rozavlea, first documented under the name of Gorzohaza in 1374. Its fine **church**, dedicated to the archangels Michael and Gabriel, was built between 1717 and 1720 in another village, then erected in Rozavlea on the site of an ancient church destroyed by the Tatars.

BOTIZA

From Rozavlea continue south for 3km to Șieu, then turn off for Botiza. It's **old church**, built in 1694, is overshadowed by the large **new church** constructed in 1974 to serve the 500 or so devout Orthodox families.

Opération Villages Roumains (OVR) runs an efficient agrotourism scheme in Botiza. Bookings can be made with local representative **George Iurca** (☏0722-942 140; botizavr@sintec.ro; house 742; r per person 50 lei, incl half-board 80 lei; ☉8am-10pm), whose house is signposted. George also runs German-, French- and English-language tours of Maramureș and Transylvania (from 260 lei per group per day; with own car 100 lei per group), rents out mountain bikes (30 lei per day) and organises fishing trips.

IEUD

The oldest wooden church in Maramureș, dating from 1364, is in Ieud, 6km south of the main road from Șieu, slightly hidden behind an overgrown cemetery. Ieud was first documented in 1365. Its fabulous Orthodox **Church on the Hill** was built from fir wood and used to house the first known document to be written in Romanian (1391–92), in which the catechism and church laws pertaining to Ieud were coded. The church was restored in 1958 and in 1997.

Ieud's second **church** is Greco-Catholic, and was built in 1717. It is unique to the region in that it has no porch. At the southern end of the village, it houses one of the largest collections of icons on glass found in Maramureș.

OVR runs a small agrotourism scheme in Ieud. You can make bookings through local representatives **Vasile Chindris** (☏0262-336 197; house 201; per person incl half-board 80 lei), **Liviu Ilea** (☏0262-336 039; house 333; per person without/with board 36/72 lei) and **Vasile Rişco** (☏0262-336 019; house 705; r incl half-board 50 lei).

MOISEI

Moisei lies 7km northeast of Săcel, at the junction of route 17C and route 18. A small town at the foot of the Rodna Massif, Moisei is known for its traditional crafts and customs. It gained regrettable fame in 1944 when retreating Hungarian (Horthyst) troops massacred local villagers.

Following the news that the front was approaching Moisei, villagers started to flee, including those forced-labour detachments stationed in the village. Occupying Hungarian forces organised a manhunt to track down the deserters. Thirty-one were captured and detained in a small camp in nearby Vișeu de Sus without food or water for three weeks. On 14 October 1944 Hungarian troops brought the 31 prisoners to a house in Moisei, locked them inside and shot them through the windows – 29 were killed. Before abandoning the village, the troops set it on fire, leaving all 125 remaining families homeless.

Only one house in Moisei survived the blaze: the one in which the prisoners were shot. Today it houses a small **museum** in tribute to those who died in the massacre. Opposite, on a hillock above the road and railway line, is a circular **monument** to the victims. The 12 upright columns symbolise sun and light. Each column is decorated with a traditional carnival mask, except for two that bear human faces based on the features of the two survivors.

The museum and monument are at the eastern end of the village. If the museum is locked, knock at the house next door and ask for the key.

Prislop Pass

Famed for its remoteness and postcard-worthy beauty, Prislop Pass is the main route from Maramureş into Moldavia. The drive is spectacular. Hikers can trek east from Borşa across the pass into Moldavia and head northeast to Câmpulung Moldovenesc and on to the monasteries of southern Bucovina; or south to the natural mineral waters of Vatra Dornei and through to the fantastic Bicaz Lake.

At 1416m a **roadside monument** marks the site of the last Tartar invasion prior to their final flight from the region in 1717. Nearby is the Hanul Prislop, site of the **Hora de la Prislop**, the major Maramureş festival, held yearly on the second Sunday in August.

MOLDAVIA

The Romania postcards you buy showing cinematically perfect forested hills and undulating valleys were most likely taken in Moldavia. The topographical, pastoral and cultural love child of Transylvania and Maramureş, Moldavia nevertheless remains an idiosyncratic tourism option, usually visited only by travellers with abundant time on their hands. Roam between painted churches, urban excesses and village retreats all connected by picturesque train rides, where the only book you'll crack open will be this one.

Iaşi

POP 400.300

Romania's second-largest city, Iaşi (pronounced 'yash') is discreetly rich with fabulous buildings, important monasteries, sprawling parks and unpretentious cultural treasures. Tragically, municipal planners didn't invoke the same discretion with the ocean of cement that partitions it all.

Moldavia's capital since 1565, and Romania's capital briefly during WWI, Iaşi is a fun, eclectic city, teeming with beautiful people, restaurants, bars and nightspots. It's also the ideal staging post for incursions on the Moldovan border, 20km away.

Iaşi Days (in the second week of October) is an unhinged street party, fuelled by a river of *must* (a sweet, fermented not-quite-wine brew).

◉ Sights

BULEVARDUL ŞTEFAN CEL MARE & AROUND

Start your tour on **Piaţa Unirii**, the main square, with a trip to the 13th-floor restaurant in **Hotel Unirea** for a bird's-eye view of Iaşi. Use the 'Panorama 13' elevator to the left of reception.

Union Museum   MUSEUM
(Muzeul Unirii; Str Alexandru Lăpuşneanu; adult/student 12/3 lei) This small, neoclassical palace on Str Alexandru Lăpuşneanu served as Alexandru Cuza's home for three years (1859–62), and later housed King Ferdinand during his WWI retreat from Bucharest. It's now a museum devoted to Cuza. Originally opened in 1959, and recently reopened after a 10-year renovation, it meticulously displays the Cuza family's opulent furniture, pictures and personal effects.

Moldavian Metropolitan Cathedral CHURCH
(Mitropolia Moldovei; B-dul Ştefan cel Mare) Southeast of Piaţa Unirii, the tree-lined B-dul Ştefan cel Mare leads to the Moldavian Metropolitan Cathedral (1833–39), with its cavernous interior painted by Gheorghe Tattarescu. In mid-October thousands of pilgrims flock here to celebrate the day of St Paraschiva, the patron saint of the cathedral and of Moldavia.

Vasile Alecsandri National Theatre
                                    HISTORIC THEATRE
Opposite the cathedral is a park, and at the far end is the Vasile Alecsandri National Theatre (1894–96). In front of it is a statue of its founder Vasile Alecsandri (1821–90), a

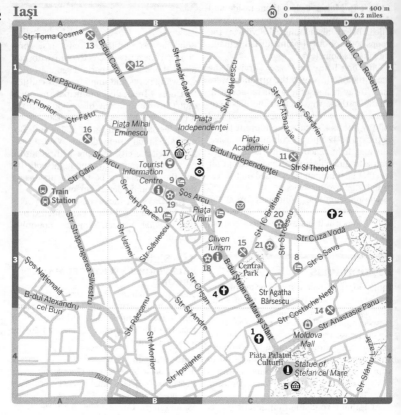

poet who single-handedly created the theatre's first repertoire with his Romanian adaptation of a French farce.

Church of the Three Hierarchs   CHURCH
(Biserica Sfinţilor Trei Ierarhi; B-dul Ştefan cel Mare) Under eternal restoration but nevertheless fabulous, the Church of the Three Hierarchs (1637–39) is unique for its mesmerising stone-patterned exterior. Built by Prince Vasile Lupu, the church was badly damaged by Tatar attacks in 1650 but later restored. Inside are the marble tombs of Prince Vasile Lupu and his family, as well as Prince Alexandru Ioan Cuza and Moldavian prince Dimitrie Cantemir.

Palatul Culturii   PALACE
(B-dul Ştefan cel Mare) At the southern end of B-dul Ştefan cel Mare stands the giant neo-Gothic Palace of Culture, built between 1906 and 1925 on the ruins of the old princely court, founded by Prince Alexandru cel Bun (r 1400–32) in the early 15th century. Its four wonderful museums are closed for a comprehensive renovation project, due to be completed in 2018.

FREE Golia Monastery   MONASTERY
(Str Cuza Vod; admission free) Fortified Golia Monastery was constructed in a late Renaissance style. The monastery's walls and the 30m Golia tower at the entrance shelter a 17th-century church, noted for its vibrant Byzantine frescos and intricately carved doorways.

PARCUL COPOU
To get to Parcul Copou (Copou Park), laid out between 1834 and 1848, catch tram 1 or 13 north from Piaţa Unirii. The park, which was established during the princely reign of Mihail Sturza, is famed for being a favourite haunt of the celebrated poet Mihai Eminescu (1850–89). He allegedly penned some of

Iaşi

his best works beneath his favourite linden tree in this park.

The tree is still standing behind a 13m-tall **monument of lions** and opposite the main entrance to the park. A bronze bust of Eminescu stands in front of it. Nearby is the **Mihai Eminescu Museum of Literature** (adult/child 4/2 lei), which recalls the life and loves of Romania's most cherished writer and poet.

🛏 Sleeping

TOP **Pensiune Fiesta & Lavric** PENSION €
CHOICE (②0232-229 961; fiestalavric@yahoo. com; Str Horia 8; s/d 125/150 lei; ❋🛜) This is hands down Iaşi's best option, with six, large, very comfortable, good-value rooms. Centrally located, there's also an on-site restaurant.

Hotel Traian HOTEL €€€
(②0232-266 666; Piaţa Unirii 1; s/d/ste 292/360/843 lei; @🛜) A friendly and elegant hotel designed by Gustave Eiffel of Paris tower fame, the high-ceilinged rooms are awash in old-world comfort, with large, modern bathrooms. Wi-fi in the lobby only.

Hotel Continental HOTEL €€
(②0232-211 846; Piaţa 14 Decembrie 1989; s/d with bathroom 112/153 lei 🛜❋) While rooms here have been freshened up, they're still decidedly on the budget end of the spectrum. Get a room away from the noisy street. Air-con is available for 15 lei.

Hotel Eden HOTEL €€
(②0332-144 486; www.hotels-eden.ro; Str Sfantu Sava 1; s/d 160/170 lei; ❋❋) An excellent three-star option, central to nearly everything. Some of the wood-furnished rooms have balconies. Breakfast is 15 lei.

Iaşi Apartment APARTMENTS €
(②0746-067 979; www.iasi-apt.com, s/d/tr from 105/105/195 lei; ❋) Manages several modern apartments with air-con, internet and cable TV smack in the city centre. Discounts for long stays. No breakfast.

🍴 Eating & Drinking

Casa Lavric ROMANIAN, MEXICAN €€
(②0232-229 960; Str Sf Atanasie 21; mains 10-40 lei) Owned by singer/musician Laura Lavric, this is the city's best Romanian restaurant, with a decent Mexican selection. The menus – including a short vegetarian page – are devoid of English, but the staff's language skills more than make up for this.

Casa Pogor ROMANIAN €€
(Str Vasile Pogor 4; mains 9-31 lei) Servers here are as lovely as its insanely cosy basement (formerly the famed Junimea wine cellar) and antique-y main dining hall. The multi-tiered terrace is beaut, too.

Casa Universitatilor ROMANIAN €
(B-dul Carol I 9; mains 6-15 lei) The simple but tasty grilled dishes and pizzas here are geared for destitute students and their grossly underpaid faculty staff. The lime-tree-festooned terrace is great for a lazy beer (4 lei).

Family Pizza PIZZA €€
(Str IC Brătianu; mains 10-20 lei) A lively, brightly lit parlour with 25 types of pizza, plus pasta and tonnes of pastries. It also delivers.

La Cao CHINESE €
(Str Arcu 8; mains 16-28 lei) Iaşi's best Chinese restaurant, with a lengthy English menu and speedy service.

Central Market MARKET €
(☺8am-4pm) Fresh fruit, vegetables, meat, cheeses and flowers at this underground market, with stairway entrances off Str Costache Negri and Str Anastasie Panu.

Terasa Corso BAR
(www.corsoterasa.ro; Str Alexandru Lăpuşneanu 11) This huge, outdoor-indoor pub is scenester paradise and Iaşi's primary social hub. Free wi-fi.

☆ Entertainment

Viper Club GAMES CLUB
(Iulius Mall; ☺24hr) A rainy-day entertainment option, inside the ubiquitous Iulius Mall, about a kilometre south of the centre. Features bowling alleys, billiards and video games.

Cinema Victoria CINEMA
(Piaţa Unirii 5; tickets 8 lei) Films shown in English with Romanian subtitles. Modern cinemas can be found in Moldova and Iulius Malls.

Filarmonica LIVE MUSIC
(www.filarmonicais.ro; Str Cuza Vodă 29; ☺box office 10am-1pm & 5-7pm Mon-Fri) Be sure to see the much-revered Iaşi State Philharmonic Orchestra if it's in town. Tickets start at 13 lei, with 50% student discounts.

Vasile Alecsandri National Theatre & Opera Română THEATRE, OPERA
(Str Agatha Bârsescu 18) Located in the same impressive neo-baroque building. For advance bookings go to the **Agenţia de Teatrala** (B-dul Ştefan cel Mare 8; ☺10am-5pm Mon-Sat). Tickets cost 18 to 22 lei, with 50% student discounts.

ⓘ Information

Cliven Turism (☑0232-258 326; www.cliven.ro; B-dul Ştefan cel Mare 8-12; ☺9am-6pm Mon-Fri, to 2pm Sat) As agents for Antrec, it can arrange rural accommodation, monastery tours and walking city tours (212 lei per group up to five).

Forte Cafe (B-dul Independenţei 27; per hr 4 lei; ☺24hr) Internet. In a passage off the footpath.

Post office (Str Cuza Vodă 10)

Raiffeisen Bank (B-dul Ştefan cel Mare 2)

Sfântu Spiridon University Hospital (☑0232-240 822, ext 193; B-dul Independenţei 1) The city's largest hospital. Walk-ins go to 'Secretariat Arhiva' on first level.

Telephone centre (Str Alexandru Lăpuşneanu; ☺9am-6pm Mon-Fri, to 1pm Sat; ☎) Has fax service and free wi-fi.

Tourist information centre (☑0232-261 990; www.turism-iasi.ro; Piaţa Unirii 12, ☺9am-6pm Mon-Fri, to 1pm Sat) A compulsory first stop, it offers excellent city maps and a free guidebook for the region.

ⓘ Getting There & Around

Air

Iaşi international airport (☑0232-271 570; www.aeroport.ro) is about 5km east of the city.

Austrian Airlines (www.aua.com) Flies to Vienna six days a week.

Carpatair (☑0232-215 295; www.carpatair.com; Str Cuza Vodă 2; ☺9am-6pm Mon-Fri, to 1pm Sat) Flights to Timişoara Monday to Saturday (from 316 lei).

Malev (www.malev.com) Flies to Budapest five days a week.

Tarom (☑0232-267 768; www.tarom.com; Şos Arcu 3-5; ☺9am-7pm Mon-Fri, to 1pm Sat) Daily flights to Bucharest for 100 to 700 lei.

Bus

The chaotic **central bus station** (Transbus Codreanu or Autogara Veche) has a number of independent companies with service to Târgu Neamţ (13 lei), Suceava (18 lei), Bacau (24 lei), Piatra Neamţ (25 lei) and Bucharest (56 lei). Daytime and overnight buses go directly to Henri Coanda airport in Bucharest (64 lei) – reserve one day in advance (☑0748-185 315). Slower buses run to Vatra Dornei (32 lei) and Braşov (48 lei).

Buses to Sibiu (68 lei) leave from Autogara Iaşi Vest, behind the large building labelled 'Auto Centre', about 1km west of the central bus station.

Private minivans to Chişinău leave from outside the Billa supermarket car park three to four times daily (40 lei, four hours); look for Moldovan plates with drivers loitering nearby. Up to eight daily (slow) buses to Chişinău depart from the central bus station (30 lei).

Car & Motorcycle

Autonom (☑0748-110 557; www.autonom.ro; B-dul Ştefan cel Mare 8-12; ☺9am-6pm Mon-Fri, to 1pm Sat) has the best car-hire rates and 24-hour assistance.

Train

Trains arrive and depart from the Gara Centrală (also called Gara Mare or Gara du Nord) on Str Garii. The **Agenţia de Voiaj CFR** (Piaţa Unirii 10; ☺8am-8pm Mon-Fri, 9am-12.30pm Sat) sells advance tickets.

There are six daily trains to Bucharest (57 lei, seven hours), one service daily each to Oradea, Galaţi and Mangalia, and four sadistically slow trains to Timişoara (78 lei, 16 to 17 hours, via Oradea), called the 'horror train' by locals.

SOUTHERN BUCOVINA

Though southern Bucovina is inexorably associated with its trove of distinctive and ceaselessly hypnotic painted churches – collectively designated a World Heritage site by Unesco in 1993 – it's also a rural paradise on a par with Maramureş, with the advantage of better transport connections. Once you've absorbed some of Europe's greatest artistic monuments, sample Romania's signature

folklore, picturesque villages, bucolic scenery and colourful inhabitants: they'll leave lasting memories that Transylvanian castles simply can't compete with.

Southern Bucovina comprises the northwestern region of present-day Moldavia; northern Bucovina is in Ukraine.

Suceava

POP 106,000

Suceava, the capital of Moldavia from 1388 to 1565, was a thriving commercial centre on the Lviv–İstanbul trading route. Today it's the seat of Suceava county and gateway to the painted churches of Bucovina.

◉ Sights

The unsightly **Casa de Cultură** (House of Culture) is at the western end of Piaţa 22 Decembrie, the city's main square. To the north is **St Dumitru's Church** (Biserica Sfântul Dumitru; 1535) built by Petru Rareş.

Southern Bukovina

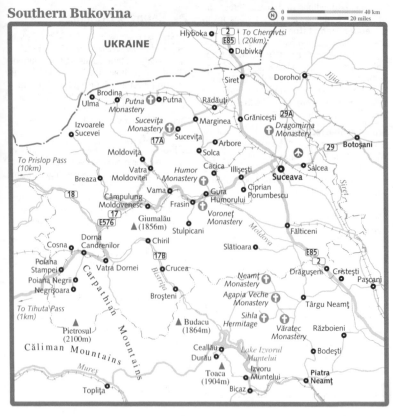

Bucovina History Museum
MUSEUM

(Muzeul Naţional al Bucovinei; Str Ştefan cel Mare 33; adult/child 6/1.50 lei) Mildly neglected, the museum nevertheless has pictures and artefacts stretching for miles, starting at the Bronze Age, touching on the likes of Vlad Ţepeş, and lavishing justifiable attention on Moldavian prince/saint/Ottoman scourge/founder of painted monasteries, Ştefan cel Mare (Stephen the Great). The presentation comes to an abrupt end at 1945, and old paintings now hang in rooms that formerly glorified the communist era.

Monastery of St John the New
MONASTERY

The Monastery of St John the New (Mănăstirea Sfântu Ioan cel Nou; 1522), off Str Mitropoliei, is well worth visiting. The paintings on the outside of the church are badly faded compared with most of the fantastical painted churches, but they're a good preview of what's to come on your trip.

City of Residence
CITADEL

Starting at McDonald's, follow the adjacent footpath along the stream, cross the little bridge and scale the 241 steps up to the **equestrian statue** (1966) of Ştefan cel Mare. Follow the footpath to the left of the statue up to the **City of Residence Citadel** (Cetatea de Scaun; admission/photo 5/10 lei; ☺9am-6pm), a fortress that held off Mehmed II, conqueror of Constantinople (İstanbul) in 1476. It's much more attractive from a distance than from the inside.

Ethnographic Museum
MUSEUM

(Str Ciprian Porumbescu 5; adult/child 6/1.50 lei) West of Piaţa 22 Decembrie is Hanul Domnesc, a marvellous 18th-century guesthouse containing a fine collection of folk costumes and typical household items.

🛏 Sleeping

TOP CHOICE **High Class Hostel**
HOSTEL €

(☏0723-782 328; www.classhostel.ro; Str Mihai Eminescu 19; per person 50 lei; 🛜) Run by Monika, a good-humoured, monastery-guiding, problem-solving force of nature, this tulip-fringed proverbial home-away-from-home is hidden on a quiet street near the centre. No breakfast, but there's a self-catering kitchen with tea and coffee all day.

TOP CHOICE **Pensiunea Giardino**
PENSION €

(☏0230-531 778; www.giardino.ro; Str Dobrogeanu Gherea 2; s/d 79/99 lei; @🛜) This immaculate three-star pension is one of the best-value options in Moldavia. Just 200m

from the bus station. Psst! 'Prices are negotiable for backpackers!' They also arrange tours (from 320 lei per group up to three people per day). No breakfast.

Irene's Hostel
HOSTEL €

(☏0744-292 588; www.ireneshostel.ro; Str Armenească 4; dm/d without bathroom 42/80 lei; ☺@) Open in 2010, in a tidy, centrally located house, Irene's has few frills, but there's new beds and a shared kitchen. No breakfast.

Villa Alice
HOTEL €

(☏0230-522 254; www.villaalice.ro; Str Simon Florea Marian 1; s/d from 90/120 lei; 🛜) These small, bright two-star rooms have comfortable beds, refrigerators, DVD players and very clean bathrooms. Some have balconies.

Hotel Balada
HOTEL €€

(☏0230-520 408; www.balada.ro; Str Mitropoliei 3; s/d/ste 210/255/400 lei; ✳@🛜) This three-storey place offers elegance and comfort over pure luxury; rooms are simply furnished. It's on a lovely quiet street.

🍴 Eating & Drinking

TOP CHOICE **B+B**
ROMANIAN €€

(Str Mihai Eminescu 18B; mains 12-36 lei) This cosy restaurant, using fresh ingredients, is a top choice for backpackers wanting a proper, stomach-distending, Romanian meal. Massive prix fixe lunches are 14 lei to 22 lei, or order from the à la carte menu. There's also pizza and a short salad page for vegetarians.

Latino
ITALIAN €€

(Str Curtea Domnească 9; mains 12-45 lei) The classy, subdued decor is accentuated by impeccable service and a dazzling menu that runs the gamut from 25 kinds of pizza – real mozzarella! – to a dozen first-rate pasta dishes (15 lei) and fresh fish (25 to 40 lei).

Pub Chagall
PUB €€

(www.chagall.ro; Str Ştefan cel Mare; mains 11-28 lei) Though it has a thick menu of pizza, chicken, pork and beef, it's mostly used as a drinking hole. Enter by going through the tunnel and down the stairs in the alley.

Giovani
INTERNATIONAL €€

(Str N Bălcescu 3; mains 11-39 lei) This is a great restaurant/cafe/pub/club conglomeration, which (depending on the time of day) serves a full menu, including pizza. They have live music on Fridays and transform into a club late on Saturdays.

Suceava

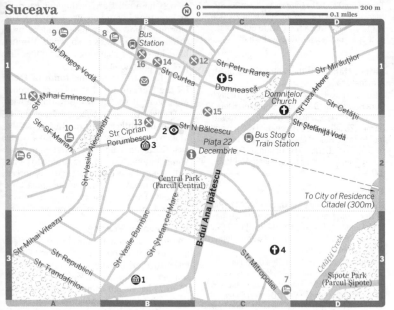

Suceava

⊙ Sights

1 Bucovina History Museum	B3
2 Casa de Cultură	B2
3 Ethnographic Museum	B2
4 Monastery of St John the New	C3
5 St Dumitru's Church	C1

🛏 Sleeping

6 High Class Hostel	A2
7 Hotel Balada	C3
8 Irene's Hostel	B1
9 Pensiunea Giardino	A1
10 Villa Alice	A2

✕ Eating

11 B+B	A1
12 Central Market	B1
13 Giovani	B2
14 Latino	B1
15 Pub Chagall	C1
16 Restaurant Cina	B1

Restaurant Cina ROMANIAN €
(Str Vasile Alecsandri 10; mains 8-21 lei) A typical Romanian menu, with salads and all
your favourite meat dishes. Also a pleasant
terrace to have a few drinks.

Central Market MARKET €
(cnr Str Petru Rareş & Str Ştefan cel Mare) Close
to the bus station.

ℹ Information

There are several ATMs on Piaţa 22 Decembrie
and along Str Ştefan cel Mare. There's no longer a
telephone office in Suceava, but you can buy payphone cards for international calls in any shop.

Games Pit (Str Mihai Eminescu 13; per hr 2 lei;
⊙24hr) Internet access.

Infoturism (☏0230-551 241; infoturism@
suceava.rdsnet.ro; Str Ştefan cel Mare 23;
⊙8am-4pm Mon-Fri) Inside the Museum of
Natural Sciences, this is the official tourism
office of Suceava county.

Post office (Str Dimitrie Onciul)

Raiffeisen Bank (Str Nicolae Bălcescu 2)

West Travel (☏0728-438 439; www.west
tourism.ro; Str Ştefan cel Mare 54; ⊙8am-7pm
Mon-Fri, 9am-2pm Sat) Offers tours, car rental,
accommodation assistance and plane tickets.

ℹ Getting There & Away

Air

Suceava's **Ştefan cel Mare airport** (www.
aerportsuceava.ro) is about 15km northeast of
the centre.

Carpatair (☏0230-529 559; www.carpatair.
com) Flies to Timişoara three times a week.

Tarom (☑0230-214 686; www.tarom.ro; Str Nicolae Bălcescu 2; ⊙7am-5pm Mon-Fri, 9am-2pm Sat) Has two daily flights to Bucharest, except Saturdays, starting at 180 lei.

Bus

The **bus station** is in the centre of town on Str Armenească.

Bus and maxitaxi services include 20 daily to Gura Humorului (8 lei), 10 to Botoşani (8 lei), 10 to Rădăuţi (8 lei), 12 to Iaşi (23 lei), five to Vatra Dornei (20 lei), three to Bucharest (52 lei) and four to Târgu Neamţ (19 lei). One daily bus goes to Chernivtsi (Cernăuţi) in Ukraine (20 lei) and a daily 6am bus leaves for Chişinău, Moldova (50 lei).

Train

The bus stop for the train station is east of Piaţa 22 Decembrie, across B-dul Ana Ipătescu, next to McDonald's. The **Agenţia de Voiaj CFR** (Str Nicolae Bălcescu 8; ⊙7.30am-8.30pm Mon-Fri) sells advance train tickets.

Daily train services from Gara Burdujeni, 5km north of the centre, (also known as Gara Principala) include nine to Gura Humorului (16 lei, 1¼ hours), seven to Vatra Dornei (24 lei, 3¼ hours), eight to Iaşi (28 lei, 2½ hours) and four Timişoara (78 lei, 13½ hours), and six to Bucharest (78 lei, seven hours). To get to Moldoviţa, change at Vama.

Bucovina Monasteries

VORONEŢ

The *Last Judgment* fresco, which fills the entire western wall of the **Voroneţ Monastery** (adult/child 3/1 lei), could be one of the most marvellous frescos in the world. At the top, angels roll up the signs of the zodiac to indicate that the time of sin is coming to an end. The middle fresco shows humanity being brought to judgment. On the left, St Paul escorts the believers, while on the right Moses brings forward the non-Christians. Souls are judged according to their deeds: good deeds are recorded by the angels, and bad deeds by the devils. The souls are represented naked because there is nothing material about them and they are unable to hide anything on Judgment Day. To the left are *Paradise* and the *Garden of Eden*. Opposite is the *Resurrection*.

On the northern wall is *Genesis,* from Adam and Eve to Cain and Abel. The southern wall features a tree of Jesse with the genealogy of biblical personalities. In the vertical fresco to the left is the story of St Nicholas and the martyrdom of St John the New (whose relics are in the Monastery of St John the New in Suceava; see p745). The vibrant, almost satiny blue pigment used throughout the frescos is known as 'Voroneţ blue', known for changing colour under different illumination.

In the narthex lies the **tomb of Daniel the Hermit**, the first abbot of Voroneţ Monastery. It was upon the worldly advice of Daniel, who told Ştefan cel Mare not to give up his battle against the Turks, that the Moldavian prince went on to win further victories against the Turks and then to build Voroneţ Monastery out of gratitude to God.

In 1785 the occupying Austrians forced Voroneţ's monks to abandon the monastery. Since 1991 the monastery has been inhabited by a small community of nuns.

🛏 Sleeping & Eating

The town of Gura Humorului is a perfect base to visit Voroneţ. Every second house takes in tourists. The usual rate per person per night in a so-called *vila* is around 50 to 75 lei. Rough camping is possible on the south bank of the Moldova River, 500m south of the bus station; follow the only path and cross the river.

Pensiunea Lions   PENSION €
(☑0230-235 226; www.motel-lions.ro, in Romanian; Str Ştefan cel Mare 39; s/d 67/88 lei; 🖥) This three-star pension-restaurant minicomplex is warm, homey and clean. The beds are decent and all rooms have a balcony. Request a room away from the noisy road. No breakfast.

Casa Doamnei   HOTEL €
(☑0735-530 753; www.casa-doamnei.ro; r 120; @) On the road to Voroneţ, this good-value option has stylish wood furniture, balconies and bathrooms with granite sinks. Voroneţ Monastery is 4km away. Breakfast is not included, but there's an on-site restaurant.

Casa Elena   VILLA €€
(☑0230-235 326; www.casaelena.ro; s/d 135/185 lei; @) A quick 3.5km trip from Gura Humorului (2km from Voroneţ Monastery), this four-star option has 47 rooms in six different villas. Amenities include a billiard room, sauna and two restaurants.

❶ Getting There & Away

See p747 for bus and train services from Suceava to Gura Humorului. A lovely option is to walk the 4km along a narrow village road to Voroneţ. The route is clearly marked and it's impossible to get lost.

HUMOR

Of all the Bucovina monasteries, **Humor Monastery** (Mănăstirea Humorului; adult/child 3/1 lei) has the most impressive interior frescos.

On the southern exterior wall of the 1530 church, you can see the life of Virgin Mary (on left), St Nicholas and the parable of the prodigal son (on right). On the porch is the *Last Judgment* and, in the first chamber inside the church, scenes of martyrdom.

Aside from hitching a ride the 6km from Gura Humorului, there are regular maxi-taxis that depart from next to the towering Best Western Hotel, at the start of the road towards the monastery.

MOLDOVIȚA

Moldovița Monastery (adult/child 3/1 lei) is in the middle of a quaint village. It's a fortified enclosure with towers and brawny gates, and a magnificent painted church at its centre. The monastery has undergone careful cleaning in recent years.

The fortifications here are actually more impressive than the frescos. On the church's southern exterior wall is a depiction of the Siege of Constantinople, while on the porch is a representation of the Last Judgment, all on a background of blue. Inside the narthex, on a wall facing the original carved iconostasis, is a portrait of Prince Petru Rareș (Moldovița's founder) and his family offering the church to Christ. All these paintings date from 1537. In the monastery's small museum is Petru Rareș' original throne and the 'Golden Apple' awarded by Unesco for the uniqueness of Bucovina's painted monasteries.

⊨ Sleeping & Eating

See www.ruraltourism.ro for some great homestays in Vama, a small village 14km south of Moldovița on the main Suceava–Vatra Dornei road.

Letitia Orsvischi Pension PENSION €
(⌨0745-869 529; letita _orsivschi@yahoo.com; Str Gării 20; s/d incl half-board 100/200) In Vama, there's a painted-egg exhibit and a small ethnographic museum. Rooms are simple but clean. Follow the signs with painted eggs. No breakfast. Only French, Romanian and a little German spoken.

Casa Alba HOTEL €
(⌨0230-340 404; www.casa-alba.suceava.ro; s/d/ste 70/90/150 lei; ⊜🛜) You certainly won't feel a monastic asceticism in this modern villa with large rooms, couches and free wi-

fi. Follow the one road heading south 5km west of Frasin and 3km east of Vama.

❶ Getting There & Away

As the time of writing, the rail line to Vatra Moldoviței, the closest station to the monastery, had been knocked out due to flooding. Repairs were not forthcoming. Your best bet is to take one of the eight daily trains from Suceava to Vama (15 lei, one hour) and hitchhike the final 15km.

SUCEVIȚA

Sucevița Monastery (adult/child 3/1 lei) is the largest of the Bucovina painted monasteries. The church inside the fortified quadrangular enclosure (built between 1582 and 1601) is almost completely covered in frescos. As you enter you first see the *Ladder of Virtues* fresco covering most of the northern exterior wall, which depicts the 30 steps to paradise. On the southern exterior wall is Jesse's genealogical tree symbolising the continuity of the Old and New Testaments. The tree grows from the reclining figure of Jesse, who is flanked by a row of ancient Greek philosophers. To the left is the Virgin, with angels holding a red veil over her head. Mysteriously, the western wall remains blank. Legend has it that the artist fell off his scaffolding and died, leaving artists of the time too scared to follow in his footsteps.

⊨ Sleeping & Eating

It's worth spending a night here and doing a little hiking in the surrounding hills. Rough camping is possible in the field across the stream from the monastery, as well as along the road from Moldovița. The road from Marginea to Sucevița is littered with *cazare* (room for rent) signs.

Ieremia Movila PENSION €
(⌨0230-417 501; www.ieremiamovila.ro, in Romanian; r 100 lei; 🅿⊜🛜) Close enough to Sucevița for views of the monastery, the rooms are surpassingly nice for the area, with great bathrooms, balconies and flat-screen TVs. On-site restaurant.

Pensiunea Emilia PENSION €
(⌨0743-117 827; Str Bercheza 173; r per person 60 lei) Of the handful of pensions in the immediate area, this one is most homey. Walk about 500m up the road opposite the monastery. No breakfast.

❶ Getting There & Away

Take one of the hourly maxitaxis from Suceava to Rădăuți (8 lei, 45 minutes), then switch to one of the southbound maxitaxis leaving hourly from an unmarked intersection about 300m east (towards Piaţa Unirii) from the bus station. Ask the driver to stop at Suceviţa.

NORTHERN DOBROGEA

In any Romania photo essay, the Northern Dobrogea region may very well have the least representation. There are no breathtaking mountains, ancient churches, striking castles or former princes with an unsettling bloodlust. Yet, despite being considered the 'least Romanian' part of the country, this is where you'll find the strongest evidence of Romania's proud connection to ancient Rome in the form of statues, busts, sarcophagi and other archaeological finds.

There are also extraordinary natural attractions here. You can soothe your body with sunshine and curative mud at the Black Sea coast (Marea Neagră). Alternatively there is the Danube Delta, a tangled web of canals, riverbeds and wetlands where fish leap out of the water to gulp the insects, birds hover above to snatch the fish, humans lurk nearby to photograph the birds, and insects converge to feast on the humans – the circle of life.

Constanţa

POP 302,000

Constanţa is the gateway to Romania's seaside activities. Sadly, price hikes have made Black Sea vacations fairly expensive, even by Western European standards. Staying in private homes (cazare) or camping can ease expenses.

Constanţa's original name, Tomis, means 'cut to pieces', in reference to Jason's beloved Medea, who cut up her brother Apsyrtus and threw the pieces into the sea near the present-day city.

After Constanţa was taken by Romania in 1877, a railway line to Bucharest was built. By the early 1900s it was a fashionable seaside resort frequented by European royalty.

The city offers a bit of everything: beaches, a picturesque Old Town, archaeological treasures and a few excellent museums.

◎ Sights

History & Archaeological Museum MUSEUM
(Piaţa Ovidiu 12; adult/child 11/5 lei) Cool that sunburn while admiring archaeological artefacts, the bones of a 2nd-century woman and mammoth tusks at Constanţa's leading

nonbeach attraction. Roman-era Tomis archaeological fragments spill over onto the surrounding square. Facing these is a glass museum, which shelters a gigantic 3rd-century **Roman mosaic** discovered in 1959. The **statue of Ovid**, erected on Piaţa Ovidiu in 1887, commemorates the Latin poet who was exiled to Constanţa in AD 8; rumour has it that he hated the place.

Art Museum & Gallery ART GALLERY
(Muzeul de Artă Populară; B-dul Tomis 84; adult/child 9/4.50 lei; ◎9am-7.30pm Mon-Fri) Mostly still-life and landscape paintings and sculptures. Contemporary exhibitions are held in an adjoining art gallery.

Naval History Museum MUSEUM
(Muzeul Marinei Române; Str Traian 53; adult/child 8/4 lei; ◎9am-5pm Wed-Sun) Housed in the old Navy high school, there's two floors of fantastic displays: recovered artefacts, costumes, ancient documents and naval items.

Planetarium PLANETARIUM
(B-dul Mamaia; adult/child 10/5 lei) Heading north towards Mamaia, you pass Constanţa's, on the southeastern shores of Lake Tăbăcăriei.

Folk Art Museum MUSEUM
(Muzeul de Artă Populară; B-dul Tomis 32; adult/child 5/2.50 lei) Filled with handicrafts, costumes and rotating temporary exhibitions.

Near the city's main intersection, B-dul Ferdinand and B-dul Tomis, is Parcul Victoriei, which has remains of the 3rd-century **Roman city wall** and the 6th-century Butchers' Tower, loads of Roman sculptures and the modern **Victory monument** (1968).

Mahmudiye Mosque (Moscheia Mahmudiye; Str Arhiepiscopiei), dating from 1910, has a 140-step minaret you can climb when the gate is unlocked. Two blocks further down the same street is an **Orthodox Cathedral** (1885). Along the promenade is the **Genoese lighthouse** (1860) and pier, with a fine view of old Constanţa.

Delphi (☎0722-336 686; www.divingdelphi.ro) provides a range of scuba-diving opportunities.

⊨ Sleeping

In high season, people meet every arriving train in Constanţa and line the roadside outside Mamaia with cazare signs; some simply jangle their keys. Room prices range from 60 to 120 lei. The rooms are usually plain, with shared bathroom and scant privacy. Always agree on a price and view the room before handing over money. The nearest camping ground is north of Mamaia (see p754).

Hotel Maria HOTEL €€
(☎0241-611 711; B-dul 1 Decembrie 1918 2D; s/d 160/200 lei; ❄☎) This modern, spotless option, across from the park facing the train station, has lots of glass, chrome and deep blues to soothe your sun-withered nerves.

Hotel Florentina HOTEL €
(☎0241-512 535; B-dul IC Brătianu 24; s 89 lei, d 95-105 lei) It's one of the better-value places in town, with clean rooms and a large breakfast, but, apart from the train/bus stations, it's not near anything. Turn left outside the stations, then left again at the massive Str IC Brătianu; it's on the right.

Hotel Class HOTEL €€
(☎0241-660 766; www.hotelclass.ro; Str Răscoala din 1907 nr 1; s/d/ste 180/190/235 lei; ❄☎) One of the swankiest places in town, everything here is new or new-looking enough to make it worth the price. Breakfast is 20 lei.

Hotel Tineretului HOTEL €
(☎0241-613 590; B-dul Tomis 24; s/d 100/120 lei) Cheap for good reason: the rooms are worn, the bathrooms woeful and the reception indifferent. However, the location is terrific.

✗ Eating & Drinking

TOP CHOICE Irish Pub INTERNATIONAL €€
(www.irishpub.ro; Str Ştefan cel Mare 1; mains 15-43 lei) The attractive, orderly wood interior and exceptional menu (one of the best in Romania) miss the true mark of an Irish pub, though you can get your pint of Guinness here. The popular terrace partially overlooks the sea.

On Plonge SEAFOOD €€
(Portul Turistic Tomis; mains 15-30 lei) This brawny portside eatery has an informal, everyman vibe and specialises in fresh fish hauled in off the boat. It gets packed on summer nights and service suffers accordingly. The views out over the port and the Old Town are stunning.

Marco Polo ITALIAN €€
(☎0241-617 537; www.marccopolo.ro; Str Mircea cel Bătrân 103; mains 17-37 lei; ☎) A swanky Italian restaurant where servers swarm to keep patrons happy. Portions are generous and the pizza, pasta, meat, fish and veggie dishes are delicious.

To Histria (33km)

Mihail Kogălniceanu Airport

Lake Tasaul

To Hârşova (49km); Năvodari ● Staţiunea Năvodari

E60
2A

● Mamaia Sat

Lake Mamaia (Siutghiol)

Ovidiu ● ● Mamaia

Lake Tăbăcăriei

A2
Valu lui Traian ● Palas ● ● Constanţa
3

To Cernavodă (45km)

Cumpăna ●

BLACK SEA

Danube & Black Sea Canal
Agigea ●

Techirghiol ● ● Eforie Nord
38 Lake Belona

● Eforie Sud
Lake Techirghiol

Tuzla ●

To Negru Vodă (31km)
E87
39

● Costineşti

Lake Tatlageac

Pecineaga ● ● Olimp
● Neptun
● Jupiter
● Cap-Aurora
To Negru Vodă (20km) ● Venus
● Saturn
● Mangalia

Lake Mangalia
Albeşti ● Limanu ● Doi Mai

Vama Veche ●

BULGARIA

To Varna (24km) ● Dunrankulak

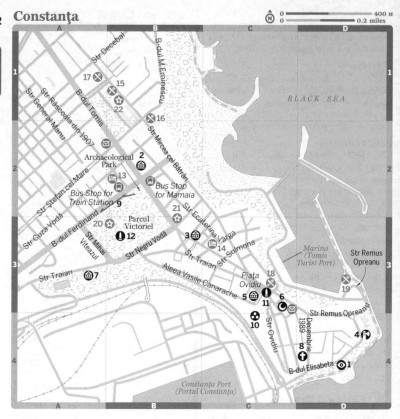

New Pizzico PIZZA €€
(www.newpizzico.ro; Piaţa Ovidiu 7; mains 11-50 lei;
🛜) Wood-fired pizza and a terrace are its
main draw, but Pizzico also offers truffles
(by request), pasta, buffalo wings, fish
(summer only) and salads. They deliver.

Café D'Art CAFE €€
(B-dul Tomis 97; mains 15-36 lei; ⊘9am-midnight)
The terrace is lovely and food is available,
but the long drinks menu (cocktails 15 lei)
makes it popular as an evening drinking
hole.

☆ Entertainment

Cinema Studio CINEMA
(www.ampmleisure.com; cnr B-bul Tomis & Str
Negru Vodă) Presents popular films.

Cinema Grădină Tomis CINEMA
(B-dul Ferdinand) In summer, films are also
screened at Cinema Grădină Tomis, an
outside cinema in Archaeological Park.

**Metamorfoze State Drama Theatre &
Opera** THEATRE/OPERA
(Str Mircea cel Bătrân 97) Tickets sold at the
ticket office (www.opera-balet-constanta.ro, in
Romanian; B-dul Tomis 97; ⊘10am-5pm Mon-Fri).
The theatre is also home to the Filarmon-
ica Marea Neagră (Black Sea Philharmonic)
and the Oleg Danovski Ballet Theatre.

ℹ Information

Banca Transilvania (B-dul Tomis 57) Changes
travellers cheques, gives unlimited cash advances on Visa and MasterCard and has an ATM.

Central post office & telephone office (B-dul
Tomis 79-81) The telephone office has free
internet and wi-fi.

County Hospital (Spitalul Judetean; ☑0241-
662 222; B-dul Tomis 145) North of the centre.

Latina Tourism (☑0241-639 713; escapade@
latina.ro; B-dul Ferdinand 70; ⊘9am-6pm Mon-
Fri, to 1pm Sat) A recommended travel agency
that can help find local accommodation.

Constanţa

⦿ Sights

Planet Games (cnr Str Ştefan cel Mare & Str Răscoala din 1907; per hr 4 lei; ⊙24hr) Internet.

❶ Getting There & Away

Air

In summer there are international flights from Athens and sometimes İstanbul to/from Constanţa's **Mihail Kogalniceanu airport** (☑0241-255 100; www.mk-airport.ro), 25km from the centre. At the time of writing, **Ryanair** (www.ryanair.com) was running summer-only flights here from Pisa and Bologna, Italy.

Tarom (☑0241-662 632; Str Ştefan cel Mare 15; ⊙8am-6pm Mon-Fri, 8.30am-12.30pm Sat) no longer flies out of Constanţa, but can book flights from Bucharest. **Carpatair** (☑0241-255 422; constanta@carpatair.com) flies to Timişoara six days a week. Its office is at Constanţa's airport.

Bus

Constanţa has two bus stations. From the **Autogara Sud** (Southern Bus Station; B-dul Ferdinand), next to the train station, buses to İstanbul

(125 lei, 10 hours) depart daily. Tickets are sold in advance from **Condor Tour** (☑0241-660 696) next to the general ticket office. Buses go to Chişinău Monday and Friday (60 lei, nine hours) at 7pm. Buses 100 and 40 go to Mamaia.

From Constanţa's **Autogara Nord** (Northern Bus Station; Str Soveja 35), just off B-dul Tomis, about 4km north of the centre, services include one daily maxitaxi to Iaşi (58 lei, eight hours) and twice hourly maxitaxis to Tulcea (26 lei, 2½ hours) from 6am to 7.30pm.

If you're travelling south along the Black Sea coast, buses are infinitely more convenient than trains. From Constanţa's train station, turn right and walk to the long queue of maxitaxis, buses and private cars destined for Mangalia, stopping at Eforie Nord, Eforie Sud, Neptun-Olimp, Venus and Saturn.

Train

Constanţa's train station is near the southern bus station at the west end of B-dul Ferdinand.

The **Agenţia de Voiaj CFR** (Aleea Vasile Canarache 4; ⊙7.30am-8.30pm Mon-Sat, to 2.30pm Sat) sells long-distance tickets only; for local train service (down the coast), buy tickets at the train station.

There are 11 to 15 daily trains to Bucharest (49 lei, 2½ to 4½ hours) and daily services to Suceava (66 lei), Cluj-Napoca, Satu Mare, Galaţi, Timişoara and other destinations. As many as 19 trains a day head from Constanţa to Mangalia (6 lei, one to 1¼ hours).

Mamaia

Mamaia is where the real action is, if by 'action' you mean pretty beaches, pretty people and pretty dreadful hangovers. This 8km strip of golden sands, restaurants and nightclubs is Romania's most popular resort. Avoid visiting in July and August, when prices spike.

🏃 Activities

Mamaia's number-one attraction is its wide, golden **beach**, which stretches the length of the resort. The further north you go, the less crowded it becomes.

Insula Ovidiu
BOAT TOUR

In summer, **boats** (return 20 lei; ⊙9am-midnight) ferry tourists across Lake Mamaia to Insula Ovidiu (Ovidiu Island), where Ovid's tomb is located. They depart every 30 minutes from the Tic-Tac wharf opposite the Staţia Cazino bus stop.

Aqua Magic
WATER PARK

(adult/under 12yr 60/40 lei) The huge Aqua Magic amusement park is about 200m from Hotel Perla, beyond Mamaia's main entrance.

Sleeping & Eating

Trying to lure tourists back during the recession, accommodation prices on the coast dropped significantly in 2010. It's impossible to say how long these deals will last. For information about rooms in private homes, see Sleeping, p750. Most private homes will be a 10- to 20-minute maxitaxi ride from the beach. **Centrul de Cazare Cazino** (☑0241-831 200) has lists of available accommodation. Booking hotel rooms through travel agencies in Constanţa can save you as much as 15% on the rack rate.

Almost every hotel has an adjoining restaurant and there are numerous fast-food stands and self-serve restaurants lining the boardwalk – all are meagre. Nightclubs start after Hotel Victoria and continue ad infinitum.

Hotel Turist HOTEL €
(☑0241-831 006; B-dul Mamaia 288; s/d 110/140 lei) Conditions here are *much* nicer than similarly priced rooms on the beach, with fridges, good beds and new bathrooms. It's close enough for those wanting the beach scene without the beach nightlife blaring through the walls. Take bus 40 from the train station.

Hotel Doina HOTEL €
(☑0241-831 815; www.hoteldoina.ro; s/d 120/150 lei) Relatively speaking, the best deal on the beach. Rooms are basic but clean. No breakfast. Frugal university students often book a double room, then cram in eight people for an extreme budget weekend at the beach. Hint, hint.

GPM Campground CAMPING GROUND €
(☑0241-831 002; sites per person 18 lei, bungalows 119-460 lei, caravans 120 lei) This fine and lively place is about 2km north of Mamaia. Call or arrive early to reserve a site near the beach. Several buses and maxitaxis, including bus 23 and maxitaxi 23E, pass by the entrance – tell the driver where you want to stop as you board the bus. The excellent self-serve restaurant is open to campers and non-campers alike.

Hotel Bulevard HOTEL €€
(☑0241-831 533; www.complexbulevard.ro; B-dul Mamaia 294; s/d three-star 191/212 lei, s/d four-star 242/276 lei; ✳☎☒) Modern and posh, offering full services and free wi-fi. Next to Hotel Turist.

ℹ Information

Every hotel has a currency exchange and ATMs are easy to find.

Asociatia de Promovare Litoral (☑0241-831 321; www.asociatia-litoral.ro) Located inside the telegondola terminus, by Hotel Perla, they can help with accommodation and tours of Dobrogea.

Expo-Litoral Turism (☑0241-555 000; www.infolitoral.ro; Constanţa Chamber of Commerce Bldg, B-dul Alexandru Lăpuşneanu 185; ⊙9am-4pm Mon-Fri) Behind a blue-glass facade, this is a highly informed and friendly private travel agency.

Post office and telephone office South of the Cazino complex on the promenade.

ℹ Getting There & Around

Tickets for trains departing from Constanţa can be bought in advance at the **Agenţia de Voiaj CFR**, adjoining the post and telephone office on the promenade in Mamaia.

The quickest way to travel between Constanţa and Mamaia is by maxitaxi. Maxitaxis 23, 23E and 301 depart regularly from Constanţa's train station, stopping at major hotels. Also, bus 40 goes to the entrance of Mamaia and a double-decker tourist bus goes from the train station to the north end of Mamaia (3 lei).

A taxi from Constanţa to Mamaia will cost about 25 lei, though some drivers try to gouge tourists for more. Agree on a price before getting in the car. Call ☑0241-953 to order a taxi.

In summer a 'train' runs up and down Mamaia's 5km-long boardwalk.

Vehicles not registered in Constanţa must pay a road tax when entering Mamaia (single entry/day pass 3/5 lei).

Neptun-Olimp

Before the 1989 revolution, the twin resort of Neptun-Olimp was the exclusive tourist complex of Romania's Communist Party. Olimp, a huge complex of hotels facing the beach, is the party place. Neptun, 1km south, is separated from the Black Sea by two small lakes amid some lush greenery.

The resort complex offers a reasonable range of activities, including tennis, windsurfing, jet-skiing, sailing, minigolf, bowling and discos.

Hotel Craiova (☑0241-701 048; www.hotelurineptun.ro, in Romanian; d 100-130 lei; ☒) is a two-star property just 75m from the beach. Rooms are a tad musty, but otherwise bright with good beds and surprisingly comfortable communist garage-sale furniture. Some have balconies and a refrigerator will cost 8 lei per day.

Hotel Slatina (☑0241-701 046; d 50-65 lei; ✴), next to Craiova, is a definite step down in quality, but acceptable for the price. Breakfast is included at both properties.

All trains travelling from Bucharest or Constanța to Mangalia stop at Halta Neptun station, midway between the two resorts and about a 15-minute walk to the hotels listed. For tickets, the **CFR office** (Str Plopilor) is inside Neptun's Hotel Apollo, northwest of Lake Neptun II.

Private maxitaxis run between the resort towns and Mangalia.

Mangalia

POP 39,600

Formerly ancient Greek Callatis, Mangalia, founded in the 6th century BC, contains several minor archaeological sites. With its many tour groups of elderly Europeans, it's not a party town.

◉ Sights

Mangalia spreads like a beach town along the coast, with nothing of note further than a few blocks inland. The train station is 1km north of the centre. Turn right as you exit and follow Șos Constanței (the main and only road you're ever likely to use, aside from the beachfront road) south. At the roundabout, turn left for Hotel Mangalia, the Izvor Hercules fountain and the beach, or go straight ahead for the pedestrianised section of Șos Constanței and most facilities, including the Callatis Archaeological Museum and the **Casă de Cultură**, which has a large socialist mural on its facade.

Callatis Archaeological Museum MUSEUM
(Str Șoseaua Constanței 26; adult/child 5/2.50 lei) It has a good collection of Roman sculptures and artefacts. Just past the high-rise building next to the museum are some remnants of a 4th-century **Roman-Byzantine necropolis**.

Palaeo-Christian basilica CHURCH
At the south side of Hotel Mangalia, along Str Izvor, are the ruins of a 6th-century Palaeo-Christian basilica and a **fountain** (Izvorul Hercules) dispensing sulphurous mineral water that, despite the smell, some people drink.

Moscheea Esmahan Sultan MOSQUE
(Sultan Esmahan Mosque; Str Oituz; admission 4 lei; ☉10am-7pm) One block east of the post office is this Turkish mosque. Built in 1525, it's surrounded by a lovely garden and well-kept cemetery.

Muzeul Poarta Callatiana MUSEUM
Located in the basement of Hotel President are the remains of the walls of the Callatis citadel, dating from the 1st to the 7th centuries.

🛏 Sleeping & Eating

Pensiune Oituz PENSION €
(☑0720-501 525; Str Oituz 11; r without bathroom 90-150 lei; ✴🛜) About 150m up the road from the mosque, and away from the beach, this modern, comfy, three-star pension has seven rooms, outfitted with flat-screen TVs, refrigerators and new bathrooms. Reception is in the travel agency downstairs. No breakfast.

Hotel Zenit HOTEL €
(☑0241-751 645; Str Teilor 7; s 95-135 lei, d 130-180 lei) A surprisingly pleasant two-star option on the promenade.

Hotel President HOTEL €€
(☑0241-755 861; www.hpresident.com; Str Treilor 6; s/d/ste from 206/281/412; ✴🛜🏊) This four-star luxury hotel is the top place to stay south of Constanța. Sea-view rooms, though higher in price, are worthwhile.

Hostel Sailor HOTEL €
(☑0241-753 492; Decembrie 1918 nr 7a; d 90 lei; ✴) At the south end of Ștefan cel Mare street, these bright, clean rooms are good value. No breakfast.

Hotel Corsa HOTEL €€
(☑0341-108 576; www.hotelcorsa.com; Str Teilor 11; s/d 260/280 lei; ✴🛜) A solid three-star option with a bar-terrace, balconies, good beds and minibars in rooms. There's a 30% discount if you stay more than three nights.

Cafe del Mar CAFE €€
(Str Treilor 4; mains 12-30 lei) A great terrace, stylish interiors and one of the most varied, fanciful menus around, including US-style buffalo wings (11 lei) and potato skins (14 lei). Next to Hotel President.

Puiu SEAFOOD €€
(mains 18-45 lei) A small, family-run seafood restaurant on far north side of the pier.

❶ Information

Most hotels have currency exchanges. Get cash advances on Visa and MasterCard at the **Banca Comercială Română** (Șos Constanței 25).

The **telephone office** (Str Ștefan cel Mare 14-15) and post office are in the same building.

ℹ Getting There & Away

Bus

Maxitaxis running up the coast from Constanţa to Vama Veche (every 20 minutes) stop at Mangalia's train station, post office and all along Şos Constanţei. Maxitaxis to Constanţa (6 lei) run from 5am to 11pm. Pay the driver. Private and city buses stop in front of the train station.

A bus to Varna, Bulgaria, leaves from the train station at 8.45am (40 lei). Call ☎0743-335 148 to reserve.

Train

The **Agenţia de Voiaj CFR** (Str Stefan cel Mare 14-15; ⏱7.30am-8.30pm Mon-Sat, to 1.30pm Sun) adjoins the central post office.

Mangalia is at the end of the line from Constanţa. In summer there are 19 daily trains between Constanţa and Mangalia (5.40 lei, one to 1¼ hours), five of which are direct to/from Bucharest Nord (58 lei, 6 hours). In summer there are also express trains to/from Iaşi, Suceava, Cluj-Napoca and Timişoara.

Danube Delta

After passing through 10 countries and absorbing countless lesser waterways, the mighty Danube River pours into the Black Sea just south of the Ukrainian border at an average of 6300 cubic metres of water per second. The Danube splits into three separate channels – Chilia, Sulina and Sfântu Gheorghe – that fan out and create a constantly evolving 4187-sq-km wetland of marshes, reed islets and sandbars, providing sanctuary for 300 species of birds and 160 species of fish. Reed marshes cover 156,300 hectares, constituting one of the world's largest single expanses of reed beds.

The Danube Delta (Delta Dunarii) is under the protection of the Administration of the Danube Delta Biosphere Reserve Authority (DDBRA), set up in response to the ecological disaster that befell the delta region during Ceauşescu's attempt to transform it into an agricultural area. Now there are 18 protected reserves (50,000 hectares) that are off limits to tourists or anglers, including the 500-year-old Leţea Forest and Europe's largest pelican colony. The areas open to visitors are a bird-watcher's paradise, with protected species such as the roller, white-tailed eagle, great white egret, mute and whooper swans, falcon and bee-eater. The delta is also on Unesco's World Heritage list.

Be sure to take food, water and lots of mosquito repellent on any expedition into the Danube Delta outside of Sulina and Sfântu Gheorghe. Warning: do not drink Danube water!

ℹ Getting Around

The Information & Ecological Education Centre (p758) in Tulcea can help book bird-watching trips.

In the delta proper it's easy to hire boats into the delta's exotic backwaters. Look for signs saying 'plimbri cu barca' (boat rides).

Hydrofoil

Hydrofoils (www.naverapide.ro) depart daily from the AFDJ Pontoon, 400m west of Hotel Delta or 200m east of the Tulcea train station. Services from Tulcea to Sulina (departing at 1.30pm, stopping in Crişan) and Sfântu Gheorghe (departing at 1.30pm, stopping in Mahmudia) take 1½ hours and cost 60 lei each way. Purchase tickets at the pontoon or on board. In high season, to guarantee a seat, reserve the night before either at the pontoon or by phone (☎0757-575 702).

Ferry

Navrom (☎0240-511 553; www.navrom.x3m.ro, in Romanian) operates passenger ferries year-round to towns and villages in the delta. Check the website or the Information & Ecological Education Centre (p758) for current information.

Navrom runs intermittent fast and slow ferries. To Sulina, the slow ferry (29 lei, four hours) departs Tulcea at 1.30pm Monday, Wednesday and Friday, returning at 7am on Tuesday, Thursday and Sunday. The fast ferry (36 lei, 2½ hours) leaves Tulcea at 1.30pm on Tuesday and Thursday, returning at 7am Wednesday and Friday.

The slow ferry to Sfântu Gheorghe (30 lei, 5½ hours) departs from Tulcea at 1.30pm on Wednesday, returning at 7am Thursday. The fast ferry (39 lei, three hours) departs Tulcea at 1.30pm on Monday and Friday, returning at 7am on Tuesday and Sunday.

Fast ferries to Periprava (43 lei, four hours) depart Tulcea at 1.30pm Monday and Wednesday, stopping at Chilia Veche. Return ferries leave Periprava at 6am Tuesday and Thursday.

Ferry tickets can be purchased at Tulcea's Navrom terminal from 11.30am to 1.30pm. There are also ticket counters on the ferries themselves.

Note that ferry schedules change frequently with the season and service is less reliable in winter.

Car

It's now possible, though not particularly cheap, to drive over the dike from Sulina to Sfântu Gheorghe. There's no public transport, so you'll have to arrange the journey through locals. This

VAMA VECHE

During the communist regime, Vama Veche (literally 'old customs point') was reserved for the staff of the Cluj-Napoca University and developed a reputation as a haven for hippies, artists and intellectuals. Even now this remote stretch of coast near the Bulgarian border holds a special place in the Romanian consciousness, conjuring up images of a bohemian paradise with desolate stretches of windswept beaches, where nudists and nonconformists of all creeds come together.

Well, sort of. Unfortunately, Vama Veche is slowly but surely moving toward the mainstream. These days, the main car park holds more than a few expensive SUVs from Bucharest. Still, there's enough of a lingering counter-culture vibe wafting in the air to make a trip here worthwhile, if this is your thing.

Despite Vama Veche's popularity, even in summer you can usually find a room. There's almost always someone standing by the road with 'cazare' sign in hand.

Stuf, off the village's main drag, is the most likeable of several beachside drinking shacks and a great place to meet fellow revellers. Tunes on the sound system range from classic AC-DC to the soundtrack of 'All That Jazz'. In a word, eclectic.

Maxitaxis serving Vama Veche run regularly from Constanţa and Mangalia.

is best done from Sulina as there are few cars available in Sfântu Gheorghe.

TULCEA
POP 92,300

Tulcea (tool-*cha*), settled by Dacians and Romans from the 7th to 1st centuries BC, is a port town and the gateway to the Danube Delta. It's usually passed through quickly en route to the delta, but it has decent restaurants and nightclubs as well as a sizeable Turkish population, giving it a refreshing multicultural flavour.

Tulcea hosts the annual **International Folk Festival of Danubian Countries** in August, when local songs, games and traditional activities are played out against a Danubian backdrop.

◉ Sights

TOP CHOICE Central Eco-Tourism Museum of the Danube Delta   AQUARIUM
(Centrul Muzeal Ecoturistic Delta Dunării; http://3d -center.ro; 14 Noiembrie nr 1; adult/student 15/5 lei) Far and away Tulcea's biggest attraction, this multimillion-euro extravaganza features dozens of aquariums filled with delta creatures big, small and crazy-looking. It's a must, especially if you're travelling with kids.

Independence Monument   MONUMENT
As you stroll along the river you'll see the Independence Monument (1904) on Citadel Hill at the far eastern end of town. You can reach this by following Str Gloriei from be-

hind the Egreta Hotel to its end. The views are superb.

Moscheia Azizie   MOSQUE
The minaret of Moscheia Azizie (Azizie Mosque; 1863) is down Str Independenţei.

Folk Art & Ethnographic Museum MUSEUM
(Str 9 Mai nr 4; adult/student 4/2 lei) This museum has Turkish and Romanian traditional costumes, rugs and carpets, and fishing nets.

Memorial   MEMORIAL
In front of the Greek Orthodox church is a memorial to the local victims of the 1989 revolution.

🛏 Sleeping

There are many areas where rough camping is permitted on the banks of the canal within a few kilometres of the city; ask at the Information & Ecological Education Centre (p758) for details.

Multiday delta tours aboard floating hotels ('boatels') is a unique, albeit pricey, way to visit the delta. Prices start at 340 lei per person per day for two-star boats and rocket up to 2200 lei for four-star boats, including full board. Check www.ddbra.ro for a list of operators.

TOP CHOICE Insula Complex   HOTEL €
(☎0240-530 908; Lake Ciuperca; s/d 80/100 lei; 🛜) Seconds from the train station on Lake Ciuperca, this two-star option has an on-site restaurant and large rooms. Turn right out of the train station and cross the bridge to the island.

Danube Delta

Map legend:
- Strictly Protected Area
- Buffer Area
- Ecological Restoration Area

Hotel Europolis   HOTEL €€
(✆0240-512 443; www.europolis.ro; Str Păcii 20; s/d 110/170 lei; ❄@) Value-conscious travellers will enjoy these newly renovated rooms with huge bathrooms. They have cable internet only. For about the same price, you can also stay at the hotel's Complexul Touristic Europolis, a resortlike place by Lake Câșla, 2km outside of Tulcea. The site is lovely, with walking trails in the thick of nature.

Hotel Select   HOTEL €€
(✆0240-506 180; www.calypsosrl.ro; Str Păcii 6; s/d 132/152 lei; ⊜❄@☎) A standard-issue modern hotel with blandly carpeted rooms and a dated '80s feel, it's nevertheless good value for its location (a block away from the port), friendly staff and excellent restaurant.

Hotel Delta   HOTEL €€
(✆0240-514 720; www.deltahotelro.com; Str Isaccei 2; s/d 3-star 220/280 lei, 4-star 280/360 lei; ⊜❄☎☒) This landmark hotel situated toward the eastern end of the port offers both three- and four-star accommodation in adjoining buildings. The three-star rooms, with air-conditioning and balcony views, are definitely better value.

✖ Eating & Drinking

There's a string of cafes and kebab and fast-food joints along Str Unirii.

Restaurant Select   ROMANIAN €€
(Str Păcii 6; mains 12-41 lei) The varied multilingual menu offers fish, frog legs, pizza and the local speciality, *tochitura Dobrogeana* (pan-fried pork with spicy sauce).

Restaurant Faleza   ROMANIAN €€
(Str Gării 34; mains 6-30 lei) Watch ferry traffic from this terrace fronting the promenade, while eating pizza, fish, traditional Romanian fare or breakfast.

Trident Pizzeria   PIZZA €€
(Str Babadag; mains 12-19 lei) An excellent spot for cheesy pizzas and fast pasta, opposite Hotel Select.

❶ Information

Anason Pharmacy (Str Babadag 8) Has an all-night dispensary.

Ibis Tours (✆0240-512 787; www.ibis-tours.ro; Str Dimitrie Sturza 6; ☉9am-6pm Mon-Sat) Arranges wildlife and bird-watching tours in the delta and Dobrogea, led by professional ornithologists, and operates two floating hotels.

Information & Ecological Education Centre (✆0240-519 214; www.deltaturism.ro; Str Portului 34a) A representative of Antrec and run by the Danube Delta Biosphere Reserve (DDBR), the centre can book accommodation in homes, hotels and pensions and help arrange tours. No fixed hours.

Post office (Str Babadag 5; ⊘7am-8pm Mon-Fri, 8am-noon Sat)

Raiffeisen Bank Directly across from Hotel Delta.

Telephone centre (⊘7am-8pm) In the same building as the post office. Free wi-fi and computer for checking email.

Tourism information centre (☑0240-519 130; www.primaria-tulcea.ro; Str Gării 26) Mainly Tulcea-focused, it also offers some Danube and boat tour assistance. It's hidden slightly back from the river promenade, next to the Capitania Portului building.

❶ Getting There & Away

The bus and train stations and the Navrom ferry terminal are adjacent to one another.

The **Agenţia de Voiaj CFR** (Str Unirii 4; ⊘8am-3.30pm Mon-Fri) is on the corner of Str Babadag. The **train station** (Str Portului) has two slow trains a day to Constanţa (18 lei, five hours) and one daily train to Bucharest (47 lei, six hours).

The **bus station** adjoins the **Navrom ferry terminal** (Str Portului). As many as 15 daily buses and maxitaxis head to Bucharest (60 lei), at least nine to Galaţi (16 lei) and one to Iaşi (60 lei). Maxitaxis to Constanţa (27 lei) leave every half-hour from 5.30am to 8pm.

TULCEA TO SULINA

Almost 64km down the shortest channel of the Danube sits Sulina, the delta's largest town. Its once sleepy and dusty esplanade has been comprehensively overhauled and now features an ATM, well-stocked markets and smart restaurants. Those seeking tranquillity and traditional delta village life can find it in nearby **Cardon**, accessible from Sulina either by a boat trip or by a far less scenic maxitaxi ride.

The Navrom ferry's first stop is at **Partizani**, from where you can find a fisher to row you to the three lakes to the north – Ta-

---

DELTA PERMITS

Though locals scoff and dismiss the idea of permits (10 lei), there are occasional checks and you will be fined 100 lei if you don't have one. If on a group excursion of any kind, these are automatically handled by the operator. If you hire a local fisher, ask to see a valid permit. If you go boating or foraging independently or simply visit a village, legally you must have one. The Tulcea Tourist Information Centre can advise on getting a permit.

---

taru, Lung and Mester. Next stop is **Maliuc**, where there is a hotel and camping ground for 80 people. North of Maliuc is **Lake Furtuna**, a snare for bird-watchers.

The next stop for the ferry is the junction with Old Danube, 1km upstream from **Crişan**. There are several pensions in the village, all charging as little as 50 lei to 60 lei per person. Try **Andrei Oprisan** (☑0240-547 034; s/d 90/120 lei) or **Pensiune Pocora** (☑0240-547 036; d 200 lei). At the main Crişana ferry dock, ask about side trips to **Mila 23** or **Caraorman**.

In Sulina, **Pensiunea Ana** (☑0724-421 976; pensiuneana@yahoo.com; r 60 lei) is run out of the home of a caring family. Breakfast is 10 lei. **Pensiune Delta Sulina** (☑0722-749 252; www.sulinaturism.ro; per person 43 lei) is a comfortable five-room place charging 16 lei for breakfast and 35 lei for dinner.

There's a camping area on the road to the beach.

For information on ferries and hydrofoils see p756.

UNDERSTAND ROMANIA

History

Ancient Romania & Dracula

Ancient Romania was inhabited by Thracian tribes, more commonly known as Dacians. The Greeks established trading colonies along the Black Sea from the 7th century BC, and the Romans conquered in AD 105–06. The slave-owning Romans brought with them their civilisation and the Latin language.

From the 10th century the Magyars (Hungarians) expanded into Transylvania, and by the 13th century all of Transylvania was under the Hungarian crown.

The Romanian-speaking principalities of Wallachia and Moldavia offered strong resistance to the Ottomans' northern expansion in the 14th and 15th centuries. Mircea the Old, Vlad Ţepeş and Ştefan cel Mare (Stephen the Great) were legendary figures in this struggle.

Vlad Drăculea, ruling prince of Wallachia from 1456 to 1462 and 1476 to 1477, posthumously gained the moniker 'Ţepeş' (Impaler) after his favoured form of punishing his enemies – impaling. A dull wooden stake was carefully inserted into the anus, driven slowly through the body avoiding vital organs, until it emerged from the mouth, resulting in hours, even days, of agony before death. He is perhaps more legendary as the inspiration for 19th-century novelist Bram Stoker's Count Dracula. (Vlad's surname, Drăculea, means 'son of the dragon', after his father, Vlad Dracul, a knight of the Order of the Dragon.)

When the Turks conquered Hungary in the 16th century, Transylvania became a vassal of the Ottoman Empire. In 1600 the three Romanian states – Transylvania, Wallachia and Moldavia – were briefly united under Mihai Viteazul (Michael the Brave). In 1687 Transylvania fell under Habsburg rule.

In 1859 Alexandru Ioan Cuza was elected to the thrones of Moldavia and Wallachia, creating a national state, which in 1862 took the name Romania. The reformist Cuza was forced to abdicate in 1866, and his place was taken by the Prussian prince Karl of Hohenzollern, who took the name Carol I. Romania declared independence from the Ottoman Empire in 1877, and, after the 1877–78 War of Independence, Dobrogea became part of Romania.

Romania in WWI & WWII

In 1916 Romania entered WWI on the side of the Triple Entente (Britain, France and Russia) with the objective of taking Transylvania – where 60% of the population was Romanian – from Austria-Hungary. The Central Powers (Germany and Austria-Hungary) occupied Wallachia. With the defeat of Austria-Hungary in 1918, the unification of Banat, Transylvania and Bucovina with Romania was finally achieved.

In the years leading to WWII, Romania, under foreign minister Nicolae Titulescu, sought security in a French alliance. On 30 August 1940 Romania was forced to cede northern Transylvania to Hungary by order of Nazi Germany and fascist Italy.

To defend the interests of the ruling classes, General Ion Antonescu forced King Carol II to abdicate in favour of his son Michael. Antonescu then imposed a fascist dictatorship. In June 1941 he joined Hitler's anti-Soviet war with gruesome results: 400,000 Romanian Jews and 36,000 Roma were murdered at Auschwitz and other camps.

On 23 August 1944 Romania suddenly changed sides, captured 53,159 German soldiers and declared war on Nazi Germany. By this act, Romania salvaged its independence and shortened the war.

Ceauşescu

After the war, the Soviet-engineered return of Transylvania enhanced the prestige of the left-wing parties, which won the parliamentary elections of November 1946. A year later the monarchy was abolished and the Romanian People's Republic was proclaimed.

Soviet troops withdrew in 1958, and after 1960 Romania adopted an independent foreign policy under two leaders: Gheorghe Gheorghiu-Dej (leader from 1952 to 1965) and his protégé Nicolae Ceauşescu (1965 to 1989).

Ceauşescu's domestic policy was chaotic and megalomaniacal. In 1974 the post of president was created for him. He placed his wife Elena, son Nicu and three brothers in important political positions during the 1980s. Some of Ceauşescu's expensive follies were projects like the Danube Canal from Agigea to Cernavo, the disruptive redevelopment of southern Bucharest (1983–89) and the 'systemisation' of agriculture by the resettlement of rural villagers into concrete apartment blocks.

The late 1980s saw workers' riots in Braşov and severe food shortages in the winter of 1988–89. But the spark that ignited Romania came on 15 December 1989, when Father Lászlo Tökés publicly condemned the dictator from his Hungarian church in Timişoara. Police attempts to arrest demonstrating parishioners failed and civil unrest quickly spread.

On 21 December in Bucharest, an address by Ceauşescu during a rally was cut short by anti-Ceauşescu demonstrators. They booed him, then retreated to the boulevard between Piaţa Universităţii and Piaţa Romană, only to be crushed hours later by police gunfire and armoured cars. The next morning thousands more demonstrators took to the streets. At midday Ceauşescu reappeared with his wife on the balcony of the Central Committee building to speak, only to be forced to flee by helicopter. The couple were arrested in Târgovişte, taken to a military base and, on 25 December, executed by a firing squad.

The National Salvation Front (FSN) swiftly took control. In May 1990 it won the country's first 'democratic' elections – some European observers reported voter coercion and intimidation in rural areas – placing Ion Iliescu at the helm as president and Petre Roman as prime minister. In Bucharest, student protests against this former communist ruler were ruthlessly squashed by 20,000 coal miners shipped in courtesy of Iliescu. Ironically when the miners returned in September 1991, it was to force the resignation of Petre Roman, who was blamed for worsening living conditions.

Modern Romania

Romania's birth as a modern nation was a difficult one. In December 1999 President Constantinescu dismissed Radul Vasile and replaced him with former National Bank of Romania governor, Mugur Isărescu. But by mid-2000 Isărescu was fighting for his political life after the opposition accused him of mismanagement of the State Property Fund. This was followed in May 2000 by the collapse of the National Fund for Investment (NFI), which saw thousands of investors lose their savings.

Romania joined the Council of Europe in 1993. The EU started accession talks with Romania in March 2000, and the country joined NATO in 2004. All this came as Romania chummed up with the USA, allowing its Iraq-bound military to set up bases and granting lucrative construction projects to American companies – something some EU members weren't happy with. In 2007 the EU granted Romania membership, though Brussels warned it would continue to monitor Romania's progress in fighting corruption and organised crime.

Romania was threatened with EU sanctions after reviews in 2007 and 2008, though none was handed down. In 2009, though minor progress had been noted, they were again reproached for lack of momentum.

People

The Romanians

Romanians make up 89% of the population; Hungarians are the next largest ethnic group (7%), followed by Roma (2%) and smaller populations of Ukrainians, Germans, Russians and Turks. Germans and Hungarians live almost exclusively in Transylvania, while Ukrainians and Russians live mainly near the Danube Delta, and Turks along the Black Sea coast.

The government estimates that only 400,000 Roma live in Romania, although other sources estimate between 1.5 and 2.5 million. A good site to learn more about the Roma is the Budapest-based **European Roma Rights Centre** (http://errc.org).

Religion

The majority of Romania's population (87%) is Eastern Orthodox Christian. The rest is made up of Protestants (6.8%), Catholics (5.6%) and Muslims (0.4%), along with some 39,000 Jehovah's Witnesses and 10,000 Jews.

Arts

Folk Art

Painting on glass and wood remains a popular folk art. Considered to be of Byzantine origin, this traditional peasant art was widespread in Romania from the 17th century onwards. Superstition and strong religious beliefs surrounded these icons, which were painted to protect a household from evil spirits.

The paintings of Nicolae Grigorescu (1838–1907) absorbed French Impressionism, and his canvases are alive with the colour of the Romanian countryside.

Sculpture

Romania's most famous sculptor is Constantin Brâncuşi (1876–1957), whose polished bronze and wood works are held by museums in Paris, New York and Canberra, as well as in Romania at the Museum of Art in Craiova and Bucharest's National Art Museum (p699).

Literature

Modern literature emerged in the mid-19th century in the shape of romantic poet Mihai Eminescu (1850–89), who captured the spirituality of the Romanian people in his work.

Music

The Romanian classical-music world is nearly synonymous with George Enescu (1881–1955), whose Romanian Rhapsodies 1 and 2 and opera *Odeipe* are generally considered classics.

Gheorghe Zamfir is Romania's main regrettable music export – a successfully self-promoting pan-flute player who inspires groans and, enigmatically, gets big sales abroad.

Cinema

The so-called 'Romanian Wave' in cinema is red hot and showing no signs of abating. Hits like Nae Caranfil's comedy *Filantropica* (2002) and Cristi Puiu's *The Death of Mr Lăzărescu* (2005) started things off, then in 2007 director Cristian Mungiu won the Cannes Film Festival's top prize with *4 Months, 3 Weeks and 2 Days*, a disturbing tale of illegal abortion in communist-era Romania, while the late Cristian Nemescu's film *California Dreamin'* also took honours.

More recent buzz-worthy films include the rare Romanian comedy *Tales from the Golden Age* (2009) by Cristian Mungiu and *Police,*

READING LIST

One of the country's best history books, Lucian Boia's excellent *Romania*, surveys Romania's past and present in a colourful, if philosophical, way. Robert Kaplan's *Balkan Ghosts* devotes a couple of key chapters to post-revolutionary Romania. Petru Popescu, who defected to the US in the 1970s, recounts his 1990s visit to his home country in *The Return* (2001), which interweaves his fascinating personal history under the Ceauşescu regime with tales from his extended family. Some of Isabel Fonseca's fascinating *Bury Me Standing* follows the Roma population in Romania. Dennis Deletant's *Ceauşescu and the Securitate* (1996) remains a scholarly classic on the outsized role of the secret police in Ceauşescu's Romania. Of course, the most famous 'Romanian' book is Bram Stoker's *Dracula*, which begins and ends in Transylvania.

Adjective by Corneliu Porumboiu, which won the Jury Prize in the *Un Certain Regard* section at Cannes in 2009. The 'wave' at Cannes continued in 2010, with Cristi Puiu's *Aurora* and Radu Muntean's *Tuesday, After Christmas* being selected for *Un Certain Regard*.

as 3700 species of plants (39 of which are endangered).

Bird life in the Danube Delta is unmatched. It is a major migration hub for numerous bird species and home to 60% of the world's small pygmy cormorant population.

Environment

The Land

Covering 237,500 sq km, Romania – shaped a bit like an agitated puffer fish – is made up of three main geographical regions, each with its particular features. The mighty Carpathian Mountains run down into the country's centre from the Ukraine, before curling northwards. West of these are large plateaus where villages and towns lie among the hills and valleys. East of the mountains are the low-lying plains (where most of the country's agricultural output comes from), which end at the Black Sea; and Europe's second-largest delta region, where the Danube spills into the sea.

Wildlife

Rural Romania has thriving animal populations that include chamois, lynx, fox, deer, wolf, bear and badger. There are 33,792 species of animals here (707 of which are vertebrates; 55 of these are endangered) as well

Food & Drink

Romanian Cuisine

In all its pork-y, potato-y, cabbage-y glory, Romanian cuisine shares many similarities with that of its neighbours and borrows liberally from the cultures that have occupied its land. It's mainly hearty, simple food laden with winter-insulating butter and cream, though new, upmarket Romanian restaurants are toying with the old formulas in interesting ways.

Mămăligă is essentially cornmeal mush that's boiled or fried, sometimes topped with cream and/or cheese, and proudly served to sceptical visitors. *Ciorbă* (soup) is the other mainstay of the Romanian diet and a powerful hangover remedy. Favourites include *ciorbă de burta* (tripe soup served with a dollop of sour cream) and *ciorbă de legume* (vegetable soup cooked with meat stock).

Other common dishes are *muşchi de vacă/porc/miel* (cutlet of beef/pork/lamb), *ficat* (liver), *piept de pui* (chicken breast)

ENVIRONMENTAL ISSUES

Romania may very well have more rubbish bins than any country on earth (look around, it's stunning) – the problem is getting people to use them. NGOs such as **Pro Natura** (www.pronatura.ro) and the **Transylvania Ecological Club** (www.greenagenda.org) work to spread word about how to diminish the impact of tourism on the country's environment.

Romania has the ongoing problem of cleaning up the pollution left by communist-era chemical plants. If you're on the train between Sighişoara and Cluj-Napoca, look out for the dilapidated, blackened plants in Copşa Mică, which until the early 1990s were so dangerous to the local community that some two-thirds of children showed signs of mental illness.

and *cabanos prajit* (fried sausages). Typical desserts include *plăcintă* (turnovers), *clătite* (crêpes) and *cozonac* (brioche).

Thanks to the Orthodox diet, you can always find some vegetarian dishes. Even outside of Orthodox feast holidays, try requesting the *meniu de post* (menus without meat or milk) for options such as *cartofi piure cu şniţele de soia* (mashed potatoes with soy schnitzels), *sarmale de post* (vegan cabbage rolls), *zacuscă de vinete cu ciuperci* (eggplant and mushroom dip/stew) and *tocăniţă de legume de post* (vegan vegetable stew). Otherwise, you may be limited to unexciting salads like *salată roşii* (tomato salad), *salată castraveţi* (cucumber salad) and *salată asortată* (mixed salad, usually just a mix of – guess what? – tomatoes and cucumbers).

Wine & Alcohol

Among the best Romanian wines are Cotnari, Murfatlar, Odobeşti, Târnave and Valea Călugărească. Red wines are called *negru* and *roşu*, white wine is *vin alb*, while *sec* means 'dry', *dulce* is 'sweet' and *spumos* translates as 'sparkling'. You'll find that Romanian semisweet is most people's idea of sweet and dry is closer to semisweet.

Ţuică is a once-filtered clear brandy made from fermented fruit (the most popular is plum), usually 30 proof. *Palincă* is similar, only it's filtered twice and is usually around 60 proof. Both of these are often made at home, with taste and strength varying wildly.

SURVIVAL GUIDE

Directory A–Z
Accommodation

Prices for Romanian accommodation dipped notably in 2010, in an attempt to lure travellers back during the recession. It's impossible to say how long these discounts will last. There are five main options: hostels, private homestays *(cazare)*, family-style guesthouse pensions *(pensiunes)*, hotels (a grab bag ranging from communist leftovers to boutique hotels) and camping grounds that usually include simple wooden huts *(căsuţe)*.

Budget permitting, aim for pensions, which are often lovingly run and offer an insight into how Romanians live. These generally cost 100 lei to 150 lei (about €25 to €35) per person, with an extra 30 lei to 45 lei (€7 to €10) for full board, and a little more in cities. The best online resource is www.ruraltourism.ro, otherwise contact **Antrec** (National Association of Rural, Ecological & Cultural Tourism; www.antrec.ro).

You'll find budget double rooms for under 150 lei (€35). Hostels cost around 45 lei to 60 lei (€11 to €14) for a dorm bed; sometimes private rooms (with shared bathroom) are available for 85 lei to 130 lei (€20 to €30). Hostels vary in quality, though most newer ones rival the better hostels in Western Europe in appeal and amenities. **Youth Hostels Romania** (www.hihostels-romania.ro) has information on HI hostels.

A frantic hotel renovation boom has resulted in a glut of new three- and four-star hotels, with a frustrating decline in one- and two-star options. The old stalwarts are hit and miss. Polished B&Bs are appearing, but still rare. Midrange hotels tend to cost 150 lei to 300 lei (€35 to €70) for a double, more so in Bucharest. Top-end places will generally cost more than 300 lei.

In-town camping is often in less-than-ideal locations, and conditions are sometimes quite shoddy. In most mountain areas there's a network of cabanas (cabins or chalets) with restaurants and dormitories. Prices are much lower than those of hotels and no reservations are required, but arrive early if the cabana is in a popular location.

Apă caldă (hot water) is finally ubiquitous, but air-conditioning is still unusual in budget places. Complimentary wi-fi is a fast-growing standard across all classes.

Prices are for high season, though in most areas there's very little difference between low and high season prices. It really pays to travel in pairs in Romania, as double rooms are often little more than singles – and occasionally they are the same price.

Hotels in cities will offer nonsmoking rooms, though not always in budget places. In rural areas, nonsmoking awareness is nascent at best.

PRICE RANGES

In this chapter prices quoted are for rooms with a private bathroom, and unless otherwise stated include breakfast. The following price indicators apply (for a high-season double room):

€€€	more than 300 lei
€€	151 to 300 lei
€	less than 150 lei

Activities

Bird-watching Europe's greatest wetlands, the Danube Delta, is home to the continent's largest pelican colony. Plus, most of the world's population of red-breasted geese (up to 70,000) winter here.

Cycling Mountain biking has taken off in recent years. Road cycling can be hair-rising as traffic zooms by.

Hiking Hiking is the number-one activity, which is not surprising considering the intensity of the Carpathians cutting across the country. The most popular places are in the Bucegi, Făgăraş and the Piatra Craiului.

Mountains Most outdoor fun is related to Romania's impressive Carpathians. Emergency rescue is provided by **Salvamont** (☎0-SALVAMONT; www.salvamont.org, in Romanian), a voluntary mountain-rescue organisation with 21 stations countrywide.

Skiing Ski and snowboard centres are popular, but ski runs tend to be fewer (and costlier) than many Bulgarian slopes. Sinaia and Poiana Braşov are the most popular ski slopes.

Business Hours

Normal business hours are listed below. Only places noticeably deviating from these hours are noted in individual listings.

Banks 9am-5pm Mon-Fri, 9am-noon Sat

Museums 9am or 10am-5pm or 6pm Tue-Sun

Restaurants 10am-midnight

Customs Regulations

Officially, you're allowed to import hard currency up to a maximum of €10,000 or the equivalent. Valuable goods over €1000 should be declared upon arrival. For foreigners, duty-free allowances for items purchased *outside* the EU are 4L of wine, 2L of spirits and 200 cigarettes, though it should be noted that wine, alcohol and cigarettes purchased inside Romania will frequently be cheaper than duty-free prices. For more information, go to www.customs.ro.

Embassies & Consulates

Unless stated otherwise, the following embassies are in Bucharest.

Australia (☎021-320 9802; B-dul Unirii 74)

Bulgaria (☎021-230 2150; www.bgembassy-romania.org; Str Rabat 5)

Canada (☎021-307 5000; bucst@international.gc.ca; Str Tuberozelor 1-3)

France (☎021-303 1000; www.ambafrance-ro.org; Str Biserica Amzei 13-15)

Germany Bucharest (☎021-202 9830; www.bukarest.diplo.de; Str Gheorghe Demetriade 6-8); Sibiu (☎0269-211 133; Str Lucian Blaga 15-17); Timişoara (☎0256-309 800; www.temeswar.diplo.de; Spl Tudor Vladmirescu 10)

Hungary (☎021-312 0073; www.mfa.gov.hu/emb/bucarest; Str Dimitrie Gerota 63-65)

Ireland (☎021-310 2131; www.embassyofireland.ro; Str Buzeşti 50-52)

Moldova (☎021-230 0474; consulat.bucuresti@msa.md; Aleea Alexandru 40)

Netherlands (☎021-208 6030; www.olanda.ro; Aleea Alexandru 20)

Serbia Bucharest (☎021-211 9871, consulate section 211 4980; ambiug@ines.ro; Calea Dorobanţilor 34); Timişoara (☎0256-490 334; gktyug@mail.dnttm.ro; Str Remus 4)

UK (☎021-201 7200; www.ukinromania.fco.gov.uk; Str Jules Michelet 24)

Ukraine (☎021-230 3671; www.ucraina.ro; B-dul Aviatorilor 24)

USA (☎021-200 3300; www.usembassy.ro; Str Tudor Arghezi 7-9)

Food

In this chapter, the following price indicators apply (for a main meal):

€€€	more than 25 lei
€€	15 to 25 lei
€	less than 15 lei

For information on Romanian cuisine, see p762.

Gay & Lesbian Travellers

In 2001 Romania became one of Europe's last countries to decriminalise homosexual activity. Bucharest has the most active gay and lesbian scene, including the emergence of GayFest in late May, which features events, films, disco nights and, sadly, counter-protests that occasionally turn violent. **Accept** (www.accept-romania.ro) is a gay-, lesbian- and transgender-rights group. There's a chatroom at http://gaybucuresti.ro.

Money

CASH

In Romania the only legal tender is the leu (plural: lei; abbreviated to RON). Notes come in denominations of one, five, 10, 50, 100, 200 and 500 – try to avoid the 200s and 500s as no one apart from hotels will give change for them. Coins come in one, five, 10, 20 and 50 bani. People sometimes still quote prices in old lei (discontinued in 2007, sporting an extra four zeros), giving hapless travellers sticker shock.

Prices are frequently quoted in euros – especially at hotels. We've quoted most prices in this chapter in Romanian lei to make on-the-ground price references easier.

ATMS

ATMs are everywhere and give 24-hour withdrawals in lei on your Cirrus, Plus, Visa, MasterCard or Eurocard. Some banks, such as Banca Comercială Română, give cash advances on credit cards in your home currency.

MONEYCHANGERS

Moneychangers are ubiquitous (avoid changers with bodyguard goons out front), but you should change currency at banks whenever possible. Dollars and euros are easiest to exchange, though British pounds are widely accepted. You often must show a passport to change money. Some changers advertise juicy rates, but subtly disguise a '9' as a '0' etc. Count your money carefully.

CREDIT CARDS & TRAVELLERS CHEQUES

Cashing travellers cheques is becoming increasingly difficult. Some branches of the Banca Comercială Română and Raiffeisen Bank, among others, will do so. Credit cards won't get you anywhere in rural areas, but they are widely accepted in larger department stores, hotels and most restaurants in cities and towns.

TIPPING

Still a relatively new concept, tipping usually amounts to rounding up to the next round number on your bill. A 10% tip is considered very generous. Increasingly, servers don't bring back small change – and sometimes large change – assuming it's a tip.

Post

A postcard or letter under 20g to Europe from Romania costs 1.60 lei and takes seven to 10 days. The postal system is reliable, if slow.

Public Holidays

Public holidays in Romania:

New Year 1 and 2 January

Catholic & Orthodox Easter Mondays March/April

Labour Day 1 May

Romanian National Day 1 December

Christmas 25 and 26 December

Telephone

Romania's telephone centres are scaling down and public phones are increasingly neglected amid the mobile-phone revolution. Mobile (cell) phones, which are preferable to landlines for many Romanians, have 10 digits, beginning with 07.

Phonecards (10 lei) can be purchased at news-stands and used in phone booths for domestic or international calls.

European mobile phones with roaming work in Romania; otherwise you can get a Romania number from Orange or Vodaphone, which have shops everywhere. The SIM card costs about 18 lei including credit; domestic calls are about 0.35 to 0.50 lei per minute.

Dial ☎971 for Romania's international operator. Romania's country code is ☎40.

Tourist Information

State tourism information centres are slowly appearing in major cities around the country. Most travel agents are geared to get you *out* of Romania, but some can help – or will try to. The best information often comes from travel-oriented accommodation such as hostels or pensions that offer day trips.

The so-called **Romanian National Tourist Office** (www.romaniantourism.ro, in Romanian) amazingly has no offices in Romania, but keeps an active **London office** (☎020 7224 3692; infouk@romaniatourism.com; 22 New Cavendish St) and **New York City office** (☎212 545 8484; infous@romaniarourism.com; 19th fl, 355 Lexington Ave).

CHANGES TO TELEPHONE NUMBERS

As of 2008 you must use area codes when dialling any landline in Romania, even if you're just across the road. This also goes for nonemergency three- and four-digit short numbers. Emergency numbers are still only three digits.

Travellers with Disabilities

Travellers with physical disabilities will find it difficult to conquer Romania. Street surfaces are sometimes uneven, ramps are substandard and specially equipped toilets and hotel rooms are uncommon. Consider joining a package tour that will cater to your specific needs. Some hotels on the Black Sea coast have wheelchair access, and spas in general may be more accustomed to disabled travellers.

Visas

Your passport's validity must extend to at least six months beyond the date you enter the country in order to obtain a visa.

Citizens of the USA, Canada, Australia, New Zealand, Japan and many other countries may travel visa-free for 90 days in Romania. EU citizens, obviously, can stay indefinitely. As visa requirements change frequently, check with the **Ministry of Foreign Affairs** (www.mae.ro) before departure.

Regular single-entry visas (€60) are valid for 90 days from the day you arrive. Transit visas (€60) can be issued for one, two or more transits. Each transit period cannot exceed five days. Transit visas are for stays of no longer than five days, and cannot be bought at the border.

To apply for a visa you need a passport, one recent passport photograph and the completed visa application form accompanied by the appropriate fee. Citizens of some countries (mainly African) need a formal invitation from a person or company in order to apply for a visa.

Check your visa requirements for Serbia and Montenegro, Hungary, Bulgaria and Ukraine if you plan on crossing those borders. If you are taking the Bucharest–St Petersburg train, you need Ukrainian and Belarusian transit visas on top of the Russian visa.

Getting There & Away
Air
AIRPORTS & AIRLINES

Tarom (Transporturile Aeriene Române, RO; www.tarom.ro) is Romania's state airline. National airline **Carpatair** (V3; ☑0256-300 900; www.carpatair.com) uses Timişoara as its hub.

Most international flights land at Bucharest's **Henri Coandă airport** (OTP; ☑021-201 4788; www.otp-airport.ro), formerly Otopeni airport. An exception is discount airline Wizz Air, which uses the capital's older **Băneasa**

airport (BBU; ☑021-232 0020; www.baneasa.aero).

Other airports receiving international flights include the following:

Cluj airport (CLJ; ☑0264-416 702; www.airport cluj.ro)

Iaşi airport (IAS; ☑0232-271 570; www.aeroport.ro)

Sibiu airport (SBZ; ☑0269-229 161; www.sibiu airport.ro, in Romanian)

Târgu Mureş airport (TGM; ☑0265-328 259; www.targumuresairport.ro)

Timişoara airport (TSR; ☑0256-493 639; www.aerotim.ro)

Major airlines flying into the country:

Air France (AF; ☑021-319 2705; www.airfrance.com)

Air Moldova (9U; ☑021-312 1258; www.airmoldova.md)

Austrian Airlines (OS; ☑021-204 2208; www.austrianair.com)

Blue Air (0B; ☑021-208 8686; www.smartflying.ro)

British Airways (BA; ☑021-303 2222; www.british-airways.com)

Carpatair (V3; ☑0256-300 900; www.carpatair.com)

ČSA (Czech Airlines; OK; ☑021-315 3205; www.csa.cz)

easyJet (U2; www.easyjet.com)

germanwings (4U; ☑0903 760 101; www.germanwings.com)

KLM (KL; ☑21-312 0149; www.klm.com)

LOT Polish Airlines (LO; ☑21-314 1096; www.lot.com)

Lufthansa (LH; ☑21-204 8410; www.lufthansa.com)

Ryan Air (FR; www.ryanair.com)

Swiss Airlines (LX; ☑21-312 0238; www.swiss.com)

Tarom (RO; ☑22-541 254, 0992 541 254; www.tarom.ro)

Turkish Airlines (TK; ☑21-311 2410; www.turkishairlines.com)

Wizz Air (W6; ☑403 6440 2000; www.wizzair.com)

Land

Expect long queues at checkpoints, particularly on weekends; bring a little food and water for the wait. Beware of unauthorised people charging dubious 'ecology', 'disinfectant' or other dodgy taxes at the border.

Bus

Romania is well linked by bus lines to Central and Western Europe as well as Turkey; see p693 for popular routes. While not as comfortable as the train, buses tend to be faster, though not always cheaper.

Eurolines (www.eurolines.ro) has a flurry of buses linking numerous cities in Romania with Western Europe. Buses to Germany cost 440 lei (€125) one way, while buses to Paris and Rome cost 310 lei to 380 lei (€90 to €110).

Many companies offer daily buses to Budapest from cities throughout Romania.

Most major cities have intermittent service to İstanbul.

Car & Motorcycle

The best advice here is to ensure your documents (personal ID, insurance, registration and visas, if required) are in order before crossing into Romania. The Green Card (a routine extension of domestic motor insurance to cover most European countries) is valid in Romania. Extra insurance can be bought at the borders.

Train

International train tickets are sold at train stations and CFR (Romanian State Railways) offices in town (look for the 'Agenţia de Voiaj CFR' signs). International tickets must be bought at least two hours prior to departure.

Those travelling on an Inter-Rail or Eurail pass still need to make seat reservations (13 lei to 17 lei, or 65 lei if using a couchette) on express trains within Romania. Even if you're not travelling with a rail pass, practically all international trains require a reservation (automatically included in tickets purchased in Romania). If you already have a ticket, you may be able to make reservations at the station an hour before departure, though it's preferable to do so at a CFR office at least one day in advance.

Getting Around
Air

State-owned carrier **Tarom** (www.tarom.ro) is Romania's main carrier. **Carpatair** (www.carpatair.com) runs domestic routes from its hub in Timişoara.

Bicycle

Cyclists have become a more frequent sight in Romania – particularly in Transylvania, Maramureş and Moldavia – but rental is not that widespread. There are generally bike and bike-repair shops in most major towns. A good place to rent one is Sinaia.

Boat

Boat is the only way of getting around much of the Danube Delta; see p756.

Bus

A mix of buses, microbuses and maxitaxis combines to form the seriously disorganised Romanian bus system. Finding updated information can be tough without local help. The slick new website www.autogari.ro gives a snapshot of domestic and international bus schedules, but it is by no means comprehensive. Some maxitaxi routes (such as Braşov–Sinaia and Sibiu–Cluj-Napoca) are more useful than others, though departure points are prone to migrating without notice. Generally it's easier to plan for train travel.

That said, fares are cheap and calculated by distance: about 1 leu per 10km.

Car & Motorcycle

Even if you're on a budget, it's well worth splitting the costs of a car – sometimes as low as 134 lei (€32) per day for short-term rental or 75 lei (€18) per day for long-term rental – and getting out into rural areas like Maramureş and Saxon Land. It's amazing how much things can change only 2km from a 'main' paved highway. Some roads are impassable without 4WD, though everything in this chapter can be reached by a Daewoo Matiz (the cheapest rental car, and a fine one), if you take extra precautions. **Autonom** (www.autonom.com) is a reliable and inexpensive agency with offices around the country. See destination sections for more car-rental recommendations.

Romania's main automobile association is the **Automobil Clubul Român** (ACR; ☏021-222 2222; www.acr.ro, in Romanian), but it's mainly for Romanians to renew licences.

Some tips:

Give yourself time Things go slower: flocks of sheep, horse carts, full-lane tractors, construction and giant potholes slow traffic.

Get a map A map is mandatory and can be found in bookshops and highway petrol stops. A good one is the Amco Press 1:750,000 *Romania* (about 10 lei).

Obey parking laws Historically, footpaths were fair game for parking your car, but this is becoming less common as the '*P cu plata*' places (meaning payment is required) proliferate in most major cities. Usually there's a payment machine nearby, but sometimes a vest-wearing bloke patrols the area selling tickets. Either way don't dilly-dally: we've heard reports of people being fined by ruthless police in the few minutes it took to wander off and purchase a ticket.

Your country's driving licence will be recognised here. There is a 0% blood-alcohol tolerance limit. Seatbelts are compulsory in the front and back; children under 12 are forbidden to sit in the front. Headlights need to be *turned on* when driving on any major roads, day or night.

Speed limits are 90km/h on major roads and 50km/h inside highway villages and towns unless otherwise noted. A few motorways allow faster driving. Speed traps – such as the video ones between Braşov and Bucharest – are common; drivers warn each other of lurking police with a flash of the headlights.

Hitching

Hitching is never entirely safe. People who do choose to hitch will be safer if they travel in pairs and let someone know where they are planning to go. That said, hitching is very popular in Romania, where people usually stand along the main roads out of a city or town. An arm-length, pat-the-dog motion is the prevailing gesture used to indicate a ride is desired, though the thumb-up signal is becoming more widespread. It's common practice to pay the equivalent of the bus fare to the driver (about 1 leu for every 10km).

Local Transport

Buses, trams and trolleybuses provide transport within most towns and cities in Romania, although many are crowded. They usually run from about 5am to midnight, although services can get thin on the ground after 7pm in more remote areas. In most cities, you'll need to purchase tickets at newspaper stands or kiosks marked *bilete* or *casă de bilete* before boarding, and validate them once aboard.

In many rural parts, the only vehicles around are horse-powered. Horse and cart, once the most popular form of transport in Romania, hit hard times in 2008 when a rash and short-sighted decision was made to ban them from major roads; they were blamed for causing up to 10% of accidents (curiously, omnipresent problems like reckless speeding and incessant mobile phone use never came up). Where still in use, many carts will stop and give you a ride, the driver expecting no more than a few cigarettes or lei in return.

Train

The punctual rail system has long been the most popular way of travelling. **Căile Ferate Române** (CFR; Romanian State Railways; www.cfr.ro) runs trains over 11,000km of track, providing services to most cities, towns and larger villages in the country.

Classes

In Romania there are four types of train, which travel at different speeds, offer varying levels of comfort and charge differently.

The cheapest trains are the sadistically slow local personal trains. *Accelerat* trains are faster, hence a tad more expensive and less crowded. Seat reservations are obligatory for all classes except personal, and are automatic when you buy your ticket. *Rapid* trains are faster still. Pricier Inter-City trains are the most comfortable, but aren't much faster than rapid trains.

Vagon de dormit (sleepers) are available between Bucharest and Cluj-Napoca, Oradea, Timişoara, Tulcea and other points. First-class sleeping compartments generally have two berths, 2nd-class sleepers generally have four berths and 2nd-class couchettes have six berths. Book these in advance.

Fares listed generally indicate one-way, 2nd-class seats on *rapid* or *accelerat* trains.

Reservations

Tickets for all but international trains can be purchased at the station up until departure. Advance tickets are also sold at an Agenţia de Voiaj CFR, a train-ticket office found in every city centre. Theoretically you can buy tickets at CFR offices up to two hours before departure. Your reservation ticket lists the code number of your train along with your assigned *vagon* (carriage) and *locul* (seat).

If you have an international ticket right through Romania, you're allowed to make stops along the route, but you must purchase a reservation ticket each time you reboard an *accelerat* or *rapid* train. If the international ticket was issued in Romania, you may also have to pay a supplement each time.

Russia Россия

Why Go?

Could there be a more iconic image of Eastern Europe than Moscow's awe-inspiring Red Square? Intimately associated with this vision is the lingering impression that Russia remains a closed-off, difficult and unfriendly place in which to travel. Nothing could be further from the truth.

Two decades on from the demise of the Soviet Union, an economically and politically resurgent Russia is a brash, exciting and fascinating place to visit. All the fruits of capitalism, including good hotels, restaurants and fully stocked shops, stand alongside things that the country has long got right, such as beautiful architecture and an elegant cultural scene of classical music and art.

Outside the major cities covered in this chapter – namely Moscow, St Petersburg, Veliky Novgorod and Kaliningrad – there are also the simple pleasures of a countryside dotted with timeless wooden cottages and deserted beaches to discover. Don't let the matter of a little visa red tape deter you.

Best Places to Stay

- » Hotel Metropol (p782)
- » Home From Home Hostel (p782)
- » Alexander House (p799)
- » Anichkov Pension (p799)
- » Chaika (p812)

Best Places to Eat

- » Delicatessen (p783)
- » Café Pushkin (p784)
- » Teplo (p803)
- » Sadko (p803)
- » Dolce Vita (p813)

When To Go
Moscow

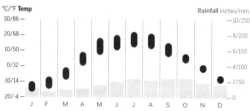

9 May Big military parades and a public holiday mark the end of WWII.

June-July Party during St Petersburg's White Nights; bask on the beaches of Kaliningrad.

December-January Winter arts festivals and snow make Moscow and St Petersburg look magical.

Fast Facts

» **Area** 16,995,800 sq km

» **Capital** Moscow

» **Telephone code** 7

» **Emergency** ambulance 03, emergency assistance 112, fire 01, police 02

Exchange Rates

Australia	A$1	R29.71
Canada	C$1	R29.26
euro	€1	R40.45
Japan	¥100	R33.93
New Zealand	NZ$1	R22.32
UK	UK£1	R45.81
USA	US$1	R28.13

Set Your Budget

» **Budget hotel room Moscow/elsewhere** R3000/1000

» **Two-course meal** R600 to R1200

» **Museum entrance** R350

» **Beer** R70

» **Metro ticket Moscow/ St Petersburg** R26/22

Resources

» **Visit Russia** (www. visitrussia.org.uk)

» **The Moscow Expat Site** (www.expat.ru)

» **Way to Russia** (www. waytorussia.net)

Connections

Bordering Belarus, Estonia, Latvia, Lithuania, Poland and Ukraine, Russia has excellent train and bus connections with the rest of Europe. Routes connecting Kaliningrad with St Petersburg will take you through the Baltic countries, while trains between Kaliningrad and Moscow head through Belarus. Trains from Kharkiv in Ukraine transit via Kursk, Oryol and Tula to terminate in Moscow. Pskov, just 30km from Estonia, is a great place to either say goodbye or hello to Russia.

ITINERARIES

Three days in Moscow

See Red Square, the Kremlin and the spectacular collection at the State Tretyakov Gallery. Also don't miss the magnificent Novodevichy Convent or a show at a contemporary gallery such as Garazh. Take a trip to Sergiev Posad or sweat it out in the luxurious Sanduny Baths.

Three days in St Petersburg

Wander up Nevsky Pr, see Palace Sq, the mighty Neva River then tour the magnificent collection of the Hermitage. Visit St Peter and Paul Fortress, the Church of the Saviour on Spilled Blood and the wonderful Russian Museum. Make an excursion either to Petrodvorets or Tsarskoe Selo.

Two days in Kaliningrad

Admire the reconstructed Gothic Cathedral, then wander along the river to the excellent World Ocean Museum. The Amber Museum is also impressive. Enjoy either the old Prussian charm of the spa town of Svetlogorsk or the sand dunes and forests of the Kurshskaya Kosa National Park.

Essential Food & Drink

» **Soups** For example, the lemony, meat *solyanka* or the hearty fish *ukha*.

» **Bliny** (pancakes) Served with *ikra* (caviar) or *tvorog* (cottage cheese).

» **Salads** A wide variety usually slathered in mayonnaise, including the chopped potato one called Olivier.

» **Pelmeni** (dumplings) Stuffed with meat and eaten with sour cream and vinegar.

» **Central Asian dishes** Try *plov* (fried rice with vegetables and lamb), *shashliky* (kebabs) or *lagman* (noodles).

» **Vodka** The quintessential Russian tipple.

» **Kvas** A refreshing, beer-like drink, or the red berry juice mix *mors*.

Highlights

1 Be awe-inspired by the massive scale and riches of **Moscow** (p772), Russia's brash, energetic capital

2 Savour the imperial past in elegant **St Petersburg** (p791), a city of colourful and often crumbling Italianate mansions, wending canals and the enormous Neva River

3 Trace Russia's roots back to **Veliky Novgorod** (p789) a tourist friendly town of with a well-preserved kremlin and many picturesque churches

4 Use **Kaliningrad** (p808) city as a base for discovering this tiny, separate piece of Russia that aims to emulate its Baltic neighbours for friendliness

5 Kick back on the pristine beaches of the **Kurshskaya Kosa National Park** (p816) and go in search of its dancing forest'

MOSCOW МОСКВА

📖 495 & 499 / POP 10.4 MILLION

Intimidating in its scale, but also exciting and unforgettable, Moscow is a place that inspires extreme passion or loathing. History, power and wild capitalism hang in the air alongside an explosion of creative energy throwing up edgy art galleries and a dynamic restaurant, bar and nightlife scene. Tchaikovsky and Chekhov are well represented at the city's theatres, but you can also see world premieres by up-and-coming composers and choreographers.

Russia's turbulent history can be traced from the sturdy stone walls of the Kremlin, which continue to occupy the founding site of Moscow, to the remains of the Soviet state scattered around the city. Institutions such as the Gulag History Museum broach subjects that were long brushed under the carpet, while contemporary artists use their work to comment on current politics. Whether you choose to stroll through a quiet neighbourhood or embrace the city's infectious buzz, few places in the world have so much to offer.

History

In the mid-12th century Yury Dolgoruky constructed the first Kremlin at a strategic spot atop Borovitsky Hill. A century later the Mongol forces of the Golden Horde burned the city to the ground and began to use Moscow to monitor the river trade and road traffic to exact tribute. Moscow's Prince Ivan acted as tax collector, earning himself the moniker 'Moneybags' (Kalita). In the process, Moscow developed into a regional capital.

Towards the end of the 15th century, the once diminutive duchy emerged as an expanding state under the reign of Grand Prince Ivan III (the Great). To celebrate his successes, he imported a team of Italian artisans for a complete renovation of the Kremlin. The city developed in concentric rings outward from this centre. Under Ivan IV (the Terrible) in the 16th century, the city earned the nickname of 'Gold-Domed Moscow' because of its multitude of monastery fortresses and magnificent churches.

In 1712 Peter the Great relocated the capital to St Petersburg, and in the early 1800s Moscow suffered further at the hands of Napoleon Bonaparte. But after the Napoleonic Wars, Moscow was feverishly rebuilt and industry prospered.

When the Bolsheviks gained control of Russia in 1917, the capital returned to Moscow. Stalin's new urban plan for the city saw historic cathedrals and monuments demolished to be replaced by a marble-bedecked metro and neo-Gothic skyscrapers. In the following decades, Moscow expanded at an exponential rate.

In the 1990s while the rest of Russia struggled to survive the collapse of communism, Moscow emerged as an enclave of affluence and was the scene of the most dramatic events of the country's political transition. Boris Yeltsin led crowds protesting the attempted coup in 1991; and two years later he ordered the army to blast the parliament into submission.

Early in the new millennium, Moscow was a target for terrorist attacks linked to the ongoing crisis in Chechnya. Over the course of several years, hundreds of people in Moscow were wounded or killed when suicide bombers attacked a theatre, a rock concert, metro stations and airplanes.

In September 2010, Yuri Luzhkov was fired as Moscow's mayor, a role he'd performed for 18 years to his and his wife's great financial gain. Under his oversight, the city has undergone a massive physical transformation. Many historic buildings have been destroyed and skyscrapers have shot up along the Moscow River. His successor, Sergei Sobyanin, Putin's former chief of staff, now has to deal with Moscow's gridlock traffic and embedded corruption.

⊙ Sights

The city's medieval heart, the Kremlin, is a triangle on the northern bank of the Moscow River. The modern city centre radiates around it and is defined by the 'garden ring' – a vast eight-lane highway that encircles Moscow's core.

The Kremlin   MUSEUM

(Map p778; 📖 495-202 3776; www.kreml.ru; adult/student R350/100; ⊙9.30am-4pm Fri-Wed; Ⓜ Aleksandrovsky Sad) The apex of Russian political power and once the centre of the Orthodox Church, the Kremlin is not only the kernel of Moscow but of the whole country. It's from here that autocratic tsars, communist dictators and modern-day presidents have done their best – and worst – for Russia.

Covering Borovitsky Hill on the north bank of the Moscow River, the Kremlin is enclosed by high walls 2.25km long, with Red Sq outside the east wall. The best views of the complex are from Sofiyskaya nab across the river.

Before entering the Kremlin, deposit bags at the left-luggage office (per bag R60, ⊙9am-

6.30pm Fri-Wed), beneath the Kutafya Tower near the main ticket office. The main ticket office is in the Alexandrovsky Garden, just off Manezhnaya pl. The entrance ticket covers admission to all five church-museums, and the Patriarch's Palace. It does not include the Armoury, the Diamond Fund Exhibition or exhibits in the Ivan the Great Bell Tower. You can buy tickets for all those places here, too.

Photography is not permitted inside the Armoury or any of the buildings on Sobornaya pl (Cathedral Sq). Visitors wearing shorts will be refused entry.

Southwest Buildings

From the Kutafya Tower, walk up the ramp and pass through the Kremlin walls beneath the **Trinity Gate Tower** (Troitskaya Bashnya). The lane to the right (south) passes the 17th-century **Poteshny Palace** (Poteshny Dvorets), where Stalin lived. The horribly out-of-place glass-and-concrete **State Kremlin Palace** (Kremlyovksy Dvorets Syezdov) houses a concert and ballet auditorium (p786), where many Western pop stars play when they are in Moscow.

Armoury

(adult/student R700/200; ⊘entry 10am, noon, 2.30pm & 4.30pm) In the Kremlin's southwestern corner is this mind-numbingly opulent collection of treasures accumulated over time by the Russian state and church. Tickets specify entry times. Highlights include Fabergé eggs and reams of royal regalia.

Diamond Fund

(Vystavka Almaznogo Fonda; ☑495-629 2036; admission R500; ⊘10am-1pm & 2-5pm Fri-Wed; Ⓜ Aleksandrovsky Sad) If the Armoury doesn't sate your diamond lust, there are more in this separate exhibition, in the same building. The lavish collection includes the largest sapphire in the world.

Sobornaya Ploshchad

On the northern side of Sobornaya pl, with five golden helmet domes and four semicircular gables facing the square, is the **Assumption Cathedral** (Uspensky Sobor), built between 1475 and 1479. As the focal church of prerevolutionary Russia, it's the burial place of most heads of the Russian Orthodox Church from the 1320s to 1700. The iconostasis dates from 1652, but its lowest level contains some older icons, including the *Virgin of Vladimir* (Vladimirskaya Bogomater), an early-15th-century Rublyov-school copy of Russia's most revered image,

FREE MOSCOW

Moscow can drain your wallet faster than an addiction to crack, but there are some things you can enjoy for free:

» March across **Red Square** (p773) and pay your respects to Lenin

» Cruise the designer shops and arcades of **GUM** (p787)

» Watch the changing of the guard in the **Alexandrovsky Garden** (p777)

» Admire the bizarre **Peter the Great statue** (p781)

» Check out the **contemporary art scene** (boxed text p777)

the *Vladimir Icon of the Mother of God* (Ikona Vladimirskoy Bogomateri).

The delicate little single-domed church beside the west door of the Assumption Cathedral is the **Church of the Deposition of the Robe** (Tserkov Rizopolozheniya), built between 1484 and 1486 by masons from Pskov.

With its two golden domes rising above the eastern side of Sobornaya pl, the 16th-century **Ivan the Great Bell Tower** (Kolokolnya Ivana Velikogo) is the Kremlin's tallest structure. Beside the bell tower stands the **Tsar Bell**, a 202-tonne monster that cracked before it ever rang. North of the bell tower is the mammoth **Tsar Cannon**, cast in 1586 but never shot.

The 1508 **Archangel Cathedral** (Arkhangelsky Sobor), at the square's southeastern corner, was for centuries the coronation, wedding and burial church of tsars. The tombs of all of Russia's rulers from the 1320s to the 1690s are here bar one (Boris Godunov, who was buried at Sergiev Posad).

Finally, the **Annunciation Cathedral** (Blagoveshchensky Sobor), at the southwest corner of Sobornaya pl and dating from 1489, contains the celebrated icons of master painter Theophanes the Greek. He probably painted the six icons at the right-hand end of the diesis row, the biggest of the six tiers of the iconostasis. *Archangel Michael* (the third icon from the left on the diesis row) and the adjacent *St Peter* are ascribed to Russian master Andrei Rublyov.

Red Square   HERITAGE AREA

(Krasnaya pl; Map p778; Ⓜ Pl Revolyutsii) Awe-inspiring Red Sq is best approached from the north through **Resurrection Gate** (Vorota Voskreseniya) – a 1995 replica of the 1680 original destroyed during Stalin's time:

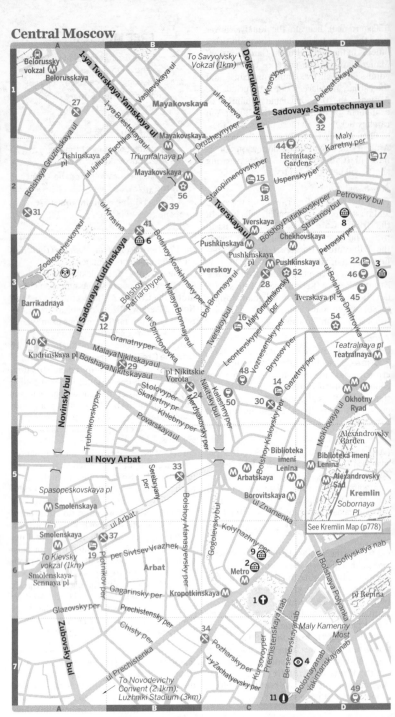

RUSSIA MOSCOW

Belorussky vokzal
Belorusskaya
1-ya Tverskaya-Yamskaya ul
To Savyolvsky Vokzal (1km)
Dolgorukovskaya ul
27
Vasilevskaya ul
ul Fadeeva
Sadovaya-Samotechnaya ul
32
Mayakovskaya
Maly Karetny per
44
17
Hermitage Gardens
Bolshaya Gruzinskaya ul
ul Julivsa Fuchika
Tishinskaya pl
1-ya Brestskaya ul
Mayakovskaya
Oruzheyny per
Staropimenovsky per
Uspensky per
ul Krasina
Triumfalnaya pl
15
18
31
Mayakovskaya
Staropimenovsky per
Tverskaya ul
56
Petrovsky bul
39
Tverskaya
Bolshoy Putinkovsky per
Strastnoy bul
8
Pushkinskaya
Chekhovskaya
Petrovsky per
41
Bolshoy Kozikhinsky per
Pushkinskaya pl
Pushkinskaya
22
3
6
Tverskoy
52
46
45
Zoologicheskaya ul
7
Bol Bronnaya ul
28
ul Bolshaya Dmitrovka
Tverskaya pl
Bolshoy Patriarshy per
Malaya Bronnaya ul
54
Barrikadnaya
Maly Gnezdnikovsky per
12
ul Spiridonovka
16
Tverskoy bul
Leontevsky per
Teatralnaya pl
Teatralnaya
Granatny per
Voznesensky per
Bryusov per
Gazetny per
Malaya Nikitskaya ul
48
14
40
Kudrinskaya pl
Malaya Nikitskaya ul
29
pl Nikitskie Vorota
Nikitsky bul
50
30
Okhotny Ryad
Bolshaya Nikitskaya ul
Stolovy per
Skatertny pr
24
Kalashny per
Merzlyakovsky per
Mokhovaya ul
Novinsky bul
Trubnikovsky per
Khlebny per
Povarskaya ul
Alexandrovsky Garden
Biblioteka imeni Lenina
Biblioteka imeni Lenina
ul Novy Arbat
33
Bolshoy Kislovsky per
Arbatskaya
Alexandrovsky Sad
Serebryany per
Gogolevsky bul
Borovitskaya
Kremlin
Spasopeskovskaya pl
Smolenskaya
ul Znamenka
Sobornaya Pl
Bolshoy Afanasyevsky per
See Kremlin Map (p778)
ul Arbat
Bolshaya Polyanka
Smolenskaya
37
Kolymazhny per
Sofiyskaya nab
To Kievsky vokzal (1km)
19
per Sivtsev Vrazhek
9
Plotnikov per
Arbat
2
Smolenskaya-Sennaya pl
Metro
Gagarinsky per
Kropotkinskaya
1
pl Repina
Glazovsky per
Prechistensky per
Maly Kamenny Most
Zubovsky bul
Chisty per
34
Pozharsky per
Prechistenskaya nab
Bersenevskaya nab
Bolotnaya nab
Yakimanskaya nab
ul Prechistenka
To Novodevichy Convent (2.1km); Luzhniki Stadium (3km)
1-ya Zachatyevsky per
Kursovoy per
4
49
11

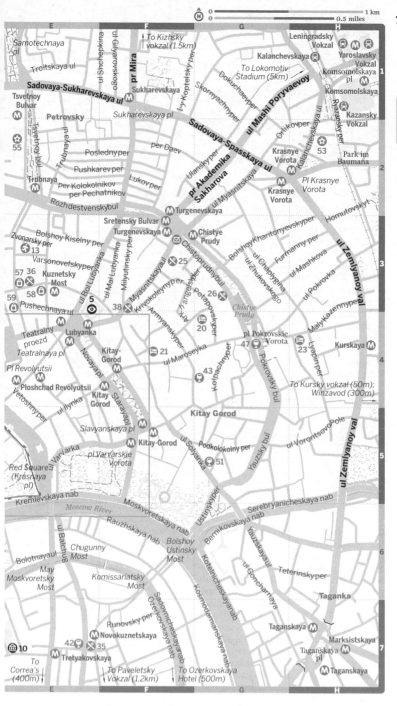

Map labels:

0 — 1 km
0 — 0.5 miles

Samotechnaya pl
Troitskaya ul
ul Gilyarovskogo
ul Shchepkina
pr Mira
To Kizhsky vokzal (1.5km)
1-y Koptelsky per
Leningradsky Vokzal
Kalanchevskaya
Yaroslavsky Vokzal
Komsomolskaya pl
Sadovaya-Sukharevskaya ul
Sukharevskaya
Tsvetnoy Bulvar
Petrovsky
Sukharevskaya pl
Skornyazhny per
Dokuchaev per
To Lokomotiv Stadium (5km)
ul Mashi Poryvaevoy
Komsomolskaya
Kazansky Vokzal
55
Trubnaya ul
Posledny per
per Daev
Ulansky per
Orlikov per
Krasnye Vorota
53
Park im Baumana
Tsvetnoy bul
Pushkarev per
Lukov per
Sadovaya-Spasskaya ul
Kalanchevskaya ul
Ryazansky per
Trubnaya
per Kolokolnikov
per Pechatnikov
pr Akademika Sakharova
ul Myasnitskaya
Pl Krasnye Vorota
Rozhdestvensky bul
Krasnye Vorota
Turgenevskaya
Homutovsky t
Sretensky Bulvar
Bolshoy Kiselny per
Zvonarsky per
Turgenevskaya
Chistye Prudy
Bolshoy Kharitonyevsky per
Furmanny per
ul Zemlyanoy val
13
Varsonofevsky per
Chistoprudny bul
ul Chaplygina
ul Mashkova
57 36
Kuznetsky Most
ul Bol Lubyanka
ul Mal Lubyanka
Milyutinsky per
Myasnitskaya ul
ul Zhukovskogo
ul Pokrovka
59
58
Pushechnaya ul
5
38
Krivokoleyny per
Armyansky per
Potapovsky per
Chistye Prudy
26
ul Pokrovka
Malykazennny per
Teatralny proezd
Lubyanka
Novaya pl
Kitay-Gorod
20
pl Pokrovskie Vorota
47
Lyapin per
23
Kurskaya
Teatralnaya pl
Pl Revolyutsii
Ploshchad Revolyutsii
Kitay Gorod
Staraya pl
21
ul Maroseyka
Kolpachny
43
Pokrovsky bul
To Kursky vokzal (50m);
Winzavod (300m)
Veroshny per
ul Ilynka
Slavyanskaya pl
Kitay-Gorod
Kitay Gorod
ul Solyanka
Podkolokolny per
Yauzsky bul
ul Vorontsovo Pole
ul Zemlyanoy val
Varvarka
pl Varvarskie Vorota
51
Red Square (Krasnaya pl)
Kremlevskaya nab
Moskvoretskaya nab
Ustinsky per
Serebryanicheskaya nab
Moscow River
Rauzhskaya nab
Bernikovskaya nab
Bolnaya ul
Balchug
Chugunny Most
Bolshoy Ustinsky Most
Kotelnicheskaya nab
Yauzskaya ul
Teterinsky per
May Moskvoretsky Most
Bolotnaya ul
Komissariatsky Most
Ozerkovskaya nab
Sadovnicheskaya nab
Kosnodamiansky nab
ul Goncharnaya
Taganka
Runovsky per
Novokuznetskaya
Taganskaya
10
42
35
Taganskaya pl
Marksistskaya
To Correa's (400m)
Tretyakovskaya
To Paveletsky Vokzal (1.2km)
To Ozerkovskaya Hotel (500m)
Taganskaya

Central Moscow

this way you get a picture-postcard view of the magnificently flamboyant **St Basil's Cathedral** (Sobor Vasilia Blazhennogo; ☑495-698 3304; adult/student R100/50; ☺11am-5pm Wed-Mon; Ⓜ︎Pl Revolyutsii) on the square's south side. Technically the Intercession Cathedral, this ultimate symbol of Russia was created between 1555 and 1561 (replacing an existing church on the site) to celebrate the capture of Kazan by Ivan the Terrible. 'St Basil's' actually refers only to the northeastern chapel, which was added later. It was built over the grave of the barefoot holy fool Vasily (Basil) the Blessed, who predicted Ivan's damnation.

Its design is the culmination of a wholly Russian style that had been developed through the building of wooden churches. Go inside to see the stark medieval wall paintings.

Lenin's Mausoleum
(☑495-623 5527; ☺10am-1pm Tue-Thu, Sat & Sun; Ⓜ︎Pl Revolyutsii) Before joining the queue at the northwestern corner of Red Sq to see Lenin's embalmed body, drop your camera at the left-luggage office in the State History Museum, as you will not be allowed to take it with you. After trooping past the oddly waxy figure, emerge from his red-and-black granite

tomb and inspect where Stalin, Brezhnev and many of communism's other heavy hitters are buried along the Kremlin wall. Visit while you can, since the former leader may eventually end up beside his mum in St Petersburg.

State History Museum
(☏495-692 3731; www.shm.ru; adult/child R250/60; ⊙10am-6pm Tue-Sat, 11am-8pm Sun; ⓜOkhotny Ryad) At the northern end of Red Sq is this museum's enormous collection covering the Russian empire from the Stone Age on. The building, dating from the late 19th century, is itself an attraction – each room is in the style of a different period or region.

Around Red Square
HERITAGE AREA
Stroll through pleasant **Alexandrovsky Garden** (Aleksandrovsky sad; Map p778) along the Kremlin's western wall. At the northern end is the **Tomb of the Unknown Soldier**, containing the remains of a soldier who died in December 1941 at kilometre 41 of Leningradskoe sh – the nearest the Nazis came to Moscow. The changing of the guard happens every hour from 10am to 7pm in summer, and to 3pm during winter. Opposite the gardens is Manezhnaya pl and the underground **Okhotny Ryad** shopping mall.

Teatralnaya pl opens out on both sides of Okhotny Ryad, 200m north of Manezhnaya pl. The northern half of the square is dominated by the **Bolshoi Theatre** (Map p778), where Tchaikovsky's *Swan Lake* was premiered (to bad reviews) in 1877; the building is looking particularly spruce after a recent renovation. On the east side of Teatralnaya pl take a moment to admire the exterior of the stunning art nouveau **Hotel Metropol** (Map p778).

State Tretyakov Gallery
MUSEUM
(Map p774; ☏499-238 1378; Lavrushinsky per 10; adult/student R300/180; ⊙10am-6.30pm Tue-Sun; ⓜTretyakovskaya) Nothing short of spectacular, the State Tretyakov Gallery holds the world's best collection of Russian icons and an outstanding collection of other prerevolutionary Russian art, particularly the works of the 19th-century *peredvizhniki* (p820).

New Tretyakov
MUSEUM
(☏499-238 1378; Krymsky val; adult/student R300/180; ⊙10am-6.30pm Tue-Sun; ⓜOktyabrsakaya) This is the premier venue for 20th-century Russian art and shouldn't be missed. Besides the plethora of socialist realism, the exhibits showcase key works by avant-garde artists like Kazimir Malevich, Vasily Kandinsky, Marc Chagall, Natalia Goncharova and Lyubov Popova. It's about 1km southwest of the main gallery, in Park Iskusstv.

Pushkin Museum of Fine Arts
MUSEUM
(Map p774; ☏495-687 7998; www.museum.ru/gmii; ul Volkhonka 12; adult/student R300/150; ⊙10am-6pm Tue-Sun; ⓜKropotkinskaya) Moscow's premier foreign-art museum displays a broad selection of European works, mostly appropriated from private collections after the revolution. They include Dutch and

---

MOSCOW'S WHITE HOT ART SCENE

Garazh (p781), which hosts the **Moscow Biennale of Contemporary Art** (www.moscowbiennale.ru), isn't the only place to take the pulse of the city's vibrant contemporary art scene. Apart from the following recommended spots also see www.artguide.ru for other options, and set your travel plans to coincide with the annual commercial gallery show **Art Moscow** (www.art-moscow.ru) and the **Kandinsky Prize** (www.kandinsky-prize.ru), an exhibition of up-and-coming Russian artists.

Proekt_Fabrika (☏499-265 3926; www.proektfabrika.ru; 18 Perevedenovsky per; admission free; ⊙10am-8pm Tue-Sun; ⓜBaumanskaya) A still-functioning paper factory is the location for this nonprofit set of gallery and performance spaces enlivened by arty graffiti and creative-industry offices.

Krasny Oktyabr Factory (Red October Factory; Map p774; admission free; ⓜKropotkinskaya) The red-brick buildings of this former chocolate factory now host **Art Strelka** (www.artstrelka.ru), **Pobeda Gallery** (pobedagallery.com) and the **Lumiere Brothers Photography Centre** (www.lumiere.ru) as well as other galleries and many trendy bars, clubs and restaurants.

Winzavod (☏495-917 4646; www.winzavod.ru; 4 Siromyatnichesky per 1; admission free; ⊙noon-8pm Tue-Sun; ⓜChkalovskaya) A former wine factory has morphed into this postindustrial complex of prestigious galleries, shops, a cinema and trendy cafe.

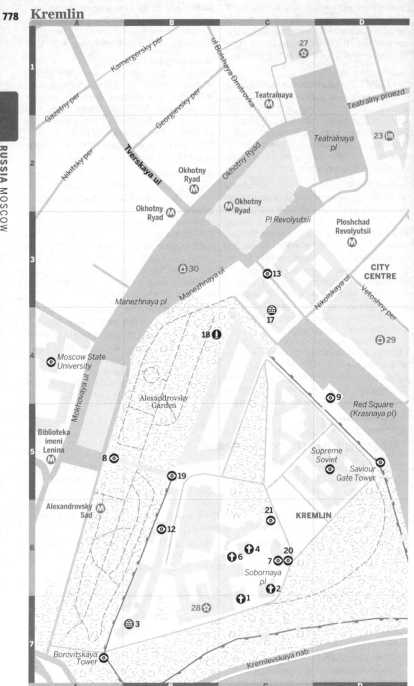

A B C D

1

Kamergersky per

Gazetny per

ul Bolshaya Dmitrovka

27

Teatralnaya
Ⓜ

Teatralny proezd

Georgievsky per

Nikitsky per

Tverskaya ul

Teatralnaya
pl

23 🏛

2

Okhotny
Ryad
Ⓜ

Okhotny Ryad

Okhotny
Ryad
Ⓜ Okhotny
Ryad

Pl Revolyutsii

Ploshchad
Revolyutsii
Ⓜ

3

Okhotny
Ryad Ⓜ

🔒30

Manezhnaya ul

13

CITY
CENTRE

Manezhnaya pl

17

Nikolskaya ul

Vetoshny per

29

18 ❗

4

Moscow State
University

Alexandrovsky
Garden

9

Red Square
(Krasnaya pl)

5

Biblioteka
imeni
Lenina
Ⓜ

Mokhovaya ul

8

Supreme
Soviet

Saviour
Gate Tower

19

Alexandrovsky
Sad Ⓜ

21

KREMLIN

6

12

6 4

7 20

2

Sobornaya
pl

1

28

3

7

Borovitskaya
Tower

Kremlevskaya nab

A B C D

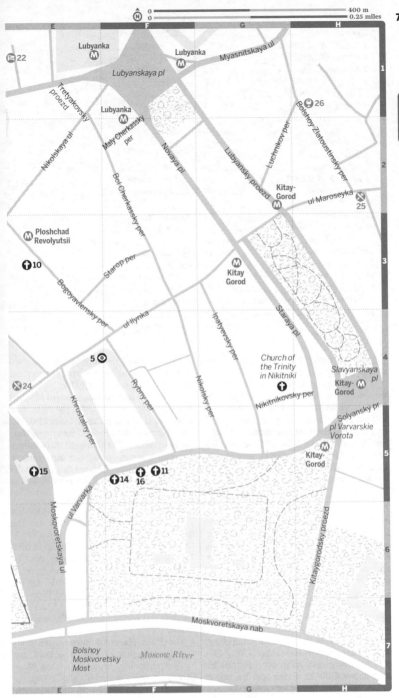

RUSSIA

Flemish masterpieces from the 17th century, several Rembrandt portraits, and the Ancient Civilisation exhibits, which include the impressive Treasures of Troy. The Pushkin's amazing collection of Impressionist and post-Impressionist paintings are found next door at the **Gallery of European & American Art of the 19th & 20th Centuries** (☑495-697 1546; ul Volkhonka 14; adult/student R300/150; ⊙10am-6pm Tue, Wed & Fri-Sun, to 8pm Thu; ⓜKropotkinskaya).

Tverskoy District   NEIGHBOURHOOD
The streets around Tverskaya ul, Moscow's main avenue, comprise the vibrant Tverskoy District, characterised by old architecture and new commerce. Small lanes such as **Kamergersky per** and **Stoleshnikov per** are among Moscow's trendiest places to sip a coffee or a beer and watch the big-city bustle.

In the midst of the swanky shops on ul Petrovka, an archway leads to a courtyard strung with barbed wire and hung with portraits of famous political prisoners. This is the entrance to the grim but compelling **Gulag History Museum** (Map p774; ☑495-621 7346; www.gmig.ru, in Russian; ul Petrovka 16; adult/student R100/20; ⊙11am-6pm Tue, Wed & Fri-Sun, noon-8pm Thu; ⓜTeatralnaya). Guides describe the vast network of labour camps that existed in the former Soviet Union and recount the horrors of camp life.

Nearby, the **Moscow Museum of Modern Art** (MMOMA; Map p774; ☑495-694 2890; www.mmoma.ru; ul Petrovka 25; adult/student R150/100; ⊙noon-7pm Tue, Wed & Fri-Sun, 1-8pm Thu; ⓜChekhovskaya) is housed in a classical 18th-century merchant's home. It contains 20th-century works by the likes of Marc Chagall, Natalia Goncharova and Vasily Kandinsky, as well as a whimsical sculpture garden.

Kitay Gorod   NEIGHBOURHOOD
This 13th-century neighbourhood was the first in Moscow to grow up outside the Kremlin walls. While its name means China Town in modern Russian, do not expect anything Chinese – the name derives from an old Russian word meaning 'wattle', for the supports used for the walls that protected the suburb. This is the heart of medieval Moscow and parts of the suburb's walls are visible.

The main places of interest are Kitay Gorod's collection of churches. Look out for the charming, brightly painted **Monastery of the Epiphany** (Map p778), opposite Ploshchad Revolyutsii metro station, and the small churches along ul Varvarka. These are the 17th-century **Monastery of the Sign** (Map p778), the 1698 **St Maxim the Blessed's Church** (Map p778) and **St Barbara's Church** (1795–1804; Map p778).

The one-time **Lubyanka Prison** (Map p774) crowning Lubyanka Hill was once the headquarters of the dreaded KGB; today it's the nerve centre of its successor, the FSB (Federal Security Service) and is closed to the public.

Art Muzeon   SCULPTURE PARK
(☑499-238 3396; ul Krymsky val 10; admission R100; ⊙9am-9pm; ⓂPark Kultury) This open-air sculpture park next to the New Tretyakov (from the metro, reach it by crossing the Moscow River) started as a collection of Soviet statues put out to pasture when they were ripped from their pedestals in the post-1991 wave of anti-Soviet feeling. They have now been joined by fascinating and diverse contemporary work. Zurab Tsereteli's monumental but controversial **Peter the Great statue** (Bersenevskaya nab; ⓂPolyanka) stands on the river bank overlooking the park.

FREE **Garazh Centre for Contemporary Culture**   GALLERY
(☑495-645 0520; www.garageccc.com; ul Obraztsova 19A; ⊙11am-9pm Mon-Thu, to 10pm Fri-Sun; ⓂMendeleyevska/Novoslobodskaya) A handsomely renovated bus depot, designed by constructivist architect Konstantin Melnikov in 1927, is the location for a fascinating foray into contemporary art. Funded by Dasha Zukova, heiress, fashion designer and partner of billionaire Roman Abramovich, this aircraft hanger–sized building includes three galleries (devoted to painting, multimedia and photography) as well as the main exhibition space, a media room,

bookshop and excellent cafe. Check the website for news of the many free events held here.

FREE **Cathedral of Christ the Saviour**   CHURCH
(Map p774; ☑495-202 4734; www.xxc.ru; ⊙10am-5pm; ⓂKropotkinskaya) Dominating the skyline along the Moscow River, this gargantuan cathedral, finished in 1997, sits on the site of an earlier and similar church of the same name, built from 1839 to 1883 to commemorate Russia's victory over Napoleon. Stalin ordered the destruction of the original and planned to replace it with a 315m-high 'Palace of Soviets' (including a 100m statue of Lenin), but the project never got off the ground – literally. Instead, for 50 years the site served an important purpose as the world's largest swimming pool.

Novodevichy Convent   CONVENT
(☑499-246 8526; adult/student R150/60; ⊙grounds 8am-8pm daily, museums 10am-5pm Wed-Mon; ⓂSportivnaya) A cluster of sparkling domes behind turreted walls on the Moscow River about 3km southwest of the Kremlin, this convent was founded in 1524 to celebrate the taking of Smolensk from Lithuania. Peter the Great imprisoned his half-sister Sofia here for her part in the Streltsy Rebellion. The oldest and most dominant building in the grounds is the white **Smolensk Cathedral**, its sumptuous interior covered in 16th-century frescos.

Adjacent to the convent, **Novodevichy Cemetery** (admission free; ⊙9am-5pm; ⓂSportivnaya) is one of Moscow's most prestigious resting places; here you will find the tombs of Chekhov, Gogol, Mayakovsky, Stanislavsky, Prokofiev, Eisenstein and Boris Yeltsin.

DON'T MISS

MOSCOW FOR CHILDREN

Apart from the following also see www.childreninmoscow.ru for more ideas.

Gorky Park (Park Kultury; ☑495-237 1266; ul Krymsky val; adult/child R80/20; ⊙10am-10pm; ⓂPark Kultury) There's always plenty to entertain kids in this vast park including fairground rides and boats on the small lakes.

Moscow Zoo (Map p774; ☑499-255 5375; www.kva-kva.ru; Yaroslavskoe shosse; adult/child R150/free; ⊙10am-7pm Tue-Sun May-Sep, to 5pm Oct-Apr; ⓂBarrikadnaya) The big cats and polar bears make it worth a visit.

Kva Kva Aqua Park (p782) There's plenty of water-based fun here for the kids among the pools and giant water slides.

Art Muzeon (p781) See all the Soviet heroes and climb around on them, too.

SERGIEV POSAD

The charming Golden Ring town of **Sergiev Posad** (Сергиев Посад), just 60km from central Moscow, is an easy day trip. The principal attraction here is the venerable 15th-century **Trinity Monastery of St Sergius** (Troitse-Sergieva Lavra; ☑496-544 5356; www.lavra.ru; admission free; ⊗10am-6pm), one of the most important and active monasteries in the Russian Orthodox religion. The fastest transport option is the express train that departs from Moscow's Yaroslavsky vokzal (R300, one hour, twice daily). Suburban trains also run every half-hour (R150, 1½ hours).

🏃 Activities

Don't leave Moscow without experiencing a good soak in one of its fancy bathhouses.

Sanduny Baths BATHHOUSE
TOP CHOICE (Map p774; ☑495-625 4631; www.sanduny.ru; Neglinnaya ul 14; private room per hr from R1300, general admission per 2hr R600-800; ⊗8am-10pm; ⓜKuznetsky Most) This is Moscow's oldest and most luxurious *banya* (hot bath).

Krasnopresnkiye Bani BATHHOUSE
(☑495-253 8690; baninapresne.ru; Stolyarny per 7; general admission R750-850; ⊗8am-10pm; ⓜUlitsa 1905 Goda) Offers an excellent, segregated *banya* as well as spa services and onsite cafe.

Kva Kva Aqua Park SWIMMING, BATHHOUSE
(☑495-258 0683; ul Krymsky val; adult/child from R830/480; ⊗10am-10pm; ⓜVDNKh, then bus N333) Around 16km north of the Kremlin is this big swimming complex with a very swanky set of saunas.

☞ Tours

Capital Tours BUS TOURS
(Map p778; ☑495-232 2442; www.capitaltours.ru; Gostiny Dvor, ul Ilyinka 4; ⓜKitay-Gorod) Offers city bus tours (adult/child R1000/500) and twice-daily tours of the Kremlin (adult/child R1550/775).

Patriarshy Dom Tours SPECIALIST TOURS
(Map p774; ☑495-795 0927; http://russiatravel-pdtours.netfirms.com; Vspolny per 6, Moscow school No 1239; ⓜBarrikadnaya) Good English-language tours on specialised subjects.

Moscow Mania WALKING TOURS
(☑916-992 46 44; www.mosmania.com; from R300) Themed itineraries with young knowledgeable guides, including fun options such as a trip up Ostankino Tower.

🛏 Sleeping

Moscow is an expensive place to stay. Be sure to book hostels and cheap hotels well ahead, or rent a room in a flat (or a whole flat). The places listed here offer nonsmoking rooms and include breakfast in the rates unless stated otherwise.

Hotel Metropol HISTORIC HOTEL €€€
TOP CHOICE (Map p778; ☑499-501 7800; www.metmos.ru; Teatralny proezd 1/4; s/d from R14,160/16,520; ✳@🖤🏊; ⓜTeatralnaya) An art nouveau masterpiece dating to 1907, the historic Metropol brings an artistic touch to every nook and cranny, from the spectacular exterior to the individually decorated rooms. Breakfast not included.

Home from Home Hostel HOSTEL €
TOP CHOICE (Map p774; ☑495-229 8018; www.home-fromhome.com; Apt 9, ul Arbat 49; dm R700-800, d R2000;@🖤; ⓜSmolenskaya) Original art and mural-painted walls create a bohemian atmosphere at this hostel; for its excellent private rooms it also goes by the name of **Bulgakov Mini-Hotel** (www.bulgakovhotel.com). Enter the courtyard from Plotnikov per and look for entrance No 2.

Assambleya Nikitskaya Hotel HOTEL €€
(Map p774; ☑495-933 5001; www.assambleya-hotels.ru; Bolshaya Nikitskaya ul 12/2; s/d from R7900/9900; ✳@🖤; ⓜOkhotny Ryad) This cosy, comfortable place offers superb location, reasonable prices and authentic Russian charm. The freshly renovated building preserves an anachronistic atmosphere, with heavy floral drapes and linens.

Artel Hotel HOTEL €€
(Map p778; ☑495-626 9008; www.artelhotel.ru; Bldg 3, 3 Teatralny pr 3; s/d from R3100/3400; 🖤) Wacky art abounds in this creative space where each room has a unique design – the cheapest ones are tiny though. Downstairs is the equally funky restaurant/bar/club/theatre space **Masterskaya** (www.mstrsk.ru).

Golden Apple BOUTIQUE HOTEL €€€
(Map p774; ☑495-980 7000; www.goldenapple.ru; ul Malaya Dmitrovka 11; s/d from R26,400/27,900; ⓜPushkinskaya; ✳@🖤) An apple theme is worked into this sophisticated boutique hotel's rooms, decorated in a minimalist, mod-

ern style. There's also a small gym, sauna and Jacuzzi. Online deals on rates make it much more affordable.

Petrovka Loft
HOTEL €€

(Map p774; ☑495-626 2210; www.petrovkaloft. com; 17/2 Petrovka ul; s & d from R3500; 🛜) Enter the courtyard and go straight ahead to find the entrance to this 10-room top-floor hotel on the left. None of the rooms are en suite but everything is pretty stylish and clean and the location is brilliant.

Hotel Akvarel
HOTEL €€

(Map p774; ☑495-502 9430; hotelakvarel.ru; Stoleshnikov per 12; s/d from R8400/10,150; ❄@🛜; Ⓜ Chekhovskaya) An intimate business-class hotel, offering 23 simple but sophisticated rooms adorned with watercolour paintings. Rates drop significantly Friday to Sunday.

East-West Hotel
HOTEL €€

(Map p774; ☑495-232 2857; www.eastwesthotel. ru; Tverskoy bul 14/4; s/d R6000/8000; ❄@🛜; Ⓜ Pushkinskaya) This small hotel, on the loveliest stretch of the Boulevard Ring, evokes the atmosphere of the 19th-century mansion it once was. It's a kitschy but charming place with 24 individually decorated rooms and a lovely fountain-filled courtyard.

Godzillas Hostel
HOSTEL €

(Map p774; ☑495-699 4223; www.godzillashostel .com; Bolshoy Karetny per 6; dm/d/tr R868/2100/ 2883; @🛜; Ⓜ Tsvetnoy bul) Moscow's biggest and most professionally run hostel, with 90 beds out over four floors. Rooms are spacious and light-filled and painted in different colours. There are also three kitchens and a comfy lounge with satellite TV.

Trans-Siberian Hostel
HOSTEL €

(Map p774; ☑495-916 2030; www.tshostel.com; Barashevsky per 12; dm R630-700, d R1750; Ⓜ Kitay-Gorod; @🛜) Snag one of the two double

ⓘ FLAT RENTAL AGENCIES

The following online agencies offer good deals, some from as low as R770 per night:

» www.cheap-moscow.com
» www.flatmates.ru/eng
» www.hofa.ru
» www.moscowapartments.net

rooms in this tiny train-themed hostel, and you're getting one of the capital's best bargains. Staff are super friendly and there's a good kitchen/lounge to hang out in.

Chocolate Hostel
HOSTEL €

(Map p774; ☑495-971 2046; www.chocohostel. com; Apt 4, Degtyarny per 15; dm from R700, tw R2200; @🛜; Ⓜ Pushkinskaya) Chocolate lovers rejoice – this charming, friendly hostel will sooth your craving. Bring your favourite brand from home for their collection. Also has a kitchen and washing machine.

Ozerkovskaya Hotel
HOTEL €€

(☑495-951 9582; www.cct.ru; Ozerkovskaya nab 50; s/d from R5940/6900; @🛜; Ⓜ Paveletskaya) Parquet floors and comfortable queen-size beds rank it above the standard post-Soviet fare. Also offers attentive service, a spa and good location (convenient for the train to Domodedovo airport).

Hotel Sverchkov 8
HOTEL €€

(Map p774; ☑495-625 4978; Sverchkov per 8; www.sverchkov-8.ru; s/d from R4800/5200; 🛜; Ⓜ Chistye Prudy) Intimate old-fashioned hotel in a graceful 18th-century building with hallways lined with plants, and paintings by local artists on the walls.

Napoleon Hostel
HOSTEL €

(Map p774; ☑495-628 6695; www.napoleonhostel. com; Maly Zlatoustinsky per 2, 4th fl; dm R500-1000; @🛜; Ⓜ Kitay-Gorod) The light-filled rooms have six to 10 wooden bunks, for a total of 47 beds (but only two toilets and two showers!), plus a clean kitchen and a comfy common room.

✖ Eating

Moscow is awash with dining options, from self-serve cafes to luxurious restaurants. Many of the city's top bars and clubs have pretty decent kitchens, too, and make for interesting places to graze during the day.

Credit cards are widely accepted and almost all restaurants have English-language menus. For the latest places to open and other reviews see http://en.restoran.ru/msk and the restaurant section of http://elementmoscow.ru.

Restaurants

TOP CHOICE Delicatessen
INTERNATIONAL €€

(Map p774; ☑495-699 3952; www.new deli.ru; Savodvaya-Karetnaya ul 20; meals R800-1000; ⏱noon-midnight Tue-Sat; Ⓜ Tsvetnoy Bulvar) Juicy homemade burgers, beetroot soup with a twist, cherry bourbon and friendly service – all great reasons for dropping by this stylish, relaxed restaurant bar tucked away in a courtyard.

TOP CHOICE **Café Pushkin** RUSSIAN €€€
(Map p774; ☑495-739 0033; Tverskoy bul 26a; business lunches R750, meals R1500-2000; ⊘24hr; ⓂPushkinskaya) The queen mother of *haute russe* dining, with an exquisite blend of Russian and French cuisines. There's a different atmosphere on each floor, including a richly decorated library and a pleasant rooftop cafe. Breakfast on the ground floor is an affordable treat.

Botanika RUSSIAN €€
(Map p774; ☑495-251 9760; Bolshaya Gruzinskaya ul 61; meals R500-700; ⊘11am-10pm; ⓂBelorusskaya) Rare is the restaurant in Moscow that is both fashionable and affordable. Somehow Botanika manages to be both, offering light, modern fare, with plenty of soups, salads and grills.

Chagall JEWISH €€
(Map p774; ☑495-926 4803; www.chagall.ru; 47/3 Bolshaya Nikitskaya ul; mains R500-700; ⊘Barrikadnaya) Inside a Jewish community centre, this convivial kosher restaurant serves tasty, freshly made dishes. The sour-sweet beef dish *esik fleish* is delicious as are the *latkes* (potato pancakes).

Moskvich RUSSIAN €€€
(☑495-705 9121; www.moskvich.su; 2/1 ul Usacheva; meals R1500-2000; ⊘noon-last guest; ⓂFrunzenskaya) Atop the stylish classic-car gallery Autoville (www.autoville.ru) is this retro-chic restaurant named after the sturdy Soviet roadster, one of which is parked in the bar. Both old and new-style Moscow dishes are on the menu and are very nicely presented.

Correa's EUROPEAN €€
(meals R600-1000; ⊘8am-midnight) Bolshaya Gruzinskaya ul (Map p774; ☑495-605 9100; Bolshaya Gruzinskaya ul 32; ⓂBelorusskaya); ul Bolshaya Ordinka (☑495-725 6035; ul Bolshaya Ordinka 40/2; ⓂTretyakovskaya) Bookings are essential for this tiny space. The menu is simple – sandwiches (R200 to R300), pizzas and grills – but everything is prepared with the freshest ingredients and the utmost care. The outlet near the Tretyakov is roomier.

Genatsvale GEORGIAN €€
(Map p774; www.restoran-genatsvale.ru; meals R600-800) Arbat (☑495-203 9453; ul Novy Arbat 11; ⓂArbatskaya); Khamovniki (☑495-202 0445; ul Ostozhenka 12/1; ⓂKropotkinskaya) Moscow's

favourite Georgian restaurant is a great setting to feast on favourites like *khachipuri* (cheesy bread), *kharcho* (rice and lamb soup) and *khinkali* (big dumplings). The original outlet on ul Ostozhenka is the more intimate of the two.

Cafes & Bakeries

Volkonsky BAKERY €
(www.wolkonsky.com; meals R300-500; ⊘8am-11pm) Tverskoy (Map p774; Bolshaya Sadovaya ul 2/46; ⓂMayakovskaya) Kitay Gorod (Map p778; ul Maroseika 4/2; ⓂKitay Gorod) The queue often runs out the door here as loyal patrons wait their turn for the city's best fresh-baked breads, pastries and pies. It's worth the wait, especially if you decide on a fruit-filled croissant or to-die-for olive bread.

Stolle RUSSIAN €
(Map p774; www.stolle.ru; meals R200-600; ⊘8am-10pm) Tverskoy (Bolshaya Sadovaya ul 8/1; ⓂMayakovskaya) Khamovniki (Malaya Pirogovskaya ul 16; ⓂSportivnaya) The selection of sweet and savoury pies sit on the counter, fresh from the oven. It may be difficult to decide (mushroom or meat? apricot or apple?), but you really can't go wrong.

Coffee Mania CAFE €€
(Map p774; www.coffeemania.ru; Bolshaya Nikitskaya ul 13; meals R600-800; ⊘24hr; ⓂAlexandrovsky Sad) The friendly, informal cafe is beloved for its homemade soups, fresh-squeezed juices and steaming cappuccino, not to mention its summer terrace overlooking the leafy courtyard of the conservatory.

Art Lebedev Café CAFE €
(Map p774; http://store.artlebedev.com/offline/lik; meals R300-600; ⊘9am-11pm) Presnaya (Bolshaya Nikitskaya ul 35B; ⓂBarrikadnaya) Chistye Prudy (22/1 Myasnitskaya ul; ⓂChistye Prudy) It's hard to resist the tempting freshly baked cakes and sweet things laid out on the counter at this cafe above a craft and design shop. The Presnaya branch is the cosier of the two.

Jagannath VEGETARIAN €
(Map p774; jagannath.ru; Kuznetsky most 11; meals R300-500; ⊘10am-11pm; ⓂKuznetsky Most; 🛜) Long-running self-serve cafe and shop. Its Indian-theme decor is more New Age-y than ethnic.

Avocado VEGETARIAN €
(Map p774; Chistoprudny bul 12/2; meals R200-400; ⊘10am-11pm; ⓂChistye Prudy; 🛜) Less atmospheric than Jagannath but with a

In capitalist Moscow, Soviet-style *stolovaya* (canteens) have been forced to modernise or close. Excellent contemporary versions of these serve-yourself cafes include **Grably** (Map p774; Pyatnitskaya ul 27; meals R200-300; ☉10am-11pm; **M**Novokuznetskaya) – this particular branch near the Tretyakov has an elaborate winter-garden seating area – and the ubiquitous **Moo-Moo** (meals R200-300; ☉9am-11pm) Basmanny (Map p774; Myasnitskaya ul 14; **M**Lubyanka); Arbat (Map p774; ul Arbat 45/24; **M**Smolenskaya), instantly recognisable from its black-and-white Holstein-print decor.

Newly minted **Stolovaya 57** (Map p778; 3rd fl, GUM, Red Sq; ☉10am-10pm; **M**Okhotny Ryad) offers a nostalgic recreation of dining in post-Stalinist Russia. The food is good – and cheap for such a fancy store. For the real deal, drop by the grandly decorated **Tsentralny** (Map p774; 1 Kudrinskaya pl; ☉10am-10pm; **M**Barrikadnaya) at the base of one of the Seven Sisters tower blocks.

more diverse menu, drawing on dishes from the world's cuisines.

🍺 **Drinking & Clubbing**

The line between cafe, bar and club in Moscow is hazy. The same place can morph from somewhere to have a quiet morning coffee to a hedonistic venue for cocktail-swilling late-night frolics. At 'in' places you'll have to brave 'face control' but, on the whole, Moscow nightlife is becoming more democratic, especially at the places we've listed.

Kvartira 44   CAFE-BAR
(Map p774; www.kv44.ru; ☉noon-2am Sun-Thu, to 6am Fri & Sat) Bolshaya Nikitskaya ul (Bolshaya Nikitskaya ul 22/2; **M**Okhotny Ryad); Zamoskvorechie (ul Malaya Yakimanka 24/8; **M**Polyanka) Somebody had the brilliant idea to convert an old Moscow apartment into a cosy bar, with tables and chairs tucked into every nook and cranny. The Zamoskvorechie outlet has live music some nights.

Mayak   CAFE-BAR
(Map p774; www.clubmayak.ru; Bolshaya Nikitskaya ul 19; meals R600-800; **M**Okhotny Ryad) Named for the Mayakovsky Theatre downstairs, this is more cafe than club. It still attracts actors, artists and writers, who come to see friendly faces, eat filling European fare and drink into the night.

Gogol   CAFE-BAR
(Map p774; www.gogolclubs.ru; Stoleshnikov per 11; cover R350; ☉24hr, concerts 9pm or 10pm Thu-Sat; **M**Chekhovskaya) Fun, informal and affordable (so surprising on swanky Stoleshnikov!), Gogol is great for food, drinks and music. In summer, the action moves out to the courtyard, where the gigantic tent is styled like an old-fashioned street scene.

Apshu   CAFE-BAR
(Map p774; Klimentovsky per 10; ☉24hr; **M**Tretyakovskaya) With decor inspired by a little fishing village on the Baltic coast, this trendy place offers inexpensive food and drinks, board games, art exhibitions, concerts... basically something for everyone.

Art Akademiya   CAFE-BAR
(Map p774; ☎495-771 7446; www.academiya.ru; 6/3 Bersenevskaya nab; ☉noon-midnight Sun-Thu, to 6am Fri & Sat) The pizza chain with all the best locations has nabbed a massive space in the Red October Factory complex for this super stylish, contemporary art-packed lounge bar. Relax on caramel leather sofas or perch at the long central bar.

Solyanka   CAFE-CLUB
(Map p774; http://s-11.ru; ul Solyanka 11; cover R500; ☉noon-midnight Sun-Wed, to 5am Fri & Sat) An 18th-century merchant's house has been revamped into this appealing hipster cafe-bar-club. Thursday to Saturday nights the biggest room is cleared for dancing, with the DJ starting up around 11pm.

Propaganda   CAFE-CLUB
(Map p778; www.propagandamoscow.com; Bolshoy Zlatoustinsky per 7; ☉noon-6am; **M**Kitay-Gorod) This long-time favourite sports exposed-brick walls and pipe ceilings. It's a cafe by day (meals R500 to R700), but at night they clear the dance floor and let the DJ do his stuff. Sunday is gay night.

Krizis Zhanra   CAFE-CLUB
(Map p774; www.kriziszhanra.ru; ul Pokrovka 16/16; ☉concerts 9pm daily, 11pm Fri & Sat; **M**Chistye Prudy) Everybody has something good to say about Krizis and what's not to love? Good cheap food, copious drinks and rockin'

COOL SPOTS FOR SUMMER DRINKS

These top chill out cafe-bars are best visited on a hot day:

Chaikhona No 1 (www.chaihona.com; ⏱noon to last customer) Hermitage Gardens (Map p774; ⓂChekhovskaya); Gorky Park (ⓂFrunzenskaya) This cool Uzbek lounge and cafe is housed in an inviting, exotic tent laid with oriental rugs and plush pillows. There's *plov* and *shashliky* on the menu.

Lebedinoe Ozero (Swan Lake; http://s-11.ru; Gorky Park; ⏱noon-2am late Apr-mid Sep; ⓂFrunzenskaya) Beside a pond with, yes, swans, this colourfully decorated place is a very happening haunt. Also offers cooling dips in a pool and Thai massage.

music every night, all of which inspires the gathered to get their groove on.

Denis Simachëv Shop & Bar CLUB

(Map p774; www.denissimachev.com; Stoleshnikov per 12/2; ⏱11am to last customer; ⓂChekhovskaya) By day, it's the boutique and cafe of the famed fashion designer of the same name. By night, it morphs into a hip-hop-happening nightclub that combines glamour and humour. Look sharp to pass face control.

Art Garbage CAFE-CLUB

(Map p774; www.art-garbage.ru; Starosadsky per 5; ⏱noon-6am; ⓂKitay-Gorod) Enter this funky club-cafe through the courtyard, which is littered with sculpture. Inside, the walls are crammed with paintings of all genres, and there are DJs or live music every night.

☆ Entertainment

To find out what's on, see the weekly magazine *element,* the entertainment section in Thursday's *Moscow Times*, or the bi-monthly edition of *Moscow in Your Pocket*.

Bolshoi Theatre BALLET, OPERA

(Map p778; ☎495-250 7317; www.bolshoi.ru; Teatralnaya pl 1; tickets R200-5000; ⓂTeatralnaya) An evening at the Bolshoi is one of Moscow's most romantic options. Both the ballet and opera companies perform a range of Russian and foreign works. Productions take place both on the main stage, now back in operation after a multiyear renovation, and the smaller New Stage (Novaya Stsena).

Kremlin Ballet Theatre BALLET

(Map p778; ☎495-928 5232; www.kremlin-gkd.ru; ul Vozdvizhenka 1; ⓂAlexandrovsky Sad) The Bolshoi does not have a monopoly on ballet in Moscow. Leading dancers also appear with the Kremlin Ballet, which performs in the State Kremlin Palace (inside the Kremlin).

Moscow International House of Music CLASSICAL MUSIC

(☎495-730 1011; www.mmdm.ru; Kosmodamianskaya nab 52/8; tickets R200-2000; ⓂPaveletskaya) This venue for the Russian Philharmonic towers over the Moscow River. It has three halls, including Svetlanov Hall, which has the largest organ in Russia.

Tchaikovsky Concert Hall CLASSICAL MUSIC

(Map p774; ☎495-232 0400; www.meloman.ru; Triumfalnaya pl 4/31; tickets R100-1000; ⓂMayakovskaya) Home to the State Symphony Orchestra, which specialises in the music of its namesake composer and other Russian classics.

MKhAT THEATRE

(Map p774; ☎495-629 8760; http://art.theatre.ru; Kamergersky per 3; ⓂTeatralnaya) Also known as the Chekhov Moscow Art Theatre, this is where method acting was founded more than 100 years ago. Watch for English-

GAY & LESBIAN MOSCOW

Sunday is gay night at Propaganda (p785). For more information see www.gay.ru/english.

Central Station MSK (Map p774; www.gaycentral.ru; Moskva ul, Yuzhny proezd, dom 4; ⏱10pm-7am Thu-Sun; ⓂKomsomolskaya) A new location and incarnation, opposite the Hilton Leningradskaya, for Moscow's biggest and best gay dance club, with drag queens, go-go boys, and a dance floor that can accommodate 800 sweaty bodies.

12 Volts (Map p774; www.12voltclub.ru; Tverskaya ul 12; meals R400-600; ⏱6pm-6am; ⓂMayakovskaya) Welcoming lesbian cafe-cum-social club, tucked in the courtyard off Tverskaya.

language versions of Russian classics performed by the American Studio.

Chinese Pilot Dzhao-Da LIVE MUSIC
(Map p778; ☎495-623 2896; www.jao-da.ru; Lubyansky proezd 25; cover R300-500; ☺concerts 10pm Thu, 11pm Fri & Sat; Ⓜ Kitay-Gorod) This divey, relaxed basement place hosts lots of different kinds of bands from around Europe and Russia, so check out the website in advance. Often has free concerts on Monday nights.

Roadhouse LIVE MUSIC
(☎499-245 5543; www.roadhouse.ru; Dovatora 8; ☺noon-midnight, concerts 9pm; Ⓜ Sportivnaya) If your dog got run over by a pick-up truck, you can find some comfort at this blues bar, around the corner from the metro station, with live music every night.

Nikulin Circus on Tsvetnoy Bulvar CIRCUS
(Map p774; ☎495-625-8970; www.circusnikulin.ru; Tsvetnoy bul 13; tickets R250-2000; ☺shows 7pm Thu-Mon & 2.30pm Sat; Ⓜ Tsvetnoy Bulvar) Named for the beloved actor, director and clown Yury Nikulin, this building has housed the circus since 1880 (though it has been thoroughly modernised). Its thematic shows are also acclaimed.

🔒 Shopping

Ul Arbat has always been a tourist attraction and is littered with souvenir shops and stalls.

GUM MALL
(Map p778; ☎495-788 4343; www.gum.ru; Krasnaya pl 3; ☺10am-10pm; Ⓜ Pl Revolyutsii) Elegant heritage building on Red Sq, packed with designer labels and good souvenir shops including the glam grocery **Gastronom No 1**.

Izmaylovo Market SOUVENIRS
(www.kremlin-izmailovo.com; Izmaylovskoye shosse; ☺9am-6pm Sat & Sun; Ⓜ Partizanskaya) Sprawling area packed with art, handmade crafts, antiques, Soviet paraphernalia and just about anything you might want for a souvenir. Emerging from the metro look for the kitsch mock Kremlin (great for photos!) to find the market and tasty shashlyk (kebab) stands.

TsUM DEPARTMENT STORE
(Map p774; www.tsum.ru; ul Petrovka 2; ☺10am-10pm Mon-Sat, 11am-10pm Sun; Ⓜ Teatralnaya) TsUM stands for Tsentralny Universalny Magazin (Central Department Store); it was built in 1909 as the Scottish-owned Muir & Merrilees. Now it's filled with luxury items including fashion by top Russian designers. Check out the chic food hall in the basement.

Muscovites are avid football (soccer) fans. The city's top teams are **Spartak** (www.spartak.com), **Lokomotiv** (www.fclm.ru), **PFC CSKA** (www.pfc-cska.com), **Dynamo** (www.fcdynamo.ru) and **FK Moskva** (www.fcmoscow.ru). Buy tickets (R150 to R6000) online at the club websites, or immediately before games, which are played at **Lokomotiv Stadium** (Bolshaya Cherkizovskaya ul 125; Ⓜ Cherkizovskaya) and **Luzhniki Stadium** (☎495-785 9717; www.luzhniki.ru; Luzhnetskaya nab 24; Ⓜ Sportivnaya).

Atlas MAPS
(Map p774; Kuznetsky most 9/10; ☺9am-8pm Mon-Fri, 10am-6pm Sat, 11am-5pm Sun; Ⓜ Kuznetsky Most) Sells city and regional maps covering the whole country.

Dom Inostrannoy Knigi BOOKS
(Map p774; Kuznetsky most 18/7; ☺9am-9pm Mon-Fri, 10am-9pm Sat, 10am-8pm Sun; Ⓜ Kuznetsky Most) Has the widest selection of literature in foreign languages.

ℹ Information
Dangers & Annoyances

Moscow is not as dangerous as paranoid locals may have you think, but as in any big city, be on your guard against pickpockets and muggers. Be particularly careful at or around metro stations at the main railway stations.

Reports of tourists being hassled by police about their documents and registration have declined. It's still wise to carry a photocopy of your passport, visa and registration stamp. If stopped by a member of the police force, do not hand over your passport! It is perfectly acceptable to show a photocopy instead.

Internet Access

Wireless access (not always free) is ubiquitous.

Cafemax (www.cafemax.ru Novoslobodskaya ul 3; per hr R120; ☺24hr; Ⓜ Novoslobodskaya) Late-night and early-morning discounts available.

Time Online (www.timeonline.ru; per hr R70-100; ☺24hr) Okhotny Ryad (Ⓜ Okhotny Ryad); Komsomolskaya (Komsomolskaya pl 3; Ⓜ Komsomolskaya) Offers copy and photo services, as well as over 100 zippy computers and free wi-fi access.

Internet Resources

Moscow Taxi (www.moscow-taxi.com) Viktor the virtual taxi driver provides extensive descriptions of sights inside and outside of Moscow, as well as hotel bookings and other tourist services.

Russia Made Easy (www.redtape.ru) Forums offer inside information on any question you might ask about the city.

Media

Reliable listings magazines in Russian include *Afisha* and *Time Out*. The following English-language media are all free:

element (www.elementmoscow.ru) Weekly newsprint magazine with restaurant reviews and concert and art exhibition listings; look out for their quarterly restaurant guide.

Moscow In Your Pocket (moscow.inyourpocket.com) Good bi-monthly booklet of listings and features available in major hotels and hostels.

Moscow News (www.moscownews.ru) This long-standing news weekly focuses on domestic and international politics and business.

Moscow Times (www.themoscowtimes.com) Best of the locally published English-language newspapers. Thursday's edition is a great source for what's happening at the weekend.

Medical Services

American Medical Centre (☎495-933 7700; www.amcenter.ru; Grokholsky per 1; ⓜPr Mira) Offers 24-hour emergency service, consultations and a full range of medical specialists, including paediatricians and dentists. Also has an onsite pharmacy with English-speaking staff.

Money

Banks, exchange counters and ATMs are common and credit cards widely accepted. Cash American Express travellers cheques at **American Express** (☎495-543 9400; Vetoshny per 17; ⓞ10am-9.30pm; ⓜTeatralnaya), which also has an ATM.

Post

Main post office (Map p774; Myasnitskaya ul 26; ⓞ8am-8pm Mon-Fri, 9am-7pm Sat & Sun; ⓜChistye Prudy)

Telephone & Fax

Payphones operate with cards that are available in the larger post offices. You can buy a local SIM card from any of the hundreds of mobile-phone shops around the city.

Central Telegraph (Tverskaya ul 7; ⓞpost 8am-10pm, telephone 24hr; ⓜOkhotny Ryad) This convenient office offers telephone, fax and internet services.

Travel Agencies

Maria Travel Agency (☎495-725 5746; ul Maroseyka 13; ⓜKitay-Gorod) Offers visa support, apartment rental and some local tours, including to the Golden Ring.

Unifest Travel (☎495-234 6555; www.unifest.ru; Komsomolsky pr 13; ⓜPark Kultury) About 500m south of the metro station, this is an on-the-ball travel company offering rail and air tickets, visa support and more.

ⓘ Getting There & Away

Air

Moscow is served by three main international airports:

Domodedovo (☎495-933 6666; www.domodedovo.ru) 48km south of the city.

Sheremetyevo (☎495-232 6565; http://svo.aero) 30km northwest of the city.

Vnukovo (495-937 5555; www.vnukovo-airport.ru) 30km southwest of the city.

For a list of carriers that serve the city see p825.

Boat

The Moscow terminus for cruises to St Petersburg is 10km northeast of the city centre at **Severny Rechnoy Vokzal** (Northern River Station; Leningradskoe shosse 51; ⓜRechnoy Vokzal). From the metro station walk 15 minutes due west, passing under Leningradskoe shosse and through a nice park.

Bus

To book a seat, go to the long-distance bus terminal, the **Shchyolkovsky bus station**

CHANGING TELEPHONE NUMBERS

Two area codes function within Moscow: ☎495 and ☎499. Gradually many old 495 numbers will be changed to 499 (with a slight change of number, in many cases). Dialling patterns for the two area codes are different:

» Within the ☎495 area code, dial seven digits, with no area code.

» Within the ☎499 area code, dial 10 digits (including ☎499).

» From ☎495 to ☎499 or vice versa, dial ☎8 + 10 digits (including appropriate area code). Although this looks like an intercity call, it is charged as a local call.

» To call a mobile phone (usually numbers starting ☎915, 916 or 926) from a landline – or vice versa – dial ☎8 + 10 digits.

(Ⓜ Shchyolkovskaya), 8km east of the city centre. Queues can be bad, so it's advisable to book ahead, especially for travel on Friday, Saturday or Sunday.

Buses tend to be crowded but are usually faster and more convenient than the *prigorodny* (suburban) trains to some Golden Ring destinations.

Train

Moscow has nine main stations. Be sure to check which Moscow station your train is using; even trains to/from the same destination may use different stations.

Belorussky vokzal (Belarus Station; Map p774; Tverskaya Zastava pl; Ⓜ Belorusskaya) For Smolensk, Kaliningrad, Minsk, Warsaw, Vilnius, Berlin; some trains to/from the Czech Republic; and suburban trains to/from the west.

Kazansky vokzal (Kazan Station; Map p774; Komsomolskaya pl; Ⓜ Komsomolskaya) For Vladimir, Nizhny Novgorod, the Ural Mountains, Siberia; the Volga; and suburban trains to/from the southeast.

Kievsky vokzal (Kyiv Station; Kievskaya pl; Ⓜ Kievskaya) For Budapest, Bucharest, Kyiv, Odessa, Prague. Also Aeroexpress services to Vnukovo airport.

Kursky vokzal (Kursk Station; pl Kurskogo vokzala; Ⓜ Kurskaya) For the Caucasus, eastern Ukraine, Crimea, Georgia, Azerbaijan. It also has some trains to/from Vladimir.

Leningradsky vokzal (Leningrad Station; Map p774; Komsomolskaya pl; Ⓜ Komsomolskaya) For Novgorod, Pskov, St Petersburg, Tallinn, Helsinki.

Paveletsky vokzal (Pavelets Station; Paveletskaya pl; Ⓜ Paveletskaya) For trains heading south, including Aeroexpress to Domodedovo airport.

Rizhsky vokzal (Rīga Station; Rizhskaya pl; Ⓜ Rizhskaya) For services to Latvia.

Savyolovsky vokzal (Savyolov Station; pl Savyolovskogo vokzala; Ⓜ Savyolovskaya) Services to/from the north, including Aeroexpress to Sheremetyevo airport.

Yaroslavsky vokzal (Yaroslavl Station; Map p774; Komsomolskaya pl; Ⓜ Komsomolskaya) For trains to Siberia, the Far East, China and Mongolia.

It is much easier to buy tickets from a travel agent (see p788) or *kassa zheleznoy dorogi* (railway ticket office) than at the train stations. Most local agencies charge a small service fee, but be careful of international travel agencies that may charge considerable mark-ups.

ⓘ Getting Around

To/From the Airport

All airports are accessible by **Aeroexpress** (www.aeroexpress.ru); these convenient train

METRO TOUR

For just R26 you can spend the day touring Moscow's magnificent metro stations. Many of the stations are marble-faced, frescoed, gilded works of art. Among our favourites are: **Komsomolskaya**, a huge stuccoed hall, its ceiling covered with mosaics depicting military heroes; **Prospekt Mira**, decorated in elegant gold-trimmed white porcelain with bas-reliefs of happy comrades; and **Mayakovskaya**, Grand Prize winner at the 1939 World's Fair in New York.

services leave from different stations depending on the airport they serve – see p828 for details. If you have a lot of luggage and you wish to take a taxi, it is highly recommended to book in advance to take advantage of fixed rates offered by most companies (usually R1000 to R1500 to/from any airport).

Public Transport

The **Moscow metro** (www.mosmetro.ru) is the easiest, quickest and cheapest way of getting around Moscow. You will rarely wait on the platform for more than two minutes, but carriages get packed during rush hour. Stations are marked outside by 'M' signs. Magnetic tickets (R26) are sold at ticket booths. Save time by buying a multiple-ride ticket (five/10/20 rides R125/240/460).

Buses, trolleybuses and trams are useful along a few radial or cross-town routes that the metro misses, and are necessary for reaching sights away from the city centre. Tickets (R28) are sold on the vehicle by a conductor.

Taxi

See the boxed text p827 for information on hailing unofficial taxis. Expect to pay R200 to R300 for a ride around the city centre. To book a taxi try:

Taxi Blues (☎ 495-243 4919; www.the-taxi.ru)

Woman Taxi (Zhenskoye Taksi; ☎ 495-662 0033; www.womantaxi.ru) Offers female drivers and child car seats.

VELIKY NOVGOROD
ВЕЛИКИЙ НОВГОРОД

☎ 8162 / POP 240,000

Between Moscow and St Petersburg, picturesque Veliky Novogord (meaning Great New Town) spans the River Volkhov. In the 12th century it was Russia's biggest city, an independent quasidemocracy with a flourishing cultural life. Today it's a pleasant provincial

SMOLENSK СМОЛЕНСК

On the upper Dnepr River, 360km southwest of Moscow, **Smolensk** (http://admin.smo lensk.ru) is one of Russia's oldest cities and has ancient walls, onion-dome cathedrals and well-landscaped parks strewn across the undulating hills. The highlight is the magnificent Assumption Cathedral, but music lovers will want to attend the renowned Glinka Festival (end of May to early June).

The best place to stay is **Hotel Tsentralnaya** (☑4812-383 604; http://smolensk-otel. keytown.com; cnr pl Lenina & ul Konenkova; s/d from R3500/4500), while a charming place to eat is **Smolenskaya Krepost** (☑4812-327 690; ul Studencheskaya 4; meals R300; ☺10am-11pm), set in the old castle walls.

Daily trains connect Smolensk with Moscow (R700, 5½ hours), Minsk (R700, four hours), Brest (R1000, eight hours), Warsaw (R2600, nine hours) and Prague (R4200, 24 hours). There's also a weekly train to Berlin (R4300, 41 hours).

town, with a magnificent historical legacy preserved in its numerous churches and museums, and the mighty walls of its kremlin.

The town's switched-on **tourist office** (☑773 074, 24hr hotline ☑8162-998 686; www.visit novgorod.ru; Sennaya pl 5; ☺9.30am-6pm) will help you get your bearings. City tours in a variety of languages can be arranged.

◉ Sights & Activities

Kremlin   HISTORIC AREA
(☺6am-midnight) On the west bank of the Volkhov, and surrounded by a pleasant wooded park, the Kremlin was first built in the 9th century, then rebuilt with brick in the 14th century; this is the version that still stands today. It houses the city's most famous sites, the highlight of which is the handsome, Byzantine **Cathedral of St Sophia** (☺8am-8pm). Finished in 1050, it is one of the oldest buildings in Russia. Services usually take place between 6pm and 8pm daily. Close by, the 15th-century **belfry** and a leaning 17th-century **clock tower** poke above the city walls. For panoramic views across the complex, climb the 41m-tall **Kokui Tower** (adult/student R100/60; ☺11am-2pm & 3-7pm Tue, Wed & Fri-Sun).

In the centre of the Kremlin stands the 16m-high, 300-tonne **Millennium of Russia Monument**. Unveiled in 1862, it's a who's who of Russian history, depicting some 127 figures – ranging from Mother Russia through to Catherine the Great. The Gothic **Chamber of Facets**, part of a palace built in 1433, has a collection of icons and lavish church booty from throughout the region, including some beautiful illuminated manuscripts; it was closed for renovation at the time of research.

Yaroslav's Court   HISTORIC AREA
Across a footbridge from the Kremlin are the remnants of an 18th-century market arcade. Beyond that is the market gatehouse, an array of churches sponsored by 13th- to 16th-century merchant guilds, and a 'road palace' built in the 18th century as a rest stop for Catherine the Great.

The 12th-century **Court Cathedral of St Nicholas** (Nikolo-Dvorishchensky sobor; adult/student R100/60; ☺10am-noon & 1-6pm Wed-Sun, closed last Fri of month) is all that remains of the early palace complex of the Novgorod princes, from which Yaroslav's Court (Yaroslavovo dvorishche) gets its name. The cathedral holds church artefacts and temporary exhibitions of local interest. Downstairs you can see fragments from the church's original frescos.

Yuriyevo   HISTORIC BUILDINGS
Hop on bus 7 or 7A opposite the tourist office heading to the village of Yuriyevo to view the picturesque 12th-century **Yuriyev Monastery** (Svyato-Yurev Myzhskoi Monastr; ☺10am-8pm) with a beautiful waterside setting. About 1km up the road is the open-air **Vitoslavlitsy Museum of Wooden Architecture** (Myzei Narodnogo Derevyannogo Zodchestva Vitoslavlitsy; adult/student R100/60; ☺park 10am-6pm, houses close 4.30pm) where you can explore some 20 or so attractive traditional timber buildings.

One hour **cruises** (R300; ☺May-Sept) from the dock below the kremlin are also recommended.

🛏 Sleeping & Eating
The tourist office can recommend homestays (around R1000 per person for a room). The rates for hotels listed here all include breakfast. During summer, open-air cafes

facing the Kremlin's west side make pleasant spots for a drink.

Hotel Volkhov
HOTEL €€

(📞225 500; www.hotel-volkhov.ru; ul Predtechenskaya 24; s/d from R1800/2700; @🛜) Centrally located and offering modern, nicely furnished rooms with lots of amenities. A sauna (extra fee) is available to guests.

Hotel Akron
HOTEL €€

(📞736 906; www.hotel-akron.ru; ul Predtechenskaya 24; s/d from R1550/2200) Similar to the Volkhov next door, but with lower prices and no elevator. Rooms have modern bathrooms, cable TV and minifridge. Friendly service is also a plus.

Park Inn Veliky Novgorod
HOTEL €€€

(📞940 910; www.parkinn.com/hotel-velikynovgorod; ul Studencheskaya 2A; r from R3500; ❄@🛜☼) Novgorod's top hotel has comfortable rooms, good service and a wealth of facilities.

Café Le Chocolat
CAFE-BAR €€

(📞739 009; www.cafelechocolate.ru; ul Lyudogoshcha 8; dishes R250-650; ◷9am-11pm) This stylish cafe-bar, with a nonsmoking section, offers some tantalising options, including dozens of sushi platters, a range of breakfasts, chocolate desserts and creative cocktails.

Ilmen
RESTAURANT, CAFE €€

(📞178 374; ul Gazon 2; cafe/restaurant meals from R50/500; ◷bistro 10am-10pm, restaurant noon-midnight) The ground floor has a little deli for takeaway snacks, and a bistro for cheap sit-down eats. Upstairs, the more formal restaurant **Holmgard** has a menu packed with Russian dishes including freshly made kebabs.

Dom Berga
RESTAURANT, CAFE €€

(📞948 838; ul Bolnaya Moskovskaya 24; cafe/restaurant meals from R50/500; ◷cafe 9am-9pm, restaurant noon-midnight) Enjoy well-prepared and reasonably priced Russian dishes in this handsome brick building near Yaroslavl's Court – again there's a choice between simple cafe and fancier restaurant.

❶ Getting There & Around

The **train station** (Novgorod-na-Volkhove; 📞775 372) is 1km west of the Kremlin, at the end of pr Karla Marksa. Three trains run daily to St Petersburg's Moscow Station (R350, three hours), and there's a night-train connection with Moscow (*platskartny/kupe* R715/1573, eight hours).

The **bus station** (📞739 979), next to the train station, serves St Petersburg (R340, four hours) at least once an hour. There's also direct buses to Pskov (R385, four hours, 8am and 4pm) and a service to Rīga (R900, 11″ hours, Wednesday and Sunday).

From the bus and train stations, take buses 4 and 20 (R10) into the city and 4 or 19 back. A taxi should cost about R100.

ST PETERSBURG
САНКТ ПЕТЕРБУРГ

📞812 / POP 4.6 MILLION

'St Petersburg is Russia, but it is not Russian.' The opinion of Nicholas II, the empire's last tsar, on his one-time capital still resonates. The city, affectionately know as Piter to locals, is a fascinating hybrid where one moment you can be clapping along to a fun Russian folk-music show in a baroque hall or sniffing incense inside a mosaic-covered Orthodox church, the next grooving on the dance floor of an underground club or posing at a contemporary-art event in a renovated bakery.

Europe's fourth-largest city is also a visual delight. The Neva River and surrounding canals reflect unbroken facades of handsome 18th- and 19th-century buildings that house a spellbinding collection of cultural storehouses, culminating in the incomparable Hermitage. It's easy to imagine how such an environment, warts and all, was the inspiration for many of Russia's greatest artists, including the writers Pushkin, Gogol and Dostoevsky, and musical maestros such as Rachmaninoff, Tchaikovsky and Shostakovich. This giant warehouse of Russian culture has more to offer the traveller than perhaps anywhere else in the country.

History

Starting with the Peter and Paul Fortress, founded on the marshy estuary of the Neva River in 1703, Peter the Great and his successors commissioned a city built to grand design by mainly European architects. By the early 19th century, St Petersburg had firmly established itself as Russia's cultural heart. But at the same time as writers, artists and musicians – such as Pushkin, Turgenev and, later, Tchaikovsky and Dostoevsky – lived in and were inspired by the city, political and social problems were on the rise.

Industrialisation brought a flood of poor workers and associated urban squalor to St Petersburg. Revolution against the monarchy was first attempted in the short-lived coup of 14 December 1825. The next revolution was in 1905, sparked by the 'Bloody

PSKOV ПСКОВ

Medieval church-studded Pskov, dominated by its mighty riverside kremlin and just 30km from Estonia, makes for an impressive first sight if you are coming over from the Baltics; or a pleasant farewell from Russia should you be headed in the opposite direction.

The **tourist office** (☎8112-724 568; www.tourism.pskov.ru; pl Lenina; ⊙10am-5pm Mon-Fri) is helpful. Lay your head at the **Hotel Rizhskaya** (☎462 223; Rizhsky pr 25; s/d R950/1700; @) and dine at **Kafe V'Gorod N** (☎737 124; Oktyabrsky pr 19; meal R200; ⊙8am-1am).

Direct trains to St Petersburg (R700, five hours) depart at ungodly hours; you're better off taking the bus (R600, 5½ hours). Night trains go to Moscow (R2000, 12 hours), Rīga (R1700, eight hours) and Vilnius (R1200, eight hours).

Two buses daily connect with Veliky Novgorod (R385, 4½ hours) and Smolensk (R700, eight to 10 hours). There are also daily services to Tallinn (R800, six hours) and Tartu (R600, four hours) in Estonia.

Sunday' of 9 January, when more than a hundred people were killed and hundreds more were injured after troops fired on a crowd petitioning the tsar outside the Winter Palace. The tsar's government limped on, until Lenin and his Bolshevik followers took advantage of Russia's disastrous involvement in WWI to instigate the third successful revolution in 1917. Again, St Petersburg (renamed a more Russian-sounding Petrograd in 1914) was at the forefront of the action.

To break with the tsarist past, the seat of government was moved back to Moscow, and St Petersburg was renamed Leningrad after the first communist leader's death in 1924. The city – by virtue of its location, three million-plus population and industry – remained one of Russia's most important, thus putting it on the front line during WWII. For 872 days Leningrad was besieged by the Germans, and one million people perished in horrendous conditions.

During the 1960s and 1970s Leningrad's bohemian spirit burned bright, fostering the likes of dissident poet Joseph Brodsky and underground rock groups such as Kino and Akvarium. In 1991, as the Soviet Union came tumbling down, the city reverted to calling itself St Petersburg.

Millions of roubles were spent on restoration for the city's tricentenary celebrations in 2003, and although the 2008 financial crash has slowed down some big construction projects, St Petersburg looks better now probably than at any other time in its history. This is one reason why Valentina Matviyenko, the city's federal governor since 2003, has been touted as a possible presidential candidate for 2012.

⊙ Sights

The Hermitage
MUSEUM

(Map p800; ☎571 3465; www.hermitagemuseum. org; Dvortsovaya pl 2; adult R400, student & under 17yr free; ⊙10.30am-6pm Tue-Sat, to 5pm Sun; Ⓜ Nevsky Pr) Mainly set in the magnificent Winter Palace, the Hermitage fully lives up to its sterling reputation. You can be absorbed by its treasures – which range from Egyptian mummies and Scythian gold to early-20th-century paintings by Matisse and Picasso – for days and still come out wishing for more.

Queues for tickets, particularly from May to August, can be horrendous. The museum can also be very busy on the first Thursday of the month, when admission is free for all. Either go late in the day when the lines are likely to be shorter or book your ticket online through the Hermitage's website. You'll be issued with a voucher that allows you to jump the queue and go straight to the ticket booth.

Joining a tour is another way to avoid queuing: call the museum's **excursions office** (☎571 8446; ⊙11am-1pm & 2-4pm); they will tell you what time to show up for the tours in English, German or French.

Dvortsovaya Ploshchad
HISTORIC AREA

(Map p800) The Hermitage's main entrance is from the Palace Square (Dvortsovaya pl), one of the city's most impressive and historic spaces. Stand back to admire the palace and the central 47.5m-high **Alexander Column**, named after Alexander I and commemorating the 1812 victory over Napoleon. Enclosing the square's south side is the **General Staff Building**, closed for renovation at the time of research: in its east wing there's an excellent branch of the Hermitage where the crowds drop away.

Church of the Saviour on Spilled Blood

CHURCH

(Spas na Krovi; Map p800; ☑315 1636; www.cathe dral.ru; Konyushennaya pl; adult/student R320/170; ⊙11am-7pm Thu-Tue Oct-Apr, 10am-8pm May-Sep; Ⓜ Nevsky Pr) This multidomed dazzler, partly modelled on St Basil's in Moscow, was built between 1883 and 1907 on the spot where Alexander II was assassinated in 1881 (hence its gruesome name). The interior's 7000 sq m of mosaics fully justify the entrance fee.

Russian Museum

MUSEUM

(Russy Muzey; Map p800; ☑595 4248; www.rusmuse um.ru; Inzhenernaya ul 4; adult/student R350/150; ⊙10am-5pm Mon, to 6pm Wed-Sun; Ⓜ Gostiny Dvor) Facing onto the elegant pl Iskusstv (Arts Sq) is the handsome Mikhailovsky Palace, now housing one of the country's finest collections of Russian art. After the Hermitage you may feel you have had your fill of art, but try your utmost to make some time for this gem of a museum. There's also a lovely garden behind the palace.

The museum owns three other city palac-es, all worth visiting if you have time, where permanent and temporary exhibitions are held: the Marble Palace (Mramorny Dvorets; Map p794; ☑312 9196; Millionnaya ul 5; adult/stu-dent R350/150; ⊙10am-5pm Wed-Mon; Ⓜ Nevsky Pr); the Mikhailovsky Castle (Mikhaylovsky Zamok; Map p800; ☑595 4248; Sadovaya ul 2; adult/student R350/150; ⊙10am-5pm Mon, to 6pm Wed-Sun; Ⓜ Gostiny Dvor), also known as

the Engineer's Castle; and the Stroganov Palace (Map p800; ☑312 9054; Nevsky pr 17; adult/student R350/150; ⊙10am-5pm Tue-Sun; Ⓜ Nevsky pr). A ticket for R600, available at each palace, covers entrance to all four with-in a 24-hour period.

St Isaac's Cathedral

MUSEUM

(Isaakievsky Sobor; Map p800; ☑315 9732; www. cathedral.ru; Isaakievskaya pl; adult/student R320/170; ⊙11am-7pm Thu-Tue; Ⓜ Sadovaya/Sen-naya Pl) The golden dome of this cathedral dominates the city skyline. Its lavish inte-rior is open as a museum, but many visitors just buy the separate ticket to climb the 262 steps up to the colonnade (R100; ⊙11am-6pm Thu-Tue) around the dome's drum to take in panoramic views.

Behind the cathedral is ploshchad Deka-bristov (Decembrists' Sq), named after the Decembrists' Uprising of 14 December 1825. Falconet's statue of Peter the Great, the Bronze Horseman, stands at the end of the square towards the river.

Yusupov Palace

MUSEUM

(Map p794; ☑314 9883; www.yusupov-palace. ru; nab reki Moyki 94; adult/student R500/380; ⊙11am-5pm; Ⓜ Sadovaya/Sennaya Pl) In a city of glittering palaces, the dazzling interiors of the Yuspov more than hold their own. Best known as the place where Rasputin met his untimely end, the palace sports a series of richly decorated rooms culminating in a

---

LOCAL KNOWLEDGE

TOP HERMITAGE SIGHTS

Dimitri Ozerkov, chief curator of the Hermitage 20/21 Project, recommends his favourite pieces from the museum's collection:

» **Egyptian mummies** (Room 100) I first visited the Hermitage when I was five or six years old. At that time what I liked the most were these mummies displayed at a low height so I could see them well and read their names, such as Pa De Ist.

» **Raphael's Loggia** (Room 227) Catherine the Great commissioned Giacomo Quarrengi in the 1780s to create this copy of a gallery she admired at the Vatican. It was made exactly to scale, so not only is it a great event of art but also of technique and design.

» **Perseus and Andromeda** (Room 246) The Hermitage has lots of works by Rubens, many of them from his studio – he was like the Damien Hirst of his day, presiding over a factory of artists. One piece that undoubtedly was done by his hand, though, is this – it's a masterpiece. You look at Medusa's eyes and you feel afraid, and the horse looks so real you feel you could touch it.

» **Dance and Music** (Room 344) From the 20th-century works, I recommend these magnificently vibrant pair of paintings by Matisse commissioned by his patron Sergei Shchukin. Originally the genitalia of the nude male dancers were shown, but [they were later] painted over. If the light is right, it's possible to see the painting as Matisse intended. It's a dilemma for the Hermitage whether to restore it to the way it was.

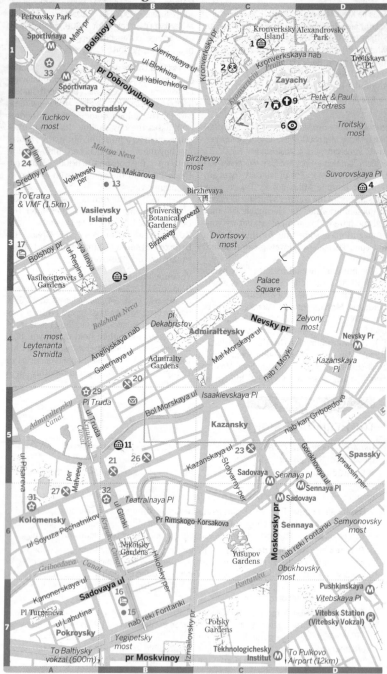

RUSSIA ST PETERSBURG

Petrovsky Park
Sportivnaya
Maly pr
Bolshoy pr
Kronverksky Alexandrovsky
Island
Park
1
Kronverksky pr
Zverinskaya ul
ul Blokhina
ul Yablochkova
2
Kronverkskaya nab
Troitskaya
Pl
pr Dobrolyubova
Sportivnaya
Petrogradsky
Zayachy
7 9
Peter & Paul
Fortress
Tuchkov
most
6
Troitsky
most
1-ya linii
24
Malaya Neva
Birzhevoy
most
Sredny pr
Volkhovsky
per
nab Makarova
13
Birzhevaya
Pl
Suvorovskaya Pl
4
To Eratra
& VMF (1.5km)
**Vasilevsky
Island**
University
Botanical
Gardens
Birzhevoy proezd
Dvortsovy
most
17
Bolshoy pr
1-ya liniya
ul Repina
Vasileostrovets
Gardens
5
Bolshaya Neva
Palace
Square
Zelyony
most
Nevsky Pr
most
Leytenanta
Shmidta
Angliyskaya nab
Galernaya ul
pl
Dekabristov
Admiralteysky
Nevsky pr
Mal Morskaya ul
Admiralty
Gardens
nab r Moyki
Kazanskaya
Pl
Admiralteysky Canal
Kryukov Canal
29
20
Pl Truda
ul Truda
Bol Morskaya ul
Isaakievskaya Pl
Kazansky
nab kan Griboedova
11
21
26
Kazanskaya ul
23
Stolyarny per
Gorokhovaya ul
Spassky
Apraksin per
27
31
32
Teatralnaya Pl
Sadovaya
Sennaya pl
Sennaya Pl
Sadovaya
Kolomensky
ul Soyuza Pechatnikov
Pr Rimskogo-Korsakova
Moskovsky pr
Sennaya
Semyonovsky
most
Griboedova Canal
Nikolsky
Gardens
Nikolsky per
Yusupov
Gardens
nab reki Fontanki
Obukhovsky
most
Pushkinskaya
Vitebskaya Pl
Kanonerskaya ul
Sadovaya ul
16
Fontanka
Vitebsk Station
(Vitebsky Vokzal)
Pl Turgeneva
ul Labutina
15
Pokroysky
nab reki Fontanki
Polsky
Gardens
Yegipetsky
most
Izmailovsky pr
Tekhnologichesky
Institut
To Pulkovo
Airport (12km)
To Baltiysky
vokzal (600m)
pr Moskvinoy

33

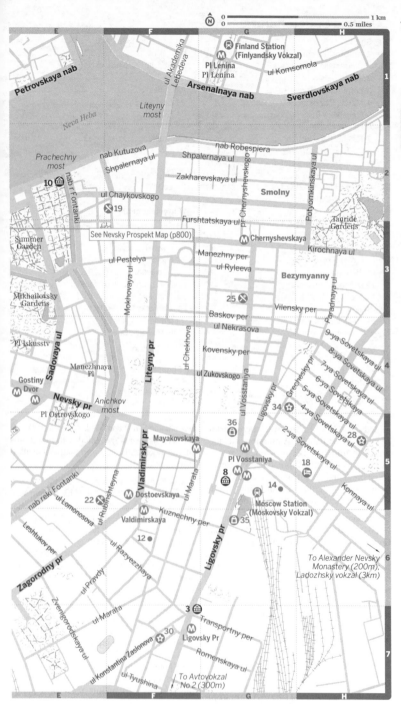

RUSSIA ST PETERSBURG

E

Petrovskaya nab

Neva Heba

Prachechny most

10 🏛

nab r Fontanki

Summer Garden

Mikhailovsky Gardens

Pl Iskusstv

Sadovaya ul

Manezhnaya Pl

🅜 Gostiny Dvor

🅜 Nevsky pr

Pl Ostrovskogo

nab reki Fontanki

ul Lomonosova

Leshtukov per

Zagorodny pr

Zvenigorodskaya ul

ul Pravdy

ul Marata

ul Konstantina Zaslonova

ul Tyushina

F

ul Akademika Lebedeva

nab Kutuzova

Shpalernaya ul

ul Chaykovskogo

❌19

See Nevsky Prospekt Map (p800)

ul Pestelya

Mokhovaya ul

ul Chekhova

Liteyny pr

Anichkov most

Vladimirsky pr

Mayakovskaya 🅜

22 ❌

🅜 Dostoevskaya

ul Rubinshteyna

Valdimirskaya 🅜

Kuznechny per

12 ●

ul Razyezzhaya

30 ✡

🅜 Ligovsky Pr

Transportny per

Romenskaya ul

To Avtovokzal No 2 (300m)

G

🅜 Finland Station (Finlyandsky Vokzal)
Pl Lenina
Pl Lenina

Arsenalnaya nab

Liteyny most

nab Robespiera

Shpalernaya ul

Zakharevskaya ul

ul Chernyshevskogo

Furshtatskaya ul

🅜 Chernyshevskaya

Manezhny per

ul Ryleeva

25 ❌

Baskov per

ul Nekrasova

Kovensky per

ul Zukovskogo

ul Vosstaniya

36 🔒

🅜

Pl Vosstaniya

8 🏛

🅜 🅜

14 ●

35 🔒

Moscow Station (Moskovsky Vokzal)

ul Marata

Ligovsky pr

3 🏛

H

0 — 1 km
0 — 0.5 miles

ul Komsomola

Sverdlovskaya nab

Potyomkinskaya ul

Smolny

Tauride Gardens

Kirochnaya ul

Bezymyanny

Paradnaya ul

Vilensky per

9-ya Sovetskaya ul

8-ya Sovetskaya ul

Grechesky pr

7-ya Sovetskaya ul

6-ya Sovetskaya ul

5-ya Sovetskaya

34 ✡

4-ya Sovetskaya

2-ya Sovetskaya ul

28 ✡

18 🏢

Konnaya ul

To Alexander Nevsky Monastery (200m); Ladozhsky vokzal (3km)

1

2

3

4

5

6

7

Central St Petersburg

Sights
1 Artillery Museum C1
Globe Gallery .... (see 3)
2 Leningradsky Zoo C1
3 Loft Project Floors F7
4 Marble Palace D2
5 Menshikov Palace B3
6 Naryshkin Bastion C2
7 Peter & Paul Fortress C2
8 Pushkinskaya 10 .... G5
9 SS Peter & Paul Cathedral C2
10 Summer Palace E2
Vodka Museum .... (see 20)
11 Yusupov Palace B5

Activities, Courses & Tours
12 Coachmen's Banya F6
13 Holiday Club Spa & Wellness B2
14 Skatprokat G5
15 Usachovskie Bani B7

Sleeping
16 Alexander House B7
17 Art Hotel Terezinni A3
Hostel Ligovsky 74 .... (see 3)
18 Hotel Repin H5

Eating
Green Room .... (see 3)
19 Olyushka & Russkye Bliny F2
20 Russian Vodkaroom No 1 .... B4
21 Sadko B5
22 Schaste E5
23 St.-Leninsbar C5
24 Stolle A2
25 Stolle G3
26 Stolle B5
27 Stolle A6

Drinking
Loft Wine Bar .... (see 3)

Entertainment
28 3L H5
Experimental Sound Gallery .... (see 8)
29 Feel Yourself Russian Folkshow A5
Fish Fabrique Nouvelle .... (see 8)
30 Griboedov F7
31 Mariinsky Concert Hall A6
32 Mariinsky Theatre B6
33 Petrovsky Stadium A1
34 Zoccolo G4

Shopping
35 Galeria G6
36 Stockman G5

gilded jewel box of a theatre, where performances are still held. Admission includes an audio tour in English or one of several other languages. At 1.45pm, tag along for the Russian-language tour *Murder of Rasputin* (adult/student R300/180), the only way to see the room where the deed was done.

Sheremetyev Palace MUSEUM
(Map p800) Facing the Fontanka Canal, the splendid Sheremetyev Palace (1750–55) houses two lovely museums. The **Museum of Music** (☎272 3898; www.theatremuseum.ru; nab reki Fontanki 34; adult/student R220/90; ⌚noon-6pm Wed-Sun; Ⓜ Gostiny Dvor) contains a collection of beautifully decorated instruments. The upstairs palace rooms have been wonderfully restored; you get a great sense of how cultured life must have been here.

In a separate wing of the palace, reached from Liteyny pr, is the charming **Anna Akhmatova Museum at the Fountain House** (☎579 7239; www.akhmatova.spb.ru; Liteyny pr 53; adult/student R200/50; ⌚10.30am-5.30pm Tue-Sun, 1-8pm Wed, closed last Wed of month; Ⓜ Mayakovskaya), filled with mementos of the poet and her family, all persecuted during Soviet times.

FREE **Summer Garden** PARK
(Letny Sad; Map p794; ⌚10am-10pm May-Sep, to 8pm Oct–mid-Apr, closed mid-late Apr; Ⓜ Gostiny Dvor) St Petersburg's prettiest park, dotted with fountains and classical statues, is a great place to relax. In its northeast corner is the modest, two-storey **Summer Palace** (Muzey Letny Dvorets Petra 1; ☎314 0374; adult/student R300/150; ⌚10am-5pm Wed-Mon early May-early Nov), built for Peter from 1710 to 1714 and best viewed from its exterior.

Peter & Paul Fortress HISTORIC BUILDINGS
(Petropavlovskaya krepost; Map p794; ☎238 4550; www.spbmuseum.ru; ⌚grounds 6am-10pm, exhibitions 11am-6pm Thu-Mon, to 5pm Tue; Ⓜ Gorkovskaya) Founded in 1703 on Zaychy Island as the original military base for the new city, this fortress was mainly used as a politi-

cal prison up to 1917: famous residents include Peter's own son Alexei, as well as Dostoyevsky, Gorky and Trotsky. Individual tickets are needed for each of the fortress' attractions, so the best deal is the combined entry ticket (adult/student R350/170, valid two days) which allows access to most of the exhibitions on the island.

At noon every day a cannon is fired from the **Naryshkin Bastion**, scaring the daylights out of unaware tourists. It's fun to walk along the **battlements** (adult/student R150/120). Most spectacular of all is the **SS Peter & Paul Cathedral** (adult/student R200/90), with its landmark needle-like golden spire and magnificent baroque interior. All Russia's tsars since Peter the Great are buried here, including Nicholas II and his family – you'll find them in an anteroom to your right as you enter. Also look out for the famously ugly pinhead **statue of Peter the Great** in the centre of the fortress.

Menshikov Palace
MUSEUM

(Menshikovsky Dvorets; Map p794; ☑323 1112; www.hermitagemuseum.org; Universitetskaya nab 15; adult/student R200/100; ⏰10.30am-6pm Tue-Sat, to 5pm Sun; Ⓜ Vasileostrovskaya) The best of many museums gathered on Vasilevsky Island is this riverside palace, built in 1707 for Peter the Great's confidant Alexander Menshikov. Now a branch of the Hermitage, it has impressively restored interiors filled with period art and furniture.

Museum of Anthropology & Ethnography
MUSEUM

(Kunstkamera; Map p800; ☑328 1412; www.kunstkamera.ru; Tamozhenny per; adult/student R250/150; ⏰11am-6pm Tue-Sun; Ⓜ Vasileostrovskaya) Established in 1714 by Peter the Great, this is the city's oldest museum. Crowds still flock to see his ghoulish collection of monstrosities, notably preserved freaks, two-headed mutant fetuses and odd body parts, although the anthropological and

RUSSIA'S MOST FAMOUS STREET

Walking **Nevsky Prospekt** (Map p800) is an essential St Petersburg experience. Starting at Dvortsovaya pl, notice the gilded spire of the **Admiralty** to your right as you head southeast down Nevsky towards the Moyka River. Across the Moyka, Rastrelli's baroque **Stroganov Palace** houses a branch of the Russian Museum, as well as a couple of restaurants and a chocolate shop masquerading as a 'museum'.

A block beyond the Moyka, on the southern side of Nevsky pr, see the great arms of the **Kazan Cathedral** (Kazansky Sobor; Kazanskaya pl 2; admission free; ⏰10am-7pm, services 10am & 6pm; Ⓜ Nevsky pr) reach out towards the avenue. It's a working cathedral, so please show some respect for the local customs if you enter.

Opposite the cathedral is the **Singer Building**, a Style Moderne (art deco) beauty restored to all its splendour when it was the headquarters of the sewing-machine company; inside is the bookshop Dom Knigi and **Café Singer** (⏰9am-11pm), serving good food and drinks with a great view over the street.

A short walk south of the cathedral, along Griboedova Canal, sits one of St Petersburg's loveliest bridges, the **Bankovsky most**. The cables of this 25.2m-long bridge are supported by four cast-iron gryphons with golden wings.

View the lavish **Grand Hotel Europe** (☑329 6000; www.grandhoteleurope.com; Mikhaylovskaya ul 1/7; Ⓜ Nevsky Pr/Gostiny Dvor), built between 1873 and 1875, redone in Style Moderne in the 1910s and completely renovated in the early 1990s. Across Nevsky pr, the historic department store **Bolshoy Gostiny Dvor** is another Rastrelli creation dating from 1757–85. Beside it stands the **clock tower** of the former Town Duma, seat of the prerevolutionary city government.

At 48 Nevsky pr, the **Passazh** department store has a beautiful arcade (note the glass ceilings), while on the corner of Sadovaya ul is the Style Moderne classic **Yeliseyevsky**, once the city's most sumptuous grocery store. The interior is closed, but its grand exterior is well worth a look.

An enormous **statue of Catherine the Great** stands at the centre of **Ploshchad Ostrovskogo**, commonly referred to as the Catherine Gardens; at the southern end of the gardens is **Aleksandrinksy Theatre**, where Chekhov's The Seagull premiered in 1896.

Nevsky pr crosses the Fontanka Canal on the **Anichkov most**, with its 1840s statues (sculpted by the German Pyotr Klodt) of rearing horses at its four corners

ST PETERSBURG'S CONTEMPORARY ART GALLERIES

St Petersburg has a thriving contemporary-art scene, with even the Hermitage diving into the 21st century with its ongoing 20/21 Project. With over 2000 works in its collection the interesting new museum and gallery **Eratra** (☏324 0809; www.erarta.com; 29-ya Liniya 2; adult/student R300/150; ☺10am-8pm Thu-Tue), on Vasilevsky Island, combines an exhibition over five floors tracing the post-WWII development of Russian art with a commercial gallery. Other commercial galleries:

Pushkinskaya 10 (Map p794; ☏764 5371; www.p-10.ru; Ligovsky pr 53; admission free; ☺3-7pm Wed-Sun; Ⓜ︎Pl Vosstaniya) An artists' squat established in 1988, this legendary locale is now a fully legit nonprofit organisation that is also home to the music clubs Fish Fabrique Nouvelle (p804) and Experimental Sound Gallery (p805). While the art centre commonly goes by the name 'Pushkinskaya 10', the entrance is through the archway at Ligovsky pr 53.

Loft Project Floors (Loft Proekt Etazhi; Map p794; www.loftprojectetagi.ru; Ligivosky pr 74; some galleries free; ☺2-10pm Tue-Sat; Ⓜ︎Ligovsky pr) Hidden away off the main road in the former Smolensky Bread Bakery, Loft Project Floors consists of four large and industrial-looking gallery spaces, the main one being **Globe Gallery** (www.globegallery.ru) next to the chic **Loft Wine Bar** (www.loftwinebar.ru). Also in the building is arty Hostel Ligovsky 74 (p799), an excellent inexpensive cafe **Green Room** (☺9am-10pm), and several shops.

ethnographic displays from around the world are pretty interesting, too.

Strelka MUSEUMS
(Map p800) Some of the best views of St Petersburg can be had from Vasilevsky Island's eastern 'nose', known as the Strelka. The two **Rostral Columns** on the point, studded with ships' prows, were oil-fired navigation beacons in the 1800s; on some holidays, such as Victory Day, gas torches are still lit on them.

Nearby the **Central Naval Museum** (Tsentralny Voenno-Morskoi Muzey; ☏328 2502; Birzhevoy proezd 4; adult/student R350/120; ☺11am-6pm Wed-Sun, closed last Thu of month; Ⓜ︎Vasileostrovskaya), housed in what was once the Stock Exchange, is a must for naval enthusiasts. Next door the **Museum of Zoology** (Zoologichesky Muzey; ☏328 0112; www.zin.ru/mus_e.htm; Universitetskaya nab 1; adult/child R150/50, Thu free; ☺11am-6pm Wed-Mon; Ⓜ︎Vasileostrovskaya) has some amazing exhibits, including a complete woolly mammoth, thawed out of the Siberian ice in 1902, and a live insect zoo.

Alexander Nevsky Monastery MONASTERY
(Ansambl Aleksandro-Nevskoi Lavra; ☏274 1702; http://lavra.spb.ru; Nevsky pr 179/2; adult/student R130/70; ☺6am-10pm; Ⓜ︎Pl Aleksandra Nevskogo) This working monastery southeast of the centre was founded in 1713 by Peter the Great, who wrongly thought this was the location where Alexander of Novgorod had beaten the Swedes in 1240. In 1797 it became a *lavra* (superior monastery).

The main reason for coming here is to see the graves of some of Russia's most famous artistic figures. The **cemeteries** (R200; ☺9.30am-5pm) are either side of the main entrance; tickets are sold in the booth on the right. The **Tikhvin Cemetery**, on the right, contains the graves of Tchaikovsky, Rimsky-Korsakov (check out his wild tomb!), Borodin, Mussorgsky and Glinka. Turn right after entering to reach the tomb of Dostoevsky. The **Lazarus Cemetery**, on the left, contains several late, great St Petersburg architects – among them Starov, Voronikhin, Quarenghi, Zakharov and Rossi.

🏃 Activities

In winter head down to Zaychy Island and watch the famous ice swimmers, or 'walruses', who start the day with a bracing dip in the water through a hole carved into the ice. In summer, the same spot sees sun worshippers out in force.

Holiday Club Spa & Wellness BATHHOUSE
(Map p794; ☏335 2200; www.sokosrestaurants.ru; Sokos Hotel Palace Bridge; Birzhevoy per 2-4, Vasilevsky Island; R600 7am-4pm Mon-Fri, R1200 4-10pm Mon-Fri, R1300 all day Sat & Sun; ☺7am-10pm; Ⓜ︎Vasileostrovskaya) Luxury spa complex with a giant swimming pool, gym and eight saunas including one built in the fashion of a Russian log house.

Coachmen's Banya BATHHOUSE
(Yaskiye Bani; Map p794; ☏312 5836; www.yamskie.ru; ul Dostoevskogo 9; admission R150-500;

men 8am-10.30pm Mon & Wed-Sun, women 8am-10.30pm daily; Ⓜ Vladimirskaya) Traditional *banya* (hot bath) with both regular and luxe sections.

Skatprokat
CYCLING

(Map p794; ☎717 6836; www.skatprokat.ru; Goncharnaya ul 7; rental per day R500; ☺24hr; Ⓜ Pl Vosstaniya) Bikes can be rented here.

Usachovskie Bani
BATHHOUSE

(Map p794; ☎714 3984; Makarenko per 12; admission R100-360; ☺women 9am-9pm Tue & Thu, 8am-10pm Sat, men 9am-9pm Wed & Fri, 8am-8pm Sun; Ⓜ Sadovaya/Sennaya Pl) Bathhouse.

VMF
SWIMMING

(☎322 4505; Sredny pr 87, Vasilevsky Island; admission R350; ☺7am-9pm; Ⓜ Vasileostrovskaya) A 50m pool.

☞ Tours

Anglo Tourismo
BOAT, WALKING

(Map p800; ☎921-989 4722; www.anglotourismo. com; nab reki Fontanki; adult/student from R500/400; Ⓜ Nevsky Prospekt). A boat tour of the canals is highly recommended, and during the main tourist season (May to October) there are plenty of boats for hire. This company's boat leaves from beside the Anichov Bridge and has English commentary. They also offer a range of walking tours.

Peter's Walking Tours
WALKING

(☎943 1229; www.peterswalk.com) Peter's band of guides can give you an insight into the city like no one else. Check the website for the departure point of the standard daily tours. Themed tours such as Dostoevsky, Rasputin, the Great October Revolution and food are available, as well as a bike tour (www.biketour. spb.ru), which leaves from Skatprokat (p798).

★☆ Festivals & Events

St Petersburg celebrates its founding on City Day (27 May) with mass festivities. During the White Nights (around the summer solstice in late June) the city parties all night.

🛏 Sleeping

Prices are high between May and September. Outside this period, rates may be 30% lower.

⬛TOP CHOICE Alexander House
BOUTIQUE HOTEL €€€

(Map p794; ☎334 3540; www.a-house. ru; nab Krukova kanala 27; s/d incl breakfast from R7340/8100, apt s/d R13,500/14,220; Ⓜ Sadovaya/Sennaya Pl; ❋@☎) Unique property offering 19 rooms each named and tastefully styled after the world's top cities. It also has a comfortable lounge area with an attached kitchen, a library, *banya,* restaurant and garden.

⬛TOP CHOICE Anichkov Pension
PENSION, APARTMENT €€

(Map p800; ☎314 7059; www.anichkov.com; Nevsky pr 64, apt 4; s/d incl breakfast from R5860/7200, apt s/d R8280/9980; @☎; Ⓜ Gostiny Dvor) The six rooms and gorgeous apartment are decorated in shades of beige and cream with walnut veneer furniture and antique-themed wallpaper. The lounge has balcony views of the bridge from which the place takes its name.

Hotel Astoria
HISTORIC HOTEL €€€

(Map p800; ☎494 5757; www.roccofortecollection. com; Bolshaya Morskaya ul 39; d/ste from R41,300/60,180; ❋@☎; Ⓜ Nevsky Pr) The very essence of old-world class and the choice of visiting VIPs. Some rooms are nonsmoking.

Hostel Ligovsky 74
HOSTEL €

(Map p794; ☎329 1274; www.hostel74.ru; Ligovsky pr 74; dm/tw/designer room R600/1500/2500; @☎) Part of Loft Project Floors (boxed text p798); the best thing about this hostel is its three great design rooms – book well ahead. Everyone gets a souvenir photo and rates include a basic breakfast at Loft Wine Bar.

Stony Island Hotel
HOTEL €€

(Map p800; ☎740 1588; www.stonyisland.ru; ul Lomonosova 1; d & tw incl breakfast from R4500;

ST PETERSBURG FOR CHILDREN

The Museum of Anthropology & Ethnography (p797) is a winner with curious kids for its display of mutants in jars, as is the Museum of Zoology (p798), with its stuffed animals. Other possibilities:

Artillery Museum (Voyenno-istorichesky Muzey Artilerii; Map p794; ☎232 0296; www. artillery-museum.ru; Alexandrovsky Park 7; adult/student R300/150; ☺11am-6pm Wed-Sun; Ⓜ Gorkovskaya) For its collection of tanks.

Leningradsky Zoo (Leningradsky Zoopark; Map p794; ☎232 4828; www.spbzoo.ru; Aleksandrovsky park 1; adult/child R300/70; ☺10am-5pm) For live animals.

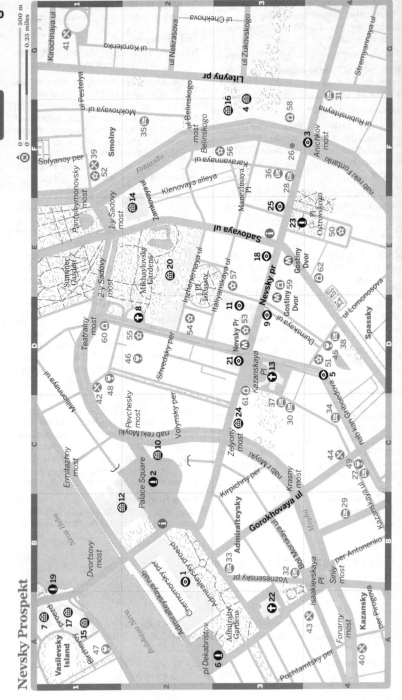

Nevsky Prospekt

✵@☎) Exposed brick walls and chic contemporary furnishings give this super central hotel the design edge. There's a slightly cheaper branch near Petrogradskaya metro station.

Art Hotel Terezinni HOTEL €€
(Map p794; ☏332 1035; www.trezzini-hotel.com; Bolshoy pr 8; s/d incl breakfast from R3300/5300; ✵☎; Ⓜ Vasileostrovskaya) All 17 rooms at this

arty hotel are very appealing, even the compact singles. Standouts are rooms 201 and 214, which have little balconies and overlook the neighbouring St Andrew's Cathedral.

Rachmaninov Antique-Hotel HOTEL €€
(Map p800; ☏327 7466; www.hotelrachmaninov. com; Kazanskaya ul 5, 3rd fl; s/d/ste incl breakfast R4400/4550/12,680; ✵@☎; Ⓜ Nevsky Pr)

WORTH A TRIP

PETRODVORETS & TSARSKOE SELO

Among the several palace estates that the tsars built around St Petersburg as country retreats, the ones not to miss are **Petrodvorets** (☑427 0073; http://peterhofmuseum.com; ul Razvodnaya 2), 29km west of St Petersburg, and **Tsarskoe Selo** (Tsar's Village; ☑465 2281; http://eng.tzar.ru; Sadovaya ul 7), 25km south of the city in the town of Pushkin.

If time is limited, Petrodvorets, also known as Peterhof, is the one to opt for, mainly because of its **Grand Cascade & Water Avenue**, a symphony of over 140 fountains and canals located in the **Lower Park** (Nizhny Park; adult/student R350/180; ◷9am-8pm Mon-Fri, to 9pm Sat & Sun). The fountains only work from mid-May to early October (11am to 5pm Monday to Friday and 11am to 6pm Saturday and Sunday), but the gilded ensemble looks marvellous at any time of the year.

Tsarskoe Selo's big draw is the baroque **Catherine Palace** (Yekaterininsky dvorets; adult/student R550/280; ◷10am-6pm Wed-Mon, closed last Mon of month), built between 1752 and 1756, but almost destroyed in WWII. The exterior and 20-odd rooms, including the dazzling Great Hall and Amber Room, have been expertly restored.

Buses and *marshrutky* (minibuses) to Petrodvorets (R50, 30 minutes) run frequently from outside metro stations Avtovo, Leninsky Pr and Pr Veteranov. There's also the K404 bus from outside the Baltisky vokzal (R50, 40 minutes). All stop near the main entrance to the Upper Garden.

From May to September, the hydrofoil **Meteor** (www.boattrip.ru; one way/return R500/800; ◷9.30am-7pm) takes the 30-minute trip every 20 to 30 minutes from the jetty in front of St Petersburg's Hermitage.

Marshrutky (R35, 30 minutes) regularly shuttle to Pushkin from outside metro Moskovskaya. Infrequent suburban trains run from St Petersburg's Vitebsk station. For Tsarskoe Selo, get off at Detskoe Selo station (R34.50) from where *marshrutky* (R15) run to the estate.

Superstylish minihotel, where minimalist decor is offset by antiques.

Polikoff Hotel
HOTEL €€

(Map p800; ☑314 7809; www.polikoff.ru; Nevsky pr 64/11; s/d incl breakfast from R3600/4860; ✳@🛜; ⓂGostiny Dvor) Entry to this smart mini-hotel is through the brown door on Karavannaya ul. It offers peach-toned, modern-furnished rooms and pleasant service.

Pio on Mokhovaya
B&B €€

(Map p800; ☑273 3585; www.hotelpio.ru; Apt 10 & 12, Mokhovaya ul 39; s/d incl breakfast R3700/4300; @; ⓂChernyshevskaya) The rooms at this appealing guesthouse are named after Italian towns. They're simply but elegantly furnished, with modern fixtures and dusky pastel-coloured walls. Sister property **Pio on Griboedov** (Map p800; apt 5, nab kanala Griboedova 35; s/d incl breakfast R3100/3400; ⓂNevsky pr) has rooms sharing bathrooms and canal views.

Cuba Hostel
HOSTEL €

(Map p800; ☑921 7115, 315 1558; www.cubahostel.ru; Kazanskaya ul 5; dm/tw R490/1250; @🛜; ⓂNevsky Pr) This funky hang-out presses all the right buttons in terms of atmosphere, friendliness, price and location. Each of the

dorms is painted a different colour, and arty design is used throughout.

Location Hostel
HOSTEL €

(Map p800; ☑490 6429; www.location-hostel.ru; Admiralteisky pr 8; dm/tw incl breakfast from R600/1400; @🛜) Spacious chic hostel – they even have Philippe Starck chairs in the well-equipped kitchen! The grand stairwell acts as a photo exhibition space for Loft Project Etazhi (boxed text, p798), where they plan to open a second hostel.

Hostel Life
HOSTEL €

(Map p800; ☑318 1808; hostel-life.ru; Nevsky pr 47; dm/tw from R700/2200; @🛜) Totally modern, this big, colourfully decorated hostel with a large lounge and kitchen is accessed from Zagorodny pr. Breakfast (R150) is cooked in the same kitchen as top Russian restaurant Palkin next door!

Hotel Repin
HOTEL €€

(Map p794; ☑717 9976; www.hotelrepin.ru; Nesky pr 136; s/d incl breakfast R3000/3700; @🛜; ⓂPl Vosstaniya) The Repin's flower-bright colours make it one of the city's more pleasant mini-hotels, with bigger-than-usual rooms (some of them nonsmoking) and a spacious lounge area hung with reproductions of the illustrious Russian artist's most famous works.

Crazy Duck
HOSTEL €

(Map p800; ☑570 4016; www.crazy-duck.com; 6B Gritsova per; dm/d or tw without bathroom from R560/1700; @🛜; MSadovaya/Sennaya Pl) Set back in a courtyard, this brightly coloured and grafittied hostel offers a super-spacious bar and decent-sized rooms.

✕ Eating

St Petersburg has a fantastic selection of restaurants and cafes, with many of the city's most successful operations also opening branches in Moscow.

TOP CHOICE Teplo
RUSSIAN €€

(Map p800; ☑570 1974; Bolshaya Morskaya ul 45; mains R260-500; 🍴; MSadovaya/Sennaya Pl) You'll instantly warm to Teplo's cosy living-room atmosphere, liberally scattered with cuddly soft toys: there's also a great kid's room. The food – roast chicken, salmon in Savoy cabbage, sweet and savoury pies and pastries baked daily – is equally comforting.

TOP CHOICE Sadko
RUSSIAN €€

(Map p794; ☑903 2373; www.sadkorst.ru; ul Glinki 2; mains R260-650; MSadovaya/Sennaya Pl) Ideal as a pre- or post-Mariinsky Theatre dining option, Sadko serves fine renditions of all the Russian favourites. It also has a lovely traditional floral design decor, a great children's room and even singing waiters!

Russian Vodkaroom No 1
RUSSIAN €€€

(Map p794; ☑570 6420; www.vodkaroom.ru; Konnogvardeysky bul 4; mains R500-1300; 🍴; MSadovaya/Sennaya Pl) Before dining in this elegant restaurant it's worth taking the English guided tour of the attached small Vodka Museum and doing a tasting of three vodkas (R450). If that whets your appetite, there are some 140 vodkas on the menu to sample.

Makarov
RUSSIAN €€

(Map p800; ☑327 0053; Manezhny per 2; mains R400-500; ⊘8am-11pm Mon-Fri, noon-11pm Sat & Sun; MChernyshevskaya) Charming place overlooking the Cathedral of the Transfiguration of our Saviour and serving traditional Russian in a relaxed setting. Also has a children's room.

Botanika
VEGETARIAN €€

(Map p800; ☑272 7011; www.cafebotanika.ru; ul Pestelya 7; mains R200-300; 🛜; MChernyshevskaya) Piter's best range of vegetarian food – from Russian salads to Indian and Japanese dishes – is offered at this stylish restaurant where the moss-green colour scheme is jazzed up with pretty decorative touches by students from the art academy across the road.

St.-Leninsbar
RUSSIAN €

(Map p794; ☑www.leninsbar.restoran.ru; Grivtsova per 7; mains R100-200; ⊘noon-midnight) Billing itself as Piter's smallest Russian Bar, this cheeky homage to Lenin is actually a great place to sample well-executed classics of Russian cuisine at Socialist prices. Their place mats also teach you how to drink vodka.

Schaste
RUSSIAN €€

(Happiness; Map p794; ☑572 2675; www.schaste-est.com; ul Rubinshteyna 15/17; mains R250-400; ⊘9am-midnight Mon-Thu, 9am-7am Fri, 10am-7am Sat, 10am-midnight Sun; MDostoevskaya/Vladimirskaya) Cherubs are the motif of this romantic cafe-bar, including on the dot-to-dot puzzles that are printed on the place mats. The food is tasty with a two/three-course lunch for R200/250 a great deal.

Stolle
RUSSIAN €

(www.stolle.ru; pies R60-100; ⊘8am-10pm); Konyushennaya per (Map p800; Konyushennaya per 1/6; MNevsky Pr); ul Dekabristov 19 (Map p794; MSadovaya/Sennaya Pl); ul Dekabristov 33 (Map p794; MSadovaya/Sennaya Pl); ul Vosstaniya (Map p794; ul Vosstaniya 32; MChernyshevskaya); Vasilevsky Island (Map p794; 1-ya linii 50; MVasileostrovskaya)

HOMESTAYS & APARTMENT RENTALS

As well as City Realty (p806), Ost-West Kontaktservice (p806) and HOFA (boxed text p783), the following can arrange apartment rentals and homestays:

Andrey & Sasha's Homestay (Map p800; ☑315 3330, 921-409 6701; asamatuga@mail.ru; nab kanala Griboedova 49; s/d without bathroom from ⊘50/70; MSadovaya/Sennaya Pl) Legendary hosts renting rooms in a couple of centrally located apartments.

Zimmer Hostels (☑973 3757; www.zimmer.ru; dm/s/d from R750/1300/2000) Has several centrally located apartments to rent as well as beds in a couple of hostels.

We can't get enough of the traditional Russian savoury and sweet pies at this chain of cafes, and we guarantee you'll also be back for more. It's easy to make a meal of it with soups and other dishes that can be ordered at the counter.

Zoom Café RUSSIAN, EUROPEAN €

(Map p800; www.cafezoom.ru; Gorokhovaya ul 22; mains R200-400; ◉🛜; MNevsky Pr) Popular boho/student hang-out with regularly changing art exhibitions. Serves unfussy tasty European and Russian food in a very relaxed ambience.

Café Idiot RUSSIAN, VEGETARIAN €€

(Map p800; ☑315 1675; nab reki Moyki 82; meals R400; ◉11am-1am; ◉🛜; MSennaya Pl) This long-running cafe charms with its prerevolutionary atmosphere. It's an ideal place to visit for a nightcap or late supper.

Olyushka & Russkye Bliny RUSSIAN €

(Map p794; Gagarinskaya ul 13; mains R70-100; ◉11am-6pm Mon-Fri; MChernyshevskaya) Authentic canteens that hark back to the simplicity of Soviet times. Olyushka serves only *pelmeni* (dumplings), all handmade, while Russkye Bliny does melt-in-the-mouth pancakes.

🍷 Drinking

With the local property market stuck in a groove, there's been a reprieve for the strip of cheapo dive bars along ul Dumskaya (Map p800); from midnight to dawn they get packed out with youthful revellers who spill onto the streets.

Barackobamabar BAR, CLUB

(Map p800; Konyushennaya pl 2; ◉11pm-6am Fri & Sat; MNevsky Pr) Head way in the back of the courtyard to find a brick ruin that's undergone a reasonably successful makeover to become an uber-cool, cover charge–free bar and dance club dedicated to the US prez. Watch this space as they plan to go nightly.

Atelierbar BAR, CAFE

(Map p800; www.atelierbar.ru; ul Lomonosova 1; ◉9am-6am; MGostiny Dvor) Attitude-free, shabby chic and youthful – just what you'd expect from the groovesters behind Cuba Hostel. During the day it's a cafe on the ground floor; late at night is when the bar/club on the two upper floors cranks up.

Other Side LIVE MUSIC

(Map p800; www.theotherside.ru; Bolshaya Konyushennaya ul 1; ◉noon to last customer; concerts 8pm Sun-Thu, 10pm or 11pm Fri & Sat; MNevsky Pr) There's live music Friday and Saturdays at this gastrobar, which serves decent food (mains R200 to R500). Most people turn up to enjoy its several beers on tap.

Grad Petrov MICROBREWERY

(Map p800; ☑326 0137; http://die-kneipe.ru; Universitetskaya nab 5; ◉noon to last customer; MVasileostrovskaya) The refreshing ales and German-style sausages are reason enough to stop by this fine microbrewery with a view across the Neva from its outdoor tables.

Stirka CAFE-BAR

(Map p800; ☑314 5371; Kazanskaya ul 26; ◉11am-1am Sun-Thu, to 4am Fri & Sat; MSadovaya/Sennaya Pl) Hipster hang-out where you can play chess or listen to the DJ, while also doing your laundry – what a good idea! A 5kg wash costs R150; the dryer R100; and a mug of excellent Vasileostrovskoe beer R120.

☆ Entertainment

The main performing arts season is September to the end of June. In summer many companies are away on tour, but plenty of performances are still staged.

Mariinsky Theatre OPERA & BALLET

(Map p794; ☑326 4141; www.mariinsky.ru; Teatralnaya pl 1; box office ◉11am-7pm; MSadovaya/Sennaya Pl) Home to the world-famous Kirov Ballet and Opera Company. A visit here is a must, if only to wallow in the sparkling glory of the interior. Use the website to book and pay for tickets in advance – either for the theatre or the acoustically splendid new concert hall (ul Pisareva 20) nearby.

Mikhaylovsky Opera & Ballet Theatre

OPERA, BALLET

(Map p800; ☑585 4305; www.mikhailovsky.ru; pl Iskusstv 1; MNevsky Pr) Challenging the Mariinksy in terms of the standards and range of its performances is this equally historic and beautifully restored theatre.

Shostakovich Philharmonia Bolshoy Zal

CLASSICAL MUSIC

(Big Hall; Map p800; ☑710 4257; www.philharmonia.spb.ru; Mikhailovskaya ul 2; MGostiny Dvor) This grand hall is one of its two venues where the renowned St Petersburg Philharmonica Symphony Orchestra plays. The other is the Maly Zal imeni Glinki (Small Hall; Map p800; ☑571 8333; Nevsky pr 30; MNevsky Pr).

Fish Fabrique Nouvelle LIVE MUSIC

(Map p794; http://vkontakte.ru/club250531; Ligovsky pr 53; cover R100-150; ◉3pm-late; MPl Vosstaniya) The new project of the legendary bar

Check out **Excess** (www.xs.gay.ru) for the latest city-specific information. The main club is **Central Station** (Map p800; www.centralstation.ru; ul Lomonosova 1/28; cover after midnight R100-300; ☺6pm-6am; ⓜGostiny Dvor), featuring two dance floors, several bars, a cafe and a souvenir shop.

3L (Tri El; Map p794; www.triel.spb.ru; 5-ya Sovetskaya ul 45; cover free-R150; ☺5pm-midnight Tue, 10pm-6am Wed-Sun; ⓜPl Vosstaniya) is a laid-back lesbian club with dancing and live music.

set in the building that's the focus of Piter's avant-garde art scene. Rock and alternative music concerts happen in the original small hall and this larger space.

Mod Club　　　　LIVE MUSIC
(Map p800; modclub.spb.ru; nab Kanala Griboedova 5; cover Fri & Sat R200; ☺6pm-6am; ⓜNevsky Pr) There's a groovy mix of live and spun music at this fun, packed place – find it set back from the street in a courtyard.

Zoccolo　　　　LIVE MUSIC
(Map p794; ☎274 9467; www.zoccolo.ru; 3-ya Sovetskaya ul 2/3; cover R200-300; ☺7pm-midnight Sun-Thu, 7pm-6am Fri & Sat, concerts 8pm; ⓜPl Vosstaniya) Has a very positive vibe and a great line-up of sounds including indie rock, Latin-hip-hop-reggae and even 'if Radiohead played punk'.

Experimental Sound Gallery　　LIVE MUSIC
(GEZ-21; Map p794; ☎764 5258; www.tac.spb.ru; Ligovsky pr 53, 3rd fl; cover R100-150; ☺concerts from 9pm; ⓜPl Vosstaniya) You know that a place called 'experimental' is going to be out there. Also catch film screenings, readings and other expressions of creativity. The attached cafe is a very groovy hang-out.

Chinese Pilot Dzhao-Da　　LIVE MUSIC
(Map p800; ☎273 7487; 7A ul Pestelya; ☺noon-midnight) Moscow's famed music club has opened a branch in St Petersburg and it's attracting some major indie talents. Jauntily decorated with green tables and red chairs, the Pilot also serves food.

Griboedov　　　　CLUB
(Map p794; www.griboedovclub.ru; Voronezhskaya ul 2a; cover R100-400; ☺5pm-6am; ⓜLigovsky Pr) This eternally hip club in an artfully converted bomb shelter is a fun place most nights. It has recently extended above ground with the groovy cafe-bar Griboedov Hill, which hosts live-music performances in the evenings.

Purga　　　　CLUB
(Map p800; www.purga-club.ru; nab reki Fontanki 11; cover R100-300; ☺4pm-6am; ⓜGostiny Dvor) Every night in one room of this intimate fun-packed club you can celebrate the new year Russian-style, while in the other a traditional wedding celebration is in full flow. There's also a branch in Moscow.

Feel Yourself Russian Folkshow　　DANCE
(Map p794; ☎312 5500; www.folkshow.ru; Nikolayevsky Palace, ul Truda 4; ticket incl drinks & snacks R1200; ☺show 6.30pm; ⓜNevsky Pr) Terrible name, but actually a very entertaining show of traditional Russian folk dancing and music by enthusiastic, professional troupes. Plus you get to enjoy the grand interior of the Nikolayevsky Palace.

🛍 Shopping

At the time of research a major new shopping mall **Galeria** (Map p794; www.galeria-spb.ru) and department store **Stockmann** (Map p800; www.stockmann.ru) were about to open near Moskovsky vokzal.

Bolshoy Gostiny Dvor　　DEPARTMENT STORE
(Map p800; www.bgd.ru; Nevsky pr 35; ⓜGostiny Dvor) The granddaddy of all St Pete's department stores is looking mighty fine after years of restoration. You'll find a great selection of nearly everything here, including fashion and souvenirs, at reasonably competitive prices.

Souvenir Fair　　　　SOUVENIRS
(Map p800; Konyushennaya pl; ☺10am-dusk; ⓜNevsky Pr) With more than 100 little stalls selling all kinds of arts, crafts and souvenirs, this is your best one-stop gift- and memento-shopping opportunity.

Tovar dlya Voennikh　　MILITARY GEAR
(Map p800; Sadovaya ul 26; ☺10am-7pm Mon-Sat; ⓜGostiny Dvor) The best place to buy cool Russian military clothes and memorabilia. Look out for the circular green-and-gold

ZENIT

Petersburgers are fanatical about local football team **Zenit** (www.fc-zenit.ru), one of the most successful in Russia. Sponsored by oil and gas giant Gazprom, their blue and white strip can be bought at shops across the city. Match tickets (R100 to R800) are sold at theatre ticket booths or at **Petrovsky Stadium** (Map p794; www.petrovsky.spb.ru; Petrovsky ostrov 2; MSportivnaya) three days before a game.

sign with Military Shop written in English; the entrance is inside the courtyard.

Anglia   BOOKS
(Map p800; nab reki Fontanki 30; ☺10am-7pm; MGostiny Dvor) English-language bookshop offering one of the city's best selections of English language books including many on Russia.

 Information

Dangers & Annoyances

Never drink tap water in St Petersburg as it could contain *Giardia lamblia,* a parasite that can cause horrific stomach cramps and nausea. Bring a water filter or stick to bottled water, which is available everywhere. If you must drink tap water, boil it for a good few minutes first.

The humidity and marshland location of St Petersburg makes it mosquito hell from May until October. Bring repellent or the standard antimosquito tablets and socket plug. Alternatively you can buy these all over the city – ask for *sredstva protif kamarov.*

Human pests include the ever-present pickpockets on Nevsky pr – be particularly vigilant around Griboedova Canal.

Sadly, racist attacks are a reality in the city. Skinhead gangs have killed an unprecedented number of mainly Caucasians and Central Asians in the past few years, and there's a climate of fear among ethnic minorities. That said, attacks in the city centre are rare, so we still encourage nonwhite travellers to visit, but suggest exercising far more caution here than anywhere else in the region. Avoid the suburbs whenever possible and try not to go out alone after dark.

Internet Access

Internet cafes and wi-fi access are common across the city.

Cafe Max (www.cafemax.ru; Nevsky pr 90/92; per hr R40; ☺24hr; MMayakovskaya) Wi-fi available here. Also has a branch in the Hermitage.

Tvoyo (Nevsky pr 66; per hr R60; ☺24hr; MGostiny Dvor) Enter from Liteyny pr.

Media

The following English-language publications are available free at many hotels, hostels, restaurants and bars across the city:

St Petersburg in Your Pocket (www.inyourpocket.com/city/st_petersburg.html) Monthly listings booklet with useful up-to-date information and short features.

St Petersburg Times (www.sptimes.ru) Published every Tuesday and Friday (when it has an indispensable listings and arts review section), this plucky little newspaper has been fearlessly telling it like it really is for over 15 years.

Medical Services

The clinics listed here are open 24 hours and have English-speaking staff:

American Medical Clinic (☎740 2090; www.amclinic.ru; nab reki Moyki 78; MSadovaya)
Medem International Clinic & Hospital (☎336 3333; www.medem.ru; ul Marata 6; MMayakovskaya)

Post

Post office branches are scattered throughout the city. All the major air-courier services are available in St Petersburg.

Central post office (Map p794; www.spbpost.ru; Pochtamtskaya ul 9; ☺24 hr; MSadovaya/Sennaya Pl) Worth visiting just to admire its elegant Style Moderne interior. The express mail service EMS Garantpost is available here.

Telephone

You can buy a local SIM card at any mobilephone shop, such as **Euroset** (www.spb.euroset.ru), a chain with branches across the city, from as little as R150 including R100 of credit.

Local phonecards *(taksfon karta)* are available from large post offices and can be used to make calls from any phone.

Tourist Information

From May to September the city sponsors 'angels' (ie guides) who roam Nevsky Pr, Palace Sq and the like ready to assist tourists.

City Tourist Information Centre (www.visit-petersburg.ru) main office (Map p800; ☎982 8253; Sadovaya ul 14/52; ☺10am-7pm Mon-Fri, noon-6pm Sat MGostiny Dvor); Hermitage booth (Map p800; Dvortsovaya pl 12; ☺10am-7pm; MNevsky Pr) There are also branches at the Pulkova-1 and Pulkova-2 air terminals (open 10am to 7pm Monday to Friday).

Travel Agencies

The following agencies have English-speaking staff:

City Realty (☑570 6342; www.cityrealtyrus sia.com; Muchnoy per 2; Ⓜ Nevsky Pr) Reliable agency that can arrange all types of accommodation, transport tickets and visas, including business ones.

Ost-West Kontaktservice (☑327 3416; www. ostwest.com; Nevsky pr 100; ☺10am-6pm Mon-Fri; Ⓜ Pl Vosstaniya) The multilingual staff here can find you an apartment to rent and organise tours and tickets.

parallel 60 (☑380 4596; www.parallel60.com; 2-ya Sovetskaya ul 1, office 501; Ⓜ Pl Vosstaniya) Friendly and efficient agency that can arrange visas, accommodation and tours.

Sindbad Travel (☑244 1000; www.sindbad. ru; 2-ya Sovetskaya ul 12; ☺9am-10pm Mon-Fri, 10am-6pm Sat & Sun; Ⓜ Pl Vosstaniya). Long-running discount air-ticket office, staffed by friendly, knowledgeable people.

Getting There & Away

Air

Pulkovo-1 (☑704 3822) and **Pulkovo-2** (☑704 3444) are, respectively, the domestic and international terminals of St Petersburg's **Pulkovo airport** (www.pulkovoairport.ru/eng). For carriers that fly to Russia, see p825. International and local airline tickets as well as train tickets can be purchased from the **Central Airline Ticket Office** (www.cavs.ru; Nevsky pr 7; ☺9am-9pm Mon-Sat, to 6pm Sun; Ⓜ Nevsky Pr).

Boat

Linking Helsinki and St Petersburg three times a week is the Finish ferry **St Peter Line** (☑322 6699; www.stpeterline.com); coming from Helsinki passengers are allowed to stay in St Petersburg visa-free for up to 72 hours. From June to August **DFDS Lisko** (☑4012-660 404; www.dfdslisco.ru) runs a weekly ferry service on the *George Ots*, travelling between Baltiysk in Russia's Kaliningrad region and St Petersburg. **Trans-Eksim** (☑4012-660 468; www.transexim.ru) also runs weekly car ferries between Baltiysk and Ust-Luga, 150km west of St Petersburg.

Bus

St Petersburg's main bus station, **Avtovokzal No 2** (☑766 5777; www.avokzal.ru, in Russian; nab Obvodnogo kanala 36; Ⓜ Ligovsky Pr) – there isn't a No 1 – has both international and European Russia services.

Buses are the cheapest way to travel to Tallinn (from R950, 7½ hours, seven daily) and Rīga (from R960, 11 hours, two daily), but for Moscow the train is a better option. There are regular buses from St Petersburg to Helsinki, Finland (from €40, eight hours, four to six daily).

Train

Apart from at stations, tickets can be purchased at the **Central Train Ticket Office** (nab kanala Griboedova 24; ☺8am-8pm Mon-Sat, to 4pm Sun; Ⓜ Nevsky Pr) and many travel agencies.

There are four main stations:

Finlyandsky vokzal (Map p794; Finland Station; pl Lenina 6; Ⓜ Ploshchad Lenina) For Helsinki.

Ladozhsky vokzal (Ladoga Station; Zhanevsky pr 73; Ⓜ Ladozhskaya) For Helsinki, the far north of Russia and towards the Urals.

Moskovsky vokzal (Moscow Station; Map p794; pl Vosstaniya; Ⓜ Pl Vosstaniya) Service to/from Moscow

Vitebsky vokzal (Vitebsk Station; Map p794; Zagorodny pr 52; Ⓜ Pushkinskaya) The Baltics, Belarus, the Czech Republic, Germany, Hungary, Poland and Ukraine.

ⓘ Getting Around

To/From the Airport

Pulkovo airport, 17km south of the centre, is easily and (very) cheaply accessed by metro and bus. From Moskovskaya metro station, bus 39 runs to Pulkovo-1, the domestic terminal, and bus 13 runs to Pulkovo-2, the international terminal. There are also plenty of *marshrutky* (minibuses). The trip takes about 15 minutes and costs just R16 to R22. Or you can take the buses and *marshrutky* K3 all the way from the airport to Sennaya pl in the city centre or K39 to pl Vosstaniya (R35). Buses stop directly outside each of the terminals.

By taxi you should be looking at around R600 to get to the city (R400 is the price from the city to the airport). Most taxi drivers will request more from foreigners, so be prepared to haggle or take the bus.

Public Transport

The **metro** (single ride/10 trips in a week R22/185; ☺5.30am-midnight) is usually the quickest way around the city. *Zhetony* (tokens) and credit-loaded cards can be bought from booths in the stations.

Marshrutkas are faster than the regular buses and trolleybuses. Costs vary with the route, but the average fare is R20 and fares are displayed prominently inside each van.

Taxi

Unofficial taxis are common; for more information see the boxed text p827.

To book a taxi call:

» **Ladybird** (☑900 0504; www.ladybird-taxi.ru) Women drivers and child car seats.

» **Peterburgskoe taksi 068** (☑068, 324 7777; www.taxi068.spb.ru)

» **Taxi Blues** (☑321 8888; www.taxiblues.ru)

KALININGRAD REGION
КАЛИНИНГРА ДСКАЯ ОБЛАСТЬ

POP 937.900

Surrounded by Poland, Lithuania and 148km of Baltic coastline, the Kaliningrad region is a Russian exclave that culturally is intimately attached to the Motherland and yet also a world apart. In this 'Little Russia' – only 15,100 sq km – you'll find plenty of fine hotels and restaurants, a youthful outlook plus all the traditions of the big parent, wrapped up in a manageable package of beautiful countryside, splendid beaches and fascinating historical sights.

The Teutonic Knights ruled the Baltic in the Middle Ages from the city of Königsburg (now Kaliningrad). After WWII, Stalin ethnically cleansed the land of all Germans, but centuries of Germanic culture and architecture were not as easily removed. In the go-ahead capital Kaliningrad, beside glitzy new shopping malls, the old cathedral has been rebuilt, and fragments of the medieval core of the city remain visible. An hour's drive north along the Baltic coast are the pine forests and Sahara-style dunes of the Kurshskaya Kosa National Park, a Unesco World Heritage site, as well as charming old Prussian seaside resorts.

Unless you're flying, to reach the Kaliningrad region from anywhere else in Russia you must have either a double- or multiple-entry Russian visa, and/or visas for its neighbouring countries. Multiple-entry visas need to be arranged in advance. Friendly, open-minded locals will only be too happy to assist you with anything else once you arrive – anyone familiar with the insular ways of big Russia will be amazed. Everyone else will be equally delighted to discover this Russian gem.

History

The indigenous pagan population of the region was conquered in the 13th century by Teutonic Knights. By 1525 the area, famous since Roman times for its amber deposits, had become the Duchy of Prussia, Europe's first Protestant state, with its capital at Königsberg. The city's liberal atmosphere attracted scholars, artists, scientists and entrepreneurs from across Europe; in 1697 Peter the Great visited as part of Russia's Grand Embassy, and the 18th-century philosopher Immanuel Kant spent all his life there.

After WWI, East Prussia was separated from the rest of Germany when Poland regained statehood. The three-month campaign by which the Red Army took it in 1945 was one of the fiercest of WWII, with hundreds of thousands of casualties on both sides. In 1946 the region was renamed Kaliningrad in honour of the recently deceased Mikhail Kalinin, one of Stalin's more vicious henchmen. Members of the surviving German population were either killed, relocated to far-flung corners of the Soviet Union or deported to Germany. The population is now predominantly Russian (77%) with less than 1% German.

In the early 1990s, following the breakup of the Soviet Union, the region struggled through extreme economic difficulties. The discovery of oil off the coast and the granting of special economic zone status have helped it turn the corner. The region is also one of only four places in Russia where casinos can be legally run – one is yet to open, however.

Although there's been talk about it, Kaliningrad's chances of becoming an independent fourth 'Baltic state' are highly unlikely: Russia would have much to lose by granting autonomy to this resource-rich region. The Baltic fleet is headquartered in Baltiysk (off limits to tourists unless on a specially arranged tour), and the area's strategic importance is key, particularly in light of recent EU expansion east. Also, the vast majority of Russians living here are proud of their Slavic heritage and ties to the Motherland.

Kaliningrad
КАЛИНИНГРАД

4012 / POP 419.000

A fascinating, affluent city, Kaliningrad is an excellent introduction to Russia's most liberal region. Interesting museums and historical sights sprout in between the shiny new shopping centres and multitude of leafy parks that soften vast swaths of brutal Soviet architecture. Plentiful transport options and good hotels mean you can use the city as a base to see the rest of the region.

Founded as a Teutonic fort in 1255, Königsberg joined the Hanseatic League in 1340, and from 1457 to 1618 was the residence of the grand masters of the Teutonic order and their successors, the dukes of Prussia. The first king of Prussia, Frederick I, was crowned here in 1701. For the next couple of centuries the city flourished, producing citizens such as the philosopher Immanuel Kant (1724–1804).

Old photos attest that Königsberg was once an architectural gem equal to Prague or Kraków. The combined destruction of WWII and the Soviet decades put paid to all that. However, there are lovely prewar residential suburbs that evoke the Prussian past, and following the successful reconstruction of the war-damaged cathedral (mainly thanks to donations from Germany), the authorities also have big plans to remodel Kaliningrad with a mix of futuristic and heritage-inspired building projects.

◉ Sights

Cathedral   CHURCH
(☑631 705; www.sobor-kaliningrad.ru; adult/student R100/50; ☺9am-5pm) A Unesco World Heritage site, the majestic red-brick Gothic cathedral dates back to 1333. For decades after WWII, its ruins rose above the once densely populated Kant Island – now all parkland dotted with sculptures. Rebuilt during the 1990s, the cathedral is occasionally used for concerts, and its ground floor has small Lutheran and Orthodox chapels. Upstairs you'll find the reconstructed carved-wood Wallenrodt Library, interesting displays of old Königsberg and objects from archaeological digs. On the top floor is an austere room with the death mask of Immanuel Kant, whose rose-marble **tomb** lies outside on the outer north side.

Fish Village   NEIGHBOURHOOD
From Kant's Island, cross the nearby **Honey Bridge**, the oldest of the city's bridges, and you'll arrive at the half-timber riverside development known as Fish Village (Ribnaya Derevnya). Disneyland-ish it may be, but this collection of hotels, shops, cafes and restaurants is a laudable attempt to reprise some of the city's destroyed architectural heritage.

The handsome **Jubilee Footbridge**, built in 2005 to celebrate the city's 750th birthday, will take you to the south bank of the river. Facing the cathedral here is the **Former Stock Exchange** (Leninsky pr 83), a fine Renaissance-style building built in the 1870s; it now houses a disco and various community clubs.

World Ocean Museum   MUSEUM
(☑340 244; www.world-ocean.ru; nab Petra Velikogo 1; adult/student R250/170, individual vessels R80/40; ☺10am-6pm Wed-Sun) Two boats and a sub can be explored at this excellent museum, strung along the banks of the Pregolya River. The highlight is the handsome former expedition vessel *Vityaz*, which during its heyday conducted many scientific studies around the world. Also part of the complex is the Maritime Hall, in a restored old

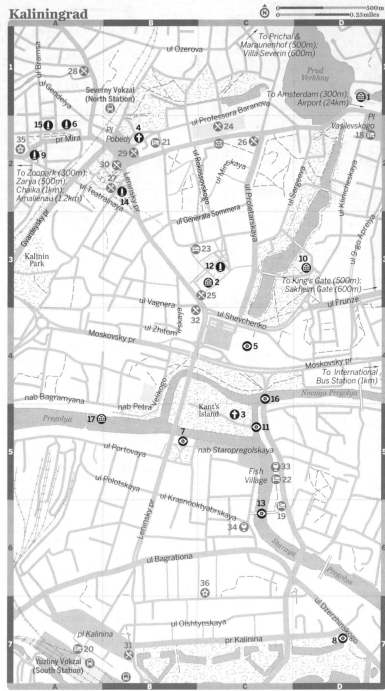

0 500m
0 0.25 miles

ul Ozerova

To Prichal &
Maraunenhof (500m);
Villa Severin (600m)

Prud
Verkhny

ul Bramsa

ul Gendelya

Severny Vokzal
(North Station)

To Amsterdam (300m);
Airport (24km)

Pl
Vasilevskogo

ul Professora Baranova

15 6

pr Mira

Pl
Pobedy

4

21

24

26

18

35

9

29

30

27

ul Teatralnaya

14

Leninsky pr

ul Rokossovskogo

ul Minskaya

ul Proletarskaya

ul Sergeeeva

ul Gvardeysky pr

To Zoopark (300m);
Zarya (500m);
Chaika (1km);
Amalienau (1.2km)

ul Generala Sommera

Kalinin
Park

23

12

2

25

10

To King's Gate (500m);
Sakheim Gate (600m)

ul Klinicheskaya

ul 9-go Aprelya

ul Vagnera

ul Zhitom

32

ul Shevchenko

ul Frunze

Moskovsky pr

5

ul Velikogo

nab Bagramyana

nab Petra

Kant's
Island

3

Moskovsky pr

To International
Bus Station (1km)

Novaya Pregolya

16

17

Pregolya

7

11

nab Staropregolskaya

Leninsky pr

ul Portovaya

ul Polotskaya

ul Krasnooktyabrskaya

Fish
Village

33

22

13

34

19

Staraya

Pregolya

ul Bagrationa

36

ul Dzerzhinskogo

pl Kalinina

ul Olshtynskaya

pr Kalinina

8

20

31

Yuzhny Vokzal
(South Station)

RUSSIA KALININGRAD

warehouse building; it has interesting displays on fishing and the sea-connected history of Kaliningrad, as well as rare archaeological finds such as the remains of a 19th-century wooden fishing boat.

Amber Museum   MUSEUM
(☑466 888; www.ambermuseum.ru; pl Vasilevskogo 1; adult/student R180/130; ☉10am-6pm Tue-Sun) On the edge of the Prud Verkny (Upper Pond), this museum has some 6000 examples of amber artworks, the most impressive being from the Soviet period. In addition to enormous pieces of jewellery containing prehistoric insects suspended within, some of the more fascinating works include an amber flute and a four-panelled amber and ivory chalice depicting Columbus, the *Niña*, the *Pinta* and the *Santa Maria*.

City Fortifications & Gates HISTORIC BUILDINGS
The Amber Museum is housed in the attractive **Dohna Tower**, a bastion of the city's old defensive ring. The adjacent **Rossgarten Gate**, one of Königsberg's city gates, contains a decent restaurant.

Several other bits of the fortifications and gates remain scattered around the city. The impressively renovated **King's Gate** (☑581

272; ul Frunze 112; adult/student R80/40; ☉11am-6pm Wed-Sun) houses a museum with cool models of old Königsberg and exhibits on the personalities who shaped the region's history. A little south of here is the twin-towered **Sackheim Gate** (cnr pr Moscovsky & Litovsky Val).

The **Friedland Gate** (pr Kalinina 6; adult/child R20/10;☉10am-5pm Tue-Sun) contains a small museum with a great map plotting the locations of the 13 original city gates. There's an intriguing arms display, and the original cobblestone road that ran through the gate is visible inside.

Amalienau & Maraunenhof NEIGHBOURHOODS
Casual strolls through the tree-lined neighbourhoods of Amalienau to the city's west along pr Mira and Maraunenhof at the north end of the Prud Verkhny are the best way to get an idea of genteel pre-WWII Königsberg. Amalienau is particularly lovely, with an eclectic range of villas; many along ul Kutuzova and the streets connecting pr Pobedy and Mira were designed by the architect Friedrich Heitmann. In Maraunenhof you'll find several appealing small hotels, as well as the German consulate, with its strikingly colourful visa section.

STATUES & MONUMENTS

A statue of Königsberg's most famous son **Immanuel Kant**, a 1992 copy of the 1864 original by Christian Rauch, stands in front of the university named after the philosopher, tucked off Leninsky pr near the Bunker Museum. Continuing northwards towards pr Mira you'll pass the **Mother Russia** monument in front of the Evropa mall; the **Fighting Bisons** by Gaul in which two of the beasts go head to head **(Peter the Great)** and the Prussian man of letters **Friedrich Schiller**. A gem of Soviet iconography is the **Cosmonaut Monument**, celebrating the local guys who went into space, while in leafy Tsentralny Park a hulking statue of **Vladimir Vysotsky**, a legendary singer from the 1960s and '70s, overlooks the amphitheatre.

History & Art Museum   MUSEUM
(☑453 844; ul Klinicheskaya 21; adult/student R70/50; ☺10am-6pm Tue-Sun) The History and Art Museum, housed in a reconstructed 1912 concert hall by the banks of the pretty Prud Nizhny (Lower Pond), is worth a visit. Though it mainly focuses on Soviet rule, the German past is not ignored in the many interesting displays. You can also see images of the castle before and during its destruction.

Bunker Museum   MUSEUM
(Muzei Blindazh; ☑536 593; Universitetskaya ul 2; adult/student R70/50; ☺10am-4pm Tue-Sun) Cross the footbridge over Prud Nizhny and walk west towards the university to discover the fascinating Bunker Museum, the buried German command post, where the city's last German commander, Otto van Lasch, capitulated to the Soviets.

Ploshchad Pobedy   SQUARE
Pl Pobedy, the modern heart of Kaliningrad, is the site of several modern shopping centres and the Russo-Byzantine **Cathedral of Christ the Saviour** (Kafedralny Sobor Khrista Spasitelya), built in 2006, its gold domes visible from many points in the city. Extending west of the square is pr Mira, lined with shops and cafes leading to some of the city's prettiest areas. Along here you'll find the zoo, **Zoopark** (☑218 924; pr Mira 26; adult/student R100/40; ☺9am-9pm Jun-Aug, 10am-5pm Sep-May), which before WWII was considered the third best in the world, but is now in a sorry state (donations accepted – and needed!).

✯ Festivals & Events

The **Baltic Season** (www.baltseasons.ru) is an international festival of arts that offers up a range of musical and theatrical productions from June to November. In August there's also the **Don Cento Jazz Festival** (www.jazz festival.ru).

🛏 Sleeping

Kaliningrad is well served with midrange and top-end hotels, while budget accommodation is thin on the ground. Unless otherwise noted all rates include breakfast.

TOP CHOICE **Radisson Hotel, Kaliningrad**
                                             HOTEL €€€
(☑593 344; www.radisson-hotels.ru/kaliningrad; pl Pobedy 10; s/d from R6250/6700; ❋@☎) The city's newest hotel offers super-spacious, stylishly decorated rooms, some with views of the nearby cathedral. Also here is the restaurant **Verres & Vers**.

TOP CHOICE **Chaika**   HOTEL €€€
(☑210 729; www.hotel-kaliningrad.ru; ul Pugacheva 13; s/d from R3900/4900; ♒❋@☎) On a leafy street near the picturesque Amalienau area is this delightful 28-room property decorated with classy heritage touches. Has a restaurant, comfy lounge and fitness room.

Heliopark Kaiserhof   HOTEL €€€
(☑592 222; www.heliopark.ru; ul Oktyabrskaya 6A; s/d from R4500/4950; ❋@☎♒) A very nicely designed and furnished hotel, with a central atrium, super-stylish rooms and a full-service spa and sauna in a separate building. Rates are almost halved Friday to Sunday.

Skipper Hotel   HOTEL €€
(Gastinitsa Shkiperskaya; ☑592 000; www.skipper hotel.ru; ul Oktyabrskaya 4A; r from R2500; ❋☎) Cute hotel with rooms with wood furnishings and river views. Attached is the pricey seafood restaurant **Langust**; breakfast is taken in a cafe in the nearby lighthouse.

Villa Severin   PENSION €€
(☑365 373; www.villa-severin.ru; ul Leningradskaya 9a; s/d from R1600/1850; ❋@☎) There's a very homely atmosphere at this pretty villa, set back from the Prud Verkny, with 10 comfortably furnished rooms including one simple

student room (R1000 without breakfast). It also has a small sauna and cafe.

Komnaty Otdykha
HOTEL €

(✆586 447; pl Kalinina; s/d R950/1500) A great job has been made of renovating these resting rooms inside the south train station, turning them into en suite accommodation. The women in charge are friendly and justifiably proud of their small hotel. To find it, turn right down the corridor after the ticket hall and walk up to the third floor. Breakfast not included.

Dona Hotel
HOTEL €€

(✆351 650; www.hoteldona.ru; pl Marshala Vasilevskogo 2; s/d from R2700/3200; ❋@✆) A pleasant place with friendly English-speaking staff. The decor is beginning to need some sprucing up, though.

Ubileiniy Luks
HOTEL €€

(✆519 024; www.ubilejny-lux.ru; ul Universitetskaya 2; r/apt from R2500/3800; ❋@✆) Atop a business centre, this hotel's 13 rooms are all enormous, and most have kitchens. Breakfast not included.

Hotel Moskva
HOTEL €€

(✆352 300; www.hotel.kaliningrad.ru; pr Mira 19; s/d from R1950/2300) Offers bright spacious rooms and a good location. Breakfast not included.

✖ Eating & Drinking

Self-caterers should visit the lively central market on ul Chernyakhovskogo or the supermarket **Viktoriya** (Kaliningrad Plaza, Leninsky pr 30; ☉10am-10pm) with branches also opposite the southern bus and train station and near Fish Village.

TOP CHOICE Dolce Vita
RUSSIAN €€€

(✆351 612; pl Marshala Vasilevskogo 2; mains R500-1000; ☉noon-midnight; ✆) Expertly prepared, inventive dishes are served at this elegant restaurant – try the 'a la Russe' selection for luxurious takes on old standards such as *pelmeni* and borsht.

Croissant Café
BAKERY €

(pr Mira 23; meals R100; ☉9am-11pm Sun-Thu, 24hr Fri & Sat) A chic baked-goods heaven. Indulge in flaky pastries, quiches, muffins, biscuits and cakes, as well as omelettes and bliny for breakfast. There are also branches in the Evropa mall as well at Leninksy pr 63 and ul Proletarskaya 79.

Kmel
RUSSIAN, MICROBREWERY €

(✆593 377; Clover City Centre mall, pl Pobedy 10; meals R350-500; ☉10am-2am) Four types of good beer are brewed at this appealing multilevel gastropub overlooking pl Pobedy. They're served alongside an interesting range of Russian and Siberian dishes including unusual ingredients such as reindeer and *omul*, a fish from Lake Baikal.

Don Chento
PIZZA €

(Sovetsky pr 9-11; meals R200-300) No need to endure depressing Soviet throwback *stolovye* (canteens) for budget meals when you can dig in at the self-serve salad bar or pick a slice of pizza at this stylish chain with several branches across the city.

Zarya
RUSSIAN €€

(✆213 929; pr Mira 43; meals R300-400; ☉10am-3am) Fashionable brasserie in the lobby of the Scala cinema that also has an attractive outdoor area. The food is reliable – try the potato pancakes with salmon caviar.

Prichal
GEORGIAN €€

(✆703 030; ul Verkhneozyornaya 2a; meals R300-500; ☉noon-1am Sun-Thu, to 2am Fri & Sat) Private huts in a pretty garden overlooking the north end of Prod Verkhny make this

RUSSIA KALININGRAD

THE RETURN OF THE CASTLE?

Königsberg's majestic castle, dating from 1255, once stood on Tsentralnaya pl. Left in ruins after WWII and dynamited out of existence in the late 1960s, it was replaced by the outstandingly ugly **Dom Sovietov** (House of Soviets). During the eyesore's construction it was discovered that the land below it was hollow, with a (now flooded) four-level underground passage connecting to the cathedral. The decaying half-finished building has never been used.

If Kaliningrad's chief planner, Alexander Bazhinm, has his way, Dom Sovietov will eventually be masked by a rebuilt castle, part of a development that would also include a clutch of modern skyscrapers and a convention centre. Even though the plan has been endorsed by no less a figure than Prime Minister Vladimir Putin (his wife Ludmilla was born in the region), the estimated US$100 million needed has yet to be raised.

spruced-up Soviet-era Georgian restaurant a memorable dining experience.

La Plas Cafe
RUSSIAN €€

(pl Pobedy 1; meals R300-400; ⊙24hr) Offering big window views onto pl Pobedy and tasty food that actually looks as good as it does on the photo menu, this round-the-clock place is a good fit for breakfast, lunch, dinner or cocktails.

Bar Verf
CAFE-BAR €

(Fish Village, ul Oktyabrskaya 4A; ⊙11am-midnight) The food is hit and miss but the ambiance is pleasant at this relaxed wine bar in Fish Village – they screen movies and provide coloured pencils and paper for you to doodle with.

First Café
CAFE-BAR

(☑644 829; ul Yepronovskaya 21; 🔊) Stylishly decorated cafe with several other locations in the city beside this branch opposite Fish Village. Serves a wide range of drinks and snacks.

☆ Entertainment

Classical concerts are occasionally held at the cathedral. Major DJs from Russia and Western Europe jet in for gigs at Kaliningrad's clubs, which open around 9pm but typically don't get going until well after midnight.

Drama & Comedy Theatre
THEATRE

(☑212 422; pr Mira 4; tickets R150-200) Plays, ballets and classical concerts are staged in this handsomely restored building.

Philharmonic Hall
CLASSICAL MUSIC

(☑448 890; ul Bogdana Khmelnitskogo 61a; tickets from R180) This beautifully restored neo-Gothic church, which has excellent acoustics, hosts organ concerts, chamber-music recitals and the occasional symphony orchestra.

Universal
CLUB

(☑952 996; www.club-universal.com; pr Mira 43; admission from R300) Kaliningrad's classiest club.

Vagonka
CLUB

(☑956 677; www.vagonka.net; Stanochnaya ul 12; admission from R150) Best option for the under-21 crowd and drinks are cheap.

Amsterdam
GAY CLUB

(www.amsterdam-club.ru; 38/11 Litovsky Val; admission free before 11pm, R200-400 after 11pm; ⊙noon-2am Mon-Thu, to 6am Fri, 8pm-6am Sat, 7pm-2am Sun) Hidden 200m down an unnamed side street off Litovsky Val; best visited on weekends.

❶ Information

The free quarterly listings magazine *Welcome to Kaliningrad*, available in hotel lobbies, has useful information in English on the city and region.

Baltma Tours (☑931 931; www.baltma.ru; pr Mira 94, 4th fl, pl Pobedy) The efficient, multilingual staff here can arrange visas, accommodation and an array of local excursions including to Yantarny, home of what was once the world's largest amber mine, and the military port city of Baltiysk, which requires a special permit to enter.

Branch post office (ul Chernyakhovskogo 32; ⊙post office 10am-2pm & 3-7pm Mon-Fri, 10am-2pm & 3-6pm Sat, internet room 10am-2pm & 3-10pm Mon-Sat) It's 600m north of pr Mira.

Emergency Hospital (☑466 989; ul Nevskogo 90; ⊙24hr)

King's Castle (☑350 782; www.kaliningrad info.ru; Hotel Kaliningrad, Leninskiy pr 81; ⊙8am-8pm Mon-Fri, 9am-4pm Sat) A private tourist agency that also operates as a tourist information centre. Offers tours of the city and to the Kurshskaya Kosa.

Königsberg.ru (www.konigsberg.ru) Web-based tour agency through which you can arrange visas, including the 72-hour express visa.

Main post office (ul Kosmonavta Leonova 22; ⊙9am-8pm Mon-Fri, 10am-6pm Sat & Sun)

Official tourism site (http://en.tourism kaliningrad.ru)

UFMS office (☑563 809; Sovetsky pr 13, Room 9) For visa queries.

❶ Getting There & Away

There are three border crossings from Poland and four from Lithuania.

Air

Khrabrovo airport (☑459 426) is 24km north of the city. There are daily flights to Moscow, St Petersburg and Rīga, as well as slightly less frequent connections to Brest, Warsaw, Kyiv, Minsk and Odessa.

Boat

DFDS Lisko (☑660 404; www.dfdslisco.ru; ul Suvorova 45) is the agent for ferry services between Baltiysk and destinations including St Petersburg, Sassnitz in Germany, and Klaipėda in Lithuania. **Trans-Exim** (☑660 468; www.tran sexim.ru; ul Suvorova 45) also runs weekly car ferries between Baltiysk and Ust-Luga, 150km west of St Petersburg. Check the websites for the latest prices and schedules.

Bus

There are two bus stations. **Yuzhny bus station** (ul Zheleznodorozhnaya 7) is next to Yuzhny vokzal. Buses depart from here to every corner of the region, including Svetlogorsk (R45, one hour, every 30 minutes). It is also the location for international bus services run by **Ecolines** (☑656 501; www.ecolines.net) to Warsaw and several German cities.

The **international bus station** (Moskovsky pr 184) has services to:

Gdansk (R500, 4½ hours, two daily)

Klaipėda (R300, four hours, two daily)

Rīga (R737, nine hours, two daily)

Tallinn (R1332, 14 hours, daily)

Vilnius (R716, eight hours, daily)

Warsaw (R750, nine hours, daily)

The best way to Svetlogorsk (R50, one hour) and Zelenogradsk (R45, 45 minutes) is via *mashrutky* from the bus stop next to Severny vokzal (North Station) on Sovetsky pr. They run about every 15 minutes or so until about 8pm.

Train

Kaliningrad's two stations are Severny vokzal (North Station) and the larger Yuzhny vokzal (South Station). All long-distance and many local trains go from Yuzhny vokzal, passing through but not always stopping at Severny vokzal.

Berlin (R4400, 14 hours, daily May to October)

Moscow (R2600 to R2900, 23 hours, three daily)

St Petersburg (R2800, 26 hours, daily)

Svetlogorsk (R60, 1½ hours, 12 daily)

Vilnius (R1600; six hours, four daily)

Zelenogradsk (R48, 30 minutes, seven daily)

ⓘ Getting Around

Tickets for trams, trolleybuses, buses and minibuses are sold on board (R10). To get to the domestic airport, take bus 144 from the bus station (R30, 30 minutes). A taxi to/from the airport is R300 with **Taxi Kaliningrad** (☑585 858; www.taxi-kaliningrad.ru).

If you're planning on touring the region, Kaliningrad is a good place to rent a car. Agencies include **City-Rent** (☑509 191; www.city-rent39. ru; Moskovsky pr 182a), which has a branch at the airport. Rates start at €26 per day.

Svetlogorsk СВЕТЛОГОРСК
☑40153 / POP 10,950

Developed in the early 20th century as a spa resort, this pleasant, slow-placed town 35km northwest of Kaliningrad has a narrow beach backed by steep sandy slopes, pretty old German houses, revamped sanatoriums, good hotels, a delightful shady forest setting scattered with artful sculptures, and a well-maintained promenade. However, if beaches

are your thing, the ones at the Kurshskaya Kosa are far nicer and cleaner.

Svetlogorsk is quite spread out. Svetlogorsk II, the train terminus, is on ul Lenina, the town's major street running east–west and bisected by ul Oktyabskaya. To the south, Kaliningradskiy pr runs past the tranquil Tikhoe pond.

There's internet access (R40 per hour) at **Svetlogorsk tourist information centre** (☑22098; http://svetlogorsk-tourism.ru; ul Karl Marksa 7a; ☉9am-7pm Mon-Fri, 10am-7pm Sat, 10am-4pm Sun) where you can also get assistance with hotel bookings, tours and car rental.

⊙ Sights

Herman Brachert House Museum   MUSEUM (Doma-Muzei Germana Brakheta; ☑21166; www.brachert.ru; ul Tokareva 7; admission R100; ☉10am-5pm Sat-Thu) A 15-minute walk west of the town centre in the village of Otradnoe is the charming Herman Brachert House Museum, the former home of the sculptor whose work can be spotted all around Svetlogorsk.

Ul Oktyabrskaya   NEIGHBOURHOOD This street is lined with handsome buildings, including the striking 25m-high **water tower** built in Jugendstil (art nouveau) style; take a peep inside the sanatorium beneath to see the colourful wall murals. Nearby, at the attractive wooden **Organ Hall** (Organniy Zal; ☑21761; organ-makarov.narod.ru; ul Kurortnaya 3; tickets R300), concerts are held throughout the week.

Between here and the seafront, a new park and cultural centre are under construction; there's also a **shopping complex** built in old Prussian style and a **glass pavilion** where you can taste the local mineral water for free.

Promenade   PROMENADE Steps or a rickety lift lead down to the seafront. Here you'll find Herman Brachert's *Nymph* statue in a mosaic-decorated shell, and at the eastern end is an impressive sundial, decorated with an eye-catching mosaic of the zodiac.

🛏 Sleeping & Eating

Hotel Universal   HOTEL **€€** (☑743 658; www.hotel-universal.ru; ul Nekrasova 3; s/d incl breakfast R1900/2200; ☞) Close to the train station and set in its own quiet grounds, this modern small hotel is nicely designed and has a variety of spacious rooms as well as a restaurant.

ℹ TRAINS ON MOSCOW TIME

It's important to note that *all* trains in Kaliningrad, including local ones, run on Moscow time, so if a train is scheduled to depart at 10am it will leave at 9am Kaliningrad time.

Lumier Art Hotel HOTEL €€€

(☏507 750; www.hotellumier.ru; per Lermontovsky 2A; r incl breakfast from R4500; ❄☎) With the cinema as its theme, the designers clearly had a lot of fun decorating this boutique hotel – the standard rooms are quite stylish and come with cable TV and DVD players. Some also have balconies. There's also a spa and restaurant, but the latter wasn't open when we visited.

Falke Hotel Resort & Spa HOTEL €€€

(☏21605; www.falke-hotel.ru; ul Lenina 16; s/d from R4700/7000; ❄@☎≋) This quietly luxurious place, about 1km east of the town centre, has fine rooms and an indoor pool (in a balmy winter garden) that is big enough for a decent swim.

Stary Doktor PENSION €€

(☏21362; www.alterdoctor.ru; ul Gagarina 12; s/d R2500/2800) In an old German home, this pension offers simple and cosy rooms.

Korvet RESTAURANT €€

(☏22040; Oktyabrskaya ul 36; pizza R200-300) This pizzeria and cafe based in the 1901 Kurhaus is a lovely place for a meal. Lounge on comfy sofas; there are rugs to keep warm if it gets too chilly. On Friday and Saturday night DJs keeping things going into the early hours.

Kafe Blinnaya CAFE €

(Oktyabrskaya ul 22; bliny R20-30; ☉9am-6pm) It's self-serve for inexpensive bliny, salads etc at this simple cafe with streetside seating. The neighbouring bar (open noon to 3am) offers table service at higher prices.

ℹ Getting There & Around

From Kaliningrad you can either take a train (R45, 1½ hours, 12 daily) to Svetlogorsk II or the faster and far more frequent buses (R45, 45 to 60 minutes), which leave from the Yuzhny vokzal bus station and outside Severny vokzal on Sovetsky pr. In Svetlagorsk, buses arrive and depart from in front of the Svetlogorsk II station.

Svetlogorsk is easy to navigate on foot or by bicycle: from May to September rent bikes

from **Eksi Tur** (ul Oktyabrskaya 10; per hr/day R50/350; ☉10am-5pm Mon-Sat).

Kurshskaya Kosa National Park КУРШСКАЯ КОСА

☏40150

Tall, windswept sand dunes and dense pine forests teeming with wildlife lie along the 98km-long Curonian Spit, which divides the tranquil Curonian Lagoon from the Baltic Sea and is a Unesco World Heritage site. The 50km of the spit that lies in Russian territory is protected within the **Kurshskaya Kosa National Park** (admission per person/car R30/200), a fascinating place to explore or to relax on pristine beaches.

Tranquil fishing and holiday villages dot the eastern coast. From south to north they are: **Lesnoy**, **Rybachy** (the largest, with a population of 1200), and **Morskoe**, which has spectacular views of the dunes from raised platforms at nearby **Vistota Efa** (42km mark).

Also don't miss the **Dancing Forest** (Tantsuyushchiy Les; 37km mark), where wind-sculpted pines do indeed appear to be frozen mid-boogie. To learn more about the park, drop by the **museum** (☏45119; 14km mark; admission R30; ☉9.30am-4.30pm Tue-Sun May-Sep, 10am-4pm Oct-Apr), where you can also see some deer and cute woodcarvings by a local artist. Call the museum to pre-arrange an excursion at the **Fringilla Field Station** (23km mark; tours R50; ☉9am-6pm Apr-Oct) a bird-ringing centre in operation since 1957, where enormous funnelled nets can trap an average of 1000 birds a day.

In Lesnoy, **Kurshskaya Kosa** (☏45242; www.holiday39rus.ru; Tsentralnaya ul 17; s/d incl breakfast from R1800/1900;@) is one of the Spit's best deals for accommodation and dining. It also has internet access and an ATM and rents bicycles (R100 per hour). Also worth checking out is **Morskoe** (☏41330; ul Dachnaya 6; r from R2350) in Morskoe.

With an early start it's possible to see most places on the Korshskaya Kosa by public transport. Four buses a day from Kaliningrad (via Zelenogradsk) head up the spit en route to Klaipėda in Lithuania. There are at least three others that shuttle between Zelenogradsk and Morskoe (R57, 50 minutes). All stop in Lesnoy and Rybachy.

For more flexibility rent a car or arrange a tour in Kaliningrad or Zelenogradsk, where a car and driver for half a day costs R1500.

UNDERSTAND RUSSIA

History

Russia's origins are rooted in countries it nowadays likes to think of as its satellites; it effectively sprang forth from Ukraine and Belarus in the Dark Ages, and took its alphabet from Bulgaria, from where Christianity also spread. The birth of the Russian state is usually identified with the founding of Novgorod in 862 AD, although from the early 13th century until 1480 Russia was effectively a colony of the Mongols.

Ivan the Terrible

Russia's medieval period was a dark and brutal time, never more so than during the reign of Ivan the Terrible (r 1547–84), whose sobriquet was well earned through his fantastically cruel punishments such as boiling his enemies alive. He also killed his son and heir in a fit of rage and is said to have blinded the architects who built St Basil's Cathedral on Red Sq.

Despite Ivan the Terrible's conquest of the Volga basin and obsession with reaching the Baltic (at that time controlled by the Lithuanians and Swedes), it was not until the Romanov dynasty (1613–1917) that Russia began its massive territorial expansion. Between the 17th and 19th centuries Siberia, the Far East, Central Asia and the Caucasus fell under Russia's sway, creating the huge country it is today.

Peter, Catherine & Later Tsars

Peter the Great (r 1689–1725) began to modernise Russia by setting up a navy, educational centres and beginning the construction of St Petersburg in 1703. Russia's capital moved north to St Petersburg from 1712, and remained there until the Bolsheviks moved it back more than two centuries later.

Catherine the Great (r 1762–96) continued Peter's legacy, in the process making Russia a world power by the mid-18th century. Her 'enlightened despotism' saw the founding of the art collection that was to become the Hermitage, a huge expansion in the sciences and arts, a correspondence with Voltaire, and the strengthening of the nation. However, it also saw her brutal suppression of a Cossack rebellion and intolerance for any institution that would threaten her authority.

Feverish capitalist development in the 19th century was undermined by successively autocratic and backwards tsars. Alexander I (r 1801–25) was preoccupied with Napoleon, who invaded Russia and got as far as Moscow in 1812, but was eventually beaten by the Russian winter. Alexander II (r 1855–81) took the brave step of freeing the serfs in 1861, but baulked at political reform, thus sowing the seeds of a revolutionary movement.

The Bolsheviks & the USSR

Nicholas II, Russia's last tsar, ascended the throne in 1894. It was his refusal to countenance serious reform that precipitated the 1917 revolution. What began as a liberal revolution was hijacked later the same year in a coup led by the Bolsheviks under Vladimir Ulyanov, aka Lenin, which resulted in the establishment of the world's first communist state.

Between 1917 and 1920 the Bolsheviks fought a bloody civil war against the 'whites', who supported the monarchy. The tsar and his family were murdered in 1918 and eventually resistance to the communists trickled out.

By the time Lenin died in 1924, Russia had become the principal member of the Union of Soviet Socialist Republics (USSR), a communist superpower absorbing some 14 neighbouring states between 1922 and 1945. Lenin's successor Josef Stalin, with single-minded brutality, forced the industrialisation of the country. Millions were killed or imprisoned under his watch. Stalin also saw Russia through the devastation of WWII, and by the time he died in 1953 the USSR had a full nuclear arsenal and half of Europe as satellite states.

The Collapse of Communism

Khrushchev (r 1957–64) began a cautious reform program and denounced Stalin before being removed and replaced by Leonid Brezhnev, whose rule (1964–82) was marked by economic stagnation and growing internal dissent. Mikhail Gorbachev's period of reform, known as perestroika, began in 1985, but it was too late to save the Soviet Union. Within six years the USSR had collapsed alongside communism, and reformer Boris Yeltsin was elected Russia's first-ever president in 1991.

Yeltsin led Russia into the roller-coaster world of cut-throat capitalism, which saw the creation of a new superclass of oligarchs – businesspeople who made billions from buying once state-owned commodities and running them as private companies – while prices soared and the rouble crashed, wiping out the meagre savings of the vast majority of the population.

On New Year's Eve 1999, with his health on the wane, Yeltsin resigned, stepping aside for Vladimir Putin, a steely-faced ex-KGB officer who was prime minister at the time. Elected president the following year, Putin had a policy of steering a careful course between reform and centralisation that made him highly popular. Russia began to recover the confidence it had lost during the Yeltsin years, and the economy boomed off the back of oil and gas exports. However, Putin's tightening of control over the media and political opponents signalled his ruthless side, as did his ordering a brutal clampdown on the independence movement in Chechnya following terrorist attacks in the capital and elsewhere in 2002 and 2004.

Russia Today

With no credible opponent, Dmitry Medvedev's election to president in March 2008 was never in doubt. Non-Russian observers worried about how 'democratic' this practically preordained outcome really was, and fretted even more in August of the same year when Russia came to blows with Georgia over the breakaway regions of Abkhazia and South Ossetia. Meanwhile, in his new role as prime minister Putin appeared to be just as much in charge of the country as he was when president.

The financial crisis of 2008 dented the bank balances of Russia's richest, but oil and gas revenues continue to generate great wealth for the country – even if not much of it trickles down out of Moscow and a handful of other big cities. In October 2010 when Medvedev sacked Yuri Luzhkov, Moscow's mayor of 18 years, some interpreted it as a move by the president to secure his power base in the run-up to the March 2012 elections. However, Putin has not ruled out that he won't stand again for a second round in the top job.

The Russians

There's some truth to the local saying 'scratch a Russian and you'll find a Tatar'. Over the centuries Russia has absorbed people from a huge number of nationalities including the Mongols, the Tatars, Siberian peoples, Ukrainians, Jews and Caucasians. This means that while the vast majority of people you meet will describe themselves as Russian, ethnic homogeneity is not always that simple.

Russians have a reputation for being dour, depressed and unfriendly. In fact, most Russians are anything but, yet find constant smiling indicative of idiocy, and ridicule pointless displays of happiness commonly seen in Western culture. Even though Russians can appear to be unfriendly and even downright rude when you first meet them (especially those working behind glass windows of any kind), their warmth is quite astounding as soon as the ice is broken. Just keep working at it.

The vast majority of Russians identify themselves as Orthodox Christians (although the proportion of those who actually practise their faith is small). Led by Patriarch Alexei II, the church has become ever more vocal in recent years, virulently condemning homosexuality, contraception and abortion.

Religious freedom exists in Russia – St Petersburg boasts the world's most northerly mosque and Buddhist temple. Prejudice against Jews exists, although this is very rarely exhibited in anything other than the odd negative comment and some deeply entrenched stereotypes. There is certainly no reason for Jewish travellers to worry about coming to Russia.

The Arts
Literature

Russia's formal literary tradition sprung to life with the poetic genius of Alexander Pushkin (1799–1837), whose epic *Yevgeny Onegin* stands out as one of Russian literature's greatest achievements. Most Russians can quote at least a few lines from this enormous, playful, philosophical poem.

Duels cut short the lives of both Pushkin and his literary heir, Mikhail Lermontov, who had the potential to equal or even surpass Pushkin's contribution – his novel *A Hero of Our Time* and his poetry spoke of incredible gifts. By the late 19th century Leo Tolstoy and Fyodor Dostoyevsky were producing some of the world's great classics – the former penning epic tapestries of Russian life such as *War and Peace* and *Anna Karenina,* the latter writing dark and troubled philosophical novels, such as *Crime and Punishment* and *The Brothers Karamazov.*

The early 20th century saw a continued literary flowering. From what was widely known as the Silver Age came the poetic talents of Alexander Blok, Anna Akhmatova and Osip Mandelstam. By the late 1920s,

For centuries Russians have made it an important part of their week to visit a *banya* (hot bath), the focus of which is the *parilka* (steam room). Here, rocks are heated by a furnace, with water poured onto them using a long-handled ladle. Often, a few drops of eucalyptus or pine oils (sometimes even beer) are added to the water, creating a scent in the burst of scalding steam that's released into the room; people are naked in the *banya* but some wear felt caps *(chapkas)* to protect their hair from the effects of the heat, and sandals *(tapki)* to protect their feet.

As they sweat it out, some bathers grab hold of a *venik* (a tied bundle of birch branches) and beat themselves or each other with it. Though it can be painful, the effect can also be pleasant and cleansing: apparently, the birch leaves (sometimes oak or, agonisingly, juniper branches) and their secretions help rid the skin of toxins. After the birch-branch thrashing, bathers run outside and, depending on their nerve, plunge into the *basseyn* (ice-cold pool) or take a cooling shower. The whole process is then repeated several times for anything up to two hours.

To take part, try the *bani* in Moscow (p782) or St Petersburg (p798).

with Stalin's grip on power was complete, all writers not spouting the party line were vilified. Dissenting writers were either shot, took their own lives, fled, or were silenced as Stalin revealed his socialist-realist model of writing, which brought novels with titles such as *Cement* and *How the Steel Was Tempered* to the toiling masses. Despite this, many writers wrote in secret, and novels such as Mikhail Bulgakov's *The Master and Margarita* and poems such as Anna Akhmatova's *Requiem* survived Stalinism to become classics.

Despite Khrushchev allowing some literary freedom (it was under his watch that Solzhenitsyn's *A Day in the Life of Ivan Denisovich*, a novella depicting life in one of Stalin's gulags, was published), censorship continued until the mid-1980s when, thanks to Mikhail Gorbachev's policy of glasnost (openness), writers who had only been published through the illegal network of *samizdat* (the home printing presses), and were thus read only by the intelligentsia, suddenly had millions of readers.

Since the demise of the Soviet Union, Russian literature has bloomed and embraced the postmodernism that was prohibited by the Soviet authorities. Current literary big hitters, all of whose books have been translated into English, include the mystery writer Boris Akunin; the surrealist Viktor Pelevin; Tatyana Tolstaya, author of the symbolic sci-fi novel *The Slynx*; and Viktor Yerofeev. The France-based expat writer Andrei Makine is also widely respected.

Music

Mikhail Glinka, composer of the operas *A Life for the Tsar* (1836) and *Ruslan and Lyudmilla* (1842) is considered the father of Russian classical music. He was born in Smolensk, where an annual festival is held in his celebration.

Composers like Nicolai Rimsky-Korsakov and Modest Mussorgsky looked to Russia's folk past for inspiration, as did Igor Stravinsky, whose *The Rite of Spring* and *The Firebird* were both influenced by Russian folk music. Other composers such as Pyotr Ilyich Tchaikovsky, Sergei Prokofiev and Sergei Rachmaninov embraced the romantic movements of Western classical music.

Prokofiev, who also left Soviet Russia but returned in 1934, wrote the scores for Eisenstein's films *Alexander Nevsky* and *Ivan the Terrible,* the ballet *Romeo and Juliet,* and *Peter and the Wolf.* His work was condemned for 'formalism' towards the end of his life.

Similarly, the ideological beliefs of Dmitry Shostakovich, who wrote brooding, bizarrely dissonant works, as well as accessible traditional classical music, led to him being alternately praised and condemned by the Soviet government. Shostakovich's Symphony no 7 – the *Leningrad* – brought him honour and international standing when it was performed by the Leningrad Philharmonic during the Siege of Leningrad.

Progressive new music surfaced only slowly in the post-Stalin era. Symphony no 1 by Alfred Schnittke, probably the most important work of this major experimental modern Russian composer, had to be premiered by its champion, conductor

RUSSIAN CINEMA

Russia has produced some of the world's most famous cinematic images – largely thanks to the father of the cinematic montage, Sergei Eisenstein, whose *Battleship Potemkin* (1925) and *Ivan the Terrible* (1944–46) are reference points for anyone serious about the history of film. Despite constant headaches with authority, Andrei Tarkovsky produced complex and iconoclastic films in the 1960s and 1970s; *The Mirror* and *Andrei Rublev* are generally considered to be his two greatest works.

In recent times Nikita Mikhalkov and Alexander Sokurov have established themselves as internationally renowned Russian directors. Mikhalkov's *Burnt by the Sun* won the Oscar for best foreign film in 1994; however the first part of his follow-up *Burnt by the Sun 2: Exodus* – a $55 million production reputed to be Russia's most expensive movie since Soviet times – was a flop in cinemas in 2010.

Alexander Sokurov has made his name producing art-house historical dramas, including *Taurus*, *Molokh* and 2002's astonishing *Russian Ark* – the only full-length film ever made using one long tracking shot. Andrei Zvyagintsev's stunning debut feature *The Return* (2003) scooped the Golden Lion at Venice.

The glossy vampire thriller *Night Watch* (2004), by Kazakhstan-born director Timur Bekmambetov, struck box-office gold both at home and abroad, leading to an equally successful sequel, *Day Watch* (2006), and to Bekmambetov being lured to Hollywood. He also directed a 2007 follow-up to the classic Soviet romantic comedy *Irony of Fate* (1975), one of Russia's all-time favourite movies.

Gennady Rozhdestvensky, in the city of Gorky (now Nizhny Novgorod) in 1974 and was not played in Moscow until 1986.

Visual Arts

Internationally, the best-known Russian artists are the avant-garde painters of the early 20th century, such as Vasily Kandinsky and Kazimir Malevich. However, most Russians will quite rightly point you towards the 'greats' of the 19th century, such as Ilya Repin and the *peredvizhniki* (wanderers) – the generation of painters who rejected the strict formalism of the St Petersburg Academy and painted realistic rural scenes with deep social messages.

Anyone visiting Russia will want to see the collections of foreign art held at St Petersburg's Hermitage and Moscow's Pushkin Museum of Fine Arts. The best galleries for Russian art are the Russian Museum in St Petersburg and Moscow's State Tretyakov Gallery.

Russia's contemporary art scene is beginning to flourish under the patronage of the country's wealthy elite. Artists worth looking out for include the cheeky Siberian artists' collective Blue Noses, and the more luxurious works of Moscow-based quartet AES+F as well as established talents such as Ilya Kabakov (whose exhibition opened Moscow's Garazh Centre for Contemporary Culture in 2008) and Aleksandr Kosolapov.

Theatre & Ballet

Since Chekhov revolutionised Russian drama in the late 19th century, Russia has seen countless innovations, from Constantin Stanislavsky, who created method acting, to Vsevolod Meyerhold, the theatrical pioneer who Stalin had arrested and murdered. Among the most celebrated contemporary theatre directors today are Kama Ginkas, who works with the Moscow Art Theatre, Pyotr Fomenko, who heads up Moscow's Pyotr Fomenko Workshop Theatre, and Lev Dodin at St Petersburg's Maly Drama Theatre.

Ballet in Russia evolved as an offshoot of French dance combined with Russian folk and peasant dance techniques. It stunned Western Europeans when it was first taken on tour during the late 19th century. Moscow's Bolshoi Theatre and St Petersburg's Mariinsky have worked hard to reinvent themselves since the end of the Soviet Union, and their productions regularly tour the world.

Sport

Since Soviet times Russia has been honing its sporting prowess, and today it continues to invest heavily in sports, developing facilities and new training programs and offering fat fees to attract top overseas coaches. Ice hockey, basketball and tennis are popular spectator sports, but top of the league is football (soccer), which is enjoying a boom pumped up by sponsorship deals with Russian big business.

The bottomless pockets of state energy giant Gazprom enabled Zenit St Petersburg to gain not only the Russian league title in 2007 but also the UEFA Cup in 2008. CSKA Moscow, funded at the time by Roman Abramovich's Sibneft, also lifted the UEFA Cup in 2005. *Football Dynamo* by Marc Bennetts is a passionate, insightful and racy read that reveals much about the fascinating yet frequently murky world of Russian soccer.

Environment

European Russia is characterised by flat fields and forests. You can take the train from one city to the other and barely pass a hill or a valley. However, the Kaliningrad region has half of the sandy Kurshskaya Kosa (Curonian Spit), the Curonian Lagoon and the world's largest supply of amber.

The disastrous environmental legacy of communism is enormous. As well as both Moscow and St Petersburg being polluted from traffic and heavy industry, the countryside is frequently blighted by crumbling and abandoned factories and other industrial plants. Environmental consciousness remains relatively low, although things are slowly changing with the emergence of a small but vocal Russian environmental movement.

For more details on the environmental problems being faced by Russia see the sites of **Greenpeace Russia** (www.greenpeace.org/russia/en) and **World Wide Fund for Nature in Russia** (www.wwf.ru/eng).

Food & Drink

Russian food, while very good, can be bland: spices are not widely used and dill is overwhelmingly the herb of choice. That said, you can eat extremely well in Russia – Caucasian food is popular throughout the country and is delicious. Moscow and St Petersburg overflow with restaurants serving cuisine from all over the world as well as top-notch renditions of national dishes.

Staples & Specialities

Russian soups are excellent. Delicious borsch (beetroot soup), *solyanka* (a soup made from pickled vegetables) and *ukha* (fish soup) are always reliable. *Pelmeni* are Russian ravioli – meat or fish parcels wrapped in dough and served with *smetana* (sour cream) – and are available everywhere. Other, more interesting possibilities are *zharkoye* (literally 'hot' – meat stew in a pot), bliny, caviar, beef stroganoff, *goluptsy* (mincemeat wrapped in cabbage leaves) and fish specialities, such as sturgeon, salmon and pikeperch.

Where to Eat & Drink

The traditional cheap *stolovoya* (canteen) has been almost entirely edged out by slick fast-food chains. Upmarket restaurants that serve the latest fashionable cuisine tend to be quite formal. In between, there's an increasing number of relaxed diner-style places in the cities, and Western-style cafes have become extremely popular. Bars and beer halls are where most Russians prefer to drink. These generally cheap places usually combine beer and hearty Russian fare, sometimes with live music.

Restaurants and bars typically open from noon to midnight, although there may be a break between afternoon and evening meals. However, they will often open later than their stated hours if the establishment is full. Smoking is allowed in practically all restaurants and bars, with a few offering nonsmoking sections.

Vegetarians & Vegans

Russia can be tough for vegetarians, and near impossible for vegans. Vegetarian possibilities include bliny with sour cream, mushrooms, cheese or savoury *tvorog* (whey); and mushroom julienne (mushrooms fried in garlic, cheese and cream). Note that Georgian restaurants generally contain a much wider selection of vegetarian dishes on their menus than the Russian menus.

SURVIVAL GUIDE

Directory A–Z

Accommodation

Budget accommodation is hard to come by in Russia, and it is strongly recommended that you book ahead for summer. During the White Nights in St Petersburg in late June, booking early is essential.

For a dorm bed in Moscow or St Petersburg, rates average between R550 and R750. A double room containing a bathroom in a budget hotel will cost anything up to R3000. Elsewhere budget hotels can be as cheap as R500 a night with shared facilities, although R1000 to R1500 is a more realistic minimum. You'll pay R1500 to R4000 for a midrange double (except in Moscow and St Petersburg, where midrange rooms start above R3000). For top-end accommodation expect to pay upwards of R4000 (R10,000 for Moscow and St Petersburg).

Rooms in this chapter come with private bathroom unless otherwise stated. Some but not all hotels have nonsmoking rooms and/or floors.

Budget ranges for Moscow and St Petersburg are:

€€€   more than R10,000

€€   R3000 to R10,000

€   less than R3000

For the rest of the country:

€€€   more than R4000

€€   R1500 to R4000

€   less than R1500

Business Hours

Russians work from early in the morning until mid-afternoon. Restaurants and bars often stay open later than their stated hours if the establishment is full. In fact, many simply say that they work *do poslednnogo klienta* (until the last customer leaves).

Banks 9am-6pm Mon-Fri

Bars & Restaurants noon-midnight

Shops 9-11am to 8-9pm

Dangers & Annoyances

Travellers have nothing to fear from Russia's 'mafia' – the increasingly respectable gangster classes are not interested in such small fry. You should, however, be very careful of pickpockets. Also be aware that there are some local gangs that can surround and rob travellers quite brazenly in broad daylight, although these are rare.

While the situation has improved slowly, many police officers and other uniformed officials are on the make – some are not much better than the people they are employed to protect the public from. If you feel you are being unfairly treated or if the police try to make you go somewhere with them, pull out your mobile phone and threaten to call your embassy (*'ya pozvonyu svoyu posolstvu'*). This will usually be sufficient to make them leave you alone. However, if they still want you to go somewhere, it's best to call your embassy immediately.

Sadly, racism is a problem in Russia. Be vigilant on the streets around Hitler's birthday (20 April), when bands of right-wing thugs have been known to roam around spoiling for a fight with anyone who doesn't look Russian. It's a sure thing that if you look like a foreigner you'll be targeted with suspicion by many (the police, in particular) at any time of year. Although it's far from a daily occurrence, Moscow and St Petersburg have seen violent attacks on non-Russians, particularly people from the Caucasus. If

---

RULES OF THE TABLE

Given its importance in Russian culture, it's drinking that is full of unspoken rules. First of all, never drink vodka without *zakuski* (snacks) – you'll get drunk otherwise, whereas (according to any Russian) that will *never* happen if you consume pickled herring or gherkins with your vodka. Once a bottle (vodka or otherwise) has been finished, it's considered rude to put it back on the table – always put it on the floor instead. Don't talk during toasts, and always appear to drink to the toast (even if you dribble it down your chin or drink nothing at all). Men should always down a vodka shot in one. Women are let off this requirement, although being able to down a large shot will garner respect from all quarters.

you stick to the main tourist areas and stay aware of what's going on around you, you should be fine.

Embassies & Consulates

See www.russianembassy.net for a full list of Russian embassies overseas.

Australia Moscow (☑495-956 6070; www.russia.embassy.gov.au; Podkolokolny per 10a/2; Ⓜ Kitay Gorod); St Petersburg (☑812-315 1100; ul Italyanskaya 1; Ⓜ Nevsky pr)

Belarus Kaliningrad (☑4012-214 412; ul Dm Donskogo 35a); Moscow (☑495-924 7031; www.embassybel.ru; Maroseyka ul 17/6, 101000; Ⓜ Kitay Gorod); St Petersburg (☑812-274 7212; ul Bonch-Bruevicha 3a; Ⓜ Chernyshevskaya)

Canada (☑495-925 6000; canadainternational.gc.ca/russia-russie/index.aspx; Starokonyushenny per 23, Moscow; Ⓜ Kropotkinskaya)

France Moscow (☑495-937 1500; www.ambafrance-ru.org/france_russie; ul Bolshaya Yakimanka 45; Ⓜ Oktyabrskaya); St Petersburg (☑812-332 2270; nab reki Moyki 15; Ⓜ Nevsky Pr)

Germany Kaliningrad (☑4012-920 230; www.kaliningrad.diplo.de; ul Leningradskaya 4); Moscow (☑495-937 9500; www.moskau.diplo.de; Mosfilmovskaya ul 56; Ⓜ Universitet, then bus 119); St Petersburg (☑812-320 2400; Furshtatskaya ul 39; Ⓜ Chernyshevskaya)

Latvia Kaliningrad (☑4012-706 755; Englesa ul 52a, Kaliningrad); Moscow (☑495-232 9760; www.am.gov.lv/en/moscow; ul Chapligina 3; Ⓜ Chistye Prudy)

Lithuania Kaliningrad (☑4012-959 486; Proletarskaya ul 133, Kaliningrad); Moscow (☑495-785 8605; ru.mfa.lt; Borisoglebsky per 10 Ⓜ Arbatskaya); St Petersburg (☑812-327 0230; ul Ryleyeva 37; Ⓜ Chernyshevskaya)

Netherlands (☑495-797 2900; www.netherlands-embassy.ru; Kalashny per 6, Moscow; Ⓜ Arbatskaya)

New Zealand (☑495-956 3579; www.nzembassy.com; Povarskaya ul 44, Moscow; Ⓜ Arbatskaya)

Poland Kaliningrad (☑4012-976 400; www.kaliningradkg.polemb.net; Kashtanovaya Alleya 51, Kaliningrad); Moscow (☑495 231 1500; www.moskwa.polemb.net; Klimashkina ul 4; Ⓜ Belorusskaya)

UK Moscow (☑495-956 7200; ukinrussia.fco.gov.uk/en; Smolenskaya nab 10; Ⓜ Smolenskaya); St Petersburg (☑812-320 3200; pl Proletarskoy Diktatury 5; Ⓜ Chernyshevskaya)

Ukraine (☑495-629 9742; www.mfa.gov.ua; Leontevsky per 18, Moscow; Ⓜ Pushkinskaya)

USA Moscow (☑495-728 5000; moscow.usembassy.gov; Bol Devyatinsky per 8; Ⓜ Barrikadnaya); St Petersburg (☑812-331 2600; ul Furshtatskaya 15; Ⓜ Chernyshevskaya)

Food

Price ranges are: budget (€; under R300), midrange (€€; R300 to R1000) and top end (€€€; over R1000).

Gay & Lesbian Travellers

Homosexuality was legalised in Russia in the early 1990s but remains a divisive issue throughout the country. Not everyone goes as far as Moscow's ex-mayor, Yury Luzhkov, who sided with ultraconservative protestors who broke up a gay parade in the capital in 2008, calling such events 'satanical'. But in general this is a conservative country, and being gay is frowned upon.

This said, there are active and relatively open gay and lesbian scenes in both Moscow and St Petersburg, and newspapers such as the *Moscow Times* and *St Petersburg Times* feature articles on gay and lesbian issues and listings for clubs, bars and events (although you shouldn't expect anything nearly as prominent as you might find in other major world centres). Away from these two major cities, the gay scene tends to be pretty much underground.

For a good overview, visit http://english.gay.ru, which has up-to-date information, good links and a resource for putting you in touch with personal guides for Moscow and St Petersburg.

Holidays

Russia's main public holidays:

New Year's Day 1 January

Russian Orthodox Christmas Day 7 January

Defender of the Fatherland Day 23 February

International Women's Day 8 March

International Labour Day/Spring Festival 1 May

Victory Day (1945) 9 May

Russian Independence Day (1991) 12 June

Unity Day 4 November

Many businesses are also closed from 1 to 7 January. Other widely celebrated holidays are **Defenders of the Motherland Day** (23 February) and **Easter Monday**.

Internet Resources

Russian Beyond the Headlines (rbth.ru) A wide-ranging online magazine with interesting features, sponsored by the daily paper *Rossiyskaya Gazeta*.

Way to Russia (www.waytorussia.net) Useful site, written and maintained by Russian backpackers.

Media

Russia is a TV country, with radio and newspapers sidelined to a greater extent than elsewhere in Europe or the US. The internet has exploded in recent years with all manner of blogs on **LiveJournal** (www.livejournal. com), the main platform for free political and cultural debate in Russia, with both the opposition and pro-government forces broadly represented.

The *Moscow Times,* a free English-language daily, has built its reputation on healthy scepticism of the Kremlin and pioneering investigative writing. Its twice-weekly sister paper, the *St Petersburg Times,* is the best source of local news from Russia's second city.

Money

The Russian currency is the rouble, written as 'рубль' and abbreviated as 'ру' or 'р'. There are 100 kopecks in a rouble, and these come in coin denominations of one (rarely seen), five, 10 and 50. Also issued in coins, roubles come in amounts of one, two, five and 10, with banknotes in values of 10, 50, 100, 500, 1000 and 5000 roubles.

Major credit and debit cards can be used in ATMs and many shops, restaurants and hotels. It's possible to exchange travellers cheques, although at a price. Euro or US dollar cash is the best to bring, and should be in pristine condition – crumpled or old notes are often refused. Most major currencies can be exchanged at change booths all over any town in Russia. Look for the sign *obmen valyut.* You may be asked for your passport.

Post

The Russian post service **Potcha Rossia** (www.russianpost.ru) gets an unfair rap. Postcards, letters and parcels sent abroad usually arrive within a couple of weeks, but there are occasional lapses. To send a postcard or letter up to 20g anywhere in the world by air costs R19 or R16.10, respectively.

Telephone

The international code for Russia is ☑7. The international access code from landline phones in Russia is ☑8, followed by ☑10 after the second tone, followed by the country code. From mobile phones, however, just dial + before the country code to place an international call.

The three main mobile-phone companies are **Beeline** (www.beeline.ru), **Megafon** (www.megafon.ru) and **MTS** (www.mts.ru).

Travellers with Disabilities

Travellers using wheelchairs aren't well catered for in Russia; there's a lack of access ramps and lifts. However, attitudes are enlightened and things are slowly changing. Major museums, such as the Hermitage and the Russian Museum, offer very good disabled access.

Visas

Everyone needs a visa to visit Russia – allow yourself at least a month before you travel to secure one. There are several types of visa, but most travellers will apply for a tourist visa, valid for 30 days from the date of entry. The process has three stages: invitation, application and registration.

Invitation

To obtain a visa, you first need an invitation. Hotels and hostels will usually issue anyone staying with them an invitation (or 'visa support') free or for a small fee (typically around €20 to €30). If you are not staying in a hotel or hostel, you will need to buy an invitation – costs typically range from €15 to €35 for a tourist visa depending on whether you require a single- or double-entry type and how quickly you need the invitation, and €45 to €270 for the various types of business visas. This can be done through most travel agents, via specialist agencies and online.

Application

Invitation in hand, you can then apply for a visa at any Russian embassy. Costs vary – anything from €35 to €350 – depending on the type of visa applied for and how quickly you need it. Rather frustratingly, Russian embassies are practically laws unto themselves, each with different fees and slightly different application rules. Avoid potential hassles by checking well in advance what these rules might be.

We highly recommended applying for your visa in your home country rather than on the road. Indeed, the rule is that you're supposed to do this, although we know from experience that some embassies and consulates can be more flexible than others.

Registration

On arrival, you should fill out an immigration card – a long white form issued by passport control; often these are given out in advance on your flight. You surrender one half of the form immediately to the passport control, while the other you keep for the duration of your stay and give up only on leaving Russia. Take good care of this as you'll need it for registration and could face problems while travelling in Russia – and certainly will on leaving – if you cannot produce it.

You must register your visa within three working days of arrival. If you're staying at a hotel, the receptionist should be able to do this for you for free or a small fee (typically R600 to R1000). Once registered, you should receive a separate slip of paper confirming the dates you'll be staying at that particular hotel. Keep this safe – that's the document that any police who stop you will need to see.

If staying in a homestay or rental apartment, you'll either need to pay a travel agency (anything from R1000 to R3200) to register your visa for you (most agencies will do this through a hotel) or make arrangements with the landlord or a friend to register you through the post office. See http://waytorussia.net/RussianVisa/Registration.html for how this can be done, as well as a downloadable form that needs to be submitted at post offices.

72-hour Visa-free Travel

If you take the St Peter Line ferry from Helsinki to St Petersburg (see p827) it's possible to visit Russia without a visa as long as you stay less than 72 hours.

Citizens of Schengen countries, the UK, Switzerland and Japan can enter Kaliningrad with an on-demand 72-hour tourist visa either via the airport or overland at the border crossings from Poland at Braniewo/Mamonovo and Bartashitsa/Bagrationovsk. These need to be arranged via local tourist agencies (see p814).

Women Travellers

The most common problem faced by foreign women in Russia is sexual harassment. It's not unusual to be propositioned in public, especially if you are walking alone at night. Unpleasant as it may be, this is rarely dangerous and a simple *'kak vam ne stydno'* ('you should be ashamed of yourself') delivered in a suitably stern manner should send anyone on their way.

That said, Russian men can also be extremely chivalrous, and will open doors, give up their seats and wherever possible help any female out to a far greater degree than their Western counterparts. Russian women are also very independent, and you won't attract attention by travelling alone as a female.

Getting There & Away

Air

Moscow's three airports (see p825) host the bulk of Russia's international flights. There are also many daily international services to St Petersburg's Pulkovo-2 airport (p825) and Kaliningrad's Khrabrovo airport (p814).

Phone numbers for the following airlines flying into Russia are for the Moscow office.

Aeroflot Russian International Airlines (☎495-223 5555; www.aeroflot.ru)

Air Berlin (☎800 555 0737; www.airberlin.com)

Air France (☎495-937 3839; www.airfrance.com)

VISA AGENCIES

Several agencies specialise in getting visas. In the US, try **Zierer Visa Services** (☎1-866 788 1100; www.zvs.com), which also has affiliates in the UK (http://uk.cibt.com), France (www.action-visas.com), Germany (www.visum-centrale.de), Australia (http://visalink.com.au), the Netherlands (www.cibt.nl), and Sweden and Denmark (www.cometconsular.com). Other agencies include **VisaHQ.com** (http://russia.visahq.com) and **Real Russia** (www.realrussia.co.uk).

Invitations can also be procured online from:

Express to Russia (www.expresstorussia.com)

Visa Able (www.visaable.com)

Way to Russia (www.waytorussia.net)

Austrian Airlines (☎495-995 0995; www. austrian.com)

Belavia (☎495-623 1084; http://belavia.by)

bmi (☎495-937 7794; www.flybmi.com)

British Airways (☎495-363 2525; www. britishairways.com)

ČSA (☎495-973 1847; www.csa.cz)

Delta (☎495-937 9090; www.delta.com)

Finnair (☎495-933 0056; www.finnair.com)

Japan Airlines (☎495-730 3070; www.jal. co.jp/en)

KLM (☎495-937 3837; www.klm.com)

LOT Polish Airlines (☎800-5082 5082; www. lot.com)

Lufthansa (☎495-980 9999; www.lufthansa. com)

Rossiya (☎495-995 2025; http://eng.pulkovo. ru/en)

SAS (☎495-775 4747; www.flysas.com)

S7 Airlines (☎495-777 9999; www.s7.ru)

Transaero Airlines (☎495-788 8080; www. transaero.com)

Land

Adjoining 13 countries, the Russian Federation has a huge number of border crossings. From Eastern Europe you are most likely to enter from Finland near Vyborg, Estonia at Narva, Latvia at Rēzekne, Belarus at Krasnoye or Ezjaryshcha, and Ukraine at Chernihiv. You can enter Kaliningrad from Lithuania and Poland at any of seven border posts.

If you're travelling to or from Russia via Belarus, you will need a transit visa and you must obtain it in advance; see p100 for details.

Sea

Ferries connect Kaliningrad with Sassnitz (Germany) and Klaipėda (Lithuania) and St Petersburg with Helsinki.

Getting Around

Air

Flying in Russia is not for the faint-hearted. Safety aside, flights can be delayed, often for hours and with no or little explanation.

A few of Russia's airlines allow you to book online. Otherwise it's no problem buying a ticket at ubiquitous *aviakassa* (ticket offices). Generally, you're better off booking

---

TRAVEL AGENCIES

Independent travellers may need to use travel agencies to secure visa invitations and to book internal travel; without Russian-language skills, it can sometimes be tricky to organise more than a simple train or plane ticket. The following agencies are recommended:

Australia

Eastern Europe/Russian Travel Centre (☎02-9262 1144; www.eetbtravel.com)

Passport Travel (☎03-9500 0444; www.travelcentre.com.au)

Russian Gateway Tours (☎02-9745 3333; www.russian-gateway.com.au)

UK

Go Russia (☎020-3355 7717; www.justgorussia.co.uk) Cultural and adventure-holiday specialist.

Regent Holidays (☎0845-277 3317; www.regent-holidays.co.uk)

Russia Experience (☎020-8566 8846; www.trans-siberian.co.uk) Very experienced and reliable.

USA

Exeter International (☎813-251 5355; www.russiatours.com) Specialises in luxury tours to Moscow and St Petersburg.

Go to Russia Travel (☎404-827 0099; www.gotorussia.com) Has offices in Atlanta, San Francisco and Moscow; offers full range of travel services.

Mir Corporation (☎206-624 7289; www.mircorp.com) Award-winning operation with many different tours, including one by steam train from Kyiv and Murmansk.

AIR TICKETS ONLINE

Sky Express (XW; ☎495-580 9360; www.skyexpress.ru/en) is a Russian low-cost carrier with services between Moscow, St Petersburg and Kaliningrad as well as several other major Russian cities. Its hub is Vnukovo airport, Moscow.

Online agencies with English interfaces specialising in Russian air tickets include **Anywayanyday** (☎495-363 6164; www.anywayanyday.com) and **Pososhok. ru** (☎495-234 8000; www.pososhok.ru).

internal flights once you arrive in Russia, where more flights and flight information are available and where prices may be lower. Fares are generally 30% cheaper (60% on major Moscow routings) for advance bookings or evening departures.

Flights between Moscow and St Petersburg go every hour; a seat costs around R3000 including taxes (one way) for a ticket bought two weeks in advance.

Boat

One of the most pleasant ways of travelling around Russia is by river. The season runs from late May through to mid-October. Numerous cruise boats ply the routes between Moscow and St Petersburg, many stopping at some of the Golden Ring cities on the way. Ferries also link Kaliningrad with St Petersburg.

Some recommended boat operators and agencies:

Infoflot (☎495-684 9188; www.infoflot.com; ul Shchepkina 28, Moscow; Ⓜ Pr Mira) The market leader with an office in St Petersburg.

Mosturflot (☎495-221 7222; www.mosturflot.ru)

Vodohod (☎495-223 96 09; www.bestrussian cruises.com)

Bus

Long-distance buses complement rather than compete with the rail network. They generally serve areas with no railway or routes on which trains are slow, infrequent or overloaded.

There's almost no need to reserve a seat – just arrive a good 30 minutes to one hour before the scheduled departure and buy a ticket. Prices are comparable to 2nd-class train fares; journey times depend on road

conditions. An extra fee may be charged for larger bags.

Marshrutky are minibuses that are quicker than the rusty old buses. Where roads are good and villages frequent, *marshrutky* can be twice as fast as buses, and are well worth the double fare.

Car & Motorcycle

You can bring your own vehicle into Russia, but expect delays, bureaucracy and the attention of the roundly hated GAI (traffic police), who take particular delight in stopping foreign cars for document checks.

To enter Russia with a vehicle you will need a valid International Driving Permit as well as the insurance and ownership documents for your car.

As you don't really need a car to get around big cities, hiring a car comes into its own for making trips out of town where public transport may not be so good. All the major agencies have offices in Moscow and St Petersburg.

Petrol comes in four main grades: 76-, 93-, 95- and 98-octane. Prices range from R22.50 to R30 per litre. Unleaded gas is available in major cities.

Driving is on the right-hand side, and at an intersection traffic coming from the right has the right of way. The speed limit is generally 60km/h in towns. The maximum legal blood-alcohol content is 0.03%. This rule is strictly enforced, so don't drink and drive.

Hitching

Hitching for free is something of an alien concept in Russia, but paying a small amount to be given a lift is a daily reality for millions. Such unofficial taxis are common in cities and while long-distance hitching is less common, it's still acceptable if the price is

UNOFFICIAL TAXIS

In St Peterburg and Moscow few people think twice about flagging down any car to request a ride. A fare is negotiated for the journey and off you go. However, proceed with caution if you are alone and/or it's late at night as there are occasional stories of violent attacks on passengers. There are plenty of official taxis now that charge reasonable rates: numbers and websites for these are listed in the transport sections for Moscow and St Petersburg.

BUYING TRAIN TICKETS ONLINE

There are several sites where you can book train tickets online, including that of **RZD** (rzd.ru, in Russian). The sites listed here are in English:

Bilet.ru (☎495-925 7571; www.bilet.ru) Partners with **Your Train** (www.poezda.net), a railway timetable search system for the Commonwealth of Independent States (CIS).

Russian Rails (☎916-202 6070; www.russianrails.com)

Trains Russia.com (☎in the US 1-404 827 0099, in Moscow 495-225 5012; www.trainsrussia.com/en/travels) Authorised US agent for RZD; tickets are issued in its Moscow office. They can then be picked up there or they can be delivered for US$15 to any address in Moscow or for US$30 to any Moscow airport or rail station, or sent via international DHL delivery to your home address.

VisitRussiacom (☎in the US 1-800 755 3080, in Moscow 495-504 1304; www.visitrussia.com)

right. Simply state your destination and ask '*skolko?*' (how much?).

Train

Russia's extensive train network is efficiently run by **Russian Railways** (www.eng.rzd.ru, in Russian). Suburban or short-distance trains (*elektrichkas*) do not require advance booking: you can buy your ticket at the *prigorodny poezd kassa* (suburban train ticket offices) at train stations.

For long-distance trains, unless otherwise specified we quote 2nd-class (*kupe*) fares. Expect 1st-class (SV) fares to be double this, and 3rd class (*platskartny*) to be about 40% less. Children under five travel free if they share a berth with an adult; otherwise, children under 10 pay a reduced fare for their own berth. On the better-class *skory* (fast) and *firmeny* (name) trains it's also possible to have two grades of *kupe* fare: with or without meals.

Reserve at least 24 hours in advance for any long-distance journey, although bookings cannot be made any earlier than 45 days before the date of departure. Over the busy summer months and holiday periods such as New Year and early May, securing berths at short notice on certain trains can be difficult. Tickets for key trains on the busy Moscow–St Petersburg route also sell out fast; keep your plans flexible and you should be able to find something.

You'll need your passport (or a photocopy) to buy tickets. You can buy tickets for others if you bring their passports or photocopies. Queues can be very long and move with interminable slowness. At service centres that exist in most big train stations you can pay a R200 surcharge and avoid the queues. Alternatively, most travel agencies will organise the reservation and delivery of train tickets for a substantial mark-up.

Serbia Србија

Best Places to Eat

» Bubi Grill (p846)
» Little Bay (p839)
» Dačo (p839)
» Ravel (p848)
» Hamam (p850)

Best Places To Stay

» Hotel Moskva (p837)
» Green Studio Hostel (p838)
» Travelling Actor (p838)
» Leopold I (p844)

Why Go?

Warm, welcoming and a hell of a lot of fun – everything you never heard about Serbia is true. Exuding a feisty mix of élan and *inat* (the Serbian trait of rebellious defiance), this country doesn't do 'mild': its capital Belgrade is one of the world's wildest party destinations, the northern town of Novi Sad hosts the rocking EXIT festival, and even its hospitality is emphatic – expect to be greeted with *rakija* and a hearty three-kiss hello.

While political correctness here is about as commonplace as a nonsmoking bar, Serbia is nevertheless a cultural crucible: the art nouveau town of Subotica revels in its proximity to Hungary, bohemian Niš echoes to the clip-clop of Roma horse-carts, and minaret-studded Novi Pazar nudges some of the most sacred sites in Serbian Orthodoxy. And in the mountainous Kopaonik and Zlatibor regions, ancient traditions coexist with après-ski bling. Forget what you think you know: come and say *zdravo* (hello)...or better yet, *živeli* (cheers)!

When To Go

Belgrade

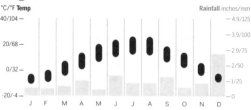

April Watch winter melt away with a scenic ride on the nostalgic Šargan 8 railway.

July–August Rock out at Novi Sad's EXIT, go wild at Guča and get jazzy at Nišville.

December–March Head for the hills of Kopaonik and Zlatibor for alpine adventure.

Fast Facts

» **Area** 77,474 sq km

» **Capital** Belgrade

» **Telephone country code** ☑381

» **Emergency** ☑92 (police), ☑93 (fire), ☑94 (ambulance)

Exchange Rates

Australia	A$1	75.00DIN
Canada	C$1	74.43DIN
euro	€1	102.07DIN
Japan	¥100	85.86DIN
New Zealand	NZ$1	56.28DIN
UK	UK£1	116.00DIN
USA	US$1	71.06DIN

Set Your Budget

» **Budget room** 2000DIN

» **Two-course meal** 1000DIN

» **Museum entry** 100DIN

» **Beer** 100DIN

» **City transport ticket** 80DIN

Resources

» **National Tourism Organisation of Serbia** (www.serbia.travel)

» **Serbia Travel Club** (www.serbiatravelers.org)

Connections

Serbia is landlocked by accessible neighbours. From the northern town of Subotica, you can travel over the Hungarian border and onwards to Budapest. The town of Vršac is only 10km from the Romanian border, and the Bulgarian border is 45 minutes from the small town of Pirot. When things are calm on the Kosovo border, €7 and three hours get you from Novi Pazar to Kosovo's capital Pristina. The Zlatibor region stretches to Bosnia & Hercegovina, allowing travellers with wheels the opportunity to take a day trip to the bridge on the River Drina. The whole of Eastern Europe feels accessible from Belgrade: Bucharest, Budapest, Ljubljana, Moscow, Sofia and Zagreb are a train ride away, and regular buses serve destinations including Banja Luka, Ljubljana, Sarajevo and Split.

ITINERARIES

One Week

Revel in three days of cultural and culinary exploration in Belgrade, allowing for at least one night of (and recovery time from) hitting the capital's legendary nightspots. Carry on to Novi Sad for day trips to the vineyards and monasteries of Fruška Gora and Sremski Karlovci.

Two Weeks

Follow the above then head north to treat your eyes to the art nouveau architecture of Subotica, before slicing south for Zlatibor's bracing mountain air en route to Ottoman-influenced Novi Pazar and the lively city of Niš.

Essential Food & Drink

» **Kajmak** Along the lines of a salty clotted cream, this dairy delight is lashed on to everything from plain bread to burgers.

» **Ćevapčići** The ubiquitous skinless sausage and *pljeskavica* (head-sized spicy hamburger) make it very easy to be a carnivore in Serbia.

» **Burek** This flaky meat, cheese or vegetable pie is eaten with yoghurt as a breakfast belly-filler or an anytime snack.

» **Žito** This is a dessert of crushed wheat and walnuts, or try *palačinke* (crepes) loaded with jam or hazelnut spread.

» **Rakija** Distilled spirit most commonly made from plums. Treat with caution: this ain't your grandpa's brandy.

Serbia Highlights

1 Marvel at Belgrade's mighty **Kalemegdan Citadel** (p831)

2 Witness the laid-back town of **Novi Sad** (p844) as it morphs into the State of EXIT every July

3 Ponder the exotic cultural fusions of Turkish-toned **Novi Pazar** (p850) in Southern Serbia

4 Steel your eardrums (and liver) at Guča's **Dragačevo Trumpet Assembly** (p852), one of the world's most frenetic music festivals

5 Escape reality in the fantastic village of **Drvengrad** (p853), built by director Emir Kusturica for indie-drama *Life is a Miracle*

6 Goggle at splendid surprises bursting from the Vojvodinian plains, like the art nouveau treasures of **Subotica** (p847)

7 Ski, hike or just take the mountain air in the magical villages of **Zlatibor** (p852)

BELGRADE БЕОГРАД

♪ 011 / POP 1.76MIL

Outspoken, adventurous, proud and audacious: Belgrade is by no means a 'pretty' capital, but its gritty exuberance makes it one of the most happening cities not only in the Balkans but all of Europe. While it hurtles towards a brighter future, its chaotic past unfolds before your eyes: socialist blocks are squeezed between art nouveau masterpieces, and remnants of the Habsburg legacy contrast with Ottoman relics.

It is here where the Sava River meets the Danube (Dunav), contemplative parkland nudges hectic urban sprawl, and where old-world culture gives way to new-world nightlife.

Grandiose coffee houses, quirky sidewalk ice-creameries and smoky dens all find rightful place along Knez Mihailova, a lively pedestrian boulevard flanked by historical buildings all the way to the ancient Kalemegdan Citadel, the crown of the city. Deeper in Belgrade's bowels are museums guarding the cultural, religious and military heritage of the country. Josip Broz Tito and other ghosts of the past have been laid to rest here.

'Belgrade' literally translates as 'White City', but Serbia's colourful capital is red hot.

History

Belgrade has been destroyed and rebuilt countless times in its 2300-year history. Celts first settled on the lumpy hill at the confluence of the Sava River and the Danube, the Romans came in the 1st century and havoc was wreaked by Goths and Huns until the area was colonised by Slavic tribes in the 6th century. In 1403 Hungary gave Belgrade to Despot Stefan Lazarević, making it the Serbian capital. The 1400s saw waves of Turkish attacks; Sultan Suleiman the Magnificent (and 300,000 soldiers) conquered Belgrade in 1521 and shipped its population to İstanbul. Belgrade continued to be fought over by Austrians, Turks and the Serbs themselves. The Karađorđević dynasty began in 1807 when Belgrade was liberated from the Turks. The Obrenović dynasty followed when Miloš Obrenović staged the Second Serbian uprising and ordered the murder of Karađorđević. Turkey finally relinquished control in 1867. In 1914 the Austro-Hungarian empire captured Belgrade; they were soon driven out, only to return more triumphantly with German help

in 1915, staying for three years. In 1918 Belgrade became the capital of Yugoslavia after the Serbs, Croats and Slovenes were united. Belgrade was bombed by both Nazis and Allies during WWII.

In the 1990s Belgrade became the stage of strong resistance against Slobodan Milošević, both underground and in the open. In 1999 NATO forces controversially bombed Belgrade for three months after Milošević refused to end the repression of Albanians in Kosovo. Belgrade bore witness to the power of protest in 2000, when citizens stormed Parliament to declaim Milošević's electoral fraud. Belgradians took to the streets again in 2008 in opposition to Kosovo's declaration of independence.

◉ Sights & Activities

FREE **Kalemegdan Citadel**   FORTRESS
Some 115 battles have been fought over imposing Kalemegdan. Fortifications began in Celtic times. The Romans extended it onto the flood plains during the settlement of 'Singidunum', Belgrade's Roman name. Much of what stands today is the product of 18th-century Austro-Hungarian and Turkish reconstructions.

Entering from Knez Mihailova brings you to the Upper Citadel. Through Stambol Gate, built by the Turks around 1750 and used for public executions, you'll find yourself in the firing line of canons and tanks; welcome to the **Military Museum** (www.muzej.mod.gov.rs; adult/child 100/50DIN; ⊙10am-5pm Tue-Sun) presenting a complete military history of the former Yugoslavia up to the 1999 NATO bombings. Captured Kosovo Liberation Army (KLA) weapons and bits of a downed American stealth fighter are on display.

City Zoo   ZOO
(www.beozoovrt.org; adult/child 350/250DIN; ⊙8am-8pm summer, 8am-4.30pm winter) The nearby City Zoo comes with an interesting anecdote reminiscent of *Twelve Monkeys*: when Nazi bombs damaged enclosures, several dangerous occupants were freed to wander the streets of Belgrade.

STARI GRAD

Architecture   NOTABLE BUILDINGS
South of the citadel along Knez Mihailova is **Stari Grad** (Old Town; www.starigrad.org.rs). This jumble of architecture covers two centuries, from when Belgrade was snatched from the dying Ottoman Empire and given a boost by the Habsburgs. People promenade along pe-

Two Days

Brunch at **Biblioteka** before exploring **Kalemegdan Citadel**. Take a leisurely stroll down the Knez Mihailova pedestrian strip, stopping at **Russian Tsar** for opulent coffee and cake. People-watch at nearby meeting-spot **Trg Republike** and check whether the **National Museum** is open, or spend the afternoon in the **Ethnographic Museum**. When hunger sets in, drift down cobblestoned **Skadarska** to enjoy traditional Serbian fare accompanied by energetic Roma violins. Leave bohemia behind with a raucous live gig at **Akademija** or join in the retro revelry at **Kafana Pavle Korčagin**.

The next day, ponder the past at **Maršal Tito's grave** before heading to **Zemun** for a seafood lunch. Back in the big smoke, enjoy dinner at historical **?** before heading to nearby **Anderground** for a heady Belgrade clubbing experience. If clubbing's not for you, opt instead for a leisurely meal at **Little Bay** for fine dining and live opera.

destrian strip **Knez Mihailova** where cafes spill onto pavements. Fine buildings include the elegant pink and white, neo-Renaissance **School of Fine Arts** (cnr Knez Mihailova & Rajićeva). Further down is the **Serbian Academy of Arts & Sciences**, an early-20th-century art nouveau building with the goddess Nike at its helm.

National Museum MUSEUM
(www.narodnimuzej.rs; Trg Republike 1A) At the other end of Knez Mihailova is Trg Republike (Republic Sq), a meeting point and outdoor exhibition space. On the square is the National Museum, which will hopefully reopen soon; lack of funding for renovations has kept it shuttered for almost 10 years.

Palace of Princess Ljubica PALACE
(Kneza Sime Markovića 8; adult/child 100/50DIN; ☺10am-5pm Tue, Wed & Fri, noon-8pm Thu, 10am-2pm Sat-Sun) This preserved Balkan-style palace was built in 1831 for the wife of Prince Miloš. Take coffee with 'the princess' (actually the museum custodian in period dress) each Saturday from noon (250DIN) as she leads you through privileged 19th-century life.

Ethnographic Museum MUSEUM
(www.etnografskimuzej.rs; Studentski Trg 13; adult/student 150/60DIN; ☺10am-5pm Tue-Sat, 9am-2pm Sun) This museum features traditional costumes, working utensils and folksy mountain-village interiors.

Museum of the Serbian Orthodox Church MUSEUM
(Kralja Petra 5; adult/child 50/20DIN; ☺8am-3pm Mon-Fri, 9am-noon Sat, 11am-1pm Sun) The Patriarchate (Patrijaršija) building houses this collection of ecclesiastical items, many of which were collected by St Sava, founder of the independent Serbian Orthodox church.

DORĆOL

Named from the Turkish words for 'four roads' (dört yol), Dorćol stretches northeast from Stari Grad to the Danube. In the days of the Ottoman occupation, Turks, Greeks, Jews, Germans, Armenians and Vlachs lived here side-by-side, bartering in a mix of languages. Today, Dorćol is a pleasant residential area but retains only a shadow of its former cosmopolitanism.

Gallery of Frescos ART GALLERY
(www.narodnimuzej.rs; Cara Uroša 20; admission 100DIN; ☺10am-5pm Tue, Wed & Fri, noon-8pm Thu & Sat, 10am-2pm Sun) The gallery features full-size replicas (and the odd original) of Byzantine Serbian church art, right down to the last scratch. Unlike the sensitive originals, these frescos can be photographed to your heart's content.

Bayrakli Mosque MOSQUE
(cnr Kralja Petra & Gospodar Jevremova) The last remaining mosque in Belgrade was built around 1575 and remains a functioning house of worship. Damage caused by riots in 2004 (a backlash against the anti-Serb pogroms in Kosovo at the time) has since been repaired.

Burial Chamber of Sheik Mustafa HISTORIC BUILDING
(cnr Braće Jugovića & Višnjićeva) This 18th-century burial chamber of a Baghdad dervish sheik is one of the few remaining pieces of Ottoman architecture in the city. Doors are locked, but the curious can window-peek from the sidewalk.

Veliko
Ratno
Ostrvo

Danube (Dunav River)

Bulevar vojvode Bojovića

34

3

6

17

7

Rige od Fere

Cara Uroša

1

5

25

47

Tadeuša Košćuška

Pariska

38

4

Vase Čarapića

54

46 15

Knez Mihailova

31

Sava River

Kneza Sime Markovića

Čubrina Venac

Ivan Begova

Vuka Karadžića

Ð Jakšića

57

19

21

10

13

Kosančićev

Pop Lukina

Cara Milice

Oblilćev Venac

Maršala

Birjuzova

48

Ušće
Park

Brankov Most

Brankova

Bulevar Mihajila Pupina

53

Jug Bogdanova

40

Karađorđeva

Gavrila Principa

Kamenička

Lomina

Zemunski put

Stari Savski Most

Železnička

20

Sadika Ramiza

Brodarska

Central
Station

Tourist
Organisation
of Belgrade

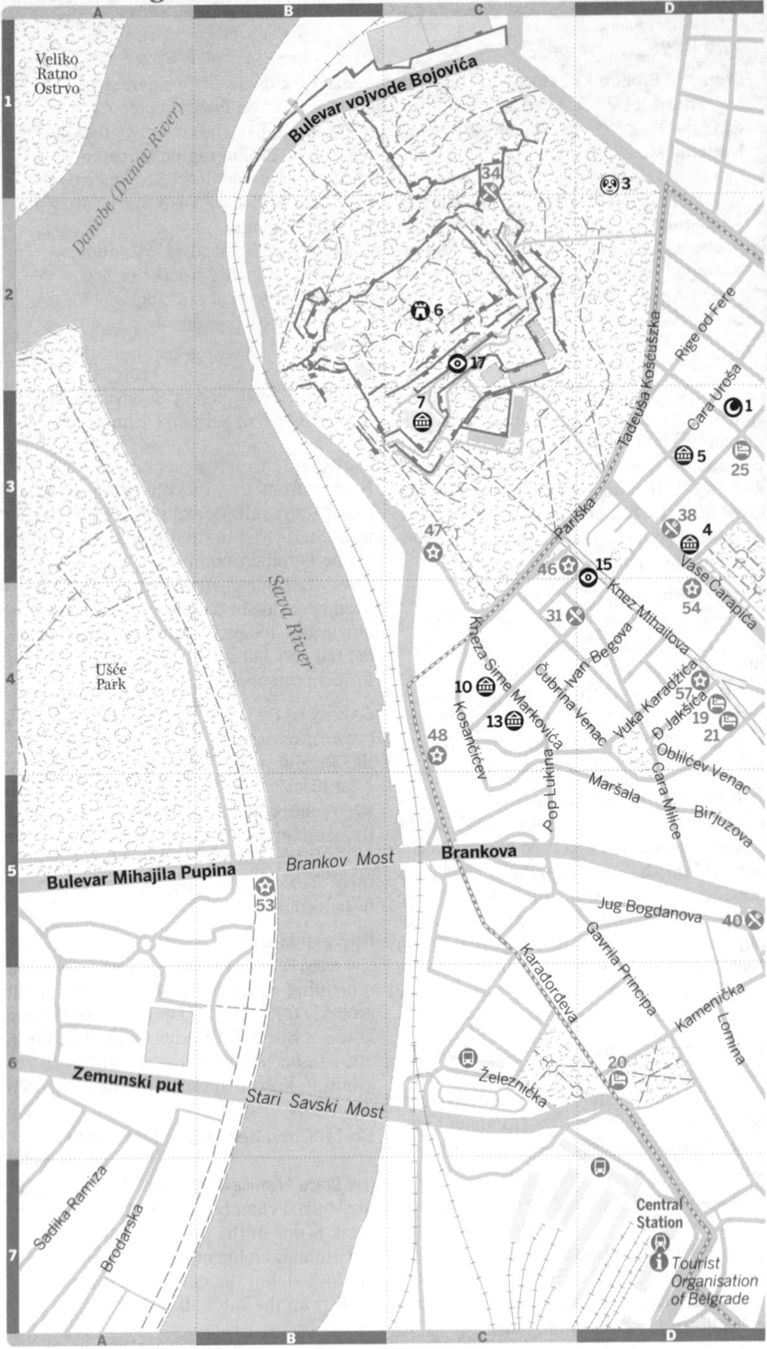

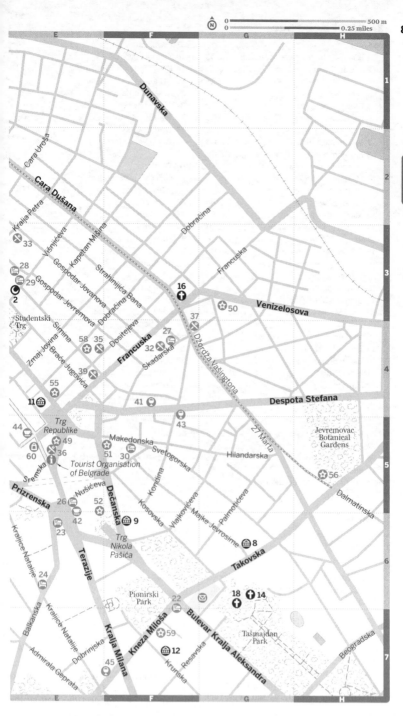

0 — 500 m
0 — 0.25 miles

Dunavska

Cara Uroša

Cara Dušana

Kralja Petra

33

Višnjićeva

28

29

Gospodar Jevremova

Gospodar Jovanova

Kapetan Mišina

Strahinjića Bana

Dobračina

Dobračina

Francuska

16

50

Venizelosova

2

Studentski Trg

Sirina

Zmaj Jovina

Braće Jugovića

Dositejeva

37

Francuska

58 35

27

32

Skadarska

Đorđa Vašingtona

39

55

11

41

Despota Stefana

43

44

Trg Republike

49

Makedonska

Svetogorska

Hilandarska

27 Marta

Jevremovac Botanical Gardens

60

36

51

30

Tourist Organisation of Belgrade

56

Dalmatinska

Sremska

Prizrenska

Kondina

Kosovska

Vlajkovićeva

Majke Jevrosime

Palmotićeva

26

52

42

Nušićeva

Dečanska

9

23

Trg Nikola Pašića

8

Takovska

24

Kraljice Natalije

Terazije

Pionirski Park

22

18

14

Kraljice Natalije

Balkanska

Dobrinjska

Kralja Milana

Kneza Miloša

59

Bulevar Kralja Aleksandra

Tašmajdan Park

Admirala Geprata

45

12

Krunska

Resavska

Beogradska

St Aleksandar Nevski Church CHURCH
(Cara Dušana 63) The first Christian church built in the area.

SKADARSKA

Skadarska or 'Skadarlija' is Belgrade's answer to Montmartre. This cobblestoned strip east of Trg Republike was the bohemian heartland at the turn of the 20th century; local *artistes* and raffish types still gather in its legion of cute restaurants and cafes. Tuck into home-style cuisine while roving Roma bands provide ambience.

CENTRAL BELGRADE

Belgrade hustles and bustles along Terazije, crowned by the majestic Hotel Moskva (p837), an art nouveau gem more than a century old.

Nikola Tesla Museum MUSEUM
(www.tesla-museum.org; Krunska 51; admission incl guided tour in English 300DIN; ⊙10am-6pm Tue-Fri, 10am-3pm Sat-Sun) Meet the man on the

FREE THRILLS

The best things in Belgrade are still free:

» Amble around **Kalemegdan Citadel** (p831).

» Explore **Stari Grad** (p831), the evocative Old Town.

» Have a splash at **Ada Ciganlija** (p837), artificial island on the Sava.

» Gasp at the sheer scale of **Sveti Sava** (p837).

» Ramble along the Danube River to **Zemun** (p843).

100DIN note at one of Belgrade's best museums. Release your inner nerd with some wondrously sci-fi-ish interactive elements.

Museum of Automobiles   MUSEUM
(Majke Jevrosime 30; adult/child 100/80DIN; ☺11am-7pm) This compelling collection of cars (all mechanically sound) and motorcycles is located in Belgrade's first public garage. Most take-for-a-spinworthy? The '57 Cadillac convertible: only 25,000km and one careful owner – President Tito.

Museum of the History of Serbia   MUSEUM
(www.imus.org.rs; Trg Nikola Pašića; adult/child 100/50DIN; ☺10am-5pm Tue-Fri) From Terazije, walk through the adjacent Nikola Pašića to this museum, home to a wealth of archaeological, ethnographic and military collections.

Sveti Marko Church   CHURCH
(Bul Kralja Aleksandra 17) Behind the main post office looms this five-domed church based on the design of Kosovo's Gračanica Monastery. It houses priceless Serbian icons and the tomb of Emperor Dušan 'The Mighty' (1308–55). Behind is a tiny white Russian Church erected by Russian refugees who fled the October Revolution.

OUTER BELGRADE

FREE **Sveti Sava**   CHURCH
(www.hramsvetogsave.com; Svetog Save) Sveti Sava is the world's biggest Orthodox church, a fact made entirely obvious looking at the city skyline from a distance or standing under its dome. The church is built on the site where the Turks apparently burnt relics of St Sava (founder of the independent Serbian Orthodox church). Work on the church interior (which has been frequently interrupted by wars) continues today.

Maršal Tito's Grave   MONUMENT
(House of Flowers; www.mij.rs; bul Mira; admission incl entry to Museum of Yugoslav History 200DIN; ☺10am-4pm Tue-Sun) A visit to Tito's mausoleum is obligatory. Also on display are thousands of elaborately designed relay batons presented to him by young 'Pioneers', plus gifts from political leaders and the voguish set of the era. Take trolleybus 40 or 41 at the south end of Parliament on Kneza Miloša. It's the second stop after it turns into bul Mira.

FREE **Ada Ciganlija**   BEACH
(www.adaciganlija.rs) In summertime, join the hordes of sea-starved locals (up to 250,000 a day) for sun and fun at this artificial island on the Sava. Cool down with a swim, kayak or windsurf after a leap from the 55-m bungee tower or a paintball fight. Take bus 53 or 56 from Zeleni Venac.

Aviation Museum   MUSEUM
(www.muzejrv.mod.gov.rs; Nikola Tesla airport; admission 450DIN; ☺8.30am-7pm Tue-Sun summer, 9am-3.30pm winter) Plane-spotters rejoice. This airport-based museum contains rare planes, a WWII collection and bits of the infamous American stealth fighter shot down in 1999.

🛏 Sleeping

Accommodation in Belgrade is the worst value for money in the country. Thankfully, more hostels have popped up while some of the crumbling classics have had face (and price) lifts.

The **Youth Hostel Association of Serbia** (Ferijalni Savez Beograd; ☏324 8550; www.serbia-hostels.org; Makedonska 22/2; ☺9am-5pm) does deals with local hotels. You need HI membership (under/over 26 500/700DIN) or an international student card.

TOP CHOICE **Hotel Moskva**   HISTORICAL HOTEL €€€
(Hotel Moscow; ☏268 6255; www.hotelmoskva.rs; Balkanska 1; s 7725-12,420DIN, d 14,000DIN, ste 14,490-18,000DIN, apt 25,000DIN; ✳🛜) Art nouveau icon and proud symbol of the best of Belgrade, the majestic Moskva has been wowing guests – including Albert Einstein, Indira Gandhi and Alfred Hitchcock – since 1906. Laden with ye olde glamour, this is the place to write your memoirs at a big old desk.

Green Studio Hostel   HOSTEL €
(☏637 562 357; www.greenstudiohostel.com; Karađorđeva 69; dm from €10, private rooms €9-30, apt €40; ✳🛜) This sunny surprise goes down as one of the best budget options in Serbia. Clean, airy and staffed by your new best

friends, it also has a handy location near the bus and train stations, as well as the best of Belgrade's attractions. Free *rakija* is one of many bonuses.

Travelling Actor PENSION €€€
(☑323 4156; www.travellingactor.rs; Gospodar Jevremova 65; d €88-98, apt €188; ❃🛜) Trip down the cobblestones and back in time at this Skadarlija boutique pension. True to its name, the gilded rooms are almost melodramatically over the top, but this luxe-campness only adds to the fun.

Hostel 360 HOSTEL €
(☑328 4523; www.threesixtyhostel.com; Knez Mihailova 21; dm/s/tw/d €15/29/44/50, apt from €75; ❃❄🛜) Hostel 360 peers down at Knez Mihailova from one of the most central spots in town. Super-tidy rooms and a garden terrace are surpassed only by spirited staff on a mission to immerse guests in local life.

Le Petit Piaf LUXURY HOTEL €€€
(☑303 5252; www.petitpiaf.com; Skadarska 34; s & d €100-120, ste €135; ❃🛜) Elegant loft rooms, refined decor and *soignée* service make this Skadarlija charmer a Parisian doppelgänger in all the right ways.

Belgrade Art Hotel BOUTIQUE HOTEL €€€
(☑331 2000; www.belgradearthotel.com; Knez Mihailova 27; tw/d 10,500/12,680DIN, apt from 17,955DIN; ❃🛜) This spanking new Italian designed hotel is everything its name suggests: stylish, refined and discerning. Soundproof windows are a godsend.

Yellowbed Hostel HOSTEL €
(☑262 8220; www.hostelyellowbed.com; Višnjićeva 3; dm from 1200DIN; ❃🛜) At times more akin to a share house than a hostel, Yellowbed is a merry choice with an ace location behind Studentski Trg. Free wireless, a terrace and balconies sweeten the deal.

Arka Barka HOSTEL €
(☑0649253507; www.arkabarka.net; bul Nikole Tesle bb; dm €15; ❃🛜) Bobbing off Ušće Park, a mere stagger from the Danube barges, this 'floating house' offers sparkling rooms in 'wake-up!' colours, party nights and fresh river breezes. It's a moderate walk, or a short ride on bus 15 or 84 from the centre.

Kasina Hotel HOTEL €€
(☑323 5575; Terazije 25; s/d standard 3598/6748DIN, comfort 6748/8148DIN, apt from 9300DIN; ❃@) Peering over at the Moskva with an obvious case of hotel envy, the Kasina nevertheless holds its own in the mid-

range department. Spacious 'comfort' rooms have been recently renovated, although 'standard' rooms have been left to languish somewhere in 1958.

Hotel Royal HOTEL €€
(☑263 4222; www.hotelroyal.rs; Kralja Petra 56; s 4280-4815DIN, d 5136-6313DIN; ❃@) While those who recall the Royal's days as a legendary cheapie will baulk at the almost doubling of rates, this is still a decent midrange option. Rooms are basic and far from sparkling, but this (very) central spot disarms with character and buzz.

Recently upgraded choices:

Hotel Prag (☑361 0422; www.hotelprag.rs; Kraljice Natalije 27; s/d from 7136/8304DIN, ste 14,144-17,331DIN; ❃@)

Hotel Excelsior (☑263 7222; www.hotel excelsior.rs; Topličin Venac 23; s 6000-8000DIN, d 9000-11,000DIN, apt 20,000-23,000DIN; ❃@)

✖ Eating

The choice is particularly overwhelming along Knez Mihailova, Kralja Petra and Makedonska.

SKADARSKA

Šešir Moj SERBIAN €€
(My Hat; Skadarska 21; meals 400-1000DIN; ⏱9am-1am) Roma bands tug the heartstrings while traditional dishes like *punjena bela vešalica* (pork stuffed with *kajmak*) buoy up the belly.

Dva Jelena SERBIAN €€
(Two Deer; www.dvajelena.com; Skadarska 32; meals 400-900DIN; ⏱11am-1am) A local icon, Dva Jelena has been dishing up hearty fare for over 180 years. Rustic, homespun and with the obligatory violin serenades, it ticks all the Skadarlija boxes.

Writers' Club FINE DINING €€€
(Klub Književnika; Francuska 7; meals 480-1030DIN; ⏱noon-1am Mon-Sat, noon-6pm Sun) The former haunt of local literati and the visiting elite (think Simone de Beauvoir and Jean-Paul Sartre), this dignified spot is still a favourite for substantial steaks and stews.

CENTRAL BELGRADE

Indulge your post- or pre-clubbing munchies in cheap bakeries around Trg Republike. **Pekara Toma** (Kolarčeva 10; snacks 50-200DIN; ⏱24hr) is a jam-packed favourite for fresh pizzas, sandwiches and salads. Forage through **Zeleni Venac Market** (cnr Brankova Prizrenska & Kraljice Natalije; ⏱6am-7pm) for DIY food. It's downhill from the Balkan Hotel towards the Sava River.

TOP CHOICE **Little Bay** FINE DINING **€€**
(www.little-bay.co.uk; Dositejeva 9a; meals 485-950DIN) It's little wonder locals and visitors have long been singing the praises of this gem: it's one of the best dining experiences you'll have in the country. Tuck yourself into a private opera box and let the duck in puff pastry (690DIN) or catfish with spinach and salsa (485DIN) melt in your mouth as a live opera singer does wonderful things to your ears.

Kafana Suvobor SERBIAN **€€**
(www.suvobor.com; Kralja Petra 70; meals 450-900DIN) Specialists in Serbian cuisine, they offer dishes like the to-die-for *rolovana pileća džigerica u slanini* (rolled chicken liver wrapped in bacon). Drool the night away on the outdoor terrace or over two levels inside.

? SERBIAN **€**
(Znak Pitanja; Kralja Petra 6; meals 450-600) Belgrade's oldest *kafana* has been attracting the bohemian set since 1823 with dishes like stuffed chicken and lamb under the iron pan (though not so much the calf's head in tripe). Its quizzical name is courtesy of a dispute with the adjacent church, which objected to the tavern naming itself in relation to a house of god ('By the Cathedral').

Kalemegdanska Terasa FINE DINING **€€€**
(328 3011; www.kalemegdanskaterasa.com; Mali Kalemegdan bb; meals 830-1700DIN; ⊘noon-1am) By the fortress, this is a literal bastion of refined dining, featuring sumptuous dishes like rolled steak and goose liver with truffle sauce. One for the romantics, and those who packed a tie.

Biblioteka INTERNATIONAL **€€**
(Terazije 27; meals 300-900DIN; ⊘7am-midnight) Buzzing outside and aptly library-ambient inside, Biblioteka is popular with locals for its extensive breakfast menu, served until 1pm.

Trattoria Košava INTERNATIONAL **€€**
(www.trattoriakosava.com; Kralja Petra 36; meals 400-1000DIN; ⊘9am-1am Mon-Fri, noon-1am Sat-Sun) Sit upstairs in lamp-lit nostalgia and tuck into gigantic serves of home-cooked Italian or Serbian classics.

OUTER BELGRADE

TOP CHOICE **Dačo** SERBIAN **€€**
(278 1009; www.kafanadaco.com; Patrisa Lumumbe 49; meals 500-1150DIN; ⊘noon-midnight Tue-Sun) Making the haul out here is like visiting the Serbian granny you never knew you had: the walls are cluttered with homey bits and bobs, chequered tablecloths adorn rickety tables and chooks strut around in the garden. And you won't have to be told twice to 'Eat! Eat!' either. Reservations recommended.

Maharaja INDIAN **€€**
(www.maharaja.rs; Ljubićka 1b; meals 640-1350DIN; ⊘noon-midnight Tue-Sun) Craving curry in a sea of *kajmak*? It's worth the trip out to one of Belgrade's only Indian restaurants, serving all the staples from tikka to tandoori. Vegetarians, predictably, will find solace here.

🍷 Drinking

In true Belgrade spirit, almost any venue fits the 'up for a drink' bill. Quiet cafes morph into drinking dens at night and then thumping clubs in the early hours. In spring and summer, action spills onto terraces and pavements.

TOP CHOICE **Kafana Pavle Korčagin** TAVERN
(240 1980; Ćirila i Metodija 2a; ⊘8pm-1am) Raise a glass to Broz Tito at this frantic, festive *kafana*. Lined with Communist memorabilia and packed to the rafters with revellers and grinning accordionists, this table-thumping throwback fills up nightly; reserve a table in advance.

Federal Association of Globe Trotters BAR
(www.usp-aur.rs; bul Despota Stefana 7/1; ⊘1pm-midnight Mon-Fri, 3pm-late Sat-Sun; 🛜) Through the big black gate and down into the basement lies one of Belgrade's coolest hangouts. Miscellaneous oddities clamour for wall space while an equally motley clientele yaks over cocktails.

Pub Brod BAR
(bul Despota Stefana 36; ⊘noon-4am) This congenial student hang-out thumbs its nose at dress codes, Top 40 and nouveau-Belgrade bling. Small and smoky inside, in summertime indie music pumps over a whooping sidewalk sprawl.

Three Carrots PUB
(Kneza Miloša 16; ⊘10am-2am Mon-Fri, noon-2am Sat, 2pm-2am Sun) Dimly lit like any Irish bar worth its quirky ceiling-hangings should be, this place pulls both pints and a cosmopolitan crowd.

Russian Tsar CAFE
(Ruski Car; www.ruskicar.net; cnr Knez Mihailova & Obilićev Venac) Whisking up decadent cakes and Russian treats since 1890, this

gold-trimmed parlour is one of Belgrade's most popular rendezvous.

Greenet
CAFE

(www.greenet.co.rs; Nušićeva 3) *The* place for local coffee connoisseurs.

☆ Entertainment
Nightclubs

Belgrade has a reputation as one of the world's top party cities, with a wild club scene limited only by imagination and hours in the day. The music is a smorgasbord of well-known European and local DJs playing house, R&B, hip hop, drum'n'bass, turbofolk and jazz.

CITY NIGHTCLUBS
Andergraund
CLUB

(Pariška 1a) The leader of the pack in a city renowned for party-hard clubbing, Andergraund has spaces on a tiered terrace on the citadel walls, but most of it is underneath in cavernous catacombs where sweaty crowds gyrate.

Akademija
LIVE MUSIC

(www.akademija.net; Rajićeva 10) Akademija has been king of Belgrade's underground scene (literally: it's in a basement) for over 20 years. Alternative crowds rock this cult institution every night, going particularly hardcore on Thursdays and Saturdays.

The Tube
CLUB

(www.thetube.rs; Simina 21; ☻Thu-Sun) Lovers of all music electronic will have a blast in this beautifully designed ex-nuclear bunker. Very upmarket and oft-crowded, despite a whopping floor space, it's worth scrubbing up for.

Bitef Art Cafe
LIVE MUSIC

(www.bitefartcafe.rs; Skver Mire Trailović 1; ☻7pm-4am) There's something for everyone at this delightful hotchpotch of a cafe-club. Funk, soul and jazz get a good airing, as do rock and classical. Regular karaoke competitions pack in the punters.

Plastic
CLUB

(www.clubplastic.rs; cnr Dalmatinska & Takovska; ☻Thu-Sat) A perennial favourite among electro-heads and booty shakers, this slick venue is frequented by top local and international DJs. In summer, head to Plastic Light, the floating version of the club on the Sava River.

Baltazar
CLUB

(www.barbaltazar.com; Karađorđeva 9; ☻Wed-Sat) There's three rooms of drinking, dancing and chilling in a space that's less Belgrade than Big Apple. If dancing around (or on)

the bar isn't your thing, flash some cash for a spot in the VIP room.

DANUBE BARGES

According to Monty Python's Michael Palin, Belgrade has so many nightclubs 'they can't fit them all on land'. Indeed: adjacent to Hotel Jugoslavija in Novi Belgrade is a 1km strip of some 20 barges. Most are closed in winter. Get there with bus 15 or 84 from Zeleni Venac or 68, 603 or 701 from Trg Republike, and get out at Hotel Jugoslavija.

Blaywatch
BARGE

(☻midnight-late) This throbbing, fleshy place gets crowded and dress codes may be enforced (sneakers bad on boys, skimpy good on girls). The crowd at this party palace is a mix of local 'beautiful people' and foreigners, all occupied with each other and the turbo tunes.

Bahus
BARGE

(www.bahus.rs; ☻10am-1pm) More posh than party, this chic alternative attracts a refined crowd who'd rather sip their cocktails than spill them down someone else's back.

Acapulco
BARGE

(www.acapulco.co.rs; noon-late) Blinged-up boys come here to flaunt their (new) money and she-accessories. Got a low turbofolk threshold? Start swimming.

SAVA RIVER BARGES

On the western bank of the Sava River is a 1.5km strip of floating bars, restaurants and discos known as 'splavs'. Most are only open in summer. Walk over Brankov Most or catch tram 7, 9 or 11.

The gigantic **Freestyler** (www.splavfree.rs; Brodarska bb; ☻11pm-5am Tue-Sun) has been a symbol of splav saturnalia for years, not least for its infamous foam parties. Nearby, **Exile** (Savski kej bb; ☻midnight-late) pounds out techno and **Sound** (Savski kej bb; ☻midnight-3am) plays house and disco to a slightly older following. For something different, try the **Povetarac** (www.povetarac.com; Brodarska bb; ☻midnight-late, 8pm-late winter), a rusting cargo ship that attracts a more indie crowd, or **20/44** (Savski kej bb; ☻7pm-4am) where you can conga to an eclectic playlist around a life-sized statue of John Cleese.

Performing Arts

For concert and theatre tickets go to **Bilet Servis** (☏303 3311; www.biletservis.co.rs; Trg Republike 5; ☻9am-9pm Mon-Fri, 9am-3pm Sat). Large venues for visiting acts include **Sava Centar** (☏220 6060; www.savacentar.com; Milentija Popovića 9, Novi Beograd; ☻box office 10am-

8pm Mon-Fri, 10am-3pm Sat) and **Belgrade Arena** (☎220 2222; www.arenabeograd.com; Bul Arsenija Čarnojevića 58, Novi Beograd; ☺10am-8pm Mon-Fri, 10am-3pm Sat).

National Theatre   THEATRE
(☎262 0946; www.narodnopozoriste.co.rs; Trg Republike; ☺box office 10am-2pm Tue-Sun) During winter, it stages operas, dramas and ballets.

Kolarčev University Concert Hall LIVE MUSIC
(☎630 550; www.kolarac.co.rs; Studentski Trg 5; ☺box office 10am-noon & 6-8pm) Home to the Belgrade Philharmonica.

Dom Omladine   LIVE MUSIC, THEATRE
(☎324 8202; www.domomladine.org; Makedonska 22; ☺box office 10am-8pm Mon-Fri, 3pm-8pm Sat) Hosts a range of mostly youth-based cultural events

**Serbian Academy of
Arts & Sciences**   LIVE MUSIC
(☎202 7200; www.sanu.ac.rs; Knez Mihailova 35; ☺concerts from 6pm Mon & Thu Oct-June) Stages free concerts and exhibitions.

Cinemas

For Hollywood blockbusters in English or with English subtitles, try the following cinemas:

Tuckwood Cineplex (☎323 6517; www.tuck. rs; Kneza Miloša 7; tickets 250/300DIN)

Dom Sindikata (☎323 4224; www.ds.co.rs; Trg Nikole Pašića 5; tickets 250/300DIN)

🔒 Shopping

Knez Mihailova is studded with global and luxury brands. Get souvenirs from Kalemegdan Park vendors, while away the hours at Zemun's Sunday morning *buvljak* (flea market) or snoop around the black market in the pedestrian passage between Zeleni Venac and Terazije. Load up on Belgrade-

themed art, clothes, books and fripperies at **Belgrade Window** (Knez Mihailova 6; ☺9am-9pm Mon-Sat) in the Belgrade Cultural Centre above the Tourist Organisation of Belgrade.

ⓘ Information

Internet Access

Net cafes come and go in Belgrade faster than you can click a mouse. Wireless is free at venues throughout the city and available at almost every hostel/hotel.

Belgrade City Library (Knez Mihailova 56; per min 2DIN; ☺8am-8pm Mon-Fri, 8am-2pm Sat)

Net Hol (Nušićeva 3; per hr 120DIN; ☺10am-2am)

Internet Resources
Belgrade City (www.beograd.rs)

Belgrade in Your Pocket (www.inyourpocket. com/serbia/belgrade)

Belgraded (www.belgraded.com)

Medical Services
Emergency Medical Assistance (☎1994; www.beograd94.rs; Bul Franše D'Eperea 5; ☺24hr) For emergencies.

Klinički Centar (☎361 7777; www.klinicki -centar.rs; Pasterova 2; ☺24hr) Medical clinic.

Prima 1 (☎361 099; www.primax.rs; Nemanjina 2; ☺24hr) All-hours pharmacy.

Money
Banca Intesa (Knez Mihailova 30; ☺8am-8pm Mon-Fri, 9am-3pm Sat)

Erste Bank (Knez Mihailova 36; ☺9am-5pm Mon-Fri, 9.30am-1.30pm Sat)

Raiffeisen Bank (Terazije 27; ☺8am-7pm Mon-Fri, 9am-3pm Sat) In the walkway linking Terazije with Trg Nikola Pašića.

Post
Central post office (☎323 8417; Takovska 2; ☺8am-7pm Mon-Fri, 8am-3pm Sat)

INTERNATIONAL BUSES FROM BELGRADE

DESTINATION	FARE (DIN)	DURATION (HOURS)	FREQUENCY
Banja Luka	2200	7½	daily
Bratislava	3810	12	Wednesday and Sunday
Ljubljana	3700	7½	daily
Podgorica	2500	nine	daily
Sarajevo	2400	eight	daily
Skopje	2100	seven	daily
Split	3900	12½	Monday to Saturday
Vienna	4660	9½	daily

INTERNATIONAL TRAINS FROM BELGRADE

DESTINATION	FARE (DIN)	DURATION (HOURS)
Bucharest	2800	14
Budapest	1590	seven
İstanbul	4525	26
Ljubljana	2327	10
Moscow	8405	50
Munich	12,102	17
Sofia	2000	11
Thessaloniki	3160	16
Vienna	6516	11
Zagreb	1990	seven

Tourist Information

Tourist Organisation of Belgrade (www.tob. co.rs) Knez Mihailova 6 (☑328 1859; ⊘9am-9pm Mon-Sat); central railway station (☑361 2732; ⊘8am-8pm Mon-Fri, 8am-4pm Sat-Sun); Terazije underpass (☑263 5622; ⊘9am-8pm Mon-Fri, 9am-4pm Sat-Sun); Nikola Tesla airport (☑209 7828; ⊘9am-9pm Mon-Sun) Helpful folk with a raft of brochures, city maps and all the info you could need.

🅐 Getting There & Away

Bus

Belgrade has two adjacent bus stations, near the eastern banks of Sava River: **BAS** (☑263 6299; www.bas.rs; Železnička 4) serves the region, while **Lasta** (☑334 8555; www.lasta. rs; Železnička 2) deals with destinations around Belgrade.

Sample domestic services include Subotica (1300DIN, three hours), Novi Sad (700DIN, one hour) Niš (1100DIN, three hours) and Novi Pazar (1200DIN, three hours), for Kosovo.

Car & Motorcycle

Several car-hire companies have offices at Nikola Tesla Airport:

Avaco (☑228 6434; www.avaco.rs; ⊘8am-8pm) Rent a Yugo!

Avis (☑209 7062; www.avis.rs; ⊘8am-8pm)

Budget (☑228 6361; www.budget.rs; ⊘8am-8pm Mon-Fri, 10am-6pm Sat, 10am-2pm Sun)

Train

The **central train station** (Savski Trg 2) has an **information office** on Platform 1, **tourist information office** (p841), **exchange bureau** (⊘6am-10pm) and **sales counter** (⊘9am-4pm Mon-Sat).

Frequent trains go to Novi Sad (288DIN, 1½ hours), Subotica (560DIN, three hours) and Niš (784DIN, four hours).

🅐 Getting Around

To/from the Airport

Nikola Tesla airport is 18km from Belgrade. The bus that connects the airport with the JAT bus terminal via the railway station wasn't running at the time of research, but will hopefully be operational again soon: see www.beg.aero for updates. Otherwise, bus 72 connects the airport with Zeleni Venac (65DIN to 100DIN, half-hourly, 5.20am to midnight from airport, 4.40am to 11.40pm from town); the cheapest tickets must be purchased from news-stands.

Don't get swallowed up by the airport taxi shark pit: unscrupulous drivers could charge you double the going rate. Ask the tourist office in the arrivals hall to call one for you. A taxi from the airport to Knez Mihailova should be around 1150DIN.

Car & Motorcycle

Parking in Belgrade is regulated by three parking zones – red (one hour, 37.50DIN), yellow (two hour, 26.50DIN per hour) and green (three hours, 21.50DIN per hour). Tickets must be bought from kiosks or via SMS (in Serbian).

Public Transport

Trams and trolleybuses ply limited routes but buses chug all over town. Tickets are 42DIN from street kiosks or 80DIN from the driver.

Tram 2 is the city circle line, connecting Kalemegdan Citadel with Trg Slavija, bus stations and the central train station.

Taxi

Move away from obvious taxi traps and flag down a distinctly labelled cruising cab, or get a local to call you one. A 5km trip costs around 415DIN.

AROUND BELGRADE

The lure of Belgrade is such that you can (happily) get stuck there. But catching a glimpse of the country beyond the capital is easy: even southern towns like Topola or Despotovac can visited as day trips from Belgrade.

Zemun ЗЕМУН

Some 6km northwest of central Belgrade, Zemun was the most southerly point of the Austro-Hungarian empire when the Turks ruled Belgrade. These days it's known for its fish restaurants and quaint, decidedly non-urban ambience.

Above the market area, up the narrow cobbled street of Grobljanska, remnants of the old village lead uphill towards **Gardoš** fortress, dating from the 9th century. Walls from the 15th-century remain, as does the **Tower of Sibinjanin Janko**, built in 1896 to celebrate the millennial anniversary of the Hungarian state and to keep an eye on the Turks. Today you can just enjoy the spectacular view.

Descending from the tower, stop in at the 1731 **Nikolajevska Church** (Njegoševa 43) to goggle at its astounding baroque iconostasis.

At the time of research, **Zemun Museum** (316 5234; Glavna 9) was still closed for renovations, which will hopefully be worth the long wait.

Zemun is a laid-back accommodation alternative to Belgrade. Floating between Zemun and Belgrade is Arka Barka (p838) barge-hostel. The lobby of the more upmarket **Hotel Skala** (307 5032; www.hotelskala.rs; Bežanijska 3; s/d/apt 6300/8100/9000DIN; ❀⊛) has sunny wi-fi-equipped rooms and a cavernous basement restaurant.

Among the many venues dishing up fish and fun along the Danube (Dunav):

Reka (261 1625; www.reka.co.rs; Kej Oslobođenja 73B; fish meals 690-1000DIN; ⊘noon-2am)

Šaran (261 8235; www.saran.co.rs; Kej Oslobođenja 53; fish meals from 1000DIN)

Venecija (307 761; Kej Oslobođenja bb; fish meals 500-1000DIN)

Zemun is a 45-minute walk from Belgrade (across Brankov Most, along Nikole Tesle and the Kej Oslobođenja waterside walkway). Alternatively take bus 15 or 84 from Zeleni Venac market, or bus 83 or 78 from the main train station.

Smederevo СМЕДЕРЕВО

The startlingly large **Smederevo Fortress** (www.tvrdjavasmederevo.com; admission 50DIN; ⊘8am-8pm), 46km southwest of Belgrade, is a 25-tower fort built under the exacting orders of Despot Đurađ Branković. After 20 years of trying, the Turks finally conquered the fortification in 1459. Massive damage was caused by the explosion of stored munitions in WWII. The fortress hosts a **theatre festival** (www.tvrdjavateatar.rs) each August.

Lovingly maintained **Smederevo Museum** (www.muzejsd.org; admission 70DIN; ⊘10am-5pm Tue-Fri, 10am-3pm Sat & Sun) is the guardian of town history, with artefacts dating from Roman times. Even without many English explanations, having a poke around is pleasant.

Regular buses (500DIN, 1½ hours, every 15 minutes) leave from Belgrade's Lasta station. The museum is a block to the left of the bus station. If you can't see the fortress just beyond across the train tracks, consult an optometrist.

VOJVODINA ВОЈВОДИНА

Home to more than 25 ethnic groups, six languages and the best of Hungarian and Serbian traditions, Vojvodina's pancake plains mask a diversity unheard of in the rest of the country. Its affable capital Novi Sad hosts the eclectic EXIT festival – the largest in southeast Europe – while the nearby hilly region of Fruška Gora keeps the noise down in hushed monasteries and ancestral vineyards. Charming Subotica, 10km from Hungary, is an oasis of art nouveau delights.

Novi Sad НОВИ САД

021 / POP 350.000

As convivial as a *rakija* toast – and at times just as carousing – Novi Sad is a chipper town with all the spoils and none of the stress of the big smoke. Locals sprawl in pretty parks and outdoor cafes, and laneway bars pack out nightly. The looming Petrovaradin Citadel keeps a stern eye on proceedings, loosening its tie each July to host Serbia's largest music festival.

◉ Sights

Petrovaradin Citadel FORTRESS

Towering over the river on a 40m-high volcanic slab, this mighty citadel – built to the

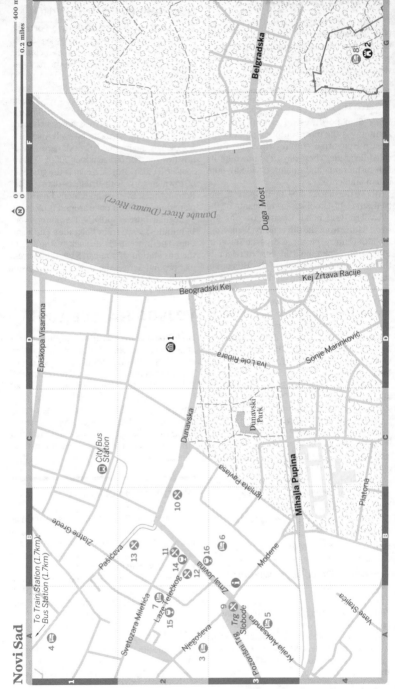

Novi Sad

400 m
0.2 miles

To Train Station (1.7km);
Bus Station (1.7km)

Danube River (Dunav River)

Belgradska

Duga Most

Kej Žrtava Racije

Beogradski Kej

Episkopa Visariona

Ive Lole Ribara

Sonje Marinković

Dunavski
Park

Dunavska

City Bus
Station

Ignjata Pavlasa

Mihajla Pupina

Platona

Zlatne Grede

Pašićeva

Zmaj Jovina

Modene

Vase Stajića

Svetozara Miletića

Laze Telečkog

Jevrejska

Njegoševa

Pozorišni trg

Kralja Aleksandra

Trg
Slobode

10

13

11
14
12

16

6

15

9

5

3

4

1

2

8

7

Novi Sad

specifics of French fortress maven Vauban – is aptly nicknamed 'Gibraltar on the Danube'. Constructed with slave labour between 1692 and 1780, the citadel's dungeons have held notable prisoners including Karađorđe (leader of the first uprising against the Turks and founder of a dynasty) and Tito...albeit not at the same time. Have a good gawk at the iconic clock tower: the size of the minute and hour hands are reversed so far-flung fishermen can tell the time.

Within the citadel walls, a **museum** (admission 100DIN; ⊙9am-5pm Tue-Sun) offers insight (sans English explanations) into the site's history.

Museum of Vojvodina   MUSEUM
(Muzej Vojvodine; www.muzejvojvodine.org.rs; Dunavska 35-7; admission 100DIN; ⊙9am-5pm Tue-Sun) This museum houses historical, archaeological and ethnological exhibits. Building 35 covers Vojvodinian history from Palaeolithic times to the late 19th century. Building 37 takes the story to 1945 with harrowing emphasis on WWI and WWII.

📷 Festivals & Events

Some festivals are worth sculpting a trip around (and booking accommodation in advance for). The biggest is EXIT Festival (p846) with blockbusting line-ups every year.

June's **Cinema City Festival** (www.cinema city.org) is an eight-day film extravaganza, while each September Novi Sad morphs into an open-air stage for the **International Festival of Street Musicians** (www.cekans.org. rs). The city has been tooting its own horn at the **Novi Sad Jazz Festival** (www.jazzns. eunet.rs) each November since 1999.

🛏 Sleeping

Leopold I   LUXURY HOTEL €€€
(☎499 7878; www.leopoldns.com; Petrovaradin Citadel; s €120, d €150-160, apt €170-390; ❋🛜) This rock-top indulgence offers rooms in Gothic, Renaissance or the (slightly) more economical modern style. Warning: the regal Leopold I apartment may induce delusions of grandeur.

Downtown   HOSTEL €
(☎69 139 7708; www.hostelnovisad.com; Njegoševa 2; dm from €9, twin €18; @) Super-friendly staff and an 'in the thick of it' location make this rambunctious, slightly ramshackle hostel a Novi Sad experience in itself.

Hotel Vojvodina   HISTORIC HOTEL €€
(☎622 122; Trg Slobode 2; s/d from 3500/5000DIN) Reeking of Communist-era retro, Novi Sad's oldest hotel (1854) isn't as slick as others, but its location overlooking the town square is unbeatable, as is the semifaded splendour of its restaurant.

Lazin Hostel   HOSTEL €
(☎63 443 703; www.lazinhostel.org; Laze Telečkog 10; dm €11-13, d/tw €15; @) Party people will appreciate this spotless, sociable spot, just a few seconds' stumble from bars and late-night eateries galore.

Hotel Zenit   HOTEL €€
(☎66 21 444; www.hotelzenit.co.rs; Zmaj Jovina 8; s 4715DIN, d 6530DIN, apt 10,030-15,190DIN; ❋🛜) With its modern glass-fronted facade, timber-bedecked interior of the Zenit is a cosy surprise. Personal service and a central location add to the charm.

Hotel Fontana   HOTEL €€
(☎621 779; Pašićeva 27; s/d/tr €37/50/66; ❋) With its pink exterior and malapropos chandeliers, this hotel is peculiar but perky. Good-sized rooms overlook the leafy courtyard.

🍴 Eating

Kod Lipa   SERBIAN €
(Svetozara Miletića 7; meals from 300DIN; ⊙7am-11pm Mon-Fri, 7am-1am Sat-Sun) This down-home

eatery has been dishing up old-school ambience alongside traditional Vojvodinian fare since the 19th century.

Caffe Pizzeria Modena INTERNATIONAL €
(www.modena-caffe.rs; Trg Slobode 4; pizzas 490-680DIN) Fill your belly as you feast your eyes in this people-watching paradise on the main square. Pizzas are above average and the huge chicken salad (560DIN) is a mouth-watering mound of goodness.

Lazina Bašta SERBIAN €
(Laze Telečkog 5; meals from 450DIN) Replete with hay bales and knick-knackery, Lazina Bašta serves up country-mouse cuisine on the most happening street in town.

Alternatively, lap up the greasy goodness at **Bubi Grill** (Dimitrija Tucovića 3; pljeskavica from 160DIN; ⊙24hr), renowned as the best in town, or lapse into a sugar coma at **Evropa** (Dunavska 6; cakes 100DIN) or **Poslastićarnica Šeherezada** (Zmaj Jovina 19; two-scoop ice cream 80DIN).

 Drinking

Laze Telečkog is lined with bars to suit every whim. Squeeze into the frenetic **London Underground Club** (Laze Telečkog 15, ⊙8am-3am) for good-timey tunes (and associated drunken sing-a-longs) or sidle next door to **Cuba Libre** (Laze Telečkog 13) and stake your spot on the narrow dance floor. The infinitely more calm **Atrium** (Laze Telečkog 2) serves drinks in a civilised (faux) library. Pour down a pint of the incongruous at the **Only Fools and Horses Pub** (Zmaj Jovina 2), complete with Trotter memorabilia.

ENTERING THE STATE OF EXIT

Home to the epic EXIT Festival (www.exitfestival.org), the Petrovaradin Fortress is stormed by thousands of revellers each July. The first festival in 2000 lasted 100 days and galvanised a generation of young Serbs against the Milošević regime, who 'exited' himself just weeks after the event. The festival has been attended in recent years by the likes of Faith No More, Chemical Brothers, Missy Elliot, Kraftwerk and Patti Smith...not to mention an annual tally of over 150,000 merrymakers from around the world.

ⓘ Information

Apoteka Pharmacy (⌨420 374; www.apoteka novisad.co.rs; Mihajla Pupina 7; ⊙24hr Mon-Sat)

Internet Club Net 21 (Zmaj Jovina 14; per hr 70DIN; ⊙24hr)

M1 Internet Caffe (Zmaj Jovina 26; per hr 60DIN; ⊙9am-11pm)

Main post office (Narodnih Heroja 2; ⊙9am-7pm Mon-Fri, 9am-2pm Sat)

Raiffeisen Bank (www.raiffeisenbank.rs; Trg Slobode 3; ⊙9am-5pm Mon-Fri, 9am-1pm Sat)

Tourist information centre (⌨661 7343; www.turizamns.rs; Ul Modene 1; ⊙7.30am-8pm Mon-Fri, 9am-5pm Sat) Ultra-helpful with maps and English info.

UniCredit Bank (www.unicreditbank.rs; Trg Slobode 3; ⊙9am-4.30pm Mon-Wed & Fri, 9am-6pm Thu)

ⓘ Getting There & Away

You can arrange flights with **JAT Airlines** (⌨457 588; www.jat.com; Mihajla Pupina 18; ⊙9am-4.30pm Mon-Fri).

The **bus station** (Bul Jaše Tomića; ⊙information counter 6am-11pm) has regular departures to Belgrade (605DIN, one hour, every 10 minutes) and Subotica (830DIN, 1½ hours), plus services to Užice (1120DIN, five hours) and Zlatibor (1210DIN, six hours). From here, four stops on bus 4 will take you to the town centre.

Frequent trains leave the **train station** (Bul Jaše Tomića 4), next door to the bus station, for Belgrade (490DIN, 1½ hours) and Subotica (390DIN, 1½ hours).

Subotica СУБОТИЦА
⌨024 / POP 148,400

Sugar-spun art nouveau marvels, a laid-back populace and a delicious sprinkling of Serbian and Hungarian flavours make this quaint town a worthy day trip or stopover.

⊙ Sights

Even the least architecturally inclined will fall for Subotica's art nouveau charms. Most sights are along the pedestrian strip of Korzo or on the main square, Trg Republike.

Town Hall HISTORIC BUILDING
(Trg Republike) Built in 1910, this behemoth of a building is a curious mix of art nouveau and something Gaudí may have had a playful dab at. If they're open, the council chambers – with exquisite stained-glass windows and elaborate decor – are not to be missed.

FRUŠKA GORA & SREMSKI KARLOVCI
ФРУШКА ГОРА & СРЕМСКИ КАРЛОВЦИ

Fruška Gora is an 80km stretch of rolling hills where monastic life has continued for centuries. Thirty-five monasteries were built here between the 15th and 18th centuries to safeguard Serbian culture and religion from the Turks. With your own wheels you can flit freely between the 16 remaining monasteries; otherwise, ask about tours at tourist offices in Novi Sad and Sremski Karlovci. Public transport gets you to villages within the park from where you can walk between sights.

An easy outing is done with a bus from Novi Sad bound for Irig; ask to be let out at the **Novo Hopovo Monastery** (150DIN, 30 minutes), a five-minute walk. From here walk or catch local buses to other points such as **Vrdnik**. Visit www.npfruskagora.co.rs for a rundown on the region; www.psdzeleznicarns.org.rs has detailed information on individual monasteries.

At the edge of Fruška Gora on the banks of the Danube (Dunav) River is the photogenic town of **Sremski Karlovci**. Lined with stunning structures like the **Orthodox cathedral** (1758-62), the baroque **Four Lions fountain** and the **Chapel of Peace** at the southern end of town (where the Turks and Austrians signed the 1699 Peace Treaty), Sremski Karlovci is also at the heart of a famed wine region. Visit the **Museum of Beekeeping & Wine Cellar** (881 071; www.muzejzivanovic.com; Mitropolita Stratimirovića 86) to try famous *bermet* wine, or drop in at any of the dozens of family-owned cellars around town. Sremski Karlovci hosts a **grape harvesting festival** every October.

Take frequent buses 61 or 62 from Novi Sad (120DIN, 30 minutes) and visit the **tourist organisation** (883 855; www.karlovci.org.rs; Patrijarha Rajačića 1; ⊘8am-6pm Mon-Fri, 10am-6pm Sat) just off the main square.

SERBIA SUBOTICA

Modern Art Gallery HISTORIC BUILDING
(www.likovnisusret.com; Park Ferenca Rajhla 5; admission 50DIN; ⊘8am-6pm Mon-Fri, 9am-noon Sat) This mansion was built in 1904 as an architect's design studio, and it shows. One of the most sumptuous buildings in Serbia, it's a vibrant flourish of mosaics, ceramic tiles, floral patterns and stained glass.

City Museum MUSEUM
(www.gradskimuzej.subotica.rs; Trg Sinagoge 3; admission 100DIN; ⊘10am-8pm Tue-Sat) Formerly housed in the Town Hall, the eclectic museum now holds exhibitions in this art nouveau residence designed by Budapest's Vago brothers.

Synagogue SYNAGOGUE
(Trg Sinagoge 2) Alas, Subotica's first art nouveau building remains shuttered and dilapidated as long-awaited renovations have failed to materialise. Grasp some of its former glory from the footpath.

⏚ Sleeping

Hotel Patria HOTEL €€
(554 500; www.hotelpatria.rs; Đure Đakovića bb; s €37-46, d €65-72, apt €93-123; ✳🛜) Renovations have turned the Patria into a topnotch midrange option, with well-appointed rooms (the presidential suite rocks a Jacuzzi), a wellness centre and a great location a few hundred metres from the train station.

Hostel Incognito HOSTEL €
(559 254; www.hostel-subotica.com; Hugo Badalića 3; s/d/tr/apt 1000/1800/2400/7000DIN; 🛜) Run by brothers Darko and Zoran, this basic but clean hostel is a couple minutes' walk from all the Subotica sights. Reception is in the restaurant downstairs.

Hotel Galleria HOTEL €€
(647 111; www.galleria-center.com; Matije Korvina 17; s & d 4009-5349DIN, s apt 6569-11,369DIN, d apt 7909-14,629DIN, presidential apt 14,629-19,429DIN; ✳🛜) These four-star rooms come over all 'gentleman's den', with warm mahogany-look fittings and beds lined with bookshelves. Find it inside the Atrium shopping plaza.

Hostel Bosa Milećević HOSTEL €
(548 290; Marije Vojnić Tošinice 7; dm per person 820DIN) Cheapie tucked well away behind Ekonomski Fakultet at Segedinski put 9-11.

✗ Eating

Ravel CAFE €
(Nušićeva 2; cakes 60-150DIN; ⊘9am-10pm Mon-Sat, 11am-10pm Sun) Dainty nibbles at *gateaux* and twee tea-taking is the name

of the game at this adorable art nouveau classic.

Boss Caffe INTERNATIONAL €
(www.bosscaffe.com; Matije Korvina 7-8) Boss' offerings include a variety of tacos (240DIN to 455DIN) and pizza with sour cream (405DN to 455DIN). It's directly behind the Modern Art Gallery.

ⓘ Information

Exchange office (train station; ⊘8am-6.30pm Mon-Sat, 8am-7pm Sun)

Pireus Bank (⊘9am-5pm Mon-Fri)

Raiffeisen Bank (⊘8am-7pm Mon-Fri, 8am-2pm Sat)

Tourist information office (☑670 350; www.visitsubotica.rs; Town Hall; ⊘8am-8pm Mon-Fri, 9am-noon Sat-Sun)

ⓘ Getting There & Away

For early birds, Subotica is an easy day trip from Belgrade. From **bus station** (Senćanski put 3) there are hourly services to Novi Sad (800DIN, two hours) and Belgrade (1200DIN, 3½ hours). Subotica's **train station** (Bose Milećević bb) has two trains to Szeged, Hungary (260DIN, 1¾ hours). Trains to Belgrade (560DIN, 3½ hours) stop at Novi Sad (400DIN, 1½ hours).

Palić ПАЛИЋ

The resort town of Palić, 8km from Subotica, is home to a 5-sq-km lake popular with boaters, fisherfolk, swimmers and afternoon amblers. In mid-July Palić hosts a **European Film Festival** (www.palicfilmfestival.com).

The **tourist information office** (☑753 111; www.palic.rs; Kanjiški put 17A; ⊘8am-6pm) can help with accommodation options.

From Subotica, take bus 6 from diagonally opposite Hotel Patria (50DIN, 20 minutes).

SOUTHERN SERBIA

Great adventures await south of Belgrade. Zlatibor's rolling hills are a peaceful privilege to explore any time of the year. Dramatic Kopaonik is a popular ski destination for Europeans in the know. Pressed against Balkan neighbours are the melding cultural heritages of the Raška region (known interchangeably by the Turkish 'Sandžak'), the last to be liberated from Ottoman rule in 1912.

The town of Novi Pazar feels more Turkish than some pockets of İstanbul, with winding streets and an Ottoman skyline spiked by minarets, yet some of Serbia's most revered Orthodox monasteries are but a cab ride away.

Topola ОПОЛА
☑034 / POP 25,292

Tiny Topola, 74km from Belgrade, is where Karađorđe – immortalised here in an imposing statue – plotted the Serbian insurrection against the Turks in 1804 and where his grandson, King Petar I, built one of the most astonishing churches in the country.

One ticket (300DIN) grants access to all the park's impressive attractions, all of which are open daily from 8am to 6pm.

Karađorđe led his rebellion from a building that is now a **museum** (Kraljice Marije). The cannon at the entrance could be heard all the way to Belgrade, summoning leaders to the room now housing the bulk of the museum's collection. The missing handle was removed by King Petar I, who made it into a crown for his 1904 coronation.

Atop Oplenac hill, the white-marble, five-domed **Church of St George** (Avenija Kralja Petra I) was built by King Petar between 1904 and 1912. Vibrant mosaics are magnificently rendered on every inch of the church with over 40 million pieces of coloured glass. Millions more adorn the Karađorđe family mausoleum under the church.

Opposite, **Petar House** was used by workers building the church, and by King Petar during his visits to inspect progress. Some humanising portraits of the royal family are exhibited here.

Your ticket allows entry to the **Winegrower's House gallery** at the park entrance.

Those with a taste for the grape will enjoy Topola's **Oplenac Vintage Festival**, held each October.

The **Tourist Organisation of Topola** (☑811 172; www.topolaoplenac.org.rs; Kneginje Zorke 13; ⊘8am-5pm Mon-Fri, 10am-5pm Sat) can provide a town map.

Day trippers can use frequent buses to and from Belgrade (600DIN, 1½ hours).

Despotovac ДЕСПОТОВАЦ
☑035 / POP 25,500

Apart from its postcard-pretty appeal, the reasons to come here are the nearby Manasija Monastery and Resava Cave.

Manasija Monastery, 2km north of Despotovac is girded by 11 custodial towers. A refuge for artists and writers fleeing the Turkish invasion of Kosovo in the first half of the 15th century, the monastery was burnt by the Turks in 1456 and further damaged in 1718 by an explosion of gunpowder stored on the premises by the Austrians. Many consider the Manasija frescos to be predecessors of the Serbian equivalent of Renaissance art.

A winding 20km beyond Despotovac, **Resavska Pećina** (Resava Cave; www.resavska pecina.rs; adult/child 270/220DIN; ☉9am-5pm Apr-Nov) has guided tours through impressive halls (featuring natural formations with names like 'Hanged Sheep' and 'Thirst for Love') taking around 40 minutes. Come prepared: temperatures average just 7°C.

A taxi will take you to both sites from town; the return trip including waiting time should be no more than 2000DIN.

Belgrade buses leave six times a day (weekdays) to Despotovac (580DIN, 2½ hours).

Niš НИШ

☑018 / POP 253,077

Niš is a lively city of curious contrasts, where Roma in horse-drawn carriages trot alongside new cars, and cocktails are sipped in cobblestoned alleys.

Niš was settled in pre-Roman times and flourished during the time of local-boy-made-good Emperor Constantine (AD 280–337). Turkish rule lasted from 1386 until 1877 despite several Serb revolts; the tower of Serbian skulls and Niš Fortress are reminders of Turkish dominion. The Nazis built one of Serbia's most notorious concentration camps here, ironically named 'the Red Cross'.

◉ Sights

Niš Fortress FORTRESS
(Jadranska; ☉24hr) While its current incarnation was built by the Turks in the 18th century, there have been forts on this site since ancient Roman times. Today it's a sprawling recreational area with restaurants, cafes, market stalls and ample space for any-time moseying. It hosts the **Nišville International Jazz Festival** (www.nisville.com) each August and **Nišomnia** (www.nisomnia.org.rs) featuring local and overseas rock and electro acts in September. Niš' main pedestrian boulevard, Obrenoviceva, stretches before the citadel.

Tower of Skulls MONUMENT
(Ćele Kula; bul Zoran Đinđić; adult/child 120/100DIN; ☉8am-8pm Tue-Sun Apr-Oct, 9am-4pm Tue-Sat, 10am-4pm Sun Nov-Mar) The Tower of Skulls is an eerie testimony to Serbian resolve. With Serbian defeat imminent at the 1809 Battle of Čegar, the Duke of Resava kamikazeed towards the Turkish defences, firing at their gunpowder stores. In doing so, he killed himself, 4000 of his men, and 10,000 Turks. The Turks still triumphed, and to deter future acts of rebellion, they beheaded, scalped and embedded the skulls of the dead Serbs in this tower. Only 58 of the initial 952 skulls remain. Contrary to Turkish intention, the tower serves as a proud monument of Serbian resistance.

FREE **Mediana** RUINS
(Bul Cara Konstantina; ☉10am-6pm Tue-Sun) Mediana, on the eastern outskirts of Niš, is what remains of Constantine's 4th-century Roman palace. Archaeological digging has so far revealed a palace, mosaics, forum and an expansive grain-storage area. There's an archaeology collection at the small **museum** (Nikole Pašića 59; adult/child 100/80DIN; ☉10am-6pm Tue-Sun).

🛏 Sleeping

The pickings remain slim for a town this size, but Niš is at least increasing its budget accommodation range.

Hostel Niš HOSTEL €
(☑513 703; www.hostelnis.rs; Dobrička 3a; dm/tw per person 1110/1610DIN; @) Perfectly central with outgoing, helpful staff, good-sized rooms and lockable storage? Winner. It's five-minute walk (towards the river) from the bus station.

Hotel Niški Cvet HOTEL €€
(☑297 700; www.niskicvet.com; Kej 29 Decembar 2; s/d €55/79, ste €76-140; ❀🔊) Top views over the Nišava River and fortress from super-slick surrounds. Prices drop on weekends.

Hostel Sweet HOSTEL €
(☑628 942 085; www.sweet-hostel.com; Milorad Veljkovića Špaje 11/4; dm/s/d/tr/q 1000/1500/2000/3000/4000DIN, apt 3000-10,000DIN; ❀🔊) This clean, genial spot has lockable storage in each room and a laid-back vibe.

Hotel Ambassador HOTEL €€
(☑501 800; www.srbijaturist.com; Trg Kralja Milana bb; s 2735-3160DIN, d 3670-4100DIN,

ste 4860; ✷@) A relic of another era, the rooms are stale but bearable.

✕ Eating & Drinking

The cobblestoned Kopitareva (Tinkers' Alley) is chock-full of fast-paced eating and drinking options, including **Flo** (Kopitareva 11; ☺7.30am-midnight Mon-Thu, 7.30am-2am Fri-Sat, 9am-midnight Sun), the speediest of them all.

Hamam   SERBIAN €€
(Tvrđava bb; meals 350-2200DIN; ☺11am-midnight) A crumbling Turkish bathhouse outside, and an elegant multi-alcove dining space inside, the wonderful Hamam offers national fare like *dimljena vešalica* (roll of smoked pork stuffed with cream cheese and almonds), pizzas and seafood.

Restoran Sindjelić   SERBIAN €
(Nikole Pasića 36; meals from 400DIN; ☺8am-1am Sun-Fri, 8am-2am Sat) Hearty traditional fare.

Cafe Reka   CAFE €
(Kej Kola Srpskih Sestara bb; ☺8am-late Wed-Sat) Kick back in a porch swing and watch the Nišava River trickle past.

Pekara Branković   BAKERY €
(Voždova Karađorđa 68; ☺24hr) Slabs of burek for 30DIN.

❶ Information

Internet cafe (Hotel Ambassador; per hr 50DIN; ☺7am-11pm)

Post office (Voždova Karađorđa 13A; ☺8am-8pm) Internet access for 50DIN per hour.

Tourist Organisation of Niš (✆521 321; www.nistourism.org.rs; Voždova Karađorđa 7; ☺7.30am-7pm Mon-Fri, 9am-1pm Sat) Located within the citadel gates.

❶ Getting There & Away

The **bus station** (Kneginje Ljubice) behind the fortress has frequent services to Belgrade (985DIN, three hours) and Brzeće (582DIN, 1½ hours) for Kopaonik, and three daily to Novi Pazar (1120DIN, four hours). There are two daily buses to Topola (930DIN, 2½ hours).

From the **train station** (Dimitrija Tucovića), there are seven trains to Belgrade (884DIN, 4½ hours) and one to Bar (2500DIN, four hours).

Novi Pazar НОВИ ПАЗАР

✆020 / POP 54,000

Novi Pazar is the cultural heartland of the Sandžak region, with a mostly Muslim population. Turkish coffee, cuisine and customs abound, yet some idyllic Orthodox sights are in the vicinity.

◉ Sights

The Old Town is lined with cafes and shops peddling Turkish desserts, meat, nuts and copperware, while just across the Raška River, cafes and restaurants flank 28 Novembar. Attempts to restore the ruined hamam (just off Maj street) have failed dismally, leaving it at the mercy of coffee-drinking men and picnickers.

The following sights are accessible by taxi; a return trip to a single site should cost around 800DIN.

Sopoćani Monastery   MONASTERY
Unesco-protected Sopoćani Monastery was built in the mid-13th century by King Uroš (who is buried here), destroyed by the Turks at the end of the 17th century and restored in the 1920s. Frescos inside the Romanesque church are prime examples of medieval art that miraculously (or perhaps divinely) survived more than two centuries exposed to the elements. The *Assumption of the Mother of God* fresco is one of the most renowned in Serbia.

Church of St Peter   CHURCH
(Petrova Crkva) Three kilometres from town on a bluff on the Kraljevo road, the small stone Church of St Peter is the oldest in Serbia and its only pre-Nemanjić church; parts of it date from the 8th century. The ancient cemetery holds the grave of a 5th-century Illyrian prince. If it's locked, ask at the nearby house to be let in.

St George Monastery   MONASTERY
(www.stupovi.rs) Visible from the Church of St Peter and dating from 1170, St George Monastery (Đurđevi Stupovi) is the result of a promise to God by Stefan Nemanja (founder of the medieval Nemanjić dynasty) that he would endow a monastery to St George if he was released from Turkish captivity. Ongoing efforts to restore the complex after extensive WWII damage are resurrecting monastic life.

🛏 Sleeping & Eating

Hotel Vrbak   HOTEL €
(✆314 548; Maršala Tita bb; s/d/apt 2000/3500/4500DIN; ☎) The Vrbak is practically a destination in its own right: a motley mash-up of architectural styles (think UFO-meets-magic mushrooms, dolled up in nouveau-cement), it's an unmissable landmark in the centre of town. Though the lofty lobby atri-

STUDENICA MONASTERY

One of the most sacred sites in Serbia, Studenica was established in the 1190s by Stefan Nemanja and developed by his sons Vukan and Stefan. Active monastic life was cultivated by St Sava and continues today, though members of this thriving little community don't mind the occasional visitor.

There are three churches within impressive white-marble walls. **Bogorodičina Crkva** (The Church of Our Lady), contains the tomb of Stefan Nemanja, brought here by his brother, Sava. Smaller **Kraljeva Crkva** (King's Church) houses the acclaimed *Birth of the Virgin* fresco.

From Novi Pazar, getting to Studenica without your own transport means travelling via Užiće (every 15 to 30 minutes from 5am) and catching a local bus from there, or negotiating a return taxi journey.

um hints at Napoleonic delusions, the rooms are clean but basic. Still, it's worth staying just so you can say you did.

Hotel Tadž   HOTEL €€
(☑311 904; Rifata Burdževića 79; s/d/apt 3000/5000/7200DIN; ❄❤) This modern, upmarket hotel has working wi-fi and a high-quality restaurant offering respite from street-eats.

Hostel Kan   HOTEL €
(Cannes; ☑315 300; Rifata Burdžovića 10; s/d/tr €15/20/30) A hostel in name but dorm-free, this slightly creaky but cosy spot opposite the Vrbak offers basic rooms with cable TV and minibars.

Kod Jonuza   GRILL €
(28 Novembar 10; meals 100-300DIN; ⊘24 hr) A no-frills facade conceals a kitchen in which something magical must be occurring: the *ćevapčići* alone will induce drool even when your meal here is but a distant memory.

🛈 Getting There & Away

Frequent buses leave the **bus station** (a five minute walk to Hotel Vrbak) to Belgrade (1000DIN, four hours). An overnight bus goes to Sarajevo (€15, seven hours) and there's one to Pristina (€7, three hours) in Kosovo.

Kopaonik КОПАОНИК
☑036
Situated around Pančićev Peak (Pančićev Vrh, 2017m) overlooking Kosovo, Serbia's prime ski resort has 44km of ski slopes served by 23 lifts and is a pleasant base for hiking. Prices plummet off season, though many places open arbitrarily or close completely.

🛏 Sleeping & Eating

Large-scale hotels with restaurants, gym facilities, pizzerias, discos and shops are the go here.

Hotel Grand   LUXURY HOTEL €€
(☑471 246; www.grand-kopaonik.com; s €51-150, d €77-224; ❤🏊) A swimming pool, fitness centre, tennis courts and ski slopes on your doorstep.

Hostel Montana   HOSTEL €
(☑062563657; www.montana.rs; dm €5-25; @) Log-cabiny good times on the cheap.

JAT Apartments   APARTMENT €€
(☑471 044; www.jatapartmani.com; apt per 1/2/3/4/5 persons from €30/34/36/50/58 plus tax; ❤) Open year-round with spacious rooms and kitchenettes.

Buongiorno Casa Montagna   PIZZA €€
Posh pizzas and daily happy hour (11am to 2.30pm) on the terrace.

Boeing   BUFFET €€
All-you-can eat buffets for that extra winter 'padding'.

🛈 Information

The resort centre is amply equipped with ATMs, shops, restaurants and a post office.

Ski Centre Kopaonik (www.skis.rs; ⊘9am-5pm) Ski passes at the base of Hotel Grand.

Skiline (www.skiline.co.uk) Books ski holidays in 'Kop'.

Tourist Centar Kopaonik (Vikend Naselje Kopaonik; www.tckopaonik.com) For assistance with all tours, packages and accommodation.

🛈 Getting There & Away

In season, there are three daily buses from Belgrade (1300DIN, five hours) and three from Niš to Brzeće (582DIN, 1½ hours). From Novi Pazar, pick up an infrequent connection in Raška; taxis from Raška cost around 1500DIN.

Zlatibor ЗЛАТИБОР

📞031 / POP 156,000

A romantic region of gentle mountains, traditions and hospitality, Zlatibor encompasses the Tara and Šargan mountains in the north and the Murtenica hills bordering Bosnia & Hercegovina. The Tržni town centre has everything you could need, but not far beyond are quaint villages where locals are oblivious to ski-bunny shenanigans.

⊙ Activities

Zlatibor's slopes are mostly mild. Major **skiing** hills are Tornik (the highest peak in Zlatibor at 1496m) and Obudovica. The **nordic skiing trail** at the northern foothill of Šumatno Brdo is 1042m at its highest point.

Several **walking trails** start, end or pass the Tržni centre. In easy reach is the **monument** in memory of local victims of German aggression in 1941; head south along Ul Sportova, cross the footbridge and follow the footpath to the monument and its spectacular views.

🛏 Sleeping & Eating

Private rooms and apartments offer more space, facilities and privacy for less money than resorts. In season they typically cost €30 to €80 for two to six people and €10 to €30 less out of season. Find them through Zlatibor Tours at the bus station or travel agents. The best meals are found in local villages, but there are a couple of good options in the town centre.

Hotel Mona Zlatibor HOTEL €€
(📞841 021; www.monazlatibor.com; Naselje Jezero 26; s & d 6950-8750DIN, apt from 8000DIN; 🛜)

This well-groomed hotel opposite the bus station does its best to keep you indoors, with a wellness centre, two restaurants and a bar.

Villa Ramović GUEST HOUSE €
(📞841 840; Jedriličarska 73; €15 pp) Rustic, romantic homestay with basic but cosy rooms.

Olimp HOTEL €€
(📞842 555; www.hotelolimp.com; Naselje Sloboda bb; d 3400-3800DIN, apt 4100DIN; 🛜) Out of the centre, this oldie but goodie offers expansive balcony views. Full board is an extra 650DIN.

Grand Zlatibor SERBIAN €€
(meals from 500DIN; ⊙11am-midnight) Warm and woody, this three-storied affair serves up suitably hearty regional dishes. Also home to the local take on an Irish bar.

Jezero INTERNATIONAL €€
(meals from 650DIN) Devour the lakeside views as you demolish plates of local and Italian fare.

Fama PIZZA €
(pizzas from 450DIN; ⊙7am-1am) The taste of new Serbia (that'd be 'pizza') in suitably modern surrounds.

❶ Information

Banka Intesa (Tržni Centar; ⊙8am-4pm Mon-Fri, 8am-noon Sat)

Igraonica Internet Caffe (Tržni centar; per hr 120DIN; ⊙9am-midnight)

Post office (Tržni centar; ⊙7am-7pm) Also has phones and maps.

Zlatibor Tours (📞845 957; bus station, Tržni centar; ⊙8am-9pm) The scarily efficient Danijela will have your homestay and tours booked before you know what hit you.

MADNESS, MADE IN SERBIA

On the surface, the **Dragačevo Trumpet Assembly** (an annual gathering of brass musicians) sounds harmless; nerdily endearing even. But this band camp this ain't: it *is*, however, the most boisterous music festival in all of Europe, if not the world.

Known simply as 'Guča', after the western Serbian village that has hosted it each August since 1961, the four-day debauch is hedonism at its most rambunctious: tens of thousands of beer-and-brass-addled visitors dance wildly *kolos* through the streets, gorging on spit-meat and slapping dinar on the sweaty foreheads of the (mostly Roma) *trubači* performers. The music itself is relentless and frenzy-fast; even Miles Davis confessed, "I didn't know you could play trumpet that way".

Sleep is a dubious proposition at Guča, but bring a tent or book ahead anyway: www.guca.rs has information on accommodation and transport.

ZLATIBOR EXCURSIONS

Tumble back in time to 19th-century Serbia at the **Open-Air Museum** (www.sirogojno. org.rs; adult/child 120/70DIN; ⊘9am-4pm Oct-Mar, 9am-7pm Apr-Sep) in the village of Sirogojno. High-roofed, fully furnished wooden houses are spread across a pleasant mountainside and are open for your exploration.

Mokra Gora is home to the village of **Drvengrad** (Küstendorf; www.mecavnik.info; Mećavnik hill; adult/child 180/100DIN; ⊘9am-9pm), built by enigmatic film-maker Emir Kusturica in 2002 for his film *Life is a Miracle*. Quirky, colourful flourishes give the village a fantastical feel. Adding to the surreal fun, the Stanley Kubrick cinema shows Kusturica's films, there's a life-size statue of Johnny Depp, and Bruce Lee St (past the church) is home to a restaurant where you can sip 'Che Guevara biorevolution juice' and goggle at some prime panoramas.

The **Šargan 8 railway** (⊘bookings 510 288 or buking.sargan8@srbrail.rs; www.serbian railways.com; adult/child 500/250DIN; ⊘10.30am & 1.25pm daily Apr-Oct, also 8am & 4.10pm depending on demand) tourist train was once part of a narrow-gauge railway linking Belgrade with Sarajevo and Dubrovnik. The joy of the 2½-hour journey is in its disorienting twists, turns and tunnels (all 22 of them).

Reach these sights via bus from Užice or on a tour with any of the agencies at Zlatibor bus station.

❶ Getting There & Around

Express buses leave the **bus stand** for Belgrade (700DIN, four hours), Novi Sad (950DIN, 6½ hours) and almost hourly to Užice (70DIN, 45 minutes, 5.50am to 11.10pm), the nearest railhead.

Without your own wheels, the easiest way to explore the region is to join locally organised tours. A return taxi from Tržni to the edge of the region costs around 2000DIN.

UNDERSTAND SERBIA

History
Early Invasions

Serbian history has been punctuated by foreign invasions from the time the Celts supplanted the Illyrians in the 4th century BC through to the arrival of the Romans 100 years later, the Slavs in the 6th century AD, the Turks in the 14th century, the Austro-Hungarians in the late 19th and early 20th centuries, and the Germans briefly in WWII. The country was locked into Eastern Europe in AD 395 when the Roman Emperor Theodosius I divided his empire, giving Serbia to the Byzantines. This was cemented in 879 when Saints Cyril and Methodius converted Serbs to the Orthodox religion.

Enter the Ottomans

Independence briefly flowered from 1217 with a 'golden age' during Stefan Dušan's reign as emperor (1346–55). Serbia declined after his death, and the pivotal Battle of Kosovo in 1389, where the Turks defeated Serbia, ushered in 500 years of Islamic rule. Early revolts were crushed but an 1815 uprising led to de facto independence that became complete in 1878.

The Land of Southern Slavs

On 28 June 1914, Austria-Hungary used the assassination of Archduke Franz Ferdinand by a Bosnian Serb as cause to invade Serbia, sparking WWI. In 1918 Croatia, Slovenia, Bosnia & Hercegovina, Vojvodina, Serbia and its Kosovo province, Montenegro, and Macedonia were joined into the Kingdom of Serbs, Croats and Slovenes; these countries became Yugoslavia (Land of Southern Slavs) in 1929.

In March 1941 Yugoslavia joined the fascist Tripartite Alliance, sparking a British-backed military coup that led to the withdrawal of support for the Axis powers; Germany reacted by bombing Belgrade. Rival resistance movements fought the Germans and each other, with the communist Partisans – led by Josip Broz Tito – gaining the upper hand. In 1945 they formed the government, abolished the monarchy and declared a federal republic including Serbia, Kosovo and Vojvodina.

Tito broke with Stalin in 1948 and Yugoslavia became a nonaligned nation, albeit bolstered by Western aid. Within the nation, growing regional inequalities and burgeoning Serbian expansionism fuelled demands by Slovenia, Croatia and Kosovo for greater autonomy. Tito's death in 1980 signalled the beginning of the rise of nationalism, stifled but long-simmering, within the republics.

A Turbulent Era

By 1986 Serbian nationalists were espousing a 'Greater Serbia', an ideology that would encompass Serbs from all republics into one state. Appropriated by Serbia's Communist Party leader Slobodan Milošević, the doctrine was fuelled by claims of the genocide of Serbs by Kosovo Albanians, leading to the abolishment of self-rule in Kosovo in 1990. Inflamed by Serbia's mounting authoritarianism and territorial claims, Croatia, Slovenia, Bosnia & Hercegovina and Macedonia seceded from the federation, sparking a series of violent conflicts known collectively as the Yugoslav Wars.

Bitter, bloody and monstrously complex, the wars – Slovenia's Ten-Day War, the Croatian War of Independence and the Bosnian War – were fought not just between breakaway forces and the majority-Serb Yugoslav Army, but along fractious ethnic and religious lines as well. Atrocities were committed on all sides: perhaps the most stunning display of savagery came with the Srebrenica massacre, Europe's largest mass murder since WWII in which 8000 Bosnian men and boys were killed under orders of Republika Srpska Army (RSA) commander Ratko Mladić and RS president Radovan Karadžić. Allegations of rape camps, ethnic cleansing and other barbarisms under Milošević's leadership saw Serbia assume the role of international pariah.

In April 1992 the remaining republics, Serbia and Montenegro, formed a 'third' Yugoslav federation without provision of autonomy for Kosovo, despite its Albanian majority. Violence erupted in January 1998.

In March 1999 peace talks failed when Serbia rejected the US-brokered Rambouillet Agreement. In response to organised resistance in Kosovo, Serbian forces engaged in ethnic cleansing in an attempt to empty the country of its Albanian population; hundreds of thousands fled into Macedonia and Albania, galvanising the US and NATO into a 78-day bombing campaign. On 12 June 1999 Serbian forces withdrew from Kosovo.

European Dawn

In the 2000 presidential elections, opposition parties led by Vojislav Koštunica declared victory, a claim denounced by Milošević. Opposition supporters from all over Serbia swarmed to Belgrade and stormed Parliament. When Russia recognised Koštunica's win, Milošević had to acknowledge defeat.

Koštunica restored ties with Europe, acknowledged Yugoslav atrocities in Kosovo and rejoined the UN. In April 2001 Milošević was arrested and extradited to the international war-crimes tribunal in The Hague.

In April 2002 a loose union of Serbia and Montenegro replaced Yugoslavia. The EU-brokered deal was intended to stabilise the region by accommodating Montenegrin demands for independence, allowing for a referendum after three years.

In March 2003 Serbia was shaken by the assassination of reformist Prime Minister Zoran Đinđić, who had been instrumental in handing Milošević to The Hague. Parliamentary elections in December 2003 saw a worrying resurgence of nationalism. Power-sharing deals installed Koštunica as head of a centre-right coalition relying on support from Milošević's Socialist Party. In June 2004 Serbia gained a new president in pro-European Boris Tadić.

On 11 March 2006 Milošević was found dead in his cell. In May, 55% of Montenegrins voted for independence from Serbia, which was formally declared the following month. The following May, 12 people (several of whom were former members of the paramilitary wing of the state security police) were found guilty of Đinđić's murder. In February 2008 Kosovo declared its independence, a move that Serbia held to be illegal. In May 2008 Tadić won 102 seats in Serbia's 250-member parliament, reaffirming Serbia's pro-European future, but the government remains fractured over how Kosovo impacts on Serbia's future with the EU. In July 2008, Karadžić was arrested for war crimes after 12 years as a fugitive; Mladić remains at large, the failure to bring him to trial another thorn in the side of Serbia's EU aspirations.

The People of Serbia

The current population is estimated at 7.3 million people. The census of 2002 revealed a population comprised of Serbs (82.9%), Hungarians (3.9%), Bosniaks (1.8%), Roma (1.4%) and others (8.9%). Around 85% of the population identify as Serbian Orthodox. The 5% Roman Catholic population are mostly Vojvodinian Hungarians. Muslims (Albanians and Slavic) comprise around 3% of the country's population.

The Arts

The survival and active rebellion of artistic expression throughout dark periods in history is a source of pride. Today creative juices flow thickly and freely, with films spawning idyllic villages (see the box, p853), art sold in cocktail bars and eclectic music events.

Literature

Bosnian-born, but a past Belgrade resident, Ivo Andrić was awarded the Nobel prize for his *Bridge over the Drina*.

Internationally acclaimed word wizard Milorad Pavić writes in many dimensions: *The Inner Side of the Wind* can be read from the back or the front, and you can read a male or female edition of his lyrical lexicon *Dictionary of the Khazars*. Novelist Momo Kapor's *A Guide to the Serbian Mentality* is an amusing peek into the national psyche. Those interested in Serbia's Roma musicians will enjoy Garth Cartwright's rollicking *Princes Amongst Men*.

Cinema

World-renowned director Emir Kusturica sets the bar on Serbian cinema with his raucous approach to story-telling. Look out for *Underground* (1995), the surreal tale of seemingly never-ending Balkan conflicts, *Time of the Gypsies* (1989), *Black Cat, White Cat* (1998) and *Life is a Miracle* (2004), about an optimistic Serbian engineer working on the Mokra Gora railway (see the box, p853).

Music

Pleh muzika (wild, haunting brass sounds influenced by Turkish and Austrian military music), also called *trubači*, is the national music. Popular examples are the soundtrack to the film *Underground* and albums by trumpet player Boban Marković. *Trubači* gets an orgiastic outing at Guča's Dragačevo Trumpet Assembly each August (see the box, p852).

Cross traditional folk with techno and you get 'turbofolk'; it was controversial during the Milošević era for its nationalist overtones but is now more mainstream fun.

Modern tastes encompass everything from wild Romani fiddlings to house, jazz, drum'n'bass, funk, reggae, rock and hip hop. Nightlife follows suit, offering every type of soundtrack.

Architecture

Ottoman, Austro-Hungarian and Serbian-Byzantine styles have fought for dominance, often over the same buildings, which have been stripped, redressed and modified over the years depending on who was in charge. Layers of Communist-era concrete aren't going anywhere in a hurry.

Environment

Serbia comprises 77,474 sq km. Midzor (2169m), on the Stara Planina range, is its highest peak. Zlatibor and Kopaonik are winter playgrounds.

Vojvodina is glass-flat agricultural land. South of the Danube (Dunav), the landscape rises through rolling green hills, which crest where the eastern outpost of the Dinaric Alps slices southeastwards across the country.

Major national parks are Kapaonik, Tara and Fruška Gora. Among Serbia's mammals are wild boar, wildcat, beaver, otters, suslik, lynx and mouflon. Around 40% of Serbia's 360 bird species are of European Conservation Concern.

Serbia faces air pollution around Belgrade and dumping of industrial waste into the Sava. Some remnants of the 1999 NATO bombings, such as factories outside Belgrade, are ecological hazards.

Serbian Cuisine

The ubiquitous snack is *burek,* a filo-pastry pie made with *sir* (cheese), *meso* (meat), *krompir* (potato) or occasionally *pečurke* (mushrooms). Eat without yoghurt if you like the 'blasphemer' tag.

Serbia is famous for grilled meats such as *ćevapčići* (rolled spicy mince), *pljeskavica* (spicy hamburger) and *ražnjići* (pork or veal shish kebabs). *Karađorđe's schnitzel* is a tubular roll of veal, stuffed with *kajmak* (curdled, salted raw milk).

Regional cuisines range from spicy Hungarian goulash in Vojvodina to Turkish kebabs in Novi Pazar, while the small central village of Ozrem takes extreme cuisine *do jaja* ('to the balls') at their annual Testicle Cooking Championships.

The further from major centres you are, the more baffled waiters will look at requests for vegetarian food. There's always vegetarian pizza, *srpska salata* (raw peppers, onions and tomatoes, seasoned with oil, vinegar and occasionally chilli), *šopska salata* (tomatoes, cucumber and onion, topped with grated white cheese) and the spicy *urnebes* (creamy paprika, cheese and garlic salad). Also try *gibanica* (cheese pie), *zeljanica* (cheese pie with spinach) or *pasulj prebranac* (cooked spiced beans).

Jelen and Lav are popular brands of *pivo* (beer). Many people distil *rakija* (brandy) from plums (*šljiva*), quince (*dunja*) or other fruits. A traditional Serbian dessert wine is *bermet* – try it in Vojvodina where recipes are passed down through generations. Viscous Turkish coffee is omnipresent, but espresso is staging a takeover bid in larger towns.

To breathe is to smoke in Serbia.

SURVIVAL GUIDE

Directory A–Z

Accommodation
More hostels are opening all the time; **Hostel World** (www.hostelworld.com) is a key website for hostel bookings.

Private rooms and apartments offer superb value and can be organised through tourist offices. 'Wild' camping is possible outside national parks.

Tax is not always automatically included in hotel rates. If you depend on internet access, check that wireless actually works. Where a room is 'nonsmoking', it does not mean that the room has not been smoked in – only that you are free not to smoke in it.

PRICE RANGES
In this chapter prices quoted are for rooms with a private bathroom, and unless otherwise stated include breakfast. The following price indicators apply (for a high-season double room):

€€€ more than €75 (7000DIN)

€€ €30 to €75 (3000DIN to 7000DIN)

€ less than €30 (3000DIN)

Activities
Serbia's national parks remain havens for hikers looking for quiet paths; Tara National Park has almost 20 marked trails ranging from a two to 18 kilometres. Climbers will enjoy the canyons of the Drina River.

It is possible to kayak and raft at Tara National Park along the Drina River; the **Drina-Tara Rafting Club** (www.raftingtara.com) and **Bodo** (www.tarabodo.com) organise rafting trips on the Tara.

The main ski resorts are Zlatibor and Kopaonik, both of which are also popular for summer hiking.

Several spots in Serbia have rich birdlife, including areas around Belgrade. Keen twitchers should contact the **League for Ornithological Action of Serbia** (www.ptica.org).

Business Hours
Banks 8am or 9am-5pm Mon-Fri, 8am-2pm Sat

Bars 8am-3am

Restaurants 8am-midnight or 1am

Shops 8am-6pm Mon-Fri, some to early afternoon Sat

Dangers & Annoyances
Travelling around Serbia is generally safe for travellers who exercise the usual caution. The exceptions can be border areas, particularly the southeast Kosovo border where Serb–Albanian tensions remain. Check the situation before attempting to cross overland, and think thrice about driving there in Serbian-plated cars.

Embassies & Consulates
A complete list of embassies and consulates in Serbia, as well as Serbian embassies around the world, is available at www.mfa.gov.rs/worldframe.htm. Countries represented in Belgrade (area code ☏011):

Albania (☏306 6642; embassy.belgrade@mfa.gov.al; Bul Kneza Aleksandra Karadjordjevica 25a)

Australia (☏330 3400; www.serbia.embassy.gov.au; 7th fl, Vladimira Popovica 38-40, New Belgrade)

Bosnia & Hercegovina (☏324 1095; bihambasada@sbb.rs; Krunska 9)

Bulgaria (☏361 3980; beostiv@eunet.rs; Birčaninova 26)

Canada (☏306 3000; bgrad@international.gc.ca; Kneza Miloša 75)

Croatia (☏367 9150; crobg@mvpei.hr; Kneza Miloša 62)

France (☏302 3500; ambafr_1@eunet.rs; Pariska 11)

Germany (☏306 4300; germany@sbb.rs; Kneza Miloša 74-6)

Hungary (☏244 0472; mission.blg@kum.hu; Krunska 72)

Netherlands (☎2023 900; bel@minbuza.nl; Simina 29)

UK (☎264 5055; ukembbg@eunet.rs; Resavska 46)

USA (☎361 9344; http://serbia.usembassy.gov; Kneza Miloša 50)

Food
In this chapter, the following price indicators apply (for a main meal):

€€€ more than €10 (1000DIN)

€€ €6 to €10 (600DIN to 1000DIN

€ less than €6 (600DIN)

Holidays
Public holidays in Serbia:

New Year 1 January

Orthodox Christmas 7 January

St Sava's Day 27 January

Statehood Day 15 February

Orthodox Good Friday April/May

Orthodox Easter Monday April/May

International Labour Days 1 and 2 May

Victory Day 9 May

St Vitus's Day 28 June

St Sava's Day, Victory Day and St Vitus's Day are working days revered as holidays.

Orthodox churches celebrate Easter between one and five weeks later than other churches.

Money
Serbia retains the dinar (DIN), though payment in euros for services and accommodation is commonplace.

ATMs are widespread and cards are accepted by established businesses. Exchange offices readily change hard currencies into dinars and back again; look for 'Menjačnica' signs. Exchange machines accept euros, US dollars and British pounds. Commission is charged for travellers cheques.

Post
Parcels should be taken unsealed to the main post office for inspection. You can receive mail, addressed poste restante, for a small charge.

Telephone
The country code is ☎381. Press the *i* button on public phones for dialling commands

in English. Calls to Europe/Australia/North America cost around 50/100/80DIN per minute. Long-distance calls can also be made from booths in post offices.

Phonecards can be bought in post offices and tobacco kiosks for 300DIN (local cards) and 600DIN (international cards). Halo Plus cards allow longer calls locally, in the former Yugoslav Republic region or internationally, depending on which category you buy. Calls to Europe/Australia/USA cost 13/40/40DIN per minute.

Mobile-phone SIM cards can be purchased at branches for around 200DIN, and recharge cards at supermarkets and kiosks. All mobile numbers in Serbia start with 06.

Tourist Information
Novi Sad and Belgrade have plenty of English material and friendly fonts of knowledge behind the desk.

In addition to the **National Tourism Organisation of Serbia** (www.serbia.travel), the **Tourist Organisation of Belgrade** (www.tob.co.rs) is a useful starting point.

Visas
Tourist visas for stays of less than 90 days aren't required by citizens of EU countries, most other European countries, Australia, New Zealand, Canada and the USA. **The Ministry of Foreign Affairs** (www.mfa.gov.rs/Visas/VisasR.htm) has full details.

Officially, all visitors must register with the police. Hotels and hostels will do this for you but if you're camping or staying in a private home, you are expected to register at the local police station within 24 hours of arrival. Unofficially? This is rarely enforced, but being unable to produce registration documents upon leaving Serbia could result in a fine.

Getting There & Away
Air
Belgrade's **Nikola Tesla Beograd Airport** (☎011 209 4444, 0648485402, 063255066; www.beg.aero) handles most international flights.

Aeroflot (SU; www.aeroflot.com)

Aerosvit (VV; www.aerosvit.com)

Air France (AF; www.airfrance.com)

Alitalia (AZ; www.alitalia.com)

Austrian Airlines (OS; www.austrian.com)

British Airways (BA; www.britishairways.com)

Czech Airlines (OK; www.czechairlines.com)

germanwings (4U; www.germanwings.com)

JAT (JU; www.jat.com)

Lufthansa (LH; www.lufthansa.com)

Montenegro Airlines (YM; www.montenegro airlines.com)

Norwegian Air Shuttle (DY; www.norwegian. no)

Olympic Airways (OA; www.olympicair.com)

Swiss International Air Lines (LX; www. swiss.com)

Tunisair (TU; www.tunisair.com)

Turkish Airlines (TK; www.thy.com)

Land

Serbia can be entered from any of its neighbours. Make sure you are registered with the police and have registration paper(s) with you when leaving (see Visas, p858 for details).

Because Serbia does not acknowledge crossing points into Kosovo as international border crossings, it may not be possible to enter Serbia from Kosovo unless you first entered Kosovo from Serbia. Check the situation with your embassy.

BUS

Bus services to Western Europe and Turkey are well developed; see p859 for details of services from Belgrade.

CAR & MOTORCYCLE

Drivers need International Driving Permits (available from your home motoring association). Vehicles need Green Card insurance, or insurance purchased at the border (from €80 a month).

Driving Serbian-plated cars into Kosovo is not advised, and often not permitted by rental agencies or insurers.

TRAIN

International rail connections leaving Serbia originate in Belgrade; see p859 for details. Heading north and west, most call at Novi Sad and Subotica. Heading east, they go via Niš.

Several trips from Serbia offer a nice slice of scenery, such as the route to Bar on the Montenegrin coast. For more information visit **Serbian Railways** (www.serbianrailways. com).

Getting Around

Bicycle

Bicycle paths are improving in larger cities like Belgrade and Novi Sad. Vojvodina is relatively flat, but main roads make for dull days. Mountainous regions such as Zlatibor offer mountain biking in summer months. Picturesque winding roads come with the downside of narrow shoulders.

Bus

Bus services are extensive, though outside major hubs sporadic connections may leave you in the lurch for a few hours. In southern Serbia particularly, you may have to double back to transport hubs.

Reservations are only worthwhile for international buses and during festivals; buses are rarely full and tickets can be purchased from the station before departure or on board.

Car & Motorcycle

The **Automobile & Motorcycle Association of Serbia** (Auto-Moto Savez Srbije; ☑011-333 1100; www.amss.org.rs; Ruzveltova 18, Belgrade) provides roadside assistance (☑987) and extensive information on its website. Drivers need International Driving Permits (available from your home motoring association).

Several car-hire companies have offices at Nikola Tesla Airport in Belgrade; see p859. Small-car hire typically costs €40 to €50 per day. Check where you are not able to take the car. Most hotels offer guests free parking. In Belgrade and other large towns you may have to purchase parking tickets from machines, kiosks or via SMS (in Serbian only).

Traffic police are everywhere and accidents are workaday. Buckle up, drive on the right, don't drink (the limit is 0.03%) and stick to speed limits (120km/h on motorways, 100km/h on dual carriageways, 80km/h on main roads and 60km/h in urban areas).

Train

Serbian Railways (☑011-361 4811; www.serbian railways.com) serves Novi Sad, Subotica and Niš from Belgrade. Enthusiasts will enjoy the Šargan 8 railway in Mokra Gora (p853).

Generally trains aren't as regular and reliable as buses, and can be murderously slow. Tickets can be booked at train stations or through travel agents.

Slovakia

Why Go?

Ancient castle ruins, traditional villages and mountainous national parks: visiting Slovakia is about experiencing a place where age-old folkways and nature still hold sway. In this compact country you can hike beside a waterfall-filled gorge one day and see nailless wooden churches in a village museum the next. The small capital, Bratislava, may not have the superlative sights of nearby Prague or Budapest, but it's abuzz with development, each new riverfront dining and entertainment complex vying to outdo the next. The rabbit-warren Old Town centre is well worth a day or two of cafe hopping.

Just make sure you also venture east. In the countryside, fortresses tower over cities and rivers, hiking trails cover the hills and well-preserved medieval towns nestle below rocky peaks. Pull up a plate of *bryndzove halušky* (sheep's-cheese dumplings) with a glass of *slivovica* (firewater-like plum brandy) and drink a toast for us – *nazdravie*!

Best Places to Eat

» Bratislavský Meštiansky Pivovar (p868)

» Kolkovna (p868)

» Salaš Krajinka (p878)

» Reštaurácia Bašta (p876)

Best Places to Stay

» Ginger Monkey Hostel (p887)

» Grand Hotel Kempinski (p885)

» Apartments Bratislava (p865)

» Hostel Blues (p865)

When To Go

Bratislava

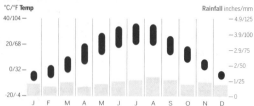

May & late September	July & August	January & February
May & late September Fewer crowds make shoulder-season travel a breeze.	**July & August** Festivals abound across the country, High Tatras hiking trails are all open.	**January & February** Peak ski season in the mountains, but many other sights are closed.

Fast Facts

» **Area** 49,035 sq km

» **Capital** Bratislava

» **Telephone area code** 02

» **Emergency** 112

Exchange Rates

Australia	A$1	€0.72
Canada	C$1	€0.71
Japan	¥100	€0.82
New Zealand	NZ$1	€0.54
UK	UK£1	€1.12
USA	US$1	€0.69

Set Your Budget

» **Budget hotel room** €30-60

» **Two-course meal** €15

» **Museum entrance** €3

» **Beer** €1.50

» **City transport ticket** €0.70

Resources

» **Kompas Maps** (www. kompas.sk)

» **Slovak Tourism Board** (www.slovakia.travel)

» **Slovakia Document Store** (www.panorama.sk)

» **What's On Slovakia** (www.whatsonslovakia. com)

Connections

Though few airlines fly into Slovakia itself, Bratislava is just 60km from the well-connected Vienna International Airport. By train from Bratislava, Budapest (three hours) and Prague (five hours) are easy to reach. Travelling further east, buses become your best bet. Connect to Zakopane, Poland (two hours) from Poprad, and to Uzhgorod, Ukraine (2½ hours) through Košice.

ITINERARIES

Three Days

Two nights in Bratislava is enough time to wander the Old Town streets, stop at a new river-park restaurant and see a museum or two. The following day is best spent on a castle excursion, either to Devín or Trenčín. Or, better yet, spend all three days hiking in the rocky High Tatra mountains, staying central in the Starý Smokovec resort town or in more off-beat Ždiar in the Belá Tatras.

One Week

After a day or two in the capital, venture east. Spend at least four nights in and around the Tatras so you can both hike to a mountain hut and take day trips to the must-see Spiš Castle ruins and medieval Levoča. You might also make time for a gentle raft ride in Pieniny. Then, for the last night or two, continue on to Bardejov to see a complete Renaissance town square, icon art and the neighbouring folk village and wooden churches.

Essential Food & Drink

» **Sheep's cheese, and more sheep's cheese** *Bryndza*, sharp, soft and spreadable; *oštiepok*, solid and ball-shaped; *korbačik*, 'little whips' or long, smoked strands; *žinčina*, a traditional sheep's-whey drink (like sour milk)

» **Schnitzel by any other name** *Vyprážaný bravčový rezeň*, breaded, fried pork steak; *Černohorský rezeň*, potato batter-coated and fried, with cheese; *gordon blu*, fried pork or chicken cutlet stuffed with ham and cheese

» **Assorted potato pancakes** Various sautéed meats, onions and peppers are stuffed *v zemiakovej placke* (in a potato pancake), like *diabolské soté* (devil's sautée), or they're topped with bryndza cheese and sour cream

» **Fruit firewater** Homemade or store-bought liquor, made from berries and pitted fruits, such as *borovička* (from juniper) and *slivovica* (from plums)

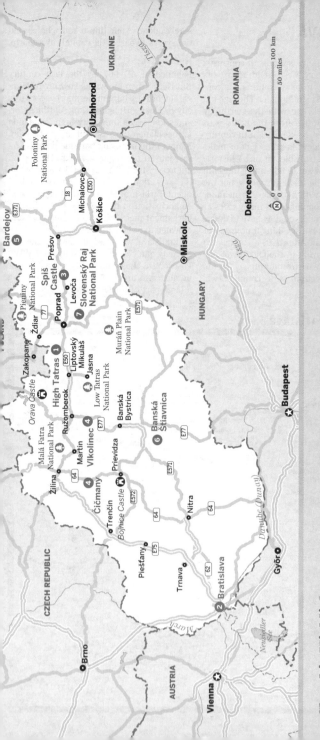

Slovakia Highlights

1 Hike between mountain huts in one of Europe's smallest alpine mountain ranges, the **High Tatras** (p880).

2 Linger over drinks at one of the myriad sidewalk and riverfront cafes in Old Town **Bratislava** (p862).

3 Wander among the 4 hectare–long ruins of **Spiš Castle** (p891), among the biggest in Europe

4 Experience the folk culture in traditional villages like **Vlkolínec** (p878) and **Čičmany** (p878)

5 Gaze on Renaissance splendour and ancient icons in **Bardejov** (p898)

6 Travel back in time at the Unesco-noted mining town of **Banská Štiavnica** (p873)

7 Climb wooden ladders past crashing waterfalls in the dramatic and challenging gorges of **Slovenský Raj National Park** (p892)

BRATISLAVA

☑ 02 / POP 428.800

Slovakia's capital city is a host of contrasts: the charming Starý Mesto (Old Town) sits across the river from a communist, concrete-block apartment jungle. The age-old castle shares a skyline with the startlingly UFO-like 'New Bridge' from the 1970s. Narrow pedestrian streets, pastel 18th-century buildings and sidewalk cafes galore make for a supremely strollable – if tiny – historic centre. You may want to pop into a museum or climb up to the castle for views, but the best thing to do with a day here is meander the alleyways, stopping in as many cafes as you dare. Be warned, you may have to dodge a German- or Italian-speaking tour group or two along the way. After that, if you haven't had enough to drink in the Old Town, one of the chichi new bar-restaurants at the up-and-coming riverfront-park complex will surely quench your thirst. Your choice; old or new, it's all part of the capital city's charm.

History

Founded in AD 907, by the 12th century Bratislava (then known as Poszony in Hungarian, or Pressburg in German) was a large city in greater Hungary. King Matthias Corvinus founded a university here, Academia Istropolitana, that is still evident today. Many of the imposing baroque palaces you see date to the reign of Austro-Hungarian empress Maria Theresa (1740–80), when the city flourished. Between the subsequent Turkish occupation of Budapest and emancipation in the mid-1800s, Hungarian parliament met locally and monarchs were crowned in St Martin's Cathedral.

'Bratislava' was officially born as the second city of a Czechoslovak state after WWI. Post WWII, the communists did a number on the town's architecture and spirit – razing a large part of the Old Town, including the

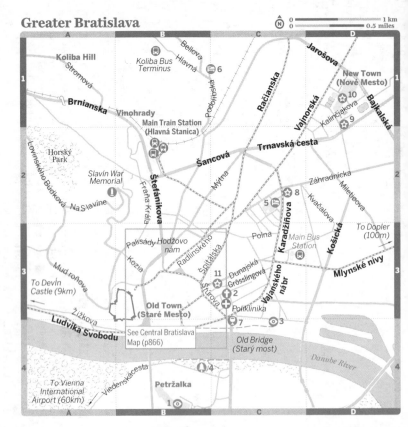

Greater Bratislava

0 — 1 km
0 — 0.5 miles

synagogue, to make way for a new highway. Today, the city is under construction once again. Look for a new (and not so cheap) hotel opening shortly on a corner near you.

◉ Sights

In addition to those mentioned here, there are a number of galleries and small museums scattered about the Old Town.

Bratislava Castle   CASTLE
(Map p866; www.snm.sk; grounds free, museum adult/child €2.50/1.25; ☺grounds 9am-9pm, museum 10am-6pm Tue-Sun) Dominating the west side of the Old Town on a hill above the Danube, the castle's look is often likened to that of an upturned table. The base of what you see today is a 1950s reconstruction; an 1811 fire left the fortress in ruins for more than a century. Renovations, begun years ago, will continue for years to come. Nevertheless, a white coat of paint has done much to improve the castle's appearance. Most of the buildings contain administrative offices. At the time of research, only a temporary-exhibit museum space was open; more will follow. In the meantime, the walls, lawns and ramparts still provide a great vantage point for city viewing.

Museum of Jewish Culture   MUSEUM
(Map p866; www.snm.sk; Židovská 17; adult/child €7/2; ☺11am-5pm Sun-Fri) The most moving of the three floors of exhibits here focuses

Greater Bratislava

◉ **Sights**
1	Aupark	B4
2	Blue Church	C3
3	Eurovea	C4
4	Sad Janka Krála Park	B4

🛏 **Sleeping**
5	Hotel-Penzión Arcus	C2
6	Penzión Zlatá Noha	C1
	Sheraton Bratislava	(see 3)

Eating
	Kolkovna	(see 3)

🍸 **Drinking**
7	Bratislava Pub Crawl	C4

🎭 **Entertainment**
8	Hlava XXII	C2
9	Ondrej Nepela Stadium	D1
10	SK Slovan Stadium	D1
11	State Puppet Theatre	C3

The most photographed sight in Bratislava is not a church or a castle, it's the bronze statue called the **Watcher** (Map p866) peeping out of an imaginary manhole below a 'Man at Work' sign at the intersection of Panská and Rybárska. He's not alone. There are several other quirky statues scattered around the old town. Look out for the **Frenchman** who leans on a park bench, the **Photographer** who stalks paparazzi-style around a corner, and the **Schöner Náci**, who tips his top hat on a main square. Look up to find other questionable characters, like a timepiece-toting monk and a rather naked imp, decorating building facades around the pedestrian centre.

on the large Jewish community and buildings lost during and after WWII. Black-and-white photos show the neighbourhood and synagogue before it was ploughed under.

St Martin's Cathedral   CHURCH
(Map p866; Dóm sv Martina; Rudnayovo nám; adult/child €2/free; ☺9-11.30am & 1-5pm Mon-Sat, 1.30-4.30pm Sun) A relatively modest interior belies the elaborate history of St Martin's Cathedral: 11 Austro-Hungarian monarchs (10 kings and one queen, Maria Theresa) were crowned in this 14th-century church. The busy motorway almost touching St Martin's follows the moat of the former city walls.

Hviezdoslavovo námestie   SQUARE
(Map p866) Embassies, restaurants and bars are the mainstay of the long, tree-lined plaza that anchors the southern end of the pedestrian zone. At the Hviezdoslavovo's east end, the ornate 1886 **Slovak National Theatre**, one of the city's opera houses, steals the show. Look also for 13th-century town ruins beneath the glass skylight just outside. The theatre is not open for tours, but ticket prices are not prohibitive. The nearby neo-baroque 1914 **Reduta Palace**, on Moštová, is under indefinite reconstruction.

Hlavné námestie   SQUARE
(Map p866) Cafe tables outline Hlavné nám, or Main Sq, the sight of numerous festival performances and a permanent crafts fair that grows exponentially at Christmas time. **Roland's Fountain**, at the square's heart, is

BRATISLAVA IN TWO DAYS

Start the morning by climbing up the ramparts of **Bratislava Castle**. The museum is under long-term construction, but from the grounds you have a view of both the barrel-tile roofs of Old Town and the concrete jungle, Petržalka. On your way back down, stop at the excellent **Museum of Jewish Culture**, and **St Martin's Cathedral**, then spend the afternoon strolling through the Old Town. Later you could feel the beat at **Aligator Rock Pub** or dine waterfront at a restaurant like **Kolkovna** in the Eurovea river complex.

Day two, trip out to **Devín Castle** to see evocative buildings and ruins from the 9th to the 18th centuries. This nearby fortress, across the river from Austria, is much more impressive than Bratislava's own.

thought to have been built in 1572 as a fire hydrant of sorts. Flanking the northeast side of the square is the 1421 **Old Town Hall**; it and the city museum contained within are under indefinite reconstruction. You'll often find a musician in traditional costume playing a *fujira* (2m-long flute) on the steps of the **Jesuit Church**.

Eurovea   NEIGHBOURHOOD
(Map p862; Pribinova) Sitting beneath a cafe umbrella or strolling along the grassy waterfront became the things to do after the Eurovea complex opened in 2010. Riverfront restaurants are the main attraction, but there's also a full shopping mall hidden within. The plaza adjoining the new Slovak National Theatre (New SND) often hosts concerts.

Apponyi Palace   MUSEUM
(Map p866; www.muzeum.bratislava.sk; Radničná 1; adult/child €6/2; ⊙10am-6pm Tue-Sun) Explore the area's winemaking heritage in the cellar exhibits of a restored 1761 palace. Upstairs the museum rooms are outfitted with period furnishings. Both sections have excellent, interactive English-language audio.

Slovak National Gallery   MUSEUM
(Map p866; Slovenská Národná Galéria; www.sng. sk; Rázusovo nábr 2; adult/child €3.50/2; ⊙10am-5pm Tue-Sun) A Stalinist modern building and an 18th-century palace make interesting co-hosts for the Slovak National Gallery. The nation's eclectic art collection contained here ranges from Gothic to graphic design.

New Bridge   TOWER
(Nový most; Map p866; www.u-f-o.sk; Viedenská cesta; observation deck adult/child €8/5; ⊙10am-11pm) Colloquially called the UFO (pronounced ew-fo) bridge, this modernist marvel from 1972 has a viewing platform, an overhyped nightclub and a restaurant with out-of-this-world prices.

Slovak National Museum   MUSEUM
(Map p866; www.snm.sk; Vajanského nábr 2; adult/child €3.50/1.50; ⊙9am-5pm Tue-Sun) Changing exhibits on the lower floors, natural history on top.

Primate's Palace   MUSEUM
(Map p866; adult/child €2/1; ⊙10am-5pm Tue-Sun) Napoleon and Austrian emperor Franz I signed the Treaty of Pressburg on 26 December 1805 here in the glittery Hall of Mirrors.

🏃 Activities

From April through September, **Slovak Shipping & Ports** (Map p866; ✆5293 2226; www.lod. sk; Fajnorovo nábr 2) runs 45-minute Bratislava return boat trips (adult/child €4/2.50) on the Danube. Its Devín sightseeing cruise (adult/child return €5.50/3.50) plies the waters to the castle, stops for one to two hours and returns to Bratislava in 30 minutes.

You can rent bikes from **Bratislava Sightseeing** (Map p866; ✆0907683112; www. bratislavasightseeing.com; Fajnorovo nábr; per hr/day €4/18; ⊙10am-6pm mid-May-mid-Sep), located in a children's playground along the waterfront. Bike tours available, too.

🧭 Tours

FREE **Be Free Tours**   WALKING TOUR
(Map p866; www.befreetours.com; Hviezdoslavovo nám; tour free; ⊙11am & 4pm Tue-Sat, 4pm Sun & Mon) Lively, two-hour-plus English tour of the Old Town, including stories and legends, leave from in front of the historic Slovak National Theatre (Historic SND).

Bratislava Culture & Information Centre   WALKING TOUR
(Map p866; ✆5443 4059; www.bkis.sk; Klobučnívcka 2; tour €14; ⊙2pm Apr-Oct, by appointment Nov-Mar) Official tourist office–run, one-hour walking tour of the Old Town in

DEVÍN CASTLE

To see a more historically complete fortress, outfitted as in olden days, take the bus beneath the New Bridge (Nový Most) to **Devín Castle** (p872), 8km outside the city.

English or German. Segway tours also available by reservation.

Oldtimer
MOTORISED TOUR

(Prešporáčik; ☑0903302817; www.tour4u.sk; Hlavné nám; adult/child from €8/4; ☺9am-7pm May-Oct, by appointment Nov-Mar) Old-fashioned cars take you around town or up to the castle; great for those who can't climb hills. Thirty- to 60-minute tours, with recorded audio in English and German.

Bratislava Pub Crawl
DRINKING TOUR

(www.befreetours.sk; Rock OK, Šafárikovo nám 4; ticket €13; ☺9.30pm Tue-Sat) Visit four different bars and clubs in one night with this backpacker-oriented tour; drink specials included.

✯ Festivals & Events

Cultural Summer Festival (www.bkis.sk) A smorgasbord of plays and performances comes to the streets and venues around town June through September.

Bratislava Jazz Days (www.bjd.sk) World-class jazz takes centre stage three days in October.

Christmas Market From 26 November, Hlavné nám fills with food and drink, crafts for sale and staged performances.

🛏 Sleeping

In recent years it's seemed as if a newer and pricier top-end hotel has opened every few minutes, including an exorbitant Kempinski. For a full accommodation listing, see www.bkis.sk. Getting a short-term rental flat in the old town (€65 to €120 per night) is a great way to stay super central without paying hotel prices; plus you can self cater. Family-run and friendly, the modern units of **Apartments Bratislava** (www.apartments bratislava.sk) are our top choice. **Bratislava Apartments** (www.bratislava-apartments.com) and **Bratislava Hotels** (www.bratislavahotels. com) are other options.

Unless noted, hostels listed have kitchen, laundry and sheets, beer and wine available, and no lockouts.

Penzión Virgo
PENSION €€

(Map p866; ☑3300 6262; www.penzionvirgo.sk; Panenská 14; s/d €65/78; ☺@) Exterior-access rooms are arranged around a courtyard; each one feels light and airy despite dark-wood floors and baroque-accent wallpaper. Sip an espresso with the breakfast buffet (€5), or cook for yourself if you opt for an apartment (€100).

Hotel Avance
HOTEL €€

(Map p866; ☑5920 8400; www.hotelavance.sk; Medená 9; r incl breakfast €99-119; P✳@☺) Thick carpeting and cushy duvets add to the comfort factor at this contemporary gem. Design-driven details include floating nightstands with cool underlighting and glass-tile mosaics in sleek bathrooms.

Sheraton Bratislava
HOTEL €€€

(Map p862; ☑3535 0000; http://www.sheraton bratislava.com; Eurovea, Pribinova 12; r €150-240, P✳@☲) One of Bratislava's newer properties, the upscale Sheraton gets points for a prime, Eurovea riverfront location. Minuses include overpriced parking and wi-fi. Watch for weekend deals.

TOP CHOICE
Hostel Blues
HOSTEL €

(Map p866; ☑0905204020; www.hostel blues.sk; Špitálska 2; dm €15-20, d €52-63; ☺@☺) Friendly, professional staff not only help you plan your days, they offer free city sightsee-

---

DON'T MISS

THE SMALLER SIGHTS

» **Blue Church** (Modrý kostol; Map p862; Bezručova 2; admission free; ☺dawn-dusk) Every surface of the 1911 Church of St Elizabeth, more commonly known as the Blue Church, is an art nouveau fantasy dressed in cool sky-blue and deeper royal blue.

» **Michael's Gate & Tower** (Map p866; Michalská brána & veža; www.muz eum.bratislava.sk; Michalská 24; adult/ child €2/1; ☺10am-6pm Tue-Sun) Climb past the five small storeys of medieval weaponry in the town's only remaining gate to a superior Old Town view from the top.

» **Museum of Clocks** (Map p866; www.muzeum.bratislava.sk; Židovská 1; adult/child €2/1; ☺10am-5pm Tue-Sun) Random old clocks, but they're contained in an interestingly narrow building.

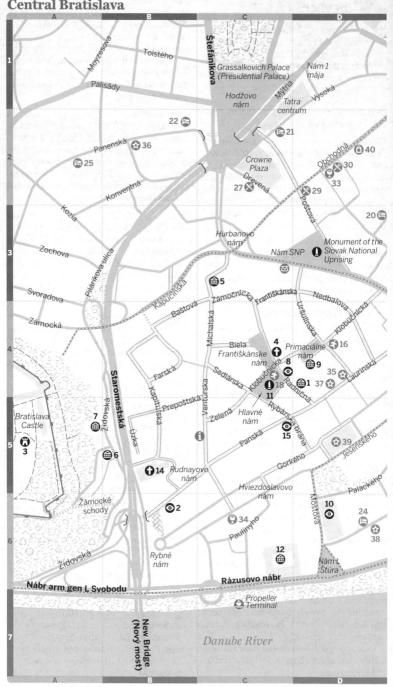

SLOVAKIA BRATISLAVA

A

B

C

D

1

Moyzesova

Tolstého

Štefánikova

Grassalkovich Palace
(Presidential Palace)

Nám 1
mája

Palisády

Hodžovo
nám

Mýtna

Vysoká

Tatra
centrum

22 🖾

🟢 36

Panenská

🖾 25

Konventná

Crowne
Plaza

Drevená

27

🖾 21

Obchodná

🔒 40

🟠 30

🖾 33

🟠 29

Poštová

20 🖾

Kozia

Zochova

Pilárikova ulica

Hurbanovo
nám

Nám SNP

Monument of the
Slovak National
Uprising

Svoradova

Kapucínska

Baštová

Zámočnícka

Františkánska

🏛 5

Nedbalova

Klobučnícka

Zámocká

Michalská

Biela
Františkánske
nám

4 ⛪

Primaciálne
nám

Ursulínska

🏛 16

35

Farská

Kapitulská

Sedlárska

8 ⊙

🏛 9

🏛 1

37 🟢

Laurinská

Bratislava
Castle

7
🏛

Židovská

Úzka

Prepoštská

Venturska

Zelená

18 🟠

🟠 11

Radničná

🟥 5
3

🏛 6

14 ⛪

Rudnayovo
nám

Hlavné
nám

Rybárska brána

🟢 39

Jesenského

Panská

15 🟠

Zámocké
schody

⊙ 2

Hviezdoslavovo
nám

Gorkého

Mostová

Palackého

10 ⊙

24 🖾

38 🟢

Židovská

Rybné
nám

🟢 34

Paulinyho

12 🏛

Nám L
Štúra

Nábr arm gen L Svobodu

Rázusovo nábr

Propeller
Terminal

New Bridge
(Nový most)

Danube River

7

ing tours. The coffeehouse-like communal space, which occasionally hosts concerts, adds to the urban apartment-living feel here. Choose from five- to 10-bed, single-sex or mixed dorms, or those with double bunk beds(!). Private rooms have their own bathrooms.

Tulip House Hotel   BOUTIQUE HOTEL €€€
(Map p866; ☎3217 1819; www.tuliphouse.sk; Štúrova 10; ste incl breakfast €150-300; P❄✳@☎) Exquisite art nouveau accents are the hallmark of this 1903 property. The decor – chocolate-brown suede headboards contrasting with plush white carpeting – is all modern elegance. Enjoy epicurean meals at pedestrian prices in the small cafe.

Hotel-Penzión Arcus   PENSION €€
(Map p862; ☎5557 2522; www.hotelarcus.sk; Moskovská 5; s/d incl breakfast €65/100; ❄☎) Because this family-run place was once an apartment building, the 13 rooms are quite varied (some with balcony, some with courtyard views). Flowery synthetic linens seem a bit outdated but bathrooms are new and sparkly white.

Downtown Backpackers   HOSTEL €
(☎5464 1191; www.backpackers.sk; Panenská 31; dm €13-20, d €45-60; ❄@☎) The first hostel in Bratislava, Backpackers is still a boozy (you enter through a bar) bohemian classic. Red-brick walls and tapestries add character, as does the fact that you have to walk through some dorm rooms to get to others.

Austria Trend   HOTEL €€
(Map p866; ☎5277 5817; www.austria-trend.sk; Vysoká 2a; r €120-150; P✳@) Newer business hotel on the edge of the Old Town.

A1 Hostel   HOSTEL €
(Map p866; ☎0944280288; http://a1hostelbratis lava.com/; Heydukova 1; dm/d €15/40; ❄☎) Little more than a super-clean, three-room flat, A1 offers quiet and camaraderie – but no kitchen.

✖ Eating

The pedestrian centre is chock-a-block with dining options priced for expense accounts and foreigners. If you want to splash out (from €20 a plate), choose a fancy-sounding foreign name (Le Monde, UpsideDown, Steakhouse etc) and go for it. What's harder to find is decent Slovak food; stick to our suggestions in the Old Town. Reasonable eateries, both sit-down and takeaway, line Obchodná street near the university. Note

BRATISLAVA EATING

Central Bratislava

that most restaurants offer lunch set menus, which can be a real steal.

TOP CHOICE **Kolkovna** CZECH & SLOVAK €€
(Map p862; ☎2091 5280; Eurovea, Pribinova 8; mains €7-12; ⊗11am-midnight) Topping the list of no less than a dozen restaurants and cafes at the riverfront Eurovea complex, Kolkovna has hearty portions and reasonable prices. Braised and roast meats are the mainstay, but there is lighter fare to go with your tank-imported draft Pilsner beer (no bottles, no preservatives). Book ahead for an outdoor table on weekend evenings.

TOP CHOICE **Bratislavský Meštiansky Pivovar** SLOVAK €€-€€€
(Map p866; ☎0944512265; Drevená 8; mains €6-12; ⊗11am-midnight Sun-Thu, until 1am Sat & Sun) Not only does this stylish microbrewery serve Bratislava's freshest beer, it offers some of the city's most creative Slovak cooking. Both after work and at weekends, crowds of young professionals fill in beneath the vaulted ceilings and stylised Old Town artwork. Reservations are never a bad idea.

U Remeselníka SLOVAK €-€€
(Map p866; Obchodná 64; mains €5-11) Small and folksy, this cellar cafe associated with the traditional ÚTuv craft store upstairs is a great place to try a trio of *halušky* (small dumplings) – with sheep's cheese and bacon, with kolbasa, and with cabbage.

Slovak Pub SLOVAK €-€€
(Map p866; Obchodná 62; mains €5-10; ⊗10am-midnight Mon-Thu, 10am-1am Fri & Sat, noon-midnight Sun) No denying that Slovak Pub, with its themed-rooms, is firmly on the tourist trail. But it does serve every traditional national dish you can think of, and the owners use cheese from their biofarm.

Divný Janko SLOVAK €-€€
(Jozefská 2; mains €4-7) A locally popular little hang-out: get your fill of tasty fried pork and chicken steaks – stuffed with pineapple,

sausage, you name it... Oh, and salads are available, too.

Činska Panda CHINESE €-€€
(Map p866; Vysoká 39; mains €5-8) And now for something completely different – an authentic and flavourful Chinese-run restaurant with solid vegetarian options. Great set lunch menus (€4).

Govinda VEGETARIAN €
(Map p866; Obchodná 30; sandwiches & meals €2.50-4; ⊗11am-8pm Mon-Fri, 11.30am-5pm Sat) Indian-inspired vegetarian meals and takeaway.

U Jakubu SLOVAK €
(Map p866; Nám SNP 24; mains €2-5; ⊗8am-6pm Mon-Fri) Self-service cafeteria with Slovak faves.

Tesco SUPERMARKET
(Map p866; Kamenné nám 1; ⊗8am-9pm Mon-Fri, 9am-7pm Sat & Sun) Humongous grocery store below ground level.

🍷 Drinking

From mid-April to October, sidewalk cafe tables sprout up in every corner of pedestrian Old Town. Any one will do for a cocktail or a coffee (no dining required). For example, several places – look for names like Verne, Bar 17 and Slang Pub – are strung out along Hviezdoslavovo. But lately *the* place to drink is riverfront at one of the many bar-restaurant-cafes in the Eurovea complex. Slovak Pub and Bratislavský Meštiansky Pivovar are also good imbibing options, and music bars can be quiet enough for a casual sip on weekdays. See p865 for a pub-crawl tour.

TOP CHOICE **Sky Bar** BAR
(Map p866; ☎5441 1244; Hviezdoslavovo nám 7) You'd never guess from the ground floor what an amazing view this seventh-storey, upscale, Old Town bar has. It's a don't-miss. Just reserve ahead for a table, or you'll be standing in tight quarters.

Kréma Gurmánov Bratislavy BAR
(Map p866; Obchodná 52) A dark cellar bar called KGB could be just the place for a clandestine tryst.

☆ Entertainment

Check **Slovak Spectator** (www.slovakspectator.com), the **Bratislava Culture & Information Centre** (www.bkis.sk) and **Kam do Mesta** (www.kamdomesta.sk) for the latest events.

BRATISLAVA FOR CHILDREN

Little ones are rarely seen at restaurants, few of which have children's menus or playgrounds. Some lodgings do provide cribs or cots. Places for kid-focused fun:

» **Bibiana** (Map p866; www.bibiana.sk; Panská 41; admission free; ⊗10am-6pm Tue-Sun) This children's library/art gallery also sponsors frequent kid-focused performances.

» **Sad Janka Krála Park** (Map p862; Viedenská cesta, Petržalka; admission free; ⊗24hr) Across the Danube from the old town, the 22-hectare waterfront park and playgrounds have room for roaming.

Nightclubs & Live Music
Cover charges for Bratislava music bars and clubs are usually quite low (free to €5). On weekends, many upscale restaurants turn into discos after 10pm; listen for the beat.

Nu Spirit BAR
(Map p866; Medená 16; ⊗10am-4am Mon-Fri, 5pm-4am Sat & Sun) Funky DJs, Brazilian rhythms, live blues drummers... this hip underground club dabbles in all the soulful sounds.

Aligator Rock Pub CLUB
(Map p866; Laurinská 7; ⊗5pm-3am Mon-Sat) One of the few places that's packed even on weeknights. Live performances at this cellar club run the gamut from Pink Floyd covers to harder-core rock.

Café Štúdio Club BAR
(Map p866; cnr Laurinská & Radničná; ⊗10am-1am Mon-Wed, to 3am Thu & Fri, 4pm-3am Sat) Bop to the oldies, or chill out to jazz; weekends there's always live music of some sort.

Apollon Club GAY & LESBIAN
(Map p866; www.apollon-gay-club.sk; Panenská 24; ⊗6pm-3am Mon-Thu, 8pm-5am Fri & Sat, 8pm-1am Sun) THE gay disco in town has two bars and three stages. Monday is karaoke; Sunday is an underwear party.

The following are outside of the centre:

Dopler CLUB
(Map p862; Prievozská 18; ⊗8pm-5am Fri & Sat) The city's biggest DJ-dance club; college-age and younger crowd.

LOCAL KNOWLEDGE

PETER LIPA: SLOVAK JAZZ GREAT

For more than 30 years singer, songwriter, musician and producer Peter Lipa has been a star on the Slovak jazz scene. He performs internationally and is a founder of the Bratislava Jazz Days festival.

What is the state of live jazz in Bratislava today?

Unfortunately, though popular, jazz still struggles to found adequate standing in our society. Other kinds of 'stage art' have state-run organizations that support performances; jazz promotion is up to the skills of people who are doing it.

What are your favourite clubs and venues?

Club Hlava XXII has opened, traditional jazz is played in Café Štúdio Club, and sometimes there are good concerts in Aligator [Rock Pub] and Nu Spirit bar.

Who are some of the voices to listen for?

Slovak Jazz Society, a private association, organises the 'New faces of Slovak Jazz' show at the beginning of December. New talents are discovered there each year. I'd recommend these experienced musicians from the younger generation: Juraj Baros, Rado Tariska, Ondrej Krajnak and Klaudius Kovac.

Hlava XXII   CLUB
(Map p862; Bazová 9; ☺3pm-3am Tue-Sat) Jam sessions, blues and world beat – live.

Sport

Bratislava's hallowed ice-hockey team, HC Slovan, plays at the **Ondrej Nepela Stadium** (Map p862; Odbojárov 9), which underwent a €40 million upgrade for the 2011 ice hockey world championship. The hometown football team plays at its namesake **SK Slovan Stadium** (Map p862; Tegelhoffa 4) nearby. Buy tickets for both online at www.ticketportal.sk.

Performing Arts

Folk dance and music ensembles, like **Sľuk** (www.sluk.sk) and **Lúčnica** (www.lucnica.sk), perform at various venues around town.

Slovak National Theatre   THEATRE
(Slovenské Národné Divadlo, SND; www.snd.sk) The national theatre company stages quality operas (Slavic and international), ballets and dramas in two venues. The gilt decorations of the landmark **Historic SND** (Map p866; Hviezdoslavovo nám; booking office cnr Jesenského & Komenského; ☺8am-5.30pm Mon-Fri, 9am-1pm Sat) is a show worth seeing in itself. The modern **New SND** (Map p862; Pribinova 17; ☺9am-5pm Mon- Fri) also contains a cafe and theatre offices.

Slovak Philharmonic   THEATRE
(www.filharmonia.sk) At the time of research the Philharmonic's home, Reduta Palace, was under indefinite reconstruction. Until finished, the state orchestra performs at the SND theatres.

 Shopping

There are several crystal, craft and jewellery stores, as well as souvenir booths, in and around Hlavné nám. Artisan galleries tend to inhabit the small alleyways of Old Town streets.

Úľuv   HANDICRAFTS
(Map p866; www.uluv.sk; Obchodná 64) For serious folk-art shopping head to the main outlet of Úľuv, the national handicraft cooperative, where there are two stores and a courtyard filled with artisans' studios.

 Information

Emergency
Emergency (☎112)
Main police station (☎159; Gunduličova 10)

Internet Access
Many local cafes have wireless internet access; Hlavné and Hviezdoslavovo squares are free wi-fi zones.

Klar-i-net (Klariská 4; per 30min €2; ☺10am-10pm Mon-Fri, 3-10pm Sat & Sun; ☻) Numerous well-equipped terminals; office services and beverages available.

Media
Slovak Spectator (www.slovakspectator.sk) English-language weekly newspaper with current affairs and event listings.

Medical Services
Poliklinika Ruzinov (☎4823 4113; Ružinovská 10) Hospital with emergency services and a 24-hour pharmacy.

WORTH THE DISCOUNT?

Bratislava City Card (1/2/3 days €10/12/15), sold at the Bratislava Culture & Information Centre, covers public transport and provides discounted museum admission. But unless you're going to take a tour or plan to see every single sight, it might not be worth it. Admission prices are cheap and the Old Town is small enough to walk.

Money

Bratislava has numerous banks and ATMs in the Old Town, with several branches on Poštova. There are also ATMs and exchange booths in the train and bus stations, and at the airport.

Tatra Banka (Dunajská 4) Staff speak excellent English.

Post

Main post office (Nám SNP 34-35)

Tourist Information

Bratislava Culture & Information Centre (BKIS; ☏16 186; www.bkis.sk; Klobučnícka 2; ⊙9am-6pm Mon-Fri, 9am-3pm Sat, 10am-3pm Sun) Official tourist office staff hoard brochures behind the counter, and seem uninterested, but keep pressing and they'll assist – a little. Small Bratislava guide available.

Bratislava Tourist Service (BTS; ☏2070 7501; www.bratislava-info.sk; Ventúrska 9; ⊙10am-8pm) A tiny, tiny place, but the young staff are obliging. Maps and knick-knacks for sale.

Websites

Bratislava City Guide (www.bratislava-city.sk) City info from the government.

Visit Bratislava (http://visit.bratislava.sk) Comprehensive city tourist board site.

Getting There & Away

Bratislava is the main hub for trains, buses and the few planes that head in and out of the country.

Air

For international airlines serving Bratislava, see p905. Keep in mind that Vienna's much busier international airport is only 60km west.

Airport Bratislava (BTS; www.airport bratislava.sk; Ivanská cesta) New terminal opened in 2010, 9km northeast of centre. Flights connect to Prague, Warsaw, UK cities and more.

Danube Wings (V5; www.danubewings.eu) The only airline with domestic service, has weekday, early-morning and evening flights to Košice.

Boat

From April through October, plying the Danube is a cruisey way to get from Bratislava to Vienna or Budapest.

Slovak Shipping & Ports (☏5293 2226; www.lod.sk; Hydrofoil Terminal, Fajnorova nábr 2) Several weekly hydrofoils to Vienna (€16 one way, 1¾ hours) and Budapest (€79 one way, four hours).

Twin City Liner (☏0903610716; www.twincity liner.com; Propeller Terminal, Rázusovo nábr) Up to four boats a day to Vienna (€17 to €28 one way, 1½ hours).

Bus

Direct destinations include cities throughout Slovakia and Europe, but the train is usually comparably priced and more convenient. For schedules, see http://cp.atlas.sk. The **Main Bus Station** (Autobusová stanica, AS; Mlynské Nivy) is 1.5km east of the old town; locals call it 'Mlynské Nivy' (the street name).

Eurobus (☏0972250305; www.eurobus.sk) Runs some international routes.

Eurolines (☏5556 7349; www.slovaklines.sk) Contact for most international buses.

Slovenská autobusová doprava (SAD; www.sad.sk) National bus company.

Train

Rail is the main way to get around Slovakia and to neighbouring countries. Intercity and Eurocity (IC/EC) trains, listed here, are the quickest. Note that *Rýclík* (R), or 'Fast' trains take longer, but run more frequently and cost less. *Osobný* (Ob)

INTERNATIONAL BUSES FROM BRATISLAVA

DESTINATION	COST (€)	DURATION (HR)	FREQUENCY (DAILY)
Vienna	8	1¼	12
Prague	16	4¼	4
Budapest	14	2½-4	8
London	81	23	1

DESTINATION	COST (€)	DURATION (HR)	FREQUENCY (DAILY)
Vienna	10	1	hourly
Prague	24	4¼	6
Budapest	14	2¾	5
Warsaw	58	10½	1
Moscow	110	37	1

trains are the milk runs. For schedules see www.cp.atlas.sk.

Main Train Station (Hlavná stanica; www.slovakrail.sk; Predštanicné nám)

ⓘ Getting Around

To/From the Airport

CITY BUS No 61 links Bratislava airport with the main train station (20 minutes).

SHUTTLE BUS A shuttle runs from the Bratislava airport to Mlynské Nivy bus station (€1) hourly weekdays from 9am to 6.50pm.

TAXI Standing taxis (over)charge about €20 to town; ask the price before you get in.

VIENNA BUS A regular bus (€9) connects Vienna airport with the Bratislava's main bus station.

Car

Numerous international car-hire companies like Hertz and Sixt have offices at the airport. Good smaller agencies include:

Advantage Car Rental (✆6241 0510; www.acr.sk) Reasonable prices include Bratislava-wide delivery.

Buchbinder (✆4363 7821; www.buchbinder.sk) In-town pick-up possible for a fee.

Car Rental 24 (✆4363 8335; www.carrental24.sk)

Public Transport

Bratislava has an extensive tram, bus and trolley-bus network; though the Old Town is small, so you won't often need it. **Dopravný Podnik Bratislava** (DPB; www.dpb.sk; Hodžovo nám; ⊙6am-7pm Mon-Fri) is the public transport company; you'll find a route map online. The office is in the underground passage beneath Hodžovo nám.

Tickets cost €0.25/0.70/1.40 for 10/60/90 minutes. Buy at newsstands and validate on board (or risk a legally enforceable €50 fine). Passes cost €3.50/6.50/8/12 for one/two/three/seven days; buy at the DPB office, validate on board.

Important lines:

Tram 13 Main Train Station to Nám L Štúra

Bus 93 Main Train Station to Hodžovo nám

Bus 206 Main Bus Station to Hodžovo nám

Bus 310 Main Bus Station to Main Train Station

Taxi

Standing cabs compulsively overcharge foreigners; an around-town trip should not cost more than €10. To save, ask someone to help you order a taxi (not all operators speak English).

AA Euro Taxi (✆16 022)

Hello Taxi (✆16 321)

Trend Taxi (✆16 302)

AROUND BRATISLAVA

One of the best sights in Bratislava is actually 9km west of the city centre. **Devín Castle** (www.muzeum.bratislava.sk; Muranská; adult/child €3/1.50; ⊙10am-5pm Tue-Fri, to 6pm Sat & Sun) was once the military plaything of 9th-century warlord Prince Ratislav. The castle

DOMESTIC TRAINS FROM BRATISLAVA

DESTINATION	COST (€)	DURATION (HR)	FREQUENCY (DAILY)
Trenčín	9	1½	3
Žilina	11	2½	4
Poprad	16	4	4
Košice	19	5½	4

PIEŠŤANY

Thermal waters bubble under much of this country, but it's Slovakia's premier spa site, **Piešťany** (www.spa-piestany.sk) that attracts most visitors. On **Kúpeľne ostrov** (Spa Island) you can swim in thermal pools, breathe seaside-like air in a salt cave and be wrapped naked in hot mud. Many of the 19th-century buildings sport a new coat of Maria-Theresa-yellow paint, others are more modern. Reserve online for a stay, or head to the *kasa* (cashier) at **Napoleon 1** (☑033-775 2198; ☑7.30am-7pm) to book a day service. **Eva Pools** (adult/child €3/2; ☑11am-5pm) and **Balnea Esplanade Hotel** (per day adult/child €15/10, 3hr €10/7; ☑8am-10pm) have public swimming. From Bratislava (87km) the train takes 1¼ hours (€4, 12 daily) and you can continue on the same route to Trenčín (€2, 45 minutes).

withstood the Turks but then was blown up in 1809 by the French. Peer at older bits that have been unearthed and tour a reconstructed palace museum. Bus 29 links Devín with Bratislava's Nový Most (New Bridge) stop, under the bridge. Austria is just across the river.

SOUTHERN SLOVAKIA

Southern Slovakia was the mining centre for greater Hungary from the 14th to the 18th centuries, but its fortunes have long since dried up. Much of the region is industrially oriented today, but the ancient mining town of Banská Štiavnica is a gem.

Banská Štiavnica

☑045 / POP 10,700

Like a fossil preserved in amber, Banská Štiavnica is a medieval wonder frozen in time. In its 16th-century heyday the town was an architectural showcase. As the minerals ran out and the mines closed, progress stopped, leaving buildings wonderfully untouched. Walking up and down among the steeply terraced hillsides now you'll see many of the same Old Town burghers' houses, churches, alleys and stairways that you would have seen then. Unesco recognised the town way back in 1972. At a mere fraction of its peak population today, the town is primarily a holiday destination, with numerous mining-related museums and an old and new castle facing each other across the steep valley.

From the train station it's a 2km climb uphill through the factories and housing blocks to Nám sv Trojice, the main, Old Town square. Buses stop 500m closer, at a crossroads, Križovatka.

◉ Sights

Wandering the steep streets gazing at the detailed architectural designs is the main attraction. Buildings aren't all in pristine condition, but the overall effect is still arresting. The numerous affiliates of the **Slovak Mining Museum** (www.muzeumbs.sk) in town include:

Open-air Mining Museum　MUSEUM
(JK Hella 12; adult/child €5/2.50; ☑8am-4pm Tue-Sun by tour) Take a trip down into a former working mine, 2km west of the centre.

Old Castle　MUSEUM
(Starozámocká 1; adult/child €3/1.50; ☑8am-4pm Tue-Sun by tour) Town history exhibits in a 16th-century stronghold.

New Castle　CASTLE
(Novozámocká 1; adult/child €3/1.50; ☑8am-4pm Tue-Sun by tour) Constructed only five years after the Old Castle; it has exhibits on the historical struggle against Turkish invasion.

⊨ Sleeping & Eating

Penzión Kachelman　PENSION €€
(☑6922 319; www.kachelman.sk; Kammerhofská 18; s/d incl breakfast €43/70; ☑) Several large Renaissance buildings combine to form a fine inn and restaurant with rustic touches. The long and varied Slovak menu (mains €5 to €12), including grilled specialties, is worth trying. It's close to the bus stop, below the Old Town centre.

Hostel 6　HOSTEL €
(☑0905106706; www.hostel6.sk; Andreja Slackovica 6; dm/d €14/30; ☑@) A hospitable little backpackers hostel with thoroughly modern amenities inside an old building. Choose from a private double, or five- or six-bed dorms. Great balcony views, full kitchen and laundry.

Penzión Príjemný Oddych　PENSION €
(☑6921 301; www.prijemnyoddych.sk; Starozámocká 3; r €30-36) Yellow walls and framed

folk embroidery keep this pension up near the Old Castle feeling light and, indeed, *prijemný* (pleasing). Small on-site restaurant, playground and sauna.

Mešianka CAFE €

(Andreja Kmeťa 2; pizzas €3-6) A place that's part pastry cafe, part pizzeria and part beer garden? May seem an odd combination, but the wood-fired pies are quite good.

ℹ Information

City Tourist Information Office (☏6949 653; www.banskastiavnica.sk; Nám sv Trojice 3; ☺8am-4pm) Semiprecious stones and minerals for sale in addition to info; beneath a branch of the mining museum. Two internet terminals (per hour €1).

ℹ Getting There & Away

Banská Štiavnica is not the easiest place to get to. Only one direct bus daily departs from Bratislava (€8, 3½ hours), at 1pm. Otherwise, all bus and train arrivals require a change in Zvolen or Banská Bystrica. Check schedules at http://cp.atlas.sk.

WEST SLOVAKIA

Snaking along the Small Carpathians on the main route northeast of Bratislava, watch for hilltop castle ruins high above the Váh River. Trenčín's magnificent reconstructed castle is one of the most impressive along this once heavily fortified stretch.

Trenčín

☏032 / POP 60,000

Looming high above the 18th- and 19th-century buildings of the Old Town, Trenčín's mighty castle has all the dark foreboding you'd want from a medieval fortress. Today's form dates from around the 15th century, but the city is much older than that. Roman legionnaires fancied the site and stationed here (they called it Laugaricio) in the 2nd century AD. You can read the inscription to prove it. Afterwards, enjoy the sidewalk cafes and lively nightlife fuelled by the town's university population. The entire centre – including two large, interlocking pedestrian squares – is easily walkable.

◉ Sights

Trenčín Castle FORTRESS

(www.muzeumtn.sk; adult/child €5/3; ☺9am-5.30pm) First noted in a Viennese chronicle

of 1069, Trenčín Castle developed through the centuries until 1790 when it was damaged by fire. Much of what you see is reconstruction, but there are remnants that date to the earliest days. From the town, climb ever more stairs to reach the lowest level of fortifications and commanding views of the Váh River plain. Two levels higher you enter the various towers and furnished palaces with one of the frequent tours (75 minutes, in Slovak only; call two days ahead to arrange an English-speaking guide). The most evocative time to visit is during festivals and on summer weekend evenings during two-hour, torchlight tours – complete with medieval sword fighting, minstrels and staged frolics.

Roman inscription ANCIENT SITE

The town's unique claim to fame is a Roman inscription of AD 179; soldier's graffiti commemorating a battle against Germanic tribes. It is actually carved into the cliff behind the **Hotel Tatra** (Ul gen MR Štefánika 2) and can only be viewed through a window in the hotel's staircase; ask at reception. The translation reads: 'To the victory of the emperor and the army which, numbering 855 soldiers, resided at Laugaricio. By order of Maximianus, legate of the 2nd auxiliary legion.'

Galéria Bazovského MUSEUM

(www.gmab.sk; Palackého 27; adult/child €2/1; ☺9am-5pm Tue-Sun) Temporary exhibits at the Galéria Bazovského represent some of the best of 20th-century Slovak and Czech art. The main collection contains works by local painter Miloš Bazovský (1899–1968).

Town Gate Tower HISTORIC BUILDING

(Mestská veža; Sládkovičova; adult/child €1/0.50; ☺10am-8pm, closed Nov-Mar) An inconspicuous glass elevator leads to the town gate entry, and six really steep flights later you emerge at a 360-degree view of the Old Town.

A few other small museums around town hold some interest, and there are historic buildings like the **Piarist Church** (Mierové nám) and the former 1913 **Synagogue** (Štúrovo nám) for exterior viewing.

🏃 Activities

Ostrov BEACH

(off Mládežnícka) Floating in the middle of the Váh river, the Ostrov (island) is Trenčín's playground. A freely accessible, small,

Trenčín

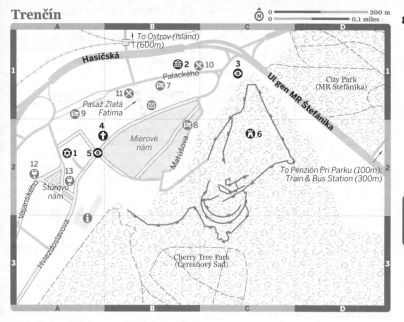

sandy beach, volleyball court, swing sets and summer concessions are part of the attraction. At the time of research an outdoor pool with water slide was under construction here.

✨ Festivals & Events

World music, jazz, rock, techno, hip hop and alternative music are all represented in one weekend in July at the **Bazant Pohoda Festival** (www.pohodafestival.sk), the largest music festival in Slovakia.

🛏 Sleeping

Penzión pri Parku PENSION €

(☏0902979814; www.penzionpriparku.sk; Kragujevackých hrdinov 7; s/d €25/33; 🛜) Mod decor fills the eclectic nook-and-cranny rooms of this Victorian building in the park. Staying here you're near both train and bus stations.

Grand Hotel HOTEL €€

(☏7434 353; www.grand-hotel.sk; Palackého 34; s/d €63/70; ✳@🛜) Perks at this super-central, contemporary hotel include free bike rental and whirlpool and sauna use. Rooms are awash in dark woods and upscale neutrals.

Penzión Svorad HOSTEL €

(☏7430 322; www.svorad-trencin.sk; Palackého 4; dm €18-32; 🛜) Peeling linoleum, thin mattresses – but oh, what castle views. This dormitory-like pension (with private bathrooms) resides in part of an old grammar school; maybe that's why the staff are so rule-obsessed.

Hotel Pod Hradom HOTEL €€
(📞7481 701; www.podhradom.sk; Matúšova 12; s €65-80, d €76-98; @) A 10-room lodging on a wee, winding street en route to the castle.

Autocamping na Ostrove CAMPING €
(📞7434 013; www.slovanet.sk/camping; Ostrov; tent site from €6, bungalow d €14) Riverside bungalow camping ground on the island has central space for tents.

✖ Eating & Drinking
Numerous restaurants and cafes line Mierové nám and Štúrovo nám; choose any one for imbibing al fresco. Quick eats are available on Palackého.

TOP CHOICE / **Reštaurácia Bašta** SLOVAK €€
(Ostrove Zamarovce; mains €5-15; ⊙24hr) Some of the freshest, cooked-to-order Slovak faves we've ever tasted – pork stuffed with spicy *klobasa*, *bryndza* (sheep's cheese) cream soup... Breakfasts are tasty, too. Well worth the walk to the Ostrov (island).

Cinema Movie Club Restaurant & Bar INTERNATIONAL €
(Palackého 33; mains €5-7; 🛜) Chicken and risotto dishes at this student haunt are quite good, but the real deal is the weekday lunch set menu (under €4).

Plzenská SLOVAK €€
(Zlatá Fatima; mains €5-13) Dig into hearty Slovak fare in pub-like surrounds off the main square. Don't forget to get a frothy glass of Czech pilsner.

Steps Bar BAR
(Sládkovičova 4-6) Both the sidewalk cafe and the upstairs bar attract a hip, college-age crowd.

Jamm Club CLUB
(Štúrovo nám 5) Hosts occasional live jazz and blues (other nights are disco).

ℹ Information
Cultural Information Centre (📞6504 294; www.visittrencin.sk; Sládkovičova 1; ⊙9am-6pm Mon-Fri, 8am-4pm Sat) Exceptionally helpful, well-informed staff give out handfuls of brochures for town and region. Good, free map available.

Library of Trenčín (Hasicska 1; ⊙7am-7pm Mon-Fri, 8am-1pm Sun) Free internet.

Main post office (Mierové nám 21)

VUB Bank (Mierové nám 37) ATM and exchange.

ℹ Getting There & Away
Riding the rails is the quickest and most cost-efficient way to get here. IC and EC trains run from Bratislava (€9, 1½ hours), Žilina (€8, one hour) and Poprad (€14, 2¾ hours), among others.

CENTRAL SLOVAKIA
The rolling hills and low, forested mountain ranges of central Slovakia are home to the shepherding tradition that defines Slovak culture. This is where the nation's Robin Hood, Juraj Jánošík, once roamed. Limited train routes means a car can be helpful for exploring the area in depth. Look roadside for farmers selling local sheep's cheese before you head off into one of the picturesque valleys.

Žilina
📞041 / POP 85,300
A Slavic tribe in the 6th century was the first to recognise Žilina's advantageous location at the intersection of several important trade routes on the Váh River. Today it's still a transit point for exploring Malá Fatra National Park, surrounding fortresses and folksy villages. It's a pleasant little city, but there isn't much to see besides the old palace-like castle on the outskirts.

From the train station in the northeast, a walk along Národná takes you through Nám A Hlinku up to Mariánské nám, the main pedestrian square.

◉ Sights
Budatín Castle PALACE
(www.pmza.sk; Topoľova 1; adult/child €1/0.50; ⊙8am-5pm Tue-Sun) The small castle, 1½km north across the Váh River, is more palace than fortress. The museum inside contains exhibits of 18th- and 19th-century decorative arts as well as wire figures made by area tinkers.

⌖ Sleeping & Eating
The information office has a list of student dorms that take travellers in July and August. Interchangeable bars and cafes lie around Mariánske and Hlinka squares.

Hotel Dubna Skala HOTEL €€
(📞5079 100; www.hoteldubnaskala.sk; Hurbanova 8; s/d €95/105; ❄🛜) Modern boutique interiors fit surprisingly well within an ornate 10th-century exterior. The well-regarded

BOJNICE & ORAVA CASTLES

Central Slovakia has numerous castles and ruins. Two of the more famous are a bit removed.

Bojnice Castle (Bojnice zámok; www.bojnicecastle.sk; adult/child €6/3; ⊙9am-5pm Tue-Sun) is straight out of a fairy-tale dream, crowned with towers and turrets and crenulated mouldings. The original 12th-century fortification got an early-20th-century redo by the Pálffy family, who modelled it on French romantic castles. The time to visit is during the International Festival of Ghosts and Ghouls in May, when costumed guides put on shows throughout the castle and grounds. The palace also gets decked out for Christmas, Valentine's Day and various medieval events. The nearby city of Prievidza has bus connections to Žilina (€3, 1¼ hours, 10 daily), Bratislava (€8, 3¼ hours, eight daily) and others. From there take local bus 3 or 7 the 3km to Bojnice, a little town with lodging and restaurants.

The classic 1922 vampire film *Nosferatu* featured the pointed towers of **Orava Castle** (Oravský hrad; www.oravamuzeum.sk; Oravský Podzámok; adult/child €6/4; ⊙8.30am-5pm, closed Apr), which rise from an impossibly narrow blade of rock. This, one of the most complete castles in Slovakia, dates from at least 1267. Later additions and reconstructions were, of course, made, most notably after a fire in 1800. The museum is chock full of weapons, folk art and period furniture. Legend has it that the castle contains one mirror where the reflection will make you beautiful, and another that will make you ugly – make sure to ask the difference. Below the castle in the tiny village of Oravsky Podzámok there's a pizza pub and a pension. Buses run at least hourly between there and Ružomberok (€2, 45 minutes), where you can transfer to the Bratislava–Košice train line. Buses run less frequently to Žilina (€2.50, 1½ hours, five daily). Another alternative is to transfer by train from the main line to a trunk line in Kraľovany (€1.50, 55 minutes, six daily).

wine-cellar restaurant here similarly juxtaposes old and new with clean white arches and stone wall accents.

Penzión Majovey   HOTEL €€
(☏5624 152; www.slovanet.sk/majovey in Slovak; Jána Milca 3; s/d €35/60) The deep coral facade and central location are more interesting than the stark white rooms here, but the bathrooms are huge. Tile floors keep things cool throughout.

Kompas Café   HOSTEL €
(☏0918481319; http://kompascafe.wordpress.com; Vojtecha Spanyola 37; dm €14) Pretty basic, two- to five-bed workers' dorms with a cafe and kitchen; 1km south of centre.

TOP
CHOICE / **Voyage Voyage**   SLOVAK €€
(Mariánske nám 191; mains €5-12) A modernized Slovak menu here includes inventive dishes like chicken filet stuffed with peaches and cheese. Don't miss the ice-cream cocktails and milkshakes.

Pizzeria Carolina   PIZZA €
(Národná 5; pizza & pasta €4-9) Outdoor cafe tables fill up fast at this student fave; dine downstairs to be near the salad bar.

❶ Information

Main post office (Sládkovičova 1)

Tourist Information Office (TIK; ☏7233 186; www.zilina.sk; Republiky 1; ⊙9am-5pm Mon-Fri, 9am-2pm Sat & Sun) Town and surrounding-area information available.

Volksbank (Národná 28) Bank and ATM near the train station.

❶ Getting There & Away

Žilina is on the main railway line between Bratislava and Košice. Four daily IC (and many more, slower, 'fast') trains head to Bratislava (€11, 2½ hours), Trenčín (€8, one hour), Poprad (€11, 1½ hours) and Košice (€14, 2¾ hours).

Around Žilina

As well as nearby Malá Fatra National Park, a few folk-culture sights within an hour of Žilina are well worth exploring.

MARTIN

The town of Martin is primarily an industrial centre, but it has a number of small museums and the country's largest *skanzen* (open-air village museum). Traditional buildings from all over the region have been moved to the **Museum of the Slovak Village** (Múzeum Slovenské Dediny; www.snm-em.sk; adult/child €2/1; ☺9am-6pm Tue-Sun). It comes complete with working *krčma* (village pub). Contact the **Tourist Information Office** (☎4234 776; www. tikmartin.sk; Štefánika 9A; ☺9am-5pm Mon-Fri) for more details. From Žilina it's easiest to take the bus the 35km to Martin (€1.50, 40 minutes, half-hourly). The village museum is 4km southeast of the city. Take local bus 10 from the main station to the last stop, Ľadovaň, and walk the remaining 1km up through the forest (or hail a taxi in town).

ČIČMANY

If you've seen a brochure or postcard of Slovakia, you've probably seen a photograph of **Čičmany** (www.cicmany.viapvt.sk); dark log homes painted with white geometric patterns fill the traditional village. This is no *skanzen*; most houses are private residences, but **Radenov House** (Čičmany 42; adult/child €2/1; ☺8am-4pm Tue-Sun) is a museum. There's a gift shop, a small restaurant and a pension in the long, narrow settlement. Buses run the 50 minutes south of Žilina (€2) five times a day; return times allow hours to wander and photograph.

VLKOLÍNEC

The folksy mountain village of **Vlkolínec** (www.vlkolinec.sk; adult/child €3/2; ☺9am-3pm), about 71km east and southeast of Žilina, is a Unesco-noted national treasure. The pastel paint and steep roofs on the 45 traditional plastered log cabins are remarkably well maintained. It's easy to imagine a *vlk* (wolf) wandering through this wooded mountainside settlement arranged along a small stream. You pay entry to walk around, and one of the buildings has been turned into a small house museum, but this is still a living village – if just barely. Of the approximately 40 residents, almost half are schoolchildren.

Three weekday-only buses make the 25-minute (€0.50) drive to Vlkolínec from the Ružomberok train station; last return is at 3:15pm. Otherwise, driving or hiking the 6km uphill from Ružomberok is the only way to get to the village. At least five direct trains a day stop in Ružomberok on their way from Bratislava (€12, 3½ hours) and Žilina (€3, one hour) to Poprad (€4, one hour).

Two kilometres west of Ružomberok, **Salaš Krajinka** (www.salaskrajinka.sk; E18; mains €4-11), is one of the country's best sheep dairy restaurants. Buy the *bryndza* and other products on-site, or sit down for a full meal in the modern-rustic dining room with a glass wall looking into the barn.

Malá Fatra National Park

☑041

Sentinel-like formations stand watch at the rocky gorge entrance to the valley filled with pine-clad slopes above. The Malá Fatra National Park (Národný park Malá Fatra) incorporates a chocolate-box-pretty, 200-sq-km swathe of its namesake mountain range. The Vrátna Valley (Vrátna dolina), 25km east of Žilina, lies at the heart of the park. From here you can access the trailheads, ski lifts and a cable car to start your exploration. The long, one-street town of Terchová is at the lower end of the valley, Chata Vrátna is at the top. The village of Štefanová lies east of the main valley road, 1km uphill from Terchová.

⊙ Sights

Statue of Juraj Jánošík   MONUMENT

Above the village of Terchová sits an immense aluminium statue of Juraj Jánošík, Slovakia's Robin Hood. In early August, much dancing, singing and feasting go on beneath his likeness during the **Jánošík Days** folk festival.

Považké Museum   MUSEUM

(www.pmza.sk; Sv Cyrila a Metoda 96, Terchová; adult/child €2/1; ☺9am-3.30pm Tue-Sun) Check out the pictures, artefacts and drawings depicting the notorious highwayman Jánošík's exploits (and gruesome death) at the small museum above the town info office. Ask for the English-language narration.

Vrátna Valley   PARK

The road to **Vrátna Valley** (www.vratna.sk) in Malá Fatra National Park runs south from Terchová through the crags of **Tiesňavy Gorge**, past picnic sites and scenic stops. A **cable car** (Vratna Výtah; return adult/child €10/7; ☺9am-4.30pm mid-Jun-Sep & mid-Dec-mid-Apr) carries you from the top of the valley to **Snilovské saddle** (1524m) below two peaks, **Chleb** (1647m) and **Velký Kriváň** (1709m). Both are on the red ridge trail, one of the most popular in the park. A hike northeast from Chleb over **Hromové** (1636m), **Poludňový grúň** (1636m) and **Stoh** (1608m) to **Medziholie saddle** (1185m) takes about 5½ hours. From there you can descend for an hour on the green trail to Štefanová village where there's a bus stop, and places to stay and eat. Note that the main summer season is July and August; during other months businesses may close for maintenance. For serious hiking, VKÚ's 1:50,000 Malá Fatra-Vrátna map (No 110) and Dajama's *Knapsacked Travel: Malá Fatra* are good.

🏃 Activities

The full complement of Vrátna Valley's 14 **ski tows and lifts** (☺8am-4pm) are open from December to April. Shacks with **ski rental** (from €12 per day) keep the same hours and are located at Starý Dvor, where **ski passes** (per day adult/child €22/15) are also for sale.

In summer, in the same parking lot, the **Organization for Sport Activities** (☑0903546600; www.splavovanie.sk; Starý Dvor; ☺9am-5pm Jul & Aug) rents mountain bikes and organises rafting trips.

🛏 Sleeping & Eating

Numerous private cottages are available for rent in the Terchová area, many listed on the information office websites. No camping is allowed in the park. The food situation in the valley isn't the best. There are a few food stands near the chairlifts and cable car, and most lodgings have restaurants. Otherwise, forage in Terchová.

Penzión Vŕšky   PENSION €€
(☑5627 300; www.penzionvrsky.sk; Vŕšky, Terchová; r €48, cottages €138-199; ☺🕾) Built in 2010 on a hill above the road to Terchová, this log-cabin lodge may seem better situated for those with cars, but it does allow backdoor access to the park. Simple-but-spotless rooms have natural wood furnishings; roomy cottages sleep six. Don't miss the restaurant's original take on Slovak food (mains €6 to €13).

Penzión Sagan   PENSION €
(☑0903744302; www.penzionsagan.sk; Štefanová 553; s/d incl breakfast €30/50; ☺🕾) Pine-clad rooms couldn't be more impeccably kept, nor could the smiling staff and fireplace in

the little restaurant be more welcoming. Look for the homely guesthouse tucked way back into Štefanová village.

Hotel Boboty   HOTEL €€
(☑5695 228; www.hotelboboty.sk; Nový Dvor; s/d €60/80; @🕾🏊) Services galore – sauna, massage, heated pool, billiards, free ski shuttle – are available at the valley's biggest lodging.

Chata Vrátna   MOUNTAIN HUT €
(☑5695 739; http://chata.vratna.org; Vrátna výťah; d/tr €22/30) Muddy hikers, giggling children and a fragrant wood-smoke aroma fill this well-worn, basic chalet near the cable car at the top of Vrátna Valley.

Reštaurácia Starý Majer   SLOVAK €
(☑5695 419; mains €5-10; ☺10am-9pm) Dig into well-done traditional sheepherders' dishes at rough-hewn outdoor tables, or inside among rustic farm implements.

Chata na Grúni   MOUNTAIN HUT €
(☑5695 324; www.chatanagruni.sk; dm €11) Hiker's hut at the top of Gruni Ski Lift; four- to six-bed dorms and self-service restaurant.

Autocamping Belá   CAMPING GROUND €
(☑5621 478; http://camping.bela.sk; camping site €4-9; ☺May–mid-Oct; 🏊) A fine camping ground with 300 sites, a heated pool and food stand. There's a bus stop in front; 5km west of Terchová.

❶ Information

Mountain Rescue Service (Horská Záchranná služba; ☑5695 232; http://his.hzs.sk/; Štefanová) Rescue service and weather info.

Terchová Tourist Information Centre (☑5695 307; www.ztt.sk; Sv Cyrila a Metoda 96, Terchová; ☺8am-4pm Mon-Fri, 10am-1pm Sat & Sun) Knick-knacks and maps for sale; ATM in building.

Turistcko-Informačna Chalupa (☑0907534354; www.uteczmesta.sk; Vrátňanská cesta, Terchová; ☺8am-8pm)

WORTH A TRIP

GOING LOCAL IN LIPTOV

From the high plain southeast of the Malá Fatra, you can see no fewer than five surrounding mountain ranges. The rolling hills and dales of the **Liptov** (www.liptov.sk) region make a lovely place to stay. From here you can easily reach most Central Slovak sights on a day trip – if you have a car (buses requires much transferring). **Jasna** (www.jasna.sk), in Low Tatras National Park, is a favourite winter playground with a relatively new summer–winter cable car. Several thermal spas are found in the area. Driving past all the farmer's stands in the region selling sheep chese, you'll know you've gone local.

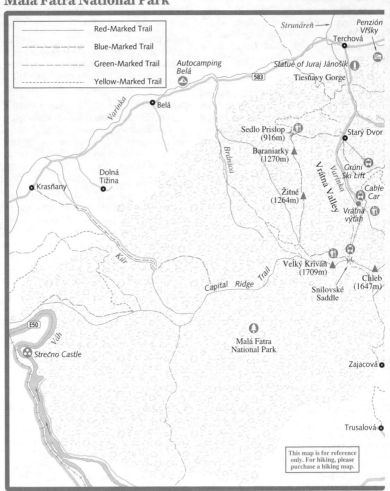

Map legend:
- Red-Marked Trail
- Blue-Marked Trail
- Green-Marked Trail
- Yellow-Marked Trail

Strunáreň

Penzión Vršky

Terchová

Autocamping Belá

583

Statue of Juraj Jánošík

Tiesňavy Gorge

Varínka

Belá

Sedlo Príslop (916m)

Starý Dvor

Baraniarky (1270m)

Branica

Dolná Tižina

Krasňany

Grúni Ski Lift

Vrátna Valley

Varínka

Žitné (1264m)

Cable Car

Vrátna výťah

Kúr

Capital Ridge Trail

Velký Kriváň (1709m)

Chleb (1647m)

Snilovské Saddle

E50

Váh

Strečno Castle

Malá Fatra National Park

Zajacová

Trusalová

This map is for reference only. For hiking, please purchase a hiking map.

Private office arranges lodging and sport activates, provides info and sells books and maps.

ⓘ Getting There & Around

Almost hourly buses link Žilina with Terchová (€1.60, 40 minutes) and valley stops, terminating near Chata Vrátna at Vrátna výťah (€2, one hour). Or you can change in Terchová for local buses. Check schedules at www.cp.atlas.sk.

EAST SLOVAKIA

Alpine peaks in Slovakia? As you look upon the snow-strewn jagged mountains rising like an apparition east of Liptovský Mikuláš, you may think you're imagining things. But there they are indeed. Hiking the High Tatras is undoubtedly the highlight of the region, but in eastern Slovakia you can also admire ancient architecture, explore castle ruins, seek out small villages and visit the country's second city.

High Tatras

🎧 052

The High Tatras (Vysoké Tatry), the tallest range in the Carpathian Mountains, tower

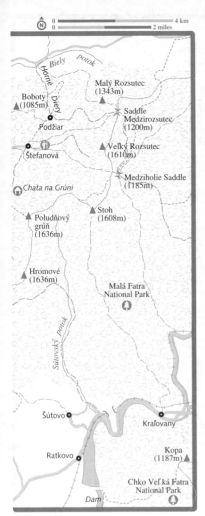

Not that the fact has arrested development on the Slovak ski slopes, much to the chagrin of watchdog groups like International Union for Conservation of Nature.

Mid-mountain, three main resort towns string west to east. Štrbské Pleso is the traditional ski centre and is most crowded, with condos and construction galore. Eleven kilometres east, Smokovec is an amalgam of the Nový (New), Starý (Old) and Horný (upper) settlements. Here you still have some turn-of-the-20th-century heyday feel, plus numerous lodging options, eateries and the most services. Five kilometres further, Tatranská Lomnica is the quaintest and the quietest village. All have mountain access by cable car, funicular or chairlift. Poprad is the closest sizeable city (with mainline train station and airport), 14km south of central Starý Smokovec.

When planning your trip, keep in mind that the highest trails are closed to snow from November to mid-June. June and July can be especially rainy; July and August are the warmest (and most crowded) months. Hotel prices and crowds are at their lowest from October to April.

☉ Sights & Activities

A 600km network of trails covers the alpine valleys and some peaks, with full-service mountain huts where hikers can stop for a meal or a rest along the way. Routes are colour coded and easy to follow. Pick up one of the numerous detailed maps and hiking guides available at bookstores and information offices. Park regulations require you to keep to the trails and refrain from picking flowers. Be aware that most of the trails are rocky and uneven, watch for sudden thunderstorms on ridges and peaks where there's no protection, and know that the assistance of the Mountain Rescue Service is not free.

over most of Eastern Europe. Some 25 peaks measure above 2500m. The massif is only 25km wide and 78km long, but photo opportunities at higher elevations are enough to get you fantasising about a career with National Geographic – pristine snowfields, ultramarine mountain lakes, crashing waterfalls and rocky slopes... Down below, traditionally thick pine forests took a beating in a serious wind storm, but the newly formed meadows are making a comeback. Since 1949 most of this jagged range has been included in the Tatra National Park (Tanap), complementing a similar park across the peaks in Poland.

SMOKOVEC RESORTS

From Starý Smokovec a **funicular railway** (www.vt.sk; adult/child return €7/5; ☉7am-7pm Jul & Aug, 8am-5pm Sep-Jun) takes you up to **Hrebienok** (1280m). From here you have a great view of the **Velká Studená Valley** and a couple of hiking options. The red **Tatranská Magistrála Trail** transects the southern slopes of the High Tatras for 65km start to finish. Bilíkova chata (p884), a log-cabin lodge and restaurant, is only a 10-minute hike from Hrebienok. Following the Magistrála east on an easy trail section to **Studený Potok** waterfalls takes about 30 minutes. Heading west instead, you could follow the

High Tatras

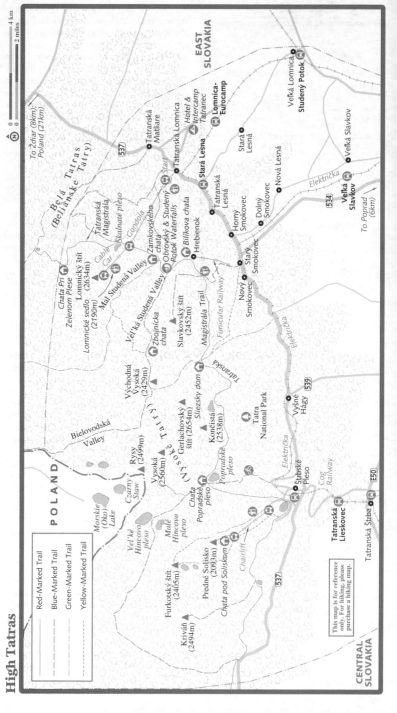

Red-Marked Trail
Blue-Marked Trail
Green-Marked Trail
Yellow-Marked Trail

This map is for reference only. For hiking, please purchase a hiking map.

Magistrála to the lakeside **Sliezsky dom** hut (two hours), down a small green connector trail, to the yellow-marked trail back to Starý Smokovec (four hours total).

Mountain climbers scale to the top of **Slavkovský štít** (2452m) via the blue trail from Starý Smokovec (seven to eight hours return). To ascend the peaks without marked hiking trails (**Gerlachovský štít** included), you must hire a guide. Contact the **Mountain Guides Society Office** (☏4422 066; www.tatraguide.sk; Starý Smokovec 38; ⊙10am-6pm Mon-Fri, noon-6pm Sat & Sun, closed weekends Oct-May); guides cost from €150, and the society runs classes too.

At the top of the funicular, tow-assist snow sledging and summer tubing are to be had at **Funpark** (Hrebienok; per ride €1.50; ⊙10am-4pm July & Aug, 9am-4pm Dec-Feb).

Rent mountain bikes at **Tatrasport** (www.tatry.net/tatrasport; Starý Smokovec 38; per day €15; ⊙8am-noon&1-6pm), above the bus-station parking lot.

TATRANSKÁ LOMNICA & AROUND

While in the Tatras, you shouldn't miss the ride to the precipitous 2634m summit of **Lomnický štít** (bring a jacket!). From Lomnica, a large **gondola** (www.vt.sk; adult/child return €13/9; ⊙8.30am-7pm Jul & Aug, to 4pm Sep-Jun) pauses mid-station at **Štart** before it takes you to the winter sports area, restaurant and lake at **Skalnaté pleso**. From there, a smaller **cable car** (www.vt.sk; adult/child return €20/14; ⊙8.30am-5.30pm Jul & Aug, to 3.30pm Sep-Jun) goes on to the summit. The second leg of the journey requires a time-reserved ticket. On sunny summer days time slots do sell out, so get in line early. You're given 50 minutes at the top to admire the views, walk the observation platforms and sip a beverage in the cafe before your return time.

One of the top Tatra day hikes starts from Skalnaté pleso, following the rocky Magistrála Trail west past amazingly open views back into the forest at **Zamkovského chata** (1½ hours), an atmospheric mountain hut and restaurant (p885). Continue down hill, along the even rockier, steeper path past the **Obrovský** and **Studený Potok** waterfalls on to Hrebienok (three hours total). From there the funicular takes you down to Starý Smokovec.

Get off the cable car at Štart and you're at **Funtools** (www.vt.sk; cable car plus 1 ride €9; ⊙9am-6pm Jun-Sep), from where you can take a fast ride down the mountain on a two-wheeled scooter, a luge-like three-wheel cart or on a four-wheel modified skateboard.

DON'T MISS

HIGH TATRA HIKES

The 65km-long **Magistrála Trail** may start at the base of the Western (Zapadné) Tatras, but most of it runs beneath the peaks (between 1300m and 1800m) of the **High Tatras**. Because there's a relatively small elevation change, the trail is accessible by cable-assisted cars and lifts, and there are huts to stop and eat at, you need not be in peak mountaineering shape to experience it. Some of our favourite routes are Skalnaté pleso to Hrebienok, Štrbské Pleso to Popradské pleso, and Skalnaté pleso to Chata pri Zelenom plese.

In recent years much winter sport development has taken place on the slopes above Tatranská Lomnica; the area now counts about 30 skiable hectares. From Skalnaté pleso a high-speed winter **quad lift** (⊙9am-4pm) hoists riders to **Lomnické sedlo**, a 2190m saddle below the summit, and access to an advanced 6km-long ski run (1300m drop). A multimillion-euro renovation also added a high-speed **six-seat chair lift** (⊙9am-4pm) from the village up to Štart, snow-making capacity and a ski-in/ski-out car park. **Vysoké Tatry** (www.vt.sk; Tatranská Lomnica 7, Tatranská Lomnica; day lift ticket adult/child €24/17; ⊙9am-3.30pm Dec-Apr) sells passes from the base of the cable car, where ski rental (from €12 per day) and lockers are also available.

ŠTRBSKÉ PLESO & AROUND

Condo and hotel development continue unabated in the village, but the namesake clear blue glacial lake (*pleso*) is surrounded by dark pine forest and rocky peaks and remains beautiful. **Row boats** (per 45min €10-15; ⊙10am-6pm May-Sep) are for rent from the dock in front of the Grand Hotel Kempinski.

In good weather the streets are overrun, as one of the most popular day hikes departs from here. Follow the red-marked **Magistrála Trail** uphill from the train station on a rocky forest trail for about 1¼ hours to **Popradské pleso**, an even more idyllic lake at 1494m. The busy mountain hut there (p885) is like a hotel, with a large, self-service restaurant. You can return to the train line by following the paved road down to the Popradské pleso stop (45 minutes). Or the Magistrála zigzags dramatically up the

ℹ️ MULTI-RESORT SKI PASSES

Recently Park Snow and Vysoký Tatry resorts, the ski concessions in Štrbské Pleso and Tatranská Lomnica respectively, have joined forces to offer multi-day, multi-resort lift passes (three days €69 per adult). The **Super Slovak Ski Pass** (http://skipass.jasna.sk) covers not only the resorts listed here, but other smaller ski areas around the country.

mountainside from Popradské pleso and then traverses east towards Sliezsky dom and the Hrebienok funicular above Starý Smokovec (four hours).

There is also a year-round **chairlift** (www. parksnow.sk; adult/child return €7.50/5; ⊙8am-3.30pm) up to **Chata pod Soliskom** (p885), from where it's a one-hour walk north along a red trail to the 2093m summit of **Predné Solisko**.

Park Snow (www.parksnow.sk; Aréal FIS; day lift ticket adult/child €24/17; ⊙8.30am-3.30pm), Štrbské Pleso's poplar ski and snowboard resort, has two chairlifts, four tow lines, 12km of easy to moderate runs, one jump and a snow-tubing area.

🛏️ Sleeping

For a full listing of Tatra lodgings, look online at www.tatryinfo.eu. Cheaper sleeps are available in small settlements like Nová Lesná down the hill or east over the ridge at Ždiar (p887) in the Belá Tatras. No wild/backcountry camping is permitted: there is a camping ground near Tatranská Lomnica. For the quintessential Slovak mountain experience, you can't beat hiking from one *chata* (a mountain hut; could be anything from a shack to a chalet) to the next, high up among the peaks. Food (optional meal service or restaurant) is always available. Beds fill up, so book ahead.

SMOKOVEC RESORTS

Look for reasonable, been-there-forever boarding houses with one-word names like 'Delta' just west of the Nový Smokovec electric train stop on the several no-name streets that run to the south.

TOP CHOICE **Penzión Tatra** PENSION €
(☎0903650802; www.tatraski.sk; Starý Smokovec 66; s/d incl breakfast €25/50; @🖥️) Big

and colourful modern rooms fill the classic 1900 alpinesque building above the train station. It's super central. Choose to have your breakfast in the large common room, or out on the terrace. Billiard table and ski storage available.

Villa Siesta HOTEL €€
(☎4423 024; www.villasiesta.sk; Nový Smokovec 88; r €52-64, ste €64-113; 🖥️) Light fills this airy, contemporary mountain villa furnished in natural hues. The full restaurant, sauna and Jacuzzi are a bonus.

Villa Mon Ami B&B €€
(☎4423 024; www.monami.sk; Nový Smokovec 31; r/apt incl breakfast €50/110; @🖥️) Scrolled ironwork beds, chandeliers and lobby fireplace make Mon Ami a romantic option. The three-story, half-timber villa is set in a park on the main drag.

Grand Hotel HOTEL €€€
(☎4870 000; www.grandhotel.sk; Starý Smokovec 38; r €90-190; 🖥️♨️) More than 100 years of history are tied up in Starý Smokovec's grande dame. Rooms could use an update.

Mountain huts above the resorts:

Bilíkova chata MOUNTAIN HUT €
(☎4422 439; www.bilikovachata.sk; Hrebienok; s/d without bathroom €25/50) Basic log-cabin hotel with full-service restaurant among the clouds; only a seven-minute walk from the Hrebienok funicular station.

Zbojnícka chata MOUNTAIN HUT €
(☎0903638000; www.zbojnickachata.sk; dm incl breakfast €15) Sixteen-bed dorm room, self-service eatery and small kitchen; at 1960m, four-plus hours' hike up from Hrebienok.

TATRANSKÁ LOMNICA & AROUND

Look for private rooms (*privat* or *zimmer frei*), from €15 per person, on the back streets south and east of the train station. You can book ahead online at www.tatry.sk and www.tanap.sk/homes.html.

Grandhotel Praha HOTEL €€
(☎4467 941; www.grandhotelpraha.sk; s/d incl breakfast €110/155; @♨️) Remember when travel was elegant and you dressed for dinner? Well, the 1899 Grandhotel's sweeping marble staircase and crystal chandeliers do. Rooms are appropriately classic, and there's a snazzy spa here, high above the village.

Penzión Encian PENSION €
(☎4467 520; www.tatry.sk/encian; Tatranská Lomnica 36; s/d €30/47; @) Steep roofs, overflowing flowerboxes and a small restaurant hearth give Encian an appropriate mountain appeal. No genuine nonsmoking rooms, and a mercurial owner.

More mountain huts and camping grounds in this area:

TOP CHOICE **Zamkovského chata** MOUNTAIN HUT €
(☎4422 636; www.zamka.sk; per person €15-20) Atmospheric wood chalet with four-bed bunk rooms and restaurant; great hike stop midway between Skalnaté Pleso and Hrebienok.

Chata pri Zelenom plese MOUNTAIN HUT €
(☎4467 420; www.zelenepleso.sk; dm €15) Fifty-bed lakeside lodging at 1540m; about 2½ hours hike east of Skalnaté Pleso, en route to the Belá Tatras.

Rijo Camping CAMPING GROUND €
(☎4467 493; www.rijocamping.eu; Stará Lesná 52; campsites €5-7.50; ⊙May-Sep) Pine trees shade much of the field at this small, tent-only site, 1km north of Stará Lesná bus stop.

Hotel & Intercamp Tatranec CAMPING GROUND €
(☎4467 092; www.hoteltatranec.com; Tatranská Lomnica 202; campsites €6-9, r €40, cabin €60) Ageing six-person cabins, motel and restaurant – with an open tent field. North of the 'T Lomnica zast' stop on the train line to Studený Potok.

ŠTRBSKÉ PLESO & AROUND

Development and crowds make staying in this village our last choice, with one grand exception.

Grand Hotel Kempinski LUXURY HOTEL €€€
(☎3262 222; www.kempinski-hightatras.com; Kupelna 6; r €199-300; ✱@≋) Far and away the swankiest Tatra accommodation: the classic, villa-like Kempinski entices high-end travellers with evening turndown service, heated marble bathroom floors and incredible lake views. Take a swim in the luxury spa and see the mountains stretch before you through two-storey glass.

Chata pod Soliskom MOUNTAIN HUT €
(☎0917655446; www.chatasolisko.sk; dm €16) Small log hostel (eight beds), nice terrace, no hiking required; next to the chairlift terminus at 1800m.

Chata Popradské pleso MOUNTAIN HUT €
(☎4492 177; www.popradskepleso.sk; dm €16, r €36-70) Sizeable mountain hotel with restaurant and bar. It's a one-hour rugged hike up from the village or a paved hike up from Popradské pleso train stop.

Eating & Drinking

The resort towns are close enough that it's easy to sleep in one and eat in another. There's at least a small grocery in each town. Nightlife is limited here; what's there is mostly in Starý Smokovec.

SMOKOVEC RESORTS

A couple of oft-changing discos are scattered around; ask for the latest when you arrive.

TOP CHOICE **Reštaurácia Svišť** SLOVAK €€
(☎4422 545; Nový Smokovec 30; mains €5-11) From hearty dumplings to beef filet with a wine reduction, this stylish Slovak restaurant does it all well – and surprisingly reasonably. At weekends you may want to reserve.

Pizzeria La Montanara ITALIAN €
(Starý Smokovec 22; mains €4-7) A local favourite, La Montanara serves good pies, pastas, soups and vegetables. It's above a grocery on the eastern edge of town.

Tatry Pub PUB
(Tatra Komplex, Starý Smokovec; ⊙3pm-1am Sun-Thu, 3pm-3am Fri & Sat; ⓦ) The official watering hole of the Mountain Guide Club is a lively place to drink, with a full schedule of dart tournaments, concerts and the like.

Cafe Hoepfner CAFE €
(Hotel Smokovec, Starý Smokovec 22; cakes €1-3) Friendly, local cafe with cakes and coffees; live jazz summer Saturday evenings.

Koliba Smokovec SLOVAK €
(Starý Smokovec 5; mains €7-15; ⊙3-10pm) A traditional rustic grill restaurant; some evening folk music.

TATRANSKÁ LOMNICA & AROUND

Hikers can carb-load at the predictable Slovak eateries by the train station.

Reštaurácia U Medveda CZECH & SLOVAK €€
(Tatranská Lomnica 88; mains €5-12) A good, off-the-beaten-track choice (south by the post office) for traditional cooking. Grilled specialties are a highlight.

Vila Park Reštaurácia
SLOVAK €€

(Hotel Vila Park, Tatranská Lomnica 40; mains €8-12) What a treat to see fresh vegetables as main ingredients and sides. Slovak dishes here have a distinct international flair.

Humno
BAR

(cable car station base; ☺10am-midnight Sun-Thu, until 3am Fri & Sat) It's a club, it's cocktail bar, it's an après-ski... With a capacity of 300, one of Lomnica's newest ventures can afford to be a little of everything.

ŠTRBSKÉ PLESO & AROUND

Food stands line the road above the train station, on the way to Aréal FIS and the chair lift.

Koliba Patria
SLOVAK €€

(southern lake shore, Štrbské pleso; mains €6-15) Come here for the lovely lakeside terrace and complex meat dishes. The trappings are definitely more refined than a typical *koliba* (rustic mountain restaurant serving Slovak sheepherder specialties).

Samoobslužná Reštaurácia
SLOVAK €

(Hotel Toliar, Štrbské pleso 21; mains €2-6; ☺7am-10pm) The self-service cafeteria has one-dish meals (goulash, chicken stir-fry etc) and vegetarian options.

ℹ Information

All three main resort towns have ATMs on the main street.

Emergency
Mountain Rescue Service (☎emergency 18 300; http://his.hzs.sk/; Starý Smokovec 23)

Internet Access
Galérka Cafe (Hotel Toliar, Štrbské Pleso 21; per hr €2; ☺8am-midnight; ☏) Two terminals available for public rental.

Townson Travel (Tatranská Lomnica 94; per hr €2; ☺9am-5pm Mon-Fri) A travel agency with one public computer.

U Michalka Café (Starý Smokovec 4; per hr €2; ☺10am-10pm; ☏) Pleasant cafe with four terminals, great tea and strudel.

Tourist Information
Note that information offices do not book rooms; they hand out a brochure listing some – not all – accommodation.

Tatra Information Office Starý Smokovec (TIK; ☎4423 440; Starý Smokovec 23; ☺8am-8pm Mon-Fri, to 1pm Sat) Largest area info office, with the most brochures.

TIK Štrbské Pleso (☎4492 391; Štrbské Pleso; ☺8am-4pm) Provides good trail info especially; uphill north from the Hotel Toliar.

TIK Tatranská Lomnica (☎4468 118; Cesta Slobody; ☺10am-6pm Mon-Fri, 9am-1pm Sat) Has the most helpful staff; opposite Penzión Encian on the main street.

Travel Agencies
T-Ski Travel (☎4423 200; www.slovakiatravel.sk; Starý Smokovec 46; ☺9am-4pm Mon-Thu, to 5pm Fri-Sun) Books lodging, arranges ski and mountain-bike programs, offers rafting and other outside-the-Tatras tours. Located at the funicular station.

Websites
High Tatras Tourist Trade Association (www.tatryinfo.eu) Comprehensive overview of area, including accommodation.

Tatra National Park (www.tanap.org) National park website.

Tatry.sk (www.tatry.sk) Official website of Tatra towns; look under 'Maps' for village layouts.

ℹ Getting There & Around

To reach the Tatras by public transport, you'll need to switch in Poprad. From there a narrow-gauge electric train makes numerous stops in the resort towns along the main road; buses go to smaller, downhill villages as well. Either way, to get between Štrbské pleso and Tatranská Lomnica, you have to change in Starý Smokovec. Check schedules at www.cp.atlas.sk.

Train
During daylight hours, electric trains (TEZ) run at least every two hours. You can buy individual TEZ tickets at stations, and block tickets (one to three used) additionally at tourist offices. Validate all on board.

BUSES FROM THE TATRAS

ROUTE	COST (€)	DURATION (MIN)	FREQUENCY (DAILY)
Poprad–Starý Smokovec	0.85	20	every 30min
Poprad–Tatranská Lomnica	1.10	30	hourly
Poprad–Štrbské pleso	1.60	60	every 45min
Tatranská Lomnica–Ždiar	1	25	8

ROUTE	COST (€)	DURATION (MIN)
Poprad–Starý Smokovec	0.70	25
Poprad–Tatranská Lomnica	0.80	25
Poprad–Štrbské pleso	1.30	75
Štrbské pleso–Starý Smokovec	1	40
Štrbské pleso–Tatranská Lomnica	0.60	10

Belá Tatras

⊘052

Travel east over the High Tatra mountain ridges and you start to hear Slovak spoken with a Polish accent. The Goral folk culture is an intricate part of the experience in the small Belianské Tatry (Belá Tatras). Traditional wooden cottages, some with striking red-and-white graphic designs, are still the building method of choice in the main village of Ždiar. A rustic, laid-back, much more local-oriented atmosphere pervades around town. From here it's an easy day trip or journey on to Poland; heck, it's almost close enough to walk.

ŽDIAR

Decorated timber cottages line long and narrow Ždiar, the oldest mountain settlement, inhabited since the 16th century. Goral traditions have been both bolstered and eroded by tourism. Several sections of the village are historical reservations, including the **Ždiar House Museum** (Ždiarsky dom; adult/child €3/1.50; ⊙10am-4pm Tue-Sun), a tiny, tiny place with colourful local costumes and furnishings.

Cross over the main road from the museum and a green trail skirts the river through **Monkova Valley** (880m), a level hike with very little elevation change. After 45 minutes the trail climbs up over **Širkové saddle** (1826m) and gets you to **Kopské saddle** (1750m) in about four hours total (seven hours return). Past this point you've crossed into the High Tatras; Chata pri Zelenom plese (p885) is an hour away and the cable car to Tatranská Lomnica is 2½ hours beyond that.

West of the main road there are two ski areas; in summer one becomes **Bikepark Bachledova** (www.skibachledova.sk; ⊙9am-4pm mid-Jul–mid-Sep). Here you can rent mountain bikes (from €5 per hour), chairlift them up the hill (€4 per ride) and thunder down.

🛏 Sleeping & Eating

Ždiar has a large number of pensions and *privaty* (here private rooms are sizeable lodgings with shared-facility rooms for rent, from €11 per person). Odds are pretty good if you just show up, or check www.zdiar.sk under *ubytovanie*.

TOP CHOICE **Ginger Monkey Hostel** HOSTEL €
(⊘4498 084; www.gingermonkey.eu; Ždiar 294; dm/d €13/30; @🛜) Crushing mountain views from a comfy old Goral-style house, hot tea at any hour, laundry, free breakfast, and a surprising sense of community... Clearly the world-travelling owner/managers have picked up a tip or two along the way. The place has a full kitchen, where a communal dinner may be cooking (by donation), or at the weekend the whole group might go out to a local eatery together. Don't just book one night; you'll end up extending. Cat, dog and chickens on site.

Penzión Kamzík PENSION €
(⊘4498 226; www.penzionkamzik.sk; Ždiar 513; s/d €13/30; 🛜) Staff at the Kamzík are every bit as cheerful as the pension's vibrant apricot exterior. Some of the modern rooms come with balconies. Small restaurant, table tennis, billiards and sauna.

Goral Krčma SLOVAK €
(⊘4498 138; Ždiar 460; mains €3-6) A traditional 'village pub' restaurant, this *krčma* serves all the regional specialities, like potato pancakes stuffed with a spicy sauté.

Rustika Pizzeria ITALIAN €
(Ždiar 334; pizza €4-6; ⊙5-10pm) Wood-fired pizza in a rambling old log house mid-village.

Ždiarsky Dom SLOVAK €
(Ždiar 55; mains €3-6) Rustic Slovak cooking next door to the little museum.

ℹ️ Information

PLP Shop (☎0903642492; Ždiar 333; ⏱9am-noon & 3-6pm) Souvenir shop, info office, bicycle rental (from €10 per day) and internet use (€2 per hour).

ℹ️ Getting There & Away

Bus is the only way to get to the Belá Tatras. Poland (open EU border) is 14km north of Ždiar. For Slovak schedules, check www.cp.atlas.sk; for Polish, see also http://strama.eu. Buses from Ždiar connect directly with Poprad (€1, one hour, 11 daily), Starý Smokovec (€1.60, 40 minutes, 11 daily), Tatranská Lomnica (€1, 30 minutes, 21 daily) and Zakopane, Poland (€2.50, 50 minutes, two daily).

Poprad

☎052 / POP 55,000

The nearest sizeable city to the High Tatras, Poprad has all the major services and is an important transport hub. Otherwise, the modern city's attraction is limited to an interesting suburb and a thermal water park. From the adjacent train and bus stations, the central pedestrian square, Nám sv Egídia, is a five-minute walk south on Alžbetina.

👁 Sights & Activities

Spišská Sobota   SQUARE

Sixteenth-century Spiš-style merchants' and artisans' houses line the Spišská Sobota town square. The suburb is 1.2km northeast of Poprad's train station.

Aqua City   BATHHOUSE

(www.aquacitypoprad.sk; Športová 1397; per day €15-30; ⏱9am-9pm) Sauna, swim, bubble and slide zones are all part of Poprad's thermal water park. Among the admirably green initiatives here, the heat and electricity derive from geothermal and solar sources.

🛏 Sleeping & Eating

There's a large Billa grocery store just east of the bus station.

Hotel Cafe Razy   PENSION €

(☎7764 101; www.hotelcaferazy.sk; Nám Sv Egídia 58; s/d €36/56) Sane and simple rooms upstairs (some wi-fi); semi-crazy pub and pizza cafe down. On the modern main square.

Penzión Sabato   B&B €€

(☎7769 580; www.sabato.sk; Sobotské nám 6, Spišská Sobota; r incl breakfast €70-110; 🛜) Exposed stone arches, cobblestone courtyard and open-hearth restaurant reveal this inn's

17th-century age – as do romantically decorated rooms.

Hotel Sobota   HOTEL €€

(☎4663 121; www.hotelsobota.sk; Kežmarská 15, Spišská Sobota; s/d incl breakfast €45/59; ❄@🛜) Modern construction with old slate-and-timber aesthetic. Full restaurant.

ℹ️ Information

City Information Centre (☎7721 700; www.poprad.sk; Dom Kultúry Štefániková 72; ⏱8am-5pm Mon-Fri, 9am-noon Sat) Town info only, lists private rooms.

ℹ️ Getting There & Away

AIR Poprad-Tatry International airport (www.airport-poprad.sk; Na Letisko 100) is 5km west of centre. Note that at the time of research it didn't receive any regular flights.

BUS Buses go to and from Levoča (€1.60, 30 minutes, hourly), Bardejov (€4.50, 2¼ hours, four daily) and Zakopane, Poland (€5, two hours, two daily).

CAR Pick-up around town is available by prearrangement from **Car Rental Tatran** (☎0903250255; www.autopozicovnatatry.sk).

TRAIN For more on the electric trains that traverse the 14km or so to the High Tatras resorts, see p905. Mainline trains run directly to Bratislava (€16, four hours, four IC trains daily), Trenčín (€14, 2¾ hours, four IC trains daily) and Košice (€5, 1½ hours, 12 daily).

Kežmarok

☎052 / POP 17,400

Snuggled beneath the broody peaks of the High Tatras, Kežmarok's pocket-sized Old Town square with distinct churches and small castle seems especially agreeable. Look for the influence of original 13th-century Germanic settlers in the architecture even today. During July the **European Folk Craft Market** – one of the nation's largest – comes to town.

From the adjacent bus and train stations, 1km northwest of the pedestrian centre, follow Dr Alexandra street to the main square, Hlavné nám. The red-and-green, pseudo-Moorish **New Evangelical Church** (cnr Toporcerova & Hviezdoslavovo; admission €2; ⏱10am-noon & 2-4pm Tue-Sat, closed Nov-Apr), c 1894, dominates the south end of town. Admission covers entry to the much more evocative **Old Wooden Evangelical Church**, built in 1717 without a single nail. It has an amazing interior of carved and painted wood, as well as an original organ.

At the other end of the square, the small, mansionlike **Kežmarok Castle** (Hradné nám 45; adult/child €3/2; ☉9am-4pm by tour) dates back to the 15th century. It's now a museum with period furniture and archaeology exhibits.

You'll find cafes aplenty around the pedestrian Hlavné nám. Our favourite *cukráreň* (pastry cafe) is 'Sweet Dream', **Sladký Sen** (Hlavné nám 90; cakes €1-3; ☉8am-6pm). The town's location makes this an easy day trip from the High Tatra resort towns or Levoča. If you decide to stay over, choose **Penzión U Jakubu** (☑4526 315; www.penzionujakuba.sk; Starý trh 39; r €30) for its folksy Slovakness, or **Hotel Club** (☑4524 051; www.hotelclubkezmarok.sk; Dr Alexandra 24; s/d €34/47; @☎) for more contemporary flair. Both have good restaurants.

Kežmarok Information Agency (☑4492 135; www.kezmarok.sk; Hlavné nám 46; ☉9am-4pm) has loads more information if you need it. From here buses are the only way to go: connect directly to Poprad (€1, 30 minutes, 16 daily), Tatranská Lomnica (€1, 30 minutes, 12 daily), Ždiar (€1.30, 40 minutes, four daily) or Levoča (€2, one hour, six daily).

Pieniny National Park

☑052

People come to the 21-sq-km **Pieniny National Park** (www.pieniny.sk) to raft the river beneath impressive 500m-tall cliffs. Along with a Polish park on the north bank, Pieniny was created in 1967 to protect Dunajec Gorge, east of the Slovak village of Červený Kláštor.

At the mouth of the gorge, a few of the rooms in the fortified 14th-century **Red Monastery** (Červený Kláštor; adult/child €2/1; ☉10am-5pm, closed Nov-Apr) hold a diminutive museum, but you're here to float. There are two departure points for a **river float trip** (☑4282 840; www.pltnictvo.sk; adult/child €10/5; ☉9am-dusk May-Oct) on Rte 243: one opposite the monastery, and another 1km upriver west of the village. Most visitors pile into one of the continually launching, traditional – and dry – *plte* (shallow, flatbottom wood rafts). But for €40 to €50 per person you can be outfitted for a wet, and slightly wilder, rubber-raft ride. Don't be expecting Class V thrills though. The Dunajec River is a fairly sedate 1½-hour experience terminating near the Slovak village of Lesnica.

To return to Červený Kláštor you can hike back the way you came, along the riverside trail through the 9km-long gorge, in a little over two hours. It's an interesting walk even if rafting is not your thing. Alternatively, 500m southeast of the river trip terminus is **Chata Pieniny** (☑4397 530; www.chatapieniny.sk; Lesnica; dm €10, meals €3-10) in Lesnica. There you can rent a bicycle for a one-way ride (€4) back through the gorge, or board a minibus that will transport you the 22km back by road (€3). In summer, the log *chata* and its restaurant are continually abuzz. Folk musicians from this distinctive region often play to the crowds. Yes, it's a bit touristy, but in a fun, very Slovak way.

There's not a lot of reason to stay over unless you're stuck, but you could pitch a tent in the field outside **Hotel Pltník** (☑4822 525; www.hotelpltnik.sk; Červený Kláštor; campsite €4-6) or check into one of the copious private rooms (signed *privaty* or *zimmer frei*) on the road in Červený Kláštor.

Though Pieniny is only 42km north of Kežmarok, getting here is a challenge unless you have a vehicle. Travel agents in the High Tatras resort towns can help you arrange scheduled trips with transport. Public buses run to Červený Kláštor from Poprad (€3, 1¾ hours), via Kežmarok (€2, 1¼ hour), only once in the morning and once in the evening. Several pedestrian bridges lead from here into Poland.

Levoča

☑053 / POP 14,700

So this is what Slovakia looked like in the 13th century... Levoča is one of the few towns to still have its ancient defences largely intact. Here high medieval walls surround Old Town buildings and cobblestone alleyways. At the centre of it all stands the pride of the country's religious art and architecture collection, the Gothic Church of St Jacob. During the Middle Ages the king of Hungary invited Saxon Germans to colonise frontier lands. Levoča became central to the resulting Slavo-Germanic Spiš region. Unesco recognised the cultural significance of the Old Town by adding it to its list of World Heritage sites at Spiš (including Spiš Castle and Spiš Chapter, in Spišské Podhradie).

From the bus stop at Nám Štefana Kluberta, follow Košicka west two blocks to the main square.

◉ Sights

Church of St Jacob CHURCH

(Chrám sv Jakuba; Nám Majstra Pavla; adult/child €3/1.50; ☺by tour 11am-4pm Mon, 8.30am-4pm Tue-Sat, 1-4pm Sun) The spindles-and-spires Church of St Jacob, built in the 14th and 15th centuries, elevates your spirit with its soaring arches, precious art and rare furnishings. Everyone comes to see the splendid 18m-high Gothic altar (1517) created by Master Pavol of Levoča. Not much is known about the sculptor, but his work is much revered. Cherubic representations of both the Last Supper and the Madonna and Child are carved into the wood-and-paint masterpiece. (This Madonna's face appeared on the original 100Sk banknote.) Buy tickets at the cashier inside the Municipal Weights House across the street from the north door. Entry is generally on the hour, but admissions are more frequent in July and August, and more sporadic off-season. The adjacent 16th-century **cage of shame** was built to punish naughty boys and girls.

Nám Majstra Pavla SQUARE

Gothic and Renaissance eye candy abound on the main square, Nám Majstra Pavla. The private **Thurzov House** (1517), at No 7, has a characteristically frenetic Spiš Renaissance roofline. No 20 is the **Master Pavol Museum**, dedicated to the works of the city's most celebrated son. The 15th-century **Historic Town Hall** (Radnica) building, centre square, is really more interesting than the limited exhibits contained within. Temporary, town-related displays are on show at No 40, **Creative Culture in Spiš** (Výtarná Kultura na Spiši), originally a municipal building, then a school. One ticket gets you into all of the last three, as they are branches of the **Spiš Museum** (www.spisskemuzeum. com; adult/child €3/1.50; ☺9am-5pm Tue-Sun).

Church of Mariánska hora CHURCH

From town you can see the Church of Mariánska hora, 2km north, where the largest Catholic pilgrimage in Slovakia takes place in early July.

⌂ Sleeping & Eating

Hotel U Leva HOTEL €€

(☑4502 311; www.uleva.sk; Nám Majstra Pavla 24; s/d/apt €50/73/99; ☺☎) Spread across two Old Town buildings, each of the 23 cleanly contemporary rooms is unique. All have muted jewel-tone walls enlivening them, and apartments come with kitchens. The fine restaurant (mains €7 to €13) combines atypical ingredients (brie, spinach) with time-honoured Slovak techniques.

Hotel Arkáda HOTEL €

(☑4512 372; www.arkada.sk; Nám Majstra Pavla 26; s/d €36/52; @☎) Furnishings in the Old Town building are mostly uninspired, but you can upgrade to a suite with antiques and arched ceilings for just €70. The cellar restaurant (mains €5 to €11) is much more atmospheric, with ancient brick vaults. Traditional and grilled dishes here attract quite a local following.

Oáza PENSION €

(☑4514 511; www.ubytovanieoaza.sk; Nová 65; dm incl breakfast €10) Simple two-bed rooms with shared bathroom, and four-bed rooms with bath and kitchen, are just what the budget doctor ordered.

Reštaurácia Slovenka SLOVAK €

(Nám Majstra Pavla 66; mains €3-7) The only place in town to get homemade *pirohy* (dumplings, somewhat akin to ravioli, stuffed with potato) topped with sheep's cheese and crackling.

Cukráren Oáza CAFE €

(Nám Majstra Pavla 28; ☺8am-8pm) Creamy cakes, pastries and ice creams served in a tropical-themed 'oasis' is quite a treat.

ℹ Information

Pretty much everything in town, including banks and post, is on the main square.

Levonet Internet Café (Nám Majstra Pavla 38; per hr €2; ☺10am-10pm)

Tourist information office (☑4513 763; www. levoca.sk; Nám Majstra Pavla 58; ☺9am-noon & 12.30-4pm) Ask for the free photocopied map.

ℹ Getting There & Away

Levoča is on the main E50 motorway between Poprad (28km) and Košice (94km). Bus travel is most practical in the area. The local bus stop at Nám Štefana Kluberta is much closer to town than the bus station, which is 1km southeast of centre. Frequent coach services take you to:

Košice (€4.50, two hours, five daily)

Poprad (€1.60, 30 minutes, hourly) Has onward, mainline train connections best for travelling to Bratislava.

Spišská Nová Ves (€1, 20 minutes, every 30 minutes) For transferring to Slovenský Raj.

Spišské Podhradie (€1, 20 minutes, 11 daily) For Spiš Castle.

Spišské Podhradie

☑ 053 / POP 3800

Stretching for 4 hectares above the village of Spišské Podhradie, the ruined Spiš Castle is undoubtedly one of largest in Europe. The ruins are certainly one of the most photographed sights in Slovakia. Two kilometres west, the medieval Spiš Chapter ecclesiastical settlement is also a Unesco World Heritage site. In between, the village itself has a few services, but not much else.

⊙ Sights

Spiš Castle   CASTLE
(Spišský hrad; www.spisskemuzeum.com; adult/child €4.50/2.50; ☺9am-7pm, closed Nov-Apr)
From the E50 motorway you catch glimpses of eerie outlines and stony ruins crowning the ridge on the eastern side of Spišské Podhradie. Can it really be that big? Indeed, Spiš Castle seems to go on forever. If the reconstructed ruins are this impressive, imagine what the fortress was once like. Be sure to get the English audio tour that brings the past into focus through story and legend.

Chronicles first mention Spiš Castle in 1209, and the remaining central **residential tower** is thought to date from that time. From there defenders are said to have repulsed the Tatars in 1241. Rulers and noble families kept adding fortifications and palaces during the 15th and 16th centuries, but by 1780 the site had already lost military significance and much was destroyed by fire. It wasn't until the 1970s that efforts were made to salvage and fortify what remained. Few structures are whole, but there's a **cistern**, a **Romanesque palace** that contains the very small museum, and the **chapel** adjacent to it. Night tours and medieval festivals take place some summer weekends.

Spiš Castle is 1km east of Spišské Podhradie, a healthy, uphill hike above the spur rail station. The easiest approach to the castle by car is off the E50 highway on the east (Prešov) side.

Spiš Chapter   MONASTERY
(Spišská Kapitula; adult/child €2/1) On the west side of Spišské Podhradie, you'll find the still-active Spiš Chapter, a 13th-century Catholic complex encircled by a 16th-century wall. Charming private Gothic houses line the single street running between the two medieval gates. The highlight is the 1273 Romanesque **St Martin's Cathedral** (Spišská Kapitula 1; admission €1; ☺10am-noon & 1-5pm

Mon-Sat), with twin towers and an ornate sanctuary. Inside are several impressive trifold-painted Gothic altars from the 15th century. Buy tickets for the cathedral and pick up a guide from the information office at Spišská Kapitula 4. If you're travelling to Spiš Chapter by bus from Levoča, get off one stop (and 1km) before Spišské Podhradie, at Kapitula.

⊨ Sleeping & Eating

This is potentially a day trip from Levoča or the High Tatras, so there's not a lot of reason to stay over. The castle has a food stand, and the village has a little grocery store.

Penzión Podzámok   PENSION €
(☑4541 755; www.penzionpodzamok.sk; Podzámková 28; r with/without bathroom €30/20) Family houses have been cobbled together to create a simple 42-bed guesthouse with a backyard view of the castle. It's in the village, north across the bridge.

Spišsky Salaš   MOUNTAIN HUT €
(☑4541 202; www.spisskysalas.sk; Levočská cesta 11; mains €3-7) Dig into lamb stew in the folksy dining room or on the covered deck, and watch the kids romp on rough-hewn play sets. The rustic log complex also has three simple rooms for rent (per person €13). It's 3km west of Spiš Chapter, on the road toward Levoča.

❶ Getting There & Away

Spišské Podhradie is 15km east of Levoča and 78km northeast of Košice.

BUS Frequent buses connect with Levoča (€1, 20 minutes), Poprad (€2.50, 50 minutes) and Košice (€4, 1½ hours).

TRAIN An inconvenient spur railway line heads to Spišské Podhradie from Spišské Vlachy (€0.50, 10 minutes, five daily), a station on the main line. Check schedules at www.cp.atlas.sk.

Slovenský Raj & Around

☑ 053

With rumbling waterfalls, steep gorges, sheer rockfaces, thick forests and hilltop meadows, Slovenský Raj lives up to the name of 'Slovak Paradise'. A few easier trails exist, but the one-way ladder-and-chain ascents make this a national park for the passionately outdoorsy. You cling to a metal rung headed straight up a precipice while an icy waterfall splashes and sprays you from a metre away. Oh, and that's after

SLOVAKIA EAST SLOVAKIA

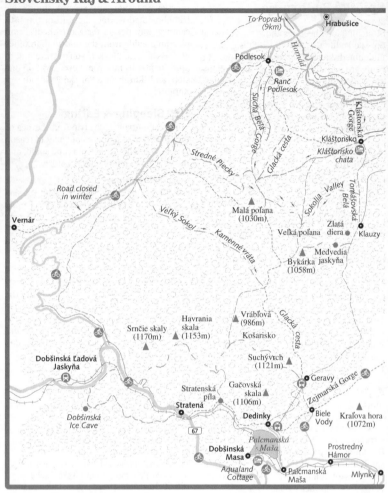

you've scrambled horizontally across a log ladder to cross the stream down below – pure exhilaration.

The nearest town of any size is the uninspiring Spišská Nová Ves, 23km southeast of Poprad. Of the three trailhead resort villages, Podlesok, outside of Hrabušice (16km southwest of Poprad), is our favourite – for its variety of hiking options, food stands, diverse lodging and sport possibilities. Čingov, 5km west of Spišská Nová Ves, also has good lodging. About 50km south, Dedinky is more of a regular village with a pub, supermarket and houses on a lake.

⊙ Sights & Activities

Before you trek, pick up VKÚ's 1:25,000 *Slovenský Raj* hiking map (No 4) or Dajama's *Knapsacked Travel: The Slovak Paradise* hiking book, available at many tourist offices and bookshops countrywide.

Slovenský Raj National Park   PARK
(Slovak Paradise; admission €1 Jul & Aug, free Sep-Jun) The national park has numerous trails that include one-way *roklina* (gorge) sections and take at least half a day. From Čingov a green trail leads up the Hornád River Gorge an hour to **Tomašovský výhľad**, a rocky outcropping and overlook that is a good short-

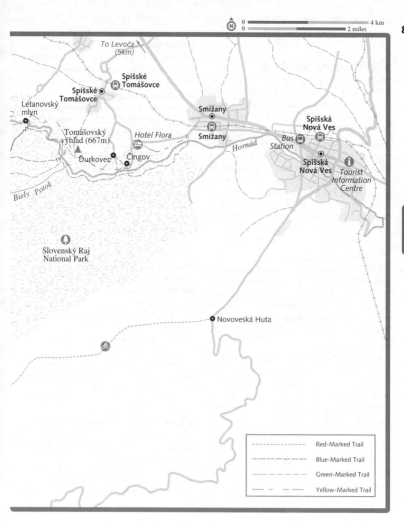

hike destination. Or continue to the green, one-way, technically aided **Kláštorisko Gorge trail**, allowing at least eight hours for the circuit.

You can also reach the Kláštorisko Gorge ascent from Podlesok (six hours). Another excellent alternative from Podlesok is to hike six to seven hours up the dramatic, ladder and technical-assist **Suchá Belá Gorge**, then east to Kláštorisko chata on a yellow then red trail. From there, take the blue trail down to the Hornád River, then follow the river gorge upstream to return to Podlesok.

One of the shortest, dramatic, technical-assist hikes starts at Biele Vody (15 minutes northeast of Dedinky via the red trail) and follows the blue-trail up **Zejmarská Gorge**. The physically fit can run, clamber and climb up in 50 minutes; others huff and puff up in 90 minutes. To get back, you can follow the green trail down to Dedinky, or there's a **chairlift** (adult/child €1/0.50; ⊘9am-5pm Jun-Aug) that works sporadically.

Dobšinská Ice Cave   CAVE
(www.ssj.sk; adult/child €7/3.50; ⊘9am-4pm Tue-Sun, closed Sep-May) The fanciful frozen formations in this Unesco-noted ice cave

are more dazzling in early June than late August. A 15-minute hike leads up to where tours begin every hour or so.

🛏 Sleeping & Eating

All the listed lodgings have restaurants. Numerous food stands and eateries and a small grocery are available in Podlesok. The biggest area supermarket is next to the bus station in Spišska Nová Ves.

Autocamp Podlesok CAMPING GROUND €
(🖉4299 165; atcpodlesok@gmail.com; Podlesok; campsites €4-8, cottages & huts per person €10; 🛜) The always-busy office at this lively camping ground provides loads of trail info and a wi-fi hotspot to check email. Pitch a tent in the big field (600 capacity) or choose from fairly up-to-date A-frame cabins, small huts and cottages with two to 12 beds and a bathroom.

TOP CHOICE | Ranč Podlesok PENSION €
(🖉0918407077; www.rancpodlesok.sk; Podlesok 5; d/tr €30/45; 🛜) A blue park trail runs behind this stone-and-log lodge and restaurant at park's edge. Spacious rooms, a giant swing set and sand volleyball add to the attraction. It's 1km past the Podlesok village area.

Penzión Lesnica PENSION €
(🖉449 1518; www.stefani.sk; Čingov 113; s/d incl breakfast €30/37) These nine simple, sunny-coloured rooms close to the trail fill up fast, so book ahead. Locals also know that the attached restaurant is one of the best local places for a Slovak repast (mains €3 to €7) – or an ice-cream sundae.

Hotel Flora HOTEL €
(🖉449 1129; www.hotelfloraslovenskyraj.sk; Čingov 110; s/d incl breakfast €30/50; 🛜) With stone-work fireplaces and leather chairs, the public spaces exude a mountain rusticicity; too

bad the rooms are plain. At least the restaurant (mains €6 to €14) has a large terrace.

Koliba Zuzana SLOVAK €-€€
(🖉0905278397; www.kolibazuzana.szm.sk; Dedinky 127; mains €3-10) Lakeside restaurant with terrace; two suites (€80) for rent upstairs.

Aqualand Cottage HOSTEL €
(🖉0948007735; www.aqualand.sk; Dobšinská Maša-Dedinky; dm €13, s/d without bathroom €25/32) A sprawling cottage-hostel with commonroom, fireplace and two kitchens across the lake from Dedinky proper.

ℹ Information

Outside Spišska Nová Ves, your lodging is often the best source of information; park info booths are open in July and August. Get cash before you arrive; there is an ATM and exchange at Spišska Nová train station. Helpful websites include www.slovenskyraj.sk and www.slovenskyraj.info.

@ve.net Internet Café (Zimná 58, Spišská Nová Ves; per hr €2; ⏰9am-6pm Mon-Fri)
Mountain Rescue Service (🖉emergency 183 00; http://his.hzs.sk)
Tourist information booth (Čingov; ⏰9am-5pm, closed Sep-Jun)
Tourist information booth (Podlesok; ⏰10am-1pm, closed Sep-Jun)
Tourist Information Centre (🖉4428 292; Letná 49, Spišská Nová Ves; ⏰8am-6pm Mon-Fri, 9am-1pm Sat, 2-6pm Sun May-Sep, 8am-5pm Mon-Fri Oct-Apr) Helps with accommodation.

ℹ Getting There & Around

Off season especially, you may consider hiring a car in Košice; connections to the park can be a chore. You'll have to transfer at least once, most likely in Spišský Štvrtok or Spišská Nová Ves. Buses run infrequently on weekends, more often in July and August. No buses run directly

BUSES FROM SPISŠKA NOVÁ VES

ROUTE	COST (€)	DURATION (MIN)	FREQUENCY (DAILY)
Poprad–Spišský Štvrtok	1	30	12 Mon-Fri
Levoča –Spišský Štvrtok	0.85	20	10 Mon-Fri
Spišský Štvrtok –Podlesok	0.85	20	2 Mon-Fri
Poprad –Spišska Nová Ves	2	45	11
Levoča –Spišska Nová Ves	0.85	20	18
Spišska Nová Ves –Čingov	0.50	15	6 Mon-Fri
Spišska Nová Ves –Podlesok	1.20	30	2 Mon-Fri
Spišska Nová Ves –Dedinky	2	90	3 Mon-Fri

between trailhead villages. Carefully check schedules at http://cp.atlas.sk.

Trains run from Spišská Nová Ves to Poprad (€1, 20 minutes, 12 daily) and Košice (€3.80. one hour, 15 daily).

Košice

☑055 / POP 235,300

An eclectic mix of Old Town architecture – modern hotels, Middle Ages churches, and art nouveau facades – lets you know this is a living city, not a relic. A handful of exhibits add to the attraction, but mostly you'll want to gather with locals on the benches near the musical fountain, or raise a glass at a sidewalk cafe. Visit during one of the summer street festivals, or enjoy the weekend nightlife, and you'll have plenty of opportunities to make new friends.

Košice received its city coat of arms in 1369 and for centuries was the eastern stronghold of the Hungarian kingdom. On 5 April 1945 the Košice Government Program – which made communist dictatorship in Czechoslovakia a virtual certainty – was announced here. Today US Steel forms the backbone of the city; you can't miss the company's influence, from the ice-hockey stadium it sponsors to the factory flare stacks on the industrial outskirts.

◉ Sights

At the time of research the East Slovak Museum was under reconstruction. Ask about it and other small exhibits at the tourist office.

Hlavná SQUARE
Most all of the sights are in or around the town's long, plaza-like main square, Hlavná. Landscaped flowerbeds surround the central **musical fountain**, across from the 1899 **State Theatre**. To the north stands a large baroque **plague column** from 1723. Look for the turn-of-the-20th-century, art nouveau **Hotel Slaviá** at No 63. No 27, **Shire Hall** (1779), is where the Košice Government Program was proclaimed in 1945; today there's a minor art gallery inside.

Cathedral of St Elizabeth CHURCH
(Dóm sv Alžbety, Hlavná; church free, attractions each €1; ⊙1-3pm Mon, 9am-5pm Tue-Fri, 9am-1pm Sat) The dark and brooding 14th-century Cathedral of St Elizabeth wins the prize for sight most likely to grace your Košice postcard home. You can't miss Europe's easternmost Gothic cathedral, which domi-

nates the square. Below the church, a **crypt** contains the tomb of Duke Ferenc Rákóczi, who was exiled to Turkey after the failed 18th-century Hungarian revolt against Austria. Don't forget to climb the 160 narrow, circular stone steps up the church's **tower** for city views. Climbing the **royal staircase** as the monarchs once did provides an interior perspective. Just to the south, the 14th-century **St Michael's Chapel** has limited entry hours.

Lower Gate Underground Museum MUSEUM
(Hlavná; adult/child €1/0.50; ⊙10am-6pm Tue-Sun) The underground remains of medieval Košice – lower gate, defence chambers, fortifications and waterways – were only uncovered during construction work in 1996. Get lost in the mazelike passages and tunnels of the archaeological excavations at the south end of the square.

Wax Museum MUSEUM
(www.waxmuseum.sk; Hlavná 3; adult/child €4/2.60; ⊙11am-3pm Mon-Fri, noon-3pm Sat, 1-3pm Sun) Fourteenth-century Urban Tower, rebuilt in the 1970s, now holds a fairly cheesy wax museum.

⊨ Sleeping

The City Information Centre has an annual town booklet that lists local accommodation, including university dorms open to the public in July and August.

Penzión Beryl HOTEL €€
(☑6998 539; www.penzionberyl.sk; Mojmírová 2; incl breakfast s €55-69, d €65-80; ☺✳✿) Modern rooms here have ecofriendly bamboo floors and earth-tone designs. A full, hot breakfast buffet includes both egg and sweet dishes. The accommodating staff can help arrange theatre tickets and car rental.

Chrysso Penzión BOUTIQUE HOTEL €€
(☑6230 450; www.penzionchrysso.sk; Zvonárska 3; s/d/apt €58/68/78; ✳✿) Think design-driven details, like silk throws and sleek leather chairs in chocolate and cream. A wine bar, terrace and restaurant downstairs are similarly stylish.

Hotel Zlatý Dukat HOTEL €€€
(☑7279 333; www.hotelzlatydukat.sk; Hlavná 16; r incl breakfast €90-195; @✿) Look through the glass floor near the reception to see the 13th-century foundations of this main-square hotel. Luxury touches include flatscreen TVs, flowers and room service.

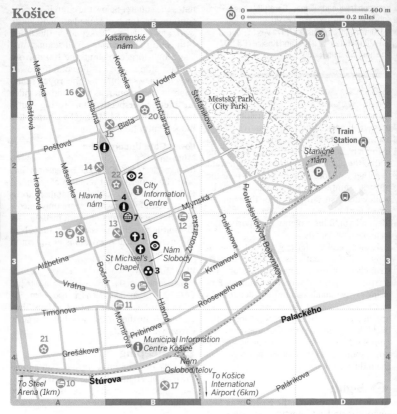

K2 HOSTEL €

(☑6255 948; Štúrova 32; s/d without bathroom €16/27) Dowdy singles and doubles, super close to the pedestrian centre. No common room or kitchen.

Penzión Slovakia PENSION €

(☑7289 820; www.penzionslovakia.sk; Orliá 6; s/d €45/55; ❄🤶) Charming city guesthouse with grill restaurant downstairs.

✕ Eating

Stará Sýpka SLOVAK €€

(Fejova 1; mains €5-11) Enjoy today's Slovak cooking in a pleasant cafe-restaurant-beer cellar that's quite popular. In summer, the courtyard terrace is the best.

Cafe Napoli ITALIAN €-€€

(Hlavná 82; mains €4-11) Stylish young locals fill up this modern Italian restaurant, taking advantage of the long cocktail list and good wine selection.

Villa Regia FINE DINING €€-€€€

(www.villaregia.sk; Dominikánske nám 3; mains €7-18) Steaks, seafood and vegetarian dishes get artistic treatment amid a rustic Old World atmosphere. The vaulted ceilings and stone walls extend to the upstairs pension rooms as well.

Karczma Mlyn SLOVAK €

(Hlavná 82; mains €3-8) A pubby place, Mlyn is good for a pint and for heaping portions of cheap and hearty traditional fare. Enter through the courtyard.

Cukráreň Aida CAFE €

(Hlavná 81; cakes €1-3; ⊙8am-10pm) The most popular ice-cream and cake shop in town; several branches on the main square.

Bagéteria CAFE €

(Hlavná 36; sandwiches €1-3) Baguette sandwiches to eat in or take out.

🍷 Drinking & Entertainment

Any of the sidewalk cafes on the main square are fine places to drink on a warm evening. The free monthly publication *Kam do Mesta* (www.kamdomesta.sk) lists in Slovak the whats, wheres and whens of the entertainment scene.

HC Pub 21   PUB
(Dominikánske nám 9) Live folk-rock plays Tuesday evenings. Otherwise, it's a convivial hockey-themed pub.

Jazz Club   CLUB
(Kováčska 39) DJs spin here most nights, but there are also occasional live concerts.

State Theatre   THEATRE
(Štátne Divadlo Košice; www.sdke.sk; Hlavná 58; ⊙box office 9am-5.30pm Mon-Fri, 10am-1pm Sat) Local opera and ballet companies stage performances in the 1899 neo-baroque theatre from September to May.

State Philharmonic Košice   LIVE MUSIC
(Štátna Filharmónia Košice; www.sfk.sk; House of the Arts, Moyzesova 66) The spring musical festival is a good time to catch performances of the city's philharmonic at the House of the Arts, but concerts take place year-round.

Steel Aréna   SPORTS
(www.steelarena.sk; Nerudova 12) A co-host venue for the 2011 ice hockey world championships; the hometown's revered team, HC Košice, plays here. Buy tickets at www.ticketportal.sk.

ⓘ Information

City Information Centre (☑6258 888; www.kosice.sk; Hlavná 59; ⊙9am-6pm Mon-Fri, 9am-1pm Sat, 1-5pm Sun Jun-Sep, closed Sun Oct-May) Ask for both the free annual town guide and the full-size colour brochure of historic sites. Good info on cultural events.

Ľudová Banka (Mlynská 29) ATM and exchange; well located between the train station and centre.

Municipal Information Centre (MIC; ☑16 168; www.mickosice.sk; Dargov Department Store; Hlavná 2; ⊙9am-8pm Mon-Sat) Souvenir and tickets sales, hidden mid-department store.

Net Club (Hlavná 9; per hr €1.60; ⊙9am-10pm) Large internet/gaming cafe.

Police station (☑159; Pribinova 6)

ⓘ Getting There & Away

Check bus and train schedules at http://cp.atlas.sk.

Air
Košice International Airport (KSC; www.airportkosice.sk) is 6km southwest of the centre. For international airlines serving Košice, see p905). **Danube Wings** (V5; www.danubewings.eu) has two daily flights to Bratislava, on weekdays only.

Bus
You can book ahead on some Ukraine-bound buses through **Eurobus** (www.eurobus.sk). Getting to Poland is easier from Poprad. Destinations include Bardejov (€4, 1¾ hours, 12 daily), Levoča (€4.50, two hours, five daily) and Uzhgorod (Ukraine; €7, two to three hours, three daily).

TRAINS FROM KOŠICE

DESTINATION	COST (€)	DURATION (HR)	FREQUENCY (DAILY)
Bratislava	19	5½	4 (IC)
Poprad (High Tatras)	5	1½	12
Spišska Nová Ves (Slovenský Raj)	3.80	1	15
Miskolc, Hungary	5	1¼	2
Lviv, Ukraine	60	12¾	1

Car

Several of the big international car-hire firms like Avis and Eurocar have representatives at the airport. It is often cheaper to rent in Bratislava, even with the added kilometres.

Buchbinder (☑0911 582 200; www.buch binder.sk) Smaller firm with good rates. Crack-erjack staff arrange gratis pick-up in the city.

🛈 Getting Around

The Old Town is small, so you probably can walk everywhere. Transport tickets (€0.60 one zone) cover most buses and trams; buy them at news-stands and validate on board. Bus 23 between the airport and the train station requires a two-zone ticket (€1).

Bardejov

☑054 / POP 33,400

The steep roofs and flat fronts of the bur-ghers' houses on Bardejov's Renaissance Old Town square appear strikingly homoge-neous at first. Look closer and you notice an ethereal sgraffito decoration or a pastel hue and plaster detail setting each apart. Unesco must have been impressed too, as it included the quiet square on its World Heri-tage list. Bardejov received its royal charter in 1376, and grew rich on trade between Po-land and Russia into the 16th century. A few local museums shed light on this region's Eastern-facing art and culture, and this is a good base for exploring further. Wooden churches in the area reflect the Carpatho-Rusyn heritage that the area shares with neighbouring parts of Ukraine and Poland. A few kilometres north in Bardejovské Kúpele you can take a cure at a thermal spa or see these churches in a traditional open-air village museum. In late 1944 heavy WWII fighting took place at the Dukla Pass on the Polish border, 54km northeast of Bardejov. Tanks still stand in the area today as a memorial.

⊙ Sights

The main square, **Radičné nám** is a sight in itself, and you can walk along the old **town walls and bastions** along Na Hradbách.

Šariš Museum   MUSEUM
(www.muzeumbardejov.sk; ⊙8am-noon & 12.30-4pm Tue-Sun) There are two local branches of the Šariš Museum worth seeing. Centre square, the **Town Hall** (Radnica; Radničné nám 48; adult/child €1.50/1) contains altarpieces and a historical collection. Built in 1509, it was the first Renaissance building in Slova-kia. At the **Icon Exposition** (Radničné nám 27; adult/child €1.50/1), more than 130 daz-zling icons and iconostases from the 16th to 19th centuries are on display. This is an excellent opportunity to see the religious art that originally decorated Greek Catholic and Orthodox wooden churches east of Bardejov.

Basilica of St Egídius   CHURCH
(Bazilika Sv Egídia; Radničné nám; adult/child €1.50/1; ⊙9.30am-5pm Mon-Fri, 10am-3pm Sat, 11.30am-3pm Sun) The interior of this 15th-century basilica is packed with 11 Gothic al-tarpieces, built from 1460 to 1510. Each has a thorough explanation in English.

🍴 Sleeping & Eating

Cafes can be found around Radničné nám.

Penzion Hradby   PENSION €
(☑0918349229; www.penzion-hradby.sk; Stöcklova 8; s/d/tr €20/28/40; 🛜) Budget digs in the heart of the Old Town: basic rooms pro-vide all you need, in view of the town walls. Rooms share a fully equipped kitchen.

el. Restaurant & Lodging   PENSION €-€€
(☑4728 404; www.el-restaurant.sk; Stöcklova 43; s/d/apt incl breakfast €30/40/70; 🛜) A myriad of chicken dishes are on the menu of the modern Slovak restaurant downstairs. Up-stairs, three bright and cheery rooms are for rent. It's very central; paid garage parking only.

Bardejov

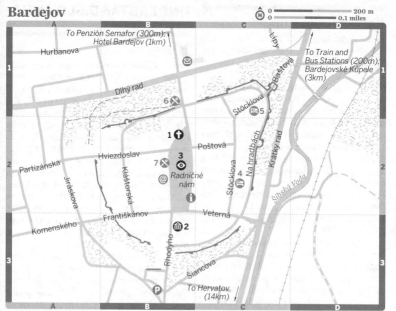

Bardejov

◉ Sights

1 Basilica of St Egídius	B2
2 Šariš Museum Icon Exposition	B3
3 Šariš Museum -Town Hall	B2

⌂ Sleeping

4 el. Restaurant & Lodging	C2
5 Penzión Hrady	C1

✖ Eating

6 La Bello	B1
7 Pohoda Café	B2

La Bello ITALIAN **€-€€**

(Radničné nám 50; mains €4-11) An atmospheric, Italianesque restaurant is the local fave. The thin-crust pizzas are all wood-fired, and grilled meat platters are equally as good.

Pohoda Café SLOVAK **€**

(Radničné nám 39; mains €3-8) This cellar restaurant is a solid choice for Slovak specialities; the bar is quite popular on weekends.

Hotel Bardejov HOTEL **€-€€**

(☑4883 487; www.hotelbardejov.sk; Toplianska ul 23; s/d/apt incl breakfast €38/50/70; 🛜) Fairly utilitarian rooms by the stream on the Old Town outskirts, but they're clean and quiet.

Penzión Semafor PENSION **€**

(☑0905830984; www.penzionsemafor.sk; Kellerova 13; s/d €30/40) Five bright doubles and an apartment in a family-run guesthouse.

🛈 Information

ČSOB (Radničné nám 7) Bank exchange and ATM.

Golem Internet Café (Radničné nám 35; per hr €2; ⏱9.30am-10.30pm Mon-Thu, 9.30am-midnight Fri, 4.30-11pm Sat & Sun)

Main post office (Dlhý rad 14)

Tourist information centre (☑4723 013; www.bardejov.sk; Radničné nám 21; ⏱9am-5.30pm Mon-Fri, 11.30am-3.30pm Sat & Sun, closed Sat & Sun Oct-Apr) Info, maps, souvenirs and guide services.

🛈 Getting There & Away

Bardejov is on a small spur train line, so buses to here are most convenient. Though you're close to Poland here, you're not near an international bus route. For those with a car, the E371 crosses into Poland north of Svidník, a town 35km east of Bardejov.

Buses go to and from Košice (€4, 1¾ hours, 12 daily), Poprad (€4.50, 2¼ hours, five daily) and Bardejovské Kúpele (€0.55, 10 minutes, 12 daily).

Bardejovské Kúpele

Three short kilometres to the north you'll find the leafy, promenade-filled spa town of **Bardejovské Kúpele**. If you want to book a service like a massage or a mineral bath (from €10), go directly to the **Spa House** (Kúpelny dom; ☑4774 225; ⊙8am-noon & 1-5pm Mon-Sat) at the top of the main pedestrian street. The town also has Slovakia's oldest *skanzen*, the **Museum of Folk Architecture** (Múzeum ľudovej architektúry; adult/child €1.30/0.70; ⊙9am-5pm Tue-Sun, to 3pm Oct-Apr). This is your best chance to see the painted interiors and iconostases of the area's nail-less wooden churches. An ancient (Unesco-listed) example from Zboj has been moved here, and a larger one built on site to hold church services.

Frequent buses connect with Bardejov. If you have a car, park in the lot by the bus station at the base of the town and walk uphill; the whole place is pedestrian-only. At the base near the colonnade, there are several restaurants and the **Tourist Information Office** (☑4744 744; www.bardejovske -kupele.sk; Kino Žriedlo; ⊙8am-5pm Mon-Fri, 10.30am-4pm Sat & Sun May-Sep, 9am-4pm Mon-Fri Oct-Apr).

UNDERSTAND SLOVAKIA

History

Slavic tribes wandered west into what would become Slovakia sometime around the 5th century; in the 9th century, the territory was part of the short-lived Great Moravian empire. It was about the same time that the Magyars (Hungarians) set up shop next door and subsequently laid claim to the whole territory. When in the early 16th century the Turks moved into Budapest, Hungarian monarchs took up residence in Bratislava (known then as Pressburg in German, and Pozsony in Hungarian). Because Slovakia was the Hungarian frontierland, many fortresses were constructed here during the Middle Ages, and can still be seen today.

It wasn't until the turn of the 20th century that the Slovak intellectuals cultivated ties with neighbouring Czechs and took their nation into the united Czechoslovakia post-WWI. The day before Hitler's troops invaded Czechoslovakia in March 1939, Slovak leaders declared Slovakia a German protectorate, and a brief period of sovereignty ensued. This was not a popular move and

---

WOODEN CHURCHES

Travelling east from Bardejov, you come to a crossroads of Western and Eastern Christianity. From the 17th to the 19th centuries, nearly 300 dark-wood, onion-domed churches were built in the region. Of the fewer than 50 that remain, eight have been recognised by Unesco. A handful celebrate the Roman Catholic or Protestant faiths, but most belong to the Eastern rites of Greek Catholicism and Orthodoxy. Typically they honour the Holy Trinity with three domes, three architectural sections and three doors on the icon screen. Richly painted icons and venerated representations of Christ and the saints decorate the iconostases, and usually every inch of the churches' interiors have also been handpainted. These can be quite the sight to behold, but it's not easy to get inside. Most of these rural village churches are remote, with extremely limited bus connections, and the doors are kept locked. Sometimes there's a map posted showing where the keeper of the key lives; sometimes he's next door, and sometimes you're out of luck. The way to guarantee seeing icons and an interior is to go to the Icon Exhibition in Bardejov, and the *skanzen* in Bardejovské Kúpele, 3km north. The church in Hervatov (c 1500) is one of the closest to Bardejov. If you're up for a further adventure, numerous resources can aid your search:

Carpathian Wooden Pearls (www.drevenechramy.sk) An illustrated map of 27 wooden churches designated national cultural treasures.

Cultural Heritage of Slovakia: Wooden Churches A comprehensive, full-colour book by Miloš Dudas with photos and church descriptions; for sale at bookstores.

Wooden Architecture in Prešovsky Kraj (www.po-kraj.sk/en) Government website that lists all the wooden churches in the Prešov prefecture (under 'Facts').

Wooden Churches near Bardejov An English-language booklet for sale at the Bardejov tourist office.

in August 1944 Slovak partisans instigated the ill-fated Slovak National Uprising (Slovenské Národné Povstanie, or SNP), a source of ongoing national pride (and innumerable street names).

After the reunification and communist takeover in 1948, power was centralised in Prague until 1989 when the Velvet Revolution brought down the iron curtain here. Elections in 1992 saw the left-leaning, nationalist Movement for a Democratic Slovakia (HZDS) come to power with Vladimír Mečiar, a former boxer, as prime minister. Scarcely a year later, without referendum, the Czechoslovak federation dissolved peacefully on 1 January 1993, bringing Slovakia its first true independence.

Despite changing government leadership that alternately rejected and embraced economic and social reforms, Slovakia was accepted into NATO and the EU by 2004, became a Schengen member state in 2007 and adopted the euro as the national currency in January 2009. Bratislava and the High Tatras were the first areas to bounce back from the subsequent global economic downturn. Investment and development are once again going strong there, but the provinces have been plagued with a series of floods that have hampered recovery.

The People of Slovakia

A deeply religious and familial people, Slovaks have strong family ties and a deep sense of folk traditions. Today Roman Catholics form the majority (about 69%), but evangelicals are also numerous and east Slovakia has many Greek Catholic and Orthodox believers. The young are warm and open, but there can be residual communist reserve within older generations. Generosity and warmth lurk just behind this stoicism. If you make friends with a family, the hospitality (and free-flowing liquor) may just knock you out. Thankfully, in the tourist industry, surly service is now the exception rather than the rule.

Government statistics estimate that Slovakia's population is 86% Slovak, 10% Hungarian and 1.7% Roma. This last figure is in some dispute as some groups estimate the Roma population to be as high as 4%, most of whom live in eastern Slovakia. The Roma are viewed by the general populace with an uncompromising suspicion – at best.

Folk Arts & Architecture

A few Slovak city-dwellers may have been put off by the clichéd image of the communist-era 'happy peasant', but traditional folk arts – from music to architecture – are still celebrated across the country. Indeed, attending one of the many village folk festivals in July and August can be the highlight of a visit: colourful costumes, upbeat traditional music (punctuated by stomps and squeals) and hearty *klobasa* and beer are all part of the fun. Two of the biggest are the Východná Folk Festival (www.obec-vychodna.sk), in the small namesake village 32km west of Poprad, and Terchová's Janošik Days, in the Malá Fatra National Park.

Traditional Slovak folk instruments include the *fujara* (a 2m-long flute), the *konkovka* (a shepherd's flute), drums and cimbalom. Today you'll likely still see a folk troupe accompanied by fiddle, bass, clarinet and sometimes trumpet or accordion. National folk companies like Lučnica (www.lucnica.sk) and Sĺuk (www.sluk.sk) perform across the country. But each microregion has its own particular melodies and costumes.

Outside of festivals, the best place to experience folk culture is at a *skanzen*, an open-air museum where examples of traditional wooden cottages and churches have been gathered in village form. The houses are fully furnished in traditional style and frequent activates, especially around holidays, focus on folk culture. The largest *skanzen*, in Martin, represents several regions and the village of Vlkolínec is like a living *skanzen*. A hillside open-air village museum in Bardejovské Kúpele sheds light on that area's far-eastern, Orthodox-leaning culture. The *skanzen* there has two good examples of the nailless wooden churches for which the area is known.

Several more of these architectural gems – built from the 16th to the 19th century with wooden onion domes outside and ornately painted walls and iconostasis inside – can be found around Bardejov; many more are further east. For more see the boxed text on p900.

The Landscape

A hilly, forested country for the most part, Slovakia sits at the heart of Europe, straddling the northwestern end of the Carpathian Mountains. With such great scenery,

TO BUILD OR NOT TO BUILD

Slovak national parks have long been mixed-use, with residential and recreational zones sharing space with more pristine areas. In some ways, this can be good. The elaborate system of cable cars, funiculars and hiker lodging in the High Tatras make the upper altitudes accessible. But recent years have seen increased development in those mountains: new high-speed chairlifts and ski runs in Tatranská Lomnica, never-ending resort construction in Štrbské Pleso... Watchdog groups like the International Union for the Conservation of Nature have protested, suggesting that national park status should be in question. But so far the government doesn't see a problem. Though the parks are less crowded than the Alps or the Rockies, tens of thousands of hikers pass through every year. Try to do your bit to keep things clean; pack out what you pack in, stay on trails and don't pick the flowers.

it's not surprising that most Slovaks spend their weekends outdoors. National parks and protected areas comprise 20% of the territory and the entire country is laced with a network of trails. You will doubtless run into a backpack-toting Slovak wherever you walk out in nature.

Not to be missed is the High Tatras (Vysoké Tatry) National Park, protecting a 12km-long rocky mountain range that seems to rise out of nowhere. The tallest peak, Gerlachovský štít, reaches an impressive 2654m, and snow could blanket the upper reaches any month. The lesser pine-clad ridges of Malá Fatra National Park are popular with local hikers and skiers. In Slovenský Raj National Park, ladders, chain assists and other technical aids make the challenging, narrow gorges and waterfalls accessible to those seeking a challenge.

Unlike the mountainous north, southwestern Slovakia is a fertile lowland stretching from the foothills of the Carpathians down to the Danube River, which forms the border with Hungary. Rivers across the country are prone to spring and autumn flooding, so pay attention to the news when travelling.

Food & Drink

Slovakia isn't known for its 'cuisine' as much as for its home cooking. Soups like *cesnaková polievka* (garlic soup), clear with croutons and cheese, and *kapustnica* (cabbage soup), with a paprika-and-pork base, start most meals. The national dish is *bryndzové halušky*, gnocchi-like dumplings topped with soft, sharp sheep's cheese and bits of bacon fat. You'll also find *bryndza* sheep cheese on potato pancakes,

in *pirohy* (dumplings) and served as a *natierka* (spread) with bread and raw onions. Don't pass up an opportunity to eat in a *salaš* or a *koliba* (rustic eateries named for traditional parts of a sheepherder's camp), where these traditional specialities are the mainstay.

Much of what you'll see on regular menus is basic central European fare: various fried meat schnitzels, hearty pork dishes and paprika-infused stews. It's all very meaty, but most towns have at least one (vegetarian-friendly) pizza place. For dessert, try *palacinka* (crepes), usually stuffed with berries and chocolate or *ovocné knedličky* (fruit dumplings).

Spirits of Slovakia

Though removed from the office setting in recent years, the Slovak drinking tradition is still going strong at home. It would be impolite to begin any visit or meal without a toast. So expect to be served a shot of *slivovica* (plum-based firewater), *borovička* (a potent berry-based clear liquor), Demänovka (a herbal liquor related to Czech Becherovka) or something of the sort.

Unlike its neighbour to the north, Slovakia is not known for its *pivo* (beer). But the full-bodied Zlatý Bažant and dark, sweet Martiner are decent.

Wine is really much more the thing here. What do oenophiles say? Oh, yes, it's highly drinkable (ie good and cheap). The Modra region squeezes out dry medium-bodied reds, like Frankovka and Kláštorné. Slovak reisling and Müller Thurgau varietals are fruity but on the dry side. Tokaj, a white dessert wine from the east, is trying (not terribly successfully, marketingwise) to give the Hungarian version of the same wine a run for its money.

SURVIVAL GUIDE

Directory A–Z
Accommodation

Bratislava has more hostels and five-star hotels than midrange accommodation. Outside the capital, you'll find a whole host of reasonable *penzióny* (guesthouses or pensions). Breakfast is usually available (sometimes included) at all lodgings, and wi-fi is common and usually free. Unless otherwise noted, all lodgings listed offer nonsmoking rooms; those with only nonsmoking are indicated with a ☻. Parking is widely available outside Bratislava.

PRICE RANGES

Note that prices listed in this chapter are for tourist season.

Budget (€) Under €60 (hostel dorms and shared-bathroom rooms, provincial guesthouses).

Midrange (€€) From €60 to €150 (pensions and hotels with restaurants or bars).

Top end (€€€) From €150 to much higher (upscale and international hotels, mostly in Bratislava).

SEASONS

May to September Tourist season countrywide; prices reflected in this guide.

October to April Off-season, rates drop dramatically (10% to 50%).

January to March Additional tourist/ski season in the mountains.

Christmas, New Year and Easter Prices 20% to 30% higher than in tourist season; reservations essential.

BOOKING RESOURCES

Lodge Yourself (www.ubytujsa.sk)

Bratislava Hotels (www.bratislavahotels.com)

Slovakia Tourist Board (www.slovakia.travel)

Activities

Hiking The Mountain Rescue Service (Horská záchranná služba; ☏18 300; http://his.hzs.sk) provides hiking and weather information in addition to aid.

Skiing Check out the snow conditions at Ski Info (www.ski.sk).

Enter any bar or restaurant during puck-pushing season (September to April) and 12 large men and an ice rink will probably be on the TV screen, even at fancy restaurants. The national team usually ranks among the world's 10 strongest, but they haven't managed to break into the Olympic top three yet. (The team was only created when Czechoslovakia dissolved in 1993.) Local club rivalries are quite heated, with the most popular teams being HC Slovan in Bratislava and HC Košice in Košice (go figure). Stoking the obsessive fires is the fact that these teams' two stadiums co-hosted the IIHF world championships in spring of 2011. Bratislava's Ondrej Nepela Arena got a big-money overhaul for the event, so it doesn't seem like the ice-hockey fever will cool down anytime soon.

Business Hours

Sight and attraction hours vary throughout the year; we've listed the opening times for tourist season, May through September, only. Schedules vary October through April; check ahead.

Unless otherwise noted within reviews, these are the standard hours for service listings in this guide.

Banks 8am-5pm Mon-Fri

Bars 11am-midnight Mon-Thu, 11am-2am Fri & Sat, 4pm-midnight Sun

Grocery stores 6.30am-6pm Mon-Fri, 7am-noon Sat

Post offices 8am-5pm Mon-Fri, 8-11am Sat

Nightclubs 4pm-4am Wed-Sun

Restaurants 10.30am-10pm

Shops 9am-6pm Mon-Fri, 9am-noon Sat

Embassies & Consulates

Australia and New Zealand do not have embassies in Slovakia; the nearest are in Vienna and Berlin respectively. The following are in Bratislava.

Canada (☏02-5920 4031; http://www.canadainternational.gc.ca/czech-tcheque/; Carlton-Savoy Building, Mostová 2)

France (☏02-5934 7111; www.france.sk; Hlavné nám 7)

Germany (☎02-5920 4400; www.pressburg.
diplo.de; Hviezdoslavovo nám 10)

Ireland (☎02-5930 9611; www.embassyofireland.
sk; Carlton-Savoy Bldg, Mostová 2)

Netherlands (☎02-5262 5081; www.holands
koweb.com; Frana Krála 5)

UK (☎02-5998 2000; http://ukinslovakia.fco.gov.
uk; Panská 16)

USA (☎02-5443 0861; http://slovakia.us
embassy.gov; Hviezdoslavovo nám 4)

Food

Restaurant review price indicators are based
on the cost of a main course.

Budget (€) Under €6.

Midrange (€€) From €6 to €12.

Top end (€€€) From €12 up.

Gay & Lesbian Travellers

Homosexuality has been legal here since
the 1960s, but this is a conservative, mostly
Catholic country. The GLBT scene is small
in Bratislava, and all but nonexistent elsewhere. Check out www.gay.sk.

Holidays

New Year's & Independence Day
1 January

Three Kings Day 6 January

Good Friday & Easter Monday March/
April

Labour Day 1 May

Victory over Fascism Day 8 May

SS Cyril & Methodius Day 5 July

SNP Day 29 August

Constitution Day 1 September

Our Lady of Sorrows Day 15 September

All Saints' Day 1 November

Christmas 24 to 26 December

Internet Access

Wi-fi is widely available at lodgings and cafes across the country. Towns will usually
have one internet cafe where the laptopless
can log on.

Money

ATMs Quite common even in smaller
towns, but shouldn't be relied upon in
villages.

Credit cards Visa and Mastercard are
accepted at most hotels and restaurants

(though only if you announce before
requesting the bill that you plan to pay
by card).

Currency Since January 2009, Slovakia's
legal tender has been the euro. But you'll
still hear reference to the former currency,
the Slovak crown, or Slovenská koruna (Sk).

Tipping 10% is fairly standard, though
some locals tip less.

Post

Post office service is reliable, but be sure to
hand your outgoing mail to a clerk; your
postcard may languish in a box for quite
some time.

Telephone

Landline numbers can have either seven or
eight digits. Mobile phone numbers (10 digits)
are often used for businesses; they start with
☎09. When dialling from abroad, you need to
drop the zero from both city area codes and
mobile phone numbers. Purchase local and
international phone cards at newsagents.

MOBILE PHONES

The country has GSM (900/1800MHz) and
3G UMTS networks operated by providers
Orange, T-Mobile and O2.

PHONE CODES

Dial out of Slovakia ☎00

Country code ☎421

Tourist Information

**Association of Information Centres of
Slovakia** (AICES; ☎16 186; www.aices.sk) Runs
an extensive network of city information
centres.

Slovak Tourist Board (www.slovakia.travel)
No Slovakia-wide information office exists;
your best bet is to go online.

Travellers With Disabilities

Slovakia lags behind many EU states in accommodation for disabled travellers. **Slovak Union for the Disabled** (www.sztp.sk)
works to change the status quo. Hotels and
restaurants have few ramps or barrier-free
rooms. There's some accessibility on public
transport, including buses that lower, and
special seating.

Visas

For a full list of visa requirements, see www.
mzv.sk (under 'Ministry' and then 'Travel').

No visa required EU citizens.

Visa-free for up to 90 days Visitors from Australia, New Zealand, Canada, Japan and the US.

Visa required South African nationals, among others.

Getting There & Away

For more travel specifics see the appropriate destination section; Bratislava and Košice are the country's main bases of entry/exit. Flights, tours and rail tickets can be booked online at lonelyplanet.com/booking.

Entering Slovakia from the EU, indeed from most of Europe, is a breeze. Lengthy custom checks make arriving from the Ukraine a bit more tedious.

Air

Bratislava's intra-European airport is small. Unless you're coming from the UK, which has a fair number of direct flights, your arrival will likely be by train. Vienna, Austria, has the nearest international air hub.

AIRPORTS

Airport Bratislava (BTS; www.airport bratislava.sk) Two dozen European destinations.

Košice International Airport (KSC; www. airportkosice.sk) Flights to Prague and Vienna.

Vienna International Airport (VIE; Schwechat; www.viennaairport.com) Austrian airport with regular bus connections to Bratislava, 60km west. Worldwide connections.

AIRLINES

The main airlines operating in Slovakia:

Austrian Airlines (OS; www.aua.com) Connects Košice with Vienna.

Czech Airlines (OK; www.czechairlines.com) Connects Prague with Bratislava and Košice.

Danube Wings (V5; www.danubewings.eu) Connects regularly with Basel, Switzerland; has summer flights to Italian and Croatian holiday destinations.

LOT Airlines (WAW; www.lot.com) Flies four days a week between Bratislava and Warsaw.

Ryanair (FR; www.ryanair.com) Connects Bratislava with numerous destinations across the UK and Italy, coastal Spain, Paris, Brussels and Stockholm.

Land

Border posts between Slovakia and fellow EU Schengen member states, Czech Republic, Hungary, Poland and Austria are nonexistent. You can come and go at will. This makes checks at the Ukrainian border all the more strident, as you will be entering the EU. By bus expect one to two hours wait; by car, much more.

BUS

Local buses connect Poprad and Ždiar with Poland. **Eurobus** (www.eurobus.sk) and **Eurolines** (www.slovaklines.sk) handle international routes across Europe from Bratislava and heading east to the Ukraine from Košice.

CAR & MOTORCYCLE

Private vehicle requirements for driving in Slovakia are registration papers, 'green card' (proof of third-party liability insurance), nationality sticker, first-aid kit and warning triangle.

TRAIN

See http://cp.atlas.sk for international and domestic train schedules. Direct trains connect Bratislava to Austria, the Czech Republic, Poland and Hungary; from Košice, trains connect to the Czech Republic, Poland, Ukraine and Russia.

River

During spring and summer, Danube riverboats offer an alternative way to get between Bratislava and Vienna or Budapest.

Getting Around
Air

Danube Wings (V5; www.danubewings.eu) offer the only domestic air service; weekdays only, between Bratislava and Košice.

Bicycle

Roads are often narrow and potholed, and in towns cobblestones and tram tracks can prove dangerous for bike riders. Bike rental is uncommon outside mountain resorts. The cost of transporting a bike by rail is usually 10% of the train ticket.

Bus

Read timetables carefully; fewer buses operate on weekends and holidays.

Cestovné poriadky (http://cp.atlas.sk) Up-to-date bus and train schedules on line.

Slovenská autobusová doprava (SAD; www.sad.sk) Comprehensive national bus network; most useful in the mountains.

Car & Motorcycle

Licences Foreign driving licences with photo ID are valid in Slovakia.

Motorway stickers (*nálepka*) Toll stickers are required on *all* green-signed motorways. Fines for not having them can be hefty. Buy at petrol stations (rental cars usually have them).

Parking City streetside parking restrictions are eagerly enforced. Always buy a ticket from a machine, attendant or newsagent in Old Town centres.

Rental Car hire is available in Bratislava and Košice primarily.

Local Transport

Towns all have good bus systems; villages have infrequent service. Bratislava and Košice additionally have trams.

Hours Public transport generally operates from 4.30am to 11.30pm daily.

Tickets City transport tickets are good for all local buses, trams and trolleybuses. Buy at newsstands and validate on board or risk serious fines (this is not a scam).

Train

Train is the way to travel in Slovakia; most places listed in this chapter are off the main Bratislava–Košice line. No online reservations.

Cestovné poriadky (http://cp.atlas.sk) Up-to-date bus and train schedules online.

Slovak Republic Railways (ŽSR; ☑18 188; www.slovakrail.sk) Far-reaching, efficient national rail service.

Slovenia

Best Places to Stay

» Antiq Hotel (p911)
» Hotel Mitra (p939)
» Hotel Triglav Bled (p923)
» Max Piran (p935)
» Celica Hostel (p915)

Best Places to Eat

» Špajza (p916)
» Pri Mari (p935)
» Restavracija Topli Val (p929)
» Restavracija Pungaršek (p924)

Why Go?

It's a pint-sized place, with a surface area of just more than 20,000 sq km and 2 million people. But 'good things come in small packages', and never was that old chestnut more appropriate than in describing Slovenia.

Slovenia has been dubbed a lot of different things by its PR machine – 'Europe in Miniature', 'The Sunny Side of the Alps', 'The Green Piece of Europe' – and they're all true. Slovenia has everything, from beaches, snowcapped mountains, hills awash in grape vines and wide plains blanketed in sunflowers to Gothic churches, baroque palaces and art nouveau public buildings. Its incredible mixture of climates brings warm Mediterranean breezes up to the foothills of the Alps, where it can snow in summer. And with more than half of its total area covered in forest, Slovenia really is one of the 'greenest' countries in the world. In recent years, it has taken on the role as Europe's activities playground.

Come for all these things but come too for the Slovenes themselves – generous, broad-minded and welcoming.

When To Go
Ljubljana

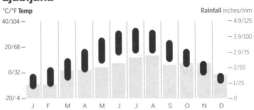

April–June Spring is a great time to be in the lowlands and the flower-carpeted valleys of Gorenjska.

September This is the month made for everything – still warm enough to swim and tailor-made for hiking.

December–March Everyone (and their grandma) dons their skis in this winter-sport mad country.

Fast Facts

» **Area** 20,273 sq km

» **Capital** Ljubljana

» **Telephone country code** 386

» **Emergency** 112

Exchange Rates

Australia	A$1	€0.72
Canada	C$1	€0.71
Japan	¥100	€0.82
New Zealand	NZ$1	€0.54
UK	UK£1	€1.12
USA	US$1	€0.69

Set Your Budget

» **Budget hotel room** €40

» **Two-course meal** €20

» **Museum entrance** €3

» **Beer in shop/bar** €1/3

» **100km by train/bus** €6.03/9.20

Resources

» **E-uprava** (http://e-uprava.gov.si/e-uprava/en/portal.euprava) Official portal with info on everything

» **Slovenian Tourist Board** (www.slovenia.info) Ambitious tourist site

Connections

Border formalities with Slovenia's three European Union neighbours – Italy, Austria and Hungary – are nonexistent and all are accessible by train and (less frequently) bus. Venice can also be reached by boat from Izola and Piran. Expect a somewhat closer inspection of your documents when travelling to/from non-EU Croatia.

ITINERARIES

One Week

Spend a couple of days in Ljubljana, then head north to unwind in Bohinj or romantic Bled beside idyllic mountain lakes. Depending on the season, take a bus or drive over the hair-raising Vršič Pass into the valley of the vivid blue Soča River and take part in some adventure sports in Bovec or Kobarid before returning to Ljubljana.

Two Weeks

Another week will allow you to see just about everything in this chapter: all of the above as well as the Karst caves at Škocjan and Postojna and the Venetian ports of Koper, Izola and Piran on the Adriatic.

Essential Food & Drink

» **Pršut** Air-dried, thinly sliced ham from the Karst region not unlike Italian prosciutto

» **Žlikrofi** Ravioli-like parcels filled with cheese, bacon and chives

» **Žganci** The Slovenian stodge of choice – groats made from barley or corn but usually *ajda* (buckwheat)

» **Potica** A kind of nut roll eaten at teatime or as a dessert

» **Wine** Distinctively Slovenian tipples include peppery red Teran from the Karst region and Malvazija, a straw-colour white wine from the coast

LJUBLJANA

🔊 01 / POP 257,675

Ljubljana (lyoob-*lya*-na) is by far Slovenia's largest and most populous city. It is also the nation's political, economic and cultural capital. As such, virtually everything of national importance begins, ends or is taking place in Ljubljana.

But it can be difficult to get a grip on the place. In many ways the city whose name *al-*

most means 'beloved' (*ljubljena*) in Slovene does not feel like an industrious municipality of national importance but a pleasant, self-contented small town. You might think that way too, especially in spring and summer when cafe tables fill the narrow streets of the Old Town and along the Ljubljanica River and street musicians entertain passers-by on pedestrian Čopova ul and Prešernov trg. Then Ljubljana becomes a little Prague or Kraków

Slovenia Highlights

① Experience the architecture, hilltop castle, green spaces and cafe life of **Ljubljana** (p909), Slovenia's beloved capital

② Wax romantic in picture-postcard **Bled** (p921), with a lake, an island and a castle as backdrop

③ Get into the outdoors or in the bluer-than-blue Soča in the majestic mountain scenery at **Bovec** (p927), one of the country's major outdoor-activities centres

④ Explore the Karst caves at **Škocjan** (p930), with scenes straight out of Jules Verne's *A Journey to the Centre of the Earth*

⑤ Swoon at the wonderful Venetian architecture of the romantic port of **Piran** (p934)

without the crowds. And you won't be disappointed with the museums and galleries, atmospheric bars and varied nightlife either.

History

Legacies of the Roman city of Emona – remnants of walls, dwellings, early churches, even a gilded statuette – can be seen everywhere. Ljubljana took its present form in the mid-12th century as Laibach under the Habsburgs, but it gained regional prominence in 1809, when it became the capital of Napoleon's short-lived 'Illyrian Provinces'. Some fine art nouveau buildings filled up the holes left by a devastating earthquake in 1895, and architect Jože Plečnik continued the remake of the city up until WWII. In recent years the city's dynamic mayor, Zoran Janković, has doubled the number of pedestrian streets, extended a great swathe of the river embankment and spanned the Ljubljanica River with two new footbridges.

◉ Sights

The oldest part of town, with the most important historical buildings and sights (including Ljubljana Castle) lies on the right (east) bank of the Ljubljanica. Center, which has the lion's share of the city's museums and galleries, is on the left (west) side of the river.

CASTLE AREA

Ljubljana Castle CASTLE
(☑306 4293; www.ljubljanafestival.si; admission free; ☺9am-11pm summer, 10am-9pm winter) Ljubljana Castle crowns a wooded hill that is the city's focal point. It's an architectural mishmash, including fortified walls dating from the early 16th century, a late-15th-century chapel and a 1970s concrete cafe. The best views are from the 19th-century **watchtower** (adult/child €5/2; ☺9am-9pm summer, 10am-6pm winter); admission includes a visit to the **Virtual Museum**, a 23-minute, 3D video tour of Ljubljana though the centuries. More interesting is the new **Slovenia History Exhibition** (with tower & Virtual Museum adult/child €8/4.80) next door, which guides you through the past via iconic objects and multimedia exhibits. The fastest way to reach the castle is via the **funicular** (vzpenjača; return adult/child €3/2; ☺9am-11pm summer, 10am-9pm winter), which ascends from Krekov trg every 10 minutes, though you can also take the hourly **tourist train** (adult/child €3/2; ☺up 9am-9pm, down 9.20am-9.20pm) from south of the tourist informa-

tion centre (TIC) on Stritarjeva ul. It takes about 15 minutes to walk to the castle via Reber ul from the Old Town.

PREŠERNOV TRG & OLD TOWN

Prešernov Trg SQUARE
This central square is dominated by the **Prešern monument** (1905), honouring national poet France Prešeren, and the salmon pink, 17th-century **Franciscan Church of the Annunciation** (☺6.40am-noon & 3-8pm). Wander north of the square along Miklošičeva c to admire the fine **art nouveau buildings**, including the landmark Grand Hotel Union at No 1, built in 1905; the former People's Loan Bank (1908) at No 4; and the colourful erstwhile Cooperative Bank from 1922 at No 8.

Triple Bridge BRIDGE
Leading southward from Prešernov trg is the small but perfectly formed Triple Bridge; prolific architect Jože Plečnik added two side bridges to the 19th-century span in 1931 to create something truly unique.

Old Town HISTORIC AREA
Ljubljana's oldest and most important district is made up of three elongated 'squares': **Mestni trg**, 'City Square' containing a copy of the baroque **Robba Fountain** (the original is now in the National Gallery) in front of the Gothic **town hall** (1718); **Stari trg** (Old Sq); and **Gornji trg** (Upper Sq).

CENTRAL MARKET AREA

Central Market MARKET
East of Prešernov trg is a lively open-air market (p917). Walk eastward along the magnificent riverside **Plečnik Colonnade** past the new **Butchers' Bridge**, with wonderful sculptures by Jakov Brdar and miniature padlocks left behind by lovers, to **Dragon Bridge** (Zmajski Most; 1901), a span guarded by four of the mythical creatures that are now the city's mascots.

Cathedral of St Nicholas CHURCH
(Dolničarjeva ul 1; ☺10am-noon & 3-6pm) Bordering the market, the 18th-century city's main church is filled with pink marble, white stucco, gilt and a panoply of baroque frescos. Check out the magnificent bronze doors (1996) on the west and south sides.

TRG FRANCOSKE REVOLUCIJE AREA

City Museum of Ljubljana MUSEUM
(☑241 25 00; www.mestnimuzej.si; Gosposka ul 15; adult/child €4/2.50; ☺10am-6pm Tue & Wed, Fri-Sun, 10am-9pm Thu) This excellent museum focuses on Ljubljana's history, culture and

politics via imaginative multimedia and interactive displays. The reconstructed Roman street dating back to the 1st century AD is worth a visit alone.

National & University Library HISTORIC BUILDING
(☑200 11 09; Turjaška ul 1; ☺9am-6pm Mon-Fri, 9am-2pm Sat) Diagonally opposite is the National & University Library, Plečnik's masterpiece completed in 1941, with its distinctive horse-head doorknobs and staircase of black marble that leads to a stunning reading room.

MUSEUM AREA

National Museum of Slovenia MUSEUM
(☑241 44 00; www.nms.si; Prešernova c 20; adult/child €3/2.50, free 1st Sun of month; ☺10am-6pm Fri-Wed, 10am-8pm Thu) Housed in an elegant 1888 building, the country's most important depository of historical items has rich archaeological and coin collections, including a Roman lapidarium and a Stone Age bone flute discovered near Cerkno in western Slovenia in 1995.

Slovenian Museum of Natural History
MUSEUM
(☑241 09 40; www2.pms-lj.si; adult/student €3/2.50, inc national museum €5/4) Housed in the same building and keeping the same hours, this museum contains the usual reassembled mammoth and whale skeletons, stuffed birds, reptiles and mammals as well as an excellent mineral collections from the 19th century.

National Gallery MUSEUM
(☑241 54 18; www.ng-slo.si; Prešernova c 24 & Cankarjeva c 20; adult/child €7/5, free 1st Sun of month; ☺10am-6pm Tue-Sun) Slovenia's foremost assembly of fine art is housed over two floors both in an old building dating to 1896 and an impressive modern wing.

Ljubljana Museum of Modern Art MUSEUM
(☑241 68 00; www.mg-lj.si; Tomšičeva ul 14; adult/student €5/2.50; ☺10am-6pm Tue-Sun) Founded

in 1948, this fine space has been given a massive facelift and is now largely given over to temporary exhibits of modern and contemporary art.

👉 Tours

Two-hour **walking tours** (adult/child €10/5; ☺10am, 2pm & 5pm Apr-Oct), combined with a ride on the funicular or the tourist train up to the castle or a cruise on the Ljubljanica, are organised by the TIC (p920). They depart daily from the town hall on Mestni trg.

🎊 Festivals & Events

There is plenty going on in and around the capital, including **Druga Godba** (www.druga godba.si), a week-long festival of alternative and world music at the Križanke in May; the **Ljubljana Festival** (www.ljubljanafestival. si), the nation's premier cultural event (music, theatre and dance) held from early July to late August; and the **International Ljubljana Marathon** (www.ljubljanskimaraton. si) in late October.

🛏️ Sleeping

The TIC (p920) has comprehensive details of private rooms (from s/d €30/50) and apartments (from d/q €55/80) though only a handful are central.

TOP CHOICE Antiq Hotel BOUTIQUE HOTEL €€€
(☑421 35 60; www.antiqhotel.si; Gornji trg 3; s €61-133, d €77-168; ✳@) Ljubljana's original boutique hotel, cobbled together from a series of townhouses in the heart of the Old Town, has 16 rooms and apartments, most of which are very spacious, and a multilevel back garden. The decor is kitsch with a smirk and there are fabulous little nooks and touches everywhere. A short distance west across the Ljubljanica is its sister, the new **Antiq Palace** (☑08-389 67 00; www.antiqpalace.com; Gosposka ul 10 & Vegova ul 5a; s/d €180/210; ✳@📶), with 13

LJUBLJANA IN TWO DAYS

From central **Prešernov trg** (p910), walk to Krekov trg and take the funicular up to **Ljubljana Castle** (p910) to get an idea of the lay of the land. After a seafood lunch at **Ribca** (p917), explore the Old Town then cross the Ljubljanica River via St James Bridge and walk north along bust-lined Vegova ul to Kongresni trg. Over a cup of something hot and a slice of something sweet at **Zvezda** (p918), plan your evening: low key at **Jazz Club Gajo** (p919), chichi at **Top: Eat & Party** (p919) or alternative at **Metelkova Mesto** (p918).

On your second day check out some of the city's excellent **museums** (p911), and then stroll or cycle through Park Tivoli, stopping for an oh-so-local horse burger at **Hot Horse** (p917) along the way.

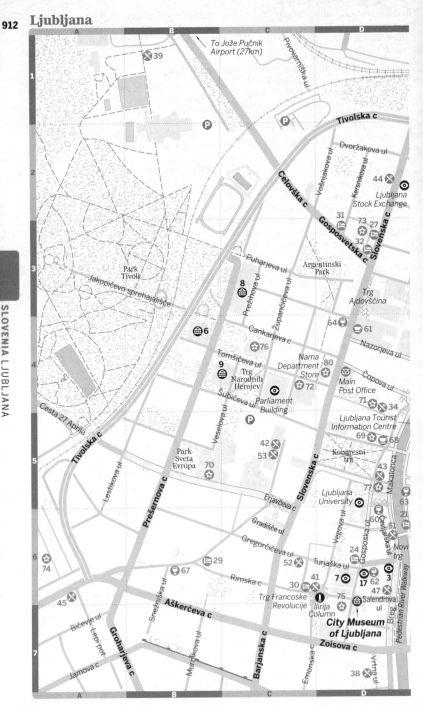

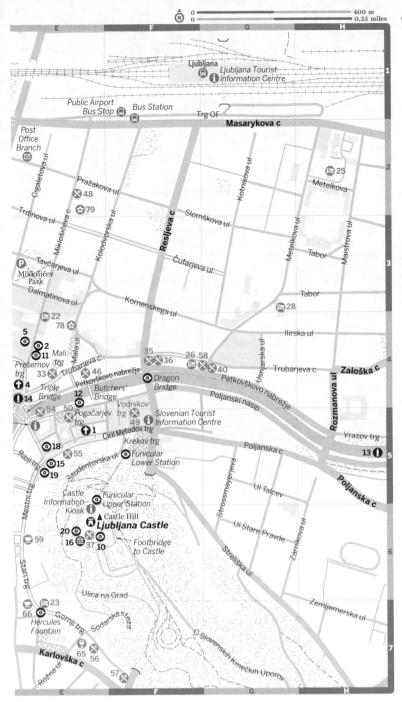

SLOVENIA LJUBLJANA

0 ___ 400 m
0 ___ 0.25 miles

Ljubljana

Ljubljana Tourist
Information Centre

Public Airport
Bus Stop   Bus Station
Trg OF

Masarykova c

Post
Office
Branch

Cigaletova ul

Pražakova ul
48
79

Trdinova ul

Miklošičeva c

Kolodvorska ul

Resljeva c

Slomškova ul

Kotnikova ul

Metelkova ul

25
Metelkova

Tabor

Maistrova ul

Tavčarjeva ul

Miklošičev
Park

Dalmatinova ul

Čufarjeva ul

Komenskega ul

Tabor

28

Ilirska ul

22
78

5
2
11

Mali
trg

Prešernov
trg   33

Mala ul

Trubarjeva c

35
36   26 58
40

Usnjarska ul

Trubarjeva c   Založka c

46

Petkovškovo nabrežje

4
14   Triple
Bridge   12

Butchers'
Bridge

Dragon
Bridge

Petkovškovo nabrežje

Poljanski nasip

Rozmanova ul

54   50
Pogačarjev
trg

Vodnikov
trg   49

Slovenian Tourist
Information Centre

1   Ciril Metodov trg

Krekov trg

Poljanska c

Vrazov trg

13

Poljanska c

18

55

15
19

Ribji trg   Študentovska ul   Funicular
Lower Station

St.rossmayerjeva

Ul Talcev

Zarnikova ul

Castle
Information
Kiosk   Funicular
Upper Station

Mestni trg   Castle Hill
Ljubljana Castle

Ul Stare Pravde

20
59   16   37   10

Footbridge
to Castle

Strelliška ul

Stari trg

Ulica na Grad

66   23

Hercules
Fountain

Gornji trg   Sodarska steza

C Slovenskih Kmečkih Uporov

Zemljemerska ul

65   56

Karlovška c

Rožna ul c

57

residential suites surrounding two courtyards of a former palace, parts of which date back to the 16th century. The suites are enormous, many retain their original features and are equipped with a full kitchen. The in-house spa facilities over two floors are the flashiest in Ljubljana.

Slamič B&B
PENSION €€

(☑433 82 33; www.slamic.si; Kersnikova ul 1; s €65-75, d €95-100; P ✳ @) It's a titch away from the action but Slamič, a B&B above a famous cafe and teahouse, offers 11 bright rooms with antique(ish) furnishings and parquet floors. Choice rooms include the ones looking onto a back garden and Nos 9 and 11 just off an enormous terrace.

Penzion Pod Lipo
PENSION €€

(☑031-809 893; www.penzion-podlipo.com; Borštnikov trg 3; d/tr/q €64/75/100; @) Sitting atop one of Ljubljana's oldest *gostilne* and a 400-year-old linden tree along Rimska c, this 10-room inn offers excellent value in a part of the city that is filling up with bars and restaurants. We love the communal kitchen, the original hardwood floors, the computer in each room and the east-facing terrace that catches the morning sun.

TOP CHOICE Celica Hostel
HOSTEL €€

(☑230 97 00; www.hostelcelica.com; Metelkova ul 8; dm €17-21, s/d/tr cell €53/56/66, 3- to 5-bed r per person €21-26, 7-bed r per person €19-23; P @ ☎) This stylishly revamped former prison (built in 1882) in Metelkova has 20 'cells', designed by as many different architects and complete with their original bars; it also has nine rooms and apartments with three to seven beds; and a packed, popular 12-bed dorm. The ground floor is home to cafes (set lunch €4.10 to €6.40; open 7am to midnight), and the hostel boasts its own gallery where everyone can show their own work. Laundry costs €7.

Ljubljana Resort
CAMPING GROUND €

(☑568 39 13; www.ljubljanaresort.si/eng; Dunajska c 270; camping adult €7-13, child €5.25-9.75; P ✳ @ ▨) This attractive 6-hectare camping ground-cum-resort 5km north of the centre also offers a 62-room hotel (singles €60 to €75, doubles €75 to €90) and a dozen stationery mobile homes (€84 to €158) accommodating up to five people. Next door is **Laguna** (www.laguna.si; adult/child from €14/10, ⊙May-to Sep), a water park with the works. Take bus 6 or 11 to the Ježica stop.

Zeppelin Hostel
HOSTEL €

(☑051-637 436; www.zeppelinhostel.com; 2 fl, Slovenska c 47; dm €18-24, d €49-60; @ ☎) Located in the historic Evropa building on the corner of Gosposvetska c, this hostel with three large and bright dorm rooms (four to eight beds) and three doubles (one en suite) is run by an affable Slovenian-Spanish couple.

Pri Mraku
HOTEL €€

(☑421 96 00; www.daj-dam.si; Rimska c 4; s €70-86, d €106-116; P ✳ @ ☎) Although it calls itself a *gostilna*, 'At Twilight' is really just a smallish hotel with 35 rooms in an old building with a garden. Rooms on the 1st and 4th floors have air-con. It's near the Križanke on Trg Francoske Revolucije – ideal for culture vultures.

Hotel Park
HOTEL €€

(☑300 25 00; www.hotelpark.si; Tabor 9; s €55-90, d €70-130; P ✳ @) A recladding outside and a facelift within has turned this 243-room tower-block hotel an even better-value central midrange choice. The 200 pleasant 'standard' and 'comfort' (air-conditioned) rooms are bright and unpretentiously well equipped. Cheaper 'hostel' rooms on the 7th and 12th floors, some of which have shared facilities (but always a toilet), cost €20 to €23 per person in a double and €17 to €19 in a quad. Students with ISIC cards get a 10% discount.

Alibi Hostel
HOSTEL €

(☑251 12 44; www.alibi.si; Cankarjevo nabrežje 27; dm €15-18, d €40-50; @ ☎) This well-situated 106-bed hostel on the Ljubljanica has brightly painted, airy dorms with four to eight wooden bunks and a dozen doubles. There's a private apartment at the top for six people. Just south of Miklošičev Park, its sister property, the smaller **Alibi M14 Hostel** (☑232 27 70; www.alibi.si; 2 fl, Miklošičeva c 14; dm €18-20, d €50-60; ✳ @ ☎), has six rooms, including a 10-bed dorm.

H2O
HOSTEL €€

(☑041-662 266; info@simbol.si; Petkovškovo nabrežje 47; dm/d/q €17/50/68; @ ☎) Also along the Ljubljanica, this six-room hostel wraps around a tiny courtyard, and one room has views of the castle. Rooms, with two to six beds, have their own kitchens.

Hotel Center
PENSION €€

(☑520 06 40, 041 263 347; www.hotelcenter.si; Slovenska c 51; s €45-55, d €60-66; @) The decor is simple and functionally modern at this new eight-room pension, but everything is spotless and you can't beat the central location.

The owners run the popular Cafe Compañeros (p918) below.

✕ Eating

TOP CHOICE Špajza
SLOVENIAN €€

(☎425 30 94; Gornji trg 28; mains €14.60-22; ⊗noon-11pm) A favourite in the Old Town, the 'Pantry' is a nicely decorated rabbit warren of a restaurant with rough-hewn tables and chairs, wooden floors, frescoed ceilings and nostalgic bits and pieces. Try the stupendous *žlikrofi* (pasta stuffed with cheese, bacon and chives; €9 to €12), mushroom dishes in season or the *kozliček iz pečiče* (oven-roasted kid; €14.60). Wines from a dozen different producers from Goriška Brda in Primorska are served.

Pri Škofu
SLOVENIAN €€

(☎426 45 08; Rečna ul 8; mains €8-22; ⊗10am-midnight Mon-Fri, noon-midnight Sat & Sun) This wonderful little place in tranquil Krakovo, south of the city centre, serves some of the best prepared local dishes and salads in Ljubljana from an ever-changing menu. Weekday set lunches are €8.

TOP CHOICE Most
INTERNATIONAL €€

(☎232 81 83; www.restavracija-most.si; Petkovškovo nabrežje 21; mains €13-23) This tastefully decorated, very welcoming restaurant at the foot of Butchers' Bridge serves international dishes that lean toward the Mediterranean. Try the saffron risotto with shrimps and porcini.

Taverna Tatjana
SEAFOOD €€

(☎421 00 87; Gornji trg 38; mains €8.50-25; ⊗5pm-midnight Mon-Sat) A wooden-beamed cottage pub with a nautical theme, this is actually a rather exclusive fish restaurant with a lovely back courtyard for the warmer months.

Čompa
SLOVENIAN €

(☎040-542 552; Trubarjeva c 40; mains €10-18; ⊗noon-3pm & 7pm-1am Mon-Sat) This new favourite Slovenian restaurant with outside seating along pedestrian Trubarjeva c serves massive platters of meats, cheese and vegetables *na žaru* (on the grill) to happy, very hungry punters.

Gostilna na Gradu
SLOVENIAN €

(☎08-205 19 30; www.nagradu.si; Grajska planota 1; dishes €4.50-10) After a wait of what seemed to be forever, the comfortable Inn at the Castle has opened in Ljubljana Castle and – joy of joys – it's serving affordable local dishes such as *jelenov golaž* (venison goulash),

skutni njoki (gnocchi with curd cheese) and *bobiči* (Istrian-style vegetarian soup).

Le Petit Restaurant
FRENCH €€

(☎426 14 88; Trg Francoske Revolucije 4; mains €12-20; ⊗7.30am-1am) Opposite the Križanke, what has always been a popular French-style cafe on French Revolution Sq has now opened a wonderful restaurant on the 1st floor with a provincial decor and menu. The pleasant, boho cafe still offers great coffee and a wide range of breakfast goodies (€2.20 to €6.50) and lunches (sandwiches €2.90 to €4.50).

Harambaša
BALKAN €

(☎041-843 106; Vrtna ul 8; dishes €4.50-6; ⊗10am-10pm Mon-Fri, noon-10pm Sat, to 6pm Sun) You'll find authentic Bosnian – Sarajevan to be precise – dishes here such as *čevapčiči* (spicy meatballs) and *pljeskavica* (meat patties) served at low tables in a charming modern cottage.

Zhong Hua
CHINESE €

(☎230 16 65; Trubarjeva c 50; mains €5.80-12.10; ⊗11am-10.30pm) This place just up from the Ljubljanica is just about the most authentic Chinese restaurant in town. Name a dish and they'll make it – and pretty authentically too. The less adventurous will to stick with rice and noodle dishes (€4.90 to €6.50).

Sokol
SLOVENIAN €

(☎439 68 55; Ciril Metodov trg 18; mains €7-20; ⊗7am-11pm Mon-Sat, 10am-11pm Sun) In an old vaulted house, traditional Slovenian food is served on heavy tables by costumed waiters. Along with traditional dishes such as *obara* (veal stew, €7) and Krvavica sausage with cabbage and turnips (€8.50), there's more exotic fare such as grilled stallion steak (€16).

Namasté
INDIAN €€

(☎425 01 59; www.restavracija-namaste.si; Breg 8; mains €6.30-17.90; ⊗11am-midnight Mon-Sat, to 10pm Sun) Should you fancy a bit of Indian, head for this place on the left bank of the Ljubljanica. You won't get high street quality curry but the thalis (from €8) and tandoori dishes (from €9) are good.

Cantina Mexicana
MEXICAN €€

(☎426 93 25; www.cantina.si; Knafljev prehod 3; mains €7.90-18.80; ⊗11am-midnight Sun-Thu, to 1am Fri & Sat) The capital's most stylish Mexican restaurant has an eye-catching red-and-blue exterior and hacienda-like decor inside. The fajitas (€8.70 to €14.30) are great.

Quick Eats

Ribca
SEAFOOD €

(📋425 15 44; Adamič-Lundrovo nabrežje 1; dishes €3.30-7.60; ⊙8am-4pm Mon-Fri, to 2pm Sat) This basement seafood bar, below the Plečnik Colonnade in Pogačarjev trg, serves tasty fried squid, sardines and herrings to hungry market-goers. Set lunch is €7.50.

Restavracija 2000
SELF-SERVICE €

(📋476 69 25; Trg Republike 1; dishes €2.15-3.70; ⊙9am-7pm Mon-Fri, to 3pm Sat) In the basement of the Maximarket department store, this self-service eatery is surprisingly upbeat, and just the ticket if you want something quick while visiting the museums.

Paninoteka
SANDWICH BAR €

(📋059-018 455; Jurčičev trg 3; soups & toasted sandwiches €3-6; ⊙8am-1am Mon-Sat, 9am-11pm Sun) Healthy sandwich creations on a lovely little square by the river with outside seating.

Ajdovo Zrno
VEGETARIAN €

(📋040-482 446; www.satwa.si; Trubarjeva c 7; soups & sandwiches €2-4, set lunch €6; ⊙10am-7pm Mon-Fri) 'Buckwheat Grain' serves soups, sandwiches, fried vegetables and lots of different salads (self-service, €3 to €10) and casseroles (€3.50). And it has terrific, freshly squeezed juices. Enter from little Mali trg.

Hot Horse
BURGERS €

(📋031-709 716; www.hot-horse.si; Park Tivoli, Celovška c 25; snacks & burgers €2.80-6; ⊙9am-6am Tue-Sun, 10am-6am Mon) This kiosk in the city's largest park supplies *Ljubljančani* with one of their favourite treats: horse burgers (€4).

Falafel
STREET FOOD €

(📋041-640 166; Trubarjeva c 40; dishes €3.50-4.50, daily menu €4.50; ⊙11am-midnight Mon-Fri, noon-midnight Sat, 1-10pm Sun) Sandwiches, salads and the eponymous falafel – ideal for veggies on the hoof (though there are meat dishes).

Nobel Burek
STREET FOOD €

(Miklošičeva c 30; burek €2, pizza slices €1.40; ⊙24hr) This hole-in-the-wall serves Slovenian-style fast food round-the-clock.

As in all European capitals, Ljubljana is awash in pizzerias (€5 to €8.50).

Pizzeria Foculus (📋421 92 95; www.foculus. com; Gregorčičeva ul 3; ⊙11am-midnight) Pick of the crop, which boasts a vaulted ceiling painted with spring and autumn leaves.

Kavalino (📋232 09 90; www.kavalino.si; Trubarjeva c 52; ⊙8am-10pm Mon-Thu, to 11pm Fri & Sat)

Trta (📋426 50 66; www.trta.si; Grudnovo nabrežje 21; ⊙11am-10pm Mon-Fri, noon-10.30pm Sat) On the right bank of the Ljubljanica.

Mirje (📋426 60 15; Tržaška c 5; ⊙10am-10pm Mon-Fri, noon-10pm Sat) Southwest of the city centre.

Self-Catering

Handy supermarkets include a large **Mercator** (Slovenska c 55; ⊙7am-9pm) southwest of the train and bus stations and a smaller, more central **Mercator branch** (Kongresni trg 9; ⊙7am-8pm Mon-Fri, 8am-3pm Sat & Sun) just up from the river.

The **Maximarket supermarket** (Trg Republike 1; ⊙9am-9pm Mon-Fri, 8am-5pm Sat) in the basement of the department store of the same name has the largest selection of food and wine in the city centre.

The **open-air market** (Pogačarjev trg & Vodnikov trg; ⊙6am-6pm Mon-Fri, to 4pm Sat summer, 6am-4pm Mon-Sat winter), held across two squares north and east of the cathedral, sells mostly fruit and vegetables and dry goods.

🍷 Drinking

Few cities of this size have central Ljubljana's concentration of inviting cafes and bars, the vast majority with outdoor seating in the warmer months.

Bars & Pubs

Nebotičnik
CAFE-BAR

(📋059-070 395; 12th fl, Štefanova ul 1; ⊙8am-3am) After a decade-long hibernation this cafe-bar with its breathtaking terrace atop Ljubljana's famed art deco Skyscraper (1933) has awakened, and the 360-degree views are still spectacular.

Pri Zelenem Zajcu
BAR

(📋031-632 992; Rožna ul 3; ⊙9am-midnight Mon-Wed & Sun, to 1am Thu & Sat, to 2am Fri) Ljubljana's only absinthe bar, 'At the Green Rabbit' to you, has its own label and relaxed vibe. It's a bit of a warren of a place (as it would be) but we're sure you'll feel comfortably frisky here.

Open Cafe
GAY & LESBIAN

(📋041-391 371; www.open.si; Hrenova ul 19; ⊙4pm-midnight) This very stylish gay cafe south of the Old Town has become the meeting point by Ljubljana's burgeoning gay culture.

Makalonca
CAFE-BAR

(📋030-362 450; Hribarjevo nabrežje 19; ⊙8am-1am Mon-Sat, 10am-10pm Sun) This cafe-bar with a 100m-long terrace within the columns of the Ljubljanica embankment is the perfect place to nurse a drink and watch the river roll by.

Žmavc
CAFE-BAR
(☎251 03 24; Rimska c 21; ⏰7.30am-1am Mon-Fri, from 10am Sat, from 6pm Sun) This super popular student hang-out west of Slovenska c, with *manga* comic-strip scenes and graffiti decorating the walls, is always voted tops in cafe-bar polls here.

Dvorni Bar
WINE BAR
(☎251 12 57; www.dvornibar.net; Dvorni trg 2; ⏰8am-1am Mon-Sat, 9am-midnight Sun) This wine bar is an excellent place to taste Slovenian vintages; it stocks more than 100 varieties and has wine tastings every second or third Wednesday of the month (check the website).

Maček
CAFE-BAR
(☎425 37 91; Krojaška ul 5; ⏰9am-12.30am Mon-Sat, to 11pm Sun) *The* place to be seen in Ljubljana on a summer afternoon, the 'Cat' is the most popular venue on the right bank of the Ljubljanica.

LP Bar
CAFE-BAR
(☎041-846 457; Novi trg 2; ⏰8am-midnight Mon-Wed & Sat, to 1am Thu & Fri, 9am-3pm Sun) Within the Academy of Arts and Sciences, LP (no relation to us!) is a civilised place for a libation, with cafe-bar, bookshop and heated seats outside. Great views of the castle.

Cafes & Teahouses

Zvezda
CAFE
(☎421 90 90; Kongresni trg 4 & Wolfova ul 14; ⏰7am-11pm Mon-Sat, 10am-8pm Sun) The 'Star' has all the usual varieties of coffee and tea but is celebrated for its shop-made cakes, especially *skutina pečena* (€2.90), an eggy cheesecake.

Čajna Hiša
TEAHOUSE
(☎421 24 44; Stari trg 3; ⏰9am-10.30pm Mon-Fri, 9am-3pm & 6-10pm Sat; 📶) If you take your cuppa seriously, come here; the appropriately named 'Tea House' offers a wide range of green and black teas and fruit tisanes (pot €2 to €3.60)

Juice Box
JUICE BAR
(☎051-614 545; Slovenska c 38; juices & smoothies €3.60-4.90; ⏰7am-8pm Mon-Fri, 8am-3pm Sat; 📶) Of the new crop of juice bars, this is the best, with some excellent fruit and vegetable combinations.

Slaščičarna Pri Vodnjaku
ICE-CREAM PARLOUR
(☎425 07 12; Stari trg 30; ⏰8am-midnight) For ice cream, the 'Confectionery by the Fountain' will surely satisfy – there are almost three-dozen flavours (per scoop €1.20), as well as teas (€2) and fresh juices (from €1.40).

☆ Entertainment

The free bimonthly **Ljubljana in Your Pocket** (www.inyourpocket.com) is your best source of information though the **Ljubljana.info** (www.ljubljana.info) has practical information and listings as well.

Nightclubs

Metelkova Mesto
CLUB
(www.metelkova.org; Masarykova c 24) 'Metelkova Town', an ex-army garrison taken over by squatters after independence, is now a free-living commune. In this two-courtyard block, idiosyncratic clubs, bars and art spaces hide behind brightly tagged doorways, coming to life generally after midnight, daily in summer and at weekends the rest of the year. Venues come in and go out; try to wade though the website or just stroll over and have a look yourself. It's just behind the Celica Hostel (p915).

Cafe Compañeros
CLUB
(☎520 06 40; Slovenska c 51; ⏰11am-5am) Raucous studenty hang-out with a lounge and terrace bar on the ground floor and a wild and crazy club with live music below.

Klub K4
CLUB
(☎438 02 61; www.klubk4.org; Kersnikova ul 4; ⏰10pm-2am Tue, 11pm-4am Wed & Thu, 11pm-6am Fri & Sat, 10pm-4am Sun) This evergreen venue in the basement of the Student Organisation of Ljubljana University (ŠOU) headquarters features rave-electronic music on Fridays and Saturdays, with other styles of music on weeknights, and a popular gay and lesbian night, K4 Roza, on Sundays. It closes in summer.

KMŠ
CLUB
(☎425 74 80; www.klubkms.si; Tržaška ul 2; ⏰8am-5am Mon-Fri, 9pm-5am Sat) Located in the deep recesses of a former tobacco factory complex, the 'Maribor Student Club' is comatose till Saturday when it turns into a lively dance place.

Bachus Center Club
CLUB
(☎241 82 40; www.bachus-center.com; Kongresni trg 3; ⏰8pm-5am Tue-Sat) This place has something for everyone, including a restaurant and bar-lounge, and attracts a mainstream crowd.

Club As
CLUB
(☎425 88 22; www.gostilnaas.si; Čopova 5a, enter from Knafljev prehod; ⏰9am-3am Wed-Sat) DJs

transform this candlelit basement bar into a pumping, crowd-pulling nightclub four nights a week.

Top: Eat & Party CLUB
(☑040-667 722; www.klubtop.si; Tomšičeva ul 2; ☺11pm-5am) This retro restaurant and cocktail bar on the 6th floor of the Nama department store becomes a popular dance venue nightly and attracts a very chi-chi crowd. Take the glass-bubble lift from along Slovenska c or the lift in the passageway linking Cankarjeva ulica and Tomšičeva ulica.

Live Music

Orto Bar LIVE MUSIC
(☑232 16 74; www.orto-bar.com; Graboličeva ul 1; ☺9pm-4am Tue & Wed, to 5am Thu-Sat) A popular bar-club for late-night drinking and dancing with occasional live music, Orto is just five minutes from Metelkova Mesto.

Hugo Barrera Club LIVE MUSIC
(☑040-177 477; Adamič Lundrovo nabrežje 5; ☺7am-2am Mon-Wed, to 3am Thu-Sat, 10am-2am Sun) Below the Plečnik Colonnade at the foot of Butchers' Bridge this new venue offers live music from the '60s, '70s and '80s four nights a week.

Sax Pub LIVE MUSIC
(☑283 9009; Eipprova ul 7; ☺noon-1am Mon, 10am-1am Tue-Sat, 4-10pm Sun) Over two decades in Trnovo, the colourful Sax has live jazz at around 9pm on Thursday or Sunday from late August to December and February to June. Canned stuff rules at other times.

Jazz Club Gajo LIVE MUSIC
(☑425 32 06; www.jazzclubgajo.com; Beethovnova ul 8; ☺7pm-2am Mon-Sat) Established in 1994, Gajo is the city's premier venue for live jazz and attracts both local and international talent. Jam sessions are at 9pm on Monday.

Roxly Cafe Bar LIVE MUSIC
(☑430 10 21, 041-399 599; www.roxly.si; Mala ul 5; ☺8am-2am Mon-Wed, to 3am Thu & Fri, 10am-3am Sat) This cafe, bar and restaurant north of the Ljubljanica features live rock music (mostly blues and rock) from 10pm two or three nights a week.

Performing Arts

Cankarjev Dom LIVE MUSIC
(☑241 71 00, box office 241 72 99; www.cd-cc.si; Prešernova c 10) is Ljubljana's premier cultural centre and has two large auditoriums (the Gallus Hall has perfect acoustics) and a dozen smaller performance spaces.

Križanke LIVE MUSIC
(☑241 60 00, box office 241 60 26; www.festival-lj.si; Trg Francoske Revolucije 1-2) Hosts concerts of the Ljubljana Festival (p911) and other events at a former 18th-century monastic complex.

Opera House OPERA, LIVE MUSIC
(☑241 17 40, box office 241 17 66; www.opera.si; Župančičeva ul 1) Opera and ballet are performed at the renovated and extended neo-Renaissance Opera House (1882).

Philharmonic Hall LIVE MUSIC
(Slovenska Filharmonija; ☑241 08 00; www.filharmonija.si; Kongresni trg 10) This concert hall dating from 1891 is home to the Slovenian Philharmonic Orchestra.

Cinema

Slovenska Kinoteka CINEMA
(☑434 25 20; www.kinoteka.si; Miklošičeva c 28) The 'Slovenian Cinematheque' screens archival art and classic films in their original languages.

❶ Information

Discount Cards

The new **Urbana-Ljubljana Tourist Card** (www.visitljubljana.si/en/ljubljana-and-more/ljubljana-tourist-card), available from the tourist offices for 24/48/72 hours (€23/30/35), offers free admission to most museums and galleries, walking and boat tours and unlimited city bus travel.

Internet Access

Web connection is available at virtually every hostel and hotel, the Slovenia Tourist Information Centre (p920; per 30min €1), the STA Travel Cafe (p920; per 20min €1) and the Student Organisation of the University of Ljubljana (p920; free). In addition:

Cyber Cafe Xplorer (☑430 19 91; Petkovškovo nabrežje 23; per 30min/hr €2.50/4; ☺10am-10pm Mon-Fri, 2-10pm Sat & Sun) Some 10 computers, wi-fi and cheap international phone calls.

DrogArt (☑439 72 70; Kolodvorska ul 20; 1st 15min free, then per 30min/hr €1/1.80; ☺10am-4pm Mon-Fri) Opposite the train station; three computers.

Portal.si Internet (☑234 46 00; Trg OF 4; per hr €4.20; ☺5.30am-10.30pm Sun-Fri, 5am-10pm Sat) In the bus station (get code from window 4); three computers.

Internet Resources

City of Ljubljana (www.ljubljana.si) Comprehensive information portal on every aspect of life and tourism.

Left Luggage

Bus station (Trg OF 4; per day €2; ☺5.30am-10.30pm Sun-Fri, 5am-10pm Sat) Window 3.

Train station (Trg OF 6; per day €2-3; ☺24hr) Coin lockers on platform 1.

Maps

Excellent free maps are available from the tourist offices. The more detailed 1:20,000-scale *Mestni Načrt Ljubljana* (Ljubljana City Map; €7.70) from **Kod & Kam** (☏600 50 80; www.kod-kam.si; Miklošičeva c 34) is available at newsstands and bookshops.

Medical Services

Central Pharmacy (Centralna Lekarna; ☏244 23 60; Prešernov trg 5; ☺7.30am-7.30pm Mon-Fri, 8am-3pm Sat)

Health Centre Ljubljana (Zdravstveni Dom Ljubljana; www.zd-lj.si; ☏472 37 00; Metelkova ul 9; ☺7.30am-7pm) For nonemergencies.

University Medical Centre Ljubljana (Univerzitetni Klinični Center Ljubljana; ☏522 50 50; www3.kclj.si; Zaloška c 2; ☺24hr) A&E service.

Money

There are ATMs at every turn, including a row of them outside the main TIC office. At the train station you'll find a **bureau de change** (☺7am-8pm) changing cash (but not travellers cheques) for no commission.

Abanka (Slovenska c 50; ☺9am-5pm Mon-Fri)

Nova Ljubljanska Banka (Trg Republike 2; ☺8am-6pm Mon-Fri)

Post

Main post office (Slovenska c 32; ☺8am-7pm Mon-Fri, to 1pm Sat) Holds poste restante for 30 days and changes money.

Post office branch (Pražakova ul 3; ☺8am-7pm Mon-Fri, to noon Sat) Just southwest of the bus and train stations.

Tourist Information

Tourist Information Centre Ljubljana Old Town (TIC; ☏306 12 15; www.visitljubljana.si; Kresija Bldg, Stritarjeva ul; ☺8am-9pm Jun-Sep, 8am-9pm Oct-May); train station (☏433 94 75; Trg OF 6; ☺8am-10pm Jun-Sep, 10am-7pm Mon-Fri, 8am-3pm Sat Oct-May) Knowledgeable and enthusiastic staff dispense information, maps and useful literature and help with accommodation.

Slovenia Tourist Information Centre (STIC; ☏306 45 76; www.slovenia.info; Krekov trg 10; ☺8am-9pm Jun-Sep, 8am-7pm Oct-May) Good source of information for the rest of Slovenia, with internet and bicycle rental also available.

Student Organisation of the University of Ljubljana

(Študentska Organizacija Univerze Ljubljani; ŠOU; ☏433 03 20, 051-373 999; www.sou-lj.si; Trubarjeva c 7; ☺9am-6pm Mon-Thu, 9am-3pm Fri) Information and free internet.

Travel Agency

STA Ljubljana (☏439 16 90, 041-612 711; www.staljubljana.com; 1st fl, Trg Ajdovščina 1; ☺10am-5pm Mon-Fri) Discount airfares for students; go online at the **STA Travel Cafe** (☺8am-midnight Mon-Sat).

❶ Getting There & Away

The bus and train stations are 800m northeast of Prešernov trg up Miklošičeva c. Ljubljana's Jože Pučnik Airport is 27km north of the city at Brnik near Kranj.

Bus

The **bus station** (☏234 46 00, information 090-934 230; www.ap-ljubljana.si; Trg OF 4; ☺5.30am-10.30pm Sun-Fri, 5am-10pm Sat) opposite the train station has bilingual info-phones. Buses serve Bohinj (€8.70, 2¼ hours, 91km, hourly) via Bled (€6.30, 1¼ hours, 57km, hourly). Those to Piran (€12, 2½ to three hours, 140km, up to five daily) go via Koper (€11.10, 1¾ to 2½ hours, 122km) and Postojna (€6, one hour, 54km, half-hourly). There's also service to Maribor (€12.40, three hours, 141km, between two and four daily).

International bus services from Ljubljana include Belgrade (€35, 7¾ hours, 537km, three times daily); Florence (€38, eight hours, 480km, 5.10am daily); Frankfurt (€86, 14 hours, 777km, 6.30pm daily) via Munich (€44, 6¾ hours, 344km); Pula (€22, 4½ hours, 249km, once daily) via Poreč (€21, three hours, 202km) and Rovinj (€21, 2½ hours, 182km); Sarajevo (€38, 10 hours, 566km, twice daily); Skopje (€50, 16 hours, 978km, twice daily); Split (€44, 10½ hours, 528km, daily in summer) via Rijeka (€17, 2½ hours, 136km); Trieste (€11.60, 2¼ hours, 106km, twice daily); and Venice–Mestre (€25, five hours, 230km, three daily).

Train

Ljubljana's **train station** (☏291 33 32; www.slo-zeleznice.si; Trg OF 6; ☺5am-10pm) has services to Koper (€10, 2½ hours, 153km, up to five daily). Alternatively you can take one of the more frequent Sežana-bound trains and change at Divača (€6.85, 1½ hours, 104km).

Ljubljana–Vienna trains (€63.20, 6¼ hours, 385km, one direct, four via Maribor daily) via Graz (€34.20, 200km, 3½ hours) are expensive, although Spar Schiene fares go as low as €29 on certain trains at certain times.

Three trains depart daily for Munich (€72, six hours, 405km). The 11.50pm departure has sleeping carriages available.

A Venice train (one way/return €25/40, four hours, 244km) via Sežana departs at 2.28am. But it's cheaper to go first to Nova Gorica (€8.50, 3½ hours, 153km, five daily), cross over on foot to the train station in Gorizia and then take an Italian train to Venice (about €9, 2½ hours).

For Zagreb (€13.40, 2½ hours, 154km) there are seven trains daily via Zidani Most. Two trains from the capital at 6.20am and 2.53pm serve Rijeka (€13.80, 2½ hours, 136km) via Postojna.

Trains to Budapest (€53.40, 8¾ hours, 451km, twice daily) go via Ptuj and Hodoš; there are 'Budapest Spezial' fares available for as low as €29 on certain trains at certain times. Belgrade (€25 to €44, 10 hours, 535km) is served by four trains a day.

ⓘ Getting Around

The cheapest way to/from Ljubljana's **Jože Pučnik Airport** (LJU; ☑04-206 19 81; www.lju-airport.si) at Brnik is by city bus (€4.10, 45 minutes, 27km) from stop 28 at the bus station. These run at 5.20am and hourly from 6.10am to 8.10pm Monday to Friday; on weekends there's a bus at 6.10am and then one every two hours from 9.10am to 7.10pm. A **private airport van** (☑040-771 771, 051- 321 414; www.airport-shuttle.si) also links Trg OF near the bus station (€5) or your hotel (€9) with the airport (30 minutes) up to 11 times daily between 5.10am and 10.30pm. A **taxi** (☑031-216 111; 059-060 777) from Center in Ljubljana will cost €40.

Ljubljana's city buses operate every five to 15 minutes from 5am (6am on Sunday) to 10.30pm, though some start as early as 3.15am and go until midnight and a couple run overnight. The flat fare (€0.80) is paid with a stored-value magnetic Urbana Card (www.jh-lj.si/urbana) which can be purchased at newsstands, tourist offices and the **LPP Information Centre** (☑430 51 75; Slovenska c 56; ⊙7am-7pm Mon-Fri) for €2; credit can then be added for from €1 to €50. The central area is perfectly walkable, though, so buses are really only necessary if you're staying way out of town.

Ljubljana Bike (per 2hr/day €1/5; ⊙8am-7pm or 9pm Apr-Oct) has two-wheelers available from locations around the city, including outside the STIC and opposite the Antiq Hotel.

JULIAN ALPS

The Julian Alps form Slovenia's dramatic northwest frontier with Italy. Triglav National Park, established in 1924, includes almost all of the Alps lying within Slovenia. The centrepiece of the park is, of course, Mt Triglav (2864m), Slovenia's highest and most sacred mountain, but there are many other peaks here reaching above 2000m. Along with an abundance of fauna and flora, the area offers a wide range of outdoor activities.

Kranj

☑04 / POP 34,620

At the foot of the Kamnik-Savinja Alps, with the snowcapped peak of Storžič (2132m) and others in full view to the north, Kranj is Slovenia's fourth-largest city. The attractive Old Town, perched on an escarpment above the confluence of the Sava and Kokra Rivers, barely measures 250m wide by 1km long.

The frequent buses between Kranj and Ljubljana's airport at nearby Brnik (€1.80, 10 minutes, 10km) make it possible to head straight to the Julian Alps without first going to the capital. While waiting for your onward bus to Bled (€3.60, 40 minutes, 29km), have a look at the **Old Town**, a 600m walk south from the bus station. On your way you'll pass the 87-room **Hotel Creina** (☑281 75 00; www.hotel-creina.si; Koroška c 5; s €60-80, d €80-100; 🅿🌸@🛜), expensive but the only game in town with bikes for rent (per hour/day €1/12). The **tourist office** (☑238 04 50; www.tourism-kranj.si; Glavni trg 2; ⊙8am-7pm Mon-Sat, 9am-6pm Sun) can find you a private room from €20 or, in summer, a bed in a student dormitory (from €15).

Pedestrianised streets lead to the **Church of St Cantianus**, with impressive frescos and stained glass. Another 300m further south, the Old Town dead-ends at the Serbian Orthodox **Plague Church**, built during a time of pestilence in 1470, and the 16th-century **defence tower** behind it. Ask the TIC about guided tours of the **tunnels** (adult/child €3/2.50; ⊙5pm Tue & Fri, 10am Sat & Sun) under the Old Town built as air-raid shelters during WWII. **Mitnica** (☑040-678 778; Tavčarjeva ul 35; ⊙7am-11pm Mon-Wed, 7am-1am Thu, 7am-2am Fri & Sat, 10am-11pm Sun) is a relaxing cafe-bar in a 16th-century toll house with a huge terrace overlooking the river.

Bled

☑04 / POP 5460

With an emerald-green lake, a picture-postcard church on a tiny island, a medieval castle clinging to a rocky cliff, and some of Slovenia's highest peaks as backdrops, Bled seems to have been designed by some god of tourism. Bled can get crowded in season, but it's always an excellent base from which to explore the mountains.

Bled

SLOVENIA JULIAN ALPS

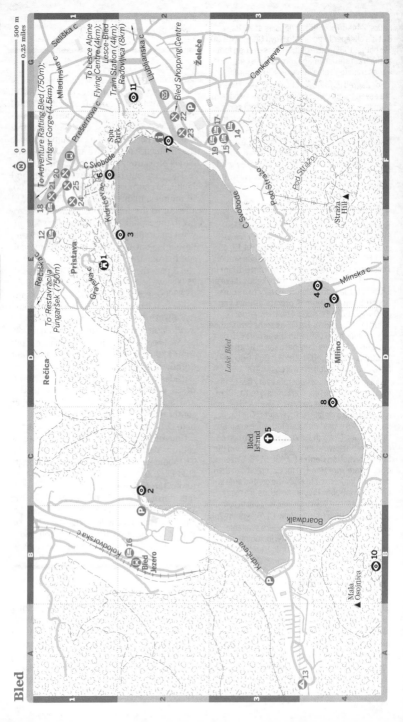

500 m
0.25 miles

Seliška c

Mladinska c

To Lešce Alpine
Flying Centre (4km);
Lesce-Bled
Train Station (4km);
Radovljica (8km)

Ljubljanska c

Bled Shopping Centre

Želeče

Cankarjeva c

To Adventure Rafting Bled (750m);
Vintgar Gorge (4.5km)

Prešernova c

Spa
Park

C Svobode

Pod Stražo

Kidričeva c

Stražo
Hill

Rečiška c

Pristava

Grajska c

Milinska c

To Restavracija
Pungaršek (750m)

Rečica

Mlino

Lake Bled

Bled
Island

Boardwalk

Kolodvorska c

Bled
Jezero

Kidričeva c

Mala
Osojnica

Bled

⊙ Sights

Lake Bled LAKE

A relaxed stroll around the 2km-by-1.4km lake shouldn't take more than a couple of hours, including the short climb to the **Osojnica viewing point** in the southwest. If you prefer, jump aboard the **tourist train** (adult/child €3/2; ⊙9am-9pm May-Oct) just south of the TIC for the 40-minute twirl around the lake.

Bled Island ISLAND, CHURCH

This tiny, tear-shaped islet is where you'll find Bled's icon, the baroque **Church of the Assumption** (⊙9am-dusk). The trip by piloted **gondola** (pletna; ☑041-427 155; per person €12) allows enough time on the island to look around and ring the 'lucky' bell; all in all, it's about 1½ hours. Do-it-yourself rowing boats for four/six people cost €10/15 per hour.

Bled Castle CASTLE, MUSEUM

(☑572 9782; www.blejski-grad.si; Grajska c 25; adult/child €7/3.50; ⊙8am-8pm summer, to 6pm

winter) Perched atop a 100m-high cliff, this castle, first mentioned a millennium ago, offers the perfect backdrop to a lake view. One of the easiest ways up on foot leads from behind Bledec Hostel. Admission includes entry to several attractions including the **museum collection** and 16th-century **chapel**.

Vintgar Gorge GORGE

(adult/child €4/2; ⊙8am-7pm mid-May–Oct) The highlight of visiting the gorge, an easy walk 4km to the northwest of the centre, is the 1600m-long wooden walkway (1893) that criss-crosses the swirling Radovna River for the first 700m or so. Thereafter the scenery becomes tamer and ends at the 16m-high **Šum Waterfall**. From June to September, a daily bus (one way/return €3.50/6.30) leaves Bled bus station for Vintgar at 10am daily, arriving at 10.30am and returning at 12.30pm. Otherwise reach it on foot via the Gostilna Vintgar, an inn just 3km away on quiet roads from the Bledec Hostel.

🏄 Activities

Agencies organise a wide range of outdoor activities in and around Bled, offering everything from mountain biking (from €28) and canyoning (€50) to paragliding (€85). One of the best trips is the Emerald River Adventure (€55), an 11-hour hiking and swimming foray into Triglav National Park and along the Soča River available from **3glav adventures** (☑041-683 184; www.3glav-adventures.com; Ljubljanska c 1; ⊙9am-noon & 4-7pm Apr-Oct). **Adventure Rafting Bled** (☑574 40 41, 051-676 008; www.adventure-rafting.si; Grajska c 21; Hrastova ul 2; ☑Apr-Oct) also organises rafting and canyoning. Both the TIC and Kompas (p925) rent bikes for €3.5/11 per hour/day.

🛏 Sleeping

Kompas (p925) has a list of private rooms and farmhouses, with singles/doubles starting at €24/38.

TOP CHOICE **Hotel Triglav Bled** BOUTIQUE HOTEL €€€

(☑575 26 10; www.hoteltriglavbled.si; Kolodvorska c 33; s €89-159, d €99-179, ste €139-209; P ❄ @ ⊛ ⊠) This bijou of a boutique hotel is in a painstakingly restored caravanserai that opened in 1906 opposite Bled Jezero train station. Many of the 22 rooms are furnished with antiques, there's an enormous sloped garden that grows the vegetables served in the 1906 terrace restaurant and the views of the lake from everywhere (including the indoor pool) are breathtaking.

RADOVLJICA

A short distance southeast of Bled and well served by bus (€1.80, 15 minutes, 8km), the sleepy town of Radovljica (pop 6025) has a particularly delightful square called **Linhartov trg** in its Old Town, where there are restored and painted houses, an interesting gallery, the fascinating **Beekeeping Museum** (⌨532 05 20; Linhartov trg 1; adult/child €3/2; ⊙10am-6pm Tue-Sun summer, 8am-3pm Tue, Thu & Fri, 10am-noon & 3-5pm Wed, Sat & Sun winter) and a **tourist office** (⌨531 53 00; www.radovljica.si; Gorenjska c 1; 9am-1pm & 2-6pm Mon-Sat summer, 9am-4pm Mon-Fri, to 1pm Sat winter). Have a meal or a drink at **Gostilna Augustin** (⌨531 41 63; Linhartov trg 15; mains €9-17), a delightful restaurant and bar with a back terrace affording views of Mt Triglav itself. The square lies 400m southeast of the bus station via Gorenjska c or just 100m up narrow Kolodvorska ul from the train station to the south.

Penzion Mayer　　　　　　PENSION €€
(⌨576 10 58; www.mayer-sp.si; Želeška c 7; s €55, d €75-80, apt €120-150; P@) This flower bedecked 12-room inn in a renovated 19th-century house has a lovely stand-alone cottage with apartments for two to four people. The Mayer's inhouse restaurant is excellent.

Garni Hotel Berc　　　　　PENSION €€
(⌨576 56 58; www.berc-sp.si; Pod Stražo 13; s €45-50, d €70-80; P@🛜) This purpose-built place, reminiscent of a Swiss chalet, has 15 rooms on two floors in a quiet location above the lake. Just opposite is a smaller branch, **Garni Penzion Berc** (⌨574 18 38; Želeška c 15; s €35-40, d €60-65), with 11 rooms.

🍃 **Camping Bled**　　　CAMPING GROUND €
(⌨575 20 00; www.camping-bled.com; Kidričeva c 10c; adult €8.50-12.50, child €5.95-8.75, huts d €30-40; P@🛜) This popular 6.5-hectare site fills a small valley at the western end of the lake. The new all-natural A-frame huts on a terrace above the site have become one of Bled's most sought-after addresses.

Traveller's Haven　　　　　HOSTEL €
(⌨041-396 545; www.travellers-haven.si; Riklijeva c 1; dm/d €19/48; @) This uber-popular hostel in a converted old villa has six rooms with between two and six beds, a great kitchen, laundry, free bikes and a chilled vibe.

Vila Gorenka　　　　　　PENSION €
(⌨574 47 22, 040-958 624; http://freeweb.siol.net/mz2; Želeška c 9; per person €17-25; P@) This budget establishment has 10 double rooms with washbasins – toilets and showers are shared – in a charming old two-story villa dating back to 1909. Some rooms on the 2nd floor have wooden balconies gazing on the lake.

Bledec Hostel　　　　　　HOSTEL €
(⌨574 52 50; www.youth-hostel-bledec.si; Grajska c 17; HI members/nonmembers dm €18/20, d €48/52; P@🛜) This well-organised HI-affiliated hostel in the shadow of the castle has dorms with four to eight beds with bathrooms, a bar and an inexpensive restaurant. A laundry service (€8.50) is available and bicycle rental is free.

🍴 **Eating**

You'll find a **Mercator** (Ljubljanska c 4; ⊙7am-8pm Mon-Sat, 8am-noon Sun) at the eastern end of Bled Shopping Centre. There's a smaller **Mercator branch** (Prešernova c 48; ⊙7am-8pm Mon-Sat, 8am-4pm Sun) close to the hostels.

TOP CHOICE **Restavracija Pungaršek**
SLOVENIAN, MEDITERRANEAN €€
(⌨059-059 136; www.pungarsek.si; Kolodvorska c 2; mains €13.50-22.50; ⊙11am-10.30pm Mon-Sat, to 6pm Sun) North of the lake and equidistant from the Hotel Triglav Bled and hostels, this upmarket restaurant is arguably Bled's finest. Mushrooms dishes are exquisite and desserts to die for. Outside seating under the pines in the warmer months.

Gostilna Pri Planincu　　SLOVENIAN, BALKAN €
(⌨574 16 13; Grajska c 8; mains €7-22; ⊙10am-10pm) 'At the Mountaineers' is a homey pub-restaurant just down the hill from the hostels, with Slovenian mains and grilled Balkan specialities such as *čevapčiči* (€8.30) and *pljeskavica z kajmakom* (Serbian-style meat patties with mascarpone-like cream cheese; €9). There's pizza upstairs.

Ostarija Peglez'n　　　　　SEAFOOD €€
(⌨574 42 18; C Svobode 19a; mains €8.50-27; ⊙noon-midnight) The most colourful restaurant in Bled, the 'Iron Inn' is just opposite the landmark Grand Hotel Toplice, with at-

The Julian Alps offer some of Europe's finest hiking. In summer 174 mountain huts (*planinska koča* or *planinski dom*) cater to hikers and none is more than five hours' walk from the next. These huts get very crowded, especially on weekends, so booking ahead is wise.

At €27 per person in a room with up to four beds or €18 in a dormitory in a Category I hut (Category II huts charge €20 and €12 respectively), the huts aren't cheap, but as they serve meals (a simple meal should cost between €4.70 and €6.20 in a Category I hut, and €3.50 and €5 in a Category II hut) you can travel light. Sturdy boots and warm clothes are indispensable, even in midsummer. Trails are generally well marked with a white-centred red circle, but you can still get lost and it's very unwise to trek alone.

For information and maps contact the area's tourist offices or the Alpine Association of Slovenia (p942) in Ljubljana.

tractively retro decor and some of the best fish dishes in town.

Pizzeria Rustika   PIZZA €
(☑576 89 00; Riklijeva c 13; pizza €5.70-9.50; ☺noon-11pm) A marble-roll down the hill from the hostels, this place has its own wood-burning oven and seating on two levels plus an outside terrace.

Slaščičarna Šmon   CAFE €
(☑574 16 16; Grajska c 3; ☺7.30am-10pm) This is the place for Bled's sweet of choice: *kremna rezina* (€2.40), a layer of vanilla custard topped with whipped cream and sandwiched neatly between two layers of flaky pastry.

❶ Information

A Propos Bar (☑574 40 44; Bled Shopping Centre, Ljubljanska c 4; per 15/30/60min €1.25/2.10/4.20; ☺8am-midnight Sun-Thu, to 1am Fri & Sat) Internet access.

Gorenjska Banka (C Svobode 15) Just north of the Park Hotel.

Kompas (☑572 75 00; www.kompas-bled.si; Bled Shopping Centre, Ljubljanska c 4; ☺8am-7pm Mon-Sat, 8am-noon & 4-7pm Sun) Private rooms and bicycles.

Post office (Ljubljanska c 10)

Tourist Information Centre Bled (☑574 11 22; www.bled.si; C Svobode 10; ☺8am-9pm Mon-Sat, 10am-6pm Sun Jul & Aug, 8am-7pm Mon-Sat, 11am-5pm Sun Mar-Jun & Sep-Oct, 8am-6pm Mon-Sat, noon-4pm Sun Nov, 8am-6pm Mon-Fri, 8am-1pm Sun Dec-Feb) Free internet access for 15 minutes or €2.50/4 per 30/60 minutes.

❶ Getting There & Around

Frequent buses to Bohinj (€3.60, 40 minutes, 29km, hourly), Ljubljana (€6.30, 1¼ hours, 57km, hourly) and Kranj (€3.60, 40 minutes,

29km, half-hourly) via Radovljica (€1.80, 15 minutes, 7km) leave from the central bus station.

Trains to Bohinjska Bistrica (€1.70, 20 minutes, 18km, eight daily) and Nova Gorica (€5.90, 1¾ hours, 79km, eight daily) use little Bled Jezero train station, which is 2km west of central Bled – handy for the Hotel Triglav Bled and the camping ground. Trains for Ljubljana (€4.50 to €6.10, 45 minutes to one hour, 51km, up to 19 daily) use Lesce-Bled train station, 4km to the east of town.

Book a taxi on ☑031-705 343.

Bohinj
☑04 / POP 5275

Lake Bohinj, a larger and less-developed glacial lake 26km to the southwest, is a world apart from Bled. Mt Triglav is visible from here and there are activities galore – from kayaking and mountain biking to hiking up Triglav via one of the southern approaches.

Bohinjska Bistrica, the area's largest village, is 6km east of the lake and only interesting for its train station. The main tourist hub on the lake is **Ribčev Laz** at the eastern end, with a supermarket, post office with an ATM and **tourist office** (☑574 60 10; www.bohinj-info.com; Ribčev Laz 48; ☺8am-8pm Mon-Sat, to 6pm Sun summer, 8am-6pm Mon-Sat, 9am-3pm Sun winter), which can help with accommodation and sells fishing licences (€25 per day for the lake, €42 catch and release in the Sava Bohinjka). Central **Alpinsport** (☑572 34 86, 041-596 079; www.alpinsport.si; Ribčev Laz 53; ☺9am or 10am-6pm or 8pm) organises a range of activities, and hires out kayaks, canoes, bikes (per hour/day €4/13.50) and other equipment from a kiosk near the stone bridge. Next door is the delightful **Church of St John the Baptist** (☺10am-noon & 4-7pm summer, by appointment other times), which contains splendid 15th- and 16th-century frescos.

The nearby village of **Stara Fužina** has an appealing little **Alpine Dairy Museum** (☑577 01 56; Stara Fužina 181; adult/child €2.50/2; ☺11am-7pm Tue-Sun Jul & Aug, 10am-noon & 4-6pm Tue-Sun Jan-Jun, Sep & Oct). Just opposite is a cheesemonger called **Planšar** (☑572 30 95; Stara Fužina 179; ☺noon-8pm summer, by appointment other times), which specialises in homemade dairy products such as hard Bohinj cheese, cottage cheese and curd pie. Just 2km east is **Studor**, a village famed for its *toplarji*, the double-linked hayrack with barns or storage areas at the top, some of which date from the 18th and 19th centuries.

One of the reasons people come to Bohinj is to hike to **Savica Waterfall** (adult/child €2.50/1.25, parking €3; ☺8am-8pm Jul & Aug; 9am-6pm Apr-Jun, Sep & Oct), which cuts deep into a gorge 60m below and is the source of Slovenia's longest river. It's a 4km hike from Camp Zlatorog in Ukanc at the lake's western end.

From early April to October, the inventively named **Tourist Boat** (☑041-434 986; adult/child 1 way €8.50/6, return €10/7; ☺10am-6pm) departs from the pier just opposite the Alpinsport kiosk every 40 minutes (between four and six times a day at other times), terminating a half-hour later at the Ukanc jetty.

The **Cows' Ball** in September is a zany weekend of folk dance, music, eating and drinking to mark the return of the cows from their high pastures down to the valleys. The **International Wildflower Festival** over two weeks in late May/early June includes guided walks and tours, traditional craft markets and concerts. For details on both, go to www.bohinj.si.

🛏 Sleeping & Eating

The tourist office can help arrange accommodation in **private rooms** (per person €13-15) and **apartments** (d €42.50-48.50, q €75-86).

Penzion Gasperin   PENSION €€
(☑059-920 382, 041-540 805; www.bohinj.si/gasperin; Ribčev Laz 36a; per person €25-35; ▣@🛈🛜) This spotless chalet-style guesthouse with 23 rooms is just 350m east of the tourist office and run by a friendly British-Slovenian couple. Most rooms have balconies.

Hotel Jezero   HOTEL €€€
(☑572 91 00; www.bohinj.si/alpinum/jezero; Ribčev Laz 51; s €60-80, d €100-140; ▣@🛈🛜🛝) Further renovations have raised the standards even higher at this 76-room place just across from the lake. It has a lovely indoor swimming pool, two saunas and a fitness centre.

Hostel Pod Voglom   HOSTEL €
(☑572 34 61; www.hostel-podvoglom.com; Ribčev Laz 60; dm €17-19, r per person with bathroom € 23-26, without bathroom € 20-22; ▣@) This budget accommodation 3km west of the centre has 122 beds in 46 somewhat frayed rooms in two buildings. The so-called Hostel Building has doubles, triples and dormitory accommodation with up to four beds and shared facilities; rooms in the Rodica Annexe, with between one and four beds, are en suite.

Camp Zlatorog   CAMPING GROUND €
(☑572 30 64; www.hoteli-bohinj.si/en; Ukanc 2; per person €7-19, tent/campervan €11/23; ☺May-Sep) This pine-shaded 2.5-hectare camping ground accommodating 500 guests is at the lake's western end, 4.5km from Ribčev Laz.

Restavracija Triglav   SLOVENIAN €€
(☑572 35 38; Stara Fužina 23; mains €10.50-17) This country-style place in nearby Stara Fužina serves up hearty Slovenian favourites like lamb and whole pig cooked on the spit and mushrooms on the grill. There's live music from 6pm daily in summer.

Center Bohinj Pizzerija   PIZZA €
(☑572 3170; www.bohinj.si/center; Ribčev Laz 50; pizza €6-10, mains €8.50-14; ☺9am-10pm) This cheap and kinda cheerful jack-of-all-trades just down from the tourist office is the only eatery in the very centre of Ribčev Laz.

🛈 Getting There & Around

Buses run regularly from Ukanc ('Bohinj Zlatorog' on most schedules) to Ljubljana (€8.70, 2¼ hours, 91km, hourly) via Ribčev Laz, Bohinjska Bistrica and Bled (€4.10, 50 minutes, 34km), with six extra buses daily between Ukanc and Bohinjska Bistrica (€2.30 20 minutes, 12km). From Bohinjska Bistrica, passenger trains to Nova Gorica (€5.20, 1¼ hours, 61km, up to nine daily) make use of a century-old tunnel under the mountains that provides the only direct option for reaching the Soča Valley. In addition there are daily auto trains *(avtovlaki)* from Bohinjska Bistrica to Podbrdo (€8.20, 10 minutes, 7km, five daily) and Most na Soči (€12.50, 40 minutes, 28km, three daily).

Kranjska Gora

☑04 / POP 1510

Nestling in the Sava Dolinka Valley about some 40km northwest of Bled, Kranjska Gora is Slovenia's largest and best-equipped ski resort. It's at its most perfect under a blanket of snow, but at other times there are endless possibilities for hiking and mountaineering in Triglav National Park, which is right on the town's doorstep to the south. Few travellers will be unimpressed by a trip over the hair-raising Vršič Pass (1611m), the gateway to the Soča Valley.

◉ Sights & Activities

Borovška c, 400m south of where the buses stop, is the heart of the village, with the endearing **Liznjek House** (☑588 19 99; Borovška 63; adult/child €2.50/1.70; ⏰10am-6pm Tue-Sat, to 5pm Sun summer, 9.30am-4pm Tue-Fri, 10am-5pm Sat & Sun winter), an 18th-century museum house with a good collection of household objects and furnishings peculiar to Gorenjska. At its western end is the **Tourist Information Centre Kranjska Gora** (☑580 94 40; www.kranjska-gora.si; Tičarjeva c 2; ⏰8am-7pm Mon-Sat, 9am-6pm Sun Jun-Sep & mid-Dec–Mar, 8am-3pm Mon-Sat Apr, May & Oct–mid-Dec). If you have time (and your own wheels), visit the new **Slovenian Mountaineering Museum** (☑583 35 01; www.planinskimuzej.si; Savska c 1; adult/child €5/3.50; ⏰9am-7pm summer, to 5pm winter) in a startlingly modern structure in Mojstrana, a village 14km to the east.

Kranjska Gora has lots of places offering ski tuition and hiring out equipment, including **ASK Kranjska Gora Ski School** (☑588 53 02; www.ask-kg.com; Borovška c 99a) in the same building as SKB Banka. Rent bikes from one of several **Sport Point** (☑588 48 83; www.sport-point.si; Borovška c 74; per hr/day €3.50/10) outlets. The men's and giant slalom **Vitranc Cup** (www.pokal-vitranc.com) are held here in early March, and the **Ski-Jumping World Cup Championships** (www.planica. info) at nearby Planica later that month.

▐ Sleeping & Eating

Accommodation costs peak from December to March and in midsummer. **Private rooms** (per person €14-24) and **apartments** (d €34-50, q €68-108) can be arranged through the tourist office.

Hotel Kotnik HOTEL **€€**
(☑588 15 64; www.hotel-kotnik.si; Borovška c 75; s €54-64, d €68-88; @) If you're not into sprawling hotels with hundreds of rooms, choose this charming, bright yellow low-rise property. It has 15 cosy rooms, a great restaurant and pizzeria, and it couldn't be more central.

Brezov Gaj PENSION **€€**
(☑588 57 90; www.brezov-gaj.si; Koroška c 7; per person €25-34; ℙ@) The 'Birch Grove' offers some of the best value in Kranjska Gora. Some of the half-dozen rooms have balco-

nies, there's a fitness room and a place to store bikes and skis.

Natura Eco Camp Kranjska Gora
CAMPING GROUND **€**
(☑064-121 966; www.naturacamp-kranjskagora.si; adult €8-10, child €5-7, cabin & tree tent €25-30) This wonderful new site some 300m from the main road on an isolated horse ranch in a forest clearing is as close to paradise as we've been for a while. Pitch a tent or stay in one of the little wooden cabins or the unique tree tents, great pouches with air mattresses suspended from the branches.

Hostel Nika HOSTEL **€**
(☑588 10 00, 031-644 209; www.porentov-dom. si; Bezje 16; dm €10-11 d €26; ℙ@) This atmospheric, very cheap place on the Sava Dolinka with 23 rooms and 68 beds in Čičare is about 800m northeast of the centre and just across the main road from the TGC Shopping Centre. It's a great starting point for walks into the mountains.

Gostilna Pri Martinu SLOVENIAN **€€**
(☑582 03 00; Borovška c 61; mains €6.50-12.50) This atmospheric tavern-restaurant in an old house just beyond Liznjek House is one of the best places to try local specialities such as *telečja obara* (veal stew; €4) and *ričet* (barley stew with smoked pork ribs; €6). Lunch is a snip at just under €7.

❶ Getting There & Away

Buses run hourly to Ljubljana (€8.70, two hours, 91km) via Jesenice (€3.10, 25 minutes, 22m), where you can change for Bled (€3.10, 30 minutes, 21km) as there's just one direct departure to Bled (€4.70, one hour, 40km) on weekdays at 9.15am. A service to Bovec (€6.70, 2¼ hours, 46km) via the Vršič Pass departs five times daily (six at the weekend) from late June to early September.

Soča Valley

The Soča Valley region is defined by the 96km-long Soča River coloured a deep, almost artificial turquoise. The valley has more than its share of historical sights, most of them related to one of the costliest battles of WWI, but the majority of visitors are here for the rafting, hiking, skiing and other active sports.

BOVEC
☑05 / POP 1810
Effectively the capital of the Soča Valley, Bovec has a great deal to offer adventure-sports

enthusiasts. With the Julian Alps above, the Soča River below and Triglav National Park all around, you could spend a week here hiking, kayaking, mountain biking and, in winter, skiing at Mt Kanin (2587m), Slovenia's highest ski station, without ever doing the same thing twice.

The compact village square, Trg Golobarskih Žrtev, has everything you'll need. There are cafes, a hotel, the **Tourist Information Centre Bovec** (☑389 64 44; www.bovec.si; Trg Golobarskih Žrtev 8; ◎8.30am-8.30pm summer, 9am-6pm winter) and a half-dozen adrenaline-raising adventure-sports companies.

🏃 Activities

Organised adventure sports (all prices per person) on offer include **canyoning** (from €45 for two hours) or **caving** (from €40 with guide). Or you could try your hand at **hydrospeed** (like riding down a river on a boogie board); you'll pay €45 to €52 for a 6km to 8km ride. A guided 10km **kayaking** tour costs from €42, or a one-day training course at €70.

From April to October, you can go **rafting** (€37/49 for a 10/20km trip). And in winter you can take a **tandem paraglider flight** (ie as a passenger accompanied by a qualified pilot; €110) from atop the Kanin cable car, 2000m above the valley floor.

The choice of operators is dizzying but the three most experienced are: **Bovec Rafting Team** (☑388 61 28, 041-338 308; www.bovec-rafting-team.com; Mala Vas 106); **Soča Rafting** (☑389 62 00, 041-724 472; www.socarafting.si; Trg Golobarskih Žrtev 14); and **Top Extreme** (☑041-620 636; www.top.si; Trg Golobarskih Žrtev 19).

🛏 Sleeping & Eating

Private rooms (per person €15-30) are easy to come by in Bovec through the TIC.

Martinov Hram PENSION €€
(☑388 62 14; www.martinov-hram.si; Trg Golobarskih Žrtev 27; s €33-48, d €54-70; P🐕🤖) This lovely guesthouse just 100m east of the centre has a dozen nicely furnished rooms and an excellent restaurant with an emphasis on game, trout and mushroom dishes.

Alp Hotel HOTEL €€
(☑388 40 00; www.alp-hotel.si; Trg Golobarskih Žrtev 48; s €48-66, d €78-98; P@🌊) This 103-room hotel is fairly good value and as central as you are going to find in Bovec. Guests get to use the swimming pool at the nearby Hotel Kanin.

Kamp Palovnik CAMPING GROUND €
(☑388 60 07; www.kamp-polovnik.com; Ledina 8; adult €6.50-7.50, child €5-5.75; ◎Apr-mid-Oct; P) Camping facilities are generally better in Kobarid, but this site about 500m southeast of the town centre is much more convenient.

Gostišče Vančar SLOVENIAN €
(☑389 60 76, 031-312 742; www.penzionvancar.com; Čezsoča 43; mains €ri6-8) This inn 3km south of Bovec is where local people go to taste such local specialities as *kalja* (a sweet-corn pudding) and *bovški krafni* ('raviolis' stuffed with dried pears, raisins and walnuts).

ℹ️ Getting There & Away

Buses to Nova Gorica (€7.50, two hours, 77km, up to five a day) go via Tolmin (€3.10, 30 minutes, 22km). A service to Kranjska Gora (€6.70, 2¼ hours, 46km) via Vršič Pass departs five times daily (six at the weekend) from late June to early September.

KOBARID

☑05 / POP 1230

Some 21km south of Bovec, quaint Kobarid (Caporetto in Italian) lies in a broad valley on the west bank of the Soča River. Although it's surrounded by mountain peaks higher than 2200m, Kobarid somehow feels more Mediterranean than alpine. The Italian border is a mere 9km to the west.

◎ Sights

Kobarid Museum MUSEUM
(☑389 00 00; www.kobariski-muzej.si; Gregorčičeva ul 10; adult/child €5/2.50; ◎9am-6pm Mon-Fri, to 7pm Sat & Sun summer, 10am-5pm Mon-Fri, 9am-6pm Sat & Sun winter) A couple of hundred metres to the southeast is this award-winning museum, devoted almost entirely to the Isonzo (Soča) Front of WWI, which formed the backdrop to Ernest Hemingway's *A Farewell to Arms*.

🏃 Activities

A free pamphlet and map titled *The Kobarid Historical Trail* outlines a 5km-long route that will take you past remnants of WWI troop emplacements to the impressive **Kozjak Stream Waterfalls** and **Napoleon Bridge** built in 1750. More ambitious is the hike outlined in the free *Pot Miru/Walk of Peace* brochure.

There are several outfits on or just off the town's main square that can organise **rafting** (€29 to €37), **canyoning**, **canoeing** and **paragliding** from April to October. They include:

A2 Rafting (☑041-641 899; www.a2rafting.eu) in a kiosk outside Apartma-Ra.

XPoint (☑388 53 08, 041-692 290; www.xpoint. si; Trg Svobode 6)

Positive Sport (☑040-654 475; www.positive -sport.com; Markova ul 2)

🛏 Sleeping

TOP CHOICE **Hotel Hvala** HOTEL
(☑389 93 00; wwww.hotel-hvala.si; Trg Svobode 1; s €72-76, d €104-112; 🅿 ❀ @) The best place to stay in town. It has 31 splendid rooms and a unique lift that takes you on a vertical tour of Kobarid.

Kamp Koren CAMPGROUND
(☑389 13 11; www.kamp-koren.si; Drežniške Ravne 33; per person pitch €9.50-11; 🅿 @ 🖴) The oldest (and, some would say, friendliest) camping ground in the valley. It's a 4-hectare site about 500m northeast of Kobarid on the left bank of the Soča River and just beyond the Napoleon Bridge with 100 pitches and six **chalets** (d/tr from €55/60).

Apartma-Ra APARTMENTS
(☑041-641 899; apartma-ra@siol.net; Gregorčičeva ul 6c; per person €15-25; 🅿 ❀ @) This welcoming little place lies between the museum and Trg Svobode and has five rooms and apartments.

🍴 Eating

In the centre of Kobarid you'll find one of Slovenia's best restaurants, which specialises in fish and seafood.

Restavracija Topli Val (☑389 93 00; wwww. hotel-hvala.si; Trg Svobode 1; mains €9.50-25; ⊙noon-10pm) Incomparable.

Hiša Franko (☑389 41 20; www.hisafranko. com; Staro Selo 1; mains €20-24; ⊙noon-3pm & 6-11pm Tue-Sun) Another slow-food phenomenon in these parts in the village of Staro Selo some 3km west of town.

ⓘ Information

Tourist Information Centre Kobarid (☑380 04 90; www.dolina-soce.com; Trg Svobode 16; ⊙9am-8pm Jul & Aug, 9am-1pm & 2-6pm Mon-Fri, 10am-1pm & 3-6pm Sat & Sun Sep-Jun) In the centre of town.

ⓘ Getting There & Around

Buses, which arrive at and depart from in front of the Cinca Marinca bar on Trg Svobode, link Kobarid with Nova Gorica (€6, 1¼ hours, 55km, up to five daily) and Ljubljana (€11.60, three hours, 131km, up to four daily) passing Most na Soči train station, which is good for Bled and Bohinj.

Buses crossing over the spectacular Vršič Pass to Kranjska Gora (€6.90, three hours, 68km) depart a couple of times a day in July and August.

NOVA GORICA
☑05 / POP 12,240

When the town of Gorica, capital of the former Slovenian province of Goriška, was awarded to the Italians after WWII, the new socialist government in Yugoslavia set out to build a model town on the eastern side of the border. They called it New Gorica and erected a chain-link barrier between the two towns. This rather flimsy 'Berlin Wall' was pulled down to great fanfare in 2004, leaving Piazza della Transalpina (or Trg z Mozaikom on the Slovenian side) straddling the border right behind Nova Gorica's train station. The latter now contains the esoteric **Museum of the Border in Gorica 1945-2004** (☑333 44 00; admission free; ⊙1-5pm Mon-Fri, 9am-5pm Sat, 10am-5pm Sun).

The helpful **Tourist Information Centre Nova Gorica** (☑330 46 00; www.novagorica -turizem.com; Bevkov trg 4; ⊙8am-8pm Mon-Fri, 9am-1pm Sat & Sun summer, 8am-6pm Mon-Fri, 9am-1pm winter) is in the Kulturni Dom (Cultural House).

One of the few inexpensive central options for overnighting, **Prenočišče Pertout** (☑330 75 50, 041-624 452; www.prenocisceper tout.com; Ul 25 Maja 23; s/d €24/34; 🅿 @) is a five-room B&B in Rožna Dolina, south of the town centre and scarcely 100m northeast of the Italian border. Some 2km east of the centre along the road to Ajdovščina, the **Siesta** (☑333 12 30; www.hotel-siesta.si; Industrijska c 5; s/d €39/49; 🅿 @) is a modern-ish 20-room hotel with bargain-basement rates.

Marco Polo (☑302 97 29; Kidričeva ul 13; mains €6-17; ⊙11am-midnight), an Italian eatery with a delightful back terrace about 250m east of the tourist office, is one of the town's best places to eat, serving pizza (€5.50 to €7.60), pasta (€6 to €12) and more-ambitious dishes.

Buses travel hourly between Nova Gorica and Ljubljana (€10.70 2½ hours, 116km) via Postojna (€6.70, 1½ hours, 63km), and up to five times daily to Bovec (€7.50, two hours, 77km) via Tolmin (€4.70, one hour, 39km).

Trains link Nova Gorica with Bohinjska Bistrica (€5.20, 1½ hours, 61km, up to seven daily), a springboard for Bled, with Postojna (€6.25, two hours, 61km, six daily) via Sežana and Divača, and with Ljubljana (€8.50, 3½ hours, 153km, five daily) via Jesenice.

SLOVENIA SOČA VALLEY

KARST & COAST

Slovenia's short coast (47km) is an area for both history and recreation. The southernmost resort town of Portorož has some decent beaches, but three important towns famed for their Venetian Gothic architecture – Koper, Izola and Piran – are the main drawcards here. En route from Ljubljana or the Soča Valley, you'll cross the Karst, a huge limestone plateau and a land of olives, ruby-red Teran wine, *pršut* (air-dried ham), old stone churches and deep subterranean caves, including Postojna and Škocjan.

Postojna

📞 05 / POP 8910

Slovenia's single most-popular tourist attraction, **Postojna Cave** (📞700 01 00; www.postojnska-jama.si; Jamska c 30; adult/child €20/12; ☉tours hourly 9am-6pm summer, 3 or 4 times from 10am daily winter) is about 1.5km northwest of the town of that name. The 5.7km-long cavern is visited on a 1½-hour tour – 4km of it by electric train and the rest on foot. Inside, impressive stalagmites and stalactites in familiar shapes stretch almost endlessly in all directions.

Just steps south of the cave's entrance is **Proteus Vivarium** (www.turizem-kras.si; adult/child €7/4.20 with cave €25/15; ☉9.30am-5.30pm May-Sep, 10.30am-3.30pm Oct-Apr), a speliobiological research station with a video introduction to underground zoology. A 45-minute tour then leads you into a small, darkened cave to peep at some of the endemic *Proteus anguinus*, a shy (and miniscule) salamander unique to Slovenia.

🛏 Sleeping & Eating

Kompas Postojna PRIVATE ROOMS €
(📞721 14 80; www.kompas-postojna.si; Titov trg 2a; r per person €17-24; ☉8am-7pm Mon-Fri, 9am-1pm Sat summer, 8am-5pm Mon-Fri, 9am-1pm Sat winter) Private rooms in town and down on the farm.

Hotel Sport HOTEL, HOSTEL €€
(📞720 22 44; www.sport-hotel.si; Kolodvorska c 1; dm €25, s/d from €55/70; P@🛜) A hotel of some sort or another since 1880, the Sport offers reasonable value for money, with 37 spic-and-span and very comfortable rooms, including five with nine dorm beds each. There's a kitchen with small eating area. It's 300m north of the centre.

Špajza SLOVENIAN €€
(📞726 45 06; Ul 1 Maja 1; mains €11-16) A welcome new addition to Postojna's limited eating scene, this attractively decorated *gostilna* 100m southeast of Kompas serves excellent local specialities.

❶ Getting There & Away

Buses from Ljubljana to Koper, Piran and Nova Gorica all stop in Postojna (€6, one hour, 54km, half-hourly). The train is less useful, as the station is 1km east of town (ie almost 3km from the caves).

Buses bound for Postojna Cave and Predjama Castle leave Postojna's train station five times a day between 9.20am and 4.10pm. The bus is free but those with train tickets take precedence. The last bus from the castle is 4.40pm and from the cave at 5.05pm. A taxi to/from the castle, including an hour's wait, will cost €30.

Škocjan Caves

📞 05

The immense system of **Škocjan Caves** (📞708 21 10; www.park-skocjanske-jame.si; Škocjan 2; adult/child €14/6), a Unesco World Heritage site since 1986, is far more captivating than the larger one at Postojna, and for many travellers a visit here will be a highlight of their trip to Slovenia. With relatively few stalactites, the attraction is the sheer depth of the awesome underground chasm, which you cross by a dizzying little footbridge. To see this you must join a guided walking tour, lasting 1½ to two hours and involving hundreds of steps and a funicular ride at the end. Tours depart hourly from 10am to 5pm from June to September, at 10am, 1pm and 3.30pm in April, May and October, and at 10am and 1pm (with an additional one at 3pm on Sunday) from November to March.

The nearest town with accommodation is **Divača** (population 1325), 5km to the northwest. **Gostilna Malovec** (📞763 12 25; Kraška 30a; s/d €32/48) has a half-dozen basic but renovated rooms in a building beside its traditional **restaurant** (mains €8-15; ☉8am to 10pm) and flashy new 20-room **hotel** (📞763 33 33; www.hotel-malovec.si; s/d €54/80; P@🛜). The nearby **Orient Express** (📞763 30 10; Kraška c 67; pizza €4.60-14; ☉11am-11pm Sun-Fri, to 2am Sat) is a popular pizzeria and pub.

Bus services running from Ljubljana to Koper and the coast stop at Divača (€7.90, 1½ hours, 82km, hourly) as do trains (€6.85, 1½ hours, 104km, hourly). A van meets incoming trains at 10am, 11.04am, 2pm and

PREDJAMA

The tiny village of Predjama (population 85), some 10km northwest of Postojna, is home to remarkable **Predjama Castle** (🏛700 01 00; www.turizem-kras.si; Predjama 1; adult/child €8/5; ☺9am-7pm summer, 10am-4pm winter), which appears to grow out of a gawping cave. The partly furnished interior spread over four floors boasts costumed wax mannequins, one of which dangles from the dripping rock-roofed torture chamber. Beneath are stalactite-adorned **caves** (adult/child €7/4.20, with castle €13/8; ☺1-hour tours 11am-5pm May-Sep), which lack Postojna's crowds but also much of its grandeur.

3.10pm and will transport those with bus or train tickets to the caves for free. Otherwise there is a large map indicating the walking route posted outside the station.

Lipica

🏛05 / POP 100

Lipica is where Austrian Archduke Charles, son of Ferdinand I, established a stud farm in 1580 to breed horses for the Spanish Riding School in Vienna. The snow-white beauties are still raised at the **Lipica Stud Farm** (🏛739 15 80; www.lipica.org; Lipica 5; adult/child €10/5), which offers equestrian fans a large variety of tours and riding presentations as well as lessons and carriage rides. Tour times are complicated; see the website for details.

The 85-room **Hotel Klub** (🏛739 15 80; s/d €32/49; P@☎) near the stud farm has a sauna and fitness centre. The nearby **Hotel Maestoso** (🏛739 15 80; s/d €80/120; P☎☀) has 68 more modern rooms.

Most people visit Lipica as a day trip from Sežana, 5km to the north, or Divača, 10km to the northeast, which are on the Ljubljana–Koper rail line. There is no public transport from either station to Lipica; a taxi will cost between €7 and €15.

Koper

🏛05 / POP 24,830

Coastal Slovenia's largest town, Koper (Capodistria in Italian) at first glance appears to be a workaday city that scarcely gives tourism a second thought. Yet its central core is delightfully medieval and far less overrun than its ritzy cousin Piran, 18km down the coast. Known as Aegida to the ancient Greeks, Koper grew rich as a key port trading salt and was the capital of Istria under the Venetian Republic during the 15th and 16th centuries. It remains Slovenia's most important port.

◉ Sights

Turn back the clock as you pass through **Muda Gate** (1516) leading into Prešernov trg and the bridge-shaped **Da Ponte Fountain** (1666). Carry on north up Župančičeva ul and then Čevljarska ul, the narrow commercial artery, to reach **Titov trg**. This fine square is dominated by the 15th-century **City Tower** (adult/child €2/1.50; ☺9am-2pm & 4-9pm), which can be reached via 204 steps. It is attached to the part-Gothic, part-Renaissance **Cathedral of the Assumption**. The Venetian Gothic and Renaissance **Praetorian Palace** (Titov trg 3; admission free; ☺9am-8pm) contains the town hall, with an old pharmacy and the tourist office on the ground floor and a ornate ceremonial hall on the 1st floor. Opposite, the splendid 1463 **Loggia**, with attached gallery. Next to it is the circular Romanesque **Rotunda of St John the Baptist**, a baptistery with ceiling fresco dating from the 12th century.

The **Koper Regional Museum** (🏛663 35 70; www.pmk-kp.si; Kidričeva ul 19; adult/child €2/1.50; ☺9am-7pm Tue-Fri, to 1pm Sat & Sun), inside the Belgramoni-Tacco Palace, contains an Italianate sculpture garden. Kidričeva ul, with its multicoloured **medieval houses**, leads west into Carpacciov trg, the former fish market with a 15th-century **salt warehouse**.

⛏ Sleeping

Museum Hostel HOSTEL, APARTMENTS €

(🏛626 18 70, 041-504 466; bozic.doris@siol.net; Muzejski trg 6; per person €20-25; ☎) This excellent-value place is more a series of bright apartments with modern kitchens and bathrooms than a hostel. Reception is at the little Museum Bife, a cafe-bar on Muzejski trg; the rooms are actually at Mladinska ul 7 and Kidričeva ul 34.

Hotel Koper HOTEL €€€

(🏛610 05 00; www.terme-catez.si; Pristaniška ul 3; s €76-92, d €120-150; ❄@☎) This 65-room property on the very edge of the historic Old Town is the only central hotel in Koper.

Koper

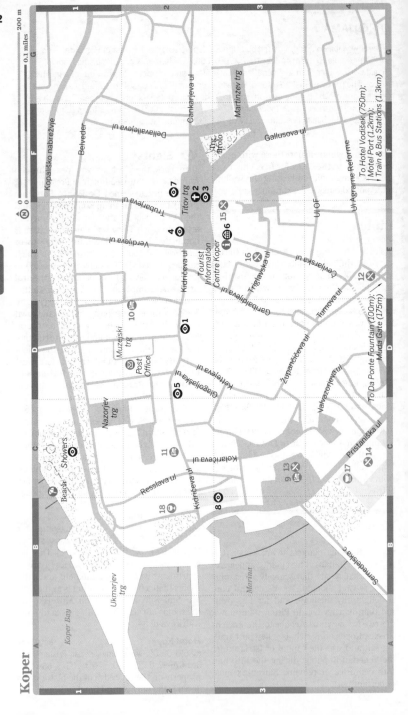

Koper

Hotel Vodišek　　　　　　　　HOTEL €€
(☑639 24 68; www.hotel-vodisek.com; Kolodvorska c 2; s €48-60, d €72-90; P❋@⊛) With 35 small but reasonably priced rooms, this place is in a shopping centre halfway between the Old Town and the train and bus stations. Bicycle use is free for guests.

Motel Port　　　　　　　　HOTEL, HOSTEL €
(☑611 75 44; www.motel-port.si; Ankaranska c 7; dm €22, s €36/49.50; ⊙Jul-Aug; P❋@⊛) On the 2nd floor of a shopping centre southeast of the Old Town, this student house, open to visitors in summer, only has 30 rooms, some of them en suite and air-conditioned and others dorm rooms with four to six beds.

✕ Eating
You'll find a small branch of the **Mercator** (Titov trg 2; ⊙7am-8pm Mon-Fri, 7am-1pm Sat, 8am-noon Sun) supermarket giant in the Old Town.

Istrska Klet Slavček　　ISTRIAN, SLOVENIAN €
(☑627 67 29; Župančičeva ul 39; dishes €3-12; ⊙7am-10pm Mon-Fri) The 'Istrian Cellar' below an 18th-century palace is one of the most colourful places for a meal in Koper's Old Town. Filling set lunches go for less than €8,

and there's local Malvazija and Teran wine from the barrel.

933

La Storia　　　　　　　　ITALIAN €€€
(☑626 20 18; www.lastoria.si; Pristaniška ul 3; mains €8.50-25) This Italian-style *trattoria* with sky-view ceiling frescos inside and a delightful covered terrace outside focuses on salads, pasta and fish dishes.

Pizzeria Atrij　　　　　　　PIZZA €€
(☑627 22 55; Čevljarska ul 8, enter from Triglavska ul 2; pizza €3-6.50; ⊙9am-9pm Mon-Fri, 10am-10pm Sat) A popular pizzeria down an alleyway no wider than your average quarterback's shoulder spread, the Atrij has a small covered garden out back.

⊊ Drinking
Kavarna Kapitanija　　　　　　CAFE
(☑040-799 000; Ukmarjev trg 8; ⊙7am-midnight Mon-Fri, 8am-midnight Sat & Sun) This attractive space, with its wide-open terrace and wicker lounges, would be even more inviting if the tacky souvenir kiosks and parked cars across the grassy strip didn't block the harbour view.

Forum　　　　　　　　　　CAFE-BAR
(Pristaniška ul 2; ⊙7am-11pm; ⊛) Cafe-bar at the northern side of the market and facing a little park and the sea; a popular local hang-out.

ⓘ Information
Banka Koper (Kidričeva ul 14)

Pina Internet Cafe (☑627 80 72; Kidričeva ul 43; per hr adult/student €4.20/1.20; ⊙noon-10pm Mon-Fri, from 4pm Sat & Sun) Central internet cafe with 10 terminals.

Post office (Muzejski trg 3)

Tourist Information Centre Koper (☑664 64 03; www.koper.si; Praetorian Palace, Titov trg 3; ⊙9am-8pm Jul & Aug, 9am-5pm Sep-Jun)

ⓘ Getting There & Away
The joint bus and train station is about 1.5km southeast of central Titov trg. To walk into town, just head north along Kolodvorska c in the direction of the cathedral's distinctive campanile (bell tower).

Buses run to Piran (€2.70, 30 minutes, 18km) every 20 minutes on weekdays and 40 minutes at weekends. Up to five daily buses daily head for Ljubljana (€11.10, 1¾ to 2½ hours, 122km), though the train is more comfortable, with four local services and two faster IC ones (€10, 2¼ hours) at 5.23am and 2.45pm.

Buses to Trieste (€3, 45 minutes, 23km, up to eight per day) run along the coast via Ankaran and Muggia between 6am and 7.30pm from Monday to Saturday. Destinations in Croatia include Rovinj (€11, three hours, 129km, 6.30pm Monday and Friday, 11am Saturday and Sunday, 3.50pm daily June to September) via Poreč (€10, two hours, 88km).

You can order a taxi on ☏040-671 086.

Izola

☏05 / POP 11.545

Overshadowed by more genteel Piran, Izola (Isola in Italian) has a certain Venetian charm, narrow old streets, and excellent (and uncrowded) waterfront restaurants. Ask the helpful **Tourist Information Centre Izola** (☏640 10 50; www.izola.eu; Sončno nabrežje 4; ◷9am-9pm Jun-Sep, 9am-5pm Mon-Fri, 10am-5pm Sat Oct-May) about **private rooms** (s €19-26, d €30-36) or, in July and August, check out the 174-bed **Riviera** (☏662 1740; branko.miklobusec@guest.arnes.si; Prekomorskih Brigad ul 7; dm €25), a student dormitory overlooking the marina. At the other end of the price range is the 52-room **Hotel Marina** (☏660 41 00; www.hotelmarina.si; Veliki trg 11; s €59-126, d €79-156; P✳@☏) on the main square and fronting the harbour. **Ribič** (☏641 83 13; www.ribic.biz; Veliki trg 3; mains €9-25; ◷8am-midnight Mon-Sat, to 10pm Sun) is a landmark seafood restaurant on the waterfront much loved by locals. Out in Izola's industrial suburbs, **Ambasada Gavioli** (☏641 8212, 041-353 722; www.myspace.com/ambasadagavioli; Industrijska c 10; ◷11pm-6am Fri & Sat) remains coastal Slovenia's top club, showcasing a procession of international and local DJs.

Frequent buses between Koper (€1.80, 15 minutes, 8km) and Piran (€2.30, 20 minutes, 10km) go via Izola.

The **Prince of Venice** (☏05-617 80 00; www.kompas-online.net) catamaran serves Venice (€50 to €70, 2½ hours) from Izola at 7.30am or 8am between one and three times a week (days vary) from April to October.

Piran

☏05 / POP 4515

Picturesque Piran (Pirano in Italian), sitting at the tip of a narrow peninsula, is everyone's favourite coastal town in Slovenia. The Old Town is a gem of Venetian Gothic architecture, but it can be a mob scene at the height of summer. Still, it's hard not to fall in love with the winding Venetian Gothic alleyways and tempting seafood restaurants. It is believed that the town's name comes from the *pyr*, Greek for fire, as fires were once lit at

Punta, the tip of the peninsula, to guide ships to the port at Aegida (now Koper).

◉ Sights

Cathedral of St George   CHURCH
(Adamičeva ul 2) Piran is watched over by the hilltop cathedral mostly dating from the 17th century. If time allows, visit the attached **Parish Museum of St George** (☏673 34 40; admission €1; ◷10am-1pm & 5-7pm Mon-Fri, 11am-7pm Sat & Sun), which contains church plate, paintings and a lapidary in the crypt. The cathedral's free-standing **bell tower** (admission €2; ◷10am-2pm & 5-8pm) dates back to 1609 and can be climbed. The octagonal **baptistery** (1650) has imaginatively recycled a 2nd-century Roman sarcophagus as a baptismal font. To the east is a 200m-long stretch of the 15th-century **town wall** complete with loopholes.

Minorite Monastery   MONASTERY
(☏673 44 17; Bolniška ul 20) Parts of this monastery to the east of Tartinijev trg date back to the 14th century; go up the steps and check out the wonderful cloister enlivened with Gregorian chant. Opposite, the **Church of Our Lady of the Snows** has a superb 15th-century arch painting of the Crucifixion.

Sergej Mašera Maritime Museum   MUSEUM
(☏671 00 40; www.pommuz-pi.si; Cankarjevo nabrežje 3; adult/student & senior/child €3.50/2.50/2.10; ◷9am-noon & 5-9pm Tue-Sun summer, 9am-5pm Tue-Sun winter) The exhibits here focus on the sea, sailing and salt-making – all crucial to Piran's development over the centuries. Check out the 2000-year-old Roman amphorae under glass on the ground floor and the impressive antique ships' models and figureheads upstairs.

Aquarium Piran   AQUARIUM
(☏673 25 72; www.aquariumpiran.com; Kidričevo nabrežje 4; adult/child €7/5; ◷9am-7pm summer, to 5pm winter) About 100m south of Tartinijev trg and facing the marina, the town's recently renovated aquarium may be on the small side, but there's a tremendous variety of sea life packed into its two-dozen tanks.

Tartinijev trg   SQUARE
At No 4 of this historic central square is the attractive 15th-century **Venetian House**, with its tracery windows and stone lion relief. When built this would have overlooked Piran's inner port, which was filled in 1894 to form the square. Tartinijev trg is named in honour of the 18th-century violinist and composer Giuseppe Tartini (1692–1770), whose statue stands in the centre.

Trg 1 Maja
SQUARE

The name of this square (1st May Sq) may sound like a socialist parade ground, but in fact it's one of Piran's most attractive squares, with a **cistern** dating from the late 18th century. Rainwater from the surrounding roofs flows into it through the fish borne by the stone putti in the corners.

Punta
HISTORIC AREA

Punta, the historical 'snout' of Piran, still has a **lighthouse**, but today's version is small and modern. Attached to it, the round, serrated tower of 18th-century **Church of St Clement** evokes the ancient beacon from which Piran got its name.

🏃 Activities

Most water-related activities take place in Portorož, but if you want to try **diving Noriksub** (☑673 22 18, 041-590 746; www.sku pinanoriksub.si; Prešernovo nabrežje 24; shore/boat dive €30/40; ⊙10am-noon & 2-6pm Tue-Sun summer, 10am-4pm Sat & Sun winter) organises shore and boat-guided dives and hires out equipment. A 'taster' course is €50.

Bicycles are available for rent from a shop in the Old Town called **Gaastra** (☑040-255 400; Vidalijeva ul 3; per day €7; ⊙9am-1pm & 5-8pm summer, to 5pm Mon-Sat winter).

🛏 Sleeping

Private rooms (s €18-31.50, d €26-48) and **apartments** (d €40-50, q €65-75) are available through the Maona Tourist Agency (p937) and the **Turist Biro** (☑673 25 09; www.turistbiro -ag.si; Tomažičeva ul 3; ⊙9am-1pm & 4-7pm Mon-Sat, 10am-1pm Sun), opposite the Hotel Piran.

TOP CHOICE Max Piran
B&B €€

(☑673 34 36, 041-692 928; www.max piran.com; Ul IX Korpusa 26; d €60-70; ❄@🛜) Piran's most romantic accommodation option has just six rooms – each bearing a woman's name rather than a number – in a delightful coral-coloured 18th-century townhouse. It's a short walk from the cathedral.

Miracolo di Mare
B&B €€

(☑921 76 60, 051-445 511; www.miracolodimare.si; Tomšičeva ul 23; s €50-55, d €60-70; @🛜) A favourite B&B, the 'Wonder of the Sea' has a dozen charming (though smallish) rooms, some of which give on to the most charming raised back garden in Piran.

Hotel Tartini
HOTEL €€€

(☑671 10 00; www.hotel-tartini-piran.com; Tartini trg 15; s €62-86, d €84-124; P❄@) This attractive, 45-room property faces Tartinijev trg and manages to catch a few sea views from the upper floors. The staff are especially friendly and helpful. If you've got the dosh, splash out on the eyrie-like suite 40a.

Alibi B11
HOSTEL €

(☑031-363 666; www.alibi.si; Bonifacijeva ul 11; per person €20-22; ⊙Apr-Dec; @🛜) The flagship of the Alibi stable is not its nicest property but has mostly doubles in eight rooms over four floors and a roof terrace in an ancient townhouse on a narrow street. Reception for all three hostels is here and there's a washing machine. Diagonally opposite is **Alibi B14** (Bonifacijeva ul 14; per person €20-22), an upbeat and colourful four-floor party place with seven rooms, each with two to four beds. More subdued is **Alibi T60** (Trubarjeva ul 60; per person €25; ❄) to the east with a fully equipped double on each of five floors. The view from the terrace of the top room is priceless. The new **Vista Apartment** (Trg 1 Maja 4; per person €25) is a two-room duplex apartment with sea views that sleeps up to eight people.

Val Hostel
HOSTEL €

(☑673 25 55; www.hostel-val.com; Gregorčičeva ul 38a; per person €22-27; @🛜) This central, partially renovated hostel has 20 rooms, with two to four beds, shared shower, kitchen and washing machine. It's a great favourite with backpackers.

Kamp Fiesa
CAMPING GROUND €

(☑674 62 30; autocamp.fiesa@siol.net; adult/child €12/4; ⊙May-Sep; P) The closest camping ground to Piran is at Fiesa, 4km by road but less than 1km by coastal trail east from the Cathedral of St George. It's tiny and crowded but right on the beach.

🍴 Eating & Drinking

There's an outdoor **fruit and vegetable market** (Zelenjavni trg; ⊙7am-2pm Mon-Sat) in the small square behind the town hall. **Mercator** (Levstikova ul 5; ⊙7am-8pm Mon-Sat, 8am-noon Sun) has a branch in the Old Town. **Ham Ham** (Cankarjevo nabrežje 19; ⊙7am-midnight) is a convenience store opposite the bus station.

TOP CHOICE Pri Mari
MEDITERRANEAN, SLOVENIAN €€

(☑673 47 35, 041-616 488; Dantejeva ul 17; mains €8.50-16; ⊙noon-11pm Tue-Sun summer, noon-10pm Tue-Sat, noon-6pm Sun winter) This stylish and welcoming restaurant run by an Italian-Slovenian couple serves the most inventive Mediterranean and Slovenian dishes in town. Be sure to book ahead.

SLOVENIA PIRAN

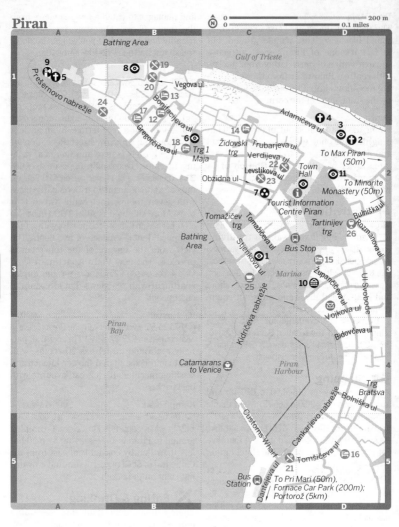

0 ____ 200 m
0 ____ 0.1 miles

Bathing Area

Gulf of Trieste

Prešernovo nabrežje

Vegova ul

Bonifacijeva ul

Gregorčičeva ul

Adamičeva ul

To Max Piran
(50m)

Trg 1
Maja

Židovski
trg

Trubarjeva ul

Verdijeva ul

Levstikova ul

Obzidna ul

Town
Hall

To Minorite
Monastery (50m)

Tourist Information
Centre Piran

Bulniška ul

Rozmanova ul

Tomažičev
trg

Tomažičeva ul

Stjenkova ul

Bathing
Area

Marina

Tartinijev
trg

Bus Stop

Županičeva ul

Ul Svobode

Kidričeva nabrežje

Piran
Bay

Piran
Harbour

Vojkova ul

Bidovčeva ul

Catamarans
to Venice

Trg
Bratsva

Bolniška ul

Customs Wharf

Cankarjevo nabrežje

Danteleva ul

Tomšičeva ul

Bus
Station

To Pri Mari (50m),
Fornače Car Park (200m);
Portorož (5km)

Riva Piran SEAFOOD €€

(☏673 22 25; Gregorčičeva ul 46; mains €8-28; ⊙11.30am-midnight) The best waterfront seafood restaurant and worth patronising is this classy place with the strip's best decor and sea views.

Galeb SEAFOOD €

(☏673 32 25; Pusterla ul 5; mains €8-11; ⊙11am-4pm & 6-11pm or midnight Wed-Mon) This excellent family-run restaurant, which has some seafront seating, is located east of the Punta lighthouse. The food is good but takes no risks.

Flora PIZZA €

(☏673 12 58; Prešernovo nabrežje 26; pizza €4-8; ⊙10am-1am summer, 10am-10pm winter) The terrace of this simple pizzeria east of the lighthouse has great views of the Adriatic.

Cafe Teater CAFE-BAR

(☏051-694 100; Stjenkova ul 1; ⊙8am-3am) Anyone who's anyone in Piran can be found at this cafe with a waterfront terrace and faux antique furnishings.

Žižola Kantina BAR

(Tartinijev trg 10; ⊙9am-2am) This simple, nautically themed bar named after the jujube

Piran

(Chinese date) that grows prolifically along the Adriatic has tables right on the main square and serves 15 different flavours of *žganje* (fruit brandy).

ⓘ Information

Banka Koper (Tartinijev trg 12)

Caffe Neptun (☑041-724 237; www.caffe neptun.com; Dantejeva ul 4; per 20min €1; ⊘7am-1am) Modern cafe near bus station with internet access; free with drink.

Maona Tourist Agency (☑673 45 20; www. maona.si; Cankarjevo nabrežje 7; ⊘9am-8pm Mon-Sat, 10am-1pm & 5-7pm Sun) Rents private rooms, organises activities and cruises.

Post office (Leninova ul 1)

Tourist Information Centre Piran (☑673 02 20, 673 44 40; www.portoroz.si; Tartinijev trg 2; ⊘9am-8pm summer, 9am-5pm winter) Housed in the impressive town hall.

ⓘ Getting There & Away

Buses from everywhere except Portorož arrive at the bus station, a 300m stroll south along the portside Cankarjevo nabrežje from Tartinijev trg. Trying to drive a car into Piran is insane; vehicles are stopped at a toll gate 200m south of the bus station, where the sensible choice is to use the huge Fornače car park (per hour/day €1.20/12) and ride the frequent shuttle bus into town.

Buses run every 20 to 40 minutes to Koper (€2.70, 30 minutes, 18km) via Izola, while five head for Trieste in Italy (€10, 1¾ hours, 36km) between 6.45am and 6.55pm Monday to Saturday. Between three and five daily buses go to Ljubljana (€12, 2½ to three hours, 140km) via Divača and Postojna.

From the southern end of Tartinijev trg, a shuttle bus (€1) goes every 15 minutes to Portorož.

Venezia Lines (☑05-674 71 60; www.venezia lines.com) catamarans sail to Venice (one way €45-55, return €64-69, 2¼ hours) at 8.30am on Wednesday from May to September. A service run by **Trieste Lines** (www.triestelines.it; one way/return €8.50/15.70) links Piran and Trieste most days during the same period.

Book a taxi on ☑031-730 700.

Portorož

☑05 / POP 2900

Portorož (Portorose in Italian), the biggest coastal resort in Slovenia, is actually quite classy for a seaside town, even along Obala, the main drag. Portorož's sandy beaches are relatively clean, and there are pleasant spas and wellness centres where you can take the waters or cover yourself in curative mud.

At the same time, the vast array of accommodation options makes Portorož a useful fallback if everything's full in Piran; the **Tourist Information Centre Portorož** (☑674 22 20; www.portoroz.si; Obala 16; ⊘9am-8pm summer, 9am-5pm winter) has listings. On the way into Portorož, the summer-only hostel **Prenočišča Korotan** (☑674 54 00; www.sd.upr. si/sdp/prenocisca; Obala 11; s/d €36/49.50; ⊘Jul & Aug; Ⓟ◉) has good-sized en-suite rooms but there's a supplement for stays of one or two nights. At the other end of the scale, the 181-room **Kempinski Palace Portorož** (☑692 70 00; www.kempinski.com/portoroz; Obala 45; s/d from €135/185; Ⓟ✳◉☏⛲), the art nouveau hotel that put Portorož on the map, has arisen phoenix-like after a protracted renovation and is now the classiest hotel in Slovenia.

There are dozens of pizzerias along Obala, but the venue of choice is **Pizzeria Figarola** (☑031-313 415; Obala 18; pizza €5.50-8.90), with a huge terrace just up from the main pier. For seafood you won't do better than at **Staro Sidro** (☑674 50 74; Obala 55; mains €8-19; ⊗noon-11pm Tue-Sun) next to the lovely (and landmark) Vila San Marco.

Kavarna Cacao (☑674 10 35; Obala 14; ⊗8am-1am Sun-Thu, to 3am Fri & Sat) wins the award as the most stylish cafe-bar on the coast and boasts a fabulous waterfront terrace. For live music on Tuesday and Friday from 10pm head for the **Kanela Bar** (☑674 61 81; Obala 14; ⊗11am-3am), a workhorse of a rock 'n' roll bar secreted between the beach and the Kavarna Cacao.

Portorož is served every 15 minutes by shuttle bus (€1) to/from Piran. Catch it along Obala.

EASTERN SLOVENIA

The rolling vine-covered hills of eastern Slovenia are attractive but much less dramatic than the Julian Alps or, indeed, the coast. If you're heading by train to Vienna via Graz in Austria it saves money to stop in lively Maribor, Slovenia's second-largest city; international tickets are very expensive per kilometre, so doing as much travelling as possible on domestic trains saves cash. While there, consider visiting postcard-perfect Ptuj less than 30km down the road.

Maribor

☑02 / POP 87,275

Slovenia's second city, chosen as the European Capital of Culture in 2012, really has no unmissable sights but oozes with charm thanks to its delightful (but tiny) Old Town. Pedestrianised central streets buzz with cafes and student life, and in late June/early July the old, riverside Lent district hosts the **Festival Lent** (http://lent.slovenija.net), a two-week extravaganza of folklore and culture.

Maribor Castle (Grajski trg 2), on the main square's northeast corner, contains a magnificent 18th-century **rococo staircase** visible from the street and the **Maribor Regional Museum** (☑228 35 51; www.pmuzej-mb.si; adult/child €3/2; ⊗9am-4pm Tue-Sat, 9am-2pm Sun), one of Slovenia's richest archaeological and ethnographical collections. To the

southwest, the **cathedral** (Slomškov trg) sits in an oasis of fountain-cooled calm. Follow little Poštna ul southward into **Glavni trg** with its 16th-century **town hall** (Glavni trg 14) and extravagant **plague pillar** erected by townspeople in gratitude for having survived the plague. A block further south down Mesarski prehod and along the Drava River's northern bank is the **Stara Trta** (Vojašniška 8), the world's oldest living grapevine. It's been a source of a dark red wine called Žametna Črnina (Black Velvet) for more than four centuries.

The **Tourist Information Centre Maribor** (☑234 66 11; www.maribor-pohorje.si; Partizanska c 6a; ⊗9am-7pm Mon-Fri, to 6pm Sat & Sun) is in a kiosk opposite the Franciscan church. For budget accommodation, try the **Lollipop Hostel** (☑040-243 160; lollipophostel@yahoo.com; Maistrova ul 17; dm €20; @), with 13 beds in two rooms a short distance from the train station and run by an affable Englishwoman. A short distance to the southeast is the **Grand Hotel Ocean** (☑234 36 73; www.hotelocean.si; Partizanska c 39; s/d €118/152; P☀@), a stunning 22-room boutique hotel named after the first train to pass through the city in 1846.

Gril Ranca (☑252 55 50; Dravska ul 10; dishes €4.80-7.50; ⊗8am-11pm Mon-Sat, noon-9pm Sun) along the Drava in Lent serves simple but scrumptious Balkan grills. For something spicier try nearby **Takos** (☑252 71 50; Mesarski prehod 3; mains €6.50-12; ⊗11am-11pm Mon-Thu, to 2.30am Fri & Sat), an atmospheric Mexican restaurant that turns into a snappy little night spot at the weekend.

Buses run to Ljubljana (€12.40, three hours, 141km) two to four times a day. Also served are Celje (€6.70, 1½ hours, 65km, four a day) and Ptuj (€3.60, 45 minutes, 27km, hourly). There are daily buses to Munich (€46, 7½ hours, 453km) at 6.30pm and 9.50pm, and one to Vienna (€29, 4½ hours, 258km) at 7.45pm. Of the two-dozen daily trains to/from Ljubljana (€8.50, 2½ hours, 156km), some seven are IC express trains costing €14.40 and taking just under two hours.

Ptuj

☑02 / POP 19,010

Rising above a wide, fairly flat valley, compact Ptuj – Poetovio to the Romans – forms a symphony of red-tile roofs best viewed from the other side of the Drava River.

⊙ Sights

Ptuj Castle CASTLE
(Na Gradu 1) Ptuj's pinnacle is well-preserved, containing the fine **Ptuj Regional Museum** (☎787 92 30; www.pok-muzej-ptuj.si; adult/child €4/2.50; ⊙9am-6pm Mon-Fri, 9am-8pm Sat & Sun summer, 9am-5pm daily winter).

✦ Festivals

Kurentovanje CARNIVAL
(www.kurentovanje.net) In February the crowds come to spot the shaggy straw men at Slovenia's foremost traditional carnival. A 'rite of spring', it is celebrated for 10 days up to Mardi Gras, or Shrove Tuesday (February or early March); the museum has some excellent Kurentovanje-related exhibits.

⊨ Sleeping

Hostel Eva HOSTEL €
(☎771 24 41, 040-226 522; www.bikeek.si; Jadranska ul 22; per person €12-17) If you're looking for budget accommodation, head for this a welcoming place that's connected to a bike shop (rental per hour/day €3.80/11) with six rooms containing two to four beds and a large, light-filled kitchen.

TOP **Hotel Mitra** HOTEL €€
CHOICE (☎787 74 55, 051-603 069; www.hotel-mitra.si; Prešernova ul 6; s €56-68, d €96-103; **P✽@☎**) If you'd like more comfort, continue walking west on Prešernova ul past a parade of cafes and bars to one of provincial Slovenia's more interesting hotels, with 26 generous-sized guestrooms and three humongous suites, lovely Oriental carpets on the original wooden floors and a wellness centre in an old courtyard cellar.

✖ Eating

Next to the town's open-air **market** (Novi trg; ⊙7am-3pm) you'll find a large **Mercator** (Novi trg 3; ⊙7.30am-7.30pm Mon-Fri, to 1pm Sat) supermarket.

Amadeus GOSTILNA €€
(☎771 70 51; Prešernova ul 36; mains €6.50-20; ⊙noon-10pm Mon-Thu, noon-11pm Fri & Sat, noon-4pm Sun) A very pleasant *gostilna* above a cafe-bar, it serves *štruklji* (dumplings with herbs and cheese, €4.50), steak and pork dishes.

Gostilna Ribič GOSTILNA €€
(☎749 06 35; Dravska ul 9; mains €9.50-20; ⊙10am-11pm Sun-Thu, to midnight Fri & Sat) The best restaurant in Ptuj has a great riverside terrace and is the ideal spot to have fish.

ℹ Information

Tourist Information Centre Ptuj (☎779 60 11; www.ptuj.info; Slovenski trg 5; ⊙8am-8pm summer, 9am-6pm winter) Facing a medieval tower in the Old Town, it has reams of information and lists of places to stay.

ℹ Getting There & Away

Buses to Maribor (€3.60, 45 minutes, 27km) run at hourly on weekdays but are less frequent on weekends. You can reach Ptuj up to nine times a day by train from Ljubljana (€8 to €10.50, 2½ hours, 155km) direct or via Zidani Most and Pragersko.

UNDERSTAND SLOVENIA

History

Slovenes can make a credible claim to having invented democracy. By the early 7th century, their Slavic ancestors had founded the Duchy of Carantania (Karantanija), based at Krn Castle (now Karnburg in Austria). Ruling dukes were elected by ennobled commoners and invested before ordinary citizens. This unique model was noted by the 16th-century French political philosopher Jean Bodin, whose work was a key reference for Thomas Jefferson when he wrote the American Declaration of Independence in 1776. Carantania (later Carinthia) was fought over by the Franks and Magyars from the 8th to 10th centuries, and later divided up among Austro-Germanic nobles and bishops. Between the late 13th and early 16th centuries, almost all the lands inhabited by Slovenes, with the exception of the Venetian-controlled coastal towns, came under the control of the Habsburgs.

Indeed, Austria ruled what is now Slovenia until 1918, apart from a brief interlude between 1809 and 1813 when Napoleon created six so-called Illyrian Provinces from Slovenian and Croatian regions and made Ljubljana the capital. Napoleon proved a popular conqueror as his relatively liberal regime de-Germanised the education system. Slovene was taught in schools for the first time, leading to an awakening of national consciousness. In tribute, Ljubljana still has a French Revolution Sq (Trg Francoske Revolucije) with a column bearing a likeness of the French emperor.

Fighting during WWI was particularly savage along the Soča Valley – the so-called Isonzo Front – which was occupied by Italy then dramatically retaken by German-led Austro-Hungarian forces. The war ended with the collapse of Austria-Hungary, which handed western Slovenia to Italy as part of postwar reparations. Northern Carinthia, including the towns of Beljak and Celovec (now Villach and Klagenfurt), voted to stay with Austria in a 1920 plebiscite. What remained of Slovenia joined fellow south (*jug*) Slavs in forming the Kingdom of Serbs, Croats and Slovenes, later Yugoslavia.

Nazi occupation in WWII was for the most part resisted by Slovenian partisans, though after Italy capitulated in 1943 the anti-partisan Slovenian Domobranci (Home Guards) were active in the west. To prevent their nemeses the communists from taking political control in liberated areas, the Domobranci threw their support behind the Germans. The war ended with Slovenia regaining Italian-held areas from Piran to Bovec, but losing Trst (Trieste) and part of Gorica (Gorizia).

In Tito's Yugoslavia, Slovenia, with only 8% of the national population, was the economic powerhouse, creating up to 20% of the national GDP. But by the 1980s the federation had become increasingly Serb-dominated, and Slovenes feared they would lose their political autonomy. In free elections, Slovenes voted overwhelmingly to break away from Yugoslavia and did so on 25 June 1991. A 10-day war that left 66 people dead followed; Yugoslavia swiftly signed a truce in order to concentrate on regaining control of coastal Croatia.

Slovenia was admitted to the UN in May 1992 and became a member of the EU in May 2004. It replaced the tolar with the euro as the national currency in January 2007.

In the national elections of October 2008, Janez Janša's coalition government was narrowly defeated by the Social Democrats under Borut Pahor, who was able to form a coalition with three minority parties. Since 2004, Slovenia has been moving towards a two-party system, with the Social Democrats and Janša's Slovenian Democratic Party as the major political forces.

The Slovenes

The population of Slovenia is largely homogeneous. Just over 83% are ethnic Slovenes, with the remainder Serbs, Croats, Bosnians, Albanians and Roma; there are also small enclaves of Italians and Hungarians, who have special deputies looking after their interests in parliament. Slovenes are ethnically Slavic, typically hardworking, multilingual and extrovert. Just under 58% of Slovenes identify themselves as Catholics.

The Arts

Slovenia's most cherished writer is the Romantic poet France Prešeren (1800–49). His patriotic yet humanistic verse was a driving force in raising Slovene national consciousness. Fittingly, a stanza of his poem 'Zdravljica' (A Toast) forms the lyrics of the national anthem.

Many of Ljubljana's most characteristic architectural features, including its recurring pyramid motif, were added by celebrated Slovenian architect Jože Plečnik (1872–1957), whose work fused classical building principles and folk-art traditions.

Postmodernist painting and sculpture were more or less dominated from the 1980s by the multimedia group Neue Slowenische Kunst (NSK) and the artists' cooperative Irwin. It also spawned the internationally known industrial-music group Laibach, whose leader, Tomaž Hostnik, died tragically in 1983 when he hanged himself from a *kozolec*, the traditional (and iconic) hayrack found only in Slovenia. Slovenia's vibrant music scene embraces rave, techno, jazz, punk, thrash-metal and *chanson* (torch songs from the likes of Vita Mavrič); the most popular local rock group is Siddharta, still going strong after 15 years. There's also been a folk-music revival: keep an ear out for the groups Katice and Katalena, who play traditional Slovenian music with a modern twist, and the vocalist Brina.

Well-received Slovenian films in recent years include *Kruh in Mleko* (Bread & Milk, 2001), the tragic story by Jan Cvitkovič of a dysfunctional small-town family, and Damjan Kozole's *Rezerni Deli* (Spare Parts, 2003) about the trafficking of illegal immigrants through Slovenia from Croatia to Italy by a couple of embittered misfits living in the southern town of Krško, site of the nation's only nuclear power plant. Much lighter fare is *Petelinji Zajtrk* (Rooster's Breakfast, 2007), a romance by Marko Naberšnik set in Gornja Radgona on the Austrian border in northeast Slovenia, and the bizarre US-made documentary *Big River Man* (John Maringouin, 2009) about an overweight dyspeptic marathon swimmer who takes on – wait for it – the Amazon and succeeds.

Environment

Slovenia is amazingly green; indeed, 58% of its total surface area is covered in forest and it's growing. Slovenia is home to almost 3200 plant species – some 70 of which are indigenous. Triglav National Park is particularly rich in native flowering plants. Among the more peculiar endemic fauna in Slovenia is a blind salamander called *Proteus anguinus* that lives deep in Karst caves, can survive for years without eating and has been called a 'living fossil'.

Slovenian Cuisine

Slovenia boasts an incredibly diverse cuisine, but except for a few national favourites such as *žlikrofi* (pasta stuffed with cheese, bacon and chives) and *jota* (hearty bean soup) and incredibly rich desserts like *gibanica*, you're not likely to encounter many of these regional specialities on menus. Dishes like *brodet* (fish soup) from the coast, *ajdovi žganci z ocvirki* (buckwheat 'porridge' with savoury pork crackling) and salad greens doused in *bučno olje* (pumpkinseed oil) are generally eaten at home.

A *gostilna* or *gostišče* (inn) or *restavracija* (restaurant) more frequently serves *rižota* (risotto), *klobasa* (sausage), *zrezek* (cutlet/steak), *golaž* (goulash) and *paprikaš* (piquant chicken or beef 'stew'). *Riba* (fish) is usually priced by the *dag* (100g). *Postrv* (freshwater trout) generally costs half the price of sea fish, though grilled squid *(lignji na žaru)* doused in garlic butter is usually a bargain.

Common in Slovenia are such Balkan favourites as *cevapčiči* (spicy meatballs of beef or pork) and *pljeskavica* (spicy meat patties), often served with *kajmak* (a type of clotted cream).

You can snack cheaply on takeaway pizza slices or pieces of *burek* (€2), flaky pastry stuffed with meat, cheese or apple. Alternatives include *štruklji* (cottage-cheese dumplings) and *palačinke* (thin sweet pancakes).

Some restaurants have *dnevno kosilo* (set lunches), including *juha* (soup), *solata* (salad) and a main course, for as low as €7.

Wine, Beer & Brandy

Distinctively Slovenian wines include peppery red Teran made from Refošk grapes in the Karst region, Cviček, a dry light red – almost rosé – wine from eastern Slovenia, and Malvazija, a straw-colour white from the coast that is light and dry. Slovenes are justly proud of their top vintages, but cheaper bar-standard 'open wine' *(odprto vino)* sold by the decilitre (100mL) is just so-so.

Pivo (beer), whether *svetlo* (lager) or *temno* (porter), is best on *točeno* (draught) but always available in cans and bottles too.

There are dozens of kinds of *žganje* (fruit brandy) available, including *češnjevec* (made with cherries), *sadjevec* (mixed fruit), *brinjevec* (juniper), *hruška* (pears, also called *viljamovka*) and *slivovka* (plums).

Like many other countries in Europe, Slovenia bans smoking across the board in all public places, including restaurants, bars and hotels.

SURVIVAL GUIDE

Directory A–Z

Accommodation

Very roughly, budget accommodation in Slovenia means a double room under €50. Midrange is €50 to €100 and top end is anything over €100. Accommodation can be a bit more expensive in Ljubljana. Unless otherwise indicated, rooms include toilet and bath or shower and breakfast. Smoking is banned in all hotels and hostels.

Camping grounds generally charge per person, whether you're in a tent or caravan. Almost all sites close from mid-October to mid-April. Camping 'rough' is illegal in Slovenia, and this law is enforced, especially around Bled and on the coast. Seek out the Slovenian Tourist Board's *Camping in Slovenia*.

Slovenia's ever-growing stable of hostels includes Ljubljana's trendy Celica and the Alibi chain found both in the capital and in Piran. Throughout the country there are student dormitories (residence halls) moonlighting as hostels for visitors in July and August. Unless stated otherwise hostel rooms share bathrooms. Hostels usually cost from €17 to €22; prices are at their highest in July and August.

Tourist information offices can usually help you find private rooms, apartments and tourist farms, or they can recommend private agencies that will. Such accommodation can appear misleadingly cheap if you overlook the 30% to 50% surcharge levied on stays of less than three nights. Also be aware that many such properties are in outlying villages with minimal (or no) public transport, and that the cheapest one-star category rooms with shared bathroom are actually very rare, so you'll usually pay well above the quoted minimum. Depending on the season you might save a little money by going directly to any house with a sign reading *sobe* or *Zimmer frei* (indicating 'rooms available' in Slovene and German). For more information check out the STB's *Friendly Countryside* pamphlet listing some 200 farms with accommodation.

Guesthouses, known as a *penzion, gostišče,* or *prenočišča,* are often cosy and better value than full-blown hotels. Beware that locally listed rates are usually quoted per person assuming double occupancy. A tourist tax – routinely from €1 per person per day – is usually not included.

Activities

EXTREME SPORTS
Several areas specialise in adrenalin-rush activities – rafting, hydro-speed, kayaking and canyoning – including Bovec (p928) and Bled (p923). Bovec is also a great place for paragliding. Gliding costs are very reasonable from Lesce near Bled. Scuba diving from Piran (p935) is also good value.

HIKING
Hiking is extremely popular, with the **Alpine Association of Slovenia** (www.pzs.si) counting more than 58,000 members and *Ljubljančani* flocking in droves to Triglav National Park (p925) on weekends. There are some 10,000km of marked trails and paths – 8250km of which are mountain trails – and more than 170 mountain huts offer comfortable trailside refuge. Ask for the STB's exhaustive *Hiking in Slovenia*.

SKIING
Skiing is a Slovenian passion, with slopes particularly crowded over the Christmas holidays and in early February. See the STB's *Slovenia Skiing* for more details.

Kranjska Gora (up to 1291m; p926) has some challenging runs, and the world record for ski-jumping was set at nearby Planica, 4km to the west. Above Lake Bohinj, Vogel (up to 1800m) is particularly scenic, as is Kanin (up to 2300m) above Bovec, which can have snow into late spring. Being relatively close to Ljubljana, Krvavec (up to 1971m), northeast of Kranj, can have particularly long lift queues.

Just west of Maribor in eastern Slovenia is a popular choice and the biggest downhill skiing area in the country. Although relatively low (336m to 1347m), the Mariborsko Pohorje is easily accessible, with very varied downhill pistes and relatively short lift queues.

OTHER ACTIVITIES
Mountain bikes are available for hire from travel agencies and some hotels at Bled, Bohinj, Bovec, Kranjska Gora and Postojna.

The Soča River near Kobarid and the Sava Bohinjka near Bohinj are great for fly-fishing April to October. Catch-and-release licences for the latter cost €42 and are sold at the tourist office.

Spas and wellness centres are very popular in Slovenia; the STB publishes a useful brochure called *Health Resorts*. Many towns (eg Portorož) have some spa complexes, and hotels often offer free or low-rate entry to their guests.

Business Hours
Most businesses post their opening times *(delovni čas)* on the door. Many shops close Saturday afternoons. A handful of grocery stores open on Sundays, including some branches of the ubiquitous Mercator supermarket chain. Most museums close on Mondays. Banks often take lunch breaks from noon or 12.30pm to 2pm or 3pm and some open on Saturday mornings. Post offices are generally open from 8am to 6pm weekdays and till noon on Saturday.

Restaurants typically open from 10pm or 11am to 10pm or 11pm. Bars stay open to midnight, though they usually have longer hours on weekends and shorter ones on Sundays.

Embassies & Consulates
Following are among the embassies and consulates in Slovenia. They are all in Ljubljana unless otherwise stated:

Australia (☎01-234 86 75; Železna c 14; ☺9am-1pm Mon-Fri)

Austria (☎01-479 07 00; Prešernova c 23; ☺8am-noon Mon-Thu, 8-10am Fri) Enter from Veselova ul.

Canada (☎01-252 44 44; 12th fl, Trg Republike 3; ☺9am-noon Mon-Fri)

Croatia Ljubljana (☎01-425 62 20; Gruberjevo nabrežje 6; ☺9am-1pm Mon-Fri); Maribor (☎02-234 66 80; Trg Svobode 3; ☺10am-1pm Mon-Fri)

France (☎01-479 04 00; Barjanska c 1; ☺8.30am-12.30pm Mon-Fri) Enter from Zoisova c 2.

Hungary (☑01-512 18 82; ul Konrada Babnika 5; ☺8am-5pm Mon-Fri)

Ireland (☑01-300 89 70; Palača Kapitelj, Poljanski nasip 6; ☺9.30am-12.30pm & 2.30-4pm Mon-Fri)

Italy Ljubljana (☑01-426 21 94; Snežniška ul 8; ☺9-11am Mon-Fri); Koper (☑05-627 37 49; Belvedere 2; ☺9-11am Mon-Fri)

Netherlands (☑01-420 14 61; Palača Kapitelj, Poljanski nasip 6; ☺9am-noon Mon-Fri)

New Zealand (☑01-580 30 55; Verovškova ul 57; ☺8am-3pm Mon-Fri)

South Africa (☑01-200 63 00; Pražakova ul 4; ☺3-4pm Tue) In the Kompas building.

UK (☑01-200 39 10; 4th fl, Trg Republike 3; ☺9am-noon Mon-Fri)

USA (☑01-200 55 00; Prešernova c 31; ☺9-11.30am & 1-3pm Mon-Fri)

Festivals & Events

Major cultural and sporting events are listed under 'Upcoming Events' on the home page of the of the **Slovenian Tourist Board** (www.slovenia.info) website and in the STB's comprehensive *Calendar of Major Events in Slovenia*, issued annually.

Food

Price ranges are: budget (€; under €15), midrange (€€; €15 to €30) and top end (€€€; over €30).

Gay & Lesbian Travellers

Roza Klub (☑01-430 47 40; Kersnikova ul 4) in Ljubljana is made up of the gay and lesbian branches of **ŠKUC** (www.skuc.org), which stands for Študentski Kulturni Center (Student Cultural Centre) but is no longer student-oriented as such.

A more or less monthly publication called **Narobe** (Upside Down; www.narobe.si) is in Slovene only, though you might be able to at least glean from the listings.

Holidays

Slovenia celebrates 14 holidays *(prazniki)* a year. If a holiday falls on a Sunday, then the following Monday becomes the holiday.

New Year 1 & 2 January

Prešeren Day (Slovenian Culture Day) 8 February

Easter & Easter Monday March/April

Insurrection Day 27 April

Labour Day holidays 1 & 2 May

National Day 25 June

Assumption Day 15 August

Reformation Day 31 October

All Saints Day 1 November

Christmas Day 25 December

Independence Day 26 December

Internet Access

Virtually every hostel and hotel now has internet access – a computer for guests' use (free or for a nominal fee), wi-fi, or both. Most cities and towns have at least one internet cafe but they usually only have a handful of terminals. The useful **e-točka** (e-points; www.e-tocke.gov.si) website lists free access terminals, wi-fi hotspots and commercial internet cafes across Slovenia.

Internet Resources

The website of the **Slovenian Tourist Board** (www.slovenia.info) is tremendously useful, as is that of **Mat'Kurja** (www.matkurja.com), a directory of Slovenian web resources. Most Slovenian towns and cities have a website accessed by typing www.town.si (or sometimes www.town-tourism.si). Especially good are **Ljubljana** (www.ljubljana.si), **Maribor** (www.maribor.si) and **Piran/Portorož** (www.portoroz.si).

Money

The official currency is the euro. Exchanging cash is simple at banks, major post offices, travel agencies and *menjalnice* (bureaux de change), although many don't accept travellers cheques. Major credit and debit cards are accepted almost everywhere, and ATMs are ubiquitous.

Post

Local mail costs €0.33 for up to 20g, while an international airmail stamp costs €0.49. Poste restante is free; address it to and pick it up from the main post office at Slovenska c 32, 1101 Ljubljana.

Telephone

Slovenia's country code is ☑386. Public telephones require a phonecard *(telefonska kartica or telekartica)*, available at post offices and some newsstands. The cheapest card (€3, 25 units) gives about 20 minutes' calling time to other European countries; the highest value is €14.60 with 300 units. Local SIM cards with €5 credit are available for €12 from **SiMobil** (www.simobil.si), for €15 from **Mobitel** (www.mobitel.si) and for just €3.99 from

EMERGENCY NUMBERS

- » **Ambulance** ☑112
- » **Fire Brigade** ☑112
- » **Police** ☑113
- » **Roadside Assistance** ☑1987

new-kid-on-the-block **Tušmobil** (www.tusmobil.si). Mobile numbers in Slovenia are identified by the prefix ☑030 and ☑040 (SiMobil), ☑031, ☑041, ☑051 and ☑071 (Mobitel) and ☑070 (Tušmobil).

Tourist Information

The Ljubljana-based **Slovenian Tourist Board** (☑01-589 85 50; www.slovenia.info; Dimičeva ul 13) has dozens of tourist information centres (TICs) in Slovenia, and seven branches abroad. See 'STB Representative Offices Abroad' on its website for details.

Visas

Citizens of virtually all European countries, as well as Australia, Canada, Israel, Japan, New Zealand and the USA, do not require visas to visit Slovenia for stays of up to 90 days. Holders of EU and Swiss passports can enter using a national identity card.

Those who do require visas (including South Africans) can get them for up to 90 days at any Slovenian embassy or consulate – see the website of the **Ministry of Foreign Affairs** (www.mzz.gov.si) for a full listing. They cost €35 regardless of the type of visa or length of validity. You'll need confirmation of a hotel booking plus one photo, and you may have to show a return or onward ticket.

Women Travellers

In the event of an emergency call the **police** (☑113) any time or the **SOS Helpline** (☑080 11 55; www.drustvo-sos.si; ☉noon-10pm Mon-Fri, 6-10pm Sat & Sun).

Getting There & Away

Air

Slovenia's only international airport receiving regular scheduled flights at present – Aerodrom Maribor does limited charters only – is Ljubljana's **Jože Pučnik Airport** (LJU; ☑04-206 1981; www.lju-airport.si) at Brnik, 27km north of Ljubljana. From there, the Slovenian flag-carrier, **Adria Airways** (JP; ☑080 13 00, 01-369 10 10; www.adria-airways.

com), serves some 30 European destinations on regularly scheduled flights, with just as many holiday spots served by charter flights in summer. Adria can be remarkably good value and includes useful connections to places like İstanbul, Pristina (Kosovo) and Tirana (Albania).

Other airlines with regularly scheduled flights to and from Ljubljana:

Air France (AF; ☑01-244 34 47; www.airfrance.com) Daily flights to Paris (CDG).

Austrian Airlines (OS; ☑04-202 01 00; www.aua.com) Multiple daily flights with Adria to Vienna.

Brussels Airlines (SN; ☑04-206 16 56; www.brusselsairlines.com) Daily flights with Adria to Brussels.

ČSA Czech Airlines (OK; ☑04-206 17 50; www.czechairlines.com) Flights to Prague.

easyJet (EZY; ☑04-206 16 77; www.easyjet.com) Low-cost daily flights to London Stansted.

Finnair (AY; ☑080 13 00; www.finnair.com) Flights to Helsinki.

JAT Airways (JU; ☑01-231 43 40; www.jat.com) Daily flights to Belgrade.

Turkish Airlines (TK; ☑04-206 16 80; www.turkishairlines.com) Flights to İstanbul.

Land
BUS

International bus destinations from Ljubljana include Serbia, Germany, Croatia, Bosnia & Hercegovina, Macedonia, Italy and Scandinavia; see p945. You can also catch buses to Italy and Croatia from coastal towns, including Piran (p937) and Koper (p933).

TRAIN

It is possible to travel to Italy, Austria, Germany, Croatia and Hungary by train; Ljubljana (p945) is the main hub, although you can, for example, hop on international trains in certain cities like Maribor and Ptuj). International train travel can be expensive. It is sometimes cheaper to travel as far as you can on domestic routes before crossing any borders.

Sea

Piran despatches ferries to Trieste daily and catamarans to Venice at least once a week in season; see p937 for details. There's also a catamaran between nearby Izola and Venice in summer months; see p934.

SLOVENIA SURVIVAL GUIDE

Getting Around

Bus

Book long-distance buses ahead of time, especially when travelling on Friday afternoons. If your bag has to go in the luggage compartment below the bus, it will cost about €1.50 extra. Check the online bus timetable on the **Avtobusna Postaja Ljubljana** (www.ap-ljubljana.si) website.

Bicycle

Bicycle rental places are generally concentrated in the more popular tourist areas such as Ljubljana, Bled, Bovec and Piran though a fair few cycle shops and repair places hire them out as well.

Car

Daily rates usually start at around €40/210 per day/week, including unlimited mileage, collision-damage waiver and theft protection. Unleaded petrol *(bencin)* costs €1.19 (95 octane) and €1.22 (98 octane), with diesel at €1.13. You must keep your headlights illuminated throughout the day. If you'll be doing a lot of driving consider buying Kod & Kam's 1:100,000 *Avtoatlas Slovenija* (€29).

Tolls are no longer paid separately on the motorways. Instead all cars must display a *vinjeta* (road-toll sticker) on the windscreen. They cost €15/30 for a week/month for cars and €7.50/25 for motorcycles and are available at petrol stations, post offices, some newsstands and tourist information centres. These stickers will already be in place on a rental car, but if you are driving your own vehicle, failure to display such a sticker risks a fine of up to €800.

Further information is available from the **Automobile Association of Slovenia** (⊡01-530 52 00; www.amzs.si).

Hitching

Hitchhiking is fairly common and legal everywhere in Slovenia except on motorways and a few major highways. But it's never totally safe and Lonely Planet doesn't recommend it.

Train

Slovenian Railways (Slovenske Železnice; ⊡01-291 33 32; www.slo-zeleznice.si) has a useful online timetable that's easy to use. Buy tickets before boarding or you'll incur a €2.50 supplement. Be aware that EuroCity (EC) and InterCity (IC) trains carry a surcharge of €1.60 on top of standard quoted fares, while InterCity Slovenia ones cost €9.50/6.30 extra in 1st/2nd class.

Ukraine Україна

Why Go?

Big, diverse and largely undiscovered, Ukraine is one of Europe's last genuine travel frontiers, a poor nation rich in colour-splashed tradition, warm-hearted people and off-the-map travel experiences.

'Ukraine' means 'land on the edge', an apt title for this slab of Eurasia in more ways than one. This is the Slavic hinterland on Europe's periphery, but it's also a country creeping towards change and modernity. One look at its renovated city centres, resurfaced roads and the infrastructure erected for the Euro 2012 soccer championships is enough to see that after two decades of independence, Ukraine is edging closer to where it aspires to be.

Most visitors head for the eclectic capital Kyiv, but architecturally rich Lviv and hedonistic Odesa are attracting ever greater numbers. Add a spot of hiking or skiing in the Carpathians and the balmy beaches of Crimea, and Ukraine becomes a much more diverse destination than many realise.

Best Places to Stay

» Sunflower B&B (p951)
» Vintage (p962)
» Leopolis Hotel (p962)
» Old Continent (p965)
» Hetman (p969)

Best Places to Eat

» Spotykach (p955)
» Pervak (p955)
» Kompot (p975)
» Masonic Restaurant (p963)
» Reflection (p967)

When to Go
Kyiv

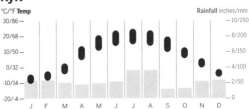

April Witness Ukraine's funny side at Odesa's Carnival Humorina festival of humour.

May Take a Sunday morning stroll through Lviv when church music wafts through streets.

December Enjoy some hearty Hutsul apresski during the Carpathian ski season.

Connections

Ukraine is well linked to its neighbours, particularly Russia and Belarus, with whom it shares the former Soviet rail system. Kyiv is connected by bus or train to Moscow, St Petersburg, Minsk, Warsaw and Budapest, as well as other Eastern European capitals. Odesa is the hub for travelling to Moldova, with several daily buses to Chişinău (both going via and avoiding Tiraspol); the city also has ferries to Bulgaria, Georgia and Turkey, though the service is erratic. From Uzhhorod it's a short journey to the international mainline into Europe at Chop, connecting Ukraine with Slovakia and Hungary. Lviv is the biggest city servicing the Polish border and an ever-increasing number of travellers are taking budget flights to Poland then crossing the border to Lviv by bus or train. It's also possible to take no-frills flights to Budapest or Bratislava, and continue to Ukraine from there by train.

ITINERARIES

One Week

Begin by sampling the charms of Kyiv before heading either south to party in Odesa or west for a more refined and relaxed time in Lviv. Alternatively, take in Kyiv and Lviv then trundle on down into the Carpathian mountains for a spot of skiing, hiking or mountain biking.

Two Weeks

Spend three days in Kyiv, two in Lviv, then pass through rocking Odesa to Crimea, making Yalta your base and being sure to visit Bakhchysaray.

Essential Food & Drink

» **Borsch** The Ukrainian national soup, which is made with beetroot, pork fat and herbs. There's also an aromatic 'green' variety, based on sorrel.

» **Salo** Basically raw pig fat, cut into slices and eaten with bread or added to soups and other dishes. Look out for the 'Ukrainian Snickers bar' – salo in chocolate

» **Varenyky** Similar to Polish pierogi – pasta pockets filled with everything from mashed potato to sour cherries.

» **Kasha** Sometimes translated as 'porridge', but usually turns out to be buckwheat drenched in milk and served for breakfast.

» **Vodka** Also known in Ukraine as horilka, it accompanies every celebration, red-letter day and get-together – in copious amounts.

AT A GLANCE

» **Currency** Hryvnya (uah)

» **Language** Ukrainian, Russian

» **Money** ATMs widespread; credit cards accepted at most hotels

» **Visas** Not required for EU, UK, US and Canadian citizens for stays of up to 90 days

Fast Facts

» **Area**: 603,550 sq km

» **Capital** Kyiv

» **Telephone country code** 380

» **Emergency** 112

Exchange Rates

Australia	A$1	8.44uah
Canada	C$1	8.36uah
euro	€1	11.48uah
Japan	¥100	9.64uah
New Zealand	NZ$1	6.33uah
UK	UK£1	13.04uah
USA	US$1	7.98uah

Set Your Budget

» **Budget room** 200uah

» **Two-course meal** 60uah

» **Museum entry** 5-15uah

» **Beer** 10-20uah

» **City transport ticket** 1-2uah

Resources

» **Brama** (www.brama.com) Useful gateway site

» **Ukraine.com** (www.ukraine.com) Up-to-date news and heaps of background information

Ukraine Highlights

1 Inspect Kyiv's collection of mummified monks by candlelight at the **Caves Monastery** (p950)

2 Take a hike up **Andriyivsky Uzviz** (p950) Kyiv's most atmospheric street

3 Do a spot of cobble-surfing in **Lviv's historical centre** (p959) packed with churches, museums and eccentric restaurants

4 Make an easy-going ascent of Ukraine's highest peak, **Hoverla** (p968)

5 Take a stroll through the island town of **Kamyanets-Podilsky** (p968) to its photogenic fortress

6 See how the medieval Tatars lived at Bakhchysaray's **Khan's Palace** (p984)

7 Head south to Ukraine's capital of hedonism, **Odesa** (p970) with its thumping nightlife and balmy Black Sea beach scene

KYIV КИЇВ

📞 044 / POP 2.7 MILLION

The ancients must have been spoilt for choice when they needed a pretty spot to settle down – at least one can't help thinking this when in Kyiv, the birthplace of Eastern Slavic civilisation, which spread from here as far as Asia's Pacific coast. Its lovely forested hills overlook the Dnipro – a river so wide that birds fall down before reaching its middle, as writer Nikolay Gogol jokingly remarked.

Those hills, numbered seven as in Rome, cradle a wonderfully eclectic city that has preserved the legacy of its former possessors – Viking chieftains turned ancient Rus princes, plus Polish and Lithuanian kings, Russian tsars and Soviet dictators. Rulers of the newly independent Ukraine are also rushing to leave their often bizarre imprint on this ancient Slavic city.

◉ Sights

Caves Monastery   MONASTERY

(www.lavra.ua; vul Sichnevoho Povstannya 21; admission Upper Lavra 20uah, Lower Lavra free; ⊙Upper Lavra 9am-7pm Apr-Sep, 9.30am-6pm Oct-Mar, Lower Lavra dawn-dusk, caves 8.30am-4.30pm) Rolling across 28 hectares of wooded slopes above the Dnipro River, the Caves Monastery Complex, also known as the Kyiv-Pechersk Lavra, deserves at least half a day. It is the most popular tourist site in the city, a highlight of visiting Ukraine and arguably the spiritual heart of the Ukrainian nation. The site is divided into the Upper Lavra (a complex of churches and museums for which entry is charged) and the Lower Lavra (the caves themselves, for which entry is free).

Entering through the Upper Lavra's Trinity Gate takes you onto a square dominated by the Trinity Gate Church and the Dormition Cathedral. Further into the complex, there is a large number of museums – many of which are of marginal interest – and the superb **Refectory Church of St Antoniy and St Feodosiy**, which contains beautifully painted frescos. There's a great view across the Dnipro from behind the church.

Continuing past the church and down under the flying buttresses will take you to the two sets of **caves** in the Lower Lavra, a few minutes' walk away; before you enter, buy a candle to light your way at a kiosk. Inside the caves, dozens of niches contain glass-topped coffins holding the blanketed bodies of the monks; believers kneel and pray at the coffins, and kiss the glass tops as well. It's all very spooky and it can be claustrophobic on a busy day (weekends are best avoided if possible).

The **excursion bureau** (📞280 3071; www.kplavra.kiev.ua, in Ukrainian), just to the left past the main entrance to the Upper Lavra, sells two-hour guided tours in various languages (375uah per group of up to 10 people). Book in advance during peak periods. Regular group tours in Russian and/or Ukrainian depart every 30 minutes (16uah per person).

St Sophia's Cathedral   CHURCH

(pl Sofiyska; admission to grounds/cathedral/bell tower 3/40/8uah; ⊙grounds 9am-7pm, cathedral 10am-6pm Thu-Tue, 10am-5pm Wed; MMaydan Nezalezhnosti) The city's oldest standing church is the magnificent St Sophia's Cathedral. Built from 1017 to 1031 and named after Hagia Sofia (Holy Wisdom) Cathedral in İstanbul, its Byzantine plan and decoration announced the new religious and political authority of Kyiv. Prince Yaroslav, the 10th-century prince under whom Kyiv reached the height of its cultural and military strength, is buried here. Perhaps the most memorable aspect of a visit is the cathedral's interior, where you'll find 11th-century mosaics and frescos.

St Volodymyr's Cathedral   CHURCH

(bul Tarasa Shevchenka 20; MUniversytet) Although not one of Kyiv's most important churches, St Volodymyr's Cathedral arguably has the prettiest interior. Built in the late 19th century to mark 900 years of Orthodox Christianity in the city, its yellow exterior and seven blue domes conform to standard Byzantine style. However, inside it breaks new ground by displaying art nouveau influences.

Andriyivsky Uzviz   HISTORIC AREA

Your visit to Kyiv wouldn't be complete without a walk along steep, cobblestoned Andriyivsky uzviz (Andrew's Descent), one of its oldest streets. It's named after Apostle Andrew who is believed to have climbed the hill here, affixed a cross to its summit and prophesied that this would be the site of a great Christian city. You can avoid the incline by taking the **funicular** (tickets 2uah; ⊙6.30am-11pm; MPoshtova Pl) to the top of the hill, where you'll find **St Michael's Monastery**, with its seven-cupola, periwinkle cathedral. Further down the street is the baroque **St Andrew's Church** (⊙10am-6.30pm Thu-Tue), built in 1754 by Italian architect Bartelomeo Rastrelli, who also designed the Winter Palace in St Petersburg.

An unmissable sight on the Uzviz is the **Museum of One Street** (Andriyivsky uzviz

2B; admission 20uah; ⊙noon-6pm Tue-Sun), a jumble-sale collection showcasing the lives of dressmakers, soldiers, a rabbi, a Syrian-born orientalist and many others who lived out their days on this one street.

Bulgakov Museum   MUSEUM
(Andriyivsky uzviz 13; tours in Russian/English 20/70uah; ⊙10am-4pm Thu-Tue; ⓂKontraktova Pl) The early home of the much-loved author of *The Master and Margarita* has become a strange and memorable museum designed as an alternative universe populated by the author's memories and characters. Mikhail Bulgakov lived here long before writing it, between 1906 and 1919, but this building was the model for the Turbin family home in *The White Guard*.

Chornobyl Museum   MUSEUM
(prov Khoryva 1; admission 10uah; ⊙10am-6pm Mon-Sat; ⓂKontraktova Pl) The Chornobyl Museum is a harrowing must-see for anyone wanting to know more about the world's worst nuclear accident. It very effectively combines two rooms of exhibits with a room of artwork and photography by those affected by the disaster.

Pyrohovo   MUSEUM
(vul Chervonopraporna; admission 15uah; ⊙museum 10am-5pm, grounds dawn-dusk) Ukraine is dotted with 'open-air' museums like this, full of life-size models of different rustic buildings. However, the Pyrohovo Museum of Folk Architecture, 12km south of Kyiv, is one of the best maintained.

Two things make it stand out. First, the quaint 17th- to 20th-century wooden churches, cottages, farmsteads and windmills are divided into seven 'villages' representing different regions. Second, in summer, workers enact different village roles, carving wood, making pottery, doing embroidery and driving horses and carts. There are also restaurants, pubs and stalls selling *shashlyk*.

The museum is near Pyrohovo village. From Lybidska metro station take *marshrutka* 172 right to the entrance. *Marshrutka* 3 and 156, as well as trolleybus 11, stop at the turn to the museum.

Museum of the Great Patriotic War   MUSEUM
(www.warmuseum.kiev.ua; vul Sichnevoho Povstannya 44; admission 10uah; ⊙10am-5pm Tue-Sun) This gloomy but atmospheric museum documents Ukrainian suffering during WWII and most memorably includes a gruesome pair of gloves made from human skin. Visible from miles around, the **Rodina Mat** (Defence of the Motherland Monument) stands right on top of the museum. Locals nickname the statue 'the Iron Lady' and 'Tin Tits'. Even if you don't like such Soviet pomposity, don't say too much: you'd be taking on a titanium woman carrying 12 tonnes of shield and sword. You can get right into her head – literally, via an elevator in the museum (200uah).

Zoloti Vorota   NOTABLE BUILDING
(Golden Gate; vul Volodymyrska; ⓂZoloti Vorota) Originally erected in 1037 but reconstructed in 1982, the Golden Gate was the original entrance into Old Kyiv. The new version of the old gate is a focal point for the city and a favoured meeting place for locals.

PinchukArtCentre   ART GALLERY
(http://pinchukartcentre.org; Arena City complex, vul Baseyna 2A; admission free; ⊙noon-9pm Tue-Sun; Ⓜpl Lva Tolstoho or Teatralna) The rotating exhibits at this world-class gallery feature elite names in the world of European contemporary art and design, all financed by billionaire mogul Viktor Pinchuk. British giants Antony Gormley and Damian Hirst were on display when we visited.

Chimera Building   NOTABLE BUILDING
(vul Bankova 10; ⓂKhreshchatyk) With its demonic-looking animals and gargoyles, the House of Chimeras is Kyiv's weirdest building. Built at the start of the 20th century by architect Vladislav Horodetsky, it's been more recently used for government receptions.

Babyn Yar   MONUMENT
(ⓂDorohozhychi) Not far from Dorohozhychi metro station, about 4km northwest of the city centre, is Babyn Yar, the location of a WWII execution site and mass grave used by the Nazis. Over 100,000 Kyiv citizens – mostly Jews – were murdered here between 1941 and 1943. The Soviet-era monument is in the wrong place. A small Jewish memorial, a menorah, better marks the spot.

🛏 Sleeping

Sunflower B&B Hotel   B&B $$$
(☏279 3846; www.sunflowerhotel.kiev.ua; vul Kostyolna 9/41; r from 1050uah; ✳@; ⓂMaydan Nezalezhnosti) The name is an oxymoron – it's more B&B than hotel – but we're not complaining. The highlight is the continental breakfast (with a warm pastry) delivered to your room, on request, by English-speaking staff.

Chillout Hostel   HOSTEL $
(☏093 332 4306; chillouthostel@gmail.com; vul Saksahanskoho 30v; dm 130uah, r without bathroom

Central Kyiv

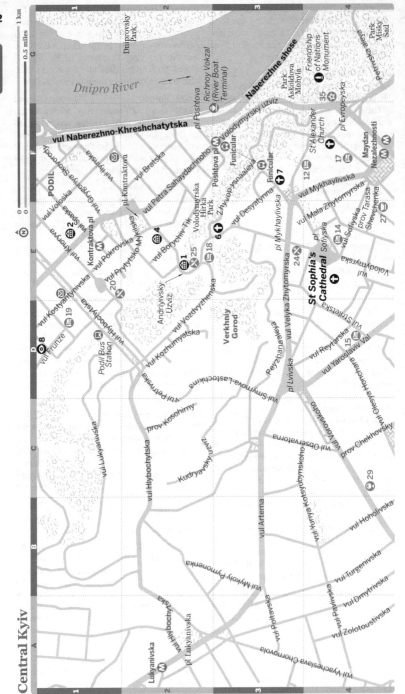

Dnipro River

Dniprovsky Park

Richnoy Vokzal (River Boat Terminal)

pl Poshtova

vul Naberezhno-Khreshchatytska

Naberezhne shose

Park Askoldova Mohyla

Friendship of Nations Monument

St Alexander Church

pl Evropeyska

Maydan Nezalezhnosti

PODIL

vul Khoryva

vul Voloska

vul Spaska

vul Hryhoriya Skovorody

vul Hlybska

vul Kontraktova

vul Bratska

pl Kontraktova

vul Petra Sahaydachnoho

Kontraktova pl

vul Pokrovska

vul Prytytsko Mykilska

vul Borychiv Tik

Volodymyrska Hirka Park

Zhytniomyrsky uzviz

Poshtova pl

Funicular

Funicular

vul Desyatynna

pl Volodymyrsky uzviz

vul Mykhaylivska

vul Mala Zhytomyrska

prov Tarasa Shevchenka

vul Sofiyska

vul Volodymyrska

pl Mykhaylivska

St Sophia's Cathedral

pl Sofiyska

vul Kostyantynivska

vul Hlybochytska

Podil Bus Station

vul Frunze

Andriyivsky Uzviz

vul Vozdvyzhenska

Verkhniy Gorod

vul Kozhumyatska

vul Petrivska

vul Smyrnova-Lastochkina

Peyzhanayeva

vul Velyka Zhytomyrska

vul Striletska

vul Reytarska

pl Lvivska

vul Yaroslaviv Val

vul Honchara

vul Lukyanivska

vul Hlybochytska

vul Lukyanivska

pl Lukyanivska

prov Kosohirny

Kudryavsky uzviz

vul Artema

vul Mykoly Pymonenka

vul Observatorna

vul Voronsoho

prov Chekhovsky

vul Olesya

vul Nunya Kotsyubynskoho

vul Hoholivska

vul Turgenivska

vul Pavlivska

vul Dmytrivska

vul Zolotoustivska

vul Poltavska

vul Vyacheslava Chornovola

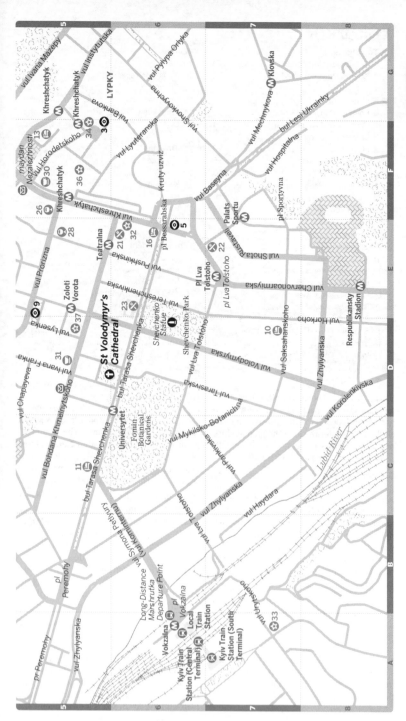

Central Kyiv

390uah; ☎) This Polish-run place has all the amenities you'd expect to find in a city-centre hostel plus balconies with Thai-style mats for chilling out. Enter through the arch at Gorkogo 22 and cross the courtyard diagonally, bearing left towards a yellow building.

Gintama Hotel　　　　　LUXURY HOTEL **$$$**
(☎278 5092; www.gintama.com.ua; vul Tryokhs-vyatytelska 9; s/d 1400/1600uah; ⊜✳☎; MMay-dan Nezalezhnosti) This friendly family-run hotel has an understated style, with smallish, individually decorated rooms tending towards the traditional, but with cleaner lines and fewer florals than usual. It's a three-minute walk from maydan Nezalezhnosti.

St Petersburg Hotel　　　HISTORIC HOTEL **$$**
(☎279 7472; www.s-peter.com.ua; bul Tarasa Shevchenka 4; s/d without bathroom 280/440uah, with bathroom from 500/680uah; MPl Lva Tol-stoho; ☎) If you're pinching pennies, this once-grand old classic is a fine option. The cheapest rooms are worn and simple, but shared showers and toilets are clean, which turns the place into a bargain, considering the central location.

Hotel Ukraine　　　　　　　HOTEL **$$**
(☎279 0347; www.ukraine-hotel.kiev.ua; vul In-stytutska 4; s/d from 660/740uah; @; MMaydan Nezalezhnosti or Khreshchatyk) This Stalin-era giant presiding over maydan Nezalezhnosti offers the best view of future revolutions, orange or otherwise. All rooms have air-con to protect you from natural and political heat.

Hyatt Regency Kyiv　　　LUXURY HOTEL **$$$**
(☎581 1234; http://kiev.regency.hyatt.com; vul Tarasova 5; r from 3600uah; ⊜✳@☎; MMaydan Nezalezhnosti) Other Ukranian hotels can only dream of having the Hyatt's view of duelling 11th-century churches. Inside everything is just as perfect, from the fabulous gym and spacious and eminently comfortable rooms, to its popular panorama bar and Grill Asia restaurant.

Radisson Blu　　　　　　LUXURY HOTEL **$$$**
(☎492 2200; www.radissonsas.com; vul Yaroslaviv Val 22; r from 3000uah; ⊜✳@; MZoloti Vorota) Before the Hyatt opened in 2007, Kyiv's first international hotel was well established as the city's best. Still, the sumptuous rooms have fluffy beds that invite entry via flying leap, and the Asian spa is a nice touch.

Most reputable agencies have websites where you can browse their apartments. Bookings are best done online or by phone; only a few firms have offices. Prices start from 500uah for a studio apartment.

The following have English-speaking representatives and accept credit cards.

» **Grata Apartments** (☑468 0757, 238 2603; www.accommodation.kiev.ua) Service-oriented firm with a good range of apartments.

» **Rentguru** (☑044 228 7509, 050 381 8586; www.uarent.com) Offers some of the cheapest (though not very central) apartments.

» **Teren Plus** (☑289 3949; www.teren.kiev.ua) Tried and true.

» **UKR Apartments** (☑234 5637, 050 311 0309; www.ukr-apartments.kiev.ua) Has a wide selection of inexpensive apartments.

Vozdvyzhensky Hotel BOUTIQUE HOTEL **$$$**
(☑531 9900; www.vozdvyzhensky.com; vul Vozdvyzhenska 60; standard s/d 1100/1400uah, superior r from 1500uah; ⊝❄@; MKontraktova pl) Tucked away in a nook just off Andriyivsky uzviz, the Vozdvyzhensky is one of Kyiv's few true boutique hotels. The 29 rooms are all individually designed and boast fine art.

Hotel Express HOTEL **$$**
(☑503 3045; www.expresskiev.com; bul Tarasa Shevchenka 38/40; s/d from 420/510uah; ❄@; MUniversytet) The Soviet-style Express has a mix of renovated and non-refurbished rooms. The cheapest have tiny beds and lack showers. Prices increase proportionally as amenities and coats of paint are added. Air-con rooms don't cost extra but you must request them.

Yaroslav Youth Hostel HOSTEL **$**
(☑331 0260; vul Yaroslavska 10; dm/d 130/300uah; MKontraktova pl) One of Kyiv's longest established hostels, this converted apartment with just three cosy rooms is located in the heart of Podil. The difference between it and its sister, Kyiv Youth Hostel, is it's much smaller and cosier – just three rooms in a converted apartment.

Sherborne Guest House BOUTIQUE HOTEL **$$$**
(☑490 9693; www.sherbornehotel.com.ua; prov Sichnevy 9, 1st entrance; s/d from 800/1000uah; ❄@; MArsenalna) A rare Ukrainian apartment-hotel, this is very salubrious both on the inside and out, with 12 internet-enabled apartments where you can cook for yourself and go about your business unhindered. The company also has other apartments throughout the centre. It's a short walk south of Arsenalna metro station along vul Sichnevoho Povstannya.

Hotel Salute HOTEL **$$$**
(☑494 1420; www.salute.kiev.ua; vul Ivana Mazepy 11b; s/d from 750/960uah; ⊝❄@; MArsenalna) Affectionately dubbed 'the grenade', the Salute features psychedelic '70s furniture and a few rooms with exceptional views of the Dnipro. For a converted Soviet hotel it has surprising benefits, like smiley receptionists and a 24-hour business centre. It's a short walk south of Arsenalna metro station along vul Sichnevoho Povstannya.

✖ Eating

TOP CHOICE **Spotykach** UKRAINIAN **$$**
(vul Volodymyrska 16; mains 80-150uah; MMaydan Nezalezhnosti) A tribute to the 1960s – a happier (and funnier) period of Soviet history – this discreetly stylish retro-Soviet place will make even a hardened dissident drop a nostalgic tear. Food is October Revolution Day banquet in the Kremlin, but with a Ukrainian twist. The eponymous *spotykach* is vodka-based liquor made with different flavours, from blackcurrant to horseradish.

Pervak RUSSIAN/UKRAINIAN **$$**
(vul Rognidenska 2; mains 60-100uah; MPl Lva Tolstoho) Kyiv's best Ukrainian restaurant masterfully creates old Kyiv (c 1900) without falling into the schmaltzy trap that dogs many a Ukrainian theme resto. The chefs boldly prepare original takes on Ukrainian classics, which are adroitly delivered to tables by waitresses in frilly, cleavage-baring country outfits.

Kyivska Perepichka STREET FOOD **$**
(vul Bohdana Khmelnytskoho 3; pastry 4uah; ⊙11am-9pm; MTeatralna) The perpetually long queue moves with a lightning speed

towards a window where two women hand out pieces of fried dough enclosing a mouth-watering sausage. An essential Kyiv experience.

Tsarske Selo
UKRAINIAN $$

(vul Sichnevoho Povstannya 42/1; mains 35-130uah; ⏰11am-1am; MArsenalna) A pure bodily delight that's well deserved by those who descend the spiritual heights of Kyivsko-Pecherska Lavra, this is Kyiv's quintessential Ukrainian theme restaurant, decorated in rustic style and filled with tour groups. Ukrainian staples are superbly done; go for borshch or varenyky stuffed with cabbage.

Shalena Mama
EUROPEAN/ASIAN $$

(vul Tereshchenkivska 4-A; mains 50-70uah; ⏰24hr; MTeatralna) This diner-like shrine to the Rolling Stones is a great place to slay the late-night munchies. The Asian-influenced food is named after Stones' tunes. Try the 'She Said Yeah' (sautéed glass noodles with white cabbage and chicken) and follow it with their massive apple strudel.

Harbuzyk
UKRAINIAN $$

(Little Pumpkin; vul Khoryva 2v; mains 30-100uah; ⏰11am-10pm; MKontraktova pl) This fun, if slightly hokey, eatery offers a great introduction to Ukrainian food without breaking the bank. Pumpkin is not just in the name: it's all over the menu, from the *mamalyha* porridge to fresh pumpkin juice. More unusual items on the drink list include birch tree sap and *kvas* (a gingery soft drink).

Svytlytsa
FRENCH/UKRAINIAN $

(Andriyivsky uzviz 136; mains 60uah; MPoshtova pl or Kontraktova pl) Once the only eatery on the *uzviz*, this ex-Soviet cafe in a wooden house reinvented itself as a French crêperie, though it keeps serving inexpensive Ukrainian fare. Yacht-themed decor and Russian pop music contribute to the overall split personality, but most patrons avoid both by choosing tables on the summer terrace – a great place for *uzviz*-watching.

Barsuk
PUB $$

(prov Kutuzova 3a; mains 60-90uah; MPecherska) Tucked away in a small lane opposite Pechersky market, 'The Badger' brings three nouvelle concepts to Kyiv – those of gastropub, organic food and open-view kitchen.

Kazbek
GEORGIAN $$

(vul Lesi Ukrainky 30a; mains 40-120; MPecherska) Don't be misled by the flashing neon lights and adjoining casino – this place is quality.

Drinking

Bars

Kupidon
PUB

(Cupid; vul Pushkinska 1-3/5; beer 14uah; meals 25-35uah; ⏰10am-11pm; MKreshchatyk) Apocalyptically dubbing itself 'the last shelter for the Ukrainian intelligensia', this is in fact a missionary station spreading Ukrainian culture in the Russian-speaking capital. Siege mentality apart, Cupid is a lovely Lviv-styled *knaypa* (pub) with an attached bookshop – a favourite drinking den for nationalist-leaning and cosmopolitan bohemians alike.

Palata No.6
BAR

(Ward No.6; vul Vorovskoho 31a; mains 40-60uah; ⏰noon-2am; MUniversytet) For a healthy dose of insanity, sneak into this well-hidden dive bar named after Anton Chekhov's short story about life in a madhouse. Dressed in doctor's white robes, stern-looking waiters nurse you with excellent steaks and apply giant syringes to pour vodka into your glass.

Baraban
PUB

(The Drum; vul Prorizna 4a; beer 14uah, mains 40-60uah; ⏰11am-11pm; MKhreshchatyk) This popular journo hangout is hard to find, but a colourful cast of regulars do so on a nightly basis. This is *the* place to talk politics and plot revolutions, and it also has decent food at good prices.

Cafes

Kaffa
COFFEE HOUSE

(prov Tarasa Shevchenka 3; ⏰; MMaydan Nezalezhnosti) The onslaught of Ukrainian and Russian coffee chains has not changed one thing: long-standing Kaffa still serves the most heart-pumping, rich-tasting brew in town. Coffees and teas from all over the world are served in a pot sufficient for two or three punters in a blissfully smoke-free, whitewashed, African-inspired interior.

Repriza
CAFE

(vul Bohdana Khmelnytskoho 40/25; ⏰8am-10pm Mon-Fri, 9am-10pm Sat & Sun; MZoloti Vorota) Not only does it have good coffee and delectable sandwiches, pastries and cakes, but Repriza also makes a fine, affordable lunch stop. There's also a branch in Podil at vul Sahaydachnoho 10.

Pasazh
COFFEE HOUSE

(off vul Khreshchatyk; ⏰8.30am-11pm Mon-Fri, 10am-11pm Sat & Sun; MKhreshchatyk) This Austrian-style coffee house is one of several cafes found on and around Pasazh, a hip street accessed through an ornate archway off vul Khreshchatyk. Great for people-watching as you tuck into its delicious cakes.

☆ Entertainment

Nightclubs

The club scene is constantly in flux, so check *What's On Kyiv* and the *Kyiv Post* for the latest big thing. Women usually get a substantial discount off the admission prices listed here.

Art Club 44 LIVE MUSIC
(www.club44.com.ua; vul Khreshchatyk 44; admission varies; ⊙10am-2am; Ⓜ Teatralna) With its jazz nights on Tuesdays, Balkan parties on Thursdays and an occasional good gig over the weekend, this venue remains a beacon for more sophisticated night creatures.

Friends of Eric CLUB
(Inside Ultramarin complex, vul Uritskoho 1a; admission 30-70uah; Ⓜ Vokzalna) As the city started coming to terms with post-Eric reality (a well-known Kyiv nightclub owner), the legendary German made an unexpected comeback with this new venue. One problem – his magic is not quite working here, and the club remains a bit soulless. It is still a good place to dance away the wee hours, especially if you're taking an early morning train.

Pomada GAY
(Lipstick; vul Zankovetskoyi 6; admission varies; ⊙6pm-6am) You know Kyiv has come a long way when we can actually publish the names of gay clubs (they used to all be underground). This is lively and centrally located, but it's the one place in town where women pay *more* to get in.

Xlib CLUB
(www.xlib.com.ua; vul Frunze 12; admission 50-100uah; Ⓜ Kontraktova Ploscha) Decidedly anti-glamorous, this hard-to-find place cooks a delicate electronic and acoustic stew for the iPod generation.

Performing Arts

Taras Shevchenko National Opera Theatre OPERA
(☑234 7165, www.opera.com.ua; vul Volodymyrska 50; tickets 20-300uah; Ⓜ Zoloti Vorota) This is a lavish theatre (1899–1901) and a performance here is a grandiose affair. True imbibers of Ukrainian culture should not miss a performance of *Zaporozhets za Dunaem* (Zaporizhzhyans Beyond the Danube), a sort of operatic, purely Ukrainian version of *Fiddler on the Roof.*

(☑279 5991; www.franko-theatre.kiev.ua, in Ukrainian; pl Ivana Franka 3; Ⓜ Khreshchatyk) Kyiv's most respected theatre has been going strong since 1888.

National Philharmonic LIVE MUSIC
(☑278 6291; www.filarmonia.com.ua; Volodymyrsky uzviz 2; ⊙box office 10am-2pm & 3-7pm; Ⓜ Maydan Nezalezhnosti) Originally the Kyiv Merchants' Assembly rooms, this beautiful building now houses the national orchestra.

❶ Information

American Medical Center (☑emergency hotline 907 600; http://amcenters.com; vul Berdychivska 1; ⊙24hr; Ⓜ Lukyanivska) Western-run medical centre with English-speaking doctors.

C-Club (Metrograd shopping mall, lowest level; per hr 15uah; ⊙9am-8am) Dozens of computers with headphones, but the place is full of gamers.

Central post office (vul Khreshchatyk 22; internet per hr 12uah; ⊙9am-7pm Mon-Fri, internet 24hr; Ⓜ Maydan Nezalezhnosti) Enter from maydan Nezalezhnosti.

Central telephone centre (vul Khreshchatyk 22; ⊙24hr; Ⓜ Maydan Nezalezhnosti)

❶ Getting There & Away

Air

Most international flights use **Boryspil International Airport** (KBP; ☑490 4777; www.airport-borispol.kiev.ua), about 35km east of the city. Many domestic flights use **Zhulyany airport** (☑242 2308; www.airport.kiev.ua, in Ukrainian), about 7km southwest of the centre. There's at least one flight a day to all major cities in Ukraine and international flights serve almost every European capital.

Plane tickets are sold at **Kiy Avia** (www.kiyavia.com; pr Peremohy 2; ⊙8am-8pm Mon-Sat, 8am-6pm Sun). There's another branch at vul Horodetskoho 4.

Bus

There are seven bus terminals, but the most useful is the **Central Bus Station** (Tsentralny Avtovokzal; pl Moskovska 3), one stop from Lybidska metro station on trolleybus 4 or 11.

Long-distance express carriers **Autolux** (☑451 8628; www.autolux.com.ua) and **Gunsel** (☑525 4505; www.gunsel.com.ua) run by far the fastest and most comfortable buses in the business. They have frequent trips to most large regional centres; most go via, or continue to,

TRAVEL AGENCIES

» **SoloEast Travel** (☎406 3500, 050 381 8656; www.tourkiev.com) Offers tickets, apartments and tours, including to Chornobyl. Probably the most helpful, friendly travel service in Kyiv, with B&B accommodation just outside the city.

» **New Logic** (☎206 2200; www.newlogic.com.ua; Leonardo Business Center, vul Bohdana Khmelnytskoho 17; MTeatralna) Great deals on Chornobyl tours for individual tourists.

» **Sam** (☎238 6020; www.sam.ua; vul Ivana Franka 40B; ⊙9am-7pm Mon-Fri, 10am-6pm Sat, 10am-4pm Sun; MUniversytet) The leading inbound operator organises sightseeing excursions, hotel bookings and trips to Chernihiv, Chornobyl and Uman.

Boryspil airport. You can book on their websites or buy tickets at the Central Bus Station or Boryspil airport.

Train

You can get pretty much everywhere in the country from Kyiv's modern **train station** (☎005; pl Vokzalna 2; MVokzalna).

Heading west, the quickest way to Lviv is on the express day train (91uah, 6½ hours, one or two daily except Mondays) or there are several overnight passenger trains (165uah, nine to 11 hours). Other western destinations include Uzhhorod (150uah, 16½ hours, four daily) and Chernivtsi (120uah, 15 hours, two daily).

Heading south, there are about four (mostly night) services to Odesa (150uah, eight to 12 hours) and one or two trains to Simferopol (180uah to 240uah, 15 hours).

You can buy tickets at the station or the **advance train ticket office** (bul Tarasa Shevchenka 38/40; ⊙7am-10pm; MUniversytet), a five-minute walk from the station.

There are international trains to/from Bucharest (25 hours), Budapest (24 hours, one daily), Bratislava (29 hours, one or two daily), Chişinău (14 to 17 hours, three daily), Minsk (11 hours, one or two daily), Moscow (14 to 16 hours, up to 17 daily) and Warsaw (17 hours, one daily).

❶ Getting Around
To/From the Airport

There is a prepaid taxi booth near the exit in the Arrivals zone, which charges 250uah to the centre. You can bargain that down to 200uah with unofficial taxis. Order a taxi by phone when going to the airport.

Catching a Polit/Atass bus is the most common way to Boryspil airport (25uah, 45 minutes to one hour). Bus 322 (marked Політ) departs from behind the train station's South Terminal every 20 to 40 minutes between 4.40am and 1.20am.

Trolleybus 9 from the train station runs to Zhulyany airport.

To/From the Train Station

The taxi drivers hanging out by the train station can be the biggest rip-off artists in Kyiv, typically charging 60uah to 100uah for what should be 30uah ride into the centre. Avoid them by walking five minutes to bul Tarasa Shevchenka or take the metro.

Public Transport

Kyiv's metro is clean, efficient, reliable and easy to use if you read Cyrillic. Many of the stations are several dozen storey underground, requiring escalator rides of seven to eight minutes! Trains run between around 6am and midnight on all three lines. Blue-green plastic tokens (*zhetony*) are sold at windows and token dispensers at station entrances. You can also get a plastic card for 7uah and top it up using terminals at every station.

Buses, trolleybuses, trams and many quicker *marshrutky* serve most routes. Tickets for buses, trams and trolleybuses cost 1.50uah and are sold at kiosks or directly from the driver or conductor.

Taxi

Expect to pay 20uah to 30uah for short (less than 5km) trips within the centre. **Troyka** (☎233 7733, 237 0047) is a reliable call-centre working with several taxi companies.

WESTERN UKRAINE

You haven't really been to Ukraine until you've been to the country's west, the Ukrainian heartland where the national culture and language are cradled with equal amounts of pride and vigilance. Here the gentle sound of Ukrainian reverberates in the medieval towns and speaking Russian will attract (not always positive) attention. The region wasn't annexed by the USSR until 1939, and somehow escaped bombing during WWII, so both the architecture and the attitudes have, for the most part, managed to avoid the Soviet influence, leaving it with a relaxed, central European feel.

Lviv ЛЬВІВ

POP 735,000

Mysterious, architecturally lovely but retaining a whiff of Sovietness, Lviv boasts that it is Ukraine's least Soviet city. It may have a point. The city's Unesco World Heritage-listed centre was built like a rich layer-cake of neoclassical architecture upon rococo, baroque, Renaissance and Gothic styles. There's nary a concrete Soviet apartment block in sight (in the centre, at least) and it has a deep-rooted coffee-house culture that is oh-so Central European.

Lviv's telephone area code for six-digit numbers is 032 and for seven-digit numbers, it's 0322.

☉ Sights

Ploshcha Rynok SQUARE

Thanks to its splendid array of buildings Lviv was declared a Unesco World Heritage Site in 1998, and this old market square lies at its heart. The square was progressively rebuilt after a major fire in the early 16th century destroyed the original. The 19th-century **ratusha** (town hall) stands in the middle of the plaza, with fountains featuring Greek gods at each of its corners. Vista junkies can climb the 65m-high neo-Renaissance **tower** (admission 5uah; ☉9am-6pm), though it's a hard slog to the top. Multilingual signs point the way to the ticket booth on the 4th floor.

House No 4, the **Black Mansion**, has one of the most striking façades. Built for an Italian merchant in 1588–89, it features a relief of St Martin on a horse. The **Kornyakt House** at No 6 is named after its original owner, a Greek merchant. An interesting row of sculpted knights along the rooftop cornice makes it a local favourite. Together, Nos 2 and 6 house the largest portion of the Lviv History Museum (p959).

Lychakivske Cemetery CEMETERY

(admission 10uah; ☉9am-6pm) Don't even think of leaving town until you've seen this amazing cemetery only a short tram ride east of the centre. This is the Père Lachaise of Eastern Europe, with the same sort of overgrown grounds and Gothic aura as the famous Parisian necropolis (but containing somewhat less well-known people). Laid out in the late 18th century, when Austrian Emperor Josef II decreed that no more burials could take place in churchyards, it's still the place Lviv's great and good are laid to rest.

Many combine a trip to the cemetery with a visit to the Museum of Folk Architecture and Life. The cemetery is one stop further on tram 7.

Museum of Folk Architecture and Life MUSEUM

(www.skansen.lviv.ua; vul Chernecha Hora 1; admission 10uah; ☉9am-dusk Tue-Sun) This open-air museum displays different regional styles of farmsteads, windmills, churches and schools that dot a huge park east of the centre. Everything is pretty spread out here and a visit involves a lot of foot work. To get to the museum, take tram 7 from vul Pidvalna up vul Lychakivska and get off at the corner of vul Mechnykova. From the stop walk 10 minutes' north on vul Krupyarska, following the signs.

Latin Cathedral CATHEDRAL

(pl Katedralna; admission 2uah) With various bits dating from between 1370 and 1480, this working cathedral is one of Lviv's most impressive churches. The church's exterior is most definitely Gothic while the heavily gilded interior, one of the city's most ornate, has a more baroque feel. The cannonball hanging by a chain off the cathedral's corner miraculously failed to penetrate its walls during a historic battle.

Dominican Cathedral CHURCH

(pl Museyna) Dominating a small square to the east of ploshcha Rynok is one of Lviv's signature sights, the large rococo dome of the Dominican Cathedral. Attached to the cathedral and to the left of the entrance is the **Museum of Religious History** (admission 5uah; ☉11am-6pm Tue-Sun), which was an atheist museum in Soviet times. The exhibition looks at all religions currently active in Ukraine and includes an 11th-century silver Byzantine reliquary said to hold the bodies of two saints.

Armenian Cathedral CHURCH

(vul Virmenska 7) One church you should not miss is the elegant 1363 Armenian Cathedral. The placid cathedral courtyard is a maze of arched passageways and squat buildings festooned with intricate Caucasian detail. Stepping into the courtyard feels like entering another era. Outside, quaint, cobbled vul Virmenska was once the heart of the old Armenian ('Virmenska' in Ukrainian) quarter.

Lviv History Museum MUSEUM

(admission 5uah to each branch; ☉all branches 10am-5.30pm Thu-Tue) Lviv's main museum is split into three collections dotted around pl Rynok. The best branch is at **No 6**. Here

Lviv

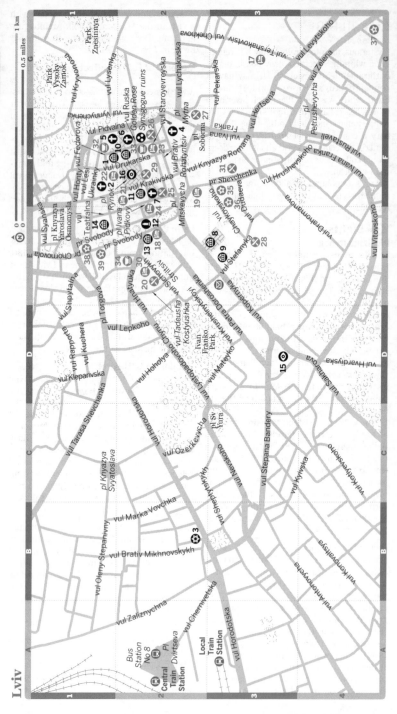

you can enjoy the Italian Renaissance inner courtyard and slide around the exquisitely decorated interior in cloth slippers on the woodcut parquetry floor made from 14 kinds of hardwood. It was also here on 22 December 1686 that Poland and Russia signed the treaty that partitioned Ukraine. **No 2** covers 19th- and 20th-century history, including two floors dedicated to the Ukrainian nationalist movement. **No 24** expounds on the city's earlier history. The highlight is an enormous painting depicting the old walled city of Lviv in the 18th century.

High Castle Hill   LANDMARK
Visiting the High Castle (Vysoky Zamok) on Castle Hill (Zamkova Hora) is a quintessential Lviv experience. The 14th-century ruined stone fort at the summit was Lviv's birthplace and offers the best vantage point of the modern city. Good times to visit are at sunset and in winter, when there are no leaves obstructing the view.

Dormition Church   CHURCH
(Uspenska Tservka; vul Pidvalna 9) This Ukrainian Orthodox church is easily distinguished by the 65m-high, triple-tiered **Kornyakt bell tower** rising beside it. The tower was named after its Greek benefactor, a merchant who was also the original owner of Kornyakt House on pl Rynok. It's well worth going inside to see the beautiful interior of the church, accessible through the gate to the right of the tower. Attached to the church is the diminutive **Three Saints Chapel**.

National Museum and Memorial to the Victims of Occupation   MUSEUM
(vul Bryullova; admission free; ⊙10am-5pm) This infamous building on vul Bryullova was used as a prison by the Poles, Nazis and Communists, but the small and very moving

ground-floor exhibition focuses on Stalinist atrocities in the early years of WWII. Left exactly as it was when the KGB bailed out in 1991, the brutally bare cells, horrific statistics posted throughout and Nazi newsreel from summer 1941 will leave few untouched.

Lvivske Museum of Beer & Brewing
MUSEUM

(www.lvivske.com; vul Kleparivska 18; admission 15uah; ⊙tours roughly every 90min 10.30am-6pm Wed-Sun) The oldest still-functioning brewery in Ukraine turns 300 in 2015, and a tasting tour through the mainly underground facilities is well worth the trek out of the centre. To reach the museum, take tram 6 to the Dobrobut stop, then walk north along vul Kleparivska for around 10 minutes.

National Museum
MUSEUM

(pr Svobody 20; admission 9uah; ⊙10am-6pm Tue-Sun) Dedicated to Ukrainian art of the 12th to 20th centuries, this extensive museum is probably only for diehard enthusiasts for Ukrainian culture. The old religious icons and medieval books are quite extraordinary, but the temporary exhibitions by local artists are of a more variable quality. Taras Shevchenko's moustachioed death mask is also here.

Museum of Ethnography, Arts & Crafts
MUSEUM

(pr Svobody 15; admission 5uah; ⊙11am-5pm Wed-Sun) Exhibits of furniture, clothing, woodcarvings, ceramics and farming implements give a basic introduction to Carpathian life.

Apteka Museum
MUSEUM

(Pharmacy Museum; vul Drukarska 2; admission 3uah; ⊙9am-6pm Mon-Fri, 10am-5pm Sat & Sun) Ukraine's only pharmacy museum is located inside a still-functioning chemist's shop dating from 1735.

Lviv Art Gallery
ART GALLERY

(vul Kopernyka 15 & vul Stefanyka 3; admission to each 10uah; ⊙11am-6pm Tue-Sat, noon-5pm Sun) Lviv's main art repository has two wings – one in the lavish **Pototsky Palace**, the other around the corner on **vul Stefanyka**.

Bernardine Church and Monastery
CHURCH

(vul Vynnychenka) Lviv's most stunning baroque interior belongs to the 17th-century Church of St Andrew.

Monument to Taras Shevchenko
MONUMENT

(pr Svobody) This statue of Taras Shevchenko, Ukraine's greatest nationalist writer, was a gift to the people of Lviv from the Ukrainian diaspora in Argentina.

🛏 Sleeping

In preparation for Euro 2012, Lviv's hotels are busy adding beds, tiling bathrooms, giving staff English lessons and generally banishing all vestiges of the Soviet past.

TOP CHOICE Vintage
BOUTIQUE HOTEL $$$

(☎235 6834; www.vintagehotel.com.ua; vul Staroyevreyska 25/27; s/d/ste 750/950/1550uah; ❄️@🛜) Lviv's first real boutique hotel is this delightfully intimate 12-room place, tucked away up a quiet street in the historical centre. Rooms ooze period style with hardwood floors, polished antique-style furniture and Victorian-style wallpaper, successfully blended with flat-screen TVs and 21st-century bathrooms. You'll be looking forward all night to the breakfast, cooked to order and served in the hotel's stylish cafe.

Leopolis Hotel
LUXURY HOTEL $$$

(☎295 9500; www.leopolishotel.com; vul Teatralna 16; s/d 1800/2000uah; ❄️@🛜) Slowly emerging as the city centre's finest place to catch some Zs, the Leopolis comes to you from the same designer who fashioned Tallinn's Telegraaf Hotel. Every guestroom in this 18th-century edifice is different, but all have a well-stocked minibar, elegant furniture and Italian marble bathrooms with underfloor heating. There's even a wheelchair-friendly room, a rarity indeed in these parts.

Kosmonaut Hostel
HOSTEL $

(☎260 1602; www.thekosmonaut.com; vul Sichovykh Striltsiv 8; dm/tw 100/250uah; ❄️🛜) Not as space-age as the branding implies, this resembles a slightly ramshackle but cool student household in Australia. That said, there are plenty of Gagarins, Lenins and other fun and scary USSR-era memorabilia scattered about the place for guests to play with (have no fear, none of the weaponry is active).

Soviet Home Hostel
HOSTEL $

(☎225 8611; www.homehostels.com.ua; vul Drukarska 3, top fl; dm/s/d 100/280/320uah; ❄️🛜) Festooned in Soviet-era junk, this friendly, 20-bed hostel is small-scale enough to not feel overcrowded yet big enough for a party crowd to form. Dorms are generously cut with not too many bunks, there's a small kitchen where the free breakfast is laid out, and the double has a less-than-sleep-inducing Lenin portrait above the bed.

Wien Hotel
HOTEL $$

(☎244 4314; www.wienhotel.lviv.ua; pr Svobody 12; s/d from 450/500uah; ❄️) Tucked behind the Wiener Kaffeehaus just off Lviv's main boulevard, cosy little Wien has 20 fresh, if slightly small, rooms. The kind reception, tasteful and elegant decor and totally agreeable pricing draw a steady stream of people in the know. The free Wiener Kaffeehaus breakfasts for guests are excellent. Book ahead as it's popular.

Grand Hotel
HOTEL $$$

(☏272 4042; www.ghgroup.com.ua; pr Svobody 13; s/d 980/1200uah; ⊕✴🅿⛱) Having rested too long on its laurels as the only real luxury show in town, the Grand is no longer top dog in Lviv. The rooms, while still holding on to their old-world flavour, are beginning to fade a bit and the service has been caught flat-footed by other more up-to-speed establishments. Fortunately its prime location on pr Svobody will never fade.

Hotel George
HOTEL $$

(☏232 6236; www.georgehotel.com.ua; pl Mitskevycha 1; r from 600uah; 🛜) Seasoned travellers to Lviv will be saddened to learn that the George is renovating and has lost its elusive 'Soviet chic' vibe. A prime candidate for a show-stopping five-star establishment, instead this gorgeous 1901 art nouveau building is receiving a crass, skin-deep makeover – plasticky, faux antique furniture clashes with the high-ceilinged period style in the rooms and cheapo carpets conceal the wonderfully creaky parquet floors.

Eurohotel
BUSINESS HOTEL $$

(☏275 7214; www.eurohotel.lviv.ua; vul Tershakovtsiv 6A; s/d from 500/600uah; ⊕✴🛜) This unexciting place is a good example of just what you can do with a surplus Soviet lumpenhotel. The 90 bog-standard but comfortable rooms are for those who want to sleep, shower and access the net, but little else.

✕ Eating

Lviv is more famous for cafes than restaurants, but the food scene has seen dramatic developments in recent years with some weird and wonderful themed restaurants popping up across the city.

TOP CHOICE ⟩ Masonic Restaurant
UKRAINIAN $$$

(Pl Rynok 14; mains before discount 300-800uah; ⊙11am-2am) It's hard to know where to start with this place. Finding it is the first obstacle – head to the 2nd floor and open door of apartment 8 (they change the numbers around occasionally to throw people off the scent). You'll be accosted by an unshaven bachelor type, into whose Soviet-era kitchen you appear to have inadvertently wandered.

Having barred your way for a few minutes he eventual opens the door to a fancy beamed restaurant full of Masonic symbols and portraits of bygone masons. The next shock is the menu – advertised as Galicia's most expensive restaurant, prices are 10 times higher than normal...so make sure you pick up a 90% discount card at Dim Lehend or Livy Bereh beforehand. The food, by the way, is great and the beer and *kvas* come in crystal vases. The loo is a candlelit Masonic throne. Ukraine's weirdest restaurant experience? Probably.

Dim Lehend
UKRAINIAN $$

(vul Staroyevreyska 48; mains 20-75uah) Dedicated entirely to the city of Lviv, there's nothing dim about the 'House of Legends'. The menu pamphlet you receive at the door is more a map to explore five floors that house a library stuffed with Lviv-themed volumes, a room showing live webcam footage of Lviv's underground river, rooms dedicated to lions and cobblestones, and another featuring the city in sounds. A GDR Trabant occupies the roof terrace, the views from which will have you reaching for your camera. Having chosen a room, the menu is a work in progress, but the coffee and desserts are bliss.

Kupol
CENTRAL EUROPEAN $$

(vul Chaykovskoho 37; mains 40-80uah; ⊙11am-9pm) This place is designed to feel like stepping back in time – to 1938 in particular, 'the year before civilisation ended' (ie before the Soviets rolled in). How well this former mansion and arts salon recreates that specific year is moot – but, goodness, the overall effect is winning. The olde-worlde interior is lined with framed letters, ocean-liner ads, antique cutlery, hampers and other memorabilia. The Polish/Austrian/Ukrainian food is delicious and beautifully garnished.

Livy Bereh
INTERNATIONAL $$

(pr Svobody 28; mains 20-80uah; ⊙10am-2am; 🅿) Buried deep beneath the Theatre of Opera and Ballet, this superb restaurant-cum-coffee house serves European fare, with a few Ukrainian and Hutsul favourites thrown in. The vibe is easy-going, the service respectful and you can even ask the waitress for pencil and paper to leave an arty memento of your visit.

Kumpel
PUB $$

(vul Vynnychenka 6; mains 20-90uah; ⊙24hr) Centred on two huge copper brewing vats cooking up Krumpel's own beer (1L for 29uah), this superb round-the-clock microbrewery restaurant has a low-lit art deco theme. The menu is heavy on international meat-and-two-veg combos, with a few local elements included.

Amadeus
FINE DINING $$

(pl Katedralna 7; mains 40-200uah) The refined interior, peaceful music and perfectly placed patio are reason enough to plop down in one of Amadeus' stylish wicker chairs. But it's the food that puts it on another level. The menu leans towards fancy European fare like fondue and risotto, but there's also stuffed baked potatoes, pizza-sized omelettes, *shashlyk* and *varenyky* (dumplings) on offer.

Veronika
FINE DINING $$

(pr Shevchenka 21; mains 40-150uah) This classy basement restaurant shares the same owners and the same menu as Amadeus. Need we say more? In addition there's a street-level *konditorei*, with criminally delicious desserts.

Puzata Khata
CAFE $

(vul Sichovykh Striltsiv 12; mains from 10uah; ⊘8am-11pm) This super-sized version of Ukraine's number-one restaurant chain stands out for its classy, Hutsul-themed interior and pure Ukrainian-rock soundtrack.

🍷 Drinking

Dzyga
CAFE

(vul Virmenska 35; ⊘9am-11.30pm) This cafe-cum-art gallery in the shadow of the Dominican Cathedral has a relaxed vibe. It's particularly popular with bohemian, alternative types, but seems to attract pretty much everyone, really. The summertime outdoor seating is gathered around the city's Monument to the Smile.

Smachna Plitka
CAFE

(vul Kurbasa 3; ⊘11am-11pm) Head down the stairs behind an anonymous wooden door in the facade of the Kurbasa Theatre to find a basement cafe that's everything you want a Central European coffee house to be – small cafe tables tucked furtively into corners, hard-to-beat coffees and beers, and turtle-necked revolutionaries filling the air with schemes.

Pid Synoyu Plyashkoyu
CAFE

(Under the Blue Bottle; vul Ruska 4; ⊘11.30am-10pm) With its nostalgia for the Polish-Austrian past and dark interior, this tiny cafe at the back of a courtyard has a cosy, secretive atmosphere. It serves sandwiches and fondues, as well as wine and coffee with pepper. It's hard to find: look for the blue bottle.

Italyansky Dvorik
CAFE

(Italian Courtyard; pl Rynok 6; ⊘10am-8pm) Even if you decide to skip the Lviv History Museum, it's worth popping in for a coffee in its aptly named inner courtyard. There's a 1uah fee to enter the courtyard.

Robert Doms Beer House
BEER HALL

(vul Kleparivska 18; ⊘noon-midnight) This fantastic beer hall is located three storeys underground in a centuries-old beer-storage vault once used by the neighbouring Lvivske brewery.

☆ Entertainment

Clubs

Kult
LIVE MUSIC

(www.kult.lviv.ua; vul Chaykovskoho 7; admission 10-20uah; ⊘noon-2am) This superb basement venue next to the Philharmonia reverberates with live Ukrainian rock music every night of the week.

Picasso
CLUB

(www.picasso.lviv.ua; vul Zelena 88; admission 15-30uah; ⊘closed Thu) Lviv's most atmospheric club, inside a former theatre, has consistently good DJs and a consistently festive crowd paying proper homage to them.

Opera, Theatre & Classical Music

Advance tickets for all Lviv's venues are sold at the **Teatralna Kasa** (Theatre Box Office; pr Svobody 37; ⊘10am-1pm & 3-5pm Mon-Sat).

Solomiya Krushelnytska Lviv Theatre of Opera & Ballet
THEATRE

(☎2728 672; www.opera.lviv.ua; pr Svobody 28). For an evening of high culture, and to enjoy the ornate building, take in a performance at this Lviv institution. For some local colour catch a performance of *Zaporozhets za Dunae*, which runs once or twice a month. The theatre shuts down for most of July and August.

Philharmonia
LIVE MUSIC

(☎741 086; www.philharmonia.lviv.ua; vul Chaykovskoho 7). If classical music is more your thing, let yourself be wooed by the sweet strains of Lviv's regional philharmonic orchestra. Things are very quiet here from July through to mid-September.

ℹ Information

Central post office (vul Slovatskoho 1)
Central telephone office (vul Petra Doroshenka 37; ⊘8.30am-7pm Mon-Fri, 9am-4pm Sat)

Chorna Medea (vul Petra Doroshenka 50; per hr 6uah; ⊘24hr) Lviv's greatest internet cafe, with drinks, Skype and cheap speedy web connection.

Tourist Information Centre (☎254 6079; www.visitlviv.net; Ratusha, pl Rynok 1; ⊘10am-7pm Mon-Fri, to 6pm Sat, to 5pm Sun)

Getting There & Away

Air

By the time you read this Lviv will have taken delivery of a shiny new **airport** (www.airport.lviv. ua) bolted together about 9km west of the centre in preparation for Euro 2012. Take trolleybus 9 to the university or *marshrutka* 95 to the centre.

You can fly from Lviv to Kyiv (four daily) and Simferopol (weekly, summer only). Book through **Kiy Avia** (272 7818; www.kiyavia.com; vul Hnyatuka 20-22; 8am-8pm Mon-Sat, to 6pm Sun).

There are currently daily flights to/from Vienna, Munich, Warsaw, Timişoara, İstanbul and Moscow.

Bus

Lviv has three bus stations of use to travellers. The extremely inconveniently located **main bus station** (Holovny Avtovokzal; vul Stryska) is 8km south of the centre. Take trolleybus 5.

From the main bus station, buses serve all major southern, eastern and central cities, including Kyiv (50uah to 90uah, nine hours, four daily), Kamyanets-Podilsky (71uah to 78uah, eight hours, twice daily) and Odesa (140uah, 15 hours, once daily). Chernivtsi (74uah, eight hours, at least twice daily) and Uzhhorod (64uah, six hours, three daily) are also served from here.

Some southbound buses depart from **bus station no 8** in front of the train station. Destinations served include Uzhhorod (50uah, 6½ hours, two daily), Odesa (daily) and Kyiv (twice daily).

Train

Lviv's train station is 2km west of the centre, connected to town by trams 1 and 9.

The quickest way to Kyiv is on an express day train (100uah, 6½ hours, daily except Tuesday). There are also at least 10 regular trains per day, many of them overnight services (150uah, nine to 11 hours). Heading south, there are trains to Uzhhorod (83uah, seven hours, at least three daily), Chop (100uah, six hours, 11 daily) and Chernivtsi (70uah, 5½ to 11 hours, four daily).

Southern destinations include Odesa (132uah, 12 hours, up to five daily) and Simferopol (190uah, three daily). International trains serve Moscow (270uah, 25 hours, up to six daily), St Petersburg (850uah, daily), Prague (390uah, daily) and Minsk (370uah, twice daily), among others.

Buy tickets from the station or the centrally located **train ticket office** (vul Hnatyuka 20; 8am-2pm & 3-8pm Mon-Sat, to 6pm Sun).

Getting Around

From the train station, take tram 1 or 9 to the southern end of pr Svobody; tram 6 will take you to the northern end. With freshly laid tram lines heading to the football stadium, new options and routes may spring up over the next couple of years.

Uzhhorod УЖГОРОД

0132 / POP 116,400

The border town of Uzhhorod (formerly Ungvar) is a mercantile place with plenty of ready charm and a good introduction to Ukraine for those arriving from the EU. Split in half by the Uzh River, which separates the new and old towns, Uzhhorod is an ideal staging post for anyone travelling to/from Slovakia or Hungary.

The old town centre lies on the northern bank of the Uzh River, which wends its way roughly east–west through town. The train and bus stations are 1km directly south. The town has skeletal tourist signposting in English, which generally points in the right direction.

Sights

Uzhhorod Castle   CASTLE

(vul Kapitalna; admission 5uah; 9am-6pm Tue-Sun) On the hill overlooking town stands the 15th-century castle with massive walls and beefy bastions built to withstand Turkish assaults. The main palace is now home to the **Transcarpathian Museum of Local Lore**, which, while not completely fabulous, does have its moments. The tranquil grounds are also fun to wander and the bastion in the northeast corner provides views across Uzhhorod.

Folk Architecture & Life Museum   MUSEUM

(vul Kapitalna; admission 10uah; 10am-6pm Wed-Mon) Next door to the castle, this is one of the tidiest and most compact open-air museums in the country, albeit on the small side. Highlights include several Hutsul cottages with their bench-lined walls, a complete timber school and the timber 18th-century Mykhaylivska Church (St Michael's Church), which was rescued from the village of Shelestovo near Mukacheve and still a working place of worship.

Sleeping & Eating

TOP CHOICE Old Continent   HOTEL $$

(669 366; www.hotel-oldcontinent. com; pl Petefi 4-6; s/d from 590/770uah;) At Uzhhorod's finest digs, the choice between 21st-century predictability, baroque opulence or swish art deco may be a difficult call as all the rooms here are immaculate, very well maintained and sumptuously cosy. English-speaking staff are courteous, the

location is bull's-eye central and there's a decent multitasking restaurant.

Hotel Atlant
HOTEL **$**

(☎614 095; www.atlant-hotel.com.ua; pl Koryatovycha 27; s 200uah, d 310-420uah; ❋🛜) These 27 European-style rooms are as sweet as can be and great value, especially the singles, which are on the top floor (no lift) and have skylights and sloping ceilings. As Uzhhorod's best deal it's popular, so book ahead if you can.

Delfin
INTERNATIONAL **$**

(nab Kyivska 3; mains 10-50uah) Locals consider this one of the better restaurants in town. European and Ukrainian dishes are served, but it's known for its grilled meats and rooftop terrace. It's at the end of the pedestrian bridge on the south side of the river. You'll have to go upstairs once you get to the building.

Kaktus Kafe
CAFE **$**

(vul Korzo 7; mains 13-41uah) Probably the most popular hang-out in town, this smoky, noisy joint is full of beer- and coffee-drinkers.

❶ Information

Coffee.net (vul Korzo 5; per hr 3uah; ⊙8am-10pm Mon-Fri, 10am-10pm Sat & Sun) Unusually stylish net cafe where the coffee comes as quickly as the web connection. Free wi-fi.

Post and telephone office (vul Mynayska 4) Has internet terminals.

Tourist office (☎613 193; www.zakarpattya tourism.info; vul Dukhnovycha 16/1; ⊙8am-5pm) Helpful and friendly office selling maps, guides and tours.

❶ Getting There & Away

Bus

Long-distance buses serve Lviv (57uah, six hours, twice daily) and Chernivtsi (100uah, 10 to 12 hours, twice daily).

Marshrutka 145 goes to Chop (7uah, 45 minutes) every 15 minutes from the side of the bus station facing the train station. Cross-border buses link Uzhhorod most usefully with Košice (100uah, three hours, three daily) in Slovakia.

Regabus (www.regabus.cz) operates overnight to Prague (490uah, 14 hours).

Train

Trains to and from Western Europe don't stop in Uzhhorod; you must go to nearby Chop. Domestic trains go to and from Lviv (83uah, seven to eight hours, four daily) and Kyiv (150uah, 16 to 19 hours, four daily).

Chernivtsi ЧЕРНІВЦІ

☑0372 / POP 252,000

Like many cities in West Ukraine, energetic Chernivtsi displays the signs of a more elegant past, most obviously in the shape of its star attraction: the phantasmagorical university building. Shabby, leafy and slightly chaotic, this Ukrainian city sometimes has a somewhat un-Slavic flavour, possibly the residue of centuries of Romanian/Moldovan influence. Renovators have been busy with the stucco and whitewash in the city centre, and some of the old Austro-Hungarian tenements are looking pretty dapper, but in general Chernivtsi remains a ramshackle place with a local student population keeping things lively.

◉ Sights

Chernivtsi University
NOTABLE BUILDING

(www.chnu.cv.ua; vul Kotsyubynskoho) University buildings are often called 'dreaming spires', but Chernivtsi's is more like a trip on LSD. This fantastic red-brick ensemble – with coloured tiles decorating its pseudo-Byzantine, pseudo-Moorish and pseudo-Hanseatic wings – is the last thing you'd expect to see here. The architect responsible was Czech Josef Hlavka, who was also behind Chernivtsi's **Former Armenian Cathedral** (vul Ukrainska 30), as well as large chunks of Vienna. He completed the university in 1882 for the Metropolitans (Orthodox Church leaders) of Bukovyna as their official residence. The Soviets later moved the university here.

The wings surround a landscaped court. To the left as you pass the gatehouse is the **Seminarska Church**, now used for concerts and ceremonies. Straight ahead stands the former main **palace residence of the Metropolitans**, housing two remarkable staircases and a fantastic, 1st-floor **Marmurovy Zal** (Marble Hall). As a public facility you can wander the buildings at will, but the best rooms are usually locked. Alternatively contact **Diana Costas** (☎584 821, 050 1764 712; tours in English 40uah), former student turned guide who will gladly show you round. Her office is in the Seminarska Church.

The university is about 1.5km northwest of the centre. Take trolleybus 2.

Kalynivsky Market
MARKET

(⊙8am-2pm) With its own police station, first-aid point and dedicated bank branches, this 33-hectare bazaar is like a town unto itself. As a conduit into Ukraine for goods from neighbouring countries, it attracts some 50,000 shoppers a day and is a frenetic, wonderful phenomenon. Take any of the numerous *marshrutky* to калинівський рунок.

🛏 Sleeping & Eating

Hotel Bukovyna   HOTEL **$$**
(☑585 625; www.bukovyna-hotel.com; vul Holovna 141; s/d/ste from 190/240/590uah; 🛜) Owing to its convenient location, its relative value for money and its large number of rooms, this jolly yellow giant has an understandably sizeable chunk of the local market. Rooms range from 'Economy', where the post-Soviet renovation is skin-deep, to 'Comfort', which come with air-con and furniture from this century.

Chernivtsi Backpackers   HOSTEL **$**
(☑099 261 3645; apt 4, vul Zankovetskoyi 25; dm 120uah; @🛜) The tourist office will tell you it doesn't exist, but Chernivtsi's only hostel is just hard to find, and once installed here, the English owner's insider tips, nights out and summer excursions into the Carpathians make this a great base. Only seven beds so book ahead.

TOP CHOICE **Reflection**   INTERNATIONAL **$$**
(vul Holovna 66; mains 40-60uah; ⊙9am-11pm) A completely atypical menu in such an unlikely city makes Reflection worth every extra kopeck. As if Waldorf and Caesar salads, vegetable fajitas, bruschetta, pesto with penne, teriyaki salad, lentil soup, pork with ripe mangoes etc weren't sufficient reminders of the culinary world you thought you'd left behind when entering regional Ukraine, there are also fresh croissants or oatmeal at breakfast.

Knaus   BEER HALL **$**
(vul Holovna 26A; mains 15-60uah) Although its menu retains a solid Russian alignment, Knaus does offer Bavarian bratwurst to accompany its range of German beers.

ℹ Information

Post office (vul Khudyakova 6)

Tourist Information Centre (☑553 684; www.chernivtsy.eu, www.guide.cv.ua; vul Holovna 16; ⊙10am-1pm & 2-6pm Mon-Fri) Runs a free city walking tour at noon each day.

ℹ Getting There & Away

Bus
The bus station is 3km southeast of the centre. Services leave for Kamyanets-Podilsky (20uah, 2½ hours, half-hourly) and Lviv (74uah, 7½ hours, at least twice daily) among others. Longer-distance services to Kyiv (90uah to 100uah,

nine hours, two daily) and Odesa (100uah, 13 hours, two daily) are also available.

Train
Mainline services include those to Kyiv (119uah, 15 hours, five daily), Odesa (170uah, 17 hours, daily) and Lviv (70uah, 5½ to 11 hours, five daily).

ℹ Getting Around

Trolleybuses 3 and 5, plus a whole host of *marshrutky*, run between the bus station and the train station. They're normally jam-packed, so be prepared to squeeze in or do a little walking.

Carpathian Mountains

One of the least-developed areas in Eastern Europe is the easternmost section of the Carpathian Mountains, which cut through the lower corner of Western Ukraine. Among the undulating ridges lives a cluster of various ethnic groups, including the Hutsuls, who, despite their clear Romanian ties, are a significant source of pride to the Ukrainian national identity.

In addition to the Hutsuls, many other mountain dwellers still live traditional lifestyles and speak in dialects coloured by the tongues of neighbouring Poland, Slovakia, Hungary and Romania. Roads are still abysmal and the economy still on crutches. Horse-drawn carts competing for pothole space with battered Ladas and wheezing old buses are a common sight.

The Carpathians are home to Ukraine's highest peak, Mt Hoverla (2062m), and its largest national park, and there are opportunities for camping, homestays, hiking, mountain biking and skiing in some superbly wild backcountry.

CARPATHIAN NATIONAL NATURE PARK
The Carpathian National Nature Park (CNNP) is Ukraine's largest at 503 sq km. Despite this status, industrial logging still takes place, and only about 25% of the park area is actually protected. Founded in 1980, the CNNP shelters wolves, brown bears, lynx, bison and deer. Hutsuls still live in the park, and the country's highest peak, Mt Hoverla, is here as well. Most come here for hiking in the summer and skiing in the winter.

Yaremche is a touristy Hutsul village, with lots of folk crafts on sale and several 'Hutsul' restaurants. It is probably the most obvious place to base yourself, as it's easy to reach and makes a good staging point for a

SKIING IN THE CARPATHIANS

The Carpathians are one of Eastern Europe's premier skiing regions and, if you're already coming this way, these slopes provide an unusual alternative to those in the continent's west. Outside pricey Bukovel, ski passes in this area are about 50 to 100uah a day, and equipment rental costs around the same. **Piligrim** (☑032-297 1899; www.piligrim.lviv.ua) and **SkiUkraine** (www.skiukraine.info) both have useful information and bookings.

In addition to the following resorts, a new $60 million resort is planned near Bystrets village, some 6km from Verkhovyna.

» **Drahobrat** (www.ski.lviv.ua/drahobrat, in Ukrainian) Want to go skiing in April? At snowy Drahobrat, 1300m above sea level, you often can. Ukraine's only truly 'Alpine' skiing spot is remote and its conditions are suitable only for the experienced; 18km from Yasinya.

» **Slavske** (www.slavsko.com.ua, in Ukrainian) This still popular resort has blue, red and black runs, but slopes tend to get bumpy and icy by the season's end; 130km south of Lviv, on the rail line to Uzhhorod.

» **Podobovets & Pylypets** (www.ski.lviv.ua/volovets-podobovets, in Ukrainian) These neighbouring resorts are slowly developing, with fewer crowds and new tow lifts, but less accommodation than other resorts. Volovets on the Kyiv–Uzhhorod line is the nearest train station, 12km away.

Mt Hoverla ascent. From the gateway town of Ivano-Frankivsk, there are dozens of buses and *marshrutky* to Yaremche (16uah, one hour). The towns of Kolomyya, Kosiv and Rakhiv are other good launch pads.

There's a wide range of accommodation, from rented rooms and cottages to hotels. The well-maintained and user-friendly **Karpaty Info** (www.karpaty.info) features hundreds of B&B, homestay and hotel listings in the region.

MOUNT HOVERLA

It's hardly the most remote trail in the Carpathians, nor the most litter-free, but the popular ascent to Ukraine's highest peak is relatively easy to achieve. On a clear day, the expansive views from Mt Hoverla are also breathtaking. Initially, the trail follows the Yaremche–Vorokta–Zaroslyak road, so how much of the way you want to hike and how much you want to cover by *marshrutka* (which go as far as Vorokhta) or taxi is up to you.

About 7km south of Vorokhta (guides know the place as 'sedmoy kilometr'), you will need to take the right fork in the road, heading west to Zaroslyak, where there's a **hotel** (☑034 344 1592; r from 80uah). En route, you will cross the CNNP boundary and pay the **entrance fee** (adult/child 15/5uah). From Zaroslyak (20km from Vorokhta) it's about 3.5km to the summit of Mt Hoverla, which is marked with a big iron cross and a huge Ukrainian national flag.

Kamyanets-Podilsky
КАМ'ЯНЕЦЬ-ПОДІЛЬСЬКИЙ
☑03849 / POP 102,000

In a country with no shortage of impressive fortresses, the unique town of Kamyanets-Podilsky still stands out for its gorgeous castle and dramatic natural beauty. The name Kamyanets refers to the massive stone island created by a sharp bend in the river Smotrych, and the resulting verdant canyon rings a charming old town guarded by a fortress straight out of a fairy tale. If Český Krumlov in the Czech Republic or Bulgaria's Veliko Tărnovo were your thing, don't miss this equally stunning double-barrelled delight.

⊙ Sights

Kamyanets-Podilsky Fortress　　FORTRESS
(adult/child 12/6uah; ⊙9am-7pm Tue-Sun, to 6pm Mon) Built of wood in the 10th to 13th centuries, then redesigned and rebuilt in stone by Italian military engineers in the 16th century, KP's fortress is a complete mishmash of styles. But the overall impression is breathtaking, and if Ukraine ever gets its act together as a tourist destination, the view from the **Turkish Bridge** leading to the fortress will become one of the country's iconic, front-page vistas. The name of the bridge is slightly misleading, as it's essentially a medieval structure whose arches were filled in and fortified by Turks in the 17th century.

The fortress is in the shape of a polygon, with nine towers of all shapes and sizes linked by a sturdy wall. In the middle of it all is a vast courtyard. The **New East Tower** (1544) is directly to your right as you enter the fortress and contains a well and a huge winch stretching 40m deep through the cliff to bring up water.

Just beyond the New East Tower, an unmarked white building houses a fantastic **museum** that romps through the history of KP and Ukraine over the last century in a jumble of nostalgia-inducing exhibits. Two revolutions bookend the collections, with the blood-red silken flags of 1917 looking symbolically more potent than the limp orange banners of 2004.

POLISH QUARTER

Under the medieval Magdeburg Laws, each of the old town's four major ethnic groups – Poles, Ukrainians, Armenians and Jews – occupied a different quarter. The focus of the old Polish Quarter is the Polish Market Square (Polsky rynok), the old town's main piazza.

Cathedral of SS Peter & Paul   CHURCH

Through a small triumphal gate in the northwest corner of the square lies this fascinating cathedral, KP's busiest place of worship. One feature of the building perfectly illustrates how the Polish and Turkish empires collided in Kamyanets-Podilsky. Built in 1580 by the Catholic Poles, the cathedral was converted into a mosque when the Turks took over in the late 17th century; they even built an adjacent 42m-high minaret. When the town was handed back to the Poles by treaty in 1699, the Turks specifically stipulated that the minaret could not be dismantled. So the Poles topped it with its current 3.5m-tall golden statue of the Virgin Mary instead.

Ratusha   NOTABLE BUILDING

(Polsky rynok) The Polish market square is lorded over by the tall 14th-century Ratusha (town hall). The renovated peach-hued building now houses three single-room museums that are of limited interest unless you are into coins, medieval justice or the Magdeburg legal system, but there is a decent bar on the ground floor. In front of the ratusha stands the enclosed **Armenian well** (1638), which looks more like a baroque chapel than a well.

Dominican Monastery   MONASTERY

(vul Dominkanska) Vul Dominikanska cuts south from the Polish Market Square, linking it with the Armenian Quarter. Here you'll find the Dominican Monastery complex, some parts of which date from the 14th

century. The buildings suffered serious damage during WWII, but are now under constant restoration. The monastery Church of St Nicholas holds services in Ukrainian and Polish throughout the day.

ARMENIAN QUARTER

The Armenian quarter is centred on the quiet Armenian Market Square, an elongated cobbled expanse to the south of the Polish Quarter.

Podillya Antiquities Museum   MUSEUM

(vul Ivano-Predtechynska 2; admission 3uah; ⊙10am-6pm Tue-Sun, to 5pm Mon) This imaginatively presented museum with English explanations takes visitors through the archaeology of Podillya in six easy steps. You begin in a Stone Age cave and end in a courtyard of sculpted Slavic gods, passing through Trypillian, Scythian and early Slav dwellings along the way.

Picture Gallery   ART GALLERY

(vul Pyatnytska 11; admission 4uah; ⊙10am-6pm Tue-Sun, to 5pm Mon) The permanent collections here are of wildly varying quality and some works are in downright wretched condition. But temporary exhibitions lift the mood and if the art on the walls doesn't impress, the elaborate parquet floors will.

Armenian Church   CHURCH

(vul Virmenska) Huge, decorative wrought iron gates keep prying tourists out of this set of 15th-century church ruins, its perimeter still weeping masonry onto the cobbles below. The reconstructed defensive bell tower is now a small Ukrainian Orthodox chapel.

🛏 Sleeping

Hotel 7 Days   HOTEL $$

(☑690 69; www.7dney.com; vul Soborna 4; s/d from 260/440uah; ✳🛜🏊) This vastly improved place in the new town impresses from the moment you walk into the air-conditioned, designer-style lobby. Staff speak English, the service is professional and the room rate includes use of the swimming pool, breakfast *and* dinner, a sure-fire deal-clincher in eatery-poor KP.

Hetman   HOTEL $$

(☑970 27; www.hetman-hotel.com.ua; Polsky Rynok 8; r/ste from 385/500uah; ✳🛜) The mammoth rooms, great location in a townhouse on the Polish Market Square and easy-going staff make this atmospheric, 14-room themed hotel worth the extra hryvna. The walls are lined with paintings of all Ukraine's Hetmans (Cossack heads of state), an 11m-long tapestry bearing the words of the national anthem hangs in the stair well and the Ukrainian restaurant (mains 20uah to 55uah) serves five types of borshch.

TIU Hostel HOSTEL $
(☎063 982 3048; vul Gagarina 69, apt 4; dm 100uah) The town's only stable backpacker hostel belongs to the TIU group, meaning a good standard of facilities and fun staff – nights out in KP and barbecues at Khotyn are regular activities. Only 10 beds so book ahead.

✖ Eating & Drinking

Kafe Pid Bramoyu UKRAINIAN $
(vul Zamkova 1A; mains 20-30uah) Although the service at this *shashlyk* restaurant-cafe can be spotty, the view overlooking the fortress never takes a day off. The menu covers all the Ukrainian basics, including *deruny* (potato pancakes) and *varenyky* (dumplings), plus fresh fish that you can pick out of their small pond.

Hostynny Dvir RUSSIAN $
(vul Troitska 1; mains 15-40uah) If you can forgive the spread-eagled bearskin pinned to the far wall, this refined restaurant has the best food in the old town, although service can be snail slow.

Stara Fortetsya UKRAINIAN $
(Vul Valy 1; mains 12-30uah) Unfortunately you can only take drinks on the balcony, perched dramatically on a 40m cliff over the gorge. Inside is where the Ukrainian food is served.

❶ Information

Post, internet & telephone office (vul Soborna 9; internet per hr 4uah; ☺post 9am-6pm Mon-Fri, to 4pm Sat, internet 8.30am-9pm Mon-Fri, 10am-10pm Sat & Sun)

Post office (vul Troitska 2; ☺9am-1pm & 2pm-6pm)

❶ Getting There & Away

Bus

Buses to Chernivtsi depart from Kamyanets-Podilsky bus station (20uah, 2½ hours, at least every 30 minutes). There are two buses per day to Lviv (80uah, 6½ hours), two night buses to Odesa (160uah, 12 hours) and one uncomfortable overnighter to Kyiv (110uah, 10 hours).

Train

The express train 177 from Kyiv is the quickest way to reach Kamyanets-Podilsky. It departs Kyiv at 4.43pm (68uah, 6½ hours). The return leg (train 178) departs Kamyanets-Podilsky at 1.55am. There's also an overnight service to and from Kyiv (88uah, 10 hours).

If coming from Lviv or Odesa, take a train to Khmelnytsky and continue by train or *marshrutka* from there. From Lviv you might also consider taking a train to Chernivtsi, and then a *marshrutka* to Kamyanets-Podilsky.

❶ Getting Around

The **bus station** is within walking distance (two blocks east) of the new town centre. The **train station** is 1km north of the bus station. Take bus 1 into the new or old town, or catch a taxi (around 20uah).

ODESA ОДЕСА

POP ONE MILLION

Odesa is a city straight from literature – an energetic, decadent boomtown. Its famous Potemkin Steps sweep down to the Black Sea and Ukraine's biggest commercial port. Behind them, a cosmopolitan cast of characters makes merry among pastel neoclassical buildings lining a geometrical grid of leafy streets.

Immigrants from all over Europe were invited to make their fortune here when Odesa was founded in the late 18th century by Russia's Catherine the Great. These new inhabitants gave Russia's southern window on the world a singular, subversive nature.

Despite its position as the capital of Ukrainian hedonism, Odesa is no Barcelona or Brighton and has a distinctly seedy feel. Prostitutes, con artists, drug dealers and the mob have all found their niche here and the city is a magnet for sex tourists, wife hunters and general ne'er-do-wells from around the world. Also, nowhere else in Ukraine do the police hassle foreigners to such an extent, something you might experience firsthand should you head to the beaches in the evening.

Odesa's telephone area code is 0482 for six-digit numbers, 048 for seven digits.

History

Catherine the Great imagined Odesa as the St Petersburg of the South. Her lover, General Grygory Potemkin, laid the groundwork for her dream in 1789 by capturing the Turkish fortress of Hadjibey, which previously stood here. However, Potemkin died before work began on the city in 1794 and his senior commanders oversaw its construction instead. The Spanish–Neapolitan general José de Ribas, after whom the main street, vul Derybasivska, is named, built the harbour. The Duc de Richelieu (Armand Emmanuel du Plessis), an aristocrat fleeing the French

Revolution, became the first governor, overseeing the city's affairs from 1803 to 1814.

In 1815, when the city became a duty-free port, things really began to boom. Its huge appetite for more labour meant the city became a refuge ('Odesa Mama') for runaway serfs, criminals, renegades and dissidents.

It was the crucible of the 1905 workers' revolution, with a local uprising and the mutiny on the battleship *Potemkin Tavrichesky*. Between 1941 and 1944 Odesa sealed its reputation as one of Stalin's 'hero' cities, when partisans sheltering in the city's catacombs during WWII put up a legendary fight against the occupying Romanian troops (allies of the Nazis).

Odesa was once a very Jewish city, too, from which its famous sense of humour presumably derives. Jews initially came to Odesa to escape persecution, but tragically suffered the same fate here. In the early 20th century they accounted for one third of the city's population, but after horrific pogroms in 1905 and 1941 hundreds of thousands emigrated. Many moved to New York's Brighton Beach, now nicknamed 'Little Odesa'.

◉ Sights & Activities

Potemkin Steps   LANDMARK
You've seen the steppe, now see the steps: the Potemkin Steps, the site of one of cinema's most famous scenes. Designed by Italian architect Franz Boffo, the last of the 192 granite steps was slotted into place in 1841. The lower steps are wider than those at the top creating an optical illusion – the steps seem to be the same width all the way up. If you don't fancy the climb back up to the top, take the free **funicular railway** (⊙8am-11pm) that runs parallel.

Vul Derybasivska   HISTORIC AREA
Odesa's main commercial street is jam-packed with restaurants, bars and, in the summer high season, tourists. At its quieter eastern end you'll discover the **De Ribas statue**, a bronze of the general who built Odesa's harbour and after whom the street is named. At the western end of the thoroughfare is the pleasant **City Garden** (Gorodskoy Sad), surrounded by several restaurants. You'll find various touristy knickknacks for sale here and you can have your photo taken with a monkey or a snake, but the main draw is people-watching.

Across the street, the swanky **Passazh shopping arcade** is the best-preserved example of the neo-renaissance architectural style that permeated Odesa in the late 19th century.

Opera & Ballet Theatre   THEATRE
(Chaykovskoho 1) The jewel in Odesa's architectural crown was designed in the 1880s by the architects who also designed the famous Vienna State Opera, namely Ferdinand Fellner and Herman Helmer. Closed for several years amid botched reconstruction efforts, the theatre reopened to great fanfare in 2007.

Bul Prymorsky   HISTORIC AREA
Sooner or later everyone gravitates to this tree-lined pedestrian zone with replica 19th-century gas lamps, park benches and more photographers armed with a small zoo of animals. At the boulevard's eastern end, you'll spot the pink and white colonnaded **City Hall**, originally the stock exchange and later the Regional Soviet Headquarters. The cannon here is a war trophy captured from the British during the Crimean War. In the square in front of the City Hall is Odesa's most photographed monument, the **Pushkin statue**.

Continuing along the boulevard, at the top of the Potemkin Steps you'll reach the **statue of the Duc de Richelieu**, Odesa's first governor, looking like a Roman in a toga. The view from here is of the passenger port, the towering Hotel Odessa and the Black Sea.

AS SEEN ON SCREEN

Regularly voted one of the most influential films of all time, Sergei Eisenstein's *Battleship Potemkin* (1925) has guaranteed Odesa cinematic immortality. The B&W classic's most renowned sequence is that of a massacre of innocent civilians on the Potemkin Steps, during which a baby in a pram is accidentally pushed off the top and bounces in agonising slow motion down the 192 stairs.

As with much great art, however, the scene is partly fiction. Sailors aboard the battleship *Potemkin Tavrichesky* did mutiny over maggot-ridden food rations while in Odesa harbour, and that mutiny did spark a revolution in 1905. However, locals running to the shore to support the sailors were never shot by tsarist troops on the steps – although they were killed elsewhere in the city.

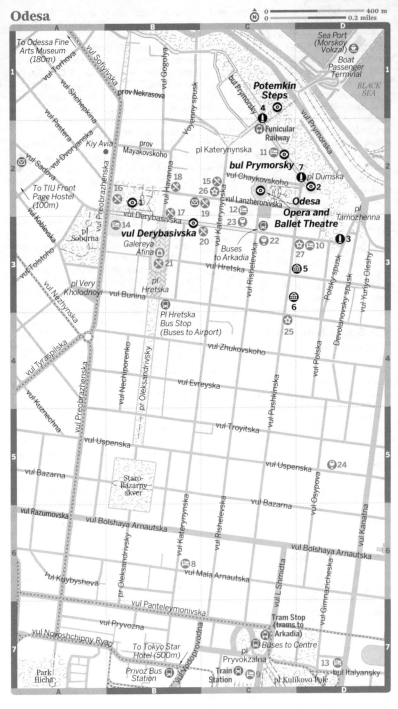

Museum of Western & Eastern Art
ART GALLERY

(www.oweamuseum.odessa.ua; vul Pushkinska 9; admission 15uah; ⊙10.30am-4pm Thu-Tue) Housed in a beautifully renovated (at least on the outside) mid-19th-century palace, the museum's star turn used to be one of 12 known versions (most likely not the original) of Caravaggio's brilliant painting *The Taking of Christ*. However, in July 2008 the canvas was cut from its frame in Ukraine's biggest art heist and only recovered by police two years later. The museum's Western Art section is currently closed indefinitely 'while security improvements are made', according to staff. Stable doors and bolting horses come to mind. The Eastern Art section has displays of porcelain and other artwork, mostly from Japan, China, Tibet and India.

Pushkin Museum
MUSEUM

(vul Pushkinska 13; admission 8uah; ⊙10am-5pm Tue-Sun Jul-Aug, Mon-Fri Sep-Jun) This is where Alexander Pushkin spent his first days in Odesa, after being exiled from Moscow by the tsar in 1823 for radical ideas. Governor Vorontsov subsequently humiliated the writer with petty administrative jobs, and it took only 13 months, an affair with Vorontsov's wife, a simultaneous affair with someone else's wife and more radical ideas for Push-

kin to be thrown out of Odesa, too. Somehow, he still found time while in town to finish the poem *The Bakhchysaray Fountain*, write the first chapter of *Eugene Onegin* and scribble the notes and moaning letters found in this humble museum.

Arkadia Beach
BEACH

An evening at Arkadia is a must when in Odesa and this is definitely the city's best place to see and be seen. Here you can play old-school arcade games, dress up like a tsar or tsarina for a photo op, or hang out in a variety of cafes, bars and clubs.

Take tram 5 from the tram stop near the train station, in front of the McDonald's on vul Panteleymonivska, to the end of the line.

🛏 Sleeping

Odesa is popular among Russians and Ukrainians, especially in July and August, but rarely are its hotels and hostels full, and turning up without a booking is still feasible, even in high season.

Mozart Hotel
HOTEL $$$

(☎377 777; www.mozart-hotel.com; vul Lanzheronivska 13; s 1104-2722uah, d 1635-3785uah; ❀❄@☎☀) As the name suggests, this top choice epitomises European luxury, with elegant furnishings and a calm, light-filled interior lurking behind its refurbished neoclassical façade.

ODESA'S APARTMENTS

Odesa's cheapest flats are offered by the 'babushka Mafia', as locals call it, whose members hang out around the train station (though not in the numbers they once did) and ask around 50uah for a room, or roughly double to triple that for a one-bedroom apartment. Otherwise contact the following agencies:

» **American Business Center** (☎777 1400; www.odessa-apartment-rentals.com; vul Derybasivska 5) Seven-day minimum stay requirement.

» **Central Vokzal Apartment Bureau** (☎727 1381; Odesa Train station; bed/apt from 50/250uah; ☺6.30am-8pm) Across from platform 4 near the station's rear exit.

» **Odessa Rent-A-Flat** (☎787 3444; www.odessarentaflat.com; vul Rishelevska. 11)

» **Odessaapts.com** (☎067 708 5501; www.odessaapts.com)

The 40 rooms are individually decorated and the location across from the Opera and Ballet Theatre is perfect.

Hotel Londonskaya　　　HOTEL $$$
(☎738 0110; www.londred.com; bul Prymorsky 11; s 1100-2910uah, d 1360-3170uah; ⊛❄☎❀) Last refurbished in the early 1990s, the rooms of Odesa's oldest luxury hotel are becoming slightly dated, but with iron-lace balustrades, stained-glass windows, parquet flooring and an inner courtyard, the place still oozes Regency charm and is still the lodgings of choice for the smart set.

Continental　　　HOTEL $$$
(☎786 0399; www.continental-hotel.com.ua; vul Derybasivska 5; s/d from 1220/1460uah; ⊛❄☎) If you're a businessperson arriving in Odesa on expenses, this smart hotel in a pretty much perfect location is probably where you'll be staying. The stylish rooms have high ceilings, exquisite oak-wood desks and plenty of unused space.

Babushka Grand Hostel　　　HOSTEL $
(☎063 070 5535; vul Mala Arnautska 60; dm from 100uah; ☎) While Odessa's other hostels are decidedly for the young, day-sleeping crowd, the wonderfully named Babushka Grand, occupying a palatial apartment near the train station, has a more laid-back, traveller vibe. The stuccoed interiors and crystal chandeliers are stunning and the staff fun.

Palladium Hotel　　　HOTEL $$
(☎728 6651; www.hotel-palladium.com.ua; bul Italyansky 4; r from 785uah; ❄☎❀) With attractive, pastel-hued rooms featuring minimalist decor and fine-textured carpets, plus a wonderful swimming pool, this definitely qualifies as a good deal for Odesa. Free admission to downstairs nightclub (closed during summer) and the summer club Itaka.

TIU Front Page Hostel　　　HOSTEL $
(☎093 566 6278; vul Koblevska 42, top fl; dm 50-120uah; @) The current owners inherited the premises from a publishing company who had wallpapered the entire place in magazine front pages, hence the name. It's definitely a party hostel with never a dull moment, so sleep here may not come easily to some.

Chillout Hostel　　　HOSTEL $
(☎063 867 7828; vul Derybasivska 5; dm from 120uah; ❄☎) Odesa's best located hostel is this modern, Polish-run affair next door to the Continental Hotel, mere stumbling distance from the city's best bars. The high-ceilinged dorms have loads of space to unpack and there's a free breakfast. Air-con means this place lives up to its name in summer.

Passazh Hotel　　　HOTEL $
(☎728 5500; www.passage.odessa.ua; vul Preobrazhenska 34; s/d from 180/230uah) The Passazh is the epitome of faded glory, but how glorious it must have been. Rooms feature lots of Soviet fixtures, awful wallpaper, saggy beds and shoddy tilework, but they are large and are fitted with old-world amenities such as full-length claw-footed bathtubs.

Tokyo Star Hotel　　　BUSINESS HOTEL $
(☎700 2191; vul Vodoprovodna 1A; s/d 100/200uah; ❄☎) This no-frills mini business hotel near the Privoz bus station is for those who use their room to sleep and wash but little else. The singles are windowless and the rooms so small that you'll be constantly climbing over a pack or suitcase. With the doubles, make sure you know your travelling companion well – very little divides the bed from the toilet and shower.

Eating

TOP CHOICE **Kompot** FRENCH **$$**
(vul Derybasivska 20; mains 40-90uah;
⊘8am-11pm) Spilling out onto busy Dery-
basivska to a jolly Gallic soundtrack, this
French-style eatery is good for any meal of
the day. Fresh pastries and an early open-
ing time are a godsend for caffeine-craving
Westerners, light lunches can be devoured
in the faux Parisian interior over a newspa-
per and you can dine out on the cobbles till
late with a bottle of something nice. Service
here can be *escargot*-paced when busy.

Balalaika RUSSIAN **$$**
(vul Katerynynska 12; mains 40-100uah; ⊘11am-
midnight) If you were looking forward to
Odesa for its Russian flavour, this brightly
lit, timber-lined restaurant decorated with
colourful Russian knick-knackery is the
place to indulge. There are Siberian *pelmeni,* imaginatively filled pancakes, heaps of
meat and fish, and a *mangal* (grill) working
overtime to supply diners with *shashlyk.*

Pulcinella ITALIAN **$$**
(vul Lanzheronivska 17; mains 30-50uah) The bright
teal interior gives this place a seaside Medi-
terranean feel, but it's the scrumptious five-
course meals that will really make you feel like
you're in southern Italy. The culinary high-
lights are the lasagne and the oven-fired pizza.

Tavriya CAFE **$**
(Galereya Afina mall, pl Hretska; mains from around
15uah; ⊘8am-10pm) This squeaky-clean food
mecca in the basement of Odesa's flashi-
est mall is the city's most popular quick eat. The *stolova* (cafeteria) has a
larger choice of dishes than the city's other
canteens, but can be a much more Ukrainian-
style push-and-shove affair, and the service
stinks.

Puzata Khata CAFE **$**
(vul Derybasivska 21; mains from 10uah; ⊘9am-
10pm) Take the lift to the 6th floor of the
Evropa shopping mall to find the Odesa
branch of this national chain. The theme
here is vaguely Greco-Black Sea, but the
serving staff still look as though they've just
stepped off the steppe. The cut-priced fare
here is as tasty as at any other branch.

Klarabara INTERNATIONAL **$$**
(City Garden; mains 35-100uah) Tucked away
in a quiet corner of the City Garden, this
classy, cosy, ivy-covered cafe and restaurant
is awash with antique furniture and fine

art. The food is a mixed bag, but every week
there's a theme menu showcasing the cuisine of this or that country.

Kumanets UKRAINIAN **$$**
(vul Havanna 7; mains 35-80uah) A kitsch little
island of Ukraine in Russian Odesa, this
veritable Ukrainian village produces afford-
able *holubtsy* (cabbage rolls), *varenyky* and
deruny (potato pancakes), in addition to
pricier mains.

Drinking

TOP CHOICE **Shkaf** BAR
(vul Derybasivska 14; ⊘7pm-late) So of-
ten in Ukraine the best watering holes are
hidden away behind unmarked doors and
buried deep below anonymous buildings.
This is definitely the case with this heaving
basement bar-cum-club, a sure-fire antidote
to Odesa's trendy beach club scene and pick-
up bars. To find it, pass through a pair of
varnished wooden doors at Derybasivska 14,
flanked by official-looking blue signs.

Shuzz LIVE MUSIC
(www.shuzz.od.ua; vul Uspenska 22; admission
30uah; ⊘5pm-3am) Occupying a former shoe
factory, this is the latest addition to Odesa's
late scene. The vibe is very laid-back here so
grab a cloudy Chernihivske Bile and chill to
whatever's playing – this is also the best al-
ternative music venue in Odesa.

Friends and Beer BAR
(vul Derybasivska 9) This charming re-created
USSR-era living room littered with photos of
Russian film stars is proof that 'Retro Soviet'
doesn't have to mean political posters and
Constructivist art. The huge TV screen is
possibly not authentic for the period, but it's
great for sports.

☆ Entertainment

Clubs

Odesa's raucous club scene is divided into
two seasons: summer (June to August) and
the rest of the year. In summer, all the ac-
tion is at Arkadia Beach, which boasts two
huge, Ibiza-style nightclubs that produce
heightened levels of madness seven days a
week. At other times of the year, the action
is closer to the city centre.

Ibiza CLUB
(www.ibiza.ua; Arkadia Beach; ⊘summer) This
white, free-form, cavelike structure is Arka-
dia's most upmarket and most expensive
club. European DJs and big-ticket Russian

and Ukrainian pop bands often play here. Ticket prices can be high when a big act is in town.

Itaka CLUB
(www.itaka-club.com.ua; Arkadia Beach; ☉summer) It's slightly more downmarket than Ibiza and consequently often rowdier (in a good way). The Greek columns and statues are a tad much, but you'll hardly care when it's 5am and you are out of your gourd. Like Ibiza, it also draws big regional pop acts.

Shede GAY
(www.shedeclub.com.ua; Derybasivska 5) One of Ukraine's best openly gay nightclubs, it has Friday and Saturday night shows beginning at 1am.

Praetoria Music Club LIVE MUSIC
(vul Lanzheronivska 26) One of the few city-centre clubs with a pulse in the summer.

Classical Music & Opera

Theatre, concert and opera tickets can be purchased at the venues or at a **Teatralna Kasa** (Theatre Kiosk; ☉9am-5pm). There's one on the corner of vul Derybasivska and vul Rishelevska.

Odessa Philharmonic Hall LIVE MUSIC
(www.odessaphilharmonic.org; vul Bunina 15; ☉closed Jul & Aug) The best regional orchestra within the former Soviet Union is the Odessa Philharmonic Orchestra, led by charismatic and energetic American conductor Hobart Earle, a former student of Leonard Bernstein. This orchestra accounts for half the symphonies put on here.

Odesa Opera and Ballet Theatre THEATRE
(www.opera-ballet.tm.odessa.ua; Chaykovskoho 1) In addition to being architecturally magnificent Odesa's magnificent theatre is also known for its marvellous acoustics. Unfortunately, the local opera company does not do justice to the theatre's impressive physical attributes, but performances are eminently affordable and the Odessa Philharmonic Orchestra performs here from time to time.

ℹ️ Information

Angar18 (vul Velika Arnautska 52; per hr 6uah; ☉24hr) Internet at any time of day, plus Skype and photocopying.

Central post office (vul Sadova 10)

Tourist Office (☎731 4808; www.odessa tourism.in.ua; bul Italyansky 11; ☉9am-1pm & 2pm-6pm Mon-Fri) Staff can book anything including hotels, all kinds of tickets and city tours. Superb website.

ℹ️ Getting There & Away

Air

Odesa airport (www.airport.od.ua) is better linked to Europe than any other Ukrainian airport besides Kyiv's. Malev, Air Baltic, Czech Airlines, Carpatair and Turkish Airlines all have regular flights here, and various regional carriers fly to Georgia, Armenia and Russia.

Domestic airline Dniproavia flies to/from Kyiv up to five times a day. **Kiy Avia** (www.kiyavia. com; vul Preobrazhenska 15; ☉8am-8pm) can sort you out with tickets and timetables.

Boat

Ferry services to and from Odesa are notoriously unreliable, with services to İstanbul (Turkey), Varna (Bulgaria) and Poti (Georgia) ceasing for months on end without explanation. Boats are in theory operated by **Ukrferry** (www.ukrferry. com). The only trustworthy passenger service (not run by Ukrferry) is the boat to Crimea (850uah, 20 hours, five to seven sailings a month). For tickets and timetables contact **London Sky Travel** (☎729 3196; www.lstravel. com.ua).

Bus

Odesa has two bus stations that are useful for travellers. The conveniently located, but slightly chaotic, **Privoz bus station** (vul Vodoprovodna), 300m west of the train station, is mainly for shorter trips.

Most international and long-haul domestic buses leave from the **long-distance bus station** (vul Kolontaevska 58), 3km west of the train station. Frequent **Gunsel** (☎326 212) and **Autolux** (☎716 4612) buses are the most comfortable and quickest way to Kyiv (125uah to 175uah, six to seven hours). Otherwise speedy *marshrutky* leave from just in front of the station building (150uah, six hours). Other destinations include Simferopol (100uah, 12 hours, six daily), Yalta (125uah, 14 hours, three daily), Lviv (140uah, 15 hours, two daily) and Chernivtsi (130uah, 13 hours, two daily) via Kamyanets-Podilsky.

There are at least 10 buses per day to Chişinău via Tiraspol, and two via Palanka (65uah, five to seven hours). The latter avoid Transdnistr.

Train

Odesa is well connected by train to all major Ukrainian, Russian and eastern European cities.

There are up to eight trains to Kyiv (110uah, 10 to 12 hours), four of which are overnighters. Other destinations include Lviv (180uah, 12 hours), Kamyanets-Podilsky (130uah, 18 hours) and Simferopol (140uah, 12 hours). Longer-distance services go to Moscow, Minsk, Rostov and (during summer only) to St Petersburg. There are still no trains to Chişinău.

❶ Getting Around

Odesa airport is about 12km southwest of the city centre, off Ovidiopilska doroha. Bus 129 goes to/from the train station; infrequent bus 117 runs to/from the pl Hretska stop.

To get to the centre from the train station (about a 20-minute walk), go to the stop near the Mc-Donald's and take any bus saying Площа Грецка (ploshcha Hretska), such as bus 148. Trolleybuses 4 and 10 trundle up vul Pushkinska before curving around to vul Prymorska past the passenger port and the foot of the Potemkin Steps.

Tram 5 goes from the train station to the long-distance bus station. From the Privoz bus station to pl Hretska take bus 220.

CRIMEA КРИМ

Rip up what you think you know about Ukraine and start from scratch – Crimea will confound any generalisations you've made about the country so far and take you into a new world of astonishing scenery, rich cultural ferment and a semitropical climate kept balmy by a warm breeze coming off the Black Sea. No wonder this peninsula has been fought over by the Greeks, Khazars, Tatars, Mongols, Huns, Genoese, Ottomans, Russians, French and British over the centuries.

The most attractive and interesting part of the peninsula is the so-called Russian Riviera – you'll understand the accuracy of the name if you're here in the summer months, when much of Moscow descends on the resorts here. In addition to the seedy resort towns of Yalta and Alupka, you'll find the fascinating palaces where modern European history was shaped in 1945 by the 'Big Three' (Stalin, Churchill and Roosevelt). But the highlight of the entire peninsula is without doubt tiny Bakhchysaray, the old Crimean Tatar capital with the dramatic setting and the perfectly preserved Khan's Palace.

History

While Crimea's early history is a palimpsest of cultural annexations from the Greeks and Scythians to the Genoese and Jews, the real crucible of the peninsula's history has been the conflict between Turkic and Slavic peoples for control.

The Mongols arrived in 1240 as they shattered Kyivan Rus, and their descendants, the Crimean Tatars, formed a khanate here,

which in later years became a vassal state of the Ottoman Empire.

While a Turkish vassal state, Crimea enjoyed much autonomy. The same was not true when the Russians arrived in 1783 and began a campaign of 'revenge' for the Tatars' slave-trading raids into Russia over the centuries. Most of the peninsula's four to five million Tatars fled to Turkey, while Russians, Ukrainians, Bulgarians and even some Germans were invited to resettle Crimea.

Much to the chagrin of its rival empires, Russia wanted to take over the faltering Ottoman Empire, and when Tsar Nicholas I sent troops into the Ottoman provinces of Moldavia and Wallachia (ostensibly to protect the Christians there) in 1854, the British and French assembled in Varna (now in Bulgaria) to protect İstanbul. Both sides lost about 250,000 soldiers in the ensuing Crimean War, many from bad medical care – to which British nurse Florence Nightingale drew attention.

By the 1860s, however, Crimea had become a chic leisure spot, thanks to Russia's imperial family building a summer estate at Livadia, on the outskirts of Yalta.

During the civil war that followed the Russian Revolution, Crimea was one of the last 'white' bastions. The Germans occupied the peninsula for three years during WWII and Crimea lost nearly half its inhabitants. In 1944 Stalin banished the entire Tatar population to Central Asia.

Throughout the Soviet era, millions came each year to Crimea, attracted by the warmth, beauty, beaches and mountain air. In 1954 Khrushchev transferred control of the peninsula to Ukraine, a sticking point today as the Crimean population still have more in common with Russia. Russia controversially uses Sevastopol as its Black Sea naval base.

Simferopol СІМФЕРОПОЛЬ

☑0652 / POP 345,000

With its odd mixture of the Levantine and the Soviet, the Crimean capital is not an unpleasant city, but there is no point lingering here as everything else on the peninsula is much more exciting – and only a short bus ride away. If you have a night to spend in Simferopol, use this opportunity to chill out in one of its quality restaurants and cafes – these are a bit of a rarity on the coast.

Simferopol

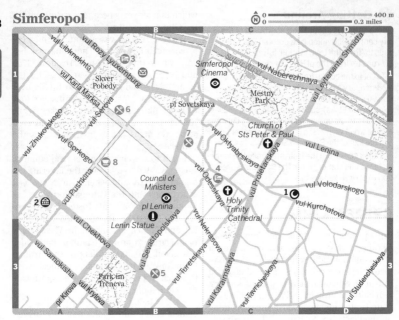

⊙ Sights

Neopolis   ANCIENT SITE

(btwn vuls Vorovskogo & Krasnoarmeyskaya)
There's little sense of history about the hilltop
site, where archaeologists have unearthed
remnants of Crimea's Scythian capital (300
BC to D 300), but it offers a good view of Simferopol in all its Soviet-constructivist glory.

Taurida Central Museum   MUSEUM

(vul Gogolya 14; admission 15uah; ⊙9am-5pm Wed-
Mon) Crimea's largest museum has a vast collection of archaeological finds and books representing different cultures that flourished
on the peninsula. Sections dedicated to the
Hellenised Goths of Feodoro princedom and
Genovese colonists are of particular interest.

Kebi-Djami Mosque   MOSQUE

(vul Kurchatova 4) This restored 16th-century
mosque dates back to the Tatar town of Ak-
Mechet (White Mosque), a predecessor of
Simferopol.

🛏 Sleeping

Hotel Valencia   HOTEL **$$**

(📞510 606; www.valencia.crimea.ua; vul Odesskaya
8; d from 400uah; ❄️🤖) Fusing Crimea and
Spain, this centrally located, friendly and
well-run hotel is justifiably popular, so book
ahead. The sole windowless 'economy' single

goes for just 150uah, but without air-con it
becomes a torture chamber in summer.

Hotel Ukraina   LUXURY HOTEL **$$**

(📞510 165; www.ukraina-hotel.biz; vul Rozy Lyuxem-
burg 7; s/d from 470/640uah; ❄️🤖) Admittedly,
the baroque public areas of this central,
forward-thinking hotel are a bit OTT, but
rooms are restrained and well finished – the
standard class in sandy ochre and red-earth
tones. Staff speak English, and there's a sauna and hammam (Turkish bath).

Soma Youth Hostel
HOSTEL **$**

(☑063 225 2896; vul Sevastopolskaya 41/6, apt 28; dm 150uah, r without bathroom 440uah; 🛜) About 15 minutes by *marshrutka* from the centre, this typical semi-clandestine Western-run hostel was operating here in the summer 2010. Cheap guided tours of Crimea's southern coast were on offer.

✗ Eating & Drinking

Cafe Motivi
MIDDLE EASTERN **$**

(Basement, vul Karla Marksa 9; mains 30-60uah, cocktails 30-45uah) This opulently decorated and moodily lit Persian restaurant is one of Simferopol's hip hangouts. The food, which consists mainly of stews and stir-fries, is delicious but usually takes ages to arrive. From Thursdays to Saturdays, locals come for the DJs and the bar rather than the food.

Grand Cafe Chekhov
RUSSIAN **$$**

(vul Chekhova 4; mains 30-80uah) In this beautifully designed oasis of whiteness and coolness, you can just imagine that Anton Pavlovich himself is treating you to classic Russian specialities, such as *ukha* fish soup and *bliny* (pancakes), at his Crimean dacha. We loved pork stir-fried with apples, cooked and served in an iron pan.

Veranda Chirakhova & Piramida
EUROPEAN **$$**

(vul Odesskaya 22/2; mains 30-70uah) This cluster of restaurants (all under the same ownership) is dominated by the open-air Chirakhova terrace with its pastel-coloured wooden furniture and comfy couches. European and Russian–Ukrainian standards are on the menu. The glassy Pyramide is for patrons to escape the winter chill.

Kofein
COFFEE HOUSE

(vul Pushkina 8; espresso 15uah, mains 35-70uah; ⊙24hr; 🛜) The 'exoticism' at this trendy African-themed cafe overdoes its appreciation of the female form. But if you can position yourself where your eyes are not being poked out by a photographed nipple, you'll find it takes its coffee seriously and turns out a good brew.

❶ Information

Central post office (vul Alexandra Nevskogo 1; internet per hr 4.50uah) Contains a telephone centre and 24-hour internet cafe.

Pro-Internet Center (vul Karla Marksa 1; per hr 4uah; ⊙24hr) Has 112 high-speed computers.

❶ Getting There & Away

Air

Simferopol airport (www.airport.crimea.ua) is 15km northwest of the centre. Aerosvit, Air Baltic, Turkish Airlines, El Al and Ukraine Airlines all fly in from abroad, as do several Russian carriers. No-frills Wizzair connects Simferopol with London Luton via Kyiv.

Kiyavia (☑272 167; www.kiyavia.crimea.ua; bul Lenina 1/7; ⊙9am-6pm Mon-Fri, 9am-5pm Sat) sells both international and domestic air tickets.

Bus

Buses to pretty much anywhere in Crimea leave from the chaotic **Kurortnaya bus station**, located on the train station square. There are frequent services to Yalta (20uah, 1½ hours, every 10 minutes), among destinations.

Locals usually catch *marshrutky* to Bakhchysaray (6uah, one hour, every 20 minutes) from the west bus station.

Train

Simferopol is Crimea's main railway junction, with five trains daily to/from Kyiv (180uah to 240uah, 15 hours) and services to/from Lviv (190uah, 21 hours, daily) and Odesa (140uah, 12 hours, daily). There are also services to Moscow, St Petersburg, Rostov-on-Don and Minsk.

Local *elektrychka* run regularly along the Crimean peninsula to/from Yevpatoriya (two hours, seven a day in each direction) and Sevastopol (two hours, seven daily in each direction). The latter service stops en route in Bakhchysaray (40 minutes).

❶ Getting Around

Marshrutka 49 shuttles between the airport, the train station, the centre and the central bus station. Trolleybus 9 (1.50uah, 30 minutes) goes from the airport to the train station. To get to the centre from here you need to take trolleybus 5 or 2 eastwards, or a *marshrutka* or bus from near McDonald's with Сільпо (Silpo) on its side.

Yalta ЯЛТА
☑0654 / POP 80,500

Like dark matter, Yalta exerts a poorly understood yet irresistible force on people in Crimea, and it seems almost anyone you meet will be heading to or escaping from the peninsula's most famous and tackiest resort town, once the preserve of tsars and artists and now...well, not.

While the city enjoys a spectacular setting with the vast Crimean Mountains rising sharply from the sea, once you start to descend towards the overdeveloped town centre,

UKRAINE CRIMEA

Yalta

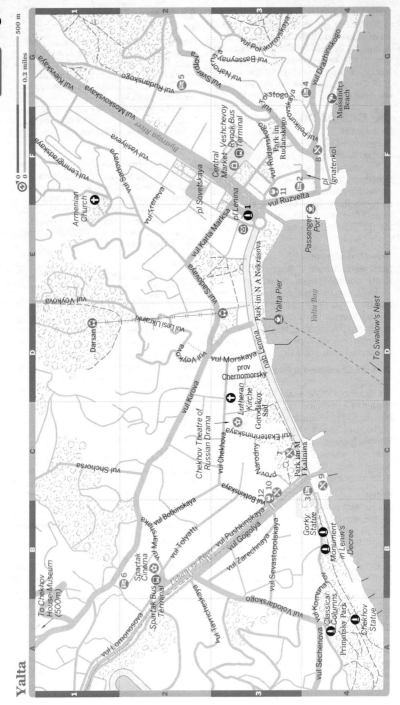

0 ——— 500 m
0 ——— 0.2 miles

Massandra Beach

Yalta Bay

To Swallow's Nest

Yalta

you'll soon realise that the journey to Yalta was one of the greatest aspects of a visit here.

◎ Sights

CITY CENTRE

Nab Lenina   SEAFRONT

The promenade, nab Lenina, stretches past numerous piers, palm trees, restaurants, boutiques and souvenir stalls to **Prymorsky Park**, where there are some carnival-type rides. The promenade starts at **ploscha Lenina**, the centre of activity. Here there are plenty of benches for people-watching under the shadow of a **statue of Lenin**. The former Soviet leader gawks at the McDonald's across the way as if it were the devil himself.

Although swimming isn't an option along the promenade, you can descend to a few short lengths of beach, which is all rocks – most of them flat and perfect for skipping along the placid, rather plain waterfront.

Chekhov House-Museum   MUSEUM

(www.chekhov.com.ua; vul Kirova 112; admission 30uah; ☉10am-5pm, last entry 4.30pm Tue-Sun Jun-Sep, Wed-Sun Sep-May) Anton Chekhov, Russia's greatest dramatist, wrote *The Cherry Orchard* and *Three Sisters* in what is now the Chekhov House-Museum. The small estate, where he entertained the likes of Chaliapin, Rachmaninov, Gorky and Tolstoy, is Yalta's only must-see sight. Take *marshrutka* 6 from Veshchevoy Rynok terminal or *marshrutka* 8 from the Spartak cinema to the Dom-Muzey Chekhova stop.

It takes 15 to 20 minutes to walk from the Spartak Cinema.

OTHER SIGHTS

Many travellers hang around in Yalta not because they're into the resorty vibe but because it makes an excellent base from which to see Crimea's spectacular historic and natural sights.

Massandra Winery   WINERY

(vul Vinodela Yegorova 9; excursion/wine-tasting 70/40uah; ☉tours every 2hr 11am-7pm) Memoirists claim that Tsar Nicholas II would always keep a flask of Massandra port hidden in his high boot during his daily walks, while his wife sipped the very same drink listening to Rasputin's prophesies. The imperial court's winery is now open to visitors. On a mandatory Russian-language excursion, you get to see the tsar's wine cellars, which contain over a million dust-covered bottles, including a 1775 Spanish Jerez de la Frontera, claimed to be the oldest preserved wine in the world. The visit ends with a tasting session.

Ay-Petri Cable Car   CABLE CAR

(Kanatnaya doroga; each way 50uah; ☉ticket office 10am-4pm, services every 20min to 5pm) On the coastal road in Miskhor, behind a cluster of market stalls, is the cable car up the cliff of Mt Ay-Petri. It's a dizzying ride across the foothills and up the mountain's sheer face, during which you overlook the coast and the sea. Views from the top are stunning, while Mt Ay-Petri's dry plateau itself feels otherworldly, or at least Central Asian. There are also several Tatar eateries. Buses 27 and 32 between Yalta and Alupka stop here.

Swallow's Nest   HISTORIC BUILDING

(Lastochkino Gnezdo; admission 5uah; ☉8am-6pm Tue-Sun) Like many movie stars, Swallow's Nest is shorter in real life than it appears in pictures. This toy-town castle is a favourite subject for Crimean postcards, but it's only big enough to house an expensive and disappointing Italian restaurant.

Instead, it's the castle's precarious perch on the sheer cliff of Cape Ay-Todor, 10km west of Yalta, that gives it a minor thrill. On the surrounding walkway, you realise that the castle actually overhangs the cliff. Although the castle looks medieval in style, it was built in 1912 for German oil magnate Baron Steingel, as a present for his mistress.

The most spectacular approach to the castle is over the water, via the ferry (20uah, up to 20 daily) that heads from Yalta pier to the beach and jetty just below Swallow's Nest.

Buses 32, 26 and 27 also pass this way, stopping directly in front of a row of souvenir stalls above the castle.

Livadia Palace   HISTORIC BUILDING
(admission 40uah ⊙10am-5.45pm Tue-Thu) It's not the most sumptuously furnished Crimean interior, but Livadia Palace reverberates with history. It's the site of the 1945 Yalta Conference, where dying US President Franklin Roosevelt and heat-allergic British Prime Minister Winston Churchill turned up to be bullied by Soviet leader Josef Stalin. While here, Churchill declared steamy Crimea 'the Riviera of Hades' – and no wonder, given the high temperatures and the company he was keeping. Stalin's insistent demands to keep Poland and other swaths of Eastern Europe shaped the face of postwar Europe. It's hard not to be awed wandering these corridors of power.

In the enormous **White Hall**, the 'Big Three' and their staff met to tacitly carve up Europe. The crucial documents, dividing Germany and ceding parts of Poland to the USSR, were signed on 11 February in the English billiard room. The most famous Yalta photograph of Churchill, Roosevelt and Stalin is hung on a wall, along with the awkward outtakes, which bring history to life.

It's upstairs, however, that Livadia's other ghosts genuinely move you. This Italian Renaissance-style building was designed as a summer residence for Russian Tsar Nicholas II in 1911. But he and his family spent just four seasons here before their arrest by Bolshevik troops in 1917 and murder in Yekaterinburg the following year. Photos and some poignant mementos of the doomed Romanovs remain in their private quarters.

Marshrutka 47a from Veshchevoy Rynok terminal and *Marshrutka* 5 (3uah, summer only) from the Spartak Cinema drop you in the palace grounds. A taxi to Livadia costs around 20uah.

🛏 Sleeping

Bristol   HISTORIC HOTEL $$$
(☑271 606, 271 603; www.hotel-bristol.com.ua; vul Ruzvelta 10; standard s/d 875/980uah; ❄) Few of us ever really need more comfort than this central, three-star establishment provides. The town's oldest hotel is in a heritage-listed, 19th-century building, but its rooms were thoughtfully renovated in 2003, many in yellow and blue hues. Throw in a good breakfast buffet and reasonable service, and your stay will usually be straightforward and uncomplicated.

Vremena Goda   HOTEL $$
(☑230 852, 234 111; www.hotel-seasons.com.ua; vul Rudanskogo 23; s/d from 570/980uah; ❄❄) For something a little special, visit this spa hotel and medical centre for its chocolate massages and mud treatments. With clean, modern lines complemented by a few art nouveau stained-glass windows, the 'Four Seasons' is within fairly easy reach (a 10- to 15-minute walk) of the high-season action.

Oreanda   HOTEL $$$
(☑274 274, 274 250; www.hotel-oreanda.com; nab Lenina 35/2; s/d 1175/1785uah; ⊜❄@❄) The crème de la Krim is favoured by oligarchs, expense-account bunnies and others who wish their wealth to be seen. Rooms are elegant and tasteful – which is more than can be said for the hotel's casino and club. However, the rooms are also small and only superior accommodation enjoys sea views.

Otdykh   B&B $
(☑353 069; www.krim-yalta.com.ua; vul Drazhinskogo 14; economy/standard d 250/475uah;❄) Hotel 'Relaxation' was a 19th-century brothel; now it's a decent enough budget *pension*. Some of the bathrooms are a bit whiffy and there's some street noise, but staff speak OK English and the location is convenient.

White Eagle   BOUTIQUE HOTEL $$
(☑327 702; prov Krutoy 13; s/d 700/800uah; ⊙summer only; ❄) Judge for yourself about the ethics of their face-control policy, which bars most Ukrainians and Russians while welcoming foreigners. Otherwise, this is a chic, relaxed residence with six air-con rooms that are comfortably and tastefully furnished.

Yalta-Intourist   HOTEL $$
(☑270 260, 270 270; www.hotel-yalta.com.ua; vul Drazhinskogo 50; s/d from 670/770uah; @❄❄) No one chooses the famous Yalta for comfort or convenience. They stay for the novelty of checking in to a 2230-bed ex-Soviet behemoth. Rooms are ordinary and the hotel is as poorly located as the neighbouring Massandra. However, given 10 bars, seven restaurants, numerous shops, a dolphinarium, a sauna, a lift to a private beach and myriad sporting activities, some guests probably never set foot off the premises.

The entire city seems to be for rent in summer. Apartments come in all shapes from four walls and a bed for 250uah to fully furnished, multibedroom cottages that may cost up to 4000uah a night. Prices drop drastically off-season – you can get a nice flat in the centre for as little as 60uah in winter.

» **Yalta Apartment** (☎050 970 9446; www.yaltaapartment.com; apt from 260uah)
English-speaking Lyudmila operates several nicely furnished flats in the heart of Yalta, at the beginning of pr Karla Marksa.

» **Travel 2 Sevastopol** (☎0506498360; www.travel2sevastopol.com) English-run, UK-based operator.

» **Black Sea Crimea** (☎in UK 07808 160 621; www.blacksea-crimea.com) Has slightly more expensive offerings.

✕ Eating & Drinking

The waterfront and adjacent street are lined with restaurants offering standard 'European' (that is, post-Soviet) menus. A myriad of Столовая signs mark cafeterias where you can choose from displayed dishes.

Khutorok La Mer UKRAINIAN $$
(vul Sverdlova 9; mains 60-170uah; ☺10am-2am)
If this is a *khutorok* (a traditional Ukranian farm), then designers must have salvaged it from the bottom of the sea. The menu is also a wild fusion of rural Ukrainian and marine themes. Nothing prevents you from ordering fried *barabulya* and cabbage *varenyki* at the same time.

Nobu JAPANESE $$$
(nab Lenina 35/2; mains 90-400uah) Unlike the Greek galera nearby, Espagnola used to be a real seafaring *caravella* that sailed as far as Georgia on the whims of Soviet cinema directors who used it as a prop. Now it stands on stilts in front of Hotel Oreanda and houses not a tapas bar but an upmarket Japanese restaurant. What else can you expect in a sushi-crazed country? It also has a separate Black Sea fish menu.

Apelsin EUROPEAN-JAPANESE $$
(nab imeni Lenina 35a; mains 30-150uah; ☺9am-midnight) A glassy structure set in a park, Apelsin is one of the few places in Yalta where you can have a decent breakfast. At other times, you can choose from an extensive menu that has a bit of everything – from standard international meat and poultry dishes to Black Sea fish and sushi.

Smak CRIMEAN TATAR $$
(vul Pushkinskaya 7a; mains 50-150uah) This simple open-air eatery and takeaway makes more than 10 different kinds of mouthwater-ing *chebureki* (10uah), an impressive array of Crimean Tatar dishes, great *shashlyks* and Black Sea fish – the latter about twice as cheap as in upmarket restaurants but of the same quality.

Pinta PUB $$
(vul Pushkinskaya 7 & vul Ignatenko 7; ☺9am-2am)
Beer drinkers, you are not forgotten in this sweet-wine kingdom! Two Pinta pubs are strategically located on both sides of the promenade. International beer brands, such as Belgian Leffe and Czech Staropramen, are on tap. Meat dishes dominate the extensive menu.

❶ Information

Dozens of tourist booths line the waterfront and around, selling reasonably priced Russian-language day trips and, occasionally, maps. Remember, some attractions don't need much commentary. Many hotels can also help with information.

Post office (pl Lenina 1; ☺8am-9pm Mon-Fri, 8am-6pm Sat, 8am-4pm Sun)

Travel2crimea.com (☎272 546; www.travel2crimea.com; Hotel Massandra, vul Drazhinsk-ogo 35; ☺9am-5pm Mon-Fri year-round, plus 9am-5pm Sat May-Sep) With years of experience, excellent English and a helpful manner, owner Igor Brudny runs a great travel service.

Ukrtelekom (vul Moskovskaya 9; internet per hr 6uah) Telephone and internet centre.

❶ Getting There & Away

Boat

Some international cruise ships now stop here, but Yalta's **passenger port** (morskoy vokzal; vul Ruzvelta 5) is largely underused. In the summer of 2010, there were two boats a week to Novorossiysk in Russia (832uah, five hours).

Bus & Trolleybus

Services depart on the longest trolleybus route in the world from Yalta's **main bus station** (vul Moskovskaya 8) to Simferopol (20uah, two hours, every 20 minutes).

ⓘ Getting Around

There are several bus and *marshrutka* stations in town. You'll arrive at the main bus station, which is about 1.5km from the waterfront. From here, trolleybuses 1, 2 and 3 go down the hill along vul Kievskaya to the centre.

Behind the main bus station, on the lower level, you'll find the buses and *marshrutky* going to the sights around Yalta. But perhaps more useful are Veshchevoy Rynok and Spartak cinema bus stations.

Bakhchysaray
БАХЧИСАРАЙ

📞 06554 / POP 27,500

A world away from the glitz and noise of the resort towns on the coast, the former capital of the Crimean khanate is an absolute must-see on any trip to the peninsula. With three stellar attractions: the Khan's Palace (which dates back to the 16th century), the still-working Uspensky Monastery built into sheer cliff walls and the 6th-century cave city of Chufut-Kale, it's worth doing an overnight trip here, not least because there are some great accommodation options and plenty of chances to taste Crimean Tatar cuisine.

◎ Sights

Khans' Palace   HISTORIC BUILDING
(Khansky Dvorets; www.hansaray.iatp.org.ua; vul Leninaya 129; admission 20uah; ⊙9am-5.30pm) When she was busy ordering the mass destruction of Bakhchysaray's mosques in the 18th and early 19th centuries, Catherine the Great spared the Khans' Palace. Her decision was reportedly based on the building being 'romantic'. While it lacks the imposing grandeur of Islamic structures in, say, İstanbul, this is a major landmark of Crimean culture and history. Erected in the 16th century under the direction of Persian, Ottoman and Italian architects, it was rebuilt a few times, but the structure still resembles the original.

Passing through the back of the finely carved, Venetian Renaissance **Demir Qapi Portal** (also called Portal Alevizo after its Italian designer who also authored parts of Moscow's Kremlin), you enter the west wing and the dimly lit **Divan Hall**. This was the seat of government where the khan and his nobles discussed laws and wars.

Through the hall lies the inner courtyard, containing two fountains. With its white marble ornately inscribed with gold leaf, the **Golden Fountain** (1733) is probably the more beautiful. However, the neighbouring **Fountain of Tears** (1764) is more famous, thanks to Alexander Pushkin's poem *The Bakhchysaray Fountain*. It's tradition that two roses – one red for love and one yellow for chagrin – are placed atop the fountain; Pushkin was the first to do this.

Behind the palace is the only surviving **harem** of the four that were traditionally attached to the palace and belonged to the khans' wives. Across the yard you can see the **Falcon Tower**.

The **Khans' Cemetery** is beside the mosque, and way back in the grounds' southeast corner is the **mausoleum of Dilara Bikez**, who may or may not be the Polish beauty who bewitched the khan.

Uspensky Monastery   MONASTERY
Stop for a moment and say 'Aah!' at possibly the cutest little church in a country absolutely jam-packed with them. Part of the small Uspensky Monastery, the gold-domed church has been built into the limestone rock of the surrounding hill, probably by Byzantine monks in the 8th or 9th century. Whitewashed monks' cells, a 'healing' fountain and tiled mosaics cling to the hillside, too.

Chufut-Kale   ANCIENT SITE
(admission 30uah; ⊙10am-5pm) Rising 200m, this long plateau houses a honeycomb of caves and structures where for centuries people have taken refuge. It's wonderful to explore, especially the burial chambers and casemates with large open 'windows' in the vertiginous northern cliff.

First appearing in historical records as Kyrk-Or (Forty Fortifications), the city was settled between the 6th and 12th centuries by Christianised descendants of Sarmatian tribes. The last powerful ruler of the Golden Horde, Tokhtamysh, sheltered here after defeat in the 1390s, and the first Crimean khanate was established at Chufut-Kale in the 15th century, before moving to nearby Bakhchysaray. After the Tatars left, Turkic-Jewish Karaites occupied the city until the mid-19th century, which won the mountain its current name of 'Jewish Fortress'.

Following the track from Uspensky, the best idea is to keep bearing right. The main entrance is not under the flat tin roof to the left of the Chufut-Kale sign, but further up the hill to the right. At this, the 14th-century main **South Gate**, you'll usually be hit for a 12uah entrance fee.

Soon after the gate, you enter a Swiss-cheese composition of carved-out rooms and steps. Behind this a stone path heads along the top of the plateau, past two locked **kenassas** (Karaite prayer houses) in a walled courtyard to the right. There is a **Karaite cultural centre and cafe** in the adjacent former house of the city's last resident, Karaite leader Avraam Firkovich.

To the left of the first intersection stands the red-tile roofed **Muslim mausoleum** (1437) of Dzhanike-Khanym, daughter of Tokhtamysh; to the right is an archway. Head left behind the mausoleum towards the cliff edge and enjoy the view into the valley below. To the right (east), a grassy track leads to two **burial chambers** in the northern side of the cliff.

From here it's hard to get lost; there are more caves until you reach the locked **East Gate**, where the road loops back on itself towards the main gate.

Zyndzhyrly Medrese   NOTABLE BUILDING
(Chain Medrese; vul Basenko 57; admission 20uah; ☉10am-6pm) Carefully restored and re-opened as a museum in 2010, the *medrese* (Muslim religious school) and the adjoining 15th-century mausoleum – where 18 members of a Crimean khan's dynasty are buried – is set to become one of Bakhchysaray's must-sees once the planned exhibition of medieval books and teaching appliances is up and running.

🍽 Sleeping & Eating

Dilara Hanum   B&B **$**
(☏050 930 4163, 065 544 7111; www.bahchisaray.net; vul Ostrovskogo 43; r 320uah) Almost under the escarpment at the end of vul Ostrovskogo, which branches off vul Lenina, this little guesthouse is 'managed by two grannies and a grandson', as their ad goes. However, Dilara is only a part-time granny and hotel manager – she is also the leader of the Crimean Tatar teachers' union and a mine of knowledge on all Tatar-related issues. Rooms look modern and come with attached bathrooms.

Efsane   B&B **$**
(☏478 61; vul Basenko 32-32a; r with/without bathroom 200/250uah) Like other hosts in Bakhcysaray, Shevkiye is a bit of a cultural ambassador for the Crimean Tatar people,

but unlike most she speaks impeccable English having taught the language to generations of local children. Cultural immersion starts at breakfast – each day a new Tatar dish is presented. Excursions, mountain treks and free cooking classes are on offer.

Villa Bakhitgul   B&B **$$**
(☏050 174 3167; www.bahitgul.com.ua; vul Basenko 32; B&B 400uah) The closest you get to a boutique hotel in Bakhchisaray, this place has two large and stylishly decorated rooms: one with dark wooden art nouveau furniture, another looking more oriental. They can organize trips to various parts of Crimea. There's free pick-up from the train or bus station.

Musafir   CRIMEAN TATAR **$**
(vul Gorkogo 21; mains 15-25uah) A specially invited Uzbek *plov* master conjures up a magic stew in the *kazan* bowl, while patrons marvel at the view of the nearby Khan's palace while squatting on Turkish-styled rugs. Apart from the usual Tatar dishes, they make excellent *yantyk* pastry and Bakhchisaray's best Turkish coffee. Enter from vul Lenina.

Aliye   CRIMEAN TATAR **$**
(vul Lesi Ukrainki; most mains 18uah) Popular with locals and tour groups, this super-friendly cafe on the main drag has Turkish-styled rugs on the upper terrace surrounded by a garden, and European tables on the lower terrace, which features an artificial waterfall.

❶ Getting There & Away

Bus

Bakhchysaray's bus station is just off the road linking Simferopol and Sevastopol, where you can a catch a bus in either direction. Frequent direct *marshrutka* go to the inconveniently located Simferopol western bus station (7uah, 30 minutes). Buses originating in Sevastopol terminate at Simferopol's train station (9uah, 50 minutes).

Elektrychka

Local trains shuffle back and forth between Sevastopol (5.60uah, 80 minutes) and Simferopol (5uah, 50 minutes) seven times a day in each direction.

❶ Getting Around

Marshrutka 2 shuttles constantly between the bus station, the train station, Khan's Palace and Uspensky monastery. A taxi ride inside the city costs 20uah.

History

Kyivan Rus

In 882 Oleh of Novgorod – of the Varangians (a Scandinavian civilisation) – declared himself ruler of Kyiv. The city prospered and grew into a large, unified Varangian state that, during its peak, stretched between the Volga River, the Danube River and Baltic Sea. By the 11th and 12th centuries, the Varangian state began to splinter into 10 rival princedoms. When the prince of Suzdal, Andriy Bogolyubov, sacked Kyiv in 1169, the end of the Varangian era was complete.

Prince Roman Mstyslavych regained control of Kyiv in 1203 and united the regions of present-day western, central and northern Ukraine. There was a period of relative prosperity under his dynamic son, King Danylo, and grandson Lev. During this time, much of eastern and southern Ukraine came under the control of the Volga-based Mongol Golden Horde. Its empire was emasculated, however, in the 14th century by the Black Death, as well as by the growing military strength of Russian, Polish and Lithuanian rulers.

Cossacks & Russian Control

By the turn of the 15th century, the uncontrolled steppe in southern Ukraine began to attract runaway serfs, criminals, Orthodox refugees and other outcasts from Poland and Lithuania. Along with a few semi-independent Tatars, the inhabitants formed self-governing militaristic communities and became known as *kazaki* (Cossacks), from the Turkic word meaning 'outlaw, adventurer or free person'. Ukrainian Cossacks eventually developed the self-ruling Cossack Hetmanate, which to some degree reasserted the concept of Ukrainian self-determination.

In 1648 Hetman Bogdan Khmelnytsky (aided by Tatar cavalry) overcame the Polish rulers at the battle of Pyliavtsi. He was forced to engage in a formal but controversial military alliance with Muscovy in 1654, but in 1660 a war broke out between Poland and Russia over control of Ukraine. This ended with treaties that granted control over Kyiv and northern Ukraine to Russia and territory to the west of the Dnipro River to the Poles.

During the course of the 18th century Russia expanded into southern Ukraine and also gained most of Western Ukraine from Poland, except for the far west, which went to the Habsburg Empire.

The 19th century saw a slow growth of nationalist sentiment, which became significant in Kyiv from the 1840s. When the tsarist authorities banned the use of Ukrainian as an official language in the capital, the movement's focus shifted to Austrian-controlled Lviv.

In 1854 Britain and France attacked Russia in the Crimean War, fearing the empire's creep to the Mediterranean Sea. The two-year war resulted in an estimated 250,000 dead on each side, but failed to check Russia's encroachment on the Mediterranean. In 1876 Russian influence over Ukraine was further cemented by Tsar Alexander II's banning of Ukrainian in print and on the stage.

The Early 20th Century

Following WWI and the collapse of tsarist power, Ukraine had a chance – but failed – to gain independence. Civil war broke out and exploded into anarchy: six different armies vied for power, and Kyiv changed hands many times within a year. Eventually Ukraine was again divided between Poland, Romania, Czechoslovakia and Russia. The Russian part became a founding member of the USSR in 1922, and later suffered immensely from a famine that killed millions in the years following Stalin's brutal collectivisation policies. Whether or not the famine was orchestrated by Stalin, who saw Ukrainian nationalism as a threat to Soviet power, remains a hotly contested matter in political and academic circles. What is in no doubt is that millions died of starvation in Ukraine between 1932 and 1933.

The Soviet Red Army rolled into Polish Ukraine in September 1939. The Germans attacked in 1941 and by the year's end controlled virtually all of Ukraine. However, Kharkiv and Kyiv were retaken by the Red Army two years later. An estimated six million Ukrainians died in WWII, which left most of the country's cities in ruin. After the war, the USSR kept the territory it had taken from Poland in 1939.

Independence

After the failed Soviet counter-coup in August 1991, the Verkhovna Rada (Supreme Council) met, and speaker Stanyslav Hurenko's memorable announcement was recorded by the *Economist* for posterity: 'Today we will vote for Ukrainian independence, because if we don't we're in the shit.' In December, some 84% of the population voted in a referendum to back the decision, and Leonid Kravchuk was elected president.

But the economy immediately hit the rocks, things seemed chaotic and people were largely dissatisfied with the results of their move for independence. Finally, the hryvnia, Ukraine's currency, was introduced in 1996, and a process of privatisation kick-started the economy. It wasn't until 1997, under President Leonid Kuchma, that inflation fell from an inconceivable 10,000% to 10%. The economy strengthened but not enough: the hryvnia felt the ripple effects hard from the 1998 Russian financial crisis, dipping 51% in value.

President Kuchma was returned to power in October 1999 after what were widely regarded as dubious elections. His credibility shrivelled further in November 2000 when a tape emerged of Kuchma having an alleged 'rid me of this turbulent priest' moment regarding Georgy Gongadze, a journalist highly critical of Kuchma's presidency, whose beheaded corpse had been discovered in a forest outside Kyiv a few months earlier.

The Orange Revolution

Kuchma was limited to two terms in power, and so he backed Viktor Yanukovych to run for office in the October 2004 presidential elections. But both the international press and the Ukrainian public were all about Viktor Yushchenko, who was poisoned (but not killed) a week before the elections, allegedly by political foes, turning his ruggedly handsome face into...well, just rugged.

Because no one carried more than 50% of the votes in the first round of elections, a run-off was scheduled for 21 November. The official results of this run-off had Yanukovych ahead by 3%, but exit polls showed Yushchenko ahead by 11%. Something wasn't quite right, and by the next day about 500,000 people had peacefully gathered on Kyiv's maydan Nezalezhnosti (Independence Sq), bearing flags, setting up tents, chanting, singing and generally having a good time. Kyiv citizens took complete strangers into their homes, and the media reported a marked drop in city crime during the span of the protest. The world was watching and officials had no choice but to annul the run-off results.

But the protesters stayed on, sometimes numbering more than one million and often withstanding freezing temperatures, until 26 December 2004, when a second run-off took place under intense international scrutiny. Yushchenko won with 52% and was inaugurated 23 January 2005, the climax to the peaceful 'Orange Revolution', so called as it was the colour of choice for the crowds supporting Yushchenko.

The Orange Glow Fades

Alas, the course of true reform never did run smooth in Ukraine (to paraphrase a *Time* magazine observation on Russia) and anyone hoping for a fairy-tale ending would be swiftly disappointed. Less than a year after they had stood shoulder to shoulder on the maydan in Kyiv, the Orange Revolution's heroes had fallen out with each other.

Anyone who's been able to follow Ukraine's political scene since the Orange Revolution probably should get out more. In the late noughties the blonde-braided Yulia Tymoshenko, a feeble president Yushenko and a resurgent Viktor Yanukovych engaged in an absurd political soap opera featuring snap elections, drawn-out coalition deals, fisticuffs in parliament and musical chairs in the prime minister's office. Russia turned off the gas at opportune moments and the West got bored and moved on. The upshot was disillusionment with the Orange Revolution among the population and then Viktor Yanukovych's victory in the April 2010 presidential elections.

The People
The National Psyche

Having endured centuries of many different foreign rulers, Ukrainians are a long-suffering people. They're nothing if not survivors; historically they've had to be, but after suffering a kind of identity theft during centuries of Russian rule, this ancient nation that 'suddenly' emerged some 20 years ago is starting to forge a new personality.

Traditionally, many patriots would unite behind a vague sense of free-spirited Cossack culture and the national poet Taras Shevchenko. This is a religious society, a superstitious society and one in which strong family and community ties still bind, and traditional gender roles persist. It's a culture where people are sometimes friendly and more generous than they can really afford to be. Paradoxically, it's also one in which remnants remain of the Soviet mentality – such as unofficial unhelpfulness and a suspicion of saying too much. As in Russia, many people lead a kind of double life: snarling, elbowing *Homo sovieticus* outside the house but generous, kind and hospitable around the kitchen table.

In patchwork Ukraine, city dwellers and farmers, east and west, young and old, Russian-speaking and Ukrainian-speaking, Hutsul and Tatar – all have very different attitudes. Broadly speaking, Russian-speaking easterners look towards Russia, while Ukrainian-speaking westerners look towards a future in Europe.

Population

As a crossroads between Europe and Asia, Ukraine has been settled by numerous ethnic groups throughout history and has a fascinating underlying mix. However, most people still describe themselves as Ukrainians and, hence, of Slavic origin. According to the last census (2001), 78% of the country's population are ethnically Ukrainian, while 17% of the population, mainly concentrated in the south and east, describe their ethnicity as Russian.

MINORITIES

Ukraine's ethnic minority groups include, in order of size, Belarusians, Moldovans, Tatars, Bulgarians, Hungarians, Romanians, Poles and Jews. Almost all of the country's 260,000 Tatars live in Crimea.

DYING NATION

Since independence, Ukraine's population has fallen more dramatically than that of any other country not affected by war, famine or plague. The number of citizens plummeted from 52 million in 1993 to around 45.8 million (possibly as low as 39 million) in 2010, as birth rates and life expectancy dropped concomitantly.

Religion

As the sheer number of churches in Ukraine attests, religion in this country is pivotal. It has provided comfort during many hard times and even shaped Ukrainian identity: when Volodymyr the Great accepted Orthodox Christianity in 989, he cast Kyivan Rus as a European, rather than Islamic Asian, state.

UKRAINE'S MANY CHURCHES

Today the country's sizeable Christian population is confusingly splintered into three Orthodox churches and one major form of Catholicism.

In the 17th century, when Ukraine came under Russian rule, so did its Orthodox Church. Even now, nearly two decades after independence, the largest Orthodox congregation in the country belongs to the Ukrainian Orthodox Church (UOC-MP), the former Ukrainian section of the Russian Orthodox Church that pays allegiance to the Moscow patriarch. There are also two smaller, breakaway Orthodox churches, which are both more 'Ukrainian' in nature. A Ukrainian Orthodox Church (UOC-KP) was formed in 1992 after independence to pay allegiance to a local Kyiv patriarch. Meanwhile, the Ukrainian Autocephalous Orthodox Church (UAOC), formed during the 19th century in western Ukraine and suppressed by the Soviets, has bounced back since independence. The two main Orthodox churches – Moscow Patriarchate and Kyiv Patriarchate – are in constant conflict and divide the country along roughly the same lines as politics and ethnic allegiance.

Five to six million Ukrainians follow another brand of Christianity. In 1596 the Union of Brest established the Uniate Church (often called the Ukrainian Catholic or Greek Catholic Church) that mixes Orthodox Christian practices with allegiance to the pope.

OTHER FAITHS

Minority faiths include Roman Catholicism, Judaism and, among Crimean Tatars, Sunni Islam. Evangelical, Buddhist, Jehovah's Witness and neo-pagan communities have also emerged since independence from the atheist USSR.

Food & Drink

'Borshch and bread – that's our food.' With this national saying, Ukrainians admit theirs is a cuisine of comfort – full of hearty, mild dishes designed for fierce winters – rather than one of gastronomic zing. Yet, while it's suffered from negative stereotypes of Soviet-style cabbage slop and pernicious pickles, Ukrainian cooking isn't bad these days. In recent years chefs have rediscovered the wholesome appeal of the national cuisine. Plenty of Ukrainian-themed restaurants offer the chance to sample local specialities made with fresh ingredients.

If Ukraine has a culinary capital, it's probably Kyiv, but there are interesting regional sidelines, too. The Hutsul people of the Carpathians favour berries and mushrooms, plus their own speciality cheese *brynza* and polenta-style *banush* or *mamalyha*. Central Asian–style Tatar cuisine spices up the menus in Crimea.

While most Ukrainians are carnivores by nature, vegetarians won't find eating out too trying, especially in the larger cities where pizza joints and international restaurants abound. Even Ukrainian cuisine can be meat-free if you stick to a fairly bland diet of *deruny* or potato-and-mushroom *varenyky*. However, it's always a good idea to specify that you want a meat-free salad and borshch is, sadly, best avoided if you're strict about your diet. Even 'vegetarian' versions are often made using beef stock.

Staples & Specialities

Borshch Locals would have you know that *borshch* (борщ) is Ukrainian – not Russian, not Polish, but Ukrainian – and there's nothing better than a steaming bowlful in winter. The main ingredients are beetroot, cabbage and herbs, but regional variations can include sausages, red kidney beans, marrow or marinated apples.

Bread Dark and white varieties of *khlib* (хліб) are available every day. Bread is often used in religious ceremonies and on special occasions. Visitors are traditionally greeted with bread and salt.

Cabbage rolls *Holubtsy* (голубці) are cabbage rolls stuffed with seasoned rice and meat and stewed in a tomato and soured cream sauce.

Kasha Pretty much any grain is called *kasha* (каша) in Ukrainian, and while the word might be used to describe what Westerners would call porridge, more commonly it turns out to be buckwheat. The latter appears as a side dish, as stuffing or as an unusual but filling breakfast gruel.

Pancakes Three types of pancake might land on your plate. *Deruny* (деруни) are potato pancakes, and are served with soured cream and vegetables or meat. *Nalysnyky* (налисники) are thin crepes, while *mlyntsy* (млинці) are thicker and smaller, like Russian *blyny*.

Varenyky Similar to Polish *pierogi*, *varenyky* (вареники) are to Ukraine what dim sum is to China and filled pasta to Italy. These small half-moon shaped dumplings have more than 50 different traditional vegetarian and meat fillings. They're usually served with soured cream.

Drinks

Ukraine produces some very quaffable beers. In fact, the beer market is booming, with many young people turning their backs on vodka in favour of it. Chernihivske, Lvivske, Slavutych and Obolon are the most popular brands.

Wines are produced in Crimea and the Transcarpathian region, though, sadly, the best wines still come from neighbouring Moldova.

On street corners in summer, you'll see small drinks tankers selling *kvas* (квас), a gingery, beer-like soft drink which is made from sugar and old black bread.

The biggest name in Ukrainian vodka is undoubtedly Nemiroff (www.nemiroff.ua).

Where To Eat & Drink

Restaurant (ресторан) and cafe (кафе) sound similar in English and Ukrainian. Some Ukrainian restaurants specialise in a particular dish, such as a *varenychna* (варенична), which serves only *varenyky*. A *stolova* (столова) is a Russian-style self-service canteen.

Be aware that prices for many meat and fish dishes are listed on the menu by weight. For example, *shashlyk* might look good value at 10uah, unless it's actually 10uah per 100g. Read the menu carefully and if in doubt, ask.

The Arts

Literature

The Ukrainian writer is Taras Shevchenko (1814–61). Born a serf and orphaned as a teenager, Shevchenko studied painting at the Academy of Arts in St Petersburg, where in 1840 he published his first work, *Kobzar* (The Bard), a book of eight romantic poems. He was exiled in 1847 for his satirical poems about Russian oppression. Today every town across the land has a Shevchenko Square or Street.

Arguably the most talented and prolific Ukrainian writer of the early 20th century was Ivan Franko, whose scholarly and moving works shed light on the issues that plague Ukrainian society. He, too, was persecuted

TOP TEN BEST READS

» *Death and the Penguin* (1996) by Andrey Kurkov

» *The White Guard* (1925) by Mikhail Bulgakov

» *Taras Bulba* (1835) by Nikolai Gogol

» *Everything is Illuminated* (2002) by Jonathan Safran Foer

» *Borderland* (1998) by Anna Reid

» *Complete Works* (reissued 2005) by Isaac Babel

» *A Short History of Tractors in Ukrainian* (2005) by Marina Lewycka

» *Street of Crocodiles* (1934) by Bruno Schulz

» *Dead Souls* (1842) by Nikolai Gogol

» *Recreations* (1998) by Yuri Andrukhovych

by the Russians. Lesya Ukrainka, a wealthy young woman whose frail health kept her indoors writing moody poetry, could be considered a Ukrainian Emily Dickinson.

Two internationally renowned authors usually claimed by Russia are Ukrainian-born. Mikhail Bulgakov's (1891–1940) first novel, *The White Guard,* is set in his native Kyiv. Nikolai Gogol's (1809–52) novels *Evenings on a Farm near Dikanka* and *Dead Souls* and short story *Taras Bulba* have links to his country of birth.

As far as contemporary writers go, Kyiv-based author Andrey Kurkov (b 1961) has been called Bulgakov's heir. His *Death and the Penguin, Penguin Lost* and *The President's Last Love* indulge in the same flights of fancy as Bulgakov's classic *The Master and Margarita.*

Cinema

Must-see pre-departure films include *Shadows of Forgotten Ancestors* (1964), a wonderfully shot (and subsequently banned) film full of shaggy Hutsul customs and symbolism from the Carpathians, and Sergei Eisenstein's *Battleship Potemkin* (1925) shot in Odesa.

Icons & Pysanky

Icons are small holy images painted on a lime-wood panel with a mix of tempera, egg yolk and hot wax. Brought to Ukraine from Constantinople by Volodymyr the Great in the 10th century and remaining the key religious art until the 17th century, icons were attributed with healing and spiritual powers.

Painted Easter eggs *(pysanky)* are an ancient Slavonic art found across Eastern Europe. Designs are drawn in wax on the eggshell – the egg is dyed one colour and the process continually repeated until a complex pattern is built up.

Painting

Ukrainian-born Ilya Repin gained international fame. His famous *Zaporizhsky Cossacks Writing a Letter to the Turkish Sultan* and other Romantic paintings are found in the Art Museum in Kharkiv.

Ivan Ayvazosky is regarded as one of the world's best seascape painters. Ethnically Armenian, he was born and lived in Feodosiya, Crimea, where hundreds of his works can be found in the Ayvazosky Museum.

Some of Ukraine's oldest frescoes are found in Kyiv's St Sophia's Cathedral.

Music

Ukrainian folk music developed as a form of storytelling. The guardians of Ukrainian folklore, *kobzary* were wandering minstrels who travelled from town to town spreading news through song while strumming their 65-string *bandura.*

Okean Elzy (www.okeanelzy.com) is one of the country's bigger music sensations. The well-respected rock group sounds a little like the Clash and has a charismatic lead singer. The most famous Ukrainian songstress of the last 40 years bar none is Sofia Rotaru (b 1947), an ethnic Moldovan born near Chernivtsi. Most of what Ukraine produces today is porno chick pop, though cross-dressing comedian/singer Verka Serduchka occupies a category all his/her own. The same is true of NYC gypsy punk outfit Gogol Bordello, whose eccentric singer, Eugene Hutz, hails from Kyiv.

Chornobyl

The Accident

In perhaps the blackest of ironies ever known to history, the world's worst nuclear disaster was the result of an unnecessary safety test. On the night of 25 April 1986, reactor No 4 at the electricity-producing Chornobyl power plant in northern Ukraine was due to be shut down for regular maintenance. Workers decided to use the opportunity to see if, in the event of a shutdown, enough electricity remained in the grid to power the systems that cooled the reactor core, and turned off the emergency cooling system. For various reasons, including a design flaw in the type of RBMK reactor at Chornobyl, operational errors and flouted safety procedures, the result of the test was a power surge, a steam explosion and a full-blown nuclear explosion. At 1.26am on the morning of 26 April 1986, the reactor blew its 500-tonne top and spewed nearly nine tonnes of radioactive material into the sky in a fireball. Fallout blew north and west, dropping mainly over Belarus, but also over Ukraine, Russia, Poland and the Baltic region. Some material also wafted over Sweden, whose scientists were the first to alert the world.

Immediate Aftermath

The Soviets initially remained silent while the emergency unfolded. Two people died in the explosion and another 29 firemen – sent in to clean up without proper radiation protection – died in the following weeks. Some 135,000 people were evacuated from the satellite town of Prypyat and a 30km radius around the plant, but were told it was only 'temporary'. Six days after the disaster, with radioactive clouds blowing over Kyiv, May Day parades in the blissfully ignorant city went ahead.

Chornobyl Today

Today the long-term effects of the disaster are still being felt and assessed. The most obvious impact has been an upsurge of thyroid cancer in children, with nearly 2000 cases reported. Studies suggest that of the 600,000 'liquidators' brought in to clean up the site, more than 4000 have died from exposure and 170,000 suffer from terminal diseases. In addition, some 35,000 sq km of forest is contaminated, and the meat, milk, vegetables and fruit produced there have higher than normal levels of radioactivity. Silt carried down the Dnipro is radioactive, although the extent is still not fully known. Birth defects, suicides, deaths from heart disease and alcoholism are also unusually high in the region. It's estimated that by 2015 the disaster will have cost the economy US$200 billion, although, of course, all the figures surrounding the disaster and its toll are disputed.

The last working reactor at Chornobyl, No 3, was finally shut down in 2000. However, reactor No 4 remains 'a monster, a monster which is always near', according to one of the 8000 scientific staff and monitors who still work on site, half of them commuting there daily from the new town of Slavutych.

After the accident, the damaged reactor and 180 tonnes of radioactive mess were hastily enclosed in a concrete-and-steel sarcophagus. However, no one really knows the state of the radioactive core inside the ruined reactor and that hastily built sarcophagus has long been crumbling. After several false starts, and a growing sense of outrage, a deal was finally signed in 2007 to begin building a secure new steel covering. Construction of this $1.7 billion shelter is being overseen by the European Bank for Reconstruction and Development (EBRD) and should be completed by 2012.

Unlikely Tourist Attraction

Chornobyl has become possibly the world's top 'dark tourism' destination, with tours becoming much easier to arrange and a little cheaper as they increase in popularity. If you're travelling alone or in a small group you'll save a lot of money by latching onto another group. Kyiv-based tour companies such as SoloEast (www.tourkiev.com), New Logic (www.newlogic.com.ua) and Sam (www.sam.ua) all run tours. Rates vary widely among travel agencies, so get several quotes.

SURVIVAL GUIDE

Directory A–Z

Accommodation

Accommodation will be your single biggest expense in Ukraine, but with the recent fall in value of the hryvnya, rooms are slightly more affordable than they once were.

PRICE RANGES

In this chapter prices quoted are for rooms with a private bathroom. The following price indicators apply (for a high-season double room):

€€€ more than 800uah

€€ 400uah to 800uah

€ less than 400uah

HOMESTAYS

Crashing with a local isn't just cheap but also a great way to get to know individual cities. Hospitality clubs such as www.couchsurfing.com and www.hospitalityclub.org have thousands of members in Ukraine.

HOSTELS

Hostelling is now a well-established sector in Ukraine's accommodation market, especially in Kyiv, Lviv and Odesa.

Hostelling Ukraine International(www.hihostels.com.ua) gathers together all of Ukraine's hostels in one place. Online booking is available. Hostels listed by **Youth Tourism & Hostels of Ukraine** (www.hostels.org.ua) tend to be in rather odd locations.

HOTELS

Ukraine has a bewildering array of hotel and room types. At the bottom are Soviet-era budget crash pads for as little as 50uah; at the top are 'six-star' overpriced luxury in OTT surroundings. Everything in between can be hit and miss, and there are no national standards to follow, so forget any star ratings you might see.

It's only worth booking ahead in Odesa and Crimea in summer, in big cities in late December and early January, and in the Carpathians from November to March.

PRIVATE RENTALS

In Crimea and Odesa you'll find people standing outside train or bus stations offering rooms in their houses or private apartment rentals. Although the numbers of *babushky* (grannies) doing so are dwindling, it's also still possible in Kyiv. Expect to pay around 250uah per night for a one-room apartment (more in Kyiv). Alternatively contact an official rental agency.

Business Hours

Business hours can be hard to pin down in Ukraine. Lunch breaks (1pm to 2pm or 2pm to 3pm) are an all-too-common throwback to Soviet days. Sunday closing is rare. Normal business hours are listed below. Only places noticeably deviating from these hours are noted in individual listings.

Banks 9am-5pm or 10am-6pm

Restaurants noon-11pm

Shops 9am-6pm, to 8pm or 9pm in big cities

Sights 9am-5pm or 6pm, closed at least one day a week

Customs Regulations

You are allowed to carry up to US$1000 when entering Ukraine without having to sign any documentation. The following can also be imported duty-free: 1L of spirits, 2L of wine, 5L of beer, 200 cigarettes or 250g of tobacco, and €50 worth of food (not exceeding 2kg).

If you exceed these limits, you'll have to sign a *deklaratsiya* (customs declaration). Be careful not to lose this completed form – you will need to present it when departing the country.

Embassies & Consulates

The following are in Kyiv (☏044) unless otherwise noted.

Australia (☏235 7586; Apt 11, vul Kominterna 18; Ⓜ Vokzalna)

Belarus (☏537 5200; vul Mykhayla Kotsyubynskoho 3; Ⓜ Universytet)

Canada (☏590 3100; www.canadainternational.gc.ca/ukraine; Yaroslaviv Val 31; Ⓜ Zoloti Vorota)

France (☏590 3600; www.ambafrance-ua.org; vul Reytarska 39; Ⓜ Zoloti Vorota)

Georgia (☏451 4353, 451 4356; vul Melnikova 83D, Section 4; Ⓜ Lukyanivska) Odesa Consulate (☏0482 726 4727; vul Tolstoho 21)

Germany (☏247 6800; vul Bohdana Khmelnytskoho 25; Ⓜ Zoloti Vorota)

Hungary (☏230 8001; vul Reytarska 33; Ⓜ Zoloti Vorota) Uzhhorod consulate (☏615 788; vul Pravoslavna 12)

Moldova (☏521 2279; www.ucraina.mfa.md; vul Sichnevoho Povstannya 6; Ⓜ Arsenalna)

Netherlands (☏490 8200; www.netherlands-embassy.com.ua; pl Kontraktova 7; Ⓜ Kontraktova ploshcha)

Poland (☏230 0700; www.polska.com.ua; vul Yaroslaviv Val 12; Ⓜ Zoloti Vorota)

Romania (☏234 5261; http://kiev.mae.ro; vul Mykhayla Kotsyubynskoho 8; Ⓜ Universytet) Odesa consulate (☏048 725 0399; http://odessa.mae.ro; vul Bazarna 31); Chernivtsi consulate (☏037 545 434; vul Skilna 16)

Russia (☏244 0961; www.embrus.org.ua; pr Vozdvkhoflotsky 27; Ⓜ Vokzalna) Kyiv consulate (☏284 6816; vul Kutuzova 8; Ⓜ Pecherska; Odesa consulate (☏048 240 164; Gagarinskoe Plato 14)

UK (☏490 3660; http://ukinukraine.fco.gov.uk/en; vul Desyatynna 9; Ⓜ Maydan Nezalezhnosti) Kyiv consulate (☏494 3418; Artyom Centre, vul Hlybochytska 4; Ⓜ Lukyanivska)

USA (☏490 0000; http://kyiv.usembassy.gov; vul Yuriya Kotsyubynskoho 10; Ⓜ Lukyanivska) Kyiv consulate (☏207 7071; vul Mykoly Pymonenka 6; Ⓜ Lukyanivska)

Food

In this chapter, the following price indicators apply (for a main meal):

€€€ more than 150uah

€€ 50uah to 150uah

€ less than 50uah

For information on Ukrainian cuisine, see p988.

Gay & Lesbian Travellers

Ukraine is generally more tolerant of homosexuality than its neighbour Russia, but that's not saying much. Out-and-proud gay views mix badly with those of the Orthodox Church, hence most people's outwardly conservative attitudes. Homosexuality is legal in Ukraine, but attitudes vary across the country. Useful gay websites include www.gayua.com, www.gay.org.ua and www.gaylvov.at.ua.

Internet Access

Internet service in Ukraine can be very intermittent, with networks and servers going down frequently. Many upmarket and midrange hotels now offer free wi-fi internet access.

Restaurants and cafes are rapidly installing wi-fi technology. Upmarket hotels often have a business centre with a couple of terminals hooked up to the internet. Internet cafes are not as common as they once were but there's usually at least one in every town. Internet cafes often double up as noisy gaming centres. Prices for internet access range from about 4uah in smaller cities to up to 12uah in Kyiv.

Money

Coins come in denominations of one, five, 10, 25 and 50 kopecks, plus the rare one hryvnia. Notes come in one, two, five, 10, 20, 50, 100, 200 and 500 hryvnya. It's virtually impossible to buy any hryvnya before you get to Ukraine.

ATMs are very common in cities, less widespread in smaller towns and nonexistent in rural areas. They accept all major cards and issue dollars as well as hryvnya.

CASH

US dollars (post-1990 issue only), the euro and Russian roubles are the easiest currencies to exchange. Banks and currency exchange offices will not accept notes with rips or tears.

CREDIT CARDS

Credit cards are increasingly accepted by upmarket hotels, restaurants and shops both in and outside Kyiv. However, Ukraine remains primarily a cash economy.

Post

The national postal service is run by **Ukrposhta** (www.ukrposhta.com). Sending a postcard or a letter up to 20g costs 5.50uah to anywhere outside Ukraine.

Mail takes about a week or less to Europe, and two to three weeks to the USA or Australia.

Public Holidays

The main public holidays in Ukraine are:

New Year's Day 1 January

Orthodox Christmas 7 January

International Women's Day 8 March

Orthodox Easter (Paskha) April

Labour Day 1-2 May

Victory Day (1945) 9 May

Constitution Day 28 June

Independence Day (1991) 24 August

Safe Travel

Despite what you may have heard, Ukraine is not a dangerous, crime-ridden place. The infamous mafia are not interested in tourists.

CRIME

Don't be overly worried about crime in Ukraine, which is normally as safe as most Western European countries. However, petty theft is a serious problem. Avoiding becoming a victim of theft is a matter of common sense: don't flash your money around and keep an eye on your wallet and belongings, particularly on public transport and in crowded situations.

Telephone

Ukraine recently simplified the way numbers are dialled, banishing Soviet-era prefixes and dialling tones for good. All numbers now start with ☏0.

PHONE CODES

Ukraine's country code is ☏0038. To call Kyiv from London, dial ☏00 38 044 and the subscriber number.

To call internationally, dial ☏0, wait for a second tone, then dial 0 again, followed by the country code, city code and number.

MOBILE PHONES

European GSM phones usually work in Ukraine. If you intend making a few calls, it's more economical to get a prepaid SIM card locally.

Toilets

A women's toilet *(tualet)* is marked with a upwards-facing triangle or ж (for *zhinochy)*; men's are marked with a downwards facing triangle, ч or м (for *cholovichy* or *muzhcheny)*.

Travellers With Disabilities

Even Kyiv, the best-equipped Ukrainian city, isn't that friendly to people with physical disabilities. The rest of the country is worse.

Visas

Tourist visas for stays of less than 90 days aren't required by citizens of the EU, Canada, the USA, Iceland, Japan, Norway, Switzerland and South Korea. Australians and New Zealanders need a visa.

Visas are required for citizens of most other countries and for anyone intending to work, study, take up permanent residency or stay for more than 90 days.

GETTING THERE & AWAY

Getting There & Away

The majority of visitors fly to Ukraine – generally to Kyiv. However, low-cost flights to neighbouring countries mean a growing number of travellers are entering the country overland. Flights, tours and rail tickets can be booked online at www.lonelyplanet.com/bookings.

Entering the Country

Your passport must be valid for at least one month beyond your intended departure from Ukraine. It must contain a visa if you need one. Border officials ask few questions these days and immigration cards were scrapped in September 2010.

Air

Low-cost airlines have struggled to find their way into Ukraine, but the situation is likely to change once Lviv's new terminal is built.

AIRPORTS & AIRLINES

Most international flights use Kyiv's main airport, **Boryspil international airport** (KBP; www.airport-borispol.kiev.ua). Other flights go to **Lviv International Airport** (LWO; www.

airport.lviv.ua) and **Odesa International Airport** (ODS; http://www.airport.odessa.ua)

Ukraine International Airlines (PS; www.flyuia.com) is Ukraine's international airline carrier. Always check this airline's rates against your country's national carrier as UIA's ticket prices are often lower. **Aerosvit** (VV; www.aerosvit.com). Also operates domestic flights.

The following airlines also fly to/from Ukraine:

Aeroflot (SU; www.aeroflot.ru)

Air Baltic (BT; www.airbaltic.com)

Air France (AF; www.airfrance.com)

Austrian Airlines (OS; www.aua.com)

British Airways (BA; www.ba.com)

Carpatair (V3; www.carpatair.com)

Czech Airlines (OK; www.czechairlines.com)

Delta (DL; www.delta.com)

El Al (LY; www.elal.co.il)

Estonian Air (OV; www.estonian-air.ee)

Finnair (AY; www.finnair.com)

germanwings (4U; www.germanwings.com)

KLM (KL; www.klm.com)

LOT (LO; www.lot.com)

Lufthansa (LH; www.lufthansa.com)

Malév (MA; www.malev.hu)

Turkish Airlines (TK; www.turkishairlines.com)

Wizzair (W6; www.wizzair.com)

Land

BORDER CROSSINGS

Crossing the border into Ukraine is a fairly straightforward, if slightly drawn-out, affair. The Poland–Ukraine and Romania–Ukraine borders are popular cigarette-smuggling routes, hence the thorough customs checks. Expect customs personnel to scrutinise your papers and search your vehicle.

BUS

Buses are slower, less frequent and less comfortable than trains for long-distance travel.

See Getting There & Away listings under cities and towns for bus transport details on fares and schedules to destinations outside Ukraine.

CAR & MOTORCYCLE

To bring your own vehicle into the country, you'll need your original registration papers (photocopies not accepted) and a 'Green Card' International Motor Insurance Cer-

A cheap way of getting to Ukraine is to take a budget flight to a neighbouring country, then cross the border by land. Poland has the most flights from Western Europe, but Hungary, Romania and Slovakia also provide a handful of options.

» **easyJet** (www.easyjet.com) This no-frills airline links the UK, France and Germany with Budapest and Krakow.

» **Jet2** (www.jet2.com) Links cities in northern England and Scotland with Krakow and Budapest.

» **Ryanair** (www.ryanair.com) This Irish budget airline connects five cities in the UK with the Polish city of Rzeszow, a mere 90km from the border with Ukraine. There are also daily flights to Budapest and Bratislava (Slovakia) from where you can continue by train.

» **Wizzair** (www.wizzair.com) Wizzair has popular direct flights to Kyiv from London Luton, but also connects the UK with Katowice and Warsaw in Poland and Cluj-Napoca in northern Romania.

Check the websites www.flycheapo.com and www.skyscanner.net for the latest flight information.

tificate. Your registration number will be noted, and you'll have to explain if leaving the country without your vehicle.

Sea

Some scheduled ferry services do exist, but as across the ex-USSR, boat services are erratic and sailings are cancelled without notice. Basing your travel plans around sea or river travel is not advisable.

Getting Around
Air

The national network mainly uses Kyiv as a hub. To fly between two Ukrainian cities you almost always have to go via the capital.

AIRLINES IN UKRAINE

Aerosvit (www.aerosvit.ua) Based at Boryspil international airport in Kyiv.

Dniproavia (www.dniproavia.com) Major domestic airline serving many routes.

Ukraine International Airlines (www.flyuia.com) Based at Boryspil international airport in Kyiv. Domestically links Kyiv, Lviv and Donetsk, but is essentially an international airline.

Ukrainian-Mediterranean Airlines (www.umairlines.com) Based at Boryspil international airport in Kyiv.

Wizzair (www.wizzair.com) Not a Ukrainian airline, but does operate one handy domestic flight between Kyiv and Simferopol.

TICKETS

Kiyavia Travel (www.kiyavia.com) has branches across the country and you can book most flights with them. The website lists timetables, prices and the aircraft that are used – all in English.

Bicycle

Cycling is a terrific way to see the real Ukraine, despite the crazed drivers and potholed roads. The Carpathians and Crimea – in that order – are particularly pleasant cycling country. Volunteers involved in the **Bikeland** (www.bikeland.com) project in the Carpathians have marked out 1300km of mountain bike trails.

Bus

Buses serve every city and small town, but are best for short trips (three hours or less) as vehicles are generally small, old and overcrowded. Tickets are sold at the bus station right up to departure and resemble shop-till receipts.

Autolux (www.autolux.ua), **Gunsel** (www.gunsel.com.ua) and **Ukrbus** (www.ukrbus.com) run main intercity routes using Westernstandard coaches. While travelling anywhere in the former Soviet Union, you are likely to encounter the *marshrutka*. These are basically minibuses that ply bus routes but stop anywhere on request. They're most common in big cities but also serve intercity routes. Fares are usually higher than on buses but journey times shorter.

UKRAINE GETTING THERE & AWAY

DIRECT TRAIN CONNECTIONS BETWEEN UKRAINE & NEIGHBOURING COUNTRIES

ROUTE	DURATION	FREQUENCY
Kyiv-Budapest	24hr	One
Lviv-Budapest	14hr	One daily
Kyiv-Minsk	11hr	One or two daily
Lviv-Minsk	13hr	One daily
Kyiv-Budapest	24hr	One daily
Lviv-Budapest	14hr	One daily
Kyiv-Chişinău	14-17hr	Three daily
Kyiv-Warsaw Wschodnia	17hr	One daily
Kyiv-Wroclaw	24hr	One daily
Lviv-Przemysl	21/2hr	Two daily
Lviv-Krakow	6hr	Two daily
Lviv-Warsaw Central	16hr	One daily
Chernivtsi-Ocniţa	6hr	One daily
Kyiv-Bucharest Nord	25hr	One daily
Kyiv-Moscow	14-16hr	Up to 17 daily
Kyiv-St Petersburg	24hr	One daily
Lviv-Moscow	24hr	Up to five daily
Lviv-St Petersburg	30hr	Odd dates, daily summer
Kyiv-Bratislava	29hr	One or two daily
Lviv-Bratislava	19hr	One or two daily

Hitching

You simply can't hitchhike around Ukraine for free. Hitching a ride is common, but it's necessary to pay drivers for the privilege. Stand at the roadside, hand up in the air, palm down.

Local Transport

Ukrainian cities are navigable by trolleybus, tram, bus and metro in Kyiv. Urban public transport systems are usually overworked and overcrowded. A ticket for one ride by bus, tram or trolleybus costs 1uah to 1.50uah. There are no return, transfer, timed or day tickets available anywhere, and tickets have to be punched on board (or ripped by the conductor).

Metro barriers take plastic tokens (zhetony), sold at counters inside stations.

Train

For long journeys, overnight train is the preferred method of travel in Ukraine. Services are incredibly punctual and you can save on accommodation costs by taking sleeper trains.

For schedules see **Ukrainian Railways** (www.uz.gov.ua, in Ukrainian). It's the official Ukrainian Railway website, but is hard to navigate. A timetable for the entire ex-USSR (in English) can be found at **Poezda.net** (www.poezda.net).

All classes have assigned places. Carriage (vahon) and bunk (mesto) numbers are printed on tickets.

SV Spalny vahon (SV) – 1st-class couchette (sleeper) compartment for two people – costs two to three times more than kupe.

Kupe 2nd-class sleeper compartment for four people – about twice as costly as platskart. Train prices quoted in this chapter are for kupe.

Platskart 3rd-class open-carriage sleeper with around 50 bunks.

TICKETS

You no longer have to show your passport when buying tickets.

Survival Guide

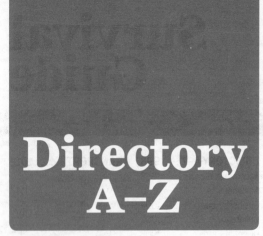

Directory A–Z

Accommodation

There's accommodation to match every budget in Eastern Europe, from Soviet-era concrete behemoths, five star luxury palaces and international hotel groups to rural campsites and homely grandmother-run private rooms. In this guide we've listed reviews by author preference and prices are quoted in the currency used in each country.

Categories

We have divided our accommodation selections into the following three categories:

Budget Bare-bones hostels and hotels, often with shared bathrooms and very limited amenities.

Midrange Hotels and guesthouses with private facilities and more often than not, television and wi-fi.

Top end Well-appointed, high-standard hotels with all the amenities and creature comforts you'd expect.

See individual country chapters to see how the price categories are broken down, as in a region as large and diverse as Eastern Europe, it's not been possible to come up with one book-wide price range for each category.

Price Icons

The price indicators in this book refer to the cost of a double room in high season, including private bathroom (any combination of toilet, bathtub, shower and washbasin) and excluding breakfast unless otherwise noted.

Reservations

Reservations are generally a good idea in high season and can usually be made by phone or, less regularly, on-

line. Hostels and cheap hotels fill up very quickly, especially in popular backpacker destinations such as Prague, Budapest and Kraków.

In most cities in Eastern Europe, there's a shortage of good-value midrange accommodation options. Some tourist offices may be able to make reservations on your behalf (some charge a small fee for this service), but in general, do not expect a Western European standard of service from tourist offices in Eastern Europe. Many countries, such as Belarus, Moldova, Ukraine and Kosovo have no tourist offices at all.

Seasons

» Rates in this guide are high season (typically July-August).

» Rates often drop outside the high season – in some cases by as much as 50%.

» In business-oriented hotels in cities, rooms are most expensive from Monday to Thursday and cheaper over the weekend.

Camping

The cheapest way to stay in Eastern Europe is to camp, and there are many camping grounds throughout the region. That said, a large proportion of the region's attractions are found in cities, where there often simply aren't any camping grounds. Most camping grounds near urban areas are large sites, intended mainly for motorists, though they're usually accessible by public transport and there's almost always space for backpackers with tents. Many camping grounds in Eastern Europe rent small on-site cabins, bungalows or caravans for double or triple the regular camping fee; in the most popular resorts all the bungalows are usually full in July and August.

The standard of camping grounds in Eastern Europe varies from country to country. They're unreliable in Romania, crowded in Slovenia and Hungary (especially on Lake Balaton), and variable in the Czech Republic, Poland, Slovakia and Bulgaria. Some countries, including Moldova and Belarus, have very few official camping grounds, though you can usually find somewhere to pitch your tent. Croatia's coast has nudist camping grounds galore (signposted FKK, the German acronym for 'naturist'); they're excellent places to stay because of their secluded locations, although they can be a bit far from other attractions.

» Camping grounds may be open from April to October, May to September, or perhaps only June to August, depending on the category of the facility, the location and demand.

» A few private camping grounds are open year-round.

» Camping in the wild is usually illegal; ask local people about the situation before you pitch your tent on a beach or in an open field.

» In Eastern Europe you are sometimes allowed to build a campfire; ask first, however.

» See p1002 for information on camping discount cards.

Farmhouses

'Village tourism', which means staying at a farmhouse, is highly developed in Estonia, Latvia, Lithuania and Slovenia, and popular in Hungary. It's like staying in a private room or pension, except that the participating farms are in picturesque rural areas and may have activities nearby such as horse riding, kayaking, skiing and cycling. See **Worldwide Opportunities on Organic Farms** (www.wwoof.org) for information about working on organic farms in exchange for room and board.

Guesthouses & Pensions

Small private pensions are now very common in parts of Eastern Europe. Priced somewhere between hotels and private rooms, pensions typically have fewer than a dozen rooms, and may sometimes have a small restaurant or bar on the premises. You'll get much more personal service at a pension than you would at a hotel, though there's a bit less privacy. Pensions can be a lifesaver if you arrive at night or on a weekend, when the travel agencies assigning private rooms are closed. Call ahead to check prices and ask about reservations – someone will usually speak some halting English, German or Russian.

Homestays & Private Rooms

Homestays are often the best and most authentic way to see daily life in Eastern Europe. It's perfectly legal to stay with someone in a private home, although in countries such as Russia where visa registration is necessary, you'll probably have to pay a travel agency to register your visa with a hotel.

In most Eastern European countries, travel agencies can arrange accommodation in private rooms in local homes. In Hungary you can get a private room almost anywhere, but in the other countries only the main tourist centres have them. Some rooms are like mini apartments, with cooking facilities and private bathrooms for the sole use of guests. Prices are low but there's often a 30% to 50% surcharge if you stay fewer than three nights. In Hungary, the Czech Republic and Croatia, higher taxation has made staying in a private room less attractive than before, but it's still good value and cheaper than a hotel.

People will frequently approach you at train or bus stations in Eastern Europe

offering a private room or a hostel bed. This can be good or bad – it's impossible to generalise. Just make sure it's not in some cardboard-quality housing project in the outer suburbs and that you negotiate a clear price. Obviously, if you are staying with strangers, you shouldn't leave your valuables behind when you go out; certainly don't leave your money, credit cards or passport.

You don't have to go through an agency or an intermediary on the street for a private room. Any house, cottage or farmhouse with *Zimmer Frei* (German), *sobe* (Slovak) or *szoba kiadó* (Hungarian) displayed outside is advertising the availability of private rooms; just knock on the door and ask if any are available.

Staying with Eastern European friends will almost certainly be a wonderful experience, thanks to the full hospitality the region is justly famous for. Make sure you bring some small gifts for your hosts – it's a deeply ingrained cultural tradition throughout the region.

Hostels

Hostels offer the cheapest roof over your head in Eastern Europe, and you don't have to be a youngster to take advantage of them. Most hostels are part of the national Youth Hostel Association (YHA), which is affiliated with the **Hostelling International** (HI; www.hihostels.com) umbrella organisation.

» Hostels affiliated with HI can be found in most Eastern European countries. A hostel card is seldom required, though you sometimes get a small discount if you have one.

» At a hostel, you get a bed for the night plus use of communal facilities; there's often a kitchen where you can prepare your own meals. You may be required to have a sleeping sheet, if you don't have one, you can usually hire one for a small fee.

» Hostels vary widely in their character and quality. The hostels in Poland tend to be extremely basic but they're inexpensive and friendly. In the Czech Republic and Slovakia, many hostels are actually fairly luxurious junior hotels with double rooms, and are often fully occupied by groups.

» A number of privately run hostels in Prague and Budapest are student dormitories that are open to travellers for six or seven weeks in summer only.

» There are many hostel guides and websites with listings, including the hostel bible, HI's *Europe*. Many hostels accept reservations by phone, fax or email, but not always during peak periods (though they might hold a bed for you for a couple of hours if you call from the train or bus station). You can also book hostels through national hostel offices.

Hotels

At the bottom end of the scale, cheap hotels may be no more expensive than private rooms or guesthouses, while at the other extreme you'll find beautifully designed boutique hotels and five-star hotels with price tags to match.

» Single rooms can be hard to find in Eastern Europe, as you are generally charged by the room and not by the number of people in it.

» The cheapest rooms sometimes have a washbasin but no bathroom, which means you'll have to go down the corridor to use the toilet and shower.

» Breakfast may be included in the price of a room, or it may be extra.

Rental Accommodation

In larger cities without a thriving hotel and hostel culture, you may find the best option is to rent an apartment from a local agency. These can often be better value than a hotel, mean you can self-cater and give you far more independence, but they can also be of varying quality and some accommodation can be far flung. The agencies operate independently and sometimes quasi-legally, so you will have no recourse if you have a disagreement with them. The agencies we have listed in this book have good reputations or we have used them ourselves.

» Cities where renting accommodation is a good idea include Prague, Budapest, Bratislava, Minsk, Kraków and Moscow.

» When dealing with agencies you've found online, never send money in advance unless you're sure they are genuine.

University Accommodation

Some universities rent out space in student halls in July and August. This is quite popular in the Baltic countries, Croatia, the Czech Republic, Hungary, Macedonia, Poland, Slovakia and Slovenia.

» Accommodation will sometimes be in single rooms (but is more commonly in doubles or triples), and cooking facilities may be available.

» Enquire at the college or university, at student-information services or at local tourist offices.

Activities

Birdwatching

The countries of Eastern Europe may not be the world's best destination for spotting our feathered friends, but birders will certainly get a look at some unusual species in Albania (p69), the Danube Delta (p756) in Romania, and several locations around Serbia (p856).

Canoeing & Kayaking

Launch a kayak, raft or canoe at one of the following waterways:

» Poland's Great Masurian Lakes (p686)

» Slovenia's Soča River (p928)

» the Czech Republic's Vltava River (p316)

» Latvia's Gauja River (p486)

» Croatia's Elafiti and Kornati Islands (p265)

» Montenegro's Bay of Kotor (p584)

Cycling

The hills and mountains of Eastern Europe can be heavy going, but this is offset by the abundance of things to see. Physical fitness is *not* a major prerequisite for cycling on the plains of eastern Hungary, but the persistent wind might slow you down. Popular holiday cycling areas in Eastern Europe include the following:

» the Šumava region and the Moravian wine country (p319) in the Czech Republic

» various routes in Hungary (p446) and Poland (p686), and the Curonian Spit (p520) in western Lithuania

» Sinaia (p764) – a great place to go mountain biking across the plateau atop the Bucegi Mountains in Romania

See p1014 for more information on bicycle touring, and the individual country chapters for rental outfits, routes and tips on places to go.

Diving

It's not the Caribbean, but the Adriatic offers its own rewards. Explore caves and shipwrecks along the coast in

Croatia (p265), Montenegro (p584, p592) and Slovenia (p935).

Extreme Sports

If medieval Old Towns, castle-topped peaks and communist monuments don't get your blood pumping, never fear – you can still get your adrenalin rush in Eastern Europe.

» In Sigulda (p486), Latvia, you'll find bungee jumping, bobsledding and skydiving.

» Bovec (p927), Slovenia, is famous for hydrospeeding, canyoning and paragliding.

Hiking

Almost every country in Eastern Europe offers excellent hiking, with well-marked trails through forests, mountains and national parks. Chalets or mountain huts in Poland, Bulgaria, Slovakia, Romania and Slovenia offer dormitory accommodation and basic meals; public transport will often take you to the trailheads. The best months for hiking are from June to September, especially late August and early September, when the summer crowds will have largely disappeared. In this book we include information about hiking in the following areas:

» High Tatras of Poland (p647) and Slovakia (p881)

» Malá Fatra of Slovakia (p881)

» Făgăraș Mountains of Romania (p727)

» Rila Mountains of Bulgaria (p160)

» Julian Alps of Slovenia (p925)

There are also many other hiking areas that are less well known, including:

» Theth (p54) in Albania

» various destinations in the Czech Republic (p319)

» a number of national parks in Macedonia (p554)

» the Bieszczady Mountains (p649) in Poland

» Tara National Park (p856) in Serbia

» Carpathian National Natural Park (p967) in Ukraine

Horse Riding

Though horse riding is possible throughout Eastern Europe, the sport is best organised – and cheapest – in Hungary, whose people, it is said locally, 'were created by God to sit on horseback'. The best horse-riding centres are on the Great Plain (Nagyalföld), though you'll also find riding schools in Transdanubia (Dunántúl) and northern Hungary; see p446 for more information. Horse riding is also very popular (and affordable) in the Baltic countries, the Czech Republic, Poland and Slovenia.

Rafting

Exciting white-water rafting is possible in spring and summer on some of Eastern Europe's most scenic rivers including:

» the Vrbas River (p138) and the River Una (p138) in Bosnia and Hercegovina (BiH)

» the Tara River (p600) in Montenegro

» the Drina (p856) in Serbia

» the Soča River (p928) in Slovenia

Rafting on the Dunajec River along the border of Poland (p649) and Slovakia (p889) is fun, but it's not a white-water experience.

Sailing

Eastern Europe's most famous yachting area is the passage between the long, rugged islands off Croatia's Dalmatian coast. Yacht tours and rentals are available, although this is certainly not for anyone on a budget. If your means are more limited try the following options:

» The Great Masurian Lakes of northeastern Poland are a good choice, as small groups can rent sailing boats by the day for very reasonable rates; try the towns of

Giżycko (p681) and Mikołajki (p681).

» Hungary's Lake Balaton is also popular among sailing enthusiasts; p418 for information on hiring boats.

Skiing

The skiing season in Eastern Europe generally lasts from early December to late March, though at higher altitudes it may extend an extra month either way. Snow conditions can vary greatly from year to year and region to region, but January and February tend to be the best (and busiest) months. Snowboarding is especially popular in Slovakia, as is cross-country skiing in the Czech Republic and Ukraine. Eastern Europe's premier skiing areas include the following:

» High Tatras of Slovakia (p880) and Poland (p648)

» Carpathian Mountains in Romania (p721) and Ukraine (p968)

» Bankso (p162) in the Rila Mountains in Bulgaria

» Slovenia's Julian Alps (p926, p927)

» Bosnian capital Sarajevo (p118) – hosted the 1984 Winter Olympics and is a growing place for skiing; you'll find some of the best-value slopes in Europe within an hour of the city

» Lesser known ski areas in Belarus (p98), Macedonia (p537), Montenegro (p600) and Serbia (p851, p852)

Thermal Baths & Saunas

» There are hundreds of thermal baths in Eastern Europe open to the public. The most affordable are in the Czech Republic, Hungary and Slovenia, and along the Black Sea in Romania.

» Among the best are the Turkish baths of Budapest (p387) in Hungary, and the fin de siècle spas of Karlovy Vary (Karlsbad; p305) in the Czech Republic.

» The Baltic countries are famous for their proliferation of saunas – both the traditional 'smoke' variety, and the clean and smokeless modern sauna. The traditionalist will find many opportunities to take in an old-style sauna in Lithuania.

» Another must for lovers of heat and sweat is the traditional Russian *banya*, where you can be beaten into cleanliness with birch twigs!

Business Hours

» Eastern Europe tends to have similar working patterns to Western Europe and North America.

» Saturday and Sunday are official days off, although only banks and offices are shut; most shops, restaurants and cafes are open every day of the week.

» Banks and offices are usually open from 9am to 5pm Monday to Friday, often with an hour or two off for lunch. They may also be open on Saturday mornings. Shops usually stay open until 7pm or later.

» During the hot summer months, some enterprises will shut for two or three hours in the early afternoon, reopening at 3pm or 4pm and working into the evening. See the individual country directories for more specific details. Reviews will only list business hours that differ from those given there.

Children

Travelling with your children in Eastern Europe will be a treat and a challenge for the whole family.

The number-one guideline for travelling with children is to avoid packing too much activity into the available time. (Actually, this should be the number-one guideline

for travelling without children too.)

The second guideline is to allow your children to help plan the trip. Sure, they may not have an opinion about Macedonia versus Montenegro or Latvia versus Lithuania, but once you arrive, they will certainly have an opinion about how they would like to spend the day. Furthermore, if your kids have helped to plan the itinerary, they will know what to look forward to and will be more engaged upon arrival.

A good resource is Lonely Planet's *Travel with Children* by Cathy Lanigan and Maureen Wheeler.

Practicalities

» In Eastern Europe most car-rental firms have children's safety seats for hire at a small cost, but it is essential that you book them in advance.

» The same goes for high chairs and cots; they're standard in many restaurants and hotels but numbers are limited.

» The choice of baby food, infant formulas, soy and cows' milk, disposable nappies and the like is often as great in the Eastern European supermarkets as it is back home.

Discount Cards

Camping Card International

The Camping Card International (CCI) is a camping-ground ID valid for a year. It can be used instead of a passport when checking in to camping grounds and includes third-party insurance. As a result, many camping grounds will offer discounts of up to 25% for card-holders. CCIs are issued by automobile associations, camping federations and, sometimes, on the spot

at camping grounds. See **Camping Card International** (www.campingcardinternational.org) for links to local organisations and lists of participating camping grounds.

Hostel Cards

No hostels in Eastern Europe require that you be a **Hostelling International** (www.hihostels.com) member, but they sometimes charge less if you have a card. Some hostels will issue one on the spot or after a few days' stay, though this might cost a bit more than getting it at home.

Senior Cards

» Many attractions offer reduced-price admission for people over 60 or 65 (or sometimes 55 for women). EU residents, especially, are eligible for discounts in many EU countries. Make sure you bring proof of age.

» For a fee of around €20, European residents aged 60 and over can get a Railplus Card as an add-on to their national rail senior pass. It entitles the holder to train-fare reductions of around 25%.

» Before leaving home, check with an agency that caters to senior travel – such as Elder Hostel (p1017) – for age-related travel packages and discounts.

Student, Youth & Teacher Cards

An International Student Identity Card (ISIC) is a plastic ID-style card that provides discounts on many forms of transport (including airlines and local transport), cheap or free admission to museums and sights, and inexpensive meals in some student cafeterias and restaurants.

If you're under 26 but not a student, you are eligible to apply for an International

Youth Travel Card (IYTC, formerly GO25), issued by the Federation of International Youth Travel Organisations, or the Euro26 card. The Euro26 card may not be recognised in Albania, Moldova, Romania, Serbia and Montenegro. Both cards go under different names in different countries and give much the same discounts and benefits as an ISIC.

An International Teacher Identity Card (ITIC) identifies the holder as an instructor and offers similar deals.

All these cards are issued by student unions, hostelling organisations or youth-oriented travel agencies; alternatively see the **International Student Travel Confederation** (www.isic.org).

Electricity

Plugs in Eastern Europe are the standard round two-pin variety, sometimes called the europlug. If your plugs are of a different design, you'll need an adapter.

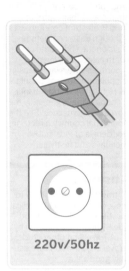

220v/50hz

Embassies & Consulates

» See the individual country directories for the addresses of embassies and consulates in Eastern Europe.

» It's important to realise what your embassy can and cannot do to help if you get into trouble while travelling abroad. Remember that you are bound by the laws of the country you are visiting. Generally speaking, your embassy cannot help much if your emergency is of your own making. It will not post bail or otherwise act to get you out of jail.

» If your documents are lost or stolen, your embassy can assist you in obtaining a new passport; this is greatly simplified if you have a photocopy of your passport. Your embassy may refer you to a lawyer or a doctor, but it is highly unlikely to provide any financial assistance, no matter what your emergency.

Gay & Lesbian Travellers

Consensual homosexual sex is legal in all of the countries of Eastern Europe. The laws on the books do not signal an open-minded approach to sexual minorities, however.

You are unlikely to raise any eyebrows by sharing a room (or a bed) with your same-sex partner. But in many countries, society frowns on overt displays of affection in any case – and even more so when it's between members of the same gender.

Many countries have online forums and gay advocacy groups. Latvia, Hungary, Poland and Russia have all had gay-pride events in recent years. Unfortunately, on most occasions, marchers were outnumbered by antigay protesters, which

often ended in arrests on both sides.

Many gays and lesbians in Eastern Europe actually oppose such parades as they provoke the majority into taking an antigay stance when they would otherwise pay no heed to the gay and lesbian population.

Despite this don't-ask-don't-tell situation, most Eastern European capitals have small, lively gay scenes, usually centred on one or two bars and clubs.

Exceptions to this rule are Tirana, Skopje, Sarajevo and Chişinău, where there is nothing gay- or lesbian-specific that is accessible to visitors.

Outside large towns, gay and lesbian life is almost nonexistent. See the individual country directories for more info.

Health

Eastern Europe poses no big health risks to travellers, though as with anywhere else in the world there are several things you should be aware of.

Availability & Cost of Health Care

Good basic health care is readily available, and pharmacists can give valuable advice and sell over-the-counter medication for minor illnesses. They can also advise when more specialised help is required and point you in the right direction.

The standard of dental care is usually good, but it is sensible to have a dental check-up before a long trip.

Medical care is not always readily available outside of major cities, but embassies, consulates and five-star hotels can usually recommend doctors or clinics. In some cases, medical supplies required in hospital may need to be bought from a pharmacy and nursing care may be limited. The usual precautions apply to help prevent transmission of hepatitis B and HIV/AIDS.

In general health-care costs are still relatively low in Eastern Europe, and tend to be more expensive in EU member states than in non-EU member states; bear in mind, however, that in most non-EU states you'll probably want to go to a private clinic for anything more than a doctor's consultation, and therefore comprehensive health insurance is essential.

Potential Illnesses or Conditions

RABIES

Spread through bites or licks from an infected animal on broken skin, rabies is always fatal unless treated promptly and is present throughout Eastern Europe. To be vaccinated, three injections are needed over a month. If you are bitten and have not been vaccinated, you will need a course of five injections starting 24 hours or as soon as possible after the injury. If you have been vaccinated, you will need fewer injections and have more time to seek medical help.

TICKBORNE ENCEPHALITIS

Spread by tick bites, tickborne encephalitis is a serious infection of the brain.

Vaccination is advised for those in risk areas who are unable to avoid tick bites (such as campers, forestry workers and walkers). Two doses of vaccine will provide protection for a year, while three doses provide up to three years' protection. Anyone walking in the Baltics and Russia for any length of time should consider vaccination, as reported cases have been steadily rising.

TRAVELLER'S DIARRHOEA

If you develop diarrhoea, be sure to drink plenty of fluids, preferably an oral rehydration solution (eg Dioralyte). A few loose stools don't require treatment, but if you start having more than four or five stools a day, you should start taking an antibiotic (usually a quinolone drug) and an antidiarrhoeal agent (such as loperamide). If diarrhoea is bloody, persists for more than 72 hours or is accompanied by fever, shaking, chills or severe abdominal pain, you should seek medical attention.

INSECT BITES & STINGS

Mosquitoes are found in most parts of Europe. They may not carry malaria but can cause irritation and infected bites. Use insect repellent, plug in anti-mosquito

devices and cover up your arms and legs in the evening.

WATER

Tap water may not be safe to drink, so it is best to stick to bottled water or boil water for 10 minutes, use water purification tablets or a filter. Do not drink water from rivers or lakes, as it may contain bacteria or viruses that can cause diarrhoea or vomiting. St Petersburg is a particular hot spot for dangerous water – *never* drink from the tap here. Brushing your teeth with tap water is very unlikely to lead to problems, but use bottled water if you want to be very safe.

Holidays

Throughout Eastern Europe, children get the summer months (usually much of July and all of August) off from school, which is one reason why this is the busiest time to go to the beach and other resorts. There are also usually breaks for Easter and Christmas; keep in mind that dates for Orthodox Christmas and Easter are different to those of their Catholic and Protestant counterparts (though Easter sometimes falls on the same date by both calendars). Even in countries with a large Muslim population, such as Bosnia & Hercegovina and Albania, school holidays generally follow these guidelines. See the individual country directories for details of local public holidays and festivals.

Insurance

A travel-insurance policy to cover theft, loss and medical problems is always a good idea. The policies written by STA Travel and other student-travel organisations are usually good value.

» Some insurance policies will specifically exclude 'dangerous activities', which can

EUROPEAN HEALTH INSURANCE CARD

Citizens of the EU, Switzerland, Iceland, Norway and Liechtenstein receive free or reduced-cost state-provided healthcare cover with the European Health Insurance Card (EHIC) for medical treatment that becomes necessary while in other EU countries. Every EU individual needs their own card. In the UK, get application forms from post offices, or download them from the Department of Health website (www.dh.gov.uk), which has comprehensive information about the card's coverage.

The EHIC does not cover private healthcare, so make sure that you are treated by a state healthcare provider. In EU countries where state-provided healthcare isn't free, you will need to pay yourself and fill in a treatment form; keep the form to claim any refunds. In general, you can claim back around 70% of the standard treatment cost.

include scuba diving, motor-cycling and even hiking.

» Some policies even exclude certain countries, so read your fine print.

» Also check that your policy covers ambulances and an emergency flight home.

» You may prefer a policy that pays doctors or hospitals directly rather than reimbursing your claims after the fact.

» Some policies ask you to call back (reverse charges) to a centre in your home country, where an immediate assessment of your problem is made.

» If you have to file a claim, make sure you keep all documentation.

» Worldwide travel insurance is available at www.lonelyplanet.com/bookings. You can buy, extend and claim online at any time – even if you're already on the road. See p1016 for information on car and motorcycle insurance.

Internet Access

With few exceptions, any decent-sized town in Eastern Europe has internet access in some shape or form. Connections may be slow, there might not be coffee and you might be sitting in a smelly room full of teenage boys playing war games – but one way or another you'll never be far from the web, even in less developed nations such as Albania and Moldova. Indeed, in some cities, internet cafes can be a social hub and a great way of meeting locals as well as other travellers. Throughout this book internet access is indicated in Sleeping and other reviews by @.

Laptop and smart phone users will be glad to know that wi-fi has taken off in Eastern Europe too, with hot spots in cafes, bars, libraries, hotels, hostels and even public places. The Baltics are particularly good – Tallinn alone has more than 300

wi-fi spots, most of them free. It's increasingly common for any high-standard or boutique hotel to have wi-fi in the rooms. Sadly, most business hotels charge for this service, while boutique and mid-range hotels are more likely to offer it for free. Locations with wi-fi access are indicated throughout this book by ☎.

Maps

» Bringing a good regional map will make things a great deal easier if you are planning a long trip taking in more than a couple of countries.

» There's a huge range available, but we recommend *Eastern Europe*, produced by Latvian publishers Jana Seta, and *Eastern Europe* from Freytag and Berndt.

» In general, buying city maps in advance is unnecessary, as nearly all large towns produce them locally for a fraction of the price you'll pay at home.

» However, maps of Eastern European capitals and other major towns are widely available from travel bookshops if you want a particularly detailed map in advance.

Money

Things have simplified in Eastern Europe, and there are no worries about 'soft' and 'hard' currencies for the most part.

The main problem you'll face is constant currency changes as you flit between the crown, złoty, rouble, lei, lev, lek, dinar and various other national currencies.

There is no longer any particular desire for 'hard' currency (the days when hoteliers would slash the rates if you paid in US dollars are long gone), and the convertibility of almost all Eastern European currencies makes

them a stable and reliable way to carry cash.

The euro remains the easiest currency to change throughout the region, and it can be used in Estonia, Kosovo, Montenegro, Slovakia and Slovenia, where it is the national currency.

Most other countries in Eastern Europe are hoping to adopt the euro in the future, though the global financial downturn has tempered enthusiasm in many quarters.

ATMs

Nearly all Eastern European countries have plenty of ATMs in their capitals and towns. Check the specific situation in your destination before setting out from the big city – and never rely entirely on being able to find an ATM.

Cash or debit cards can be used throughout Eastern Europe at ATMs linked to international networks such as Cirrus and Maestro.

The major advantage of using ATMs is that you don't pay commission charges to exchange money, although you might pay a bank fee. The exchange rate is usually at a better rate than that offered for travellers cheques or cash exchanges.

If you choose to rely on plastic, go for two different cards – this allows one to be used as backup in the case of loss, or more commonly, if a bank does not accept one card.

Better still is a combination of cards and travellers cheques so you have something to fall back on if there are no ATMs in the area, or they accept local cards only.

Cash

The two most favoured currencies throughout Eastern Europe are the euro and the US dollar.

Although it's not difficult to exchange other major world currencies in big cities, you are at the mercy of the exchange office and its rates.

A far better option is to change your money into euros or US dollars before you leave home.

Credit Cards

As purchase tools, credit cards are still not as commonly used as they are in Western Europe, but cards such as Amex, Visa and MasterCard are gaining ground. You'll be able to use them at upmarket restaurants, shops, hotels, car-rental firms, travel agencies and many petrol stations.

Bear in mind that if you use a credit card for purchases, exchange rates may have changed by the time your bill is processed, which can work out to your advantage or disadvantage.

Charge-card companies such as Amex, and to a lesser extent Diners Club, have offices in most countries in Eastern Europe, and because they treat you as a customer of the company rather than of the bank that issued the card, they can generally replace a lost card within 24 hours.

The cards' major drawback is that they're not widely accepted off the beaten track. Credit cards such as Visa and MasterCard are more widely accepted because they tend to charge merchants lower commissions.

See the warning on p1007 about credit card scams.

Moneychangers

Never exchange your hard-earned cash without first shopping around for a decent rate. If you happen to be in a tourist area, you will be offered crappy rates everywhere; for example around the Charles Bridge in Prague. In this case, don't bother shopping around – just leave for a less-touristed neighbourhood.

Border crossings, airports and train stations are typically places where rates aren't great, but many people change money out of necessity.

Tipping

Tipping practices vary from country to country and often from place to place. In general, you can't go wrong if you add 10% onto your bill at a restaurant.

Porters at upmarket hotels will appreciate a few euros for their efforts. In fashionable venues in urban centres, the wait staff will expect this; in rural locations you might astonish your server. See the individual country chapters for specific advice.

Travellers Cheques

The benefit of using travellers cheques rather than cash is the protection they offer from theft. But this old-school travel tool has lost its once enormous popularity, as more and more travellers prefer to withdraw cash from ATMs as they go along.

Keep in mind that banks usually charge from 1% to 2% commission to change travellers cheques (up to 5% in Bulgaria, Estonia, Latvia, Lithuania and Romania), and opening hours are sometimes limited.

Always check the commission and rate before signing a travellers cheque or handing over any cash.

Amex and Thomas Cook representatives cash their own travellers cheques without commission, but both give poor rates of exchange. If you're changing more than US$20, you're usually better off going to a bank and paying the standard 1% to 2% commission to change there.

Western Union

If everything goes horribly wrong – your money, travellers cheques and credit cards are all stolen – don't despair. While it's a terrible (and highly unusual) situation, a friend or relative back home will be able to wire money to you anywhere in Eastern Europe via Western Union (WU). We don't bother listing WU representatives in this guide as there are literally thousands of them; just look for the distinctive yellow and black sign. The sender is given a code that they communicate to you, then you take the code to the nearest office, along with your passport, to receive your cash.

Photography & Video

» Eastern Europe was once notorious for its photographic restrictions – taking shots of anything 'strategic', such as bridges or train stations, was strictly forbidden. These days local officials are much less paranoid, but you need to use common sense when it comes to taking photos.

» Photographing military installations, for example, is never a good idea anywhere in the world. Most importantly, have the courtesy to ask permission before taking close-up photos of people. Be aware that museums often demand that you buy permission to photograph or video their displays.

» Digital memory, film and camera equipment is available everywhere in Eastern Europe, though you'll have a better selection in larger towns. Avoid buying film at tourist sites in Eastern Europe as it will certainly be more expensive than in normal photography shops.

» Lonely Planet's guide to *Travel Photography* covers all aspects of travel photography and shows you how to develop your skills to capture the perfect picture.

Post

Both the efficiency and cost of the national postal systems in Eastern Europe vary enormously. There seems to be no set rules, but EU countries are likely to be faster, more reliable and more expensive than the non-EU states.

Postal service from Belarus, Moldova, Montenegro, Russia and Ukraine is slow, but the mail usually reaches its destination eventually. For added assurance and speed, most of these countries offer an express service. The only country where it is not advised to use the state-run postal service to send parcels is Albania.

To send a parcel from Eastern Europe you usually have to take it unwrapped to a main post office; parcels weighing over 2kg often must be taken to a special customs post office. The post-office staff will usually wrap the parcels for you. The staff may ask to see your passport and note the number on the form; if you don't have a return address within the country put the address of any large tourist hotel.

Poste restante is an unreliable, not to mention increasingly unnecessary, communication method. If you desperately need something posted to you, do your research – find a friend of a friend who could receive the mail at their address, or ask nicely at a hotel you plan to stay at. You can also have mail sent to you at Amex offices if you have an Amex card or are carrying its travellers cheques.

Details of post offices are given for cities and towns in the individual country chapters, and postage costs given in the country directories.

Safe Travel

Eastern Europe is as safe – or unsafe – as any other part of the developed world. If you can handle yourself in the big cities of Western Europe, North America or Australia, you'll have little trouble dealing with the less pleasant side of Eastern Europe. Look purposeful, keep alert and you'll be OK.

Some locals will regale you with tales of how dangerous their city is and recount various cases of muggings, break-ins, kidnappings etc, often involving Roma or other popular scapegoats (other Eastern Europeans will tell you horror stories about the Romanians and Albanians). Most of these stories are overblown and exaggerated and you are unlikely to have any threatening encounters.

Corruption

Low-level corruption is disappearing fast, and is now rare for travellers to encounter. Do not pay bribes to people in official positions, such as police, border guards, train conductors and ticket inspectors.

Be aware, however, that these anachronistic systems still exist in Belarus, Moldova, Russia and Transdniestr. If corrupt cops want to hold you up because some obscure stamp is missing from your documentation or on some other pretext, just let them and consider the experience an integral part of your trip. Insisting on calling your embassy is always a good move; officers are likely to receive some grief if their superiors learn they are harassing tourists.

If you're taken to the police station for questioning, you'll have the opportunity to observe the quality of justice in that country from the inside. In most cases, the more senior officers will eventually let you go (assuming, of course, you haven't committed a real crime).

If you do have to pay a fine or supplementary charge, insist on a proper receipt before turning over any money; this is now law in Hungary, for example, where traffic police were once notorious for demanding 'gifts' from motorists guilty of some alleged infraction. In all of this, try to maintain your cool, as any threats from you will only make matters worse.

Drugs

Always treat drugs with a great deal of caution. There are a lot of drugs available in the region, but that doesn't mean they are legal. The continual fighting in the former Yugoslavia in the 1990s forced drug traffickers to seek alternative routes from Asia to Western Europe, sometimes crossing through Hungary, Slovakia, the Czech Republic and Poland. Now EU members, these countries do not look lightly upon drug use.

Landmines

BiH (p144) and Kosovo (p459) still have landmines in remote areas. Ask locals for the latest situation, and stick to established roads and paths in places where mines are still a problem.

Scams

A word of warning about credit cards: fraudulent shopkeepers have been known to make several charge-slip imprints with your credit card when you're not looking and then simply copy your signature from the authorised slip.

There have also been reports of these unscrupulous people making quick and very hi-tech duplicates of credit- or debit-card information with a machine. If your card leaves your possession for longer than you think necessary, consider cancelling it.

Now that most Eastern European currencies have reached convertibility, there is no longer a black market for currency exchange in this region. The days of getting five times the official rate for cash on the streets of Warsaw and Bucharest are well and truly over.

Anyone who approaches you offering such a deal (an uncommon occurrence these days) is an outright thief, trying to get their hands on your money, either by scamming you or by simply taking it.

Theft

Theft is definitely a problem in Eastern Europe, and the threat comes from both local thieves and fellow travellers. The most important things to guard are your passport, other documents, tickets and money – in that order.

It's always best to carry these items in a sturdy pouch on your belt or under your shirt. Train-station lockers or luggage-storage counters are useful to store your luggage (but not valuables) while you get your bearings in a new town. Be very suspicious of people who offer to help you operate your locker.

Always be wary of snatch thieves and lessen your risk by taking simple precautions. Cameras and shoulder bags are great for these people, who sometimes operate from motorcycles or scooters, slashing the strap before you have a chance to react.

A small daypack is more secure, but watch your rear and don't keep valuables in the outside pockets. Loop the strap around your leg while seated at bars or cafes.

Pickpockets are most active in dense crowds, especially in busy train stations and on public transport during peak hours. A common ploy in the Budapest and Prague metros has been for a group of well-dressed young people to surround you, chattering away while one of the group zips through your pockets or purse.

Be careful even in hotels: don't leave valuables lying around in your room. Carry your own padlock for hostel lockers and always use them.

Parked cars containing luggage or other bags are prime targets for petty criminals in most cities, and cars with foreign number plates and/or rental-agency stickers attract particular attention. While driving in cities, beware of snatch thieves when you pull up at the lights – keep doors locked and windows rolled up.

In the case of theft or loss, always report the incident to the police and ask for a statement; otherwise your travel-insurance company won't pay up.

Violence

It's unlikely that travellers will encounter any violence while in Eastern Europe. Be aware, however, that many countries in the region have thriving neo-Nazi movements, which tend to target local Roma populations as well as black and Asian travellers.

Russian neo-Nazis have been known to seek out fights with nonwhite people on Hitler's birthday (20 April); St Petersburg in particular has seen an extraordinary amount of violence against ethnic minorities, and not only on this date.

Telephone

Telephone services in Eastern Europe are generally excellent. The mobile phone is king across the region, though most cities have a huge number of call centres too; they're increasingly the domain of entrepreneurs who offer discounted rates, although there are also state-run call centres, which are often in the same building as the main post office. Here you can usually make your call from one of the booths inside an enclosed area, paying the cashier as you leave. Public telephones are almost always found at post offices.

Mobile Phones

» The expansion of mobile-phone use in Eastern Europe has been phenomenal, and this can be great for travellers too.

» If you plan to spend more than a week or so in any one country, consider buying a SIM card to slip into your phone, although you'll need to check with your provider at home that your handset has been unlocked.

» SIM cards can cost as little as €5 and can be topped up with cards available at supermarkets and mobile-phone dealers.

» Alternatively, if you have roaming, your phone will usually switch automatically over to a local network. This can be expensive if you use the phone a great deal, but can be very useful for ad hoc and emergency use.

Phone Codes

» Every country's international dialling code and international access code is given in the Fast Facts section at the beginning of each chapter. If area codes are used within a country, they are listed directly under each town's name.

» To call abroad from a landline you simply dial the international access code for the country you are calling

---

SOLO TRAVELLERS

Eastern Europe is a great place to travel alone. Relatively low hostel and restaurant prices mean that it won't break the bank, and the entire region is unthreatening and well set up for lone travellers. If you want to take a break from going it alone, the best place to find some company is at hostels, which are set up to allow the guests to mix and mingle. Indeed, you may pick up a travelling companion who is heading in your direction. Other places to meet fellow travellers are internet cafes and expat bars (usually the ubiquitous Irish pubs).

from (most commonly ✔00 in Eastern Europe, but ✔8-10 in Belarus and Russia).

» From a mobile phone simply dial + followed by the country code, the city code and the local number.

» To make a domestic call to another city in the same country, you generally need to dial the area code (with the initial zero) and the number; however, in some countries the area code is an integral part of the phone number, and must be dialled every time – even if you're just calling next door.

Phonecards

» Local telephone cards – available from post offices, telephone centres, newsstands or retail outlets – are used everywhere in the region. In any given country, there's a wide range of local and international phonecards available. For local calls you're usually better off with a local phonecard.

Time

Eastern Europe spans three time zones: Central European Time (GMT+1), Eastern European Time (GMT+2) and Moscow Time (GMT+3). At noon in New York, it's 6pm in Warsaw, 7pm in Minsk and 8pm in Moscow.

» All countries employ daylight savings. Clocks are put forward an hour at the start of daylight savings, usually on the last Sunday in March.

They are set back one hour on the last Sunday in October.

» Note that the 24-hour clock is widely used in Eastern Europe, though not always conversationally.

Toilets

» Toilets have improved enormously in the past decade across the region. The vast majority of toilets you use will be modern, sit down, flushing toilets.

» In Russia, Belarus, Ukraine and Moldova, however, you can expect to find smelly and rather unpleasant squat toilets in bus and train stations, though they are very rare in restaurants or hotels.

» Public toilets have improved too, though you'll need to pay a small fee to use most public toilets in Eastern Europe.

» Using hotel or restaurant facilities is nearly always free and one way to ensure you'll be using a clean bathroom.

Tourist Information

» The provision of tourist information varies enormously. While countries that have successfully realised their potential as holiday destinations have developed a network of excellent tourist information centres (TICs), there are still many countries that take little or no interest in the economic benefits tourism can bring.

» Countries in the latter category are Ukraine, Belarus and Moldova. Russia is similarly badly organised, though there are unhelpful TICs in Moscow and St Petersburg.

» Among the best prepared are Slovakia, Slovenia, Croatia, the Czech Republic, Hungary, Poland and Bulgaria, many of which have tourist offices abroad as well as throughout the country.

» The Baltic countries, Montenegro, Romania, Albania and Macedonia fall in a middle category of places actively trying to encourage tourism, but whose efforts remain rather obscure at the moment. See individual country chapters for details of local TICs.

Travellers with Disabilities

Eastern Europe is a real mixed bag for less-able travellers. While individual museums and hotels are slowly being brought up to

EASTERN EUROPE TIME ZONES

TIME ZONE	LOCATIONS
Central Europe (GMT+1 hour)	Albania, BiH, Croatia, Czech Republic, Hungary, Kosovo, Macedonia, Montenegro, Poland, Serbia, Slovakia and Slovenia.
Eastern Europe (GMT+2 hours)	Belarus, Bulgaria, Estonia, Kaliningrad, Latvia, Lithuania, Moldova, Romania and Ukraine.
Moscow (GMT+3 hours)	Moscow and St Petersburg.

Western European standards of accessibility, there is little coordinated effort to improve things regionally.

In general, wheelchair-accessible rooms are available only at top-end hotels (and are limited, so be sure to book in advance). Rental cars and taxis may be accessible, but public transport rarely is. Most major museums and sites have disabled access, although there are many exceptions.

If you have a physical disability, get in touch with your national support organisation (preferably the travel officer if there is one) and ask about the countries you plan to visit. The organisations often have libraries devoted to travel, including access guides, and staff can put you in touch with travel agencies who specialise in tours for the disabled.

In the UK, the **Royal Association for Disability & Rehabilitation** (Radar; ☑ in the UK 020-7250 3222; www.radar.org.uk) is a very helpful association and sells a number of publications for people with disabilities.

Visas

Visas have become a thing of the past for many travellers in Eastern Europe, though sadly they are still a reality for anyone wanting to explore the region's eastern extremities – all visitors to Russia and Belarus still require a visa, while several nationalities still require visas for Moldova and Ukraine. See individual country chapters for more detail.

In line with the Schengen Agreement, there are no longer strict passport controls at the borders between most EU countries, but procedures between EU and non-EU countries can still be fairly thorough.

If you do get a visa, it's important to remember that it has an expiration date, and

you'll be refused entry after that period has elapsed. Consulates sometimes issue visas on the spot, although some levy a 50% to 100% surcharge for 'express service'. If there's a choice between getting a visa in advance and on the border, go for the former option if you have the time. They're often cheaper in your home country and this can save on bureaucratic procedure.

Decide in advance if you want a tourist or transit visa; transit visas, usually valid for just 48 or 72 hours, are often cheaper and issued faster, but it's usually not possible to extend a transit visa or change it to a tourist visa.

Some countries require visitors to register with the local authorities within 48 hours of arrival, supposedly so they know where you are staying. If you're staying at a hotel or other official accommodation, the administration will take care of this registration for you.

If you're staying with friends, relatives or in a private room, you're supposed to register with the police yourself. In some cases, this is a formality that is never enforced, so you can skip it. In other cases (such as Russia), you can be fined if you do not go through the motions.

Obtaining registration through the proper channels is a major hassle, often requiring fluent language skills, a pile of documents and several hours of negotiation. You are better off paying a local travel agency for the registration instead of trying to do it yourself.

The hassles created by losing your passport and visa can be considerably reduced if you have a record of its number and issue date or, even better, photocopies of the relevant data pages. A photocopy of your birth certificate can also be useful.

Women Travellers

Women travellers will find that Eastern Europe is a safe and welcoming place to travel, whether you're in a group, with a mate, or on your own.

That is not to say that sexual harassment does not exist, however. It is not unusual for women to be propositioned by strangers on the street. As a rule, foreigners are still a little exotic and therefore attract more attention, but this attention is rarely dangerous, and is easily deflected with a shake of the head and a firm 'no'. (Use the local language if you can, but English usually works fine too.)

In Muslim countries, women travelling solo will certainly be of interest or curiosity to both local men and women. In Albania and BiH, women may feel self-conscious in bars and cafes, which are usually populated only by men. Unmarried men rarely have contact with women outside their family unit, and so may shower travelling women with too much attention. (In such areas, women travelling with a male companion will often experience the opposite, and may need to pinch themselves as a reminder that yes, they actually exist.)

Work

The massive eastwards expansion of the EU in recent years has meant that EU citizens have free rein to work in many countries in the region. However, with unemployment still a problem, Eastern European countries aren't always keen on handing out jobs to foreigners.

If you're not an EU citizen, the paperwork involved in arranging a work permit can be almost impossible, especially for temporary work.

That doesn't prevent enterprising travellers from topping up their funds occasionally – and they don't always have to do this illegally. If you do find a temporary job in Eastern Europe, though, the pay is likely to be low. Do it for the experience, not to earn your fortune.

Teaching English is the easiest way to make some extra cash, but the market is saturated in places such as Prague and Budapest. You'll probably be much more successful in less popular places such as Sofia and Bucharest.

If you play an instrument or have other artistic talents, you could try working the streets. As every Peruvian pipe player knows, busking is fairly common in Eastern European cities such as Prague, Budapest and Ljubljana. Some countries may require municipal permits for this sort of thing, so talk to other street artists before you start.

Work Your Way Around the World by Susan Griffith gives good, practical advice on a wide range of issues. The publisher Vacation Work has some useful titles, including *The Directory of Summer Jobs Abroad,* edited by David Woodworth. *Working Holidays* by Ben Jupp (Central Bureau for Educational Visits & Exchanges in the UK) is another good source, as is *Now Hiring! Jobs in Eastern Europe* by Clarke Canfield (Perpetual Press).

Organising a volunteer-work placement is another great way to gain a deeper insight into local culture. In some instances volunteers are paid a living allowance, sometimes they work for their keep, and sometimes they are required to pay to undertake the program.

Several websites can help you search for volunteer work opportunities in Eastern Europe. The **Coordinating Committee for International Voluntary Service** (www.unesco.org/ccivs) is an umbrella organisation, with over 140 member organisations worldwide. It's useful if you want to find out about your country's national volunteer placement agency. Check the Transitions Abroad website and **Serve Your World** (www.serveyourworld. com) to search for vacancies and other volunteering opportunities in Eastern Europe.

Transport

GETTING THERE & AWAY

While not quite as well connected to the rest of the world as Western Europe, Eastern Europe is still a cinch to get to from almost anywhere in the world, whether it be overland, by boat or by air. This section outlines the major transport routes into the region from the rest of Europe and beyond.

Flights, tours and rail tickets can be booked online at www. lonelyplanet.com/bookings.

Entering Eastern Europe

All Eastern European countries require travellers to have a valid passport, preferably with at least six months between the time of departure and the passport's expiration date.

EU travellers from countries that issue national identity cards are increasingly using them to travel within the EU, although it's impossible to use them as sole travel documents outside the EU.

Visas are another thing to consider. Some countries require certain nationalities to buy a document allowing entry between certain dates. Specifically, Belarus and Russia require all nationalities to obtain visas, while Aussie and Kiwi travellers also need visas to enter Moldova and Ukraine. Other nationalities may have additional requirements; see p1010 or the individual country directories for details.

Air

Airports & Airlines

Moscow (Russia), Prague (Czech Republic), Budapest (Hungary) and Warsaw (Poland) are the region's best-connected air hubs. They all have transatlantic flights as well as plenty of flights from Western Europe; they are also well served by budget airlines. Other smaller hubs are St Petersburg (Russia), Rīga (Latvia), Timişoara (Romania), Zagreb (Croatia), Kyiv (Ukraine) and Bratislava (Slovakia), all of which have regular flights to many European cities. Most of the small hubs also have budget-airline connections, although as a rule the further east you go the fewer there are.

NATIONAL AIRLINES

Almost every country in Eastern Europe has its own national carrier. Most of these airlines provide direct flights to major cities across Western Europe.

Adria Airways (www.adria -airways.com)

Aeroflot (www.aeroflot.ru)

Aerosvit Ukrainian Airline (www.aerosvit.com)

airBaltic (www.airbaltic.com)

Belavia (www.belavia.by)

BH Airlines (www.bhairlines. ba)

Bulgaria Air (www.air.bg)

Croatia Airlines (www. croatiaairlines.hr)

CLIMATE CHANGE & TRAVEL

Every form of transport that relies on carbon-based fuel generates CO_2, the main cause of human-induced climate change. Modern travel is dependent on aeroplanes, which might use less fuel per kilometre per person than most cars but travel much greater distances. The altitude at which aircraft emit gases (including CO_2) and particles also contributes to their climate change impact. Many websites offer 'carbon calculators' that allow people to estimate the carbon emissions generated by their journey and, for those who wish to do so, to offset the impact of the greenhouse gases emitted with contributions to portfolios of climate-friendly initiatives throughout the world. Lonely Planet offsets the carbon footprint of all staff and author travel.

Czech Airlines (www.csa.cz)

Estonian Air (www.estonian
-air.ee)

Jat Airways (www.jat.com)

Kosova Airlines (www.
kosovaairlines.com)

LOT Polish Airlines (www.
lot.com)

MAT Airways (www.matair
ways.com.mk)

Malév (www.malev.hu)

Moldavian Airlines (www.
mdv.md)

Tarom (www.tarom.ro)

Ukraine International
Airlines (www.flyuia.com)

INTERNATIONAL AIRLINES
The invaluable travellers
website **flycheapo** (www.
flycheapo.com) is a great resource to see which budget
airlines fly where.

Look out for some of the
following airlines, which
provide the biggest selection
of flights to/from Eastern
Europe:

Air Berlin (www.airberlin.com)

Air France (www.airfrance.
com)

Alitalia (www.alitalia.com)

Austrian Airlines (www.
austrian.com)

Baboo (www.flybaboo.com)

Belle Air (www.belleair.it)

Blue Air (www.blueair-web.
com)

bmibaby (www.bmibaby.com)

British Airways (www.
ba.com)

Carpatair (www.carpatair.com)

Delta (www.delta.com)

easyJet (www.easyjet.com)

El Al (www.elal.co.il)

Emirates (www.emirates.com)

Finnair (www.finnair.com)

flybe.com (www.flybe.com)

flythomascook (www.
flythomascook.com)

germanwings (www.german
wings.com)

Iberia (www.iberia.com)

Jet2.com (www.jet2.com)

KLM (www.klm.com)

Lufthansa (www.lufthansa.
com)

Meridiana fly (www.meridi
ana.it)

Norwegian (www.norwegian.
com)

Ryanair (www.ryanair.com)

SAS (www.flysas.com)

SmartWings (www.smart
wings.net)

Swiss International
Airlines (www.swiss.com)

TAP (www.flytap.com)

United Airlines (www.united.
com)

Vueling (www.vueling.com)

Wind Jet (www.volawindjet.it)

Wizz Air (www.wizzair.com)

Land

Bus

Buses are never a great option for long-distance travel;
fares have been undercut
even by airlines recently.
However, not all places are
served by budget airlines,
so buses are always a useful
fall back if travelling from
Western Europe, and they are
reliably cheap.

Eurolines (www.eurolines.
com) has a vast network with
member companies in many
Eastern European countries
and offers innumerable
routes across the continent.

Ecolines (www.ecolines.
net) also runs buses between
Eastern and Western Europe.

See individual country
chapters for details of specific bus services.

Car & Motorcycle

Travelling by car or motorcycle into Eastern Europe
gives travellers an immense
amount of freedom and is
generally worry-free.

If you're driving a car into
Eastern Europe, keep in mind
some insurance packages, especially those covering rental
cars, do not include all European countries. Be sure to
ask the agency to insure the
car in all the countries where
you plan to travel. It's outright
forbidden to take rental cars
into certain countries.

See p1015 for more on
travelling by car or motorcycle throughout Europe.

Train

There are numerous routes
into Eastern Europe by train,
mostly from Western Eu-
rope. The big railway hubs in
Eastern Europe are Prague
(Czech Republic), Budapest
(Hungary), Bucharest (Ro-
mania), Belgrade (Serbia)
and Moscow (Russia).

Albania is unique in
Eastern Europe, as it has no
international train services
at all, while Montenegro
has a single line that heads
into Serbia. See individual
country chapters for train
services to Western Europe
and Turkey.

From Asia, the Trans-
Siberian, Trans-Mongolian
and Trans-Manchurian
Railways connect Moscow to
the Russian Far East, Ulaan-
baatar (Mongolia), Beijing
(China) and Pyongyang
(North Korea). Central Asian
cities such as Tashkent (Uz-
bekistan) and Almaty (Ka-
zakhstan) are also regularly
connected by long-distance
trains to Moscow.

Sea

The expansion of budget
airlines into Eastern Europe
has made travelling into the
region so far less finan-
cially attractive, but ferries
are still an atmospheric and
inexpensive way to travel.

Boats from several com-
panies regularly connect Italy
with Croatia, Slovenia, Montenegro and Albania; there
are also services between
Corfu (Greece) and Albania.
A car-passenger ferry links
Odesa (Ukraine) and İstanbul
(Turkey).

From Scandinavia, ferries
ply the Gulf of Finland and
the wide Baltic Sea, connecting Helsinki and Stockholm
with Tallinn (Estonia), St
Petersburg (Russia) and Rīga
(Latvia). In Poland, Gdańsk

and Gdynia are linked to Sweden and Denmark.

See individual country chapters for details.

GETTING AROUND

The borders between Serbia and Kosovo, and Russia and Belarus can be problematic; see p858 and p1014, respectively, for details.

The Schengen Agreement, which allows for passport-free travel within a large chunk of Europe, includes Czech Republic, Slovakia, Hungary, Slovenia, Poland,Estonia, Latvia and Lithuania. Bulgaria and Romania are both scheduled to join the area at a date in the future that is yet to be finalised.

Air

The major Eastern European cities are connected by a full schedule of regular flights within the region, and with the advent of low-cost airlines, prices are seriously competitive with trains and even buses.

Particularly well-connected regional airports include Moscow and St Petersburg (Russia), Prague (Czech Republic), Budapest (Hungary), Warsaw (Poland), Rīga (Latvia), Timişoara (Romania) and Zagreb (Croatia).

Many countries offer domestic flights, although there is rarely a need to fly internally unless you are in a particular rush. Russia is the exception; flying from either Moscow or St Petersburg to Kaliningrad saves the trouble of getting a double-entry Russian visa (p808). If you travel to Kaliningrad by boat or land, you are given an exit stamp, making your single-entry visa invalid.

Bicycle

Eastern Europe is compact enough to make it ideal for a cycling trip and mountainous enough to ensure that it will be challenging.

If you are planning a tour of the region by bike, contact one of these helpful cycling clubs:

» **Cyclists' Touring Club** (CTC; www.ctc.org.uk) Offers members an information service on all matters associated with cycling, including maps, cycling conditions, itineraries and detailed routes.

» **European Cyclists' Federation** (www.ecf.com) Advocates bike-friendly policies and organises tours. Also manages EuroVelo, a project to create bike routes across the continent.

One major drawback to cycling in Eastern Europe is the exhaust fumes put out by Eastern European vehicles, especially buses and trucks. Roads in the southern Balkans – particularly Albania, Bosnia and Hercegovina (BiH), Serbia, Macedonia and Montenegro – can be terrible, and there's also a small risk of landmines and unexploded ordnance in Kosovo and BiH.

Hire

Except in a few of the more visited regions, it can be difficult to hire bikes in Eastern Europe. The best spots are often camping grounds and resort hotels during the summer months, or travel agencies in the major cities.

Transporting a Bicycle

You should be able to take your bicycle on plane trips. You can either take it apart and pack all the pieces in a bike bag or box, or simply wheel it to the check-in desk, where it should be treated as a piece of check-in luggage.

If your bicycle and other luggage exceed your weight allowance, ask about alternatives, as you may otherwise find yourself being charged a fortune for excess baggage.

AT YOUR OWN RISK

There is effectively no border between Russia and Belarus. In theory, it's possible to enter Belarus by train and leave it for Russia – or go to Russia and back from Belarus – without going through passport control, and therefore without needing a visa for the country you're sneaking into. However, a hotel won't take you without a visa, so you'd have to stay with friends or rent an apartment, and if your visa-less documents are checked on the street (unlikely unless you're a troublemaker or a person of colour), you will be deported.

If you do not receive a migration card when entering Russia, contact your embassy immediately upon arrival to find out how to get one. If you do not receive an entry stamp, go to the local OVIR (Visa and Registration) office in Russia – but bring a full supply of patience.

A much better option if you plan to travel from Belarus into Russia is to ensure you have a valid visa for Russia as well. This will be stamped by Belarusian control on entry to Belarus and, under the terms of the Russian-Belarusian 'one state' agreement, is valid as an entry stamp for Russia. Keep your immigration card from Belarus and use it when you leave Russia, as they are valid in both countries.

Within Western Europe, bikes can usually be transported on trains as luggage, subject to a fairly small supplementary fee. If it's possible, book tickets in advance.

Tours

Plenty of companies offer organised cycling tours of Eastern Europe. These specialised companies generally plan the itinerary, organise accommodation and transport luggage, making life a lot simpler for cyclists:

» **BaltiCCycle** (www.baltic cycle.eu) Promotes cycling in the Baltic countries and provides information on routes, maps and bike rental.

» **Experience Plus** (www. experienceplus.com) Runs cycling tours throughout the region, including cycling Croatia, cycling the Danube from Budapest to the Black Sea, and cycling through the heart of the Balkans.

» **First Light Bicycle Tours** (www.firstlightbicycletours. com) Offers several cycling tours in the Czech Republic, as well as one epic journey from Kraków to Budapest. Self-guided tours are also available.

» **Top Bicycle** (www.topbicy cle.com) This Czech company offers cycling tours of the Czech Republic and Slovakia, as well as more-extensive tours around the region.

» **Velo Touring** (www. velo-touring.hu) Based in Budapest, this company offers tours of Austria and Hungary, as well as bike rentals for those who want to go it alone.

Boat

Eastern Europe's massive rivers and myriad canals, lakes and seas provide rich opportunities for boat travel, although in almost all cases these are very much pleasure cruises rather than particularly practical ways to get around. Boat travel is usually

far more expensive than the equivalent bus or train journey, but that's not necessarily the point.

Bus

Buses are a viable alternative to the rail network in most Eastern European countries. Generally they tend to complement the rail system rather than duplicate it, though in some countries – notably Hungary, the Czech Republic and Slovakia – you'll almost always have a choice between the two options.

Buses tend to be best for shorter hops, getting around cities and reaching remote rural villages. They are often the only option in mountainous regions.

In general, buses are slightly cheaper and slower than trains; in Russia, Poland, Hungary, the Czech Republic and Slovakia they cost about the same.

The ticketing system varies in each country, but advance reservations are rarely necessary. On long-distance buses you can usually pay upon boarding, although it's safest to buy your ticket in advance at the station.

The only company covering the majority of the region is **Eurolines** (www.eurolines. com). See the individual country chapters for more details about long-distance buses.

Car & Motorcycle

Travelling with your own vehicle allows you increased flexibility and the option to get off the beaten track. However, cars can be inconvenient in city centres when you have to negotiate strange one-way systems or find somewhere to park in the narrow streets of Old Towns.

Theft from vehicles is a problem in many parts of the region – never leave valuables in your car.

Russia, Belarus and Ukraine still remain tediously difficult places to drive into – border controls can take a long time and bribes are often the order of the day.

It is not recommended to drive a rental car from Serbia into Kosovo, and vice versa.

Driving Licence & Documentation

Proof of ownership of a private vehicle (a Vehicle Registration Document for British-registered cars) should always be carried when touring Europe.

An EU driving licence may be used throughout most of Eastern Europe, as may North American and Australian ones. If you want to be extra cautious – or if you have any other type of licence – you should obtain an International Driving Permit (IDP) from your local motoring organisation.

Always double-check which type of licence is required in your chosen destination before departure.

Every vehicle travelling across an international border should display a sticker that shows the country of registration.

Fuel & Spare Parts

Fuel prices vary considerably from country to country, though they rarely bear any relation to the general cost of living. Relatively affluent Slovenia, for example, has very cheap fuel, while the opposite is true in inexpensive Hungary.

Savings can be made if you fill up in the right place. Russia is the cheapest spot, followed by Romania, which has prices half those of neighbouring Hungary. Motoring organisations in your home country can give more details.

Unleaded petrol of 95 or 98 octane is widely available throughout Eastern Europe, though it may not be stocked at the odd station on back roads or outside main cities in Russia.

Unleaded petrol is usually slightly cheaper than super (premium grade). Look for the pump with green markings and the word *Bleifrei*, German for 'unleaded'. Diesel is usually significantly cheaper than petrol in Eastern Europe.

Good-quality petrol is easy to find in the Baltic countries, but stations seem to be placed somewhat erratically. Several may be located within a few kilometres of each other, then there may not be any for incredibly long stretches. Make sure you fill up your tank wherever possible – especially if you are travelling off the main highways.

Spare parts for Western cars are widely available from garages and dealerships around the region, although this is less the case in Belarus, Moldova and Ukraine, and of course in more rural areas.

Hire

Hiring a car in Eastern Europe is now a totally straightforward procedure and can be done hassle-free, even in Albania or Belarus where you might imagine it would still be problematic.

The big international companies will give you reliable service and a good standard of vehicle. Prebooked rates are generally lower than walk-in rates at rental offices, but either way you'll pay about 20% to 40% more than in Western Europe.

Local companies will usually offer lower prices than the multinationals, but it's best to only use local companies with good reputations – try asking at your hotel.

The big chain companies sometimes offer the flexibility of allowing you to pick up the vehicle from one place and drop it off at another at no additional charge.

If you're coming from North America, Australia or New Zealand, ask your airline if it has any special deals for rental cars in Eastern Europe, or check the ads in the weekend travel sections of major newspapers. You can often find very competitive deals.

Bear in mind that many companies will not allow you to take cars into certain countries. Russia, Belarus, Moldova and Albania all regularly feature on forbidden lists – there's usually a way around this, but check in advance with the car-hire firm you're planning to use.

You should be able to make advance reservations online. See the following:

» **Avis** (www.avis.com)
» **Budget** (www.budget.com)
» **Europcar** (www.europcar.com)
» **Hertz** (www.hertz.com)

Insurance

Third-party motor insurance is compulsory throughout the EU. For non-EU countries make sure you check the requirements with your insurer. For more information contact the **Association of British Insurers** (www.abi.org.uk).

You should get your insurer to issue a Green Card (which may cost extra), an internationally recognised proof of insurance, and check that it lists all the countries you intend to visit.

If the Green Card doesn't list one of the countries you're visiting and your insurer cannot (or will not) add it, you will have to take out separate third-party cover at the border of the country in question. This may be the case for Bulgaria, Russia and the Baltic countries. Allow extra time at borders to purchase insurance.

The European Accident Statement is available from your insurance company and allows each party at an accident to record information for insurance purposes. The Association of British Insurers has more details. Never sign an accident statement you cannot understand – insist on a translation and sign only if it's acceptable.

Taking out a European breakdown-assistance policy, such as the Five Star Service with **AA** (www.theaa.com) or the Eurocover Motoring Assistance with **RAC** (www.rac.co.uk), is a good investment.

Non-Europeans might find it cheaper to arrange for international coverage with their own national motoring organisation before leaving home. Ask your motoring organisation for details about reciprocal services offered by affiliated organisations around Europe.

Road Rules

Motoring organisations can supply members with country-by-country information on motoring regulations, or they may produce motoring guidebooks for general sale.

Driving in Eastern Europe can be much more dangerous than in Western Europe. Driving at night can be particularly hazardous in rural areas as the roads are often narrow and winding, and you may encounter horse-drawn vehicles, cyclists, pedestrians and domestic animals. In the event of an accident, you're supposed to notify the police and file an insurance claim.

If your car has significant body damage from a previous accident, point this out to customs upon arrival in the country and have it noted somewhere. Damaged vehicles may only be allowed to leave the country with police permission.

Standard international road signs are used in Eastern Europe. When driving in the region, keep the following rules in mind:

» Drive on the right-hand side of the road and overtake on the left.
» Don't overtake more than one car at a time.
» Seatbelts are mandatory for the driver and all passengers.
» Motorcyclists (and their passengers) must wear a helmet.
» Children under 12 and intoxicated passengers are

not allowed to sit in the front seat in most countries.

» Drink-driving is a serious offence – most Eastern European countries have a 0% blood-alcohol concentration (BAC) limit.

» When two roads of equal importance intersect, the vehicle coming from the right has right of way unless signs indicate otherwise; in many countries this rule also applies to cyclists, so take care.

» Trams have priority at crossroads and when they are turning right.

» Don't pass a tram that's stopping to let off passengers until everyone is out and the doors have closed again.

» Never pass a tram on the left or stop within 1m of tram tracks. A police officer who sees you blocking a tram route by waiting to turn left will flag you over.

» It's usually illegal to stop or park at the top of slopes, in front of pedestrian crossings, at bus or tram stops, on bridges or at level crossings.

» Speed limits are posted, and are generally:

* 110km/h or 120km/h on motorways
* 100km/h on highways
* 80km/h on secondary and tertiary roads
* 50km/h or 60km/h in built-up areas

» Motorcycles are usually limited to 90km/h on motorways, and vehicles with trailers to 80km/h.

Traffic police usually administer fines on the spot; always ask for a receipt.

Almost everywhere in Europe it is compulsory to carry a red warning triangle, which you must use when parking on a highway in an emergency. If you don't use the triangle and another vehicle hits you from behind, you will be held responsible.

A first-aid kit and a fire extinguisher are also required in most Eastern European countries, while a spare-bulb kit and headlamp converters are recommended. Contact the RAC or the AA for more information.

Hitching

Hitching is never entirely safe in any country and we don't recommend it. Travellers who decide to hitch should understand they are taking a small but potentially serious risk.

As long as public transport remains cheap in Eastern Europe, hitching is more for the adventure than for the transport. In the former Soviet Union, Albania and Romania, drivers expect riders to pay the equivalent of a bus fare. In Romania traffic is light, motorists are probably not going far, and you'll often face small vehicles overloaded with passengers.

If you want to give it a try, remember the following key points:

» Hitch in pairs; it will be safer.

» Solo women should never hitch.

» Don't hitch from city centres; take public transport to suburban exit routes.

» Make a clearly written cardboard sign indicating your intended destination, remembering to use the local name for the town or city (Praha not Prague, or Warszawa not Warsaw).

» Don't let your luggage be put in the boot, only sit next to a door you can open and ask drivers where they are going before you say where you're going.

» Always let someone know where you're going before heading off.

» Travellers considering hitching as a way of getting around can find destination-based information and rideshare options at the **Backpackers Ultimate Guide to Europe** (www.bugeurope.com) and the useful **Hitchhikers** (www.hitchhikers.org) which connects hitchhikers and drivers worldwide.

Local Transport

Public transport in Eastern Europe has been developed to a far greater extent than in Western Europe. There are excellent metro networks in Moscow and St Petersburg (Russia), Warsaw (Poland), Prague (Czech Republic), Kyiv (Ukraine), Minsk (Belarus), Budapest (Hungary) and Bucharest (Romania) as well as rudimentary ones in Sofia (Bulgaria) and Belgrade (Serbia).

One form of transport that doesn't exist in Western Europe is the shared minibus (*marshrutka* in the former Soviet Union, *furgon* in the Balkans). These quick but cramped minibuses are used throughout Eastern Europe as both inter- and intracity transport. St Petersburg would cease to function without them, and it's also the most likely way you'll travel between mountain towns in Albania.

Trolleybuses are another phenomenon of Eastern Europe. Although slow, they are environmentally friendly (being powered by electricity) and can be found throughout the former Soviet Union.

Trams are also popular, though they vary greatly in speed and modernity. Those in Russia are borderline antiques, which seem to derail on a daily basis, while Prague's fleet of sleek trams have electronic destination displays and automated announcements.

Tours

A package tour is generally worth considering only if your time is limited or you have a special interest such as skiing, canoeing, sailing, horse riding, cycling or spa treatments.

Cruises on the Danube are an exciting and romantic way to see Europe's most famous river, but they tend to be on the expensive side.

Most tour prices are for double occupancy, which means singles have to share a double room with someone of the same sex or pay a supplement to have the room to themselves.

Some experienced operators in Eastern Europe include the following:

» **Regent Holidays** (www. regent-holidays.co.uk) UK-based company offers comprehensive individual and group tours, which take in everything from a two-week Hanseatic Baltic tour to city breaks in Minsk and tours of Albania.

» **Baltic Holidays** (www. balticholidays.com) Exclusively runs tours of the Baltic region and northwest Russia, including weekend city breaks, family holidays, spa breaks and activity tours. Custom itineraries follow themes such as Soviet or Jewish heritage.

» **Eastern Europe Russian Travel Centre** (www.eetb travel.com) Australian-based company offers dozens of upmarket tours to the whole region, but particularly Russia; they also offer river cruises.

» **Trans-Siberian Experience** (www.trans-siberian. co.uk) This backpackers' travel organisation offers specialised trips in Russia.

» **Elder Hostel** (www.elder hostel.org) Offers educational tours for people over 50 throughout Russia, the Baltic countries, the Balkans and Central Europe.

Train

Trains are the most atmospheric, comfortable and fun way to make long overland journeys in Eastern Europe. All major cities are on the rail network, and it's perfectly feasible for train travel to be your only form of intercity transport. In general trains run like clockwork, and you can expect to arrive pretty

much to the timetabled minute.

If you're travelling overnight (which is nearly always the case when you're going between countries), you'll get a bed reservation included in the price of your ticket, although you may have to pay a few euros extra for the bedding once on board.

Each wagon is administered by a steward, who will look after your ticket and – crucially, if you arrive during the small hours – make sure that you get off at the correct stop.

Each wagon has a toilet and washbasin at either end – the state of cleanliness varies. Be aware that toilets may be closed while the train is at a station and a good 30 minutes before you arrive in a big city.

Overnight trains also have the benefit of saving you a night's accommodation. It's a great way to meet locals – and it's not unusual to be invited to stay for a night or two with people who shared your cabin.

If you plan to travel extensively by train, it might be worth checking the following resources:

» **Thomas Cook European Rail Timetable** (www. thomascookpublishing.com) A complete listing of train schedules that indicates where supplements apply or where reservations are necessary; it's updated monthly and you can order it online from Thomas Cook Publishing.

» **Rail Europe** (www. raileurope.com) Provides information on fares and passes as well as schedules for the most popular routes in Europe.

» **DB Bahn** (www. reiseauskunft.bahn.de) A particularly useful resource of timetables and fares for trains all across Eastern Europe; the website is available in many languages, including English.

Classes

The system of classes in Eastern Europe is similar to that in Western Europe. Short trips, or longer ones that don't involve sleeping on the train, are usually seated like a normal train – benches (on suburban trains) or aeroplane-style seats (on smarter intercity services).

There are generally three classes of sleeping accommodation on trains – each country has a different name for them, but for the sake of simplicity, we'll call them 3rd, 2nd and 1st class.

Third class Generally consists of six berths in each compartment and is the cheapest option; although you may feel your privacy has been slightly invaded. In the former Soviet Union, 3rd class is called *platskartny* and does not have compartments; instead, there's just one open-plan carriage with beds everywhere. Third-class is not widely available.

Second class Known as *kupeyny* in the former Soviet Union, 2nd class has four berths in a closed compartment. If there are two of you, you will share your accommodation with two others. However, if there are three of you, you'll often have the compartment to yourselves.

First class SV or *myagky* in the former Soviet Union is a treat, although you are paying for space rather than decor. Here you'll find two berths in a compartment, usually adorned with plastic flowers to remind you what you've paid for.

While it's reasonably priced, train travel costs more than bus travel in some countries. First-class tickets are double the price of 2nd-class tickets, which are in turn approximately twice the price of 3rd-class tickets.

Reservations

It's always advisable to buy a ticket in advance. Seat reservations are also recommended, but are only necessary if the timetable specifies one is required. On busy routes and during the summer, however, always try to reserve a seat several days in advance.

You can book most routes in the region from any main station in Eastern Europe.

For peace of mind, you may prefer to book tickets via travel agencies before you leave home, although this will be more expensive than booking on arrival.

Safety

Trains, while generally safe, can attract petty criminals. Carry your valuables on you at all times – don't even go to the bathroom without taking your cash, wallet and passport.

If you are sharing a compartment with others, you'll have to decide whether or not you trust them. If there's any doubt, be very cautious about leaving the compartment. At night, make sure your door is locked from the inside.

If you have a compartment to yourself, you can ask the steward to lock it while you go to the dining car or go for a wander outside when the train is stopped. However, be aware that most criminals strike when they can easily disembark from the train, and on occasions the stewards are complicit.

In the former Soviet Union, the open-plan 3rd-class accommodation is by far the most vulnerable to thieves.

Train Passes

Not all countries in Eastern Europe are covered by rail passes, but passes do include a number of destinations and so can be worthwhile if you are concentrating your travels on a particular part of the region. These are available online or through most travel agents. Check out the excellent summary of available passes, and their pros and cons, at **Man In**

Seat Sixty-one (www.seat61.com/Railpass.htm).

Keep in mind that all passes offer discounted 'youth' prices for travellers who are under 26 years of age on the first day of travel. Those aged four to 11 are eligible for a child rate. Discounted fares are also available if you are travelling in a group of two to five people (although you must always travel together).

In the USA, you can buy passes through **Rail Europe** (www.raileurope.com); in Australia you can use either **Rail Plus** (www.railplus.com.au) or Rail Europe.

BALKAN FLEXIPASS

The Balkan Flexipass includes Bulgaria, Romania, Greece, Serbia, Montenegro, Macedonia and Turkey. This pass is not available to anyone who is a resident of Europe, Morocco, Turkey, or any of the countries of the former Soviet Union. It's valid for 1st-class travel only. In the USA, Rail Europe charges US$260/156/130 per adult/youth/child for five days of 1st-class travel within one month; passes with 10 or 15 days of travel are also available.

EURAIL GLOBAL

The famous **Eurail** (www.eurail.com) pass allows the greatest flexibility for 'overseas' visitors only – if you are a resident of Europe, check out the InterRail Pass. The Eurail Global pass allows unlimited travel in 21 countries, including Croatia, the Czech Republic, Hungary, Romania and Slovenia. The pass is valid for a designated period of time, ranging from 15 days (adult/youth/child US$688/447/345) to three months (adult/youth/child US$1928/1256/965).

Alternatively, if you don't plan to travel quite so intensively but you still want the range of countries, consider the Eurail Global Flexi, which allows for 10 or 15 travel days over the course of two months. The Flexi is

suitably more affordable: the 10-day pass goes for US$811/530/407 per adult/youth/child from Rail Europe.

EURAIL SELECT

Again, only non-European residents can purchase this pass, which covers travel in three, four or five neighbouring countries, which you choose from the 18 available. Your Eastern European options include Bulgaria, Croatia, the Czech Republic, Hungary, Montenegro, Romania, Serbia and Slovenia. Note that Bulgaria, Serbia and Montenegro count as one country for Eurail pass purposes, as do Croatia and Slovenia, so the clever traveller can get six countries for the price of three.

From Rail Europe this would be US$434/283/218 per adult/youth/child for five days of travel in two months; adult and child fares are for 1st class, while the youth fare is only for 2nd class. Additional countries and additional days of travel are available for higher cost.

EUROPEAN EAST PASS

The European East Pass can be purchased by anyone not permanently resident in Europe and the former Soviet Union. The pass is valid for travel in Austria, the Czech Republic, Hungary, Slovakia and Poland, and offers five days of travel in a one-month period. It also includes bonuses such as Danube River cruises.

European East is sold in North America, Australia and the UK. Rail Europe charges US$307/214 for 1st-/2nd-class travel (half-price for children), with extra rail days available for purchase.

INTERRAIL GLOBAL

These passes are available to European residents of more than six months' standing (passport identification is required), although residents of Turkey and parts of North Africa can also buy them. Terms and conditions vary slightly from country to country, but the InterRail pass is not valid for travel within your country of residence. For complete information, check out the **InterRail** (www.interrail.net) website.

InterRail Global allows unlimited travel in 30 European countries, including BiH, Bulgaria, Croatia, the Czech Republic, Hungary, Macedonia, Montenegro, Poland, Romania, Serbia, Slovakia and Slovenia. The consecutive pass is valid for unlimited travel within a period of 22 days or one month. The Flexi version of InterRail allows for five or 10 rail days within a designated time period.

Interrail offers 22 days of unlimited 2nd-class travel for €469/309/240 per adult/youth/child. Ten 2nd-class rail days in the same time period go for €359/239/180.

INTERRAIL & EURAIL COUNTRY PASSES

If you are intending to travel extensively within any one country, you might consider purchasing a Country Pass (InterRail if you are an EU resident, Eurail if not). The Eurail Country Pass is available for Bulgaria, Croatia, the Czech Republic, Hungary, Poland, Romania and Slovenia. The InterRail Country Pass is available for all of those countries, plus Serbia and Slovakia. The passes and prices vary for each country, so check out the websites listed earlier for more information. You'll probably need to travel extensively to recoup your money, but the passes will save you the time and hassle of buying individual tickets that don't require reservations. Some of these countries also offer national rail passes; see individual country chapters for more information.

WANT MORE?

For in-depth language information and handy phrases, check out Lonely Planet's *Eastern Europe Phrasebook*, *Baltic Phrasebook* and *Ukrainian Phrasebook*. You'll find them at **shop. lonelyplanet.com**, or you can buy Lonely Planet's iPhone phrasebooks at the Apple App Store.

Language

This chapter offers basic vocabulary to help you get around Eastern Europe. If you read our coloured pronunciation guides as if they were English, you'll be understood. Note that the stressed syllables are indicated with italics. Although most Eastern European languages use the Roman alphabet, it's also worth familiarising yourself with the Cyrillic alphabet (see p1034) so you can read menus, maps and street signs that are in Cyrillic.

Some of the phrases in this chapter have both polite and informal forms (indicated by the abbreviations 'pol' and 'inf' respectively). Use the polite form when addressing older people, officials or service staff. The abbreviations 'm' and 'f' indicate masculine and feminine gender respectively.

ALBANIAN

There are two main dialects of Albanian – Tosk (spoken in southern Albania, Greece, Italy and Turkey) and Gheg (spoken in northern Albania, Kosovo and the surrounding areas of Serbia, Montenegro and Macedonia). Tosk is the official language of Albania and is also used in this chapter.

Note that ew is pronounced as 'ee' with rounded lips, uh as the 'a' in 'ago', dh as the 'th' in 'that', dz as the 'ds' in 'adds', and zh as the 's' in 'pleasure'. Also, ll and rr are pronounced stronger than when they are written as single letters.

Basics

Hello.	*Tungjatjeta.*	toon·dya·tye·ta
Goodbye.	*Mirupafshim.*	mee·roo·paf·sheem
Excuse me.	*Më falni.*	muh *fal*·nee
Sorry.	*Më vjen keq.*	muh vyen kech
Please.	*Ju lutem.*	yoo *loo*·tem
Thank you.	*Faleminderit.*	fa·le·meen·*de*·reet
Yes./No.	*Po./Jo.*	po/yo

What's your name?
Si quheni? see *choo*·he·nee

My name is ...
Unë quhem ... oo·nuh *choo*·hem ...

Do you speak English?
A flisni anglisht? a *flees*·nee ang·*leesht*

I don't understand.
Unë nuk kuptoj. oo·nuh nook koop·*toy*

Accommodation

campsite	*vend kampimi*	vend kam·*pee*·mee
guesthouse	*bujtinë*	booy·*tee*·nuh
hotel	*hotel*	ho·*tel*
youth hostel	*fjetore për të rinj*	fye·*to*·re puhr tuh reeny

Signs – Albanian	
Hyrje	Entrance
Dalje	Exit
Hapur	Open
Mbyllur	Closed
E Ndaluar	Prohibited
Nevojtorja	Toilets

Numbers – Albanian

1	një	nyuh
2	dy	dew
3	tre	tre
4	katër	ka·tuhr
5	pesë	pe·suh
6	gjashtë	dyash·tuh
7	shtatë	shta·tuh
8	tetë	te·tuh
9	nëntë	nuhn·tuh
10	dhjetë	dhye·tuh

Do you have a ... room?	A keni një dhomë ...?	a ke·nee nyuh dho·muh ...
single	teke	te·ke
double	dopjo	dop·yo

How much is it per ...?	Sa kushton për një ...?	sa koosh·ton puhr nyuh ...
night	natë	na·tuh
person	njeri	nye·ree

Eating & Drinking

Is there a vegetarian restaurant near here?
A ka ndonjë restorant vegjetarian këtu afër? — a ka ndo·nyuh res·to·rant ve·dye·ta·ree·an kuh·too a·fuhr

What would you recommend?
Çfarë më rekomandoni? — chfa·ruh muh re·ko·man·do·nee

I'll have ...
Dua ... — doo·a ...

Cheers!
Gëzuar! — guh·zoo·ar

I'd like the ..., please.	Më sillni ..., ju lutem.	muh seell·nee ... yoo loo·tem
bill	faturën	fa·too·ruhn
menu	menunë	me·noo·nuh

(bottle of) beer	(shishe) birrë	(shee·she) bee·rruh
(cup of) coffee/tea	(filxhan) kafe/çaj	(feel·dyan) ka·fe/chai
water	ujë	oo·yuh
(glass of) wine	(gotë) verë	(go·tuh) ve·ruh

breakfast	mëngjes	muhn·dyes
lunch	drekë	dre·kuh
dinner	darkë	dar·kuh

Emergencies

Help!	Ndihmë!	ndeeh·muh
Go away!	Ik!	eek

Call ...!	Thirrni ...!	theerr·nee ...
a doctor	doktorin	dok·to·reen
the police	policinë	po·lee·tsee·nuh

I'm lost.
Kam humbur rrugën. — kam hoom·boor rroo·guhn

I'm ill.
Jam i/e sëmurë. (m/f) — yam ee/e suh·moo·ruh

Where are the toilets?
Ku janë banjat? — koo ya·nuh ba·nyat

Shopping & Services

I'm looking for ...
Po kërkoj për ... — po kuhr·koy puhr ...

How much is it?
Sa kushton? — sa koosh·ton

That's too expensive.
Është shumë shtrenjtë. — uhsh·tuh shoo·muh shtreny·tuh

market	treg	treg
post office	posta	pos·ta
tourist office	zyrë turistike	zew·ra too·rees·tee·ke

Transport & Directions

Where's the ...?
Ku është ...? — koo uhsh·tuh ...

What's the address?
Cila është adresa? — tsee·la uhsh·tuh a·dre·sa

Can you show me (on the map)?
A mund të ma tregoni (në hartë)? — a moond tuh ma tre·go·nee (nuh har·tuh)

One ... ticket (to Shkodër), please.	Një biletë ... (për në Shkodër), ju lutem.	nyuh bee·le·tuh ... (puhr nuh shko·duhr) yoo loo·tem
one-way	për vajtje	puhr vai·tye
return	kthimi	kthee·mee

boat	anija	a·nee·ya
bus	autobusi	a·oo·to·boo·see
plane	aeroplani	a·e·ro·pla·nee
train	treni	tre·nee

BULGARIAN

Bulgarian is written in the Cyrillic alphabet which is very similar to that used in Russian (see p1034).

Vowels in unstressed syllables are generally pronounced shorter and weaker than they are in stressed syllables. Note that uh is pronounced as the 'a' in 'ago' and zh as the 's' in 'pleasure'.

Basics

Hello.	Здравейте.	zdra·vey·te
Goodbye.	Довиждане.	do·veezh·da·ne
Excuse me.	Извинете.	iz·vee·ne·te
Sorry.	Съжалявам.	suh·zhal·ya·vam
Please.	Моля.	mol·ya
Thank you.	Благодаря.	bla·go·dar·ya
Yes./No.	Да./Не.	da/ne

What's your name?
Как се казвате/   kak se *kaz*·va·te/
казваш? (pol/inf)   *kaz*·vash

My name is ...
Казвам се ...   *kaz*·vam se ...

Do you speak English?
Говорите ли   go·*vo*·ree·te lee
английски?   ang·*lees*·kee

I don't understand.
Не разбирам.   ne raz·*bee*·ram

Accommodation

campsite	къмпинг	*kuhm*·peeng
guesthouse	пансион	pan·see·*on*
hotel	хотел	ho·*tel*
youth hostel	общежитие	ob·shte·*zhee*·tee·ye

Do you have a ... room?	Имате ли стая с ...?	ee·ma·te lee *sta*·ya s ...
single	едно легло	ed·no leg·*lo*
double	едно голямо легло	ed·*no* go·*lya*·mo leg·*lo*

Numbers – Bulgarian

1	един	ed·*een*
2	два	dva
3	три	tree
4	четири	che·tee·ree
5	пет	pet
6	шест	shest
7	седем	se·dem
8	осем	o·sem
9	девет	de·vet
10	десет	de·set

How much is it per ...?	Колко е на ...?	*kol*·ko e na ...
night	вечер	ve·cher
person	човек	cho·vek

Eating & Drinking

Do you have vegetarian food?
Имате ли   ee·ma·te lee
вегетерианска   ve·ge·te·ree·*an*·ska
храна?   hra·*na*

What would you recommend?
Какво ще   kak·*vo* shte
препоръчате?   pre·po·*ruh*·cha·te

I'll have ...
Ще взема ...   shte *vze*·ma ...

Cheers!
Наздраве!   na·*zdra*·ve

I'd like the ..., please.	Дайте ми ..., моля.	*dai*·te mee ... *mol*·ya
bill	сметката	*smet*·ka·ta
menu	менюто	men·*yoo*·to

(bottle of) beer	(шише) бира	(shee·*she*) *bee*·ra
(cup of) coffee/tea	(чаша) кафе/чай	(*chas*·ha) ka·*fe*/chai
water	вода	vo·*da*
(glass of) wine	(чаша) вино	(*cha*·sha) *vee*·no

breakfast	закуска	za·*koos*·ka
lunch	обед	o·bed
dinner	вечеря	ve·*cher*·ya

Emergencies

Help!	Помощ!	po·mosht
Go away!	Махайте се!	ma·hai·te se

Call ...!	Повикайте …!	po·vee·kai·te …
a doctor	лекар	le·kar
the police	полицията	po·lee·tsee·ya·ta

I'm lost.
Загубих се. — za·goo·beeh se

I'm ill.
Болен/Болна — bo·len/bol·na
съм. (m/f) — suhm

Where are the toilets?
Къде има тоалетни? — kuh·de ee·ma to·a·let·nee

Shopping & Services

I'm looking for ...
Търся … — tuhr·sya …

How much is it?
Колко струва? — kol·ko stroo·va

That's too expensive.
Скъпо е. — skuh·po e

bank	банка	ban·ka
post office	поща	po·shta
tourist office	бюро за туристическа информация	byoo·ro za too·ree·stee·ches·ka een·for·ma·tsee·ya

Transport & Directions

Where's the ...?
Къде се намира …? — kuh·de se na·mee·ra …

What's the address?
Какъв е адресът? — ka·kuhv e ad·re·suht

Can you show me (on the map)?
Можете ли да ми покажете (на картата)? — mo·zhe·te lee da mee po·ka·zhe·te (na kar·ta·ta)

One ... ticket (to Varna), please.	Един билет … (за Варна), моля.	e·deen bee·let … (za var·na) mol·ya
one-way	в едната посока	v ed·na·ta po·so·ka
return	за отиване и връщане	za o·tee·va·ne ee vruhsh·ta·ne

boat	корабът	ko·ra·buht
bus	автобусът	av·to·boo·suht
plane	самолетът	sa·mo·le·tuht
train	влакът	vla·kuht

CROATIAN & SERBIAN

Linguists commonly refer to the varieties spoken in Croatia, Serbia, Bosnia & Hercegovina, Montenegro and Kosovo with the umbrella term 'Serbo-Croatian', while acknowledging dialectical differences between them. Serbian uses both the Cyrillic alphabet (see p1034) and the Roman alphabet. In this chapter, we've indicated significant differences between Croatian and Serbian with (C) and (S) respectively.

Note that r is rolled and that zh is pronounced as the 's' in 'pleasure'.

Basics

Hello.	Bog. (C)	bog
	Zdravo. (S)	zdra·vo
Goodbye.	Zbogom.	zbo·gom
Excuse me.	Oprostite.	o·pro·sti·te
Sorry.	Žao mi je.	zha·o mi ye
Please.	Molim.	mo·lim
Thank you.	Hvala.	hva·la
Yes.	Da.	da
No.	Ne.	ne

What's your name?
Kako se zovete/ zoveš? (pol/inf) — ka·ko se zo·ve·te/ zo·vesh

My name is ...
Zovem se … — zo·vem se …

Do you speak English?
Govorite/Govoriš li engleski? (pol/inf) — go·vo·ri·te/go·vo·rish li en·gle·ski

I don't understand.
Ja ne razumijem. — ya ne ra·zu·mi·yem

Accommodation

campsite	kamp	kamp
guesthouse	privatni smještaj	pri·vat·ni smyesh·tai
hotel	hotel	ho·tel
youth hostel	prenočište za mladež	pre·no·chish·te za mla·dezh

Signs – Croatian & Serbian	
Ulaz/Улаз	Entrance
Izlaz/Излаз	Exit
Otvoreno/Отворено	Open
Zatvoreno/Затворено	Closed
Zabranjeno/Забрањено	Prohibited
Zahodi/Тоалети	Toilets

Numbers – Croatian & Serbian

1	jedan	ye·dan
2	dva	dva
3	tri	tri
4	četiri	che·ti·ri
5	pet	pet
6	šest	shest
7	sedam	se·dam
8	osam	o·sam
9	devet	de·vet
10	deset	de·set

Do you have a ... room?	Imate li ... sobu?	i·ma·te li ... so·bu
single	jedno-krevetnu	yed·no·kre·vet·nu
double	dvokrevetnu	dvo·kre·vet·nu
How much is it per ...?	Koliko stoji po ...?	ko·li·ko sto·yi po ...
night	noći	no·chi
person	osobi	o·so·bi

Eating & Drinking

What would you recommend?
Što biste preporučili?   shto bi·ste pre·po·ru·chi·li

Do you have vegetarian food?
Da li imate
vegetarijanski obrok?   da li i·ma·te
ve·ge·ta·ri·yan·ski o·brok

I'll have ...
Želim naručiti ...   zhe·lim na·ru·chi·ti ...

Cheers!
Živjeli!   zhi·vye·li

I'd like the ..., please.	Mogu li dobiti ..., molim?	mo·gu li do·bi·ti ... mo·lim
bill	račun	ra·chun
menu	jelovnik	ye·lov·nik
(bottle of) beer	(boca) piva	(bo·tsa) pi·va
(cup of) coffee/tea	(šalica/ šoljica) kave/čaja (C/S)	(sha·lee·tsa/ sho·lyee·tsa) ka·ve/cha·ya
water	voda	vo·da
(glass of) wine	(čaša) vina	(cha·sha) vi·na
breakfast	doručak	do·ru·chak
lunch	ručak	ru·chak
dinner	večera	ve·che·ra

Emergencies

Help!   Upomoć!   u·po·moch

Go away!   Maknite se!   mak·ni·te se

Call ...!	Zovite ...!	zo·vi·te ...
a doctor	liječnika (C) lekara (S)	li·yech·ni·ka le·ka·ra
the police	policiju	po·li·tsi·yu

I'm lost.
Izgubio/Izgubila
sam se. (m/f)   iz·gu·bi·o/iz·gu·bi·la
sam se

I'm ill.
Ja sam bolestan/
bolesna. (m/f)   ya sam bo·le·stan/
bo·le·sna

Where are the toilets?
Gdje se nalaze
zahodi/toaleti? (C/S)   gdye se na·la·ze
za·ho·di/to·a·le·ti

Shopping & Services

I'm looking for ...
Tražim ...   tra·zhim

How much is it?
Koliko stoji/
košta? (C/S)   ko·li·ko sto·yi/
kosh·ta

That's too expensive.
To je preskupo.   to ye pre·sku·po

bank	banka	ban·ka
post office	poštanski ured	po·shtan·skee oo·red
tourist office	turistička agencija	tu·ris·tich·ka a·gen·tsi·ya

Transport & Directions

Where's the ...?
Gdje je ...?   gdye ye ...

What's the address?
Koja je adresa?   ko·ya ye a·dre·sa

Can you show me (on the map)?
Možete li mi to
pokazati (na karti)?   mo·zhe·te li mi to
po·ka·za·ti (na kar·ti)

One ... ticket (to Sarajevo), please.	Jednu ... kartu (do Sarajeva), molim.	yed·nu ... kar·tu (do sa·ra·ye·va) mo·lim
one-way	jedno-smjernu	yed·no·smyer·nu
return	povratnu	po·vrat·nu

boat	brod	brod
bus	autobus	a·u·to·bus
plane	zrakoplov (C)	zra·ko·plov
	avion (S)	a·vi·on
train	vlak/voz (C/S)	vlak/voz

CZECH

An accent mark over a vowel in written Czech indicates it's pronounced as a long sound.

Note that air is pronounced as in 'hair', aw as in 'law', oh as the 'o' in 'note', ow as in 'how', uh as the 'a' in 'ago', kh as in the Scottish *loch*, and zh as the 's' in 'pleasure'. Also, r is rolled in Czech and the apostrophe (') indicates a slight y sound.

Basics

Hello.	Ahoj.	uh·hoy
Goodbye.	Na shledanou.	nuh·skhle·duh·noh
Excuse me.	Promiňte.	pro·min'·te
Sorry.	Promiňte.	pro·min'·te
Please.	Prosím.	pro·seem
Thank you.	Děkuji.	dye·ku·yi
Yes./No.	Ano./Ne.	uh·no/ne

What's your name?
| Jak se jmenujete/ | yuhk se yme·nu·ye·te/ |
| jmenuješ? (pol/inf) | yme·nu·yesh |

My name is ...
| Jmenuji se ... | yme·nu·yi se ... |

Do you speak English?
| Mluvíte anglicky? | mlu·vee·te uhn·glits·ki |

I don't understand.
| Nerozumím. | ne·ro·zu·meem |

Accommodation

campsite	tábořiště	ta·bo·rzhish·tye
guesthouse	penzion	pen·zi·on
hotel	hotel	ho·tel
youth hostel	mládežnická	mla·dezh·nyits·ka
	ubytovna	u·bi·tov·nuh

Signs – Czech	
Vchod	Entrance
Východ	Exit
Otevřeno	Open
Zavřeno	Closed
Zakázáno	Prohibited
Záchody/Toalety	Toilets

Do you have a ... room?
	Máte ... pokoj?	ma·te ... po·koy
single	jednolůžkový	yed·no·loozh·ko·vee
double	dvoulůžkový	dvoh·loozh·ko·vee

How much is it per ...?
	Kolik to stojí ...?	ko·lik to sto·yee ...
night	na noc	nuh nots
person	za osobu	zuh o·so·bu

Eating & Drinking

What would you recommend?
| Co byste doporučil/ | tso bis·te do·po·ru·chil/ |
| doporučila? (m/f) | do·po·ru·chi·luh |

Do you have vegetarian food?
| Máte vegetariánská | ma·te ve·ge·tuh·ri·ans·ka |
| jídla? | yeed·luh |

I'll have ...
| Dám si ... | dam si ... |

Cheers!
| Na zdraví! | nuh zdruh·vee |

I'd like the ..., please.	Chtěl/ Chtěla bych ..., prosím. (m/f)	khtyel/ khtye·luh bikh ... pro·seem
bill	účet	oo·chet
menu	jídelníček	yee·del·nyee·chek
(bottle of) beer	(láhev) piva	(la·hef) pi·vuh
(cup of) coffee/tea	(šálek) kávy/čaje	(sha·lek) ka·vi/chuh·ye
water	voda	vo·duh
(glass of) wine	(skleničku) vína	(skle·nyich·ku) vee·nuh
breakfast	snídaně	snee·duh·nye
lunch	oběd	o·byed
dinner	večeře	ve·che·rzhe

Emergencies

Help!	Pomoc!	po·mots
Go away!	Běžte pryč!	byezh·te prich
Call ...!	Zavolejte ...!	zuh·vo·ley·te ...
a doctor	lékaře	lair·kuh·rzhe
the police	policii	po·li·tsi·yi

Numbers – Czech		
1	*jeden*	ye·den
2	*dva*	dvuh
3	*tři*	trzhi
4	*čtyři*	chti·rzhi
5	*pět*	pyet
6	*šest*	shest
7	*sedm*	se·dm
8	*osm*	o·sm
9	*devět*	de·vyet
10	*deset*	de·set

I'm lost.
Zabloudil/   zuh·bloh·dyil/
Zabloudila jsem. (m/f)   zuh·bloh·dyi·luh ysem

I'm ill.
Jsem nemocný/   ysem ne·mots·nee/
nemocná. (m/f)   ne·mots·na

Where are the toilets?
Kde jsou toalety?   gde ysoh to·uh·le·ti

Shopping & Services

I'm looking for ...
Hledám ...   hle·dam ...

How much is it?
Kolik to stojí?   ko·lik to sto·yee

That's too expensive.
To je moc drahé.   to ye mots druh·hair

bank	*banka*	buhn·kuh
post office	*pošta*	posh·tuh
tourist office	*turistická*	tu·ris·tits·ka
	informační	in·for·muhch·nyee
	kancelář	kuhn·tse·larzh

Transport & Directions

Where's the ...?
Kde je ...?   gde ye ...

What's the address?
Jaká je adresa?   yuh·ka ye uh·dre·suh

Can you show me (on the map)?
Můžete mi to   moo·zhe·te mi to
ukázat (na mapě)?   u·ka·zuht (nuh muh·pye)

One ... ticket	*... jízdenku*	... yeez·den·ku
to (Telč),	*do (Telče),*	do (tel·che)
please.	*prosim.*	pro·seem
one-way	*Jedno-*	yed·no-
	směrnou	smyer·noh
return	*Zpáteční*	zpa·tech·nyee

bus	*autobus*	ow·to·bus
plane	*letadlo*	le·tuhd·lo
train	*vlak*	vluhk

ESTONIAN

Double vowels in written Estonian indicate they are pronounced as long sounds.

Note that air is pronounced as in 'hair', aw as in 'law', ea as in 'ear', eu as in 'nurse', ew as 'ee' with rounded lips, oh as the 'o' in 'note', ow as in 'how', uh as the 'a' in 'ago', kh as in the Scottish *loch*, and zh as the 's' in 'pleasure'.

Basics

Hello.	*Tere.*	te·re
Goodbye.	*Nägemist.*	nair·ge·mist
Excuse me.	*Vabandage. (pol)*	va·ban·da·ge
	Vabanda. (inf)	va·ban·da
Sorry.	*Vabandust.*	va·ban·dust
Please.	*Palun.*	pa·lun
Thank you.	*Tänan.*	tair·nan
Yes.	*Jaa.*	yaa
No.	*Ei.*	ay

What's your name?
Mis on teie nimi?   mis on tay·e ni·mi

My name is ...
Minu nimi on ...   mi·nu ni·mi on ...

Do you speak English?
Kas te räägite   kas te rair·git·te
inglise keelt?   ing·kli·se keylt

I don't understand.
Ma ei saa aru.   ma ay saa a·ru

Eating & Drinking

What would you recommend?
Mida te soovitate?   mi·da te saw·vit·tat·te

Do you have vegetarian food?
Kas teil on taimetoitu?   kas tayl on tai·met·toyt·tu

I'll have a ...
Ma tahaksin ...   ma ta·hak·sin ...

Cheers!
Terviseks!   tair·vi·seks

Signs – Estonian	
Sissepääs	Entrance
Väljapääs	Exit
Avatud/Lahti	Open
Suletud/Kinni	Closed
WC	Toilets

I'd like the ..., please.	Ma sooviksin ..., palun.	ma saw·vik·sin ... pa·lun
bill	arvet	ar·vet
menu	menüüd	me·newt
(bottle of) beer	(pudel) õlut	(pu·del) uh·lut
(cup of) coffee/tea	(tass) kohvi/teed	(tas) kokh·vi/teyd
water	vesi	ve·si
(glass of) wine	(klaas) veini	(klaas) vay·ni
breakfast	hommikusöök	hom·mi·ku·seuk
dinner	õhtusöök	uhkh·tu·seuk
lunch	lõuna	luh·u·na

Numbers – Estonian

1	üks	ewks
2	kaks	kaks
3	kolm	kolm
4	neli	ne·li
5	viis	vees
6	kuus	koos
7	seitse	say·tse
8	kaheksa	ka·hek·sa
9	üheksa	ew·hek·sa
10	kümme	kewm·me

One ... ticket (to Pärnu), please.	Üks ... pilet (Pärnusse), palun.	ewks ... pi·let (pair·nus·se) pa·lun
one-way	ühe otsa	ew·he o·tsa
return	edasi-tagasi	e·da·si·ta·ga·si
boat	laev	laiv
bus	buss	bus
plane	lennuk	len·nuk
train	rong	rongk

Emergencies

Help!	Appi!	ap·pi
Go away!	Minge ära!	ming·ke air·ra
Call ...!	Kutsuge ...!	ku·tsu·ge ...
a doctor	arst	arst
the police	politsei	po·li·tsay

I'm lost.
Ma olen ära eksinud.   ma o·len air·ra ek·si·nud

Where are the toilets?
Kus on WC?   kus on ve·se

Shopping & Services

I'm looking for ...
Ma otsin ...   ma o·tsin

How much is it?
Kui palju see maksab?   ku·i pal·yu sey mak·sab

That's too expensive.
See on liiga kallis.   sey on lee·ga kal·lis

bank	pank	pank
market	turg	turg
post office	postkontor	post·kont·tor

Transport & Directions

Where's the ...?
Kus on ...?   kus on ...

Can you show me (on the map)?
Kas te näitaksite mulle (kaardil)?   kas te nair·i·tak·sit·te mul·le (kaar·dil)

HUNGARIAN

A symbol over a vowel in written Hungarian indicates it's pronounced as a long sound. Double consonants should be drawn out a little longer than in English.

Note that aw is pronounced as in 'law', eu as in 'nurse', ew as 'ee' with rounded lips, and zh as the 's' in 'pleasure'. Also, r is rolled in Hungarian and the apostrophe (') indicates a slight y sound.

Basics

Hello.	Szervusz. (sg) Szervusztok. (pl)	ser·vus ser·vus·tawk
Goodbye.	Viszlát.	vis·lat
Excuse me.	Elnézést kérek.	el·ney·zeysht key·rek
Sorry.	Sajnálom.	shoy·na·lawm
Please.	Kérem. (pol) Kérlek. (inf)	key·rem keyr·lek
Thank you.	Köszönöm.	keu·seu·neum
Yes.	Igen.	i·gen
No.	Nem.	nem

What's your name?
Mi a neve/neved? (pol/inf)   mi o ne·ve/ne·ved

My name is ...
A nevem ...   o ne·vem ...

Do you speak English?
Beszél/Beszélsz   be·seyl/be·seyls
angolul? (pol/inf)   on·gaw·lul

I don't understand.
Nem értem.   nem eyr·tem

Accommodation

campsite	*kemping*	kem·ping
guesthouse	*panzió*	pon·zi·āw
hotel	*szálloda*	sal·law·do
youth hostel	*ifjúsági szálló*	if·yū·sha·gi sal·lāw

Do you have a ... room?	*Van Önnek kiadó egy ... szobája?*	von eun·nek ki·o·dāw ed' ... saw·ba·yo
single	*egyágyas*	ej·a·dyosh
double	*duplaágyas*	dup·lo·a·dyosh

How much is it per ...?	*Mennyibe kerül egy ...?*	men'·nyi·be ke·rewl ej ...
night	*éjszakára*	ey·so·ka·ro
person	*főre*	fēū·re

Eating & Drinking

What would you recommend?
Mit ajánlana?   mit o·yan·lo·no

Do you have vegetarian food?
Vannak Önöknél   von·nok eu·neuk·neyl
vegetáriánus ételek?   ve·ge·ta·ri·a·nush ey·te·lek

I'll have ...
... kérek.   ... key·rek

Cheers! (to one person)
Egészségedre!   e·geys·shey·ged·re

Cheers! (to more than one person)
Egészségetekre!   e·geys·shey·ge·tek·re

I'd like the ...	*... szeretném.*	... se·ret·neym
bill	*A számlát*	o sam·lat
menu	*Az étlapot*	oz eyt·lo·pawt

Signs – Hungarian

Bejárat	Entrance
Kijárat	Exit
Nyitva	Open
Zárva	Closed
Tilos	Prohibited
Toalett	Toilets

Numbers – Hungarian

1	*egy*	ej
2	*kettő*	ket·tēū
3	*három*	ha·rawm
4	*négy*	neyj
5	*öt*	eut
6	*hat*	hot
7	*hét*	heyt
8	*nyolc*	nyawlts
9	*kilenc*	ki·lents
10	*tíz*	teez

(bottle of) beer	*(üveg) sör*	(ew·veg) sheur
(cup of) coffee/tea	*(csésze) kávé/tea*	(chey·se) ka·vey/te·o
water	*víz*	veez
(glass of) wine	*(pohár) bor*	(paw·har) bawr

breakfast	*reggeli*	reg·ge·li
lunch	*ebéd*	e·beyd
dinner	*vacsora*	vo·chaw·ro

Emergencies

Help!	*Segítség!*	she·geet·sheyg
Go away!	*Menjen innen!*	men·yen in·nen
Call a doctor!	*Hívjon orvost!*	heev·yawn awr·vawsht
Call the police!	*Hívja a rendőrséget!*	heev·yo o rend·ēūr·shey·get

I'm lost.
Eltévedtem.   el·tey·ved·tem

I'm ill.
Rosszul vagyok.   raws·sul vo·dyawk

Where are the toilets?
Hol a vécé?   hawl o vey·tsey

Shopping & Services

I'm looking for ...
Keresem a ...   ke·re·shem o ...

How much is it?
Mennyibe kerül?   men'·nyi·be ke·rewl

That's too expensive.
Ez túl drága.   ez tūl dra·go

market	*piac*	pi·ots
post office	*postahivatal*	pawsh·to·hi·vo·tol
tourist office	*turistairoda*	tu·rish·to·i·raw·do

Transport & Directions

Where's the ...?
Hol van a ...?   hawl von o ...

What's the address?
Mi a cím?   mi o tseem

Can you show me (on the map)?
Meg tudja mutatni   meg *tud*·yo *mu*·tot·ni
nekem (a térképen)?   ne·kem (o *teyr*·key·pen)

One ... ticket to (Eger), please.	*Egy ... jegy (Eger)be.*	ej ... yej (e·ger)·be
one-way	*csak oda*	chok aw·do
return	*oda-vissza*	aw·do·vis·so
bus	*busz*	bus
plane	*repülőgép*	re·pew·lēū·geyp
train	*vonat*	vaw·not

LATVIAN

A line over a vowel in written Latvian indicates it's pronounced as a long sound.

Note that air is pronounced as in 'hair', aw as in 'law', ea as in 'ear', ow as in 'how', wa as in 'water', dz as the 'ds' in 'adds', and zh as the 's' in 'pleasure'. The apostrophe (') indicates a slight y sound.

Basics

Hello.	*Sveiks.*	svayks
Goodbye.	*Atā.*	a·taa
Excuse me.	*Atvainojiet.*	at·vai·nwa·yeat
Sorry.	*Piedodiet.*	pea·dwa·deat
Please.	*Lūdzu.*	loo·dzu
Thank you.	*Paldies.*	pal·deas
Yes./No.	*Jā./Nē.*	yaa/nair

What's your name?
Kā Jūs sauc?   kaa yoos sowts

My name is ...
Mani sauc ...   ma·ni sowts ...

Do you speak English?
Vai Jūs runājat   vai yoos ru·*naa*·yat
angliski?   *ang*·li·ski

I don't understand.
Es nesaprotu.   es ne·sa·prwa·tu

Eating & Drinking

What would you recommend?
Ko Jūs iesakat?   kwa yoos ea·sa·kat

Do you have vegetarian food?
Vai Jums ir veģetārie   vai yums ir ve·dye·taa·rea
ēdieni?   air·dea·ni

I'll have a ...
Man lūdzu vienu ...   man loo·dzu vea·nu ...

Cheers!
Priekā!   prea·kaa

I'd like the ..., please.	*Es vēlos ..., lūdzu.*	es vair·lwas ... loo·dzu
bill	*rēķinu*	rair·tyi·nu
menu	*ēdienkarti*	air·dean·kar·ti
(bottle of) beer	*(pudeli) alu*	*(pu*·de·li) a·lu
(cup of) coffee/tea	*(tasi) kafijas/ tējas*	*(ta*·si) ka·fi·yas/ tair·yas
water	*ūdeni*	oo·de·ni
(glass of) wine	*(glāzi) vīnu*	*(glaa*·zi) vee·nu
breakfast	*brokastis*	brwa·ka·stis
lunch	*pusdienas*	pus·dea·nas
dinner	*vakariņas*	va·ka·ri·nyas

Emergencies

Help!	*Palīgā!*	pa·lee·gaa
Go away!	*Ej prom!*	ay prwam
Call a doctor!	*Zvani ārstam!*	zva·ni aar·stam
Call the police!	*Zvani policijai!*	zva·ni po·li·tsi·yai

I'm lost.
Esmu apmaldījies.   es·mu ap·mal·dee·yeas

Where are the toilets?
Kur ir tualetes?   kur ir tu·a·le·tes

Shopping & Services

I'm looking for ...
Es meklēju ...   es mek·lair·yu ...

How much is it?
Cik maksā?   tsik mak·saa

That's too expensive.
Tas ir par dārgu.   tas ir par daar·gu

Numbers – Latvian

1	*viens*	veans
2	*divi*	di·vi
3	*trīs*	trees
4	*četri*	che·tri
5	*pieci*	pea·tsi
6	*seši*	se·shi
7	*septiņi*	sep·ti·nyi
8	*astoņi*	as·twa·nyi
9	*deviņi*	de·vi·nyi
10	*desmit*	des·mit

bank	*banka*	ban·ka
market	*tirgus*	tir·gus
post office	*pasts*	pasts

Transport & Directions

Where's the ...?
Kur ir ...?   kur ir ...

Can you show me (on the map)?
Vai Jūs varat man   vai yoos va·rat man
parādīt (uz kartes)?   pa·raa·deet (uz kar·tes)

One ... ticket	*Vienu ... biļeti*	vea·nu ... bi·lye·ti
(to Jūrmala),	*(uz Jūrmalu),*	(uz yoor·ma·lu)
please.	*lūdzu.*	loo·dzu
one-way	*vienvirziena*	vean·vir·zea·na
return	*turp-atpakaļ*	turp·at·pa·kal'

boat	*laiva*	lai·va
bus	*autobus*	ow·to·bus
plane	*lidmašīna*	lid·ma·shee·na
train	*vilciens*	vil·tseans

LITHUANIAN

Symbols on vowels in written Lithuanian indicate they are pronounced as long sounds.

Note that aw is pronounced as in 'law', ea as in 'ear', ow as in 'how', wa as in 'water', dz as the 'ds' in 'adds', and zh as the 's' in 'pleasure'.

Basics

Hello.	*Sveiki.*	svay·ki
Goodbye.	*Viso gero.*	vi·so ge·ro
Excuse me.	*Atleiskite.*	at·lays·ki·te
Sorry.	*Atsiprašau.*	at·si·pra·show
Please.	*Prašau.*	pra·show
Thank you.	*Ačiū.*	aa·choo
Yes./No.	*Taip./Ne.*	taip/ne

What's your name?
Koks jūsų vardas?   kawks yoo·soo var·das

My name is ...
Mano vardas ...   ma·no var·das ...

Do you speak English?
Ar kalbate angliškai?   ar kal·ba·te aang·lish·kai

I don't understand.
Aš nesuprantu.   ash ne·su·pran·tu

Eating & Drinking

What would you recommend?
Ką jūs rekomenduo-   kaa yoos re·ko·men·dwo·
tumėte?   tu·mey·te

Do you have vegetarian food?
Ar turite vegetariško   ar tu·ri·te ve·ge·taa·rish·ko
maisto?   mais·to

I'll have a ...
Aš užsisakysiu ...   ash uzh·si·sa·kee·syu ...

Cheers!
Į sveikatą!   ee svay·kaa·taa

I'd like the ...,	*Aš*	ash
please.	*norėčiau ...*	no·rey·chyow ...
bill	*sąskaitos*	saas·kai·taws
menu	*meniu*	me·nyu

(bottle of)	*(butelio)*	(bu·te·lyo)
beer	*alaus*	a·lows
(cup of)	*(puodelio)*	(pwa·dey·lyo)
coffee/tea	*kavos/*	ka·vaws/
	arbatos	ar·baa·tos
water	*vandens*	van·dens
(glass of)	*(taurės)*	(tow·reys)
wine	*vyno*	vee·no

breakfast	*pusryčių*	pus·ree·chyoo
lunch	*lančo*	lan·cho
dinner	*pietų*	pea·too

Emergencies

Help!	*Padėkit!*	pa·dey·kit
Go away!	*Eikit iš čia!*	ay·kit ish chya

Signs – Lithuanian

Įėjimas	Entrance
Išėjimas	Exit
Atidara	Open
Uždara	Closed
Patogumai	Toilets

Numbers – Lithuanian		
1	*vienas*	vea·nas
2	*du*	du
3	*trys*	trees
4	*keturi*	ke·tu·ri
5	*penki*	pen·ki
6	*šeši*	she·shi
7	*septyni*	sep·tee·ni
8	*aštuoni*	ash·twa·ni
9	*devyni*	de·vee·ni
10	*dešimt*	de·shimt

Call ...!	*Iškvieskit ...!*	ish·kveas·kit ...
a doctor	*gydytoją*	gee·dee·to·ya
the police	*policiją*	po·li·tsi·ya

I'm lost.
Aš pasiklydau.   ash pa·si·klee·dow

Where are the toilets?
Kur yra tualetai?   kur ee·ra tu·a·le·tai

Shopping & Services

I'm looking for ...
Aš ieškau ...   ash eash·kow ...

How much is it?
Kiek kainuoja?   keak kain·wo·ya

That's too expensive.
Per brangu.   per bran·gu

bank	*bankas*	baan·kas
market	*turgus*	tur·gus
post office	*paštas*	paash·tas

Transport & Directions

Where's the ...?
Kur yra ...?   kur ee·ra ...

Can you show me (on the map)?
Ar galite   ar gaa·li·te
parodyti man   pa·raw·dee·ti maan
(žemėlapyje)?   (zhe·mey·la·pee·ye)

One ... ticket (to Kaunas), please.	*Vieną bilietą ... (į Kauną), prašau.*	vea·naa bi·lye·taa ... (ee kow·naa) pra·show
one-way	*į vieną pusę*	ee vea·naa pu·sey
return	*į abi puses*	ee a·bi pu·ses

boat	*laivas*	lai·vas
bus	*autobusas*	ow·to·bu·sas
plane	*lėktuvas*	leyk·tu·vas
train	*traukinys*	trow·ki·nees

MACEDONIAN

Macedonian is written in the Cyrillic alphabet which is very similar to that used in Serbian (see p1034).

Note that dz is pronounced as the 'ds' in 'adds', r is rolled, and zh as the 's' in 'pleasure'.

Basics

Hello.	Здраво.	zdra·vo
Goodbye.	До гледање.	do gle·da·nye
Excuse me.	Извинете.	iz·vi·ne·te
Sorry.	Простете.	pros·te·te
Please.	Молам.	mo·lam
Thank you.	Благодарам.	bla·go·da·ram
Yes.	Да.	da
No.	Не.	ne

What's your name?
Како се викате/   ka·ko se vi·ka·te/
викаш? (pol/inf)   vi·kash

My name is ...
Јас се викам ...   yas se vi·kam ...

Do you speak English?
Зборувате ли англиски?   zbo·ru·va·te li an·glis·ki

I don't understand.
Јас не разбирам.   yas ne raz·bi·ram

Accommodation

campsite	камп	kamp
guesthouse	приватно сместување	*pri*·vat·no smes·*tu*·va·nye
hotel	хотел	*ho*·tel
youth hostel	младинско преноќиште	*mla*·din·sko pre·*no*·kyish·te

Do you have a ... room?	Дали имате ... соба?	da·li *i*·ma·te ... *so*·ba
single	едно-креветна	ed·no·*kre*·vet·na
double	двокреветна	dvo·*kre*·vet·na

How much is it per ...?	Која е цената за ...?	*ko*·ya e *tse*·na·ta za ...
night	ноќ	noky
person	еден	e·den

Signs – Macedonian

Влез	Entrance
Излез	Exit
Отворено	Open
Затворено	Closed
Забрането	Prohibited
Клозети	Toilets

Eating & Drinking

What would you recommend?
Што препорачувате вие? — shto pre·po·ra·chu·va·te vi·e

Do you have vegetarian food?
Дали имате вегетаријанска храна? — da·li i·ma·te ve·ge·ta·ri·yan·ska hra·na

I'll have ...
Јас ќе земам ... — yas kye ze·mam ...

Cheers!
На здравје! — na zdrav·ye

I'd like the ..., please.	Ве молам ...	ve mo·lam ...
bill	сметката	smet·ka·ta
menu	мени	me·ni

(bottle of) beer	(шише) пиво	(shi·she) pi·vo
(cup of) coffee/tea	(шоља) кафе/чај	(sho·lya) ka·fe/chai
water	вода	vo·da
(glass of) wine	(чаша) вино	(cha·sha) vi·no

breakfast	појадок	po·ya·dok
lunch	ручек	ru·chek
dinner	вечера	ve·che·ra

Emergencies

Help!	Помош!	po·mosh
Go away!	Одете си!	o·de·te si

Call ...!	Викнете ...!	vik·ne·te ...
a doctor	лекар	le·kar
the police	полиција	po·li·tsi·ya

I'm lost.
Се загубив. — se za·gu·biv

I'm ill.
Јас сум болен/ болна. (m/f) — yas sum bo·len/ bol·na

Where are the toilets?
Каде се тоалетите? — ka·de se to·a·le·ti·te

Shopping & Services

I'm looking for ...
Барам ... — ba·ram ...

How much is it?
Колку чини тоа? — kol·ku chi·ni to·a

That's too expensive.
Тоа е многу скапо. — to·a e mno·gu ska·po

market	пазар	pa·zar
post office	пошта	posh·ta
tourist office	туристичко биро	tu·ris·tich·ko·to bi·ro

Transport & Directions

Where's the ...?
Каде е ...? — ka·de e ...

What's the address?
Која е адресата? — ko·ya e ad·re·sa·ta

Can you show me (on the map)?
Можете ли да ми покажете (на картава)? — mo·zhe·te li da mi po·ka·zhe·te (na kar·ta·va)

One ... ticket (to Ohrid), please.	Еден ... (за Охрид), ве молам.	e·den ... (za oh·rid) ve mo·lam
one-way	билет во еден правец	bi·let vo e·den pra·vets
return	повратен билет	pov·ra·ten bi·let

boat	брод	brod
bus	автобус	av·to·bus
plane	авион	a·vi·on
train	воз	voz

Numbers – Macedonian

1	еден	e·den
2	два	dva
3	три	tri
4	четири	che·ti·ri
5	пет	pet
6	шест	shest
7	седум	se·dum
8	осум	o·sum
9	девет	de·vet
10	десет	de·set

CYRILLIC ALPHABET

Cyrillic	Pronunciation	
А а	a	as in 'father';
		as in 'ago' if not stressed (Russian)
Б б	b	as in 'but'
В в	v	as in 'van'
Г г	g	as in 'go';
	h	as in 'hot' (Ukrainian)
Ѓ г	g	as in 'go' (Ukrainian)
Ѓ ѓ	gy	as the 'gu' in 'legume' (Macedonian)
Д д	d	as in 'dog'
Ђ ђ	dy	as the 'j' in 'joke' (Serbian)
Е е	e	as in 'there'
	ye	as in 'yet' if not stressed (Russian)
Ё ё	yo	as in 'yore' (Russian)
Є є	ye	as in 'yet' (Ukrainian)
Ж ж	zh	as the 's' in 'measure'
З з	z	as in 'zoo'
Ѕ ѕ	dz	as the 'ds' in 'suds' (Macedonian)
И и	i	as the 'ee' in 'meet';
		as the 'i' in 'ill' (Ukrainian)
І і	i	as in 'hit' (Ukrainian)
Ї ї	yi	as in 'yield' (Ukrainian)
Й й	y	as in 'boy'
Ј ј	y	as in 'young'
К к	k	as in 'kind'
Ќ ќ	ky	as the 'cu' in 'cure' (Macedonian)
Л л	l	as in 'lamp'
Љ љ	ly	as the 'lli' in 'million'
М м	m	as in 'mat'
Н н	n	as in 'not'
Њ њ	ny	as the 'ny' in 'canyon'
О о	o	as the 'a' in 'water';
		as the 'a' in 'ago' if not stressed (Russian)
П п	p	as in 'pick'
Р р	r	as in 'rub' (rolled)
С с	s	as in 'sing'
Т т	t	as in 'ten'
Ћ ћ	ch	as in 'cheese' (Serbian)
У у	u	as in 'rule'
Ф ф	f	as in 'fan'
Х х	h	as in 'hot';
	kh	as the 'ch' in 'Bach' (Russian, Ukrainian)
Ц ц	ts	as in 'bits'
Ч ч	ch	as in 'church'
Џ џ	dzh	as the 'dg' in 'lodge'
Ш ш	sh	as in 'shop'
Щ щ	shch	as 'shch' in 'fresh chips' (Russian, Ukrainian);
	sht	as the '-shed' in 'pushed' (Bulgarian)
Ъ ъ	uh	as the 'a' in 'ago' (Bulgarian)
ъ		'hard' sign (Russian)
Ы ы	y	as the 'i' in 'ill' (Russian)
ь	'	'soft' sign (indicates that the preceding consonant is pronounced with a slight 'y' sound)
Э э	e	as in 'end' (Russian)
Ю ю	yu	as 'you'
Я я	ya	as in 'yard'

POLISH

Polish vowels are generally pronounced short. Nasal vowels are pronounced as though you're trying to force the air through your nose, and are indicated with n or m following the vowel.

Note that ow is pronounced as in 'how', kh as in the Scottish *loch*, and zh as the 's' in 'pleasure'. Also, r is rolled in Polish and the apostrophe (') indicates a slight y sound.

Excuse me.	*Przepraszam.*	pshe·*pra*·sham
Sorry.	*Przepraszam.*	pshe·*pra*·sham
Please.	*Proszę.*	*pro*·she
Thank you.	*Dziękuję.*	jyen·*koo*·ye
Yes.	*Tak.*	tak
No.	*Nie.*	nye

What's your name?

Jak się pan/pani	yak shye pan/*pa*·nee
nazywa? (m/f pol)	na·*zi*·va
Jakie się nazywasz? (inf)	yak shye na·*zi*·vash

My name is ...

Nazywam się ...	na·*zi*·vam shye ...

Basics

Hello.	*Cześć.*	cheshch
Goodbye.	*Do widzenia.*	do vee·*dze*·nya

(bottle of) beer	*(butelka) piwa*	(boo·*tel*·ka) *pee*·va
(cup of) coffee/tea	*(filiżanka) kawy/herbaty*	(fee·lee·*zhan*·ka) *ka*·vi/her·*ba*·ti
water	*woda*	*vo*·da
(glass of) wine	*(kieliszek) wina*	(kye·lee·*shek*) *vee*·na
breakfast	*śniadanie*	shnya·*da*·nye
lunch	*obiad*	o·byad
dinner	*kolacja*	ko·*la*·tsya

Signs – Polish

Wejście	Entrance
Wyjście	Exit
Otwarte	Open
Zamknięte	Closed
Wzbroniony	Prohibited
Toalety	Toilets

Do you speak English?
Czy pan/pani mówi po angielsku? (m/f) — chi pan/*pa*·nee *moo*·vee po an·*gyel*·skoo

I don't understand.
Nie rozumiem. — nye ro·*zoo*·myem

Accommodation

campsite	*kamping*	*kam*·peeng
guesthouse	*pokoje gościnne*	po·*ko*·ye gosh·*chee*·ne
hotel	*hotel*	*ho*·tel
youth hostel	*schronisko młodzieżowe*	skhro·*nees*·ko mwo·jye·*zho*·ve
Do you have a ... room?	*Czy jest pokój ...?*	chi yest *po*·kooy ...
single	*jedno-osobowy*	yed·no-o·so·*bo*·vi
double	*z podwójnym łóżkiem*	z pod·*vooy*·nim *woozh*·kyem
How much is it per ...?	*Ile kosztuje za ...?*	ee·le kosh·*too*·ye za ...
night	*noc*	nots
person	*osobę*	o·*so*·be

Eating & Drinking

What would you recommend?
Co by pan polecił? (m) — tso bi pan po·*le*·cheew
Co by pani poleciła? (f) — tso bi *pa*·nee po·le·*chee*·wa

Do you have vegetarian food?
Czy jest żywność wegetariańska? — chi yest *zhiv*·noshch ve·ge·tar·*yan'*·ska

I'll have ...
Proszę ... — *pro*·she ...

Cheers!
Na zdrowie! — na *zdro*·vye

I'd like the ..., please.	*Proszę o ...*	*pro*·she o ...
bill	*rachunek*	ra·*khoo*·nek
menu	*jadłospis*	ya·*dwo*·spees

Emergencies

Help!	*Na pomoc!*	na *po*·mots
Go away!	*Odejdź!*	o·*deyj*
Call ...!	*Zadzwoń po ...!*	zad·*zvon'* po ...
a doctor	*lekarza*	le·*ka*·zha
the police	*policję*	po·*lee*·tsye

I'm lost.
Zgubiłem/ Zgubiłam się. (m/f) — zgoo·*bee*·wem/ zgoo·*bee*·wam shye

I'm ill.
Jestem chory/a. (m/f) — *yes*·tem *kho*·ri/a

Where are the toilets?
Gdzie są toalety? — gjye som to·a·*le*·ti

Shopping & Services

I'm looking for ...
Szukam ... — *shoo*·kam

How much is it?
Ile to kosztuje? — ee·le to kosh·*too*·ye

That's too expensive.
To jest za drogie. — to yest za *dro*·gye

Numbers – Polish		
1	*jeden*	*ye*·den
2	*dwa*	dva
3	*trzy*	tshi
4	*cztery*	*chte*·ri
5	*pięć*	pyench
6	*sześć*	sheshch
7	*siedem*	*shye*·dem
8	*osiem*	*o*·shyem
9	*dziewięć*	*jye*·vyench
10	*dziesięć*	*jye*·shench

market	targ	tark
post office	urząd pocztowy	oo·zhond poch·to·vi
tourist office	biuro turystyczne	byoo·ro too·ris·tich·ne

Transport & Directions

Where's the ...?
Gdzie jest ...?   gjye yest ...

What's the address?
Jaki jest adres?   ya·kee yest ad·res

Can you show me (on the map)?
Czy może pan/pani mi pokazać (na mapie)? (m/f)   chi mo·zhe pan/pa·nee mee po·ka·zach (na ma·pye)

One ... ticket (to Katowice), please.	Proszę bilet ... (do Katowic).	pro·she bee·let ... (do ka·to·veets)
one-way	w jedną stronę	v yed·nom stro·ne
return	powrotny	po·vro·tni

boat	łódź	wooj
bus	autobus	ow·to·boos
plane	samolot	sa·mo·lot
train	pociąg	po·chonk

ROMANIAN

Romanian is the official language of Romania and Moldova (where it's called Moldovan).

Note that ew is pronounced as 'ee' with rounded lips, oh as the 'o' in 'note', ow as in 'how', uh as the 'a' in 'ago', and zh as the 's' in 'pleasure'. The apostrophe (') indicates a very short, unstressed i (almost silent).

Basics

Hello.	Bună ziua.	boo·nuh zee·wa
Goodbye.	La revedere.	la re·ve·de·re
Excuse me.	Scuzaţi-mă.	skoo·za·tsee·muh
Sorry.	Îmi pare rău.	ewm' pa·re ruh·oo
Please.	Vă rog.	vuh rog
Thank you.	Mulţumesc.	mool·tsoo·mesk
Yes.	Da.	da
No.	Nu.	noo

What's your name?
Cum vă numiţi?   koom vuh noo·meets'

My name is ...
Numele meu este ...   noo·me·le me·oo yes·te ...

Do you speak English?
Vorbiţi engleza?   vor·beets' en·gle·za

I don't understand.
Eu nu înţeleg.   ye·oo noo ewn·tse·leg

Accommodation

campsite	teren de camping	te·ren de kem·peeng
guesthouse	pensiune	pen·syoo·ne
hotel	hotel	ho·tel
youth hostel	hostel	hos·tel

Do you have a ... room?	Aveţi o cameră ...?	a·vets' o ka·me·ruh ...
single	de o persoană	de o per·so·a·nuh
double	dublă	doo·bluh

How much is it per ...?	Cît costă ...?	kewt kos·tuh ...
night	pe noapte	pe no·ap·te
person	de persoană	de per·so·a·nuh

Eating & Drinking

What would you recommend?
Ce recomandaţi?   che re·ko·man·dats'

Do you have vegetarian food?
Aveţi mâncare vegetariană?   a·ve·tsi mewn·ka·re ve·je·ta·rya·nuh

I'll have ...
Aş dori ...   ash do·ree ...

Cheers!
Noroc!   no·rok

I'd like the ..., please.	Vă rog, aş dori ...	vuh rog ash do·ree ...
bill	nota de plată	no·ta de pla·tuh
menu	meniul	me·nee·ool

Numbers – Romanian		
1	unu	oo·noo
2	doi	doy
3	trei	trey
4	patru	pa·troo
5	cinci	cheench'
6	şase	sha·se
7	şapte	shap·te
8	opt	opt
9	nouă	no·wuh
10	zece	ze·che

(bottle of) beer	(sticlă de) bere	(stee·kluh de) be·re
(cup of) coffee/tea	(o ceaşcă de) cafea/ceai	(o che·ash·kuh de) ka·fe·a/che·ai
water	apă	a·puh
(glass of) wine	(pahar de) vin	(pa·har de) veen

breakfast	micul dejun	mee·kool de·zhoon
lunch	dejun	de·zhoon
dinner	cină	chee·nuh

Emergencies

Help!	Ajutor!	a·zhoo·tor
Go away!	Pleacă!	ple·a·kuh

Call ...!	Chemaţi ...!	ke·mats' ...
a doctor	un doctor	oon dok·tor
the police	poliţia	po·lee·tsya

I'm lost.
M-am rătăcit.   mam ruh·tuh·cheet

I'm ill.
Mă simt rău.   muh seemt ruh·oo

Where are the toilets?
Unde este o toaletă?   oon·de yes·te o to·a·le·tuh

Shopping & Services

I'm looking for ...
Caut ...   kowt ...

How much is it?
Cât costă?   kewt kos·tuh

That's too expensive.
E prea scump.   ye pre·a skoomp

market	piaţă	pya·tsuh
post office	poşta	posh·ta
tourist office	biroul de informaţii turistice	bee·ro·ool de een·for·ma·tsee too·rees·tee·che

Transport & Directions

Where's the ...?
Unde este ...?   oon·de yes·te ...

What's the address?
Care este adresa?   ka·re yes·te a·dre·sa

Can you show me (on the map)?
Puteţi să-mi arătaţi (pe hartă)?   poo·te·tsi suh·mi a·ruh·tats' (pe har·tuh)

One ... ticket (to Cluj), please.	Un bilet ... (până la Cluj),vă rog.	oon bee·let ... (pew·nuh la kloozh) vuh rog
one-way	dus	doos
return	dus-întors	doos ewn·tors

boat	vapor	va·por
bus	autobuz	ow·to·booz
plane	avion	a·vyon
train	tren	tren

RUSSIAN

The Cyrillic alphabet, with Roman-letter equivalents and pronunciation guides, is shown on p1034.

Note that kh is pronounced as in the Scottish *loch* and zh as the 's' in 'pleasure'. Also, r is rolled in Russian and the apostrophe (') indicates a slight y sound.

Basics

Hello.	Здравствуйте.	zdrast·vuyt·ye
Goodbye.	До свидания.	da svee·dan·ya
Excuse me./ Sorry.	Извините, пожалуйста.	eez·vee·neet·ye pa·zhal·sta
Please.	Пожалуйста.	pa·zhal·sta
Thank you.	Спасибо	spa·see·ba
Yes./No.	Да./Нет.	da/nyet

Signs – Russian	
Вход	Entrance
Выход	Exit
Открыто	Open
Закрыто	Closed
Запрещено	Prohibited
Туалет	Toilets

What's your name?
Как вас зовут?   kak vaz za·*vut*

My name is ...
Меня зовут …   meen·*ya* za·*vut* …

Do you speak English?
Вы говорите   vi ga·va·*reet*·ye
по-английски?   pa·an·*glee*·skee

I don't understand.
Я не понимаю.   ya nye pa·nee·*ma*·yu

Accommodation

campsite	кемпинг	*kyem*·peeng
guesthouse	пансионат	pan·see·a·*nat*
hotel	гостиница	ga·*stee*·neet·sa
youth hostel	общежитие	ap·shee·*zhi*·tee·ye

Do you have a ... room? У вас есть …? u vas yest' …

| single | одноместный номер | ad·nam·*yes*·ni *no*·meer |
| double | номер с двуспальней кроватью | *no*·meer z dvu·*spaln*·yey kra·*vat*·yu |

How much is it ...? Сколько стоит за …? skol'·ka *sto*·eet za …

| for two people | двоих | dva·*eekh* |
| per night | ночь | noch' |

Eating & Drinking

What would you recommend?
Что вы   shto vi
рекомендуете?   ree·ka·meen·*du*·eet·ye

Do you have vegetarian food?
У вас есть овощные   u vas yest' a·vashch·*ni*·ye
блюда?   *blyu*·da

I'll have ...
…, пожалуйста.   … pa·*zhal*·sta

Cheers!
Пей до дна!   pyey da dna

I'd like the ..., please. Я бы хотел/ хотела … (m/f) ya bi khat·*yel*/ khat·*ye*·la …

| bill | счёт | shot |
| menu | меню | meen·*yu* |

(bottle of) beer	(бутылка) пива	(bu·*til*·ka) *pee*·va
(cup of) coffee/tea	(чашка) кофе/чаю	(*chash*·ka) kof·ye/*cha*·yu
water	вода	va·*da*
(glass of) wine	(рюмка) вина	(*ryum*·ka) vee·*na*

Numbers – Russian

1	один	a·*deen*
2	два	dva
3	три	tree
4	четыре	chee·*ti*·ree
5	пять	pyat'
6	шесть	shest'
7	семь	syem'
8	восемь	*vo*·seem'
9	девять	dye·*veet*'
10	десять	dye·*seet*'

breakfast	завтрак	*zaf*·trak
lunch	обед	ab·*yet*
dinner	ужин	*u*·zhin

Emergencies

Help! Помогите! pa·ma·*gee*·tye

Go away! Идите ee·*deet*·ye
отсюда! at·*syu*·da

Call ...! Вызовите …! *vi*·za·veet·ye …

| a doctor | врача | vra·*cha* |
| the police | милицию | mee·*leet*·si·yu |

I'm lost.
Я потерялся/   ya pa·teer·*yal*·sa/
потерялась. (m/f)   pa·teer·*ya*·las'

I'm ill.
Я болею.   ya bal·*ye*·yu

Where are the toilets?
Где здесь туалет?   gdye zdyes' tu·al·*yet*

Shopping & Services

I'd like ...
Я бы хотел/   ya bi khat·*yel*/
хотела … (m/f)   khat·*ye*·la …

How much is it?
Сколько стоит?   skol'·ka *sto*·eet

That's too expensive.
Это очень дорого.   e·ta o·*cheen*' *do*·ra·ga

bank	банк	bank
market	рынок	*ri*·nak
post office	почта	*poch*·ta
tourist office	туристическое бюро	tu·rees·*tee*·chee·ska·ye byu·*ro*

Transport & Directions

Where's the ...?
Где (здесь) ...?   gdye (zdyes') ...

What's the address?
Какой адрес?   ka·koy a·drees

Can you show me (on the map)?
Покажите мне,   pa·ka·zhi·tye mnye
пожалуйста (на карте).   pa·zhal·sta (na kart·ye)

One ... ticket (to Novgorod), please.	Билет ... (на Новгород).	beel·yet ... (na nov·ga·rat)
one-way	в один конец	v a·deen kan·yets
return	в оба конца	v o·ba kant·sa

boat	параход	pa·ra·khot
bus	автобус	af·to·bus
plane	самолёт	sa·mal·yot
train	поезд	po·yeest

SLOVAK

An accent mark over a vowel in written Slovak indicates it's pronounced as a long sound.

Note that air is pronounced as in 'hair', aw as in 'law', oh as the 'o' in 'note', ow as in 'how', uh as the 'a' in 'ago', dz as the 'ds' in 'adds', kh as in the Scottish *loch*, and zh as the 's' in 'pleasure'. The apostrophe (') indicates a slight y sound.

Basics

Hello.	Dobrý deň.	do·bree dyen'
Goodbye.	Do videnia.	do vi·dye·ni·yuh
Excuse me.	Prepáčte.	pre·pach·tye
Sorry.	Prepáčte.	pre·pach·tye
Please.	Prosím.	pro·seem
Thank you.	Ďakujem	dyuh·ku·yem
Yes.	Áno.	a·no
No.	Nie.	ni·ye

Signs – Slovak	
Vchod	Entrance
Východ	Exit
Otvorené	Open
Zatvorené	Closed
Zakázané	Prohibited
Záchody/Toalety	Toilets

What's your name?
Ako sa voláte?   uh·ko suh vo·la·tye

My name is ...
Volám sa ...   vo·lam suh ...

Do you speak English?
Hovoríte po   ho·vo·ree·tye po
anglicky?   uhng·lits·ki

I don't understand.
Nerozumiem.   nye·ro·zu·myem

Accommodation

campsite	táborisko	ta·bo·ris·ko
guesthouse	penzión	pen·zi·awn
hotel	hotel	ho·tel
youth hostel	nocľaháreň pre mládež	nots·lyuh·ha·ren' pre mla·dyezh

Do you have a single room?
Máte jedno-   ma·tye yed·no-
posteľovú izbu?   pos·tye·lyo·voo iz·bu

Do you have a double room?
Máte izbu s   ma·tye iz·bu s
manželskou   muhn·zhels·koh
postelou?   pos·tye·lyoh

How much is it per ...?	Koľko to stojí na ...?	kol'·ko to sto·yee nuh ...
night	noc	nots
person	osobu	o·so·bu

Eating & Drinking

What would you recommend?
Čo by ste mi   cho bi stye mi
odporučili?   od·po·ru·chi·li

Do you have vegetarian food?
Máte vegetariánske   ma·tye ve·ge·tuh·ri·yan·ske
jedlá?   yed·la

I'll have ...
Dám si ...   dam si ...

Cheers!
Nazdravie!   nuhz·druh·vi·ye

I'd like the ..., please.	Prosím si ...	pro·seem si ...
bill	účet	oo·chet
menu	jedálny lístok	ye·dal·ni lees·tok

(bottle of) beer	(fľaša) piva	(flyuh·shuh) pi·vuh
(cup of) coffee/tea	(šálka) kávy/čaju	(shal·kuh) ka·vi/chuh·yu
water	voda	vo·duh
(glass of) wine	(pohár) vína	(po·har) vee·nuh

Numbers – Slovak

1	jeden	ye·den
2	dva	dvuh
3	tri	tri
4	štyri	shti·ri
5	päť	pet'
6	šesť	shest'
7	sedem	se·dyem
8	osem	o·sem
9	deväť	dye·vet'
10	desať	dye·suht'

breakfast	raňajky	ruh·nyai·ki
lunch	obed	o·bed
dinner	večera	ve·che·ruh

Emergencies

| Help! | Pomoc! | po·mots |
| Go away! | Choďte preč! | khod'·tye prech |

Call ...!	Zavolajte ...!	zuh·vo·lai·tye ...
a doctor	lekára	le·ka·ruh
the police	políciu	po·lee·tsi·yu

I'm lost.
Stratil/Stratila   struh·tyil/struh·tyi·luh
som sa. (m/f)   som suh

I'm ill.
Som chorý/chorá. (m/f)   som kho·ree/kho·ra

Where are the toilets?
Kde sú tu záchody?   kdye soo tu za·kho·di

Shopping & Services

I'm looking for ...
Hľadám ...   hlyuh·dam ...

How much is it?
Koľko to stojí?   kol'·ko to sto·yee

That's too expensive.
To je príliš drahé.   to ye pree·lish druh·hair

market	trh	trh
post office	pošta	posh·tuh
tourist office	turistická	tu·ris·tits·ka
	kancelária	kuhn·tse·la·ri·yuh

Transport & Directions

Where's the ...?
Kde je ...?   kdye ye ...

What's the address?
Aká je adresa?   uh·ka ye uh·dre·suh

Can you show me (on the map)?
Môžete mi ukázať   mwo·zhe·tye mi u·ka·zuht'
(na mape)?   (nuh muh·pe)

One ... ticket	Jeden ... lístok	ye·den ... lees·tok
(to Poprad),	(do Popradu),	(do pop·ruh·du)
please.	prosím.	pro·seem
one-way	jedno-	yed·no-
	smerný	smer·nee
return	spiatočný	spyuh·toch·nee

bus	autobus	ow·to·bus
plane	lietadlo	li·ye·tuhd·lo
train	vlak	vluhk

SLOVENE

We've used the symbols oh (as the 'o' in 'note') and ow (as in 'how') to help you pronounce vowels followed by the letters l and v in written Slovene – at the end of a syllable these combinations produce a sound similar to the 'w' in English.

Note also that uh is pronounced as the 'a' in 'ago', zh as the 's' in 'pleasure', r is rolled, and the apostrophe (') indicates a slight y sound.

Basics

Hello.	Zdravo.	zdra·vo
Goodbye.	Na svidenje.	na svee·den·ye
Excuse me.	Dovolite.	do·vo·lee·te
Sorry.	Oprostite.	op·ros·tee·te
Please.	Prosim.	pro·seem
Thank you.	Hvala.	hva·la
Yes.	Da.	da
No.	Ne.	ne

What's your name?
Kako vam/ti   ka·ko vam/tee
je ime? (pol/inf)   ye ee·me

My name is ...
Ime mi je ...   ee·me mee ye ...

Signs – Slovene

Vhod	Entrance
Izhod	Exit
Odprto	Open
Zaprto	Closed
Prepovedano	Prohibited
Stranišče	Toilets

Numbers – Slovene		
1	*en*	en
2	*dva*	dva
3	*trije*	tree·ye
4	*štirje*	shtee·rye
5	*pet*	pet
6	*šest*	shest
7	*sedem*	se·dem
8	*osem*	o·sem
9	*devet*	de·vet
10	*deset*	de·set

Do you speak English?
Ali govorite a·lee go·vo·ree·te
angleško? ang·lesh·ko

I don't understand.
Ne razumem. ne ra·zoo·mem

Accommodation

campsite	*kamp*	kamp
guesthouse	*gostišče*	gos·teesh·che
hotel	*hotel*	ho·tel
youth hostel	*mladinski hotel*	mla·deen·skee ho·tel

Do you have a ... room?	*Ali imate ... sobo?*	a·lee ee·ma·te ... so·bo
single	*enoposteljno*	e·no·pos·tel'·no
double	*dvoposteljno*	dvo·pos·tel'·no

How much is it per ...?	*Koliko stane na ...?*	ko·lee·ko sta·ne na ...
night	*noč*	noch
person	*osebo*	o·se·bo

Eating & Drinking

What would you recommend?
Kaj priporočate? kai pree·po·ro·cha·te

Do you have vegetarian food?
Ali imate a·lee ee·ma·te
vegetarijansko hrano? ve·ge·ta·ree·yan·sko hra·no

I'll have ...
Jaz bom ... yaz bom ...

Cheers!
Na zdravje! na zdrav·ye

I'd like the ..., please.	*Želim ..., prosim.*	zhe·leem ... pro·seem
bill	*račun*	ra·choon
menu	*jedilni list*	ye·deel·nee leest

(bottle of) beer	*(steklenica) piva*	(stek·le·nee·tsa) pee·va
(cup of) coffee/tea	*(skodelica) kave/čaja*	(sko·de·lee·tsa) ka·ve/cha·ya
water	*voda*	vo·da
(glass of) wine	*(kozarec) vina*	(ko·za·rets) vee·na

breakfast	*zajtrk*	zai·tuhrk
lunch	*kosilo*	ko·see·lo
dinner	*večerja*	ve·cher·ya

Emergencies

Help!	*Na pomoč!*	na po·moch
Go away!	*Pojdite stran!*	poy·dee·te stran

Call ...!	*Pokličite ...!*	pok·lee·chee·te ...
a doctor	*zdravnika*	zdrav·nee·ka
the police	*policijo*	po·lee·tsee·yo

I'm lost.
Izgubil/ eez·goo·beew/
Izgubila sem se. (m/f) eez·goo·bee·la sem se

I'm ill.
Bolan/Bolna sem. (m/f) bo·lan/boh·na sem

Where are the toilets?
Kje je stranišče? kye ye stra·neesh·che

Shopping & Services

I'm looking for ...
Iščem ... eesh·chem ...

How much is this?
Koliko stane? ko·lee·ko sta·ne

That's too expensive.
To je predrago. to ye pre·dra·go

market	*tržnica*	tuhrzh·nee·tsa
post office	*pošta*	posh·ta
tourist office	*turistični urad*	too·rees·teech·nee oo·rad

Transport & Directions

Where's the ...?
Kje je ...? kye ye ...

What's the address?
Na katerem naslovu je? na ka·te·rem nas·lo·voo ye

Can you show me (on the map)?
Mi lahko pokažete mee lah·ko po·ka·zhe·te
(na zemljevidu)? (na zem·lye·vee·doo)

One ... ticket to (Koper), please.	... *vozovnico do (Kopra), prosim.*	... vo·*zov*·nee·tso do (*ko*·pra) *pro*·seem
one-way	*Enosmerno*	e·no·*smer*·no
return	*Povratno*	pov·*rat*·no
boat	*ladja*	*lad*·ya
bus	*avtobus*	av·to·boos
plane	*letalo*	le·*ta*·lo
train	*vlak*	vlak

UKRAINIAN

Ukrainian is written in the Cyrillic alphabet which is very similar to that used in Russian (see p1034).

Vowels in unstressed syllables are generally pronounced shorter and weaker than they are in stressed syllables. Note that kh is pronounced as in the Scottish *loch* and zh as the 's' in 'pleasure'. The apostrophe (') indicates a slight y sound.

Basics

Hello.	Добрий день.	*do*·bry den'
Goodbye.	До побачення.	do po·*ba*·chen·nya
Excuse me.	Вибачте.	vy·*bach*·te
Sorry.	Перепрошую.	pe·re·*pro*·shu·yu
Please.	Прошу.	*pro*·shu
Thank you.	Дякую.	*dya*·ku·yu
Yes.	Так.	tak
No.	Ні.	ni

What's your name?
Як вас звати? — yak vas zva·ty

My name is ...
Мене звати … — me·*ne* zva·ti ...

Do you speak English?
Ви розмовляєте англійською мовою? — vy roz·mow·*lya*·ye·te an·*hliys*·ko·yu *mo*·vo·yu

I don't understand.
Я не розумію. — ya ne ro·zu·*mi*·yu

Accommodation

Do you have any rooms available?
У вас є вільні номери? — u vas ye *vil*'·ni no·*me*·ri

How much is it per night/person?
Скільки коштує номер за ніч/особу? — *skil*'·ky ko·*shtu*·ye *no*·mer za nich/o·*so*·bu

Signs – Ukrainian

Вхід	Entrance
Вихід	Exit
Відчинено	Open
Зачинено	Closed
Заборонено	Prohibited
Туалет	Toilets

campsite	кемпінг	*kem*·pinh
double room	номер на двох	*no*·mer na dvokh
hotel	готель	ho·*tel*'
single room	номер на одного	*no*·mer na o·dno·ho
youth hostel	молодіжний гуртожиток	mo·lo·*dizh*·ni hur·*to*·zhi·tok

Eating & Drinking

What do you recommend?
Що Ви порадите? — shcho vy po·*ra*·dy·te

I'm a vegetarian.
Я вегетаріанець/ вегетаріанка. (m/f) — ya ve·he·ta·ri·a·*nets*'/ ve·he·ta·ri·*an*·ka

I'd like ...
Я візьму … — ya viz'·*mu* ...

Cheers!
Будьмо! — *bud*'·mo

beer	пиво	*pi*·vo
bill	рахунок	ra·*khu*·nok
breakfast	сніданок	sni·*da*·nok
coffee	кава	*ka*·va
dinner	вечеря	ve·*che*·rya
lunch	обід	o·*bid*
market	ринок	*ri*·nok
menu	меню	me·*nyu*
restaurant	ресторан	re·sto·*ran*
tea	чай	chai
wine	вино	vi·*no*
water	вода	vo·*da*

Emergencies

Help!
Допоможіть! — do·po·mo·*zhit*'

Go away!
Іди/Ідіть звідси! (pol/inf) — i·*di*/i·*dit*' *zvid*·si

I'm lost.
Я заблукав/ заблукала. (m/f) — ya za·blu·*kaw*/ za·blu·*ka*·la

Call a doctor!
Викличте лікаря!   *vi*·klich·te *li*·ka·rya!

Call the police!
Викличіть міліцію!   *vi*·kli·chit' mi·*li*·tsi·yu

I'm ill.
Мені погано.   me·*ni* po·*ha*·no

Where's the toilet?
Де туалети?   de tu·a·le·ti

Shopping & Services

I'd like to buy ...
Я б хотів/хотіла   ya b kho·*tiw*/kho·*ti*·la
купити ... (m/f)   ku·*pi*·ti ...

How much is it?
Скільки це (він/вона)   *skil'*·ki tse (vin/vo·*na*)
коштує? (m/f)   *ko*·shtu·ye?

That's too expensive.
Це надто дорого.   tse *nad*·to *do*·ro·ho

ATM	банкомат	ban·ko·*mat*
market	ринок	*ri*·nok
post office	пошта	*po*·shta
tourist office	туристичне бюро	tu·ri·*stich*·ne byu·*ro*

Transport & Directions

Where is ...?
Де ...?   de ...

1	один	o·*din*
2	два	dva
3	три	tri
4	чотири	cho·*ti*·ri
5	п'ять	pyat'
6	шість	shist'
7	сім	sim
8	вісім	*vi*·sim
9	дев'ять	*de*·vyat'
10	десять	*de*·syat'

What's the address?
Яка адреса?   ya·*ka* a·*dre*·sa

Can you show me (on the map)?
Ви можете показати,   vi *mo*·zhe·te po·ka·*za*·ti
мени (на карти)?   me·*ni* (na *kar*·ti)

I want to go to ...
Мені треба їхати   me·*ni* tre·ba yi·kha·ti
до ...   do ...

bus	автобус	aw·*to*·bus
one-way ticket	квиток в один бік	kvi·*tok* v o·*din* bik
plane	літак	li·*tak*
return ticket	зворотний квиток	zvo·*ro*·tni kvi·*tok*
train	поїзд	*po*·yizd

behind the scenes

SEND US YOUR FEEDBACK

We love to hear from travellers – your comments keep us on our toes and help make our books better. Our well-travelled team reads every word on what you loved or loathed about this book. Although we cannot reply individually to postal submissions, we always guarantee that your feedback goes straight to the appropriate authors, in time for the next edition. Each person who sends us information is thanked in the next edition – and the most useful submissions are rewarded with a free book.

Visit **lonelyplanet.com/contact** to submit your updates and suggestions or to ask for help. Our award-winning website also features inspirational travel stories, news and discussions.

Note: We may edit, reproduce and incorporate your comments in Lonely Planet products such as guidebooks, websites and digital products, so let us know if you don't want your comments reproduced or your name acknowledged. For a copy of our privacy policy visit lonelyplanet.com/privacy.

OUR READERS

Many thanks to the travellers who used the last edition and wrote to us with helpful hints, useful advice and interesting anecdotes:
Yoram Adriaanse, Bernhard, Geoff Block, Denis Bodnar, Ana Flavia Borges, Anette Jeroen Bruggeman, Munthe & Jan Bruusgaard, Albrecht Eisen, Bård Magnus Fauske, Lorraine Federico, Fiona Gall, Heiko Günther, Graham Hamilton, Mathilda Hermansson, Nancy Kinlock, Ken Levine, Catherine Leung, Robert Lismanis, Lorel Martin, Marvin, Ken Merk, Peter Moselund, Mick Nishikawa, Ivan Petryshyn, Innes Rothel, Karlis Rozenkrons, Tim Schoof, John Soar, Reinier Spreen, Thomas Staempfli, Jason Stewart, Richard Stow, Julian Timm, David Torrance, Gayna Vetter, Lisa Warner, Jeffrey White, Martins Zaprauskis

AUTHOR THANKS

Tom Masters

An enormous thanks to my 18 co-authors on this book, whose hard work tramping the backstreets of Eastern Europe and passion for new discovery made them such a pleasure to work with. Thanks to Anna Tyler, Jo Potts, Imogen Bannister and all the inhouse teams at Lonely Planet. In Belarus a big thank you to Leonid, Anna, Sasha and Alyona in Minsk, to Vera and Nina in Brest and the kind employees of the Chagall Museum in Vitebsk for their help on a difficult day.

Brett Atkinson

Thanks to my Czech friends and drinking partners who again conspired to make a globetrotting Kiwi feel right at home. Special thanks to Greg and Francie in Olomouc, and at Lonely Planet thanks to Jo Potts for the editorial support and to coordinating author Tom Masters and the carto team for bringing the whole shebang together. Finally, love and special thanks to Carol and to Mum and Dad.

Carolyn Bain

Big Baltic hugs to friends who shared with me the pleasure of their company on parts of this trip, especially Graham Harris, Brandon Presser and Tallinn's finest tea-meister, Steve Kokker. I am again indebted to Steve for his friendship, kindness and immense local wisdom. Thanks to others who generously helped out with tips and company around the country, including Geli Lillemaa, Sirli Kalep and Andrew Meek.

Mark Baker

On the ground in Hungary, my gratitude goes out to the helpful people at Tourinform and to my friend in Pécs, Krisztina Koncz, who introduced me to Villány's wonderful wines and even took the day off to show me around

Szeged. Thanks also to my commissioning editors Jo Potts and Anna Tyler for choosing me as an author and cheerfully answering questions as they arose. A special thanks to coordinating author Tom Masters for his patience and calmness.

Jayne D'Arcy

Thanks to fellow travellers Peter van der Brugghen and Marja Exterkate, familiar faces Mario Qytyku and Scott Logan, colleagues Carolyn Bain and Peter Dragicevich, and Lawrence and Mia Marzouk in Kosovo. Thanks to Tawan Sierek for the laughs during my third (!) visit to Butrint, to my dearest partner Sharik Billington for making sure young Miles was fed, watered and schooled until we were all together again, and to Miles. You guys rock.

Chris Deliso

My research was greatly expedited by many people. Special thanks are due to Happie Datt and Mayor Milosim Vojneski in Makedonski Brod, Petar and family in Dihovo, Risto and Anita in Elšani and Zoran Grozdanovski in Ohrid. My gratitude also extends to to Blagoja Samakoski for his assistance in Prilep and around. Mayor Aleksandar Panov in Kavadarci, and Mitko, our skipper on Lake Tikveš, should also be credited. Finally, coordinating author Tom Masters and Lonely Planet's editors Jo Potts and Anna Tyler, the ever-helpful Imogen Bannister, and Herman So and his mapmaking team also deserve a hearty thanks.

Marc Di Duca

When researching in Ukraine, you're never short of people bending over backwards to help you along the way. Firstly, a huge thanks to Ukraine expert Greg Bloom for all his support and a mammoth дякую to my parents-in-law Mykola and Vira for taking care of son Taras while I was on the road. Big thanks also go to Yuri, Maria and family in Uzhhorod, Markiyan, Yarema and Ihor in Lviv, Viktor in Yaremche, Marcus in Odesa and last, but certainly not least, my wife, Tanya, for all the days we spend apart.

Peter Dragičević

Thanks to Hayley Wright, Jack Delf and Amy Watson for helpful tips and contacts. Special thanks to Michael Woodhouse for finding Belgrade's campest accommodation and generally making the first week of research so enjoyable.

Lisa Dunford

Most heartfelt thanks go to my dear friends Saša, Fero, Šimon and Sara Petriska, Edita and Anton Augustin. Thank you too, to Andrea Sarkany, Miro, Vera and Jan Zachar, Jennifer Josifek, and Jess at the Ginger Money, for your hospitality and guidance. I appreciate all the time put in by Tom Masters and the rest of

the crew that worked on this book. And Billy, you're the best travel companion ever.

Mark Elliott

Many thanks to Snezhan in Trebinje, Vlaren at Tvrdoš Monastery, Semir in Blagaj, Nermen, Žika, Sanila and Narmina in Mostar, Branislav in Višegrad and so many more, including the mysterious 'angel' who provided me with such insights to the Belašnica highland villages then disappeared without my ever knowing his name. As ever my greatest thanks go to my endlessly inspiring wife, Dani Systermans, and to my unbeatable parents who, three decades ago, had the crazy idea of driving me to Bosnia in the first place.

Steve Fallon

Thanks to Tatjana Radovič and Petra Stušek at the Ljubljana Tourist Board and Lucija Jager at the Slovenian Tourist Board. Slovenian Railways' Marino Fakin, Tone Plankar at the Ljubljana bus station and Tomaž Škofic of Adria Airways helped with transport and Dušan Brejc of the Wine Association of Slovenia with the right vintage(s). It was wonderful catching up with mates Domen Kalajžič of 3glav Adventures, Bled, and Aleš Hvala of Hotel Hvala, Kobarid. As always, my efforts here are dedicated to my partner, Michael Rothschild.

Anna Kaminski

Many thanks to everyone who helped me on my Lithuania journey, including all of the too-numerous-to-mention-individually tourist office and Litinterp staff. A special thank you to Mikael for the late, late Vilnius nights, to Gintaras for his insider tips on Kaunas, to Justas and Milda for the memorable Klaipeda dinner, and to Luisė and Juozas for the smoked eel and boundless hospitality in Nida, yet again.

Anja Mutić

Hvala mama, for your home cooking and contagious laughter. *Gracias* to the Barcelona family. *Obrigada*, Hoji, for always being there. A huge *hvala* to my friends in Croatia who gave me endless contacts and recommendations. Lidija, you're always full of great ideas! Special thanks to Viviana Vukelić and her team at HTZ. A thank you also goes to Tom Masters for his flexibility. Finally, to the inspiring memory of my late father who travels with me still.

Leif Pettersen

In Romania, a hearty thanks goes to Monica Zavoianu in Suceava, Iulian Cozma in Brașov, Duncan Crombie & Josephine Postema in Sibiu, the folks at Retro Hostel in Cluj and Craig Turp in Bucharest. In Moldova, I'm indebted to Rali Roesing, Sandy and Andy Smith, Josh Boissevain and, as always, Marisha Waters and Vitalie Eremia. And general gratitude to anyone who forced their țuică into my hands. Unsurprisingly, I don't remember any of your names.

Brandon Presser

Paldies first and foremost to my pal Aleks Karlsons for his help and hospitality. Thanks also to Richard Baerug and Karlis Celms. Hey Emma: 'what? you don't like thank yous?' In Lonely Planet–land, props to the savvy production staff, Jo Potts, Anna Tyler, Imogen Bannister, and my talented co-authors – especially coordinating author, Tom Masters, and hostess-with-the-mostest, the illustrious Carolyn Bain.

Tim Richards

As always, I'm indebted to the professional staff of Poland's tourist offices, who perform their jobs with enthusiasm and skill. I also give thanks to the national train company PKP; their trains aren't always fast, but they're usually on time. Much love to my Polish friends – particularly Ewa, Magda, Gosia and Andrzej – for their continued good company. Thanks to artist Tomasz Moczek and his friends Marcin and Kuba, with whom I spent a pleasant hour drinking beer in the sunshine within a crumbling former brewery in Wrocław, while talking about gnomes; and to Belarusian sailor Aleksandr, who kept me company on a train journey between Giżycko and Białystok. Cheers also to Ania and Jaime, who I met via Twitter and shared a drink with at a Lublin pub. Finally, to the unseen hotel staff who prepared my packed breakfasts when (often) catching an insanely early train – I salute you!

Simon Richmond

In Moscow, *bolshoi spasibo* to Mirjana Vesentin for her hospitality and company on my culinary travels around the city. Leonid Ragozin was also a great help as was Roxane Chatounovski. Cheers to the fearless expat explorers Bina and Thomas – I loved your story about Vegas. As always, Sasha and Andrey were fabulous hosts in St Petersburg, where I also must thank Peter and Valery for their company and input.

Tamara Sheward

Alas, it's impossible to attempt to thank everyone here, so to be brutally specific, *hvala* and *živeli* to: Nevenka and Bane Šuvakov, Lazar Pašćanović, Benn and Olya, the good folk at Downtown Novi Sad (wrenched-out tooth notwithstanding), the Green Studio girls, Yellowbed kitchen-party people, Mick Muck, Cath Lanigan, David Collins and Tony Jackson for getting me in this fine mess to begin with, and the exceptionally patient and sage Brandon Presser. Dušan, *hvala na svemu moj divan durak*.

Richard Watkins

Many thanks to Martin Nedelchev for the dinner and perhaps too much *rakia*. Thanks also go to Rositsa, Albena and all the girls at Zig Zag Holidays and the staff at Odysseia-In for their assistance in Sofia. I'd also like to thank Maya Todorova and Milko Belberov at the Rusenski Lom Nature Park Office, the helpful staff at the tourist offices in Burgas, Plovdiv and Ruse and taxi driver Emil Kukov for his world-weary wit.

ACKNOWLEDGMENTS

Climate map data adapted from Peel MC, Finlayson BL & McMahon TA (2007) 'Updated World Map of the Köppen-Geiger Climate Classification', *Hydrology and Earth System Sciences*, 11, 163344. Many thanks to the following for the use of their content: Prague Transit Map © DP Praha

Cover photograph: St Basil's Cathedral, Moscow, Russia. Many of the images in this guide are available for licensing from Lonely Planet Images: www.lonelyplanetimages.com.

THIS BOOK

Many people have helped to create this 11th edition of Lonely Planet's *Eastern Europe* guidebook, which is part of Lonely Planet's Europe series. Other titles in this series include *Western Europe*, *Mediterranean Europe*, *Central Europe*, *Scandinavia* and *Europe on a Shoestring*. Lonely Planet also publishes phrasebooks for these regions. This guidebook was commissioned in Lonely Planet's London office, and produced by the following:

Commissioning Editors Jo Potts, Anna Tyler

Coordinating Editor Justin Flynn

Coordinating Cartographer Anita Bahn

Coordinating Layout Designer Jacqui Saunders

Managing Editors Sasha Baskett, Kirsten Rawlings

Managing Cartographers Herman So, Anthony Phelan, Amanda Sierp, Adrian Persoglia

Managing Layout Designer Jane Hart

Assisting Editors Eli Arduca, Judith Bamber, Pete Cruttenden, Cathryn Game, Gabrielle Innes, Kate James, Andi Lien, Sonya Mithen, Kristin Odijk, Gabbi Stefanos

Assisting Cartographers Andras Bogdanovits, Piotr Czajkowski, Katalin Dadi-Racz, Xavier Di Toro, Mick Garrett, Karen Grant, Eve Kelly, Ross Macaw, Angus McNab, Maritza Kolega, Valentina Kremenchutskaya

Cover Research Naomi Parker

Internal Image Research Aude Vauconsant

Language Content Branislava Vladisavljevic

Thanks to Ryan Evans, Gerard Walker, Lisa Knights, Trent Paton, Martine Power, Sophie Ward

BEHIND THE SCENES

index

000 Map pages
000 Photo pages

how to use this book

These symbols will help you find the listings you want:

👁	Sights	🎎	Festivals & Events	☆	Entertainment
🏃	Activities	🛏	Sleeping	🛍	Shopping
🍃	Courses	🍴	Eating	ℹ	Information/Transport
👉	Tours	🍷	Drinking		

These symbols give you the vital information for each listing:

☑	Telephone Numbers	🔊	Wi-Fi Access	🚌	Bus
⏱	Opening Hours	🏊	Swimming Pool	⛴	Ferry
P	Parking	🥗	Vegetarian Selection	M	Metro
⊖	Nonsmoking	📖	English-Language Menu	S	Subway
❄	Air-Conditioning	👪	Family-Friendly	⊖	London Tube
@	Internet Access	🐾	Pet-Friendly	🚊	Tram
				🚆	Train

Reviews are organised by author preference.

Look out for these icons:

TOP CHOICE	Our author's recommendation
FREE	No payment required
🍃	A green or sustainable option

Our authors have nominated these places as demonstrating a strong commitment to sustainability – for example by supporting local communities and producers, operating in an environmentally friendly way, or supporting conservation projects.

Map Legend

Sights
- 🏖 Beach
- ☸ Buddhist
- 🏰 Castle
- ✝ Christian
- 🕉 Hindu
- ☪ Islamic
- ✡ Jewish
- 🗿 Monument
- 🏛 Museum/Gallery
- 🏚 Ruin
- 🍷 Winery/Vineyard
- 🦁 Zoo
- 👁 Other Sight

Activities, Courses & Tours
- 🤿 Diving/Snorkelling
- 🛶 Canoeing/Kayaking
- ⛷ Skiing
- 🏄 Surfing
- 🏊 Swimming/Pool
- 🚶 Walking
- 🏄 Windsurfing
- 🎯 Other Activity/Course/Tour

Sleeping
- 🛏 Sleeping
- ⛺ Camping

Eating
- 🍴 Eating

Drinking
- ☕ Drinking
- ☕ Cafe

Entertainment
- 🎭 Entertainment

Shopping
- 🛍 Shopping

Information
- 📮 Post Office
- ℹ Tourist Information

Transport
- ✈ Airport
- 🛂 Border Crossing
- 🚌 Bus
- ⊕ Cable Car/Funicular
- ⊖ Cycling
- ⊖ Ferry
- Ⓜ Metro
- ⊖ Monorail
- P Parking
- S S-Bahn
- 🚕 Taxi
- ⊕ Train/Railway
- ⊕ Tram
- ⊖ Tube Station
- Ⓤ U-Bahn
- • Other Transport

Routes
- Tollway
- Freeway
- Primary
- Secondary
- Tertiary
- Lane
- Unsealed Road
- Plaza/Mall
- Steps
- Tunnel
- Pedestrian Overpass
- Walking Tour
- Walking Tour Detour
- Path

Boundaries
- International
- State/Province
- Disputed
- Regional/Suburb
- Marine Park
- Cliff
- Wall

Population
- 🔴 Capital (National)
- ◉ Capital (State/Province)
- 🔴 City/Large Town
- 🔵 Town/Village

Geographic
- 🏠 Hut/Shelter
- 🚨 Lighthouse
- 👁 Lookout
- ▲ Mountain/Volcano
- 🌴 Oasis
- 🌳 Park
-)(Pass
- 🌳 Picnic Area
- 💧 Waterfall

Hydrography
- River/Creek
- Intermittent River
- Swamp/Mangrove
- Reef
- Canal
- Water
- Dry/Salt/Intermittent Lake
- Glacier

Areas
- Beach/Desert
- Cemetery (Christian)
- Cemetery (Other)
- Park/Forest
- Sportsground
- Sight (Building)
- Top Sight (Building)

Tim Richards

Poland Tim spent a year teaching English in Kraków in 1994–95, having transferred with an international teaching organisation from a two-year stint in Egypt. He was fascinated by the massive post-communism transition affecting every aspect of Polish life, and by surviving remnants of the Cold War days. He's since returned to Poland repeatedly for Lonely Planet, deepening his continued relationship with this beautiful, complex country. When he's not on the road for Lonely Planet, Tim is a freelance journalist living in Melbourne, Australia, writing on various topics, particularly travel and the arts. You can see more of his writing in his collection of essays about his Polish experiences, the Kindle e-book *We Have Here the Homicide* and also at iwriter.com.au.

Simon Richmond

Russia After studying Russian history and politics at university, Simon's first visit to the country was in 1994, when he wandered goggle-eyed around gorgeous St Petersburg, and peeked at Lenin's mummified corpse in Red Square. He's since travelled the breadth of the nation from Kamchatka in the far east to Kaliningrad in the far west, stopping off at many points between. An award-winning writer and photographer, Simon is the co-author of the first and subsequent editions of Lonely Planet's *Trans-Siberian Railway* as well as editions 3, 4 and 5 of *Russia*. You can also check Simon's website at www.simonrichmond.com.

Read more about Simon at:
lonelyplanet.com/members/simonrichmond

Tamara Sheward

Serbia After years of freelance travel writing, rock'n'roll journalism and insalubrious authordom, Tamara leapt at the chance to join the Lonely Planet ranks in 2009 as presenter of LPTV's *Roads Less Travelled: Cambodia* documentary. Taking on the decidedly less leech-infested Serbia for this book was a natural fit for a half-Russian Australian girl with a penchant for Cyrillic, ćevapčići and homemade spirits, although getting trapped in a derelict Tito-era lift did test pan-Slavic relations somewhat. As befitting someone who believes that mayonnaise, sour cream and cheese does a salad make, Tamara has extensively travelled in and written about the Balkans, the Caucasus and Russia, and will continue to do so, as soon as the brain cells she lost at Guča are rejuvenated.

Richard Watkins

Bulgaria Richard studied ancient history at Oxford, and his first job after university was teaching conversational English to college students in Sofia. He tried teaching for a while in Singapore, but found travelling much more fun, and he has returned to Bulgaria several times since, discovering something new each time. This was his fifth (or sixth?) visit, and this time he finally got to see distant, sleepy Vidin and the forested riverbank of Romania across the wide brown Danube. Richard has written for Lonely Planet since 2003 and his previous books include two editions of Lonely Planet *Bulgaria* as well as *Poland*, *Best of Prague*, *Best of Kraków* and *Eastern Europe*.

Mark Elliott

Bosnia & Hercegovina British-born travel-writer Mark Elliott was only 11 when his family first dragged him to Sarajevo and stood him in the now defunct concrete footsteps of Gavrilo Princip. Fortunately no Austro-Hungarian emperors were passing at the time. He has since visited virtually every corner of BiH supping fine Hercegovinian wines with master vintners, talking philosophy with Serb monks and Sufi mystics and drinking more Bosnian coffee than any healthy stomach should be subjected to. When not travel-writing he lives a blissfully quiet life in suburban Belgium with the lovely Danielle, who he met while jamming blues harmonica in a Turkmenistan club.

Steve Fallon

Slovenia Steve has been travelling to Slovenia since the early 1990s, when almost everyone but the Slovenes had never heard of the place. Never mind, it was his own private Idaho for over a decade. Though *on še govori slovensko kot jamski človek* (he still speaks Slovene like a caveman), Steve considers part of his soul to be Slovenian and returns as often as he can for a glimpse of the Julian Alps in the sun, a dribble of *bučno olje* and a dose of the dual.

Anna Kaminski

Lithuania Anna was born in the Soviet Union, has been travelling to the Baltics and Ukraine since the tender age of three, and remembers a time when all the Lenin statues were not just nostalgic remains of the Soviet past. A jill-of-all-trades, a former healthcare worker/translator/legal assistant, she was sucked into the heady world of travel writing in 2007 and intends to be a glorified vagrant for years to come. Over the last three years, travel-writing assignments have taken her from the hedonistic Baltic shore to remnants of extermination camps, Vilnius bars and the ruins of a once-mighty empire. Anna enjoys seeing Russia and the Baltics from the dual perspective of a communist kid and a Western traveller. An incorrigible foodie, she actually enjoys Lithuania's signature dish – the zeppelin.

Anja Mutić

Croatia It's been more than 18 years since Anja left her native Croatia. The journey took her to several countries before she made New York City her base 11 years ago. But the roots are a'calling. She's been returning to Croatia frequently for work and play, intent on discovering a new place on every visit. On her last trip, she loved exploring Hvar's lavender-dotted interior. See everthenomad.com for more about Anja.

Read more about Anja at:
lonelyplanet.com/members/anjamutic

Leif Pettersen

Moldova, Romania In 2003, after nine years of feigning interest in electronic payments for the US Federal Reserve System, Leif – from Minneapolis, Minnesota – was 'Kramered' into being a homeless, shameless, godless freelance travel writer by an unbalanced friend. Leif's weakness for pretty girls first brought him to Romania in 2004, where he's since lived and/or travelled for two cumulative years. He's repeatedly visited every notable patch of grass in Romania and Moldova, making dear friends, except for Romania's Neo-Nazi Party who publicly denounced him in 2008, calling him a 'slimeball' and 'human piece of garbage'. (True story.) Leif writes an almost award-winning, 'slightly caustic' blog, where he dishes on travel writing, Romania, Italy's woeful internet and his remarkable-gift-for-hyphenation.

Brandon Presser

Latvia His wanderlust bigger than his wallet, Brandon earned his backpacker stripes after an epic overland adventure from Morocco to Finland. He then joined the glamourous ranks of eternal nomadism as a fulltime travel writer, and has since contributed to more than 20 Lonely Planet titles. He co-authored *Estonia, Latvia & Lithuania* and was delighted to return to the Baltic where he put his Harvard art history degree to good use while checking out Rīga's surplus of evocative art nouveau architecture.

Mark Baker

Hungary Mark first came to Eastern Europe in the mid-'80s as a grad student in international affairs. Those were the dark days of the dying communist regimes, yet even then he was hooked by the region's quirky history, beauty and cheap booze. He's lived in Prague for the better part of 20 years, and is a frequent traveller throughout the region (and now has a special fondness for Hungary). After working as a fulltime journalist for The Economist Group and Radio Free Europe, he's found permanent employment as a freelance travel writer and is co-author of Lonely Planet *Prague* and Lonely Planet *Romania*, among other titles.

Jayne D'Arcy

Albania, Kosovo Counting Albania's highlights every two years for the past six has led Jayne to the startling conclusion that Albania resembles a robust child's growth chart. Taking advantage of the growth are cyclists in remote corners, hikers turning the 'Accursed Mountains' into a 'must-hike' and backpacker hostels opening in the hottest spots. When she's not taking photos of vintage folding bikes in Albania, Jayne also writes about the southern hemisphere (*Southeast Asia on a Shoestring* and *Australia*) and rides her own vintage folding bike around Melbourne, Australia.

Chris Deliso

Macedonia American travel writer and journalist Chris Deliso has been exploring widely in the Balkans ever since finishing a Master's in Byzantine History at Oxford University, back in 1999. He's lived in Greece, Turkey and, for the most part, Macedonia – a country that still continues to surprise him on a daily basis. In researching the present guide, Chris checked out new nightspots in Skopje's revitalised old town, gazed out from beatific mountaintop monasteries, and hopped boulders while fending off freshwater crabs in Macedonia's rushing rivers. Chris has contributed to several other Lonely Planet guidebooks, including *Greece*, *Bulgaria* and *Western Balkans*. See www.chrisdeliso.com for more about Chris' work.

Read more about Chris at:
lonelyplanet.com/members/chrisdeliso

Marc Di Duca

Ukraine Driven by an urge to discover Eastern Europe's wilder side, Marc first hit Kyiv one dark, snow-flecked night in early 1998. Several prolonged stints, countless near misses with Kyiv's metro doors and many bottles of *horilka* later, he still never misses a chance to fine-tune his Russian while exploring far-flung corners of this immense land. An established travel author, Marc has penned guides to Moscow and Lake Baikal, as well as working on Lonely Planet's *Trans-Siberian Railway* and *Russia* books.

Peter Dragičević

Montenegro Among the two dozen or so Lonely Planet books that Peter's co-written are the first ever *Montenegro* country guide, *Western Balkans* and the two previous editions of this title. While it was family ties that first drew him to the Balkans, it's the history, natural beauty, convoluted politics, cheap *rakija* and intriguing people that keep bringing him back. This trip's highlight was a particularly dramatic trek through the clouds to the Njegoš monument on the top of Mt Lovćen.

Lisa Dunford

Slovakia A fascination with Eastern Europe has gripped Lisa since childhood, probably because her grandfather emigrated from the Carpathian mountains that were a part of Hungary, then Czechoslovakia and now are in the Ukraine. She studied in Budapest junior year at university and post graduation worked for the Agency for International Development at the US embassy in Bratislava. While living in Slovakia, Lisa danced with the country as it became an independent nation, learned the language and made life-long friends. Now a freelance writer, she returns often. Lisa has contributed to numerous books for Lonely Planet, including *Czech & Slovak Republics*, *Hungary* and *Central Europe*.

OUR STORY

A beat-up old car, a few dollars in the pocket and a sense of adventure. In 1972 that's all Tony and Maureen Wheeler needed for the trip of a lifetime – across Europe and Asia overland to Australia. It took several months, and at the end – broke but inspired – they sat at their kitchen table writing and stapling together their first travel guide, *Across Asia on the Cheap*. Within a week they'd sold 1500 copies. Lonely Planet was born.

Today, Lonely Planet has offices in Melbourne, London and Oakland, with more than 600 staff and writers. We share Tony's belief that 'a great guidebook should do three things: inform, educate and amuse'.

OUR WRITERS

Tom Masters

Coordinating Author & Belarus Tom has been travelling in Eastern Europe since the age of 14 when he spent a summer with Bulgarian family friends in newly post-communist Sofia. Since then he has lived in St Petersburg, travelled the Baltic coast with Greenpeace, worked on documentaries throughout the region for the BBC and the Discovery Channel and slept on more overnight trains than he can remember. The region may have changed enormously in the two decades since his first trip, but Belarus, where he returned for this book, remains defiantly Soviet. Tom lives in Berlin and can be found online at www.tommasters.net.

Read more about Tom at:
lonelyplanet.com/members/tommasters

Brett Atkinson

Czech Republic Brett Atkinson has been travelling to Eastern Europe for more than 20 years, honeymooning in Bosnia, Croatia and Hungary, writing about the legacy of the communist era, and enjoying more than a few local beers. For his fourth extended research trip to the Czech Republic, he dived into Prague's emerging visual arts scene, trekked the spectacular valleys of the Bohemian Switzerland region, and continued to marvel at sunsets above Prague Castle. When he's not on the road for Lonely Planet, Brett's at home in Auckland, planning his next overseas sojourn with wife Carol. He's contributed to more than 20 Lonely Planet titles, and travelled to more than 60 countries. See www.brett-atkinson.net for details of his latest writing and travels.

Carolyn Bain

Estonia Melbourne-born Carolyn got her first glimpse behind the Iron Curtain in Poland in early 1989, while a student in Denmark. It was the year communism unravelled throughout Eastern Europe, and thus began her fascination. In 1991, while studying Russian and politics at university, she was overjoyed when her 'Soviet Politics' class had to change its name to 'The Soviet Union & Beyond'. Since then, on regular visits to the Baltic region she has applauded the renewed independence and flourishing creativity. Among other destinations, she has covered Sweden and Denmark for Lonely Planet, but Estonia holds a special place in her heart for combining the best of Eastern Europe and Scandinavia and coming up with something heartwarmingly unique.

OVER MORE
PAGE WRITERS

Published by Lonely Planet Publications Pty Ltd
ABN 36 005 607 983
11th edition – Oct 2011
ISBN 978 1 74179 675 9
© Lonely Planet 2011   Photographs © as indicated 2011
10 9 8 7 6 5 4 3 2 1
Printed in Singapore

Although the authors and Lonely Planet have taken all reasonable care in preparing this book, we make no warranty about the accuracy or completeness of its content and, to the maximum extent permitted, disclaim all liability arising from its use.